2019
STANDARD POSTAGE STAMP CATALOGUE

ONE HUNDRED AND SEVENTY-FIFTH EDITION IN SIX VOLUMES

VOLUME 3B

H-I

EDITOR	Donna Houseman
MANAGING EDITOR	Charles Snee
EDITOR EMERITUS	James E. Kloetzel
SENIOR EDITOR /NEW ISSUES & VALUING	Martin J. Frankevicz
SENIOR VALUING ANALYST	Steven R. Myers
SENIOR EDITOR	Timothy A. Hodge
ADMINISTRATIVE ASSISTANT/CATALOGUE LAYOUT	Eric Wiessinger
PRINTING AND IMAGE COORDINATOR	Stacey Mahan
SENIOR GRAPHIC DESIGNER	Cinda McAlexander
SALES DIRECTOR	David Pistello
SALES DIRECTOR	Eric Roth

Released June 2018
Includes New Stamp Listings through the April 2018 *Linn's Stamp News Monthly* Catalogue Update

AMOS MEDIA

911 Vandemark Road, Sidney, OH 45365-4129
Publishers of *Linn's Stamp News, Linn's Stamp News Monthly, Coin World* and *Coin World Monthly.*

Table of Contents

See the following volumes for other country listings:
Volume 1A: United States, United Nations, Abu Dhabi-Australia; Volume 1B: Austria-B
Volume 2A: C-Cur; Volume 2B: Cyp-F
Volume 3A: G
Volume 4A: J-L; Volume 4B: M
Volume 5A: N-Phil; Volume 5B: Pit-Sam
Volume 6A: San-Tete; Volume 6B: Thai-Z

Scott Catalogue Mission Statement

The Scott Catalogue Team exists to serve the recreational, educational and commercial hobby needs of stamp collectors and dealers.

We strive to set the industry standard for philatelic information and products by developing and providing goods that help collectors identify, value, organize and present their collections.

Quality customer service is, and will continue to be, our highest priority. We aspire toward achieving total customer satisfaction.

Copyright Notice

Trademark Notice

ISBN 978-0-89487-547-2

Library of Congress Card No. 2-3301

Acknowledgments

Our appreciation and gratitude go to the following individuals who have assisted us in preparing information included in this year's Scott Catalogues. Some helpers prefer anonymity. These individuals have generously shared their stamp knowledge with others through the medium of the Scott Catalogue.

Those who follow provided information that is in addition to the hundreds of dealer price lists and advertisements and scores of auction catalogues and realizations that were used in producing the catalogue values. It is from those noted here that we have been able to obtain information on items not normally seen in published lists and advertisements. Support from these people goes beyond data leading to catalogue values, for they also are key to editorial changes.

A special acknowledgment to Liane and Sergio Sismondo of The Classic Collector for their assistance and knowledge sharing that have aided in the preparation of this year's Standard and Classic Specialized Catalogues.

Roland Austin
Jim Bardo (Bardo Stamps)
William Barclay (South Sudan Philatelic Society)
John Birkinbine II
Helmut Blaschczyk
Roger S. Brody
Tina & John Carlson (JET Stamps)
Henry Chlanda
Bob Coale
David & Julia Crawford
Tony L. Crumbley (Carolina Coin & Stamp, Inc.)
Christopher Dahle
Tony Davis
Ubaldo Del Toro
Leon Djerahian
Bob & Rita Dumaine (Sam Houston Duck Co.)
Sister Theresa Durand
Paul G. Eckman
George Epstein (Allkor Stamp Co.)
Robert A. Fisher
Jeffrey M. Forster
Robert S. Freeman
Ernest E. Fricks
Michael Fuchs
Bob Genisol (Sultan Stamp Center)
Stan Goldfarb
Allen Grant (Rushstamps (Retail) Ltd.)
Daniel E. Grau
Robin Harris
Bruce Hecht (Bruce L. Hecht Co.)
Peter Hoffman
John Hotchner
Armen Hovsepian (Armenstamp)
Doug Iams
Eric Jackson
John Jamieson (Saskatoon Stamp and Coin)
Peter Jeannopoulos
William A. Jones
Allan Katz (Ventura Stamp Co.)
Lewis Kaufman (The Philatelic Foundation)
Patricia Kaufmann (Confederate Stamp Alliance)
Jon Kawaguchi (Ryukyu Philatelic Specialist Society)
Roland Kretschmer
William V. Kriebel (Brazil Philatelic Association)
Frederick P. Lawrence
John R. Lewis (The William Henry Stamp Co.)
Ulf Lindahl
Ignacio Llach (Filatelia Llach S.L.)
Marilyn R. Mattke
William K. McDaniel
Mauricio Mejia
Gary Morris (Pacific Midwest Co.)
Peter Mosiondz, Jr.
Bruce M. Moyer (Moyer Stamps & Collectibles)
Richard H. Muller
Scott Murphy (Professional Stamp Experts)
Leonard Nadybal
Dr. Tiong Tak Ngo
Gerald Nylander
Nik & Lisa Oquist
Dr. Everett Parker
Don Peterson (International Philippine Philatelic Society)
Stanley M. Piller (Stanley M. Piller & Associates)
Virgil Pirvulescu
Todor Drumev Popov
Peter W. W. Powell
Bob Prager (Gary Posner, Inc.)
Siddique Mahmudur Rahman
Ghassan D. Riachi
Mehrdad Sadri (Persiphila)
Sabah Jawad Salih
Theodosios Sampson PhD
Alexander Schauss (Schauss Philatelics)
Michael Schreiber
Jeff Siddiqui
Sergio & Liane Sismondo (The Classic Collector)
Jay Smith
Kenneth Thompson
Peter Thy
Scott R. Trepel (Robert A. Siegel Auction Galleries, Inc.)
Dan Undersander (United Postal Stationery Society)
Herbert R. Volin
Philip T. Wall
Giana Wayman
Don White (Dunedin Stamp Centre)
Ralph Yorio
Val Zabijaka
Michal Zika

SCOTT

What's new for 2019 Scott Standard Volume 3B?

Greetings, Fellow Scott Catalog User:

This year celebrates another milestone in the 150-year history of the Scott catalogs. The 2019 volumes are the 175th edition of the Scott *Standard Postage Stamp Catalogue*. Vol. 3B includes listings for countries of the world H through I. Listings for countries of the world beginning with the letter G can be found in Vol. 3A.

In the Hong Kong listings, the editors completed a line-by-line review that yielded more than 1,650 value changes. This year, the focus was on postage issues from the mid-1970s to the present. For the most part, values for unused stamps show declines through the mid-1990s. Values for used high-denomination stamps, in contrast, show gains. Values for selected modern definitive sets were adjusted to better reflect market values for individual stamps within those sets. In some cases, the overall set totals did not change appreciably. In general, values for more recent issues rise 10 percent or somewhat more. A representative example is the 2003 Miniature Landscapes set of four (Scott 1040-1041), which moves from $4 in mint never-hinged condition and $3.50 in used condition in 2018 to $4.50 and $4, respectively, this year.

Hong Kong's 2003 Miniature Landscapes set of four (Scott 1040-1041) moves from $4 in mint never-hinged condition and $3.50 in used condition in 2018 to $4.50 and $4, respectively, this year.

Somewhat more than 750 value changes are recorded for India. This year's focus was on issues up to the mid-1960s. A mixture of increases and decreases is seen, with some robust upward adjustments for selected early classics. For example, the 1854 ½-anna Queen Victoria (Scott 1) advances from $1,200 unused in 2018 to $3,250 this year.

The listings for Indonesia stamps received a line-by-line review that resulted in almost 3,300 value changes. A few increases are sprinkled among the changes, but overall values reflect a weakening of this market. The 1999-2000 Millennium set of two stamps and two souvenir sheets increases slightly. The values for the two-stamp set (Scott 1878-1879) move to $1.25 mint and 75¢ used, from $1 and 50¢, respectively. The sheet of 20 plus 20 labels (1879a) jumps from $22.50 both mint and used to $25. The set of two souvenir sheets (1880-1881) rockets to $20 used, from $8. The mint value remains unchanged at $20. Several footnoted values also were updated.

Ireland comes in with about 1,750 value changes. The editors concentrated on stamps issued from the late 1930s through the first half of 2001. Modest declines are the norm, but there are some notable scattered increases. The 29-penny deep rose lilac of 1982 (Scott 475) in used condition jumps from 80¢ last year to $2 this year. The 1997 £1 Greenland White-fronted Goose (1319) takes wing, advancing from $6 mint and used in 2018 to $7.50 both ways in the 2019 catalog.

The editors resumed their comprehensive review of Israel begun last year. Picking up with issues of 1995, more than 1,700 value changes were recorded. Values are down 10 percent to 20 percent, but some increases are seen among more popular topicals and self-adhesive definitives. The 1998 Children's Pets sheet of six doubles in value, from $2 mint and used last year to $4 both ways this year. Selected modern postage issues in imperforate form are now footnoted and valued.

Editorial enhancements for Vol. 3B

Heligoland: Illustrations have been added for the three types found on the 1867-68 (Scott 1-4), 1869-71 (5-6), 1873 (7-12), 1874 (13), and 1875 (14-19) Queen Victoria stamps. On type I, the curl below the chignon is rounded; on type II the curl resembles an upside-down question mark; and on type III the curl is hooked.

Hungary: A scarce error of the 1888 5-kreuzer Crown of St. Stephen, with the "5" doubled and inverted, has been added as Scott 25a.

India: A small number of color varieties were added to classic-period listings. New Scott 15c is a yellow variety of the 1855 2-anna buff Diadem with Maltese Crosses. An orange variety of the 1865 2a brownish orange Diadem with Maltese Crosses enters the 2019 catalog as Scott 23c. The rare presentation booklet containing the 1948 Mahatma Gandhi set of four (Scott 203-206) with "Specimen" overprints is now footnoted with a value of $13,000. The error variety of the 1973 15-naye paise International Red Cross Centenary (Scott 373) with the red cross omitted also is newly footnoted, with a value of $25,000.

Italy: New enlarged images have been added for Italy Scott 93, 111, and 123 to make it easier for collectors to determine the correct Scott number for the original 1906 15-centesimo slate Victor Emmanuel III stamp (93) and the redrawn (111) and re-engraved (123) versions of this denomination.

Italy - Trieste: Several new images were added to the listings of Trieste Zone A in Vol. 3B of the 2018 Scott Standard catalog. These stamps bear the overprint "A.M.G./F.T.T." and were issued jointly by the Allied Military Government of the United States and Great Britain following World War II, from 1947 through 1954. More than 30 new images have been added to Vol. 3B of the 2019 Scott Standard catalog.

As always, we encourage you to pay special attention to the Number Additions, Deletions & Changes found on page 809 in this volume. We also suggest reading the catalog introduction, which includes an abundance of useful information.

Enjoy this wonderful hobby every day!

Donna Houseman

Donna Houseman/Catalogue Editor

Addresses, Telephone Numbers, Web Sites, E-Mail Addresses of General & Specialized Philatelic Societies

Collectors can contact the following groups for information about the philately of the areas within the scope of these societies, or inquire about membership in these groups. Aside from the general societies, we limit this list to groups that specialize in particular fields of philately, particular areas covered by the Scott Standard Postage Stamp Catalogue, and topical groups. Many more specialized philatelic society exist than those listed below. These addresses are updated yearly, and they are, to the best of our knowledge, correct and current. Groups should inform the editors of address changes whenever they occur. The editors also want to hear from other such specialized groups not listed. Unless otherwise noted all website addresses begin with http://

American Philatelic Society
100 Match Factory Place
Bellefonte PA 16823-1367
Ph: (814) 933-3803
www.stamps.org
E-mail: apsinfo@stamps.org

American Stamp Dealers Association, Inc.
P.O. Box 692
Leesport PA 19553
Ph: (800) 369-8207
www.americanstampdealer.com
E-mail: asda@americanstampdealer.com

National Stamp Dealers Association
Richard Kostka, President
3643 Private Road 18
Pinckneyville IL 62274-3426
Ph: (800) 875-6633 or (618) 357-5497
www.nsdainc.org
E-mail: nsda@nsdainc.org

International Society of Worldwide Stamp Collectors
Joanne Berkowitz, MD
P.O. Box 19006
Sacramento CA 95819
www.iswsc.org
E-mail: executivedirector@iswsc.org

Royal Philatelic Society
41 Devonshire Place
London, W1G 6JY
UNITED KINGDOM
www.rpsl.org.uk
E-mail: secretary@rpsl.org.uk

Royal Philatelic Society of Canada
P.O. Box 69080
St. Clair Post Office
Toronto, ON, M4T 3A1
CANADA
Ph: (888) 285-4143
www.rpsc.org
E-mail: info@rpsc.org

Young Stamp Collectors of America
Janet Houser
100 Match Factory Place
Bellefonte PA 16823-1367
Ph: (814) 933-3820
www.stamps.org/ysca/intro.htm
E-mail: ysca@stamps.org

Philatelic Research Resources

(The Scott editors encourage any additional research organizations to submit data for inclusion in this listing category)

American Philatelic Research Library
Scott Tiffney
100 Match Factory Place
Bellefonte PA 16823
Ph: (814) 933-3803
www.stamplibrary.org
E-mail: libraryestamps.org

Institute for Analytical Philately, Inc.
P.O. Box 8035
Holland MI 49422-8035
Ph: (616) 399-9299
www.analyticalphilately.org
E-mail: info@analyticalphilately.org

The Western Philatelic Library
P.O. Box 2219
1500 Partridge Ave.
Sunnyvale CA 94087
Ph: (408) 733-0336
www.fwpf.org

Groups focusing on fields or aspects found in worldwide philately (some might cover U.S. area only)

American Air Mail Society
Stephen Reinhard
P.O. Box 110
Mineola NY 11501
www.americanairmailsociety.org
E-mail: sreinhard1@optonline.net

American First Day Cover Society
Douglas Kelsey
P.O. Box 16277
Tucson AZ 85732-6277
Ph: (520) 321-0880
www.afdcs.org
E-mail: afdcs@afdcs.org

American Revenue Association
Eric Jackson
P.O. Box 728
Leesport PA 19533-0728
Ph: (610) 926-6200
www.revenuer.org
E-mail: eric@revenuer.com

American Topical Association
Vera Felts
P.O. Box 8
Carterville IL 62918-0008
Ph: (618) 985-5100
www.americantopicalassn.org
E-mail: americantopical@msn.com

Christmas Seal & Charity Stamp Society
John Denune
234 E. Broadway
Granville OH 43023
Ph: (740) 587-0276
www.seal-society.org
E-mail: john@christmasseals.net

Errors, Freaks and Oddities Collectors Club
Scott Shaulis
P.O. Box 549
Murrysville PA 15668-0549
Ph: (724) 733-4134
www.efocc.org
E-mail: Scott@shaulisstamps.com

First Issues Collectors Club
Kurt Streepy, Secretary
3128 E. Mattatha Drive
Bloomington IN 47401
www.firstissues.org
E-mail: secretary@firstissues.org

International Society of Reply Coupon Collectors
Peter Robin
P.O. Box 353
Bala Cynwyd PA 19004
E-mail: peterrobin@verizon.net

The Joint Stamp Issues Society
Richard Zimmermann
29A Rue Des Eviats
Lalaye F-67220
FRANCE
www.philarz.net
E-mail: richard.zimmermann@club-internet.fr

National Duck Stamp Collectors Society
Anthony J. Monico
P.O. Box 43
Harleysville PA 19438-0043
www.ndscs.org
E-mail: ndscs@ndscs.org

No Value Identified Club
Albert Sauvanet
Le Clos Royal B, Boulevard des Pas Enchantes
St. Sebastien-sur Loire, 44230
FRANCE
E-mail: alain.vailly@irin.univ nantes.fr

The Perfins Club
Ken Masters
111 NW 94th Street Apt. 102
Kansas City MO 64155-2993
Ph: (816) 835-5907
www.perfins.org
E-mail: kmasters@aol.com

Postage Due Mail Study Group
John Rawlins
13, Longacre
Chelmsford, CM1 3BJ
UNITED KINGDOM
E-mail: john.rawlins2@ukonline.co.uk.

Post Mark Collectors Club
Bob Milligan
7014 Woodland Oaks
Magnolia TX 77354
Ph: (281) 259-2735
www.postmarks.org
E-mail: bob.milligan@gmail.net

Postal History Society
Gary Wayne Loew
P.O. Box 468101
Atlanta GA 31146-8101
www.postalhistorysociety.org
E-mail: garywloew@gmail.com

Precancel Stamp Society
Dick Kalmbach
2658 Iron Works Drive
Buford GA 30519
Ph: (610) 248-8844
www.precancels.com
E-mail: promo@precancels.com

United Postal Stationery Society
Stuart Leven
1659 Branham Lane Suite F-307
San Jose CA 95118-2291
www.upss.org
E-mail: poststat@gmail.com

United States Possessions Philatelic Society
Daniel F. Ring
P.O. Box 113
Woodstock IL 60098
www.uspps.net
E-mail: danielfring@hotmail.com

Groups focusing on U.S. area philately as covered in the Standard Catalogue

Canal Zone Study Group
Tom Brougham
737 Neilson St.
Berkeley CA 94707
www.CanalZoneStudyGroup.com
E-mail: czsgsecretary@gmail.com

Carriers and Locals Society
Martin Richardson
P.O. Box 74
Grosse Ile MI 48138
www.pennypost.org
E-mail: martinr362@aol.com

Confederate Stamp Alliance
Patricia A. Kaufmann
10194 N. Old State Road
Lincoln DE 19960
Ph. (302) 422-2656
www.csalliance.org
E-mail: trishkauf@comcast.net

Hawaiian Philatelic Society
Gawwon Sugimura
P.O. Box 10115
Honolulu HI 96816-0115
E-mail: hiphilsoc@gmail.com

Plate Number Coil Collectors Club
Gene Trinks
16415 W. Desert Wren Court
Surprise AZ 85374
Ph: (623) 322-4619
www.pnc3.org
E-mail: gctrinks@cox.net

Ryukyu Philatelic Specialist Society
Laura Edmonds, Secy.
P.O. Box 240177
Charlotte NC 28224-0177
Ph: (336) 509-3739
www.ryukyustamps.org
E-mail: secretary@ryukyustamps.org

United Nations Philatelists
Blanton Clement, Jr.
P.O. Box 146
Morrisville PA 19067-0146
www.unpi.com
E-mail: bclemjunior@gmail.com

United States Stamp Society
Executive Secretary
Larry Ballantyne
P.O. Box 6634
Katy TX 77491-6634
www.usstamps.org

U.S. Cancellation Club
Roger Curran
20 University Avenue
Lewisburg PA 17837
E-mail: rcurran@dejazzd.com

U.S. Philatelic Classics Society
Rob Lund
2913 Fulton St.
Everett WA 98201-3733
www.uspcs.org
E-mail: membershipchairman@uspcs.org

Groups focusing on philately of foreign countries or regions

Aden & Somaliland Study Group
Gary Brown
P.O. Box 106
Briar Hill, Victoria, 3088
AUSTRALIA
E-mail: garyjohn951@optushome.com.au

American Society of Polar Philatelists (Antarctic areas)
Alan Warren
P.O. Box 39
Exton PA 19341-0039
www.polarphilatelists.org

Andorran Philatelic Study Circle
D. Hope
17 Hawthorn Drive
Stalybridge, Cheshire, SK15 1UE
UNITED KINGDOM
www.andorranpsc.org.uk
E-mail: andorranpsc@btinternet.com

Australian States Study Circle of The Royal Sydney Philatelic Club
Ben Palmer
GPO 1751
Sydney, N.S.W., 2001
AUSTRALIA
www.philas.org.au/states

Austria Philatelic Society
Ralph Schneider
P.O. Box 23049
Belleville IL 62223
Ph: (618) 277-6152
www.austriaphilatelicsociety.com
E-mail: rschneiderstamps@att.net

Bechuanalands and Botswana Society
Neville Midwood
69 Porlock Lane
Furzton, Milton Keynes, MK4 1JY
UNITED KINGDOM
www.nevsoft.com
E-mail: bbsoc@nevsoft.com

Bermuda Collectors Society
John Pare
405 Perimeter Road
Mount Horeb WI 53572
www.bermudacollectorssociety.com
E-mail: pare16@mhtc.net

Brazil Philatelic Association
William V. Kriebel
1923 Manning St.
Philadelphia PA 19103-5728
www.brazilphilatelic.org
E-mail: info@brazilphilatelic.org

British Caribbean Philatelic Study Group
Duane Larson
2 Forest Blvd.
Park Forest IL 60466
www.bcpsg.com
E-mail: dlarson283@aol.com

The King George VI Collectors Society (British Commonwealth)
Brian Livingstone
21 York Mansions, Prince of Wales Drive
London, SW11 4DL
UNITED KINGDOM
www.kg6.info
E-mail: livingstone484@btinternet.com

British North America Philatelic Society (Canada & Provinces)
Andy Ellwood
10 Doris Avenue
Gloucester, ON, KIT 3W8
CANADA
www.bnaps.org
E-mail: secretary@bnaps.org

British West Indies Study Circle
John Seidl
4324 Granby Way
Marietta GA 30062
Ph: (404) 229-6863
www.bwisc.org
E-mail: john.seidl@gmail.com

Burma Philatelic Study Circle
Michael Whittaker
1, Ecton Leys, Hillside
Rugby, Warwickshire, CV22 5SL
UNITED KINGDOM
www.burmastamps.homecall.co.uk
E-mail: manningham8@mypostoffice.co.uk

Cape and Natal Study Circle
Dr. Guy Dillaway
P.O. Box 181
Weston MA 02493
www.nzsc.demon.co.uk

Ceylon Study Circle
R. W. P. Frost
42 Lonsdale Road, Cannington
Bridgwater, Somerset, TA5 2JS
UNITED KINGDOM
www.ceylonsc.org
E-mail: rodney.frost@tiscali.co.uk

Channel Islands Specialists Society
Richard Flemming
64, Falconers Green, Burbage
Hinckley, Leicestershire, LE10 2SX
UNITED KINGDOM
www.ciss1950.org.uk
E-mail: secretary@ciss1950.org.uk

China Stamp Society
H. James Maxwell
1050 West Blue Ridge Blvd.
Kansas City MO 64145-1216
www.chinastampsociety.org
E-mail: president@chinastampsociety.org

Colombia/Panama Philatelic Study Group (COPAPHIL)
Thomas P. Myers
P.O. Box 522
Gordonsville VA 22942
www.copaphil.org
E-mail: tpmphil@hotmail.com

Association Filatelic de Costa Rica
Giana Wayman (McCarty)
SJO 4935, P.O. Box 025723
Miami FL 33102-5723
E-mail: scotland@racsa.co.cr

Society for Costa Rica Collectors
Dr. Hector R. Mena
P.O. Box 14831
Baton Rouge LA 70808
www.socorico.org
E-mail: hrmena@aol.com

International Cuban Philatelic Society
Ernesto Cuesta
P.O. Box 34434
Bethesda MD 20827
www.cubafil.org
E-mail: ecuesta@philat.com

Cuban Philatelic Society of America ®
P.O. Box 141656
Coral Gables FL 33114-1656
www.cubapsa.com
E-mail: cpsa.usa@gmail.com

Cyprus Study Circle
Colin Dear
10 Marne Close, Wem
Shropshire, SY4 5YE
UNITED KINGDOM
www.cyprusstudycircle.org/index.htm
E-mail: colindear@talktalk.net

Society for Czechoslovak Philately
Tom Cossaboom
P.O. Box 4124
Prescott AZ 86302
Ph: (928) 771-9097
www.csphilately.org
E-mail: klfck1@aol.com

Danish West Indies Study Unit of the Scandinavian Collectors Club
Arnold Sorensen
7666 Edgedale Drive
Newburgh IN 47630
Ph: (812) 480-6532
www.scc-online.org
E-mail: valbydwi@hotmail.com

East Africa Study Circle
Michael Vesey-Fitzgerald
Gambles Cottage, 18 Clarence Road
Lyndhurst, SO43 7AL
UNITED KINGDOM
www.easc.org.uk
E-mail: secretary@easc.org.uk

Egypt Study Circle
Mike Murphy
109 Chadwick Road
London, SE15 4PY
UNITED KINGDOM
Trent Ruebush: North American Agent
E-mail: tkruebrush@gmail.com
www.egyptstudycircle.org.uk
E-mail: egyptstudycircle@hotmail.com

Estonian Philatelic Society
Juri Kirsimagi
29 Clifford Ave.
Pelham NY 10803
Ph: (914) 738-3713

Ethiopian Philatelic Society
Ulf Lindahl
21 Westview Place
Riverside CT 06878
Ph: (203) 722-0769
http://ethiopianphilatelicsociety.weebly.com
E-mail: ulindahl@optonline.net

Falkland Islands Philatelic Study Group
Carl J. Faulkner
615 Taconic Trail
Williamstown MA 01267-2745
Ph: (413) 458-4421
www.fipsg.org.uk
E-mail: cfaulkner@taconicwilliamstown.com

Faroe Islands Study Circle
Norman Hudson
40 Queen's Road, Vicar's Cross
Chester, CH3 5HB
UNITED KINGDOM
www.faroeislandssc.org
E-mail: jntropics@hotmail.com

Former French Colonies Specialist Society
COLFRA
BP 628
75367 Paris, Cedex 08
FRANCE
www.colfra.org
E-mail: secretaire@colfra.org

France & Colonies Philatelic Society
Edward Grabowski
111 Prospect St., 4C
Westfield NJ 07090
www.franceandcolps.org
E-mail: edjjg@alum.mit.edu

Gibraltar Study Circle
Susan Dare
22, Byways Park, Strode Road,
Clevedon, North Somerset, BS21 6UR
UNITED KINGDOM
www.gibraltarstudycircle.wordpress.com
E-mail: smldare@yahoo.co.uk

Germany Philatelic Society
P.O. Box 6547
Chesterfield MO 63006
www.germanyphilatelicusa.org

Plebiscite-Memel-Saar Study Group of the German Philatelic Society
Clayton Wallace
100 Lark Court
Alamo CA 94507
E-mail: claytonwallace@comcast.net

Great Britain Collectors Club
Steve McGill
10309 Brookhollow Circle
Highlands Ranch CO 80129
www.gbstamps.com/gbcc
E-mail: steve.mcgill@comcast.net

International Society of Guatemala Collectors
Jaime Marckwordt
449 St. Francis Blvd.
Daly City CA 94015-2136
www.guatemalastamps.com
E-mail:
membership@guatamalastamps.com

Haiti Philatelic Society
Ubaldo Del Toro
5709 Marble Archway
Alexandria VA 22315
www.haitiphilately.org
E-mail: u007ubi@aol.com

Federacion Filatelica de la Republica de Honduras (Honduran Philatelic Federation, FFRH)
Mauricio Mejia
Apartado postal 1465
Tegucigalpa
HONDURAS

Hong Kong Stamp Society
Ming W. Tsang
P.O. Box 206
Glenside PA 19038
www.hkss.org
E-mail: hkstamps@yahoo.com

Society for Hungarian Philately
Alan Bauer
P.O. Box 3024
Andover MA 01810
Ph: (978) 682-0242
www.hungarianphilately.org
E-mail: alan@hungarianstamps.com

India Study Circle
John Warren
P.O. Box 7326
Washington DC 20044
Ph: (202) 488-7443
www.indiastudycircle.org
E-mail: jw-kbw@earthlink.net

Indian Ocean Study Circle
E. S. Hutton
29 Patermoster Close
Waltham Abby, Essex, EN9 3JU
UNITED KINGDOM
www.indianoceanstudycircle.com
E-mail: secretary@indianoceanstudycircle.com

Society of Indo-China Philatelists
Ron Bentley
2600 N. 24th St.
Arlington VA 22207
www.sicp-online.org
E-mail: ron.bentley@verizon.net

Iran Philatelic Study Circle
Mehdi Esmaili
P.O. Box 750096
Forest Hills NY 11375
www.iranphilatelic.org
E-mail: m.esmaili@earthlink.net

Eire Philatelic Association (Ireland)
David J. Brennan
P.O. Box 704
Bernardsville NJ 07924
www.eirephilatelicassoc.org
E-mail: brennan704@aol.com

Society of Israel Philatelists
Jacqueline Baca
100 Match Factory Place
Bellefonte PA 16823-1367
Ph: (814) 933-3803 ext. 212
www.israelstamps.com
E-mail: israelstamps@gmail.com

Italy and Colonies Study Circle
Richard Harlow
7 Duncombe House, 8 Manor Road
Teddington, TW11 8BE
UNITED KINGDOM
www.icsc.pwp.blueyonder.co.uk
E-mail: richardharlow@outlook.com

International Society for Japanese Philately
William Eisenhauer
P.O. Box 230462
Tigard OR 97281
www.isjp.org
E-mail: secretary@isjp.org

Korea Stamp Society
John Talmage
P.O. Box 6889
Oak Ridge TN 37831
www.koreastampsociety.org
E-mail: jtalmage@usit.net

Latin American Philatelic Society
Jules K. Beck
30½ St. #209
St. Louis Park MN 55426-3551

Liberian Philatelic Society
William Thomas Lockard
P.O. Box 106
Wellston OH 45692
Ph: (740) 384-2020
E-mail: tlockard@zoomnet.net

Liechtenstudy USA (Liechtenstein)
Paul Tremaine
410 SW Ninth St.
Dundee OR 97115
Ph: (503) 538-4500
www.liechtenstudy.org
E-mail: editor@liechtenstudy.org

Lithuania Philatelic Society
John Variakojis
8472 Carlisle Court
Burr Ridge IL 60527
Ph: (630) 974-6525
www.lithuanianphilately.com/lps
E-mail: variakojis@sbcglobal.net

Luxembourg Collectors Club
Gary B. Little
7319 Beau Road
Sechelt, BC, V0N 3A8
CANADA
lcc.luxcentral.com
E-mail: gary@luxcentral.com

Malaya Study Group
David Tett
4 Amenbury Court
Harpenden Herts,
Wheathampstead Herts AL5 2BU
UNITED KINGDOM
www.m-s-g.org.uk
E-mail: davidtett@aol.com

Malta Study Circle
Rodger Evans
Ravensbourne, Hook Heath Road
Woking, Surrey, GU22 0LB
UNITED KINGDOM
www.maltastudycircle.org.uk
E-mail: carge@hotmail.co.uk

Mexico-Elmhurst Philatelic Society International
Eric Stovner
P.O. Box 10097
Santa Ana CA 92711-0097
www.mepsi.org
E-mail: treasurer@mepsi.org

Asociacion Mexicana de Filatelia AMEXFIL
Alejando Grossman
Jose Maria Rico, 129, Col. Del Valle
Mexico City DF, 03100
MEXICO
www.amexfil.mx
E-mail: amexfil@gmail.com

Society for Moroccan and Tunisian Philately S.P.L.M.
206, bld Pereire
Paris 75017
FRANCE
splm-philatelie.org
E-mail: splm206@aol.com

Nepal & Tibet Philatelic Study Group
Ken Goss
2643 Wagner Place
EL Dorado Hills CA 95762
Ph: (510) 207-5369
www.fuchs-online.com/ntpsc/
E-mail: kfgoss@comcast.net

American Society for Netherlands Philately
Hans Kremer
50 Rockport Court
Danville CA 94526
Ph: (925) 820-5841
www.asnp1975.com
E-mail: hkremer@usa.net

New Zealand Society of Great Britain
Michael Wilkinson
121 London Road
Sevenoaks, Kent, TN13 1BH
UNITED KINGDOM
www.nzsgb.org.uk
E-mail: mwilkin799@aol.com

Nicaragua Study Group
Erick Rodriguez
11817 SW 11th St.
Miami FL 33184-2501
clubs.yahoo.com/clubs/
nicaraguastudygroup
E-mail: nsgsec@yahoo.com

Society of Australasian Specialists/Oceania
David McNamee
P.O. Box 37
Alamo CA 94507
www.sasoceania.org
E-mail: treasurer@sasoceania.org

Orange Free State Study Circle
J. R. Stroud
24 Hooper Close
Burnham-on-sea, Somerset, TA8 1JQ
UNITED KINGDOM
orangefreestatephilately.org.uk
E-mail: richard@richardstroud.plus.com

Pacific Islands Study Circle
John Ray
24 Woodvale Ave.
London, SE25 4AE
UNITED KINGDOM
www.pisc.org.uk
E-mail: secretary@pisc.org.uk

Pakistan Philatelic Study Circle
Jeff Siddiqui
P.O. Box 7002
Lynnwood WA 98046
E-mail: jeffsiddiqui@msn.com

Asociacion Filatelica de Panama (ASOFILPA)
Edward D. Vianna
Apartado Postal 0819-03400
El Dorado, Panama
PANAMA
www.asociacionfilatelicadepanama.
blogspot.com
E-mail: asofilpa@gmail.com

Papuan Philatelic Society
Steven Zirinsky
P.O. Box 49, Ansonia Station
New York NY 10023
Ph: (718) 706-0616
www.communigate.co.uk/york/pps
E-mail: szirinsky@cs.com

International Philippine Philatelic Society
Donald J. Peterson
P.O. Box 122
Brunswick MD 21716
Ph: (301) 834-6419
www.theipps.info
E-mail: dpeterson4526@gmail.com

Pitcairn Islands Study Group
Dr. Everett L. Parker
117 Cedar Breeze South
Glenburn ME 04401-1734
Ph: (207) 573-1686
www.pisg.net
E-mail: eparker@hughes.net

Polonus Philatelic Society (Poland)
Daniel Lubelski
P.O. Box 2212
Benicia CA 94510
Ph: (419) 410-9115
www.polonus.org
E-mail: info@polonus.org

International Society for Portuguese Philately
Clyde Homen
1491 Bonnie View Road
Hollister CA 95023-5117
www.portugalstamps.com
E-mail: ispp1962@sbcglobal.net

Rhodesian Study Circle
William R. Wallace
P.O. Box 16381
San Francisco CA 94116
www.rhodesianstudycircle.org.uk
E-mail: bwall8rscr@earthlink.net

Rossica Society of Russian Philately
Alexander Kolchinsky
1506 Country Lake Drive
Champaign IL 6821-6428
www.rossica.org
E-mail: alexander.kolchinsky@rossica.org

St. Helena, Ascension & Tristan Da Cunha Philatelic Society
Dr. Everett L. Parker
117 Cedar Breeze South
Glenburn ME 04401-1734
Ph: (207) 573-1686
www.shatps.org
E-mail: eparker@hughes.net

St. Pierre & Miquelon Philatelic Society
James R. (Jim) Taylor
2335 Paliswood Road SW
Calgary, AB, T2V 3P6
CANADA
www.stamps.org/spm

Asociacion Filatelica Salvadorena
Joseph D. Hahn
301 Rolling Ridge Drive, Apt. 111
State College PA 16801-6149
www.elsalvadorphilately.org
E-mail: joehahn100@hotmail.com

Fellowship of Samoa Specialists
Donald Mee
23 Leo St.
Christchurch, 8051
NEW ZEALAND
www.samoaexpress.org
E-mail: donanm@xtra.co.nz

Sarawak Specialists' Society
Stephen Schumann
2417 Cabrillo Drive
Hayward CA 94545
Ph: (510) 785-4794
www.britborneostamps.org.uk
E-mail: stephen.schumann@att.net

Scandinavian Collectors Club
Steve Lund
P.O. Box 16213
St. Paul MN 55116
www.scc-online.org
E-mail: steve88h@aol.com

Slovakia Stamp Society
Jack Benchik
P.O. Box 555
Notre Dame IN 46556

Philatelic Society for Greater Southern Africa
Alan Hanks
34 Seaton Drive
Aurora, ON, L4G 2K1
CANADA
www.psgsa.thestampweb.com

South Sudan Philatelic Society
William Barclay
1370 Spring Hill Road
South Londonderry VT 05155
E-mail: barclayphilatelics@gmail.com

Spanish Philatelic Society
Robert H. Penn
1108 Walnut Drive
Danielsville PA 18038
Ph: (610) 844-8963
E-mail: roberthpenn43@gmail.com

Sudan Study Group
David Sher
5 Ellis Park Road
Toronto, ON, M6S2V1
CANADA
www.sudanstamps.org
e-mail: sh3603@hotmail.com

American Helvetia Philatelic Society (Switzerland, Liechtenstein)
Richard T. Hall
P.O. Box 15053
Asheville NC 28813-0053
www.swiss-stamps.org
E-mail: secretary2@swiss-stamps.org

Tannu Tuva Collectors Society
Ken R. Simon
P.O. Box 385
Lake Worth FL 33460-0385
Ph: (561) 588-5954
www.tuva.tk
E-mail: yurttuva@yahoo.com

Society for Thai Philately
H. R. Blakeney
P.O. Box 25644
Oklahoma City OK 73125
E-mail: HRBlakeney@aol.com

Transvaal Study Circle
Chris Board
36 Wakefield Gardens
London, SE19 2NR
UNITED KINGDOM
www.transvaalstamps.org.uk
E-mail: c.board@macace.net

Ottoman and Near East Philatelic Society (Turkey and related areas)
Bob Stuchell
193 Valley Stream Lane
Wayne PA 19087
www.oneps.org
E-mail: rstuchell@msn.com

Ukrainian Philatelic & Numismatic Society
Martin B. Tatuch
5117 8th Road N.
Arlington VA 22205-1201
www.upns.org
E-mail: treasurer@upns.org

Vatican Philatelic Society
Sal Quinonez
1 Aldersgate, Apt. 1002
Riverhead NY 11901-1830
Ph: (516) 727-6426
www.vaticanphilately.org

British Virgin Islands Philatelic Society
Giorgio Migliavacca
P.O. Box 7007
St. Thomas VI 00801-0007
www.islandsun.com/category/collectables/
E-mail: issun@candwbvi.net

West Africa Study Circle
Martin Bratzel
1233 Virginia Ave.
Windsor, ON, N8S 2Z1
CANADA
www.wasc.org.uk
E-mail: marty_bratzel@yahoo.ca

Western Australia Study Group
Brian Pope
P.O. Box 423
Claremont, Western Australia, 6910
AUSTRALIA
www.wastudygroup.com
E-mail: black5swan@yahoo.com.au

Yugoslavia Study Group of the Croatian Philatelic Society
Michael Lenard
1514 N. Third Ave.
Wausau WI 54401
Ph: (715) 675-2833
E-mail: mjlenard@aol.com

Topical Groups

Americana Unit
Dennis Dengel
17 Peckham Road
Poughkeepsie NY 12603-2018
www.americanaunit.org
E-mail: ddengel@americanaunit.org

Astronomy Study Unit
John Budd
728 Sugar Camp Way
Brooksville FL 34604
Ph: (352) 345-4799
www.astronomystudyunit.net
E-mail: jwgbudd@gmail.com

Bicycle Stamps Club
Steve Andreasen
2000 Alaskan Way, Unit 157
Seattle WA 98121
E-mail: steven.w.andreasen@gmail.com

Biology Unit
Alan Hanks
34 Seaton Drive
Aurora, ON, L4G 2K1
CANADA
Ph: (905) 727-6993

Bird Stamp Society
S. A. H. (Tony) Statham
Ashlyns Lodge, Chesham Road,
Berkhamsted, Hertfordshire HP4 2ST
UNITED KINGDOM
www.bird-stamps.org/bss
E-mail: tony.statham@sky.com

Captain Cook Society
Jerry Yucht
8427 Leale Ave.
Stockton CA 95212
www.captaincooksociety.com
E-mail: US@captaincooksociety.com

The CartoPhilatelic Society
Marybeth Sulkowski
2885 Sanford Ave, SW, #32361
Grandville MI 49418-1342
www.mapsonstamps.org
E-mail: secretary@mapsonstamps.org

Casey Jones Railroad Unit
Jeff Lough
2612 Redbud Lane, Apt. C
Lawrence KS 66046
www.uqp.de/cjr/index.htm
E-mail: jeffydplaugh@gmail.com

Cats on Stamps Study Unit
Robert D. Jarvis
2731 Teton Lane
Fairfield CA 94533
www.catstamps.info
E-mail: bobmarci@aol.com

Chemistry & Physics on Stamps Study Unit
Dr. Roland Hirsch
20458 Water Point Lane
Germantown MD 20874
www.cpossu.org
E-mail: rfhirsch@cpossu.org

Chess on Stamps Study Unit
Ray C. Alexis
608 Emery St.
Longmont CO 80501
E-mail: chessstuff911459@aol.com

Christmas Philatelic Club
Jim Balog
P.O. Box 744
Geneva OH 44041
www.christmasphilatelicclub.org
E-mail: jpb4stamps@windstream.net

Cricket Philatelic Society
A. Melville-Brown, President
11 Weppons, Ravens Road
Shoreham-by-Sea
West Sussex, BN43 5AW
UNITED KINGDOM
www.cricketstamp.net
E-mail: mel.cricket.100@googlemail.com

Dogs on Stamps Study Unit
Morris Raskin
202A Newport Road
Monroe Township NJ 08831
Ph: (609) 655-7411
www.dossu.org
E-mail: mraskin@cellurian.com

Earth's Physical Features Study Group
Fred Klein
515 Magdalena Ave.
Los Altos CA 94024
epfsu.jeffhayward.com

Ebony Society of Philatelic Events and Reflections, Inc. (African-American topicals)
Manuel Gilyard
800 Riverside Drive, Suite 4H
New York NY 10032-7412
www.esperstamps.org
E-mail: gilyardmani@aol.com

Europa Study Unit
Tonny E. Van Loij
3002 S. Xanthia St.
Denver CO 80231-4237
Ph: (303) 752-0189
www.europastudyunit.org
E-mail: tvanloij@gmail.com

Fine & Performing Arts
Deborah L. Washington
6922 S. Jeffery Blvd., #7 - North
Chicago IL 60649
E-mail: brasslady@comcast.net

Fire Service in Philately
John Zaranek
81 Hillpine Road
Cheektowaga NY 14227-2259
Ph: (716) 668-3352
E-mail: jczaranek@roadrunner.com

Gay & Lesbian History on Stamps Club
Joe Petronie
P.O. Box 190842
Dallas TX 75219-0842
www.facebook.com/glhsc
E-mail: glhsc@aol.com

Gems, Minerals & Jewelry Study Unit
Mrs. Gilberte Proteau
138 Lafontaine
Beloeil QC J3G 2G7
CANADA
Ph: (978) 851-8283
E-mail: gilberte.ferland@sympatico.ca

Graphics Philately Association
Mark H. Winnegrad
P.O. Box 380
Bronx NY 10462-0380
www.graphics-stamps.org
E-mail: indybrucel@yahoo.com

Journalists, Authors & Poets on Stamps
Clete Delvaux
800 East River Drive
De Pere WI 54115
E-mail: cdelvaux@msn.com

Lighthouse Stamp Society
Dalene Thomas
1805 S Balsam St., #106
Lakewood CO 80232
Ph: (303) 986-6620
www.lighthousestampsociety.org
E-mail: dalene@lighthousestampsociety.org

Lions International Stamp Club
John Bargus
108-2777 Barry Road RR 2
Mill Bay, BC, V0R 2P2
CANADA
Ph: (250) 743-5782

Mahatma Gandhi On Stamps Study Circle
Pramod Shivagunde
Pratik Clinic, Akluj
Solapur, Maharashtra, 413101
INDIA
E-mail: drnanda@bom6.vsnl.net.in

Masonic Study Unit
Gene Fricks
25 Murray Way
Blackwood NJ 08012-4400
E-mail: genefricks@comcast.net

Mathematical Study Unit
Monty Strauss
4209 88th St.
Lubbock TX 79423-2941
www.mathstamps.org
E-mail: montystrauss@gmail.com

Medical Subjects Unit
Dr. Frederick C. Skvara
P.O. Box 6228
Bridgewater NJ 08807
E-mail: fcskvara@optonline.net

Military Postal History Society
Ed Dubin
1 S. Wacker Drive, Suite 3500
Chicago IL 60606
www.militaryPHS.org
E-mail: dubine@comcast.net

Mourning Stamps and Covers Club
James Camak, Jr.
3801 Acapulco Ct.
Irving TX 75062
www.mscc.ms
E-mail: jamescamak7@gmail.com

Napoleonic Age Philatelists
Ken Berry
4117 NW 146th St.
Oklahoma City OK 73134-1746
Ph: (405) 748-8646
www.nap-stamps.org
E-mail: krb4117@att.net

Old World Archeological Study Unit
Caroline Scannell
11 Dawn Drive
Smithtown NY 11787-1761
www.owasu.org
E-mail: editor@owasu.org

Petroleum Philatelic Society International
Feitze Papa
922 Meander Dr.
Walnut Creek CA 94598-4239
E-mail: oildad@astound.net

Rotary on Stamps Unit
Gerald L. Fitzsimmons
105 Calle Ricardo
Victoria TX 77904
rotaryonstamps.org
E-mail: glfitz@suddenlink.net

Scouts on Stamps Society International
Woodrow (Woody) Brooks
498 Baldwin Road
Akron OH 44312
Ph: (330) 612-1294
www.sossi.org
E-mail: rfrank@sossi.org

Ships on Stamps Unit
Les Smith
302 Conklin Ave.
Penticton, BC, V2A 2T4
CANADA
Ph: (250) 493-7486
www.shipsonstamps.org
E-mail: lessmith440@shaw.ca

Space Unit
David Blog
P.O. Box 174
Bergenfield NJ 07621
www.space-unit.com
E-mail: davidblognj@gmail.com

Sports Philatelists International
Mark Maestrone
2824 Curie Place
San Diego CA 92122-4110
www.sportstamps.org
Email: president@sportstamps.org

Stamps on Stamps Collectors Club
Alf Jordan
156 W. Elm St.
Yarmouth ME 04096
www.stampsonstamps.org
E-mail: ajordan1@maine.rr.com

Windmill Study Unit
Walter J. Hollien
607 N. Porter St.
Watkins Glenn NY 14891-1345
Ph: (607) 229-3541
www.windmillworld.com
E-mail: whollien@earthlink.net

Wine On Stamps Study Unit
David Wolfersberger
768 Chain Ridge Road
St. Louis MO 63122-3259
Ph: (314) 961-5032
www.wine-on-stamps.org
E-mail: dewolf2@swbell.net

Women on Stamps Study Unit
Hugh Gottfried
2232 26th St.
Santa Monica CA 90405-1902
E-mail: hgottfried@adelphia.net

Expertizing Services

The following organizations will, for a fee, provide expert opinions about stamps submitted to them. Collectors should contact these organizations to find out about their fees and requirements before submiting philatelic material to them. The listing of these groups here is not intended as an endorsement by Amos Media Co.

General Expertizing Services

American Philatelic Expertizing Service (a service of the American Philatelic Society)
100 Match Factory Place
Bellefonte PA 16823-1367
Ph: (814) 237-3803
Fax: (814) 237-6128
www.stamps.org
E-mail: twhorn@stamps.org
Areas of Expertise: Worldwide

B. P. A. Expertising, Ltd.
P.O. Box 1141
Guildford, Surrey, GU5 0WR
UNITED KINGDOM
E-mail: sec@bpaexpertising.org
Areas of Expertise: British Commonwealth, Great Britain, Classics of Europe, South America and the Far East

Philatelic Foundation
22 E. 35th St., 4th Floor
New York NY 10016
Ph: (212) 221-6555
Fax: (212) 221-6208
www.philatelicfoundation.org
E-mail: philatelicfoundation@verizon.net
Areas of Expertise: U.S. & Worldwide

Philatelic Stamp Authentication and Grading, Inc.
P.O. Box 41-0880
Melbourne FL 32941-0880
Customer Service: (305) 345-9864
www.psaginc.com
E-mail: info@psaginc.com
Areas of Expertise: U.S., Canal Zone, Hawaii, Philippines, Canada & Provinces

Professional Stamp Experts
P.O. Box 539309
Henderson NV 89053-9309
Ph: (702) 776-6522
www.gradingmatters.com
www.psestamp.com
E-mail: info@gradingmatters.com
Areas of Expertise: Stamps and covers of U.S., U.S. Possessions, British Commonwealth

Royal Philatelic Society Expert Committee
41 Devonshire Place
London, W1N 1PE
UNITED KINGDOM
www.rpsl.org.uk/experts.html
E-mail: experts@rpsl.org.uk
Areas of Expertise: Worldwide

Expertizing Services Covering Specific Fields or Countries

China Stamp Society Expertizing Service
1050 W. Blue Ridge Blvd.
Kansas City MO 64145
Ph: (816) 942-6300
E-mail: hjmesq@aol.com
Areas of Expertise: China

Confederate Stamp Alliance Authentication Service
Gen. Frank Crown, Jr.
P.O. Box 278
Capshaw AL 35742-0396
Ph: (302) 422-2656
Fax: (302) 424-1990
www.csalliance.org
E-mail: csaas@knology.net
Areas of Expertise: Confederate stamps and postal history

Errors, Freaks and Oddities Collectors Club Expertizing Service
138 East Lakemont Drive
Kingsland GA 31548
Ph: (912) 729-1573
Areas of Expertise: U.S. errors, freaks and oddities

Estonian Philatelic Society Expertizing Service
39 Clafford Lane
Melville NY 11747
Ph: (516) 421-2078
E-mail: esto4@aol.com
Areas of Expertise: Estonia

Hawaiian Philatelic Society Expertizing Service
P.O. Box 10115
Honolulu HI 96816-0115
Areas of Expertise: Hawaii

Hong Kong Stamp Society Expertizing Service
P.O. Box 206
Glenside PA 19038
Fax: (215) 576-6850
Areas of Expertise: Hong Kong

International Association of Philatelic Experts United States Associate members:

Paul Buchsbayew
119 W. 57th St.
New York NY 10019
Ph: (212) 977-7734
Fax: (212) 977-8653
Areas of Expertise: Russia, Soviet Union

William T. Crowe
P.O. Box 2090
Danbury CT 06813-2090
E-mail: wtcrowe@aol.com
Areas of Expertise: United States

John Lievsay
(see American Philatelic Expertizing Service and Philatelic Foundation)
Areas of Expertise: France

Robert W. Lyman
P.O. Box 348
Irvington on Hudson NY 10533
Ph and Fax: (914) 591-6937
Areas of Expertise: British North America, New Zealand

Robert Odenweller
P.O. Box 401
Bernardsville NJ 07924-0401
Ph and Fax: (908) 766-5460
Areas of Expertise: New Zealand, Samoa to 1900

Sergio Sismondo
The Regency Tower, Suite 1109
770 James Street
Syracuse NY 13203
Ph: (315) 422-2331
Fax: (315) 422-2956
Areas of Expertise: British East Africa, Cameroons, Cape of Good Hope, Canada, British North America

International Society for Japanese Philately Expertizing Committee
132 North Pine Terrace
Staten Island NY 10312-4052
Ph: (718) 227-5229
Areas of Expertise: Japan and related areas, except WWII Japanese Occupation issues

International Society for Portuguese Philately Expertizing Service
P.O. Box 43146
Philadelphia PA 19129-3146
Ph and Fax: (215) 843-2106
E-mail: s.s.washburne@worldnet.att.net
Areas of Expertise: Portugal and Colonies

Mexico-Elmhurst Philatelic Society International Expert Committee
Expert Committee Administrator
Marc E. Gonzales
P.O. Box 29040
Denver CO 80229-0040
www.mepsi.org/expertization
Areas of Expertise: Mexico

Ukrainian Philatelic & Numismatic Society Expertizing Service
30552 Dell Lane
Warren MI 48092-1862
Areas of Expertise: Ukraine, Western Ukraine

V. G. Greene Philatelic Research Foundation
P.O. Box 204, Station Q
Toronto, ON, M4T 2M1
CANADA
Ph: (416) 921-2073
Fax: (416) 921-1282
www.greenefoundation.ca
E-mail: vggfoundation@on.aibn.com
Areas of Expertise: British North America

Information on Catalogue Values, Grade and Condition

Catalogue Value

The Scott Catalogue value is a retail value; that is, an amount you could expect to pay for a stamp in the grade of Very Fine with no faults. Any exceptions to the grade valued will be noted in the text. The general introduction on the following pages and the individual section introductions further explain the type of material that is valued. The value listed for any given stamp is a reference that reflects recent actual dealer selling prices for that item.

Dealer retail price lists, public auction results, published prices in advertising and individual solicitation of retail prices from dealers, collectors and specialty organizations have been used in establishing the values found in this catalogue. Amos Media Co. values stamps, but Amos Media is not a company engaged in the business of buying and selling stamps as a dealer.

Use this catalogue as a guide for buying and selling. The actual price you pay for a stamp may be higher or lower than the catalogue value because of many different factors, including the amount of personal service a dealer offers, or increased or decreased interest in the country or topic represented by a stamp or set. An item may occasionally be offered at a lower price as a "loss leader," or as part of a special sale. You also may obtain an item inexpensively at public auction because of little interest at that time or as part of a large lot.

Stamps that are of a lesser grade than Very Fine, or those with condition problems, generally trade at lower prices than those given in this catalogue. Stamps of exceptional quality in both grade and condition often command higher prices than those listed.

Values for pre-1900 unused issues are for stamps with approximately half or more of their original gum. Stamps with most or all of their original gum may be expected to sell for more, and stamps with less than half of their original gum may be expected to sell for somewhat less than the values listed. On rarer stamps, it may be expected that the original gum will be somewhat more disturbed than it will be on more common issues. Post-1900 unused issues are assumed to have full original gum. From breakpoints in most countries' listings, stamps are valued as never hinged, due to the wide availability of stamps in that condition. These notations are prominently placed in the listings and in the country information preceding the listings. Some countries also feature listings with dual values for hinged and never-hinged stamps.

Grade

A stamp's grade and condition are crucial to its value. The accompanying illustrations show examples of Very Fine stamps from different time periods, along with examples of stamps in Fine to Very Fine and Extremely Fine grades as points of reference. When a stamp seller offers a stamp in any grade from fine to superb without further qualifying statements, that stamp should not only have the centering grade as defined, but it also should be free of faults or other condition problems.

FINE stamps (illustrations not shown) have designs that are quite off center, with the perforations on one or two sides very close to the design but not quite touching it. There is white space between the perforations and the design that is minimal but evident to the unaided eye. Imperforate stamps may have small margins, and earlier issues may show the design just touching one edge of the stamp design. Very early perforated issues normally will have the perforations slightly cutting into the design. Used stamps may have heavier than usual cancellations.

FINE-VERY FINE stamps will be somewhat off center on one side, or slightly off center on two sides. Imperforate stamps will have two margins of at least normal size, and the design will not touch any edge. For perforated stamps, the perfs are well clear of the design, but are still noticeably off center. *However, early issues of a country may be printed in such a way that the design naturally is very close to the edges. In these cases, the perforations may cut into the design very slightly.* Used stamps will not have a cancellation that detracts from the design.

VERY FINE stamps will be just slightly off center on one or two sides, but the design will be well clear of the edge. The stamp will present a nice, balanced appearance. Imperforate stamps will be well centered within normal-sized margins. *However, early issues of many countries may be printed in such a way that the perforations may touch the design on one or more sides. Where this is the case, a boxed note will be found defining the centering and margins of the stamps being valued.* Used stamps will have light or otherwise neat cancellations. This is the grade used to establish Scott Catalogue values.

EXTREMELY FINE stamps are close to being perfectly centered. Imperforate stamps will have even margins that are slightly larger than normal. Even the earliest perforated issues will have perforations clear of the design on all sides.

Amos Media Co. recognizes that there is no formally enforced grading scheme for postage stamps, and that the final price you pay or obtain for a stamp will be determined by individual agreement at the time of transaction.

Condition

Grade addresses only centering and (for used stamps) cancellation. *Condition* refers to factors other than grade that affect a stamp's desirability.

Factors that can increase the value of a stamp include exceptionally wide margins, particularly fresh color, the presence of selvage, and plate or die varieties. Unusual cancels on used stamps (particularly those of the 19th century) can greatly enhance their value as well.

Factors other than faults that decrease the value of a stamp include loss of original gum, regumming, a hinge remnant or foreign object adhering to the gum, natural inclusions, straight edges, and markings or notations applied by collectors or dealers.

Faults include missing pieces, tears, pin or other holes, surface scuffs, thin spots, creases, toning, short or pulled perforations, clipped perforations, oxidation or other forms of color changelings, soiling, stains, and such man-made changes as reperforations or the chemical removal or lightening of a cancellation.

Grading Illustrations

On the following two pages are illustrations of various stamps from countries appearing in this volume. These stamps are arranged by country, and they represent early or important issues that are often found in widely different grades in the marketplace. The editors believe the illustrations will prove useful in showing the margin size and centering that will be seen on the various issues.

In addition to the matters of margin size and centering, collectors are reminded that the very fine stamps valued in the Scott catalogues also will possess fresh color and intact perforations, and they will be free from defects.

Examples shown are computer-manipulated images made from single digitized master illustrations.

Stamp Illustrations Used in the Catalogue

It is important to note that the stamp images used for identification purposes in this catlaogue may not be indicative of the grade of stamp being valued. Refer to the written discussion of grades on this page and to the grading illustrations on the following two pages for grading information.

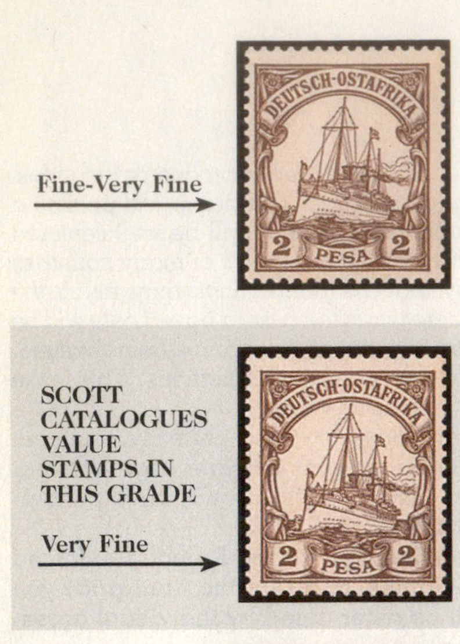

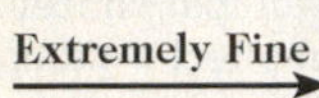

Fine-Very Fine →

SCOTT CATALOGUES VALUE STAMPS IN THIS GRADE

Very Fine →

Extremely Fine →

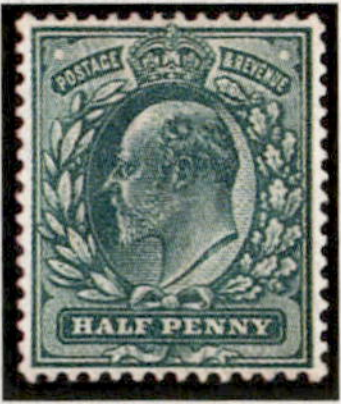

SCOTT CATALOGUES VALUE STAMPS IN THIS GRADE

Very Fine

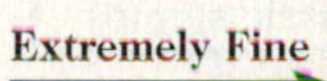

Fine-Very Fine

SCOTT CATALOGUES VALUE STAMPS IN THIS GRADE

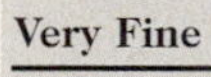

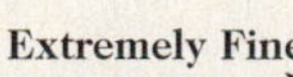

For purposes of helping to determine the gum condition and value of an unused stamp, Scott presents the following chart which details different gum conditions and indicates how the conditions correlate with the Scott values for unused stamps. Used together, the Illustrated Grading Chart on the previous pages and this Illustrated Gum Chart should allow catalogue users to better understand the grade and gum condition of stamps valued in the Scott catalogues.

Gum Categories:	MINT N.H.	ORIGINAL GUM (O.G.)				NO GUM
	Mint Never Hinged *Free from any disturbance*	 **Lightly Hinged** *Faint impression of a removed hinge over a small area*	 **Hinge Mark or Remnant** *Prominent hinged spot with part or all of the hinge remaining*	**Large part o.g.** *Approximately half or more of the gum intact*	**Small part o.g.** *Approximately less than half of the gum intact*	**No gum** *Only if issued with gum*
Commonly Used Symbol:	★★	★	★	★	★	(★)
Pre-1900 Issues (Pre-1881 for U.S.)	*Very fine pre-1900 stamps in these categories trade at a premium over Scott value*			Scott Value for "Unused"		Scott "No Gum" listings for selected unused classic stamps
From 1900 to breakpoints for listings of never-hinged stamps	Scott "Never Hinged" listings for selected unused stamps	Scott Value for "Unused" (Actual value will be affected by the degree of hinging of the full o.g.)				
From breakpoints noted for many countries	Scott Value for "Unused"					

Never Hinged (NH; ★★): A never-hinged stamp will have full original gum that will have no hinge mark or disturbance. The presence of an expertizer's mark does not disqualify a stamp from this designation.

Original Gum (OG; ★): Pre-1900 stamps should have approximately half or more of their original gum. On rarer stamps, it may be expected that the original gum will be somewhat more disturbed than it will be on more common issues. Post-1900 stamps should have full original gum. Original gum will show some disturbance caused by a previous hinge(s) which may be present or entirely removed. The actual value of a post-1900 stamp will be affected by the degree of hinging of the full original gum.

Disturbed Original Gum: Gum showing noticeable effects of humidity, climate or hinging over more than half of the gum. The significance of gum disturbance in valuing a stamp in any of the Original Gum categories depends on the degree of disturbance, the rarity and normal gum condition of the issue and other variables affecting quality.

Regummed (RG; (★)): A regummed stamp is a stamp without gum that has had some type of gum privately applied at a time after it was issued. This normally is done to deceive collectors and/or dealers into thinking that the stamp has original gum and therefore has a higher value. A regummed stamp is considered the same as a stamp with none of its original gum for purposes of grading.

Catalogue Listing Policy

It is the intent of Amos Media Co. to list all postage stamps of the world in the *Scott Standard Postage Stamp Catalogue*. The only strict criteria for listing is that stamps be decreed legal for postage by the issuing country and that the issuing country actually have an operating postal system. Whether the primary intent of issuing a given stamp or set was for sale to postal patrons or to stamp collectors is not part of our listing criteria. Scott's role is to provide basic comprehensive postage stamp information. It is up to each stamp collector to choose which items to include in a collection.

It is Scott's objective to seek reasons why a stamp should be listed, rather than why it should not. Nevertheless, there are certain types of items that will not be listed. These include the following:

1. Unissued items that are not officially distributed or released by the issuing postal authority. If such items are officially issued at a later date by the country, they will be listed. Unissued items consist of those that have been printed and then held from sale for reasons such as change in government, errors found on stamps or something deemed objectionable about a stamp subject or design.

2. Stamps "issued" by non-existent postal entities or fantasy countries, such as Nagaland, Occusi-Ambeno, Staffa, Sedang, Torres Straits and others. Also, stamps "issued" in the names of legitimate, stamp-issuing countries that are not authorized by those countries.

3. Semi-official or unofficial items not required for postage. Examples include items issued by private agencies for their own express services. When such items are required for delivery, or are valid as prepayment of postage, they are listed.

4. Local stamps issued for local use only. Postage stamps issued by governments specifically for "domestic" use, such as Haiti Scott 219-228, or the United States non-denominated stamps, are not considered to be locals, since they are valid for postage throughout the country of origin.

5. Items not valid for postal use. For example, a few countries have issued souvenir sheets that are not valid for postage. This area also includes a number of worldwide charity labels (some denominated) that do not pay postage.

6. Egregiously exploitative issues such as stamps sold for far more than face value, stamps purposefully issued in artificially small quantities or only against advance orders, stamps awarded only to a selected audience such as a philatelic bureau's standing order customers, or stamps sold only in conjunction with other products. All of these kinds of items are usually controlled issues and/or are intended for speculation. These items normally will be included in a footnote.

7. Items distributed by the issuing government only to a limited group, club, philatelic exhibition or a single stamp dealer or other private company. These items normally will be included in a footnote.

8. Stamps not available to collectors. These generally are rare items, all of which are held by public institutions such as museums. The existence of such items often will be cited in footnotes.

The fact that a stamp has been used successfully as postage, even on international mail, is not in itself sufficient proof that it was legitimately issued. Numerous examples of so-called stamps from non-existent countries are known to have been used to post letters that have successfully passed through the international mail system.

There are certain items that are subject to interpretation. When a stamp falls outside our specifications, it may be listed along with a cautionary footnote.

A number of factors are considered in our approach to analyzing how a stamp is listed. The following list of factors is presented to share with you, the catalogue user, the complexity of the listing process.

Additional printings — "Additional printings" of a previously issued stamp may range from an item that is totally different to cases where it is impossible to differentiate from the original. At least a minor number (a small-letter suffix) is assigned if there is a distinct change in stamp shade, noticeably redrawn design, or a significantly different perforation measurement. A major number (numeral or numeral and capital-letter combination) is assigned if the editors feel the "additional printing" is sufficiently different from the original that it constitutes a different issue.

Commemoratives — Where practical, commemoratives with the same theme are placed in a set. For example, the U.S. Civil War Centennial set of 1961-65 and the Constitution Bicentennial series of 1989-90 appear as sets. Countries such as Japan and Korea issue such material on a regular basis, with an announced, or at least predictable, number of stamps known in advance. Occasionally, however, stamp sets that were released over a period of years have been separated. Appropriately placed footnotes will guide you to each set's continuation.

Definitive sets — Blocks of numbers generally have been reserved for definitive sets, based on previous experience with any given country. If a few more stamps were issued in a set than originally expected, they often have been inserted into the original set with a capital-letter suffix, such as U.S. Scott 1059A. If it appears that many more stamps than the originally allotted block will be released before the set is completed, a new block of numbers will be reserved, with the original one being closed off. In some cases, such as the U.S. Transportation and Great Americans series, several blocks of numbers exist. Appropriately placed footnotes will guide you to each set's continuation.

New country — Membership in the Universal Postal Union is not a consideration for listing status or order of placement within the catalogue. The index will tell you in what volume or page number the listings begin.

"No release date" items — The amount of information available for any given stamp issue varies greatly from country to country and even from time to time. Extremely comprehensive information about new stamps is available from some countries well before the stamps are released. By contrast some countries do not provide information about stamps or release dates. Most countries, however, fall between these extremes. A country may provide denominations or subjects of stamps from upcoming issues that are not issued as planned. Sometimes, philatelic agencies, those private firms hired to represent countries, add these later-issued items to sets well after the formal release date. This time period can range from weeks to years. If these items were officially released by the country, they will be added to the appropriate spot in the set. In many cases, the specific release date of a stamp or set of stamps may never be known.

Overprints — The color of an overprint is always noted if it is other than black. Where more than one color of ink has been used on overprints of a single set, the color used is noted. Early overprint and surcharge illustrations were altered to prevent their use by forgers.

Personalized Stamps — Since 1999, the special service of personalizing stamp vignettes, or labels attached to stamps, has been offered to customers by postal administrations of many countries. Sheets of these stamps are sold, singly or in quantity, only through special orders made by mail, in person, or through a sale on a computer website with the postal administrations or their agents for which an extra fee is charged, though some countries offer to collectors at face value personalized stamps having generic images in the vignettes or on the attached labels. It is impossible for any catalogue to know what images have been chosen by customers. Images can be 1) owned or created by the customer, 2) a generic image, or 3) an image pulled from a library of stock images on the stamp creation website. It is also impossible to know the quantity printed for any stamp having a particular image. So from a valuing standpoint, any image is equivalent to any other image for any personalized stamp having the same catalogue number. Illustrations of personalized stamps in the catalogue are not always those of stamps having generic images.

Personalized items are listed with some exceptions. These include:

1. Stamps or sheets that have attached labels that the customer cannot personalize, but which are nonetheless marketed as "personalized," and are sold for far more than the franking value.
2. Stamps or sheets that can be personalized by the customer, but where a portion of the print run must be ceded to the issuing country for sale to other customers.
3. Stamps or sheets that are created exclusively for a particular commercial client, or clients, including stamps that differ from any similar stamp that has been made available to the public.
4. Stamps or sheets that are deliberately conceived by the issuing authority that have been, or are likely to be, created with an excessive number of different face values, sizes, or other features that are changeable.
5. Stamps or sheets that are created by postal administrations using the same system of stamp personalization that has been put in place for use by the public that are printed in limited quantities and sold above face value.
6. Stamps or sheets that are created by licensees not directly affiliated or controlled by a postal administration.

Excluded items may or may not be footnoted.

Se-tenants — Connected stamps of differing features (se-tenants) will be listed in the format most commonly collected. This includes pairs, blocks or larger multiples. Se-tenant units are not always symmetrical. An example is Australia Scott 508, which is a block of seven stamps. If the stamps are primarily collected as a unit, the major number may be assigned to the multiple, with minors going to each component stamp. In cases where continuous-design or other unit se-tenants will receive significant postal use, each stamp is given a major Scott number listing. This includes issues from the United States, Canada, Germany and Great Britain, for example.

Understanding the Listings

On the opposite page is an enlarged "typical" listing from this catalogue. Below are detailed explanations of each of the highlighted parts of the listing.

1 Scott number — Scott catalogue numbers are used to identify specific items when buying, selling or trading stamps. Each listed postage stamp from every country has a unique Scott catalogue number. Therefore, Germany Scott 99, for example, can only refer to a single stamp. Although the Scott catalogue usually lists stamps in chronological order by date of issue, there are exceptions. When a country has issued a set of stamps over a period of time, those stamps within the set are kept together without regard to date of issue. This follows the normal collecting approach of keeping stamps in their natural sets.

When a country issues a set of stamps over a period of time, a group of consecutive catalogue numbers is reserved for the stamps in that set, as issued. If that group of numbers proves to be too few, capital-letter suffixes, such as "A" or "B," may be added to existing numbers to create enough catalogue numbers to cover all items in the set. A capital-letter suffix indicates a major Scott catalogue number listing. Scott generally uses a suffix letter only once. Therefore, a catalogue number listing with a capital-letter suffix will seldom be found with the same letter (lower case) used as a minor-letter listing. If there is a Scott 16A in a set, for example, there will seldom be a Scott 16a. However, a minor-letter "a" listing may be added to a major number containing an "A" suffix (Scott 16Aa, for example).

Suffix letters are cumulative. A minor "b" variety of Scott 16A would be Scott 16Ab, not Scott 16b.

There are times when a reserved block of Scott catalogue numbers is too large for a set, leaving some numbers unused. Such gaps in the numbering sequence also occur when the catalogue editors move an item's listing elsewhere or have removed it entirely from the catalogue. Scott does not attempt to account for every possible number, but rather attempts to assure that each stamp is assigned its own number.

Scott numbers designating regular postage normally are only numerals. Scott numbers for other types of stamps, such as air post, semi-postal, postal tax, postage due, occupation and others have a prefix consisting of one or more capital letters or a combination of numerals and capital letters.

2 Illustration number — Illustration or design-type numbers are used to identify each catalogue illustration. For most sets, the lowest face-value stamp is shown. It then serves as an example of the basic design approach for other stamps not illustrated. Where more than one stamp use the same illustration number, but have differences in design, the design paragraph or the description line clearly indicates the design on each stamp not illustrated. Where there are both vertical and horizontal designs in a set, a single illustration may be used, with the exceptions noted in the design paragraph or description line.

When an illustration is followed by a lower-case letter in parentheses, such as "A2(b)," the trailing letter indicates which overprint or surcharge illustration applies.

Illustrations normally are 70 percent of the original size of the stamp. Oversized stamps, blocks and souvenir sheets are reduced even more. Overprints and surcharges are shown at 100 percent of their original size if shown alone, but are 70 percent of original size if shown on stamps. In some cases, the illustration will be placed above the set, between listings or omitted completely. Overprint and surcharge illustrations are not placed in this catalogue for purposes of expertizing stamps.

3 Paper color — The color of a stamp's paper is noted in italic type when the paper used is not white.

4 Listing styles — There are two principal types of catalogue listings: major and minor.

Major listings are in a larger type style than minor listings. The catalogue number is a numeral that can be found with or without a capital-letter suffix, and with or without a prefix.

Minor listings are in a smaller type style and have a small-letter suffix or (if the listing immediately follows that of the major number) may show only the letter. These listings identify a variety of the major item. Examples include perforation and shade differences, multiples (some souvenir sheets, booklet panes and se-tenant combinations), and singles of multiples.

Examples of major number listings include 16, 28A, B97, C13A, 10N5, and 10N6A. Examples of minor numbers are 16a and C13Ab.

5 Basic information about a stamp or set — Introducing each stamp issue is a small section (usually a line listing) of basic information about a stamp or set. This section normally includes the date of issue, method of printing, perforation, watermark and, sometimes, some additional information of note. *Printing method, perforation and watermark apply to the following sets until a change is noted.* Stamps created by overprinting or surcharging previous issues are assumed to have the same perforation, watermark, printing method and other production characteristics as the original. Dates of issue are as precise as Scott is able to confirm and often reflect the dates on first-day covers, rather than the actual date of release.

6 Denomination — This normally refers to the face value of the stamp; that is, the cost of the unused stamp at the post office at the time of issue. When a denomination is shown in parentheses, it does not appear on the stamp. This includes the non-denominated stamps of the United States, Brazil and Great Britain, for example.

7 Color or other description — This area provides information to solidify identification of a stamp. In many recent cases, a description of the stamp design appears in this space, rather than a listing of colors.

8 Year of issue — In stamp sets that have been released in a period that spans more than a year, the number shown in parentheses is the year that stamp first appeared. Stamps without a date appeared during the first year of the issue. Dates are not always given for minor varieties.

9 Value unused and Value used — The Scott catalogue values are based on stamps that are in a grade of Very Fine unless stated otherwise. Unused values refer to items that have not seen postal, revenue or any other duty for which they were intended. Pre-1900 unused stamps that were issued with gum must have at least most of their original gum. Later issues are assumed to have full original gum. From breakpoints specified in most countries' listings, stamps are valued as never hinged. Stamps issued without gum are noted. Modern issues with PVA or other synthetic adhesives may appear ungummed. Unused self-adhesive stamps are valued as appearing undisturbed on their original backing paper. Values for used self-adhesive stamps are for examples either on piece or off piece. For a more detailed explanation of these values, please see the "Catalogue Value," "Condition" and "Understanding Valuing Notations" sections elsewhere in this introduction.

In some cases, where used stamps are more valuable than unused stamps, the value is for an example with a contemporaneous cancel, rather than a modern cancel or a smudge or other unclear marking. For those stamps that were released for postal and fiscal purposes, the used value represents a postally used stamp. Stamps with revenue cancels generally sell for less.

Stamps separated from a complete se-tenant multiple usually will be worth less than a pro-rated portion of the se-tenant multiple, and stamps lacking the attached labels that are noted in the listings will be worth less than the values shown.

10 Changes in basic set information — Bold type is used to show any changes in the basic data given for a set of stamps. These basic data categories include perforation gauge measurement, paper type, printing method and watermark.

11 Total value of a set — The total value of sets of three or more stamps issued after 1900 are shown. The set line also notes the range of Scott numbers and total number of stamps included in the grouping. The actual value of a set consisting predominantly of stamps having the minimum value of 25 cents may be less than the total value shown. Similarly, the actual value or catalogue value of se-tenant pairs or of blocks consisting of stamps having the minimum value of 25 cents may be less than the catalogue values of the component parts.

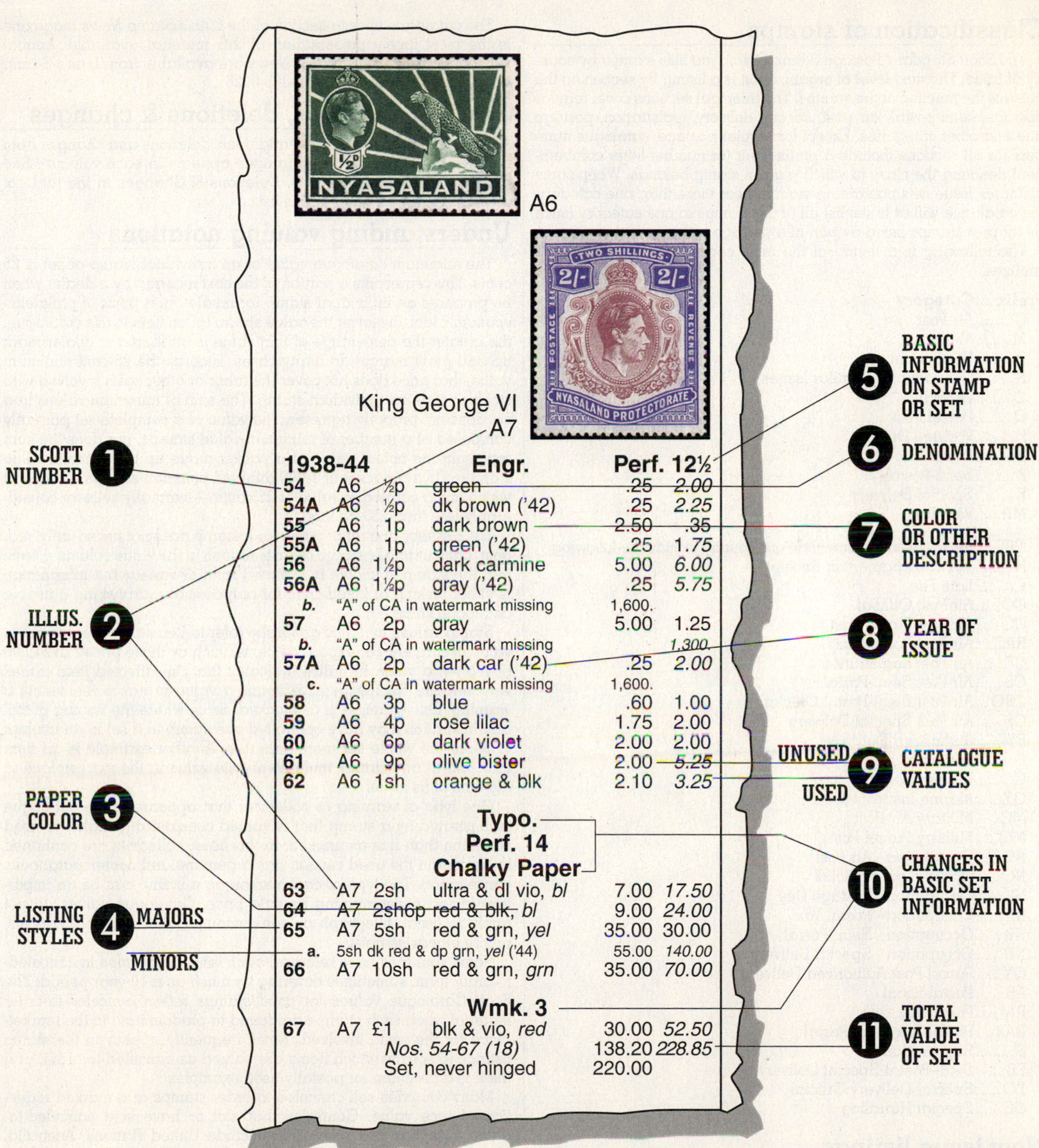
NYASALAND
A6
TWO SHILLINGS
2/- 2/-
POSTAGE
REVENUE
NYASALAND PROTECTORATE
King George VI
A7
1938-44 Engr. Perf. 12½
54 A6 ½p green .25 2.00
54A A6 ½p dk brown ('42) .25 2.25
55 A6 1p dark brown 2.50 .35
55A A6 1p green ('42) .25 1.75
56 A6 1½p dark carmine 5.00 6.00
56A A6 1½p gray ('42) .25 5.75
b. "A" of CA in watermark missing 1,600.
57 A6 2p gray 5.00 1.25
b. "A" of CA in watermark missing 1,300.
57A A6 2p dark car ('42) .25 2.00
c. "A" of CA in watermark missing 1,600.
58 A6 3p blue .60 1.00
59 A6 4p rose lilac 1.75 2.00
60 A6 6p dark violet 2.00 2.00
61 A6 9p olive bister 2.00 5.25
62 A6 1sh orange & blk 2.10 3.25
Typo.
Perf. 14
Chalky Paper
63 A7 2sh ultra & dl vio, bl 7.00 17.50
64 A7 2sh6p red & blk, bl 9.00 24.00
65 A7 5sh red & grn, yel 35.00 30.00
a. 5sh dk red & dp grn, yel ('44) 55.00 140.00
66 A7 10sh red & grn, grn 35.00 70.00
Wmk. 3
67 A7 £1 blk & vio, red 30.00 52.50
Nos. 54-67 (18) 138.20 228.85
Set, never hinged 220.00
SCOTT NUMBER 1
ILLUS. NUMBER 2
PAPER COLOR 3
LISTING STYLES 4 MAJORS
MINORS
5 BASIC INFORMATION ON STAMP OR SET
6 DENOMINATION
7 COLOR OR OTHER DESCRIPTION
8 YEAR OF ISSUE
UNUSED
USED
9 CATALOGUE VALUES
10 CHANGES IN BASIC SET INFORMATION
11 TOTAL VALUE OF SET

Special Notices

Classification of stamps

The *Scott Standard Postage Stamp Catalogue* lists stamps by country of issue. The next level of organization is a listing by section on the basis of the function of the stamps. The principal sections cover regular postage, semi-postal, air post, special delivery, registration, postage due and other categories. Except for regular postage, catalogue numbers for all sections include a prefix letter (or number-letter combination) denoting the class to which a given stamp belongs. When some countries issue sets containing stamps from more than one category, the catalogue will at times list all of the stamps in one category (such as air post stamps listed as part of a postage set).

The following is a listing of the most commonly used catalogue prefixes.

Prefix ....Category
C.........Air Post
M........Military
P.........Newspaper
N.........Occupation - Regular Issues
O........Official
Q........Parcel Post
J..........Postage Due
RA......Postal Tax
B.........Semi-Postal
E.........Special Delivery
MR......War Tax

Other prefixes used by more than one country include the following:
H.........Acknowledgment of Receipt
I..........Late Fee
CO......Air Post Official
CQ......Air Post Parcel Post
RAC....Air Post Postal Tax
CF......Air Post Registration
CB......Air Post Semi-Postal
CBO...Air Post Semi-Postal Official
CE......Air Post Special Delivery
EY.......Authorized Delivery
S.........Franchise
G........Insured Letter
GY......Marine Insurance
MC.....Military Air Post
MQ.....Military Parcel Post
NC......Occupation - Air Post
NO......Occupation - Official
NJ........Occupation - Postage Due
NRA....Occupation - Postal Tax
NB......Occupation - Semi-Postal
NE......Occupation - Special Delivery
QY......Parcel Post Authorized Delivery
AR......Postal-fiscal
RAJ.....Postal Tax Due
RAB....Postal Tax Semi-Postal
F.........Registration
EB.......Semi-Postal Special Delivery
EO......Special Delivery Official
QE......Special Handling

New issue listings

Updates to this catalogue appear each month in the *Linn's Stamp News* monthly magazine. Included in this update are additions to the listings of countries found in the *Scott Standard Postage Stamp Catalogue* and the *Specialized Catalogue of United States Stamps and Covers*, as well as corrections and updates to current editions of this catalogue.

From time to time there will be changes in the final listings of stamps from the *Linn's Stamp News* magazine to the next edition of the catalogue. This occurs as more information about certain stamps or sets becomes available.

The catalogue update section of the *Linn's Stamp News* magazine is the most timely presentation of this material available. Annual subscriptions to *Linn's Stamp News* are available from Linn's Stamp News, Box 926, Sidney, OH 45365-0926.

Number additions, deletions & changes

A listing of catalogue number additions, deletions and changes from the previous edition of the catalogue appears in each volume. See Catalogue Number Additions, Deletions & Changes in the table of contents for the location of this list.

Understanding valuing notations

The *minimum catalogue value* of an individual stamp or set is 25 cents. This represents a portion of the cost incurred by a dealer when he prepares an individual stamp for resale. As a point of philatelic-economic fact, the lower the value shown for an item in this catalogue, the greater the percentage of that value is attributed to dealer mark up and profit margin. In many cases, such as the 25-cent minimum value, that price does not cover the labor or other costs involved with stocking it as an individual stamp. The sum of minimum values in a set does not properly represent the value of a complete set primarily composed of a number of minimum-value stamps, nor does the sum represent the actual value of a packet made up of minimum-value stamps. Thus a packet of 1,000 different common stamps — each of which has a catalogue value of 25 cents — normally sells for considerably less than 250 dollars!

The *absence of a retail value* for a stamp does not necessarily suggest that a stamp is scarce or rare. A dash in the value column means that the stamp is known in a stated form or variety, but information is either lacking or insufficient for purposes of establishing a usable catalogue value.

Stamp values in *italics* generally refer to items that are difficult to value accurately. For expensive items, such as those priced at $1,000 or higher, a value in italics indicates that the affected item trades very seldom. For inexpensive items, a value in italics represents a warning. One example is a "blocked" issue where the issuing postal administration may have controlled one stamp in a set in an attempt to make the whole set more valuable. Another example is an item that sold at an extreme multiple of face value in the marketplace at the time of its issue.

One type of warning to collectors that appears in the catalogue is illustrated by a stamp that is valued considerably higher in used condition than it is as unused. In this case, collectors are cautioned to be certain the used version has a genuine and contemporaneous cancellation. The type of cancellation on a stamp can be an important factor in determining its sale price. Catalogue values do not apply to fiscal, telegraph or non-contemporaneous postal cancels, unless otherwise noted.

Some countries have released back issues of stamps in canceled-to-order form, sometimes covering as much as a 10-year period. The Scott Catalogue values for used stamps reflect canceled-to-order material when such stamps are found to predominate in the marketplace for the issue involved. Notes frequently appear in the stamp listings to specify which items are valued as canceled-to-order, or if there is a premium for postally used examples.

Many countries sell canceled-to-order stamps at a marked reduction of face value. Countries that sell or have sold canceled-to-order stamps at *full* face value include United Nations, Australia, Netherlands, France and Switzerland. It may be almost impossible to identify such stamps if the gum has been removed, because official government canceling devices are used. Postally used examples of these items on cover, however, are usually worth more than the canceled-to-order stamps with original gum.

Abbreviations

Scott uses a consistent set of abbreviations throughout this catalogue to conserve space, while still providing necessary information.

COLOR ABBREVIATIONS

amb.	amber	crim.	crimson	ol	olive
anil.	aniline	cr	cream	olvn.	olivine
ap	apple	dk	dark	org	orange
aqua	aquamarine	dl	dull	pck	peacock
az	azure	dp	deep	pnksh	pinkish
bis	bister	db	drab	Prus.	Prussian
bl	blue	emer	emerald	pur	purple
bld	blood	gldn.	golden	redsh	reddish
blk	black	grysh	grayish	res	reseda
bril	brilliant	grn	green	ros	rosine
brn	brown	grnsh	greenish	ryl	royal
brnsh	brownish	hel	heliotrope	sal	salmon
brnz.	bronze	hn	henna	saph	sapphire
brt	bright	ind	indigo	scar.	scarlet
brnt.	burnt	int	intense	sep	sepia
car	carmine	lav	lavender	sien.	sienna
cer	cerise	lem	lemon	sil	silver
chlky	chalky	lil	lilac	sl	slate
cham	chamois	lt	light	stl	steel
chnt.	chestnut	mag.	magenta	turq.	turquoise
choc	chocolate	man.	manila	ultra	ultramarine
chr	chrome	mar.	maroon	Ven.	Venetian
cit	citron	mv	mauve	ver	vermilion
cl	claret	multi	multicolored	vio	violet
cob.	cobalt	mlky	milky	yel	yellow
cop.	copper	myr.	myrtle	yelsh	yellowish

When no color is given for an overprint or surcharge, black is the color used. Abbreviations for colors used for overprints and surcharges include: "(B)" or "(Blk)," black; "(Bl)," blue; "(R)," red; and "(G)," green.

Additional abbreviations in this catalogue are shown below:

Adm.	Administration
AFL	American Federation of Labor
Anniv.	Anniversary
APS	American Philatelic Society
Assoc.	Association
ASSR.	Autonomous Soviet Socialist Republic
b.	Born
BEP	Bureau of Engraving and Printing
Bicent.	Bicentennial
Bklt.	Booklet
Brit	British
btwn.	Between
Bur.	Bureau
c. or ca.	Circa
Cat.	Catalogue
Cent.	Centennial, century, centenary
CIO	Congress of Industrial Organizations
Conf.	Conference
Cong.	Congress
Cpl.	Corporal
CTO	Canceled to order
d.	Died
Dbl.	Double
EDU	Earliest documented use
Engr.	Engraved
Exhib.	Exhibition
Expo.	Exposition
Fed.	Federation
GB	Great Britain
Gen.	General
GPO	General post office
Horiz.	Horizontal
Imperf.	Imperforate
Impt.	Imprint
Intl.	International
Invtd.	Inverted
L	Left
Lieut., lt.	Lieutenant
Litho.	Lithographed
LL	Lower left
LR	Lower right
mm	Millimeter
Ms.	Manuscript
Natl.	National
No.	Number
NY	New York
NYC	New York City
Ovpt.	Overprint
Ovptd.	Overprinted
P	Plate number
Perf.	Perforated, perforation
Phil.	Philatelic
Photo.	Photogravure
PO	Post office
Pr.	Pair
P.R.	Puerto Rico
Prec.	Precancel, precanceled
Pres.	President
PTT	Post, Telephone and Telegraph
R	Right
Rio	Rio de Janeiro
Sgt.	Sergeant
Soc.	Society
Souv.	Souvenir
SSR	Soviet Socialist Republic, see ASSR
St.	Saint, street
Surch.	Surcharge
Typo.	Typographed
UL	Upper left
Unwmkd.	Unwatermarked
UPU	Universal Postal Union
UR	Upper Right
US	United States
USPOD	United States Post Office Department
USSR	Union of Soviet Socialist Republics
Vert.	Vertical
VP	Vice president
Wmk.	Watermark
Wmkd.	Watermarked
WWI	World War I
WWII	World War II

Examination

Amos Media Co. will not comment upon the genuineness, grade or condition of stamps, because of the time and responsibility involved. Rather, there are several expertizing groups that undertake this work for both collectors and dealers. Neither will Amos Media Co. appraise or identify philatelic material. The company cannot take responsibility for unsolicited stamps or covers sent by individuals.

All letters, E-mails, etc. are read attentively, but they are not always answered due to time considerations.

How to order from your dealer

When ordering stamps from a dealer, it is not necessary to write the full description of a stamp as listed in this catalogue. All you need is the name of the country, the Scott catalogue number and whether the desired item is unused or used. For example, "Japan Scott 422 unused" is sufficient to identify the unused stamp of Japan listed as "422 A206 5y brown."

Basic Stamp Information

A stamp collector's knowledge of the combined elements that make a given stamp issue unique determines his or her ability to identify stamps. These elements include paper, watermark, method of separation, printing, design and gum. On the following pages each of these important areas is briefly described.

Paper

Paper is an organic material composed of a compacted weave of cellulose fibers and generally formed into sheets. Paper used to print stamps may be manufactured in sheets, or it may have been part of a large roll (called a web) before being cut to size. The fibers most often used to create paper on which stamps are printed include bark, wood, straw and certain grasses. In many cases, linen or cotton rags have been added for greater strength and durability. Grinding, bleaching, cooking and rinsing these raw fibers reduces them to a slushy pulp, referred to by paper makers as "stuff." Sizing and, sometimes, coloring matter is added to the pulp to make different types of finished paper.

After the stuff is prepared, it is poured onto sieve-like frames that allow the water to run off, while retaining the matted pulp. As fibers fall onto the screen and are held by gravity, they form a natural weave that will later hold the paper together. If the screen has metal bits that are formed into letters or images attached, it leaves slightly thinned areas on the paper. These are called watermarks.

When the stuff is almost dry, it is passed under pressure through smooth or engraved rollers - dandy rolls - or placed between cloth in a press to be flattened and dried.

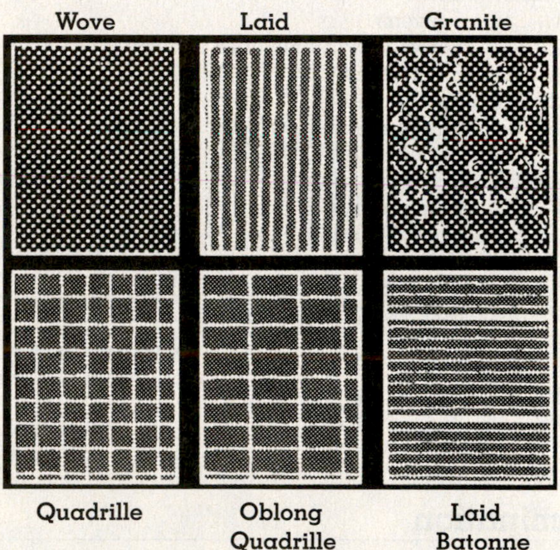

Stamp paper falls broadly into two types: wove and laid. The nature of the surface of the frame onto which the pulp is first deposited causes the differences in appearance between the two. If the surface is smooth and even, the paper will be of fairly uniform texture throughout. This is known as *wove paper*. Early papermaking machines poured the pulp onto a continuously circulating web of felt, but modern machines feed the pulp onto a cloth-like screen made of closely interwoven fine wires. This paper, when held to a light, will show little dots or points very close together. The proper name for this is "wire wove," but the type is still considered wove. Any U.S. or British stamp printed after 1880 will serve as an example of wire wove paper.

Closely spaced parallel wires, with cross wires at wider intervals, make up the frames used for what is known as *laid paper*. A greater thickness of the pulp will settle between the wires. The paper, when held to a light, will show alternate light and dark lines. The spacing and the thickness of the lines may vary, but on any one sheet of paper they are all alike. See Russia Scott 31-38 for examples of laid paper.

Batonne, from the French word meaning "a staff," is a term used if the lines in the paper are spaced quite far apart, like the printed ruling on a writing tablet. Batonne paper may be either wove or laid. If laid, fine laid lines can be seen between the batons.

Quadrille is the term used when the lines in the paper form little squares. *Oblong quadrille* is the term used when rectangles, rather than squares, are formed. Grid patterns vary from distinct to extremely faint. See Mexico-Guadalajara Scott 35-37 for examples of oblong quadrille paper.

Paper also is classified as thick or thin, hard or soft, and by color. Such colors may include yellowish, greenish, bluish and reddish.

Brief explanations of other types of paper used for printing stamps, as well as examples, follow.

Colored — Colored paper is created by the addition of dye in the paper-making process. Such colors may include shades of yellow, green, blue and red. *Surface-colored papers*, most commonly used for British colonial issues in 1913-14, are created when coloring is added only to the surface during the finishing process. Stamps printed on surface-colored paper have white or uncolored backs, while true colored papers are colored through. See Jamaica Scott 71-73.

Pelure — Pelure paper is a very thin, hard and often brittle paper that is sometimes bluish or grayish in appearance. See Serbia Scott 169-170.

Native — This is a term applied to handmade papers used to produce some of the early stamps of the Indian states. Stamps printed on native paper may be expected to display various natural inclusions that are normal and do not negatively affect value. Japanese paper, originally made of mulberry fibers and rice flour, is part of this group. See Japan Scott 1-18.

Manila — This type of paper is often used to make stamped envelopes and wrappers. It is a coarse-textured stock, usually smooth on one side and rough on the other. A variety of colors of manila paper exist, but the most common range is yellowish-brown.

Silk — Introduced by the British in 1847 as a safeguard against counterfeiting, silk paper contains bits of colored silk thread scattered throughout. The density of these fibers varies greatly and can include as few as one fiber per stamp or hundreds. U.S. revenue Scott R152 is a good example of an easy-to-identify silk paper stamp.

Silk-thread paper has uninterrupted threads of colored silk arranged so that one or more threads run through the stamp or postal stationery. See Great Britain Scott 5-6 and Switzerland Scott 14-19.

Granite — Filled with minute cloth or colored paper fibers of various colors and lengths, granite paper should not be confused with either type of silk paper. Austria Scott 172-175 and a number of Swiss stamps are examples of granite paper.

Chalky — A chalk-like substance coats the surface of chalky paper to discourage the cleaning and reuse of canceled stamps, as well as to provide a smoother, more acceptable printing surface. Because the designs of stamps printed on chalky paper are imprinted on what is often a water-soluble coating, any attempt to remove a cancellation will destroy the stamp. *Do not soak these stamps in any fluid.* To remove a stamp printed on chalky paper from an envelope, wet the paper from underneath the stamp until the gum dissolves enough to release the stamp from the paper. See St. Kitts-Nevis Scott 89-90 for examples of stamps printed on this type of chalky paper.

India — Another name for this paper, originally introduced from China about 1750, is "China Paper." It is a thin, opaque paper often used for plate and die proofs by many countries.

Double — In philately, the term double paper has two distinct meanings. The first is a two-ply paper, usually a combination of a thick and a thin sheet, joined during manufacture. This type was used experimentally as a means to discourage the reuse of stamps.

The design is printed on the thin paper. Any attempt to remove a cancellation would destroy the design. U.S. Scott 158 and other Banknote-era stamps exist on this form of double paper.

The second type of double paper occurs on a rotary press, when the end of one paper roll, or web, is affixed to the next roll to save time feeding the paper through the press. Stamp designs are printed over the joined paper and, if overlooked by inspectors, may get into post office stocks.

Goldbeater's Skin — This type of paper was used for the 1866 issue of Prussia, and was a tough, translucent paper. The design was printed in reverse on the back of the stamp, and the gum applied over the printing. It is impossible to remove stamps printed on this type of paper from the paper to which they are affixed without destroying the design.

Ribbed — Ribbed paper has an uneven, corrugated surface made by passing the paper through ridged rollers. This type exists on some copies of U.S. Scott 156-165.

Various other substances, or substrates, have been used for stamp manufacture, including wood, aluminum, copper, silver and gold foil, plastic, and silk and cotton fabrics.

Watermarks

Watermarks are an integral part of some papers. They are formed in the process of paper manufacture. Watermarks consist of small designs, formed of wire or cut from metal and soldered to the surface of the mold or, sometimes, on the dandy roll. The designs may be in the form of crowns, stars, anchors, letters or other characters or symbols. These pieces of metal - known in the paper-making industry as "bits" - impress a design into the paper. The design sometimes may be seen by holding the stamp to the light. Some are more easily seen with a watermark detector. This important tool is a small black tray into which a stamp is placed face down and dampened with a fast-evaporating watermark detection fluid that brings up the watermark image in the form of dark lines against a lighter background. These dark lines are the thinner areas of the paper known as the watermark. Some watermarks are extremely difficult to locate, due to either a faint impression, watermark location or the color of the stamp. There also are electric watermark detectors that come with plastic filter disks of various colors. The disks neutralize the color of the stamp, permitting the watermark to be seen more easily.

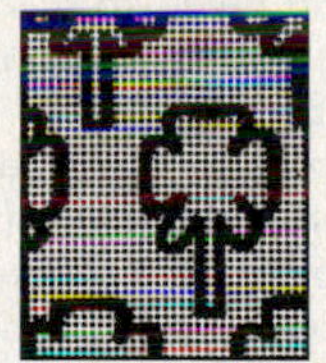

Multiple watermarks of Crown Agents and Burma

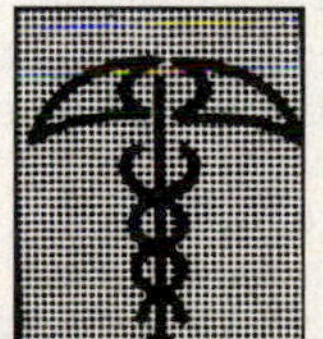
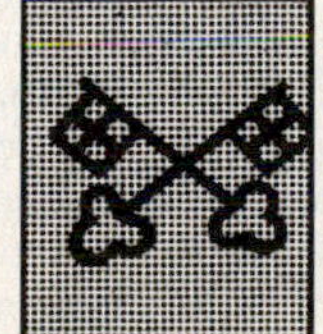
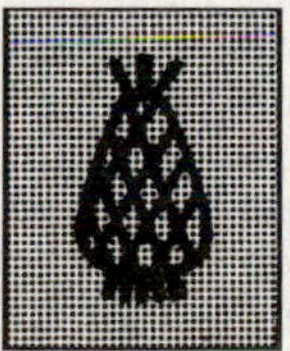

Watermarks of Uruguay, Vatican City and Jamaica

WARNING: Some inks used in the photogravure process dissolve in watermark fluids (Please see the section on Soluble Printing Inks). Also, see "chalky paper."

Watermarks may be found normal, reversed, inverted, reversed and inverted, sideways or diagonal, as seen from the back of the stamp. The relationship of watermark to stamp design depends on the position of the printing plates or how paper is fed through the press. On machine-made paper, watermarks normally are read from right to left. The design is repeated closely throughout the sheet in a "multiple-watermark design." In a "sheet watermark," the design appears only once on the sheet, but extends over many stamps. Individual stamps may carry only a small fraction or none of the watermark.

"Marginal watermarks" occur in the margins of sheets or panes of stamps. They occur on the outside border of paper (ostensibly outside the area where stamps are to be printed). A large row of letters may spell the name of the country or the manufacturer of the paper, or a border of lines may appear. Careless press feeding may cause parts of these letters and/or lines to show on stamps of the outer row of a pane.

Soluble Printing Inks

WARNING: Most stamp colors are permanent; that is, they are not seriously affected by short-term exposure to light or water. Many colors, especially of modern inks, fade from excessive exposure to light. There are stamps printed with inks that dissolve easily in water or in fluids used to detect watermarks. Use of these inks was intentional to prevent the removal of cancellations. Water affects all aniline inks, those on so-called safety paper and some photogravure printings - all such inks are known as fugitive colors. *Removal from paper of such stamps requires care and alternatives to traditional soaking.*

Separation

"Separation" is the general term used to describe methods used to separate stamps. The three standard forms currently in use are perforating, rouletting and die-cutting. These methods are done during the stamp production process, after printing. Sometimes these methods are done on-press or sometimes as a separate step. The earliest issues, such as the 1840 Penny Black of Great Britain (Scott 1), did not have any means provided for separation. It was expected the stamps would be cut apart with scissors or folded and torn. These are examples of imperforate stamps. Many stamps were first issued in imperforate formats and were later issued with perforations. Therefore, care must be observed in buying single imperforate stamps to be certain they were issued imperforate and are not perforated copies that have been altered by having the perforations trimmed away. Stamps issued imperforate usually are valued as singles. However, imperforate varieties of normally perforated stamps should be collected in pairs or larger pieces as indisputable evidence of their imperforate character.

PERFORATION

The chief style of separation of stamps, and the one that is in almost universal use today, is perforating. By this process, paper between the stamps is cut away in a line of holes, usually round, leaving little bridges of paper between the stamps to hold them together. Some types of perforation, such as hyphen-hole perfs, can be confused with roulettes, but a close visual inspection reveals that paper has been removed. The little perforation bridges, which project from the stamp when it is torn from the pane, are called the teeth of the perforation.

As the size of the perforation is sometimes the only way to differentiate between two otherwise identical stamps, it is necessary to be able to accurately measure and describe them. This is done with a perforation gauge, usually a ruler-like device that has dots or graduated lines to show how many perforations may be counted in the space of two centimeters. Two centimeters is the space universally adopted in which to measure perforations.

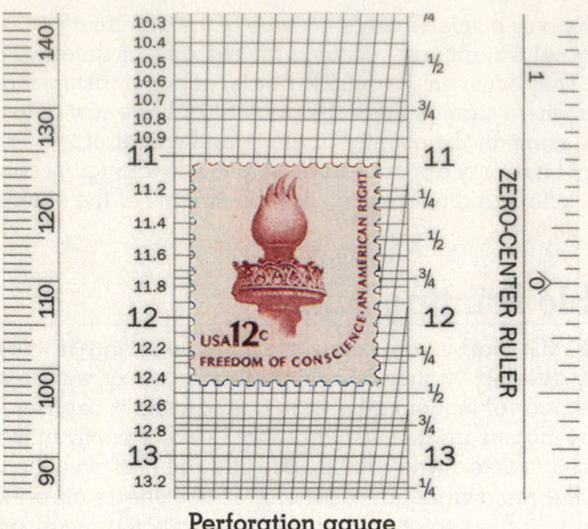

Perforation gauge

To measure a stamp, run it along the gauge until the dots on it fit exactly into the perforations of the stamp. If you are using a graduated-line perforation gauge, simply slide the stamp along the surface until the lines on the gauge perfectly project from the center of the bridges or holes. The number to the side of the line of dots or lines that fit the stamp's perforation is the measurement. For example, an "11" means that 11 perforations fit between two centimeters. The description of the stamp therefore is "perf. 11." If the gauge of the perforations on the top and bottom of a stamp differs from that on the sides, the result is what is known as *compound perforations*. In measuring compound perforations, the gauge at top and bottom is always given first, then the sides. Thus, a stamp that measures 11 at top and bottom and 10½ at the sides is "perf. 11 x 10½." See U.S. Scott 632-642 for examples of compound perforations.

Stamps also are known with perforations different on three or all four sides. Descriptions of such items are clockwise, beginning with the top of the stamp.

A perforation with small holes and teeth close together is a "fine perforation." One with large holes and teeth far apart is a "coarse perforation." Holes that are jagged, rather than clean-cut, are "rough perforations." *Blind perforations* are the slight impressions left by the perforating pins if they fail to puncture the paper. Multiples of stamps showing blind perforations may command a slight premium over normally perforated stamps.

The term *syncopated perfs* describes intentional irregularities in the perforations. The earliest form was used by the Netherlands from 1925-33, where holes were omitted to create distinctive patterns. Beginning in 1992, Great Britain has used an oval perforation to help prevent counterfeiting. Several other countries have started using the oval perfs or other syncopated perf patterns.

A new type of perforation, still primarily used for postal stationery, is known as microperfs. Microperfs are tiny perforations (in some cases hundreds of holes per two centimeters) that allows items to be intentionally separated very easily, while not accidentally breaking apart as easily as standard perforations. These are not currently measured or differentiated by size, as are standard perforations.

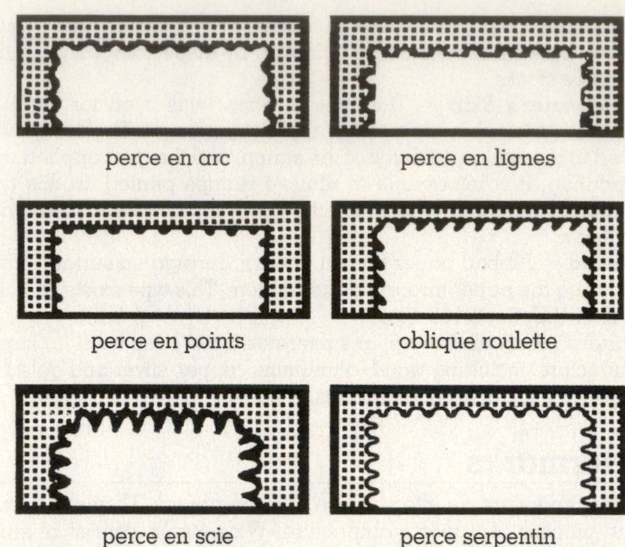

ROULETTING

In rouletting, the stamp paper is cut partly or wholly through, with no paper removed. In perforating, some paper is removed. Rouletting derives its name from the French roulette, a spur-like wheel. As the wheel is rolled over the paper, each point makes a small cut. The number of cuts made in a two-centimeter space determines the gauge of the roulette, just as the number of perforations in two centimeters determines the gauge of the perforation.

The shape and arrangement of the teeth on the wheels varies. Various roulette types generally carry French names:

Perce en lignes - rouletted in lines. The paper receives short, straight cuts in lines. This is the most common type of rouletting. See Mexico Scott 500.

Perce en points - pin-rouletted or pin-perfed. This differs from a small perforation because no paper is removed, although round, equidistant holes are pricked through the paper. See Mexico Scott 242-256.

Perce en arc and *perce en scie* - pierced in an arc or saw-toothed designs, forming half circles or small triangles. See Hanover (German States) Scott 25-29.

Perce en serpentin - serpentine roulettes. The cuts form a serpentine or wavy line. See Brunswick (German States) Scott 13-18.

Once again, no paper is removed by these processes, leaving the stamps easily separated, but closely attached.

DIE-CUTTING

The third major form of stamp separation is die-cutting. This is a method where a die in the pattern of separation is created that later cuts the stamp paper in a stroke motion. Although some standard stamps bear die-cut perforations, this process is primarily used for self-adhesive postage stamps. Die-cutting can appear in straight lines, such as U.S. Scott 2522, shapes, such as U.S. Scott 1551, or imitating the appearance of perforations, such as New Zealand Scott 935A and 935B.

Printing Processes

ENGRAVING (Intaglio, Line-engraving, Etching)

Master die — The initial operation in the process of line engraving is making the master die. The die is a small, flat block of softened steel upon which the stamp design is recess engraved in reverse.

Master die

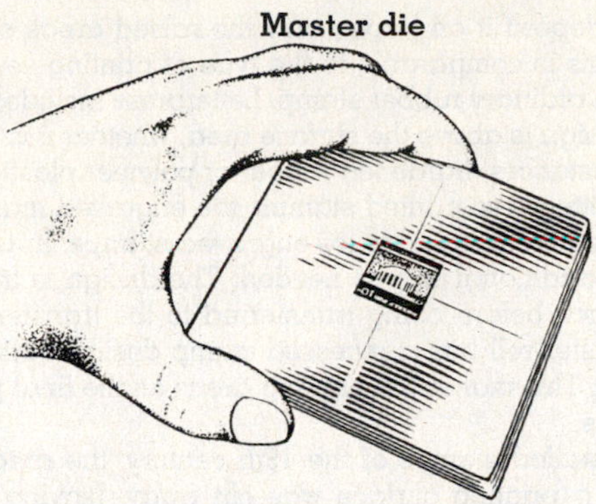

Photographic reduction of the original art is made to the appropriate size. It then serves as a tracing guide for the initial outline of the design. The engraver lightly traces the design on the steel with his graver, then slowly works the design until it is completed. At various points during the engraving process, the engraver hand-inks the die and makes an impression to check his progress. These are known as progressive die proofs. After completion of the engraving, the die is hardened to withstand the stress and pressures of later transfer operations.

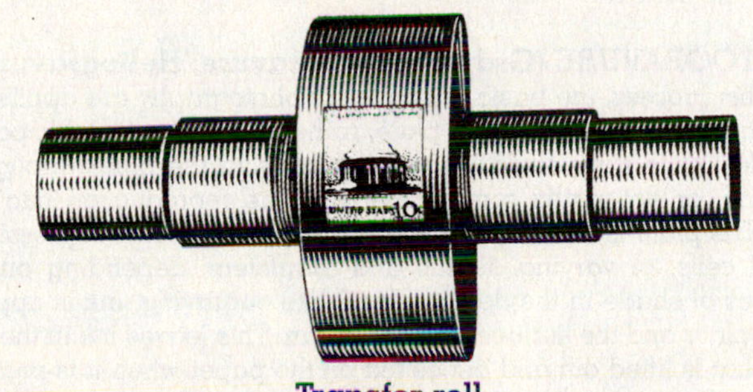

Transfer roll

Transfer roll — Next is production of the transfer roll that, as the name implies, is the medium used to transfer the subject from the master die to the printing plate. A blank roll of soft steel, mounted on a mandrel, is placed under the bearers of the transfer press to allow it to roll freely on its axis. The hardened die is placed on the bed of the press and the face of the transfer roll is applied to the die, under pressure. The bed or the roll is then rocked back and forth under increasing pressure, until the soft steel of the roll is forced into every engraved line of the die. The resulting impression on the roll is known as a "relief" or a "relief transfer." The engraved image is now positive in appearance and stands out from the steel. After the required number of reliefs are "rocked in," the soft steel transfer roll is hardened.

Different flaws may occur during the relief process. A defective relief may occur during the rocking in process because of a minute piece of foreign material lodging on the die, or some other cause. Imperfections in the steel of the transfer roll may result in a breaking away of parts of the design. This is known as a relief break, which will show up on finished stamps as small, unprinted areas. If a damaged relief remains in use, it will transfer a repeating defect to the plate. Deliberate alterations of reliefs sometimes occur. "Altered reliefs" designate these changed conditions.

Plate — The final step in pre-printing production is the making of the printing plate. A flat piece of soft steel replaces the die on the bed of the transfer press. One of the reliefs on the transfer roll is positioned over this soft steel. Position, or layout, dots determine the correct position on the plate. The dots have been lightly marked on the plate in advance. After the correct position of the relief is determined, the design is rocked in by following the same method used in making the transfer roll. The difference is that this time the image is being transferred from the transfer roll, rather than to it. Once the design is entered on the plate, it appears in reverse and is recessed. There are as many transfers entered on the plate as there are subjects printed on the sheet of stamps. It is during this process that double and shifted transfers occur, as well as re-entries. These are the result of improperly entered images that have not been properly burnished out prior to rocking in a new image.

Modern siderography processes, such as those used by the U.S. Bureau of Engraving and Printing, involve an automated form of rocking designs in on preformed cylindrical printing sleeves. The same process also allows for easier removal and re-entry of worn images right on the sleeve.

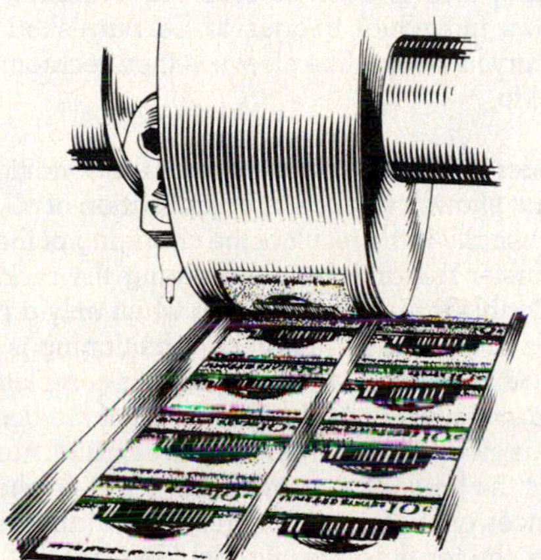

Transferring the design to the plate

Following the entering of the required transfers on the plate, the position dots, layout dots and lines, scratches and other markings generally are burnished out. Added at this time by the siderographer are any required *guide lines, plate numbers* or other *marginal markings.* The plate is then hand-inked and a proof impression is taken. This is known as a plate proof. If the impression is approved, the plate is machined for fitting onto the press, is hardened and sent to the plate vault ready for use.

On press, the plate is inked and the surface is automatically wiped clean, leaving ink only in the recessed lines. Paper is then forced under pressure into the engraved recessed lines, thereby receiving the ink. Thus, the ink lines on engraved stamps are slightly raised, and slight depressions (debossing) occur on the back of the stamp. Prior to the advent of modern high-speed presses and more advanced ink formulations, paper had to be dampened before receiving the ink. This sometimes led to uneven shrinkage by the time the stamps were perforated, resulting in improperly perforated stamps, or misperfs. Newer presses use drier paper, thus both *wet* and *dry printings* exist on some stamps.

Rotary Press — Until 1914, only flat plates were used to print engraved stamps. Rotary press printing was introduced in 1914, and slowly spread. Some countries still use flat-plate printing.

After approval of the plate proof, older *rotary press plates* require additional machining. They are curved to fit the press cylinder. "Gripper slots" are cut into the back of each plate to receive the "grippers," which hold the plate securely on the press. The plate is then hardened. Stamps printed from these bent rotary press plates are longer or wider than the same stamps printed from flat-plate presses. The stretching of the plate during the curving process is what causes this distortion.

Re-entry — To execute a re-entry on a flat plate, the transfer roll is re-applied to the plate, often at some time after its first use on the press. Worn-out designs can be resharpened by carefully burnishing out the original image and re-entering it from the transfer roll. If the original impression has not been sufficiently removed and the transfer roll is not precisely in line with the remaining impression, the resulting double transfer will make the re-entry obvious. If the registration is true, a re-entry may be difficult or impossible to distinguish. Sometimes a stamp printed from a successful re-entry is identified by having a much sharper and clearer impression than its neighbors. With the advent of rotary presses, post-press re-entries were not possible. After a plate was curved for the rotary press, it was impossible to make a re-entry. This is because the plate had already been bent once (with the design distorted).

However, with the introduction of the previously mentioned modern-style siderography machines, entries are made to the preformed cylindrical printing sleeve. Such sleeves are dechromed and softened. This allows individual images to be burnished out and re-entered on the curved sleeve. The sleeve is then rechromed, resulting in longer press life.

Double Transfer — This is a description of the condition of a transfer on a plate that shows evidence of a duplication of all, or a portion of the design. It usually is the result of the changing of the registration between the transfer roll and the plate during the rocking in of the original entry. Double transfers also occur when only a portion of the design has been rocked in and improper positioning is noted. If the worker elected not to burnish out the partial or completed design, a strong double transfer will occur for part or all of the design.

It sometimes is necessary to remove the original transfer from a plate and repeat the process a second time. If the finished re-worked image shows traces of the original impression, attributable to incomplete burnishing, the result is a partial double transfer.

With the modern automatic machines mentioned previously, double transfers are all but impossible to create. Those partially doubled images on stamps printed from such sleeves are more than likely re-entries, rather than true double transfers.

Re-engraved — Alterations to a stamp design are sometimes necessary after some stamps have been printed. In some cases, either the original die or the actual printing plate may have its "temper" drawn (softened), and the design will be re-cut. The resulting impressions from such a re-engraved die or plate may differ slightly from the original issue, and are known as "re-engraved." If the alteration was made to the master die, all future printings will be consistently different from the original. If alterations were made to the printing plate, each altered stamp on the plate will be slightly different from each other, allowing specialists to reconstruct a complete printing plate.

Dropped Transfers — If an impression from the transfer roll has not been properly placed, a dropped transfer may occur. The final stamp image will appear obviously out of line with its neighbors.

Short Transfer — Sometimes a transfer roll is not rocked its entire length when entering a transfer onto a plate. As a result, the finished transfer on the plate fails to show the complete design, and the finished stamp will have an incomplete design printed. This is known as a "short transfer." U.S. Scott No. 8 is a good example of a short transfer.

TYPOGRAPHY (Letterpress, Surface Printing, Flexography, Dry Offset, High Etch)

Although the word "Typography" is obsolete as a term describing a printing method, it was the accepted term throughout the first century of postage stamps. Therefore, appropriate Scott listings in this catalogue refer to typographed stamps. The current term for this form of printing, however, is "letterpress."

As it relates to the production of postage stamps, letterpress printing is the reverse of engraving. Rather than having recessed areas trap the ink and deposit it on paper, only the raised areas of the design are inked. This is comparable to the type of printing seen by inking and using an ordinary rubber stamp. Letterpress includes all printing where the design is above the surface area, whether it is wood, metal or, in some instances, hardened rubber or polymer plastic.

For most letterpress-printed stamps, the engraved master is made in much the same manner as for engraved stamps. In this instance, however, an additional step is needed. The design is transferred to another surface before being transferred to the transfer roll. In this way, the transfer roll has a recessed stamp design, rather than one done in relief. This makes the printing areas on the final plate raised, or relief areas.

For less-detailed stamps of the 19th century, the area on the die not used as a printing surface was cut away, leaving the surface area raised. The original die was then reproduced by stereotyping or electrotyping. The resulting electrotypes were assembled in the required number and format of the desired sheet of stamps. The plate used in printing the stamps was an electroplate of these assembled electrotypes.

Once the final letterpress plates are created, ink is applied to the raised surface and the pressure of the press transfers the ink impression to the paper. In contrast to engraving, the fine lines of letterpress are impressed on the surface of the stamp, leaving a debossed surface. When viewed from the back (as on a typewritten page), the corresponding line work on the stamp will be raised slightly (embossed) above the surface.

PHOTOGRAVURE (Gravure, Rotogravure, Heliogravure)

In this process, the basic principles of photography are applied to a chemically sensitized metal plate, rather than photographic paper. The design is transferred photographically to the plate through a halftone, or dot-matrix screen, breaking the reproduction into tiny dots. The plate is treated chemically and the dots form depressions, called cells, of varying depths and diameters, depending on the degrees of shade in the design. Then, like engraving, ink is applied to the plate and the surface is wiped clean. This leaves ink in the tiny cells that is lifted out and deposited on the paper when it is pressed against the plate.

Gravure is most often used for multicolored stamps, generally using the three primary colors (red, yellow and blue) and black. By varying the dot matrix pattern and density of these colors, virtually any color can be reproduced. A typical full-color gravure stamp will be created from four printing cylinders (one for each color). The original multicolored image will have been photographically separated into its component colors.

Modern gravure printing may use computer-generated dot-matrix screens, and modern plates may be of various types including metal-coated plastic. The catalogue designation of Photogravure (or "Photo") covers any of these older and more modern gravure methods of printing.

For examples of the first photogravure stamps printed (1914), see Bavaria Scott 94-114.

LITHOGRAPHY (Offset Lithography, Stone Lithography, Dilitho, Planography, Collotype)

The principle that oil and water do not mix is the basis for lithography. The stamp design is drawn by hand or transferred from engraving to the surface of a lithographic stone or metal plate in a greasy (oily) substance. This oily substance holds the ink, which will later be transferred to the paper. The stone (or plate) is wet with an acid fluid, causing it to repel the printing ink in all areas not covered by the greasy substance.

Transfer paper is used to transfer the design from the original stone or plate. A series of duplicate transfers are grouped and, in turn, transferred to the final printing plate.

Photolithography — The application of photographic processes to lithography. This process allows greater flexibility of design, related to use of halftone screens combined with line work. Unlike photogravure or engraving, this process can allow large, solid areas to be printed.

Offset — A refinement of the lithographic process. A rubber-covered blanket cylinder takes the impression from the inked lithographic plate. From the "blanket" the impression is *offset* or transferred to the paper. Greater flexibility and speed are the principal reasons offset printing has largely displaced lithography. The term "lithography" covers both processes, and results are almost identical.

EMBOSSED (Relief) Printing

Embossing, not considered one of the four main printing types, is a method in which the design first is sunk into the metal of the die. Printing is done against a yielding platen, such as leather or linoleum. The platen is forced into the depression of the die, thus forming the design on the paper in relief. This process is often used for metallic inks.

Embossing may be done without color (see Sardinia Scott 4-6); with color printed around the embossed area (see Great Britain Scott 5 and most U.S. envelopes); and with color in exact registration with the embossed subject (see Canada Scott 656-657).

HOLOGRAMS

For objects to appear as holograms on stamps, a model exactly the same size as it is to appear on the hologram must be created. Rather than using photographic film to capture the image, holography records an image on a photoresist material. In processing, chemicals eat away at certain exposed areas, leaving a pattern of constructive and destructive interference. When the photoresist is developed, the result is a pattern of uneven ridges that acts as a mold. This mold is then coated with metal, and the resulting form is used to press copies in much the same way phonograph records are produced.

A typical reflective hologram used for stamps consists of a reproduction of the uneven patterns on a plastic film that is applied to a reflective background, usually a silver or gold foil. Light is reflected off the background through the film, making the pattern present on the film visible. Because of the uneven pattern of the film, the viewer will perceive the objects in their proper three-dimensional relationships with appropriate brightness.

The first hologram on a stamp was produced by Austria in 1988 (Scott 1441).

FOIL APPLICATION

A modern technique of applying color to stamps involves the application of metallic foil to the stamp paper. A pattern of foil is applied to the stamp paper by use of a stamping die. The foil usually is flat, but it may be textured. Canada Scott 1735 has three different foil applications in pearl, bronze and gold. The gold foil was textured using a chemical-etch copper embossing die. The printing of this stamp also involved two-color offset lithography plus embossing.

THERMOGRAPHY

In the 1990s stamps began to be enhanced with thermographic printing. In this process, a powdered polymer is applied over a sheet that has just been printed. The powder adheres to ink that lacks drying or hardening agents and does not adhere to areas where the ink has these agents. The excess powder is removed and the sheet is briefly heated to melt the powder. The melted powder solidifies after cooling, producing a raised, shiny effect on the stamps. See Scott New Caledonia C239-C240.

COMBINATION PRINTINGS

Sometimes two or even three printing methods are combined in producing stamps. In these cases, such as Austria Scott 933 or Canada 1735 (described in the preceding paragraph), the multiple-printing technique can be determined by studying the individual characteristics of each printing type. A few stamps, such as Singapore Scott 684-684A, combine as many as three of the four major printing types (lithography, engraving and typography). When this is done it often indicates the incorporation of security devices against counterfeiting.

INK COLORS

Inks or colored papers used in stamp printing often are of mineral origin, although there are numerous examples of organic-based pigments. As a general rule, organic-based pigments are far more subject to varieties and change than those of mineral-based origin.

The appearance of any given color on a stamp may be affected by many aspects, including printing variations, light, color of paper, aging and chemical alterations.

Numerous printing variations may be observed. Heavier pressure or inking will cause a more intense color, while slight interruptions in the ink feed or lighter impressions will cause a lighter appearance. Stamps printed in the same color by water-based and solvent-based inks can differ significantly in appearance. This affects several stamps in the U.S. Prominent Americans series. Hand-mixed ink formulas (primarily from the 19th century) produced under different conditions (humidity and temperature) account for notable color variations in early printings of the same stamp (see U.S. Scott 248-250, 279B, for example). Different sources of pigment can also result in significant differences in color.

Light exposure and aging are closely related in the way they affect stamp color. Both eventually break down the ink and fade colors, so that a carefully kept stamp may differ significantly in color from an identical copy that has been exposed to light. If stamps are exposed to light either intentionally or accidentally, their colors can be faded or completely changed in some cases.

Papers of different quality and consistency used for the same stamp printing may affect color appearance. Most pelure papers, for example, show a richer color when compared with wove or laid papers. See Russia Scott 181a, for an example of this effect.

The very nature of the printing processes can cause a variety of differences in shades or hues of the same stamp. Some of these shades are scarcer than others, and are of particular interest to the advanced collector.

Luminescence

All forms of tagged stamps fall under the general category of luminescence. Within this broad category is fluorescence, dealing with forms of tagging visible under longwave ultraviolet light, and phosphorescence, which deals with tagging visible only under shortwave light. Phosphorescence leaves an afterglow and fluorescence does not. These treated stamps show up in a range of different colors when exposed to UV light. The differing wavelengths of the light activates the tagging material, making it glow in various colors that usually serve different mail processing purposes.

Intentional tagging is a post-World War II phenomenon, brought about by the increased literacy rate and rapidly growing mail volume. It was one of several answers to the problem of the need for more automated mail processes. Early tagged stamps served the purpose of triggering machines to separate different types of mail. A natural outgrowth was to also use the signal to trigger machines that faced all envelopes the same way and canceled them.

Tagged stamps come in many different forms. Some tagged stamps have luminescent shapes or images imprinted on them as a form of security device. Others have blocks (United States), stripes, frames (South Africa and Canada), overall coatings (United States), bars (Great Britain and Canada) and many other types. Some types of tagging are even mixed in with the pigmented printing ink (Australia Scott 366, Netherlands Scott 478 and U.S. Scott 1359 and 2443).

The means of applying taggant to stamps differs as much as the intended purposes for the stamps. The most common form of tagging is a coating applied to the surface of the printed stamp. Since the taggant ink is frequently invisible except under UV light, it does not interfere with the appearance of the stamp. Another common application is the use of phosphored papers. In this case the paper itself either has a coating of taggant applied before the stamp is printed, has taggant applied during the papermaking process (incorporating it into the fibers), or has the taggant mixed into the coating of the paper. The latter method, among others, is currently in use in the United States.

Many countries now use tagging in various forms to either expedite mail handling or to serve as a printing security device against counterfeiting. Following the introduction of tagged stamps for public use in 1959 by Great Britain, other countries have steadily joined the parade. Among those are Germany (1961); Canada and Denmark (1962); United States, Australia, France and Switzerland (1963); Belgium and Japan (1966); Sweden and Norway (1967); Italy (1968); and Russia (1969). Since then, many other countries have begun using forms of tagging, including Brazil, China, Czechoslovakia, Hong Kong, Guatemala, Indonesia, Israel, Lithuania, Luxembourg, Netherlands, Penrhyn Islands, Portugal, St. Vincent, Singapore, South Africa, Spain and Sweden to name a few.

In some cases, including United States, Canada, Great Britain and Switzerland, stamps were released both with and without tagging. Many of these were released during each country's experimental period. Tagged and untagged versions are listed for the aforementioned countries and are noted in some other countries' listings. For at least a few stamps, the experimentally tagged version is worth far more than its untagged counterpart, such as the 1963 experimental tagged version of France Scott 1024.

In some cases, luminescent varieties of stamps were inadvertently created. Several Russian stamps, for example, sport highly fluorescent ink that was not intended as a form of tagging. Older stamps, such as early U.S. postage dues, can be positively identified by the use of UV light, since the organic ink used has become slightly fluorescent over time. Other stamps, such as Austria Scott 70a-82a (varnish bars) and Obock Scott 46-64 (printed quadrille lines), have become fluorescent over time.

Various fluorescent substances have been added to paper to make it appear brighter. These optical brightners, as they are known, greatly affect the appearance of the stamp under UV light. The brightest of these is known as Hi-Brite paper. These paper varieties are beyond the scope of the Scott Catalogue.

Shortwave UV light also is used extensively in expertizing, since each form of paper has its own fluorescent characteristics that are impossible to perfectly match. It is therefore a simple matter to detect filled thins, added perforation teeth and other alterations that involve the addition of paper. UV light also is used to examine stamps that have had cancels chemically removed and for other purposes as well.

Gum

The Illustrated Gum Chart in the first part of this introduction shows and defines various types of gum condition. Because gum condition has an important impact on the value of unused stamps, we recommend studying this chart and the accompanying text carefully.

The gum on the back of a stamp may be shiny, dull, smooth, rough, dark, white, colored or tinted. Most stamp gumming adhesives use gum arabic or dextrine as a base. Certain polymers such as polyvinyl alcohol (PVA) have been used extensively since World War II.

The *Scott Standard Postage Stamp Catalogue* does not list items by types of gum. The *Scott Specialized Catalogue of United States Stamps and Covers* does differentiate among some types of gum for certain issues.

Reprints of stamps may have gum differing from the original issues. In addition, some countries have used different gum formulas for different seasons. These adhesives have different properties that may become more apparent over time.

Many stamps have been issued without gum, and the catalogue will note this fact. See, for example, United States Scott 40-47. Sometimes, gum may have been removed to preserve the stamp. Germany Scott B68, for example, has a highly acidic gum that eventually destroys the stamps. This item is valued in the catalogue with gum removed.

Reprints and Reissues

These are impressions of stamps (usually obsolete) made from the original plates or stones. If they are valid for postage and reproduce obsolete issues (such as U.S. Scott 102-111), the stamps are *reissues.* If they are from current issues, they are designated as *second, third,* etc., *printing.* If designated for a particular purpose, they are called *special printings.*

When special printings are not valid for postage, but are made from original dies and plates by authorized persons, they are *official reprints. Private reprints* are made from the original plates and dies by private hands. An example of a private reprint is that of the 1871-1932 reprints made from the original die of the 1845 New Haven, Conn., postmaster's provisional. *Official reproductions* or imitations are made from new dies and plates by government authorization. Scott will list those reissues that are valid for postage if they differ significantly from the original printing.

The U.S. government made special printings of its first postage stamps in 1875. Produced were official imitations of the first two stamps (listed as Scott 3-4), reprints of the demonetized pre-1861 issues (Scott 40-47) and reissues of the 1861 stamps, the 1869 stamps and the then-current 1875 denominations. Even though the official imitations and the reprints were not valid for postage, Scott lists all of these U.S. special printings.

Most reprints or reissues differ slightly from the original stamp in some characteristic, such as gum, paper, perforation, color or watermark. Sometimes the details are followed so meticulously that only a student of that specific stamp is able to distinguish the reprint or reissue from the original.

Remainders and Canceled to Order

Some countries sell their stock of old stamps when a new issue replaces them. To avoid postal use, the *remainders* usually are canceled with a punch hole, a heavy line or bar, or a more-or-less regular-looking cancellation. The most famous merchant of remainders was Nicholas F. Seebeck. In the 1880s and 1890s, he arranged printing contracts between the Hamilton Bank Note Co., of which he was a director, and several Central and South American countries. The contracts provided that the plates and all remainders of the yearly issues became the property of Hamilton. Seebeck saw to it that ample stock remained. The "Seebecks," both remainders and reprints, were standard packet fillers for decades.

Some countries also issue stamps *canceled-to-order (CTO),* either in sheets with original gum or stuck onto pieces of paper or envelopes and canceled. Such CTO items generally are worth less than postally used stamps. In cases where the CTO material is far more prevalent in the marketplace than postally used examples, the catalogue value relates to the CTO examples, with postally used examples noted as premium items. Most CTOs can be detected by the presence of gum. However, as the CTO practice goes back at least to 1885, the gum inevitably has been soaked off some stamps so they could pass as postally used. The normally applied postmarks usually differ slightly from standard postmarks, and specialists are able to tell the difference. When applied individually to envelopes by philatelically minded persons, CTO material is known as *favor canceled* and generally sells at large discounts.

Cinderellas and Facsimiles

Cinderella is a catch-all term used by stamp collectors to describe phantoms, fantasies, bogus items, municipal issues, exhibition seals, local revenues, transportation stamps, labels, poster stamps and many other types of items. Some cinderella collectors include in their collections local postage issues, telegraph stamps, essays and proofs, forgeries and counterfeits.

A *fantasy* is an adhesive created for a nonexistent stamp-issuing authority. Fantasy items range from imaginary countries (Occusi-Ambeno, Kingdom of Sedang, Principality of Trinidad or Torres Straits), to non-existent locals (Winans City Post), or nonexistent transportation lines (McRobish & Co.'s Acapulco-San Francisco Line).

On the other hand, if the entity exists and could have issued stamps (but did not) or was known to have issued other stamps, the items are considered *bogus* stamps. These would include the Mormon postage stamps of Utah, S. Allan Taylor's Guatemala and Paraguay inventions, the propaganda issues for the South Moluccas and the adhesives of the Page & Keyes local post of Boston.

Phantoms is another term for both fantasy and bogus issues.

Facsimiles are copies or imitations made to represent original stamps, but which do not pretend to be originals. A catalogue illustration is such a facsimile. Illustrations from the Moens catalogue of the last century were occasionally colored and passed off as stamps. Since the beginning of stamp collecting, facsimiles have been made for collectors as space fillers or for reference. They often carry the word "facsimile," "falsch" (German), "sanko" or "mozo" (Japanese), or "faux" (French) overprinted on the face or stamped on the back. Unfortunately, over the years a number of these items have had fake cancels applied over the facsimile notation and have been passed off as genuine.

Forgeries and Counterfeits

Forgeries and counterfeits have been with philately virtually from the beginning of stamp production. Over time, the terminology for the two has been used interchangeably. Although both forgeries and counterfeits are reproductions of stamps, the purposes behind their creation differ considerably.

Among specialists there is an increasing movement to more specifically define such items. Although there is no universally accepted terminology, we feel the following definitions most closely mirror the items and their purposes as they are currently defined.

Forgeries (also often referred to as *Counterfeits*) are reproductions of genuine stamps that have been created to defraud collectors. Such spurious items first appeared on the market around 1860, and most old-time collections contain one or more. Many are crude and easily spotted, but some can deceive experts.

An important supplier of these early philatelic forgeries was the Hamburg printer Gebruder Spiro. Many others with reputations in this craft included S. Allan Taylor, George Hussey, James Chute, George Forune, Benjamin & Sarpy, Julius Goldner, E. Oneglia and L.H. Mercier. Among the noted 20th-century forgers were Francois Fournier, Jean Sperati and the prolific Raoul DeThuin.

Forgeries may be complete replications, or they may be genuine stamps altered to resemble a scarcer (and more valuable) type. Most forgeries, particularly those of rare stamps, are worth only a small fraction of the value of a genuine example, but a few types, created by some of the most notable forgers, such as Sperati, can be worth as much or more than the genuine. Fraudulently produced copies are known of most classic rarities and many medium-priced stamps.

In addition to rare stamps, large numbers of common 19th- and early 20th-century stamps were forged to supply stamps to the early packet trade. Many can still be easily found. Few new philatelic forgeries have appeared in recent decades. Successful imitation of well-engraved work is virtually impossible. It has proven far easier to produce a fake by altering a genuine stamp than to duplicate a stamp completely.

Counterfeit (also often referred to as *Postal Counterfeit* or *Postal Forgery*) is the term generally applied to reproductions of stamps that have been created to defraud the government of revenue. Such items usually are created at the time a stamp is current and, in some cases, are hard to detect. Because most counterfeits are seized when the perpetrator is captured, postal counterfeits, particularly used on cover, are usually worth much more than a genuine example to specialists. The first postal counterfeit was of Spain's 4-cuarto carmine of 1854 (the real one is Scott 25). Apparently, the counterfeiters were not satisfied with their first version, which is now very scarce, and they soon created an engraved counterfeit, which is common. Postal counterfeits quickly followed in Austria, Naples, Sardinia and the Roman States. They have since been created in many other countries as well, including the United States.

An infamous counterfeit to defraud the government is the 1-shilling Great Britain "Stock Exchange" forgery of 1872, used on telegraph forms at the exchange that year. The stamp escaped detection until a stamp dealer noticed it in 1898.

Fakes

Fakes are genuine stamps altered in some way to make them more desirable. One student of this part of stamp collecting has estimated that by the 1950s more than 30,000 varieties of fakes were known. That number has grown greatly since then. The widespread existence of fakes makes it important for stamp collectors to study their philatelic holdings and use relevant literature. Likewise, collectors should buy from reputable dealers who guarantee their stamps and make full and prompt refunds should a purchased item be declared faked or altered by some mutually agreed-upon authority. Because fakes always have some genuine characteristics, it is not always possible to obtain unanimous agreement among experts regarding specific items. These students may change their opinions as philatelic knowledge increases. More than 80 percent of all fakes on the philatelic market today are regummed, reperforated (or perforated for the first time), or bear forged overprints, surcharges or cancellations.

Stamps can be chemically treated to alter or eliminate colors. For example, a pale rose stamp can be re-colored to resemble a blue shade of high market value. In other cases, treated stamps can be made to resemble missing color varieties. Designs may be changed by painting, or a stroke or a dot added or bleached out to turn an ordinary variety into a seemingly scarcer stamp. Part of a stamp can be bleached and reprinted in a different version, achieving an inverted center or frame. Margins can be added or repairs done so deceptively that the stamps move from the "repaired" into the "fake" category.

Fakers have not left the backs of the stamps untouched either. They may create false watermarks, add fake grills or press out genuine grills. A thin India paper proof may be glued onto a thicker backing to create the appearance an issued stamp, or a proof printed on cardboard may be shaved down and perforated to resemble a stamp. Silk threads are impressed into paper and stamps have been split so that a rare paper variety is added to an otherwise inexpensive stamp. The most common treatment to the back of a stamp, however, is regumming.

Some in the business of faking stamps have openly advertised fool-proof application of "original gum" to stamps that lack it, although most publications now ban such ads from their pages. It is believed that very few early stamps have survived without being hinged. The large number of never-hinged examples of such earlier material offered for sale thus suggests the widespread extent of regumming activity. Regumming also may be used to hide repairs or thin spots. Dipping the stamp into watermark fluid, or examining it under longwave ultraviolet light often will reveal these flaws.

Fakers also tamper with separations. Ingenious ways to add margins are known. Perforated wide-margin stamps may be falsely represented as imperforate when trimmed. Reperforating is commonly done to create scarce coil or perforation varieties, and to eliminate the naturally occurring straight-edge stamps found in sheet margin positions of many earlier issues. Custom has made straight-edged stamps less desirable. Fakers have obliged by perforating straight-edged stamps so that many are now uncommon, if not rare.

Another fertile field for the faker is that of overprints, surcharges and cancellations. The forging of rare surcharges or overprints began in the 1880s or 1890s. These forgeries are sometimes difficult to detect, but experts have identified almost all. Occasionally, overprints or cancellations are removed to create non-overprinted stamps or seemingly unused items. This is most commonly done by removing a manuscript cancel to make a stamp resemble an unused example. "SPECIMEN" overprints may be removed by scraping and repainting to create non-overprinted varieties. Fakers use inexpensive revenues or pen-canceled stamps to generate unused stamps for further faking by adding other markings. The quartz lamp or UV lamp and a high-powered magnifying glass help to easily detect removed cancellations.

The bigger problem, however, is the addition of overprints, surcharges or cancellations - many with such precision that they are very difficult to ascertain. Plating of the stamps or the overprint can be an important method of detection.

Fake postmarks may range from many spurious fancy cancellations to a host of markings applied to transatlantic covers, to adding normally appearing postmarks to definitives of some countries with stamps that are valued far higher used than unused. With the increased popularity of cover collecting, and the widespread interest in postal history, a fertile new field for fakers has come about. Some have tried to create entire covers. Others specialize in adding stamps, tied by fake cancellations, to genuine stampless covers, or replacing less expensive or damaged stamps with more valuable ones. Detailed study of postal rates in effect at the time a cover in question was mailed, including the analysis of each handstamp used during the period, ink analysis and similar techniques, usually will unmask the fraud.

Restoration and Repairs

Scott bases its catalogue values on stamps that are free of defects and otherwise meet the standards set forth earlier in this introduction. Most stamp collectors desire to have the finest copy of an item possible. Even within given grading categories there are variances. This leads to a controversial practice that is not defined in any universal manner: stamp *restoration*.

There are broad differences of opinion about what is permissible when it comes to restoration. Carefully applying a soft eraser to a stamp or cover to remove light soiling is one form of restoration, as is washing a stamp in mild soap and water to clean it. These are fairly accepted forms of restoration. More severe forms of restoration include pressing out creases or removing stains caused by tape. To what degree each of these is acceptable is dependent upon the individual situation. Further along the spectrum is the freshening of a stamp's color by removing oxide build-up or the effects of wax paper left next to stamps shipped to the tropics.

At some point in this spectrum the concept of *repair* replaces that of restoration. Repairs include filling thin spots, mending tears by reweaving or adding a missing perforation tooth. Regumming stamps may have been acceptable as a restoration or repair technique many decades ago, but today it is considered a form of fakery.

Restored stamps may or may not sell at a discount, and it is possible that the value of individual restored items may be enhanced over that of their pre-restoration state. Specific situations dictate the resultant value of such an item. Repaired stamps sell at substantial discounts from the value of sound stamps.

Terminology

Booklets — Many countries have issued stamps in small booklets for the convenience of users. This idea continues to become increasingly popular in many countries. Booklets have been issued in many sizes and forms, often with advertising on the covers, the panes of stamps or on the interleaving.

The panes used in booklets may be printed from special plates or made from regular sheets. All panes from booklets issued by the United States and many from those of other countries contain stamps that are straight edged on the sides, but perforated between. Others are distinguished by orientation of watermark or other identifying features. Any stamp-like unit in the pane, either printed or blank, that is not a postage stamp, is considered to be a *label* in the catalogue listings.

Scott lists and values booklet panes. Modern complete booklets also are listed and valued. Individual booklet panes are listed only when they are not fashioned from existing sheet stamps and, therefore, are identifiable from their sheet stamp counterparts.

Panes usually do not have a used value assigned to them because there is little market activity for used booklet panes, even though many exist used and there is some demand for them.

Cancellations — The marks or obliterations put on stamps by postal authorities to show that they have performed service and to prevent their reuse are known as cancellations. If the marking is made with a pen, it is considered a "pen cancel." When the location of the post office appears in the marking, it is a "town cancellation." A "postmark" is technically any postal marking, but in practice the term generally is applied to a town cancellation with a date. When calling attention to a cause or celebration, the marking is known as a "slogan cancellation." Many other types and styles of cancellations exist, such as duplex, numerals, targets, fancy and others. See also "precancels," below.

Coil Stamps — These are stamps that are issued in rolls for use in dispensers, affixing and vending machines. Those coils of the United States, Canada, Sweden and some other countries are perforated horizontally or vertically only, with the outer edges imperforate. Coil stamps of some countries, such as Great Britain and Germany, are perforated on all four sides and may in some cases be distinguished from their sheet stamp counterparts by watermarks, counting numbers on the reverse or other means.

Covers — Entire envelopes, with or without adhesive postage stamps, that have passed through the mail and bear postal or other markings of philatelic interest are known as covers. Before the introduction of envelopes in about 1840, people folded letters and wrote the address on the outside. Some people covered their letters with an extra sheet of paper on the outside for the address, producing the term "cover." Used airletter sheets, stamped envelopes and other items of postal stationery also are considered covers.

Errors — Stamps that have some major, consistent, unintentional deviation from the normal are considered errors. Errors include, but are not limited to, missing or wrong colors, wrong paper, wrong watermarks, inverted centers or frames on multicolor printing, inverted or missing surcharges or overprints, double impressions, missing perforations, unintentionally omitted tagging and others. Factually wrong or misspelled information, if it appears on all examples of a stamp, are not considered errors in the true sense of the word. They are errors of design. Inconsistent or randomly appearing items, such as misperfs or color shifts, are classified as freaks.

Color-Omitted Errors — This term refers to stamps where a missing color is caused by the complete failure of the printing plate to deliver ink to the stamp paper or any other paper. Generally, this is caused by the printing plate not being engaged on the press or the ink station running dry of ink during printing.

Color-Missing Errors — This term refers to stamps where a color or colors were printed somewhere but do not appear on the finished stamp. There are four different classes of color-missing errors, and the catalog indicates with a two-letter code appended to each such listing what caused the color to be missing. These codes are used only for the United States' color-missing error listings.

FO = A *foldover* of the stamp sheet during printing may block ink from appearing on a stamp. Instead, the color will appear on the back of the foldover (where it might fall on the back of the selvage or perhaps on the back of the stamp or another stamp). FO also will be used in the case of foldunders, where the paper may fold underneath the other stamp paper and the color will print on the platen.

EP = A piece of *extraneous paper* falling across the plate or stamp paper will receive the printed ink. When the extraneous paper is removed, an unprinted portion of stamp paper remains and shows partially or totally missing colors.

CM = A misregistration of the printing plates during printing will result in a *color misregistration*, and such a misregistraion may result in a color not appearing on the finished stamp.

PS = *A perforation shift* after printing may remove a color from the finished stamp. Normally, this will occur on a row of stamps at the edge of the stamp pane.

Measurements – When measurements are given in the Scott catalogues for stamp size, grill size or any other reason, the first measurement given is always for the top and bottom dimension, while the second measurement will be for the sides (just as perforation gauges are measured). Thus, a stamp size of 15mm x 21mm will indicate a vertically oriented stamp 15mm wide at top and bottom, and 21mm tall at the sides. The same principle holds for measuring or counting items such as U.S. grills. A grill count of 22x18 points (B grill) indicates that there are 22 grill points across by 18 grill points down.

Overprints and Surcharges — Overprinting involves applying wording or design elements over an already existing stamp. Overprints can be used to alter the place of use (such as "Canal Zone" on U.S. stamps), to adapt them for a special purpose ("Porto" on Denmark's 1913-20 regular issues for use as postage due stamps, Scott J1-J7) or to commemorate a special occasion (United States Scott 647-648).

A *surcharge* is a form of overprint that changes or restates the face value of a stamp or piece of postal stationery.

Surcharges and overprints may be handstamped, typeset or, occasionally, lithographed or engraved. A few hand-written overprints and surcharges are known.

Personalized Stamps — In 1999, Australia issued stamps with se-tenant labels that could be personalized with pictures of the customer's choice. Other countries quickly followed suit, with some offering to print the selected picture on the stamp itself within a frame that was used exclusively for personalized issues. As the picture used on these stamps or labels vary, listings for such stamps are for any picture within the common frame (or any picture on a se-tenant label), be it a "generic" image or one produced especially for a customer, almost invariably at a premium price.

Precancels — Stamps that are canceled before they are placed in the mail are known as precancels. Precanceling usually is done to expedite the handling of large mailings and generally allow the affected mail pieces to skip certain phases of mail handling.

In the United States, precancellations generally identified the point of origin; that is, the city and state. This information appeared across the face of the stamp, usually centered between parallel lines. More recently, bureau precancels retained the parallel lines, but the city and state designations were dropped. Recent coils have a service inscription that is present on the original printing plate. These show the mail service paid for by the stamp. Since these stamps are not intended to receive further cancellations when used as intended, they are considered precancels. Such items often do not have parallel lines as part of the precancellation.

In France, the abbreviation *Affranchts* in a semicircle together with the word *Postes* is the general form of precancel in use. Belgian precancellations usually appear in a box in which the name of the city appears. Netherlands precancels have the name of the city enclosed between concentric circles, sometimes called a "lifesaver." Precancellations of other countries usually follow these patterns, but may be any arrangement of bars, boxes and city names.

Precancels are listed in the Scott catalogues only if the precancel changes the denomination (Belgium Scott 477-478); if the precanceled stamp is different from the non-precanceled version (such as untagged U.S. precancels); or if the stamp exists only precanceled (France Scott 1096-1099, U.S. Scott 2265).

Proofs and Essays — Proofs are impressions taken from an approved die, plate or stone in which the design and color are the same as the stamp issued to the public. Trial color proofs are impressions taken from approved dies, plates or stones in colors that vary from the final version. An essay is the impression of a design that differs in some way from the issued stamp. "Progressive die proofs" generally are considered to be essays.

Provisionals — These are stamps that are issued on short notice and intended for temporary use pending the arrival of regular issues. They usually are issued to meet such contingencies as changes in government or currency, shortage of necessary postage values or military occupation.

During the 1840s, postmasters in certain American cities issued stamps that were valid only at specific post offices. In 1861, postmasters of the Confederate States also issued stamps with limited validity. Both of these examples are known as "postmaster's provisionals."

Se-tenant — This term refers to an unsevered pair, strip or block of stamps that differ in design, denomination or overprint.

Unless the se-tenant item has a continuous design (see U.S. Scott 1451a, 1694a) the stamps do not have to be in the same order as shown in the catalogue (see U.S. Scott 2158a).

Specimens — The Universal Postal Union required member nations to send samples of all stamps they released into service to the International Bureau in Switzerland. Member nations of the UPU received these specimens as samples of what stamps were valid for postage. Many are overprinted, handstamped or initial-perforated "Specimen," "Canceled" or "Muestra." Some are marked with bars across the denominations (China-Taiwan), punched holes (Czechoslovakia) or back inscriptions (Mongolia).

Stamps distributed to government officials or for publicity purposes, and stamps submitted by private security printers for official approval, also may receive such defacements.

The previously described defacement markings prevent postal use, and all such items generally are known as "specimens."

Tete Beche — This term describes a pair of stamps in which one is upside down in relation to the other. Some of these are the result of intentional sheet arrangements, such as Morocco Scott B10-B11. Others occurred when one or more electrotypes accidentally were placed upside down on the plate, such as Colombia Scott 57a. Separation of the tete-beche stamps, of course, destroys the tete beche variety.

Pronunciation Symbols

ə .... banana, collide, abut

ˈə, ˌə .... humdrum, abut

ə .... immediately preceding \l\, \n\, \m\, \ŋ\, as in battle, mitten, eaten, and sometimes open \ˈō-pᵊm\, lock and key \-ᵊŋ-\; immediately following \l\, \m\, \r\, as often in French table, prisme, titre

ər .... further, merger, bird

ˈər-, ˈə-r .... as in two different pronunciations of hurry \ˈhər-ē, ˈhə-rē\

a .... mat, map, mad, gag, snap, patch

ā .... day, fade, date, aorta, drape, cape

ä .... bother, cot, and, with most American speakers, father, cart

ȧ .... father as pronounced by speakers who do not rhyme it with *bother*; French patte

au̇ .... now, loud, out

b .... baby, rib

ch .... chin, nature \ˈnā-chər\

d .... did, adder

e .... bet, bed, peck

ˈē, ˌē .... beat, nosebleed, evenly, easy

ē .... easy, mealy

f .... fifty, cuff

g .... go, big, gift

h .... hat, ahead

hw .... whale as pronounced by those who do not have the same pronunciation for both *whale* and *wail*

i .... tip, banish, active

ī .... site, side, buy, tripe

j .... job, gem, edge, join, judge

k .... kin, cook, ache

k̲ .... German ich, Buch; one pronunciation of loch

l .... lily, pool

m .... murmur, dim, nymph

n .... no, own

ⁿ .... indicates that a preceding vowel or diphthong is pronounced with the nasal passages open, as in French *un bon vin blanc* \œⁿ-bōⁿ-vaⁿ-bläⁿ\

ŋ .... sing \ˈsiŋ\, singer \ˈsiŋ-ər\, finger \ˈfiŋ-gər\, ink \ˈiŋk\

ō .... bone, know, beau

ȯ .... saw, all, gnaw, caught

œ .... French boeuf, German Hölle

œ̄ .... French feu, German Höhle

ȯi .... coin, destroy

p .... pepper, lip

r .... red, car, rarity

s .... source, less

sh .... as in shy, mission, machine, special (actually, this is a single sound, not two); with a hyphen between, two sounds as in *grasshopper* \ˈgras-ˌhä-pər\

t .... tie, attack, late, later, latter

th .... as in thin, ether (actually, this is a single sound, not two); with a hyphen between, two sounds as in *knighthood* \ˈnīt-ˌhu̇d\

t̲h̲ .... then, either, this (actually, this is a single sound, not two)

ü .... rule, youth, union \ˈyün-yən\, few \ˈfyü\

u̇ .... pull, wood, book, curable \ˈkyu̇r-ə-bəl\, fury \ˈfyu̇r-ē\

ue .... German füllen, hübsch

ue̅ .... French rue, German fühlen

v .... vivid, give

w .... we, away

y .... yard, young, cue \ˈkyü\, mute \ˈmyüt\, union \ˈyün-yən\

ʸ .... indicates that during the articulation of the sound represented by the preceding character the front of the tongue has substantially the position it has for the articulation of the first sound of *yard*, as in French *digne* \dēnʸ\

z .... zone, raise

zh .... as in vision, azure \ˈa-zhər\ (actually, this is a single sound, not two); with a hyphen between, two sounds as in *hogshead* \ˈhȯgz-ˌhed, ˈhägz-\

\ .... slant line used in pairs to mark the beginning and end of a transcription: \ˈpen\

ˈ .... mark preceding a syllable with primary (strongest) stress: \ˈpen-mən-ˌship\

ˌ .... mark preceding a syllable with secondary (medium) stress: \ˈpen-mən-ˌship\

\- .... mark of syllable division

( ) .... indicate that what is symbolized between is present in some utterances but not in others: *factory* \ˈfak-t(ə-)rē\

÷ .... indicates that many regard as unacceptable the pronunciation variant immediately following: *cupola* \ˈkyü-pə-lə, ÷-ˌlō\

Currency Conversion

Country	Dollar	Pound	S Franc	Yen	HK $	Euro	Cdn $	Aus $
Australia	1.2490	1.7757	1.3430	0.0114	0.1597	1.5546	1.0142	—
Canada	1.2315	1.7508	1.3242	0.0113	0.1575	1.5329	—	0.9860
European Union	0.8034	1.1422	0.8639	0.0073	0.1027	—	0.6524	0.6432
Hong Kong	7.8201	11.118	8.4087	0.0715	—	9.7338	6.3501	6.2611
Japan	109.38	155.51	117.61	—	13.987	136.15	88.819	87.574
Switzerland	0.9300	1.3222	—	0.0085	0.1189	1.1576	0.7552	0.7446
United Kingdom	0.7034	—	0.7563	0.0064	0.0899	0.8755	0.5712	0.5632
United States	—	1.4217	1.0753	0.0091	0.1279	1.2447	0.8120	0.8006

Country	Currency	U.S. $ Equiv.
Gabon	Community of French Africa (CFA) franc	.0019
Gambia	dalasy	.0209
Georgia	lari	.4030
Germany	euro	1.2447
Ghana	cedi	.2219
Gibraltar	pound	1.4217
Great Britain	pound	1.4217
Alderney	pound	1.4217
Guernsey	pound	1.4217
Jersey	pound	1.4217
Isle of Man	pound	1.4217
Greece	euro	1.2447
Mount Athos	euro	1.2447
Greenland	Danish krone	.1673
Grenada	East Caribbean dollar	.3704
Grenada Grenadines	East Caribbean dollar	.3704
Guatemala	quetzal	.1361
Guinea	franc	.0001
Guinea-Bissau	CFA franc	.0019
Guyana	dollar	.0048

Source: ***xe.com,*** *Feb. 1, 2018. Figures reflect values as of Feb. 1, 2018.*

COMMON DESIGN TYPES

Pictured in this section are issues where one illustration has been used for a number of countries in the Catalogue. Not included in this section are overprinted stamps or those issues which are illustrated in each country. Because the location of Never Hinged breakpoints varies from country to country, some of the values in the listings below will be for unused stamps that were previously hinged.

EUROPA

Europa, 1956

The design symbolizing the cooperation among the six countries comprising the Coal and Steel Community is illustrated in each country.

Belgium	*496-497*
France	*805-806*
Germany	*748-749*
Italy	*715-716*
Luxembourg	*318-320*
Netherlands	*368-369*

Nos. 496-497 (2)	9.00	.70
Nos. 805-806 (2)	5.25	1.00
Nos. 748-749 (2)	7.30	1.20
Nos. 715-716 (2)	9.25	1.25
Nos. 318-320 (3)	65.50	42.00
Nos. 368-369 (2)	72.50	1.75
Set total (13) Stamps	168.80	47.90

Europa, 1958

"E" and Dove — CD1

European Postal Union at the service of European integration.

1958, Sept. 13

Belgium	527-528
France	889-890
Germany	790-791
Italy	750-751
Luxembourg	341-343
Netherlands	375-376
Saar	317-318

Nos. 527-528 (2)	4.25	.60
Nos. 889-890 (2)	1.65	.55
Nos. 790-791 (2)	3.65	.65
Nos. 750-751 (2)	1.05	.60
Nos. 341-343 (3)	1.35	.90
Nos. 375-376 (2)	2.50	.75
Nos. 317-318 (2)	1.05	2.30
Set total (15) Stamps	15.50	6.35

Europa, 1959

6-Link Enless Chain — CD2

1959, Sept. 19

Belgium	536-537
France	929-930
Germany	805-806
Italy	791-792
Luxembourg	354-355
Netherlands	379-380

Nos. 536-537 (2)	1.55	.60
Nos. 929-930 (2)	1.40	.80
Nos. 805-806 (2)	1.55	.65
Nos. 791-792 (2)	.80	.50
Nos. 354-355 (2)	2.65	1.00
Nos. 379-380 (2)	9.90	1.25
Set total (12) Stamps	17.85	4.80

Europa, 1960

19-Spoke Wheel CD3

First anniversary of the establishment of C.E.P.T. (Conference Europeenne des Administrations des Postes et des Telecommunications.) The spokes symbolize the 19 founding members of the Conference.

1960, Sept.

Belgium	553-554
Denmark	379
Finland	376-377
France	970-971
Germany	818-820
Great Britain	377-378
Greece	688
Iceland	327-328
Ireland	175-176
Italy	809-810
Luxembourg	374-375
Netherlands	385-386
Norway	387
Portugal	866-867
Spain	941-942
Sweden	562-563
Switzerland	400-401
Turkey	1493-1494

Nos. 553-554 (2)	1.25	.55
No. 379 (1)	.55	.50
Nos. 376-377 (2)	1.70	1.80
Nos. 970-971 (2)	.50	.50
Nos. 818-820 (3)	2.25	1.50
Nos. 377-378 (2)	8.00	5.00
No. 688 (1)	5.00	2.00
Nos. 327-328 (2)	1.30	1.85
Nos. 175-176 (2)	47.50	27.50
Nos. 809-810 (2)	.50	.50
Nos. 374-375 (2)	1.00	.80
Nos. 385-386 (2)	3.65	1.50
No. 387 (1)	1.25	1.25
Nos. 866-867 (2)	2.25	1.25
Nos. 941-942 (2)	1.50	.75
Nos. 562-563 (2)	1.05	.55
Nos. 400-401 (2)	1.25	.65
Nos. 1493-1494 (2)	2.10	1.35
Set total (34) Stamps	82.60	49.80

Europa, 1961

19 Doves Flying as One — CD4

The 19 doves represent the 19 members of the Conference of European Postal and Telecommunications Administrations C.E.P.T.

1961-62

Belgium	572-573
Cyprus	201-203
France	1005-1006
Germany	844-845
Great Britain	382-384
Greece	718-719
Iceland	340-341
Italy	845-846
Luxembourg	382-383
Netherlands	387-388
Spain	1010-1011
Switzerland	410-411
Turkey	1518-1520

Nos. 572-573 (2)	.75	.50
Nos. 201-203 (3)	*2.10*	*1.20*
Nos. 1005-1006 (2)	.50	.50
Nos. 844-845 (2)	.60	.75
Nos. 382-384 (3)	.75	.75
Nos. 718-719 (2)	.80	.50
Nos. 340-341 (2)	1.10	1.60
Nos. 845-846 (2)	.50	.50
Nos. 382-383 (2)	.55	.55
Nos. 387-388 (2)	.55	.50
Nos. 1010-1011 (2)	.70	.55
Nos. 410-411 (2)	1.25	.60
Nos. 1518-1520 (3)	2.45	1.30
Set total (29) Stamps	12.60	9.80

Europa, 1962

Young Tree with 19 Leaves CD5

The 19 leaves represent the 19 original members of C.E.P.T.

1962-63

Belgium	582-583
Cyprus	219-221
France	1045-1046
Germany	852-853
Greece	739-740
Iceland	348-349
Ireland	184-185
Italy	860-861
Luxembourg	386-387
Netherlands	394-395
Norway	414-415
Switzerland	416-417
Turkey	1553-1555

Nos. 582-583 (2)	.65	.65
Nos. 219-221 (3)	*76.25*	*6.75*
Nos. 1045-1046 (2)	.60	.50
Nos. 852-853 (2)	.70	.80
Nos. 739-740 (2)	2.25	1.15
Nos. 348-349 (2)	.85	.85
Nos. 184-185 (2)	2.00	.50
Nos. 860-861 (2)	1.00	.55
Nos. 386-387 (2)	.75	.55
Nos. 394-395 (2)	1.40	.75
Nos. 414-415 (2)	2.25	2.25
Nos. 416-417 (2)	1.65	1.00
Nos. 1553-1555 (3)	*3.00*	1.55
Set total (28) Stamps	93.35	17.85

Europa, 1963

Stylized Links, Symbolizing Unity — CD6

1963, Sept.

Belgium	598-599
Cyprus	229-231
Finland	419
France	1074-1075
Germany	867-868
Greece	768-769
Iceland	357-358
Ireland	188-189
Italy	880-881
Luxembourg	403-404
Netherlands	416-417
Norway	441-442
Switzerland	429
Turkey	1602-1603

Nos. 598-599 (2)	1.60	.55
Nos. 229-231 (3)	*64.00*	*9.40*
No. 419 (1)	1.25	.55
Nos. 1074-1075 (2)	.60	.50
Nos. 867-868 (2)	.50	.55
Nos. 768-769 (2)	5.25	1.90
Nos. 357-358 (2)	1.20	1.20
Nos. 188-189 (2)	4.75	3.25
Nos. 880-881 (2)	.50	.50
Nos. 403-404 (2)	.75	.55
Nos. 416-417 (2)	2.25	1.00
Nos. 441-442 (2)	4.75	3.00
No. 429 (1)	.90	.60
Nos. 1602-1603 (2)	1.40	.60
Set total (27) Stamps	89.70	24.15

Europa, 1964

Symbolic Daisy — CD7

5th anniversary of the establishment of C.E.P.T. The 22 petals of the flower symbolize the 22 members of the Conference.

1964, Sept.

Austria	738
Belgium	614-615
Cyprus	244-246
France	1109-1110
Germany	897-898
Greece	801-802
Iceland	367-368
Ireland	196-197
Italy	894-895
Luxembourg	411-412
Monaco	590-591
Netherlands	428-429
Norway	458
Portugal	931-933
Spain	1262-1263
Switzerland	438-439
Turkey	1628-1629

No. 738 (1)	1.20	.80
Nos. 614-615 (2)	1.40	.60
Nos. 244-246 (3)	*32.25*	*5.10*
Nos. 1109-1110 (2)	.50	.50
Nos. 897-898 (2)	.50	.50
Nos. 801-802 (2)	5.00	1.90
Nos. 367-368 (2)	1.40	1.15
Nos. 196-197 (2)	17.00	4.25
Nos. 894-895 (2)	.50	.50
Nos. 411-412 (2)	.75	.55
Nos. 590-591 (2)	2.50	.70
Nos. 428-429 (2)	1.80	.60
No. 458 (1)	4.50	4.50
Nos. 931-933 (3)	*10.00*	*2.00*
Nos. 1262-1263 (2)	1.30	.80
Nos. 438-439 (2)	1.60	.50
Nos. 1628-1629 (2)	2.65	1.35
Set total (34) Stamps	84.85	26.30

Europa, 1965

Leaves and "Fruit" CD8

1965

Belgium	636-637
Cyprus	262-264
Finland	437
France	1131-1132
Germany	934-935
Greece	833-834
Iceland	375-376
Ireland	204-205
Italy	915-916
Luxembourg	432-433
Monaco	616-617
Netherlands	438-439
Norway	475-476
Portugal	958-960
Switzerland	469
Turkey	1665-1666

Nos. 636-637 (2)	.50	.50
Nos. 262-264 (3)	*25.35*	*6.00*
No. 437 (1)	1.25	.55
Nos. 1131-1132 (2)	.70	.55
Nos. 934-935 (2)	.50	.50
Nos. 833-834 (2)	2.25	1.15
Nos. 375-376 (2)	2.50	1.75
Nos. 204-205 (2)	16.00	3.35
Nos. 915-916 (2)	.50	.50
Nos. 432-433 (2)	.75	.55
Nos. 616-617 (2)	3.25	1.65
Nos. 438-439 (2)	.75	.55
Nos. 475-476 (2)	4.00	3.10
Nos. 958-960 (3)	*10.00*	*2.75*
No. 469 (1)	1.15	.25
Nos. 1665-1666 (2)	3.50	2.10
Set total (32) Stamps	72.95	25.80

Europa, 1966

Symbolic Sailboat — CD9

1966, Sept.

Andorra, French	172
Belgium	675-676
Cyprus	275-277
France	1163-1164
Germany	963-964

Country	Nos.
Greece	862-863
Iceland	384-385
Ireland	216-217
Italy	942-943
Liechtenstein	415
Luxembourg	440-441
Monaco	639-640
Netherlands	441-442
Norway	496-497
Portugal	980-982
Switzerland	477-478
Turkey	1718-1719

No. 172 (1)	3.00	3.00
Nos. 675-676 (2)	.80	.50
Nos. 275-277 (3)	*4.75*	*2.75*
Nos. 1163-1164 (2)	.55	.50
Nos. 963-964 (2)	.50	.55
Nos. 862-863 (2)	2.25	1.05
Nos. 384-385 (2)	4.50	3.50
Nos. 216-217 (2)	6.75	2.00
Nos. 942-943 (2)	.50	.50
No. 415 (1)	.40	.35
Nos. 440-441 (2)	.70	.55
Nos. 639-640 (2)	2.00	.65
Nos. 441-442 (2)	1.50	.65
Nos. 496-497 (2)	5.00	3.00
Nos. 980-982 (3)	*9.75*	2.25
Nos. 477-478 (2)	1.60	.60
Nos. 1718-1719 (2)	3.35	1.75
Set total (34) Stamps	47.90	24.15

Europa, 1967

Cogwheels
CD10

1967

Country	Nos.
Andorra, French	174-175
Belgium	688-689
Cyprus	297-299
France	1178-1179
Germany	969-970
Greece	891-892
Iceland	389-390
Ireland	232-233
Italy	951-952
Liechtenstein	420
Luxembourg	449-450
Monaco	669-670
Netherlands	444-447
Norway	504-505
Portugal	994-996
Spain	1465-1466
Switzerland	482
Turkey	B120-B121

Nos. 174-175 (2)	10.75	6.25
Nos. 688-689 (2)	1.05	.55
Nos. 297-299 (3)	*4.25*	*2.50*
Nos. 1178-1179 (2)	.55	.50
Nos. 969-970 (2)	.55	.55
Nos. 891-892 (2)	3.75	1.00
Nos. 389-390 (2)	3.00	2.00
Nos. 232-233 (2)	5.90	2.30
Nos. 951-952 (2)	.60	.50
No. 420 (1)	.45	.40
Nos. 449-450 (2)	1.00	.70
Nos. 669-670 (2)	2.75	.70
Nos. 444-447 (4)	5.00	1.85
Nos. 504-505 (2)	3.25	2.75
Nos. 994-996 (3)	*9.50*	1.85
Nos. 1465-1466 (2)	.50	.50
No. 482 (1)	.70	.25
Nos. B120-B121 (2)	3.50	2.75
Set total (38) Stamps	57.05	27.90

Europa, 1968

Golden Key with C.E.P.T. Emblem
CD11

1968

Country	Nos.
Andorra, French	182-183
Belgium	705-706
Cyprus	314-316
France	1209-1210
Germany	983-984
Greece	916-917
Iceland	395-396
Ireland	242-243
Italy	979-980
Liechtenstein	442
Luxembourg	466-467
Monaco	689-691
Netherlands	452-453
Portugal	1019-1021
San Marino	687
Spain	1526
Switzerland	488
Turkey	1775-1776

Nos. 182-183 (2)	16.50	10.00
Nos. 705-706 (2)	1.25	.50
Nos. 314-316 (3)	*2.90*	*2.50*
Nos. 1209-1210 (2)	.85	.55
Nos. 983-984 (2)	.50	.55
Nos. 916-917 (2)	3.75	1.65
Nos. 395-396 (2)	3.00	2.20
Nos. 242-243 (2)	3.30	2.25
Nos. 979-980 (2)	.50	.50
No. 442 (1)	.45	.40
Nos. 466-467 (2)	.80	.70
Nos. 689-691 (3)	*5.40*	.95
Nos. 452-453 (2)	2.10	.70
Nos. 1019-1021 (3)	*9.75*	2.10
No. 687 (1)	.55	.35
No. 1526 (1)	.25	.25
No. 488 (1)	.45	.25
Nos. 1775-1776 (2)	5.00	2.00
Set total (35) Stamps	57.30	28.40

Europa, 1969

"EUROPA" and "CEPT"
CD12

Tenth anniversary of C.E.P.T.

1969

Country	Nos.
Andorra, French	188-189
Austria	837
Belgium	718-719
Cyprus	326-328
Denmark	458
Finland	483
France	1245-1246
Germany	996-997
Great Britain	585
Greece	947-948
Iceland	406-407
Ireland	270-271
Italy	1000-1001
Liechtenstein	453
Luxembourg	475-476
Monaco	722-724
Netherlands	475-476
Norway	533-534
Portugal	1038-1040
San Marino	701-702
Spain	1567
Sweden	814-816
Switzerland	500-501
Turkey	1799-1800
Vatican	470-472
Yugoslavia	1003-1004

Nos. 188-189 (2)	18.50	12.00
No. 837 (1)	.65	.30
Nos. 718-719 (2)	.75	.50
Nos. 326-328 (3)	*3.00*	*2.25*
No. 458 (1)	.75	.75
No. 483 (1)	3.50	.75
Nos. 1245-1246 (2)	.55	.50
Nos. 996-997 (2)	.80	.50
No. 585 (1)	.25	.25
Nos. 947-948 (2)	5.00	1.50
Nos. 406-407 (2)	4.20	2.40
Nos. 270-271 (2)	3.50	2.00
Nos. 1000-1001 (2)	.50	.50
No. 453 (1)	.45	.45
Nos. 475-476 (2)	.95	.50
Nos. 722-724 (3)	*10.50*	2.00
Nos. 475-476 (2)	2.60	1.15
Nos. 533-534 (2)	3.75	2.35
Nos. 1038-1040 (3)	17.75	2.40
Nos. 701-702 (2)	.90	.90
No. 1567 (1)	.25	.25
Nos. 814-816 (3)	4.00	2.85
Nos. 500-501 (2)	1.85	.60
Nos. 1799-1800 (2)	3.85	2.25
Nos. 470-472 (3)	.75	.75
Nos. 1003-1004 (2)	4.00	4.00
Set total (51) Stamps	93.55	44.65

Europa, 1970

Interwoven Threads
CD13

1970

Country	Nos.
Andorra, French	196-197
Belgium	741-742
Cyprus	340-342
France	1271-1272
Germany	1018-1019
Greece	985, 987
Iceland	420-421
Ireland	279-281
Italy	1013-1014
Liechtenstein	470
Luxembourg	489-490
Monaco	768-770
Netherlands	483-484
Portugal	1060-1062
San Marino	729-730
Spain	1607
Switzerland	515-516
Turkey	1848-1849
Yugoslavia	1024-1025

Nos. 196-197 (2)	20.00	8.50
Nos. 741-742 (2)	1.10	.55
Nos. 340-342 (3)	*2.70*	*2.75*
Nos. 1271-1272 (2)	.65	.50
Nos. 1018-1019 (2)	.60	.50
Nos. 985,987 (2)	7.75	2.00
Nos. 420-421 (2)	6.00	4.00
Nos. 279-281 (3)	7.50	2.50
Nos. 1013-1014 (2)	.50	.50
No. 470 (1)	.45	.45
Nos. 489-490 (2)	.80	.55
Nos. 768-770 (3)	*6.35*	2.10
Nos. 483-484 (2)	2.50	1.15
Nos. 1060-1062 (3)	*9.75*	2.35
Nos. 729-730 (2)	.90	.55
No. 1607 (1)	.25	.25
Nos. 515-516 (2)	1.85	.60
Nos. 1848-1849 (2)	5.00	2.25
Nos. 1024-1025 (2)	.80	.80
Set total (40) Stamps	75.45	32.85

Europa, 1971

"Fraternity, Cooperation, Common Effort"
CD14

1971

Country	Nos.
Andorra, French	205-206
Belgium	803-804
Cyprus	365-367
Finland	504
France	1304
Germany	1064-1065
Greece	1029-1030
Iceland	429-430
Ireland	305-306
Italy	1038-1039
Liechtenstein	485
Luxembourg	500-501
Malta	425-427
Monaco	797-799
Netherlands	488-489
Portugal	1094-1096
San Marino	749-750
Spain	1675-1676
Switzerland	531-532
Turkey	1876-1877
Yugoslavia	1052-1053

Nos. 205-206 (2)	20.00	7.75
Nos. 803-804 (2)	1.30	.55
Nos. 365-367 (3)	*2.60*	*3.25*
No. 504 (1)	5.00	.75
No. 1304 (1)	.45	.40
Nos. 1064-1065 (2)	.60	.50
Nos. 1029-1030 (2)	4.00	1.80
Nos. 429-430 (2)	5.00	3.75
Nos. 305-306 (2)	4.50	1.50
Nos. 1038-1039 (2)	.65	.50
No. 485 (1)	.45	.45
Nos. 500-501 (2)	1.00	.65
Nos. 425-427 (3)	*.80*	*.80*
Nos. 797-799 (3)	*15.00*	2.80
Nos. 488-489 (2)	2.50	1.15
Nos. 1094-1096 (3)	*9.75*	1.75
Nos. 749-750 (2)	.65	.55
Nos. 1675-1676 (2)	.75	.55
Nos. 531-532 (2)	1.85	.65
Nos. 1876-1877 (2)	5.60	2.50
Nos. 1052-1053 (2)	.50	.50
Set total (43) Stamps	82.95	33.10

Europa, 1972

Sparkles, Symbolic of Communications
CD15

1972

Country	Nos.
Andorra, French	210-211
Andorra, Spanish	62
Belgium	825-826
Cyprus	380-382
Finland	512-513
France	1341
Germany	1089-1090
Greece	1049-1050
Iceland	439-440
Ireland	316-317
Italy	1065-1066
Liechtenstein	504
Luxembourg	512-513
Malta	450-453
Monaco	831-832
Netherlands	494-495
Portugal	1141-1143
San Marino	771-772
Spain	1718
Switzerland	544-545
Turkey	1907-1908
Yugoslavia	1100-1101

Nos. 210-211 (2)	21.00	7.00
No. 62 (1)	45.00	45.00
Nos. 825-826 (2)	.95	.55
Nos. 380-382 (3)	*5.95*	*4.25*
Nos. 512-513 (2)	7.00	1.40
No. 1341 (1)	.50	.35
Nos. 1089-1090 (2)	1.30	.50
Nos. 1049-1050 (2)	2.00	1.55
Nos. 439-440 (2)	2.90	2.65
Nos. 316-317 (2)	13.00	4.50
Nos. 1065-1066 (2)	.55	.50
No. 504 (1)	.45	.45
Nos. 512-513 (2)	.95	.65
Nos. 450-453 (4)	1.05	1.40
Nos. 831-832 (2)	5.00	1.40
Nos. 494-495 (2)	3.25	1.15
Nos. 1141-1143 (3)	*9.75*	1.50
Nos. 771-772 (2)	.70	.50
No. 1718 (1)	.50	.40
Nos. 544-545 (2)	1.65	.60
Nos. 1907-1908 (2)	7.50	3.00
Nos. 1100-1101 (2)	1.20	1.20
Set total (44) Stamps	132.15	80.50

Europa, 1973

Post Horn and Arrows
CD16

1973

Country	Nos.
Andorra, French	219-220
Andorra, Spanish	76
Belgium	839-840
Cyprus	396-398
Finland	526
France	1367
Germany	1114-1115
Greece	1090-1092
Iceland	447-448
Ireland	329-330
Italy	1108-1109
Liechtenstein	528-529
Luxembourg	523-524
Malta	469-471
Monaco	866-867
Netherlands	504-505
Norway	604-605
Portugal	1170-1172
San Marino	802-803
Spain	1753
Switzerland	580-581
Turkey	1935-1936
Yugoslavia	1138-1139

Nos. 219-220 (2)	20.00	11.00
No. 76 (1)	.65	.55
Nos. 839-840 (2)	1.00	.65
Nos. 396-398 (3)	*4.25*	*3.85*
No. 526 (1)	1.25	.55
No. 1367 (1)	1.25	.75
Nos. 1114-1115 (2)	.90	.50
Nos. 1090-1092 (3)	2.10	1.40
Nos. 447-448 (2)	6.65	3.35

Nos. 329-330 (2)	5.25	2.00
Nos. 1108-1109 (2)	.50	.50
Nos. 528-529 (2)	.60	.60
Nos. 523-524 (2)	.90	.75
Nos. 469-471 (3)	.90	1.20
Nos. 866-867 (2)	15.00	2.40
Nos. 504-505 (2)	2.85	1.10
Nos. 604-605 (2)	6.25	2.40
Nos. 1170-1172 (3)	*13.00*	2.15
Nos. 802-803 (2)	*1.00*	.60
No. 1753 (1)	.35	.25
Nos. 580-581 (2)	1.55	.60
Nos. 1935-1936 (2)	10.00	4.50
Nos. 1138-1139 (2)	1.15	1.10
Set total (46) Stamps	97.35	42.75

Europa, 2000

CD17

2000

Albania....2621-2622
Andorra, French....522
Andorra, Spanish....262
Armenia....610-611
Austria....1814
Azerbaijan....698-699
Belarus....350
Belgium....1818
Bosnia & Herzegovina (Moslem)....358
Bosnia & Herzegovina (Serb)....111-112
Croatia....428-429
Cyprus....959
Czech Republic....3120
Denmark....1189
Estonia....394
Faroe Islands....376
Finland....1129
Aland Islands....166
France....2771
Georgia....228-229
Germany....2086-2087
Gibraltar....837-840
Great Britain (Jersey)....935-936
Great Britain (Isle of Man)....883
Greece....1959
Greenland....363
Hungary....3699-3700
Iceland....910
Ireland....1230-1231
Italy....2349
Latvia....504
Liechtenstein....1178
Lithuania....668
Luxembourg....1035
Macedonia....187
Malta....1011-1012
Moldova....355
Monaco....2161-2162
Poland....3519
Portugal....2358
Portugal (Azores)....455
Portugal (Madeira)....208
Romania....4370
Russia....6589
San Marino....1480
Slovakia....355
Slovenia....424
Spain....3036
Sweden....2394
Switzerland....1074
Turkey....2762
Turkish Rep. of Northern Cyprus....500
Ukraine....379
Vatican City....1152

Nos. 2621-2622 (2)	11.00	11.00
No. 522 (1)	2.00	1.00
No. 262 (1)	1.60	.70
Nos. 610-611 (2)	4.75	4.75
No. 1814 (1)	1.40	1.40
Nos. 698-699 (2)	6.00	6.00
No. 350 (1)	1.75	1.75
No. 1818 (1)	1.40	.60
No. 358 (1)	4.75	4.75
Nos. 111-112 (2)	110.00	110.00
Nos. 428-429 (2)	6.25	6.25
No. 959 (1)	2.10	1.40
No. 3120 (1)	1.20	.40
No. 1189 (1)	3.50	2.25
No. 394 (1)	1.25	1.25
No. 376 (1)	2.40	2.40
No. 1129 (1)	2.00	.60
No. 166 (1)	2.00	1.10
No. 2771 (1)	1.25	.40
Nos. 228-229 (2)	9.00	9.00
Nos. 2086-2087 (2)	4.15	1.90
Nos. 837-840 (4)	5.50	5.30
Nos. 935-936 (2)	2.40	2.40
No. 883 (1)	1.75	1.75
No. 363 (1)	1.90	1.90
Nos. 3699-3700 (2)	6.50	2.50
No. 910 (1)	1.60	1.60
Nos. 1230-1231 (2)	4.35	4.35
No. 2349 (1)	1.50	.40
No. 504 (1)	5.00	2.40
No. 1178 (1)	2.25	1.75
No. 668 (1)	1.50	1.50
No. 1035 (1)	1.40	.85
No. 187 (1)	3.00	3.00
Nos. 1011-1012 (2)	4.35	4.35
No. 355 (1)	3.50	3.50
Nos. 2161-2162 (2)	2.80	1.40
No. 3519 (1)	1.10	.50
No. 2358 (1)	1.25	.65
No. 455 (1)	1.25	.50
No. 208 (1)	1.25	.50
No. 4370 (1)	2.50	1.25
No. 6589 (1)	2.00	.85
No. 1480 (1)	1.00	1.00
No. 355 (1)	1.25	.55
No. 424 (1)	3.25	1.60
No. 3036 (1)	.75	.40
No. 2394 (1)	3.00	2.25
No. 1074 (1)	2.10	.75
No. 2762 (1)	2.00	2.00
No. 500 (1)	2.50	2.50
No. 379 (1)	4.50	3.00
No. 1152 (1)	1.25	1.25
Set total (68) Stamps	260.00	227.40

The Gibraltar stamps are similar to the stamp illustrated, but none have the design shown above. All other sets listed above include at least one stamp with the design shown, but some include stamps with entirely different designs. Bulgaria Nos. 4131-4132, Guernsey Nos. 802-803 and Yugoslavia Nos. 2485-2486 are Europa stamps with completely different designs.

PORTUGAL & COLONIES
Vasco da Gama

Fleet Departing CD20

Fleet Arriving at Calicut — CD21

Embarking at Rastello CD22

Muse of History CD23

San Gabriel, da Gama and Camoens CD24

Archangel Gabriel, the Patron Saint CD25

Flagship San Gabriel — CD26

Vasco da Gama — CD27

Fourth centenary of Vasco da Gama's discovery of the route to India.

1898

Azores....93-100
Macao....67-74
Madeira....37-44
Portugal....147-154
Port. Africa....1-8
Port. Congo....75-98
Port. India....189-196
St. Thomas & Prince Islands....170-193
Timor....45-52

Nos. 93-100 (8)	122.00	76.25
Nos. 67-74 (8)	136.00	96.75
Nos. 37-44 (8)	44.55	34.00
Nos. 147-154 (8)	169.30	43.45
Nos. 1-8 (8)	24.75	21.70
Nos. 75-98 (24)	50.50	34.45
Nos. 189-196 (8)	20.25	12.95
Nos. 170-193 (24)	38.75	34.30
Nos. 45-52 (8)	19.50	8.75
Set total (104) Stamps	625.60	362.60

Pombal
POSTAL TAX
POSTAL TAX DUES

Marquis de Pombal — CD28

Planning Reconstruction of Lisbon, 1755 — CD29

Pombal Monument, Lisbon — CD30

Sebastiao Jose de Carvalho e Mello, Marquis de Pombal (1699-1782), statesman, rebuilt Lisbon after earthquake of 1755. Tax was for the erection of Pombal monument. Obligatory on all mail on certain days throughout the year. Postal Tax Dues are inscribed "Multa."

1925

Angola.... RA1-RA3, RAJ1-RAJ3
Azores.... RA9-RA11, RAJ2-RAJ4
Cape Verde.... RA1-RA3, RAJ1-RAJ3
Macao.... RA1-RA3, RAJ1-RAJ3
Madeira.... RA1-RA3, RAJ1-RAJ3
Mozambique.... RA1-RA3, RAJ1-RAJ3
Nyassa.... RA1-RA3, RAJ1-RAJ3
Portugal.... RA11-RA13, RAJ2-RAJ4
Port. Guinea.... RA1-RA3, RAJ1-RAJ3
Port. India.... RA1-RA3, RAJ1-RAJ3
St. Thomas & Prince Islands.... RA1-RA3, RAJ1-RAJ3
Timor.... RA1-RA3, RAJ1-RAJ3

Nos. RA1-RA3,RAJ1-RAJ3 (6)	6.60	6.60
Nos. RA9-RA11,RAJ2-RAJ4 (6)	6.60	9.30
Nos. RA1-RA3,RAJ1-RAJ3 (6)	6.00	5.40
Nos. RA1-RA3,RAJ1-RAJ3 (6)	18.50	10.50
Nos. RA1-RA3,RAJ1-RAJ3 (6)	4.35	12.45
Nos. RA1-RA3,RAJ1-RAJ3 (6)	2.40	2.55
Nos. RA1-RA3,RAJ1-RAJ3 (6)	52.50	38.25
Nos. RA11-RA13,RAJ2-RAJ4 (6)	5.80	5.20
Nos. RA1-RA3,RAJ1-RAJ3 (6)	3.30	2.70
Nos. RA1-RA3,RAJ1-RAJ3 (6)	3.45	3.45
Nos. RA1-RA3,RAJ1-RAJ3 (6)	3.60	3.60
Nos. RA1-RA3,RAJ1-RAJ3 (6)	2.10	3.90
Set total (72) Stamps	115.20	103.90

Vasco da Gama CD34

Mousinho de Albuquerque CD35

Dam CD36

Prince Henry the Navigator CD37

Affonso de Albuquerque CD38

Plane over Globe CD39

1938-39

Angola....274-291, C1-C9
Cape Verde....234-251, C1-C9
Macao....289-305, C7-C15
Mozambique....270-287, C1-C9
Port. Guinea....233-250, C1-C9
Port. India....439-453, C1-C8
St. Thomas & Prince Islands.... 302-319, 323-340, C1-C18
Timor....223-239, C1-C9

Nos. 274-291,C1-C9 (27)	132.90	22.85
Nos. 234-251,C1-C9 (27)	100.00	31.20
Nos. 289-305,C7-C15 (26)	701.70	135.60
Nos. 270-287,C1-C9 (27)	63.45	11.20
Nos. 233-250,C1-C9 (27)	88.05	30.70
Nos. 439-453,C1-C8 (23)	74.75	25.50
Nos. 302-319,323-340,C1-C18 (54)	319.25	190.35
Nos. 223-239,C1-C9 (26)	149.25	73.15
Set total (237) Stamps	1,629.	520.55

Lady of Fatima

Our Lady of the Rosary, Fatima, Portugal — CD40

1948-49

Angola....315-318
Cape Verde....266
Macao....336
Mozambique....325-328
Port. Guinea....271
Port. India....480
St. Thomas & Prince Islands....351
Timor....254

Nos. 315-318 (4)	68.00	17.25
No. 266 (1)	8.50	4.50
No. 336 (1)	40.00	12.00
Nos. 325-328 (4)	73.25	16.85
No. 271 (1)	3.25	3.00
No. 480 (1)	2.50	2.25
No. 351 (1)	7.25	6.50
No. 254 (1)	2.75	2.75
Set total (14) Stamps	205.50	65.10

A souvenir sheet of 9 stamps was issued in 1951 to mark the extension of the 1950 Holy Year. The sheet contains: Angola No. 316, Cape Verde No. 266, Macao No. 336, Mozambique No. 325, Portuguese Guinea No. 271, Portuguese India Nos. 480, 485, St. Thomas & Prince Islands No. 351, Timor No. 254. The sheet also contains a portrait of Pope Pius XII and is inscribed "Encerramento do

Ano Santo, Fatima 1951." It was sold for 11 escudos.

Holy Year

Church Bells and Dove CD41

Angel Holding Candelabra CD42

Holy Year, 1950.

1950-51

Angola 331-332
Cape Verde 268-269
Macao 339-340
Mozambique 330-331
Port. Guinea 273-274
Port. India 490-491, 496-503
St. Thomas & Prince Islands 353-354
Timor 258-259

Nos. 331-332 (2)	7.60	1.35
Nos. 268-269 (2)	4.75	2.20
Nos. 339-340 (2)	55.00	12.50
Nos. 330-331 (2)	3.00	1.10
Nos. 273-274 (2)	3.50	2.60
Nos. 490-491,496-503 (10)	12.80	5.40
Nos. 353-354 (2)	7.50	4.40
Nos. 258-259 (2)	3.75	3.25
Set total (24) Stamps	97.90	32.80

A souvenir sheet of 8 stamps was issued in 1951 to mark the extension of the Holy Year. The sheet contains: Angola No. 331, Cape Verde No. 269, Macao No. 340, Mozambique No. 331, Portuguese Guinea No. 275, Portuguese India No. 490, St. Thomas & Prince Islands No. 354, Timor No. 258, some with colors changed. The sheet contains doves and is inscribed 'Encerramento do Ano Santo, Fatima 1951.' It was sold for 17 escudos.

Holy Year Conclusion

Our Lady of Fatima — CD43

Conclusion of Holy Year. Sheets contain alternate vertical rows of stamps and labels bearing quotation from Pope Pius XII, different for each colony.

1951

Angola 357
Cape Verde 270
Macao 352
Mozambique 356
Port. Guinea 275
Port. India 506
St. Thomas & Prince Islands 355
Timor 270

No. 357 (1)	5.25	1.50
No. 270 (1)	1.50	1.25
No. 352 (1)	37.50	10.00
No. 356 (1)	2.25	1.00
No. 275 (1)	1.00	.65
No. 506 (1)	1.60	1.00
No. 355 (1)	2.50	2.00
No. 270 (1)	2.00	1.75
Set total (8) Stamps	53.60	19.15

Medical Congress

CD44

First National Congress of Tropical Medicine, Lisbon, 1952. Each stamp has a different design.

1952

Angola 358
Cape Verde 287
Macao 364
Mozambique 359
Port. Guinea 276
Port. India 516
St. Thomas & Prince Islands 356
Timor 271

No. 358 (1)	1.50	.50
No. 287 (1)	.70	.50
No. 364 (1)	9.75	4.25
No. 359 (1)	1.25	.55
No. 276 (1)	.45	.35
No. 516 (1)	4.75	2.00
No. 356 (1)	.30	.30
No. 271 (1)	1.00	1.00
Set total (8) Stamps	19.70	9.45

Postage Due Stamps

CD45

1952

Angola J37-J42
Cape Verde J31-J36
Macao J53-J58
Mozambique J51-J56
Port. Guinea J40-J45
Port. India J47-J52
St. Thomas & Prince Islands J52-J57
Timor J31-J36

Nos. J37-J42 (6)	4.05	3.15
Nos. J31-J36 (6)	2.80	2.30
Nos. J53-J58 (6)	17.45	6.85
Nos. J51-J56 (6)	1.80	1.55
Nos. J40-J45 (6)	2.55	2.55
Nos. J47-J52 (6)	6.10	6.10
Nos. J52-J57 (6)	4.15	4.15
Nos. J31-J36 (6)	6.20	3.50
Set total (48) Stamps	45.10	30.15

Sao Paulo

Father Manuel da Nobrega and View of Sao Paulo — CD46

Founding of Sao Paulo, Brazil, 400th anniv.

1954

Angola 385
Cape Verde 297
Macao 382
Mozambique 395
Port. Guinea 291
Port. India 530
St. Thomas & Prince Islands 369
Timor 279

No. 385 (1)	.80	.50
No. 297 (1)	.70	.60
No. 382 (1)	14.00	3.00
No. 395 (1)	.40	.30
No. 291 (1)	.35	.25
No. 530 (1)	.80	.40
No. 369 (1)	.80	.60
No. 279 (1)	.85	.70
Set total (8) Stamps	18.70	6.35

Tropical Medicine Congress

CD47

Sixth International Congress for Tropical Medicine and Malaria, Lisbon, Sept. 1958. Each stamp shows a different plant.

1958

Angola 409
Cape Verde 303
Macao 392
Mozambique 404
Port. Guinea 295
Port. India 569
St. Thomas & Prince Islands 371
Timor 289

No. 409 (1)	3.50	1.10
No. 303 (1)	5.50	2.10
No. 392 (1)	8.00	3.00
No. 404 (1)	2.50	.85
No. 295 (1)	2.75	1.10
No. 569 (1)	1.75	.75
No. 371 (1)	2.75	2.25
No. 289 (1)	3.00	2.75
Set total (8) Stamps	29.75	13.90

Sports

CD48

Each stamp shows a different sport.

1962

Angola 433-438
Cape Verde 320-325
Macao 394-399
Mozambique 424-429
Port. Guinea 299-304
St. Thomas & Prince Islands 374-379
Timor 313-318

Nos. 433-438 (6)	5.50	3.20
Nos. 320-325 (6)	15.25	5.20
Nos. 394-399 (6)	74.00	14.60
Nos. 424-429 (6)	5.70	2.45
Nos. 299-304 (6)	4.95	2.15
Nos. 374-379 (6)	6.75	3.20
Nos. 313-318 (6)	6.40	3.70
Set total (42) Stamps	118.55	34.50

Anti-Malaria

Anopheles Funestus and Malaria Eradication Symbol — CD49

World Health Organization drive to eradicate malaria.

1962

Angola 439
Cape Verde 326
Macao 400
Mozambique 430
Port. Guinea 305
St. Thomas & Prince Islands 380
Timor 319

No. 439 (1)	1.75	.90
No. 326 (1)	1.40	.90
No. 400 (1)	6.50	2.00
No. 430 (1)	1.40	.40
No. 305 (1)	1.25	.45
No. 380 (1)	2.00	1.50
No. 319 (1)	.75	.60
Set total (7) Stamps	15.05	6.75

Airline Anniversary

Map of Africa, Super Constellation and Jet Liner — CD50

Tenth anniversary of Transportes Aereos Portugueses (TAP).

1963

Angola 490
Cape Verde 327
Mozambique 434
Port. Guinea 318
St. Thomas & Prince Islands 381

No. 490 (1)	1.00	.35
No. 327 (1)	1.10	.70
No. 434 (1)	.40	.25
No. 318 (1)	.65	.35
No. 381 (1)	.70	.60
Set total (5) Stamps	3.85	2.25

National Overseas Bank

Antonio Teixeira de Sousa — CD51

Centenary of the National Overseas Bank of Portugal.

1964, May 16

Angola 509
Cape Verde 328
Port. Guinea 319
St. Thomas & Prince Islands 382
Timor 320

No. 509 (1)	.90	.30
No. 328 (1)	1.10	.75
No. 319 (1)	.65	.40
No. 382 (1)	.70	.50
No. 320 (1)	.75	.60
Set total (5) Stamps	4.10	2.55

ITU

ITU Emblem and the Archangel Gabriel — CD52

International Communications Union, Cent.

1965, May 17

Angola 511
Cape Verde 329
Macao 402
Mozambique 464
Port. Guinea 320
St. Thomas & Prince Islands 383
Timor 321

No. 511 (1)	1.25	.65
No. 329 (1)	2.10	1.40
No. 402 (1)	5.00	2.00
No. 464 (1)	.45	.25
No. 320 (1)	1.90	.75
No. 383 (1)	1.50	1.00
No. 321 (1)	1.50	.90
Set total (7) Stamps	13.70	6.95

National Revolution

CD53

40th anniv. of the National Revolution. Different buildings on each stamp.

1966, May 28

Angola 525
Cape Verde 338
Macao 403
Mozambique 465
Port. Guinea 329
St. Thomas & Prince Islands 392
Timor 322

No. 525 (1)	.50	.25
No. 338 (1)	.60	.45
No. 403 (1)	5.00	2.00
No. 465 (1)	.50	.30
No. 329 (1)	.55	.35
No. 392 (1)	.75	.50
No. 322 (1)	1.50	.90
Set total (7) Stamps	9.40	4.75

Navy Club

CD54

Centenary of Portugal's Navy Club. Each stamp has a different design.

1967, Jan. 31

Angola	527-528
Cape Verde	339-340
Macao	412-413
Mozambique	478-479
Port. Guinea	330-331
St. Thomas & Prince Islands	393-394
Timor	323-324

Nos. 527-528 (2)	1.75	.75
Nos. 339-340 (2)	2.00	1.40
Nos. 412-413 (2)	9.50	3.75
Nos. 478-479 (2)	1.40	.65
Nos. 330-331 (2)	1.20	.90
Nos. 393-394 (2)	3.20	1.25
Nos. 323-324 (2)	4.00	2.00
Set total (14) Stamps	23.05	10.70

Admiral Coutinho

CD55

Centenary of the birth of Admiral Carlos Viegas Gago Coutinho (1869-1959), explorer and aviation pioneer. Each stamp has a different design.

1969, Feb. 17

Angola	547
Cape Verde	355
Macao	417
Mozambique	484
Port. Guinea	335
St. Thomas & Prince Islands	397
Timor	335

No. 547 (1)	.85	.35
No. 355 (1)	.35	.25
No. 417 (1)	3.75	1.50
No. 484 (1)	.25	.25
No. 335 (1)	.35	.25
No. 397 (1)	.50	.35
No. 335 (1)	1.10	.85
Set total (7) Stamps	7.15	3.80

Administration Reform

Luiz Augusto Rebello da Silva — CD56

Centenary of the administration reforms of the overseas territories.

1969, Sept. 25

Angola	549
Cape Verde	357
Macao	419
Mozambique	491
Port. Guinea	337
St. Thomas & Prince Islands	399
Timor	338

No. 549 (1)	.35	.25
No. 357 (1)	.35	.25
No. 419 (1)	5.00	1.00
No. 491 (1)	.25	.25
No. 337 (1)	.25	.25
No. 399 (1)	.45	.45
No. 338 (1)	.40	.25
Set total (7) Stamps	7.05	2.70

Marshal Carmona

CD57

Birth centenary of Marshal Antonio Oscar Carmona de Fragoso (1869-1951), President of Portugal. Each stamp has a different design.

1970, Nov. 15

Angola	563
Cape Verde	359
Macao	422
Mozambique	493
Port. Guinea	340
St. Thomas & Prince Islands	403
Timor	341

No. 563 (1)	.45	.25
No. 359 (1)	.55	.35
No. 422 (1)	2.25	1.25
No. 493 (1)	.40	.25
No. 340 (1)	.35	.25
No. 403 (1)	.75	.45
No. 341 (1)	.25	.25
Set total (7) Stamps	5.00	3.05

Olympic Games

CD59

20th Olympic Games, Munich, Aug. 26-Sept. 11. Each stamp shows a different sport.

1972, June 20

Angola	569
Cape Verde	361
Macao	426
Mozambique	504
Port. Guinea	342
St. Thomas & Prince Islands	408
Timor	343

No. 569 (1)	.65	.25
No. 361 (1)	.65	.30
No. 426 (1)	3.25	1.00
No. 504 (1)	.30	.25
No. 342 (1)	.45	.25
No. 408 (1)	.35	.25
No. 343 (1)	.50	.50
Set total (7) Stamps	6.15	2.80

Lisbon-Rio de Janeiro Flight

CD60

50th anniversary of the Lisbon to Rio de Janeiro flight by Arturo de Sacadura and Coutinho, March 30-June 5, 1922. Each stamp shows a different stage of the flight.

1972, Sept. 20

Angola	570
Cape Verde	362
Macao	427
Mozambique	505
Port. Guinea	343
St. Thomas & Prince Islands	409
Timor	344

No. 570 (1)	.35	.25
No. 362 (1)	1.50	.30
No. 427 (1)	22.50	7.50
No. 505 (1)	.25	.25
No. 343 (1)	.25	.25
No. 409 (1)	.35	.25
No. 344 (1)	.25	.40
Set total (7) Stamps	25.45	9.20

WMO Centenary

WMO Emblem — CD61

Centenary of international meterological cooperation.

1973, Dec. 15

Angola	571
Cape Verde	363
Macao	429
Mozambique	509
Port. Guinea	344
St. Thomas & Prince Islands	410
Timor	345

No. 571 (1)	.45	.25
No. 363 (1)	.65	.30
No. 429 (1)	6.25	1.75
No. 509 (1)	.30	.25
No. 344 (1)	.45	.35
No. 410 (1)	.60	.50
No. 345 (1)	1.75	2.00
Set total (7) Stamps	10.45	5.40

FRENCH COMMUNITY

Upper Volta can be found under Burkina Faso in Vol. 1

Madagascar can be found under Malagasy in Vol. 3

Colonial Exposition

People of French Empire CD70

Women's Heads CD71

France Showing Way to Civilization CD72

"Colonial Commerce" CD73

International Colonial Exposition, Paris.

1931

Cameroun	213-216
Chad	60-63
Dahomey	97-100
Fr. Guiana	152-155
Fr. Guinea	116-119
Fr. India	100-103
Fr. Polynesia	76-79
Fr. Sudan	102-105
Gabon	120-123
Guadeloupe	138-141
Indo-China	140-142
Ivory Coast	92-95
Madagascar	169-172
Martinique	129-132
Mauritania	65-68
Middle Congo	61-64
New Caledonia	176-179
Niger	73-76
Reunion	122-125
St. Pierre & Miquelon	132-135
Senegal	138-141
Somali Coast	135-138
Togo	254-257
Ubangi-Shari	82-85
Upper Volta	66-69
Wallis & Futuna Isls.	85-88

Nos. 213-216 (4)	23.00	18.25
Nos. 60-63 (4)	22.00	22.00
Nos. 97-100 (4)	26.00	26.00
Nos. 152-155 (4)	22.00	22.00
Nos. 116-119 (4)	19.75	19.75
Nos. 100-103 (4)	18.00	*18.00*
Nos. 76-79 (4)	30.00	30.00
Nos. 102-105 (4)	19.00	19.00
Nos. 120-123 (4)	17.50	17.50
Nos. 138-141 (4)	19.00	19.00
Nos. 140-142 (3)	12.00	11.50
Nos. 92-95 (4)	22.50	22.50
Nos. 169-172 (4)	7.90	5.00
Nos. 129-132 (4)	21.00	21.00
Nos. 65-68 (4)	22.00	22.00
Nos. 61-64 (4)	20.00	18.50
Nos. 176-179 (4)	24.00	24.00
Nos. 73-76 (4)	21.50	21.50
Nos. 122-125 (4)	22.00	22.00
Nos. 132-135 (4)	24.00	24.00
Nos. 138-141 (4)	20.00	20.00
Nos. 135-138 (4)	22.00	22.00
Nos. 254-257 (4)	22.00	22.00
Nos. 82-85 (4)	21.00	21.00
Nos. 66-69 (4)	19.00	19.00
Nos. 85-88 (4)	35.00	35.00
Set total (103) Stamps	552.15	542.50

Paris International Exposition
Colonial Arts Exposition

"Colonial Resources" CD74 CD77

Overseas Commerce CD75

Exposition Building and Women CD76

"France and the Empire" CD78

Cultural Treasures of the Colonies CD79

Souvenir sheets contain one imperf. stamp.

1937

Cameroun	217-222A
Dahomey	101-107
Fr. Equatorial Africa	27-32, 73
Fr. Guiana	162-168
Fr. Guinea	120-126
Fr. India	104-110
Fr. Polynesia	117-123
Fr. Sudan	106-112
Guadeloupe	148-154
Indo-China	193-199
Inini	41
Ivory Coast	152-158
Kwangchowan	132
Madagascar	191-197
Martinique	179-185
Mauritania	69-75
New Caledonia	208-214
Niger	77-83
Reunion	167-173
St. Pierre & Miquelon	165-171
Senegal	172-178
Somali Coast	139-145
Togo	258-264
Wallis & Futuna Isls.	89

Nos. 217-222A (7)	18.80	20.30
Nos. 101-107 (7)	23.60	27.60
Nos. 27-32, 73 (7)	28.10	32.10
Nos. 162-168 (7)	22.50	24.50
Nos. 120-126 (7)	24.00	28.00
Nos. 104-110 (7)	21.15	36.50
Nos. 117-123 (7)	58.50	75.00
Nos. 106-112 (7)	23.60	27.60
Nos. 148-154 (7)	19.55	21.05
Nos. 193-199 (7)	17.70	19.70
No. 41 (1)	21.00	27.50
Nos. 152-158 (7)	22.20	26.20
No. 132 (1)	9.25	11.00
Nos. 191-197 (7)	19.25	21.75
Nos. 179-185 (7)	19.95	21.70
Nos. 69-75 (7)	20.50	24.50
Nos. 208-214 (7)	39.00	50.50
Nos. 73-83 (11)	42.70	46.70
Nos. 167-173 (7)	21.70	23.20
Nos. 165-171 (7)	49.60	64.00
Nos. 172-178 (7)	21.00	23.80
Nos. 139-145 (7)	25.60	32.60
Nos. 258-264 (7)	20.40	20.40
No. 89 (1)	28.50	37.50
Set total (154) Stamps	618.15	743.70

Curie

Pierre and Marie Curie CD80

40th anniversary of the discovery of radium. The surtax was for the benefit of the Intl. Union for the Control of Cancer.

1938

Cameroun.. B1
Cuba..B1-B2
Dahomey.. B2
France.. B76
Fr. Equatorial Africa........................ B1
Fr. Guiana.. B3
Fr. Guinea.. B2
Fr. India.. B6
Fr. Polynesia.. B5
Fr. Sudan.. B1
Guadeloupe.. B3
Indo-China.. B14
Ivory Coast.. B2
Madagascar.. B2
Martinique.. B2
Mauritania.. B3
New Caledonia.. B4
Niger.. B1
Reunion.. B4
St. Pierre & Miquelon........................ B3
Senegal.. B3
Somali Coast.. B2
Togo.. B1

No. B1 (1)	10.00	10.00
Nos. B1-B2 (2)	12.00	3.35
No. B2 (1)	9.50	9.50
No. B76 (1)	21.00	12.50
No. B1 (1)	24.00	24.00
No. B3 (1)	13.50	13.50
No. B2 (1)	8.75	8.75
No. B6 (1)	10.00	10.00
No. B5 (1)	20.00	20.00
No. B1 (1)	12.50	12.50
No. B3 (1)	11.00	10.50
No. B14 (1)	12.00	12.00
No. B2 (1)	11.00	7.50
No. B2 (1)	11.00	11.00
No. B2 (1)	13.00	13.00
No. B3 (1)	7.75	7.75
No. B4 (1)	16.50	17.50
No. B1 (1)	15.00	15.00
No. B4 (1)	14.00	14.00
No. B3 (1)	21.00	22.50
No. B3 (1)	10.50	10.50
No. B2 (1)	7.75	7.75
No. B1 (1)	20.00	20.00
Set total (24) Stamps	311.75	293.10

Caillie

Rene Caillie and Map of Northwestern Africa — CD81

Death centenary of Rene Caillie (1799-1838), French explorer. All three denominations exist with colony name omitted.

1939

Dahomey..108-110
Fr. Guinea..161-163
Fr. Sudan..113-115
Ivory Coast..160-162
Mauritania..109-111
Niger..84-86
Senegal..188-190
Togo..265-267

Nos. 108-110 (3)	1.20	3.60
Nos. 161-163 (3)	1.20	3.20
Nos. 113-115 (3)	1.20	3.20
Nos. 160-162 (3)	1.05	2.55
Nos. 109-111 (3)	1.05	3.80
Nos. 84-86 (3)	1.05	2.35
Nos. 188-190 (3)	1.05	2.90
Nos. 265-267 (3)	1.05	3.30
Set total (24) Stamps	8.85	24.90

New York World's Fair

Natives and New York Skyline CD82

1939

Cameroun..223-224
Dahomey..111-112
Fr. Equatorial Africa........................78-79
Fr. Guiana..169-170
Fr. Guinea..164-165
Fr. India..111-112
Fr. Polynesia..124-125
Fr. Sudan..116-117
Guadeloupe..155-156
Indo-China..203-204
Inini..42-43
Ivory Coast..163-164
Kwangchowan..133-134
Madagascar..209-210
Martinique..186-187
Mauritania..112-113
New Caledonia..215-216
Niger..87-88
Reunion..174-175
St. Pierre & Miquelon........................205-206
Senegal..191-192
Somali Coast..179-180
Togo..268-269
Wallis & Futuna Isls.........................90-91

Nos. 223-224 (2)	2.80	2.40
Nos. 111-112 (2)	1.60	3.20
Nos. 78-79 (2)	1.60	3.20
Nos. 169-170 (2)	2.60	2.60
Nos. 164-165 (2)	1.60	3.20
Nos. 111-112 (2)	3.00	*8.00*
Nos. 124-125 (2)	4.80	4.80
Nos. 116-117 (2)	1.60	3.20
Nos. 155-156 (2)	2.50	2.50
Nos. 203-204 (2)	2.05	2.05
Nos. 42-43 (2)	7.50	9.00
Nos. 163-164 (2)	1.50	3.00
Nos. 133-134 (2)	2.50	2.50
Nos. 209-210 (2)	1.50	2.50
Nos. 186-187 (2)	2.35	2.35
Nos. 112-113 (2)	1.40	2.80
Nos. 215-216 (2)	3.35	3.35
Nos. 87-88 (2)	1.40	2.80
Nos. 174-175 (2)	2.80	2.80
Nos. 205-206 (2)	4.80	6.00
Nos. 191-192 (2)	1.40	2.80
Nos. 179-180 (2)	1.40	2.80
Nos. 268-269 (2)	1.40	2.80
Nos. 90-91 (2)	6.00	6.00
Set total (48) Stamps	63.45	86.65

French Revolution

Storming of the Bastille CD83

French Revolution, 150th anniv. The surtax was for the defense of the colonies.

1939

Cameroun..B2-B6
Dahomey..B3-B7
Fr. Equatorial Africa.......... B4-B8, CB1
Fr. Guiana........................ B4-B8, CB1
Fr. Guinea..B3-B7
Fr. India..B7-B11
Fr. Polynesia................... B6-B10, CB1
Fr. Sudan..B2-B6
Guadeloupe..B4-B8
Indo-China.................... B15-B19, CB1
Inini..B1-B5
Ivory Coast..B3-B7
Kwangchowan..B1-B5
Madagascar........................ B3-B7, CB1
Martinique..B3-B7
Mauritania..B4-B8
New Caledonia.................. B5-B9, CB1
Niger..B2-B6
Reunion........................... B5-B9, CB1
St. Pierre & Miquelon........................B4-B8
Senegal........................... B4-B8, CB1
Somali Coast..B3-B7
Togo..B2-B6
Wallis & Futuna Isls.........................B1-B5

Nos. B2-B6 (5)	60.00	60.00
Nos. B3-B7 (5)	47.50	47.50
Nos. B4-B8,CB1 (6)	120.00	120.00
Nos. B4-B8,CB1 (6)	79.50	79.50
Nos. B3-B7 (5)	47.50	47.50
Nos. B7-B11 (5)	28.75	*32.50*
Nos. B6-B10,CB1 (6)	122.50	122.50
Nos. B2-B6 (5)	50.00	50.00
Nos. B4-B8 (5)	50.00	50.00
Nos. B15-B19,CB1 (6)	85.00	85.00
Nos. B1-B5 (5)	80.00	100.00
Nos. B3-B7 (5)	43.75	43.75
Nos. B1-B5 (5)	46.25	46.25
Nos. B3-B7,CB1 (6)	65.50	65.50
Nos. B3-B7 (5)	52.50	52.50
Nos. B4-B8 (5)	42.50	42.50
Nos. B5-B9,CB1 (6)	101.50	101.50
Nos. B2-B6 (5)	60.00	60.00
Nos. B5-B9,CB1 (6)	87.50	87.50
Nos. B4-B8 (5)	67.50	72.50
Nos. B4-B8,CB1 (6)	56.50	56.50
Nos. B3-B7 (5)	45.00	45.00
Nos. B2-B6 (5)	42.50	42.50
Nos. B1-B5 (5)	95.00	95.00
Set total (128) Stamps	1,577.	1,606.

Plane over Coastal Area CD85

All five denominations exist with colony name omitted.

1940

Dahomey.. C1-C5
Fr. Guinea.. C1-C5
Fr. Sudan.. C1-C5
Ivory Coast.. C1-C5
Mauritania.. C1-C5
Niger.. C1-C5
Senegal.. C12-C16
Togo.. C1-C5

Nos. C1-C5 (5)	4.00	4.00
Nos. C1-C5 (5)	4.00	4.00
Nos. C1-C5 (5)	4.00	4.00
Nos. C1-C5 (5)	3.80	3.80
Nos. C1-C5 (5)	3.50	3.50
Nos. C1-C5 (5)	3.50	3.50
Nos. C12-C16 (5)	3.50	3.50
Nos. C1-C5 (5)	3.15	3.15
Set total (40) Stamps	29.45	29.45

Defense of the Empire

Colonial Infantryman — CD86

1941

Cameroun..B13B
Dahomey..B13
Fr. Equatorial Africa........................B8B
Fr. Guiana..B10
Fr. Guinea..B13
Fr. India..B13
Fr. Polynesia..B12
Fr. Sudan..B12
Guadeloupe..B10
Indo-China..B19B
Inini..B7
Ivory Coast..B13
Kwangchowan..B7
Madagascar..B9
Martinique..B9
Mauritania..B14
New Caledonia..B11
Niger..B12
Reunion..B11
St. Pierre & Miquelon........................B8B
Senegal..B14
Somali Coast..B9
Togo..B10B
Wallis & Futuna Isls.........................B7

No. B13B (1)	1.60
No. B13 (1)	1.20
No. B8B (1)	3.50
No. B10 (1)	1.40
No. B13 (1)	1.40
No. B13 (1)	1.25
No. B12 (1)	3.50
No. B12 (1)	1.40
No. B10 (1)	1.00
No. B19B (1)	1.60
No. B7 (1)	1.75
No. B13 (1)	1.25
No. B7 (1)	.85
No. B9 (1)	1.50
No. B9 (1)	1.40
No. B14 (1)	.95
No. B12 (1)	1.40
No. B11 (1)	1.60
No. B8B (1)	4.50
No. B14 (1)	1.25
No. B9 (1)	1.60
No. B10B (1)	1.10
No. B7 (1)	2.40
Set total (23) Stamps	39.40

Each of the CD86 stamps listed above is part of a set of three stamps. The designs of the other two stamps in the set vary from country to country. Only the values of the Common Design stamps are listed here.

Colonial Education Fund

CD86a

1942

Cameroun..CB3
Dahomey..CB4
Fr. Equatorial Africa........................CB5
Fr. Guiana..CB4
Fr. Guinea..CB4
Fr. India..CB3
Fr. Polynesia..CB4
Fr. Sudan..CB4
Guadeloupe..CB3
Indo-China..CB5
Inini..CB3
Ivory Coast..CB4
Kwangchowan..CB4
Malagasy..CB5
Martinique..CB3
Mauritania..CB4
New Caledonia..CB4
Niger..CB4
Reunion..CB4
St. Pierre & Miquelon........................CB3
Senegal..CB5
Somali Coast..CB3
Togo..CB3
Wallis & Futuna..CB3

No. CB3 (1)	1.10	
No. CB4 (1)	.80	5.50
No. CB5 (1)	.80	
No. CB4 (1)	1.10	
No. CB4 (1)	.40	5.50
No. CB3 (1)	.90	
No. CB4 (1)	2.00	
No. CB4 (1)	.40	5.50
No. CB3 (1)	1.10	
No. CB5 (1)	1.10	
No. CB3 (1)	1.25	
No. CB4 (1)	1.00	5.50
No. CB4 (1)	1.00	
No. CB5 (1)	.65	
No. CB3 (1)	1.00	
No. CB4 (1)	.80	
No. CB4 (1)	2.25	
No. CB4 (1)	.35	
No. CB4 (1)	.90	
No. CB3 (1)	7.00	
No. CB5 (1)	.80	6.50
No. CB3 (1)	.70	
No. CB3 (1)	.35	
No. CB3 (1)	2.25	
Set total (24) Stamps	30.00	28.50

Cross of Lorraine & Four-motor Plane CD87

1941-5

Cameroun..C1-C7
Fr. Equatorial Africa...............C17-C23
Fr. Guiana..C9-C10
Fr. India..C1-C6
Fr. Polynesia..C3-C9
Fr. West Africa..C1-C3
Guadeloupe..C1-C2
Madagascar..C37-C43

Martinique..............................C1-C2
New Caledonia.........................C7-C13
Reunion.................................C18-C24
St. Pierre & Miquelon................C1-C7
Somali Coast............................C1-C7

Nos. C1-C7 (7)	6.30	6.30
Nos. C17-C23 (7)	10.40	6.35
Nos. C9-C10 (2)	3.80	3.10
Nos. C1-C6 (6)	9.30	*15.00*
Nos. C3-C9 (7)	13.75	10.00
Nos. C1-C3 (3)	9.50	3.90
Nos. C1-C2 (2)	3.75	2.50
Nos. C37-C43 (7)	5.60	3.80
Nos. C1-C2 (2)	3.00	1.60
Nos. C7-C13 (7)	8.85	7.30
Nos. C18-C24 (7)	7.05	5.00
Nos. C1-C7 (7)	11.60	9.40
Nos. C1-C7 (7)	13.95	11.10
Set total (71) Stamps	106.85	85.35

Somali Coast stamps are inscribed "Djibouti".

Transport Plane CD88

Caravan and Plane CD89

1942

Dahomey...................................C6-C13
Fr. Guinea................................C6-C13
Fr. Sudan..................................C6-C13
Ivory Coast...............................C6-C13
Mauritania................................C6-C13
Niger..C6-C13
Senegal...................................C17-C25
Togo...C6-C13

Nos. C6-C13 (8)	7.15
Nos. C6-C13 (8)	5.75
Nos. C6-C13 (8)	8.00
Nos. C6-C13 (8)	11.15
Nos. C6-C13 (8)	9.75
Nos. C6-C13 (8)	6.90
Nos. C17-C25 (9)	9.45
Nos. C6-C13 (8)	6.75
Set total (65) Stamps	64.90

Red Cross

Marianne CD90

The surtax was for the French Red Cross and national relief.

1944

Cameroun......................................B28
Fr. Equatorial Africa.......................B38
Fr. Guiana.....................................B12
Fr. India.......................................B14
Fr. Polynesia..................................B13
Fr. West Africa.................................B1
Guadeloupe....................................B12
Madagascar....................................B15
Martinique......................................B11
New Caledonia................................B13
Reunion...B15
St. Pierre & Miquelon......................B13
Somali Coast..................................B13
Wallis & Futuna Isls...........................B9

No. B28 (1)	2.00	1.60
No. B38 (1)	1.60	1.20
No. B12 (1)	1.75	1.25
No. B14 (1)	1.50	1.25
No. B13 (1)	2.00	1.60
No. B1 (1)	6.50	4.75
No. B12 (1)	1.40	1.00
No. B15 (1)	.90	.90
No. B11 (1)	1.20	1.20
No. B13 (1)	1.50	1.50
No. B15 (1)	1.60	1.10
No. B13 (1)	2.40	2.40
No. B13 (1)	1.75	2.00
No. B9 (1)	4.50	3.25
Set total (14) Stamps	30.60	25.00

Eboue

CD91

Felix Eboue, first French colonial administrator to proclaim resistance to Germany after French surrender in World War II.

1945

Cameroun.............................296-297
Fr. Equatorial Africa...............156-157
Fr. Guiana.............................171-172
Fr. India...............................210-211
Fr. Polynesia..........................150-151
Fr. West Africa.........................15-16
Guadeloupe............................187-188
Madagascar............................259-260
Martinique.............................196-197
New Caledonia........................274-275
Reunion.................................238-239
St. Pierre & Miquelon...............322-323
Somali Coast..........................238-239

Nos. 296-297 (2)	2.40	1.95
Nos. 156-157 (2)	2.55	2.00
Nos. 171-172 (2)	2.45	2.00
Nos. 210-211 (2)	2.20	1.95
Nos. 150-151 (2)	3.60	2.85
Nos. 15-16 (2)	2.40	2.40
Nos. 187-188 (2)	2.05	1.60
Nos. 259-260 (2)	2.00	1.45
Nos. 196-197 (2)	2.05	1.55
Nos. 274-275 (2)	3.40	3.00
Nos. 238-239 (2)	2.40	2.00
Nos. 322-323 (2)	4.40	3.45
Nos. 238-239 (2)	2.45	2.10
Set total (26) Stamps	34.35	28.30

Victory

Victory — CD92

European victory of the Allied Nations in World War II.

1946, May 8

Cameroun...C8
Fr. Equatorial Africa.......................C24
Fr. Guiana.......................................C11
Fr. India...C7
Fr. Polynesia...................................C10
Fr. West Africa...................................C4
Guadeloupe.......................................C3
Indo-China......................................C19
Madagascar.....................................C44
Martinique...C3
New Caledonia.................................C14
Reunion...C25
St. Pierre & Miquelon.........................C8
Somali Coast......................................C8
Wallis & Futuna Isls............................C1

No. C8 (1)	1.60	1.20
No. C24 (1)	1.60	1.25
No. C11 (1)	1.75	1.25
No. C7 (1)	1.00	4.00
No. C10 (1)	2.75	2.00
No. C4 (1)	1.60	1.20
No. C3 (1)	1.25	1.00
No. C19 (1)	1.00	.55
No. C44 (1)	1.00	.35
No. C3 (1)	1.30	1.00
No. C14 (1)	1.50	1.25
No. C25 (1)	1.10	.90
No. C8 (1)	2.10	2.10
No. C8 (1)	1.75	1.40
No. C1 (1)	2.50	1.90
Set total (15) Stamps	23.80	21.35

Chad to Rhine

Leclerc's Departure from Chad — CD93

Battle at Cufra Oasis — CD94

Tanks in Action, Mareth — CD95

Normandy Invasion — CD96

Entering Paris — CD97

Liberation of Strasbourg — CD98

"Chad to the Rhine" march, 1942-44, by Gen. Jacques Leclerc's column, later French 2nd Armored Division.

1946, June 6

Cameroun..................................C9-C14
Fr. Equatorial Africa..................C25-C30
Fr. Guiana................................C12-C17
Fr. India....................................C8-C13
Fr. Polynesia.............................C11-C16
Fr. West Africa............................C5-C10
Guadeloupe..................................C4-C9
Indo-China................................C20-C25
Madagascar...............................C45-C50
Martinique....................................C4-C9
New Caledonia..........................C15-C20
Reunion....................................C26-C31
St. Pierre & Miquelon..................C9-C14
Somali Coast..............................C9-C14
Wallis & Futuna Isls.....................C2-C7

Nos. C9-C14 (6)	12.05	9.70
Nos. C25-C30 (6)	14.70	10.80
Nos. C12-C17 (6)	12.65	10.35
Nos. C8-C13 (6)	12.80	*15.00*
Nos. C11-C16 (6)	17.55	13.40
Nos. C5-C10 (6)	16.05	11.95
Nos. C4-C9 (6)	12.00	9.60
Nos. C20-C25 (6)	6.40	6.40
Nos. C45-C50 (6)	10.30	8.40
Nos. C4-C9 (6)	8.85	7.30
Nos. C15-C20 (6)	13.40	11.90
Nos. C26-C31 (6)	10.25	6.55
Nos. C9-C14 (6)	17.30	14.35
Nos. C9-C14 (6)	18.10	12.65
Nos. C2-C7 (6)	13.75	10.45
Set total (90) Stamps	196.15	158.80

UPU

French Colonials, Globe and Plane — CD99

Universal Postal Union, 75th anniv.

1949, July 4

Cameroun...C29
Fr. Equatorial Africa.........................C34
Fr. India...C17
Fr. Polynesia....................................C20
Fr. West Africa..................................C15
Indo-China.......................................C26
Madagascar......................................C55
New Caledonia..................................C24
St. Pierre & Miquelon........................C18
Somali Coast.....................................C18
Togo..C18
Wallis & Futuna Isls..........................C10

No. C29 (1)	8.00	4.75
No. C34 (1)	16.00	12.00
No. C17 (1)	11.50	8.75
No. C20 (1)	20.00	15.00
No. C15 (1)	12.00	8.75
No. C26 (1)	4.75	4.00
No. C55 (1)	4.00	2.75
No. C24 (1)	7.50	5.00
No. C18 (1)	20.00	12.00
No. C18 (1)	14.00	10.50
No. C18 (1)	8.50	7.00
No. C10 (1)	12.50	8.25
Set total (12) Stamps	138.75	98.75

Tropical Medicine

Doctor Treating Infant CD100

The surtax was for charitable work.

1950

Cameroun...B29
Fr. Equatorial Africa.........................B39
Fr. India...B15
Fr. Polynesia....................................B14
Fr. West Africa....................................B3
Madagascar......................................B17
New Caledonia..................................B14
St. Pierre & Miquelon........................B14
Somali Coast.....................................B14
Togo..B11

No. B29 (1)	7.25	5.50
No. B39 (1)	7.25	5.50
No. B15 (1)	6.00	4.00
No. B14 (1)	10.50	8.00
No. B3 (1)	9.50	7.25
No. B17 (1)	5.50	5.50
No. B14 (1)	6.75	5.25
No. B14 (1)	14.00	13.00
No. B14 (1)	7.75	6.25
No. B11 (1)	5.00	3.50
Set total (10) Stamps	79.50	63.75

Military Medal

Medal, Early Marine and Colonial Soldier — CD101

Centenary of the creation of the French Military Medal.

1952

Cameroun...322
Comoro Isls...39
Fr. Equatorial Africa.........................186

Fr. India 233
Fr. Polynesia 179
Fr. West Africa 57
Madagascar 286
New Caledonia 295
St. Pierre & Miquelon 345
Somali Coast 267
Togo 327
Wallis & Futuna Isls. 149

No. 322 (1)	7.25	3.25
No. 39 (1)	50.00	40.00
No. 186 (1)	8.00	5.50
No. 233 (1)	5.50	7.00
No. 179 (1)	13.50	10.00
No. 57 (1)	8.75	6.50
No. 286 (1)	3.75	2.50
No. 295 (1)	6.50	6.00
No. 345 (1)	12.00	12.00
No. 267 (1)	9.00	8.00
No. 327 (1)	5.50	4.75
No. 149 (1)	9.50	7.00
Set total (12) Stamps	139.25	112.50

Liberation

Allied Landing, Victory Sign and Cross of Lorraine — CD102

Liberation of France, 10th anniv.

1954, June 6

Cameroun C32
Comoro Isls. C4
Fr. Equatorial Africa C38
Fr. India C18
Fr. Polynesia C22
Fr. West Africa C17
Madagascar C57
New Caledonia C25
St. Pierre & Miquelon C19
Somali Coast C19
Togo C19
Wallis & Futuna Isls. C11

No. C32 (1)	7.25	4.75
No. C4 (1)	35.00	20.00
No. C38 (1)	12.00	8.00
No. C18 (1)	11.00	8.00
No. C22 (1)	10.00	8.00
No. C17 (1)	12.00	5.50
No. C57 (1)	3.25	2.00
No. C25 (1)	7.50	5.00
No. C19 (1)	20.00	12.00
No. C19 (1)	10.50	8.50
No. C19 (1)	7.00	5.50
No. C11 (1)	12.50	8.25
Set total (12) Stamps	148.00	95.50

FIDES

Plowmen CD103

Efforts of FIDES, the Economic and Social Development Fund for Overseas Possessions (Fonds d' Investissement pour le Developpement Economique et Social). Each stamp has a different design.

1956

Cameroun 326-329
Comoro Isls. 43
Fr. Equatorial Africa 189-192
Fr. Polynesia 181
Fr. West Africa 65-72
Madagascar 292-295
New Caledonia 303
St. Pierre & Miquelon 350
Somali Coast 268-269
Togo 331

Nos. 326-329 (4)	6.90	3.20
No. 43 (1)	2.25	1.60
Nos. 189-192 (4)	3.20	1.65
No. 181 (1)	4.00	2.00
Nos. 65-72 (8)	16.00	6.35
Nos. 292-295 (4)	2.25	1.20
No. 303 (1)	1.90	1.10
No. 350 (1)	5.50	3.50
Nos. 268-269 (2)	5.35	3.15
No. 331 (1)	4.25	2.10
Set total (27) Stamps	51.60	25.85

Flower

CD104

Each stamp shows a different flower.

1958-9

Cameroun 333
Comoro Isls. 45
Fr. Equatorial Africa 200-201
Fr. Polynesia 192
Fr. So. & Antarctic Terr. 11
Fr. West Africa 79-83
Madagascar 301-302
New Caledonia 304-305
St. Pierre & Miquelon 357
Somali Coast 270
Togo 348-349
Wallis & Futuna Isls. 152

No. 333 (1)	1.60	.80
No. 45 (1)	5.50	4.50
Nos. 200-201 (2)	3.60	1.60
No. 192 (1)	6.50	4.00
No. 11 (1)	8.75	7.50
Nos. 79-83 (5)	10.45	5.60
Nos. 301-302 (2)	1.60	.60
Nos. 304-305 (2)	8.00	3.00
No. 357 (1)	4.25	2.10
No. 270 (1)	4.25	1.40
Nos. 348-349 (2)	1.10	.50
No. 152 (1)	4.50	2.50
Set total (20) Stamps	60.10	34.10

Human Rights

Sun, Dove and U.N. Emblem CD105

10th anniversary of the signing of the Universal Declaration of Human Rights.

1958

Comoro Isls. 44
Fr. Equatorial Africa 202
Fr. Polynesia 191
Fr. West Africa 85
Madagascar 300
New Caledonia 306
St. Pierre & Miquelon 356
Somali Coast 274
Wallis & Futuna Isls. 153

No. 44 (1)	11.00	11.00
No. 202 (1)	2.40	1.25
No. 191 (1)	13.00	8.75
No. 85 (1)	2.40	2.00
No. 300 (1)	.80	.40
No. 306 (1)	2.00	1.50
No. 356 (1)	3.50	2.50
No. 274 (1)	3.50	2.10
No. 153 (1)	5.75	4.00
Set total (9) Stamps	44.35	33.50

C.C.T.A.

CD106

Commission for Technical Cooperation in Africa south of the Sahara, 10th anniv.

1960

Cameroun 339
Cent. Africa 3
Chad 66
Congo, P.R. 90
Dahomey 138
Gabon 150
Ivory Coast 180
Madagascar 317
Mali 9
Mauritania 117
Niger 104
Upper Volta 89

No. 339 (1)	1.60	.75
No. 3 (1)	1.90	.65
No. 66 (1)	1.90	.50
No. 90 (1)	1.00	1.00
No. 138 (1)	.50	.25
No. 150 (1)	1.40	1.10
No. 180 (1)	1.10	.50
No. 317 (1)	.60	.30
No. 9 (1)	1.20	.50
No. 117 (1)	.75	.40
No. 104 (1)	.85	.45
No. 89 (1)	.65	.40
Set total (12) Stamps	13.45	6.80

Air Afrique, 1961

Modern and Ancient Africa, Map and Planes — CD107

Founding of Air Afrique (African Airlines).

1961-62

Cameroun C37
Cent. Africa C5
Chad C7
Congo, P.R. C5
Dahomey C17
Gabon C5
Ivory Coast C18
Mauritania C17
Niger C22
Senegal C31
Upper Volta C4

No. C37 (1)	1.00	.50
No. C5 (1)	1.00	.55
No. C7 (1)	1.00	.25
No. C5 (1)	1.75	.90
No. C17 (1)	.80	.40
No. C5 (1)	11.00	6.00
No. C18 (1)	2.00	1.25
No. C17 (1)	2.50	1.25
No. C22 (1)	1.75	.90
No. C31 (1)	.80	.30
No. C4 (1)	3.50	1.75
Set total (11) Stamps	27.10	14.05

Anti-Malaria

CD108

World Health Organization drive to eradicate malaria.

1962, Apr. 7

Cameroun B36
Cent. Africa B1
Chad B1
Comoro Isls. B1
Congo, P.R. B3
Dahomey B15
Gabon B4
Ivory Coast B15
Madagascar B19
Mali B1
Mauritania B16
Niger B14
Senegal B16
Somali Coast B15
Upper Volta B1

No. B36 (1)	1.00	.45
No. B1 (1)	1.40	1.40
No. B1 (1)	1.25	.50
No. B1 (1)	4.00	4.00
No. B3 (1)	1.40	1.00
No. B15 (1)	.75	.75
No. B4 (1)	1.00	1.00
No. B15 (1)	1.25	1.25
No. B19 (1)	.75	.50
No. B1 (1)	1.25	.60
No. B16 (1)	.80	.80
No. B14 (1)	.60	.60
No. B16 (1)	1.10	.65
No. B15 (1)	7.00	7.00
No. B1 (1)	.75	.70
Set total (15) Stamps	24.30	21.20

Abidjan Games

CD109

Abidjan Games, Ivory Coast, Dec. 24-31, 1961. Each stamp shows a different sport.

1962

Cent. Africa 19-20, C6
Chad 83-84, C8
Congo, P.R. 103-104, C7
Gabon 163-164, C6
Niger 109-111
Upper Volta 103-105

Nos. 19-20,C6 (3)	3.90	2.60
Nos. 83-84,C8 (3)	6.30	1.55
Nos. 103-104,C7 (3)	3.85	1.80
Nos. 163-164,C6 (3)	5.00	3.00
Nos. 109-111 (3)	2.60	1.10
Nos. 103-105 (3)	2.80	1.75
Set total (18) Stamps	24.45	11.80

African and Malagasy Union

Flag of Union CD110

First anniversary of the Union.

1962, Sept. 8

Cameroun 373
Cent. Africa 21
Chad 85
Congo, P.R. 105
Dahomey 155
Gabon 165
Ivory Coast 198
Madagascar 332
Mauritania 170
Niger 112
Senegal 211
Upper Volta 106

No. 373 (1)	2.00	.75
No. 21 (1)	1.25	.60
No. 85 (1)	1.25	.25
No. 105 (1)	1.50	.50
No. 155 (1)	1.25	.90
No. 165 (1)	1.60	1.25
No. 198 (1)	2.10	.75
No. 332 (1)	.80	.80
No. 170 (1)	.75	.50
No. 112 (1)	.80	.40
No. 211 (1)	.80	.50
No. 106 (1)	1.10	.75
Set total (12) Stamps	15.20	7.95

Telstar

Telstar and Globe Showing Andover and Pleumeur-Bodou — CD111

First television connection of the United States and Europe through the Telstar satellite, July 11-12, 1962.

1962-63

Andorra, French 154
Comoro Isls. C7
Fr. Polynesia C29
Fr. So. & Antarctic Terr. C5
New Caledonia C33
St. Pierre & Miquelon C26
Somali Coast C31
Wallis & Futuna Isls. C17

No. 154 (1)	2.00	1.60
No. C7 (1)	5.00	3.00
No. C29 (1)	11.50	8.00

No. C5 (1)	29.00	21.00
No. C33 (1)	25.00	18.50
No. C26 (1)	6.00	4.50
No. C31 (1)	1.00	1.00
No. C17 (1)	3.50	3.50
Set total (8) Stamps	83.00	61.10

Freedom From Hunger

World Map and Wheat Emblem CD112

U.N. Food and Agriculture Organization's "Freedom from Hunger" campaign.

1963, Mar. 21

Cameroun	B37-B38
Cent. Africa	B2
Chad	B2
Congo, P.R.	B4
Dahomey	B16
Gabon	B5
Ivory Coast	B16
Madagascar	B21
Mauritania	B17
Niger	B15
Senegal	B17
Upper Volta	B2

Nos. B37-B38 (2)	2.25	.75
No. B2 (1)	1.25	1.25
No. B2 (1)	2.00	.50
No. B4 (1)	1.40	1.00
No. B16 (1)	.80	.80
No. B5 (1)	1.00	1.00
No. B16 (1)	1.50	1.50
No. B21 (1)	.60	.45
No. B17 (1)	.80	.80
No. B15 (1)	.60	.60
No. B17 (1)	.80	.50
No. B2 (1)	.75	.70
Set total (13) Stamps	13.75	9.85

Red Cross Centenary

CD113

Centenary of the International Red Cross.

1963, Sept. 2

Comoro Isls.	55
Fr. Polynesia	205
New Caledonia	328
St. Pierre & Miquelon	367
Somali Coast	297
Wallis & Futuna Isls.	165

No. 55 (1)	9.50	7.00
No. 205 (1)	15.00	12.00
No. 328 (1)	8.00	6.75
No. 367 (1)	12.00	5.50
No. 297 (1)	6.25	6.25
No. 165 (1)	4.00	3.50
Set total (6) Stamps	54.75	41.00

African Postal Union, 1963

UAMPT Emblem, Radio Masts, Plane and Mail CD114

Establishment of the African and Malagasy Posts and Telecommunications Union.

1963, Sept. 8

Cameroun	C47
Cent. Africa	C10
Chad	C9
Congo, P.R.	C13
Dahomey	C19
Gabon	C13
Ivory Coast	C25
Madagascar	C75
Mauritania	C22
Niger	C27
Rwanda	36
Senegal	C32
Upper Volta	C9

No. C47 (1)	2.25	1.00
No. C10 (1)	1.90	.85
No. C9 (1)	2.40	.60
No. C13 (1)	1.40	.75
No. C19 (1)	.75	.25
No. C13 (1)	1.90	.80
No. C25 (1)	2.50	1.50
No. C75 (1)	1.25	.80
No. C22 (1)	1.50	.60
No. C27 (1)	1.25	.60
No. 36 (1)	.90	.55
No. C32 (1)	1.75	.50
No. C9 (1)	1.50	.75
Set total (13) Stamps	21.25	9.55

Air Afrique, 1963

Symbols of Flight — CD115

First anniversary of Air Afrique and inauguration of DC-8 service.

1963, Nov. 19

Cameroun	C48
Chad	C10
Congo, P.R.	C14
Gabon	C18
Ivory Coast	C26
Mauritania	C26
Niger	C35
Senegal	C33

No. C48 (1)	1.25	.40
No. C10 (1)	2.40	.60
No. C14 (1)	1.60	.60
No. C18 (1)	1.40	.65
No. C26 (1)	1.00	.50
No. C26 (1)	.70	.25
No. C35 (1)	.90	.50
No. C33 (1)	2.00	.65
Set total (8) Stamps	11.25	4.15

Europafrica

Europe and Africa Linked — CD116

Signing of an economic agreement between the European Economic Community and the African and Malagasy Union, Yaounde, Cameroun, July 20, 1963.

1963-64

Cameroun	402
Cent. Africa	C12
Chad	C11
Congo, P.R.	C16
Gabon	C19
Ivory Coast	217
Niger	C43
Upper Volta	C11

No. 402 (1)	2.25	.60
No. C12 (1)	2.50	1.75
No. C11 (1)	2.00	.50
No. C16 (1)	1.60	1.00
No. C19 (1)	1.40	.75
No. 217 (1)	1.10	.35
No. C43 (1)	.85	.50
No. C11 (1)	1.50	.80
Set total (8) Stamps	13.20	6.25

Human Rights

Scales of Justice and Globe CD117

15th anniversary of the Universal Declaration of Human Rights.

1963, Dec. 10

Comoro Isls.	56
Fr. Polynesia	206
New Caledonia	329
St. Pierre & Miquelon	368
Somali Coast	300
Wallis & Futuna Isls.	166

No. 56 (1)	9.50	7.50
No. 205 (1)	15.00	12.00
No. 329 (1)	7.00	6.00
No. 368 (1)	7.00	3.50
No. 300 (1)	8.50	8.50
No. 166 (1)	8.00	7.50
Set total (6) Stamps	55.00	45.00

PHILATEC

Stamp Album, Champs Elysees Palace and Horses of Marly CD118

Intl. Philatelic and Postal Techniques Exhibition, Paris, June 5-21, 1964.

1963-64

Comoro Isls.	60
France	1078
Fr. Polynesia	207
New Caledonia	341
St. Pierre & Miquelon	369
Somali Coast	301
Wallis & Futuna Isls.	167

No. 60 (1)	4.50	4.00
No. 1078 (1)	.25	.25
No. 206 (1)	15.00	10.00
No. 341 (1)	6.50	6.50
No. 369 (1)	11.00	8.00
No. 301 (1)	7.75	7.75
No. 167 (1)	3.50	3.50
Set total (7) Stamps	48.50	40.00

Cooperation

CD119

Cooperation between France and the French-speaking countries of Africa and Madagascar.

1964

Cameroun	409-410
Cent. Africa	39
Chad	103
Congo, P.R.	121
Dahomey	193
France	1111
Gabon	175
Ivory Coast	221
Madagascar	360
Mauritania	181
Niger	143
Senegal	236
Togo	495

Nos. 409-410 (2)	2.50	.50
No. 39 (1)	1.00	.55
No. 103 (1)	1.00	.25
No. 121 (1)	.80	.35
No. 193 (1)	.80	.35
No. 1111 (1)	.25	.25
No. 175 (1)	.90	.60
No. 221 (1)	1.10	.35
No. 360 (1)	.60	.25
No. 181 (1)	.60	.35
No. 143 (1)	.80	.40
No. 236 (1)	1.60	.85
No. 495 (1)	.70	.25
Set total (14) Stamps	12.65	5.30

ITU

Telegraph, Syncom Satellite and ITU Emblem CD120

Intl. Telecommunication Union, Cent.

1965, May 17

Comoro Isls.	C14
Fr. Polynesia	C33
Fr. So. & Antarctic Terr.	C8
New Caledonia	C40
New Hebrides	124-125
St. Pierre & Miquelon	C29
Somali Coast	C36
Wallis & Futuna Isls.	C20

No. C14 (1)	20.00	10.00
No. C33 (1)	80.00	52.50
No. C8 (1)	200.00	160.00
No. C40 (1)	10.00	8.00
Nos. 124-125 (2)	40.50	34.00
No. C29 (1)	20.00	10.00
No. C36 (1)	15.00	9.00
No. C20 (1)	21.00	15.00
Set total (9) Stamps	406.50	298.50

French Satellite A-1

Diamant Rocket and Launching Installation — CD121

Launching of France's first satellite, Nov. 26, 1965.

1965-66

Comoro Isls.	C16a
France	1138a
Reunion	359a
Fr. Polynesia	C41a
Fr. So. & Antarctic Terr.	C10a
New Caledonia	C45a
St. Pierre & Miquelon	C31a
Somali Coast	C40a
Wallis & Futuna Isls.	C23a

No. C16a (1)	11.00	11.00
No. 1138a (1)	.65	.65
No. 359a (1)	3.50	3.00
No. C41a (1)	14.00	14.00
No. C10a (1)	29.00	24.00
No. C45a (1)	7.00	7.00
No. C31a (1)	12.50	12.50
No. C40a (1)	7.00	7.00
No. C23a (1)	9.25	9.25
Set total (9) Stamps	93.90	88.40

French Satellite D-1

D-1 Satellite in Orbit — CD122

Launching of the D-1 satellite at Hammaguir, Algeria, Feb. 17, 1966.

1966

Comoro Isls.	C17
France	1148

Fr. Polynesia C42
Fr. So. & Antarctic Terr. C11
New Caledonia C46
St. Pierre & Miquelon C32
Somali Coast C49
Wallis & Futuna Isls. C24

No. C17 (1)	4.00	4.00
No. 1148 (1)	.25	.25
No. C42 (1)	7.00	4.75
No. C11 (1)	57.50	40.00
No. C46 (1)	2.25	2.00
No. C32 (1)	8.00	6.00
No. C49 (1)	4.25	2.75
No. C24 (1)	3.50	3.50
Set total (8) Stamps	86.75	63.25

Air Afrique, 1966

Planes and Air Afrique Emblem — CD123

Introduction of DC-8F planes by Air Afrique.

1966

Cameroun C79
Cent. Africa C35
Chad C26
Congo, P.R. C42
Dahomey C42
Gabon C47
Ivory Coast C32
Mauritania C57
Niger C63
Senegal C47
Togo C54
Upper Volta C31

No. C79 (1)	.80	.25
No. C35 (1)	1.00	.40
No. C26 (1)	1.00	.25
No. C42 (1)	1.00	.25
No. C42 (1)	.75	.25
No. C47 (1)	.90	.35
No. C32 (1)	1.00	.60
No. C57 (1)	.80	.30
No. C63 (1)	.65	.35
No. C47 (1)	.80	.30
No. C54 (1)	.80	.25
No. C31 (1)	.75	.50
Set total (12) Stamps	10.25	4.05

African Postal Union, 1967

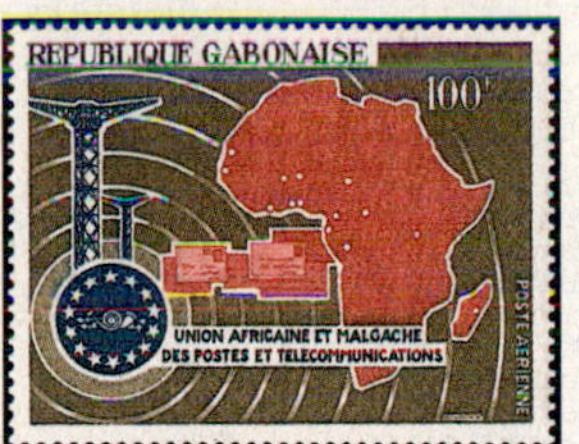

Telecommunications Symbols and Map of Africa — CD124

Fifth anniversary of the establishment of the African and Malagasy Union of Posts and Telecommunications, UAMPT.

1967

Cameroun C90
Cent. Africa C46
Chad C37
Congo, P.R. C57
Dahomey C61
Gabon C58
Ivory Coast C34
Madagascar C85
Mauritania C65
Niger C75
Rwanda C1-C3
Senegal C60
Togo C81
Upper Volta C50

No. C90 (1)	2.40	.65
No. C46 (1)	2.25	.85
No. C37 (1)	2.00	.60
No. C57 (1)	1.60	.60
No. C61 (1)	1.75	.95
No. C58 (1)	2.25	.95
No. C34 (1)	3.50	1.50
No. C85 (1)	1.25	.60
No. C65 (1)	1.25	.60
No. C75 (1)	1.40	.60
Nos. C1-C3 (3)	2.30	1.25
No. C60 (1)	1.75	.50
No. C81 (1)	1.90	.30
No. C50 (1)	1.80	.70
Set total (16) Stamps	27.40	10.65

Monetary Union

Gold Token of the Ashantis, 17-18th Centuries — CD125

West African Monetary Union, 5th anniv.

1967, Nov. 4

Dahomey 244
Ivory Coast 259
Mauritania 238
Niger 204
Senegal 294
Togo 623
Upper Volta 181

No. 244 (1)	.65	.65
No. 259 (1)	.85	.40
No. 238 (1)	.45	.25
No. 204 (1)	.45	.25
No. 294 (1)	.60	.25
No. 623 (1)	.60	.25
No. 181 (1)	.65	.35
Set total (7) Stamps	4.25	2.40

WHO Anniversary

Sun, Flowers and WHO Emblem CD126

World Health Organization, 20th anniv.

1968, May 4

Afars & Issas 317
Comoro Isls. 73
Fr. Polynesia 241-242
Fr. So. & Antarctic Terr. 31
New Caledonia 367
St. Pierre & Miquelon 377
Wallis & Futuna Isls. 169

No. 317 (1)	3.00	3.00
No. 73 (1)	2.75	2.00
Nos. 241-242 (2)	22.00	12.75
No. 31 (1)	62.50	47.50
No. 367 (1)	4.00	2.25
No. 377 (1)	10.00	8.00
No. 169 (1)	6.50	4.50
Set total (8) Stamps	110.75	80.00

Human Rights Year

Human Rights Flame — CD127

1968, Aug. 10

Afars & Issas 322-323
Comoro Isls. 76
Fr. Polynesia 243-244
Fr. So. & Antarctic Terr. 32
New Caledonia 369
St. Pierre & Miquelon 382
Wallis & Futuna Isls. 170

Nos. 322-323 (2)	6.75	4.00
No. 76 (1)	3.50	3.50
Nos. 243-244 (2)	24.00	14.00
No. 32 (1)	55.00	47.50
No. 369 (1)	2.75	1.50
No. 382 (1)	8.00	5.50
No. 170 (1)	3.75	3.75
Set total (9) Stamps	103.75	79.75

2nd PHILEXAFRIQUE

CD128

Opening of PHILEXAFRIQUE, Abidjan, Feb. 14. Each stamp shows a local scene and stamp.

1969, Feb. 14

Cameroun C118
Cent. Africa C65
Chad C48
Congo, P.R. C77
Dahomey C94
Gabon C82
Ivory Coast C38-C40
Madagascar C92
Mali C65
Mauritania C80
Niger C104
Senegal C68
Togo C104
Upper Volta C62

No. C118 (1)	3.25	1.25
No. C65 (1)	1.90	1.90
No. C48 (1)	2.40	1.00
No. C77 (1)	2.00	1.75
No. C94 (1)	2.25	2.25
No. C82 (1)	2.25	2.25
Nos. C38-C40 (3)	14.50	14.50
No. C92 (1)	1.75	.85
No. C65 (1)	1.75	1.00
No. C80 (1)	1.90	.75
No. C104 (1)	2.75	1.90
No. C68 (1)	2.00	1.40
No. C104 (1)	2.25	.45
No. C62 (1)	4.00	3.25
Set total (16) Stamps	44.95	34.50

Concorde

Concorde in Flight CD129

First flight of the prototype Concorde supersonic plane at Toulouse, Mar. 1, 1969.

1969

Afars & Issas C56
Comoro Isls. C29
France C42
Fr. Polynesia C50
Fr. So. & Antarctic Terr. C18
New Caledonia C63
St. Pierre & Miquelon C40
Wallis & Futuna Isls. C30

No. C56 (1)	26.00	16.00
No. C29 (1)	24.00	16.00
No. C42 (1)	.75	.35
No. C50 (1)	55.00	35.00
No. C18 (1)	55.00	37.50
No. C63 (1)	27.50	20.00
No. C40 (1)	30.00	11.00
No. C30 (1)	15.00	10.00
Set total (8) Stamps	233.25	145.85

Development Bank

Bank Emblem — CD130

African Development Bank, fifth anniv.

1969

Cameroun 499
Chad 217
Congo, P.R. 181-182
Ivory Coast 281
Mali 127-128
Mauritania 267
Niger 220
Senegal 317-318
Upper Volta 201

No. 499 (1)	.80	.25
No. 217 (1)	.70	.25
Nos. 181-182 (2)	.80	.50
No. 281 (1)	.70	.40
Nos. 127-128 (2)	1.00	.50
No. 267 (1)	.60	.25
No. 220 (1)	.60	.30
Nos. 317-318 (2)	1.55	.50
No. 201 (1)	.65	.30
Set total (12) Stamps	7.40	3.25

ILO

ILO Headquarters, Geneva, and Emblem — CD131

Intl. Labor Organization, 50th anniv.

1969-70

Afars & Issas 337
Comoro Isls. 83
Fr. Polynesia 251-252
Fr. So. & Antarctic Terr. 35
New Caledonia 379
St. Pierre & Miquelon 396
Wallis & Futuna Isls. 172

No. 337 (1)	2.75	2.00
No. 83 (1)	1.25	.75
Nos. 251-252 (2)	24.00	12.50
No. 35 (1)	15.00	10.00
No. 379 (1)	2.25	1.10
No. 396 (1)	8.50	5.50
No. 172 (1)	3.00	2.90
Set total (8) Stamps	56.75	34.75

ASECNA

Map of Africa, Plane and Airport CD132

10th anniversary of the Agency for the Security of Aerial Navigation in Africa and Madagascar (ASECNA, Agence pour la Securite de la Navigation Aerienne en Afrique et a Madagascar).

1969-70

Cameroun 500
Cent. Africa 119
Chad 222
Congo, P.R. 197
Dahomey 269
Gabon 260
Ivory Coast 287
Mali 130
Niger 221
Senegal 321
Upper Volta 204

No. 500 (1)	2.00	.60
No. 119 (1)	2.25	.80
No. 222 (1)	1.00	.25
No. 197 (1)	2.00	.40
No. 269 (1)	.90	.55
No. 260 (1)	1.75	.75
No. 287 (1)	.90	.40
No. 130 (1)	.90	.40
No. 221 (1)	1.25	.70
No. 321 (1)	1.60	.50
No. 204 (1)	1.75	1.00
Set total (11) Stamps	16.30	6.35

U.P.U. Headquarters

CD133

New Universal Postal Union headquarters, Bern, Switzerland.

1970

Afars & Issas 342
Algeria 443
Cameroun 503-504
Cent. Africa 125
Chad 225
Comoro Isls. 84
Congo, P.R. 216
Fr. Polynesia 261-262
Fr. So. & Antarctic Terr. 36
Gabon 258
Ivory Coast 295
Madagascar 444
Mali 134-135
Mauritania 283
New Caledonia 382
Niger 231-232
St. Pierre & Miquelon 397-398
Senegal 328-329
Tunisia 535
Wallis & Futuna Isls. 173

No. 342 (1)	2.50	1.40
No. 443 (1)	1.10	.40
Nos. 503-504 (2)	2.60	.55
No. 125 (1)	1.90	.70
No. 225 (1)	1.00	.25
No. 84 (1)	5.50	2.00
No. 216 (1)	.80	.25
Nos. 261-262 (2)	20.00	10.00
No. 36 (1)	40.00	27.50
No. 258 (1)	.90	.55
No. 295 (1)	1.10	.50
No. 444 (1)	.55	.25
Nos. 134-135 (2)	1.05	.50
No. 283 (1)	.60	.30
No. 382 (1)	3.00	1.50
Nos. 231-232 (2)	1.20	.60
Nos. 397-398 (2)	28.00	17.00
Nos. 328-329 (2)	1.55	.55
No. 535 (1)	.60	.25
No. 173 (1)	4.00	4.00
Set total (26) Stamps	117.95	69.05

De Gaulle

CD134

First anniversary of the death of Charles de Gaulle, (1890-1970), President of France.

1971-72

Afars & Issas 356-357
Comoro Isls. 104-105
France 1325a
Fr. Polynesia 270-271
Fr. So. & Antarctic Terr. 52-53
New Caledonia 393-394
Reunion 380a
St. Pierre & Miquelon 417-418
Wallis & Futuna Isls. 177-178

Nos. 356-357 (2)	12.50	7.50
Nos. 104-105 (2)	9.00	5.75
No. 1325a (1)	3.00	2.50
Nos. 270-271 (2)	51.50	29.50
Nos. 52-53 (2)	40.00	29.50
Nos. 393-394 (2)	23.00	11.75
No. 380a (1)	9.25	8.00
Nos. 417-418 (2)	40.00	30.00
Nos. 177-178 (2)	24.00	16.25
Set total (16) Stamps	212.25	140.75

African Postal Union, 1971

UAMPT Building, Brazzaville, Congo — CD135

10th anniversary of the establishment of the African and Malagasy Posts and Telecommunications Union, UAMPT. Each stamp has a different native design.

1971, Nov. 13

Cameroun C177
Cent. Africa C89
Chad C94
Congo, P.R. C136
Dahomey C146
Gabon C120
Ivory Coast C47
Mauritania C113
Niger C164
Rwanda C8
Senegal C105
Togo C166
Upper Volta C97

No. C177 (1)	2.00	.50
No. C89 (1)	2.25	.85
No. C94 (1)	1.50	.50
No. C136 (1)	1.60	.75
No. C146 (1)	1.75	.80
No. C120 (1)	1.75	.70
No. C47 (1)	2.00	1.00
No. C113 (1)	1.20	.65
No. C164 (1)	1.25	.60
No. C8 (1)	2.75	2.25
No. C105 (1)	1.60	.50
No. C166 (1)	1.25	.40
No. C97 (1)	1.50	.70
Set total (13) Stamps	22.40	10.20

West African Monetary Union

African Couple, City, Village and Commemorative Coin — CD136

West African Monetary Union, 10th anniv.

1972, Nov. 2

Dahomey 300
Ivory Coast 331
Mauritania 299
Niger 258
Senegal 374
Togo 825
Upper Volta 280

No. 300 (1)	.65	.25
No. 331 (1)	1.00	.50
No. 299 (1)	.75	.25
No. 258 (1)	.55	.30
No. 374 (1)	.50	.30
No. 825 (1)	.60	.25
No. 280 (1)	.60	.25
Set total (7) Stamps	4.65	2.10

African Postal Union, 1973

Telecommunications Symbols and Map of Africa — CD137

11th anniversary of the African and Malagasy Posts and Telecommunications Union (UAMPT).

1973, Sept. 12

Cameroun 574
Cent. Africa 194
Chad 294
Congo, P.R. 289
Dahomey 311
Gabon 320
Ivory Coast 361
Madagascar 500
Mauritania 304
Niger 287
Rwanda 540
Senegal 393
Togo 849
Upper Volta 297

No. 574 (1)	1.75	.40
No. 194 (1)	1.25	.75
No. 294 (1)	1.75	.40
No. 289 (1)	1.60	.50
No. 311 (1)	1.25	.55
No. 320 (1)	1.40	.75
No. 361 (1)	2.50	1.00
No. 500 (1)	1.10	.35
No. 304 (1)	1.10	.40
No. 287 (1)	.90	.60
No. 540 (1)	3.75	2.00
No. 393 (1)	1.60	.50
No. 849 (1)	1.00	.35
No. 297 (1)	1.25	.70
Set total (14) Stamps	22.20	9.25

Philexafrique II — Essen

CD138

CD139

Designs: Indigenous fauna, local and German stamps. Types CD138-CD139 printed horizontally and vertically se-tenant in sheets of 10 (2x5). Label between horizontal pairs alternately commemorates Philexafrique II, Libreville, Gabon, June 1978, and 2nd International Stamp Fair, Essen, Germany, Nov. 1-5.

1978-1979

Benin C286a
Central Africa C201a
Chad C239a
Congo Republic C246a
Djibouti C122a
Gabon C216a
Ivory Coast C65a
Mali C357a
Mauritania C186a
Niger C292a
Rwanda C13a
Senegal C147a
Togo C364a

No. C286a (1)	9.00	8.50
No. C201a (1)	7.50	7.50
No. C239a (1)	8.00	4.00
No. C246a (1)	7.00	7.00
No. C122a (1)	8.50	8.50
No. C216a (1)	6.50	4.00
No. C65a (1)	9.00	9.00
No. C357a (1)	5.00	3.00
No. C186a (1)	4.50	4.00
No. C292a (1)	6.00	5.00
No. C13a (1)	4.00	4.00
No. C147a (1)	10.00	4.00
No. C364a (1)	3.00	1.50
Set total (13) Stamps	88.00	70.00

BRITISH COMMONWEALTH OF NATIONS

The listings follow established trade practices when these issues are offered as units by dealers. The Peace issue, for example, includes only one stamp from the Indian state of Hyderabad. The U.P.U. issue includes the Egypt set. Pairs are included for those varieties issued with bilingual designs se-tenant.

Silver Jubilee

Windsor Castle and King George V CD301

Reign of King George V, 25th anniv.

1935

Antigua 77-80
Ascension 33-36
Bahamas 92-95
Barbados 186-189
Basutoland 11-14
Bechuanaland Protectorate 117-120
Bermuda 100-103
British Guiana 223-226
British Honduras 108-111
Cayman Islands 81-84
Ceylon 260-263
Cyprus 136-139
Dominica 90-93
Falkland Islands 77-80
Fiji 110-113
Gambia 125-128
Gibraltar 100-103
Gilbert & Ellice Islands 33-36
Gold Coast 108-111
Grenada 124-127
Hong Kong 147-150
Jamaica 109-112
Kenya, Uganda, Tanzania 42-45
Leeward Islands 96-99
Malta 184-187
Mauritius 204-207
Montserrat 85-88
Newfoundland 226-229
Nigeria 34-37
Northern Rhodesia 18-21
Nyasaland Protectorate 47-50
St. Helena 111-114
St. Kitts-Nevis 72-75
St. Lucia 91-94
St. Vincent 134-137
Seychelles 118-121
Sierra Leone 166-169
Solomon Islands 60-63
Somaliland Protectorate 77-80
Straits Settlements 213-216
Swaziland 20-23
Trinidad & Tobago 43-46
Turks & Caicos Islands 71-74
Virgin Islands 69-72

The following have different designs but are included in the omnibus set:

Great Britain 226-229
Offices in Morocco (Sp. Curr.) 67-70
Offices in Morocco (Br. Curr.) 226-229
Offices in Morocco (Fr. Curr.) 422-425
Offices in Morocco (Tangier) 508-510
Australia 152-154
Canada 211-216
Cook Islands 98-100
India 142-148
Nauru 31-34
New Guinea 46-47
New Zealand 199-201
Niue 67-69
Papua 114-117
Samoa 163-165
South Africa 68-71
Southern Rhodesia 33-36
South-West Africa 121-124

Nos. 77-80 (4)	20.25	*23.25*
Nos. 33-36 (4)	58.50	*127.50*
Nos. 92-95 (4)	25.00	*46.00*
Nos. 186-189 (4)	30.00	46.80
Nos. 11-14 (4)	11.60	*21.25*
Nos. 117-120 (4)	15.75	*36.00*
Nos. 100-103 (4)	16.80	*58.50*
Nos. 223-226 (4)	18.35	35.50
Nos. 108-111 (4)	15.25	*16.35*
Nos. 81-84 (4)	21.60	*24.50*
Nos. 260-263 (4)	10.40	21.60
Nos. 136-139 (4)	39.75	*34.40*
Nos. 90-93 (4)	18.85	19.85
Nos. 77-80 (4)	55.00	14.75
Nos. 110-113 (4)	15.25	27.90
Nos. 125-128 (4)	12.20	*25.25*
Nos. 100-103 (4)	28.75	42.75
Nos. 33-36 (4)	36.80	*67.00*
Nos. 108-111 (4)	25.75	*78.10*
Nos. 124-127 (4)	16.70	*40.60*
Nos. 147-150 (4)	59.00	18.75
Nos. 109-112 (4)	17.00	39.00
Nos. 42-45 (4)	8.75	*11.00*
Nos. 96-99 (4)	35.75	49.60
Nos. 184-187 (4)	22.00	33.70
Nos. 204-207 (4)	47.60	58.25
Nos. 85-88 (4)	10.25	*30.25*
Nos. 226-229 (4)	17.50	12.05
Nos. 34-37 (4)	13.25	*59.75*
Nos. 18-21 (4)	16.75	16.25
Nos. 47-50 (4)	39.75	*80.25*
Nos. 111-114 (4)	31.15	*33.25*
Nos. 72-75 (4)	11.55	*18.50*
Nos. 91-94 (4)	16.00	*20.80*
Nos. 134-137 (4)	9.45	*21.25*
Nos. 118-121 (4)	17.50	*32.50*
Nos. 166-169 (4)	24.25	*56.00*
Nos. 60-63 (4)	27.25	38.00
Nos. 77-80 (4)	17.00	*48.25*
Nos. 213-216 (4)	15.00	*25.10*
Nos. 20-23 (4)	6.80	18.25
Nos. 43-46 (4)	14.05	27.75
Nos. 71-74 (4)	8.40	14.50
Nos. 69-72 (4)	25.00	55.25
Nos. 226-229 (4)	5.15	*4.40*

Nos. 67-70 (4) 14.35 *26.10*
Nos. 226-229 (4) 8.20 *28.90*
Nos. 422-425 (4) 3.90 2.00
Nos. 508-510 (3) 18.80 *23.85*
Nos. 152-154 (3) 45.75 60.35
Nos. 211-216 (6) 24.85 13.35
Nos. 98-100 (3) 9.65 *12.00*
Nos. 142-148 (7) 28.85 14.00
Nos. 31-34 (4) 9.90 *9.90*
Nos. 46-47 (2) 4.35 1.70
Nos. 199-201 (3) 21.75 *31.75*
Nos. 67-69 (3) 11.30 *26.50*
Nos. 114-117 (4) 9.20 *17.00*
Nos. 163-165 (3) 4.40 5.50
Nos. 68-71 (4) 57.00 *155.00*
Nos. 33-36 (4) 27.75 *45.25*
Nos. 121-124 (4) 13.00 *36.10*
Set total (245) Stamps 1,322. 2,140.

Coronation

Queen Elizabeth and King George VI
CD302

1937

Aden 13-15
Antigua 81-83
Ascension 37-39
Bahamas 97-99
Barbados 190-192
Basutoland 15-17
Bechuanaland Protectorate 121-123
Bermuda 115-117
British Guiana 227-229
British Honduras 112-114
Cayman Islands 97-99
Ceylon 275-277
Cyprus 140-142
Dominica 94-96
Falkland Islands 81-83
Fiji 114-116
Gambia 129-131
Gibraltar 104-106
Gilbert & Ellice Islands 37-39
Gold Coast 112-114
Grenada 128-130
Hong Kong 151-153
Jamaica 113-115
Kenya, Uganda, Tanzania 60-62
Leeward Islands 100-102
Malta 188-190
Mauritius 208-210
Montserrat 89-91
Newfoundland 230-232
Nigeria 50-52
Northern Rhodesia 22-24
Nyasaland Protectorate 51-53
St. Helena 115-117
St. Kitts-Nevis 76-78
St. Lucia 107-109
St. Vincent 138-140
Seychelles 122-124
Sierra Leone 170-172
Solomon Islands 64-66
Somaliland Protectorate 81-83
Straits Settlements 235-237
Swaziland 24-26
Trinidad & Tobago 47-49
Turks & Caicos Islands 75-77
Virgin Islands 73-75

The following have different designs but are included in the omnibus set:

Great Britain 234
Offices in Morocco (Sp. Curr.) 82
Offices in Morocco (Fr. Curr.) 439
Offices in Morocco (Tangier) 514
Canada 237
Cook Islands 109-111
Nauru 35-38
Newfoundland 233-243
New Guinea 48-51
New Zealand 223-225
Niue 70-72
Papua 118-121
South Africa 74-78
Southern Rhodesia 38-41
South-West Africa 125-132

Nos. 13-15 (3) 2.70 *5.65*
Nos. 81-83 (3) 1.85 *8.00*
Nos. 37-39 (3) 2.75 *2.75*
Nos. 97-99 (3) 1.05 *3.05*
Nos. 190-192 (3) 1.10 1.95
Nos. 15-17 (3) 1.15 *3.00*
Nos. 121-123 (3) .95 3.35
Nos. 115-117 (3) 1.25 5.00
Nos. 227-229 (3) 1.45 3.05
Nos. 112-114 (3) 1.20 2.40
Nos. 97-99 (3) 1.10 2.70
Nos. 275-277 (3) 8.25 10.35
Nos. 140-142 (3) 3.75 6.50
Nos. 94-96 (3) .85 2.40
Nos. 81-83 (3) 2.90 *2.30*
Nos. 114-116 (3) 1.50 *5.75*
Nos. 129-131 (3) .95 3.95
Nos. 104-106 (3) 2.25 6.45
Nos. 37-39 (3) .85 *2.15*
Nos. 112-114 (3) 3.10 *10.00*
Nos. 128-130 (3) 1.00 .85
Nos. 151-153 (3) 23.00 12.50
Nos. 113-115 (3) 1.25 1.25
Nos. 60-62 (3) 1.00 2.35
Nos. 100-102 (3) 1.55 4.00
Nos. 188-190 (3) 1.25 1.60
Nos. 208-210 (3) 2.05 3.75
Nos. 89-91 (3) 1.00 3.35
Nos. 230-232 (3) 7.00 2.80
Nos. 50-52 (3) 3.25 8.50
Nos. 22-24 (3) .95 2.25
Nos. 51-53 (3) 1.05 1.30
Nos. 115-117 (3) 1.45 2.05
Nos. 76-78 (3) .95 2.05
Nos. 107-109 (3) 1.05 2.05
Nos. 138-140 (3) .80 *4.75*
Nos. 122-124 (3) 1.20 *1.90*
Nos. 170-172 (3) 1.95 5.65
Nos. 64-66 (3) .90 2.00
Nos. 81-83 (3) 1.10 *3.40*
Nos. 235-237 (3) 3.25 1.60
Nos. 24-26 (3) 1.05 1.75
Nos. 47-49 (3) 1.00 1.00
Nos. 75-77 (3) 1.30 1.15
Nos. 73-75 (3) 2.20 6.90

No. 234 (1) .25 .25
No. 82 (1) .80 .80
No. 439 (1) .35 .25
No. 514 (1) .55 .55
No. 237 (1) .35 .25
Nos. 109-111 (3) .85 .80
Nos. 35-38 (4) 1.10 *5.50*
Nos. 233-243 (11) 41.90 30.40
Nos. 48-51 (4) 1.40 *7.90*
Nos. 223-225 (3) 1.40 *2.75*
Nos. 70-72 (3) .80 *2.05*
Nos. 118-121 (4) 1.60 *5.25*
Nos. 74-78 (5) 9.25 10.80
Nos. 38-41 (4) 3.55 15.50
Nos. 125-132 (8) 5.00 8.40
Set total (189) Stamps 172.65 262.95

Peace

King George VI and Parliament Buildings, London
CD303

Return to peace at the close of World War II.

1945-46

Aden 28-29
Antigua 96-97
Ascension 50-51
Bahamas 130-131
Barbados 207-208
Bermuda 131-132
British Guiana 242-243
British Honduras 127-128
Cayman Islands 112-113
Ceylon 293-294
Cyprus 156-157
Dominica 112-113
Falkland Islands 97-98
Falkland Islands Dep. 1L9-1L10
Fiji 137-138
Gambia 144-145
Gibraltar 119-120
Gilbert & Ellice Islands 52-53
Gold Coast 128-129
Grenada 143-144
Jamaica 136-137
Kenya, Uganda, Tanzania 90-91
Leeward Islands 116-117
Malta 206-207
Mauritius 223-224
Montserrat 104-105
Nigeria 71-72
Northern Rhodesia 46-47
Nyasaland Protectorate 82-83
Pitcairn Islands 9-10
St. Helena 128-129
St. Kitts-Nevis 91-92
St. Lucia 127-128
St. Vincent 152-153
Seychelles 149-150
Sierra Leone 186-187
Solomon Islands 80-81
Somaliland Protectorate 108-109
Trinidad & Tobago 62-63
Turks & Caicos Islands 90-91
Virgin Islands 88-89

The following have different designs but are included in the omnibus set:

Great Britain 264-265
Offices in Morocco (Tangier) 523-524
Aden
  Kathiri State of Seiyun 12-13
  Qu'aiti State of Shihr and Mukalla 12-13
Australia 200-202
Basutoland 29-31
Bechuanaland Protectorate 137-139
Burma 66-69
Cook Islands 127-130
Hong Kong 174-175
India 195-198
  Hyderabad 51-53
New Zealand 247-257
Niue 90-93
Pakistan-Bahawalpur O16
Samoa 191-194
South Africa 100-102
Southern Rhodesia 67-70
South-West Africa 153-155
Swaziland 38-40
Zanzibar 222-223

Nos. 28-29 (2) .95 2.50
Nos. 96-97 (2) .50 *.80*
Nos. 50-51 (2) .80 *2.00*
Nos. 130-131 (2) .50 1.40
Nos. 207-208 (2) .50 1.10
Nos. 131-132 (2) .55 .55
Nos. 242-243 (2) 1.05 *1.40*
Nos. 127-128 (2) .50 .50
Nos. 112-113 (2) .80 .80
Nos. 293-294 (2) .60 *2.10*
Nos. 156-157 (2) .90 .70
Nos. 112-113 (2) .50 .50
Nos. 97-98 (2) .90 1.35
Nos. 1L9-1L10 (2) 1.30 1.00
Nos. 137-138 (2) .50 *1.75*
Nos. 144-145 (2) .50 .95
Nos. 119-120 (2) .75 *1.00*
Nos. 52-53 (2) .50 *1.10*
Nos. 128-129 (2) 1.85 *3.75*
Nos. 143-144 (2) .50 *.95*
Nos. 136-137 (2) .80 *12.50*
Nos. 90-91 (2) .65 .65
Nos. 116-117 (2) .50 1.50
Nos. 206-207 (2) .65 2.00
Nos. 223-224 (2) .50 1.05
Nos. 104-105 (2) .50 .50
Nos. 71-72 (2) .70 *2.75*
Nos. 46-47 (2) 1.25 *2.00*
Nos. 82-83 (2) .50 .50
Nos. 9-10 (2) 1.40 1.40
Nos. 128-129 (2) .65 .70
Nos. 91-92 (2) .50 .50
Nos. 127-128 (2) .50 .60
Nos. 152-153 (2) .50 .50
Nos. 149-150 (2) .55 .50
Nos. 186-187 (2) .50 .50
Nos. 80-81 (2) .50 1.50
Nos. 108-109 (2) .70 .50
Nos. 62-63 (2) .50 .50
Nos. 90-91 (2) .50 .50
Nos. 88-89 (2) .50 .50

Nos. 264-265 (2) .50 .50
Nos. 523-524 (2) 1.50 3.00
Nos. 12-13 (2) .50 .90
Nos. 12-13 (2) .50 *1.25*
Nos. 200-202 (3) 1.60 *3.00*
Nos. 29-31 (3) 2.10 2.60
Nos. 137-139 (3) 2.05 *4.75*
Nos. 66-69 (4) 1.60 1.30
Nos. 127-130 (4) 2.00 1.85
Nos. 174-175 (2) 6.75 3.15
Nos. 195-198 (4) 5.60 5.50
Nos. 51-53 (3) 1.50 1.70
Nos. 247-257 (11) 3.95 3.90
Nos. 90-93 (4) 1.70 *2.20*
No. O16 (1) 5.50 *7.00*
Nos. 191-194 (4) 2.05 1.00
Nos. 100-102 (3) 1.20 4.00
Nos. 67-70 (4) 1.40 1.75
Nos. 153-155 (3) 1.85 3.25
Nos. 38-40 (3) 2.40 *5.50*
Nos. 222-223 (2) .65 1.00
Set total (151) Stamps 75.20 116.95

Silver Wedding

King George VI and Queen Elizabeth
CD304 CD305

1948-49

Aden 30-31
  Kathiri State of Seiyun 14-15
  Qu'aiti State of Shihr and Mukalla 14-15
Antigua 98-99
Ascension 52-53
Bahamas 148-149
Barbados 210-211
Basutoland 39-40
Bechuanaland Protectorate 147-148
Bermuda 133-134
British Guiana 244-245
British Honduras 129-130
Cayman Islands 116-117
Cyprus 158-159
Dominica 114-115
Falkland Islands 99-100
Falkland Islands Dep. 1L11-1L12
Fiji 139-140
Gambia 146-147
Gibraltar 121-122
Gilbert & Ellice Islands 54-55
Gold Coast 142-143
Grenada 145-146
Hong Kong 178-179
Jamaica 138-139
Kenya, Uganda, Tanzania 92-93
Leeward Islands 118-119
Malaya
  Johore 128-129
  Kedah 55-56
  Kelantan 44-45
  Malacca 1-2
  Negri Sembilan 36-37
  Pahang 44-45
  Penang 1-2
  Perak 99-100
  Perlis 1-2
  Selangor 74-75
  Trengganu 47-48
Malta 223-224
Mauritius 229-230
Montserrat 106-107
Nigeria 73-74
North Borneo 238-239
Northern Rhodesia 48-49
Nyasaland Protectorate 85-86
Pitcairn Islands 11-12
St. Helena 130-131
St. Kitts-Nevis 93-94
St. Lucia 129-130
St. Vincent 154-155
Sarawak 174-175
Seychelles 151-152
Sierra Leone 188-189
Singapore 21-22
Solomon Islands 82-83
Somaliland Protectorate 110-111
Swaziland 48-49
Trinidad & Tobago 64-65
Turks & Caicos Islands 92-93
Virgin Islands 90-91
Zanzibar 224-225

The following have different designs but are included in the omnibus set:

Great Britain 267-268
  Offices in Morocco (Sp. Curr.) 93-94
  Offices in Morocco (Tangier) 525-526
Bahrain 62-63
Kuwait 82-83
Oman 25-26
South Africa 106
South-West Africa 159

Nos. 30-31 (2) 40.40 47.25
Nos. 14-15 (2) 17.85 *16.00*
Nos. 14-15 (2) 18.55 *12.50*
Nos. 98-99 (2) 13.55 *15.75*
Nos. 52-53 (2) 55.55 50.45
Nos. 148-149 (2) 45.25 40.30
Nos. 210-211 (2) 18.35 13.05
Nos. 39-40 (2) 52.80 *55.25*
Nos. 147-148 (2) 42.85 *47.75*
Nos. 133-134 (2) 47.75 *55.25*
Nos. 244-245 (2) 24.25 *28.45*
Nos. 129-130 (2) 25.25 *53.20*
Nos. 116-117 (2) 25.25 *33.50*
Nos. 158-159 (2) 58.50 *78.05*
Nos. 114-115 (2) 25.25 *32.75*
Nos. 99-100 (2) 112.10 76.10
Nos. 1L11-1L12 (2) 4.25 6.00
Nos. 139-140 (2) 17.00 11.50
Nos. 146-147 (2) 21.25 21.25
Nos. 121-122 (2) 61.00 *78.00*
Nos. 54-55 (2) 14.25 *26.25*
Nos. 142-143 (2) 35.25 48.20
Nos. 145-146 (2) 21.75 21.75
Nos. 178-179 (2) 283.50 96.50
Nos. 138-139 (2) 27.85 *60.25*
Nos. 92-93 (2) 50.25 *67.75*
Nos. 118-119 (2) 7.00 8.25
Nos. 128-129 (2) 29.25 *53.25*
Nos. 55-56 (2) 35.25 *50.25*
Nos. 44-45 (2) 35.75 *62.75*
Nos. 1-2 (2) 35.40 *49.75*
Nos. 36-37 (2) 28.10 *38.20*
Nos. 44-45 (2) 28.00 *38.05*
Nos. 1-2 (2) 40.50 37.80

Nos. 99-100 (2) 27.80 37.75
Nos. 1-2 (2) 33.50 58.00
Nos. 74-75 (2) 30.25 25.30
Nos. 47-48 (2) 35.25 62.75
Nos. 223-224 (2) 40.55 45.25
Nos. 229-230 (2) 17.75 45.25
Nos. 106-107 (2) 9.25 18.25
Nos. 73-74 (2) 17.85 22.80
Nos. 238-239 (2) 35.30 45.75
Nos. 48-49 (2) 92.80 90.25
Nos. 85-86 (2) 18.25 30.25
Nos. 11-12 (2) 44.75 48.50
Nos. 130-131 (2) 32.80 42.80
Nos. 93-94 (2) 11.25 7.25
Nos. 129-130 (2) 22.25 45.25
Nos. 154-155 (2) 27.75 30.25
Nos. 174-175 (2) 50.40 52.90
Nos. 151-152 (2) 16.25 45.75
Nos. 188-189 (2) 24.75 26.25
Nos. 21-22 (2) 116.00 45.40
Nos. 82-83 (2) 13.40 13.40
Nos. 110-111 (2) 8.40 8.75
Nos. 48-49 (2) 40.30 47.75
Nos. 64-65 (2) 32.75 38.25
Nos. 92-93 (2) 11.25 16.25
Nos. 90-91 (2) 16.25 22.25
Nos. 224-225 (2) 29.60 38.00

Nos. 267-268 (2) 30.40 25.25
Nos. 93-94 (2) 20.10 25.35
Nos. 525-526 (2) 23.10 29.25
Nos. 62-63 (2) 38.50 57.75
Nos. 82-83 (2) 45.50 45.50
Nos. 25-26 (2) 46.00 47.50
No. 106 (1) .90 1.25
No. 159 (1) 1.10 .35
Set total (136) Stamps 2,461. 2,674.

U.P.U.

Mercury and Symbols of Communications — CD306

Plane, Ship and Hemispheres — CD307

Mercury Scattering Letters over Globe CD308

U.P.U. Monument, Bern CD309

Universal Postal Union, 75th anniversary.

1949

Aden 32-35
Kathiri State of Seiyun....16-19
Qu'aiti State of Shihr and Mukalla 16-19
Antigua 100-103
Ascension 57-60
Bahamas 150-153
Barbados 212-215
Basutoland....41-44
Bechuanaland Protectorate....149-152
Bermuda....138-141
British Guiana....246-249
British Honduras....137-140
Brunei....79-82
Cayman Islands....118-121
Cyprus....160-163
Dominica....116-119
Falkland Islands 103-106
Falkland Islands Dep....1L14-1L17
Fiji....141-144
Gambia....148-151
Gibraltar....123-126
Gilbert & Ellice Islands....56-59
Gold Coast....144-147
Grenada....147-150
Hong Kong 180-183
Jamaica....142-145
Kenya, Uganda, Tanzania....94-97
Leeward Islands....126-129
Malaya
Johore....151-154
Kedah....57-60
Kelantan....46-49
Malacca....18-21
Negri Sembilan....59-62
Pahang....46-49
Penang....23-26
Perak....101-104
Perlis....3-6
Selangor....76-79
Trengganu....49-52
Malta....225-228
Mauritius....231-234
Montserrat....108-111
New Hebrides, British....62-65
New Hebrides, French....79-82
Nigeria....75-78
North Borneo....240-243
Northern Rhodesia....50-53
Nyasaland Protectorate....87-90
Pitcairn Islands....13-16
St. Helena....132-135
St. Kitts-Nevis....95-98
St. Lucia....131-134
St. Vincent....170-173
Sarawak....176-179
Seychelles....153-156
Sierra Leone....190-193
Singapore....23-26
Solomon Islands....84-87
Somaliland Protectorate....112-115
Southern Rhodesia....71-72
Swaziland....50-53
Tonga....87-90
Trinidad & Tobago....66-69
Turks & Caicos Islands....101-104
Virgin Islands....92-95
Zanzibar....226-229

The following have different designs but are included in the omnibus set:

Great Britain....276-279
Offices in Morocco (Tangier)....546-549
Australia....223
Bahrain....68-71
Burma....116-121
Ceylon....304-306
Egypt....281-283
India....223-226
Kuwait....89-92
Oman....31-34
Pakistan-Bahawalpur 26-29, O25-O28
South Africa....109-111
South-West Africa....160-162

Nos. 32-35 (4) 5.85 8.45
Nos. 16-19 (4) 2.75 5.50
Nos. 16-19 (4) 2.60 4.20
Nos. 100-103 (4) 3.60 7.70
Nos. 57-60 (4) 11.10 9.00
Nos. 150-153 (4) 5.35 9.30
Nos. 212-215 (4) 4.40 14.15
Nos. 41-44 (4) 4.75 10.00
Nos. 149-152 (4) 3.35 7.25
Nos. 138-141 (4) 4.75 6.15
Nos. 246-249 (4) 2.75 4.20
Nos. 137-140 (4) 3.30 6.35
Nos. 79-82 (4) 9.50 8.45
Nos. 118-121 (4) 3.60 7.25
Nos. 160-163 (4) 4.60 10.70
Nos. 116-119 (4) 2.30 5.65
Nos. 103-106 (4) 14.00 17.10
Nos. 1L14-1L17 (4) 14.60 14.50
Nos. 141-144 (4) 3.35 14.75
Nos. 148-151 (4) 3.10 7.10
Nos. 123-126 (4) 5.90 8.75
Nos. 56-59 (4) 4.30 13.00
Nos. 144-147 (4) 2.55 10.35
Nos. 147-150 (4) 2.15 3.55
Nos. 180-183 (4) 57.25 18.25
Nos. 142-145 (4) 2.25 2.45
Nos. 94-97 (4) 2.90 3.40
Nos. 126-129 (4) 3.05 9.60
Nos. 151-154 (4) 4.70 8.90
Nos. 57-60 (4) 4.80 12.00
Nos. 46-49 (4) 4.25 12.65
Nos. 18-21 (4) 4.25 17.30
Nos. 59-62 (4) 3.50 10.75
Nos. 46-49 (4) 3.00 7.25
Nos. 23-26 (4) 5.10 11.75
Nos. 101-104 (4) 3.65 10.75
Nos. 3-6 (4) 3.95 14.25
Nos. 76-79 (4) 4.90 12.30
Nos. 49-52 (4) 4.95 9.75
Nos. 225-228 (4) 4.50 4.85
Nos. 231-234 (4) 4.35 6.70
Nos. 108-111 (4) 3.40 3.85
Nos. 62-65 (4) 1.60 4.25
Nos. 79-82 (4) 24.25 24.25
Nos. 75-78 (4) 2.80 9.25
Nos. 240-243 (4) 7.15 6.50
Nos. 50-53 (4) 5.00 6.50
Nos. 87-90 (4) 4.05 4.05
Nos. 13-16 (4) 18.50 16.50
Nos. 132-135 (4) 4.85 7.10
Nos. 95-98 (4) 3.35 4.70
Nos. 131-134 (4) 2.55 3.85
Nos. 170-173 (4) 2.20 5.05
Nos. 176-179 (4) 8.15 10.85
Nos. 153-156 (4) 3.25 4.10
Nos. 190-193 (4) 3.00 5.10
Nos. 23-26 (4) 18.00 13.20
Nos. 84-87 (4) 4.05 4.90
Nos. 112-115 (4) 3.95 8.70
Nos. 71-72 (2) 1.95 2.25
Nos. 50-53 (4) 2.80 4.65
Nos. 87-90 (4) 3.00 5.25
Nos. 66-69 (4) 3.15 3.15
Nos. 101-104 (4) 2.70 4.10
Nos. 92-95 (4) 2.60 5.90
Nos. 226-229 (4) 5.45 13.50

Nos. 276-279 (4) 1.35 1.00
Nos. 546-549 (4) 3.20 10.15
No. 223 (1) .60 .55
Nos. 68-71 (4) 4.75 16.50
Nos. 116-121 (6) 7.30 5.35
Nos. 304-306 (3) 3.35 4.25
Nos. 281-283 (3) 5.75 2.70
Nos. 223-226 (4) 27.25 10.50
Nos. 89-92 (4) 6.10 10.25
Nos. 31-34 (4) 5.55 15.75
Nos. 26-29,O25-O28 (8) 2.00 42.00
Nos. 109-111 (3) 2.20 3.00
Nos. 160-162 (3) 3.00 5.50
Set total (313) Stamps 460.00 695.30

University

Arms of University College CD310

Alice, Princess of Athlone CD311

1948 opening of University College of the West Indies at Jamaica.

1951

Antigua....104-105
Barbados....228-229
British Guiana....250-251
British Honduras....141-142
Dominica....120-121
Grenada....164-165
Jamaica....146-147
Leeward Islands....130-131
Montserrat....112-113
St. Kitts-Nevis....105-106
St. Lucia....149-150
St. Vincent....174-175
Trinidad & Tobago....70-71
Virgin Islands....96-97

Nos. 104-105 (2) 1.35 3.75
Nos. 228-229 (2) 1.85 1.55
Nos. 250-251 (2) 1.10 1.25
Nos. 141-142 (2) 1.40 2.20
Nos. 120-121 (2) 1.40 1.75
Nos. 164-165 (2) 1.20 1.60
Nos. 146-147 (2) .90 .70
Nos. 130-131 (2) 1.35 4.00
Nos. 112-113 (2) .85 1.50
Nos. 105-106 (2) .90 1.50
Nos. 149-150 (2) 1.40 1.50
Nos. 174-175 (2) 1.00 2.15
Nos. 70-71 (2) .75 .75
Nos. 96-97 (2) 1.50 3.75
Set total (28) Stamps 16.95 27.95

Coronation

Queen Elizabeth II — CD312

1953

Aden....47
Kathiri State of Seiyun....28
Qu'aiti State of Shihr and Mukalla....28
Antigua....106
Ascension....61
Bahamas....157
Barbados....234
Basutoland....45
Bechuanaland Protectorate....153
Bermuda....142
British Guiana....252
British Honduras....143
Cayman Islands....150
Cyprus....167
Dominica....141
Falkland Islands....121
Falkland Islands Dependencies....1L18
Fiji....145
Gambia....152
Gibraltar....131
Gilbert & Ellice Islands....60
Gold Coast....160
Grenada....170
Hong Kong....184
Jamaica....153
Kenya, Uganda, Tanzania....101
Leeward Islands....132
Malaya
Johore....155
Kedah....82
Kelantan....71
Malacca....27
Negri Sembilan....63
Pahang....71
Penang....27
Perak....126
Perlis....28
Selangor....101
Trengganu....74
Malta....241
Mauritius....250
Montserrat....127
New Hebrides, British....77
Nigeria....79
North Borneo....260
Northern Rhodesia....60
Nyasaland Protectorate....96
Pitcairn Islands....19
St. Helena....139
St. Kitts-Nevis....119
St. Lucia....156
St. Vincent....185
Sarawak....196
Seychelles....172
Sierra Leone....194
Singapore....27
Solomon Islands....88
Somaliland Protectorate....127
Swaziland....54
Trinidad & Tobago....84
Tristan da Cunha....13
Turks & Caicos Islands....118
Virgin Islands....114

The following have different designs but are included in the omnibus set:

Great Britain....313-316
Offices in Morocco (Tangier)....579-582
Australia....259-261
Bahrain....92-95
Canada....330
Ceylon....317
Cook Islands....145-146
Kuwait....113-116
New Zealand....280-284
Niue....104-105
Oman....52-55
Samoa....214-215
South Africa....192
Southern Rhodesia....80
South-West Africa....244-248
Tokelau Islands....4

No. 47 (1) 1.25 1.25
No. 28 (1) .75 1.50
No. 28 (1) 1.10 .60
No. 106 (1) .40 .75
No. 61 (1) 1.25 2.75
No. 157 (1) 1.40 .75
No. 234 (1) 1.00 .25
No. 45 (1) .50 .60
No. 153 (1) .75 .35
No. 142 (1) .85 .50
No. 252 (1) .45 .25
No. 143 (1) .60 .40
No. 150 (1) .40 1.75
No. 167 (1) 1.60 .75
No. 141 (1) .40 .40
No. 121 (1) .90 1.50
No. 1L18 (1) 1.80 1.40
No. 145 (1) 1.00 .60
No. 152 (1) .50 .50
No. 131 (1) .50 .50
No. 60 (1) .65 2.25
No. 160 (1) 1.00 .25

No. 170 (1)	.30	.25
No. 184 (1)	6.00	.35
No. 153 (1)	.70	.25
No. 101 (1)	.40	.25
No. 132 (1)	1.00	*2.25*
No. 155 (1)	1.40	.30
No. 82 (1)	2.25	.60
No. 71 (1)	1.60	1.60
No. 27 (1)	1.10	*1.50*
No. 63 (1)	1.40	.65
No. 71 (1)	2.25	.25
No. 27 (1)	1.75	.30
No. 126 (1)	1.60	.25
No. 28 (1)	1.75	*4.00*
No. 101 (1)	1.75	.25
No. 74 (1)	1.50	1.00
No. 241 (1)	.50	.25
No. 250 (1)	1.00	.25
No. 127 (1)	.65	.50
No. 77 (1)	.75	.60
No. 79 (1)	.45	.25
No. 260 (1)	2.00	1.00
No. 60 (1)	.70	.25
No. 96 (1)	.75	.75
No. 19 (1)	2.25	2.25
No. 139 (1)	1.25	1.25
No. 119 (1)	.35	.25
No. 156 (1)	.70	.35
No. 185 (1)	.50	.30
No. 196 (1)	2.00	*1.75*
No. 172 (1)	.80	.80
No. 194 (1)	.40	.40
No. 27 (1)	2.50	.40
No. 88 (1)	1.00	1.00
No. 127 (1)	.40	.25
No. 54 (1)	.30	.25
No. 84 (1)	.25	.25
No. 13 (1)	1.00	1.75
No. 118 (1)	.40	*1.10*
No. 114 (1)	.40	*1.00*
Nos. 313-316 (4)	16.35	5.95
Nos. 579-582 (4)	7.40	5.20
Nos. 259-261 (3)	4.60	3.25
Nos. 92-95 (4)	15.25	12.75
No. 330 (1)	.25	.25
No. 317 (1)	1.50	.25
Nos. 145-146 (2)	2.65	2.65
Nos. 113-116 (4)	16.00	8.50
Nos. 280-284 (5)	5.65	6.85
Nos. 104-105 (2)	1.60	1.60
Nos. 52-55 (4)	15.25	6.50
Nos. 214-215 (2)	2.10	1.00
No. 192 (1)	.30	.25
No. 80 (1)	7.25	7.25
Nos. 244-248 (5)	3.00	2.35
No. 4 (1)	2.75	2.75
Set total (106) Stamps	169.00	118.45

Separate designs for each country for the visit of Queen Elizabeth II and the Duke of Edinburgh.

Royal Visit 1953

1953

Aden 62
Australia 267-269
Bermuda 163
Ceylon 318
Fiji 146
Gibraltar 146
Jamaica 154
Kenya, Uganda, Tanzania 102
Malta 242
New Zealand 286-287

No. 62 (1)	.65	1.25
Nos. 267-269 (3)	2.35	1.90
No. 163 (1)	.50	.25
No. 318 (1)	1.25	.25
No. 146 (1)	.65	.35
No. 146 (1)	.50	.30
No. 154 (1)	.50	.25
No. 102 (1)	.50	.25
No. 242 (1)	.35	.25
Nos. 286-287 (2)	.50	.50
Set total (13) Stamps	7.75	5.55

West Indies Federation

Map of the Caribbean CD313

Federation of the West Indies, April 22, 1958.

1958

Antigua 122-124
Barbados 248-250
Dominica 161-163
Grenada 184-186
Jamaica 175-177
Montserrat 143-145
St. Kitts-Nevis 136-138
St. Lucia 170-172
St. Vincent 198-200
Trinidad & Tobago 86-88

Nos. 122-124 (3)	5.80	3.80
Nos. 248-250 (3)	1.60	*2.90*
Nos. 161-163 (3)	1.95	1.85
Nos. 184-186 (3)	1.50	1.20
Nos. 175-177 (3)	2.65	3.45
Nos. 143-145 (3)	2.35	1.35
Nos. 136-138 (3)	3.00	1.85
Nos. 170-172 (3)	2.05	2.80
Nos. 198-200 (3)	1.50	1.75
Nos. 86-88 (3)	.75	.90
Set total (30) Stamps	23.15	21.85

Freedom from Hunger

Protein Food CD314

U.N. Food and Agricultural Organization's "Freedom from Hunger" campaign.

1963

Aden 65
Antigua 133
Ascension 89
Bahamas 180
Basutoland 83
Bechuanaland Protectorate 194
Bermuda 192
British Guiana 271
British Honduras 179
Brunei 100
Cayman Islands 168
Dominica 181
Falkland Islands 146
Fiji 198
Gambia 172
Gibraltar 161
Gilbert & Ellice Islands 76
Grenada 190
Hong Kong 218
Malta 291
Mauritius 270
Montserrat 150
New Hebrides, British 93
North Borneo 296
Pitcairn Islands 35
St. Helena 173
St. Lucia 179
St. Vincent 201
Sarawak 212
Seychelles 213
Solomon Islands 109
Swaziland 108
Tonga 127
Tristan da Cunha 68
Turks & Caicos Islands 138
Virgin Islands 140
Zanzibar 280

No. 65 (1)	1.50	1.75
No. 133 (1)	.35	.35
No. 89 (1)	1.00	.50
No. 180 (1)	.65	.65
No. 83 (1)	.50	.25
No. 194 (1)	.50	.50
No. 192 (1)	1.00	.50
No. 271 (1)	.45	.25
No. 179 (1)	.60	.25
No. 100 (1)	3.25	2.25
No. 168 (1)	.55	.30
No. 181 (1)	.30	.30
No. 146 (1)	10.50	2.50
No. 198 (1)	3.50	2.25
No. 172 (1)	.50	.25
No. 161 (1)	4.00	2.25
No. 76 (1)	1.40	.40
No. 190 (1)	.30	.25
No. 218 (1)	47.50	7.50
No. 291 (1)	2.00	2.00
No. 270 (1)	.50	.50
No. 150 (1)	.55	.45
No. 93 (1)	.60	.25
No. 296 (1)	1.90	.75
No. 35 (1)	10.00	4.50
No. 173 (1)	2.25	1.10
No. 179 (1)	.40	.40
No. 201 (1)	.90	.50
No. 212 (1)	1.60	*1.75*
No. 213 (1)	.85	.35
No. 109 (1)	3.00	.85
No. 108 (1)	.50	.50
No. 127 (1)	.60	.35
No. 68 (1)	.75	.35
No. 138 (1)	.50	.25
No. 140 (1)	.50	.50
No. 280 (1)	1.50	.80
Set total (37) Stamps	107.25	39.40

Red Cross Centenary

Red Cross and Elizabeth II CD315

1963

Antigua 134-135
Ascension 90-91
Bahamas 183-184
Basutoland 84-85
Bechuanaland Protectorate 195-196
Bermuda 193-194
British Guiana 272-273
British Honduras 180-181
Cayman Islands 169-170
Dominica 182-183
Falkland Islands 147-148
Fiji 203-204
Gambia 173-174
Gibraltar 162-163
Gilbert & Ellice Islands 77-78
Grenada 191-192
Hong Kong 219-220
Jamaica 203-204
Malta 292-293
Mauritius 271-272
Montserrat 151-152
New Hebrides, British 94-95
Pitcairn Islands 36-37
St. Helena 174-175
St. Kitts-Nevis 143-144
St. Lucia 180-181
St. Vincent 202-203
Seychelles 214-215
Solomon Islands 110-111
South Arabia 1-2
Swaziland 109-110
Tonga 134-135
Tristan da Cunha 69-70
Turks & Caicos Islands 139-140
Virgin Islands 141-142

Nos. 134-135 (2)	1.00	*2.00*
Nos. 90-91 (2)	6.75	3.35
Nos. 183-184 (2)	2.30	2.80
Nos. 84-85 (2)	1.20	.90
Nos. 195-196 (2)	.95	.85
Nos. 193-194 (2)	3.00	2.80
Nos. 272-273 (2)	1.05	.80
Nos. 180-181 (2)	1.00	2.50
Nos. 169-170 (2)	1.10	*3.00*
Nos. 182-183 (2)	.70	*1.05*
Nos. 147-148 (2)	18.00	5.50
Nos. 203-204 (2)	3.25	2.80
Nos. 173-174 (2)	.75	1.00
Nos. 162-163 (2)	6.25	5.40
Nos. 77-78 (2)	2.00	*3.50*
Nos. 191-192 (2)	.80	.50
Nos. 219-220 (2)	35.00	7.35
Nos. 203-204 (2)	.75	*1.65*
Nos. 292-293 (2)	2.50	4.75
Nos. 271-272 (2)	.90	.90
Nos. 151-152 (2)	1.00	.80
Nos. 94-95 (2)	1.00	.50
Nos. 36-37 (2)	6.50	5.50
Nos. 174-175 (2)	1.70	2.30
Nos. 143-144 (2)	.90	.90
Nos. 180-181 (2)	1.25	1.25
Nos. 202-203 (2)	.90	.90
Nos. 214-215 (2)	1.10	.90
Nos. 110-111 (2)	1.25	1.15
Nos. 1-2 (2)	1.25	1.25
Nos. 109-110 (2)	1.10	1.10
Nos. 134-135 (2)	1.00	1.25
Nos. 69-70 (2)	1.15	.80
Nos. 139-140 (2)	.85	.75
Nos. 141-142 (2)	.80	1.25
Set total (70) Stamps	111.00	74.00

Shakespeare

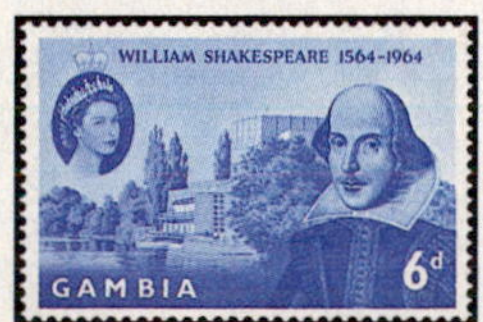

Shakespeare Memorial Theatre, Stratford-on-Avon — CD316

400th anniversary of the birth of William Shakespeare.

1964

Antigua 151
Bahamas 201
Bechuanaland Protectorate 197
Cayman Islands 171
Dominica 184
Falkland Islands 149
Gambia 192
Gibraltar 164
Montserrat 153
St. Lucia 196
Turks & Caicos Islands 141
Virgin Islands 143

No. 151 (1)	.35	.25
No. 201 (1)	.60	.35
No. 197 (1)	.35	.35
No. 171 (1)	.35	.30
No. 184 (1)	.35	.35
No. 149 (1)	1.60	.50
No. 192 (1)	.35	.25
No. 164 (1)	.65	.55
No. 153 (1)	.35	.25
No. 196 (1)	.45	.25
No. 141 (1)	.40	.25
No. 143 (1)	.45	.45
Set total (12) Stamps	6.25	4.10

ITU

ITU Emblem CD317

Intl. Telecommunication Union, cent.

1965

Antigua 153-154
Ascension 92-93
Bahamas 219-220
Barbados 265-266
Basutoland 101-102
Bechuanaland Protectorate 202-203
Bermuda 196-197
British Guiana 293-294
British Honduras 187-188
Brunei 116-117
Cayman Islands 172-173
Dominica 185-186
Falkland Islands 154-155
Fiji 211-212
Gibraltar 167-168
Gilbert & Ellice Islands 87-88
Grenada 205-206
Hong Kong 221-222
Mauritius 291-292
Montserrat 157-158
New Hebrides, British 108-109
Pitcairn Islands 52-53
St. Helena 180-181
St. Kitts-Nevis 163-164
St. Lucia 197-198
St. Vincent 224-225
Seychelles 218-219
Solomon Islands 126-127
Swaziland 115-116
Tristan da Cunha 85-86
Turks & Caicos Islands 142-143
Virgin Islands 159-160

Nos. 153-154 (2)	1.45	1.35
Nos. 92-93 (2)	1.90	1.30
Nos. 219-220 (2)	1.35	1.50
Nos. 265-266 (2)	1.50	1.25
Nos. 101-102 (2)	.85	.65
Nos. 202-203 (2)	1.10	.75
Nos. 196-197 (2)	2.15	*2.25*
Nos. 293-294 (2)	.60	.55
Nos. 187-188 (2)	.75	.75
Nos. 116-117 (2)	1.75	1.75
Nos. 172-173 (2)	1.00	.85
Nos. 185-186 (2)	.55	.55
Nos. 154-155 (2)	6.75	3.15
Nos. 211-212 (2)	2.00	1.05
Nos. 167-168 (2)	9.00	5.95
Nos. 87-88 (2)	.85	.60
Nos. 205-206 (2)	.50	.50
Nos. 221-222 (2)	24.50	3.80
Nos. 291-292 (2)	1.20	.65
Nos. 157-158 (2)	1.25	1.15
Nos. 108-109 (2)	.65	.50
Nos. 52-53 (2)	6.25	4.30
Nos. 180-181 (2)	.80	.60
Nos. 163-164 (2)	.60	.60
Nos. 197-198 (2)	1.25	1.25
Nos. 224-225 (2)	.80	.90
Nos. 218-219 (2)	.90	.60
Nos. 126-127 (2)	.70	.55
Nos. 115-116 (2)	.75	.75
Nos. 85-86 (2)	1.00	.65
Nos. 142-143 (2)	.75	.50
Nos. 159-160 (2)	.85	.85
Set total (64) Stamps	76.30	42.40

Intl. Cooperation Year

ICY Emblem CD318

1965

Antigua	155-156
Ascension	94-95
Bahamas	222-223
Basutoland	103-104
Bechuanaland Protectorate	204-205
Bermuda	199-200
British Guiana	295-296
British Honduras	189-190
Brunei	118-119
Cayman Islands	174-175
Dominica	187-188
Falkland Islands	156-157
Fiji	213-214
Gibraltar	169-170
Gilbert & Ellice Islands	104-105
Grenada	207-208
Hong Kong	223-224
Mauritius	293-294
Montserrat	176-177
New Hebrides, British	110-111
New Hebrides, French	126-127
Pitcairn Islands	54-55
St. Helena	182-183
St. Kitts-Nevis	165-166
St. Lucia	199-200
Seychelles	220-221
Solomon Islands	143-144
South Arabia	17-18
Swaziland	117-118
Tristan da Cunha	87-88
Turks & Caicos Islands	144-145
Virgin Islands	161-162

Nos. 155-156 (2)	.55	.50
Nos. 94-95 (2)	1.30	1.40
Nos. 222-223 (2)	.65	1.90
Nos. 103-104 (2)	.75	.85
Nos. 204-205 (2)	.85	1.00
Nos. 199-200 (2)	2.05	1.25
Nos. 295-296 (2)	.65	.60
Nos. 189-190 (2)	.60	.55
Nos. 118-119 (2)	.85	.85
Nos. 174-175 (2)	1.00	.75
Nos. 187-188 (2)	.55	.55
Nos. 156-157 (2)	6.00	1.65
Nos. 213-214 (2)	1.95	1.25
Nos. 169-170 (2)	1.25	*2.75*
Nos. 104-105 (2)	.85	.60
Nos. 207-208 (2)	.50	.50
Nos. 223-224 (2)	22.00	3.10
Nos. 293-294 (2)	.70	.70
Nos. 176-177 (2)	.80	.65
Nos. 110-111 (2)	.50	.50
Nos. 126-127 (2)	12.00	12.00
Nos. 54-55 (2)	6.35	4.50
Nos. 182-183 (2)	.95	.50
Nos. 165-166 (2)	.70	.60
Nos. 199-200 (2)	.55	.55
Nos. 220-221 (2)	.90	.65
Nos. 143-144 (2)	.70	.60
Nos. 17-18 (2)	1.20	.50
Nos. 117-118 (2)	.75	.75
Nos. 87-88 (2)	1.05	.65
Nos. 144-145 (2)	.65	.50
Nos. 161-162 (2)	.65	.50
Set total (64) Stamps	70.80	44.20

Churchill Memorial

Winston Churchill and St. Paul's, London, During Air Attack CD319

1966

Antigua	157-160
Ascension	96-99
Bahamas	224-227
Barbados	281-284
Basutoland	105-108
Bechuanaland Protectorate	206-209
Bermuda	201-204
British Antarctic Territory	16-19
British Honduras	191-194
Brunei	120-123
Cayman Islands	176-179
Dominica	189-192
Falkland Islands	158-161
Fiji	215-218
Gibraltar	171-174
Gilbert & Ellice Islands	106-109
Grenada	209-212
Hong Kong	225-228
Mauritius	295-298
Montserrat	178-181
New Hebrides, British	112-115
New Hebrides, French	128-131
Pitcairn Islands	56-59
St. Helena	184-187
St. Kitts-Nevis	167-170
St. Lucia	201-204
St. Vincent	241-244
Seychelles	222-225
Solomon Islands	145-148
South Arabia	19-22
Swaziland	119-122
Tristan da Cunha	89-92
Turks & Caicos Islands	146-149
Virgin Islands	163-166

Nos. 157-160 (4)	3.05	3.05
Nos. 96-99 (4)	10.00	6.40
Nos. 224-227 (4)	2.30	*3.20*
Nos. 281-284 (4)	3.00	4.45
Nos. 105-108 (4)	2.80	3.25
Nos. 206-209 (4)	2.50	2.50
Nos. 201-204 (4)	4.00	*4.75*
Nos. 16-19 (4)	37.85	18.00
Nos. 191-194 (4)	2.45	1.30
Nos. 120-123 (4)	7.65	6.55
Nos. 176-179 (4)	3.10	3.65
Nos. 189-192 (4)	1.15	1.15
Nos. 158-161 (4)	12.75	9.55
Nos. 215-218 (4)	4.40	3.00
Nos. 171-174 (4)	3.05	5.30
Nos. 106-109 (4)	1.50	1.30
Nos. 209-212 (4)	1.10	1.10
Nos. 225-228 (4)	52.50	11.40
Nos. 295-298 (4)	4.05	4.05
Nos. 178-181 (4)	1.60	1.55
Nos. 112-115 (4)	2.30	1.00
Nos. 128-131 (4)	10.25	10.25
Nos. 56-59 (4)	11.00	6.75
Nos. 184-187 (4)	1.85	1.95
Nos. 167-170 (4)	1.70	1.70
Nos. 201-204 (4)	1.50	1.50
Nos. 241-244 (4)	1.50	1.75
Nos. 222-225 (4)	3.20	3.60
Nos. 145-148 (4)	1.50	1.60
Nos. 19-22 (4)	2.95	2.20
Nos. 119-122 (4)	1.70	2.55
Nos. 89-92 (4)	5.95	2.70
Nos. 146-149 (4)	1.60	1.75
Nos. 163-166 (4)	1.90	1.90
Set total (136) Stamps	209.70	136.70

Royal Visit, 1966

Queen Elizabeth II and Prince Philip CD320

Caribbean visit, Feb. 4 - Mar. 6, 1966.

1966

Antigua	161-162
Bahamas	228-229
Barbados	285-286
British Guiana	299-300
Cayman Islands	180-181
Dominica	193-194
Grenada	213-214
Montserrat	182-183
St. Kitts-Nevis	171-172
St. Lucia	205-206
St. Vincent	245-246
Turks & Caicos Islands	150-151
Virgin Islands	167-168

Nos. 161-162 (2)	3.50	2.60
Nos. 228-229 (2)	3.05	3.05
Nos. 285-286 (2)	3.00	2.00
Nos. 299-300 (2)	3.35	1.60
Nos. 180-181 (2)	3.45	1.80
Nos. 193-194 (2)	3.00	.60
Nos. 213-214 (2)	.80	.50
Nos. 182-183 (2)	1.70	1.00
Nos. 171-172 (2)	.80	.75
Nos. 205-206 (2)	1.50	1.35
Nos. 245-246 (2)	2.75	1.35
Nos. 150-151 (2)	1.20	.55
Nos. 167-168 (2)	1.75	1.75
Set total (26) Stamps	29.85	18.90

World Cup Soccer

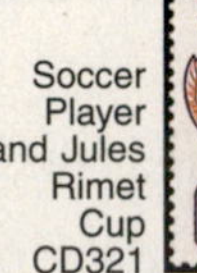

Soccer Player and Jules Rimet Cup CD321

World Cup Soccer Championship, Wembley, England, July 11-30.

1966

Antigua	163-164
Ascension	100-101
Bahamas	245-246
Bermuda	205-206
Brunei	124-125
Cayman Islands	182-183
Dominica	195-196
Fiji	219-220
Gibraltar	175-176
Gilbert & Ellice Islands	125-126
Grenada	230-231
New Hebrides, British	116-117
New Hebrides, French	132-133
Pitcairn Islands	60-61
St. Helena	188-189
St. Kitts-Nevis	173-174
St. Lucia	207-208
Seychelles	226-227
Solomon Islands	167-168
South Arabia	23-24
Tristan da Cunha	93-94

Nos. 163-164 (2)	.80	.85
Nos. 100-101 (2)	2.50	2.00
Nos. 245-246 (2)	.65	.65
Nos. 205-206 (2)	1.75	1.75
Nos. 124-125 (2)	1.30	1.25
Nos. 182-183 (2)	.75	.65
Nos. 195-196 (2)	1.20	.75
Nos. 219-220 (2)	1.70	.60
Nos. 175-176 (2)	1.85	1.75
Nos. 125-126 (2)	.70	.60
Nos. 230-231 (2)	.65	*.95*
Nos. 116-117 (2)	1.00	1.00
Nos. 132-133 (2)	7.00	7.00
Nos. 60-61 (2)	5.50	5.00
Nos. 188-189 (2)	1.25	.60
Nos. 173-174 (2)	.85	.80
Nos. 207-208 (2)	1.15	.90
Nos. 226-227 (2)	.85	.85
Nos. 167-168 (2)	1.10	1.10
Nos. 23-24 (2)	1.90	.55
Nos. 93-94 (2)	1.25	.80
Set total (42) Stamps	35.70	30.40

WHO Headquarters

World Health Organization Headquarters, Geneva — CD322

1966

Antigua	165-166
Ascension	102-103
Bahamas	247-248
Brunei	126-127
Cayman Islands	184-185
Dominica	197-198
Fiji	224-225
Gibraltar	180-181
Gilbert & Ellice Islands	127-128
Grenada	232-233
Hong Kong	229-230
Montserrat	184-185
New Hebrides, British	118-119
New Hebrides, French	134-135
Pitcairn Islands	62-63
St. Helena	190-191
St. Kitts-Nevis	177-178
St. Lucia	209-210
St. Vincent	247-248
Seychelles	228-229
Solomon Islands	169-170
South Arabia	25-26
Tristan da Cunha	99-100

Nos. 165-166 (2)	1.15	.55
Nos. 102-103 (2)	6.60	3.35
Nos. 247-248 (2)	.80	.80
Nos. 126-127 (2)	1.35	1.35
Nos. 184-185 (2)	2.25	1.20
Nos. 197-198 (2)	.75	.75
Nos. 224-225 (2)	4.70	3.30
Nos. 180-181 (2)	6.50	4.50
Nos. 127-128 (2)	.80	.70
Nos. 232-233 (2)	.80	.50
Nos. 229-230 (2)	11.25	2.30
Nos. 184-185 (2)	1.00	1.00
Nos. 118-119 (2)	.75	.50
Nos. 134-135 (2)	8.75	8.75
Nos. 62-63 (2)	7.25	6.50
Nos. 190-191 (2)	3.50	1.50
Nos. 177-178 (2)	.65	.65
Nos. 209-210 (2)	.80	.80
Nos. 247-248 (2)	1.15	1.05
Nos. 228-229 (2)	1.25	.75
Nos. 169-170 (2)	.95	.80
Nos. 25-26 (2)	2.10	.70
Nos. 99-100 (2)	1.90	1.25
Set total (46) Stamps	67.00	43.55

UNESCO Anniversary

"Education" — CD323

"Science" (Wheat ears & flask enclosing globe). "Culture" (lyre & columns). 20th anniversary of the UNESCO.

1966-67

Antigua	183-185
Ascension	108-110
Bahamas	249-251
Barbados	287-289
Bermuda	207-209
Brunei	128-130
Cayman Islands	186-188
Dominica	199-201
Gibraltar	183-185
Gilbert & Ellice Islands	129-131
Grenada	234-236
Hong Kong	231-233
Mauritius	299-301
Montserrat	186-188
New Hebrides, British	120-122
New Hebrides, French	136-138
Pitcairn Islands	64-66
St. Helena	192-194
St. Kitts-Nevis	179-181
St. Lucia	211-213
St. Vincent	249-251
Seychelles	230-232
Solomon Islands	171-173
South Arabia	27-29
Swaziland	123-125
Tristan da Cunha	101-103
Turks & Caicos Islands	155-157
Virgin Islands	176-178

Nos. 183-185 (3)	1.90	*2.50*
Nos. 108-110 (3)	11.00	5.80
Nos. 249-251 (3)	2.35	2.35
Nos. 287-289 (3)	2.50	2.15
Nos. 207-209 (3)	3.80	*3.90*
Nos. 128-130 (3)	4.65	5.40
Nos. 186-188 (3)	2.50	1.50
Nos. 199-201 (3)	1.60	.75
Nos. 183-185 (3)	6.50	3.25
Nos. 129-131 (3)	2.50	*2.45*
Nos. 234-236 (3)	1.10	1.20
Nos. 231-233 (3)	69.50	17.50
Nos. 299-301 (3)	2.10	1.50
Nos. 186-188 (3)	2.40	2.40
Nos. 120-122 (3)	1.90	1.90
Nos. 136-138 (3)	7.75	7.75
Nos. 64-66 (3)	7.10	4.75
Nos. 192-194 (3)	5.25	3.65
Nos. 179-181 (3)	.90	.90
Nos. 211-213 (3)	1.15	1.15
Nos. 249-251 (3)	2.30	1.35
Nos. 230-232 (3)	2.40	2.40
Nos. 171-173 (3)	2.00	1.50
Nos. 27-29 (3)	5.50	5.50
Nos. 123-125 (3)	1.45	1.45
Nos. 101-103 (3)	2.00	1.40
Nos. 155-157 (3)	1.05	.90
Nos. 176-178 (3)	1.40	1.30
Set total (84) Stamps	156.55	88.55

Silver Wedding, 1972

Queen Elizabeth II and Prince Philip — CD324

Designs: borders differ for each country.

1972

Anguilla	161-162
Antigua	295-296
Ascension	164-165
Bahamas	344-345
Bermuda	296-297
British Antarctic Territory	43-44
British Honduras	306-307
British Indian Ocean Territory	48-49

Brunei 186-187
Cayman Islands 304-305
Dominica 352-353
Falkland Islands 223-224
Fiji 328-329
Gibraltar 292-293
Gilbert & Ellice Islands 206-207
Grenada 466-467
Hong Kong 271-272
Montserrat 286-287
New Hebrides, British 169-170
New Hebrides, French 188-189
Pitcairn Islands 127-128
St. Helena 271-272
St. Kitts-Nevis 257-258
St. Lucia 328-329
St.Vincent 344-345
Seychelles 309-310
Solomon Islands 248-249
South Georgia 35-36
Tristan da Cunha 178-179
Turks & Caicos Islands 257-258
Virgin Islands 241-242

Nos. 161-162 (2)	1.30	*1.50*
Nos. 295-296 (2)	.50	.50
Nos. 164-165 (2)	.70	.70
Nos. 344-345 (2)	.60	.60
Nos. 296-297 (2)	.50	*.65*
Nos. 43-44 (2)	7.75	6.10
Nos. 306-307 (2)	.80	.80
Nos. 48-49 (2)	2.00	1.00
Nos. 186-187 (2)	.70	.70
Nos. 304-305 (2)	.75	.75
Nos. 352-353 (2)	.65	.65
Nos. 223-224 (2)	1.00	1.15
Nos. 328-329 (2)	.70	.70
Nos. 292-293 (2)	.50	.50
Nos. 206-207 (2)	.50	.50
Nos. 466-467 (2)	.70	.70
Nos. 271-272 (2)	1.70	1.50
Nos. 286-287 (2)	.55	.55
Nos. 169-170 (2)	.50	.50
Nos. 188-189 (2)	1.05	1.05
Nos. 127-128 (2)	.90	.85
Nos. 271-272 (2)	.70	1.20
Nos. 257-258 (2)	.65	.50
Nos. 328-329 (2)	.75	.75
Nos. 344-345 (2)	.55	.55
Nos. 309-310 (2)	.95	.95
Nos. 248-249 (2)	.50	.50
Nos. 35-36 (2)	1.40	1.40
Nos. 178-179 (2)	.70	.70
Nos. 257-258 (2)	.50	.50
Nos. 241-242 (2)	.50	.50
Set total (62) Stamps	31.55	29.50

Princess Anne's Wedding

Princess Anne and Mark Phillips — CD325

Wedding of Princess Anne and Mark Phillips, Nov. 14, 1973.

1973

Anguilla 179-180
Ascension 177-178
Belize 325-326
Bermuda 302-303
British Antarctic Territory 60-61
Cayman Islands 320-321
Falkland Islands 225-226
Gibraltar 305-306
Gilbert & Ellice Islands 216-217
Hong Kong 289-290
Montserrat 300-301
Pitcairn Islands 135-136
St. Helena 277-278
St. Kitts-Nevis 274-275
St. Lucia 349-350
St. Vincent 358-359
St. Vincent Grenadines 1-2
Seychelles 311-312
Solomon Islands 259-260
South Georgia 37-38
Tristan da Cunha 189-190
Turks & Caicos Islands 286-287
Virgin Islands 260-261

Nos. 179-180 (2)	.55	.55
Nos. 177-178 (2)	.60	.60
Nos. 325-326 (2)	.50	.50
Nos. 302-303 (2)	.50	.50
Nos. 60-61 (2)	1.10	1.10
Nos. 320-321 (2)	.50	.50
Nos. 225-226 (2)	.70	.60
Nos. 305-306 (2)	.55	.55
Nos. 216-217 (2)	.50	.50
Nos. 289-290 (2)	2.65	2.00
Nos. 300-301 (2)	.65	.65
Nos. 135-136 (2)	.70	.60
Nos. 277-278 (2)	.50	.50
Nos. 274-275 (2)	.50	.50
Nos. 349-350 (2)	.50	.50
Nos. 358-359 (2)	.50	.50
Nos. 1-2 (2)	.50	.50
Nos. 311-312 (2)	.70	.70
Nos. 259-260 (2)	.70	.70
Nos. 37-38 (2)	.75	.75
Nos. 189-190 (2)	.50	.50
Nos. 286-287 (2)	.50	.50
Nos. 260-261 (2)	.50	.50
Set total (46) Stamps	15.65	14.80

Elizabeth II Coronation Anniv.

CD326

CD327

CD328

Designs: Royal and local beasts in heraldic form and simulated stonework. Portrait of Elizabeth II by Peter Grugeon. 25th anniversary of coronation of Queen Elizabeth II.

1978

Ascension 229
Barbados 474
Belize 397
British Antarctic Territory 71
Cayman Islands 404
Christmas Island 87
Falkland Islands 275
Fiji 384
Gambia 380
Gilbert Islands 312
Mauritius 464
New Hebrides, British 258
New Hebrides, French 278
St. Helena 317
St. Kitts-Nevis 354
Samoa 472
Solomon Islands 368
South Georgia 51
Swaziland 302
Tristan da Cunha 238
Virgin Islands 337

No. 229 (1)	2.00	2.00
No. 474 (1)	1.35	1.35
No. 397 (1)	1.40	1.75
No. 71 (1)	6.00	6.00
No. 404 (1)	2.00	2.00
No. 87 (1)	3.50	*4.00*
No. 275 (1)	4.00	5.50
No. 384 (1)	1.75	1.75
No. 380 (1)	1.50	1.50
No. 312 (1)	1.25	1.25
No. 464 (1)	2.75	2.75
No. 258 (1)	1.75	1.75
No. 278 (1)	3.50	3.50
No. 317 (1)	1.75	1.75
No. 354 (1)	1.00	1.00
No. 472 (1)	2.00	2.00
No. 368 (1)	2.50	2.50
No. 51 (1)	3.00	3.00
No. 302 (1)	1.75	1.75
No. 238 (1)	1.50	1.50
No. 337 (1)	1.80	1.80
Set total (21) Stamps	48.05	50.40

Queen Mother Elizabeth's 80th Birthday

CD330

Designs: Photographs of Queen Mother Elizabeth. Falkland Islands issued in sheets of 50; others in sheets of 9.

1980

Ascension 261
Bermuda 401
Cayman Islands 443
Falkland Islands 305
Gambia 412
Gibraltar 393
Hong Kong 364
Pitcairn Islands 193
St. Helena 341
Samoa 532
Solomon Islands 426
Tristan da Cunha 277

No. 261 (1)	.40	.40
No. 401 (1)	.45	.75
No. 443 (1)	.40	.40
No. 305 (1)	.40	.40
No. 412 (1)	.40	.50
No. 393 (1)	.35	.35
No. 364 (1)	1.10	1.25
No. 193 (1)	.60	.60
No. 341 (1)	.50	.50
No. 532 (1)	.55	.55
No. 426 (1)	.50	.50
No. 277 (1)	.45	.45
Set total (12) Stamps	6.10	6.65

Royal Wedding, 1981

Prince Charles and Lady Diana — CD331

CD331a

Wedding of Charles, Prince of Wales, and Lady Diana Spencer, St. Paul's Cathedral, London, July 29, 1981.

1981

Antigua 623-627
Ascension 294-296
Barbados 547-549
Barbuda 497-501
Bermuda 412-414
Brunei 268-270
Cayman Islands 471-473
Dominica 701-705
Falkland Islands 324-326
Falkland Islands Dep. 1L59-1L61
Fiji 442-444
Gambia 426-428
Ghana 759-764
Grenada 1051-1055
Grenada Grenadines 440-443
Hong Kong 373-375
Jamaica 500-503
Lesotho 335-337
Maldive Islands 906-909
Mauritius 520-522
Norfolk Island 280-282
Pitcairn Islands 206-208
St. Helena 353-355
St. Lucia 543-549
Samoa 558-560
Sierra Leone 509-518
Solomon Islands 450-452
Swaziland 382-384
Tristan da Cunha 294-296
Turks & Caicos Islands 486-489
Caicos Island 8-11
Uganda 314-317
Vanuatu 308-310
Virgin Islands 406-408

Nos. 623-627 (5)	6.55	2.55
Nos. 294-296 (3)	1.00	1.00
Nos. 547-549 (3)	.90	.90
Nos. 497-501 (5)	10.95	10.95
Nos. 412-414 (3)	2.00	2.00
Nos. 268-270 (3)	2.15	*4.50*
Nos. 471-473 (3)	1.20	1.30
Nos. 701-705 (5)	8.35	2.35
Nos. 324-326 (3)	1.65	1.70
Nos. 1L59-1L61 (3)	1.45	1.45
Nos. 442-444 (3)	1.35	1.35
Nos. 426-428 (3)	.80	.80
Nos. 759-764 (9)	6.20	6.20
Nos. 1051-1055 (5)	9.85	1.85
Nos. 440-443 (4)	2.35	2.35
Nos. 373-375 (3)	3.05	2.85
Nos. 500-503 (4)	1.45	1.35
Nos. 335-337 (3)	.90	.90
Nos. 906-909 (4)	1.55	1.55
Nos. 520-522 (3)	2.75	2.75
Nos. 280-282 (3)	1.35	1.35
Nos. 206-208 (3)	1.10	1.10
Nos. 353-355 (3)	.85	.85
Nos. 543-549 (5)	8.50	8.50
Nos. 558-560 (3)	.85	.85
Nos. 509-518 (10)	15.50	15.50
Nos. 450-452 (3)	1.25	1.25
Nos. 382-384 (3)	1.30	1.25
Nos. 294-296 (3)	.90	.90
Nos. 486-489 (4)	2.20	2.20
Nos. 8-11 (4)	5.00	5.00
Nos. 314-317 (4)	3.30	3.00
Nos. 308-310 (3)	1.15	1.15
Nos. 406-408 (3)	1.10	1.10
Set total (131) Stamps	110.80	94.65

Princess Diana

CD332

CD333

Designs: Photographs and portrait of Princess Diana, wedding or honeymoon photographs, royal residences, arms of issuing country. Portrait photograph by Clive Friend. Souvenir sheet margins show family tree, various people related to the princess. 21st birthday of Princess Diana of Wales, July 1.

1982

Antigua 663-666
Ascension 313-316
Bahamas 510-513
Barbados 585-588
Barbuda 544-547
British Antarctic Territory 92-95
Cayman Islands 486-489
Dominica 773-776
Falkland Islands 348-351
Falkland Islands Dep. 1L72-1L75
Fiji 470-473
Gambia 447-450
Grenada 1101A-1105
Grenada Grenadines 485-491
Lesotho 372-375
Maldive Islands 952-955
Mauritius 548-551
Pitcairn Islands 213-216
St. Helena 372-375
St. Lucia 591-594
Sierra Leone 531-534
Solomon Islands 471-474
Swaziland 406-409
Tristan da Cunha 310-313
Turks and Caicos Islands 531-534
Virgin Islands 430-433

Nos. 663-666 (4)	8.25	7.35
Nos. 313-316 (4)	3.50	3.50
Nos. 510-513 (4)	6.00	3.85
Nos. 585-588 (4)	3.40	3.25
Nos. 544-547 (4)	9.75	7.70
Nos. 92-95 (4)	5.30	3.45
Nos. 486-489 (4)	*4.75*	*2.70*
Nos. 773-776 (4)	7.05	7.05
Nos. 348-351 (4)	2.95	2.95
Nos. 1L72-1L75 (4)	2.50	2.60
Nos. 470-473 (4)	3.25	2.95
Nos. 447-450 (4)	2.85	2.85
Nos. 1101A-1105 (7)	16.05	15.55

Nos. 485-491 (7)	17.65	17.65
Nos. 372-375 (4)	4.00	4.00
Nos. 952-955 (4)	5.50	3.90
Nos. 548-551 (4)	5.50	5.50
Nos. 213-216 (4)	2.15	2.15
Nos. 372-375 (4)	2.95	2.95
Nos. 591-594 (4)	9.90	9.90
Nos. 531-534 (4)	7.20	7.20
Nos. 471-474 (4)	2.90	2.90
Nos. 406-409 (4)	3.85	2.25
Nos. 310-313 (4)	3.65	1.45
Nos. 486-489 (4)	2.20	2.20
Nos. 430-433 (4)	3.00	3.00
Set total (110) Stamps	146.05	130.80

250th anniv. of first edition of Lloyd's List (shipping news publication) & of Lloyd's marine insurance.

CD335

Designs: First page of early edition of the list; historical ships, modern transportation or harbor scenes.

1984

Ascension	351-354
Bahamas	555-558
Barbados	627-630
Cayes of Belize	10-13
Cayman Islands	522-526
Falkland Islands	404-407
Fiji	509-512
Gambia	519-522
Mauritius	587-590
Nauru	280-283
St. Helena	412-415
Samoa	624-627
Seychelles	538-541
Solomon Islands	521-524
Vanuatu	368-371
Virgin Islands	466-469

Nos. 351-354 (4)	2.90	2.55
Nos. 555-558 (4)	4.15	2.95
Nos. 627-630 (4)	6.10	5.15
Nos. 10-13 (4)	2.65	2.65
Nos. 522-526 (5)	9.30	8.45
Nos. 404-407 (4)	3.50	3.65
Nos. 509-512 (4)	5.30	4.90
Nos. 519-522 (4)	4.20	4.30
Nos. 587-590 (4)	8.95	8.95
Nos. 280-283 (4)	2.40	2.35
Nos. 412-415 (4)	2.40	2.40
Nos. 624-627 (4)	2.75	2.55
Nos. 538-541 (4)	5.25	5.25
Nos. 521-524 (4)	4.65	3.95
Nos. 368-371 (4)	2.40	2.40
Nos. 466-469 (4)	4.25	4.25
Set total (65) Stamps	71.15	66.70

Queen Mother 85th Birthday

CD336

Designs: Photographs tracing the life of the Queen Mother, Elizabeth. The high value in each set pictures the same photograph taken of the Queen Mother holding the infant Prince Henry.

1985

Ascension	372-376
Bahamas	580-584
Barbados	660-664
Bermuda	469-473
Falkland Islands	420-424
Falkland Islands Dep.	1L92-1L96
Fiji	531-535
Hong Kong	447-450
Jamaica	599-603
Mauritius	604-608
Norfolk Island	364-368
Pitcairn Islands	253-257
St. Helena	428-432
Samoa	649-653
Seychelles	567-571
Zil Elwannyen Sesel	101-105
Solomon Islands	543-547
Swaziland	476-480
Tristan da Cunha	372-376
Vanuatu	392-396

Nos. 372-376 (5)	4.65	4.65
Nos. 580-584 (5)	7.70	6.45
Nos. 660-664 (5)	8.00	6.70
Nos. 469-473 (5)	9.40	9.40
Nos. 420-424 (5)	7.35	6.65
Nos. 1L92-1L96 (5)	8.00	8.00
Nos. 531-535 (5)	6.15	6.15
Nos. 447-450 (4)	9.50	8.50
Nos. 599-603 (5)	6.15	7.00
Nos. 604-608 (5)	11.80	11.80
Nos. 364-368 (5)	5.05	5.05
Nos. 253-257 (5)	5.25	5.95
Nos. 428-432 (5)	5.25	5.25
Nos. 649-653 (5)	8.65	7.80
Nos. 567-571 (5)	8.70	8.70
Nos. 101-105 (5)	7.15	7.15
Nos. 543-547 (5)	3.95	3.95
Nos. 476-480 (5)	8.00	7.50
Nos. 372-376 (5)	5.40	5.40
Nos. 392-396 (5)	5.25	5.25
Set total (99) Stamps	141.35	137.30

Queen Elizabeth II, 60th Birthday

CD337

1986, April 21

Ascension	389-393
Bahamas	592-596
Barbados	675-679
Bermuda	499-503
Cayman Islands	555-559
Falkland Islands	441-445
Fiji	544-548
Hong Kong	465-469
Jamaica	620-624
Kiribati	470-474
Mauritius	629-633
Papua New Guinea	640-644
Pitcairn Islands	270-274
St. Helena	451-455
Samoa	670-674
Seychelles	592-596
Zil Elwannyen Sesel	114-118
Solomon Islands	562-566
South Georgia	101-105
Swaziland	490-494
Tristan da Cunha	388-392
Vanuatu	414-418
Zambia	343-347

Nos. 389-393 (5)	2.80	3.30
Nos. 592-596 (5)	2.75	*3.70*
Nos. 675-679 (5)	3.35	3.20
Nos. 499-503 (5)	4.65	*5.15*
Nos. 555-559 (5)	4.55	5.60
Nos. 441-445 (5)	3.95	*4.95*
Nos. 544-548 (5)	3.00	3.00
Nos. 465-469 (5)	8.75	6.75
Nos. 620-624 (5)	2.75	2.70
Nos. 470-474 (5)	2.10	2.10
Nos. 629-633 (5)	3.70	3.70
Nos. 640-644 (5)	4.50	4.50
Nos. 270-274 (5)	2.70	2.70
Nos. 451-455 (5)	3.05	3.05
Nos. 670-674 (5)	2.90	2.90
Nos. 592-596 (5)	2.70	2.70
Nos. 114-118 (5)	2.25	2.25
Nos. 562-566 (5)	2.90	2.90
Nos. 101-105 (5)	3.30	3.65
Nos. 490-494 (5)	2.30	2.30
Nos. 388-392 (5)	3.00	3.00
Nos. 414-418 (5)	3.10	3.10
Nos. 343-347 (5)	1.75	1.75
Set total (115) Stamps	76.80	78.95

Royal Wedding

Marriage of Prince Andrew and Sarah Ferguson CD338

1986, July 23

Ascension	399-400
Bahamas	602-603
Barbados	687-688
Cayman Islands	560-561
Jamaica	629-630
Pitcairn Islands	275-276
St. Helena	460-461
St. Kitts	181-182
Seychelles	602-603
Zil Elwannyen Sesel	119-120
Solomon Islands	567-568
Tristan da Cunha	397-398
Zambia	348-349

Nos. 399-400 (2)	1.60	1.60
Nos. 602-603 (2)	2.75	2.75
Nos. 687-688 (2)	2.25	1.25
Nos. 560-561 (2)	1.70	*2.35*
Nos. 629-630 (2)	1.35	1.35
Nos. 275-276 (2)	2.40	2.40
Nos. 460-461 (2)	1.05	1.05
Nos. 181-182 (2)	1.50	1.50
Nos. 602-603 (2)	2.50	2.50
Nos. 119-120 (2)	2.30	2.30
Nos. 567-568 (2)	1.00	1.00
Nos. 397-398 (2)	1.40	1.40
Nos. 348-349 (2)	1.10	1.30
Set total (26) Stamps	22.90	22.75

Queen Elizabeth II, 60th Birthday

Queen Elizabeth II & Prince Philip, 1947 Wedding Portrait — CD339

Designs: Photographs tracing the life of Queen Elizabeth II.

1986

Anguilla	674-677
Antigua	925-928
Barbuda	783-786
Dominica	950-953
Gambia	611-614
Grenada	1371-1374
Grenada Grenadines	749-752
Lesotho	531-534
Maldive Islands	1172-1175
Sierra Leone	760-763
Uganda	495-498

Nos. 674-677 (4)	8.00	8.00
Nos. 925-928 (4)	5.50	6.20
Nos. 783-786 (4)	23.15	23.15
Nos. 950-953 (4)	7.25	7.25
Nos. 611-614 (4)	8.25	7.90
Nos. 1371-1374 (4)	6.80	6.80
Nos. 749-752 (4)	6.75	6.75
Nos. 531-534 (4)	5.25	5.25
Nos. 1172-1175 (4)	6.25	6.25
Nos. 760-763 (4)	6.30	6.30
Nos. 495-498 (4)	8.50	8.50
Set total (44) Stamps	92.00	92.35

Royal Wedding, 1986

CD340

Designs: Photographs of Prince Andrew and Sarah Ferguson during courtship, engagement and marriage.

1986

Antigua	939-942
Barbuda	809-812
Dominica	970-973
Gambia	635-638
Grenada	1385-1388
Grenada Grenadines	758-761
Lesotho	545-548
Maldive Islands	1181-1184
Sierra Leone	769-772
Uganda	510-513

Nos. 939-942 (4)	7.00	*8.75*
Nos. 809-812 (4)	14.55	14.55
Nos. 970-973 (4)	7.25	7.25
Nos. 635-638 (4)	8.55	8.55
Nos. 1385-1388 (4)	8.30	8.30
Nos. 758-761 (4)	9.00	9.00
Nos. 545-548 (4)	7.45	7.45
Nos. 1181-1184 (4)	8.45	8.45
Nos. 769-772 (4)	5.35	5.35
Nos. 510-513 (4)	9.25	10.00
Set total (40) Stamps	85.15	87.65

Lloyds of London, 300th Anniv.

CD341

Designs: 17th century aspects of Lloyds, representations of each country's individual connections with Lloyds and publicized disasters insured by the organization.

1986

Ascension	454-457
Bahamas	655-658
Barbados	731-734
Bermuda	541-544
Falkland Islands	481-484
Liberia	1101-1104
Malawi	534-537
Nevis	571-574
St. Helena	501-504
St. Lucia	923-926
Seychelles	649-652
Zil Elwannyen Sesel	146-149
Solomon Islands	627-630
South Georgia	131-134
Trinidad & Tobago	484-487
Tristan da Cunha	439-442
Vanuatu	485-488

Nos. 454-457 (4)	5.00	5.00
Nos. 655-658 (4)	8.90	4.95
Nos. 731-734 (4)	12.50	8.35
Nos. 541-544 (4)	8.00	*6.60*
Nos. 481-484 (4)	5.45	3.85
Nos. 1101-1104 (4)	4.25	4.25
Nos. 534-537 (4)	11.00	7.85
Nos. 571-574 (4)	8.35	8.35
Nos. 501-504 (4)	8.70	7.15
Nos. 923-926 (4)	9.40	9.40
Nos. 649-652 (4)	13.10	13.10
Nos. 146-149 (4)	11.25	11.25
Nos. 627-630 (4)	7.00	4.45
Nos. 131-134 (4)	6.30	3.70
Nos. 484-487 (4)	10.25	6.35
Nos. 439-442 (4)	7.60	7.60
Nos. 485-488 (4)	5.90	5.90
Set total (68) Stamps	142.95	118.10

Moon Landing, 20th Anniv.

CD342

Designs: Equipment, crew photographs, spacecraft, official emblems and report profiles created for the Apollo Missions. Two stamps in each set are square in format rather than like the stamp shown; see individual country listings for more information.

1989

Ascension	468-472
Bahamas	674-678
Belize	916-920
Kiribati	517-521
Liberia	1125-1129
Nevis	586-590
St. Kitts	248-252
Samoa	760-764
Seychelles	676-680
Zil Elwannyen Sesel	154-158
Solomon Islands	643-647
Vanuatu	507-511

Nos. 468-472 (5)	9.40	8.60
Nos. 674-678 (5)	23.00	19.70
Nos. 916-920 (5)	22.85	18.10
Nos. 517-521 (5)	12.50	12.50
Nos. 1125-1129 (5)	8.50	8.50
Nos. 586-590 (5)	7.50	7.50

Nos. 248-252 (5)	8.00	8.00
Nos. 760-764 (5)	9.60	9.05
Nos. 676-680 (5)	16.05	16.05
Nos. 154-158 (5)	26.85	26.85
Nos. 643-647 (5)	9.00	6.75
Nos. 507-511 (5)	9.90	9.90
Set total (60) Stamps	163.15	151.50

Queen Mother, 90th Birthday

CD343

CD344

Designs: Portraits of Queen Elizabeth, the Queen Mother. See individual country listings for more information.

1990

Ascension 491-492
Bahamas 698-699
Barbados 782-783
British Antarctic Territory 170-171
British Indian Ocean Territory 106-107
Cayman Islands 622-623
Falkland Islands 524-525
Kenya 527-528
Kiribati 555-556
Liberia 1145-1146
Pitcairn Islands 336-337
St. Helena 532-533
St. Lucia 969-970
Seychelles 710-711
Zil Elwannyen Sesel 171-172
Solomon Islands 671-672
South Georgia 143-144
Swaziland 565-566
Tristan da Cunha 480-481

Nos. 491-492 (2)	4.75	4.75
Nos. 698-699 (2)	5.25	5.25
Nos. 782-783 (2)	4.00	3.70
Nos. 170-171 (2)	6.75	6.75
Nos. 106-107 (2)	18.00	18.50
Nos. 622-623 (2)	4.00	*5.50*
Nos. 524-525 (2)	4.75	4.75
Nos. 527-528 (2)	7.00	7.00
Nos. 555-556 (2)	4.75	4.75
Nos. 1145-1146 (2)	3.25	3.25
Nos. 336-337 (2)	4.25	4.25
Nos. 532-533 (2)	5.25	5.25
Nos. 969-970 (2)	5.25	5.25
Nos. 710-711 (2)	6.60	6.60
Nos. 171-172 (2)	8.25	8.25
Nos. 671-672 (2)	5.00	*5.30*
Nos. 143-144 (2)	5.50	6.50
Nos. 565-566 (2)	4.35	4.35
Nos. 480-481 (2)	5.60	5.60
Set total (38) Stamps	112.55	115.55

Queen Elizabeth II, 65th Birthday, and Prince Philip, 70th Birthday

CD345

CD346

Designs: Portraits of Queen Elizabeth II and Prince Philip differ for each country. Printed in sheets of 10 + 5 labels (3 different) between. Stamps alternate, producing 5 different triptychs.

1991

Ascension 506a
Bahamas 731a
Belize 970a
Bermuda 618a
Kiribati 572a
Mauritius 734a
Pitcairn Islands 349a
St. Helena 555a
St. Kitts 319a
Samoa 791a
Seychelles 724a
Zil Elwannyen Sesel 178a
Solomon Islands 689a
South Georgia 150a
Swaziland 587a
Vanuatu 541a

No. 506a (1)	3.50	3.75
No. 731a (1)	4.00	4.00
No. 970a (1)	3.75	3.75
No. 618a (1)	3.50	*4.00*
No. 572a (1)	4.00	4.00
No. 734a (1)	3.75	3.75
No. 349a (1)	3.25	3.25
No. 555a (1)	2.75	2.75
No. 319a (1)	3.00	3.00
No. 791a (1)	4.25	4.25
No. 724a (1)	5.00	5.00
No. 178a (1)	6.50	6.50
No. 689a (1)	3.75	3.75
No. 150a (1)	4.75	7.00
No. 587a (1)	4.25	4.25
No. 541a (1)	2.50	2.50
Set total (16) Stamps	62.50	65.50

Royal Family Birthday, Anniversary

CD347

Queen Elizabeth II, 65th birthday, Charles and Diana, 10th wedding anniversary: Various photographs of Queen Elizabeth II, Prince Philip, Prince Charles, Princess Diana and their sons William and Henry.

1991

Antigua 1446-1455
Barbuda 1229-1238
Dominica 1328-1337
Gambia 1080-1089
Grenada 2006-2015
Grenada Grenadines 1331-1340
Guyana 2440-2451
Lesotho 871-875
Maldive Islands 1533-1542
Nevis 666-675
St. Vincent 1485-1494
St. Vincent Grenadines 769-778
Sierra Leone 1387-1396
Turks & Caicos Islands 913-922
Uganda 918-927

Nos. 1446-1455 (10)	21.70	20.05
Nos. 1229-1238 (10)	125.00	119.50
Nos. 1328-1337 (10)	30.20	30.20
Nos. 1080-1089 (10)	24.65	24.40
Nos. 2006-2015 (10)	25.45	22.10
Nos. 1331-1340 (10)	23.85	23.35
Nos. 2440-2451 (12)	21.40	21.15
Nos. 871-875 (5)	13.55	13.55
Nos. 1533-1542 (10)	28.10	28.10
Nos. 666-675 (10)	25.65	25.65
Nos. 1485-1494 (10)	26.75	25.90
Nos. 769-778 (10)	25.40	25.40
Nos. 1387-1396 (10)	26.55	26.55
Nos. 913-922 (10)	27.50	25.30
Nos. 918-927 (10)	26.60	26.60
Set total (147) Stamps	472.35	457.80

Queen Elizabeth II's Accession to the Throne, 40th Anniv.

CD348

Various photographs of Queen Elizabeth II with local Scenes.

1992

Antigua 1513-1518
Barbuda 1306-1311
Dominica 1414-1419
Gambia 1172-1177
Grenada 2047-2052
Grenada Grenadines 1368-1373
Lesotho 881-885
Maldive Islands 1637-1642
Nevis 702-707
St. Vincent 1582-1587
St. Vincent Grenadines 829-834
Sierra Leone 1482-1487
Turks and Caicos Islands 978-987
Uganda 990-995
Virgin Islands 742-746

Nos. 1513-1518 (6)	15.00	*15.10*
Nos. 1306-1311 (6)	125.25	83.65
Nos. 1414-1419 (6)	12.50	12.50
Nos. 1172-1177 (6)	16.60	16.35
Nos. 2047-2052 (6)	15.95	15.95
Nos. 1368-1373 (6)	17.00	15.35
Nos. 881-885 (5)	11.90	11.90
Nos. 1637-1642 (6)	17.55	17.55
Nos. 702-707 (6)	13.80	13.80
Nos. 1582-1587 (6)	14.40	14.40
Nos. 829-834 (6)	19.65	19.65
Nos. 1482-1487 (6)	22.50	22.50
Nos. 913-922 (10)	27.50	25.30
Nos. 990-995 (6)	19.50	19.50
Nos. 742-746 (5)	15.50	15.50
Set total (92) Stamps	364.60	319.00

CD349

1992

Ascension 531-535
Bahamas 744-748
Bermuda 623-627
British Indian Ocean Territory 119-123
Cayman Islands 648-652
Falkland Islands 549-553
Gibraltar 605-609
Hong Kong 619-623
Kenya 563-567
Kiribati 582-586
Pitcairn Islands 362-366
St. Helena 570-574
St. Kitts 332-336
Samoa 805-809
Seychelles 734-738
Zil Elwannyen Sesel 183-187
Solomon Islands 708-712
South Georgia 157-161
Tristan da Cunha 508-512
Vanuatu 555-559
Zambia 561-565

Nos. 531-535 (5)	6.10	6.10
Nos. 744-748 (5)	6.90	4.70
Nos. 623-627 (5)	7.40	*7.55*
Nos. 119-123 (5)	22.75	19.25
Nos. 648-652 (5)	7.60	6.60
Nos. 549-553 (5)	5.95	5.90
Nos. 605-609 (5)	5.15	*5.50*
Nos. 619-623 (5)	5.10	5.25
Nos. 563-567 (5)	9.10	9.10
Nos. 582-586 (5)	3.85	3.85
Nos. 362-366 (5)	5.35	5.35
Nos. 570-574 (5)	5.70	5.70
Nos. 332-336 (5)	6.60	5.50
Nos. 805-809 (5)	8.10	6.15
Nos. 734-738 (5)	10.80	10.80
Nos. 183-187 (5)	9.40	9.40
Nos. 708-712 (5)	5.00	5.30
Nos. 157-161 (5)	5.60	5.90
Nos. 508-512 (5)	8.75	8.30
Nos. 555-559 (5)	3.65	3.65
Nos. 561-565 (5)	5.60	5.60
Set total (105) Stamps	154.45	145.45

Royal Air Force, 75th Anniversary

CD350

1993

Ascension 557-561
Bahamas 771-775
Barbados 842-846
Belize 1003-1008
Bermuda 648-651
British Indian Ocean Territory 136-140
Falkland Is. 573-577
Fiji 687-691
Montserrat 830-834
St. Kitts 351-355

Nos. 557-561 (5)	15.60	14.60
Nos. 771-775 (5)	24.65	21.45
Nos. 842-846 (5)	13.65	12.35
Nos. 1003-1008 (6)	16.55	16.50
Nos. 648-651 (4)	9.65	*10.45*
Nos. 136-140 (5)	16.10	16.10
Nos. 573-577 (5)	10.85	10.85
Nos. 687-691 (5)	17.75	17.40
Nos. 830-834 (5)	14.35	14.35
Nos. 351-355 (5)	24.45	23.95
Set total (50) Stamps	163.60	158.00

Royal Air Force, 80th Anniv.

Design CD350 Re-inscribed

1998

Ascension 697-701
Bahamas 907-911
British Indian Ocean Terr 198-202
Cayman Islands 754-758
Fiji 814-818
Gibraltar 755-759
Samoa 957-961
Turks & Caicos Islands 1258-1265
Tuvalu 763-767
Virgin Islands 879-883

Nos. 697-701 (5)	16.10	16.10
Nos. 907-911 (5)	13.60	12.65
Nos. 136-140 (5)	16.10	16.10
Nos. 754-758 (5)	15.25	15.25
Nos. 814-818 (5)	14.00	12.75
Nos. 755-759 (5)	9.70	9.70
Nos. 957-961 (5)	16.70	15.90
Nos. 1258-1265 (2)	27.50	27.50
Nos. 763-767 (5)	9.75	9.75
Nos. 879-883 (5)	15.00	15.00
Set total (47) Stamps	153.70	150.70

End of World War II, 50th Anniv.

CD351

CD352

1995

Ascension 613-617
Bahamas 824-828
Barbados 891-895
Belize 1047-1050
British Indian Ocean Territory 163-167
Cayman Islands 704-708
Falkland Islands 634-638
Fiji 720-724
Kiribati 662-668
Liberia 1175-1179
Mauritius 803-805
St. Helena 646-654
St. Kitts 389-393
St. Lucia 1018-1022
Samoa 890-894
Solomon Islands 799-803
South Georgia 198-200
Tristan da Cunha 562-566

Nos. 613-617 (5)	21.50	21.50

Nos. 824-828 (5)	22.00	18.70
Nos. 891-895 (5)	14.20	11.90
Nos. 1047-1050 (4)	6.05	5.90
Nos. 163-167 (5)	16.25	16.25
Nos. 704-708 (5)	17.65	13.95
Nos. 634-638 (5)	18.65	17.15
Nos. 720-724 (5)	17.50	14.50
Nos. 662-668 (7)	16.30	16.30
Nos. 1175-1179 (5)	15.25	11.15
Nos. 803-805 (3)	7.50	7.50
Nos. 646-654 (9)	26.10	26.10
Nos. 389-393 (5)	13.60	13.60
Nos. 1018-1022 (5)	14.25	11.15
Nos. 890-894 (5)	14.25	13.50
Nos. 799-803 (5)	14.75	14.75
Nos. 198-200 (3)	14.50	15.50
Nos. 562-566 (5)	20.10	20.10
Set total (91) Stamps	290.40	269.50

UN, 50th Anniv.

CD353

1995

Bahamas	839-842
Barbados	901-904
Belize	1055-1058
Jamaica	847-851
Liberia	1187-1190
Mauritius	813-816
Pitcairn Islands	436-439
St. Kitts	398-401
St. Lucia	1023-1026
Samoa	900-903
Tristan da Cunha	568-571
Virgin Islands	807-810

Nos. 839-842 (4)	7.15	6.40
Nos. 901-904 (4)	7.00	5.75
Nos. 1055-1058 (4)	4.70	4.70
Nos. 847-851 (5)	5.40	5.45
Nos. 1187-1190 (4)	9.65	9.65
Nos. 813-816 (4)	3.90	3.90
Nos. 436-439 (4)	8.15	8.15
Nos. 398-401 (4)	6.15	6.15
Nos. 1023-1026 (4)	7.50	7.25
Nos. 900-903 (4)	9.35	8.20
Nos. 568-571 (4)	13.50	13.50
Nos. 807-810 (4)	7.45	7.45
Set total (49) Stamps	89.90	86.55

Queen Elizabeth, 70th Birthday

CD354

1996

Ascension	632-635
British Antarctic Territory	240-243
British Indian Ocean Territory	176-180
Falkland Islands	653-657
Pitcairn Islands	446-449
St. Helena	672-676
Samoa	912-916
Tokelau	223-227
Tristan da Cunha	576-579
Virgin Islands	824-828

Nos. 632-635 (4)	5.30	5.30
Nos. 240-243 (4)	10.50	8.90
Nos. 176-180 (5)	11.50	11.50
Nos. 653-657 (5)	13.55	11.20
Nos. 446-449 (4)	8.60	8.60
Nos. 672-676 (5)	12.70	12.70
Nos. 912-916 (5)	11.50	11.50
Nos. 223-227 (5)	10.50	10.50
Nos. 576-579 (4)	8.35	8.35
Nos. 824-828 (5)	11.30	11.30
Set total (46) Stamps	103.80	99.85

Diana, Princess of Wales (1961-97)

CD355

1998

Ascension	696
Bahamas	901A-902
Barbados	950
Belize	1091
Bermuda	753
Botswana	659-663
British Antarctic Territory	258
British Indian Ocean Terr.	197
Cayman Islands	752A-753
Falkland Islands	694
Fiji	819-820
Gibraltar	754
Kiribati	719A-720
Namibia	909
Niue	706
Norfolk Island	644-645
Papua New Guinea	937
Pitcairn Islands	487
St. Helena	711
St. Kitts	437A-438
Samoa	955A-956
Seycelles	802
Solomon Islands	866-867
South Georgia	220
Tokelau	252B-253
Tonga	980
Niuafo'ou	201
Tristan da Cunha	618
Tuvalu	762
Vanuatu	718A-719
Virgin Islands	878

No. 696 (1)	5.25	5.25
Nos. 901A-902 (2)	5.30	5.30
No. 950 (1)	5.00	5.00
No. 1091 (1)	5.00	5.00
No. 753 (1)	5.00	5.00
Nos. 659-663 (5)	8.25	8.80
No. 258 (1)	6.25	6.25
No. 197 (1)	5.50	5.50
Nos. 752A-753 (3)	7.40	7.40
No. 694 (1)	5.00	5.00
Nos. 819-820 (2)	5.25	5.25
No. 754 (1)	4.75	4.75
Nos. 719A-720 (2)	4.85	4.85
No. 909 (1)	1.75	1.75
No. 706 (1)	5.50	5.50
Nos. 644-645 (2)	5.25	5.25
No. 937 (1)	6.50	6.50
No. 487 (1)	4.75	4.75
No. 711 (1)	4.25	4.25
Nos. 437A-438 (2)	5.15	5.15
Nos. 955A-956 (2)	7.00	7.00
No. 802 (1)	6.25	6.25
Nos. 866-867 (2)	5.40	5.40
No. 220 (1)	4.50	5.00
Nos. 252B-253 (2)	5.50	5.50
No. 980 (1)	5.75	5.75
No. 201 (1)	6.50	6.50
No. 618 (1)	5.00	5.00
No. 762 (1)	4.00	4.00
Nos. 718A-719 (2)	8.00	8.00
No. 878 (1)	4.50	4.50
Set total (46) Stamps	168.35	169.40

Wedding of Prince Edward and Sophie Rhys-Jones

CD356

1999

Ascension	729-730
Cayman Islands	775-776
Falkland Islands	729-730
Pitcairn Islands	505-506
St. Helena	733-734
Samoa	971-972
Tristan da Cunha	636-637
Virgin Islands	908-909

Nos. 729-730 (2)	4.50	4.50
Nos. 775-776 (2)	4.95	4.95
Nos. 729-730 (2)	14.00	14.00
Nos. 505-506 (2)	7.00	7.00
Nos. 733-734 (2)	5.00	5.00
Nos. 971-972 (2)	5.00	5.00
Nos. 636-637 (2)	7.50	7.50
Nos. 908-909 (2)	7.50	7.50
Set total (16) Stamps	55.45	55.45

1st Manned Moon Landing, 30th Anniv.

CD357

1999

Ascension	731-735
Bahamas	942-946
Barbados	967-971
Bermuda	778
Cayman Islands	777-781
Fiji	853-857
Jamaica	889-893
Kiribati	746-750
Nauru	465-469
St. Kitts	460-464
Samoa	973-977
Solomon Islands	875-879
Tuvalu	800-804
Virgin Islands	910-914

Nos. 731-735 (5)	12.80	12.80
Nos. 942-946 (5)	14.10	14.10
Nos. 967-971 (5)	8.65	7.75
No. 778 (1)	9.00	9.00
Nos. 777-781 (5)	9.25	9.25
Nos. 853-857 (5)	9.25	8.45
Nos. 889-893 (5)	8.30	7.18
Nos. 746-750 (5)	8.85	8.85
Nos. 465-469 (5)	8.90	10.15
Nos. 460-464 (5)	12.00	12.00
Nos. 973-977 (5)	13.45	13.30
Nos. 875-879 (5)	7.50	7.50
Nos. 800-804 (5)	7.45	7.45
Nos. 910-914 (5)	11.75	11.75
Set total (66) Stamps	141.25	139.53

Queen Mother's Century

CD358

1999

Ascension	736-740
Bahamas	951-955
Cayman Islands	782-786
Falkland Islands	734-738
Fiji	858-862
Norfolk Island	688-692
St. Helena	740-744
Samoa	978-982
Solomon Islands	880-884
South Georgia	231-235
Tristan da Cunha	638-642
Tuvalu	805-809

Nos. 736-740 (5)	15.50	15.50
Nos. 951-955 (5)	13.75	12.65
Nos. 782-786 (5)	8.35	8.35
Nos. 734-738 (5)	30.00	28.25
Nos. 858-862 (5)	12.80	13.25
Nos. 688-692 (5)	10.30	10.30
Nos. 740-744 (5)	16.15	16.15
Nos. 978-982 (5)	12.50	12.10
Nos. 880-884 (5)	7.50	7.00
Nos. 231-235 (5)	29.75	30.00
Nos. 638-642 (5)	18.00	18.00
Nos. 805-809 (5)	8.65	8.65
Set total (60) Stamps	183.25	180.20

Prince William, 18th Birthday

CD359

2000

Ascension	755-759
Cayman Islands	797-801
Falkland Islands	762-766
Fiji	889-893
South Georgia	257-261
Tristan da Cunha	664-668
Virgin Islands	925-929

Nos. 755-759 (5)	15.50	15.50
Nos. 797-801 (5)	11.15	10.90
Nos. 762-766 (5)	24.60	22.50
Nos. 889-893 (5)	12.90	12.90
Nos. 257-261 (5)	29.00	28.75
Nos. 664-668 (5)	21.50	21.50
Nos. 925-929 (5)	14.50	14.50
Set total (35) Stamps	129.15	126.55

Reign of Queen Elizabeth II, 50th Anniv.

CD360

2002

Ascension	790-794
Bahamas	1033-1037
Barbados	1019-1023
Belize	1152-1156
Bermuda	822-826
British Antarctic Territory	307-311
British Indian Ocean Territory	239-243
Cayman Islands	844-848
Falkland Islands	804-808
Gibraltar	896-900
Jamaica	952-956
Nauru	491-495
Norfolk Island	758-762
Papua New Guinea	1019-1023
Pitcairn Islands	552
St. Helena	788-792
St. Lucia	1146-1150
Solomon Islands	931-935
South Georgia	274-278
Swaziland	706-710
Tokelau	302-306
Tonga	1059
Niuafo'ou	239
Tristan da Cunha	706-710
Virgin Islands	967-971

Nos. 790-794 (5)	14.10	14.10
Nos. 1033-1037 (5)	15.25	15.25
Nos. 1019-1023 (5)	13.15	13.15
Nos. 1152-1156 (5)	12.65	12.25
Nos. 822-826 (5)	18.00	18.00
Nos. 307-311 (5)	25.00	25.00
Nos. 239-243 (5)	19.40	19.40
Nos. 844-848 (5)	13.25	13.25
Nos. 804-808 (5)	23.00	22.00
Nos. 896-900 (5)	6.65	6.65
Nos. 952-956 (5)	16.65	16.65
Nos. 491-495 (5)	18.75	18.75
Nos. 758-762 (5)	19.50	19.50
Nos. 1019-1023 (5)	14.50	14.50
No. 552 (1)	9.25	9.25
Nos. 788-792 (5)	19.75	19.75
Nos. 1146-1150 (5)	12.25	12.25
Nos. 931-935 (5)	12.40	12.40
Nos. 274-278 (5)	28.00	28.50
Nos. 706-710 (5)	12.75	12.75
Nos. 302-306 (5)	14.50	14.50
No. 1059 (1)	8.50	8.50
No. 239 (1)	8.75	8.75
Nos. 706-710 (5)	18.50	18.50
Nos. 967-971 (5)	16.50	16.50
Set total (113) Stamps	391.00	390.10

Queen Mother Elizabeth (1900-2002)

CD361

2002

Ascension....................................799-801
Bahamas 1044-1046
Bermuda......................................834-836
British Antarctic Territory..........312-314
British Indian Ocean Territory........245-247
Cayman Islands.........................857-861
Falkland Islands 812-816
Nauru..499-501
Pitcairn Islands.........................561-565
St. Helena 808-812
St. Lucia 1155-1159
Seychelles 830
Solomon Islands........................945-947
South Georgia 281-285
Tokelau 312-314
Tristan da Cunha.......................715-717
Virgin Islands.............................979-983

Nos. 799-801 (3)	8.85	8.85
Nos. 1044-1046 (3)	9.10	9.10
Nos. 834-836 (3)	12.25	12.25
Nos. 312-314 (3)	19.25	19.25
Nos. 245-247 (3)	17.35	17.35
Nos. 857-861 (5)	15.00	15.00
Nos. 812-816 (5)	28.50	28.50
Nos. 499-501 (3)	16.00	16.00
Nos. 561-565 (5)	15.25	15.25
Nos. 808-812 (5)	12.00	12.00
Nos. 1155-1159 (5)	13.00	13.00
No. 830 (1)	6.50	6.50
Nos. 945-947 (3)	9.25	9.25
Nos. 281-285 (5)	19.50	19.50
Nos. 312-314 (3)	11.85	11.85
Nos. 715-717 (3)	16.25	16.25
Nos. 979-983 (5)	23.50	23.50
Set total (63) Stamps	253.40	253.40

Head of Queen Elizabeth II

CD362

2003

Ascension...822
Bermuda..865
British Antarctic Territory.....................322
British Indian Ocean Territory 261
Cayman Islands...................................878
Falkland Islands 828
St. Helena 820
South Georgia 294
Tristan da Cunha.................................731
Virgin Islands.....................................1003

No. 822 (1)	12.50	12.50
No. 865 (1)	50.00	50.00
No. 322 (1)	10.00	10.00
No. 261 (1)	11.00	11.00
No. 878 (1)	14.00	14.00
No. 828 (1)	9.00	9.00
No. 820 (1)	9.00	9.00
No. 294 (1)	8.50	8.50
No. 731 (1)	10.00	10.00
No. 1003 (1)	10.00	10.00
Set total (10) Stamps	144.00	144.00

Coronation of Queen Elizabeth II, 50th Anniv.

CD363

2003

Ascension.....................................823-825
Bahamas 1073-1075
Bermuda.......................................866-868
British Antarctic Territory..........323-325
British Indian Ocean Territory 262-264
Cayman Islands.........................879-881
Jamaica 970-972
Kiribati 825-827
Pitcairn Islands..........................577-581
St. Helena 821-823
St. Lucia 1171-1173
Tokelau 320-322
Tristan da Cunha.......................732-734
Virgin Islands..........................1004-1006

Nos. 823-825 (3)	12.50	12.50
Nos. 1073-1075 (3)	13.00	13.00
Nos. 866-868 (2)	14.25	14.25
Nos. 323-325 (3)	26.00	26.00
Nos. 262-264 (3)	28.00	28.00
Nos. 879-881 (3)	19.25	19.25
Nos. 970-972 (3)	10.00	10.00
Nos. 825-827 (3)	13.50	13.50
Nos. 577-581 (5)	14.40	14.40
Nos. 821-823 (3)	7.25	7.25
Nos. 1171-1173 (3)	8.75	8.75
Nos. 320-322 (3)	17.25	17.25
Nos. 732-734 (3)	16.75	16.75
Nos. 1004-1006 (3)	25.00	25.00
Set total (43) Stamps	225.90	225.90

Prince William, 21st Birthday

CD364

2003

Ascension...826
British Indian Ocean Territory 265
Cayman Islands...........................882-884
Falkland Islands 829
South Georgia 295
Tokelau 323
Tristan da Cunha.................................735
Virgin Islands..........................1007-1009

No. 826 (1)	7.25	7.25
No. 265 (1)	8.00	8.00
Nos. 882-884 (3)	6.95	6.95
No. 829 (1)	13.50	13.50
No. 295 (1)	8.50	8.50
No. 323 (1)	7.25	7.25
No. 735 (1)	6.00	6.00
Nos. 1007-1009 (3)	10.00	10.00
Set total (12) Stamps	67.45	67.45

British Commonwealth of Nations

Dominions, Colonies, Territories, Offices and Independent Members

Comprising stamps of the British Commonwealth and associated nations.

A strict observance of technicalities would bar some or all of the stamps listed under Burma, Ireland, Kuwait, Nepal, New Republic, Orange Free State, Samoa, South Africa, South-West Africa, Stellaland, Sudan, Swaziland, the two Transvaal Republics and others but these are included for the convenience of collectors.

1. Great Britain

Great Britain: Including England, Scotland, Wales and Northern Ireland.

2. The Dominions, Present and Past

AUSTRALIA

The Commonwealth of Australia was proclaimed on January 1, 1901. It consists of six former colonies as follows:

New South Wales
Victoria
Queensland
Tasmania
South Australia
Western Australia

The following islands and territories are, or have been, administered by Australia: Australian Antarctic Territory, Christmas Island, Cocos (Keeling) Islands, Nauru, New Guinea, Norfolk Island, Papua.

CANADA

The Dominion of Canada was created by the British North America Act in 1867. The following provinces were former sepa- rate colonies and issued postage stamps:

British Columbia and Vancouver Island
Newfoundland
New Brunswick
Nova Scotia
Prince Edward Island

FIJI

The colony of Fiji became an independent nation with dominion status on Oct. 10, 1970.

GHANA

This state came into existence Mar. 6, 1957, with dominion status. It consists of the former colony of the Gold Coast and the Trusteeship Territory of Togoland. Ghana became a republic July 1, 1960.

INDIA

The Republic of India was inaugurated on January 26, 1950. It succeeded the Dominion of India which was proclaimed August 15, 1947, when the former Empire of India was divided into Pakistan and the Union of India. The Republic is composed of about 40 predominantly Hindu states of three classes: governor's provinces, chief commissioner's provinces and princely states. India also has various territories, such as the Andaman and Nicobar Islands.

The old Empire of India was a federation of British India and the native states. The more important princely states were autonomous. Of the more than 700 Indian states, these 43 are familiar names to philatelists because of their postage stamps.

CONVENTION STATES

Chamba
Faridkot
Gwalior
Jhind
Nabha
Patiala

FEUDATORY STATES

Alwar
Bahawalpur
Bamra
Barwani
Bhopal
Bhor
Bijawar
Bundi
Bussahir
Charkhari
Cochin
Dhar
Dungarpur
Duttia
Faridkot (1879-85)
Hyderabad
Idar
Indore
Jaipur
Jammu
Jammu and Kashmir
Jasdan
Jhalawar
Jhind (1875-76)
Kashmir
Kishangarh
Kotah
Las Bela
Morvi
Nandgaon
Nowanuggur
Orchha
Poonch
Rajasthan
Rajpeepla
Sirmur
Soruth
Tonk
Travancore
Wadhwan

NEW ZEALAND

Became a dominion on September 26, 1907. The following islands and territories are, or have been, administered by New Zealand:

Aitutaki
Cook Islands (Rarotonga)
Niue
Penrhyn
Ross Dependency
Samoa (Western Samoa)
Tokelau Islands

PAKISTAN

The Republic of Pakistan was proclaimed March 23, 1956. It succeeded the Dominion which was proclaimed August 15, 1947. It is made up of all or part of several Moslem provinces and various districts of the former Empire of India, including Bahawalpur and Las Bela. Pakistan withdrew from the Commonwealth in 1972.

SOUTH AFRICA

Under the terms of the South African Act (1909) the self-governing colonies of Cape of Good Hope, Natal, Orange River Colony and Transvaal united on May 31, 1910, to form the Union of South Africa. It became an independent republic May 3, 1961.

Under the terms of the Treaty of Versailles, South-West Africa, formerly German South-West Africa, was mandated to the Union of South Africa.

SRI LANKA (CEYLON)

The Dominion of Ceylon was proclaimed February 4, 1948. The island had been a Crown Colony from 1802 until then. On May 22, 1972, Ceylon became the Republic of Sri Lanka.

3. Colonies, Past and Present; Controlled Territory and Independent Members of the Commonwealth

Aden
Aitutaki
Anguilla
Antigua
Ascension
Bahamas
Bahrain
Bangladesh
Barbados
Barbuda
Basutoland
Batum
Bechuanaland
Bechuanaland Prot.
Belize
Bermuda
Botswana
British Antarctic Territory
British Central Africa
British Columbia and Vancouver Island
British East Africa
British Guiana

British Honduras
British Indian Ocean Territory
British New Guinea
British Solomon Islands
British Somaliland
Brunei
Burma
Bushire
Cameroons
Cape of Good Hope
Cayman Islands
Christmas Island
Cocos (Keeling) Islands
Cook Islands
Crete,
 British Administration
Cyprus
Dominica
East Africa & Uganda
 Protectorates
Egypt
Falkland Islands
Fiji
Gambia
German East Africa
Gibraltar
Gilbert Islands
Gilbert & Ellice Islands
Gold Coast
Grenada
Griqualand West
Guernsey
Guyana
Heligoland
Hong Kong
Indian Native States
 (see India)
Ionian Islands
Jamaica
Jersey
Kenya
Kenya, Uganda & Tanzania
Kuwait
Labuan
Lagos
Leeward Islands
Lesotho
Madagascar
Malawi
Malaya
 Federated Malay States
 Johore
 Kedah
 Kelantan
 Malacca
 Negri Sembilan
 Pahang
 Penang
 Perak
 Perlis
 Selangor
 Singapore
 Sungei Ujong
 Trengganu
Malaysia
Maldive Islands
Malta
Man, Isle of
Mauritius
Mesopotamia
Montserrat
Muscat
Namibia
Natal
Nauru
Nevis
New Britain
New Brunswick
Newfoundland
New Guinea
New Hebrides
New Republic
New South Wales
Niger Coast Protectorate
Nigeria
Niue
Norfolk Island
North Borneo
Northern Nigeria
Northern Rhodesia
North West Pacific Islands
Nova Scotia
Nyasaland Protectorate
Oman
Orange River Colony
Palestine
Papua New Guinea
Penrhyn Island
Pitcairn Islands
Prince Edward Island
Queensland
Rhodesia
Rhodesia & Nyasaland
Ross Dependency
Sabah
St. Christopher
St. Helena
St. Kitts
St. Kitts-Nevis-Anguilla
St. Lucia
St. Vincent
Samoa
Sarawak
Seychelles
Sierra Leone
Solomon Islands
Somaliland Protectorate
South Arabia
South Australia
South Georgia
Southern Nigeria
Southern Rhodesia
South-West Africa
Stellaland
Straits Settlements
Sudan
Swaziland
Tanganyika
Tanzania
Tasmania
Tobago
Togo
Tokelau Islands
Tonga
Transvaal
Trinidad
Trinidad and Tobago
Tristan da Cunha
Trucial States
Turks and Caicos
Turks Islands
Tuvalu
Uganda
United Arab Emirates
Victoria
Virgin Islands
Western Australia
Zambia
Zanzibar
Zululand

POST OFFICES IN FOREIGN COUNTRIES

Africa
 East Africa Forces
 Middle East Forces
Bangkok
China
Morocco
Turkish Empire

Colonies, Former Colonies, Offices, Territories Controlled by Parent States

Belgium

Belgian Congo
Ruanda-Urundi

Denmark

Danish West Indies
Faroe Islands
Greenland
Iceland

Finland

Aland Islands

France

COLONIES PAST AND PRESENT, CONTROLLED TERRITORIES

Afars & Issas, Territory of
Alaouites
Alexandretta
Algeria
Alsace & Lorraine
Anjouan
Annam & Tonkin
Benin
Cambodia (Khmer)
Cameroun
Castellorizo
Chad
Cilicia
Cochin China
Comoro Islands
Dahomey
Diego Suarez
Djibouti (Somali Coast)
Fezzan
French Congo
French Equatorial Africa
French Guiana
French Guinea
French India
French Morocco
French Polynesia (Oceania)
French Southern & Antarctic Territories
French Sudan
French West Africa
Gabon
Germany
Ghadames
Grand Comoro
Guadeloupe
Indo-China
Inini
Ivory Coast
Laos
Latakia
Lebanon
Madagascar
Martinique
Mauritania
Mayotte
Memel
Middle Congo
Moheli
New Caledonia
New Hebrides
Niger Territory
Nossi-Be
Obock
Reunion
Rouad, Ile
Ste.-Marie de Madagascar
St. Pierre & Miquelon
Senegal
Senegambia & Niger
Somali Coast
Syria
Tahiti
Togo
Tunisia
Ubangi-Shari
Upper Senegal & Niger
Upper Volta
Viet Nam
Wallis & Futuna Islands

POST OFFICES IN FOREIGN COUNTRIES

China
Crete
Egypt
Turkish Empire
Zanzibar

Germany

EARLY STATES

Baden
Bavaria
Bergedorf
Bremen
Brunswick
Hamburg
Hanover
Lubeck
Mecklenburg-Schwerin
Mecklenburg-Strelitz
Oldenburg
Prussia
Saxony
Schleswig-Holstein
Wurttemberg

FORMER COLONIES

Cameroun (Kamerun)
Caroline Islands
German East Africa
German New Guinea
German South-West Africa
Kiauchau
Mariana Islands
Marshall Islands
Samoa
Togo

Italy

EARLY STATES

Modena
Parma
Romagna
Roman States
Sardinia
Tuscany
Two Sicilies
  Naples
  Neapolitan Provinces
  Sicily

FORMER COLONIES, CONTROLLED TERRITORIES, OCCUPATION AREAS

Aegean Islands
  Calimno (Calino)
  Caso
  Cos (Coo)
  Karki (Carchi)
  Leros (Lero)
  Lipso
  Nisiros (Nisiro)
  Patmos (Patmo)
  Piscopi
  Rodi (Rhodes)
  Scarpanto
  Simi
  Stampalia
Castellorizo
Corfu
Cyrenaica
Eritrea
Ethiopia (Abyssinia)
Fiume
Ionian Islands
  Cephalonia
  Ithaca
  Paxos
Italian East Africa
Libya
Oltre Giuba
Saseno
Somalia (Italian Somaliland)
Tripolitania

POST OFFICES IN FOREIGN COUNTRIES "ESTERO"*

Austria
China
  Peking
  Tientsin
Crete
Tripoli
Turkish Empire
  Constantinople
  Durazzo
  Janina
Jerusalem
Salonika
Scutari
Smyrna
Valona

*Stamps overprinted "ESTERO" were used in various parts of the world.

Netherlands

Aruba
Caribbean Netherlands
Curacao
Netherlands Antilles (Curacao)
Netherlands Indies
Netherlands New Guinea
St. Martin
Surinam (Dutch Guiana)

Portugal

COLONIES PAST AND PRESENT, CONTROLLED TERRITORIES

Angola
Angra
Azores
Cape Verde
Funchal
Horta
Inhambane
Kionga
Lourenco Marques
Macao
Madeira
Mozambique
Mozambique Co.
Nyassa
Ponta Delgada
Portuguese Africa
Portuguese Congo
Portuguese Guinea
Portuguese India
Quelimane
St. Thomas & Prince Islands
Tete
Timor
Zambezia

Russia

ALLIED TERRITORIES AND REPUBLICS, OCCUPATION AREAS

Armenia
Aunus (Olonets)
Azerbaijan
Batum
Estonia
Far Eastern Republic
Georgia
Karelia
Latvia
Lithuania
North Ingermanland
Ostland
Russian Turkestan
Siberia
South Russia
Tannu Tuva
Transcaucasian Fed. Republics
Ukraine
Wenden (Livonia)
Western Ukraine

Spain

COLONIES PAST AND PRESENT, CONTROLLED TERRITORIES

Aguera, La
Cape Juby
Cuba
Elobey, Annobon & Corisco
Fernando Po
Ifni
Mariana Islands
Philippines
Puerto Rico
Rio de Oro
Rio Muni
Spanish Guinea
Spanish Morocco
Spanish Sahara
Spanish West Africa

POST OFFICES IN FOREIGN COUNTRIES

Morocco
Tangier
Tetuan

Dies of British Colonial Stamps

DIE A:

1. The lines in the groundwork vary in thickness and are not uniformly straight.
2. The seventh and eighth lines from the top, in the groundwork, converge where they meet the head.
3. There is a small dash in the upper part of the second jewel in the band of the crown.
4. The vertical color line in front of the throat stops at the sixth line of shading on the neck.

DIE B:

1. The lines in the groundwork are all thin and straight.
2. All the lines of the background are parallel.
3. There is no dash in the upper part of the second jewel in the band of the crown.
4. The vertical color line in front of the throat stops at the eighth line of shading on the neck.

DIE I:

1. The base of the crown is well below the level of the inner white line around the vignette.
2. The labels inscribed "POSTAGE" and "REVENUE" are cut square at the top.
3. There is a white "bud" on the outer side of the main stem of the curved ornaments in each lower corner.
4. The second (thick) line below the country name has the ends next to the crown cut diagonally.

DIE Ia.	DIE Ib.
1 as die II.	1 and 3 as die II.
2 and 3 as die I.	2 as die I.

DIE II:

1. The base of the crown is aligned with the underside of the white line around the vignette.
2. The labels curve inward at the top inner corners.
3. The "bud" has been removed from the outer curve of the ornaments in each corner.
4. The second line below the country name has the ends next to the crown cut vertically.

British Colonial and Crown Agents Watermarks

Wmk. 1
Crown and C C

Wmk. 2
Crown and C A

Wmk. 3
Multiple Crown and C A

Wmk. 4
Multiple Crown and Script C A

Wmk. 4a

Wmk. 46

Wmk. 314
St. Edward's Crown and C A Multiple

Wmk. 373

Wmk. 384

Wmk. 406

Watermarks 1 to 4, 314, 373, 384 and 406, common to many British territories, are illustrated here to avoid duplication.

The letters "CC" of Wmk. 1 identify the paper as having been made for the use of the Crown Colonies, while the letters "CA" of the others stand for "Crown Agents." Both Wmks. 1 and 2 were used on stamps printed by De La Rue & Co.

Wmk. 3 was adopted in 1904; Wmk. 4 in 1921; Wmk. 46 in 1879; Wmk. 314 in 1957; Wmk. 373 in 1974; Wmk. 384 in 1985; Wmk 406 in 2008.

In Wmk. 4a, a non-matching crown of the general St. Edwards type (bulging on both sides at top) was substituted for one of the Wmk. 4 crowns which fell off the dandy roll. The non-matching crown occurs in 1950-52 printings in a horizontal row of crowns on certain regular stamps of Johore and Seychelles, and on various postage due stamps of Barbados, Basutoland, British Guiana, Gold Coast, Grenada, Northern Rhodesia, St. Lucia, Swaziland and Trinidad and Tobago. A variation of Wmk. 4a, with the non-matching crown in a horizontal row of crown-CA-crown, occurs on regular stamps of Bahamas, St. Kitts-Nevis and Singapore.

Wmk. 314 was intentionally used sideways, starting in 1966. When a stamp was issued with Wmk. 314 both upright and sideways, the sideways varieties usually are listed also – with minor numbers. In many of the later issues, Wmk. 314 is slightly visible.

Wmk. 373 is usually only faintly visible.

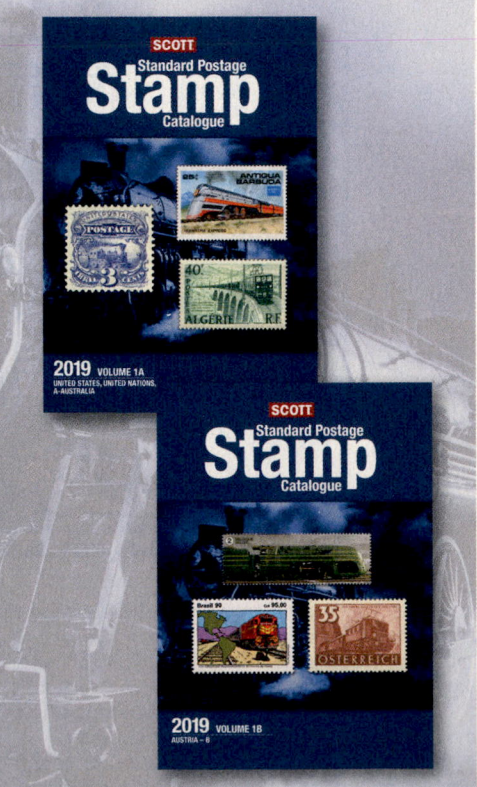

HAITI

'hā-tē

LOCATION — Western part of Hispaniola
GOVT. — Republic
AREA — 10,714 sq. mi.
POP. — 6,884,264 (1999 est.)
CAPITAL — Port-au-Prince

100 Centimes = 1 Piaster (1906)
100 Centimes = 1 Gourde

Catalogue values for unused stamps in this country are for Never Hinged items, beginning with Scott 370 in the regular postage section, Scott B2 in the semi-postal section, Scott C33 in the air post section, Scott CB9 in the air post semi-postal section, Scott CO6 in the air post official section, Scott CQ1 in the air post parcel post seciton, Scott E1 in the special delivery section, Scott J21 in the postage due section, Scott Q1 in the parcel post section, Scott RA1 in the postal tax section, and Scott RAC1 in the air post postal tax section.

ISSUES OF THE REPUBLIC

Watermark

Wmk. 131 — RH

Liberty Head — A1

On A3 (Nos. 18, 19) there are crossed lines of dots on face. On A4 the "5" is 3mm wide, on A1 2½mm wide.

1881 Unwmk. Typo. *Imperf.*

1 A1 1c vermilion, *yelsh* 10.00 5.50
2 A1 2c violet, *pale lil* 12.00 5.50
3 A1 3c gray bister, *pale bis* 22.50 8.00
4 A1 5c yel green, *grnsh* 35.00 16.00
5 A1 7c deep blue, *grysh* 24.00 4.00
6 A1 20c red brown, *yelsh* 85.00 30.00
Nos. 1-6 (6) 188.50 69.00
Set, never hinged 384.00

Nos. 1-6 were printed from plate I, Nos. 7-13 from plates II and III.

1882 *Perf. 13½*

7 A1 1c dp ver, *dp yelsh* ('83) 6.25 2.10
a. Vert. pair imperf. btwn. 200.00 *250.00*
8 A1 2c dp purple, *pale lil* ('83) 12.00 3.25
a. 2c dark violet, *white* ('84) 13.00 6.50
b. As "a," vert. pair, imperf between 175.00 *250.00*
c. As "a.," horiz. pair, imperf between 175.00 *250.00*
d. 2c red violet, *pale lilac* ('85) 8.00 2.60
e. As "d," vert. pair, imperf between 175.00 *275.00*
f. As "d," horiz. pair, imperf between 175.00 *275.00*
9 A1 3c gray bister, *pale bis* 12.50 3.25
10 A1 5c blue grn, *grnsh* 9.00 1.60
a. 5c yellow green, *greenish* ('85) 8.50 1.40
b. 5c deep green, *greenish* ('85) 8.50 1.40
c. As "b," horiz. pair, imperf between 190.00 *275.00*
11 A1 7c deep blue, *grysh* ('85) 11.50 2.10
a. Horiz. pair, imperf. between 150.00 *250.00*
12 A1 7c ultra, *grysh* ('85) 17.50 3.25
a. Vert. pair, imperf. between 150.00 *250.00*
13 A1 20c pale brn, *yelsh* ('86) 17.50 4.50
a. Vert. pair, imperf between 175.00 *275.00*
b. 20c red brown, *yellowish* ('84) 21.00 8.00
c. As "b," vert. pair, imperf between 150.00 *300.00*
d. As "b," horiz. pair, imperf between 150.00 *300.00*
Nos. 7-13 (7) 86.25 20.05
Set, never hinged 189.00

Stamps perf. 14, 16 are postal forgeries.

A3

A4

1886-87 *Perf. 13½*

18 A3 1c vermilion, *yelsh* 5.75 2.00
a. Horiz. pair, imperf. vert. 175.00 175.00
b. Horiz. pair, imperf. between 200.00 190.00
19 A3 2c dk violet, *lilac* 42.50 7.00
20 A4 5c green ('87) 20.00 2.75
Nos. 18-20 (3) 68.25 11.75
Set, never hinged 137.00

General Louis Etienne Félicité Salomon — A5

1887 Engr. *Perf. 14*

21 A5 1c lake .40 .30
22 A5 2c violet 1.00 .70
23 A5 3c blue .70 .45
24 A5 5c green 50.00 .55
a. Double impression *2,250.*
Nos. 21-24 (4) 52.10 2.00
Set, never hinged 89.00

Imperfs. of Nos. 21-24 are plate proofs. Value per pair, $50.

Nos. 21-22 are known overprinted "R:S:" and postally used. Neither is known unused. Overprint is of a provisional or revolutionary government.

No. 23 Handstamp Surcharged in Red

1890

25 A5 2c on 3c blue 3.50 3.00
Never hinged 15.00
a. Inverted surcharge 30.00 *40.00*
b. Double surcharge 30.00 *40.00*
c. Double surcharge, one inverted — *37.50*
d. Pair, one without surcharge 100.00

Missing letters are frequently found. This applies to succeeding surcharged issues.

Coat of Arms — A7

1891 *Perf. 13*

26 A7 1c violet 1.00 .30
27 A7 2c blue 1.50 .30
28 A7 3c gray lilac 2.00 .45
a. 3c slate 1.75 .55
29 A7 5c orange 5.50 .50
30 A7 7c red 20.00 2.75
Nos. 26-30 (5) 30.00 4.30
Set, never hinged 85.25

Nos. 26-30 exist imperf. Value of unused pairs, each $50.

The 2c, 3c and 7c exist imperf. vertically. Value, each $50 and up.

No. 28 Surcharged Like No. 25 in Red

1892

31 A7 2c on 3c gray lilac 3.00 2.00
Never hinged 10.00
a. 2c on 3c slate 3.50 2.25
b. Inverted surcharge 24.00
c. Double surcharge 32.50
d. Pair, one without surcharge 32.50

Coat of Arms (Leaves Drooping) — A9

1892-95 Engr., Litho. (20c) *Perf. 14*

32 A9 1c lilac .40 .25
b. Double impression *500.00*
33 A9 2c deep blue .50 .25
34 A9 3c gray .70 .45
35 A9 5c orange 2.75 .50
36 A9 7c red .50 .25
a. Imperf., pair 30.00
37 A9 20c brown 1.40 1.00
Nos. 32-37 (6) 6.25 2.70
Set, never hinged 15.75

Nos. 32, 33, 35 exist in horiz. pairs, imperf. vert., Nos. 33, 35, in vert. pairs, imperf. horiz. No. 32 exists imperf. It is a proof.

1896 Engr. *Perf. 13½*

38 A9 1c light blue .55 *.70*
39 A9 2c red brown .65 *1.20*
40 A9 3c lilac brown .55 *1.20*
41 A9 5c slate green .65 *1.20*
42 A9 7c dark gray .90 *1.75*
43 A9 20c orange 1.10 *2.25*
Nos. 38-43 (6) 4.40 8.30
Set, never hinged 27.50

Nos. 32-37 are 23¾mm high, Nos. 38-43 23¼mm to 23½mm. The "C" is closed on Nos. 32-37, open on Nos. 38-43. Other differences exist. The stamps of the two issues may be readily distinguished by their colors and perfs.

Nos. 38-43 exist imperf. and in horiz. pairs, imperf. vert. The 1c, 3c, 5c, 7c exist in vert. pairs, imperf. horiz. or imperf. between. The 5c, 7c exist in horiz. pairs, imperf. between. Value of unused pairs, $9 and up.

Nos. 37, 43 Surcharged Like No. 25 in Red

1898

44 A9 2c on 20c brown 3.00 *6.00*
Never hinged 10.00
a. Inverted surcharge 27.50
b. Double surcharge 32.50
45 A9 2c on 20c orange 1.75 1.40
Never hinged 6.00
a. Inverted surcharge 10.00
b. Double surcharge 27.50
c. Double surcharge, one inverted 35.00

No. 45 exists in various part perf. varieties.

Coat of Arms — A11

1898 Wmk. 131 *Perf. 11*

46 A11 1c ultra 2.50 *5.00*
47 A11 2c brown carmine .55 .40
48 A11 3c dull violet 2.50 *5.00*
49 A11 5c dark green .55 .40
a. Double impression *600.00*
50 A11 7c gray 5.00 *10.00*
51 A11 20c orange 10.00 *20.00*
Nos. 46-51 (6) 21.10 *40.80*
Set, never hinged 42.00

Nos. 46-51 exist imperforate. They are plate proofs. Value, pair $30-$40 each.

Pres. T. Augustin Simon Sam — A12

Coat of Arms — A13

1898-99 Unwmk. *Perf. 12*

52 A12 1c ultra .25 .25
53 A13 1c yel green ('99) .25 .25
54 A12 2c deep orange .25 .25
55 A13 2c car lake ('99) .25 .25
56 A12 3c green .25 .25
57 A13 4c red .25 .25
58 A12 5c red brown .25 .25
59 A13 5c pale blue ('99) .25 .25
60 A12 7c gray .25 .25
61 A13 8c carmine .25 .25
62 A13 10c orange red .25 .25
63 A13 15c olive green .60 .45
64 A12 20c black .60 .45
65 A12 50c rose brown 1.00 .50
66 A12 1g red violet 2.25 2.00
Nos. 52-66 (15) 7.20 6.15
Set, never hinged 21.66

Nos. 52-66 imperf are color plate proofs.

For overprints see Nos. 67-81, 110-124, 169, 247-248.

Stamps of 1898-99 Handstamped in Black

1902

67 A12 1c ultra .60 *1.50*
a. Inverted overprint 3.50
b. Pair, one without overprint *40.00*
68 A13 1c yellow green .45 .30
a. Inverted overprint 3.50
b. Double overprint 30.00
c. Pair, one without overprint 50.00
69 A12 2c deep orange .80 *1.50*
a. Inverted overprint 4.50
b. Double overprint 6.00
c. Pair, one without overprint *50.00*
70 A13 2c carmine lake .45 .30
a. Inverted overprint 4.00
b. Double overprint 6.00
71 A12 3c green .45 .45
a. Inverted overprint 3.50
72 A13 4c red .60 *.90*
a. Inverted overprint 3.50
b. Double overprint 6.00
c. Pair, one without overprint 50.00
73 A12 5c red brown 1.25 *6.00*
a. Inverted overprint 6.00
74 A13 5c pale blue .45 .45
a. Inverted overprint 3.75
b. Double overprint 20.00
75 A12 7c gray .95 .95
a. Inverted overprint 4.00
b. Double overprint 6.00
76 A13 8c carmine .95 *8.50*
a. Inverted overprint 5.00
b. Double overprint 6.00
77 A13 10c orange red .95 *1.50*
a. Inverted overprint 6.00
b. Double overprint 6.00
78 A13 15c olive green 5.00 *7.00*
a. Inverted overprint 18.00
b. Double overprint 10.00
79 A12 20c black 5.00 *6.00*
a. Inverted overprint 14.00
b. Double overprint 16.00
80 A12 50c rose brown 17.50 *37.50*
a. Inverted overprint 45.00
81 A12 1g red violet 25.00 *60.00*
a. Inverted overprint 120.00
b. Pair, one without overprint 150.00
Nos. 67-81 (15) 60.40 132.85

Many forgeries exist of this overprint.

Specialists have called into question the existence of the double-overprint errors listed for this set except Nos. 68b and 74b. The editors would like to see documented evidence of the existence of Nos. 69b, 70b, 72b, 75b, 76b, 77b, 78b, 79b and 81b.

Centenary of Independence Issues

Coat of Arms — A14

Francois-Dominique Toussaint L'Ouverture — A15

Emperor Jean Jacques Dessalines A16

Pres. Alexandre Sabes Pétion A17

1903, Dec. 31 Engr. *Perf. 13¼, 14*

82 A14 1c green .35 .35

Center Engr., Frame Litho.

No.	Type	Description	Unused	Used
83	A15	2c rose & blk	1.25	*3.00*
84	A15	5c dull blue & blk	1.25	*3.00*
85	A16	7c plum & blk	1.25	*3.00*
86	A16	10c yellow & blk	1.25	*3.00*
87	A17	20c slate & blk	1.25	*3.00*
88	A17	50c olive & blk	1.25	*3.00*
		Nos. 82-88 (7)	7.85	18.35

Nos. 82 to 88 exist imperforate.

Nos. 83-88 exist with centers inverted. Some are known with head omitted.

Forgeries exist both perforated and imperf and constitute the great majority of Nos. 83-88 offered in the marketplace. Stamps perforated 13½ are forgeries. Many forgeries exist with heads lithographed instead of engraved.

Same Handstamped in Blue

1904

No.	Type	Description	Unused	Used
89	A14	1c green	.50	1.50
90	A15	2c rose & blk	.50	1.50
91	A15	5c dull blue & blk	.50	1.50
92	A16	7c plum & blk	.50	1.50
93	A16	10c yellow & blk	.50	1.50
94	A17	20c slate & blk	.50	1.50
95	A17	50c olive & blk	.50	1.50
		Nos. 89-95 (7)	3.50	10.50

Two dies were used for the handstamped overprint on Nos. 89-95. Letters and figures are larger on one than on the other. All values exist imperforate.

Pres. Pierre Nord-Alexis — A18

1904 Engr. *Perf. 13¼, 14*

No.	Type	Description	Unused	Used
96	A18	1c green	.35	.35
97	A18	2c carmine	.35	.35
98	A18	5c dark blue	.35	.35
99	A18	10c orange brown	.35	.35
100	A18	20c orange	.35	.35
101	A18	50c claret	.35	.35
a.		Tête bêche pair	*500.00*	
		Nos. 96-101 (6)	2.10	2.10

Used values are for c-t-o's. Postally used examples are worth considerably more.

Nos. 96-101 exist imperforate. Value, set $10.

This issue, and the overprints and surcharges, exist in horiz. pairs, imperf. vert., and in vert. pairs, imperf. horiz.

For overprints and surcharges see Nos. 102-109, 150-161, 170-176, 217-218, 235-238, 240-242, 302-303.

Forgeries of Nos. 96, 101, 101a exist.

Some specialists believe No. 101a is a proof. Research is ongoing.

Reprints or very accurate imitations of this issue exist, including No. 101a. Some are printed in very bright colors on very white paper and are found both perforated and imperforate. The original stamps are perf. 13¼ or 14, the reprints (forgeries) perf 13½, as well as numerous other perforations, including compound perfs.

Same Handstamped in Blue like Nos. 89-95

1904

No.	Type	Description	Unused	Used
102	A18	1c green	.60	1.50
103	A18	2c carmine	.60	1.50
104	A18	5c dark blue	.60	1.50
105	A18	10c orange brown	.60	1.50
106	A18	20c orange	.60	1.50
107	A18	50c claret	.60	1.50
		Nos. 102-107 (6)	3.60	9.00

The note after No. 95 applies also to Nos. 102-107. All values exist imperf.

Forgeries exist.

Regular Issue of 1904 Handstamp Surcharged in Black

1906, Feb. 20

No.	Type	Description	Unused	Used
108	A18	1c on 20c orange	.35	.25
a.		1c on 50c claret	*950.00*	
109	A18	2c on 50c claret	.35	.25

No. 108a is known only with inverted surcharge.

Forgeries exist.

Nos. 52-66 Handstamped in Red

1906

No.	Type	Description	Unused	Used
110	A12	1c ultra	1.40	.95
a.		Inverted overprint	3.00	
111	A13	1c yellow green	.75	.75
a.		Inverted overprint	—	
112	A12	2c deep orange	2.50	2.25
a.		Inverted overprint	3.00	*25.00*
113	A13	2c carmine lake	1.50	1.25
a.		Inverted overprint	3.00	
114	A12	3c green	1.50	1.25
a.		Inverted overprint	3.00	*10.00*
115	A13	4c red	5.75	4.50
a.		Pair, one without overprint	200.00	
116	A12	5c red brown	7.00	5.50
a.		Inverted overprint	10.00	
117	A13	5c pale blue	1.10	.60
a.		Inverted overprint	3.75	
118	A12	7c gray	5.00	4.50
a.		Inverted overprint	20.00	
119	A13	8c carmine	1.10	1.00
a.		Inverted overprint	5.00	
b.		Double overprint	60.00	
c.		Pair, one without overprint	100.00	
120	A13	10c orange red	2.00	1.25
a.		Inverted overprint	6.00	
b.		Pair, one without overprint	100.00	*150.00*
121	A13	15c olive green	2.50	1.25
a.		Inverted overprint	18.00	
122	A12	20c black	5.75	4.50
123	A12	50c rose brown	5.50	3.50
a.		Inverted overprint	45.00	
124	A12	1g red violet	15.00	10.00
a.		Inverted overprint	120.00	
		Nos. 110-124 (15)	58.35	43.05

The ink used in this overprint is fugitive and will bleed in water.

Forgeries of this overprint are plentiful.

Coat of Arms — A19

President Nord-Alexis A20

Market at Port-au-Prince A21

Sans Souci Palace — A22

Independence Palace at Gonaives — A23

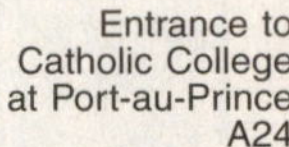

Entrance to Catholic College at Port-au-Prince A24

Monastery and Church at Port-au-Prince A25

Seat of Government at Port-au-Prince A26

Presidential Palace at Port-au-Prince A27

For Foreign Postage (centimes de piastre)

1906-13 *Perf. 12*

No.	Type	Description	Unused	Used
125	A19	1c de p green	.35	.25
126	A20	2c de p ver	.45	.25
127	A21	3c de p brown	.60	.25
128	A21	3c de p org yel ('11)	6.00	6.00
129	A22	4c de p car lake	.60	.35
130	A22	4c de p lt ol grn ('13)	25.00	25.00
131	A20	5c de p dk blue	2.50	.30
132	A23	7c de p gray	1.75	.85
133	A23	7c de p org red ('13)	65.00	65.00
134	A24	8c de p car rose	1.75	.80
135	A24	8c de p ol grn ('13)	55.00	42.50
136	A25	10c de p org red	1.25	.30
137	A25	10c de p red brn ('13)	27.50	22.50
138	A26	15c de p sl grn	2.25	.90
139	A26	15c dp p yel ('13)	20.00	12.00
140	A20	20c de p blue grn	2.25	.90
141	A19	50c de p red	3.25	2.25
142	A19	50c de p org yel ('13)	20.00	12.00
143	A27	1p claret	7.25	4.50
144	A27	1p red ('13)	13.00	11.00
		Nos. 125-144 (20)	255.75	207.90

All 1906 values exist imperf. These are plate proofs.

For overprints and surcharges see Nos. 177-195, 213-216, 239, 245, 249-260, 263, 265-277, 279-284, 286-301, 304.

Nord-Alexis A28

Coat of Arms — A29

For Domestic Postage (centimes de gourde)

1906-10

No.	Type	Description	Unused	Used
145	A28	1c de g blue	.35	.25
146	A29	2c de g org yel	.45	.25
147	A29	2c de g lemon ('10)	.65	.25
148	A28	3c de g slate	.40	.25
149	A29	7c de g green	1.25	.45
		Nos. 145-149 (5)	3.10	1.45

For overprints see Nos. 196-197.

Regular Issue of 1904 Handstamp Surcharged in Red like Nos. 108-109

1907

No.	Type	Description	Unused	Used
150	A18	1c on 5c dk bl	.40	.35
151	A18	1c on 20c org	.40	.25
152	A18	2c on 10c org brn	.40	.40
153	A18	2c on 50c claret	.50	.40

Black Surcharge

No.	Type	Description	Unused	Used
154	A18	1c on 5c dk bl	.50	.40
155	A18	1c on 10c org brn	.50	.25
156	A18	2c on 20c org	.40	.40

Brown Surcharge

No.	Type	Description	Unused	Used
157	A18	1c on 5c dk bl	1.50	1.25
158	A18	1c on 10c org brn	1.50	1.25
159	A18	2c on 20c org	5.00	4.00
160	A18	2c on 50c claret	27.50	22.50

Violet Surcharge

No.	Type	Description	Unused	Used
161	A18	1c on 20c org	150.00	

The handstamps are found sideways, diagonal, inverted and double.

Forgeries exist.

A30

President Antoine T. Simon — A31

1910 For Foreign Postage

No.	Type	Description	Unused	Used
162	A30	2c de p rose red & blk	.65	.50
163	A30	5c de p bl & blk	13.00	1.00
164	A30	20c de p yel grn & blk	12.50	12.50

For Domestic Postage

No.	Type	Description	Unused	Used
165	A31	1c de g lake & blk	.30	.25
		Nos. 162-165 (4)	26.45	14.25

For overprint and surcharges see Nos. 198, 262, 278, 285.

A32

A33

Pres. Cincinnatus Leconte — A34

1912

No.	Type	Description	Unused	Used
166	A32	1c de g car lake	.40	.40
167	A33	2c de g dp org	.50	.40

For Foreign Postage

No.	Type	Description	Unused	Used
168	A34	5c de p dp blue	.90	.40
		Nos. 166-168 (3)	1.80	1.20

For overprints see Nos. 199-201.

Stamps of Preceding Issues Handstamped Vertically

1914 On No. 61

No.	Type	Description	Unused	Used
169	A13	8c carmine	20.00	13.00

On Nos. 96-101

No.	Type	Description	Unused	Used
170	A18	1c green	47.50	35.00
171	A18	2c carmine	47.50	35.00
172	A18	5c dk blue	.75	.50
173	A18	10c orange brn	.75	.50

174 A18 20c orange 1.25 .60
175 A18 50c claret 3.00 1.50
Nos. 170-175 (6) 100.75 73.10

Perforation varieties of Nos. 172-175 exist.
No. 175 overprinted "T. M." is a revenue stamp. The letters are the initials of "Timbre Mobile."

On No. 107

176 A18 50c claret *10,000. 13,000.*

Horizontally on Stamps of 1906-13

177 A19 1c de p green .55 .45
178 A20 2c de p ver .75 .45
179 A21 3c de p brown 1.25 .65
180 A21 3c de p org yel .55 .45
181 A22 4c de p car lake 1.25 .65
182 A22 4c de p lt ol grn 3.00 1.60
183 A23 7c de p gray 2.75 2.75
184 A23 7c de p org red 7.25 6.75
185 A24 8c de p car rose 5.00 4.50
186 A24 8c de p ol grn 9.25 9.00
187 A25 10c de p org red 1.50 .65
188 A25 10c de p red brn 4.00 2.50
189 A26 15c de p sl grn 4.25 3.75
190 A26 15c de p yellow 3.00 1.60
191 A20 20c de p bl grn 3.75 1.40
192 A19 50c de p red 6.50 6.00
193 A19 50c de p org yel 11.00 10.00
194 A27 1p claret 6.50 6.00
195 A27 1p red 12.00 11.00
196 A29 2c de g lemon .55 .45
197 A28 3c de g slate .55 .45
Nos. 177-197 (21) 85.20 71.05

On No. 164

198 A30 20c de p yel grn & blk 3.75 3.50

Vertically on Nos. 166-168

199 A32 1c de g car lake .50 .40
200 A33 2c de g dp org .65 .50
201 A34 5c de p dp blue 1.10 .40
Nos. 199-201 (3) 2.25 1.30

Two handstamps were used for the overprints on Nos. 169-201. They may be distinguished by the short and long foot of the "L" of "GL" and the position of the first "1" in "1914" with regard to the period above it. Both handstamps are found on all but Nos. 176, 294, 295, 306, 308.

Handstamp Surcharged

On Nos. 141 and 143

213 A19 1c de p on 50c de p red .50 .40
214 A27 1c de p on 1p claret .65 .50

On Nos. 142 and 144

215 A19 1c de p on 50c de p org yel .65 .50
216 A27 1c de p on 1p red .65 .50

Handstamp Surcharged

On Nos. 100 and 101

217 A18 7c on 20c orange .50 .25
218 A18 7c on 50c claret .45 .25

The initials on the preceding handstamps are those of Gen. Oreste Zamor; the date is that of his triumphal entry into Port-au-Prince.

Pres. Oreste Zamor

Coat of Arms

Pres. Tancrède Auguste

Owing to the theft of a large quantity of this 1914 issue, while in transit from the printers, the stamps were never placed on sale at post offices. A few stamps have been canceled through carelessness of favor. Value, set of 10, $8.50.

Preceding Issues Handstamp Surcharged in Carmine or Blue

1915-16 — On Nos. 98-101

235 A18 1c on 5c dk bl (C) 2.00 2.25
236 A18 1c on 10c org brn .60 .75
237 A18 1c on 20c orange .60 .75
238 A18 1c on 50c claret .60 .75

On No. 132

239 A23 1c on 7c de p gray (C) .60 .75

On Nos. 106-107

240 A18 1c on 20c orange 1.50 1.50
241 A18 1c on 50c claret 3.50 1.50
242 A18 1c on 50c cl (C) *125.00 150.00*
Nos. 235-242 (8) 134.40 158.25

Nos. 240-242 are known with two types of the "Post Paye" overprint. No. 237 with red surcharge and any stamps with violet surcharge are unofficial.

> Values for Nos. 245-308 are for examples with the boxed "Gourde" surcharge partially on the stamp. Examples upon which this surcharge is fully present on the stamp command substantial premiums.

No. 143 Handstamp Surcharged in Red

1917-19

245 A27 2c on 1p claret .50 .50

Stamps of 1906-14 Handstamp Surcharged in Various Colors

1c, 5c

On Nos. 123-124

247 A12 1c on 50c (R) 90.00 40.00
248 A12 1c on 1g (R) 90.00 40.00

On #127, 129, 134, 136, 138, 140-141

249 A22 1c on 4c de p (Br) .65 .75
250 A25 1c on 10c de p (Bl) .65 .75
252 A20 1c on 20c de p (R) .65 .75
253 A20 1c on 20c de p (Bk) .65 .75
254 A19 1c on 50c de p (R) .65 .75
255 A19 1c on 50c de p (Bk) .65 .75
256 A21 2c on 3c de p (R) .65 .75
257 A24 2c on 8c de p (R) .65 .75
258 A24 2c on 8c de p (Bk) .65 .75
259 A26 2c on 15c de p (R) .65 .75
260 A20 2c on 20c de p (R) .65 .75
Nos. 249-260 (11) 7.15 8.25

The 1c on 10c de p stamp in black is actually a blue ink which bled into the stamps.

On Nos. 164, 128

262 A30 1c on 20c de p (Bk) 3.75 3.50
263 A21 2c on 3c de p (R) .60 .75

On #130, 133, 135, 137, 139, 142, 144

265 A22 1c on 4c de p (R) .70 .85
266 A23 1c on 7c de p (Br) .70 .85
267 A26 1c on 15c de p (R) .70 .85
268 A19 1c on 50c de p (Bk) 2.25 2.75
269 A27 1c on 1p (Bk) 2.25 2.75
270 A24 2c on 8c de p (R) .70 .85
271 A25 2c on 10c de p (Br) .70 .85
272 A26 2c on 15c de p (R) .70 .85
274 A25 5c on 10c de p (Bk) .70 .85
275 A26 5c on 15c de p (R) 5.50 6.75
Nos. 265-275 (10) 14.90 18.20

"O. Z." Stamps of 1914 Handstamp Surcharged in Red or Brown

276 A26 1c on 15c de p sl grn .70 .85
277 A20 1c on 20c de p bl grn .70 .85
278 A30 1c on 20c de p yel grn & blk .70 .85
279 A27 1c on 1p claret (Br) .70 .85
280 A27 1c on 1p claret 2.25 2.75
281 A27 5c on 1p red (Br) .70 .85
Nos. 276-281 (6) 5.75 7.00

Srchd. in Violet, Green, Red, Magenta or Black 1 ct and 2 cts as in 1917-19 and

1919-20

282 A22 2c on 4c de p car lake (V) .70 .85
283 A24 2c on 8c de p car rose (G) .70 .85
284 A24 2c on 8c de p ol grn (R) .70 .85
285 A30 2c on 20c de p yel grn & blk (R) .85 1.10
286 A19 2c on 50c de p red (G) .70 .85
288 A19 2c on 50c de p red (R) .70 .85
289 A19 2c on 50c de p org yel (R) .70 .85
290 A27 2c on 1p claret (R) 3.50 4.00
291 A27 2c on 1p red (R) 2.25 2.75
292 A21 3c on 3c de p brn (R) .70 .85
293 A23 3c on 7c de p org red (R) .70 .85
294 A21 5c on 3c de p brn (R) .70 .85
295 A21 5c on 3c de p org yel (R) 2.25 2.75
296 A22 5c on 4c de p car lake (R) .70 .85
297 A22 5c on 4c de p ol grn (R) .70 .85
298 A23 5c on 7c de p gray (V) .70 .85
299 A23 5c on 7c de p org red (V) .70 .85
300 A25 5c on 10c de p org red (V) .70 .85
301 A26 5c on 15c de p yel (M) .70 .85
Nos. 282-301 (19) 19.35 23.35

Nos. 217 and 218 Handstamp Surcharged with New Value in Magenta

302 A18 5c on 7c on 20c orange .60 .75
303 A18 5c on 7c on 50c claret 3.50 4.00

No. 187 Handstamp Surcharged in Magenta

304 A25 5c de p on 10c de p .60 .75

Postage Due Stamps of 1906-14 Handstamp Surcharged in Black or Magenta (#308)

On Stamp of 1906

305 D2 5c on 50c ol gray 15.00 15.00

On Stamp of 1914

306 D2 5c on 10c violet .60 .75
307 D2 5c on 50c olive gray .60 .75
308 D2 5c on 50c ol gray (M) 2.50 2.00
Nos. 305-308 (4) 18.70 18.50

Nos. 299 with red surcharge and 306-307 with violet are trial colors or essays.

Allegory of Agriculture A40

Allegory of Commerce A41

1920, Apr. — Engr. — *Perf. 12*

310 A40 3c deep orange .40 .40
311 A40 5c green .40 .40
312 A41 10c vermilion .50 .40
313 A41 15c violet .50 .40
314 A41 25c deep blue .65 .50
Nos. 310-314 (5) 2.45 2.10
Set, never hinged 18.50

Nos. 311-313 overprinted "T. M." are revenue stamps. The letters are the initials of "Timbre Mobile."

President Louis J. Borno — A42

Christophe's Citadel — A43

Old Map of West Indies — A44

Borno — A45

National Capitol — A46

1924, Sept. 3

315 A42 5c deep green .40 .25
316 A43 10c carmine .40 .25
317 A44 20c violet blue .90 .40
318 A45 50c orange & blk .90 .40
319 A46 1g olive green 1.60 .50
Nos. 315-319 (5) 4.20 1.80
Set, never hinged 25.00

For surcharges see Nos. 359, C4A.

Coffee Beans and Flowers — A47

1928, Feb. 6

320 A47 35c deep green 3.75 .60

For surcharge see No. 337.

Pres. Louis Borno — A48

1929, Nov. 4

321 A48 10c carmine rose .50 .40

Signing of the "Frontier" treaty between Haiti and the Dominican Republic.

Presidents Salomon and Vincent — A49

Pres. Sténio Vincent — A50

1931, Oct. 16

322 A49 5c deep green 1.30 .50
323 A50 10c carmine rose 1.30 .50

50th anniv. of Haiti's joining the UPU.

President Vincent — A52

Aqueduct at Port-au-Prince A53

Fort National — A54

Palace of Sans Souci — A55

Christophe's Chapel at Milot — A56

King's Gallery, Citadel — A57

Vallières Battery — A58

1933-40

325 A52 3c orange .30 .25
326 A52 3c dp ol grn ('39) .30 .25
327 A53 5c green .30 .25
a. 5c emerald ('38) .30 .25
b. 5c bright green ('39) .30 .25
c. 5c brown olive ('40) .50 .25
329 A54 10c rose car .50 .25
a. 10c vermilion .65 .25
330 A54 10c red brn ('40) .50 .25
331 A55 25c blue .90 .25
332 A56 50c brown 2.50 .55
333 A57 1g dark green 2.50 .55
334 A58 2.50g olive bister 4.50 .90
Nos. 325-334 (9) 12.30 3.50
Set, never hinged 70.00

For surcharges see Nos. 357-358, 360.

Alexandre Dumas, His Father and Son — A59

1935, Dec. 29 Litho. *Perf. 11½*

335 A59 10c rose pink & choc .90 .40
336 A59 25c blue & chocolate 1.60 .50
Nos. 335-336,C10 (3) 7.00 3.40
Set, never hinged 70.00

Visit of a delegation from France to Haiti.
No. 335 exists imperf and in horiz. pair, imperf. between. No. 336 exists as pair, imperf horiz.

No. 320 Surcharged in Red

1939, Jan. 24 *Perf. 12*

337 A47 25c on 35c dp grn .90 .40

Statue of Liberty, Map of Haiti and Flags of American Republics A60

1941, June 30 Engr. *Perf. 12*

338 A60 10c rose carmine 1.00 .50
339 A60 25c dark blue .90 .40
Nos. 338-339,C12-C13 (4) 8.40 2.40
Set, never hinged 25.00

3rd Inter-American Caribbean Conf., held at Port-au-Prince.

Patroness of Haiti, Map and Coat of Arms — A61

1942, Dec. 8 Size: 26x36¼mm

340 A61 3c dull violet .40 .25
341 A61 5c brt green .50 .25
342 A61 10c rose car .50 .25
343 A61 15c orange .65 .50
344 A61 20c brown .65 .50
345 A61 25c deep blue 1.40 .50
346 A61 50c red orange 1.75 .70
347 A61 2.50g olive black 4.75 1.10

Size: 32x45mm

348 A61 5g purple 14.00 9.00
Nos. 340-348,C14-C18 (14) 30.30 15.10
Set, never hinged 80.00

Issued in honor of Our Lady of Perpetual Help, patroness of Haiti.
For surcharges see Nos. 355-356.

Adm. Hammerton Killick and Destruction of "La Crête-à-Pierrot" — A62

1943, Sept. 6

349 A62 3c orange .40 .25
350 A62 5c turq green .50 .40
351 A62 10c carmine rose .50 .40
352 A62 25c deep blue .65 .40
353 A62 50c olive 1.40 .50
354 A62 5g brown black 5.75 3.00
Nos. 349-354,C22-C23 (8) 11.45 6.95
Set, never hinged 40.00

Nos. 343 and 345 Surcharged with New Value and Bars in Red

1944, July 19

355 A61 10c on 15c orange .40 .25
356 A61 10c on 25c dp blue .40 .25
Set, never hinged 10.00

Nos. 319, 326 and 334 Surcharged with New Values and Bars in Red

1944-45

357 A52 2c on 3c dp ol grn .30 .25
358 A52 5c on 3c dp ol grn .40 .40
359 A46 10c on 1g ol grn .50 .40
a. Surcharged "01.0" 1.50 *3.00*
360 A58 20c on 2.50g ol bis .50 .40
Nos. 357-360 (4) 1.70 1.45
Set, never hinged 20.00

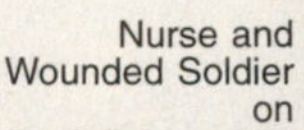

Nurse and Wounded Soldier on Battlefield — A63

1945, Feb. 20 Cross in Rose

361 A63 3c gray black .25 .25
362 A63 5c dk blue grn .25 .25
363 A63 10c red orange .30 .25
364 A63 20c black brn .30 .25
365 A63 25c deep blue .40 .25
366 A63 35c orange .50 .25
367 A63 50c car rose .50 .25
368 A63 1g olive green .90 .40
369 A63 2.50g pale violet 2.50 .50
Nos. 361-369,C25-C32 (17) 18.75 7.55
Set, never hinged 80.00

Issued to honor the Intl. Red Cross. 20c, 1g, 2.50g, Aug. 14. Others, Feb. 20.
For overprints and surcharges see Nos. 456-457, C153-C160.

Catalogue values for unused stamps in this section, from this point to the end of the section, are for Never Hinged items.

Col. François Capois — A64

Unwmk.

1946, July 18 Engr. *Perf. 12*

370 A64 3c red orange .25 .25
371 A64 5c Prus green .25 .25
372 A64 10c red .25 .25
373 A64 20c olive black .25 .25
374 A64 25c deep blue .30 .25
375 A64 35c orange .40 .25
376 A64 50c red brown .50 .40
377 A64 1g olive brown .50 .40
378 A64 2.50g gray 1.30 .50
Nos. 370-378,C35-C42 (17) 9.60 6.15

For surcharges see Nos. 383, 392, C43-C45, C49-C51, C61-C62. For overprint see Nos. 483, Q4.

Jean Jacques Dessalines — A65

1947-54

379 A65 3c orange yel .25 .25
380 A65 5c green .25 .25
380A A65 5c dp vio ('54) .65 .25
381 A65 10c carmine rose .25 .25
382 A65 25c deep blue .40 .25
Nos. 379-382,C46 (6) 2.20 1.50

No. 375 Surcharged with New Value and Rectangular Block in Black

1948

383 A64 10c on 35c orange .40 .25

Arms of Port-au-Prince A66

Engraved and Lithographed

1950, Feb. 12 *Perf. 12½*

384 A66 10c multicolored .40 .25
Nos. 384,C47-C48 (3) 2.20 1.25

200th anniv. (in 1949) of the founding of Port-au-Prince.

Nos. RA10-RA12 and RA16 Surcharged or Overprinted in Black

1950, Oct. 4 Unwmk. *Perf. 12*

No.	Type	Description	Unused	Used
385	PT2	3c on 5c ol gray	.25	.25
386	PT2	5c green	.40	.25
387	PT2	10c on 5c car rose	.40	.25
388	PT2	20c on 5c blue	.50	.50
		Nos. 385-388,C49-C51 (7)	4.30	3.55

75th anniv. (in 1949) of the UPU.

Exist with inverted or double surcharge and 10c on 5c green.

Cacao — A67

1951, Sept. 3 Photo. *Perf. 12½*

No.	Type	Description	Unused	Used
389	A67	5c dark green	.40	.25
		Nos. 389,C52-C54 (4)	27.15	4.75

Pres. Paul E. Magloire and Day Nursery, Saline — A68

Design: 10c, Applying asphalt.

1953, May 4 Engr. *Perf. 12*

No.	Type	Description	Unused	Used
390	A68	5c green	.25	.25
391	A68	10c rose carmine	.30	.25
		Nos. 390-391,C57-C60 (6)	3.80	2.35

No. 375 Surcharged in Black

1953, Apr. 7

No.	Type	Description	Unused	Used
392	A64	50c on 35c orange	.50	.40

Gen. Pierre Dominique Toussaint L'Ouverture, 1743-1803, liberator.

J. J. Dessalines and Paul E. Magloire — A69

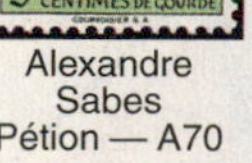

Alexandre Sabes Pétion — A70

Battle of Vertieres — A71

Design: No. 395, Larmartiniere. No. 396, Boisrond-Tonnerre. No. 397, Toussaint L'Ouverture. No. 399, Capois. No. 401, Marie Jeanne and Lamartiniere leading attack.

1954, Jan. 1 Photo. *Perf. 11½*

Portraits in Black

No.	Type	Description	Unused	Used
393	A69	3c blue gray	.25	.25
394	A70	5c yellow green	.30	.25
395	A70	5c yellow green	.30	.25
396	A70	5c yellow green	.40	.30
397	A70	5c yellow green	.30	.25
398	A69	10c crimson	.30	.25
399	A70	15c rose lilac	.40	.25
		Perf. 12½		
400	A71	25c dark gray	.40	.25
401	A71	25c deep orange	.40	.25
		Nos. 393-401 (9)	3.05	2.30
		Nos. 393-401,C63-C70,C71-C74 (21)	14.90	10.65

150th anniv. of Haitian independence. See Nos. C95-C96.

Mme. Yolette Magloire — A72

1954, Jan. 1 *Perf. 11½*

No.	Type	Description	Unused	Used
402	A72	10c orange	.30	.25
403	A72	10c blue	.30	.25
		Nos. 402-403,C75-C80 (8)	6.75	5.20

Henri Christophe, Paul Magloire and Citadel A73

Tomb and Arms of Henri Christophe — A74

Perf. 13½x13

1954, Dec. 6 Litho. Unwmk.

No.	Type	Description	Unused	Used
404	A73	10c carmine	.25	.25
		Perf. 13		
405	A74	10c red, blk & car	.30	.25
		Nos. 404-405,C81-C90 (12)	15.10	8.85

Restoration of Christophe's Citadel.

J. J. Dessalines — A75

1955-57 Photo. *Perf. 11½*

No.	Type	Description	Unused	Used
406	A75	3c ocher & blk	.25	.25
407	A75	5c pale vio & blk ('56)	.25	.25
408	A75	10c rose & blk	.25	.25
a.		10c salmon pink & black ('57)	.25	.25
409	A75	25c chalky bl & blk ('56)	.30	.25
a.		25c blue & black ('57)	.30	.25
		Nos. 406-409,C93-C94 (6)	1.55	1.50

For surcharges, see Nos. 454-455.

Pres. Magloire and Dessalines Memorial, Gonaives — A76

1955, Aug. 1

No.	Type	Description	Unused	Used
410	A76	10c deep blue & blk	.40	.25
411	A76	10c crimson & blk	.40	.25
		Nos. 410-411,C97-C98 (4)	2.10	1.00

21st anniv. of the new Haitian army.

Nos. 410-411 were printed in a single sheet of 20 (5x4). The two upper rows are of No. 410, the two lower No. 411, providing five se-tenant pairs. Value 85 cents.

Flamingo A77

Mallard A78

1956, Apr. 14 Photo. *Perf. 11½*

Granite Paper

No.	Type	Description	Unused	Used
412	A77	10c blue & ultra	2.25	.30
413	A78	25c dk grn & bluish grn	3.25	.45
		Nos. 412-413,C99-C104 (8)	43.40	6.80

Immanuel Kant — A79

1956, July 19 *Perf. 12*

Granite Paper

No.	Type	Description	Unused	Used
414	A79	10c brt ultra	.30	.25
		Nos. 414,C105-C107 (4)	2.45	1.40

10th anniv. of the 1st Inter-American Philosophical Congress.

Zim Waterfall — A80

1957, Dec. 16 Unwmk. *Perf. 11½*

Granite Paper

No.	Type	Description	Unused	Used
415	A80	10c orange & blue	.30	.25
		Nos. 415,C108-C111 (5)	4.70	3.00

For surcharge & overprint see Nos. CB49, CQ2.

J. J. Dessalines and Dessalines Memorial, Gonaives — A81

1958, July 1 Photo.

No.	Type	Description	Unused	Used
416	A81	5c yel grn & blk	.25	.25

Bicentenary of birth of J. J. Dessalines.

See Nos. 470-471, C112, C170. For overprints see Nos. 480-482, C183-C184, CQ1, Q1-Q3.

"Atomium" — A82

View of Brussels Exposition A83

Perf. 13x13½, 13½x13

1958, July 22 Litho. Unwmk.

No.	Type	Description	Unused	Used
417	A82	50c brown	.40	.25
418	A83	75c brt green	.40	.25
419	A82	1g purple	.75	.25
420	A83	1.50g red orange	.75	.40
		Nos. 417-420,C113-C114 (6)	5.05	2.50

Issued for the Universal and International Exposition at Brussels.

For surcharges see Nos. B2-B3, CB9.

Sylvio Cator — A84

1958, Aug. 16 Photo. *Perf. 11½*

Granite Paper

No.	Type	Description	Unused	Used
421	A84	5c green	.25	.25
422	A84	10c brown	.25	.25
423	A84	20c lilac	.25	.25
		Nos. 421-423,C115-C118 (7)	4.15	2.50

30th anniversary of the world championship record broad jump of Sylvio Cator.

U. S. Satellite — A85

Designs: 20c, Emperor penguins. 50c, Modern observatory. 1g, Ocean exploration.

1958, Oct. 8 *Perf. 14x13½*

No.	Type	Description	Unused	Used
424	A85	10c brt bl & brn red	.30	.25
425	A85	20c black & dp org	1.40	.50
426	A85	50c grn & rose brn	.75	.30
427	A85	1g black & blue	.80	.30
		Nos. 424-427,C119-C121 (7)	9.35	2.75

Issued for the International Geophysical Year 1957-58.

President François Duvalier — A86

Engraved and Lithographed

1958, Oct. 22 Unwmk. *Perf. 11½*

Commemorative Inscription in Ultramarine

No.	Type	Description	Unused	Used
428	A86	10c blk & dp pink	.30	.25
429	A86	50c blk & lt grn	.40	.25
430	A86	1g blk & brick red	.50	.40
431	A86	5g blk & sal	2.40	1.50
		Nos. 428-431,C122-C125 (8)	10.90	6.50

1st anniv. of the inauguration of Pres. Dr. François Duvalier. See note on souvenir sheets after No. C125.

1958 Nov. 20

Without Commemorative Inscription

No.	Type	Description	Unused	Used
432	A86	5c blk & lt vio bl	.25	.25
433	A86	10c blk & dp pink	.25	.25
434	A86	20c blk & yel	.25	.25
435	A86	50c blk & lt grn	.30	.25
436	A86	1g blk & brick red	.50	.40
437	A86	1.50g blk & rose pink	.65	.50
438	A86	2.50g blk & gray vio	.90	.50
439	A86	5g blk & sal	1.60	1.10
		Nos. 432-439,C126-C132 (15)	13.35	8.15

For surcharges see Nos. B13, B22-B24.

Map of Haiti — A87

1958, Dec. 5 Photo. *Perf. 11½*

Granite Paper

440 A87 10c rose pink	.25	.25
441 A87 25c green	.30	.25
Nos. 440-441,C133-C135 (5)	1.85	1.40

Tribute to the UN. See No. C135a. For overprints and surcharges see Nos. 442-443, B4-B5, CB11-CB12.

Nos. 440-441 Overprinted

Overprint reads "10th ANNIVERSARY OF THE / UNIVERSAL DECLARATION / OF HUMAN RIGHTS" in: a, English; b, French; c, Spanish; d, Portuguese.

1959, Jan. 28

442 Block of 4	.35	.35
a.-d. A87 10c any single	.25	.25
443 Block of 4	.90	.70
a.-d. A87 25c any single	.25	.25
Nos. 442-443,C136-C138 (5)	14.75	14.55

10th anniv. of the signing of the Universal Declaration of Human Rights.

Pope Pius XII and Children — A88

50c, Pope praying. 2g, Pope on throne.

1959, Feb. 28 Photo. *Perf. 14x13½*

444 A88 10c vio bl & ol	.25	.25
445 A88 50c green & dp brn	.40	.25
446 A88 2g dp claret & dk brn	.90	.50
Nos. 444-446,C139-C141 (6)	3.45	2.05

Issued in memory of Pope Pius XII.
For surcharges see Nos. B6-B8.

Abraham Lincoln — A89

1959, May 12 Photo. *Perf. 12*

447 A89 50c lt bl & deep claret	.40	.25
Nos. 447,C142-C144 (4)	2.50	1.55

Sesquicentennial of the birth of Abraham Lincoln. Imperf. pairs exist.
For surcharges see No. B9, CB16-CB18.

Chicago's Skyline and Dessables House — A90

Jean Baptiste Dessables and Map of American Midwest, c. 1791 — A91

Design: 50c, Discus thrower and flag of Haiti.

1959, Aug. 27 Unwmk. *Perf. 14*

448 A90 25c blk brn & lt bl	.40	.25
449 A90 50c multicolored	.50	.40
450 A91 75c brown & blue	.65	.50
Nos. 448-450,C145-C147 (6)	4.70	2.30

3rd Pan American Games, Chicago, 8/27-9/7.

For surcharges see Nos. B10-B12, CB19-CB21.

No. 449 Overprinted

1960, Feb. 29

451 A90 50c multicolored	1.60	1.20
Nos. 451,C148-C150 (4)	7.65	7.25

8th Olympic Winter Games, Squaw Valley, Calif., Feb. 18-29, 1960.

Uprooted Oak Emblem and Hands — A92

1960, Apr. 7 Litho. *Perf. 12½x13*

452 A92 10c salmon & grn	.25	.25
453 A92 50c violet & mag	.40	.25
Nos. 452-453,C151-C152 (4)	1.55	1.15

World Refugee Year, July 1, 1959-June 30, 1960. See Nos. 489-490, C191-C192. For surcharges see Nos. B14-B17, B28-B29, CB24-CB27, CB45-CB46.

No. 406 Surcharged with New Values

1960, Apr. 27 Photo. *Perf. 11½*

454 A75 5c on 3c ocher & blk	.25	.25
455 A75 10c on 3c ocher & blk	.35	.25

No. 369 Surcharged or Overprinted in Red: "28eme ANNIVERSAIRE"

1960, May 8 Engr. *Perf. 12*

Cross in Rose

456 A63 1g on 2.50g pale vio	.90	.50
457 A63 2.50g pale violet	1.40	1.00
Nos. 456-457,C153-C160 (10)	7.30	5.35

28th anniversary of the Haitian Red Cross.

Claudinette Fouchard, Miss Haiti, Sugar Queen — A93

Sugar Queen and: 20c, Sugar harvest. 50c, Beach. 1g, Sugar plantation.

Perf. 11½

1960, May 30 Photo. Unwmk.

Granite Paper

458 A93 10c ol bis & vio	.25	.25
459 A93 20c red brn & blk	.30	.25
460 A93 50c brt bl & brn	.75	.25
461 A93 1g green & brn	1.75	.25
Nos. 458-461,C161-C162 (6)	6.20	1.75

Haitian sugar industry.

Olympic Victors, Athens, 1896, Melbourne Stadium and Olympic Flame A94

Designs: 20c, Discus thrower and Rome stadium. 50c, Pierre de Coubertin and victors, Melbourne, 1956. 1g, Athens stadium, 1896.

1960, Aug. 18 Photo. *Perf. 12*

462 A94 10c black & org	.25	.25
463 A94 20c dk blue & crim	.25	.25
464 A94 50c green & ocher	.65	.25
465 A94 1g dk brn & grnsh bl	.80	.65
Nos. 462-465,C163-C165 (7)	5.60	2.50

17th Olympic Games, Rome, Aug. 25-Sept. 11. For surcharges see Nos. B18-B19, CB28-CB29.

Occide Jeanty and Score from "1804" A95

20c, Occide Jeanty and National Capitol.

1960, Oct. 19 *Perf. 14x14½*

466 A95 10c orange & red lilac	.25	.25
467 A95 20c blue & red lilac	.35	.25
468 A95 50c green & sepia	.50	.40
Nos. 466-468,C166-C167 (5)	2.35	1.40

Cent. of the birth of Occide Jeanty, composer. Printed in sheets of 12 (3x4) with commemorative inscription and opening bars of "1804," Jeanty's military march, in top margin.

UN Headquarters, NYC — A96

1960, Nov. 25 Engr. *Perf. 10½*

469 A96 1g green & blk	.50	.40
Nos. 469,C168-C169 (3)	1.40	1.05

15th anniv. of the UN.
No. 469 exists with center inverted.
For surcharges see Nos. B20-B21, CB30-CB31, CB35-CB36.

Dessalines Type of 1958

Perf. 11½

1960, Nov. 5 Unwmk. Photo.

Granite Paper

470 A81 10c red org & blk	.25	.25
471 A81 25c ultra & blk	.35	.25
Nos. 470-471,C170 (3)	.85	.75

Alexandre Dumas Père and Musketeer — A97

5c, Map of Haiti & birthplace of General Alexandre Dumas, horiz. 50c, Alexandre Dumas, father & son, French & Haitian flags, horiz.

1961, Feb. 10 *Perf. 11½*

Granite Paper

472 A97 5c lt blue & choc	.25	.25
473 A97 10c rose, blk & sep	.25	.25
474 A97 50c dk blue & crim	.40	.25
Nos. 472-474,C177-C179 (6)	3.35	1.60

Gen. Dumas (Alexandre Davy de la Pailleterie), born in Jeremie, Haiti, and his son and grandson, French authors.

Three Pirates — A98

Tourist publicity: 5c, Map of Tortuga. 15c, Pirates. 20c, Privateer in battle. 50c, Pirate with cutlass in rigging.

1961, Apr. 4 Litho. *Perf. 12*

475 A98 5c blue & yel	.25	.25
476 A98 10c lake & yel	.25	.25
477 A98 15c ol grn & org	.25	.25
478 A98 20c choc & org	.30	.25
479 A98 50c vio bl & org	.40	.25
Nos. 475-479,C180-C182 (8)	2.75	2.15

For surcharges and overprints see Nos. 484-485, C186-C187.

Nos. 416, 470-471 and 378 Overprinted: "Dr. F. Duvalier / Président / 22 Mai 1961"

1961, May 22 Photo. *Perf. 11½*

480 A81 5c yel grn & blk	.25	.25
481 A81 10c red org & blk	.25	.25
482 A81 25c ultra & blk	.25	.25

Engr.

Perf. 12

483 A64 2.50g gray	1.10	.60
Nos. 480-483,C183-C185 (7)	2.75	2.25

Re-election of Pres. Francois Duvalier.

No. 475 Surcharged: "EXPLORATION SPATIALE JOHN GLENN," Capsule

1962, May 10 Litho.

484 A98 50c on 5c bl & yel	.50	.40
485 A98 1.50g on 5c bl & yel	1.40	1.00
Nos. 484-485,C186-C187 (4)	3.80	2.80

U.S. achievement in space exploration and for the 1st orbital flight of a US astronaut, Lt. Col. John H. Glenn, Jr., Feb. 20, 1962.

Malaria Eradication Emblem — A99

Design: 10c, Triangle pointing down.

Unwmk.

1962, May 30 Litho. *Perf. 12*

486 A99 5c crimson & dp bl .25 .25
487 A99 10c red brn & emer .25 .25
488 A99 50c blue & crimson .40 .25
Nos. 486-488,C188-C190 (6) 2.05 1.65

WHO drive to eradicate malaria.

Sheets of 12 with marginal inscription.

For surcharges see Nos. B25-B27, CB42-CB44.

WRY Type of 1960 Dated "1962"

1962, June 22 *Perf. 12½x13*

489 A92 10c lt blue & org .25 .25
490 A92 50c rose lil & ol grn .40 .40
Nos. 489-490,C191-C192 (4) 1.40 1.30

Issued to publicize the plight of refugees. For souvenir sheet see note after Nos. C191-C192.

Haitian Scout Emblem — A100

5c, 50c, Scout giving Scout sign. 10c, Lord and Lady Baden-Powell, horiz.

Perf. 14x14½, 14½x14

1962, Aug. 6 Photo.

491 A100 3c blk, ocher & pur .25 .25
492 A100 5c cit, red brn & blk .25 .25
493 A100 10c ocher, blk & grn .25 .25
494 A100 25c maroon, ol & bl .25 .25
495 A100 50c violet, grn & red .40 .25
Nos. 491-495,C193-C195 (8) 2.80 2.30

22nd anniv. of the Haitian Boy Scouts.

For surcharges and overprints see Nos. B31-B34, C196-C199.

TIMBRE MOBILE, etc.

From 1970 through 1979 postage and airmail stamps were overprinted for use as revenue stamps. The overprints used were: "TIMBRE MOBILE," "TIMBRE DE SOLIDARITE," "SOLIDARITE," "TIMBRE SOLIDARITE," "OBLIGATION PELIGRE."

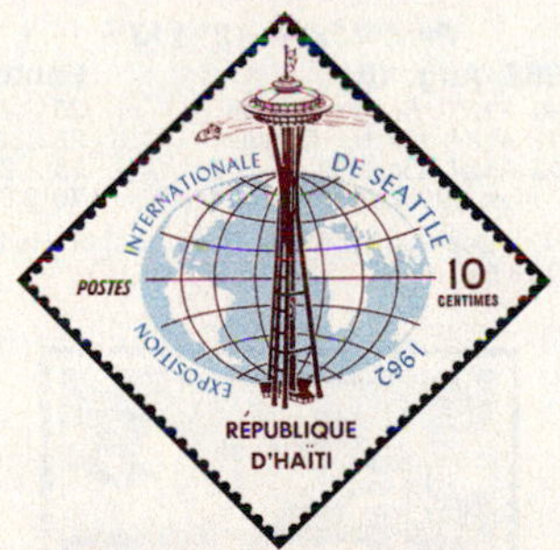

Space Needle, Space Capsule and Globe — A101

1962, Nov. 19 Litho. *Perf. 12½*

496 A101 10c red brn & lt bl .25 .25
497 A101 20c vio bl & pink .25 .25
498 A101 50c emerald & yel .40 .25
499 A101 1g car & lt grn .50 .40
Nos. 496-499,C200-C202 (7) 3.10 2.20

"Century 21" International Exposition, Seattle, Wash., Apr. 21-Oct. 21.

For overprints see Nos. 503-504, C206-C207.

Plan of Duvalier Ville and Stamp of 1904 — A102

1962, Dec. 10 Photo. *Perf. 14x14½*

500 A102 5c vio, yel & blk .25 .25
501 A102 10c car rose, yel & blk .25 .25
502 A102 25c bl gray, yel & blk .35 .25
Nos. 500-502,C203-C205 (6) 3.25 1.90

Issued to publicize Duvalier Ville.

For surcharge see No. B30.

Nos. 498-499 with Vertical Overprint in Black

1963, Jan. 23 Litho. *Perf. 12½*

503 A101 50c emerald & yel .65 .40
a. Claret overprint, horiz. .65 .40
504 A101 1g car & lt grn 1.40 .50
a. Claret overprint, horiz. 1.40 .50
Nos. 503-504,C206-C207 (4) 5.20 2.60
Nos. 503a-504a,C206a-C207a (4) 5.20 2.60

"Peaceful Uses of Outer Space." The black vertical overprint has no outside frame lines and no broken shading lines around capsule. Nos. 503a and 504a were issued Feb. 20.

Symbolic Harvest A103

1963, July 12 Photo. *Perf. 13x14*

505 A103 10c orange & blk .25 .25
506 A103 20c bluish grn & blk .25 .25
Nos. 505-506,C208-C209 (4) 1.40 1.15

FAO "Freedom from Hunger" campaign.

J. J. Dessalines — A104

1963, Oct. 17 *Perf. 14x14½*

507 A104 5c tan & ver .25 .25
508 A104 10c yellow & blue .25 .25
Nos. 507-508,C214-C215 (4) 1.00 1.00

For overprints see Nos. 509, C216-C217.

No. 508 Overprinted: "FETE DES MERES / 1964"

1964, July 22

509 A104 10c yellow & blue .25 .25
Nos. 509,C216-C218 (4) 1.65 1.15

Issued for Mother's Day, 1964.

Weight Lifter — A105

Design: 50c, Hurdler.

1964, Nov. 12 Photo. *Perf. 11½*

Granite Paper

510 A105 10c lt bl & dk brn .25 .25
511 A105 25c salmon & dk brn .25 .25
512 A105 50c pale rose lil & dk brn .40 .25
Nos. 510-512,C223-C226 (7) 2.85 2.15

18th Olympic Games, Tokyo, Oct. 10-25. Printed in sheets of 50 (10x5), with map of Japan in background extending over 27 stamps.

For surcharges see Nos. B35-B37, CB51-CB54.

Madonna of Haiti and International Airport, Port-au-Prince A106

1964, Dec. 15 *Perf. 14½x14*

513 A106 10c org yel & blk .25 .25
514 A106 25c bl grn & blk .25 .25
515 A106 50c brt yel grn & blk .40 .25
516 A106 1g vermilion & blk .50 .40
Nos. 513-516,C227-C229 (7) 3.85 2.45

Nos. 513-516 Overprinted in Black

1965, Feb. 11

517 A106 10c org, yel & blk .25 .25
518 A106 25c blue grn & blk .25 .25
519 A106 50c brt yel grn & blk .40 .25
520 A106 1g vermilion & blk .50 .40
Nos. 517-520,C230-C232 (7) 3.45 2.50

Unisphere, NY World's Fair — A107

20c, "Rocket Thrower" by Donald De Lue.

1965, Mar. 22 Photo. *Perf. 13½*

521 A107 10c grn, yel ol & dk red .25 .25
522 A107 20c plum & orange .25 .25
523 A107 50c dk brn, dk red, yel & grn .40 .25
Nos. 521-523,C233-C235 (6) 4.20 3.30

New York World's Fair, 1964-65.

Merchantmen — A108

1965, May 13 Unwmk. *Perf. 11½*

524 A108 10c blk, lt grn & red .25 .25
525 A108 50c blk, lt bl & red .40 .25
Nos. 524-525,C236-C237 (4) 1.80 1.25

The merchant marine.

ITU Emblem, Old and New Communication Equipment — A109

1965, Aug. 16 Litho. *Perf. 13½*

526 A109 10c gray & multi .25 .25
527 A109 25c multicolored .40 .25
528 A109 50c multicolored .50 .25
Nos. 526-528,C242-C245 (7) 4.55 2.50

Cent. of the ITU.

For overprints see Nos. 537-539, C255-C256.

Statue of Our Lady of the Assumption A110

Designs: 5c, Cathedral of Port-au-Prince, horiz. 10c, High altar.

Perf. 14x13, 13x14

1965, Nov. 19 Photo.

Size: 39x29mm, 29x39mm

529 A110 5c multicolored .25 .25
530 A110 10c multicolored .25 .25
531 A110 25c multicolored .30 .25
Nos. 529-531,C246-C248 (6) 4.60 3.65

200th anniv. of the Metropolitan Cathedral of Port-au-Prince.

Passionflower A111

Flowers: 5c, 15c, American elder. 10c, Okra.

1965, Dec. 20 Photo. *Perf. 11½*

Granite Paper

532 A111 3c dk vio, lt vio bl & grn .25 .25
533 A111 5c grn, lt bl & yel .25 .25
534 A111 10c multicolored .25 .25
a. "0.10" omitted
535 A111 15c grn, pink & yel .70 .25
536 A111 50c dk vio, yel & grn 1.40 1.10
Nos. 532-536,C249-C254 (11) 15.45 7.15

For surcharges see Nos. 566, B38-B40, CB55-CB56.

Nos. 526-528 Overprinted in Red: "20e. Anniversaire / UNESCO"

1965, Aug. 27 Litho. *Perf. 13½*

537 A109 10c gray & multi .30 .25
538 A109 25c yel brn & multi .35 .35
539 A109 50c pale grn & multi .70 .70
Nos. 537-539,C255-C256 (5) 5.35 2.65

20th anniversary of UNESCO.

Amulet — A112

Ceremonial Stool — A113

Perf. 14x½x14, 14x14½

1966, Mar. 14 Photo. Unwmk.

540 A112 5c grnsh bl, blk & yel .25 .25
541 A113 10c multi .25 .25
542 A112 50c scar, yel & blk .40 .25
Nos. 540-542,C257-C259 (6) 3.45 2.35

For overprints and surcharges see Nos. 543, 567-570, C260-C261, C280-C281.

No. 541 Overprinted in Red "Hommage / a Hailé Sélassiéler / 24-25 Avril 1966"

1966, Apr. 24

543 A113 10c multi .30 .25
Nos. 543,C260-C262 (4) 2.35 1.70

Visit of Emperor Haile Selassie of Ethiopia, Apr. 24-25.

Space Rendezvous of Gemini VI and VII, Dec. 15, 1965 A114

1966, May 3 *Perf. 13½*

544 A114 5c vio bl, brn & lt bl .25 .25
545 A114 10c pur, brn & lt bl .25 .25
546 A114 25c grn, brn & lt bl .30 .25
547 A114 50c dk red, brn & lt bl .40 .25
Nos. 544-547,C263-C265 (7) 2.75 2.15

Walter M. Schirra, Thomas P. Stafford, Frank A. Borman, James A. Lovell and Gemini VI.

For overprint see No. 584.

Soccer Ball within Wreath and Pres. Duvalier A115

Design: 10c, 50c, Soccer player within wreath and Duvalier.

Lithographed and Photogravure

1966, June 16 *Perf. 13x13½*

Portrait in Black; Gold Inscription; Green Commemorative Inscription in Two Lines

548 A115 5c pale sal & grn .25 .25
549 A115 10c lt ultra & grn .25 .25
550 A115 15c lt grn & grn .25 .25
551 A115 50c pale lil rose & grn .40 .25

Green Commemorative Inscription in 3 Lines; Gold Inscription Omitted

552 A115 5c pale sal & grn .25 .25
553 A115 10c lt ultra & grn .25 .25
554 A115 15c lt grn & grn .25 .25
555 A115 50c pale lil rose & grn .40 .25
Nos. 548-555,C266-C269 (12) 4.40 3.65

Caribbean Soccer Festival, June 10-22. Nos. 548-551 also for the Natl. Soccer Championships, May 8-22.

For surcharges and overprint see Nos. 578-579, C288, CB57.

"ABC," Boy and Girl — A116

10c, Scout symbols. 25c, Television set, book and communications satellite, horiz.

Perf. 14x13½, 13½x14

1966, Oct. 18 Litho. & Engr.

556 A116 5c grn, sal pink & brn .25 .25
557 A116 10c red brn, lt brn & blk .25 .25
558 A116 25c grn, bl & dk vio .25 .25
Nos. 556-558,C270-C272 (6) 2.30 1.90

Issued to publicize education through literacy, Scouting and by audio-visual means.

Dr. Albert Schweitzer, Maps of Alsace and Gabon — A117

Designs: 10c, Dr. Schweitzer and pipe organ. 20c, Dr. Schweitzer and Albert Schweitzer Hospital, Deschapelles, Haiti.

Perf. 12½x13

1967, Apr. 20 Photo. Unwmk.

559 A117 5c pale lil & multi .25 .25
560 A117 10c buff & multi .25 .25
561 A117 20c gray & multi .40 .25
Nos. 559-561,C273-C276 (7) 3.45 2.75

Issued in memory of Dr. Albert Schweitzer (1875-1965), medical missionary to Gabon, theologian and musician.

Watermelon and J. J. Dessalines — A118

1967, July 4 Photo. *Perf. 12½*

562 A118 5c shown .25 .25
563 A118 10c Cabbage .25 .25
564 A118 20c Tangerine 1.25 .25
565 A118 50c Chayote 2.00 .25
Nos. 562-565,C277-C279 (7) 11.25 5.75

No. 532 Surcharged

1967, Aug. 21 Photo. *Perf. 11½*

566 A111 50c on 3c multi .30 .25
Nos. 566,B38-B40,CB55-CB56 (6) 2.25 1.90

12th Boy Scout World Jamboree, Farragut State Park, Idaho, Aug. 1-9.

Nos. 540-542 Overprinted and Surcharged

Perf. 14½x14, 14x14½

1967, Aug. 30 Photo.

567 A112 5c grnsh bl, blk & yel .25 .25
568 A113 10c multi .25 .25
569 A112 50c scar, yel & blk .25 .25
570 A112 1g on 5c multi .50 .40
Nos. 567-570,C280-C281 (6) 2.60 2.10

EXPO '67 Intl. Exhibition, Montreal, 4/28-10/27.

Pres. Duvalier and Brush Turkey A119

1967, Sept. 22 Photo. *Perf. 14x13*

571 A119 5c car rose & gold .25 .25
572 A119 10c ultra & gold .25 .25
573 A119 25c dk red brn & gold .25 .25
574 A119 50c dp red lil & gold .40 .25
Nos. 571-574,C282-C284 (7) 3.40 2.60

10th anniversary of Duvalier revolution.

Writing Hands A120

Designs: 10c, Scout emblem and Scouts, vert. 25c, Audio-visual teaching of algebra.

1967, Dec. 11 Litho. *Perf. 11½*

575 A120 5c multicolored .25 .25
576 A120 10c multicolored .25 .25
577 A120 25c dk grn, lt bl & yel .25 .25
Nos. 575-577,C285-C287 (6) 2.15 1.90

Issued to publicize the importance of education.

For surcharges see Nos. CB58-CB60.

Nos. 552 and 554 Surcharged

Lithographed and Photogravure

1968, Jan. 18 *Perf. 13x13½*

578 A115 50c on 15c .85 .25
579 A115 1g on 5c 1.00 .85
Nos. 578-579,C288,CB57 (4) 6.50 4.60

19th Olympic Games, Mexico City, Oct. 12-27.

The 1968 date is missing on 2 stamps in every sheet of 50.

Caiman Woods, by Raoul Dupoux A121

1968, Apr. 22 Photo. *Perf. 12*

Size: 36x26mm

580 A121 5c multi .25 .25
581 A121 10c rose red & multi .25 .25
582 A121 25c multi .25 .25
583 A121 50c dl lil & multi .40 .25
Nos. 580-583,C289-C295 (11) 6.60 5.00

Caiman Woods ceremony during the Slaves' Rebellion, Aug. 14, 1791.

No. 547 Overprinted

1968, Apr. 19 Photo. *Perf. 13½*

584 A114 50c dk red, brn & lt bl .90 .80
Nos. 584,C296-C298 (4) 5.40 2.90

10th Winter Olympic Games, Grenoble, France, Feb. 6-18, 1968.

Monument to the Unknown Maroon — A122

1968, May 22 *Perf. 11½*

Granite Paper

585 A122 5c bl & blk .25 .25
586 A122 10c rose brn & blk .25 .25
587 A122 20c vio & blk .25 .25
588 A122 25c lt ultra & blk .25 .25
589 A122 50c brt bl grn & blk .40 .25
Nos. 585-589,C299-C301 (8) 3.10 2.40

Unveiling of the monument to the Unknown Maroon, Port-au-Prince.

For surcharges see Nos. 610 and C324-C325.

Palm Tree and Provincial Coats of Arms — A123

Madonna, Papal Arms and Arms of Haiti — A124

Design: 25c, Cathedral, arms of Pope Paul VI and arms of Haiti.

Perf. 13x14, 12½x13½

1968, Aug. 16 Photo.

590 A123 5c grn & multi .25 .25
591 A124 10c brn & multi .25 .25
592 A124 25c multi .25 .25
Nos. 590-592,C302-C305 (7) 3.70 3.00

Consecration of the Bishopric of Haiti, 10/28/66.

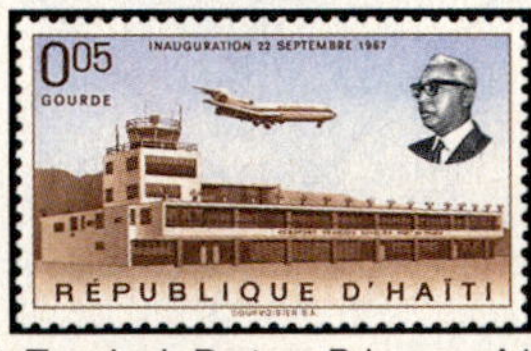

Air Terminal, Port-au-Prince — A125

1968, Sept. 22 Photo. *Perf. 11½*

Portrait in Black

593 A125 5c brn & lt ultra .25 .25
594 A125 10c brn & lt bl .25 .25
595 A125 25c brn & pale lil .25 .25
Nos. 593-595,C306-C308 (6) 2.70 2.30

Inauguration of the Francois Duvalier Airport in Port-au-Prince.

Slave Breaking Chains, Map of Haiti, Torch, Conch — A126

1968, Oct. 28 Litho. *Perf. 14½x14*
596 A126 5c brn, lt bl & brt pink .25 .25
597 A126 10c brn, lt ol & brt pink .25 .25
598 A126 25c brn, bis & brt pink .25 .25
Nos. 596-598,C310-C313 (7) 3.10 2.50

Slaves' Rebellion, of 1791.

Children Learning to Read A127

10c, Children watching television. 50c, Hands setting volleyball and sports medal.

1968, Nov. 14 *Perf. 11½*
599 A127 5c multi .25 .25
600 A127 10c multi .25 .25
601 A127 50c multi .40 .25
Nos. 599-601,C314-C316 (6) 2.45 1.90

Issued to publicize education through literacy, audio-visual means and sport.
For surcharges see Nos. B41-B42, CB61-CB62.

Winston Churchill — A128

Churchill: 5c, as painter. 10c, as Knight of the Garter. 15c, and soldiers at Normandy. 20c, and early seaplane. 25c, and Queen Elizabeth II. 50c, and Big Ben, London.

1968, Dec. 23 Photo. *Perf. 13*
602 A128 3c gold & multi .25 .25
603 A128 5c gold & multi .25 .25
604 A128 10c gold & multi .25 .25
605 A128 15c gold & multi .25 .25
606 A128 20c gold & multi .25 .25
607 A128 25c gold & multi .25 .25
608 A128 50c gold & multi .40 .25
Nos. 602-608,C319-C322 (11) 4.25 3.50

Exist imperf. For surcharge see No. 828.

1968 Winter Olympics, Grenoble A128a

Designs: 5c, 1.50g, Peggy Fleming, US, figure skating. 10c, Harold Groenningen, Norway, cross-country skiing. 20c, Belousova & Protopopov, USSR, pairs figure skating. 25c, Toini Gustafsson, Sweden, cross country skiing. 50c, Eugenio Monti, Italy, 4-man bobsled. 2g, Erhard Keller, Germany, speed skating. 4g, Jean-Claude Killy, France, downhill skiing.

1968, Nov. 11 Litho. *Perf. 14x13½*
609 A128a 5c brt bl & multi .25 .25
609A A128a 10c bl grn & multi .25 .25
609B A128a 20c brt rose & multi .25 .25
609C A128a 25c sky bl & multi .25 .25
609D A128a 50c ol bis & multi .45 .30
609E A128a 1.50g vio & multi 1.10 .65

Size: 36x65mm
Perf. 12x12½
609F A128a 2g emer grn & multi 2.25 2.25
Nos. 609-609F (7) 4.80 4.20

Souvenir Sheet
609G A128a 4g brn & multi 20.00 20.00

No. 609G contains one 36x65mm stamp. Nos. 609F-609G are airmail. No. 609G exists imperf. with green, brown and blue margin.

No. 589 Surcharged

1969, Feb. 21 Photo. *Perf. 11½*
610 A122 70c on 50c .50 .40
Nos. 610,C324-C325 (3) 1.80 1.30

Blue-headed Euphonia — A129

Birds of Haiti: 10c, Hispaniolan trogon. 20c, Palm chat. 25c, Stripe-headed tanager. 50c, Like 5c.

1969, Feb. 26 *Perf. 13½*
611 A129 5c lt grn & multi 2.00 .50
612 A129 10c yel & multi 2.00 .50
613 A129 20c cream & multi 2.25 .50
614 A129 25c lt lil & multi 2.50 .60
615 A129 50c lt gray & multi 3.50 .60
Nos. 611-615,C326-C329 (9) 28.50 9.45

For overprints see Nos. C344A-C344D.

Olympic Marathon Winners, 1896-1968 — A130

Designs: Games location, date, winner, country and time over various stamp designs. Souvenir sheets do not show location, date, country or time.

1969, May 16 *Perf. 12½x12*
Size: 66x35mm (Nos. 616, 616C, 616F, 616N)
616 A130 5c like Greece #124 .25 .25
616A A130 10c like France #124 .25 .25
616B A130 15c US #327 .25 .25
616C A130 20c like Great Britain #142 .50 .40
616D A130 20c Sweden #68 .50 .40
616E A130 25c Belgium #B49 .80 .40
616F A130 25c like France #198 .80 .40
616G A130 25c Netherlands #B30 .80 .40
616H A130 30c US #718 .90 .40
616I A130 50c Germany #B86 1.40 1.00
616J A130 60c Great Britain #274 1.75 1.00
616K A130 75c like Finland #B110 2.50 2.00
616L A130 75c like Australia #277 2.50 2.00
616M A130 90c Italy #799 2.75 2.00
616N A130 1g like Japan #822 3.75 3.00
616O A130 1.25g like Mexico #C328 5.00 4.00
Nos. 616-616O (16) 24.70 18.15

Souvenir Sheets
616P A130 1.50g US #718, diff. 16.00 16.00

Imperf
616Q A130 1.50g Germany #B86, diff. 16.00 16.00

Nos. 616H-616O are airmail. Nos. 616P-616Q contain one 66x35mm stamp. A 2g souvenir sheet exists, perf. & imperf. Value, each $9.

Power Lines and Light Bulb — A131

1969, May 22 Litho. *Perf. 13x13½*
617 A131 20c lilac & blue .25 .25

Issued to publicize the Duvalier Hydroelectric Station. See Nos. C338-C340.

Learning to Write — A132

Designs: 10c, children playing, vert. 50c, Peace poster on educational television, vert.

1969, Aug. 12 Litho. *Perf. 13½*
618 A132 5c multi .25 .25
619 A132 10c multi .25 .25
620 A132 50c multi .25 .25
Nos. 618-620,C342-C344 (6) 2.35 1.90

Issued to publicize national education.

ILO Emblem A133

1969, Sept. 22 *Perf. 14*
621 A133 5c bl grn & blk .25 .25
622 A133 10c brn & blk .25 .25
623 A133 20c vio bl & blk .25 .25
Nos. 621-623,C345-C347 (6) 3.10 1.95

50th anniv. of the ILO.

Apollo Space Missions — A133a

Designs: 10c, Apollo 7 rendezvous of command module, third stage. 15c, Apollo 7, preparation for re-entry. 20c, Apollo 8, separation of third stage. 25c, Apollo 8, mid-course correction. 70c, Apollo 8, approaching moon. 1g, Apollo 8, orbiting moon, Christmas 1968, vert. 1.25, Apollo 8, leaving moon. 1.50g, Apollo 8, crew, vert. 1.75g, 2g, Apollo 11, first lunar landing.

1969, Oct. 6 *Perf. 12x12½*
624 A133a 10c brt rose & multi .25 .25
624A A133a 15c vio & multi .25 .25
624B A133a 20c ver & multi .25 .25
624C A133a 25c emer grn & multi .25 .25
624D A133a 70c brt bl & multi .25 .25
624E A133a 1g bl grn & multi .55 .30
624F A133a 1.25g dk bl & multi .65 .40
624G A133a 1.50g dp rose lil & multi .80 .50

Souvenir Sheets
624H A133a 1.75g grn & multi 12.00 12.00
624I A133a 2g sky bl & multi 12.00 12.00
Nos. 624-624I (10) 27.25 26.45

Nos. 624D-624I are airmail. Nos. 624-624I exist imperf. in different colors.

Papilio Zonaria — A134

Butterflies: 20c, Zerene cesonia cynops. 25c, Papilio machaonides.

1969, Nov. 14 Photo. *Perf. 13½*
625 A134 10c pink & multi 2.25 .75
626 A134 20c gray & multi 4.00 3.00
627 A134 25c lt bl & multi 6.00 3.00
Nos. 625-627,C348-C350 (6) 52.25 19.75

Martin Luther King, Jr. A135

1970, Jan. 12 Litho. *Perf. 12½x13½*
628 A135 10c bis, red & blk .25 .25
629 A135 20c grnsh bl, red & blk .25 .25
630 A135 25c brt rose, red & blk .25 .25
Nos. 628-630,C351-C353 (6) 3.20 2.45

Martin Luther King, Jr. (1929-1968), American civil rights leader.

Laeliopsis Dominguensis — A136

Haitian Orchids: 20c, Oncidium Haitiense. 25c, Oncidium calochilum.

1970, Apr. 3 Litho. *Perf. 13x12½*
631 A136 10c yel, lil & blk .25 .25
632 A136 20c lt bl grn, yel & brn 2.00 2.00
633 A136 25c bl & multi 2.50 2.00
Nos. 631-633,C354-C356 (6) 15.50 10.50

UPU Monument and Map of Haiti — A137

Designs: 25c, Propeller and UPU emblem, vert. 50c, Globe and doves.

1970, June 23 Photo. *Perf. 11½*
634 A137 10c blk, brt grn & ol bis .25 .25
635 A137 25c blk, brt rose & ol bis .25 .25
636 A137 50c blk & bl .35 .25
Nos. 634-636,C357-C359 (6) 2.80 2.10

16th Cong. of the UPU, Tokyo, Oct. 1-Nov. 16, 1970.
For overprints see Nos. 640, C360-C362.

Map of Haiti, Dam and Pylon — A138

Design: 20c, Map of Haiti, Dam and Generator.

1970 Litho. *Perf. 14x13½*

637 A138 20c lt grn & multi .25 .25
638 A138 25c lt bl & multi .25 .25

François Duvalier Central Hydroelectric Plant.
For surcharges see Nos. B43-B44, RA40-RA41.

Apollo 12 — A138a

No. 639, Lift-off. No. 639A, 2nd stage ignition. No. 639B, Docking preparations. No. 639C, Heading for moon. No. 639E, Lunar exploration. No. 639F, Landing on Moon. No. 639G, Lift-off from Moon. No. 639H, 3rd stage separation. No. 639I, Lunar module, crew. No. 639J, Lunar orbital activities. No. 639K, Leaving Moon orbit. No. 639L, In Earth orbit. No. 639M, Re-entry. No. 639N, Landing at sea. No. 639O, Docking with lunar module.

1970, Sept. 7 *Perf. 13½x14*

639 A138a 5c multi .25 .25
639A A138a 10c multi .25 .25
639B A138a 15c multi .25 .25
639C A138a 20c multi .35 .25
639D A138a 25c like 639B .45 .25
639E A138a 25c multi .25 .25
639F A138a 30c multi .65 .25
639G A138a 30c multi .45 .25
639H A138a 40c multi .90 .35
639I A138a 40c multi .55 .25
639J A138a 50c multi 1.10 .80
639K A138a 50c multi .65 .35
639L A138a 75c multi 1.10 .75
639M A138a 1g multi 1.50 1.25
639N A138a 1.25g multi 2.25 1.50
639O A138a 1.50g multi 2.40 2.00
Nos. 639-639O (16) 13.35 9.25

Nos. 639E, 639G, 639I, 639K-639O are airmail. Nos. 639-639O exist imperf. with brighter colors. Value, unused $16.
For overprints see Nos. 656-656O.

No. 636 Overprinted in Red with UN Emblem and: "XXVe ANNIVERSAIRE / O.N.U."

1970, Dec. 14 Photo. *Perf. 11½*

640 A137 50c blk & bl .35 .25
Nos. 640,C360-C362 (4) 2.30 1.60

UN, 25th anniv.

Fort Nativity, Drawing by Columbus A139

1970, Dec. 22

641 A139 3c dk brn & buff .25 .25
642 A139 5c dk grn & pale grn .30 .25

Christmas 1970.

Ascension, by Castera Bazile — A140

Paintings: 5c, Man with Turban, by Rembrandt. 20c, Iris in a Vase, by Van Gogh. 50c, Baptism of Christ, by Castera Bazile. No. 647, Young Mother Sewing, by Mary Cassatt. No. 648, The Card Players, by Cezanne.

Size: 20x40mm

1971, Apr. 29 Litho. *Perf. 12x12½*

643 A140 5c multi .25 .25
644 A140 10c multi .25 .25

Perf. 13x12½
Size: 25x37mm

645 A140 20c multi .25 .25

Perf. 12x12½
Size: 20x40mm

646 A140 50c multi .50 .25
Nos. 643-646,C366-C368 (7) 3.65 2.70

Souvenir Sheets
Imperf

647 A140 3g multi 5.00 5.00
648 A140 3g multi 5.00 5.00

No. 647 contains one stamp, size: 20x40mm, No. 648 size: 25x37mm.
Nos. 643-646, C366-C368 exist imperf in changed colors.

Soccer Ball — A141

Design: No. 651, 1g, 5g, Jules Rimet cup.

1971, June 14 Photo. *Perf. 11½*

649 A141 5c salmon & blk .25 .25
650 A141 50c tan & blk .50 .35
651 A141 50c rose pink, blk & gold .50 .35
652 A141 1g lil, blk & gold .65 .45
653 A141 1.50g gray & blk .80 .55
654 A141 5g gray, blk & gold 2.40 1.60
Nos. 649-654 (6) 5.10 3.55

Souvenir Sheet
Imperf

655 Sheet of 2 12.00 8.50
a. A141 70c light violet & black 4.00 3.00
b. A141 1g light green, blue & gold 4.00 3.00

9th World Soccer Championships for the Jules Rimet Cup, Mexico City, May 30-June 21, 1970. The surface tint of the sheets of 50 (10x5) of Nos. 649-654 includes a map of Brazil covering 26 stamps. Positions 27, 37 and 38 inscribed "Brasilia," "Santos," "Rio de Janeiro" respectively. On soccer ball design the 4 corner stamps are inscribed "Pele."
Nos. 655a and 655b have portions of map of Brazil in background; No. 655a inscribed "Pele" and "Santos," No. 655b "Brasilia."

Nos. 639-639O Ovptd. in Gold or Red

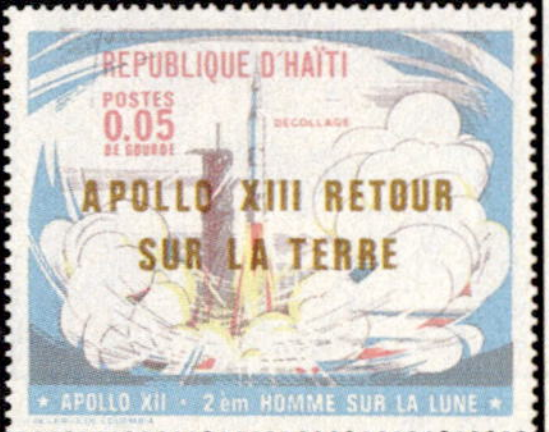

1971, Mar. 15

656 A138a 5c multi (G) .25 .25
656A A138a 10c multi (G) .25 .25
656B A138a 15c multi (G) .25 .25
656C A138a 20c multi (G) .35 .25
656D A138a 25c multi (R) .45 .25
656E A138a 25c multi (R) .25 .25
656F A138a 30c multi (R) .65 .25
656G A138a 30c multi (R) .45 .25
656H A138a 40c multi (R) .90 .35
656I A138a 40c multi (R) .55 .35
656J A138a 50c multi (R) 1.10 .35
656K A138a 50c multi (R) .65 .35
656L A138a 75c multi (R) 1.10 .40
656M A138a 1g multi (R) 1.50 .50
656N A138a 1.25g multi (R) 2.25 .75
656O A138a 1.50g multi (R) 2.40 .75
Nos. 656-656O (16) 13.35 5.80

Nos. 656E, 656G, 656I, 656K-656O are airmail.
Nos. 656-656O exist imperf. overprinted in silver. Value, unused $16.

J. J. Dessalines — A142

1972, Apr. 28 Photo. *Perf. 11½*

657 A142 5c grn & blk .25 .25
658 A142 10c brt bl & blk .25 .25
659 A142 25c org & blk .25 .25
Nos. 657-659,C378-C379 (5) 2.20 1.65

See Nos. 697-700, C448-C458, 727, C490-C493, C513-C514. For surcharges see Nos. 692, 705-709, 724-726, C438, C512.

"Sun" and EXPO '70 Emblem — A143

1972, Oct. 27 Photo. *Perf. 11½*

660 A143 10c ocher, yel & grn .25 .25
661 A143 25c ocher, yel & lake .25 .25
Nos. 660-661,C387-C390 (6) 3.00 2.10

EXPO '70 International Exposition, Osaka, Japan, Mar. 15-Sept. 13, 1970.

Gold Medalists, 1972 Summer Olympics, Munich — A143a

Designs: 5c, L. Linsenhoff, dressage, W. Ruska, judo. 10c, S. Kato, gymnastics, S.Gould, women's swimming. 20c, M. Peters, women's pentathlon, K. Keino, steeplechase. 25c, L. Viren, 5,000, 10,000m races, R. Milburn, 110m hurdles. No. 662D, D. Morelon, cycling, J. Akii-Bua, 400m hurdles. No. 662E, R. Williams, long jump. 75c, G. Mancinelli, equestrian. 1.50g, W. Nordwig, pole vault. 2.50g, K. Wolferman, javelin. 5g, M. Spitz, swimming.

1972, Dec. 29 *Perf. 13½*

662 A143a 5c multicolored .25 .25
662A A143a 10c multicolored .25 .25
662B A143a 20c multicolored .25 .25
662C A143a 25c multicolored .25 .25
662D A143a 50c multicolored .25 .25
662E A143a 50c multicolored .70 .25
662F A143a 75c multicolored 1.00 .25
662G A143a 1.50g multicolored 1.50 .70
662H A143a 2.50g multicolored 3.00 1.10
662I A143a 5g multicolored 5.75 1.60
Nos. 662-662I (10) 13.20 5.15

Nos. 662E-662I are airmail.

Basket Vendors A144

Designs: 80c, 2.50g, Postal bus.

1973, Jan. Photo. *Perf. 11½*

665 A144 50c blk & multi .35 .25
666 A144 80c blk & multi .45 .35
667 A144 1.50g blk & multi .70 .45
668 A144 2.50g blk & multi 1.50 .80
Nos. 665-668 (4) 3.00 1.85

20th anniv. of Caribbean Travel Assoc.

Space Exploration

A set of 12 stamps for US-USSR space exploration, the same overprinted for the centenary of the UPU and 3 overprinted in silver for Apollo 17 exist but we have no evidence that they were printed with the approval of the Haitian postal authorities. Value, $10 and $6, respectively.

Micromelo Undata A145

Marine life: 10c, Nemaster rubiginosa. 25c, Cyerce cristallina. 50c, Desmophyllum riisei, horiz.

1973, Sept. 4 Litho. *Perf. 14*

669 A145 5c shown .25 .25
670 A145 10c multicolored .25 .25
671 A145 25c multicolored .50 .25
672 A145 50c multicolored 1.00 .25
Nos. 669-672,C395-C398 (8) 8.90 2.20

For surcharge see No. C439.

Gramma Loreto — A146

50c, Acanthurus coeruleus.

1973 *Perf. 13½*

673 A146 10c shown .50 .25
674 A146 50c multicolored .65 .50
Nos. 673-674,C399-C402 (6) 8.00 4.55

For surcharges see Nos. 693, C440.

Soccer Stadium A147

Design: 20c, Haiti No. 654.

1973, Nov. 29 *Perf. 14x13*

675 A147 10c bis, blk & emer .25 .25
676 A147 20c rose lil, blk & tan .25 .25
Nos. 675-676,C407-C410 (6) 5.50 3.80

Caribbean countries preliminary games of the World Soccer Championships, Munich, 1974.

Jean Jacques Dessalines — A148

1974, Apr. 22 Photo. *Perf. 14*

677 A148 10c lt bl & emer .25 .25
678 A148 20c rose & blk .25 .25
679 A148 25c yel & vio .25 .25
Nos. 677-679,C411-C414 (7) 3.05 2.35

For surcharges see Nos. 694, C443.

Nicolaus Copernicus A149

Design: 10c, Symbol of heliocentric system.

1974, May 24 Litho. Perf. 14x13½
680 A149 10c multi .25 .25
681 A149 25c brt grn & multi .25 .25
Nos. 680-681,C415-C419 (7) 3.15 2.35

For overprint and surcharges see Nos. 695, C444, C460-C463.

Pres. Jean-Claude Duvalier — A151

1974 Photo. Perf. 14x13½
689 A151 10c grn & gold .25 .25
690 A151 20c car rose & gold .30 .25
691 A151 50c bl & gold .40 .25
Nos. 689-691,C421-C426 (9) 7.40 4.60

For surcharge and overprints see Nos. C445, C487-C489.

Audubon Birds

In 1975 or later various sets of bird paintings by Audubon were produced by government employees without official authorization. They were not sold by the Haiti post office and were not valid for postage. The first set consisted of 23 values and was sold in 1975. A second set containing some of the original stamps and some new stamps appeared unannounced several years later. More sets may have been printed as there are 75 different stamps. These consist of 5 denominations each for the 15 designs.

Perf and imperf souvenir sheets picturing Audubon were also produced.

Nos. 659, 673 and 679-680 Surcharged with New Value and Bar

Perf. 11½, 13½, 14, 14x13½

1976 Photo.; Litho.
692 A142 80c on 25c .55 .35
693 A146 80c on 10c .55 .35
694 A148 80c on 25c .55 .35
695 A149 80c on 10c .55 .35
Nos. 692-695 (4) 2.20 1.40

Haiti No. C11 and Bicentennial Emblem — A152

1976, Apr. 22 Photo. Perf. 11½
Granite Paper
696 A152 10c multi .25 .25
Nos. 696,C434-C437 (5) 4.70 3.30

American Bicentennial.

Dessalines Type of 1972

1977 Photo. Perf. 11½
697 A142 10c rose & blk .25 .25
698 A142 20c lemon & blk .25 .25
699 A142 50c vio & blk .35 .25
700 A142 50c tan & blk .35 .25
Nos. 697-700 (4) 1.20 1.00

Dessalines Type of 1972 Surcharged in Black or Red

1978 Photo. Perf. 11½
705 A142 1g on 20c (#698) .65 .35
706 A142 1g on 1.75g (#C454) .65 .35
707 A142 1.25g on 75c (#C448) .65 .35
708 A142 1.25g on 1.50g (#C453) .65 .35
709 A142 1.25g on 1.50g (#C453; R) .65 .35
Nos. 705-709 (5) 3.25 1.75

Rectangular bar obliterates old denomination on Nos. 705-709 and "Par Avion" on Nos. 706-709.

J. C. Duvalier Earth Telecommunications Station — A153

Designs: 20c, Video telephone. 50c, Alexander Graham Bell, vert.

1978, June 19 Litho. Perf. 13½
710 A153 10c multi .25 .25
711 A153 20c multi .25 .25
712 A153 50c multi .35 .25
Nos. 710-712,C466-C468 (6) 2.70 2.10

Centenary of first telephone call by Alexander Graham Bell, Mar. 10, 1876.

Athletes' Inaugural Parade — A154

1978, Sept. 4 Litho. Perf. 13½x13
713 A154 5c shown .25 .25
714 A154 25c Bicyclists .25 .25
715 A154 50c Pole Vault .40 .25
Nos. 713-715,C469-C471 (6) 6.60 4.10

21st Olympic Games, Montreal, 7/17-8/1/76.

Mother Nursing Child — A155

1979, Jan. 15 Photo. Perf. 14x14½
716 A155 25c multi .25 .25
Nos. 716,C472-C473 (3) 1.60 1.15

Inter-American Children's Inst., 50th anniv.

Mother Feeding Child — A156

1979, May 11 Photo. Perf. 11½
717 A156 25c multi .25 .25
718 A156 50c multi .35 .25
Nos. 717-718,C474-C476 (5) 3.60 2.55

30th anniversary of CARE (Cooperative for American Relief Everywhere).

Human Rights Emblem — A157

1979, July 20 Litho. Perf. 14
719 A157 25c multi .30 .25
Nos. 719,C477-C479 (4) 3.30 2.30

30th anniversary of declaration of human rights.

Anti-Apartheid Year Emblem, Antenor Firmin, "On the Equality of Human Races" A158

1979, Nov. 22 Photo. Perf. 12x11½
720 A158 50c tan & black .50 .25
Nos. 720,C480-C482 (4) 4.35 2.30

Anti-Apartheid Year (1978).

Children Playing, IYC Emblem A159

1979, Dec. 19 Photo. Perf. 12
721 A159 10c multi .25 .25
722 A159 25c multi .25 .25
723 A159 50c multi .40 .25
Nos. 721-723,C483-C486 (7) 8.50 4.65

International Year of the Child.

Nos. C379, C449, C454 Surcharged

1980 Photo. Perf. 11½
Granite Paper
724 A142 1g on 2.50g lil & blk .55 .45
725 A142 1.25g on 80c emer & blk .65 .55
726 A142 1.25g on 1.75g rose & blk .65 .55
Nos. 724-726 (3) 1.85 1.55

Dessalines Type of 1972

1980, Aug. 27 Photo. Perf. 11½
Granite Paper
727 A142 25c org yel & blk .30 .25
Nos. 727,C490-C493 (5) 5.10 3.70

Henry Christophe Citadel — A160

1980, Dec. 2 Litho. Perf. 12½x12
728 A160 5c shown .25 .25
729 A160 25c Sans Souci Palace .25 .25
730 A160 50c Vallieres market .35 .25
Nos. 728-730,C494-C498 (8) 5.60 4.25

World Tourism Conf., Manila, Sept. 27.
For surcharges see Nos. 738, C511.

Soccer Players, World Cup, Flag of Uruguay (1930 Champion) — A161

1980, Dec. 30 Litho. Perf. 14
731 A161 10c shown .25 .25
732 A161 20c Italy, 1934 .25 .25
733 A161 25c Italy, 1938 .25 .25
Nos. 731-733,C499-C506 (11) 10.25 6.90

World Cup Soccer Championship, 50th anniv.
For surcharges see Nos. 741, 829.

Going to Church, by Gregoire Etienne A162

Paintings: 5c, Woman with Birds and Flowers, by Hector Hyppolite, vert. 20c, Street Market, by Petion Savain. 25c, Market Vendors, by Michele Manuel.

1981, May 12 Photo. Perf. 11½
734 A162 5c multi .25 .25
735 A162 10c multi .25 .25
736 A162 20c multi .25 .25
737 A162 25c multi .25 .25
Nos. 734-737,C507-C510 (8) 5.65 4.25

For surcharges see Nos. 739-740.

Nos. 728, 734-735, 732 Surcharged

Perf. 12½x12, 14, 11½

1981, Dec. 30 Litho., Photo.
738 A160 1.25g on 5c multi .65 .55
739 A162 1.25g on 5c multi .65 .55
740 A162 1.25g on 10c multi .65 .55
741 A161 1.25g on 20c multi .65 .55
Nos. 738-741,C511-C512 (6) 4.45 3.60

10th Anniv. of Pres. Duvalier Reforms — A163

1982, June 21 Photo. Perf. 11½x12
Granite Paper
742 A163 25c yel grn & blk .25 .25
743 A163 50c olive & blk .35 .25
744 A163 1g rose & blk .55 .45
745 A163 1.25g bl & blk .65 .55
746 A163 2g org red & blk 1.10 .85
747 A163 5g org & blk 2.40 1.60
Nos. 742-747 (6) 5.30 3.95

Nos. 742, 744-746 Overprinted in Blue: "1957-1982 / 25 ANS DE REVOLUTION"

1982, Nov. 29 Photo. Perf. 11½x12
Granite Paper
748 A163 25c yel grn & blk .25 .25
749 A163 1g rose & blk .55 .45
750 A163 1.25g blue & blk .65 .55
751 A163 2g org red & blk 1.10 .85
Nos. 748-751 (4) 2.55 2.10

25th anniv. of revolution.

Scouting Year A164

5c, Building campfire. 10c, Baden-Powell, vert. 25c, Boat building.

Perf. 13½x14, 14x13½

1983, Feb. 26 **Litho.**

752	A164	5c multi	.25	.25
753	A164	10c multi	.25	.25
754	A164	25c multi	.25	.25
755	A164	50c like 10c	.50	.25
756	A164	75c like 25c	1.25	.25
757	A164	1g like 5c	1.50	.30
758	A164	1.25g like 25c	2.00	.35
759	A164	2g like 10c	2.75	.60
		Nos. 752-759 (8)	8.75	2.50

Nos. 756-759 airmail.
For surcharge see No. 827.

Patroness of Haiti — A165

1983, Mar. 9 **Litho.** ***Perf. 14***

760	A165	10c multi	.25	.25
761	A165	20c multi	.25	.25
762	A165	25c multi	.25	.25
763	A165	50c multi	.25	.25
764	A165	75c multi	.35	.25
765	A165	1g multi	.60	.25
766	A165	1.25g multi	.70	.30
767	A165	1.50g multi	1.00	.35
768	A165	1.75g multi	1.40	.40
769	A165	2g multi	1.75	.50
770	A165	5g multi	2.75	1.00
a.		Souvenir sheet, 116x90mm	*37.50*	*37.50*
j.		Souvenir sheet, 90x116mm	*37.50*	*37.50*
		Nos. 760-770 (11)	9.55	4.05

Centenary of the Miracle of Our Lady of Perpetual Help. Nos. 764-770 airmail.
For surcharge see No. 875.

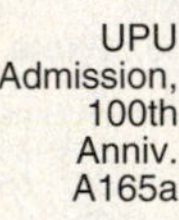

UPU Admission, 100th Anniv. A165a

10c, L.F. Salomon, J.C. Duvalier. 25c, No. 1, UPU emblem.

1983, June 10 **Litho.** ***Perf. 15x14***

770B	A165a	5c shown	.50	.25
770C	A165a	10c multi	.50	.25
770D	A165a	25c multi	.50	.25
770E	A165a	50c like 5c	.50	.25
770F	A165a	75c like 10c	.60	.25
770G	A165a	1g like 5c	.80	.25
770H	A165a	1.25g like 25c	1.00	.30
770I	A165a	2g like 25c	1.60	.40
		Nos. 770B-770I (8)	6.00	2.20

Nos. 770F-770I airmail.
For surcharge see No. 825.

1982 World Cup — A166

Games and scores: 5c, Argentina, Belgium. 10c, Northern Ireland, Yugoslavia. 20c, England, France. 25c, Spain, Northern Ireland. 50c, Italy (champion). 1g, Brazil, Scotland. 1.25g, Northern Ireland, France. 1.50g, Poland, Cameroun. 2g, Italy, Germany. 2.50g, Argentina, Brazil.
Nos. 776-780 airmail, horiz.

1983, Nov. 22 **Litho.** ***Perf. 14***

771	A166	5c multicolored	.25	.25
772	A166	10c multicolored	.25	.25
773	A166	20c multicolored	.25	.25
774	A166	25c multicolored	.25	.25
775	A166	50c multicolored	.35	.25
776	A166	1g multicolored	.55	.45
777	A166	1.25g multicolored	.65	.55
778	A166	1.50g multicolored	.95	.65
779	A166	2g multicolored	1.10	.85
780	A166	2.50g multicolored	1.40	1.10
		Nos. 771-780 (10)	6.00	4.85

For surcharge see No. 826.

Haiti Postage Stamp Centenary — A167

1984, Feb. 28 **Litho.** ***Perf. 14½***

781	A167	5c #1	.30	.25
782	A167	10c #2	.30	.25
783	A167	25c #3	.30	.25
784	A167	50c #5	.30	.25
785	A167	75c Liberty, Salomon	.45	.25
786	A167	1g Liberty, Salomon	.60	.35
787	A167	1.25g Liberty, Duvalier	.70	.40
788	A167	2g Liberty, Duvalier	1.10	.75
		Nos. 781-788 (8)	4.05	2.75

Nos. 785-788 airmail.
For surcharge see No. 826A.

A168

25c, Broadcasting equipment, horiz. 1g, Drum. 2g, Globe.

1984, May 30 **Photo.** ***Perf. 11½***

Granite Paper

789	A168	25c multicolored	.25	.25
790	A168	50c like 25c	.35	.25
791	A168	1g multicolored	.55	.45
792	A168	1.25g like 1g	.65	.55
793	A168	2g multicolored	1.10	.85
794	A168	2.50g like 2g	1.40	1.10
		Nos. 789-794 (6)	4.30	3.45

World Communications Year.

A169

5c, Javelin, running, pole vault, horiz. 25c, Hurdles, horiz. 1g, Long jump.

1984, July 27 **Granite Paper**

795	A169	5c multicolored	.25	.25
796	A169	10c like 5c	.25	.25
797	A169	25c multicolored	.25	.25
798	A169	50c like 25c	.75	.25
799	A169	1g multicolored	1.25	.95
800	A169	1.25g like 1g	1.75	1.25
801	A169	2g like 1g	2.40	1.75
		Nos. 795-801 (7)	6.90	4.95

Souvenir Sheet

802	A169	2.50g like 1g	15.00	10.00

1984 Summer Olympics. No. 802 exists imperf. Value $15.
For surcharge see No. 874.

Arrival of Europeans in America, 500th Anniv. — A170

The Unknown Indian, detail or full perspective of statue. Nos. 807-809 are vert. and airmail.

1984, Dec. 5 **Litho.** ***Perf. 14***

803	A170	5c multi	.55	.45
804	A170	10c multi	.55	.45
805	A170	25c multi	.55	.45
806	A170	50c multi	.90	.60
807	A170	1g multi	1.10	.60
808	A170	1.25g multi	1.75	.90
809	A170	2g multi	6.00	3.00
a.		Souvenir sheet of #806, 809	16.00	16.00
		Nos. 803-809 (7)	11.40	6.45

For surcharge see No. 881.

Simon Bolivar and Alexander Petion — A171

Designs: 25c, 1.25g, 7.50g, Portraits reversed. 50c, 4.50g, Bolivar, flags of Grand Colombian Confederation member nations.

1985, Aug. 30 ***Perf. 13½x14***

810	A171	5c multi	.30	.25
811	A171	25c multi	.30	.25
812	A171	50c multi	.35	.25
813	A171	1g multi	.55	.30
814	A171	1.25g multi	.60	.45
815	A171	2g multi	1.10	.85
816	A171	7.50g multi	3.25	*3.75*
		Nos. 810-816 (7)	6.45	6.10

Souvenir Sheet

Imperf

817	A171	4.50g multi	3.50	2.50

Nos. 813-817 airmail.
For surcharge see No. 876.

Arrival of Europeans in America, 500th Anniv. — A172

Designs: 10c, 25c, 50c, Henri, cacique of Bahoruco, hero of the Spanish period, 1492-1625. 1g, 1.25g, 2g, Henri in tropical forest.

1986, Apr. 11 **Litho.** ***Perf. 14***

818	A172	10c multi	1.00	.35
819	A172	25c multi	1.00	.35
820	A172	50c multi	1.00	.35
821	A172	1g multi	1.75	.45
822	A172	1.25g multi	2.50	.50
823	A172	2g multi	3.75	.75
		Nos. 818-823 (6)	11.00	2.75

Nos. 821-823 are airmail. A 3g souvenir sheet exists picturing Henri in tropical forest. Value $16.
For surcharge see No. 883.

Nos. 770B, 771, 781, 756, C322, C500 Surcharged

1986, Apr. 18

825	A165a	25c on 5c No. 770B	.30	.25
826	A166	25c on 5c No. 771	.30	.25
826A	A167	25c on 5c No. 781	.30	.25
827	A164	25c on 75c No. 756	.30	.25
828	A128	25c on 1.50g No. C322	.30	.25
829	A161	25c on 75c No. C500	.30	.25
		Nos. 825-829 (6)	1.80	1.50

Intl. Youth Year — A173

1986, May 20 **Litho.** ***Perf. 14x15***

830	A173	10c Afforestation	.25	.25
831	A173	25c IYY emblem	.25	.25
832	A173	50c Girl Guides	.35	.25
833	A173	1g like 10c	.55	.45
834	A173	1.25g like 25c	.65	.55
835	A173	2g like 50c	1.10	.85
		Nos. 830-835 (6)	3.15	2.60

Souvenir Sheet

836	A173	3g multi	*12.50*	*12.50*

Nos. 833-836 are airmail.
For surcharge see No. 873.

UNESCO, 40th Anniv. (in 1986) — A174

1987, May 29 **Photo.** ***Perf. 11½***

Granite Paper

837	A174	10c multi	.25	.25
838	A174	25c multi	.25	.25
839	A174	50c multi	.35	.25
840	A174	1g multi	.55	.45
841	A174	1.25g multi	.70	.55
842	A174	2.50g multi	1.40	1.10
		Nos. 837-842 (6)	3.50	2.85

Souvenir Sheet

Granite Paper

843	A174	2g multi	*3.00*	*3.00*

Nos. 840-842 are airmail.
For surcharge see No. 882.

Charlemagne Peralte, Resistance Leader — A175

1988, Oct. 18 **Litho.** ***Perf. 14***

844	A175	25c multi	.25	.25
845	A175	50c multi	.35	.25
846	A175	1g multi	.55	.45
847	A175	2g multi	1.10	.85
a.		Souvenir sheet of 1	7.50	7.50
848	A175	3g multi	1.75	1.40
		Nos. 844-848 (5)	4.00	3.20

Nos. 846-848, 847a are airmail.

Slave Rebellion, 200th Anniv. A176

Design: 1g, 2g, 3g, Slaves around fire, vert.

1991, Aug. 22 **Litho.** ***Perf. 12x11½***

849	A176	25c brt grn & multi	.60	.30
850	A176	50c pink & multi	1.00	.50

Perf. 11½x12

851	A176	1g blue & multi	2.00	1.00
852	A176	2g yellow & multi	4.00	2.00
a.		Souv. sheet of 2, #850 & 852	*27.50*	*27.50*
853	A176	3g buff & multi	7.50	3.50
		Nos. 849-853 (5)	15.10	7.30

Nos. 851-853 are airmail.

Discovery of America, 500th Anniv. A177

Designs: 25c, 50c, Ships at anchor, men coming ashore, native. 1g, 2g, 3g, Ships, beached long boats, vert.

1993, July 30 **Litho.** ***Perf. 11½***

854	A177	25c green & multi	.60	.35
855	A177	50c yellow & multi	.85	.40
856	A177	1g blue & multi	1.25	.75
857	A177	2g pink & multi	2.75	1.25
a.		Souvenir sheet of 2, #856-857	*500.00*	*500.00*

858 A177 3g org yel & multi 6.00 3.75
Nos. 854-858 (5) 11.45 6.50

Nos. 856-858, 857a are airmail.

25th Genl. Assembly of the Organization of American States A178

Designs: 50c, 75c, 7.50g, Emblem, map of Haiti. 1g, 2g, 3g, 5g, Emblems, map of North, South America, vert.

Perf. 14x12½, 12½x14

1995, June 25 **Litho.**

859 A178 50c violet & multi .40 .25
860 A178 75c green & multi .60 .30
861 A178 1g gray blue & multi .75 .45
862 A178 2g lilac rose & multi 1.50 .85
863 A178 3g green & multi 2.00 1.40
864 A178 5g violet & multi 3.25 1.90
Nos. 859-864 (6) 8.50 5.15

Souvenir Sheet

Imperf

865 A178 7.50g green blue & multi *10.00 10.00*

UN, 50th Anniv. A179

Designs: 50c, 75c, Dove holding UN, Haitian flags. 1g, 2g, 3g, 5g, Haitian, UN flags, dove carrying olive branch.

1995, Nov. 24 **Litho.** ***Perf. 12x11½***

866 A179 50c blue & multi *.50 .30*
867 A179 75c lilac & multi *.75 .40*
868 A179 1g apple green & multi *1.00 .60*
869 A179 2g yellow & multi *2.25 1.00*
870 A179 3g org brn & multi *3.50 1.50*
871 A179 5g blue green & multi *5.75 3.00*
Nos. 866-871 (6) *13.75 6.80*

Souvenir Sheet

872 A179 5g multicolored *16.50 16.50*

Nos. 868-872 are airmail.

Nos. 766, 800, 814, 834 Surcharged

1996 ***Perfs., Etc., as Before***

873 A173 1g on 1.25g #834 *.75 .60*
874 A169 2g on 1.25g #800 *1.50 1.00*
875 A165 3g on 1.25g #766 *2.25 1.50*
876 A171 3g on 1.25g #814 *2.50 1.50*
Nos. 873-876 (4) *7.00 4.60*

Size and location of surcharge varies. Nos. 873, 875-876 are airmail.

1996 Summer Olympic Games, Atlanta — A180

1996, Aug. 2 **Litho.** ***Perf. 14***

877 A180 3g Hurdler .75 .45
878 A180 10g Athlete up close 2.50 1.60

Volleyball Federation, 1996 Summer Olympics, Atlanta — A181

No. 879: a, 50c, Three players in yellow shirts. b, 75c, Three players in red shirts. c, 1g, Two players in white shirts, torch. d, 2g, Players in yellow, in red.
15g, Player in red.

1996, Aug. 2

879 A181 Sheet of 4, #a.-d. 17.50 17.50

Souvenir Sheet

880 A181 15g multicolored 17.50 17.50

Volleyball, cent. (No. 880).

Nos. 803, 818, 837 Surcharged

1996, Nov. **Litho.** ***Perfs. as Before***

881 A170 1g on 5c #803 *.75 .60*
882 A174 4g on 10c #837 *3.00 2.00*
883 A172 6g on 10c #818 *4.00 3.00*
Nos. 881-883 (3) *7.75 5.60*

Size and location of surcharge varies.

Christmas A182

Paintings: 2g, The Virgin and Infant, by Jacopo Bellini. 3g, Adoration of the Shepherds, by Strozzi. 6g, Virgin and the Infant, by Giovanni Bellini. 10g, Virgin and the Infant, by Francesco Mazzola. No. 888, Adoration of the Magi, by Gentile da Fabriano.
No. 889 The Nativity, by Jan de Beer, horiz.

1996, Dec. 16 **Litho.** ***Perf. 13½x14***

884 A182 2g multicolored *.50 .30*
885 A182 3g multicolored *.75 .60*
886 A182 6g multicolored *1.50 1.25*
887 A182 10g multicolored *3.00 1.50*
888 A182 25g multicolored *6.50 7.00*
Nos. 884-888 (5) *12.25 10.65*

Souvenir Sheet

Perf. 14x13½

889 A182 25g multicolored *10.00 10.00*

UNICEF, 50th Anniv. — A183

1997, Jan. 28 ***Perf. 14***

890 A183 4g green & multi *1.25 .75*
891 A183 5g pink & multi *1.75 1.00*
892 A183 6g blue & multi *2.25 1.50*
893 A183 10g brown & multi *3.75 2.00*
894 A183 20g bister & multi *7.00 3.50*
Nos. 890-894 (5) 16.00 8.75

Souvenir Sheet

895 A183 25g like #890-894, vert. *10.00 10.00*

Nos. 890-894 were each issued in sheets of 6.

Grimm's Fairy Tales — A184

No. 896, No. 902a, 2g, Sleeping Beauty. No. 897, No. 902b, 3g, Snow White. No. 898, No. 902c, 4g, Prince awakening Sleeping Beauty. No. 899, No. 902d, 6g, Old man sleeping from "The Drink of Life." No. 900, No. 902e, 10g, Cinderella. No. 901, No. 902f, 20g, Old man awakened after taking drink.
No. 903, Cottage of the Seven Dwarfs, horiz.

1998, Jan. 5 **Litho.** ***Perf. 13½***

896 A184 2g multicolored *1.50 1.50*
897 A184 3g multicolored *2.00 2.00*
898 A184 4g multicolored *2.50 2.50*
899 A184 6g multicolored *4.00 4.00*
900 A184 10g multicolored *7.00 7.00*
901 A184 20g multicolored *14.00 14.00*
Nos. 896-901 (6) 31.00 31.00

Size: 38x50mm

Perf. 14

902 A184 Sheet of 6, #a.-f. *35.00 35.00*

Souvenir Sheet

903 A184 25g multicolored *27.50 27.50*

Abstract paintings A185

2g, "Coconut on Pastel Stairs," by Luce Turnier. 3g, "Ogou," by Rose Marie Desruisseau. 5g, "Lantern," by Hilda Williams. 6g, Woman using artist's brush and palette.
15g, Fish, flower and geometric design with faces, snakes by Philippe Dodard.

1998, Oct. 30 **Litho.** ***Perf. 12½***

904 A185 2g multicolored *3.00 1.50*
905 A185 3g multicolored *5.00 2.00*
906 A185 5g multicolored *7.00 2.75*
907 A185 6g multicolored *12.00 4.00*
Nos. 904-907 (4) *27.00 10.25*

Souvenir Sheet

Perf. 13

908 A185 15g multicolored *40.00 35.00*

Tourism. Nos. 904-907 exist in imperf. souvenir sheet of 4. No. 908 contains one 28x36mm stamp.

Birds A186

Designs: 2g, Priotelus roseigaster. 4g, Xenoligeo mantana. 10g, Phoenicophilus poliocephalus. 20g, Phoenicopterus ruber.

1999, Aug. 27 **Litho.** ***Perf. 14***

909 A186 2g multicolored *.75 .75*
910 A186 4g multicolored *1.50 1.50*
911 A186 10g multicolored *4.00 4.00*
912 A186 20g multicolored *7.00 8.00*
a. Souvenir sheet, #909-912 *15.00 15.00*
Nos. 909-912 (4) *13.25 14.25*

Nos. 911-912 are airmail.

Worldwide Fund for Nature — A187

No. 913: a, 2g, Hyla vasta. b, 4g, Head of Hyla vasta. c, 2g, Cyclura ricordii. d, 4g, Head of Cyclura ricordii.

1999, Aug. 27 **Litho.** ***Perf. 14***

913 A187 Block of 4, #a.-d. 3.00 3.00

Issued in sheets of 16 (4x4) and 8 (2x4).

Souvenir Sheet

Protection of Natural Resources — A188

1999 **Litho.** ***Perf. 13¾***

914 A188 20g multicolored 7.50 7.50

A188a Christmas A188b

1999 **Photo.** ***Perf. 11¾***

Panel Color

914A A188a 1g Prussian blue .75 .75
914B A188a 3g red brown 1.00 1.00
914C A188a 5g dark blue *2.50 2.50*
914D A188b 10g dk purple *4.00 4.00*
914E A188b 15g red *5.00 5.00*
914F A188b 20g blue *7.50 7.50*
g. Souvenir sheet, #915A-915F *25.00 25.00*
Nos. 914A-914F (6) 14.45 14.45

Nos. 914D-914F are airmail.

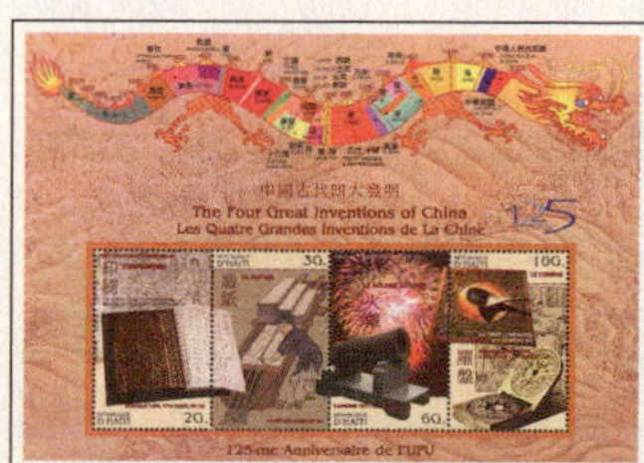

Chinese Inventions — A189

No. 915, 2g, Movable type. No. 916, 3g, Paper. No. 917, 6g, Gunpowder, cannon. No. 918, 10g, Compass.

1999, Dec. 20 **Litho.** ***Perf. 13¾***

915-918 Set of 4 *30.00 30.00*
a. A189 Souv. sheet, #915-918 *20.00 20.00*

UPU, 125th anniv.

Tourism A190

Designs: 2g, Pirogue. 3g, Smiling girl. 4g, Zim Pond, vert. 5g, Ardadins Island, vert. 6g, Gingerbread House. 10g, National Palace.20g, Peligre Reservoir, vert.

Perf. 14¼x14½, 14½x14¼

2000, June 5 Litho.

919-925	A190	Set of 7	*11.00*	*11.00*
a.	Souv. sheet, #919-925 + label		*12.50*	*12.50*

Souvenir Sheet

926	A190	25g Boat "Pays," vert.	*12.00*	*12.00*

1801 Constitution, Bicent. A191

Designs: 1g, 2g, 5g, 10g, 25g, 50g, Toussaint L'Ouverture and 1801 Constitution.

No. 933: a, Toussaint L'Ouverture. b, 1801 Constitution.

2001 Litho. *Perf. 13¾x13¼*

927	A191	1g multi	*.50*	*.50*
928	A191	2g multi	*.50*	*.50*
929	A191	5g multi	*.50*	*.50*
930	A191	10g multi	*2.00*	*1.25*
931	A191	25g multi	*4.00*	*2.25*
932	A191	50g multi	*8.00*	*3.75*
		Nos. 927-932 (6)	8.75	8.75

Souvenir Sheet

Perf. 12¾

933	A191	25g Sheet of 2, #a-b	*75.00*	*75.00*

Nos. 929-932 are airmail. No. 933 contains two 25x29mm stamps.

Toussaint L'Ouverture (c. 1743-1803) A192

Background color: 1g, Green. 2g, Brown. 3g, Yellow green. 5g, Red brown. 6g, blue. 10g, Violet.

2003, Apr. 7 Litho. *Perf. 13*

934-939	A192	Set of 6	*30.00*	*30.00*

Souvenir Sheet

Imperf

940	A192	15g multi	*50.00*	*50.00*

Pope John Paul II and Pope Benedict XVI Stamps

In 2005 a set of 8 face-different stamps with the image of John Paul II and 8 face different stamps with the image of Benedict XVI were printed without official authorization. They were printed in sheetlets numbered 1-40, with either three or six stamps per sheet. Selvage of various sheets containing the same stamps bear text in either French, English, Latin, Polish, Italian or Spanish. They were not sold by the Haiti post office and were not valid for postage.

The following items inscribed "Republic of Haiti" have been declared "illegal" by Haitian postal authorities:

Sheets of six 8g stamps depicting Pope John Paul II, and Pope Benedict XVI.

Sheets of six 10g stamps depicting Pope John Paul II, and Pope Benedict XVI.

Sheets of six 15g stamps depicting Pope John Paul II, and Pope Benedict XVI.

Sheet of three 20g stamps depicting Pope John Paul II.

Sheet of three 30g stamps depicting Pope John Paul II.

Sheets of two 25g stamps depicting Pope Benedict XVI (2 different).

A sheet of seven stamps of various denominations and two labels and a sheet of eight 25g stamp and one label commemorating the Jan. 12, 2010 Haiti earthquake have been determined to be bogus issues.

SEMI-POSTAL STAMPS

Pierre de Coubertin SP1

Engraved & Litho (flag)

1939, Oct. 3 Unwmk. *Perf. 12*

B1	SP1	10c + 10c multi	27.50	27.50
		Nos. B1,CB1-CB2 (3)	77.50	77.50

Pierre de Coubertin, organizer of the modern Olympic Games. The surtax was used to build a Sports Stadium at Port-au-Prince.

Catalogue values for unused stamps in this section, from this point to the end of the section, are for Never Hinged items.

Nos. 419-420 Surcharged in Deep Carmine

Perf. 13x13½, 13½x13

1958, Aug. 30 Litho. Unwmk.

B2	A82	1g + 50c purple	2.50	2.40
B3	A83	1.50g + 50c red org	2.50	2.40
		Nos. B2-B3,CB9 (3)	7.50	7.20

The surtax was for the Red Cross. Overprint arranged horizontally on No. B3.

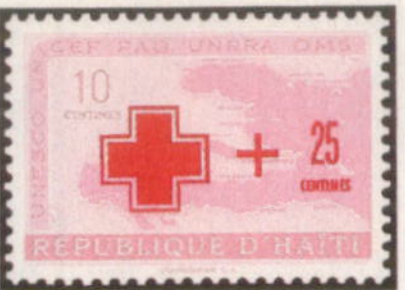

Nos. 440-441 Srchd. in Red

1959, Apr. 7 Photo. *Perf. 11½*

Granite Paper

B4	A87	10c + 25c rose pink	.40	.25
B5	A87	25c + 25c green	.40	.35

Nos. 444-446 Surcharged Like Nos. B2-B3 in Red

Perf. 14x13½

B6	A88	10c + 50c vio bl & ol	.75	.50
B7	A88	50c + 50c grn & dp brn	.75	.60
B8	A88	2g + 50c dp cl & dk brn	1.25	1.00
		Nos. B6-B8,CB10-CB15 (9)	7.65	7.00

The surtax was for the Red Cross.

No. 447 Surcharged Diagonally

Unwmk.

1959, July 23 Photo. *Perf. 12*

B9	A89	50c + 20c lt bl & dp cl	.85	.85
		Nos. B9,CB16-CB18 (4)	4.05	4.05

Issued for the World Refugee Year, July 1, 1959-June 30, 1960.

Nos. 448-450 Surcharged in Dark Carmine

1959, Oct. 30 *Perf. 14*

B10	A90	25c + 75c blk brn & lt bl	.65	.60
B11	A90	50c + 75c multi	.90	.60
B12	A91	75c + 75c brn & bl	.90	.60
		Nos. B10-B12,CB19-CB21 (6)	5.45	4.80

The surtax was for Haitian athletes.

On No. B12, surcharge lines are spaced to total depth of 16mm.

No. 436 Surcharged in Red: "Hommage a l'UNICEF +G. 0,50"

Engraved and Lithographed

1960, Feb. 2 *Perf. 11½*

B13	A86	1g + 50c blk & brick red	.90	.90
		Nos. B13,CB22-CB23 (3)	3.65	3.65

UNICEF.

Nos. 452-453 Surcharged with Additional Value and Overprinted "ALPHABETISATION" in Red or Black

Perf. 12½x13

1960, July 12 Litho. Unwmk.

B14	A92	10c + 20c sal & grn (R)	.35	.25
B15	A92	10c + 30c sal & grn	.40	.25
B16	A92	50c + 20c vio & mag (R)	.40	.25
B17	A92	50c + 30c vio & mag	.55	.50
		Nos. B14-B17,CB24-CB27 (8)	4.55	3.70

Olympic Games Issue

Nos. 464-465 Surcharged with Additional Value

1960, Sept. 9 Photo. *Perf. 12*

B18	A94	50c + 25c grn & ocher	.40	.25
B19	A94	1g + 25c dk brn & grnsh bl	.50	.40
		Nos. B18-B19,CB28-CB29 (4)	1.95	1.45

No. 469 Surcharged: "UNICEF +25 centimes"

1961, Jan. 14 Engr. *Perf. 10½*

B20	A96	1g + 25c grn & blk	.50	.40
		Nos. B20,CB30-CB31 (3)	1.55	1.20

UNICEF.

No. 469 Surcharged: "OMS SNEM +20 CENTIMES"

1961, Dec. 11

B21	A96	1g + 20c grn & blk	.55	.50
		Nos. B21,CB35-CB36 (3)	4.40	4.35

Haiti's participation in the UN malaria eradication drive.

Nos. 434, 436 and 438 Surcharged in Black or Red

(Surcharge arranged to fit shape of stamp.)

1961-62 Engr. & Litho. *Perf. 11½*

B22	A86	20c + 25c blk & yel	.30	.25
B23	A86	1g + 50c blk & brick red (R) ('62)	.50	.50
B24	A86	2.50g + 50c blk & gray vio (R) ('62)	.90	.60
		Nos. B22-B24,CB37-CB41 (8)	5.55	5.20

The surtax was for the benefit of the urban rehabilitation program in Duvalier Ville.

Nos. 486-488 Surcharged: "+25 centimes"

1962, Sept. 13 Litho. *Perf. 12*

B25	A99	5c + 25c crim & dp bl	.30	.25
B26	A99	10c + 25c red brn & emer	.30	.25
B27	A99	50c + 25c bl & crim	.40	.25
		Nos. B25-B27,CB42-CB44 (6)	2.15	1.65

Nos. 489-490 Surcharged in Red: "+0.20"

1962 Unwmk. *Perf. 12½x13*

B28	A92	10c + 20c bl & org	.30	.25
B29	A92	50c + 20c rose lil & ol grn	.40	.40
		Nos. B28-B29,CB45-CB46 (4)	1.60	1.45

No. 502 Surcharged: "ALPHABETISATION" and "+0,10"

1963, Mar. 15 Photo. *Perf. 14x14½*

B30	A102	25c + 10c bl gray, yel & blk	.25	.25
		Nos. B30,CB47-CB48 (3)	1.15	.90

Nos. 491-494 Surcharged and Overprinted in Black or Red

Overprint includes Olympic Emblem and: "JEUX OLYMPIQUES / D'HIVER / INNSBRUCK 1964"

Perf. 14x14½, 14½x14

1964, July 27 Unwmk.

B31	A100	50c + 10c on 3c (R)	.60	.40
B32	A100	50c + 10c on 5c	.60	.40
B33	A100	50c + 10c on 10c (R)	.60	.40
B34	A100	50c + 10c on 25c	.60	.40
		Nos. B31-B34,CB49 (5)	3.30	2.40

9th Winter Olympic Games, Innsbruck, Austria, Jan. 20-Feb. 9, 1964. The 10c surtax went for charitable purposes.

Nos. 510-512 Surcharged: "+ 5c." in Black

1965, Mar. 15 Photo. *Perf. 11½*
Granite Paper

B35	A105 10c + 5c lt bl & dk brn	.25	.25
B36	A105 25c + 5c sal & dk brn	.30	.25
B37	A105 50c + 5c pale rose lil & dk brn	.50	.40
	Nos. B35-B37,CB51-CB54 (7)	3.15	2.45

Nos. B35-B37 and CB51-CB54 also exist with this surcharge (without period after "c") in red. They also exist with a similar black surcharge which lacks the period and is in a thinner, lighter type face.

Nos. 533 and 535-536 Surcharged and Overprinted with Haitian Scout Emblem and "12e Jamboree / Mondial 1967" Like Regular Issue

1967, Aug. 21 Photo. *Perf. 11½*

B38	A111 10c + 10c on 5c multi	.25	.25
B39	A111 15c + 10c multi	.25	.25
B40	A111 50c + 10c multi	.30	.25
	Nos. B38-B40,CB55-CB56 (5)	1.85	1.50

12th Boy Scout World Jamboree, Farragut State Park, Idaho, Aug. 1-9. The surcharge on No. B38 includes 2 bars through old denomination.

Nos. 600-601 Surcharged in Red

Surcharge includes with new value, Red Cross and: "50ème. Anniversaire / de la Ligue des / Sociétés de la / Croix Rouge".

1969, June 25 Litho. *Perf. 11½*

B41	A127 10c + 10c multi	.25	.25
B42	A127 50c + 20c multi	.50	.40
	Nos. B41-B42,CB61-CB62 (4)	2.15	1.55

50th anniv. of the League of Red Cross Societies.

Nos. 637-638 Surcharged with New Value and: "INAUGURATION / 22-7-71"

1971, Aug. 3 Litho. *Perf. 14x13½*

B43	A138 20c + 50c multi	.45	.35
B44	A138 25c + 1.50g multi	.80	.45

Inauguration of the François Duvalier Central Hydroelectric Plant, July 22, 1971.

AIR POST STAMPS

Plane over Port-au-Prince — AP1

1929-30 Unwmk. Engr. *Perf. 12*

C1	AP1 25c dp grn ('30)	.50	.40
C2	AP1 50c dp vio	.65	.40
C3	AP1 75c red brn ('30)	1.75	1.25
C4	AP1 1g dp ultra	1.90	1.60
	Nos. C1-C4 (4)	4.80	3.65

No. 317 Surcharged in Red

1933, July 6

C4A	A44 60c on 20c vio blue	75.00	80.00

Non-stop flight of Capt. J. Errol Boyd and Robert G. Lyon from New York to Port-au-Prince.

Plane over Christophe's Citadel — AP2

1933-40

C5	AP2 50c org brn	5.25	1.00
C6	AP2 50c ol grn ('35)	4.00	1.00
C7	AP2 50c car rose ('37)	3.50	2.00
C8	AP2 50c blk ('38)	2.00	1.00
C8A	AP2 60c choc ('40)	1.10	.50
C9	AP2 1g ultra	1.75	.50
	Nos. C5-C9 (6)	17.60	6.00

For surcharge see No. C24.

Dumas Type of Regular Issue

1935, Dec. 29 Litho. *Perf. 11½*

C10	A59 60c brt vio & choc	4.50	2.50

Visit of delegation from France to Haiti.

Arms of Haiti and Portrait of George Washington — AP4

1938, Aug. 29 Engr. *Perf. 12*

C11	AP4 60c deep blue	.70	.40

150th anniv. of the US Constitution.

Caribbean Conference Type of Regular Issue

1941, June 30

C12	A60 60c olive	3.25	.85
C13	A60 1.25g purple	3.25	.65

Madonna Type of Regular Issue

1942, Dec. 8 *Perf. 12*

C14	A61 10c dk olive	.40	.25
C15	A61 25c brt ultra	.50	.40
C16	A61 50c turq grn	.90	.40
C17	A61 60c rose car	1.40	.50
C18	A61 1.25g black	2.50	.50
	Nos. C14-C18 (5)	5.70	2.05

Souvenir Sheets

C19	A61 Sheet of 2, #C14, C16	5.00	5.00
a.	Imperf	25.00	25.00
C20	A61 Sheet of 2, #C15, C17	5.00	5.00
a.	Imperf	25.00	25.00
C21	A61 Sheet of 1, #C18	5.00	5.00
a.	Imperf	25.00	25.00

Our Lady of Perpetual Help, patroness of Haiti.

Killick Type of Regular Issue

1943, Sept. 6

C22	A62 60c purple	.65	.40
C23	A62 1.25g black	1.60	1.60

No. C8A Surcharged with New Value and Bars in Red

1944, Nov. 25

C24	AP2 10c on 60c choc	.50	.40
a.	Bars at right vertical	2.40	
b.	Double surcharge	75.00	

Red Cross Type of Regular Issue

1945 Cross in Rose

C25	A63 20c yel org	.40	.25
C26	A63 25c brt ultra	.40	.25
C27	A63 50c ol blk	.40	.25
C28	A63 60c dl vio	.50	.25
C29	A63 1g yellow	1.40	.40
C30	A63 1.25g carmine	1.25	.40
C31	A63 1.35g green	1.25	.60
C32	A63 5g black	7.25	2.50
	Nos. C25-C32 (8)	12.85	4.90

Issue dates: 1g, Aug. 14; others, Feb. 20.
For surcharges see Nos. C153-C160.

Catalogue values for unused stamps in this section, from this point to the end of the section, are for Never Hinged items.

Franklin D. Roosevelt — AP11

1946, Feb. 5 Unwmk. *Perf. 12*

C33	AP11 20c black	.40	.25
C34	AP11 60c black	.50	.25

Capois Type of Regular Issue

1946, July 18 Engr.

C35	A64 20c car rose	.25	.25
C36	A64 25c dk grn	.25	.25
C37	A64 50c orange	.25	.25
C38	A64 60c purple	.40	.25
C39	A64 1g gray blk	.50	.25
C40	A64 1.25g red vio	.75	.40
C41	A64 1.35g black	.80	.50
C42	A64 5g rose car	2.40	1.20
	Nos. C35-C42 (8)	5.60	3.35

For surcharges see Nos. C43-C45, C49-C51, C61-C62.

Nos. C37 and C41 Surcharged with New Value and Bar or Block in Red or Black

1947-48

C43	A64 5c on 1.35g (R) ('48)	.60	.40
C44	A64 30c on 50c	.50	.40
C45	A64 30c on 1.35g (R)	.50	.40
	Nos. C43-C45 (3)	1.60	1.20

Dessalines Type of 1947-54 Regular Issue

1947, Oct. 17 Engr.

C46	A65 20c chocolate	.40	.25

Christopher Columbus and Fleet — AP14

Pres. Dumarsais Estimé and Exposition Buildings — AP15

1950, Feb. 12 *Perf. 12½*

C47	AP14 30c ultra & gray	.90	.50
C48	AP15 1g black	.90	.50

200th anniversary (in 1949) of the founding of Port-au-Prince.

Nos. C36, C39 and C41 Surcharged or Overprinted in Carmine

1950, Oct. 4 *Perf. 12*

C49	A64 30c on 25c dk grn	.40	.30
a.	30c on 1g gray black	75.00	
C50	A64 1g gray blk	.60	.50
a.	"P" of overprint omitted	65.00	60.00
C51	A64 1.50g on 1.35g blk	1.75	1.50
	Nos. C49-C51 (3)	2.75	2.30

75th anniv. (in 1949) of the UPU.

Bananas AP16

Coffee AP17

Sisal — AP18

1951, Sept. 3 Photo. *Perf. 12½*

C52	AP16 30c dp org	2.25	.40
C53	AP17 80c dk grn & sal pink	5.50	.60
C54	AP18 5g gray	19.00	3.50
	Nos. C52-C54 (3)	26.75	4.50

For surcharge see No. C218.

Isabella I — AP19

1951, Oct. 12 *Perf. 13*

C55	AP19 15c brown	.30	.25
C56	AP19 30c dull blue	.40	.40

Queen Isabella I of Spain, 500th birth anniv.

Type of Regular Issue

20c, Cap Haitien Roadstead. 30c, Workers' housing, St. Martin. 1.50g, Restored cathedral. 2.50g, School lunchroom.

1953, May 4 Engr. *Perf. 12*

C57	A68 20c dp bl	.25	.25
C58	A68 30c red brn	.40	.25
C59	A68 1.50g gray blk	.85	.50
C60	A68 2.50g violet	1.75	.85
	Nos. C57-C60 (4)	3.25	1.85

Nos. C38 and C41 Surcharged in Black

1953, May 18

C61	A64 50c on 60c pur	.40	.25
a.	Double surcharge	200.00	200.00
C62	A64 50c on 1.35g blk	.40	.25
a.	Double surcharge	200.00	

150th anniv. of the adoption of the natl. flag.

Dessalines and Magloire Type and

Henri Christophe — AP21

No. C64, Toussaint L'Ouverture. No. C65, Dessalines. No. C66, Petion. No. C67, Boisrond-Tonerre. No. C68, Petion. No. C69, Lamartiniere.

1954, Jan. 1 Photo. *Perf. 11½*

C63	AP21 50c shown	.50	.25
C64	AP21 50c multicolored	.50	.25
C65	AP21 50c multicolored	.50	.25
C66	AP21 50c multicolored	.50	.25
C67	AP21 50c multicolored	.50	.25
C68	AP21 1g multicolored	.80	.50
C69	AP21 1.50g multicolored	1.50	1.00
C70	A69 7.50g multicolored	5.50	5.00
	Nos. C63-C70 (8)	10.30	7.75

See Nos. C95-C96.

Marie Jeanne and Lamartinière Leading Attack — AP23

Design: Nos. C73, C74, Battle of Vertieres.

1954, Jan. 1 *Perf. 12½*

C71 AP23 50c black .40 .25
C72 AP23 50c carmine .40 .25
C73 AP23 50c ultra .40 .25
C74 AP23 50c sal pink .40 .25
Nos. C71-C74 (4) 1.60 1.00

150th anniv. of Haitian independence.

Mme. Magloire Type of Regular Issue

1954, Jan. 1 *Perf. 11½*

C75 A72 20c red org .25 .25
C76 A72 50c brown .40 .40
C77 A72 1g gray grn .50 .40
C78 A72 1.50g crimson .75 .50
C79 A72 2.50g bl grn 1.25 .90
C80 A72 5g gray 3.00 2.25
Nos. C75-C80 (6) 6.15 4.70

Christophe Types of Regular Issue

1954, Dec. 6 Litho. *Perf. 13½x13*

Portraits in Black

C81 A73 50c orange .40 .25
C82 A73 1g blue .80 .50
C83 A73 1.50g green 1.10 .65
C84 A73 2.50g gray 1.75 .90
C85 A73 5g rose car 3.25 1.90

Perf. 13

Flag in Black and Carmine

C86 A74 50c orange .40 .25
C87 A74 1g dp bl .75 .45
C88 A74 1.50g bl grn 1.10 .65
C89 A74 2.50g gray 1.75 .90
C90 A74 5g red org 3.25 1.90
Nos. C81-C90 (10) 14.55 8.35

Fort Nativity, Drawing by Christopher Columbus — AP27

1954, Dec. 14 Engr. *Perf. 12*

C91 AP27 50c dk rose car .65 .50
C92 AP27 50c dk gray .65 .50

Dessalines Type of 1955-57 Issue

Perf. 11½

1955, July 14 Unwmk. Photo.

C93 A75 20c org & blk .25 .25
C94 A75 20c yel grn & blk .25 .25

For overprint see No. C183a.

Portrait Type of 1954 Dates omitted

Design: J. J. Dessalines.

1955, July 19 Portrait in Black

C95 AP21 50c gray .40 .25
C96 AP21 50c blue .40 .25

Dessalines Memorial Type of Regular Issue

1955, Aug. 1

C97 A76 1.50g gray & blk .65 .25
C98 A76 1.50g grn & blk .65 .25

Types of 1956 Regular Issue and

Car and Coastal View — AP30

Designs: No. C100, 75c, Plane, steamship and Haiti map. 1g, Car and coastal view. 2.50g, Flamingo. 5g, Mallard.

1956, Apr. 14 Unwmk. *Perf. 11½*

Granite Paper

C99 AP30 50c hn brn & lt bl .70 .25
C100 AP30 50c blk & gray .45 .25
C101 AP30 75c dp grn & bl grn .95 .50
C102 AP30 1g ol grn & lt bl .80 .30
C103 A77 2.50g dp org & org 14.00 1.75
C104 A78 5g red & buff 21.00 3.00
Nos. C99-C104 (6) 37.90 6.05

For overprint see No. C185.

Kant Type of Regular Issue

1956, July 19 Photo. *Perf. 12*

Granite Paper

C105 A79 50c chestnut .40 .25
C106 A79 75c dp yel grn .50 .40
C107 A79 1.50g dp magenta 1.25 .50
a. Miniature sheet of 3 8.00 5.00
Nos. C105-C107 (3) 2.15 1.15

No. C107a exists both perf. and imperf. Each sheet contains Nos. C105, C106 and a 1.25g gray black of same design.

Waterfall Type of Regular Issue

1957, Dec. 16 *Perf. 11½*

Granite Paper

C108 A80 50c grn & grnsh bl .25 .25
C109 A80 1.50g ol grn & grnsh bl .65 .40
C110 A80 2.50g dk bl & brt bl 1.00 .60
C111 A80 5g bluish blk & saph 2.50 1.50
Nos. C108-C111 (4) 4.40 2.75

For surcharge and overprint see Nos. CB49, CQ2.

Dessalines Type of Regular Issue

1958, July 2

C112 A81 50c org & blk .65 .40

For overprints see Nos. C184, CQ1.

Brussels Fair Types of Regular Issue, 1958

Perf. 13x13½, 13½x13

1958, July 22 Litho. Unwmk.

C113 A82 2.50g pale car rose 1.25 .50
C114 A83 5g bright blue 1.50 .85
a. Souv. sheet of 2, #C113-C114, imperf. 5.50 5.00

For surcharge see No. CB9.

Sylvio Cator — AP33

1958, Aug. 16 Photo. *Perf. 11½*

Granite Paper

C115 AP33 50c green .25 .25
C116 AP33 50c blk brn .25 .25
C117 AP33 1g org brn .50 .40
C118 AP33 5g gray 2.40 .85
Nos. C115-C118 (4) 3.40 1.75

30th anniversary of the world championship record broad jump of Sylvio Cator.

IGY Type of Regular Issue, 1958

Designs: 50c, US Satellite. 1.50g, Emperor penguins. 2g, Modern observatory.

1958, Oct. 8 *Perf. 14x13½*

C119 A85 50c dp ultra & brn red .60 .25
C120 A85 1.50g brn & crim 3.25 .75
C121 A85 2g dk bl & crim 2.25 .40
a. Souv. sheet of 4, #427, C119-C121, imperf. 8.00 7.50
Nos. C119-C121 (3) 6.10 1.40

President Francois Duvalier AP34

Commemorative Inscription in Ultramarine

Engraved and Lithographed

1958, Oct. 22 Unwmk. *Perf. 11½*

C122 AP34 50c blk & rose 1.00 .25
C123 AP34 2.50g blk & ocher 1.40 .60
C124 AP34 5g blk & rose lil 1.90 1.25
C125 AP34 7.50g blk & lt bl grn 3.00 2.00
Nos. C122-C125 (4) 7.30 4.10

See note after No. 431.

Souvenir sheets of 3 exist, perf. and imperf., containing one each of Nos. C124-C125 and No. 431. Sheets measure 132x77mm. with marginal inscription in ultramarine. Value, $6.25 each.

For surcharges see Nos. CB37-CB39.

Same Without Commemorative Inscription

1958, Nov. 20

C126 AP34 50c blk & rose .40 .25
C127 AP34 1g blk & vio .50 .25
C128 AP34 1.50g blk & pale brn .75 .40
C129 AP34 2g blk & rose pink 1.00 .40
C130 AP34 2.50g blk & ocher 1.00 .50
C131 AP34 5g blk & rose lil 2.00 1.25
C132 AP34 7.50g blk & lt bl grn 3.00 1.60
Nos. C126-C132 (7) 8.65 4.65

For surcharges see Nos. CB22-CB23, CB40-CB41.

Type of Regular Issue and

Flags of Haiti and UN — AP35

Perf. 11½

1958, Dec. 5 Unwmk. Photo.

Granite Paper

C133 AP35 50c pink, car & ultra .40 .25
C134 A87 75c brt bl .40 .25
C135 A87 1g brown .50 .40
a. Souv. sheet of 2, #C133, C135, imperf. 3.50 3.50
Nos. C133-C135 (3) 1.30 .90

For surcharges see Nos. CB10-CB12.

Nos. C133-C135 Overprinted

Overprint reads "10th ANNIVERSARY OF THE UNIVERSAL DECLARATION OF HUMAN RIGHTS" in: a, English; b, French; c, Spanish; d, Portuguese.

1959, Jan. 28

C136 Block of 4 2.75 2.75
a.-d. AP35 50c any single .60 .60
C137 Block of 4 3.75 3.75
a.-d. A87 75c any single .80 .80
C138 Block of 4 7.00 7.00
a.-d. A87 1g any single 1.50 1.50
Nos. C136-C138 (3) 13.50 13.50

Pope Pius XII — AP36

1.50g, Pope praying. 2.50g, Pope on throne.

1959, Feb. 28 Photo. *Perf. 14x13½*

C139 AP36 50c grn & lil .25 .25
C140 AP36 1.50g ol & red brn .65 .40
C141 AP36 2.50g pur & dk bl 1.00 .40
Nos. C139-C141 (3) 1.90 1.05

Issued in memory of Pope Pius XII.
For surcharges see Nos. CB13-CB15.

Lincoln Type of Regular Issue, 1959

Designs: Various Portraits of Lincoln.

1959, May 12 *Perf. 12*

C142 A89 1g lt grn & chnt .50 .40
C143 A89 2g pale lem & sl grn .75 .50
C144 A89 2.50g buff & vio bl .85 .40
a. Min. sheet of 4, #447, C142-C144, imperf. 3.00 2.75
Nos. C142-C144 (3) 2.10 1.30

Imperf. pairs exist.
For surcharges see Nos. CB16-CB18.

Pan American Games Types of Regular Issue

Designs: 50c, Jean Baptiste Dessables and map of American Midwest, c. 1791. 1g, Chicago's skyline and Dessables house. 1.50g, Discus thrower and flag of Haiti.

Unwmk.

1959, Aug. 27 Photo. *Perf. 14*

C145 A91 50c hn brn & aqua .75 .25
C146 A90 1g lil & aqua 1.00 .40
C147 A90 1.50g multi 1.40 .50
Nos. C145-C147 (3) 3.15 1.15

For surcharges see Nos. CB19-CB21.

Nos. C145-C147 Overprinted like No. 451

1960, Feb. 29

C148 A91 50c hn brn & aqua 1.40 1.40
C149 A90 1g lil & aqua 1.90 1.90
C150 A90 1.50g multi 2.75 2.75
Nos. C148-C150 (3) 6.05 6.05

WRY Type of Regular Issue, 1960

1960, Apr. 7 Litho. *Perf. 12½x13*

C151 A92 50c bl & blk .40 .25
C152 A92 1g lt grn & mar .50 .40
a. Souv. sheet of 4, #452-453, C151-C152, imperf. 6.50 6.00

See Nos. C191-C192. For surcharges see Nos. CB24-CB27, CB45-CB46.

Nos. C31, C28 and 369 Surcharged or Overprinted in Red: "28ème ANNIVERSAIRE"

1960, May 8 Engr. *Perf. 12*

Cross in Rose

C153 A63 20c on 1.35g grn .40 .25
C154 A63 50c on 60c dl vio .65 .40
C155 A63 50c on 1.35g grn .40 .40
C156 A63 50c on 2.50g pale vio .40 .40
C157 A63 60c dl vio .40 .40
C158 A63 1g on 1.35g grn .70 .50
C159 A63 1.35g green .65 .50
C160 A63 2g on 1.35g grn 1.40 1.00
Nos. C153-C160 (8) 5.00 3.85

28th anniv. of the Haitian Red Cross. Additional overprint "Avion" on No. C156.

Sugar Type of Regular Issue

Miss Fouchard &: 50c, Harvest. 2.50g, Beach.

Perf. 11½

1960, May 30 Unwmk. Photo.

Granite Paper

C161 A93 50c lil rose & brn .90 .25
C162 A93 2.50g ultra & brn 2.25 .50

Olympic Type of Regular Issue

Designs: 50c, Pierre de Coubertin, Melbourne stadium and Olympic Flame. 1.50g, Discus thrower and Rome stadium. 2.50g, Victors' parade, Athens, 1896, and Melbourne, 1956.

1960, Aug. 18 *Perf. 12*

C163 A94 50c mar & bis .65 .25
C164 A94 1.50g rose car & yel grn 1.40 .40
C165 A94 2.50g sl grn & mag 1.60 .45
a. Souv. sheet of 2, #465, C165, imperf. 5.50 5.50
Nos. C163-C165 (3) 3.65 1.10

For surcharges see Nos. CB28-CB29.

Jeanty Type of Regular Issue

50c, Occide Jeanty and score from "1804." 1.50g, Occide Jeanty and National Capitol.

1960, Oct. 19 *Perf. 14x14½*

C166 A95 50c yel & bl .50 .25
C167 A95 1.50g lil rose & sl grn .75 .25

Printed in sheets of 12 (3x4) with inscription and opening bars of "1804," Jeanty's military march, in top margin.

UN Type of Regular Issue, 1960

1960, Nov. 25 Engr. *Perf. 10½*

C168 A96 50c red org & blk .40 .25
C169 A96 1.50g dk bl & blk .50 .40
a. Souv. sheet of 3, #469, C168-C169, imperf. 3.25 3.25

For surcharges see Nos. CB30-CB31, CB35-CB36.
Nos. C168-C169 exist with centers inverted.

Dessalines Type of Regular Issue

1960, Nov. 5 Photo. *Perf. 11½*

Granite Paper

C170 A81 20c gray & blk .25 .25

For overprint see No. C183.

Sud-Caravelle Jet Airliner and Orchid — AP37

Designs: 50c, Boeing 707 jet airliner, facing left, and Kittyhawk. 1g, Sud-Caravelle jet airliner and Orchid. 1.50g, Boeing 707 jet airliner and air post stamp of 1933.

1960, Dec. 17 Photo. Unwmk.
Granite Paper

C171 AP37 20c dp ultra & car .25 .25
C172 AP37 50c rose brn & grn .50 .25
C173 AP37 50c brt grnsh bl & ol grn .50 .25
C174 AP37 50c gray & grn .50 .25
C175 AP37 1g gray ol & ver 1.60 .25
C176 AP37 1.50g brt pink & dk bl 1.25 .30
a. Souv. sheet of 3, #C174-C176, imperf. 4.00 4.00
Nos. C171-C176 (6) 4.60 1.55

Issued for Aviation Week, Dec. 17-23.

Nos. C172-C174 are dated 17 Decembre 1903.

For overprints and surcharges see Nos. CB32-CB34, CO1-CO5.

Dumas Type of Regular Issue

Designs: 50c, The Three Musketeers and Dumas père, horiz 1g, The Lady of the Camellias and Dumas fils. 1.50g, The Count of Monte Cristo and Dumas père.

1961, Feb. 10 Photo. *Perf. 11½*
Granite Paper

C177 A97 50c brt bl & blk .60 .25
C178 A97 1g blk & red .75 .25
C179 A97 1.50g brt grn & bl blk 1.10 .35
Nos. C177-C179 (3) 2.45 .85

Type of Regular Issue, 1961

Tourist publicity: 20c, Privateer in Battle. 50c, Pirate with cutlass in rigging. 1g, Map of Tortuga.

1961, Apr. 4 Litho. *Perf. 12*

C180 A98 20c dk bl & yel .30 .25
C181 A98 50c brt pur & org .55 .25
C182 A98 1g Prus grn & yel .45 .40
Nos. C180-C182 (3) 1.30 .90

For overprint and surcharge see Nos. C186-C187.

Nos. C170, C112 and C101 Overprinted: "Dr. F. Duvalier Président 22 Mai 1961"

1961, May 22 Photo. *Perf. 11½*

C183 A81 20c gray & blk .25 .25
a. On No. C93
C184 A81 50c org & blk .25 .25
C185 AP30 75c dp grn & bl grn .40 .40
Nos. C183-C185 (3) .90 .90

Re-election of Pres. Francois Duvalier.

No. C182 Overprinted or Surcharged

Overprint or Surcharge includes Capsule and: "EXPLORATION SPATIALE JOHN GLENN".

1962, May 10 Litho. *Perf. 12*

C186 A98 1g Prus grn & yel .50 .40
C187 A98 2g on 1g Prus grn & yel 1.40 1.00

See note after No. 485.

Malaria Type of Regular Issue

Designs: 20c, 1g, Triangle pointing down. 50c, Triangle pointing up.

1962, May 30 Unwmk.

C188 A99 20c lilac & red .25 .25
C189 A99 50c emer & rose car .40 .25
C190 A99 1g org & dk vio .50 .40
a. Souv. sheet of 3 3.00 3.00
Nos. C188-C190 (3) 1.15 .90

Sheets of 12 with marginal inscription.

No. C190a contains stamps similar to Nos. 488 and C189-C190 in changed colors and imperf. Issued July 16.

A similar sheet without the "Contribution . . ." inscription was issued May 30.

For surcharges see Nos. CB42-CB44.

WRY Type of 1960 Dated "1962"

1962, June 22 *Perf. 12½x13*

C191 A92 50c lt bl & red brn .35 .25
C192 A92 1g bister & blk .40 .40

A souvenir sheet exists containing one each of Nos. 489-490, C191-C192, imperf. Value, $5.50.

For surcharges see Nos. CB45-CB46.

Boy Scout Type of 1962

Designs: 20c, Scout giving Scout sign. 50c, Haitian Scout emblem. 1.50g, Lord and Lady Baden-Powell, horiz.

Perf. 14x14½, 14½x14

1962, Aug. 6 Photo. Unwmk.

C193 A100 20c multi .25 .25
C194 A100 50c multi .50 .40
C195 A100 1.50g multi .65 .40
Nos. C193-C195 (3) 1.40 1.05

A souvenir sheet contains one each of Nos. C194-C195 imperf. Value, $5.50.

A similar sheet inscribed in gold, "Epreuves De Luxe," was issued Dec. 10. Value $3.

Nos. 495 and C193-C195 Overprinted: "AÉROPORT INTERNATIONAL 1962"

1962, Oct. 26 *Perf. 14x14½, 14½x14*

C196 A100 20c multi, #C193 .25 .25
C197 A100 50c multi, #495 .40 .25
C198 A100 50c multi, #C194 .40 .25
C199 A100 1.50g multi, #C195 .60 .40
Nos. C196-C199 (4) 1.65 1.15

Proceeds from the sale of Nos. C196-C199 were for the construction of new airport at Port-au-Prince. The overprint on No. C197 has "Poste Aérienne" added.

Seattle Fair Type of 1962

Design: Denomination at left, "Avion" at right.

1962, Nov. 19 Litho. *Perf. 12½*

C200 A101 50c blk & pale lil .40 .25
C201 A101 1g org brn & gray .60 .40
C202 A101 1.50g red lil & org .70 .40
Nos. C200-C202 (3) 1.70 1.05

An imperf. sheet of two exists containing one each of Nos. C201-C202 with simulated gray perforations. Size: 133x82mm. Value, $5.50.

Street in Duvalier Ville and Stamp of 1881 — AP38

1962, Dec. 10 Photo. *Perf. 14x14½*
Stamp in Dark Brown

C203 AP38 50c orange .50 .25
C204 AP38 1g blue .90 .40
C205 AP38 1.50g green 1.00 .50
Nos. C203-C205 (3) 2.40 1.15

Issued to publicize Duvalier Ville.
For surcharges see Nos. CB47-CB48.

Nos. C201-C202 Overprint in Black

1963, Jan. 23 Litho. *Perf. 12½*

C206 A101 1g org brn & gray 1.40 .60
a. Claret overprint, horiz. 1.40 .60
C207 A101 1.50g red lil & org 1.75 1.10
a. Claret overprint, horiz. 1.75 1.10

"Peaceful Uses of Outer Space." The black vertical overprint has no outside frame lines and no broken shading lines around capsule. Nos. C206a and C207a were issued Feb. 20.

Hunger Type of Regular Issue

Perf. 13x14

1963, July 12 Unwmk. Photo.

C208 A103 50c lil rose & blk .40 .25
C209 A103 1g lt ol grn & blk .50 .40

Dag Hammarskjold and UN Emblem — AP39

Lithographed and Photogravure

1963, Sept. 28 *Perf. 13½x14*
Portrait in Slate

C210 AP39 20c buff & brn .25 .25
C211 AP39 50c lt bl & car .40 .25
a. Souvenir sheet of 2 3.50 3.50
C212 AP39 1g pink & bl .40 .25
C213 AP39 1.50g gray & grn .65 .50
Nos. C210-C213 (4) 1.70 1.25

Dag Hammarskjold, Sec. Gen. of the UN, 1953-61. Printed in sheets of 25 (5x5) with map of Sweden extending over 9 stamps in second and third vertical rows. No. C211a contains 2 imperf. stamps: 50c blue and carmine and 1.50g ocher and brown with map of southern Sweden in background.

For overprints see Nos. C219-C222, C238-C241, CB50.

Dessalines Type of Regular Issue, 1963

1963, Oct. 17 Photo. *Perf. 14x14½*

C214 A104 50c bl & lil rose .25 .25
C215 A104 50c org & grn .25 .25

Nos. C214-C215 and C53 Overprinted in Black or Red: "FETE DES MERES / 1964"

1964, July 22 *Perf. 14x14½, 12½*

C216 A104 50c bl & lil rose .40 .25
C217 A104 50c org & grn .40 .25
C218 AP17 1.50g on 80c dk grn & sal pink (R) .60 .40
a. Inverted surcharge 20.00
Nos. C216-C218 (3) 1.40 .90

Issued for Mother's Day, 1964.

Nos. C210-C213 Overprinted in Red

Lithographed and Engraved

1964, Oct. 2 *Perf. 13½x14*
Portrait in Slate

C219 AP39 20c buff & brn .40 .25
C220 AP39 50c lt bl & car .40 .25
C221 AP39 1g pink & bl .60 .40
C222 AP39 1.50g gray & grn .70 .50
Nos. C219-C222,CB50 (5) 3.50 2.65

Cent. (in 1963) of the Intl. Red Cross.

Olympic Type of Regular Issue

No. C223, Weight lifter. Nos. C224-C226, Hurdler.

1964, Nov. 12 Photo. *Perf. 11½*
Granite Paper

C223 A105 50c pale lil & dk brn .40 .25
C224 A105 50c pale grn & dk brn .40 .25
C225 A105 75c buff & dk brn .50 .40
C226 A105 1.50g gray & dk brn .65 .50
a. Souv. sheet of 4 2.60 2.50
Nos. C223-C226 (4) 1.95 1.40

Printed in sheets of 50 (10x5), with map of Japan in background extending over 27 stamps.

No. C226a contains four imperf. stamps similar to Nos. C223-C226 in changed colors and with map of Tokyo area in background.

For surcharges see Nos. CB51-CB54.

Airport Type of Regular Issue, 1964

1964, Dec. 15 *Perf. 14½x14*

C227 A106 50c org & blk .40 .25
C228 A106 1.50g brt lil rose & blk .65 .45
C229 A106 2.50g lt vio & blk 1.40 .60
Nos. C227-C229 (3) 2.45 1.30

Same Overprinted "1965"

1965, Feb. 11 Photo.

C230 A106 50c org & blk .40 .25
C231 A106 1.50g brt lil rose & blk .65 .40
C232 A106 2.50g lt vio & blk 1.00 .70
Nos. C230-C232 (3) 2.05 1.35

World's Fair Type of Regular Issue, 1965

Designs: 50c, 1.50g, "Rocket Thrower" by Donald De Lue. 5g, Unisphere, NY World's Fair.

1965, Mar. 22 Unwmk. *Perf. 13½*

C233 A107 50c dp bl & org .40 .25
C234 A107 1.50g gray & org .50 .40
C235 A107 5g multi 2.40 1.90
Nos. C233-C235 (3) 3.30 2.55

Merchant Marine Type of Regular Issue, 1965

1965, May 13 Photo. *Perf. 11½*

C236 A108 50c blk, lt grnsh bl & red .40 .25
C237 A108 1.50g blk, lt vio & red .75 .50

Nos. C210-C213 Overprinted

Lithographed and Photogravure

1965, June 26 *Perf. 13½x14*
Portrait in Slate

C238 AP39 20c buff & brn .25 .25
C239 AP39 50c lt bl & car .40 .25
C240 AP39 1g pink & bl .50 .40
C241 AP39 1.50g gray & grn .65 .50
Nos. C238-C241 (4) 1.80 1.40

20th anniversary of the United Nations.

ITU Type of Regular Issue

Perf. 13½

1965, Aug. 16 Unwmk. Litho.

C242 A109 50c multi .40 .25
C243 A109 1g multi .50 .40
C244 A109 1.50g bl & multi 1.00 .50
C245 A109 2g pink & multi 1.50 .60
Nos. C242-C245 (4) 3.40 1.75

A souvenir sheet, released in 1966, contains 50c and 2g stamps resembling Nos. C242 and C245, with simulated perforations. Value $15.00.

For overprints see Nos. C255-C256.

Cathedral Type of Regular Issue, 1965

Designs: 50c, Cathedral, Port-au-Prince, horiz. 1g, High Altar. 7.50g, Statue of Our Lady of the Assumption.

Perf. 14x13, 13x14

1965, Nov. 19 Photo.
Size: 39x29mm, 29x39mm

C246 A110 50c multi .40 .25
C247 A110 1g multi .65 .40

Size: 38x52mm

C248 A110 7.50g multi 2.75 2.25
Nos. C246-C248 (3) 3.80 2.90

Flower Type of Regular Issue

No. C249, 5g, Passionflower. Nos. C250, C252, Okra. Nos. C251, C253, American elder.

1965, Dec. 20 Photo. *Perf. 11½*
Granite Paper

C249 A111 50c dk vio, yel & grn 1.10 .25
C250 A111 50c multi 1.10 .25
C251 A111 50c grn, gray & yel 1.10 .25
C252 A111 1.50g multi 1.90 1.40
C253 A111 1.50g grn, tan & yel 1.90 1.40
C254 A111 5g dk vio, yel grn & grn 5.50 1.50
Nos. C249-C254 (6) 12.60 5.05

For surcharges see Nos. CB55-CB56.

Nos. C242-C243 Overprinted in Red: "20e. Anniversaire / UNESCO"

1965, Aug. 27 Litho. *Perf. 13½*
C255 A109 50c lt vio & multi 1.40 .50
C256 A109 1g citron & multi 2.60 .85

20th anniversary of UNESCO.
The souvenir sheet noted below No. C245 was also overprinted "20e. Anniversaire / UNESCO" in red. Value, $20.

Culture Types of Regular Issue and

Modern Painting — AP40

Designs: 50c, Ceremonial stool. 1.50g, Amulet.

Perf. 14x14½, 14½x14, 14
1966, Mar. 14 Photo. Unwmk.
C257 A113 50c lil, brn & brnz .40 .25
C258 A112 1.50g brt rose lil, yel & blk .65 .50
C259 AP40 2.50g multi 1.50 .85
Nos. C257-C259 (3) 2.55 1.60

For overprints and surcharge see Nos. C260-C262, C280-C281.

Nos. C257-C259 Overprinted in Black or Red: "Hommage / a Hailé Sélassié Ier / 24-25 Avril 1966"

1966, Apr. 24
C260 A112 50c (R) .40 .25
C261 A113 1.50g (vert. ovpt.) .65 .50
C262 AP40 2.50g (R) 1.00 .70
Nos. C260-C262 (3) 2.05 1.45

See note after No. 543.

Walter M. Schirra, Thomas P. Stafford, Frank A. Borman, James A. Lovell and Gemini VI and VII — AP41

1966, May 3 *Perf. 13½*
C263 AP41 50c vio bl, brn & lt bl .40 .25
C264 AP41 1g grn, brn & lt bl .50 .40
C265 AP41 1.50g car, brn & bl .65 .50
Nos. C263-C265 (3) 1.55 1.15

See No. 547.
For overprints see Nos. C296-C298.

Soccer Type of Regular Issue

Portrait in Black; Gold Inscription; Green Commemorative Inscription in Two Lines

Designs: 50c, Pres. Duvalier and soccer ball within wreath. 1.50g, President Duvalier and soccer player within wreath.

Lithographed and Photogravure
1966, June 16 *Perf. 13x13½*
C266 A115 50c lt ol grn & plum .40 .25
C267 A115 1.50g rose & plum .65 .50

Green Commemorative Inscription in 3 Lines; Gold Inscription Omitted
C268 A115 50c lt ol grn & plum .40 .40
C269 A115 1.50g rose & plum .65 .50
Nos. C266-C269 (4) 2.10 1.65

Caribbean Soccer Festival, June 10-22. Nos. C266-C267 also for the National Soccer Championships, May 8-22.
For overprint and surcharge see Nos. C288, CB57.

Education Type of Regular Issue

Designs: 50c, "ABC", boy and girl. 1g, Scout symbols. 1.50g, Television set, book and communications satellite, horiz.

Perf. 14x13½, 13½x14
Litho. and Engraved
1966, Oct. 18
C270 A116 50c grn, yel & brn .40 .25
C271 A116 1g dk brn, org & blk .50 .40
C272 A116 1.50g grn, bl grn & dk bl .65 .50
Nos. C270-C272 (3) 1.55 1.15

Schweitzer Type of Regular Issue

Designs (Schweitzer and): 50c, 1g, Albert Schweitzer Hospital, Deschapelles, Haiti. 1.50g, Maps of Alsace and Gabon. 2g, Pipe organ.

Perf. 12½x13
1967, Apr. 20 Photo. Unwmk.
C273 A117 50c multi .50 .40
C274 A117 1g multi .50 .40
C275 A117 1.50g lt bl & multi .65 .50
C276 A117 2g multi .90 .70
Nos. C273-C276 (4) 2.55 2.00

Fruit-Vegetable Type of Regular Issue, 1967

1967, July 4 Photo. *Perf. 12½*
C277 A118 50c Watermelon 2.00 .25
C278 A118 1g Cabbage 2.50 2.00
C279 A118 1.50g Tangerine 3.00 2.50
Nos. C277-C279 (3) 7.50 4.75

No. C258 Overprinted or Surcharged Like EXPO '67 Regular Issue

1967, Aug. 30 Photo. *Perf. 14½x14*
C280 A112 1.50g multi .60 .40
C281 A112 2g on 1.50g multi .75 .55

Issued to commemorate EXPO '67 International Exhibition, Montreal, Apr. 28-Oct. 27.

Duvalier Type of Regular Issue, 1967

1967, Sept. 22 Photo. *Perf. 14x13*
C282 A119 1g brt grn & gold .50 .40
C283 A119 1.50g vio & gold .65 .50
C284 A119 2g org & gold 1.10 .70
Nos. C282-C284 (3) 2.25 1.60

Education Type of Regular Issue, 1967

50c, Writing hands. 1g, Scout emblem and Scouts, vert. 1.50g, Audio-visual teaching of algebra.

1967, Dec. 11 Litho. *Perf. 11½*
C285 A120 50c multi .25 .25
C286 A120 1g multi .50 .40
C287 A120 1.50g multi .65 .50
Nos. C285-C287 (3) 1.40 1.15

For surcharges see Nos. CB58-CB60.

No. C269 Overprinted

Lithographed and Photogravure
1968, Jan. 18 *Perf. 13x13½*
C288 A115 1.50g rose & plum 1.40 1.00

See note after No. 579.

Caiman Woods Type of Regular Issue

1968, Apr. 22 Photo. *Perf. 12*
Size: 36x26mm
C289 A121 50c multi .40 .25
C290 A121 1g multi .50 .40

Perf. 12½x13½
Size: 49x36mm
C291 A121 50c multi .40 .25
C292 A121 1g multi .50 .40
C293 A121 1.50g multi .75 .60
C294 A121 2g gray & multi .90 .70
C295 A121 5g multi 2.00 1.40
Nos. C289-C295 (7) 5.45 4.00

Nos. C263-C265 Overprinted

1968, Apr. 19 *Perf. 13½*
C296 AP41 50c multi .70 .40
C297 AP41 1g multi 1.40 .60
C298 AP41 1.50g multi 2.40 1.10
Nos. C296-C298 (3) 4.50 2.10

See note after No. 584.

Monument Type of Regular Issue

1968, May 22 *Perf. 11½*
Granite Paper
C299 A122 50c ol bis & blk .40 .25
C300 A122 1g brt rose & blk .50 .40
C301 A122 1.50g org & blk .80 .50
Nos. C299-C301 (3) 1.70 1.15

For surcharges see Nos. C324-C325.

Types of Regular Bishopric Issue

50c, Palm tree & provincial coats of arms. 1g, 2.50g, Madonna, papal arms & arms of Haiti. 1.50g, Cathedral, arms of Pope Paul VI & arms of Haiti.

Perf. 13x14, 12½x13½
1968, Aug. 16 Photo.
C302 A123 50c lil & multi .40 .25
C303 A124 1g multi .50 .40
C304 A124 1.50g multi .65 .50
C305 A124 2.50g multi 1.40 1.10
Nos. C302-C305 (4) 2.95 2.25

Airport Type of Regular Issue

50c, 1.50g, 2.50g, Front view of air terminal.

1968, Sept. 22 Photo. *Perf. 11½*
Portrait in Black
C306 A125 50c rose lake & pale vio .40 .25
C307 A125 1.50g rose lake & bl .65 .50
C308 A125 2.50g rose lake & lt grnsh bl .90 .80
Nos. C306-C308 (3) 1.95 1.55

Pres. Francois Duvalier — AP42

Embossed & Typo. on Gold Foil
1968, Sept. 22 *Die Cut Perf. 14*
C309 AP42 30g black & red *40.00 50.00*

Freed Slaves' Type of Regular Issue

1968, Oct. 28 Litho. *Perf. 14½x14*
C310 A126 50c brn, lil & brt pink .40 .25
C311 A126 1g brn, yel grn & brt pink .50 .40
C312 A126 1.50g brn, lt vio bl & brt pink .65 .50
C313 A126 2g brn, lt grn & brt pink .80 .60
Nos. C310-C313 (4) 2.35 1.75

Education Type of Regular Issue, 1968

50c, 1.50g, Children watching television. 1g, Hands throwing ball, and sports medal.

1968, Nov. 14 *Perf. 11½*
C314 A127 50c multi .40 .25
C315 A127 1g multi .50 .40
C316 A127 1.50g multi .65 .50
Nos. C314-C316 (3) 1.55 1.15

For surcharges see Nos. CB61-CB62.

Jan Boesman and his Balloon — AP43

1968, Nov. 28 Litho. *Perf. 13½*
C317 AP43 70c lt yel grn & sepia .65 .50
C318 AP43 1.75g grnsh bl & sepia 1.40 1.00

Dr. Jan Boesman's balloon flight, Mexico City, Nov. 1968.

Miniature Sheet

Cachet of May 2, 1925 Flight — AP44

Black Cachets, Magenta Inscriptions and Rose Lilac Background

1968, Nov. 28 Litho. *Perf. 13½x14*
C318A AP44 Sheet of 12 13.00 *13.00*
b. 70c 2 Mai 1925 .70 *.80*
c. 70c 2 Septembre 1925 .70 *.80*
d. 70c 28 Mars 1927 .70 *.80*
e. 70c 12 Juillet 1927 .70 *.80*
f. 70c 13 Septembre 1927 .70 *.80*
g. 70c 6 Fevrier 1928 .70 *.80*

Galiffet 1784 balloon flight and pioneer flights of the 1920's. No. C318A contains 2 each of Nos. C318b-C318g. The background of the sheet shows in white outlines a balloon and the inscription "BALLON GALIFFET 1784." The design of each stamp shows a different airmail cachet, date of a special flight and part of the white background design.

Churchill Type of Regular Issue

Churchill: 50c, and early seaplane. 75c, and soldiers at Normandy. 1g, and Queen Elizabeth II. 1.50g, and Big Ben, London. 3g, and coat of arms, horiz.

1968, Dec. 23 Photo. *Perf. 13*
C319 A128 50c gold & multi .40 .25
C320 A128 75c gold & multi .50 .40
C321 A128 1g gold & multi .65 .50
C322 A128 1.50g gold & multi .80 .60
Nos. C319-C322 (4) 2.35 1.75

Souvenir Sheet
Perf. 12½x13, Imperf.
C323 A128 3g sil, blk & red 6.00 6.00

Nos. C319-C322 exist imperf. Value, $6.
No. C323 contains one horizontal stamp.
For surcharge, see No. C515. size: 38x25½mm.

Nos. C299-C300 Surcharged

1969, Feb. 21 Photo. *Perf. 11½*
C324 A122 70c on 50c .50 .40
C325 A122 1.75g on 1g .80 .50

Bird Type of Regular Issue

Birds of Haiti: 50c, Hispaniolan trogon. 1g, Black-cowled oriole. 1.50g, Stripe-headed tanager. 2g, Striated woodpecker.

1969, Feb. 26 *Perf. 13½*

No.	Type	Description	Unused	Used
C326	A129	50c multi	3.00	.85
C327	A129	1g lt bl & multi	3.75	1.40
C328	A129	1.50g multi	4.50	2.00
C329	A129	2g gray & multi	5.00	2.50
		Nos. C326-C329 (4)	16.25	6.75

For overprints see Nos. C344A-C344D.

Electric Power Type of 1969

1969, May 22 Litho. *Perf. 13x13½*

No.	Type	Description	Unused	Used
C338	A131	20c dk bl & lil	.25	.25
C339	A131	25c grn & rose red	.25	.25
C340	A131	25c rose red & grn	.25	.25
		Nos. C338-C340 (3)	.75	.75

Education Type of 1969

Designs: 50c, Peace poster on educational television, vert. 1g, Learning to write. 1.50g, Playing children, vert.

1969, Aug. 12 Litho. *Perf. 13½*

No.	Type	Description	Unused	Used
C342	A132	50c multi	.30	.25
C343	A132	1g multi	.50	.40
C344	A132	1.50g multi	.80	.50
		Nos. C342-C344 (3)	1.60	1.15

Nos. C326-C329 Overprinted

1969, Aug. 29 Photo. *Perf. 13½*

No.	Type	Description	Unused	Used
C344A	A129	50c multi	1.25	1.25
C344B	A129	1g lt bl & multi	2.40	2.40
C344C	A129	1.50g multi	4.50	4.50
C344D	A129	2g gray & multi	5.75	5.75
		Nos. C344A-C344D (4)	13.90	13.90

ILO Type of Regular Issue

1969, Sept. 22 *Perf. 14*

No.	Type	Description	Unused	Used
C345	A133	25c red & blk	.30	.25
C346	A133	70c org & blk	.65	.25
C347	A133	1.75g brt pur & blk	1.40	.70
		Nos. C345-C347 (3)	2.35	1.20

Butterfly Type of Regular Issue

50c, Danaus eresimus kaempfferi. 1.50g, Anaea marthesia nemesis. 2g, Prepona antimache.

1969, Nov. 14 Photo. *Perf. 13½*

No.	Type	Description	Unused	Used
C348	A134	50c multi	7.00	3.00
C349	A134	1.50g multi	13.00	4.00
C350	A134	2g yel & multi	20.00	6.00
		Nos. C348-C350 (3)	40.00	13.00

King Type of Regular Issue

1970, Jan. 12 Litho. *Perf. 12½x13½*

No.	Type	Description	Unused	Used
C351	A135	50c emer, red & blk	.45	.25
C352	A135	1g brick red, red & blk	.80	.60
C353	A135	1.50g brt bl, red & blk	1.20	.85
		Nos. C351-C353 (3)	2.45	1.70

Orchid Type of Regular Issue

Haitian Orchids: 50c, Tetramicra elegans. 1.50g, Epidendrum truncatum. 2g, Oncidium desertorum.

1970, Apr. 3 Litho. *Perf. 13x12½*

No.	Type	Description	Unused	Used
C354	A136	50c buff, brn & mag	2.00	.25
C355	A136	1.50g multi	3.50	2.50
C356	A136	2g lilac & multi	5.25	3.50
		Nos. C354-C356 (3)	10.75	6.25

UPU Type of Regular Issue

Designs: 50c, Globe and doves. 1.50g, Propeller and UPU emblem, vert. 2g, UPU Monument and map of Haiti.

1970, June 23 Photo. *Perf. 11½*

No.	Type	Description	Unused	Used
C357	A137	50c blk & vio	.35	.25
C358	A137	1.50g multi	.65	.45
C359	A137	2g multi	.95	.65
a.		Souvenir sheet of 3, #C357-C359, imperf.	2.50	2.25
		Nos. C357-C359 (3)	1.95	1.35

Nos. C357-C359a Overprinted in Red with UN Emblem and: "XXVe ANNIVERSAIRE / O.N.U."

1970, Dec. 14 Photo. *Perf. 11½*

No.	Type	Description	Unused	Used
C360	A137	50c blk & vio	.35	.25
C361	A137	1.50g multi	.65	.45
C362	A137	2g multi	.95	.65
a.		Souvenir sheet of 3	3.50	3.00
		Nos. C360-C362 (3)	1.95	1.35

United Nations, 25th anniversary.

Haitian Nativity AP45

1970, Dec. 22

No.	Type	Description	Unused	Used
C363	AP45	1.50g sepia & multi	.65	.45
C364	AP45	1.50g ultra & multi	.65	.45
C365	AP45	2g multi	1.10	.65
		Nos. C363-C365 (3)	2.40	1.55

Christmas 1970.

Painting Type of Regular Issue

Paintings: 50c, Nativity, by Rigaud Benoit. 1g, Head of a Negro, by Rubens. 1.50g, Ascension, by Castera Bazile (like No. 648).

1971, Apr. 29 Litho. *Perf. 12x12½*

Size: 20x40mm

No.	Type	Description	Unused	Used
C366	A140	50c multi	.50	.25
C367	A140	1g multi	.80	.65
C368	A140	1.50g multi	1.10	.80
		Nos. C366-C368 (3)	2.40	1.70

Nos. C366-C368 exist imperf in changed colors.

Balloon and Haiti No. C2 — AP46

No. C370, as #C369. No. C373, Haiti #C2. 1g, 1.50g, Supersonic transport & Haiti #C2.

1971, Dec. 22 Photo. *Perf. 11½*

No.	Type	Description	Unused	Used
C369	AP46	20c bl, red org & blk	.30	.25
C370	AP46	50c ultra, red org & blk	.50	.25
C371	AP46	1g org & blk	1.25	.35
C372	AP46	1.50g lil rose & blk	1.90	.45
		Nos. C369-C372 (4)	3.95	1.30

Souvenir Sheet

Imperf

No.	Type	Description	Unused	Used
C373	AP46	50c brt grn & blk	9.00	4.50

40th anniv. (in 1969) of air post service in Haiti.

For overprints see Nos. C374-C377, C380-C386.

Nos. C369-C372 Overprinted

1972, Mar. 17 *Perf. 11½*

No.	Type	Description	Unused	Used
C374	AP46	20c multi	.25	.25
C375	AP46	50c multi	.35	.35
C376	AP46	1g org & blk	.55	.45
C377	AP46	1.50g lil rose & blk	.65	.55
		Nos. C374-C377 (4)	1.80	1.60

14th INTERPEX, NYC, Mar. 17-19.

Dessalines Type of Regular Issue

1972, Apr. 28 Photo. *Perf. 11½*

No.	Type	Description	Unused	Used
C378	A142	50c yel grn & blk	.35	.25
C379	A142	2.50g lil & blk	1.10	.65

For surcharge see No. C438.

Nos. C369-C372 Overprinted

1972, May 4

No.	Type	Description	Unused	Used
C380	AP46	20c multi	.25	.25
C381	AP46	50c multi	.35	.25
C382	AP46	1g org & blk	.45	.35
C383	AP46	1.50g lil rose & blk	.65	.45
		Nos. C380-C383 (4)	1.70	1.30

HAIPEX, 5th Congress.

Nos. C370-C372 Overprinted

1972, July

No.	Type	Description	Unused	Used
C384	AP46	50c multi	.35	.25
C385	AP46	1g org & blk	.45	.35
C386	AP46	1.50g lil rose & blk	.65	.45
		Nos. C384-C386 (3)	1.45	1.05

Belgica '72, International Philatelic Exhibition, Brussels, June 24-July 9.

Tower of the Sun, EXPO '70 Emblem AP47

1972, Oct. 27

No.	Type	Description	Unused	Used
C387	AP47	50c bl, lake & dk bl	.35	.25
C388	AP47	1g bl, lake & red	.55	.35
C389	AP47	1.50g bl, lake & brn	.65	.45
C390	AP47	2.50g bl, lake & grn	.95	.55
		Nos. C387-C390 (4)	2.50	1.60

EXPO '70 International Exposition, Osaka, Japan, Mar. 15-Sept. 13, 1970.

For surcharges see Nos. C447-C447A.

Souvenir Sheets

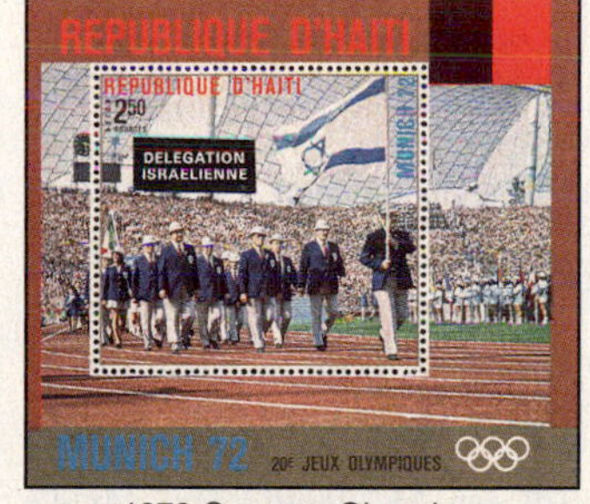

1972 Summer Olympics, Munich — AP47a

Designs: 2.50g, Israeli delegation, opening ceremony in Munich Stadium. 5g, Assassinated Israeli athlete David Berger.

1973 *Perf. 13½*

No.	Type	Description	Unused	Used
C390A	AP47a	2.50g multi	2.00	2.00
C390B	AP47a	5g multi	2.25	1.50

No. C390B contains one 22½x34mm stamp.

Headquarters and Map of Americas — AP48

1973, May 11 Litho. *Perf. 14½*

No.	Type	Description	Unused	Used
C391	AP48	50c dk bl & multi	.35	.25
C392	AP48	80c multi	.50	.35
C393	AP48	1.50g vio & multi	.60	.45
C394	AP48	2g brn & multi	.85	.55
		Nos. C391-C394 (4)	2.30	1.60

70th anniversary (in 1972) of the Panamerican Health Organization.

Marine Life Type of Regular Issue

50c, Platypodia spectabilis, horiz. 85c, Goniaster tessellatus. 1.50g, Stephanocyathus diadema, horiz. 2g, Phyllangia americana.

1973, Sept. 4 *Perf. 14*

No.	Type	Description	Unused	Used
C395	A145	50c multicolored	1.00	.25
C396	A145	85c multicolored	1.40	.25
C397	A145	1.50g multicolored	2.00	.30
C398	A145	2g multicolored	2.50	.40
		Nos. C395-C398 (4)	6.90	1.20

For surcharge see No. C439.

Fish Type of Regular Issue

Tropical fish: 50c, Gramma melacara. 85c, Holacanthus tricolor. 1.50g, Liopropoma rubre. 5g, Clepticus parrai.

1973 *Perf. 13½*

No.	Type	Description	Unused	Used
C399	A146	50c multicolored	.65	.50
C400	A146	85c multicolored	.80	.65
C401	A146	1.50g multicolored	1.40	.75
C402	A146	5g multicolored	4.00	1.90
		Nos. C399-C402 (4)	6.85	3.80

For surcharge see No. C440.

Haitian Flag AP49

Nos. C404, C405, Haitian flag and coat of arms. No. C406, Flag and Pres. Jean-Claude Duvalier.

1973, Nov. 18 *Perf. 14½x14*

Size: 35x22½mm

No.	Type	Description	Unused	Used
C403	AP49	80c blk & red	.45	.35
C404	AP49	80c red & blk	.45	.35

Perf. 14x13½

Size: 42x27mm

No.	Type	Description	Unused	Used
C405	AP49	1.85g blk & red	.95	.65
C406	AP49	1.85g red & blk	.95	.65
		Nos. C403-C406 (4)	2.80	2.00

For overprints and surcharges see Nos. C427-C428, C432-C433, C441-C442.

Soccer Type of Regular Issue

50c, 80c, Soccer Stadium. 1.75g, 10g, Haiti #654.

1973, Nov. 29 *Perf. 14x13*

No.	Type	Description	Unused	Used
C407	A147	50c multi	.35	.25
C408	A147	80c multi	.45	.35
C409	A147	1.75g multi	.95	.45
C410	A147	10g multi	3.25	2.25
		Nos. C407-C410 (4)	5.00	3.30

Dessalines Type of 1974

1974, Apr. 22 Photo. *Perf. 14*

No.	Type	Description	Unused	Used
C411	A148	50c brn & grnsh bl	.35	.25
C412	A148	80c gray & brn	.45	.35
C413	A148	1g lt grn & mar	.55	.45
C414	A148	1.75g lil & ol brn	.95	.55
		Nos. C411-C414 (4)	2.30	1.60

For surcharge see No. C443.

Copernicus Type of 1974

Designs: No. C415, 80c, 1.50g, 1.75g, Symbol of heliocentric system. No. C416, 1g, 2.50g, Nicolaus Copernicus.

1974, May 24 Litho. *Perf. 14x13½*

C415	A149	50c org & multi	.35	.25
C416	A149	50c yel & multi	.35	.25
C417	A149	80c multi	.45	.35
C418	A149	1g multi	.55	.45
C419	A149	1.75g brn & multi	.95	.55
		Nos. C415-C419 (5)	2.65	1.85

Souvenir Sheet

Imperf

C420	Sheet of 2	2.50	2.50
a.	A149 1.50g light green & multi	.90	.90
b.	A149 2.50g deep orange & multi	1.40	1.40

For overprint and surcharges see Nos. C444, C460-C463.

Pres. Duvalier Type of 1974

1974 Photo. *Perf. 14x13½*

C421	A151	50c vio brn & gold	.35	.25
C422	A151	80c rose red & gold	.45	.35
C423	A151	1g red lil & gold	.65	.45
C424	A151	1.50g Prus bl & gold	1.00	.65
C425	A151	1.75g brt vio & gold	1.25	.65
C426	A151	5g ol grn & gold	2.75	1.50
		Nos. C421-C426 (6)	6.45	3.85

For surcharge and overprints see Nos. C445, C487-C489.

Nos. C405-C406 Surcharged in Violet Blue

1975, July 15 Litho. *Perf. 14x13½*

C427	AP49	80c on 1.85g, #C405	1.50	1.50
C428	AP49	80c on 1.85g, #C406	1.50	1.50

Nos. C405-C406 Overprinted in Blue

1975, July 15 Litho. *Perf. 14x13½*

C432	AP49	1.85g blk & red	.95	.65
C433	AP49	1.85g red & blk	.95	.65

Centenary of Universal Postal Union. "100 ANS" in 2 lines on No. C433.

Names of Haitian Participants at Siege of Savannah — AP50

1976, Apr. 22 Photo. *Perf. 11½*

Granite Paper

C434	AP50	50c multi	.35	.25
C435	AP50	80c multi	.55	.35
C436	AP50	1.50g multi	.80	.55
C437	AP50	7.50g multi	2.75	1.90
		Nos. C434-C437 (4)	4.45	3.05

American Bicentennial.

Stamps of 1972-74 Surcharged with New Value and Bar in Black or Violet Blue

Photogravure; Lithographed

1976 *Perf. 11½, 13½, 14x13½, 14*

C438	A142	80c on 2.50g, #C379	.55	.35
C439	A145	80c on 85c, #C396	.55	.35
C440	A146	80c on 85c, #C400	.55	.35
C441	AP49	80c on 1.85g, #C405	.55	.35
C442	AP49	80c on 1.85g, #C406	.55	.35
C443	A148	80c on 1.75g, #C414 (VB)	.55	.35
C444	A149	80c on 1.75g, #C419 (VB)	.55	.35
C445	A151	80c on 1.75g, #C425	.55	.35
C446	AP50	80c on 1.50g, #C436	.55	.35
C447	AP47	80c on 1.50g, #C389	.55	.35
C447A	AP47	80c on 2.50g #C390	.55	.35
		Nos. C438-C447A (11)	6.05	3.85

Black surcharge of Nos. C441-C442 differs from the violet blue surcharge of Nos. C427-C428 in type face, arrangement of denomination and bar, and size of bar (10x6mm).

Dessalines Type of 1972

1976-77 Photo. *Perf. 11½*

Granite Paper

C448	A142	75c yel & blk	.35	.35
C449	A142	80c emer & blk	.35	.35
C450	A142	1g bl & blk	.45	.35
C451	A142	1g red brn & blk	.55	.45
C452	A142	1.25g yel grn & blk	.45	.35
C453	A142	1.50g bl gray & blk	.45	.35
C454	A142	1.75g rose & blk	.55	.45
C455	A142	2g yel & blk	.65	.55
C457	A142	5g bl grn & blk	1.75	1.10
C458	A142	10g ocher & blk	3.50	2.10
		Nos. C448-C458 (10)	9.05	6.40

Issued: 75c, 80c, No. C451, 1,75g, 5g, 10g, 1977.

Nos. C415-C416, C418-C419 Overprinted or Surcharged in Black, Dark Blue or Green

1977, July 6 Litho. *Perf. 14x13½*

C460	A149	1g (Bk)	.45	.35
C461	A149	1.25g on 50c (DB)	.55	.45
C462	A149	1.25g on 50c (G)	.55	.45
C463	A149	1.25g on 1.75g (Bk)	.55	.45
		Nos. C460-C463 (4)	2.10	1.70

Charles A. Lindbergh's solo transatlantic flight from NY to Paris, 50th anniv.

Telephone Type of 1978

Designs: 1g, Telstar over globe. 1.25g, Duvalier Earth Telecommunications Station. 2g, Wall telephone, 1890, vert.

1978, June 19 Litho. *Perf. 13½*

C466	A153	1g multi	.45	.35
C467	A153	1.25g multi	.55	.45
C468	A153	2g multi	.85	.55
		Nos. C466-C468 (3)	1.85	1.35

Olympic Games Type of 1978

Montreal Olympic Games' Emblem and: 1.25g, Equestrian. 2.50g,Basketball. 5g, Yachting.

1978, Sept. 4 Litho. *Perf. 13½x13*

C469	A154	1.25g multi	.70	.60
C470	A154	2.50g multi	1.50	1.25
C471	A154	5g multi	3.50	1.50
		Nos. C469-C471 (3)	5.70	3.35

Children's Institute Type, 1979

Designs: 1.25g, Mother nursing child. 2g, Nurse giving injection.

1979, Jan. 15 Photo. *Perf. 14x14½*

C472	A155	1.25g multi	.55	.35
C473	A155	2g multi	.80	.55

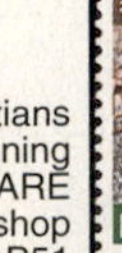
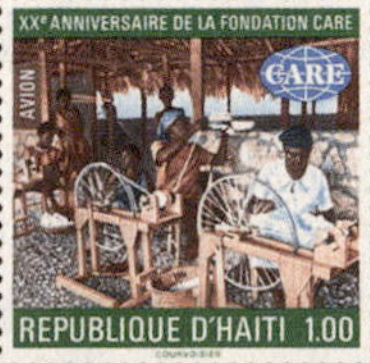

Haitians Spinning Cotton, CARE Workshop AP51

1979, May 11 Photo. *Perf. 11½*

C474	AP51	1g multi	.65	.55
C475	AP51	1.25g multi	.95	.65
C476	AP51	2g multi	1.40	.85
		Nos. C474-C476 (3)	3.00	2.05

30th anniversary of CARE.

Human Rights Type of 1979

1979, July 20 Litho. *Perf. 14*

C477	A157	1g multi	.65	.55
C478	A157	1.25g multi	.95	.65
C479	A157	2g multi	1.40	.85
		Nos. C477-C479 (3)	3.00	2.05

Anti-Apartheid Year Type of 1979

1979, Nov. 22 Photo. *Perf. 12x11½*

C480	A158	1g yel grn & blk	1.00	.55
C481	A158	1.25g bl & blk	1.10	.65
C482	A158	2g gray olive	1.75	.85
		Nos. C480-C482 (3)	3.85	2.05

IYC Type of 1979

1979, Dec. 19 Photo. *Perf. 12*

C483	A159	1g multi	.65	.55
C484	A159	1.25g multi	.95	.65
C485	A159	2.50g multi	2.50	1.10
C486	A159	5g multi	3.50	1.60
		Nos. C483-C486 (4)	7.60	3.90

Nos. C421, C424-C425 Overprinted

1980, May 17 Photo. *Perf. 14x13½*

C487	A151	50c multi	.35	.25
C488	A151	1.50g multi	.95	.45
C489	A151	1.75g multi	1.20	.55
		Nos. C487-C489 (3)	2.50	1.25

Wedding of Pres. Duvalier, May 27.

Dessalines Type of 1972

1980, Aug. 27 Photo. *Perf. 11½*

Granite Paper

C490	A142	1g gray vio & blk	.55	.45
C491	A142	1.25g sal pink & blk	.65	.55
C492	A142	2g pale grn & blk	1.20	.85
C493	A142	5g lt bl & blk	2.40	1.60
		Nos. C490-C493 (4)	4.80	3.45

For surcharge see No. C512.

Tourism Type

1980, Dec. 2 Litho. *Perf. 12½x12*

C494	A160	1g like #728	.55	.45
C495	A160	1.25g like #729	.65	.55
C496	A160	1.50g Carnival dancers	.95	.55
C497	A160	2g Vendors	1.20	.85
C498	A160	2.50g like #C497	1.40	1.10
		Nos. C494-C498 (5)	4.75	3.50

For surcharge see No. C511.

Soccer Type of 1980

50c, Uruguay, 1950. 75c, Germany, 1954. 1g, Brazil, 1958. 1.25g, Brazil, 1962. 1.50g, Gt. Britain, 1966. 1.75g, Brazil, 1970. 2g, Germany, 1974. 5g, Argentina, 1978.

1980, Dec. 30 Litho. *Perf. 14*

C499	A161	50c multi	.35	.25
C500	A161	75c multi	.45	.35
C501	A161	1g multi	.65	.45
C502	A161	1.25g multi	.80	.55
C503	A161	1.50g multi	1.10	.65
C504	A161	1.75g multi	1.25	.85
C505	A161	2g multi	1.40	.95
C506	A161	5g multi	3.50	2.10
		Nos. C499-C506 (8)	9.50	6.15

Painting Type of 1981

1981, May 12 Photo. *Perf. 11½*

C507	A162	50c like #734	.35	.25
C508	A162	1.25g like #735	.65	.55
C509	A162	2g like #736	1.25	.85
C510	A162	5g like #737	2.40	1.60
		Nos. C507-C510 (4)	4.65	3.25

Nos. C496, C493 Surcharged

Perf. 12½x12, 11½

1981, Dec. 30 Litho., Photo.

C511	A160	1.25g on 1.50g multi	.65	.55
C512	A142	2g on 5g multi	1.20	.85

Dessalines Type of 1972

1982, Jan. 25 Photo. *Perf. 11½*

Granite Paper

C513	A142	1.25g lt brn & blk	.65	.55
C514	A142	2g lilac & blk	1.20	.85

No. C320 Surcharged

2000? Photo. *Perf. 13*

C515	A128	3g on 75c #C320	—	—

AIR POST SEMI-POSTAL STAMPS

Coubertin Semipostal Type of 1939

Unwmk.

1939, Oct. 3 Engr. *Perf. 12*

CB1	SP1	60c + 40c multi	25.00	25.00
CB2	SP1	1.25g + 60c multi	25.00	25.00

Mosquito and National Sanatorium — SPAP2

1949, July 22 Cross in Carmine

CB3	SPAP2	20c + 20c sep	11.00	6.00
CB4	SPAP2	30c + 30c dp grn	11.00	6.00
CB5	SPAP2	45c + 45c lt red brn	11.00	6.00
CB6	SPAP2	80c + 80c pur	11.00	6.00
CB7	SPAP2	1.25g + 1.25g car rose	11.00	6.00
a.		Souvenir sheet	40.00	25.00
CB8	SPAP2	1.75g + 1.75g bl	11.00	6.00
a.		Souvenir sheet	40.00	25.00
		Nos. CB3-CB8 (6)	66.00	36.00

The surtax was used for fighting tuberculosis and malaria.

Catalogue values for unused stamps in this section, from this point to the end of the section, are for Never Hinged items.

No. C113 Surcharged in Deep Carmine

1958, Aug. 30 Litho. *Perf. 13x13½*

CB9	A82	2.50g + 50c	2.50	2.40

The surtax was for the Red Cross.

Similar Surcharge in Red on One Line on Nos. C133-C135

1959, Apr. 7 Photo. *Perf. 11½*

Granite Paper

CB10	AP35	50c + 25c pink, car & ultra	.40	.40
CB11	A87	75c + 25c brt bl	.50	.50
CB12	A87	1g + 25c brn	.75	.75

Nos. C139-C141 Surcharged Like No. CB9 in Red

CB13	AP36	50c + 50c grn & lil	1.00	1.00
CB14	AP36	1.50g + 50c ol & red brn	1.00	1.00
CB15	AP36	2.50g + 50c pur & dk bl	1.25	1.25
		Nos. CB10-CB15 (6)	4.90	4.90

Surtax for the Red Cross.

Nos. C142-C144 Surcharged Diagonally

1959, July 23 Unwmk. Perf. 12
CB16 A89 1g + 20c 1.00 1.00
CB17 A89 2g + 20c 1.10 1.10
CB18 A89 2.50g + 20c 1.10 1.10
Nos. CB16-CB18 (3) 3.20 3.20

World Refugee Year, July 1, 1959-June 30, 1960. A similar surcharge of 50c was applied horizontally to stamps in No. C144a. Value $25.

C145-C147 Surcharged in Dark Carmine

1959, Oct. 30 Photo. Perf. 14
CB19 A91 50c + 75c hn brn & aqua 1.00 1.00
CB20 A90 1g + 75c lil & aqua 1.00 1.00
CB21 A90 1.50g + 75c multi 1.00 1.00
Nos. CB19-CB21 (3) 3.00 3.00

The surtax was for Haitian athletes.

On No. CB19, surcharge lines are spaced to total depth of 16mm.

Nos. C129-C130 Surcharged in Red: "Hommage a l'UNICEF +G. 0,50"

Engraved and Lithographed
1960, Feb. 2 Perf. 11½
CB22 AP34 2g + 50c 1.00 1.00
CB23 AP34 2.50g + 50c 1.75 1.75

Issued to honor UNICEF.

Nos. C151-C152 Surcharged and Overprinted: "ALPHABETISATION" in Red or Black.

1960, July 12 Litho. Perf. 12½x13
CB24 A92 50c + 20c (R) .40 .40
CB25 A92 50c + 30c .65 .55
CB26 A92 1g + 20c (R) .90 .75
CB27 A92 1g + 30c .90 .75
Nos. CB24-CB27 (4) 2.85 2.45

Olympic Games Issue
Nos. C163-C164 Surcharged

1960, Sept. 9 Photo. Perf. 12
CB28 A94 50c + 25c .40 .25
CB29 A94 1.50g + 25c .65 .55

Nos. C168-C169 Surcharged: "UNICEF +25 centimes"

1961, Jan. 14 Engr. Perf. 10½
CB30 A96 50c + 25c red org & blk .40 .25
CB31 A96 1.50g + 25c dk bl & blk .65 .55

Nos. C171, C175-C176 Surcharged

1961, Sept. 30 Photo. Perf. 11½
CB32 AP37 20c + 25c .40 .30
CB33 AP37 1g + 25c .50 .40
CB34 AP37 1.50g + 25c .60 .60
Nos. CB32-CB34 (3) 1.50 1.30

Issued to commemorate the 18th Boy Scout World Conference, Lisbon, Sept. 19-24, 1961.

The surtax was for the Red Cross. Additional proceeds from the sale of Nos. CB32-CB34 benefited the Port-au-Prince airport project.

The same surcharge was also applied to No. C176a. Value $3.

Nos. C168-C169 Surcharged: "OMS SNEM +20 CENTIMES"

1961, Dec. 11 Engr. Perf. 10½
CB35 A96 50c + 20c 1.60 1.60
CB36 A96 1.50g + 20c 2.25 2.25

Issued to publicize Haiti's participation in the UN malaria eradication drive.

Nos. C123, C126-C127 and C131-C132 Surcharged in Black or Red

Engraved and Lithographed
1961-62 Perf. 11½
CB37 AP34 50c + 25c .25 .25
CB38 AP34 1g + 50c .35 .35
CB39 AP34 2.50g + 50c (R) ('62) .65 .65
CB40 AP34 5g + 50c 1.10 1.10
CB41 AP34 7.50g + 50c (R) ('62) 1.50 1.50
Nos. CB37-CB41 (5) 3.85 3.85

The surtax was for the benefit of the urban rehabilitation program in Duvalier Ville.

Nos. C188-C190 Surcharged: "+25 centimes"

1962, Sept. 13 Litho. Perf. 12
CB42 A99 20c + 25c .25 .25
CB43 A99 50c + 25c .40 .25
CB44 A99 1g + 25c .50 .40
Nos. CB42-CB44 (3) 1.15 .80

Nos. C191-C192 Surcharged in Red: "+0.20"

1962 Perf. 12½x13
CB45 A92 50c + 20c .40 .40
CB46 A92 1g + 20c .50 .40

Nos. C203 and C205 Surcharged: "ALPHABETISATION" and "+0, 10"

1963, Mar. 15 Photo. Perf. 14x14½
CB47 AP38 50c + 10c .40 .25
CB48 AP38 1.50g + 10c .50 .40

No. C110 Surcharged in Red

Surcharge includes Olympic Emblem and: "JEUX OLYMPIQUES / D'HIVER / INNSBRUCK 1964".

1964, July 27 Photo. Perf. 11½
CB49 A80 2.50g + 50c + 10c .90 .80

See note after No. B34. The 50c+10c surtax went for charity.

No. C213 Surcharged in Red

Engraved and Photogravure
1964, Oct. 2 Perf. 13½x14
CB50 AP39 2.50g + 1.25g on 1.50g 1.40 1.25

Issued to commemorate the centenary (in 1963) of the International Red Cross.

Nos. C223-C226 Surcharged: "+ 5c."

1965, Mar. 15 Photo. Perf. 11½
CB51 A105 50c + 5c pale lil & dk brn .40 .25
CB52 A105 50c + 5c pale grn & dk brn .40 .25
CB53 A105 75c + 5c buff & dk brn .50 .40
CB54 A105 1.50g + 5c gray & dk brn .80 .65
Nos. CB51-CB54 (4) 2.10 1.45

The souvenir sheet No. C226a was surcharged "+25c." Value, $8.

See note following No. B37.

Nos. C251 and C253 Surcharged and Overprinted

Overprint includes Haitian Scout Emblem and "12e Jamboree / Mondial 1967" Like Regular Issue.

1967, Aug. 21 Photo. Perf. 11½
CB55 A111 50c + 10c multi .50 .40
CB56 A111 1.50g + 50c multi .65 .50

See note after No. B40.

No. C269 Surcharged Like Regular Issue

Lithographed and Photogravure
1968, Jan. 18 Perf. 13x13½
CB57 A115 2.50g + 1.25g on 1.50g 3.25 2.50
a. Double surcharge 15.00
b. Inverted surcharge 25.00

See note after No. 579.

Nos. C285-C287 Surcharged "CULTURE + 10"

1968, July 4 Litho. Perf. 11½
CB58 A120 50c + 10c multi .40 .25
CB59 A120 1g + 10c multi .50 .40
CB60 A120 1.50g + 10c multi .65 .50
Nos. CB58-CB60 (3) 1.55 1.15

Nos. C314 and C316 Surcharged in Red

Surcharge includes Red Cross and: "50ème. Anniversaire / de la Ligue des / Sociétés de la / Croix Rouge".

1969, June 25 Litho. Perf. 11½
CB61 A127 50c + 20c multi .50 .40
CB62 A127 1.50g + 25c multi .90 .50

League of Red Cross Societies, 50th anniv.

AIR POST OFFICIAL STAMPS

Nos. C172-C176 and C176a Overprinted: "OFFICIEL"

Perf. 11½
1961, Mar. Unwmk. Photo.
CO1 AP37 50c rose brn & grn .60
CO2 AP37 50c brt grnsh bl & ol grn .60
CO3 AP37 50c gray & grn .60
CO4 AP37 1g gray ol & ver .85
CO5 AP37 1.50g brt pink & dk bl 1.40
a. Sheet of 3 3.75
Nos. CO1-CO5 (5) 4.05

Nos. CO1-CO5a only available canceled.

Catalogue values for unused stamps in this section, from this point to the end of the section, are for Never Hinged items.

Jean Jacques Dessalines — OA1

1962, Mar. 7 Photo. Perf. 14x14½
Size: 20½x38mm
CO6 OA1 50c dk bl & sepia .50 .40
CO7 OA1 1g lt bl & maroon .80 .50
CO8 OA1 1.50g bister & bl 1.00 .70

Size: 30x40mm
CO9 OA1 5g rose & ol grn 2.75 2.40
Nos. CO6-CO9 (4) 5.05 4.00

Inscription at bottom of No. CO9 is in 2 lines.

AIR POST PARCEL POST STAMPS

Catalogue values for unused stamps in this section are for Never Hinged items.

Nos. C112 and C111 Overprinted in Red

Perf. 11½
1960, Nov. 21 Unwmk. Photo.
CQ1 A81 50c orange & black .50 .40
CQ2 A80 5g bluish blk & saph 3.50 2.60

Type of Parcel Post Stamps, 1961
Inscribed "Poste Aerienne"

1961, Mar. 24 Perf. 14
CQ3 PP1 2.50g yel grn & mar 2.00 1.40
CQ4 PP1 5g org & green 2.50 1.60

SPECIAL DELIVERY STAMP

The catalogue value for the unused stamp in this section is for Never Hinged.

Postal Administration Building — SD1

Unwmk.
1953, May 4 Engr. Perf. 12
E1 SD1 25c vermilion .70 .50

POSTAGE DUE STAMPS

D1

1898, Aug. Unwmk. Engr. Perf. 12
J1 D1 2c black 1.00 .75
J2 D1 5c red brown 1.50 1.00
J3 D1 10c brown orange 2.00 1.50
J4 D1 50c slate 3.00 2.50
Nos. J1-J4 (4) 7.50 5.75

For overprints see Nos. J5-J9, J14-J16.

Stamps of 1898 Handstamped like Nos. 67-81

1902 Black Overprint
J5 D1 2c black 2.50 1.50
J6 D1 5c red brown 2.50 1.50
J7 D1 10c brown orange 2.50 1.50
J8 D1 50c slate 12.00 7.00

Red Overprint
J9 D1 2c black 3.50 3.50
Nos. J5-J9 (5) 23.00 15.00

Nos. J5-J9 exist with inverted overprint.

D2

1906
J10 D2 2c dull red 1.50 1.00
J11 D2 5c ultra 2.75 2.50
J12 D2 10c violet 2.75 2.50
J13 D2 50c olive gray 11.50 7.50
Nos. J10-J13 (4) 18.50 13.50

For surcharges and overprints see Nos. 305-308, J17-J20.

Preceding Issues Handstamped like Nos. 169-201

1914 On Stamps of 1898
J14 D1 5c red brown 1.50 1.10
J15 D1 10c brown orange 1.50 1.10
J16 D1 50c slate 6.00 5.50
Nos. J14-J16 (3) 9.00 7.70

On Stamps of 1906
J17 D2 2c dull red 1.25 1.00
J18 D2 5c ultra 2.25 2.25
J19 D2 10c violet 7.50 5.50
J20 D2 50c olive gray 45.00 45.00
Nos. J17-J20 (4) 56.00 53.75

The note after No. 201 applies to Nos. J14-J20 also.
Nos. J14-J20 exist with inverted overprint.

Catalogue values for unused stamps in this section, from this point to the end of the section, are for Never Hinged items.

Unpaid Letter — D3

1951, July Litho. *Perf. 11½*
J21 D3 10c carmine .25 .25
J22 D3 20c red brown .25 .25
J23 D3 40c green .40 .40
J24 D3 50c orange yellow .50 .50
Nos. J21-J24 (4) 1.40 1.40

PARCEL POST STAMPS

Catalogue values for unused stamps in this section are for Never Hinged items.

Nos. 416, 470-471 and 378 Overprinted in Red

Photogravure, Engraved
Perf. 11½, 12
1960, Nov. 21 Unwmk.
Q1 A81 5c yel grn & blk .25 .25
Q2 A81 10c red org & blk .25 .25
Q3 A81 25c ultra & black .40 .25
Q4 A64 2.50g gray 2.75 2.40
Nos. Q1-Q4 (4) 3.65 3.15

Coat of Arms — PP1

Unwmk.
1961, Mar. 24 Photo. *Perf. 14*
Q5 PP1 50c bister & purple .50 .40
Q6 PP1 1g pink & dark blue .80 .50

See Nos. CQ3-CQ4.

POSTAL TAX STAMPS

Catalogue values for unused stamps in this section are for Never Hinged items.

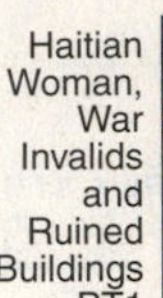

Haitian Woman, War Invalids and Ruined Buildings PT1

Unwmk.
1944, Aug. 16 Engr. *Perf. 12*
RA1 PT1 5c dull purple 1.40 .60
RA2 PT1 5c dark blue 1.40 .60
RA3 PT1 5c olive green 1.40 .60
RA4 PT1 5c black 1.40 .60

1945, Dec. 17
RA5 PT1 5c dark green 1.40 .60
RA6 PT1 5c sepia 1.40 .60
RA7 PT1 5c red brown 1.40 .60
RA8 PT1 5c rose carmine 1.40 .60
Nos. RA1-RA8 (8) 11.20 4.80

The proceeds from the sale of Nos. RA1 to RA8 were for United Nations Relief.

George Washington, J.J. Dessalines and Simón Bolivar — PT2

1949, Sept. 20
RA9 PT2 5c red brown .50 .40
RA10 PT2 5c olive gray .50 .40
RA11 PT2 5c blue .50 .40
RA12 PT2 5c green .50 .40
RA13 PT2 5c violet .50 .40
RA14 PT2 5c black .50 .40
RA15 PT2 5c orange .50 .40
RA16 PT2 5c carmine rose .50 .40
Nos. RA9-RA16 (8) 4.00 3.20

Bicentenary of Port-au-Prince.
For overprint and surcharges see #385-388.

Helicopter Inspection of Hurricane Damage — PT3

1955, Jan. 3 Photo. *Perf. 11½*
RA17 PT3 10c bright green .25 .25
RA18 PT3 10c bright blue .25 .25
RA19 PT3 10c gray black .25 .25
RA20 PT3 10c orange .25 .25
RA21 PT3 20c rose carmine .35 .25
RA22 PT3 20c deep green .35 .25
Nos. RA17-RA22 (6) 1.70 1.50

Helicopter — PT4

1955, May 3
RA23 PT4 10c black, *gray* .25 .25
RA24 PT4 20c violet blue, *blue* .30 .25

The surface tint of the sheets of 50, (10x5) of Nos. RA23-RA24, RAC1-RAC2 includes a map of Haiti's southern peninsula which extends over the three center rows of stamps. The tax was for reconstruction.

See Nos. RAC1-RAC2.

PT5

1959-60 Unwmk. Photo. *Perf. 11½*
Size: 38x22½mm
RA25 PT5 5c green .25 .25
RA26 PT5 5c black ('60) .25 .25
RA27 PT5 10c red .25 .25
Nos. RA25-RA27 (3) .75 .75

1960-61 Size: 28x17mm
RA28 PT5 5c green .25 .25
RA29 PT5 10c red .25 .25
RA30 PT5 10c blue ('61) .25 .25
Nos. RA28-RA30 (3) .75 .75

PT6

1963, Sept. *Perf. 14½x14*
Size: 13½x21mm
RA31 PT6 10c red orange .25 .25
RA32 PT6 10c bright blue .25 .25
RA33 PT6 10c olive .25 .25
Nos. RA31-RA33,RAC6-RAC8 (6) 1.50 1.50

1966-69 Photo. *Perf. 14x14½*
Size: 17x25mm
RA34 PT6 10c bright green .25 .25
RA35 PT6 10c violet .25 .25
RA36 PT6 10c violet blue .25 .25
RA37 PT6 10c brown ('69) .25 .25
Nos. RA34-RA37,RAC9-RAC15 (11) 2.75 2.75

Nos. RA25-RA37 represent a tax for a literacy campaign.
See Nos. RA42-RA45, RAC20-RAC22.

Duvalier de Peligre Hydroelectric Works — PT7

1970-72
RA38 PT7 20c violet & olive .25 .25
RA39 PT7 20c ultra & blk ('72) .25 .25

See Nos. RA46, RAC16-RAC19, RAC23.

Nos. 637-638 Surcharged: "ALPHABETISATION +10"

1971, Dec. 23 Litho. *Perf. 14x13½*
RA40 A138 20c + 10c multi .35 .25
a. Inverted surcharge 2.00
RA41 A138 25c + 10c multi .35 .25

Tax was for the literacy campaign.

"CA" Type of 1963
1972-74 Photo. *Perf. 14x14½*
Size: 17x25mm
RA42 PT6 5c violet blue .25 .25
RA43 PT6 5c deep carmine .25 .25
RA44 PT6 5c ultra ('74) .25 .25
RA45 PT6 5c carmine rose ('74) .25 .25
Nos. RA42-RA45 (4) 1.00 1.00

Tax was for literacy campaign.

Hydroelectric Type of 1970
1980 Photo. *Perf. 14x14½*
RA46 PT7 25c choc & green .25 .25

AIR POST POSTAL TAX STAMPS

Catalogue values for unused stamps in this section are for Never Hinged items.

Helicopter Type of 1955
1955 Unwmk. Photo. *Perf. 11½*
RAC1 PT4 10c red brn, *pale sal* .30 .25
RAC2 PT4 20c rose pink, *pink* .35 .25

See note after No. RA24.

Type of Postal Tax Stamps, 1960-61
1959 Size: 28x17mm
RAC3 PT5 5c yellow .25 .25
RAC4 PT5 10c dull salmon .25 .25
RAC5 PT5 10c blue .25 .25
Nos. RAC3-RAC5 (3) .75 .75

Type of Postal Tax Stamps, 1963
1963, Sept. *Perf. 14½x14*
Size: 13½x21mm
RAC6 PT6 10c dark gray .25 .25
RAC7 PT6 10c violet .25 .25
RAC8 PT6 10c brown .25 .25
Nos. RAC6-RAC8 (3) .60 .60

1966-69 *Perf. 14x14½*
Size: 17x25mm
RAC9 PT6 10c orange .25 .25
RAC10 PT6 10c sky blue .25 .25
RAC11 PT6 10c yellow ('69) .25 .25
RAC12 PT6 10c carmine ('69) .25 .25
RAC13 PT6 10c gray grn ('69) .25 .25
RAC14 PT6 10c lilac ('69) .25 .25
RAC15 PT6 10c dp claret ('69) .25 .25
Nos. RAC9-RAC15 (7) 1.40 1.40

Nos. RAC3-RAC15, RAC20-RAC21 represent a tax for a literacy campaign.

Hydroelectric Type of 1970
1970-74
RAC16 PT7 20c tan & slate .25 .25
RAC17 PT7 20c brt bl & dl vio .25 .25
RAC18 PT7 25c sal & bluish blk ('74) .25 .25
RAC19 PT7 25c yel ol & bluish blk ('74) .25 .25
Nos. RAC16-RAC19 (4) 1.00 1.00

"CA" Type of 1963
1973 Photo. *Perf. 14x14½*
Size: 17x26mm
RAC20 PT6 10c brn & blue .35 .25
RAC21 PT6 10c brn & green .35 .25
RAC22 PT6 10c brn & orange .35 .25
Nos. RAC20-RAC22 (3) 1.05 .75

Hydroelectric Power Type of 1970
1979(?) Photo. *Perf. 14x14½*
RAC23 PT7 25c blue & vio brn .25 .25

HATAY

hä-'tī

LOCATION — Northwest of Syria, bordering on Mediterranean Sea
GOVT. — Semi-independent republic
AREA — 10,000 sq. mi. (approx.)
POP. — 273,350 (1939)
CAPITAL — Antioch

Alexandretta, a semi-autonomous district of Syria under French mandate, was renamed Hatay in 1938 and transferred to Turkey in 1939.

100 Santims = 1 Kurush
40 Paras = 1 Kurush (1939)

Stamps of Turkey, 1931-38, Surcharged in Black

On A77

On A78

1939 Unwmk. *Perf. 11½x12*

1	A77	10s	on 20pa dp org	1.75	.35
a.			"Sent" instead of "Sant"	135.00	25.00
2	A78	25s	on 1ku dk sl grn	2.00	.35
a.			Small "25"	14.00	1.75
3	A78	50s	on 2ku dk vio	2.00	.35
a.			Small "50"	6.50	2.25
4	A77	75s	on 2½ku green	1.75	.40
5	A78	1ku	on 4ku slate	10.00	4.25
6	A78	1ku	on 5ku rose red	5.50	1.40
7	A78	1½ku	on 3ku brn org	3.50	1.25
8	A78	2½ku	on 4ku slate	4.00	1.00
9	A78	5ku	on 8ku brt blue	6.00	1.25
10	A77	12½ku	on 20ku ol grn	7.00	2.00
11	A77	20ku	on 25ku Prus bl	13.50	7.25
			Nos. 1-11 (11)	57.00	19.85
			Set, never hinged	115.00	

Map of Hatay — A1

Lions of Antioch A2

Flag of Hatay A3

Post Office A4

1939 Unwmk. Typo. *Perf. 12*

12	A1	10p	orange & aqua	2.50	.75
13	A1	30p	lt vio & aqua	2.50	.75
14	A1	1½ku	olive & aqua	2.50	.75
15	A2	2½ku	turq grn	3.00	1.00
16	A2	3ku	light blue	3.00	1.00
17	A2	5ku	chocolate	3.00	1.00
18	A3	6ku	brt blue & car	3.75	1.25
19	A3	7½ku	dp grn & car	4.25	1.40
20	A3	12ku	violet & car	5.00	1.40
21	A3	12½ku	dk blue & car	4.50	1.50
22	A4	17½ku	brown car	8.00	3.00
23	A4	25ku	olive brn	9.00	3.50
24	A4	50ku	slate blue	18.00	8.75
			Nos. 12-24 (13)	69.00	26.05
			Set, never hinged	146.00	

Stamps of 1939 Overprinted in Black

1939

25	A1	10p	orange & aqua	2.00	.90
a.			Overprint reading up	32.50	
26	A1	30p	lt vio & aqua	2.00	.90
27	A1	1½ku	ol & aqua	2.75	1.00
28	A2	2½ku	turq grn	2.75	1.00
29	A2	3ku	light blue	3.00	1.00
30	A2	5ku	chocolate	3.75	1.40
a.			Overprint inverted	32.50	
31	A3	6ku	brt bl & car	4.00	1.40
32	A3	7½ku	dp grn & car	4.50	2.25
33	A3	12ku	vio & car	4.25	1.50
34	A3	12½ku	dk bl & car	4.75	1.50
35	A4	17½ku	brn car	6.00	2.50
a.			Overprint inverted	32.50	
36	A4	25ku	olive brn	10.00	4.75
37	A4	50ku	slate blue	21.00	11.00
			Nos. 25-37 (13)	70.75	31.10
			Set, never hinged	145.00	

The overprint reads "Date of annexation to the Turkish Republic, June 30, 1939."

On Nos. 25-27, the overprint reads down. On Nos. 28-37, it is horizontal.

POSTAGE DUE STAMPS

Postage Due Stamps of Turkey, 1936, Surcharged or Overprinted in Black

1939 Unwmk. *Perf. 11½*

J1	D6	1ku	on 2ku lt bl	4.00	.95
J2	D6	3ku	bright violet	4.50	1.50
J3	D6	4ku	on 5ku Prus bl	4.75	1.75
J4	D6	5ku	on 12ku brt rose	5.25	1.75
J5	D6	12ku	bright rose	57.50	40.00
			Nos. J1-J5 (5)	76.00	45.95
			Set, never hinged	162.00	

Castle at Antioch D1

1939 Typo. *Perf. 12*

J6	D1	1ku	red orange	4.75	1.75
J7	D1	3ku	dk olive brown	5.50	2.00
J8	D1	4ku	turqoise green	6.00	2.25
J9	D1	5ku	slate black	7.00	2.75
			Nos. J6-J9 (4)	23.25	8.75
			Set, never hinged	43.00	

Nos. J6-J9 Overprinted in Black like Nos. 25-37

1939

J10	D1	1ku	red orange	4.50	1.75
J11	D1	3ku	dk olive brown	5.50	2.00
J12	D1	4ku	turqoise green	5.75	2.25
J13	D1	5ku	slate black	8.00	3.00
a.			Overprint inverted	42.50	
			Nos. J10-J13 (4)	23.75	9.00
			Set, never hinged	44.00	

HELIGOLAND

'he-lə-gō-,land

LOCATION — An island in the North Sea near the northern coast of Germany
GOVT. — Former British Possession
AREA — ¼ sq. mi.
POP. — 2,307 (1900)

Great Britain ceded Heligoland to Germany in 1890. It became part of Schleswig-Holstein province. Stamps of Heligoland were superseded by those of the German Empire.

16 Schillings = 1 Mark
100 Pfennig = 1 Mark = 1 Schilling (1875)

REPRINTS

Most Heligoland issues were extensively reprinted between 1875 and 1895, and these comprise the great majority of Heligoland stamps in the marketplace. Such reprints sell for much less than the originals, usually for $1-$2 each. All stamps on surfaced paper with glossy white gum, and small hole perforations are reprints from Leipzig. All stamps perforated 14 are reprints from Hamburg. Reprints from Berlin are discussed after each listing. Expertization of Heligoland issues is strongly recommended by the editors.

Some Heligoland issues were officially reprinted for the Philatelic Archive in Bonn. A few have become available to the public and are exceedingly scarce.

Queen Victoria
A1 A2

A2a

A3

Type I

Type II

Type III

Type I: Curl below chignon is rounded
Type II: Curl resembles an upside-down question mark
Type III: Curl is hooked

All stamps with a different head type from the listing are reprints.

Typo., Head Embossed

1867-68 Unwmk. *Rouletted 10*

1	A1	½sch	bl grn & rose, I	350.00	*1,000.*
1A	A2	½sch	bl grn & rose, II	800.00	*1,700.*
2	A1	1sch	rose & dp grn, I	190.00	*200.00*
3	A3	2sch	rose & pale grn, I	20.00	*65.00*
4	A3	6sch	gray grn & rose, I	20.00	*475.00*

All genuine stamps have a ridge that appears as a very faint gray line near the rouletting, best viewed under angled light. The ridge must be visible on at least one margin. Reprints lack the ridge. The 2sch and 6sch perforated exist only as reprints.

1869-71 *Perf. 13½x14¼*

Thick Soft Paper

5	A2	½sch	ol grn & car rose, II	125.00	*160.00*
6	A2a	1sch	red & yel grn, III	175.00	*300.00*

Berlin reprints have comparatively poor printing quality. The thin frame line inside the text is broken and often merges with the thick frame line.

A4

1873 Thick Quadrille Paper

7	A4	¼sch	pale rose & pale grn, I	35.00	*2,250.*
a.			¼sch dp carmine & pale yel grn	*325.00*	*2,250.*
8	A4	¼sch	yel grn & rose, I	135.00	*3,600.*
9	A2	½sch	brt grn & rose, II	125.00	*210.00*
10	A4	¾sch	gray grn & pale rose, I	50.00	*2,250.*
11	A2a	1sch	rose & yel grn, III	210.00	*425.00*
12	A4	1½sch	yel grn & rose, I	95.00	*325.00*

Reprints are never on quadrille paper.

1874 Thin Wove Paper

13	A4	¼sch	rose & yel grn, I	17.50	

Berlin reprints are head type 2.

A5

A6

A7

1875 Wove Paper

14	A5	1pf	dk rose & dk grn, II	20.00	*600.00*
15	A5	2pf	yel grn & dk rose, II	21.00	*875.00*
16	A6	5pf	dk rose & dk grn, II	23.00	*21.00*
17	A6	10pf	blue grn & red, II	17.00	*37.50*
a.			10pf yel green & dark rose	110.00	*27.50*
b.			10pf lt green & pink red	140.00	*25.00*
18	A7	25pf	rose & dk grn, II	24.00	*30.00*
a.			25pf dk rose & dk green	24.00	*30.00*
19	A7	50pf	grn & brick red, II	26.00	*85.00*
a.			50pf dl grn & dk rose	65.00	*37.50*

Under UV the red in Berlin reprints glows orange. Originals remain dull.

There are no reprints of Nos. 16-19.

Coat of Arms — A8

1876-88 Typo.

20	A8	3pf	dp grn & dl red	275.00	*1,600.*
a.			3pf green & bright red ('77)	175.00	*1,000.*

No.	Type	Denom.	Color	Unused	Used
21	A8	20pf	ver & brt yel grn ('88)	15.00	*32.50*
a.			20pf ver & yel grn ('87)	425.00	*47.50*
b.			20pf lila rose & grn ('82)	240.00	*125.00*
c.			20pf salmon & yel grn ('85)	425.00	*65.00*
d.			20pf vio car & yel grn ('76)	240.00	*125.00*
e.			20pf lila rose & dk grn ('80)	240.00	*125.00*

The coat-of-arms on Nos. 20, 21 and sub-varieties is printed in three colors: varying shades of yellow, red and green.

The 3pf has been reprinted. Reprints usually have a paler red. However some Berlin reprints are the same shade as the originals. Expertizing is strongly recommended.

A9

A10

1879 **Typo.**

No.	Type	Denom.	Color	Unused	Used
22	A9	1m	dp grn & car	225.00	*225.00*
a.			1m blue green & salmon	225.00	*240.00*
b.			1m dark green & ver	80.00	
23	A10	5m	blue grn & sal	225.00	*1,200.*

Perf. 11½

No.	Type	Denom.	Color	Unused	Used
24	A9	1m	dp grn & car	1,500.	—
25	A10	5m	bl grn & rose red	1,500.	—
a.			Horiz. pair, imperf. vert.	*6,000.*	

Nos. 13, 22b, 24 and 25 were never placed in use. Forged cancellations of Nos. 1-23 are plentiful.

Heligoland stamps were replaced by those of the German Empire in 1890.

HONDURAS

hän-ˈdur-əs

LOCATION — Central America, between Guatemala on the north and Nicaragua on the south
GOVT. — Republic
AREA — 43,277 sq. mi.
POP. — 5,997,327 (1999 est.)
CAPITAL — Tegucigalpa

8 Reales = 1 Peso
100 Centavos = 1 Peso (1878)
100 Centavos = 1 Lempira (1933)

Catalogue values for unused stamps in this country are for Never Hinged items, beginning with Scott 344 in the regular postage section, Scott B1 in the semi-postal section, Scott C144 in the airpost section, Scott CB5 in the airpost semi-postal section, Scott CE3 in the airpost special delivery section, Scott CO110 in the airpost official section, and Scott RA6 in the postal tax section.

Values for unused stamps are for examples with original gum as defined in the catalogue introduction. Very fine examples of the locally printed Nos. 95-110, 127, 140, 151-210C, and 218-279 will have margins clear of the perforations but will be noticeably off center.

Watermark

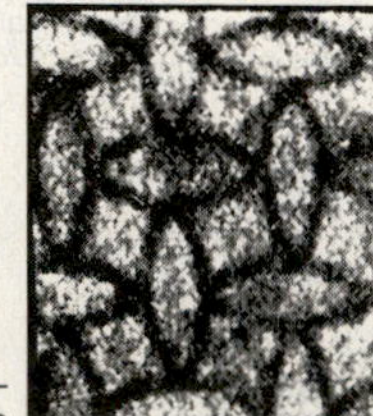
Wmk. 209 — Multiple Ovals

Coat of Arms — A1

1865, Dec. Unwmk. Litho. *Imperf.*

No.	Type	Denom.	Color	Unused	Used
1	A1	2r	black, *green*	.65	*250.00*
2	A1	2r	black, *pink*	.65	*250.00*

Comayagua

Tegucigalpa

Medio real = ½ real
Un real = 1 real
Dos reales = 2 reales

Comayagua Issue

1877, May **Red Surcharge**

No.	Type	Surcharge	Unused	Used
3	A1	½r on 2r blk, *grn*	70.00	

Blue Surcharge

No.	Type	Surcharge	Unused	Used
5	A1	2r on 2r blk, *grn*	150.00	—
6	A1	2r on 2r blk, *pink*	*475.00*	—

Black Surcharge

No.	Type	Surcharge	Unused	Used
7	A1	1r on 2r blk, *grn*	150.00	
8	A1	2r on 2r blk, *grn*	*800.00*	
9	A1	2r on 2r blk, *pink*	500.00	

No. 5 may exist only as the base for No. 13a.

Tegucigalpa Issue

1877, July **Black Surcharge**

No.	Type	Surcharge	Unused	Used
13	A1	1r on 2r blk, *grn*	15.00	*35.00*
a.		Surcharged on #5	*1000.*	
14	A1	1r on 2r blk, *pink*	*80.00*	
16	A1	2r on 2r blk, *pink*	—	

Blue Surcharge

No.	Type	Surcharge	Unused	Used
18	A1	½r on 2r blk, *grn*	*80.00*	
19	A1	½r on 2r blk, *pink*	*25.00*	
20	A1	1r on 2r blk, *pink*	*35.00*	
23	A1	2r on 2r blk, *pink*	15.00	*25.00*

Red Surcharge

No.	Type	Surcharge	Unused	Used
24	A1	½r on 2r blk, *grn*	15.00	*35.00*
25	A1	½r on 2r blk, *pink*	60.00	

Only the stamps valued or dashed used are known to have been postally used. Nos. 3 and 7 may have been postally used, but to date no examples are recorded used. The other listed stamps were sold as remainders. No covers bearing Nos. 3 to 25 are known.

The blue surcharges range from light blue to violet black. The black surcharge has no tinge of blue. The red surcharges range from light to dark carmine. Some exist double or inverted, but genuine errors are rare. Normal cancel is a blue or black 7-bar killer. Target cancels on Nos. 1-24 are forgeries. Surcharges and cancels have been extensively forged.

Regular Issue

President Francisco Morazán — A4

Printed by National Bank Note Co. of N.Y.
Thin, hard paper, colorless gum
Various Frames

1878, July **Engr.** ***Perf. 12***

No.	Type	Denom.	Color	Unused	Used
30	A4	1c	violet	.50	.50
31	A4	2c	brown	.50	.50
32	A4	½r	black	5.00	.50
33	A4	1r	green	25.00	.50
34	A4	2r	deep blue	3.00	*5.00*
35	A4	4r	vermilion	5.00	*10.00*
36	A4	1p	orange	6.00	*25.00*
			Nos. 30-36 (7)	45.00	*42.00*

Various counterfeit cancellations exist on Nos. 30-36. Most used copies of Nos. 35-36 offered are actually 35a-36a with fake or favor cancels.

Printed by American Bank Note Co. of N.Y.
Re-Issue Soft paper, yellowish gum
Various Frames

1889

No.	Type	Denom.	Color	Unused
30a	A4	1c	deep violet	*10.00*
31a	A4	2c	red brown	.25
32a	A4	½r	black	.25
33a	A4	1r	blue green	.25
34a	A4	2r	ultramarine	*5.00*
35a	A4	4r	scarlet vermilion	.25
36a	A4	1p	orange yellow	.25
			Nos. 30a-36a (7)	16.25

Although Nos. 30a-36a were not intended for postal use, they were valid, and genuine cancels are known on Nos. 31a-34a.

Arms of Honduras — A5

1890, Jan. 6

No.	Type	Denom.	Color	Unused	Used
40	A5	1c	yellow green	.30	.30
41	A5	2c	red	.30	.30
42	A5	5c	blue	.30	.30
43	A5	10c	orange	.35	*.40*
44	A5	20c	ocher	.35	*.40*
45	A5	25c	rose red	.35	*.40*
46	A5	30c	purple	.50	*.60*
47	A5	40c	dark blue	.50	*.80*
48	A5	50c	brown	.55	*.80*
49	A5	75c	blue green	.55	*2.00*
50	A5	1p	carmine	.70	*2.25*
			Nos. 40-50 (11)	4.75	*8.55*

The tablets and numerals of Nos. 40 to 50 differ for each denomination.

For overprints see Nos. O1-O11.

Used values of Nos. 1-110 are for stamps with genuine cancellations applied while the stamps were valid. Various counterfeit cancellations exist.

A6

President Luis Bográn — A7

1891, July 31

No.	Type	Denom.	Color	Unused	Used
51	A6	1c	dark blue	.30	.30
52	A6	2c	yellow brown	.30	.30
53	A6	5c	blue green	.30	.30
54	A6	10c	vermilion	.30	.30
55	A6	20c	brown red	.30	.30
56	A6	25c	magenta	.40	*.55*
57	A6	30c	slate	.40	*.55*
58	A6	40c	blue green	.40	*.55*
59	A6	50c	black brown	.50	*.80*
60	A6	75c	purple	.50	*1.25*
61	A6	1p	brown	.75	*1.60*
62	A7	2p	brn & black	2.25	*5.00*
a.			Head inverted	225.00	
63	A7	5p	pur & black	2.00	*5.75*
a.			Head inverted	60.00	
64	A7	10p	green & blk	2.00	*5.75*
a.			Head inverted	75.00	
			Nos. 51-64 (14)	10.70	*23.30*

Nos. 62, 64 exist with papermakers watermark.

For overprints see Nos. O12-O22.

Columbus Sighting Honduran Coast — A8

1892, July 31

No.	Type	Denom.	Color	Unused	Used
65	A8	1c	slate	.40	*.45*
66	A8	2c	deep blue	.40	*.45*
67	A8	5c	yellow green	.40	*.45*
68	A8	10c	blue green	.40	*.45*
69	A8	20c	red	.40	*.45*
70	A8	25c	orange brown	.50	*.55*
71	A8	30c	ultramarine	.50	*.60*
72	A8	40c	orange	.50	*.90*
73	A8	50c	brown	.65	*.85*
74	A8	75c	lake	.75	*1.25*
75	A8	1p	purple	.75	*1.40*
			Nos. 65-75 (11)	5.65	*7.80*

Discovery of America by Christopher Columbus, 400th anniv.

General Trinidad Cabanas — A9

1893, Aug.

No.	Type	Denom.	Color	Unused	Used
76	A9	1c	green	.25	*1.50*
77	A9	2c	scarlet	.25	*1.50*
78	A9	5c	dark blue	.25	*1.50*
79	A9	10c	orange brn	.25	*1.50*
80	A9	20c	brown red	.25	*1.50*
81	A9	25c	dark blue	.30	*1.50*
82	A9	30c	red orange	.50	*1.50*
83	A9	40c	black	.50	*1.50*
84	A9	50c	olive brn	.50	*1.50*
85	A9	75c	purple	.75	*1.50*
86	A9	1p	deep magenta	.75	*1.75*
			Nos. 76-86 (11)	4.55	*16.75*

"Justice" — A10

1895, Feb. 15

No.	Type	Denom.	Color	Unused	Used
87	A10	1c	vermilion	.30	.30
88	A10	2c	deep blue	.30	.30
89	A10	5c	slate	.35	*.50*
90	A10	10c	brown rose	.45	*.50*
91	A10	20c	violet	.45	*.50*
92	A10	30c	deep violet	.45	*.85*
93	A10	50c	olive brown	.55	*1.25*
94	A10	1p	dark green	.60	*1.60*
			Nos. 87-94 (8)	3.45	*5.80*

The tablets and numerals of Nos. 76-94 differ for each denomination.

President Celio Arias — A11

1896, Jan. 1 **Litho.** ***Perf. 11½***

No.	Type	Denom.	Color	Unused	Used
95	A11	1c	dark blue	.30	*.35*
96	A11	2c	yellow brn	.30	*.35*
97	A11	5c	purple	1.10	.30
a.			5c red violet	.60	*1.10*
98	A11	10c	vermilion	.40	.40
a.			10c red	4.50	*4.50*
99	A11	20c	emerald	.75	.50
a.			20c deep green		
100	A11	30c	ultramarine	.65	*.70*
101	A11	50c	rose	.90	*1.00*
102	A11	1p	black brown	1.25	*1.50*
			Nos. 95-102 (8)	5.65	*5.10*

Counterfeits are plentiful. Nos. 95-102 exist imperf. between horiz. or vertically.

Originals of Nos. 95 to 102 are on both thin, semi-transparent paper and opaque paper; reprints are on thicker, opaque paper and usually have a black cancellation "HONDURAS" between horizontal bars.

Railroad Train — A12

1898, Aug. 1

No.	Type	Description	Unused	Used
103	A12	1c brown	.50	.25
104	A12	2c rose	.50	.25
105	A12	5c dull ultra	1.00	.25
b.		5c red violet (error)	1.50	.70
106	A12	6c red violet	.90	.25
b.		6c dull rose		
107	A12	10c dark blue	1.00	.30
108	A12	20c dull orange	1.25	.75
109	A12	50c orange red	2.00	1.25
110	A12	1p blue green	4.00	3.00
		Nos. 103-110 (8)	11.15	6.30

Excellent counterfeits of Nos. 103-110 exist.
For overprints see Nos. O23-O27.

Laid Paper

No.	Type	Value	Unused	Used
103a	A12	1c	1.00	.70
104a	A12	2c	1.25	.70
105a	A12	5c	1.60	.70
106a	A12	6c	1.60	.75
107a	A12	10c	1.60	1.00
		Nos. 103a-107a (5)	7.05	3.85

General Santos Guardiola — A13

1903, Jan. 1 Engr. *Perf. 12*

No.	Type	Description	Unused	Used
111	A13	1c yellow grn	.35	.25
112	A13	2c carmine rose	.35	.30
113	A13	5c blue	.35	.30
114	A13	6c dk violet	.35	.30
115	A13	10c brown	.40	.30
116	A13	20c dull ultra	.45	.40
117	A13	50c vermilion	1.25	1.10
118	A13	1p orange	1.25	1.10
		Nos. 111-118 (8)	4.75	4.05

"PERMITASE" handstamped on stamps of 1896-1903 was applied as a control mark by the isolated Pacific Coast post office of Amapala to prevent use of stolen stamps.

President José Medina — A14

1907, Jan. 1 *Perf. 14*

No.	Type	Description	Unused	Used
119	A14	1c dark green	.25	.25
120	A14	2c scarlet	.25	.25
120A	A14	2c carmine	9.00	5.50
121	A14	5c blue	.30	.30
122	A14	6c purple	.35	.30
a.		6c dark violet	.80	.60
123	A14	10c gray brown	.40	.35
124	A14	20c ultra	.90	.85
a.		20c blue violet	110.00	110.00
125	A14	50c deep lake	1.10	1.10
126	A14	1p orange	1.50	1.50
a.		1p orange yellow	—	
		Nos. 119-126 (9)	14.05	10.40

All values of the above set exist imperforate, imperforate horizontally and in horizontal pairs, imperforate between. No. 124a imperf is worth only 10% of the listed perforated variety.
For surcharges see Nos. 128-130.

1909 Typo. *Perf. 11½*

No.	Type	Description	Unused	Used
127	A14	1c green	1.25	1.00
a.		Imperf., pair	4.00	4.00
b.		Printed on both sides	7.50	10.00

The 1909 issue is roughly typographed in imitation of the 1907 design. It exists pin perf. 8, 13, etc.

No. 124 Handstamp Surcharged in Black, Green or Red

1910, Nov. *Perf. 14*

No.	Type	Description	Unused	Used
128	A14	1c on 20c ultra	8.50	6.00
129	A14	5c on 20c ultra (G)	8.50	6.00
130	A14	10c on 20c ultra (R)	8.50	6.00
		Nos. 128-130 (3)	25.50	18.00

As is usual with handstamped surcharges inverts and double exist.

Honduran Scene — A15

1911, Jan. Litho. *Perf. 14, 12 (1p)*

No.	Type	Description	Unused	Used
131	A15	1c violet	.35	.25
132	A15	2c green	.35	.25
a.		Perf. 12	5.00	1.25
133	A15	5c carmine	.40	.25
a.		Perf. 12	8.00	3.50
134	A15	6c ultramarine	.50	.30
135	A15	10c blue	.60	.40
136	A15	20c yellow	.60	.50
137	A15	50c brown	2.00	1.75
138	A15	1p olive green	2.50	2.00
		Nos. 131-138 (8)	7.30	5.70

For overprints and surcharges see Nos. 139, 141-147, O28-O47.

No. 132a Overprinted in Red

1911, Sept. 19 *Perf. 12*

No.	Type	Description	Unused	Used
139	A15	2c green	20.00	18.00
a.		Inverted overprint	24.00	22.50

90th anniversary of Independence.
Counterfeit overprints on perf. 14 stamps exist.

President Manuel Bonilla — A16

1912, Feb. 1 Typo. *Perf. 11½*

No.	Type	Description	Unused	Used
140	A16	1c orange red	12.00	12.00

Election of Pres. Manuel Bonilla.

Stamps of 1911 Surcharged in Black, Red or Blue

a

b

1913 Litho. *Perf. 14*

No.	Type	Description	Unused	Used
141	A15(a)	2c on 1c violet	1.25	.75
a.		Double surcharge		3.25
b.		Inverted surcharge	4.50	
c.		Double surch., one invtd.	6.75	
d.		Red surcharge	40.00	40.00
142	A15(b)	2c on 1c violet	7.00	5.75
a.		Inverted surcharge	14.00	
143	A15(b)	2c on 10c blue	2.75	2.25
a.		Double surcharge	5.75	5.75
b.		Inverted surcharge		
144	A15(b)	2c on 20c yellow	7.00	6.75
145	A15(b)	5c on 1c violet	2.50	.75
146	A15(b)	5c on 10c bl (Bl)	2.75	1.50
147	A15(b)	6c on 1c violet	2.75	2.25
		Nos. 141-147 (7)	26.00	20.00

Counterfeit surcharges exist.

Terencio Sierra — A17

Bonilla — A18

ONE CENTAVO:
Type I — Solid border at sides below numerals.
Type II — Border of light and dark stripes.

1913-14 Typo. *Perf. 11½*

No.	Type	Description	Unused	Used
151	A17	1c dark brn, I	.25	.25
a.		1c brown, type II	.75	.45
152	A17	2c carmine	.25	.25
153	A18	5c blue	.40	.25
154	A18	5c ultra ('14)	.40	.25
155	A18	6c gray vio	.50	.25
156	A18	6c purple ('14)	.40	.25
a.		6c red lilac	.60	.35
157	A17	10c blue	.75	.75
158	A17	10c brown ('14)	1.25	.50
159	A17	20c brown	1.00	.75
160	A18	50c rose	2.00	2.00
161	A18	1p gray green	2.25	2.25
		Nos. 151-161 (11)	9.45	7.75

For overprints and surcharges see Nos. 162-173, O48-O57.

Surcharged in Black or Carmine

1914

No.	Type	Description	Unused	Used
162	A17	1c on 2c carmine	.75	.75
163	A17	5c on 2c carmine	1.25	.90
164	A18	5c on 6c gray vio	2.00	2.00
165	A17	10c on 2c carmine	2.00	2.00
166	A18	10c on 6c gray vio	2.00	2.00
a.		Double surcharge	10.00	
167	A18	10c on 6c gray vio (C)	2.00	2.00
168	A18	10c on 50c rose	6.50	5.00
		Nos. 162-168 (7)	16.50	14.65

No. 158 Surcharged

1915

No.	Type	Description	Unused	Used
173	A17	5c on 10c dk brn	2.50	1.75

Ulua Bridge — A19

Bonilla Theater — A20

1915-16 Typo.

No.	Type	Description	Unused	Used
174	A19	1c chocolate	.25	.25
175	A19	2c carmine	.25	.25
a.		Tête bêche pair	1.00	1.00
176	A20	5c bright blue	.25	.25
177	A20	6c deep purple	.35	.25
178	A19	10c dull blue	.75	.25
179	A19	20c red brown	1.25	1.00
a.		Tête bêche pair	4.00	4.00
180	A20	50c red	1.50	1.50
181	A20	1p yellow grn	2.50	2.50
		Nos. 174-181 (8)	7.10	6.25

For overprints & surcharges see Nos. 183, 231-232, 237, 239-240, 285, 292, C1-C13, C25, C28, C31, C36, C57, CO21, CO30-CO32, CO42, O58-O65.

Imperf., Pairs

No.	Type	Value	Unused	Used
174a	A19	1c	2.00	2.00
175b	A19	2c	2.00	2.00
176a	A20	5c	3.50	
178a	A19	10c	3.50	
179b	A19	20c	5.25	
180b	A20	50c	7.00	
181a	A20	1p	8.75	8.75

Francisco Bertrand — A21

1916, Feb. 1

No.	Type	Description	Unused	Used
182	A21	1c orange	2.00	2.00

Election of Pres. Francisco Bertrand.
Unauthorized reprints exist.

Official Stamp No. O60 Overprinted

1918

No.	Type	Description	Unused	Used
183	A20	5c bright blue	2.00	1.50
a.		Inverted overprint	5.00	5.00

Statue to Francisco Morazán — A22

1919 Typo.

No.	Type	Description	Unused	Used
184	A22	1c brown	.25	.25
a.		Printed on both sides	2.00	
b.		Imperf., pair	.70	
185	A22	2c carmine	.25	.25
186	A22	5c lilac rose	.25	.25
187	A22	6c brt purple	.25	.25
188	A22	10c dull blue	.25	.25
189	A22	15c light blue	.75	.25
190	A22	15c dark violet	.60	.25
191	A22	20c orange brn	1.00	.30
a.		20c gray brown	10.00	.30
b.		Imperf., pair	2.75	
192	A22	50c light brown	4.00	2.50
a.		Imperf. pair	15.00	
193	A22	1p yellow green	7.50	*20.00*
a.		Imperf., pair	20.00	
b.		Printed on both sides	9.00	
c.		Tête bêche pair	15.00	
		Nos. 184-193 (10)	15.10	24.55

See note on handstamp following No. 217.
Unauthorized reprints exist.
For overprints and surcharges see Nos. 201-210C, 230, 233, 235-236, 238, 241-243, 287, 289, C58, C61, CO23, CO25, CO33, CO36-CO38, CO39, CO40, O66-O74.

"Dawn of Peace" — A23

1920, Feb. 1 **Size: 27x21mm**
194 A23 2c rose 2.50 2.50
a. Tête bêche pair 15.00 12.50
b. Imperf., pair 15.00 12.50

Size: 51x40mm

195 A23 2c gold 10.00 10.00
196 A23 2c silver 10.00 10.00
197 A23 2c bronze 10.00 10.00
198 A23 2c red 12.00 12.00
Nos. 194-198 (5) 44.50 44.50

Assumption of power by Gen. Rafael Lopez Gutierrez.
Nos. 195-198 exist imperf.
Unauthorized reprints of Nos. 195-198 exist.

Type of 1919, Dated "1920"

1921
201 A22 6c dark violet 10.00 *5.00*
a. Tête bêche pair 15.00
b. Imperf., pair 15.00

Unauthorized reprints exist.

No. 185 Surcharged in Antique Letters

1922
202 A22 6c on 2c carmine .40 .40
a. "ALE" for "VALE" 2.00 2.00
b. Comma after "CTS" 2.00 2.00
c. Without period after "CTS" 2.00 2.00
d. "CT" for "CTS" 2.00 2.00
e. Double surcharge 4.25
f. Inverted surcharge 4.25

Stamps of 1919 Surcharged in Roman Figures and Antique Letters in Green

1923
203 A22 10c on 1c brown 1.50 1.50
204 A22 50c on 2c carmine 2.00 2.00
a. Inverted surcharge 10.00 10.00
b. "HABILTADO" 6.00 6.00

Surcharged in Black or Violet Blue

205 A22 1p on 5c lil rose (Bk) 3.50 3.50
a. "PSEO" 20.00 20.00
b. Inverted surcharge 20.00 20.00
206 A22 1p on 5c lil rose (VB) 20.00 20.00
a. "PSEO" 70.00

On Nos. 205-206, "Habilitado Vale" is in Antique letters, "Un Peso" in Roman.

No. 185 Surcharged in Roman Letters in Green

207 A22 6c on 2c carmine 3.50 2.75

Nos. 184-185 Surcharged in Roman Letters in Green

208 A22 10c on 1c brown 1.75 1.25
a. "DIES" 6.00
b. "DEIZ" 6.00
c. "DEIZ CAS" 6.00
d. "TTS" for "CTS" 6.00
e. "HABILTADO" 6.00
f. "HABILITAD" 6.00
g. "HABILITA" 6.00
h. Inverted surcharge 30.00
209 A22 50c on 2c carmine 3.75 2.75
a. "CAT" for "CTA" 10.00
b. "TCA" for "CTA" 10.00
c. "TTS" for "CTS" 10.00
d. "CAS" for "CTS" 10.00
e. "HABILITADO" 10.00

Surcharge on No. 209 is found in two spacings between value and HABILITADO: 5mm (illustrated) and 1½mm.

No. 186 Surcharged in Antique Letters in Black

210 A22 1p on 5c lil rose 25.00 *25.00*
a. "PFSO" 75.00

In the surcharges on Nos. 202 to 210 there are various wrong font, inverted and omitted letters.

No. 184 Surcharged in Large Antique Letters in Green

210C A22 10c on 1c brown 15.00 15.00
d. "DIFZ" 55.00 55.00

Dionisio de Herrera — A24

1924, June **Litho.** ***Perf. 11, 11½***
211 A24 1c olive green .30 .25
212 A24 2c deep rose .35 .25
213 A24 6c red violet .40 .25
214 A24 10c blue .40 .25
215 A24 20c yellow brn .80 .35
216 A24 50c vermilion 1.75 1.10
217 A24 1p emerald 4.00 2.75
Nos. 211-217 (7) 8.00 5.20

In 1924 a facsimile of the signatures of Santiago Herrera and Francisco Caceres, covering four stamps, was handstamped in violet to prevent the use of stamps that had been stolen during a revolution.
Imperfs exist.
For overprints and surcharges see Nos. 280-281, 290-291, C14-C24, C26-C27, C29-C30, C32-C35, C56, C60, C73-C76, CO1-CO5, CO22, CO24, CO28-CO29, CO34-CO35, CO38A, CO39A, CO41, CO43, O75-O81.

Pres. Miguel Paz Baraona — A25

1925, Feb. 1 **Typo.** ***Perf. 11½***
218 A25 1c dull blue 2.00 2.00
a. 1c dark blue 2.00 2.00
219 A25 1c car rose 5.00 5.00
a. 1c brown carmine 5.00 5.00
220 A25 1c olive brn 14.00 14.00
a. 1c orange brown 14.00 14.00
b. 1c dark brown 14.00 14.00
c. 1c black brown 14.00 14.00
221 A25 1c buff 12.00 12.00
222 A25 1c red 60.00 60.00
223 A25 1c green 40.00 40.00
Nos. 218-223 (6) 133.00 133.00

Imperf

225 A25 1c dull blue 5.50 5.50
a. 1c dark blue 5.50 5.50
226 A25 1c car rose 8.75 8.75
a. 1c brown carmine 8.75 8.75
227 A25 1c olive brn 8.75 8.75
a. 1c orange brown 8.75 8.75
b. 1c deep brown 8.75 8.75
c. 1c black brown 8.75 8.75
228 A25 1c buff 8.75 8.75
229 A25 1c red 60.00 60.00
229A A25 1c green 27.50 27.50
Nos. 225-229A (6) 119.25 119.25

Inauguration of President Baraona.
Counterfeits and unauthorized reprints exist.

No. 187 Overprinted in Black and Red

1926, June ***Perf. 11½***
230 A22 6c brt purple 1.50 1.25

Many varieties of this two-part overprint exist: one or both inverted or double, and various combinations. Value, each $10.

Nos. 177 and 187 Overprinted in Black or Red

1926
231 A20 6c deep pur (Bk) 2.00 2.00
a. Inverted overprint 5.50 5.50
b. Double overprint 5.50 5.50
232 A20 6c deep pur (R) 2.50 2.50
a. Double overprint 5.00 5.00
233 A22 6c lilac (Bk) .60 .60
a. 6c violet .75 .75
b. Inverted overprint 5.00 5.00
c. Double overprint 5.00 5.00
d. Double ovpt., one inverted 5.00 5.00
e. "192" 7.50 7.50
f. Double ovpt., both inverted 7.50 7.50

No. 230 Overprinted

235 A22 6c violet 20.00 20.00
a. "1926" inverted 20.00 20.00
b. "Habilitado" triple, one invtd. 20.00 20.00

No. 188 Surcharged in Red or Black

236 A22 6c on 10c blue (R) .50 .25
c. Double surcharge 5.00 4.00
d. Without bar
e. Inverted surcharge 4.00 3.50
f. "Vale" omitted
g. "6cts" omitted
h. "cts" omitted
k. Black surcharge *55.00 55.00*

Nos. 175 and 185 Overprinted in Green

237 A19 2c carmine .25 .25
a. Tête bêche pair 4.00 4.00
b. Double overprint 2.00 1.40
c. "HARILITADO" 2.00 1.40
d. "1926" only 2.75 2.75
e. Double overprint, one inverted 2.75 2.75
f. "1926" omitted 3.50 3.50
g. Triple overprint, two inverted 5.25 5.25
h. Double on face, one on back 5.25 5.25
238 A22 2c carmine .25 .25
a. "HARILITADO" .90 .90
b. Double overprint 1.40 1.40
c. Inverted overprint 2.00 2.00

No. 177 Overprinted in Red

1927 **Large Numerals, 12x5mm**
239 A20 6c deep purple 25.00 25.00
a. "1926" over "1927" 35.00 35.00
b. Invtd. ovpt. on face of stamp, normal ovpt. on back 30.00

No. 179 Surcharged

1927
240 A19 6c on 20c brown .75 .75
a. Tête bêche pair 2.75 2.75
c. Interted surcharge 2.50 2.50
d. Double surcharge 8.50 8.50

Nos. 8 and 10 in the setting have no period after "cts" and No. 50 has the "t" of "cts" inverted.

Nos. 189-191 Surcharged

241 A22 6c on 15c blue 27.50 27.50
a. "c" of "cts" omitted
242 A22 6c on 15c vio .70 .70
a. Double surcharge 1.75 1.75
b. Double surch., one invtd. 2.00 2.00
c. "L" of "Vale" omitted
243 A22 6c on 20c yel brn .60 .60
a. 6c on 20c deep brown
b. "6" omitted 1.75 1.75
c. "Vale" and "cts" omitted 3.50 3.50
Nos. 240-243 (4) 29.55 29.55

On Nos. 242 and 243 stamps Nos. 12, 16 and 43 in the setting have no period after "cts" and No. 34 often lacks the "s." On No. 243 the "c" of "cts" is missing on stamp No. 38. On No. 241 occur the varieties "ct" or "ts" for "cts." and no period.

Southern Highway — A26

Ruins of Copán — A27

Pine Tree — A28

Presidential Palace — A29

Ponciano Leiva — A30

Pres. M.A. Soto — A31

Lempira — A32

Map of Honduras — A33

President Juan Lindo — A34

Statue of Columbus — A35

1927-29 Typo. Wmk. 209
244 A26 1c ultramarine .30 .25
a. 1c blue .30 .25
245 A27 2c carmine .30 .25
246 A28 5c dull violet .30 .25
247 A28 5c bl gray ('29) 25.00 7.00
248 A29 6c blue black .75 .50
a. 6c gray black .75 .50
249 A29 6c dark bl ('29) .40 .25
a. 6c light blue .40 .25
250 A30 10c blue .70 .25
251 A31 15c deep blue 1.00 .50
252 A32 20c dark blue 1.25 .60
253 A33 30c dark brown 1.50 1.00
254 A34 50c light blue 2.50 1.50
255 A35 1p red 5.00 2.50
Nos. 244-255 (12) 39.00 14.85

In 1929 a quantity of imperforate sheets of No. 249 were stolen from the Litografia Nacional. Some of them were perforated by sewing machine and a few copies were passed through the post. To prevent the use of stolen stamps of the 1927-29 issues they were declared invalid and the stock on hand was overprinted "1929 a 1930."

For overprints and surcharges see Nos. 259-278, CO19-CO20B.

Pres. Vicente Mejia Colindres and Vice-Pres. Rafael Diaz Chávez — A36

President Mejia Colindres — A37

1929, Feb. 25
256 A36 1c dk carmine 3.00 3.00
257 A37 2c emerald 3.00 3.00

Installation of Pres. Vicente Mejia Colindres. Printed in sheets of ten.

Nos. 256 and 257 were surreptitiously printed in transposed colors. They were not regularly issued.

Stamps of 1927-29 Overprinted in Various Colors

1929, Oct.
259 A26 1c blue (R) .25 .25
a. 1c ultramarine (R) .50 .25
b. Double overprint 2.50 1.75
c. As "a", double overprint 2.50 1.75
260 A26 1c blue (Bk) 6.50 6.50
a. 1c ultramarine (Bk)
261 A27 2c car (R Br) 3.50 3.50
a. Double overprint
262 A27 2c car (Bl Gr) 1.00 1.00
a. Double overprint
263 A27 2c car (Bk) 1.00 .50
264 A27 2c car (V) .50 .25
a. Double overprint
b. Double ovpt., one inverted
265 A27 2c org red (V) 1.50
266 A28 5c dl vio (R) .40 .30
a. Double overprint (R+V)
267 A28 5c bl gray (R) 1.00 .75
a. Double overprint (R+Bk)
269 A29 6c gray blk (R) 2.50 2.00
a. Double overprint 6.00 6.00
272 A29 6c dk blue (R) .40 .25
a. 6c light blue (R) .40 .25
b. Double overprint 2.00 2.00
c. Double overprint (R+V)
273 A30 10c blue (R) .40 .25
a. Double overprint 2.50 1.75
274 A31 15c dp blue (R) .50 .25
a. Double overprint 3.50 2.50
275 A32 20c dark bl (R) .50 .35
276 A33 30c dark brn (R) .75 .60
a. Double overprint 3.50 2.50
277 A34 50c light bl (R) 2.00 1.00
278 A35 1p red (V) 5.00 2.50
Nos. 259-278 (17) 27.70 20.25

Nos. 259-278 exist in numerous shades. There are also various shades of the red and violet overprints. The overprint may be found reading upwards, downwards, inverted, double, triple, tête bêche or combinations.

Status of both 6c stamps with overprint in black is questioned.

A38

1929, Dec. 10
279 A38 1c on 6c lilac rose .70 .70
a. "1992" for "1929"
b. "9192" for "1929"
c. Surcharge reading down 8.00
d. Dbl. surch., one reading down

Varieties include "1992" reading down and pairs with one surcharge reading down, double or with "1992."

No. 214 Surcharged in Red

Perf. 11, 11½

1930, Mar. 26 Unwmk.
280 A24 1c on 10c blue .35 .30
a. "1093" for "1930" 1.40
b. "tsc" for "cts" 1.40
281 A24 2c on 10c blue .35 .30
a. "tsc" for "cts" 2.00
b. "Vale 2" omitted

Official Stamps of 1929 Overprinted in Red or Violet

1930, Mar. Wmk. 209 *Perf. 11½*
282 O1 1c blue (R) .50 .50
a. Double overprint 2.00 2.00
284 O1 2c carmine (V) .90 .90

Stamps of 1915-26 Overprinted in Blue

On No. 174

1930, July 19 Unwmk.
285 A19 1c chocolate .30 .25
a. Double overprint 1.00 1.00
b. Inverted overprint 1.40 1.40
c. Dbl. ovpt., one inverted 1.40 1.40

On No. 184

287 A22 1c brown 15.00 15.00
a. Double overprint
c. Inverted overprint

On No. 204

289 A22 50c on 2c carmine 100.00 90.00
b. Inverted surcharge

On Nos. 211 and 212

290 A24 1c olive green .25 .25
a. Double overprint 1.75 1.75
b. Inverted overprint 1.75 1.75
d. On No. O75 12.00
291 A24 2c carmine rose .25 .25
a. Double overprint 1.75 1.75
b. Inverted overprint 1.75 1.75

On No. 237

292 A19 2c car (G & Bl) 100.00 100.00

From Title Page of Government Gazette, First Issue — A39

1930, Aug. 11 Typo. Wmk. 209
295 A39 2c orange 2.00 2.00
296 A39 2c ultramarine 2.00 2.00
297 A39 2c red 2.00 2.00
Nos. 295-297 (3) 6.00 6.00

Publication of the 1st newspaper in Honduras, cent. The stamps were on sale and available for postage on Aug. 11th, 1930, only. Not more than 5 examples of each color could be purchased by an applicant.

Nos. 295-297 exist imperf. and part-perforate. Unauthorized reprints exist.

For surcharges see Nos. CO15-CO18A.

Paz Baraona — A40

Manuel Bonilla — A41

Lake Yojoa — A42

View of Palace at Tegucigalpa — A43

Mayan Stele at Copán — A45

Christopher Columbus — A46

Discovery of America — A47

Loarque Bridge — A48

City of Amapala — A44

Unwmk.

1931, Jan. 2 Engr. *Perf. 12*
298 A40 1c black brown .75 .25
299 A41 2c carmine rose .75 .25
300 A42 5c dull violet 1.00 .25
301 A43 6c deep green 1.00 .25
302 A44 10c brown 1.50 .25
303 A45 15c dark blue 2.00 .30
304 A46 20c black 3.50 .40
305 A47 50c olive green 4.50 1.50
306 A48 1p slate black 9.00 2.50
Nos. 298-306 (9) 24.00 5.95

Regular Issue of 1931 Overprinted in Black or Various Colors

1931
307 A40 1c black brown .40 .30
308 A41 2c carmine rose .60 .30
309 A45 15c dark blue 1.00 .30
310 A46 20c black 2.50 .40

Overprinted

311 A42 5c dull violet .50 .30
312 A43 6c deep green .50 .30
315 A44 10c brown 1.50 .35
316 A47 50c olive green 8.00 5.00
317 A48 1p slate black 10.00 7.50
Nos. 307-317 (9) 25.00 14.75
Nos. 307-317,C51-C55 (14) 50.00 35.75

The overprint is a control mark. It stands for "Tribunal Superior de Cuentas" (Superior Tribunal of Accounts).

Overprint varieties include: inverted; double; double, one or both inverted; on back; pair, one without overprint; differing colors (6c exists with overprint in orange, yellow and red).

President Carías and Vice-President Williams — A49

1933, Apr. 29
318 A49 2c carmine rose .50 .35
319 A49 6c deep green .75 .40
320 A49 10c deep blue 1.00 .50
321 A49 15c red orange 1.25 .75
Nos. 318-321 (4) 3.50 2.00

Inauguration of Pres. Tiburcio Carias Andino and Vice-Pres. Abraham Williams, Feb. 1, 1933.

Columbus' Fleet and Flag of the Race — A50

Wmk. 209

1933, Aug. 3 Typo. *Perf. 11½*
322 A50 2c ultramarine 1.00 .65
323 A50 6c yellow 1.00 .65
324 A50 10c lemon 1.40 .85

Perf. 12
325 A50 15c violet 2.00 1.50
326 A50 50c red 4.00 3.50
327 A50 1 l emerald 7.00 7.00
Nos. 322-327 (6) 16.40 14.15

"Day of the Race," an annual holiday throughout Spanish-American countries. Also for the 441st anniv. of the sailing of Columbus to the New World, Aug. 3, 1492.

Masonic Temple, Tegucigalpa — A51

Designs: 2c, President Carias. 5c, Flag. 6c, Tomás Estrada Palma.

Unwmk.

1935, Jan. 12 Engr. *Perf. 12*

328 A51 1c green .40 .25
329 A51 2c carmine .40 .25
330 A51 5c dark blue .40 .25
331 A51 6c black brown .40 .25
a. Vert. pair, imperf. btwn. 20.00 20.00
Nos. 328-331 (4) 1.60 1.00
Nos. 328-331,C77-C83 (11) 15.20 6.60

Gen. Carías Bridge — A55

1937, June 4

332 A55 6c car & ol green .90 .40
333 A55 21c grn & violet 1.50 .65
334 A55 46c orange & brn 2.10 1.50
335 A55 55c ultra & black 3.00 2.40
Nos. 332-335 (4) 7.50 4.95

Prolongation of the Presidential term to Jan. 19, 1943.

Seal of Honduras A56

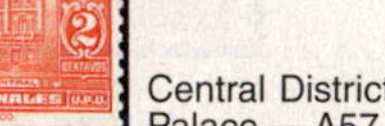

Central District Palace — A57

Designs: 3c, Map of Honduras. 5c, Bridge of Choluteca. 8c, Flag.

1939, Mar. 1 *Perf. 12½*

336 A56 1c orange yellow .25 .25
337 A57 2c red orange .25 .25
338 A57 3c carmine .30 .25
339 A57 5c orange .30 .25
340 A56 8c dark blue .50 .25
Nos. 336-340 (5) 1.60 1.25
Nos. 336-340,C89-C98 (15) 15.45 8.90

Nos. 336-340 exist imperf.
For overprints see Nos. 342-343.

Nos. 336 and 337 Overprinted in Green

1944 *Perf. 12½*

342 A56 1c orange yellow .30 .30
a. Inverted overprint 5.00 5.00
343 A57 2c red orange 1.25 .75
a. Inverted overprint 5.00 5.00

Catalogue values for unused stamps in this section, from this point to the end of the section, are for Never Hinged items.

International Peace Movement — A58

1984, Feb. 15 Litho. *Perf. 12*

344 A58 78c multi .85 .65
345 A58 85c multi .95 .30
346 A58 95c multi 1.00 .35
347 A58 1.50 l multi 1.75 .55
348 A58 2 l multi 2.10 .70
349 A58 5 l multi 5.50 1.75
Nos. 344-349 (6) 12.15 4.30

Central American Aeronautics Corp., 25th Anniv. — A59

Designs: 2c, Edward Warner Award issued by the Intl. Civil Aviation Organization, vert. 5c, Corp. emblem, flags of Guatemala, Honduras, El Salvador, Costa Rica and Panama. 60c, Transmission tower, plane. 75c, Corp. emblem, vert. 1 l, 1.50 l, Emblem, flags, diff.

1987, Feb. 26 Litho. *Perf. 12*

350 A59 2c multi .25 .25
351 A59 5c multi .25 .25
352 A59 60c multi .75 .35
353 A59 75c multi .95 .40
354 A59 1 l multi 1.25 .55
Nos. 350-354 (5) 3.45 1.80

Souvenir Sheet

355 A59 1.50 l multi 3.00 3.00

Housing Institute (INVA), 30th Anniv. A60

1987, Oct. 9 Litho. *Perf. 13½*

356 A60 5c shown .30 .25
357 A60 95c Map, emblem, text 1.00 .40

EXFILHON '88 — A61

1988, Sept. 11 Litho. *Imperf.*

358 A61 3 l dl red brn & brt ultra 4.50 4.50

1988 Summer Olympics, Seoul — A62

1988, Sept. 30 Litho. *Imperf.*

359 A62 4 l multi 4.75 4.75
Nos. 359,C772-C773 (3) 7.05 5.65

Luis Bogran Technical Institute, Cent. A63

85c, Cogwheel, map, flag of Honduras.

1990, Sept. 28 Litho. *Perf. 10½*

360 A63 20c multicolored .25 .25
361 A63 85c multicolored .65 .40

Size: 114x82mm

Imperf

362 A63 2 l like #360 2.00 1.40
Nos. 360-362 (3) 2.90 2.05

Nos. 360-361 are airmail.

America Issue A64

UPAE emblem, land and seascapes showing produce and fish.

1990, Oct. 31 Litho. *Perf. 13½*

363 A64 20c multi, vert. .80 .25
364 A64 1 l multicolored 1.60 .30

1992 Winter Olympics, Albertville — A65

3 l, Cross-country skiing.

1992, Feb. 17

365 A65 50c shown .60 .25
366 A65 3 l multicolored 2.25 1.25

A66

Mother's Day (Paintings): 20c, Saleswoman, by Manuel Rodriguez. 50c, The Grandmother and Baby, by Rodriguez. 5 l, Saleswomen, by Maury Flores.

1992, May 21 Litho. *Perf. 13½*

367 A66 20c shown .40 .25
368 A66 50c multicolored .65 .25
369 A66 5 l multicolored 3.25 2.00
Nos. 367-369 (3) 4.30 2.50

Butterflies A67

Designs: 25c, Melitaeinae chlosyne janais. 85c, Heliconiinae agrilus vanillae. 3 l, Morphinae morpho granadensis. 5 l, Heliconiinae dryadula phalusa.

1992, June 22

370 A67 25c multicolored .50 .25
371 A67 85c multicolored 1.25 .40
372 A67 3 l multicolored 4.50 1.25

Size: 108x76mm

Imperf

373 A67 5 l multicolored 6.00 5.25
Nos. 370-373 (4) 12.25 7.15

1992 Summer Olympics, Barcelona — A68

1992, Mar. 16 Litho. *Perf. 13½*

374 A68 20c Running .40 .25
375 A68 50c Tennis .80 .25
376 A68 85c Soccer 1.20 .40
Nos. 374-376 (3) 2.40 .90

Japanese Overseas Cooperation Volunteers in Honduras, 20th Anniv. — A69

Designs: 1.40 l, Volunteers working on Japanese letter, vert. 4.30 l, Folding screen showing Mayan Gods. 5.40 l, Men, women of Honduras in traditional costumes, volunteer.

1995, Sept. 20 Litho. *Perf. 13½*

377 A69 1.40 l multicolored .50 .40
378 A69 4.30 l multicolored 1.50 1.25
379 A69 5.40 l multicolored 1.75 1.50
Nos. 377-379 (3) 3.75 3.15

Nos. 378-379 are airmail.

Birds — A70

Designs: 1.40 l, Buteo jamaicensis. 1.50 l, Ramphastos sulfuratus. 2 l, Dendrocygna autumnalis. 2.15 l, Micrastur semitorquatus. 3 l, Polyporus plancus. 5.40 l, 10 l, Sarcoramphus papa.

1997, Apr. 29 Litho. *Perf. 13½*

380 A70 1.40 l multicolored .85 .55
381 A70 1.50 l multicolored .95 .60
382 A70 2 l multicolored 1.20 .80
383 A70 2.15 l multicolored 1.40 .90
a. Pair, #382, 383 3.50 2.50
384 A70 3 l multicolored 1.75 1.25
a. Pair, #380, 384 3.50 3.50
385 A70 5.40 l multicolored 3.25 2.00
a. Pair, #381, 385 5.00 5.00
Nos. 380-385 (6) 9.40 6.10

Size: 50x73mm

Imperf

386 A70 20 l multicolored 7.25 6.00

Nos. 380-385 were printed in panes of 30 (5x6), with one value comprising the top three rows and another the bottom three rows. Thus, each pane contains five setenant pairs.
No. 386 is airmail.

No. RA8 Surcharged in Gold

1999, June 25 Litho. *Perf. 13½*

387 PT6 2.60 l on 1c .65 .35
388 PT6 7.85 l on 1c 1.90 .95
389 PT6 10.65 l on 1c 2.60 1.25
390 PT6 11.55 l on 1c 2.75 1.40
391 PT6 12.45 l on 1c 3.00 1.50
392 PT6 13.85 l on 1c 3.50 1.75
Nos. 387-392 (6) 14.40 7.20

For surcharges, see C1199//C1206.

Inauguration of Pres. Juan Orlando Hernández — A71

Designs: No. 393, 50 l, Honduras coat of arms. No. 394, 50 l, Isla Conejo, horiz. 100 l, Pres. Hernández wearing sash, flag of Honduras. 150 l, Pres. Hernánadez, with arm raised, horiz. 200 l, Pres. Hernández wearing sash, waving.

2014, June 4 Litho. *Perf. 13½*
393-397 A71 Set of 5 57.50 57.50

SEMI-POSTAL STAMPS

Catalogue values for unused stamps in this section are for Never Hinged items.

Indiginous Musical Instruments — SP1

No. B1: a, Garífuna drum. b, Flutes. c, Toltec drum. d, Hornpipe. e, Maya drum. f, Conch shell.

2000, Apr. 7 Litho. *Perf. 13¼*
B1 Sheet of 6, "Pro filatelia" in black 16.00 16.00
a.-f. SP1 10 l + 1 l Any single 2.50 2.50
g. As #B1, "Pro filatelia" in gold 17.50 17.50

See Nos. C1073, C1209.

AIR POST STAMPS

Regular Issue of 1915-16 Overprinted in Black, Blue or Red

1925 Unwmk. *Perf. 11½*
C1 A20 5c lt blue (Bk) 87.50 87.50
C2 A20 5c lt blue (Bl) 300.00 300.00
a. Inverted overprint *400.00*
b. Vertical overprint *600.00*
c. Double overprint *800.00*
C3 A20 5c lt blue (R) *7,250.*

Value for No. C3 is for an example without gum.

C4 A19 10c dk blue (R) 175.00
a. Inverted overprint 325.00
b. Overprint tête bêche, pair *800.00*
C5 A19 10c dk blue (Bk) *1,100.*
C6 A19 20c red brn (Bk) 175.00 175.00
a. Inverted overprint 250.00
b. Tête bêche pair 400.00
c. Overprint tête bêche, pair *725.00*
d. "AFRO" *1,400.*
e. Double overprint *600.00*
C7 A19 20c red brn (Bl) 175.00 175.00
a. Inverted overprint *700.00*
b. Tête bêche pair *1,000*
c. Vertical overprint 900.00
C8 A20 50c red (Bk) 450.00 300.00
a. Inverted overprint *550.00*
b. Overprint tête bêche, pair *900.00*
C9 A20 1p yel grn (Bk) 600.00 600.00

Surcharged in Black or Blue

C10 A19 25c on 1c choc 125.00 125.00
a. Inverted surcharge 700.00
C11 A20 25c on 5c lt bl (Bl) 225.00 225.00
a. Inverted surcharge 700.00
b. Double inverted surcharge *675.00*
C12 A19 25c on 10c dk bl *125,000.*
C13 A19 25c on 20c brn (Bl) 200.00 200.00
a. Inverted surcharge 325.00
b. Tête bêche pair 450.00

Counterfeits of Nos. C1-C13 are plentiful.

Monoplane and Lisandro Garay
AP1

1929, June 5 Engr. *Perf. 12*
C13C AP1 50c carmine 2.25 1.75

No. 216 Surcharged in Blue

1929 *Perf. 11, 11½*
C14 A24 25c on 50c ver 5.00 3.50

In the surcharges on Nos. C14 to C40 there are various wrong font and defective letters and numerals, also periods omitted.

Nos. 215-217 Surcharged in Green, Black or Red

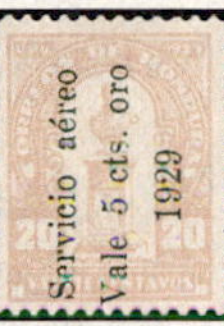

1929, Oct.
C15 A24 5c on 20c yel brn (G) 1.40 1.40
a. Double surcharge (R+G) 45.00
C16 A24 10c on 50c ver (Bk) 2.25 1.90
C17 A24 15c on 1p emer (R) 3.50 3.50
Nos. C15-C17 (3) 7.15 6.80

Nos. 214 and 216 Surcharged Vertically in Red or Black

a

b

1929, Dec. 10
C18 A24(a) 5c on 10c bl (R) .60 .60
C19 A24(b) 20c on 50c ver 1.00 1.00
a. "1299" for "1929" 190.00
b. "cts. cts." for "cts. oro." 190.00
c. "r" of "Aereo" omitted 2.00
d. Horiz. pair, imperf. btwn. 20.00

Nos. 214, 215 and 180 Surcharged in Various Colors

1930, Feb.
C20 A24 5c on 10c (R) .50 .50
a. "1930" reading down 3.50
b. "1903" for "1930" 3.50
c. Surcharge reading down 10.00
d. Double surcharge 14.00
e. Dbl. surch., one downward 14.00
C21 A24 5c on 10c (Y) *450.00 450.00*
C22 A24 5c on 20c (Bl) 125.00 125.00
C23 A24 10c on 20c (Bk) .75 .75
a. "0" for "10" 3.50
b. Double surcharge 8.75
c. Dbl. surch., one downward 12.00
d. Horiz. pair, imperf. btwn. 70.00
C24 A24 10c on 20c (V) *750.00 750.00*
a. "0" for "10" *1,600.*
C25 A20 25c on 50c (Bk) .95 .95
a. "Internaoicnal" 3.50
b. "o" for "oro" 3.50
c. Inverted surcharge 17.50
d. As "a," invtd. surch. *175.00*
e. As "b," invtd. surch. *175.00*

Surcharge on Nos. C20-C24 are vertical.

Nos. 214, 215 and 180 Surcharged

1930, Apr. 1
C26 A24 5c on 10c blue .50 .50
a. Double surcharge 9.50
b. "Servicioa" 3.50
C27 A24 15c on 20c yel brn .55 .55
a. Double surcharge 7.00
C28 A20 20c on 50c red, surch. reading down .95 .95
a. Surcharge reading up 7.00
Nos. C26-C28 (3) 2.00 2.00

Nos. C22 and C23 Surcharged Vertically in Red

1930
C29 A24 10c on 5c on 20c (Bl+R) .90 .90
a. "1930" reading down 9.00 9.00
b. "1903" for "1930" 9.00 9.00
c. Red surcharge, reading down 14.00
C30 A24 10c on 10c on 20c (Bk+R) 87.50 87.50
a. "0" for "10" 190.00

No. 181 Surcharged as No. C25 and Re-surcharged

C31 A20 50c on 25c on 1p grn 4.25 4.25
a. "Internaoicnal" 7.00
b. "o" for "oro" 7.00
c. 25c surcharge inverted 17.50 17.50
d. 50c surcharge inverted 17.50 17.50
e. As "a" and "c"
f. As "a" and "d"
g. As "b" and "c"
h. As "b" and "d"
Nos. C29-C31 (3) 92.65 92.65

No. 215 Surcharged in Dark Blue

1930, May 22
C32 A24 5c on 20c yel brn 1.25 1.00
a. Double surcharge 5.25 5.25
b. Horiz. pair, imperf. btwn. 60.00 60.00
c. Vertical pair, imperf. between 20.00 20.00

Nos. O78-O80 Surcharged in Various Colors

1930
C33 A24 5c on 10c (R) 450.00 350.00
a. "1930" reading down *1,500.*
b. "1903" for "1930" *1,500.*
C34 A24 5c on 20c (Bl) 400.00 400.00
C35 A24 25c on 50c (Bk) 225.00 225.00
a. 55c on 50c vermilion 325.00 325.00

No. C35 exists with inverted surcharge.

No. O64 Surcharged like No. C28
C36 A20 20c on 50c red, surcharge reading down *350.00 350.00*
a. Surcharge reading up *350.00 350.00*
b. Dbl. surch., reading down *350.00 350.00*
c. Dbl. surch., reading up *350.00 350.00*

No. O87 Overprinted

1930, Feb. 21 Wmk. 209 *Perf. 11½*
C37 O1 50c yel, grn & blue 1.40 1.25
a. "Internacionai" 5.25
b. "luternacional" 5.25
c. Double overprint 5.25

Nos. O86-O88 Overprinted in Various Colors

1930, May 23
C38 O1 20c dark blue (R) 1.10 .85
a. Double overprint 8.75
b. Triple overprint 12.00
C39 O1 50c org, grn & bl (Bk) 1.10 .90
C40 O1 1p buff (Bl) 1.40 1.25
a. Double overprint 10.50
Nos. C38-C40 (3) 3.60 3.00

National Palace
AP3

Unwmk.
1930, Oct. 1 Engr. *Perf. 12*
C41 AP3 5c yel orange .50 .30
C42 AP3 10c carmine .75 .60
C43 AP3 15c green 1.00 .75
C44 AP3 20c dull violet 1.25 .60
C45 AP3 1p light brown 4.00 4.00
Nos. C41-C45 (5) 7.50 6.25

Overprinted in Various Colors

1931 *Perf. 12*
C51 AP3 5c yel orange (R) *2.00 1.50*
C52 AP3 10c carmine (Bk) *3.00 2.50*
C53 AP3 15c green (Br) *5.00 4.00*
C54 AP3 20c dull vio (O) *5.00 4.25*
C55 AP3 1p lt brown (G) *10.00 8.75*
Nos. C51-C55 (5) *25.00 21.00*

See note after No. 317.

Stamps of Various Issues Surcharged in Blue or Black (#C59)

1931, Oct. On No. 215 *Perf. 11½*
C56 A24 15c on 20c yel brn 3.50 2.75
a. Horiz. pair, imperf. btwn. 42.50
b. Green surcharge 20.00 20.00

On No. O64
C57 A20 15c on 50c red 4.25 3.50
a. Inverted surcharge 10.50 10.50

On No. O72
C58 A22 15c on 20c brn 4.25 4.25
a. Vert. pair, imperf. between 12.00

On Nos. C57 and C58 the word "OFICIAL" is canceled by two bars.

On No. O88

Wmk. 209

C59 O1 15c on 1p buff 4.25 4.25
- *a.* Vert. pair, imperf. horiz. 25.00
- *b.* "Servicio" 14.00 14.00

The varieties "Vaie" for "Vale," "aereo" with circumflex accent on the first "e" and "Interior" with initial capital "I" are found on Nos. C56, C58-C59. No. C57 is known with initial capital in "Interior."

A similar surcharge, in slightly larger letters and with many minor varieties, exists on Nos. 215, O63, O64 and O73. The authenticity of this surcharge is questioned.

Nos. 215, O73, O87-O88 Surcharged in Green, Red or Black

1931, Nov. Unwmk.

C60 A24 15c on 20c (G) 3.50 2.75
- *a.* Inverted surcharge 6.25
- *b.* "XI" omitted 6.25
- *c.* "X" for "XI" 6.25
- *d.* "PI" for "XI" 6.25

C61 A22 15c on 50c (R) 3.50 2.75
- *a.* "XI" omitted 6.75
- *b.* "PI" for "XI" 6.75
- *c.* Double surcharge 20.00 20.00

On No. C61 the word "OFICIAL" is not barred out.

Wmk. 209

C62 O1 15c on 50c (Bk) 2.75 2.50
- *a.* "1391" for "1931" 10.50 10.50
- *b.* Double surcharge 8.75 8.75

C63 O1 15c on 1p (Bk) 2.50 2.25
- *a.* "1391" for "1931" 12.50
- *b.* Surcharged on both sides 7.00

Nos. O76-O78 Surcharged in Black or Red

1932 Unwmk. *Perf. 11, 11½*

C73 A24 15c on 2c .80 .80
- *a.* Double surcharge 5.50
- *b.* Inverted surcharge 4.25
- *c.* "Ae" of "Aero" omitted 1.00
- *d.* On No. 212 (no "Official")

C74 A24 15c on 6c .80 .80
- *a.* Double surcharge 3.50
- *b.* Horiz. pair, imperf. btwn. 17.50
- *c.* "Aer" omitted
- *d.* "A" omitted 1.00
- *e.* Inverted surcharge 3.50

C75 A24 15c on 10c (R) .80 .80
- *a.* Double surcharge 5.50
- *b.* Inverted surcharge 3.50
- *c.* "r" of "Aereo" omitted 1.00

Same Surcharge on No. 214 in Red

C76 A24 15c on 10c dp bl *150.00 100.00*

There are various broken and missing letters in the setting.

A similar surcharge with slightly larger letters exists.

Post Office and National Palace — AP4

View of Tegucigalpa — AP5

Designs: 15c, Map of Honduras. 20c, Mayol Bridge. 40c, View of Tegucigalpa. 50c, Owl. 1 l, Coat of Arms.

1935, Jan. 10 *Perf. 12*

C77 AP4 8c blue .25 .25
C78 AP5 10c gray .25 .25
C79 AP5 15c olive gray .40 .25
C80 AP5 20c dull green .50 .25
C81 AP5 40c brown .70 .25
C82 AP4 50c yellow 8.25 1.60
C83 AP4 1 l green 3.25 2.75
Nos. C77-C83 (7) 13.55 5.35

Flags of US and Honduras — AP11

Engr. & Litho.

1937, Sept. 17 Unwmk.

C84 AP11 46c multicolored 2.75 1.40

US Constitution, 150th anniv.

Comayagua Cathedral AP12

Founding of Comayagua AP13

Alonzo Cáceres and Pres. Carías — AP14

Lintel of Royal Palace AP15

1937, Dec. 7 Engr.

C85 AP12 2c copper red .25 .25
C86 AP13 8c dark blue .35 .25
C87 AP14 15c slate black .70 .70
C88 AP15 50c dark brown 4.25 2.75
Nos. C85-C88 (4) 5.55 3.95

City of Comayagua founding, 400th anniv.
For surcharges see Nos. C144-C146.

Mayan Stele at Copán AP16

Mayan Temple, Copán AP17

Designs: 15c, President Carias. 30c, José C. de Valle. 40c, Presidential House. 46c, Lempira. 55c, Church of Our Lady of Suyapa. 66c, J. T. Reyes. 1 l, Hospital at Choluteca. 2 l, Ramón Rosa.

1939, Mar. 1 *Perf. 12½*

C89 AP16 10c orange brn .25 .25
C90 AP16 15c grnsh blue .30 .25
C91 AP17 21c gray .50 .25
C92 AP16 30c dk blue grn .55 .25
C93 AP17 40c dull violet 1.00 .25
C94 AP16 46c dk gray brn 1.00 .65
C95 AP16 55c green 1.25 1.00
- *a.* Imperf., pair 22.50

C96 AP16 66c black 1.75 1.25
C97 AP16 1 l olive grn 3.00 1.00
C98 AP16 2 l henna red 4.25 2.50
Nos. C89-C98 (10) 13.80 7.45

For surcharges see Nos. C118-C119, C147-C152.

Souvenir Sheets

AP26

14c, Francisco Morazan. 16c, George Washington. 30c, J. C. de Valle. 40c, Simon Bolivar.

1940, Apr. 13 Engr. *Perf. 12*

Centers of Stamps Lithographed

C99 AP26 Sheet of 4 10.00 10.00
- *a.* 14c black, yellow, ultra & rose 1.40 1.40
- *b.* 16c black, yellow, ultra & rose 1.75 1.75
- *c.* 30c black, yellow, ultra & rose 2.40 2.40
- *d.* 40c black, yellow, ultra & rose 2.75 2.75

Imperf

C100 AP26 Sheet of 4 16.00 16.00
- *a.* 14c black, yellow, ultra & rose 2.25 2.25
- *b.* 16c black, yellow, ultra & rose 2.75 2.75
- *c.* 30c black, yellow, ultra & rose 4.00 4.00
- *d.* 40c black, yellow, ultra & rose 4.50 4.50

Pan American Union, 50th anniv.
For overprints see Nos. C153-C154, C187.

Air Post Official Stamps of 1939 Overprinted in Red

1940, Oct. 12 *Perf. 12½*

C101 OA2 2c dp bl & green .25 .25
C102 OA2 5c dp blue & org .25 .25
C103 OA2 8c deep bl & brn .30 .30
C104 OA2 15c dp blue & car .50 .50
C105 OA2 46c dp bl & ol grn .80 .80
C106 OA2 50c dp bl & vio .90 .90
C107 OA2 1 l dp bl & red brn 3.75 3.75
C108 OA2 2 l dp bl & red org 7.50 7.50
Nos. C101-C108 (8) 14.25 14.25

Erection and dedication of the Columbus Memorial Lighthouse.

Air Post Official Stamps of 1939 Overprinted in Black

1941, Aug. 2

C109 OA2 5c deep bl & org 3.00 .25
C110 OA2 8c dp blue & brn 5.00 .25
- *a.* Overprint inverted 225.00

Nos. CO44, CO47-CO51 Surcharged in Black

1941, Oct. 28

C111 OA2 3c on 2c .40 .25
C112 OA2 8c on 2c .50 .50
C113 OA2 8c on 15c .50 .25
C114 OA2 8c on 46c .60 .60
C115 OA2 8c on 50c .75 .50
C116 OA2 8c on 1 l 1.25 .70
C117 OA2 8c on 2 l 2.00 1.50
Nos. C111-C117 (7) 6.00 4.30

Once in each sheet a large "h" occurs in "ocho."

Nos. C90, C94 Surcharged in Red

1942, July 14

C118 AP16 8c on 15c .70 .30
- *a.* "Cerreo" 2.00 2.00
- *b.* Double surcharge 25.00 25.00
- *c.* As "a," double surcharge *175.00*

C119 AP16 16c on 46c .70 .30
- *a.* "Cerreo" 2.00 2.00

Plaque AP27

Morazán's Tomb, San Salvador — AP28

Designs: 5c, Battle of La Trinidad. 8c, Morazán's birthplace. 16c, Statue of Morazán. 21c, Church where Morazán was baptized. 1 l, Arms of Central American Federation. 2 l, Gen. Francisco Morazán.

1942, Sept. 15 *Perf. 12*

C120 AP27 2c red orange .25 .25
C121 AP27 5c turq green .25 .25
C122 AP27 8c sepia .25 .25
C123 AP28 14c black .40 .30
C124 AP27 16c olive gray .25 .25
C125 AP27 21c light blue 1.00 .65
C126 AP27 1 l brt ultra 3.00 2.25
C127 AP28 2 l dl ol brn 7.50 7.25
Nos. C120-C127 (8) 12.90 11.45

Gen. Francisco Morazan (1799-1842).
For surcharges see Nos. C349-C350.

Coat of Arms AP35

Cattle AP36

Bananas — AP37

Pine Tree — AP38

Tobacco Plant AP39

Orchid AP40

Coco Palm — AP41

Map of Honduras AP42

Designs: 2c, Flag. 8c, Rosario. 16c, Sugar cane. 30c, Oranges. 40c, Wheat. 1 l, Corn. 2 l, Map of Americas.

1943, Sept. 14 *Perf. 12½*

C128 AP35 1c light grn .25 .25
C129 AP35 2c blue .25 .25
C130 AP36 5c green .30 .25
C131 AP37 6c dark bl grn .25 .25
C132 AP36 8c lilac .30 .25
C133 AP38 10c lilac brn .30 .25
C134 AP39 15c dp claret .35 .25
C135 AP38 16c dark red .35 .25
C136 AP40 21c deep blue .75 .25
C137 AP39 30c org brown .60 .25
C138 AP40 40c red orange .60 .25
C139 AP41 55c black 1.10 .60
C140 AP41 1 l dark olive 1.75 1.40
C141 AP37 2 l brown red 5.25 4.00
C142 AP42 5 l orange 13.00 13.00
a. Vert. pair, imperf. btwn. 150.00
Nos. C128-C142 (15) 25.40 21.75

Pan-American School of Agriculture AP50

1944, Oct. 12 *Perf. 12*

C143 AP50 21c dk blue grn .40 .25

Inauguration of the Pan-American School of Agriculture, Tegucigalpa.

Catalogue values for unused stamps in this section, from this point to the end of the section, are for Never Hinged items.

Air Post Stamps of 1937-39 Surcharged in Red or Green

1945, Mar. 13 *Perf. 11, 12½*

C144 AP15 1c on 50c dk brn .25 .25
C145 AP12 2c on 2c cop red .25 .25
C146 AP14 8c on 15c sl blk .25 .25
C147 AP16 10c on 10c org brown (G) .45 .30
C148 AP16 15c on 15c grnsh blue (G) .30 .25
C149 AP17 30c on 21c gray (G) 4.50 3.00
C150 AP17 40c on 40c dull violet (G) 2.25 1.25
C151 AP16 1 l on 46c dk gray brown (G) 2.25 1.75
C152 AP16 2 l on 66c blk (G) 4.50 3.00
Nos. C144-C152 (9) 15.00 10.30

Nos. C99 and C100 Overprinted in Red
Souvenir Sheets

1945, Oct. 1 *Perf. 12*

C153 AP26 Sheet of 4 4.00 3.00

Imperf

C154 AP26 Sheet of 4 6.50 4.25

Allied Nations' victory and Germany's unconditional surrender, May 8, 1945.

Seal of Honduras AP51

Arms of Gracias and Trujillo AP52

Franklin D. Roosevelt ("F.D.R." under Column) AP53

Arms of San Miguel de Heredia de Tegucigalpa AP54

Designs (Coats of Arms): 5c, Comayagua and San Jorge de Olancho. 15c, Province of Honduras and San Juan de Puerto Caballas. 21c, Comayagua and Tencoa. 1 l, Jerez de la Frontera de Choluteca and San Pedro de Zula.

Perf. 12½

1946, Oct. 15 **Unwmk.** **Engr.**

C155 AP51 1c red .25 .25
a. Vert. pair, imperf. between 17.50
b. Imperf., pair 70.00
C156 AP52 2c red orange .25 .25
a. Imperf., pair 70.00
C157 AP52 5c violet .45 .25
C158 AP53 8c brown 1.60 .50
a. Horiz. pair, imperf. btwn. 70.00
C159 AP52 15c sepia .80 .25
C160 AP52 21c deep blue .90 .30
a. Horiz. pair, imperf. btwn. 15.00
b. Imperf., pair 70.00
C161 AP52 1 l green 3.25 1.25
C162 AP54 2 l dark grn 5.00 2.00
Nos. C155-C162 (8) 12.50 5.05

No. C158 commemorates the death of Franklin D. Roosevelt and the Allied victory over Japan in World War II.

Type AP53 Redrawn ("Franklin D. Roosevelt" under Column) AP59

1947, Oct. *Perf. 12½*

C163 AP59 8c brown .50 .35
a. Vert. pair, imperf. between 87.50
b. Horiz. pair, imperf. btwn. 175.00
c. Perf. 12x6 175.00

Map, Ancient Monuments and Conference Badge AP60

1947, Oct. 20 *Perf. 11x12½*

Various Frames

C164 AP60 16c green .40 .25
C165 AP60 22c orange yel .30 .25
C166 AP60 40c orange .65 .35
C167 AP60 1 l deep blue 1.10 .90
C168 AP60 2 l lilac 4.00 3.50
C169 AP60 5 l brown 10.50 8.00
Nos. C164-C169 (6) 16.95 13.25

1st Intl. Archeological Conf. of the Caribbean.

For overprints and surcharges see Nos. C181-C186, C351, C353-C354, C379, C544.

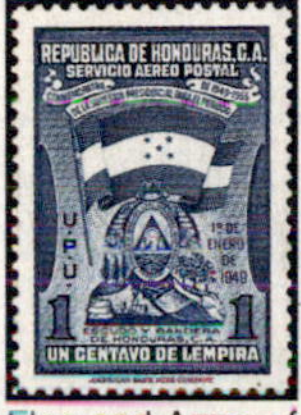
Flag and Arms of Honduras AP61

Juan Manuel Galvez AP62

J. M. Galvez, Gen. Tiburcio Carias A. and Julio Lozano AP63

National Stadium AP64

Designs: 5c, 15c, Julio Lozano. 9c, Juan Manuel Galvez. 40c, Custom House. 1 l, Recinto Hall. 2 l, Gen. Tiburcio Carias A. 5 l, Galvez and Lozano.

Various frames inscribed: "Conmemorativa de la Sucesion Presidencial para el Periodo de 1949-1955."

1949, Sept. 17 **Engr.** *Perf. 12*

C170 AP61 1c deep blue .25 .25
C171 AP62 2c rose car .25 .25
C172 AP62 5c deep blue .25 .25
C173 AP62 9c sepia .25 .25
C174 AP62 15c red brown .25 .25
C175 AP63 21c gray black .45 .25
C176 AP64 30c olive gray .60 .25
C177 AP64 40c slate gray .90 .25
C178 AP61 1 l red brown 1.40 .40
C179 AP62 2 l violet 3.25 1.50
C180 AP64 5 l rose car 9.25 5.50
Nos. C170-C180 (11) 17.10 9.40

Presidential succession for the 1949-1955 term.

For overprints and surcharges see Nos. C188-C197, C206-C208, C346, C355, C419-C420, C478, C545.

Nos. C164-C169 Overprinted in Carmine

1951, Feb. 26 *Perf. 11x12½*

C181 AP60 16c green .50 .40
a. Inverted overprint 45.00 45.00
C182 AP60 22c orange yel .65 .55
a. Inverted overprint 45.00
C183 AP60 40c orange .65 .55
C184 AP60 1 l deep blue 2.00 1.75
C185 AP60 2 l lilac 3.75 3.25
a. Inverted overprint 60.00
C186 AP60 5 l brown 32.50 29.00
Nos. C181-C186 (6) 40.05 35.50

Souvenir Sheets

Same Overprint in Carmine on Nos. C99 and C100

Perf. 12

C187 AP26 Sheet of 4 8.00 4.75
a. Imperf. 250.00 250.00

UPU, 75th anniv. (in 1949).

Nos. C170 to C179 Overprinted in Carmine

1951, Feb. 27 *Perf. 12*

C188 AP61 1c deep blue .25 .25
C189 AP62 2c rose car .25 .25
C190 AP62 5c deep blue .25 .25
C191 AP62 9c sepia .25 .25
C192 AP62 15c red brown .25 .25
C193 AP63 21c gray black .25 .25
C194 AP64 30c olive gray .60 .30
C195 AP64 40c slate gray .90 .60
C196 AP61 1 l red brown 2.25 1.50
C197 AP62 2 l violet 7.25 5.00
Nos. C188-C197 (10) 12.50 8.90

Founding of Central Bank, July 1, 1950.

Discovery of America AP65

Queen Isabella I — AP66

2c, 1 l, Columbus at court. 8c, Surrender of Granada. 30c, Queen Isabella offering her jewels.

Perf. 13½x14, 14x13½

1952, Oct. 11 **Engr.** **Unwmk.**

C198 AP65 1c red org & blk .25 .25
C199 AP65 2c bl & red brn .25 .25
C200 AP65 8c dk grn & dk brn .25 .25
C201 AP66 16c dk bl & blk .40 .25
C202 AP65 30c pur & dk grn .70 .70
C203 AP65 1 l dp car & blk 1.75 1.40
C204 AP65 2 l brn & vio 4.25 3.50
C205 AP66 5 l rose lil & ol 9.25 8.75
Nos. C198-C205 (8) 17.10 15.35

500th birth anniv. of Isabella I of Spain.

For overprints and surcharges see Nos. C209-C221, C377-C378, C404-C406, C489, CO52-CO59.

No. C175 Surcharged in Carmine

1953, May 13 *Perf. 12*
C206 AP63 5c on 21c gray blk .25 .25
C207 AP63 8c on 21c gray blk .55 .25
C208 AP63 16c on 21c gray blk .95 .25
Nos. C206-C208 (3) 1.75 .75

Nos. CO52-CO54 Surcharged "HABILITADO 1953" and New Value in Red

1953, Dec. 8 *Perf. 13½x14, 14x13½*
C209 AP65 10c on 1c .25 .25
a. Inverted surcharge 50.00 50.00
C210 AP65 12c on 1c .25 .25
C211 AP65 15c on 2c .30 .25
C212 AP65 20c on 2c .50 .30
C213 AP65 24c on 2c .50 .30
a. Inverted surcharge 50.00 50.00
C214 AP65 25c on 2c .50 .30
C215 AP65 30c on 8c .60 .30
C216 AP65 35c on 8c .70 .45
C217 AP65 50c on 8c .80 .45
C218 AP65 60c on 8c 1.00 .90

Same Overprint on Nos. CO57-CO59

C219 AP65 1 l dk grn & dk brown 3.00 2.25
C220 AP65 2 l bl & red brn 6.75 5.50
C221 AP66 5 l red org & blk 16.00 13.00
a. Date inverted 150.00
Nos. C209-C221 (13) 31.15 24.50

Flags of UN and Honduras AP67

2c, UN emblem. 3c, UN building. 5c, Shield. 15c, Juan Manuel Galvez. 30c, UNICEF. 1 l, UNRRA. 2 l, UNESCO. 5 l, FAO.

Engraved; Center of 1c Litho.

1953, Dec. 18 *Perf. 12½*

Frames in Black

C222 AP67 1c ultra & vio bl .25 .25
C223 AP67 2c blue .25 .25
C224 AP67 3c rose lilac .25 .25
C225 AP67 5c green .25 .25
C226 AP67 15c red brown .40 .25
C227 AP67 30c brown .85 .50
C228 AP67 1 l dp carmine 6.75 4.50
C229 AP67 2 l orange 8.75 6.25
C230 AP67 5 l blue green 19.00 15.00
Nos. C222-C230 (9) 36.75 27.50

Issued to honor the United Nations.
For overprints and surcharges see Nos. C231-C249, C331-C335, C472, C490, CO60-CO68.

Nos. CO60-CO66 Overprinted in Red

1955, Feb. 23 **Unwmk.** *Perf. 12½*

Frames in Black

C231 AP67 1c ultra & vio bl .25 .25
C232 AP67 2c dp blue grn .25 .25
C233 AP67 3c orange .25 .25
C234 AP67 5c dp carmine .25 .25
C235 AP67 15c dk brown .35 .35
C236 AP67 30c purple 1.00 .90
C237 AP67 1 l olive gray 20.00 15.00

Overprint exists inverted on 1c, 3c.

Nos. C231 to C233 Surcharged in Black

C238 AP67 8c on 1c .25 .25
C239 AP67 10c on 2c .25 .25
C240 AP67 12c on 3c .25 .25
Nos. C231-C240 (10) 23.10 18.00

50th anniv. of the founding of Rotary International (Nos. C231-C240).

Nos. CO60-CO63, C226-C230 Overprinted

1956, July 14 **Unwmk.** *Perf. 12½*

Frames in Black

C241 AP67 1c ultra & vio bl .25 .25
C242 AP67 2c dp bl grn .25 .25
C243 AP67 3c orange .25 .25
C244 AP67 5c dp car .30 .25
C245 AP67 15c red brn .35 .30
C246 AP67 30c brown .55 .40
C247 AP67 1 l dp car 4.00 2.75
C248 AP67 2 l orange 5.75 4.75
C249 AP67 5 l bl grn 15.00 14.00
Nos. C241-C249 (9) 26.70 23.20

10th anniv. of UN (in 1955). The red "OFICIAL" overprint was not obliterated.
The "ONU" overprint exists inverted on 1c, 3c, 5c and 1-lempira.

Basilica of Suyapa AP68

Pres. Julio Lozano Diaz — AP69

3c, Southern Highway. 4c, Genoveva Guardiola de Estrada Palma. 5c, Maria Josefa Lastiri de Morazan. 8c, Landscape and cornucopia (5-Year Plan). 10c, National Stadium. 12c, US School. 15c, Central Bank. 20c, Legislative Palace. 25c, Development Bank (projected). 30c, Toncontin Airport. 40c, Juan Ramon Molina Bridge. 50c, Peace Monument. 60c, Treasury Palace. 1 l, Blood bank. 2 l, Communications Building. 5 l, Presidential Palace.

Engraved; #C255 Litho.

1956, Oct. 3 *Perf. 13x12½, 12½x13*
C250 AP68 1c black & vio bl .25 .25
C251 AP69 2c black & dk bl .25 .25
C252 AP68 3c black & brown .25 .25
C253 AP69 4c black & lilac .25 .25
C254 AP69 5c black & dk red .25 .25
C255 AP68 8c brown & multi .25 .25
C256 AP67 10c black & emer .25 .25
C257 AP68 12c black & green .25 .25
C258 AP68 15c dk red & blk .30 .25
C259 AP68 20c black & ultra .30 .25
C260 AP69 24c black & lil .35 .25
C261 AP68 25c black & green .40 .25
C262 AP68 30c blk & car rose .40 .25
C263 AP68 40c blk & red brn .50 .25
C264 AP69 50c blk & bl grn .60 .35
C265 AP68 60c blk & org .80 .45
C266 AP68 1 l blk & rose vio 2.00 1.00
C267 AP69 2 l black & mag 3.75 2.25
C268 AP69 5 l blk & brn car 9.00 5.00
Nos. C250-C268 (19) 20.40 12.55

Issued to publicize the Five-Year Plan.
For overprints and surcharges see Nos. C414-C418, C491-C493, C537-C538, C542, C550.
Types AP68 and AP69 in different colors, overprinted "OFICIAL," see Nos. CO69-CO87.

Flag of Honduras AP70

Designs: 2c, 8c, Monument and mountains. 10c, 15c, 1 l, Lempira. 30c, 2 l, Coat of arms.

1957, Oct. 21 **Litho.** *Perf. 13*

Frames in Black

C269 AP70 1c buff & ultra .25 .25
C270 AP70 2c org, pur & emer .25 .25
C271 AP70 5c pink & ultra .25 .25
C272 AP70 8c org, vio & ol .25 .25
C273 AP70 10c violet & brown .25 .25
C274 AP70 12c lt grn & ultra .25 .25
C275 AP70 15c green & brown .30 .25
C276 AP70 30c pink & slate .45 .25
C277 AP70 1 l blue & brown 2.00 1.50
C278 AP70 2 l lt grn & slate 3.75 3.00
Nos. C269-C278 (10) 8.00 6.50

First anniv. of the October revolution.
For overprints and surcharge, see Nos. C551, CO88-CO97.

Control marks were handstamped in violet on many current stamps in July and August, 1958, following fire and theft of stamps at Tegucigalpa in April.

All post offices were ordered to honor only stamps overprinted with the facsimile signature of their departmental revenue administrator. Honduras has 18 departments.

Flags of Honduras and US — AP71

1958, Oct. 2 **Engr.** *Perf. 12*

Flags in National Colors

C279 AP71 1c light blue .25 .25
C280 AP71 2c red .25 .25
C281 AP71 5c green .25 .25
C282 AP71 10c brown .25 .25
C283 AP71 20c orange .40 .25
C284 AP71 30c deep rose .45 .25
C285 AP71 50c gray .60 .40
C286 AP71 1 l orange yel 1.25 1.00
C287 AP71 2 l gray olive 2.40 2.00
C288 AP71 5 l vio blue 5.50 4.00
Nos. C279-C288 (10) 11.60 8.90

Honduras Institute of Inter-American Culture. The proceeds were intended for the Binational Center, Tegucigalpa.
For overprints see Nos. C320-C324.

Abraham Lincoln — AP72

Lincoln's Birthplace AP73

Designs: 3c, 50c, Gettysburg Address. 5c, 1 l, Freeing the slaves. 10c, 2 l, Assassination. 12c, 5 l, Memorial, Washington.

1959, Feb. 12 **Unwmk.** *Perf. 13½*

Flags in National Colors

C289 AP72 1c green .25 .25
C290 AP73 2c dark blue .25 .25
C291 AP73 3c purple .25 .25
C292 AP73 5c dk carmine .25 .25
C293 AP73 10c black .30 .25
C294 AP73 12c dark brown .30 .25
C295 AP72 15c red orange .40 .25
C296 AP73 25c dull pur .60 .40
C297 AP73 50c ultra .75 .65
C298 AP73 1 l red brown 1.50 1.40
C299 AP73 2 l gray olive 2.40 1.75
C300 AP73 5 l ocher 5.50 5.00
a. Miniature sheet 10.00 10.00
Nos. C289-C300 (12) 12.75 10.95

Birth sesquicentennial of Abraham Lincoln.
No. C300a contains one each of the 1c, 3c, 10c, 25c, 1 l and 5 l, imperf.
For overprints and surcharges see Nos. C316-C319, C325-C330, C345, C347-C348, C352, C356-C364, C494-C495, C539-C541, C552-C553.
Types AP72 and AP73 in different colors, overprinted "OFICIAL," see Nos. CO98-CO109.

Constitution AP74

Designs: 2c, 12c, Inauguration of Pres. Villeda Morales, horiz. 3c, 25c, Pres. Ramon Villeda Morales. 5c, 50c, Allegory of Second Republic (Torch and olive branches).

Engr.; Seal Litho. on 1c, 10c

1959, Dec. 21 *Perf. 13½*
C301 AP74 1c red brn, car & ultra .25 .25
C302 AP74 2c bister brn .25 .25
C303 AP74 3c ultra .25 .25
C304 AP74 5c orange .25 .25
C305 AP74 10c dl grn, car & ultra .25 .25
C306 AP74 12c rose red .35 .25
C307 AP74 25c dull lilac .85 .25
C308 AP74 50c dark blue 1.40 .50
Nos. C301-C308 (8) 3.85 2.25

Second Republic of Honduras, 2nd anniv.
For surcharge see No. C543.

King Alfonso XIII and Map AP75

Designs: 2c, 1906 award of King Alfonso XIII of Spain. 5c, Arbitration commission delivering its award, 1907. 10c, Intl. Court of Justice. 20c, Verdict of the Court, 1960. 50c, Pres. Morales, Foreign Minister Puerto and map. 1 l, Pres. Davila and Pres. Morales.

1961, Nov. 18 **Engr.** *Perf. 14½x14*
C309 AP75 1c dark blue .25 .25
C310 AP75 2c magenta .25 .25
C311 AP75 5c deep green .25 .25
C312 AP75 10c brn orange .25 .25
C313 AP75 20c vermilion .40 .35
C314 AP75 50c brown 1.00 .55
C315 AP75 1 l vio black 1.50 1.00
Nos. C309-C315 (7) 3.90 2.90

Judgment of the Intl. Court of Justice at The Hague, Nov. 18, 1960, returning a disputed territory to Honduras from Nicaragua.

Nos. C295-C297 and CO105 Surcharged

1964, Apr. 7 *Perf. 13½*

Flags in National Colors

C316 AP72 6c on 15c red org .25 .25
C317 AP73 8c on 25c dull pur .25 .25
C318 AP73 10c on 50c ultra .30 .25
C319 AP73 20c on 25c black .75 .40
Nos. C316-C319 (4) 1.55 1.15

The red "OFICIAL" overprint on No. C319 was not obliterated.
See Nos. C345-C355, C419-C421.

Nos. C279-C281, C284 and C287 Overprinted: "FAO / Lucha Contra / el Hambre"

1964, Mar. 23 **Unwmk.** *Perf. 12*

Flags in National Colors

C320 AP71 1c light blue .25 .25
C321 AP71 2c red .25 .25
C322 AP71 5c green .25 .25

C323 AP71 30c deep rose 1.10 .75
C324 AP71 2 l gray olive 5.75 5.50
Nos. C320-C324 (5) 7.60 7.00

FAO "Freedom from Hunger Campaign" (1963).

Nos. CO98-CO101, CO104 and CO106 Overprinted in Blue or Black

Overprint reads: "IN MEMORIAM / JOHN F. KENNEDY / 22 NOVEMBRE 1963"

1964, May 29 ***Perf. 13½***

Flags in National Colors

C325 AP72 1c ocher (Bl) .25 .25
C326 AP73 2c gray ol (Bl) .25 .25
C327 AP73 3c red brn (Bl) .35 .25
C328 AP73 5c ultra (Bk) .50 .30
C329 AP72 15c dk brn (Bl) 2.00 1.25
C330 AP73 50c dk car (Bl) 10.50 6.25
Nos. C325-C330 (6) 13.85 8.55

Pres. John F. Kennedy (1917-63). The red "OFICIAL" overprint was not obliterated. The same overprint was applied to the stamps in miniature sheet No. C300a and seal of Honduras and Alliance for Progress emblem added in margin. Value $65.

Nos. C222-C224, C226 and CO67 Overprinted with Olympic Rings and "1964"

Engr.; Center of 1c Litho.

1964, July 23 ***Perf. 12½***

Frames in Black

C331 AP67 1c ultra & vio bl .25 .25
C332 AP67 2c blue .25 .25
C333 AP67 3c rose lilac .25 .25
C334 AP67 15c red brown .50 .50
C335 AP67 2 l lilac rose 6.25 6.25
Nos. C331-C335 (5) 7.50 7.50

18th Olympic Games, Tokyo, Oct. 10-25. The red "OFICIAL" overprint on No. C335 was not obliterated.

The same overprint was applied in black to the 6 stamps in No. CO108a, with additional rings and "1964" in margins of souvenir sheet. Value $50.

View of Copan AP76

Designs: 2c, 12c, Stone marker from Copan. 5c, 1 l, Mayan ball player (stone). 8c, 2 l, Olympic Stadium, Tokyo.

Unwmk.

1964, Nov. 27 **Photo.** ***Perf. 14***

Black Design and Inscription

C336 AP76 1c yellow grn .25 .25
C337 AP76 2c pale rose lil .25 .25
C338 AP76 5c light ultra .25 .25
C339 AP76 8c bluish green .30 .25
C340 AP76 10c buff .40 .30
C341 AP76 12c lemon .60 .35
C342 AP76 1 l light ocher 1.60 1.25
C343 AP76 2 l pale ol grn 4.25 3.50
C344 AP76 3 l rose 4.75 4.00
Nos. C336-C344 (9) 12.65 10.40

18th Olympic Games, Tokyo, Oct. 10-25. Perf. and imperf. souvenir sheets of four exist containing one each of Nos. C338-C339, C341 and C344. Size: 129x110mm. Values: perf $40; imperf $50.

For overprints, see Nos. CO111-CO119.

Nos. C292, C174, CO106, CO104, C124-C125, C165, CO105, C167-C168 and C178 Surcharged

1964-65

C345 AP73 4c on 5c dk car, bl & red .25 .25
C346 AP62 10c on 15c red brn .25 .25
C347 AP73 10c on 50c dk car, bl & red .25 .25
C348 AP72 12c on 15c dk brn, bl & red .30 .25
C349 AP27 12c on 16c ol gray .30 .25
C350 AP27 12c on 21c lt blue .30 .25
C351 AP60 12c on 22c org yel .30 .25
C352 AP73 12c on 25c blk, bl & red .30 .25
C353 AP60 30c on 1 l dp blue .50 .25
C354 AP60 40c on 2 l lilac ('65) .70 .50
C355 AP61 40c on 1 l red brn ('65) .70 .30
Nos. C345-C355 (11) 4.15 3.05

The red "OFICIAL" overprint on Nos. C347-C348 and C352 was not obliterated.

Nos. C289, CO99, C291-C292, C295-C296, CO106 and C299-C300 Overprinted in Black or Green

Overprint reads: "Toma de Posesión / General / Oswaldo López A. / Junio 6, 1965"

1965, June 6 **Engr.** ***Perf. 13½***

Flags in National Colors

C356 AP72 1c green .25 .25
C357 AP73 2c gray ol (G) .25 .25
C358 AP73 3c purple (G) .25 .25
C359 AP73 5c dk car (G) .25 .25
C360 AP72 15c red orange .35 .35
C361 AP73 25c dull pur (G) .50 .50
C362 AP73 50c dk car (G) 1.00 1.00
C363 AP73 2 l gray olive (G) 4.00 4.00
C364 AP73 5 l ocher (G) 9.50 9.50
Nos. C356-C364 (9) 16.35 16.35

Inauguration of Gen. Oswaldo López Arellano as president. The red "OFICIAL" overprint on Nos. C357 and C362 was not obliterated.

Ambulance and Maltese Cross AP77

Designs (Maltese Cross and): 5c, Hospital of Knights of Malta. 12c, Patients treated in village. 1 l, Map of Honduras.

1965, Aug. 30 **Litho.** ***Perf. 12x11***

C365 AP77 1c ultra .40 .25
C366 AP77 5c dark green .45 .30
C367 AP77 12c dark brown .60 .50
C368 AP77 1 l brown 2.40 1.90
Nos. C365-C368 (4) 3.85 2.95

Knights of Malta; campaign against leprosy.

Father Manuel de Jesus Subirana — AP78

Designs: 1c, Jicaque Indian. 2c, Preaching to the Indians. 10c, Msgr. Juan de Jesus Zepeda. 12c, Pope Pius IX. 20c, Tomb of Father Subirana, Yore. 1 l, Mission church. 2 l, Jicaque mother and child.

Perf. 13½x14

1965, July 27 **Litho.** **Unwmk.**

C369 AP78 1c multicolored .25 .25
C370 AP78 2c multicolored .25 .25
C371 AP78 8c multicolored .25 .25
C372 AP78 10c multicolored .25 .25
C373 AP78 12c multicolored .25 .25
C374 AP78 20c multicolored .45 .30
C375 AP78 1 l multicolored 2.00 1.50
C376 AP78 2 l multicolored 4.00 3.00
a. Souv. sheet of 4, #C371, C373, C375-C376 20.00 20.00
Nos. C369-C376 (8) 7.70 6.05

Centenary (in 1964) of the death of Father Manuel de Jesus Subirana (1807-64), Spanish missionary to the Central American Indians.

For overprints and surcharges see Nos. C380-C386, C407-C413, C487-C488, C554.

Nos. C198-C199, C168 Overprinted

Overprint reads: "IN MEMORIAM / Sir Winston Churchill / 1874-1965."

1965, Dec. 20 **Engr.** ***Perf. 13½x14***

C377 AP65 1c red org & blk .30 .30
C378 AP65 2c blue & red brn .80 .80
C379 AP60 2 l lilac 7.00 7.00
Nos. C377-C379 (3) 8.10 8.10

Sir Winston Spencer Churchill (1874-1965), statesman and World War II leader.

Nos. C369-C375 Overprinted

1966, Mar. 10 **Litho.** ***Perf. 13½x14***

C380 AP78 1c multicolored .25 .25
C381 AP78 2c multicolored .25 .25
C382 AP78 8c multicolored .25 .25
C383 AP78 10c multicolored .25 .25
C384 AP78 12c multicolored .30 .25
C385 AP78 20c multicolored .35 .35
C386 AP78 1 l multicolored 3.25 3.25
Nos. C380-C386 (7) 4.90 4.85

Visit of Pope Paul VI to the UN, New York City, Oct. 4, 1965.

Stamp of 1866, #1 — AP79

Tomas Estrada Palma — AP80

Post Office, Tegucigalpa AP81

Designs: 2c, Air post stamp of 1925, #C1. 5c, Locomotive. 6c, 19th cent. mail transport with mules. 7c, 19th cent. mail room. 8c, Sir Rowland Hill. 9c, Modern mail truck. 10c, Gen. Oswaldo Lopez Arellano. 12c, Postal emblem. 15c, Heinrich von Stephan. 20c, Mail plane. 30c, Flag of Honduras. 40c, Coat of Arms. 1 l, UPU monument, Bern. 2 l, José Maria Medina.

Perf. 14½x14, 14x14½

1966, May 31 **Litho.** **Unwmk.**

C387 AP79 1c gold, blk & grnsh gray .25 .25
C388 AP79 2c org, blk & lt bl .25 .25
C389 AP80 3c brt rose, gold & dp plum .25 .25
C390 AP81 4c bl, gold & blk .25 .25
C391 AP81 5c pink, gold & blk .75 .25
C392 AP81 6c lil, gold & blk .25 .25
C393 AP81 7c lt bl grn, gold & black .25 .25
C394 AP80 8c lt bl, gold & blk .25 .25
C395 AP81 9c lt ultra, gold & black .25 .25
C396 AP80 10c cit, gold & blk .25 .25
C397 AP79 12c gold, blk, yel & emerald .25 .25
C398 AP80 15c brt pink, gold & dp claret .40 .40
C399 AP81 20c org, gold & blk .45 .45
C400 AP79 30c gold & bl .55 .55
C401 AP79 40c multi .90 .80
C402 AP79 1 l emer, gold & dk green 2.00 1.50
C403 AP80 2 l gray, gold & black 4.25 4.25
a. Souv. sheet of 6, #C387-C388, C396-C397, C402-C403 6.75 6.75
Nos. C387-C403 (17) 11.80 10.70

Centenary of the first Honduran postage stamp. No. C403a exists perf. and imperf. See No. CE3. For surcharges see Nos. C473-C474, C479, C486, C496.

Nos. CO53, C201, C204 Overprinted

Overprint reads: "CAMPEONATO DE FOOTBALL Copa Mundial 1966 Inglaterra-Alemania Wembley, Julio 30"

Perf. 13½x14, 14x13½

1966, Nov. 25 **Engr.**

C404 AP65 2c brown & vio .25 .25
C405 AP66 16c dk bl & blk .30 .30
C406 AP65 2 l brn & vio 8.50 8.50
Nos. C404-C406 (3) 9.05 9.05

Final game between England and Germany in the World Soccer Cup Championship, Wembley, July 30, 1966. The overprint on the 2c and 2 l is in 5 lines, it is in 8 lines on the 16c. There is no hyphen between "Inglaterra" and "Alemania" on the 16c.

Nos. C369-C371 and C373-C376 Overprinted in Red

Overprint reads: "CONMEMORATIVA / del XX Aniversario / ONU 1966".

1967, Jan. 31 **Litho.** ***Perf. 13½x14***

C407 AP78 1c multicolored .25 .25
C408 AP78 2c multicolored .25 .25
C409 AP78 8c multicolored .30 .30
C410 AP78 12c multicolored .50 .40
C411 AP78 20c multicolored .65 .55
C412 AP78 1 l multicolored 1.50 1.50
C413 AP78 2 l multicolored 3.50 3.25
Nos. C407-C413 (7) 6.95 6.50

UN, 20th anniversary.

Nos. C250, C252, C258, C261 and C267 Overprinted in Red

Overprint reads: "Siméon Cañas y Villacorta / Libertador de los esclavos / en Centro America / 1767-1967"

1967, Feb. 27 **Engr.**

C414 AP68 1c blk & vio bl .25 .25
C415 AP68 3c blk & brown .25 .25
C416 AP68 15c dk red & blk .35 .35
C417 AP68 25c blk & grn 1.00 .70
C418 AP69 2 l blk & mag 2.75 2.50
Nos. C414-C418 (5) 4.60 4.05

Birth bicentenary of Father José Siméon Canas y Villacorta, D.D. (1767-1838), emancipator of the Central American slaves. The overprint is in 6 lines on the 2 l, in 4 lines on all others.

Nos. C178-C179 and CE2 Surcharged

1967

C419 AP61 10c on 1 l .35 .25
C420 AP62 10c on 2 l .35 .25
C421 APSD1 10c on 20c .35 .25
Nos. C419-C421 (3) 1.05 .75

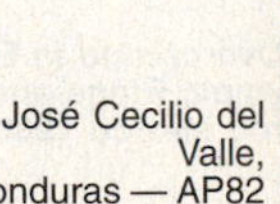

José Cecilio del Valle, Honduras — AP82

Designs: 12c, Ruben Dario, Nicaragua. 14c, Batres Montufar, Guatemala. 20c, Francisco Antonio Gavidia, El Salvador. 30c, Juan Mora Fernandez, Costa Rica. 40c, Federation Emblem with map of Americas. 50c, Map of Central America.

1967, Aug. 4 **Litho.** ***Perf. 13***

C422 AP82 11c gold, dp ultra & blk .25 .25
C423 AP82 12c lt bl, yel & blk .25 .25
C424 AP82 14c sil, grn & blk .25 .25
C425 AP82 20c pink, grn & blk .25 .25
C426 AP82 30c bluish lil, yel & black .40 .35
C427 AP82 40c pur, lt bl & gold .70 .70
C428 AP82 50c lem, grn & car rose .70 .70
Nos. C422-C428 (7) 2.80 2.75

Founding of the Federation of Central American Journalists.

For surcharges see Nos. C475-C476.

Olympic Rings, Flags of Mexico and Honduras AP83

Olympic Rings and Winners of 1964 Olympics: 2c, Like 1c. 5c, Italian flag and boxers. 10c, French flag and women skiers. 12c, German flag and equestrian team. 50c, British flag and women runners. 1 l, US flag and runners (Bob Hayes).

1968, Mar. 4 Litho. *Perf. 14x13½*

C429	AP83	1c gold & multi	.25	.25
C430	AP83	2c gold & multi	.25	.25
C431	AP83	5c gold & multi	.25	.25
C432	AP83	10c gold & multi	.30	.25
C433	AP83	12c gold & multi	.50	.25
C434	AP83	50c gold & multi	3.25	3.25
C435	AP83	1 l gold & multi	6.25	6.25
		Nos. C429-C435 (7)	11.05	10.75

19th Olympic Games, Mexico City, Oct. 12-27.
Exist imperf. Value $45.
Perf. and imperf. souvenir sheets of 2 exist containing 20c and 40c stamps in design of 1c. Values: perf $8; imperf $16.
For surcharge see No. C499.

John F. Kennedy, Rocket at Cape Kennedy AP84

ITU Emblem and: 2c, Radar and telephone. 3c, Radar and television set. 5c, Radar and globe showing Central America. 8c, Communications satellite. 10c, 20c, like 1c.

1968, Nov. 28 *Perf. 14x13½*

C436	AP84	1c vio & multi	.25	.25
C437	AP84	2c sil & multi	.25	.25
C438	AP84	3c multicolored	.35	.35
C439	AP84	5c org & multi	.40	.40
C440	AP84	8c multicolored	.50	.50
C441	AP84	10c olive & multi	.55	.55
C442	AP84	20c multicolored	.70	.70
		Nos. C436-C442 (7)	3.00	3.00

ITU, cent. A 30c in design of 2c, a 1 l in design of 5c and a 1.50 l in design of 1c exist; also two souvenir sheets, one containing 10c, 50c and 75c, the other one 1.50 l.
For overprints see Nos. C446-C453.

Nos. C436, C441-C442 Overprinted: "In Memoriam / Robert F. Kennedy / 1925-1968"

1968, Dec. 23

C446	AP84	1c vio & multi	.25	.25
C447	AP84	10c olive & multi	.50	.50
C448	AP84	20c multicolored	.80	.80
		Nos. C446-C448 (3)	1.55	1.55

In memory of Robert F. Kennedy. Same overprint was also applied to a 1.50 l and to a souvenir sheet containing one 1.50 l. Value, souvenir sheet $6.

Nos. C437-C440 Overprinted in Blue or Red with Olympic Rings and: "Medalias de Oro / Mexico 1968"

1969, Mar. 3

C450	AP84	2c multi (Bl)	.50	.50
C451	AP84	3c multi (Bl)	1.00	1.00
C452	AP84	5c multi (Bl)	1.50	1.50
C453	AP84	8c multi (R)	2.00	2.00
		Nos. C450-C453 (4)	5.00	5.00

Gold medal winners in 19th Olympic Games, Mexico City. The same red overprint was also applied to a 30c and a 1 l. The souvenir sheet of 3 noted after No. C442 exists with this overprint in black. Value, souvenir sheet $6.

Rocket Blast-off AP85

Designs: 10c, Close-up view of moon. 12c, Spacecraft, horiz. 20c, Astronaut and module on moon, horiz. 24c, Lunar landing module.

Perf. 14½x13½, 13½x14

1969, Oct. 29

C454	AP85	5c multicolored	.25	.25
C455	AP85	10c multicolored	.30	.30
C456	AP85	12c multicolored	.40	.40
C457	AP85	20c multicolored	.50	.50
C458	AP85	24c multicolored	1.00	1.00
		Nos. C454-C458 (5)	2.45	2.45

Man's first landing on the moon, July 20, 1969. A 30c showing re-entry of capsule, a 1 l in design of 20c and a 1.50 l in design of 24c exist. Two souvenir sheets exist, one containing Nos. C454-C455 and 1.50 l, and the other No. C456, 30c and 1 l.
For the safe return of Apollo 13, overprints were applied in 1970 to Nos. C454-C458, the 3 unlisted denominations and the 2 souvenir sheets. Value of 2 souvenir sheets $20.
For overprints and surcharges see Nos. C500-C504, C555.

Nos. C224, C393, C395, C422, C424, CE2 and C178 Surcharged

1970, Feb. 20 Engr.; Litho.

C472	AP67	4c on 3c blk & rose lil	.25	.25
C473	AP81	5c on 7c multi	.25	.25
C474	AP81	10c on 9c multi	.30	.25
C475	AP82	10c on 11c multi	.30	.25
C476	AP82	12c on 14c multi	.35	.25
C477	APSD1	12c on 20c blk & red	.35	.25
C478	AP61	12c on 1 l red brn	.35	.25
		Nos. C472-C478 (7)	2.15	1.75

No. CE3 Overprinted "HABILITADO"

1970 Litho. *Perf. 14x14½*

C479	AP81	20c bis brn, brn & gold	.75	.35

Julio Adolfo Sanhueza AP86

Emblems, Map and Flag of Honduras — AP87

Designs: 8c, Rigoberto Ordoñez Rodriguez. 12c, Forest Fire Brigade emblem (with map of Honduras) and emblems of fire fighters, FAO and Alliance for Progress, horiz. 1 l, Flags of Honduras, UN and US, Arms of Honduras and emblems as on 12c.

Perf. 14½x14, 14x14½

1970, Aug. 15 Litho.

C480	AP86	5c gold, emer & ind	.30	.25
C481	AP86	8c gold, org brn & indigo	.40	.25
C482	AP87	12c bl & multi	.50	.25
C483	AP87	20c yel & multi	.70	.25
C484	AP87	1 l gray & multi	3.50	1.75
a.		Souvenir sheet of 5	3.00	2.00
		Nos. C480-C484 (5)	5.40	2.75

Campaign against forest fires and in memory of the men who lost their lives fighting forest fires. No. C484a contains 5 imperf. stamps with simulated perforations and without gum similar to Nos. C480-C484. Sold for 1.45 l.
For surcharges see Nos. C497-C498.

Hotel Honduras Maya AP88

1970, Oct. 24 Litho. *Perf. 14*

C485	AP88	12c sky blue & blk	.30	.25

Hotel Honduras Maya, Tegucigalpa, opening.

Stamps of 1952-1968 Surcharged

1971 Litho.; Engr.

C486	AP79	4c on 1c (#C387)	.25	.25
C487	AP78	5c on 1c (#C369)	.30	.25
C488	AP78	8c on 2c (#C370)	.65	.30
C489	AP65	10c on 2c (#C199)	.80	.40
C490	AP67	10c on 3c (#C224)	.80	.40
a.		Inverted surcharge	.80	.40
C491	AP68	10c on 3c (#C252)	.80	.40
C492	AP68	10c on 3c (#CO71)	.80	.40
C493	AP69	10c on 2c (#C251)	.80	.40
C494	AP73	10c on 2c (#CO99)	.80	.40
C495	AP73	10c on 3c (#CO100)	.80	.40
C496	AP80	10c on 3c (#C389)	.80	.40
C497	AP87	15c on 12c (#C482)	1.00	.55
C498	AP87	30c on 12c (#C482)	1.25	.80
C499	AP83	40c on 50c (#C434)	2.10	1.60
C500	AP85	40c on 24c (#C458)	2.10	1.60
		Nos. C486-C500 (15)	14.05	8.55

Red "OFICIAL" overprint was not obliterated on Nos. C492, C494-C495.
No. C491 exists with inverted surcharge.

Nos. C454, C456-C458 Ovptd. & Srchd.

Perf. 14½x13½, 13½x14½

1972, May 15 Litho.

C501	AP85	5c multi	1.50	.50
C502	AP85	12c multi	2.50	1.25
C503	AP85	1 l on 20c multi	6.00	3.25
C504	AP85	2 l on 24c multi	10.00	6.50
		Nos. C501-C504 (4)	20.00	11.50

Masonic Grand Lodge of Honduras, 50th anniv. Overprint varies to fit stamp shape.

Soldier's Bay, Guanaja AP89

5c, Taps, vert. 6c, Yojoa Lake. 7c, Banana Carrier, by Roberto Aguilar, vert. 8c, Military parade. 9c, Orchid, national flower, vert. 12c, Soldier with machine gun. 15c, Sunset over beach. 20c, Litter bearers. 30c, Landscape, by Antonio Velasquez. 40c, Ruins of Copan. 50c, Girl from Huacal, by Pablo Zelaya Sierra. 1 l, Trujillo Bay. 2 l, Orchid, national flower, vert.

1972, May 19 *Perf. 13*

C505	AP89	4c shown	.25	.25
C506	AP89	5c multi	.25	.25
C507	AP89	6c multi	.25	.25
C508	AP89	7c multi	.25	.25
C509	AP89	8c multi	.25	.25
C510	AP89	9c multi	.25	.25
C511	AP89	10c like 9c, vert.	.25	.25
C512	AP89	12c multi	.25	.25
C513	AP89	15c multi	.30	.25
C514	AP89	20c multi	.30	.25
C515	AP89	30c multi	.50	.25
C516	AP89	40c multi	.75	.40
a.		Souv. sheet of 4, #C508, C513, C515-C516	2.00	2.00
C517	AP89	50c multi	.60	.35
a.		Souv. sheet of 4, #C506-C507, C514, C517	2.00	2.00
C518	AP89	1 l multi	1.50	1.00
a.		Souv. sheet of 4, #C505, C509, C512, C518	2.75	2.75
C519	AP89	2 l multi	4.00	3.00
a.		Souv. sheet of 3, #C510-C511, C519	6.50	6.50
		Nos. C505-C519,CE4 (16)	10.65	7.85

Sesquicentennial of independence (stamps inscribed 1970).
For surcharge see No. CE5.

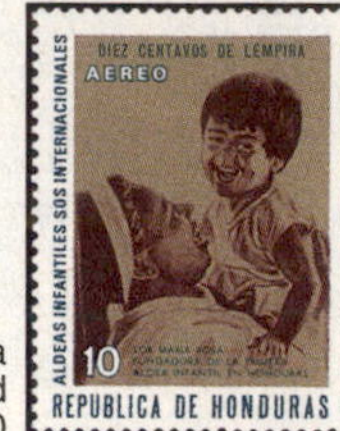

Sister Maria Rosa and Child — AP90

Designs: 15c, SOS Children's Village emblem, horiz. 30c, Father José Trinidad Reyes. 40c, Kennedy Center, first SOS village in Central America, horiz. 1 l, Boy.

Perf. 13½x13, 13x13½

1972, Nov. 10 Photo.

C520	AP90	10c grn, gold & brn	.25	.25
C521	AP90	15c grn, gold & brn	.25	.25
C522	AP90	30c grn, gold & brn	.40	.25
C523	AP90	40c grn, gold & brn	.50	.25
C524	AP90	1 l grn, gold & brn	2.00	1.50
		Nos. C520-C524 (5)	3.40	2.50

Children's Villages in Honduras (Intl. SOS movement to save homeless children).
For overprints and surcharges see Nos. C531, C534-C536, C546-C549, C556, C560-C561.

Map of Honduras and Society Emblem AP91

Design: 12c, Map of Honduras, emblems of National Geographic Institute and Interamerican Geodesic Service.

1973, Mar. 27 Litho. *Perf. 13*

C525	AP91	10c multicolored	.55	.30
C526	AP91	12c multicolored	.65	.30

25th annivs. of Natl. Cartographic Service (10c) and of joint cartographic work (12c).
For overprints and surcharges see Nos. C532-C533, C557-C558.

Juan Ramón Molina AP92

Designs: 8c, Illustration from Molina's book "Habitante de la Osa." 1 l, Illustration from "Tierras Mares y Cielos." 2 l, "UNESCO."

1973, Apr. 17 Litho. *Perf. 13½*

C527	AP92	8c brn org, blk & red brn	.25	.25
C528	AP92	20c brt bl & multi	.65	.25
C529	AP92	1 l green & multi	1.50	1.00
C530	AP92	2 l org & multi	3.25	2.75
a.		Sheet of 4	6.00	6.00
		Nos. C527-C530 (4)	5.65	4.25

Molina (1875-1908), poet, and 25th anniv. (in 1971) of UNESCO. No. C530a contains 4 stamps similar to Nos. C527-C530. Exists perf. & imperf.
For surcharge see No. C559.

Nos. C520-C523, C525-C526 Overprinted in Red or Black

Overprint reads: "Censos de Población y Vivienda, marzo 1974. 1974, Año Mundial de Población"

Perf. 13½x13, 13x13½, 13

1973, Dec. 28 **Photo; Litho.**

C531 AP90 10c multi (R) .25 .25
C532 AP91 10c multi (B) .25 .25
C533 AP91 12c multi (B) .25 .25
C534 AP90 15c multi (R) .25 .25
C535 AP90 30c multi (R) .30 .25
C536 AP90 40c multi (R) .35 .35
Nos. C531-C536 (6) 1.65 1.60

1974 population and housing census; World Population Year. The overprint is in 7 lines on vertical stamps, in 5 lines on horizontal.

Issues of 1947-59 Surcharged in Red or Black

Perf. 13x12½, 13½, 11x12½, 12

1974, June 28 **Engr.**

C537 AP68 2c on 1c (#C250) (R) .25 .25
C538 AP68 2c on 1c (#CO69) .25 .25
C539 AP72 2c on 1c (#C289) .25 .25
C540 AP72 2c on 1c (#CO98) .25 .25
C541 AP72 3c on 1c (#C289) .25 .25
C542 AP68 3c on 1c (#C250) (R) .25 .25
C543 AP74 1 l on 50c (#C308) 1.40 1.40
C544 AP60 1 l on 2 l (#C168) 1.40 1.40
C545 AP62 1 l on 2 l (#C179) (R) 1.40 1.40
Nos. C537-C545 (9) 5.70 5.70

Red "OFICIAL" overprint was not obliterated on Nos. C538 and C540.

Nos. C520-C523 Ovptd. in Bright Green

Overprint reads: "1949-1974 SOS Kinderdorfer International Honduras-Austria"

1974, July 25 **Photo.**

C546 AP90 10c grn, gold & brn .25 .25
C547 AP90 15c grn, gold & brn .25 .25
C548 AP90 30c grn, gold & brn .25 .25
C549 AP90 40c grn, gold & brn .35 .35
Nos. C546-C549 (4) 1.10 1.10

25th anniversary of Children's Villages in Honduras. Overprint in 6 lines on 10c and 30c, in 4 lines on 15c and 40c.

Stamps of 1956-73 Surcharged

1975, Feb. 24 **Litho.; Engr.**

C550 AP68 16c on 1c (#C250) .25 .25
C551 AP70 16c on 1c (#C269) .25 .25
C552 AP72 16c on 1c (#C289) .25 .25
C553 AP72 16c on 1c (#CO98) .25 .25
C554 AP78 16c on 1c (#C369) .30 .30
C555 AP85 18c on 12c (#C456) .40 .25
C556 AP90 18c on 10c (#C520) .25 .25
C557 AP91 18c on 10c (#C525) .25 .25
C558 AP91 18c on 12c (#C526) .25 .25
C559 AP92 18c on 8c (#C527) .25 .25
C560 AP90 50c on 30c (#C522) .75 .50
C561 AP90 1 l on 30c (#C522) 1.25 .90
Nos. C550-C561,CE5 (13) 6.70 4.80

Denominations not obliterated on Nos. C551, C553-C558, C560-C561; "OFICIAL" overprint not obliterated on No. C553.

For surcharges, see Nos. C1197, C1198, C1200.

Flags of Germany and Austria AP93

Designs (Flags): 2c, Belgium & Denmark. 3c, Spain & France. 4c, Hungary & Russia. 5c, Great Britain & Italy. 10c, Norway & Sweden. 12c, Honduras. 15c, US & Switzerland. 20c, Greece & Portugal. 30c, Romania & Serbia. 1 l, Egypt & Netherlands. 2 l, Luxembourg & Turkey.

1975, June 18 **Litho.** ***Perf. 13***

Gold & Multicolored; Colors Listed are for Shields

C562 AP93 1c lilac .25 .25
C563 AP93 2c gold .25 .25
C564 AP93 3c rose gray .25 .25
C565 AP93 4c light blue .25 .25
C566 AP93 5c yellow .25 .25
C567 AP93 10c gray .25 .25
C568 AP93 12c lilac rose .25 .25
C569 AP93 15c bluish green .35 .35
C570 AP93 20c bright blue .40 .40
C571 AP93 30c pink .75 .75
C572 AP93 1 l salmon 1.75 1.75
C573 AP93 2 l yellow green 3.75 3.75
Nos. C562-C573 (12) 8.75 8.75

Souvenir Sheet

C574 AP93 Sheet of 12 *12.00 12.00*

UPU, cent. (in 1974). No. C574 contains 12 stamps similar to Nos. C562-C573 with shields in different colors.

Humuya Youth Center and Mrs. Arellano AP94

Designs (Portrait of First Lady, Gloria de Lopez Arellano, IWY Emblem and): 16c, Jalteva Youth Center. 18c, Mrs. Arellano (diff. portrait) and IWY emblem. 30c, El Carmen de San Pedro Sula Youth Center. 55c, Flag of National Social Welfare Organization, vert. 1 l, La Isla sports and recreational facilities. 2 l, Women's Social Center.

1976, Mar. 5 **Litho.** ***Perf. 13½***

C575 AP94 8c sal & multi .25 .25
C576 AP94 16c yel & multi .25 .25
C577 AP94 18c pink & multi .25 .25
C578 AP94 30c org & multi .45 .45
C579 AP94 55c multicolored .70 .70
C580 AP94 1 l multicolored 1.50 1.50
C581 AP94 2 l multicolored 2.75 2.75
Nos. C575-C581 (7) 6.15 6.15

International Women's Year (1975).

For surcharges see Nos. C736-C737, C781, C798, C886, C887, C919, C1203.

"CARE" and Globe AP95

Designs: 1c, 16c, 30c, 55c, 1 l, Care package and globe, vert. Others like 5c.

1976, May 24 **Litho.** ***Perf. 13½***

C582 AP95 1c blk & lt blue .25 .25
C583 AP95 5c rose brn & blk .25 .25
C584 AP95 16c black & org .25 .25
C585 AP95 18c lemon & blk .25 .25
C586 AP95 30c blk & blue .35 .35
C587 AP95 50c yel grn & blk .50 .50
C588 AP95 55c blk & buff .50 .50
C589 AP96 70c brt rose & blk .70 .70
C590 AP95 1 l blk & lt grn 1.25 1.25
C591 AP95 2 l ocher & blk 2.40 2.40
Nos. C582-C591 (10) 6.70 6.70

20th anniversary of CARE in Honduras.

For surcharges see Nos. C735, C738, C788, C888, C922, C1105.

Fawn in Burnt-out Forest — AP96

Forest Protection: 16c, COHDEFOR emblem (Corporacion Hondureña de Desarollo Forestal). 18c, Forest, horiz. 30c, 2 l, Live and burning trees. 50c, like 10c. 70c, Emblem. 1 l, Young forest, horiz.

1976, May 28 **Litho.** ***Perf. 13½***

C592 AP96 10c multicolored .25 .25
C593 AP96 16c multicolored .25 .25
C594 AP96 18c multicolored .25 .25
C595 AP96 30c grn & multi .50 .25
C596 AP96 50c multicolored .75 .30
C597 AP96 70c brn & multi 1.00 .40
C598 AP96 1 l yel & multi 2.00 .75
C599 AP96 2 l vio & multi 3.50 3.50
Nos. C592-C599,CE6 (9) 9.50 6.50

For surcharges see Nos. C784, C787, C917, C1100.

"Sons of Liberty" — AP97

American Bicentennial: 2c, Raising flag of "Liberty and Union." 3c, Bunker Hill flag. 4c, Washington's Cruisers' flag. 5c, 1st Navy Jack. 6c, Flag of Honduras over Presidential Palace, Tegucigalpa. 18c, US flag over Capitol. 55c, Grand Union flag. 2 l, Bennington flag. 3 l, Betsy Ross and her flag.

1976, Aug. 29 **Litho.** ***Perf. 12***

C601 AP97 1c multicolored .25 .25
C602 AP97 2c multicolored .25 .25
C603 AP97 3c multicolored .25 .25
C604 AP97 4c multicolored .25 .25
C605 AP97 5c multicolored .25 .25
C606 AP97 6c multicolored .25 .25
C607 AP97 18c multicolored .30 .35
C608 AP97 55c multicolored .75 .70
a. Souv. sheet of 4, #C603, C606-C608 *2.00 2.00*
C609 AP97 2 l multicolored 2.25 2.25
a. Souv. sheet of 3, #C601, C604, C609 *4.50 4.50*
C610 AP97 3 l multicolored 4.75 4.75
a. Souv. sheet of 3, #C602, C605, C610 *5.50 5.50*
Nos. C601-C610 (10) 9.55 9.55

For surcharges see Nos. C883-C884, C885, C889, C1102.

King Juan Carlos of Spain — AP98

Designs: 16c, Queen Sophia. 30c, Queen Sophia and King Juan Carlos. 2 l, Arms of Honduras and Spain, horiz.

1977, Sept. 13 **Litho.** ***Perf. 14***

C611 AP98 16c multicolored .25 .25
C612 AP98 18c multicolored .25 .25
C613 AP98 30c multicolored .30 .25
C614 AP98 2 l multicolored 2.10 2.10
Nos. C611-C614 (4) 2.90 2.85

Visit of King and Queen of Spain.

For surcharges see Nos. C890, C918, C1107.

Mayan Steles, Exhibition Emblems AP99

Designs: 18c, Giant head. 30c, Statue. 55c, Sun god. 1.50 l, Mayan pelota court.

1978, Apr. 28 **Litho.** ***Perf. 12***

C615 AP99 15c multi .25 .25
C616 AP99 18c multi .45 .45
C617 AP99 30c multi .65 .65
C618 AP99 55c multi 1.25 1.25

Imperf

C619 AP99 1.50 l multi 4.00 4.00
Nos. C615-C619 (5) 6.60 6.60

Honduras '78 Philatelic Exhibition.

For overprints and surcharges see Nos. C642-C645, C786, C920, C924, CB6.

Del Valle's Birthplace AP100

Designs: 14c, La Merced Church, Choluteca, where del Valle was baptized. 15c, Baptismal font, vert. 20c, Del Valle reading independence acts. 25c, Portrait, documents, map of Central America. 40c, Portrait, vert. 1 l, Monument, Central Park, Choluteca, vert. 3 l, Bust, vert.

1978, Apr. 11 **Litho.** ***Perf. 14***

C620 AP100 8c multicolored .25 .25
C621 AP100 14c multicolored .25 .25
C622 AP100 15c multicolored .25 .25
C623 AP100 20c multicolored .25 .25
C624 AP100 25c multicolored .30 .30
C625 AP100 40c multicolored .40 .40
C626 AP100 1 l multicolored 1.25 1.25
C627 AP100 3 l multicolored 4.00 4.00
Nos. C620-C627 (8) 6.95 6.95

Bicentenary of the birth of José Cecilio del Valle (1780-1834), Central American patriot and statesman.

For surcharges see Nos. C739, C793, C795, C886A, C1098.

Rural Health Center AP101

Designs: 6c, Child at water pump. 10c, Los Laureles Dam, Tegucigalpa. 20c, Rural aqueduct. 40c, Teaching hospital, Tegucigalpa. 2 l, Parents and child. 3 l, National vaccination campaign. 5 l, Panamerican Health Organization Building, Washington, DC.

1978, May 10 **Litho.** ***Perf. 14***

C628 AP101 5c multicolored .25 .25
C629 AP101 6c multicolored .25 .25
C630 AP101 10c multicolored .25 .25
C631 AP101 20c multicolored .25 .25
C632 AP101 40c multicolored .45 .45
C633 AP101 2 l multicolored 1.90 1.90
C634 AP101 3 l multicolored 3.00 3.00
C635 AP101 5 l multicolored 4.50 4.50
Nos. C628-C635 (8) 10.85 10.85

75th anniv. of Panamerican Health Organization (in 1977).

For surcharges see Nos. C783, C783A.

Luis Landa and his "Botanica" AP102

Designs (Luis Landa and): 16c, Map of Honduras showing St. Ignacio. 18c, Medals received by Landa. 30c, Landa's birthplace in St. Ignacio. 2 l, Brassavola (orchid), national flower. 3 l, Women's Normal School.

1978, Aug. 29 **Photo.** ***Perf. 13x13½***

C636 AP102 14c multicolored .25 .25
C637 AP102 16c multicolored .25 .25
C638 AP102 18c multicolored .25 .25
C639 AP102 30c multicolored .40 .25
C640 AP102 2 l multicolored 3.00 1.00
C641 AP102 3 l multicolored 3.50 3.50
Nos. C636-C641 (6) 7.65 5.50

Prof. Luis Landa (1875-1975), botanist.

For surcharges see Nos. C740, C794, C888A, C923, C1099.

Nos. C615-C618 Overprinted in Red

Overprint includes Argentina '78 Soccer Cup Emblem and: "Argentina Campeon / Holanda Sub-Campeon / XI Campeonato Mundial / de Football".

1978, Sept. 6 Litho. *Perf. 12*

C642	AP99 15c multicolored	.25	.25
C643	AP99 18c multicolored	.35	.25
C644	AP99 30c multicolored	.45	.40
C645	AP99 55c multicolored	1.00	.65
	Nos. C642-C645 (4)	2.05	1.55

Argentina's victory in World Cup Soccer Championship. Same overprint was applied to No. C619. Value $45.

For surcharges, see No. C924, C1079.

Central University and Coat of Arms — AP103

Designs show for each denomination a 19th century print and a contemporary photograph of same area (except 1.50 l, 5 l): No. C647, University City. 8c, Manuel Bonilla Theater. No. C650, Court House, vert. No. C651, North Boulevard highway intersection, vert. No. C652, Natl. Palace. No. C653, Presidential Palace. 20c, Hospital. 40c, Cathedral of Tegucigalpa. 50c, View of Tegucigalpa. 1.50 l, Aerial view of Tegucigalpa. No. C660, Arms of San Miguel de Tegucigalpa, 18th cent., vert. No. C661, Pres. Marco Aurelio Soto (1846-1908) (painting), vert.

1978, Sept. 29

C646	AP103 6c black & brn	.25	.25
C647	AP103 6c multicolored	.25	.25
a.	Pair, #C646-C647	.25	.25
C648	AP103 8c black & brn	.25	.25
C649	AP103 8c multicolored	.25	.25
a.	Pair, #C648-C649	.25	.25
C650	AP103 10c black & brn	.25	.25
C651	AP103 10c multicolored	.25	.25
a.	Pair, #C650-C651	.30	.30
C652	AP103 16c black & brn	.25	.25
C653	AP103 16c multicolored	.25	.25
a.	Pair, #C652-C653	.50	.50
C654	AP103 20c black & brn	.30	.25
C655	AP103 20c multicolored	.30	.25
a.	Pair, #C654-C655	.60	.60
C656	AP103 40c black & brn	.75	.45
C657	AP103 40c multicolored	.75	.45
a.	Pair, #C656-C657	1.60	1.60
C658	AP103 50c black & brn	1.00	.50
C659	AP103 50c multicolored	1.00	.50
a.	Pair, #C658-C659	2.10	2.10
C660	AP103 5 l black & brn	6.75	6.75
C661	AP103 5 l multicolored	6.75	6.75
a.	Pair, #C660-C661	14.00	14.00
	Nos. C646-C661 (16)	19.60	17.90

Souvenir Sheet

C662	AP103 1.50 l multi	2.75	2.75

400th anniv. of the founding of Tegucigalpa.

In the listing the first number is for the 19th cent. design, the second for the 20th cent. design.

For overprints and surcharges see Nos. C724-C725, C740A-C746, C766-C769, C779-C780, C1094-C1095, C1103-C1104.

Goalkeeper — AP104

Designs: Various soccer scenes.

1978, Nov. 26 Litho. *Perf. 12*

C663	AP104 15c multi, vert.	.25	.25
C664	AP104 30c multi	.30	.30
C665	AP104 55c multi, vert.	.60	.60
C666	AP104 1 l multi	1.40	1.40
C667	AP104 2 l multi	2.50	2.50
	Nos. C663-C667 (5)	5.05	5.05

7th Youth Soccer Championship, Nov. 26.

For surcharge see No. C797.

UPU Emblem — AP105

2c, Postal emblem of Honduras. 25c, Dr. Ramon Rosa, vert. 50c, Pres. Marco Aurelio Soto, vert.

1979, Apr. 1 Litho. *Perf. 12*

C668	AP105 2c multicolored	.25	.25
C669	AP105 15c multicolored	.25	.25
C670	AP105 25c multicolored	.25	.25
C671	AP105 50c multicolored	.40	.40
	Nos. C668-C671 (4)	1.15	1.15

Centenary of Honduras joining UPU.

Rotary Emblem and "50" AP106

1979, Apr. 26 Litho. *Perf. 14*

C672	AP106 3c multi	.25	.25
C673	AP106 5c multi	.25	.25
C674	AP106 50c multi	.50	.50
C675	AP106 2 l multi	1.75	1.75
	Nos. C672-C675 (4)	2.75	2.75

Rotary Intl. of Honduras, 50th anniv.

For surcharge see No. C884A, C1096.

Map of Caratasca Lagoon AP107

Designs: 10c, Fort San Fernando de Omoa. 24c, Institute anniversary emblem, vert. 5 l, Map of Santanilla islands.

1979, Sept. 15 Litho. *Perf. 13½*

C676	AP107 5c multi	.25	.25
C677	AP107 10c multi	.25	.25
C678	AP107 24c multi	.25	.25
C679	AP107 5 l multi	4.00	4.00
	Nos. C676-C679 (4)	4.75	4.75

Panamerican Institute of History and Geography, 50th anniversary.

For surcharge see No. C891.

General Post Office, 1979 — AP108

UPU Membership Cent.: 3 l, Post Office, 19th cent.

1980, Feb. 20 Litho. *Perf. 12*

C680	AP108 24c multi	.25	.25
C681	AP108 3 l multi	2.75	2.75

For surcharge see No. C925.

Workers in the Field, IYC Emblem AP109

5c, Landscape, vert. 15c, Sitting boy, vert. 20c, IYC emblem, vert. 30c, Beach scene. 1 l, UNICEF and IYC emblems, vert.

1980, Dec. 9 Litho. *Perf. 14½*

C682	AP109 1c shown	.25	.25
C683	AP109 5c multicolored	.25	.25
C684	AP109 15c multicolored	.25	.25
C685	AP109 20c multicolored	.25	.25
C686	AP109 30c multicolored	.45	.45
	Nos. C682-C686 (5)	1.45	1.45

Souvenir Sheet

C687	AP109 1 l multicolored	1.50	1.50

International Year of the Child (1979).

Maltese Cross, Hill AP110

2c, Penny Black. 5c, Honduras type A1. 10c, Honduras type A1. 15c, Postal emblem. 20c, Flags of Honduras, Gt. Britain.
1 l, Honduras #C402.

1980, Dec. 17

C688	AP110 1c shown	.25	.25
C689	AP110 2c multicolored	.25	.25
C690	AP110 5c multicolored	.25	.25
C691	AP110 10c multicolored	.25	.25

Size: 47x34mm

C692	AP110 15c multicolored	.25	.25
C693	AP110 20c multicolored	.25	.25
	Nos. C688-C693 (6)	1.50	1.50

Souvenir Sheet

C694	AP110 1 l multicolored	2.50	2.50

Sir Rowland Hill (1795-1879), originator of penny postage. No. C694 contains one stamp 47x34mm.

Intibucana Mother and Child — AP111

Inter-American Women's Commission, 50th Anniv.: 2c, Visitacion Padilla, Honduras Section founder. 10c, Maria Trinidad del Cid, Section member. 1 l, Emblem, horiz.

1981, June 15 Litho. *Perf. 14½*

C695	AP111 2c multicolored	.25	.25
C696	AP111 10c multicolored	.25	.25
C697	AP111 40c multicolored	.30	.30
C698	AP111 1 l multicolored	.80	.80
	Nos. C695-C698 (4)	1.60	1.60

Bernardo O'Higgins, by Jose Gil de Castro — AP112

Paintings of O'Higgins: 16c, Liberation of Chile, by Cosme San Martin, horiz. 20c, Portrait of Ambrosio O'Higgins (father). 1 l, Abdication of Office, by Antonio Caro, horiz.

1981, June 29

C699	AP112 16c multicolored	.25	.25
C700	AP112 20c multicolored	.25	.25
C701	AP112 30c multicolored	.25	.25
C702	AP112 1 l multicolored	1.00	.50
	Nos. C699-C702 (4)	1.75	1.25

For surcharges see Nos. C785, C888B, C1106.

CONCACAF 81 Soccer Cup — AP113

1981, Dec. 30 Litho. *Perf. 14*

C703	AP113 20c Emblem	.60	.25
C704	AP113 50c Player	1.25	.35
C705	AP113 70c Flags	1.90	1.00
C706	AP113 1 l Stadium	2.75	1.50
	Nos. C703-C706 (4)	6.50	3.10

Souvenir Sheet

C707	AP113 1.50 l like #C703	2.25	2.25

For overprint see No. C797.

50th Anniv. of Air Force (1981) AP114

Designs: 3c, Curtiss CT-32 Condor. 15c, North American NA-16. 25c, Chance Vought F4U-5. 65c, Douglas C47. 1 l Cessna A37-B. 2 l, Super Mystere SMB-11.
1.55 l, Helicopter.

1983, Jan. 14 Litho. *Perf. 12*

C708	AP114 3c multi	.25	.25
C709	AP114 15c multi	.25	.25
C710	AP114 25c multi	.35	.25
C711	AP114 65c multi	.65	.35
C712	AP114 1 l multi	1.00	.50
C713	AP114 2 l multi	2.00	1.75
	Nos. C708-C713 (6)	4.50	3.35

Souvenir Sheet

C714	AP114 1.55 l multi	4.00	4.00

For surcharges see Nos. C884B, C1097.

UPU Executive Council Membership, 3rd Anniv. — AP115

16c, UPU monument. 18c, 18th UPU Congress emblem. 30c, Natl. Postal Service emblem. 55c, Rio de Janeiro. 2 l, Dove on globe.

1983, Jan. 14

C715	AP115 16c multicolored	.25	.25
C716	AP115 18c multicolored	.25	.25
C717	AP115 30c multicolored	.35	.35
C718	AP115 55c multicolored	.50	.50
C719	AP115 2 l multicolored	2.00	2.00
	Nos. C715-C719 (5)	3.35	3.35

Souvenir Sheet

C720	AP115 1 l like 2 l	2.50	2.50

For surcharges see Nos. C921, C1204.

Natl. Library and Archives Centenary (1980) AP116

1983, Feb. 11 Litho. *Perf. 12*

C721	AP116 9c Library	.30	.25
C722	AP116 1 l Books	1.10	.40

For surcharge see No. C1101.

Intl. Year of the Disabled (1979) AP117

1983, Feb. 11

C723 AP117 25c Emblem .40 .25

No. C657a Ovptd. in Red "CONMEMORATIVA DE LA VISITA / DE SS. JUAN PABLO II / 8 de marzo de 1983"

1983, Mar. 8

C724 AP103 40c blk & brn 3.00 2.50
C725 AP103 40c multicolored 3.00 2.50
a. Pair, #C724-C725 6.00 5.00

Visit of Pope John Paul II.

Literacy Campaign (1980) — AP118

40c, Hands, open book. 1.50 l, People holding books.

1983, May 18 Litho. *Perf. 12*

C726 AP118 40c multi .50 .45
C727 AP118 1.50 l multi 2.25 1.90

World Food Day, Oct. 16, 1981 — AP119

65c, Produce, emblem.

1983, May 18

C728 AP119 65c multicolored 1.00 1.00

20th Anniv. of Inter-American Development Bank (1980) — AP120

1 l, Comayagua River Bridge. 2 l, Luis Bogran Technical Institute of Physics.

1983, June 17 Litho. *Perf. 12*

C729 AP120 1 l multi 1.50 .50
C730 AP120 2 l multi 2.75 1.00

2nd Anniv. of Return to Constitutional Government — AP121

1984, Jan. 27 Litho. *Perf. 12*

C731 20c Arms, text .25 .25
C732 20c Pres. Suazo Cordova .25 .25
a. AP121 Pair, #C731-C732 .80 .80

La Gaceta Newspaper Sesquicentenary (1980) — AP122

1984, May 25 Litho. *Perf. 12*

C733 AP122 10c multicolored .35 .35
C734 AP122 20c multicolored .35 .35

Nos. C582, C575-C576 Surcharged

1985, June 26 Litho. *Perf. 13½*

C735 AP95 5c on 1c #C582 .25 .25
C736 AP94 10c on 8c #C575 .25 .25
C737 AP94 20c on 16c #C576 .25 .25
C738 AP95 1 l on 1c #C582 1.00 .40
Nos. C735-C738 (4) 1.75 1.15

Nos. C621, C636, C647a Surcharged

Litho., Photo. (No. C740)

1986, Aug. 21 *Perfs. as before*

C739 AP100 50c on 14c #C621 .45 .25
C740 AP102 60c on 14c #C636 .55 .30
C740A AP103 85c on 6c #C646 .80 .55
C740B AP103 85c on 6c #C647 .80 .55
c. Pair, #C740A-C740B 1.75 1.50
C741 AP103 95c on 6c #C646 .90 .60
C742 AP103 95c on 6c #C647 .90 .60
a. Pair, #C741-C742 2.00 1.75
Nos. C739-C742 (6) 4.40 2.85

Black bar obliterating old values on Nos. C739-C740 also cover "aereo."

Nos. C656-C657 Overprinted in Red

No. C743

No. C744

No. C745

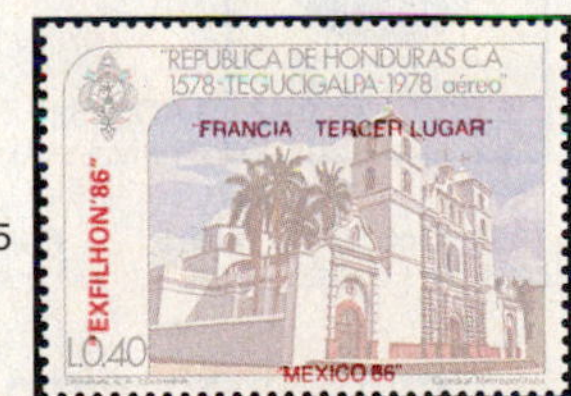

No. C746

1986, Sept. 12 Litho. *Perf. 12*

C743 AP103 40c No. C656 .40 .25
C744 AP103 40c No. C657 .40 .25
C745 AP103 40c No. C657 .40 .25
C746 AP103 40c No. C656 .40 .25
a. Block of 4, #C743-C746 2.00

AP123

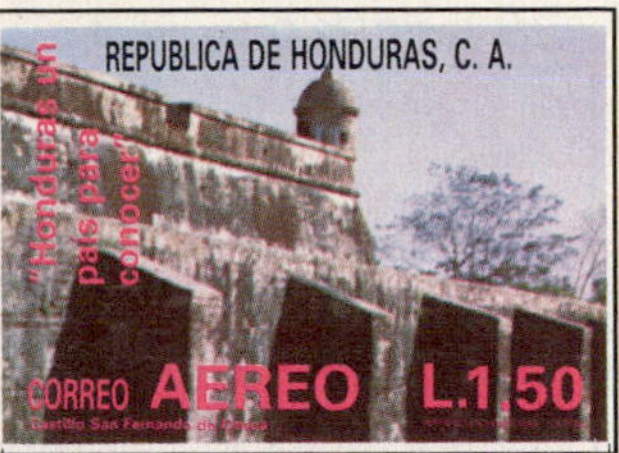

San Fernando de Omoa Castle — AP124

20c, Phulapanzak Falls. 78c, Bahia Isls. beach. 85c, Bahia Isls. cove. 95c, Yojoa Lake. 1 l, Woman painting pottery.

Perf. 13½x14, 14x13½

1986, Nov. 10 Litho.

C747 AP123 20c multi, vert. .25 .25
C748 AP123 78c multi 1.10 .55
C749 AP123 85c multi 1.25 .55
C750 AP123 95c multi, vert. 1.40 .65
C751 AP123 1 l multi, vert. 1.50 .70

Size: 84x59mm

Imperf

C752 AP124 1.50 l multi 2.75 2.75
Nos. C747-C752 (6) 8.25 5.45

For overprint see No. C782.

AP125

National flag, Pres. Jose Azcona Hoyo.

1987, Feb. 2 Litho. *Perf. 13½*

C753 AP125 20c grn & multi .30 .25
C754 AP125 85c red & multi 1.25 .85

Democratic government, 1st anniv.

Flora — AP126

10c, Eupatorium cyrillinelsonii. 20c, Salvia ernesti-vargasii. 95c, Robinsonella erasmi-sosae.

1987, July 8 Litho. *Perf. 13½x14*

C755 AP126 10c multicolored .25 .25
C756 AP126 20c multicolored .45 .45
C757 AP126 95c multicolored 1.40 .75
Nos. C755-C757 (3) 2.10 1.45

Birds — AP127

50c, Eumomota superciliosa. 60c, Ramphastos sulfuratus. 85c, Amazona autumnalis.

1987, Sept. 10 Litho. *Perf. 13½x14*

C758 AP127 50c multicolored 2.00 .50
C759 AP127 60c multicolored 2.25 .50
C760 AP127 85c multicolored 4.00 1.10
Nos. C758-C760 (3) 8.25 2.10

AP128

1987, Dec. 10 Litho. *Perf. 13½*

C761 AP128 1 l blk, brt yel & dark red 1.25 .50

Natl. Autonomous University of Honduras, 30th anniv.

AP129

1987, Dec. 23 Litho. *Perf. 13½*

C762 AP129 20c red & dk ultra .50 .25

Natl. Red Cross, 50th anniv.

AP130

1988, Jan. 27 Litho. *Perf. 13½*

C763 AP130 95c brt blue & org yel 1.10 .45

17th regional meeting of Lions Intl.

Atlantida Bank, 75th Anniv. AP131

Main offices: 10c, La Ceiba, Atlantida, 1913. 85c, Tegucigalpa, 1988.

1988, Feb. 10

C764 AP131 10c multi .25 .25
C765 AP131 85c mutli .90 .40
a. Souv. sheet of 2, #358-359, imperf. 1.25 1.25

No. C765a sold for 1 l.

No. C649a Surcharged

1988, June 9 Litho. *Perf. 12*

C766 AP103 20c on 8c #C648 .90 .90
C767 AP103 20c on 8c #C649 .90 .90
a. Pair, #C766-C767 2.00 2.00

No. C647a Surcharged

1988, July 8 **Litho.** ***Perf. 12***
C768 AP103 5c on 6c #C646 .30 .30
C769 AP103 5c on 6c #C647 .30 .30
a. Pair, #C768-C769 .80 .80

Postman AP132

Tegucigalpa Postmark on Stampless Cover, 1789 — AP133

1988, Sept. 11 **Litho.** ***Perf. 13½***
C770 AP132 85c dull red brn 1.40 .40
C771 AP133 2 l dull red brn & ver 3.00 1.00

EXFILHON '88.

Summer Olympics Type of 1988

85c, Running, vert. 1 l, Baseball, soccer, basketball.

1988, Sept. 30 **Litho.** ***Perf. 13½***

Size: 28x33mm

C772 A62 85c multi 1.10 .40

Size: 36x27mm

C773 A62 1 l multi 1.20 .50

Discovery of America, 500th Anniv. (in 1992) AP134

Pre-Colombian pottery artifacts: 10c, Footed vase, vert. 25c, Bowl. 30c, Footed bowl. 50c, Pitcher, vert. 1 l, Rectangular footed bowl.

1988 **Litho.** ***Perf. 13½***
C774 AP134 10c multicolored .30 .25
C775 AP134 25c multicolored .75 .25
C776 AP134 30c multicolored .90 .30
C777 AP134 50c multicolored 1.50 .50
Nos. C774-C777 (4) 3.45 1.30

Size: 115x83mm

Imperf

C778 AP134 1 l multicolored 3.25 3.25

Nos. C653a and C576 Surcharged

1988 **Litho.** ***Perf. 12, 13½***
C779 AP103 10c on 16c #C652 .25 .25
C780 AP103 10c on 16c #C653 .25 .25
a. Pair, #C779-C780 .50 .50
C781 AP94 50c on 16c #C576 .80 .40
Nos. C779-C781 (3) 1.30 .90

Nos. C779-C780 exist with double surcharge.
Issued: 10c, Apr. 7, 50c, May 25.

No. C752 Overprinted

1989, July 14 **Litho.** ***Imperf.***
C782 AP124 1.50 l multi 2.75 2.75

French revolution, bicent.

Nos. C629 and C593 Surcharged

I

II

1989 **Litho.** ***Perf. 14, 13½***
C783 AP101 15c on 6c, I 1.50 .25
C783A AP101 15c on 6c, II 2.00 .25
C784 AP96 1 l on 16c 1.50 .95
Nos. C783-C784 (3) 5.00 1.45

Issue date: 1 l, June 15.

Nos. C699 and C616 Surcharged

1989, Dec. 15 **Litho.** ***Perf. 14½, 12***
C785 AP112 20c on 16c #C699 .95 .25
C786 AP99 95c on 18c #C616 2.75 .50

No. C786 exists with inverted surcharge.
Issued: No. C785, 12/15; No. C786, 12/28.

Nos. C594 and C585 Surcharged with New Denomination and "IV Juegos / Olimpicos / Centroamericanos"

1990, Jan. 12 ***Perf. 13½***
C787 AP96 75c on 18c #C594 (S) 1.10 .85
C788 AP95 85c on 18c #C585 1.25 .95

No. C787 exists with double and inverted surcharge.

World Wildlife Fund — AP135

Various Mono ateles: No. C790, Adult, young. No. C791, Adult hanging, diff. No. C792, Adult, young, diff.

1990, Apr. 18 **Litho.** ***Perf. 13½***
C789 AP135 10c shown 3.75 2.50
C790 AP135 10c multi 3.75 2.50
C791 AP135 20c multi 6.00 4.00
C792 AP135 20c multi 6.50 4.50
Nos. C789-C792 (4) 20.00 13.50

No. C621 Surcharged

1990, Feb. 8 **Litho.** ***Perf. 14***
C793 AP100 20c on 14c multi .40 .25

Nos. C621 and C636 Surcharged "50 Aniversario / IHCI" / 1939-1989

1990, Mar. 29
C794 AP102 20c on 14c No. C636 .25 .25
C795 AP100 1 l on 14c No. C621 .65 .40

No. C665 Surcharged

1990, June 14 **Litho.** ***Perf. 12***
C796 AP104 1 l on 55c multi 1.00 .40

World Cup Soccer Championships, Italy.

No. C707 Ovptd. in Margin

Overprint includes Character Trademark and: "CAMPEONATO MUNDIAL DE FUTBOL Italia '90".

Souvenir Sheet

1990, June 14 ***Perf. 14***
C797 AP113 1.50 l multi 1.50 .80

No. C577 Surcharged in Black

1990, Feb. 22 **Litho.** ***Perf. 13½***
C798 AP94 20c on 18c multi .50 .25

FAO, 45th Anniv. — AP136

1990, Oct. 16 **Litho.** ***Perf. 13½***
C799 AP136 95c yel, blk, bl, grn 1.00 .75

17th Interamerican Congress of Industry and Construction — AP137

20c, Map, vert. 1 l, Jose Cecilio Del Valle Palace.

1990, Nov. 21 **Litho.** ***Perf. 13½***
C800 AP137 20c multi .25 .25
C801 AP137 1 l multi .75 .45

AP138

Christmas — AP139

95c, Madonna and Child, vert. 3 l, Poinsettia.

1990, Nov. 30 **Litho.** ***Perf. 13½***
C802 AP138 20c shown .75 .25
C803 AP138 95c multicolored 1.25 .40

Size: 112x82mm

Imperf

C804 AP139 3 l multicolored 2.75 2.00
Nos. C802-C804 (3) 4.75 2.65

Salesian Order in Honduras, 80th Anniv. AP140

75c, St. John Bosco. 1 l, Natl. Youth Sanctuary.

1990, Dec. 28 **Litho.** ***Perf. 13½***
C805 AP140 75c multi .60 .30
C806 AP140 1 l multi .80 .50

Pres. Rafael Leonardo Callejas — AP141

1991, Jan. 31
C807 AP141 30c Taking oath .25 .25
C808 AP141 2 l Portrait 1.25 .90

Moths and Butterflies AP142

85c, Strymon melinus. 90c, Diorina sp. 1.50 l, Hyalophora cecropia. 5 l, Papilio polixenes.

1991, Feb. 28 **Litho.** ***Perf. 13½***
C809 AP142 85c multi 1.60 .40
C810 AP142 90c multi 2.00 .50
C811 AP142 1.50 l multi 3.25 .70

Size: 114x82mm

Imperf

C812 AP142 5 l multi 6.50 4.00
Nos. C809-C812 (4) 13.35 5.60

Notary Day — AP143

1991, May 22 **Litho.** ***Perf. 13½***
C813 AP143 50c multicolored .85 .25

Rafael Heliodoro Valle, Birth Cent. — AP144

1991, July 26 **Litho.** ***Perf. 13½***

C815 AP144 2 l pale pink & blk 1.40 .90

Churches AP145

Discovery of America, 500th Anniv. emblem and: 30c, Church of St. Manuel of Colohete, Gracias. 95c, Church of Our Lady of Mercy, Gracias. 1 l, Comayagua Cathedral.

1991, Aug. 30 **Litho.** ***Perf. 13½***

C816 AP145 30c multicolored .25 .25
C817 AP145 95c multicolored .70 .25
C818 AP145 1 l multicolored .85 .45
Nos. C816-C818 (3) 1.80 .95

Latin American Institute, 25th Anniv. AP146

1991, June 20

C819 AP146 1 l multicolored .70 .40

Flowers AP147

30c, Rhyncholaelia glauca. 50c, Oncidium splendidum, vert. 95c, Laelia anceps, vert. 1.50 l, Cattleya skinneri.

1991, Apr. 30

C820 AP147 30c multicolored .40 .25
C821 AP147 50c multicolored .55 .40
C822 AP147 95c multicolored .75 .70
C823 AP147 1.50 l multicolored 1.40 1.10
Nos. C820-C823 (4) 3.10 2.45

Espamer '91, Buenos Aires AP148

1991, July 1

C824 AP148 2 l multicolored 2.25 .80

Size: 101x82mm

Imperf

C825 AP148 5 l like #C824 5.50 3.50

Discovery of America, 500th anniv. (in 1992).

11th Pan American Games, Havana AP149

30c, Equestrian. 85c, Judo. 95c, Men's swimming. 5 l, Women's swimming.

1991, Aug. 8

C826 AP149 30c multicolored .25 .25
C827 AP149 85c multicolored .60 .40
C828 AP149 95c multicolored .75 .40

Size: 114x83mm

Imperf

C829 AP149 5 l multicolored 3.50 3.50
Nos. C826-C829 (4) 5.10 4.55

Pre-Columbian Culture — AP150

UPAEP emblem, artifacts and: 25c, ears of corn. 40c, ear of corn, map. 1.50 l, map.

1991, Sept. 30 **Litho.** ***Perf. 13½***

C830 AP150 25c multicolored .25 .25
C831 AP150 40c multicolored .75 .40
C832 AP150 1.50 l multicolored 1.50 .60
Nos. C830-C832 (3) 2.50 1.25

4th Intl. Congress on Control of Insect Pests AP151

Designs: 30c, Tactics to control pests. 75c, Integration of science. 1 l, Cooperation between farmers and scientists. 5 l, Pests and biological controls.

1991, Nov. 22

C833 AP151 30c multicolored .40 .25
C834 AP151 75c multicolored 1.10 .55
C835 AP151 1 l multicolored 2.10 .85

Size: 115x83mm

Imperf

C836 AP151 5 l multicolored 3.25 3.25
Nos. C833-C836 (4) 6.85 4.90

America Issue AP152

90c, Sighting land. 1 l, Columbus' ships. 2 l, Ship, map, birds.

1992, Jan. 27 **Litho.** ***Perf. 13½***

C837 AP152 90c multicolored .75 .60
C838 AP152 1 l multicolored .85 .75
C839 AP152 2 l multicolored 1.60 1.25
Nos. C837-C839 (3) 3.20 2.60

Christmas AP153

2 l, Poinsettias in rooster vase.

1991, Dec. 19

C840 AP153 1 l shown .75 .40
C841 AP153 2 l multicolored 1.50 .90

Honduran Savings Insurance Company, 75th Anniv. AP154

1992, Jan. 17

C842 AP154 85c multicolored .75 .30
C843 AP154 1 l Priest saying mass 1.25 .40

Size: 115x83mm

Imperf

C844 AP154 5 l like #C842 4.50 3.25
Nos. C842-C844 (3) 6.50 3.95

First mass in New World, 490th anniv. (No. C843). Taking possession of new continent, 490th anniv. (Nos. C842, C844).

Pres. Rafael Leonardo Callejas, 2nd Year in Office AP155

Callejas with: 20c, Italian president Francesco Cossiga. 2 l, Pope John Paul II.

1992, Jan. 27 **Litho.** ***Perf. 13½***

C845 AP155 20c black & purple .25 .25
C846 AP155 2 l black & multi 1.40 .80

Flowers AP156

20c, Bougainvillea glabra. 30c, Canna indica. 75c, Epiphyllum. 95c, Sobralia macrantha.

1992, July 25 **Litho.** ***Perf. 13½***

C847 AP156 20c multicolored .40 .25
C848 AP156 30c multicolored .45 .25
C849 AP156 75c multicolored 1.20 .45
C850 AP156 95c multicolored 2.00 .65
Nos. C847-C850 (4) 4.05 1.60

Gen. Francisco Morazan Hydroelectric Complex — AP157

1992, Aug. 17

C851 AP157 85c Dam face, vert. .75 .30
C852 AP157 4 l Rear of dam 3.00 1.60

AP158

1992, Aug. 24

C853 AP158 95c black & multi .65 .55
C854 AP158 95c multicolored .65 .55

Intl. Conference on Agriculture, 50th anniv.

AP159

Gen. Francisco Morazan (1792-1842): 5c, Morazan mounted on horseback. 10c, Statue of Morazan. 50c, Watch and sword, horiz. 95c, Portrait of Josefa Lastiri de Morazan. 5 l, Portrait of Morazan in uniform.

1992, Sept. 18 **Litho.** ***Perf. 13½***

C855 AP159 5c blk, purple blk .30 .25
C856 AP159 10c multicolored .35 .25
C857 AP159 50c multicolored .45 .25
C858 AP159 95c multicolored 1.20 .35

Size: 76x108mm

Imperf

C859 AP159 5 l multicolored 4.00 2.25
Nos. C855-C859 (5) 6.30 3.35

Children's Day — AP160

Paintings of children: 25c, Musicians. 95c, Boy, dog standing in doorway. 2 l, Flower girl.

1992, Sept. 7

C860 AP160 25c multicolored .25 .25
C861 AP160 95c multicolored .60 .30
C862 AP160 2 l multicolored 1.25 .80
Nos. C860-C862 (3) 2.10 1.35

Intl. Conference on Nutrition AP161

1992, Sept. 30 **Litho.** ***Perf. 13½***

C863 AP161 1.05 l multicolored .75 .45

Pan-American Agricultural School, 50th Anniv. — AP162

20c, Bee keepers. 85c, Woman, goats. 1 l, Plowing. 2 l, Man with tool, vert.

1992, Oct. 9

C864 AP162 20c multicolored .25 .25
C865 AP162 85c multicolored .50 .30
C866 AP162 1 l multicolored .60 .40
C867 AP162 2 l multicolored 1.25 .80
Nos. C864-C867 (4) 2.60 1.75

Exfilhon '92 — AP163

Birds: 1.50 l, F. triquilidos. 2.45 l, Ara macao. 5 l, Quetzal pharomachrus mocinno.

1992, Oct. 2

C868 AP163 1.50 l multicolored 1.75 1.50
C869 AP163 2.45 l multicolored 2.75 2.40

Size: 76x108mm

Imperf

C870 AP163 5 l multicolored 7.50 4.50
Nos. C868-C870 (3) 12.00 8.40

Discovery of America, 500th anniv.

America Issue — AP164

UPAEP emblem and: 35c, Native settlement. 5 l, Explorers meeting natives in boats.

1992, Oct. 30 Litho. *Perf. 13½*

C871 AP164	35c multicolored	.25	.25
C872 AP164	5 l multicolored	2.75	2.00

Printed on both thick and thin paper.

Discovery of America, 500th Anniv. — AP165

Details from First Mass, by Roque Zelaya: 95c, Ships off-shore. 1 l, Holding services with natives, horiz. 2 l, Natives, countryside, temples, horiz.

1992, Oct. 30

C873 AP165	95c multicolored	.50	.40
C874 AP165	1 l multicolored	.65	.45
C875 AP165	2 l multicolored	1.25	1.00
	Nos. C873-C875 (3)	2.40	1.85

City of El Progreso, Cent. AP166

1992, Oct. 17

C876 AP166	1.55 l multicolored	1.75	.55

First Road Conservation Congress of Panama and Central America — AP167

85c, Bulldozer on highway.

1992, Nov. 16 *Perf. 13½*

C878 AP167	20c shown	.30	.25
C879 AP167	85c multicolored	.55	.30

Pan-American Health Organization, 90th Anniv. — AP168

1992, Nov. 27

C880 AP168	3.95 l multicolored	2.25	1.75

Christmas AP169

Paintings by Roque Zelaya: 20c, Crowd watching people climb pole in front of church, vert. 85c, Nativity scene.

1992, Nov. 24

C881 AP169	20c multicolored	.30	.25
C882 AP169	85c multicolored	.70	.30

1992-93

Perfs. and Printing Methods as Before

C883	AP97	20c on 1c #C601	.45	.25
C884	AP97	20c on 3c #C603	.55	.25
C884A	AP106	20c on 3c #C672	.55	.25
C884B	AP114	20c on 3c #C708	.40	.25
C885	AP97	20c on 6c #C606	.40	.25
C886	AP94	20c on 8c #C575	.40	.25
C886A	AP100	20c on 8c #C620	.25	.25
C887	AP94	50c on 16c #C576	.40	.25
C888	AP95	50c on 16c #C584	.40	.25
C888A	AP102	50c on 16c #C637	.40	.25
C888B	AP112	50c on 16c #C699	.40	.25
C889	AP97	85c on 18c #C607	.55	.30
C890	AP98	85c on 18c #C612	.65	.30
C891	AP107	85c on 24c #C678	.65	.30
		Nos. C883-C891 (14)	6.45	3.65

Size and location of surcharge varies.

Issued: No. C883, 12/18/92; No. C889, 1/22/93; No. C885, 3/8/93; No. C888A, 9/7/93; No. C888, 9/13/93; No. C890, 9/24/93; No. C891, 10/1/93; No. C884A, 10/5/93; No. C884B, 10/8/93; Nos. C884, C886A, 10/21/93; No. C886, 10/29/93; Nos. C887, C888B, 11/3/93.

No. C601 Surcharged Intl. Court of Justice Decision on Border Dispute Between Honduras & El Salvador AP170

Designs: 90c, Pres. of El Salvador and Pres. Callejas of Honduras, vert. 1.05 l, Country flags, map of Honduras and El Salvador.

1993, Feb. 24 Litho. *Perf. 13½*

C893 AP170	90c multicolored	.50	.30
C894 AP170	1.05 l multicolored	.65	.40

Third year of Pres. Callejas' term.

Mother's Day — AP171

Paintings of a mother and child, by Sandra Pendrey: 50c, Red blanket. 95c, Green blanket.

1993, May 5 Litho. *Perf. 13½*

C895 AP171	50c multi	.40	.25
C896 AP171	95c multi	1.25	.30

Endangered Animals — AP172

85c, Manatee, horiz. 2.45 l, Puma, horiz. 10 l, Jaguar.

1993, May 14 *Perf. 13½*

C897 AP172	85c multi	.75	.50
C898 AP172	2.45 l multi	1.75	1.25
C899 AP172	10 l multi	6.50	4.00
	Nos. C897-C899 (3)	9.00	5.75

Natl. Symbols AP173

25c, Ara macao. 95c, Odocoileus virginianus.

1993, June 25 Litho. *Perf. 13½*

C900 AP173	25c multi	1.50	.95
C901 AP173	95c multi	2.00	1.25

First Brazilian Postage Stamps, 150th Anniv. AP174

1993, Sept. 10 Litho. *Perf. 13½*

C902 AP174	20c Brazil No. 1	.30	.25
C903 AP174	50c Brazil No. 2	.40	.25
C904 AP174	95c Brazil No. 3	.55	.40
	Nos. C902-C904 (3)	1.25	.90

Departments in Honduras — AP175

Various scenes, department name: No. C905a, Atlantida. b, Colon. c, Cortes. d, Choluteca. e, El Paraiso. f, Francisco Morazan.

No. C906a, Comayagua. b, Copan. c, Intibuca. d, Islas de la Bahia. e, Lempira. f, Ocotepeque.

No. C907a, La Paz. b, Olancho. c, Santa Barbara. d, Valle. e, Yoro. f, Gracias a Dios.

1993, Sept. 20 *Perf. 13½*

C905 AP175	20c Strip of 6, #a.-f.	1.75	1.75
C906 AP175	50c Strip of 6, #a.-f.	3.00	3.00
C907 AP175	1.50 l Strip of 6, #a.-f.	7.00	7.00
	Nos. C905-C907 (3)	11.75	11.75

No. C906 is vert.

UN Development Program AP177

1993, Oct. 19

C911 AP177	95c multicolored	.50	.35

Christmas AP178

1993, Nov. 5

C912 AP178	20c Church	.25	.25
C913 AP178	85c Woman, flowers	.45	.30

Nos. C577, C585, C593, C611, C616, C638, C643, C680, C716 Surcharged

1993

Perfs. and Printing Methods as Before

C917	AP96	50c on 16c #C593	.30	.25
C918	AP98	50c on 16c #C611	.30	.25
C919	AP94	50c on 18c #C577	.30	.25
C920	AP99	50c on 18c #C616	.30	.25
C921	AP115	50c on 18c #C716	.55	.40
C922	AP95	85c on 18c #C585	.55	.40
C923	AP102	85c on 18c #C638	.55	.40
C924	AP99	85c on 18c #C643	.55	.40
C925	AP108	85c on 24c #C680	.55	.40
		Nos. C917-C925 (9)	3.95	3.00

Size and location of surcharge varies.

Issued: Nos. C917-C918, 11/12; Nos. C920, C924, 11/23; Nos. C921, C925, 11/30; Nos. C922-C923, 12/3; No. C919, 12/10.

Fish AP179

20c, Pomacanthus arcuatus. 85c, Holacanthus ciliaris. 3 l, Chaetodon striatus.

1993, Dec. 7 Litho. *Perf. 13½*

C931 AP179	20c multicolored	.30	.25
C932 AP179	85c multicolored	.80	.50
C933 AP179	3 l multicolored	2.50	1.90
	Nos. C931-C933 (3)	3.60	2.65

Famous Men — AP180

25c, Ramon Rosa. 65c, Jesus Aguilar Paz. 85c, Augusto C. Coello.

1993, Nov. 17

C934 AP180 25c multicolored .25 .25
C935 AP180 65c multicolored .30 .25
C936 AP180 85c multicolored .40 .30
Nos. C934-C936 (3) .95 .80

Pres. Rafael Leonardo Callejas, 4th Year in Office
AP181

95c, Wife, Norma, planting tree, vert.

1994, Jan. 21 Litho. *Perf. 13½*

C937 AP181 95c multicolored .50 .30
C938 AP181 1 l multicolored .75 .30

AP182

1994, Mar. 8 Litho. *Perf. 13 ½*

C939 AP182 1 l multicolored .80 .30

Intl. Year of the Family.

AP183

1994, Oct. 24 Litho. *Perf. 13½*

C940 AP183 1 l multicolored .80 .30

Intl. Conference on Peace and Development in Central America, Tegucigalpa.

Christmas
AP184

Paintings by Gelasio Gimenez: 95c, Madonna and Child. 1 l, Holy Family.

1994, Dec. 15 Litho. *Perf. 13½*

C941 AP184 95c multicolored .80 .30
C942 AP184 1 l multicolored .80 .40

UN, 50th Anniv. — AP185

Designs: 1 l, The Sowing: Ecological Family, by Elisa Dulcey. 2 l, Family Scene, by Delmer Mejia. 3 l, UN emblem, "50."

1995, Jan. 17

C943 AP185 1 l multicolored .50 .50
C944 AP185 2 l multicolored .85 .85
C945 AP185 3 l multicolored 1.40 1.40
Nos. C943-C945 (3) 2.75 2.75

Pres. Carlos Roberto Reina, 1st Anniv. of Taking Office
AP186

Designs: 80c, Beside flag, vert. 1 l, Summit meeting of area presidents & vice presidents.

1995, Jan. 27

C946 AP186 80c multicolored .30 .30
C947 AP186 95c multicolored .40 .30
C948 AP186 1 l multicolored .45 .40
Nos. C946-C948 (3) 1.15 1.00

America Issue
AP187

Postal vehicles.

1995, Feb. 28 Litho. *Perf. 13½*

C949 AP187 1.50 l Van 1.00 .55
C950 AP187 2 l Motorcycle 1.25 .70

Miniature Sheet

Mushrooms — AP188

1 l: a, Marasmius cohaerens. b, Lepista nuda. c, Polyporus pargamenus. d, Fomes. e, Paneolus sphinctrinus. f, Hygrophorus aurantiaca.

1.50 l, vert: g, Psathyrella. h, Amanita rubescens. i, Boletellus russelli. j, Boletus frostii. k, Marasmius spegazzinii. l, Fomes annosus.

2 l, vert: m, Craterellus cornucopioides. n, Amanita. o, Auricularia delicata. p, Psilocybe cubensis. q, Clavariadelphus pistilaris. r, Boletus regius.

2.50 l: s, Scleroderma aurantium. t, Amanita praegraveolens. u, Cantharellus cibarius. v, Geastrum triplex. w, Russula emetica. x, Boletus pinicola.

3 l: y, Fomes versicolor. z, Cantharellus pupurascens. aa, Lyophyllum decastes. ab, Pleurotus ostreatus. ac, Boletus ananas. ad, Amanita caesarea.

1995, Apr. 7

C951 AP188 Sheet of 30, #a.-ad. 35.00 35.00

FAO, 50th Anniv.
AP189

1995, May 25 Litho. *Perf. 13½*

C952 AP189 3 l multicolored 1.25 .40

CARE, 50th Anniv.
AP190

Designs: 1.40 l, Family, farm. No. C954, Orchid, wildlife, couple working in soil. No. C955, Couple in vegetable garden.

1995, Aug. 4 Litho. *Perf. 13½*

C953 AP190 1.40 l multicolored .50 .50
C954 AP190 5.40 l multicolored 2.10 2.10
C955 AP190 5.40 l multicolored 2.10 2.10
Nos. C953-C955 (3) 4.70 4.70

El Puente Archaeological Park — AP191

1995, Aug. 8 *Imperf.*

C956 AP191 20 l multicolored 8.50 6.25

America Issue
AP192

1.40 l, Kinosternon scorpioides. 4.54 l, Alpinia purpurata, vert. 10 l, Polyborus plancus, vert.

1995, Oct. 10 Litho. *Perf. 13½*

C957 AP192 1.40 l multicolored .50 .50
C958 AP192 4.54 l multicolored 1.60 1.60
C959 AP192 10 l multicolored 3.50 3.50
Nos. C957-C959 (3) 5.60 5.60

Reptiles and Amphibians — AP193

No. C960, Iguana iguana. No. C961, Agalychnis.

1995, Nov. 10 Litho. *Perf. 13*

C960 AP193 5.40 l multicolored 2.10 2.00
C961 AP193 5.40 l multicolored 2.10 2.00

Christmas
AP194

1.40 l, Bell, vert. 5.40 l, Nativity figurines. 6.90 l, Carved deer, vert.

1995, Dec. 4 Litho. *Perf. 13½*

C962 AP194 1.40 l multi .50 .60
C963 AP194 5.40 l multi 2.25 2.25
C964 AP194 6.90 l multi 2.50 2.50
Nos. C962-C964 (3) 5.25 5.35

Integration System of Central America
AP195

1.40 l, Map of Central America, Tegucigalpa Protocol, 1991. 4.30 l, Functions listed, 1993. 5.40 l, 17th Summit of Presidents of Central America.

1996, Feb. 19 Litho. *Perf. 13½*

C965 AP195 1.40 l multicolored .50 .50
C966 AP195 4.30 l multicolored 1.60 1.60
C967 AP195 5.40 l multicolored 2.00 2.00
Nos. C965-C967 (3) 4.10 4.10

UN Fight Against Drug Trafficking and Abuse, 10th Anniv.
AP196

Designs: 1.40 l, Stylized picture of minds on drugs. 5.40 l, Person with butterfly for brain, vert. 10 l, Musical score, "Viva la Vida."

1996, May 3

C968 AP196 1.40 l multicolored .40 .40
C969 AP196 5.40 l multicolored 1.75 1.75
C970 AP196 10 l multicolored 2.75 2.75
Nos. C968-C970 (3) 4.90 4.90

Arrival of the Garifunas in Honduras, Bicent.
AP197

Designs: 1.40 l, Headdress, vert. 5.40 l, Dancers, men playing drums. 10 l, Drums.

1996, June 13 Litho. *Perf. 13½*

C971 AP197 1.40 l multicolored .40 .25
C972 AP197 5.40 l multicolored 1.50 1.00
C973 AP197 10 l multicolored 2.75 1.50
Nos. C971-C973 (3) 4.65 2.75

EXFILHON '96, 7th Philatelic Exhibition
AP198

No. C974, Steam locomotive. No. C975, Passenger railcar.

1996, July 12 Litho. *Perf. 13½*

C974 AP198 5.40 l multi 2.50 2.00
C975 AP198 5.40 l multi 2.50 2.00

73x52mm

Imperf

C976 AP198 20 l +2 l like #C974 10.50 10.50
Nos. C974-C976 (3) 15.50 14.50

6th Central American Games
AP199

1996, Aug. 30 Litho. *Perf. 13½*

C977 AP199 4.30 l Soccer 1.50 .60
C978 AP199 4.54 l Volleyball 1.50 .65
C979 AP199 5.40 l Mascot, vert. 1.50 .75
Nos. C977-C979 (3) 4.50 2.00

Scouting in Honduras, 75th Anniv.
AP200

1996, Oct. 25 Litho. *Perf. 13½*

C980 AP200 2.15 l Emblems .50 .25
C981 AP200 5.40 l Emblem, vert. 1.40 .60
C982 AP200 6.90 l Scout feeding deer, vert. 2.10 .80
Nos. C980-C982 (3) 4.00 1.65

HONDURAS AEREO L 3.00

Christmas
AP201

Poinsettia and: 1.40 l, Candles. 5.40 l, Candles, vert.

1996, Dec. 23 Litho. *Perf. 13½*

C983	AP201	1.40 l	multicolored	.65	.25
C984	AP201	3 l	shown	1.25	.50
C985	AP201	5.40 l	multicolored	2.10	.95
	Nos. C983-C985 (3)			4.00	1.70

Traditional Costumes AP202

America issue: 4.55 l, Man in costume. 5.40 l, Woman in costume. 10 l, Couple in costumes.

1997, Jan. 17 Litho. *Perf. 13½*

C986	AP202	4.55 l	multicolored	1.10	.50
C987	AP202	5.40 l	multicolored	1.40	.65
C988	AP202	10 l	multicolored	3.50	1.10
	Nos. C986-C988 (3)			6.00	2.25

Honduras Plan, 20th Anniv., Intl. Plan, 60th Anniv. AP203

Children's paintings: 1.40 l, Outdoor scene, children swimming, vert. 5.40 l, Girl standing beside lake, fish. 9.70 l, People working between buildings.

1997, Feb. 7 Litho. *Perf. 13½*

C989	AP203	1.40 l	multicolored	.50	.25
C990	AP203	5.40 l	multicolored	1.50	.70
C991	AP203	9.70 l	multicolored	3.00	2.50
	Nos. C989-C991 (3)			5.00	3.45

Heinrich von Stephan (1831-97) AP205

1997, May 9 Litho. *Perf. 13½*

C995	AP205	5.40 l	multicolored	1.50	.55

World Population Day AP206

Designs: 6.90 l, Child's drawing of people outside, trees, houses.

1997, July 11 Litho. *Perf. 13½*

C996	AP206	1.40 l	shown	.75	.50
C997	AP206	6.90 l	multicolored	2.50	1.25

Butterflies AP207

Designs: 1 l, Rothchildia forbesi. 1.40 l, Parides photinus. 2.15 l, Morpho peleides. 3 l, Eurytides marcellus. 4.30 l, Parides iphidamas. 5.40 l, Danaus plexippus. 20 l+2 l, Hamadryas arinome.

1997, July 31

C998	AP207	1 l	multi	.50	.25
C999	AP207	1.40 l	multi	.50	.25
C1000	AP207	2.15 l	multi	.90	.25
C1001	AP207	3 l	multi	1.25	.25
C1002	AP207	4.30 l	multi	1.60	.65
C1003	AP207	5.40 l	multi	2.25	.85

Imperf

Size: 80x53mm

C1004	AP207	20 l +2 l	multi	7.50	5.50
	Nos. C998-C1004 (7)			14.50	8.00

For surcharge see No. C1175.

St. Teresa of Jesus, Death Cent. — AP208

1997, Aug. 20 Litho. *Perf. 13½*

C1005	AP208	1.40 l	shown	.85	.25
C1006	AP208	5.40 l	Portrait, diff.	1.75	.60

Astronomical Observatory AP209

Designs: 5.40 l, Statue of Father Jose Trinidad Reyes. 10 l, Woman with book leading child up steps.

1997, Sept. 19 Litho. *Perf. 13½*

C1007	AP209	1.40 l	multicolored	.40	.25
C1008	AP209	5.40 l	multicolored	1.25	.60
C1009	AP209	10 l	multicolored	2.25	1.10
	Nos. C1007-C1009 (3)			3.90	1.95

Alma Mater Foundation, 150th anniv., Autonomous University, 40th anniv.

Alcoholics Anonymous in Honduras, 37th anniv. — AP210

1997, Oct. 27

C1010	AP210	5.40 l	multicolored	2.00	.60

Diana, Princess of Wales (1961-97) AP211

1.40 l, Portrait, vert. 5.40 l, Diana dressed to walk through mine field, warning sign. 20 l, Mother Teresa, Princess Diana.

1997, Oct. 15

C1011	AP211	1.40 l	multi	.40	.25
C1012	AP211	5.40 l	multi	1.60	.70

Size: 51x78mm

Imperf

C1013	AP211	20 l	multi	6.00	4.25
	Nos. C1011-C1013 (3)			8.00	5.20

Christmas AP212

1.40 l, Christ of Picacho. 5.40 l, Virgin of Suyapa.

1997, Dec. 2 Litho. *Perf. 13½*

C1014	AP212	1.40 l	multi	.40	.40
C1015	AP212	5.40 l	multi	1.60	.85

Mascot — AP213

C1016: a, Basketball. b, At bat, baseball. c, Soccer. d, Racquetball. e, Spiking volleyball. f, Setting volleyball. g, Bowling. h, Table tennis. i, Rings over map of Central America. j, Pitching, baseball.

No. C1017: a, Kicking, karate. b, Chopping, karate. c, Bowing, karate. d, Wrestling. e, Weight lifting. f, Boxing. g, Body building. h, Fencing. i, Program cover. j, Shooting.

No. C1018: a, Riding bicycle. b, Riding bicycle by shoreline. c, Swimming. d, Water polo. e, Hurdles. f, Gymnastics. g, Riding horse. h, Tennis. i, Program cover with mascot. j, Chess.

1997 Sheets of 10

C1016	AP213	1.40 l	#a.-j.	5.00	5.00
C1017	AP213	1.50 l	#a.-j.	5.50	5.50
C1018	AP213	2.15 l	#a.-j.	7.00	7.00

6th Central American Games, San Pedro Sula.

Fish AP214

1.40 l, Cichlasoma dovii. 2 l, Cichlasoma spilurum. 3 l, Cichlasoma spilurum facing right. 5.40 l, Astyanay fasciatus.

1997 Litho. *Perf. 13½*

C1019	AP214	1.40 l	multicolored	.50	.30
C1020	AP214	2 l	multicolored	.75	.40
C1021	AP214	3 l	multicolored	1.20	.50
C1022	AP214	5.40 l	multicolored	2.10	.90
	Nos. C1019-C1022 (4)			4.55	2.10

Marine Life, Islas de la Bahía (Bay Islands) — AP215

Designs: a, Balistes vetula. b, Haemudon plumieri. c, Pomacanthus paru. d, Juvenile halichoeres garnoti. e, Pomacanthus arcuatus. f, Holacanthus ciliaris. g, Diver's face, pseud opterogorgia. h, Diver's oxygen tanks, pseud opterogorgia. i, Dendrogya cylindrus. j, Holocentrus adscensionis. k, Dendrogya cylindrus, diff. l, Stegastes fuscus. m, Gorgonia mariae. n, Pillar coral. o, Pomacanthus arcuatus, diff. p, Holocentrus adscensionis, diff. q, Eusmilia fastigiata. r, Scarus coelestinus. s, Pillar coral, diff. t, Lachnolaimus masimus.

1998, Mar. 13 Litho. *Perf. 13½*

Sheet of 20

C1023	AP215	2.50 l	#a.-t.	16.00	16.00

Bancahsa, 50th anniv.

Exists imperf. Value, $30.

America Issue AP216

No. C1024, Post Office headquarters. No. C1025, Postman on motorcycle.

1998, May 29 Litho. *Perf. 13½*

C1024	AP216	5.40 l	multi	1.60	.80
C1025	AP216	5.40 l	multi	1.60	.80

Maya Artifacts — AP217

Designs: 1 l, Large carving on temple. 1.40 l, Stele of Mayan king. 2.15 l, Large stelae. 5.40 l, Small ornamental carving. 20 l, Maya Ruins, Copán.

1998, June 19 Litho. *Perf. 13½*

C1026	AP217	1 l	multi	.30	.25
C1027	AP217	1.40 l	multi	.55	.25
C1028	AP217	2.15 l	multi	2.00	.25
C1029	AP217	5.40 l	multi	2.10	.55

Size: 78x52mm

Imperf

C1030	AP217	20 l	multi	6.50	3.00
	Nos. C1026-C1030 (5)			11.45	4.30

1998 World Cup Soccer Championships, France — AP218

No. C1032, Players, vert.

No. C1033: a, Stadium, Tegucigalpa. b, St. Denis Stadium, France.

1998, July 3 Litho. *Perf. 13½*

C1031	AP218	5.40 l	shown	1.50	.70
C1032	AP218	10 l	multi	3.00	1.50

Imperf

C1033	AP218	10 l	Pair, #a.-b.	8.25	7.00

No. C1033 contains two 53x42mm stamps. No. C1033 also issued rouletted between the stamps; value the same.

Reptiles AP219

Designs: 1.40 l, Green iguana. 2 l, Rattlesnake. 3 l, Two iguanas. 5.40 l, Coral snake. 20 l + 2 l, Marine turtle.

1998, July 31 Litho. *Perf. 13½*

C1034	AP219	1.40 l	multi	.45	.35
C1035	AP219	2 l	multi	.75	.60
C1036	AP219	3 l	multi	.95	.75
C1037	AP219	5.40 l	multi	1.90	1.25

Size: 77x52mm

Imperf

C1038	AP219	20 l +2 l	multi	7.00	4.50
	Nos. C1034-C1038 (5)			11.05	7.45

Christmas AP220

Designs: 3 l, Girl taking ornament from bird, vert. 5.40 l, Christ Child asleep on bed of holly, dove, stars. 10 l, Boy with lantern leading donkey, cabin in the snow, vert.

1998, Dec. 8 Litho. *Perf. 13½*

C1039 AP220 3 l multicolored .70 .30
C1040 AP220 5.40 l multicolored 1.25 .60
C1041 AP220 10 l multicolored 2.25 1.25
Nos. C1039-C1041 (3) 4.20 2.15

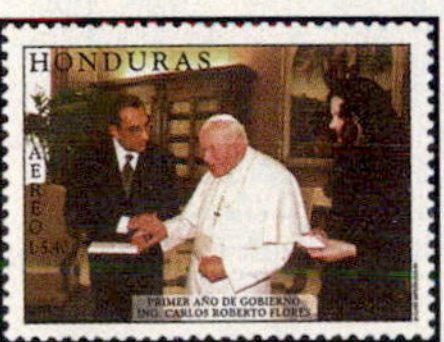

Pres. Carlos Roberto Flores, 1st Anniv. of Taking Office AP221

Designs: 5.40 l, Pres. and Mrs. Flores, Pope John Paul II. 10 l, Portrait of Pres., Mrs. Flores, vert.

1999, Jan. 27 Litho. *Perf. 13½*

C1042 AP221 5.40 l multicolored 1.40 .55
C1043 AP221 10 l multicolored 2.10 1.00

Hurricane Mitch — AP222

No. C1044: a, Men working to clean up. b, Helicopter distributing aid. c, Vehicles under water, North Zone. d, Tipper Gore, Mary de Flores cleaning. e, Working to save banana crop. f, Destruction of Tegucigalpa. g, Cars, buses, trucks blocked by rock slide. h, Destruction of Comayagüela. i, Streets of Comayagüela. j, Oriental Zone. k, Loading debris, help from Mexico. l, Streets of Limpieza. m, Pres. Flores with Pres. Chirac of France. n, Business district of Comayagüela. o, Flooding, Tegucigalpa. p, Car in street, Comayagüela.

No. C1045: a, Central Zone. b, South Zone. c, Prince Felipe de Borbon, Mary de Flores. d, Small child crying. e, Cleaning up debris, Comayagüela. f, Families, man carrying baby, North Zone. g, Two men looking at destruction of building, Tegucigalpa. h, Man, child, woman wading in water, North Zone. i, Destruction in rural area. j, Cars piled up, concrete abutment along roadway. k, Cars, buildings along roadway. l, Mexican troops, airplane. m, Boys swimming. n, Pres. & Mrs. Flores, Hillary Clinton. o, People walking over rubble and debris, South Zone. p, Pres. Flores, former US Pres. George Bush.

1999, Feb. 19 *Rouletted*

Sheets of 16

C1044 AP222 5.40 l #a.-p. 18.00 18.00
C1045 AP222 5.40 l #a.-p. 18.00 18.00

For surcharges, see Nos. C1207, C1208.

Famous Honduran Women — AP223

America Issue: 2.60 l, Maria del Pilar Salinas (b. 1914), scholar. 7.30 l, Clementina Suarez (1902-91), poet, writer. 10.65 l, Mary Flake de Flores, first lady of Honduras.

1999, Apr. 20 Litho. *Perf. 13½*

C1046 AP223 2.60 l multi .55 .25
C1047 AP223 7.30 l multi 1.50 .75
C1048 AP223 10.65 l multi 2.25 1.10
Nos. C1046-C1048 (3) 4.30 2.10

Dated 1998.

Mother's Day AP224

Designs: 20 l, Police officer Orellana breastfeeding baby, vert. 30 l, Paphiopedilum urbanianum. 50 l, Miltoniopsis vexillaria.

1999, May 14 Litho. *Perf. 13½*

C1049 AP224 20 l multicolored 4.25 3.50
C1050 AP224 30 l multicolored 6.25 4.25
C1051 AP224 50 l multicolored 10.50 7.25
Nos. C1049-C1051 (3) 21.00 15.00

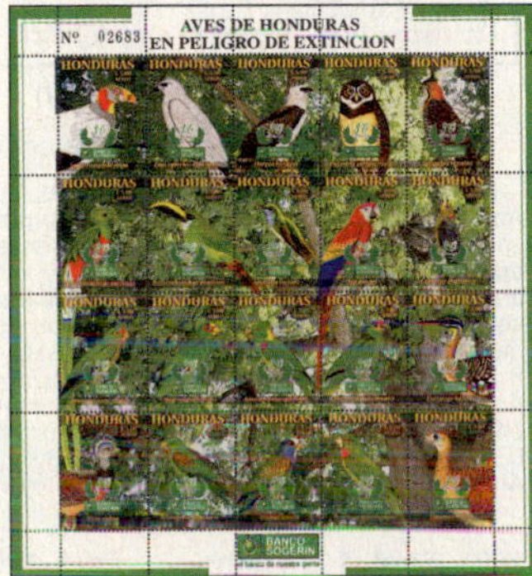

Endangered Birds — AP225

No. C1052, 5 l: a, Sarcoramphus papa. b, Leucopternis albicollis. c, Harpia harpyja. d, Pulsatrix perspicallata. e, Spizaetus ornatus. f, Pharomarchrus mocinno. g, Aulacorhynchus prasinus. h, Amazilia luciae. i, Ara macao. j, Centurus pygmaeus.

3 l: k, Aratinga canicularis. l, Amazona albifrons. m, Amazona auropalliata. n, Amazona autumnalis. o, Eurypyga helias. p, Crax rubra. q, Brotogeris jugularis. r, Pionus senilis. s, Aratinga rubritorques. t, Tinamus major.

No. C1053: a, Jaberu mycteria. b, Chondrohierax uncinatus. c, Pharomachrus mocinno. d, Ramphastos sulfuratus.

1999, July 8

C1052 AP225 Sheeet of 20, #a.-t. 20.00 18.50
C1053 AP225 10 l Sheet of 4, #a.-d. 9.00 7.50

Banco Sogerin, 30th anniv.

Inter-American Development Bank, 40th Anniv. — AP226

1999, Nov. 22 Litho. *Perf. 13½*

C1054 AP226 18.30 l multi 3.75 2.00

For surcharge see No. C1249.

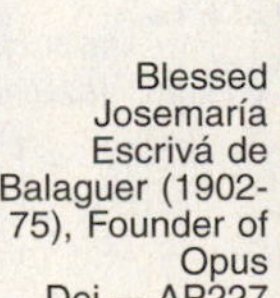

Blessed Josemaría Escrivá de Balaguer (1902-75), Founder of Opus Dei — AP227

1999, Nov. 29

C1055 AP227 2.60 l multi .60 .30
C1056 AP227 16.40 l multi 3.25 2.00

Millennium AP228

Designs: 2 l, Salvador Moncada, discoverer of nitric oxide in blood, vert. 8.65 l, Albert Einstein, vert. 10 l, Wilhelm Röntgen, vert. 14.95 l, George Stephenson and locomotive "Rocket."

1999, Oct. 18

C1057 AP228 2 l multi .90 .40
C1058 AP228 8.65 l multi 1.75 1.10
C1059 AP228 10 l multi 2.25 1.25
C1060 AP228 14.95 l multi 3.75 2.50
Nos. C1057-C1060 (4) 8.65 5.25

National Congress, 175th Anniv. AP229

Designs: 4.30, Statue of Francisco Morazán. 10 l, Congress President Rafael Pineda Ponce, Congress Building.

1999, Dec. 17 Litho. *Perf. 13¼*

C1061 AP229 4.30 l multi 1.00 .50
C1062 AP229 10 l multi 2.25 1.10

AP230

Nos. C606-C607 Surcharged Holy Year 2000 — AP231

Holy Year Emblem and: 4 l, Pope John Paul II, people. 4.30 l, St. Peter. 6.90 l, Jesus, Jerusalem, horiz. 7.30 l, John Paul II, crowd, horiz. 10 l, John Paul II giving blessing. 14 l, Pres. Carlos Roberto Flores, John Paul II.

2000, Jan. 1 Litho. *Perf. 13¼*

C1063 AP230 4 l multi 1.25 .60
C1064 AP230 4.30 l shown 9.50 3.00
C1065 AP230 6.90 l multi 2.00 1.00
C1066 AP230 7.30 l multi 2.25 1.10
C1067 AP230 10 l multi 3.00 1.50
C1068 AP231 14 l shown 3.50 1.75

Nos. C1064, C1068 Redrawn

C1069 AP230 4.30 l multi 1.25 .75
C1070 AP231 14 l multi 3.75 2.00
Nos. C1063-C1070 (8) 26.50 11.70

No. C1067 issued in sheets of 6, with picture of John Paul II in selvage. No. C1069 has "HONDURAS" in yellow; No. C1064 in white. No. C1070 has "HONDURAS" at right, reading up; No. C1068 at top.

2nd Anniv. of Inauguration of Pres. Flores — AP232

Pres. Flores and: 10 l, Conference delegates. 10.65 l, Mario Hung Pacheco.

2000, Jan. 27

C1071 AP232 10 l multi 2.50 1.25
C1072 AP232 10.65 l multi 3.00 1.40

Musical Instruments Type of Semi-postals of 2000

No. 1073, vert.: a, 1.40 l, Marimba, denomination at L. b, 1.40 l, Marimba, denomination at L. c, 1.40 l, Ayotl. d, 10 l, Maya drum. e, 10 l, Teponaxtle. f, 2.60 l, Maracas. g, 2.60 l, Güiro. h, 2.60 l, Chinchín. i, 2.60 l, Raspador. j, 2.60 l, Horse's jawbone. k, 3 l, Green zoomorphic whistle. l, 3 l, Aztec drum. m, 3 l, One-tone zoomorphic whistle. n, 3 l, Two-tone zoomorphic whistle. o, 3 l, Tun. p, 4 l, Gourd. q, 4 l, Deer hide drum. r, 4 l, Guacalitos. s, 4 l, Five musicians, marimba. t, 4 l, Four musicians, marimba.

2000, Apr. 7 Litho. *Perf. 13¼*

C1073 SP1 Sheet of 20, #a-t 25.00 22.50

Paintings of Pablo Zelaya Sierra — AP233

No. C1074: a, 2 l, Green City (building and tree). b, 2 l, Old Woman With Rosary. c, 2 l, Rural Women (women with jars). d, 2 l, Woman With Green Robe. e, 2 l, City. f, 1.40 l, Shoulders of a Man. g, 1.40 l, Goat. h, 1.40 l, Spanish City. i, 1.40 l, Woman With Chignon. j, 1.40 l, Woman With Calabash. k, 2.60 l, Goat and Birds. l, 2.60 l, Tree Trunks. m, 2.60 l, Nuns. n, 2.60 l, Archers. o, 2.60 l, Moon and Boats. p, 2.60 l, Bust. q, 10 l, Still-life. r, 10 l, Composition With Books. s, 2.60 l, Landscape. t, 2.60 l, Head, Fan and Book.

2000, July 1

C1074 AP233 Sheet of 20, #a-t 22.50 22.50

Airmail Anniv. Type of Semi-postals

Designs: 7.30 l, #C12. 10 l, Thomas Canfield Pounds, owner of Central American Airline, vert. 10.65 l, Pres. Rafael López Gutiérrez, signer of first airmail contract, vert.

2000, July 7 Size: 35x25mm

C1075 SP2 7.30 l multi 1.60 .85

Size: 25x35mm

C1076 SP2 10 l multi 2.25 1.10
C1077 SP2 10.65 l multi 2.40 1.25
Nos. C1075-C1077 (3) 6.25 3.20

America Issue, A New Millennium Without Arms — AP234

Designs: 10 l, Sobralia macrantha, No guns. 10.65 l, Peace dove, No soldiers. 14 l, Train, No bombs, no more terrorism, horiz.

2000, July 28 Litho. *Perf. 13¼*
C1078-C1080 AP234 Set of 3 9.00 7.00

2000 Summer Olympics, Sydney AP235

Designs: 2.60 l, Soccer players Ivan Guerrero, Mario Chirinos. 10.65 l, Swimmer Ramon Valle, vert. 12.45 l, Runner Gina Coello.

No. C1084: a, 4.30 l, Swimmer. b, 4.30 l, Soccer player Danilo Turcios. c, 10.65 l, Runner Pedro Ventura. d, 12.45 l, Soccer player David Suazo.

2000, Sept. 13
C1081-C1083 AP235 Set of 3 11.00 8.50

Souvenir Sheet

C1084 AP235 Sheet of 4, #a-d 12.00 12.00

No. C1084 exists imperf. Value, $18.

Intl. Voluntarism Year — AP236

Emblem, people and: 2.60 l, White-crowned parrot. 10.65 l, Telipogon ampliflorus.

2000, Dec. 5
C1085-C1086 AP236 Set of 2 3.25 2.25

Christmas AP237

Designs: 2.60 l, Madonna and child. 7.30 l, Nativity, vert. 14 l, Carpet painter.

2000, Dec. 18
C1087-C1089 AP237 Set of 3 5.00 3.25

America Issue, Birds — AP238

Designs: 2.60 l, Amazona auropalliata caribea. 4.30 l, Columbina passerina, horiz. 10.65 l, Ara macao. 20 l, Aguila harpia.

2001, Feb. 16 Litho. *Perf. 13¼*
C1090-C1093 AP238 Set of 4 10.00 8.25

Nos. C584, C593, C606, C611, C646-C647, C652-C653, C699 Surcharged — c

Nos. C620, C672, C708, C721 Surcharged — d

Nos. C584, C612, C637 Surcharged
No. C637 Surcharged — e

Methods and Perfs. as Before

2001

C1094	AP103(c)	2 l on 16c #C652		.35	.25
C1095	AP103(c)	2 l on 16c #C653		.35	.25
a.	Pair, #C1094-C1095			.70	.35
C1096	AP106(d)	2.60 l on 3c #C672		.45	.25
C1097	AP114(d)	2.60 l on 3c #C708		.45	.25
C1098	AP100(d)	2.60 l on 8c #C620		.45	.25
C1099	AP102(e)	2.60 l on 16c #C637		.45	.25
C1100	AP96(c)	3 l on 16c #C593		.55	.25
C1101	AP116(d)	4 l on 9c #C721		.70	.35
C1102	AP97(c)	4.30 l on 6c #C606		.75	.35
C1103	AP103(c)	7.30 l on 6c #C646		1.25	.60
C1104	AP103(c)	7.30 l on 6c #C647		1.25	.60
a.	Pair, #C1103-C1104			2.50	1.20
C1105	AP95(c)	10 l on 16c #C584		1.75	.90
C1106	AP112(c)	10.65 l on 16c #C699		1.90	.95
C1107	AP98(c)	14 l on 16c #C611		3.00	1.25
	Nos. C1094-C1107 (14)			13.65	6.75

Size and location of surcharge varies. Issued: Nos. C1096-C1099, 3/26; others, 4/3.

Oscar Cardinal Rodriguez — AP239

No. C1108: a, 2.60 l, With father, 1946. b, 2.60 l, In Sanctuary of Our Lady of Suyapa. c, 2.60 l, As seminarian, 1964. d, 2.60 l, Installation as archbishop. e, 2.60 l, Ordination, 1960. f, 2.60 l, At Vatican, Feb. 21, 2001. g, 2.60 l, At mass in Guatemala, 1970. h, 2.60 l, Standing behind Honduran flag. i, 2.60 l, With Pope John Paul II, 1993. j, 2.60 l, Returning to Honduras as Cardinal. k, 2.60 l, Giving address as Cardinal, Mar. 10, 2001. l, 10.65 l, With Pope and woman, 1993. m, 10.65 l, Papal audience, Feb. 23, 2001. n, 10.65 l, Celebration of the Eucharist. o, 10.65 l, Kneeling before Pope, 1993. p, 10.65 l, Installation as Cardinal, Feb. 21, 2001. q, 15 l, Installation as Cardinal, St. Peter's Square.

2001, May 9 Litho. *Perf. 13¼*
C1108 AP239 Sheet of 17, #a-q 30.00 30.00

Stamp sizes: Nos. C1108a-C1108j, 29x40mm; C1108k-C1108p, 49x40mm; C1108q, 163x131mm. No. C1108 exists imperf. Value $30.

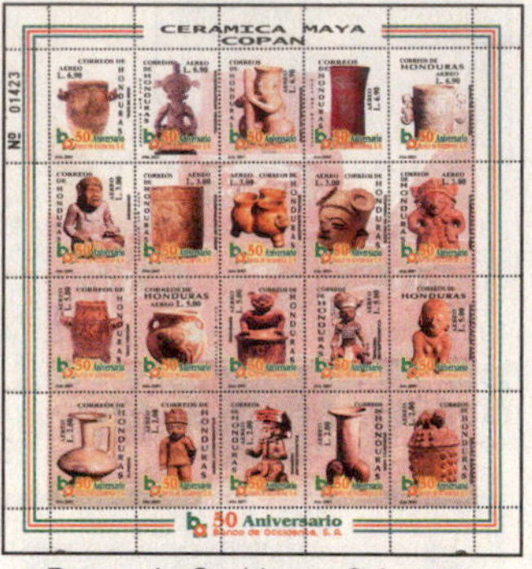

Banco de Occidente, S.A., 50th Anniv. — AP240

Mayan ceramics: a, 2 l, Flower pot. b, 2 l, Anthropomorphic jar. c, 2 l, Anthropomorphic cover. d, 2 l, Cylindrical vase. e, 2 l, Censer tripod. f, 3 l, Scribe. g, 3 l, Cylindrical jar with anthropomorphic figures. h, 3 l, Three-part container. i, 3 l, Ceramic face. j, 3 l, Anthropomorphic jar, diff. k, 5 l, Three-legged vessel. l, 5 l, Pot with handles. m, 5 l, Censer. n, 5 l, Anthropomorphic cover. o, 5 l, Anthropomorphic jar, diff. p, 6.90 l, Pot with handles, diff. q, 6.90 l, Anthropomorphic cover, diff. r, 6.90 l, Anthropomorphic jar, diff. s, 6.90 l, Red cylindrical container. t, 6.90 l, Decorated container.

2001, Sept. 1 Litho. *Perf. 13¼*
C1109 AP240 Sheet of 20, #a-t 26.00 26.00

UN High Commissioner for Refugees, 50th Anniv. — AP241

Designs: 2.60 l, Refugee and child, vert. 10.65 l, Refugees running.

2001
C1110-C1111 AP241 Set of 2 4.00 3.00

Souvenir Sheet

Juan Ramon Molina Bridge — AP242

No. C1112: a, 2.60 l, Aerial view from end. b, 10 l, Close-up view from side. c, 10.65 l, Aerial view from side. d, 13.65 l, Side view showing river.

2001, Dec. 20 Litho. *Rouletted 6½*
C1112 AP242 Sheet of 4, #a-d 15.00 15.00

Stamp sizes: No. C1112b, 152x93mm; others, 40x30mm.

America Issue — Wildlife AP243

Designs: 10 l, Bird, Yojoa Lake. 10.65 l, Iguana, Cisne Islands. 20 l, Chrysina quetzalcoatli, Morpho sp., Pulaphanzhak Cataracts.

2002, Jan. 31 *Perf. 13¼*
C1113-C1115 AP243 Set of 3 13.00 13.00

Pan-American Health Organization, Cent. — AP244

2002, Apr. 7
C1116 AP244 10 l multi 3.25 3.25

Miguel R. Pastor, Central District Mayor — AP245

Central District emblem and: a, 1.40 l, Cathedral of San Miguel, statues, birds (57x35mm). b, 1.40 l, Chimpanzee throwing banana peel in trash can (57x35mm). c, 1.40 l, Municipal building (57x35mm). d, 2.60 l, Mayor Pastor, flags (27x35mm). e, 2.60 l, Mayor Pastor under tree (27x35mm). f, 2.60 l, Mayor Pastor with old woman (27x35mm). g, 2.60 l, Mayor Pastor with crowd (27x35mm). h, 2.60 l, Mayor Pastor planting seedling (27x35mm). i, 2.60 l, Mayor Pastor and family (27x35mm). j, 10 l, Municipal council (57x35mm). k, 10 l, Mayor with guests (57x35mm). l, 10.65 l, Cathedral of San Miguel, statues, birds (114x75mm).

2002, June 13 Litho. *Perf. 13¼*
C1117 AP245 Sheet of 12, #a-l 16.00 16.00

Souvenir Sheet

Discovery of Honduras, 500th Anniv. — AP246

No. C1118: a, 10.65 l, Boat on shore, jungle. b, 12.45 l, Natives on shore. c, 13.65 l, Spaniards coming ashore. d, 20 l, Spanish ship.

2002, Aug. 14
C1118 AP246 Sheet of 4, #a-d 9.00 9.00

Exfilhon 2002.

Souvenir Sheet

Christianity in Honduras, 500th Anniv. — AP247

No. C1119: a, 2.60 l, Natives and cross. b, 3 l, Santa Barbara Trujillo Fort. c, 10 l, 400 Years of History, by Mario Castillo. d, 10 l, Spaniards on shore, ships at sea.

2002, Aug. 14
C1119 AP247 Sheet of 4, #a-d 5.00 5.00

America issue.

Banco del Pais, 10th Anniv. AP248

2002, Sept. 5 **Litho.** ***Perf. 13¼***

C1120 AP248 2 l multi .25 .25
a. Block of 10 3.00 3.00
C1121 AP248 2.60 l multi .50 .50
a. Block of 10 4.25 4.25
C1122 AP248 10 l multi 1.75 1.75
a. Sheet of 30 45.00 45.00
C1123 AP248 10.65 l multi 2.00 2.00
a. Sheet of 30 50.00 50.00
Nos. C1120-C1123 (4) 4.50 4.50

Backgrounds of Nos. C1120-C1123 show a flag on a staff and clouds in the blocks and and the flag on the sheets, giving each stamp a different background.

Orchids AP249

Designs: 1.40 l, Vanilla planifolia. 2.60 l, Lycaste virginalis. 3 l, Coelia bella. 4.30 l, Chysis laevis. 8.65 l, Myrmecophila bryslana. 10 l, Rhyncolaelia digbyana.
20 l, Mormodes aromatica.

2002, Sept. 25 **Litho.** ***Perf. 13¼***
C1124-C1129 AP249 Set of 6 7.00 7.00

Size: 96x66mm

Imperf

C1130 AP249 20 l multi 6.00 6.00

for surcharges see Nos. C1241, C1243, C1252-C1253.

Christmas AP250

Designs: 2.60 l, Creche scene. 10.65 l, Holy Family. 14 l, People at recreation of nativity scene.

2002, Nov. 25
C1131-C1133 AP250 Set of 3 4.00 4.00

National Children's Foundation AP251

Designs: 2.60 l, Children. 10 l, Elderly people. 10.65 l, Symbols of Honduras, vert.

2002, Dec. 6
C1134-C1136 AP251 Set of 3 3.50 3.50

Insects — AP252

No. C1137: a, 2 l, Chrysina spectabilis. b, 2 l, Chrysina strasseni. c, 2 l, Viridimicus omoaensis. d, 2 l, Hoplopyga liturata. e, 2.60 l, Chrysina cusuquensis. f, 2.60 l, Calomacraspis haroldi. g, 2.60 l, Pelidnota strigosa. h, 2.60 l, Odontocheila tawahka. i, 3 l, Chrysina cavei. j, 3 l, Macropoides crassipes. k, 3 l, Pelidnota velutipes. l, 3 l, Tragidion cyanovestis. m, 4 l, Chrysina pastori. n, 4 l, Platycoelia humeralis. o, 4 l, Phanaeus eximius. p, 4 l, Acanthoderes cavei. q, 10.65 l, Chrysina quetzalcoatli. r, 10.65 l, Cyclocephala abrelata. s, 10.65 l, Aegithus rufipennis. t, 10.65 l, Callipogon barbatum.

No. C1138 — Chrysina spp.: a, Eggs. b, Larva. b, Pupa.

2003, Feb. 20
C1137 AP252 Sheet of 20, #a-t 17.00 17.00

Souvenir Sheet

C1138 AP252 10 l Sheet of 3, #a-c 6.00 6.00

Banco Atlantida, 90th anniv. (No. C1137).

World Food Program AP253

Designs: 2.60 l, Children with food. 6.90 l, Child with food. 10.65 l, Child with bowl and spoon.

2003, May 15
C1139-C1141 AP253 Set of 3 3.50 3.50

For surcharge see No. C1196.

Souvenir Sheet

Pontificate of John Paul II, 25th Anniv., and 20th Anniv. of Visit to Honduras — AP254

No. C1142: a, 13.65 l, Pope giving blessing. b, 14.55 l, Pope at airport. c, 15.45 l, Pope with staff. d, 16.65 l, Pope with rosary beads.

2003, Oct. 10 ***Perf. 10½***
C1142 AP254 Sheet of 4, #a-d 11.00 11.00

For surcharges, See Nos. C1299-C1300.

Regional Sanitary Agricultural Organization, 50th Anniv. — AP255

Designs: 2.60 l, Eggs, sliced meat. 10 l, Eye, map of Central America, corn. 10.65 l, Emblem, map of Central America. 14 l, Vegetables. 20 l, Corn, tomato, fish.

2003, Oct. 24 ***Perf. 13¼***
C1143-C1147 AP255 Set of 5 10.00 10.00

Bridges Built by Japan — AP256

No. C1148: a, 3 l, Ilama Bridge, Santa Bárbara. b, 3 l, Sol Naciente Bridge, Choluteca. c, 4.30 l, Río Hondo Bridge, Francisco Morazán. d, 4.30 l, El Chile Bridge, Central District. e, 4.30 l, Iztoca Bridge, Choluteca. f, 10 l, La Democracia Bridge, near El Progreso. g, 10 l, Guasaule Bridge, Honduras-Nicaragua border. 20 l, Juan Ramón Molina Bridge, Tegucigalpa (168x109mm).

2003, Nov. 25 **Litho.** ***Perf. 13¼***
C1148 AP256 Sheet of 7, #a-h + label 10.00 10.00

Telethon Honduras AP257

Telethon emblem and: 1.40 l, Flag on staff. 2.60 l, Hand, flag in light blue. 7.30 l, Hand, flag in dark blue. 10 l, Map.

2003, Dec. 4
C1149-C1152 AP257 Set of 4 3.50 3.50

For surcharges see Nos. C1244-C1245, C1247.

Christmas AP258

Designs: 10.65 l, Angel. 14 l, Holy Family in manger.

2003, Dec. 8
C1153-C1154 AP258 Set of 2 4.00 4.00

Souvenir Sheet

Endangered Birds — AP259

No. C1155: a, 10 l, Arantinga strenua. b, 10.65 l, Falco deiroleucus. c, 14 l, Spizaetus melanoleucos. d, 20 l, Amazona xantholora.

2004, May 13
C1155 AP259 Sheet of 4, #a-d 10.00 10.00

Exfilhon 2004.

Endangered Animals — AP260

Designs: 85c, Pecari tajacu. 1.40 l, Mazama americana. 2 l, Tamandua mexicana, vert. 2.60 l, Felis concolor. No. C1160, Tamandua mexicana, vert. No. C1161, Felis concolor. No. C1162, Mazama americana. No. C1163, Bradypus variegatus. 4.30 l, Pecari tajacu. 7.85 l, Agalychinis challidryas, vert. 10.65 l, Bradypus variegatus. 14.95 l, Agalchinis challidryas, vert.

No. C1168, vert.: a, Mono titi. b, Cebus capucinus. c, Ateles geoffroyi. d, Alouatta palliata.

2004, May 24 **Litho.** ***Perf. 13¼***

C1156 AP260 85c multi .25 .25
C1157 AP260 1.40 l multi .25 .25
C1158 AP260 2 l multi .40 .40
C1159 AP260 2.60 l multi .45 .45
C1160 AP260 3 l multi .55 .55
C1161 AP260 3 l multi .55 .55
C1162 AP260 4 l multi .60 .60
C1163 AP260 4 l multi .60 .60
C1164 AP260 4.30 l multi .65 .65
C1165 AP260 7.85 l multi 1.40 1.40
C1166 AP260 10.65 l multi 2.10 2.10
C1167 AP260 14.95 l multi 3.00 3.00
Nos. C1156-C1167 (12) 10.80 10.80
C1168 AP260 10 l Sheet of 4, #a-d 7.50 7.50

Nos. C1156-C1158, C1161, C1163, and C1165 were each printed in souvenir sheets of 4.

For surcharges see Nos. C1239-C1240, C1242, C1254-C1255.

Shells AP261

Designs: Nos. C1169, C1174f, Voluta polypleura. Nos. C1170, C1174d, Strombus gallus. Nos. C1171, C1174a, Charonia variegata, Terebra taurina. Nos. C1172, C1174e, Spondylus americanus. Nos. C1173, C1174c, Strombus raninus. No. C1174b, Man blowing conch shell.

2004, July 19 **Litho.** ***Perf. 13¼***

C1169 AP261 85c multi .25 .25
C1170 AP261 1.40 l multi .40 .25
C1171 AP261 2 l multi .55 .35
C1172 AP261 2.60 l multi .70 .55
C1173 AP261 10.65 l multi 2.10 2.10
Nos. C1169-C1173 (5) 4.00 3.50

Miniature Sheet

C1174 Sheet of 6 11.00 11.00
a.-b. AP261 4 l Either single .75 .75
c.-d. AP261 5 l Either single .95 .95
e.-f. AP261 20 l Either single 3.75 3.75

For surcharges see Nos. C1246, C1248, C1250-C1251.

No. C1004 Surcharged in Red

2004, Aug. 13 **Litho.** ***Imperf.***
C1175 AP207 50 l on 20 l+2 l multi 9.00 9.00

Miniature Sheet

Banco Fichosa, Sponsor of National Soccer Team — AP262

No. C1176: a, 4.30 l, Players, Honduras flag. b, 10.65 l, Team. c, 14 l, Saúl Martinez, David Suazo. d, 20 l, Amado Guevara.

2004, Sept. 3 **Litho.** ***Perf. 13¼***
C1176 AP262 Sheet of 4, #a-d 6.50 6.50

Christmas AP263

Designs: 2.60 l, Flight into Egypt. 7.85 l, Santa Claus on ornament. 10.65 l, Three Kings. 20 l, Holy Family.

2004, Nov. 23 **Litho.** ***Perf. 13¼***
C1177-C1180 AP263 Set of 4 7.50 7.50
C1178a Sheet of 4 #C1178 6.50 6.50

For surcharges see Nos. C1224-C1227.

AP264

National Unity — AP265

2005, Feb. 3
C1181 AP264 10 l multi 1.10 1.10
C1182 AP265 20 l multi 2.25 2.25

Rotary International, Cent. — AP266

Rotary International emblem and: 2.60 l, Rafael Diaz Chávez, Paul Harris and Jorge Fidel Durón. 5 l, "100 años," vert. 8 l, Globe and arrows. 10.65 l, Map of Honduras, PolioPlus emblem. 14 l, Mayan sculpture.

2005, Feb. 23
C1183-C1187 AP266 Set of 5 5.25 5.25

Pope John Paul II (1920-2005) AP267

Pope: 10 l, Wearing white vestments. 15 l, Wearing colored vestments. 20 l, Holding crucifix.

2005, Apr. 15 **Litho.** ***Perf. 13¼***
C1188-C1189 AP267 Set of 2 3.25 3.25

Souvenir Sheet

C1190 Sheet of 2 #C1190a 5.25 5.25
a. AP267 20 l multi, 29x42mm 2.50 2.50

Honduran Medical Review, 75th Anniv. — AP268

Designs: 3 l, House. 5 l, Bird. 12 l, Jaguar. 30 l, Flowers.

No. C1195: a, Macaws. b, Macaw in banana tree. c, Rooster. d, Turkeys and hens.

2005, May 18
C1191-C1194 AP268 Set of 4 6.50 6.50

Souvenir Sheet

C1195 AP268 25 l Sheet of 4, #a-d 13.00 13.00

Nos. 390-392, B1, C550, C552, C553, C576, C715, C1044-C1045, C1140 and RA8 Surcharged

"X" Obliterators — f

Box Obliterator and "Aereo" — g

Box Obliterator — h

Methods and Perfs as Before

2005, June 3
C1196 AP253(f) 3 l on 6.90 l #C1140 .30 .30
C1197 AP72(f) 5 l on 16c on 1c #C552 .55 .55
C1198 AP72(f) 5 l on 16c on 1c #C553 .55 .55
C1199 PT6(g) 10 l on 13.85 l on 1c #392 1.10 1.10
C1200 AP68(f) 14 l on 16c on 1c #C550 1.50 1.50
C1201 PT6(g) 20 l on 13.85 l on 1c #392 2.10 2.10
C1202 PT6(g) 25 l on 11.55 l on 1c #390 2.75 2.75
C1203 AP94(f) 30 l on 16c #C576 3.25 3.25
C1204 AP115(f) 35 l on 16c #C715 3.75 3.75
C1205 PT6(g) 40 l on 11.55 l on 1c #390 4.25 4.25
C1206 PT6(g) 50 l on 12.45 l on 1c #391 5.50 5.50
Nos. C1196-C1206 (11) 25.60 25.60

Sheets

C1207 Sheet of 16 (#C1044) 15.00 15.00
a.-p. AP222(h) 8 l on 5.40 l any single .90 .90
C1208 Sheet of 16 (#C1045) 15.00 15.00
a.-p. AP222(h) 8 l on 5.40 l any single .90 .90
C1209 Sheet of 6 (#B1) 10.00 10.00
a.-f. SP1(f) 15 l on 10 l +1 l any single 1.60 1.60
g. As No. C1209, on No. B1g 10.00 10.00

Size, location and font of surcharges and obliterators vary on types "f" and "h."

Honduras — Japan Diplomatic Relations, 70th Anniv. AP269

Designs: 8 l, Actors in play. 15 l, Emblem of Japanese-Central American Year. 30 l, National Congress, Japanese Princess Sayako.

No. C1213: a, Japanese ceramics. b, Flowers. c, Mayan ceramics. d, Mount Fuji, Japan and Pico Bonito National Park, Honduras.

2005, Aug. 9 **Litho.** ***Perf. 13¼***
C1210-C1212 AP269 Set of 3 7.00 7.00

Souvenir Sheet

C1213 AP269 25 l Sheet of 4, #a-d 13.00 13.00

Gen. José Trinidad Cabañas (1805-71) AP270

Cabañas: 3 l, With green panel at bottom. 8 l, With university buildings, horiz. 15 l, In oval frame.

2005, Sept. 12
C1214-C1216 AP270 Set of 3 3.25 3.25

Honduras, Water Capital — AP271

Water droplet and: 30 l, Heart, butterfly, Sanaa and Ras-hon emblems. 50 l, Heart.

2005, Sept. 28
C1217 AP271 30 l multi 4.00 4.00

Souvenir Sheet

C1218 AP271 50 l multi 9.00 9.00

Souvenir Sheet

America Issue — Endangered Mushrooms — AP272

No. C1219: a, 20 l, Hygrophorus marzuolus. b, 25 l, Lactarius deliciosus. c, 30 l, Boletus pinophilus. d, 50 l, Gyromitra esculenta.

2005
C1219 AP272 Sheet of 4, #a-d 17.00 17.00

AP273

Mail Transport AP274

Designs: 5 l, Charles Lindbergh, PAA emblem. 25 l, Postal rail car, 1920. 30 l, First Honduran postal car, 1914.

50 l, Sikorsky S-38 airplane, PAA emblem, horiz.

2005, Dec. 6 **Litho.** ***Perf. 13¼***
C1220 AP273 5 l multi .65 .65
C1221 AP274 25 l multi 3.00 3.00
C1222 AP274 30 l multi 3.75 3.75
Nos. C1220-C1222 (3) 7.40 7.40

Imperf

Size: 89x64mm

C1223 AP273 50 l multi 6.50 6.50

Nos. C1177-C1179 Surcharged

2005 Litho. *Perf. 13¼*

C1224 AP263 3 l on 2.60 l #C1177 .35 .35
C1225 AP263 15 l on 7.85 l #C1178 1.90 1.90
C1226 AP263 25 l on 7.85 l #C1178 3.50 3.50
C1227 AP263 50 l on 10.65 l #C1179 6.75 6.75
Nos. C1224-C1227 (4) 12.50 12.50

No. C1226 has a thick wavy line obliterator and was issued in sheets of four.

2006 Winter Olympics, Turin — AP275

Skier and: 20 l, Turin Olympics emblem, Olympic rings. 50 l, Olympic rings.

2006, Jan. 24
C1228-C1229 AP275 Set of 2 9.00 9.00

Forgiveness of Honduran Debts by Foreign Nations — AP276

Designs: 14 l, Structure 4, Copán Ruins. 15 l, Flags of nations forgiving debts. 30 l, Honduras Pres. Ricardo Maduro, vert.

2006, Jan. 26
C1230-C1232 AP276 Set of 3 12.50 12.50

Cortés Chamber of Commerce and Industry, 75th Anniv. — AP277

Anniversary and Chamber of Commerce emblem and: 20 l, Gears. 35 l, The Forger, sculpture by J. Zelaya, horiz. 50 l, El Industrial, mural by A. Martínez.

2006
C1233-C1235 AP277 Set of 3 13.00 13.00

Diplomatic Relations Between Honduras and Brazil, Cent. AP278

Designs: 20 l, Flags of Honduras and Brazil. 30 l, Baron of Rio Branco (1845-1912) Brazilian diplomat, vert.

2006 Litho. *Perf. 13¼*
C1236-C1237 AP278 Set of 2 6.50 6.50

Miniature Sheet

Honduran Friendship With Japan — AP279

No. C1238: a, 10 l, Children learning about Chagas disease. b, 15 l, Teacher and children. c, 20 l, Japanese naval vessels and flag. d, 25 l, Sailors in dress uniforms.

2006
C1238 AP279 Sheet of 4, #a-d 7.50 7.50

Nos. C1054, C1124-C1125, C1127-C1128, C1149-C1151, C1159, C1162, C1164, C1166-C1167, C1169-C1170, C1172-C1173 Surcharged

Methods and Perfs As Before

2007 ?

C1239 AP260 2 l on 2.60 l #C1159 .25 .25
C1240 AP260 2 l on 4 l #C1162 .25 .25
C1241 AP249 2 l on 8.65 l #C1128 .25 .25
C1242 AP260 2 l on 10.65 l #C1166 .25 .25
C1243 AP249 3 l on 1.40 l #C1124 .35 .35
C1244 AP257 3 l on 1.40 l #C1149 .35 .35
C1245 AP257 3 l on 2.60 l #C1150 .35 .35
C1246 AP261 3 l on 2.60 l #C1172 .35 .35
C1247 AP257 3 l on 7.30 l #C1151 .35 .35
C1248 AP261 3 l on 10.65 l #C1173 .35 .35
C1249 AP226 3 l on 18.30 l #C1054 .35 .35
C1250 AP261 5 l on 85c #C1169 .55 .55
C1251 AP261 5 l on 1.40 l #C1170 .55 .55
C1252 AP249 5 l on 2.60 l #C1125 .55 .55
C1253 AP249 5 l on 4.30 l #C1127 .55 .55
C1254 AP260 5 l on 4.30 l #C1164 .55 .55
C1255 AP260 5 l on 14.95 l #C1167 .55 .55
Nos. C1239-C1255 (17) 6.75 6.75

Constitution, 25th Anniv. — AP280

Designs: 5 l, Leaders of the Legislative, Executive and Judicial branches of government. 10 l, 1824 Constituent Assembly Building. 15 l, Presidential House, 1922-91, vert. 20 l, Legislative Building.

2007 Litho. *Perf. 13¼*
C1256-C1259 AP280 Set of 4 6.50 6.50

Miniature Sheet

Central Bank of Honduras, 50th Anniv. — AP281

No. C1260 — Central Bank of Honduras emblem and paintings: a, 5 l, Holocausto, by César Rendón. b, 10 l, La Novia, by Miguel Angel Ruiz Matute. c, 15 l, Ayer, Hoy y Mañana, by Felipe Bouchard. d, 20 l, Paisaje de Tegucigalpa, by Mario Castillo. e, 25 l, Dinamismo, by Benigno Gómez. f, 30 l, Guitarras en Descanso, by Dante Lazzaroni.

2007
C1260 AP281 Sheet of 6, #a-f 13.50 13.50

Adjudication of "Four Cardinal Points" Police Torture Case — AP282

2007, Oct. 18 Litho. *Perf. 13¼*
C1261 AP282 50 l multi 9.50 9.50

Printed in sheets of 2.

Miniature Sheets

Launch of Sputnik I, 50th Anniv. — AP283

No. C1262: a, 25 l, Sputnik launch vehicle, pale blue background (30x40mm). b, 35 l, Sputnik I, yellow background (30x40mm). c, 50 l, Sputnik orbiting Earth, pale green background (60x40mm).

No. C1263: a, 25 l, As #C1262a, pale green background. b, 35 l, As #C1262b, pale blue background. c, 50 l, As #C1262c, yellow background.

2007, Nov. 30
C1262 AP283 Sheet of 3, #a-c 14.50 14.50
C1263 AP283 Sheet of 3, #a-c 25.00 25.00

Miniature Sheet

Paintings by Gaye-Darléne Bidart de Satulsky — AP284

No. C1264: a, 3 l, Medusa de las Islas. b, 3 l, Nido de Amor. c, 3 l, Guitarrista Isleño. d, 5 l, "M" Hombre Cruz. e, 5 l, Amor a Martillazos. f, 5 l, Sor María Rosa. g, 5 l, Isleña, Luna y Mar. h, 5 l, Clementina Suárez. i, 5 l, La Naranjera.

2008
C1264 AP284 Sheet of 9, #a-i 7.50 7.50

Miniature Sheet

America Issue — AP285

No. C1265: a, 2 l, Factory workers and sewing machine. b, 3 l, Energy savings mascot. c, 5 l, School children. d, 10 l, Children in native costumes.

2008
C1265 AP285 Sheet of 4, #a-d 3.00 3.00

2008 Summer Olympics, Beijing AP286

Designs: 3 l, Olympic torch. No. C1267, 5 l, Judo. No. C1268, 5 l, Runners. 25 l, Soccer.

2008, July 30
C1266-C1269 AP286 Set of 4 4.00 4.00

Juan Ramón Molina (1875-1908), Poet — AP287

Designs: 10 l, Molina, mermaid and ship. 25 l, Molina.

2008, Oct. 30
C1270-C1271 AP287 Set of 2 4.50 4.50

Miniature Sheet

Treaty of Amity, Commerce and Navigation Between Honduras and Mexico, Cent. — AP288

No. C1272: a, 5 l, Sailor and ship. b, 10 l, Hands, flags and maps. c, 15 l, Handshake, double helix of flags, horiz. d, 20 l, Flags and "100 Años de Amistad." e, 25 l, "100" and colors of flags, horiz. f, 50 l, Parrot and eagle, horiz.

2008 Litho. ***Perf. 13¼***

C1272 AP288 Sheet of 6, #a-f + 3 labels 15.00 15.00

España Normal School, Villa Ahumada, 58th Anniv. AP289

Designs: 2 l, School. 5 l, School emblem.

2009, Aug. 28 Litho. ***Perf. 13¼***

C1273-C1274 AP289 Set of 2 .85 .85

America Issue AP290

Traditional toys and games: 3 l, Hopscotch. 10 l, Kite. 20 l, Top. 50 l, Children playing soccer, jumping rope and flying kite.

2009, Aug. 28

C1275-C1278 AP290 Set of 4 8.75 8.75

President's House AP291

Dove, Map of Honduras AP292

Interim President Roberto Micheletti Baín — AP293

2009, Dec. 3

C1279 AP291 3 l multi .35 .35
C1280 AP292 15 l multi 1.75 1.75
C1281 AP293 20 l multi 2.25 2.25
Nos. C1279-C1281 (3) 4.35 4.35

2010 World Cup Soccer Championships, South Africa — AP294

Designs: 5 l, Child playing soccer. 20 l, Honduras soccer team. 25 l, Emblem of Honduras soccer team.

2009, Dec. 3

C1282-C1284 AP294 Set of 3 6.00 6.00

2010 World Cup Soccer Championships, South Africa — AP295

2010 World Cup emblem, Ficohsa Bank emblem, stadium and flag of: 3 l, Chile. 5 l, Switzerland. 14 l, Spain.

No. C1288, vert.: a, 2010 World Cup emblem, World Cup trophy. b, 2010 World Cup emblem.

2010, May Litho. ***Perf. 13¼***

C1285-C1287 AP295 Set of 3 2.75 2.75

Souvenir Sheet

C1288 AP295 20 l Sheet of 2, #a-b 5.00 5.00

America Issue, National Symbols AP296

Designs: 5 l, Flag and coat of arms of Honduras. 25 l, Odocoileus virginianus. 50 l, Ara macao.

2010, Nov.

C1289-C1291 AP296 Set of 3 13.00 13.00

Maria Auxiliadora Institute, Cent. — AP297

Designs: 10 l, Virgin Mary and Jesus, "100" with hearts replacing zeroes. 50 l, Virgin Mary and Jesus.

2010, Nov.

C1292-C1293 AP297 Set of 2 9.50 9.50

Christmas AP298

Designs: 3 l, Angel and lamb. 20 l, Adoration of the Magi.

50 l, Locomotive with Christmas decorations, horiz.

2010, Nov. ***Perf. 13¼***

C1294-C1295 AP298 Set of 2 2.75 2.75

Imperf

Size: 90x63mm

C1296 AP298 50 l multi 6.25 6.25

Postal Union of the Americas, Spain and Portugal (UPAEP), Cent. — AP299

Designs: 5 l, Mayan sculpture. 25 l, Yum Kax, Mayan agricultural deity.

2011, Mar. 23 ***Perf. 13½x13¼***

C1297-C1298 AP299 Set of 2 4.00 4.00

No. C1142 Surcharged

Method and Perf. As Before

2011, May 2

C1299	Sheet of 4	11.00	11.00
a.	AP254 5 l on 13.65 l #C1142a	2.00	2.00
b.	AP254 5 l on 14.55 l #C1142b	2.00	2.00
c.	AP254 10 l on 15.45 l #C1142c	3.00	3.00
d.	AP254 10 l on 16.65 l #C1142d	3.00	3.00
C1300	Sheet of 4	22.50	22.50
a.	AP254 15 l on 13.65 l #C1142a	4.00	4.00
b.	AP254 15 l on 14.55 l #C1142b	4.00	4.00
c.	AP254 20 l on 15.45 l #C1142c	6.00	6.00
d.	AP254 20 l on 16.65 l #C1142d	6.00	6.00

Inscribed across the stamps of the sheet is the text "Beato Juan Pablo 01/05/2011" on No. C1299 and "Beatificacion 01/05/2011" on No. C1300.

AP300

Diplomatic Relations Between Honduras and South Korea, 50th Anniv. — AP301

Designs: 5 l, Presidents and flags of Honduras and South Korea.

No. C1302: a, Korean vase. b, Mayan calendar. c, Korean statue of Buddha. d, Honduran bowl. e, Korean sundial. f, Mayan stele.

2012, Apr. 25 Litho. ***Perf. 13¼***

C1301 AP300 5 l multi .95 .95

Miniature Sheet

C1302 AP301 2 l Sheet of 6, #a-f 2.00 2.00

National Library and Archives, 132nd Anniv. AP302

Designs: 2 l, Pres. Porfirio Lobo Sosa, Tulio Mariano Gonzales, Minister of Sport, Culture and Art.

No. C1304: a, 8 l, Pres. Marco A. Soto (1846-1908). b, 8 l, Old Mint Building (National Library). c, 8 l, Old Presidential House (National Archives). d, 12 l, Antonio R. Vallejo (1844-1914), founder of National Library and Archives. e, 12 l, Ramón Rosa (1848-93), governmental minister. f, 12 l, Juan Ramón Molina (1875-1908), writer.

2012, Oct. 10

C1303 AP302 2 l multi .40 .40

Miniature Sheet

C1304 AP302 Sheet of 6, #a-f, + 3 labels 6.25 6.25

Blanca Jeannette Kawas (1946-95), Murdered Environmental Activist — AP303

Designs: No. C1305, 20 l, Kawas. No. C1306, 20 l, Kawas, vert.

No. C1307 — Scenes from Blanca Jeannette Kawas National Park: a, 15 l, Beach, denomination in white. b, 15 l, Beach, denomination in black. c, 15 l, Birds on boat. d, 25 l, Buildings on shore. e, 25 l, Aerial view of cove. f, 25 l, River shore and forest.

2013, Feb. 8

C1305-C1306 AP303 Set of 2 4.50 4.50

Miniature Sheet

C1307 AP303 Sheet of 6, #a-f, + 3 labels 13.00 13.00

Wildlife Conservation — AP304

Designs: No. C1308, 5 l, Río Cangrejal. No. C1309, 5 l, Iguana iguana. 8 l, Amanita caesarea. vert. No. C1311, 10 l, Isla de El Tigre. No. C1312, 10 l, Bothriechis schlegelii. 15 l, Athene cunicularia. 30 l, Siproeta stelenes. 50 l, Amazilia luciae.

2014, June Litho. ***Perf. 13½***

C1308-C1315 AP304 Set of 8 16.00 16.00

Christmas AP305

Designs: 5 l, Ribbon and star. 25 l, Angel, lamb and Holy Family, vert. 30 l, Candles and poinsettias, vert.

2014, Oct. 15 Litho. ***Perf. 13½***

C1316-C1318 AP305 Set of 3 6.75 6.75

Convention on the Rights of the Child, 25th Anniv. AP306

Designs: 2 l, Child, facing left. 5 l, Clock face. 10 l, Child, facing right chin on knees. 15 l, Child, head on knees with hand up. 35 l, Child, facing forward. 40 l, Whole clock.

2014, Nov. 25 Litho. *Perf. 13½*
C1319-C1324 AP306 Set of 6 12.00 12.00

Alfredo Hawit Banegas, 2011-2012 President of CONCACAF, and CONCACAF Emblem — AP307

2014, Dec. 1 Litho. *Perf. 13½*
C1325 AP307 10 l multi .95 .95

San Fernando de Omoa Fortress — AP308

Designs: 5 l, Coat of Arms of King Ferdinand VI. 10 l, King Ferdinand VI of Spain. 25 l, Fortress, horiz. 50 l, Ship and fortress, horiz.

2015, Jan. 20 Litho. *Perf. 13½*
C1326-C1329 AP308 Set of 4 8.75 8.75

Cooperation Between Japan and Central American Integration System Countries — AP309

Designs: No. C1330, 2 l, Emblem, flag of Japan, schools and children. No. C1331, 2 l, Emblem, flag of Japan, Japanese volunteer with baby. No. C1332, 5 l, Emblem, flag of Japan, public works projects. No. C1333, 5 l, Emblem, flags of Japan and Honduras, Japanese and Honduran foods. No. C1334, 10 l, Flags of Japan and Honduras, Friendship Bridge. No. C1335, 10 l, Flags of Japan and Honduras, El Puente Archaeological Park. 15 l, Emblem, flags of Japan and Honduras, judokas. 50 l, Emblem.

2015, Feb. 9 Litho. *Perf. 13½*
C1330-C1337 AP309 Set of 8 9.25 9.25

Environmental Protection AP310

Designs: No. C1338, 5 l, Miner at El Mochito mine. No. C1339, 5 l, Cuero y Salado Wildlife Refuge. No. C1340, 5 l, Light bulb. No. C1341, 5 l, Amazilia luciae. No. C1342, 10 l, Jepidochelys olivacea. No. C1343, 10 l, Stream in Nombre de Dios National Park. No. C1344, 10 l, Forest in Merendón Mountains. No. C1345, 10 l, Sky and forest in Merendón Mountains.

2015, Apr. 10 Litho. *Perf. 13½*
C1338-C1345 AP310 Set of 8 5.50 5.50

Peruvian People and Places AP311

Designs: No. C1346, 5 l, César Vallejo (1892-1938), poet. No. C1347, 5 l, Chabuca Granda (1920-83), singer. No. C1348, 5 l, Enrique Zileri (1931-2014), magazine publisher, vert. No. C1349, 10 l, Machu Picchu, vert. No. C1350, 10 l, Andrés Townsend (1915-94), novelist and politician, vert. 15 l, Túpac Amaru II (1738-81), leader of indigenous people's uprising, vert. 25 l, José Luis Bustamente y Rivero (1894-1989), president of Peru, vert. 35 l, Miguel Grau (1834-79), Peruvian admiral, vert.

2015, May 29 Litho. *Perf. 13¼*
C1346-C1353 AP311 Set of 8 10.00 10.00

AP312

Interamerican Commission on Sustainable Development AP313

Designs: No. C1354, Wind generators. No. C1355, Reservoir. 10 l, Farmers in field. 25 l, Shell.

2015 Litho. *Perf. 13¼*

C1354	AP312	5 l multi	.45	.45
C1355	AP312	5 l multi	.45	.45
C1356	AP312	10 l multi	.90	.90
C1357	AP313	25 l multi	2.25	2.25
	Nos. C1354-C1357 (4)		4.05	4.05

AP314

Knights of the Holy Sepulchre in Tegucigalpa, 50th Anniv. — AP315

Designs: No. C1358, Religious procession. No. C1359, Crucifixion icon. No. C1360, Religious procession, diff. No. C1361, Knights wearing suits. No. C1362, Head of Jesus icon. 15 l, Religious procession and crowd. 25 l, Emblem.

2016, Apr. 15 Litho. *Perf. 13¼*

C1358	AP314	5 l multi	.45	.45
C1359	AP315	5 l multi	.45	.45
C1360	AP314	10 l multi	.90	.90
C1361	AP314	10 l multi	.90	.90
C1362	AP315	10 l multi	.90	.90
C1363	AP315	15 l multi	1.40	1.40
C1364	AP315	25 l multi	2.25	2.25
	Nos. C1358-C1364 (7)		7.25	7.25

Honduran Postal Service AP316

Designs: 2 l, Honducor emblem, post office interior. No. C1366, 5 l, EMS Honduras emblem. No. C1367, 5 l, Honducor emblem, post office and mail delivery vehicle. No. C1368, 10 l, Honducor emblem. No. C1369, 10 l, ExportaFácil emblem. 15 l, Honducor emblem, post office, mail delivery vehicle and postal worker delivering package.

2016, Apr. 26 Litho. *Perf. 13¼*
C1365-C1370 AP316 Set of 6 4.25 4.25

Tourism AP317

Tourism emblem and: No. C1371, 5 l, Sculpture of head, Ciudad Blanca. No. C1372, 5 l, Fisherman, Lago de Yojoa. No. C1373, 5 l, Cacao pods. No. C1374, 5 l, Coffee berries. No. C1375, 5 l, Pico Bonito zip line, vert. No. C1376, 10 l, Church, Comayagua. No. C1377, 10 l, Los Naranjos Park, vert. No. C1378, 10 l, Person near Pulhapanzak Waterfall, vert. No. C1379, 10 l, "Somos tierra, somos mar, somos gente, somos corazón, somos Honduras," vert. No. C1380, 15 l, Turtle in water, Guanaja Island. No. C1381, 15 l, Emblem for Kaha Kamasa archaeological site, Ciudad Blanca, vert. 25 l, Sculpture, Copán archaeological site.

2016, June 28 Litho. *Perf. 13¼*
C1371-C1382 AP317 Set of 12 10.50 10.50

Honduras Bar Association, Cent. — AP318

2016, Aug. 9 Litho. *Perf. 13¼*
C1383 AP318 25 l blk & ochre 2.25 2.25

Francisco Morazán University, 60th Anniv. AP319

60th anniv. emblem and: No. C1384, 10 l, Arts and culture. No. C1385, 10 l, Sports. No. C1386, 10 l, University emblem and National Pedagogical University emblem, vert. No. C1387, 15 l, National Pedagogical University Building. No. C1388, 15 l, Morazán (1792-1842), President of Honduras, book and butterflies. 25 l, Morazán, hands, flag of Honduras, vert.

2016, Nov. 4 Litho. *Perf. 13¼*
C1384-C1389 AP319 Set of 6 7.50 7.50

AP320

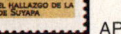

AP321

Archdiocese of Tegucigalpa, Cent. — AP322

Designs: No. C1390, Religious procession with statue of Virgin Mary. No. C1391, President of the Republic of China in Cathedral with Archbishop and others. No. C1392, Religious procession with statue of Crucifixion. No. C1393, Bishops of Tegucigalpa from 1916-2016, vert. No. C1394, Oscar Cardinal Rodríguez and Pope Francis, vert. No. C1395, Virgin of Suyapa, 270th anniv. of discovery, vert. 15 l, Basilica of Our Lady of Suyapa. 25 l, Cathedral retable depicting St. Michael, vert. 50 l, Angel, Basilica, chalice and host.

2017, Apr. 8 Litho. *Perf. 13¼*

C1390	AP320	5 l multi	.45	.45
C1391	AP320	5 l multi	.45	.45
C1392	AP320	5 l multi	.45	.45
C1393	AP320	10 l multi	.85	.85
C1394	AP320	10 l multi	.85	.85
C1395	AP321	10 l multi	.85	.85
C1396	AP320	15 l multi	1.40	1.40
C1397	AP320	25 l multi	2.25	2.25
C1398	AP322	50 l multi	4.25	4.25
	Nos. C1390-C1398 (9)		11.80	11.80

Bonn Challenge AP323

Designs: 10 l, Motagua River and Bonn Challenge emblem. 25 l, Bonn Challenge emblem.

2017, June 7 Litho. *Perf. 13½*
C1399-C1400 AP323 Set of 2 3.00 3.00

National Electrical Power Company, 60th Anniv. AP324

Designs: 2 l, Patuca III Power Plant. No. C1402, 5 l, San Nicolas Substation. No. C1403, 5 l, Cañaveral Hydroelectric Project. 8 l, Amarateca Substation. No. C1405, 10 l, 60th anniversary emblem and building. No. C1406, 10 l, Worker fixing street lamp, vert. No. C1407, 10 l, Workers fixing transmission lines, vert. 15 l, El Cajón Dam. 25 l, People examining fluorescent light bulb. 50 l, 60th anniversary emblem, wind generators, houses, transmission towers.

2017, July 28 Litho. *Perf. 13½*
C1401-C1410 AP324 Set of 10 12.00 12.00

AIR POST SEMI-POSTAL STAMPS

No. C13C Surcharged in Black

Unwmk.

1929, June 5 Engr. *Perf. 12*

CB1 AP1 50c + 5c carmine .65 .30
CB2 AP1 50c + 10c carmine .70 .35
CB3 AP1 50c + 15c carmine .95 .55
CB4 AP1 50c + 20c carmine 1.40 .75
Nos. CB1-CB4 (4) 3.70 1.95

Catalogue values for unused stamps in this section, from this point to the end of the section, are for Never Hinged items.

Souvenir Sheet

Airmail Pilot Sumner B. Morgan and Airplane — SP2

2000, July 7

CB5 SP2 50 l + 5 l multi 18.00 18.00

First airmail flight in Honduras, 75th anniv., EXFILHON 2000. See Nos. C1075-C1077.

No. C619 Surcharged With New Value in Black and 2000 Sydney Olympics Emblem in Red

2000, Sept. 13 Litho. *Imperf.*

CB6 AP99 48.50 l +1.50 l multi 24.00 15.00

AIR POST SPECIAL DELIVERY STAMPS

No. CO52 Surcharged in Red

Perf. 13½x14

1953, Dec. 8 Engr. Unwmk.

CE1 AP65 20c on 1c 3.00 1.50

Transport Plane APSD1

1956, Oct. 3 *Perf. 13x12½*

CE2 APSD1 20c black & red .80 .50

Surcharges on No. CE2 (see Nos. C421, C477) eliminate its special delivery character.

Catalogue values for unused stamps in this section, from this point to the end of the section, are for Never Hinged items.

Stamp Centenary Type of Air Post Issue

Design: 20c, Mailman on motorcycle.

1966, May 31 Litho. *Perf. 14x14½*

CE3 AP81 20c bis brn, brn & gold 1.00 .50

Centenary (in 1965) of the first Honduran postage stamp.

The "HABILITADO" overprint on No. CE3 (see No. C479) eliminates its special delivery character.

Independence Type of Air Post Issue

1972, May 19 Litho. *Perf. 13*

CE4 AP89 20c Corsair plane .70 .35

No. CE4 Surcharged

1975

CE5 AP89 60c on 20c 2.00 .85

Forest Protection Type of Air Post

1976, May 28 Litho. *Perf. 13½*

CE6 AP96 60c Stag in forest 1.00 .55

AIR POST OFFICIAL STAMPS

Official Stamps Nos. O78 to O81 Overprinted in Red, Green or Black

1930 *Perf. 11, 11½*

CO1 A24 10c deep blue (R) 1.25 1.25
CO2 A24 20c yellow brown 1.25 1.25
a. Vert. pair, imperf. btwn. 14.00
CO3 A24 50c vermilion (Bk) 1.40 1.40
CO4 A24 1p emerald (R) 1.25 1.25
Nos. CO1-CO4 (4) 5.15 5.15

No. O77 Surcharged in Green

CO5 A24 5c on 6c red vio 1.00 1.00
a. "1910" for "1930" 2.75 2.75
b. "1920" for "1930" 2.75 2.75

The overprint exists in other colors and on other denominations but the status of these is questioned.

Official Stamps of 1931 Overprinted

1931 Unwmk. *Perf. 12*

CO6 O2 1c ultra .35 .35
CO7 O2 2c black brown .85 .85
CO8 O2 5c olive gray 1.00 1.00
CO9 O2 6c orange red 1.00 1.00
a. Inverted overprint 24.00 24.00
CO10 O2 10c dark green 1.25 1.25
CO11 O2 15c olive brown 2.00 1.75
a. Inverted overprint 20.00 20.00
CO12 O2 20c red brown 2.00 1.75
CO13 O2 50c gray violet 1.40 1.40
CO14 O2 1p deep orange 2.00 1.75
Nos. CO6-CO14 (9) 11.85 11.10

In the setting of the overprint there are numerous errors in the spelling and punctuation, letters omitted and similar varieties.

This set is known with blue overprint. A similar overprint is known in larger type, but its status has not been fully determined.

Postage Stamps of 1918-30 Surcharged Type "a" or Type "b" (#CO22-CO23) in Green, Black, Red and Blue

a

b

1933 Wmk. 209, Unwmk.

CO15 A39 20c on 2c #295 (G) 3.25 3.25
CO16 A39 20c on 2c #296 (G) 3.25 3.25
CO17 A39 20c on 2c #297 (G) 3.25 3.25
CO17A A39 40c on 2c #295 2.00 2.00
CO18 A39 40c on 2c #297 (G) 7.00 7.00
CO18A A39 40c on 2c #297 4.25 4.25
CO19 A28 40c on 5c #246 4.25 4.25
CO19A A28 40c on 5c #247 7.00 7.00
CO20 A28 40c on 5c #266 15.00 15.00
CO20A A28 40c on 5c #267 9.00 9.00
CO20B A28 40c on 5c #267 (R) 14.00 14.00
CO21 A20 70c on 5c #183 3.00 3.00
CO22 A24 70c on 10c #214 (R) 3.25 3.25
CO23 A22 1 l on 20c #191 (Bl) 3.25 3.25
CO24 A24 1 l on 50c #216 (Bl) 14.00 14.00
CO25 A22 1.20 l on 1p #193 (Bl) 1.00 1.00
Nos. CO15-CO25 (16) 96.75 96.75

Official Stamps of 1915-29 Surcharged Type "a" or Type "b" (#CO28-CO29, CO33-CO41, CO43) in Black, Red, Green, Orange, Carmine or Blue

CO26 O1 40c on 5c #O84 (Bk) 1.00 1.00
CO27 O1 40c on 5c #O84 (R) 25.00 25.00
CO28 A24 60c on 6c #O77 (Bk) .70 .70
CO29 A24 60c on 6c #O77 (G) 25.00 25.00
CO30 A20 70c on 5c #O60 (Bk) 5.25 5.25
CO31 A19 70c on 10c #O62 (R) 9.00 9.00
CO32 A19 70c on 10c #O62 (Bk) 7.75 7.75
CO33 A22 70c on 10c #O70 (R) 4.50 4.00
CO34 A24 70c on 10c #O78 (O) 3.50 3.50
CO35 A24 70c on 10c #O78 (C) 4.50 4.50
CO36 A22 70c on 15c #O71 (R) 87.50 87.50
CO37 A22 90c on 10c #O70 (R) 5.25 5.25
CO38 A22 90c on 15c #O71 (R) 8.00 8.00
CO38A A24 1 l on 2c #O76 1.40 1.40
CO39 A22 1 l on 20c #O72 2.50 2.50
CO39A A24 1 l on 20c #O79 3.75 3.75
CO40 A22 1 l on 50c #O73 1.90 1.90
CO41 A24 1 l on 50c #O80 4.25 4.25
CO42 A20 1.20 l on 1p #O65 9.00 7.00
CO43 A24 1.20 l on 1p #O81 3.00 3.00
Nos. CO26-CO43 (20) 212.75 210.25

Varieties of foregoing surcharges exist.

Merchant Flag and Seal of Honduras OA2

1939, Feb. 27 Unwmk. *Perf. 12½*

CO44 OA2 2c dp blue & grn .25 .25
CO45 OA2 5c dp blue & org .25 .25
CO46 OA2 8c dp blue & brn .25 .25
CO47 OA2 15c dp blue & car .30 .25
CO48 OA2 46c dp blue & ol grn .40 .30
CO49 OA2 50c dp blue & vio .50 .30
CO50 OA2 1 l dp blue & red brn 1.75 1.25
CO51 OA2 2 l dp blue & red org 3.75 2.25
Nos. CO44-CO51 (8) 7.45 5.10

For overprints and surcharges see Nos. C101-C117.

Types of Air Post Stamps of 1952 Ovptd. in Red

Perf. 13½x14, 14x13½

1952 Engr. Unwmk.

CO52 AP65 1c rose lil & ol .25 .25
CO53 AP65 2c brown & vio .25 .25
CO54 AP65 8c dp car & blk .25 .25
CO55 AP66 16c pur & dk grn .25 .25
CO56 AP65 30c dk bl & blk .50 .50
CO57 AP65 1 l dk grn & dk brown 1.75 1.75
CO58 AP65 2 l bl & red brn 3.50 3.50
CO59 AP66 5 l red org & blk 8.50 8.50
Nos. CO52-CO59 (8) 15.25 15.25

Queen Isabella I of Spain, 500th birth anniv.

For overprints and surcharge, see Nos. CE1, CO110.

No. C222 and Types of Air Post Stamps of 1953 Overprinted in Red

Engraved; Center of 1c Litho.

1953, Dec. 18 *Perf. 12½*

Frames in Black

CO60 AP67 1c ultra & vio bl .25 .25
CO61 AP97 2c dp blue grn .25 .25
CO62 AP67 3c orange .25 .25
CO63 AP67 5c dp carmine .25 .25
CO64 AP67 15c dk brown .25 .25
CO65 AP67 30c purple .45 .35
CO66 AP67 1 l olive gray 4.00 2.25
CO67 AP67 2 l lilac rose 5.00 3.00
CO68 AP67 5 l ultra 11.50 7.00
Nos. CO60-CO68 (9) 22.20 13.85

Issued to honor the United Nations.

Types of Air Post Stamps Overprinted in Red

Engraved; 8c Lithographed

1956, Oct. 3 *Perf. 13x12½*

CO69 AP68 1c blk & brn car .25 .25
CO70 AP69 2c black & mag .25 .25
CO71 AP68 3c blk & rose vio .25 .25
CO72 AP69 4c black & org .25 .25
CO73 AP69 5c black & bl grn .25 .25
CO74 AP68 8c violet & multi .25 .25
CO75 AP68 10c blk & red brn .25 .25
CO76 AP68 12c blk & car rose .25 .25
CO77 AP68 15c carmine & blk .25 .25
CO78 AP68 20c black & ol brn .25 .25
CO79 AP69 24c black & blue .25 .25
CO80 AP68 25c blk & rose vio .25 .25
CO81 AP68 30c black & grn .25 .25
CO82 AP68 40c blk & red org .25 .25
CO83 AP69 50c blk & brn red .30 .30
CO84 AP68 60c blk & rose vio .40 .40
CO85 AP68 1 l black & brn 1.40 1.10
CO86 AP69 2 l black & dk bl 2.75 2.25
CO87 AP69 5 l black & vio bl 5.75 5.25
Nos. CO69-CO87 (19) 14.10 12.80

Nos. C269-C278 Overprinted Vertically in Red (Horizontally on Nos. CO89 and CO91)

1957, Oct. 21 Litho. *Perf. 13*

Frames in Black

CO88 AP70 1c buff & aqua .25 .25
CO89 AP70 2c org, pur & emer .25 .25
CO90 AP70 5c pink & ultra .25 .25
a. Inverted overprint

CO91 AP70 8c orange, vio & ol .25 .25
CO92 AP70 10c violet & brn .25 .25
CO93 AP70 12c lt grn & ultra .25 .25
CO94 AP70 15c green & brn .25 .25
CO95 AP70 30c pink & sl .55 .25
CO96 AP70 1 l blue & brn 1.40 1.00
CO97 AP70 2 l lt grn & sl 2.75 2.25
Nos. CO88-CO97 (10) 6.45 5.25

Types of Lincoln Air Post Stamps 1959 Overprinted in Red

1959 Engr. *Perf. 13½*
Flags in National Colors

CO98 AP72 1c ocher .25 .25
CO99 AP73 2c gray olive .25 .25
a. Inverted overprint
CO100 AP73 3c red brown .25 .25
CO101 AP73 5c ultra .25 .25
CO102 AP73 10c dull purple .25 .25
a. Overprint omitted
CO103 AP73 12c red orange .25 .25
CO104 AP72 15c dark brown .25 .25
CO105 AP73 25c black .25 .25
CO106 AP73 50c dark car .30 .25
CO107 AP73 1 l purple .75 .65
CO108 AP73 2 l dark blue 1.40 1.10
a. Min. sheet of 6, 2c, 5c, 12c, 15c, 50c, 2 l, imperf. 3.00 3.00
CO109 AP73 5 l green 4.50 3.75
Nos. CO98-CO109 (12) 8.95 7.75

Catalogue values for unused stamps in this section, from this point to the end of the section, are for Never Hinged items.

No. CO55 Overprinted: "IN MEMORIAM / Sir Winston / Churchill / 1874-1965"

1965, Dec. 20 *Perf. 14x13½*
CO110 AP66 16c purple & dk grn 1.00 1.00

See note after No. C379.

Nos. C336-C344 Ovptd. in Red

1965 Photo. *Perf. 14*
Black Design and Inscription

CO111 AP76 1c yellow green .25 .25
CO112 AP76 2c pale rose lil .25 .25
CO113 AP76 5c light ultra .25 .25
CO114 AP76 8c bluish grn .25 .25
CO115 AP76 10c buff .30 .30
CO116 AP76 12c lemon .35 .35
CO117 AP76 1 l light ocher 4.00 4.00
CO118 AP76 2 l pale ol grn 8.75 8.75
CO119 AP76 3 l rose 11.00 11.00
Nos. CO111-CO119 (9) 25.40 25.40

OFFICIAL STAMPS

Type of Regular Issue of 1890 Overprinted in Red

1890 Unwmk. *Perf. 12*
O1 A5 1c pale yellow .25
O2 A5 2c pale yellow .25
O3 A5 5c pale yellow .25
O4 A5 10c pale yellow .25
O5 A5 20c pale yellow .25
O6 A5 25c pale yellow .25
O7 A5 30c pale yellow .25
O8 A5 40c pale yellow .25
O9 A5 50c pale yellow .25
O10 A5 75c pale yellow .25
O11 A5 1p pale yellow .25
Nos. O1-O11 (11) 2.75

Type of Regular Issue of 1891 Overprinted in Red

1891
O12 A6 1c yellow .25
O13 A6 2c yellow .25
O14 A6 5c yellow .25
O15 A6 10c yellow .25
O16 A6 20c yellow .25
O17 A6 25c yellow .25
O18 A6 30c yellow .25
O19 A6 40c yellow .25
O20 A6 50c yellow .25
O21 A6 75c yellow .25
O22 A6 1p yellow .25
Nos. O12-O22 (11) 2.75

Nos. O1 to O22 were never placed in use. Cancellations were applied to remainders. They exist with overprint inverted, double, triple and omitted; also, imperf. and part perf.

Regular Issue of 1898 Overprinted

1898-99 *Perf. 11½*
O23 A12 5c dl ultra .40
O24 A12 10c dark bl .80
O25 A12 20c dull org 1.25
O26 A12 50c org red 2.40
O27 A12 1p blue grn 3.00
Nos. O23-O27 (5) 7.85

Counterfeits of basic stamps and of overprint exist.

Regular Issue of 1911 Overprinted

1911-15 *Perf. 12, 14*
Carmine Overprint

O28 A15 1c violet 1.50 .65
a. Inverted overprint 2.40 2.40
b. Double overprint 2.00
O29 A15 6c ultra 2.50 2.00
a. Inverted overprint 2.75 2.75
O30 A15 10c blue 1.50 1.25
a. "OFICAIL" 2.50
b. Double overprint 3.50
O31 A15 20c yellow 15.00 12.00
O32 A15 50c brown 8.00 7.00
O33 A15 1p ol grn 12.00 10.00
Nos. O28-O33 (6) 40.50 32.90

Black Overprint

O34 A15 2c green 1.00 .70
a. "CIFICIAL" 5.00
O35 A15 5c carmine 1.50 1.00
a. Perf. 12 7.50 5.00
O36 A15 6c ultra 4.50 4.50
O37 A15 10c blue 4.00 4.00
O38 A15 20c yellow 5.00 5.00
O39 A15 50c brown 5.50 4.00
Nos. O34-O39 (6) 21.50 19.20

Counterfeits of overprint of Nos. O28-O39 exist.

With Additional Surcharge

1913-14
O40 A15 1c on 5c car 1.75 1.50
O41 A15 2c on 5c car 2.00 1.50
O42 A15 10c on 1c vio 4.00 3.50
a. "OFICIAL" inverted 7.50
O43 A15 20c on 1c vio 3.00 2.50
Nos. O40-O43 (4) 10.75 9.00

On No. O40 the surcharge reads "1 cent." Nos. O40-O43 exist with double surcharge.

No. O43 Surcharged Vertically in Black, Yellow or Maroon

1914
O44 A15 10c on 20c on 1c 20.00 20.00
a. Maroon surcharge 20.00 20.00
O45 A15 10c on 20c on 1c (Y) 40.00 40.00

No. O35 Surcharged

1915
O46 A15 10c on 5c car *20.00 20.00*

No. O39 Surcharged

O47 A15 20c on 50c brn 5.00 5.00

Regular Issues of 1913-14 Overprinted in Red or Black

1915 *Perf. 11½*
O48 A17 1c brn (R) .40 .40
a. "OFICAIL" 5.00
O49 A17 2c car (Bk) .40 .40
a. "OFICAIL" 5.00
b. Double overprint 4.00
O50 A18 5c ultra (Bk) .45 .45
a. "OFIC" 4.00
O51 A18 5c ultra (R) 1.00 1.00
a. "OFIC"
b. "OFICAIL" 5.00
O52 A18 6c pur (Bk) 1.50 1.50
a. 6c red lil (Bk)
O53 A17 10c brn (Bk) 1.25 1.25
O54 A17 20c brn (Bk) 3.00 3.00
O55 A17 20c brn (R) 3.00 3.00
a. Double overprint (R+Bk) 10.00
b. "OFICAIL" 5.00
O56 A18 50c rose (Bk) 6.00 6.00
Nos. O48-O56 (9) 17.00 17.00

The 10c blue has the overprint "OFICIAL" in different type from the other stamps of the series. It is stated that forty stamps were overprinted for the Postmaster General but the stamp was never put in use or on sale at the post office.

No. 152 Surcharged

O57 A17 1c on 2c car 2.00 2.00
a. "0.10" for "0.01" 4.25 4.25
b. "0.20" for "0.01" 4.25 4.25
c. Double surcharge 8.50 8.50
d. As "a," double surcharge 77.50
e. As "b," double surcharge 77.50

Regular Issue of 1915-16 Overprinted in Black or Red

1915-16
O58 A19 1c choc (Bk) .25 .25
O59 A19 2c car (Bk) .25 .25
a. Tête bêche pair 1.25 1.25
b. Double overprint 2.00
c. Double overprint, one inverted 2.00
d. "b" and "c" in tête bêche pair
O60 A20 5c brt blue (R) .30 .30
a. Inverted overprint 3.00
O61 A20 6c deep pur (R) .40 .40
a. Black overprint 3.00
b. Inverted overprint 2.00 2.00
O62 A19 10c dl bl (R) .40 .40
O63 A19 20c red brn (Bk) .60 .60
a. Tête bêche pair 2.50
O64 A20 50c red (Bk) 1.75 1.75
O65 A20 1p yel grn (C) 3.75 3.75
Nos. O58-O65 (8) 7.70 7.70

The 6c, 10c and 1p exist imperf.

Regular Issue of 1919 Overprinted

1921
O66 A22 1c brown *2.25 2.25*
a. Inverted overprint 3.00 3.00
O67 A22 2c carmine *6.50 6.50*
a. Inverted overprint 3.00 3.00
O68 A22 5c lilac rose *6.50 6.50*
a. Inverted overprint 3.00
O69 A22 6c brt vio .50 .50
a. Inverted overprint
O70 A22 10c dull blue .60 .60
a. Double overprint
O71 A22 15c light blue .70 .70
a. Inverted overprint 2.00
b. Double ovpt., one inverted 4.00
O72 A22 20c brown 1.00 1.00
O73 A22 50c light brown 1.50 1.50
O74 A22 1p yellow green 3.00 3.00
Nos. O66-O74 (9) 22.55 22.55

Regular Issue of 1924 Overprinted

1924 *Perf. 11, 11½*
O75 A24 1c olive brn .25 .25
O76 A24 2c deep rose .25 .25
O77 A24 6c red vio .30 .30
O78 A24 10c deep bl .45 .45
O79 A24 20c yel brn .60 .60
O80 A24 50c vermilion 1.25 1.25
O81 A24 1p emerald 2.00 2.00
Nos. O75-O81 (7) 5.10 5.10

J. C. del Valle — O1

Designs: 2c, J. R. Molina. 5c, Coffee tree. 10c, J. T. Reyes. 20c, Tegucigalpa Cathedral. 50c, San Lorenzo Creek. 1p, Radio station.

1929 Litho. Wmk. 209 *Perf. 11½*
O82 O1 1c blue .25 .25
O83 O1 2c carmine .25 .25
a. 2c rose .25 .25
O84 O1 5c purple .35 .35
O85 O1 10c emerald .50 .35
O86 O1 20c dk bl .60 .60
O87 O1 50c org, grn & bl 1.00 1.00
O88 O1 1p buff 1.75 1.75
Nos. O82-O88 (7) 4.70 4.55

Nos. O82-O88 exist imperf.

For overprints and surcharges see Nos. 282, 284, C37-C40, C59, C62-C63, CO26-CO27.

View of Tegucigalpa O2

1931 Unwmk. Engr. *Perf. 12*

O89 O2 1c ultra .30 .25
O90 O2 2c black brn .30 .25
O91 O2 5c olive gray .35 .25
O92 O2 6c orange red .40 .30
O93 O2 10c dark green .50 .35
O94 O2 15c olive brn .65 .40
O95 O2 20c red brown .75 .50
O96 O2 50c gray vio 1.00 .65
O97 O2 1p dp orange 1.75 1.75
Nos. O89-O97 (9) 6.00 4.70

For overprints see Nos. CO6-CO14, O98-O105.

Official Stamps of 1931 Overprinted in Black

1936-37

O98 O2 1c ultra .25 .25
O99 O2 2c black brn .25 .25
a. Inverted overprint 10.00
O100 O2 5c olive gray .30 .30
O101 O2 6c red orange .40 .40
O102 O2 10c dark green .40 .40
O103 O2 15c olive brown .50 .50
a. Inverted overprint 5.00
O104 O2 20c red brown 1.00 1.00
a. "1938-1935" —
O105 O2 50c gray violet 4.00 3.00
Nos. O98-O105 (8) 7.10 6.10

Double overprints exist on 1c and 2c. No. O97 with this overprint is fraudulent.

POSTAL TAX STAMPS

Red Cross — PT1

Engr.; Cross Litho.

1941, Aug. 1 Unwmk. *Perf. 12*

RA1 PT1 1c blue & carmine .25 .25

Obligatory on all domestic or foreign mail, the tax to be used by the Honduran Red Cross.

Francisco Morazán — PT2

1941, Aug. 1 Engr.

RA2 PT2 1c copper brown .40 .25

Francisco Morazan, 100th anniv. of death.

Mother and Child — PT3

1945 Engr.; Cross Litho.

RA3 PT3 1c ol brn, car & bl .25 .25

The tax was for the Honduran Red Cross.

Similar to Type of 1945

Large Red Cross

1950

RA4 PT3 1c olive brn & red .25 .25

The tax was for the Honduran Red Cross.

Henri Dunant — PT4

1959 *Perf. 13x13½*

RA5 PT4 1c blue & red .25 .25

The tax was for the Red Cross.

Catalogue values for unused stamps in this section, from this point to the end of the section, are for Never Hinged items.

Henri Dunant — PT5

No. RA7, as PT5, but redrawn; country name panel at bottom, value at right, "El poder . . ." at top.

1964, Dec. 15 Litho. *Perf. 11*

RA6 PT5 1c brt grn & red .25 .25
RA7 PT5 1c brown & red .25 .25

The tax was for the Red Cross.

Nurse and Patient — PT6

1969, June Litho. *Perf. 13½*

RA8 PT6 1c light blue & red .25 .25

The tax was for the Red Cross.

For surcharges see Nos. 387-391, C1199, C1201-C1202, C1205-C1206.

HONG KONG

'hän̩,kän̩

LOCATION — A peninsula and island in southeast China at the mouth of the Canton River

GOVT. — Special Administrative Area of China (PRC) (as of 7/1/97)

AREA — 426 sq. mi.

POP. — 6,847,125 (1999 est.)

CAPITAL — Victoria

100 Cents = 1 Dollar

Catalogue values for unused stamps in this country are for Never Hinged items, beginning with Scott 174 in the regular postage section, Scott B1 in the semi-postal section and Scott J13 in the postage due section.

Watermark

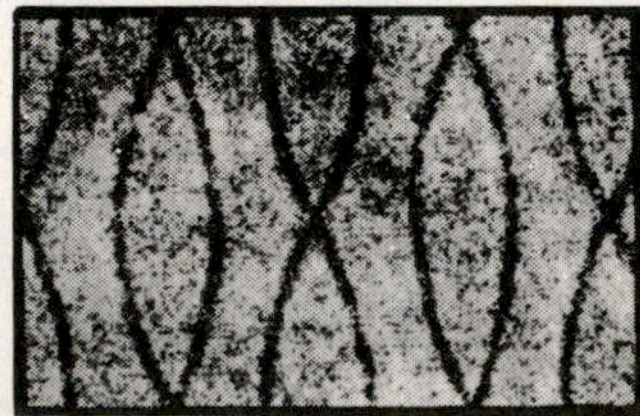

Wmk. 340

Values for unused stamps are for examples with original gum as defined in the catalogue introduction. Very fine examples of Nos. 1-25, 29-48, 61-66d and 69-70a will have perforations touching the design on at least one side due to the narrow spacing of the stamps on the plates. Stamps with perfs clear of the design on all four sides are scarce and will command higher prices.

Queen Victoria — A1

Unwmk.

1862, Dec. 8 Typo. *Perf. 14*

1 A1 2c pale brown 500.00 110.00
a. 2c deep brown 675.00 160.00
2 A1 8c buff 725.00 80.00
3 A1 12c blue 625.00 55.00
4 A1 18c lilac 625.00 50.00
5 A1 24c green 1,000. 110.00
6 A1 48c rose 2,600. 325.00
7 A1 96c gray 3,500. 400.00

1863-80 Wmk. 1

8 A1 2c brn ('65) 120.00 7.75
a. 2c deep brown ('64) 325.00 32.50
9 A1 2c dull rose ('80) 225.00 37.50
a. 2c rose 250.00 32.50
10 A1 4c slate 110.00 8.75
a. 4c greenish grey 325.00 45.00
b. 4c bluish slate 450.00 25.00
11 A1 5c ultra ('80) 775.00 52.50
12 A1 6c lilac 425.00 17.50
a. 6c violet 625.00 18.00
13 A1 8c org buff ('65) 525.00 12.50
a. 8c bright orange 450.00 15.00
b. 8c brownish orange 475.00 15.00
14 A1 10c violet ('80) 825.00 17.00
15 A1 12c light blue 30.00 8.00
a. 12c light greenish blue 1,100. 37.50
b. 12c deep blue 275.00 13.00
16 A1 16c yel ('77) 1,750. 62.50
17 A1 18c lilac ('66) 6,750. 275.00
18 A1 24c grn ('65) 575.00 11.00
a. 24c deep green 1,250. 32.50
19 A1 30c vermilion 1,000. 14.50
20 A1 30c violet ('71) 250.00 5.00
21 A1 48c rose car 900.00 30.00
22 A1 48c brn ('80) 1,200. 100.00
23 A1 96c bis ('65) *77,500.* 725.00
24 A1 96c gray ('66) 1,300. 62.50

Imperfs. are plate proofs.

1874 *Perf. 12½*

25 A1 4c slate 11,000. 250.00

See Nos. 36-49. For surcharges or overprints on stamps of type A1 see Nos. 29-35B, 51-56, 61-66, 69-70.

A2

A3

A4

1874 Engr. Wmk. 1 *Perf. 15½x15*

26 A2 $2 sage green 375.00 67.50
27 A3 $3 violet 350.00 52.50
28 A4 $10 rose 7,750. 675.00

Nos. 26-28 are revenues which were used postally. Used values are for postally canceled examples. Black "Paid All" cancels are fiscal usage.

See Nos. 57-59. For surcharges see Nos. 50, 67. For type surcharged see No. 60.

Nos. 17 and 20 Surcharged in Black

1876 *Perf. 14*

29 A1 16c on 18c lilac 1,850. 140.00
30 A1 28c on 30c violet 1,300. 47.50

Stamps of 1863-80 Surcharged in Black

1879-80

31 A1 5c on 8c org ('80) 900.00 100.00
a. Inverted surcharge *20,000.*
b. Double surcharge *20,000.*
32 A1 5c on 18c lilac 800.00 62.50
33 A1 10c on 12c pale blue 1,000. 50.00
a. 10c on 12c blue 1,450. 100.00
b. Double surcharge *47,500.*
34 A1 10c on 16c yellow 5,500. 140.00
a. Inverted surcharge *90,000.*
b. Double surcharge *72,500.*
35 A1 10c on 24c grn ('80) 1,850. 95.00

Most examples of No. 31a are damaged.

Nos. 16-17 Surcharged in Black

No. 35B Surcharged in Black

1879

35A A5 3c on 16c on card *325.* *2,200.*
Stamp off card 475.
35B A5 5c on 18c on card *350.* *2,600.*
Stamp off card 475.
35C A6 3c on 5c on 18c on card *8,500.* *9,500.*
Stamp off card *8,000.* *8,250.*

Nos. 35A-35C were sold affixed to postal cards. Most used examples are found off card so values are given for these.

Type of 1862

1882-1902 Wmk. 2 *Perf. 14*

36b A1 2c carmine ('84) 50.00 2.75
37 A1 2c green ('00) 27.50 1.00
38 A1 4c slate ('96) 28.00 2.75
39 A1 4c car rose ('00) 20.00 1.00
40 A1 5c ultramarine 45.00 1.00
41 A1 5c yellow ('00) 26.00 8.00
42 A1 10c lilac 925.00 21.00
43 A1 10c green 160.00 2.00
a. 10c blue green 1,700. 37.50
44 A1 10c vio, *red* ('91) 42.50 1.75
45 A1 10c ultra ('00) 50.00 2.25
46 A1 12c blue ('02) 46.00 *67.50*
47 A1 30c gray grn ('91) 100.00 26.00
a. 30c yellow green 135.00 42.50
48 A1 30c brown ('01) 57.50 26.00
a. Pair, imperf. 2,000.
Nos. 36b-48 (13) 1,578. 163.00

No. 47 has fugitive ink. Both colors will turn dull green upon soaking.

The 2c rose, perf 12, is a proof.

No. 28 Surcharged in Black

1880 Wmk. 1 *Perf. 15½x15*

50 A4 12c on $10 rose 900.00 325.00

Surcharged in Black

1885-91 **Wmk. 2** ***Perf. 14***

51 A1 20c on 30c ver 160.00 6.75
a. Double surcharge — —
52 A1 20c on 30c gray grn ('91) 90.00 *140.00*
a. 20c on 30c yellow green 150.00 160.00
53 A1 50c on 48c brown 300.00 65.00
54 A1 50c on 48c lil ('91) 225.00 *300.00*
55 A1 $1 on 96c ol gray 675.00 82.50
56 A1 $1 on 96c vio, *red* ('91) 700.00 325.00

For overprints see Nos. 61-63.

Types of 1874 and

A7

1890-1902 **Wmk. 2** ***Perf. 14***

56A A7 2c dull purple 150.00 40.00

Wmk. 1

57 A2 $2 gray green 400.00 250.00
58 A3 $3 lilac ('02) 575.00 525.00
59 A4 $10 gray grn ('92) *11,500.* *10,500.*
Fiscal cancellation *500.00*

Due to a shortage of 2c postage stamps, No. 56A was authorized for postal use December 24-30, 1890.

Fake postmarks are known on No. 59. Beware also of fiscal cancels altered to resemble postal cancels.

For surcharge see No. 68.

Type of 1874 Surcharged in Black

1891, Jan. 1 **Wmk. 2**

60 A4 $5 on $10 vio, *red* 350.00 110.00

Nos. 36b, 44 Overprinted

a

b

1891, Jan. 1

60A A1 2c carmine (a) 900.00 350.00
60B A1 2c carmine (b) 375.00 190.00
a. Inverted overprint *9,000.*
60C A1 10c vio, *red* (a) *1,600.* 425.00

Nos. 60A-60C were overprinted for use as fiscal stamps, "S.O." denoting "Stamp Office" and "S.D." denoting "Stamp Duty." They were authorized for postal use Jan. 1, 1891-1893. Examples of No. 60A with "O" changed to "D" in manuscript are known.

Forged overprints are often encountered. Expertization is required.

Nos. 52, 54 and 56 Handstamped with Chinese characters

g

h

i

61 A1 (g) 20c on 30c yellow green 52.50 12.50
a. 20c on 30c dull green 50.00 11.00
b. "20 CENTS" double *24,000.* *24,000.*
62 A1 (h) 50c on 48c 75.00 5.00
63 A1 (i) $1 on 96c 400.00 21.00
a. Chinese inscriptions both sides *750.00*

No. 61 may be found with Chinese character 2mm, 2½mm or 3mm high.

The handstamped Chinese surcharges on Nos. 61-63 exist in several varieties including inverted, double, triple, misplaced, omitted and (on No. 63) on both front and back.

Nos. 43 and 20 Surcharged

1891

64 A1 7c on 10c green 90.00 9.50
a. Double surcharge *6,250.* *1,250.*
b. Antique "t" in "cents" 675.00 150.00
c. Small "t" in "cents" 650.00 145.00
On cover —

Wmk. 1

65 A1 14c on 30c violet 180.00 77.50

Beware of faked varieties.

No. 36 Overprinted in Black

1841
Hong Kong
JUBILEE
1891

1891, Jan. 22 **Wmk. 2**

66 A1 2c rose *375.00* 130.00
a. Double overprint *17,500.* *13,500.*
b. "U" of "JUBILEE" shorter *775.00* 200.00
c. "J" of "JUBILEE" shorter *775.00* 200.00
d. Tall "K" in "KONG" *1,250.* 450.00
g. "1841" omitted *7,500.*

50th anniversary of the colony.

Beware of faked varieties. Value for 66a are for doubling clearly seperated & visible. Overprint nearly over each other are valued much less. No. 66g is from a shift of a single row or 12 of the overprint.

No. 26 Surcharged (Chinese Handstamped)

1897, Sept. **Wmk. 1** ***Perf. 15½x15***

67 A2 $1 on $2 sage green 200.00 125.00
a. Without Chinese surcharges 4,000. 3,750.
b. Diagonal Chinese surcharge omitted *29,500.*

On No. 57

Perf. 14

68 A2 $1 on $2 gray green 225.00 140.00
a. Without Chinese surcharges 1,900. *1,700.*
b. Diagonal Chinese surcharge omitted *22,000.*
c. Vertical Chinese surcharge omitted —
Handstamped "SPECIMEN" 150.00

Handstamp Surcharged in Black

1898 **Wmk. 2**

69 A1 10c on 30c gray grn 72.50 *87.50*
a. Large Chinese surcharge *1,400.* *1,400.*
b. Without Chinese surcharge 550.00 *1,200.*
70 A1 $1 on 96c black 240.00 32.50
a. Without Chinese surcharge 3,000. *4,000.*
Overprinted "SPECIMEN" 625.00

The Chinese surcharge is added separately. See notes below Nos. 61-63. The small Chinese surcharge is illustrated.

King Edward VII — A10

1903 **Wmk. 2**

71 A10 1c brown & lilac 2.25 .55
72 A10 2c gray green 20.00 2.10
73 A10 4c violet, *red* 23.00 .45
74 A10 5c org & gray grn 22.00 9.50
75 A10 8c vio & blk 14.50 1.75
76 A10 10c ultra & lil, *bl* 62.50 1.40
77 A10 12c red vio & gray grn, *yel* 11.50 5.75
78 A10 20c org brn & blk 62.50 4.75
79 A10 30c blk & gray grn 62.50 24.00
80 A10 50c red vio & gray grn 65.00 62.50
81 A10 $1 ol grn & lil 110.00 26.00
82 A10 $2 scar & black 300.00 350.00
83 A10 $3 dp bl & blk 375.00 *400.00*
84 A10 $5 blue grn & lil 550.00 575.00
85 A10 $10 org & blk, *bl* 1,100. 450.00
Nos. 71-85 (15) 2,781. 1,914.

1904-11 **Wmk. 3**

Ordinary or Chalky Paper

86 A10 1c brown ('10) 9.00 1.00
a. Booklet pane of 4
87 A10 2c gray green 22.50 2.75
88 A10 2c deep green 42.00 1.50
a. Booklet pane of 4
b. Booklet pane of 12
89 A10 4c violet, *red* 34.00 .50
90 A10 4c carmine 18.00 .40
a. Booklet pane of 4
b. Booklet pane of 12
91 A10 5c org & gray grn 62.50 17.50
a. Chalky paper ('06) 22.50 6.50
92 A10 6c red vio & org ('07) 34.00 8.25
93 A10 8c vio & blk ('07) 18.00 1.75
94 A10 10c ultra & lil, *bl* 32.00 1.25
95 A10 10c ultramarine 57.50 .50
96 A10 12c red vio & gray grn, *yel* ('07) 22.00 7.75
97 A10 20c org brn & blk 67.50 4.00
a. Chalky paper ('06) 62.50 3.50
98 A10 20c ol grn & vio ('11) 50.00 50.00
99 A10 30c blk & gray grn 62.50 32.50
a. Chalky paper ('06) 62.50 22.50
100 A10 30c org & vio ('11) 62.50 42.50
101 A10 50c red vio & gray green 105.00 15.50
a. Chalky paper ('06) 90.00
102 A10 50c blk, *grn* ('11) 52.50 19.00
103 A10 $1 ol grn & lil 190.00 42.00
a. Chalky paper ('06) 160.00
104 A10 $2 scar & black 400.00 160.00
a. Chalky paper ('06) 325.00 125.00
105 A10 $2 blk & car ('10) 350.00 440.00
106 A10 $3 dp bl & blk 300.00 325.00
107 A10 $5 bl grn & lil 425.00 450.00
108 A10 $10 org & blk, *bl* 1,700. 1,450.
a. Chalky paper ('06) 1,800. 1,100.
Nos. 86-108 (23) 4,117. 3,074.

Nos. 86, 88, 90, 94 and 95 are on ordinary paper only. Nos. 92, 93, 96, 98, 100, 102, 105, 106 and 107 are on chalky paper and the others of the issue are on both papers.

The 4c, 5c, 8c, 12c 20c, 50c, $2 and $5 denominations of type A10 are expressed in colored letters or numerals and letters on a colorless background.

King George V
A11 A12

A13

A14

A15

Type I

Type II

Two Types of 25c:

I: A short vertical stroke crosses the bottom of the top Chinese character in the left label.

II: The vertical stroke is absent from the character.

1912-14 **Ordinary Paper**

109 A11 1c brown 4.50 .60
a. Booklet pane of 12
110 A11 2c deep green 12.00 .40
a. Booklet pane of 12
111 A12 4c carmine 6.50 .40
a. Booklet pane of 12
b. Booklet pane of 4
112 A13 6c orange 6.00 2.25
113 A12 8c gray 27.50 8.00
114 A11 10c ultramarine 27.50 .35

Chalky Paper

115 A14 12c vio, *yel* 9.00 *10.00*
116 A14 20c ol grn & vio 12.00 1.50
117 A15 25c red vio & dl vio (I) ('14) 32.50 *32.50*
118 A13 30c org & violet 29.00 8.50
119 A14 50c black, *bl grn*, white back 25.00 2.00
a. 50c black, *emerald* 27.50 10.00
b. 50c black, *bl grn*, ol back 1,100. 27.50
c. 50c black, *emer*, ol back 32.50 10.00
120 A11 $1 blue & vio, *bl* 50.00 5.75
121 A14 $2 black & red 175.00 70.00
122 A13 $3 vio & green 250.00 100.00
123 A14 $5 red & grn, *grn* 625.00 350.00
a. $5 red & grn, *bl grn*, ol back 1,150. 375.00
124 A13 $10 blk & vio, *red* 575.00 95.00
Nos. 109-124 (16) 1,867. 687.25

For overprints see British Offices in China Nos. 1-27.

1914, May **Surface-colored Paper**

125 A14 12c violet, *yel* 10.00 *18.00*
126 A14 50c black, *green* 30.00 4.00
127 A14 $5 red & grn, *grn* 525.00 350.00
Nos. 125-127 (3) 565.00 372.00

Stamp of 1912-14 Redrawn (Type II)

1919, Aug. **Chalky Paper**

128 A15 25c red vio & dl vio 250.00 80.00

Types of 1912-14 Issue

1921-37 **Ordinary Paper** **Wmk. 4**

129 A11 1c brown 1.25 .50
130 A11 2c deep green 4.00 .75
131 A11 2c gray ('37) 22.50 8.00
132 A12 3c gray ('31) 10.00 1.50
133 A12 4c rose red 5.50 1.00
134 A12 5c violet ('31) 18.00 .40
135 A12 8c gray 21.00 *37.50*
136 A12 8c orange 5.75 2.00
137 A11 10c ultramarine 7.50 .45

Chalky Paper

138 A14 12c vio, *yel* ('33) 20.00 4.00
139 A14 20c ol grn & dl vio 8.50 .40
140 A15 25c red vio & dl vio, redrawn 7.50 1.50
141 A13 30c yel & violet 12.00 1.75
142 A13 50c blk, *emerald* 24.00 .45
143 A11 $1 ultra & vio, *bl* 45.00 .60
144 A14 $2 black & red 135.00 7.50
145 A13 $3 dl vio & grn ('26) 190.00 67.50
146 A14 $5 red & grn, *emer* ('25) 475.00 77.50
Nos. 129-146 (18) 1,013. 213.30

Common Design Types pictured following the introduction.

Silver Jubilee Issue
Common Design Type

1935, May 6 Engr. *Perf. 11x12*

147 CD301 3c black & ultra 3.50 3.00
148 CD301 5c indigo & grn 9.00 3.50
149 CD301 10c ultra & brn 18.00 4.00
150 CD301 20c brn vio & ind 28.50 8.25
Nos. 147-150 (4) 59.00 18.75
Set, never hinged 110.00

Coronation Issue
Common Design Type

1937, May 12 *Perf. 11x11½*

151 CD302 4c deep green 3.50 5.75
152 CD302 15c dark carmine 8.50 2.75
153 CD302 25c deep ultra 11.00 4.00
Nos. 151-153 (3) 23.00 12.50
Set, never hinged 32.50

King George VI — A16

1938-52 Typo. *Perf. 14*

Ordinary Paper

154 A16 1c brown 1.00 *2.00*
a. Double printed *7,500.*
155 A16 2c gray 1.00 .25
156 A16 4c orange 5.00 4.00
157 A16 5c green .60 .25
157B A16 8c brn red ('41) 1.00 *1.75*
c. Imperf., pair 60,000. —
d. Period after cents
158 A16 10c violet 4.00 .60
159 A16 15c carmine 1.00 .30
159A A16 20c gray ('46) .60 .30
159B A16 20c rose red ('48) 7.00 .45
160 A16 25c ultramarine 14.50 2.75
160A A16 25c gray ol ('46) 4.25 *2.75*
161 A16 30c olive bister 75.00 1.90
161B A16 30c lt ultra ('46) 3.50 .25

Chalky Paper

162 A16 50c red violet 6.00 .40
b. Ordinary paper 8.50 .75
162C A16 80c lilac rose ('48) 3.25 .70
163 A16 $1 lilac & ultra 4.25 2.50
a. Ordinary paper 11.00 *16.00*
163B A16 $1 dp org & grn ('46) 26.00 1.00
c. Ordinary paper 13.50 .30
164 A16 $2 dp org & grn 40.00 20.00
164A A16 $2 vio & red ('46) 27.50 .60
b. Ordinary paper 25.00 6.75
165 A16 $5 lilac & red 35.00 *30.00*
165A A16 $5 grn & vio ('46) 60.00 3.50
b. Ordinary paper 25.00 17.00
166 A16 $10 grn & vio 350.00 97.50
166A A16 $10 vio & ultra ('46) 100.00 12.50
b. Ordinary paper 70.00 32.50
Nos. 154-166A (23) 770.45 186.25
Set, never hinged 1,200.

Coarse Impressions
Ordinary Rough-Surfaced Paper

1941-46 *Perf. 14½x14*

155a A16 2c gray .90 *4.25*
156a A16 4c orange ('46) 2.50 2.00
157a A16 5c green 1.75 *3.00*
158a A16 10c violet 4.75 .25
161a A16 30c dull olive bister 14.00 6.75
162a A16 50c red lilac 15.00 .75
Nos. 155a-162a (6) 38.90 17.00
Set, never hinged 80.00

A17

1938, Jan. 11 **Wmk. 4**

167 A17 5c green 60.00 15.00

No. 167 is a revenue stamp officially authorized to be sold and used for postal purposes. Used Jan. 11-20, 1938. The used price is for the stamp on cover. CTO covers exist.

Street Scene — A18

Hong Kong Bank — A22

Liner and Junk — A19

Nos. C672, C678, C708 Surcharged University of Hong Kong — A20

Nos. C575-C576, C603, C620, C699 Surcharged Harbor — A21

China Clipper and Seaplane A23

Perf. 13½x13, 13x13½

1941, Feb. 26 Engr. Wmk. 4

168 A18 2c sepia & org 4.00 1.75
169 A19 4c rose car & vio 4.75 3.50
170 A20 5c yel grn & blk 1.75 .35
171 A21 15c red & black 4.75 2.75
172 A22 25c dp blue & dk brn 9.50 6.50
173 A23 $1 brn org & brt bl 25.00 9.25
Nos. 168-173 (6) 49.75 24.10
Set, never hinged 80.00

Centenary of British rule.

Catalogue values for unused stamps in this section, from this point to the end of the section, are for Never Hinged items.

Peace Issue

Phoenix Rising from Flames A24

1946, Aug. 29 *Perf. 13x12½*

174 A24 30c car & dp blue 3.00 2.40
175 A24 $1 car & brown 3.75 .75
Set, hinged 4.00

Return to peace after WWII.

Silver Wedding Issue
Common Design Types

Perf. 14x14½

1948, Dec. 22 Photo. Wmk. 4

178 CD304 10c purple 3.50 1.50

Engr.; Name Typo.

Perf. 11½x11

179 CD305 $10 rose car 280.00 95.00
Set, hinged 225.00

UPU Issue
Common Design Types

Engr.; Name Typo. on 20c & 30c

1949, Oct. 10 *Perf. 13½, 11x11½*

180 CD306 10c violet 3.75 1.00
181 CD307 20c deep car 13.50 4.75
182 CD308 30c indigo 12.00 5.00
183 CD309 80c red violet 28.00 7.50
Nos. 180-183 (4) 57.25 18.25
Set, hinged 23.00

Coronation Issue
Common Design Type

1953, June 2 Engr. *Perf. 13½x13*

184 CD312 10c pur & blk 6.00 .35
Hinged 2.25

Elizabeth II — A25

1954-60 Typo. *Perf. 13½x14*

185 A25 5c orange 1.60 .25
a. Imperf., pair *2,250.*
186 A25 10c violet 2.00 .25
187 A25 15c green 4.00 1.75
188 A25 20c brown 5.50 .30
189 A25 25c rose red 5.00 2.25
190 A25 30c gray 4.50 .25
191 A25 40c blue 5.75 .40
192 A25 50c red violet 6.00 .25
193 A25 65c lt gray ('60) 20.00 11.00
194 A25 $1 org & green 7.00 .25
195 A25 $1.30 bl & ver ('60) 22.50 1.60
196 A25 $2 violet & red 11.00 .60
197 A25 $5 green & vio 72.50 2.25
198 A25 $10 violet & ultra 62.50 7.50
Nos. 185-198 (14) 229.85 28.90
Set, hinged 110.00

Nos. 185-187 are on ordinary paper; Nos. 188-198 on chalky paper. No. 191 exists as imperf, but is a printer's trial. Value, $600.

Arms of University A26

Perf. 11½x12

1961, Sept. 11 Photo. Wmk. 314

199 A26 $1 bl, blk, red, grn & gold 7.25 2.00
a. Gold omitted 2,000.

University of Hong Kong, 50th anniv.

Queen Victoria Statue, Victoria Park, Hong Kong — A27

1962, May 4 *Perf. 14*

200 A27 10c car rose & black .60 .25
201 A27 20c blue & black 1.75 *2.00*
202 A27 50c bister & black 4.25 .45
Nos. 200-202 (3) 6.60 2.70

1st postage stamps of Hong Kong, cent.

Queen Elizabeth II — A28

Wmk. 314 Upright

1962, Oct. 4 Photo. *Perf. 14½x14*

Size: 17x21mm

203 A28 5c red orange .85 .50
a. Booklet pane of 4 4.00
204 A28 10c purple 1.60 .25
a. Booklet pane of 4 7.50
205 A28 15c green 3.75 1.90
206 A28 20c red brown 2.75 .25
a. Booklet pane of 4 14.00
207 A28 25c lilac rose 3.75 *4.25*
208 A28 30c dark blue 2.75 .25
209 A28 40c Prus green 5.25 .65
210 A28 50c crimson 1.90 .30
a. Booklet pane of 4 25.00
211 A28 65c ultramarine 19.00 2.00
212 A28 $1 dark brown 25.00 .40

Perf. 14x14½

Size: 25½x30½mm

Portrait in Natural Colors

213 A28 $1.30 sky blue 3.00 .25
a. Ocher (sash) omitted 70.00
b. Yellow omitted 70.00
214 A28 $2 fawn 5.25 1.00
a. Yellow and ocher (sash) omitted 275.00
b. Yellow omitted 70.00
215 A28 $5 orange 13.00 1.25
a. Ocher (sash) omitted 60.00
216 A28 $10 green 25.00 2.50
217 A28 $20 violet blue 85.00 21.00
Nos. 203-217 (15) 197.85 36.75

1966-72 Wmk. 314 Sideways

203b A28 5c ('67) .55 *1.00*
204b A28 10c ('67) .65 *.75*
205a A28 15c ('67) 1.75 *3.00*
206b A28 20c 1.50 *2.50*
207a A28 25c ('67) 2.75 *4.00*
208a A28 30c ('70) 7.50 4.00
209a A28 40c ('67) 3.50 3.50
210b A28 50c ('67) 2.50 *3.00*
211a A28 65c ('67) 5.00 *8.50*
212a A28 $1 ('67) 11.00 1.50
213c A28 $1.30 ('72) 9.00 3.00
214c A28 $2 ('71) 9.00 3.25
215b A28 $5 ('71) 50.00 27.50
217a A28 $20 ('72) 120.00 80.00
Nos. 203b-217a (14) 224.70 145.50

Most of the A28 type issue werereissued in 1971-73 on glazed paper. These are all valued higher than the listed stamps.

Freedom from Hunger Issue
Common Design Type

Perf. 14x14½

1963, June 4 Photo. Wmk. 314

218 CD314 $1.30 green 47.50 7.50

Red Cross Centenary Issue
Common Design Type

1963, Sept. 2 Litho. *Perf. 13*

219 CD315 10c black & red 2.50 .35
220 CD315 $1.30 ultra & red 32.50 7.00

ITU Issue
Common Design Type

1965, May 17 *Perf. 11x11½*

221 CD317 10c red lil & yel 2.00 .30
222 CD317 $1.30 apple grn & turq blue 22.50 3.50

Intl. Cooperation Year Issue
Common Design Type

1965, Oct. 25 *Perf. 14½*

223 CD318 10c blue grn & cl 2.00 .35
224 CD318 $1.30 lt violet & grn 20.00 2.75

Churchill Memorial Issue
Common Design Type

1966, Jan. 24 Photo. *Perf. 14*

Design in Black, Gold and Carmine Rose

225 CD319 10c bright blue 2.75 .25
226 CD319 50c green 3.25 .40
227 CD319 $1.30 brown 17.50 3.25
228 CD319 $2 violet 29.00 7.50
Nos. 225-228 (4) 52.50 11.40

WHO Headquarters Issue
Common Design Type

1966, Sept. 20 Litho. *Perf. 14*

229 CD322 10c multicolored 2.25 .30
230 CD322 50c multicolored 9.00 2.00

UNESCO Anniversary Issue
Common Design Type

1966, Dec. 1 Litho. *Perf. 14*

231 CD323 10c "Education" 3.00 .25
232 CD323 50c "Science" 14.00 1.25
233 CD323 $2 "Culture" 52.50 16.00
Nos. 231-233 (3) 69.50 17.50

Three Rams' Heads A29

Lunar New Year: $1.30, Three rams.

1967, Jan. 17 Photo. *Perf. 14*

234 A29 10c red, citron & grn 2.00 .60
235 A29 $1.30 red, cit & brt grn 30.00 8.00

Outline of Telephone with Map of South East Asia and Australia
A30

1967, Mar. 30 Photo. *Perf. 12½*
236 A30 $1.30 dk red & blue 17.00 2.75

Completion of the Hong Kong-Malaysia link of the South East Asia Commonwealth Cable, SEACOM.

Monkeys
A31

Lunar New Year: $1.30, Two monkey families.

1968, Jan. 23 Wmk. 314 *Perf. 14*
237 A31 10c crim, blk & gold 2.25 .50
238 A31 $1.30 crim, blk & gold 26.00 7.00

Liner and New Sea Terminal
A32

Seacraft: 20c, Pleasure launch and sailing cruiser. 40c, Vehicle ferry. 50c, Passenger ferry. $1, Sampan. $1.30, Junk.

Perf. 13x12½
1968, Apr. 24 Litho. Unwmk.
239 A32 10c multicolored 2.00 .25
240 A32 20c sky blue, bis & black 3.00 1.00
241 A32 40c org, rose lil & black 8.50 6.75
242 A32 50c brt red, emer & black 6.50 1.00
243 A32 $1 yel, cop red & black 11.00 4.00
244 A32 $1.30 dk bl, brt pink & black 30.00 5.00
Nos. 239-244 (6) 61.00 18.00

Bauhinia Blakeana — A33

Perf. 14x14½
1968, Sept. 25 Photo. Wmk. 314
245 A33 65c shown 8.50 .50
a. Wmkd. sideways ('72) 47.50 17.50
246 A33 $1 Coat of Arms 8.50 .55
a. Wmkd. sideways ('71) 8.50 2.50

Human Rights and "Lamp of Life"
A34

1968, Nov. 20 Litho. *Perf. 13½*
247 A34 10c green, org & blk 1.25 .50
248 A34 50c magenta, yel & blk 4.75 2.00

International Human Rights Year.

Cock
A35

Design: $1.30, Cock, vert.

Perf. 13x13½, 13½x13
1969, Feb. 11 Photo. Unwmk.
249 A35 10c brn, blk, org & red 4.00 1.50
a. Red omitted 400.00
250 A35 $1.30 ocher, blk, org & red *47.50* *9.50*

Lunar New Year, Feb. 17, 1969.

Chinese University Seal — A36

1969, Aug. 26 Unwmk. *Perf. 13*
251 A36 40c multicolored 6.50 3.00

Chinese University of Hong Kong, founded 1963.

Radar, Globe and Satellite
A37

Perf. 14x14½
1969, Sept. 24 Photo. Wmk. 314
252 A37 $1 scar, blk, sil & bl 18.50 6.00

Opening of the satellite earth station (connected through the Indian Ocean satellite Intelsat III) on Stanley Peninsula, Hong Kong.

Chow — A38

Lunar New Year (Year of the Dog): $1.30, Chow, horiz.

1970, Jan. 28 *Perf. 14*
253 A38 10c black & multi *3.50* .80
254 A38 $1.30 green & multi *60.00* 8.50

Emblem — A39

25c, Emblem and Chinese junks, horiz.

Perf. 13½x13, 13x13½
1970, Mar. 14 Litho. Wmk. 314
255 A39 15c multicolored .60 .60
256 A39 25c multicolored 1.50 1.50

EXPO '70 Intl. Exposition, Osaka, Japan, Mar. 15-Sept. 13.

"A Compassionate Ship on the Bitter Sea" — A40

1970, Apr. 9 Photo. *Perf. 14*
257 A40 10c yel green & multi 1.00 .30
258 A40 50c scarlet & multi 3.25 1.50

Centenary of the Tung Wah Group of Hospitals (including schools and various charitable organizations).

A.P.Y. Emblem — A41

1970, Aug. 5 Litho. Wmk. 314
259 A41 10c yellow & multi 1.25 .50

Issued for Asian Productivity Year.

Boar
A42

Perf. 13x13½
1971, Jan. 20 Photo. Unwmk.
260 A42 10c yel grn, gold & black *3.25* 1.25
261 A42 $1.30 vio, gold & blk *36.00* *6.00*

Lunar New Year.

Scout Emblem and "60" — A43

Perf. 14x14½
1971, July 23 Litho. Wmk. 314
262 A43 10c red, yel & blk .80 .25
263 A43 50c blue, emer & blk 3.25 1.00
264 A43 $2 vio, lil rose & blk 16.50 9.00
Nos. 262-264 (3) 20.55 10.25

60th anniversary of Hong Kong Boy Scouts.

Festival Emblem
A44

Symbolic Flower
A45

Festival of Hong Kong: 50c, Dancers, horiz.

1971, Nov. 2 *Perf. 14*
265 A44 10c lilac & orange 1.25 .25

Perf. 14½
266 A45 50c lilac & multi 3.25 .90
267 A45 $1 lilac & multi 8.50 6.00
Nos. 265-267 (3) 13.00 7.15

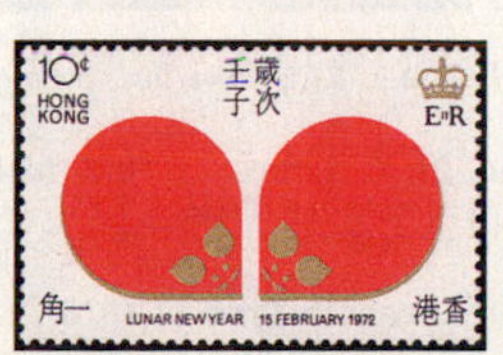

Rats
A46

Perf. 13½x13
1972, Feb. 8 Photo. Unwmk.
268 A46 10c blk, red & gold *3.00* .50
269 A46 $1.30 blk, gold & red *33.00* 6.00

Lunar New Year.

Cross Harbor Tunnel Entrance — A47

Perf. 14x14½
1972, Oct. 20 Litho. Wmk. 314
270 A47 $1 multicolored 5.75 1.75

Inauguration of Cross Harbor Tunnel linking Victoria and Kowloon.

Silver Wedding Issue, 1972
Common Design Type

Design: Queen Elizabeth II, Prince Philip, phoenix and dragon.

1972, Nov. 20 Photo. *Perf. 14x14½*
271 CD324 10c citron & multi .60 .25
272 CD324 50c gray & multi 1.10 *1.25*

Ox
A48

Lunar New Year: 10c, Ox, vert.

1973, Feb. 3 *Perf. 14*
273 A48 10c dk brown & red 2.75 .50
274 A48 $1.30 dk brn, yel & org 8.00 5.75

Elizabeth II — A49

Wmk. 314 Upright; Sideways (15c, 30c, 40c)
1973, June 12 Photo. *Perf. 14½x14*
Size: 20x24mm
275 A49 10c orange .85 .50
d. Watermark sideways (coil) 1.50 1.50
276 A49 15c olive green 7.00 *7.50*
277 A49 20c bright purple 1.75 .30
278 A49 25c deep brown 8.00 7.50
279 A49 30c ultramarine .90 .50
280 A49 40c blue green 2.75 2.75
281 A49 50c red 1.25 .50
282 A49 65c dp bister 12.50 11.50
283 A49 $1 dk slate green 2.00 .65

Perf. 14x14½
Wmk. 314 Sideways
Size: 28x32mm
284 A49 $1.30 dk pur & yel 6.00 .75
285 A49 $2 dp brn & lt grn 7.50 1.00
286 A49 $5 dk vio bl & rose 10.00 3.00

Photo. & Embossed
287 A49 $10 dk sl green & pink 12.00 8.00
288 A49 $20 black & rose 21.00 18.50
Nos. 275-288 (14) 93.50 62.95

1975-78 Wmk. 373 *Perf. 14½x14*
Size: 20x24mm
275a A49 10c orange .50 .30
c. Booklet pane of 4 ('76) 2.00
276a A49 15c olive green 13.50 11.00
c. Booklet pane of 4 70.00
277a A49 20c bright purple .50 .25
c. Booklet pane of 4 ('76) 2.00
278a A49 25c deep brown 16.00 15.00
279a A49 30c ultramarine .75 .70
280a A49 40c blue green 1.00 *1.75*
281a A49 50c red 2.50 .75
c. Booklet pane of 4 11.00
Complete booklet, 2 #275c, 276c, 2 #277c, 281c 90.00
282a A49 65c deep bister 18.00 11.00
283a A49 $1 dark slate green 2.50 .75

Perf. 14x14½
Size: 28x32mm
284a A49 $1.30 dark purple & yel 2.25 .45
285a A49 $2 dp brn & lt grn 2.75 1.10
286a A49 $5 dk vio bl & rose ('78) 4.25 2.00
287a A49 $10 dk sl grn & pink ('78) 4.75 *6.00*

288a A49 $20 black & rose ('78) *7.25* *11.00*
Nos. 275a-288a (14) 76.50 62.05

No. 288a exists imperf. Value, pair $750.
See Nos. 314-327.

Princess Anne's Wedding Issue
Common Design Type
Wmk. 314

1973, Nov. 14 Litho. *Perf. 14*
289 CD325 50c ocher & multi .65 .25
290 CD325 $2 lilac & multi 2.00 1.75

Chinese Character "Hong" — A50

Designs: 50c, "Kong." $1, "Festival."

1973, Nov. 23 Litho. *Perf. 14½x14*
291 A50 10c red & green .50 .25
292 A50 50c plum & red 1.50 .90
293 A50 $1 emerald & plum 3.75 3.00
Nos. 291-293 (3) 5.75 4.15

Festival of Hong Kong 1973.

Tiger A51

Lunar New Year: $1.30, Tiger, vert.

Perf. 14½x14, 14x14½
1974, Jan. 8 Wmk. 314
294 A51 10c green & multi 3.00 .50
295 A51 $1.30 lilac & multi 13.00 12.00

Chinese Opera Mask — A52

Designs: Chinese opera masks.

1974, Feb. 1 Photo. *Perf. 12x12½*
296 A52 10c black, red & org .55 .25
297 A52 $1 multicolored 5.00 3.75
298 A52 $2 black, org & gold 10.00 8.00
a. Souvenir sheet of 3, #296-298, perf. 14x13 *60.00* *50.00*
Nos. 296-298 (3) 15.55 12.00

Hong Kong Arts Festival.

Carrier Pigeons A53

Cent. of UPU: 50c, Symbolic globe in envelope. $2, Hands holding letters.

1974, Oct. 9 Litho. *Perf. 14*
299 A53 10c blue, grn & blk .50 .25
a. Unwatermarked 35.00
300 A53 50c magenta & multi 2.00 .40
301 A53 $2 violet & multi 4.25 3.00
Nos. 299-301 (3) 6.75 3.65

Rabbit A54

Lunar New Year: $1.30, Two rabbits.

1975, Feb. 5 Wmk. 314 *Perf. 14*
302 A54 10c silver & red 1.25 .50
a. Unwatermarked 1.40 1.00
303 A54 $1.30 gold & green 6.75 6.75
a. Unwatermarked 7.50 *9.50*

Queen Elizabeth II, Prince Philip, Hong Kong Arms — A55

Wmk. 373

1975, Apr. 30 Litho. *Perf. 13½*
304 A55 $1.30 blue & multi 3.25 1.90
305 A55 $2 yellow & multi 4.50 4.25

Royal Visit 1975.

Mid-Autumn Festival — A56

Abstract Designs: $1, Dragon Boat Festival (boats). $2, Tin Hau Festival (ships with flags).

1975, July 31 Unwmk. *Perf. 14*
306 A56 50c rose lil & multi 2.75 .75
307 A56 $1 brt grn & multi 10.00 2.50
308 A56 $2 orange & multi 27.50 9.00
a. Souv. sheet of 3, #306-308 *110.00* *55.00*
Nos. 306-308 (3) 40.25 12.25

Hong Kong Festivals, 1975.

Brown Laughing Thrush — A57

Birds: $1.30, Chinese bulbul. $2, Black-capped kingfisher.

1975, Oct. 29 Litho. Wmk. 373
309 A57 50c lt blue & multi 2.50 .75
310 A57 $1.30 pink & multi 9.00 5.50
311 A57 $2 yellow & multi 17.50 10.00
Nos. 309-311 (3) 29.00 16.25

Dragon A58

Lunar New Year: $1.30, like 20c, pattern reversed.

1976, Jan. 21 Litho. *Perf. 14½*
312 A58 20c gold, pur & lilac 1.10 .45
313 A58 $1.30 gold, red & grn 6.75 2.75

Queen Elizabeth Type of 1973
Wmk. 373 (#320-323), Unwmkd.
1976-81 Photo. *Perf. 14½x14*
Size: 20x24mm
314 A49 10c orange 24.00 10.00
316 A49 20c bright purple 3.50 1.25
318 A49 30c ultramarine 8.00 2.25
320 A49 60c lt violet ('77) 1.75 *2.50*
321 A49 70c yellow ('77) 1.75 .75
322 A49 80c brt mag ('77) 2.25 *3.25*
323 A49 90c sepia ('81) 9.00 2.75

Size: 28x32mm
Perf. 14x14½
324 A49 $2 dp brn & lt grn 10.50 4.00
325 A49 $5 dk vio bl & rose 17.00 7.50

Photo. & Embossed
326 A49 $10 dk sl grn & pink 90.00 42.50
327 A49 $20 black & rose 175.00 65.00
Nos. 314-327 (11) 342.75 141.75

"60" and Girl Guides Emblem A59

$1.30, "60," tents and Girl Guides emblem.

1976, Apr. 23 Wmk. 314 *Perf. 14½*
328 A59 20c silver & multi 1.00 .25
329 A59 $1.30 silver & multi 5.50 4.00

60th anniv. of Hong Kong Girl Guides.

"Postal Services" (in Chinese) — A60

Designs: $1.30, General Post Office, 1911-1976. $2, New G.P.O., 1976.

1976, Aug. 11 Litho. Wmk. 373
330 A60 20c gray, grn & blk .75 .25
331 A60 $1.30 gray, red & black 3.50 1.50
332 A60 $2 gray, yel & black 6.00 4.00
Nos. 330-332 (3) 10.25 5.75

Opening of new GPO building.

Snake A61

Lunar New Year: $1.30, Snake & branch face left.

1977, Jan. 6 *Perf. 13½*
333 A61 20c multicolored .75 .25
334 A61 $1.30 multicolored 4.75 3.50

Streetcars — A63

Designs: 60c, Star ferryboat. $1.30, Funicular railway. $2, Junk and sampan.

1977, June 30 Wmk. 373 *Perf. 13½*
338 A63 20c multicolored .60 .25
339 A63 60c multicolored 1.50 2.00
340 A63 $1.30 multicolored 2.75 2.00
341 A63 $2 multicolored 3.25 3.50
Nos. 338-341 (4) 8.10 7.75

Tourist publicity.

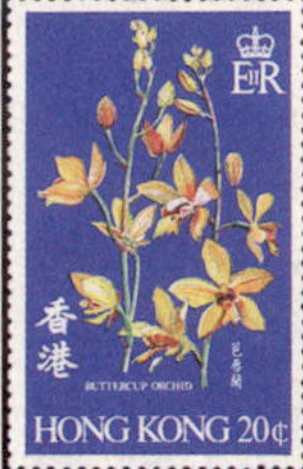

Buttercup Orchid — A64

$1.30, Lady's-slipper. $2, Susan orchid.

1977, Oct. 12 Litho. *Perf. 14*
342 A64 20c blue & multi 1.50 .30
343 A64 $1.30 yellow & multi 4.00 1.75
344 A64 $2 green & multi 7.00 4.50
Nos. 342-344 (3) 12.50 6.55

Queen Dotting Eye of Dragon, 1975 Visit — A62

20c, Presentation of the orb. $2, Orb, vert.

1977, Feb. 7 Litho.
335 A62 20c multicolored .55 .25
336 A62 $1.30 multicolored 1.35 .85
337 A62 $2 multicolored 1.75 1.50
Nos. 335-337 (3) 3.65 2.60

25th anniv. of the reign of Elizabeth II.

Horse and Chinese Character "Ma" — A65

1978, Jan. 26 Litho. *Perf. 14½*
345 A65 20c multicolored .75 .25
346 A65 $1.30 multicolored 4.00 4.00

Lunar New Year.

Elizabeth II — A66

1978, June 2 Litho. *Perf. 14x14½*
347 A66 20c carmine & dk blue .45 .25
348 A66 $1.30 dk blue & carmine 1.60 *1.75*

25th anniv. of coronation of Elizabeth II.

Boy and Girl A67

Design: $1.30, Ring-around-a-rosy.

1978, Nov. 8 Wmk. 373 *Perf. 14½*
349 A67 20c multicolored .25 .25
350 A67 $1.30 multicolored 1.50 *2.00*

Centenary of Po Leung Kuk, society for help and education of orphans and poor children.

Electronics — A68

Industries: $1.30, Toy (bear and drum). $2, Garment (mannequins).

1979, Jan. 9 Litho. *Perf. 14½*
351 A68 20c multicolored .30 .25
352 A68 $1.30 multicolored 1.00 *1.60*
353 A68 $2 multicolored 1.10 *2.00*
Nos. 351-353 (3) 2.40 *3.85*

Precis Orithya — A69

Butterflies: $1, Graphium sarpedon. $1.30, Heliophorus epicles phoenicoparyphus. $2, Danaus genutia.

1979, June 20 Photo. Unwmk.
354 A69 20c multicolored .90 .25
355 A69 $1 multicolored 1.60 .65
356 A69 $1.30 multicolored 1.75 1.50
357 A69 $2 multicolored 2.00 3.25
Nos. 354-357 (4) 6.25 5.65

Cross Section of Station A70

Mass Transit Railroad: $1.30, Front, rear and side views of train. $2, Map of routes.

1979, Oct. 1 Litho. *Perf. 13½*
358 A70 20c multicolored .50 .25
359 A70 $1.30 multicolored 1.60 .55
360 A70 $2 multicolored 2.10 *2.50*
Nos. 358-360 (3) 4.20 3.30

Ching Chung Koon Temple, Tuen Mun — A71

Rural Architecture: 20c, Tsui Shing Lau Pagoda, Sheung Cheung Wai, vert. $1.30, Village house, Sai O.

Perf. 13x13½, 13½x13
1980, May 14 Litho. Wmk. 373
361 A71 20c multicolored .35 .25
362 A71 $1.30 multicolored 1.25 1.00
363 A71 $2 multicolored 1.60 *2.00*
Nos. 361-363 (3) 3.20 3.25

Queen Mother Elizabeth Birthday Issue
Common Design Type

1980, Aug. 4 Litho. *Perf. 14*
364 CD330 $1.30 multicolored 1.10 *1.25*

Botanical Gardens — A72

1980, Nov. 12 Litho. *Perf. 13½*
365 A72 20c shown .30 .25
366 A72 $1 Ocean Park .65 .35
367 A72 $1.30 Kowloon Park .75 .75
368 A72 $2 Country Park 1.40 *2.00*
Nos. 365-368 (4) 3.10 3.35

Epinephelus Akaara — A73

$1, Nemipterus virgatus. $1.30, Choerodon azurio. $2, Scarus ghobban.

1981, Jan. 28 Litho. *Perf. 13½*
369 A73 20c shown .25 .25
370 A73 $1 multicolored .65 .45
371 A73 $1.30 multicolored .80 .60
372 A73 $2 multicolored 1.25 *2.00*
Nos. 369-372 (4) 2.95 3.30

Royal Wedding Issue
Common Design Type

1981, July 29 Photo. *Perf. 14*
373 CD331 20c Bouquet .25 .25
374 CD331 $1.30 Charles .55 .35
375 CD331 $5 Couple 2.25 2.25
Nos. 373-375 (3) 3.05 2.85

Public Housing Development A74

Various public housing developments.

1981, Oct. 14 Litho. *Perf. 13½*
376 A74 20c multicolored .25 .25
377 A74 $1 multicolored .70 .40
378 A74 $1.30 multicolored 1.00 .65
379 A74 $2 multicolored 1.25 *1.75*
a. Souvenir sheet of 4, #376-379 6.00 6.00
Nos. 376-379 (4) 3.20 3.05

Port of Hong Kong A75

Various views of Port of Hong Kong.

1982, Jan. 12 Litho. *Perf. 14½*
380 A75 20c multicolored .60 .25
381 A75 $1 multicolored 1.60 1.10
382 A75 $1.30 multicolored 1.75 1.60
383 A75 $2 multicolored 2.10 *2.50*
Nos. 380-383 (4) 6.05 5.45

Five-banded Civet — A76

$1, Pangolin. $1.30, Chinese porcupine. $5, Barking deer.

1982, May 4 Litho. *Perf. 14½*
384 A76 20c shown .30 .25
385 A76 $1 multicolored .60 .45
386 A76 $1.30 multicolored 1.10 .85
387 A76 $5 multicolored 3.00 *3.25*
Nos. 384-387 (4) 5.00 4.80

Queen Elizabeth II
A77 A78

Perf. 14½x14
1982, Aug. 30 Photo. Wmk. 373
388 A77 10c yellow & dk red .80 .60
389 A77 20c blue vio & vio 1.00 1.00
390 A77 30c orange & pur 1.50 .30
391 A77 40c lt blue & red 1.50 .30
392 A77 50c pale grn & brn 1.50 .30
393 A77 60c gray & brt mag 2.75 2.00
394 A77 70c brt org & dk grn 2.75 .90
395 A77 80c gray ol & brn ol 2.75 3.00
396 A77 90c grnsh bl & grn 4.50 .60
397 A77 $1 brt pink & brn org 2.50 .30
398 A77 $1.30 rose vio & dk bl 4.00 .30
399 A77 $2 buff & blue 6.50 1.00

Photo. & Embossed
Perf. 14x14½
400 A78 $5 lemon & lake 8.00 2.50
401 A78 $10 brn & blk brn 9.00 5.00
402 A78 $20 lt blue & lake 15.00 14.00
403 A78 $50 gray & lake 36.00 29.00
Nos. 388-403 (16) 100.05 61.10

Nos. 388 and 397 also issued in coils.

1985-87 Unwmk.
388a A77 10c .75 *1.50*
389a A77 20c 20.00 16.00
391a A77 40c 1.00 1.00
392a A77 50c 1.00 .30
393a A77 60c 1.60 1.10
394a A77 70c 3.50 1.00
395a A77 80c 3.75 3.50
396a A77 90c 4.75 .75
397a A77 $1 1.90 .40
398b A77 $1.30 2.50 .45
398A A77 $1.70 brt yel grn & dp bl 4.50 1.50
399a A77 $2 4.00 1.50
400a A78 $5 10.00 3.75
401a A78 $10 10.00 5.00
402a A78 $20 11.00 7.50
403a A78 $50 32.50 26.00
Nos. 388a-403a (16) 112.75 71.25

Issued: $1.30, 6/13/86; $1.70, 9/2/86; 20c, 6/87; others, 10/10/85.

3rd Far East and South Pacific Games for the Disabled A79

Perf. 14x14½
1982, Oct. 31 Litho. Wmk. 373
404 A79 30c Table tennis .50 .25
405 A79 $1 Racing .90 1.00
406 A79 $1.30 Basketball 2.60 1.75
407 A79 $5 Archery 4.25 *6.00*
Nos. 404-407 (4) 8.25 9.00

Performing Arts — A80

1983, Jan. 26 Litho. *Perf. 14½x14*
408 A80 30c Dancing .50 .25
409 A80 $1.30 Theater 1.75 1.25
410 A80 $5 Music 4.50 *5.00*
Nos. 408-410 (3) 6.75 6.50

A81

1983, Mar. 14 *Perf. 14½x13½*
411 A81 30c Aerial view .75 .25
412 A81 $1 Liverpool Bay 1.75 1.10
413 A81 $1.30 Flag 2.00 1.25
414 A81 $5 Queen Elizabeth II 4.50 *6.25*
Nos. 411-414 (4) 9.00 8.85

Commonwealth Day.

Views by Night A82

30c, Victoria Harbor. $1, Space Museum. $1.30, Chinese New Year Fireworks. $5, Jumbo Restaurant.

1983, Aug. 17 Litho. *Perf. 14½*
415 A82 30c multicolored 1.50 .60
416 A82 $1 multicolored 3.50 1.75
417 A82 $1.30 multicolored 4.50 2.25
418 A82 $5 multicolored 14.50 11.00
Nos. 415-418 (4) 24.00 15.60

Royal Observatory Centenary — A83

40c, Technical facilities. $1, Wind measurement. $1.30, Temperature measurement. $5, Earthquake measurement.

1983, Nov. 23 Litho. *Perf. 14½*
419 A83 40c multicolored .80 .30
420 A83 $1 multicolored 2.25 1.50
421 A83 $1.30 multicolored 2.50 1.50
422 A83 $5 multicolored 7.75 *8.00*
Nos. 419-422 (4) 13.30 11.30

Training Plane, Dorado A84

$1, Hong Kong Clipper seaplane. $1.30, Jumbo jet, Kai Tak Airport. $5, Baldwin Brothers balloon, vert.

1984, Mar. 7 Wmk. 373 *Perf. 13½*
423 A84 40c shown 1.80 .30
424 A84 $1 multicolored 2.25 1.50
425 A84 $1.30 multicolored 2.75 1.50
426 A84 $5 multicolored 7.75 9.75
Nos. 423-426 (4) 14.55 13.05

Map of Hong Kong, 19th Cent. A85

Various maps.

1984, June 21 Litho. *Perf. 14*
427 A85 40c multicolored 1.10 .35
428 A85 $1 multicolored 1.75 1.40
429 A85 $1.30 multicolored 2.75 2.00
430 A85 $5 multicolored 10.00 *12.00*
Nos. 427-430 (4) 15.60 15.75

Chinese Lanterns
A86

1984, Sept. 6 Litho. *Perf. 13½x13*
431 A86 40c Rooster 1.25 .50
432 A86 $1 Bull 3.00 1.75
433 A86 $1.30 Butterfly 4.00 2.00
434 A86 $5 Fish 10.00 *12.00*
Nos. 431-434 (4) 18.25 16.25

Jockey Club Centenary — A87

40c, Supporting health care. $1, Supporting disabled. $1.30, Supporting the arts. $5, Supporting Ocean Park.

1984, Nov. 21 Litho. *Perf. 14½*
435 A87 40c multicolored 1.35 .40
436 A87 $1 multicolored 2.75 1.75
437 A87 $1.30 multicolored 3.50 2.00
438 A87 $5 multicolored 8.00 *11.00*
a. Souvenir sheet of 4, #435-438 27.50 27.50
Nos. 435-438 (4) 15.60 15.15

Historic Buildings
A88

40c, Hung Sing Temple. $1, St. John's Cathedral. $1.30, Old Supreme Court Building. $5, Wan Chai Post Office.

Perf. 13½
1985, Mar. 14 Unwmk. Litho.
439 A88 40c multicolored .95 .30
440 A88 $1 multicolored 1.90 1.60
441 A88 $1.30 multicolored 2.40 1.75
442 A88 $5 multicolored 6.75 *8.50*
Nos. 439-442 (4) 12.00 12.15

Intl. Dragon Boat Festival
A89

Perf. 13½x13
1985, June 19 Wmk. 373 Litho.
443 A89 40c multicolored .60 .30
444 A89 $1 multicolored 2.00 1.50
445 A89 $1.30 multicolored 3.25 1.75
446 A89 $5 multicolored 10.00 *11.00*
a. Strip of 4, #443-446 *30.00 30.00*
b. Souvenir sheet of 4, #443-446, perf. 13x12½ *30.00 30.00*
Nos. 443-446 (4) 15.85 14.55

Nos. 443-446 when placed together form a continuous design.

Queen Mother 85th Birthday Issue
Common Design Type

40c, At Glamis Castle, age 9. $1, On balcony with Princes William and Charles. $1.30, Photograph by Cecil Beaton,1980. $5, Holding Prince Henry.

1985, Aug. 7 Litho. *Perf. 14½x14*
447 CD336 40c multicolored .65 .25
448 CD336 $1 multicolored 1.60 1.25
449 CD336 $1.30 multicolored 2.00 1.25
450 CD336 $5 multicolored 5.25 *5.75*
Nos. 447-450 (4) 9.50 8.50

Indigenous Flowers — A90

40c, Melastoma. 50c, Chinese lily. 60c, Grantham's camellia. $1.30, Narcissus. $1.70, Bauhinia. $5, Chinese New Year flower.

1985, Sept. 25 Litho. *Perf. 13½*
451 A90 40c multicolored 1.75 .30
452 A90 50c multicolored 2.00 .50
453 A90 60c multicolored 2.50 1.50
454 A90 $1.30 multicolored 3.50 1.50
455 A90 $1.70 multicolored 3.75 1.75
456 A90 $5 multicolored 7.25 *11.00*
Nos. 451-456 (6) 20.75 16.55

See No. 898.

Modern Architecture — A91

50c, Hong Kong Academy for Performing Arts. $1.30, Exchange Square, vert. $1.70, Hong Kong Bank Hdqtrs., vert. $5, Hong Kong Coliseum.

1985, Nov. 27 *Perf. 15*
457 A91 50c multicolored .65 .25
458 A91 $1.30 multicolored 1.25 .80
459 A91 $1.70 multicolored 1.90 1.00
460 A91 $5 multicolored 6.00 6.00
Nos. 457-460 (4) 9.80 8.05

Halley's Comet
A92

50c, Comet, solar system. $1.30, Edmond Halley. $1.70, Hong Kong, trajectory. $5, Comet, Earth.

1986, Feb. 26 Litho. *Perf. 13½x13*
461 A92 50c multi 1.35 .25
462 A92 $1.30 multi 2.00 1.25
463 A92 $1.70 multi 3.25 1.50
464 A92 $5 multicolored 9.00 *10.00*
a. Souvenir sheet of 4, #461-464 28.00 28.00
Nos. 461-464 (4) 15.60 13.00

Queen Elizabeth II 60th Birthday
Common Design Type

Designs: 50c, At the wedding of Cecillia Bowes-Lyon, Brompton Parish Church, 1939. $1, Most Noble Order of the Garter, service at St. George's Chapel, Windsor Castle, 1977. $1.30, State visit, 1975. $1.70, Queen Mother's 80th birthday celebration, Royal Lodge, Windsor, 1980. $5, Visiting Crown Agents' offices, 1983.

1986, Apr. 21 *Perf. 14½*
465 CD337 50c scar, blk & sil .45 .25
466 CD337 $1 ultra & multi 1.00 .35
467 CD337 $1.30 green & multi 1.35 .50
468 CD337 $1.70 violet & multi 1.45 .65
469 CD337 $5 rose vio & multi 4.50 5.00
Nos. 465-469 (5) 8.75 6.75

EXPO '86, Vancouver — A93

50c, Transportation. $1.30, Finance. $1.70, Trade. $5, Communications.

1986, July 18 Litho. *Perf. 13½*
470 A93 50c multicolored .90 .30
471 A93 $1.30 multicolored 1.60 1.00
472 A93 $1.70 multicolored 2.50 1.50
473 A93 $5 multicolored 6.75 *8.00*
Nos. 470-473 (4) 11.75 10.80

Fishing Vessels
A94

Designs: 50c, Hand-liner sampan. $1.30, Stern trawler. $1.70, Long liner junk. $5, Junk trawler.

1986, Sept. 24 Litho.
474 A94 50c multicolored .80 .25
475 A94 $1.30 multicolored 1.60 1.00
476 A94 $1.70 multicolored 3.25 1.25
477 A94 $5 multicolored 6.75 *8.00*
Nos. 474-477 (4) 12.40 10.50

19th Cent. Paintings — A95

50c, Possibly, Second puan khequa, by Spoilum. $1.30, Chinese woman, artist unknown. $1.70, Self-portrait at age 52, by Kwan Kiu Chin. $5, Possibly, Wife of a merchant, by George Chinnery.

1986, Dec. 9 Litho. *Perf. 14*
478 A95 50c multicolored .45 .25
479 A95 $1.30 multicolored 1.45 1.25
480 A95 $1.70 multicolored 1.75 1.50
481 A95 $5 multicolored 4.75 *6.25*
Nos. 478-481 (4) 8.40 9.25

New Year (Year of the Hare)
A96

Embroideries of various rabbits.

1987, Jan. 21 Litho. *Perf. 13½x14*
482 A96 50c multicolored .90 .30
483 A96 $1.30 multicolored 1.45 1.25
484 A96 $1.70 multicolored 1.75 1.25
485 A96 $5 multicolored 6.25 *6.50*
a. Souvenir sheet of 4, #482-485 40.00 40.00
Nos. 482-485 (4) 10.35 9.30

19th Century Paintings in the Hong Kong Museum of Art and Shanghai Banking Corp.
A97

Scenes: 50c, A Village Square, Hong Kong Island, 1838, by Auguste Borget (1809-1877). $1.30, Boat Dwellers in Kowloon Bay, 1838, by Borget. $1.70, Flagstaff House, Lt. Governor D'Aguilar's Residence, 1846, by Murdoch Bruce. $5, A View of Wellington Street, late 19th century, by C. Andrasi.

1987, Apr. 23 Litho. *Perf. 14*
486 A97 50c multicolored .90 .25
487 A97 $1.30 multicolored 2.25 1.40
488 A97 $1.70 multicolored 2.75 1.50
489 A97 $5 multicolored 8.00 *10.50*
Nos. 486-489 (4) 13.90 13.65

Elizabeth II, Hong Kong Waterfront
A98

Queen, Natl. Landmarks
A99

Type I — Darker Shading Under Chin

Type II — Lighter Shading Under Chin

Designs: $5, Tsim Shah Tsui, Kowloon. $10, Victoria Harbor. $20, Legislative Council Building. $50, Government House.

Type I

1987, July 13 Litho. *Perf. 14½x14*
No date inscription below design
490 A98 10c yel grn, gray & blk .80 *.90*
491 A98 40c bluish grn, lt yel & blk 1.75 *2.25*
492 A98 50c brn org, buff & blk 1.00 .30
493 A98 60c lt blue, pale rose & blk 2.25 1.25
494 A98 70c vio, pale rose & blk 2.00 1.00
495 A98 80c brt rose lil, lt blue & blk 2.75 2.10
496 A98 90c pink, pale beige & blk 2.75 1.00
497 A98 $1 brt lem & blk 2.25 .70
498 A98 $1.30 rose clar, brt yel grn & blk 3.00 .80
499 A98 $1.70 lt blue & blk 3.00 .80
500 A98 $2 yel grn, cream & blk 3.00 1.40

Perf. 14
501 A99 $5 grn, lt grn & blk 3.00 2.25
502 A99 $10 brn, yel brn & blk 8.50 5.25
503 A99 $20 rose vio, lil & blk 13.00 12.00
504 A99 $50 sep, gray & blk 20.00 *28.00*
Nos. 490-504 (15) 69.05 60.00

Type II
No date inscription below design

1988, Sept. 1
490a A98 10c .75 .60
491a A98 40c 1.75 1.75
492a A98 50c 1.50 .55
493a A98 60c 1.75 1.10
494a A98 70c 2.00 .80
495a A98 80c 2.00 2.25
496a A98 90c 2.25 1.00
497a A98 $1 8.50 1.75
498a A98 $1.30 3.50 1.25
499a A98 $1.70 9.00 2.00
500a A98 $2 3.50 1.10
501a A99 $5 5.00 2.50
502a A99 $10 13.00 5.50
503a A99 $20 18.00 12.00
504a A99 $50 37.50 20.00
Nos. 490a-504a (15) 110.00 54.15

See Nos. 532-533, 592-593, 629.

1989, Aug. 1 Inscribed "1989"
490b A98 10c 1.00 *1.25*
491b A98 40c 2.75 2.75
492b A98 50c 1.25 .90
493b A98 60c 1.75 .30
494b A98 70c 2.50 2.25
495b A98 80c 2.00 1.60
496b A98 90c 1.75 1.25
497b A98 $1 2.25 .90
498b A98 $1.30 4.00 2.50
500b A98 $2 2.50 .60
501b A99 $5 7.00 2.00
502b A99 $10 10.00 6.00
503b A99 $20 14.00 12.00
504b A99 $50 21.00 *22.50*
Nos. 490b-504b (14) 73.75 56.80

1990 Inscribed "1990"
490c A98 10c 1.00 *1.25*
491c A98 40c 2.75 2.75
492c A98 50c 1.25 .90
493c A98 60c 1.75 .30
494c A98 70c 2.50 2.25
495c A98 80c 2.00 1.60
496c A98 90c 1.75 1.25
497c A98 $1 2.25 .90
498c A98 $1.30 4.00 2.50
500c A98 $2 2.50 .60
501c A99 $5 7.00 2.00
502c A99 $10 10.00 6.00
e. Souv. sheet of 1 *110.00*

503c A99 $20 14.00 12.00
504c A99 $50 21.00 *22.50*
Nos. 490c-504c (14) 73.75 56.80

No. 502e was issued in conjunction with the New Zealand 1990 World Stamp Exhibition with NZ 1990 inscriptions and related design in the sheet selvage.

No. 502e issued 8/24.

1991 **Inscribed "1991"**

490d A98 10c 1.10 *1.25*
492d A98 50c 2.00 .90
493d A98 60c 2.50 .30
494d A98 70c 3.25 2.25
495d A98 80c 3.25 1.60
496d A98 90c 2.40 1.25
497d A98 $1 3.25 .90
499d A98 $1.70 3.50 *4.50*
500d A98 $2 3.50 .60
501d A99 $5 8.75 2.00
502d A99 $10 12.00 6.50
f. Souv. sheet of 1, PHILANIPPON selvage *47.50* *27.50*
g. As "f," Olympics selvage *22.50* *17.50*
503d A99 $20 20.00 12.00
504d A99 $50 20.00 *22.50*
Nos. 490d-504d (13) 85.50 56.55

Nos. 502f-502g were were issued to commemorate Hong Kong's participation in PHILANIPPON '91 and the sponsorship of the 1992 Olympics Games by the Hong Kong Post Office, respectively. The selvage of each sheets bears a distinctive design and inscriptions. See No. 629.

Issued: No. 502f, 11/16; 502g, 12/4.

Nethersole Hospital, Cent. — A100

50c, Hospital, 1887. $1.30, Patients, staff. $1.70, Technology, 1987. $5, Treatment.

1987, Sept. 8 ***Perf. 14½***

505 A100 50c multicolored 1.25 .25
506 A100 $1.30 multicolored 2.75 1.40
507 A100 $1.70 multicolored 3.25 1.50
508 A100 $5 multicolored 9.00 9.00
Nos. 505-508 (4) 16.25 12.15

Natl. Flag A101

Map of Hong Kong A101a

Coil Stamps

1987, July 13 ***Perf. 15x14***

No date inscription below design

509 A101 10c shown 1.75 *2.25*
a. Inscribed "1989" 1.50 1.50
b. Inscribed "1990" 1.50 1.50
c. Inscribed "1991" 1.50 1.50
510 A101a 50c blk, dl ol & lake 2.00 *2.75*
a. Inscribed "1989" 1.50 1.50

Issued: Nos. 509a, 510a, 8/1/89.

See Nos. 611-614.

Folk Costumes — A102

1987, Nov. 18 ***Perf. 13½***

511 A102 50c multicolored .60 .25
512 A102 $1.30 multi, diff. 1.60 1.10
513 A102 $1.70 multi, diff. 1.75 1.40
514 A102 $5 multi, diff. 5.75 *6.75*
Nos. 511-514 (4) 9.70 9.50

New Year (Year of the Dragon) A103

1988, Jan. 27 **Litho.** ***Perf. 13½***

515 A103 50c multicolored .80 .30
516 A103 $1.30 multi, diff. 2.00 .90
517 A103 $1.70 multi, diff. 2.25 1.35
518 A103 $5 multi, diff. 4.50 *5.00*
a. Souv. sheet of 4, #515-518 *18.00* *18.00*
Nos. 515-518 (4) 9.55 7.55

See No. 838e.

Indigenous Birds — A104

50c, White-breasted kingfisher. $1.30, Fukien niltava. $1.70, Black kite. $5, Pied kingfisher.

1988, Apr. 20 ***Perf. 13½x14***

519 A104 50c multicolored 1.10 .30
520 A104 $1.30 multicolored 2.25 1.25
521 A104 $1.70 multicolored 2.45 1.50
522 A104 $5 multicolored 5.75 *6.50*
Nos. 519-522 (4) 11.55 9.55

Indigenous Trees — A105

50c, Chinese banyan. $1.30, Bauhinia blakeana. $1.70, Cotton tree. $5, Schima.

1988, June 16 **Litho.** ***Perf. 13½***

523 A105 50c multicolored .30 .25
524 A105 $1.30 multicolored 1.00 .65
525 A105 $1.70 multicolored 1.25 .75
526 A105 $5 multicolored 3.50 *4.75*
a. Souv. sheet of 4, #523-526 *16.00* *12.00*
Nos. 523-526 (4) 6.05 6.40

See No. 923. See note after No. 940.

Peak Tramway, Victoria, Cent. — A106

Various views of Hong Kong and the tram line.

1988, Aug. 4 **Litho.** ***Perf. 15***

527 A106 50c multicolored .50 .25
528 A106 $1.30 multi, diff. 1.00 1.00
529 A106 $1.70 multi, diff. 1.10 *1.25*
530 A106 $5 multi, diff. 3.50 *4.75*
a. Souvenir sheet of 4, #527-530 *12.00* *12.00*
Nos. 527-530 (4) 6.10 7.25

Catholic Cathedral, Caine Road, Cent. — A107

1988, Sept. 30 **Litho.** ***Perf. 14***

531 A107 60c multicolored 1.60 1.60

Queen and Waterfront Type of 1987 Type II

1988, Sept. 1 **Litho.** ***Perf. 14½x14***

No date inscription below design

532 A98 $1.40 multicolored 4.00 3.00
a. Inscribed "1989" 4.00 1.10
b. Inscribed "1990" 4.00 1.10
533 A98 $1.80 multicolored 4.50 1.50
a. Inscribed "1989" 4.50 .75
b. Inscribed "1990" 4.50 .75
c. Inscribed "1991" 4.50 .75

Issued: No. 532a, 533a, 8/1/89, 532b, 533b, 1990; No. 533c, 4/2/91.

New Year (Year of the Snake) A108

1989, Jan. 18 **Litho.** ***Perf. 13½x14***

534 A108 60c multicolored .75 .25
535 A108 $1.40 multi, diff. 1.75 .70
536 A108 $1.80 multi, diff. 2.00 .90
a. Bklt. pane, 5 each #534, 536 14.00
537 A108 $5 multi, diff. 5.50 *6.75*
a. Souv. sheet of 4, #534-537 *16.50* *11.50*
Nos. 534-537 (4) 10.00 8.60

See No. 838g.

Cheung Chau Bun Festival — A109

60c, Girl, doll. $1.40, Girl. $1.80, Festival paper god. $5, Bun tower gate.

1989, May 4 **Unwmk.** ***Perf. 13½***

538 A109 60c multicolored .60 .25
539 A109 $1.40 multicolored 1.25 .80
540 A109 $1.80 multicolored 1.75 .90
541 A109 $5 multicolored 4.50 *5.50*
Nos. 538-541 (4) 8.10 7.45

Modern Art — A110

60c, Twin, sculpture by Cheung Yee (b. 1936). $1.40, Figures, painted by Luis Chan (b. 1905). $1.80, Lotus, sculpture by Van Lau (b. 1933). $5, Zen, painted by Lui Shou-kwan (1919-1975).

1989, July 19 ***Perf. 12x13***

542 A110 60c multicolored .60 .25
543 A110 $1.40 multicolored 1.35 .80
544 A110 $1.80 multicolored 1.75 .95
545 A110 $5 multicolored 3.50 *4.50*
Nos. 542-545 (4) 7.20 6.50

Hong Kong People — A111

Designs: 60c, Youth holding autumn festival decoration, lunar year festival dragon. $1.40, Shadow boxer, horse racing. $1.80, Office and construction workers. $5, Two women, two men (ethnic multiplicity).

1989, Sept. 6 ***Perf. 13x14½***

546 A111 60c multicolored .70 .25
547 A111 $1.40 multicolored 2.10 .80
548 A111 $1.80 multicolored 2.25 .90
549 A111 $5 multicolored 4.75 *7.50*
Nos. 546-549 (4) 9.80 9.45

See No. 762.

Construction Projects A112

60c, University of Science and Technology. 70c, Cultural center. $1.30, Eastern Harbor Crossing. $1.40, Bank of China. $1.80, Convention center. $5, Light rail transit.

1989, Oct. 5 **Unwmk.** ***Perf. 13***

550 A112 60c multicolored .55 .25
551 A112 70c multicolored .60 .40
552 A112 $1.30 multicolored 1.10 1.10
553 A112 $1.40 multicolored 1.25 .80
554 A112 $1.80 multicolored 1.40 1.10
555 A112 $5 multicolored 6.50 *8.00*
Nos. 550-555 (6) 11.40 11.65

Visit of the Prince and Princess of Wales — A113

Portraits and view of Hong Kong: 60c, Charles and Diana. $1.40, Diana. $1.80, Charles. $5, Couple wearing formal attire.

1989, Nov. 8 **Wmk. 340** ***Perf. 14½***

556 A113 60c multicolored 1.50 .30
557 A113 $1.40 multicolored 2.50 1.10
558 A113 $1.80 multicolored 1.75 1.10
559 A113 $5 multicolored 7.50 7.50
a. Souvenir sheet of 1 16.50 13.50
Nos. 556-559 (4) 13.25 10.00

New Year 1990 (Year of the Horse) A114

Perf. 13½x12½

1990, Jan. 23 **Unwmk.**

560 A114 60c multicolored .80 .35
561 A114 $1.40 multi, diff. 1.90 1.25
562 A114 $1.80 multi, diff. 2.10 1.25
a. Bklt. pane, 3 each 60c, $1.80 8.75
Complete booklet, 2 #562a 17.50
563 A114 $5 multi, diff. 6.50 *9.50*
a. Souvenir sheet of 4, #560-563 18.00 13.00
Nos. 560-563 (4) 11.30 12.35

Examples of No. 562a ovptd. with marginal inscription were released on May 3 to publicize Stamp World London '90.

See No. 838k.

Intl. Cuisine — A115

1990, Apr. 26 Litho. *Perf. 12½x13*

No.	Type	Denom.	Description	Unused	Used
564	A115	60c	Chinese	.65	.25
565	A115	70c	Indian	.65	.50
566	A115	$1.30	Chinese, diff.	1.10	1.25
567	A115	$1.40	Thai	1.10	.70
568	A115	$1.80	Japanese	1.40	1.00
569	A115	$5	French	4.75	*7.50*
			Nos. 564-569 (6)	9.65	11.20

Pollutants — A116

Wmk. 340

1990, June 5 Litho. *Perf. 14½*

No.	Type	Denom.	Description	Unused	Used
570	A116	60c	Air	.45	.25
571	A116	$1.40	Noise	.95	.70
572	A116	$1.80	Water	1.60	.70
573	A116	$5	Land	3.50	*3.75*
			Nos. 570-573 (4)	6.50	5.40

World Environment Day.

Electrification of Hong Kong, Cent. — A117

Views of Hong Kong and streetlights.

1990, Oct. 2 Litho. *Perf. 14½*

No.	Type	Denom.	Description	Unused	Used
574	A117	60c	1890	.60	.25
575	A117	$1.40	1940	1.25	.90
576	A117	$1.80	1960	1.40	.90
577	A117	$5	1980	3.00	*4.25*
a.			Souvenir sheet of 2, #575, 577	6.75	6.75
			Complete booklet, 4 #577a	27.50	
			Nos. 574-577 (4)	6.25	6.30

Christmas — A118

60c, Dove, holly. $1.40, Skyline, snowman. $1.80, Santa Claus' hat, skyscraper. $2, Children, Santa Claus. $5, Candy cane, skyline.

1990, Nov. 8

No.	Type	Denom.	Description	Unused	Used
578	A118	50c	shown	.25	.25
579	A118	60c	multicolored	.35	.25
580	A118	$1.40	multicolored	.90	.45
581	A118	$1.80	multicolored	1.00	.55
582	A118	$2	multicolored	1.45	1.40
583	A118	$5	multicolored	3.50	*5.50*
			Nos. 578-583 (6)	7.45	8.40

New Year 1991 (Year of the Sheep) A119

Different embroidered rams.

1991, Jan. 24 Litho. *Perf. 13½x12½*

No.	Type	Denom.	Description	Unused	Used
584	A119	60c	multicolored	.40	.25
585	A119	$1.40	multicolored	.95	.60
586	A119	$1.80	multicolored	1.10	.75
a.			Bklt. pane, 3 each #584, 586	6.50	
			Complete booklet, 2 #586a	13.00	
587	A119	$5	multicolored	3.50	*5.25*
a.			Souv. sheet of 4, #584-587	9.00	9.00
			Nos. 584-587 (4)	5.95	6.85

See No. 838j.

Education — A120

80c, Kindergarten. $1.80, Primary & secondary. $2.30, Vocational. $5, Tertiary.

Perf. 13½x13

1991, Apr. 18 Litho. Unwmk.

No.	Type	Denom.	Description	Unused	Used
588	A120	80c	multicolored	.40	.25
589	A120	$1.80	multicolored	1.25	.70
590	A120	$2.30	multicolored	1.50	1.25
591	A120	$5	multicolored	4.00	*5.25*
			Nos. 588-591 (4)	7.15	7.45

Queen and Waterfront Type of 1987

Type II

1991, Apr. 2 Litho. *Perf. 14½x14*

No.	Type	Denom.	Description	Unused	Used
592	A98	$1.20	multicolored	3.00	*3.50*
593	A98	$2.30	multicolored	3.00	*3.50*

Transportation A121

80c, Rickshaw. 90c, Bus. $1.70, Ferry. $1.80, Tram. $2.30, Mass transit railway. $5, Hydrofoil.

1991, June 6 Unwmk. *Perf. 14*

No.	Type	Denom.	Description	Unused	Used
594	A121	80c	multicolored	.45	.30
595	A121	90c	multicolored	.75	.60
596	A121	$1.70	multicolored	1.25	1.00
597	A121	$1.80	multicolored	1.50	.80
598	A121	$2.30	multicolored	2.25	2.00
599	A121	$5	multicolored	4.00	*6.00*
			Nos. 594-599 (6)	10.20	10.70

A122

Royal postboxes with contemporary envelopes: 80c, Stamp of Type A1, Queen Victoria. $1.70, Stamps of Type A10, King Edward VII. $1.80, #149, King George V. $2.30, Stamps of Type A16, King George VI. $5, $10, Stamp of Type A98, Queen Elizabeth II.

1991, Aug. 25 Litho. *Perf. 14*

No.	Type	Denom.	Description	Unused	Used
600	A122	80c	multicolored	.60	.30
601	A122	$1.70	multicolored	1.25	1.00
602	A122	$1.80	multicolored	1.75	.80
603	A122	$2.30	multicolored	1.50	1.75
604	A122	$5	multicolored	4.00	*7.00*
			Nos. 600-604 (5)	9.10	10.85

Souvenir Sheet

No.	Type	Denom.	Description	Unused	Used
605	A122	$10	multicolored	14.00	*16.00*

Hong Kong Post Office, 150th anniv.

See No. 792.

Historic Landmarks A123

80c, Bronze Buddha. $1.70, Peak Pavilion. $1.80, Clock Tower. $2.30, Catholic Cathedral. $5, Wong Tai Sin Temple.

1991, Oct. 24

No.	Type	Denom.	Description	Unused	Used
606	A123	80c	mag & blk	.65	.25
607	A123	$1.70	brt grn & blk	1.10	.55
608	A123	$1.80	brt pur & blk	1.75	.60
609	A123	$2.30	brt blue & blk	1.25	.75
610	A123	$5	brt org & blk	4.25	*6.75*
			Nos. 606-610 (5)	9.00	8.90

Map of Hong Kong Type

1992, Mar. 26 Photo. *Perf. 14½x14*

Coil Stamps

Color of Map

No.	Type	Denom.	Description	Unused	Used
611	A101a	80c	red lilac	*1.50*	*3.25*
612	A101a	90c	blue	*1.50*	*2.00*
613	A101a	$1.80	brt yel grn	*2.00*	*2.75*
614	A101a	$2.30	red brown	*2.25*	*3.75*
			Nos. 611-614 (4)	*7.25*	*11.75*

Inscribed 1991.

New Year 1992 (Year of the Monkey) A125

Various embroidery designs of monkeys.

1992, Jan. 22 Litho. *Perf. 14½*

No.	Type	Denom.	Description	Unused	Used
615	A125	80c	multicolored	.35	.25
616	A125	$1.80	multicolored	.90	.60
617	A125	$2.30	multicolored	1.50	1.50
a.			Bklt. pane, 3 ea #615, 617	6.25	
			Complete booklet, 2 #617a	14.00	
618	A125	$5	multicolored	3.50	*6.50*
a.			Sheet of 4, #615-618	12.00	12.00
			Nos. 615-618 (4)	6.25	8.85

See No. 838i.

Queen Elizabeth II's Accession to the Throne, 40th Anniv.

Common Design Type

Unwmk.

1992, Feb. 11 Litho. *Perf. 14*

No.	Type	Denom.	Description	Unused	Used
619	CD349	80c	multicolored	.35	.25
620	CD349	$1.70	multicolored	.60	.60
621	CD349	$1.80	multicolored	.65	.40
622	CD349	$2.30	multicolored	1.00	1.00
623	CD349	$5	multicolored	2.50	*3.00*
			Nos. 619-623 (5)	5.10	5.25

1992 Summer Olympics, Barcelona — A126

80c, Running. $1.80, Swimming and javelin. $2.30, Cycling. $5, High jump.

1992, Apr. 2 Litho. *Perf. 14½*

Black Inscription

No.	Type	Denom.	Description	Unused	Used
624	A126	80c	multi	.40	.25
625	A126	$1.80	multi	1.00	.70
626	A126	$2.30	multi	1.50	1.50
627	A126	$5	multi	2.75	4.50
			Nos. 624-627 (4)	5.65	6.95

Souvenir Sheet

No.	Description	Unused	Used
628	Sheet of 4	8.00	8.00
a.	A126 80c red inscription	.25	.25
b.	A126 $1.80 green inscription	.65	.65
c.	A126 $2.30 blue inscription	1.05	1.05
d.	A126 $5 orange yellow inscription	1.90	1.90
e.	Sheet of 4 with inscription in margin	5.75	5.75

Issue date: No. 628e, July 25. New inscription on No. 628e sheet margin reads "To Commemorate the Opening of the 1992 Summer Olympic Games 25 July 1992" in English and Chinese.

Queen and Landmarks Type of 1987

Souvenir Sheet

Perf. 14

1992, May 22 Litho. Type II

No.	Type	Denom.	Description	Unused	Used
629	A99	$10	lt violet & black	6.50	6.50

World Columbian Stamp Expo '92.

A127

Perf. 15x14

1992-97 Photo. Unwmk.

Color of Chinese Inscription

No.	Type	Denom.	Description	Unused	Used
630	A127	10c	pink	.35	.40
630A	A127	20c	black	1.00	*1.50*
631	A127	50c	red orange	.35	.30
632	A127	60c	blue	2.00	1.50
633	A127	70c	red lilac	2.00	1.25
634	A127	80c	rose	.45	.35
635	A127	90c	gray green	.45	.50
636	A127	$1	org brn	.45	.25
637	A127	$1.10	carmine	2.00	1.25
638	A127	$1.20	violet	.55	.35
639	A127	$1.30	dark blue	2.25	1.10
640	A127	$1.40	apple green	1.75	1.00
641	A127	$1.50	brown	2.00	1.50
642	A127	$1.60	green	1.75	1.00
643	A127	$1.70	ultramarine	1.25	.90
644	A127	$1.80	rose lilac	1.50	.55
645	A127	$1.90	green	1.50	1.25
646	A127	$2	blue green	1.75	.55
647	A127	$2.10	claret	2.50	2.75
648	A127	$2.30	gray	2.50	.70
649	A127	$2.40	dark blue	3.00	2.00
650	A127	$2.50	olive green	1.75	2.00
a.			Sheet of 6, 2 #647, 4 #650	12.00	
d.			Booklet pane, 2 #647, 4 #650	12.00	
651	A127	$2.60	dark brown	2.25	2.00
651A	A127	$3.10	salmon	2.00	1.00
l.			Sheet of 6, 2 #642, 4 #651A	11.50	
o.			Booklet pane, 2 #642, 4 #651A	11.50	
651B	A127	$5	bright green	3.00	2.00
k.			Souvenir sheet of 1	7.00	5.00
m.			Sheet of 6, 4 #639, 2 #651B	15.00	
n.			Booklet pane, 4 #639, 2 #651B	15.00	
p.			Souvenir booklet, #650d, 651Ao, 651Bn	38.50	

Size: 25x30mm

Perf. 14½x14

No.	Type	Denom.	Description	Unused	Used
651C	A127	$10	brown	5.00	2.50
h.			Souvenir sheet of 1	5.00	6.00
651D	A127	$20	orange red	7.00	4.25
651E	A127	$50	gray	14.00	10.50
			Nos. 630-651E (28)	66.35	45.20

Issued: 20c, $1.30, $1.90, $2.40, 11/1/93; No. 651Bk, 2/18/94; No. 651Ch, 8/16/94; $1.10, $1.50, $2.10, $2.60, 6/1/95; $1.40, $1.60, $2.50, $3.10, 9/2/96; No. 651Bp, 2/14/97; others, 6/16/92.

10c, 50c, 80c, 90c, $1, $1.20, $1.30, $1.50, $1.60, $1.80, $1.90, $2.10, 2.30, $2.40, $2.50, $2.60, $3.10 also issued in coils. These have numbers on the back of every fifth stamp.

No. 651Bk issued for Hong Kong '94; No. 651Ch for Conference of Commonwealth Postal Administrations.

Nos. 650a, 651Al, 651Bm are 130x85mm.

Nos. 650d, 651Ao, 651Bn are 180x130mm and are rouletted at left.

See Nos. 656, 677-678, 683, 688, 724, 729, 738, 743, 756-757.

1993-96 Litho. *Perf. 15x14*

No.	Type	Denom.	Description	Unused	Used
636a	A127	$1	Litho.	1.00	1.00
b.			As "a," bklt. pane of 10	10.00	
638a	A127	$1.20	Litho.	1.00	1.00
b.			As "a," bklt. pane of 10	10.00	
			Complete booklet, #638b	10.00	
639a	A127	$1.30	Litho.	.65	.65
b.			As "a," booklet pane of 10	6.50	
645a	A127	$1.90	Litho.	1.25	1.25
b.			As "a," bklt. pane of 10	12.50	
647a	A127	$2.10	Litho.	1.25	1.25
b.			As "a," bklt. pane of 10	12.50	
			Complete booklet, #647b	12.50	
649a	A127	$2.40	Litho.	1.25	1.25
b.			As "a," bklt. pane of 10	12.50	
650b	A127	$2.50	Litho.	1.25	1.25
c.			As "b," booklet pane of 10	12.50	
651f	A127	$2.60	Litho.	1.25	1.25
g.			As "f," bklt. pane of 10	12.50	
			Complete booklet, #651g	12.50	
651Ai	A127	$3.10	Litho.	1.25	1.25
j.			As "i," booklet pane of 10	12.50	
			Nos. 636a-651Ai (9)	10.15	10.15

Chinese characters on Nos. 636a, 638a, 645a, 647a, 649a, 651f are lighter in shade and contrast less with the background color than characters on Nos. 636, 638, 645, 647, 649, 651.

Issued: No. 636a, 12/14/93; Nos. 645a, 649a, 12/28/93; Nos. 638a, 647a, 651f, 6/1/95; Nos. 639a, 650a, 651Ai, 9/2/96.

Stamp Collecting — A128

Stamps and: 80c, Perforation gauge, #559, 586a. $1.80, Canceler, #66, stamp tongs. $2.30, Magnifying glass, #174, 180, 181. $5, Watermark detector, Type A1.

1992, July 15 Litho. *Perf. 14½*

652 A128 80c multicolored .35 .25
653 A128 $1.80 multicolored .75 .65
654 A128 $2.30 multicolored 1.10 1.10
655 A128 $5 multicolored 2.25 *3.50*
Nos. 652-655 (4) 4.45 5.50

See note after No. 940.

Queen Type of 1992
Souvenir Sheet
Perf. 14½x14
1992, Sept. 1 Photo. Unwmk.
Background Color

656 A127 $10 blue 6.00 6.00

Kuala Lumpur Philatelic Exhibition '92. Size of stamp: 25x30mm.

Chinese Opera — A129

80c, Principal male role. $1.80, Martial role. $2.30, Principal female role. $5, Comic role.

1992, Sept. 24 Litho. *Perf. 13½*

657 A129 80c multicolored 1.10 .30
658 A129 $1.80 multicolored 1.90 1.50
659 A129 $2.30 multicolored 2.25 2.25
660 A129 $5 multicolored 4.25 *8.00*
Nos. 657-660 (4) 9.50 12.05

Greetings Stamps — A130

1992, Nov. 19 Litho. *Perf. 14½*

661 A130 80c Hearts .35 .25
662 A130 $1.80 Stars .70 .50
663 A130 $2.30 Presents .80 .80
664 A130 $5 Balloons 1.90 *3.00*
a. Bklt. pane of 6, #662-664, 3 #661 6.50 5.00
Complete booklet, 2 #664a 13.00
Nos. 661-664 (4) 3.75 4.55

New Year 1993 (Year of the Rooster) A131

Various embroidery designs of a rooster.

1993, Jan. 7 Litho. *Perf. 13½*

665 A131 80c multicolored .30 .25
666 A131 $1.80 multicolored .70 .50
667 A131 $2.30 multicolored 1.10 1.10
a. Bklt. pane, 3 ea #665, 667 5.00
Complete booklet, 2 #667a 10.00
668 A131 $5 multicolored 2.75 3.75
a. Souvenir sheet of 4, #665-668 7.50 7.50
Nos. 665-668 (4) 4.85 5.60

See No. 838h.

Chinese String Instruments A132

1993, Apr. 14 Litho. *Perf. 14½*

669 A132 80c Pipa .45 .25
670 A132 $1.80 Erhu .80 .70
671 A132 $2.30 Ruan 1.25 1.10
672 A132 $5 Gehu 2.50 *3.25*
Nos. 669-672 (4) 5.00 5.30

Coronation of Queen Elizabeth II, 40th Anniv. A133

Different views of Hong Kong with portraits of Queen that appear on Types A25, A28, A49 and A127.

1993, June 3 Litho. *Perf. 14*

673 A133 80c multicolored .40 .25
674 A133 $1.80 multicolored .80 .75
675 A133 $2.30 multicolored 1.10 1.10
676 A133 $5 multicolored 2.75 *3.75*
Nos. 673-676 (4) 5.05 5.85

Queen Type of 1992
Souvenir Sheets
1993, July 6 Litho. *Perf. 14½x14*
Background Color

677 A127 $10 brown 7.00 7.00

1993, Aug. 12 Background Color

678 A127 $10 bright blue 6.50 6.50

Hong Kong '94 Stamp Exhibition. Nos. 677-678 contain a 25x30mm stamp.

No. 678 exists with gold, silver or red overprints with the Hong Kong Philatelic Society emblem and Chinese characters. These sheets were sold only at various philatelic exhibitions.

Science and Technology — A134

Designs: 80c, Education, Hong Kong University of Science and Technology. $1.80, Public presentation, Hong Kong Science Museum. $2.30, Achievement regognition, Governor's Award. $5, World class telecommunications, telecommunications industry.

1993, Sept. 8 *Perf. 14½*

679 A134 80c multicolored .25 .25
680 A134 $1.80 multicolored .60 .40
681 A134 $2.30 multicolored .80 .80
682 A134 $5 multicolored 1.90 *3.00*
Nos. 679-682 (4) 3.55 4.45

Queen Type of 1992
Souvenir Sheet
1993, Oct. 5 Litho. *Perf. 14½x14*
Background Color

683 A127 $10 bright green 4.25 4.25

Bangkok '93 Stamp Exhibition. No. 683 contains one 25x30mm stamp.

Goldfish A135

$1, Red calico egg-fish. $1.90, Red cap oranda. $2.40, Red & white fringetail. $5, Black & gold dragon-eye.

1993, Nov. 17 Litho. *Perf. 14½*

684 A135 $1 multicolored .50 .35
685 A135 $1.90 multicolored .80 .50
686 A135 $2.40 multicolored 1.25 1.10
687 A135 $5 multicolored 3.25 *5.00*
a. Souvenir sheet of 4, #684-687 10.00 10.00
Nos. 684-687 (4) 5.80 6.95

Queen Type of 1992
Perf. 15x14
1994, Jan. 27 Photo. Wmk. 373

688 Souvenir booklet 22.50 22.50
a. A127 Sheet of #630, 5 #646 7.25 7.25
b. A127 Sheet of #643, 5 #644 7.25 7.25
c. A127 Sheet of 5 #636, #651B 7.25 7.25

First Hong Kong stamps, 130th anniv. No. 688 sold for $38.

Year of the Dog A136

Various embroidery designs of dogs.

1994, Jan. 27 Litho. *Perf. 14½*

689 A136 $1 multicolored .35 .25
690 A136 $1.90 multicolored .75 .50
691 A136 $2.40 multicolored 1.00 .80
a. Bklt. pane, 3 ea #689, 691 6.00
Complete booklet, 2 #691a 12.00
692 A136 $5 multicolored 2.25 *4.50*
a. Souvenir sheet of 4, #689-692 10.00 10.00
Nos. 689-692 (4) 4.35 6.05

See No. 838f.

Royal Hong Kong Police Force, 150th Anniv. — A137

Designs: $1, Traffic policeman, woman. $1.20, Marine policeman. $1.90, Male, female officers of 1950. $2, Policeman holding M-16. $2.40, Policemen, 1906, pre-1920. $5, Policemen, 1900.

1994, May 4 Litho. *Perf. 13½*

693 A137 $1 multicolored .35 .30
694 A137 $1.20 multicolored .45 .50
695 A137 $1.90 multicolored .65 .50
696 A137 $2 multicolored 1.00 .80
697 A137 $2.40 multicolored 1.50 1.25
698 A137 $5 multicolored 3.25 *4.00*
Nos. 693-698 (6) 7.20 7.35

Traditional Chinese Festivals — A138

Designs: $1, Dragon Boat Festival. $1.90, Lunar New Year. $2.40, Seven Sisters Festival. $5, Mid-Autumn Festival.

1994, June 8 Litho. *Perf. 14*

699 A138 $1 multicolored .35 .25
700 A138 $1.90 multicolored .75 .65
701 A138 $2.40 multicolored 1.25 1.10
702 A138 $5 multicolored 2.25 *4.00*
Nos. 699-702 (4) 4.60 6.00

XV Commonwealth Games, Victoria, BC, Canada — A139

Unwmk.
1994, Aug. 25 Litho. *Perf. 14*

703 A139 $1 Swimming .25 .25
704 A139 $1.90 Lawn bowling .90 .50
705 A139 $2.40 Gymnastics 1.10 .80
706 A139 $5 Weight lifting 1.75 *3.00*
Nos. 703-706 (4) 4.00 4.55

Dr. James Legge (1815-97), Religious Leader, Translator — A140

1994, Oct. 5 Litho. *Perf. 14*

707 A140 $1 multicolored 1.00 1.00

Corals — A141

1994, Nov. 17 Litho. *Perf. 14*

708 A141 $1 Alcyonium .30 .25
709 A141 $1.90 Zoanthus .50 .45
710 A141 $2.40 Tubastrea .65 .55
711 A141 $5 Platygyra 1.50 *2.75*
a. Souv. sheet of 4, #708-711 6.50 6.50
Nos. 708-711 (4) 2.95 4.00

See No. 916.

New Year 1995 (Year of the Boar) A142

Various embroidery designs of pigs.

1995, Jan. 17 Litho. *Perf. 14½*

712 A142 $1 multicolored .40 .35
713 A142 $1.90 multicolored .85 .65
714 A142 $2.40 multicolored 1.10 .75
a. Bklt. pane, 3 each #712, 714 6.00
Complete booklet, 2 #714a 12.00
715 A142 $5 multicolored 2.25 *3.50*
a. Souvenir sheet of 4, #712-715 7.50 7.50
Nos. 712-715 (4) 4.60 5.25

See No. 838d.

Intl. Sporting Events A143

Designs: $1, Hong Kong Rugby Sevens. $1.90, China Sea Race. $2.40, Intl. Dragon Boat Races. $5, Hong Kong Intl. Horse Races.

1995, Mar. 22 Litho. *Perf. 14½*

716 A143 $1 multicolored .50 .25
717 A143 $1.90 multicolored .80 .80
718 A143 $2.40 multicolored 1.25 1.25
719 A143 $5 multicolored 2.50 *3.75*
Nos. 716-719 (4) 5.05 6.05

Traditional Buildings — A144

Litho. & Engr.
1995, May 24 *Perf. 13½*

720 A144 $1 Tsui Shing Lau .40 .25
721 A144 $1.90 Sam Tung UK .75 .45
722 A144 $2.40 Lo Wai .85 .50
723 A144 $5 Man Shek Tong 2.00 *3.00*
Nos. 720-723 (4) 4.00 4.20

Queen Type of 1992
Souvenir Sheet

1995, Aug. 25 Litho. *Perf. 14*
Background Color

724 A127 $10 carmine 5.50 5.50

Singapore '95 World Stamp Exhibition. No. 724 contains one 25x30mm stamp.

Royal Hong Kong Regiment (1854-1995) — A145

$1.20, Modern Regimental Badge, vert. $2.10, Current flag. $2.60, Former flag. $5, Royal Hong Kong Defense Force, 1951 soldier's badge, vert.

1995, Aug. 16 Litho. *Perf. 14½*

725 A145 $1.20 multicolored .50 .30
726 A145 $2.10 multicolored .60 .50
727 A145 $2.60 multicolored .80 .80
728 A145 $5 multicolored 2.00 *3.00*
Nos. 725-728 (4) 3.90 4.60

Queen Type of 1992
Souvenir Sheet

1995, Oct. 9 Litho. *Perf. 14*
Background Color

729 A127 $10 brown 6.25 *7.00*

End of World War II, 50th anniv. No. 729 contains one 25x30mm stamp.

Hong Kong Movie Stars A146

$1.20, Bruce Lee. $2.10, Leung Sing-Por. $2.60, Yam Kim-Fai. $5, Lin Dai.

1995, Nov. 15 Litho. *Perf. 13½*

730 A146 $1.20 multi 1.75 .80
731 A146 $2.10 multi 2.75 1.25
732 A146 $2.60 multi 3.75 2.00
733 A146 $5 multi 5.50 5.50
Nos. 730-733 (4) 13.75 9.55

New Year 1996 (Year of the Rat) A147

Various embroidery designs of rats.

1996, Jan. 31 Litho. *Perf. 13½*

734 A147 $1.20 multicolored .30 .30
735 A147 $2.10 multicolored .55 .55
736 A147 $2.60 multicolored .70 .70
a. Bklt. pane, 3 ea #734, 736 3.75
Complete booklet, 2 #736a 7.50
737 A147 $5 multicolored 1.50 1.50
a. Souvenir sheet of 4, #734-737 5.00 5.00
Nos. 734-737 (4) 3.05 3.05

See No. 838a.

Queen Type of 1992
Souvenir Sheet
Unwmk.

1996, Feb. 23 Litho. *Perf. 14*

738 A127 $10 org & grn 7.00 7.00

Hong Kong '97 Stamp Exhibition. No. 738 contains one 25x30mm stamp.

1996 Summer Olympics, Atlanta — A148

1996, Mar. 20 Litho. *Perf. 13½*

739 A148 $1.20 Gymnastics .30 .30
740 A148 $2.10 Diving .70 .70
741 A148 $2.60 Running .90 .90
742 A148 $5 Basketball 1.60 *2.75*
Nos. 739-742 (4) 3.50 4.65

Souvenir Sheet

742A Sheet of 4, #742b-742e 4.00 4.00
f. As #742A, different sheet margin 4.75 4.75

No. 742Af shows Olympic gold medal at top of sheet margin.

Nos. 748-751 have denominations in color and Olympic rings in gold. Nos. 739-742 have denominations in black, Olympic rings in different colors. No. 742Ab-742Ae have gold Olympic rings.

No. 742f issued 7/19/96.

Queen Type of 1992
Souvenir Sheet
Unwmk.

1996, May 18 Litho. *Perf. 14*

743 A127 $10 brt grn & bl vio 4.00 4.00

Hong Kong '97 Stamp Exhibition. No. 743 contains one 25x30mm stamp.

Archaeological Finds — A149

$1.20, Painted pottery basin. $2.10, Stone "Yue". $2.60, Stone "GE". $5, Pottery tripod.

1996, June 26 Litho. *Perf. 13½*

744 A149 $1.20 multicolored .40 .30
745 A149 $2.10 multicolored .55 .55
746 A149 $2.60 multicolored .80 *.90*
747 A149 $5 multicolored 1.50 *2.25*
Nos. 744-747 (4) 3.25 4.00

1996 Summer Olympic Games Type

1996, July 19 Litho. *Perf. 14x14½*
Color of Denomination

748 A148 $1.20 like #739, red .35 .25
749 A148 $2.10 like #740, blue .40 *.50*
750 A148 $2.60 like #741, green .75 *.85*
751 A148 $5 like #742, org 1.50 *2.50*
Nos. 748-751 (4) 3.00 *4.10*

Nos. 748-751 have denominations in color and Olympic rings in gold. Nos. 739-742 have denonminations in black, Olympic rings in different colors.

Mountains in Hong Kong — A150

$1.30, Pat Sing Leng. $2.50, Ma On Shan. $3.10, Lion Rock, vert. $5, Lantau Peak, vert.

Unwmk.

1996, Sept. 24 Litho. *13½x14*

752 A150 $1.30 multi .50 .45

Perf. 14x14½, 14½x14

753 A150 $2.50 multi 1.00 1.00
754 A150 $3.10 multi 1.25 1.25

Perf. 14x13½

755 A150 $5 multi 1.90 3.75
Nos. 752-755 (4) 4.65 6.45

No. 753 is 40x36mm, No. 754 36x40mm.

See Nos. 899, 905.

Queen Type of 1992
Souvenir Sheets

1996 Photo. Unwmk. *Perf. 14*

756 A127 $10 red & grn 3.25
757 A127 $10 brn & dk brn 3.75

Issued: No. 756, 10/16; No. 757, 10/29.

Visit Hong Kong '97 Stamp Exhibition (No. 756). 1996 Summer Olympic Games, Atlanta (No. 757). Nos. 756-757 each contain one 25x30mm stamp.

Urban Heritage A151

Designs: $1.30, Main building, University of Hong Kong, 1912. $2.50, Western Market, 1906. $3.10, Old Pathological Institute, 1905. $5, Flagstaff House, 1846.

Litho. & Engr.

1996, Nov. 20 *Perf. 13½*

758 A151 $1.30 multicolored .40 .60
759 A151 $2.50 multicolored .70 .80
760 A151 $3.10 multicolored .80 *.90*
761 A151 $5 multicolored 1.35 *2.00*
Nos. 758-761 (4) 3.25 4.30

Hong Kong People Type of 1989
Souvenir Sheet
Perf. 13x13½

1997, Jan. Photo. Unwmk.

762 A111 $5 like No. 549 1.90 1.90

No. 762 contains one 23x33mm stamp that has darker colors and a different perf. than No. 549.

Panoramic Views of Hong Kong Skyline — A152

Nos. 763-775: Various daytime views from harbor.

Nos. 776-778, Various nighttime views from harbor.

Perf. 13½x13

1997, Jan. 26 Litho. Unwmk.
Background Color

763 A152 10c pink .25 .25
764 A152 20c vermilion .25 .25
765 A152 50c orange .25 *.35*
766 A152 $1 orange yellow .25 .25
767 A152 $1.20 olive .30 .30
768 A152 $1.30 apple green .35 .35
a. Booklet pane of 10 3.50
Complete booklet, #768a 3.50
769 A152 $1.40 green .30 *.40*
770 A152 $1.60 blue green .35 *.45*
771 A152 $2 green blue .50 .50
772 A152 $2.10 blue .50 *.60*
773 A152 $2.50 purple .55 *.90*
a. Booklet pane of 10 5.50
Complete booklet, #773a 5.50
774 A152 $3.10 rose .70 .70
a. Booklet pane of 10 7.00
Complete booklet, #774a 7.00
c. Sheet of 4, #771-774 2.50 2.50
775 A152 $5 orange 1.25 1.25
a. Sheet of 13, #763-775 5.75 5.75

Size: 28x33mm
Perf. 14x13½

776 A152 $10 blue 2.50 2.50
a. Souv. sheet of 1 (Series #4) *8.00*
b. Souv. sheet of 1 (Series #5) *8.00*
c. Souv. Sheet of 1 (Sheet #12) 3.00 3.00
d. Souv. sheet of 1, perf14x13¼ (Sheet #14) 2.60 2.60
777 A152 $20 bl, pur & rose 5.25 5.25
778 A152 $50 purple & rose 13.00 13.00
a. Sheet of 3, #776-778 *22.00*
Nos. 763-778 (16) 26.55 27.30

Hong Kong '97 (Nos. 776a-776b). 1996 Atlanta Paralympic Games (No. 776c). 13th Asian Games, Bangkok, Thailand (No. 774c). China 1999 World Philatelic Exhibition (No. 776d).

Perforations are alternating small and large holes.

Nos. 775a and 778a are continuous designs.

Issued: No. 776a, 2/12; No. 776b, 2/16; No. 774c, 3/27/99; No. 776d, 8/21/99.

See note after No. 940.

Coil Stamps
Photo. *Perf. 14½x14*

763a A152 10c .25 *.50*
765a A152 50c .25 *.70*
768b A152 $1.30 .45 *.70*
770a A152 $1.60 .50 *.70*
773b A152 $2.50 .80 *.75*
774b A152 $3.10 1.00 *1.25*
Nos. 763a-774b (6) 3.25 *4.60*

These have numbers on back of every fifth stamp.

Perforations are the same size.

New Year 1997 (Year of the Ox) A153

Various designs of oxen.

Perf. 14½

1997, Feb. 27 Litho. Unwmk.
Background Color

780 A153 $1.30 pink .30 .30
781 A153 $2.50 orange yellow .65 .65
782 A153 $3.10 green .80 .80
a. Booklet pane, 3 each #780a, 782b 6.00
Complete booklet, 2 #782a 12.00
783 A153 $5 blue 1.25 1.75
a. Souvenir sheet of 4, #780-783 4.50 4.50
Nos. 780-783 (4) 3.00 3.50

See Nos. 838b, 838c.

Perf. 13½

780a A153 $1.30 .50 .50
781a A153 $2.50 .90 .90
782b A153 $3.10 1.10 1.10
783b A153 $5 1.75 2.25
c. Souvenir sheet of 4, #780a-781a, 782b-783b 4.50 4.50

Migratory Birds — A154

$1.30, Yellow-breasted bunting. $2.50, Great knot. $3.10, Falcated teal. $5, Black-faced spoonbill.

Perf. 13½

1997, Apr. 27 Unwmk. Photo.

784 A154 $1.30 multicolored .30 .30
785 A154 $2.50 multicolored .65 .65
786 A154 $3.10 multicolored .80 .80
787 A154 $5 multicolored 1.25 *1.75*
Nos. 784-787 (4) 3.00 3.50

Landmarks — A155

$1.30, Hong Kong Stadium. $2.50, The Peak Tower. $3.10, Hong Kong Convention & Exhibition Center. $5, The Lantau Link (bridge).

1997, May 18 *Perf. 13½*

788 A155 $1.30 multicolored .30 .30
789 A155 $2.50 multicolored .75 .75
790 A155 $3.10 multicolored 1.00 1.00
791 A155 $5 multicolored 1.75 *2.25*
a. Souvenir sheet of 1 2.25 2.25
Nos. 788-791 (4) 3.80 4.30

Opening of the Lantau Link (bridge) (No. 791a).

Nos. 788-791 and 791a also exist perf 14x14½. Values are the same.

Royal Postbox Type of 1991
Souvenir Sheet

1997, June 30 Litho. *Perf. 11½*

792 A122 $5 like No. 604 1.75 1.75

No. 792 contains one 19x29mm stamp.

Special Administrative Region of People's Republic of China

First Issue Under Chinese Administration A156

Sights and symbols of Hong Kong: $1.30, Chinese architecture. $1.60, Modern buildings, methods of transportation. $2.50, Skyscrapers, Hong Kong Convention & Exhibition Center. $2.60, Cargo ship entering port. $3.10, Chinese junks, dolphins jumping in water. $5, Hibiscus flower.

1997, July 1 Litho. *Perf. 12x12½*

793	A156	$1.30	multicolored	.35	.35
794	A156	$1.60	multicolored	.40	.40
795	A156	$2.50	multicolored	.65	.65
796	A156	$2.60	multicolored	.70	.70
797	A156	$3.10	multicolored	.80	.80
798	A156	$5	multicolored	1.25	1.25
a.			Souvenir sheet of 1	1.25	1.25
			Nos. 793-798 (6)	4.15	4.15

1997 World Bank Group/Intl. Monetary Fund Annual Meetings — A157

Designs: $1.30, Finance, banking. $2.50, Investment, stock exchange. $3.10, Trade, telecommunications. $5, Infrastructure, transport.

Perf. 14½

1997, Sept. 21 Litho. Unwmk.

799	A157	$1.30	multicolored	.35	.35
800	A157	$2.50	multicolored	.70	.70
801	A157	$3.10	multicolored	.90	.90
802	A157	$5	multicolored	1.40	1.40
			Nos. 799-802 (4)	3.35	3.35

Shells — A158

1997, Nov. 9 Photo. *Perf. 13½*

803	A158	$1.30	Clam	.40	.40
804	A158	$2.50	Cowrie	.70	.70
805	A158	$3.10	Cone	.90	.90
806	A158	$5	Murex	1.40	1.40
			Nos. 803-806 (4)	3.40	3.40

New Year 1998 (Year of the Tiger) A159

Various embroidery designs of tigers.

1998, Jan. 4 Litho. *Perf. 13½*

807	A159	$1.30	multicolored	.35	.35
808	A159	$2.50	multicolored	.75	.75
809	A159	$3.10	multicolored	.95	.95
a.			Bklt. pane, 6 ea #807, 809	9.00	
			Complete booklet, #809a	8.00	
810	A159	$5	multicolored	1.50	1.50
a.			Souvenir sheet, #807-810	4.75	4.75
			Nos. 807-810 (4)	3.55	3.55

See No. 838.

Star Ferry, Cent. A160

Star Ferry during: $1.30, 1900's. $2.50, 1910's-1920's. $3.10, 1920's-1950's. $5, Mid-1950's on.

1998, Apr. 26 Photo. *Perf. 13½*

811	A160	$1.30	multicolored	.40	.40
812	A160	$2.50	multicolored	.85	.85
813	A160	$3.10	multicolored	1.05	1.05
814	A160	$5	multicolored	1.60	1.60
			Nos. 811-814 (4)	3.90	3.90

Nos. 811-814 also exist perf 14½ from a booklet of one each sold only at "Australia '99" International Stamp Exhibition for $25.

Souvenir Sheet

The Closing of Kai Tak Airport — A161

1998, July 5 Photo. *Perf. 13½*

815	A161	$5	multicolored	2.25	2.25

New Hong Kong Airport A162

$1.30, Passengers on terminal's moving sidewalks. $1.60, Couple entering Automated People Mover. $2.50, Airport Railway, Tsing Ma Bridge. $2.60, Terminal building, Airmail Center. $3.10, Aircraft gates. $5, Terminal departure level.

1998, July 5 *Perf. 14*

816	A162	$1.30	multicolored	.40	.40
817	A162	$1.60	multicolored	.45	.45
818	A162	$2.50	multicolored	.70	.70
819	A162	$2.60	multicolored	.80	.80
820	A162	$3.10	multicolored	.90	.90
821	A162	$5	multicolored	1.40	1.40
a.			Souvenir sheet of 1	2.00	2.00
b.			Block of 6, #816-821	5.25	5.25

See note after No. 940.

A163

Scouting in Hong Kong: Rope tied in various knots, different scouting divisions: $1.30, Grasshopper Scouts, Cub Scouts. $2.50, Tower, tents, Boy Scouts, Girl Scouts. $3.10, Helicopter, sailboats, Venture Scouts. $5, City buildings, Rover Scouts, adult leaders.

Unwmk.

1998, July 26 Litho. *Perf. 14*

822	A163	$1.30	multicolored	.40	.40
823	A163	$2.50	multicolored	.70	.70
824	A163	$3.10	multicolored	1.00	1.00
825	A163	$5	multicolored	1.50	1.50
			Nos. 822-825 (4)	3.60	3.60

A164

Hong Kong designs.

1998, Sept. 20 Litho. *Perf. 13½*

826	A164	$1.30	Graphic	.40	.40
827	A164	$2.50	Product	.75	.75
828	A164	$3.10	Interior	.95	.95
829	A164	$5	Fashion	1.40	1.40
			Nos. 826-829 (4)	3.50	3.50

Kites — A165

1998, Nov. 15 Litho. *Perf. 13½*

830	A165	$1.30	Dragonfly	.40	.40
831	A165	$2.50	Dragon	.85	.85
832	A165	$3.10	Butterfly	1.10	1.10
833	A165	$5	Goldfish	1.60	1.60
a.			Souvenir sheet, #830-833	4.00	4.00
			Nos. 830-833 (4)	3.95	3.95

A166

New Year 1999 (Year of the Rabbit): White rabbit with flower designs in various positions.

1999, Jan. 31 Photo. *Perf. 14x13½*

834	A166	$1.30	yel org & multi	.40	.40
			Scratched panel		.40
a.			Sheet of 10	4.00	
835	A166	$2.50	green & multi	.75	.75
			Scratched panel		.40
a.			Sheet of 10	7.50	
836	A166	$3.10	orange & multi	.90	.90
			Scratched panel		.40
a.			Sheet of 10	9.25	
837	A166	$5	red lilac & multi	1.45	1.45
			Scratched panel		.40
a.			Sheet of 10	14.50	
			Nos. 834-837 (4)	3.50	3.50

Nos. 834-837 are printed with a layering of gold "scratch off" ink, which, when removed, reveals a Chinese greeting.

New Year Types of 1987-98

Designs: a, Like #734. b, Like #780. c, Like #783. d, Like #712. e Like 515. f, Like #691. g, Like #534. h, Like #668. i, Like #615. j, Like #584. k, Like #560. #a.-k. have 4 Chinese characters at UL instead of crown and ER.

1999, Feb. 21 Litho. *Perf. 13½*

Sheet of 12

838	$1.30 #a.-k, #807 + label	7.75	7.75

Design in label and sheet selvage is engraved.

Intl. Year of Older Persons — A167

$1.30, Calligraphy. $2.50, Bird raising. $3.10, Playing Go. $5, Voluntary services.

Perf. 14½

1999, Mar. 14 Litho. Unwmk.

839	A167	$1.30	multicolored	.40	.40
840	A167	$2.50	multicolored	.75	.75
841	A167	$3.10	multicolored	.90	.90
842	A167	$5	multicolored	1.45	1.45
			Nos. 839-842 (4)	3.50	3.50

Souvenir Sheet

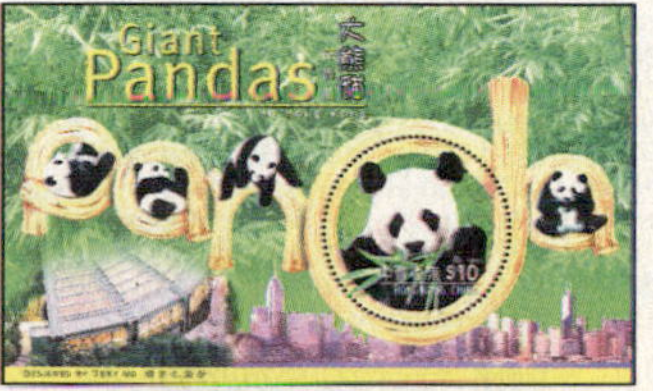

Giant Pandas in Hong Kong — A168

1999, Apr. 25 Litho. *Perf. 14¼*

843	A168	$10	multicolored	3.75	3.75

No. 843 contains one circular stamp 38mm in diameter.

Public Transport — A169

1999, May 23

844	A169	$1.30	Bus	.45	.45
845	A169	$2.40	Minibus	.90	.90
846	A169	$2.50	Tram	.95	.95
847	A169	$2.60	Taxi	1.00	1.00
848	A169	$3.10	Airport express	1.15	1.15
			Nos. 844-848 (5)	4.45	4.45

Hong Kong and Singapore Tourism — A170

Designs: $1.20, Hong Kong Harbor. $1.30, Singapore Skyline. $2.50, Giant Buddha, Hong Kong. $2.60, Merlion, Sentosa Island, Singapore. $3.10, Hong Kong street scene. $5, Bugis Junction, Singapore.

Perf. 13¼

1999, July 1 Litho. Unwmk.

849	A170	$1.20	multicolored	.35	.35
850	A170	$1.30	multicolored	.40	.40
851	A170	$2.50	multicolored	.70	.70
852	A170	$2.60	multicolored	.70	.70
853	A170	$3.10	multicolored	.85	.85
854	A170	$5	multicolored	1.75	1.75
a.			Souvenir sheet, #849-854	4.75	4.75
			Nos. 849-854 (6)	4.75	4.75

See Singapore Nos. 896-902.

People's Republic of China, 50th Anniv. — A171

Designs: $1.30, Flags of People's Republic and Hong Kong Special Administrative District. $2.50 Bauhinia blakeana flower, Hong Kong skyline. $3.10, Dragon dance. $5, Fireworks.

Perf. 14¼ Syncopated

1999, Oct. 1 **Photo.**

Granite Paper

855 A171 $1.30 multicolored .50 .50
856 A171 $2.50 multicolored 1.00 1.00
857 A171 $3.10 multicolored 1.10 1.10
858 A171 $5 multicolored 1.90 1.90
a. Block or strip of 4, #855-858 4.50 4.50

Issued in sheets of 4 blocks or strips and individually in sheets of 20.

Landmarks — A172

10c, Museum of Tea Ware. 20c, St. John's Cathedral. 50c, Legislative Council building. $1, Tai Fu Tai. $1.20, Wong Tai Sin Temple. $1.30, Victoria Harbor. $1.40, Hong Kong Railway Museum. $1.60, Tsim Sha Tsui Clock Tower. $2, Happy Valley Racecourse. $2.10, Kowloon-Canton Railway. $2.50, Chi Lin Nunnery. $3.10, Buddha at Po Lin Monastery. $5, Aw Boon Haw Gardens. $10, Tsing Ma Bridge. $20, Hong Kong Convention & Exhibition Center. $50, Hong Kong Intl. Airport.

Perf. 13x13¾ Syncopated

1999, Oct. 18 **Photo.**

Granite Paper

859 A172 10c blue & multi .30 .25
a. Booklet pane of 1 .35
860 A172 20c blue & multi .30 .25
a. Booklet pane of 1 .35
861 A172 50c blue & multi .30 .25
a. Booklet pane of 1 .35
862 A172 $1 blue & multi .30 .25
a. Booklet pane of 1 .60
863 A172 $1.20 blue & multi .35 .30
a. Booklet pane of 1 .70
864 A172 $1.30 blue & multi .40 .35
a. Booklet pane of 1 .80
865 A172 $1.40 blue & multi .40 .35
a. Booklet pane of 1 .80
b. Booklet pane of 10 4.00 —
Booklet, #865b 4.00
866 A172 $1.60 blue & multi .45 .40
a. Booklet pane of 1 .90
867 A172 $2 blue & multi .55 .50
a. Booklet pane of 1 1.10
868 A172 $2.10 blue & multi .60 .55
a. Booklet pane of 1 1.20
869 A172 $2.50 blue & multi .65 .60
a. Booklet pane of 1 1.30
870 A172 $3.10 blue & multi .85 .75
a. Booklet pane of 1 1.75
871 A172 $5 blue & multi 1.50 1.25
a. Booklet pane of 1 3.00
Souv. booklet, #859a-871a 14.00
b. Sheet of 13, #859-871 6.00 6.00
c. Souvenir sheet of 1 (Definitive #4) 1.50 1.50
d. Souv. sheet of 1 (Definitive #6) 1.50 1.50

Size: 26x32mm

Perf. 13¼

872 A172 $10 blue & multi 2.75 2.50
a. Souv. sheet of 1 (Definitive #1) 2.75 2.75
b. Souv. sheet of 1 (Exhibition #1) 4.00 4.00
c. Souv. sheet of 1 (Exhibition #2) 2.75 2.75
d. Souv. sheet of 1 (Definitive #2) 2.75 2.75
e. Souv. sheet of 1 (Definitive #5) 2.75 2.75
873 A172 $20 blue & multi 5.50 5.00
874 A172 $50 blue & multi 14.00 12.50
a. Sheet of 3, #872-874 22.00 22.00
Nos. 859-874 (16) 29.20 26.05

Coil Stamps

Perf. 15x13½ Syncopated

Size: 18x22mm

874B A172 10c blue & multi .60 .40
874C A172 50c blue & multi .60 .40
874D A172 $1.30 blue & multi .90 .55
874E A172 $1.60 blue & multi 1.00 .65
874F A172 $2.50 blue & multi 1.50 .95
874G A172 $3.10 blue & multi 1.90 1.20
Nos. 874B-874G (6) 6.50 4.15

Nos. 872a-872b are Syncopated perf 14x14¼. No. 872c is Syncopated perf 13¼x13. No. 872d is Syncopated perf 14x14½. No. 872e is Syncopated perf 13¼x13.

Issued: No. 872a, 1/31/00; No. 872b, 2/10/00; No. 872c, 4/15/00; No. 872d, 12/2/00; No. 871c, 4/21/01; No. 872e, 8/1/01; Nos. 874B-874E, 874G, 10/18/99; No. 874F, 10/18/99; No. 871d, 1/19/02. No. 865b, 4/1/02.

See note after No. 940.
See also Nos. 917, 965-973, 991-993, 1083

Chinese White Dolphin — A173

Various views of dolphin.

1999, Nov. 14 **Litho.** *Perf. 14½*

Granite Paper

875 A173 $1.30 green & multi .60 .60
876 A173 $2.50 bl grn & multi 1.00 1.00
877 A173 $3.10 blue & multi 1.25 1.25
878 A173 $5 pur & multi 1.75 1.75

Souvenir Sheet

879 Sheet of 4, #a.-d. 4.75 4.75

Nos. 875-878 have Worldwide Fund for Nature (WWF) emblem; Nos. 879a-879d do not.

See No. 900.

Souvenir Sheet

Millennium — A174

No. 880: a, Dragon boat races, skyline. b, Bridge, birds.

Perf. 14¼ Syncopated

1999, Dec. 31 **Photo.**

Granite Paper

880 A174 $5 Sheet of 2, #a.-b. 6.00 6.00

New Millennium Children's Stamp Design Contest Winners — A175

Designs: $1.30, Scales. $2.50, Children planting tree on planet. $3.10, Planets. $5, Inhabited planets, space shuttle, rocket.

2000, Jan. 1 **Granite Paper**

881 A175 $1.30 multi .45 .45
882 A175 $2.50 multi .85 .85
883 A175 $3.10 multi .95 .95
884 A175 $5 multi 1.75 1.75
Nos. 881-884 (4) 4.00 4.00

Victoria Harbor A176

Litho. & Embossed with Foil Application

2000, Jan. 1 *Perf. 13¼*

885 A176 $50 gold & multi 22.50 22.50

New Year 2000 (Year of the Dragon) — A177

Various dragons.

Perf. 14¼ Syncopated

2000, Jan. 23 **Litho.**

Granite Paper

886 A177 $1.30 multi .40 .40
887 A177 $2.50 multi .75 .75
888 A177 $3.10 multi .85 .85
889 A177 $5 multi 1.45 1.45
a. Souvenir sheet of 1, imperf. 15.00 15.00
b. Souvenir sheet, #886-889 4.00 4.00
Nos. 886-889 (4) 3.45 3.45

See Nos. 1030a, 1431a, 1479a, 1480a.

Museums and Libraries — A178

Designs: $1.30, Heritage Museum. $2.50, Central Library. $3.10, Museum of Coastal Defense. $5 Museum of History.

Perf. 14½x14¼

2000, Mar. 26 **Photo.**

Granite Paper

890 A178 $1.30 multi .60 .35
891 A178 $2.50 multi 1.30 .95
892 A178 $3.10 multi 1.25 1.00
893 A178 $5 multi 2.25 2.25
a. Block, #890-893 8.00 8.00
Nos. 890-893 (4) 5.40 4.55

Nos. 890-893 issued in sheets of 24. No. 893a issued only in sheet containing 4 blocks.

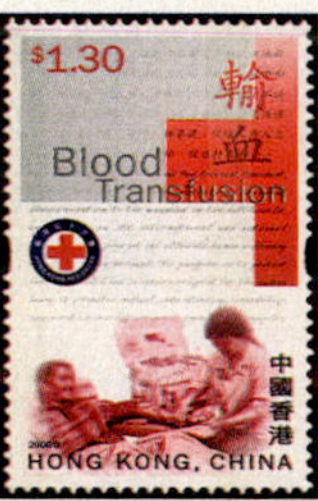

Red Cross — A179

Designs: $1.30, Blood transfusion. $2.50, Special education. $3.10, Disaster relief. $5, Voluntary service.

Perf. 14¼ Syncopated

2000, May 7 **Photo.**

Granite Paper

894 A179 $1.30 multi .45 .45
895 A179 $2.50 multi .85 .85
896 A179 $3.10 multi .95 .95
897 A179 $5 multi 1.75 1.75
a. Souvenir sheet, #894-897 4.25 4.25
Nos. 894-897 (4) 4.00 4.00

Flower Type of 1989, Mountain Type of 1996 Inscribed "Hong Kong, China," and Dolphin Type of 1999

Perf. 14¼ Syncopated

2000, June 17 **Photo.**

Granite Paper

898 A90 $5 Booklet pane of 1, like #455 4.50 4.50
899 A150 $5 Booklet pane of 1, like #755 4.50 4.50
900 A173 $5 Booklet pane of 1, like #879d 4.50 4.50
Booklet, #898-900 13.50

Hong Kong 2001 Stamp Exhibition. Booklet sold for $35.

Insects — A180

Designs: $1.30, Pyrops candelarius. $2.50, Macromidia ellenae. $3.10, Troides helena spilotia. $5, Chiridopsis bowringi.

Perf. 13½x13¼ Syncopated

2000, July 16 **Litho.**

Granite Paper

901-904 A180 Set of 4 4.50 4.50
904a Souvenir sheet, #901-904 4.50 4.50

Mountain Type of 1996 Inscribed "Hong Kong, China"

Souvenir Sheet

Perf. 13¼ Syncopated

2000, Aug. 12 **Photo.**

Granite Paper

905 A150 $10 Like #754 4.50 4.00

Hong Kong 2001 Stamp Exhibition.

2000 Summer Olympics, Sydney — A181

Designs: $1.30, Cycling, badminton. $2.50, Table tennis, running. $3.10, Judo, rowing. $5, Swimming, sailboarding.

Perf. 14¼ Syncopated

2000, Aug. 27 **Litho.**

Granite Paper

906-909 A181 Set of 4 4.50 3.75

Birds A182

2000, Sept. 30 **Photo.**

Granite Paper

910 Booklet pane of 2 4.50
a. A182 $1.30 Yellow-breasted bunting 1.50 1.50
b. A182 $2.50 Great knot 3.00 3.00
911 Booklet pane of 2 6.50
a. A182 $3.10 Falcated teal 2.50 2.50
b. A182 $5 Black-faced spoonbill 4.00 4.00
Booklet, #910-911 11.00

Booklet containing Nos. 910-911 sold for $25.

Chinese General Chamber of Commerce, Cent. — A183

Designs: $1.30, Hong Kong in 1900. $2.50, Headquarters buildings. $3.10, People reading notice for distribution of relief funds. $5, Hand with computer mouse, currency symbols.

Perf. 13¾ Syncopated

2000, Oct. 22 **Litho.**

Granite Paper

912-915 A183 Set of 4 4.50 3.75

Coral Type of 1994 Inscribed "Hong Kong, China"
Souvenir Sheet
Perf. 13¼ Syncopated

2000, Nov. 25 **Photo.**
Granite Paper
916 A141 $10 Like #709 5.00 4.00

Landmarks Type of 1999
Souvenir Sheet
Litho. & Holography

2000, Dec. 31
917 A172 $20 Like #873 8.00 8.00

Soaking in water may affect hologram.

New Year 2001 (Year of the Snake) — A184

Various snakes. Denominations: $1.30, $2.50, $3.10, $5.

Perf. 14½ Sync.

2001, Jan. 1 **Photo.**
918-921 A184 Set of 4 4.50 4.00
921a Souvenir sheet of 1, imperf. 2.50 2.50
921b Souvenir sheet, #918-921 4.75 4.75

See Nos. 1030b, 1431b, 1479b, 1480b.

Souvenir Sheet

Opening of Hong Kong 2001 Stamp Exhibition — A185

No. 922: a, Year of the Dragon. b, Year of the Snake.

Litho. & Embossed with Foil Application

2001, Feb. 1 ***Perf. 13¼***
922 A185 $50 Sheet of 2, #a-b 45.00 45.00

Indiginous Trees Type of 1988 Inscribed "Hong Kong, China"

2001 Photo. ***Perf. 14¼ Syncopated***
Granite Paper
923 A105 $5 multi, sheetlet #5 2.25 2.25
a. Sheetlet #6 2.25 2.25
b. Sheetlet #7 2.25 2.25
c. Sheetlet #8 2.25 2.25

Issued: No. 923, 2/2; No. 923a, 2/3; No. 923b, 2/4; No. 923c, 2/5. No. 923b with gold overprint in margin reading "To commemorate the FIAP Day of HONG KONG 2001 Stamp Exhibition on 4th February, 2001" is a private emission.

See note after No. 940 for unsyncopated stamp.

Greetings — A186

Designs: $1.30, Maple leaves. $1.60, Swans. $2.50, Chicks. $2.60, Cherry blossoms. $3.10, Bamboo. $5, Snow-covered plant.

Stamps + Labels

2001, Feb. 1 **Photo.**
Granite Paper
924-929 A186 Set of 6 5.75 4.75

See note after Nos. 934-937.

Hong Kong Water Supply, 150th Anniv. — A187

Designs: $1.30, Tai Tam Tuk Reservoir. $2.50, Plover Cove Reservoir. $3.10, Pipelines. $5, Beakers, chemical symbols.

2001, Mar. 18 **Litho. & Embossed**
Granite Paper
930-933 A187 Set of 4 5.00 4.00
933a Block of 4, #930-933 6.00 6.00

Movie Stars A188

Designs: $1.30, Ng Cho-fan (1911-93) and Pak Yin (1920-87). $2.50, Sun Ma Si-tsang (1916-97) and Tang Bik-wan (1926-91). $3.10, Cheung Wood-yau (1910-85) and Wong Man-lei (1913-98). $5, Mak Bing-wing (1915-84) and Fung Wong-nui (1925-92).

2001, Apr. 8 **Litho.**
Granite Paper
934-937 A188 Set of 4 4.25 3.25
937a Block of 4, #934-937 4.50 4.50

Values are for stamps with surrounding selvage.

On June 12, 2001 Hong Kong sold for $120 limited numbers of a sheet containing 18 examples of the $1.30 stamp, No. 924. The 18 labels to the right of the stamps on this sheet differ from those found on examples of No. 924 sold on the stamp's original date of issue, and the 18 labels to the left of the stamps depict Chinese celebrities.

Dragon Boat Races A189

Dragon boats and: No. 938, $5, Sydney Opera House. No. 939, Hong Kong Convention and Exhibition Center.

2001, June 25 **Litho.** ***Perf. 14x14½***
Granite Paper
938-939 A189 Set of 2 3.75 2.75
939a Souvenir sheet, #938-939 3.75 3.75

See Australia Nos. 1977-1978.

Emblem of 2008 Summer Olympics, Beijing — A190

2001, July 14 **Photo.** ***Perf. 13x13¼***
940 A190 $1.30 multi + label 1.25 1.25

No. 940 printed in sheets of 12 stamp + label pairs with one large central label. See People's Republic of China No. 3119, Macao No. 1067. No. 940 with different label is from People's Republic of China No. 3119a.

On July 21, 2001 Hong Kong sold a booklet containing stamps with a face value of $12.40 for $30. The stamps are the Indigenous Trees type of 1988 with the inscription "Hong Kong, China." The first pane in the booklet contained $1.30 and $2.50 stamps, and those on the second pane contained $3.10 and $5 stamps.

On Aug. 25, 2001 Hong Kong sold a booklet containing stamps with a face value of $30 for $65. The first pane in the booklet contained four stamps with a face value of $1.80 of the Stamp Collecting type of 1992 with the inscription "Hong Kong, China." The second pane contained two $3.10 perf. 13½x13 stamps on granite paper of type A152, and two $3.10 perf. 13¾ syncopated stamps on granite paper of type A172. The third pane contained four $2.60 perf. 14¼ stamps on granite paper of type A162.

Tea Culture — A191

Various tea services and background colors of: $1.30, Lilac. $2.50, Orange brown. $3.10, Bright orange. $5, Green.

Perf. 14¼x14½ Syncopated

2001, Sept. 9 **Litho.**
944-947 A191 Set of 4 4.25 3.75

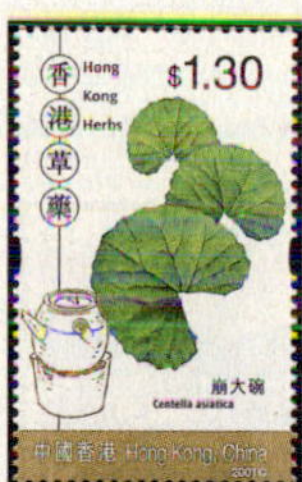

Herbs — A192

Designs: $1.30, Centella asiatica. $2.50, Lobelia chinensis. $3.10, Gardenia jasminoides. $5, Scutellaria indica.

Perf. 14½ Syncopated

2001, Oct. 7 **Granite Paper** **Litho.**
948-951 A192 Set of 4 4.25 3.75

Children's Stamp Coloring Contest — A193

Designs: $1.30, Bear. $2.50, Penguin. $3.10, Flower. $5, Bee.

Granite Paper

Die Cut Perf. 13¾x13¼ Sync.

2001, Nov. 18 **Self-Adhesive**
952-955 A193 Set of 4 5.00 4.00
955a Souvenir sheet, #952-955 5.00 5.00

New Year 2002 (Year of the Horse) — A194

Various horses. Denominations: $1.30, $2.50, $3.10, $5.

2002, Jan. 13 ***Perf. 14½ Syncopated***
Granite Paper
956-959 A194 Set of 4 4.25 3.75
959a Souvenir sheet of 1, imperf. 2.50 2.50
959b Souvenir sheet, #956-959 4.75 4.75

See Nos. 1030c, 1431c, 1479c, 1480c.

Souvenir Sheet

New Year 2002 (Year of the Horse) — A195

No. 960: a, Snake. b, Horse.

Litho. & Embossed with Foil Application

2002, Feb. 9 ***Perf. 13¼***
960 A195 $50 Sheet of 2, #a-b 42.50 42.50

Works of Art — A196

Details from: $1.30, Lines in Motion, by Chui Tze-hung. $2.50, Volume and Time, by Hon Chi-fun. $3.10, Bright Sun, by Aries Lee. $5, Midsummer, by Irene Chou.

Perf. 14½ Syncopated

2002, Feb. 24 **Litho.**
Granite Paper
961-964 A196 Set of 4 4.50 3.50

Landmarks Type of 1999

Designs: $1.40, Hong Kong Railway Museum. $1.80, Hong Kong Stadium. $1.90, Western Market. $2.40, Kwun Yam statue, Repulse Bay. $3, Peak Tower. $13, Hong Kong Cultural Center.

Perf. 13x13¾ Syncopated

2002, Apr. 1 **Photo.**
Granite Paper
965 A172 $1.80 blue & multi .50 .50
966 A172 $1.90 blue & multi .55 .55
967 A172 $2.40 blue & multi .65 .65
a. Booklet pane of 10 6.50 —
Complete booklet, #967a 6.50
968 A172 $3 blue & multi .85 .85
a. Booklet pane of 10 8.50 —
Complete booklet, #968a 8.50

Size: 26x32mm

Perf. 13¼ Syncopated

969 A172 $13 blue & multi 4.00 4.00
Nos. 965-969 (5) 6.55 6.55

Coil Stamps

Size: 18x22mm

Perf. 14¾x13¼ Syncopated

970 A172 $1.40 blue & multi 1.05 .50
971 A172 $1.80 blue & multi 1.35 .80
972 A172 $2.40 blue & multi 1.75 1.00
973 A172 $3 blue & multi 2.25 1.50
Nos. 970-973 (4) 6.40 3.80

Cyberindustry in Hong Kong — A197

Designs: $1.40, Innovation. $2.40, Connectivity. $3, Trend. $5, Strength.

Perf. 13¾ Syncopated

2002, Apr. 14 **Litho.**

Granite Paper

974-977 A197 Set of 4 4.00 3.50
977a Block of 4, #974-977 4.50 4.50

A booklet of two panes, one containing one each of Nos. 974 and 976, and another containing one each of Nos. 975 and 977, sold for $30. Value, $11.

2002 World Cup Soccer Championships, Japan and Korea — A198

No. 978: a, Goalie. b, Crowd and players.

Perf. 12 Syncopated

2002, May 16 **Photo.**

978 Horiz. pair, with central label 2.00 2.00
a.-b. A198 $1.40 Either single 1.00 1.00

No. 978 was printed in sheets of 5 pairs and five different labels.

A souvenir sheet containing Nos. 978a-978b, People's Republic of China No. 3198, and Macao Nos. 1091a-1091b exists.

Corals A199

Designs: $1.40, North Atlantic pink tree, Pacific orange cup, and North Pacific horn corals. $2.40, North Atlantic giant orange tree, and Black corals. $3, Dendronepthea gigantea and Dendronepthea corals. $5, Tubastrea and Echinogorgia corals.

Perf. 13¾x14 Syncopated

2002, May 19 **Litho.**

Granite Paper

979-982 A199 Set of 4 4.50 4.00
982a Souvenir sheet, #979-982 5.00 5.00

On May 10, 2003, Hong Kong sold a booklet with a face value of $11.80 for $25. The first pane contains Nos. 979-980 perf 13¼x13. The second pane contains Nos. 981-982, perf 13¼x13.

See Canada Nos. 1948-1951.

Beijing — Kowloon Through Trains A200

Train and: $1.40, Hong Kong commercial buildings. $2.40, Wuhan-Changjiang Bridge, Wuchang. $3, Shaolin Monastery Pagodas, Zhengzhou. $5, Temple of Heaven, Beijing.

2002, June 9 *Perf. 14¼ Syncopated*

Granite Paper

983-986 A200 Set of 4 4.25 3.75
986a Horiz. strip of 4, #983-986 5.00 5.00

Hong Kong Special Administrative Region, 5th Anniv. — A201

Designs: $1.40, White dolphins, corals. $2.40, Students, bauhinia flowers. $3, Flying cranes, Hong Kong International Airport. $5, Flags of Hong Kong and People's Republic of China, fireworks over skyline.

2002, July 1 **Granite Paper**

987-990 A201 Set of 4 4.50 4.00
990a Souvenir sheet, #987-990 4.50 4.50

Landmarks Type of 1999 with Pink Denomination and Country Name

Souvenir Sheet

Design: Tsing Ma Bridge.

Perf. 13¼ Syncopated

2002, July 27 **Photo.**

Granite Paper

991 A172 $10 pink & multi 4.25 3.75

Philakorea 2002.

Landmarks Type of 1999 With Olive Green Denomination and Country Name

Souvenir Sheet

Design: Tsing Ma Bridge.

Perf. 13¼ Syncopated

2002, Aug. 24 **Photo.**

Granite Paper

992 A172 $10 ol green & multi 4.50 4.00

Amphilex 2002 Intl. Stamp Exhibition, Amsterdam.

Landmarks Type of 1999 With Buff Background

Souvenir Sheet

Design: Tsing Ma Bridge.

2002, Sept. 7

993 A172 $10 blue, buff & multi 4.50 4.00

Rocks A202

Designs: $1.40, Ping Chau (siltstone). $2.40, Port Island (conglomerate). $3, Po Pin Chau (tuff). $5, Lamma Island (granite).

Perf. 13¼x12¾

2002, Sept. 15 **Litho.**

994-997 A202 Set of 4 4.75 4.25
997a Souvenir sheet, #994-997 4.75 4.75

Portions of the designs were applied by a thermographic process, producing a shiny, raised effect.

Eastern and Western Cultures A203

Designs: 10c, Radar screen, luopan. 20c, Calculator, abacus. 50c, Incense coil, stained glass window. $1, Chair, Chinese bed. $1.40, Dim sum, loaves of bread. $1.80, Silverware, chopsticks and spoon. $1.90, Canned drinks, tea caddies. $2, Western and Eastern wedding cakes. $2.40, Erhu, violin. $2.50, Letter boxes, internet. $3, Sailboats, dragon boat. $5, Tiled roof, glass wall. $10, Ballet, Chinese opera. $13, Chess, Xiangqi. $20, Christmas decorations, lanterns. $50, Eastern and Western sculptures.

Perf. 13¼x13 Syncopated

2002, Oct. 14 **Photo.**

Granite Paper

998 A203 10c multi .30 .25
999 A203 20c multi .30 .25
1000 A203 50c multi .30 .25
1001 A203 $1 multi .35 .35
1002 A203 $1.40 multi .45 .40
a. Booklet pane of 10 4.50
Complete booklet, #1002a 4.50
1003 A203 $1.80 multi .60 .50
a. Booklet pane of 10 ('03) 6.00 —
Complete booklet, #1003a 6.00
1004 A203 $1.90 multi .65 .50
1005 A203 $2 multi .65 .50
1006 A203 $2.40 multi .75 .55
a. Booklet pane of 10 7.50
Complete booklet, #1006a 7.50
1007 A203 $2.50 multi .80 .60
1008 A203 $3 multi .90 .80
a. Booklet pane of 10 9.00
Complete booklet, #1008a 9.00
1009 A203 $5 multi 1.75 1.25
a. Souvenir sheet, #998-1009 8.00 8.00
b. Booklet pane, #998-1009 8.00
Complete booklet, #1009b 8.00

Size: 40x24mm

Perf. 14¾ Syncopated

1010 A203 $10 multi 3.00 1.40
1011 A203 $13 multi 3.75 1.75
1012 A203 $20 multi 7.00 3.00
1013 A203 $50 multi 16.00 7.50
a. Souvenir sheet #1010-1013 30.00 30.00
Nos. 998-1013 (16) 37.55 19.85

Coil Stamps

Size: 22x19mm

Perf. 13¼x14¾ Syncopated

1014 A203 $1.40 multi 1.60 1.00
1015 A203 $1.80 multi 2.00 1.40
1016 A203 $2.40 multi 3.00 2.00
1017 A203 $3 multi 4.00 3.00
Nos. 1014-1017 (4) 10.60 7.40

No. 1003a issued 10/7/04.

Christmas — A204

Designs: $1.40, Christmas tree. $2.40, Ornament. $3, Snowman. $5, Bell.

Photo. with Hologram Applied

Perf. 13½ Syncopated

2002, Nov. 24 **Granite Paper**

1018-1021 A204 Set of 4 4.50 4.00
1021a Block or strip of 4, #1018-1021 4.75 4.75

Perforations within the stamp outline the designs.

Hong Kong Disneyland A205

Designs: $1.40, Main Street. $2.40, Fantasyland. $3, Adventureland. $5, Tomorrowland.

Perf. 13¾ Syncopated

2003, Jan. 12 **Litho. & Embossed**

Granite Paper

1022-1025 A205 Set of 4 5.00 4.50
1025a Souvenir sheet, #1022-1025 5.50 5.50

New Year 2003 (Year of the Ram) — A206

Various rams: $1.40, $2.40, $3, $5.

Perf. 14¼ Syncopated

2003, Jan. 19 **Litho.**

Granite Paper

1026-1029 A206 Set of 4 4.75 4.25
1029a Souvenir sheet of 1, imperf. 3.00 3.00
1029b Souvenir sheet, #1026-1029 4.75 4.75

See Nos. 1030d, 1431d, 1479d, 1480d.

New Year Types of 2000-03

2003, Jan. 19 **Litho.** *Perf. 12¾x13¼*

Flocked Paper

1030 Block of 4 15.00 15.00
a. A177 $10 Like #888 3.75 3.75
b. A184 $10 Like #920 3.75 3.75
c. A194 $10 Like #957 3.75 3.75
d. A206 $10 Like #1029 3.75 3.75

Souvenir Sheet

New Year 2003 (Year of the Ram) — A207

No. 1031: a, Horse. b, Ram.

Litho. & Embossed with Foil Application

2003, Jan. 19 *Perf. 13¼*

1031 A207 $50 Sheet of 2, #a-b 42.50 42.50

Traditional Trades and Handicrafts — A208

Designs: $1.40, Letter writing. $1.80, Bird cage making, vert. $2.40, Qipao tailoring. $2.50, Hairdressing, vert. $3, Dough figurine making, vert. $5, Olive selling.

Perf. 13½x14 Syncopated, 13½ Syncopated (vert. stamps)

2003, Mar. 13 **Litho.**

Granite Paper

1032-1037 A208 Set of 6 6.00 5.00
1037a Souvenir sheet, #1032-1037 6.00 6.00

Souvenir Sheet

Hong Kong 2004 Stamp Expo — A209

2003, Apr. 8 *Perf. 13¼ Syncopated*

Granite Paper

1038 A209 $10 multi 4.50 4.00

Souvenir Sheet

Master-of-Nets Garden, Suzhou — A210

2003, June 27 **Granite Paper**

1039 A210 $10 multi 4.50 4.00

See No. 1456f.

Miniature Landscapes — A211

Plants: $1.40, Fukien tea. $2.40, Hedge sageretia. $3, Fire-thorn, vert. $5, Chinese hackberry, vert.

Perf. 13¾x12¾ Syncopated, 12¾x13¾ Syncopated

2003, July 17 **Photo.**

Granite Paper

1040-1043 A211 Set of 4 4.50 4.00

Aquarium Fish A212

Various fish: $1.40, $2.40, $3, $5.

2003, Aug. 7 ***Perf. 14¼ Syncopated***

Granite Paper

With Fish-Shaped Holes in Paper

1044-1047 A212 Set of 4 5.00 4.25
1047a Block of 4, #1044-1047 5.50 5.50

A213

Heartwarming A214

Perf. 13¾ Syncopated

2003, Sept. 10 **Litho.**

Inscribed "Local Mail Postage"

Granite Paper

1048 A213 ($1.40) multi .60 .50
1049 A214 ($1.40) multi .60 .50
a. Sheet of 16 + 17 labels ('04) 19.50 19.50

Inscribed "Air Mail Postage"

1050 A213 ($3) multi 1.60 1.10
1051 A214 ($3) multi 1.60 1.10
a. Sheet, 4 each #1048-1051, + 17 labels 18.00 18.00
Nos. 1048-1051 (4) 4.40 3.20

No. 1049a issued 10/7/04. No. 1049a sold for $50 and has a 2004 Olympic Games theme on the labels. A similar sheet issued in 2005 with labels having a Lions Club Convention theme, sold for $108 in conjunction with other items, and was not available separately.

See Nos. 1594-1597.

Birds A215

Designs: $1.40, Pied avocet. $2.40, Horned grebe. $3, Black-throated diver. $5, Great crested grebe.

Perf. 12½ Syncopated

2003, Oct. 4 **Litho. & Engr.**

Granite Paper

1052-1055 A215 Set of 4 4.50 4.00
1055a Booklet pane, #1052-1055 5.25 —
Complete booklet, 2 #1055a 10.50

See Sweden No. 2469.

Souvenir Sheet

Hong Kong 2004 Stamp Expo — A216

Perf. 13¼ Syncopated

2003, Oct. 14 **Litho.**

Granite Paper

1056 A216 $10 multi 4.75 4.75
1056a Sheet, 2 each #1038, 1056, + 2 labels 32.50 32.50

No. 1056a was issued 1/30/04 and sold for $80. Labels could be personalized.

Percussion Instruments — A217

Designs: $1.40, Drum. $2.40, Clappers. $3, Cymbals. $5, Gongs. $13, Chimes.

Perf. 13½x13¼ Syncopated

2003, Nov. 6 **Photo.**

1057-1060 A217 Set of 4 4.00 3.50

Souvenir Sheet

Perf. 13¾x13¼ Syncopated

1061 A217 $13 multi 4.50 4.00

No. 1061 contains one 35x45mm stamp.

Launch of First Manned Chinese Spacecraft — A218

No. 1062: a, Astronaut, Shenzhou spacecraft. b, Rocket lift-off.

2003, Oct. 16 **Photo.** ***Perf. 13x13¼***

1062 A218 $1.40 Pair, #a-b 2.00 2.00

A booklet containing No. 1062, People's Republic of China No. 3314 and Macao No. 1128a exists. The booklet sold for a premium over face value.

UNESCO World Heritage Sites in People's Republic of China — A219

Designs: $1.40, Potala Palace, vert. (27x75mm). $1.80, Imperial Palace of the Ming and Qing Dynasties. $2.40, Mausoleum of the First Qin Emperor. $2.50, Mount Huangshan, vert. $3, Old Town of Lijiang, vert. $5, Jiuzhaigou Valley (75x27mm).

Perf. 13¼ Syncopated

2003, Nov. 25 **Litho.**

Granite Paper

1063 A219 $1.40 multi .60 .55
a. Perf. 13¼x13¼x13¼x13 Syncopated .60 .55

Perf. 13x13¼ Syncopated

1064 A219 $1.80 multi .75 .70
a. Perf. 13x13¼x12½x13¼ Syncopated .75 .70
1065 A219 $2.40 multi .90 .85
a. Perf. 12½x13¼ Syncopated .90 .85

Perf. 13 Syncopated

1066 A219 $2.50 multi 1.05 .90
a. Perf. 13x13x13x13¼ Syncopated 1.05 .90
b. Perf. 13¼x13x13x13 Syncopated 1.05 .90
c. Perf. 13¼x13x13x13¼ Syncopated 1.05 .90
1067 A219 $3 multi 1.25 1.10
a. Perf. 12½x13x13x13 Syncopated 1.25 1.10

Perf. 13x12¾ Syncopated

1068 A219 $5 multi 2.00 1.75
a. Perf. 13x12¾x13 and 13¼x13 Syncopated 2.00 1.75
b. Perf. 13 Syncopated 2.00 1.75
c. Miniature sheet (see note below) 19.50 19.50
Nos. 1063-1068 (6) 6.55 5.85

No. 1068c contains one each of Nos. 1063a, 1064, 1065, 1066a, 1066b, 1066c, 1067a, 1068b and two each of Nos. 1063, 1064a, 1065a, 1067 and 1068a. Perfs for the minor varieties are for the measurement that comprises the longest part of each side, as the sides of some stamps have sections with varying perf measurements. Approximately one half of the bottom row of perfs on No. 1068a is perf. 13 while the other half is perf. 13¼.

Development of Public Housing — A220

Various buildings.

Perf. 13¼x13 Syncopated

2003, Dec. 11 **Photo.**

Granite Paper

1069 A220 $1.40 org & multi .60 .45
a. Tete-beche pair 1.20 .90
1070 A220 $2.40 yel & multi .85 .70
a. Tete-beche pair 1.75 1.40
1071 A220 $3 pur & multi 1.50 .95
a. Tete-beche pair 3.00 1.90
1072 A220 $5 red & multi 2.25 1.50
a. Tete-beche pair 4.50 3.00
Nos. 1069-1072 (4) 5.20 3.60

New Year 2004 (Year of the Monkey) — A221

Various monkeys: $1.40, $2.40, $3, $5.

Perf. 13½x13¼ Syncopated

2004, Jan. 4 **Litho.**

Granite Paper

1073-1076 A221 Set of 4 4.00 4.00
1076a Souvenir sheet of 1, imperf. 2.25 2.25
1076b Souvneir sheet, #1073-1076 4.00 4.00

See Nos. 1253a, 1431e, 1479e, 1480e.

Souvenir Sheet

New Year 2004 (Year of the Monkey) — A222

No. 1077: a, Ram. b, Monkey.

Litho. & Embossed with Foil Application

2004, Jan. 4 ***Perf. 13¼***

1077 A222 $50 Sheet of 2, #a-b 35.00 35.00

Souvenir Sheets

New Year Puddings and Greeting — A223

New Year Puddings With Two Greetings — A224

New Year Parade — A225

Jade — A226

Fire Dragon Dance — A227

No. 1079: a, Same Chinese text as on No. 1078 when viewed from directly above (top character with long curved line at bottom). b, Text different from that on No. 1078 when viewed from directly above.

2004 Litho. ***Perf. 13¼ Syncopated***

Granite Paper

1078 A223 $10 multi 4.00 4.00
1079 A224 $10 Sheet of 2, #a-b 5.00 5.00
1080 A225 $10 multi 4.00 4.00
1081 A226 $10 multi 4.00 4.00
1082 A227 $10 multi 4.00 4.00
Nos. 1078-1082 (5) 21.00 21.00

2004 Hong Kong Stamp Expo. Issued: Nos. 1078-1079, 1/30; No. 1080, 1/31; No. 1081, 2/1; No. 1082, 2/2.

Nos. 1079a and 1079b show the same two Chinese texts, but the texts appear different depending on the angle at which one views the stamps. Under magnification it can be seen that the two Chinese texts are printed differently to achieve this effect.

Landmarks Type of 1999 With Red Violet Denomination and Country Name

No. 1083: a, Museum of Tea Ware. b, St. John's Cathedral. c, Legislative Council Building. d, Tai Fu Tai. e, Wong Tai Sin Temple. f, Victoria Harbor. g, Hong Kong Railway Museum. h, Tsim Sha Tsui Clock Tower. i, Hong Kong Stadium. j, Western Market. k, Happy Valley Racecourse. l, Kowloon-Canton Railway. m, Repulse Bay. n, Chi Lin Nunnery. o, Peak Tower. p, Buddha at Po Lin Monastery. q, Aw Boon Haw Gardens. r, Tsing Ma Bridge. s, Hong Kong Cultural Center. t, Hong Kong Convention and Exhibition Center. u, Hong Kong Intl. Airport.

Perf. 13x13¾ Syncopated

2004, Feb. 3 Photo.

Granite Paper

1083 Sheet of 21 10.00 10.00
a.-u. A172 $1.40 Any single, red vio & multi (23x27mm) .45 .45

2004 Hong Kong Stamp Expo.

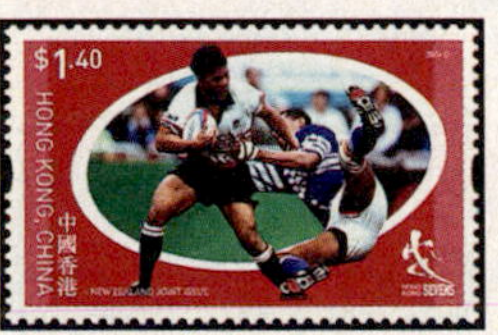

Rugby Sevens A228

Designs: $1.40, Hong Kong Sevens. $2.40, New Zealand Sevens. $3, Hong Kong Stadium. $5, Westpac Stadium, Wellington, New Zealand.

Perf. 13¼x14¼ Syncopated

2004, Feb. 25 Litho.

Granite Paper

1084-1087 A228 Set of 4 4.25 4.25
1087a Block of 4, #1084-1087 5.25 5.25

Children's Games and Activities — A229

Designs: $1.40, Scissors, Paper, Stone. $2.40, Chinese chess. $3, Blowing bubbles. $5, Hopscotch.

2004, Apr. 7 Granite Paper

1088-1091 A229 Set of 4 4.00 3.50
1091a Block of 4, #1088-1091 4.00 4.00

Souvenir Sheet

Chen Clan Academy — A230

Perf. 13½x13¼ Syncopated

2004, May 6

1092 A230 $10 multi 4.00 3.50

See No. 1456g.

Trams in Hong Kong, Cent. — A231

Various trams and tickets: $1.40, Green ticket. $2.40, Brown ticket. $3, Blue ticket. No. 1096, $5, Yellow ticket.

No. 1097, Olive ticket.

2004, May 27 Granite Paper

1093-1096 A231 Set of 4 4.00 3.50
1096a Souvenir sheet, #1093-1096 4.00 4.00

Souvenir Sheet

1097 A231 $5 multi 1.60 1.60

People's Liberation Army Forces of Hong Kong — A232

Inscriptions: $1.40, The Powerful and Civilized Military Force. $1.80, Social Services. $2.40, Open Day. $2.50, Army. $3, Navy. $5, Air Force.

Perf. 13¼x14 Syncopated

2004, June 30 Litho.

Granite Paper

1098 A232 $1.40 multi .45 .45
a. Booklet pane of 4 2.60 —
1099 A232 $1.80 multi .65 .65
a. Booklet pane of 4 3.25 —
1100 A232 $2.40 multi .80 .80
a. Booklet pane of 4 4.25 —
1101 A232 $2.50 multi .85 .85
a. Booklet pane of 4 4.75 —
1102 A232 $3 multi 1.05 1.05
a. Booklet pane of 4 5.50 —
1103 A232 $5 multi 1.60 1.60
a. Booklet pane of 4 8.50 —
Complete booklet, #1098a-1103a 29.00
Nos. 1098-1103 (6) 5.40 5.40

Complete booklet sold for $85.

Relay Race — A233

Diving — A234

Volleyball — A235

Cycling — A236

Badminton — A237

No. 1104: a, Runners in blocks. b, Runners. c, Runner taking baton. d, Runner at finish.

No. 1105: a, Diver on board. b, Diver with legs tucked in. c, Diver with arms and legs extended. d, Diver entering water.

No. 1106: a, Player making save. b, Player leaping to get ball. c, Player striking ball above net. d, Player trying to block ball.

No. 1107: a, Cyclists, denomination at left. b, Cyclist at right, denomination at left. c, Cyclists, denomination at right. d, Cyclist with arms extended.

No. 1108: a, Bird above head, racquet at shoulder level. b, Bird at shoulder level, racquet at knee level. c, Bird and racquet above head. d, Player with face covered by arm.

Perf. 13½x13¼ Syncopated

2004, July 20 Granite Paper

1104 A233 $1.40 Horiz. strip of 4, #a-d 1.75 1.75
1105 A234 $1.40 Horiz. strip of 4, #a-d 1.75 1.75
1106 A235 $1.40 Horiz. strip of 4, #a-d 1.75 1.75
1107 A236 $1.40 Horiz. strip of 4, #a-d 1.75 1.75
1108 A237 $1.40 Horiz. strip of 4, #a-d 1.75 1.75
e. Miniature sheet, #1104-1108 8.75 8.75

Souvenir Sheet

2004 Summer Olympics, Athens — A238

No. 1109: a, Runner without clothes. b, Runner with clothes.

2004, Aug. 13 Granite Paper

1109 A238 $5 Sheet of 2, #a-b 3.75 3.75

Deng Xiaoping (1904-97), Chinese Leader — A239

No. 1110: a, Saluting flags. b, Watching fireworks.

$10, Three photographs.

2004, Aug. 22 ***Perf. 13x13¼***

1110 A239 $1.40 Horiz. pair, #a-b 1.00 1.00

Souvenir Sheet

1111 A239 $10 multi 4.25 4.25

Hong Kong Currency — A240

Obverse and reverse of: $1.40, 1863 one mil bronze coin. $2.40, 1866 twenty cent silver coin. $3, 1935 one dollar banknotes. No. 1115, $5, 1997 one thousand dollar gold coin commemorating establishment of Special Administrative Region.

No. 1116, $5, 1993 ten dollar coin.

Perf. 13¼x14 Syncopated

2004, Sept. 2 Granite Paper

1112-1115 A240 Set of 4 4.25 4.25
1115a Miniature sheet, #1112-1115 4.25 4.25

Souvenir Sheet

1116 A240 $5 multi 2.50 2.50

Pearl River Delta Region Development — A241

Designs: $1.40, Men and bridge. $2.40, Men and crane. $3, Tourist attractions. $5, Men and buildings.

2004, Oct. 19 Granite Paper

1117-1120 A241 Set of 4 4.00 4.00
1120a Block of 4, #1117-1120 4.75 4.75

No. 1120a printed in sheets of 4 blocks.

Mushrooms A242

Designs: $1.40, Straw mushrooms. $2.40, Red-orange mushrooms. $3, Violet marasmius. No. 1124, $5, Lingzhi mushrooms.

No. 1125, Hexagon fungi.

Perf. 13½x13¼ Syncopated

2004, Nov. 23 Granite Paper

1121-1124 A242 Set of 4 4.25 4.25
1124a Souvenir sheet, #1121-1124 4.25 4.25

Souvenir Sheet

1125 A242 $5 multi 2.10 2.10

Letters of the Alphabet — A243

Nos. 1126 and 1127 — Upper half of letters made with common household items: a, Clothespin. b, Scissors. c, Lamp. d, Plastic cap for glue bottle. e, Steaming rack. f, Caliper with ruler. g, Bolt of padlock. h, Bamboo ladder. i, Flashlight. j, Toilet brush. k, Stapler. l, Sock. m, Draftsman's triangle. n, Nail clippers. o, Rubber band. p, Strainer. q, Link from chain. r, Sunglasses. s, Clothes hanger. t, Wooden broom. u, Sandals. v, Compass. w, Corkscrew. x, Faucet. y, Fork. z, Paint roller.

Perf. 13¼x13 Syncopated

2005, Jan. 4 Litho.

Granite Paper (#1126)

1126 A243 Sheet of 30 (see footnote) 13.00 13.00
a.-z. $1.40 Any single .45 .45

Self-Adhesive

Serpentine Die Cut 12½ Syncopated

1127 A243 Sheet of 30 (see footnote) 14.00
a.-z. $1.40 Any single .45 .45

Each sheet contains one of each letter and an additional example of a, e, i and o stamps.

Covers were prepared in 2006 with se-tenant strips spelling "KUNG," "HEI," "FAT" and "CHOY," which are not found in No. 1126.

New Year 2005 (Year of the Rooster) — A244

Various roosters with background colors of: $1.40, Orange. $2.40, Green. $3, Dark red. $5, Blue.

2005, Jan. 30 ***Perf. 14¼ Syncopated***
Granite Paper

1128-1131 A244 Set of 4		4.25	4.25
1128a	Dated "2011," perf. 13½x13¼ syncopated (1431)	.50	.50
1131a	Souvenir sheet of 1, imperf.	2.25	2.25
1131b	Souvenir sheet, #1128-1131	4.25	4.25

Issued: No. 1128a, 1/22/11. See No. 1253b, 1479f, 1480f.

Souvenir Sheet

New Year 2005 (Year of the Rooster) — A245

No. 1132: a, Monkey. b, Rooster.

Litho. & Embossed With Foil Application

2005, Jan. 30 ***Perf. 13¼***

1132 A245 $50 Sheet of 2, #a-b 35.00 35.00

Fairy Tales by Hans Christian Andersen (1805-75) A246

Designs: $1.40, The Ugly Duckling. $2.40, The Little Mermaid. $3, The Little Match Girl. $5, The Emperor's New Clothes.

Perf. 13¾ Syncopated

2005, Mar. 22 **Litho. & Embossed**
Granite Paper

1133-1136 A246 Set of 4		*10.00*	*10.00*
1133a	Souvenir sheet of 4	*5.25*	*5.25*
1134a	Souvenir sheet of 4	*9.00*	*9.00*
1135a	Souvenir sheet of 4	*12.00*	*12.00*
1136a	Souvenir sheet of 4	*19.50*	*19.50*

Souvenir Sheet

Hong Kong Skyline, Sydney Opera House — A247

Perf. 13½ Syncopated

2005, Apr. 21 **Litho.**
Granite Paper

1137 A247 $10 multi 4.00 4.00

Pacific Explorer 2005 World Stamp Expo, Sydney.

Goldfish A248

Designs: $1.40, Variegated pearl-scale. $2.40, Red and white swallow-tail. $3, Pale bronze egg-phoenix. No. 1141, $5, Blue wenyu.

No. 1142, $5, Red and white dragon-eye.

Perf. 13¼x14 Syncopated

2005, May 12 **Granite Paper**

1138-1141 A248 Set of 4		4.25	4.25
1141a	Souvenir sheet, #1138-1141	4.25	4.25

Souvenir Sheet

1142 A248 $5 multi *10.00 10.00*

No. 1142 contains one 45x35mm stamp.

Maritime Expeditions of Zheng He, 600th Anniv. A249

No. 1143 — Ships and: a, Zheng He (1371-1433), explorer. b, Giraffe, ceramics. c, Compass wheel.

$10, Zheng He on ship.

2005, June 28 ***Perf. 13x13¼***

1143	Horiz. strip of 3	2.10	2.10
a.-c.	A249 $1.40 Any single	.70	.70

Souvenir Sheet

Perf. 13¼

1144 A249 $10 multi 5.00 5.00

No. 1144 contains one 50x30mm stamp.

Creative Industries A250

Designs: $1.40, Circles, squares and triangles (advertising). $2.40, Numerals, letters and symbols (computer and digital industries). $3, Vertical and horizontal lines (broadcasting industries). $5, Curved brushstrokes (arts and crafts).

Perf. 14x14¼ Syncopated

2005, July 21 **Litho.**
Granite Paper

1145-1148 A250 Set of 4		4.50	4.50
1148a	Block of 4 with selvage, #1145-1148	4.50	4.50
1148b	Booklet pane, 2 #1148a	9.00	—
	Complete booklet, 2 #1148b	18.00	

Each block of 4 in the booklet has a different arrangement. Rouletting separates the blocks within each booklet pane.

Great Inventions of Ancient China — A251

Designs: $1.40, Compass. $2.40, Printing. $3, Gunpowder. $5, Papermaking.

Perf. 13¼x14¼ Syncopated

2005, Aug. 18

1149-1152 A251 Set of 4		4.25	4.25
1152a	Miniature sheet, 4 each #1149-1152	17.00	17.00

Opening of Hong Kong Disneyland A252

Designs: $1.40, Mickey and Minnie Mouse. $2.40, Dumbo. $3, Simba and Nala. No. 1156, $5, Pluto.

Nos. 1157, 1158, Mickey Mouse.

Perf. 13¾x13½ Syncopated

2005, Sept. 12 **Litho.**
Granite Paper (#1153-1157)

1153-1156 A252 Set of 4		5.00	5.00
1156a	Souvenir sheet, #1153-1156	5.00	5.00

Souvenir Sheets

1157 A252 $5 multi 2.25 2.25

Litho. & Embossed with Foil Application

1158 A252 $50 gold & multi 21.50 21.50

Souvenir Sheet

Qiantang Tidal Bore — A253

Perf. 13¼ Syncopated

2005, Sept. 16 **Litho.**

1159 A253 $10 multi 4.25 4.25

See No. 1456a.

Fishing Villages A254

Desings: $1.40, Tai O, Hong Kong. $2.40, Aldeia da Carrasqueira, Portugal. $3, Tai O, diff. $5, Aldeia da Carrasqueira, diff.

Perf. 14¼x14 Syncopated

2005, Oct. 18

1160-1163 A254 Set of 4		4.50	4.50
1163a	Miniature sheet, 4 each #1160-1163	18.00	18.00

See Portugal Nos. 2767-2768.

Popular Singers — A255

Designs: $1.40, Wong Ka Kui. $1.80, Danny Chan. $2.40, Roman Tam. $3, Leslie Cheung. $5, Anita Mui.

Perf. 13½x13¼ Syncopated

2005, Nov. 8 **Granite Paper**

1164-1168 A255 Set of 5 5.00 5.00

Because of concerns about the licensing of the images of the singers in foreign countries, the philatelic bureau did not make Nos. 1164-1168 available by mail order to foreign customers. The stamps were freely available to any purchasers over the counter.

New Year 2006 (Year of the Dog) — A256

Designs: $1.40, Golden retriever. $2.40, Pekingese. $3, German shepherd. $5, Beagle.

Perf. 13½x13¼ Syncopated

2006, Jan. 15 **Litho.**
Granite Paper

1169-1172 A256 Set of 4		4.00	4.00
1172a	Souvenir sheet of #1172, imperf.	2.75	2.75
1172b	Souvenir sheet, #1169-1172	4.00	4.00

See Nos. 1253c, 1431f. 1479g, 1480g.

Souvenir Sheet

New Year 2006 (Year of the Dog) — A257

No. 1173: a, Rooster. b, Dog.

Litho. & Embossed with Foil Application

2006, Jan. 15 ***Perf. 13½x13¼***

1173 A257 $50 Sheet of 2, #a-b 40.00 40.00

Chinese Lanterns — A258

No. 1174: a, $1.40, Lotus Fairy lantern. $1.80, Narcissus lantern. $2.40, Peacock lantern.

$5, Boys holding Dragon lantern.

Perf. 12¾x13¼ Syncopated

2006, Feb. 12 **Litho.**
Granite Paper (#1174)

1174 A258 Horiz. strip of 3, #a-c 2.75 2.75

Souvenir Sheet

Perf. 13¼ Syncopated

1175 A258 $5 multi 3.00 3.00

No. 1175 contains one 35x46mm stamp.

Teddy Bears in Costumes A259

Teddy bears in various costumes.

Perf. 13¾ Syncopated

2006, Mar. 30 **Granite Paper**

1176 A259 $1.40 multi		.45	.45
1177 A259 $1.80 multi		.65	.65
a.	Booklet pane, #1176-1177	2.00	—
1178 A259 $2.40 multi		.75	.75
1179 A259 $2.50 multi		.80	.80
a.	Booklet pane, #1178-1179	3.00	—

1180 A259 $3 multi 1.00 1.00
1181 A259 $5 multi 1.60 1.60
a. Booklet pane, #1180-1181 4.75 —
Complete booklet, #1177a, 1179a, 1181a 9.75
b. Souvenir sheet, #1176-1181, + central label 5.25 5.25
Nos. 1176-1181 (6) 5.25 5.25

Complete booklet sold for $30.

Souvenir Sheet

Gongbei Rock, Mount Taishan — A260

2006, May 4 ***Perf. 14¼ Syncopated***
Granite Paper

1182 A260 $10 multi 3.75 3.75

See No. 1456i.

Souvenir Sheet

Washington 2006 World Philatelic Exhibition — A261

Perf. 13¼x12¾ Syncopated
2006, May 27 **Granite Paper**

1183 A261 $10 multi 3.75 3.75

Chinese Idioms A262

Idioms: $1.40, Respect makes successful marriage. $2.40, Reading is always rewarding. $3, Prepare for success. $5, All in the same boat.

Perf. 13¾ Syncopated
2006, June 15 **Granite Paper**

1184-1187 A262 Set of 4 4.00 4.00
1187a Souvenir sheet, #1184-1187 4.00 4.00

Attractions in Hong Kong's Districts — A263

Designs: No. 1188, $1.40, Central Police Station Historical Compound, Peak Tram, International Finance Center, Central and Western District. No. 1189, $1.40, Victoria Park, Island Eastern Corridor, Hong Kong Museum of Coastal Defense, Eastern District. No. 1190, $1.40, Floating restaurant, Murray House, Ocean Park, Southern District. No. 1191, $1.40, Hong Kong Convention and Exhibition Center, Old Wan Chai Post Office, Lovers' Rock, Wan Chai District. No. 1192, $1.40, Hong Kong Cultural Center, Temple Street, Yuen Po Bird Garden, Yau Tsim Mong District. No. 1193, $1.40, Wong Tai Sin Temple, Lion Rock, Chi Lin Nunnery, Wong Tai Sin District. No. 1194, $1.40, Lei Yue Mun Seafood Bazaar, buildings, Child-giving Rocks, Kwun Tong District. No. 1195, $1.40, Computer shopping center, Lingnan Garden, Festival Walk, Sham Shui Po District. No. 1196, $1.40, Kowloon Walled City Park, Wonderful Worlds of Whampoa, Sung Wong Toi, Kowloon City District. No. 1197, $1.40, Seafood Street, Tai Long Wan, Lions Nature Education Center Shell House, Sai Kung District. No. 1198, $1.40, Lantau Link View Point, Kwai Chung Container Terminals, Tsing Ma Bridge, Kwai Tsing District. No. 1199, $1.40, Lookout Tower, Lam Tsuen Wishing Tree, Tai Po Waterfront Park, Tai Po District. No. 1200, $1.40, Fung Ying Seen Koon, Chung Ying Street, Pak Hok Lam, North District. No. 1201, $1.40, Sam Tung Uk Museum, Yuen Yuen Institute, Tai Mo Shan Country Park, Tsuen Wan District. No. 1202, $1.40, Amah Rock, Shing Mun River Promenade, Che Kung Temple, Sha Tin District. No. 1203, $1.40, Hong Kong Gold Coast, Ching Chung Koon, Tsing Shan Monastery, Tuen Mun District. No. 1204, $1.40, Mai Po Nature Reserve, birds over farm, Chinese cakes, Yuen Long District. No. 1205, $1.40, Tian Tan Buddha, Cheung Chau Bun Festival, Tai O, Islands District.

2006, July 18 ***Perf. 13½ Syncopated***
Granite Paper

1188-1205 A263 Set of 18 8.00 8.00
1205a Souvenir sheet, #1188-1205 8.00 8.00

Fireworks A264

Designs: No. 1206, $5, No. 1208a, $50, Fireworks over Hong Kong Harbor. No. 1207, $5, No. 1208b, $50, Fireworks over Prater Ferris Wheel, Vienna, Austria.

2006, Aug. 22 **Litho.** ***Perf. 14***

1206-1207 A264 Set of 2 3.00 3.00

Souvenir Sheet
Photo. With Glass Beads Affixed

1208 A264 $50 Sheet of 2, #a-b 35.00 35.00
c. Sheet, Austria #2060b, Hong Kong #1208a 40.00 40.00

See Austria No. 2060.

No. 1208c sold for €12.40 in Austria and for $120 in Hong Kong, and is identical to Austria No. 2060c.

Intl. Day of Peace — A265

Chinese characters and: $1.40, Flower and "Love." $1.80, Origami crane and "Peace." $2.40, Four-leaf clover and "Hope." $3, Tree and "Caring." $5, Earth and "Harmony."

Perf. 13½x13¼ Syncopated
2006, Sept. 21 **Litho.**
Granite Paper

1209-1213 A265 Set of 5 4.50 4.50
1213a Souvenir sheet, #1209-1213 4.50 4.50

Government Vehicles — A266

Designs: $1.40, Correctional Services security bus. $1.80, Customs Department X-ray scanning vehicle. $2.40, Fire Department hydraulic platform pumper truck. $2.50, Government Flying Service Super Puma helicopter. $3, Police Department traffic patrol motorcycle. $5, Immigration Department launch.

Perf. 13¼x14½ Syncopated
2006, Oct. 19 **Litho.**
Granite Paper

1214-1219 A266 Set of 6 5.50 5.50
1219a Sheet, 3 each #1214-1219 16.50 16.50

Dr. Sun Yat-sen (1866-1925), Republic of China President — A267

Photographs from: $1.40, 1883. $2.40, 1912. $3, 1916. No. 1223, $5, 1922. No. 1224, $5, 1924 (hands visible).

Perf. 13¼x13 Syncopated
2006, Nov. 12 **Granite Paper**

1220-1223 A267 Set of 4 4.25 4.25

Souvenir Sheet

1224 A267 $5 multi 3.00 3.00

A booklet containing two panes, one containing Nos. 1220-1221, and one containing Nos. 1222-1223 sold for $25.

Heartwarming A268

No. 1225, Hearts. No. 1226, Bottles. No. 1227, Flowers. No. 1228, Drink glasses.

Perf. 13½ Syncopated
2006, Nov. 28 **Granite Paper**
Inscribed "Local Mail Postage"

1225 A268 ($1.40) multi .40 .40
a. Sheet of 8 + 8 labels 3.25 3.25
1226 A268 ($1.40) multi .40 .40
a. Sheet of 20 + 21 labels 12.50 12.50

Inscribed "Air Mail Postage"

1227 A268 ($3) multi .90 .90
1228 A268 ($3) multi .90 .90
a. Sheet, 5 each #1225-1228, + 21 labels 13.00 13.00
b. Sheet of 20 + 21 labels 27.50 27.50
Nos. 1225-1228 (4) 2.60 2.60

Issued: Nos. 1226a, 1228b, 5/2/08; No. 1225a, 2/14/12. Labels on Nos. 1225a, 1226a and 1228b could not be personalized. Nos. 1226a and 1228b sold as a set for $154.

No. 1225a is impregnated with a rose scent.

Birds — A269

Designs: 10c, White-bellied sea eagle. 20c, Collared scops owl. 50c, Scarlet minivet. $1, Common kingfisher. $1.40, Fork-tailed sunbird. $1.80, Roseate tern. $1.90, Black-faced spoonbill. $2, Little egret. $2.40, Greater painted snipe. $2.50, Barn swallow. $3, Red-whiskered bulbul. $5, Long-tailed shrike. $10, White wagtail. $13, Northern shoveler. $20, Common magpie. $50, Dalmatian pelican.

Perf. 13x13¾ Syncopated
2006, Dec. 31 **Photo.**
Granite Paper
Size: 22x26mm

1229 A269 10c multi .25 .25
1230 A269 20c multi .25 .25
1231 A269 50c multi .25 .25
1232 A269 $1 multi .25 .25
1233 A269 $1.40 multi .35 .35
a. Booklet pane of 10 3.50 —
Complete booklet, #1233a 3.50
1234 A269 $1.80 multi .45 .45
a. Booklet pane of 10 4.50 —
Complete booklet, #1234a 4.50
1235 A269 $1.90 multi .50 .50
1236 A269 $2 multi .55 .55
1237 A269 $2.40 multi .60 .60
a. Booklet pane of 10 6.00 —
Complete booklet, #1237a 6.00
1238 A269 $2.50 multi .65 .65
1239 A269 $3 multi .80 .80
a. Booklet pane of 10 8.00 —
Complete booklet, #1239a 8.00
1240 A269 $5 multi 1.40 1.40
a. Miniature sheet, #1229-1240 6.25 6.25
b. Booklet pane, #1229-1240 6.25 —
Complete booklet, #1240b 6.25

Size: 25x30mm
Perf. 13½x13¼ Syncopated

1241 A269 $10 multi 2.60 2.60
a. Souvenir sheet of 1 2.60 2.60
1242 A269 $13 multi 3.50 3.50
1243 A269 $20 multi 5.25 5.25
1244 A269 $50 multi 13.00 13.00
a. Souvenir sheet, #1241-1244 25.00 25.00
Nos. 1229-1244 (16) 30.65 30.65

Coil Stamps
Size: 17x21mm
Perf. 14¾x13½ Syncopated

1245 A269 $1.40 multi .80 .80
1246 A269 $1.80 multi 1.00 1.00
1247 A269 $2.40 multi 1.35 1.35
1248 A269 $3 multi 1.75 1.75
Nos. 1245-1248 (4) 4.90 4.90

Nos. 1241-1244 have microperforations around denominations.

Issued: No. 1241a, 9/21/10.

New Year 2007 (Year of the Pig) — A270

Various pigs with background colors of: $1.40, Brown. $2.40, Orange red. $3, Green. $5, Rose.

2007, Feb. 4 ***Perf. 13½ Syncopated***
Granite Paper

1249-1252 A270 Set of 4 3.25 3.25
1249a Dated "2011," perf. 13½x13¼ syncopated (1431) .35 .35
1252a Souvenir sheet of #1252, imperf. 2.00 2.00
1252b Souvenir sheet, #1249-1252 3.75 3.75

Issued: No. 1249a, 1/22/11. See Nos. 1253d, 1479h, 1480h.

New Year Types of 2004-07

2007, Feb. 4 **Litho.** ***Perf. 13x13½***
Flocked Paper

1253 Block of 4 11.00 11.00
a. A221 $10 Like #1075 2.75 2.75
b. A244 $10 Like #1128 2.75 2.75
c. A256 $10 Like #1170 2.75 2.75
d. A270 $10 Like #1251 2.75 2.75

Souvenir Sheet

New Year 2007 (Year of the Pig) — A271

No. 1254: a, Beagle. b, Pig and piglet.

Litho. & Embossed With Foil Application

2007, Feb. 4 ***Perf. 13¼***

1254 A271 $50 Sheet of 2, #a-b 27.50 27.50

Scouting, Cent. — A272

Designs: $1.40, Campfire, Lord Robert Baden-Powell. $2.40, Hong Kong Scouting emblem, compass. $3, Backpack, knot. $5, Scouts, tent.

Litho. With Foil Application
Perf. 13¼x14¼ Syncopated

2007, Mar. 1 Granite Paper

1255-1258 A272 Set of 4 3.50 3.50
1258a Souvenir sheet, #1255-1258 3.50 3.50

Children's Games and Puzzles A273

Designs: $1.40, Find the difference between the two rabbits. $1.80, Color in the dotted areas. $2.40, Maze. $2.50, Follow lines to hunt for Easter Eggs. $3, Find the ten rabbits. $5, Look for a star.

Perf. 13¾ Syncopated

2007, Mar. 22 Litho.
Granite Paper

1259-1264 A273 Set of 6 4.50 4.50
1264a Souvenir sheet, #1259-1264 4.50 4.50

A booklet containing three panes, containing Nos. 1259-1260, 1261-1262, and 1263-1264 respectively, sold for $36.

Souvenir Sheet

Stone Forest, Shilin — A274

Perf. 13¼x14¼ Syncopated

2007, May 3 Granite Paper

1265 A274 $10 multi 3.00 3.00

See No. 1456h.

Chinese Martial Arts A275

Designs: $1.40, Southern Lion Dance. $2.40, Nanquan. $3, Northern Lion Dance. $5, Beitui.

Litho. with Foil Application

2007, May 22

1266-1269 A275 Set of 4 3.25 3.25
1269a Souvenir sheet, #1266-1269 3.25 3.25

Butterflies — A276

Designs: $1.40, Faunis eumeus. $1.80, Prioneris philonome. $2.40, Polyura nepenthes. $3, Tajuria maculata. $5, Acraea issoria.

Perf. 13½ Syncopated

2007, June 14 Litho.
Granite Paper

1270-1274 A276 Set of 5 3.75 3.75

A booklet containing two panes, one containing Nos. 1270-1272 and the other containing Nos. 1273-1274, sold for $38.

Return of Hong Kong to China, 10th Anniv. A277

Perf. 13x12¾ Syncopated

2007, July 1 Photo.

1275 A277 $1.40 multi .80 .80

A souvenir sheet containing No. 1275 and People's Republic of China Nos. 3594-3596 sold for $12.95.

A278

Hong Kong Special Administrative Region, 10th Anniv. — A279

Designs: $1.40, Ten children with joined hands. $1.80, Banner on Hong Kong Heritage Museum. $2.40, Vehicles on Tsing Ma Bridge. $2.50, Ten birds over Hong Kong Wetland Park. $3, Two International Finance Center Building and Moon. $5, Fireworks over Hong Kong.

No. 1282: a, "7" over Bank of China Tower, fireworks over Cheung Kong Center. b, Fireworks over smaller buildings. c, Fireworks over smaller buildings, Two International Finance Center Building at right.

Perf. 13½x14¼ Syncopated

2007, July 1 Granite Paper Litho.

1276-1281 A278 Set of 6 4.75 4.75

Litho. With Foil Application and Hologram
Perf. 13½

1282 A279 $10 Sheet of 3, #a-c 8.25 8.25

Souvenir Sheet

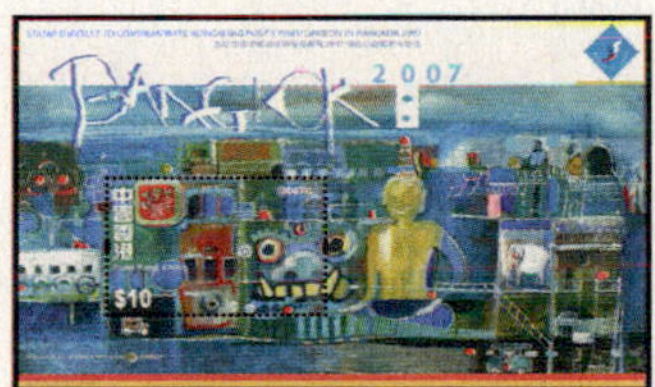

Bangkok 2007 Asian International Stamp Exhibition — A280

Perf. 13½x14¼ Syncopated

2007, Aug. 3 Litho.
Granite Paper

1283 A280 $10 multi 3.00 3.00

Civic Education A281

Designs: $1.40, Human rights. $2.40, Rule of law. $3, Social participation. $5, Corporate citizenship.

2007, Aug. 23 ***Perf. 13 Syncopated***
Granite Paper

1284-1287 A281 Set of 4 3.25 3.25
1287a Miniature sheet, 4 each #1284-1287 13.00 13.00

Declared Monuments — A282

Designs: $1.40, Tin Hau Temple, Causeway Bay. $1.80, Old Wan Chai Post Office. $2.40, Former Central Police Station Compound. $2.50, Former Yamen Building of Kowloon Walled City. $3, Kun Lung Gate Tower, Lung Yeuk Tau. $5, Tang Lung Chau Lighthouse.

Litho. & Engr.

2007, Sept. 20 ***Perf. 14x13¼***
Granite Paper

1288-1293 A282 Set of 6 4.50 4.50
1293a Miniature sheet, #1288-1293 4.50 4.50

Christmas — A283

Designs: $1.40, Stocking. $2.40, Gingerbread man-shaped egg tart. $3, Bell decorated with neon lights. $5, Snowman with Chinese vest.

2007, Oct. 11 Litho. ***Perf. 13x13½***
Granite Paper

1294-1297 A283 Set of 4 3.25 3.25

Woodwork — A284

Designs: No. 1298, $5, Zitan armchair with dragon design, China, denomination at left. No. 1299, $5, Modern Finnish bowls, denomination at right.

Perf. 13½x14¼ Syncopated

2007, Nov. 2 Granite Paper

1298-1299 A284 Set of 2 3.00 3.00
1299a Souvenir sheet, #1298-1299 3.25 3.25

See Finland No. 1298.

Heartwarming A285

Designs: No. 1300, Birds and flowers. No. 1301, Firecrackers. No. 1302, Gifts and balloons. No. 1303, Slippers.

Perf. 13½ Syncopated

2007, Dec. 28 Litho.
Granite Paper

Inscribed "Local Mail Postage"

1300 A285 ($1.40) multi .40 .40
1301 A285 ($1.40) multi .40 .40

Inscribed "Air Mail Postage"

1302 A285 ($3) multi 1.00 1.00
1303 A285 ($3) multi 1.00 1.00
a. Sheet, 5 each #1300-1303 + 21 labels 14.00 14.00

New Year 2008 (Year of the Rat) — A286

Various rats with background colors of: $1.40, Blue. $2.40, Green. $3, Orange red. $5, Brown.

Perf. 13½x13¼ Syncopated

2008, Jan. 26 Litho.
Granite Paper

1304-1307 A286 Set of 4 4.00 4.00
1304a Dated "2011" (1431) .45 .45
1307a Souvenir sheet of #1307, imperf. 2.40 2.40
1307b Souvenir sheet, #1304-1307 4.50 4.50

Issued: No. 1304a, 1/22/11. See Nos. 1432a, 1479i, 1480i.

Souvenir Sheet

New Year 2008 (Year of the Rat) — A287

No. 1308: a, Pig. b, Rat.

Litho. & Embossed With Foil Application

2008, Jan. 26 ***Perf. 13¼***

1308 A287 $50 Sheet of 2, #a-b 30.00 30.00

Souvenir Sheet

Huanglong — A288

Perf. 14¼ Syncopated

2008, Feb. 28 Litho.
Granite Paper

1309 A288 $10 multi 3.00 3.00

See No. 1456d.

Flowers A289

Designs: $1.40, Chinese hibiscus. $1.80, Tree cotton. $2.40, Allamandas. $2.50, Azaleas. $3, Indian lotus. $5, Morning glories.

Perf. 13½x13¼ Syncopated

2008, Mar. 14 Granite Paper

1310-1315 A289 Set of 6 6.00 6.00
1315a Souvenir sheet, #1310-1315 6.00 6.00

Paper Folding Art — A290

Designs: $1.40, Bauhinia blossoms. $1.80, Bear, horiz. $2.40, Lunar New Year decorations. $2.50, Lotus flowers and rainbow, horiz. $3, Koalas, monkey with banana. $5, Christmas party scene, horiz.

Perf. 14¼x13½, 13½x14¼ Syncopated

2008, May 22

1316-1321 A290 Set of 6 6.00 6.00
1321a Souvenir sheet, #1316-1321 6.00 6.00

Jellyfish — A291

Designs: $1.40, Flower hat jellyfish. $1.80, Octopus jellyfish, horiz. $2.40, Brown sea nettle. $2.50, Moon jellyfish, horiz. $3, Lion's mane jellyfish. $5, Pacific sea nettle.

Perf. 14¼ Syncopated

2008, June 12 **Litho.**

Granite Paper

1322-1327 A291 Set of 6 6.25 6.25
1327a Souvenir sheet, #1322-1327 6.25 6.25

Stamps have a glow-in-the dark coating on the jellyfish illustrations. A booklet containing panes of Nos. 1322-1323, 1324-1325, and 1326-1327, sold for $36.

Giant Pandas A292

Designs: $1.40, Ying Ying, Le Le, and hearts. $2.40, Ying Ying and leaves. $3, Le Le and panda heads. $5, Ying Ying, Le Le, and circles.

2008, July 1 ***Perf. 13¾ Syncopated***

Granite Paper

1328-1331 A292 Set of 4 5.00 5.00
1331a Sheet, 2 each # 1328-1331, + 4 labels 10.00 10.00

Hong Kong, Venue for 2008 Summer Olympic Equestrian Events — A293

Desings: $1.40, Horse and rider jumping fence. $2.40, Dressage. $3, Horse and rider jumping over water obstacle. $5, Horse and rider at medal stand.

Perf. 13¼x14 Syncopated

2008, Aug. 9 **Granite Paper**

1332-1335 A293 Set of 4 4.00 4.00
1335a Souvenir sheet, #1332-1335 4.00 4.00

Souvenir Sheet

Praga 2008 World Stamp Exhibition — A294

Perf. 13¼x14¼ Syncopated

2008, Sept. 12 **Litho.**

Granite Paper

1336 A294 $10 multi 3.75 3.75

Big Head Buddha Mask, Hong Kong — A295

Chwibari Mask, Korea — A296

Perf. 13¼x14 Syncopated

2008, Nov. 6 **Granite Paper**

1337 A295 $5 multi 2.00 2.00
1338 A296 $5 multi 2.00 2.00
a. Souvenir sheet, #1337-1338 4.00 4.00

See South Korea No. 2299.

The Judiciary A297

Designs: $1.40, Statue of Justice. $2.40, Court of Final Appeal. $3, Judicial robes for various courts. $5, Chief Justice's mace.

Perf. 13¾ Syncopated

2008, Nov. 27 **Granite Paper**

1339-1342 A297 Set of 4 4.25 4.25
1342a Souvenir sheet, #1339-1342 4.25 4.25

New Year 2009 (Year of the Ox) — A298

Various oxen with background colors of: $1.40, Purple. $2.40, Brown. $3, Green. $5, Blue.

Perf. 13½x13¼ Syncopated

2009, Jan. 17 **Litho.**

Granite Paper

1343-1346 A298 Set of 4 4.25 4.25
1346a Souvenir sheet of #1346, imperf. 2.00 2.00
1346b Souvenir sheet, #1343-1346 4.25 4.25

See Nos. 1431g, 1432b, 1479j, 1480j.

Souvenir Sheet

New Year 2009 (Year of the Ox) — A299

No. 1347: a, Rat. b, Ox.

Litho. & Embossed With Foil Application

2009, Jan. 17 ***Perf. 13¼***

1347 A299 $50 Sheet of 2, #a-b 40.00 40.00

Souvenir Sheet

Mount Tianshan — A300

Perf. 14¼ Syncopated

2009, Feb. 24 **Litho.**

Granite Paper

1348 A300 $10 multi 4.00 4.00

See No. 1456c.

Souvenir Sheet

Peony and Bauhinia Flowers — A301

2009, Apr. 7 ***Perf. 13¼ Syncopated***

Granite Paper

1349 A301 $5 multi 1.75 1.75

China 2009 World Stamp Exhibition, Luoyang.

Souvenir Sheet

Tangram Figure — A302

2009, May 14 ***Perf. 13¼***

Granite Paper

1350 A302 $50 multi + 2 labels 15.00 15.00

Hong Kong 2009 Intl. Stamp Exhibition.

Items in Hong Kong Museums — A303

Designs: $1.40, Poem by Wang Duo, Hong Kong Museum of Art. $1.80, Landscape, painting by Wang Yuanqi, Hong Kong Museum of Art. $2.40, Calligraphy by Wang Xizhi, Art Museum of the Chinese University of Hong Kong. $2.50, Bird in Moonlight, painting by Gao Qifeng, Hong Kong Heritage Museum. $3, Flower and Butterfly, fan painting by Ju Lian, Hong Kong Heritage Museum, horiz. (50x30mm). $5, Drawing by Gu Huai, University Museum and Art Gallery of the University of Hong Kong, horiz. (50x30mm).

Perf. 13½x13¼ Syncopated

2009, May 16 **Granite Paper**

1351-1356 A303 Set of 6 5.25 5.25
1356a Souvenir sheet, #1351-1356 5.75 5.75

Heartwarming A304

Designs: No. 1357, Flowers. No. 1358, Lion. No. 1359, Birthday hats. No. 1360, Butterflies and heart.

Perf. 13½ Syncopated

2009, June 25 **Granite Paper**

Inscribed "Local Mail Postage"

1357 A304 ($1.40) multi .90 .90
1358 A304 ($1.40) multi .90 .90

Inscribed "Air Mail Postage"

1359 A304 ($3) multi 2.00 2.00
1360 A304 ($3) multi 2.00 2.00
a. Sheet of 12, 3 each #1357-1360, + 12 labels 17.50 17.50
Nos. 1357-1360 (4) 5.80 5.80

Labels on No. 1360a could not be personalized.

Customs and Excise Service, Cent. A305

Designs: $1.40, Officer with drug-sniffing dog and baggage inspectors of 1960s. $2.40, Mobile x-ray vehicle scanner and Sheng Shui Customs Station, 1935. $3, Patrol boats. $5, Officers raising flag.

Perf. 13¼x13 Syncopated

2009, Sept. 17 **Litho.**

Granite Paper

1361-1364 A305 Set of 4 4.00 4.00
1364a Souvenir sheet, #1361-1364 4.00 4.00

A booklet containing two panes, one with Nos. 1361-1362, and the other with Nos. 1363-1364, sold for $36.

A306

People's Republic of China, 60th Anniv. — A307

Designs: $1.40, Cogwheels, Victoria Harbor, Hong Kong and Tiananmen Square, Beijing. $1.80, Flag of People's Republic of China, Forever Blooming Bauhinia statue, Hong Kong. $2.40, Dove, Olympic Stadium, Beijing. $2.50, Shenzhou-7 on launch pad. $3, Doves, Temple of Heaven. $5, Dragon, Great Wall of China.

No. 1371: a, Emblem of People's Republic of China, Tiananmen Square. b, Emblem of Hong Kong, Hong Kong skyline at night.

2009, Oct. 1 ***Perf. 13¼***

Granite Paper (A306)

1365-1370 A306 Set of 6 5.75 5.75
1370a Souvenir sheet, #1365-1370 6.25 6.25

Souvenir Sheet

Perf. 13

1371 A307 $5 Sheet of 2, #a-b 4.50 4.50

Soccer A308

Soccer player from: $1.40, Hong Kong. $2.40, Hong Kong, diff. $3, Brazil. $5, Brazil, diff.

Perf. 13¼x14¼ Syncopated

2009, Nov. 5 **Granite Paper**

1372-1375 A308 Set of 4 4.00 4.00
1375a Souvenir sheet, #1372-1375 4.00 4.00

See Brazil No. 3114.

2009 East Asia Games, Hong Kong A309

Designs: No. 1376, $1.40, Judo, rowing and rugby. No. 1377, $1.40, Wushu, track, badminton and shooting. No. 1378, $2.40, Squash, basketball, field hockey and swimming. No. 1379, $2.40, Cycling, weight lifting and tennis. No. 1380, $3, Bowling, windsurfing, soccer and taekwondo. No. 1381, $3, Dancing, table tennis, volleyball and billiards.

Litho. With Foil Application

2009, Dec. 5 ***Perf. 14¼ Syncopated***

Granite Paper

1376-1381 A309 Set of 6 4.50 4.50
1381a Souvenir sheet, #1376-1381 4.50 4.50

Stonecutters Bridge — A310

Designs: $1.40, View of bridge tower from water level. $2.40, Aerial view of bridge, horiz. $3, View of bridge from water level, horiz. $5, Aerial view of bridge tower.

Perf. 14½x14 Syncopated, 14x14½ Syncopated

2009, Dec. 17 **Litho.**

Granite Paper

1382-1385 A310 Set of 4 4.50 4.50
1385a Souvenir sheet, #1382-1385 4.50 4.50

New Year 2010 (Year of the Tiger) — A311

Various tigers with background colors of: $1.40, Red. $2.40, Green. $3, Blue. $5, Orange.

Perf. 13½x13¼ Syncopated

2010, Feb. 6 **Granite Paper**

1386-1389 A311 Set of 4 4.50 4.50
1386a Dated "2011" (1431) .50 .50
1389a Souvenir sheet of #1389, imperf. 1.90 1.90
1389b Souvenir sheet, #1386-1389 4.50 4.50

Issued: No. 1386a, 1/22/11. See Nos. 1432c, 1479k, 1480k.

Souvenir Sheet

New Year 2010 (Year of the Tiger) — A312

No. 1390: a, Ox. b, Tiger.

Litho. & Embossed With Foil Application

2010, Feb. 6 ***Perf. 13¾***

1390 A312 $50 Sheet of 2, #a-b 27.50 27.50

Souvenir Sheet

Fujian Tulou UNESCO World Heritage Site — A313

Perf. 13¼ Syncopated

2010, Mar. 18 **Litho.**

Granite Paper

1391 A313 $10 multi 4.00 4.00

See No. 1456e.

Expo 2010, Shanghai — A314

Designs: $1.40, Dragon dance. $2.40, Hong Kong on green leaf. $3, Tsing Ma Bridge, Hong Kong. $5, Smart Card chip, head, Hong Kong skyline.

2010, Apr. 27 ***Perf. 13¼ Syncopated***

Granite Paper

1392-1395 A314 Set of 4 3.50 3.50
1395a Souvenir sheet, #1392-1395 3.50 3.50

No. 1395a was printed in sheet containing four souvenir sheets.

Souvenir Sheet

London 2010 Intl. Philatelic Exhibition — A315

2010, May 8 **Litho.** **Granite Paper**

1396 A315 $10 multi 3.25 3.25

Hong Kong Street Scenes A316

Designs: No. 1397, $1.40, Pottinger Street. No. 1398, $1.40, Nathan Road. No. 1399, $2.40, Hollywood Road. No. 1400, $2.40, Temple Street. No. 1401, $3, Des Voeux Road West. No. 1402, $3, Stanley Market.

Perf. 13¾ Syncopated

2010, June 24 **Granite Paper**

1397-1402 A316 Set of 6 4.00 4.00
1402a Souvenir sheet, #1397-1402 4.00 4.00

Intl. Year of Biodiversity — A317

Designs: $1.40, Macropodus hongkongensis. $2.40, Liuixalus romeri. $3, Sinopora hongkongensis. $5, Fukienogomphus choifongae.

Perf. 13¼x14¼ Syncopated

2010, July 15 **Litho.**

Granite Paper

1403-1406 A317 Set of 4 3.25 3.25
1406a Souvenir sheet, #1403-1406 3.50 3.50

Railways in Hong Kong, Cent. — A318

Designs: $1.40, Steam train, Hong Kong Railway Museum. $1.80, Diesel train, clock tower of Kowloon-Canton Railway Terminus. $2.40, Electric train, Hung Hom Terminus. $2.50, Mass Transit Railway train, International Finance Center. $3, Kowloon-Guangzhou through train, Mass Transit Railway Hung Hom Station. $5, Airport Express train, aerial view of Hong Kong International Airport.

$20, Steam train, Hong Kong Railway Museum, diff.

Perf. 13½x13¼ Syncopated

2010, Sept. 28 **Litho.**

Granite Paper

1407-1412 A318 Set of 6 4.50 4.50
1412a Souvenir sheet, #1407-1412 4.50 4.50

Souvenir Sheet

Litho. With Three-Dimensional Plastic Affixed

1413 A318 $20 multi 6.25 6.25

No. 1413 contains one 37x51mm stamp.

A booklet containing three panes, containing Nos. 1407-1408, 1409-1410, and 1411-1412 respectively, sold for $36.

Winning Entries in Children's Stamp Design Contest — A319

Designs: $1.40, "Harbor of Hong Kong." $2.40, "Beautiful Hong Kong." $3, "Hong Kong is Fun." $5, "City Beat."

Perf. 13¼x13½ Syncopated

2010, Oct. 21 **Litho.**

Granite Paper

1414-1417 A319 Set of 4 3.50 3.50
1417a Souvenir sheet, #1414-1417 3.50 3.50

Renovation of Old Neighborhoods — A320

Designs: $1.40, Rehabilitation. $2.40, Revitalization. $3, Preservation. $5, Redevelopment.

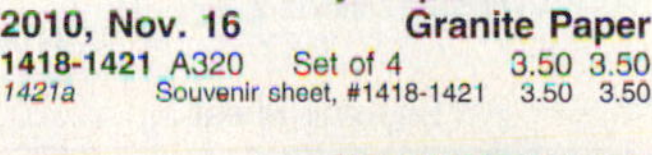

Perf. 13¾ Syncopated

2010, Nov. 16 **Granite Paper**

1418-1421 A320 Set of 4 3.50 3.50
1421a Souvenir sheet, #1418-1421 3.50 3.50

Lighthouses A321

Map and: $1.40, Cape D'Aguilar Lighthouse. $1.80, Old Green Island Lighthouse. $2.40, New Green Island Lighthouse. $3, Tang Lung Chau Lighthouse. $5, Waglan Lighthouse.

Perf. 13½x13¼ Syncopated

2010, Dec. 29 **Litho.**

Granite Paper

1422-1426 A321 Set of 5 4.00 4.00
1426a Souvenir sheet of 5, #1422-1426 4.00 4.00

New Year 2011 (Year of the Rabbit) — A322

Various rabbits with background color of: $1.40, Green. $2.40, Blue. $3, Brown. $5, Red.

Perf. 13½x13¼ Syncopated

2011, Jan. 22 Granite Paper

1427-1430	A322 Set of 4	3.75	3.75
1430a	Souvenir sheet of #1430, imperf.	1.60	1.60
1430b	Souvenir sheet of 4, #1427-1430	3.75	3.75

See Nos. 1432d, 1479l, 1480l.

New Year Types of 2000-11

Perf. 13½x13¼ Syncopated

2011, Jan. 22 Litho.

Granite Paper

1431	Sheet of 12, #1128a, 1249a, 1304a, 1386a, 1427, 1431a-1431g	6.00	6.00
a.	A177 $1.40 Dragon	.50	.50
b.	A184 $1.40 Snake	.50	.50
c.	A194 $1.40 Horse	.50	.50
d.	A206 $1.40 Ram (like #1028)	.50	.50
e.	A221 $1.40 Monkey (like #1076)	.50	.50
f.	A256 $1.40 Dog (like #1170)	.50	.50
g.	A298 $1.40 Ox (like #1344)	.50	.50

Flocked Paper

Perf. 13½x13¼

1432	Block of 4	13.00	13.00
a.	A286 $10 Rat	3.25	3.25
b.	A298 $10 Ox	3.25	3.25
c.	A311 $10 Tiger	3.25	3.25
d.	A322 $10 Rabbit	3.25	3.25

Souvenir Sheet

New Year 2011 (Year of the Rabbit) — A323

No. 1433: a, Tiger. b, Rabbit.

Litho. & Embossed With Foil Application

2011, Jan. 22 *Perf. 13¾*

1433	A323 $50 Sheet of 2, #a-b	32.50	32.50

Souvenir Sheet

Powered Flight in Hong Kong, Cent. — A324

No. 1434: a, Drawing of first aircraft. b, Photograph of first flight.

Perf. 13¼ Syncopated

2011, Mar. 18 Litho.

Granite Paper

1434	A324 $3 Sheet of 2, #a-b	1.75	1.75

A325

Volunteerism — A326

Designs: $1.40, Leaf, child's notebook page. $2.40, Volunteer recruitement web page. $3, E-mail message, children. No. 1438, $5, Written reminder on calendar page.

Perf. 13½x13¼ Syncopated

2011, Mar. 29 Granite Paper

1435-1438	A325 Set of 4	3.50	3.50

Souvenir Sheet

Perf.

1439	A326 $5 shown	1.50	1.50

Green Living — A327

Growing plant and: $1.40, Water faucet, Earth in water droplet. $2.40, Cloud, tree, Earth. $3, Fluorescent lightbulb, Earth under lampshade. No. 1443, $5, Recycling emblem, recyclable items, Earth.

No. 1444, $5, Growing plant on Earth.

2011, Apr. 14 *Perf. 13¾ Syncopated*

Granite Paper

1440-1443	A327 Set of 4	3.50	3.50

Souvenir Sheet

1444	A327 $5 multi	1.50	1.50

Hong Kong General Chamber of Commerce, 150th Anniv. A328

Designs: $1.40, Old Hong Kong Club Building. $2.40, Wharf. $3, Handshake, Good Citizen Award Certificate. $5, Chamber of Commerce members in China near train, 1978.

2011, May 26 Litho.

Granite Paper

1445-1448	A328 Set of 4	3.25	3.25
1448a	Souvenir sheet of 4, #1445-1448	3.25	3.25

Chinese Idioms — A329

Idioms: Nos. 1449, 1454a, $1.40, Mutual help in hard times. Nos. 1450, 1454b, $1.80, Water drops wear away rocks. Nos. 1451, 1454c, $2.40, Practice makes perfect. Nos. 1452, 1454d, $3, Save to give. Nos. 1453, 1454e, $5, As deft as a master butcher.

Perf. 13¼x14¼ Syncopated

2011, June 28 Granite Paper

Multicolored Designs

1449-1453	A329 Set of 5	3.50	3.50

Stamp Designs With Gray Areas

1454	A329 Sheet of 5, #a-e	3.50	3.50

No. 1454 was sold with a sheet of multicolored self-adhesive stickers that could be placed over corresponding gray areas on the souvenir sheet. Value for No. 1454 is for sheet without stickers attached.

Souvenir Sheet

Dunhuang Grottoes — A330

Perf. 13½x13¼ Syncopated

2011, Aug. 2 Granite Paper

1455	A330 $10 multi	2.60	2.60

See No. 1456b.

Chinese Scenery Types of 2003-11

Miniature Sheet

Perf. 13¼x13½ Syncopated, 13¼ Syncopated (#1456a), 13½x13¼ Syncopated (#1456b, 1456i), 13¼x13 Syncopated (#1456d)

2011, Aug. 2 Litho.

Granite Paper

1456	Sheet of 9	6.25	6.25
a.	A253 $2.40 Qiantang Bore	.65	.65
b.	A330 $2.40 Dunhuang Grottoes	.65	.65
c.	A300 $2.40 Mount Tianshan	.65	.65
d.	A288 $2.40 Huanglong	.65	.65
e.	A313 $2.40 Fujian Tulou	.65	.65
f.	A210 $2.40 Master-of-Nets Garden	.65	.65
g.	A230 $2.40 Chen Clan Academy	.65	.65
h.	A274 $2.40 Shilin	.65	.65
i.	A260 $2.40 Mount Taishan	.65	.65

Souvenir Sheet

Hong Kong Postal Service, 170th Anniv. — A331

Litho. & Embossed With Foil Application

Perf. 13½ Syncopated

2011, Aug. 25 Granite Paper

1457	A331 $10 multi	2.60	2.60

University of Hong Kong, Cent. — A332

University crest and: $1.40, Main Building, 1910, and golden trowel. $1.80, Main Building, 1912, and University Bazaar poster. $2.40, Union Building, 1919, Main Building, and statue of Dr. Sun Yat-sen. $2.50, Main Building, 1946, and mace. $3, Main Building and West Gate, 1940s, and inkstand. No. 1463, $5, Courtyard and Main Building, 2011, University arms. No. 1464, $5, Letters patent, vert.

Perf. 13¼x13 Syncopated

2011, Sept. 5 Litho.

Granite Paper

1458-1463	A332 Set of 6	4.25	4.25

Souvenir Sheet

Perf. 13¾x14¼ Syncopated

1464	A332 $5 multi	1.40	1.40

A booklet containing two panes, containing Nos. 1458-1460 and 1461-1463, respectively, sold for $45.

Chinese Revolution, Cent. — A333

Designs: $1.40, Monument to the 72 Martyrs of Huanghuagang. $2.40, Wuchang Uprising. $3, Revolution leaders Cai Yuanpei, Zhang Taiyan, Huang Xing and Song Jiaoren. No. 1468, $5, Dr. Sun Yat-sen assuming office of Provisional President.

No. 1469, $5, horiz. — Dr. Sun Yat-sen and: a, Central School. b, Proclamation of the Three Principles of the People.

Perf. 13½x13¼ Syncopated

2011, Oct. 10 Granite Paper

1465-1468	A333 Set of 4	3.25	3.25

Souvenir Sheet

Perf. 13¼x13 Syncopated

1469	A333 $5 Sheet of 2, #a-b	2.75	2.75

Handicrafts A334

Artisan creating: No. 1470, $5, Dough figurines, Hong Kong. No. 1471, $5, Painted Easter egg, Romania.

Perf. 13¼ Syncopated

2011, Nov. 24 Granite Paper

1470-1471	A334 Set of 2	2.60	2.60
1471a	Souvenir sheet of 2, #1470-1471	2.60	2.60

See Romania Nos. 5311-5312.

Items in Hong Kong Museums — A335

Designs: $1.40, Forehead headdress used in opera, *The Sounds of Battle.* $1.80, Qipao, 1920s-1930s. $2.40, Silver-footed bowl decorated in repousse, horiz. $2.50, Sequined reversible palace costume, horiz. $3, Green glazed barrel for herbal tea, horiz. $5, Traditional baby carrier with head support, horiz.

Perf. 13¾x14¼ Syncopated, 14¼x13¾ Syncopated

2011, Dec. 6 Granite Paper

1472-1477	A335 Set of 6	4.25	4.25
1477a	Souvenir sheet of 6, #1472-1477	4.25	4.25

Souvenir Sheet

Tamar Development Project — A336

Perf. 13¼ Syncopated

2011, Dec. 15 Litho.

Granite Paper

1478 A336 $10 multi 3.00 3.00

New Year Types of 2000-11

No. 1479: a, Dragon, green background. b, Snake, orange brown background. c, Horse, red background. d, Ram, dull red background. e, Monkey, blue green background. f, Rooster, blue background. g, Dog, green background. h, Pig, dull red background. i, Rat, blue background. j, Ox, red brown background. k, Tiger, blue green background. l, Rabbit, orange brown background.

No. 1480: a, Dragon, blue background. b, Snake, red background. c, Horse, green background. d, Ram, orange brown background. e, Monkey, green background. f, Rooster, orange background. g, Dog, red violet background. h, Pigs, red brown background. i, Rat, brown background. j, Ox, lilac background. k, Tiger, green background. l, Rabbit, dull green background.

Perf. 13½x13¼ Syncopated

2012, Jan. 14 Litho.

Granite Paper

Animals in Silver and Gold

1479	Sheet of 12	7.00	7.00
a.	A177 $1.40 multi	.55	.55
b.	A184 $1.40 multi	.55	.55
c.	A194 $1.40 multi	.55	.55
d.	A206 $1.40 multi	.55	.55
e.	A221 $1.40 multi	.55	.55
f.	A244 $1.40 multi	.55	.55
g.	A256 $1.40 multi	.55	.55
h.	A270 $1.40 multi	.55	.55
i.	A286 $1.40 multi	.55	.55
j.	A298 $1.40 multi	.55	.55
k.	A311 $1.40 multi	.55	.55
l.	A322 $1.40 multi	.55	.55
1480	Sheet of 12	7.00	7.00
a.	A177 $1.40 multi	.55	.55
b.	A184 $1.40 multi	.55	.55
c.	A194 $1.40 multi	.55	.55
d.	A206 $1.40 multi	.55	.55
e.	A221 $1.40 multi	.55	.55
f.	A244 $1.40 multi	.55	.55
g.	A256 $1.40 multi	.55	.55
h.	A270 $1.40 multi	.55	.55
i.	A286 $1.40 multi	.55	.55
j.	A298 $1.40 multi	.55	.55
k.	A311 $1.40 multi	.55	.55
l.	A322 $1.40 multi	.55	.55

Souvenir Sheet

New Year 2012 (Year of the Dragon) — A337

No. 1481: a, Rabbit. b, Dragon.

Litho. & Embossed With Foil Application

2012, Jan. 14 ***Perf. 14x13¾***

1481 A337 $50 Sheet of 2, #a-b 30.00 30.00

New Year 2012 (Year of the Dragon) A338

Various dragons with background colors of: $1.40, Orange. $2.40, Red violet. $3, Purple. $5, Green.

$10, Dragon, red background. $50, Dragon, multicolored background.

Litho. With Foil Application

2012, Jan. 14 ***Perf. 13¼ Syncopated***

Granite Paper

1482-1485 A338 Set of 4 3.50 3.50

Souvenir Sheets

1486 A338 $10 multi 3.00 3.00

Litho.

Silk-faced Paper

1487 A338 $50 multi 15.00 15.00

Nos. 1487 and 1488 each contain one 45x45mm stamp. See No. 1700a.

Queen's College, 150th Anniv. A339

2012, Mar. 27 ***Perf.***

1488	Sheet of 4	10.50	10.50
a.	A339 $10 Litho., text at top in tan, denomination in black, glitter on shield frame	2.60	2.60
b.	A339 $10 Litho., text at top in claret, denomination in tan, lacquer on part of design	2.60	2.60
c.	A339 $10 Litho. & embossed, text at top in tan, denomination in black	2.60	2.60
d.	A339 $10 Litho & embossed with foil application, denomination and building in gold	2.60	2.60

Souvenir Sheet

Litho.

1489 A339 $10 Text at top in tan, denomination in black 2.60 2.60

Art — A340

Designs: $1.40, Douglas Castle, painting by unknown Chinese artist. $2.40, Crab, sculpture by Cheung Yee. $3, The Racecourse - Amateur Jockeys Close to a Carriage, painting by Edgar Degas. $5, The Horse, sculpture by Raymond Duchamp-Villon.

Perf. 13 Syncopated

2012, May 3 Litho.

Granite Paper

1490-1493 A340 Set of 4 3.00 3.00
1493a Souvenir sheet of 4, #1490-1493 3.00 3.00

See France Nos. 4201-4205.

Festivals — A341

Designs: $1.40, Tin Hau Festival. $2.40, Kwun Yum Festival. $3, Birthday of the Buddha. No. 1497, $5, Tuen Ng Festival.

No. 1498, $5, Mid-autumn Festival.

Perf. 13¾x14 Syncopated

2012, May 22 Granite Paper

1494-1497 A341 Set of 4 3.00 3.00

Souvenir Sheet

1498 A341 $5 multi 1.40 1.40

Working Dogs A342

Designs: $1.40, Beagle (quarantine detector dog) and emblem of Agriculture, Fisheries and Conservation Department. $1.80, German shepherd (correctional services dog) and emblem of Correctional Services Department. $2.40, English Springer spaniel (customs detector dog) and emblem of Customs and Excise Department. $2.50, Labrador retriever (fire investigation dog) and emblem of Fire Services Department. $3, Labrador retriever (quarantine detector dog) and emblem of Food and Environmental Hygiene Department. No. 1504, $5, Malinois (police dog) and emblem of Police Force.

No. 1505, Beagle, German shepherd, English Springer spaniel, Labrador retrievers, and Malinois.

Perf. 13½x14¼ Syncopated

2012, June 6 Granite Paper

1499-1504 A342 Set of 6 4.25 4.25

Souvenir Sheet

Perf. 13¼x13 Syncopated

1505 A342 $5 multi 1.40 1.40

No. 1505 contains one 100x40mm stamp. A booklet containing panes of Nos. 1499-1500, 1501-1502, and 1503-1504, respectively, sold for $45.

Souvenir Sheet

Hong Kong Special Administrative Region, 15th Anniv. — A343

No. 1506 — Various Hong Kong landmarks and panel in: a, Blue. b, Yellow. c, Green.

Perf. 13½x13 Syncopated

2012, June 25 Granite Paper

1506 A343 $5 Sheet of 3, #a-c 4.00 4.00

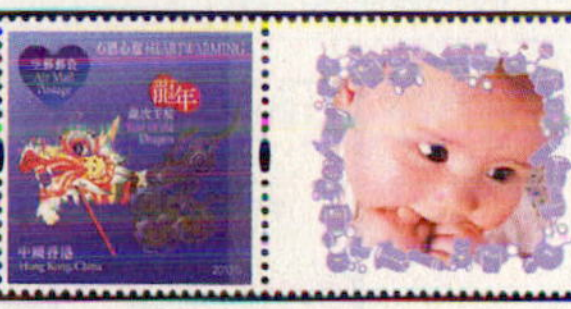

On June 19, 2012, Hong Kong issued the stamps pictured above, having franking values of $1.40 and $3 respectively. The stamps were each printed in sheets of 12 + 12 non-personalizable labels depicting various infants. The sheets sold for $40 and $66 respectively. Sheets with other non-personalizable label designs were made available later.

2012 Summer Olympics, London A344

Designs: $1.40, Windsurfing, rowing, "2." $2.40, Badminton, archery, "0." $3, Table tennis, cycling, "1." $5, Swimming, track, "2."

2012, July 27 ***Perf. 13¾ Syncopated***

1507-1510 A344 Set of 4 3.00 3.00
1510a Souvenir sheet of 4, #1507-1510 3.00 3.00

Delicacies — A345

Designs: $1.40, Egg tart and milk tea. $2.40, Wontons. $3, Roast goose. $5, Crab.

Perf. 14¼x14 Syncopated

2012, Aug. 30 Granite Paper

1511-1514 A345 Set of 4 3.00 3.00
1514a Souvenir sheet of 4, #1511-1514 3.00 3.00

Souvenir Sheet

Great Wall of China — A346

Granite Paper

Perf. 13¼x14 Syncopated

Litho. & Silk-screened

2012, Sept. 17

1515 A346 $10 multi 2.60 2.60

Signs of the Zodiac — A347

Designs: Nos. 1516, 1528, Capricorn. Nos. 1517, 1529, Aquarius. Nos. 1518, 1530, Pisces. Nos. 1519, 1531, Aries. Nos. 1520, 1532, Taurus. Nos. 1521, 1533, Gemini. Nos. 1522, 1534, Cancer. Nos. 1523, 1535, Leo. Nos. 1524, 1536, Virgo. Nos. 1525, 1537, Libra. Nos. 1526, 1538, Scorpio. Nos. 1527, 1539, Sagittarius.

Granite Paper (#1516-1527)

Perf. 14 Syncopated

2012, Nov. 1 Litho.

1516	A347 $1.40 multi	.35	.35
1517	A347 $1.40 multi	.35	.35
1518	A347 $1.40 multi	.35	.35
1519	A347 $1.40 multi	.35	.35
1520	A347 $1.40 multi	.35	.35
1521	A347 $1.40 multi	.35	.35
1522	A347 $1.40 multi	.35	.35
1523	A347 $1.40 multi	.35	.35
1524	A347 $1.40 multi	.35	.35
1525	A347 $1.40 multi	.35	.35
1526	A347 $1.40 multi	.35	.35
1527	A347 $1.40 multi	.35	.35
a.	Souvenir sheet of 12, #1516-1527	4.25	4.25
	Nos. 1516-1527 (12)	4.20	4.20

Self-Adhesive

Die Cut Perf. 14 Syncopated

1528	A347 $1.40 multi	.35	.35
1529	A347 $1.40 multi	.35	.35
1530	A347 $1.40 multi	.35	.35
1531	A347 $1.40 multi	.35	.35
1532	A347 $1.40 multi	.35	.35
1533	A347 $1.40 multi	.35	.35
1534	A347 $1.40 multi	.35	.35
1535	A347 $1.40 multi	.35	.35
1536	A347 $1.40 multi	.35	.35
1537	A347 $1.40 multi	.35	.35
1538	A347 $1.40 multi	.35	.35
1539	A347 $1.40 multi	.35	.35
a.	Vert. coil strip of 12, #1528-1539	4.25	
b.	Booklet pane of 12, #1528-1539	4.25	
	Nos. 1528-1539 (12)	4.20	4.20

A sheet containing Nos. 1516-1527 + 12 non-personalizable labels sold for $40. Sheets containing eight stamps of any of Nos. 1516-1527 + eight non-personalizable labels sold for $30 each.

Insects A348

Designs: $1.40, Spittle bug. $1.80, Flower mantid. $2.40, Mangrove China-mark moth. $2.25, White dragontail butterfly. $3, Four-spot midget damselfly. $5, Hong Kong bent-winged firefly.

Perf. 13¼x14 Syncopated

2012, Nov. 22 Granite Paper

1540-1545 A348 Set of 6 4.25 4.25
1545a Souvenir sheet of 6, #1540-1545 4.25 4.25

Hong Kong Postage Stamps, 150th Anniv. A349

Designs: $1.40, Hong Kong #1, quill and inkwell. $1.80, Hong Kong #2, fountain pen. $2.40, Hong Kong #3, ball-point pen. $2.50, Hong Kong #4, typewriter. $3, Hong Kong #5, computer keyboard. $5, Hong Kong #6, quick response code.
$10, Hong Kong #7, bar code, horiz.

Granite Paper

2012, Dec. 8 ***Perf. 13¾ Syncopated***

1546-1551 A349 Set of 6 4.25 4.25
1548a Booklet pane of 3, #1546-1548 2.75 —
1551a Booklet pane of 3, #1549-1551 5.25 —

Souvenir Sheet

Perf. 13½ Syncopated

1552 A349 $10 multi 2.60 2.60
a. Booklet pane of 1 5.00 —
Complete booklet, #1548a, 1551a, 1552a 13.00

No. 1552 contains one 67x24mm stamp. Complete booklet sold for $50.

New Year 2013 (Year of the Snake) A350

Designs: $1.40, Paper-cutting of snake. $2.40, Painting of snake. $3, Seal carvings depicting snake and Chinese character for snake. $5, Jade carving of snake.
No. 1557: a, Dragon and clouds, green background. b, Snake.
No. 1558, Snake, hexagons with Chinese characters. No. 1559, Snake, no hexagons.

Perf. 13¼x14 Syncopated

2013, Jan. 26 Litho.

Granite Paper

1553-1556 A350 Set of 4 3.00 3.00

Litho. With Foil Application (#1557a, 1558), Litho. With Metal Affixed (#1557b)

Perf. 13¼ Syncopated

1557 A350 $50 Sheet of 2, #a-b 26.00 26.00

Souvenir Sheets

1558 A350 $10 multi 2.60 2.60

Litho.

On Silk-faced Paper

1559 A350 $50 multi 13.00 13.00

Nos. 1558 and 1559 each contain one 45x45mm stamp. See No. 1700b.

On Dec. 8, 2012, Hong Kong issued the stamp pictured above, having franking values of $1.40. The stamp was printed in sheets of 12 + 12 non-personalizable labels depicting various items. The sheet sold for $40. A similar stamp, having the franking value of $3, and depicting the same items found on No. 1550, was printed in sheets of 8 + 8 non-personalizable labels. The sheet sold for $55.

On Feb. 12, 2013, Hong Kong issued the stamps pictured above, having franking values of $1.40 and $3 respectively. The stamps were each printed in sheets of 12 + 12 non-personalizable labels depicting various flowers. The sheets sold for $40 and $66 respectively. A sheet of the $1.40 value with other non-personalizable label designs was made available later.

International Red Cross, 150th Anniv. — A351

Designs: $1.40, Airplane, Red Cross worker with person. $2.40, Red Cross tent, worker bandaging arm. $3, Red Cross worker talking to people. $5, World map, worker carrying supplies.

Perf. 13¾ Syncopated

2013, Feb. 28 Litho.

Granite Paper

1560-1563 A351 Set of 4 3.00 3.00
1563a Souvenir sheet of 4, #1560-1563 3.00 3.00

Children and Pets — A352

Children and: $1.40, Dog. $1.80, Cat. $2.40, Tortoise. $2.50, Guinea pig. $3, Rabbit. $5, Hamster.

2013, Mar. 28 Litho.

Granite Paper

1564-1569 A352 Set of 6 4.25 4.25
1569a Souvenir sheet of 6, #1564-1569 4.25 4.25

On Mar. 28, 2013, Hong Kong issued the stamps pictured above, having franking values of $1.40 and $3 respectively. The stamps were each printed in sheets of 8 + 8 non-personalizable labels depicting children and dogs or children and rabbits. The sheets sold for $30 and $55 respectively.

Revitalization of Historic Buildings — A353

Designs: $1.40, YHA Mei Ho House Youth Hostel. $1.80, Yuen Yuen Institute "Fong Yuen Study Hall." $2.40, Jao Tsung-I Academy. $2.50, Hong Kong Baptist University School of Chinese Medicine - Lui Seng Chun. $3, Tai O Heritage Hotel. $5, SCAD Hong Kong.

Perf. 13¼x14¼ Syncopated

2013, May 7 Granite Paper

1570-1575 A353 Set of 6 4.25 4.25
1575a Souvenir sheet of 6, #1570-1575 4.25 4.25

A booklet containing panes of Nos. 1570-1571, 1572-1573, and 1574-1575, respectively sold for $45.

Souvenir Sheets

Kai Tak Cruise Terminal — A354

Perf. 13¼x13 Syncopated

2013, June 11 Litho.

Granite Paper

1576 A354 $10 multi 2.60 2.60

Litho. With Foil Application

1577 A354 $20 multi 5.25 5.25

Chinese and Western Wedding Customs — A355

Designs: $1.40, Chinese bride and groom in traditional outfits bowing. $1.80, Western bride in gown and groom in tuxedo exchanging vows. $2.40, Items in Chinese wedding gift presentation. $2.50, Western wedding cake. $3, Chinese bride and groom, dragon and phoenix. $5, Western bride and groom, wedding bells, flowered archway.
$10, Chinese and Western couples, bangles depicting dragon and phoenix, wedding rings, horiz.

Perf. 13¾x13¼ Syncopated

2013, July 23 Litho.

Granite Paper

1578-1583 A355 Set of 6 4.25 4.25

Souvenir Sheet

Perf. 13¼x13 Syncopated

1584 A355 $10 multi 2.60 2.60

No. 1584 contains one 100x40mm stamp.

On July 23, 2013, Hong Kong issued the stamps pictured above, having franking values of $1.40 and $5 respectively. The stamps were each printed in sheets of 8 + 8 with non-personalizable labels depicting various wedding items. The sheets sold for $30 and $55 respectively.

Souvenir Sheet

Old Town of Lijiang UNESCO World Heritage Site, People's Republic of China — A356

Perf. 14 Syncopated

2013, Aug. 22 Litho. & Embossed

Granite Paper

1585 A356 $10 multi 2.60 2.60

Buses — A357

Designs: $1.40, 1947 Tilling Stevens bus. $1.80, 1949 Daimler A bus. $2.40, 1975 Albion Coach. $2.50, 1988 Leyland Olympian 11m bus. $3, 1995, Volvo Olympian 11m bus. No. 1591, $5, 1997 Dennis Trident bus.
No. 1592, $5, Euro V bus, horiz. $20, Euro V bus, diff. horiz.

Perf. 13½x13¼ Syncopated

2013, Sept. 24 Litho.

Granite Paper

1586-1591 A357 Set of 6 4.25 4.25

Souvenir Sheets

Perf. 13¾x14 Syncopated

1592 A357 $5 multi 1.40 1.40

Litho. With Three-Dimensional Plastic Affixed

Perf. 13¾x14 Syncopated

1593 A357 $20 multi 5.25 5.25

Nos. 1592 and 1593 each contain one 100x40mm stamp. A booklet containing panes of Nos. 1586-1588, 1589-1591 and 1592, respectively, sold for $50.

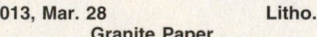

Heartwarming Types of 2003 Redrawn Removing White Chinese Characters and "Heartwarming" and

A358

A359

Size: 30x30mm
Granite Paper

Perf. 13¼ Syncopated

2013, Oct. 1 **Litho.**

Inscribed "Local Mail Postage"

1594 A214 ($1.70) multi .45 .45
a. Booklet pane of 10 4.50 —
Complete booklet, #1594a 4.50

Inscribed "Air Mail Postage"

1595 A213 ($3.70) multi .95 .95
a. Booklet pane of 10 9.50 —
Complete booklet, #1595a 9.50

Coil Stamps
Inscribed "Local Mail Postage"

Perf. 15x14 Syncopated

1596 A358 ($1.70) multi .45 .45
1597 A359 ($3.70) multi .95 .95

Works of Handicapped Artists — A360

Designs: $1.70, Thanksgiving, painting by Chan Tung Mui. $2.90, Always By Your Side, photograph by Cheng Kai Man. $3.70, The Vitality of Hong Kong, painting, by Ko Nam. $5, How Are You, painting by Liu Tung Mui.

Perf. 13¼x14¼ Syncopated
Litho. & Thermography

2013, Oct. 15 **Granite Paper**

1598-1601 A360 Set of 4 3.50 3.50
1601a Souvenir sheet of 4, #1598-1601 3.50 3.50

New Technologies — A361

Designs: $1.70, Green technology. $2.20, Information and communication technology. $2.90, Chinese medicine. $3.10, Biotechnology. $3.70, Nanotechnology and advanced materials. $5, Radio frequency identification.

Perf. 14x14¼ Syncopated

2013, Nov. 19 **Litho.**

Granite Paper

1602-1607 A361 Set of 6 4.75 4.75
1607a Souvenir sheet of 6, #1602-1607 4.75 4.75

Hong Kong Legislative Council — A362

Designs: $1.70, New Legislative Council Complex. $2.90, Old Legislative Council Building. $3.70, Chamber in New Legislative Council Complex. $5, President's Chair in Old Legislative Council Building.

Perf. 13½x13¼ Syncopated

2013, Dec. 5 **Litho.**

Granite Paper

1608-1611 A362 Set of 4 3.50 3.50
1611a Souvenir sheet of 4, #1608-1611 3.50 3.50

New Year 2014 (Year of the Horse) A363

Designs: $1.70, Horse made of fabric. $2.90, Wood carving of horse. $3.70, Metal sculpture of horse. $5, Lacquer ware horse.
No. 1616: a, Snake. b, Horse.
$10, Horse (with gold emblem at right). No. 1618, Horse (without gold emblem at right).

Perf. 13¼x14¼ Syncopated

2014, Jan. 11 **Litho.**

Granite Paper

1612-1615 A363 Set of 4 3.50 3.50

Litho. With Foil Application (#1616a), Litho. With Metal Affixed (#1616b)

Perf. 13¼x12¾ Syncopated

1616 A363 $50 Sheet of 2, #a-b 26.00 26.00

Souvenir Sheets
Litho. With Foil Application

Perf. 13¼ Syncopated

1617 A363 $10 multi 2.60 2.60

Litho.
On Silk-Faced Granite Paper

1618 A363 $50 multi 13.00 13.00

Nos. 1617-1618 each contain one 45x45mm stamp. Imperforate examples of No. 1617 with silver lines replacing the perforations were given away as gifts to standing order customers and are not valid for postage.
See No. 1700c.

On Jan. 11, 2014, Hong Kong issued the stamps pictured above, having franking values of $1.70 and $3.70 respectively. The stamps were each printed in sheets of 12 + 12 non-personalizable labels depicting various images. The sheets sold for $42 and $70 respectively.

Heartwarming A364

Designs: No. 1619, Champagne flutes. No. 1620, Birthday cake and candle. No. 1621, Flower held by man and woman. No. 1622, People watching fireworks. No. 1623, Birthday party decorations, gifts, birthday cake and candle. No. 1624, Family, balloons and hearts.

Litho. With Foil Application

2014, Jan. 23 ***Perf. 13¼ Syncopated***

Granite Paper

Inscribed "Local Mail Postage"

1619 A364 ($1.70) multi .45 .45
1620 A364 ($1.70) multi .45 .45
1621 A364 ($1.70) multi .45 .45

Inscribed "Air Mail Postage"

1622 A364 ($3.70) multi .95 .95
1623 A364 ($3.70) multi .95 .95
1624 A364 ($3.70) multi .95 .95
a. Sheet of 12, 2 each #1619-1624, + 12 labels 8.50 8.50
Nos. 1619-1624 (6) 4.20 4.20

Dinosaurs — A365

Designs: $1.70, Daxiatitan binglingi. $2.20, Microraptor gui. $2.90, Lufengosaurus magnus. $3.10, Tuojiangosaurus multispinus. $3.70, Protoceratops andrewsi. $5, Yangchuanosaurus shangyouensis.

Perf. 13½x13¼ Syncopated

2014, Feb. 20 **Litho.**

Granite Paper

1625-1630 A365 Set of 6 4.75 4.75
1630a Souvenir sheet of 6, #1625-1630 4.75 4.75

A booklet containing panes of Nos. 1625-1626, 1627-1628 and 1629-1630, respectively sold for $48.

Weather Phenomena A366

Designs: $1.70, Rainbow. $2.20, Frost. $2.90, Cloud. $3.10, Lightning. $3.70, Fog. No. 1636, $5, Rain.
Nos. 1637, $5, 1638, $20, Typhoon.

Perf. 13¾ Syncopated

2014, Mar. 27 **Litho.**

Granite Paper

1631-1636 A366 Set of 6 4.75 4.75

Souvenir Sheets

Perf. 13¼ Syncopated

1637 A366 $5 multi 1.40 1.40

Litho. With Three-Dimensional Plastic Affixed

1638 A366 $20 multi 5.25 5.25

Nos. 1637 and 1638 each contain one 45x45mm stamp. A booklet containing panes of Nos. 1631-1633 and 1634-1636 repsectively sold for $53.

Souvenir Sheet

Old General Post Office Building — A367

Litho., Sheet Margin Litho. With Foil Application

Perf. 14x13¾ Syncopated

2014, Apr. 29 **Granite Paper**

1639 A367 $20 multi 5.25 5.25

No. 1639 was also sold in a commemorative booklet that sold for $60. The sheet in that booklet was placed in a stamp mount. Values are for sheets without booklet.

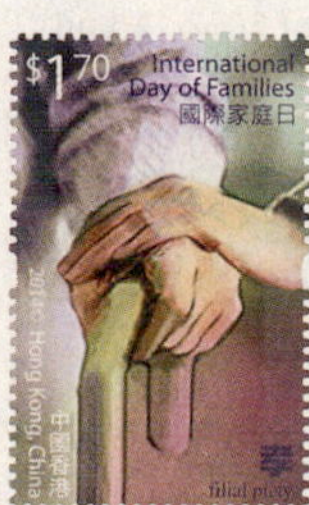
International Day of Families — A368

Clasped hands and words at lower right: $1.70, Filial piety. $2.90, Love. $3.70, Harmony. $5, Care.

Perf. 13½x13¼ Syncopated

2014, May 15 **Litho.**

Granite Paper

1640-1643 A368 Set of 4 3.50 3.50
1643a Souvenir sheet of 4, #1640-1643 3.50 3.50

Paintings by Wu Guanzhong (1919-2010) — A369

Designs: $1.70, Victoria Harbour, 2002. $2.20, Memories of Home, 1991. $2.90, Waterway, 1997, vert. (30x45mm). $3.10, Faces Unchanged, 2001, vert. (30x45mm). $3.70, Two Swallows, 1981. $5, The Farthest Corner of the World, 2009, vert. (30x45mm). $10, At Rest, 2010.

Perf. 13¼x13½ Syncopated, 13¼ Syncopated (Vert. Stamps)

2014, June 17 **Litho.**

Granite Paper

1644-1649 A369 Set of 6 4.75 4.75

Souvenir Sheet

Perf. 13¼x13

1650 A369 $10 multi 2.60 2.60

No. 1650 contains one 130x68mm stamp.

Earth Features — A370

Designs: 10c, North Ninepin Island. 20c, Basalt Island. 50c, Tai Long Wan. $1, Po Pin Chau. $1.70, High Island Reservoir East Dam. $2, Port Island. $2.20, Wong Chuk Kok Tsui. $2.30, Bride's Pool. $2.90, Lan Kwo Shui. $3.10, Lung Lok Shui. $3.70, Kang Lau Shek. $5, Ap Chau. $10, Sharp Island. $15.50, High Island. $20, Lai Chi Chong. $50, Pak Sha Tau Tsui.

Perf. 12¾x13¾ Syncopated

2014, July 24 **Litho.**

Granite Paper (#1651-1670)
Size: 25x29mm

1651 A370 10c multi .25 .25
1652 A370 20c multi .25 .25
1653 A370 50c multi .25 .25
1654 A370 $1 multi .25 .25
1655 A370 $1.70 multi .45 .45
1656 A370 $2 multi .50 .50
1657 A370 $2.20 multi .55 .55
1658 A370 $2.30 multi .60 .60
1659 A370 $2.90 multi .75 .75
1660 A370 $3.10 multi .80 .80
1661 A370 $3.70 multi .95 .95
1662 A370 $5 multi 1.40 1.40
a. Souvenir sheet of 12, #1651-1662 7.00 7.00

Size: 29x34mm

Perf. 13¼x13 Syncopated

1663 A370 $10 multi 2.60 2.60
1664 A370 $15.50 multi 4.00 4.00
1665 A370 $20 multi 5.25 5.25
1666 A370 $50 multi 13.00 13.00
a. Souvenir sheet of 4, #1663-1666 25.00 25.00
Nos. 1651-1666 (16) 31.85 31.85

Coil Stamps
Size: 20x24mm

Perf. 15x15½ Syncopated

1667 A370 $1.70 multi .45 .45
1668 A370 $2.20 multi .55 .55
1669 A370 $2.90 multi .75 .75
1670 A370 $3.70 multi .95 .95
Nos. 1667-1670 (4) 2.70 2.70

Booklet Stamps
Self-Adhesive
Size: 25x29mm

Die Cut Perf. 12¾x13¾ Syncopated

1671 A370 $1.70 multi .45 .45
a. Booklet pane of 10 4.50
1672 A370 $2.20 multi .55 .55
a. Booklet pane of 10 5.50
1673 A370 $2.90 multi .75 .75
a. Booklet pane of 10 7.50

1674	A370	$3.70 multi	.95	.95
a.		Booklet pane of 10	9.50	
		Nos. 1671-1674 (4)	2.70	2.70

Nos. 1662-1666 have microperforations in the denominations.

Cantonese Opera Costumes — A371

Designs: $1.70, Great Han costume. $2.20, Gown with sloping collar. $2.90, Dress for young ladies. $3.10, Military uniform for soldiers. $3.70, Python ceremonial robe. $5, Gown with a vertical collar.
$10, Joint investiture, horiz.

Perf. 13½x13¼ Syncopated
2014, Aug. 21 Litho.
Granite Paper

1675-1680 A371 Set of 6 5.00 5.00

Souvenir Sheet
Perf. 13¾x14

1681 A371 $10 multi 2.60 2.60

No. 1681 contains one 100x40mm stamp.

Souvenir Sheet

Hong Kong 2015 Intl. Stamp Exhibition — A372

Litho. With Foil Application
Perf. 13½x13¼ Syncopated
2014, Sept. 18 Granite Paper

1682	A372	$20 multi	5.25	5.25
a.		With 2015 copyright date (#1750a)	5.50	5.50

Issued: No. 1682a, 11/23/15.

Local Foods of Hong Kong and Malaysia — A373

Flower and: $1.70, Egg waffle. $2.90, Nasi lemak. $3.70, Poon choi. $5, Satay.

Perf. 13½x13¼ Syncopated
2014, Oct. 9 Granite Paper Litho.

1683-1686	A373	Set of 4	3.50	3.50
1686a		Souvenir sheet of 4, #1683-1686	3.50	3.50

See Malaysia Nos. 1510-1513.

Christmas — A374

Designs: Nos. 1687, 1691, $1.70, Santa Claus and reindeer. Nos. 1688, 1692, $2.90, Reindeer. Nos. 1689, 1693, $3.70, Snowman and birds. Nos. 1690, 1694, $5, Angel and snowmen.

Perf. 13½ Syncopated
2014, Nov. 4 Litho.
Granite Paper (#1687-1690)

1687-1690	A374	Set of 4	3.50	3.50
1690a		Souvenir sheet of 4, #1687-1690	3.50	3.50

Self-Adhesive
Die Cut Perf. 13½ Syncopated

1691-1694	A374	Set of 4	3.50	3.50
1694a		Souvenir sheet of 4, #1691-1694	3.50	

On Dec. 4, 2014, Hong Kong issued the stamps pictured above, having franking values of $1.70 and $3.70 respectively. The stamps were each printed in sheets of 8 + 8 non-personalizable labels depicting various Christmas images. The sheets sold for $32 and $60 respectively.

Souvenir Sheet

China Danxia UNESCO World Heritage Site — A375

Perf. 13½x13¼ Syncopated
Litho. & Silk-Screened
2014, Dec. 4 Granite Paper

1695 A375 $10 multi 2.60 2.60

New Year Types of 2012-14 and

New Year 2015 (Year of the Ram) A376

Designs: $1.70, Celadon ram figurine. $2.90, Gold glazed ceramic ram. $3.70, Clay ram. $5, Jade ram.

No. 1700: a, Like #1483. b, Like #1554. c, Like #1612. d, Like #1699.
No. 1701, Cloisonné ram (gold emblem at right). No. 1702, Cloisonné ram (without gold emblem at right).
No. 1703: a, Horse. b, Ram.

Perf. 13¼ Syncopated
2015, Jan. 24 Litho.
Granite Paper

1696-1699 A376 Set of 4 3.50 3.50

Litho. & Embossed With Foil Application

1700	Block of 4	10.50	10.50
a.	A338 $10 multi	2.60	2.60
b.	A350 $10 multi	2.60	2.60
c.	A363 $10 multi	2.60	2.60
d.	A376 $10 multi	2.60	2.60

Souvenir Sheets

1701 A376 $10 multi 2.60 2.60

Litho.
Silk-Faced Granite Paper

1702 A376 $50 multi 13.00 13.00

Litho. With Foil Application (#1703a), Litho. With Metal Affixed (#1703b)
Granite Paper

1703 A376 $50 Sheet of 2, #a-b 26.00 26.00

Nos. 1701-1702 each contain one 45x45mm stamp.

On Jan. 24, 2015, Hong Kong issued the stamps pictured above, having franking values of $1.70 and $3.70 respectively. The stamps were each printed in sheets of 12 + 12 non-personalizable labels. The sheets sold for $42 and $70 respectively.

Hearts — A377

Heart-shaped items: No. 1704, Lollipop. No. 1705, Decorated cake. No. 1706, Eggs on slice of bread. No. 1707, Four-leaf clovers. No. 1708, Party balloons. No. 1709, Photograph frame.

Perf. 13¼ Syncopated
2015, Feb. 12 Litho. & Embossed
Granite Paper
Inscribed "Local Mail Postage"

1704	A377 ($1.70) multi	.45	.45
1705	A377 ($1.70) multi	.45	.45
1706	A377 ($1.70) multi	.45	.45

Inscribed "Air Mail Postage"

1707	A377 ($3.70) multi	.95	.95
1708	A377 ($3.70) multi	.95	.95
1709	A377 ($3.70) multi	.95	.95
a.	Souvenir sheet of 12, 2 each #1704-1709, + 12 labels	8.50	8.50
	Nos. 1704-1709 (6)	4.20	4.20

Astronomical Phenomena A378

Designs: $1.70, Solar eclipse. $2.20, Meteor shower. $2.90, Comet. $3.10, Variation in Saturn's ring tilt. $3.70, Sunspot. $5, Moon-planet conjunction.
$10, $20, Lunar Eclipse.

Perf. 13¾x14 Syncopated
2015, Mar. 17 Litho.
Granite Paper

1710-1715	A378	Set of 6	5.00	5.00
1715a		Horiz. strip of 6, #1710-1715	5.00	5.00

Souvenir Sheets
Perf. 14x13¾ Syncopated

1716 A378 $10 multi 2.60 2.60

Litho. With Foil Application

1717 A378 $20 multi 5.25 5.25

A booklet containing panes of Nos. 1710-1712, 1713-1715 and 1716, respectively sold for $60.

Promulgation of the Basic Law, 25th Anniv. — A379

Flags of People's Republic of China and Hong Kong, people and: $1.70, Legislators, government officials and buildings. $2.90, Shenzhen Bay Bridge. $3.70, Return of Hong Kong Monument, Forever Blooming Bauhinia sculpture. $5, Spiral Lookout Tower, Tai Po.

Perf. 13¼x13½ Syncopated
2015, Apr. 2 Litho.
Granite Paper

1718-1721	A379	Set of 4	3.50	3.50
1721a		Souvenir sheet of 4, #1718-1721	3.50	3.50

Sports — A380

Designs: $1.70, Cycling. $2.20, Table tennis. $2.90, Soccer. $3.10, Track. $3.70, Badminton. $5, Swimming.

Perf. 13½x13¼ Syncopated
2015, Apr. 23 Litho.
Granite Paper

1722-1727	A380	Set of 6	5.00	5.00
1727a		Souvenir sheet of 6, #1722-1727	5.00	5.00

Governmental Ships — A381

Designs: $1.70, Customs and Excise Department Sector Patrol Launch. $2.20, Department of Health Port Quarantine Launch. $2.90, Environmental Protection

Department Marine Monitoring Vessel. $3.10, Fire Services Department Fireboat. $3.70, Police Force Training Launch. $5, Marine Department Hydrographic Survey Launch.
$10, Sector Patrol Launch, Port Quarantine Launch, Marine Monitoring Vessel, Fireboat, Training Launch and Hydrographic Survey Launch.

Perf. 13¼x14¼ Syncopated
2015, May 21 Litho.
Granite Paper

1728-1733 A381 Set of 6 5.00 5.00
1733a Souvenir sheet of 18, 3 each #1728-1733 15.00 15.00

Souvenir Sheet
Perf. 14 Syncopated

1734 A381 $10 multi 2.60 2.60

No. 1734 contains one 75x40mm stamp.
A booklet containing panes of Nos. 1728-1729, 1730-1731 and 1732-1733, respectively sold for $50.

Souvenir Sheet

Honghe Hani Rice Terrace UNESCO World Heritage Site — A382

Perf. 13¾x13½ Syncopated
2015, June 18 Litho. & Embossed
Granite Paper

1735 A382 $10 multi 2.60 2.60

Chinese and Foreign Folklore A383

Designs: Nos. 1736, 1742a, $1.70, The Old Man Who Moved Mountains. Nos. 1737, 1742b, $2.20, The Tortoise and the Hare. Nos. 1738, 1742c, $2.90, The Little Engine That Could. Nos. 1739, 1742d, $3.10, The Wild Swans. Nos. 1740, 1742e, $3.70, The Three Little Pigs. Nos. 1741, 1742f, $5, The Parable of the Pipeline.

Perf. 13¾ Syncopated
2015, July 16 Litho.
Granite Paper (#1736-1741)

1736-1741 A383 Set of 6 5.00 5.00
1741a Souvenir sheet of 6, #1736-1741 5.00 5.00

Self-Adhesive
Die Cut Perf. 13¼ Syncopated

1742 A383 Sheet of 6, #a-f 5.00 5.00

Souvenir Sheet

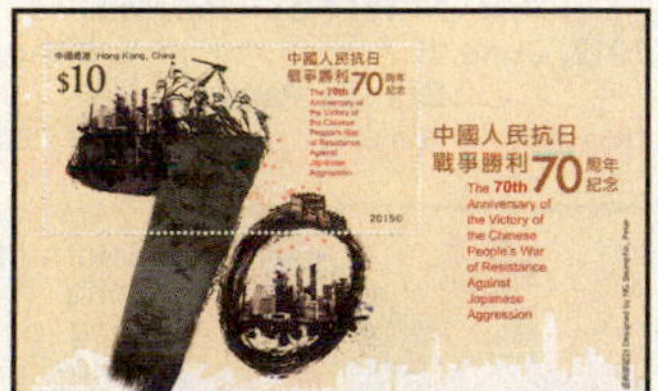

End of World War II, 70th Anniv. — A384

Perf. 14 Syncopated
2015, Sept. 2 Litho.
Granite Paper

1743 A384 $10 multi 2.60 2.60

Souvenir Sheet

Relocation of Court of Final Appeal — A385

Perf. 14 Syncopated
Litho. & Embossed
2015, Sept. 30 Granite Paper

1744 A385 $10 multi 2.60 2.60

World Post Day A386

Shadow pigeons made of hands, various cancels and map of: $1.70, Oceania. $2.90, Indian Ocean and East Africa. $3.70, East Asia. $5, Europe.

Perf. 13¼x14¼ Syncopated
2015, Oct. 9 Litho.
Granite Paper

1745-1748 A386 Set of 4 3.50 3.50
1748a Souvenir sheet of 4, #1745-1748 3.50 3.50

Souvenir Sheets

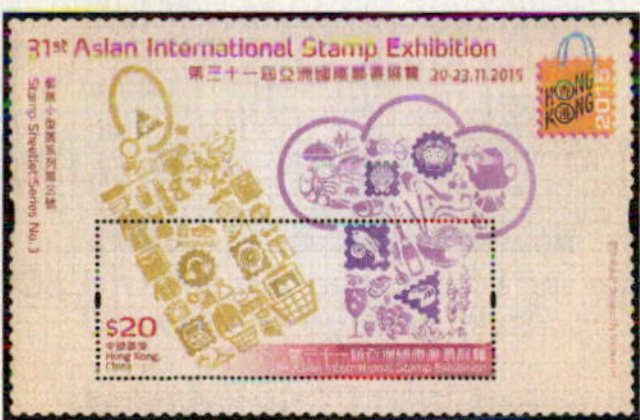

A387

Hong Kong 2015 Intl. Stamp Exhibition — A388

Litho. With Foil Application
2015 ***Perf. 13½x13¼ Syncopated***
Granite Paper

1749 A387 $20 multi 5.25 5.25
1750 A388 $20 multi 5.25 5.25
a. Booklet pane of 3, #1682a, 1749, 1750 16.50 —
Complete booklet, #1750a 16.50

Issued: No. 1749, 11/20; Nos. 1750, 1750a, 11/23. The edges of the souvenir sheet margins on Nos. 1749 and 1750 are perf. 6½ syncopated. The perforations around the souvenir sheet margins of items in the booklet are perf. 13¼ syncopated. Complete booklet sold for $65.

Ancient Chinese Scientists — A389

Designs: $1.70, Zhang Heng (78-139), and seismoscope. $2.90, Zu Chongzhi (429-500), and calculation of pi. $3.70, Guo Shoujing (1231-1316), and simplified armilla. $5, Li Shizhen (1518-93), and Compendium of Materia Medica.

Perf. 13½x13¼ Syncopated
2015, Dec. 8 Litho.
Granite Paper

1751-1754 A389 Set of 4 3.50 3.50
1754a Souvenir sheet of 4, #1751-1754 3.50 3.50

New Year 2016 (Year of the Monkey) A390

Designs: $1.70, Monkey holding peach. $2.90, Monkey. $3.70, Silver monkey. $5, Beijing Opera Sun Wukong monkey mask.
$10, Monkey holding peach, diff.
No. 1760, Like $10.
No. 1761: a, Ram. b, Monkey.

Perf. 13¼x14¼ Syncopated
2016, Jan. 16 Litho.
Granite Paper

1755-1758 A390 Set of 4 3.50 3.50

Souvenir Sheets
Litho. With Foil Application
Perf. 13¼ Syncopated

1759 A390 $10 multi 2.60 2.60

Litho.
Silk-Faced Granite Paper

1760 A390 $50 multi 13.00 13.00

Litho. With Foil Application (#1761a), Litho. with Metal Affixed (#1761b)
Granite Paper

1761 A390 $50 Sheet of 2, #a-b 26.00 26.00

Nos. 1759-1760 each contain one 45x45mm stamp.

On Jan. 16, 2016, Hong Kong issued the stamps pictured above, having franking values of $1.70 and $3.70 respectively. The stamps were each printed in sheets of 12 + 12 non-personalizable labels. The sheets sold for $42 and $70 respectively.

Hong Kong Girl Guides, Cent. A391

Designs: $1.70, First Aid, AIDS Knowledge, Environmental Protection and Community Health badges, girl wearing current Girl Guides uniform. $2.90, Against Corruption, Book Lover, Friendship and Thrift badges, girl wearing Brownie uniform of 1970s. $3.70, Orienteering, Country Walking, Basic Survival and Star Gazing badges, girl wearing Sea Ranger's uniform from 1940s-1970s. $5, Artist, Signaller, Craft and Knotter badges, girl wearing Brownie uniform from 1920s-1930s.

Perf. 13¼ Syncopated
2016, Feb. 22 Litho.
Granite Paper

1762-1765 A391 Set of 4 3.50 3.50
1765a Souvenir sheet of 4, #1762-1765, perf. 13¼x14¼ syncopated 3.50 3.50

Syncopation on No. 1765a differs from that on Nos. 1762-1765. A booklet containing panes of Nos. 1762-1763 and 1764-1765 respectively sold for $45.

Public Architecture — A392

Designs: $1.70, Hong Kong Museum of Coastal Defense. $2.70, Victoria Park Swimming Pool. $2.90, Sai Kung Waterfront Park. $3.10, Ping Shan Tin Shui Wai Leisure and Cultural Building. $3.70, Hong Kong Wetland Park. $5, Electrical and Mechanical Services Department Headquarters.

Perf. 13¼ Syncopated
2016, Mar. 31 Litho.
Granite Paper

1766-1771 A392 Set of 6 4.75 4.75
1771a Souvenir sheet of 6, #1766-1771 4.75 4.75

St. John Ambulance Brigade, Cent. — A393

Designs: $1.70, Ambulance, medic treating child. $2.90, Medic treating fallen runner. $3.70, Dentistry for wheelchair-bound patient. $5, First aid training for teenagers.

Perf. 13¼x13½ Syncopated
2016, Apr. 14 Litho.
Granite Paper

1772-1775 A393 Set of 4 3.50 3.50
1775a Souvenir sheet of 4, #1772-1775 3.50 3.50

A booklet containing panes of Nos. 1772-1773 and 1774-1775 respectively sold for $45.

Souvenir Sheet

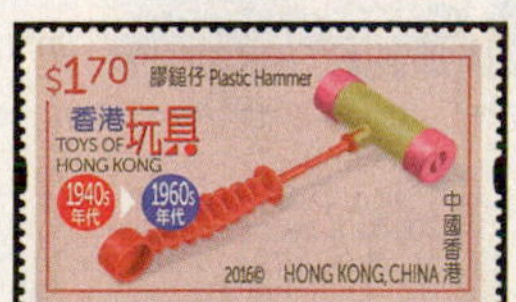

Grand Canal World Heritage Site, People's Republic of China — A394

Perf. 14 Syncopated
2016, May 10 Litho. & Embossed
Granite Paper

1776 A394 $10 multi 2.60 2.60

Toys Made in Hong Kong From 1940s-1960s — A395

Designs: $1.70, Plastic hammer. $2.20, Paper dolls. $2.90, Water pistol. $3.10, Miniature plastic swords. $3.70, Yellow plastic ducks. $5, Tin frog.

Perf. 13¼x14¼ Syncopated

2016, June 8 Litho.

Granite Paper

1777-1782 A395 Set of 6 4.75 4.75
1782a Miniature sheet of 18, 3 each #1777-1782 14.50 14.50

Souvenir Sheet

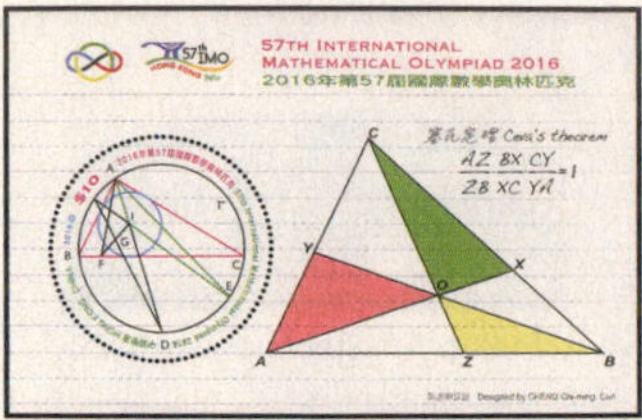

Ceva's Theorem — A396

2016, July 6 Litho. *Perf.*

Granite Paper

1783 A396 $10 multi 2.60 2.60

57th International Mathematical Olympiad, Hong Kong.

2016 Summer Olympics, Rio de Janeiro A397

Designs: $1.70, Track and cycling. $2.90, Table tennis and badminton. $3.70, Windsurfing and swimming. $5, Golf and swimming.

Litho. With Foil Application

2016, Aug. 5 *Perf. 13¾ Syncopated*

Granite Paper

1784-1787 A397 Set of 4 3.50 3.50
1787a Souvenir sheet of 4, #1784-1787 3.50 3.50

Tribute to Teachers — A398

Designs: $1.70, Hearts and open book. $2.90, Teacher and students. $3.70, Trophy. $5, Teacher and student.
$10, Mortarboard and books.

Perf. 13½x13¼ Syncopated

2016, Sept. 6 Litho.

Granite Paper

1788-1791 A398 Set of 4 3.50 3.50

Souvenir Sheet

1792 A398 $10 multi 2.60 2.60

Lantau Trail A399

Designs and trail segment: Nos. 1793, 1805, $1.70, Mui Wo Ferry Pier (Mui Wo to Nam Shan). Nos. 1794, 1806, $1.70, Stone chalets (Nam Shan to Pak Kung Au). Nos. 1795, 1807, $1.70, Lantau Peak (Pak Kung Au to Ngong Ping). Nos. 1796, 1808, $1.70, Wisdom Path and Statue of Buddha (Ngong Ping to Sham Wat Road). Nos. 1797, 1809, $1.70, Kneecap Peak (Sham Wat Road to Man Cheung Po). Nos. 1798, 1810, $1.70, Tai O fishing village (Man Cheung Po to Tai O). Nos. 1799, 1811, $1.70, Fan Lau Fort (Tai O to Kau Ling Chung). Nos. 1800, 1812, $1.70, Lantau South Obelisk (Kau Ling Chung to Shek Pik). Nos. 1801, 1813, $1.70, Shek Pik Reservoir (Shek Pik to Shui Hau). Nos. 1802, 1814, $1.70, Shui Hau Wan (Shui Hau to Tung Chung Road). Nos. 1803, 1815, $1.70, Waterfall (Tung Chung Road to Pui O). Nos. 1804, 1816, $1.70, Pui O Beach, Sunset Peak, Lin Fa Shan (Pui O to Mui Wo).

Perf. 13¼ Syncopated

2016, Oct. 13 Litho.

Granite Paper

1793-1804 A399 Set of 12 5.25 5.25

Litho. With Foil Application

1804a Souvenir sheet of 12, #1793-1804 5.25 5.25

Booklet Stamps Self-Adhesive

Die Cut Perf. 13¼ Syncopated

Litho.

1805-1816 A399 Set of 12 5.25 5.25
1816a Booklet pane of 12, #1805-1816 5.25

Sun Yat-sen (1866-1925), President of the Republic of China — A400

Sun Yat-sen and: $1.70, Government Central School. $2.90, Alice Memorial Hospital and College of Medicine, vert. $3.70, Hong Kong Hotel, vert. $5, Main Building of University of Hong Kong.

Perf. 13¼ Syncopated

2016, Nov. 12 Litho.

Granite Paper

1817-1820 A400 Set of 4 3.50 3.50
1820a Souvenir sheet of 4, #1817-1820 3.50 3.50

A booklet containing panes of Nos. 1817-1818 and 1819-1820 respectively sold for $45.

Pencil Drawings by Kong Kai-Ming — A401

Designs: $1.70, Airport Tunnel, Hung Hom. $2.20, Argyle Street, Mong Kok. $2.90, Kwun Tong MTR Station. $3.10, Wan Chai Tram Depot. $3.70, Canton Road. $5, Zoroastrian Church, Causeway Bay.
$10, Aberdeen.

Perf. 13½ Syncopated

2016, Dec. 6 Litho. & Engr.

Granite Paper

1821-1826 A401 Set of 6 4.75 4.75

Souvenir Sheet

Perf. 13½x13¾

1827 A401 $10 multi 2.60 2.60

No. 1827 contains one 60x43mm stamp.

New Year 2017 (Year of the Rooster) A402

Designs: $1.70, Rooster made of fabric. $2.90, Tin rooster. $3.70, Rooster made of seashells. $5, Silver rooster.
$10, Embroidered rooster, diff.
No. 1833, Like $10.
No. 1834: a, Monkey. b, Rooster.

Perf. 13¼x14¼ Syncopated

2017, Jan. 7 Litho.

Granite Paper

1828-1831 A402 Set of 4 3.50 3.50

Souvenir Sheets

Litho. With Foil Application

Perf. 13¼ Syncopated

1832 A402 $10 multi 2.60 2.60

Litho.

Silk-Faced Granite Paper

1833 A402 $50 multi 13.00 13.00

Litho. With Foil Application (#1834a), Litho. with Metal Affixed (#1834b)

Granite Paper

1834 A402 $50 Sheet of 2, #a-b 26.00 26.00

Nos. 1832-1833 each contain one 45x45mm stamp.

On Jan. 7, 2017, Hong Kong issued the stamps pictured above, having franking values of $1.70 and $3.70 respectively. The stamps were each printed in sheets of 12 + 12 non-personalizable labels. The sheets sold for $42 and $70 respectively.

Souvenir Sheet

Kaiping Diaolou and Villages UNESCO World Heritage Site — A403

Perf. 13x13¼ Syncopated

2017, Feb. 16 Litho. & Embossed

Granite Paper

1835 A403 $10 multi 2.60 2.60

Revitalization of Historic Buildings — A404

Designs: $1.70, Viva Blue House. $2.20, Oi! Arts Center. $2.90, Green Hub. $3.10, Stone Houses Family Garden. $3.70, PMQ. $5, Mallory Street Revitalization Project.

Litho. With Foil Application

Perf. 13¼x14¼ Syncopated

2017, Apr. 25 Granite Paper

1836-1841 A404 Set of 6 4.75 4.75
1841a Souvenir sheet of 6, #1836-1841 4.75 4.75

A booklet containing panes of Nos. 1836-1837, 1838-1839 and 1840-1841, respectively sold for $50.

Outdoor Activities — A405

Inscriptions: $1.70, Picnic and barbecue. $2.20, Cycling. $2.90, Visiting heritage sites. $3.10, Beach fun. $3.70, Hiking. $5, Outdoor photography.

Perf. 13½x13¼ Syncopated

2017, May 2 Litho.

Granite Paper

1842-1847 A405 Set of 6 4.75 4.75
1847a Souvenir sheet of 6, #1842-1847 4.75 4.75

Numbered Typhoon Signals, Cent. — A406

Inscriptions: $1.70, Standby signal No. 1. $2.20, Strong wind signal No. 3. $2.90, Gale or storm signal No. 8. $3.70, Increasing gale or storm signal No. 9. $5, Hurricane signal No. 10.
$10, Hoisting of hurricane signal No. 10, horiz.

Perf. 13½x13¼ Syncopated

Litho. & Silk-Screened

2017, June 13 Granite Paper

1848-1852 A406 Set of 5 4.00 4.00

Souvenir Sheet

Perf. 14¼x14 Syncopated

1853 A406 $10 multi 2.60 2.60

A booklet containing panes of Nos. 1848-1850 and 1851-1852, respectively sold for $48. No. 1853 contains one 63x34mm stamp.

Souvenir Sheet

Stationing of People's Liberation Army in Hong Kong, 20th Anniv. — A407

Perf. 14¼x14 Syncopated

2017, June 20 Litho.

Granite Paper

1854 A407 $10 multi 2.60 2.60

Return of Hong Kong to People's Republic of China, 20th Anniv. A408

Perf. 13 Syncopated

2017, July 1 Photo.

1855 A408 $1.70 multi .45 .45

See People's Republic of China Nos. 4455-4457.

Hong Kong Special Administrative Region, 20th Anniv. — A409

Designs: $1.70, Buildings and flags of Hong Kong and People's Republic of China. $2.90, Athletes, violinist, dancer and actors. $3.70, Buildings and doves. $5, People releasing balloons.

Litho. With Foil Application
Perf. 14x13¼ Syncopated
2017, July 1 Granite Paper

1856-1859 A409 Set of 4 3.50 3.50
1859a Souvenir sheet of 4, #1856-1859 3.50 3.50

Five Senses A410

Designs: $1.70, Hearing. $2.20, Sight. $2.90, Smell. $3.70, Taste. $5, Touch.
$10, Children experiencing the five senses, horiz.

Litho. & Thermography ($1.70, $5), Litho.
Perf. 13¾ Syncopated
2017, July 18 Granite Paper

1860-1864 A410 Set of 5 4.00 4.00
1864a Souvenir sheet of 15, 3 each #1860-1864 12.00 12.00

Souvenir Sheet
Perf. 14¼x14 Syncopated

1865 A410 $10 multi 2.60 2.60

No. 1861 has a circular die cut hole punched out to simulate camera lens. No. 1862 is impregnated with a peach scent. No. 1863 has vanilla-flavored gum. No. 1865 contains one 105x60mm stamp.

Rare Flora — A411

Designs: $1.70, Ilex graciliflora. $2.90, Bulbophyllum bicolor. $3.70, Begonia hongkongensis. $5, Illicium angustisepalum.

Perf. 13¾ Syncopated
2017, Aug. 17 Litho.
Granite Paper

1866-1869 A411 Set of 4 3.50 3.50
1869a Souvenir sheet of 4, #1866-1869 3.50 3.50

Paintings and Calligraphy by Jao Tsung-I (1917-2018) A412

Designs: $1.70, Pine Trees in Huangshan. $2.20, Pine Trees and Arhat. $2.90, Five Character Couplet in Official Script. $3.10, Victoria Peak After the Rain. $3.70, Avalokitesvara After the Style of Tang Dynasty. $5, Calligraphy in Bronze Script.
$10, Four-screen Lotus Set, horiz.

Perf. 14¼x14 Syncopated
2017, Sept. 5 Litho.
Granite Paper

1870-1875 A412 Set of 6 4.75 4.75
1875a Souvenir sheet of 12, 2 each #1870-1875 9.50 9.50

Souvenir Sheet
Perf. 14x14¼ Syncopated

1876 A412 $10 multi 2.60 2.60

No. 1876 contains one 75x65mm stamp.

Shopping Areas — A413

Designs: $1.70, Goldfish Market. $2.20, Chinese Medicine Street. $2.90, Jade Market. $3.10, Kitchenware Street. $3.70, Flower Market. $5, Yau Ma Tei Wholesale Fruit Market.

Perf. 13¼x12¾ Syncopated
2017, Sept. 19 Litho.
Granite Paper

1877-1882 A413 Set of 6 4.75 4.75
1882a Souvenir sheet of 6, #1877-1882 4.75 4.75

Qipaos — A414

Qipao from: $1.70, 1920s. $2.20, 1930s. $2.90, 1940s. $3.10, 1950s. $3.70, 1960s. $5, 1970s.
$10, $20, Contemporary qipao.

Perf. 13½x13¼ Syncopated
2017, Oct. 17 Litho.
Granite Paper (#1883-1889)

1883-1888 A414 Set of 6 4.75 4.75
1888a Souvenir sheet of 18, 3 each #1883-1888 14.50 14.50

Souvenir Sheet
Perf. 12¾x13

1889 A414 $10 multi 2.60 2.60

On Taffeta-Faced Paper

1890 A414 $20 multi 5.25 5.25

Nos. 1889-1890 each contain one 35x78mm stamp. A booklet containing panes of Nos. 1883-1885, 1886-1888, and 1889, respectively sold for $60.

Bamboo Carvings — A415

Designs: $1.70, Cricket cage, by Xu Subai, 1959. $2.20, Lingzhi fungus and narcissus, c. 1723-35 (50x30mm). $2.90, Brushpot, 18th cent. (50x30mm). $3.10, Incense holder, 17th-18th cent. $3.70, Water container, c. 1662-1722 (50x30mm). $5, Jar, c. 1736-95 (50x30mm).

Perf. 13½x13¼ Syncopated
2017, Nov. 14 Litho. & Embossed
Granite Paper

1891-1896 A415 Set of 6 4.75 4.75
1896a Souvenir sheet of 6, #1891-1896 4.75 4.75

SEMI-POSTAL STAMPS

Catalogue values for unused stamps in this section are for Never Hinged items.

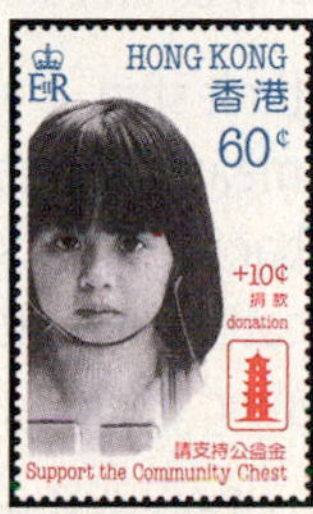

Community Chest of Hong Kong — SP1

No. B1, Girl. No. B2, Elderly woman. No. B3, Blind youth. No. B4, Mother and child.

1988, Nov. 30 Litho. *Perf. 14½*

B1 SP1 60c +10c multi .50 *.90*
B2 SP1 $1.40 +20c multi .60 *1.00*
B3 SP1 $1.80 +30c multi 1.40 *1.50*
B4 SP1 $5 +$1 multi 3.50 *4.00*
Nos. B1-B4 (4) 6.00 *7.40*

Surtax for the social welfare organization.

POSTAGE DUE STAMPS

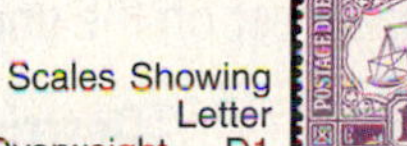

Scales Showing Letter Overweight — D1

1923, Dec. Typo. Wmk. 4 *Perf. 14*

J1 D1 1c brown 2.75 .70
a. Chalky paper, wmkd. sideways 1.60 *3.50*
J2 D1 2c green 42.50 11.00
J3 D1 4c red 52.50 7.25
J4 D1 6c orange 34.00 13.50
J5 D1 10c ultramarine 28.00 9.00
Nos. J1-J5 (5) 159.75 41.45
Set, never hinged 300.00

No. J1a issued Mar. 21, 1956.

1938-47 *Perf. 14*

J6 D1 2c gray 6.75 *10.00*
J7 D1 4c orange yellow 10.00 *5.25*
J8 D1 6c carmine 3.50 5.75
J9 D1 8c fawn ('46) 3.00 *34.00*
J10 D1 10c violet 19.00 .55
J11 D1 20c black ('46) 3.75 2.50
J12 D1 50c blue ('47) 40.00 13.50
Nos. J6-J12 (7) 86.00 71.55
Set, never hinged 190.00

Nos. J6-J7 and J10 exist on both ordinary and chalky paper.

Catalogue values for unused stamps in this section, from this point to the end of the section, are for Never Hinged items.

Wmk. 314 Sideways
1965-69 *Perf. 14*
Chalk-surfaced Paper

J13 D1 4c orange yellow 9.00 *32.50*
J14 D1 5c orange ver ('69) 3.75 *5.25*
a. 5c carmine, wmk. upright ('67) 4.00 *5.00*
J15 D1 10c purple ('67) 4.75 *8.50*
J16 D1 20c black 10.00 3.00
J17 D1 50c dark blue 37.50 8.00
a. Wmk. upright ('70) 50.00 11.50
Nos. J13-J17 (5) 65.00 57.25

Size of 5c, 21x18mm.; others, 22x18mm.

Wmk. 314 Upright
1972-74 *Perf. 13½x14*
Glazed Ordinary Paper

J18 D1 5c red brown ('74) 3.00 *6.00*

Perf. 14x14½

J19 D1 10c lilac 7.00 5.00
J20 D1 20c black 8.50 7.00
J21 D1 50c dull blue 6.00 *11.00*
Nos. J18-J21 (4) 24.50 29.00

1978 Wmk. 373

J22 D1 10c lilac 1.00 *6.00*
f. Chalk-surfaced paper 1.00 *2.25*
J22A D1 20c black 1.50 *7.50*
g. Chalk-surfaced paper 1.75 *2.50*
J22B D1 50c dull blue 1.50 *6.00*
h. Chalk-surfaced paper 1.75 *3.00*
J22C D1 $1 yellow 14.00 14.00
i. Chalk-surfaced paper 1.50 *4.25*
Nos. J22-J22C (4) 18.00 33.50

Size of $1, 20½x17mm; others, 22x18mm. Issued: Nos. J22-J22C, 3/19; J22f-J22i, 12/15.

1986, Jan. 11 Unwmk.
Chalk-surfaced Paper

J22D D1 50c dull blue 2.25 *5.75*
J22E D1 $1 yellow 3.00 *8.00*

D2

Perf. 14x15
1986, Mar. 25 Litho. Unwmk.

J23 D2 10c light green .25 *.70*
J24 D2 20c dark red brown .25 *.70*
J25 D2 50c lilac .25 .25
J26 D2 $1 light orange .25 .30
J27 D2 $5 grayish blue 1.00 *1.75*
J28 D2 $10 rose red 2.00 *3.50*
Nos. J23-J28 (6) 4.00 *7.20*

D3

Perf. 14x14¾
2004, Sept. 23 Litho. Unwmk.

J29 D3 10c dark blue .25 *.50*
J30 D3 20c blue .25 *.50*
J31 D3 50c orange .30 .25
J32 D3 $1 pink .65 *.75*
J33 D3 $5 olive green 1.60 *1.75*
J34 D3 $10 cerise 3.50 3.50
Nos. J29-J34 (6) 6.55 7.25

OCCUPATION STAMPS

Issued under Japanese Occupation

Japan No. 325 Surcharged in Black

Japan No. 259 Surcharged in Black

Japan No. 261 Surcharged in Black

Wmk. 257
1945, Apr. Typo. *Perf. 13*

N1 A144 1½y on 1s org brn 37.50 32.00
N2 A84 3y on 2s ver 12.50 *27.50*

N3	A86	5y on 5s brn lake	1,000.	160.00
		Nos. N1-N3 (3)	1,050.	219.50

No. N1 has eleven characters.

HORTA

'hor-tə

LOCATION — An administrative district of the Azores, consisting of the islands of Pico, Fayal, Flores and Corvo
GOVT. — A district of the Republic of Portugal
AREA — 305 sq. mi.
POP. — 49,000 (approx.)
CAPITAL — Horta

1000 Reis = 1 Milreis

King Carlos — A1

Chalk-surfaced Paper

Perf. 11½, 12½, 13½

1892-93 Typo. Unwmk.

1	A1	5r yellow	2.00	1.50
2	A1	10r reddish violet	2.00	1.75
3	A1	15r chocolate	2.00	2.00
4	A1	20r lavender	6.00	3.00
5	A1	25r dp grn, perf. 11½	5.00	1.00
	a.	Perf. 13½	5.75	3.75
6	A1	50r blue	7.00	3.00
	a.	Perf. 13½	9.00	5.25
7	A1	75r carmine	8.00	4.00
8	A1	80r yellow green	9.00	7.50
9	A1	100r brn, *yel* ('93)	35.00	10.00
	a.	Perf. 12½	125.00	90.00
10	A1	150r car, *rose* ('93)	55.00	32.50
11	A1	200r dk bl, *bl* ('93)	60.00	32.50
12	A1	300r dk bl, *sal* ('93)	70.00	35.00
		Nos. 1-12 (12)	261.00	133.75

Bisects of No. 1 were used in Aug. 1894. Value, on newsprint, $16.

The reprints have shiny white gum and clean-cut perforation 13½. The white paper is thinner than that of the originals. Value unused, $12 each.

King Carlos — A2

1897-1905 ***Perf. 11½***

Name and Value in Black Except 500r

13	A2	2½r gray	.50	.30
14	A2	5r orange	.50	.30
15	A2	10r lt green	.50	.30
16	A2	15r brown	5.75	4.00
17	A2	15r gray grn ('99)	1.25	.80
18	A2	20r gray violet	1.75	.85
19	A2	25r sea green	2.25	.45
20	A2	25r car rose ('99)	.90	.50
21	A2	50r blue	3.00	.70
22	A2	50r ultra ('05)	18.00	7.00
23	A2	65r slate blue ('98)	.70	.55
24	A2	75r rose	2.00	.95
25	A2	75r brn, *yel* ('05)	20.00	10.00
26	A2	80r violet	1.25	1.10
27	A2	100r dk blue, *bl*	1.75	.95
28	A2	115r org brn, *pink* ('98)	4.00	1.50
29	A2	130r gray brn, *buff* ('98)	4.00	1.50
30	A2	150r lt brn, *buff*	4.00	1.50
31	A2	180r sl, *pnksh* ('98)	4.00	1.75
32	A2	200r red vio, *pale lil*	12.00	4.00
33	A2	300r dk blue, *rose*	18.00	7.00
34	A2	500r blk & red, *bl*	20.00	8.50
		Nos. 13-34 (22)	126.10	54.50

Stamps of Portugal replaced those of Horta.

HUNGARY

ˈhəŋ-gə-ˌrē

LOCATION — Central Europe
GOVT. — Republic
AREA — 35,911 sq. mi.
POP. — 10,186,372 (1999 est.)
CAPITAL — Budapest

Prior to World War I, Hungary together with Austria comprised the Austro-Hungarian Empire. The Hungarian post became independent on May 1, 1867. During 1850-1871 stamps listed under Austria were also used in Hungary. Copies showing clear Hungarian cancels sell for substantially more.

100 Krajczár (Kreuzer) = 1 Forint 100 Fillér = 1 Korona (1900) 100 Fillér = 1 Pengö (1926) 100 Fillér = 1 Forint (1946)

Catalogue values for unused stamps in this country are for Never Hinged items, beginning with Scott 503 in the regular postage section, Scott B92 in the semi-postal section, Scott C35 in the airpost section, Scott CB1 in the airpost semi-postal section, Scott F1 in the registrtation section, Scott J130 in the postage due section, and Scott Q9 in the parcel post section.

Watermarks

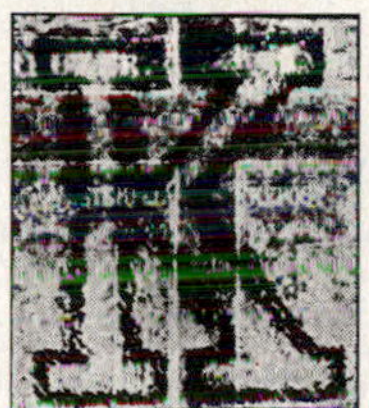

Wmk. 91 — "ZEITUNGS-MARKEN" in Double-lined Capitals across the Sheet

Wmk. 106 — Multiple Star

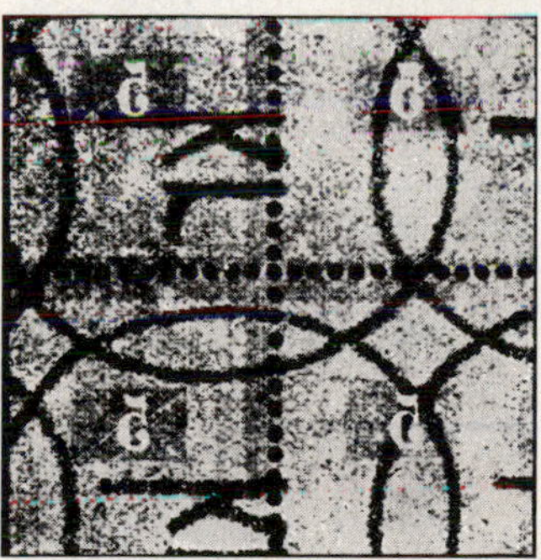

Wmk. 132 — kr in Oval

Wmk. 133 — Four Double Crosses

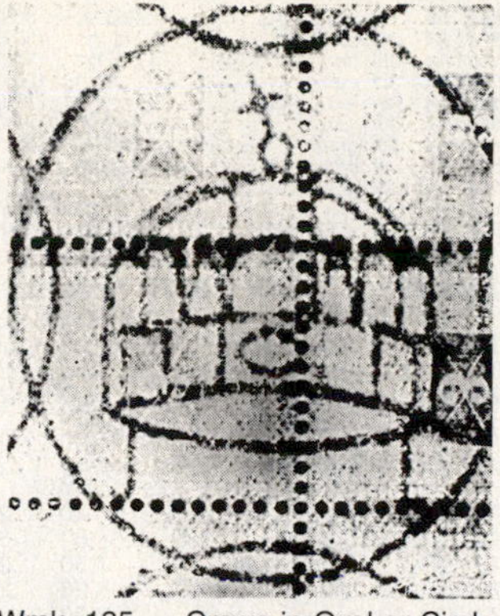

Wmk. 135 — Crown in Oval or Circle, Sideways

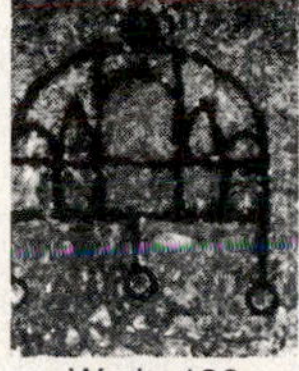

Wmk. 136

Wmk. 136a

Wmk. 137 — Double Cross

Wmk. 210 — Double Cross on Pyramid

Wmk. 266 — Double Barred Cross, Wreath and Crown

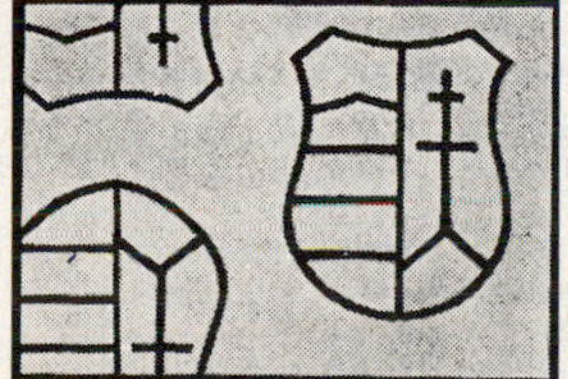

Wmk. 283 — Double Barred Cross on Shield, Multiple

Watermarks 132, 135, 136 and 136a can be found normal, reversed, inverted, or reversed and inverted.

Values for unused stamps are for examples with original gum as defined in the catalogue introduction. Very fine examples of Nos. 1-12 will have perforations touching the framelines on one or two sides due to imperfect perforating methods. Stamps with perfs clear on all four sides are very scarce and will command substantial premiums.

Issues of the Monarchy

Franz Josef I — A1

1871 Unwmk. Litho. *Perf. 9½*

1	A1	2k orange	325.00	100.00
a.		2k yellow	1,200.	250.00
2	A1	3k lt green	1,000.	600.00
3	A1	5k rose	450.00	25.00
a.		5k brick red	900.00	75.00
4	A1	10k blue	1,250.	100.00
a.		10k pale blue	1,400.	150.00
5	A1	15k yellow brn	1,250.	125.00
6	A1	25k violet	1,000.	200.00
a.		25k bright violet	1,500.	300.00

The first printing of No. 1, in dark yellow, was not issued because of spots on the King's face. A few stamps were used at Pest in 1873. Value, $3,000.

1871-72 Engr.

7	A1	2k orange	40.00	7.50
a.		2k yellow	175.00	20.00
b.		Bisect on cover		—
8	A1	3k green	125.00	25.00
a.		3k blue green	150.00	30.00
9	A1	5k rose	110.00	1.75
a.		5k brick red	200.00	8.00
10	A1	10k deep blue	300.00	10.00
11	A1	15k brown	475.00	15.00
a.		15k copper brown	—	1,500.
b.		15k black brown	875.00	85.00
12	A1	25k lilac	200.00	40.00
		Nos. 7-12 (6)	1,250.	99.25

Reprints are perf. 11½ and watermarked "kr" in oval. Value, set $225.

Crown of St. Stephen — A2

1874-76 *Perf. 13*

13	A2	2k red violet	30.00	2.00
a.		2k violet	35.00	2.50
14	A2	3k yellow green	30.00	2.00
a.		3k blue green	37.50	2.50
15	A2	5k red	10.00	.50
a.		5k brick red	45.00	1.50
b.		5k lilac red	15.00	.75
c.		5k rose	10.00	.40
16	A2	10k blue	35.00	.75
17	A2	20k grnsh gray	700.00	9.00
a.		20k gray	750.00	10.00
		Nos. 13-17 (5)	805.00	14.25
		Perf. 11½		
13b	A2	2k red violet	45.00	5.00
c.		2k violet	—	6.00
d.		2k rose lilac	75.00	4.50
e.		2k gray blue	60.00	3.75
14b	A2	3k yellow green	50.00	4.00
c.		3k blue green	60.00	5.00
15d	A2	5k red	60.00	1.00
e.		5k rose	50.00	.75
16a	A2	10k blue	75.00	5.00
17b	A2	20k gray	700.00	45.00
		Perf. 13x11½		
13f	A2	2k red violet	180.00	30.00
g.		2k rose lilac	200.00	30.00
14d	A2	3k yellow green	125.00	4.50
15f	A2	5k lilac red	250.00	12.00
g.		5k rose	300.00	15.00
16b	A2	10k blue	250.00	6.00
17c	A2	20k gray	800.00	50.00
		Perf. 11½x13		
13h	A2	2k red violet	60.00	5.00
i.		2k rose lilac	100.00	4.00
j.		2k gray blue	75.00	3.75
15h	A2	5k red	75.00	1.00
17d	A2	20k gray	—	100.00
		Perf. 9½		
14e	A2	3k green	*7,500.*	*2,500.*

All examples of the 5k perf 9½ are counterfeit.

1881 Wmk. 132 *Perf. 11½*

18	A2	2k lilac	3.50	.40
a.		2k violet	3.50	.40
b.		2k gray blue	4.50	.50
19	A2	3k blue green	3.50	.40
a.		3k yellow green	4.50	.60
20	A2	5k rose	2.50	.25
21	A2	10k blue	6.00	.40
a.		10k pale blue	7.00	.60
22	A2	20k gray	4.50	.65
a.		20k greenish gray	5.00	.75
		Nos. 18-22 (5)	20.00	2.10
		Perf. 13		
18c	A2	2k violet	150.00	20.00
d.		2k gray blue	120.00	10.00
19b	A2	3k blue green	90.00	4.00
c.		3k yellow green	100.00	5.50
20a	A2	5k rose	120.00	4.00
21b	A2	10k blue	75.00	5.00
22b	A2	20k gray	350.00	15.00
		Perf. 13x11½		
18e	A2	2k violet	—	40.00
19d	A2	3k blue green	160.00	6.00
e.		3k yellow green	—	8.00
20b	A2	5k rose	—	15.00
21c	A2	10k blue	—	8.00
22c	A2	20k gray	—	12.50
		Perf. 11½x13		
18f	A2	2k violet	200.00	9.00
g.		2k gray blue	180.00	6.00
19f	A2	3k blue green	—	60.00
g.		3k yellow green	—	75.00
20c	A2	5k rose	150.00	1.00
21d	A2	10k blue	—	1.75
22d	A2	20k gray	—	40.00
		Perf. 12x11½		
18h	A2	2k lilac	1.00	.25
i.		2k violet	15.00	1.20
19h	A2	3k blue green	1.00	.25
20d	A2	5k rose	2.50	.25
21e	A2	10k blue	3.00	.25
22e	A2	20k gray	300.00	7.50

Crown of St. Stephen — A3

Design A3 has an overall burelage of colored vertical lines. Compare with design N3.

1888-98 Typo. *Perf. 12x11¾*

Numerals in Black

22A A3 1k black, one plate 1.25 .30
c. "1" printed separately 15.00 3.00
23 A3 2k red violet 1.50 .50
24 A3 3k green 1.75 .40
25 A3 5k rose 2.00 .25
a. "5" double, inverted *1,750.*
26 A3 8k orange 6.00 .60
a. "8" double 150.00
27 A3 10k blue 5.00 1.25
28 A3 12k brown & green 12.50 1.00
29 A3 15k claret & blue 10.00 .40
30 A3 20k gray 7.50 2.00
31 A3 24k brn vio & red 22.50 1.25
32 A3 30k ol grn & brn 25.00 .35
33 A3 50k red & org 40.00 1.50

Numerals in Red

34 A3 1fo gray bl & sil 175.00 2.25
Nos. 22A-34 (13) 310.00 12.05

Perf. 11½

22i A3 1k black, one plate 1.00 .40
j. "1" printed separately 500.00 125.00
23i A3 2k red violet 600.00 50.00
24i A3 3k green 60.00 20.00
25i A3 5k rose 60.00 20.00
26i A3 8k orange 10.00 .75
27i A3 10k blue 1,750. 750.00
28i A3 12k brown & green 12.50 2.00
29i A3 15k claret & green 14.00 .40
30i A3 20k gray 2,000. 900.00
31i A3 24k brn vio & red 25.00 2.00
32i A3 30k ol grn & brn 275.00 .50
33i A3 50k red & org 40.00 3.00
34i A3 1fo gray blue & sil 190.00 3.00
35 A3 3fo lilac brn & gold 25.00 12.00

1898-99 *Perf. 12x11½*

Numerals in Black

Wmk. 135 (Oval)

35A A3 1k black 1.50 .50
36 A3 2k violet 6.00 .50
37 A3 3k green 4.00 .60
38 A3 5k rose 5.00 .40
39 A3 8k orange 17.50 4.00
40 A3 10k blue 5.00 1.00
41 A3 12k red brn & grn 75.00 9.00
42 A3 15k rose & blue 5.00 .75
43 A3 20k gray 35.00 2.00
44 A3 24k vio brn & red 6.00 4.75
45 A3 30k ol grn & brn 40.00 1.50
46 A3 50k dull red & org 100.00 15.00
Nos. 35A-46 (12) 300.00 40.00

Perf. 11½

35Ab A3 1k black 40.00 7.50
36a A3 2k violet 125.00 20.00
37a A3 3k green 100.00 15.00
38a A3 5k rose 140.00 15.00
39a A3 8k orange 250.00 120.00
40a A3 10k blue 150.00 60.00
41a A3 12k red brn & grn 375.00 100.00
42a A3 15k rose & blue 250.00 60.00
43a A3 20k gray 375.00 75.00
44a A3 24k vio brn & red 450.00 200.00
45a A3 30k ol grn & brn 250.00 60.00
46a A3 50k dull red & org 500.00 250.00

Wmk. 135 (Circle)

Perf. 12x11½

35Ac A3 1k black 14.00 2.50
36b A3 2k violet 7.50 1.50
37b A3 3k green 8.50 2.00
38b A3 5k rose 10.00 1.00
39b A3 8k orange 50.00 25.00
40b A3 10k blue 75.00 4.00
41b A3 12k red brn & grn 60.00 30.00
42b A3 15k rose & blue 250.00 4.00
43b A3 20k gray 5.00 6.00
44b A3 24k vio brn & red 1,250. 45.00
45b A3 30k ol grn & brn 5.00 4.00
46b A3 50k dull red & org 15.00 35.00

Perf. 11½

35Ad A3 1k black 50.00 15.00
36c A3 2k violet 200.00 25.00
37c A3 3k green 200.00 40.00
38c A3 5k rose 100.00 15.00
39c A3 8k orange 80.00 12.50
40c A3 10k blue 450.00 80.00
41c A3 12k red brn & grn 750.00 300.00
42c A3 15k rose & blue 450.00 200.00
43c A3 20k gray 1,500. 350.00
44c A3 24k vio brn & red 2,250. 600.00
45c A3 30k ol grn & brn 750.00 150.00
46c A3 50k dull red & org 500.00 400.00

In the watermark with circles, a four-pointed star and "VI" appear four times in the sheet in the large spaces between the intersecting circles. The paper with the circular watermark is often yellowish and thinner than that with the oval watermark.

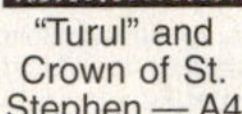

"Turul" and Crown of St. Stephen — A4

Franz Josef I Wearing Hungarian Crown — A5

1900-04 Wmk. 135 *Perf. 12x11½*

Numerals in Black

47 A4 1f gray .75 .30
a. 1f dull lilac .75 .30
48 A4 2f olive yel 1.00 .75
49 A4 3f orange .75 .25
50 A4 4f violet 1.00 .25
a. Booklet pane of 6 *60.00*
51 A4 5f emerald 2.50 .25
a. Booklet pane of 6 *35.00*
52 A4 6f claret 1.50 .60
a. 6f violet brown 2.50 .50
53 A4 6f bister ('01) 20.00 1.20
54 A4 6f olive grn ('02) 7.50 .50
55 A4 10f carmine 4.00 .25
a. Booklet pane of 6 *35.00*
56 A4 12f violet ('04) 2.00 1.25
57 A4 20f brown ('01) 4.00 .60
58 A4 25f blue 5.00 .60
a. Booklet pane of 6 *60.00*
59 A4 30f orange brn 24.00 .25
60 A4 35f red vio ('01) 14.00 1.00
a. Booklet pane of 6 *100.00*
61 A4 50f lake 12.00 1.00
62 A4 60f green 45.00 .30
63 A5 1k brown red 37.50 .75
64 A5 2k gray blue ('01) 600.00 22.50
65 A5 3k sea green 90.00 3.75
66 A5 5k vio brown ('01) 125.00 40.00
Nos. 47-66 (20) 997.50 76.35

The watermark on Nos. 47 to 66 is always the circular form of Wmk. 135 described in the note following No. 46.

Pairs imperf between of Nos. 47-49, 51 were favor prints made for an influential Budapest collector. Value, $90 each.

For overprints & surcharges see Nos. B35-B52, 2N1-2N3, 6N1-6N6, 6NB127N1-7N6, 7NB1, 10N1.

Perf. 11½

47b A4 1f gray 350.00 80.00
48a A4 2f olive yel 350.00 60.00
49a A4 3f orange 100.00 20.00
50b A4 4f violet 225.00 12.50
51b A4 5f emerald 50.00 3.75
52b A4 6f claret — 60.00
53a A4 6f bister ('01) — 110.00
54a A4 6f olive grn ('02) — 300.00
55b A4 10f carmine 400.00 25.00
56a A4 12f violet ('04) 250.00 80.00
57a A4 20f brown ('01) — 150.00
58b A4 25f blue — 75.00
59a A4 30f orange brn — 125.00
60b A4 35f red vio ('01) — 275.00
61a A4 50f lake 400.00 75.00
62a A4 60f green 600.00 150.00
63a A5 1k brown red 175.00 15.00
64a A5 2k gray blue ('01) — 600.00
65a A5 3k sea green — *4,000.*
66a A5 5k vio brown ('01) — 1,000.

1908-13 Wmk. 136 *Perf. 15*

67 A4 1f slate .30 .25
68 A4 2f olive yellow .25 .25
69 A4 3f orange .30 .25
70 A4 5f emerald .30 .25
c. Booklet pane of 6 *100.00*
71 A4 6f olive green .30 .25
72 A4 10f carmine .40 .25
c. Booklet pane of 6 *100.00*
73 A4 12f violet .40 .25
74 A4 16f gray green ('13) .50 .50
75 A4 20f dark brown 7.50 .25
76 A4 25f blue 6.25 .25
77 A4 30f orange brown 7.50 .25
78 A4 35f red violet 10.00 .25
79 A4 50f lake 3.00 .30
80 A4 60f green 9.00 .25
81 A5 1k brown red 12.50 .25
82 A5 2k gray blue 90.00 .40
83 A5 5k violet brown 125.00 9.00
Nos. 67-83 (17) 273.50 13.45

Nos. 67-73, 75-83 exist imperf. Value, set $1,000.

1904-05 Wmk. 136a *Perf. 12x11½*

67a A4 1f slate 2.50 *2.50*
68a A4 2f olive yellow 5.00 .30
69a A4 3f orange 2.00 .40
70a A4 5f emerald 4.00 .25
71a A4 6f olive green 2.50 .40
72a A4 10f carmine 7.50 .25
73a A4 12f violet 4.00 3.00
75a A4 20f dark brown 20.00 1.00
76a A4 25f blue 40.00 1.00
77a A4 30f orange brown 9.00 .40
78a A4 35f red violet 22.50 .40
79a A4 50f lake 15.00 4.00
c. 50f magenta 1.00 *10.00*
80a A4 60f green 250.00 .40
81a A5 1k brown red 250.00 .75
82a A5 2k gray blue *900.00* 50.00
c. Perf. 11½ *2,000.* 150.00
83a A5 5k violet brown 240.00 75.00
Nos. 67a-83a (16) *1,774.* 140.05

1906 *Perf. 15*

67b A4 1f slate 2.50 .50
68b A4 2f olive yellow 1.75 .25
69b A4 3f orange 2.25 .25
70b A4 5f emerald 2.00 .25
71b A4 6f olive green 2.00 .25
72b A4 10f carmine 2.50 .25
73b A4 12f violet 4.00 .25
75b A4 20f dark brown 10.00 .30
76b A4 25f blue 8.00 .30
77b A4 30f orange brown 10.00 .25
78b A4 35f red violet 50.00 .25
79b A4 50f lake 5.00 1.00
80b A4 60f green 62.50 .25
81b A5 1k brown red 60.00 .60
82b A5 2k gray blue 225.00 8.00
Nos. 67b-82b (15) 447.50 12.95

1913-16 Wmk. 137 Vert. *Perf. 15*

84 A4 1f slate .25 .25
85 A4 2f olive yellow .25 .25
86 A4 3f orange .25 .25
87 A4 5f emerald .50 .25
88 A4 6f olive green .25 .25
89 A4 10f carmine .25 .25
90 A4 12f violet, *yel* .30 .25
91 A4 16f gray green .35 .90
92 A4 20f dark brown 1.00 .25
93 A4 25f ultra 1.20 .25
94 A4 30f orange brown .90 .25
95 A4 35f red violet .90 .25
96 A4 50f lake, *blue* .30 .25
a. Cliché of 35f in plate of 50f 325.00 —
97 A4 60f green 5.75 2.00
98 A4 60f green, *salmon* .80 .30
99 A4 70f red brn, *grn* ('16) .25 .25
100 A4 80f dull violet ('16) .25 .25
101 A5 1k dull red 2.50 .25
102 A5 2k dull blue 4.25 .25
103 A5 5k violet brown 20.00 5.00
Nos. 84-103 (20) 40.50 12.20

Nos. 89-97, 99-103 exist imperf. Value, set $1,200.

For overprints and surcharges see Nos. 2N1-2N3, 6N1-6N6, 6NB12, 7N1-7N6, 7NB1, 10N1.

Wmk. 137 Horiz.

84a A4 1f slate .75 .60
85a A4 2f olive yellow 2.00 .40
87a A4 5f emerald .50 .25
88a A4 6f olive green 1.00 .25
89b A4 10f carmine 1.00 .25
90a A4 12f violet, *yellow* 2.00 .25
92a A4 20f dark brown 6.25 .25
94a A4 30f orange brown 50.00 .25
95a A4 35f red violet 200.00 .25
96b A4 50f lake, *blue* 15.00 6.25
97a A4 60f green 4.25 1.75
98a A4 60f green, *salmon* 1.50 .25
101a A5 1k dull red 16.00 .25
102a A5 2k dull blue 100.00 1.00
Nos. 84a-102a (14) 400.25 12.25

A5a

Wmk. 137 Vert.

1916, July 1 *Perf. 15*

103A A5a 10f violet brown .25 .25

Although issued as a postal savings stamp, No. 103A was also valid for postage. Used value is for postal usage.

Exists imperf. Value $10.

For overprints and surcharges see Nos. 2N59, 5N23, 6N50, 8N13, 10N42.

Queen Zita — A6

Charles IV — A7

1916, Dec. 30

104 A6 10f violet 1.25 1.25
105 A7 15f red 1.25 1.25

Coronation of King Charles IV and Queen Zita on Dec. 30, 1916.

Exist imperf. Value, set $20.

During 1921-24 the two center rows of panes of various stamps then current were punched with three holes forming a triangle. These were sold at post offices. Collectors and dealers who wanted the stamps unpunched would have to purchase them through the philatelic agency at a 10% advance over face value.

Harvesting (White Numerals) — A8

1916

106 A8 10f rose .75 .25
107 A8 15f violet .75 .25

Exist imperf. Value, set $20.

For overprints and surcharges see Nos. B56-B57, 2N4-2N5, 5N1.

Harvesting Wheat — A9

Parliament Building at Budapest — A10

1916-18 Wmk. 137 Vert. *Perf. 15*

108 A9 2f brown orange .25 .25
109 A9 3f red lilac .25 .25
110 A9 4f slate gray ('18) .25 .25
111 A9 5f green .25 .25
112 A9 6f grnsh blue .25 .25
113 A9 10f rose red 1.40 .25
114 A9 15f violet .25 .25
115 A9 20f gray brown .25 .25
116 A9 25f dull blue .30 .25
117 A9 35f brown .25 .25
118 A9 40f olive green .25 .25

Perf. 14
Wmk. 137 Horiz.

No.	Type	Description	Unused	Used
119	A10	50f red vio & lil	.25	.25
120	A10	75f brt bl & pale bl	.25	.25
121	A10	80f grn & pale grn	.25	.25
122	A10	1k red brn & claret	.25	.25
123	A10	2k ol brn & bister	.25	.25
124	A10	3k dk vio & indigo	.60	.25
125	A10	5k dk brn & lt brn	.60	.25
126	A10	10k vio brn & vio	1.20	.25
		Nos. 108-126 (19)	7.60	4.75

Nos. 108-126 exist imperf. Value, set $100.

See Nos. 335-377, 388-396. For overprints and surcharges see Nos. 153-167, C1-C5, J76-J99, 1N1-1N21, 1N26-1N30, 1N33, 1N36-1N39, 2N6-2N27, 2N33-2N38, 2N41, 2N43-2N48, 4N1-4N4, 5N2-5N17, 6N7-6N24, 6N29-6N39, 7N7-7N30, 7N38, 7N41-7N42, 8N1-8N4, 9N1-9N2, 9N4, 10N2-10N16, 10N25-10N29, 10N31, 10N33-10N41, 11N1-15, 11N20-24, 11N27, 11N30, 11N32-33.

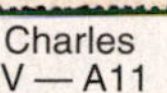

Charles IV — A11

Queen Zita — A12

1918 Wmk. 137 Vert. *Perf. 15*

No.	Type	Description	Unused	Used
127	A11	10f scarlet	.55	.35
128	A11	15f deep violet	.55	.35
129	A11	20f dark brown	.55	.35
130	A11	25f brt blue	.55	.35
131	A12	40f olive green	.55	.35
132	A12	50f lilac	.55	.35
		Nos. 127-132 (6)	3.30	2.10

Exist Imperf. Value, set $35.

For overprints see Nos. 168-173, 1N32, 1N34-1N35, 2N28-2N32, 2N39-2N40, 2N42, 2N49-2N51, 5N18-5N22, 6N25-6N28, 6N40-6N43, 7N31-7N37, 7N39-7N40, 8N5, 9N3, 10N17-10N21, 10N30, 10N32, 11N16-19, 11N25-26, 11N28-29, 11N31.

Issues of the Republic

Hungarian Stamps of 1916-18 Overprinted in Black

1918-19 Wmk. 137 *Perf. 15, 14*

On Stamps of 1916-18

No.	Type	Description	Unused	Used
153	A9	2f brown orange	.25	.25
154	A9	3f red lilac	.25	.25
155	A9	4f slate gray	.25	.25
156	A9	5f green	.25	.25
157	A9	6f grnsh blue	.25	.25
158	A9	10f rose red	.25	.25
159	A9	20f gray brown	.25	.25
162	A9	40f olive green	.25	.25
163	A10	1k red brn & claret	.25	.25
164	A10	2k ol brn & bis	.25	.25
165	A10	3k dk violet & ind	.40	1.00
166	A10	5k dk brn & lt brn	2.00	5.00
167	A10	10k vio brn & vio	.65	1.50

On Stamps of 1918

No.	Type	Description	Unused	Used
168	A11	10f scarlet	.25	.25
169	A11	15f deep violet	.25	.25
170	A11	20f dark brown	.25	.25
171	A11	25f brt blue	.25	.25
172	A12	40f olive green	.30	.60
173	A12	50f lilac	.25	.30
		Nos. 153-173 (19)	7.10	11.90

Nos. 153-164 exist imperf. Value, set $90.

Nos. 153-162, 168-173 exist with overprint inverted. Value, each $6.

A13

A14

1919-20 *Perf. 15*

No.	Type	Description	Unused	Used
174	A13	2f brown orange	.25	.25
176	A13	4f slate gray	.25	.25
177	A13	5f yellow grn	.25	.25
178	A13	6f grnsh blue	.25	.25
179	A13	10f red	.25	.25
180	A13	15f violet	.25	.25
181	A13	20f dark brown	.25	.25
182	A13	20f green ('20)	.25	.25
183	A13	25f dull blue	.25	.25
184	A13	40f olive green	.25	.25
185	A13	40f rose red ('20)	.25	.25
186	A13	45f orange	.25	.25

Perf. 14

No.	Type	Description	Unused	Used
187	A14	50f brn vio & pale vio	.25	.25
188	A14	60f brown & bl ('20)	.25	.25
189	A14	95f dk bl & bl	.25	.25
190	A14	1k red brn	.25	.25
191	A14	1k dk bl & dull bl ('20)	.25	.25
192	A14	1.20k dk grn & grn	.25	.25
193	A14	1.40k yellow green	.25	.25
194	A14	2k ol brn & bis	.25	.25
195	A14	3k dk vio & ind	.25	.25
196	A14	5k dk brn & brn	.25	.85
197	A14	10k vio brn & red vio	.50	.75
		Nos. 174-197 (23)	6.00	6.85

The 3f red lilac, type A13, was never regularly issued without overprint (Nos. 204 and 312). In 1923 a small quantity was sold by the Government at public auction. Value $3.

For overprints see Nos. 203-222, 306-330, 1N40, 2N52-2N58, 6N44-6N49, 8N6-8N12, 10N22-10N24, 11N34-35.

Nos. 174, 177-179, 181-197 exist imperf. Value set $60.

Issues of the Soviet Republic

Karl Marx — A15

Sándor Petőfi — A16

Ignác Martinovics — A17

György Dózsa — A18

Friedrich Engels — A19

Wmk. 137 Horiz.

1919, June 12 Litho. *Perf. 12½x12*

No.	Type	Description	Unused	Used
198	A15	20f rose & brown	.50	1.00
199	A16	45f brn org & dk grn	.50	1.00
200	A17	60f blue gray & brn	4.00	4.00
201	A18	75f claret & vio brn	4.00	4.00
202	A19	80f olive db & blk brn	4.00	4.00
		Nos. 198-202 (5)	13.00	14.00

Used values are for favor cancels.

Exist imperf. Value, Set $150.

Wmk. Vertical

No.	Type	Description	Unused	Used
198a	A15	20f	7.50	10.00
199a	A16	45f	7.50	10.00
200a	A17	60f	7.50	10.00
201a	A18	75f	7.50	10.00
202a	A19	80f	25.00	25.00
		Nos. 198a-202a (5)	55.00	

Nos. 198a-202a were not used postally. Used examples are favor canceled.

Stamps of 1919 Overprinted in Red

1919, July 21 Typo. *Perf. 15*

No.	Type	Description	Unused	Used
203	A13	2f brown orange	.25	.25
204	A13	3f red lilac	.25	.25
205	A13	4f slate gray	.25	.25
206	A13	5f yellow green	.25	.25
207	A13	6f grnsh blue	.25	.25
208	A13	10f red	.25	.25
209	A13	15f violet	.25	.25
210	A13	20f dark brown	.25	.25
211	A13	25f dull blue	.25	.25
212	A13	40f olive green	.25	.25
213	A13	45f orange	.25	.25

Overprinted in Red

Perf. 14

No.	Type	Description	Unused	Used
214	A14	50f brn vio & pale vio	.25	.30
215	A14	95f dk blue & blue	.25	.30
216	A14	1k red brown	.25	.30
217	A14	1.20k dk grn & grn	.25	.40
218	A14	1.40k yellow green	.25	.40
219	A14	2k ol brn & bister	.40	1.25
220	A14	3k dk vio & ind	.65	1.00
221	A14	5k dk brn & brn	.50	.80
222	A14	10k vio brn & red vio	.75	1.75
		Nos. 203-222 (20)	6.30	9.25

"Magyar Tanacsköztarsasag" on Nos. 198 to 222 means "Hungarian Soviet Republic."

Nos. 203-218, 221-222 exist imperf. Value, set $125.

Issues of the Kingdom

Stamps of 1919 Overprinted in Black

1919, Nov. 16

No.	Type	Description	Unused	Used
306	A13	5f green	.65	1.00
307	A13	10f rose red	.65	1.00
308	A13	15f violet	.65	1.00
309	A13	20f gray brown	.65	1.00
310	A13	25f dull blue	.65	1.00
		Nos. 306-310 (5)	3.25	5.00

Issued to commemorate the Romanian evacuation. The overprint reads: "Entry of the National Army-November 16, 1919."

Forged overprints exist.

Nos. 203 to 213 Overprinted in Black

1920, Jan. 26 *Perf. 15*

No.	Type	Description	Unused	Used
311	A13	2f brown orange	1.25	1.60
312	A13	3f red lilac	.25	.30
313	A13	4f slate gray	1.25	1.60
314	A13	5f yellow green	.25	.25
315	A13	6f blue green	.25	.40
316	A13	10f red	.25	.25
317	A13	15f violet	.25	.25
318	A13	20f dark brown	.25	.25
319	A13	25f dull blue	.25	.30
320	A13	40f olive green	1.50	2.00
321	A13	45f orange	1.50	2.00

Nos. 214 to 222 Overprinted in Black

Perf. 14

No.	Type	Description	Unused	Used
322	A14	50f brn vio & pale vio	1.50	2.00
323	A14	95f dk bl & bl	1.50	2.00
324	A14	1k red brown	1.50	2.00
325	A14	1.20k dk grn & grn	1.50	2.50
326	A14	1.40k yellow green	1.50	2.50
327	A14	2k ol brn & bis	8.50	17.50
328	A14	3k dk vio & ind	8.50	17.50
329	A14	5k dk brn & brn	.25	.50
330	A14	10k vio brn & red vio	8.50	17.50
		Nos. 311-330 (20)	40.50	73.20

Counterfeit overprints exist.

Types of 1916-18 Issue

Denomination Tablets Without Inner Frame on Nos. 350 to 363

1920-24 Wmk. 137 *Perf. 15*

No.	Type	Description	Unused	Used
335	A9	5f brown orange	.25	.25
336	A9	10f red violet	.25	.25
337	A9	40f rose red	.25	.25
338	A9	50f yellow green	.25	.25
339	A9	50f blue vio ('22)	.25	.25
340	A9	60f black	.25	.25
341	A9	1k green ('22)	.25	.25
342	A9	1½k brown vio ('22)	.25	.25
343	A9	2k grnsh blue ('22)	.25	.25
344	A9	2½k dp green ('22)	.25	.25
345	A9	3k brown org ('22)	.25	.25
346	A9	4k lt red ('22)	.25	.25
347	A9	4½k dull violet ('22)	.25	.25
348	A9	5k dp brn ('22)	.25	.25
349	A9	6k dark blue ('22)	.25	.25
350	A9	10k brown ('23)	.25	.25
351	A9	15k slate ('23)	.25	.25
352	A9	20k red vio ('23)	.25	.25
353	A9	25k orange ('23)	.25	.25
354	A9	40k gray grn ('23)	.25	.25
355	A9	50k dark blue ('23)	.25	.25
356	A9	100k claret ('23)	.25	.25
357	A9	150k dk grn ('23)	.30	.25

358	A9	200k green ('23)	.30	.25
359	A9	300k rose red ('24)	.80	.30
360	A9	350k violet ('23)	1.50	.30
361	A9	500k dark gray ('24)	2.50	.30
362	A9	600k olive bis ('24)	2.50	.30
363	A9	800k org yel ('24)	2.50	.30

Perf. 14

364	A10	2.50k bl & gray bl	.25	.25
365	A10	3.50k gray	.25	.25
366	A10	10k brown ('22)	.50	.25
367	A10	15k dk gray ('22)	.25	.25
368	A10	20k red vio ('22)	.25	.25
369	A10	25k orange ('22)	.25	.25
370	A10	30k claret ('22)	.75	.25
371	A10	40k gray grn ('22)	.75	.25
372	A10	50k dp blue ('22)	.75	.25
373	A10	100k yel brn ('22)	.75	.25
374	A10	400k turq bl ('23)	.75	.30
375	A10	500k brt vio ('23)	1.10	.25
376	A10	1000k lilac ('24)	1.50	.25
377	A10	2000k car ('24)	2.00	.60
		Nos. 335-377 (43)	26.00	11.40

Nos. 372 to 377 have colored numerals.

Nos. 335-338, 340, 350-365, 368, 370, 372-377 exist imperf. Value, set $200.

Madonna and Child — A23

1921-25 **Typo.** ***Perf. 12***

378	A23	50k dk brn & bl	.25	.25
379	A23	100k ol bis & yel brn	.40	.35

Wmk. 133

380	A23	200k dk bl & ultra	.40	.25
381	A23	500k vio brn & vio	.75	.40
382	A23	1000k vio & red vio	1.00	.35
383	A23	2000k grnsh bl & vio	1.75	.50
384	A23	2500k ol brn & buff	2.00	.25
385	A23	3000k brn red & vio	2.00	.25
386	A23	5000k dk grn & yel grn	2.00	.25
a.		Center inverted	*16,000.*	*12,000.*
387	A23	10000k gray vio & pale bl	2.00	.25
		Nos. 378-387 (10)	12.55	3.10

Nos. 380-387 exist imperf. Value, set of 8 $175.

Issue dates: 50k, 100k, Feb. 27, 1921; 2500k, 10,000k, 1925; others, 1923.

Types of 1916-18

Denomination Tablets Without Inner Frame on Nos. 388-394

1924 **Wmk. 133** ***Perf. 15***

388	A9	100k claret	.40	.25
389	A9	200k yellow grn	.25	.25
390	A9	300k rose red	.30	.35
391	A9	400k deep blue	.30	.35
392	A9	500k dark gray	.40	.25
393	A9	600k olive bister	.45	.25
a.		"800" in upper right corner	110.00	260.00
394	A9	800k org yel	.50	.25

Perf. 14½x14

395	A10	1000k lilac	1.50	.25
396	A10	2000k carmine	2.00	.25
		Nos. 388-396 (9)	6.10	2.45

Nos. 395 and 396 have colored numerals.

Exist imperf. Value, set $37.50.

Maurus Jókai (1825-1904), Novelist A24

1925, Feb. 1 **Unwmk.** ***Perf. 12***

400	A24	1000k dp grn & blk brn	1.75	3.25
401	A24	2000k lt brn & blk brn	.80	1.00
402	A24	2500k dk bl & blk brn	1.75	3.25
		Nos. 400-402 (3)	4.30	7.50

Exist imperf. Value, set $90.

Crown of St. Stephen A25

Matthias Cathedral A26

Palace at Budapest — A27

Perf. 14x14¼, 15

1926-27 **Wmk. 133** **Litho.**

403	A25	1f dk gray	.45	.25
404	A25	2f lt blue	.55	.25
405	A25	3f orange	.55	.25
406	A25	4f violet	.65	.25
407	A25	6f lt green	.90	.25
408	A25	8f lilac rose	1.60	.25

Typo.

409	A26	10f deep blue	2.75	.25
410	A26	16f dark violet	2.25	.25
411	A26	20f carmine	2.75	.25
412	A26	25f lt brown	2.75	.25

Perf. 14¼x14

413	A27	32f dp vio & brt vio	4.25	.25
414	A27	40f dk blue & blue	5.00	.25
		Nos. 403-414 (12)	24.45	3.00

See Nos. 428-436. For surcharges see Nos. 450-456, 466-467.

Nos. 403-414, 418-421 exist imperf. Value, set $250.

Madonna and Child — A28

1926-27 **Engr.** ***Perf. 14***

415	A28	1p violet	15.00	.65
416	A28	2p red	17.50	.85
417	A28	5p blue ('27)	17.50	4.00
		Nos. 415-417 (3)	50.00	5.50

Exist imperf. Value, set $400.

Palace at Budapest A29

1926-27 **Typo.** ***Perf. 14x14¼***

418	A29	30f blue grn ('27)	4.00	.25
419	A29	46f ultra ('27)	5.25	.30
420	A29	50f brown blk ('27)	6.00	.25
421	A29	70f scarlet	9.75	.25
		Nos. 418-421 (4)	25.00	1.05

For surcharge see No. 480.

St. Stephen — A30

1928-29 **Engr.** ***Perf. 15***

422	A30	8f yellow grn	.65	.30
423	A30	8f rose lake ('29)	.65	.30
424	A30	16f orange red	.85	.30
425	A30	16f violet ('29)	.85	.30
426	A30	32f ultra	2.50	4.00
427	A30	32f bister ('29)	2.50	4.00
		Nos. 422-427 (6)	8.00	9.20

890th death anniversary of St. Stephen, the first king of Hungary.

Exist imperf. Value, set $300.

Types of 1926-27 Issue

Perf. 14x14¼, 15

1928-30 **Typo.** **Wmk. 210**

428	A25	1f black	.25	.25
429	A25	2f blue	.35	.25
430	A25	3f orange	.35	.25
431	A25	4f violet	.45	.25
432	A25	6f blue grn	.60	.25
433	A25	8f lilac rose	1.25	.25
434	A26	10f dp blue ('30)	4.50	.25
435	A26	16f violet	1.50	.25
436	A26	20f dull red	1.25	.25
		Nos. 428-436 (9)	10.50	2.25

On Nos. 428-433 the numerals have thicker strokes than on the same values of the 1926-27 issue.

Exist imperf. Value, set $110.

Palace at Budapest — A31

Type A31 resembles A27 but the steamer is nearer the right of the design. A31, A29 & A27 are similar but the frame borders are different.

1928-31 ***Perf. 14¼x14***

437	A31	30f lt grn ('31)	4.00	.25
438	A31	32f red violet	4.00	.25
439	A31	40f deep blue	5.00	.25
440	A31	46f apple green	4.50	.25
441	A31	50f ocher ('31)	4.50	.25
		Nos. 437-441 (5)	22.00	1.25

Exist imperf. Value, set $110.

Admiral Nicholas Horthy — A32

1930, Mar. 1 **Litho.** ***Perf. 15***

445	A32	8f myrtle green	.75	.25
446	A32	16f purple	1.00	.25
447	A32	20f carmine	6.00	1.10
448	A32	32f olive brown	4.00	1.25
449	A32	40f dull blue	7.00	.50
		Nos. 445-449 (5)	18.75	3.35

10th anniv. of the election of Adm. Nicholas Horthy as Regent, Mar. 1, 1920.

Exist imperf. Value, set, $200.

Stamps of 1926-28 Surcharged

1931, Jan. 1 ***Perf. 14¼, 15***

450	A25	2f on 3f orange	.50	*.40*
451	A25	6f on 8f magenta	.50	.25
a.		Perf. 14x14¼	30.00	*30.00*
452	A26	10f on 16f violet	.50	.25

Wmk. 133

453	A25	2f on 3f orange	2.50	5.00
a.		Perf. 14x14¼	3.00	*6.00*
454	A25	6f on 8f magenta	2.00	4.00
a.		Perf. 14x14¼	50.00	100.00
455	A26	10f on 16f dk vio	1.75	3.50
a.		Perf. 14x14¼	2.00	*4.00*
456	A26	20f on 25f lt brn	1.25	2.50
a.		Perf. 14x14¼	1.25	2.25
		Nos. 450-456 (7)	9.00	15.90

For surcharges see Nos. 466-467.

St. Elizabeth A33

Ministering to Children A34

Wmk. 210

1932, Apr. 21 **Photo.** ***Perf. 15***

458	A33	10f ultra	.75	.25
459	A33	20f scarlet	.75	.25

Perf. 14

460	A34	32f deep violet	1.50	2.50
461	A34	40f deep blue	2.00	1.00
		Nos. 458-461 (4)	5.00	4.00

700th anniv. of the death of St. Elizabeth of Hungary.

Exist imperf. Value, set $100.

Madonna, Patroness of Hungary — A35

1932, June 1 ***Perf. 12***

462	A35	1p yellow grn	30.00	.25
463	A35	2p carmine	30.00	.40
464	A35	5p deep blue	42.50	3.00
465	A35	10p olive bister	42.50	22.50
		Nos. 462-465 (4)	145.00	26.15

Exist imperf. Value, set $1,000.

Nos. 451 and 454 Surcharged

1932, June 14 **Wmk. 210** ***Perf. 15***

466	A25	2f on 6f on 8f mag	.25	.25

Wmk. 133

467	A25	2f on 6f on 8f mag	50.00	100.00

Imre Madách — A36

Designs: 2f, Janos Arany. 4f, Dr. Ignaz Semmelweis. 6f, Baron Lorand Eotvos. 10f, Count Stephen Szechenyi. 16f, Ferenc Deak. 20f, Franz Liszt. 30f, Louis Kossuth. 32f, Stephen Tisza. 40f, Mihaly Munkacsy. 50f, Alexander Csoma. 70f, Farkas Bolyai.

1932 **Wmk. 210** ***Perf. 15***

468	A36	1f slate violet	.25	.25
469	A36	2f orange	.25	.25
470	A36	4f ultra	.25	.25
471	A36	6f yellow grn	.25	.25
472	A36	10f Prus green	.35	.25
473	A36	16f dull violet	.35	.25
474	A36	20f deep rose	.30	.25
475	A36	30f brown	.50	.25
476	A36	32f brown vio	.70	.25
477	A36	40f dull blue	.85	.25
478	A36	50f deep green	1.10	.25
479	A36	70f cerise	1.50	.25
		Nos. 468-479 (12)	6.65	3.00
		Set, never hinged	11.50	

Issued in honor of famous Hungarians.

Exist imperf. Value, set $125.

See Nos. 509-510.

No. 421 Surcharged

1933, Apr. 15 **Wmk. 133** ***Perf. 14***

480	A29	10f on 70f scarlet	3.00	.40
		Never hinged	6.00	

Leaping Stag and Double Cross — A47

Wmk. 210

1933, July 10 **Photo.** ***Perf. 15***

481	A47	10f dk green	.75	.80
482	A47	16f violet brn	2.00	*2.50*
483	A47	20f car lake	1.50	1.25

484	A47	32f yellow	5.00	*6.00*
485	A47	40f deep blue	5.00	4.00
		Nos. 481-485 (5)	14.25	14.55
		Set, never hinged	27.50	

Boy Scout Jamboree at Gödöllö, Hungary, July 20 - Aug. 20, 1933.
Exists imperf. Value, set $150.

Souvenir Sheet

Franz Liszt — A48

1934, May 6 ***Perf. 15***

486	A48	20f lake	70.00	90.00
		Never hinged	140.00	

2nd Hungarian Phil. Exhib., Budapest, and Jubilee of the 1st Hungarian Phil. Soc. Sold for 90f, including entrance fee. Size: 64x76mm.
Exists imperf. Value $2,500.

Francis II Rákóczy (1676-1735), Prince of Transylvania
A49

1935, Apr. 8 ***Perf. 12***

487	A49	10f yellow green	.90	.50
488	A49	16f brt violet	5.00	3.75
489	A49	20f dark carmine	2.00	1.50
490	A49	32f brown lake	7.00	7.25
491	A49	40f blue	8.50	8.50
		Nos. 487-491 (5)	23.40	21.50
		Set, never hinged	42.50	

Exists imperf. Value, set $400.

Cardinal Pázmány — A50

Signing the Charter — A51

1935, Sept. 25

492	A50	6f dull green	1.10	1.00
493	A51	10f dark green	.25	.25
494	A50	16f slate violet	1.50	1.60
495	A50	20f magenta	.25	.40
496	A51	32f deep claret	2.50	3.25
497	A51	40f dark blue	2.00	3.25
		Nos. 492-497 (6)	7.60	9.75
		Set, never hinged	15.00	

Tercentenary of the founding of the University of Budapest by Peter Cardinal Pázmány.
Exists imperf. Value, set $400.

Ancient City and Fortress of Buda — A52

Guardian Angel over Buda — A53

Shield of Buda, Cannon and Massed Flags — A54

First Hungarian Soldier to Enter Buda — A55

1936, Sept. 2 ***Perf. 11½x12½***

498	A52	10f dark green	.40	.25
499	A53	16f deep violet	2.50	*3.50*
500	A54	20f car lake	.40	.25
501	A55	32f dark brown	2.50	*3.25*
502	A52	40f deep blue	2.50	*3.25*
		Nos. 498-502 (5)	8.30	10.50
		Set, never hinged	16.00	

250th anniv. of the recapture of Budapest from the Turks.
Exists imperf. Value, set $400.

Catalogue values for unused stamps in this section, from this point to the end of the section, are for Never Hinged items.

Budapest International Fair — A56

1937, Feb. 22 ***Perf. 12***

503	A56	2f deep orange	.25	.25
504	A56	6f yellow green	.40	.25
505	A56	10f myrtle green	.55	.25
506	A56	20f deep cerise	1.25	.40
507	A56	32f dark violet	2.00	.55
508	A56	40f ultra	1.60	.80
		Nos. 503-508 (6)	6.05	2.50

Exist imperf. Value, set $250.

Portrait Type of 1932

5f, Ferenc Kolcsey. 25f, Mihaly Vorosmarty.

1937, May 5 ***Perf. 15***

509	A36	5f brown orange	.80	.25
510	A36	25f olive green	1.60	.25

Exist imperf. Value, set $400.

Pope Sylvester II, Archbishop Astrik — A59

Designs: 2f, 16f, Stephen the Church builder. 4f, 20f, St. Stephen enthroned. 5f, 25f, Sts. Gerhardt, Emerich, Stephen. 6f, 30f, St. Stephen offering holy crown to Virgin Mary. 10f, same as 1f. 32f, 50f, Portrait of St. Stephen. 40f, Madonna and Child. 70f, Crown of St. Stephen.

See designs A75-A77 for smaller stamps of designs similar to Nos. 521-524, but with slanted "MAGYAR KIR POSTA."

1938, Jan. 1 ***Perf. 12***

511	A59	1f deep violet	.40	.25
512	A59	2f olive brown	.40	.25
513	A59	4f brt blue	.80	.25
514	A59	5f magenta	1.25	.25
515	A59	6f dp yel grn	1.60	.25
516	A59	10f red orange	1.25	.25
517	A59	16f gray violet	2.00	.55
518	A59	20f car lake	1.25	.25
519	A59	25f dark green	1.60	.80
520	A59	30f olive bister	2.50	.25
521	A59	32f dp claret, *buff*	2.50	2.00
522	A59	40f Prus green	2.50	.25
523	A59	50f rose vio, *grnsh*	2.75	.25
524	A59	70f ol grn, *bluish*	4.50	.55
		Nos. 511-524 (14)	25.30	6.40

900th anniv. of the death of St. Stephen.
Exists imperf. Value, set $400.
For overprints see Nos. 535-536.

Admiral Horthy — A67

1938, Jan. 1 ***Perf. 12½x12***

525	A67	1p peacock green	2.75	.25
526	A67	2p brown	3.25	.35
527	A67	5p sapphire blue	4.00	1.90
		Nos. 525-527 (3)	10.00	2.50

Exist imperf. Value, set $475.

Souvenir Sheet

St. Stephen — A68

1938, May 22 Wmk. 210 ***Perf. 12***

528	A68	20f carmine lake	32.50	25.00

3rd Hungarian Phil. Exhib., Budapest. Sheet sold only at exhibition with 1p ticket.
Exists imperf. Value $4,500.

College of Debrecen
A69

Three Students — A71

George Marothy — A73

10f, 18th cent. view of College. 20f, 19th cent. view of College. 40f, Stephen Hatvani.

Perf. 12x12½, 12½x12

1938, Sept. 24 **Wmk. 210**

529	A69	6f deep green	.40	.25
530	A69	10f brown	.40	.25
531	A71	16f brown car	.40	.30
532	A69	20f crimson	.40	.25
533	A73	32f slate green	1.10	.75
534	A73	40f brt blue	1.10	.60
		Nos. 529-534 (6)	3.80	2.40

Founding of Debrecen College, 400th anniv.
Exists imperf. Value $300.

Types of 1938 Overprinted in Blue (#535) or Carmine (#536)

a

b

1938 ***Perf. 12***

535	A59(a)	20f sal pink	2.00	1.60
536	A59(b)	70f brn, *grnsh*	2.00	1.60
a.		Overprint omitted	*12,500.*	*7,500.*

Restoration of the territory ceded by Czechoslovakia.
Exists imperf. Value $135.
Forgeries exist of No. 536a.

Crown of St. Stephen
A75

St. Stephen
A76

Madonna, Patroness of Hungary
A77

Coronation Church, Budapest
A78

Reformed Church, Debrecen
A79

Cathedral, Esztergom
A80

Deak Square Evangelical Church, Budapest — A81

Cathedral of Kassa — A82

Wmk. 210

1939, June 1 Photo. ***Perf. 15***

537	A75	1f brown car	.25	.25
538	A75	2f Prus green	.25	.25
539	A75	4f ocher	.25	.25
540	A75	5f brown violet	.25	.25
541	A75	6f yellow green	.25	.25
542	A75	10f bister brn	.25	.25
543	A75	16f rose violet	.25	.25
544	A76	20f rose red	.25	.25
545	A77	25f blue gray	.25	.25

Perf. 12

546 A78 30f red violet .40 .25
547 A79 32f brown .25 .25
548 A80 40f greenish blue .40 .25
549 A81 50f olive .50 .25
550 A82 70f henna brown .50 .25
Nos. 537-550 (14) 4.30 3.50

See Nos. 521-524, 578-596. For overprints see Nos. 559-560.
Exists imperf. Value, set $250.

Girl Scout Sign and Olive Branch — A83

6f, Scout lily, Hungary's shield, Crown of St. Stephen. 10f, Girls in Scout hat & national headdress. 20f, Dove & Scout emblems.

1939, July 20 Photo. *Perf. 12*

551 A83 2f brown orange .50 .35
552 A83 6f green .50 .35
553 A83 10f brown .80 .45
554 A83 20f lilac rose 1.25 .80
Nos. 551-554 (4) 3.05 1.95

Girl Scout Jamboree at Gödöllö.
Exists imperf. Value, set $300.

Admiral Horthy at Szeged, 1919 — A87

Admiral Nicholas Horthy A88

Cathedral of Kassa and Angel Ringing "Bell of Liberty" A89

1940, Mar. 1

555 A87 6f green .25 .25
556 A88 10f ol blk & ol bis .25 .25
557 A89 20f brt rose brown .80 .55
Nos. 555-557 (3) 1.30 1.05

20th anniversary of the election of Admiral Horthy as Regent of Hungary.
Exists imperf. Value, set $100.

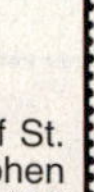

Crown of St. Stephen A90

1940, Sept. 5

558 A90 10f dk green & yellow .40 .40

Issued in commemoration of the recovery of northeastern Transylvania from Romania.
Exists imperf. Value $25.

Nos. 542, 544 Overprinted in Red or Black

1941, Apr. 21 *Perf. 15*

559 A75 10f bister brn (R) .60 .30
560 A76 20f rose red (Bk) .60 .35

Return of the Bacska territory from Yugoslavia.
Exist imperf. Value, set $50.

Admiral Nicholas Horthy — A92

Wmk. 210

1941, June 18 Photo. *Perf. 12*

570 A92 1p dk green & buff .25 .25
571 A92 2p dk brown & buff .50 .40
572 A92 5p dk rose vio & buff 2.00 1.00
Nos. 570-572 (3) 2.75 1.65

Exist imperf. Value, set $75.
See Nos. 597-599.

Count Stephen Széchenyi A93

Count Széchenyi and Royal Academy of Science A94

Representation of the Narrows of Kazán — A95

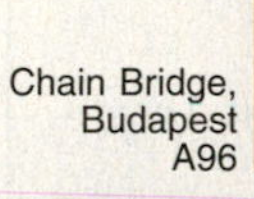

Chain Bridge, Budapest A96

Mercury, Train and Boat — A97

1941, Sept. 21

573 A93 10f dk olive grn .40 .40
574 A94 16f olive brown .40 .40
575 A95 20f carmine lake .40 .40
576 A96 32f red orange .70 .40
577 A97 40f royal blue 1.00 .40
Nos. 573-577 (5) 2.90 2.00

Count Stephen Szechenyi (1791-1860).
Exist imperf. Value, set $250.

Types of 1939

Perf. 12x12½, 12½x12, 15

1941-43 Wmk. 266

578 A75 1f rose lake ('42) .25 .25
579 A75 3f dark brown .25 .25
580 A75 5f violet gray ('42) .25 .25
581 A75 6f lt green ('42) .25 .25
582 A75 8f slate grn .25 .25
583 A75 10f olive brn ('42) .25 .25
584 A75 12f red orange .25 .25
585 A76 20f rose red ('42) .25 .25
586 A76 24f brown violet .25 .25
587 A78 30f lilac ('42) .25 .25
588 A82 30f rose red ('43) .25 .25
589 A80 40f blue green ('42) .25 .25
590 A79 40f gray black ('43) .25 .25
591 A81 50f olive grn ('42) .25 .25
592 A80 50f brt blue ('43) .25 .25
593 A82 70f copper red ('42) .25 .25
594 A81 70f gray green ('43) .25 .25
595 A77 80f brown bister .40 .25
596 A78 80f bister brn ('43) .25 .25
Nos. 578-596 (19) 4.90 4.75

Exist imperf. Value, set $350.

Horthy Type of 1941

Perf. 12x12½

1941, Dec. 18 Wmk. 266

597 A92 1p dk green & buff .80 .25
598 A92 2p dk brown & buff .25 .25
599 A92 5p dk rose vio & buff .55 .25
Nos. 597-599 (3) 1.60 .75

Exist imperf. Value, set $60.

Stephen Horthy — A98

1942, Oct. 15 *Perf. 12*

600 A98 20f black .40 .40

Death of Stephen Horthy (1904-42), son of Regent Nicholas Horthy, who died in a plane crash.
Exists imperf. Value $40.

Arpád — A99

A109

Portraits: 2f, King Ladislaus I. 3f, Miklós Toldi. 4f, János Hunyadi. 5f, Paul Kinizsi. 6f, Count Miklós Zrinyi. 8f, Francis II Rákóczy. 10f, Count Andrew Hadik. 12f, Arthur Görgei. 18f, 24f, Virgin Mary, Patroness of Hungary.

1943-45 *Perf. 15*

601 A99 1f grnsh black .25 .25
602 A99 2f red orange .25 .25
603 A99 3f ultra .25 .25
604 A99 4f brown .25 .25
605 A99 5f vermilion .25 .25
606 A99 6f slate blue .25 .25
607 A99 8f dk ol grn .25 .25
608 A99 10f brown .25 .25
609 A99 12f dp blue grn .25 .25
610 A99 18f dk gray .25 .25
611 A109 20f chestnut brn .40 .25
612 A99 24f rose violet .25 .25
613 A109 30f brt carmine .25 .25
614 A109 50f blue .25 .25
615 A109 80f yellow brn .25 .25
616 A109 1p green .25 .25
616A A109 2p brown ('45) .25 .40
616B A109 5p dk red violet ('45) .25 .80
Nos. 601-616B (18) 4.65 5.20

Exist imperf. Value, set $150.
For overprints and surcharges see Nos. 631-658, 660-661, 664, 666-669, 671-672, 674-677, 679, 680, 682, 685-689, 691-698, 801-803, 805-806, 810-815, F2, Q2-Q3, Q7.

Message to the Shepherds A110

20f, Nativity. 30f, Adoration of the Magi.

1943, Dec. 1 *Perf. 12x12½*

617 A110 4f dark green .25 .25
618 A110 20f dull blue .25 .25
619 A110 30f brown orange .25 .25
Nos. 617-619 (3) .75 .75

Exist imperf. Value, set $150.

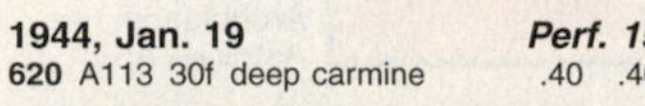

St. Margaret — A113

1944, Jan. 19 *Perf. 15*

620 A113 30f deep carmine .40 .40

Canonization of St. Margaret of Hungary.
Exists imperf. Value $40.
For surcharges see Nos. 662, 673A.

Kossuth with Family — A114

Lajos Kossuth — A117

Honvéd Drummer A115

Design: 30f, Kossuth orating.

1944, Mar. 20 *Perf. 12½x12, 12x12½*

621 A114 4f yellow brown .25 .25
622 A115 20f dk olive grn .25 .25
623 A115 30f henna brown .25 .25
624 A117 50f slate blue .25 .25
Nos. 621-624 (4) 1.00 1.00

Louis (Lajos) Kossuth (1802-94).
Exist imperf. Value, set $200.
For surcharges see Nos. B175-B178.

St. Elizabeth — A118

Portraits: 24f, St. Margaret. 30f, Elizabeth Szilágyi. 50f, Dorothy Kanuizsai. 70f, Susanna Lórántffy. 80f, Ilona Zrinyi.

1944, Aug. 1 *Perf. 15*

625 A118 20f olive .25 .25
626 A118 24f rose violet .25 .25
627 A118 30f copper red .25 .25
628 A118 50f dark blue .25 .25
629 A118 70f orange red .25 .25
630 A118 80f brown car .25 .25
Nos. 625-630 (6) 1.50 1.50

Exist imperf. Value, set $120.
For overprints and surcharges see Nos. 659, 663, 665, 670, 673, 678, 681, 683-684, 690, 804, 807-809, F1, F3, Q1, Q4-Q6, Q8.

Issues of the Republic

Types of Hungary, 1943 Surcharged in Carmine

1945, May 1 Wmk. 266

Blue Surface-tinted Paper

631 A99 10f on 1f grnsh blk 1.50 1.50
632 A99 20f on 3f ultra 1.50 1.50
633 A99 30f on 4f brown 1.50 1.50
634 A99 40f on 6f slate bl 1.50 1.50
635 A99 50f on 8f dk ol grn 1.50 1.50
636 A99 1p on 10f brown 1.50 1.50
637 A99 150f on 12f dp bl grn 1.50 1.50
638 A99 2p on 18f dk gray 1.50 1.50
639 A109 3p on 20f chnt brn 1.50 1.50
640 A99 5p on 24f rose vio 1.50 1.50
641 A109 6p on 50f blue 1.50 1.50
642 A109 10p on 80f yel brn 1.50 1.50
643 A109 20p on 1p green 1.50 1.50

Yellow Surface-tinted Paper

644 A99 10f on 1f grnsh blk 1.50 1.50
645 A99 20f on 3f ultra 1.50 1.50
646 A99 30f on 4f brown 1.50 1.50
647 A99 40f on 6f slate bl 1.50 1.50
648 A99 50f on 8f dk ol grn 1.50 1.50
649 A99 1p on 10f brown 1.50 1.50
650 A99 150f on 12f dp bl grn 1.50 1.50
651 A99 2p on 18f dk gray 1.50 1.50
652 A109 3p on 20f chnt brn 1.50 1.50
653 A99 5p on 24f rose vio 1.50 1.50
654 A109 6p on 50f blue 1.50 1.50
655 A109 10p on 80f yel brn 1.50 1.50
656 A109 20p on 1p green 1.50 1.50
Nos. 631-656 (26) 39.00 39.00

Hungary's liberation.

Types of Hungary, 1943-45, Surcharged in Carmine or Black

1945 Blue Surface-tinted Paper

No.	Type	Description	Unused	Used
657	A99	10f on 4f brn (C)	.25	.25
658	A99	10f on 10f brn (C)	.45	.45
659	A118	20f on 20f ol (C)	.25	.25
660	A99	28f on 5f ver	.25	.25
661	A109	30f on 30f brt car	.25	.25
662	A113	30f on 30f dp car	.25	.25
663	A118	30f on 30f cop red	.25	.25
664	A99	40f on 10f brown	.25	.25
665	A118	1p on 70f org red	.25	.25
666	A109	1p on 80f yel brn (C)	.25	.25
667	A99	2p on 4f brown	.25	.25
668	A109	2p on 2p brn (C)	.25	.25
669	A109	4p on 30f brt car	.25	.25
670	A118	8p on 20f olive	.25	.25
671	A99	10p on 2f red org	8.00	8.00
672	A109	10p on 80f yel brn	.25	.25
673	A118	20p on 30f cop red	.25	.25

Same Surcharge with Thinner Unshaded Numerals of Value

No.	Type	Description	Unused	Used
673A	A113	300p on 30f dp car	.25	.25

Surcharged as Nos. 657-673 Yellow Surface-tinted Paper

No.	Type	Description	Unused	Used
674	A99	10f on 12f dp bl grn (C)	.25	.25
675	A99	20f on 1f grnsh blk (C)	.25	.25
676	A99	20f on 18f dk gray (C)	.25	.25
a.		Double surcharge		
677	A99	40f on 24f rose vio (C)	.25	.25
678	A118	40f on 24f rose vio (C)	.25	.25
679	A109	42f on 20f chnt brn (C)	.25	.25
680	A109	50f on 50f bl (C)	.25	.25
681	A118	50f on 50f bl (C)	.25	.25
682	A99	60f on 8f dk ol grn (C)	.25	.25
683	A118	80f on 24f rose vio	.25	.25
684	A118	80f on 80f brn car (C)	.25	.25
685	A109	1p on 20f chnt brn	.25	.25
686	A109	1p on 1p grn (C)	.25	.25
687	A99	150f on 6f sl bl (C)	.90	.90
688	A99	1.60p on 12f dp bl grn	.25	.25
689	A99	3p on 3f ultra (C)	.25	.25
690	A118	3p on 50f dk bl	.25	.25
691	A99	5p on 8f dk ol grn	.25	.25
692	A109	5p on 5p dk red vio (C)	.25	.25
693	A109	6p on 50f blue	.25	.25
694	A109	7p on 1p grn	.25	.25
695	A99	9p on 1f grnsh blk	.25	.25

Same Surcharge with Thinner, Unshaded Numerals of Value

No.	Type	Description	Unused	Used
696	A99	40p on 8f dk ol grn	.25	.25
697	A99	60p on 18f dk gray	.25	.25
698	A99	100p on 12f dp bl grn	.25	.25
		Nos. 657-698 (43)	19.35	19.35

Various shades and errors of overprint exist on Nos. 657-698.

These surface-tinted stamps exist without surcharge, but were not so issued.

Mining A124

Designs: 1.60p, Manufacturing. 2p, Railroading. 3p, Construction. 5p, Agriculture. 8p, Communications. 10p, Architecture. 20p, Writing.

Wmk. 266

1945, Sept. 11 Photo. *Perf. 12*

No.	Type	Description	Unused	Used
700	A124	40f gray black	5.50	6.50
701	A124	1.60p olive bis	5.50	6.50
702	A124	2p slate green	5.50	6.50
703	A124	3p dark purple	5.50	6.50
704	A124	5p dark red	5.50	6.50
705	A124	8p brown	5.50	6.50
706	A124	10p deep claret	5.50	6.50
707	A124	20p slate blue	5.50	6.50
		Nos. 700-707 (8)	44.00	52.00

World Trade Union Conf., Paris, Sept. 25 to Oct. 10, 1945.

Exist imperf. Value, set $500.

"Reconstruction" — A132

1945-46

No.	Type	Description	Unused	Used
708	A132	12p brown olive	.25	.25
709	A132	20p brt green	.25	.25
710	A132	24p orange brn	.25	.25
711	A132	30p gray black	.25	.25
712	A132	40p olive green	.25	.25
713	A132	60p red orange	.25	.25
714	A132	100p orange yel	.25	.25
715	A132	120p brt ultra	.25	.25
716	A132	140p brt red	.55	.65
717	A132	200p olive brn	.25	.25
718	A132	240p brt blue	.25	.25
719	A132	300p dk carmine	.25	.25
720	A132	500p dull green	.25	.25
721	A132	1000p red violet	.25	.25
722	A132	3000p brt red ('46)	.25	.25
		Nos. 708-722 (15)	4.05	4.15

Nos. 708-721 exist tête bêche. Value: $16.

Exist imperf. Value, set $200.

"Liberation" A133

1946, Feb. 12

No.	Type	Description	Unused	Used
723	A133	3ez p dark red	.25	.25
724	A133	15ez p ultra	.25	.25

Exist imperf. Value, set $50.

Postrider — A134

Photo.; Values Typo.

1946 *Perf. 15*

No.	Type	Description	Unused	Used
725	A134	4ez p brown org	.25	.25
726	A134	10ez p brt red	.25	.25
727	A134	15ez p ultra	.25	.25
728	A134	20ez p dk brown	.25	.25
729	A134	30ez p red violet	.25	.25
730	A134	50ez p gray black	.25	.25
731	A134	80ez p brt ultra	.25	.25
732	A134	100ez p rose car	.25	.25
733	A134	160ez p gray green	.25	.25
734	A134	200ez p yellow grn	.25	.25
735	A134	500ez p red	.25	.25
736	A134	640ez p olive bis	.25	.25
737	A134	800ez p rose violet	.25	.25
		Nos. 725-737 (13)	3.25	3.25

Exist imperf. Value, set $60.

Abbreviations:

Ez (Ezer) = Thousand
Mil (Milpengo) = Million
Mlrd (Milliard) = Billion
Bil (Billio-pengo) = Trillion

Arms of Hungary — A135

1946 Wmk. 210

No.	Type	Description	Unused	Used
738	A135	1mil p vermilion	.25	.25
a.		"1" in center omitted	600.00	
739	A135	2mil p ultra	.25	.25
740	A135	3mil p brown	.25	.25
741	A135	4mil p slate gray	.25	.25
742	A135	5mil p rose violet	.25	.25
743	A135	10mil p green	.25	.25
744	A135	20mil p carmine	.25	.25
745	A135	50mil p olive	.25	.25

Arms and Post Horn
A136 A137

No.	Type	Description	Unused	Used
746	A136	100mil p henna brn	.25	.25
747	A136	200mil p henna brn	.25	.25
748	A136	500mil p henna brn	.25	.25
749	A136	1000mil p henna brn	.25	.25
750	A136	2000mil p henna brn	.25	.25
751	A136	3000mil p henna brn	.25	.25
752	A136	5000mil p henna brn	.25	.25
753	A136	10,000mil p henna brn	.25	.25
754	A136	20,000mil p henna brn	.25	.25
755	A136	30,000mil p henna brn	.25	.25
756	A136	50,000mil p henna brn	.25	.25

Denomination in Carmine

No.	Type	Description	Unused	Used
757	A137	100mlrd p olive	.25	.25
758	A137	200mlrd p olive	.25	.25
759	A137	500mlrd p olive	.25	.25

Dove and Letter — A138

Denomination in Carmine

No.	Type	Description	Unused	Used
760	A138	1bil p grnsh blk	.25	.25
761	A138	2bil p grnsh blk	.25	.25
763	A138	5bil p grnsh blk	.25	.25
764	A138	10bil p grnsh blk	.25	.25
765	A138	20bil p grnsh blk	.25	.25
766	A138	50bil p grnsh blk	.25	.25
767	A138	100bil p grnsh blk	.25	.25
768	A138	200bil p grnsh blk	.25	.25
769	A138	500bil p grnsh blk	.25	.25
770	A138	1000bil p grnsh blk	.25	.25
771	A138	10,000bil p grnsh blk	.25	.25
772	A138	50,000bil p grnsh blk	.25	.25
773	A138	100,000bil p grnsh blk	.25	.25
774	A138	500,000bil p grnsh blk	.25	.25

Denomination in Black

No.	Type	Description	Unused	Used
775	A137	5ez ap green	.25	.25
776	A137	10ez ap green	.25	.25
777	A137	20ez ap green	.25	.25
778	A137	50ez ap green	.25	.25
779	A137	80ez ap green	.25	.25
780	A137	100ez ap green	.25	.25
781	A137	200ez ap green	.25	.25
782	A137	500ez ap green	.25	.25
783	A137	1mil ap vermilion	.25	.25
784	A137	5mil ap vermilion	.25	.25
		Nos. 738-784 (46)	11.50	11.50

Denominations are expressed in "ado" or "tax" pengos.

Nos. 738-784 exist imperf. Value, set $400.

Early Steam Locomotive A139

Designs: 20,000ap, Recent steam locomotive. 30,000ap, Electric locomotive. 40,000ap, Diesel locomotive.

1946, July 15 Wmk. 266 *Perf. 12*

No.	Type	Description	Unused	Used
785	A139	10,000ap vio brn	5.00	5.00
786	A139	20,000ap dk blue	5.00	5.00
787	A139	30,000ap dp yel grn	5.00	5.00
788	A139	40,000ap rose car	5.00	5.00
b.		"40,000 ap" omitted	3,500.	
		Nos. 785-788 (4)	20.00	20.00

Centenary of Hungarian railways.

Exist imperf. Value, set $700.

Industry A143

Agriculture A144

1946 Wmk. 210 Photo. *Perf. 15*

No.	Type	Description	Unused	Used
788A	A143	8f henna brn	.25	.25
789	A143	10f henna brn	.30	.25
790	A143	12f henna brn	.25	.25
791	A143	20f henna brn	.30	.25
792	A143	30f henna brn	.40	.25
793	A143	40f henna brn	.40	.25
794	A143	60f henna brn	.40	.25
795	A144	1fo dp yel grn	.75	.25
796	A144	1.40fo dp yel grn	.75	.25
797	A144	2fo dp yel grn	1.25	.25
798	A144	3fo dp yel grn	5.50	.25
799	A144	5fo dp yel grn	1.50	.25
800	A144	10fo dp yel grn	3.00	.35
		Nos. 788A-800 (13)	15.05	3.35

For surcharges see Nos. Q9-Q11.

Exist imperf. Value, set $175.

Stamps and Types of 1943-45 Ovptd. in Carmine or Black to Show Class of Postage for which Valid

a

b

"Any." or "Nyomtatv." = Printed Matter.
"Hl" or "Helyi levél" = Local Letter.
"Hlp." or "Helyi lev.-lap" = Local Postcard.
"Tl." or "Távolsági levél" =Domestic Letter.
"Tlp." or "Távolsági lev.-lap" = Domestic Postcard.

1946 Wmk. 266

No.	Type	Description	Unused	Used
801	A99(a)	"Any 1." on 1f (#601;C)	.25	.25
802	A99(a)	"Any 2." on 1f (#601;C)	.25	.25
803	A99(b)	"Nyomtatv. 20gr" on 60f on 8f (#682;Bk + C)	.25	.25
804	A118(a)	"Hl. 1" on 50f (#628;C)	.25	.25
805	A99(a)	"Hl. 2" on 40f on 10f (#664;C + Bk)	.25	.25
806	A99(b)	"Helyi levél" on 10f brn, *bl* (Bk)	.25	.25
807	A118(a)	"Hlp.1" on 8p on 20f (#670;C + Bk)	.25	.25
808	A118(a)	"Hlp.2." on 8p on 20f (#670;C + Bk)	.25	.25
809	A118(b)	"Helyi lev.-lap" on 20f ol, *bl* (C)	.25	.25
810	A99(a)	"Tl.1" on 10f (#608;Bk)	.25	.25
811	A99(a)	"Tl.2." on 10f on 4f (#657;Bk + C)	.25	.25
812	A99(b)	"Tavolsagi level" on 18f (#610;C)	.25	.25
813	A99(a)	"Tlp.1." on 4f (#604;Bk)	.25	.25
814	A99(a)	"Tlp.2." on 4f (#604;Bk)	.25	.25
815	A99(b)	"Tavolsagi lev.-lap" on 4f (#604;Bk)	.25	.25
		Nos. 801-815 (15)	3.75	3.75

Nos. 806, 809 not issued without overprint.

György Dózsa — A145

Designs: 10f, Antal Budai-Nagy. 12f, Tamas Esze. 20f, Ignac Martinovics. 30f, Janos Batsanyi. 40f, Lajos Kossuth. 60f, Mihaly Tancsics. 1fo, Sandor Petőfi. 2fo, Andreas Ady. 4fo, Jozsef Attila.

1947, Mar. 15 Photo. Wmk. 210

No.	Type	Description	Unused	Used
816	A145	8f rose brown	.25	.25
817	A145	10f deep ultra	.35	.25
818	A145	12f deep brown	.30	.25
819	A145	20f dk yel grn	.40	.25
820	A145	30f dk ol bis	.50	.25
821	A145	40f brown car	.70	.25
822	A145	60f cerise	.70	.25
823	A145	1fo dp grnsh bl	.80	.25
824	A145	2fo dk violet	1.75	.35
825	A145	4fo grnsh black	2.75	.50
		Nos. 816-825 (10)	8.50	2.85

Exist imperf. Value, set $175.

Peace and Agriculture — A155

1947, Sept. 22 *Perf. 12*

No.	Type	Description	Unused	Used
826	A155	60f bright red	1.00	.25
a.		"60f." omitted	1,500.	

Peace treaty.

Exists imperf. Value, set $120.

Postal Savings Emblem — A156

60f, Postal Savings Bank, Budapest.

1947, Oct. 31

No.	Type	Value	Color	Unused	Used
827	A156	40f	rose brown	.50	.25
828	A156	60f	brt rose car	.50	.25

Savings Day, Oct. 31, 1947.
Exist imperf. Value, set $50.

Hungarian Flag — A157

1848 Printing Press A158

Barred Window and Dove — A159

1848 Shako, Sword and Trumpet A160

"On your feet Hungarian, the Homeland is Calling!" A161

Arms of Hungary — A162

Perf. 12½x12, 12x12½

1948 Wmk. 283 Photo.

No.	Type	Value	Color	Unused	Used
829	A157	8f	dk rose red	.30	.25
830	A158	10f	ultra	.40	.25
831	A159	12f	copper brn	.75	.25
832	A160	20f	deep green	1.50	.25
833	A161	30f	olive brown	1.00	.25
834	A157	40f	dk vio brn	1.25	.25
835	A161	60f	carmine lake	1.50	.25
a.			Printed on both sides	1,100.	
836	A162	1fo	brt ultra	1.50	.25
837	A162	2fo	red brown	2.50	.25
838	A162	3fo	green	5.00	.25
839	A162	4fo	scarlet	7.50	.25
			Nos. 829-839 (11)	23.20	2.75

Cent. of the beginning of Hungary's war for independence.
No. 834 is inscribed "Kossuth," No. 835 "Petofi."
Exist imperf. Value, set $300.

Baron Lorand Eötvös A163

1948, July 27

No.	Type	Value	Color	Unused	Used
840	A163	60f	deep red	1.50	.50

Roland Eötvös, physicist, birth cent.
Exists imperf. Value $100.

Hungarian Workers — A164

1948, Oct. 17 Wmk. 283 *Perf. 12*

No.	Type	Value	Color	Unused	Used
841	A164	30f	dk carmine rose	1.00	.50
a.			Sheet of 4	32.50	32.50

The 17th Trade Union Congress, Budapest, October 1948. No. 841a was sold for 2 forint.
Exist imperf. Value: single $25; sheet of 4 $2,000.

Marx Stamp of 1919 and Crowd Carrying Flags — A165

Petőfi Stamp of 1919 and Flags — A166

1949, Mar. 19 Flags in Carmine

No.	Type	Value	Color	Unused	Used
842	A165	40f	brown	.75	.50
843	A166	60f	olive gray	.75	.50

1st Hungarian Soviet Republic, 30th anniv.
Exist imperf. Value, set $50.

Workers of the Five Continents and Flag — A167

1949, June 29 *Perf. 12x12½*

Flag in Red

No.	Type	Value	Color	Unused	Used
844	A167	30f	yellow brown	4.00	4.00
845	A167	40f	brown violet	4.00	4.00
846	A167	60f	lilac rose	4.00	4.00
847	A167	1fo	violet blue	4.00	4.00
			Nos. 844-847 (4)	16.00	16.00

2nd Congress of the World Federation of Trade Unions, Milan, 1949.
Exist imperf. Value, set $125.

Sándor Petőfi — A168

Perf. 12½x12

1949, July 31 Engr. Unwmk.

No.	Type	Value	Color	Unused	Used
848	A168	40f	claret	.95	.35
849	A168	60f	dark red	.75	.35
850	A168	1fo	deep blue	.90	.35
			Nos. 848-850 (3)	2.60	1.05

Cent. of the death of Sándor Petőfi, poet.
Exist imperf. Value, set $30.

See Nos. 867-869.

Youth of Three Races — A169

Designs: 30f, Three fists. 40f, Soldier breaking chain. 60f, Soviet youths carrying flags. 1fo, Young workers displaying books.

Perf. 12½x12

1949, Aug. 14 Photo. Wmk. 283

No.	Type	Value	Color	Unused	Used
851	A169	20f	dk violet brn	1.25	1.25
a.			20f blue green	4.00	4.00
852	A169	30f	blue green	1.50	1.50
a.			30f violet brown	4.00	4.00
853	A169	40f	olive bister	2.00	2.00
a.			40f ultramarine	4.00	4.00
854	A169	60f	rose pink	1.50	1.50
855	A169	1fo	ultra	2.75	2.75
a.			1fo olive bister	4.00	4.00
b.			Souv. sheet of 5, #851a-853a, 854, 855a	35.00	35.00
			Nos. 851-855 (5)	9.00	9.00

World Festival of Youth and Students, Budapest, Aug. 14-28, 1949.
Exist imperf. Value, set $100. No. 855b imperf, $2,000.

Arms of Hungarian People's Republic A170

Arms in Bister, Carmine, Blue and Green

1949 Wmk. 283

No.	Type	Value	Color	Unused	Used
856	A170	20f	green	1.25	.50
a.			Unwatermarked	1.75	.80
857	A170	60f	carmine	1.25	.30
a.			Unwatermarked	1.10	.30
858	A170	1fo	blue	2.50	1.10
a.			Unwatermarked	1.25	.60
			Nos. 856-858 (3)	5.00	1.90

Adoption of the Hungarian People's Republic constitution.
Nos. 856-858 exist imperf. Value, set $175. Nos. 856a-858a also exist imperf. Value, set $200.
Nos. 856-858 exist with papermaker's watermark. These sell for the same.

Symbols of the UPU — A171

1949, Nov. 1 *Perf. 12x12½*

No.	Type	Value	Color	Unused	Used
859	A171	60f	rose red	.50	.50
a.			Booklet pane of 6	10.00	
860	A171	1fo	blue	.50	.50
a.			Booklet pane of 6	14.00	
			Nos. 859-860,C63 (3)	2.50	2.50

75th anniv. of the UPU.
Nos. 859 and 860 exist imperf. and stamps from 859a and 860a in horiz. pairs, imperf. between. Values: set $15; pairs, imperf between $10.
See No. C63, C81.

Chain Bridge A172

1949, Nov. 20 Wmk. 283

No.	Type	Value	Color	Unused	Used
861	A172	40f	blue green	.50	.30
862	A172	60f	red brown	.50	.35
863	A172	1fo	blue	.50	.35
			Nos. 861-863,C64-C65 (5)	5.00	5.00

Cent. of the opening of the Chain Bridge at Budapest to traffic.
Exist imperf. Value, set $12.
For souvenir sheet see No. C66.

Joseph V. Stalin — A173

Perf. 12½x12

1949, Dec. 21 Engr. Unwmk.

No.	Type	Value	Color	Unused	Used
864	A173	60f	dark red	1.00	.25
865	A173	1fo	deep blue	1.00	.30
866	A173	2fo	brown	2.00	.50
			Nos. 864-866 (3)	4.00	1.05

70th anniv. of the birth of Joseph V. Stalin.
Exist imperf. Value, set $15.
See Nos. 1034-1035.

Petőfi Type of 1949

1950, Feb. 5 *Perf. 12½x12*

No.	Type	Value	Color	Unused	Used
867	A168	40f	brown	.75	.35
868	A168	60f	dark carmine	.40	.25
869	A168	1fo	dark green	.40	.25
			Nos. 867-869 (3)	1.55	.85

Exist imperf. Value, set $30.

Philatelic Museum, Budapest A174

Perf. 12x12½

1950, Mar. 12 Photo. Wmk. 283

No.	Type	Value	Color	Unused	Used
870	A174	60f	gray & brown	8.00	8.00

20th anniv. of the establishment of the Hungarian PO Phil. Museum.
Exists imperf. Value $90.
See No. C68.

Coal Mining A175

Designs: 10f, Heavy industry. 12f, Power production. 20f, Textile industry. 30f, "Cultured workers." 40f, Mechanized agriculture. 60f, Village cooperative. 1fo, Train. 1.70fo, "Holiday." 2fo, Defense. 3fo, Shipping. 4fo, Livestock. 5fo, Engineering. 10fo, Sports.

1950 Wmk. 283

No.	Type	Value	Color	Unused	Used
871	A175	8f	gray	.75	.25
872	A175	10f	claret	.75	.25
873	A175	12f	orange ver	1.00	.25
874	A175	20f	blue green	1.25	.25
875	A175	30f	rose violet	1.25	.25
876	A175	40f	sepia	1.50	.25
877	A175	60f	red	2.00	.25
878	A175	1fo	gray brn, yel & lil	3.00	.25
879	A175	1.70fo	dk grn & yel	8.50	.25
880	A175	2fo	vio brn & cr	4.00	.25
881	A175	3fo	slate & cream	8.50	.25
882	A175	4fo	blk brn & sal	47.50	1.25
883	A175	5fo	rose vio & yel	22.50	.30
884	A175	10fo	dk brn & yel	47.50	6.00
			Nos. 871-884 (14)	150.00	10.30
			Hinged set	80.00	

Issued to publicize Hungary's Five Year Plan.
Exist imperf. Value, set $450.
See Nos. 945-958.

Citizens Welcoming Liberators — A176

1950, Apr. 4 Unwmk. *Perf. 12*

885 A176 40f gray black	1.00	.35
886 A176 60f rose brown	1.00	.25
887 A176 1fo deep blue	1.00	.25
888 A176 2fo brown	1.00	.35
Nos. 885-888 (4)	4.00	1.20

Fifth anniversary of Hungary's liberation.
Exist imperf. Value, set $50.

Chess Players A177

Design: 1fo, Iron Workers Union building and chess emblem.

1950, Apr. 9 Wmk. 106

889 A177 60f deep magenta	2.75	.60
890 A177 1fo deep blue	4.75	1.10
Nos. 889-890,C69 (3)	14.75	4.20

World Chess Championship Matches, Budapest.
Exist imperf. Value, set (3) $200.

Workers Symbolizing International Proletariat — A178

Design: 60f, Blast furnace, tractor, workers holding Maypole.

1950, May 1

891 A178 40f orange brown	1.50	.35
892 A178 60f rose carmine	1.50	.25
893 A178 1fo deep blue	2.00	.50
Nos. 891-893 (3)	5.00	1.10

Issued to publicize Labor Day, May 1, 1950.
Exist imperf. Value, set $75.

Liberty, Cogwheel, Dove and Globes — A179

Design: 60f, Three workers and flag.

Inscribed: "1950. V. 10.-24."

1950, May 10 Photo. *Perf. 12x12½*

894 A179 40f olive green	1.50	.35
895 A179 60f dark carmine	1.25	.25
Nos. 894-895,C70 (3)	4.35	1.25

Meeting of the World Federation of Trade Unions, Budapest, May 1950.
Exist imperf. Value, set $70.

Doctor Inspecting Baby's Bath — A180

Children's Day: 30f, Physical Culture. 40f, Education. 60f, Boys' Camp. 1.70fo, Model plane building.

1950, June 4 Wmk. 106

896	A180	20f gray & brn	2.00	1.70
897	A180	30f brn & rose lake	.85	.30
898	A180	40f indigo & dk grn	.85	.30
899	A180	60f SZABAD	1.10	.30
a.		UTANPOTLASUNK . .	*950.00*	*750.00*
900	A180	1.70fo dp grn & gray	2.00	.90
		Nos. 896-900 (5)	6.80	3.50

Exist imperf. Value, set $60.

Youths Marching on Globe — A181

Working Man and Woman — A182

30f, Foundry worker. 60f, Workers on Mt. Gellert. 1.70fo, Worker, peasant & student; flags.

Inscribed: Budapest 1950. VI. 17-18.

Perf. 12x12½, 12½x12

1950, June 17

901	A181	20f dark green	1.00	.30
902	A181	30f deep red org	.30	.25
903	A182	40f dark brown	.45	.25
904	A182	60f deep claret	1.00	.25
905	A182	1.70fo dark olive grn	1.25	.40
		Nos. 901-905 (5)	4.00	1.45

Issued to publicize the First Congress of the Working Youth, Budapest, June 17-18, 1950.
Exist imperf. Value, set $60.

Peonies — A183

Designs: 40f, Anemones. 60f, Pheasant's-eye. 1fo, Geraniums. 1.70fo, Bluebells.

Engraved and Lithographed
Perf. 12½x12

1950, Aug. 20 Unwmk.

906	A183	30f rose brn, rose pink & grn	1.25	.30
907	A183	40f dk green, lil & yel	1.60	.30
908	A183	60f red brn, yel & grn	2.00	.30
909	A183	1fo pur, red & grn	4.00	1.25
910	A183	1.70fo dk violet & grn	4.00	1.00
		Nos. 906-910 (5)	12.85	3.15

Exist imperf. Value, set $60.

Miner — A184

Designs: 60f, High speed lathe. 1fo, Prefabricated building construction.

Perf. 12x12½

1950, Oct. 7 Photo. Wmk. 106

911 A184 40f brown	1.00	.35
912 A184 60f carmine rose	1.25	.25
913 A184 1fo brt blue	2.25	.25
Nos. 911-913 (3)	4.50	.85

2nd National Exhibition of Inventions.
Exist imperf. Value, set $35.

Gen. Josef Bem and Battle at Piski A185

Perf. 12½x12

1950, Dec. 10 Engr. Unwmk.

914 A185 40f dark brown	1.25	.50
915 A185 60f deep carmine	1.00	.25
916 A185 1fo deep blue	1.50	.50
Nos. 914-916 (3)	3.75	1.25

Gen. Josef Bem, death centenary.
Exist imperf. Value, set $25.
See No. C80.

Signing Petition A186

Peace Demonstrator Holding Dove — A187

1fo, Mother and Children with soldier.

Wmk. 106

1950, Nov. 23 Photo. *Perf. 12*

917 A186 40f ultra & red brn	15.00	14.00
918 A187 60f red org & dk grn	5.00	4.00
919 A186 1fo ol grn & dk brn	15.00	14.00
Nos. 917-919 (3)	35.00	32.00

Exist imperf. Value, set $80.

Women Swimmers A188

Designs: 20f, Vaulting. 1fo, Mountain climbing. 1.70fo, Basketball. 2fo, Motorcycling.

1950, Dec. 2 *Perf. 12x12½*

920	A188	10f blue & gray	.30	.25
921	A188	20f sal & dk brn	.30	.25
922	A188	1fo olive & grn	.75	.25
923	A188	1.70fo ver & brn car	1.00	.25
924	A188	2fo salmon & pur	1.75	.30
		Nos. 920-924,C82-C86 (10)	13.85	5.00

Exist imperf. Value, set (10) $100.

Canceled to Order

The government stamp agency started about 1950 to sell canceled sets of new issues. Values in the second ("used") column are for these canceled-to-order stamps. Postally used stamps are worth more.

The practice was to end Apr. 1, 1991.

A189

Worker, Peasant, Soldier and Party Flag — A190

60f, Matthias Rakosi & allegory. 1fo, House of Parliament, columns of workers & banner.

Inscribed: "Budapest * 1951 * Februar 24."

1951, Feb. 24 *Perf. 12½x12, 12x12½*

925 A189 10f yellow green	.75	.35
926 A190 30f brown	.90	.40
927 A190 60f carmine rose	1.25	.70
928 A189 1fo blue	1.75	1.00
Nos. 925-928 (4)	4.65	2.45

2nd Congress of the Hungarian Workers' Party.
Exist imperf. Value, set $40.

Mare and Foal — A191

Designs: 30f, Sow and shoats. 40f, Ram and ewe. 60f, Cow and calf.

1951, Apr. 5 *Perf. 12x12½*

929 A191 10f ol bis & rose brn	1.10	.25
930 A191 30f rose brn & ol bis	1.25	.55
931 A191 40f dk green & brn	1.25	.55
932 A191 60f brown org & brn	1.50	.35
Nos. 929-932,C87-C90 (8)	18.35	5.10

Issued to encourage increased livestock production.
Exist imperf. Value, set (8) $100.

Flags of Russia and Hungary — A192

Russian Technician Teaching Hungarians A193

1951, Apr. 4 *Perf. 12½x12, 12x12½*

933 A192 60f brnsh carmine	1.25	.25
934 A193 1fo dull violet	1.25	.50

Issued to publicize the "Month of Friendship" between Hungary and Russia, 1951.
Exist imperf. Value, set $30.

Worker Holding Olive Branch and Mallet A194

Workers Carrying Flags — A195

1fo, Workers approaching Place of Heroes.

Perf. 12x12½, 12½x12

1951, May 1 Photo. Wmk. 106

935 A194 40f brown 1.10 .90
936 A195 60f scarlet 1.10 .25
937 A194 1fo blue 1.25 .60
Nos. 935-937 (3) 3.45 1.75

Issued to publicize Labor Day, May 1, 1951.
Exist imperf. Value, set $30.

Leo Frankel — A196

Paris Street Fighting, 1871 — A197

1951, May 20

938 A196 60f dark brown 1.00 .25
939 A197 1fo blue & red 1.25 .40

80th anniv. of the Commune of Paris.
Exist imperf. Value, set $28.

Children of Various Races — A198

Designs: 40f, Boy and girl at play. 50f, Street car and Girl Pioneer. 60f, Chemistry students. 1.70fo, Pioneer bugler.

Inscribed: "Nemzetkozi Gyermeknap 1951"

1951, June 3 *Perf. 12½x12*

940 A198 30f dark brown .60 .25
941 A198 40f green .60 .25
942 A198 50f brown red .60 .25
943 A198 60f plum .85 .35
944 A198 1.70fo blue 1.10 1.00
Nos. 940-944 (5) 3.75 2.10

International Day of Children, 6/3/51.
Exist imperf. Value, set $40.

5-Year-Plan Type of 1950

Designs as before.

1951-52 Wmk. 106 *Perf. 12x12½*

945 A175 8f gray .45 .25
946 A175 10f claret .60 .25
947 A175 12f orange ver .50 .25
948 A175 20f blue green .60 .25
949 A175 30f rose violet .60 .25
950 A175 40f sepia 1.25 .25
951 A175 60f red 1.25 .25
952 A175 1fo gray brn, yel & lil 1.50 .25
953 A175 1.70fo dk grn & yel 1.50 .25
954 A175 2fo vio brn & cr 2.25 .25
955 A175 3fo slate & cream 3.00 .25
956 A175 4fo blk brn & sal 4.00 .35
957 A175 5fo rose vio & yel ('52) 5.00 .80
958 A175 10fo dk brn & yel ('52) 15.00 3.25
Nos. 945-958 (14) 37.50 7.15

Maxim Gorky — A199

Perf. 12½x12

1951, June 17 Engr. Unwmk.

959 A199 60f copper red .40 .25
960 A199 1fo deep blue .25 .40
961 A199 2fo rose violet 1.10 .45
Nos. 959-961 (3) 1.75 1.10

15th anniversary of the death of Gorky.
Exist imperf. Value, set $25.

Budapest Buildings

Railroad Workshop A200

Building in Lehel Street A201

Suburban Bus Terminal A202

Rakosi House of Culture A203

George Kilian Street School A204

Central Construction Headquarters A205

Design Size: 22x18mm

1951 Wmk. 106 Photo. *Perf. 15*

962 A200 20f green .55 .25
963 A201 30f red orange .55 .25
964 A202 40f brown .55 .25
965 A203 60f red .75 .25
966 A204 1fo blue 1.00 .25
967 A205 3fo deep plum 3.00 .25
Nos. 962-967 (6) 6.40 1.50

Exist imperf. Value, set $100.
See Nos. 1004-1011, 1048-1056C.

1958 Design Size: 21x17mm

962a A200 20f green .65 .25
963a A201 30f red orange 1.10 .25
964a A202 40f brown .95 .25
965a A203 60f red 1.40 .25
966a A204 1fo blue 1.40 .25
967a A205 3fo deep plum 3.00 .25
Nos. 962a-967a (6) 8.50 1.50

Tractor Manufacture A206

30f, Fluoroscope examination. 40f, Checking lathework. 60f, Woman tractor operator.

1951, Aug. 20 *Perf. 12x12½*

968 A206 20f black brown .25 .25
969 A206 30f deep blue .25 .25
970 A206 40f crimson rose .65 .25
971 A206 60f brown .80 .25
Nos. 968-971,C91-C93 (7) 5.50 2.35

The successful conclusion of the first year under Hungary's 5-year plan.
Exist imperf. Value, set $50.

Soldiers of the People's Army — A207

1951, Sept. 29

972 A207 1fo brown 1.00 .25

Issued to publicize Army Day, Sept. 29, 1951. See No. C94.
Exist imperf. Value (with C94) $30.

Stamp of 1871, Portrait Replaced by Postmark — A208

Perf. 12½x12

1951, Sept. 12 Engr. Unwmk.

973 A208 60f olive green 4.00 4.00
Nos. 973,B207-B208 (3) 30.00 30.00

80th anniv. of Hungary's 1st postage stamp.
See Nos. C95, CB13-CB14.
Exist imperf. Value, set (3) $60.

Cornflower — A209

40f, Lily of the Valley. 60f, Tulip. 1fo, Poppy. 1.70fo, Cowslip.

1951, Nov. 4 Engr. & Litho.

974 A209 30f shown .75 .25
975 A209 40f multi 3.00 .75
976 A209 60f multi .75 .25
977 A209 1fo multi 2.00 .25
978 A209 1.70fo multi 2.00 .30
Nos. 974-978 (5) 8.50 1.80

Exist imperf. Value, set $50.

Storming of the Winter Palace A210

Designs: 60f, Lenin speaking to soldiers. 1fo, Lenin and Stalin.

Perf. 12x12½

1951, Nov. 7 Photo. Wmk. 106

979 A210 40f gray green 1.00 .50
980 A210 60f deep blue 1.25 .25
981 A210 1fo rose lake 1.75 .40
Nos. 979-981 (3) 4.00 1.15

34th anniversary of the Russian Revolution.
Exist imperf. Value, set $40.

Marchers Passing Stalin Monument — A211

1951, Dec. 16 Wmk. 106

982 A211 60f henna brown 1.50 .60
983 A211 1fo deep blue 1.50 .60

Joseph V. Stalin, 72nd birthday.
Exist imperf. Value, set $30.

Grand Theater, Moscow A212

Views of Moscow: 1fo, Lenin Mausoleum. 1.60fo, Kremlin.

1952, Feb. 20 *Perf. 12*

984 A212 60f ol grn & rose brn .65 .25
985 A212 1fo lil rose & ol brn 1.00 .35
986 A212 1.60fo red brn & ol 2.00 .65
Nos. 984-986 (3) 3.65 1.25

Hungarian-Soviet Friendship Month.
Exist imperf. Value, set $30.

Rakosi and Farmers A213

Matyas Rakosi — A214

Design: 2fo, Rakosi and Workers.

Perf. 12x12½, 12½x12

1952, Mar. 9 Engr. Unwmk.

987 A213 60f deep plum .80 .25
988 A214 1fo dk red brown .90 .25
989 A213 2fo dp violet blue 1.90 .55
Nos. 987-989 (3) 3.60 1.05

60th anniv. of the birth of Matyas Rakosi, communist leader.
Exist imperf. Value, set $35.

Lajos Kossuth and Speech at Debrecen A215

Designs: 30f, Sándor Petőfi. 50f, Gen. Josef Bem. 60f, Mihaly Tancsics. 1fo, Gen. János Damjanich. 1.50fo, Gen. Jozsef Nagysandor.

1952, Mar. 15 *Perf. 12x12½*

990 A215 20f green .25 .25
991 A215 30f rose violet .25 .25
992 A215 50f grnsh blk .25 .25
993 A215 60f brown car .35 .25
994 A215 1fo blue 1.00 .25
995 A215 1.50fo redsh brown 1.10 .45
Nos. 990-995 (6) 3.20 1.70

Heroes of the 1848 revolution.
Exist imperf. Value, set $32.50.
Nos. 990-995 also exist perf 12. Value, set $300.

No. B204 Surcharged in Black with Bars Obliterating Inscription and Surtax

Perf. 12½x12

1952, Apr. 27 Photo. Wmk. 283

996 SP121 60f magenta 42.50 42.50

Budapest Philatelic Exhibition. Counterfeits exist.

Girl Drummer Leading Parade A216

Designs: 60f, Workers and soldier. 1fo, Worker, flag-encircled globe and dove.

Perf. 12x12½

1952, May 1 Photo. Wmk. 106

997 A216 40f dk grn & dull red 1.50 .50
998 A216 60f dk red brn & dull red 1.00 .25
999 A216 1fo sepia & dull red 1.50 .30
Nos. 997-999 (3) 4.00 1.05

Issued to publicize Labor Day, May 1, 1952.
Exist imperf. Value, set $60.

Runner — A217

Designs: 40f, Swimmer. 60f, Fencer. 1fo, Woman gymnast.

1952, May 26 ***Perf. 11***

1000 A217 30f dark red brown .85 .25
1001 A217 40f deep green .85 .25
1002 A217 60f deep lilac rose 1.25 .25
1003 A217 1fo deep blue 1.40 .50
Nos. 1000-1003,C107-C108 (6) 8.95 3.50

Issued to publicize Hungary's participation in the Olympic Games, Helsinki, 1952.
Exist imperf. Value, set (6) $75.

Building Types of 1951

Buildings: 8f, School, Stalinvarost. 10f, Szekesfehervar Station. 12f, Building, Ujpest. 50f, Metal works, Inotai. 70f, Grain elevator, Hajdunanas. 80f, Tiszalok dam. 4fo, Miners' union headquarters. 5fo, Workers' apartments, Ujpest.

Design Size: 22x18mm

1952 Wmk. 106 ***Perf. 15***

1004 A202 8f green .45 .25
1005 A200 10f purple .45 .25
1006 A202 12f carmine .45 .25
1007 A202 50f gray blue .65 .25
1008 A202 70f yellow brn 1.25 .25
1009 A200 80f maroon 1.25 .25
1010 A202 4fo olive grn 4.00 .25
1011 A202 5fo gray black 6.00 .25
Nos. 1004-1011 (8) 14.50 2.00

Exist imperf. Value, set $140.

1958 Design Size: 21x17mm

1004a A202 8f green .50 .25
1005a A200 10f purple 2.50 .25
1006a A202 12f carmine .60 .25
1007a A202 50f gray blue .90 .25
1008a A202 70f yellow brn .90 .25
1009a A200 80f maroon 1.40 .25
1010a A202 4fo olive grn 4.00 .25
1011a A202 5fo gray black 5.50 .25
Nos. 1004a-1011a (8) 16.30 2.00

Approaching Train — A218

Railroad Day: 1fo, Railroad Construction.

1952, Aug. 10 ***Perf. 12x12½***

1012 A218 60f red brown 1.10 .35
1013 A218 1fo deep olive grn 1.40 .40

Exist imperf. Value, set $30.

Coal Excavator A219

Miners' Day: 1fo, Coal breaker.

1952, Sept. 7

1014 A219 60f brown 1.00 .25
1015 A219 1fo dark green 1.25 .30

Exist imperf. Value, set $25.

Lajos Kossuth — A220

Design: 60f, Kossuth statue.

1952, Sept. 19 ***Perf. 12½x12***

1016 A220 40f ol brn, *pink* .50 .25
1017 A220 60f black brn, *bl* .75 .25
1018 A220 1fo purple, *citron* 1.25 .25
Nos. 1016-1018 (3) 2.50 .75

150th anniv. of the birth of Lajos Kossuth.
Exist imperf. Value, set $35.

Janos Hunyadi — A221

Portraits: 30f, Gyorgy Dozsa. 40f, Miklos Zrinyi. 60f, Ilona Zriuyi. 1fo, Bottyan Vak. 1.50fo, Aurel Stromfeld.

1952, Sept. 28 Engr. Unwmk.

1019 A221 20f purple .25 .25
1020 A221 30f dark green .25 .25
1021 A221 40f indigo .25 .25
1022 A221 60f dk violet brn .55 .30
1023 A221 1fo dk blue grn .80 .40
1024 A221 1.50fo dark brown 1.90 1.00
Nos. 1019-1024 (6) 4.00 2.45

Army Day, Sept. 28, 1952.
Exist imperf. Value, set $50.

Lenin and Conference at Smolny Palace A222

Designs: 60f, Stalin and Cavalry Attack. 1fo, Marx, Engels, Lenin and Stalin.

1952, Nov. 7 Wmk. 106

Portraits in Olive Gray

1025 A222 40f deep claret 1.75 .50
1026 A222 60f gray 1.25 .25
1027 A222 1fo rose red 2.00 .35
Nos. 1025-1027 (3) 5.00 1.10

Russian Revolution, 35th anniversary.
Exist imperf. Value, set $50.

Peasant Woman Holding Wheat — A223

Peace Meeting A224

Perf. 12½x12, 12x12½

1952, Nov. 22

1028 A223 60f brn red, *citron* 1.00 .30
1029 A224 1fo brown, *blue* 1.00 .45

Third Hungarian Peace Congress, 1952.
Exist imperf. Value, set $25.

Subway Construction A225

Design: 1fo, Station and map.

1953, Jan. 19 Photo. ***Perf. 12x12½***

1030 A225 60f dk slate green 1.75 .60
1031 A225 1fo brown red 2.25 .90

Completion of the Budapest subway extension.
Exist imperf. Value, set $25.

Tank and Flag — A226

60f, Map of Central Europe and Soldier.

1953, Feb. 18

1032 A226 40f dark car rose 1.75 .40
1033 A226 60f chocolate 1.75 .70

Battle of Stalingrad, 10th anniversary.
Exist imperf. Value, set $25.

Stalin — A227

Two types of No. 1035. Type I: "MAGYAR POSTA" on solid background. Type II: "MAGYAR POSTA" on background of vertical lines.

Perf. 12x11½

1953 Engr. Wmk. 106

1034 A227 60f pur blk 1.25 .50

Souvenir Sheet

1035 A227 2fo pur blk, Type II 27.50 27.50
a. Type I 600.00 300.00

Death of Joseph Stalin (1879-1953).
Exist imperf. Values: 60f $20; No. 1035 $150; No. 1035a $450.
Issue dates: No. 1034, Mar. 27; No. 1035, Mar. 9.

Workers' Rest Home, Galyateto A228

Designs: 40f, Home at Mecsek. 50f, Parad Mineral Baths. 60f, Home at Kekes. 70f, Balatonfured Mineral Baths.

1953, Apr. Photo. ***Perf. 12x12½***

1036 A228 30f fawn .50 .25
1037 A228 40f deep blue .50 .25
1038 A228 50f dk olive bis .50 .25
1039 A228 60f dp yellow grn .50 .25
1040 A228 70f scarlet .50 .25
Nos. 1036-1040,C121-C122 (7) 4.40 1.90

Exist imperf. Value, set (7) $60.

Young Workers with Red Flags — A229

1953, May 1 ***Perf. 12½x12***

1041 A229 60f brn & red, *yel* 1.00 .25

Issued to publicize Labor Day, May 1, 1953.
Exist imperf. Value $25.

Karl Marx — A230

1953, May 1 Engr. ***Perf. 11½x12***

1042 A230 1fo black, *pink* 1.50 .25
a. Perf 12½x12 250.00 60.00

70th anniv. of the death of Karl Marx. See No. 1898.
Exist imperf. Value $30.

Insurgents in the Forest — A231

30f, Drummer & fighters. 40f, Battle scene. 60f, Cavalry attack. 1fo, Francis Rákóczy II.

1953, June 14 Photo. ***Perf. 11***

1043 A231 20f dk ol grn & org red, *grnsh* .30 .25
1044 A231 30f vio brn & red org 1.00 .25
1045 A231 40f gray bl & red org, *pink* 1.10 .25
1046 A231 60f dk ol brn & org, *yel* 2.25 .55
1047 A231 1fo dk red brn & org red, *yel* 3.00 .75
Nos. 1043-1047 (5) 7.65 2.05

250th anniv. of the Insurrection of 1703.
Exist imperf. Value $45.

Building Types of 1951

Buildings: 8f, Day Nursery, Ozd. 10f, Medical research institute, Szombathely. 12f, Apartments, Komlo. 20f, Department store, Ujpest. 30f, Brick factory, Maly. 40f, Metropolitan hospital. 50f, Sports building, Stalinvaros. 60f, Post office, Csepel. 70f, Blast furnace, Diosgyor. 1.20fo, Agricultural school, Ajkacsinger Valley. 1.70fo, Iron Works School, Csepel. 2fo, Optical works house of culture.

Design Size: 22x18mm

1953 Wmk. 106 ***Perf. 15***

1048 A204 8f olive green .90 .25
1049 A204 10f purple 1.25 .25
1050 A205 12f rose car 1.50 .25
1051 A204 20f dark green .90 .25
1052 A204 30f orange 1.75 .25
1053 A204 40f dark brown 3.00 .25
1054 A205 50f blue violet 3.50 .25
1055 A205 60f rose red 3.25 .25
1056 A204 70f yel brn 4.00 .25
1056A A205 1.20fo red 4.00 .25
1056B A204 1.70fo blue 3.00 .25
1056C A204 2fo green 7.50 .25
Nos. 1048-1056C (12) 34.55 3.00

Exist imperf. Value, set $175.

Design Size: 21x17mm

1958

1048a A204 8f olive green 1.50 .25
1049a A204 10f purple — .75
1050a A205 12f rose car 2.25 .25
1051a A204 20f dark green 2.25 .25
1052a A204 30f orange 2.25 .25
1053a A204 40f dark brown 2.25 .25
1054a A205 50f blue violet 2.25 .25

1055a	A205	60f	rose red	3.25	.25
1056a	A204	70f	yel brn	4.00	.25
1056Aa	A205	1.20fo	red	3.50	.25
1056Ba	A204	1.70fo	blue	2.25	.25
1056Ca	A204	2fo	green	7.50	.25
		Nos. 1048a-1056Ca (12)		33.25	3.50

Exist imperf. Value, set $150.

Bicycling — A232

1953, Aug. 20 *Perf. 11*

1057	A232	20f	shown	.25	.25
1058	A232	30f	Swimming	.25	.25
1059	A232	40f	Calisthenics	.25	.25
1060	A232	50f	Discus	.40	.25
1061	A232	60f	Wrestling	.50	.25
	Nos. 1057-1061,C123-C127 (10)			13.15	5.25

Opening of the People's Stadium, Budapest.
Exist imperf. Value, set (10) $90.

Kazar Costume A233

Provincial Costumes: 30f, Ersekcsanad. 40f, Kalocsa. 60f, Sioagard. 1fo, Sarkoz. 1.70fo, Boldog. 2fo, Orhalom. 2.50fo, Hosszuheteny.

1953, Sept. 12 **Engr.** *Perf. 12*

1062	A233	20f	blue green	1.25	.50
1063	A233	30f	chocolate	1.50	.50
1064	A233	40f	ultra	2.00	.50
1065	A233	60f	red	3.00	1.50
1066	A233	1fo	grnsh blue	3.50	1.50
1067	A233	1.70fo	brt green	4.00	2.00
1068	A233	2fo	car rose	7.00	3.00
1069	A233	2.50fo	purple	9.00	6.50
	Nos. 1062-1069 (8)			31.25	16.00

Exist imperf. Value, set $100.
See No. 1189.

Lenin — A234

Designs: 60f, Lenin and Stalin at meeting. 1fo, Lenin, facing left.

1954, Jan. 21 **Wmk. 106** *Perf. 12*

1073	A234	40f	dk blue grn	1.50	.75
1074	A234	60f	black brown	1.50	.25
1075	A234	1fo	dk car rose	2.00	.65
	Nos. 1073-1075 (3)			5.00	1.65

30th anniversary, death of Lenin.
Exist imperf. Value, set $50.

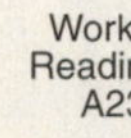
Worker Reading A235

Revolutionary and Red Flag — A236

Design: 1fo, Soldier.

Perf. 12x12½, 12½x12

1954, Mar. 21 **Photo.**

1076	A235	40f	gray blue & red	3.50	.50
1077	A236	60f	brown & red	3.50	.50
1078	A235	1fo	gray & red	3.50	.50
	Nos. 1076-1078 (3)			10.50	1.50

35th anniversary of the "First Hungarian Communist Republic."
Exist imperf. Value, set $60.

Blood Test — A237

Designs: 40f, Mother receiving newborn baby. 60f, Medical examination of baby.

1954, Mar. 8 *Perf. 12*

1079	A237	30f	brt blue	.25	.25
1080	A237	40f	brown bister	.45	.25
1081	A237	60f	purple	.55	.25
	Nos. 1079-1081,C146-C148 (6)			6.05	2.90

Exist imperf. Value, set $65.

Maypole — A238

Design: 60f, Flag bearer.

1954, May 1 *Perf. 12½x12*

1082	A238	40f	olive	.50	.25
1083	A238	60f	orange red	.50	.30

Issued to publicize Labor Day, May 1, 1954.
Exist imperf. Value, set $25.

Farm Woman with Fruit A239

1954, May 24 *Perf. 12*

1084	A239	60f	red orange	.80	.25

3rd Congress of the Hungarian Workers Party, Budapest, May 24, 1954.
Exists imperf. Value, set $20.

Natl. Museum, Budapest — A240

Designs: 60f, Arms of People's Republic. 1fo, Dome of Parliament Building.

1954, Aug. 20 *Perf. 12½x12*

1085	A240	40f	brt blue	1.00	.35
1086	A240	60f	redsh brown	1.00	.25
1087	A240	1fo	dark brown	1.50	.25
	Nos. 1085-1087 (3)			3.50	.85

People's Republic Constitution, 5th anniv.
Exist imperf. Value, set $30.

Peppers A241

Fruit: 50f, Tomatoes. 60f, Grapes. 80f, Apricots. 1fo, Apples. 1.20fo, Plums. 1.50fo, Cherries. 2fo, Peaches.

1954, Sept. 11 **Engr., Litho.**

Fruit in Natural Colors

1088	A241	40f	gray blue	.50	.25
1089	A241	50f	plum	.50	.25
1090	A241	60f	gray blue	.60	.25
1091	A241	80f	chocolate	1.40	.25
1092	A241	1fo	rose violet	1.75	.25
1093	A241	1.20fo	dull blue	1.40	.25
1094	A241	1.50fo	plum	2.25	.75
1095	A241	2fo	gray blue	1.75	.40
	Nos. 1088-1095 (8)			10.15	2.65

National agricultural fair.
Exist imperf. Value, set $50.

Maurus Jokai — A242

1954, Oct. 17 **Engr.**

1096	A242	60f	dk brown olive	1.00	.25
1097	A242	1fo	deep claret	1.50	.75

50th anniv. of the death of Maurus Jokai, writer.
Exist imperf. Value, set $25.
No. 1097 in violet blue is from the souvenir sheet, No. C157.

Janos Apaczai Csere A243

Scientists: 10f, Csoma Sandor Korosi. 12f, Anyos Jedlik. 20f, Ignaz Semmelweis. 30f, Janos Irinyi. 40f, Frigyes Koranyi. 50f, Armin Vambery. 60f, Karoly Than. 1fo, Otto Herman. 1.70fo, Tivadar Puskas. 2fo, Endre Hogyes.

1954, Dec. 5 **Photo.** *Perf. 12x12½*

1098	A243	8f	dk vio brn, *yel*	.25	.25
1099	A243	10f	brn, car, *pink*	.25	.25
1100	A243	12f	gray, *bl*	.25	.25
1101	A243	20f	brn, *yel*	.25	.25
1102	A243	30f	vio bl, *pink*	.25	.25
1103	A243	40f	dk grn, *yel*	.25	.25
1104	A243	50f	red brn, *pale grn*	.25	.25
1105	A243	60f	blue, *pink*	.25	.25
1106	A243	1fo	olive	.35	.25
1107	A243	1.70fo	rose brn, *yel*	.85	.35
1108	A243	2fo	blue green	1.50	.45
	Nos. 1098-1108 (11)			4.70	3.05

Exist imperf. Value, set $45.

Readers in Industrial Library — A244

Industry A245

1fo, Agriculture. 2fo, Liberation monument.

1955, Apr. 4 *Perf. 12½x12, 12x12½*

1109	A244	40f	dk car & ol brn	.75	.35
1110	A245	60f	dk green & red	.75	.25
1111	A245	1fo	choc & grn	1.00	.25
1112	A244	2fo	blue grn & brn	1.25	.35
	Nos. 1109-1112 (4)			3.75	1.20

10th anniversary of Hungary's liberation.
Exist imperf. Value, set $35.

Date, Flags, Grain Elevator and Tractor A246

1955, May 1 *Perf. 12x12½*

1113	A246	1fo	rose carmine	.80	.25

Labor Day, May 1, 1955.
Exist imperf. Value, set $20.

Government Printing Plant — A247

1955, May 28 **Wmk. 106**

1114	A247	60f	gray grn & hn brn	.50	.25

Centenary of the establishment of the government printing plant.
Exist imperf. Value, set $20.

Young Citizens and Hungarian Flag — A248

1955, June 15 *Perf. 12*

1115	A248	1fo	red brown	.65	.25

Issued to publicize the second national congress of the Hungarian Youth Organization.
Exist imperf. Value, set $20.

Truck Farmer A249

10f, Fisherman. 12f, Bricklayer. 20f, Radio assembler. 30f, Woman potter. 40f, Railwayman & train. 50f, Clerk & scales. 60f, Postman emptying mail box. 70f, Cattle & herdsman. 80f, Textile worker. 1fo, Riveter. 1.20fo, Carpenter. 1.40fo, Streetcar conductor. 1.70fo, Herdsman & pigs. 2fo, Welder. 2.60fo, Woman tractor driver. 3fo, Herdsman in national costume & horse. 4fo, Bus driver. 5fo, Lineman. 10fo, Coal miner.

1955 **Wmk. 106** *Perf. 12x12½*

1116	A249	8f	chestnut	.25	.25
1117	A249	10f	Prus green	.25	.25
1118	A249	12f	red orange	.25	.25
1119	A249	20f	olive green	.40	.25
1120	A249	30f	dark red	.35	.25
1121	A249	40f	brown	.40	.25
1122	A249	50f	violet bl	.40	.25
1123	A249	60f	brown red	.50	.25
1124	A249	70f	olive	.80	.25
1125	A249	80f	purple	.50	.25
1126	A249	1fo	blue	1.00	.25
1127	A249	1.20fo	olive bis	1.20	.25
1128	A249	1.40fo	deep green	1.00	.25
1129	A249	1.70fo	purple	1.00	.25

1130 A249 2fo rose brown 1.00 .25
1131 A249 2.60fo vermilion 1.50 .25
1132 A249 3fo green 2.25 .25
1133 A249 4fo peacock blue 2.00 .25
1134 A249 5fo orange brown 2.00 .25
1135 A249 10fo violet 1.75 .55
Nos. 1116-1135 (20) 18.80 5.30

Exist imperf. Value, set $120.

For surcharges see Nos. B211-B216.

Postrider Blowing Horn — A250

1955, June 25 ***Perf. 12½x12***
1136 A250 1fo rose violet .50 .25

Hungarian Postal Museum, 25th anniv.

Exists tete-beche. Value: 2½ times the value of a single.

Exists imperf. Value $25.

Mihaly Csokonai Vitez A251

1fo, Mihaly Vorosmarty. 2fo, Attila József.

1955, July 28 ***Perf. 12***
1137 A251 60f olive black 1.25 .30
1138 A251 1fo dark blue 1.25 .40
1139 A251 2fo rose brown 1.50 .65
Nos. 1137-1139 (3) 4.00 1.35

Issued to honor three Hungarian poets.

Exist imperf. Value $35.

Bela Bartok — A252

1955, Oct. 9
1140 A252 60f light brown 1.00 .25
Nos. 1140,C168-C169 (3) 6.50 3.50

10th anniversary of the death of Bela Bartok, composer.

Exist imperf. Value, set (3) $30.

Diesel Train A253

Designs: 60f, Bus. 80f, Motorcycle. 1fo, Truck. 1.20fo, Steam locomotive. 1.50fo, Dump truck. 2fo, Freighter.

1955, Dec. 20 ***Perf. 14½***
1141 A253 40f grn & vio brn .25 .25
1142 A253 60f dp grn & ol .25 .25
1143 A253 80f ol grn & brn .25 .25
1144 A253 1fo ocher & grn .30 .25
1145 A253 1.20fo salmon & blk .90 .25
1146 A253 1.50fo grnsh blk & red brn 1.25 .25
1147 A253 2fo aqua & brown 2.00 .55
Nos. 1141-1147 (7) 5.20 2.05

Exist imperf. Value, set $50.

Puli (Sheepdog) — A254

Puli and Steer A255

Hungarian Pointer — A256

Hungarian Dogs: 60f, Pumi (sheepdog). 1fo, Retriever with fowl. 1.20fo, Kuvasz (sheepdog). 1.50fo, Komondor (sheepdog) and cottage. 2fo, Komondor (head).

Perf. 11x13 (A254), 12
1956, Mar. 17 **Engr. & Litho.**
1148 A254 40f yel, blk & red .25 .25
1149 A255 50f blue, bis & blk .25 .25
1150 A254 60f yel grn, blk & red .25 .25
1151 A256 80f bluish grn, ocher & blk .25 .30
1152 A256 1fo turq, ocher & blk .40 .25
1153 A254 1.20fo salmon, blk & chnt .75 .25
1154 A255 1.50fo ultra, blk & buff 1.75 .35
1155 A254 2fo cerise, blk & chnt 2.50 .55
Nos. 1148-1155 (8) 6.40 2.45

Exist imperf. Value, set $45.

Pioneer Emblem A257

Perf. 12x12½
1956, June 2 **Photo.** **Wmk. 106**
1156 A257 1fo red .50 .25
1157 A257 1fo gray .50 .25

Pioneer movement, 10th anniversary.

Exist imperf. Value, set $27.50.

Janos Hunyadi Statue — A258

1956, Aug. 12 ***Perf. 12***
1158 A258 1fo brown, *yelsh* 1.00 .35

500th anniv. of the defeat of the Turks at the battle of Pecs under Janos Hunyadi.

Printed in sheets of 50 with alternate vertical rows inverted and center row of perforation omitted, providing 25 tête bêche pairs, of which 5 are imperf. between. Values for tete-beche pairs: unused $3; used $1.50. Values for tete-beche pairs, imperf between: unused $6; used $250.

Exists imperf. Value $35. Tête bêche pair also exists imperf. Value, $100.

Miner — A259

1956, Sept. 2
1159 A259 1fo dark blue .50 .25

Issued in honor of Miners' Day 1956.

Exists imperf. Value $15.

Kayak Racer A260

Sports: 30f, Horse jumping hurdle. 40f, Fencing. 60f, Women hurdlers. 1fo, Soccer. 1.50fo, Weight lifting. 2fo, Gymnastics. 3fo, Basketball.

1956, Sept. 25 **Wmk. 106** ***Perf. 11***
Figures in Brown Olive
1160 A260 20f lt blue .25 .25
1161 A260 30f lt olive grn .25 .25
1162 A260 40f deep orange .25 .25
1163 A260 60f bluish grn .25 .25
1164 A260 1fo vermilion .35 .25
1165 A260 1.50fo blue violet .65 .25
1166 A260 2fo emerald .80 .30
1167 A260 3fo rose lilac 1.40 .40
Nos. 1160-1167 (8) 4.20 2.20

16th Olympic Games at Melbourne, Nov. 22-Dec. 8, 1956.

Exist imperf. Value, set $75.

Franz Liszt A261

Portrait: No. 1169, Frederic Chopin facing left.

1956, Oct. 7 **Photo.** ***Perf. 12x12½***
1168 A261 1fo violet blue 2.50 2.50
1169 A261 1fo magenta 2.50 2.50
a. Pair, #1168-1169 6.00 6.00

29th Day of the Stamp. Sold only at the Philatelic Exhibition together with entrance ticket for 4fo.

Exist imperf. Value, pair $25.

Janos Arany — A262

1957, Sept. 15 **Wmk. 106** ***Perf. 12***
1170 A262 2fo bright blue 1.00 .50

75th anniv. of the death of Janos Arany, poet.

Exists imperf. Value $15.

Arms of Hungary A263

1957, Oct. 1
1171 A263 60f brt red .75 .25
1172 A263 1fo dp yellow grn .75 .25

Exists imperf. Value, set $25.

Trade Union Congress Emblem A264

1957, Oct. 4
1173 A264 1fo dk carmine .50 .25

4th Intl. Trade Union Cong., Leipzig, 10/4-15.

Exists imperf. Value $15.

Dove and Colors of Communist Countries — A265

Design: 1fo, Lenin.

1957, Nov. 7 **Litho.** ***Perf. 12***
1174 A265 60f gray, blk & multi .50 .25
a. Perf 11 2.50 .25
1175 A265 1fo ol bis & indigo .50 .35
a. Perf 11 2.50 .25

Russian Revolution, 40th anniversary.

Exist imperf. Value, set $25.

Komarom Tumbler Pigeons A266

Pigeons: 40f, Two short-beaked Budapest pigeons. 60f, Giant domestic pigeon. 1fo, Three Szeged pigeons. 2fo, Two Hungarian fantails.

Perf. 12x12½
1957-58 **Photo.** **Wmk. 106**
1176 A266 30f yel grn, cl & ocher .25 .25
1177 A266 40f ocher & blk .25 .25
1178 A266 60f blue & gray .25 .25
1179 A266 1fo gray & red brn .25 .25
1180 A266 2fo brt pink & gray .60 .40
Nos. 1176-1180,C175 (6) 2.50 1.90

Intl. Pigeon Exhibition, Budapest, 12/14-16.

Exist imperf. Value, set (6) $35.

Issued: 30f, 1/12/58; others, 12/14/57.

Television Station — A267

1958, Feb. 22 **Engr.** ***Perf. 11***
1181 A267 2fo rose violet 1.25 .75
a. Perf. 12 7.50 7.50

Souvenir Sheet

1182 A267 2fo green 42.50 42.50

Issued to publicize the television industry. No. 1182 sold for 25fo.
Exist imperf. Values: single $15; souvenir sheet $125.

Mother and Child A268

Designs: 30f, Old man feeding pigeons. 40f, School boys. 60f, "Working ants and fiddling grasshopper." 1fo, Honeycomb and bee. 2fo, Handing over money.

1958, Mar. 9 **Photo.** ***Perf. 12***
1183 A268 20f yel grn & ol gray .25 .25
1184 A268 30f lt olive & mar .25 .25
1185 A268 40f yel bis & brn .50 .25
1186 A268 60f rose car & grnsh blk .50 .25
1187 A268 1fo ol gray & dk brn .75 .25
1188 A268 2fo org & ol gray 1.25 .35
Nos. 1183-1188 (6) 3.50 1.60

Issued to publicize the value of savings and insurance.
Exist imperf. Value, set $40.

Kazar Costume Type of 1953
Souvenir Sheet

1958, Apr. 17 **Engr.** ***Perf. 12***
1189 A233 10fo magenta 27.50 27.50

Issued for the Universal and International Exposition at Brussels.
Exists imperf. Value $60.

Arms of Hungary A269

1958, May 23 **Litho.** **Wmk. 106**
Arms in Original Colors
1190 A269 60f lt red brn & red .25 .25
1191 A269 1fo gray grn & grn .50 .25
1192 A269 2fo gray & dk brn .80 .25
Nos. 1190-1192 (3) 1.55 .75

1st anniv. of the law amending the constitution.
Exist imperf. Value, set $20.

Youth Holding Book — A270

1958, June 14 **Photo.** ***Perf. 12½x12***
1193 A270 1fo brown carmine .75 .50

5th Hungarian Youth Festival at Keszthely.
Printed with alternating label, inscribed: V. IFJUSAGI TALALKOZO KESZTHELY 1958.
Exists imperf. Value, with label $15.

Post Horn and Town Hall, Prague — A271

1958, June 30
1194 A271 60f green .50 .25
a. Pair, #1194, C184 1.00 1.00

Conference of Postal Ministers of Communist Countries at Prague, June 30-July 8.
Exists imperf. Value, $7. In pair with No. C184 imperf, value $15.

Dolomite Flax — A272

Hungarian Thistles — A273

30f, Kitaibelia vitifolia. 60f, Crocuses. 1fo, Hellebore. 2fo, Lilies. 2.50fo, Pinks. 3fo, Dog roses.

Perf. 11x13, 12½x12 (A273)
1958, Aug. 12 **Photo.** **Wmk. 106**
1195 A272 20f red vio & yel 1.00 .25
1196 A272 30f blue, yel & grn .25 .25
1197 A273 40f brown & bis .25 .25
1198 A273 60f bl grn & pink .30 .25
1199 A273 1fo rose car & yel grn .55 .25
1200 A273 2fo grn & yel .95 .25
1201 A272 2.50fo vio bl & pink 1.10 .45
1202 A272 3fo green & pink 1.90 .70
a. Souv. sheet of 4, perf. 12 35.00 *35.00*
Nos. 1195-1202 (8) 6.30 2.65

No. 1202a and a similar imperf. sheet were issued for the International Philatelic Congress at Brussels, Sept. 15-17, 1958. They contain the triangular 20f, 30f, 2.50fo and 3fo stamps printed in different colors. Sheets measure 111x111mm. and are printed on unwatermarked, linen-finish paper. Background of stamps, marginal inscriptions and ornaments in green. No. 1202a also exists perf. 11. Value, $45.
Exist imperf. Value, set $35. Value of 1202a imperf, $75.

Paddle, Ball and Olive Branch A274

Designs: 30f, Table tennis player, vert. 40f, Wrestlers, vert. 60f, Wrestlers, horiz. 1fo, Water polo player, vert. 2.50fo, High dive, vert. 3fo, Swimmer.

1958, Aug. 30 **Wmk. 106** ***Perf. 12***
1203 A274 20f rose red, *pnksh* .25 .25
1204 A274 30f olive, *grnsh* .25 .25
1205 A274 40f mag, *yel* .25 .25
1206 A274 60f brown, *bluish* .40 .25
1207 A274 1fo ultra, *bluish* .45 .25
1208 A274 2.50fo dk red, *yel* 1.10 .30
1209 A274 3fo grnsh bl, *grnsh* 1.40 .50
Nos. 1203-1209 (7) 4.10 2.05

Intl. Wrestling and European Swimming and Table Tennis Championships, held at Budapest.
Exist imperf. Value, set $25.

Red Flag — A275

Design: 2fo, Hand holding newspaper.

1958, Nov. 21 ***Perf. 12½x12***
1210 A275 1fo brown & red .25 .25
1211 A275 2fo dk gray bl & red .55 .25

40th anniversary of the founding of the Hungarian Communist Party and newspaper.
Exist imperf. Value, set $15.

Satellite, Sputnik and American Rocket A276

Designs: 10f, Eötvös Torsion Balance and Globe. 20f, Deep sea exploration. 30f, Icebergs, penguins and polar light. 40f, Soviet Antarctic camp and map of Pole. 60f, "Rocket" approaching moon. 1fo, Sun and observatory.

1959, Mar. 14 ***Perf. 12x12½***
Size: 32x21mm
1212 A276 10f car rose & sepia .35 .25
1213 A276 20f brt blue & gray .25 .25
1214 A276 30f dk slate grn & bis .40 .25

Perf. 12
Size: 35x26mm
1215 A276 40f slate bl & lt bl .25 .25

Perf. 15
Size: 58x21mm
1216 A276 60f Prus bl & lemon .45 .25

Perf. 12
Size: 35x26mm
1217 A276 1fo scarlet & yel .70 .30
1218 A276 5fo brn & red brn 1.60 .80
Nos. 1212-1218 (7) 4.00 2.35

Intl. Geophysical Year. See No. 1262.
Exist imperf. Value, set $20.

"Revolution" — A277

1959, Mar. 21 ***Perf. 12½x12***
1219 A277 20f vio brn & red .25 .25
1220 A277 60f blue & red .25 .25
1221 A277 1fo brown & red .60 .25
Nos. 1219-1221 (3) 1.10 .75

40th anniv. of the proclamation of the Hungarian Soviet Republic.
Exist imperf. Value, set $15.

Rose — A278

1959, May 1 **Photo.** ***Perf. 11***
1222 A278 60f lilac, dp car & grn .40 .25
1223 A278 1fo lt brn, dl red & grn .60 .25

Issued for Labor Day, May 1, 1959.
Exist imperf. Value, set $15.

Early Locomotive — A279

Designs: 30f, Diesel coach. 40f, Early semaphore, vert. 60f, Csonka automobile. 1fo, Icarus bus. 2fo, First Lake Balaton steamboat. 2.50fo, Stagecoach.

1959, May 26 **Litho.** ***Perf. 14½x15***
1224 A279 20f multi .25 .25
1225 A279 30f multi .25 .25
1226 A279 40f multi .25 .25
1227 A279 60f multi .25 .25
1228 A279 1fo multi .25 .25
1229 A279 2fo multi .25 .25
1230 A279 2.50fo multi 1.25 .30
Nos. 1224-1230,C201 (8) 4.75 3.05

Transport Museum, Budapest.
Exist imperf. Value, set (8) $25.

Perf. 10½x11½
1959, May 29 **Wmk. 106**
1231 A279 2.50fo multi 2.00 2.00

Designer's name on No. 1231. Printed in sheets of four with four labels to commemorate the congress of the International Federation for Philately in Hamburg. Value $15.
Exist imperf. Values: paid with label $15; sheetlet $100.

Post Horn and World Map — A280

1959, June 1 **Photo.** ***Perf. 12***
1232 A280 1fo cerise .75 .30

Postal Ministers Conference, Berlin.
Printed in sheets of 25 stamps with 25 alternating gray labels showing East Berlin Opera House.
Exists imperf. Value: in pair with label, $15.

Great Cormorant A281

Birds: 20f, Little egret and nest. 30f, Purple heron and nest. 40f, Great egret. 60f, White spoonbill. 1fo, Gray heron. 2fo, Squacco heron and nest. 3fo, Glossy ibis.

1959, June 14
1233 A281 10f green & indigo .25 .25
1234 A281 20f gray bl & ol grn .25 .25
1235 A281 30f org, grnsh blk & vio .25 .25
1236 A281 40f dark grn & gray .25 .25
1237 A281 60f dp cl & pale rose .35 .25
1238 A281 1fo dp bl grn & blk .50 .25
1239 A281 2fo dp orange & gray .85 .30
1240 A281 3fo bister & brn lake 1.50 .70
Nos. 1233-1240 (8) 4.20 2.50

Exist imperf. Value, set $30.

Warrior, 10th Century — A282

Designs: 20f, Warrior, 15th century. 30f, Soldier, 18th century. 40f, Soldier, 19th century. 60f, Cavalry man, 19th century. 1fo, Fencer, assault. 1.40fo, Fencer on guard. 3fo, Swordsman saluting.

1959, July 11

1241 A282 10f gray & blue .25 .25
1242 A282 20f gray & dull yel .25 .25
1243 A282 30f gray & gray vio .25 .25
1244 A282 40f gray & ver .25 .25
1245 A282 60f gray & rose lil .25 .25
1246 A282 1fo ind & lt bl grn .30 .25
1247 A282 1.40fo orange & blk .60 .25
1248 A282 3fo blk & ol grn .90 .70
Nos. 1241-1248 (8) 3.05 2.45

24th World Fencing Championships, Budapest.
Exist imperf. Value, set $25.

Sailboat, Lake Balaton — A283

40f, Vintager & lake, horiz. 60f, Bathers. 1.20fo, Fishermen. 2fo, Summer guests & ship.

1959, July 11 Photo. Wmk. 106

1249 A283 30f blue, *yel* .25 .25
1250 A283 40f carmine rose .25 .25
1251 A283 60f dp red brown .25 .25
1252 A283 1.20fo violet .30 .25
1253 A283 2fo red org, *yel* .60 .50
Nos. 1249-1253,C202-C205 (9) 2.90 2.55

Issued to publicize Lake Balaton and the opening of the Summer University.
Exist imperf. Value, set (9) $25.

Haydn's Monogram A284

Esterhazy Palace A285

Haydn and Schiller Monograms — A286

Design: 1fo, Joseph Haydn and score.

1959, Sept. 20 Wmk. 106 *Perf. 12*

1254 A284 40f dp claret & yel .25 .25
1255 A285 60f Prus bl, gray & yel .75 .75
1256 A284 1fo dk vio, lt brn & org .65 .25

Designs: 40f, Schiller's monogram. 60f, Pegasus rearing from flames. 1fo, Friedrich von Schiller.

1257 A284 40f olive grn & org .25 .25
1258 A285 60f violet bl & lil .40 .25
1259 A284 1fo dp cl & org brn .80 .25
Nos. 1254-1259 (6) 3.10 2.00

Souvenir Sheet
Imperf

1260 A286 Sheet of 2 17.50 17.50
a. 3fo magenta 3.50 3.50
b. 3fo green 3.50 3.50

150th anniv. of the death of Joseph Haydn, Austrian composer, Nos. 1254-1256; 200th anniv. of the birth of Friedrich von Schiller, German poet and dramatist, Nos. 1257-1259; No. 1260 honors both Haydn and Schiller.
Nos. 1254-1260 exist imperf. Value, set $20.

Shepherd — A287

1959, Sept. 25 Engr. *Perf. 12*

1261 A287 2fo deep claret 1.50 1.50
a. With ticket 2.25 2.25

Day of the Stamp and Natl. Stamp Exhib. Issued in sheets of 8 with alternating ticket. The 4fo sale price marked on the ticket was the admission fee to the Natl. Stamp Exhib.
Exist imperf. Values: single $6; single with ticket $15.

Type of 1959 Overprinted in Red

1959, Sept. 24 Photo. *Perf. 15*

1262 A276 60f dull bl & lem .65 .25
a. Overprint omitted 3,000.

Landing of Lunik 2 on moon, Sept. 14.
Exists imperf. Value $10.

Handing over Letter A288

1959, Oct. 4 Litho. *Perf. 12*

1263 A288 60f multicolored .60 .25

Intl. Letter Writing Week, Oct. 4-10.
Exists imperf. Value $12.50.

Szamuely and Lenin — A289

Designs: 40f, Aleksander Pushkin. 60pf, Vladimir V. Mayakovsky. 1fo, Hands holding peace flag.

1959, Nov. 14 Photo. Wmk. 106

1264 A289 20f dk red & bister .25 .25
1265 A289 40f brn & rose lil, *bluish* .25 .25
1266 A289 60f dk blue & bis .55 .25
1267 A289 1fo bl, car, buff, red & grn .55 .30
Nos. 1264-1267 (4) 1.60 1.05

Soviet Stamp Exhibition, Budapest.
Exists imperf. Value $20.

European Swallowtail A290

Butterflies: 30f, Arctia hebe, horiz. 40f, Lysandra hylas, horiz. 60f, Apatura ilia.

Perf. 11½x12, 12x11½

1959, Nov. 20

Butterflies in Natural Colors

1268 A290 20f blk & yel grn .25 .25
1269 A290 30f lt blue & blk .35 .25
1270 A290 40f dk gray & org brn .35 .25
1271 A290 60f dk gray & dl yel .45 .25
Nos. 1268-1271,C206-C208 (7) 6.05 2.35

Exist imperf. Value, set (7) $30.

Worker with Banner — A291

Design: 1fo, Congress flag.

1959, Nov. 30 *Perf. 14½*

1272 A291 60f brown, grn & red .25 .25
1273 A291 1fo brn, red, red & grn .25 .25

Issued to commemorate the 7th Congress of the Hungarian Socialist Workers' Party.
Exist imperf. Value, set $15.

Teacher Reading Fairy Tales — A292

Fairy Tales: 30f, Sleeping Beauty. 40f, Matt, the Goose Boy. 60f, The Cricket and the Ant. 1fo, Mashenka and the Three Bears. 2fo, Hansel and Gretel. 2.50fo, Pied Piper. 3fo, Little Red Riding Hood.

1959, Dec. 15 Litho. *Perf. 11½*

Designs in Black

1274 A292 20f gray & multi .25 .25
1275 A292 30f brt pink .25 .25
1276 A292 40f lt blue grn .25 .25
1277 A292 60f lt blue .45 .25
1278 A292 1fo yellow .75 .25
1279 A292 2fo brt yellow grn .75 .25
1280 A292 2.50fo orange 1.10 .40
1281 A292 3fo crimson 1.10 .60
Nos. 1274-1281 (8) 4.90 2.50

Exist imperf. Value, set $20.

Sumeg Castle — A293

Castles: 20fr, Tata. 30f, Diosgyor. 60f, Saros-Patak. 70f, Nagyvazsony. 1.40fo, Siklos. 1.70fo, Somlo. 3fo, Csesznek, vert. 5fo, Koszeg, vert. 10fo, Sarvar, vert.

Wmk. 106

1960, Feb. 1 Photo. *Perf. 14½*

Size: 21x17½mm

1282 A293 8f purple .25 .25
1283 A293 20f dk yel grn .25 .25
1284 A293 30f orange brn .25 .25
1285 A293 60f rose red .25 .25
1286 A293 70f emerald .35 .25

Perf. 12x11½, 11½x12

Size: 28x21mm, 21x28mm

1287 A293 1.40fo ultra .85 .25
1288 A293 1.70fo dl vio, "Somlo" 1.00 .25
b. "Somlyo" 1.50 .25
1289 A293 3fo red brown 1.75 .30
1290 A293 5fo yellow green 2.25 .30
1291 A293 10fo car rose 3.00 .60
Nos. 1282-1291 (10) 10.20 2.95

Exist imperf. Value, set $90.

Tinted Paper

Perf. 14½

Size: 21x17½mm

1282a A293 8f pur, *bluish* .25 .25
1283a A293 20f dk yel grn, *grnsh* .25 .25
1284a A293 30f org brn, *yel* .35 .25
1285a A293 60f rose red, *pnksh* .25 .25
1286a A293 70f emer, *bluish* .65 .25

Perf. 12x11½

Size: 28x21mm

1287a A293 1.40fo ultra, *bluish* .70 .25
1288a A293 1.70fo dull vio, *bluish* .90 .25
Nos. 1282a-1288a (7) 3.35 1.75

Exist imperf. Value, set $30.
See Nos. 1356-1365, 1644-1646.

Halas Lace — A294

Designs: Various Halas lace patterns.

Sizes: 20f, 60f, 1fo, 3fo: 27x37mm
30f, 40f, 1.50fo, 2fo: 37½x43½mm

Wmk. 106

1960, Feb. 15 Litho. *Perf. 11½*

Inscriptions in Orange

1292 A294 20f brown black .25 .25
1293 A294 30f violet .25 .25
1294 A294 40f Prus blue .40 .25
1295 A294 60f dark brown .50 .25
1296 A294 1fo dark green .80 .30
1297 A294 1.50fo green 1.00 .40
1298 A294 2fo dark blue 1.75 .60
1299 A294 3fo dk carmine 3.00 .80
Nos. 1292-1299 (8) 7.95 3.10

Exist imperf. Value, set $25.
See Nos. 1570-1577.

Inscriptions in Orange

1960, Sept. 3 Souvenir Sheet

1300 A294 Sheet of 4 + 4 labels 16.00 16.00
a. 3fo brown olive 3.25 3.25
b. 3fo bright violet 3.25 3.25
c. 3fo emerald 3.25 3.25
d. 3fo bright blue 3.25 3.25

Fédération Internationale de Philatélie Congress, Warsaw, Sept. 3-11. No. 1300 contains 4 stamps and 4 alternating labels, printed in colors of adjoining stamps.
Exists imperf. Value $100.

Cross-country Skier — A295

Sports: 40f, Ice hockey player. 60f, Ski jumper. 80f, Woman speed skater. 1fo, Downhill skier. 1.20fo, Woman figure skater.

1960, Feb. 29 Photo. Perf. 11½x12
Inscriptions and Figures in Bister

1301 A295 30f deep blue .25 .25
1302 A295 40f brt green .25 .25
1303 A295 60f scarlet .25 .25
1304 A295 80f purple .25 .25
1305 A295 1fo brt grnsh blue .60 .25
1306 A295 1.20fo brown red .70 .45
Nos. 1301-1306,B217 (7) 4.05 2.05

8th Olympic Winter Games, Squaw Valley, Calif., Feb. 18-29, 1960.
Exists imperf. Value $20.

Clara Zetkin — A296

Portraits: No. 1308, Kato Haman. No. 1309, Lajos Tüköry. No. 1310, Giuseppe Garibaldi. No. 1311, István Türr. No. 1312, Ottó Herman. No. 1313, Ludwig van Beethoven. No. 1314, Ferenc Mora. No. 1315, Istvan Toth Bucsoki. No. 1316, Donat Banki. No. 1317, Abraham G. Pattantyus. No. 1318, Ignaz Semmelweis. No. 1319, Frédéric Joliot-Curie. No. 1320, Ferenc Erkel. No. 1321, Janos Bolyai. No. 1322, Lenin.

1960 Photo. Perf. 10½
1307 A296 60f lt red brn .25 .25

Engr.
1308 A296 60f pale purple .25 .25
1309 A296 60f rose red .25 .25
1310 A296 60f violet .25 .25
1311 A296 60f blue green .25 .25
1312 A296 60f blue .25 .25
1313 A296 60f gray brown .25 .25
1314 A296 60f salmon pink .25 .25
1315 A296 60f gray .25 .25
1316 A296 60f rose lilac .25 .25
1317 A296 60f green .25 .25
1318 A296 60f violet blue .25 .25
1319 A296 60f brown .25 .25
1320 A296 60f rose brown .25 .25
1321 A296 60f grnsh blue .25 .25
1322 A296 60f dull red .25 .25
Nos. 1307-1322 (16) 4.00 4.00

Nos. 1307-1308 commemorate International Women's Day, Mar. 8.
Exists imperf. Value $55.

Flower and Quill — A297

Wmk. 106
1960, Apr. 2 Photo. Perf. 12
1323 2fo brn, yel & grn 1.25 1.25
a. A297 With ticket 1.50 1.50

Issued for the stamp show of the National Federation of Hungarian Philatelists. The olive green 4fo ticket pictures the Federation's headquarters and served as entrance ticket to the show. Printed in sheets of 35 stamps and 35 tickets.
Exists imperf. Value, stamp + ticket, $15.

Soviet Capt. Ostapenko Statue — A298

Designs: 60f, Youth holding flag, horiz.

Perf. 12½x11½, 11½x12½
1960, Apr. 4
1324 A298 40f dp carmine & brn .35 .25
1325 A298 60f red brn, red & grn .65 .25

Hungary's liberation from the Nazis, 15th anniv.
Exist imperf. Value, set $12.50.

Boxers — A299

Sports: 10f, Rowers. 30f, Archer. 40f, Discus thrower. 50f, Girls playing ball. 60f, Javelin thrower. 1fo, Rider. 1.40fo, Wrestlers. 1.70fo, Swordsmen. 3fo, Hungarian Olympic emblem.

1960, Aug. 21 Perf. 11½x12
Designs in Ocher and Black
1326 A299 10f blue .25 .25
1327 A299 20f salmon .25 .25
1328 A299 30f lt violet .25 .25
1329 A299 40f yellow .25 .25
1330 A299 50f deep pink .25 .25
1331 A299 60f gray .25 .25
1332 A299 1fo pale brn vio .25 .25
1333 A299 1.40fo lt violet bl .25 .25
1334 A299 1.70fo ocher .45 .25
1335 A299 3fo multi 1.00 .50
Nos. 1326-1335,B218 (11) 4.70 3.05

17th Olympic Games, Rome, 8/25-9/11.
Exist imperf. Value, set $20.

Souvenir Sheet

Romulus and Remus Statue and Olympic Flame — A300

1960, Aug. 21
1336 A300 10fo multicolored 20.00 20.00

Winter and Summer Olympic Games, 1960.
Exists imperf. Value $40.

Woman of Mezokovesd Writing Letter — A301

Perf. 11½x12
1960, Oct. 15 Photo. Wmk. 106
1337 A301 2fo multicolored 1.40 1.40
a. With ticket 1.75 1.75

Day of the Stamp and Natl. Stamp Exhib. Issued in sheets of 8 with alternating ticket. The 4fo sale price marked on the ticket was the admission fee to the Natl. Stamp Exhib.
Exists imperf. Value, stamp + ticket, $12.50.

The Turnip, Russian Fairy Tale — A302

Fairy Tales: 30f, Snow White and the Seven Dwarfs. 40f, The Miller, His Son and the Donkey. 60f, Puss in Boots. 80f, The Fox and the Raven. 1fo, The Maple-Wood Pipe. 1.70fo, The Fox and the Stork. 2fo, Momotaro (Japanese).

1960, Dec. 1 Perf. 11½x12
1338 A302 20f multi .25 .25
1339 A302 30f multi .25 .25
1340 A302 40f multi .25 .25
1341 A302 60f multi .25 .25
1342 A302 80f multi .25 .25
1343 A302 1fo multi .35 .25
1344 A302 1.70fo multi .65 .35
1345 A302 2fo multi 1.00 .50
Nos. 1338-1345 (8) 3.25 2.35

Exist imperf. Value, set $20.

Brown Bear — A303

Animals: 20f, Kangaroo. 30f, Bison. 60f, Elephants. 80fr, Tiger with cubs. 1fo, Ibex. 1.40fo, Polar bear. 2fo, Zebra and young. 2.60fo, Bison cow with calf. 3fo, Main entrance to Budapest Zoological Gardens. 30f, 60f, 80f, 1.40fo, 2fo, 2.60fo are horizontal.

1961, Feb. 24 Perf. 11½x12
1346 A303 20f orange & blk .25 .25
1347 A303 30f yel grn & blk brn .25 .25
1348 A303 40f org brn & brn .25 .25
1349 A303 60f lil rose & gray .25 .25
1350 A303 80f gray & yel .25 .25
1351 A303 1fo blue grn & brn .30 .25
1352 A303 1.40fo grnsh bl, gray & blk .60 .25
1353 A303 2fo pink & black .50 .25
1354 A303 2.60fo brt vio & brn 1.00 .40
1355 A303 3fo multicolored 1.40 .75
Nos. 1346-1355 (10) 5.05 3.15

Issued for the Budapest Zoo.
Exist imperf. Value, set $25.

Castle Type of 1960

10f, Kisvárda. 12f, Szigliget. 40f, Simon Tornya. 50f, Füzér. 80f, Egervár. 1fo, Vitány. 1.20fo, Sirok. 2fo, Boldogkö. 2.60fo, Hollókö. 4fo, Eger.

1961, Mar. 3 Photo. Perf. 14½
Size: 21x17½mm
1356 A293 10f orange brn .25 .25
1357 A293 12f violet blue .25 .25
1358 A293 40f brt green .25 .25
1359 A293 50f brown .25 .25
1360 A293 80f dull claret .25 .25

Perf. 12x11½
Size: 28x21mm
1361 A293 1fo brt blue .25 .25
1362 A293 1.20fo rose violet .25 .25
1363 A293 2fo olive bister .40 .25
1364 A293 2.60fo dull blue .60 .25
1365 A293 4fo brt violet .75 .25
Nos. 1356-1365 (10) 3.50 2.50

Exist imperf. Value, set $65.

Child Chasing Butterfly — A304

40f, Man on operating table. 60f, Ambulance & stretcher. 1fo, Traffic light & scooter. 1.70fo, Syringe. 4fo, Emblem of Health Information Service (torch & serpent).

1961, Mar. 17 Litho. Perf. 10½
Cross in Red
Size: 18x18mm
1366 A304 30f org brn & blk .25 .25
1367 A304 40f bl grn, bl & sepia .25 .25

Size: 25x30mm
1368 A304 60f multi .25 .25
1369 A304 1fo multi .25 .25
1370 A304 1.70fo multi .45 .25
1371 A304 4fo gray & yel grn 1.25 .50
Nos. 1366-1371 (6) 2.70 1.75

Health Information Service.
Exist imperf. Value, set $20.

Ferenc Rozsa, Journalist — A305

Portraits: No. 1373, Gyorgy Kilian. No. 1374, Jozsef Rippl-Ronai. No. 1375, Sandor Latinka. No. 1376, Maté Zalka. No. 1377, Jozsef Katona.

Wmk. 106, Unwmk.
1961 Photo. Perf. 12
1372 A305 1fo red brown .25 .25
1373 A305 1fo greenish blue .25 .25
1374 A305 1fo rose brown .25 .25
1375 A305 1fo olive bister .25 .25
1376 A305 1fo olive green .25 .25
1377 A305 1fo maroon .25 .25
Nos. 1372-1377 (6) 1.50 1.50

Press Day (No. 1372); the inauguration of the Gyorgy Kilian Sports Movement (No. 1373); birth cent. of Jozsef Rippl-Ronai, painter (No. 1374); Sandor Latinka, revolutionary leader, 75th death anniv. (No. 1375); Mate Zalka, author and revolutionist (No. 1376); Jozsef Katona, dramatist (No. 1377).
Nos. 1374, 1375, 1377 are unwmkd. Others in this set have wmk. 106.
Exist imperf. Value, set $30.

Yuri A. Gagarin and Vostok 1 — A306

Design: 1fo, Launching Vostok 1.

Perf. 11½x12
1961, Apr. 25 Wmk. 106
1381 A306 1fo dk bl & bis brn .75 .50
1382 A306 2fo dp ultra & bis brn 3.25 1.25

1st man in space, Yuri A. Gagarin, 4/12/61.
Exist imperf. Value, set $60.

Roses — A307

Design: 2fo, as 1fo, design reversed.

1961, Apr. 29 Perf. 12½x11½
1383 A307 1fo grn & dp car .25 .25
1384 A307 2fo grn & dp car .80 .25
a. Pair, #1383-1384 1.50 .30

Issued for May Day, 1961.
Exist imperf. Value, No. 1384a $20.

"Venus" and Moon A308

Designs: Various Stages of Rocket.

1961, May 24 Wmk. 106 *Perf. 15*

1385	A308 40f grnsh bl, bis & blk	.80	.80
1386	A308 60f brt bl, bis & blk	.80	.80
1387	A308 80f ultra & blk	.80	.80

Perf. 11¼x11

1388	A308 2fo violet & yel	1.60	1.60
	Nos. 1385-1388 (4)	4.00	4.00

Soviet launching of the Venus space probe, Feb. 12, 1961. Exist imperf. Value, set $30. No. 1388 was also printed in sheets of four, perf. and imperf. Size: 130x76mm. Value: perf $16; imperf $200.

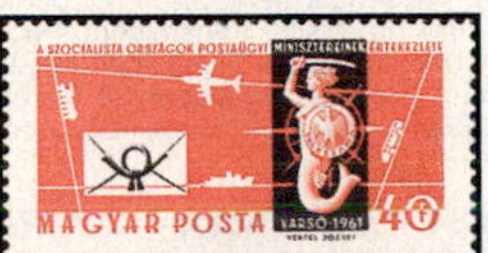
Warsaw Mermaid, Letter and Sea, Air and Land Transport — A309

Mermaid and: 60f, Television screen and antenna. 1fo, Radio.

1961, June 19 Photo. *Perf. 13½*

1389	A309 40f red org & blk	.25	.25
1390	A309 60f lilac & blk	.25	.25
1391	A309 1fo brt blue & blk	.60	.25
	Nos. 1389-1391 (3)	1.10	.75

Conference of Postal Ministers of Communist Countries held at Warsaw.
Exist imperf. Value, set $15.

Flag and Parliament — A310

Designs: 1.70fo, Orchid. 2.60fo, Small tortoise-shell butterfly. 3fo, Goldfinch.

1961, June 23 *Perf. 11*

Background in Silver

1392	A310	1fo grn, red & blk	.40	.35
1393	A310	1.70fo red & multi	.50	.45
1394	A310	2.60fo purple & multi	.75	.75
1395	A310	3fo blue & multi	1.00	1.00

1961, Aug. 19

Background in Gold

1396	A310	1fo green & blk	.35	.30
1397	A310	1.70fo red & multi	.50	.40
1398	A310	2.60fo purple & multi	.75	.75
1399	A310	3fo blue & multi	1.00	1.00
		Nos. 1392-1399 (8)	5.25	5.00

Issued to publicize the International Stamp Exhibition, Budapest, Sept. 23-Oct. 3, 1961.
Nos. 1392-1399 each printed in sheets of 4.
In gold background issue the top left inscription is changed on 1fo and 3fo.
Exist imperf. Values: set $35; sheetlet set $200.

George Stephenson A311

Winged Wheel, Steering Wheel and Road A312

Design: 2fo, Jenő Landler.

Perf. 12½x11½

1961, July 4 Photo. Wmk. 106

1400	A311 60f yellow olive	.30	.25
1401	A312 1fo blue & bister	.30	.25
1402	A311 2fo yellow brown	.50	.35
	Nos. 1400-1402 (3)	1.10	.85

Conference of Transport Ministers of Communist Countries held at Budapest.
Exist imperf. Value, set $20.

Soccer A313

1961, July 8 Unwmk. *Perf. 14½*

1403	A313 40f shown	.25	.25
1404	A313 60f Wrestlers	.25	.25
1405	A313 1fo Gymnast	.30	.25
	Nos. 1403-1405 (3)	.80	.75

50th anniv. of the Steel Workers Sport Club (VASAS). See No. B219.
Exist imperf. Value, set of 4 (with B219) $20.

Galloping Horses — A314

40f, Hurdle Jump. 60f, Two trotters. 1fo, Three trotters. 1.70fo, Mares & foals. 2fo, Race horse "Baka." 3fo, Race horse "Kincsem."

1961, July 22

1406	A314	30f multi	.25	.25
1407	A314	40f multi	.25	.25
1408	A314	60f multi	.35	.25
1409	A314	1fo multi	.35	.25
1410	A314	1.70fo multi	.50	.25
1411	A314	2fo multi	1.40	.30
1412	A314	3fo multi	1.60	.65
		Nos. 1406-1412 (7)	4.70	2.20

Exist imperf. Value, set $25.

Keyboard, Music and Liszt Silhouette A315

Liszt Monument, Budapest A316

Designs: 2fo, Academy of Music, Budapest, and bar of music. 10fo, Franz Liszt.

1961, Oct. 2 Unwmk. *Perf. 12*

1413	A315 60f gold & blk	.35	.25
1414	A316 1fo dark gray	.60	.25
1415	A315 2fo dk bl & gray grn	.75	.40
	Nos. 1413-1415 (3)	1.70	.90

Souvenir Sheet

1416	A316 10fo multi	11.00	9.50

150th anniv. of the birth, and the 75th anniv. of the death of Franz Liszt, composer.
Exist imperf. Value: set $20; souvenir sheet $30.

Lenin — A317

1961, Oct. 22 *Perf. 11½*

1417	A317 1fo deep brown	.40	.25

22nd Congress of the Communist Party of the USSR, Oct. 17-31.
Exist imperf. Value $5.

Monk's Hood — A318

30f, Centaury. 40f, Blue iris. 60f, Thorn apple. 1fo, Purple hollyhock. 1.70fo, Hop. 2fo, Poppy. 3fo, Mullein.

Wmk. 106

1961, Nov. 4 Photo. *Perf. 12*

1418	A318	20f shown	.25	.25
1419	A318	30f multi	.25	.25
1420	A318	40f multi	.25	.25
1421	A318	60f multi	.55	.25
1422	A318	1fo multi	.30	.25
1423	A318	1.70fo multi	.40	.25
1424	A318	2fo multi	.95	.30
1425	A318	3fo multi	1.50	.60
		Nos. 1418-1425 (8)	4.45	2.40

Exist imperf. Value, set $20.

Nightingale — A319

Birds: 40f, Great titmouse. 60f, Chaffinch, horiz. 1fo, Eurasian jay. 1.20fo, Golden oriole, horiz. 1.50fo, European blackbird, horiz. 2fo, Yellowhammer, 3fo, Lapwing, horiz.

1961, Dec. 18 Unwmk. *Perf. 12*

1426	A319	30f multi	.25	.25
1427	A319	40f multi	.25	.25
1428	A319	60f multi	.25	.25
1429	A319	1fo multi	.25	.25
1430	A319	1.20fo multi	.25	.25
1431	A319	1.50fo multi	.45	.25
1432	A319	2fo multi	.55	.25
1433	A319	3fo multi	.75	.35
		Nos. 1426-1433 (8)	3.00	2.10

Exist imperf. Value, set $20.

Mihaly Karolyi — A320

1962, Mar. 18

1434	A320 1fo black	.25	.25

Mihaly Karolyi, (1875-1955), Prime Minister of Hungarian Republic (1918-19).
Exists imperf. Value $4.

1962, Mar. 29

Portrait: No. 1435, Ferenc Berkes.

1435	A320 1fo red brown	.25	.25

Fifth Congress of the Hungarian Cooperative Movement, and to honor Ferenc Berkes, revolutionary. See Nos. 1457, 1459.

Exists imperf. Value $4.

Map of Europe, Train Signals and Emblem — A321

1962, May 2 Photo.

1436	A321 1fo blue green	.25	.25

14th Intl. Esperanto Cong. of Railway Men.
Exists imperf. Value $2.

Xiphophorus Helleri A322

Tropical Fish: 30f, Macropodus opercularis. 40f, Lebistes reticulatus. 60f, Betta splendens. 80f, Puntius tetrazona. 1fo, Pterophyllum scalare. 1.20fo, Mesogonistius chaetodon. 1.50fo, Aphyosemion australe. 2fo, Hyphessobrycon innesi. 3fo, Symphysodon aequifasciata haraldi.

1962, May 5 *Perf. 11½x12*

Fish in Natural Colors, Black Inscriptions

1437	A322	20f blue	.25	.25
1438	A322	30f citron	.25	.25
1439	A322	40f lt blue	.25	.25
1440	A322	60f lt yellow grn	.25	.25
1441	A322	80f blue green	.30	.25
1442	A322	1fo brt bl grn	.25	.25
1443	A322	1.20fo blue green	.30	.25
1444	A322	1.50fo grnsh blue	.55	.25
a.		"1962" twice in design	2.00	2.00
1445	A322	2fo green	.70	.25
1446	A322	3fo gray grn & yel	1.50	1.00
		Nos. 1437-1446 (10)	4.60	3.25

On No. 1444a, the year date appears both to the left and below the value inscription. On No. 1444, it appears only to the left of the value.
Exist imperf. Value, set $25.

Globe, Soccer Ball and Flags of Colombia and Uruguay — A323

Goalkeeper — A324

Flags of: 40f, USSR and Yugoslavia. 60f, Switzerland and Chile. 1fo, Germany and Italy. 1.70fo, Argentina and Bulgaria. 3fo, Brazil and Mexico.

Unwmk.

1962, May 21 Photo. *Perf. 11*

Flags in National Colors

1447	A323	30f rose & bis	.30	.25
1448	A323	40f pale grn & bis	.35	.25
1449	A323	60f pale lil & bis	.55	.30
1450	A323	1fo blue & bis	.90	.30
1451	A323	1.70fo ocher & bis	1.25	.35
1452	A323	3fo pink & blue bis	1.90	.50
		Nos. 1447-1452,B224,C209A (8)	8.65	3.00

Souvenir Sheet

Perf. 12

1453	A324	10fo multicolored	7.00	7.00

World Cup Soccer Championship, Chile, May 30-June 17.

Exist imperf. Value: set (8) $25; souvenir sheet $25.

Type of 1961 and

Johann Gutenberg A325

No. 1456, Miklós Misztófalusi Kis, Hungarian printer (1650-1702). No. 1457, Jozsef Pach. No. 1458, András Cházár. No. 1459, Dr. Ferenc Hutyra. No. 1460, Gábor Egressy & National Theater.

1962 Unwmk. Photo. *Perf. 12*

1455	A325	1fo blue black	.25	.25
1456	A325	1fo red brown	.25	.25
1457	A320	1fo blue	.25	.25
1458	A325	1fo violet	.25	.25
1459	A320	1fo deep blue	.30	.25
1460	A325	1fo rose red	.40	.25
		Nos. 1455-1460 (6)	1.70	1.50

Cent. of Printers' and Papermakers' Union (Nos. 1455-1456). 75th anniv. of founding, by Joszef Pech, of Hungarian Hydroelectric Service (No. 1457). András Cházár, founder of Hungarian deaf-mute education (No. 1458). Dr. Ferenc Hutyra, founder of Hungarian veterinary medicine (No. 1459). 125th anniv. of National Theater (No. 1460).

Exist imperf. Value, set $20.

Malaria Eradication Emblem — A327

1962, June 25 *Perf. 15*

1461	A327	2.50fo lemon & blk	.75	.50
a.		2.50fo grn & blk, sheet of 4, perf. 11	4.00	3.75

WHO drive to eradicate malaria.

Imperfs exist. Values: single (lemon) $9; single (green) $10; green sheetlet of 4 $50.

Imperf. sheets with control numbers exist.

Sword-into-Plowshare Statue, United Nations, NY — A328

1962, July 7 *Perf. 12*

1462	A328	1fo brown	.25	.25

World Congress for Peace and Disarmament, Moscow, July 9-14.

Exists imperf. Value $1.25.

Floribunda Rose — A329

Festival Emblem — A330

1962 *Perf. 12½x11½*

Various Roses in Natural Colors

1465	A329	20f orange brn	.30	.30
1466	A329	40f slate grn	.50	.30
1467	A329	60f violet	.50	.30
1468	A329	80f rose red	.75	.30
1469	A329	1fo dark green	.90	.35
1470	A329	1.20fo orange	.95	.35
1471	A329	2fo dk blue grn	2.10	.45
1472	A330	3fo multi	1.00	1.00
		Nos. 1465-1472 (8)	7.00	3.35

No. 1472 was issued for the 8th World Youth Festival, Helsinki, July 28-Aug. 6.

Exist imperf. Value, set $57.50.

Weight Lifter — A331

1962, Sept. 16 *Perf. 12*

1473	A331	1fo copper red	.50	.25

European Weight Lifting Championships.

Exists imperf. Value $3.

Oil Derrick and Primitive Oil Well — A332

Perf. 12x11½

1962, Oct. 8 Photo. Unwmk.

1474	A332	1fo green	.50	.25

25th anniv. of the Hungarian oil industry.

Exists imperf. Value $1.50.

Racing Motorcyclist — A333

Designs: 30f, Stunt racing. 40f, Uphill race. 60f, Cyclist in curve. 1fo, Start. 1.20fo, Speed racing. 1.70fo, Motorcyclist with sidecar. 2fo, Motor scooter. 3fo, Racing car.

1962, Dec. 28 *Perf. 11*

1475	A333	20f multi	.25	.25
1476	A333	30f multi	.25	.25
1477	A333	40f multi	.25	.25
1478	A333	60f multi	.25	.25
1479	A333	1fo multi	.40	.25
1480	A333	1.20fo multi	.45	.25
1481	A333	1.70fo multi	.75	.25
1482	A333	2fo multi	.85	.30
1483	A333	3fo multi	1.00	.75
		Nos. 1475-1483 (9)	4.45	2.80

Exist imperf. Value, set $20.

Ice Skater — A334

Designs: 20f-3fo, Various figure skating and ice dancing positions. 20f, 3fo horiz. 10fo, Figure skater and flags of participating nations.

Perf. 12x11½, 11½x12

1963, Feb. 5 Photo. Unwmk.

1484	A334	20f multi	.25	.25
1485	A334	40f multi	.25	.25
1486	A334	60f multi	.35	.25
1487	A334	1fo multi	.45	.30
1488	A334	1.40fo multi	.65	.40
1489	A334	2fo multi	1.00	.45
1490	A334	3fo multi	1.60	.75
		Nos. 1484-1490 (7)	4.55	2.65

Souvenir Sheet

Perf. 11½x12

1491	A334	10fo multi	6.50	6.50

European Figure Skating and Ice Dancing Championships, Budapest, Feb. 5-10.

Exist imperf. Value: set $20; souvenir sheet $80.

János Batsányi (1763-1845) — A335

No. 1493, Helicon Monument. No. 1494, Actors before Szeged Cathedral. No. 1495, Leo Weiner, composer. No. 1496, Ferenc Entz,horticulturist. No. 1497, Ivan Markovits, inventor of Hungarian shorthand,1863. No. 1498, Dr. Frigyes Koranyi. No. 1499, Ferenc Erkel (1810-93), composer. No. 1500, Geza Gardonyi (1863-1922), writer of Hungarian historical novels for youth. No. 1501, Pierre de Coubertin, Frenchman, reviver of Olympic Games. No. 1502, Jozsef Eötvös, author, philosopher, educator. No. 1503, Budapest Industrial Fair emblem. No. 1504, Stagecoach and Arc de Triomphe, Paris. No. 1505, Hungary map and power lines. No. 1506, Roses.

1963 Unwmk. *Perf. 11*

1492	A335	40f dk car rose	.25	.25
1493	A335	40f blue	.25	.25
1494	A335	40f violet blue	.25	.25
1495	A335	40f olive	.25	.25
1496	A335	40f emerald	.25	.25
1497	A335	40f dark blue	.25	.25
1498	A335	60f dull violet	.25	.25
1499	A335	60f bister brn	.25	.25
1500	A335	60f gray green	.25	.25
1501	A335	60f red brown	.40	.25
1502	A335	60f lilac	.25	.25
1503	A335	1fo purple	.25	.25
1504	A335	1fo rose red	.25	.25
1505	A335	1fo gray	.25	.25
1506	A335	2fo multi	.50	.25
		Nos. 1492-1506 (15)	4.15	3.75

No. 1493, 10th Youth Festival, Keszthely. No. 1494, Outdoor plays, Szeged. No. 1495, Budapest Music Competition. No. 1496, Cent. of professional horticultural training. No. 1498, 50th anniv. of the death of Prof. Koranyi, pioneer in fight against tuberculosis. No. 1499, Erkel Memorial Festival, Gyula. No. 1501, 10th anniv. of the People's Stadium, Budapest. No. 1502, 150th anniv. of birth of Jozsef Eötvös, organizer of modern public education in Hungary. No. 1504, Paris Postal Conf., 1863. No. 1505, Rural electrification. No. 1506, 5th Natl. Rose Show.

Exist imperf. Value, set $50.

Ship and Chain Bridge, Budapest — A336

Bus and Parliament A337

20f, Trolley. 30f, Sightseeing bus & Natl. Museum. 40f, Bus & trailer. 50f, Railroad tank car. 60f, Trolley bus. 70f, Railroad mail car. 80f, Motorcycle messenger. No. 1516, Mail plane, vert. No. 1517, Television transmitter, Miskolc, vert. 1.40fo, Mobile post office. 1.70fo, Diesel locomotive. 2fo, Mobile radio transmitter & stadium. 2.50fo, Tourist bus. 2.60fo, Passenger train. 3fo, P.O. parcel conveyor. 4fo, Television transmitters, Pecs, vert. 5fo, Hydraulic lift truck & mail car. 6fo, Woman teletypist. 8fo, Map of Budapest & automatic dial phone. 10fo, Girl pioneer &woman letter carrier.

1963-64 Photo. *Perf. 11*

1507	A336	10f brt blue	.25	.25
1508	A336	20f dp yellow grn	.25	.25
1509	A336	30f violet	.25	.25
1510	A336	40f orange	.25	.25
1511	A336	50f brown	.25	.25
1512	A336	60f crimson	.25	.25
1513	A336	70f olive gray	.25	.25
1514	A336	80f red brn ('64)	.25	.25

Perf. 12x11½, 11½x12

1515	A337	1fo rose claret	.25	.25
1516	A337	1.20fo orange brn	.80	.60
1517	A337	1.20fo dp vio ('64)	.25	.25
1518	A337	1.40fo dp yel grn	.25	.25
1519	A337	1.70fo maroon	.25	.25
1520	A337	2fo grnsh blue	.35	.25
1521	A337	2.50fo lilac	1.20	.25
1522	A337	2.60fo olive	1.25	.25
1523	A337	3fo dk blue ('64)	.25	.25
1524	A337	4fo blue ('64)	.35	.25
1525	A337	5fo ol brn ('64)	.45	.25
1526	A337	6fo dk ol bis ('64)	.55	.25
1527	A337	8fo red lilac ('64)	.80	.25
1528	A337	10fo emerald ('64)	1.25	.75
		Nos. 1507-1528 (22)	10.25	6.35

Size of 20f, 60f: 20½-21x16¾-17mm.

Minute inscription in lower margin includes year date, number of stamp in set and designer's name (Bokros F. or Legrady S.).

Exist imperf. Value, set $60.

See Nos. 1983-1983B, 2201-2204.

Size: 21½x16½mm

1965-67 Coil Stamps *Perf. 14*

1508a	A336	20f deep yellow green	.30	.25
1512a	A336	60f crimson ('67)	.50	.25

Black control number on back of every 3rd stamp.

Motorboat — A338

Girl, Steamer and Castle — A339

Design: 60f, Sailboat.

1963, July 13 *Perf. 11*

1529	A338	20f sl grn, red & blk	.25	.25
1530	A339	40f multicolored	.25	.25
1531	A338	60f bl, blk, brn & org	.60	.25
		Nos. 1529-1531 (3)	1.10	.75

Centenary of the summer resort Siofok.

Exist imperf. Value, set $20.

Child with Towel and Toothbrush — A340

Designs: 40f, Child with medicines. 60f, Girls of 3 races. 1fo, Girl and heart. 1.40fo, Boys of 3 races. 2fo, Medical examination of child. 3fo, Hands shielding plants.

1963, July 27 *Perf. 12x11½*

1532 A340 30f multi .25 .25
1533 A340 40f multi .25 .25
1534 A340 60f multi .25 .25
1535 A340 1fo multi .25 .25
1536 A340 1.40fo multi .35 .25
1537 A340 2fo multi .40 .25
1538 A340 3fo multi 1.20 .40
Nos. 1532-1538 (7) 2.95 1.90

Centenary of the International Red Cross.
Exist imperf. Value, set $17.50.

Karancsság Woman — A341

Provincial Costumes: 30f, Kapuvár man. 40f, Debrecen woman. 60f, Hortobágy man. 1fo, Csököly woman. 1.70fo, Dunántul man. 2fo, Buják woman. 2.50fo, Alföld man. 3fo, Mezőkövesd bride.

1963, Aug. 18 Engr. *Perf. 11½*

1539 A341 20f claret .25 .25
1540 A341 30f green .25 .25
1541 A341 40f brown .25 .25
1542 A341 60f brt blue .30 .25
1543 A341 1fo brown red .45 .25
1544 A341 1.70fo purple .50 .35
1545 A341 2fo dk blue grn .65 .35
1546 A341 2.50fo dk carmine .75 .65
1547 A341 3fo violet blue 1.60 .65
Nos. 1539-1547 (9) 5.00 3.25

Popular Art Exhibition in Budapest.
Exist imperf. Value, set $40.

Slalom and 1964 Olympic Emblem — A342

Sports: 60f, Downhill skiing. 70f, Ski jump. 80f, Biathlon. 1fo, Figure skating pair. 2fo, Ice hockey. 2.60fo, Speed ice skating. 10fo, Skier and mountains, vert.

1963-64 Photo. *Perf. 12*

1964 Olympic Emblem in Black and Red

1548 A342 40f yel grn & bis .25 .25
1549 A342 60f violet & bis .25 .25
1550 A342 70f ultra & bis .25 .25
1551 A342 80f emer & bis .25 .25
1552 A342 1fo brn org & bis .25 .25
1553 A342 2fo brt blue & bis .40 .25
1554 A342 2.60fo rose lake & bis .60 .40
Nos. 1548-1554,B234 (8) 2.95 2.20

Souvenir Sheet

Perf. 11½x12

1555 A342 10fo grnsh bl, red & brn ('64) 5.50 5.50

9th Winter Olympic Games, Innsbruck, Austria, Jan. 29-Feb. 9, 1964.
Exist imperf. Value: set (8) $20; souvenir sheet $20.

Four-Leaf Clover — A343

Good Luck Symbols: 20f, Calendar and mistletoe, horiz. 30f, Chimneysweep and clover. 60f, Top hat, pig and clover. 1fo, Clown with balloon and clover, horiz. 2fo, Lanterns, mask and clover.

Perf. 12x11½, 11½x12

1963, Dec. 12 Photo. Unwmk.

Sizes: 28x22mm (20f, 1fo); 22x28mm (40f); 28x39mm (30f, 60f, 2fo)

1556 A343 20f multi .25 .25
1557 A343 30f multi .25 .25
1558 A343 40f multi .25 .25
1559 A343 60f multi .25 .25
1560 A343 1fo multi .25 .25
1561 A343 2fo multi .45 .25
Nos. 1556-1561,B235-B236 (8) 2.90 2.10

New Year 1964.
Exist imperf. Value, set $15.
The 20f and 40f issued in booklet panes of 10, perf. and imperf.; sold for 2 times and 1½ times face respectively.

Moon Rocket — A344

U.S. & USSR Spacecraft: 40f, Venus space probe. 60f, Vostok I, horiz. 1fo, Friendship 7. 1.70fo, Vostok III & IV. 2fo, Telstar 1 & 2, horiz. 2.60fo, Mars I. 3fo, Radar, rockets and satellites, horiz.

1964, Jan. 8 *Perf. 11½x12, 12x11½*

1562 A344 30f grn, yel & brnz .25 .25
1563 A344 40f pur, bl & sil .25 .25
1564 A344 60f bl, blk, yel, sil & red .25 .25
1565 A344 1fo dk brn, red & sil .35 .25
1566 A344 1.70fo vio bl, blk, tan & red .70 .25
1567 A344 2fo sl grn, yel & sil .70 .25
1568 A344 2.60fo dp bl, yel & brnz .70 .45
1569 A344 3fo dp vio, lt bl & sil 1.00 .50
Nos. 1562-1569 (8) 4.20 2.45

Achievements in space research.
Exist imperf. Value, set $15.

Lace Type of 1960

Various Halas Lace Designs.
Sizes: 20f, 2.60fo: 38x28mm. 30f, 40f, 60f, 1fo, 1.40fo, 2fo: 38x45mm.

Engr. & Litho.

1964, Feb. 28 *Perf. 11½*

1570 A294 20f emerald & blk .25 .25
1571 A294 30f dull yel & blk .25 .25
1572 A294 40f deep rose & blk .25 .25
1573 A294 60f olive & blk .25 .25
1574 A294 1fo red org & blk .35 .25
1575 A294 1.40fo blue & blk .45 .25
1576 A294 2fo bluish grn & blk .55 .25
1577 A294 2.60fo lt vio & blk .85 .45
Nos. 1570-1577 (8) 3.20 2.20

Exist imperf. Value, set $35.

Special Anniversaries-Events Issue

Imre Madach (1823-64) — A345

Shakespeare A346

Karl Marx and Membership Card of International Working Men's Association — A347

Michelangelo — A348

Lajos Kossuth and György Dózsa — A349

Budapest Fair Buildings — A350

No. 1579, Ervin Szabo. No. 1580, Writer Andras Fay (1786-1864). No. 1581, Aggtelek Cave scene. No. 1582, Excavating bauxite. No. 1584, Equestrian statue, Szekesfehervar. No. 1585, Bowler. No. 1586, Waterfall and forest. No. 1587, Architect Miklos Ybl (1814-91) and Budapest Opera. No. 1590, Armor, saber, sword & foil. No. 1592, Galileo Galilei. No. 1593, Women basketball players. No. 1595, Two runners breaking tape.

Perf. 11½x12, 12x11½, 11

1964 Photo. Unwmk.

Inscribed: "ÉVFORDULÓK-ESEMÉNYEK"

1578 A345 60f brt purple .25 .25
1579 A345 60f olive .25 .25
1580 A345 60f olive grn .25 .25
1581 A346 60f bluish grn .25 .25
1582 A346 60f Prus blue .25 .25
1583 A347 60f rose red .25 .25
1584 A348 60f slate blue .25 .25
1585 A345 1fo car rose .25 .25
a. With Olympic rings bottom tab 1.00 1.00
1586 A346 1fo dull blue grn .25 .25
1587 A348 1fo orange brn .25 .25
1588 A349 1fo ultra .25 .25
1589 A350 1fo brt green .25 .25
1590 A345 2fo yellow brn .25 .25
1591 A346 2fo magenta .35 .25
1592 A346 2fo red brown .25 .25
1593 A346 2fo brt blue .25 .25
1594 A348 2fo gray brown .30 .25
1595 A348 2fo brown red .25 .25
Nos. 1578-1595 (18) 4.65 4.50

No. 1579, Municipal libraries, 60th anniv., and librarian Szabo (1877-1918). No. 1582, Bauxite mining in Hungary, 30th year. No. 1583, Cent. of 1st Socialist Intl. No. 1584, King Alba Day in Székesfehérvár. No. 1585, 1st European Bowling Championship, Budapest. No. 1586, Cong. of Natl. Forestry Federation. No. 1588, City of Cegléd, 600th anniv. No. 1589, Opening of 1964 Budapest Intl. Fair. No. 1590, Hungarian Youth Fencing Association, 50th anniv. Nos. 1591-1592, Shakespeare and Galileo, 400th birth anniversaries. No. 1593, 9th European Women's Basketball Championship. No. 1594, Michelangelo's 400th death anniv. No. 1595, 50th anniv. of 1st Hungarian-Swedish athletic meet.
Exists imperf. Value, set $100. No. 1585a imperf value $350.

Eleanor Roosevelt — A351

Design, horiz.: a, d, Portrait at right. b, c, Portrait at left.

1964, Apr. 27 *Perf. 12½*

1596 A351 2fo gray, black & buff .30 .25

Miniature Sheet

Perf. 11

1597 Sheet of 4 3.00 2.75
a. A351 2fo dp claret, brn & blk .65 .65
b. A351 2fo dk bl, brn & blk .65 .65
c. A351 2fo grn, brn & blk .65 .65
d. A351 2fo olive, brn & blk .65 .65

Exist imperf. Value: single $7; souvenir sheet $20.

Fencing — A352

Sport: 40f, Women's gymnastics. 60f, Soccer. 80f, Equestrian. 1fo, Running. 1.40fo, Weight lifting. 1.70fo, Gymnast on rings. 2fo, Hammer throw and javelin. 2.50fo, Boxing.

1964, June 12 Photo. *Perf. 11*

Multicolored Design and Inscription

1598 A352 30f lt ver .25 .25
1599 A352 40f blue .25 .25
1600 A352 60f emerald .25 .25
1601 A352 80f tan .25 .25
1602 A352 1fo yellow .25 .25
1603 A352 1.40fo bis brn .25 .25
1604 A352 1.70fo bluish gray .30 .25
1605 A352 2fo gray grn .35 .25
1606 A352 2.50fo vio gray .55 .40
Nos. 1598-1606,B237 (10) 3.30 3.15

18th Olympic Games, Tokyo, Oct. 10-25.
Exist imperf. Value, set (10) $20.

Elberta Peaches A353

Peaches: 40h, Blossoms (J. H. Hale). 60h, Magyar Kajszi. 1fo, Mandula Kajszi. 1.50fo, Borsi Rozsa. 1.70fo, Blossoms (Alexander). 2fo, Champion. 3fo, Mayflower.

1964, July 24 *Perf. 11½*

1607 A353	40f multi	.25	.25
1608 A353	60f multi	.25	.25
1609 A353	1fo multi	.25	.25
1610 A353	1.50fo multi	.25	.25
1611 A353	1.70fo multi	.25	.25
1612 A353	2fo multi	.35	.25
1613 A353	2.60fo multi	.45	.30
1614 A353	3fo multi	.65	.50
	Nos. 1607-1614 (8)	2.70	2.30

National Peach Exhibition, Szeged.
Exist imperf. Value, set $30.

Crossing Street in Safety Zone — A354

60f, "Watch out for Children" (child & ball). 1fo, "Look before Crossing" (mother & child).

1964, Sept. 27 *Perf. 11*

1615 A354	20f multicolored	.25	.25
1616 A354	60f multicolored	.25	.25
1617 A354	1fo lilac & multi	.60	.25
	Nos. 1615-1617 (3)	1.10	.75

Issued to publicize traffic safety.
Exist imperf. Value, set $20.

Souvenir Sheet

Voskhod 1 and Globe — A355

1964, Nov. 6 *Perf. 12x11½*

1618 A355	10fo multicolored	3.75	3.50

Russian space flight of Vladimir M. Komarov, Boris B. Yegorov and Konstantine Feoktistov.
Exists imperf. Value $32.50.

Arpad Bridge — A356

Danube Bridges, Budapest: 30f, Margaret Bridge. 60f, Chain Bridge. 1fo, Elizabeth Bridge. 1.50fo, Freedom Bridge. 2fo, Petőfi Bridge. 2.50fo, Railroad Bridge.

1964, Nov. 21 **Photo.** *Perf. 11x11½*

1619 A356	20f multi	.25	.25
1620 A356	30f multi	.25	.25
1621 A356	60f multi	.25	.25
1622 A356	1fo multi	.25	.25
1623 A356	1.50fo multi	.30	.25
1624 A356	2fo multi	.50	.25
1625 A356	2.50fo multi	.85	.40
	Nos. 1619-1625 (7)	2.65	1.90

Opening of the reconstructed Elizabeth Bridge. See No. C250.
Exist imperf. Value, set $30.

Ring-necked Pheasant and Hunting Rifle — A357

Designs: 30f, Wild boar. 40f, Gray partridges. 60f, Varying hare. 80f, Fallow deer. 1fo, Mouflon. 1.70fo, Red deer. 2fo, Great bustard. 2.50fo, Roebuck and roe deer. 3fo, Emblem of National Federation of Hungarian Hunters (antlers).

1964, Dec. 30 **Photo.** *Perf. 12x11½*

1626 A357	20f multi	.25	.25
1627 A357	30f multi	.25	.25
1628 A357	40f multi	.25	.25
1629 A357	60f multi	.25	.25
1630 A357	80f multi	.25	.25
1631 A357	1fo multi	.25	.25
1632 A357	1.70fo multi	.25	.25
1633 A357	2fo multi	.30	.25
1634 A357	2.50fo multi	.50	.30
1635 A357	3fo multi	.75	.50
	Nos. 1626-1635 (10)	3.30	2.80

Exist imperf. Value, set $30.

Castle Type of 1960

3fo, Czesznek, vert. 4fo, Eger. 5fo, Koszeg, vert.

1964 *Perf. 11½x12, 12x11½*

Size: 21x28mm, 28x21mm

1644 A293	3fo red brown	1.00	.25
1645 A293	4fo brt violet	1.50	.25
1646 A293	5fo yellow grn	1.50	.25
	Nos. 1644-1646 (3)	4.00	.75

Equestrian, Gold and Bronze Medals — A358

Medals: 30f, Women's gymnastics, silver & bronze. 50f, Small-bore rifle, gold & bronze. 60f, Water polo, gold. 70f, Shot put, bronze. 80f, Soccer, gold. 1fo, Weight lifting, 1 bronze, 2 silver. 1.20fo, Canoeing, silver. 1.40fo, Hammer throw, silver. 1.50fo, Wrestling, 2 gold. 1.70fo, Javelin, 2 silver. 3fo, Fencing, 4 gold.

1965, Feb. 20 *Perf. 12*

Medals in Gold, Silver or Bronze

1647 A358	20f lt ol grn & dk brn	.25	.25
1648 A358	30f vio & dk brn	.25	.25
1649 A358	50f olive & dk brn	.25	.25
1650 A358	60f lt bl & red brn	.25	.25
1651 A358	70f lt gray & red brn	.25	.25
1652 A358	80f yel grn & dk brn	.25	.25
1653 A358	1fo lil, vio & red brn	.25	.25
1654 A358	1.20fo lt bl, ultra & red brn	.25	.25
1655 A358	1.40fo gray & red brn	.25	.25
1656 A358	1.50fo tan, lt brn & red brn	.25	.25
1657 A358	1.70fo pink & red brn	.50	.25
1658 A358	3fo grnsh blue & brn	.70	.55
	Nos. 1647-1658 (12)	3.70	3.30

Victories by the Hungarian team in the 1964 Olympic Games, Tokyo, Oct. 10-25.
Exist imperf. Value, set $20.

Arctic Exploration A359

Designs: 30f, Radar tracking rocket, ionosphere research. 60f, Rocket and earth with reflecting layer diagrams, atmospheric research. 80f, Telescope and map of Milky Way, radio astronomy. 1.50fo, Earth, compass rose and needle, earth magnetism. 1.70fo, Weather balloon and lightning, meteorology. 2fo, Aurora australis and penguins, arctic research. 2.50fo, Satellite, earth and planets, space research. 3fo, IQSY emblem and world map. 10fo, Sun with flares and corona, snow crystals and rain.

Perf. 11½x12

1965, Mar. 25 **Photo.** **Unwmk.**

1659 A359	20f blue, org & blk	.25	.25
1660 A359	30f gray, blk & emer	.25	.25
1661 A359	60f lilac, blk & yel	.25	.25
1662 A359	80f lt grn, yel & blk	.25	.25
1663 A359	1.50fo lemon, bl & blk	.25	.25
1664 A359	1.70fo blue, pink & blk	.25	.25
1665 A359	2fo ultra, sal & blk	.25	.25
1666 A359	2.50fo org brn, yel & blk	.40	.25
1667 A359	3fo lt bl, cit & blk	.70	.40
	Nos. 1659-1667 (9)	2.85	2.40

Souvenir Sheet

1668 A359	10fo ultra, org & blk	2.50	2.50

Intl. Quiet Sun Year, 1964-65.
Exist imperf. Value: set $15; souvenir sheet $25.

Chrysanthemums A360

30f, Peonies. 50f, Carnations. 60f, Roses. 1.40fo, Lilies. 1.70fo, Anemones. 2fo, Gladioli. 2.50fo, Tulips. 3fo, Mixed flower bouquet.

1965, Apr. 4

Flowers in Natural Colors

1669 A360	20f gold & gray	.25	.25
1670 A360	30f gold & gray	.25	.25
1671 A360	50f gold & gray	.25	.25
1672 A360	60f gold & gray	.25	.25
1673 A360	1.40fo gold & gray	.25	.25
1674 A360	1.70fo gold & gray	.25	.25
1675 A360	2fo gold & gray	.25	.25
1676 A360	2.50fo gold & gray	.30	.25
1677 A360	3fo gold & gray	.60	.50
	Nos. 1669-1677 (9)	2.65	2.50

20th anniversary of liberation from the Nazis.
Exist imperf. Value, set $15.

"Head of a Combatant" by Leonardo da Vinci — A361

Perf. 11½x12

1965, May 4 **Photo.** **Unwmk.**

1678 A361	60f bister & org brn	.30	.25

Issued to publicize the First International Renaissance Conference, Budapest.
Exists imperf. Value $9.

Nikolayev, Tereshkova and View of Budapest — A362

1965, May 10 *Perf. 11*

1679 A362	1fo dull blue & brn	.40	.25

Visit of the Russian astronauts Andrian G. Nikolayev and Valentina Tereshkova (Mr. & Mrs. Nikolayev) to Budapest.
Exists imperf. Value $10.

ITU Emblem, Old and New Communication Equipment A363

1965, May 17

1680 A363	60f violet blue	.25	.25

Cent. of the ITU.
Exists imperf. Value $7.

Souvenir Sheet

Austrian WIPA Stamp of 1933 — A363a

1965, June 4 **Photo.** *Perf. 11*

1681 A363a	Sheet of 2 + 2 labels	3.50	3.50
a.	2fo gray & deep ultra	1.50	1.50

1965 Vienna Intl. Phil. Exhib. WIPA, 6/4-13.
Exists imperf. Value $30.

Marx and Lenin, Crowds with Flags — A364

1965, June 15 *Perf. 11½x12*

1682 A364	60f red, blk & yel	.25	.25

6th Conference of Ministers of Post of Socialist Countries, Peking, June 21-July 15.
Exists imperf. Value $9.

ICY Emblem and Pulley — A365

1965, June 25

1683 A365	2fo dark red	.25	.25
a.	Min. sheet of 4, perf. 11	2.25	2.25

Intl. Cooperation Year, 1965. No. 1683a contains rose red, olive, Prussian green and violet stamps.
Exists imperf. Value: single $6; sheetlet of 4 $30.

Musical Clown — A366

Circus Acts: 20f, Equestrians. 40f, Elephant. 50f, Seal balancing ball. 60f, Lions. 1fo, Wild-cat jumping through burning hoops. 1.50fo, Black leopards. 2.50fo, Juggler. 3fo, Leopard and dogs. 4fo, Bear on bicycle.

1965, July 26 Photo. *Perf. 11½x12*

1684	A366	20f	multi	.25	.25
1685	A366	30f	multi	.25	.25
1686	A366	40f	multi	.25	.25
1687	A366	50f	multi	.25	.25
1688	A366	60f	multi	.25	.25
1689	A366	1fo	multi	.25	.25
1690	A366	1.50fo	multi	.25	.25
1691	A366	2.50fo	multi	.35	.25
1692	A366	3fo	multi	.40	.25
1693	A366	4fo	multi	.50	.40
		Nos. 1684-1693 (10)		3.00	2.65

Exist imperf. Value, set $20.

Dr. Semmelweis A367

1965, Aug. 20 Photo. Unwmk.

1694 A367 60f red brown .25 .25

Dr. Ignaz Philipp Semmelweis (1818-1865), discoverer of the cause of puerperal fever and introduced antisepsis into obstetrics.

Exists imperf. Value $6.

Runner — A368

Sport: 30f, Swimmer at start. 50f, Woman diver. 60f, Gymnastics. 80f, Tennis. 1.70fo, Fencing. 2fo, Volleyball. 2.50fo, Basketball. 4fo, Water polo. 10fo, People's Stadium, Budapest, horiz.

1965, Aug. 20 *Perf. 11*

Size: 38x38mm

1695	A368	20f	multi	.25	.25
1696	A368	30f	blue & red brn	.25	.25
1697	A368	50f	bl grn, blk & red brn	.25	.25
1698	A368	60f	vio, blk & red brn	.25	.25
1699	A368	80f	tan, ol & red brn	.25	.25
1700	A368	1.70fo	multi	.25	.25
1701	A368	2fo	multi	.30	.25
1702	A368	2.50fo	gray, blk & red brn	.45	.25
1703	A368	4fo	bl, red brn & blk	.75	.45
		Nos. 1695-1703 (9)		3.00	2.45

Souvenir Sheet

Perf. 12x11½

1704 A368 10fo bis, red brn & gray 3.00 2.75

Intl. College Championships, "Universiade," Budapest. No. 1704 contains one 38x28mm stamp.

Exist imperf. Value: set $25; souvenir sheet $30.

Hemispheres and Warsaw Mermaid — A369

1965, Oct. 8 Photo. *Perf. 12x11½*

1705 A369 60f brt blue .35 .25

Sixth Congress of the World Federation of Trade Unions, Warsaw.

Exists imperf. Value $6.

Phyllocactus Hybridus A370

Flowers from Botanical Gardens: 30f, Cattleya Warszewiczii (orchid). 60f, Rebutia calliantha. 70f, Paphiopedilum hybridium. 80f, Opuntia cactus. 1fo, Laelia elegans (orchid). 1.50fo, Christmas cactus. 2fo, Bird-of-paradise flower. 2.50fo, Lithops Weberi. 3fo, Victoria water lily.

1965, Oct. 11 *Perf. 11½x12*

1706	A370	20f	gray & multi	.25	.25
1707	A370	30f	gray & multi	.25	.25
1708	A370	60f	gray & multi	.25	.25
1709	A370	70f	gray & multi	.25	.25
1710	A370	80f	gray & multi	.25	.25
1711	A370	1fo	gray & multi	.25	.25
1712	A370	1.50fo	gray & multi	.25	.25
1713	A370	2fo	gray & multi	.25	.25
1714	A370	2.50fo	gray & multi	.40	.25
1715	A370	3fo	gray & multi	.60	.35
		Nos. 1706-1715 (10)		3.00	2.60

Exist imperf. Value, set $22.

"The Black Stallion" A371

Tales from the Arabian Nights: 30f, Shahriar and Scheherazade. 50f, Sinbad's Fifth Voyage (ship). 60f, Aladdin, or The Wonderful Lamp. 80f, Harun al-Rashid. 1fo, The Flying Carpet. 1.70fo, The Fisherman and the Genie. 2fo, Ali Baba and the Forty Thieves. 3fo, Sinbad's Second Voyage (flying bird).

1965, Dec. 15 Litho. *Perf. 11½*

1716	A371	20f	multi	.25	.25
1717	A371	30f	multi	.25	.25
1718	A371	50f	multi	.25	.25
1719	A371	60f	multi	.25	.25
1720	A371	80f	multi	.25	.25
1721	A371	1fo	multi	.25	.25
1722	A371	1.70fo	multi	.35	.25
1723	A371	2fo	multi	.45	.25
1724	A371	3fo	multi	.75	.45
		Nos. 1716-1724 (9)		3.05	2.45

Exist imperf. Value, set $22.50.

Congress Emblem A372

1965, Dec. 9 Photo. *Perf. 11½x12*

1725 A372 2fo dark blue .30 .25

Fifth Congress of the International Federation of Resistance Fighters (FIR), Budapest.

Exists imperf. Value $6.

Callimorpha Dominula A373

1966, Feb. 1 Photo. *Perf. 11½x12*

Various Butterflies in Natural Colors; Black Inscription

1726	A373	20f	lt aqua	.25	.25
1727	A373	60f	pale violet	.25	.25
1728	A373	70f	tan	.25	.25
1729	A373	80f	lt ultra	.25	.25
1730	A373	1fo	gray	.25	.25
1731	A373	1.50fo	emerald	.40	.25
1732	A373	2fo	dull rose	.30	.25
1733	A373	2.50fo	bister	.45	.30
1734	A373	3fo	blue	.70	.50
		Nos. 1726-1734 (9)		3.10	2.55

Exist imperf. Value, set $30.

Lal Bahadur Shastri A374

Designs: 60f, Bela Kun. 2fo, Istvan Széchenyi and Chain Bridge.

Lithographed; Photogravure (#1736)

1966 *Perf. 11½x12, 12x11½*

1735	A374	60f	red & black	.25	.25
1736	A374	1fo	brt violet	.25	.25
1737	A374	2fo	dull yel, buff & sepia	.25	.25
		Nos. 1735-1737 (3)		.75	.75

Kun (1886-1939), communist labor leader; Shastri (1904-66), Indian Prime Minister; Count Istvan Széchenyi (1791-1860), statesman.

Exist imperf. Value, set $12.

See Nos. 1764-1765, 1769-1770.

Luna 9 — A375

Design: 3fo, Luna 9 sending signals from moon to earth, horiz.

1966, Mar. 12 Photo. *Perf. 12*

1738	A375	2fo	violet, blk & yel	.45	.25
1739	A375	3fo	lt ultra, blk & yel	.85	.60

1st soft landing on the moon by the Russian satellite Luna 9, Feb. 3, 1966.

Exist imperf. Value, set $12.

Crocus — A376

Flowers: 30f, Cyclamen. 60f, Ligularia sibirica. 1.40fo, Lilium bulbiferum. 1.50fo, Snake's head. 3fo, Snapdragon and emblem of Hungarian Nature Preservation Society.

Flowers in Natural Colors

1966, Mar. 12 *Perf. 11*

1740	A376	20f	brown	.25	.25
1741	A376	30f	aqua	.25	.25
1742	A376	60f	rose claret	.25	.25
1743	A376	1.40fo	gray	.30	.25
1744	A376	1.50fo	ultra	.45	.25
1745	A376	3fo	mag & sepia	.65	.40
		Nos. 1740-1745 (6)		2.15	1.65

Exist imperf. Value, set $20.

Birds in Natural Colors

Designs: 20f, Barn swallows. 30f, Long-tailed tits. 60f, Red crossbill and pine cone. 1.40fo, Middle spotted woodpecker. 1.50fo, Hoopoe feeding young. 3fo, Forest preserve, lapwing and emblem of National Forest Preservation Society.

1966, Apr. 16

1746	A376	20f	brt green	.25	.25
1747	A376	30f	vermilion	.25	.25
1748	A376	60f	brt green	.40	.25
1749	A376	1.40fo	vio blue	.90	.25
1750	A376	1.50fo	blue	1.00	.40
1751	A376	3fo	brn, mag & grn	1.25	.75
		Nos. 1746-1751 (6)		4.05	2.15

Nos. 1740-1751 issued to promote protection of wild flowers and birds.

Exist imperf. Value, set $30.

Locomotive, 1847; Monoplane, 1912; Autobus, 1911; Steamer, 1853, and Budapest Railroad Station, 1846 — A377

Designs: 2fo, Transportation, 1966: electric locomotive V.43; turboprop airliner IL-18; Ikarusz autobus; Diesel passenger ship, and Budapest South Railroad Station.

1966, Apr. 2 Photo. *Perf. 12*

1752	A377	1fo	yel, brn & grn	.25	.25
1753	A377	2fo	pale grn, bl & brn	.35	.25

Re-opening of the Transport Museum, Budapest.

Exist imperf. Value, set $15.

Bronze Order of Labor — A378

Decorations: 30f, Silver Order of Labor. 50f, Banner Order, third class. 60f, Gold Order of Labor. 70f, Banner Order, second class. 1fo, Red Banner Order of Labor. 1.20fo, Banner Order, first class. 2fo, Order of Merit. 2.50fo, Hero of Socialist Labor. Sizes: 20f, 30f, 60f, 1fo, 2fo, 2.50fo: 19½x38mm. 50f: 21x29mm. 70f, 25x31mm. 1.20fo: 28x38mm.

1966, Apr. 2 Unwmk. *Perf. 11*

Decorations in Original Colors

1754	A378	20f	dp ultra	.25	.25
1755	A378	30f	lt brown	.25	.25
1756	A378	50f	blue green	.25	.25
1757	A378	60f	violet	.25	.25
1758	A378	70f	carmine	.25	.25
1759	A378	1fo	violet bl	.25	.25
1760	A378	1.20fo	brt blue	.25	.25
1761	A378	2fo	olive	.25	.25
1762	A378	2.50fo	dull blue	.35	.25
			Nos. 1754-1762 (9)	2.35	2.25

Exist imperf. Value, set $15.

Portrait Type of 1966 and

Dubna Nuclear Research Institute — A379

WHO Headquarters, Geneva — A380

Designs: No. 1764, Pioneer girl. No. 1765, Tamás Esze (1666-1708), military hero. No. 1767, Old view of Buda and UNESCO emblem. No. 1768, Horse-drawn fire pump and emblem of Sopron Fire Brigade. No. 1769, Miklos Zrinyi (1508-66), hero of Turkish Wars. No. 1770, Sandor Koranyi (1866-1944), physician and scientist.

1966 Litho. *Perf. 11½x12*

1763	A379	60f	blue grn & blk	.25	.25
1764	A374	60f	multicolored	.25	.25
1765	A374	60f	brt bl & blk	.25	.25
1766	A380	2fo	lt ultra & blk	.25	.25
1767	A380	2fo	lt blue & pur	.25	.25
1768	A380	2fo	orange & blk	.25	.25
1769	A374	2fo	ol bis & brn	.25	.25
1770	A374	2fo	multicolored	.25	.25
			Nos. 1763-1770 (8)	2.00	2.00

No. 1763, 10th anniv. of the United Institute for Nuclear Research, Dubna, USSR; No. 1764, 20th anniv. of Pioneer Movement; No. 1766, Inauguration of the WHO Headquarters, Geneva; No. 1767, 20th anniv. of UNESCO and 72nd session of Executive Council, Budapest, May 30-31; No. 1768, Cent. of Volunteer Fire Brigade.

Exist imperf. Value, set $50.

Hungarian Soccer Player and Soccer Field — A381

Designs (Views of Soccer play): 30f, Montevideo 1930 (Uruguay 4, Argentina 2). 60f, Rome 1934 (Italy 2, Czechoslovakia 1). 1fo, Paris 1938 (Italy 4, Hungary 2). 1.40fo, Rio de Janeiro 1950 (Uruguay 2, Brazil 1). 1.70fo, Bern 1954 (Germany 3, Hungary 2). 2fo, Stockholm 1958 (Brazil 5, Sweden 2). 2.50fo, Santiago 1962 (Brazil 3, Czechoslovakia 1).

Souvenir Sheet

1966, May 16 Photo. *Perf. 11½x12*

1771	A381	10fo	multi	3.25	3.00

Exists imperf. Value $30.

Jules Rimet, Cup and Soccer Ball — A382

1966, June 6 *Perf. 12x11½*

1772	A382	20f	blue & multi	.25	.25
1773	A382	30f	orange & multi	.25	.25
1774	A382	60f	multi	.25	.25
1775	A382	1fo	multi	.25	.25
1776	A382	1.40fo	multi	.25	.25
1777	A382	1.70fo	multi	.25	.25
1778	A382	2fo	multi	.25	.25
1779	A382	2.50fo	multi	.60	.40
			Nos. 1772-1779,B258 (9)	3.35	2.65

World Cup Soccer Championship, Wembley, England, July 11-30.

Exist imperf. Value, set (9) $22.75.

European Red Fox — A383

Hunting Trophies: 60f, Wild boar. 70f, Wildcat. 80f, Roebuck. 1.50fo, Red deer. 2.50fo, Fallow deer. 3fo, Mouflon.

1966, July 4 Photo. *Perf. 11½x12*

Animals in Natural Colors

1780	A383	20f	gray & lt brn	.25	.25
1781	A383	60f	buff & gray	.25	.25
1782	A383	70f	lt bl & gray	.25	.25
1783	A383	80f	pale grn & yel bis	.25	.25
1784	A383	1.50fo	pale lem & brn	.35	.25
1785	A383	2.50fo	gray & brn	.60	.35
1786	A383	3fo	pale pink & gray	.95	.50
			Nos. 1780-1786 (7)	2.90	2.10

The 80f and 1.50fo were issued with and without alternating labels, which show date and place when trophy was taken; the 2.50fo was issued only with labels, 20f, 60f, 70f and 3fo without labels only.

Nos. 1780-1786 exist imperf. Value, set $25.

Discus Thrower and Matthias Cathedral A384

30f, High jump & Agriculture Museum. 40f, Javelin (women's) & Parliament. 50f, Hammer throw, Mt. Gellert & Liberty Bridge. 60f, Broad jump & view of Buda. 1fo, Shot put & Chain Bridge. 2fo, Pole vault & Stadium. 3fo, Long distance runners & Millenium Monument.

1966, Aug. 30 Photo. *Perf. 12x11½*

1787	A384	20f	grn, brn & org	.25	.25
1788	A384	30f	multi	.30	.25
1789	A384	40f	multi	.25	.25
1790	A384	50f	multi	.25	.25
1791	A384	60f	multi	.25	.25
1792	A384	1fo	multi	.25	.25
1793	A384	2fo	multi	.50	.25
1794	A384	3fo	multi	.75	.50
			Nos. 1787-1794 (8)	2.80	2.25

8th European Athletic Championships, Budapest, Aug. 30-Sept. 4. See No. C261.

Exist imperf. Value, set $18.

Girl in the Forest by Miklos Barabas A385

Paintings: 1fo, Mrs. Istvan Bitto by Miklos Barabas (1810-98). 1.50fo, Hunyadi's Farewell by Gyula Benczur (1844-1920). 1.70fo, Reading Woman by Gyula Benczur, horiz. 2fo, Woman with Fagots by Mihaly Munkacsi (1844-1900). 2.50fo, Yawning Boy by Mihaly Munkacsi. 3fo, Lady in Violet by Pal Szinyei Merse (1845-1920). 10fo, Picnic in May by Pal Szinyei Merse, horiz.

1966, Dec. 9 *Perf. 12½*

Gold Frame

1795	A385	60f	multi	.25	.25
1796	A385	1fo	multi	.25	.25
1797	A385	1.50fo	multi	.40	.25
1798	A385	1.70fo	multi	.40	.25
1799	A385	2fo	multi	.40	.25
1800	A385	2.50fo	multi	.45	.25
1801	A385	3fo	multi	.90	.80
			Nos. 1795-1801 (7)	3.05	2.30

Souvenir Sheet

1802	A385	10fo	multi	6.00	6.00

Issued to honor Hungarian painters. Size of stamp in No. 1802: 56x51mm.

Exist imperf. Value: set $20; souvenir sheet $30.

Vostoks 3 and 4 — A386

Space Craft: 60f, Gemini 6 and 7. 80f, Vostoks 5 and 6. 1fo, Gemini 9 and target rocket. 1.50fo, Alexei Leonov walking in space. 2fo, Edward White walking in space. 2.50fo, Voskhod. 3fo, Gemini 11 docking Agena target.

1966, Dec. 29 *Perf. 11*

1803	A386	20f	multi	.25	.25
1804	A386	60f	multi	.25	.25
1805	A386	80f	multi	.25	.25
1806	A386	1fo	multi	.25	.25
1807	A386	1.50fo	multi	.30	.25
1808	A386	2fo	multi	.30	.25
1809	A386	2.50fo	multi	.50	.30
1810	A386	3fo	multi	.75	.50
			Nos. 1803-1810 (8)	2.85	2.30

American and Russian twin space flights.

Exist imperf. Value, set $17.

Pal Kitaibel and Kitaibelia Vitifolia — A387

Flowers of the Carpathian Basin: 60f, Dentaria glandulosa. 1fo, Edraianthus tenuifolius. 1.50fo, Althaea pallida. 2fo, Centaurea mollis. 2.50fo, Sternbergia colchiciflora. 3fo, Iris Hungarica.

1967, Feb. 7 Photo. *Perf. 11½x12*

Flowers in Natural Colors

1811	A387	20f	rose, blk & gold	.25	.25
1812	A387	60f	green	.25	.25
1813	A387	1fo	violet gray	.25	.25
1814	A387	1.50fo	blue	.25	.25
1815	A387	2fo	light olive	.25	.25
1816	A387	2.50fo	gray grn	.45	.30
1817	A387	3fo	yellow grn	.75	.50
			Nos. 1811-1817 (7)	2.45	2.05

Pal Kitaibel (1757-1817), botanist, chemist and physician.

Exist imperf. Value, set $18.

Militiaman A388

1967, Feb. 18 Photo. *Perf. 11½x12*

1818	A388	2fo	blue gray	.40	.25

Workers' Militia, 10th anniversary.

Exists imperf. Value $3.

Mme. Du Barry and Louis XV, by Gyula Benczur (1844-1920) — A390

Painting: 10fo, Milton dictating "Paradise Lost" to his daughters, by Soma Orlai Petrics.

Souvenir Sheet

1967, May 6 Photo. *Perf. 12½*

1819	A390	10fo	multi	5.00	5.00

Exists imperf. Value $30.

1967, June 22 Gold Frame

Paintings: 60f, Franz Liszt by Mihaly Munkacsi (1844-1900). 1fo, Samuel Lanyi, self-portrait, 1840. 1.50fo, Lady in Fur-lined Jacket by Jozsef Borsos (1821-83). 1.70fo, The Lovers, by Pal Szinyei Merse (1845-1920). 2fo, Portrait of Szidonia Deak, 1861, by Alajos Gyorgyi (1821-63). 2.50fo, National Guardsman, 1848, by Jozsef Borsos.

1820	A390	60f	multi	.25	.25
1821	A390	1fo	multi	.25	.25
1822	A390	1.50fo	multi	.25	.25
1823	A390	1.70fo	multi, horiz.	.30	.25
1824	A390	2fo	multi	.35	.25

1825 A390 2.50fo multi .45 .25
1826 A390 3fo multi .75 .70
Nos. 1820-1826 (7) 2.60 2.20

Issued to honor Hungarian painters. No. 1819 commemorates AMPHILEX 67 and the F.I.P. Congress, Amsterdam, May 11-21. No. 1819 contains one 56x50mm stamp.
Exist imperf. Value, set $20.
See Nos. 1863-1870, 1900-1907, 1940-1947.

Map of Hungary, Tourist Year Emblem, Plane, Train, Car and Ship A391

1967, May 6 ***Perf. 12x11½***
1827 A391 1fo brt blue & blk .35 .25

International Tourist Year, 1967.
Exists imperf. Value $6.

S.S. Ferencz Deak, Schönbüchel Castle, Austrian Flag — A392

Designs: 60f, Diesel hydrobus, Bratislava Castle and Czechoslovak flag. 1fo, Diesel ship Hunyadi, Buda Castle and Hungarian flag. 1.50fo, Diesel tug Szekszard, Golubac Fortress and Yugoslav flag. 1.70fo, Towboat Miskolc, Vidin Fortress and Bulgarian flag. 2fo, Cargo ship Tihany, Galati shipyard and Romanian flag. 2.50fo, Hydrofoil Siraly I, Izmail Harbor and Russian flag.

1967, June 1 ***Perf. 11½x12***
Flags in National Colors

1828 A392 30f lt blue grn .50 .35
1829 A392 60f orange brn .80 .40
1830 A392 1fo grnsh blue 1.25 .40
1831 A392 1.50fo lt green 2.25 .90
1832 A392 1.70fo blue 4.00 1.25
1833 A392 2fo rose lilac 5.00 1.75
1834 A392 2.50fo lt olive grn 7.00 1.90
Nos. 1828-1834 (7) 20.80 6.95

25th session of the Danube Commission.
Exists imperf. Value, set $250.

Poodle A393

Collie — A394

1fo, Hungarian pointer. 1.40fo, Fox terriers. 2fo, Pumi, Hungarian sheep dog. 3fo, German shepherd. 4fo, Puli, Hungarian sheep dog.

1967, July 7 **Litho.** ***Perf. 12***
1835 A393 30f multi .25 .25
1836 A394 60f multi .25 .25
1837 A393 1fo multi .25 .25
1838 A394 1.40fo multi .25 .25
1839 A393 2fo multi .35 .25
1840 A394 3fo multi .60 .35
1841 A393 4fo multi .95 .60
Nos. 1835-1841 (7) 2.90 2.20

Exist imperf. Value, set $20.

Sterlets A395

Fish: 60f, Pike perch. 1fo, Carp. 1.70fo, European catfish. 2fo, Pike. 2.50fo, Rapfin.

1967, Aug. 22 **Photo.** ***Perf. 12x11½***
1842 A395 20f multi .25 .25
1843 A395 60f bister & multi .25 .25
1844 A395 1fo multi .25 .25
1845 A395 1.70fo multi .25 .25
1846 A395 2fo green & multi .30 .25
1847 A395 2.50fo gray & multi .75 .55
Nos. 1842-1847,B263 (7) 2.95 2.25

14th Cong. of the Intl. Federation of Anglers (C.I.P.S.), Dunaujvaros, Aug. 20-28.
Exist imperf. Value, set $15.

Prince Igor, by Aleksandr Borodin — A396

Opera Scenes: 30f, Freischütz, by Karl Maria von Weber. 40f, The Magic Flute, by Mozart. 60f, Prince Bluebeard's Castle, by Bela Bartok. 80f, Carmen, by Bizet, vert. 1fo, Don Carlos, by Verdi, vert. 1.70fo, Tannhäuser, by Wagner, vert. 3fo. Laszlo Hunyadi, by Ferenc Erkel, vert.

1967, Sept. 26 **Photo.** ***Perf. 12***
1848 A396 20f multi .25 .25
1849 A396 30f multi .25 .25
1850 A396 40f multi .25 .25
1851 A396 60f multi .25 .25
1852 A396 80f multi .25 .25
1853 A396 1fo multi .25 .25
1854 A396 1.70fo multi .45 .30
1855 A396 3fo multi 1.00 .70
Nos. 1848-1855 (8) 2.95 2.50

Exist imperf. Value, set $15.

Teacher, Students and Stone from Pecs University, 14th Century A397

1967, Oct. 9 **Photo.** ***Perf. 11½x12***
1856 A397 2fo gold & dp grn .40 .25

600th anniv. of higher education in Hungary; University of Pecs was founded in 1367.
Exists imperf. Value $5.

Eötvös University, and Symbols of Law and Justice — A398

1967, Oct. 12 ***Perf. 12x11½***
1857 A398 2fo slate .40 .25

300th anniv. of the School of Political Science and Law at the Lorand Eötvös University, Budapest.
Exists imperf. Value $5.

Lenin as Teacher, by Sandor Legrady A399

Paintings by Sandor Legrady: 1fo, Lenin. 3fo, Lenin, Revolutionaries.

1967, Oct. 31 ***Perf. 12½***
1858 A399 60f gold & multi .25 .25
1859 A399 1fo gold & multi .25 .25
1860 A399 3fo gold & multi .60 .25
Nos. 1858-1860 (3) 1.10 .75

50th anniv. of the Russian October Revolution.
Exist imperf. Value, set $8.

Venera 4 Landing on Venus — A400

1967, Nov. 6 ***Perf. 12***
1861 A400 5fo gold & multi 1.25 1.10

Landing of the Russian automatic space station Venera 4 on the planet Venus.
Exists imperf. Value $9.

Souvenir Sheet

19th Century Mail Coach and Post Horn — A401

Photogravure; Gold Impressed
1967, Nov. 21 ***Perf. 12½***
1862 A401 10fo multicolored 2.50 2.50

Hungarian Postal Administration, cent.
Exists imperf. Value $35.

Painting Type of 1967

Paintings: 60f, Brother and Sister by Adolf Fenyes (1867-1945). 1fo, Wrestling Boys by Oszkar Glatz (1872-1958). 1.50fo, "October" by Karoly Ferenczy (1862-1917). 1.70fo, Women at the River Bank by Istvan Szönyi (1894-1960), horiz. 2fo, Godfather's Breakfast by Istvan Csok (1865-1961). 2.50fo, "Eviction Notice" by Gyula Derkovits (1894-1934). 3fo, Self-portrait by M. T. Csontvary Kosztka (1853-1919). 10fo, The Apple Pickers by Bela Uitz (1887-).

1967, Dec. 21 **Photo.** ***Perf. 12½***
1863 A390 60f multi .25 .25
1864 A390 1fo multi .25 .25
1865 A390 1.50fo multi .25 .25
1866 A390 1.70fo multi .25 .25
1867 A390 2fo multi .30 .25
1868 A390 2.50fo multi .40 .25
1869 A390 3fo multi .70 .45
Nos. 1863-1869 (7) 2.40 1.95

Miniature Sheet

1870 A390 10fo multi 2.75 2.50

Issued to honor Hungarian painters.
Exists imperf. Value: set $15; souvenir sheet $22.

Biathlon — A402

Sport (Olympic Rings and): 60f, Figure skating, pair. 1fo, Bobsledding. 1.40fo, Slalom. 1.70fo, Women's figure skating. 2fo, Speed skating. 3fo, Ski jump. 10fo, Ice hockey.

1967, Dec. 30 **Photo.** ***Perf. 12½***
Souvenir Sheet

1871 A402 10fo lilac & multi 2.50 2.00

Exists imperf. Value $18.

1968, Jan. 29 ***Perf. 11***
1872 A402 30f multi .25 .25
1873 A402 60f multi .25 .25
1874 A402 1fo multi .25 .25
1875 A402 1.40fo rose & multi .25 .25
1876 A402 1.70fo multi .25 .25
1877 A402 2fo multi .30 .25
1878 A402 3fo ol & multi .80 .30
Nos. 1872-1878,B264 (8) 3.05 2.10

10th Winter Olympic Games, Grenoble, France, Feb. 6-18. No. 1871 contains one 43x43mm stamp.
Exist imperf. Value, set (8) $15.

A403

Design: 2fo, Kando Statue, Miskolc, Kando Locomotive and Map of Hungary.

1968, Mar. 30 **Photo.** ***Perf. 11½x12***
1879 A403 2fo dark blue .40 .25

Kalman Kando (1869-1931), engineer, inventor of Kando locomotive.
Exists imperf. Value $4.

Domestic Cat A404

60f, Cream Persian. 1fo, Smoky Persian. 1.20fo, Domestic kitten. 1.50fo, White Persian. 2fo, Brown-striped Persian. 2.50fo, Siamese. 5fo, Blue Persian.

1968, Mar. 30 ***Perf. 11***
1880 A404 20f shown .25 .25
1881 A404 60f multi .25 .25
1882 A404 1fo multi .25 .25
1883 A404 1.20fo multi .25 .25
1884 A404 1.50fo multi .30 .25
1885 A404 2fo multi .30 .25
1886 A404 2.50fo multi .60 .25
1887 A404 5fo multi 1.25 .55
Nos. 1880-1887 (8) 3.45 2.30

Exist imperf. Value, set $20.

Zoltan Kodaly, by Sandor Légrády — A405

1968, Apr. 17 Photo. *Perf. 12½*

1888	A405	5fo gold & multi	1.00	.75

Kodaly (1882-1967), composer & musicologist.
Exists imperf. Value $6.

White Storks — A406

Birds: 50f, Golden orioles. 60f, Imperial eagle. 1fo, Red-footed falcons. 1.20fo, Scops owl. 1.50fo, Great bustard. 2fo, European bee-eaters. 2.50fo, Graylag goose.

1968, Apr. 25

Birds in Natural Colors

1889	A406	20f	ver & lt ultra	.25	.25
1890	A406	50f	ver & gray	.25	.25
1891	A406	60f	ver & lt bl	.25	.25
1892	A406	1fo	ver & yel grn	.25	.25
1893	A406	1.20fo	ver & brt grn	.25	.25
1894	A406	1.50fo	ver & lt vio	.25	.25
1895	A406	2fo	ver & pale lil	.55	.30
1896	A406	2.50fo	ver & bl grn	1.10	.50
	Nos. 1889-1896 (8)			3.15	2.30

International Bird Preservation Congress.
Exists imperf. Value, set $25.

City Hall, Kecskemét — A407

1968, Apr. 25 *Perf. 12x11½*

1897	A407	2fo brown orange	.30	.25

600th anniversary of Kecskemét.
Exists imperf. Value $4.

Marx Type of 1953

1968, May 5 Engr. *Perf. 12*

1898	A230	1fo claret	.25	.25

Karl Marx (1818-1883).
Exists imperf. Value $5.

Student and Agricultural College — A408

1968, May 24 Photo. *Perf. 12x11½*

1899	A408	2fo dk olive green	.30	.25

150th anniv. of the founding of the Agricultural College at Mosonmagyaróvár.
Exists imperf. Value $4.

Painting Type of 1967

Paintings: 40f, Girl with Pitcher, by Goya (1746-1828). 60f, Head of an Apostle, by El Greco (c. 1541-1614). 1fo, Boy with Apple Basket and Dogs, by Pedro Nunez (1639-1700), horiz. 1.50fo, Mary Magdalene, by El Greco. 2.50fo, The Breakfast, by Velazquez (1599-1660), horiz. 4fo, The Virgin from The Holy Family, by El Greco. 5fo, The Knife Grinder, by Goya. 10fo, Portrait of a Girl, by Palma Vecchio (1480-1528).

1968, May 30 *Perf. 12½*

1900	A390	40f multi	.25	.25
1901	A390	60f multi	.25	.25
1902	A390	1fo multi	.25	.25
1903	A390	1.50fo multi	.25	.25
1904	A390	2.50fo multi	.50	.25
1905	A390	4fo multi	.70	.25
1906	A390	5fo multi	1.00	.35
	Nos. 1900-1906 (7)		3.20	1.85

Souvenir Sheet

1907	A390	10fo multi	3.25	3.00

Issued to publicize art treasures in the Budapest Museum of Fine Arts and to publicize an art exhibition.
Exist imperf. Values: set of 7, $15; souvenir sheet $22.50.

Lake Balaton at Badacsony — A409

Views on Lake Balaton: 40f like 20f. 60f, Tihanyi Peninsula. 1fo, Sailboats at Almadi. 2fo, Szigliget Bay.

1968-69 Litho. *Perf. 12*

1908	A409	20f multi	.25	.25
1908A	A409	40f multi ('69)	.25	.25
b.		Bklt. pane, #1909, 1911, 2 each #1908A, 1910	.75	
c.		Bklt. pane, #1909-1911, 3 #1908A	.75	
d.		Bklt. pane, #1911, 3 #1908A, 2 #1909	.75	
1909	A409	60f multi	.25	.25
1910	A409	1fo multi	.25	.25
1911	A409	2fo multi	.45	.25
	Nos. 1908-1911 (5)		1.45	1.25

Exist imperf. Value, set $20.

Locomotive, Type 424 — A410

1968, July 14 Photo. *Perf. 12x11½*

1912	A410	2fo gold, lt bl & slate	.60	.25

Centenary of the Hungarian State Railroad.
Exists imperf. Value $8.

Horses Grazing — A411

Designs: 40f, Horses in storm. 60f, Horse race on the steppe. 80f, Horsedrawn sleigh. 1fo, Four-in-hand and rainbow. 1.40fo, Farm wagon drawn by 7 horses. 2fo, One rider driving five horses. 2.50fo, Campfire on the range. 4fo, Coach with 5 horses.

1968, July 25 *Perf. 11*

1913	A411	30f multi	.25	.25
1914	A411	40f multi	.25	.25
1915	A411	60f multi	.25	.25
1916	A411	80f multi	.25	.25
1917	A411	1fo multi	.25	.25
1918	A411	1.40fo multi	.30	.25
1919	A411	2fo multi	.30	.25
1920	A411	2.50fo multi	.40	.25
1921	A411	4fo multi	.75	.45
	Nos. 1913-1921 (9)		3.00	2.45

Horse breeding on the Hungarian steppe (Puszta).

Exist imperf. Value, set $40.

Mihály Tompa (1817-68), Poet — A412

1968, July 30 Photo. *Perf. 12x11½*

1922	A412	60f blue black	.25	.25

Exists imperf. Value $4.

Festival Emblem, Bulgarian and Hungarian National Costumes — A413

1968, Aug. 3 Litho. *Perf. 12*

1923	A413	60f multicolored	.30	.25

Issued to publicize the 9th Youth Festival for Peace and Friendship, Sofia, Bulgaria.
Exists imperf. Value $5.

Souvenir Sheet

Runners and Aztec Calendar Stone — A414

1968, Aug. 21 Photo. *Perf. 12½*

1924	A414	10fo multicolored	2.50	2.25

19th Olympic Games, Mexico City, 10/12-27.
Exists imperf. Value $20.

Scientific Society Emblem — A415

Perf. 12½x11½

1968, Dec. 10 Photo.

1925	A415	2fo brt blue & blk	.35	.25

Society for the Popularization of Scientific Knowledge.
Exists imperf. Value $4.

Hesperis — A416

Garden Flowers: 60f, Pansy. 80f, Zinnias. 1fo, Morning-glory. 1.40fo, Petunia. 1.50fo, Portulaca. 2fo, Michaelmas daisies. 2.50fo, Dahlia.

1968, Oct. 29 *Perf. 11½x12*

Flowers in Natural Colors

1926	A416	20f	gray	.25	.25
1927	A416	60f	lt green	.25	.25
1928	A416	80f	bluish lilac	.25	.25
1929	A416	1fo	buff	.25	.25
1930	A416	1.40fo	lt grnsh bl	.25	.25
1931	A416	1.50fo	lt blue	.25	.25
1932	A416	2fo	pale pink	.30	.25
1933	A416	2.50fo	lt blue	.60	.40
	Nos. 1926-1933 (8)			2.40	2.15

Exist imperf. Value, set $15.

Pioneers Saluting Communist Party — A417

Children's Paintings: 60f, Four pioneers holding banner saluting Communist Party. 1fo, Pioneer camp.

1968, Nov. 16 Photo. *Perf. 12x11½*

1934	A417	40f buff & multi	.25	.25
1935	A417	60f buff & multi	.25	.25
1936	A417	1fo buff & multi	.30	.25
	Nos. 1934-1936 (3)		.80	.75

50th anniv. of the Communist Party of Hungary. The designs are from a competition among elementary school children.
Exist imperf. Value, set $15.

Workers, Monument by Z. Olcsai-Kiss — A418

Design: 1fo, "Workers of the World Unite!" poster by N. Por, vert.

Perf. 11½x12, 12x11½

1968, Nov. 24 Photo.

1937	A418	1fo gold, red, & blk	.25	.25
1938	A418	2fo gold & multi	.25	.25

Communist Party of Hungary, 50th anniv.
Exist imperf. Value, set $15.

Human Rights Flame — A419

1968, Dec. 10 *Perf. 12½x11½*

1939	A419	1fo dark red brown	.40	.25

International Human Rights Year.
Exists imperf. Value $4.

Painting Type of 1967

Italian Paintings: 40f, Esterhazy Madonna, by Raphael. 60f, The Annunciation, by Bernardo Strozzi. 1fo, Portrait of a Young Man, by Raphael. 1.50fo, The Three Graces, by Battista Naldini. 2.50fo, Portrait of a Man, by Sebastiano del Piombo. 4fo, The Doge Marcantonio Trevisani, by Titian. 5fo, Venus, Cupid and Jealousy, by Angelo Bronzino. 10fo, Bathsheba Bathing, by Sebastiano Ricci, horiz.

1968, Dec. 10 Photo. *Perf. 12½*

1940 A390 40f multi .25 .25
1941 A390 60f multi .25 .25
1942 A390 1fo multi .25 .25
1943 A390 1.50fo multi .25 .25
1944 A390 2.50fo multi .30 .25
1945 A390 4fo multi .60 .25
1946 A390 5fo multi .80 .35
Nos. 1940-1946 (7) 2.70 1.85

Miniature Sheet

Perf. 11

1947 A390 10fo multi 2.75 2.50

Issued to publicize art treasures in the Budapest Museum of Fine Arts. No. 1947 contains one stamp size of stamp: 62x45mm.

Exist imperf. Value: set $18; souvenir sheet $22.

1869 and 1969 Emblems of Athenaeum Press — A420

1969, Jan. 27 *Perf. 12½x11½*

1948 A420 2fo gold, gray, lt bl & blk .40 .25

Centenary of Athenaeum Press, Budapest.

Exists imperf. Value $3.50.

Endre Ady (1877-1919), Lyric Poet — A421

1969, Jan. 27 *Perf. 11½x12*

1949 A421 1fo multicolored .40 .25

Exists imperf. Value $4.

Olympic Medal and Women's Javelin — A422

Olympic Medal and: 60f, Canadian singles (canoeing). 1fo, Soccer. 1.20fo, Hammer throw. 2fo, Fencing. 3fo, Greco-Roman Wrestling. 4fo, Kayak single. 5fo, Equestrian. 10fo, Head of Mercury by Praxiteles and Olympic torch.

1969, Mar. 7 Photo. *Perf. 12*

1950 A422 40f multi .25 .25
1951 A422 60f multi .25 .25
1952 A422 1fo multi .25 .25
1953 A422 1.20fo multi .25 .25
1954 A422 2fo multi .25 .25
1955 A422 3fo multi .30 .25
1956 A422 4fo multi .70 .25
1957 A422 5fo multi .75 .45
Nos. 1950-1957 (8) 3.00 2.20

Souvenir Sheet

Litho. *Perf. 11½*

1958 A422 10fo multi 2.75 2.75

Victories won by the Hungarian team in the 1968 Olympic Games, Mexico City, Oct. 12-27, 1968. No. 1958 contains one 45x33mm stamp.

Exist imperf. Value: set $20; souvenir sheet $22.

1919 Revolutionary Poster — A423

Revolutionary Posters: 60f, Lenin. 1fo, Man breaking chains. 2fo, Industrial worker looking at family and farm. 3fo, Militia recruiter. 10fo, Shouting revolutionist with red banner, horiz.

1969, Mar. 21 Photo. *Perf. 11½x12*

Gold Frame

1960 A423 40f red & black .25 .25
1961 A423 60f red & black .25 .25
1962 A423 1fo red & black .25 .25
1963 A423 2fo black, gray & red .25 .25
1964 A423 3fo multicolored .35 .25
Nos. 1960-1964 (5) 1.35 1.25

Souvenir Sheet

Perf. 12½

1965 A423 10fo red, gray & blk 1.50 1.50

50th anniv. of the proclamation of the Hungarian Soviet Republic.

Exist imperf. Values: set $15; souvenir sheet $15.

The 60f red lilac with 4-line black printing on back was given away by the Hungarian PO. Value $1, mint or canceled.

No. 1965 contains one 51x38½mm stamp.

Jersey Tiger A424

Butterflies and Moths: 60f, Eyed hawk moth. 80f, Painted lady. 1fo, Tiger moth. 1.20fo, Small fire moth. 2fo, Large blue. 3fo, Belted oak egger. 4fo, Peacock.

1969, Apr. 15 Litho. *Perf. 12*

1966 A424 40f shown .25 .25
1967 A424 60f multi .25 .25
1968 A424 80f multi .25 .25
1969 A424 1fo multi .25 .25
1970 A424 1.20fo multi .25 .25
1971 A424 2fo multi .35 .25
1972 A424 3fo multi .65 .45
1973 A424 4fo multi .90 .50
Nos. 1966-1973 (8) 3.15 2.45

Exist imperf. Value, set $20.

ILO Emblem A426

1969, May 22 Photo. *Perf. 12x11½*

1974 A426 1fo car lake & lake .40 .25

50th anniv. of the ILO.

Exist imperf. Value $5.

Black Pigs, by Paul Gauguin A427

French Paintings: 60f, These Women, by Toulouse-Lautrec, horiz. 1fo, Venus in the Clouds, by Simon Vouet. 2fo, Lady with Fan, by Edouard Manet, horiz. 3fo, La Petra Camara (dancer), by Théodore Chassériau. 4fo, The Cowherd, by Constant Troyon, horiz. 5fo, The Wrestlers, by Gustave Courbet. 10fo, Pomona, by Nicolas Fouché.

1969, May 28 Photo. *Perf. 12½*

1975 A427 40f multicolored .25 .25
1976 A427 60f multicolored .25 .25
1977 A427 1fo multicolored .25 .25
1978 A427 2fo multicolored .30 .25
1979 A427 3fo multicolored .50 .25
1980 A427 4fo multicolored .70 .25
1981 A427 5fo multicolored 1.00 .50
Nos. 1975-1981 (7) 3.25 2.00

Miniature Sheet

1982 A427 10fo multicolored 4.00 4.00

Art treasures in the Budapest Museum of Fine Arts. No. 1982 contains one 40x62mm stamp.

Exist imperf. Value: set $17.50; souvenir sheet $17.50.

Hotel Budapest — A428

1969, May Photo. *Perf. 11*

1983 A428 1fo brown .30 .25

Exists imperf. Value $15.

Budapest Post Office 100 — A429

Coil Stamps

1970, Aug. 3 *Perf. 14*

1983A A429 40f gray .40 .25
1983B A428 1fo brown .50 .25

Black control number on back of every 5th stamp.

Arms and Buildings of Vac A430

Towns of the Danube Bend: 1fo, Szentendre. 1.20fo, Visegrad. 3fo, Esztergom.

1969, June 9 Litho. *Perf. 12*

1984 A430 40f multi .25 .25
a. Bklt. pane, #1985, 1987, 4 #1984 2.75
b. Bklt. pane, #1986, 3 #1984, 2 #1985 2.75
1985 A430 1fo multi .25 .25
1986 A430 1.20fo multi .25 .25
1987 A430 3fo multi .30 .25
Nos. 1984-1987 (4) 1.05 1.00

Stamps in booklet panes Nos. 1984a-1984b come in two arrangements.

Exist imperf. Value, set $15.

"PAX" and Men Holding Hands — A431

1969, June 17 Photo. *Perf. 11½x12*

1988 A431 1fo lt bl, dk bl & gold .30 .25

20th anniversary of Peace Movement.

Exists imperf. Value $5.

The Scholar, by Rembrandt A432

1969, Sept. 15 *Perf. 11½x12*

1989 A432 1fo sepia .50 .25

Issued to publicize the 22nd International Congress of Art Historians, Budapest.

Exists imperf. Value $5.

Fossilized Zelkova Leaves — A433

Designs: 60f, Greenockit calcite sphalerite crystals. 1fo, Fossilized fish, clupea hungarica. 1.20fo, Quartz crystals. 2fo, Ammonite. 3fo, Copper. 4fo, Fossilized turtle, placochelys placodonta. 5fo, Cuprite crystals.

1969, Sept. 21 Photo.

1990 A433 40f red, gray & sep .25 .25
1991 A433 60f violet, yel & blk .25 .25
1992 A433 1fo blue, tan & brn .25 .25
1993 A433 1.20fo emer, gray & lil .25 .25
1994 A433 2fo ol, tan & brn .25 .25
1995 A433 3fo org, brt & dk grn .30 .25
1996 A433 4fo dull blk grn, brn & blk .55 .30
1997 A433 5fo multicolored .90 .40
Nos. 1990-1997 (8) 3.00 2.20

Centenary of the Hungarian State Institute of Geology.

Exists imperf. Value, set $18.

Steeplechase — A434

Designs: 60f, Fencing. 1fo, Pistol shooting. 2fo, Swimmers at start. 3fo, Relay race. 5fo, Pentathlon.

1969, Sept. 15 Photo. *Perf. 12x11½*

1998 A434 40f blue & multi .25 .25
1999 A434 60f multi .25 .25
2000 A434 1fo multi .25 .25
2001 A434 2fo violet & multi .30 .25
2002 A434 3fo lemon & multi .50 .30
2003 A434 5fo bluish grn, gold & dk red .75 .50
Nos. 1998-2003 (6) 2.30 1.80

Hungarian Pentathlon Championships.

Exists imperf. Value, set $15.

First Hungarian Postal Card — A435

1969, Oct. 1

2004	A435	60f ver & ocher	.30	.25

Centenary of the postal card. Hungary and Austria both issued cards in 1869.
Exists imperf. Value $5.

Mahatma Gandhi — A436

1969, Oct. 1 ***Perf. 11½x12***

2005	A436	5fo green & multi	1.50	.70

Mohandas K. Gandhi (1869-1948), leader in India's fight for independence.
Exists imperf. Value $8.

World Trade Union Emblem A437

1969, Oct. 17 Photo. ***Perf. 12x11½***

2006	A437	2fo fawn & dk blue	.30	.25

Issued to publicize the 7th Congress of the World Federation of Trade Unions.
Exists imperf. Value $5.

Janos Balogh Nagy, Self-portrait A438

1969, Oct. 17 ***Perf. 11½x12***

2007	A438	5fo gold & multi	1.50	.80

Janos Balogh Nagy (1874-1919), painter.
Exists imperf. Value $7.50.

St. John the Evangelist, by Anthony Van Dyck — A439

Dutch Paintings: 60f, Three Fruit Pickers (by Pieter de Molyn?). 1fo, Boy Lighting Pipe, by Hendrick Terbrugghen. 2fo, The Feast, by Jan Steen. 3fo, Woman Reading Letter, by Pieter de Hooch. 4fo, The Fiddler, by Dirk Hals. 5fo, Portrait of Jan Asselyn, by Frans Hals. 10fo, Mucius Scaevola before Porsena, by Rubens and Van Dyck.

1969-70 Photo. ***Perf. 12½***

2008	A439	40f multi	.25	.25
2009	A439	60f multi	.25	.25
2010	A439	1fo multi	.25	.25
2011	A439	2fo multi	.25	.25
2012	A439	3fo multi	.40	.25
2013	A439	4fo multi	.50	.30
2014	A439	5fo multi	1.00	.50
		Nos. 2008-2014 (7)	2.90	2.05

Miniature Sheet

2015	A439	10fo multi	3.25	3.25

Treasures in the Museum of Fine Arts, Budapest and the Museum in Eger.
Exist imperf. Value: set $15; souvenir sheet $25.
Issued: 40f-5fo, 12/2/69; 10fo, 1/70.

Kiskunfelegyhaza Circling Pigeon — A440

1969, Dec. 12 Photo. ***Perf. 11½x12***

2016	A440	1fo multicolored	.40	.25

Issued to publicize the International Pigeon Show, Budapest, Dec. 1969.
Exists imperf. Value $5.

Subway A441

1970, Apr. 3 Photo. ***Perf. 12***

2017	A441	1fo blk, lt grn & ultra	.40	.25

Opening of new Budapest subway.
Exists imperf. Value $7.50.

Souvenir Sheet

Panoramic View of Budapest 1945 and 1970, and Soviet Cenotaph — A442

1970, Apr. 3 ***Perf. 12x11½***

2018	A442	Sheet of 2	2.75	2.50
a.		5fo "1945"	1.00	1.00
b.		5fo "1970"	1.00	1.00

25th anniv. of the liberation of Budapest.
Exists imperf. Value $25.

Cloud Formation, Satellite, Earth and Receiving Station — A443

1970, Apr. 8 Litho. ***Perf. 12***

2019	A443	1fo dk bl, yel & blk	.30	.25

Centenary of the Hungarian Meteorological Service.
Exists imperf. Value $5.

Lenin Statue, Budapest — A444

Design: 2fo, Lenin portrait.

1970, Apr. 22 Photo. ***Perf. 11***

2020	A444	1fo gold & multi	.25	.25
2021	A444	2fo gold & multi	.25	.25

Lenin (1870-1924), Russian communist leader.
Exist imperf. Value, set $10.

Franz Lehar and "Giuditta" Music — A445

1970, Apr. 30 Photo. ***Perf. 12***

2022	A445	2fo multicolored	.50	.25

Franz Lehar (1870-1948), composer.
Exists imperf. Value $7.50.

Samson and Delilah, by Michele Rocca A446

Paintings: 60f, Joseph Telling Dream, by Giovanni Battista Langetti. 1fo, Clio, by Pierre Mignard. 1.50fo, Venus and Satyr, by Sebastiano Ricci, horiz. 2.50fo, Andromeda, by Francesco Furini. 4fo, Venus, Adonis and Cupid, by Luca Giordano. 5fo, Allegorical Feast, by Corrado Giaquinto. 10fo, Diana and Callisto, by Abraham Janssens, horiz.

1970, June 2 Photo. ***Perf. 12½***

2023	A446	40f gold & multi	.25	.25
2024	A446	60f gold & multi	.25	.25
2025	A446	1fo gold & multi	.25	.25
2026	A446	1.50fo gold & multi	.25	.25
2027	A446	2.50fo gold & multi	.30	.25
2028	A446	4fo gold & multi	.60	.30
2029	A446	5fo gold & multi	.75	.50
		Nos. 2023-2029 (7)	2.65	2.05

Miniature Sheet

Perf. 11

2030	A446	10fo gold & multi	3.50	3.00

No. 2030 contains one 63x46mm horizontal stamp.
Exist imperf. Values: set $15; souvenir sheet $20.

Beethoven Statue, by Janos Pasztor, at Martonvasar A447

1970, June 27 Litho. ***Perf. 12***

2031	A447	1fo plum, gray grn & org yel	.75	.25

Ludwig van Beethoven, composer. The music in the design is from his Sonatina No. 1.
Exists imperf. Value $7.50.

Foundryman A448

1970, July 28 Litho. ***Perf. 12***

2032	A448	1fo multicolored	.40	.25

200th anniversary of the first Hungarian steel foundry at Diosgyor, now the Lenin Metallurgical Works.
Exists imperf. Value $5.

King Stephen I — A449

1970, Aug. 19 Photo. ***Perf. 11½x12***

2033	A449	3fo multicolored	1.00	.50

Millenary of the birth of Saint Stephen, first King of Hungary.
Exists imperf. Value $5.

Women's Four on Lake Tata and Tata Castle — A450

1970, Aug. 19 Litho. ***Perf. 12***

2034	A450	1fo multicolored	.35	.25

17th European Women's Rowing Championships, Lake Tata.
Exists imperf. Value $5.

Mother Giving Bread to her Children, FAO Emblem — A451

1970, Sept. 21 Litho. ***Perf. 12***

2035	A451	1fo lt blue & multi	.40	.25

7th European Regional Cong. of the UNFAO, Budapest, Sept. 21-25.
Exists imperf. Value $5.

Boxing and Olympic Rings A452

Designs (Olympic Rings and): 60f, Canoeing. 1fo, Fencing. 1.50fo, Water polo. 2fo, Woman gymnast. 2.50fo, Hammer throwing. 3fo, Wrestling. 5fo, Swimming, butterfly stroke.

1970, Sept. 26 Photo. *Perf. 11*

2036	A452	40f	lilac & multi	.25	.25
2037	A452	60f	sky blue & multi	.25	.25
2038	A452	1fo	orange & multi	.25	.25
2039	A452	1.50fo	multi	.25	.25
2040	A452	2fo	multi	.25	.25
2041	A452	2.50fo	multi	.30	.25
2042	A452	3fo	multi	.40	.25
2043	A452	5fo	multi	.60	.40
			Nos. 2036-2043 (8)	2.55	2.15

75th anniv. of the Hungarian Olympic Committee. The 5fo also publicizes the 1972 Olympic Games in Munich.
Exist imperf. Value, set $15.

Flame and Family A453

1970, Sept. 28 Litho. *Perf. 12*

2044	A453	1fo	ultra, org & emer	.40	.25

5th Education Congress, Budapest.
Exists imperf. Value $5.

Chalice, by Benedek Suky, 1440 — A454

Hungarian Goldsmiths' Art: 60f, Altar burette, 1500. 1fo, Nadasdy goblet, 16th century. 1.50fo, Coconut goblet, 1600. 2fo, Silver tankard, by Mihaly Toldalaghy, 1623. 2.50fo, Communion cup of Gyorgy Rakoczy I, 1670. 3fo, Tankard, 1690. 4fo, Bell-flower cup, 1710.

1970, Oct. Photo. *Perf. 12*

2045	A454	40f	gold & multi	.25	.25
2046	A454	60f	gold & multi	.25	.25
2047	A454	1fo	gold & multi	.30	.25
2048	A454	1.50fo	gold & multi	.35	.25
2049	A454	2fo	gold & multi	.45	.25
2050	A454	2.50fo	gold & multi	.55	.30
2051	A454	3fo	gold & multi	.90	.35
2052	A454	4fo	gold & multi	1.10	.50
			Nos. 2045-2052 (8)	4.15	2.40

Exist imperf. Value, set $15.

Virgin and Child, by Giampietrino — A455

Paintings from Christian Museum, Esztergom: 60f, "Love" (woman with 3 children), by Gregorio Lazzarini. 1fo, Legend of St. Catherine, by Master of Bat. 1.50fo, Adoration of the Shepherds, by Francesco Fontebasso, horiz. 2.50fo, Adoration of the Kings, by Master of Aranyosmarot. 4fo, Temptation of St. Anthony the Hermit, by Jan de Cock. 5fo, St. Sebastian, by Marco Palmezzano. 10fo, Lady with the Unicorn, by Painter of Lombardy.

1970, Dec. 7 Photo. *Perf. 12½*

2053	A455	40f	silver & multi	.25	.25
2054	A455	60f	silver & multi	.25	.25
2055	A455	1fo	silver & multi	.25	.25
2056	A455	1.50fo	silver & multi	.25	.25
2057	A455	2.50fo	silver & multi	.40	.25
2058	A455	4fo	silver & multi	.65	.30
2059	A455	5fo	silver & multi	.90	.40
			Nos. 2053-2059 (7)	2.95	1.95

Souvenir Sheet

2060	A455	10fo	silver & multi	3.00	2.75

No. 2060 contains one 50½x56mm stamp.
Exist imperf. Values: set $15; souvenir sheet $17.50.

Monument to Hungarian Martyrs, by A. Makrisz — A456

1970, Dec. 30 Photo. *Perf. 12x11½*

2061	A456	1fo	ultra & sepia	.40	.25

The 25th anniversary of the liberation of the concentration camps at Auschwitz, Mauthausen and Dachau.
Exists imperf. Value $5.

"Souvenir Sheets"

Beginning in 1971, the government stamp agency, as well as a number of other state sanctioned organizations, have created souvenir sheets that do not have postal validity. These are not listed in this catalogue.

Marseillaise, by Francois Rude — A457

1971, Mar. 18 Litho. *Perf. 12*

2062	A457	3fo	bister & green	.40	.25

Centenary of the Paris Commune.
Exists imperf. Value $5.

Béla Bartók (1881-1945), Composer A458

Design: No. 2064, András L. Achim (1871-1911), peasant leader.

1971

2063	A458	1fo	gray & dk car	.55	.25
2064	A458	1fo	gray & green	.25	.25

Issued: No. 2063, Mar. 25; No. 2064, Apr. 17.
Exist imperf. Value, set $10.

Györ Castle, 1594 A459

1971, Mar. 27

2065	A459	2fo	lt blue & multi	.40	.25

700th anniversary of Györ.
Exists imperf. Value $5.

Bison Hunt — A460

Designs: 60f, Wild boar hunt. 80f, Deer hunt. 1fo, Falconry. 1.20fo, Felled stag and dogs. 2fo, Bustards. 3fo, Net fishing. 4fo, Angling.

1971, May Photo. *Perf. 12*

2066	A460	40f	ver & multi	.25	.25
2067	A460	60f	plum & multi	.25	.25
2068	A460	80f	multi	.25	.25
2069	A460	1fo	lilac & multi	.25	.25
2070	A460	1.20fo	multi	.25	.25
2071	A460	2fo	multi	.25	.25
2072	A460	3fo	multi	.40	.30
2073	A460	4fo	green & multi	.55	.40
			Nos. 2066-2073 (8)	2.45	2.20

World Hunting Exhibition, Budapest, Aug. 27-30. See No. C313.
Exist imperf. Value, set $20.

Souvenir Sheet

Portrait of a Man, by Dürer — A461

1971, May 21 *Perf. 12½*

2074	A461	10fo	gold & multi	2.75	2.50

Albrecht Dürer (1471-1528), German painter and etcher.
Exists imperf. Value $20.

Carnation and Pioneers' Emblem — A462

1971, June 2 Photo. *Perf. 12*

2075	A462	1fo	dark red & multi	.40	.25

Hungarian Pioneers' Organization, 25th anniv.
Exists imperf. Value $5.

FIR Emblem, Resistance Fighters — A463

1971, July 3

2076	A463	1fo	brown & multi	.40	.25

International Federation of Resistance Fighters (FIR), 20th anniversary.
Exists imperf. Value $5.

Walking in Garden, Tokyo School A464

Japanese Prints from Museum of East Asian Art, Budapest: 60f, Geisha in Boat, by Yeishi (1756-1829). 1fo, Woman with Scroll, by Yeishi. 1.50fo, Courtesans, by Kiyonaga (1752-1815). 2fo, Awabi Fisher Women, by Utamaro (1753-1806). 2.50fo, Seated Courtesan, by Harunobu (1725-1770). 3fo, Peasant Woman Carrying Fagots, by Hokusai (1760-1849). 4fo, Women and Girls Walking, by Yeishi.

1971, July 9 *Perf. 12½*

2077	A464	40f	gold & multi	.25	.25
2078	A464	60f	gold & multi	.25	.25
2079	A464	1fo	gold & multi	.25	.25
2080	A464	1.50fo	gold & multi	.25	.25
2081	A464	2fo	gold & multi	.25	.25
2082	A464	2.50fo	gold & multi	.30	.25
2083	A464	3fo	gold & multi	.50	.25
2084	A464	4fo	gold & multi	.75	.45
			Nos. 2077-2084 (8)	2.80	2.20

Exist imperf. Value, set $15.

Locomotive, Map of Rail System and Danube — A465

1971, July 15 **Litho.** *Perf. 12*

2086	A465	1fo	multi	.40	.25

125th anniversary of first Hungarian railroad between Pest and Vac.
Exists imperf. Value $7.50.

Griffin Holding Ink Balls A466

1971, Sept. 11 **Photo.** *Perf. 12x11½*

2087	A466	1fo	multicolored	.75	.75

Centenary of stamp printing in Hungary. Printed se-tenant with 2 labels showing printing presses of 1871 and 1971 and Hungary Nos. P1 and 1171. Value unused, $1.
Exists imperf. Value, strip $12.50.

OIJ Emblem and Printed Page — A467

1971, Sept. 21 *Perf. 11½x12*

2088	A467	1fo	dk bl, bl & gold	.40	.25

25th anniversary of the International Organization of Journalists (OIJ).
Exists imperf. Value $5.

Josef Jacob Winterl and Barren Strawberry — A468

Plants: 60f, Bromeliaceae. 80f, Titanopsis calcarea. 1fo, Periwinkle. 1.20fo, Gymnocalycium. 2fo, White water lily. 3fo, Iris arenaria. 5fo, Peony.

1971, Oct. 29 **Litho.** *Perf. 12*

2089	A468	40f	lt vio & multi	.25	.25
2090	A468	60f	gray & multi	.25	.25
2091	A468	80f	multi	.25	.25
2092	A468	1fo	multi	.25	.25
2093	A468	1.20fo	lilac & multi	.25	.25
2094	A468	2fo	gray & multi	.30	.25
2095	A468	3fo	multi	.50	.25
2096	A468	5fo	multi	.75	.40
			Nos. 2089-2096 (8)	2.80	2.15

Bicentenary of Budapest Botanical Gardens.
Exist imperf. Value, set $17.50.

Galloping — A469

Equestrian Sports: 60f, Trotting. 80f, Horses fording river. 1fo, Jumping. 1.20fo, Start. 2fo, Polo. 3fo, Steeplechase. 5fo, Dressage.

1971, Nov. 22 **Photo.** *Perf. 12*

2097	A469	40f	blue & multi	.25	.25
2098	A469	60f	ocher & multi	.25	.25
2099	A469	80f	olive & multi	.25	.25
2100	A469	1fo	red & multi	.25	.25
2101	A469	1.20fo	multi	.25	.25
2102	A469	2fo	multi	.30	.25
2103	A469	3fo	violet & multi	.50	.30
2104	A469	5fo	blue & multi	.75	.50
			Nos. 2097-2104 (8)	2.80	2.30

Exist imperf. Value, set $15.

Beheading of Heathen Chief Koppany A470

Designs: 60f, Samuel Aba pursuing King Peter. 1fo, Basarad's victory over King Charles Robert. 1.50fo, Strife between King Salomon and Prince Geza. 2.50fo, Founding of Obuda Church by King Stephen I and Queen Gisela. 4fo, Reconciliation of King Koloman and his brother Almos. 5fo, Oradea Church built by King Ladislas I. 10fo, Funeral of Prince Emeric and blinding of Vazul.

1971, Dec. 10 **Litho.**

2105	A470	40f	buff & multi	.25	.25
2106	A470	60f	buff & multi	.25	.25
2107	A470	1fo	buff & multi	.25	.25
2108	A470	1.50fo	buff & multi	.25	.25
2109	A470	2.50fo	buff & multi	.25	.25
2110	A470	4fo	buff & multi	.50	.30
2111	A470	5fo	buff & multi	.75	.50
			Nos. 2105-2111 (7)	2.50	2.05

Miniature Sheet

Perf. 11½

2112	A470	10fo	buff & multi	3.00	2.75

History of Hungary, from miniatures from Illuminated Chronicle of King Louis the Great, c. 1370. No. 2112 contains one stamp (size 44½x52mm).
Exist imperf. Value: set $15; souvenir sheet $17.50.

Equality Year Emblem A471

1971, Dec. 30 **Litho.** *Perf. 12*

2113	A471	1fo	bister & multi	.40	.25

Intl. Year Against Racial Discrimination.
Exists imperf. Value $5.

Ice Hockey and Sapporo '72 Emblem — A472

Sport and Sapporo '72 Emblem: 60f, Men's slalom. 80f, Women's figure skating. 1fo, Ski jump. 1.20fo, Long-distance skiing. 2fo, Men's figure skating. 3fo, Bobsledding. 4fo, Biathlon. 10fo, Buddha.

1971, Dec. 30 *Perf. 12*

2114	A472	40f	black & multi	.25	.25
2115	A472	60f	black & multi	.25	.25
2116	A472	80f	black & multi	.25	.25
2117	A472	1fo	black & multi	.25	.25
2118	A472	1.20fo	black & multi	.25	.25
2119	A472	2fo	black & multi	.35	.25
2120	A472	3fo	black & multi	.50	.30
2121	A472	4fo	black & multi	.75	.50
			Nos. 2114-2121 (8)	2.85	2.30

Souvenir Sheet

Perf. 11½

2122	A472	10fo	gold & multi	2.75	2.50

11th Winter Olympic Games, Sapporo, Japan, Feb. 3-13, 1972. No. 2122 contains one 86x48mm stamp.
Exist imperf. Value: set $15; souvenir sheet $20.

Hungarian Locomotive — A473

Locomotives: 60f, Germany. 80f, Italy. 1fo, Soviet Union. 1.20fo, Japan. 2fo, Great Britain. 4fo, Austria. 5fo, France.

1972, Feb. 23 **Photo.** *Perf. 12x11½*

2123	A473	40f	multi	.25	.25
2124	A473	60f	ocher & multi	.25	.25
2125	A473	80f	multi	.25	.25
2126	A473	1fo	olive & multi	.25	.25
2127	A473	1.20fo	ultra & multi	.35	.30
2128	A473	2fo	ver & multi	.25	.25
2129	A473	4fo	multi	.75	.25
2130	A473	5fo	multi	1.25	.45
			Nos. 2123-2130 (8)	3.60	2.25

Exist imperf. Value, set $20.

Janus Pannonius, by Andrea Mantegna A474

1972, Mar. 27 **Litho.** *Perf. 12*

2131	A474	1fo	gold & multi	.40	.25

Janus Pannonius (Johannes Czezmiczei, 1434-1472), humanist and poet.
Exists imperf. Value $5.

Mariner 9 — A475

Design: No. 2133, Mars 2 and 3 spacecraft.

1972, Mar. 30 **Photo.** *Perf. 11½x12*

2132	A475	2fo	dk blue & multi	.45	.45
2133	A475	2fo	multi	.45	.45
a.			Strip #2132-2133 + label	1.75	1.75

Exploration of Mars by Mariner 9 (US), and Mars 2 and 3 (USSR). Issued in sheets containing 4 each of Nos. 2132-2133 and 4 labels inscribed in Hungarian, Russian and English.
Exist imperf. Values: strip $5, sheetlet $25.

13th Century Church Portal — A476

1972, Apr. 11

2134	A476	3fo	greenish black	.40	.25

Centenary of the Society for the Protection of Historic Monuments.
Exists imperf. Value $7.50.

Hungarian Greyhound — A477

Hounds: 60f, Afghan hound (head). 80f, Irish wolfhound. 1.20fo, Borzoi. 2fo, Running greyhound. 4fo, Whippet. 6fo, Afghan hound.

1972, Apr. 14 **Litho.** *Perf. 12*

2135	A477	40f	multi	.25	.25
2136	A477	60f	brown & multi	.25	.25
2137	A477	80f	multi	.25	.25
2138	A477	1.20fo	multi	.25	.25
2139	A477	2fo	multi	.30	.25
2140	A477	4fo	multi	.70	.25
2141	A477	6fo	multi	1.10	.60
			Nos. 2135-2141 (7)	3.10	2.10

Exist imperf. Value, set $25.

József Imre, Emil Grósz, László Blaskovics (Ophthalmologists) — A478

Design: 2fo, Allvar Gullstrand, V. P. Filatov, Jules Gonin, ophthalmologists.

1972, Apr. 17

2142	A478	1fo	red, brn & blk	.40	.25
2143	A478	2fo	blue, brn & blk	.95	.45

First European Ophthalmologists' Congress, Budapest.
Exist imperf. Value, set $15.

Girl Reading and UNESCO Emblem A479

1972, May 27 **Photo.** *Perf. 11½x12*

2144	A479	1fo	multicolored	.40	.25

International Book Year 1971.
Exists imperf. Value $5.

Roses — A480

1972, June 1
2145 A480 1fo multicolored .40 .25

15th Rose Exhibition, Budapest.
Exists imperf. Value $5.

George Dimitrov A481

1972, June 18 Litho. *Perf. 12*
2146 A481 3fo black & multi .40 .25

90th anniversary, birth of George Dimitrov (1882-1949), communist leader.
Exists imperf. Value $5.

Souvenir Sheet

St. Martin and the Beggar, Stained-glass Window — A482

1972, June 20 *Perf. 10½*
2147 A482 10fo multi 2.75 2.50

Belgica 72, International Philatelic Exhibition, Brussels, June 24-July 9.
Exists imperf. Value $20.

Gyorgy Dozsa (1474-1514), Peasant Leader — A483

1972, June 25 Photo. *Perf. 11½x12*
2148 A483 1fo red & multi .40 .25

Exists imperf. Value $5.

Olympic Rings, Soccer — A484

Designs (Olympic Rings and): 60f, Water polo. 80f, Javelin, women's. 1fo, Kayak, women's. 1.20fo, Boxing. 2fo, Gymnastics, women's. 5fo, Fencing.

1972, July 15 *Perf. 11*

2149	A484	40f	multi	.25	.25
2150	A484	60f	multi	.25	.25
2151	A484	80f	multi	.25	.25
2152	A484	1fo	lilac & multi	.25	.25
2153	A484	1.20fo	blue & multi	.25	.25
2154	A484	2fo	multi	.40	.25
2155	A484	5fo	green & multi	.75	.50
	Nos. 2149-2155,B299 (8)			2.90	2.30

20th Olympic Games, Munich, Aug. 26-Sept. 11. See No. C325.
Exist imperf. Value, set $17.50.

Prince Geza Selecting Site of Székesfehérvár — A485

Designs: 60f, St. Stephen, first King of Hungary. 80f, Knights (country's defense). 1.20fo, King Stephen dictating to scribe (legal organization). 2fo, Sculptor at work (education). 4fo, Merchants before king (foreign relations). 6fo, View of castle and town of Székesfehérvár, 10th century. 10fo, King Andreas II presenting Golden Bull to noblemen.

1972, Aug. 20 Photo. *Perf. 12*

2156	A485	40f	slate & multi	.25	.25
2157	A485	60f	multi	.25	.25
2158	A485	80f	lilac & multi	.25	.25
2159	A485	1.20fo	multi	.25	.25
2160	A485	2fo	bister & multi	.40	.25
2161	A485	4fo	blue & multi	.55	.25
2162	A485	6fo	purple & multi	.75	.50
	Nos. 2156-2162 (7)			2.70	2.00

Souvenir Sheet

Perf. 12½

2163 A485 10fo black & multi 3.00 3.00

Millennium of the town of Székesfehérvár; 750th anniv. of the Golden Bull granting rights to lesser nobility.
Different printings of Nos. 2157 and 2160 have the year date at the lower left and lower right.
No. 2163 contains one 94x45mm stamp.
Exist imperf. Value: set $15; souvenir sheet $15.

Parliament, Budapest A486

Design: 6fo, Session room of Parliament.

1972, Aug. 20 Litho.
2164 A486 5fo dk blue & multi .60 .25
2165 A486 6fo multicolored .75 .30

Constitution of 1949.
Exist imperf. Value, set $12.50.

Eger, 17th Century View, and Bottle of Bull's Blood — A487

Design: 2fo, Contemporary view of Tokay and bottle of Tokay Aszu.

1972, Aug. 21 Litho. *Perf. 12*
2166 A487 1fo buff & multi .30 .25
2167 A487 2fo green & multi .65 .25

1st World Wine Exhibition, Budapest, Aug. 1972.
Exist imperf. Value, set $12.50.

Georgikon Emblems, Grain, Potato Flower — A488

1972, Sept. 3
2168 A488 1fo multi .40 .25

175th anniv. of the founding of the Georgikon at Keszthely, the 1st scientific agricultural academy.
Exists imperf. Value $5.

Vase with Bird — A489

Herend Porcelain: 60f, Covered candy dish. 80f, Vase with flowers and butterflies. 1fo, Plate with Mexican landscape. 1.20fo, Covered dish. 2fo, Teapot, cup and saucer. 4fo, Plate with flowers. 5fo, Baroque vase showing Herend factory.

1972, Sept. 15
Sizes: 23x46mm (40f, 80f, 2fo, 5fo); 33x36mm, others

2169	A489	40f	gray & multi	.25	.25
2170	A489	60f	ocher & multi	.25	.25
2171	A489	80f	multi	.25	.25
2172	A489	1fo	multi	.25	.25
2173	A489	1.20fo	green & multi	.25	.25
2174	A489	2fo	multi	.30	.25
2175	A489	4fo	red & multi	.50	.30
2176	A489	5fo	multi	.70	.50
	Nos. 2169-2176 (8)			2.75	2.30

Herend china factory, founded 1839.
Exist imperf. Value, set $15.

UIC Emblem and M-62 Diesel Locomotive — A490

1972, Sept. 19 Photo. *Perf. 11½x12*
2177 A490 1fo dark red .40 .25

50th anniversary of International Railroad Union Congress, Budapest, Sept. 19.
Exist imperf. Value $10.

"25" and Graph — A491

1972, Sept. *Perf. 11½x12*
2178 A491 1fo yellow & brown .40 .25

Planned national economy, 25th anniv.
Exists imperf. Value $5.

Budapest, 1972 — A492

No. 2179, View of Obuda, 1872. No. 2181, Buda, 1872. No. 2183, Pest, 1872. Nos. 2182, 2184, Budapest, 1972.

1972, Sept. 26 *Perf. 12x11½*

2179	A492	1fo	Prus bl & rose car	.25	.25
2180	A492	1fo	rose car & Prus bl	.25	.25
a.			Pair, #2179-2180	.40	.25
2181	A492	2fo	ocher & olive	.30	.25
2182	A492	2fo	olive & ocher	.30	.25
a.			Pair, #2181-2182	.75	.35
2183	A492	3fo	green & lt brn	.40	.25
2184	A492	3fo	lt brown & grn	.40	.25
a.			Pair, #2183-2184	1.25	.50
	Nos. 2179-2184 (6)			1.90	1.50

Centenary of unification of Obuda, Buda and Pest into Budapest.
Exist imperf. Value, set in pairs $20.

Ear and Congress Emblem A493

1972, Oct. 3 *Perf. 11½x12*
2185 A493 1fo brown, yel & blk .40 .25

11th Intl. Audiology Cong., Budapest.
Exists imperf. Value $6.

Flora Martos — A494

Portrait: No. 2187, Miklós Radnóti.

1972 Photo. *Perf. 11½x12*
2186 A494 1fo green & multi .25 .25
2187 A494 1fo brown & multi .25 .25

Flora Martos (1897-1938), Hungarian labor leader, & Miklós Radnóti (1909-44), poet.
Exist imperf. Value, set $6.
Issued: No. 2186, Nov. 5; No. 2187, Nov. 11.

Muses, by Jozsef Rippl-Ronai A495

Stained-glass Windows, 19th-20th Centuries: 60f, 16th century scribe, by Ferenc Sebesteny. 1fo, Flight into Egypt, by Karoly Lotz and Bertalan Székely. 1.50fo, Prince Arpad's Messenger, by Jenö Percz. 2.50fo, Nativity, by Lili Sztehlo. 4fo, Prince Arpad and Leaders, by Karoly Kernstock. 5fo, King Matthias and Jester, by Jenö Haranghy.

1972, Nov. 15 *Perf. 12*

2188	A495	40f multi	.25	.25
2189	A495	60f multi	.25	.25
2190	A495	1fo multi	.25	.25
2191	A495	1.50fo multi	.25	.25
2192	A495	2.50fo multi	.35	.25
2193	A495	4fo multi	.65	.30
2194	A495	5fo multi	1.10	.50
		Nos. 2188-2194 (7)	3.10	2.05

Exist imperf. Value, set $15.

Weaver, Cloth and Cogwheel — A496

1972, Nov. 27 **Litho.** *Perf. 12*

2195	A496	1fo silver & multi	.40	.25

Opening of Museum of Textile Techniques, Budapest.
Exists imperf. Value $6.

Main Square, Szarvas — A497

1fo, Modern buildings, Salgotarjan.

1972 **Litho.** *Perf. 11*

2196	A497	40f brown & orange	.25	.25
2197	A497	1fo dk & lt blue	.25	.25

Exist imperf. Value, set $15.

Vineyard, Tokaj — A498

3fo, Tokaj and vineyard. 4fo, Esztergom Cathedral. 7fo, Town Hall, Kaposvar. 20fo, Veszprem.

1973 *Perf. 12x11½*

2198	A498	3fo dk & lt green	.40	.25
2199	A498	4fo red brn & org	.50	.25
2200	A498	7fo blue vio & lil	1.00	.25
2200A	A498	20fo multicolored	2.50	.40
		Nos. 2196-2200A (6)	4.90	1.65

Exist imperf. Value, set $40.
See Nos. 2330-2335.

Type of 1963-64
Coil Stamps

Designs as before.

1972, Nov. **Photo.** *Perf. 14*
Size: 21½x17½mm, 17½x21½mm

2201	A336	2fo blue green	.40	.25
2202	A336	3fo dark blue	.55	.25
2203	A336	4fo blue, vert.	.75	.25
2204	A336	6fo bister	1.10	.35
		Nos. 2201-2204 (4)	2.80	1.10

Black control number on back of every 5th stamp.
Minute inscription centered in lower margin: "Legrady Sandor."

Arms of Soviet Union — A498a

1972, Dec. 30 **Photo.** *Perf. 11½x12*

2205	A498a	1fo multicolored	.40	.25

50th anniversary of Soviet Union.
Exists imperf. Value $10.

Petőfi Speaking at Pilvax Cafe A499

2fo, Portrait. 3fo, Petőfi on horseback, 1848-49.

1972, Dec. 30 **Engr.** *Perf. 12*

2206	A499	1fo rose carmine	.25	.25
2207	A499	2fo violet	.35	.25
2208	A499	3fo Prus green	.45	.25
		Nos. 2206-2208 (3)	1.05	.75

Sesquicentennial of the birth of Sandor Petőfi (1823-49), poet and revolutionary.
Exist imperf. Value, set $15.

Postal Zone Map of Hungary and Letter-carrying Crow — A500

1973, Jan. 1 **Litho.** *Perf. 12*

2209	A500	1fo red & black	.40	.25

Introduction of postal code system.
Exists imperf. Value $6.

Imre Madách (1823-64), Poet and Dramatist A501

1973, Jan. 20 **Photo.** *Perf. 11½x12*

2210	A501	1fo multicolored	.40	.25

Exists imperf. Value $6.

Busho Mask — A502

Designs: Various Busho masks.

1973, Feb. 17 **Litho.** *Perf. 12*

2211	A502	40f bistre brn & multi	.25	.25
2212	A502	60f turq grn & multi	.25	.25
2213	A502	80f lilac & multi	.25	.25
2214	A502	1.20fo ol grn & multi	.25	.25
2215	A502	2fo dl mauve & multi	.30	.25
2216	A502	4fo turq grn & multi	.50	.30
2217	A502	6fo lilac & multi	.75	.40
		Nos. 2211-2217 (7)	2.55	1.95

Busho Walk at Mohacs, ancient ceremony to drive out winter.
Exist imperf. Value, set $15.

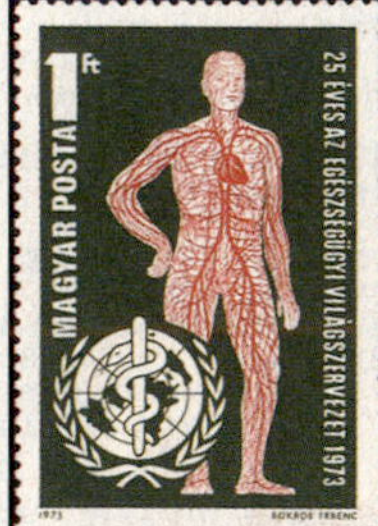

Nicolaus Copernicus A503

1973, Feb. 19 **Engr.** *Perf. 12*

2218	A503	3fo bright ultra	.75	.50

Printed with alternating label showing heliocentric system and view of Torun.
Exists imperf. Value $12.50.

Vascular System and WHO Emblem A504

1973, Apr. 16 **Photo.** *Perf. 12*

2219	A504	1fo sl grn & brn red	.40	.25

25th anniv. of WHO.
Exists imperf. Value $6.

Tank, Rocket, Radar, Plane, Ship and Soldier A505

1973, May 9 **Litho.** *Perf. 12*

2220	A505	3fo blue & multi	.50	.25

Philatelic Exhibition of Military Stamp Collectors of Warsaw Treaty Member States. No. 2220 was printed with alternating label showing flags of Warsaw Treaty members.
Exists imperf. Value $12.50.

Hungary No. 1396 and IBRA '73 Emblem — A506

No. 2222, No. 1397, POLSKA '73. No. 2223, No. 1398, IBRA '73. No. 2224, No. 1399, POLSKA. No. 2225, No. B293a, IBRA. No. 2226, No. B293b, POLSKA. No. 2227, No. B293c, IBRA. No. 2228, No. B293d, POLSKA.

1973, May 11 **Litho.** *Perf. 12*

2221	A506	40f shown	.25	.25
2222	A506	60f multi	.25	.25
2223	A506	80f multi	.25	.25
2224	A506	1fo multi	.25	.25
2225	A506	1.20fo multi	.25	.25
2226	A506	2fo multi	.25	.25
2227	A506	4fo multi	.50	.30
2228	A506	5fo multi	.75	.40
		Nos. 2221-2228 (8)	2.75	2.20

Publicity for IBRA '73 International Philatelic Exhibition, Munich, May 11-20; and POLSKA '73, Poznan, Aug. 15-Sept. 2. See No. C345.
Exist imperf. Value, set $17.50.

Typesetting, from "Orbis Pictus," by Comenius A507

3fo, Printer & wooden screw press, woodcut from Hungarian translation of Gospels.

1973, June 5 **Photo.** *Perf. 11½x12*

2229	A507	1fo black & gold	.25	.25
2230	A507	3fo black & gold	.40	.25

500th anniv. of book printing in Hungary.
Exist imperf. Value, set $11.

Storm over Hortobagy Puszta, by Csontvary — A508

Paintings: 60f, Mary's Well, Nazareth. 1fo, Carriage Ride by Moonlight in Athens, vert. 1.50fo, Pilgrimage to Cedars of Lebanon, vert. 2.50fo, The Lonely Cedar. 4fo, Waterfall at Jajce. 5fo, Ruins of Greek Theater at Taormina. 10fo, Horseback Riders on Shore.

1973, June 18 *Perf. 12½*

2231	A508	40f gold & multi	.25	.25
2232	A508	60f gold & multi	.25	.25
2233	A508	1fo gold & multi	.25	.25
2234	A508	1.50fo gold & multi	.25	.25
2235	A508	2.50fo gold & multi	.40	.25
2236	A508	4fo gold & multi	.65	.35
2237	A508	5fo gold & multi	.80	.50
		Nos. 2231-2237 (7)	2.85	2.10

Souvenir Sheet

2238	A508	10fo gold & multi	3.50	3.00

Paintings by Tivadar Kosztka Csontvary (1853-1919). No. 2238 contains one stamp (size: 90x43mm).
Exist imperf. Value: set $15; souvenir sheet $20.

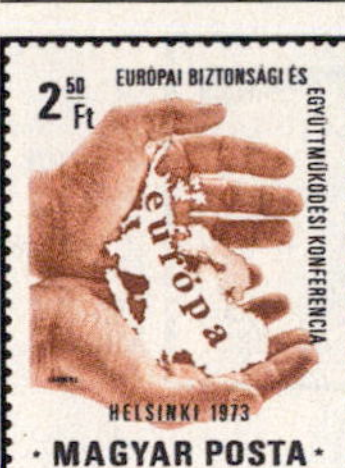
Hands Holding Map of Europe — A509

1973, July 3 Photo. *Perf. 11½x12*
2239 A509 2.50fo blk & gldn brn 3.00 3.00
a. Sheetlet of 4 + 2 labels 10.00 9.00

Conference for European Security and Cooperation. Helsinki, July 1973. No. 2239 was printed in a sheetlet of 4 stamps and 2 blue labels showing conference sites.
Exists imperf. Value, sheetlet $125.

Flowers — A510

1973, Aug. 4

2240	A510	40f	Provence roses	.25	.25
2241	A510	60f	Cyclamen	.25	.25
2242	A510	80f	Lungwort	.25	.25
2243	A510	1.20fo	English daisies	.25	.25
2244	A510	2fo	Buttercups	.30	.25
2245	A510	4fo	Violets	.70	.30
2246	A510	6fo	Poppies	1.00	.50
			Nos. 2240-2246 (7)	3.00	2.05

Exist imperf. Value, set $15.

"Let's be Friends in Traffic" — A511

Designs: 60f, "Not even one drink." 1fo, "Light your bicycle."

1973, Aug. 18 Photo. *Perf. 12x11½*

2247	A511	40f	green & orange	.25	.25
2248	A511	60f	purple & orange	.25	.25
2249	A511	1fo	indigo & orange	.25	.25
			Nos. 2247-2249 (3)	.75	.75

To publicize traffic rules.
Exist imperf. Value $15.

Adoration of the Kings A512

Paintings: 60f, Angels playing violin and lute. 1fo, Adoration of the Kings. 1.50fo, Annunciation. 2.50fo, Angels playing organ and harp. 4fo, Visitation of Mary. 5fo, Legend of St. Catherine of Alexandria. 10fo, Nativity.

1973, Nov. 3 Photo. *Perf. 12½*

2250	A512	40f	gold & multi	.25	.25
2251	A512	60f	gold & multi	.25	.25
2252	A512	1fo	gold & multi	.25	.25
2253	A512	1.50fo	gold & multi	.25	.25
2254	A512	2.50fo	gold & multi	.40	.25
2255	A512	4fo	gold & multi	.60	.30
2256	A512	5fo	gold & multi	.80	.50
			Nos. 2250-2256 (7)	2.80	2.05

Souvenir Sheet
Perf. 11

2257 A512 10fo gold & multi 3.00 2.75

Paintings by Hungarian anonymous early masters from the Christian Museum at Esztergom. No. 2257 contains one 49x74mm stamp.
Exist imperf. Value: set $15; souvenir sheet $15.

Mihaly Csokonai Vitez — A513

1973, Nov. 17 Photo. *Perf. 11½x12*
2258 A513 2fo bister & multi .35 .25

Mihaly Csokonai Vitez (1773-1805), poet.
Exists imperf. Value $5.

José Marti and Cuban Flag — A514

1973, Nov. 30
2259 A514 1fo dk brn, red & bl .40 .25

Marti (1853-95), Cuban natl. hero and poet.
Exists imperf. Value $5.

Barnabas Pesti (1920-44), Member of Hungarian Underground Communist Party — A515

1973, Nov. 30
2260 A515 1fo blue, brn & buff .40 .25

Exists imperf. Value $5.

Women's Double Kayak — A516

Designs: 60f, Water polo. 80f, Men's single kayak. 1.20fo, Butterfly stroke. 2fo, Men's fours kayak. 4fo, Men's single canoe. 6fo, Men's double canoe.

1973, Dec. 29 Litho. *Perf. 12x11*

2261	A516	40f	red & multi	.25	.25
2262	A516	60f	blue & multi	.25	.25
2263	A516	80f	multicolored	.25	.25
2264	A516	1.20fo	green & multi	.25	.25
2265	A516	2fo	car & multi	.35	.25
2266	A516	4fo	violet & multi	.45	.30
2267	A516	6fo	multicolored	.50	.50
			Nos. 2261-2267 (7)	2.30	2.05

Hungarian victories in water sports at Tampere and Belgrade.
Exist imperf. Value, set $17.50.

Souvenir Sheet

Map of Europe — A517

1974, Jan. 15 Photo. *Perf. 12x11½*
2268 A517 Sheet of 2 + label 8.50 8.00
a. 5fo multicolored 2.25 2.25

European Peace Conference (Arab-Israeli War), Geneva, Jan. 1974.
Exists imperf. Value $110.

Lenin — A518

1974, Jan. 21 Photo. *Perf. 11½x12*
2269 A518 2fo gold, dull bl & brn .50 .25

50th anniv. of the death of Lenin (1870-1924).
Exists imperf. Value $6.

Jozsef Boczor, Imre Békés, Tamás Elek — A519

1974, Feb. 21 *Perf. 12½*
2270 A519 3fo brown & multi .40 .25

30th anniversary of the death in France of Hungarian resistance fighters.
Exists imperf. Value $6.

Comecon Building, Moscow and Flags A520

1974, Feb. 26 Photo. *Perf. 12x11½*
2271 A520 1fo multicolored .40 .25

25th anniversary of the Council of Mutual Economic Assistance.
Exists imperf. Value $7.50.

Bank Emblem, Coins and Banknote A521

1974, Mar. 1 *Perf. 11½x12*
2272 A521 1fo lt green & multi .40 .25

25th anniversary of the State Savings Bank.
Exists imperf. Value $5.

Spacecraft on Way to Mars — A522

Designs: 60f, Mars 2 over Mars. 80f, Mariner 4. 1fo, Mars and Mt. Palomar Observatory. 1.20fo, Soft landing of Mars 3. 5fo, Mariner 9 with Mars satellites Phobos and Deimos.

1974, Mar. 11 Photo. *Perf. 12½*

2273	A522	40f	gold & multi	.25	.25
2274	A522	60f	silver & multi	.25	.25
2275	A522	80f	gold & multi	.25	.25
2276	A522	1fo	silver & multi	.25	.25
2277	A522	1.20fo	gold & multi	.25	.25
2278	A522	5fo	silver & multi	.75	.40
			Nos. 2273-2278,C347 (7)	2.75	2.15

Exploration of Mars. See No. C348.
Exist imperf. Value, set (7) $15.

Salvador Allende (1908-73), Pres. of Chile — A523

1974, Mar. 27 Photo. *Perf. 11½x12*
2279 A523 1fo black & multi .40 .25

Exists imperf. Value $5.

Mona Lisa, by Leonardo da Vinci A524

1974, Apr. 19 *Perf. 12½*
2280 A524 4fo gold & multi 6.25 6.00

Exists imperf. Value $20. Exhibition of the Mona Lisa in Asia.
Printed in sheets of 6 stamps and 6 labels with commemorative inscription. Value, $65.
Exist imperf. Value: single with labels $20; sheetlet $150.

Souvenir Sheet

Issue of 1874 and Flowers — A525

a, Mallow. b, Aster. c, Daisy. d, Columbine.

1974, May 11 Litho. *Perf. 11½*
2281 A525 Sheet of 4 2.75 2.75
a.-d. 2.50fo any single .50 .50

Centenary of the first issue inscribed "Magyar Posta" (Hungarian Post).
Exists imperf. Value, sheet of 4 $20.

Carrier Pigeon, World Map, UPU Emblem — A526

1974, May 22 Litho. *Perf. 12*

2282	A526	40f shown	.25	.25
2283	A526	60f Mail coach	.25	.25
2284	A526	80f Old mail automobile	.25	.25
2285	A526	1.20fo Balloon post	.35	.25
2286	A526	2fo Mail train	.45	.25
2287	A526	4fo Mail bus	1.00	.40
		Nos. 2282-2287,C349 (7)	3.80	2.55

Centenary of the Universal Postal Union.
Exist imperf. Value, set $20.

Dove of Basel, Switzerland No. 3L1, 1845 — A527

1974, June 7 Photo. *Perf. 11½x12*

2288	A527	3fo gold & multi	1.25	1.25

INTERNABA 1974 Philatelic Exhibition, Basel, June 7-16. No. 2288 issued in sheets of 3 stamps and 3 labels showing Internaba 1974 emblem. Size: 104x125mm.
Exist imperf. Values: single $8; sheet $25.

Chess Players, from 13th Century Manuscript A528

Designs: 60f, Chess players, 15th century English woodcut. 80f, Royal chess party, 15th century Italian chess book. 1.20fo, Chess players, 17th century copper engraving by Selenus. 2fo, Farkas Kempelen's chess playing machine, 1769. 4fo, Hungarian Grand Master Geza Maroczy (1870-1951). 6fo, View of Nice and emblem of 1974 Chess Olympiad.

1974, June 6 Litho. *Perf. 12*

2289	A528	40f multi	.25	.25
2290	A528	60f multi	.25	.25
2291	A528	80f multi	.25	.25
2292	A528	1.20fo multi	.30	.25
2293	A528	2fo multi	.45	.25
2294	A528	4fo multi	1.10	.30
2295	A528	6fo multi	1.75	.50
		Nos. 2289-2295 (7)	4.35	2.05

50th anniv. of Intl. Chess Federation and 21st Chess Olympiad, Nice, June 6-30.
Exist imperf. Value, set $125.

Souvenir Sheet

Cogwheel Railroad — A529

Designs: a, Passenger train, 1874. b, Freight train, 1874. c, Electric train, 1929-73. d, Twin motor train, 1973.

1974, June 25 Litho. *Perf. 12*

2296	A529	Sheet of 4	3.50	3.25
a.-d.		2.50fo, any single	.50	.50

Cent. of Budapest's cogwheel railroad.
Exist imperf. Value, sheet $30.

Congress Emblem (Globe and Parliament) — A530

1974, Aug. 18 Photo. *Perf. 12*

2297	A530	2fo silver, dk & lt bl	.40	.25

4th World Congress of Economists, Budapest, Aug. 19-24.
Exists imperf. Value $5.

Bathing Woman, by Károly Lotz A531

Paintings of Nudes: 60f, Awakening, by Károly Brocky. 1fo, Venus and Cupid, by Brocky, horiz. 1.50fo, After the Bath, by Lotz. 2.50fo, Resting Woman, by Istvan Csok, horiz. 4fo, After the Bath, by Bertalan Szekely. 5fo, "Devotion," by Erzsebet Korb. 10fo, Lark, by Pál Szinyei Merse.

1974, Aug. *Perf. 12½*

2298	A531	40f gold & multi	.25	.25
2299	A531	60f gold & multi	.25	.25
2300	A531	1fo gold & multi	.25	.25
2301	A531	1.50fo gold & multi	.30	.25
2302	A531	2.50fo gold & multi	.35	.25
2303	A531	4fo gold & multi	.70	.25
2304	A531	5fo gold & multi	.90	.40
		Nos. 2298-2304 (7)	3.00	1.90

Souvenir Sheet

Perf. 11

2305	A531	10fo gold & multi	3.25	3.00

No. 2305 contains one stamp (45x70mm).
Exist imperf. Value: set $20; souvenir sheet $20.

Mimi, by Béla Czóbel A532

1974, Sept. 4

2306	A532	1fo multicolored	.50	.25

91st birthday of Béla Czóbel, Hungarian painter.
Exists imperf. Value $6.

Intersputnik Tracking Station — A533

High Voltage Line "Peace" and Pipe Line "Friendship" A534

Perf. 11½x12, 12x11½

1974, Sept. 5 Litho.

2307	A533	1fo blue & violet	.25	.25
2308	A534	3fo multicolored	.60	.25

Technical assistance and cooperation between Hungary and USSR, 25th anniv.
Exist imperf. Value, set $10.

Pablo Neruda — A535

1974, Sept. 11 Photo. *Perf. 11½x12*

2309	A535	1fo multicolored	.40	.25

Pablo Neruda (Neftali Ricar do Reyes, 1904-1973), Chilean poet.
Exists imperf. Value $5.

Sweden No. 1 and Lion from Royal Palace, Stockholm A536

1974, Sept. 21 *Perf. 12x11½*

2310	A536	3fo ultra, yel grn & gold	1.50	1.50

Stockholmia 74 Intl. Philatelic Exhibition, Stockholm, Sept. 21-29. No. 2310 issued in sheets of 3 stamps and 3 labels showing Stockholmia emblem. White margin inscribed "UPU" multiple in white. Size: 126x104mm. Value $6.50.
Exists imperf. Value: single $7.50; sheetlet $22.50.

Tank Battle and Soldier with Anti-tank Grenade — A537

1974, Sept. 28 Litho. *Perf. 12*

2311	A537	1fo gold, orange & blk	.25	.25
		Nos. 2311,C351-C352 (3)	.95	.75

Army Day.
Exist imperf. Value, set (3) $15.

Segner and Segner Crater on Moon A538

1974, Oct. 5

2312	A538	3fo multicolored	.75	.25

270th anniversary of the birth of Janos Andras Segner, naturalist. No. 2312 printed se-tenant with label arranged checkerwise in sheet. Label shows Segner wheel.
Exists imperf. Value, with label $12.50.

Rhyparia Purpurata — A539

Lepidoptera: 60f, Melanargia galathea. 80f, Parnassius Apollo. 1fo, Celerio euphorbia. 1.20fo, Catocala fraxini. 5fo, Apatura iris. 6fo, Palaeochrysophanus hyppothoe.

1974, Nov. 11 Photo. *Perf. 12½*

2313	A539	40f multicolored	.25	.25
2314	A539	60f violet & multi	.25	.25
2315	A539	80f multicolored	.25	.25
2316	A539	1fo brown & multi	.25	.25
2317	A539	1.20fo blue & multi	.25	.25
2318	A539	5fo purple & multi	.75	.30
2319	A539	6fo multicolored	1.00	.40
		Nos. 2313-2319 (7)	3.00	1.95

Exist imperf. Value, set $17.50.

Motherhood A540

1974, Dec. 24 Litho. *Perf. 12*

2320	A540	1fo lt blue, blk & yel brn	.40	.25

Exists imperf. Value $5.

Robert Kreutz — A541

1974, Dec. 24

2321	A541	1fo shown	.30	.25
2322	A541	1fo István Pataki	.30	.25

30th death anniv. of anti-fascist martyrs Kreutz (1923-44) and Pataki (1914-44).
Exist imperf. Value, set $10.

Puppy
A542

Young Animals: 60f, Siamese kittens, horiz. 80f, Rabbit. 1.20fo, Foal, horiz. 2fo, Lamb. 4fo, Calf, horiz. 6fo, Piglet.

1974, Dec. 30

2323 A542 40f lt blue & multi .25 .25
2324 A542 60f multicolored .25 .25
2325 A542 80f olive & multi .25 .25
2326 A542 1.20fo green & multi .25 .25
2327 A542 2fo brown & multi .30 .25
2328 A542 4fo orange & multi .70 .30
2329 A542 6fo violet & multi 1.10 .50
Nos. 2323-2329 (7) 3.10 2.05

Exist imperf. Value, set $15.
See Nos. 2403-2409.

Building Type of 1972

4fo, Szentendre. 5fo, View of Szolnok across Tisza River. 6fo, Skyscraper, Dunaújváros. 8fo, Church and city hall, Vac. 10fo, City Hall, Kiskunfélegyháza. 50fo, Church (Turkish Mosque), Hunyadi Statue & TV tower, Pecs.

1974-80 Litho. *Perf. 12x11½*

2330 A498 4fo red brn & pink .60 .25
2331 A498 5fo dk blue & ultra .75 .25
2332 A498 6fo dk brn & org .90 .25
2333 A498 8fo dk & brt grn 1.25 .25
2334 A498 10fo brown & yel 1.75 .25
2335 A498 50fo multi 6.00 1.25
Nos. 2330-2335 (6) 11.25 2.50

Exist imperf. Value, set $95.
Issued: 8fo, 12/7; 10fo, 50fo, 12/30; 5fo, 3/8/75; 6fo, 6/10/75; 4fo, 6/20/80.

Hospital, Lambarene — A544

60f, Dr. Schweitzer, patient & microscope. 80f, Patient arriving by boat. 1.20fo, Hospital supplies arriving by ship. 2fo, Globe, Red Cross, carrier pigeons. 4fo, Nobel Peace Prize medal. 6fo, Portrait & signature of Dr. Schweitzer, organ pipes & "J. S. Bach."

1975, Jan. 14 Photo. *Perf. 12*

2340 A544 40f gold & multi .25 .25
2341 A544 60f gold & multi .25 .25
2342 A544 80f gold & multi .25 .25
2343 A544 1.20fo gold & multi .25 .25
2344 A544 2fo gold & multi .25 .25
2345 A544 4fo gold & multi .60 .30
2346 A544 6fo lil & multi .80 .45
Nos. 2340-2346 (7) 2.65 2.00

Dr. Albert Schweitzer (1875-1965), medical missionary and musician, birth centenary.
Exist imperf. Value, set $15.

Farkas Bolyai — A545

1975, Feb. 7 Litho. *Perf. 11½x12*

2347 A545 1fo gray & red brown .25 .25

Bolyai (1775-1856), mathematician.
Exists imperf. Value $7.

Mihály Károlyi
A546

1975, Mar. 4 Litho. *Perf. 12*

2348 A546 1fo lt blue & brown .40 .25

Birth centenary of Count Mihály Károlyi (1875-1955), prime minister, 1918-1919.
Exists imperf. Value $5.

Woman, IWY Emblem
A547

1975, Mar. 8 *Perf. 12x11½*

2349 A547 1fo aqua & black .40 .25

International Women's Year 1975.
Exists imperf. Value $5.

"Let us Build up the Railroads" — A548

Posters: 60f, "Bread starts here." 2fo, "Hungarian Communist Party-a Party of Action." 4fo, "Heavy Industry-secure base of Three-year Plan." 5fo, "Our common interest-a developed socialist society."

1975, Mar. 17 Photo. *Perf. 11*

2350 A548 40f red & multi .25 .25
2351 A548 60f red & multi .25 .25
2352 A548 2fo red & multi .25 .25
2353 A548 4fo red & multi .40 .25
2354 A548 5fo red & multi .50 .30
Nos. 2350-2354 (5) 1.65 1.30

Hungary's liberation from Fascism, 30th anniv.
Exist imperf. Value, set $15.

Arrow, 1915, Pagoda and Mt. Fuji — A549

Antique Cars: 60f, Swift, 1911, Big Ben and Tower of London. 80f, Model T Ford, 1908, Capitol and Statue of Liberty. 1fo, Mercedes, 1901, Towers of Stuttgart. 1.20fo, Panhard Levassor, 1912, Arc de Triomphe and Eiffel Tower. 5fo, Csonka, 1906, Fishermen's Bastion and Chain Bridge. 6fo, Emblems of Hungarian Automobile Club, Alliance Internationale de Tourisme and Federation Internationale de l'Automobile.

1975, Mar. 27 Litho. *Perf. 12*

2355 A549 40f lt blue & multi .25 .25
2356 A549 60f lt green & multi .25 .25
2357 A549 80f pink & multi .25 .25
2358 A549 1fo lilac & multi .25 .25
2359 A549 1.20fo orange & multi .25 .25
2360 A549 5fo ultra & multi .65 .30
2361 A549 6fo lilac rose & multi 1.00 .50
Nos. 2355-2361 (7) 2.90 2.05

Hungarian Automobile Club, 75th anniv.
Exist imperf. Value, set $17.50.

The Creation of Adam, by Michelangelo — A550

1975, Apr. 23 Photo. *Perf. 12½*

2362 A550 10fo gold & multi 3.50 3.25

Michelangelo Buonarroti (1475-1564), Italian painter, sculptor and architect.
Exists imperf. Value $22.50.

Academy of Science
A551

Designs: 2fo, Dates "1975 1825." 3fo, Count Istvan Szechenyi.

1975, May 5 Litho. *Perf. 12*

2363 A551 1fo green & multi .25 .25
2364 A551 2fo green & multi .30 .25
2365 A551 3fo green & multi .50 .30
Nos. 2363-2365 (3) 1.05 .80

Sesquicentennial of Academy of Science, Budapest, founded by Count Istvan Szechenyi.
Exists imperf. Value, set $15.

Emblem of 1980 Olympics and Proposed Moscow Stadium — A553

1975, May 8 Photo. *Perf. 11½x12*

2366 A553 5fo lt blue & multi 1.50 1.25

Socfilex 75 Intl. Philatelic Exhibition, Moscow, 5/8-18. No. 2366 issued in sheets of 3 stamps and 3 labels showing Socfilex 75 emblem (War Memorial, Berlin-Treptow).
Exists imperf. Value: single with label $12.50; sheetlet $45.

France No. 1100 and Venus of Milo — A554

1975, June 3 Photo. *Perf. 11½x12*

2367 A554 5fo lilac & multi 1.50 1.25

ARPHILA 75 International Philatelic Exhibition, Paris, June 6-16. No. 2367 issued in sheets of 3 stamps and 3 labels showing ARPHILA 75 emblem.
Exists imperf. Value: single with label $10; sheetlet $35.

Early Transformer, Kando Locomotive, 1902, Pylon — A555

1975, June 10 Litho. *Perf. 12*

2368 A555 1fo multicolored .40 .25

Hungarian Electrotechnical Association, 75th anniversary.
Exists imperf. Value $12.50.

Epée, Saber, Foil and Globe — A556

1975, July 11

2369 A556 1fo multicolored .40 .25

32nd World Fencing Championships, Budapest, July 11-20.
Exists imperf. Value $10.

Souvenir Sheet

Whale Pavilion, Oceanexpo 75 — A557

1975, July 21 Photo. *Perf. 12½*

2370 A557 10fo gold & multi 3.00 2.75

Oceanexpo 75, International Exhibition, Okinawa, July 20, 1975-Jan. 1976.
Exists imperf. Value $30.

Dr. Agoston Zimmermann (1875-1963), Veterinarian
A558

1975, Sept. 4 Litho. *Perf. 12*

2371 A558 1fo brown & blue .40 .25

Exists imperf. Value $7.50.

Symbolic of 14 Cognate Languages
A559

1975, Sept. 9

2372 A559 1fo gold & multi .40 .25

International Finno-Ugrian Congress.

Exists imperf. Value $6.

Voters — A560

Design: No. 2374, Map of Hungary with electoral districts.

1975, Oct. 1

2373 A560 1fo multicolored .30 .25
2374 A560 1fo multicolored .30 .25

Hungarian Council System, 25th anniv. Exist imperf. Value, set $11.

Fish and Waves (Ocean Pollution) A561

Designs: 60f, Skeleton hand reaching for rose in water glass. 80f, Fish gasping for raindrop. 1fo, Carnation wilting in polluted soil. 1.20fo, Bird dying in polluted air. 5fo, Sick human lung and smokestack. 6fo, "Stop Pollution" (raised hand protecting globe from skeleton hand).

1975, Oct. 16 Litho. *Perf. 11½*

2375 A561 40f multi .25 .25
2376 A561 60f multi .25 .25
2377 A561 80f multi .25 .25
2378 A561 1fo multi .25 .25
2379 A561 1.20fo multi .25 .25
2380 A561 5fo multi .60 .30
2381 A561 6fo multi .85 .40
Nos. 2375-2381 (7) 2.70 1.95

Environmental Protection. Exist imperf. Value, set $15.

Mariska Gárdos (1885-1973) A562

Portraits: No. 2383, Imre Mezö (1905-56). No. 2384, Imre Tarr (1900-37).

1975, Nov. 4 Litho. *Perf. 12*

2382 A562 1fo black & red org .25 .25
2383 A562 1fo black & red org .25 .25
2384 A562 1fo black & red org .25 .25
Nos. 2382-2384 (3) .75 .75

Famous Hungarians, birth anniversaries. Exist imperf. Value, set $15.

Treble Clef, Organ and Orchestra — A563

1975, Nov. 14

2385 A563 1fo multicolored .40 .25

Franz Liszt Musical Academy, centenary. Exists imperf. Value $10.

Szigetcsep Icon — A564

Virgin and Child, 18th Century Icons: 60f, Grabóc. 1fo, Esztergom. 1.50fo, Vatoped. 2.50fo, Tottos. 4fo, Gyor. 5fo, Kazan.

1975, Nov. 25 Photo. *Perf. 12½*

2386 A564 40f gold & multi .25 .25
2387 A564 60f gold & multi .25 .25
2388 A564 1fo gold & multi .25 .25
2389 A564 1.50fo gold & multi .25 .25
2390 A564 2.50fo gold & multi .35 .25
2391 A564 4fo gold & multi .70 .30
2392 A564 5fo gold & multi .90 .60
Nos. 2386-2392 (7) 2.95 2.15

Exist imperf. Value, set $15.

Members' Flags, Radar, Mother and Child — A565

1975, Dec. 15 Litho. *Perf. 12*

2393 A565 1fo multicolored .40 .25

20th anniversary of the signing of the Warsaw Treaty (Bulgaria, Czechoslovakia, German Democratic Rep., Hungary, Poland, Romania, USSR).
Exists imperf. Value $6.

Ice Hockey, Winter Olympics' Emblem — A566

Designs (Emblem and): 60f, Slalom. 80f, Ski race. 1.20fo, Ski jump. 2fo, Speed skating. 4fo, Cross-country skiing. 6fo, Bobsled. 10fo, Figure skating, pair.

1975, Dec. 29 Photo. *Perf. 12x11½*

2394 A566 40f silver & multi .25 .25
2395 A566 60f silver & multi .25 .25
2396 A566 80f silver & multi .25 .25
2397 A566 1.20fo silver & multi .25 .25
2398 A566 2fo silver & multi .35 .25
2399 A566 4fo silver & multi .70 .30
2400 A566 6fo silver & multi .90 .50
Nos. 2394-2400 (7) 2.95 2.05

Souvenir Sheet

Perf. 12½

2401 A566 10fo silver & multi 3.25 3.00

12th Winter Olympic Games, Innsbruck, Austria, Feb. 4-15, 1976. No. 2401 contains one stamp (59x36mm).
Exist imperf. Value: set $15; souvenir sheet $15.

"P," 5-pengö and 500-pengö Notes — A567

1976, Jan. 16 Litho. *Perf. 12*

2402 A567 1fo multicolored .40 .25

Hungarian Bank Note Co., 50th anniversary. Exists imperf. Value $9.

Animal Type of 1974

Young Animals: 40f, Wild boars, horiz. 60f, Squirrels. 80f, Lynx, horiz. 1.20fo, Wolves. 2fo, Foxes, horiz. 4fo, Bears. 6fo, Lions, horiz.

1976, Jan. 26

2403 A542 40f multi .25 .25
2404 A542 60f blue & multi .25 .25
2405 A542 80f multi .25 .25
2406 A542 1.20fo multi .25 .25
2407 A542 2fo violet & multi .30 .25
2408 A542 4fo yellow & multi .65 .30
2409 A542 6fo multi .75 .40
Nos. 2403-2409 (7) 2.70 1.95

Exist imperf. Value, set $15.

A.G. Bell, Telephone, Molniya I and Radar — A568

1976, Mar. 10 Litho. *Perf. 11½x12*

2410 A568 3fo multicolored .75 .75

Centenary of first telephone call by Alexander Graham Bell, Mar. 10, 1876. Issued in sheets of 4.
Exists imperf. Value: single $4; sheetlet $15.

Battle of Kuruc-Labantz — A569

Paintings: 60f, Meeting of Rakoczi and Tamas Esze, by Endre Veszpremi. 1fo, Diet of Onod, by Mor Than. 2fo, Camp of the Kurucs. 3fo, Ilona Zrinyi (Rakoczi's mother), vert. 4fo, Kuruc officers, vert. 5fo, Prince Francis II Rakoczy, by Adam Manyoki, vert. Painters of 40f, 2fo, 3fo, 4fo, are unknown.

1976, Mar. 27 Photo. *Perf. 12½*

2411 A569 40f gold & multi .25 .25
2412 A569 60f gold & multi .25 .25
2413 A569 1fo gold & multi .30 .25
2414 A569 2fo gold & multi .60 .25
2415 A569 3fo gold & multi .85 .25
2416 A569 4fo gold & multi 1.25 .30
2417 A569 5fo gold & multi 1.60 .50
Nos. 2411-2417 (7) 5.10 2.05

Francis II Rakoczy (1676-1735), leader of Hungarian Protestant insurrection, 300th birth anniversary.
Exist imperf. Value, set $20.

Standard Meter, Hungarian Meter Act — A570

2fo, Istvan Krusper, his vacuum balance, standard kilogram. 3fo, Interferometer & rocket.

1976, Apr. 5 *Perf. 11½x12*

2418 A570 1fo multicolored .25 .25
2419 A570 2fo multicolored .30 .25
2420 A570 3fo multicolored .50 .30
Nos. 2418-2420 (3) 1.05 .80

Introduction of metric system in Hungary, cent.
Exist imperf. Value, set $20.

US No. 1353 and Independence Hall, Philadelphia — A571

Photogravure and Foil Embossed

1976, May 29 *Perf. 11½x12*

2421 A571 5fo blue & multi 1.40 1.25

Interphil 76 International Philatelic Exhibition, Philadelphia, Pa., May 29-June 6. No. 2421 issued in sheets of 3 stamps and 3 labels showing bells. Size: 115x125mm.
Exists imperf. Value: single with label $8.50; sheetlet $25.

"30" and Various Pioneer Activities — A572

1976, June 5 Litho. *Perf. 12*

2422 A572 1fo multicolored .40 .25

Hungarian Pioneers, 30th anniversary. Exists imperf. Value $5.

Trucks, Safety Devices, Trade Union Emblem — A573

1976, June *Perf. 12½*

2423 A573 1fo multicolored .40 .25

Labor safety. Exists imperf. Value $5.

Intelstat 4, Montreal Olympic Emblem, Canadian Flag — A574

Designs: 60f, Equestrian. 1fo, Butterfly stroke. 2fo, One-man kayak. 3fo, Fencing. 4fo, Javelin. 5fo, Athlete on vaulting horse.

1976, June 29 Photo. *Perf. 11½x12*
2424 A574 40f dk blue & multi .25 .25
2425 A574 60f slate grn & multi .25 .25
2426 A574 1fo blue & multi .25 .25
2427 A574 2fo green & multi .35 .25
2428 A574 3fo brown & multi .45 .25
2429 A574 4fo bister & multi .60 .30
2430 A574 5fo maroon & multi .75 .40
Nos. 2424-2430 (7) 2.90 1.95

21st Olympic Games, Montreal, Canada, July 17-Aug. 1. See No. C365.
Exist imperf. Value, set $20.

Denmark No. 2 and Mermaid, Copenhagen — A575

1976, Aug. 19 Photo. *Perf. 11½x12*
2431 A575 3fo multicolored 1.25 1.25

HAFNIA 76 Intl. Phil. Exhib., Copenhagen, Aug. 20-29. No. 2431 issued in sheets of 3 stamps and 3 labels showing HAFNIA emblem.
Exists imperf. Value: single with label $6; sheetlet $17.50.

Souvenir Sheet

Discovery of Body of Lajos II, by Bertalan Székely — A576

1976, Aug. 27 Photo. *Perf. 12½*
2432 A576 20fo multicolored 3.00 2.75

450th anniversary of the Battle of Mohacs against the Turks.
Exists imperf. Value $17.50.

Flora, by Titian — A577

1976, Aug. 27
2433 A577 4fo gold & multi .75 .25

Titian (1477-1576), Venetian painter.
Exists imperf. Value $9.

Hussar, Herend China — A578

1976, Sept. 28 Litho. *Perf. 12*
2434 A578 4fo multicolored .75 .25

Herend China manufacture, sesqui.
Exists imperf. Value $7.50.

Daniel Berzsenyi (1776-1836), Poet — A579

1976, Sept. 28
2435 A579 2fo black, gold & yel .40 .25

Exists imperf. Value $5.

Pal Gyulai (1826-1909), Poet and Historian — A580

1976, Sept. 28
2436 A580 2fo orange & black .40 .25

Exists imperf. Value $5.

Tuscany No. 1 and Emblem — A581

1976, Oct. 13 Photo. *Perf. 11½x12*
2437 A581 5fo orange & multi 1.75 1.75

ITALIA 76 International Philatelic Exhibition, Milan, Oct. 14-24. No. 2437 issued in sheets of 3 stamps and 3 labels showing Italia 76 emblem. Size: 106x127mm.

Exists imperf. Value: single with label $8; sheetlet $25.

Jozsef Madzsar, M.D. — A582

Labor leaders: No. 2439, Ignac Bogar (1876-1933), secretary of printers' union. No. 2440, Rudolf Golub (1901-44), miner.

1976, Nov. 4 Litho. *Perf. 12*
2438 A582 1fo deep brown & red .25 .25
2439 A582 1fo deep brown & red .25 .25
2440 A582 1fo deep brown & red .25 .25
Nos. 2438-2440 (3) .75 .75

Exist imperf. Value, set $15.

Science and Culture House, Georgian Dancer, Hungarian and USSR Flags — A583

1976, Nov. 4 *Perf. 12½x12*
2441 A583 1fo multicolored .40 .25

House of Soviet Science and Culture, Budapest, 2nd anniversary.
Exists imperf. Value $5.

Koranyi Sanitarium and Statue — A584

1976, Nov. 11 *Perf. 12*
2442 A584 2fo multicolored .40 .25

Koranyi TB Sanitarium, founded by Dr. Frigyes Koranyi, 75th anniversary.
Exists imperf. Value $5.

Locomotive, 1875, Enese Station — A585

Designs: 60f, Steam engine No. 17, 1885, Rabatamasi Station. 1fo, Railbus, 1925, Fertoszentmiklos Station. 2fo, Express steam engine, Kapuvar Station. 3fo, Engine and trailer, 1926, Gyor Station. 4fo, Eight-wheel express engine, 1934, and Fertoboz Station. 5fo, Raba-Balaton engine, Sopron Station.

1976, Nov. 26 Litho. *Perf. 12*
2443 A585 40f multicolored .25 .25
2444 A585 60f multicolored .25 .25
2445 A585 1fo multicolored .25 .25
2446 A585 2fo multicolored .30 .25
2447 A585 3fo multicolored .50 .25
2448 A585 4fo multicolored .70 .35
2449 A585 5fo multicolored .90 .50
Nos. 2443-2449 (7) 3.15 2.10

Gyor-Sopron Railroad, centenary.
Exist imperf. Value, set $20.

Poplar, Oak, Pine and Map of Hungary — A586

1976, Dec. 14
2450 A586 1fo multicolored .40 .25

Millionth hectare of reforestation.
Exists imperf. Value $7.50.

Weight Lifting and Wrestling, Silver Medals — A587

60f, Kayak, men's single & women's double. 1fo, Horse vaulting. 4fo, Women's fencing. 6fo, Javelin. 20fo, Water polo.

1976, Dec. 14 Photo. *Perf. 11½x12*
2451 A587 40f multicolored .25 .25
2452 A587 60f multicolored .25 .25
2453 A587 1fo multicolored .25 .25
2454 A587 4fo multicolored .75 .30
2455 A587 6fo multicolored .90 .50
Nos. 2451-2455 (5) 2.40 1.55

Souvenir Sheet
Perf. 12½x11½
2456 A587 20fo multicolored 3.25 3.25

Hungarian medalists in 21st Olympic Games.
Exist imperf. Value: set $15; souvenir sheet $15.

Spoonbills — A588

Birds: 60f, White storks. 1fo, Purple herons. 2fo, Great bustard. 3fo, Common cranes. 4fo, White wagtails. 5fo, Garganey teals.

1977, Jan. 3 Litho. *Perf. 12*
2457 A588 40f multicolored .25 .25
2458 A588 60f multicolored .25 .25
2459 A588 1fo multicolored .25 .25
2460 A588 2fo multicolored .40 .25
2461 A588 3fo multicolored .45 .30
2462 A588 4fo multicolored .90 .40
2463 A588 5fo multicolored 1.10 .50
Nos. 2457-2463 (7) 3.60 2.20

Birds from Hortobagy National Park.
Exist imperf. Value, set $17.50.

1976 World Champion Imre Abonyi Driving Four-in-hand — A589

Designs: 60f, Omnibus on Boulevard, 1870. 1fo, One-horse cab at Budapest Railroad Station, 1890. 2fo, Mail coach, Buda to Vienna route. 3fo, Covered wagon of Hajduszoboszlo. 4fo, Hungarian coach, by Jeremias Schemel, 1563. 5fo, Post chaise, from a Lübeck wood panel, 1430.

1977, Jan. 31 Litho. *Perf. 12x11½*

2464	A589 40f multicolored	.25	.25
2465	A589 60f multicolored	.25	.25
2466	A589 1fo multicolored	.25	.25
2467	A589 2fo multicolored	.30	.25
2468	A589 3fo multicolored	.30	.25
2469	A589 4fo multicolored	.50	.35
2470	A589 5fo multicolored	.70	.45
	Nos. 2464-2470 (7)	2.55	2.05

History of the coach.
Exist imperf. Value, set $17.50.

Peacock A590

Birds: 60f, Green peacock. 1fo, Congo peacock. 3fo, Argus pheasant. 4fo, Impeyan pheasant. 6fo, Peacock pheasant.

1977, Feb. 22 Litho. *Perf. 12*

2471	A590 40f multicolored	.25	.25
2472	A590 60f multicolored	.25	.25
2473	A590 1fo multicolored	.25	.25
2474	A590 3fo multicolored	.40	.25
2475	A590 4fo multicolored	.60	.30
2476	A590 6fo multicolored	.90	.50
	Nos. 2471-2476 (6)	2.65	1.80

Exist imperf. Value, set $17.50.

Newspaper Front Page, Factories A591

1977, Mar. 3 Litho. *Perf. 12*

2477 A591 1fo gold, black & ver .40 .25

Nepszava newspaper, centenary.
Exists imperf. Value $5.

Flowers, by Mihaly Munkacsy A592

Flowers, by Hungarian Painters: 60f, Jakab Bogdany. 1fo, Istvan Csok, horiz. 2fo, Janos Halapy. 3fo, Jozsef Rippl-Ronai, horiz. 4fo, Janos Tornyai. 5fo, Jozsef Koszta.

1977, Mar. 18 Photo. *Perf. 12½*

2478	A592 40f gold & multi	.25	.25
2479	A592 60f gold & multi	.25	.25
2480	A592 1fo gold & multi	.25	.25
2481	A592 2fo gold & multi	.30	.25
2482	A592 3fo gold & multi	.40	.25
2483	A592 4fo gold & multi	.55	.30
2484	A592 5fo gold & multi	.75	.50
	Nos. 2478-2484 (7)	2.75	2.05

Exist imperf. Value, set $20.

Newton and Double Convex Lens A593

1977, Mar. 31 Litho. *Perf. 12*

2485 A593 3fo tan & multi 1.00 .80

Isaac Newton (1643-1727), natural philosopher and mathematician, 250th death anniversary. No. 2485 issued in sheets of 4 stamps and 4 blue and black labels showing illustration from Newton's "Principia Mathematica," and Soviet space rocket.
Exists imperf. Value: single with label $6; sheetlet $25.

Janos Vajda (1827-97), Poet — A594

1977, May 2 Litho. *Perf. 12*

2486 A594 1fo green, cream & blk .40 .25

Exists imperf. Value $5.

Netherlands No. 1 and Tulips — A595

1977, May 23 Photo. *Perf. 11½x12*

2487 A595 3fo multicolored 1.60 1.60

AMPHILEX '77, Intl. Stamp Exhib., Amsterdam, May 26-June 5. Issued in sheets of 3 stamps + 3 labels showing Amphilex poster. Value, $5.
Exist imperf. Value: single with label $10; sheetlet $35.

Scene from "Wedding at Nagyrede" A596

1977, June 14 Litho. *Perf. 12*

2488 A596 3fo multicolored .50 .25

State Folk Ensemble, 25th anniversary.
Exists imperf. Value $5.

Souvenir Sheet

Bath of Bathsheba, by Rubens — A597

1977, June 14 Photo. *Perf. 11*

2489 A597 20fo multicolored 5.00 5.00

Peter Paul Rubens (1577-1640), Flemish painter.
Exists imperf. Value $45.

Medieval View of Sopron, Fidelity Tower, Arms A598

1977, June 25 Litho. *Perf. 12x11½*

2490 A598 1fo multicolored 1.40 1.40

700th anniv. of Sopron. Printed se-tenant with label showing European Architectural Heritage medal awarded Sopron in 1975.
Exists imperf. Value, single with label $15.

Race Horse Kincsem A599

1977, July 16 Litho. *Perf. 12*

2491 A599 1fo multicolored 1.00 .90

Sesquicentennial of horse racing in Hungary. Printed se-tenant with label showing portrait of Count Istvan Szechenyi and vignette from his 1827 book "Rules of Horse Racing in Hungary."
Exists imperf. Value, single with label $15.

German Democratic Republic No. 370 — A600

1977, Aug. 18 Photo. *Perf. 12x11½*

2492 A600 3fo multicolored 1.25 1.10

SOZPHILEX 77 Philatelic Exhibition, Berlin, Aug. 19-28. No. 2492 issued in sheets of 3 stamps and 3 labels showing SOZPHILEX emblem.
Exist imperf. Value: single with label $5; sheetlet $15.

Scythian Iron Bell, 6th Century B.C. — A601

Panel, Crown of Emperor Constantin Monomakhos — A602

Designs: No. 2494, Bronze candlestick in shape of winged woman, 12th-13th centuries. No. 2495, Centaur carrying child, copper aquamanile, 12th century. No. 2496, Gold figure of Christ, from 11th century Crucifix. Designs show art treasures from Hungarian National Museum, founded 1802.

1977, Sept. 3 Litho. *Perf. 12*

2493	A601 2fo multicolored	.75	.75
2494	A601 2fo multicolored	.75	.75
2495	A601 2fo multicolored	.75	.75
2496	A601 2fo multicolored	.75	.75
a.	Horiz. strip of 4, #2493-2496	3.00	3.00

Souvenir Sheet

2497 A602 10fo multicolored 3.50 3.00

50th Stamp Day.
Exist imperf. Value: strip of 4 $15; souvenir sheet $17.50.

Sputnik A603

Spacecraft: 60f, Skylab. 1fo, Soyuz-Salyut 5. 3fo, Luna 24. 4fo, Mars 3. 6fo, Viking.

1977, Sept. 20

2498	A603 40f multicolored	.25	.25
2499	A603 60f multicolored	.25	.25
2500	A603 1fo multicolored	.25	.25
2501	A603 3fo multicolored	.40	.25
2502	A603 4fo multicolored	.65	.35
2503	A603 6fo multicolored	.90	.45
	Nos. 2498-2503 (6)	2.70	1.80

Space explorations, from Sputnik to Viking. See No. C375.
Exist imperf. Value, set $15.

Janos Szanto Kovacs (1852-1908), Agrarian Movement Pioneer A604

Ervin Szabo (1877-1918), Revolutionary Workers' Movement Pioneer A605

1977, Nov. 4 Litho. Perf. 12
2504 A604 1fo red & black .30 .25
2505 A605 1fo red & black .30 .25

Exist imperf. Value, set $10.

Monument to Hungarian October Revolutionists, Omsk — A606

1977, Nov. 4
2506 A606 1fo black & red .40 .25

60th anniv. of Russian October Revolution.
Exists imperf. Value $5.

Hands and Feet Bathed in Thermal Spring — A607

1977, Nov. 1
2507 A607 1fo multicolored .40 .25

World Rheumatism Year.
Exists imperf. Value $7.50.

Endre Ady — A608

1977, Nov. 22 Engr. Perf. 12
2508 A608 1fo violet blue .40 .35

Endre Ady (1877-1919), lyric poet. Issued in sheets of 4.
Exists imperf. Value $5. Sheetlet $25.

Lesser Panda — A609

Designs: 60f, Giant panda. 1fo, Asiatic black bear. 4fo, Polar bear. 6fo, Brown bear.

1977, Dec. 16 Litho. Perf. 11½x12
2509 A609 40f yellow & multi .25 .25
2510 A609 60f yellow & multi .25 .25
2511 A609 1fo yellow & multi .35 .25
2512 A609 4fo yellow & multi .75 .30
2513 A609 6fo yellow & multi 1.00 .50
Nos. 2509-2513 (5) 2.60 1.55

Exist imperf. Value $17.50.

Souvenir Sheet

Flags and Ships along Intercontinental Waterway — A610

Flags: a, Austria. b, Bulgaria. c, Czechoslovakia. d, France. e, Luxembourg. f, Yugoslavia. g, Hungary. h, Fed. Rep. of Germany. i, Romania. j, Switzerland. k, USSR.

1977, Dec. 28 Litho. Perf. 12
2514 A610 Sheet of 11 8.00 7.75
a.-k. 2fo, any single 1.00 1.00

European Intercontinental Waterway: Danube, Main and Rhine.
Exists imperf. Value $125.

Lancer, 17th Century A611

Hussars: 60f, Kuruts, 1710. 1fo, Baranya, 1762. 2fo, Palatine officer, 1809. 4fo, Sandor, 1848. 6fo, Trumpeter, 5th Honved Regiment, 1900.

1978, Jan. Litho. Perf. 11½x12
2515 A611 40f lilac & multi .25 .25
2516 A611 60f yel grn & multi .25 .25
2517 A611 1fo red & multi .25 .25
2518 A611 2fo dull bl & multi .35 .25
2519 A611 4fo olive bis & multi .70 .30
2520 A611 6fo gray & multi 1.10 .50
Nos. 2515-2520 (6) 2.90 1.80

Exist imperf. Value, set $15.

School of Arts and Crafts A612

1978, Mar. 31 Litho. Perf. 12
2521 A612 1fo multicolored .40 .25

School of Arts and Crafts, 200th anniv.
Exists imperf. Value $6.

Soccer Players, Flags of West Germany and Poland — A613

Designs (Various Soccer Scenes and Flags): No. 2523, Hungary and Argentina. No. 2524, France and Italy. No. 2525, Tunisia and Mexico. No. 2526, Sweden and Brazil. No. 2527, Spain and Austria. No. 2528, Peru and Scotland. No. 2529, Iran and Netherlands. Flags represent first round of contestants. 20fo, Argentina '78 emblem.

1978, May 25 Litho. Perf. 12
2522 A613 2fo multicolored .25 .25
2523 A613 2fo multicolored .25 .25
2524 A613 2fo multicolored .25 .25
2525 A613 2fo multicolored .25 .25
2526 A613 2fo multicolored .25 .25
2527 A613 2fo multicolored .25 .25
2528 A613 2fo multicolored .55 .30
2529 A613 2fo multicolored .90 .40
Nos. 2522-2529 (8) 2.95 2.20

Souvenir Sheet

Perf. 11½

2530 A613 20fo multicolored 3.75 3.75

Argentina '78 11th World Cup Soccer Championships, Argentina, June 2-25.
Exist imperf. Values: set $15; souvenir sheet $17.50.

Vase, Star and Glass Blower's Tube A614

1978, May 20 Litho. Perf. 12
2531 A614 1fo multicolored .40 .25

Ajka Glass Works, centenary.
Exist imperf. Value $6.

Canada No. 1 and Trillium — A615

1978, June 2
2532 A615 3fo multicolored 1.00 .90

CAPEX '78, Canadian International Philatelic Exhibition, Toronto, Ont., June 9-18. Issued in sheets of 3 stamps and 3 labels showing CAPEX '78 emblem.
Exists imperf. Value: single with label $5; sheetlet $15.

Souvenir Sheets

Explorers and Their Ships — A616

No. 2533: a, Leif Ericson. b, Columbus. c, Vasco da Gama. d, Magellan. No. 2534: a, Drake. b, Hudson. c, Cook. d, Peary.

1978, June 10 Litho. Perf. 12x11½
2533 A616 Sheet of 4 3.25 3.00
a.-d. 2fo, any single .70 .70
2534 A616 Sheet of 4 3.25 3.00
a.-d. 2fo, any single .70 .70

Exist imperf. Value: set of 2 sheets $75.

Diesel Train, Pioneer's Kerchief — A617

1978, June 10 Perf. 12
2535 A617 1fo multicolored .40 .25

30th anniversary of Pioneer Railroad.
Exists imperf. Value $7.

Congress Emblem as Flower — A618

Design: No. 2537, Congress emblem, "Cuba" and map of Cuba.

1978, June
2536 A618 1fo multi .25 .25
2537 A618 1fo multi .25 .25
a. Pair, #2536-2537 .50 .30

11th World Youth Festival, Havana.
Exist imperf. Value $12.50.

WHO Emblem, Stylized Body and Heart — A619

1978, Aug. 21 Litho. Perf. 12
2538 A619 1fo multicolored .40 .25

Drive against hypertension.
Exists imperf. Value $7.50.

Clenched Fist, Dove and Olive Branch — A620

1978, Sept. 1 Litho. Perf. 12
2539 A620 1fo gray, red & black .40 .25

Publication of review "Peace and Socialism," 20th anniversary.
Exists imperf. Value $5.

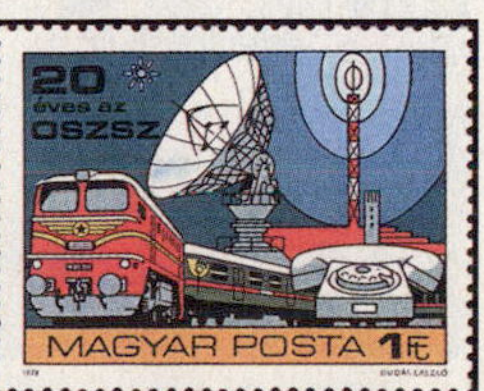

Train, Telephone, Space Communication — A621

1978, Sept. 8 Litho. Perf. 12
2540 A621 1fo multicolored .40 .25

20th anniv. of Organization for Communication Cooperation of Socialist Countries.
Exists imperf. Value $5.

"Toshiba" Automatic Letter Sorting Machine — A622

1978, Sept. 15 Litho. ***Perf. 11½x12***

2541 A622 1fo multicolored .50 .25

Introduction of automatic letter sorting. No. 2541 printed with se-tenant label showing bird holding letter.

Exists imperf. Value: single with label $12.50.

Eros Offering Grapes, Villa Hercules A623

Roman Mosaics Found in Hungary: No. 2543, Tiger (Villa Hercules, Budapest). No. 2544, Bird eating berries (Balacapuszta). No. 2545, Dolphin (Aquincum). 10fo, Hercules aiming at Centaur fleeing with Deianeira (Villa Hercules).

Photogravure and Engraved

1978, Sept. 16 ***Perf. 11½***

2542 A623 2fo multicolored 1.50 1.25
2543 A623 2fo multicolored 1.50 1.25
2544 A623 2fo multicolored 1.50 1.25
2545 A623 2fo multicolored 1.50 1.25
Nos. 2542-2545 (4) 6.00 5.00

Souvenir Sheet

2546 A623 10fo multicolored 9.00 8.50

Stamp Day. No. 2546 contains one stamp (52x35mm).

Exist imperf. Value: set $70; souvenir sheet $125.

Count Imre Thököly — A624

1978, Oct. 1 Photo. ***Perf. 12½***

2547 A624 1fo black & yellow .40 .25

300th anniv. of Hungary's independence movement, led by Imre Thököly (1657-1705).

Exists imperf. Value $5.

Souvenir Sheet

Hungarian Crown Jewels — A625

1978, Oct. 10

2548 A625 20fo gold & multi 6.00 6.00

Return of Crown Jewels from US, 1/6/78.

Exists imperf. Value $30.

"The Red Coach" A626

1978, Oct. 21 Litho. ***Perf. 12***

2549 A626 3fo red & black .50 .25

Gyula Krudy, 1878-1933, novelist.

Exists imperf. Value $6.

St. Ladislas I Reliquary, Györ Cathedral A627

1978, Nov. 15 ***Perf. 11½x12½***

2550 A627 1fo multicolored .40 .25

Ladislas I (1040-1095), 900th anniversary of accession to throne of Hungary.

Exists imperf. Value $6.

Miklos Jurisics Statue, Köszeg — A628

1978, Nov. 15 ***Perf. 12***

2551 A628 1fo multicolored .40 .25

650th anniversary of founding of Köszeg.

Exists imperf. Value $5.

Samu Czaban and Gizella Berzeviczy — A629

Photogravure and Engraved

1978, Nov. 24 ***Perf. 11½x12***

2552 A629 1fo brown, buff & red .50 .25

Samu Czaban (1878-1942) and Gizella Berzeviczy (1878-1954), Communist teachers during Soviet Republic (1918-1919).

Exists imperf. Value $5.

Communist Party Emblem A630

1978, Nov. 24 Litho. ***Perf. 12***

2553 A630 1fo gray, red & blk .40 .25

Hungarian Communist Party, 60th anniv.

Exists imperf. Value $5.

Woman Cutting Bread A631

Ceramics by Margit Kovacs (1902-1976): 2fo, Woman with pitcher. 3fo, Potter.

1978, Nov. 30 Litho. ***Perf. 11½x12***

2554 A631 1fo multicolored .25 .25
2555 A631 2fo multicolored .30 .25
2556 A631 3fo multicolored .70 .60
Nos. 2554-2556 (3) 1.25 1.10

Exist imperf. Value, set $15.

Virgin and Child, by Dürer A632

Dürer Paintings: 60f, Adoration of the Kings, horiz. 1fo, Self-portrait, 1500. 2fo, St. George. 3fo, Nativity, horiz. 4fo, St. Eustatius. 5fo, The Four Apostles. 20fo, Dancing Peasant Couple, 1514 (etching).

1979, Jan. 8 Photo. ***Perf. 12½***

2557 A632 40f gold & multi .25 .25
2558 A632 60f gold & multi .25 .25
2559 A632 1fo gold & multi .25 .25
2560 A632 2fo gold & multi .30 .25
2561 A632 3fo gold & multi .35 .25
2562 A632 4fo gold & multi .70 .30
2563 A632 5fo gold & multi .80 .60
Nos. 2557-2563 (7) 2.90 2.15

Souvenir Sheet

Litho.

2564 A632 20fo buff & brown 3.50 3.25

Albrecht Dürer (1471-1528), German painter and engraver.

Exist imperf. Value: set $15; souvenir sheet $35.

Human Rights Flame — A633

1979, Feb. 8 Litho. ***Perf. 11½x12***

2565 A633 1fo dk & lt blue 1.25 1.25

Universal Declaration of Human Rights, 30th anniversary. No. 2565 issued in sheets of 12 stamps (3x4) and 4 labels. Alternating horizontal rows inverted.

Exists imperf. Value $10. Strip of 3 $40, Sheetlet $60.

Child at Play — A634

IYC Emblem and: No. 2567, Family. No. 2568, 3 children (international friendship).

1979, Feb. 26 ***Perf. 12***

2566 A634 1fo multicolored .75 .75
2567 A634 1fo multicolored .75 .75
2568 A634 1fo multicolored 6.50 5.50
Nos. 2566-2568 (3) 8.00 7.00

Exist imperf. Value, set $22.50.

Soldiers of the Red Army, by Bela Uitz A635

1979, Mar. 21 Litho. ***Perf. 12***

2569 A635 1fo silver, blk & red .40 .25

60th anniv. of Hungarian Soviet Republic.

Exists imperf. Value $5.

Calvinist Church, Nyirbator — A636

1979, Mar. 28 ***Perf. 11***

2570 A636 1fo brown & yellow .40 .25

700th anniv. of Nyirbator. See No. 2601.

Exists imperf. Value $10.

Chessmen, Gold Cup, Flag — A637

1979, Apr. 12 Litho. ***Perf. 12***

2571 A637 3fo multicolored 1.00 .50

Hungarian victories in 23rd Chess Olympiad, Buenos Aires, 1978.

Exists imperf. Value $15.

Alexander Nevski Cathedral, Sofia, Bulgaria No. 1 — A638

1979, May 18 Litho. ***Perf. 11½x12***

2572 A638 3fo multicolored .75 .75

Philaserdica '79 Philatelic Exhibition, Sofia, Bulgaria, May 18-27. No. 2572 issued in sheets of 3 stamps and 3 labels showing Philaserdica emblem and arms of Sofia.

Exist imperf. Value: single with label $5.50; sheetlet $17.50.

Stephenson's Rocket, 1829, IVA '79 Emblem — A639

Railroad Development: 60f, Siemens' first electric locomotive, 1879. 1fo, "Pioneer," Chicago & Northwestern Railroad, 1836. 2fo, Orient Express, 1883. 3fo, Trans-Siberian train, 1898. 4fo, Express train on Tokaido line, 1964. 5fo, Transrapid-O5 train, exhibited 1979. 20fo, Map of European railroad network.

1979, June 8 Litho. *Perf. 12x11½*

2573 A639 40f multi .25 .25
2574 A639 60f multi .25 .25
2575 A639 1fo multi .25 .25
2576 A639 2fo multi .30 .25
2577 A639 3fo multi .45 .25
2578 A639 4fo multi .60 .45
2579 A639 5fo multi .90 .50
Nos. 2573-2579 (7) 3.00 2.20

Souvenir Sheet

Perf. 12½x11½

2580 A639 20fo multi 4.00 3.75

Intl. Transportation Exhibition (IVA '79), Hamburg. No. 2580 contains one 47x32mm stamp.
Exist imperf. Value: set $17.50; souvenir sheet $35.

Natural Gas Pipeline and Compressor A640

2fo, Lenin power station & dam, Dnepropetrovsk & pylon. 3fo, Comecon Building, Moscow, & star symbolizing 10 member states.

1979, June 26 *Perf. 11½x12*

2581 A640 1fo multi .25 .25
2582 A640 2fo multi .25 .25
2583 A640 3fo multi .40 .25
Nos. 2581-2583 (3) .90 .75

30th anniversary of the Council of Mutual Economic Assistance, Comecon.
Exist imperf. Value, set $15.

Zsigmond Moricz (1879-1942), Writer, by Jozsef Ripple-Ronai A641

1979, June 29 *Perf. 12*

2584 A641 1fo multi .40 .25

Exists imperf. Value $5.

Town Hall, Helsinki, Finnish Flag, Moscow '80 Emblem A642

Designs (Moscow '80 Emblem and): 60f, Colosseum, Rome, Italian flag. 1fo, Asakusa Temple, Tokyo, Japanese flag. 2fo, Mexico City Cathedral, Mexican flag. 3fo, Our Lady's Church, Munich, German flag. 4fo, Skyscrapers, Montreal, Canadian flag. 5fo, Lomonosov University, Misha the bear and Soviet flag.

1979, July 31 *Perf. 12x11½*

2585 A642 40f multi .25 .25
2586 A642 60f multi .25 .25
2587 A642 1fo multi .25 .25
2588 A642 2fo multi .25 .25
2589 A642 3fo multi .30 .25
2590 A642 4fo multi .40 .30
2591 A642 5fo multi .70 .45
Nos. 2585-2591 (7) 2.40 2.00

Pre-Olympic Year.
Exist imperf. Value, set $20.

Boy with Horse and Greyhounds, by Janos Vaszary — A643

Paintings of Horses: 60f, Coach and Five, by Karoly Lotz. 1fo, Boys on Horseback, by Celesztin Pallya. 2fo, Farewell, by Lotz. 3fo, Horse Market, by Pallya. 4fo, Wanderer, by Bela Ivanyi-Grunwald. 5fo, Ready for the Hunt, by Karoly Sterio.

1979, Aug. 11 Photo. *Perf. 12½*

2592 A643 40f multi .25 .25
2593 A643 60f multi .25 .25
2594 A643 1fo multi .25 .25
2595 A643 2fo multi .25 .25
2596 A643 3fo multi .40 .25
2597 A643 4fo multi .50 .30
2598 A643 5fo multi .75 .40
Nos. 2592-2598 (7) 2.65 1.95

Exist imperf. Value, set $20.

Sturgeons, Map of Danube, "Calypso" — A644

1979, Aug. 11

2599 A644 3fo multi .50 .25

Environmental protection of rivers and seas.
Exists imperf. Value $6.

Pentathlon A645

1979, Aug. 12 Litho. *Perf. 12*

2600 A645 2fo multi .50 .25

Pentathlon World Championship, Budapest, Aug. 12-18.
Exists imperf. Value $5.

Architecture Type of 1979

Design: Vasvar Public Health Center.

1979, Aug. 15 Litho. *Perf. 11*

2601 A636 40f grn & blk .40 .25

700th anniversary of Vasvar.
Exists imperf. Value $10.

Denarius of Stephen I, 1000-1038, Reverse A646

Hungarian Coins: 2fo, Copper coin of Bela III, 1172-1196. 3fo, Golden groat of King Louis the Great, 1342-1382. 4fo, Golden forint of Matthias I, 1458-1490. 5fo, Silver gulden of Wladislaw II, 1490-1516.

Engraved and Photogravure

1979, Sept. 3 *Perf. 12x11½*

2602 A646 1fo multi .25 .25
2603 A646 2fo multi .25 .25
2604 A646 3fo multi .35 .25
2605 A646 4fo multi .50 .40
2606 A646 5fo multi 1.00 .70
Nos. 2602-2606 (5) 2.35 1.85

9th International Numismatic Congress, Berne, Switzerland.
Exist imperf. Value, set $15.

Souvenir Sheet

Unofficial Stamp, 1848 — A647

1979, Sept. 15 Litho. *Perf. 12*

2607 A647 10fo dk brown, blk & red 2.75 2.50

Stamp Day.
Exists imperf. Value $20.

Souvenir Sheet

Gyor-Sopron-Ebenfurt rail service, cent. — A648

Designs: a, Elbel Locomotive. b, Type 424 steam engine. c, "War Locomotive." d, Hydraulic diesel locomotive.

1979, Oct. 19 Litho. *Perf. 12*

2608 A648 Sheet of 4 3.25 3.00
a.-d. A648 5fo any single .65 .65

Exists imperf. Value $27.50

Vega-Chess, by Victor Vasarely A649

1979, Oct. 29

2609 A649 1fo multi .40 .25

Exists imperf. Value $15.

International Savings Day — A650

1979, Oct. 29 Litho. *Perf. 12*

2610 A650 1fo multi .40 .25

Exists imperf. Value $5.

Otter — A651

Wildlife Protection: 60f, Wild cat. 1fo, Pine marten. 2fo, Eurasian badger. 4fo, Polecat. 6fo, Beech marten.

1979, Nov. 20

2611 A651 40f multi .25 .25
2612 A651 60f multi .25 .25
2613 A651 1fo multi .25 .25
2614 A651 2fo multi .30 .25
2615 A651 4fo multi .60 .25
2616 A651 6fo multi .90 .60
Nos. 2611-2616 (6) 2.55 1.85

Exist imperf. Value, set $15.

Tom Thumb, IYC Emblem A652

IYC Emblem and Fairy Tale Scenes: 60f, The Ugly Duckling. 1fo, The Fisherman and the Goldfish. 2fo, Cinderella. 3fo, Gulliver's Travels. 4fo, The Little Pigs and the Wolf. 5fo, Janos the Knight. 20fo, The Fairy Ilona.

1979, Dec. 29 Litho. *Perf. 12x11½*

2617 A652 40f multi .25 .25
2618 A652 60f multi .25 .25
2619 A652 1fo multi .25 .25
2620 A652 2fo multi .35 .25
2621 A652 3fo multi .50 .30
2622 A652 4fo multi .70 .30
2623 A652 5fo multi 1.00 .60
Nos. 2617-2623 (7) 3.30 2.20

Souvenir Sheet

2624 A652 20fo multi 3.75 3.50

Exist imperf. Value: set $17.50; souvenir sheet $22.50.

Trichodes Apairius and Yarrow — A653

Insects Pollinating Flowers: 60f, Bumblebee and blanketflower. 1fo, Red admiral butterfly and daisy. 2fo, Cetonia aurata and rose. 4fo, Graphosoma lineatum and petroselinum hortense. 6fo, Chlorophorus varius and thistle.

1980, Jan. 25 Litho. *Perf. 12*

2625 A653 40f multi .25 .25
2626 A653 60f multi .25 .25
2627 A653 1fo multi .25 .25
2628 A653 2fo multi .35 .25
2629 A653 4fo multi .50 .25
2630 A653 6fo multi .75 .30
Nos. 2625-2630 (6) 2.35 1.55

Exist imperf. Value, set $17.50.

Hanging Gardens of Semiramis, 6th Century B.C., Map showing Babylon — A654

Seven Wonders of the Ancient World (and Map): 60f, Temple of Artemis, Ephesus, 6th century B.C. 1fo, Zeus, by Phidias, Olympia. 2fo, Tomb of Maussolos, Halikarnassos, 3rd century B.C. 3fo, Colossos of Rhodes. 4fo, Pharos Lighthouse, Alexandria, 3rd century B.C. 5fo, Pyramids, 26th-24th centuries B.C.

1980, Feb. 29 Litho. *Perf. 12x11½*

2631 A654 40f multi .25 .25
2632 A654 60f multi .25 .25
2633 A654 1fo multi .25 .25
2634 A654 2fo multi .30 .25
2635 A654 3fo multi .40 .25
2636 A654 4fo multi .60 .35
2637 A654 5fo multi .85 .60
Nos. 2631-2637 (7) 2.90 2.20

Exist imperf. Value, set $17.50.

Tihany Benedictine Abbey and Deed — A655

1980, Mar. 19 Litho. *Perf. 12*

2638 A655 1fo multi .40 .25

Benedictine Abbey, Tihany, 925th anniversary of deed (oldest document in Hungarian).
Exists imperf. Value $5.

Gabor Bethlen, Copperplate Print — A656

1980, Mar. 19

2639 A656 1fo multi .40 .25

Gabor Bethlen (1580-1629), Prince of Transylvania (1613-29) and King of Hungary (1620-29).
Exists imperf. Value $5.

Easter Casket of Garamszentbenedek, 15th Century (Restoration) — A657

1980, Mar. 19

2640 A657 1fo shown .25 .25
2641 A657 2fo Three Marys .25 .25
2642 A657 3fo Apostle James .35 .35
2643 A657 4fo Thaddeus .55 .55
2644 A657 5fo Andrew .75 .55
Nos. 2640-2644 (5) 2.15 1.95

Exist imperf. Value, set $15.

Liberation from Fascism, 35th Anniversary A658

1980, Apr. 3 Litho. *Perf. 12*

2645 A658 1fr multi .40 .25

Exists imperf. Value $5.

Jozsef Attila, Poet and Lyricist — A659

1980, Apr. 11

2646 A659 1fo rose car & olive .40 .25

Exists imperf. Value $5.
See No. 2675.

Hungarian Postal Museum, 50th anniv. — A660

1980, Apr. 28 *Perf. 11½x12*

2647 A660 1fo multi 1.90 1.50

Features Hungary No. 386a.
Exists imperf. Value $20.

Two Pence Blue, Mounted Guardsman, London 1980 Emblem — A661

1980, Apr. 30 *Perf. 11½x12*

2648 A661 3fo multi 1.00 1.00

London 1980 International Stamp Exhibition, May 6-14. No. 2648 issued in sheets of 3 stamps and 3 labels showing London 1980 emblem and arms of city. Size: 104x125mm.
Exists imperf. Value: single with label $5; sheetlet $15.

Norway No. B51, Mother with Child, by Gustav Vigeland — A662

1980, June 9 Litho. *Perf. 11½x12*

2649 A662 3fo multi 1.00 1.00

NORWEX '80 Stamp Exhibition, Oslo, June 13-22. No. 2649 issued in sheets of 3 stamps and 3 labels showing NORWEX emblem. Size: 108x125mm.
Exists imperf. Value: single with label $5; sheetlet $15.

Margit Kaffka (1880-1918), Writer — A663

1980, June 9 *Perf. 12*

2650 A663 1fo blk & pur, *cr* .40 .25

Exists imperf. Value $6.

Zoltan Schönherz (1905-42), Anti-fascist Martyr — A664

1980, July 25 Litho.

2652 A664 1fo multi .40 .25

Exists imperf. Value $5.

Dr. Endre Hogyes and Congress Emblem A665

1980, July 25

2653 A665 1fo multi .40 .25

28th International Congress of Physiological Sciences, Budapest, Dr. Hogyes (1847-1906) first described equilibrium reflex-curve and modified Pasteur's rabies vaccine.
Exists imperf. Value $5.

Decanter, c. 1850 — A666

1980, Sept. Litho. *Perf. 12*

2654 A666 1fo shown .25 .25
2655 A666 2fo Decorated glass .35 .35
2656 A666 3fo Stem glass .65 .65
Nos. 2654-2656 (3) 1.25 1.25

Souvenir Sheet

2657 A666 10fo Pecs glass 2.50 2.25

53rd Stamp Day.
Exist imperf. Value: set $12.50; souvenir sheet $15.

Bertalan Por, Self-portrait A667

1980, Nov. 4 Litho. *Perf. 12*

2658 A667 1fo Artist (1880-1964) .40 .25

Exists imperf. Value $5.

Graylag Goose — A668

60f, Black-crowned night heron. 1fo, Shoveler. 2fo, Chlidonias leucopterus. 4fo, Great crested grebe. 6fo, Black-necked stilt.
20fo, Great white heron.

1980, Nov. 11 *Perf. 11½x12*

2659 A668 40f shown .25 .25
2660 A668 60f multicolored .25 .25
2661 A668 1fo multicolored .25 .25
2662 A668 2fo multicolored .30 .25
2663 A668 4fo multicolored .60 .30
2664 A668 6fo multicolored 1.00 .50
Nos. 2659-2664 (6) 2.65 1.80

Souvenir Sheet

2665 A668 20fo multicolored 4.25 4.00

European Nature Protection Year. No. 2665 contains one stamp (37x59mm).
Exist imperf. Value: set $22.50; souvenir sheet $30.

Souvenir Sheet

Dove on Map of Europe — A669

1980, Nov. 11 ***Perf. 12½x11½***
2666 A669 20fo multi 4.50 4.00

European Security and Cooperation Conference, Madrid.
Exists imperf. Value $30.

Johannes Kepler and Model of his Theory — A670

1980, Nov. 21 **Litho.** ***Perf. 12***
2667 A670 1fo multi .50 .25

Johannes Kepler (1571-1630), German astronomer, 350th anniversary of death. No. 2667 printed se-tenant with label showing rocket and satellites orbiting earth.
Exists imperf. Value, single with label $12.50.

Karoly Kisfaludy (1788-1830), Poet and Dramatist A671

1980, Nov. 21
2668 A671 1fo brn red & dull brn .40 .25

Exists imperf. Value $5.

UN Headquarters, New York — A672

UN membership, 25th anniversary: 60f, Geneva headquarters. 1fo, Vienna headquarters. 2fo, UN & Hungary flags. 4fo, UN, Hungary arms. 6fo, World map.

Photogravure and Engraved

1980, Dec. 12 ***Perf. 11½x12***
2669 A672 40f shown .25 .25
2670 A672 60f multicolored .25 .25
2671 A672 1fo multicolored .25 .25
2672 A672 2fo multicolored .30 .25
2673 A672 4fo multicolored .55 .35
2674 A672 6fo multicolored .90 .55
Nos. 2669-2674 (6) 2.50 1.90

Exist imperf. Value, set $20.

Attila Type of 1980

Ferenc Erdei (1910-71), economist & statesman.

1980, Dec. 23 **Litho.** ***Perf. 12***
2675 A659 1fo dk green & brown .40 .25

Exists imperf. Value $5.

Bela Szanto — A674

1981, Jan. 31 **Litho.** ***Perf. 12***
2676 A674 1fo multi .40 .25

Bela Szanto (1881-1951), labor movement leader.
Exists imperf. Value $5.
See Nos. 2698, 2724, 2767.

Count Lajos Batthyany A675

1981, Feb. 14
2677 A675 1fo multi .40 .25

Count Lajos Batthyany (1806-1849), prime minister, later executed.
Exists imperf. Value $6.

Bela Bartok (1881-1945), Composer A677

Design: b, Cantata Profana illustration.

1981, Mar. 25 **Litho.** ***Perf. 12½***
2685 Sheet of 2 2.50 2.50
a.-b. A677 10fo any single 1.25 1.25

Exists imperf. Value $20.

Telephone Exchange System Cent. — A678

1981, Apr. 29 **Litho.** ***Perf. 12***
2686 A678 2fo multi .40 .25

Exists imperf. Value $5.

Belling Stag — A679

1981, Apr. 29
2687 A679 2fo multi .40 .25

Exists imperf. Value $5.

Flag of the House of Arpad, 11th Cent. A680

60f, Hunyadi family, 15th cent. 1fo, Gabor Bethlen, 1600. 2fo, Ferenc Rakoczi II, 1716. 4fo, Honved, 1848. 6fo, Troop flag, 1919.

1981, Apr. 29
2688 A680 40f shown .25 .25
2689 A680 60f multicolored .25 .25
2690 A680 1fo multicolored .25 .25
2691 A680 2fo multicolored .25 .25
2692 A680 4fo multicolored .60 .25
2693 A680 6fo multicolored .80 .35
Nos. 2688-2693 (6) 2.40 1.60

Exist imperf. Value, set $15.

Red Cross and Ambulance Vehicles A681

Map of Europe and J. Henry Dunant (Red Cross Founder) — A682

1981, May 4
2694 A681 2fo multi .40 .25

Souvenir Sheet

Perf. 12½x11½

2695 A682 20fo multi 3.00 3.00

Hungarian Red Cross cent. (2fo); 3rd European Red Cross Conf., Budapest, May 4-7 (20fo).
Exist imperf. Value: single $5; souvenir sheet $22.50.

Souvenir Sheet

1933 WIPA Exhibition Seals — A683

1981, May 15 ***Perf. 12x12½***
2696 A683 Sheet of 4 2.75 2.75
a.-d. 5fo any single .65 .65

WIPA 1981 Phil. Exhib., Vienna, May 22-31.
Exists imperf. Value $20.

Stephenson and his Nonpareil — A684

1981, June 12 **Litho.** ***Perf. 12***
2697 A684 2fo multi .40 .25

George Stephenson (1781-1848), British railroad engineer, birth bicentenary.
Exists imperf. Value $6.

Famous Hungarians Type

Bela Vago (1881-1939), anti-fascist martyr.

1981, Aug. 7 **Litho.** ***Perf. 12***
2698 A674 2fo ocher & brn ol .40 .25

Exists imperf. Value $5.

Alexander Fleming (1881-1955), Discoverer of Penicillin — A686

1981, Aug. 7
2699 A686 2fo multi .40 .25

Exists imperf. Value $7.50.

Bridal Chest A687

Bridal chests: 1fo, Szentgal, 18th cent. 2fo, Hodmezovasar-hely, 19th cent.
10fo, Bacs County, 17th cent.

1981, Sept. 12 **Litho.** ***Perf. 12***
2700 A687 1fo multicolored .25 .25
2701 A687 2fo multicolored .30 .25

Souvenir Sheet

2702 A687 10fo multicolored 1.75 1.75

54th Stamp Day. No. 2702 contains one stamp (44x25mm).
Exist imperf. Values: Nos. 2700-2701 $12.50; No. 2702 $20.

Calvinist College, Papa, 450th Anniv. A688

1981, Oct. 3 **Litho.** ***Perf. 12***
2703 A688 2fo multi .40 .25

Exists imperf. Value $5.

World Food Day — A689

1981, Oct. 16
2704 A689 2fo multi .40 .25

Exists imperf. Value $6.

Passenger Ship Rakoczi, 1964, No. 1834 — A690

Sidewheelers and Hungarian stamps: No. 2705, Franz I, #1828. No. 2706, Arpad, #1829. No. 2707, Szechenyi, #1830. No. 2708, Grof Szechenyi Istvan, #1831. No. 2709, Sofia, #1832. No. 2710, Felszabadulas, #1833. No. 2712, Hydrofoil Solyom, #1830.

1981, Nov. 25 *Perf. 12x11½*

2705	A690	1fo multicolored	.25	.25
2706	A690	1fo multicolored	.25	.25
2707	A690	2fo multicolored	.30	.25
2708	A690	2fo multicolored	.30	.25
2709	A690	4fo multicolored	.65	.30
2710	A690	6fo multicolored	.95	.50
2711	A690	8fo shown	1.25	.65
		Nos. 2705-2711 (7)	3.95	2.45

Souvenir Sheet

Perf. 13

2712 A690 20fo multicolored 3.00 3.00

European Danube Commission, 125th anniv.

Exist imperf. Value: set $20; souvenir sheet $25.

Souvenir Sheet

Natl. Costumes — A691

Perf. 12½x11½

1981, Nov. 18 **Litho.**

2713	A691	Sheet of 4	2.00	1.90
a.		1fo Slovakian	.25	.25
b.		2fo German	.40	.35
c.		3fo Croatian	.60	.60
d.		4fo Romanian	.80	.75

Exists imperf. Value $20.

Christmas 1981 — A692

Sculptures: 1fo, Mary Nursing the Infant Jesus, by Margit Kovacs. 2fo, Madonna of Csurgo.

1981, Dec. 4 *Perf. 12½x11½*

2714	A692	1fo multi	.25	.25
2715	A692	2fo multi	.40	.25

Exist imperf. Value, set $10.

Pen Pals, by Norman Rockwell A693

Norman Rockwell Illustrations: No. 2717, Courting Under the Clock at Midnight. No. 2718, Maiden Voyage. No. 2719, Threading the Needle.

1981, Dec. 29 *Perf. 11½x12*

2716	A693	1fo shown	.25	.25
2717	A693	2fo multicolored	.25	.25
2718	A693	2fo multicolored	.25	.25
2719	A693	4fo multicolored	.45	.25
		Nos. 2716-2719,C435-C437 (7)	3.25	2.65

Exist imperf. Value, set (7) $17.50.

Souvenir Sheet

La Toilette, by Pablo Picasso (1881-1973) — A694

1981, Dec. 29 **Litho.** *Perf. 11½*

2720 A694 20fo multicolored 3.50 3.50

Exists imperf. Value $50.

25th Anniv. of Worker's Militia A695

1982, Jan. 26 **Litho.** *Perf. 12*

2721	A695	1fo Shooting practice	.25	.25
2722	A695	4fo Members, 3 generations	.50	.35

Exist imperf. Value, set $10.

10th World Trade Union Congress — A696

1982, Feb. 12 **Litho.** *Perf. 12x11½*

2723 A696 2fo multicolored .40 .25

Exists imperf. Value $5.

Famous Hungarians Type

Gyula Alpári (1882-1944), anti-fascist martyr.

1982, Mar. 24 *Perf. 12*

2724 A674 2fo multicolored .40 .25

Exists imperf. Value $5.

Robert Koch — A698

1982, Mar. 24 **Litho.** *Perf. 12*

2725 A698 2fo multicolored .40 .25

TB Bacillus centenary.

Exists imperf. Value $6.

1982 World Cup — A699

Designs: Hungary in competition with other World Cup teams.

No. 2733: a, Barcelona Stadium. b, Madrid Stadium.

1982, Apr. 16 *Perf. 11*

2726	A699	1fo Egypt, 1934	.25	.25
2727	A699	1fo Italy, 1938	.25	.25
2728	A699	2fo Germany, 1954	.25	.25
2729	A699	2fo Mexico, 1958	.25	.25
2730	A699	4fo England, 1962	.45	.25
2731	A699	6fo Brazil, 1966	.70	.40
2732	A699	8fo Argentina, 1978	.90	.55
		Nos. 2726-2732 (7)	3.05	2.20

Souvenir Sheet

2733		Sheet of 2	3.00	3.00
a.-b.		A699 10fo any single	1.40	1.40

No. 2733 contains 44x44mm stamps.

Exist imperf. Value: set $17; souvenir sheet $20.

European Table Tennis Championship, Budapest, Apr. 17-25 — A700

1982, Apr. 16 **Litho.** *Perf. 11½x12*

2734 A700 2fo multi .40 .25

Exists imperf. Value $5.

Roses A701

1982, Apr. 30 *Perf. 12*

2735	A701	1fo Pascali	.25	.25
2736	A701	1fo Michele Meilland	.25	.25
2737	A701	2fo Diorama	.30	.25
2738	A701	2fo Wendy Cussons	.30	.25
2739	A701	3fo Blue Moon	.40	.25
2740	A701	3fo Invitation	.40	.25
2741	A701	4fo Tropicana	.60	.30
		Nos. 2735-2741 (7)	2.50	1.80

Souvenir Sheet

2742 A701 10fo Bouquet 2.50 2.50

No. 2742 contains one stamp (34x59mm, perf. 11).

Exist imperf. Value: set $17.50; souvenir sheet $30.

25 Years of Space Travel — A702

No. 2743, Columbia shuttle, 1981. No. 2744, Armstrong, Apollo 11, 1969. No. 2745, A. Leonov, Voskhod 2, 1965. No. 2746, Yuri Gagarin, Vostok. No. 2747, Laika, Sputnik 2, 1957. No. 2748, Sputnik I, 1957. No. 2749, Space researcher K.E. Tsiolkovsky.

1982, May 18 **Photo.** *Perf. 11½*

2743	A702	1fo multicolored	.25	.25
2744	A702	1fo multicolored	.25	.25
2745	A702	2fo multicolored	.30	.25
2746	A702	2fo multicolored	.30	.25
2747	A702	4fo multicolored	.55	.35
2748	A702	4fo multicolored	.55	.35
2749	A702	6fo multicolored	.90	.50
		Nos. 2743-2749 (7)	3.10	2.20

Exist imperf. Value, set $15.

A703

1982, May 7 **Litho.** *Perf. 12*

2750 A703 2fo multi .50 .25

George Dimitrov (1882-1947), 1st prime minister of Bulgaria. SOZPHILEX '82 Stamp Exhib., Sofia, Bulgaria, May. No. 2750 se-tenant with label showing Bulgarian 1300th anniv. emblems.

Exists imperf. Value, with label $12.50.

Diosgyor paper mill, bicent. — A704

1982, May 27 **Litho.** *Perf. 12x11½*

2751 A704 2fo multi .40 .25

Exists imperf. Value $5.

First Rubik's Cube World Championship, Budapest, June 5 — A705

1982, June 4 *Perf. 11½x12*

2752 A705 2fo multi .40 .25

Exists imperf. Value $6.

Souvenir Sheet

George Washington, by F. Kemmelmeyer — A706

Washington's 250th Birth Anniv.: a, Michael Kovats de Fabricy (1724-1779), Cavalry Commandant, by Sandor Finta.

1982, July 2 **Litho.** *Perf. 11*

2753	A706	Sheet of 2	2.50	2.50
a.-b.		5fo any single	.75	.75

Exists imperf. Value $17.50.

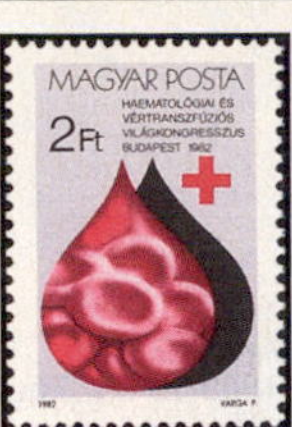

World Hematology Congress, Budapest — A707

1982, July 30 *Perf. 12½x11½*

2754 A707 2fo multi .40 .25

Exists imperf. Value $6.

Zirc Abbey, 800th Anniv. — A708

1982, Aug. 19 *Perf. 11½x12*

2755 A708 2fo multi .40 .25

Exists imperf. Value $5.

KNER Printing Office, Gyoma, Centenary — A709

1982, Sept. 23 Litho. *Perf. 12x11½*

2756 A709 2fo Emblem .40 .25

Exists imperf. Value $5.

AGROFILA '82 Intl. Agricultural Stamp Exhibition, Godollo — A710

1982, Sept. 24 *Perf. 11½x12*

2757 A710 5fo Map 1.60 1.60

Issued in sheets of 3 stamps and 3 labels showing Godollo Agricultural University, emblem. Size: 109x127mm. Value, $5.

Exist imperf. Value: single with label $10; sheetlet $35.

Public Transportation Sesquicentennial — A711

1982, Oct. 5 Litho. *Perf. 12x11½*

2758 A711 2fo multi .40 .25

Exists imperf. Value $15.

Vuk and a Bird — A712

Scenes from Vuk the Fox Cub, Cartoon by Attila Dargay.

1982, Nov. 11 *Perf. 12½*

2759	A712	1fo shown	.25	.25
2760	A712	1fo Dogs	.25	.25
2761	A712	2fo Rooster	.25	.25
2762	A712	2fo Owl	.25	.25
2763	A712	4fo Geese	.50	.30
2764	A712	6fo Frog	.70	.55
2765	A712	8fo Master fox	1.00	.70
		Nos. 2759-2765 (7)	3.20	2.55

Exist imperf. Value, set $17.50.

Engineering Education Bicentenary A713

2fo, Budapest Polytechnical University.

1982, Oct. 13 *Perf. 12*

2766 A713 2fo multicolored .40 .25

Exists imperf. Value $5.

Famous Hungarians Type

Gyorgy Boloni (1882-1959), writer and journalist.

1982, Oct. 29

2767 A674 2fo multi .40 .25

Exists imperf. Value $5.

October Revolution, 65th Anniv. — A715

1982, Nov. 5 Litho. *Perf. 11½x12*

2768 A715 5fo Lenin .75 .40

Exists imperf. Value $6.

Works of Art in Hungarian Chapel, Vatican — A716

Designs: No. 2769, St. Stephen, first King of Hungary (1001-1038). No. 2770, Pope Sylvester II making donation to St. Stephen. No. 2771, Pope Callixtus III ordering noon victory bell ringing by St. John of Capistrano, 1456. No. 2772, Pope Paul VI showing Cardinal Lekai location of Hungarian Chapel. No. 2773, Pope John Paul II consecrating chapel, 1980. No. 2774, Madonna and Child. Nos. 2769, 2774 sculptures by Imre Varga; others by Amerigo Tot. Nos. 2770-2773, size 37x18mm, in continuous design in block of 4 between Nos. 2769 and 2774.

1982, Nov. 30 *Perf. 12x11½*

2769	A716	2fo multi	.55	.55
2770	A716	2fo multi	.55	.55
2771	A716	2fo multi	.55	.55
2772	A716	2fo multi	.55	.55
2773	A716	2fo multi	.55	.55
2774	A716	2fo multi	.55	.55
a.		Block of 6, #2769-2774	4.00	4.00

Exist imperf. Value, block $15.

Souvenir Sheet

Zoltan Kodaly (1882-1967), Composer — A717

1982, Dec. 16 *Perf. 11½*

2775 A717 20fo multi 2.75 2.75

Exists imperf. Value $17.50.

A718

Perf. 12½x11½

1982, Dec. 16 **Litho.**

2776 A718 2fo multi .40 .25

New Year 1983.

Exists imperf. Value $5.

A719

Design: Johann Wolfgang Goethe (1749-1832), German poet, by Heinrich Kolbe.

1982, Dec. 29 *Perf. 11½x12½*

Souvenir Sheet

2777 A719 20fo multi 2.75 2.75

Exists imperf. Value $27.50.

10th Anniv. of Postal Code — A720

1983, Jan. 24 *Perf. 11½x12*

2778 A720 2fo multi .40 .25

Exists imperf. Value $5.

3rd Budapest Spring Festival, Mar. 18-27 A721

2fo, Ship of Peace, by Engre Szasz.

1983, Mar. 18 Litho. *Perf. 12x11½*

2779 A721 2fo multicolored .40 .25

Exists imperf. Value $5.

Gyula Juhasz (1883-1937), Poet — A722

1983, Apr. 15 *Perf. 12*

2780 A722 2fo multi .40 .25

Exists imperf. Value $5.

City of Szentgotthard, 800th Anniv. — A723

2fo, Monastery, seal, 1489.

1983, May 4 Litho. *Perf. 11½*

2781 A723 2fo multicolored .40 .25

Exists imperf. Value $5.

Malomto Lake, Tapolca — A724

1983, May 17 *Perf. 11½x12*

2782 A724 5fo multi .80 .80

TEMBAL '83 Intl. Topical Stamp Exhibition, Basel, May 21-29. Issued in sheets of 3 stamps and 3 labels.

Exists imperf. Value: single with label $4; sheetlet $15.

Souvenir Sheet

5th Interparliamentary Union Conference on European Cooperation, Budapest, May 30-June 5 — A725

20fo, Budapest Parliament.

1983, May 30 **Litho.** ***Perf. 12½***
2783 A725 20fo multi 3.50 3.25

Exists imperf. Value $20.

Jeno Hamburger (1883-1936) A726

1983, May 31 ***Perf. 12***
2784 A726 2fo multi .45 .25

Exists imperf. Value $5.

Lady with Unicorn, by Raphael (1483-1517) A727

Paintings: No. 2786, Joan of Aragon. No. 2787, Granduca Madonna. No. 2788, Madonna and Child with St. John. 4fo, La Muta. 6fo, La Valeta. 8fo, La Fornarina. 20fo, Esterhazy Madonna.

Perf. 11½x12½
1983, June 29 **Litho.**

2785	A727	1fo multi	.25	.25
2786	A727	1fo multi	.25	.25
2787	A727	2fo multi	.25	.25
2788	A727	2fo multi	.25	.25
2789	A727	4fo multi	.45	.30
2790	A727	6fo multi	.65	.30
2791	A727	8fo multi	.75	.45
		Nos. 2785-2791 (7)	2.85	2.05

Souvenir Sheet

2792 A727 20fo multi 3.00 3.00

No. 2792 contains one stamp (24x37mm).
Exist imperf. Value: set $17.50; souvenir sheet $17.50.

Simon Bolivar (1783-1830) A728

1983, July 22 **Litho.** ***Perf. 12***
2793 A728 2fo multi .40 .25

Exists imperf. Value $5.

Istvan Vagi (1883-1940), Anti-fascist Martyr A729

1983, July 22 ***Perf. 11½x12½***
2794 A729 2fo multi .45 .25

Exists imperf. Value $5.

68th World Esperanto Congress, Budapest, July 30-Aug. 6 — A730

1983, July 29 ***Perf. 12***
2795 A730 2fo multi .40 .25

Exists imperf. Value $6.

Souvenir Sheet

Martin Luther (1483-1546) — A731

1983, Aug. 12 ***Perf. 12½***
2796 A731 20fo multi 2.75 2.50

Exists imperf. Value $20.

Birds — A732

Designs: Protected birds of prey and World Wildlife Fund emblem

1983, Aug. 18 ***Perf. 11½x12***

2797	A732	1fo Aquila heliaca	.25	.25
2798	A732	1fo Aquila pomarina	.25	.25
2799	A732	2fo Haliaetus albicilla	.75	.25
2800	A732	2fo Falco vespertinus	.75	.25
2801	A732	4fo Falco cherrug	1.00	.30
2802	A732	6fo Buteo lagopus	1.25	.35
2803	A732	8fo Buteo buteo	1.50	.75
		Nos. 2797-2803 (7)	5.75	2.40

Exist imperf. Value, set $20.

29th Intl. Apicultural Congress, Budapest, Aug. 25-31 — A733

1fo, Bee collecting pollen.

1983, Aug. 25 ***Perf. 12***
2804 A733 1fo multi .40 .25

Exists imperf. Value $6.

Fruit, by Bela Czobel (1883-1976) — A734

1983, Sept. 15 **Litho.** ***Perf. 12x11½***
2805 A734 2fo multi .40 .25

Exists imperf. Value $5.

World Communications Year — A735

No. 2806, Telecommunications, Earth Satellite. No. 2807, Intersputnik Earth Station. 2fo, TMM-81 Telephone Service. 3fo, Intelligent Terminal System. 5fo, OCR Optical Reading Instrument. 8fo, Teletext. 20fo, Molniya Communications Satellite.

1983, Oct. 7 **Litho.** ***Perf. 11½x12***

2806	A735	1fo multi	.25	.25
2807	A735	1fo multi	.25	.25
2808	A735	2fo multi	.25	.25
2809	A735	3fo multi	.40	.25
2810	A735	5fo multi	.70	.40
2811	A735	8fo multi	1.10	.65
		Nos. 2806-2811 (6)	2.95	2.05

Souvenir Sheet
Perf. 12x12½

2812 A735 20fo multi 3.00 3.00

Exist imperf. Value: set $15; souvenir sheet $15.

34th Intl. Astronautical Federation Congress — A736

1983, Oct. 10 **Photo.** ***Perf. 12***
2813 A736 2fo multi .75 .25

Exists imperf. Value $5.

SOZPHILEX 83, Moscow — A737

1983, Oct. 14 **Litho.** ***Perf. 12***
2814 A737 2fo Kremlin .50 .50

Issued in sheets of 3 stamps and 3 labels showing emblem. Size: 101x133mm.
Exists imperf. Value: single with label $5; sheetlet $16.

Mihaly Babits (1883-1941), Poet and Translator — A738

1983, Nov. 25
2815 A738 2fo multi .40 .25

Exists imperf. Value $5.

Souvenir Sheet

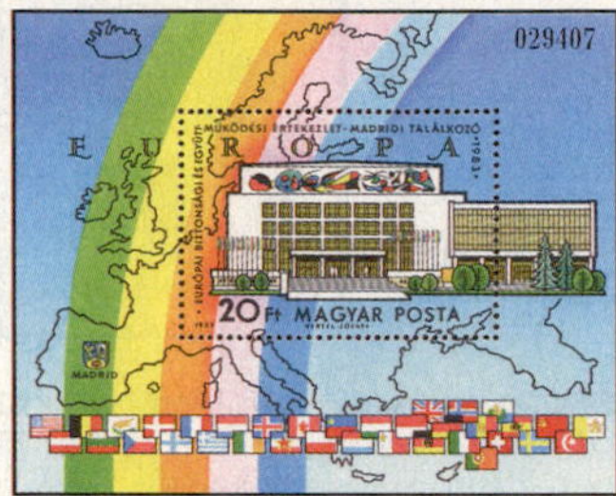

European Security and Cooperation Conference, Madrid — A739

Perf. 12½x11½
1983, Nov. 10 **Litho.**
2816 A739 20fo multi 3.75 3.75

Exists imperf. Value $17.50.

1984 Winter Olympics, Sarajevo — A740

Designs: Ice dancers representing the seven phases of a figure cut: No. 2817, Emblem upper right. No. 2818, Emblem upper left. No. 2819, Arms extended. No. 2820, Arms bent. No. 2821, Man looking down. No. 2822, Girl looking up.

1983, Dec. 22 **Litho.** ***Perf. 12x12½***

2817	A740	1fo multicolored	.25	.25
2818	A740	1fo multicolored	.25	.25
2819	A740	2fo multicolored	.25	.25
2820	A740	2fo multicolored	.25	.25
2821	A740	4fo multicolored	.55	.30
2822	A740	4fo multicolored	.55	.30
2823	A740	6fo multicolored	.85	.45
a.		Strip of 7, #2817-2823	3.00	2.00

Souvenir Sheet
Perf. 12½

2824 A740 20fo multicolored 3.00 3.00

No. 2824 contains one 49x39mm stamp.
Exist imperf. Value: strip $20; souvenir sheet $20.

Christmas A741

Designs: 1fo, Madonna with Rose, Kassa, 1500. 2fo, Altar piece, Csikmenasag, 1543.

1983, Dec. 13 **Litho.** ***Perf. 11½x12***

2825	A741	1fo multi	.25	.25
2826	A741	2fo multi	.50	.25

Exist imperf. Value, set $10.

Resorts and Spas — A742

1fo, Zanka, Lake Balaton. 2fo, Hajduszoboszlo. 5fo, Heviz.

1983, Dec. 18

2827 A742 1fo multicolored .25 .25
2828 A742 2fo multicolored .30 .25
2829 A742 5fo multicolored .70 .35
Nos. 2827-2829 (3) 1.25 .85

Exist imperf. Value, set $15.

Virgin with Six Saints, by Giovanni Battista Tiepolo — A743

Rest During Flight into Egypt, by Giovanni Domenico Tiepolo — A744

Paintings Stolen and Later Recovered, Museum of Fine Arts, Budapest: b, Esterhazy Madonna, by Raphael. c, Portrait of Giorgione, 16th cent. d, Portrait of a Woman, by Tintoretto. e, Pietro Bempo, by Raphael. f, Portrait of a Man, by Tintoretto.

1984, Feb. 16 ***Perf. 12½x12***

2839 Sheet of 7 3.75 3.75
a.-f. A743 2fo multi .35
g. A744 8fo multi 1.50

Exists imperf. Value $35.

Energy Conservation A745

1984, Mar. 30 Litho. ***Perf. 11½x12***

2840 A745 1fo multi .40 .25

Exists imperf. Value $5.

A746

Design: 2fo, Sandor Korosi Csoma (1784-1842), Master of Tibetan Philology.

1984, Mar. 30 ***Perf. 11½x12½***

2841 A746 2fo multi .40 .25

Stamps with silver inscription and with back inscription "Gift of the Hungarian Post" issued to members of Natl. Fed. of Hungarian Philatelists. Value $1.50.
Exists imperf. Value $5.

Miniature Sheet

No. 1900 — A747

Designs: b, No. 1346. c, No. 1259.

1984, Apr. 20 Litho. ***Perf. 12x11½***

2842 A747 Sheet of 3 + 3 labels 2.75 2.75
a.-c. 4fo multi .70

Espana '84; Ausipex '84; Philatelia '84.
Exists imperf. Value $20.

Post-Roman Archaeological Discoveries — A748

No. 2843, Round gold disc hair ornaments, Rakamaz. No. 2844, Saber belt plates, Szolnok-Strazsahalom and Galgocz. No. 2845, Silver disc hair ornaments, Sarospatak. No. 2846, Swords. 4fo, Silver and gold bowl, Ketpo. 6fo, Bone walking stick handles, Hajdudorog and Szabadbattyan. 8fo, Ivory saddle bow, Izsak; bit, stirrups, Muszka.

1984, May 15 ***Perf. 12***

2843 A748 1fo dk brn & tan .25 .25
2844 A748 1fo dk brn & tan .25 .25
2845 A748 2fo dk brn & tan .25 .25
2846 A748 2fo dk brn & tan .25 .25
2847 A748 4fo dk brn & tan .50 .25
2848 A748 6fo dk brn & tan .75 .30
2849 A748 8fo dk brn & tan 1.00 .40
Nos. 2843-2849 (7) 3.25 1.95

Exist imperf. Value, set $15.

View of Cracow — A749

1984, May 21 Litho. ***Perf. 12½x11½***

2850 A749 2fo multi .25 .25

Permanent Committee of Posts and Telecommunications, 25th Session, Cracow.
Exists imperf. Value $5.

Butterflies A750

No. 2851, Epiphille dilecta. No. 2852, Agra sara. No. 2853, Morpho cypris. No. 2854, Ancylusis formossissima. No. 2855, Danaus chrysippus. No. 2856, Catagramma cynosura. No. 2857, Ornithoptera paradisea.

1984, June 7 ***Perf. 11½x12***

2851 A750 1fo multicolored .25 .25
2852 A750 1fo multicolored .25 .25
2853 A750 2fo multicolored .25 .25
2854 A750 2fo multicolored .25 .25
2855 A750 4fo multicolored .50 .25
2856 A750 6fo multicolored .75 .30
2857 A750 8fo multicolored 1.00 .45
Nos. 2851-2857 (7) 3.25 2.00

Exist imperf. Value, set $20.

A751

Archer, by Kisfaludy Strobl (1884-1975).

1984, July 26 Litho. ***Perf. 12½x11½***

2858 A751 2fo cream, red brn .30 .25

Exists imperf. Value $5.

A752

1984, July 26

2859 A752 2fo gold, blk, red brn .25 .25

Akos Hevesi (1884-1937), revolutionary. See Nos. 2884-2885, 2910, 2915, 2962.
Exists imperf. Value $5.

Kepes Ujsag Peace Festival — A753

1984, Aug. 3 Litho. ***Perf. 12½x11½***

2860 A753 2fo Map, building .60 .25

Exists imperf. Value $5.

Aerobatic Championship A754

2fo, Plane, map.

1984, Aug. 14

2861 A754 2fo multicolored .30 .25

Exists imperf. Value $5.

Horse Team World Championship, Szilvasvarad, Aug. 17-20 — A755

2fo, Horse-drawn wagon.

1984, Aug. 17 ***Perf. 12***

2862 A755 2fo multicolored .30 .25

Exists imperf. Value $5.

Budapest Riverside Hotels — A756

No. 2863, Atrium Hyatt. No. 2864, Duna Intercontinental. No. 2865, Forum. No. 2866, Thermal Hotel, Margaret Island. No. 2867, Hilton. No. 2868, Gellert.
No. 2869, Hilton, diff.

1984, Sept.

2863 A756 1fo multicolored .25 .25
2864 A756 2fo multicolored .25 .25
2865 A756 4fo multicolored .50 .25
2866 A756 4fo multicolored .50 .25
2867 A756 5fo multicolored .70 .35
2868 A756 8fo multicolored 1.00 .50
Nos. 2863-2868 (6) 3.20 1.85

Souvenir Sheet

2869 A756 20fo multicolored 2.75 2.75

Exist imperf. Value: set $15; souvenir sheet $20.

14th Conference of Postal Ministers, Budapest — A757

2fo, Building, post horn.

1984, Sept. 10 ***Perf. 12½x11½***

2870 A757 2fo multi .25 .25

Exists imperf. Value $5.

57th Stamp Day A758

1fo, Four-handled vase, Zsolnay. 2fo, Platter, vert. 10fo, #19 on cover.

1984, Sept. 21 ***Perf. 12***

2871 A758 1fo multi .25 .25
2872 A758 2fo multi .80 .25

Souvenir Sheet

2872A A758 10fo multi 2.50 2.50

No. 2872A contains one stamp (44x27mm, perf. 11).
Exist imperf. Value: set $12.50; souvenir sheet $20.

Edible Mushrooms A759

No. 2873, Boletus edulis. No. 2874, Marasmius oreades. No. 2875, Morchella esculenta. No. 2876, Agaricus campester. No. 2877, Macrolepiota procera. No. 2878, Cantharellus cibarius. No. 2879, Armillariella mellea.

Photogravure and Engraved

1984, Oct. ***Perf. 12x11½***

2873 A759 1fo multicolored .35 .25
2874 A759 1fo multicolored .35 .25
2875 A759 2fo multicolored .60 .25
2876 A759 2fo multicolored .60 .25
2877 A759 3fo multicolored .90 .25

2878 A759 3fo multicolored .90 .25
2879 A759 4fo multicolored 1.25 .30
Nos. 2873-2879 (7) 4.95 1.80

Exist imperf. Value, set $15.

Budapest Opera House Centenary — A760

1fo, Fresco by Mor Than. 2fo, Hallway. 5fo, Auditorium.
20fo, Building.

1984, Sept. 27 ***Perf. 12x11½***

2880 A760 1fo multi .25 .25
2881 A760 2fo multi .25 .25
2882 A760 5fo multi .65 .30
Nos. 2880-2882 (3) 1.15 .80

Souvenir Sheet

2883 A760 20fo multi 2.75 2.75

No. 2883 contains one stamp (49x40mm, perf. 12½).
Exist imperf. Value: set $15; souvenir sheet $20.

Famous Hungarians Type of 1984

No. 2884, Bela Balazs, writer (1884-1949); No. 2885, Kato Haman, labor leader (1884-1936).

1984, Dec. 3 Litho. ***Perf. 12½x11½***

2884 A752 2fo multi .25 .25
2885 A752 2fo multi .25 .25

Exist imperf. Value, set $10.

Madonna and Child, Trensceny A763

1984, Dec. 17 Litho. ***Perf. 11½x12***

2886 A763 1fo multi .30 .30

Exists imperf. Value $5.

Owls — A764

Photogravure and Engraved

1984, Dec. 28 ***Perf. 12½x11½***

2887 A764 1fo Athene Noctua .25 .25
2888 A764 1fo Tyto alba .25 .25
2889 A764 2fo Strix aluco .25 .25
2890 A764 2fo Asio otus .25 .25
2891 A764 4fo Nyctea scadiaca .45 .30
2892 A764 6fo Strix uralensis .75 .40
2893 A764 8fo Bubo bubo .90 .50
Nos. 2887-2893 (7) 3.10 2.20

Exist imperf. Value, set $15.

Torah Crown, Buda — A765

19th Cent. Art from Jewish Museum, Budapest: No. 2895, Chalice, Moscow. No. 2896, Torah shield, Vienna. No. 2897, Chalice, Warsaw. No. 2898, Container, Augsburg. No. 2899, Candlestick holder, Warsaw. No. 2900, Money box, Pest.

1984, Dec. Litho. ***Perf. 12***

2894 A765 1fo shown .25 .25
2895 A765 1fo multicolored .25 .25
2896 A765 2fo multicolored .25 .25
2897 A765 2fo multicolored .25 .25
2898 A765 4fo multicolored .55 .25
2899 A765 6fo multicolored .80 .35
2900 A765 8fo multicolored 1.10 .45
Nos. 2894-2900 (7) 3.45 2.05

Exist imperf. Value, set $15.

Souvenir Sheet

Hungarian Olympic Committee, 90th Anniv. — A766

1985, Jan. 2 Photo. ***Perf. 12x12½***

2901 A766 20fo Long jump 3.00 3.00

Exists imperf. Value $20.

Novi Sad, Yugoslavia — A767

Danube Bridges: No. 2903, Baja. No. 2904, Arpad Bridge, Budapest. No. 2905, Bratislava, Czechoslovakia. 4fo, Reichsbrucke, Vienna. 6fo, Linz, Austria. 8fo, Regensburg, Fed. Rep. of Germany. 20fo, Elizabeth Bridge, Budapest, and map.

1985, Feb. 12 Litho. ***Perf. 12x11½***

2902 A767 1fo multi .25 .25
2903 A767 1fo multi .25 .25
2904 A767 2fo multi .25 .25
2905 A767 2fo multi .25 .25
2906 A767 4fo multi .50 .25
2907 A767 6fo multi .75 .40
2908 A767 8fo multi 1.00 .45
Nos. 2902-2908 (7) 3.25 2.10

Souvenir Sheet

Perf. 12½

2909 A767 20fo multi 3.00 3.00

Exist imperf. Value: set $15; souvenir sheet $20.
For surcharge, see No. 4333.

Famous Hungarians Type of 1984

Design: Laszlo Rudas (1885-1950), communist philosopher.

1985, Feb. 21 ***Perf. 12½x11½***

2910 A752 2fo gold & brn .25 .25

Exists imperf. Value $5.

Intl. Women's Day, 75th Anniv. A769

1985, Mar. 5 Photo. ***Perf. 11½x12½***

2911 A769 2fo gold & multi .30 .25

Exists imperf. Value $5.

OLYMPHILEX '85, Lausanne A770

1985, Mar. 14 Litho. ***Perf. 11½x12***

2912 A770 4fo No. B81 .50 .25
2913 A770 5fo No. B82 .65 .30

Exist imperf. Value, set $10.

Souvenir Sheet

Liberation of Hungary From German Occupation Forces, 40th Anniv. — A771

Design: Liberty Bridge, Budapest and silhouette of the Liberation Monument on Gellert Hill illuminated by fireworks.

1985, Mar. 28 ***Perf. 12½***

2914 A771 20fo multi 2.75 2.75

Exists imperf. Value $20.

Famous Hungarians Type of 1984

Design: Gyorgy Lukacs (1885-1971) communist philosopher, educator.

1985, Apr. 12 ***Perf. 12½x11½***

2915 A752 2fo gold & brn .40 .25

Exists imperf. Value $5.

Totfalusi Bible, 300th Anniv. — A773

1985, Apr. 25 ***Perf. 12***

2916 A773 2fo gold & black .40 .25

1st Bible printed in Hungarian by Nicolas Totfalusi Kis (1650-1702), publisher, in 1685.
Exists imperf. Value $5.

Lorand Eotvos Univ., 350th Anniv. — A774

Design: Archbishop Peter Pazmany (1570-1637), founder.

1985, May 14

2917 A774 2fo magenta & gray .50 .25

No. 2917 printed se-tenant with label picturing obverse and reverse of university commemorative medal.
Exists imperf. Value, with label $5.

A775

1985, May 25

2918 A775 2fo multi .50 .25

26th European Boxing Championships, Budapest.
Exists imperf. Value $6.

Intl. Youth Year — A776

1985, May 29 ***Perf. 11½x12***

2919 A776 1fo Girl's soccer .25 .25
2920 A776 2fo Windsurfing .25 .25
2921 A776 2fo Aerobic exercise .25 .25
2922 A776 4fo Karate .45 .25
2923 A776 4fo Go-kart racing .45 .25
2924 A776 5fo Hang gliding .65 .25
2925 A776 6fo Skateboarding .70 .35
Nos. 2919-2925 (7) 3.00 1.85

Exist imperf. Value, set $15.

Electro-magnetic High-speed Railway — A777

EXPO '85, Tsukuba, Japan: futuristic technology: 4fo, Fuyo (robot) Theater.

1985, May 29 ***Perf. 12x11½***

2926 A777 2fo shown .30 .25
2927 A777 4fo multicolored .70 .25

Exist imperf. Value, set $12.50.

Audubon Birth Bicentenary A778

Audubon illustrations: No. 2928, Colaptes cafer. No. 2929, Bombycilla garrulus. No.

2930, Dryocopus pileatus. No. 2931, Icterus galbula.

1985, June 19 ***Perf. 12***

2928	A778 2fo multicolored		.30	.25
2929	A778 2fo multicolored		.30	.25
2930	A778 2fo multicolored		.30	.25
2931	A778 4fo multicolored		.55	.30
	Nos. 2928-2931,C446-C447 (6)		2.90	1.90

Exist imperf. Value, set (6) $20.

Mezohegyes Stud Farm, Bicent. — A779

Horses: No. 2932, Nonius-36, 1883, a dark chestnut. No. 2933, Furioso-23, 1889, a light chestnut. No. 2934, Gidrian-1, 1935, a blond breed. No. 2935, Ramses-3, 1960, gray sporting horse. No. 2936, Krozus-1, 1970, chestnut sporting horse.

1985, June 28

2932	A779 1fo multi	.25	.25
2933	A779 2fo multi	.25	.25
2934	A779 4fo multi	.55	.25
2935	A779 4fo multi	.55	.25
2936	A779 6fo multi	.85	.35
	Nos. 2932-2936 (5)	2.45	1.35

Exist imperf. Value, set $15.

Prevention of Nuclear War — A780

Design: Illustration of a damaged globe and hands, by Imre Varga (b. 1923), 1973 Kossuth prize-winner.

1985, June 28 ***Perf. 11½x12***

2937 A780 2fo multi .50 .25

Intl. Physician's Movement for the Prevention of Nuclear War, 5th Congress.

Exists imperf. Value $6.

European Music Year — A781

Composers and instruments: 1fo, George Frideric Handel (1685-1759), kettle drum, horn. 2fo, Johann Sebastian Bach (1685-1750), Thomas Church organ. No. 2940, Luigi Cherubini (1760-1842), harp, bass viol, baryton. No. 2941, Frederic Chopin (1810-1849), piano, 1817. 5fo, Gustav Mahler (1860-1911), pardessus de viole, kettle drum, double horn. 6fo, Erkel Ferenc (1810-1893), bass tuba, violin.

1985, July 10 ***Perf. 11***

2938	A781 1fo multi	.25	.25
2939	A781 2fo multi	.25	.25
2940	A781 4fo multi	.50	.25
2941	A781 4fo multi	.50	.25
2942	A781 5fo multi	.65	.25
2943	A781 6fo multi	.75	.30
	Nos. 2938-2943 (6)	2.90	1.55

Exist imperf. Value, set $17.50.

Souvenir Sheet

12th World Youth Festival, Moscow — A782

20fo, Emblem, Red Square.

1985, July 22 ***Perf. 12½***

2944 A782 20fo multi 2.75 2.50

Exists imperf. Value $27.50.

Souvenir Sheet

Helsinki Agreement, 10th Anniv. — A783

20fo, Finlandia Hall, Helsinki.

1985, Aug. 1 ***Perf. 11***

2945 A783 20fo multi 3.00 3.00

Exists imperf. Value $27.50.

World Tourism Day — A784

2fo, Key, globe, heart.

Perf. 12½x11½

1985, Sept. 27 **Litho.**

2946 A784 2fo multi .30 .25

Exists imperf. Value $5.

COMNET '85 — A785

4fo, Computer terminal.

1985, Oct. 1 ***Perf. 11½***

2947 A785 4fo multi .60 .30

3rd Computer Sciences Conference, Budapest, Oct. 1-4.

Exists imperf. Value $5.

Souvenir Sheet

Danube River, Budapest Bridges — A786

1985, Oct. 15 ***Perf. 12***

2948 A786 20fo multi 3.50 3.50

European Security and Cooperation Conference and Cultural Forum, Budapest, Oct. 15-Nov. 25. Exists inscribed "Kuturalis Forum Resztvevoi Tiszteletere" in gold on front and "Gift of the Hungarian Post" on back. Not valid for postage.

Exists imperf. Value $30.

16-17th Century Ceramics — A787

1fo, Faience water jar and dispenser, 1609. 2fo, Tankard, 1670. 10fo, Hexagonal medicine jar, 1774.

1985, Oct. 18 ***Perf. 12½x11½***

2949	A787 1fo multi	.25	.25
2950	A787 2fo multi	.80	.25

Souvenir Sheet

2951 A787 10fo multi 1.75 1.75

EUROPHILEX '85, Oct. 14-31.

Exist imperf. Value: set $10; souvenir sheet $20.

Italy No. 799, view of Rome — A788

1985, Oct. 21 ***Perf. 12x11½***

2952 A788 5fo multi .90 .90

Italia '85, Rome, Oct. 25-Nov. 3.

Issued in sheets of 3 stamps and 3 labels showing emblem.

Exists imperf. Value: single with label $5.50; sheetlet $17.50.

UN, 40th Anniv. — A789

4fo, Dove, globe, emblem.

1985, Oct. 24 ***Perf. 11½x12***

2953 A789 4fo multicolored .50 .30

Exists imperf. Value $5.

Indigenous Lilies — A790

No. 2954, Lilium bulbiferum. No. 2955, Lilium martagon. No. 2956, Erythronium dens-canis. No. 2957, Fritillaria meleagris. No. 2958, Lilium tigrinum. No. 2959, Hemerocallis lilio-asphodelus. No. 2960, Bulbocodium vernum.

Photogravure and Engraved

1985, Oct. 28 ***Perf. 12x11½***

2954	A790 1fo multicolored	.25	.25
2955	A790 2fo multicolored	.25	.25
2956	A790 2fo multicolored	.25	.25
2957	A790 4fo multicolored	.55	.25
2958	A790 4fo multicolored	.55	.25
2959	A790 5fo multicolored	.70	.30
2960	A790 6fo multicolored	.85	.35
	Nos. 2954-2960 (7)	3.40	1.90

Exists imperf. Value, set $20.

Christmas 1985 — A791

1985, Nov. 6 **Litho.** ***Perf. 13½x13***

2961 A791 2fo Youths caroling .30 .25

Exists imperf. Value $5.

Famous Hungarians Type of 1984

Design: Istvan Ries (1885-1950), Minister of Justice (1949), labor movement.

1985, Nov. 11 ***Perf. 12½x11½***

2962 A752 2fo gold & ol brn .25 .25

Exists imperf. Value $5.

Motorcycle Centenary — A793

No. 2963, Fantic Sprinter, 1984. No. 2964, Suzuki Katana GSX, 1983. No. 2965, Harley-Davidson Duo-Glide, 1960. No. 2966, Rudge-Whitworth, 1935. No. 2967, BMW R47, 1927. No. 2968, NSU, 1910. No. 2969, Daimler, 1885.

Photogravure & Engraved

1985, Dec. 28 ***Perf. 11½x12***

2963	A793 1fo multicolored	.25	.25
2964	A793 2fo multicolored	.25	.25
2965	A793 2fo multicolored	.25	.25
2966	A793 4fo multicolored	.45	.25
2967	A793 4fo multicolored	.45	.25
2968	A793 5fo multicolored	.60	.25
2969	A793 6fo multicolored	.70	.25
	Nos. 2963-2969 (7)	2.95	1.75

Exist imperf. Value, set $18.

Bela Kun (1886-1939), Communist Party Founder — A794

Perf. 12½x11½

1986, Feb. 20 **Litho.**

2970 A794 4fo multi .50 .30

Exist imperf. Value $5.

Souvenir Sheet

US Shuttle Challenger — A795

1986, Feb. 21 ***Perf. 11½***

2971 A795 20fo multi 3.25 3.25

Memorial to the US astronauts who died when the Challenger exploded during takeoff, Jan. 28.

Exist imperf. Value $20.

Halley's Comet — A796

No. 2972, US ICE satellite, dinosaurs. No. 2973, USSR Vega and Bayeaux tapestry detail, 1066, France. No. 2974, Japanese Suisei and German engraving, 1507. No. 2975, European Space Agency Giotto and The Three Magi, tapestry by Giotto. No. 2976, USSR Astron and Apianis constellation, 1531. No. 2977, US space shuttle and Edmond Halley.

Perf. 11½x13½

1986, Feb. 14 **Litho.**

2972 A796 2fo multi .25 .25
2973 A796 2fo multi .25 .25
2974 A796 2fo multi .25 .25
2975 A796 4fo multi .45 .25
2976 A796 4fo multi .45 .25
2977 A796 6fo multi .80 .35
Nos. 2972-2977 (6) 2.45 1.60

Exist imperf. Value, set $17.50.

Seeing-eye Dog, Red Cross — A797

Perf. 12½x11½

1986, Mar. 20 **Litho.**

2978 A797 4fo multi .50 .25

Assistance for the blind.

Exists imperf. Value $12.50.

Soccer Players in Blue and Red Uniforms — A798

1986, Apr. 2 ***Perf. 11***

Color of Uniforms

2979 A798 2fo shown .25 .25
2980 A798 2fo blue & green .25 .25
2981 A798 4fo red & black .55 .25
2982 A798 4fo yellow & red .55 .25
2983 A798 4fo yellow & green .55 .25
2984 A798 6fo orange & white .75 .30
Nos. 2979-2984 (6) 2.90 1.55

Souvenir Sheet

Perf. 12½

2985 A798 20fo Victors 3.50 3.50

1986 World Cup Soccer Championships, Mexico. No. 2979 contains one stamp (size: 41x32mm). Also exists with added inscription "In honor of the winner . . ." and red control number. Value $90.

Exist imperf. Value: set $17.50; souvenir sheet $17.50.

Buda Castle Cable Railway Station Reopening — A799

1986, Apr. 30 ***Perf. 11½x12***

2986 A799 2fo org, brn & pale yel .40 .25

Exists imperf. Value $5.

Souvenir Sheet

A800

AMERIPEX '86, Chicago, May 22-June 1: a, Yankee doodle rose. b, America rose. c, George Washington, statue by Gyula Bezeredy (1858-1935), Budapest.

1986, Apr. 30 ***Perf. 12½x11½***

2987 A800 Sheet of 3 3.25 3.00
a.-b. 5fo any single .75 .75
c. 10fo multi 1.50 1.50

Size of No. 2987c: 27x74mm.

Exists imperf. Value $25.

Folk Dolls — A801

1986, May 6 ***Perf. 11½x12***

2988 A801 4fo multi .50 .30

Hungary Days in Tokyo.

Exists imperf. Value $5.

Andras Fay (1786-1864), Author, Politician — A802

Lithographed and Engraved

1986, May 29 ***Perf. 12***

2989 A802 4fo beige & fawn 1.25 1.25

Printed se-tenant with label picturing First Hungarian Savings Bank Union, founded by Fay.

Exists imperf. Value, with label $9.

Automobile, Cent. A803

No. 2990, 1961 Ferrari Tipo 156, 1985 race car. No. 2991, 1932 Alfa Romeo Tipo B, 1984 race car. No. 2992, 1936 Volkswagen, 1986 Porsche 959. No. 2993, 1902 Renault 14CV, 1985 Renault 5 GT Turbo. No. 2994, 1899 Fiat 3½, 1985 Fiat Ritmo. 6fo, 1886 Daimler, 1986 Mercedes-Benz 230SE.

1986, July 24 **Litho.** ***Perf. 12***

2990 A803 2fo multi .25 .25
2991 A803 2fo multi .25 .25
2992 A803 2fo multi .25 .25
2993 A803 4fo multi .55 .25
2994 A803 4fo multi .55 .25
2995 A803 6fo multi .85 .35
Nos. 2990-2995 (6) 2.70 1.60

Exists imperf. Value, set $17.50.

Wasa, 1628, Warship — A804

1986, Aug. 15 **Litho.** ***Perf. 11½x12***

2996 A804 2fo multi .70 .70

STOCKHOLMIA '86, 8/28-9/7. Printed se-tenant with label (size: 27x34mm) picturing exhibition emblem. Printed in sheets of 3.

Exists imperf. Value: single with label $6; sheetlet $20.

14th Intl. Cancer Congress, Budapest — A805

Design: Moritz Kaposi (1837-1902), Austrian cancer researcher.

1986, Aug. 21 ***Perf. 12½x11½***

2997 A805 4fo multicolored .50 .30

Exists imperf. Value $9.

Recapture of Buda Castle, by Gyula Benczur (1844-1920) — A806

1986, Sept. 2 ***Perf. 12***

2998 A806 4fo multicolored .60 .30

Recapture of Buda from the Turks, 300th anniv.

Exists imperf. Value $6.

Tranquility — A807

Hope — A808

Stamp Day: Paintings by Endre Szasz.

1986, Sept. 5

2999 A807 2fo shown .40 .25
3000 A807 2fo Confidence .40 .25

Souvenir Sheet

Perf. 11½

3001 A808 10fo shown 2.00 2.00

Exist imperf. Value: set $15; souvenir sheet $25.

5th Intl. Conference on Oriental Carpets, Vienna and Budapest A809

4fo, Anatolia crivelli, 15th cent.

1986, Sept. 17 **Litho.** ***Perf. 11***

3002 A809 4fo multi .60 .30

Exists imperf. Value $5.

Franz Liszt, Composer A810

1986, Oct. 21 **Engr.** ***Perf. 12***

3003 A810 4fo grayish green .50 .30

Exists imperf. Value $5.

Intl. Peace Year — A811

1986, Oct. 24 **Litho.**
3004 A811 4fo multicolored .75 .30

No. 3004 printed se-tenant with label. Exists imperf. Value, with label $20.

Souvenir Sheet

Hofburg Palace, Vienna, and Map — A812

1986, Nov. 4 ***Perf. 11***
3005 A812 20fo multicolored 3.00 2.75

European Security and Cooperation Conference, Vienna.
Exists imperf. Value $30.

Fruits A813

Photogravure & Engraved

1986, Nov. 25 ***Perf. 12x11½***
3006 A813 2fo Sour cherries .25 .25
3007 A813 2fo Apricots .25 .25
3008 A813 4fo Peaches .50 .25
3009 A813 4fo Raspberries .50 .25
3010 A813 4fo Apples .50 .25
3011 A813 6fo Grapes .80 .35
Nos. 3006-3011 (6) 2.80 1.60

Exist imperf. Value, set $17.50.

Natl. Heroes — A814

Designs: No. 3012, Jozseph Pogany (1886-1939), journalist, martyr. No. 3013, Ferenc Munnich (1886-1967), prime minister, 1958-61.

1986 **Litho.** ***Perf. 12½x11½***
3012 A814 4fo multi .65 .30
3013 A814 4fo multi .65 .30

Issued: No. 3012, Nov. 6; No. 3013, Nov. 14.
Exist imperf. Value, set $10.

World Communist Youth Fed., 12th Congress A815

1986, Nov. 21 ***Perf. 12***
3014 A815 4fo multi .50 .30

Exist imperf. Value $5.

Castles — A816

2fo, Forgach, Szecseny. 3fo, Savoya, Rackeve. 4fo, Batthyany, Kormend. 5fo, Szechenyi, Nagycenk. 6fo, Rudnyanszky, Nagyteteny. 7fo, Esterhazy, Papa. 8fo, Szapary, Buk. 10fo, Festetics, Keszthely. 12fo, Dory Castle, Mihalyi. 20fo, Brunswick, Martonvasar. 30fo, De la Motte, Nosvaj. 40fo, L'Huillier-Coborg, Edeleny. 50fo, Teleki-Degenfeld, Szirak. 70fo, Magochy, Pacin. 100fo, Eszterhazy, Fertod.

Perf. 12x11½, 11½x12½ (7fo)

1986-91 **Litho.**
3015 A816 2fo multi .25 .25
3016 A816 3fo multi .25 .25
3017 A816 4fo multi .25 .25
3018 A816 5fo multi .30 .25
3019 A816 6fo multi .35 .25
3020 A816 7fo multi .50 .30
3021 A816 8fo multi .50 .30
3022 A816 10fo multi .85 .40
3023 A816 12fo multi .90 .50
3024 A816 20fo multi 1.75 .75
3025 A816 30fo multi 2.25 1.10
3026 A816 40fo multi 3.00 1.60
3027 A816 50fo multi 4.00 1.90
3028 A816 70fo multi 5.00 2.75
3029 A816 100fo multi 8.00 4.00
Nos. 3015-3029 (15) 28.15 14.85

The 7fo, 12fo are inscribed "Magyarország."
Issued: 2fo-6fo, 8fo, 11/28; 10fo, 20fo-30fo, 100fo, 5/28/87; 40fo-70fo, 7/30/87; 7fo, 6/27/91; 12fo, 9/6/91.
Exist imperf. Value, set $175.
For overprint see No. 3320.

Festetics Castle, Keszthely — A816a

1989-92 **Litho. & Engr.** ***Perf. 12***
3030 A816a 10fo brn blk & yel ochre 1.50 .85

Litho.

3031 A816a 15fo lt grn & brn 1.10 .65

The 15fo is inscribed "Magyarország."
Issued: 10fo, Feb. 28; 15fo, Mar. 27, 1992.
No. 3030 exist imperf. Value $110.

Wildlife Conservation A817

No. 3035, Felis silvestris. No. 3036, Lutra lutra. No. 3037, Mustela erminea. No. 3038, Sciurus vulgaris. No. 3039, Erinaceus concolor. No. 3040, Emys orbicularis.

1986, Dec. 15 ***Perf. 12***
3035 A817 2fo multi .30 .25
3036 A817 2fo multi .30 .25
3037 A817 2fo multi .30 .25
3038 A817 4fo multi .55 .30
3039 A817 4fo multi .55 .30
3040 A817 6fo multi .80 .40
Nos. 3035-3040 (6) 2.80 1.75

Exist imperf. Value, set $17.50.

Portraits of Hungarian Kings in the Historical Portrait Gallery — A818

King and reign: No. 3041, St. Steven, 997-1038. No. 3042, Geza I, 1074-1077. No. 3043, St. Ladislas, 1077-1095. No. 3044, Bela III, 1172-1196. No. 3045, Bela IV, 1235-1270.

1986, Dec. 10 ***Perf. 11½x12***
3041 A818 2fo multi .30 .25
3042 A818 2fo multi .30 .25
3043 A818 4fo multi .60 .30
3044 A818 4fo multi .60 .30
3045 A818 6fo multi .90 .45
Nos. 3041-3045 (5) 2.70 1.55

Exist imperf. Value, set $17.50.
See Nos. 3120-3122.

Fungi — A819

No. 3046, Amanita phalloides. No. 3047, Inocybe patouillardi. No. 3048, Amanita muscarla. No. 3049, Omphalotus olearius. No. 3050, Amanita pantherina. No. 3051, Gyromitra esculenta.

Lithographed and Engraved

1986, Dec. 30 ***Perf. 11½***
3046 A819 2fo multicolored .30 .25
3047 A819 2fo multicolored .30 .25
3048 A819 2fo multicolored .30 .25
3049 A819 4fo multicolored .55 .30
3050 A819 4fo multicolored .55 .30
3051 A819 6fo multicolored .80 .40
Nos. 3046-3051 (6) 2.80 1.75

Exist imperf. Value, set $17.50.

Saltwater Fish — A820

No. 3052, Colisa fasciata. No. 3053, Pseudotropheus zebra. No. 3054, Iriatherina werneri. No. 3055, Aphyosemion multicolor. No. 3056, Papiliochromis ramirezi. No. 3057, Hyphessobrycon erythrostigma.

1987, Jan. 15 **Photo.** ***Perf. 11½***
3052 A820 2fo multicolored .30 .25
3053 A820 2fo multicolored .30 .25
3054 A820 2fo multicolored .30 .25
3055 A820 4fo multicolored .55 .30
3056 A820 4fo multicolored .55 .30
3057 A820 6fo multicolored .80 .40
Nos. 3052-3057 (6) 2.80 1.75

Exist imperf. Value, set $20.

Seated Woman, 1918, by Bela Uitz (1887-1972), Painter — A821

1987, Mar. 6 **Litho.** ***Perf. 12***
3058 A821 4fo multicolored .50 .30

Exists imperf. Value $5.

Abstract, 1960, by Lajos Kassak (1887-1967) A822

1987, Mar. 20
3059 A822 4fo black & red .50 .30

Exists imperf. Value $5.

Medical Pioneers — A823

Designs: 2fo, Hippocrates (460-377 B.C.), Greek physician. No. 3061, Avicenna or Ibn Sina (A.D. 980-1037), Islamic pharmacist, diagnostician. No. 3062, Ambroise Pare (1510-1590), French surgeon. No. 3063, William Harvey (1578-1657), English physician, anatomist. 6fo, Ignaz Semmelweis (1818-1865), Hungarian obstetrician.

1987, Mar. 31
3060 A823 2fo black & dk red brn .30 .25
3061 A823 4fo black & dk grn .55 .30
3062 A823 4fo black & steel bl .55 .30
3063 A823 4fo black & olive blk .55 .30
3064 A823 6fo black & grn blk .80 .40
Nos. 3060-3064 (5) 2.75 1.55

Exists imperf. Value, set $17.50.

Neolithic and Copper Age Artifacts — A824

Designs: 2fo, Urn, Hodmezovasarhely. No. 3066, Altar, Szeged. No. 3067, Deity, Szegvar-Tuzkoves. 5fo, Vase, Center.

1987, Apr. 15 **Litho.** ***Perf. 12***
3065 A824 2fo pale bl grn & sep .25 .25
3066 A824 4fo buff & sepia .55 .30
3067 A824 4fo pale org & sepia .55 .30
3068 A824 5fo pale yel grn & sep .80 .40
Nos. 3065-3068 (4) 2.15 1.25

Exists imperf. Value, set $17.50.

Souvenir Sheet

Esztergom Cathedral Treasury Reopening — A825

20fo, Calvary of King Matthias.

1987, Apr. 28 *Perf. 11*
3069 A825 20fo multi 3.50 3.50

No. 3069 margin pictures the Horn Chalice of King Sigismund, Rhineland, 1408 (UL), Crozier of Archbishop Miklos Olah, Hungary, c. 1490 (UR), Monstrance of Imre Eszterhazy, by Gaspar Meichl, Vienna, 1728 (LL), and the Chalice of Matthias, Hungary, c. 1480.
Exists imperf. Value $25.

Hungarian First Aid Assoc., Cent. — A826

4fo, Ambulances, 1887-1987.

1987, May 5 *Perf. 11½x12*
3070 A826 4fo multicolored .50 .30

Exists imperf. Value $5.

Souvenir Sheet

CAPEX '87, Toronto — A827

Stamp exhibitions: b, OLYMPHILEX '87, Rome. c, HAFNIA '87, Copenhagen.

1987, May 20 **Litho.** *Perf. 11*
3071 A827 Sheet of 3 + 3 labels 3.50 2.75
a.-c. 5fo any single 1.25 .90

Exists imperf. Value $17.50.

Jozsef Marek (1886-1952), Veterinarian — A828

1987, May 25 *Perf. 12x11½*
3072 A828 4fo multicolored .50 .30

Veterinary education, bicent.
Exists imperf. Value $5.

Teleki's African Expedition, Cent. — A829

1987, June 10
3073 A829 4fo multicolored .50 .30

Samuel Teleki (1845-1916), explorer.
Exists imperf. Value $5.

Woodcut by Abraham von Werdt, 18th Cent. — A830

Litho. & Engr.

1987, June 25 *Perf. 12*
3074 A830 4fo beige & sepia .50 .30

Hungarian Printing, Paper and Press Workers' Union, 125th anniv.
Exists imperf. Value $5.

Antarctic Research, 75th Anniv. — A831

Helicopter Landing, Mirnij Research Station — A832

Map, explorer and scene: No. 3075, James Cook (1728-1779) and ship. No. 3076, Fabian von Bellingshausen (1778-1852) and seals. No. 3077, Ernest H. Shackleton (1874-1922) and penguins. No. 3078, Roald Amundsen (1872-1928) discovering South Pole, dog team. No. 3079, Robert F. Scott (1868-1912) and ship. No. 3080, Richard E. Byrd (1888-1957) and Floyd Bennett monoplane.

1987, June 30 **Litho.**
3075 A831 2fo multi .30 .25
3076 A831 2fo multi .30 .25
3077 A831 2fo multi .30 .25
3078 A831 4fo multi .55 .30
3079 A831 4fo multi .55 .30
3080 A831 6fo multi .80 .40
Nos. 3075-3080 (6) 2.80 1.75

Souvenir Sheet

Perf. 11½

3081 A832 20fo multi 3.00 3.00

Exist imperf. Value: set $20; souvenir sheet $40.

Railway Officers Training Institute, Cent. — A833

1987, Sept. 4 **Litho.** *Perf. 11½x12*
3082 A833 4fo blue & black .75 .50

Exists imperf. Value $5.

Stamp Day, 60th Anniv. — A834

Masonry of the medieval Buda Castle: 2fo, Flowers, dolphin. 4fo, Arms of King Matthias. 10fo, "ONDIDIT/GENEROSVM" inscribed on capital.

Litho. & Engr.

1987, Sept. 18 *Perf. 12*
3083 A834 2fo lt blue & dk blue .35 .25
3084 A834 4fo lt grn & dk grn .70 .45

Souvenir Sheet

Perf. 11

3085 A834 10fo multicolored 1.75 1.75

Exist imperf. Value: set $12.50; souvenir sheet $25.

A835

1987, Sept. 30 **Litho.** *Perf. 12*
3086 A835 4fo multi .80 .50
a. Se-tenant with label .80 .50

No 3086 printed in sheet of 50 and in sheet of 25 plus 25 labels picturing 13th cent. church at Gyongyospata which houses the altar.
Exists imperf. Value $10; with label $30.

A836

Orchids A837

No. 3087, Cypripedium calceolus. No. 3088, Orchis purpurea. No. 3089, Himantoglossum hircinum. No. 3090, Ophrys scolopax cornuta. No. 3091, Cephalanthera rubra. No. 3092, Epipactis atrorubens.

1987, Oct. 29 **Litho.** *Perf. 11*
3087 A836 2fo multicolored .35 .25
3088 A836 2fo multicolored .35 .25
3089 A836 4fo multicolored .60 .50
3090 A836 4fo multicolored .65 .50
3091 A836 5fo multicolored .75 .60
3092 A836 6fo multicolored .80 .75
Nos. 3087-3092 (6) 3.50 2.85

Miniature Sheet

3093 A837 20fo shown 3.50 3.25

Exist imperf. Value: set $20; souvenir sheet $35.

1988 Winter Olympics, Calgary — A838

No. 3094, Speed skating. No. 3095, Cross-country skiing. No. 3096, Biathlon. No. 3097, Ice hockey. No. 3098, 4-Man bobsled. No. 3099, Ski-jumping.
No. 3100, Slalom.

1987, Nov. 24
3094 A838 2fo multicolored .35 .25
3095 A838 2fo multicolored .35 .25
3096 A838 4fo multicolored .65 .40
3097 A838 4fo multicolored .65 .40
3098 A838 4fo multicolored .65 .40
3099 A838 6fo multicolored 1.00 .65
Nos. 3094-3099 (6) 3.65 2.35

Souvenir Sheet

3100 A838 20fo multicolored 3.50 3.25

Exist imperf. Value: set $15; souvenir sheet $20.

Souvenir Sheet

U.S.-Soviet Summit, Dec. 7-10 — A839

1987, Dec. 7 *Perf. 12*
3101 A839 20fo Shaking hands 3.50 3.25

Meeting of Gen. Secretary Gorbachev and Pres. Reagan to discuss and sign nuclear arms reduction treaty.
Exists imperf. Value $20.

Fairy Tales — A840

Designs: No. 3102, The White Crane, from Japan. No. 3103, The Fox and the Crow, Aesop's Fables. No. 3104, The Tortoise and the Hare, Aesop's Fables. No. 3105, The Ugly Duckling, by Hans Christian Andersen. No. 3106, The Steadfast Tin Soldier, by Andersen.

1987, Dec. 11
3102 A840 2fo multi .40 .25
3103 A840 2fo multi .40 .25
3104 A840 4fo multi .75 .50
3105 A840 4fo multi .75 .50
3106 A840 6fo multi 1.00 .75
Nos. 3102-3106 (5) 3.30 2.25

Exist imperf. Value, set $17.50.

Count Ferdinand von Zeppelin (1838-1917), Designer of Dirigibles — A841

No. 3107, LZ-2, 1905. No. 3108, LZ-4, 1908. No. 3109, LZ-10, Schwaben, 1911. No. 3110, LZ-127, Graf Zeppelin, 1928.

1988, Jan. 29 Litho. *Perf. 12*

3107	A841	2fo blue	.40	.25
3108	A841	4fo brown	.80	.45
3109	A841	4fo lilac	.90	.45
3110	A841	8fo green	1.50	1.00
		Nos. 3107-3110 (4)	3.60	2.15

Exist imperf. Value, set $17.50.

1988 World Figure Skating Championships, Budapest — A842

Various athletes wearing period costumes: No. 3111, Male, 20th cent. No. 3112, Male, (cap), 19th cent. No. 3113, Male (hat), 18th cent. No. 3114, Woman, c. 1930. No. 3115, Woman (contemporary). No. 3116, Pair. No. 3117, Death spiral.

1988, Feb. 29 Photo. *Perf. 11½*

3111	A842	2fo multicolored	.35	.25
3112	A842	2fo multicolored	.35	.25
3113	A842	4fo multicolored	.60	.40
3114	A842	4fo multicolored	.60	.40
3115	A842	5fo multicolored	.75	.50
3116	A842	6fo multicolored	1.00	.65
		Nos. 3111-3116 (6)	3.65	2.45

Souvenir Sheet

Perf. 12x11½

3117	A842	20fo multicolored	3.50	3.25

No. 3117 contains one 37x52mm stamp. Exist imperf. Value: set $17.50; souvenir sheet $20.

Illes Monus (1888-1944), Party Leader — A843

1988, Mar. 11 Litho. *Perf. 11½x12*

3118	A843	4fo multi	.50	.50

Exists imperf. Value $4.

See Nos. 3152, 3160.

Miniature Sheet

Postmaster's Coat, Hat and Post Horn, 18th Cent. — A844

1988, Mar. 18 Litho. *Perf. 13*

3119	A844	4fo + 4 labels	1.25	1.25

Intl. stamp exhibitions, 1988. No. 3119 contains 4 labels picturing exhibition emblems: JUVALUX '88, Luxembourg, Mar. 29-Apr. 4 (UL), SYDPEX '88, Sydney, Australia, July 30-Aug.7 (UR), FINLANDIA '88, Helsinki, Finland, June 1-12 (LR), and PRAGA '88, Prague, Czechoslovakia, Aug. 26-Sept. 4 (LL). Exists imperf. Value $25.

King Type of 1986

Portraits of Hungarian kings in the Historical Portrait Gallery. King and reign: 2fo, Charles Robert (1308-1342). 4fo, Louis I (1342-1382). 6fo, Sigismund (1387-1437).

1988, Mar. 31 *Perf. 11½x12*

3120	A818	2fo pale grn, sep & red	.30	.25
3121	A818	4fo pale ultra, sep & red	.60	.45
3122	A818	6fo pale vio, sep & red	.90	.65
		Nos. 3120-3122 (3)	1.80	1.35

Exists imperf. Value, set $17.50.

1988 Summer Olympics, Seoul — A845

1988, Apr. 20 Litho. *Perf. 13½x13*

3123	A845	2fo Rowing	.30	.25
3124	A845	4fo Hurdling	.60	.45
3125	A845	4fo Fencing	.60	.45
3126	A845	6fo Boxing	.90	.65
		Nos. 3123-3126 (4)	2.40	1.80

Souvenir Sheet

Perf. 12½

3127	A845	20fo Tennis	3.75	3.25

Exist imperf. Value: set $15; souvenir sheet $25.

Computer Animation A846

Design: Graphic from the computer-animated film *Dilemma*, 1972, by graphic artist Janos Kass (b. 1927) and cartoon film director John Halas (b. 1912).

1988, May 12 *Perf. 12*

3128	A846	4fo black, pur & ver	.50	.25

Exists imperf. Value $6.

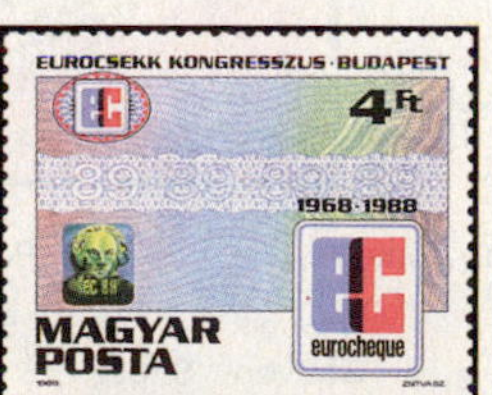

Eurocheck Congress, June 10, Budapest — A847

1988, June 10 Litho. *Perf. 12*

3129	A847	4fo multicolored	.50	.25

Eurocheck as legal tender, 20th anniv. Exists imperf. Value $6.

Sovereign of the Seas — A848

No. 3131, Santa Maria. No. 3132, Mayflower. No. 3133, Jylland. No. 3134, St. Jupat.

1988, June 30

3130	A848	2fo shown	.35	.25
3131	A848	2fo multicolored	.35	.25
3132	A848	2fo multicolored	.35	.25
3133	A848	4fo multicolored	.75	.50
3134	A848	6fo multicolored	1.10	.80
		Nos. 3130-3134 (5)	2.90	2.05

Exist imperf. Value, set $17.50.

Fight Drug Abuse — A849

1988, July 7 Litho. *Perf. 12*

3135	A849	4fo multicolored	.65	.25

Exists imperf. Value $6.

Ducks A850

No. 3136, Anas crecca. No. 3137, Bucephala clangula. No. 3138, Anas penelope. No. 3139, Netta rufina. No. 3140, Anas strepera.

No. 3141, Anas platyrhynchos.

1988, July 29 Litho. *Perf. 13x13½*

3136	A850	2fo multicolored	.30	.25
3137	A850	2fo multicolored	.30	.25
3138	A850	4fo multicolored	.65	.45
a.		Pane of 10 #3136 + 10 #3138 with gutter btwn.	12.00	
		Complete booklet, #3138a, with text and cover in either English or German	12.00	
3139	A850	4fo multicolored	.65	.50
3140	A850	6fo multicolored	1.10	.65
		Nos. 3136-3140 (5)	3.00	2.10

Souvenir Sheet

Perf. 12½x11½

3141	A850	20fo multicolored	4.75	3.50

No. 3141 contains one 52x37mm stamp. Exist imperf. Value: set $17.50; souvenir sheet $30.

For surcharges see Nos. 3199-3200.

Antique Toys — A851

No. 3142, Train. No. 3143, See-saw. No. 3144, Pecking chickens. No. 3145, String-manipulated soldier.

1988, Aug. 12 *Perf. 12*

3142	A851	2fo multi	.30	.25
3143	A851	2fo multi	.30	.25
3144	A851	4fo +2fo multi	1.00	.65
3145	A851	5fo multi	.85	.55
		Nos. 3142-3145 (4)	2.45	1.70

Surtax for youth philately programs. Exist imperf. Value, set $15.

Calvinist College, Debrecen, 450th Anniv. — A852

1988, Aug. 16 Litho. *Perf. 13½x13*

3146	A852	4fo multi	.40	.25

Exists imperf. Value $5.

A853

1988, Aug. 30 *Perf. 12*

3147	A853	4fo multi	.40	.25

58th American Society of Travel Agents World Congress, Oct. 23-29, Budapest. Exists imperf. Value $7.50.

P.O. Officials Training School, Cent. — A854

1988, Sept. 9 Litho. *Perf. 12*

3148	A854	4fo Badge on collar	.40	.25

Exists imperf. Value $6.

Gabor Baross (1848-1892), Minister of Commerce and Communication — A855

Portrait and: 2fo, Postal Savings Bank, Budapest, emblem and postal savings stamp. 4fo, Telephone and telegraph apparatus, registration label and cancellations. 10fo, East Railway Station, Budapest.

1988, Sept. 16

3149	A855	2fo multi	.30	.25
3150	A855	4fo multi	.65	.50

Souvenir Sheet

Perf. 11½

3151	A855	10fo multi	2.25	2.00

No. 3151 contains one 50x29mm stamp. Exist imperf. Value: set $12.50; souvenir sheet $35.

Famous Hungarians Type of 1988

Gyula Lengyel (1888-1941), political writer.

1988, Oct. 7 *Perf. 11½x12*

3152	A843	4fo multi	.40	.25

Exists imperf. Value $5.

Christmas — A857

Perf. 12½x11½

1988, Nov. 10 **Litho.**
3153 A857 2fo multi .30 .25

Exists imperf. Value $5.

Nobel Prize Winners — A858

Designs: No. 3154, Richard Adolf Zsigmondy (1865-1929), Germany, chemistry (1925). No. 3155, Robert Barany (1876-1936), Austria, medicine (1914). No. 3156, Georg von Hevesy (1885-1966), Hungary, chemistry (1943). No. 3157, Albert Szent-Gyorgyi (1893-1986), Hungary-US, medicine (1937). No. 3158, Georg von Bekesy (1899-1972), US, medicine (1961). 6fo, Denis Gabor (1900-1979), Great Britain, physics (1971).

Litho. & Engr.

1988, Nov. 30 ***Perf. 12***
3154 A858 2fo red brown .35 .25
3155 A858 2fo green .35 .25
3156 A858 2fo deep claret .35 .25
3157 A858 4fo rose lake .60 .40
3158 A858 4fo steel blue .60 .40
3159 A858 6fo sepia .75 .65
Nos. 3154-3159 (6) 3.00 2.20

Exist imperf. Value, set $17.

Famous Hungarians Type of 1988

Arpad Szakasits (1888-1965), party leader.

1988, Dec. 6 ***Perf. 11½x12***
3160 A843 4fo multicolored .40 .25

Exists imperf. Value $5.

Souvenir Sheet

Medals Won by Hungarian Athletes at the 1988 Seoul Olympic Games — A860

1988, Dec. 19 **Litho.** ***Perf. 12***
3161 A860 20fo multicolored 3.75 3.50

Exists imperf. Value $20.

Silver and Cast Iron — A861

No. 3162, Teapot, Pest, 1846. No. 3163, Coffee pot, Buda, 18th cent. No. 3164, Sugar bowl, Pest, 1822. No. 3165, Cast iron plate, Romania, 1850.

1988, Dec. 28 **Litho. & Engr.**
3162 A861 2fo multicolored .35 .25
3163 A861 2fo multicolored .35 .25
3164 A861 4fo multicolored .65 .45
3165 A861 5fo multicolored .85 .55
Nos. 3162-3165 (4) 2.20 1.50

Exist imperf. Value, set $15.

Postal Savings Bank Inauguration — A862

1989, Jan. 20 **Litho.** ***Perf. 12x11½***
3166 A862 5fo royal blue, blk & silver .50 .25

Exists imperf. Value $5.

Kalman Wallisch (1889-1934), Labor Leader — A863

1989, Feb. 28 **Litho.** ***Perf. 12***
3167 A863 3fo dk red & brt bl .40 .25

Exists imperf. Value $5.
See No. 3170.

A864

1989, Mar. 3 ***Perf. 13x13½***
3168 A864 3fo multicolored .40 .25

World Indoor Sports Championships, Budapest, Mar. 3-5.
Exists imperf. Value $5.

Souvenir Sheet

Interparliamentary Union Cent. and 81st Session, Budapest, Mar. 13-18 — A865

a, Parliament, Big Ben & Tower Bridge, London. b, Parliament & Chain Bridge, Budapest.

1989, Mar. 13 **Litho.** ***Perf. 11***
3169 A865 Sheet of 2 3.75 3.50
a.-b. 10fo any single 1.75 1.60

Exists with red inscriptions and control number. Value $75.
Exists imperf. Value $25.

Famous Hungarians Type of 1989

Janos Gyetvai (1889-1967), journalist, diplomat.

1989, Apr. 7 **Litho.** ***Perf. 12***
3170 A863 3fo dark red & brt grn .40 .25

Exists imperf. Value $5.

Stud Farm at Babolna, 200th Anniv. — A867

Horses: a, O Bajan. b, Meneskari Csikos. c, Gazal II.

1989, May 18 **Litho.** ***Perf. 12***
3171 A867 Strip of 3 1.75 1.10
a.-c. 3fo any single .55 .35

Exists imperf. Value, strip $15.

ART '89, May 23-27, Budapest A868

1989, May 23 ***Perf. 12x11½***
3172 A868 5fo multi .50 .25

Exhibition for disabled artists.
Exists imperf. Value $5.

Flower Arrangements — A869

1989, May 31 ***Perf. 12***
3173 A869 2fo multi, vert. .35 .25
3174 A869 3fo multi, vert. .40 .30
3175 A869 3fo shown .40 .30
3176 A869 5fo multi, diff. .85 .50
3177 A869 10fo multi, vert. 1.50 1.00
Nos. 3173-3177 (5) 3.50 2.35

Exist imperf. Value, set $15.

French Revolution, Bicent. A870

1989, June 1 ***Perf. 12***
3178 A870 5fo brt blue, blk & red .50 .30

Souvenir Sheet

Perf. 11½

3179 A870 20fo like 5fo 3.50 3.25

No. 3179 contains one 50x30mm stamp.
Exist imperf. Value: single $12.50; souvenir sheet $22.50.

Medieval Church of the Csolts Near Veszto — A871

1989, June 15 **Litho.** ***Perf. 12***
3180 A871 3fo multi .50 .25

Exists imperf. Value $5.

Photography, 150th Anniv. — A872

1989, June 15
3181 A872 5fo multi .50 .25

Exists imperf. Value $5.

Old Mills — A873

Designs: 2fo, Water mill, Turistvandi, 18th cent. 3fo, Horse-driven mill, Szarvas, 1836. 5fo, Windmill, Kiskunhalas, 18th cent. 10fo, Water wheel on the Drava River.

1989, June 20
3182 A873 2fo multi .30 .25
3183 A873 3fo multi .45 .30
3184 A873 5fo multi .75 .50
3185 A873 10fo multi 1.50 1.00
Nos. 3182-3185 (4) 3.00 2.05

Exist imperf. Value, set $15.

Souvenir Sheet

1st Moon Landing, 20th Anniv. — A874

1989, July 12 **Litho.** ***Perf. 12½***
3186 A874 20fo multi 3.75 3.50

Exists imperf. Value $20.

Gliders — A875

1989, July 20 ***Perf. 12***
3187 A875 3fo Futar .45 .30
3188 A875 5fo Cimbora .80 .60

17th Intl. Old Timers Rally, Budakeszi Airport, and 60th anniv. of glider flying in Hungary.
Exist imperf. Value, set $15.

Reptiles A876

Designs: 2fo, Lacerta agilis. 3fo, Lacerta viridis. No. 3191, Vipera rakosiensis. No. 3192, Natrix natrix. 10fr, Emys orbicularis.

1989, July 26 *Perf. 11*
3189 A876 2fo multicolored .25 .25
3190 A876 3fo multicolored .45 .25
3191 A876 5fo multicolored .70 .40
3192 A876 5fo multicolored .70 .40
3193 A876 10fo multicolored 1.25 .75
Nos. 3189-3193 (5) 3.35 2.05

Exist imperf. Value, set $20.

31st Modern Pentathlon World Championships, Aug. 30-Sept. 4, Budapest — A877

1989, July 31 *Perf. 13½x13*
3194 A877 5fo multi .50 .25

Exists imperf. Value $5.

Caves — A878

10th World Speleology Congress, Aug. 13-20, Sofia: 3fo, Baradla. 5fo, Szemlohegy. 10fo, Anna. 12fo, Lake Cave of Tapolca.

1989, Aug. 14 **Litho.** *Perf. 11*
3195 A878 3fo multi .30 .25
3196 A878 5fo multi .55 .40
3197 A878 10fo multi .90 .70
3198 A878 12fo multi 1.25 .80
Nos. 3195-3198 (4) 3.00 2.15

Exist imperf. Value, set $15.

Nos. 3136 and 3138 Surcharged

No. 3199

No. 3200

1989, Aug. 14 *Perf. 13x13½*
3199 A850 3fo on 2fo #3136 2.00 1.75
3200 A850 5fo on 4fo #3138 2.00 1.75
a. Pane of 10 #3199 + pane of 10 #3200 with gutter between 20.00
Complete booklet, #3200a, with text and cover in either English or German 35.00

A879

1989, Aug. 24 *Perf. 12*
3201 A879 5fo multi .50 .25

Third World Two-in-Hand Carriage-driving Championships, Balatonfenyves, Aug. 24-27.
Exists imperf. Value $5.

A880

Nurses: 5fo, Zsuzsanna Kossuth (1820-1854) and emblem. 10fo, Florence Nightingale (1820-1910) and medal awarded in her name by the Red Cross.

1989, Sept. 8 **Litho.** *Perf. 12*
3202 A880 5fo multi .65 .40
3203 A880 10fo multi 1.10 .75

Stamp Day. See No. B341.
Exist imperf. Value, set $12.50.

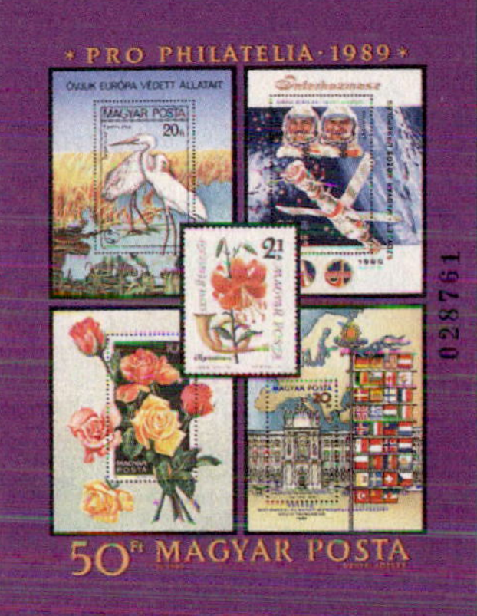

Pro-Philatelia 1989 — A881

1989, Oct. 10 **Litho.** *Imperf.*
3204 A881 50fo #2665, C426, 2742, 3005, B233 6.25 5.75

Dismantling of the Electronic Surveillance System (Iron Curtain) on the Hungary-Austria Border — A882

1989, Oct. 30 *Perf. 11*
3205 A882 5fo multi 1.00 .50

Exists imperf. Value $6.

Conquest of Hungary, by Mor Than — A883

1989, Oct. 31
3206 A883 5fo multi .60 .25

Arpad, chief who founded the 1st Magyar dynasty of Hungary in 889.
Exists imperf. Value $5.

Christmas — A884

1989, Nov. 10 **Litho.** *Perf. 11½x12*
3207 A884 3fo Flight to Egypt .45 .25

Exists imperf. Value $5.

Jawaharlal Nehru — A885

Litho. & Engr.

1989, Nov. 14 *Perf. 12*
3208 A885 3fo buff & rose brn 1.00 .25

Jawaharlal Nehru, 1st prime minister of independent India.
Exists imperf. Value $5.

Modern Art (Paintings) A886

3fo, *Mike*, by Dezso Korniss. 5fo, *Sunrise*, by Lajos Kassak. 10fo, *Grotesque Burial*, by Endre Balint. 12fo, *Memory of Toys*, by Tihamer Gyarmathy.

1989, Dec. 18 **Litho.** *Perf. 12*
3209 A886 3fo multicolored .35 .25
3210 A886 5fo multicolored .65 .50
3211 A886 10fo multicolored 1.40 .95
3212 A886 12fo multicolored 1.60 1.10
Nos. 3209-3212 (4) 4.00 2.80

Exist imperf. Value, set $20.

Medical Pioneers — A887

No. 3213, Galen (129-c.199), Greek physician. No. 3214, Paracelsus (1493-1541), German alchemist. 4fo, Andreas Vesalius (1514-64), Belgian anatomist. 6fo, Rudolf Virchow (1821-1902), German pathologist. 10fo, Ivan Petrovich Pavlov (1849-1936), Russian physiologist.

1989, Dec. 29 **Engr.** *Perf. 12*
3213 A887 3fo olive gray .40 .25
3214 A887 3fo brown .40 .25
3215 A887 4fo black .70 .45
3216 A887 6fo intense black .85 .55
3217 A887 10fo brown violet 1.40 .80
Nos. 3213-3217 (5) 3.75 2.30

Exist imperf. Value, set $20.

Hungarian Savings Bank, 150th Anniv. — A888

1990, Jan. 11 **Litho.**
3218 A888 5fo multicolored .75 .45

Exists imperf. Value $8.

A889

1990, Jan. 15 *Perf. 12*
3219 A889 5fo brown & sepia .75 .45

Singer Sewing Machine, 25th anniv.
Exists imperf. Value $7.

A890

3fo, Telephone, Budapest Exchange. 5fo, Mailbox and main p.o., Budapest, c. 1900.

1990, Jan. 29
3220 A890 3fo multicolored .40 .25
3221 A890 5fo multicolored .60 .30

Coil Stamps

Size: 17x22mm

Perf. 14

Photo.

3222 A890 3fo multi .40 .25
3223 A890 5fo shown .60 .30
Nos. 3220-3223 (4) 2.00 1.10

Nos. 3220-3221 inscribed "Pj 1989." Nos. 3222-3223 inscribed "1989."
Nos. 3220-3221 exist imperf. Value, set $20.

A891

Protected bird species: No. 3224, Alcedo atthis. No. 3225, Pyrrhula pyrrhula. No. 3226, Dendrocopos syriacus. No. 3227, Upupa epops. No. 3228, Merops apiaster. 10fo, Coracias garrulus.

1990, Feb. 20 **Litho.** *Perf. 11½x12*
3224 A891 3fo multicolored .45 .30
3225 A891 3fo multicolored .45 .30
3226 A891 3fo multicolored .45 .30
3227 A891 5fo multicolored .75 .50
3228 A891 5fo multicolored .75 .50
3229 A891 10fo multicolored 1.50 1.00
Nos. 3224-3229 (6) 4.35 2.90

Exist imperf. Value, set $20.

A892

Flowers of the continents (Africa): No. 3230, Leucadendron. No. 3231, Protea compacta. No. 3232, Leucadendron spissifolium. No. 3233, Protea barbigera. No. 3234, Protea lepidocarpodendron. 10fr, Protea cynaroides. 20fo, Montage of African flowers.

1990, Mar. 14 Litho. *Perf. 12*

3230	A892	3fo multicolored	.40	.25
3231	A892	3fo multicolored	.40	.25
3232	A892	3fo multicolored	.40	.25
3233	A892	5fo multicolored	.70	.40
3234	A892	5fo multicolored	.70	.40
3235	A892	10fo multicolored	1.25	.85
		Nos. 3230-3235 (6)	3.85	2.40

Souvenir Sheet

Perf. 12½x12

3236	A892	20fo multicolored	3.75	3.75

No. 3236 contains one 27x38mm stamp.
See Nos. 3278-3283, 3371-3375, 3377-3381, 3451-3455.
Exist imperf. Value: set $20; souvenir sheet $30.

A893

Portraits of Hungarian kings in the Historical Portrait Gallery. King and reign: No. 3237, Janos Hunyadi (c. 1407-1409). No. 3238, Mathias Hunyadi (1443-1490).

1990, Apr. 6 Litho. *Perf. 11½x12*

3237	A893	5fo multicolored	.70	.40
3238	A893	5fo multicolored	.70	.40
a.		Pair, #3237-3238	1.40	1.00

Exist imperf. Value, pair $12.50.

Souvenir Sheet

A894

Litho. & Engr.

1990, Apr. 17 *Perf. 12½x12*

3239	A894	20fo black & buff	3.75	3.25

Penny Black 150th anniv., Stamp World London '90.
Exists imperf. Value $22.50.

Karoli Bible, 400th Anniv. — A895

1990, Apr. 24 Litho.

3240	A895	8fo Gaspar Karoli	1.00	.70

No. 3240 printed se-tenant with label picturing Bible frontispiece.
Exists imperf. Value, with label $12.50.

1990 World Cup Soccer Championships, Italy — A896

Various athletes.

1990, Apr. 27 *Perf. 11½x12*

3241	A896	3fo Dribble	.30	.25
3242	A896	5fo Heading the ball	.55	.35
3243	A896	5fo Kick	.55	.35
3244	A896	8fo Goal attempt	.80	.55
3245	A896	8fo Dribble, diff.	.80	.55
3246	A896	10fo Dribble, diff.	1.00	.75
		Nos. 3241-3246 (6)	4.00	2.80

Souvenir Sheet

Perf. 12½

3247	A896	20fo Dribble, diff.	3.50	3.50

No. 3247 contains one 32x42mm stamp.
Exist imperf. Value: set $20; souvenir sheet $20.

Kelemen Mikes (1690-1761), Writer — A897

1990, May 31 Litho. *Perf. 13½x13*

3248	A897	8fo black & gold	1.10	.75

Exists imperf. Value $5.

Noemi and Beni Ferenczy, Birth Cent. — A898

Designs: 3fo, Painting by Noemi Ferenczy. 5fo, Sculpture by Beni Ferenczy.

1990, June 18 Litho. *Perf. 12*

3249	A898	3fo multicolored	.30	.25
3250	A898	5fo multicolored	.50	.30

Exist imperf. Value, set $10.

Ferenc Kazinczy (1759-1831), Hungarian Language Reformer A899

1990, July 18 Litho. *Perf. 12*

3251	A899	8fo multicolored	.60	.40

Exists imperf. Value $5.

Ferenc Kolcsey (1790-1838), Poet — A900

1990, Aug. 3

3252	A900	8fo multicolored	.60	.40

Exists imperf. Value $7.50.

New Coat of Arms A901

1990, Aug. 17 Litho. *Perf. 13½x13*

3253	A901	8fo multicolored	.60	.40

Souvenir Sheet

Perf. 11

3254	A901	20fo multicolored	4.00	4.00

No. 3254 contains one 34x50mm stamp.
A souvenir sheet like No. 3254 was released with a hologram as the stamp. The sheet exists with black or red control numbers on the reverse. Values: with black numbers $175; with red numbers $300.
Exist imperf. Value: single $15; souvenir sheet $30.

Grapes and Wine Producing Areas — A902

Grapes and Growing Area: 3fo, Cabernet franc, Hajos-Vaskut. 5fo, Cabernet sauvignon, Villany-Siklos. No. 3257, Italian Riesling, Badacsony. No. 3258, Kadarka, Szekszard. No. 3259, Leanyka, Eger. 10fo, Furmint, Tokaj-Hegyalja.

1990, Aug. 31 *Perf. 13x13½*

3255	A902	3fo multicolored	.25	.25
3256	A902	5fo multicolored	.45	.30
3257	A902	8fo multicolored	.65	.45
3258	A902	8fo multicolored	.65	.45
3259	A902	8fo multicolored	.65	.45
3260	A902	10fo multicolored	.85	.60
		Nos. 3255-3260 (6)	3.50	2.50

Exist imperf. Value, set $25.
See Nos. 3580-3582, 3656-3657, 3704-3705, 3773-3774, 3832-3833, 3938-3939, 4037-4039.

Paintings by Endre Szasz A903

1990, Oct. 12 Litho. *Perf. 12*

3261	A903	8fo Feast	.70	.45
3262	A903	12fo Message	1.10	.65

Stamp Day. See No. B344.
Exist imperf. Value, set $17.50.

Prehistoric Animals A904

1990, Nov. 16 Litho. *Perf. 12*

3263	A904	3fo Tarbosaurus	.25	.25
3264	A904	5fo Brontosaurus	.40	.25
3265	A904	5fo Stegosaurus	.40	.25
3266	A904	5fo Dimorphodon	.40	.25
3267	A904	8fo Platybelodon	.70	.35
3268	A904	10fo Mammoth	.85	.40
		Nos. 3263-3268 (6)	3.00	1.75

Exist imperf. Value, set $20.

Intl. Literacy Year — A905

1990, Nov. 21 *Perf. 13x13½*

3269	A905	10fo multicolored	1.40	.65

Exist imperf. Value $5.

Budapest Stamp Museum, 60th Anniv. — A906

1990, Nov. 23 *Perf. 12½*

3270	A906	5fo brn red & grn	.50	.30

Exist imperf. Value $5.

Souvenir Sheet

Thurn & Taxis Postal System, 500th Anniv. — A907

1990, Nov. 30 Litho. *Perf. 12½x12*

3271 A907 50fo multicolored *10.00 10.00*

Antique Clocks — A908

No. 3272, Travelling clock, 1576. No. 3273, Table clock, 1643. No. 3274, Mantel clock, 1790. No. 3275, Table clock, 1814.

1990, Dec. 14 *Perf. 12*

3272 A908 3fo multicolored .25 .25
3273 A908 5fo multicolored .45 .30
3274 A908 5fo multicolored .45 .30
3275 A908 10fo multicolored .85 .60
Nos. 3272-3275 (4) 2.00 1.45

Exist imperf. Value, set $17.50.

Madonna with Child by Botticelli — A909

1990, Dec. 14 *Perf. 12½x11½*

3276 A909 5fo multicolored .50 .25

Exists imperf. Value $5.

Lorand Eotvos (1848-1919) and Torsion Pendulum A910

1991, Jan. 31 Litho. *Perf. 11*

3277 A910 12fo multicolored 1.10 .65

Exists imperf. Value $10.

Flowers of the Continents Type

Flowers of the Americas: No. 3278, Mandevilla splendens. No. 3279, Lobelia cardinalis. No. 3280, Cobaea scandens. No. 3281, Steriphoma paradoxa. No. 3282, Beloperone guttata.

No. 3283, Flowers of the Americas.

1991, Feb. 28 Litho. *Perf. 12*

3278 A892 5fo multicolored .35 .25
3279 A892 7fo multicolored .45 .30
3280 A892 7fo multicolored .45 .30
3281 A892 12fo multicolored .75 .50
3282 A892 15fo multicolored 1.00 .70
Nos. 3278-3282 (5) 3.00 2.05

Souvenir Sheet

Perf. 11

3283 A892 20fo multicolored 3.50 1.75

No. 3283 contains one 27x44mm stamp. Exist imperf. Value: set $20; souvenir sheet $50.

Post Office, Budapest A911

Designs: 7fo, Post Office, Pecs.

Perf. 11½x12½

1991, Mar. 22 Litho.

3284 A911 5fo multicolored 5.50 4.00
3285 A911 7fo multicolored 6.50 4.50
a. Pair, #3284-3285 13.00 11.00

Admission to CEPT. Exist imperf. Value, pair $40.

Europa — A912

12fo, Ulysses probe. 30fo, Cassini-Huygens probe.

1991, Apr. Litho. *Perf. 12½*

3286 A912 12fo multi *4.00* 2.00
3287 A912 30fo multi *8.00* 6.00

Exist imperf. Value, set $35.

Budapest Zoological and Botanical Gardens, 125th Anniv. — A913

1991, May 15 *Perf. 13½x13*

3288 A913 7fo Gorilla .60 .35
3289 A913 12fo Rhinoceros .85 .60
3290 A913 12fo Toucan .85 .60
3291 A913 12fo Polar bear .85 .60
3292 A913 20fo Orchid 1.40 1.00
Nos. 3288-3292 (5) 4.55 3.15

Exist imperf. Value, set $20.

A915

1991, June 13 *Perf. 13x13½*

3294 A915 12fo multicolored 1.00 .60

44th World Fencing Championships, Budapest.
Exists imperf. Value $7.50.

Images of the Virgin and Child in Hungarian Shrines A916

Designs: 7fo, Mariapocs. No. 3296, Mariagyud. No. 3297, Celldomolk. No. 3298, Mariaremete. 20fo, Esztergom.

1991, June 17 *Perf. 12½*

3295 A916 7fo multicolored .55 .35
3296 A916 12fo multicolored .85 .60
3297 A916 12fo multicolored .85 .60
3298 A916 12fo multicolored .85 .60
3299 A916 20fo multicolored 1.40 1.00
Nos. 3295-3299 (5) 4.50 3.15

Compare with design A927.
Exist imperf. Value, set $20.

Souvenir Sheet

Visit of Pope John Paul II, Aug. 16-20, 1991 — A917

Litho. & Engr.

1991, July 15 *Perf. 12*

3300 A917 50fo multicolored 4.50 3.50

Exists imperf. Value $25.

Karoly Marko (1791-1860), Painter — A918

1991, June 17 *Perf. 12*

3301 A918 12fo multicolored 1.25 .75

Exists imperf. Value $7.50.

Basketball, Cent. — A919

1991, June 27 Litho. *Perf. 12*

3302 A919 10fo multicolored 1.25 .75

Exists imperf. Value $8.

Otto Lilienthal's First Glider Flight, Cent. — A920

Aircraft of aviation pioneers: 7fo, Otto Lilienthal. 12fo, Wright Brothers. 20fo, Alberto Santos-Dumont. 30fo, Aladar Zselyi.

1991, June 27

3303 A920 7fo multi .50 .35
3304 A920 12fo multi .80 .65
3305 A920 20fo multi 1.40 1.00
3306 A920 30fo multi 2.00 1.50
Nos. 3303-3306 (4) 4.70 3.50

Exist imperf. Value, set $20.

3rd Intl. Hungarian Philological Congress A921

1991, Aug. 12 Litho. *Perf. 13½x13*

3307 A921 12fo multicolored 1.50 .65

Exists imperf. Value $6.

A922

1991, Sept. 6 Engr. *Perf. 12*

3308 A922 12fo dark red .65 .45

Count Istvan Szechenyi (1791-1860), founder of Academy of Sciences.
Exists imperf. Value $6.

A923

Wolfgang Amadeus Mozart (1756-91).

1991, Sept. 6 Litho.

3309 A923 12fo As child 1.00 .50
3310 A923 20fo As adult 2.00 .80

Souvenir Sheet

3311 A923 30fo +15fo, in red coat 4.00 2.50

Stamp Day. No. 3311 contains one 30x40mm stamp.
Exist imperf. Value: set $25; souvenir sheet $60.

Telecom '91 — A924

1991, Sept. 30 Litho. *Perf. 12*

3312 A924 12fo multicolored .90 .50

6th World Forum and Exposition on Telecommunications, Geneva, Switzerland. Exists imperf. Value $7.50.

A925

1991, Oct. 30 Litho. *Perf. 13½x13*

3313 A925 12fo multicolored 1.75 .50

Sovereign Order of the Knights of Malta. Exists imperf. Value, set $7.50.

A926

Early explorers and Discovery of America, 500th anniv. (in 1992): 7fo, Sebastian Cabot, Labrador Peninsula, Nova Scotia. No. 3315, Amerigo Vespucci, South American region. No. 3316, Hernando Cortez, Mexico. 15fo, Ferdinand Magellan, Straits of Magellan. 20fo, Francisco Pizarro, Peru, Andes Mountain region. 30fo, Christopher Columbus and coat of arms.

1991, Oct. 30 *Perf. 12*

3314 A926 7fo multicolored .50 .25
3315 A926 12fo multicolored .80 .45
3316 A926 12fo multicolored .80 .45
3317 A926 15fo multicolored 1.00 .60
3318 A926 20fo multicolored 1.40 .75
Nos. 3314-3318 (5) 4.50 2.50

Souvenir Sheet

3319 A926 30fo multicolored 2.50 2.00

No. 3319 contains one 26x37mm stamp.
Exist imperf. Value: set $25; souvenir sheet $60.

No. 3023 Overprinted in Brown

1991, Oct. 22 Litho. *Perf. 12x11½*

3320 A816 12fo multicolored 1.25 .90

Anniversary of Hungarian revolution, 1956.

Christmas — A927

Images of the Virgin and Child from: 7fo, Mariapocs. 12fo, Mariaremete.

1991, Nov. 20 *Perf. 13½x13*

3322 A927 7fo multicolored .65 .25
3323 A927 12fo multicolored 1.10 .45

Nos. 3322-3323 issued in sheets of 20 plus 20 labels.
Exist imperf. Value, set $14.

A928

1991, Nov. 20 *Perf. 12*

3324 A928 12fo multicolored .90 .45

Fight for human rights. Exist imperf. Value $20.

A929

7fo, Cross-country skiing. 12fo, Slalom skiing. 15fo, Four-man bobsled. 20fo, Ski jump. 30fo, Hockey.
No. 3330, Pairs figure skating.

1991, Dec. 6 *Perf. 13½x13*

3325 A929 7fo multicolored .35 .25
3326 A929 12fo multicolored .70 .30
3327 A929 15fo multicolored .80 .45
3328 A929 20fo multicolored 1.10 .60
3329 A929 30fo multicolored 1.60 .85
Nos. 3325-3329 (5) 4.55 2.45

Souvenir Sheet

Perf. 12½x11½

3330 A929 30fo multicolored 2.50 2.00

1992 Winter Olympics, Albertville.
Exist imperf. Value: set $20; souvenir sheet $20.

Souvenir Sheet

First Hungarian Postage Stamp, 120th Anniv. — A930

1991, Dec. 20 Litho. *Perf. 12x12½*

3331 A930 50fo No. 6 4.00 3.00

Piarist Order in Hungary, 350th Anniv. — A931

1992, Jan. 22 *Perf. 13½x13*

3332 A931 10fo multicolored .85 .40

World Heritage Village of Holloko A932

1992, Jan. 22 *Perf. 12*

3333 A932 15fo multicolored 1.50 .60

1992 Summer Olympics, Barcelona — A933

1992, Feb. 26 Litho. *Perf. 13½x13*

3334 A933 7fo Swimming .90 .75
3335 A933 9fo Cycling 1.40 .85
3336 A933 10fo Gymnastics 1.50 1.00
3337 A933 15fo Running 2.75 1.60
Nos. 3334-3337 (4) 6.55 4.20

Discovery of America, 500th Anniv. — A934

Expo '92, Seville: No. 3338, Map shaped as Indian, Columbus' fleet. No. 3339, Face-shaped map of ocean, sailing ship. No. 3340, Map shaped as European face, ship. No. 3341, Map, square, protractor, compass.

1992, Mar. 27 Litho. *Perf. 12*

3338 A934 10fo multicolored .90 .35
3339 A934 10fo multicolored .90 .35
3340 A934 15fo multicolored .90 .55
3341 A934 15fo multicolored 1.25 .55
Nos. 3338-3341 (4) 3.95 1.80

A935

Design: 15fo, Jozsef Cardinal Mindszenty (1892-1975), Leader of Hungarian Catholic Church.

1992, Mar. 27 *Perf. 12½x11½*

3342 A935 15fo red, brn & buff 1.10 .60

A936

1992, Mar. 27 *Perf. 13½x13*

3343 A936 15fo multicolored 1.10 .60

Jan Amos Komensky (Comenius), writer, 400th birth anniv.

Maya Indian Sculpture — A937

40fo, Indian sculpture, diff.

1992, Apr. 14 Litho. *Perf. 13½x13*

3344 A937 15fo multicolored *2.50* 1.00
3345 A937 40fo multicolored *7.25* 3.00

Europa. Discovery of America, 500th anniversary.

European Gymnastics Championships, Budapest — A938

1992, May 15 Litho. *Perf. 12*

3346 A938 15fo multicolored 1.10 .60

A939

1992, June 26 Litho. *Perf. 13½x13*

3347 A939 15fo multicolored 1.00 .50

St. Margaret, 750th Anniv. (in 1991). No. 3347 printed with se-tenant label.

A940

Protected birds: 9fo, Falco cherrug. 10fo, Hieraaetus pennatus. 15fo, Circaetus gallicus. 40fo, Milvus milvus.

1992, June 26 *Perf. 13x13½*

3348 A940 9fo multicolored .40 .25
3349 A940 10fo multicolored .60 .25
3350 A940 15fo multicolored .85 .50
3351 A940 40fo multicolored 1.60 1.00
Nos. 3348-3351 (4) 3.45 2.00

Raoul Wallenberg, Swedish Diplomat, 80th Anniv. of Birth — A941

1992, July 30 Litho. *Perf. 12*
3352 A941 15fo gray & red 1.50 .45

Theodore von Karman (1881-1963), Physicist and Aeronautical Engineer — A942

Design: 40fo, John von Neumann (1903-1957), mathematician.

1992, Aug. 3 Litho. *Perf. 12x11½*
3353 A942 15fo multicolored .45 .25
3354 A942 40fo multicolored 1.90 .70

3rd World Congress of Hungarians A943

1992, Aug. 3 *Perf. 13½x13*
3355 A943 15fo multicolored .80 .35

Telecom '92 — A945

1992, Oct. 6 Litho. *Perf. 12½x11½*
3360 A945 15fo multicolored .80 .35

Stamp Day — A946

No. 3361, Coat of arms, vert. No. 3363, like #3362, inscribed "65. Belyegnap". No. 3364, Postilion.

1992, Sept.4 *Perf. 12*
3361 A946 10fo +5fo multi 1.00 .80
3362 A946 15fo shown 1.00 .40
3363 A946 15fo +5fo multi 1.50 .85
Nos. 3361-3363 (3) 3.50 2.05

Souvenir Sheet

3364 A946 50fo +20fo multi 4.50 3.25

Eurofilex '92 (Nos. 3361, 3363-3364). Nos. 3361, 3363 printed with se-tenant label. No. 3364 contains one 40x30mm stamp.

Famous Men — A947

Designs: 10fo, Stephen Bathory (1533-1586), Prince of Transylvania and King of Poland. 15fo, Stephen Bocskay (1557-1606), Prince of Transylvania. 40fo, Gabriel Bethlen (1580-1629), Prince of Transylvania and King of Hungary.

1992, Oct. 28 Litho. *Perf. 12*
3365 A947 10fo multicolored .40 .25
3366 A947 15fo multicolored .70 .30
3367 A947 40fo multicolored 1.25 .85
Nos. 3365-3367 (3) 2.35 1.40

Postal Uniforms — A948

Designs: 10fo, Postrider, 1703-1711. 15fo, Letter carrier, 1874.

1992, Nov. 20 *Perf. 13½x13*
3368 A948 10fo multicolored .65 .30
3369 A948 15fo multicolored 1.00 .50

Christmas A949

Litho. & Engr.

1992, Nov. 20 *Perf. 12*
3370 A949 15fo blue & black 1.00 .50

Flowers of the Continents Type of 1990

Flowers of Australia: 9fo, Clianthus formosus. 10fo, Leschenaultia biloba. 15fo, Anigosanthos manglesii. 40fo, Comesperma ericinum. 50fo, Bouquet of flowers.

1992, Nov. 20 Litho.
3371 A892 9fo multicolored .50 .25
3372 A892 10fo multicolored .55 .40
3373 A892 15fo multicolored .75 .50
3374 A892 40fo multicolored 1.75 1.25
Nos. 3371-3374 (4) 3.55 2.40

Souvenir Sheet

Perf. 12½

3375 A892 50fo multicolored 5.00 3.75

No. 3375 contains one 32x41mm stamp.

1992 European Chess Championships A950

1992, Oct. 28 *Perf. 11*
3376 A950 15fo multicolored 1.25 .35

Flowers of the Continents Type of 1990

Flowers of Asia: No. 3377, Dendrobium densiflorum. No. 3378, Arachnis flos-aeris. No. 3379, Lilium speciosum. No. 3380, Meconopsis aculeata. 50fo, Bouquet of flowers.

1993, Jan. 27 Litho. *Perf. 13½x13*
3377 A892 10fo multicolored .45 .25
3378 A892 10fo multicolored .45 .25
3379 A892 15fo multicolored 1.00 .50
3380 A892 15fo multicolored 1.00 .50
Nos. 3377-3380 (4) 2.90 1.50

Souvenir Sheet

Perf. 12½

3381 A892 50fo multicolored 11.00 3.25

No. 3381 contains one 32x41mm stamp.

Scythian Archaeological Artifacts — A951

1993, Feb. 25 Litho. *Perf. 13x13½*
3382 A951 10fo Horse standing .50 .25
3383 A951 17fo Horse lying down 1.00 .25

Hungarian Rowing Association, Cent. — A952

1993, Feb. 25 Litho. *Perf. 12*
3384 A952 17fo multicolored .75 .25

Missale Romanum of Matthias Corvinus (Matyas Hunyadi, King of Hungary) — A953

Design: 40fo, Illuminated page.

1993, Mar. 12 Litho. *Perf. 12*
3385 A953 15fo multicolored 1.25 .40

Souvenir Sheet

3386 A953 40fo multicolored 7.00 6.00

No. 3386 contains one 60x38mm stamp. See Belgium Nos. 1474, 1476.

Motocross World Championships A954

1993, May 5 Litho. *Perf. 11½x12*
3387 A954 17fo multicolored .75 .25

Europa — A955

Buildings designed by Imre Makovecz: 17fo, Roman Catholic Church, Paks. 45fo, Hungarian Pavilion, Expo '92, Seville.

1993, May 5 *Perf. 13x13½*
3388 A955 17fo multicolored *1.50* .50
3389 A955 45fo multicolored *2.75* 1.25

Heliocentric Solar System, Copernicus — A956

1993, May 5 *Perf. 12*
3390 A956 17fo multicolored .90 .25

Polska '93. No. 3390 issued in sheets of 8 + 4 labels.

Edible Mushrooms A957

10fo, Ramaria botrytis. 17fo, Craterellus cornucopioides. 45fo, Amanita caesarea.

1993, June 18 Litho. *Perf. 13½x13*
3391 A957 10fo multicolored .40 .25
3392 A957 17fo multicolored .70 .25
3393 A957 45fo multicolored 2.25 .80
Nos. 3391-3393 (3) 3.35 1.30

St. Christopher, by Albrecht Durer — A958

1993, June 18 *Perf. 12*
3394 A958 17fo sil, blk & buff .65 .25

Year of the Elderly.

City of Mohacs, 900th Anniv. — A959

1993, June 18 *Perf. 13½x13*
3395 A959 17fo buff, mar & red brn .65 .25

Hungarian State Railways, 125th Anniv. A960

1993, June 18 *Perf. 13x13½*
3396 A960 17fo lt blue & blue .65 .25

Comedians A961

1993, July 28 Litho. *Perf. 12*
3397 A961 17fo Kalman Latabar .75 .25
3398 A961 30fo Charlie Chaplin 1.25 .65

Butterflies A962

10fo, Limenitis populi. 17fo, Aricia artaxerxes. 30fo, Plebejides pylaon.

1993, July 28 *Perf. 13½x13*
3399 A962 10fo multicolored .30 .25
3400 A962 17fo multicolored .70 .25
3401 A962 30fo multicolored 1.25 .65
Nos. 3399-3401 (3) 2.25 1.15

Souvenir Sheet

Helsinki Conference on European Security and Cooperation, 20th Anniv. — A963

1993, July 28 *Perf. 12*
3402 A963 50fo multicolored 3.00 3.00

Intl. Solar Energy Society Congress, Budapest — A964

Perf. 12½x11½
1993, Aug. 23 Litho.
3403 A964 17fo multicolored .65 .25

No. 3403 printed se-tenant with label.

Writers — A965

Designs: No. 3404, Laszlo Nemeth (1901-75). No. 3405, Dezso Szabo (1879-1945). No. 3406, Antal Szerb (1901-45).

1993, Aug. 23 *Perf. 12*
3404 A965 17fo blue .50 .25
3405 A965 17fo blue .50 .25
3406 A965 17fo blue .50 .25
Nos. 3404-3406 (3) 1.50 .75

School of Agronomy, Pannon Agricultural Univ., 175th Anniv. — A966

1993, Oct. 22 Litho. *Perf. 12*
3407 A966 17fo multicolored .60 .30

Ships A967

10fo, Steamer with sails. 30fo, Battleship.

1993, Oct. 27 *Perf. 13x13½*
3408 A967 10fo multicolored .35 .25
3409 A967 30fo multicolored 1.00 .50
a. Pair, #3408-3409 1.60 .70

Prehistoric Man — A968

1993, Oct. 27 *Perf. 13½x13*
3410 A968 17fo Skull fragment .75 .30
3411 A968 30fo Stone tool 1.25 .50

Souvenir Sheet

Roman Roads — A969

1993, Oct. 27 *Perf. 11*
3412 A969 50fo multicolored 2.75 1.50

Christmas A970

Altarpiece: 10fo, Virgin and Christ Child, Cathedral of Szekesfehervar, by F. A. Hillebrant.

1993, Nov. 24 *Perf. 13½x13*
3413 A970 10fo multicolored .50 .25

Sights of Budapest — A971

Designs: 17fo, Szechenyi Chain Bridge. 30fo, Opera House. 45fo, Matthias Church, vert.

Photo. & Engr.
1993, Dec. 16 *Perf. 12*
3414 A971 17fo lt grn & dk grn 1.10 .55
3415 A971 30fo lt mag & dk mag 1.75 .65
3416 A971 45fo lt brn & dk brn 2.75 1.50
Nos. 3414-3416 (3) 5.60 2.70

Expo '96.

József Antall (1932-93) — A972

1993 Litho. *Perf. 11*
3417 A972 19fo multicolored .80 .40
a. Souvenir sheet of 1 1.50 1.50

For surcharge, see No. 4167.

ICAO, 50th Anniv. A973

1994, Jan. 13 *Perf. 13x13½*
3418 A973 56fo multicolored 1.90 .95

1994 Winter Olympics, Lillehammer — A974

1994, Jan. 13 *Perf. 12*
3419 A974 12fo Downhill skiing .40 .25
3420 A974 19fo Ice hockey .70 .30

Easter — A975

Design: Golgotha, by Mihaly Munkacsy.

1994, Feb. 17 Litho. *Perf. 11½x12*
3421 A975 12fo multicolored .50 .25

A976

Artists: 12fo, Gyula Benczur (1844-1920). 19fo, Mihaly Munkacsy (1844-1900).

1994, Feb. 17
3422 A976 12fo multicolored .40 .25
3423 A976 19fo multicolored .65 .30

Lajos Kossuth (1802-94) A977

1994, Feb. 17
3424 A977 19fo multicolored .65 .30

Gen. Joseph Bem (1794-1850) A978

1994, Mar. 10 *Perf. 12*
3425 A978 19fo multicolored .75 .30

Otis Tarda — A979

World Wildlife Fund: No. 3426, Female, male with feathers ruffled in mating dance. No. 3427, Nestlings, female on nest. No. 3428, Nestlings, female standing. No. 3429, Three flying.

1994, Mar. 14
3426 A979 10fo multicolored .75 .40
3427 A979 10fo multicolored .75 .40
3428 A979 10fo multicolored .75 .40
3429 A979 10fo multicolored .75 .40
a. Block of 4, #3426-3429 3.50 3.00

A980

Europa: 19fo, Sailing steamer Tegetthoff, Franz-Joseph Land, Julius Payer (1842-1915), Austrian explorer. 50fo, Mark Aurel Stein (1862-1943), explorer, archeologist, geographer, Asian scenes.

1994, Apr. 1 Litho. *Perf. 13x13½*
3430 A980 19fo multicolored 2.00 .50
3431 A980 50fo multicolored 3.00 1.25

Austro-Hungarian Arctic Expedition, 120th anniv. (No. 3430).

A981

No. 3432, Baron Miklos Josika (1794-1865), Novelist. No. 3433, Balint Balassi (1551-94), poet.

1994, May 19 Litho. *Perf. 12*
3432 A981 19fo gray .65 .30
3433 A981 19fo rose lake .65 .30

Creation of Magyar Hungary, 1100th Anniv. (in 1996) — A982

Designs: No. 3434, Two soldiers on horseback. No. 3435, Soldier on white horse, others in background with flags. No. 3436, Soldier on black horse, others in background. No. 3437, Man with staff, oxen pulling carts. No. 3438, Oxen pulling royal cart. No. 3439, Man with staff on shoulder, oxen with packs. No. 3440,

Minstrels, bard celebrating. No. 3441, Soldiers preparing to sacrifice white horse. No. 3442, Shaman before fire, headsman.

1994-96

3434 A982 19fo multicolored .85 .30
3435 A982 19fo multicolored .85 .30
3436 A982 19fo multicolored .85 .30
a. Strip of 3, #3434-3436 3.00 3.00
3437 A982 22fo multicolored .85 .30
3438 A982 22fo multicolored .85 .30
3439 A982 22fo multicolored .85 .30
a. Strip of 3, #3437-3439 3.00 3.00
3440 A982 24fo multicolored .85 .30
3441 A982 24fo multicolored .85 .30
3442 A982 24fo multicolored .85 .30
a. Strip of 3, #3440-3442 3.00 3.00
Nos. 3434-3442 (9) 7.65 2.70

Souvenir Sheet

3442B A982 195fo multicolored 20.00 16.00

Nos. 3436a, 3439a, 3442a are continuous design. No. 3436a sold for 59fo.
Nos. 3435, 3438, 3441 are 60x40mm.
No. 3442B contains one each of Nos. 3436a, 3439a, 3442a.
Issued: Nos. 3434-3436, 5/19/94; Nos. 3437-3439, 2/23/95; Nos. 3440-3442, 2/29/96, No. 3442B, 4/18/96.

Intl. Olympic Committee, Cent. — A985

Designs: 12fo, 1896, 1992 medals. No. 3444, Flag, runners, Olympic flame. No. 3445, Athens Stadium, 1896. 35fo, Pierre de Coubertin (1863-1937), first president.

1994, June 16 Litho. *Perf. 12½*

3443 A985 12fo multicolored .45 .25
3444 A985 19fo multicolored .65 .30
3445 A985 19fo multicolored .65 .30
3446 A985 35fo multicolored 1.25 .60
Nos. 3443-3446 (4) 3.00 1.45

1994 World Cup Soccer Championships, US — A986

US flag, soccer players and: No. 3447, Elvis Presley. No. 3448, Marilyn Monroe. No. 3449, John Wayne.

1994, June 16 *Perf. 12*

3447 A986 19fo multicolored .65 .30
3448 A986 19fo multicolored .65 .30
3449 A986 35fo multicolored 1.25 .60
Nos. 3447-3449 (3) 2.55 1.20

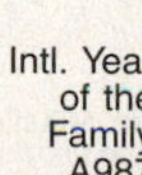

Intl. Year of the Family A987

1994, July 21 Litho. *Perf. 11*

3450 A987 19fo multicolored .65 .30

Flowers of the Continents Type of 1990

Flowers of Europe: 12fo, Leucojum aestivum. 19fo, Helianthemum nummularium. 35fo, Eryngium alpinum. 50fo, Thlaspi rotundifolium. 100fo, Bouquet of European flowers.

1994, Aug. 18 Litho. *Perf. 11½x12*

3451 A892 12fo multicolored .40 .25
3452 A892 19fo multicolored .65 .35
3453 A892 35fo multicolored 1.25 .60
3454 A892 50fo multicolored 1.60 .85
Nos. 3451-3454 (4) 3.90 2.05

Souvenir Sheet

Perf. 12½

3455 A892 100fo multicolored 4.00 2.50

No. 3455 contains one 32x41mm stamp.

UPU, 120th Anniv. A988

UPU emblem and: 19fo, Heinrich Von Stephan (1831-97). 35fo, Mihaly Gervay (1819-96).
No. 3458: a, Von Stephan, vert. b, Gervay, vert.

1994, Sept. 9 Litho. *Perf. 12*

3456 A988 19fo multicolored .55 .30
3457 A988 35fo multicolored 1.00 .50

Souvenir Sheet of 2

3458 A988 50fo +25fo, #a.-b. 4.50 2.25

Stamp Day, 67th anniv.
No. 3458 with printing in the margin on the back of the sheet, "140 éves az Egyetemes Postaegyesület / A Magyar Posta köszönt a bélyeg-elofizetoket!", was given as a gift to standing order customers in 2014.

Folk Designs — A989

Various ornate designs.

1994-96 Litho. *Perf. 11½x12*

3459 A989 1fo bl vio & blk .25 .25
3460 A989 2fo multi .25 .25
3461 A989 3fo multi .25 .25
3461A A989 9fo multi .25 .25
3462 A989 11fo multi .35 .25
3463 A989 12fo multi .35 .25
3463A A989 13fo grn, red & blk .25 .25
3464 A989 14fo multi .25 .25
3465 A989 16fo bl, red & blk .30 .25
3466 A989 17fo red & blk .30 .25
3467 A989 19fo multi .50 .25
3468 A989 22fo multi .35 .25
3469 A989 24fo multi .40 .25
3470 A989 32fo multi .95 .50
3471 A989 35fo multi 1.00 .50
3472 A989 38fo multi .65 .30
3473 A989 40fo multi 1.40 .55
3474 A989 50fo multi 1.75 .70
3475 A989 75fo multi 1.50 .65
3476 A989 80fo multi 1.75 .70
3477 A989 300fo multi 6.25 2.60
3478 A989 500fo multi 10.00 4.50
Nos. 3459-3478 (22) 29.30 14.25

Issued: 11fo, 12fo, 19fo, 32fo, 35fo, 40fo, 50fo, 10/10/94; 1fo, 1/10/95; 2fo, 3fo, 9fo, 14fo, 22fo, 38fo, 4/3/95; 13fo, 16fo, 17fo, 24fo, 75fo, 80fo, 7/1/96.
See Nos. 3561, 3615, 3630, 3644-3646, 3649-3650. For surcharge see No. 3583.

Souvenir Sheet

Summit Meeting of the Conference for European Security & Cooperation — A990

1994, Sept. 10 Litho. *Perf. 12*

3479 A990 100fo Budapest 3.50 2.50

Holocaust, 50th Anniv. — A991

1994, Oct. 20

3480 A991 19fo multicolored .80 .30

Buildings in Budapest A992

No. 3481, Vajdahunyadvar Castle. No. 3482, Nemzeti Museum. No. 3483, Muszaki Palace.

1994, Nov. 17 Engr.

3481 A992 19fo violet .55 .30
3482 A992 19fo green .55 .30
3483 A992 19fo brown .55 .30
Nos. 3481-3483 (3) 1.65 .90

Christmas — A993

1994, Nov. 17 Litho.

3484 A993 12fo shown .45 .25
3485 A993 35fo Flight into Egypt 1.40 .60

Hungarian Shipping Co., Cent. — A994

Design: 22fo, Early steamer Francis Joseph I, cargo ship Baross.

1995, Jan. 24 Litho. *Perf. 13*

3486 A994 22fo multicolored .65 .30

Easter — A995

1995, Mar. 7 *Perf. 12*

3487 A995 14fo black & lilac .45 .25

Hungarian Shipping — A996

Designs: 14fo, Tug-wheeled steamship, map of first navigable section of the Tisza, view of Szeged. 60fo, Pal Vasarhelyi, Tisza survey ship, surveyor.

1995, Mar. 7 *Perf. 13*

3488 A996 14fo multicolored .45 .25
3489 A996 60fo multicolored 2.00 1.00

A997

1995, Apr. 7 *Perf. 12*

3490 A997 22fo multicolored .65 .30

Natl. Meteorological Service, 125th anniv.

FAO, 50th Anniv. — A998

1995, Apr. 7

3491 A998 22fo multicolored .80 .30

European Nature Conservation Year — A999

No. 3492, Crane, frog, flowers. No. 3493, Squirrel, insect. No. 3494, Bird, berries, flowers. No. 3495, Butterfly, hedgehog, flowers.

1995, May 9 Litho. *Perf. 13½x13*

3492 A999 14fo multicolored .55 .25
3493 A999 14fo multicolored .55 .25
3494 A999 14fo multicolored .55 .25
3495 A999 14fo multicolored .55 .25
a. Strip of 4, #3492-3495 3.00 2.50

Peace & Liberty — A1000

1995, May 9

3496 A1000 22fo multicolored *3.50* .40

Europa.

Hungarian Olympic Committee, Cent. — A1001

22fo, Diver, Pierre de Coubertin. 60fo, Javelin. 100fo, Fencing.

1995, June 12 Litho. *Perf. 12*

3497 A1001 22fo multicolored .60 .30
3498 A1001 60fo multicolored 1.60 .80
3499 A1001 100fo multicolored 2.75 1.40
Nos. 3497-3499 (3) 4.95 2.50

St. Ladislas I (1040?-1095) A1002

1995, June 12
3500 A1002 22fo multicolored .60 .30

Laszlo Almasy, Sahara Researcher, Birth Cent. — A1003

1995, Aug. 22 Litho. *Perf. 13x13½*
3501 A1003 22fo multicolored .75 .30

Odon Lechner, Architect, 150th Birth Anniv. — A1004

Design: 22fo, Museum of Applied Arts, Lechner.

Litho. & Engr.
1995, Aug. 22 *Perf. 12*
3502 A1004 22fo multicolored .75 .30

Contemporary Paintings A1005

No. 3503, Abstract, by Laszlo Moholy-Nagy (1895-1946). No. 3504, Woman with a violin, by Aurel Bernath (1895-1982).

1995, Sept. 18 Litho.
3503 A1005 22fo multicolored .75 .30
3504 A1005 22fo multicolored .75 .30

Eotvos College, Cent. — A1006

60fo, Eotvos College, Josef Eotvos (1813-71), statesman, writer, educational leader.

1995, Sept. 18
3505 A1006 60fo red brn, blk 1.60 .80

Stamp Day A1007

Designs: 22fo, Horse-drawn mail chaise. 40fo, Jet, map. 100fo + 30fo, Man, boys looking at stamp album, vert.

1995, Sept. 29 Litho. *Perf. 13½x13*
3506 A1007 22fo multicolored .60 .30
3507 A1007 40fo multicolored 1.10 .55

Souvenir Sheet
Perf. 12x12½
3508 A1007 100fo +30fo multi 3.50 2.50

Buildings of Budapest A1008

No. 3509, Nyugati Palyaudvar. No. 3510, Vigado.

1995 Engr. *Perf. 12*
3509 A1008 22fo dark olive brn 1.00 .30
3510 A1008 22fo deep claret 1.00 .30

UN, 50th Anniv. A1009

1995, Oct. 24 Litho. *Perf. 11*
3511 A1009 60fo multicolored 1.75 .80

Christmas — A1010

Children's designs: 14fo, Spark thrower. 60fo, The Three Magi.

1995, Nov. 16 *Perf. 12*
3512 A1010 14fo multicolored .40 .25
3513 A1010 60fo multicolored 1.60 .80

Nobel Prize Fund Established, Cent. — A1011

1995, Nov. 16
3514 A1011 100fo Medals 3.00 1.40

No. 3514 is printed se-tenant with label.

St. Elizabeth of Hungary Bathing Lepers — A1012

1995, Nov. 16 *Perf. 13*
3515 A1012 22fo multicolored .80 .30

No. 3515 is printed se-tenant with label.

A1013

Archaeological Finds from Karos: a, Gold and silver saber. b, Badge.

1996, Mar. 14 Litho. *Perf. 13½x13*
3516 A1013 24fo #a.-b. + 2 labels 2.00 .55

Souvenir Sheet

Pannonhalma, Benedictine Monastery, 1000th Anniv. — A1014

1996, Mar. 21 Engr. *Perf. 12*
3517 A1014 100fo deep violet 5.50 3.50

Sheet margin is litho. and multicolored.

1996 Summer Olympics, Atlanta A1015

1996, Apr. 18 Litho. *Perf. 11½x12*
3518 A1015 24fo Swimming .55 .30
3519 A1015 50fo Tennis 1.10 .60
3520 A1015 75fo Kayak 1.75 .85
Nos. 3518-3520 (3) 3.40 1.75

National Productivity A1016

1996, Apr. 18 Litho. *Perf. 12*
3521 A1016 24fo multicolored .55 .30

Natl. Writers Assoc., Cent. — A1017

1996, Apr. 18 *Perf. 12x11½*
3522 A1017 50fo multicolored 1.10 .60

Budapest Subway, Cent. — A1018

1996, May 2 *Perf. 12*
3523 A1018 24fo multicolored .80 .30

Famous Women A1019

Europa: 24fo, Queen Gizella. 75fo, Bavarian Princess Elisabeth Wittelsbach.

1996, May 2 Litho. *Perf. 12*
3524 A1019 24fo multicolored *1.50* .50
3525 A1019 75fo multicolored *3.50* 1.25

Pannonhalma, Benedictine Monastery, 1000th Anniv. A1020

Designs: 17fo, Entrance to cathedral. 24fo, Monks in northern wing.

1996, June 21 Engr. *Perf. 12*
3526 A1020 17fo red brown .60 .25
3527 A1020 24fo dark blue .90 .30

See Nos. 3536-3537.

Intl. Anti-Drug Day — A1021

1996, June 21 Litho. *Perf. 14*
3528 A1021 24fo multicolored .65 .30

Hungarian Developers of Technolgy — A1022

Inventor, invention: 24fo, Denes Mihaly (1894-1953), Telehor. 50fo, Jozsef Biro Laszlo (1899-1985), mass-produced ball-point pen. 75fo, Zoltan Bay (1900-92), lunar radar set.

1996, June 21 *Perf. 12x11½*
3529 A1022 24fo multicolored .55 .30
3530 A1022 50fo multicolored 1.10 .60
3531 A1022 75fo multicolored 1.75 .85
Nos. 3529-3531 (3) 3.40 1.75

Hungarian Railways, 150th Anniv. — A1023

Designs: 17fo, 303-Series steam tender locomotive. No. 3533, 325-Series locomotive. No. 3534, "Pest," steam locomotive made by Cokerill and Co.

1996, July 12 *Perf. 13½x13*
3532 A1023 17fo multicolored .55 .25
3533 A1023 24fo multicolored .70 .30
3534 A1023 24fo multicolored 1.50 .30
Nos. 3532-3534 (3) 2.75 .85

Second European Congress of Mathematicians A1024

1996, July 12 *Perf. 12*
3535 A1024 24fo multicolored .55 .30

Pannonhalma, Benedictine Monastery, Type of 1996

Designs: 17fo, Refectory. 24fo, Main library.

1996, Aug. 12 **Engr.** *Perf. 12*
3536 A1020 17fo dark brown .60 .25
3537 A1020 24fo dark green .90 .25

Nature Expo '96 A1025

No. 3538, Egretta alba. No. 3539, Iris sibirica. No. 3540, Lynx lynx. No. 3541, Ropalopus ungaricus.

1996, Aug. 12 **Litho.** *Perf. 12x11½*
3538 A1025 13fo multi .25 .25
3539 A1025 13fo multi .25 .25
3540 A1025 13fo multi .25 .25
3541 A1025 13fo multi 1.20 1.20
a. Block of 4, #3538-3541 2.00 2.00

A1026

1996, Aug. 12 *Perf. 12*
3542 A1026 24fo No. 4 1.00 .25

Hungarian postage stamps, 125th anniv.

Issued in miniature sheets of 6 stamps in two columns of 3 separated by a column of labels. Values, stamp plus label $1.50, miniature sheet $7.50.

A1027

Stamp Day, Budapest '96: 17fo, Prince Arpad, people from 14th cent. "Vienna Picture Chronicle," man stirring liquid in pot. 24fo, Prince on horseback, archer.

150fo+50fo, #601, first page from "The Deeds of Hungarians."

1996, Aug. 21 **Litho.** *Perf. 11½x12*
3543 A1027 17fo multicolored .60 .25
3544 A1027 24fo multicolored .90 .25

Souvenir Sheet

Perf. 12x12½

3545 A1027 150fo +50fo multi 5.50 3.00

Steamships on Lake Balaton, 150th Anniv. — A1028

Steamer Kisfaludy.

1996, Sept. 17 **Litho.** *Perf. 12*
3548 A1028 17fo multicolored .60 .25

Hungarian Revolution, 40th Anniv. — A1029

Newspaper clippings and: 13fo, People marching. 16fo, Troops on back of truck. 17fo, Two men with guns. 24fo, Imre Nagy addressing people.

40fo, Nagy Cabinet.

1996, Oct. 23 **Litho.** *Perf. 12*
3549 A1029 13fo multicolored .35 .25
3550 A1029 16fo multicolored .40 .25
3551 A1029 17fo multicolored .40 .25
3552 A1029 24fo multicolored .60 .25
Nos. 3549-3552 (4) 1.75 1.00

Souvenir Sheet

3553 A1029 40fo multicolored 4.00 2.25

Souvenir Sheet

1996 Summer Olympic Games, Atlanta — A1030

1996, Oct. 22
3554 A1030 150fo multicolored 4.50 2.25

A1036

1996, Nov. 14 **Litho.** *Perf. 11½x12*
3555 A1036 24fo multicolored .40 .20

Miklos Wesselenyi (1796-1850), writer.

A1037

1996, Nov. 14 *Perf. 13½x13*
3556 A1037 24fo multicolored .40 .25

UNICEF, 50th anniv.

Christmas A1038

Paintings: 17fo, Mary with Infant Jesus and Two Angels, by Matteo di Giovanni. 24fo, Adoration of the Kings, by unknown painter of Salsburg.

1996, Nov. 14 *Perf. 12*
3557 A1038 17fo multicolored .35 .25
3558 A1038 24fo multicolored .65 .25

Hungarian Literature — A1039

Designs: No. 3559, Scenes from "The Umbrella of St. Peter," Kalman Mikszath (1847-1910). No. 3560, Scenes of men and dogs from "Abel in the Vast Trackless Forest" and "Matthias the Ice-breaker," Aron Tamasi (1897-1966).

1997, Jan. 16 **Litho.** *Perf. 12x11½*
3559 A1039 27fo multicolored .50 .25
3560 A1039 27fo multicolored .50 .25

Folk Art Type of 1994

1997, Mar. 26 *Perf. 11½x12*
3561 A989 27fo multicolored .65 .25

Coat of Arms of Budapest and Counties — A1040

No. 3562: a, Hajdú-Bihar. b, Baranya. c, Bács-Kiskun. d, Békés. e, Borsod-Abaúj-Zemplén.

No. 3563: a, Fejér. b, Györ-Moson-Sopron. c, Heves. d, Jász-Nagykun-Szolnok. e, Komárom-Esztergom. f, Nógrád.

No. 3564: a, Pest. b, Somogy. c, Toina. d, Vas. e, Veszprém. f, Zala.

No. 3565: a, Budapest. b, Csongrád. c, Szabolcs-Szatmár-Bereg.

1997, Mar. 26 *Perf. 11½x12*
3562 A1040 27fo Sheet of 5, #a.-e. + label 5.00 3.25
3563 A1040 27fo Sheet of 6, #a.-f. 6.25 4.25
3564 A1040 27fo Sheet of 6, #a.-f. 6.25 4.25
3564G A1040 27fo Hajdu-Bihar 5.00 5.00

Size: 51x33mm

3565 A1040 27fo Sheet of 3, #a.-c. 2.25 1.75

No. 3564G is 51x33mm and has the same design as No. 3562a which has a se-tenant label, but lacks the perforations separating these items. Nos. 3262a-3262e, 3563a-3563f, 3564a-3564f, 3565a-3565c were also printed in individual sheets. Value, set of singles (20): mint $11; used $4.

A1041

Youth Stamps — A1042

Designs: 20fo, Scouting emblem, tents, sailboat, waterfall. 27fo+10fo, Knights on horseback from "Toldi," by Janos Arany.

1997, Apr. 23 *Perf. 12*
3566 A1041 20fo multicolored .50 .25
3567 A1042 27fo +10fo multi 1.25 .35

A1043

1997, Apr. 23 *Perf. 13½x13*
3568 A1043 90fo multicolored 1.60 .80

World Meeting of Custom Directors.

A1044

1997, Apr. 23 **Engr.** *Perf. 12*
3569 A1044 80fo deep violet 2.00 .70

St. Adalbert (956-997). See Germany No. 1964, Poland No. 3307, Czech Republic No. 3012, Vatican City No. 1040..

Stories and Legends A1045

Europa: 27fo, Hunters on horseback shooting bow and arrow at deer. 90fo, Preparing body in sarcophagus of Prince Geza.

1997, May 5 Litho. *Perf. 13x13½*
3570 A1045 27fo multicolored 1.25 .40
3571 A1045 90fo multicolored 2.50 .90

African Animals A1046

16fo, Oryx gazella. No. 3573, Equus burchelli. No. 3574, Diceros bicornis. 27fo, Panthera leo.
90fo, Loxodonta africana.

1997, May 5 *Perf. 12*
3572 A1046 16fo multicolored .30 .25
3573 A1046 20fo multicolored .60 .25
3574 A1046 20fo multicolored .60 .25
3575 A1046 27fo multicolored 1.00 .30
Nos. 3572-3575 (4) 2.50 1.05

Souvenir Sheet

3576 A1046 90fo multicolored 4.50 3.00

A1047

1997, June 8 Litho. *Perf. 12*
3577 A1047 90fo multicolored 1.60 .70

Polish Queen Jadwiga (1373-99).

A1048

World Congress on Stress, Budapest: Janos (Hans) Selye (1907-82), founder of theory of stress, face of person under stress.

1997, July 1
3578 A1048 90fo multicolored 1.75 .70

Indigenous Fish — A1049

Designs: a, Gymnocephalus schraetzer. b, Cottus gobio. c, Alburnoides bipunctatus. d, Cobitis taenia.

1997, June 6 Litho. *Perf. 13x13½*
3579 A1049 20fo Strip of 4, #a.-d. 2.50 1.25

Grapes and Wine Producing Areas Type of 1990

Grapes and growing area: No. 3580, Nemes kadarka, Great Kiskoros. No. 3581, Teitfürtü ezerjo, Mor. No. 3582, Harslevelu, Gyongyos.

1997, Aug. 12 Litho. *Perf. 13x13½*
3580 A902 27fo multicolored .50 .25
3581 A902 27fo multicolored .50 .25
3582 A902 27fo multicolored 1.00 .25
Nos. 3580-3582 (3) 2.00 .75

No. 3469 Surcharged in Red

1997, July 10 Litho. *Perf. 11½x12*
3583 A989 60fo on 24fo multi 1.00 .45

Christmas A1050

20fo, Holy family. 27fo, Adoration of the Magi.

1997, Oct. 31 Litho. *Perf. 13x13½*
3584 A1050 20fo multicolored .40 .25
3585 A1050 27fo multicolored .60 .25

World Weight Lifting Championships, Thailand A1051

1997, Nov. 12 *Perf. 12*
3586 A1051 90fo multicolored 1.60 .65

Zsigmond Szechenyi, African Explorer A1052

1998, Jan. 22 Litho. *Perf. 12*
3587 A1052 60fo multicolored 1.60 .45

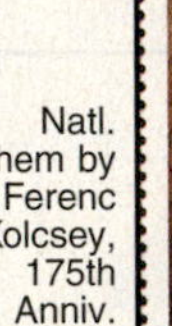

Natl. Anthem by Ferenc Kolcsey, 175th Anniv. A1053

1998, Jan. 22
3588 A1053 75fo multicolored 1.60 .55

1998 Winter Olympic Games, Nagano — A1054

1998, Jan. 22 *Perf. 13½x13*
3589 A1054 30fo Downhill skiing .75 .30
3590 A1054 100fo Snowboarding 1.25 .85

Valentine's Day — A1055

1998, Feb. 11 *Perf. 11½x12*
3591 A1055 24fo multicolored .65 .25

A1056

1998, Feb. 11 *Perf. 12*
3592 A1056 50fo multicolored 1.75 .50

Leo Szilard (1898-1964), physicist.

A1057

Balint Postas (Post Office Mascot) in front of printed material: 23fo, Holding letter. 24fo, Bowing. 30fo, Standing straight with arms outstretched. 65fo, Flying.

1998, Feb. 11 *Perf. 11½x12*
3593 A1057 23fo multicolored .50 .25
3594 A1057 24fo multicolored .50 .25
3595 A1057 30fo multicolored .65 .30
3596 A1057 65fo multicolored 1.40 .65
Nos. 3593-3596 (4) 3.05 1.45

A1058

Easter — A1059

1998, Mar. 13 Litho. *Perf. 13½x13*
3597 A1058 24fo Stylized egg .55 .25

Perf. 11

3598 A1059 30fo Christ's resurrection .65 .25

1848-49 Revolution, War of Independence, 150th Anniv. — A1060

23fo, Sandor Petofi (1823-49), poet, handwriting, tricolor. 24fo, Mihaly Tancsics, writer & politician, ink well. 30fo, Lajos Kossuth (1802-94), seal.

1998, Mar. 13 *Perf. 12*
3599 A1060 23fo multicolored .40 .25
3600 A1060 24fo multicolored .50 .25
3601 A1060 30fo multicolored .60 .25
Nos. 3599-3601 (3) 1.50 .75

See Nos. 3640-3643.

Art Nouveau — A1061

Ceramics: 20fo, Vase with relief design of young girl picking flowers, 1899. 24fo, Flower holder with peacock-eyed butterflies, 1901. 30fo, Vase with tulip stems, 1899. 95fo, Round container with legs, 1912.

1998, Mar. 31 Litho. *Perf. 12*
3602 A1061 20fo multi, vert. .35 .25
Complete booklet, 10 #3602 3.25
3603 A1061 24fo multi .40 .25
Complete booklet, 10 #3603 3.75
3604 A1061 30fo multi, vert. .50 .25
Complete booklet, 10 #3604 4.75
3605 A1061 95fo multi 1.50 .70
Nos. 3602-3605 (4) 2.75 1.45

Postal Regulation, 250th Anniv. — A1062

Designs: 24fo+10fo, Courier of 1748, detail of postal route connecting counties of Zala and Gyor. 30fo+10fo, Mounted courier, blowing post horn, script of regulation.
150fo, Horse-drawn postal coach, detail of postal route.

1998, Apr. 10
3606 A1062 24fo +10fo multi .75 .45
3607 A1062 30fo +10fo multi 1.25 .60

Souvenir Sheet

3608 A1062 150fo multicolored 5.00 2.50

Stamp Day.

Animals of the Americas A1063

23fo, Bison bison. No. 3610, Ursus horribilis. No. 3611, Alligator mississippiensis. 30fo, Leopardus pardalis.
150fo, Loddigesia mirabilis.

1998, Apr. 30
3609 A1063 23fo multicolored .75 .35
3610 A1063 24fo multicolored .75 .35
3611 A1063 24fo multicolored .75 .35
3612 A1063 30fo multicolored 1.00 .45
Nos. 3609-3612 (4) 3.25 1.50

Souvenir Sheet

3613 A1063 150fo multicolored 5.00 2.50

Gyorgy Jendrassik, Engineer, Birth Cent. A1064

1998, May 4 Engr.
3614 A1064 100fo dark blue 1.50 .75

Folk Designs Type of 1994

1998, June 5 Litho. *Perf. 11½x12*
3615 A989 5fo multicolored .40 .25

1998 Canoe-Kayak World Championships, Szeged — A1065

1998, June 5 *Perf. 12*
3616 A1065 30fo multicolored .50 .25

1998 World Cup Soccer Championships, France — A1066

Different soccer players.

1998, June 5
3617 A1066 30fo multicolored .45 .25
3618 A1066 110fo multicolored 1.60 .80
a. Pair, 3617-3618 2.10 1.00

1998 European Track & Field Championships, Budapest — A1067

1998, June 5 *Perf. 12x11*
3619 A1067 24fo Hurdles .35 .25
3620 A1067 65fo Pole vault .95 .50
3621 A1067 80fo Hammer throw 1.25 .60
Nos. 3619-3621 (3) 2.55 1.35

Gabor Baross (1848-92), Postal Administrator A1068

1998, June 5 *Perf. 12*
3622 A1068 60fo multicolored .90 .45

A1069

1998, July 31 **Litho.** *Perf. 12*
3623 A1069 24fo multicolored .60 .25
Complete booklet, 10 #3623 10.00

Széchenyi Hill Children's Railway, 50th anniv.

A1070

1998, July 31 *Perf. 12x11½*
3624 A1070 65fo multicolored 1.25 .50

World Congress of Computer Technology, Budapest.

Natl. Holidays — A1071

Europa: 50fo, Sculptures, Festival of the 1956 Revolution, Proclamation of the Republic, 1989, October 23. 60fo, Sheaf of grain, Natl. arms, National Day, August 20.

1998, Aug. 19 **Litho.** *Perf. 12*
3625 A1071 50fo multicolored 1.50 .65
3626 A1071 60fo multicolored 2.25 .85

A1072

1998, Aug. 19
3627 A1072 100fo multicolored 1.40 .70

World Federation of Hungarians, 60th Anniv.

National Parks A1073

Various flora, fauna, explorer of given region: 24fo, Dr. Miklós Udvardy, Hortobágy Natl. Park. 70fo, Adám Boros, Kiskunság Natl. Park.

1998, Oct. 6 **Litho.** *Perf. 12*
3628 A1073 24fo multicolored .50 .25
3629 A1073 70fo multicolored 1.25 .50

See Nos. 3654-3655, 3689-3690, 3745-3747, 3689-3690, 4072.

Folk Designs Type of 1994

1998 **Litho.** *Perf. 11½x12*
3630 A989 200fo multicolored 5.00 .70

Christmas A1074

Designs: 20fo, Painting, "Visit of the Shepherds," by Agnolo Bronzino (1503-72). 24fo, Artwork, "Mary Upon the Throne with the Infant," by Carlo Crivelli (1430?-94?), vert.

1998, Oct. 30 *Perf. 12x11½, 11½x12*
3631 A1074 20fo multicolored .40 .25
Complete booklet, 10 #3631 3.75
3632 A1074 24fo multicolored .45 .25
Complete booklet, 10 #3632 6.50

See No. 3676.

Easter A1075

1999, Feb. 11 **Litho.** *Perf. 12*
3633 A1075 27fo Decorated eggs .35 .25
3634 A1075 32fo Shroud of Turin .75 .25

No. 3634 is 38x53mm.

Intl. Year of the Elderly A1076

1999, Feb. 11 *Perf. 12½x13½*
3635 A1076 32fo multicolored .75 .25

Sailing Ships A1077

32fo, Novara. 79fo, Phoenix. 110fo, Galley, 15th cent.

1999, Feb. 11 *Perf. 12*
3636 A1077 32fo multi .40 .25
3637 A1077 79fo multi 1.00 .50
3638 A1077 110fo multi 1.40 .70
Nos. 3636-3638 (3) 2.80 1.45

Souvenir Sheet

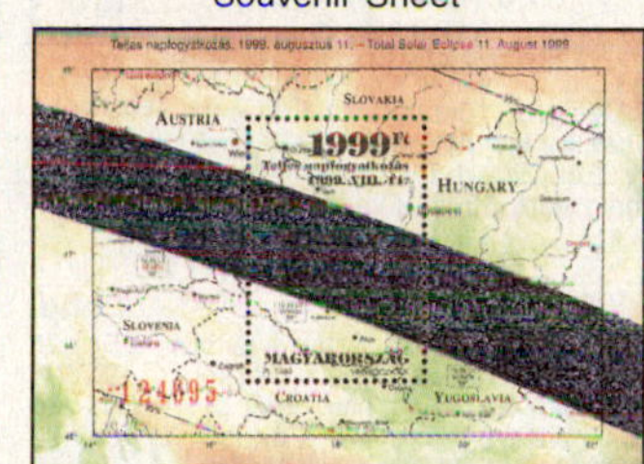

Total Solar Eclipse, Aug. 11 — A1078

1999, Feb. 11
3639 A1078 1999fo multi 22.00 22.00

No. 3639 contains a holographic image. Soaking in water may affect the hologram.

Revolution of 1848-49 Type of 1998

24fo, Sword, Artúr Görgey (1818-1916), general. 27fo, Military decoration, Lajos Batthyány (1806-49), premier of 1st Hungarian ministry. 32fo, Military decoration, Jósef Bem (1794-1850), Polish General who joined Hungarian army.
100fo, Battle scene.

1999, Mar. 12
3640 A1060 24fo multicolored .45 .25
3641 A1060 27fo multicolored .55 .25
3642 A1060 32fo multicolored .60 .25
Nos. 3640-3642 (3) 1.60 .75

Souvenir Sheet

3643 A1060 100fo multicolored 4.00 2.00

No. 3643 contains one 45x28mm stamp.

Folk Designs Type of 1994

1999 **Litho.** *Perf. 12½*
3644 A989 24fo multicolored .40 .25
3645 A989 65fo red & black 1.10 .30
3646 A989 90fo multicolored 2.00 .55
Nos. 3644-3646 (3) 3.50 1.10

Nos. 3644-3646 are inscribed "1999."

Entrance into NATO — A1079

1999, Mar. 12 **Litho.** *Perf. 12x11½*
3647 A1079 110fo multicolored 1.60 .55

Souvenir Sheet

1999 Modern Pentathlon World Championships, Budapest — A1080

1999, Mar. 24 *Perf. 12½*
3648 A1080 100fo multicolored 3.50 1.75

Folk Designs Type of 1994

Various ornate designs.

1999, Apr. 19 **Litho.** *Perf. 11½x12*
3649 A989 79fo multicolored 1.60 .45
3650 A989 100fo multicolored 2.40 .60

A1081

1999, May 3 *Perf. 12*
3651 A1081 50fo slate & bister .85 .30

Ferenc Pápai Páriz (1649-1716).

A1082

1999, May 3
3652 A1082 100fo multicolored 1.75 .65

Ferencvárosi Torna Sport Club, cent.

World Science Conference A1082a

1999, May 3 **Litho.** *Perf. 11½x12½*
3652A A1082a 65fo multicolored 2.00 .60

Council of Europe, 50th Anniv. A1083

1999, May 4 *Perf. 13x13¼*
3653 A1083 50fo multicolored 2.00 .50

National Parks Type of 1998

Europa: 27fo, Aggteleki National Park. 32fo, Bükki National Park.

1999, May 6 *Perf. 12*
3654 A1073 27fo multicolored 3.50 1.40
3655 A1073 32fo multicolored 5.00 3.25

Grapes and Wine Producing Areas Type of 1990

Grapes, growing area and: 24fo, Castle ruins, Somló region. 27fo, 17th cent. view of Sopron.

1999, May 6 Litho. *Perf. 12¼x12½*
3656 A902 24fo multi, horiz. .70 .25
3657 A902 27fo multi, horiz. 1.10 .30

Animals of Asia A1085

Designs: 27fo, Tigris regalis. 32fo, Ailuropodus melanoleucus. 52fo, Panthera pardus. 79fo, Pongo pygmaeus.
100fo, Aix galericulata.

1999, May 6 *Perf. 12*
3658 A1085 27fo multicolored .50 .25
3659 A1085 32fo multicolored .65 .30
3660 A1085 52fo multicolored .95 .40
3661 A1085 79fo multicolored 1.90 .50
Nos. 3658-3661 (4) 4.00 1.45

Souvenir Sheet

3662 A1085 100fo multicolored 6.50 5.00

No. 3662 contains one 50x30mm stamp.

Queen Maria Theresa's Introduction of Mail Coach Service, 250th Anniv. A1086

Stamp Day: 32fo+15fo, Decree by Maria Theresa, coach, street. 52fo+20fo, People entering coach, woman with letters, portion of decree.
150fo, Horse-drawn coach arriving a station.

1999, May 21 Litho. *Perf. 12½x12¼*
3663 A1086 32fo +15fo multi .80 .75
3664 A1086 52fo +20fo multi 1.40 1.00

Souvenir Sheet

3665 A1086 150fo multicolored 4.50 4.00

No. 3665 contains one 32x42mm stamp.

Red Poppy — A1087

32fo, Stalkless gentian.

1999, July 7 Litho. *Perf. 12x11½*
3666 A1087 27fo shown 1.00 .40
3667 A1087 32fo multi 1.50 .70

Compare with types A1644-A1645. See Nos. 3805-3806.

George Cukor (1899-1983), Film Director — A1088

1999, July 7 Litho. *Perf. 12*
3668 A1088 50fo multicolored 1.25 .40

UPU, 125th Anniv. A1089

1999, Aug. 13 Litho. *Perf. 12*
3669 A1089 32fo multicolored 1.25 .85

Issued in sheets of 3. Value $4.50.

Frankfurt Book Fair — A1090

1999, Sept. 9 Litho. *Perf. 12*
3670 A1090 40fo multicolored 1.75 .25

Antique Furniture A1091

Designs: 10fo, Chair, 17th cent, vert. 20fo, Chair by Károly Lingel, 1915, vert. 50fo, Chair by Pál Esterházy, vert. 70fo, Upholstered chair, vert. 100fo, Couch by Lajos Kozma.

Perf. 11½x12, 12x11½
1999, Oct. 7 Litho.
3671 A1091 10fo bister & dk brn .25 .25
3672 A1091 20fo grn & dk grn .40 .25
3673 A1091 50fo blue & dk bl .80 .30
3674 A1091 70fo red & dk red 1.25 .35
3675 A1091 100fo brn & dk brn 1.75 .50
Nos. 3671-3675 (5) 4.45 1.65

Nos. 3671-3673, 3675 exist dated "2001."
See Nos. 3711-3721, 3737-3743, 3790-3791, 3821-3823, 3960-3965, 4134, 4184.

Bronzino Christmas Painting Type of 1998 and

Magi — A1092

Madonna and Child, Stained Glass by Miksa Róth — A1093

1999, Oct. 15 *Perf. 12x11½, 11½x12*
3676 A1074 24fo multi .65 .25
Complete booklet, 10 #3676 10.00
3677 A1092 27fo multi .85 .25
Complete booklet, 10 #3677 9.50
3678 A1093 32fo multi 1.00 .25
Complete booklet, 10 #3678 10.00
Nos. 3676-3678 (3) 2.50 .75

Jenö Wigner (1902-95), Winner of 1963 Nobel Physics Prize — A1094

1999, Nov. 3 *Perf. 12*
3679 A1094 32fo blue 1.00 .30

Souvenir Sheet

Chain Bridge, 150th Anniv. — A1095

1999, Nov. 3
3680 A1095 150fo multi 3.25 2.25

Hungarian Millennium A1096

Designs: 28fo, 30fo, Coronation scepter. 34fo, 40fo, Millennium flag.

2000 Litho. *Perf. 12x11½*
3681 A1096 28fo multi .80 .25
3682 A1096 30fo multi .80 .25
3683 A1096 34fo multi .80 .25
3684 A1096 40fo multi 1.10 .25
Nos. 3681-3684 (4) 3.50 1.00

Coronation of Stephen I, Hungarian conversion to Christianity, 1000th anniv.
Issued: 30fo, 40fo, 1/1; 28fo, 24fo, 2/24.
No. 3681 exists dated 2001.
See No. 3744.

Souvenir Sheet

Famous Hungarians — A1097

No. 3685: a, 30fo, Miklós Misztófalusi Kis (1650-1702), scientist. b, 40fo, Anyos Jedlik (1800-95), physicist. c, 50fo, Jeno Kvassay (1850-1919), engineer. d, 80fo, Jeno Barcsay (1900-88), painter.

2000, Jan. 11 *Perf. 11½x12*
3685 A1097 Sheet of 4, #a.-d. 4.00 3.75

Souvenir Sheet

Literary and Theatrical Personalities — A1098

No. 3686: a, Mihály Vörösmarty (1800-55), dramatist. b, Mari Jászai (1850-1926), actress. c, Sándor Márai (1900-89), writer. d, Lujza Blaha (1850-1926), actress. e, Lorinc Szabó (1900-57), writer.

2000, Feb. 24 *Perf. 12*
3686 A1098 50fo Sheet of 5, #a.-e. 4.00 3.50

A1099

Easter — A1100

2000, Mar. 20
3687 A1099 26fo multi .50 .25
3688 A1100 28fo multi .75 .30

National Parks Type of 1998

Designs: 29fo, Bluethroat, Siberian iris, ornithologist György Breuer (1887-1955), Ferto-Hanság Park. 34fo, Black stork, fritillary, scientist Pál Kitaibel (1757-1817), Duna-Dráva Park.

2000, Mar. 20 Litho. *Perf. 12*
3689 A1073 29fo multi .60 .25
Complete booklet, 10 #36892 5.50
3690 A1073 34fo multi 1.00 .35
Complete booklet, 10 #3690 7.50

Ferihegy Airport, 50th Anniv. — A1101

2000, May 3 *Perf. 12x11½*
3691 A1101 136fo multi 2.00 1.00

István Türr (1825-1908) and Canal Boat — A1102

2000, May 9 *Perf. 12*
3692 A1102 80fo multi 1.50 .70

Expo 2000, Hanover.

Australian Wildlife — A1103

2000, May 9
3693 A1103 26fo shown .30 .25
3694 A1103 28fo Opossum .35 .25
3695 A1103 83fo Koala 1.10 .30
3696 A1103 90fo Red kangaroo 1.00 .35
Nos. 3693-3696 (4) 2.75 1.15

Souvenir Sheet

3697 A1103 110fo Platypus 4.00 2.25

Souvenir Sheet

Millennium — A1104

Litho., Hologram in Margin
2000, May 9
3698 A1104 2000fo multi 25.00 25.00

Soaking in water may affect the hologram.

Europa, 2000
Common Design Type and

A1105

2000, May 9 **Litho.**
3699 A1105 34fo multi 2.75 .75
3700 CD17 54fo multi 3.75 1.75

Stamp Day — A1106

26fo, Queen Gisela in coronation gown. 28fo, King Stephen I in coronation gown.

2000, May 18
3701 A1106 26fo multi .75 .45
3702 A1106 28fo multi 1.25 .65

Austria No. 4 and Bisect A1107

2000, May 18
3703 A1107 110fo multi 1.75 1.75

WIPA 2000 Philatelic Exhibition, Vienna.

Grapes and Wine Producing Areas Type of 1990

Grapes and: 29fo, Winery building, Balatonfüred-Csopak region, horiz. 34fo, Storage containers, Aszár-Neszmély region, horiz.

2000, May 25 ***Perf. 13¼x13***
3704 A902 29fo multi .65 .35
3705 A902 34fo multi 1.10 .40

Houses of Worship A1108

Designs: No. 3706, 30fo, Abbey Church, Ják. No. 3707, 30fo, Reformed Church, Tákos. No. 3708, 30fo, St. Antal's Church, Eger. No. 3709, 30fo, Deák Evangelical Church, Budapest. 120fo, Dohany Synagogue, Budapest.

2000 **Litho.** ***Perf. 12***
3706-3710 A1108 Set of 5 3.00 3.00

Issued: 120fo, 9/19; others 6/30. See Israel No. 1416.

Furniture Type of 1999

Designs: 2fo, Wooden chair, 1838, vert. 3fo, 19th cent. chair, vert. 4fo, Chair by Géza Maróti, 1900, vert. 5fo, Chair by Odon Farago, 1900, vert. 6fo, Chair by Márton Kovács, 1893, vert. 9fo, 18th cent. chair from Dunapataj, vert. 26fo, 1850 chair, vert. 29fo, 19th cent. chair with animal designs, vert. 30fo, Chair by Károly Nagy, 1935, vert. 80fo, 1840-50 chair, vert. 90fo, Chair by Lajos Kozma, 1928, vert.

2000 ***Perf. 11½x12***
3711-3721 A1091 Set of 11 4.50 2.00

Issued: 2fo, 3fo, 9fo, 26fo, 29fo, 30fo, 6/30; others, 10/9.

Hungarian Aviation, 90th Anniv. A1109

2000, Aug. 18 ***Perf. 12¾x12¼***
3722 A1109 120fo multi 1.75 1.50

Souvenir Sheets

Hungarian History — A1110

No. 3723: a, King with orb, knights. b, St. Laszlo with sword. c, St. Elizabeth, Mongol invasion. d, King Sigismund, knight on horseback. e, Janos Hunuyadi and Janos Kapisztran.

No. 3724: a, King Matthias. b, Crucifixion scene, Miklos Zrinyi. c, Trumpeter on horseback, battle scenes. d, Gabor Bethlen (in black hat). e, Peer Parmany, university.

2000, Aug. 18 ***Perf. 12***
3723 A1110 Sheet of 5 5.00 3.50
a.-e. 50fo Any single .70 .35
3724 A1110 Sheet of 5 5.00 3.50
a.-e. 50fo Any single .70 .35

See Nos. 3770-3771.

A1111

A1112

Christmas A1113

2000, Oct. 16 ***Perf. 12¼x11½***
3725 A1111 26fo shown .40 .25

Perf. 13¼x13
3726 A1112 28fo shown .65 .25
Booklet, 10 #3726 7.00
3727 A1112 29fo Christmas tree .65 .25

Perf. 12
3728 A1113 34fo shown .70 .25
Booklet, 10 #3728 8.00
Nos. 3725-3728 (4) 2.40 1.00

European Convention on Human Rights, 50th Anniv. — A1114

2000, Nov. 3 ***Perf. 12½***
3729 A1114 50fo multicolored .75 .50

2000 Summer Olympics, Sydney A1115

Sports and total of medals won: 30fo, Shooting, three bronzes. 40fo, Weight lifting, six silvers. 80fo, Men's rings, eight golds. 120fo, Rowing, total count.

2000, Nov. 22 ***Perf. 12***
3730-3732 A1115 Set of 3 1.50 1.50

Souvenir Sheet
3733 A1115 120fo multi 3.00 1.75

European Language Year A1116

2001, Jan. 15 **Litho.** ***Perf. 13x13¼***
3734 A1116 100fo multi 1.25 1.25

Souvenir Sheet

Greetings — A1117

No. 3735: a, Bugler on pig. b, Man, woman, flower. c, Baby in cradle. d, Clown. e, Mother and child.

2001, Feb. 9 ***Perf. 11½x12***
3735 A1117 36fo Sheet of 5, #a-f 2.50 2.00

World Speed Skating Championships, Budapest — A1118

2001, Feb. 9 **Litho.** ***Perf. 13***
3736 A1118 140fo multi 1.75 1.75

Furniture Type of 1999

Designs: 1fo, Three-legged stool, by János Vincze, 1910, vert. 7fo, 1853 chair, vert. 8fo, 19th cent. chair, vert. 31fo, Like No. 3717, vert. 40fo, Armchair by Ignác Alpár, 1896, vert. 60fo, Armchair by Ferenc Steindl, 1840, vert. 200fo, Settee by Sebestyén Vogel, 1810.

2001 ***Perf. 11½x12, 12x11½***
3737-3743 A1091 Set of 7 4.25 1.50

Issued: 31fo, 3/5; others, 2/9.

Hungarian Millennium Type of 2000

2001, Mar. 5 ***Perf. 12x11½***
3744 A1096 36fo Millennium flag 1.00 .25

National Parks Type of 1998

Designs: 28fo, Balaton. 36fo, Körös-maros. 70fo, Duna-Ipoly.

2001, Mar. 5 ***Perf. 12***
3745-3747 A1073 Set of 3 1.75 1.50

Easter A1119

2001, Mar. 5 ***Perf. 13***
3748 A1119 28fo multi .50 .25

Locomotives — A1120

Designs: 31fo, Mk. 48. 36fo, 490. 100fo, 394. 150fo, C50.

2001, Apr. 13 ***Perf. 13¼x13***
3749-3752 A1120 Set of 4 3.25 3.25

Esztergom Archbishopric, 1000th Anniv. — A1121

2001, Apr. 18 ***Perf. 12***
3753 A1121 124fo multi 1.50 1.25

Organizations — A1122

No. 3754: a, 70fo, Emblems of European and Mediterranean Plant Protection Organization and Intl. Plant Protection Convention. b, 80fo, UN High Commissioner for Refugees, 50th anniv.

2001, Apr. 18 ***Perf. 13¼x13***
3754 A1122 Horiz. pair, #a-b 1.75 1.50

Europa A1123

Designs: 36fo, Open chest with water. 90fo, Split globe with water.

2001, May 9 ***Perf. 12***
3755-3756 A1123 Set of 2 3.25 1.75

Animals A1124

Designs: 28fo, Phoca hispida. 36fo, Canis lupus. 70fo, Testudo hermanni. 90fo, Alcedo atthis ispida.
200fo, Cervus elaphus.

2001, May 9 ***Perf. 12***
3757-3760 A1124 Set of 4 2.50 2.50

Souvenir Sheet
3761 A1124 200fo multi 3.00 2.25

A1125

Stamp Day — A1126

Designs: 36fo, #N2. 90fo, #2.
200fo+40fo, Pigeon Post, by Miklos Barabás.

2001, May 25 ***Perf. 12¼x11½***
3762-3763 A1125 Set of 2 1.75 1.50
a. Sheet, 6 each # 3762-3763 10.50 9.00

Souvenir Sheet

Perf. 12½

3764 A1126 200fo +40fo multi 3.50 2.75

European Water Polo Championships A1127

2001, June 14 ***Perf. 13½x13***
3765 A1127 150fo multi 2.00 1.00

Intl. Scouting Conference — A1128

2001, June 21 ***Perf. 12***
3766 A1128 150fo multi 2.00 1.00

World Youth Track and Field Championships, Debrecen — A1129

2001, July 12 Litho. ***Perf. 13x13¼***
3767 A1129 140fo multi 1.50 1.00

Artist's Colony, Gödöllö, Cent. — A1130

Fészek Arts Club, Cent. — A1131

2001, July 12 ***Perf. 12***
3768 A1130 100fo multi 1.00 .50
3769 A1131 150fo blue & blk 1.50 .75

Hungarian History Type of 2000

Souvenir Sheets

No. 3770: a, Prince Francis II Rákóczy, swordsman on horseback, Ilona Zrinyi. b, Rider from Royal Horse Guard, Castle at Munkács, Queen Maria Theresa. c, Count Stephen Széchenyi, Chain Bridge. d, Lajos Kossuth, Artúr Görgey with sword on horseback, battle scene. e, Poet János Arany, Parliament building.

No. 3771: a, World War I soldier on horseback, outline map of Hungary and lost parts of empire, Hungarian people. b, Albert Szent-Gyorgi and chemistry equipment. c, Chain Bridge, World War II soldiers, Bishop Vilmos Apor. d, Pictures of 1956 revolution, Polish-Hungarian Solidarity banner. e, Barbed wire, children representing Hungary's future, Hungarian millennium flag.

2001, Aug. 15
3770 A1110 Sheet of 5 5.00 2.50
a.-e. 50fo Any single 1.00 .35
3771 A1110 Sheet of 5 5.00 2.50
a.-e. 50fo Any single 1.00 .35

Souvenir Sheet

Crown of St. Stephen — A1132

Litho. & Embossed

2001, Aug. 15 ***Perf. 13x12¾***
3772 A1132 2001fo multi 22.00 22.00

Grapes and Wine Producing Areas Type of 1990

Grapes and: 60fo, Pannonhalma Abbey, Pannonhalma-Sokoróalja region, horiz. 70fo, Spherical observatory and Red Chapel, Balatonboglár, horiz.

2001, Aug. 17 Litho. ***Perf. 13¼x13***
3773-3774 A902 Set of 2 1.50 .75

Attempt To Create World's Largest Stamp Mosaic — A1133

2001, Oct. 9 ***Perf. 12***
3775 A1133 10fo multi .30 .25

Maria Valeria Bridge Reconstruction — A1134

2001, Oct. 11 ***Perf. 13¼x13***
3776 A1134 36fo multi .50 .50

See Slovakia No. 388.

Christmas A1135

2001, Oct. 16 ***Perf. 12***
3777 A1135 36fo multi .50 .25

State Printers, 150th Anniv. — A1136

2001, Nov. 23 Litho. ***Perf. 13¼x13***
3778 A1136 150fo multi 1.75 .75

2002 Winter Olympics, Salt Lake City — A1137

2002, Feb. 8 Litho. ***Perf. 12***
3779 A1137 160fo multi 2.50 .90

Souvenir Sheet

History of the Bicycle — A1138

No. 3780: a, Large-wheeled bicycle and rider, c. 1880. b, Tricycle, early 1900s. c, Károly Iszer (1860-1929), Budapest Sport Club chairman and bicycle. d, Tandem bicycle.

2002, Feb. 20 ***Perf. 11½x12¼***
3780 A1138 40fo Sheet of 4, #a-d 2.50 1.75

Souvenir Sheet

Hungarian — Ottoman Battles of 1552 — A1139

No. 3781: a, 50fo, Siege of Eger Castle (25x30mm). b, 50fo, Battle of Temesvár (25x30mm). c, 100fo+50fo, Battle of Drégely Castle (40x30mm).

2002, Feb. 20 ***Perf. 12***
3781 A1139 Sheet of 3, #a-c 4.00 2.75

Easter — A1140

2002, Mar. 14 ***Perf. 11½x12¼***
3782 A1140 30fo multi .50 .25

Airplanes Designed by Hungarians — A1141

Designs: 180fo, Libelle, by János adorján, 1910. 190fo, Magyar Lloyd, by Tibor Melczer, 1914.

2002, Mar. 14 ***Perf. 12½***
3783-3784 A1141 Set of 2 4.00 2.25

See Nos. 3831-3832, 3968-3969.

Famous Hungarians A1142

Designs: 33fo, Lajos Kossuth (1802-94), leader of Hungarian independence movement. 134fo, János Bolyai (1802-60), mathematician. 150fo, Gyula Illyés (1902-83), writer.

2002, Mar. 14 ***Perf. 13x13½***
3785-3787 A1142 Set of 3 4.00 1.75

Souvenir Sheet

Parliament Building, Cent. — A1143

2002, Mar. 14 ***Perf. 11½x12¼***
3788 A1143 500fo multi 6.50 5.50

Souvenir Sheet

Opening of National Theater — A1144

2002, Mar. 14
3789 A1144 500fo multi 6.00 5.25

Furniture Type of 1999

Designs: 33fo, Chair, 1809, vert. 134fo, Theater armchair, 1900.

2002, Mar. 28 ***Perf. 11½x12, 12x11½***
3790-3791 A1091 Set of 2 2.50 1.00

Environmental Protection — A1145

2002, Mar. 28 ***Perf. 12***
3792 A1145 158fo multi 1.60 .80

Souvenir Sheet

Founding of Hungarian National Museum and National Széchényi Library, Bicent. — A1146

No. 3793: a, Mihály Apafi psalter, 1686. b, Illuminated letter from Graduale Pars II. c, Standard of the Civil Guard of Pest, 1848. d, Basin for holy water, 12th cent.

2002, Apr. 29
3793 A1146 150fo Sheet of 4, #a-d 7.50 7.50

Halas Lace, Cent. — A1147

Designs: 100fo, Tablecloth with Two Deer, by Mrs. Béla Bazala, 1916. 110fo, Swan Tablecloth, by Erno Stepanek, 1930. 140fo, Jancsi and Iluska, by Antal Tar, 1935.

Litho. & Embossed

2002, May 3 ***Perf. 12***
3794-3796 A1147 Set of 3 4.00 1.75

Europa A1148

2002, May 9 Litho. ***Perf. 11***
3797 A1148 62fo multi *1.50* 1.50

2002 World Cup Soccer Championships, Japan and Korea — A1149

2002, May 9 ***Perf. 13x13½***
3798 A1149 160fo multi + label 2.00 1.60

Fauna A1150

Designs: 30fo, Felis sylvestris. 38fo, Podarcis taurica. 110fo, Garrulus glandarius. 160fo, Rosalia alpina.
500fo, Acipenser ruthenus.

2002, May 9 ***Perf. 12***
3799-3802 A1150 Set of 4 4.00 1.75

Souvenir Sheet

3803 A1150 500fo multi 6.00 5.00

Greetings — A1151

No. 3804: a, Etesd meg! b, Megszülettem! c, Sok boldogságot! d, Ontözd meg! e, Ennyire szeretlek!

Serpentine Die Cut 12¼x12¾

2002, May 29 Self-Adhesive
3804 Booklet pane of 5 2.50
a.-e. A1151 38fo Any single .50 .25

Flower Type of 1999

Designs: 30fo, Red poppy. 38fo, Stalkless gentian.

2002, June 24 ***Perf. 12¼x11½***
3805-3806 A1087 Set of 2 1.00 .35

Art — A1152

Designs: 62fo, Kodobálók, by Károly Ferenczy. 188fo, Táncosno, sculpture by Ferenc Megyessy, vert.

Perf. 12¾x12¼, 12¼x12¾

2002, June 24
3807-3808 A1152 Set of 2 3.00 1.25

UNESCO World Heritage Sites — A1153

Designs: 100fo, Budapest. 150fo, Hollóko. 180fo, Caves of Aggtelek Karst, horiz.

2002, June 24 ***Perf. 12***
3809-3811 A1153 Set of 3 4.50 2.25

See Nos. 3881-3882, 4073.

Kalocsa Archbishopric, 1000th Anniv. — A1154

2002, Aug. 1 Litho. ***Perf. 13¼x12½***
3812 A1154 150fo multi 1.50 .75

Medical Congresses A1155

No. 3813: a, 100fo, 38th European Diabetes Association Congress. b, 150fo, 16th European Arm and Shoulder Surgeons Congress.

2002, Aug. 23 ***Perf. 13x13¼***
3813 A1155 Vert. pair, #a-b 3.00 2.50

Printed in sheets of two pairs. Value $5.50.

Ceramics by Margit Kovács — A1156

No. 3814: a, 33fo, Madonna and Child, 1938. b, 38fo, Mother and Children, 1953. 400fo+200fo, St. George, 1936.

2002, Oct. 3 ***Perf. 13¼x13***
3814 A1156 Pair, #a-b 1.00 .35

Souvenir Sheet

Perf. 12¼x11½

3815 A1156 400fo +200fo multi 6.00 6.00

Stamp Day. No. 3814 printed in sheets of two pairs. Value $1.75. No. 3815 contains one 25x36mm stamp.

Christmas A1157

Designs: 30fo, Adoration of the Magi. 38fo, Bethlehem.

Litho. with Foil Application

2002, Oct. 30 ***Perf. 12***
3816-3817 A1157 Set of 2 1.25 .35

See No. 4006.

World Gymnastics Championships, Debrecen — A1158

2002, Nov. 20 Litho. ***Perf. 13x13¼***
3818 A1158 160fo multi 1.60 .80

Hungarian and Turkish Buildings — A1159

Designs: 40fo, Rakoczi House, Tekirdag, Turkey. 110fo, Gazi Kassim Pasha Mosque, Pécs, Hungary.

2002, Dec. 2 Litho. ***Perf. 13½x13¼***
3819-3820 A1159 Set of 2 1.50 .75

See Turkey No. 2844.

Furniture Type of 1999

Designs: 32fo, Wooden chair with carved back, 19th cent., vert. 35fo, Armchair, 18th cent., vert. 65fo, Armchair with carved back, 1920, vert.

2003, Jan. 30 ***Perf. 11½x12¼***
3821-3823 A1091 Set of 3 1.75 .70

Scientists A1160

Designs: 32fo, John von Neumann (1903-57), mathematician, and computer pioneer. 40fo, Rezsö Soó (1903-80), botanist. 60fo, Károly Zipernowsky (1853-1942), electrical engineer.

2003, Feb. 12 ***Perf. 13x13¼***
3824 A1160 32fo multicolored .35 .25
3825 A1160 40fo multicolored 6.00 6.00
3826 A1160 60fo multicolored .60 .60
Nos. 3824-3826 (3) 6.95 6.85

Souvenir Sheet

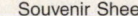

Herend Porcelain — A1161

No. 3827: a, Platter with floral design, Frankenthal coffee set. b, Vase with floral design, coffee set. c, Vase with ram's head handles. d, Shell-shaped bowl, pitcher.

2003, Feb. 12 ***Perf. 12***
3827 A1161 150fo Sheet of 4, #a-d 6.00 6.00

Defeat of Royal Hungarian Army, 60th Anniv. — A1162

2003, Feb. 15 ***Perf. 12¼x12½***
3828 A1162 40fo multi .60 .25

Easter — A1163

2003, Mar. 14
3829 A1163 32fo multi .50 .25

Nemzeti Sport, Cent. — A1164

2003, Mar. 14 ***Perf. 13x13¼***
3830 A1164 150fo multi + label 2.00 .75

Airplanes Type of 2002

Designs: 142fo, Gerle 13, by Antal Bánhidi, 1933. 160fo, L-2 Róma, by Árpád Lampich, 1925.

2003, Mar. 20 ***Perf. 12½***
3831-3832 A1141 Set of 2 3.50 1.50

Hotels — A1165

Designs: 110fo, Rogner Hotel, Héviz. 120fo, Hélia Hotel, Budapest.

2003, Mar. 20
3833-3834 A1165 Set of 2 2.50 1.10

See Nos. 3883-3884.

Souvenir Sheet

Extreme Sports — A1166

No. 3835: a, 100fo, BMX cycling. b, 100fo, Snowboarding. c, 100fo, Parachuting. d, 100fo+50fo, Kayaking.

2003, Mar. 20 ***Perf. 12***
3835 A1166 Sheet of 4, #a-d 4.50 4.50

Greetings
A1167

No. 3836: a, Church. b, Two flowers. c, One flower. d, Easter eggs. e, Candles in window, Christmas tree.

Serpentine Die Cut 12¾

2003, Mar. 20 **Self-Adhesive**
3836 Booklet pane of 5 2.00
a.-e. A1167 40fo Any single .40 .25

Souvenir Sheet

Space Shuttle Columbia — A1168

2003, Apr. 9 ***Perf. 12***
3837 A1168 500fo multi 5.00 2.50

World Ice Hockey Championships, Budapest — A1169

2003, Apr. 10 ***Perf. 13x13¼***
3838 A1169 110fo multi + label 1.10 .55

Budapest Sports Arena — A1170

2003, Apr. 10
3839 A1170 120fo multi + label 1.25 .60

Souvenir Sheet

Ratification of European Union Accession Treaty — A1171

2003, Apr. 14 ***Perf. 12***
3840 A1171 500fo multi 7.50 7.50

Policeman on Motorcycle and Emergency Phone Number
A1172

2003, Apr. 24
3841 A1172 65fo multi .65 .35

Stamp Day — A1173

Designs: 35fo, Statue of woman with legs crossed. 40fo, Statue of woman with hand on chin.
400fo+100fo, Fountain.

2003, May 6 ***Perf. 13¼x13***
3842-3843 A1173 Set of 2 .75 .40

Souvenir Sheet

Perf. 12¾x13

3844 A1173 400fo +100fo multi 7.00 5.00

No. 3844 contains one 31x40mm stamp.

Souvenir Sheet

Uprising Against Hapsburgs of Ferenc Rákóczi II, 400th Anniv. — A1174

No. 3845: a, Swords and scabbards. b, Coins. c, Banner, pipes and drums. d, Guns.

2003, May 6 ***Perf. 12***
3845 A1174 120fo Sheet of 4, #a-d 6.50 5.50

Europa — A1175

2003, May 9
3846 A1175 65fo multi 1.75 1.75

Fauna
A1176

Designs: 35fo, Mustela eversmanni. 40fo, Calandrella brachydactyla. 100fo, Hyla arborea. 110fo, Misgurnus fossilis.
500fo, Eresus cinnabarinus.

2003, May 9
3847-3850 A1176 Set of 4 4.00 1.75

Souvenir Sheet

3851 A1176 500fo multi 6.00 5.00

Grapes and Wine Producing Areas Type of 1990

Grapes and: 60fo, Bükkalja region, horiz. 130fo, Balaton-felvidéki region, horiz.

2003, June 6 ***Perf. 13¼x12½***
3852-3853 A902 Set of 2 2.50 1.00

Souvenir Sheet

Robe of St. László — A1177

2003, June 13 ***Perf. 12***
3854 A1177 300fo multi 4.25 3.00

Art
A1178

Designs: 32fo, Sculpture by Imre Varga, vert. 60fo, Mostar Bridge, by Tivadar Csontváry Kosztka.

Perf. 12½x13¼, 13¼x12½

2003, July 18
3855-3856 A1178 Set of 2 1.50 .50

Souvenir Sheet

Sports History — A1179

No. 3857: a, Ferenc Puskás Stadium Budapest, 50th anniv. b, Hungary vs. England soccer match, 50th anniv.

2003, July 18 ***Perf. 11½x12¼***
3857 A1179 250fo Sheet of 2, #a-b 5.75 5.00

European Union Membership
A1180

2003 **Litho.** ***Perf. 12x11½***
3858 A1180 115fo shown 1.40 .60
3859 A1180 130fo Clock at 11:35 1.60 .70

Issued: 115fo, 9/16; 130fo, 10/18.
See Nos. 3877-3878.

Nutrition
A1181

2003, Sept. 16 ***Perf. 12***
3860 A1181 120fo multi 1.50 .60

European Automobile-free Day — A1182

2003, Sept. 16
3861 A1182 150fo multi 1.50 .75

Reszo Soó (1903-80), Botanist
A1183

2003, Sept. 23
3862 A1183 44fo multi .55 .25

Book Printing — A1184

Designs: No. 3863, 44fo, Hungarian Illuminated Chronicle, 1358. No. 3864, 44fo, Ritual of Zhou, China.

2003, Sept. 30
3863-3864 A1184 Set of 2 1.40 .45

See People's Republic of China Nos. 3309-3310.

Souvenir Sheet

Ferenc Deák (1803-76), Statesman — A1185

2003, Oct. 18
3865 A1185 500fo multi 6.00 5.00

Christmas — A1186

Designs: 35fo, Reindeer. 44fo, Angels, Christmas tree, houses.

2003, Oct. 31 ***Perf. 11½x12***
3866-3867 A1186 Set of 2 1.00 .40

Souvenir Sheet

World Science Forum, Budapest — A1187

2003, Nov. 7 **Litho.** ***Perf. 12***
3868 A1187 500fo multi 6.00 5.00

Locomotives Type of 2001

Designs: 120fo, Muki Diesel locomotive, Kemence Forest Railway. 150fo, Rezét steam locomotive, Gemenc Forest Railway.

2004, Feb. 4 ***Perf. 13¼x13***
3869-3870 A1120 Set of 2 3.00 3.00

Famous Men — A1188

Designs: 40fo, Bálint Balassi (1554-94), poet. 44fo, József Bajza (1804-58), poet. 80fo, János András Segner (1704-77), physicist.

2004, Feb. 4 ***Perf. 13***
3871-3873 A1188 Set of 3 2.25 .85

Souvenir Sheet

Dogs — A1189

No. 3874: a, 100fo, Puli. b, 100fo, Hungarian greyhound. c, 100fo, Mudi. d, 100fo+50fo, Vizsla.

2004, Feb. 19 ***Perf. 12***
3874 A1189 Sheet of 4, #a-d 5.50 4.50

Surtax on No. 3874d for youth philately.

Souvenir Sheet

Festivals — A1190

No. 3875: a, Busójárás Carnival. b, Virágkarnevál (Flower Carnival). c, Borfesztivál (Wine Festival). d, Fesztiválok Karneválok (Festivals and Carnivals).

2004, Feb. 19
3875 A1190 60fo Sheet of 4, #a-d 3.25 2.40

European Ministerial Conference on the Information Society — A1191

No. 3876 — Color of panel and "e:" a, Red violet. b, Dark blue. c, Green. d, Orange.

2004, Feb. 26 ***Perf. 13¼x13***
3876 A1191 40fo Block of 4, #a-d 3.00 2.25

European Union Membership (Clock) Type of 2003

2004 ***Perf. 12x11½***
3877 A1180 100fo Clock at 11:48 1.25 .50
3878 A1180 190fo Clock at 11:57 2.25 .90

Issued: 100fo, 3/5; 190fo, 4/19.

Tenth World Indoor Track and Field Championships, Budapest A1192

2004, Mar. 5 ***Perf. 13x13¼***
3879 A1192 120fo multi 1.50 .60

Easter — A1193

2004, Mar. 18 **Litho.**
3880 A1193 48fo multi .50 .25

World Heritage Sites Type of 2002

Designs: 150fo, Abbey of Pannonhalma. 170fo, Hortobágy National Park, horiz.

2004, Mar. 18 ***Perf. 12***
3881-3882 A1153 Set of 2 3.75 1.60

Hotels Type of 2003

Designs: 120fo, Bük Thermal and Sports Hotel, Bükfürdo. 150fo, Aqua-Sol Hotel, Hajdúszoboszló.

2004, Mar. 18
3883-3884 A1165 Set of 2 3.25 1.25

Holocaust, 60th Anniv. A1194

2004, Apr. 16 ***Perf. 13x13¼***
3885 A1194 160fo multi 1.90 .75

Souvenir Sheet

Zsolnay Porcelain, 150th Anniv. — A1195

No. 3886: a, Vase with handles. b, Small vase, vessel with horse and rider top. c, Vase. d, Mocha set.

2004, Apr. 20 **Litho.** ***Perf. 12***
3886 A1195 160fo Sheet of 4, #a-d 7.00 7.00

Police Boat and Emergency Phone Number A1196

2004, Apr. 23 **Litho.** ***Perf. 13x13¼***
3887 A1196 48fo multi .60 .35

Souvenir Sheet

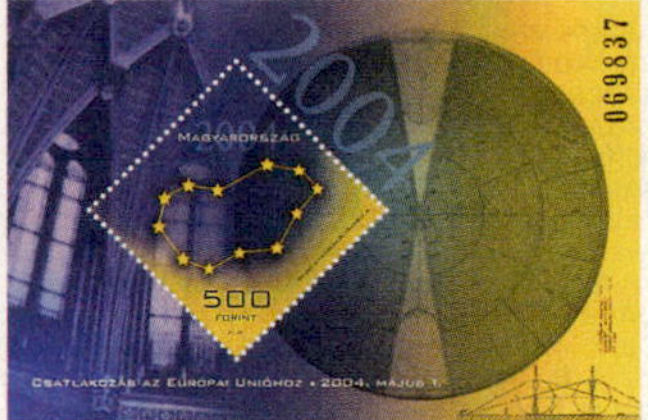

Admission to European Union — A1197

2004, Apr. 30 ***Perf. 12***
3888 A1197 500fo multi 5.25 5.25

Expansion of the European Union — A1198

No. 3889: a, 120fo, Stars and flowers. b, 150fo, Stars, map of Europe, flags of nations entering European Union.

2004, May 1 **Litho.**
3889 A1198 Horiz. pair, #a-b 3.25 2.75

European Parliament Elections A1199

2004, May 7 ***Perf. 12½x13½***
3890 A1199 150fo multi 1.75 .70

Europa A1200

2004, May 7 ***Perf. 12***
3891 A1200 160fo multi 2.25 1.00

Fauna A1201

Designs: 48fo, Nannospalax leucodon. 65fo, Panurus biarmicus. 90fo, Ablepharus kitaibelii fitzingeri. 120fo, Huso huso.
500fo, Anthaxia hungarica.

2004, May 7
3892-3895 A1201 Set of 4 4.00 1.50

Souvenir Sheet

3896 A1201 500fo multi 5.25 5.25

Stamp Day — A1202

Designs: 48fo, Walls and Doors, sculpture by Erzsébet Schaár. 65fo, Translucent Red Circle, painting by Tihamér Gyarmathy.
400fo+200fo, The Wasp King, painting by Béla Kondor.

2004, May 7 **Litho.** ***Perf. 12¼x12¾***
3897-3898 A1202 Set of 2 2.10 .55

Souvenir Sheet

Perf. 12¾x12¼

3899 A1202 400fo +200fo multi 7.25 5.75

No. 3899 contains one 41x31mm stamp.

FIFA (Fédération Internationale de Football Association), Cent. — A1203

2004, May 21 **Litho.** ***Perf. 13¼x13***
3900 A1203 100fo multi 1.25 .45

Central European Catholics' Day — A1204

No. 3901: a, Basilica, Mariazell, Austria. b, Statue of Madonna, Mariazell. c, Statue of Madonna and Child, Mariazell. d, Statue of Madonna, Celldömölk, Hungary. e, Framed painting of Madonna and Child, Mariazell. f, Statue of Mary of Kiscell, Obuda Parish, Hungary.

2004, May 21 **Litho.** ***Perf. 11½x12***
3901 A1204 100fo Sheet of 6, #a-f 6.50 5.75

Information Technology A1205

2004, June 28 ***Perf. 13x13¼***
3902 A1205 120fo multi 1.25 .60

Theodor Herzl (1860-1904), Zionist Leader A1206

2004, July 6 **Litho.** ***Perf. 12***
3903 A1206 150fo multi 2.25 .75

See Austria No. 1960, Israel No. 1566.

2004 Summer Olympics, Athens — A1207

Designs: 90fo, Canoeing. 130fo, Volleyball. 150fo, Running.

2004, July 13

3904-3906	A1207	Set of 3	3.75	1.75

A1208

A1209

A1210

A1211

A1212

A1213

A1214

Folkloriada Festival — A1215

2004, Aug. 12

3907	Block of 10 + 10 labels	10.00	10.00
a.	A1208 65fo dark blue	.75	.40
b.	A1208 65fo orange	.75	.40
c.	A1209 65fo orange brown	.75	.40
d.	A1209 65fo purple	.75	.40
e.	A1210 65fo carmine	.75	.40
f.	A1211 65fo orange brown	.75	.40
g.	A1212 65fo orange brown	.75	.40
h.	A1213 65fo Prussian blue	.75	.40
i.	A1214 65fo green	.75	.40
j.	A1215 65fo orange brown	.75	.40
k.	Sheet, #3907	32.00	32.00

No. 3907k has labels that could be personalized. The personalized sheet sold for 1600fo.

Chess History — A1216

No. 3908 — Beginning of text, square color, piece (if any): a, A sakkjáték, tan, black rook. b, A magyaroknak, brown. c, A magyar történelem, tan, black bishop. d, A magyar sakkirodalom, brown, black king. e, A XVIII. században, tan, black queen. f, Az elso, brown. g, Az 1839-ben, tan, black knight. h, A XIX. század, brown, black rook. i, A magyar sakkfeladványszerok, brown, black pawn. j, Három, a XIX. század, tan, black pawn. k, Maróczy Géza, brown, black pawn. l, Két kiváló, tan, black pawn. m, A levelezási, brown, black bishop. n, A sakkélet, tan, black pawn. o, A férfi országos, brown, black pawn. p, A II. világháború tan után sokáig, black pawn. q, A nol sakkozás, tan. r, 1958-ban már, brown. s, A sakkozók, tan, black knight. t, 1951-ben indult, brown. u, A XX. századnak, tan. v, A II. világháború utá feladvány, brown. w, A XX. században, tan. x, A XX. század elején, brown. y, A világ sakkéletét, brown. z, A két világháború között, tan. aa, A háború után, brown. ab, A férfi sakkolimpián, tan. ac, A nemzetek közti, brown, black pawn. ad, 1957-ben a hollandiai, tan. ae, A noi sakkolimpiákon, brown. af, A XIX. és XX. században, tan. ag, Sakkirodalom nélkül, tan. ah, A XX. század magyar, brown. ai, A széles sakkozó, tan, white bishop. aj, A Magyar Sakkszövetség, brown. ak, Barcza Gedeon, tan, white pawn. al, Szábo László, brown. am, Portisch Lajos, tan. an, Adorján András, brown. ao, Sax Gyula, brown. ap, Ribli Zoltán, tan. aq, Lékó Péter, brown. ar, Almási Zoltán, tan. as, Bilek, István, brown. at, A két világháború közti, tan, white knight. au, Az olimpiákon többször, brown. av, Sok kiváló magyar, tan. aw, Polgár Zsuzsa, tan, white pawn. ax, Polgár Judit, brown, white pawn. ay, Polgár Zsófia, tan, white pawn. az, Lángos Józsa, brown, white pawn. ba, Veroci Zsuzsa, tan. bb, Ivánka Mária, brown, white pawn. bc, Mádl Ildikó, tan, white pawn. bd, Országos bajnoki, brown, white pawn. be, Sakkozásunk a XXI. századot, brown, white rook. bf, A sakkozással, tan, white knight. bg, A magyar sakkozás, brown, white bishop. bh, Minden összefoglaló,tan, white king. bi, A jelen munkában, brown, white queen. bj, Elek Ferenc, tan. bk, Katkó (Regos) Imre, brown. bl, Gróf Pongrácz Arnold, tan, white rook.

2004, Sept. 24

3908	Sheet of 64	42.50	42.50
a.-bl.	A1216 50fo Any single	.60	.40

Souvenir Sheet

Admission to European Union — A1217

No. 3909 — Large stars and time of small clock: a, 11:20. b, 11:35. c, 11:48. d, 11:57.

2004, Oct. 8 ***Perf. 12x11½***

3909	A1217	100fo Sheet of 4, #a-d	5.50	4.00

Istvan Bocskay (1557-1606), Leader of 1604-06 Rebellion — A1218

2004, Nov. 11 Litho. ***Perf. 11½x12***

3910	A1218	120fo multi	1.25	.60

Intl. Organization of Supreme Audit Institutions, 18th Congress, Budapest A1219

2004, Oct. 11 ***Perf. 11¼***

3911	A1219	150fo multi	1.50	.75

Christmas Type of 2002 and

A1220

A1221

A1222

A1223

A1224

A1225

A1226

A1227

A1228

A1229

A1230

A1231

A1232

A1233

A1234

Christmas — A1235

No. 3915: Various Christmas cookies.

Litho. With Foil Application

2004 ***Perf. 12***

3912	A1157	48fo Bethlehem	.50	.25

Litho.

Perf. 11¼

3913	Sheet of 20 + 20 labels	30.00	16.50
a.	A1220 48fo multi + label	1.25	.40
b.	A1221 48fo multi + label	1.25	.40
c.	A1222 48fo multi + label	1.25	.40
d.	A1223 48fo multi + label	1.25	.40
e.	A1224 48fo multi + label	1.25	.40
f.	A1225 48fo multi + label	1.25	.40
3914	Sheet of 20 + 20 labels	30.00	16.50
a.	A1226 48fo multi + label	1.25	.40
b.	A1227 48fo multi + label	1.25	.40
c.	A1228 48fo multi + label	1.25	.40

d. A1229 48fo multi + label 1.25 .40
e. A1230 48fo multi + label 1.25 .40
f. A1231 48fo multi + label 1.25 .40
g. A1232 48fo multi + label 1.25 .40
h. A1233 48fo multi + label 1.25 .40
i. A1234 48fo multi + label 1.25 .40
3915 A1235 48fo Sheet of 20, #a-t, + 20 labels 30.00 16.50

Issued: No. 3912, 10/28; Nos. 3913-3915, 11/3.

No. 3913 contains 5 No. 3913b, 3 No. 3913c, 4 each Nos. 3913a, 3913e, 2 each Nos. 3913d, 3913f. Background colors on some stamps differ slightly.

No. 3914 contains Nos. 3914d, 3914e, 4 each Nos. 3914a, 3914b, 2 each Nos. 3914c, 3914f, 3914g, 3914h, 3914i.

Nos. 3913-3915 could be personalized, with each sheet selling for 2000fo.

Sándor Korösi Csoma (1784-1842), Philologist and Sir Marc Aurel Stein (1862-1943), Archaeologist A1236

2004, Nov. 3 Litho. *Perf. 13x13¼*
3916 A1236 80fo multi 1.25 .40

Natura 2000 — A1237

2004, Dec. 3 *Perf. 11½x12*
3917 A1237 100fo multi 1.10 .55

Zodiac — A1238

No. 3918: a, Capricorn (goat). b, Aquarius (water bearer). c, Pisces (fish). d, Aries (ram). e, Taurus (bull). f, Gemini (twins). g, Cancer (crab). h, Leo (lion). i, Virgo (virgin). j, Libra (scales). k, Scorpio (scorpion). l, Sagittarius (archer).

2005, Jan. 3 Litho. *Perf. 11¼*
3918 A1238 50fo Sheet of 12, #a-l 10.00 7.50
m. Sheet of 20 #3918a + 20 labels 29.00 —
n. Sheet of 20 #3918b + 20 labels 29.00 —
o. Sheet of 20 #3918c + 20 labels 29.00 —
p. Sheet of 20 #3918d + 20 labels 29.00 —
q. Sheet of 20 #3918e + 20 labels 29.00 —
r. Sheet of 20 #3918f + 20 labels 29.00 —
s. Sheet of 20 #3918g + 20 labels 29.00 —
t. Sheet of 20 #3918h + 20 labels 29.00 —
u. Sheet of 20 #3918i + 20 labels 29.00 —
v. Sheet of 20 #3918j + 20 labels 29.00 —
w. Sheet of 20 #3918k + 20 labels 29.00 —
x. Sheet of 20 #3918l + 20 labels 29.00 —

Nos. 3918m-3918x each sold for 2100fo and had labels that could be personalized.

Rotary International, Cent. — A1239

2005, Feb. 4 *Perf. 13¼x13*
3919 A1239 130fo multi 1.60 .70

Souvenir Sheet

Cats — A1240

No. 3920: a, 100fo, Siamese, silhouette of cat sitting. b, 100fo, Maine Coon cat, silhouette of cat with arched back and thin tail. c, 100fo, Persian, silhouette of cat with large tail. d, 100fo+50fo, Domestic cat, silhouette of cat walking.

2005, Feb. 4 *Perf. 12x11½*
3920 A1240 Sheet of 4, #a-d 4.75 4.75

Easter — A1241

2005, Feb. 21 *Perf. 12*
3921 A1241 50fo multi .55 .25

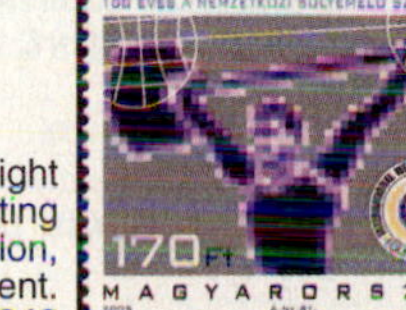

Intl. Weight Lifting Federation, Cent. A1242

2005, Mar. 3 *Perf. 12¼x12½*
3922 A1242 170fo multi 1.90 .95

Sándor Iharos (1930-96), Runner A1243

2005, Mar. 10 *Perf. 13x13¼*
3923 A1243 90fo multi 1.00 .50

Souvenir Sheet

Opening of Palace of Arts, Budapest — A1244

2005, Mar. 10 *Perf. 12*
3924 A1244 500fo multi 5.50 5.50

World Theater Day — A1245

2005, Mar. 21 *Perf. 11¼*
3925 A1245 50fo multi .80 .25

See No. 4198.

Compass and Map of Hungary — A1246

No. 3926: a, Compass at right, map of western Hungary. b, Compass at left, map of eastern Hungary.

2005, Apr. 1 Litho. *Perf. 11¼*
3926 A1246 50fo Pair, #a-b, + 2 labels 2.00 1.10
c. Sheet of 20, 10 each #3926a-3926b, + 20 labels 40.00 —

No. 3926c sold for 2100fo. Labels on sheets of 3926 and 3926c could be personalized. Compare with No. 4054.

Writers A1247

Designs: 90fo, Jeno Rejto (1905-43), novelist, playwright. 140fo, Attila József (1905-37), poet.

2005, Apr. 11 Litho. *Perf. 13x13¼*
3927-3928 A1247 Set of 2 2.75 1.25

Police Helicopter and Emergency Phone Number A1248

2005, Apr. 22 *Perf. 13x13¼*
3929 A1248 85fo multi .90 .45

End of World War II, 60th Anniv. A1249

2005, May 6 *Perf. 13*
3930 A1249 150fo multi 1.60 .80

Farm Animals A1250

Designs: 50fo, Hungarian gray bull. 70fo, Hungarian spotted cow. 100fo, Hortobágy Racka sheep. 110fo, Cigája sheep. 500fo, Mangalica pigs.

2005, May 9 *Perf. 13x13¼*
3931-3934 A1250 Set of 4 3.75 1.60

Souvenir Sheet

3935 A1250 500fo multi 6.50 5.00

No. 3935 contains one 41x32mm stamp.

Souvenir Sheet

Europa — A1251

No. 3936 — Plate of Chicken Paprika and Dumplings with: a, Flowers at UR. b, Flowers at UL.

2005, May 9 *Perf. 12*
3936 A1251 160fo Sheet, 2 each #a-b 7.75 6.25

The top and bottom rows of stamps in the sheet are tete-beche.

Souvenir Sheet

Pope John Paul II (1920-2005) — A1252

2005, May 18
3937 A1252 500fo multi 6.00 5.00

Grapes and Wine Producing Areas Type of 1990

Designs: 120fo, Pintes grapes, Zala region, horiz. 140fo, Kunleány grapes, Csongrád region, horiz.

2005, May 25 *Perf. 13¼x12½*
3938-3939 A902 Set of 2 3.25 1.40

Church, Ják, and Ornament From Cluny Abbey, France A1253

2005, May 25 *Perf. 13x13¼*
3940 A1253 110fo multi 1.60 .55

Souvenir Sheet

Consecration of St. Stephen's Basilica, Budapest, Cent. — A1254

2005, May 25 *Perf. 12¾x13*
3941 A1254 500fo multi 6.00 5.00

Miniature Sheet

Budapest Tourist Attractions — A1255

No. 3942: a, Hallway and exhibits, Postal Museum. b, #386a and die of vignette, Stamp Museum, horiz. c, Agriculture Museum, Vajdahunyad Castle. d, Ethnographic Museum, horiz. e, Sándor Palace, horiz.

Perf. 11½x12, 12x11½ (horiz. stamps)

2005, May 25
3942 A1255 100fo Sheet of 5, #a-e, + 5 labels 6.50 5.00

First Hungarian in Space, 25th Anniv. — A1256

2005, May 26 ***Perf. 12½***
3943 A1256 130fo multi 1.25 .65

A1257

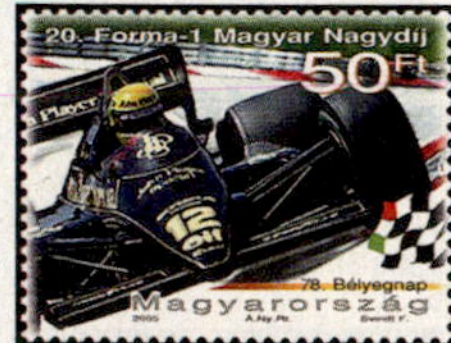

Formula I Auto Racing in Hungary, 20th Anniv. (in 2006) A1258

Designs: Nos. 3944, 3947, Hungaroring Race Track. No. 3945, Car No. 12. No. 3946, Driver in red car.

2005 Litho. ***Perf. 11¼***
3944 A1257 50fo multi + label .50 .25

Perf. 13x13¼

3945 A1258 50fo multi .75 .25
3946 A1258 90fo multi 1.25 .45

Souvenir Sheet

Perf. 13x12¾

3947 A1258 500fo +200fo multi 7.75 7.00

78th Stamp Day (Nos. 3945-3947). Issued: Nos. 3944, 3947, 7/18; Nos. 3945-3946, 6/17. Labels on No. 3944 could be personalized.

Souvenir Sheet

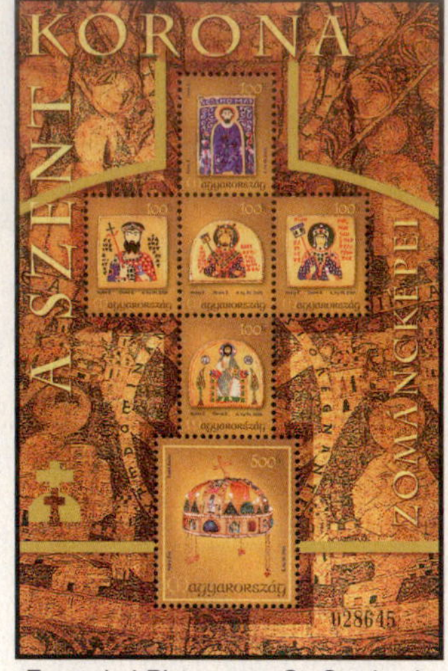

Enameled Pictures on St. Stephen's Crown — A1259

No. 3948: a, 100fo, St. Thomas (20x26mm). b, 100fo, King Géza I (in square panel with black lettering) (20x26mm). c, 100fo, Byzantine Emperor Michael Ducas (in arched panel with red lettering) (20x26mm). d, 100fo, Byzantine Emperor Constantine (in square panel with red lettering) (20x26mm). e, 100fo, Jesus Christ (in arched panel with no lettering) (20x26mm). f, 500fo, St. Stephen's Crown (30x36mm).

2005, Aug. 19 Litho. ***Perf. 12x11½***
3948 A1259 Sheet of 6, #a-f 11.50 10.50

First Hungarian Mail Vehicle, Cent. A1260

2005, Sept. 15 ***Perf. 11¼x11***
3949 A1260 50fo multi .50 .25

Trash Recycling A1261

2005, Sept. 15 ***Perf. 13x13¼***
3950 A1261 140fo multi 1.75 .70

World Wrestling Championships, Budapest — A1262

2005, Sept. 26 ***Perf. 13***
3951 A1262 150fo multi 1.75 .75

Ferenc Farkas (1905-2000), Composer — A1263

2005, Sept. 30 ***Perf. 13x13¼***
3952 A1263 100fo multi 1.75 .50

World Science Forum, Budapest A1264

2005, Sept. 30
3953 A1264 120fo multi 1.75 .60

See No. 4052.

Hungarian University of Craft and Design, 125th Anniv. A1265

2005, Oct. 19 ***Perf. 12***
3954 A1265 90fo multi 1.25 .45

The Three Magi — A1266

Christmas A1267

No. 3956: a, Candle. b, Apple. c, Heart-shaped ornament. d, Teddy bear.

Litho. with Foil Application

2005, Oct. 19 ***Perf. 12¾x12¼***
3955 A1266 50fo blue .75 .25

Self-Adhesive

Litho.

Serpentine Die Cut 12¾

3956 Booklet pane of 4 3.25
a.-d. A1267 50fo Any single .80 .25

House of the Future A1268

2005, Dec. 16 Litho. ***Perf. 12***
3957 A1268 100fo multi 1.25 .45

Hungarian News Agency, 125th Anniv. — A1269

2006, Jan. 1 Litho. ***Perf. 12x11½***
3958 A1269 90fo multi 1.10 .45

2006 Winter Olympics, Turin A1270

2006, Feb. 10 ***Perf. 13¼***
3959 A1270 200fo multi 3.25 1.00

Furniture Type of 1999

Designs: 52fo, Like #3790, vert. 75fo, Chair with heart carved in back, 1893, vert. 212fo, Like #3791. 300fo, Settee, 18th cent. 500fo, Rococo settee, c. 1880. 1000fo, Vassily chair, by Marcel Breuer, 1925.

2006 ***Perf. 11½x12¼***
3960 A1091 52fo bl & dk bl .50 .25
3961 A1091 75fo org brn & brn .70 .35

Perf. 12¼x11½

3962 A1091 212fo grn & dk grn 2.00 1.00

Perf. 12¾x12¼

3963 A1091 300fo red & dk red 3.00 1.50
3964 A1091 500fo bl & dk bl 5.00 2.50
3965 A1091 1000fo ol & dk ol 10.00 5.00
Nos. 3960-3965 (6) 21.20 10.60

Issued: 52fo, 75fo, 212fo, 3/16; others, 5/19.

World Heritage Sites — A1271

Designs: 52fo, Early Christian Necropolis, Pecs. 90fo, Ferto-Neuseidler Lake Cultural Landscape, horiz.

2006, Mar. 16 ***Perf. 12***
3966-3967 A1271 Set of 2 1.75 .75

Airplanes Type of 2002

Designs: 120fo, Boeing 767-200ER. 140fo, Lockheed Sirius 8A.

2006, Mar. 16
3968-3969 A1141 Set of 2 3.25 1.40

Easter — A1272

2006, Mar. 22
3970 A1272 52fo multi .50 .25

Union of European Football Associations Congress, Budapest A1273

2006, Mar. 22 ***Perf. 13x13¼***
3971 A1273 170fo multi 2.25 .85

Sándor Légrády (1906-87), Stamp Designer, and Vignette of Unissued Stamp — A1274

2006, Mar. 30 Litho. ***Perf. 12x11½***
3972 A1274 75fo multi 1.00 .35

Ilona Sasváriné-Paulik (1954-99), Paralymic Athlete — A1275

2006, Mar. 30 ***Perf. 13x13¼***
3973 A1275 185fo multi 2.00 .85

László Detre (1906-74), Astronomer — A1276

2006, Mar. 30 ***Perf. 12***
3974 A1276 212fo multi 2.75 1.00

Wi-fi Technology A1277

2006, Mar. 30 ***Perf. 13x13¼***
3975 A1277 240fo multi 2.50 1.10

Orchid — A1278

Rose — A1279

Lily — A1280

Tulip — A1281

Gerbera Daisy — A1282

Rose — A1283

Rose — A1284

Rose — A1285

Butterfly and Wedding Rings — A1286

Butterfly and Rose — A1287

Daisy and Rubber Duck — A1288

Daisy and Blue Booties — A1289

Daisy and Pink Booties — A1290

Daisy and Rattle — A1291

Rose — A1292

Clematis — A1293

2006 Litho. ***Perf. 11¼***

3976	Vert. strip of 5 + 5 labels	12.50	12.50
a.	A1278 52fo multi + label	2.00	.35
b.	A1279 52fo multi + label	2.00	.35
c.	A1280 52fo multi + label	2.00	.35
d.	A1281 52fo multi + label	2.00	.35
e.	A1282 52fo multi + label	2.00	.35
	Sheet, 4 each #3976a-3976e	45.00	45.00
3977	Strip of 3 + 3 labels	2.50	.50
a.	A1283 52fo multi + label	.75	.50
b.	A1284 52fo multi + label	.75	.50
c.	A1285 52fo multi + label	.75	.50
	Sheet, 7 each #3977a-3977b, 6 #3977c	20.00	20.00
3978	Pair + 2 labels	2.00	2.00
a.	A1286 52fo multi + label	1.00	.50
b.	A1287 52fo multi + label	1.00	.50
	Sheet, 10 each #3978a-3978b	20.00	20.00
3979	Block or strip of 4 + 4 labels	12.00	12.00
a.	A1288 52fo multi + label	2.00	.50
b.	A1289 52fo multi + label	2.00	.50
c.	A1290 52fo multi + label	2.00	.50
d.	A1291 52fo multi + label	2.00	.50
	Sheet, 3 each #3979b-39779c, 7 each #3977a, 3977d	55.00	—
3980	Pair + 2 labels	5.00	5.00
a.	A1292 90fo multi + label	2.00	.50
b.	A1293 90fo multi + label	2.00	.50
	Sheet, 10 each #3980a-3980b	60.00	—
	Nos. 3976-3980 (5)	34.00	32.00

Issued: Nos. 3976, 3977, 5/4, others, 5/19. Background colors of stamps in full sheets varies. Labels could be personalized for an additional fee.

Compare with Nos. 4092, 4199, 4298.

Battle of Belgrade, 550th Anniv. — A1294

2006, May 9 ***Perf. 13½x12½***
3981 A1294 120fo multi 1.75 .65

2006 World Cup Soccer Championships, Germany — A1295

2006, May 9 ***Perf. 13x13¼***
3982 A1295 170fo multi 3.50 .90

Europa — A1296

2006, May 9 ***Perf. 12***
3983 A1296 190fo multi 2.25 1.10

Printed in sheets of 4, with each stamp rotated 90 degrees to create circle of faces. Value $9.50.

Horses A1297

Breeds: 75fo, Shagya Arab. 90fo, Furioso (Mezohegyes halfbreed). 140fo, Gidran. 160fo, Nonius.

No. 3988: a, Huçul. b, Lippizaner. c, Kisbér halfbreed.

2006, May 9
3984-3987 A1297 Set of 4 5.50 2.25

Souvenir Sheet

3988 A1297 200fo Sheet of 3, #a-c 7.00 3.00

Margin of No. 3988 is embossed.

Composers — A1298

Designs: No. 3989, 90fo, George Enescu (1881-1955), and Romanian flag. No. 3990, 90fo, Béla Bartók (1881-1945) and Hungarian flag.

2006, June 8 ***Perf. 13x13¼***
3989-3990 A1298 Set of 2 2.25 .85

See Romania No. 4838.

Miskolc Intl. Opera Festival A1299

2006, June 15 ***Perf. 13¼x13***
3991 A1299 190fo multi 2.25 .85

Souvenir Sheet

Budapest Museum of Fine Arts, Cent. — A1300

No. 3992: a, Esterházy Madonna, by Raphael. b, Mary Magdalene, by El Greco. c, Equestrian statue, by Leonardo da Vinci, horiz. d, Three Fishing Boats, by Claude Monet, horiz.

2006, June 23 Litho. ***Perf. 12***
3992 A1300 200fo Sheet of 4, #a-d 9.00 4.00

The Four Virtues, Frescoes From Castle Museum, Esztergom — A1301

Iconostasis, Szentendre Cathedral — A1302

No. 3993: a, Bölcsesség and Mértékletesség. b, Allhatatosság and Igazságosság.

2006, June 23 *Perf. 13¼x13*
3993 A1301 52fo Horiz. pair, #a-b 1.50 .50

Souvenir Sheet
Perf. 12
3994 A1302 400fo +200fo multi 6.50 5.50

Stamp Day.

Emblem of Border Guard and Falcon A1303

2006, June 27 *Perf. 12*
3995 A1303 170fo multi 1.75 .80

European Swimming Championships, Budapest — A1304

Designs: 90fo, Synchronized swimmers and diver. 180fo, Swimmers and fish.

2006, July 27 *Perf. 13x13¼*
3996-3997 A1304 Set of 2 2.75 1.25

Contemporary Art — A1305

Designs: 120fo, Child with Model Aircraft, by László Fehér. 140fo, Circle Dance, sculpture by István Haraszty, vert. 160fo, Aequilibrium, tapestry by Zsuzsa Péreli, vert.

2006, July 27 *Perf. 13x13¼, 13¼x13*
3998-4000 A1305 Set of 3 4.50 2.00

Hungaroring Race Track, 20th Anniv. — A1306

2006, Aug. 3 *Perf. 13x13¼*
4001 A1306 75fo multi 1.00 .40

Souvenir Sheet

Budapest Zoo, 140th Anniv. — A1307

2006, Aug. 9 **Litho.** *Perf. 12*
4002 A1307 500fo multi 5.50 2.40

Souvenir Sheet

Consecration of Esztergom Basilica, 150th Anniv. — A1308

2006, Aug. 18
4003 A1308 500fo multi 5.50 2.40

Miniature Sheet

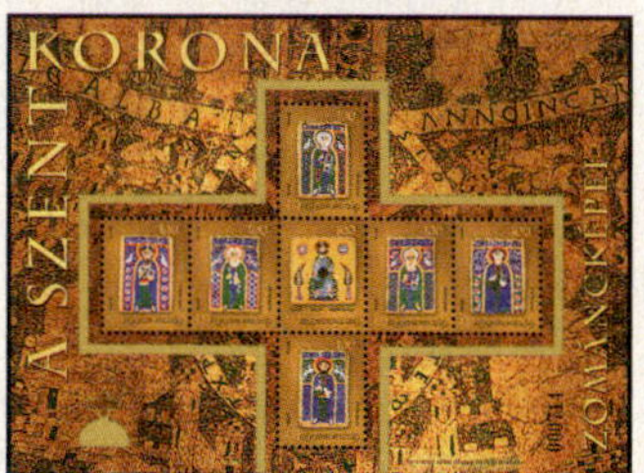

Enamel Paintings on St. Stephen's Crown — A1309

No. 4004: a, St. John (scsiohs inscription at top). b, St. Andrew (scsandreas) c, St. Peter (scspetrvs). d, God. e, St. Paul (scspavlus). f, St. Philip (scsphilipvs). g, St. Jacob (scsiacobvs).

Litho. (Foil Application on Sheet Margin)

2006, Aug. 18 *Perf. 12x11½*
4004 A1309 100fo Sheet of 7, #a-g 8.00 4.00

Souvenir Sheet

1956 Revolution, 50th Anniv. — A1310

2006, Oct. 20 **Litho.** *Perf. 13x12¾*
4005 A1310 500fo multi 5.50 3.00

No. 4005 has a die cut hole in the middle of the flag.

Christmas Type of 2002

52fo, Adoration of the Magi.

Litho. With Foil Application

2006, Oct. 27 *Perf. 12*
4006 A1157 52fo multi .60 .25

Souvenir Sheet

1956 Melbourne Summer Olympics, 50th Anniv. — A1311

2006, Nov. 13 **Litho.** *Perf. 12*
4007 A1311 500fo László Papp 5.25 2.60

Hungarian Red Cross, 125th Anniv. A1312

2006, Nov. 24 *Perf. 12¼x11½*
4008 A1312 100fo multi 1.10 .55

Launch of Sputnik 1 and Sputnik 2, 50th Anniv. — A1313

2007, Feb. 6 **Litho.** *Perf. 12*
4009 A1313 350fo multi 3.75 1.90

Easter — A1314

2007, Feb. 9 *Perf. 12¼x12¾*
4010 A1314 62fo multi .65 .30

Famous Men — A1315

Designs: 107fo, János Ferencsik (1907-84), conductor. 135fo, Count Lajos Batthyány (1807-49), prime minister.

2007, Feb. 9 *Perf. 12*
4011-4012 A1315 Set of 2 2.50 1.25

Rural Life — A1316

Designs: 62fo, Man with bottle and woman with glass. 95fo, Girl with flowers and birds. 242fo, Man cooking fish over fire.

2007, Feb. 9 *Perf. 12¼x11½*
4013-4015 A1316 Set of 3 4.25 2.10

Customs and Finance Guards, 140th Anniv. A1317

2007, Mar. 10 *Perf. 12*
4016 A1317 180fo multi 2.00 1.00

Diets A1318

Designs: 210fo, Prince John Sigismund of Transylvania and Torda Church. 230fo, Prince Ferenc Rákóczi II and Marosvásárhely Castle

2007, Apr. 10 *Perf. 13¼x12½*
4017-4018 A1318 Set of 2 5.00 2.50

Diet of Torda, 450th anniv.; Diet of Marosvásárhely, 300th anniv.

Souvenir Sheet

The Boys of Paul Street, Novel by Ferenc Molnár (1878-1952) — A1319

No. 4019: a, 160fo, Molnar. b, 160fo, Posted handbill. c, 160fo+30fo, Boy in red shirt. d, 160fo+30fo, Boy in green shirt.

2007, Apr. 10 *Perf. 12*
4019 A1319 Sheet of 4, #a-d 8.00 8.00

A1320

A1321

A1322

Rendeljen Személyes bélyeget a Magyar Postától! Telefon: 06 40 46 46 46 BELFÖLD MAGYARORSZÁG

A1323

A1324

A1325

A1326

A1327

A1328

A1329

A1330

A1331

Graduation — A1332

No. 4020: a, Two hot air balloons. b, Graduate pulled by balloon, arch of books, diploma, hot air balloon. c, Graduation cap, hot air balloon, graduate. d, Three graduates, hot air balloon. e, Hot air balloon, graduate pulled by balloon, two graduates standing on books. f, Graduate on path, graduate holding portfolio. g, Diploma, two graduates standing on books. h, Diploma on path, bottom half of graduate at upper right. i, Three graduates on path. j, Arch of books, diploma, inkwell, quill pen, path. k, Two graduates on path. l, Inkwell, quill pen, three books. m, Graduate with magnifying glass, path. n, Graduate with magnifying glass. o, Diploma on path, legs of two graduates, path. p, Graduate carrying portfolio, diploma on arch of books. q, Arch of books, diploma, inkwell, quill pen. r, Arch of books, diploma. s, Inkwell, quill pen, graduate. t, Diploma on path, graduate at right, legs of graduate at top.

2007, Apr. 16 — Litho. — *Perf. 11¼*

4020 A1320 (62fo) Sheet of 20, #a-t, + 20 labels — 20.00 14.00
4021 Block of 8 + 8 labels — 8.00 8.00
- a. A1321 (62fo) multi + label — 1.00 .50
- b. A1322 (62fo) multi + label — 1.00 .50
- c. A1323 (62fo) multi + label — 1.00 .50
- d. A1324 (62fo) multi + label — 1.00 .50
- e. A1325 (62fo) multi + label — 1.00 .50
- f. A1326 (62fo) multi + label — 1.00 .50
- g. A1327 (62fo) multi + label — 1.00 .50
- h. A1328 (62fo) multi + label — 1.00 .50
- Sheet, 3 each #4021a-4021d, 2 each #4021e-4021h, + 20 labels — 20.00 20.00

4022 Pair + 2 labels — 2.00 2.00
- a. A1329 (62fo) multi + label — 1.00 .50
- b. A1330 (62fo) multi + label — 1.00 .50
- Sheet, 10 each #4022a-4022b, + 20 labels — 20.00 20.00

4023 Pair + 2 labels — 2.10 2.10
- a. A1331 (95fo) multi + label — 1.00 .50
- b. A1332 (95fo) multi + label — 1.00 .50
- Sheet, 10 each #4023a-4023b, + 20 labels — 21.00 21.00

Labels on Nos. 4020-4023 could be personalized for an additional fee.

Stamp Day
A1333

Designs: 62fo, St. Elizabeth of Hungary (1207-31) caring for the sick. 95fo, St. Elizabeth caring for poor.
500fo+200fo, St. Emeric (1007-31) praying.

2007, Apr. 27 — Litho. — *Perf. 13*

4024-4025 A1333 Set of 2 — 1.75 .85

Souvenir Sheet

Perf. 13x12¾

4026 A1333 500fo +200fo multi — 8.00 8.00

No. 4026 contains one 40x32mm stamp.

Television Broadcasting in Hungary, 50th Anniv. — A1334

2007, May 9 — *Perf. 13x13½*

4027 A1334 160fo multi — 1.75 .85

Souvenir Sheet

Europa — A1335

No. 4028: a, Scouts in canoe. b, Scouts and Brownsea Island commemorative stone.

2007, May 9 — *Perf. 12*

4028 A1335 210fo Sheet, 2 each #a-b — 9.25 4.50

Scouting, cent.

Dogs
A1336

Designs: 62fo, Komondor. 150fo, Transylvanian hound. 180fo, Kuvasz. 240fo, Pumis. 600fo, Hungarian vizsla.

2007, May 9 — *Perf. 13x13½*

4029-4032 A1336 Set of 4 — 7.00 3.50

Souvenir Sheet

Perf. 12

4033 A1336 600fo multi — 6.50 3.25

11th Intl. Cave Rescue Conference, Aggtelek-Jósvafo — A1337

2007, May 15 — Litho. — *Perf. 12*

4034 A1337 200fo multi — 2.25 1.10

Academy of Music Building, Budapest, Cent. — A1338

2007, May 18

4035 A1338 250fo multi — 2.75 1.40

Souvenir Sheet

National Gallery, 50th Anniv. — A1339

No. 4036: a, The Mystical Betrothal of St. Catherine, c. 1490. b, View of Rome, by Károly Markó the Elder, 1835. c, October, by Károly Ferenczy, 1903. d, Picnic in May, by Pál Szinyei Merse, 1873, horiz.

2007, May 23 — *Perf. 12*

4036 A1339 150fo Sheet of 4, #a-d — 6.50 3.25

Grapes and Wine Producing Areas Type of 1990

Designs: 95fo, Cirfandli grapes, Pecs region. 140fo, Ezerfürtü grapes, Etyek-Buda region. 260fo, Zenit grapes, Tolna region.

2007, May 25 — *Perf. 12½x13¼*

4037-4039 A902 Set of 3 — 5.50 2.75

Emblem of Border Guard and German Shepherd
A1340

2007, June 27 — Litho. — *Perf. 12*

4040 A1340 107fo multi — 1.25 .60

Personalized Stamp Types of 2004-05 Redrawn With "Belföld" Instead of Denomination and

Pens — A1341

A1342

A1343

A1344

A1345

A1346 A1347

A1348

A1349

A1350

Doorknockers
A1351

Chain Bridge, Budapest — A1352

Parliament, Budapest — A1353

Buda Castle, Budapest — A1354

Heroes Square, Budapest — A1355

Fisherman's Bastion, Budapest — A1356

No. 4043: a, Quill pen, open inkwell, ink spots, green background. b, Brown fountain pen with point on flourish of "M," brown background. c, Open and closed black and gold fountain pens, green background. d, Black and gold fountain pen with point on flourish of "M," green background. e, Ball-point pen, pen point at LL, pink background. f, Cap of black and gold pen, green background. g, Brown fountain head with flat circular tip on nib, open inkwell, brown background. h, Black and gold pen with pen point at UL, pink background. i, Black and gold fountain pen, pen point at LR, green background. j, Ball-point pen, pen point at LR, pink background. k, Fountain pen and quill, green background. l, Fountain pen, pen point at LR, brown background. m, Brown fountain pen, inkwell, brown background. n, Inkwell, quill, fountain pen, ink spots, green background. o, Plunger and clip of black ball-point pen, pink background. p, Quills, quill pen, ink spots, green background. q, Closed inkwell, pen nib, quill, ink spots, green background. r, Two fountain pens, brown background. s, Black and gold fountain pen and cap, green background. t, Tip of ball-point pen with point on flourish of "M," pink background.

2007 Litho. *Perf. 11¼*

4041 Sheet of 20 + 20 labels 20.00 20.00
a. A1220 (62fo) multi + label 1.00 .80
b. A1221 (62fo) multi + label 1.00 .80
c. A1222 (62fo) multi + label 1.00 .80
d. A1223 (62fo) multi + label 1.00 .80
e. A1224 (62fo) multi + label 1.00 .80
f. A1225 (62fo) multi + label 1.00 .80
4042 Block or horiz. strip of 4 + 4 labels 4.00 4.00
a. A1288 (62fo) multi + label 1.00 .80
b. A1289 (62fo) multi + label 1.00 .80
c. A1290 (62fo) multi + label 1.00 .80
d. A1291 (62fo) multi + label 1.00 .80
Sheet of 20, 7 each #4042a, 4042d, 3 each #4042b, 4042c, + 20 labels 20.00 20.00
4043 A1341 Sheet of 20 + 20 labels 20.00 20.00
a.-t. (62fo) Any single + label 1.00 .80
4044 Block of 10 + 10 labels 10.00 10.00
a. A1342 (62fo) multi + label 1.00 .80
b. A1343 (62fo) multi + label 1.00 .80
c. A1344 (62fo) multi + label 1.00 .80
d. A1345 (62fo) multi + label 1.00 .80
e. A1346 (62fo) multi + label 1.00 .80
f. A1347 (62fo) multi + label 1.00 .80
g. A1348 (62fo) multi + label 1.00 .80
h. A1349 (62fo) multi + label 1.00 .80
i. A1350 (62fo) multi + label 1.00 .80
j. A1351 (62fo) multi + label 1.00 .80
Sheet of 20, 2 each #4044a-4044j, + 20 labels 20.00 20.00
4045 Vert. strip of 5 + 5 labels 5.00 5.00
a. A1352 (62fo) multi + label 1.00 .80
b. A1353 (62fo) multi + label 1.00 .80
c. A1354 (62fo) multi + label 1.00 .80
d. A1355 (62fo) multi + label 1.00 .80
e. A1356 (62fo) multi + label 1.00 .80
Sheet of 20, 4 each #4045a-4045e, + 20 labels 20.00 20.00
Nos. 4041-4045 (5) 59.00 59.00

Issued: No. 4041, 9/27; others, 7/16.

No. 4041 contains 4 each Nos. 4041a, 4041e, 2 each Nos. 4041d, 4041f, 5 No. 4041b and 3 No. 4041c. Background colors on some stamps differ slightly. Labels could be personalized for an additional fee.

Zoltán Kodály (1882-1967), Composer — A1357

2007, July 16 *Perf. 13x13¼*
4046 A1357 200fo multi 2.25 1.10

Hungarian University Sports Federation, Cent. — A1358

2007, July 30 *Perf. 11½x12*
4047 A1358 360fo multi 4.00 2.00

Dolomite Flax — A1359 Pasque Flower — A1360

Booklet Stamps

Serpentine Die Cut 10¾x10½

2007, Aug. 1 Self-Adhesive
4048 A1359 (230fo) multi 2.50 1.25
a. Booklet pane of 4 + 4 etiquettes 10.00
4049 A1360 (260fo) multi 3.00 1.50
a. Booklet pane of 4 + 4 etiquettes 12.00

Souvenir Sheet

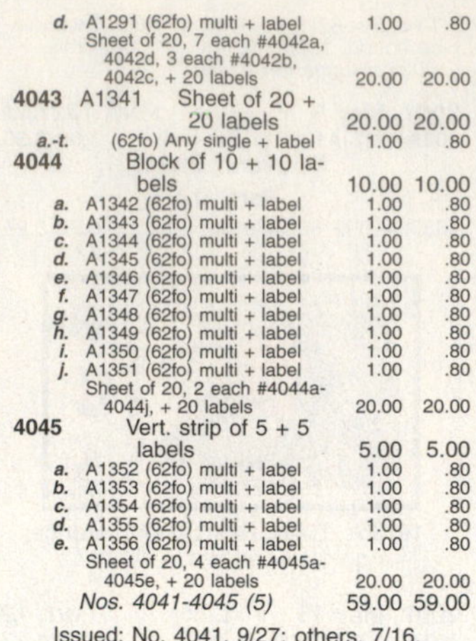

Enamel Paintings on St. Stephen's Crown — A1361

No. 4050: a, St. Cosmas (light blue robe). b, St. George (holding spear and shield). c, Archangel Michael (holding staff).

Litho. (Litho. With Foil Application in Sheet Margin)

2007, Aug. 17 *Perf. 12x11½*
4050 A1361 300fo Sheet of 3, #a-c 10.00 5.00

János Selye (1907-82), Stress Researcher — A1362

Perf. 13¼x12¾

2007, Aug. 23 Litho.
4051 A1362 400fo multi 4.50 2.25

Second World Stress Conference, Budapest.

World Science Forum Type of 2005 Redrawn

2007, Sept. 27 *Perf. 13x13¼*
4052 A1264 230fo multi 2.60 1.25

Christmas — A1363

No. 4053: a, Annunciation. b, Holy Family and Shepherds. c, Adoration of the Magi.

2007, Oct. 19 *Perf. 12*
4053 A1363 62fo Horiz. strip of 3, #a-c 2.50 1.25

Compass and Map Type of 2005 Redrawn With "Belföld" Instead of Denomination

No. 4054: a, Compass at right, map of western Hungary. b, Compass at left, map of eastern Hungary.

2008, Feb. 8 Litho. *Perf. 11¼*
4054 A1246 (70fo) Pair, #a-b, + 2 labels 1.60 1.60
Sheet of 18 #4054a, 17 #4054b, + 35 labels 28.00 —

Labels could be personalized.

Easter
A1364

2008, Feb. 27 *Perf. 12*
4055 A1364 70fo multi .80 .40

King Matthias, 550th Anniv. of Election — A1365

King Matthias, arms and: 70fo, Fountain. 100fo, Castle and horses. 600fo+200fo, King and Queen on throne.

2008, Mar. 13
4056-4057 A1365 Set of 2 2.10 1.10

Souvenir Sheet

4058 A1365 600fo +200fo multi 10.00 10.00

Stamp Day. No. 4058 contains one 40x30mm stamp.

General Károly Knezich (1808-49)
A1366

2008, Mar. 14 *Perf. 13x12½*
4059 A1366 380fo multi 4.75 2.40

Miniature Sheet

Transportation — A1367

No. 4060: a, 150fo, Automobile. b, 150fo, Ship. c, 150fo+30fo, Train. d, 150fo+30fo, Airplane.

2008, Mar. 14 *Perf. 12*
4060 A1367 Sheet of 4, #a-d 8.25 8.25

Romany Dancer and Musicians
A1368

German Dancer and Accordion
A1369

2008 *Perf. 13½x13*
4061 A1368 260fo multi 3.25 1.60
4062 A1369 275fo multi 3.50 1.75

Hungarian ethnic minorities. Issued: 260fo, 4/8; 275fo, 5/9.

2008 Summer Olympics, Beijing
A1370

Designs: 70fo, Water polo. 100fo, Wrestling. 170fo, Fencing.

2008, Apr. 16 *Perf. 13x13¼*
4063-4065 A1370 Set of 3 4.25 2.10

Miniature Sheet

Europa — A1371

No. 4066: a, 100fo, Letter in envelope, capital "A." b, 230fo, Pen nib.

2008, May 9 ***Perf. 12***
4066 A1371 Sheet, 2 each #a-b 8.25 4.25

Stamps on bottom row are tete-beche in relation to the top row.

Indigenous Animals A1372

Designs: 145fo, Hungarian giant rabbit. 150fo, Hungarian domestic goat. 170fo, Cikta sheep. 310fo, Hungarian donkey.
600fo, Water buffalo.

2008, May 9
4067-4070 A1372 Set of 4 9.50 4.75

Souvenir Sheet

4071 A1372 600fo multi 7.50 3.75

National Parks Type of 1998

Design: Orség National Park.

2008, May 16
4072 A1073 220fo multi 3.00 1.50

UNESCO World Heritage Sites Type of 2002

Design: Tokaj Wine Region.

2008, May 16
4073 A1153 290fo multi 3.75 1.90

UEFA Euro 2008 Soccer Championships, Austria and Switzerland A1373

2008, May 16 ***Perf. 13½x13***
4074 A1373 250fo multi 3.25 1.60

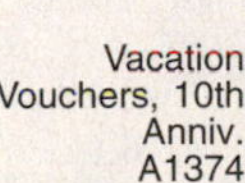
Vacation Vouchers, 10th Anniv. A1374

2008, May 20 ***Perf. 12x11½***
4075 A1374 70fo multi .90 .45

A1375

A1376

A1377

A1378

A1379

Philavillage A1380

2008 ***Perf. 12, 13¼x13 (#4077)***
4076 A1375 100fo multi 1.40 .70
4077 A1376 100fo multi 1.40 .70
4078 A1377 100fo multi 1.40 .70
4079 A1378 100fo multi 1.40 .70
4080 A1379 100fo multi 1.40 .70
4081 A1380 100fo multi 1.40 .70
Nos. 4076-4081 (6) 8.40 4.20

Issued: Nos. 4076-4077, 6/6; Nos. 4078-4079, 6/20; Nos. 4080-4081, 7/10. Stamps also served as game pieces for Philavillage board game.

A1381

A1382

A1383

A1384

A1385

Philavillage A1386

2008 **Litho.** ***Perf. 12***
4082 A1381 100fo multi 1.25 .60
4083 A1382 100fo multi 1.25 .60

Perf. 13x13¼, 13¼x13 (#4086)

4084 A1383 100fo multi 1.10 .55
4085 A1384 100fo multi 1.10 .55
4086 A1385 100fo multi .95 .50
4087 A1386 100fo multi .95 .50
Nos. 4082-4087 (6) 6.60 3.30

Issued: Nos. 4082-4083, 9/2; Nos. 4084-4085, 10/9; Nos. 4086-4087, 11/5. Stamps also served as game pieces for Philavillage board game.

Hungarian Illuminated Chronicle, 650th Anniv. — A1387

Litho. & Embossed With Foil Application

2008, June 20 ***Perf. 12***
4088 A1387 400fo multi 5.50 2.75

Souvenir Sheet

Debrecen and Veszprém Zoos, 50th Anniv. — A1388

No. 4089: a, Giraffes, cranes, hippopotamus, camel (Debrecen). b, Camel, crane, lion, zebra, rhinoceros, flamingo (Veszprém).

2008, Aug. 14 **Litho.** ***Perf. 12***
4089 A1388 260fo Sheet of 2, #a-b 6.50 3.25

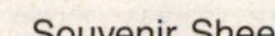
Souvenir Sheet

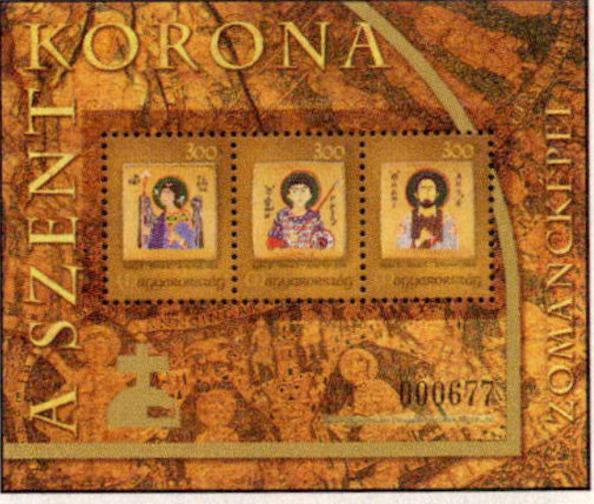

Enamel Paintings on St. Stephen's Crown — A1389

No. 4090: a, Archangel Gabriel (holding staff). b, St. Demeter (with shield and spear). c, St. Damian (with beard).

Litho. (Litho. With Foil Application in Sheet Margin)

2008, Aug. 19 ***Perf. 12x11½***
4090 A1389 300fo Sheet of 3, #a-c 11.50 5.75

Miklós Zrinyi (1508-66), Military Leader A1390

2008, Sept. 5 **Litho.** ***Perf. 13x13¼***
4091 A1390 190fo multi 2.25 1.10

Flowers Types of 2006 Redrawn With "Belföld" Instead of Denomination

2008, Sept. 2 **Litho.** ***Perf. 11¼***
4092 Vert. strip of 5 + 5 labels 4.25 4.25
a. A1278 (70fo) multi + label .85 .85
b. A1279 (70fo) multi + label .85 .85
c. A1280 (70fo) multi + label .85 .85
d. A1281 (70fo) multi + label .85 .85
e. A1282 (70fo) multi + label .85 .85
Sheet, 4 each #4092a-4092e, + 20 labels 17.00 —

Background colors of stamps in full sheets varies. Labels could be personalized for an additional fee.

Archangel Gabriel, Sculpture by György Zala (1858-1937) A1391

2008, Sept. 25 **Litho.** ***Perf. 13¼x13***
4093 A1391 200fo multi 2.25 1.10

Synagogues A1392

Designs: 200fo, Synagogue, Szeged. 250fo, Synagogue of the Jewish Theological Seminary, Budapest.

2008, Sept. 25 ***Perf. 12½x13¼***
4094-4095 A1392 Set of 2 5.00 2.50

Cat — A1393

Bear — A1394

Rabbit — A1395

Lion — A1396

Giraffe — A1397

2008, Oct. 9 ***Perf. 11¼***
4096 Vert. strip of 5 + 5 labels 3.75 3.75
a. A1393 (70fo) multi .75 .40
b. A1394 (70fo) multi .75 .40
c. A1395 (70fo) multi .75 .40
d. A1396 (70fo) multi .75 .40
e. A1397 (70fo) multi .75 .40
Sheet, 4 each #4096a-4096e, + 20 labels 15.00 15.00

Labels on No. 4096 could be personalized for an additional fee.

Souvenir Sheet

Ferenc Puskás (1927-2006), Player on 1952 Hungarian Olympic Soccer Team — A1398

2008, Oct. 28 ***Perf. 12***
4097 A1398 600fo multi 6.00 3.00

Christmas A1399

Art by György Konecsni (1908-70): 70fo, Nativity. 100fo, Adoration of the Magi.

2008, Oct. 28 ***Perf. 12¼x11½***
4098-4099 A1399 Set of 2 1.75 .85

Edward Teller (1908-2003), Nuclear Physicist — A1400

2008, Nov. 3 ***Perf. 13x13¼***
4100 A1400 250fo multi 2.40 1.25

Ludovika Academy, 200th Anniv. — A1401

2008, Nov. 5 ***Perf. 13¼x13***
4101 A1401 300fo multi 3.00 1.50

Crocus — A1402

Scilla — A1403

2009, Feb. 24 **Litho.** ***Perf. 11½x12***
4102 A1402 (75fo) multi .65 .30
4103 A1403 (100fo) multi .85 .40

Self-Adhesive

Serpentine Die Cut 10x10¼
4104 A1402 (75fo) multi .65 .30
Nos. 4102-4104 (3) 2.15 1.00

Easter — A1404

2009, Feb. 24 ***Perf. 12x12½***
4105 A1404 75fo multi .65 .30

Franciscan Order, 800th Anniv. — A1405

2009, Feb. 24 ***Perf. 12***
4106 A1405 100fo multi .85 .40

1909 Flights of Louis Blériot, Cent. — A1406

No. 4107: a, Flight across English Channel. b, Flight at Kisrákoson, Hungary.

2009, Mar. 12
4107 A1406 105fo Horiz. pair, #a-b, + central label 2.00 1.00

Souvenir Sheet

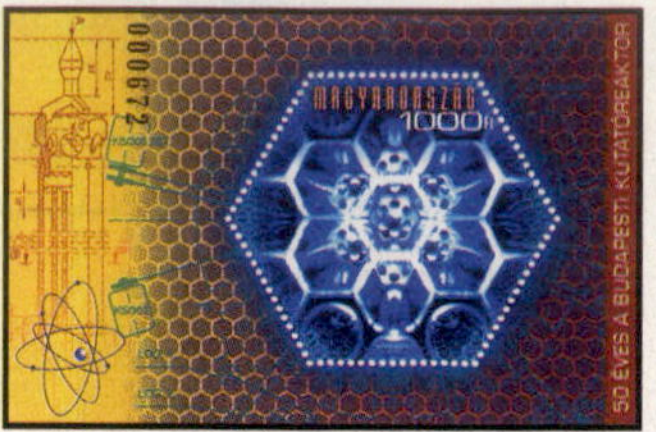
Budapest Research Reactor, 50th Anniv. — A1407

2009, Mar. 25 ***Perf. 11¼***
4108 A1407 1000fo multi 9.25 4.50

Preservation of Polar Regions and Glaciers — A1408

Designs: Nos. 4109, 4113, 75fo, Ursus maritimus and walruses. Nos. 4110, 4114, 130fo, Ovibos moschatus. Nos. 4111, 4115, 145fo, Uncia uncia. Nos. 4112, 4116, 275fo, Aptenodytes patagonicus.

No. 4117: a, Ursus maritimus. b, Alopex lagopus.

2009, Mar. 27 **Litho.** ***Perf. 12½x12***
4109-4112 A1408 Set of 4 5.75 3.00

Litho. & Silk-screened
4113-4116 A1408 Set of 4 5.75 3.00

Souvenir Sheet
4117 A1408 260fo Sheet of 2, #a-b 4.75 2.40

Portions of the designs of Nos. 4113-4117 that were applied by the silk-screen process have a silvery shine when viewed at an angle.

Joseph Haydn (1732-1809), Composer — A1409

2009, Apr. 2 **Litho.** ***Perf. 13x13¼***
4118 A1409 300fo red & black 2.75 1.40

Locomotives — A1410

Designs: 75fo, Mk48 Diesel locomotive. 100fo, C 50 Diesel locomotive. 125fo, MD 40 Diesel locomotive. 275fo, Morgó steam locomotive.

2009, Apr. 2 ***Perf. 13¼x13***
4119-4122 A1410 Set of 4 5.25 2.60

Souvenir Sheet

Ferenc Kazinczy (1759-1831), Writer — A1411

2009, Apr. 2 ***Perf. 13x12¾***
4123 A1411 600fo multi 5.50 2.75

Miniature Sheet

Elek Benedek (1859-1929), Fable Writer and Translator — A1412

No. 4124: a, 100fo, Arabian man, chicken and bees. b, 100fo, Three pigs. c, 100fo+50fo, Cat in king's robes. d, 100fo+50fo, Benedek.

2009, Apr. 2 ***Perf. 12x12½***
4124 A1412 Sheet of 4, #a-d 4.75 2.40

Miklós Radnóti (1909-44), Poet — A1413

2009, May 5 ***Perf. 13¼x13***
4125 A1413 280fo multi 2.60 1.25

Souvenir Sheet

Europa — A1414

No. 4126: a, 100fo, Galileo Galilei and Galileo space probe. b, 230fo, Planets.

2009, May 8 ***Perf. 12***
4126 A1414 Sheet, 2 each #a-b 6.25 6.25

Intl. Year of Astronomy.

John Calvin (1509-64), Theologian and Religious Reformer A1415

2009, May 22 ***Perf. 13¼x13***
4127 A1415 200fo multi 2.00 1.00

Donát Bánki (1859-1922), Inventor of Carburetor — A1416

2009, June 5

4128 A1416 300fo multi 3.00 1.50

Visegrád, 1000th Anniv. A1417

Designs: 75fo, Column and entableture. 100fo, Solomon Tower, octagonal column, carved head.

600fo+200fo, Summer Palace, fountain, monument, Madonna and Child.

2009, June 5 ***Perf. 13x13¼***

4129-4130 A1417 Set of 2 1.75 .85

Souvenir Sheet

4131 A1417 600fo +200fo multi 7.75 4.00

Stamp Day.

Discovery of Statue of Virgin Mary, Máriabesnyo, 250th Anniv. — A1418

2009, Aug. 14 ***Perf. 13¼x12***

4132 A1418 200fo multi 2.10 1.10

Bishopric of Pécs, 1000th Anniv. — A1419

2009, Aug. 19 ***Perf. 12***

4133 A1419 100fo multi 1.10 .55

Furniture Type of 1999

Design like No. 3791.

2009, Sept. 4 Litho. ***Perf. 12¼x11½***

4134 A1091 230fo blue green 2.40 1.25

Building, Pecs — A1420

Calvary Hill, Pecs — A1421

City Hall, Szechenyi Square, Pecs — A1422

Sts. Peter and Paul Cathedral, Pecs — A1423

Building, Pecs — A1424

Hungarian Academy of Sciences, Sculpture, Pecs — A1425

Synagogue, Pecs — A1426

Sts. Peter and Paul Cathedral, Pecs — A1427

Door Knocker and Handle, Pecs — A1428

Klimó Library, Pecs — A1429

National Theater, Pecs — A1430

Zsolnay Fountain, Pecs — A1431

Roof, Pecs — A1432

Street, Pecs — A1433

Necropolis, Pecs — A1434

Post Office Roof, Pecs — A1435

Mosque, Pecs — A1436

Barbican, Pecs — A1437

Mosque and Minaret, Pecs — A1438

Sculpture, Pecs — A1439

2009, Sept. 4 Litho. ***Perf. 11¼***

4135 Sheet of 20 + 20 labels 16.00 16.00

- *a.* A1420 (75fo) multi + label .80 .80
- *b.* A1421 (75fo) multi + label .80 .80
- *c.* A1422 (75fo) multi + label .80 .80
- *d.* A1423 (75fo) multi + label .80 .80
- *e.* A1424 (75fo) multi + label .80 .80
- *f.* A1425 (75fo) multi + label .80 .80
- *g.* A1426 (75fo) multi + label .80 .80
- *h.* A1427 (75fo) multi + label .80 .80
- *i.* A1428 (75fo) multi + label .80 .80
- *j.* A1429 (75fo) multi + label .80 .80
- *k.* A1430 (75fo) multi + label .80 .80
- *l.* A1431 (75fo) multi + label .80 .80
- *m.* A1432 (75fo) multi + label .80 .80
- *n.* A1433 (75fo) multi + label .80 .80
- *o.* A1434 (75fo) multi + label .80 .80
- *p.* A1435 (75fo) multi + label .80 .80
- *q.* A1436 (75fo) multi + label .80 .80
- *r.* A1437 (75fo) multi + label .80 .80
- *s.* A1438 (75fo) multi + label .80 .80
- *t.* A1439 (75fo) multi + label .80 .80

Labels could be personalized for an additional fee.

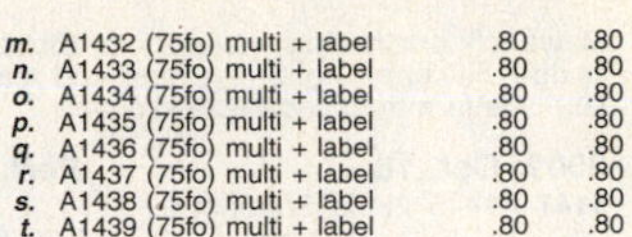

Opening of Border Between Austria and Hungary, 20th Anniv. A1440

2009, Sept. 10 Litho. ***Perf. 12***

4136 A1440 210fo multi 2.40 1.25

See Austria No. 2219, Germany No. 2548.

Rainbow, by Jòzsef Egry (1883-1951) — A1441

2009, Sept. 10 ***Perf. 13¼x12½***

4137 A1441 275fo multi 3.00 1.50

Louis Braille (1809-52), Educator of the Blind — A1442

Litho. & Embossed

2009, Oct. 15 ***Perf. 13¼x13***

4138 A1442 200fo multi 2.25 1.10

A1443

Christmas A1444

2009, Oct. 15 Litho. ***Perf. 12***

4139 A1443 75fo multi .80 .40

Perf. 12x11½

4140 A1444 100fo blue & yel org 1.10 .55

Miniature Sheet

Hungarian-Japanese Jubilee Year — A1445

No. 4141: a, Hungarian flask. b, Mount Fuji, horiz. c, Jar from Japanese tea service. d,

Matyo folk embroidery, Hungary. e, Elizabeth Bridge, Hungary, horiz. f, Crane and leaves fabric pattern from Japanese kimono.

2009, Oct. 16 *Perf. 12*

4141 A1445 260fo Sheet of 6, #a-f 17.00 8.50

See Japan No. 3167.

Ajka Crystal — A1446

2009, Oct. 28

4142 A1446 300fo multi 3.25 1.60

World Science Forum, Budapest A1447

2009, Nov. 5 *Perf. 13x13¼*

4143 A1447 100fo multi 1.10 .55

Filaclub Characters A1448

No. 4144: a, Bogi Fila. b, Levi Fila. c, Pötyi Fila.

2009, Dec. 4

4144 Horiz. strip of 3 .70 .35
a.-c. A1448 20fo Any single .25 .25

Promotion of children's philately.

Hassan Jakovali Mosque, Pecs — A1449

Calvary Hill, Pecs — A1450

National Theater, Pecs — A1451

Hungarian Academy of Sciences, Pecs — A1452

Barbican, Pecs — A1453

Synagogue, Pecs — A1454

Statue of St. Francis of Assisi, by György Bársony, Pecs — A1455

Interior of National Theater, Pecs — A1456

Statue of Janus Pannonius, by Sándor Rétfalvi, Pecs — A1457

County Hall, Pecs — A1458

Post Office, Pecs — A1459

St. Peter and Paul Cathedral, Pecs — A1460

St. Peter and Paul Cathedral, Pecs — A1461

Statue of the Holy Trinity, by György Kiss, Pecs — A1462

Mosque of Pasha Gazi Kasim, Pecs — A1463

University Gate, Pecs — A1464

Necropolis, Pecs — A1465

Zsolnay Fountain, Pecs — A1466

Klimó Library, Pecs — A1467

Statue of Tivadar Csontváry Kosztka, Zsolnay Vase, Pecs — A1468

Reformed Church, Pecs — A1469

Tettye Ruins, Pecs — A1470

Lutheran Church, Pecs — A1471

City Hall, Pecs — A1472

Symbol Sculpture, by Victor Vasarely, Pecs — A1473

2010, Jan. 10 **Litho.** *Perf. 12*

4145	Sheet of 25	20.00	10.00
a.	A1449 (75fo) multi	.80	.40
b.	A1450 (75fo) multi	.80	.40
c.	A1451 (75fo) multi	.80	.40
d.	A1452 (75fo) multi	.80	.40
e.	A1453 (75fo) multi	.80	.40
f.	A1454 (75fo) multi	.80	.40
g.	A1455 (75fo) multi	.80	.40
h.	A1456 (75fo) multi	.80	.40
i.	A1457 (75fo) multi	.80	.40
j.	A1458 (75fo) multi	.80	.40
k.	A1459 (75fo) multi	.80	.40
l.	A1460 (75fo) multi	.80	.40
m.	A1461 (75fo) multi	.80	.40
n.	A1462 (75fo) multi	.80	.40
o.	A1463 (75fo) multi	.80	.40
p.	A1464 (75fo) multi	.80	.40
q.	A1465 (75fo) multi	.80	.40
r.	A1466 (75fo) multi	.80	.40
s.	A1467 (75fo) multi	.80	.40
t.	A1468 (75fo) multi	.80	.40
u.	A1469 (75fo) multi	.80	.40
v.	A1470 (75fo) multi	.80	.40
w.	A1471 (75fo) multi	.80	.40
x.	A1472 (75fo) multi	.80	.40
y.	A1473 (75fo) multi	.80	.40

Pecs, 2010 European Cultural Capital.

2010 Winter Olympics, Vancouver A1474

2010, Feb. 5

4146 A1474 260fo multi 2.60 1.40

Izidor Kner (1860-1935), Publisher — A1475

2010, Feb. 5 *Perf. 12x13¼*

4147 A1475 295fo multi 3.00 1.50

Budapest Landmarks A1476

Designs: 295fo, Tympanum of Humanities Building, Loránd Eötvös University, Budapest. 400fo, Elisabeth Tower, Budapest.

2010, Feb. 19 *Perf. 12½x12*

4148-4149 A1476 Set of 2 7.00 3.50

Loránd Eötvös University, 375th anniv., Elisabeth Tower, cent.

Easter A1477

2010, Mar. 1

4150 A1477 80fo multi .85 .40

Republican Guard Regiment, 250th Anniv. A1478

2010, Mar. 1 *Perf. 13x13¼*
4151 A1478 320fo multi 3.25 1.60

Souvenir Sheet

Ferenc Erkel (1810-93), Composer — A1479

2010, Mar. 26 *Perf. 12*
4152 A1479 500fo multi 5.25 2.60

Stamp Day — A1480

Sites in Sopron: 80fo, Saint Ursula's Church, Church of the Virgin Mary. 105fo, Sculptur of the Virgin Mary, Gates of Faith, horiz.
500fo+200fo, Statue of the Holy Trinity.

2010, Mar. 26 *Perf. 12x12½, 12½x12*
4153-4154 A1480 Set of 2 1.90 .95

Souvenir Sheet

4155 A1480 500fo +200fo multi 7.25 3.50

Surtax on No. 4155 for Natl. Association of Hungarian Stamp Collectors.

Hungarian Documents on Paper, 700th Anniv. A1481

2010, Apr. 8 *Perf. 13x13¼*
4156 A1481 140fo multi 1.40 .70

Chronicle of the Ways of the Hungarians, by Gáspár Heltai (c. 1510-74), Writer — A1482

2010, Apr. 8 *Perf. 13¼x13*
4157 A1482 240fo multi 2.50 1.25

Expo 2010, Shanghai — A1483

Gömböc in various positions with stamps numbered in lower left: Nos. 4158a, 4158ae, 1. Nos. 4158b, 4158af, 2. Nos. 4158c, 4158ag, 3. Nos. 4158d, 4158ah, 2 squared (4). Nos. 4158e, 4158ai, 5. Nos. 4158f, 4158aj, 2*3 (6). Nos. 4158g, 4158ak, 7. Nos. 4158h, 4158al, 2 cubed (8). Nos. 4158i, 4158am, 3 squared (9). Nos. 4158j, 4158an, 2*5 (10). Nos. 4158k, 4158ao, 11. Nos. 4158l, 4158ap, 2 squared * 3 (12). Nos. 4158m, 4158aq, 13. Nos. 4158n, 4158ar, 2*7 (14). Nos. 4158o, 4158as, 3*5 (15). Nos. 4158p, 4158at, 2 to the fourth power (16). Nos. 4158q, 4158au, 17. Nos. 4158r, 4158av, 2*9 (18). Nos. 4158s, 4158aw, 19. Nos. 4158t, 4158ax, 2 squared * 5 (20). Nos. 4158u, 4158ay, 3*7 (21). Nos. 4158v, 4158az, 2*11 (22). Nos. 4158w, 4158ba, 23. Nos. 4158x, 4158bb, 2 cubed * 3 (24). Nos. 4158y, 4158bc, 5 squared (25). Nos. 4158z, 4158bd, 2*13 (26). Nos. 4158aa, 4158be, 3 cubed (27). Nos. 4158ab, 4158bf, 2 squared * 7 (28). Nos. 4158ac, 4158bg, 29. Nos. 4158ad, 4158bh, 2*3*5 (30).

2010, Apr. 30 **Litho.** *Perf. 12*
4158 Sheet of 30 30.00 30.00
a.-ad. A1483 100fo Any single 1.00 .50
ae.-bh. A1483 100fo Any booklet single, perf. 12 horiz. at top 1.00 .50
Complete booklet, #4158ae-4158bh 30.00

Miniature Sheet

The Tragedy of Man, Play by Imre Madách, 150th Anniv. — A1484

No. 4159 — Scenes from play: a, 105fo, Adam and Eve in Garden of Eden (denomination in white). b, 105fo, Men and women in London (denomination in black). c, 105fo+50fo, Men and women in Rome (denomination at bottom in white). d, 105fo+50fo, Woman in Prague (denomination at top in white).

2010, May 3 *Perf. 13x13¼*
4159 A1484 Sheet of 4, #a-d 4.75 2.40

Surtax for supporting youth stamp collecting.

2010 World Cup Soccer Championships, South Africa — A1485

2010, May 7 *Perf. 11*
4160 A1485 325fo multi 3.00 1.50

Intl. Year of Biodiversity A1486

Designs: 80fo, Spermophilus citellus. 110fo, Phyllomorpha lacinata. 215fo, Parus caeruleus. 350fo, Vipera ursinii rakosiensis.
500fo, Iris aphylla ssp. hungarica.

2010, May 7 *Perf. 12½x12*
4161-4164 A1486 Set of 4 7.00 3.50

Souvenir Sheet
Perf. 12

4165 A1486 500fo multi 4.75 2.40

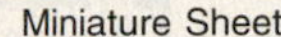

Miniature Sheet

Europa — A1487

No. 4166 — Vackor the Bear: a, Holding plant. b, Picking fruit.

2010, May 7 *Perf. 12*
4166 A1487 150fo Sheet, 2 each #a-b 5.50 2.75

No. 3417a Surcharged in Red

Method and Perf. As Before
2010, June 18
4167 A972 200fo on 19fo multi (R) 1.75 .90

Election of Prime Minister József Antall, 20th anniv.

Frédéric Chopin (1810-49), Composer — A1488

2010, June 18 **Litho.** *Perf. 12½*
4168 A1488 240fo multi 2.10 1.10

Self-Portrait of Miklós Barabás (1810-98) A1489

2010, June 18 *Perf. 12½x13¼*
4169 A1489 365fo multi 3.25 1.60

World Triathlon Championships, Budapest — A1490

2010, July 2 **Litho.** *Perf. 13x13¼*
4170 A1490 280fo multi 2.50 1.25

European Swimming League Championships, Budapest and Lake Balaton — A1491

2010, July 2 *Perf. 13¼x13*
4171 A1491 300fo multi 2.60 1.40

25th Hungarian Formula 1 Grand Prix — A1492

2010, July 30 *Perf. 12*
4172 A1492 230fo multi 2.10 1.10

Synagogues A1493

Designs: 110fo, Nagykoros Synagogue. 175fo, New Synagogue, Szolnok.

2010, Sept. 6 *Perf. 12½x13¼*
4173-4174 A1493 Set of 2 2.60 1.40

Hungarian Gymnastics Federation, 125th Anniv. — A1494

2010, Sept. 24 **Litho.** *Perf. 12x12½*
4175 A1494 140fo multi 1.40 .70

Christmas A1495

Designs: 80fo, Madonna and Child. 105fo, Angels making music, horiz.

Litho. With Foil Application
2010, Oct. 28 *Perf. 12*
4176-4177 A1495 Set of 2 1.90 .95

Embroidery — A1496

Designs: 80fo, Termeh embroidery designs, Yazd, Iran. 240fo, Jazgyian embroidery designs, Hungary.

2010, Nov. 10 Litho. ***Perf. 12½x12***
4178-4179 A1496 Set of 2 3.25 1.60

See Iran No. 3027.

Souvenir Sheet

Rudolf Kárpáti (1920-99), Fencing Gold Medalist at 1960 Summer Olympics — A1497

2010, Dec. 10 ***Perf. 12***
4180 A1497 500fo multi 4.75 2.40

Sándor Püski (1911-2009), Book Publisher A1498

2011, Feb. 4 Litho. ***Perf. 12x12½***
4181 A1498 270fo multi 2.75 1.40

Hungarian Presidency of the Council of the European Union — A1499

2011, Feb. 7 ***Perf. 12***
4182 A1499 90fo multi .90 .45

Visegrád Group, 20th Anniv. — A1500

2011, Feb. 15
4183 A1500 240fo multi 2.40 1.25

See Czech Republic No. 3490, Poland No. 4001, Slovakia No. 611.

Furniture Type of 1999

Design like No. 3738.

2011, Mar. 1 Litho. ***Perf. 11½x12¼***
4184 A1091 225fo green 2.40 1.25

Hungarian Golgotha, Textile Art by Erzsébet Szekeres A1501

2011, Mar. 1 ***Perf. 12***
4185 A1501 90fo multi .95 .45

Easter.

Tourist Attractions A1502

Designs: 160fo, Pauline Piarist Church, Sátoraljaújhely. 220fo, Royal Palace of Gödöllo.

2011, Mar. 4 ***Perf. 12½x12***
4186-4187 A1502 Set of 2 4.00 2.00

Vasas Sport Club, Cent. A1503

2011, Mar. 16
4188 A1503 315fo multi 3.50 1.75

Entertainers — A1504

Designs: 250fo, Rodolfo (Rezso Gács) (1911-87), magician. 340fo, Lajos Básti (1911-77), actor. 370fo, Manyi Kiss (1911-71), actress.

2011, Mar. 28 ***Perf. 12***
4189-4191 A1504 Set of 3 10.50 5.25

Stamp Day — A1505

Buildings in Balatonfüred: 90fo, Anna Grand Hotel. 115fo, Heart Hospital.
600fo+200fo, Vaszary Villa.

2011, Apr. 8 ***Perf. 12x12½***
4192-4193 A1505 Set of 2 2.25 1.10

Souvenir Sheet

4194 A1505 600fo +200fo multi 9.00 9.00

Balatonfüred, 800th anniv. Surtax on No. 4194 is for National Federation of Hungarian Philatelists.

Miniature Sheet

City Park, Budapest — A1506

No. 4195: a, 160fo, Buildings and animals of Budapest Zoo and Botanical Garden. b, 160fo, Vajdahunyad Castle. c, 160fo+50fo, Amusement Park. d, 160fo+50fo, Ice rink.

2011, Apr. 8 ***Perf. 12***
4195 A1506 Sheet of 4, #a-d 8.25 8.25

Surtax on Nos. 5195c-4195d for youth philately.

Souvenir Sheet

First Manned Space Flight, 50th Anniv. — A1507

2011, Apr. 12 ***Perf. 12x12½***
4196 A1507 600fo multi 6.50 3.25

Souvenir Sheet

Crown of St. Stephen — A1508

Litho. & Embossed With Foil Application

2011, Apr. 25 ***Perf. 13x12¾***
4197 A1508 2011fo multi 22.00 11.00
a. As #4197, with inscriptions added in sheet margin 15.00 7.50

Enactment of new Fundamental Law for Hungary. A souvenir sheet with red serial number and affixed glass crystals sold for 5000fo. A souvenir sheet like No. 4197a, with red serial number, affixed glass crystals and inscriptions of "Otéves Magyarsrszág Alaptörvénye" and "2016. Aprilis 25." was released in limited quantities in 2016 and sold for 5990fo.

Issued: No. 4197a, 4/25/16. Sheet margin of No. 4197a has black serial number and added inscriptions of "Otéves Magyarsrszág Alaptörvénye" and "2016. Aprilis 25."

World Theater Day Type of 2005 and Butterfly Types of 2006 Redrawn With "Belföld" Instead of Denomination

2011, Apr. 26 Litho. ***Perf. 11¼***
4198 A1245 (90fo) multi + label 1.00 .50
Sheet of 20 + 20 labels 20.00 20.00
4199 Pair + 2 labels 2.00 2.00
a. A1286 (90fo) multi + label 1.00 .50
b. A1287 (90fo) multi + label 1.00 .50
Sheet of 20, 10 each #4199a-4199b + 20 labels 20.00 20.00

Labels on Nos. 4198-4199 could be personalized for an extra fee.

Fruit and Blossoms A1509

Designs: 145fo, Apples. 310fo, Pears.

2011, May 6 ***Perf. 12***
4200-4201 A1509 Set of 2 5.00 2.50

See Nos. 4238-4239, 4322-4323.

Butterflies A1510

Designs: 80fo, Apatura metis. 105fo, Melanargia russiae. 255fo, Arctia caja. 370fo, Proserpinus proserpina.
600fo, Lycaena dispar.

2011, May 6 ***Perf. 13x13¼***
4202-4205 A1510 Set of 4 8.75 4.50

Souvenir Sheet

Perf. 13x12¾

4206 A1510 600fo multi 6.50 3.25

No. 4206 contains one 40x32mm stamp.

Miniature Sheet

Europa — A1511

No. 4207: a, Orség area forest in summer. b, Forest in Visegrád Mountains in winter.

2011, May 6 ***Perf. 12***
4207 A1511 200fo Sheet of 4, 2 each #a-b 8.75 4.50

Intl. Year of Forests.

Paintings A1512

Designs: 195fo, Small Girl with Geranium, by József Koszta (1861-1949). 345fo, Female Profile, Zorka, by József Rippi-Rónai (1861-1927).

2011, May 18 ***Perf. 13½x13***
4208-4209 A1512 Set of 2 6.00 3.00

Items in Hungarian Museums A1513

Various items from and building for: 280fo, Rákóczi Museum, Sárospatak. 385fo, Várpalota Museum of Chemistry.

2011, May 18 ***Perf. 12***
4210-4211 A1513 Set of 2 7.25 3.75

Pannon Philharmonic Orchestra, Pécs, 200th Anniv. — A1514

2011, June 2 **Litho.**
4212 A1514 330fo multi 3.75 1.90

Budapest Spas A1515

Spa and statue at: 240fo, Lukács Spa. 250fo, Gellért Spa.

2011, July 7 ***Perf. 12½x12***
4213-4214 A1515 Set of 2 5.25 2.60

István Bibó (1911-79), Politician A1516

2011, Aug. 5 ***Perf. 12x12½***
4215 A1516 345fo multi 3.75 1.90

Souvenir Sheet

Franz Liszt (1811-86), Composer — A1517

2011, Aug. 19 ***Perf. 12¾x13***
4216 A1517 600fo multi 5.75 3.00

Christmas A1518

Creche scenes and Catholic churches in: 90fo, Nagykarácsony. 115fo, Vörs.

Litho. With Foil Application

2011, Oct. 27 ***Perf. 12***
4217-4218 A1518 Set of 2 1.90 .95

Bell and Christmas Ornament — A1519

Christmas Ornament and Gift Box — A1520

2011, Oct. 27 **Litho.** ***Perf. 11¼***
4219 Pair + 2 labels 1.60 1.60
a. A1519 (90fo) multi + label .80 .40
b. A1520 (90fo) multi + label .80 .40
Sheet of 20, 10 each #4219a-4219b + 20 labels 16.00 16.00

Labels on Nos. 4219 could be personalized for an extra fee.

World Science Forum, Budapest A1521

2011, Nov. 3 **Litho.** ***Perf. 13x13¼***
4220 A1521 270fo multi 2.50 1.25

St. Martin of Tours (c. 316-97) A1522

2011, Nov. 11 ***Perf. 12***
4221 A1522 160fo multi 1.50 .75

Morning Sunshine, by Károly Ferenczy (1862-1917) A1523

2012, Feb. 8 ***Perf. 12***
4222 A1523 420fo multi 4.00 2.00

Greek Orthodox Diocese of Hajdúdorog, Cent. — A1524

2012, Feb. 17 ***Perf. 13¼x12½***
4223 A1524 380fo multi 3.50 1.75

Easter — A1525

2012, Feb. 24 ***Perf. 12¼x12¾***
4224 A1525 105fo multi .95 .50

University Centenaries — A1526

Buildings at: 180fo, Tivadar Puskás Technical School of Telecommunications, Budapest. 270fo, University of Debrecen, Debrecen.

2012, Mar. 22 ***Perf. 12½x12***
4225-4226 A1526 Set of 2 4.00 2.00

Budapest Baths A1527

Designs: 235fo, Király Baths. 260fo, Rudas Baths.

2012, Mar. 22
4227-4228 A1527 Set of 2 4.50 2.25

Performing Artists A1528

Designs: 395fo, Zoltán Várkonyi (1912-79), actor and director. 425fo, Katalin Karády (1910-90), actress and singer.

2012, Mar. 27
4229-4230 A1528 Set of 2 7.25 3.75

Launch of Masat 1, First Hungarian Satellite A1529

2012, Apr. 12 ***Perf. 13¼x13***
4231 A1529 310fo multi 3.00 1.50

Souvenir Sheet

Sinking of the Titanic, Cent. — A1530

No. 4232: a, Two aft smokestacks (denomination at UL). b, Two fore smokestacks (denomination at UR).

Litho. & Embossed

2012, Apr. 13 ***Perf. 12***
4232 A1530 800fo Sheet of 2, #a-b 15.00 7.50

Miniature Sheet

Hungarian Scout Association, Cent. — A1531

No. 4233: a, 105fo, Scouts, emblem of 1933 International Jamboree, Gödöllö. b, 105fo, Scout praying at cross, Scout sign. c, 105fo+50fo, Leaf, Scouts putting up tent. d, 105fo+50fo, Scout trefoil, Scouts bandaging boy's leg.

2012, Apr. 20 **Litho.** ***Perf. 13¼x13***
4233 A1531 Sheet of 4, #a-d 5.00 5.00

Surtax on Nos. 4233c-4233d for youth philately.

Protected Birds A1532

Designs: 80fo, Aquila heliaca. 140fo, Haliaeetus albicilla. 180fo, Falco vespertinus. 345fo, Falco cherrug.

2012, May 4 ***Perf. 13x13¼***
4234-4237 A1532 Set of 4 7.00 3.50

See No. 4246.

Fruit and Blossoms Type of 2011

Designs: 185fo, Sour cherries. 230fo, Rose apricots.

2012, May 9 ***Perf. 12***
4238-4239 A1509 Set of 2 3.50 1.75

Miniature Sheet

Europa — A1533

No. 4240: a, Peppers and grapes. b. Items in Library of Abbey of Pannonhalma.

2012, May 9 ***Perf. 12½x12***
4240 A1533 235fo Sheet of 4, 2 each #a-b 8.00 4.00

Raoul Wallenberg (1912-47), Swedish Diplomat Who Saved Jews in World War II — A1534

2012, May 10 ***Perf. 12***
4241 A1534 340fo multi 3.00 1.50

See Sweden No. 2693.

"Belföld" — A1535

2012, May 14 ***Perf. 11***
4242 A1535 (175fo) green + label 1.50 .75
Sheet of 28+28 labels 42.00 21.00

Labels could be personalized for an additional fee. The label shown is one of a number of generic labels produced.

Solidarity Between Generations — A1536

2012, May 17 ***Perf. 12½x12***
4243 A1536 200fo multi 1.75 .85

Souvenir Sheet

Smokehouses and Pottery — A1537

No. 4244: a, Felsoszönok, Hungary smokehouse at left, pitcher, two lidded jars. b, Filovci, Slovenia smokehouse at right, jug, colander.

2012, May 25
4244 A1537 260fo Sheet of 2, #a-b 4.50 2.25

See Slovenia No. 948.

2012 European Soccer Championships, Poland and Ukraine — A1538

2012, June 8 ***Perf. 12***
4245 A1538 270fo multi 2.40 1.25

Protected Birds Type of 2012

Souvenir Sheet

2012, June 15 ***Perf. 12½x12***
4246 A1532 500fo Buteo buteo 4.25 2.10

Battle of Rozgony, 700th Anniv. — A1539

2012, June 15 ***Perf. 12x12½***
4247 A1539 370fo multi 3.25 1.60

2012 Summer Olympics, London — A1540

Designs: 315fo, Swimming. 360fo, Kayaking.

2012, June 22 ***Perf. 12***
4248-4249 A1540 Set of 2 5.75 3.00

A1541

Stamp Day — A1542

Designs: 80fo, Kalocsa embroidery. 130fo, Peppers, Paprika Museum, Kaposi. 600fo+200fo, Chalice.

2012, July 6 ***Perf. 12***
4250-4251 A1541 Set of 2 1.90 .95

Souvenir Sheet

Perf. 12¾x13

4252 A1542 600fo +200fo multi 6.75 3.50

Surtax on No. 4252 is for National Federation of Hungarian Philatelists.

Miniature Sheet

Famous Men — A1543

No. 4253: a, Istvan Orkény (1912-79), writer. b, Sir Georg Solti (1912-97), conductor. c, Géza Ottlik (1912-90), writer. d, János Szentágothai (1912-94), anatomist.

2012, July 6 ***Perf. 12x12½***
4253 A1543 105fo Sheet of 4, #a-d 3.75 1.90

Synagogues A1544

Synagogue in: 300fo, Baja. 400fo, Kiskunhalas.

2012, Sept. 4 ***Perf. 12***
4254-4255 A1544 Set of 2 6.50 3.25

Sixth World Congress of Finno-Ugric People, Siófók — A1545

2012, Sept. 5 ***Perf. 12½x12***
4256 A1545 290fo multi 2.75 1.40

Miniature Sheet

Parliament Building, 110th Anniv. — A1546

No. 4257: a, Statues, panel in tan at right. b, Speaker's dais and coats of arms, panel in brown at bottom. c, Speaker's chair, panel in gray green at right. d, Decorative arches, panel in gray green at bottom. e, Wall sculpture of horse and rider, panel in tan at bottom. f, Chamber, panel in gray at right. g, Coat of arms, panel in beige at right. h, Chamber, panel in brown at bottom.

2012, Oct. 8 ***Perf. 13¼***
4257 A1546 Sheet of 8 + central label 14.50 7.25
a.-h. 200fo Any single 1.75 .90

An embossed sheet with a lacquered finish was printed in a limited edition and sold for 3200fo.

Christmas A1547

Litho. With Foil Application

2012, Oct. 26 ***Perf. 12***
4258 A1547 130fo multi 1.25 .60

No. 4258 was printed in sheets of 4.

Souvenir Sheet

Benedictine Abey, Tihany — A1548

2012, Oct. 26 Litho. ***Perf. 12x12½***
4259 A1548 600fo multi 5.50 2.75

Souvenir Sheet

Miklos Prison, Kosice, Slovakia — A1549

2013, Jan. 25 ***Perf. 12***
4260 A1549 600fo multi 5.50 2.75

Kosice, 2013 European Capital of Culture.

József Galamb (1881-1955), Mechanical Engineer, and Ford Model Ts — A1550

2013, Feb. 5
4261 A1550 145fo multi 1.40 .70

Dr. Miklós Ujvárosi (1913-81), Botanist A1551

2013, Feb. 5 ***Perf. 12½x12***
4262 A1551 395fo multi 3.75 1.90

Composers A1552

Designs: 165fo, Richard Wagner (1813-83). 325fo, Giuseppe Verdi (1813-1901).

2013, Mar. 5 ***Perf. 13x13¼***
4263-4264 A1552 Set of 2 4.25 2.10

A1553

A1554

A1555

A1556

A1557

A1558

A1559

A1560

A1561

A1562

A1563

A1564

A1565

A1566

2013, Mar. 5 Litho. *Perf. 12¼x12¾*

4265	Horiz. pair	1.50	.75
a.	A1553 85fo multi	.75	.35
b.	A1554 85fo multi	.75	.35
4266	Horiz. pair	1.90	1.00
a.	A1555 110fo multi	.95	.50
b.	A1556 110fo multi	.95	.50
4267	Sheet of 12	9.00	4.25
a.	A1553 85fo multi	.75	.35
b.	A1554 85fo multi	.75	.35
c.	A1557 85fo multi	.75	.35
d.	A1558 85fo multi	.75	.35
e.	A1559 85fo multi	.75	.35
f.	A1560 85fo multi	.75	.35
g.	A1561 85fo multi	.75	.35
h.	A1562 85fo multi	.75	.35
i.	A1563 85fo multi	.75	.35
j.	A1564 85fo multi	.75	.35
k.	A1565 85fo multi	.75	.35
l.	A1566 85fo multi	.75	.35

Easter. Nos. 4265a and 4265b have lithographed dots in rows with the red dots on the white portions of the eggs near the side being large. Nos. 4267a and 4267b were printed with stochastic lithography, with red dots that are smaller, and appearing to be randomly placed rather than in rows.

Tourist Attractions A1567

Designs: 85fo, Szeged Cathedral. 195fo, Water Tower, Margaret Island, vert. 325fo, Springhouse, Orfu, vert.

2013 *Perf. 12½x12, 12x12½*
4268-4270 A1567 Set of 3 5.50 2.75

Issued: 85fo, 325fo, 5/3; 195fo, 3/5.

European Judo Championships, Budapest — A1568

2013, Apr. 2 *Perf. 13x13¼*
4271 A1568 360fo multi 3.25 1.60

Széchenyi Thermal Baths A1569

Buildings, baths and: 145fo, Statue of nude woman. 165fo, Mosaic of nude woman.

2013, Apr. 2 *Perf. 12½x12*
4272-4273 A1569 Set of 2 2.75 1.40

Mammals A1570

Designs: 110fo, Mustela erminea. 140fo, Sorex minutus. 230fo, Lynx lynx. 390fo, Myotis myotis.
600fo, Erinaceus roumanicus.

2013, Apr. 9 Litho. *Perf. 12*
4274-4277 A1570 Set of 4 7.75 4.00

Souvenir Sheet

4278 A1570 600fo multi 5.50 2.75

Stamp Day — A1571

Attractions in Székesfehérvár: 85fo, Bishops Fountain, Statue of St. Astrik of Pannonhalma. 110fo, City Hall, Statue of Justice, horiz. 500fo+200fo, Cistercian Church.

2013, Apr. 26 *Perf. 13¼x13, 13x13¼*
4279-4280 A1571 Set of 2 1.75 .85

Souvenir Sheet

Perf. 12¾x13

4281 A1571 500fo +200fo multi 6.25 3.25

No. 4281 contains one 32x40mm stamp. Surtax on No. 4281 is for National Federation of Hungarian Philatelists.

Miniature Sheet

Europa — A1572

No. 4282: a, 1914 Csonka parcel delivery van. b, Modern Ford postal van.

2013, May 3 *Perf. 13x13¼*
4282 A1572 235fo Sheet of 4, 2 each #a-b 8.50 4.25

Items in Hungarian Museums A1573

Designs: 250fo, Calcite crystals, Calcite Crystal Museum, Fertorákos. 400fo, Lamps, Lamp Museum, Zsámbék.

2013, May 3
4283-4284 A1573 Set of 2 5.75 3.00

Nos. 4283-4284 were printed in sheets of 4. The designs, when viewed through red and blue glasses, become three-dimensional.

Locomotives — A1574

Designs: 195fo, V43 Szili electric locomotive. 445fo, M61 Nohab Diesel-electric locomotive.

2013, June 5 *Perf. 12*
4285-4286 A1574 Set of 2 6.00 3.00

Souvenir Sheet

Fabric Designs Depicting Peacocks — A1575

No. 4287 — Peacock from: a, Hungarian embroidered pillow cover (white background). b, Azeri woven horse blanket (tan background).

2013, June 15 *Perf. 13x13¼*
4287 A1575 300fo Sheet of 2, #a-b 5.50 2.75

See Azerbaijan No. 1028.

Miniature Sheet

Sándor Weöres (1913-89), Writer — A1576

No. 4288: a, 110fo, Writer. b, 110fo, Frog playing flute. c, 110fo+50fo, Upside-down girl. d, 110fo+50fo, Castle.

2013, June 20 *Perf. 12x12½*
4288 A1576 Sheet of 4, #a-d 5.00 5.00

Surtax for support of youth philately.

World Fencing Championships, Budapest — A1577

2013, July 4 *Perf. 11*
4289 A1577 300fo multi + label 2.75 1.40

Hungarian Skiing Association, Cent. — A1578

Serpentine Die Cut 10x10¼
2013, July 15 Self-Adhesive
4290 A1578 500fo multi 4.50 2.25

World Wrestling Championships, Budapest — A1579

2013, Aug. 2 *Perf. 13¼x12½*
4291 A1579 360fo multi 3.25 1.60

Géza Gárdonyi (1863-1922), Writer A1580

2013, Aug. 14 *Perf. 12½x13¼*
4292 A1580 425fo multi 3.75 1.90

Souvenir Sheet

Saints — A1581

No. 4293 — Paintings from Cathedral of St. Martin, Spisska Kapitula, Slovakia: a, St. Laszlo, denomination at LR. b, St. Imre (Emeric), denomination at UL. c, St. Stephen, denomination at bottom center.

2013, Aug. 14 Litho. *Perf. 12*
4293 A1581 600fo Sheet of 3, #a-c 16.00 8.00
d. As #4293, litho. with foil application 16.00 8.00

A lithographed green monocolored sheet of type A1581 that was not valid for postage was sold together with Nos. 4293 and 4293d in a package costing 4100fo.

Miniature Sheet

Dome Hall of Parliament Building — A1582

No. 4294: a, Main staircases. b, Scepter. c, Dome, denomination at UR. d, Dome, diff., denomination at UL. e, Glass windows at UL. f, Glass windows at UR. g, Soldiers at display of Hungarian crown. h, Statues atop pillars.

2013, Sept. 3 Litho. *Perf. 13¼*
4294 A1582 Sheet of 8 + central label 18.00 9.00
a.-h. 250fo Any single 2.25 1.10

Woman Gathering a Bundle of Hay on a Collective Farm, Photograph by Robert Capa (1913-54) — A1583

2013, Oct. 2 ***Perf. 12***
4295 A1583 310fo multi 3.00 1.50

The Source of Art, Painting by Aladár Körösfoi-Kriesch (1863-1920) — A1584

2013, Oct. 2 ***Perf. 13¼x12½***
4296 A1584 315fo multi 3.00 1.50

Souvenir Sheet

Budapest Water Summit — A1585

2013, Oct. 4 ***Perf. 13¼x13***
4297 A1585 365fo multi 3.50 1.75

Rose — A1586

Rose — A1587

Rose — A1588

2013, Oct. 8 **Litho.** ***Perf. 11¼***
4298 Strip of 3 + 3 labels 3.00 1.50
a. A1586 (110fo) multi + label 1.00 .50
b. A1587 (110fo) multi + label 1.00 .50
c. A1588 (110fo) multi + label 1.00 .50
Sheet, 7 each #4298a, 4298c, 6 #4298b 20.00 20.00

Labels could be personalized for an additional fee. Compare with No. 3977.

MTK Sports Club, 125th Anniv. — A1589

2013, Nov. 5 **Litho.** ***Perf. 13¼x13***
4299 A1589 400fo blue & dk bl 3.75 1.90

Christmas A1590

Decorated gingerbread cookies in shape of: 85fo, Christmas tree. 110fo, Star of Bethlehem, horiz. 140fo, Angel.

2013, Nov. 5 **Litho.** ***Die Cut***

Self-Adhesive

4300 A1590 85fo multi .80 .40
a. Booklet pane of 5 4.00
4301 A1590 110fo multi 1.00 .50
a. Booklet pane of 5 5.00
4302 A1590 140fo multi 1.25 .65
a. Booklet pane of 5 6.25
Nos. 4300-4302 (3) 3.05 1.55

Miniature Sheet

New Year 2014 (Year of the Horse) — A1591

No. 4303 — Horse: a, Galloping, head at right. b, Galloping, head at left. c, Grooming itself. d, Grazing.

2014, Jan. 6 **Litho.** ***Perf. 12½x12¼***
4303 A1591 110fo Sheet of 4, #a-d 4.00 2.00

Hungarian Maltese Charity, 25th Anniv. A1592

Litho. & Embossed

2014, Feb. 4 ***Perf. 12***
4304 A1592 300fo multi 2.60 1.40

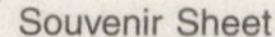

Souvenir Sheet

Beatified Hungarians — A1593

No. 4305: a, Blessed Zoltán Lajos Meszlényi (1892-1951), bishop of Esztergom. b, Blessed Istvan Sándor (1914-53), monk. c, Blessed Szilárd Bogdánffy (1911-53), clandestine bishop of Oradea, Romania.

2014, Feb. 25 **Litho.** ***Perf. 12***
4305 A1593 400fo Sheet of 3, #a-c 11.00 5.50
d. As No. 4305, litho. with foil application 11.00 5.50

A lithographed blue monocolored sheet of type A1593 that was not valid for postage was only sold together with Nos. 4305 and 4305d in a package that sold for 3990fo.

Miniature Sheet

Baby Animals Recently Born at the Budapest Zoo — A1594

No. 4306: a, Sempala, the giraffe (zsiráf). b, Sid, the two-toes sloth (kétujjú lajhár. c, Jakab, the Barbary sheep (sörényes juh). d, Moira, the orangutan. e, Bangita, the blackbuck (Indiai antilop). f, Maszat, the prairie dog (prérikutya). g, Mazsola, the ground cuscus (földi kuszkusz). h, Rozi, the meerkat (szurikata). i, Gizmó, the ring-tailed lemur (gyurusfarkú maki). j, Skipper, the African penguin (pápaszemes pingvin). k, Kiran, the Asiatic lion (Perzsa oroszlán). l, Willow, the common wombat (csupaszorrú vombat).

2014, Mar. 4 **Litho.** ***Perf. 12***
4306 A1594 115fo Sheet of 12, #a-l 12.50 6.25

Klári Tolnay (1914-98), Actress — A1595

Annie Fischer (1914-95), Pianist — A1596

2014, Mar. 5 **Litho.** ***Perf. 12x12½***
4307 A1595 260fo multi 2.40 1.25
4308 A1596 285fo multi 2.60 1.25

Nos. 4307-4308 were each printed in sheets of 4.

A1597

Easter — A1598

No. 4310 — Stations of the Cross in Roman numerals: a, I. b, II. c, III. d, IV. e, V. f, VI. g, VII. h, VIII. i, IX. j, X. k, XI. l, XII. m, XIII. n, XIV. o, XV.

Litho. With Foil Application

2014, Mar. 28 ***Perf. 12***
4309 A1597 115fo multi 1.10 .55

Miniature Sheet

4310 A1598 90fo Sheet of 15, #a-o 12.00 6.00

Souvenir Sheet

Wenckheim Palace, Szabadkigyós, Designed by Miklós Ybl (1814-91) — A1599

2014, Apr. 4 **Litho.** ***Perf. 12x12½***
4311 A1599 1000fo multi 9.00 4.50

Stamp Day A1600

Buildings in Debrecen: 115fo, Kölcsey Center. 145fo, Small Reformed Church, vert. 600fo+200fo, Great Reformed Church, vert.

Perf. 13x13¼, 13¼x13

2014, Apr. 25 **Litho.**
4312-4313 A1600 Set of 2 2.40 1.25

Souvenir Sheet

Perf. 12¾x13

4314 A1600 600fo +200fo multi 7.25 7.25

Examples of No. 4314 with a red serial number and a quartz crystal affixed to the sheet margin were printed in limited quantities

Souvenir Sheet

Canonization of Popes John XXIII and John Paul II — A1601

No. 4315: a, Pope John XXIII. b, Pope John Paul II.

2014, Apr. 27 Litho. *Perf. 12x12½*
4315 A1601 250fo Sheet of 2, #a-b 4.50 2.25

Hands of Holocaust Survivor Holding Uprooted Plant — A1602

2014, Apr. 28 Litho. *Perf. 13¼x13*
4316 A1602 375fo multi 3.50 1.75

Jewish Ghetto Decrees, 70th anniv. (start of Holocaust for Hungarian Jews).

Béni Egressy (1814-51), Composer A1603

2014, May 9 Litho. *Perf. 12*
4317 A1603 200fo multi 1.75 .90

No. 4317 was printed in sheets of 4.

Miniature Sheet

Europa — A1604

No. 4318: a, Hurdy-gurdy (gardon). b, Mouth harp (doromb).

2014, May 9 Litho. *Perf. 11½x12*
4318 A1604 250fo Sheet of 4, 2 each #a-b 9.00 4.50

2014 World Cup Soccer Championships, Brazil — A1605

2014, June 4 Litho. *Perf. 11½x12*
4319 A1605 145fo multi 1.25 .65

Tripartitum, Compilation of Hungarian Law, by István Werboczy, 500th Anniv. — A1606

2014, July 4 Litho. *Perf. 13¼x13*
4320 A1606 330fo multi 3.00 1.50

No. 4320 was printed in sheets of 4.

World War I, Cent. A1607

2014, July 28 Litho. *Perf. 13¼x13*
4321 A1607 440fo multi 3.75 1.90

Fruit and Blossoms Type of 2011

Designs: 245fo, Plums. 260fo, Strawberries.

2014, Aug. 6 Litho. *Perf. 14¼*
4322-4323 A1509 Set of 2 4.25 2.10

Souvenir Sheet

Repatriation of the Sevso Treasure — A1608

No. 4324: a, Plate with central design of hunters (30x45mm). b, Plate with central geometric design, Dionysius ewer, basin (60x50mm). c, Basin, ewer with geometric design, container (30x45mm).

Litho. & Embossed With Foil Application

2014, Aug. 25 *Perf. 12*
4324 A1608 1000fo Sheet of 3, #a-c 25.00 12.50

Imperforate examples of No. 4324 are from a limited printing.

Synagogues — A1609

Designs: 285fo, Miskolc Synagogue. 330fo, Mád Synagogue.

2014, Sept. 2 Litho. *Perf. 12*
4325-4326 A1609 Set of 2 5.25 2.60

Nos. 4325-4326 each were printed in sheets of 4.

Insects A1610

Designs: 90fo, Dendroleon pantherinus. 115fo, Mantispa styriaca. 405fo, Carabus auronitens. 445fo, Stilbum cyanurum. 600fo, Aeshna viridis.

Litho., Litho. With Foil Application (#4329-4330)

2014, Sept. 9 *Perf. 12*
4327-4330 A1610 Set of 4 8.75 4.50

Souvenir Sheet

4331 A1610 600fo multi 5.00 2.50

Miniature Sheet

Motorcycles — A1611

No. 4332: a, 1932 Csepel WM98. b, 1942 Mátra 100. c, 1948 Csepel Túra 100. d, 1953 Csepel 250. e, 1953 Csepel 125 T. f, 1957 Pannonia TLT. g, 1961 Danuvia 125. h, 1961 Berva. i, 1963 Danuvia Moto-cross. j, 1964 Pannonia T5 Export. k, 1969 Pannonia P10H. l, 1969, Pannonia P20.

2014, Sept. 9 Litho. *Perf. 12½x12*
4332 A1611 90fo Sheet of 12, #a-l 9.00 4.50

No. 2909 Surcharged
Souvenir Sheet

Method and Perf. As Before

2014, Oct. 3
4333 A767 300fo on 20fo #2909 2.50 1.25

Seat of Danube Commission in Budapest, 60th anniv.

Miniature Sheet

Speaker's Reception Halls in House of Parliament — A1612

No. 4334: a, Blue sofa and chairs, table, fireplace. b, Wooden cabinet. c, Mantelpiece clock. d, Circle in diamond wall decoration. e, Framed wall decoration. f, Triangular cabinet top. g, Columns and arches wall decoration. h, Red sofa and chairs, table.

2014, Oct. 3 Litho. *Perf. 13¼*
4334 A1612 200fo Sheet of 8, #a-h, + central label 13.00 6.50

2014 European Women's Handball Championships, Hungary and Croatia — A1613

2014, Nov. 6 Litho. *Perf. 13x13¼*
4335 A1613 145fo multi 1.25 .60

Railway Wheel Assembly — A1614

2014, Nov. 6 Litho. *Perf. 11½x12¼*
4336 A1614 200fo multi 1.60 .80

Abrahám Ganz (1814-67), foundry owner, patent holder for casting railway wheels.

Christmas A1615

2014, Nov. 18 Litho. *Perf. 14*
4337 A1615 145fo multi 1.25 .60

34th Racing Pigeon Olympiad, Budapest A1616

Racing pigeon: 115fo, First Lady and Heroes' Square. 145fo, Mr. Villám and Fishermen's Bastion.

No. 4340: a, Jr. Villám and Liberty Statue. b, Release of pigeons, horiz.

2015, Jan. 16 Litho. *Perf. 14*
4338-4339 A1616 Set of 2 1.90 .95

Souvenir Sheet

Perf. 13½x13, 13x13½
4340 A1616 450fo Sheet of 2, #a-b 6.75 3.50

UNICEF in Hungary, 40th Anniv. — A1617

2015, Feb. 5 Litho. *Perf. 11¼*
4341 A1617 500fo multi 3.75 1.90

Third World Conference on Disaster Risk Reduction, Sendai City, Japan — A1618

2015, Feb. 19 Litho. *Perf. 14*
4342 A1618 330fo multi 2.40 1.25

Miniature Sheet

New Year 2015 (Year of the Goat) — A1619

No. 4343 — Goat with background color of: a, Buff. b, Dark blue.

Perf. 11½x12¼

2015, Feb. 19 Litho.
4343 A1619 285fo Sheet of 4, 2 each #a-b 8.25 4.25

Nos. 4343a and 4343b are tete-beche within the sheet.

Easter — A1620

No. 4344 — Easter egg with: a, Maroon background. b, Cream background.

2015, Mar. 5 Litho. *Perf. 11½x12*
4344 A1620 115fo Horiz. pair, #a-b 1.75 .85

Bánk Bán, Play by József Katona, 200th Anniv. — A1621

2015, Mar. 19 Litho. *Perf. 14*
4345 A1621 275fo multi 2.10 1.10

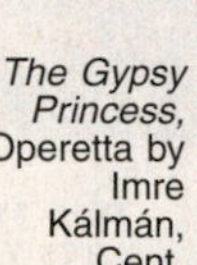

The Gypsy Princess, Operetta by Imre Kálmán, Cent. A1622

2015, Mar. 19 Litho. *Perf. 14*
4346 A1622 375fo multi 2.75 1.40

Zita Szeleczky (1915-99), Actress A1623

2015, Apr. 10 Litho. *Perf. 12½x12*
4347 A1623 150fo multi 1.10 .55

No. 4347 was printed in sheets of 4.

Use of M62 Locomotive, 50th Anniv. — A1624

2015, Apr. 16 Litho. *Perf. 13x13¼*
4348 A1624 420fo multi 3.25 1.60

Scheduled Bus Service in Budapest, Cent. — A1625

2015, Apr. 16 Litho. *Perf. 14x13¾*
4349 A1625 475fo multi 3.50 1.75

Frank Sinatra (1915-98), Singer — A1626

2015, May 8 Litho. *Perf. 12*
4350 A1626 200fo multi 1.50 .75

No. 4350 was printed in sheets of 4, with adjacent stamps rotated 90 degrees.

Edith Piaf (1915-63), Singer — A1627

2015, May 8 Litho. *Perf. 12x12½*
4351 A1627 325fo multi 2.40 1.25

No. 4351 was printed in sheets of 4.

Europa — A1628

No. 4352 — Toys: a, Dolls, hussar on horseback, castle. b, Dolls, blacksmith and horse-drawn cart.

2015, May 8 Litho. *Perf. 12½x12*
4352 A1628 285fo Horiz. pair, #a-b 4.25 2.10

No. 4352 was printed in sheets containing 2 pairs.

2015 European Women's Basketball Championships, Hungary and Romania A1629

2015, June 4 Litho. *Perf. 13¼x13*
4353 A1629 390fo multi 2.75 1.40

Souvenir Sheet

Pax, Mosaic by Miksa Roth (1865-1944) — A1630

2015, June 4 Litho. *Perf. 13¼x13*
4354 A1630 1000fo multi 7.00 3.50

Examples of No. 4354 with green serial number, imperforate with red serial number, and a monochrome design, were printed in limited quantities.

Ujpest Torna Egylet Sports Club, 130th Anniv. — A1631

2015, June 19 Litho. *Perf. 13¼x13*
4355 A1631 400fo multi 2.75 1.40

Stamp Day — A1632

Buildings in Tata: 115fo, Bell Tower. 145fo, Tata Castle.
600fo+300fo, Statue of St. John the Baptist, Old Lake, József Eötvös High School.

2015, June 26 Litho. *Perf. 12x12½*
4356-4357 A1632 Set of 2 1.90 .95

Souvenir Sheet

4358 A1632 600fo +300fo multi 6.25 6.25

Surtax on No. 4358 is for promotion of philately.

Items in Hungarian Museums A1633

Designs: 200fo, Chest, pottery jug, Flóris Rómer (1815-89), founder of Museum of Art and History, Gyor. 270fo, Ceramic items from Zsolnay Collection of the Janus Pannonius Museum, Pécs.

2015, July 3 Litho. *Perf. 12½x12*
4359-4360 A1633 Set of 2 3.25 1.60

Nos. 4359-4360 were each printed in sheets of 4.

Vigadó Concert Hall, Budapest, 150th Anniv. — A1634

2015, July 24 Litho. *Perf. 14x13¾*
4361 A1634 285fo multi 2.10 1.10

Flowers A1635

Designs: 115fo, Iris bucharica. 215fo, Paeonia suffruticosa.

2015, Aug. 7 Litho. *Perf. 14*
4362-4363 A1635 Set of 2 2.40 1.25

Souvenir Sheet

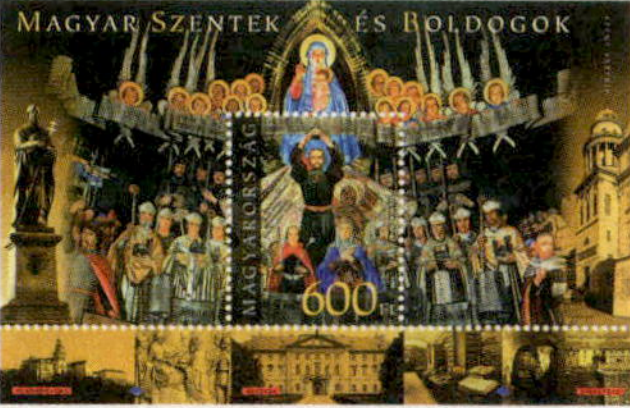

St. Astrik Offering Crown to St. Stephen and Queen Gisela — A1636

2015, Aug. 7 Litho. *Perf. 12*
4364 A1636 600fo multi 4.50 2.25
a. As #4364, litho. with foil application 4.50 2.25

A lithographed sheet with the vignette in brown that was not valid for postage was printed in limited quantities and only sold together with Nos. 4364 and 4364a in a package that sold for 2790fo.

Albert Einstein's General Theory of Relativity, Cent. — A1637

2015, Sept. 7 Litho. *Perf. 13¼x12½*
4365 A1637 285fo multi 2.10 1.10

Kálmán Széll (1843-1915), Prime Minister — A1638

2015, Oct. 1 Litho. *Perf. 14*
4366 A1638 145fo multi 1.10 .55

Miniature Sheet

Hunting Hall and Delegation Room in House of Parliament — A1639

No. 4367: a, Hunting Hall (dining room) with windows at right. b, Painting of Buda and Attilla fighting bison, clock and doors. c, Chandelier and arches. d, Doors. e, Door under arch. f, Stained-glass window depicting dragons. g, Painting of coronation of Franz Joseph I. h, Tables in meeting room.

2015, Oct. 1 Litho. *Perf. 12*
4367 A1639 250fo Sheet of 8, #a-h, + central label 14.50 7.25

International Telecommunication Union, 150th Anniv. — A1640

2015, Oct. 12 Litho. *Perf. 11*
4368 A1640 375fo multi + label 2.75 1.40

2015 ITU Conference, Budapest.

Hungarian Academy of Sciences, 150th Anniv. A1641

2015, Nov. 10 Engr. *Perf. 12½x12*
4369 A1641 500fo brown 3.50 1.75

Miniature Sheet

Space Achievements — A1642

No. 4370: a, Drawing of Soviet space capsule, cosmonaut in blue space suit spacewalking. b, New Horizons space probe, denomination at LL. c, Drawing of dog in space helmet, bone, space capsule. d, Astronaut Edward White spacewalking. e, Cosmonaut Alexei Leonov spacewalking. f, Drawing of rocket, antenna on planet. g, Dawn space probe, denomination at UL. h, Drawing of monkey in space helmet.

2015, Nov. 10 Litho. *Perf. 14*
4370 A1642 115fo Sheet of 8, #a-h 6.25 3.25

Christmas A1643

Serpentine Die Cut 10¼x10
2015, Nov. 10 Litho.
Self-Adhesive
4371 A1643 (115fo) multi .85 .40

Litho. With Foil Application
Serpentine Die Cut 10x9½
4372 A1643 (115fo) multi .85 .40

No. 4372 was printed in sheets of 4.

Stalkless Gentian A1644

Red Poppy — A1645

2016, Jan. 22 Litho. *Perf. 12x11½*
4373 A1644 (305fo) multi 2.25 1.10
4374 A1645 (355fo) multi 2.50 1.25

Dated 2015. Compare with type A1087.

István Tömörkény (1866-1917), Writer — A1646

2016, Jan. 22 Litho. *Perf. 12x12½*
4375 A1646 340fo multi 2.40 1.25

Miniature Sheet

New Year 2016 (Year of the Monkey) — A1647

No. 4376 — Color of monkey: a, Black. b, Red.

2016, Feb. 8 Litho. *Perf. 12*
4376 A1647 300fo Sheet of 4, 2 each #a-b 8.50 4.25

Nos. 4376a and 4376b are tete-beche within the sheet.

Easter A1648

2016, Mar. 4 Litho. *Perf. 14*
4377 A1648 115fo multi .85 .40

József Simándy (1916-97), Opera Singer A1649

2016, Mar. 4 Litho. *Perf. 12½x12*
4378 A1649 150fo multi 1.10 .55

St. Martin of Tours (316-97) A1650

Litho. With Foil Application
2016, Mar. 18 *Perf. 14*
4379 A1650 115fo multi .85 .40

Count István Széchenyi (1791-1860) Statesman A1651

2016, Apr. 8 Litho. *Perf. 12x12½*
4380 A1651 225fo multi 1.75 .85

Europa A1652

2016, May 6 Litho. *Perf. 12½x12*
4381 A1652 305fo multi 2.25 1.10

Think Green Issue.

Stamp Day — A1653

Attractions in Szombathely: 115fo, Funerary stele of the Sempronius family, Roman Emperor Constantius Chlorus proclaiming law in Savaria (Szombathely). 145fo, Holy Trinity statue, chancel of Szombathely Cathedral.
600fo+300fo, St. Martin of Tours, capital of Roman column, horiz.

2016, May 6 Litho. *Perf. 14*
4382-4383 A1653 Set of 2 1.90 .95

Souvenir Sheet
Perf. 14x13½
4384 A1653 600fo +300fo multi 6.50 3.25

Hungarian Interchurch Aid, 25th Anniv. A1654

Litho. & Embossed
2016, May 17 *Perf. 14*
4385 A1654 145fo blue & orange 1.10 .55

2016 European Soccer Championships, France — A1655

2016, June 3 Litho. *Perf. 12½x12*
4386 A1655 340fo multi 2.40 1.25

Items in Hungarian Museums A1656

Designs: 355fo, Chess pieces, Chess Museum, Heves. 395fo, Pipes, Pipe Museum, Ibafa.

2016, June 3 Litho. *Perf. 12*
4387-4388 A1656 Set of 2 5.25 2.60

Nos. 4387-4388 comes in sheets of 4.

Geological Treasures A1657

Designs: 115fo, Daphnogene polymorpha fossil. 145fo, Raskya vetusta fossil. 600fo, Glyptostrobus europaeus fossil.

2016, June 8 Litho. *Perf. 12½x12*
4389-4390 A1657 Set of 2 1.90 .95

Souvenir Sheet
4391 A1657 600fo multi 4.25 2.10

Miniature Sheet

Exterior Details of House of Parliament — A1658

No. 4392: a, Tower and upper stories, sky at top, light chestnut panel at left. b, Dome, lavender gray panel at right. c, Tower, bridge in background, greenish slate panel at right. d, Dome, brownish gray panel at left. e, Tower and rooftop, ochre panel at right. f, Gargoyles and root spires, light chestnut panel at left. g, Statues on pillars, light olive gray panel at right. h, Statues on pillars, roof, light red brown panel at right.

2016, June 8 Litho. *Perf. 12*
4392 A1658 200fo Sheet of 8, #a-h, + central label 11.50 5.75

Jan Jessinius (1566-1621), Physician and Professor of Anatomy — A1659

Photo. & Engr.

2016, June 22 ***Perf. 11¼x11¾***
4393 A1659 280fo multi + label 2.00 1.00

See Czech Republic No. 3677, Poland No. 4232, Slovakia No. 743.

Miniature Sheet

Fire Fighting — A1660

No. 4394: a, 150fo, Károly Koszeghi-Mártony (1783-1848), inventor of compressed air breathing system, fire wagon. b, 150fo, Count Odön Széchenyi (1839-1922), chief officer of Budapest Fire Brigade, fire wagon. c, 150fo+75fo, Kornél Szilvay (1890-1957), inventor of dry fire extinguisher, fire truck. d, 150fo+75fo, Fire fighter and Heros Aquadux-X 4000 fire truck.

2016, June 22 **Litho.** ***Perf. 12***
4394 A1660 Sheet of 4, #a-d 5.25 2.60

Surtax for youth philately.

2016 Summer Olympics, Rio de Janeiro A1661

Designs: 115fo, Swimming. 355fo, Kayaking.

2016, July 7 **Litho.** ***Perf. 12½x12***
4395-4396 A1661 Set of 2 3.50 1.75

First Horse Tramway in Pest, 150th Anniv. A1662

2016, July 8 **Litho.** ***Perf. 13¼x13***
4397 A1662 200fo multi 1.50 .75

Introduction of M40 Locomotive in Hungary, 50th Anniv. — A1663

2016, July 8 **Litho.** ***Perf. 12***
4398 A1663 260fo multi 1.90 .95

Miniature Sheet

Baby Animals Recently Born at the Budapest Zoo — A1664

No. 4399: a, Rudi, the African forest buffalo (vörös kafferbivaly). b, Adolf, the Javan surili (Javai langur). c, Ocsi, the northern bald ibis (tarvarjú). d, Bulan, the Visayan warty pig (Cebu-szigeti disznó). e, Panka, the greater rhea (nandu). f, Batty, the Lyle's flying fox (Lyle-repülőkutya). g, Gátor, the Dalmatian pelican (borzas gödény). h, Evita, the mhorr gazelle (mhorr gazella). i, Nefriti, the night monkey (éji majom). j, Lóránt, the red-fronted macaw (vörösfülü ara). k, Dalma, the dhole (ázsiai vadkutya). l, Kia, the eyelash viper (schlegel-lándzsakígyó.

2016, Aug. 9 **Litho.** ***Perf. 12***
4399 A1664 115fo Sheet of 12, #a-l 10.00 5.00

Souvenir Sheet

Budapest Zoo, 150th Anniv. — A1665

2016, Aug. 9 **Litho.** ***Perf. 13¼x13***
4400 A1665 1000fo multi 7.25 3.50

Examples of No. 4400 with a green serial number, and imperforate with a red serial number were printed in limited quantities.

Souvenir Sheet

Hungarian Royalty — A1666

No. 4401: a, Blessed King Charles IV (1887-1922) (26x33mm). b, Crown of St. Stephen, orb, scepter and sword (35x41mm). c, Queen Zita (1892-1989) (26x33mm).

Perf. 11½x12, 13 (#4401b)

2016, Aug. 17 **Litho.**
4401 A1666 200fo Sheet of 3, #a-c 4.50 2.25
a. As No. 4401, litho. & embossed with foil application 4.50 2.25

Coronation of King Charles IV, cent. A lithographed black monocolor sheet of type A1666 that was not valid for postage was sold together with Nos 4401 and 4401a in a package costing 3990fo.

Souvenir Sheet

Battle of Szigetvár, 450th Anniv. — A1667

No. 4402: a, Zrinski's Charge from the Szigetvár Fortress, by Bertalan Székely. b, Szigetvár coat of arms.

Perf. 13¼x13x13¼x14

2016, Sept. 5 **Litho.**
4402 A1667 300fo Sheet of 2, #a-b 4.50 2.25

See Croatia No. 1004.

Souvenir Sheet

Leaders of the Battle of Szigetvár — A1668

No. 4403: a, Nikola Zrinski (1508-66). b, Suleiman the Magnificent (1495-1566).

Perf. 13¼x13x13¼x14

2016, Sept. 5 **Litho.**
4403 A1668 300fo Sheet of 2, #a-b 4.50 2.25

See Turkey No. 3522.

Ulmus Minor — A1669

2016, Sept. 8 **Litho.** ***Perf. 12x12½***
4404 A1669 115fo multi .85 .40

Károly Simonyi (1916-2001), Physicist and Electrical Engineer — A1670

2016, Oct. 5 **Litho.** ***Perf. 12½x12***
4405 A1670 400fo multi 3.00 1.50

Souvenir Sheet

Revolution of 1956, 60th Anniv. — A1671

2016, Oct. 21 **Litho.** ***Perf.***
4406 A1671 800fo multi 5.75 3.00

Royal Wedding Garments — A1672

No. 4407 — Garment of: a, King Louis II, brown purple denomination. b, Queen Mary, red denomination.

2016, Nov. 8 **Litho.** ***Perf. 12½x12***
4407 A1672 250fo Pair, #a-b 3.50 1.75

Printed in sheets containing two each Nos. 4407a-4407b.

Souvenir Sheet

City With Various European Landmarks — A1673

2016, Nov. 8 **Litho.** ***Perf. 12¼***
4408 A1673 600fo multi 4.25 2.10

Christmas — A1674

Die Cut Perf. 11½

2016, Nov. 8 **Typo.**

Self-Adhesive

4409 A1674 (115fo) blue & org yel .80 .40
4410 A1674 (115fo) blue & gold .80 .40

No. 4409 has four die cut diagonal lines in the vignette. No. 4410 was printed in vertical strips of 5.

Souvenir Sheet

Budapest Water Summit — A1675

2016, Nov. 21 **Litho.** ***Perf. 13¼x13***
4411 A1675 400fo multi 2.75 1.40

New Year 2017 (Year of the Rooster) — A1676

No. 4412: a, Gold rooster. b, Blue rooster.

Litho. With Foil Application

2017, Jan. 27 ***Perf. 11½x12***
4412 A1676 335fo Pair, #a-b 4.75 2.40

Printed in sheets containing two each Nos. 4412a-4412b.

Dove and Barbed Wire — A1677

2017, Feb. 1 **Litho.** ***Perf. 14***
4413 A1677 360fo multi 2.50 1.25

Remembrance of victims of Soviet Gulag and GUPVI labor camps.

Regiomontanus (1436-76), Astronomer, and Frontispiece of *Epitome of the Almagest* — A1678

2017, Feb. 3 **Litho.** ***Perf. 13¾***
4414 A1678 235fo multi 1.60 .80

Arrival of Regiomontanus in Hungary, 550th anniv.

Easter — A1679

Die Cut Perf. 11½
2017, Mar. 6 **Litho.**
Self-Adhesive
4415 A1679 120fo multi .85 .40

Claudio Monteverdi (1567-1643), Composer — A1680

2017, Mar. 6 **Litho.** ***Perf. 12***
4416 A1680 210fo multi 1.50 .75

No. 4416 was printed in sheets of 4.

Zoltán Fábri (1917-94), Film Director — A1681

2017, Mar. 6 **Litho.** ***Perf. 12***
4417 A1681 300fo multi 2.10 1.10

No. 4417 was printed in sheets of 4, with each stamp rotated 90 degrees from each adjacent stamp.

Lions Club International, Cent. — A1682

2017, Apr. 3 **Litho.** ***Perf. 14***
4418 A1682 120fo multi .85 .40

Zoltán Kodály (1882-1967), Composer — A1683

2017, Apr. 3 **Litho.** ***Perf. 11½x12***
4419 A1683 155fo multi 1.10 .55

No. 4419 was printed in sheets of 4.

2017 World Aquatics Championships, Budapest and Lake Balaton — A1684

2017, Apr. 5 **Litho.** ***Perf. 14***
4420 A1684 435fo multi 3.00 1.50

Protestant Reformation, 500th Anniv. — A1685

Designs: 290fo, Statue of Gáspár Károli (c. 1530-91), translator of Bible into Hungarian, printing press, Bible, alpha, omega and quill pen. 445fo, Reformed College of Debrecen, Lamb of God, horiz.
800fo, Martin Luther nailing 95 Theses to church door, Sacred Heart.

2017, Apr. 20 **Litho.** ***Perf. 14***
4421-4422 A1685 Set of 2 5.25 2.60

Souvenir Sheet
Perf. 13¼x13
4423 A1685 800fo multi 5.75 3.00

Hungarian Postal Service, 150th Anniv. — A1686

Designs: 5fo, Handstamps used from 1867-1945. 10fo, Horse-drawn parcel delivery cart used from 1867-1958. 30fo, Mail box, 1894. 100fo, Post office sign used from 1875-1945. 200fo, Postman's cap, 1895.300fo, Posthorn, 19th cent.

Die Cut Perf. 11½
2017, May 4 **Litho.**
Self-Adhesive

4424 A1686 5fo multi .25 .25
4425 A1686 10fo multi .25 .25
4426 A1686 30fo multi .25 .25
4427 A1686 100fo multi .75 .35
4428 A1686 200fo multi 1.50 .75
4429 A1686 300fo multi 2.25 1.10
Nos. 4424-4429 (6) 5.25 2.95

Miniature Sheet

Postal Transportation — A1687

No. 4430: a, Horse-drawn parcel delivery cart. b, Postman with János Csonka motorized tricycle. c, Postmen on Cespel bicycles. d, Postal rail car, postman on Danuvia motorcycle. e, Barkas mail van and airplane. f, Nissan ENV 200 electric mail van.

2017, May 4 **Litho.** ***Perf. 14***
4430 A1687 120fo Sheet of 6, #a-f 5.25 2.60

Hungarian Postal Service, 150th anniv.

Nagybánya Landscape with the Gutin Mountains, by Béla Iványi Grünwald (1867-1940) A1688

2017, May 5 **Litho.** ***Perf. 12***
4431 A1688 375fo multi 2.75 1.40

No. 4431 was printed in sheets of 4.

Europa A1689

No. 4432: a, Andrássy Castle, Tiszadob. b, Nádasdy Castle, Nádasdladány.

2017, May 5 **Litho.** ***Perf. 12***
4432 A1689 335fo Pair, #a-b 5.00 2.50

Printed in sheets containing two pairs.

Souvenir Sheet

Holy Roman Empress Maria Theresa (1717-80) — A1690

2017, May 12 **Litho.** ***Perf. 13¼x13***
4433 A1690 495fo multi 3.75 1.90

See Austria No. 2677, Croatia No. 1038, Slovenia No. 1219, Ukraine No. 1093.

Hungarian Stamps, 150th Anniv. — A1691

No. 4434: a, Unissued stamp designed for independent Hungary in 1848. b, Austria #27. c, Hungary #3. d, Hungary #14.

2017, June 1 **Litho.** ***Perf. 12***
4434 Vert. strip of 4 8.00 4.00
a.-d. A1691 275fo Any single 2.00 1.00

Printed in sheets containing two strips.

Owls A1692

Designs: 200fo, Tyto alba. 360fo, Strix aluco. 390fo, Asio otus. 410fo, Athene noctua. 600fo, Otus scops.

2017, July 3 **Litho.** ***Perf. 14***
4435-4438 A1692 Set of 4 10.00 5.00

Souvenir Sheet
4439 A1692 600fo multi 4.50 2.25

Miniature Sheet

János Arany (1817-82), Writer — A1693

No. 4440 — Illustrations by Mihály Zichy of scenes from ballads by Arany: a, 120fo, The Hero of Bor (Bor Vitéz). b, The Bards of Wales (A Walesi Bárdok). c, 120fo+75fo, Mistress Agnes (Agnes Asszony). d, 120fo+75fo, The Mother of King Matthias (Mátyás Anyja).

2017, July 10 **Litho.** ***Perf. 13x13¼***
4440 A1693 Sheet of 4, #a-d 5.00 2.50

Surtax for youth philately.

Souvenir Sheet

1867 Stamps of the Austro-Hungarian Empire — A1694

No. 4441: a, 120fo, Austria #29. b, 450fo, Austria #33.

2017, Aug. 25 **Litho.** ***Perf. 13¼x13***
4441 A1694 Sheet of 2, #a-b 4.50 2.25

See Austria No. 2690.

"Belföld" — A1695

2017, Sept. 1 Litho. *Perf. 11*
4442 A1695 (120fo) gold + label .95 .45

Labels could be personalized for an additional fee. The label shown is one of a number of generic labels produced.

Miniature Sheet

Old Eastern European Automobiles — A1696

No. 4443: a, Warszawa 220, Poland. b, Moszkvics 407, Russia. c, GAZ-12 ZIM, Russia. d, Trabant P 50, German Democratic Republic. e, Tatra 2-603, Czechoslovakia. f, Wartburg 311, German Democratic Republic.

Litho. & Embossed
2017, Sept. 1 *Perf. 12*
4443 A1696 120fo Sheet of 6, #a-f 5.75 3.00

Daughters of King Béla IV — A1697

No. 4444: a, St. Margaret (1242-70). b, St. Kinga (1224-92). c, Blessed Yolanda (c. 1235-98).

2017, Sept. 1 Litho. *Perf. 13¼x13*
4444 A1697 400fo Sheet of 3, #a-c 9.50 4.75

Synagogues A1698

Designs: 210fo, Gyor Synagogue. 235fo, Pécs, Synagogue, horiz.

Perf. 13x13¼, 13¼x13
2017, Sept. 5 Litho.
4445-4446 A1698 Set of 2 3.50 1.75

Flórián Albert (1941-2011), Soccer Player, and Recipient of 1967 Ballon d'Or Trophy — A1699

2017, Sept. 15 Litho. *Perf. 14*
4447 A1699 300fo multi 2.25 1.10

Magda Szabó (1917-2007), Writer — A1700

Litho. & Embossed
2017, Oct. 5 *Perf. 14*
4448 A1700 435fo multi 3.25 1.60

Stamp Day A1701

Designs: 120fo, Archduke Joseph Karl (1833-1905) and Military Merit Cross with war decoration. 155fo, 1890 shako and 1904 saber, vert.
550fo+300fo, Stefánia Palace, Budapest.

2017, Nov. 3 Litho. *Perf. 14*
4449-4450 A1701 Set of 2 2.10 1.10

Souvenir Sheet
4451 A1701 500fo +300fo multi 6.25 3.25

Christmas A1702

Die Cut Perf. 11½
2017, Nov. 3 Typo.
Self-Adhesive
4452 A1702 (120fo) gold & black .90 .45

Typo. With Foil Application
4453 A1702 (120fo) gold & black .90 .45

On No. 4453, the gold is more reflective of light than No. 4452.
No. 4453 is printed in miniature sheets of 5 + label.

Statue From Piarist Secondary School, Budapest A1703

2017, Nov. 15 Litho. *Perf. 14*
4454 A1703 200fo multi 1.50 .75

Piarist Secondary School, 300th anniv.

Postcrossing A1704

2018, Feb. 2 Litho. *Perf. 12*
4455 A1704 120fo multi 1.00 .50

No. 4455 was printed in sheets of 4.

2018 Winter Olympics, PyeongChang, South Korea — A1705

2018, Feb. 2 Litho. *Perf. 13¼x13*
4456 A1705 445fo multi 3.75 1.90

New Year 2018 (Year of the Dog) — A1706

No. 4457 — Dog with background color of: a, Light blue. b, Scarlet.

2018, Feb. 6 Litho. *Perf. 12*
4457 A1706 400fo Pair, #a-b 6.50 3.25

Printed in sheets containing two each Nos. 4457a-4457b.

SEMI-POSTAL STAMPS

Issues of the Monarchy

"Turul" and St. Stephen's Crown — SP1

Franz Josef I Wearing Hungarian Crown — SP2

Wmk. Double Cross (137)
1913, Nov. 20 Typo. *Perf. 14*

B1	SP1	1f	slate	.40	.25
B2	SP1	2f	olive yellow	.40	.25
B3	SP1	3f	orange	.40	.25
B4	SP1	5f	emerald	.40	.25
B5	SP1	6f	olive green	.40	.25
B6	SP1	10f	carmine	.60	.25
B7	SP1	12f	violet, *yellow*	.50	.25
B8	SP1	16f	gray green	.75	.25
B9	SP1	20f	dark brown	3.00	.40
B10	SP1	25f	ultra	1.75	.25
B11	SP1	30f	org brn	2.00	.25
B12	SP1	35f	red violet	2.00	.25
B13	SP1	50f	lake, *blue*	3.75	.60
B14	SP1	60f	grn, *sal*	3.75	.50
B15	SP2	1k	dull red	25.00	2.00
B16	SP2	2k	dull blue	75.00	40.00
B17	SP2	5k	violet brown	30.00	30.00
	Nos. B1-B17 (17)			150.10	76.25

Nos. B1-B17 were sold at an advance of 2f over face value, as indicated by the label at bottom. The surtax was to aid flood victims.
For overprints see Nos. 5NB1-5NB10, 6NB1-6NB11.
Exist imperf. Value, set $1,000.

Semi-Postal Stamps of 1913 Surcharged in Red, Green or Brown

a

b

1914

B18	SP1(a)	1f	slate	.25	.25
B19	SP1(a)	2f	olive yel	.25	.25
B20	SP1(a)	3f	orange	.25	.25
B21	SP1(a)	5f	emerald	.25	.25
B22	SP1(a)	6f	olive green	.25	.25
B23	SP1(a)	10f	carmine (G)	.35	.25
B24	SP1(a)	12f	violet, *yel*	.25	.25
B25	SP1(a)	16f	gray green	.30	.25
B26	SP1(a)	20f	dark brown	.90	.25
B27	SP1(a)	25f	ultra	.90	.25
B28	SP1(a)	30f	orange brn	1.10	.25
B29	SP1(a)	35f	red violet	1.90	.25
B30	SP1(a)	50f	lake, *bl*	1.50	.50
B31	SP1(a)	60f	grn, *sal*	2.00	.55
B32	SP2(b)	1k	dull red (Br)	60.00	25.00
B33	SP2(b)	2k	dull blue	37.50	26.00
B34	SP2(b)	5k	violet brn	30.00	21.00
	Nos. B18-B34 (17)			137.95	76.05

Exist imperf. Value, set $800.

Regular Issue of 1913 Surcharged in Red or Green

c

d

1915, Jan. 1

B35	A4(c)	1f	slate	.25	.25
B36	A4(c)	2f	olive yel	.25	.25
B37	A4(c)	3f	orange	.25	.25
B38	A4(c)	5f	emerald	.25	.25
B39	A4(c)	6f	olive grn	.25	.25
B40	A4(c)	10f	carmine (G)	.25	.25
B41	A4(c)	12f	violet, *yel*	.25	.25
B42	A4(c)	16f	gray green	.25	.25
B43	A4(c)	20f	dark brown	.25	.25
B44	A4(c)	25f	ultra	.25	.25
B45	A4(c)	30f	orange brn	.40	.25
B46	A4(c)	35f	red violet	.45	.25
B47	A4(c)	50f	lake, *bl*	.65	.25
a.	On No. 96a			*5,000.*	
B48	A4(c)	60f	green, *salmon*	.80	.30
B49	A5(d)	1k	dull red	1.10	3.00
B50	A5(d)	2k	dull blue	3.00	7.50
B51	A5(d)	5k	violet brown	9.50	17.50

Surcharged as Type "c" but in Smaller Letters

B52	A4	60f	green, *salmon*	2.25	1.25
	Nos. B35-B52 (18)			20.65	32.80

Nos. B18-B52 were sold at an advance of 2f over face value. The surtax to aid war widows and orphans.
Exist imperf. Value, set $200.

Soldiers Fighting SP3 SP4

Eagle with Sword — SP5

1916-17 *Perf. 15*

B53	SP3	10f + 2f rose red	.25	.30
B54	SP4	15f + 2f dull violet	.25	.30
B55	SP5	40f + 2f brn car ('17)	.25	.40
	Nos. B53-B55 (3)		.75	1.00

Exist imperf. Value, set $15.
For overprints and surcharge see Nos. B58-B60. 1NB1-1NB3, 2NB1-2NB6, 4NJ1, 5NB11-5NB13, 6NB13-6NB15, 7NB2-7NB3, 9NB1, 10NB1-10NB4, 11NB1-B4.

Nos. 106-107 Surcharged in Red

1917, Sept. 15

B56 A8 10f + 1k rose	.60	*1.00*
B57 A8 15f + 1k violet	.60	*1.00*

Nos. B56 and B57 were issued in connection with the War Exhibition of Archduke Josef.

Issues of the Republic

Semi-Postal Stamps of 1916-17 Overprinted in Black

1918

B58 SP3 10f + 2f rose red	.25	.25
B59 SP4 15f + 2f dull violet	.25	.25
B60 SP5 40f + 2f brown car	.25	.25
Nos. B58-B60 (3)	.75	.75

Nos. B58-B60 exist with inverted overprint. Exist imperf. Value, set $12.50.

Postally used examples of Nos. B69-B174 sell for more.

Issues of the Kingdom

Released Prisoner Walking Home — SP7

Prisoners of War — SP8

Homecoming of Soldier — SP9

Wmk. 137 Vert. or. Horiz.

1920, Mar. 10 *Perf. 12*

B69a SP7 40f + 1k dull red	1.75	3.50
B70a SP8 60f + 2k gray brown	3.00	6.00
B71 SP9 1k + 5k dk blue	1.75	3.50
Nos. B69a-B71 (3)	6.50	13.00
Set, never hinged	18.50	

The surtax was used to help prisoners of war return home from Siberia.
Exist imperf. Value, set $100.

Statue of Petőfi — SP10

Griffin — SP11

Sándor Petőfi — SP12

Petőfi Dying — SP13

Petőfi Addressing People — SP14

1923, Jan. 23 ***Perf. 14 (10k, 40k), 12***

B72 SP10 10k slate green	.50	*1.00*
B73 SP11 15k dull blue	1.00	*2.75*
B74 SP12 25k gray brown	.50	*1.00*
B75 SP13 40k brown violet	1.50	3.00
B76 SP14 50k violet brown	1.50	3.00
Nos. B72-B76 (5)	5.00	10.75
Set, never hinged	10.00	

Birth centenary of the Hungarian poet Sándor Petőfi. The stamps were on sale at double face value, for a limited time and in restricted quantities, after which the remainders were given to a charitable organization.
Exist imperf. Value, set $100.

Child with Symbols of Peace — SP15

Mother and Infant — SP16

Instruction in Archery — SP17

Wmk. 133

1924, Apr. 8 **Engr.** ***Perf. 12***

B77 SP15 300k dark blue	1.50	*4.00*
a. Perf. 11½	35.00	30.00
B78 SP16 500k black brown	1.50	*4.00*
B79 SP17 1000k black green	1.50	*4.00*
Nos. B77-B79 (3)	4.50	*12.00*
Set, never hinged	12.00	

Each stamp has on the back an inscription stating that it was sold at a premium of 100 per cent over the face value.
Exist imperf. Value, set $90.

Parade of Athletes SP18

Skiing — SP19

Skating — SP20

Diving — SP21

Fencing SP22

Scouts Camping — SP23

Soccer SP24

Hurdling — SP25

Perf. 12, 12½ and Compound

1925 **Typo.** **Unwmk.**

B80 SP18 100k bl grn & brn	2.25	*2.00*
B81 SP19 200k lt brn & myr grn	2.90	*2.50*
B82 SP20 300k dark blue	3.50	*3.50*
B83 SP21 400k dp bl & dp grn	3.80	*3.50*
B84 SP22 500k pur brn	7.50	*10.00*
B85 SP23 1000k red brown	6.25	*7.00*
B86 SP24 2000k brown violet	7.50	*7.50*
B87 SP25 2500k olive brown	7.50	*9.00*
Nos. B80-B87 (8)	41.20	*45.00*
Set, never hinged	75.00	

These stamps were sold at double face value, plus a premium of 10 per cent on orders sent by mail. They did not serve any postal need and were issued solely to raise funds to aid athletic associations. An inscription regarding the 100 per cent premium is printed on the back of each stamp.
Exist imperf. Value, set $450.

St. Emerich SP26

Sts. Stephen and Gisela SP27

St. Ladislaus SP28

Sts. Gerhardt and Emerich SP29

1930, May 15 **Wmk. 210** ***Perf. 14***

B88 SP26 8f + 2f deep green	.45	.40
B89 SP27 16f + 4f brt violet	.65	*.60*
B90 SP28 20f + 4f deep rose	1.90	*2.00*
B91 SP29 32f + 8f ultra	2.50	*4.50*
Nos. B88-B91 (4)	5.50	*7.50*
Set, never hinged	11.00	

900th anniv. of the death of St. Emerich, son of Stephen I, king, saint and martyr.
Exist imperf. Value, set $150.

Catalogue values for unused stamps in this section, from this point to the end of the section, are for Never Hinged items.

St. Ladislaus — SP30

Holy Sacrament SP31

SP32

1938 May 16 **Photo.** ***Perf. 12***

B92 SP30 16f + 16f dull slate bl	3.00	3.00
B93 SP31 20f + 20f dk car	3.00	3.00

Souvenir Sheet

B94 SP32 Sheet of 7	50.00	32.50
a. 6f + 6f St. Stephen	4.00	3.00
b. 10f + 10f St. Emerich	4.00	3.00
c. 16f + 16f slate blue (B92)	4.00	3.00
d. 20f + 20f dark carmine (B93)	4.00	3.00

e.	32f + 32f St. Elizabeth	4.00	3.00
f.	40f + 40f St. Maurice	4.00	3.00
g.	50f + 50f St. Margaret	4.00	3.00

Printed in sheets measuring 136½x155mm. Nos. B94c and B94d are slightly smaller than B92 and B93.

Eucharistic Cong. in Budapest, May, 1938.

Exist imperf. Value: set $125; souvenir sheet $3,750.

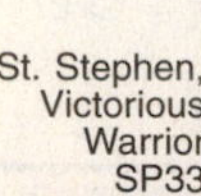

St. Stephen, Victorious Warrior SP33

St. Stephen, Offering Crown SP34

SP35

1938, Aug. 12 *Perf. 12*

B95	SP33	10f + 10f violet brn	3.00	3.00
B96	SP34	20f + 20f red org	3.00	3.00

Souvenir Sheet

B97	SP35	Sheet of 7	32.50	20.00
	a.	6f + 6f St. Stephen the Missionary	3.25	2.00
	b.	10f + 10f violet brown (B95)	3.25	2.00
	c.	16f + 16f Seated Upon Throne	3.25	2.00
	d.	20f + 20f red orange (B96)	3.25	2.00
	e.	32f + 32f Receives Bishops and Monks	3.25	2.00
	f.	40f + 40f St. Gisela, St. Stephen and St. Emerich	3.25	2.00
	g.	50f + 50f St. Stephen on Bier	3.25	2.00

Death of St. Stephen, 900th anniversary.

No. B97 is on brownish paper, Nos. B95-B96 on white.

Nos. B95-B97 exist imperf. Values: Nos. B95-B96 $150; No. B97 $4,500.

Statue Symbolizing Recovered Territories SP36

Castle of Munkács SP37

Admiral Horthy Entering Komárom SP38

Cathedral of Kassa SP39

Girl Offering Flowers to Soldier — SP40

1939, Jan. 16

B98	SP36	6f + 3f myrtle grn	1.00	.65
B99	SP37	10f + 5f olive grn	.65	.45
B100	SP38	20f + 10f dark red	.65	.45
B101	SP39	30f + 15f grnsh blue	1.25	.80
B102	SP40	40f + 20f dk bl gray	1.75	.80
		Nos. B98-B102 (5)	5.30	3.15

The surtax was for the aid of "Hungary for Hungarians" patriotic movement.

Exist imperf. Value, set $175.

Memorial Tablets SP41

Gáspár Károlyi, Translator of the Bible into Hungarian SP42

Albert Molnár de Szenci, Translator of the Psalms SP43

Prince Gabriel Bethlen — SP44

Susanna Lórántffy — SP45

Perf. 12x12½, 12½x12

1939 **Photo.** **Wmk. 210**

B103	SP41	6f + 3f green	.70	.70
B104	SP42	10f + 5f claret	1.00	1.00
B105	SP43	20f + 10f cop red	1.00	1.00
B106	SP44	32f + 16f bister	1.00	1.00
B107	SP45	40f + 20f chalky blue	1.00	1.00
		Nos. B103-B107 (5)	4.70	4.70

Souvenir Sheets

Perf. 12

B108	SP44	32f olive & vio brn	30.00	15.00

Imperf

B109	SP44	32f bl grn, cop red & gold	30.00	15.00

National Protestant Day. The surtax was used to erect an Intl. Protestant Institute.

The souvenir sheets sold for 1.32p each.

Nos. B103-B108 exist imperf. Values: Nos. B103-B107 $350; No. B108 $4,000.

Issue dates: Nos. B103-B107, Oct. 2. Nos. B108-B109, Oct. 27.

Boy Scout Flying Kite — SP47

Allegory of Flight — SP48

Archangel Gabriel from Millennium Monument, Budapest, and Planes — SP49

1940, Jan. 1 *Perf. 12½x12*

B110	SP47	6f + 6f yellow grn	.75	1.00
B111	SP48	10f + 10f chocolate	.95	1.25
B112	SP49	20f + 20f copper red	1.40	1.25
		Nos. B110-B112 (3)	3.10	3.50

The surtax was used for the Horthy National Aviation Fund.

Exist imperf. Value, set $150.

Souvenir Sheet

SP50

Wmk. 210

1940, May 6 **Photo.** *Perf. 12*

B113	SP50	20f + 1p dk blue grn	6.00	6.00

Exist imperf. Value $4,500.

Soldier Protecting Family from Floods SP51

1940, May

B114	SP51	10f + 2f gray brown	.40	.25
B115	SP51	20f + 4f orange red	.40	.25
B116	SP51	20f + 50f red brown	1.25	1.25
		Nos. B114-B116 (3)	2.05	1.75

The surtax on Nos. B113-B116 was used to aid flood victims.

Exist imperf. Value, set $200.

Hunyadi Coat of Arms SP52

King Matthias SP54

Hunyadi Castle SP53

Equestrian Statue of King Matthias SP55

Corvin Codex — SP56

Equestrian Statue of King Matthias — SP57

1940 *Perf. 12½x12, 12x12½*

B117	SP52	6f + 3f blue grn	.60	.60
B118	SP53	10f + 5f gldn brn	.60	.60
B119	SP54	16f + 8f dk ol bis	.80	.80
B120	SP55	20f + 10f brick red	.80	.80
B121	SP56	32f + 16f dk gray	1.25	1.10
		Nos. B117-B121 (5)	4.05	3.90

Souvenir Sheet

B122	SP57	20f + 1p dk bl grn & pale grn	6.00	6.00

King Matthias (1440-1490) at Kolozsvar, Transylvania. The surtax was used for war relief.

Nos. B117-B122 exist imperf. Values: Nos. B117-B121 $250; No. B122 $4,500.

Issued: Nos. B117-B121, July 1. No. B122. Nov. 7.

Hungarian Soldier — SP58

20f+50f, Virgin Mary and Szekley, symbolizing the return of transylvania. 32f+50f, Szekley Mother Offering Infant Son to the Fatherland.

1940, Dec. 2 **Photo.** *Perf. 12½x12*

B123	SP58	10f + 50f dk blue grn	1.25	1.25
B124	SP58	20f + 50f brown car	1.40	1.40
B125	SP58	32f + 50f yellow brn	1.60	1.60
		Nos. B123-B125 (3)	4.25	4.25

Occupation of Transylvania. The surtax was for the Pro-Transylvania movement.

Exist imperf. Value, set $225.

Symbol for Drama SP61

Symbol for Sculpture — SP62

Symbols: 16f+16f, Art. 20f+20f, Literature.

1940, Dec. 15 ***Perf. 12x12½, 12½x12***

B126	SP61 6f + 6f dark green		1.40	1.25
B127	SP62 10f + 10f olive bis		1.40	1.25
B128	SP62 16f + 16f dk violet		1.40	1.25
B129	SP61 20f + 20f fawn		1.40	1.25
	Nos. B126-B129 (4)		5.60	5.00

Souvenir Sheet

1941, Jan. 5 ***Imperf.***

B130	Sheet of 4	6.00	6.00
a.	SP61 6f + 6f olive brown	1.25	1.25
b.	SP62 10f + 10f henna brown	1.25	1.25
c.	SP62 16f + 16f dk blue green	1.25	1.25
d.	SP61 20f + 20f rose violet	1.25	1.25

Surtax on Nos. B126-B130 was used for the Pension and Assistance Institution for Artists.

Nos. B126-B129 exist imperf. Value, set $70.

Winged Head of Pilot — SP66

Designs: 10f+10f, Boy Scout with model plane. 20f+20f, Glider in flight. 32f+32f, Our Lady of Loreto, patroness of Hungarian pilots.

1941, Mar. 24 ***Perf. 12x12½***

B131	SP66 6f + 6f grn olive	.55	.50
B132	SP66 10f + 10f dp claret	.55	.50
B133	SP66 20f + 20f org ver	.65	.60
B134	SP66 32f + 32f turq blue	1.60	1.50
	Nos. B131-B134 (4)	3.35	3.10

The surtax was used to finance civilian and army pilot training through the Horthy National Aviation Fund.

Exist imperf. Value, set $270.

Infantry SP70

12f+18f, Heavy artillery. 20f+30f, Plane and tanks. 40f+60f, Cavalryman and cyclist.

1941, Dec. 1 **Photo.** **Wmk. 266**

Inscribed: "Honvedeink Karacsonyara 1941"

B135	SP70 8f + 12f dk green	.50	.50
B136	SP70 12f + 18f olive grn	.50	.50
B137	SP70 20f + 30f slate	.60	.60
B138	SP70 40f + 60f red brown	.60	.60
	Nos. B135-B138 (4)	2.20	2.20

The surtax was for the benefit of the Army.

Exist imperf. Value, set $275.

Soldier and Emblem SP74

1941, Dec. 1

B139	SP74 20f + 40f dark red	2.25	2.25

The surtax was for the soldiers' Christmas.

Exists imperf. Value $70.

Aviator and Plane — SP75

Planes and Ghostly Band of Old Chiefs SP76

Plane and Archer SP77

Aviators and Plane — SP78

1942, Mar. 15 ***Perf. 12½x12, 12x12½***

B140	SP75 8f + 8f dark green	.80	.80
B141	SP76 12f + 12f sapphire	.80	.80
B142	SP77 20f + 20f brown	.80	.80
B143	SP78 30f + 30f dark red	.80	.80
	Nos. B140-B143 (4)	3.20	3.20

The surtax aided the Horthy National Aviation Fund.

Exist imperf. Value, set $270.

Blood Transfusion — SP79

Designs: 8f+32f, Bandaging wounded soldier. 12f+50f, Radio and carrier pigeons. 20f+1p, Widows and orphans.

1942, Sept. 1 ***Perf. 12½x12***

B144	SP79 3f + 18f dk ol & red	1.40	1.40
B145	SP79 8f + 32f dp brn & red	1.40	1.40
B146	SP79 12f + 50f dp cl & red	1.40	1.40
B147	SP79 20f + 1p slate bl & red	1.40	1.40
	Nos. B144-B147 (4)	5.60	5.60

The surtax aided the Hungarian Red Cross. Sheets of 10. Value, set $85.

Exist imperf. Value, set $300.

Widow of Stephen Horthy — SP83

Red Cross Nurse Aiding Soldier SP84

Magdalene Horthy Mother of Stephen Horthy — SP85

1942, Dec. 1 ***Perf. 13, Imperf.***

B148	SP83 6f + 1p vio bl & red	3.00	3.00
a.	Sheet of 4	27.50	27.50
B149	SP84 8f + 1p dk ol grn & red	3.00	3.00
a.	Sheet of 4	27.50	27.50
B150	SP85 20f + 1p dk red brn & red	3.00	3.00
a.	Sheet of 4	27.50	27.50
	Nos. B148-B150 (3)	9.00	9.00

The surtax aided the Hungarian Red Cross.

King Ladislaus I

SP86 SP87

1942, Dec. 21 **Wmk. 266** ***Perf. 12***

B151	SP86 6f + 6f olive gray	.90	*.90*
B152	SP87 8f + 8f green	.90	*.90*
B153	SP86 12f + 12f dull violet	.90	*.90*
B154	SP87 20f + 20f Prus green	.90	*.90*
B155	SP86 24f + 24f brown	.90	*.90*
B156	SP87 30f + 30f rose car	.90	*.90*
	Nos. B151-B156 (6)	5.40	5.40

900th anniv. of the birth of St. Ladislaus (1040-95), the 700th anniv. of the beginning of the country's reconstruction by King Béla IV (1206-70) and the 600th anniv. of the accession of King Lajos the Great (1326-82).

The surtax aided war invalids and their families.

Exist imperf. Value, set $350.

Archer on Horseback SP92

Knight with Sword and Shield — SP93

Old Magyar Arms — SP94

Designs: 3f+1f, 4f+1f, Warrior with shield and battle ax. 12f+2f, Knight with lance, 20f+2f, Musketeer. 40f+4f, Hussar. 50f+6f, Artilleryman.

1943

B157	SP92 1f + 1f dk gray	.25	.35
B158	SP93 3f + 1f dull violet	.50	*.80*
B159	SP93 4f + 1f lake	.25	.35
B160	SP93 8f + 2f green	.25	.35
B161	SP92 12f + 2f bister brn	.25	.35
B162	SP93 20f + 2f dp claret	.25	.35
B163	SP92 40f + 4f gray vio	.25	.35
B164	SP93 50f + 6f org brn	.25	.35
B165	SP94 70f + 8f slate blue	.40	.35
	Nos. B157-B165 (9)	2.65	3.60

The surtax aided war invalids.

Exist imperf. Value, set $270.

Model Glider — SP101

Gliders — SP102

White-tailed Sea Eagle and Planes — SP103

ME-109E Fighter and Gliders — SP104

1943, July 17

B166	SP101 8f + 8f green	.80	*1.00*
B167	SP102 12f + 12f royal blue	.80	*1.00*
B168	SP103 20f + 20f chestnut	.80	*1.00*
B169	SP104 30f + 30f rose car	.80	*1.00*
	Nos. B166-B169 (4)	3.20	4.00

The surtax aided the Horthy National Aviation Fund.

Exist imperf. Value, set $270.

Stephen Horthy SP105

1943, Aug. 16

B170	SP105 30f + 20f dp rose vio	.55	.50

The surtax aided the Horthy National Aviation Fund.

Exists imperf. Value $70.

Nurse and Soldier SP106

Designs: 30f+30f, Soldier, nurse, mother and child. 50f+50f, Nurse keeping lamp alight. 70f+70f, Wounded soldier and tree shoot.

1944, Mar. 1 **Cross in Red**

B171	SP106 20f + 20f brown	.50	.40
B172	SP106 30f + 30f henna	.50	.40
B173	SP106 50f + 50f brown vio	.55	.40
B174	SP106 70f + 70f Prus blue	.55	.40
	Nos. B171-B174 (4)	2.10	1.60

The surtax aided the Hungarian Red Cross.

Exist imperf. Value, set $270.

Issues of the Republic

Types of 1944 Surcharged in Red or Black

a

b

1945, July 23 **Wmk. 266** *Perf. 12*

B175 A115(a) 3p + 9p on 20f dk ol grn, *yel* 1.00 .80
B176 A114(b) 4p + 12p on 4f yel brn, *bl* (Bk) 1.00 .80
B177 A117(b) 8p + 24p on 50f sl bl, *yel* 1.00 .80
B178 A115(a) 10p + 30p on 30f hn brn, *bl* (Bk) 1.00 .80
Nos. B175-B178 (4) 4.00 3.20

The surtax was for the Peoples Universities. "Béke" means "peace".

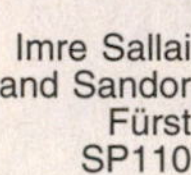

Imre Sallai and Sandor Fürst
SP110

Designs: 3p+3p, L. Kabok and Illes Monus. 4p+4p, Ferenc Rozsa and Zoltan Schonerz. 6p+6p, Anna Koltai and Mrs. Paul Knurr. 10p+10p, George Sarkozi and Imre Nagy. 15p+15p, Vilmos Tartsay and Jeno Nagy. 20p+20p, Janos Kiss and Andreas Bajcsy-Zsilinszky. 40p+40p, Endre Sagvari and Otto Hoffmann.

1945, Oct. 6 **Photo.**

B179 SP110 2p + 2p yel brn 1.75 1.75
B180 SP110 3p + 3p dp red 1.75 1.75
B181 SP110 4p + 4p dk pur 1.75 1.75
B182 SP110 6p + 6p dk yel grn 1.75 1.75
B183 SP110 10p + 10p dp car 1.75 1.75
B184 SP110 15p + 15p dk sl grn 1.75 1.75
B185 SP110 20p + 20p dk brn 1.75 1.75
B186 SP110 40p + 40p dp bl 1.75 1.75
Nos. B179-B186 (8) 14.00 14.00

The surtax was for child welfare.
Exist imperf. Value, set $175.

Andreas Bajcsy-Zsilinszky and Eagle — SP111

1945, May 27

B187 SP111 1p + 1p dk brn vio .90 *.90*

1st anniv. of the death of Andreas Bajcsy-Zsilinszky, hanged by the Nazis for anti-fascist activities.
Exists imperf. Value $135.

Lion with Broken Shackles
SP112

1946, May 1

B188 SP112 500ez p + 500ez p 2.25 2.25
B189 SP112 1mil p + 1mil p 2.25 2.25
B190 SP112 1.5mil p + 1.5mil p 2.25 2.25
B191 SP112 2mil p + 2mil p 2.25 2.25
Nos. B188-B191 (4) 9.00 9.00

75th anniv. of Hungary's 1st postage stamp. The surtax was for the benefit of postal employees.
Exist imperf. Value, set $135.

"Agriculture" Holding Wheat — SP113

1946, Sept. 7 **Photo.**

B192 SP113 30f + 60f dp yel grn 5.00 *7.00*
B193 SP113 60f + 1.20fo rose brn 5.00 *7.00*
B194 SP113 1fo + 2fo dp blue 5.00 *7.00*
Nos. B192-B194 (3) 15.00 *21.00*

1st Agricultural Congress and Exhibition.
Exist imperf. Value, set $325.

Physician with Syringe — SP114

Designs: 12f+50f, Physician examining X-ray picture. 20f+50f, Nurse and child. 60f+50f, Prisoner of war starting home.

Perf. 12½x12

1947, May 16 **Wmk. 210**

B195 SP114 8f + 50f ultra 4.25 *5.00*
B196 SP114 12f + 50f choc 4.25 *5.00*
B197 SP114 20f + 50f dk grn 4.25 *5.00*
B198 SP114 60f + 50f dk red 1.00 1.25
Nos. B195-B198 (4) 13.75 *16.25*

The surtax was for charitable purposes.
Exist imperf. Value, set $400.

Franklin D. Roosevelt and Freedom of Speech Allegory
SP115

Pres. F. D. Roosevelt and Allegory: 12f+12f, Freedom of Religion. 20f+20f, Freedom from Want. 30f+30f, Freedom from Fear.

1947, June 11 **Photo.** *Perf. 12x12½*

Portrait in Sepia

B198A SP115 8f + 8f dk red 4.00 *5.25*
B198B SP115 12f + 12f dp grn 4.00 *5.25*
B198C SP115 20f + 20f brown 4.00 *5.25*
B198D SP115 30f + 30f blue 4.00 *5.25*
Nos. B198A-B198D,CB1-CB1C (8) 33.00 *42.00*

Exist imperf. Value, set $250.
Nos. B198A-B198D and CB1-CB1C were also printed in sheets of 4 of each denomination (size: 117x96mm). Value, set of 8, $700. Exist imperf. Value $900.
A souvenir sheet exists, containing one each of Nos. B198A-B198D with border inscriptions and decorations in brown. Size: 161x122mm. Value $125. Also printed in tête-bêche souvenir sheets of 4. Value $800. Exists imperf. Value $250.

Lenin — SP118

Designs: 60f+60f, Soviet Cenotaph, Budapest. 1fo+1fo, Joseph V. Stalin.

1947, Oct. 29 **Photo.** **Wmk. 283**

B199 SP118 40f + 40f ol grn & org brn 4.50 5.50
B200 SP118 60f + 60f red & sl bl 2.00 2.00
B201 SP118 1fo + 1fo vio & brn blk 4.50 5.50
Nos. B199-B201 (3) 11.00 13.00

The surtax was for the Hungarian-Soviet Cultural Association.
Exist imperf. Value, set $475.

XVI Century Mail Coach
SP119

1947, Dec. 21 *Perf. 12x12½*

B202 SP119 30f (+ 50f) hn brn 9.50 10.00
Sheet of 4 55.00 55.00

Stamp Day. The surtax paid admission to a philatelic exhibition in any of eight Hungarian towns, where the stamps were sold.
No. B202 exists imperf. Values: single $800; sheetlet of 4 $4,500.

Globe and Carrier Pigeon — SP120

1948, Oct. 17 *Perf. 12½x12*

B203 SP120 30f (+ 1fo) grnsh bl 6.50 6.50
Sheet of 4 45.00 45.00

5th Natl. Hungarian Stamp Exhib., Budapest. Each stamp sold for 1.30 forint, which included admission to the exhibition.
Exists imperf. Value: single $450; sheetlet $2,250.

Woman Worker — SP121

1949, Mar. 8

B204 SP121 60f + 60f magenta 2.50 2.50

Intl. Woman's Day, Mar. 8, 1949. The surtax was for the Democratic Alliance of Hungarian Women.
Exists imperf. Value $70.

Aleksander S. Pushkin — SP122

SP123

1949, June 6 **Photo.**

B205 SP122 1fo + 1fo car lake 10.00 10.00

Souvenir Sheet

Perf. 12½x12, Imperf

B206 SP123 1fo + 1fo red vio & car lake 15.00 15.00

150th anniversary of the birth of Aleksander S. Pushkin. The surtax was for the Hungarian-Russian Culture Society.
No. B205 exists imperf. Value $220.

IMPERFORATE STAMPS

Through 1991, most semi-postal stamps were also issued imperforate. Where these items form part of a larger set with regular issues, values for imperfs will be included in that of the sets to which they belong, footnoted in the Regular Issues section. For Nos. B207-B345, values for imperfs will be given only for those items not included in sets with regular issues.

1st Stamp Type

Perf. 12½x12

1951, Oct. 6 **Engr.** **Unwmk.**

B207 A208 1fo + 1fo red 12.00 12.00
B208 A208 2fo + 2fo blue 14.00 14.00

Exists imperf.

Postwoman Delivering Mail — SP124

1953, Nov. 1 **Wmk. 106** *Perf. 12*

B209 SP124 1fo + 1fo blue grn 4.00 1.25
B210 SP124 2fo + 2fo rose vio 4.00 1.25

Stamp Day, Nov. 1, 1953.
Exist imperf. Value, set $60.

Stamps of 1955 Surcharged in Red or Lake

1957, Jan. 31 **Photo.** *Perf. 12x12½*

B211 A249 20f + 20f olive grn .25 .25
B212 A249 30f + 30f dk red (L) .40 .25
a. Red (cross) inverted 450.00
B213 A249 40f + 40f brown .45 .40
B214 A249 60f + 60f brn red (L) .55 .45
B215 A249 1fo + 1fo blue 1.20 1.00
B216 A249 2fo + 2fo rose brn 2.00 1.40
Nos. B211-B216 (6) 4.85 3.75

The surtax was for the Hungarian Red Cross.
Exist imperf. Value, set $135.

Winter Olympic Type of 1960

Design: Olympic Games emblem.

Perf. 11½x12

1960, Feb. 29 **Wmk. 106**

B217 A295 2fo + 1fo multi 1.75 .35

Exists imperf.

Olympic Type of 1960

Design: 2fo+1fo, Romulus and Remus.

Perf. 11½x12

1960, Aug. 21 **Photo.** **Wmk. 106**

B218 A299 2fo + 1fo multi 1.25 .30

Exists imperf.

Sport Club Type of 1961

Sport: 2fo+1fo, Sailboats.

1961, July 8 **Unwmk.** *Perf. 14½*

B219 A313 2fo + 1fo multi .40 .25

Exists imperf.

St. Margaret's Island and Danube — SP125

Views of Budapest: No. B221, Fishermen's Bastion. No. B222, Coronation Church and Chain Bridge. No. B223, Mount Gellert.

Unwmk.

1961, Sept. 24 Photo. *Perf. 12*

B220 SP125 2fo + 1fo multi 1.50 1.50
B221 SP125 2fo + 1fo multi 1.50 1.50
B222 SP125 2fo + 1fo multi 1.50 1.50
B223 SP125 2fo + 1fo multi 1.50 1.50
a. Horiz. strip of 4, #B220-B223 6.00 6.00

Stamp Day, 1961, and Budapest Intl. Stamp Exhibition.
No. B223a has a continuous design.
Exist imperf. Value, strip $32.
Miniature presentation sheets, perf. and imperf., contain one each of Nos. B220-B223; size: 204x66½mm. Value for both sheets, $2,000.

Soccer Type of Regular Issue, 1962

Design: Flags of Spain and Czechoslovakia.

1962, May 21 *Perf. 11*
Flags in Original Colors

B224 A323 4fo + 1fo lt grn & bis 2.00 .75

Exists imperf.

Austrian Stamp of 1850 with Pesth Postmark SP126

Stamps: No. B226, #201. No. B227, #C164. No. B228, #C208.

Lithographed and Engraved

1962, Sept. 22 Unwmk. *Perf. 11*
Design and Inscription in Dark Brown

B225 SP126 2fo + 1fo yellow 1.40 1.40
B226 SP126 2fo + 1fo pale pink 1.40 1.40
B227 SP126 2fo + 1fo pale blue 1.40 1.40
B228 SP126 2fo + 1fo pale yel grn 1.40 1.40
a. Horiz. strip of 4, #B225-B228 6.75 6.75
b. Souv. sheet of 4, #B225-B228 8.00 8.00

35th Stamp Day and 10th anniv. of Mabeosz, the Hungarian Phil. Fed.
Exist imperf. Value: strip $23; souvenir sheet $45.

Emblem, Cup and Soccer Ball — SP127

1962, Nov. 18 Photo. *Perf. 11½x12*

B229 SP127 2fo + 1fo multi .80 .50

Winning of the "Coupe de l'Europe Centrale" by the Steel Workers Sport Club (VASAS) in the Central European Soccer Championships.
Exists imperf. Value $6.

Stamp Day — SP128

No. B230, Hyacinth. No. B231, Narcissus. No. B232, Chrysanthemum. No. B233, Tiger lily.

1963, Oct. 24 *Perf. 11½x12*
Size: 32x43mm

B230 SP128 2fo + 1fo multi .50 .50
B231 SP128 2fo + 1fo multi .50 .50
B232 SP128 2fo + 1fo multi .50 .50
B233 SP128 2fo + 1fo multi .50 .50
a. Horiz. strip of 4, #B230-B233 3.00 3.00
b. Min. sheet of 4, #B230-B233 3.50 3.50

No. B233b contains 25x32mm stamps, perf. 11.
Exist imperf. Value: strip $20; miniature sheet $35.

Winter Olympic Type of 1963

Design: 4fo+1fo, Bobsledding.

1963, Nov. 11 *Perf. 12*

B234 A342 4fo + 1fo grnsh bl & bis .70 .30

Exists imperf.

New Year Type of Regular Issue

Good Luck Symbols: 2.50fo+1.20fo, Horseshoe, mistletoe and clover. 3fo+1.50fo, Pigs, clover and balloon, horiz.

Perf. 12x11½, 11½x12
1963, Dec. 12 Photo. Unwmk.
Sizes: 28x39mm (#B235); 28x22mm (#B206)

B235 A343 2.50fo + 1.20fo multi .50 .25
B236 A343 3fo + 1.50fo multi .70 .35

The surtax was for the modernization of the Hungarian Postal and Philatelic Museum.
Exist imperf.

Olympic Type of Regular Issue

Design: 3fo+1fo, Water polo.

1964, June 12 *Perf. 11*

B237 A352 3fo + 1fo multi .60 .75

Exists imperf.

Exhibition Hall — SP129

1964, July 23 Photo.

B238 SP129 3fo + 1.50fo blk, red org & gray .60 .35

Tennis Exhibition, Budapest Sports Museum.
Exists imperf. Value $8.

Twirling Woman Gymnast SP130

No. B239, Lilac. No. B240, Mallards. No. B241, Gymnast. No. B242, Rocket & globe.

1964, Sept. 4 *Perf. 11½x12*
Size: 27x38mm

B239 SP130 2fo + 1fo multi 1.00 1.00
B240 SP130 2fo + 1fo multi 1.00 1.00
B241 SP130 2fo + 1fo multi 1.00 1.00
B242 SP130 2fo + 1fo multi 1.00 1.00
a. Horiz. strip of 4, #B239-B242 4.00 4.00
b. Souv. sheet of 4, #B239-B242 4.00 4.00

37th Stamp Day and Intl. Topical Stamp Exhib., IMEX. No. B242b contains 4 20x28mm stamps, perf. 11.
Exist imperf. Value: strip $17.50; souvenir sheet $32.50.

13th Century Tennis SP131

History of Tennis: 40f+10f, Indoor tennis, 16th century. 60f+10f, Tennis, 18th century. 70f+30f, Tennis court and castle. 80f+40f, Tennis court, Fontainebleau (buildings). 1fo+50f, Tennis, 17th century. 1.50fo+50f, W. C. Wingfield, Wimbledon champion 1877, and Wimbledon Cup. 1.70fo+50f, Davis Cup, 1900. 2fo+1fo, Bela Kehrling (1891-1937), Hungarian champion.

Lithographed and Engraved

1965, June 15 Unwmk. *Perf. 12*

B243 SP131 30f + 10f mar, *dl org* .25 .25
B244 SP131 40f + 10f blk, *pale lil* .25 .25
B245 SP131 60f + 10f grn, *ol* .25 .25
B246 SP131 70f + 30f lil, *brt grn* .25 .25
B247 SP131 80f + 40f dk bl, *lt vio* .40 .25
B248 SP131 1fo + 50f grn, *yel* .50 .25
B249 SP131 1.50fo + 50f sep, *lt ol grn* .50 .25
B250 SP131 1.70fo + 50f ind, *lt bl* .75 .25
B251 SP131 2fo + 1fo dk red, *lt grn* .85 .30
Nos. B243-B251 (9) 4.00 2.30

Exist imperf. Value, set $20.

Flood Scene SP132

10fo+5fo, Relief commemorating 1838 flood.

1965, Aug. 14 Photo. *Perf. 12x11½*

B252 SP132 1fo + 50f org brn & bl .30 .30

Souvenir Sheet

B253 SP132 10fo + 5fo gldn brn & buff 2.75 2.75

Surtax for aid to 1965 flood victims.
Exist imperf. Value: No. B252 $6; No. B253 $20.

Geranium Stamp of 1950 (No. 909) SP133

Stamp Day: No. B255, #120. No. B256, #1489. No. B257, #1382.

Perf. 12x11½
1965, Oct. 30 Photo. Unwmk.
Stamps in Original Colors

B254 SP133 2fo + 1fo gray & dk bl .65 .60
B255 SP133 2fo + 1fo gray & red .65 .60
B256 SP133 2fo + 1fo gray & ocher .65 .60
B257 SP133 2fo + 1fo gray & vio .65 .60
a. Horiz. strip of 4, #B254-B257 3.00 3.00
b. Souv. sheet of 4, #B254-B257 3.50 3.25

No. B257b contains 32x23mm stamps, perf. 11.
Exist imperf. Value: No. B257a $15; No. B257b $25.

Soccer Type of Regular Issue

Design: 3fo+1fo, Championship emblem and map of Great Britain showing cities where matches were held.

1966, June 6 Photo. *Perf. 12x11½*

B258 A382 3fo + 1fo multi 1.00 .50

Exists imperf.

Woman Archer and Danube at Visegrad SP134

Stamp Day: No. B260, Gloria Hungariae grapes and Lake Balaton. No. B261, Red poppies and ruins of Diosgyor Castle. No. B262, Russian space dogs Ugolek and Veterok.

1966, Sept. 16 Photo. *Perf. 12x11½*

B259 SP134 2fo + 50f multi .60 .60
B260 SP134 2fo + 50f multi .60 .60
B261 SP134 2fo + 50f multi .60 .60
B262 SP134 2fo + 50f multi .60 .60
a. Horiz. strip of 4, #B259-B262 2.75 2.75
b. Souv. sheet of 4, #B259-B262 2.75 2.75

No. B262b contains 4 29x21mm stamps, perf. 11.
Exist imperf. Value: B262a $15; B262b $30.

Anglers, C.I.P.S. Emblem and View of Danube SP135

1967, Aug. 22 Photo. *Perf. 12x11½*

B263 SP135 3fo + 1fo multi .90 .45

See note after No. 1847.
Exists imperf.

Olympic Type of Regular Issue

Indoor stadium & Winter Olympics emblem.

1968, Jan. 29 Photo. *Perf. 11*

B264 A402 4fo + 1fo multi .70 .30

Exists imperf.

Jug, Western Hungary, 1618 SP136

Hungarian Earthenware: No. B266, Tiszafüred vase, 1847. No. B267, Toby jug, 1848. No. B268, Decorative Baja plate, 1870. No. B269a, Jug, Northern Hungary, 1672. No. B269b, Decorative Mezőcsat plate, 1843. No. B269c, Decorative Moragy plate, 1860. No. B269d, Pitcher, Debrecen, 1793.

1968, Oct. 5 Litho. *Perf. 12*

B265 SP136 1fo + 50f ultra & multi .50 .50
B266 SP136 1fo + 50f sky bl & multi .50 .50
B267 SP136 1fo + 50f sepia & multi .50 .50
B268 SP136 1fo + 50f yel brn & multi .50 .50
Nos. B265-B268 (4) 2.00 2.00

Miniature Sheet

B269 Sheet of 4 2.75 2.50
a. SP136 2fo + 50f ultra & multi .45 .40
b. SP136 2fo + 50f yel brn & multi .45 .40
c. SP136 2fo + 50f olive & multi .45 .40
d. SP136 2fo + 50f brt rose & multi .45 .40

Issued for 41st Stamp Day. No. B269 contains 4 25x36mm stamps. See Nos. B271-B275.
Exist imperf. Value: Nos. B265-B268 $15; No. B269 $15.

Suspension Bridge, Buda Castle and Arms of Budapest — SP137

Lithographed and Engraved

1969, May 22 *Perf. 12*

B270 SP137 5fo + 2fo sep, pale yel & gray 1.00 1.00

Budapest 71 Philatelic Exposition.
Exists imperf. Value $7.50.

Folk Art Type of 1968

Hungarian Wood Carvings: No. B271, Stirrup cup from Okorag, 1880. No. B272, Jar with flower decorations from Felsőtiszavidek, 1898. No. B273, Round jug, Somogyharsagy, 1935. No. B274, Two-legged jug, Alföld, 1740. No. B275a, Carved panel (farm couple), Csorna, 1879. No. B275b, Tankard, Okany, 1914. No. B275c, Round jar with soldiers, Sellye, 1899. No. B275d, Square box with 2 women, Lengyeltoti, 1880.

1969, Sept. 13 **Litho.** *Perf. 12*

B271 SP136 1fo + 50f rose cl & multi .60 .60
B272 SP136 1fo + 50f dp bis & multi .60 .60
B273 SP136 1fo + 50f bl & multi .60 .60
B274 SP136 1fo + 50f lt bl grn & multi .60 .60
Nos. B271-B274 (4) 2.40 2.40

Miniature Sheet

B275 Sheet of 4 2.75 2.50
a. SP136 2fo + 50f ultra & multi .50 .45
b. SP136 2fo + 50f brn org & multi .50 .45
c. SP136 2fo + 50f lt brn & multi .50 .45
d. SP136 2fo + 50f bl grn & multi .50 .45

Issued for the 42nd Stamp Day. No. B275 contains 4 stamps (size: 25x36mm).
Exists imperf. Value: B271-B274 $15; B275 $15.

Fishermen's Bastion, Coronation Church and Chain Bridge — SP138

Designs: No. B277, Parliament and Elizabeth Bridge. No. B278, Castle and Margaret Bridge.

1970, Mar. 7 **Litho.** *Perf. 12*

B276 SP138 2fo + 1fo gldn brn & multi .60 .60
B277 SP138 2fo + 1fo bl & multi .60 .60
B278 SP138 2fo + 1fo lt vio & multi .60 .60
Nos. B276-B278 (3) 1.80 1.80

Budapest 71 Philatelic Exhibition, commemorating the centenary of Hungarian postage stamps.
Exist imperf. Value, set $15.

King Matthias I Corvinus SP139

Initials and Paintings from Bibliotheca Corvina: No. B280, Letter "A." No. B281, Letter "N." No. B282, Letter "O." No. B283a, Ransanus Speaking before King Matthias. No. B283b, Scholar and letter "Q." No. B283c, Portrait of Appianus and letter "C." No. B283d, King David and letter "A."

1970, Aug. 22 **Photo.** *Perf. 11½x12*

B279 SP139 1fo + 50f multi .40 .40
B280 SP139 1fo + 50f multi .40 .40
B281 SP139 1fo + 50f multi .40 .40
B282 SP139 1fo + 50f multi .40 .40
Nos. B279-B282 (4) 1.60 1.60

Miniature Sheet

B283 Sheet of 4 2.75 2.50
a.-d. SP139 2fo + 50f, any single .50 .45

Issued for the 43rd Stamp Day. No. B283 contains 4 stamps (size: 22½x32mm).
Exist imperf. Value: B279-B282 $15; B283 $20.

View of Buda, 1470 — SP140

No. B285, Buda, 1600. No. B286, Buda and Pest, about 1638. No. B287, Buda and Pest, 1770. No. B288a, Buda, 1777. No. B288b, Buda, 1850. No. B288c, Buda, 1895. No. B288d, Budapest, 1970.

1971, Feb. 26 **Litho.** *Perf. 12*

B284 SP140 2fo + 1fo blk & yel .60 .60
B285 SP140 2fo + 1fo blk & pink .60 .60
B286 SP140 2fo + 1fo blk & pale grn .60 .60
B287 SP140 2fo + 1fo blk & pale sal .60 .60
Nos. B284-B287 (4) 2.40 2.40

Souvenir Sheet

Perf. 10½

B288 Sheet of 4 2.50 2.25
a. SP140 2fo + 1fo blk & pale sal .50 .45
b. SP140 2fo + 1fo blk & pale grn .50 .45
c. SP140 2fo + 1fo blk & lilac .50 .45
d. SP140 2fo + 1fo blk & pink .50 .45

Budapest 71 Intl. Stamp Exhib. for the cent. of Hungarian postage stamps, Budapest, Sept. 4-12. No. B288 contains 4 stamps, size: 39½x18mm.
Exist imperf. Value: Nos. B284-B287 $15; No. B288 $15.

Iris and #P1 SP141

Designs: No. B290, Daisy and #199. No. B291, Poppy and #391. No. B292, Rose and #B128. No. B293a, Carnations and #B200. No. B293b, Dahlia and #1068. No. B293c, Tulips and #C196. No. B293d, Anemones and #C251.

1971, Sept. 4 **Photo.** *Perf. 12x11½*

B289 SP141 2fo + 1fo sil & multi .70 .70
B290 SP141 2fo + 1fo sil & multi .70 .70
B291 SP141 2fo + 1fo sil & multi .70 .70
B292 SP141 2fo + 1fo sil & multi .70 .70
Nos. B289-B292 (4) 2.80 2.80

Souvenir Sheet

Perf. 11½

B293 Sheet of 4 2.75 2.50
a.-d. SP141 2fo + 1fo, any single .50 .45

Cent. of 1st Hungarian postage stamps and in connection with Budapest 71 Intl. Stamp Exhib., Sept. 4-12.
Exist imperf. Value: Nos. B289-B292 $16; No. B293 $25.

Miskólcz Postmark, 1818-43 — SP142

Postmarks: No. B295, Szegedin, 1827-48. No. B296, Esztergom, 1848-51. No. B297, Budapest 1971 Exhibition. No. B298a, Paar family signet, 1593. No. B298b, Courier letter, 1708. No. B298c, First well-known Hungarian postmark "V. TOKAI," 1752. No. B298d, Letter, 1705.

1972, May *Perf. 12x11½*

B294 SP142 2fo + 1fo blue & blk .70 .70
B295 SP142 2fo + 1fo yel & blk .70 .70
B296 SP142 2fo + 1fo yel grn & blk .70 .70
B297 SP142 2fo + 1fo ver & multi .70 .70
Nos. B294-B297 (4) 2.80 2.80

Souvenir Sheet

B298 Sheet of 4 2.50 2.25
a. SP142 2fo + 1fo yel grn & multi .50 .45
b. SP142 2fo + 1fo brn & multi .50 .45
c. SP142 2fo + 1fo ultra & multi .50 .45
d. SP142 2fo + 1fo red & multi .50 .45

9th Congress of National Federation of Hungarian Philatelists (Mabeosz). No. B298 contains 4 stamps (size: 32x23mm).
Exist imperf. Value: Nos. B294-B297 $15; No. B298 $17.50.

Olympic Type of Regular Issue

Design: Wrestling and Olympic rings.

1972, July 15 **Photo.** *Perf. 11*

B299 A484 3fo + 1fo multi .50 .30

Exists imperf.

Historic Mail Box, Telephone and Molniya Satellite — SP143

Design: No. B301, Post horn, Tokai postmark, and Nos. 183, 1802, 1809.

1972, Oct. 27 **Litho.** *Perf. 12*

B300 SP143 4fo + 2fo grn & multi .80 .70
B301 SP143 4fo + 2fo bl & multi .80 .70

Reopening of the Post and Philatelic Museums, Budapest.
Exist imperf. Value, set $15.

Bird on Silver Disk, 10th Century SP144

Treasures from Hungarian Natl. Museum. No. B303, Ring with serpent's head, 11th cent. No. B304, Lovers, belt buckle, 12th cent. No. B305, Flower, belt buckle, 15th cent. No. B306a, Opal pendant, 16th cent. No. B306b, Jeweled belt buckle, 18th cent. No. B306c, Flower pin, 17th cent. No. B306d, Rosette pendant, 17th cent.

1973, Sept. 22 **Litho.** *Perf. 12*

B302 SP144 2fo + 50f brn & multi .65 .65
B303 SP144 2fo + 50f brt rose lil & multi .65 .65
B304 SP144 2fo + 50f dk bl & multi .65 .65
B305 SP144 2fo + 50f grn & multi .65 .65
Nos. B302-B305 (4) 2.60 2.60

Souvenir Sheet

B306 Sheet of 4 2.50 2.50
a. SP144 2fo + 50f brown & multi .35 .35
b. SP144 2fo + 50f car & multi .35 .35
c. SP144 2fo + 50f ol grn & multi .35 .35
d. SP144 2fo + 50f brt bl & multi .35 .35

46th Stamp Day. No. B306 contains 4 stamps (size: 25x35mm).
Exist imperf. Value: Nos. B302-B305 $15; No. B306 $20.

Gothic Wall Fountain SP145

Visegrad Castle and Bas-reliefs — SP146

Designs: No. B308, Wellhead, Anjou period. No. B309, Twin lion-head wall fountain. B310, Fountain with Hercules riding dolphin. No. B311a, Raven panel. No. B311b, Visegrad Madonna. B311c, Lion panel. No. B311d, Visegrad Castle. Designs show artworks from Visegrad Palace of King Matthias Corvinus I, 15th century.

1975, Sept. 13 **Litho.** *Perf. 12*

Multicolored and:

B307 SP145 2fo + 1fo green 1.50 1.50
B308 SP145 2fo + 1fo ver 1.50 1.50
B309 SP145 2fo + 1fo blue 1.50 1.50
B310 SP145 2fo + 1fo lilac 1.50 1.50
a. Horizontal strip of 4 6.00 6.00

Souvenir Sheet

B311 SP146 Sheet of 4 7.50 7.50
a. 2fo + 1fo 21x32mm 1.40 1.40
b. 2fo + 1fo 47x32mm 1.40 1.40
c. 2fo + 1fo 21x32mm 1.40 1.40
d. 2fo + 1fo 99x32mm 1.40 1.40

European Architectural Heritage Year 1975 and 48th Stamp Day.
Exist imperf. Value: Nos. B307-B310 $125; No. B311 $100.

Knight SP147

Gothic Sculptures, Buda Castle — SP148

Gothic sculptures from Buda Castle: No. B313, Armor-bearer. No. B314, Apostle. No. B315, Bishop.

1976 **Photo.** *Perf. 12*

B312 SP147 2.50 + 1fo shown .60 .60
B313 SP147 2.50 + 1fo multi .60 .60
B314 SP147 2.50 + 1fo multi .60 .60
B315 SP147 2.50 + 1fo multi .60 .60
a. Horizontal strip of 4, #B312-B315 2.75 2.75

Souvenir Sheet

Designs: a, Man with hat. b, Woman with wimple. c, Man with cloth cap. d, Man with fur hat.

B316 SP148 Sheet of 4 3.00 3.00
a.-d. 2.50 + 1fo any single .55 .55

49th Stamp Day.

No. B316 issued in connection with 10th Congress of National Federation of Hungarian Philatelists (Mabeosz).

Exist imperf. Value: Nos. B312-B315 $15; No. B316 $20.

Issued: No. B316, 5/22; Nos. B312-B315, 9/4.

Young Runners SP149

1977, Apr. 2 Litho. *Perf. 12*
B317 SP149 3fo + 1.50fo multi .85 .85

Sports promotion among young people.
Exists imperf. Value $5.

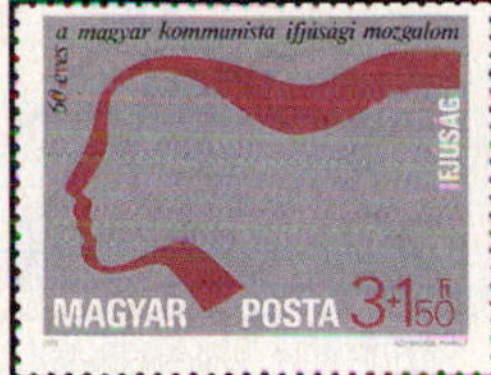
Young Man and Woman, Profiles SP150

1978, Apr. 1 Litho. *Perf. 12*
B318 SP150 3fo + 1.50fo multi 1.25 1.25

Hungarian Communist Youth Movement, 60th anniversary.
Exists imperf. Value $10.

"Generations," by Gyula Derkovits SP151

1978, May 6 Litho. *Perf. 12*
B319 SP151 3fo + 1.50fo multi .90 .90

Szocfilex '78, Szombathely. No. B319 printed in sheets of 3 stamps and 3 labels showing Szocfilex emblem.
Exists imperf. Value: single $5; sheetlet $15.

Girl Reading Book, by Ferenc Kovacs SP152

1979, Mar. 31 Litho. *Perf. 12*
B320 SP152 3fo + 1.50fo blk & ultra .45 .45

Surtax was for Junior Stamp Exhibition, Bekescsaba.
Exists imperf. Value $5.

Watch Symbolizing Environmental Protection SP153

1980, Apr. 3 Litho. *Perf. 12*
B321 SP153 3fo + 1.50fo multi .70 .70

Surtax was for Junior Stamp Exhibition, Dunaujvaros.
Exists imperf. Value $5.

International Year of the Disabled — SP154

1981, May 15 Litho. *Perf. 12*
B322 SP154 2fo + 1fo multi .45 .45

Exists imperf. Value $6.

Youths and Factory — SP155

1981, May 29 *Perf. 12x11½*
B323 SP155 4fo + 2fo multi .80 .80

Young Communist League, 10th Congress, Budapest, May 29-31.
Exists imperf. Value $7.

European Junior Tennis Cup, July 25-Aug. 1 — SP156

1982, Apr. 2 Litho. *Perf. 12x11½*
B324 SP156 4fo + 2fo multi .80 .80

Exists imperf. Value $5.

Souvenir Sheet

SP157

Perf. 12½x11½
1982, June 11 Litho.
B325 SP157 20fo + 10fo multi 4.00 4.00

PHILEXFRANCE '82 Stamp Exhibition, Paris, June 11-21.
Exists imperf. Value $15.

55th Stamp Day — SP158

Budapest Architecture and Statues: No. B326, Fishermen's Bastion, Janos Hunyadi (1403-1456). No. B327, Parliament, Ferenc Rakoczi the Second (1676-1735).

1982, Sept. 10 Litho. *Perf. 12*
B326 SP158 4fo + 2fo multi .90 .90
B327 SP158 4fo + 2fo shown .90 .90

Exist imperf. Value, set $15.

Souvenir Sheet

Parliament, Chain Bridge, Buda Castle, Budapest — SP159

1982, Sept. 10 *Perf. 11½*
B328 SP159 20fo + 10fo multi 3.75 3.75

European Security and Cooperation Conference, 10th anniv.
Exists imperf. Value $24.

21st Junior Stamp Exhibition, Baja, Mar. 31-Apr. 9 — SP160

1983, Mar. 31 Litho. *Perf. 12x11½*
B329 SP160 4fo + 2fo multi .90 .90

Surtax was for show.
Exists imperf. Value $6.

56th Natl. Stamp Day SP161

Budapest Architecture (19th Cent. Engravings by) — Rudolph Alt, H. Luders (No. B331): No. B330, Old Natl. Theater. No. B331, Municipal Concert Hall.
No. B332, Holy Trinity Square.

1983, Sept. 9 Litho. *Perf. 12*
B330 SP161 4fo + 2fo multi .90 .90
B331 SP161 4fo + 2fo multi .90 .90

Souvenir Sheet
Lithographed and Engraved
Perf. 11

B332 SP161 20fo + 10fo multi 3.75 3.75

No. B332 contains one stamp (28x45mm).
Exist imperf. Value: Nos. B330-B331 $15; No. B332 $20.

Mother & Child — SP162

1984, Apr. 2 Litho. *Perf. 12½x11½*
B333 SP162 4fo + 2fo multi .75 .75

Surtax was for children's foundation.
Exists imperf. Value $10.

SP163

Little Red Riding Hood, by the Brothers Grimm.

1985, Apr. 2 Litho. *Perf. 11½x12*
B334 SP163 4fo + 2fo multi .75 .75

Jacob (1785-1863) and Wilhelm (1786-1859) Grimm, fabulists and philologists.
Exists imperf. Value $8.

Natl. SOS Children's Village Assoc., 3rd Anniv. SP164

1985, Dec. 10 Litho. *Perf. 11*
B335 SP164 4fo + 2fo multi .75 .75

Surtax for natl. SOS Children's Village.
Exists imperf. Value $7.

Natl. Young Pioneers Org., 40th Anniv. SP165

1986, May 30 *Perf. 11½x12½*
B336 SP165 4fo + 2fo multi .75 .60

Exists imperf. Value $6.

Souvenir Sheet

Budapest Natl. Theater — SP166

Lithographed and Engraved

1986, Oct. 10 *Perf. 11*
B337 SP166 20fo + 10fo tan, brn & buff 4.00 4.00

Surtax benefited natl. theater construction. Exists imperf. Value $20.

Natl. Communist Youth League, 30th Anniv. — SP167

1987, Mar. 20 *Perf. 13½x13*
B338 SP167 4fo + 2fo multi .60 .60

Exists imperf. Value $6.

Souvenir Sheet

SOCFILEX '88, Aug. 12-21, Kecskemet — SP168

1988, Mar. 10 **Litho.** *Perf. 11½*
B339 SP168 20fo +10fo multi 4.50 4.50

Surtax for SOCFILEX '88. Exists imperf. Value $20.

Sky High Tree, a Tapestry by Erzsebet Szekeres SP169

1989, Apr. 12 **Litho.** *Perf. 12*
B340 SP169 5fo +2fo multi 1.50 1.50

Surtax to promote youth philately. Exist imperf. Value, set $7.

Souvenir Sheet

Battle of Solferino, by Carlo Bossoli — SP170

1989, Sept. 8 **Litho.** *Perf. 10½*
B341 SP170 20fo +10fo multi 3.75 3.75

Stamp Day. Exists imperf. Value $35.

Souvenir Sheet

Martyrs of Arad, Arad, Romania, 1849 — SP171

1989, Oct. 6 *Perf. 11½x12½*
B342 SP171 20fo +10fo multi 3.75 3.75

Surtax to fund production of another statue. Exists imperf. Value $20.

Teacher's Training High School, Sarospatak Municipal Arms — SP172

1990, Mar. 30 **Litho.** *Perf. 12x11½*
B343 SP172 8fo +4fo multi 2.00 2.00

28th Youth Stamp Exhib., Sarospatak, Apr. 6-22. Exists imperf. Value $9.

Souvenir Sheet

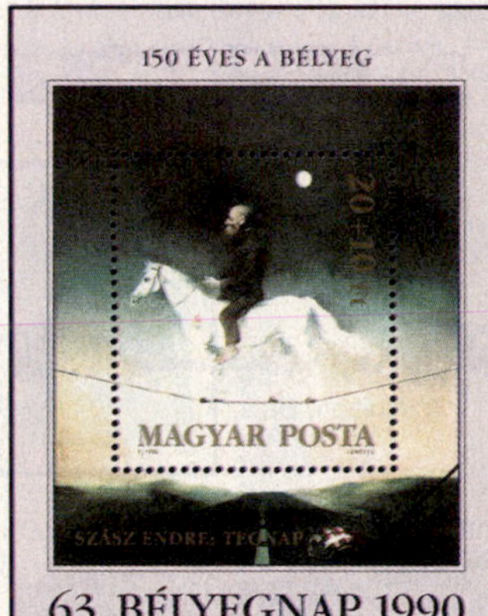

Yesterday, by Endre Szasz — SP173

1990, Oct. 12 **Litho.** *Perf. 12*
B344 SP173 20fo +10fo multi 4.50 4.50

Stamp Day. Surtax for National Federation of Hungarian Philatelists. Exists imperf. Value $30.

Tapestry, Peter and the Wolf, by Gabriella Hajnal — SP174

1991, Apr. 30 **Litho.** *Perf. 12*
B345 SP174 12fo +6fo multi 1.75 1.75

Surtax to promote youth philately. Exists imperf. Value $8.

Children's Drawings SP175

Designs: 9fo + 4fo, Girl holding flower, vert. 10fo + 4fo, Child standing beneath sun. 15fo + 4fo, Boy wearing crown, vert.

1992, May 15 **Litho.** *Perf. 12*
B346 SP175 9fo +4fo multi 1.10 1.10
B347 SP175 10fo +4fo multi 1.25 1.25
B348 SP175 15fo +4fo multi 1.65 1.65
Nos. B346-B348 (3) 4.00 4.00

Surtax for children's welfare.

Souvenir Sheet

1992 Summer Olympics, Barcelona — SP176

1992, Sept. 4 **Litho.** *Perf. 12*
B349 SP176 50fo +20fo multi 3.50 3.00

Textile Art, by Erzsebet Szekeres SP177

No. B350, Outdoor scene. No. B351, Tree of life.

1993, Apr. 14 **Litho.** *Perf. 12*
B350 SP177 10fo +5fo multi .60 .40
B351 SP177 17fo +8fo multi 1.60 1.00

Stamp Day SP178

Stamp designers, stamps: 10fo + 5fo, Zoltan Nagy (1916-1987), #1062. 17fo + 5fo, Sandor Legrady (1906-1987), #523. 50fo + 20fo, Ferenc Helbing (1870-1959), #465.

1993, Sept. 10 **Litho.** *Perf. 12*
B352 SP178 10fo +5fo multi .75 .30
B353 SP178 17fo +5fo multi 1.00 .45

Souvenir Sheet

B354 SP178 50fo +20fo multi 3.25 1.75

No. B354 contains one 35x27mm stamp.

The Little Prince, by Antoine de Saint-Exupery SP179

1994, Apr. 1 **Litho.** *Perf. 13½x13*
B355 SP179 19fo +5fo multi 2.00 2.00

Surtax for children's welfare.

Poem, "John the Hero," 150th Anniv. SP180

1995, Apr. 7 **Litho.** *Perf. 12*
B356 SP180 22fo +10fo multi 1.00 .60

Surtax to promote youth philately.

Olympiafila '95, Budapest — SP181

No. B357, Yellow rings. No. B358, Purple rings.

1995, June 12 **Litho.** *Perf. 11*
B357 SP181 22fo +11fo multi 1.10 .50
B358 SP181 22fo +11fo multi 1.10 .50
a. Pair, #B357-B358 2.50 1.50

No. B358a also sold in a strip of 3 pairs in a booklet.

World Festival of Puppet Players, Budapest SP182

Laszlo Vitez puppet and ghost puppet.

1996, June 21 **Litho.** *Perf. 12*
B359 SP182 24fo +10fo multi 1.00 .75

Oder River Flood of 1997 SP183

No. B360, Flower in water.

1997, Sept. 12 **Litho.** *Perf. 12*
B360 SP183 27fo +100fo multi 2.25 .95

Surtax is for aid to flood victims.

Stamp Day SP184

Early postman using: 27fo + 5fo, Motorized tricycle. 55fo + 5fo, Experimental registered letter-receiving machine, vert. 90fo + 30fo, Postal van.

1997, Sept. 19

B361 SP184 27fo +5fo multi .75 .25
B362 SP184 55fo +5fo multi 1.50 .45

Souvenir Sheet

B363 SP184 90fo +30fo multi 7.00 3.75

Souvenir Sheet

Revolution of 1848 — SP185

Design: Seven members of movement, newspaper *Nemzeti dal.*

1998, Mar. 13 Litho. *Perf. 12*

B364 SP185 150fo +50fo multi 4.50 1.75

Surtax to promote youth philately.

Youth Stamp SP186

1999, Mar. 12 Litho. *Perf. 12*

B365 SP186 52fo +25fo multi 1.50 .75

István Fekete (1900-70), Writer — SP187

2000, Jan. 11 Litho. *Perf. 12*

B366 SP187 60fo +30fo multi 2.00 2.00

Surtax for youth philately.

Hunphilex 2000 Stamp Exhibition, Budapest SP188

2000, Jan. 11

B367 SP188 200fo +100fo multi 4.00 3.00

Surtax to support stamp exhibition.

Souvenir Sheet

Hunphilex 2000 Stamp Exhibition, Budapest — SP189

No. B368, Coronation robe.

2000, Aug. 18 Litho. *Perf. 12*

B368 SP189 200fo +100fo multi 3.75 2.75
a. Sheet of 2 9.00 5.75

Star Over Eger, by Geza Gardonyi SP190

2001, Jan. 15 Litho. *Perf. 13¼x13*

B369 SP190 60fo +30fo multi 1.75 .50

Surtax for youth philately.

Campaign Against Breast Cancer — SP191

2005, Sept. 29 Litho. *Perf. 12*

B370 SP191 90fo +50fo multi 2.50 2.00

Victory in First Grand Prix Race by Ferenc Szisz (1873-1944) — SP192

2006, May 9 Litho. *Perf. 13x13¼*

B371 SP192 120fo +50fo multi 2.00 2.00

Smile, by Zita Zagyi SP193

2008, May 20 Litho. *Perf. 13x13¼*

B372 SP193 100fo + 50fo multi 1.90 1.90

Design was a winner in a children's art contest. Surtax for Hungarian Ambulance Service.

Togetherness — SP194

2009, Aug. 31

B373 SP194 75fo +50fo multi 1.40 1.40

Surtax for Crisis Foundation.

Hungarian Red Cross — SP195

2010, Mar. 1 Litho. *Perf. 12¼x12¾*

B374 SP195 105fo + 55fo multi 1.75 1.75

Surtax for Red Cross.

Interlocking Hands — SP196

2010, Nov. 24 Litho. *Perf. 13x13¼*

B375 SP196 (80fo) +100fo multi 1.75 1.75

Surtax for victims of Hungarian Red Sludge disaster of Oct. 4, 2010.

Child and Heart SP197

2011, Mar. 1 Litho. *Perf. 12½x12*

B376 SP197 (90fo) +50fo multi 1.75 1.75

Surtax for Intl. Children's Safety Service. For overprint, see No. B379.

Souvenir Sheet

William Shakespeare (1564-1616), Writer — SP198

No. B377 — Characters from *Hamlet*: a, Queen Gertrude. b, Hamlet.

2014, Apr. 25 Litho. *Perf. 13¼*

B377 SP198 200fo +50fo Sheet of 2, #a-b 4.50 4.50

Surtax for youth philately.

Souvenir Sheet

Publication of Poem *Matyi, the Goose Boy*, by Mihály Fazekas, 200th Anniv. — SP199

2015, Mar. 24 Litho. *Perf. 14x13½*

B378 SP199 400fo +150fo multi 4.25 4.25

Surtax for youth philately.

No. B376 Overprinted in Green

2015, May 29 Litho. *Perf. 12½x12*

B379 SP197 (115fo) +50fo multi 1.25 1.25

Intl. Children's Safety Service, 25th anniv.

AIR POST STAMPS

Issues of the Monarchy

Nos. 120, 123 Surcharged in Red or Blue

Wmk. 137

1918, July 4 Typo. *Perf. 14*

C1 A10 1k 50f on 75f (R) 25.00 *27.50*
C2 A10 4k 50f on 2k (Bl) 25.00 *27.50*

Counterfeits exist.
Exist imperf. Value, set $350.

No. 126 Surcharged

1920, Nov. 7

C3 A10 3k on 10k (G) 1.40 *2.25*
C4 A10 8k on 10k (R) 1.40 *2.25*
C5 A10 12k on 10k (Bl) 1.40 *2.25*
Nos. C3-C5 (3) 4.20 6.75
Set, never hinged 7.50

Icarus — AP3

1924-25 *Perf. 14*

C6 AP3 100k red brn & red 1.25 *2.50*
C7 AP3 500k bl grn & yel grn 1.25 *2.50*
C8 AP3 1000k bis brn & brn 1.25 *2.50*
C9 AP3 2000k dk bl & lt bl 1.25 *2.50*

Wmk. 133

C10 AP3 5000k dl vio & brt vio 2.00 *2.50*
C11 AP3 10000k red & dl vio 2.00 *4.00*
Nos. C6-C11 (6) 9.00 16.50
Set, never hinged 20.00

Issue dates: 100k-2000k, 4/11/24. Others, 4/20/25.
Exist imperf. Value, set $100.
Forgeries exist.
For surcharges see Nos. J112-J116.

Mythical "Turul" AP4

"Turul" Carrying Messenger AP5

1927-30 Engr. *Perf. 14*

C12 AP4	4f orange ('30)	.25	*.40*
C13 AP4	12f deep green	.45	*.40*
C14 AP4	16f red brown	.45	*.40*
C15 AP4	20f carmine	.45	*.40*
C16 AP4	32f brown vio	1.75	1.20
C17 AP4	40f dp ultra	1.40	.80
C18 AP5	50f claret	1.40	.80
C19 AP5	72f olive grn	1.90	1.20
C20 AP5	80f dp violet	1.90	1.20
C21 AP5	1p emerald ('30)	2.25	.50
C22 AP5	2p red ('30)	4.50	3.00
C23 AP5	5p dk blue ('30)	16.50	*27.50*
	Nos. C12-C23 (12)	33.20	37.80
	Set, never hinged	55.00	

Exist imperf. Value, set $250.

"Turul" Carrying Messenger — AP6

1931, Mar. 27 Overprinted

C24 AP6	1p orange (Bk)	40.00	*65.00*
C25 AP6	2p dull vio (G)	40.00	*65.00*
	Set, never hinged	160.00	

Exist imperf. Value, set $375.

Monoplane over Danube Valley — AP7

Worker Welcoming Plane, Double Cross and Sun Rays — AP8

Spirit of Flight on Plane Wing AP9

"Flight" Holding Propeller AP10

Wmk. 210

1933, June 20 Photo. *Perf. 15*

C26 AP7	10f blue green	2.00	.40
C27 AP7	16f purple	2.00	.40

Perf. 12½x12

C28 AP8	20f carmine	4.50	.75
C29 AP8	40f blue	4.00	1.25
C30 AP9	48f gray black	9.50	2.00
C31 AP9	72f bister brn	20.00	3.00
C32 AP10	1p yellow grn	25.00	3.00
C33 AP10	2p violet brn	47.50	18.00
C34 AP10	5p dk gray	85.00	*150.00*
	Nos. C26-C34 (9)	199.50	178.80
	Set, never hinged	375.00	

Exist imperf. Value, set $2,600.

Catalogue values for unused stamps in this section, from this point to the end of the section, are for Never Hinged items.

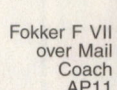

Fokker F VII over Mail Coach AP11

Plane over Parliament AP12

Airplane AP13

1936, May 8 *Perf. 12x12½*

C35 AP11	10f brt green	.80	.40
C36 AP11	20f crimson	.80	.40
C37 AP11	36f brown	.90	.40
C38 AP12	40f brt blue	.90	.40
C39 AP12	52f red org	3.25	.85
C40 AP12	60f brt violet	20.00	2.00
C41 AP12	80f dk sl grn	4.00	.60
C42 AP13	1p dk yel grn	4.75	.55
C43 AP13	2p brown car	7.50	2.00
C44 AP13	5p dark blue	24.00	19.50
	Nos. C35-C44 (10)	66.90	27.10
	Set, hinged	27.50	

Exist imperf. Value, set $675.

Issues of the Republic

Loyalty Tower, Sopron — AP14

Designs: 20f, Cathedral of Esztergom. 50f, Liberty Bridge, Budapest. 70f, Palace Hotel, Lillafüred. 1fo, Vajdahunyad Castle, Budapest. 1.40fo, Visegrád Fortress on the Danube. 3fo, Lake Balaton. 5fo, Parliament Building, Budapest.

Perf. 12½x12

1947, Mar. 5 Photo. Wmk. 210

C45 AP14	10f rose lake	.45	.50
C46 AP14	20f gray green	.50	.50
C47 AP14	50f copper brn	.60	.50
C48 AP14	70f olive grn	.70	.50
C49 AP14	1fo gray blue	.90	.50
C50 AP14	1.40fo brown	1.75	.50
C51 AP14	3fo green	2.00	.50
C52 AP14	5fo rose violet	5.50	1.00
	Nos. C45-C52 (8)	12.40	4.50

Exist imperf. Value, set $250.

Johannes Gutenberg and Printing Press AP22

Designs: 2f, Columbus. 4f, Robert Fulton. 5f, George Stephenson. 6f, David Schwarz and Ferdinand von Zeppelin. 8f, Thomas A. Edison. 10f, Louis Bleriot. 12f, Roald Amundsen. 30f, Kalman Kando. 40f, Alexander S. Popov.

Perf. 12x12½

1948, May 15 Wmk. 283

C53 AP22	1f orange red	.25	.25
C54 AP22	2f dp magenta	.30	.30
C55 AP22	4f blue	.30	.30
C56 AP22	5f orange brn	.35	.35
C57 AP22	6f green	.40	.40
C58 AP22	8f dp red vio	.40	.40
C59 AP22	10f brown	.50	.50
C60 AP22	12f blue grn	.55	.55
C61 AP22	30f brown rose	2.00	2.00
C62 AP22	40f blue violet	2.40	2.40
	Nos. C53-C62 (10)	7.45	7.45

Explorers and inventors.
Exist imperf. Value, set $120.

See Nos. CB3-CB12.

IMPERFORATE STAMPS

Through 1991, most air post stamps stamps were also issued imperforate. Where these items form part of a larger set with regular issues, values for imperfs will be included in that of the sets to which they belong, footnoted in the Regular Issues section. For Nos. C63-C452, values for imperfs will be given only for those items not included in sets with regular issues.

UPU Type

1949, Nov. 1

C63 A171	2fo orange brn	1.50	1.50
a.	Booklet pane of 6	37.50	

75th anniv. of the UPU. See No. C81.
Exists imperf.

Chain Bridge Type and

Symbols of Labor — AP25

1949, Nov. 20

C64 A172	1.60fo scarlet	1.75	*2.00*
C65 A172	2fo olive	1.75	*2.00*

Souvenir Sheet

Perf. 12½x12

C66 AP25	50fo car lake	350.00	350.00

Opening of the Chain Bridge, Budapest, cent.
No. C66 exists imperf. Value $5,500.

Postman and Mail Carrying Vehicles AP26

1949, Dec. 11 *Perf. 12*

C67 AP26	50f lilac gray	6.00	6.00
	Sheet of 4	40.00	30.00

Stamp Day, 1949.
Exists imperf. Value: single $100; sheet $525.

Plane, Globe, Stamps and Stagecoach — AP27

1950, Mar. 12 *Perf. 12x12½*

C68 AP27	2fo red brn & yel	12.00	12.00

20th anniv. of the establishment of the Hungarian Post Office Philatelic Museum.
Exists imperf. Value $50.

Chess Emblem, Globe and Plane AP28

1950, Apr. 9 Wmk. 106 *Perf. 12*

C69 AP28	1.60fo brown	7.25	2.50

World Chess Championship Matches, Budapest.
Exists imperf.

Globes, Parliament Building and Chain Bridge — AP29

1950, May 16 *Perf. 12x12½*

C70 AP29	1fo red brown	1.60	.65

Meeting of the World Federation of Trade Unions, Budapest, May 1950.
Exists imperf.

Statue of Liberty and View of Budapest — AP30

Designs: 30f, Crane and apartment house. 70f, Steel mill. 1fo, Stalinyec tractor. 1.60fo, Steamship. 2fo, Reaping-threshing machine. 3fo, Passenger train. 5fo, Matyas Rakosi Steel Mill, Csepel. 10fo, Budaörs Airport.

Perf. 12½x12

1950, Oct. 29 Engr. Unwmk.

C71 AP30	20f claret	.65	.25
C72 AP30	30f blue vio	.65	.25
C73 AP30	70f violet brn	.25	.25
C74 AP30	1fo yellow brn	.25	.25
C75 AP30	1.60fo ultra	.70	.25
C76 AP30	2fo red org	.75	.25
C77 AP30	3fo olive blk	1.00	.50
C78 AP30	5fo gray blue	2.00	1.00
C79 AP30	10fo chestnut	6.25	1.75
	Nos. C71-C79 (9)	12.50	4.75

See Nos. C167 and C172.
Exist imperf. Value, set $100.

Bem Type

Souvenir Sheet

1950, Dec. 10 Engr. *Imperf.*

C80 A185	2fo deep plum	42.50	42.50

Stamp Day and Budapest Stamp Exhibition.

UPU Type of 1949

Perf. 12x12½, Imperf.

1950, July 2 Photo. Wmk. 106

C81 A171	3fo dk car & dk brn	40.00	40.00
	Sheet of 4	525.00	525.00

Exists imperf. Value: single $80; sheet of 4 $600.

Sports Type

Designs: 30f, Volleyball. 40f, Javelin-throwing. 60f, Sports badge. 70f, Soccer. 3fo, Glider meet.

1950, Dec. 2

C82 A188	30f lilac & magenta	.50	.25
C83 A188	40f olive & indigo	.75	.25
C84 A188	60f ol, dk brn & org red	1.25	.40
C85 A188	70f gray & dk brn	2.75	.55
C86 A188	3fo buff & dk brn	4.50	2.25
	Nos. C82-C86 (5)	9.75	3.70

Exist imperf.

Livestock Type

1951, Apr. 5 Photo. *Perf. 12x12½*

C87 A191 20f Mare & foal 2.00 .30
C88 A191 70f Sow & shoats 2.25 .70
C89 A191 1fo Ram & ewe 3.75 .90
C90 A191 1.60fo Cow & calf 5.25 1.50
Nos. C87-C90 (4) 13.25 3.40

Exist imperf.

Telegraph Linemen AP34

Designs: 1fo, Workers on vacation. 2fo, Air view of Stalin Bridge.

1951, Aug. 20

C91 AP34 70f henna brown .85 .30
C92 AP34 1fo blue green .95 .35
C93 AP34 2fo deep plum 1.75 .70
Nos. C91-C93 (3) 3.55 1.35

Successful conclusion of the 1st year under Hungary's 5-year plan.
Exist imperf.

Tank Column — AP35

1951, Sept. 29 *Perf. 12½x12*

C94 AP35 60f deep blue 1.00 .25

Army Day, Sept. 29, 1951
Exists imperf.

1st Stamp Type
Souvenir Sheet

1951, Oct. 6 Engr. Unwmk.

C95 A208 60f olive green 75.00 65.00

Stamp exhibition to commemorate the 80th anniv. of Hungary's 1st postage stamp.
Exists imperf. Value $200.
Twelve hundred copies in rose lilac, perf. and imperf., were presented to exhibitors and members of the arranging committee of the exhibition. Value, each $1,600.

Avocet — AP37

Hungarian Birds: 30f, White stork. 40f, Golden oriole. 50f, Kentish plover. 60f, Black-winged stilt. 70f, Lesser gray shrike. 80f, Great bustard. 1fo, Redfooted falcon. 1.40fo, European bee-eater. 1.60fo, Glossy ibis. 2.50fo, Great white egret.

Perf. 13x11

1952, Mar. 16 Photo. Wmk. 106

Birds in Natural Colors

C96 AP37 20f emer, *grnsh* .25 .25
C97 AP37 30f sage grn, *grysh* .25 .25
C98 AP37 40f brown, *cr* .35 .25
C99 AP37 50f orange, *cr* .40 .25
C100 AP37 60f dp car .50 .25
C101 AP37 70f red org, *cr* .60 .35
C102 AP37 80f olive, *cr* .80 .45
C103 AP37 1fo dp blue, *bluish* 1.00 .55
C104 AP37 1.40fo gray, *grysh* 2.00 .65
C105 AP37 1.60fo org brn, *cr* 2.50 .85
C106 AP37 2.50fo rose vio, *cr* 3.50 1.25
Nos. C96-C106 (11) 12.15 5.35

Exist imperf. Value, set $100.

Olympic Games Type

Designs: 1.70fo, hammer thrower; 2fo, Stadium, Budapest.

1952, May 26 *Perf. 11*

C107 A217 1.70fo dp red orange 2.10 1.00
C108 A217 2fo olive brown 2.50 1.25

Issued to publicize Hungary's participation in the Olympic Games, Helsinki, 1952.
Exists imperf.

Leonardo da Vinci — AP39

1952, June 15 *Perf. 12½x12*

C109 AP39 1.60fo shown 1.50 1.00
C110 AP39 2fo Victor Hugo 2.00 1.10

Exist imperf. Value, set $35.

AP40

AP41

20f, Red squirrel. 30f, Hedgehog. 40f, Hare. 50f, Beech marten. 60f, Otter. 70f, Red fox. 80f, Fallow deer. 1fo, Roe deer. 1.50fo, Boar. 2fo, Red deer.

1953, Mar. 4 *Perf. 12x12½*

C111 AP40 20f multi .50 .25
C112 AP41 30f multi .65 .25
C113 AP41 40f multi .65 .30
C114 AP40 50f multi .80 .40
C115 AP41 60f multi 1.00 .45
C116 AP41 70f multi 1.00 .50
C117 AP40 80f multi 1.25 .75
C118 AP41 1fo multi 1.60 1.00
C119 AP41 1.50fo multi 4.00 1.25
C120 AP40 2fo multi 4.50 1.50
Nos. C111-C120 (10) 15.95 6.65

Exist imperf. Value, set $75.

Type of Regular Issue

Designs: 1fo, Children at Balaton Lake. 1.50fo, Workers' Home at Lillafured.

1953, Apr. 19 *Perf. 12*

C121 A228 1fo brt grnsh blue .65 .25
C122 A228 1.50fo dp red lilac 1.25 .40

Exist imperf.

People's Stadium Type

1953, Aug. 20 *Perf. 11*

C123 A232 80f Water polo 1.00 .25
C124 A232 1fo Boxing 2.00 .25
C125 A232 2fo Soccer 2.25 .80
C126 A232 3fo Track 2.50 .95
C127 A232 5fo Stadium 3.75 1.75
Nos. C123-C127 (5) 11.50 4.00

Exist imperf.

No. C125 Overprinted in Black

1953, Dec. 3

C128 A232 2fo green & brown 27.50 25.00

Hungary's success in the soccer matches at Wembley, England, Nov. 25, 1953. Counterfeits exist.
Exists imperf. Value $300.

Janos Bihari and Scene from Verbunkos AP44

Portraits: 40f, Ferenc Erkel. 60f, Franz Liszt. 70f, Mihaly Mosonyi. 80f, Karl Goldmark. 1fo, Bela Bartok. 2fo, Zoltan Kodaly.

1953, Dec. 5 Photo. *Perf. 12*

Frames and Portraits in Brown

C129 AP44 30f blue gray .35 .25
C130 AP44 40f orange .35 .25
C131 AP44 60f green .55 .25
C132 AP44 70f red .45 .30
C133 AP44 80f gray blue .50 .40
C134 AP44 1fo olive bis 1.00 .60
C135 AP44 2fo violet 1.50 1.25
Nos. C129-C135 (7) 4.70 3.30

Hungarian composers.
Exists imperf. Value, set $40.

Carrot Beetle — AP45

May (or June) Beetle AP46

Designs: Various beetles. 60f, Bee.

Perf. 12½x12, 12x12½

1954, Feb. 6 Wmk. 106

C136 AP45 30f dp org & dk brn .50 .25
C137 AP46 40f grn & dk brn .60 .25
C138 AP46 50f rose brn & blk .85 .30
C139 AP46 60f vio, dk brn & yel .85 .45
C140 AP45 80f grnsh gray, pur & rose 1.25 .70
C141 AP45 1fo ocher & blk 1.75 .80
C142 AP46 1.20fo dl grn & dk brn 2.10 1.00
C143 AP46 1.50fo ol brn & dk brn 3.25 1.25
C144 AP46 2fo hn brn & dk brn 4.25 1.50
C145 AP45 3fo bl grn & dk brn 5.50 2.00
Nos. C136-C145 (10) 20.90 8.50

Exists imperf. Value, set $110.

Lunchtime at the Nursery AP47

Designs: 1.50fo, Mother taking child from doctor. 2fo, Nurse and children.

1954, Mar. 8 *Perf. 12*

C146 AP47 1fo olive green 1.00 .40
C147 AP47 1.50fo red brown 1.40 .50
C148 AP47 2fo blue green 2.40 1.25
Nos. C146-C148 (3) 4.80 2.15

Exist imperf.

Model Glider Construction — AP48

Boy Flying Model Glider AP49

Designs: 60f, Gliders. 80f, Pilot leaving plane. 1fo, Parachutists. 1.20fo, Biplane. 1.50fo, Plane over Danube. 2fo, Jet planes.

1954, June 25 *Perf. 11*

C149 AP48 40f brn, ol & dk bl gray .30 .25
C150 AP49 50f gray & red brn .40 .25
C151 AP48 60f red brn & dk bl gray .40 .25
C152 AP49 80f violet & sep .45 .25
C153 AP48 1fo brn & dk bl gray .65 .25
C154 AP49 1.20fo olive & sep 1.00 .25
C155 AP48 1.50fo cl & dk bl gray 1.25 .50
C156 AP49 2fo blue & dk brn 1.90 .50
Nos. C149-C156 (8) 6.35 2.50

Exist imperf. Value, set $75.

Jokai Type
Souvenir Sheet

1954, Oct. 17 Engr. *Perf. 12½x12*

C157 A242 1fo violet blue 37.50 37.50

Stamp Day. Exists imperforate. Value $90.

Children on Sled — AP51

Skaters AP52

50f, Ski racer. 60f, Ice yacht. 80f, Ice hockey. 1fo, Ski jumper. 1.50fo, Downhill ski racer. 2fo, Man and woman exhibition-skating.

1955 Photo. *Perf. 12*

C158 AP51	40f multi		.55	.25
C159 AP52	50f multi		.35	.25
C160 AP51	60f multi		.35	.25
C161 AP52	80f multi		.45	.25
C162 AP51	1fo multi		1.10	.30
C163 AP52	1.20fo multi		1.10	.30
C164 AP51	1.50fo multi		2.75	.60
C165 AP52	2fo multi		3.25	.50
	Nos. C158-C165 (8)		9.90	2.70

Exist imperf. Value, set $75.
Issued: 1.20fo, 2fo, Jan. 27; others Feb. 26.

Government Printing Plant Type
Souvenir Sheet

1955, May 28 *Perf. 12x12½*

C166 A247 5fo hn brn & gray grn 32.50 32.50

Cent. of the establishment of the government printing plant.
Exists imperf. Value $160.

No. C78 Printed on Aluminum Foil
Perf. 12½x12

1955, Oct. 5 Engr. Unwmk.

C167 AP30 5fo gray blue 15.00 12.50

Intl. Cong. of the Light Metal Industry and for 20 years of aluminum production in Hungary.
Exists imperf. Value $100.

Bartok Type
Wmk. 106

1955, Oct. 9 Photo. *Perf. 12*

C168 A252	1fo gray green	2.00	1.25
C169 A252	1fo violet brn	3.50	2.00
a.	With ticket	15.00	12.50

10th anniv. of the death of Bela Bartok, composer. No. C169a was issued for the Day of the Stamp, Oct. 16, 1955. The 5fo sales price, marked on the attached ticket, was the admission fee to any one of 14 simultaneous stamp shows.
Exist imperf. Value, set with ticket, $135.

"Esperanto" — AP55

Lazarus Ludwig Zamenhof AP56

1957, June 8

C170 AP55	60f red brown	.50	.25
C171 AP56	1fo dark green	.50	.30

10th anniversary of the death of L. L. Zamenhof, inventor of Esperanto.
Exist imperf. Value $30.

Type of 1950
Design: 20fo, Budaörs Airport.

Perf. 12½x12

1957, July 18 Engr. Unwmk.

C172 AP30	20fo dk slate grn	10.00	10.00
	Punched 3 holes	11.00	11.00

A few days after issuance, stocks of No. C172 were punched with three holes and used on domestic surface mail.
Exist imperf. Value $70.

Courier and Fort Buda AP57

Design: No. C174, Plane over Budapest.

Wmk. 106

1957, Oct. 13 Photo. *Perf. 12*

C173 AP57	1fo ol bis & brn, *buff*	1.00	1.00
C174 AP57	1fo ol bis & dp cl, *buff*	1.00	1.00
a.	Strip of #C173-C174 + label	2.50	2.50

Stamp Day, Oct. 20th. The triptych sold for 6fo.
Exists imperf. Value, strip $30.

Type of Regular Pigeon Issue
Design: 3fo, Two carrier pigeons.

1957, Dec. 14 *Perf. 12x12½*

C175 A266 3fo red, grn, gray & blk .90 .50

Exists imperf.

Hungarian Pavilion, Brussels — AP58

Designs: 40f, Map, lake and local products. 60f, Parliament. 1fo, Chain Bridge, Budapest. 1.40fo, Arms of Hungary and Belgium. 2fo, Fountain, Brussels, vert. 3fo, City Hall, Brussels vert. 5fo, Exposition emblem.

Perf. 14½x15

1958, Apr. 17 Litho. Wmk. 106

C176 AP58	20f red org & red brn	.25	.25
C177 AP58	40f lt blue & brn	.25	.25
C178 AP58	60f crimson & sep	.25	.25
C179 AP58	1fo bis & red brn	.25	.25
C180 AP58	1.40fo dull vio & multi	.40	.25
C181 AP58	2fo gldn brn & dk brn	.40	.25
C182 AP58	3fo bl grn & sep	1.50	.40
C183 AP58	5fo gray ol, blk, red, bl & yel	1.90	.60
	Nos. C176-C183 (8)	5.20	2.50

Universal and Intl. Exposition at Brussels.
Exist imperf. Value, set $20.

View of Prague and Morse Code AP59

1958, June 30 Photo. *Perf. 12x12½*

C184 AP59 1fo rose brown .35 .25

See No. 1194a for se-tenant pair.
Conference of Postal Ministers of Communist Countries at Prague, June 30-July 8.
Exists imperf.

Post Horn, Pigeon and Pen AP60

No. C185, Stamp under magnifying glass.

1958, Oct. 25 Wmk. 106 *Perf. 12*

C185 AP60	1fo dp car & bis	1.00	1.00
C186 AP60	1fo yel grn & bis	1.00	1.00
a.	Strip, #C185-C186 + label	2.50	2.50

Natl. Stamp Exhib., Budapest, 10/25-11/2.
No. C185 inscribed: "XXXI Belyegnap 1958."
Exist imperf. Value, strip $25.

1958, Oct. 26

Designs: 60f, as No. C186. 1fo, Ship, plane, locomotive and pen surrounding letter.

C187 AP60	60f dp plum & grysh buff	.40	.25
C188 AP60	1fo bl & grysh buff	.60	.25

Issued for Letter Writing Week.
Exist imperf. Value, set $18.

Plane over Heroes' Square Budapest — AP61

Design: 5fo, Plane over Tower of Sopron.

Perf. 12½x12

1958, Nov. 3 Engr. Wmk. 106

C189 AP61	3fo gray, rose vio & red	1.25	.60
C190 AP61	5fo gray, dk bl & red	1.50	.90

40th anniv. of Hungarian air post stamps.
Exist imperf. Value, set $20.

Same Without Commemorative Inscription

Plane over: 20f, Szeged. 30f, Sarospatak. 70f, Gyor. 1fo, Budapest, Opera House. 1.60fo, Veszprém. 2fo, Budapest, Chain Bridge. 3fo, Sopron. 5fo, Heroes' Square, Budapest. 10fo, Budapest, Academy of Science and Parliament. 20fo, Budapest.

1958, Dec. 31 Engr. Wmk. 106
Yellow Paper and Vermilion Inscriptions

C191 AP61	20f green	.25	.25
C192 AP61	30f violet	.25	.25
C193 AP61	70f brown vio	.25	.25
C194 AP61	1fo blue	.40	.25
C195 AP61	1.60fo purple	.40	.25
C196 AP61	2fo Prus green	.50	.25
C197 AP61	3fo brown	1.00	.25
C198 AP61	5fo olive green	1.50	.25
C199 AP61	10fo dark blue	2.25	.35
C200 AP61	20fo brown	4.25	.75
	Nos. C191-C200 (10)	11.05	3.10

Exist imperf. Value, set $60.

Transport Type of Regular Issue
Design: 3fo, Early plane.

1959, May Litho. *Perf. 14½x15*

C201 A279 3fo dl lil, blk, yel & brn 2.00 1.25

Exist imperf.

Tihany — AP62

Designs: 70f, Ship. 1fo, Heviz and water lily. 1.70fo, Sailboat and fisherman statue.

1959, July 15 Photo. *Perf. 11½x12*

C202 AP62	20f brt green	.25	.25
C203 AP62	70f brt blue	.25	.25
C204 AP62	1fo ultra & car rose	.25	.25
C205 AP62	1.70fo red brn, *yel*	.50	.30
	Nos. C202-C205 (4)	1.25	1.05

Issued to publicize Lake Balaton and the opening of the Summer University.
Exist imperf.

Moth-Butterfly Type of 1959

Butterflies: 1fo, Lycaena virgaureae. 2fo, Acherontia atropos, horiz. 3fo, Red admiral.

Perf. 11½x12, 12x11½

1959, Nov. 20 Wmk. 106
Butterflies in Natural Colors

C206 A290	1fo black & lt bl grn	.90	.25
C207 A290	2fo black & lilac	1.50	.35
C208 A290	3fo dk gray & emer	2.25	.75
	Nos. C206-C208 (3)	4.65	1.35

Exist imperf.

Souvenir Sheet

Rockets in Orbit, Gagarin, Titov & Glenn — AP63

Perf. 11, Imperf.

1962, Mar. 29 Unwmk.

C209 AP63 10fo multi 14.00 14.00

Cosmonants Yuri A. Gagarin and Gherman Titov, USSR and astronaut John H. Glenn, Jr., US.
Exists imperf. Value $40.

Soccer Type of 1962
Flags of Hungary and Great Britain.

1962, May 21 Photo. *Perf. 11*
Flags in National Colors

C209A A323 2fo greenish bister 1.40 .30

Exists imperf.

Glider and Lilienthal's 1898 Design — AP64

Designs: 30f, Icarus and Aero Club emblem. 60f, Light monoplane and 1912 aerobatic plane. 80f, Airship GZ-1 and Montgolfier balloon. 1fo, IL-18 Malev and Wright 1903 plane. 1.40fo, Stunt plane and Nyesterov's 1913 plane. 2fo, Helicopter and Asboth's 1929 helicopter. 3fo, Supersonic bomber and Zhukovski's turbomotor. 4fo, Space rocket and Tsiolkovsky's rocket.

1962, July 19 Unwmk. *Perf. 15*

C210 AP64	30f blue & dull yel	.25	.25
C211 AP64	40f yel grn & ultra	.25	.25
C212 AP64	60f ultra & ver	.25	.25
C213 AP64	80f grnsh bl & sil	.25	.25
C214 AP64	1fo lilac, sil & bl	.25	.25
C215 AP64	1.40fo blue & org	.25	.25
C216 AP64	2fo bluish grn & brn	.25	.25
C217 AP64	3fo vio, sil & bl	.50	.25
C218 AP64	4fo grn, sil & blk	.80	.35
	Nos. C210-C218 (9)	3.05	2.35

Issued to show flight development: "From Icarus to the Space Rocket."
Exist imperf. Value, set $20.

AP65

Design: 1fo, Earth, TV Screens and Rockets. 2fo, Andrian G. Nikolayev, Pavel R. Popovich and rockets.

1962, Sept. 4 *Perf. 12*

C219		1fo dk bl & org brn	.70	.35
C220		2fo dk bl & org brn	.80	.55
a	AP65	Pair, #C219-C220	1.75	.90

First group space flight of Vostoks 3 and 4, Aug. 11-15, 1962. Printed in alternating horizontal rows.

Exist imperf. Value $16.

John H. Glenn, Jr. AP66

Astronauts: 40f, Yuri A. Gagarin. 60f, Gherman Titov. 1.40fo, Scott Carpenter. 1.70fo, Andrian G. Nikolayev. 2.60fo, Pavel R. Popovich. 3fo, Walter Schirra.

1962, Oct. 27 *Perf. 12x11½*

Portraits in Bister

C221	AP66	40f purple	.25	.25
C222	AP66	60f dark green	.25	.25
C223	AP66	1fo dark bl grn	.25	.25
C224	AP66	1.40fo dark brown	.25	.25
C225	AP66	1.70fo deep blue	.30	.25
C226	AP66	2.60fo violet	.65	.30
C227	AP66	3fo red brown	1.10	.45
		Nos. C221-C227 (7)	3.05	2.00

Issued to honor the first seven astronauts and in connection with the Astronautical Congress in Paris.

Exist imperf. Value, set $15.

Eagle Owl — AP67

Birds: 40f, Osprey. 60f, Marsh harrier. 80f, Booted eagle. 1fo, African fish eagle. 2fo, Lammergeier. 3fo, Golden eagle. 4fo, Kestrel.

1962, Nov. 18 **Litho.** *Perf. 11½*

Birds in Natural Colors

C228	AP67	30f yel grn & blk	.25	.25
C229	AP67	40f org yel & blk	.25	.25
C230	AP67	60f bister & blk	.25	.25
C231	AP67	80f lt grn & blk	.25	.25
C232	AP67	1fo ol bis & blk	.25	.25
C233	AP67	2fo bluish grn & blk	.35	.25
C234	AP67	3fo lt vio & blk	.65	.30
C235	AP67	4fo dp org & blk	1.25	.50
		Nos. C228-C235 (8)	3.50	2.30

Exist imperf. Value, set $25.

Radio Mast and Albania No. 623 AP68

Designs (Communication symbols and rocket stamps of various countries): 30f, Bulgaria #C77, vert. 40f, Czechoslovakia #1108. 50f, Communist China #380. 60f, North Korea. 80f, Poland #875. 1fo, Hungary #1386. 1.20fo, Mongolia #189, vert. 1.40fo, DDR #580. 1.70fo, Romania #1200. 2fo, Russia #2456, vert. 2.60fo, North Viet Nam.

Perf. 12x11½, 11½x12

1963, May 9 **Photo.** **Unwmk.**

Stamp Reproductions in Original Colors

C236	AP68	20f olive green	.25	.25
C237	AP68	30f rose lake	.25	.25
C238	AP68	40f violet	.25	.25
C239	AP68	50f brt blue	.25	.25
C240	AP68	60f orange brn	.25	.25
C241	AP68	80f ultra	.25	.25
C242	AP68	1fo dull red brn	.25	.25
C243	AP68	1.20fo aqua	.25	.25
C244	AP68	1.40fo olive	.25	.25
C245	AP68	1.70fo brown olive	.25	.25
C246	AP68	2fo rose lilac	.30	.25
C247	AP68	2.60fo bluish green	.60	.40
		Nos. C236-C247 (12)	3.40	3.15

5th Conference of Postal Ministers of Communist Countries, Budapest.

Exist imperf. Value, set $20.

Souvenir Sheet

Globe and Spaceships — AP69

Perf. 11½x12, Imperf.

1963, July 13 **Unwmk.**

C248	AP69	10fo dk & lt blue	8.00	7.00

Space flights of Valeri Bykovski, June 14-19, and Valentina Tereshkova, 1st woman cosmonaut, June 16-19, 1963.

Exists imperf. Value $25.

Souvenir Sheet

Mt. Fuji and Stadium — AP70

1964, Sept. 22 **Photo.** *Perf. 11½x12*

C249	AP70	10fo multi	4.00	3.50

18th Olympic Games, Tokyo, Oct. 10-24.

Exists imperf. Value $20.

Bridge Type of 1964

Souvenir Sheet

Design: Elizabeth Bridge.

1964, Nov. 21 **Photo.** *Perf. 11*

C250	A356	10fo silver & dp grn	3.75	3.50

No. C250 contains one 59x20mm stamp.

Exists imperf. Value $100.

Lt. Col. Alexei Leonov in Space — AP71

Design: 2fo, Col. Pavel Belyayev, Lt. Col. Alexei Leonov and Voskhod 2.

1965, Apr. 17 **Photo.** *Perf. 11½x12*

C251	AP71	1fo violet & gray	.45	.25
C252	AP71	2fo rose claret & ocher	1.10	.65

Space flight of Voskhod 2 and of Lt. Col. Alexei Leonov, the first man floating in space.

Exists imperf. Value, set $15.

Mariner IV (USA) — AP72

New achievements in space research: 30f, San Marco satellite, Italy. 40f, Molniya satellite, USSR. 60f, Moon rocket, 1965, USSR. 1fo, Shapir rocket, France. 2.50fo, Zond III satellite, USSR. 3fo, Syncom III satellite, US. 10fo, Rocket sending off satellites, horiz.

1965, Dec. 31 **Photo.** *Perf. 11*

C253	AP72	20f ultra, blk & org yel	.25	.25
C254	AP72	30f brn, vio & yel	.25	.25
C255	AP72	40f vio, brn & pink	.25	.25
C256	AP72	60f lt pur, blk & org yel	.25	.25
C257	AP72	1fo red lil, blk & buff	.30	.25
C258	AP72	2.50fo rose cl, blk & gray	.60	.35
C259	AP72	3fo bl grn, blk & bis	.75	.60
		Nos. C253-C259 (7)	2.65	2.20

1965, Dec. 20 **Souvenir Sheet**

C260	AP72	10fo brt bl, yel & dk ol	3.50	3.00

Exist imperf. Value: Nos. C253-C259 $20; No. C260 $25.

Sport Type of Regular Issue

Souvenir Sheet

10fo, Women hurdlers and Ferihegy airport.

1966, Sept. 4 **Photo.** *Perf. 12x11½*

C261	A384	10fo brt bl, brn & red	3.00	3.00

Exists imperf. Value $20.

Plane over Helsinki — AP73

Plane over Cities Served by Hungarian Airlines: 50f, Athens. 1fo, Beirut. 1.10fo, Frankfort on the Main. 1.20fo, Cairo. 1.50fo, Copenhagen. 2fo, London. 2.50fo, Moscow. 3fo, Paris. 4fo, Prague. 5fo, Rome. 10fo, Damascus. 20fo, Budapest.

1966-67 **Photo.** *Perf. 12x11½*

C262	AP73	20f brown org	.25	.25
C263	AP73	50f brown	.25	.25
C264	AP73	1fo blue	.25	.25
C265	AP73	1.10fo black	.25	.25
C266	AP73	1.20fo orange	.25	.25
C267	AP73	1.50fo blue grn	.25	.25
C268	AP73	2fo brt blue	.30	.25
C269	AP73	2.50fo brt red	.30	.25
C270	AP73	3fo yel grn	.40	.25
C271	AP73	4fo brown red	.40	.25
C272	AP73	5fo brt pur	.25	.25
C273	AP73	10fo violet bl ('67)	.25	.25
C274	AP73	20fo gray ol ('67)	.40	.25
		Nos. C262-C274 (13)	3.80	3.25

Exist imperf. Value, set $90.

See No. C276.

Souvenir Sheet

Icarus Falling — AP73a

1968, May 11 **Photo.** *Perf. 11*

C275	AP73a	10fo multicolored	2.75	2.50

In memory of the astronauts Edward H. White, US, Vladimir M. Komarov and Yuri A. Gagarin, USSR.

Exists imperf. Value $20.

Type of 1966-67 without "Legiposta" Inscription

Design: 2.60fo, Malev Airlines jet over St. Stephen's Cathedral, Vienna.

1968, July 4 **Photo.** *Perf. 12x11½*

C276	AP73	2.60fo violet	.50	.25

50th anniv. of regular airmail service between Budapest and Vienna.

Exists imperf. Value $12.50.

Women Swimmers and Aztec Calendar Stone — AP74

Aztec Calendar Stone, Olympic Rings and; 60f, Soccer. 80f, Wrestling. 1fo, Canoeing. 1.40fo, Gymnast on rings. 3fo, Fencing. 4fo, Javelin.

1968, Aug. 21 **Photo.** *Perf. 12*

C277	AP74	20f brt bl & multi	.25	.25
C278	AP74	60f green & multi	.25	.25
C279	AP74	80f car rose & multi	.25	.25
C280	AP74	1fo grnsh bl & multi	.25	.25
C281	AP74	1.40fo violet & multi	.25	.25
C282	AP74	3fo brt lilac & multi	.65	.35
C283	AP74	4fo green & multi	1.00	.55
		Nos. C277-C283,CB31 (8)	3.25	2.50

Issued to publicize the 19th Olympic Games, Mexico City, Oct. 12-27.

Exist imperf. Value, set (8) $20.

Souvenir Sheet

Apollo 8 Trip Around the Moon — AP75

1969, Feb. **Photo.** *Perf. 12½*

C284	AP75	10fo multi	2.00	2.00

Man's 1st flight around the moon, Dec. 21-27, 1968.

Exists imperf. Value $20.

Soyuz 4 and 5, and Men in Space AP76

Design: No. C286, Soyuz 4 and 5.

1969, Mar. 21 Photo. *Perf. 12x11½*

C285 AP76 2fo multi .35 .35
C286 AP76 2fo dk bl, lt bl & red .35 .35
a. Strip, # C285-C286 + label .85

First team flights of Russian spacecraft Soyuz 4 and 5, Jan. 16, 1969.
Exist imperf. Value, strip $8.

Journey to the Moon, by Jules Verne — AP77

Designs: 60f, Tsiolkovski's space station. 1fo, Luna 1. 1.50fo, Ranger 7. 2fo, Luna 9 landing on moon. 2.50fo, Apollo 8 in orbit around moon. 3fo, Soyuz 4 and 5 docking in space. 4fo, Lunar landing module landing on moon. 10fo, Apollo 11 astronauts on moon and lunar landing module.

1969 Photo. *Perf. 12x11½*

C287 AP77 40f multi .25 .25
C288 AP77 60f multi .25 .25
C289 AP77 1fo multi .25 .25
C290 AP77 1.50fo multi .25 .25
C291 AP77 2fo multi .25 .25
C292 AP77 2.50fo multi .25 .25
C293 AP77 3fo multi .50 .25
C294 AP77 4fo multi .75 .40
Nos. C287-C294 (8) 2.75 2.15

Souvenir Sheet

Perf. 11

C295 AP77 10fo multi 4.00 4.00

Moon landing issue. See note after Algeria No. 427.
No. C295 contains one 74x49mm stamp. Issued: Nos. C287-C294, 11/1; No. C295, 8/15.
Exist imperf. Value: Nos. C287-C294 $15; No. C295 $30.

Daimler, 1886 — AP78

Automobiles: 60f, Peugeot, 1894. 1fo, Benz, 1901. 1.50fo, Cudell mail truck, 1902. 2fo, Rolls Royce, 1908. 2.50fo, Model T Ford, 1908. 3fo, Vermorel, 1912. 4fo, Csonka mail car, 1912.

1970, Feb. 28 Photo. *Perf. 12*

C296 AP78 40f ocher & multi .25 .25
C297 AP78 60f multi .25 .25
C298 AP78 1fo red & multi .25 .25
C299 AP78 1.50fo bl & multi .25 .25
C300 AP78 2fo multi .25 .25
C301 AP78 2.50fo vio & multi .30 .25
C302 AP78 3fo multi .40 .30
C303 AP78 4fo multi .70 .50
Nos. C296-C303 (8) 2.65 2.30

Exist imperf. Value, set $15.

American Astronauts on Moon — AP79

No. C305, Soyuz 6, 7 and 8 in space.

1970, Mar. 20 Photo. *Perf. 11*

C304 AP79 3fo blue & multi .75 .75
C305 AP79 3fo car rose & multi .75 .75

Landing of Apollo 12 on the moon, Nov. 14, 1969, and group flight of Russian spacecraft Soyuz 6, 7 & 8, Oct. 11-13, 1969.
Nos. C304-C305 issued in sheets of 4. Size: 112½x78mm.
Exist imperf. Value: set $17.50; sheets of 4 $40.

"Rain at Foot of Fujiyama," by Hokusai, and Pavilion — AP80

3fo, Sun Tower, Peace Bell and globe.

1970, Apr. 30 Photo. *Perf. 12½*

C306 AP80 2fo multi .75 .75
C307 AP80 3fo multi .75 .75

Issued to publicize EXPO '70 International Exhibition, Osaka, Japan, Mar. 15-Sept. 13.
Exist imperf. Value, set $10.

Miniature Sheets

Phases of Apollo 13 Moon Flight — AP81

Vignettes of No. C308: Apollo 13 over moon; return to earth; capsule with parachutes; capsule floating, aircraft carrier and helicopter.
Vignettes of No. C309: Soyuz 9 on way to launching pad; launching of Soyuz 9 capsule in orbit; cosmonauts Andrian Nikolayev and Vitaly Sevastyanov.
Vignettes of No. C310: Luna 16 approaching moon; module on moon; landing; nose cone on ground.
Vignettes of No. C311: Lunokhod 1 on moon; trajectories of Luna 17 around earth and moon.

1970-71 Litho. *Perf. 11½*

C308 AP81 Sheet of 4 2.00 2.00

Photo.

C309 AP81 Sheet of 4 2.00 2.00
C310 AP81 Sheet of 4 ('71) 2.00 2.00
C311 AP81 Sheet of 4 ('71) 2.00 2.00

Nos. C308-C311 were valid for postage only as full sheets. Each contains four 2.50fo vignettes.
No. C308 for the aborted moon flight and safe return of Apollo 13, 4/11-17/70.
No. C309 for the 424-hour flight of Soyuz 9, 6/1-9.
No. C310 for Luna 16, the unmanned, automated moon mission, 9/12-24/70.
No. C311 for Luna 17, unmanned, automated moon mission, 11/10-17/70.
Exist imperf. Value, set $70.
Issued: No. C308, 6/10; No. C309, 9/4; No. C310, 1/15; No. C311 3/8.

Souvenir Sheet

American Astronauts on Moon — AP82

1971, Mar. 31 *Perf. 12½*

C312 AP82 10fo multi 2.00 2.00

Apollo 14 moon landing, 1/31-2/9/71.
Exists imperf. Value $20.
See Nos. C315, C326-C328.

Hunting Type of Regular Issue

Souvenir Sheet

Design: 10fo, Red deer group.

1971, Aug. 27 Photo. *Perf. 11*

C313 A460 10fo multi 3.00 2.50

No. C313 contains one 70x45mm stamp.
Exists imperf. Value $35.

Souvenir Sheet

Astronauts Volkov, Dobrovolsky and Patsayev — AP83

1971, Oct. 4 Photo. *Perf. 12½*

C314 AP83 10fo multi 2.00 2.00

In memory of the Russian astronauts Vladislav N. Volkov, Lt. Col. Georgi T. Dobrovolsky and Victor I. Patsayev, who died during the Soyuz 11 space mission, June 6-30, 1971.
Exists imperf. Value $15.

Apollo 14 Type of 1971

Souvenir Sheet

10fo, American Lunar Rover on moon.

1972, Jan. 20 Photo. *Perf. 12½*

C315 AP82 10fo multi 2.00 2.00

Apollo 15 moon mission, 7/26-8/7/71.
Exists imperf. Value $15.

Soccer and Hungarian Flag — AP84

Various Scenes from Soccer and Natl. Flags of: 60f, Romania. 80f, DDR. 1fo, Great Britain. 1.20fo, Yugoslavia. 2fo, USSR. 4fo, Italy. 5fo, Belgium.

1972, Apr. 29

C316 AP84 40f gold & multi .25 .25
C317 AP84 60f gold & multi .25 .25
C318 AP84 80f gold & multi .25 .25
C319 AP84 1fo gold & multi .25 .25
C320 AP84 1.20fo gold & multi .25 .25
C321 AP84 2fo gold & multi .30 .25
C322 AP84 4fo gold & multi .75 .40
C323 AP84 5fo gold & multi 1.10 .70
a. Sheet of 8, #C316-C323 3.75 2.75
Nos. C316-C323 (8) 3.40 2.60

European Soccer Championships for the Henri Delaunay Cup.
Exist imperf. Value: set $45; sheet $45.
Nos. C316-C321 were later issued individually in sheets of 20 and in partly changed colors.

Souvenir Sheet

Olympic Rings and Globe — AP85

1972, June 10 Photo. *Perf. 12½*

C324 AP85 10fo multi 4.00 4.00

20th Olympic Games, Munich, 8/26-9/11.
Exists imperf. Value $80.

Olympic Type of Regular Issue

Souvenir Sheet

Design: Equestrian and Olympic Rings.

1972, July 15 Photo. *Perf. 12½*

C325 A484 10fo multi 2.50 2.50

20th Olympic Games, Munich, Aug. 26-Sept. 11. No. C325 contains one 43x43mm stamp.
Exists imperf. Value $20.

Apollo 14 Type of 1971

Souvenir Sheets

Design: 10fo, Astronaut in space, Apollo 16 capsule and badge.

1972, Oct. 10 Photo. *Perf. 12½*

C326 AP82 10fo blue & multi 2.75 2.75

Apollo 16 US moon mission, 4/15-27/72.
Exists imperf. Value $20.

1973, Jan. 15

Design: Astronaut exploring moon, vert.

C327 AP82 10fo blue & multi 3.00 3.00

Apollo 17 US moon mission, Dec. 7-19, 1972. No. C327 contains one vertical stamp.
Exists imperf. Value $20.

1973, Mar. 12 Photo. *Perf. 12½*

C328 AP82 10fo Venera 8 2.00 2.00

Venera 8 USSR space mission, Mar. 27-July 22, 1972.
Exists imperf. Value $15.

Equestrian (Pentathlon), Olympic Rings and Medal — AP86

Designs (Olympic Rings and Medals): 60f, Weight lifting. 1fo, Canoeing. 1.20fo, Swimming, women's. 1.80fo, Boxing. 4fo, Wrestling. 6fo, Fencing. 10fo, Allegorical figure lighting flame, vert.

1973, Mar. 31

C329 AP86 40f multi .25 .25
C330 AP86 60f multi .25 .25
C331 AP86 1fo blue & multi .25 .25
C332 AP86 1.20fo multi .25 .25
C333 AP86 1.80fo multi .30 .25
C334 AP86 4fo multi .65 .30
C335 AP86 6fo multi 1.00 .50
Nos. C329-C335 (7) 2.95 2.05

Souvenir Sheet

Perf. 11

C336 AP86 10fo blue & multi 3.75 3.75

Hungarian medalists at 20th Olympic Games. No. C336 contains one 44x71mm stamp.
Exist imperf. Value: Nos. C329-C335 $15; No. C336 $60.

Wrens — AP87

60f, Rock thrush. 80f, Robins. 1fo, Firecrests. 1.20fo, Linnets. 2fo, Blue titmice. 4fo, White-spotted blue throat. 5fo, Gray wagtails.

1973, Apr. 16 Litho. *Perf. 12*

C337	AP87	40f shown	.25	.25
C338	AP87	60f multi	.25	.25
C339	AP87	80f multi	.25	.25
C340	AP87	1fo multi	.25	.25
C341	AP87	1.20fo multi	.25	.25
C342	AP87	2fo multi	.35	.25
C343	AP87	4fo multi	.60	.25
C344	AP87	5fo multi	.75	.35
		Nos. C337-C344 (8)	2.95	2.10

Exist imperf. Value $20.

Exhibition Type of Regular Issue
Souvenir Sheet

10fo, Bavaria #1 with mill wheel cancellation; Munich City Hall, TV Tower and Olympic tent.

1973, May 11 Litho. *Perf. 11*

C345 A506 10fo multi 2.25 2.25

No. C345 contains one 83x45mm stamp.
Exists imperf. Value $20.

Souvenir Sheet

Skylab over Earth — AP88

1973, Oct. 16 Photo. *Perf. 12½*

C346 AP88 10fo dk bl, lt bl & yel 2.25 2.25

First US manned space station.
Exists imperf. Value $15.

Space Type of Regular Issue

Designs: 6fo, Mars "canals" and Giovanni V. Schiaparelli. 10fo, Mars 7 spacecraft.

1974, Mar. 11 Photo. *Perf. 12½*

C347 A522 6fo gold & multi .75 .50

Souvenir Sheet

C348 A522 10fo gold & multi 2.50 2.50

Exist imperf. Value, souvenir sheet $17.50.

UPU Type of 1974

Designs: a, Mail coach. b, Old mail automobile. c, Jet. d, Apollo 15.

1974, May 22 Litho. *Perf. 12*

C349 A526 6fo UPU emblem and TU-154 jet 1.25 .90

Souvenir Sheet

C350 Sheet of 4 2.50 2.50
a.-d. A526 2.50fo, any single .40 .40

No. C350 has bister UPU emblem in center where 4 stamps meet.
Exist imperf. Value, souvenir sheet $35.

Army Day Type of 1974

Designs: 2fo, Ground-to-air missiles, vert. 3fo, Parachutist, helicopter, supersonic jets.

1974, Sept. 28 Litho. *Perf. 12*

C351 A537 2fo gold, emer & blk .25 .25
C352 A537 3fo gold, blue & blk .45 .25

Exist imperf.

Carrier Pigeon, Elizabeth Bridge, Mt. Gellert — AP89

1975, Feb. 7 Litho. *Perf. 12*

C353 AP89 3fo multi 1.00 1.00

Carrier Pigeons' Olympics, Budapest, Feb. 7-9. No. C353 printed checkerwise with black and violet coupon showing Pigeon Olympics emblem.
Exists imperf. Value $12.

Sputnik 2, Apollo-Soyuz Emblem AP90

Spacecraft and Apollo-Soyuz Emblem: 60f, Mercury-Atlas 5. 80f, Lunokhod I on moon. 1.20fo, Lunar rover, Apollo 15 mission. 2fo, Soyuz take-off, Baikonur. 4fo, Apollo take-off, Cape Kennedy. 6fo, Apollo-Soyuz link-up. 10fo, Apollo, Soyuz, American and Russian flags over earth, horiz.

1975, July 7 Photo. *Perf. 12x11½*

C354	AP90	40f silver & multi	.25	.25
C355	AP90	60f silver & multi	.25	.25
C356	AP90	80f silver & multi	.25	.25
C357	AP90	1.20fo silver & multi	.25	.25
C358	AP90	2fo silver & multi	.25	.25
C359	AP90	4fo silver & multi	.45	.30
C360	AP90	6fo silver & multi	.75	.45
		Nos. C354-C360 (7)	2.45	2.00

Souvenir Sheet
Perf. 12½

C361 AP90 10fo blue & multi 2.50 2.25

Apollo Soyuz space test project (Russo-American cooperation), launching July 15; link-up July 17. No. C361 contains one 59x38mm stamp.
Exist imperf. Value: Nos. C354-C360 $15; No. C361 $22.50.

Souvenir Sheet

Map of Europe and Cogwheels — AP91

1975, July 30 Litho. *Perf. 12½*

C362 AP91 10fo multi 4.00 3.25

European Security and Cooperation Conference, Helsinki, July 30-Aug. 1.
Exists imperf. Value $50.

Souvenir Sheet

Hungary Nos. 1585, 1382, 2239, 2280, C81 — AP92

1975, Sept. 9 Photo. *Perf. 12½*

C363 AP92 10fo multi 2.75 2.50

30 years of stamps.

Exists imperf. Value $20.
A similar souvenir sheet with blue margin, no denomination and no postal validity was released for the 25th anniversary of Filatelica Hungarica.

Souvenir Sheet

Paintings by Károly Lotz and János Halápi — AP93

1976, Mar. 19 Photo. *Perf. 12½*

C364 AP93 Sheet of 2 3.25 2.50
a. 5fo Horses in Storm 1.00 1.00
b. 5fo Morning at Tihany 1.00 1.00

Tourist publicity. Nos. C364a and C364b are imperf. between.
Exists imperf. Value $30.

Souvenir Sheet

Montreal Olympic Stadium — AP94

1976, June 29 Litho. *Perf. 12½*

C365 AP94 20fo red, gray & blk 3.75 3.75

21st Olympic Games, Montreal, Canada, July 17-Aug. 1.
Exists imperf. Value $27.50.

US Mars Mission AP95

60f, Viking in space. 1fo, Viking on Mars. 2fo, Venus, rocket take-off. 3fo, Venera 9 in space. 4fo, Venera 10, separation in space. 5fo, Venera on Venus. 20fo, Viking 1 landing on Mars, vert.

1976, Nov. 11 Photo. *Perf. 11*

C366	AP95	40f silver & multi	.25	.25
C367	AP95	60f silver & multi	.25	.25
C368	AP95	1fo silver & multi	.25	.25
C369	AP95	2fo silver & multi	.25	.25
C370	AP95	3fo silver & multi	.35	.25
C371	AP95	4fo silver & multi	.55	.30
C372	AP95	5fo silver & multi	.75	.40
		Nos. C366-C372 (7)	2.65	1.95

Souvenir Sheet
Perf. 12½

C373 AP95 20fo black & multi 3.00 2.75

US-USSR space missions. No. C373 contains one stamp (size: 41x64mm).
Exist imperf. Value: Nos. C366-C372 $15; No. C373 $20.

Hungary No. CB33 — AP96

1977, Apr. Litho. *Perf. 11½x12*

C374 AP96 3fo multi 1.50 1.50

European stamp exhibitions. Issued in sheets of 3 stamps and 3 labels. Labels show exhibition emblems respectively: 125th anniversary of Brunswick stamps, Brunswick, May 5-8; Regiofil XII, Lugano, June 17-19; centenary of San Marino Stamps, Riccione, Aug. 27-29.
Exists imperf. Value: single $20; sheetlet $30.

Space Type 1977
Souvenir Sheet

Design: 20fo, Viking on Mars.

1977, Sept. 20 Litho. *Perf. 11½*

C375 A603 20fo multi 2.75 2.75

Exists imperf. Value $15.

Souvenir Sheet

"EUROPA," Map and Dove — AP97

1977, Oct. 3 *Perf. 12½*

C376 AP97 20fo multi 4.50 4.50

European Security Conference, Belgrade, Oct.-Nov.
Exists imperf. Value $25.

TU-154, Malev over Europe AP98

Planes, Airlines, Maps: 1.20fo, DC-8, Swissair, Southeast Asia. 2fo, IL-62, CSA, North Africa. 2.40fo, A 300B Airbus, Lufthansa, Northwest Europe. 4fo, Boeing 747, Pan Am, North America. 5fo, TU-144, Aeroflot, Northern Europe. 10fo, Concorde, Air France, South America. 20fo, IL-86, Aeroflot, Northeast Asia.

1977, Oct. 26 Litho. *Perf. 11½x12*
Size: 32x21mm

C377	AP98	60f orange & blk	.25	.25
C378	AP98	1.20fo violet & blk	.35	.25
C379	AP98	2fo yellow & blk	.35	.25
C380	AP98	2.40fo bl grn & blk	.50	.25
C381	AP98	4fo ultra & blk	.50	.25
C382	AP98	5fo dp rose & blk	.70	.25
C383	AP98	10fo blue & blk	1.25	.40

Perf. 12x11½
Size: 37½x29mm

C384 AP98 20fo green & blk 1.40 .90
Nos. C377-C384 (8) 5.30 2.80

Exist imperf. Value, set $35.

Montgolfier Brothers and Balloon, 1783 — AP99

Designs: 60f, David Schwarz and airship, 1850. 1fo, Alberto Santos-Dumont and airship flying around Eiffel Tower, 1901. 2fo, Konstantin E. Tsiolkovsky, airship and Kremlin, 1857.

3fo, Roald Amundsen, airship Norge, Polar bears and map, 1872. 4fo, Hugo Eckener, Graf Zeppelin over Mt. Fuji, 1930. 5fo, Count Ferdinand von Zeppelin, Graf Zeppelin over Chicago, 1932. 20fo, Graf Zeppelin over Budapest, 1931.

1977, Nov. 1 Photo. *Perf. 12x11½*

C385	AP99	40f gold & multi	.25	.25
C386	AP99	60f gold & multi	.25	.25
C387	AP99	1fo gold & multi	.25	.25
C388	AP99	2fo gold & multi	.25	.25
C389	AP99	3fo gold & multi	.40	.25
C390	AP99	4fo gold & multi	.50	.30
C391	AP99	5fo gold & multi	.75	.50
		Nos. C385-C391 (7)	2.65	2.05

Souvenir Sheet

Perf. 12½

C392	AP99	20fo silver & multi	2.75	2.50

History of airships. No. C392 contains one 60x36mm stamp.
Exist imperf. Value: Nos. C385-C391 $15; No. C392 $25.

Moon Station — AP100

Science Fiction Paintings by Pal Varga: 60f, Moon settlement. 1fo, Spaceship near Phobos. 2fo, Exploration of asteroids. 3fo, Spaceship in gravitational field of Mars. 4fo, Spaceship and rings of Saturn. 5fo, Spaceship landing on 3rd Jupiter moon.

1978, Mar. 10 Litho. *Perf. 11*

C393	AP100	40f multi	.25	.25
C394	AP100	60f multi	.25	.25
C395	AP100	1fo multi	.25	.25
C396	AP100	2fo multi	.25	.25
C397	AP100	3fo multi	.40	.25
C398	AP100	4fo multi	.50	.30
C399	AP100	5fo multi	.75	.40
		Nos. C393-C399 (7)	2.65	1.95

Exist imperf. Value, set $15.

Louis Bleriot and La Manche AP101

60f, J. Alcock & R. W. Brown, Vickers Vimy, 1919. 1fo, A. C. Read, Navy Curtiss NC-4, 1919. 2fo, H. Köhl, G. Hünefeld, J. Fitzmaurice, Junkers W33, 1928. 3fo, A. Johnson, J. Mollison, Gipsy Moth, 1930. 4fo, G. Endresz, S. Magyar, Lockheed Sirius, 1931. 5fo, W. Gronau, Dornier WAL, 1932. 20fo, Wilbur & Orville Wright & their plane.

1978, May 10 Litho. *Perf. 12*

C400	AP101	40f multi	.25	.25
C401	AP101	60f multi	.25	.25
C402	AP101	1fo multi	.25	.25
C403	AP101	2fo multi	.25	.25
C404	AP101	3fo multi	.40	.25
C405	AP101	4fo multi	.55	.30
C406	AP101	5fo multi	.85	.40
		Nos. C400-C406 (7)	2.80	1.95

Souvenir Sheet

C407	AP101	20fo multi	3.00	2.75

75th anniv. of 1st powered flight by Wright brothers. No. C407 contains one 75x25mm stamp.
Exist imperf. Value: Nos. C400-C406 $15; No. C407 $25.

Souvenir Sheet

Jules Verne and "Voyage from Earth to Moon" — AP102

1978, Aug. 21 *Perf. 12½x11½*

C408	AP102	20fo multi	3.00	2.75

Jules Verne (1828-1905), French science fiction writer.
Exists imperf. Value $25.

Vladimir Remek Postmarking Mail on Board Salyut 6 — AP103

1978, Sept. 1 Photo. *Perf. 11½x12*

C409	AP103	3fo multi	1.50	1.50

PRAGA '78 International Philatelic Exhibition, Prague, Sept. 8-17. Issued in sheets of 3 stamps and 3 labels, showing PRAGA '78 emblem and Golden Tower, Prague. FISA emblems in margin.
Exists imperf. Value: single $4.50; sheetlet $15.

Ski Jump — AP104

Lake Placid '80 Emblem and: 60f, 20fo, Figure skating, diff. 1fo, Downhill skiing. 2fo, Ice hockey. 4fo, Bobsledding. 6fo, Cross-country skiing.

1979, Dec. 15 Litho. *Perf. 12*

C410	AP104	40f multi	.25	.25
C411	AP104	60f multi	.25	.25
C412	AP104	1fo multi	.25	.25
C413	AP104	2fo multi	.30	.25
C414	AP104	4fo multi	.60	.30
C415	AP104	6fo multi	1.00	.55
		Nos. C410-C415 (6)	2.65	1.85

Souvenir Sheet

C416	AP104	20fo multi	2.75	2.75

13th Winter Olympic Games, Lake Placid, NY, Feb. 12-24, 1980.
Exist imperf. Value: Nos. C410-C415 $20; No. C416 $25.

Soviet and Hungarian Cosmonauts AP105

1980, May 27 Litho. *Perf. 11½x12*

C417	AP105	5fo multi	.60	.25

Intercosmos cooperative space program.
Exists imperf. Value $20.

Women's Handball, Moscow '80 Emblem, Olympic Rings — AP106

1980, June 16 Photo. *Perf. 11½x12*

C418	AP106	40f shown	.25	.25
C419	AP106	60f Double kayak	.25	.25
C420	AP106	1fo Running	.25	.25
C421	AP106	2fo Gymnast	.25	.25
C422	AP106	3fo Equestrian	.40	.25
C423	AP106	4fo Wrestling	.55	.35
C424	AP106	5fo Water polo	.65	.50
		Nos. C418-C424 (7)	2.60	2.10

Souvenir Sheet

C425	AP106	20fo Torch bearers	3.00	3.00

22nd Summer Olympic Games, Moscow, July 19-Aug. 3.
See No. C427.
Exist imperf. Value: Nos. C418-C424 $20; No. C425 $17.50.

Souvenir Sheet

Cosmonauts Bertalan Farkes and Valery Kubasov, Salyut 6-Soyuz 35 and 36 — AP107

1980, July 12 Litho. *Perf. 12½*

C426	AP107	20fo multi	3.25	3.00

Intercosmos cooperative space program (USSR-Hungary).
Exists imperf. Value $25.

Olympic Type of 1980

Souvenir Sheet

20fo, Greek Frieze and gold medal.

1980, Sept. 26 Litho. *Perf. 12½*

C427	AP106	20fo multi	3.25	3.00

Olympic Champions.
Exists imperf. Value $20.

Kalman Kittenberger (1881-1958), Zoologist and Explorer — AP108

40f, Cheetah. 60f, Lion. 1fo, Leopard. 2fo, Rhinoceros. 3fo, Antelope. 4fo, African elephant.

1981, Mar. 6 Photo. *Perf. 11½*

C427A	AP108	40f multi	.25	.25
C427B	AP108	60f multi	.25	.25
C427C	AP108	1fo multi	.25	.25
C427D	AP108	2fo multi	.35	.25
C427E	AP108	3fo multi	.55	.25
C427F	AP108	4fo multi	.65	.30
C427G	AP108	5fo shown	.85	.40
		Nos. C427A-C427G (7)	3.15	1.95

Exist imperf. Value, set $20.

Graf Zeppelin over Tokyo, First Worldwide Flight, Aug. 7-Sept. 4, 1929 — AP109

Graf Zeppelin Flights (Zeppelin and): 2fo, Icebreaker Malygin, Polar flight, July 24-31, 1931. 3fo, Nine Arch Bridge, Hortobagy, Hungary, Mar. 28-30, 1931. 4fo, Holsten Tor, Lubeck, Baltic Sea, May 12-15, 1931. 5fo, Tower Bridge, England, Aug. 18-20, 1931. 6fo, Federal Palace, Chicago World's Fair, 50th crossing of Atlantic, Oct. 14-Nov. 2, 1933. 7fo, Lucerne, first flight across Switzerland, Sept. 26, 1929.

Perf. 12½x11½

1981, Mar. 16 Litho.

C428	AP109	1fo multi	.25	.25
C429	AP109	2fo multi	.25	.25
C430	AP109	3fo multi	.40	.25
C431	AP109	4fo multi	.55	.35
C432	AP109	5fo multi	.65	.40
C433	AP109	6fo multi	.75	.55
C434	AP109	7fo multi	.85	.60
		Nos. C428-C434 (7)	3.70	2.65

LURABA '81, First Aviation and Space Philatelic Exhibition, Lucerne, Switzerland, Mar. 20-29. No. C434 se-tenant with label showing exhibition emblem.
Exist imperf. Value, set $15.

Illustrator Type of 1981

Illustrations by A. Lesznai: 4fo, At the End of the Village. 5fo, Dance. 6fo, Sunday.

1981, Dec. 29 Litho. *Perf. 11½x12*

C435	A693	4fo multicolored	.55	.50
C436	A693	5fo multicolored	.70	.55
C437	A693	6fo multicolored	.80	.60
		Nos. C435-C437 (3)	2.05	1.65

Exist imperf.

Manned Flight Bicentenary AP110

Various hot air balloons.

1983, Apr. 5 Litho. *Perf. 12x11½*

C438	AP110	1fo 1811	.25	.25
C439	AP110	1fo 1896	.25	.25
C440	AP110	2fo 1904	.25	.25
C441	AP110	2fo 1977	.25	.25
C442	AP110	4fo 1981	.50	.25
C443	AP110	4fo 1982	.50	.25
C444	AP110	5fo 1981	.70	.35
		Nos. C438-C444 (7)	2.70	1.85

Souvenir Sheet

Perf. 12½

C445	AP110	20fo 1983	2.75	2.75

No. C445 contains one 39x49mm stamp.
Exist imperf. Value: Nos. C438-C444 $15; No. C445 $20.

Audubon Type of 1985

4fo, Colaptes auratus. 6fo, Richmondena cardinalis.

1985, June 19 Litho. *Perf. 12*

C446	A778	4fo multi	.60	.35
C447	A778	6fo multi	.85	.50

Exist imperf.

Aircraft — AP111

1fo, Lloyd CII. 2fo, Brandenburg Cl. 4fo, UFAG Cl. 10fo, Gerle 13. 12fo, WM 13.

1988, Aug. 31 Litho. *Perf. 11*

C448	AP111	1fo multi	.25	.25
C449	AP111	2fo multi	.30	.25
C450	AP111	4fo multi	.50	.35
C451	AP111	10fo multi	1.40	.90
C452	AP111	12fo multi	1.60	1.10
		Nos. C448-C452 (5)	4.05	2.85

Exist imperf. Value, set $30.

AIR POST SEMI-POSTAL STAMPS

Catalogue values for unused stamps in this section are for Never Hinged items.

Roosevelt Type of Semipostal Stamps, 1947

F. D. Roosevelt, Plane and Place: 10f+10f, Casablanca. 20f+20f, Tehran. 50f+50f, Yalta (map). 70f+70f, Hyde Park.

Perf. 12x12½

1947, June 11 Photo. Wmk. 210

Portrait in Sepia

CB1	SP115	10f + 10f red vio	4.25	*5.25*
CB1A	SP115	20f + 20f brn ol	4.25	*5.25*
CB1B	SP115	50f + 50f vio	4.25	*5.25*
CB1C	SP115	70f + 70f blk	4.25	*5.25*
		Nos. CB1-CB1C (4)	17.00	21.00

Exist imperf.

A souvenir sheet contains one each of Nos. CB1-CB1C with border inscriptions and decorations in gray. Size: 161x122mm. Value $125. Exists imperf. Value $225.

See note below Nos. B198A-B198D.

Souvenir Sheet

Chain Bridge, Budapest — SPAP1

Perf. 12x12½

1948, May 15 Photo. Wmk. 283

CB1D	SPAP1	2fo + 18fo brn car	120.00	120.00

Exists imperf. Value $2,500.

Souvenir Sheet

Chain Bridge — SPAP2

1948, Oct. 16

CB2	SPAP2	3fo + 18fo dp grnsh bl	120.00	120.00

Exists imperf. Value $2,500.

Type of Air Post Stamps of 1948

Portraits at Right

Writers: 1f, William Shakespeare. 2f, Francois Voltaire. 4f, Johann Wolfgang von Goethe. 5f, Lord Byron. 6f, Victor Hugo. 8f, Edgar Allen Poe. 10f, Sandor Petőfi. 12f, Mark Twain. 30f, Count Leo Tolstoy. 40f, Maxim Gorky.

1948, Oct. 16 Photo.

CB3	AP22	1f dp ultra	.25	.25
CB4	AP22	2f rose carmine	.25	.25
CB5	AP22	4f dp yellow grn	.25	.25
CB6	AP22	5f dp rose lilac	.35	.35
CB7	AP22	6f deep blue	.35	.35
CB8	AP22	8f olive brn	.35	.35
CB9	AP22	10f red	.50	.45
CB10	AP22	12f deep violet	.50	.45
CB11	AP22	30f orange brn	1.75	1.50
CB12	AP22	40f sepia	2.25	1.75
		Nos. CB3-CB12 (10)	6.80	5.95

Sold at a 50 per cent increase over face, half of which aided reconstruction of the Chain Bridge and the other half the hospital for postal employees.

Exist imperf. Value, set $100.

1st Stamp Type

Souvenir Sheets

Perf. 12½x12

1951, Sept. 12 Engr. Unwmk.

CB13	A208	1fo + 1fo red	75.00	75.00
CB14	A208	2fo + 2fo blue	75.00	75.00

Exist imperf. Value, each $175.

Children Inspecting Stamp Album — SPAP3

2fo+2fo, Children at stamp exhibition.

Perf. 12x12½

1952, Oct. 12 Photo. Wmk. 106

CB15	SPAP3	1fo + 1fo blue	10.00	10.00
CB16	SPAP3	2fo + 2fo brn red	10.00	10.00

Stamp week, Oct. 11-19, 1952.

Exist imperf. Value, set $100.

Globe and Mailbox SPAP4

Designs: 1fo+50f, Mobile post office. 2fo+1fo, Telegraph pole. 3fo+1.50fo, Radio. 5fo+2.50fo, Telephone. 10fo+5fo, Post horn.

1957, June 20 *Perf. 12x12½, 12*

Cross in Red

Size: 32x21mm

CB17	SPAP4	60f + 30f bis brn	.55	.25
CB18	SPAP4	1fo + 50f lilac	.75	.35
CB19	SPAP4	2fo + 1fo org ver	1.00	.45
CB20	SPAP4	3fo + 1.50fo blue	1.50	.70
CB21	SPAP4	5fo + 2.50fo gray	2.25	1.75

Size: 46x31mm

CB22	SPAP4	10fo + 5fo pale grn	4.50	4.00
		Nos. CB17-CB22 (6)	10.55	7.50

The surtax was for the benefit of hospitals for postal and telegraph employees.

Exist imperf. Value, set $70.

Parachute of Fausztusz Verancsics, 1617 SPAP5

History of Hungarian Aviation: No. CB24, Balloon of David Schwarz, 1897. No. CB25, Monoplane of Ernő Horvath, 1911. No. CB26, PKZ-2 helicopter, 1918.

Engraved and Lithographed

1967, May 6 *Perf. 10½*

CB23	SPAP5	2fo + 1fo sep & yel	.50	.50
CB24	SPAP5	2fo + 1fo sep & lt bl	.50	.50
CB25	SPAP5	2fo + 1fo sep & lt grn	.50	.50
CB26	SPAP5	2fo + 1fo sep & pink	.50	.50
a.		Horiz. strip of 4, #CB23-CB26	2.75	2.75
b.		Souv. sheet of 4, #CB23-CB26	3.00	2.75

"AEROFILA 67" International Airmail Exhibition, Budapest, Sept. 3-10.

Exist imperf. Value: strip $20; souvenir sheet $40.

1967, Sept. 3

Aviation, 1967: No. CB27, Parachutist. No. CB28, Helicopter Mi-1. No. CB29, TU-154 jet. No. CB30, Space station Luna 12.

CB27	SPAP5	2fo + 1fo slate & lt grn	.50	.50
CB28	SPAP5	2fo + 1fo slate & buff	.50	.50
CB29	SPAP5	2fo + 1fo slate & yel	.50	.50
CB30	SPAP5	2fo + 1fo slate & pink	.50	.50
a.		Horiz. strip of 4, #CB27-CB30	2.75	2.75
b.		Souv. sheet of 4, #CB27-CB30	3.75	3.75

Issued to commemorate (in connection with AEROFILA 67) the 7th Congress of FISA (Fédération Internationale des Sociétés Aérophilatéliques) and the 40th Stamp Day.

Exist imperf. Value: strip $20; souvenir sheet $35.

Olympic Games Airmail Type

Design: 2fo+1fo, Equestrian.

1968, Aug. 21 Photo. *Perf. 12*

CB31	AP74	2fo + 1fo multi	.35	.35

Exists imperf.

1st Hungarian Airmail Letter, 1918, Plane — SPAP6

Designs: No. CB33, Letter, 1931, and Zeppelin. No. CB34, Balloon post letter, 1967, and balloon. No. CB35, Letter, 1969, and helicopter.

No. CB36: a, #C1. b, #C7. c, #C305. d, #C312.

1974, Oct. 19 Litho. *Perf. 12*

CB32	SPAP6	2fo + 1fo multi	.95	.95
CB33	SPAP6	2fo + 1fo multi	.95	.95
a.		Pair, #CB32-CB33	2.00	2.00
CB34	SPAP6	2fo + 1fo multi	.95	.95
CB35	SPAP6	2fo + 1fo multi	.95	.95
a.		Pair, #CB34-CB35	2.00	2.00
		Nos. CB32-CB35 (4)	3.80	3.80

Souvenir Sheet

CB36		Sheet of 4	3.50	3.50
a.-d.		SPAP6 2fo+1fo any single	.50	.50

AEROPHILA, International Airmail Exhibition, Budapest, Oct. 19-27.

No. CB36 contains 4 35x25mm stamps.

Exist imperf. Value: set of 2 pairs $35; souvenir sheet $30.

SPECIAL DELIVERY STAMPS

Issue of the Monarchy

SD1

1916 Typo. Wmk. 137 *Perf. 15*

E1	SD1	2f gray green & red	.25	.25

Exists imperf. Value $7.50.

For overprints and surcharges see Nos. 1NE1, 2NE1, 4N5, 5NE1, 6NE1, 7NE1, 8NE1, 10NE1, 11NE1, 11NJ7-J8.

Issues of the Republic

Special Delivery Stamp of 1916 Overprinted

1919

E2	SD1	2f gray green & red	.25	*.75*

Exists imperf. Value $12.50.

General Issue

SD2

1919

E3	SD2	2f gray green & red	.25	*.75*

Exists imperf. Value $10.

REGISTRATION STAMPS

Catalogue values for unused stamps in this section are for Never Hinged items.

Nos. 625, 609 and 626 Overprinted in Carmine

a

b

"Ajl." or "Ajánlás" = Registered Letter.

1946 Wmk. 266 *Perf. 15*

F1	A118(a)	"Ajl.1." on 20f	.25	.25
a.		"Ajl.1."	50.00	
F2	A99(a)	"Ajl.2." on 12f	.25	.25
F3	A118(b)	"Ajánlás" on 24f	.25	.25
		Nos. F1-F3 (3)	.75	.75

Hellebore — R1

2011, May 2 Litho. *Perf. 12¼x12¾*

F4	R1	(315fo) multi	3.50	1.75

POSTAGE DUE STAMPS

Issues of the Monarchy

D1

Perf. 11½, 11¾x12

1903 Typo. Wmk. 135

J1	D1	1f green & blk	.50	.50
J2	D1	2f green & blk	3.00	1.50
J3	D1	5f green & blk	15.00	6.50
J4	D1	6f green & blk	12.00	6.00
J5	D1	10f green & blk	80.00	3.00
J6	D1	12f green & blk	2.50	2.50
J7	D1	20f green & blk	20.00	1.50
J8	D1	50f green & blk	16.00	12.50
J9	D1	100f green & blk	1.00	1.00
		Nos. J1-J9 (9)	150.00	35.00

See Nos. J10-J26, J28-J43. For overprints and surcharges see Nos. J27, J44-J50, 1NJ1-1NJ5, 2NJ1-2NJ16, 4NJ2-4NJ3, 5NJ1-5NJ8,

6NJ1-6NJ9, 7NJ1-7NJ4, 9NJ1-9NJ3, 10NJ1-10NJ6, 11NJ1-J6.

1908-09 Wmk. 136 *Perf. 15*

J10 D1 1f green & black .75 .50
J11 D1 2f green & black 1.00 .50
J12 D1 5f green & black 2.50 .75
J13 D1 6f green & black 1.50 .50
J14 D1 10f green & black 1.50 .50
J15 D1 12f green & black 1.25 .50
J16 D1 20f green & black 10.00 .50
c. Center inverted 9,000. *9,000.*
J17 D1 50f green & black 1.75 .75
Nos. J10-J17 (8) 20.25 4.50

1905 Wmk. 136a *Perf. 11½x12*

J12a D1 5f green & black 175.00 70.00
J13a D1 6f green & black 14.00 7.50
J14a D1 10f green & black 175.00 5.00
J15a D1 12f green & black 25.00 16.00
J17a D1 50f green & black 6.00 2.50
J18 D1 100f green & black 5.00

1906 *Perf. 15*

J11b D1 2f green & black 3.50 3.50
J12b D1 5f green & black 2.50 2.00
J13b D1 6f green & black 2.50 2.00
J14b D1 10f green & black 15.00 .60
J15b D1 12f green & black .75 .60
J16b D1 20f green & black 25.00 .60
d. Center inverted *9,000.* *9,000.*
J17b D1 50f green & black 1.00 1.00
Nos. J11b-J17b (7) 50.25 10.30

1914 Wmk. 137 Horiz. *Perf. 15*

J19 D1 1f green & black .35 .25
J20 D1 2f green & black .25 .25
J21 D1 5f green & black .40 .40
J22 D1 6f green & black .80 .60
J23 D1 10f green & black .90 .70
J24 D1 12f green & black .40 .25
J25 D1 20f green & black .35 .25
J26 D1 50f green & black .70 .25
Nos. J19-J26 (8) 4.15 2.95

1914 Wmk. 137 Vert.

J20a D1 2f green & black 57.50 57.50
J21a D1 5f green & black 4.50 4.50
J22a D1 6f green & black 9.00 7.50
J25a D1 20f green & black *2,250.* *900.00*
J26a D1 50f green & black 2.50 2.50

During 1921-24, a number of Postage Due stamps were punched with three holes prior to sale. See note following No. 105 in the Regular Postage section.

No. J9 Surcharged in Red

1915 Wmk. 135

J27 D1 20f on 100f grn & blk .50 2.00
a. On No. J18, Wmk. 136a 15.00 *37.50*

1915-22 Wmk. 137

J28 D1 1f green & red .25 .25
J29 D1 2f green & red .25 .25
J30 D1 5f green & red .35 .25
J31 D1 6f green & red .25 .25
J32 D1 10f green & red .25 .25
J33 D1 12f green & red .25 .25
J34 D1 15f green & red .35 *.50*
J35 D1 20f green & red .25 .25
J36 D1 30f green & red .25 .25
J37 D1 40f green & red ('20) .25 .25
J38 D1 50f green & red ('20) .25 .25
a. Center inverted 60.00
J39 D1 120f green & red ('20) .25 .25
J40 D1 200f green & red ('20) .25 .25
J41 D1 2k green & red ('22) .25 *.90*
J42 D1 5k green & red ('22) .25 .25
J43 D1 50k green & red ('22) .50 .30
Nos. J28-J43 (16) 4.45 4.95

Issues of the Republic

Postage Due Stamps of 1914-18 Overprinted in Black

1918-19 On Issue of 1914

J44 D1 50f green & black 3.00 5.50

On Stamps and Type of 1915-18

J45 D1 2f green & red .25 .75
J46 D1 3f green & red .25 .75
a. "KOZTARSASAG" omitted *650.00*
J47 D1 10f green & red .25 .75
J48 D1 20f green & red .25 .75
J49 D1 40f green & red .25 .75
a. Inverted overprint 60.00 60.00
J50 D1 50f green & red .25 .75
a. Center and overprint inverted 75.00 75.00
Nos. J44-J50 (7) 4.50 10.00

Issues of the Kingdom

D3

1919-20 Typo.

J65 D3 2f green & black .25 .50
a. Inverted center 2,200.
J66 D3 3f green & black .25 .50
J67 D3 20f green & black .25 .50
J68 D3 40f green & black .25 .50
J69 D3 50f green & black .25 .50
Nos. J65-J69 (5) 1.25 2.50

Postage Due Stamps of this type have been overprinted "Magyar Tancskztarsasag" but have not been reported as having been issued without the additional overprint "heads of wheat."

For overprints see Nos. J70-J75.

Additional Overprint in Black

1920

J70 D3 2f green & black .85 1.50
J71 D3 3f green & black .85 1.50
J72 D3 10f green & black 1.40 2.50
J73 D3 20f green & black .85 1.50
J74 D3 40f green & black .85 1.50
J75 D3 50f green & black .85 1.50
Nos. J70-J75 (6) 5.65 10.00

Postage Issues Surcharged

a

b

c

1921-25 Red Surcharge

J76 A9(a) 100f on 15f violet .25 .25
J77 A9(a) 500f on 15f violet .25 .25
J78 A9(b) 2½k on 10f red vio .25 *.25*
J79 A9(b) 3k on 15f violet .25 *.25*
J80 A9(c) 6k on 1½k violet .25 *1.50*
J81 A9(b) 9k on 40f ol grn .25 *.25*
J82 A9(c) 10k on 2½k green .25 *1.25*
J83 A9(b) 12k on 60f blk brn .25 *.25*
J84 A9(c) 15k on 1½k vio .25 *.25*
J85 A9(c) 20k on 2½k grn .25 *1.10*
J86 A9(c) 25k on 1½k vio .25 *.25*
J87 A9(c) 30k on 1½k vio .25 *.25*
J88 A9(c) 40k on 2½k grn .25 *1.25*
J89 A9(c) 50k on 1½k vio .25 *.25*
J90 A9(c) 100k on 4½k dl vio .25 .25
J91 A9(c) 200k on 4½k dl vio .25 .25
J92 A9(c) 300k on 4½k dl vio .25 .25
J93 A9(c) 500k on 2k grnsh bl .60 .25
J94 A9(c) 500k on 3k org brn 2.10 .30
J95 A9(c) 1000k on 2k grnsh bl 1.20 .25
J96 A9(c) 1000k on 3k org brn 1.75 .25
J97 A9(c) 2000k on 2k grnsh bl 1.20 .40
J98 A9(c) 2000k on 3k org brn 2.10 .35
J99 A9(c) 5000k on 5k brown .90 *1.75*
Nos. J76-J99 (24) 14.10 11.90

Year of issue: 6k, 15k, 25k, 30k, 50k, 1922. 10k, 20k, 40k, 100k - No. J93, Nos. J95, J97, 1923. 5,000k, 1924. Nos. J94, J96, J98, 1925. Others, 1921.

D6

Perf. 14x14½, 15

1926 Wmk. 133 Litho.

J100 D6 1f rose red .25 .25
J101 D6 2f rose red .25 .25
J102 D6 3f rose red .30 .60
J103 D6 4f rose red .25 .25
J104 D6 5f rose red 1.75 *2.50*
J105 D6 8f rose red .25 .25
J106 D6 10f rose red 1.25 .25
J107 D6 16f rose red .30 .25
J108 D6 32f rose red .50 .25
J109 D6 40f rose red .75 .25
J110 D6 50f rose red .90 .40
J111 D6 80f rose red 1.25 .65
Nos. J100-J111 (12) 8.00 6.15

Exist imperf. Value, set $100.

See Nos. J117-J123. For surcharges see Nos. J124-J129.

Nos. C7-C11 Surcharged in Red or Green

1926 Wmk. 137 *Perf. 14*

J112 AP3 1f on 500k (R) .25 .30
J113 AP3 2f on 1000k (G) .25 .30
J114 AP3 3f on 2000k (R) .25 .30

Wmk. 133

J115 AP3 5f on 5000k (G) .65 *1.50*
J116 AP3 10f on 10000k (G) .50 *1.10*
Nos. J112-J116 (5) 1.90 *3.50*

Type of 1926 Issue

1928-32 Wmk. 210 *Perf. 15*

J117 D6 2f rose red .25 .25
J118 D6 4f rose red ('32) .25 .25
J119 D6 8f rose red .25 .25
J120 D6 10f rose red .25 .25
J121 D6 16f rose red .35 .25
J122 D6 20f rose red .60 .25
J123 D6 40f rose red .50 .25
Nos. J117-J123 (7) 2.45 1.75

Exist imperf. Value, set $60.

Postage Due Stamps of 1926 Surcharged in Black

1931-33 Wmk. 133

J124 D6 4f on 5f rose red .25 .25
J125 D6 10f on 16f rose red 1.50 *3.75*
J126 D6 10f on 80f rose red ('33) .30 .25
J127 D6 12f on 50f rose red ('33) .35 .25
J128 D6 20f on 32f rose red .35 .30
Nos. J124-J128 (5) 2.75 *4.80*

Surcharged on No. J121

1931 Wmk. 210 *Perf. 15*

J129 D6 10f on 16f rose red .85 *1.25*

Catalogue values for unused stamps in this section, from this point to the end of the section, are for Never Hinged items.

Figure of Value — D7

1934 Photo. Wmk. 210

J130 D7 2f ultra .25 .25
J131 D7 4f ultra .25 .25
J132 D7 6f ultra .25 .25
J133 D7 8f ultra .25 .25
J134 D7 10f ultra .25 .25
J135 D7 12f ultra .25 .25
J136 D7 16f ultra .25 .25
J137 D7 20f ultra .40 .25
J138 D7 40f ultra .60 .25
J139 D7 80f ultra 2.00 .50
Nos. J130-J139 (10) 4.75 2.75

Exist imperf. Value, set $60.

Coat of Arms and Post Horn — D8

1941

J140 D8 2f brown red .25 .25
J142 D8 4f brown red .25 .25
J143 D8 6f brown red .25 .25
J144 D8 8f brown red .25 .25
J145 D8 10f brown red .25 .25
J146 D8 12f brown red .30 .25
J147 D8 16f brown red .40 .25
J148 D8 20f brown red .50 .25
J150 D8 40f brown red .75 .25
Nos. J140-J150 (9) 3.20 2.25

Exist imperf. Value, set $25.

1941-44 Wmk. 266

J151 D8 2f brown red .25 .25
J152 D8 3f brown red .25 .25
J153 D8 4f brown red .25 .25
J154 D8 6f brown red .25 .25
J155 D8 8f brown red .25 .25
J156 D8 10f brown red .25 .25
J157 D8 12f brown red .25 .25
J158 D8 16f brown red .25 .25
J159 D8 18f brown red ('44) .25 .25
J160 D8 20f brown red .25 .25
J161 D8 24f brown red .25 .25
J162 D8 30f brown red ('44) .25 .25
J163 D8 36f brown red ('44) .25 .25
J164 D8 40f brown red .25 .25
J165 D8 50f brown red .25 .25
J166 D8 60f brown red ('44) .30 .25
Nos. J151-J166 (16) 4.05 4.00

Exist imperf. Value, set $30.

For surcharges see Nos. J167-J185.

Issues of the Republic

Types of Hungary Postage Due Stamps, 1941-44, Surcharged in Carmine

1945 Wmk. 266 Photo. *Perf. 15*

Blue Surface-tinted Paper

J167 D8 10f on 2f brn red .25 .25
J168 D8 10f on 3f brn red .25 .25
J169 D8 20f on 4f brn red .25 .25
J170 D8 20f on 6f brn red 9.50 9.50
J171 D8 20f on 8f brn red .25 .25
J172 D8 40f on 12f brn red .25 .25
J173 D8 40f on 16f brn red .25 .25
J174 D8 40f on 18f brn red .25 .25
J175 D8 60f on 24f brn red .25 .25
J176 D8 80f on 30f brn red .25 .25
J177 D8 90f on 36f brn red .25 .25
J178 D8 1p on 10f brn red .25 .25
J179 D8 1p on 40f brn red .25 .25
J180 D8 2p on 20f brn red .25 .25
J181 D8 2p on 50f brn red .25 .25
J182 D8 2p on 60f brn red .25 .25

Surcharged in Black, Thicker Type

J183 D8 10p on 3f brn red .25 .25
J184 D8 12p on 8f brn red .25 .25
J185 D8 20p on 24f brn red .25 .25
Nos. J167-J185 (19) 14.00 14.00

D9

1946-50 Wmk. 210 *Perf. 15*

Numerals in Deep Magenta

J186 D9 4f magenta .50 .25
J187 D9 10f magenta 1.25 .25
J188 D9 20f magenta .50 .25
J189 D9 30f magenta .50 .25
J190 D9 40f magenta .75 .25
J191 D9 50f mag ('50) 2.25 .50
J192 D9 60f magenta 1.50 .25
J193 D9 1.20fo magenta 2.25 .25
J194 D9 2fo magenta 3.75 .30
Nos. J186-J194 (9) 13.25 2.55

1951 Wmk. 106

Numerals in Deep Magenta

J194A D9 4f magenta .25 .25
J194B D9 10f magenta .25 .25
J194C D9 20f magenta 1.25 .25
j. "fiellr" 35.00 7.50
J194D D9 30f magenta 1.50 .25
J194E D9 40f magenta .50 .25

J194F D9 50f magenta 1.00 .25
J194G D9 60f magenta .85 .25
J194H D9 1.20fo magenta 3.50 .25
J194I D9 2fo magenta 3.00 .25
Nos. J194A-J194I (9) 12.10 2.25

Nos. J194A-J194I are found in both large format (about 18x22mm) and small (about 17x21mm).

Revenue Stamps with Blue Surcharge — D10

Paper with Vertical Lines in Green

1951 Unwmk. Typo. *Perf. 14½x15*

J195 D10 8f dark brown .25 .25
J196 D10 10f dark brown .25 .25
J197 D10 12f dark brown .40 .40
Nos. J195-J197 (3) .90 .90

D11

1951 Wmk. 106 Photo. *Perf. 14½*

J198 D11 4f brown .25 .25
J199 D11 6f brown .25 .25
J200 D11 8f brown .25 .25
J201 D11 10f brown .25 .25
J202 D11 14f brown .35 .25
J203 D11 20f brown .25 .25
J204 D11 30f brown .25 .25
J205 D11 40f brown .25 .25
J206 D11 50f brown .25 .25
J207 D11 60f brown .30 .25
J208 D11 1.20fo brown .30 .25
J209 D11 2fo brown .50 .30
Nos. J198-J209 (12) 3.45 3.05

Exist imperf. Value, set $30.

D12

Photo., Numeral Typo. in Black

1953 Numerals 3mm High

J210 D12 4f dull green .25 .25
J211 D12 6f dull green .25 .25
J212 D12 8f dull green .25 .25
J213 D12 10f dull green .25 .25
J214 D12 12f dull green .25 .25
J215 D12 14f dull green .25 .25
J216 D12 16f dull green .25 .25
J217 D12 20f dull green .25 .25
J218 D12 24f dull green .25 .25
J219 D12 30f dull green .25 .25
J220 D12 36f dull green .25 .25
J221 D12 40f dull green .25 .25
J222 D12 50f dull green .25 .25
J223 D12 60f dull green .25 .25
J224 D12 70f dull green .25 .25
J225 D12 80f dull green .30 .25

Numerals 4½mm High

J226 D12 1.20fo dull green .40 .25
J227 D12 2fo dull green .75 .25
a. Small "2" (3mm high) 4.00 2.00
Nos. J210-J227 (18) 5.20 4.50

1st Hungarian postage due stamp, 50th anniv.
Exist imperf. Value, set $30.

D13

Photo., Numeral Typo. in Black on Nos. J228-J243

1958 Wmk. 106 *Perf. 14½*

Size: 21x16½mm

J228 D13 4f red .25 .25
J229 D13 6f red .25 .25
J230 D13 8f red .25 .25
J231 D13 10f red .25 .25
J232 D13 12f red .25 .25
J233 D13 14f red .25 .25
J234 D13 16f red .25 .25
J235 D13 20f red .25 .25
J236 D13 24f red .25 .25
J237 D13 30f red .25 .25
J238 D13 36f red .25 .25
J239 D13 40f red .25 .25
J240 D13 50f red .25 .25
J241 D13 60f red .25 .25
J242 D13 70f red .25 .25
J243 D13 80f red .25 .25

Perf. 12

Size: 31x21mm

J244 D13 1.20fo dk red brn .35 .25
J245 D13 2fo dk red brn .50 .25
Nos. J228-J245 (18) 4.85 4.50

Exist imperf. Value, set $15.

Photo., Numeral Typo. in Black on Nos. J246-J261

1965-69 Unwmk. *Perf. 11½*

Size: 21x16½mm

J246 D13 4f red .25 .25
J247 D13 6f red .25 .25
J248 D13 8f red .25 .25
J249 D13 10f red .25 .25
J250 D13 12f red .25 .25
J251 D13 14f red .25 .25
J252 D13 16f red .25 .25
J253 D13 20f red .25 .25
J254 D13 24f red .25 .25
J255 D13 30f red .25 .25
J256 D13 36f red .25 .25
J257 D13 40f red .25 .25
J258 D13 50f red .25 .25
J259 D13 60f red .25 .25
J260 D13 70f red .25 .25
J261 D13 80f red .25 .25

Perf. 11½x12

Size: 31x21mm

J262 D13 1fo dk red brn ('69) .25 .25
J263 D13 1.20fo dk red brn .25 .25
J264 D13 2fo dk red brn .30 .25
J265 D13 4fo dk red brn ('69) .50 .25
Nos. J246-J265 (20) 5.30 5.00

Mail Plane and Truck — D14

Designs: 20f, Money order canceling machine. 40f, Scales in self-service P.O. 80f, Automat for registering parcels. 1fo, Keypunch operator. 1.20fo, Mail plane and truck. 2fo, Diesel mail train. 3fo, Mailman on motorcycle with sidecar. 4fo, Rural mail delivery. 8fo, Automatic letter sorting machine. 10fo, Postman riding motorcycle.

1973-85 Photo. *Perf. 11*

Size: 21x18mm

J266 D14 20f brown & ver .25 .25
J267 D14 40f dl bl & ver .25 .25
J268 D14 80f violet & ver .25 .25
J269 D14 1fo ol grn & ver .25 .25

Perf. 12x11½

Size: 28x22mm

J270 D14 1.20fo green & ver .25 .25
J271 D14 2fo lilac & ver .25 .25
J272 D14 3fo brt blue & ver .25 .25
J273 D14 4fo org brn & ver .35 .25
J274 D14 8fo dp mag & dk red 1.00 .30
J275 D14 10fo grn & dk red 1.10 .35
Nos. J266-J275 (10) 4.20 2.65

Issued: 20f-4fo, 12/1973; 8fo, 10fo, 12/16/85.

Postal History — D15

Designs: Excerpt from 18th cent. letter, innovations in letter carrying: 1fo, Foot messenger, 16th cent. 4fo, Post rider, 17th cent. 6fo, Horse-drawn mail coach, 18th cent. 8fo, Railroad mail car, 19th cent. 10fo, Mail truck, 20th cent. 20fo, Airplane, 20th cent.

1987, Dec. 10 Litho. *Perf. 12*

J276 D15 1fo multicolored .25 .25
J277 D15 4fo multicolored .55 .30
J278 D15 6fo multicolored .75 .45
J279 D15 8fo multicolored 1.00 .60
J280 D15 10fo multicolored 1.25 .65
J281 D15 20fo multicolored 2.25 1.25
Nos. J276-J281 (6) 6.05 3.50

OFFICIAL STAMPS

During 1921-24, a number of Official stamps were punched with three holes prior to sale. See note following No. 105 in the Regular Postage section.

O1

1921-23 Wmk. 137 Typo. *Perf. 15*

O1 O1 10f brn vio & blk .25 .25
O2 O1 20f ol brn & blk .25 .25
a. "HIVATALOS" inverted 10,000.
O3 O1 60f blk brn & blk .25 .25
O4 O1 100f dl rose & blk .25 .25
O5 O1 250f bl & blk .25 .25
O6 O1 350f gray & blk .25 .25
O7 O1 500f lt brn & blk .25 .25
O8 O1 1000f lil brn & blk .25 .25
O9 O1 5k brn ('23) .25 .25
O10 O1 10k choc ('23) .25 .25
O11 O1 15k gray blk ('23) .25 .25
O12 O1 25k org ('23) .25 .25
O13 O1 50k brn & red ('22) .25 .25
O14 O1 100k bis & red ('22) .25 .25
O15 O1 150k grn & red ('23) .25 .25
O16 O1 300k dl red & red ('23) .25 .25
O17 O1 350k vio & red ('23) .30 .25
O18 O1 500k org & red ('22) .30 .25
O19 O1 600k ol bis & red ('23) .80 .60
O20 O1 1000k bl & red ('22) 1.20 .25
Nos. O1-O20 (20) 6.60 5.35

Counterfeits of No. O2a exist.

Stamps of 1921 Surcharged in Red

1922

O21 O1 15k on 20f ol brn & blk .25 .25
O22 O1 25k on 60f blk brn & blk .25 .25

Stamps of 1921 Overprinted in Red

1923

O23 O1 350k gray & blk .25 .25

With Additional Surcharge of New Value in Red

O24 O1 150k on 100f dl rose & blk .30 .25
O25 O1 2000k on 250f bl & blk 1.50 .40
Nos. O23-O25 (3) 2.05 .90

Three-Hole Punch

1923-24

Paper with Gray Moiré on Face

O26 O1 500k org & red ('23) 2.10 .25
O27 O1 1000k bl & red ('23) 2.10 .25
O28 O1 3000k vio & red ('24) 2.10 1.25
O29 O1 5000k bl & red ('24) 2.40 1.50
Nos. O26-O29 (4) 8.70 3.25

1924 Wmk. 133

O30 O1 500k orange & red 1.40 1.00
O31 O1 1000k blue & red 1.40 1.00

NEWSPAPER STAMPS

Issues of the Monarchy

St. Stephen's Crown and Post Horn
N1 N2

Litho. (#P1), Typo. (#P2)

1871-72 Unwmk. *Imperf.*

P1 N1 (1k) ver red 50.00 20.00
P2 N2 (1k) rose red ('72) 20.00 6.00
a. (1k) vermilion 10.00 2.00
b. Printed on both sides

Reprints of No. P2 are watermarked. Value, $450.

Letter with Crown and Post Horn — N3

1874

P3 N3 1k orange 3.75 .35

1881 Wmk. "kr" in Oval (132)

P4 N3 1k orange 1.25 .25
a. 1k lemon yellow 16.00 3.50
b. Printed on both sides

1898 Wmk. 135

P5 N3 1k orange 1.25 .25

See watermark note after No. 46.

N5

1900 Wmk. Crown in Circle (135)

P6 N5 (2f) red orange .75 .25

1905 Wmk. Crown (136a)

P7 N5 (2f) red orange 1.00 .25
a. Wmk. 136 ('08) 1.00 .25

1914-22 Wmk. Double Cross (137)

P8 N5 (2f) orange .25 .25
a. Wmk. horiz. 4.50 3.75
P9 N5 (10f) deep blue ('20) .25 .25
P10 N5 (20f) lilac ('22) .25 .25
Nos. P8-P10 (3) .75 .75

For overprints and surcharges see Nos. 1NJ6-1NJ10, 1NP1, 2NP1, 5NP1, 6NP1, 8NP1, 10NP1, 11NP1.

NEWSPAPER TAX STAMPS

Issues of the Monarchy

NT1

NT2

Wmk. 91; Unwmk. from 1871

1868 Typo. *Imperf.*

PR1 NT1 1k blue 4.00 1.00
a. Pair, one sideways
PR2 NT2 2k brown 20.00 10.00
a. 2k red brown 275.00 47.50

NT3

1868

PR2B NT3 1k blue *50,000. 11,000.*

No. PR2B was issued for the Military Border District only. All used stamps are precanceled (newspaper text printed on the stamp). A similar 2k was not issued.

1889-90 Wmk. "kr" in Oval (132)

PR3 NT1 1k blue 2.00 .80
PR4 NT2 2k brown 5.50 5.00

1898 Wmk. Crown in Oval (135)

PR5 NT1 1k blue 6.00 7.50

These stamps did not pay postage, but represented a fiscal tax collected by the postal authorities on newspapers.

Nos. PR3 and PR5 have a tall "k" in "kr."

PARCEL POST STAMPS

Nos. 629, 613, 612, 615, 630, 667 and Type of 1943-45 Overprinted in Black or Carmine

a

b

"Cs." or "Csomag"=Parcel

1946 Wmk. 266 *Perf. 15*

Q1 A118 "Cs. 5-1." on 70f .25 .25
Q2 A109 "Cs. 5-1." on 30f 22.50 20.00
Q3 A99 "Cs. 5-2." on 24f .25 .25
Q4 A118 "Cs. 10-1." on 70f .25 .25
Q5 A118 "Cs. 10-1." on 80f 27.50 26.00
Q6 A118 "Cs. 10-2." on 80f .25 .25
Q7 A99 "Csomag 5kg." on 2p on 4f (C+Bk) .25 .25
Q8 A118 "Csomag 10kg." on 30f copper red, *bl* .25 .25
Nos. Q1-Q8 (8) 51.50 47.50

No. Q8 was not issued without overprint.

Catalogue values for unused stamps in this section, from this point to the end of the section, are for Never Hinged items.

No. 796 Surcharged with New Value in Red or Black

1954 Wmk. 210

Q9 A144 1.70fo on 1.40fo 1.40 .25
Q10 A144 2fo on 1.40fo (Bk) 1.60 .30
Q11 A144 3fo on 1.40fo 2.00 .50
Nos. Q9-Q11 (3) 5.00 1.05
Set, hinged 1.80

OCCUPATION STAMPS

Issued under French Occupation

ARAD ISSUE

The overprints on this issue have been extensively forged. Even the inexpensive values are difficult to find with genuine overprints. Values are for genuine overprints. Collectors should be aware that stamps sold "as is" are likely to be forgeries, and unexpertized collections should be assumed to consist of mostly forged stamps. Education plus working with knowledgeable dealers is mandatory in this collecting area. More valuable stamps should be expertized.

Stamps of Hungary Overprinted in Red or Blue

On Issue of 1916-18

1919 Wmk. 137 *Perf. 15, 14*

1N1 A9 2f brn org (R) 1.60 1.60
1N2 A9 3f red lil (R) .75 .75
1N3 A9 5f green (R) 20.00 20.00
1N4 A9 6f grnsh bl (R) 1.90 1.90
a. Inverted overprint 30.00 30.00
1N5 A9 10f rose red 4.00 4.00
1N6 A9 15f violet (R) 1.75 1.75
a. Double overprint 50.00 50.00
1N7 A9 20f gray brn (R) 50.00 50.00
1N8 A9 35f brown (R) 65.00 65.00
1N9 A9 40f ol grn (R) 37.50 37.50
1N10 A10 50f red vio & lil 6.00 6.00
1N11 A10 75f brt bl & pale bl 2.00 2.00
1N12 A10 80f grn & pale grn 2.75 2.75
1N13 A10 1k red brn & cl 15.00 15.00
1N14 A10 2k ol brn & bis 3.00 3.00
a. Inverted overprint 50.00 50.00
1N15 A10 3k dk vio & ind 17.50 17.50
1N16 A10 5k dk brn & lt brn 13.50 13.50
1N17 A10 10k vio brn & vio 70.00 70.00
Nos. 1N1-1N17 (17) 312.25 312.25

With Additional Surcharges

a

b

c

d

1N18 A9 (a) 45f on 2f brn org 8.00 8.00
1N19 A9 (b) 45f on 2f brn org 8.00 8.00
1N20 A9 (c) 50f on 3f red lil 8.00 8.00
1N21 A9 (d) 50f on 3f red lil 8.00 8.00
Nos. 1N18-1N21 (4) 32.00 32.00

Overprinted On Issue of 1918

1N22 A11 10f scarlet (Bl) 60.00 60.00
1N23 A11 20f dk brn .90 .90
1N24 A11 25f brt bl 2.40 2.40
a. Inverted overprint 30.00 30.00
1N25 A12 40f ol grn 3.25 3.25
Nos. 1N22-1N25 (4) 66.55 66.55

Ovptd. On Issue of 1918-19, Overprinted "Koztarsasag"

1N26 A9 2f brn org 2.00 2.00
a. Inverted overprint 50.00 50.00
1N27 A9 4f slate gray 2.00 2.00
1N28 A9 5f green .60 .60
1N29 A9 6f grnsh bl 12.00 12.00
a. Inverted overprint 30.00 30.00
1N30 A9 10f rose red (Bl) 60.00 60.00
1N31 A9 20f gray brn 15.00 15.00
1N32 A11 25f brt bl 2.75 2.75
a. Inverted overprint 30.00 30.00
1N33 A9 40f ol grn 2.00 2.00
1N34 A12 40f ol grn 60.00 60.00
a. Inverted overprint 125.00 125.00
1N35 A12 50f lilac 8.00 8.00
1N36 A10 1k red brn & cl (Bl) 3.25 3.25
1N37 A10 3k dk vio & ind (Bl) 15.00 15.00
Nos. 1N26-1N37 (12) 182.60 182.60

No. 1N36 With Additional Surcharge

e

f

1N38 A10 (e) 10k on 1k 13.50 13.50
1N39 A10 (f) 10k on 1k 13.50 13.50

On Issue of 1919 Inscribed "MAGYAR POSTA"

1N40 A13 5f red (R) 55.00 55.00
1N41 A13 10f red (Bl) 6.50 6.50

SEMI-POSTAL STAMPS

Hungarian Semi-Postal Stamps of 1916-17 Overprinted "Occupation francaise" in Blue or Red

1919 Wmk. 137 *Perf. 15*

1NB1 SP3 10f + 2f rose red 65.00 65.00
1NB2 SP4 15f + 2f dl vio (R) 9.50 9.50
1NB3 SP5 40f + 2f brn car 12.50 12.50
Nos. 1NB1-1NB3 (3) 87.00 87.00

SPECIAL DELIVERY STAMP

Hungarian Special Delivery Stamp of 1916 Overprinted "Occupation francaise"

1919 Wmk. 137 *Perf. 15*

1NE1 SD1 2f gray green & red .60 .60

POSTAGE DUE STAMPS

Hungarian Postage Due Stamps of 1915 Overprinted "Occupation francaise"

1919 Wmk. 137 *Perf. 15*

1NJ1 D1 2f green & red 7.50 7.50
1NJ2 D1 10f green & red 4.00 4.00
1NJ3 D1 12f green & red 32.50 32.50
1NJ4 D1 15f green & red 42.50 42.50
1NJ5 D1 20f green & red 3.00 3.00

Hungarian Newspaper Stamp of 1914 Surcharged

Occupation française
12 Porto 12

1NJ6 N5 12f on 2f orange 8.00 8.00
1NJ7 N5 15f on 2f orange 8.00 8.00
1NJ8 N5 30f on 2f orange 8.00 8.00
a. Double surcharge 50.00 50.00
1NJ9 N5 50f on 2f orange 8.00 8.00
1NJ10 N5 100f on 2f orange 8.00 8.00
Nos. 1NJ1-1NJ10 (10) 129.50 129.50

NEWSPAPER STAMP

Hungarian Newspaper Stamp of 1914 Overprinted "Occupation francaise"

1919 Wmk. 137 *Imperf.*

1NP1 N5 (2f) orange 1.25 1.25

ISSUED UNDER ROMANIAN OCCUPATION

FIRST DEBRECEN ISSUE

The overprints on this issue have been extensively forged. Even the inexpensive values are difficult to find with genuine overprints. The more extensive note before No. 1N1 also applies to Nos. 2N1-2NP16.

Hungarian Stamps of 1913-19 Overprinted in Blue, Red or Black

1919 Wmk. 137 *Perf. 15, 14½x14*

On Stamps of 1913

2N1 A4 2f ol yel *90.00 90.00*
2N2 A4 3f orange *125.00 125.00*
2N3 A4 6f ol grn (R) 50.00 50.00

On Stamps of 1916

2N4 A8 10f rose 75.00 75.00
2N5 A8 15f violet (Bk) 65.00 65.00

On Stamps of 1916-18

2N6 A9 2f brown org 1.50 1.50
2N7 A9 3f red lilac .70 .70
2N8 A9 5f green 4.75 4.75
2N9 A9 6f grnsh bl (R) 1.60 1.60
2N10 A9 15f violet (Bk) .80 .80
a. Red overprint 75.00 75.00
2N11 A9 20f gray brn *125.00 125.00*
2N12 A9 25f dull bl (Bk) 4.50 4.50
2N13 A9 35f brown 60.00 60.00
2N14 A9 40f olive grn 3.75 3.75
2N15 A10 50f red vio & lil 8.25 8.25
2N16 A10 75f brt bl & pale bl (Bk) 2.00 2.00
2N17 A10 80f grn & pale grn (R) 3.50 3.50
2N18 A10 1k red brn & cl 4.75 4.75
2N19 A10 2k ol brn & bis (Bk) 1.75 1.75
2N20 A10 3k dk vio & ind (R) 30.00 30.00
a. Blue overprint *65.00 65.00*
b. Black overprint *250.00 250.00*
2N21 A10 5k dk brn & lt brn (Bk) 27.50 27.50
2N22 A10 10k vio brn & vio *160.00 160.00*

With New Value Added

2N23 A9 35f on 3f red lil 2.00 2.00
2N24 A9 45f on 2f brn org 2.00 2.00
2N25 A10 3k on 75f brt bl & pale bl (Bk) 4.00 4.00
2N26 A10 5k on 75f brt bl & pale bl (Bk) 3.75 3.75
2N27 A10 10k on 80f grn & pale grn (R) 3.50 3.50

On Stamps of 1918

2N28 A11 10f scarlet 60.00 60.00
2N28A A11 15f violet (R) 75.00 75.00
b. Black overprint 125.00 125.00
2N29 A11 20f dk brn (R) 6.25 6.25
a. Black overprint 30.00 30.00
b. Blue overprint 75.00 75.00
2N30 A11 25f brt blue (R) 7.00 7.00
a. Black overprint 75.00 75.00
2N31 A12 40f ol grn 3.00 3.00
2N32 A12 50f lilac 50.00 50.00

On Stamps of 1918-19, Overprinted "Koztarsasag"

2N33 A9 2f brn org 3.00 3.00
2N34 A9 3f red lilac 65.00 65.00
2N35 A9 4f sl gray (R) 1.75 1.75
2N36 A9 5f green .65 .65
2N37 A9 6f grnsh bl (R) 30.00 30.00
2N38 A9 10f rose red 37.50 37.50
2N39 A11 10f scarlet 25.00 25.00
2N40 A11 15f dp vio (Bk) 45.00 45.00
a. Red overprint 125.00 125.00
2N41 A9 20f gray brn 3.25 3.25
2N42 A11 20f dk brn (Bk) 37.50 37.50
b. Red overprint 50.00 50.00

2N43 A9 40f olive grn 1.75 1.75
2N44 A10 1k red brn & cl 2.75 2.75
2N45 A10 2k ol brn & bis (Bk) 60.00 60.00
a. Blue overprint 125.00 125.00
2N46 A10 3k dk vio & ind (R) 9.75 9.75
a. Blue overprint 60.00 60.00
b. Black overprint *200.00 200.00*
2N47 A10 5k dk & lt brn (Bk) *225.00 225.00*
2N48 A10 10k vio brn & vio *500.00 500.00*
2N49 A11 25f brt bl (R) 3.25 3.25
a. Black overprint 25.00 25.00
2N50 A12 40f olive grn *125.00 125.00*
2N51 A12 50f lilac 2.25 2.25

On Stamps of 1919

2N52 A13 5f green .50 .50
2N53 A13 6f grnsh bl (Bk) 22.50 22.50
2N54 A13 10f red .25 .25
2N55 A13 20f dk brown .25 .25
2N56 A13 25f dl bl (Bk) 1.25 1.25
2N56A A13 40f ol grn 125.00 125.00
2N57 A13 45f orange 15.00 15.00
2N57A A14 95f dk bl & bl 125.00 125.00
2N57B A14 1.20k dk grn & grn 125.00 125.00
2N57C A14 1.40k yel grn 125.00 125.00

No. 2N58

2N58 A14 5k dk brn & brn 3,000. 3,000.

#2N58 is handstamped. Counterfeits exist. Expertization is required.

On No. 103A

2N59 A5a 10f violet brn (R) 50.00 50.00

On No. 208

2N60 A13 10f red 75.00 75.00
Nos. 2N1-2N57,2N59-2N60 (61) 2,530. 2,530.

SEMI-POSTAL STAMPS

Hungary Nos. B36, B37 Overprinted like Regular Issues in Blue

1919 Wmk. 137 *Perf. 14*

2NB1 A4(c) 2f olive yellow 125.00 125.00
2NB1A A4(c) 3f orange 125.00 125.00

Same Overprint in Blue or Black on Hungary Nos. B53--B55

1919 Wmk. 137 *Perf. 15*

2NB1B SP3 10f + 2f rose red 4.00 4.00
2NB2 SP4 15f + 2f dl vio (Bk) 17.00 17.00
2NB3 SP5 40f + 2f brn car 11.00 11.00
Nos. 2NB1B-2NB3 (3) 32.00 32.00

Same Overprint on Hungary Nos. B58-B60 (with "Köztarsasag")

1919

2NB4 SP3 10f + 2f rose red 42.50 42.50
2NB5 SP4 15f + 2f dl vio (Bk) 75.00 75.00
2NB6 SP5 40f + 2f brn car 32.50 32.50
Nos. 2NB4-2NB6 (3) 150.00 150.00

SPECIAL DELIVERY STAMP

Hungarian Special Delivery Stamp of 1916 Overprinted like Regular Issues

1919 Wmk. 137 *Perf. 15*

2NE1 SD1 2f gray grn & red (Bl) 3.00 3.00

POSTAGE DUE STAMPS

Hungarian Postage Due Stamps of 1914-19 Overprinted in Black like Regular Issues

1919 Wmk. 137 *Perf. 15*

On Stamp of 1914

2NJ1 D1 50f grn & blk *125.00 125.00*

On Stamps of 1915

2NJ2 D1 1f green & red 62.50 62.50
2NJ3 D1 2f green & red 2.00 2.00
2NJ4 D1 5f green & red *225.00 225.00*
2NJ5 D1 6f green & red *125.00 125.00*
2NJ6 D1 10f green & red .80 .80
2NJ7 D1 12f green & red *125.00 125.00*
2NJ8 D1 15f green & red 20.00 20.00
2NJ9 D1 20f green & red 4.50 4.50
2NJ10 D1 30f green & red 13.50 13.50

On Stamps of 1918-19, Overprinted "Koztarsasag"

2NJ11 D1 2f green & red 25.00 25.00
2NJ12 D1 3f green & red 30.00 30.00
2NJ13 D1 10f green & red 30.00 30.00
2NJ14 D1 20f green & red 30.00 30.00
2NJ15 D1 40f green & red 30.00 30.00
2NJ16 D1 50f green & red 30.00 30.00
Nos. 2NJ1-2NJ16 (16) 878.30 878.30
Nos. 2NJ1-2NJ13,2NJ15-2NJ16 (15) 848.30

NEWSPAPER STAMP

Hungarian Newspaper Stamp of 1914 Overprinted like Regular Issues

1919 Wmk. 137 *Imperf.*

2NP1 N5 (2f) orange (Bl) .55 .55
a. Inverted overprint 50.00 50.00
b. Double overprint 125.00 125.00

SECOND DEBRECEN ISSUE

Complete forgeries exist of this issue and are often found in large multiples or even complete sheets. Values are for genuine stamps.

Mythical "Turul" — OS5

Throwing Lariat OS6

Hungarian Peasant OS7

1920 Unwmk. Typo. *Perf. 11½*

3N1 OS5 2f lt brown 2.25 2.25
3N2 OS5 3f red brown 2.25 2.25
3N3 OS5 4f gray 2.25 2.25
3N4 OS5 5f lt green .50 .50
3N5 OS5 6f slate 2.25 2.25
3N6 OS5 10f scarlet .50 .50
3N7 OS5 15f dk violet 3.00 3.00
3N8 OS5 20f dk brown .60 .60
3N9 OS6 25f ultra 1.25 1.25
3N10 OS6 30f buff .65 .65
3N11 OS6 35f claret 1.25 1.25
3N12 OS6 40f olive grn .75 .75
3N13 OS6 45f salmon 1.00 1.00
3N14 OS6 50f pale vio .75 .75
3N15 OS6 60f yellow grn .90 .90
3N16 OS6 75f Prus blue .75 .75
3N17 OS7 80f gray grn .85 .85
3N18 OS7 1k brown red 3.00 3.00
3N19 OS7 2k chocolate 3.00 3.00
3N20 OS7 3k brown vio 2.25 2.25
3N21 OS7 5k bister brn 2.25 2.25
3N22 OS7 10k dull vio 2.25 2.25
Nos. 3N1-3N22 (22) 34.50 34.50

Thick, Glazed Paper

3N23 OS5 2f lt brown 3.00 3.00
3N24 OS5 3f red brown 3.00 3.00
3N25 OS5 4f gray 3.00 3.00
3N26 OS5 5f lt green 3.00 3.00
3N27 OS5 6f slate 3.00 3.00
3N28 OS5 10f scarlet .75 .75
3N29 OS5 15f dk vio 3.00 3.00
3N30 OS5 20f dk brown 1.00 1.00
3N31 OS7 80f gray grn 1.50 1.50
3N32 OS7 1k brown red 4.00 4.00
3N33 OS7 1.20k orange 8.00 8.00
3N34 OS7 2k chocolate 4.50 4.50
Nos. 3N23-3N34 (12) 37.75 37.75

SEMI-POSTAL STAMPS

Carrying Wounded — SP1

1920 Unwmk. Typo. *Perf. 11½*

3NB1 SP1 20f green 1.25 1.25
3NB2 SP1 50f gray brn 2.25 2.25
3NB3 SP1 1k blue green 2.25 2.25
3NB4 SP1 2k dk green 2.25 2.25

Colored Paper

3NB5 SP1 20f green, *bl* 3.00 3.00
3NB6 SP1 50f brn, *rose* 3.00 3.00
3NB7 SP1 1k dk grn, *grn* 3.00 3.00
Nos. 3NB1-3NB7 (7) 17.00 17.00

POSTAGE DUE STAMPS

D1

1920 Typo. *Perf. 15*

3NJ1 D1 5f blue green 1.50 1.50
3NJ2 D1 10f blue green 1.50 1.50
3NJ3 D1 20f blue green .75 .75
3NJ4 D1 30f blue green .75 .75
3NJ5 D1 40f blue green 1.25 1.25
Nos. 3NJ1-3NJ5 (5) 5.75 5.75

TEMESVAR ISSUE

Issued under Romanian Occupation

Forgeries exist of the inverted and color error surcharges.

Hungary Nos. 108, 155, 109, 111, E1 Surcharged

1919 Wmk. 137 *Perf. 15*

4N1 A9 30f on 2f brn org (Bl) .40 .40
a. Red surcharge 2.00 2.00
b. Inverted surcharge (R) 25.00 25.00
4N2 A9 1k on 4f sl gray (R) .30 .30
4N3 A9 150f on 3f rod lil (Bk) .25 .25
4N4 A9 150f on 5f grn (Bk) .40 .40
4N5 SD1 3k on 2f gray grn & red (Bk) 2.00 2.00
a. Blue surcharge .80 .80
Nos. 4N1-4N5 (5) 3.35 3.35

POSTAGE DUE STAMPS

D1

D2

1919 Wmk. 137 *Perf. 15*

4NJ1 D1 40f on 15f + 2f vio (Bk) .50 .50
a. Red surcharge 2.00 2.00
4NJ2 D2 60f on 2f grn & red (Bk) 2.50 2.50
a. Red surcharge 8.00 8.00
4NJ3 D2 60f on 10f grn & red (Bk) 1.25 1.25
a. Red surcharge 4.00 4.00
Nos. 4NJ1-4NJ3 (3) 4.25 4.25

FIRST TRANSYLVANIA ISSUE

Issued under Romanian Occupation

The scarcer values of this issue have been extensively forged. Genuine common values are more easily found.

Issued in Kolozsvar (Cluj)

Hungarian Stamps of 1916-18 Overprinted

1919 Wmk. 137 *Perf. 15, 14*

On Stamp of 1916, White Numerals

5N1 A8 15b violet 4.75 4.75

On Stamps of 1916-18

5N2 A9 2b brown org .25 .25
5N3 A9 3b red lilac .25 .25
5N4 A9 5b green .25 .25
5N5 A9 6b grnsh blue .40 .40
5N5A A9 10b rose red 60.00 60.00
5N6 A9 15b violet .25 .25
5N7 A9 25b dull blue .25 .25
5N8 A9 35b brown .25 .25
5N9 A9 40b olive grn .50 .50
5N10 A10 50b red vio & lil 1.00 1.00
5N11 A10 75b brt bl & pale bl .30 .30
5N12 A10 80b grn & pale grn .25 .25
5N13 A10 1 l red brn & cl .25 .25
5N14 A10 2 l ol brn & bis .60 .60
5N15 A10 3 l dk vio & ind 3.50 3.50
5N16 A10 5 l dk brn & lt brn 2.50 2.50
5N17 A10 10 l vio brn & vio 3.00 3.00

On Stamps of 1918

5N18 A11 10b scarlet 40.00 40.00
5N19 A11 15b dp violet 20.00 20.00
5N20 A11 20b dk brown .25 .25
a. Gold overprint 75.00 75.00
b. Silver overprint 75.00 75.00
5N21 A11 25b brt blue .65 .65
5N22 A12 40b olive grn .30 .30

On No. 103A

5N23 A5a 10b violet brn .35 .35
Nos. 5N1-5N23 (24) 140.10 140.10

SEMI-POSTAL STAMPS

Hungarian Semi-Postal Stamps of 1913-17 Overprinted like Regular Issues

On Issue of 1913

1919 Wmk. 137 *Perf. 14*

5NB1 SP1 1 l on 1f slate 27.50 27.50
5NB2 SP1 1 l on 2f ol yel 70.00 70.00
5NB3 SP1 1 l on 3f org 37.50 37.50
5NB4 SP1 1 l on 5f emer 3.25 3.25
5NB5 SP1 1 l on 10f car 4.50 4.50
5NB6 SP1 1 l on 12f vio,*yel* 16.00 16.00
5NB7 SP1 1 l on 16f gray grn 6.25 6.25

5NB8 SP1 1 l on 25f ultra 60.00 60.00
5NB9 SP1 1 l on 35f red vio 10.00 10.00
5NB10 SP2 1 l on 1k dl red 60.00 60.00

On Issue of 1916-17

Perf. 15

5NB11 SP3 10b + 2b rose red .25 .25
5NB12 SP4 15b + 2b dull vio .25 .25
5NB13 SP5 40b + 2b brn car .25 .25
Nos. 5NB1-5NB13 (13) 295.75 295.75

SPECIAL DELIVERY STAMP

Hungarian Special Delivery Stamp of 1916 Overprinted like Regular Issues

1919 Wmk. 137 ***Perf. 15***

5NE1 SD1 2b gray grn & red .30 .30

POSTAGE DUE STAMPS

Hungarian Postage Due Stamps of 1914-18 Overprinted like Regular Issues

On Stamp of 1914

1919 Wmk. 137 ***Perf. 15***

5NJ1 D1 50b green & blk 13.00 13.00

On Stamps of 1915

5NJ2 D1 1b green & red *350.00 350.00*
5NJ3 D1 2b green & red .70 .70
5NJ4 D1 5b green & red 60.00 60.00
5NJ5 D1 10b green & red .45 .45
5NJ6 D1 15b green & red 20.00 20.00
5NJ7 D1 20b green & red .40 .40
5NJ8 D1 30b green & red 30.00 30.00
Nos. 5NJ1-5NJ8 (8) 474.55 474.55

NEWSPAPER STAMP

Hungarian Newspaper Stamp of 1914 Overprinted like Regular Issues

1919 Wmk. 137 ***Imperf.***

5NP1 N5 2b orange 3.75 3.75

SECOND TRANSYLVANIA ISSUE

The scarcer values of this issue have been extensively forged. Genuine common values are more easily found.

Issued in Nagyvarad (Oradea)

Hungarian Stamps of 1916-19 Overprinted

1919 Wmk. 137 ***Perf. 15, 14***

On Stamps of 1913-16

6N1 A4 2b olive yel 7.00 7.00
6N2 A4 3b orange 13.00 13.00
6N3 A4 6b olive grn 1.75 1.75
6N4 A4 16b gray grn 37.50 37.50
6N5 A4 50b lake, *bl* 1.75 1.75
6N6 A4 70b red brn & grn 26.00 26.00

On Stamp of 1916 (White Numerals)

6N6A A8 15b violet 125.00 125.00

On Stamps of 1916-18

6N7 A9 2b brown org .25 .25
6N8 A9 3b red lilac .25 .25
6N9 A9 5b green .30 .30
6N10 A9 6b grnsh blue 1.60 1.60
6N11 A9 10b rose red 2.10 2.10
6N12 A9 15b violet .25 .25
6N13 A9 20b gray brn 20.00 20.00
6N14 A9 25b dull blue .30 .30
6N15 A9 35b brown .45 .45
6N16 A9 40b olive grn .30 .30
6N17 A10 50b red vio & lil .60 .60
6N18 A10 75b brt bl & pale bl .25 .25
6N19 A10 80b grn & pale grn .30 .30
6N20 A10 1 l red brn & cl .75 .75
6N21 A10 2 l ol brn & bis .25 .25
6N22 A10 3 l dk vio & ind 6.50 6.50
6N23 A10 5 l dk brn & lt brn 3.25 3.25
6N24 A10 10 l vio brn & vio 1.50 1.50

On Stamps of 1918

6N25 A11 10b scarlet 3.25 3.25
6N26 A11 20b dk brown .25 .25
6N27 A11 25b brt blue .75 .75
6N28 A12 40b olive grn 1.10 1.10

On Stamps of 1918-19, Overprinted "Koztarsasag"

6N29 A9 2b brown org 4.00 4.00
6N30 A9 3b red lilac .25 .25
6N31 A9 4b slate gray .25 .25
6N32 A9 5b green .50 .50
6N33 A9 6b grnsh bl 3.00 3.00
6N34 A9 10b rose red 17.50 17.50
6N35 A9 20b gray brn 2.50 2.50
6N36 A9 40b olive grn .50 .50
6N37 A10 1 l red brn & cl .25 .25
6N38 A10 3 l dk vio & ind .75 .75
6N39 A10 5 l dk brn & lt brn 4.50 4.50
6N40 A11 10b scarlet *75.00 75.00*
6N41 A11 20b dk brown 4.50 4.50
6N42 A11 25b brt blue 1.25 1.25
6N43 A12 50b lilac .25 .25

On Stamps of 1919

Inscribed "MAGYAR POSTA"

6N44 A13 5b yellow grn .25 .25
6N45 A13 10b red .25 .25
6N46 A13 20b dk brown .40 .40
6N47 A13 25b dull blue 2.00 2.00
6N48 A13 40b olive grn .65 .65
6N49 A14 5 l dk brn & brn 6.50 6.50

On No. 103A

6N50 A5a 10b violet brn .85 .85
Nos. 6N1-6N50 (51) 382.45 382.45

SEMI-POSTAL STAMPS

Hungarian Semi-Postal Stamps of 1913-17 Overprinted like Regular Issues

On Stamps of 1913

1919 Wmk. 137 ***Perf. 14***

6NB1 SP1 1 l on 1f slate 2.25 2.25
6NB2 SP1 1 l on 2f olive yel 8.50 8.50
6NB3 SP1 1 l on 3f orange 2.75 2.75
6NB4 SP1 1 l on 5f emerald .25 .25
6NB5 SP1 1 l on 6f olive grn 2.25 2.25
6NB6 SP1 1 l on 10f carmine .30 .30
6NB7 SP1 1 l on 12f vio, *yel* 60.00 60.00
6NB8 SP1 1 l on 16f gray grn 2.50 2.50
6NB9 SP1 1 l on 20f dk brn 11.00 11.00
6NB10 SP1 1 l on 25f ultra 7.50 7.50
6NB11 SP1 1 l on 35f red vio 7.75 7.75

On Stamp of 1915

Wmk. 135 ***Perf. 11½***

6NB12 A4 5b emerald 20.00 20.00

On Stamps of 1916-17

Wmk. 137 ***Perf. 15***

6NB13 SP3 10b + 2b rose red 1.25 1.25
6NB14 SP4 15b + 2b dull vio .45 .45
6NB15 SP5 40b + 2b brn car .25 .25
Nos. 6NB1-6NB15 (15) 127.00 127.00

SPECIAL DELIVERY STAMP

Hungarian Special Delivery Stamp of 1916 Overprinted like Regular Issues

1919 Wmk. 137 ***Perf. 15***

6NE1 SD1 2b gray grn & red .40 .40

POSTAGE DUE STAMPS

Hungarian Postage Due Stamps of 1915 Overprinted like Regular Issues

1919 Wmk. 137 ***Perf. 15***

6NJ1 D1 1b green & red 30.00 30.00
6NJ2 D1 2b green & red .25 .25
6NJ3 D1 5b green & red 9.75 9.75
6NJ4 D1 6b green & red 6.75 6.75
6NJ5 D1 10b green & red .25 .25
6NJ6 D1 12b green & red 1.50 1.50
6NJ7 D1 15b green & red 1.50 1.50
6NJ8 D1 20b green & red .25 .25
6NJ9 D1 30b green & red 1.60 1.60
Nos. 6NJ1-6NJ9 (9) 51.85 51.85

On Hungary No. J27

Perf. 11½x12

Wmk. 135

6NJ10 D1 20b on 100b grn & blk 350.00 350.00

NEWSPAPER STAMP

Hungarian Newspaper Stamp of 1914 Overprinted like Regular Issues

1919 Wmk. 137 ***Imperf.***

6NP1 N5 2b orange .45 .45

FIRST BARANYA ISSUE

Issued under Serbian Occupation

The scarcer values of this issue have been extensively forged. Genuine common values are more easily found.

Hungarian Stamps of 1913-18 Overprinted in Black or Red

On A4, A9, A11, A12

On A10

1919 Wmk. 137 ***Perf. 15***

On Issue of 1913-16

7N1 A4 6f olive grn (R) .90 .90
7N2 A4 50f lake, *bl* .25 .25
7N3 A4 60f grn, *salmon* .75 .75
7N4 A4 70f red brn & grn (R) 2.00 2.00
7N5 A4 70f red brn & grn (Bk) .25 .25
7N6 A4 80f dl vio (R) 3.25 3.25

On Issue of 1916-18

7N7 A9 2f brown org (Bk) 4.25 4.25
7N8 A9 2f brown org (R) .25 .25
7N9 A9 3f red lilac (Bk) .25 .25
7N10 A9 3f red lilac (R) .80 .80
7N11 A9 5f green (Bk) .80 .80
7N12 A9 5f green (R) .25 .25
7N13 A9 6f grnsh bl (Bk) 1.75 1.75
7N14 A9 6f grnsh bl (R) 2.00 2.00
7N15 A9 15f violet .35 .35
7N16 A9 20f gray brn 20.00 20.00
7N17 A9 25f dull blue 3.50 3.50
7N18 A9 35f brown 5.75 5.75
7N19 A9 40f olive grn 20.00 20.00
7N20 A10 50f red vio & lil 2.00 2.00
7N21 A10 75f brt bl & pale bl .40 .40
7N22 A10 80f grn & pale grn .65 .65
7N23 A10 1k red brn & cl .55 .55
7N24 A10 2k ol brn & bis .65 .65
7N25 A10 3k dk vio & ind .65 .65
7N26 A10 5k dk brn & lt brn 1.25 1.25
7N27 A10 10k vio brn & vio 4.00 *4.00*

7N28 A9 45f on 2f brn org .35 .35
7N29 A9 45f on 5f green .25 .25
7N30 A9 45f on 15f violet .25 .25

On Issue of 1918

7N31 A11 10f scarlet (Bk) .25 .25
7N32 A11 20f dk brn (Bk) .25 .25
7N34 A11 25f dp blue (Bk) 1.90 1.90
7N35 A11 25f dp blue (R) 1.10 1.10
7N36 A12 40f olive grn (Bk) 4.50 4.50
7N37 A12 40f olive grn (R) 30.00 30.00

On Issue of 1918-19 (Koztarsasag)

7N38 A9 2f brown org (Bk) 3.50 3.50
7N39 A12 40f ol grn (Bk) *125.00 125.00*
7N40 A12 40f olive grn (R) 20.00 20.00

With New Value Added

7N41 A9 45f on 2f brn org (Bk) 2.00 2.00
7N42 A9 45f on 2f brn org (R) .45 .45

The overprints were set in groups of 25. In each group two stamps have the figures "1" of "1919" with serifs.

SEMI-POSTAL STAMPS

Hungarian Semi-Postal Stamps Overprinted Regular Issue First Type On Stamp of 1915

1919 Wmk. 137 ***Perf. 15***

7NB1 A4 50f + 2f lake, *bl* 16.00 16.00

On Stamps of 1916

7NB2 SP3 10f + 2f rose red .30 .30
7NB3 SP4 15f + 2f dull vio .40 .40
Nos. 7NB1-7NB3 (3) 16.70 16.70

SPECIAL DELIVERY STAMP

SD1

1919 Wmk. 137 ***Perf. 15***

7NE1 SD1 105f on 2f gray grn & red 1.25 1.25

POSTAGE DUE STAMPS

Overprinted or Surcharged on Hungary Nos. J29, J32, J35

1919 Wmk. 137 ***Perf. 15***

7NJ1 D1 2f green & red 3.75 3.75
7NJ2 D1 10f green & red 1.25 1.25
7NJ3 D1 20f green & red 1.60 1.60

With New Value Added

7NJ4 D1 40f on 2f grn & red 1.50 1.50
Nos. 7NJ1-7NJ4 (4) 8.10 8.10

SECOND BARANYA ISSUE

The scarcer values of this issue have been extensively forged. Genuine common values are more easily found.

Hungarian Stamps of 1916-19 Surcharged in Black and Red

1919 On Stamps of 1916-18

8N1 A9 20f on 2f brn org 4.25 4.25
8N2 A9 50f on 5f green 2.00 2.00
8N3 A9 150f on 15f violet 2.00 2.00
8N4 A10 200f on 75f brt bl & pale bl .75 .75

On Stamp of 1918-19, Overprinted "Koztarsasag"

8N5 A11 150f on 15f dp vio .50 .50

On Stamps of 1919

8N6 A13 20f on 2f brn org .35 .35
8N7 A13 30f on 6f grnsh bl .70 .70
8N8 A13 50f on 5f yel grn .25 .25
8N9 A13 100f on 25f dull bl .25 .25
8N10 A13 100f on 40f ol grn .25 .25
8N11 A13 100f on 45f orange 1.10 1.10
8N12 A13 150f on 20f dk brn 1.40 1.40

On No. 103A

8N13 A5a 10f on 10f vio brn .75 .75
Nos. 8N1-8N13 (13) 14.55 14.55

SPECIAL DELIVERY STAMP

Hungarian Special Delivery Stamp of 1916 Surcharged like Regular Issues

1919 Wmk. 137 *Perf. 15*
8NE1 SD1 10f on 2f gray grn & red .65 .65

NEWSPAPER STAMP

Hungarian Newspaper Stamp of 1914 Surcharged like Regular Issues

1919 Wmk. 137 *Imperf.*
8NP1 N5 10f on 2f orange .80 .80

TEMESVAR ISSUES

Issued under Serbian Occupation

Forgeries exist of the inverted and color error surcharges.

Hungarian Stamps of 1916-18 Surcharged in Black, Blue or Brown

a

b

1919
9N1 A9(a) 10f on 2f brn org (Bl) .25 .25
a. Black surcharge 15.00 15.00
9N2 A9(b) 30f on 2f brn org .25 .25
a. Inverted surcharge 75.00 75.00
9N3 A11(b) 50f on 20f dk brn (Bl) .25 .25
a. Inverted surcharge
9N4 A9(b) 1k 50f on 15f vio .30 .30
a. Brown surcharge .75 .75
b. Double surcharge (Bk) 50.00 50.00
Nos. 9N1-9N4 (4) 1.05 1.05

SEMI-POSTAL STAMP

Hungarian Semi-Postal Stamp of 1916 Surcharged in Blue

1919 Wmk. 137 *Perf. 15*
9NB1 SP3 45f on 10f + 2f rose red .25 .25

POSTAGE DUE STAMPS

Hungarian Postage Due Stamps of 1915 Surcharged

1919 Wmk. 137 *Perf. 15*
9NJ1 D1 40f on 2f grn & red .80 .80
9NJ2 D1 60f on 2f grn & red .80 .80
9NJ3 D1 100f on 2f grn & red .80 .80
Nos. 9NJ1-9NJ3 (3) 2.40 2.40

BANAT, BACSKA ISSUE

Issued under Serbian Occupation

Postal authorities at Temesvar applied these overprints. The stamps were available for postage, but were chiefly used to pay postal employees' salaries.

The overprints on this issue have been extensively forged. Even the inexpensive values are difficult to find with genuine overprints. The more extensive note before 1N1 also applies to Nos. 10N1-10NP1.

Hungarian Stamps of 1913-19 Overprinted in Black or Red

a

b

1919

Type "a" on Stamp of 1913

10N1 A4 50f lake, *blue* 4.00 4.00

Type "a" on Stamps of 1916-18

10N2 A9 2f brown org 4.00 4.00
10N3 A9 3f red lilac 4.00 4.00
10N4 A9 5f green 4.00 4.00
10N5 A9 6f grnsh blue 4.00 4.00
10N6 A9 15f violet 4.00 4.00
10N7 A9 35f brown 35.00 35.00

Type "b"

10N8 A10 50f red vio & lil (R) 30.00 30.00
10N9 A10 75f brt bl & pale bl 4.00 4.00
10N10 A10 80f grn & pale grn 4.00 4.00
a. Red overprint 37.50 37.50
10N11 A10 1k red brn & cl 4.00 4.00
10N12 A10 2k ol brn & bis 4.00 4.00
a. Red overprint 37.50 37.50
10N14 A10 3k dk vio & ind 65.00 65.00
10N15 A10 5k dk brn & lt brn 4.00 4.00
10N16 A10 10k vio brn & vio 4.00 4.00

Type "a" on Stamps of 1918

10N17 A11 10f scarlet 4.00 4.00
10N18 A11 20f dk brown 4.00 4.00
10N19 A11 25f brt blue 4.00 4.00
10N20 A12 40f olive grn 4.00 4.00
10N21 A12 50f lilac 4.00 4.00

Type "a" on Stamps of 1919 Inscribed "Magyar Posta"

10N22 A13 10f red *30.00 30.00*
10N23 A13 20f dk brown *30.00 30.00*
10N24 A13 25f dull blue *37.50 37.50*

Type "a" on Stamps of 1918-19 Overprinted "Koztarsasag"

10N25 A9 4f slate gray 3.50 3.50
10N26 A9 4f sl gray (R) 42.50 42.50
10N27 A9 5f green 4.00 4.00
10N28 A9 6f grnsh blue 4.00 4.00
10N29 A9 10f rose red 30.00 30.00
10N30 A11 15f dp violet 30.00 30.00
10N31 A9 20f gray brn 30.00 30.00
10N32 A11 25f brt blue 30.00 30.00
10N33 A9 40f olive grn 3.50 3.50
10N34 A9 40f ol grn (R) 32.50 32.50

Type "b"

10N35 A10 1k red brn & cl 4.00 4.00
10N36 A10 2k ol brn & bis 30.00 30.00
10N37 A10 3k dk vio & ind 30.00 30.00
10N38 A10 5k dk brn & lt brn 30.00 30.00
10N39 A10 10k vio brn & vio 30.00 30.00

Type "a" on Temesvár Issue

10N40 A9 10f on 2f brn org (Bl & Bk) 4.00 4.00
10N41 A9 1k50f on 15f vio 4.00 4.00

10N42 A5a 50f on 10f vio brn 4.00 4.00
a. Red overprint 75.00 75.00
Nos. 10N1-10N42 (41) *641.50 641.50*

SEMI-POSTAL STAMPS

Semi-Postal Stamps of 1916-17 Overprinted Type "a" in Black

1919
10NB1 SP3 10f + 2f rose red 4.00 4.00
10NB2 SP4 15f + 2f dull vio 4.00 4.00
10NB3 SP5 40f + 2f brn car 4.00 4.00

Same Overprint on Temesvar Issue

10NB4 SP3 45f on 10f + 2f rose red (Bl & Bk) 4.00 4.00
Nos. 10NB1-10NB4 (4) 16.00 16.00

SPECIAL DELIVERY STAMP

Hungary No. E1 Surcharged in Black

1919
10NE1 SD1 30f on 2f gray grn & red 4.00 4.00
a. Red overprint 75.00 75.00

POSTAGE DUE STAMPS

Postage Due Stamps of 1914-15 Overprinted Type "a" in Black

1919
10NJ1 D1 2f green & red 4.00 4.00
10NJ2 D1 10f green & red 4.00 4.00
10NJ3 D1 15f green & red 32.50 32.50
10NJ4 D1 20f green & red 4.00 4.00
10NJ5 D1 30f green & red 30.00 30.00
10NJ6 D1 50f green & blk 30.00 30.00
Nos. 10NJ1-10NJ6 (6) 104.50 104.50

NEWSPAPER STAMP

Stamp of 1914 Overprinted Type "a" in Black

1919
10NP1 N5 (2f) orange 4.00 4.00

SZEGED ISSUE

The "Hungarian National Government, Szeged, 1919," as the overprint reads, was an anti-Bolshevist government which opposed the Soviet Republic then in control at Budapest.

The overprints on this issue have been extensively forged. Even the inexpensive stamps are difficult to find with genuine overprints. The more extensive note before No. 1N1 also applies to Szeged Nos. 11N1-11NP1.

Hungary Stamps of 1916-19 Overprinted in Green, Red and Blue

On Stamps of 1916-18

1919 *Perf. 15, 14*
11N1 A9 2f brn org (G) 2.25 2.25
11N2 A9 3f red lilac (G) .75 .75
11N3 A9 5f green 2.75 2.75
11N4 A9 6f grnsh blue 32.50 32.50
11N5 A9 15f violet 3.50 3.50
11N6 A10 50f red vio & lil 19.00 19.00
11N7 A10 75f brt bl & pale bl 4.25 4.25
11N8 A10 80f grn & pale grn 18.00 18.00
11N9 A10 1k red brn & cl (G) 2.25 2.25
11N10 A10 2k ol brn & bis 4.75 4.75
11N11 A10 3k dk vio & ind 7.25 7.25
11N12 A10 5k dk brn & lt brn 60.00 60.00
11N13 A10 10k vio brn & vio 60.00 60.00

With New Value Added

11N14 A9 45f on 3f red lil (R & G) .80 .80
11N15 A10 10k on 1k red brn & cl (Bl & G) 8.00 8.00

On Stamps of 1918

11N16 A11 10f scarlet (G) 2.50 2.50
11N17 A11 20f dk brown .60 .60
11N18 A11 25f brt blue 22.50 22.50
11N19 A12 40f olive grn 11.00 11.00

On Stamps of 1918-19 Overprinted "Koztarsasag"

11N20 A9 3f red lil (G) 42.50 42.50
11N21 A9 4f slate gray 11.00 11.00
11N22 A9 5f green 25.00 25.00
11N23 A9 6f grnsh blue 15.00 15.00
11N24 A9 10f rose red (G) 32.50 32.50
11N25 A11 10f scarlet) 30.00 30.00
11N26 A11 15f dp violet 10.00 10.00
11N27 A9 20f gray brown 50.00 50.00
11N28 A11 20f dk brown 65.00 65.00
11N29 A11 25f brt blue 20.00 20.00
11N30 A9 40f olive 2.25 2.25
11N31 A12 50f lilac 1.75 1.75
11N32 A10 3k dk vio & ind 37.50 37.50

With New Value Added

11N33 A9 20f on 2f brn org (R & G) .80 .80

On Stamps of 1919 Inscribed "Magyar Posta"

11N34 A13 20f dk brown 60.00 60.00
11N35 A13 25f dull blue 1.75 1.75
Nos. 11N1-11N35 (35) 667.70 667.70

SEMI-POSTAL STAMPS

Szeged Overprint on Semi-Postal Stamps of 1916-17 in Green or Red

1919
11NB1 SP3 10f + 2f rose red (G) .85 .85
11NB2 SP4 15f + 2f dl vio (R) 3.75 3.75
11NB3 SP5 40f + 2f brn car (G) 10.00 10.00

With Additional Overprint "Koztarsasag"

11NB4 SP5 40f + 2f brn car (Bk & G) 15.00 15.00
Nos. 11NB1-11NB4 (4) 29.60 29.60

SPECIAL DELIVERY STAMP

Szeged Overprint on Special Delivery Stamp of 1916 in Red

1919
11NE1 SD1 2f gray grn & red 11.00 11.00

POSTAGE DUE STAMPS

Szeged Overprint on Stamps of 1915-18 in Red

1919
11NJ1 D1 2f green & red 3.00 3.00
11NJ2 D1 6f green & red 9.75 9.75
11NJ3 D1 10f green & red 3.75 3.75
11NJ4 D1 12f green & red 4.75 4.75
11NJ5 D1 20f green & red 6.00 6.00
11NJ6 D1 30f green & red 9.00 9.00

Surcharged in Red

11NJ7 SD1 50f on 2f gray grn & red 2.75 2.75
11NJ8 SD1 100f on 2f gray grn & red 2.75 2.75
Nos. 11NJ1-11NJ8 (8) 41.75 41.75

NEWSPAPER STAMP

Szeged Overprint on Stamp of 1914 in Green

1919 Wmk. 137 *Imperf.*
11NP1 N5 (2f) orange .85 .85

ICELAND

'is-lənd

LOCATION — Island in the North Atlantic Ocean, east of Greenland
GOVT. — Republic
AREA — 39,758 sq. mi.
POP. — 272,069 (1997)
CAPITAL — Reykjavik

Iceland became a republic on June 17, 1944. Formerly this country was united with Denmark under the government of King Christian X who, as a ruling sovereign of both countries, was assigned the dual title of king of each. Although the two countries were temporarily united in certain affairs beyond the king's person, both were acknowledged as sovereign states.

96 Skillings = 1 Rigsdaler
100 Aurar (singular "Eyrir") = 1 Krona (1876)

Catalogue values for unused stamps in this country are for Never Hinged items, beginning with Scott 246 in the regular postage section, Scott B7 in the semi-postal section and Scott C21 in the air post section.

Watermarks

Wmk. 112 — Crown

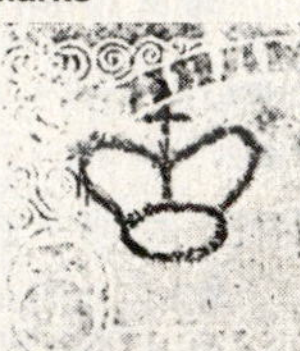
Wmk. 113 — Crown

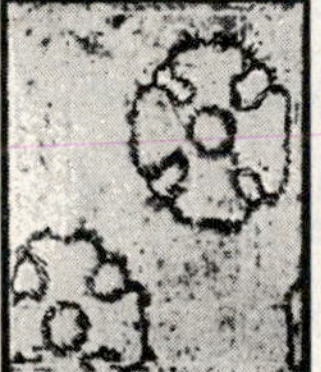
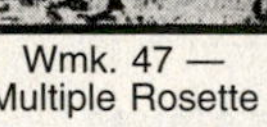
Wmk. 47 — Multiple Rosette

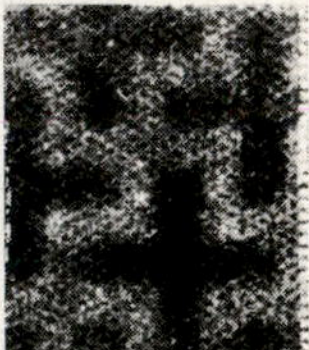
Wmk. 114 — Multiple Crosses

Wmk. 409 — State Shield

Wmk. 410 — State Arms

Values for unused stamps are for examples with original gum as defined in the catalogue introduction. Very fine examples of Nos. 1-33A and O1-O12 will have centering with perforations clear of the framelines but with design noticeably off center, and Nos. 1-7 and O1-O3 additionally will have some irregular or shorter perforations. Well centered stamps are quite scarce and will command higher prices.

A1

Perf. 14x13½

1873 Typo. Wmk. 112

No.	Type	Description	Unused	Used
1	A1	2s ultra	1,050.	*2,150.*
a.		Imperf.	625.	
2	A1	4s dark car	175.	*900.*
a.		Imperf.	625.	—
3	A1	8s brown	325.	*1,150.*
a.		Imperf.	350.	
4	A1	16s yellow	1,450.	*2,200.*
a.		Imperf.	400.	
		Perf. 12½		
5	A1	3s gray	475.	*1,450.*
a.		Imperf.	750.	
6	A1	4s carmine	1,400.	*2,000.*
7	A1	16s yellow	140.	*625.*

False and favor cancellations are often found on Nos. 1-7. Values are considerably less than those shown.

A2

1876

No.	Type	Description	Unused	Used
8	A2	5a blue	475.00	*1,000.*
		Perf. 14x13½		
9	A2	5a blue	425.00	*900.00*
a.		Imperf.	2,450.	
10	A2	6a gray	150.00	35.00
11	A2	10a carmine	225.00	8.00
a.		Imperf.	625.00	*750.00*
12	A2	16a brown	140.00	65.00
13	A2	20a dark violet	35.00	*500.00*
a.		20a light violet	1,100.	500.00
14	A2	40a green	100.00	*225.00*

Fake and favor cancellations are almost always found on No. 13, and value is considerably less than that shown.

Beware of unused color-faded examples of No. 13 described as No. 13a. Expertization is recommended.

Small "3" — A3

1882-98

No.	Type	Description	Unused	Used
15	A3	3a orange	62.50	30.00
16	A2	5a green	67.50	14.00
17	A2	20a blue	325.00	50.00
a.		20a ultramarine	800.00	275.00
18	A2	40a red violet	70.00	47.50
a.		Perf. 13 ('98)	*5,000.*	
19	A2	50a bl & car ('92)	90.00	*100.00*
20	A2	100a brn & vio ('92)	92.50	*140.00*
		Nos. 15-20 (6)	707.50	381.50

See note after No. 68.

Large "3" — A3a

1896-1901 ***Perf. 13***

No.	Type	Description	Unused	Used
21	A3	3a orange ('97)	125.00	12.00
22	A3a	3a yellow ('01)	8.50	*22.50*
23	A2	4a rose & gray ('99)	18.00	*20.00*
24	A2	5a green	4.00	3.00
25	A2	6a gray ('97)	17.50	*19.00*
26	A2	10a carmine ('97)	17.00	3.00
27	A2	16a brown	75.00	*110.00*
28	A2	20a dull blue ('98)	45.00	40.00
a.		20a dull ultramarine	575.00	45.00
29	A2	25a yel brn & bl ('00)	22.50	*32.50*
30	A2	50a bl & car ('98)	450.00	*750.00*

See note after No. 68.
For surcharges see Nos. 31-33A, 45-68.

Black and Red Surcharge

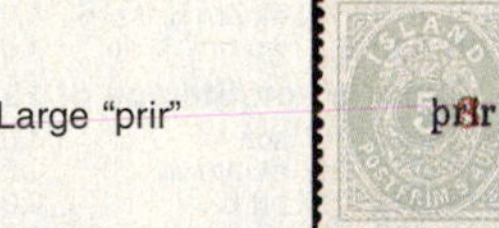
Large "prir"

1897 ***Perf. 13***

No.	Type	Description	Unused	Used
31	A2	3a on 5a green	675.	575.
a.		Perf. 14x13½		*2,300.*
b.		Inverted surcharge	*1,500.*	*1,250.*
c.		As "a," inverted surcharge		*7,500.*

Large "prir" is 6.1mm to 6.3mm wide by 3.5mm tall.

Small "prir"

No.	Type	Description	Unused	Used
32	A2	3a on 5a green	700.	575.
a.		Inverted surcharge	1,250.	1,050.
b.		Perf. 14x13½	*12,500.*	*2,250.*
c.		In vert. pair with #31	1,750.	1,500.
d.		As "b," in vert. pair with #31a		—

All 5 known unused examples of No. 32b lack gum.
Small "prir" is 5.5mm to 5.6mm wide by 3.1mm tall.

Black Surcharge

Large "prir"

No.	Type	Description	Unused	Used
33	A2	3a on 5a green	1,000.	750.
b.		Inverted surcharge	1,500.	1,250.

Large "prir" is 6.1mm to 6.3mm wide by 3.5mm tall.

Small "prir"

No.	Type	Description	Unused	Used
33A	A2	3a on 5a green	1,100.	750.
c.		Inverted surcharge	1,800.	1,500.

Excellent counterfeits are known.
Small "prir" is 5.5mm to 5.6mm wide by 3.1mm tall.

King Christian IX — A4

1902-04 Wmk. 113 ***Perf. 13***

No.	Type	Description	Unused	Used
34	A4	3a orange	6.25	4.00
35	A4	4a gray & rose	4.00	1.40
36	A4	5a yel green	42.50	1.10
37	A4	6a gray brown	22.50	11.00
38	A4	10a car rose	6.50	1.10
39	A4	16a chocolate	8.50	*11.00*
40	A4	20a deep blue	3.50	*4.50*
a.		Inscribed "PJONUSTA"	90.00	*160.00*
41	A4	25a brn & grn	4.00	*7.00*
42	A4	40a violet	4.50	*7.00*
43	A4	50a gray & bl blk	6.25	*25.00*
44	A4	1k sl bl & yel brn	7.50	*10.50*
44A	A4	2k olive brn & brt blue ('04)	29.00	*75.00*
44B	A4	5k org brn & slate blue ('04)	150.00	*230.00*
		Nos. 34-44B (13)	295.00	*388.60*

For surcharge see No. 142.

Stamps of 1882-1901 Overprinted

1902-03 Wmk. 112 ***Perf. 13***

Red Overprint

No.	Type	Description	Unused	Used
45	A2	5a green	1.40	*10.50*
a.		Inverted overprint	80.00	*105.00*
b.		"I" before Gildi omitted	175.00	250.00
c.		'03-'03	750.00	
d.		02'-'03	625.00	850.00
e.		Pair, one without overprint	175.00	
46	A2	6a gray	1.20	*10.50*
a.		Double overprint	140.00	
b.		Inverted overprint	80.00	
c.		'03-'03	525.00	
d.		02'-'03	525.00	
e.		Pair, one with invtd. ovpt.	400.00	
f.		Pair, one without overprint	225.00	
g.		As "f", inverted	400.00	
47	A2	20a dull blue	1.20	*12.50*
a.		Inverted overprint	85.00	*110.00*
b.		"I" before Gildi omitted	175.00	
c.		02'-'03	1,500.	
48	A2	25a yel brn & bl	1.20	*19.00*
a.		Inverted overprint	75.00	*85.00*
b.		'03-'03	450.00	
c.		02'-'03	450.00	675.00
d.		Double overprint	175.00	

Black Overprint

No.	Type	Description	Unused	Used
49	A3	3a orange	240.00	*525.00*
b.		Inverted overprint	375.00	850.00
c.		"I" before Gildi omitted	575.00	
d.		'03-'03	625.00	
e.		02'-'03	625.00	
50	A3a	3a yellow	1.40	*2.50*
a.		Double overprint	400.00	
b.		Inverted overprint	85.00	*105.00*
c.		"I" before Gildi omitted	625.00	
d.		02'-'03	750.00	
51	A2	4a rose & gray	40.00	*57.50*
a.		Double overprint	525.00	
b.		Inverted overprint	120.00	
c.		Dbl. ovpt., one invtd.	400.00	
d.		"I" before Gildi omitted	290.00	
e.		'03-'03	525.00	700.00
f.		02'-'03	525.00	
g.		Pair, one with invtd. ovpt.	400.00	
52	A2	5a green	350.00	*925.00*
a.		Inverted overprint	400.00	*975.00*
b.		Pair, one without overprint	510.00	
c.		As "b", inverted	625.00	
53	A2	6a gray	750.00	*1,150.*
a.		Inverted overprint	800.00	
b.		Pair, one without overprint	800.00	
c.		Double overprint	1,150.	
54	A2	10a carmine	1.40	*12.50*
a.		Inverted overprint	75.00	110.00
b.		Pair, one without overprint	210.00	

No.	Type	Description	Unused	Used
55	A2	16a brown	26.00	*40.00*
a.		Inverted overprint	175.00	
b.		"I" before Gildi omitted	350.00	
c.		'03-'03	700.00	
d.		02'-'03	625.00	
56	A2	20a dull blue	*10,000.*	
a.		Inverted overprint	*9,600.*	
57	A2	25a yel brn & bl	*10,500.*	
a.		Inverted overprint	*14,500.*	
58	A2	40a red vio	1.20	*40.00*
a.		Inverted overprint	90.00	
59	A2	50a bl & car	3.50	*70.00*
a.		Double overprint	250.00	
b.		02'-'03	850.00	
c.		'03-'03	850.00	

Perf. 14x13½

Red Overprint

No.	Type	Description	Unused	Used
60	A2	5a green	2,100.	—
a.		'03-'03	—	
b.		02'-'03	*45,500.*	
61	A2	6a gray	2,100.	—
a.		02'-'03	—	
62	A2	20a blue	*5,750.*	—
b.		02'-'03	—	

Black Overprint

No.	Type	Description	Unused	Used
63	A3	3a orange	1,350.	*2,100.*
a.		Inverted overprint	1,750.	
b.		02'-'03	2,500.	
c.		'03-'03	2,750.	
64	A2	10a carmine	*9,750.*	—
65	A2	16a brown	1,500.	*2,100.*
a.		Inverted overprint	1,900.	
b.		02'-'03	2,300.	
d.		'03-'03	*22,000.*	
65C	A2	20a dull blue	*9,100.*	—
a.		Inverted overprint	*15,500.*	
66	A2	40a red vio	21.00	*105.00*
a.		Inverted overprint	250.00	—
b.		'03-'03	525.00	
c.		02'-'03	525.00	
67	A2	50a bl & car	55.00	*140.00*
a.		Inverted overprint	350.00	
b.		'03-'03	475.00	
c.		02'-'03	475.00	800.00
d.		As "c," inverted	—	
68	A2	100a brn & vio	60.00	*80.00*
a.		Inverted overprint	210.00	
b.		02'-'03	575.00	800.00
c.		'03-'03	850.00	

"I GILDI" means "valid."

In 1904 Nos. 20, 22-30, 45-59 (except 49, 52, 53, 56 and 57) and No. 68 were reprinted for the Postal Union. The reprints are perforated 13 and have watermark type 113. Value $120 each. Without overprint, $250 each.

Kings Christian IX and Frederik VIII — A5

Typo., Center Engr.

1907-08 Wmk. 113 *Perf. 13*

No.	Type	Description	Unused	Used
71	A5	1e yel grn & red	1.75	1.40
72	A5	3a yel brn & ocher	4.75	1.75
73	A5	4a gray & red	3.00	1.75
74	A5	5a green	95.00	1.40
75	A5	6a gray & gray brn	60.00	4.00
76	A5	10a scarlet	150.00	1.60
77	A5	15a red & green	7.50	1.25
78	A5	16a brown	9.75	*40.00*
79	A5	20a blue	8.00	5.75
80	A5	25a bis brn & grn	7.00	*12.00*
81	A5	40a claret & vio	7.00	*15.00*
82	A5	50a gray & vio	7.00	*15.00*
83	A5	1k blue & brn	32.50	*70.00*
84	A5	2k dk brn & dk grn	37.50	*80.00*
85	A5	5k brn & slate	175.00	*350.00*
		Nos. 71-85 (15)	605.75	*600.90*
		Set, never hinged	1,800.	

See Nos. 99-107.

For surcharges and overprints see Nos. 130-138, 143, C2, O69.

Jon Sigurdsson — A6

1911 Typo. and Embossed

No.	Type	Description	Unused	Used
86	A6	1e olive green	2.50	2.00
87	A6	3a light brown	5.00	*15.00*
88	A6	4a ultramarine	1.75	*1.75*
89	A6	6a gray	14.50	*25.00*
90	A6	15a violet	15.00	2.00
91	A6	25a orange	25.00	*50.00*
		Nos. 86-91 (6)	63.75	*95.75*
		Set, never hinged	190.00	

Sigurdsson (1811-79), statesman and author.
For surcharge see No. 149.

Frederik VIII — A7

1912, Feb. 17

No.	Type	Description	Unused	Used
92	A7	5a green	30.00	12.00
93	A7	10a red	30.00	12.00
94	A7	20a pale blue	45.00	18.00
95	A7	50a claret	9.50	*35.00*
96	A7	1k yellow	30.00	*75.00*
97	A7	2k rose	30.00	*75.00*
98	A7	5k brown	160.00	*225.00*
		Nos. 92-98 (7)	334.50	*452.00*
		Set, never hinged	825.00	

For surcharges and overprints see Nos. 140-141, O50-O51.

Type of 1907-08

Typo., Center Engr.

1915-18 Wmk. 114 *Perf. 14x14½*

No.	Type	Description	Unused	Used
99	A5	1e yel grn & red	8.00	*18.00*
100	A5	3a bister brn	4.00	3.00
101	A5	4a gray & red	4.00	*9.50*
102	A5	5a green	100.00	1.40
103	A5	6a gray & gray brn	22.50	*130.00*
104	A5	10a scarlet	3.50	1.25
107	A5	20a blue	225.00	22.50
		Nos. 99-107 (7)	367.00	*185.65*
		Set, never hinged	1,150.	

Revenue cancellations consisting of "TOLLUR" boxed in frame are found on stamps used to pay the tax on parcel post packages entering Iceland.

Christian X — A8

1920-22 Typo.

No.	Type	Description	Unused	Used
108	A8	1e yel grn & red	1.25	*1.25*
		Revenue cancellation		9.00
109	A8	3a bister brn	8.50	*17.50*
		Revenue cancellation		9.00
110	A8	4a gray & red	5.75	2.50
		Revenue cancellation		9.00
111	A8	5a green	2.25	5.75
		Revenue cancellation		17.50
112	A8	5a ol green ('22)	5.75	1.75
		Revenue cancellation		6.75
113	A8	6a dark gray	15.00	8.50
		Revenue cancellation		14.00
114	A8	8a dark brown	8.50	2.50
		Revenue cancellation		12.00
115	A8	10a red	3.00	*12.00*
		Revenue cancellation		22.50
116	A8	10a green ('21)	4.00	2.00
		Revenue cancellation		9.00
117	A8	15a violet	40.00	1.40
		Revenue cancellation		9.00
118	A8	20a deep blue	3.50	*19.00*
		Revenue cancellation		22.50
119	A8	20a choc ('22)	65.00	1.75
		Revenue cancellation		9.00
120	A8	25a brown & grn	17.50	2.00
		Revenue cancellation		9.00
121	A8	25a red ('21)	17.00	*57.50*
		Revenue cancellation		4.25
122	A8	30a red & green	52.50	3.50
		Revenue cancellation		9.00
123	A8	40a claret	40.00	3.50
		Revenue cancellation		9.00
124	A8	40a dk bl ('21)	80.00	15.00
		Revenue cancellation		10.50
125	A8	50a dk gray & cl	190.00	12.00
		Revenue cancellation		13.50
126	A8	1k dp bl & dk brn	110.00	1.75
		Revenue cancellation		1.75
127	A8	2k ol brn & myr green	250.00	35.00
		Revenue cancellation		3.50
128	A8	5k brn & ind	57.50	17.50
		Revenue cancellation		3.50
		Nos. 108-128 (21)	977.00	*223.65*
		Set, never hinged	4,400.	

See Nos. 176-187, 202.

For surcharges and overprints see Nos.139, 150, C1, C9-C14, O52, O70-O71.

A9

A10

A11

1921-25 Wmk. 113 *Perf. 13*

No.	Type	Description	Unused	Used
130	A9	5a on 16a brown	4.00	*30.00*
		Revenue cancellation		35.00
131	A11	5a on 16a brown	2.50	*8.50*
		Revenue cancellation		22.50
132	A10	20a on 25a brn & green	8.00	8.50
a.		Double surcharge	—	
133	A11	20a on 25a bis brn & green	4.50	*8.50*
134	A9	20a on 40a violet	8.00	*20.00*
135	A11	20a on 40a cl & vio	15.00	*23.00*
		Revenue cancellation		17.50
137	A9	30a on 50a gray & bl blk ('25)	35.00	*37.50*
		Revenue cancellation		20.00
138	A9	50a on 5k org brn & sl bl ('25)	65.00	52.50
		Revenue cancellation		21.00
		Nos. 130-138 (8)	142.00	*188.50*
		Set, never hinged	480.00	

No. 111 Surcharged

1922 Wmk. 114 *Perf. 14x14½*

No.	Type	Description	Unused	Used
139	A8	10a on 5a green	8.00	3.50
		Revenue cancellation		35.00

Nos. 95-96, 44A, 85 Surcharged

1924-30 Wmk. 113 *Perf. 13*

No.	Type	Description	Unused	Used
140	A7	10k on 50a ('25)	300.00	*450.00*
		Revenue cancellation		35.00
141	A7	10k on 1k	375.00	*625.00*
		Revenue cancellation		75.00
142	A4	10k on 2k ('29)	80.00	32.50
		Revenue cancellation		11.00
143	A5	10k on 5k ('30)	450.00	575.00
		Revenue cancellation		35.00
		Nos. 140-143 (4)	1,205.	1,683.
		Set, never hinged	3,000.	

Landing the Mail — A12

Designs: 7a, 50a, Landing the mail. 10a, 35a, View of Reykjavik. 20a, Museum building.

Perf. 14x15

1925, Sept. 12 Typo. Wmk. 114

No.	Type	Description	Unused	Used
144	A12	7a yel green	45.00	7.50
		Revenue cancellation		5.75
145	A12	10a dp bl & brn	45.00	.85
		Revenue cancellation		5.75
146	A12	20a vermilion	45.00	.85
		Revenue cancellation		4.50
147	A12	35a deep blue	70.00	9.50
		Revenue cancellation		3.50
148	A12	50a yel grn & brn	70.00	1.75
		Revenue cancellation		1.75
		Nos. 144-148 (5)	275.00	20.45
		Set, never hinged	850.00	

No. 91 Surcharged

1925 Wmk. 113 *Perf. 13*

No.	Type	Description	Unused	Used
149	A6	2k on 25a orange	160.00	*140.00*
		Revenue cancellation		17.50

No. 124 Surcharged in Red

1926

No.	Type	Description	Unused	Used
150	A8	1k on 40a dark blue	150.00	35.00
		Revenue cancellation		25.00

Parliament Building A15

Designs: 5a, Viking ship in storm. 7a, Parliament meeting place, 1690. 10a, Viking funeral. 15a, Vikings naming land. 20a, The dash for Thing. 25a, Gathering wood. 30a, Thingvalla Lake. 35a, Iceland woman in national costume. 40a, Iceland flag. 50a, First Althing, 930 A.D. 1k, Map of Iceland. 2k, Winter-bound home. 5k, Woman spinning. 10k, Viking Sacrifice to Thor.

Perf. 12½x12

1930, Jan. 1 Litho. Unwmk.

No.	Type	Description	Unused	Used
152	A15	3a dull vio & gray vio	3.75	*10.00*
153	A15	5a dk bl & sl grn	3.75	*10.00*
154	A15	7a grn & gray grn	3.25	*10.00*
155	A15	10a dk vio & lilac	10.00	*18.00*
156	A15	15a dp ultra & bl gray	2.75	*11.00*
157	A15	20a rose red & sal	45.00	*90.00*
a.		Double impression	350.00	

158 A15 25a dk brn & lt brn 7.50 *15.00*
159 A15 30a dk grn & sl grn 6.50 *15.00*
160 A15 35a ultra & bl gray 7.50 *15.00*
161 A15 40a dk ultra, red & slate grn 6.50 *15.00*
162 A15 50a red brn & cinn 70.00 *150.00*
163 A15 1k ol grn & gray green 60.00 *150.00*
164 A15 2k turq bl & gray green 70.00 *175.00*
165 A15 5k org & yellow 50.00 *140.00*
166 A15 10k mag & dl rose 50.00 *140.00*
Nos. 152-166 (15) 396.50 *964.00*
Set, never hinged 850.00

Millenary of the "Althing," the Icelandic Parliament, oldest in the world.
Imperfs were privately printed.
For overprints see Nos. O53-O67.

Gullfoss (Golden Falls) — A30

1931-32 Unwmk. Engr. *Perf. 14*
170 A30 5a gray 14.00 1.10
171 A30 20a red 12.00 .25
172 A30 35a ultramarine 24.00 16.00
Revenue cancellation 2.25
173 A30 60a red lil ('32) 15.00 1.50
174 A30 65a red brn ('32) 2.50 1.25
175 A30 75a grnsh bl ('32) 95.00 32.50
Revenue cancellation 5.00
Nos. 170-175 (6) 162.50 52.60
Set, never hinged 460.00

Issued: 5a-35a, Dec. 15; 60a-75a, May 30.

Type of 1920 Christian X Issue Redrawn

Perf. 14x14½

1931-33 Typo. Wmk. 114
176 A8 1e yel grn & red 1.00 *1.75*
Revenue cancellation 3.00
177 A8 3a bister brown 15.00 *15.00*
Revenue cancellation 8.00
178 A8 4a gray & red 2.50 2.50
Revenue cancellation 7.00
179 A8 6a dark gray 1.75 *5.00*
Revenue cancellation 7.00
180 A8 7a yel grn ('33) .65 *1.75*
Revenue cancellation 9.50
181 A8 10a chocolate 140.00 1.40
Revenue cancellation 7.00
182 A8 25a brn & green 17.50 4.25
Revenue cancellation 3.50
183 A8 30a red & green 30.00 7.00
Revenue cancellation 8.00
184 A8 40a claret 240.00 21.00
Revenue cancellation 12.00
185 A8 1k dk bl & lt brn 40.00 7.50
Revenue cancellation 3.50
186 A8 2k choc & dk grn 240.00 80.00
Revenue cancellation 8.00
187 A8 10k yel grn & blk 250.00 210.00
Revenue cancellation 17.50
Nos. 176-187 (12) 978.40 357.15
Set, never hinged 4,300.

On the redrawn stamps the horizontal lines of the portrait and the oval are closer together than on the 1920 stamps and are crossed by many fine vertical lines.
See No. 202.

Dynjandi Falls — A31

Mount Hekla — A32

Perf. 12½

1935, June 28 Engr. Unwmk.
193 A31 10a blue 24.00 .25
Never hinged 80.00
Revenue cancellation 24.00
194 A32 1k greenish gray 42.50 .25
Never hinged 140.00
Revenue cancellation 5.75

Matthias Jochumsson — A33

1935, Nov. 11
195 A33 3a gray green .75 *4.00*
Revenue cancellation 4.00
196 A33 5a gray 14.00 1.40
Revenue cancellation 17.50
197 A33 7a yel green 20.00 2.40
Revenue cancellation 7.00
198 A33 35a blue .60 *1.40*
Revenue cancellation 7.00
Nos. 195-198 (4) 35.35 *9.20*
Set, never hinged 115.00

Birth cent. of Matthias Jochumsson, poet.
For surcharges see Nos. 212, 236.

King Christian X — A34

1937, May 14 *Perf. 13x12½*
199 A34 10a green 2.40 *25.00*
200 A34 30a brown 2.40 *10.50*
201 A34 40a claret 2.40 *10.50*
Nos. 199-201 (3) 7.20 *46.00*
Set, never hinged 12.00

Reign of Christian X, 25th anniv.

Christian X Type of 1931-33

1937 Unwmk. Typo. *Perf. 11½*
202 A8 1e yel grn & red .80 *2.50*
Never hinged 2.40

Geyser
A35 A36

1938-47 Engr. *Perf. 14*
203 A35 15a dp rose vio 6.00 *12.00*
Revenue cancellation 24.00
a. Imperf., pair *1,250.*
Never hinged 1,600.
204 A35 20a rose red 24.00 .25
Revenue cancellation 17.50
205 A35 35a ultra .70 *1.10*
Revenue cancellation 22.50
206 A36 40a dk brn ('39) 14.00 *27.50*
Revenue cancellation 90.00
207 A36 45a brt ultra ('40) .80 *1.10*
Revenue cancellation 1.75
208 A36 50a dk slate grn 21.00 1.10
Revenue cancellation 22.50
208A A36 60a brt ultra ('43) 5.75 1.10
c. Perf. 11½ ('47) 3.00 *12.00*
Never hinged (#208Ac) 7.50
208B A36 1k indigo ('45) 9.50 .50
d. Perf. 11½ ('47) 3.00 *12.00*
Never hinged (#208Bd) 7.50
Nos. 203-208B (8) 81.75 *44.65*
Set, never hinged 215.00

University of Iceland A37

1938, Dec. 1 *Perf. 13½*
209 A37 25a dark grn 7.50 *16.00*
210 A37 30a brown 7.50 *16.00*
211 A37 40a brt red vio 7.50 *16.00*
Nos. 209-211 (3) 22.50 *48.00*
Set, never hinged 37.50

20th anniversary of independence.

No. 198 Surcharged with New Value

1939, Mar. 17 *Perf. 12½*
212 A33 5a on 35a blue .80 *1.60*
Never hinged 1.40
a. Double surcharge *250.00*
Never hinged 525.00

Trylon and Perisphere A38

Leif Ericsson's Ship and Route to America A39

Statue of Thorfinn Karlsefni — A40

1939 Engr. *Perf. 14*
213 A38 20a crimson 3.50 *7.00*
214 A39 35a bright ultra 4.00 *8.50*
215 A40 45a bright green 4.25 *12.00*
216 A40 2k dark gray 52.50 *150.00*
Nos. 213-216 (4) 64.25 *177.50*
Set, never hinged 110.00

New York World's Fair.
For overprints see Nos. 232-235.

Codfish — A41

Herring — A42

Flag of Iceland — A43

1939-45 Engr. *Perf. 14, 14x13½*
217 A41 1e Prussian blue .45 *4.50*
a. Perf. 14x13½ 1.75 5.75
218 A42 3a dark violet .45 *1.25*
a. Perf. 14x13½ 2.40 *8.50*
219 A41 5a dark brown .45 .45
c. Perf. 14x13½ 2.75 1.75
220 A42 7a dark green 4.75 *10.50*
221 A42 10a green ('40) 35.00 1.25
b. Perf. 14x13½ 65.00 4.00
Never hinged 210.00
222 A42 10a slate gray ('45) .25 .25
223 A42 12a dk grn ('43) .45 .90
224 A41 25a brt red ('40) 29.00 .60
b. Perf. 14x13½ 57.50 3.00
Never hinged (#224b) 190.00
225 A41 25a hn brn ('45) 1.25 .45
226 A42 35a carmine ('43) .60 .70
227 A41 50a dk bl grn ('43) .70 .25

Typo.
228 A43 10a car & ultra 2.50 1.75
Nos. 217-228 (12) 75.85 *22.85*
Set, never hinged 250.00

Statue of Thorfinn Karlsefni — A44

1939-45 Engr. *Perf. 14*
229 A44 2k dark gray 3.00 .50
230 A44 5k dk brn ('43) 22.50 .60
231 A44 10k brn yel ('45) 12.00 2.50
Nos. 229-231 (3) 37.50 3.60
Set, never hinged 92.50

1947 *Perf. 11½*
229a A44 2k 8.00 1.75
230a A44 5k 29.00 2.40
231a A44 10k 12.00 *45.00*
Nos. 229a-231a (3) 49.00 *49.15*
Set, never hinged 160.00

New York World's Fair Issue of 1939 Overprinted "1940" in Black

1940, May 11 *Perf. 14*
232 A38 20a crimson 8.00 *29.00*
233 A39 35a bright ultra 8.00 *29.00*
234 A40 45a bright green 8.00 *29.00*
235 A40 2k dark gray 100.00 *510.00*
Nos. 232-235 (4) 124.00 *597.00*
Set, never hinged 240.00

No. 195 Surcharged in Red

1941, Mar. 6 *Perf. 12½*
236 A33 25a on 3a gray green 1.00 *1.60*
Never hinged 1.60

Statue of Snorri Sturluson — A45

1941, Nov. 17 Engr. *Perf. 14*
237 A45 25a rose red 1.20 *2.50*
238 A45 50a deep ultra 1.75 *5.25*
239 A45 1k dk olive grn 1.75 *5.25*
Nos. 237-239 (3) 4.70 13.00
Set, never hinged 8.50

Snorri Sturluson, writer and historian, 700th death anniv.

Republic

Jon Sigurdsson — A46

1944, June 17 *Perf. 14x13½*
240 A46 10a gray black .50 *1.00*
241 A46 25a dk red brn .50 *1.00*
242 A46 50a slate grn .50 *1.00*
243 A46 1k blue black .85 *1.00*
244 A46 5k henna 2.50 *12.50*
245 A46 10k golden brn 35.00 *100.00*
Nos. 240-245 (6) 39.85 *116.50*
Set, never hinged 95.00

Founding of Republic of Iceland, June 17, 1944.

Catalogue values for unused stamps in this section, from this point to the end of the section, are for Never Hinged items.

A47

A48

Eruption of Hekla Volcano: 35a, 60a, Close view of Hekla.

Unwmk.

1948, Dec. 3 Engr. *Perf. 14*
246 A47 12a dark vio brn .25 *.60*
247 A48 25a green 1.75 .25
248 A47 35a carmine rose .50 .35
249 A47 50a brown 2.50 .25
250 A47 60a bright ultra 8.25 4.75
251 A48 1k orange brown 12.00 .25
252 A48 10k violet black 60.00 .50
Nos. 246-252 (7) 85.25 6.95
Set, hinged 40.00

For surcharge see No. 283.

Pack Train and UPU Monument, Bern — A49

UPU, 75th Anniv.: 35a, Reykjavik. 60a, Map. 2k, Thingvellir Road.

1949, Oct. 9

253 A49 25a dark green .35 *.60*
254 A49 35a deep carmine .35 *.60*
255 A49 60a blue .65 *1.40*
256 A49 2k orange red 1.60 1.50
Nos. 253-256 (4) 2.95 *4.10*

Trawler — A50

Designs: 20a, 75a, 1k, Tractor plowing. 60a, 5k, Flock of sheep. 5a, 90a, 2k, Vestmannaeyjar harbor.

1950-54 *Perf. 13*

257 A50 5a dk brn ('54) .25 .25
258 A50 10a gray .50 .60
259 A50 20a brown .50 .60
260 A50 25a car ('54) .25 .25
261 A50 60a green 17.50 *23.00*
262 A50 75a red org ('52) .70 .25
263 A50 90a carmine .70 .70
264 A50 1k chocolate 7.50 .25
265 A50 1.25k red vio ('52) 23.00 .45
266 A50 1.50k deep ultra 16.00 .60
267 A50 2k purple 30.00 .45
268 A50 5k dark grn 45.00 1.50
Nos. 257-268 (12) 141.90 28.90
Set, hinged 50.00

For surcharges see Nos. B12-B13.

Jon Arason — A51

1950, Nov. 7 *Perf. 14*

269 A51 1.80k carmine 3.50 *4.25*
270 A51 3.30k green 2.50 *3.50*

Bishop Jon Arason, 400th anniv. of death.

Mail Delivery, 1776 — A52

Design: 3k, Airmail, 1951.

1951, May 13

271 A52 2k deep ultra 3.00 3.00
272 A52 3k dark purple 4.25 4.25

175th anniv. of Iceland's postal service.

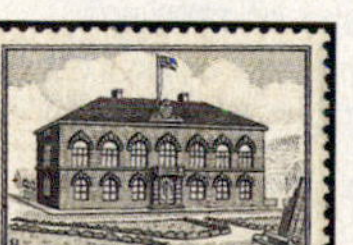

Parliament Building — A53

1952, Apr. 1 *Perf. 13x12½*

273 A53 25k gray black 200.00 17.50
Hinged 85.00

Sveinn Björnsson — A54

1952, Sept. 1 *Perf. 13½*

274 A54 1.25k deep blue 3.00 .25
275 A54 2.20k deep green .75 *4.75*
276 A54 5k indigo 10.00 1.75
277 A54 10k brown red 45.00 30.00
Nos. 274-277 (4) 58.75 36.75

Sveinn Björnsson, 1st President of Iceland.

Reykjabok — A55

Designs: 70a, Lettering manuscript. 1k, Corner of 15th century manuscript, "Stjorn." 1.75k, Reykjabok. 10k, Corner from law manuscript.

1953, Oct. 1 *Perf. 13½x13*

278 A55 10a black .25 .25
279 A55 70a green .30 .30
280 A55 1k carmine .50 .25
281 A55 1.75k blue 30.00 1.75
282 A55 10k orange brn 13.00 1.40
Nos. 278-282 (5) 44.05 3.95

No. 248 Surcharged With New Value and Bars in Black

1954, Mar. 31 *Perf. 14*

283 A47 5a on 35a car rose .35 .35
a. Bars omitted 90.00
b. Inverted surcharge 250.00

Hannes Hafstein — A56

Portraits: 2.45k, in oval. 5k, fullface.

1954, June 1 **Engr.** *Perf. 13*

284 A56 1.25k deep blue 4.75 .70
285 A56 2.45k dark green 24.00 *35.00*
286 A56 5k carmine 26.00 3.00
Nos. 284-286 (3) 54.75 *38.70*

Appointment of the first native minister to Denmark, 50th anniv.

Icelandic Wrestling — A57

1955, Aug. 9 **Unwmk.** *Perf. 14*

287 A57 75a shown .35 .25
288 A57 1.25k Diving .60 .30

See Nos. 300-301.

Skoga Falls — A58

Ellidaar Power Plant — A59

Waterfalls: 60a, Goda. 2kr, Detti. 5kr, Gull. Electric Power Plants: 1.50kr, Sogs. 2.45kr, Andakilsar. 3kr, Laxar.

Perf. 11½, 13½x14 (A59)

1956, Apr. 4 **Unwmk.**

289 A58 15a vio blue .25 .25
290 A59 50a dull green .30 .25
291 A59 60a brown 3.50 *4.75*
292 A59 1.50k violet 32.50 .25
293 A59 2k sepia 1.75 .60
294 A59 2.45k gray black 7.00 *11.00*
295 A59 3k dark blue 6.00 1.20
296 A58 5k dark green 15.00 2.25
Nos. 289-296 (8) 66.30 20.55

Telegraph-Telephone Emblem and Map — A60

1956, Sept. 29 **Engr.** *Perf. 13*

297 A60 2.30k ultramarine .35 *1.10*

Telegraph and Telephone service in Iceland, 50th anniv.

Northern Countries Issue

Whooper Swans — A60a

1956, Oct. 30 *Perf. 12½*

298 A60a 1.50k rose red .60 *1.10*
299 A60a 1.75k ultra 9.25 *12.00*

To emphasize the bonds among Denmark, Finland, Iceland, Norway and Sweden.

Sports Type of 1955

1.50k, Icelandic wrestling. 1.75k, Diving.

1957, Apr. 1 **Engr.** *Perf. 14*

300 A57 1.50k carmine 1.40 .25
301 A57 1.75k ultramarine .70 .25

Type of 1952 Air Post Stamps, Plane Omitted

Glaciers: 2k, Snaefellsjokull. 3k, Eiriksjokull. 10k, Oraefajokull.

1957, May 8 *Perf. 13½x14*

302 AP16 2k green 4.75 .30
303 AP16 3k dark blue 5.25 .30
304 AP16 10k reddish brn 7.00 .45
Nos. 302-304 (3) 17.00 1.05

Bessastadir, President's Residence A61

1957, Aug. 1 **Engr.** **Unwmk.**

305 A61 25k gray blk 25.00 5.00

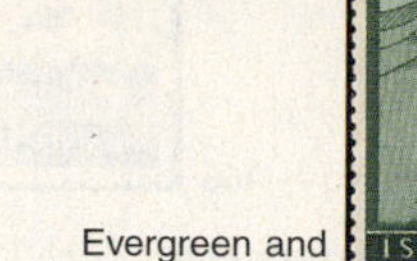

Evergreen and Volcanoes — A62

1957, Sept. 4 *Perf. 13½x13*

306 A62 35a shown .25 .25
307 A62 70a Birch .25 .25

Issued to publicize a reforestation program.

Jonas Hallgrimsson — A63

1957, Nov 16

308 A63 5k grn & blk 1.75 .60

150th birth anniv. of Jonas Hallgrimsson, poet.

Willow Herb — A64

1958, July 8 **Litho.** **Unwmk.**

309 A64 1k shown .25 .50
310 A64 2.50k Wild pansy .50 .50

Icelandic Pony — A65

1958, Sept. 27 **Engr.**

311 A65 10a gray black .25 .25
312 A65 2.25k brown .60 .35

See No. 324.

Flag — A66

Perf. 13½x14

1958, Dec. 1 Litho. Unwmk.

Size: 17½x21mm

313 A66 3.50k brt ultra & red 2.50 .75

Size: 23x26½mm

314 A66 50k brt ultra & red 7.00 7.00

40th anniversary of Icelandic flag.

Old Icelandic Government Building — A67

1958, Dec. 9 Photo. *Perf. 11½*

315 A67 2k deep green .50 .50
316 A67 4k deep brown .60 .60

See Nos. 333-334.

Jon Thorkelsson Teaching — A68

1959, May 5 Engr. *Perf. 13½*

317 A68 2k green .60 *.70*
318 A68 3k dull purple .80 *.90*

Death bicentenary of Jon Thorkelsson, headmaster of Skaholt.

Sockeye Salmon A69

Eider Ducks — A70

Design: 25k, Gyrfalcon.

1959-60 Engr. *Perf. 14*

319 A69 25a dark blue .25 .25
320 A70 90a chestnut & blk .30 .25
321 A70 2k olive grn & blk .65 .25
322 A69 5k gray green 10.00 1.25

Litho. *Perf. 11½*

323 A70 25k dl pur, gray & yel 15.00 16.00
Nos. 319-323 (5) 26.20 *18.00*

Issued: 25k, Mar. 1, 1960; others, Nov. 25.

Pony Type of 1958

1960, Apr. 7 Engr. *Perf. 13½x13*

324 A65 1k dark carmine .60 .35

"The Outlaw" by Einar Jonsson — A71

1960, Apr. 7 *Perf. 14*

325 A71 2.50k reddish brn .30 .30
326 A71 4.50k ultramarine .80 1.10

World Refugee Year, 7/1/59-6/30/60.

Common Design Types pictured following the introduction.

Europa Issue, 1960

Common Design Type

1960, Sept. 18 Photo. *Perf. 11½*

Size: 32½x22mm

327 CD3 3k grn & lt grn .65 .45
328 CD3 5.50k dk bl & lt bl .65 1.40

Wild Geranium — A72

Flowers: 50a, Bellflower. 2.50k, Dandelion. 3.50k, Buttercup.

1960-62 Photo. *Perf. 11½*

329 A72 50a gray grn, grn & violet ('62) .25 .25
330 A72 1.20k sep, vio & grn .25 .25
331 A72 2.50k brn, yel & grn .25 .25
332 A72 3.50k dl bl, yel & green ('62) .60 .60
Nos. 329-332 (4) 1.35 1.35

See Nos. 363-366, 393-394.

Building Type of 1958

1961, Apr. 11 Unwmk. *Perf. 11½*

333 A67 1.50k deep blue .30 .25
334 A67 3k dark carmine .30 .25

Jon Sigurdsson — A73

Typographed and Embossed

1961, June 17 *Perf. 12½x14*

335 A73 50a crimson .25 .25
336 A73 3k dark blue 1.50 1.25
337 A73 5k deep plum .60 .55
Nos. 335-337 (3) 2.35 2.05

Jon Sigurdsson (1811-1879), statesman and scholar.

Reykjavik A74

1961, Aug. 18 Photo. *Perf. 11½*

338 A74 2.50k blue & grn .60 .30
339 A74 4.50k lilac & vio bl 1.00 .50

Municipal charter of Reykjavik, 175th anniv.

Europa Issue, 1961

Common Design Type

1961, Sept. 18 Size: 32x22½mm

340 CD4 5.50k multicolored .55 .80
341 CD4 6k multicolored .55 .80

Benedikt Sveinsson — A75

University of Iceland — A76

Design: 1.40k, Björn M. Olsen.

1961, Oct. 6 Photo. *Perf. 11½*

342 A75 1k red brown .25 .25
343 A75 1.40k ultramarine .25 .25
344 A76 10k green 1.40 .60
a. Souv. sheet of 3, #342-344, imperf. 1.00 *2.25*
Nos. 342-344 (3) 1.90 1.10

50th anniv. of the University of Iceland; Benedikt Sveinsson (1827-1899), statesman; and Björn M. Olsen (1850-1919), first rector.

Production Institute — A77

New Buildings: 4k, Fishing Research Institute. 6k, Farm Bureau.

1962, July 6 Unwmk. *Perf. 11½*

345 A77 2.50k ultramarine .35 .25
346 A77 4k dull green .50 .25
347 A77 6k brown .65 .30
Nos. 345-347 (3) 1.50 .80

Europa Issue, 1962

Common Design Type

1962, Sept. 17 *Perf. 11½*

Size: 32½x22½mm

348 CD5 5.50k yel, lt grn & brn .25 .25
349 CD5 6.50k lt grn, grn & brn .60 .60

Map Showing Submarine Telephone Cable — A78

1962, Nov. 20 Granite Paper

350 A78 5k multicolored 1.10 .60
351 A78 7k grn, lt bl & red .60 .45

Inauguration of the submarine telephone cable from Newfoundland, via Greenland and Iceland to Scotland.

Sigurdur Gudmundsson, Self-portrait — A79

5.50k, Knight slaying dragon, Romanesque door from Valthjofsstad Church, ca. 1200 A.D.

1963, Feb. 20 Photo. *Perf. 11½*

352 A79 4k bis brn & choc .60 .45
353 A79 5.50k gray ol & brn .45 .45

National Museum of Iceland, cent., and its first curator, Sigurdur Gudmundsson.

Herring Boat — A80

1963, Mar. 21

354 A80 5k multicolored .80 .30
355 A80 7.50k multicolored .25 .25

FAO "Freedom from Hunger" campaign.

View of Akureyri A81

1963, July 2 Unwmk. *Perf. 11½*

356 A81 3k gray green .25 *.50*

Europa Issue, 1963

Common Design Type

1963, Sept. 16 Size: 32½x23mm

357 CD6 6k org brn & yel .60 .60
358 CD6 7k blue & yellow .60 .60

M.S. Gullfoss A82

1964, Jan. 17 Photo. *Perf. 11½*

359 A82 10k ultra, blk & gray 2.40 1.75
a. Accent on 2nd "E" omitted 35.00 *47.50*

Iceland Steamship Company, 50th anniv.

Scout Emblem and "Be Prepared" — A83

1964, Apr. 24

360 A83 3.50k multicolored .60 .45
361 A83 4.50k multicolored .60 .45

Issued to honor the Boy Scouts.

Icelandic Coat of Arms — A84

1964, June 17 *Perf. 11½*

362 A84 25k multicolored 3.00 2.50

20th anniversary, Republic of Iceland.

Flower Type of 1960-62

Flowers: 50a, Eight-petal dryas. 1k, Crowfoot (Ranunculus glacialis). 1.50k, Buck bean. 2k, Clover (trifolium repens).

Flowers in Natural Colors

1964, July 15

363 A72 50a vio bl & lt vio bl .30 .25
364 A72 1k gray & dk gray .30 .25
365 A72 1.50k brn & pale brn .30 .25
366 A72 2k ol & pale olive .30 .25
Nos. 363-366 (4) 1.20 1.00

Europa Issue, 1964

Common Design Type

1964, Sept. 14 Photo. *Perf. 11½*

Granite Paper

Size: 22½x33mm

367 CD7 4.50k golden brn, yel & Prus grn .70 .45
368 CD7 9k bl, yel & dk brn .70 .70

Jumper — A85

1964, Oct. 20 Unwmk. *Perf. 11½*
369 A85 10k lt grn & blk 1.25 .90

18th Olympic Games, Tokyo, Oct. 10-25.

ITU Emblem A86

1965, May 17 Photo. *Perf. 11½*
370 A86 4.50k green .95 .60
371 A86 7.50k bright ultra .25 .25

ITU, centenary.

Surtsey Island, April 1964 — A87

1.50k, Underwater volcanic eruption, Nov. 1963, vert. 3.50k, Surtsey, Sept. 1964.

1965, June 23 Unwmk. *Perf. 11½*
372 A87 1.50k bl, bis & blk .70 .70
373 A87 2k multicolored .70 .70
374 A87 3.50k bl, blk & red .85 .70
Nos. 372-374 (3) 2.25 2.10

Emergence of a new volcanic island off the southern coast of Iceland.

Europa Issue, 1965
Common Design Type

1965, Sept. 27 Photo. *Perf. 11½*
Size: 33x22½mm
375 CD8 5k tan, brn & brt grn 1.50 1.00
376 CD8 8k brt grn, brn & yel green 1.00 .75

Einar Benediktsson A88

Engr. & Litho.
1965, Nov. 16 *Perf. 14*
377 A88 10k brt blue & brn 3.50 *4.50*

Einar Benediktsson, poet (1864-1940).

White-tailed Sea Eagle — A89

National Costume — A90

1965-66 Photo. *Perf. 11½*
378 A89 50k multicolored 12.00 12.00
379 A90 100k multicolored 9.50 8.50

Issued: No. 378, 4/26/66; No. 379, 12/3/65.

West Iceland — A91

1966, Aug. 4 Photo. *Perf. 11½*
380 A91 2.50k shown .35 .45
381 A91 4k North Iceland .65 .45
382 A91 5k East Iceland .90 .45
383 A91 6.50k South Iceland .70 .45
Nos. 380-383 (4) 2.60 1.80

Europa Issue, 1966
Common Design Type

1966, Sept. 26 Photo. *Perf. 11½*
Size: 22½x33mm
384 CD9 7k grnsh bl, lt bl & red *2.25 1.75*
385 CD9 8k brn, buff & red *2.25 1.75*

Literary Society Emblem A92

1966, Nov. 18 Engr. *Perf. 11½*
386 A92 4k ultramarine .35 .30
387 A92 10k vermilion .85 .60

Icelandic Literary Society, 150th anniv.

Common Loon — A93

1967, Mar. 16 Photo. *Perf. 11½*
388 A93 20k multicolored 6.00 6.00

Europa Issue, 1967
Common Design Type

1967, May 2 Photo. *Perf. 11½*
Size: 22½x33mm
389 CD10 7k yel, brn & dk bl *1.50 1.00*
390 CD10 8k emer, gray & dk bl *1.50 1.00*

Old and New Maps of Iceland and North America A94

1967, June 8 Photo. *Perf. 11½*
391 A94 10k blk, tan & lt bl .35 *.45*

EXPO '67 Intl. Exhibition, Montreal, Apr. 28-Oct. 27, 1967. The old map, drawn about 1590 by Sigurdur Stefansson, is at the Royal Library, Copenhagen.

Symbols of Trade, Fishing, Husbandry and Industry A95

1967, Sept. 14 Photo. *Perf. 11½*
392 A95 5k dk bl, yel & emerald .35 .25

Icelandic Chamber of Commerce, 50th anniv.

Flower Type of 1960-62

Flowers: 50a, Saxifraga oppositifolia. 2.50k, Orchis maculata.

1968, Jan. 17 Photo. *Perf. 11½*
Flowers in Natural Colors
393 A72 50a green & dk brn .25 .25
394 A72 2.50k dk brn, yel & grn .35 .35

Europa Issue, 1968
Common Design Type

1968, Apr. 29 Photo. *Perf. 11½*
Size: 33½x23mm
395 CD11 9.50k dl yel, car rose & blk *1.75 1.20*
396 CD11 10k brt yel grn, blk & org *1.25 1.00*

Right-hand Driving — A96

1968, May 21 Photo. *Perf. 11½*
397 A96 4k yellow & brn .35 .25
398 A96 5k lt reddish brn .35 .25

Introduction of right-hand driving in Iceland, May 26, 1968.

Fridrik Fridriksson, by Sigurjón Olafsson — A97

1968, Sept. 5 Photo. *Perf. 11½*
399 A97 10k sky bl & dk gray .45 *.55*

Rev. Fridrik Fridriksson (1868-1961), founder of the YMCA in Reykjavik and writer.

Reading Room, National Library — A98

1968, Oct. 30 Photo. *Perf. 11½*
Granite Paper
400 A98 5k yellow & brn .25 .25
401 A98 20k lt bl & dp ultra 1.25 1.25

Natl. Library, Reykjavik, sesquicentennial.

Prime Minister Jon Magnusson (1859-1926) — A99

1968, Dec. 12 Granite Paper
402 A99 4k carmine lake .35 .25
403 A99 50k dark brown 3.50 *4.50*

50th anniversary of independence.

Nordic Cooperation Issue

Five Ancient Ships — A99a

1969, Feb. 28 Engr. *Perf. 12½*
404 A99a 6.50k vermilion .60 .45
405 A99a 10k bright blue .70 .60

50th anniv. of the Nordic Society and centenary of postal cooperation among the northern countries. The design is taken from a coin found at the site of Birka, an ancient Swedish town. See also Denmark Nos. 454-455, Finland No. 481, Norway Nos. 523-524, and Sweden Nos. 808-810.

Europa Issue, 1969
Common Design Type

1969, Apr. 28 Photo. *Perf. 11½*
Size: 32½x23mm
406 CD12 13k pink & multi *3.75 2.00*
407 CD12 14.50k yel & multi *.45 .40*

Flag of Iceland and Rising Sun — A100

1969, June 17 Photo. *Perf. 11½*
408 A100 25k gray, gold, vio bl & red 1.00 .60
409 A100 100k lt bl, gold, vio bl & red 6.00 6.00

25th anniversary, Republic of Iceland.

Boeing 727 A101

Design: 12k, Rolls Royce 400.

1969, Sept. 3 Photo. *Perf. 11½*
410 A101 9.50k dk bl & sky bl .60 .70
411 A101 12k dk bl & ultra .60 .70

50th anniversary of Icelandic aviation.

Snaefellsjökull Mountain A102

1970, Jan. 6 Photo. *Perf. 11½*
412 A102 1k shown .25 .25
413 A102 4k Laxfoss .35 .35
414 A102 5k Hattver, vert. .45 .35
415 A102 20k Fjardargill, vert. 1.75 .75
Nos. 412-415 (4) 2.80 1.70

First Meeting of Icelandic Supreme Court A103

1970, Feb. 16 Photo. *Perf. 11½*
416 A103 6.50k multicolored .30 .25

Icelandic Supreme Court, 50th anniv.

Column from "Skarosbók," 1363 (Law Book) — A104

Icelandic Manuscripts: 15k, Preface to "Flateyjarbók" (History of Norwegian Kings), 1387-1394. 30k, Initial from "Flateyjarbók" showing Harald Fairhair cutting fetters of Dofri.

1970, Mar. 20 Photo. *Perf. 11½*
417 A104 5k multicolored .25 .25
418 A104 15k multicolored .65 .65
419 A104 30k multicolored 1.25 1.25
Nos. 417-419 (3) 2.15 2.15

Europa Issue, 1970
Common Design Type

1970, May 4 Photo. *Perf. 11½*
Size: 32x22mm
420 CD13 9k brn & yellow *2.50 1.50*
421 CD13 25k brt grn & bister *3.50 2.50*

Nurse — A105

Grimur Thomsen — A106

The Rest, by Thorarinn B. Thorlaksson A107

1970, June 19 Photo. *Perf. 11½*

422 A105 7k ultra & lt bl .45 .25
423 A106 10k ind & lt grnsh bl .35 *.45*
424 A107 50k gold & multi 1.75 1.50
Nos. 422-424 (3) 2.55 2.20

50th anniv. (in 1969) of the Icelandic Nursing Association (No. 422); 150th birth anniv. of Grimur Thomsen (1820-1896), poet (No. 423); Intl. Arts Festival, Reykjavik, June 1970 (No. 424).

Saxifraga Oppositifolia A108

Lakagigar A109

1970, Aug. 25 Photo. *Perf. 11½*

425 A108 3k multicolored .30 .30
426 A109 15k multicolored 1.10 1.10

European Nature Conservation Year.

UN Emblem and Map of Iceland A110

1970, Oct. 23 Photo. *Perf. 11½*

427 A110 12k multicolored .55 *.65*

25th anniversary of United Nations.

"Flight," by Asgrimur Jonsson A111

1971, Mar. 26 Photo. *Perf. 11½*

428 A111 10k multicolored .85 .85

Joint northern campaign for the benefit of refugees.

Europa Issue, 1971

Common Design Type

1971, May 3 Photo. *Perf. 11½*

Size: 33x22mm

429 CD14 7k rose cl, yel & blk *2.25 1.75*
430 CD14 15k ultra, yel & blk *2.75 2.00*

Postal Checking Service Emblem A112

1971, June 22 Photo. *Perf. 11½*

431 A112 5k vio bl & lt blue .25 .25
432 A112 7k dk grn & yel grn .30 .25

Introduction of Postal Checking Service, Apr. 30, 1971.

Tryggvi Gunnarsson — A113

Design: 30k, Patriotic Society emblem.

1971, Aug. 19 Photo. *Perf. 11½*

433 A113 30k lt bl & vio blk 1.25 .95
434 A113 100k gray & vio blk 6.00 6.00

Icelandic Patriotic Society, cent.; Tryggvi Gunnarsson (1835-1917), founder and president.

Haddock Freezing Plant — A114

Fish Industry: 7k, Cod fishing. 20k, Shrimp canning plant.

1971, Nov. 18

435 A114 5k multicolored .25 .25
436 A114 7k multicolored .25 .25
437 A114 20k green & multi 1.10 .70
Nos. 435-437 (3) 1.60 1.20

Herdubreid Mountain — A115

Engr. & Litho.

1972, Mar. 9 *Perf. 14*

438 A115 250k blue & multi .60 .30

Europa Issue 1972

Common Design Type

1972, May 2 Photo. *Perf. 11½*

Size: 22x32mm

439 CD15 9k lt vio & multi *1.00 .90*
440 CD15 13k yel grn & multi *1.90 1.75*

"United Municipalities" — A116

1972, June 14 Photo. *Perf. 11½*

441 A116 16k multicolored .25 .25

Legislation for local government, cent.

Chessboard, World Map, Rook — A117

1972, July 2 Litho. *Perf. 13*

442 A117 15k lt ol & multi .45 .45

World Chess Championship, Reykjavik, July-Sept. 1972.

Hothouse Tomatoes A118

Designs: 12k, Steam valve and natural steam. 40k, Hothouse roses.

1972, Aug. 23 Photo. *Perf. 11½*

443 A118 8k Prus bl & multi .25 .25
444 A118 12k green & multi .25 .25
445 A118 40k dk pur & multi 1.40 1.20
Nos. 443-445 (3) 1.90 1.70

Hothouse gardening in Iceland, using natural steam and hot springs.

Iceland and the Continental Shelf — A119

1972, Sept. 27 Litho. *Perf. 13*

446 A119 9k blue & multi .25 .25

To publicize Iceland's offshore fishing rights.

Europa Issue 1973

Common Design Type

1973, Apr. 30 Photo. *Perf. 11½*

Size: 32½x22mm

447 CD16 13k vio & multi *5.75 2.75*
448 CD16 25k olive & multi *.90 .60*

Iceland No. 1 and Messenger — A120

Designs (First Issue of Iceland and): 15k, No. 5 and pony train. 20k, No. 2 and mailboat "Esja." 40k, No. 3 and mail truck. 80k, No. 4 and Beech-18 mail plane.

Litho. & Engr.

1973, May 23 *Perf. 13x13½*

449 A120 10k dl bl, blk & ultra .30 .30
450 A120 15k grn, blk & gray .25 .25
451 A120 20k maroon, blk & car .25 .25
452 A120 40k vio, blk & brn .25 .25
453 A120 80k olive, blk & yel 1.40 1.00
Nos. 449-453 (5) 2.45 2.05

Centenary of Iceland's first postage stamps.

Nordic Cooperation Issue

Nordic House, Reykjavik A120a

1973, June 26 Engr. *Perf. 12½*

454 A120a 9k multicolored .45 .25
455 A120a 10k multicolored 1.40 1.10

A century of postal cooperation among Denmark, Finland, Iceland, Norway and Sweden, and in connection with the Nordic Postal Conference, Reykjavik.

Ásgeir Ásgeirsson, (1894-1972),President of Iceland 1952-1968 — A121

Perf. 13x13½

1973, Aug. 1 Wmk. 409 Engr.

456 A121 13k carmine .45 .25
457 A121 15k blue .25 *.25*

Islandia 73 Emblem A122

20k, Islandia 73 emblem; diff. arrangement.

Perf. 11½

1973, Aug. 31 Photo. Unwmk.

458 A122 17k gray & multi .45 .45
459 A122 20k brn, ocher & yel .35 .45

Islandia 73 Philatelic Exhibition, Reykjavik, Aug. 31-Sept. 9.

Man and WMO Emblem — A123

1973, Nov. 14 Photo. *Perf. 12½*

460 A123 50k silver & multi .70 .60

Intl. meteorological cooperation, cent.

The Settlement, Tapestry by Vigdis Kristjansdottir A124

Designs: 13k, Establishment of Althing, painting by Johannes Johannesson, horiz. 15k, Gudbrandur Thorlakkson, Bishop ofHolar 1571-1627. 17k, Age of Sturlungar (Fighting Vikings), drawing by Thorvaldur Skulason. 20k, Stained glass window honoring Hallgrimur Petursson (1614-74), hymn writer. 25k, Illumination from Book of Flatey, 14th century. 30k, Conversion to Christianity (altarpiece, Skalholt), mosaic by Nina Tryggvadottir. 40k, Wood carving (family and plants), 18th century. 60k, Curing the Catch, cement bas-relief. 70k, Age of Writing (Saemundur Riding Seal), sculpture by Asmundur Sveinsson. 100k, Virgin and Child with Angels, embroidered antependium, Stafafell Church, 14th century, horiz.

1974 Photo. *Perf. 11½*

461 A124 10k multicolored .25 .25
462 A124 13k multicolored .25 .25
463 A124 15k multicolored .25 .25
464 A124 17k multicolored .35 .25
465 A124 20k multicolored .35 .25
466 A124 25k multicolored .25 .25
467 A124 30k multicolored .90 .70
468 A124 40k multicolored 1.15 .90
469 A124 60k multicolored 1.15 1.15
470 A124 70k multicolored 1.15 1.00
471 A124 100k multicolored 1.50 .70
Nos. 461-471 (11) 7.55 5.95

1100th anniv. of settlement of Iceland. Issued: 10k, 13k, 30k, 70k, 3/12; 17k, 25k, 100k, 6/11; 15k, 20k, 40k, 60k, 7/16.

Horseback Rider, Wood, 17th Century — A125

Europa: 20k, "Through the Sound Barrier," contemporary bronze by Asmundur Sveinsson.

1974, Apr. 29 Photo. Perf. 11½

472 A125 13k brn red & multi .35 .35
473 A125 20k gray & multi 1.00 1.00

Clerk Selling Stamps, UPU Emblem A126

Design: 20k, Mailman delivering mail.

1974, Oct. 9 Photo. Perf. 11½

474 A126 17k ocher & multi .35 .35
475 A126 20k olive & multi .35 .35

Centenary of Universal Postal Union.

Volcanic Eruption, Heimaey, Jan. 23, 1973 — A127

Design: 25k, Volcanic eruption, night view.

1975, Jan. 23 Photo. Perf. 11½

476 A127 20k multicolored .70 .45
477 A127 25k multicolored .35 .35

Europa Issue

Bird, by Thorvaldur Skulason A128

Sun Queen, by Johannes S. Kjarval — A129

1975, May 12 Photo. Perf. 11½

478 A128 18k multicolored .35 .35
479 A129 23k gold & multi 1.10 .70

Stephan G. Stephansson A130

1975, Aug. 1 Engr. Perf. 13

480 A130 27k green & brn .55 .35

Stephan G. Stephansson (1853-1927), Icelandic poet and settler in North America; centenary of Icelandic emigration to North America.

Petursson, by Hjalti Thorsteinsson A131

Einar Jonsson, Self-portrait A132

23k, Arni Magnusson, by Hjalti Thorsteinsson. 30k, Jon Eiriksson, sculpture by Olafur Olafsson.

1975, Sept. 18 Engr. Perf. 13

481 A131 18k sl grn & indigo .25 .60
482 A131 23k Prussian blue .25 .25
483 A131 30k deep magenta .25 .25
484 A132 50k indigo .50 .25
Nos. 481-484 (4) 1.25 1.35

Famous Icelanders: Hallgrimur Petursson (1614-1674), minister and religious poet; Arni Magnusson (1663-1730), historian, registrar and manuscript collector; Jon Eiriksson (1728-1787), professor of law and cabinet member; Einar Jonsson (1874-1954), sculptor, painter and writer.

Red Cross A133

1975, Oct. 15 Photo. Perf. 11½x12

485 A133 23k multicolored .45 .45

Icelandic Red Cross, 50th anniversary.

Abstract Painting, by Nina Tryggvadottir A134

1975, Oct. 15 Perf. 12x12½

486 A134 100k multicolored 1.25 .60

International Women's Year 1975.

Thorvaldsen Statue, by Thorvaldsen — A135

1975, Nov. 19 Photo. Perf. 11½

487 A135 27k lt vio & multi .80 .45

Centenary of Thorvaldsen Society, a charity honoring Bertel Thorvaldsen (1768-1844), sculptor.

Saplings Growing in Bare Landscape A136

1975, Nov. 19 Perf. 12x11½

488 A136 35k multicolored .60 .45

Reforestation.

Lang Glacier, by Asgrimur Jonsson A137

1976, Mar. 18 Photo. Perf. 11½

489 A137 150k gold & multi 1.75 1.50

Asgrimur Jonsson (1876-1958), painter.

Wooden Bowl — A138

Europa: 45k, Spinning wheel, vert.

1976, May 3 Photo. Perf. 11½

490 A138 35k ver & multi 1.25 .90
491 A138 45k blue & multi 1.25 1.25

No. 9 with First Day Cancel — A139

1976, Sept. 22 Photo. Perf. 11½
Granite Paper

492 A139 30k bis, blk & gray bl .35 .45

Centenary of aurar stamps.

Decree Establishing Postal Service — A140

45k, Conclusion of Decree with signatures.

1976, Sept. 22 Engr. Perf. 13

493 A140 35k dark brown .45 .35
494 A140 45k dark blue .70 .45

Iceland's Postal Service, bicentenary.

Federation Emblem, People — A141

1976, Dec. 2 Photo. Perf. 12½
Granite Paper

495 A141 100k multicolored 1.10 .70

Icelandic Federation of Labor, 60th anniv.

Five Water Lilies — A142

Photo. & Engr.

1977, Feb. 2 Perf. 12½

496 A142 35k brt grn & multi .80 .60
497 A142 45k ultra & multi .80 .60

Nordic countries cooperation for protection of the environment and 25th Session of Nordic Council, Helsinki, Feb. 19.

Ofaerufoss, Eldgja — A143

Europa: 85k, Kirkjufell Mountain, seen from Grundarfjord.

1977, May 2 Photo. Perf. 12

498 A143 45k multicolored 3.25 .90
499 A143 85k multicolored 1.25 .35

Harlequin Duck — A144

1977, June 14 Photo. Perf. 11½

500 A144 40k multicolored .55 .45

Wetlands conservation, European campaign.

Society Emblem — A145

1977, June 14

501 A145 60k vio bl & ultra .75 .65

Federation of Icelandic Cooperative Societies, 75th anniversary.

Hot Springs, Therapeutic Bath, Emblem A146

1977, Nov. 16 Photo. Perf. 11½

502 A146 90k multicolored .65 .55

World Rheumatism Year.

Stone Marker — A147

1977, Dec. 12 Engr. Perf. 11½

503 A147 45k dark blue .90 .65

Touring Club of Iceland, 50th anniversary.

Thorvaldur Thoroddsen, (1855-1921), Geologist, Scientist and Writer — A148

Design: 60k, Briet Bjarnhedinsdottir (1856-1940), Founder of Icelandic Women's Association and Reykjavik city councillor.

1977, Dec. 12 Engr. *Perf. 11½*

504 A148 50k brn & slate grn .25 .25
505 A148 60k grn & vio brn .80 .60

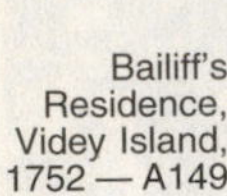

Bailiff's Residence, Videy Island, 1752 — A149

Europa: 120k, Husavik Church, 1906.

1978, May 2 Photo. *Perf. 11½*

506 A149 80k multicolored *1.40 .60*
507 A149 120k multi, vert. *3.00 .80*

Alexander Johannesson, Junkers Planes — A150

100k, Fokker Friendship plane over mountains.

1978, June 21 Photo. *Perf. 12½*

508 A150 60k multicolored .55 .30
509 A150 100k multicolored .55 .55

50th anniv. of domestic flights in Iceland.

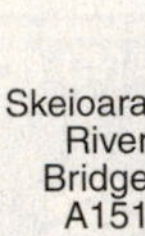

Skeioara River Bridge A151

1978, Aug. 17 Photo. *Perf. 11½*

510 A151 70k multicolored .30 .30

Lava Near Mt. Hekla, by Jon Stefansson — A152

1978, Nov. 16 Photo. *Perf. 12*

511 A152 1000k multicolored 4.00 3.50

Jon Stefansson (1881-1962), Icelandic painter.

Ship to Shore Rescue A153

1978, Dec. 1 Engr. *Perf. 13*

512 A153 60k black .30 .30

National Life Saving Assoc., 50th anniv.

Halldor Hermannsson (1878-1958), Historian, Librarian — A154

1978, Dec. 1

513 A154 150k indigo .55 .45

Lighthouse A155

1978, Dec. 1 Photo. *Perf. 11½*

514 A155 90k multicolored .55 .45

Centenary of Icelandic lighthouses.

Telephone, c. 1900 — A156

Europa: 190k, Post horn and satchel.

1979, Apr. 30 Photo. *Perf. 11½*

515 A156 110k multicolored *1.75 .45*
516 A156 190k multicolored *2.90 .70*

Jon Sigurdsson and Ingibjorg Einarsdottir A157

1979, Nov. 1 Engr. *Perf. 13x12½*

517 A157 150k black .60 .60

Jon Sigurdsson (1811-1879), Icelandic statesman and leader in independence movement.

Excerpt from Olafs Saga Helga — A158

1979, Nov. 1 Photo. *Perf. 11½*

518 A158 200k multicolored .80 .55

Snorri Sturluson (1178-1241), Icelandic historian and writer.

Children with Flowers ICY Emblem A159

1979, Sept. 12

519 A159 140k multicolored .80 .55

International Year of the Child.

A160

Icelandic Arms, before 1904 and 1904-1919.

1979, Sept. 12

520 A160 500k multicolored 1.40 .90

Home rule, 75th anniversary.

A161

Designs: 80k, Ingibjorg H. Bjarnason (1867-1941). 100k, Bjarni Thorsteinsson (1861-1938), composer. 120k, Petur Gudjohnsen (1812-77), organist. 130k, Sveinbjorn Sveinbjornson (1847-1927), composer. 170k, Torfhildur Holm (1845-1918), poet.

1979 Engr. *Perf. 13*

521 A161 80k rose violet .25 .25
522 A161 100k black .25 .25
523 A161 120k rose carmine .25 .25
524 A161 130k sepia .45 .45
525 A161 170k carmine rose .55 .45
Nos. 521-525 (5) 1.75 1.65

Issued: 80k, 170k, Aug. 3; others, Dec. 12.

Canis Familiaris — A162

Design: 90k, Alopex lagopus.

1980, Jan. 24

526 A162 10k black .25 .25
527 A162 90k sepia .25 .25

See Nos. 534-536, 543-545, 552, 553, 556-558, 610-612.

Jon Sveinsson Nonni (1857-1944), Writer — A163

Europa: 250k, Gunnar Gunnarsson (1889-1975), writer.

1980, Apr. 28 Photo. *Perf. 11½*

Granite Paper

528 A163 140k dl rose & blk *.90 .45*
529 A163 250k tan & blk *1.25 .70*

Mountain Ash Branch and Berries — A164

1980, July 8 Photo. *Perf. 12½*

530 A164 120k multicolored .35 .35

Year of the Tree.

Laugardalur Sports Complex, Reykjavik A165

1980, July 8 Engr. *Perf. 13x12½*

531 A165 300k slate green .70 .55

1980 Olympic Games.

Carved and Painted Cabinet Door, 18th Cent. — A166

Nordic Cooperation: 180k, Embroidered cushion, 19th cent.

1980, Sept. 9 Photo. *Perf. 11½*

Granite Paper

532 A166 150k multicolored .60 .45
533 A166 180k multicolored .70 .55

Animal Type of 1980

Designs: 160k, Sebastes marinus. 170k, Fratercula arctica. 190k, Phoca vitulina.

1980, Oct. 16 Engr. *Perf. 13*

534 A162 160k rose violet .85 .25
535 A162 170k black .95 .70
536 A162 190k dark brown .25 .35
Nos. 534-536 (3) 2.05 1.30

Radio Receiver, 1930 — A168

1980, Nov. 20 Photo. *Perf. 12½*

Granite Paper

537 A168 400k multicolored 1.10 .45

State Broadcasting Service, 50th anniv.

University Hospital, 50th Anniversary A169

1980, Nov. 20 *Perf. 11½*

538 A169 200k multicolored .45 .45

A170

Design: 170a, Magnus Stephensen (1762-1833), Chief Justice. 190a, Finnur Magnusson (1781-1847), Privy Archives keeper.

1981, Feb. 24 Engr. *Perf. 13*

539 A170 170a bright ultra .55 .45
540 A170 190a olive green .55 .45

Europa Issue

Europa — A171

180a, Luftur the Sorcerer. 220a, Sea witch.

1981, May 4 Photo. Perf. 11½
Granite Paper

541 A171 180a multicolored 1.25 .80
542 A171 220a multicolored 1.25 .80

Animal Type of 1980

Designs: 50a, Troglodytes troglodytes. 100a, Pluvialis apricaria. 200a, Corvus corax.

1981, Aug. 20 Engr. Perf. 13

543 A162 50a brown .25 .25
544 A162 100a blue .25 .25
545 A162 200a black .25 .25
Nos. 543-545 (3) .75 .75

Intl. Year of the Disabled — A173

1981, Sept. 29 Photo. Perf. 11½

546 A173 200a multicolored .30 .25

Skyggnir Earth Satellite Station, First Anniv. — A174

1981, Sept. 29 Photo. Perf. 11½

547 A174 500a multicolored 1.25 .60

Hauling the Line, by Gunnlaugur Scheving (1904-1972) A175

1981, Oct. 21 Photo. Perf. 11½

548 A175 5000a multi 5.75 3.50

Christian Missionary Work in Iceland Millennium A176

1981, Nov. 24 Engr. Perf. 13

549 A176 200a dark violet .35 .35

Christmas A177

1981, Nov. 24 Photo. Perf. 12½
Granite Paper

550 A177 200a Leaf bread .70 .70
551 A177 250a Leaf bread, diff. .70 .55

Animal Type of 1980

Designs: 20a, Buccinum undatum, vert. 600a, Chlamys islandica.

1982, Mar. 23 Engr. Perf. 13

552 A162 20a copper brn .25 .25
553 A162 600a vio brown .90 .45

Europa Issue

First Norse Settlement, 874 — A179

450a, Discovery of North America, 1000.

1982, May 3 Photo. Perf. 11½
Granite Paper

554 A179 350a shown 5.25 1.25
555 A179 450a multi 5.25 1.25

Animal Type of 1980

Designs: 300a, Ovis aries, vert. 400a, Bos taurus, vert. 500a, Felis catus, vert.

1982, June 3 Engr. Perf. 13

556 A162 300a brown .80 .45
557 A162 400a lake .60 .35
558 A162 500a gray .25 .25
Nos. 556-558 (3) 1.65 1.05

Kaupfelag Thingeyinga Cooperative Society Centenary — A181

1982, June 3

559 A181 1000a black & red .90 .45

Man Riding Iceland Pony — A182

1982, July 1 Photo. Perf. 11½
Granite Paper

560 A182 700a multicolored .80 .35

Centenary of School of Agriculture, Holar A183

1982, July 1 Granite Paper

561 A183 1500a multi 1.25 .70

Mount Herdubreid, by Isleifur Konradsson (1889-1972) A184

1982, Sept. 8 Photo. Perf. 11½
Granite Paper

562 A184 800a multicolored .70 .55

UN World Assembly on Aging, 7/26-8/6.

Borbjorg Sveinsdottir (1828-1903) — A185

1982, Sept. 8 Engr. Perf. 13

563 A185 900a red brown .55 .45

Borbjorg Sveinsdottir (1828-1903), midwife and Univ. founder.

Souvenir Sheet

NORDIA '84 — A186

Photo. & Engr.

1982, Oct. 7 Perf. 13½

564 A186 Sheet of 2 5.00 5.00
a. 400a Reynistaour Monastery seal 2.50 2.50
b. 800a Bingeyrar 2.50 2.50

NORDIA '84 Intl. Stamp Exhibition, Reykjavik, July 3-8, 1984. Sold for 18k.
See No. 581.

Christmas A187

Score from The Night was Such a Splendid One.

1982, Nov. 16 Photo. Perf. 11½
Granite Paper

565 A187 3k Birds .90 .55
566 A187 3.50k Bells 1.00 .55

Caltha Palustris — A188

8k, Lychnis alpina. 10k, Potentilla palustris. 20k, Myosotis scorpioides.

1983, Feb. 10 Photo.
Granite Paper

567 A188 7.50k shown .55 .55
568 A188 8k multicolored .90 .55
569 A188 10k multicolored 1.25 .55
570 A188 20k multicolored 2.50 .90
Nos. 567-570 (4) 5.20 2.55

See Nos. 586-587, 593-594, 602-605, 663-664.

Nordic Cooperation A189

1983, Mar. 24 Granite Paper

571 A189 4.50k Mt. Sulur 1.20 .75
572 A189 5k Urrida Falls 1.20 .75

Europa Issue

Thermal Energy Projects — A190

1983, May 5 Granite Paper

573 A190 5k shown 3.00 1.40
574 A190 5.50k multi, diff. 22.50 2.00

Fishing Industry A191

1983, June 8 Engr. Perf. 13x12½

575 A191 11k Fishing boats .30 .30
576 A191 13k Fishermen 1.40 .80

Bicentenary of Skaftareldar Volcanic Eruption A192

15k, Volcano, by Finnur Jonsson.

1983, June 8 Photo. Perf. 11½
Granite Paper

577 A192 15k multicolored .75 .55

Skiing — A193

1983, Sept. 8 Photo. Perf. 11½

578 A193 12k shown .85 .55
579 A193 14k Running 1.00 .75

World Communications Year — A194

1983, Sept. 8 Perf. 12½

580 A194 30k multi 2.40 1.25

NORDIA '84 Type of 1982

Souvenir Sheet

Bishops' Seals: 8k, Magnus Eyjolfsson of Skalholt, 1477-90. 12k, Ogmundur Palsson of Skalhot, 1521-40.

Photo. & Engr.

1983, Oct. 6 Perf. 13½

581 Sheet of 2 6.50 6.50
a. A186 8k violet blue & black 3.25 3.25
b. A186 12k pale green & black 3.25 3.25

Sold for 30k.

Christmas — A195

1983, Nov. 10 Photo. Perf. 11½
Granite Paper

582 A195 6k Virgin and Child .90 .55
583 A195 6.50k Angel .90 .55

Pres. Kristjan Eldjarn (1916-82) — A196

Perf. 14x13½
1983, Dec. 6 Engr. Wmk. 410

584 A196 6.50k brn carmine .90 .70
585 A196 7k dark blue .35 .25

Flower Type of 1983

6k, Rosa pimpinellifolia. 25k, Potentilla anserium.

Perf. 11½
1984, Mar. 1 Photo. Unwmk.
Granite Paper

586 A188 6k multicolored .90 .45
587 A188 25k multicolored 1.25 .45

Europa 1959-84 A197

1984, May 3

588 A197 6.50k grnsh bl & blk *2.40 .75*
589 A197 7.50k rose & black *1.25 .75*

Souvenir Sheet

A198

Design: Abraham Ortelius' map of Northern Europe, 1570.

Photo. & Engr.
1984, June 6 Perf. 14x13½

590 A198 40k multi 15.00 15.00

NORDIA '84 Intl. Stamp Exhibition, Reykjavik, July 3-8. Sold for 60k.

A199

1984, June 17 Photo. Perf. 11½
Granite Paper

591 A199 50k Flags 5.75 3.00

40th Anniv. of Republic.

Good Templars Headquarters, Akureyri — A200

1984, July 18 Engr. Perf. 13

592 A200 10k green .70 .45

Order of the Good Templars, centenary in Iceland, temperance org.

Flower Type of 1983

6.50k, Loiseleuria procumbens. 7.50k, Arctostaphylos uva-ursi.

1984, Sept. 11 Photo. Perf. 11½
Granite Paper

593 A188 6.50k multicolored .55 .30
594 A188 7.50k multicolored .55 .30

Christmas — A201

600a, Madonna and Child. 650a, Angel, Christmas rose.

1984, Nov. 29 Photo.

595 A201 600a multicolored .65 .30
596 A201 650a multicolored .65 .45

Gudbrand's Bible, 400th Anniv. — A202

1984, Nov. 29 Engr. Perf. 12½x13

597 A202 6.50k Text .65 .30
598 A202 7.50k Illustration .45 *.55*

First Icelandic Bible.

Confederation of Employers, 50th Anniv. — A203

1984, Nov. 9 Photo. Perf. 12x12½
Granite Paper

599 A203 30k Building blocks 1.40 1.25

Bjorn Bjarnarson (1853-1918) — A204

40k, New gallery building, horiz.

1984, Nov. 9 Photo. Perf. 11½
Granite Paper

600 A204 12k shown .60 .60
601 A204 40k multicolored 2.10 1.25

Natl. Gallery centenary.

Flower Type of 1983
1985, Mar. 20 Photo. Perf. 11½
Granite Paper

602 A188 8k Rubus saxatilis .90 .35
603 A188 9k Veronica fruticans .90 .35
604 A188 16k Lathyrus japonicus 2.50 .55
605 A188 17k Draba alpina .70 .55
Nos. 602-605 (4) 5.00 1.80

Music Year Emblem, Woman Playing the Langspil — A205

Europa: 7.50k, Man playing the Icelandic violin.

1985, May 3 Photo. Perf. 11½
Granite Paper

606 A205 6.50k multicolored *3.00 .75*
607 A205 7.50k multicolored *3.00 .95*

Natl. Horticulture Soc., Cent. — A206

1985, June 20 Photo. Perf. 12

608 A206 20k Sorbus intermedia 1.00 .55

Intl. Youth Year — A207

1985, June 20 Photo. Perf. 11½

609 A207 25k Icelandic girl 1.25 .95

Animal Type of 1980

Designs: 700a, Todarodes sagittatus. 800a, Hyas araneus. 900a, Tealia felina.

1985, Sept. 10 Engr. Perf. 13

610 A162 700a brn carmine .25 *.30*
611 A162 800a dk brown .35 .25
612 A162 900a carmine 1.25 .45
Nos. 610-612 (3) 1.85 1.00

Hannes Stephensen (1799-1856), Cleric, Politician, Translator — A209

Famous men: 30k, Jon Gudmudsson (1807-1875), editor, politician.

1985, Sept. 10 Engr.

613 A209 13k dp magenta .65 .45
614 A209 30k deep violet 1.60 .75

Yearning to Fly, by Johannes S. Kjarval (1885-1972), Reykjavik Natl. Museum A210

1985, Oct. 15 Photo. Perf. 12x11½

615 A210 100k multi 5.75 4.75

A211

Abstract ice crystal paintings, by Snorri Sveinn Fridriksson (b. 1934).

1985, Nov. 14 Photo. Perf. 11½

616 A211 8k Crucifix .80 .35
617 A211 9k Pine Trees .80 .55

Christmas.

Birds — A212

1986, Mar. 19 Photo. Perf. 11½
Granite Paper

618 A212 6k Motacilla alba .25 .25
619 A212 10k Anas acuta 1.75 .60
620 A212 12k Falco columbarius 1.25 .60
621 A212 15k Alca torda .70 .45
Nos. 618-621 (4) 3.95 1.90

See Nos. 642-645, 665-666, 671-672, 686-687, 721-722.

Europa Issue

Natl. Parks — A213

1986, May 5

622 A213 10k Skaftafell *11.00 1.10*
623 A213 12k Jokulsargljufur *4.75 1.40*

Nordic Cooperation Issue A214

Sister towns: 10k, Stykkishólmur. 12k, Seydisfjördur.

1986, May 27 Perf. 11½

624 A214 10k multicolored 1.10 .75
625 A214 12k multicolored 1.10 .75

Natl. Bank, Cent. A215

13k, Headquarters, Reykjavik. 250k, Bank-note reverse, 1928.

1986, July 1 Engr. Perf. 14

626 A215 13k black .90 .70
627 A215 250k red brn 9.50 8.50

Reykjavik Bicent. A216

10k, City seal, 1815. 12k, View from bank, illustration, 1856. 13k, Laugardalur hot water brook. 40k, City Theater.

1986, Aug. 18 Engr. *Perf. 13½x14*
628 A216 10k red .70 .35
629 A216 12k brown .70 .35
630 A216 13k green .70 .55
631 A216 40k blue 1.75 1.40
Nos. 628-631 (4) 3.85 2.65

Introduction of the Telephone in Iceland, 80th Anniv. — A217

10k, Morse receiver, 1906. 20k, Handset, microchip, 1986.

1986, Sept. 29 Photo. *Perf. 11½*
Granite Paper
632 A217 10k multicolored .45 .35
633 A217 20k multicolored 1.10 .60

Souvenir Sheet

Hvita River Crossing, Loa, 1836, by Auguste Mayer — A218

Photo. & Engr.
1986, Oct. 9 *Perf. 14*
634 A218 20k bluish black 5.25 5.25

Stamp Day. Sold for 30k to benefit philatelic organizations. See Nos. 646, 667.

Christmas — A219

Paintings by Bjoerg Thorsteinsdottir: 10k, Christmas at Peace. 12k, Christmas Night.

1986, Nov. 13 Photo. *Perf. 12*
635 A219 10k multicolored 1.00 .45
636 A219 12k multicolored .45 .45

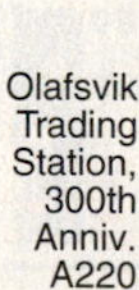

Olafsvik Trading Station, 300th Anniv. A220

50k, Merchantman Svanur, 1777.

1987, Mar. 26 Engr. *Perf. 14x13½*
637 A220 50k bluish black 2.50 1.25

Keflavik Intl. Airport Terminal Inauguration — A221

1987, Apr. 14 Photo. *Perf. 12x11½*
638 A221 100k multi 4.50 1.75

Europa Issue

— A222

Designs: Stained Glass Windows by Leifur Breidfjoerd, Fossvogur Cemetery Chapel: 12k, Christ carrying the cross. 15k, Soldiers, peace dove.

1987, May 4 Photo. *Perf. 12x11½*
639 A222 12k multicolored *2.00 .70*
640 A222 15k multicolored *2.00 .70*

Rasmus Christian Rask (1787-1832), Danish Linguist — A223

1987, June 10 Engr. *Perf. 13½*
641 A223 20k black .90 .70

Preservation of the Icelandic language.

Bird Type of 1986

13k, Asio flammeus. 40k, Turdus iliacus. 70k, Haematopus ostralegus. 90k, Anas platyrhynchos.

1987, Sept. 16 Photo. *Perf. 11½*
Granite Paper
642 A212 13k multicolored 1.25 .45
643 A212 40k multicolored 2.00 .60
644 A212 70k multicolored 2.75 .95
645 A212 90k multicolored 4.50 1.50
Nos. 642-645 (4) 10.50 3.50

Stamp Day Type of 1986
Souvenir Sheet

Trading Station of Djupivogur in 1836, by Auguste Mayer.

1987, Oct. 9 Engr. *Perf. 13½x14*
646 A218 30k black 5.50 5.50

Stamp Day. Sold for 45k to benefit the Stamp and Postal History Fund.

Dental Protection — A226

1987, Oct. 9 Photo. *Perf. 11½x12*
Granite Paper
647 A226 12k multicolored .55 .45

Eagle — A227

Guardian Spirits of the North, East, South and West.

Perf. 13 on 3 sides
1987, Oct. 9 Engr.
Booklet Stamps
648 A227 13k shown .60 .60
649 A227 13k Dragon .60 .60
650 A227 13k Bull .60 .60
651 A227 13k Giant .60 .60
a. Block of 4, #648-651 2.50 2.50
b. Bklt. pane of 12, 3 #651a 7.50 —

Legend of Heimskringla, the story of the Norse kings. Haraldur Gormsson, king of Denmark, deterred from invading Iceland after hearing of the guardian spirits.
See Nos. 656-659, 677, 688-695.

Christmas — A228

1987, Oct. 21 Photo. *Perf. 11½x12*
652 A228 13k Fir branch .65 .25
653 A228 17k Candle flame .65 .45

Steinn Steinarr (1908-1958) A229

Poets: 21k, David Stefansson (1895-1964).

1988, Feb. 25 Photo. *Perf. 12*
654 A229 16k multi .80 .35
655 A229 21k multi .80 .65

Guardian Spirit Type of 1987
Perf. 13 on 3 sides
1988, May 2 Engr.
Booklet Stamps
656 A227 16k Eagle .60 .60
657 A227 16k Dragon .60 .60
658 A227 16k Bull .60 .60
659 A227 16k Giant .60 .60
a. Block of 4, #656-659 2.50 2.50
b. Bklt. pane of 12, 3 #659a 7.50 —

Europa Issue

Modern Communication — A230

16k, Data transmission system. 21k, Facsimile machine.

1988, May 2 Photo. *Perf. 12x11½*
660 A230 16k multicolored *1.00 .60*
661 A230 21k multicolored *4.25 2.00*

1988 Summer Olympics, Seoul A231

1988, June 9 Photo. *Perf. 12*
Granite Paper
662 A231 18k Handball .70 .60

Flower Type of 1983
1988, June 9 *Perf. 11½*
Granite Paper
663 A188 10k Vicia cracca .55 .30
664 A188 50k Thymus praecox 3.00 .80

Bird Type of 1986
1988, Sept. 21 Photo. *Perf. 11½*
Granite Paper
665 A212 5k Limosa limosa .45 .25
666 A212 30k Clangula hyemalis 1.75 .80

Stamp Day Type of 1986
Souvenir Sheet

Nupsstadur Farm, Fljotshverfi, 1836, by Auguste Mayer.

1988, Oct. 9 Engr. *Perf. 14*
667 A218 40k black 4.75 4.75

Stamp Day. Sold for 60k to benefit the Stamp and Postal History Fund.

WHO, 40th Anniv. — A234

1988, Nov. 3 Photo. *Perf. 11½x12*
Granite Paper
668 A234 19k multicolored .80 .45

Christmas A235

1988, Nov. 3 *Perf. 11½*
Granite Paper
669 A235 19k Fisherman at sea 1.00 .30
670 A235 24k Ship, buoy 1.25 1.25

Bird Type of 1986

19k, Phalaropus lobatus. 100k, Plectrophenax nivalis.

1989, Feb. 2 Photo.
671 A212 19k multicolored 1.00 .35
672 A212 100k multicolored 5.25 1.40

Women's Folk Costumes — A236

1989, Apr. 20 Photo. *Perf. 11½x12*
Granite Paper
673 A236 21k Peysufot 1.75 .70
674 A236 26k Upphlutur 1.75 .90

Nordic cooperation.

Europa 1989 A237

Children's games.

1989, May 30 Photo. *Perf. 11½*
Granite Paper
675 A237 21k Sailing toy boats *5.25 1.25*
676 A237 26k Hoop, stick pony *5.25 1.25*

Guardian Spirit Type of 1987
1989, June 27 Engr. *Perf. 13*
677 A227 500k Dragon 17.00 7.00

Landscapes A238

35k, Mt. Skeggi, Arnarfjord. 45k, Thermal spring, Namaskard.

1989, Sept. 20 Photo. *Perf. 11½*
Granite Paper
678 A238 35k multicolored 1.40 .55
679 A238 45k multicolored 1.75 .55

See Nos. 713-714, 728, 737.

Agricultural College at Hvanneyri, Cent. A239

1989, Sept. 20 **Engr.** ***Perf. 14***
680 A239 50k multi 1.40 1.00

Souvenir Sheet

NORDIA '91 — A240

Detail of *A Chart and Description of Northern Routes and Wonders to Be Found in the Nordic Countries,* 1539, by Olaus Magnus (1490-1557).

1989, Oct. 9 ***Perf. 12½***
681 A240 Sheet of 3 9.50 9.50
a.-c. 30k any single 3.00 3.00

Stamp Day. Sold for 130k to benefit the exhibition.
See Nos. 715, 740.

Natural History Soc., Cent. A241

Flowers or fish and: 21k, Stefan Stefansson (1863-1921), botanist and founder. 26k, Bjarni Saemundsson (1867-1940), chairman.

1989, Nov. 9 **Photo.** ***Perf. 11½***
Granite Paper
682 A241 21k multi .85 .85
683 A241 26k multi .90 .90

Christmas — A242

Paintings like stained-glass windows by Johannes Johannesson (b. 1921): 21k, Madonna and Child. 26k, Three Wise Men.

1989, Nov. 9 **Granite Paper**
684 A242 21k multi 1.20 .35
685 A242 26k multi 1.20 1.10

Bird Type of 1986

21k, Anas penelope. 80k, Anser brachyrhynchus.

1990, Feb. 15 **Granite Paper**
686 A212 21k multicolored 1.75 .70
687 A212 80k multicolored 4.00 1.60

Guardian Spirit Type of 1987
Perf. 13 on 3 Sides

1990, Feb. 15 **Engr.**
688 A227 5k Eagle .25 .25
689 A227 5k Dragon .25 .25
690 A227 5k Bull .25 .25
691 A227 5k Giant .25 .25
a. Block of 4, #688-691 1.00 1.00
692 A227 21k Eagle .60 .60
693 A227 21k Dragon .60 .60
694 A227 21k Bull .60 .60
695 A227 21k Giant .60 .60
a. Block of 4, #692-695 2.50 2.50
b. Block of 8, #688-695 5.00 5.00
c. Bklt. pane, 2 each #691a, 695a 7.50 7.50

Famous Women — A243

No. 696, Gudrun Larusdottir (1880-1938), author and politician, by Halldor Petursson. No. 697, Ragnhildur Petursdottir (1880-1961), educator, by Asgrimur Jonsson.

1990, Mar. 22 **Litho.** ***Perf. 13½x14***
696 A243 21k multicolored .70 .60
697 A243 21k multicolored .70 .60

Europa 1990 A244

Old and new post offices in Reykjavik and letter scales.

1990, May 7 **Photo.** ***Perf. 12x11½***
Granite Paper
698 A244 21k 1915 *3.75* .90
699 A244 40k 1989 *3.75* 2.00

Sports — A245

No. 700, Archery. No. 701, Soccer. No. 706, Golf. No. 707, Icelandic wrestling. No. 708, Volleyball. No. 709, Skiing. No. 710, Running. No. 711, Team handball. No. 711A, Swimming. No. 711B, Weight lifting.

1990-94 **Litho.** ***Perf. 13x14½***
700 A245 21k multicolored .80 .55
701 A245 21k multicolored .80 .55
706 A245 26k multicolored .80 .60
707 A245 26k multicolored .90 .60

Perf. 13½x14½
Photo.
708 A245 30k multicolored 1.25 .70
709 A245 30k multicolored 1.25 .70
710 A245 30k multicolored 1.00 .55
711 A245 30k multicolored 1.00 .55

Litho.
Perf. 14x14½
711A A245 30k multicolored 1.00 .45
711B A245 30k multicolored 1.00 .45
Nos. 700-711B (10) 9.80 5.70

Issued: Nos. 700-701, 6/28; Nos. 706-707, 8/14/91; Nos. 708-709, 2/20/92; Nos. 710-711, 3/10/93; Nos. 711A-711B, 2/25/94.

European Tourism Year — A246

1990, Sept. 6 **Litho.** ***Perf. 13½***
712 A246 30k multicolored .95 .60

Landscape Type of 1989

1990, Sept. 6 **Photo.** ***Perf.***
713 A238 25k Hvitserkur 1.20 .60
714 A238 200k Lomagnupur 6.75 2.25

NORDIA '91 Map Type of 1989
Souvenir Sheet

Detail of 1539 Map by Olaus Magnus: a, Dania. b, Gothia. c, Gotlandia.

Perf. 12x12½

1990, Oct. 9 **Lith & Engr.**
715 A240 Sheet of 3 12.50 12.50
a.-c. 40k any single 4.00 4.00

Stamp Day. Sold for 170k to benefit the exhibition.

Christmas A247

1990, Nov. 8 ***Perf. 13½x13***
716 A247 25k shown 1.40 .55
717 A247 30k Carolers 1.40 .95

Bird Type of 1986

1991, Feb. 7 **Photo.** ***Perf. 11½***
Granite Paper
721 A212 25k Podiceps auritus 1.25 .45
722 A212 100k Sula bassana 5.75 1.20

Landscape Type of 1989

1991, Mar. 7 **Photo.** ***Perf. 11½***
Granite Paper
728 A238 10k Vestrahorn .55 .30
737 A238 300k Kverkfjoll 10.00 3.50

Europa A248

1991, Apr. 29 **Litho.** ***Perf. 14***
738 A248 26k Weather map *7.00* 1.00
739 A248 47k Solar panels *3.50* 2.00

NORDIA '91 Map Type of 1989
Souvenir Sheet

Detail of 1539 Map by Olaus Magnus: a, Iceland's west coast. b, Islandia. c, Mare Glacial.

Litho. & Engr.

1991, May 23 ***Perf. 12½***
740 A240 Sheet of 3 14.00 14.00
a.-c. 50k any single 4.50 4.50

Sold for 215k to benefit the exhibition.

Jokulsarlon Lagoon A249

Design: 31k, Strokkur hot spring.

1991, May 23 **Litho.** ***Perf. 15x14***
741 A249 26k multicolored 1.75 .80
742 A249 31k multicolored 1.75 .90

Ragnar Jonsson (1904-1984), Patron of the Arts — A250

70k, Pall Isolfsson (1893-1974), musician, vert.

1991, Aug. 14 **Litho.** ***Perf. 14***
743 A250 60k multicolored 1.75 1.20
744 A250 70k multicolored 2.50 1.40

Ships A251

Designs: a, Soloven, schooner, 1840. b, Arcturus, steamer with sails, 1858. c, Gullfoss, steamer, 1915. d, Esja II, diesel ship, 1939.

1991, Oct. 9 **Litho.** ***Perf. 14***
745 Block or strip of 4 27.50 27.50
a.-d. A251 30k any single 3.50 1.75
e. A251 Bklt. pane, 2 #745 55.00

Issued in sheet of 8. No. 745e is distinguished from sheet of 8 by rouletted selvage at left.
See Nos. 803-806.

College of Navigation, Reykjavik, Cent. A252

1991, Oct. 9 ***Perf. 13½***
746 A252 50k multicolored 1.50 1.25

Christmas — A253

Paintings by Eirikur Smith (b. 1925): 30k, Christmas star. 35k, Star over winter landscape.

1991, Nov. 7 **Litho.** ***Perf. 13½***
747 A253 30k multicolored 1.20 .45
748 A253 35k multicolored 1.20 .90

Europa A254

Map and: No. 749, Viking longboat of Leif Eriksson. No. 750, Sailing ship of Columbus.

1992, Apr. 6 **Litho.** ***Perf. 13½x14***
749 A254 55k multicolored *5.00* *2.25*
750 A254 55k multicolored *5.00* *2.25*

Souvenir Sheet
751 A254 Sheet of 2, #749-750 *13.50* *8.00*

First landing in the Americas by Leif Erikson (No. 749). Discovery of America by Christopher Columbus, 500th anniv. (No. 750).
Stamps on No. 751 printed in continuous design. Nos. 749-750 have borders.

Export Trade and Commerce A255

Designs: 35k, Fishing boat, fish.

1992, June 16 **Litho.** ***Perf. 13½***
752 A255 30k multicolored 1.25 .45
753 A255 35k multicolored 1.25 .90

Bridges A256

1992, Oct. 9 **Litho.** ***Perf. 13½***
754 A256 5k Fnjoska, 1908 .25 .25
755 A256 250k Olfusa, 1891 8.50 5.25

See Nos. 766-767.

Mail Trucks A257

No. 756, Mail transport car RE 231, 1933. No. 757, Ford bus, 1946. No. 758, Ford Model TT truck, 1920-26. No. 759, Citroen snowmobile, 1929.

1992, Oct. 9 *Perf. 14*

756	A257 30k shown		2.40	1.20
757	A257 30k multicolored		2.40	1.20
758	A257 30k multicolored		2.40	1.20
759	A257 30k multicolored		2.40	1.20
a.	Block or strip of 4, #756-759		9.75	9.75
b.	Bklt. pane, 2 ea #756-759		30.00	

Issued in sheets of 8. No. 759b has rouletted selvage at left.

See Nos. 820-823.

Christmas — A258

Paintings by Bragi Asgeirsson: 35k, Sun over mountains.

1992, Nov. 9 Litho. *Perf. 13½x13*

760	A258 30k shown	1.25	.45
761	A258 35k multicolored	1.25	1.25

Falco Rusticolus — A259

5k, Adult, two young. 10k, Adult feeding. 20k, Adult, head up. 35k, Adult.

1992, Dec. 3 Photo. *Perf. 11½*

Granite Paper

762	A259 5k multi	2.30	.55
763	A259 10k multi	2.90	1.20
764	A259 20k multi	2.90	1.40
765	A259 35k multi	2.90	2.40
	Nos. 762-765 (4)	11.00	5.55

Bridges Type of 1992

90k, Hvita, 1928. 150k, Jokulsa a Fjollum, 1947.

1993, Mar. 10 Litho. *Perf. 13½x13*

766	A256 90k multi	2.75	1.60
767	A256 150k multi	5.00	2.25

Nordica '93 — A260

Designs: 30k, The Blue Lagoon therapeutic bathing area, hot water plant, Svartsengi. 35k, Perlan hot water storage tanks, restaurant.

1993, Apr. 26 Litho. *Perf. 13½x13*

768	A260 30k multicolored	1.25	.65
769	A260 35k multicolored	1.40	1.25

Sculptures — A261

Europa: 35k, Sailing, by Jon Gunnar Arnason. 55k, Hatching of the Jet, by Magnus Tomasson.

1993, Apr. 26 *Perf. 13x13½*

770	A261 35k multicolored	1.75	1.25
771	A261 55k multicolored	2.90	2.50

Souvenir Sheet

Italian Group Flight, 60th Anniv. — A262

1993, Oct. 9 Litho. *Perf. 13½*

772	A262 Sheet of 3, #a.-c.	7.00	7.00
a.	10k #C12	.60	.60
b.	50k #C13	2.40	2.40
c.	100k #C14	4.00	4.00

No. 772 sold for 200k.

Seaplanes — A263

No. 773, Junkers F-13 (D463). No. 774, Waco YKS-7 (TF-ORN). No. 775, Grumman G-21A/JRF-5 (RVK). No. 776, PBY-5 Catalina (TF-ISP).

1993, Oct. 9 *Perf. 14*

773	A263 30k multicolored	2.50	1.00
774	A263 30k multicolored	2.50	1.00
775	A263 30k multicolored	2.50	1.00
776	A263 30k multicolored	2.50	1.00
a.	Block or strip of 4, #773-776	10.00	10.00
b.	Bklt. pane, 2 ea #773-776	22.50	

No. 776b is distinguished from sheet of 8 by rouletted selvage at left.

Issued in sheet of 8.

See Nos. 838-841.

Christmas A264

30k, Adoration of the Magi. 35k, Virgin and Child.

1993, Nov. 8 Litho. *Perf. 12½*

777	A264 30k multicolored	1.25	.55
778	A264 35k multicolored	1.25	1.25

Intl. Year of the Family A265

1994, Feb. 25 Litho. *Perf. 13½x13*

779	A265 40k multicolored	1.25	.70

Voyages of St. Brendan (484-577) A266

Europa: 35k, St. Brendan, Irish monks sailing pact volcano. 55k, St. Brendan on island with sheep, monks in boat.

1994, Apr. 18 Litho. *Perf. 14½x14*

780	A266 35k multicolored	2.50	1.10
	Booklet, 10 #780	25.00	
781	A266 55k multicolored	2.75	1.40
	Booklet, 10 #781	27.50	
a.	Miniature sheet of 2, #780-781	5.75	4.25

See Ireland Nos. 923-924; Faroe Islands Nos. 264-265.

Icelandic Art and Culture A267

No. 782, Music. No. 783, Crafts. No. 784, Film making. No. 785, Ballet, modern dance. No. 786, Theatre.

1994, May 25 Litho. *Perf. 13½x13*

782	A267 30k multicolored	1.00	.70
783	A267 30k multicolored	1.00	.70
784	A267 30k multicolored	1.00	.70
785	A267 30k multicolored	1.00	.70
786	A267 30k multicolored	1.00	.70
	Nos. 782-786 (5)	5.00	3.50

Independence, 50th anniv.

Gisli Sveinsson (1880-1959), Politician — A268

1994, June 14 *Perf. 14*

787	A268 30k multicolored	1.00	.60

Proclamation of new constitution, 50th anniv.

Souvenir Sheet

Republic of Iceland, 50th Anniv. — A269

Presidents of Iceland: a, Sveinn Bjornsson (1881-1952). b, Asgeir Asgeirsson (1894-1972). c, Kristjan Eldjarn (1916-82). d, Vigdis Finnbogadottir (b. 1930).

1994, June 17 Photo. *Perf. 11½*

Granite Paper

788	A269 Sheet of 4, #a.-d.	7.00	7.00
a.-d.	50k any single	1.75	1.75

Souvenir Sheet

Stamp Day — A270

Designs: a, Boy, girl with stamp album. b, Nos. 672, 713, portions of other Icelandic stamps. c, Girl, elderly man looking at globe.

1994, Oct. 7 Litho. *Perf. 13½*

789	A270 Sheet of 3	7.00	7.00
a.	30k multicolored	1.75	1.75
b.	35k multicolored	1.75	1.75
c.	100k multicolored	3.50	3.50

No. 789 sold for 200k for the benefit of the Stamp and Postal History Fund.

Christmas A271

1994, Nov. 9 Litho. *Perf. 14½*

790	A271 30k Woman, stars	1.00	.45
791	A271 35k Man, stars	1.25	1.25

ICAO, 50th Anniv. A272

1994, Nov. 9 *Perf. 13½x14*

792	A272 100k multicolored	3.50	2.00

A273

1995, Mar. 14 Litho. *Perf. 13*

793	A273 35k multicolored	1.25	.80

Salvation Army in Iceland, cent.

A274

1995, Mar. 14

794	A274 90k multicolored	4.25	1.75

Town of Seydisfjordur, cent.

1995 Men's Team Handball World Championships, Iceland — A275

Federation emblem, handball and: No. 795, Geyser, landscape. No. 796, Silhouette of building, landscape. No. 797, Volcano, lake. No. 798, Inlet, sunlight on water.

1995, Mar. 14 Litho. *Perf. 14*

795	A275 35k multicolored	1.75	1.10
796	A275 35k multicolored	1.75	1.10
797	A275 35k multicolored	1.75	1.10
798	A275 35k multicolored	1.75	1.10
a.	Block or strip of 4, #795-798	7.25	7.00
b.	Booklet pane, 2 #798a	17.50	
	Complete booklet, #798b	17.50	

Nos. 795-798 issued in sheets of 8 containing 2 each. No. 798b is separated from booklet by rouletted selvage at left, and sold for 480k in the complete booklet.

Norden 1995 — A276

Designs: 30k, Turf farmhouses, church. 35k, Volcano, Fjallsjokull glacier.

1995, May 5 Litho. ***Perf. 13½x13***
799 A276 30k multicolored .80 .40
Booklet, 10 #799 8.00
800 A276 35k multicolored 1.40 1.00

Spell-Broken, by Einar Jonsson (1874-1954) — A277

1995, May 5 ***Perf. 13x13½***
801 A277 35k brown & multi *1.10 1.00*
Booklet, 10 #801 *12.60*
802 A277 55k blue & multi *2.00 1.75*
Booklet, 10 #802 *20.00*

Europa.

Ship Type of 1991

No. 803, SS Laura. No. 804, MS Dronning Alexandrine. No. 805, MS Laxfoss. No. 806, MS Godafoss III.

1995, June 30 Litho. ***Perf. 14***
803 A251 30k multi 1.20 .90
804 A251 30k multi 1.20 .90
805 A251 30k multi 1.20 .90
806 A251 30k multi 1.20 .90
a. Block or strip of 4, #803-806 5.00 4.50
b. Bklt. pane, 2 ea #803-806 10.00
Prestige booklet, #806b 16.00

No. 806b is distinguished from sheet of 8 by rouletted selvage at left.
Issued in sheets of 8.
Prestige booklet sold for 400k.

Luxembourg-Reykjavik, Iceland Air Route, 40th Anniv. — A278

1995, Sept. 18 Litho. ***Perf. 13½***
807 A278 35k multicolored 1.25 1.10

See Luxembourg No. 936.

Birds A279

25k, Acanthis flammea. 250k, Gallinago gallinago.

1995, Sept. 18 ***Perf. 13½***
808 A279 25k multicolored .80 .65
809 A279 250k multicolored 8.50 6.00

Souvenir Sheet

Nordia '96, Reykjavik — A280

Design: Hraunfossar Waterfalls, Hvita River.

1995, Oct. 9 ***Perf. 13½x14***
810 A280 Sheet of 2, #a.-b. 7.00 7.00
a. 10k multicolored 2.50 2.50
b. 150k multicolored 4.50 4.50

See No. 830.

Christmas A281

1995, Nov. 8 Litho. ***Perf. 13½***
811 A281 30k Snowman, woman 1.00 .60
812 A281 35k Three trees 1.10 .90

UN, 50th Anniv. — A282

1995, Nov. 8 ***Perf. 13x13½***
813 A282 100k multicolored 3.25 2.50

Water Birds A283

Designs: 20k, Phalacrocorax carbo. 40k, Bucephala islandica.

1996, Feb. 7 Litho. ***Perf. 13½***
814 A283 20k multicolored 1.00 .55
815 A283 40k multicolored 1.25 1.00

See Nos. 834-835.

Paintings A284

100k, Seamen in a Boat, by Gunnlaugur Scheving (1904-72). 200k, At the Washing Springs, by Kristín Jónsdóttir (1888-1959).

1996, Feb. 7
816 A284 100k multicolored 3.00 2.40
817 A284 200k multicolored 5.25 4.50

Famous Women A285

Europa: 35k, Halldóra Bjarnadóttir (1873-1981), educator. 55k, Olafía Jóhannsdóttir (1863-1924), representative of women's rights, temperance affairs.

1996, Apr. 18 Litho. ***Perf. 14½***
818 A285 35k multicolored *1.25 .80*
Booklet, 10 #818 *12.50*
819 A285 55k multicolored *1.45 1.25*
Booklet, 10 #819 *14.50*

Postal Vehicle Type of 1992

Designs: No. 820, 1931 Buick. No. 821, 1933 Studebaker bus with destination sign, Reykjavik Municipal Bus Service. No. 822, Orange 1937 Ford bus, Iceland Motor Coach Service. No. 823, Red 1946 REO bus, Post and Telecommunications.

1996, May 13 Litho. ***Perf. 14***
820 A257 35k multicolored 1.25 .85
821 A257 35k multicolored 1.25 .85
822 A257 35k multicolored 1.25 .85
823 A257 35k multicolored 1.25 .85
a. Block or strip of 4, #820-823 5.00 5.00
b. Bklt. pane, 2 ea #820-823 10.00 10.00
Souvenir booklet, #823b 12.00

No. 823a issued in sheets of 8 stamps. No. 823b has rouletted selvage at left.

1996 Summer Olympic Games, Atlanta A286

1996, June 25 Litho. ***Perf. 12½***
824 A286 5k Running .25 .25
825 A286 25k Javelin .70 .40
826 A286 45k Long jump 1.40 1.10
827 A286 65k Shot put 2.10 1.50
Nos. 824-827 (4) 4.45 3.25

Order of the Sisters of St. Joseph in Iceland, Cent. — A287

1996, Sept. 17 Litho. ***Perf. 14½x13***
828 A287 65k multicolored 1.75 1.75

Reykjavik School, 150th Anniv. A288

1996, Sept. 17 ***Perf. 12½x13***
829 A288 150k multicolored 4.25 3.50

Nordia '96 Type of 1995

Design: Godafoss Waterfalls, Skjalfandafljot River.

1996, Oct. 9 Litho. ***Perf. 13½x14***
830 A280 Sheet of 3, #a.-c. 10.50 10.50
a. 45k multicolored 3.50 3.50
b. 65k multicolored 3.50 3.50
c. 90k multicolored 3.50 3.50

Reykjavik Cathedral, Bicent. — A289

1996, Nov. 5 ***Perf. 14***
831 A289 45k multicolored 1.40 1.10

Christmas — A290

Artifacts from Natl. Museum of Iceland: 35k, Figurine of Madonna and Child carved from walrus tusk. 45k, Pax showing Nativity.

1996, Nov. 5 ***Perf. 13½***
832 A290 35k multicolored 1.10 .60
a. Booklet pane of 10 11.00
Booklet, #832a 11.00
833 A290 45k multicolored 1.40 1.25

Bird Type of 1996

10k, Mergus serrator. 500k, Anas crecca.

1997, Apr. 2 Litho. ***Perf. 13½***
834 A283 10k multicolored .45 .35
835 A283 500k multicolored 14.00 12.00

Paintings A291

150k, Song of Iceland, by Svavar Guthnason. 200k, The Harbor, by Thorvaldur Skúlason.

1997, Mar. 6 Litho. ***Perf. 14***
836 A291 150k multicolored 4.75 4.00
837 A291 200k multicolored 5.75 4.50

Airplane Type of 1993

No. 838, De Havilland DH-89A (TF-ISM). No. 839, Stinson SR 8B Reliant (TF-RVB). No. 840, Douglas DC-3 (TF-ISH). No. 841, De Havilland DHC-6 Twin Otter (TF-REG).

1997, Apr. 15 Litho. ***Perf. 14***
838 A263 35k multicolored 1.25 .90
839 A263 35k multicolored 1.25 .90
840 A263 35k multicolored 1.25 .90
841 A263 35k multicolored 1.25 .90
a. Block or strip of 4, #838-841 5.00 5.00
b. Booklet pane, 2 each #838-841 10.00
Booklet, #841b 10.00

Issued in sheet of 8.
No. 841b has rouletted selvage at left.

European Games A292

1997, May 13 Litho. ***Perf. 14½***
842 A292 35k Hurdles 1.10 .70
843 A292 45k Sailing 1.40 1.10

Europa A293

Stories and legends by Asgrimur Jonsson: 45k, Couple on galloping horse. 65k, Old woman reaching for children.

1997, May 13 ***Perf. 13½***
844 A293 45k multicolored *1.60 1.25*
Complete booklet of 10 *16.00*
845 A293 65k multicolored *2.50 1.75*
Complete booklet of 10 *25.00*

Union of Graphic Workers, Cent. — A294

1997, Sept. 3 Litho. ***Perf. 13½***
846 A294 90k multicolored 2.75 2.25

ÍSLAND 100⁰⁰
LEIKFÉLAG REYKJAVÍKUR 100 ÁRA

Reykjavik Theater, Cent. — A295

1997, Sept. 3 ***Perf. 13½x14***
847 A295 100k multicolored 2.75 2.25

Stamp Day — A296

Icelandic row boats: a, Gideon, eight-oared lugger, 1836. b, Breidafjördur double-ended transport, 1904. c, Engey, six-oared craft, 1912.

1997, Oct. 9 Litho. *Perf. 15*
848 A296 Sheet of 3 10.00 10.00
a. 35k multicolored 2.25 2.25
b. 100k multicolored 3.50 3.50
c. 65k multicolored 4.00 4.00

Christmas A297

1997, Nov. 5 Litho. *Perf. 13½x13*
849 A297 35k Magi 1.00 .60
a. Booklet pane of 10 10.00
Booklet, #849a 10.00
850 A297 45k Nativity 1.40 .90

Rural Postman A298

Litho. & Engr.

1997, Nov. 5 *Perf. 13½*
851 A298 50k multicolored 1.50 1.25

1998 Winter Olympic Games, Nagano A299

1998, Jan. 22 Litho. *Perf. 13½*
852 A299 35k Downhill skier 1.00 .70
853 A299 45k Cross country skier 1.40 1.25

Nordic Stamps A300

1998, Mar. 5 Litho. *Perf. 13½x13*
854 A300 35k Sailboats 1.25 .70
855 A300 45k Power boats 1.75 1.40

Fish — A301

5k, Cyclopterus lumpus. 10k, Gadus morhua. 60k, Raja batis. 300k, Anarhicus lupus.

1998, Apr. 16
856 A301 5k multicolored .45 .45
857 A301 10k multicolored .45 .45
858 A301 60k multicolored 2.25 2.25
859 A301 300k multicolored 8.50 8.50
a. Min. sheet of 4, #856-859 11.00 11.00
Nos. 856-859 (4) 11.65 11.65

Intl. Year of the Ocean (No. 859a).
See Nos. 871-872, 915-916, 928-929.

National Holidays and Festivals A302

Independence Day, June 17th: 45k, Children standing at attention, flag. 65k, Monument, parade.

1998, May 12 Litho. *Perf. 14½*
860 A302 45k multicolored *1.50 1.00*
Complete booklet, 10 #860 *15.00*
861 A302 65k multicolored *2.10 1.50*
Complete booklet, 10 #861 *21.00*

Europa.

Minerals — A303

1998, Sept. 3 Litho. *Perf. 13½*
862 A303 35k Stilbite 1.20 .90
863 A303 45k Scolecite 1.40 1.10

See Nos. 885-886.

Leprosy Hospital, Laugarnes A304

1998, Sept. 3 *Perf. 13½x14*
864 A304 70k multicolored 2.00 1.60

First Icelandic Postage Stamp, 125th Anniv. — A305

1998, Oct. 9 Litho. *Perf. 13½*
865 A305 35k multicolored 1.20 .80

Agricultural Tools — A306

1998, Oct. 9 *Perf. 15*
866 A306 Sheet of 3 7.50 7.50
a. 35k Turf scythe 1.75 1.75
b. 65k Hay mower 2.50 2.50
c. 100k Manure mincer 3.25 3.25

Stamp Day.

Christmas, Children's Drawings — A307

35k, Black cat, homes, mountains. 45k, Angels, Christmas tree, moon and stars.

1998, Nov. 5 Litho. *Perf. 13x13½*
867 A307 35k multicolored 1.10 .90
a. Booklet pane of 10 11.00
Complete booklet, #867a 11.00
868 A307 45k multicolored 1.25 1.10

Universal Declaration of Human Rights, 50th Anniv. — A308

1998, Nov. 5 *Perf. 14½*
869 A308 50k multicolored 1.60 1.60

Jón Leifs (1899-1968), Composer — A309

1999, Jan. 22 Litho. *Perf. 14½*
870 A309 35k multicolored 1.25 1.25

Fish Type of 1998

35k, Pleuronectez platessa. 55k, Clupea harengus.

1999, Jan. 22 *Perf. 14½x15*
871 A301 35k multicolored 1.40 .90
872 A301 55k multicolored 1.60 1.60

Marine Mammals — A311

Designs: 35k, Orcinus orca. 45k, Physeter macrocephalus. 65k, Balaenoptera musculus. 85k, Phocoena phocoena.

1999, Mar. 4 Litho. *Perf. 14½*
873 A311 35k multicolored 1.40 .90
874 A311 45k multicolored 1.75 1.10
875 A311 65k multicolored 2.25 1.90
876 A311 85k multicolored 3.00 2.40
a. Sheet of 4, #873-876 8.00 8.00
Nos. 873-876 (4) 8.40 6.30

See Nos. 911-914, 945-948. For surcharge see No. 944.

Locomotive A312

Perf. 13 on 2 or 3 Sides
1999, Apr. 15 Booklet Stamps
877 A312 25k green & multi 3.50 3.50
878 A312 50k brown & multi 1.25 1.25
a. Booklet pane, 1 #877, 3 #878 7.50
Complete booklet, #878a 7.50
879 A312 75k Ship 2.50 2.50
a. Booklet pane of 4 10.00
Complete booklet, #879a 10.00
Nos. 877-879 (3) 7.25 7.25

See Nos. 908-909.

Council of Europe, 50th Anniv. A313

1999, Apr.15 *Perf. 13x13½*
880 A313 35k multicolored 1.20 .90

Mushrooms A314

35k, Suillus grevillei. 75k, Agaricus campestris.

1999, May 20 Litho. *Perf. 14½*
881 A314 35k multicolored 1.10 1.10
882 A314 75k multicolored 2.25 2.25

See Nos. 898-899, 957-958, 1021-1022, 1087-1088.

National Parks — A315

1999, May 20 *Perf. 13¼*
883 A315 50k Skutustadagigar *1.40 1.40*
a. Booklet pane of 10 *14.00*
Complete booklet, #883a *14.00*
884 A315 75k Vid Arnarstapa *2.50 2.00*
a. Booklet pane of 10 *25.00*
Complete booklet, #884a *26.00*

Europa.

Minerals Type of 1998

1999, Sept. 9 Litho. *Perf. 14¾*
885 A303 40k Calcite 1.25 1.25
886 A303 50k Heulandite 1.75 1.75

Nature Conservation A316

1999, Sept. 9 Litho. *Perf. 14¼*
887 A316 35k "Hreinar" 1.25 1.25
888 A316 35k "Markviss" 1.25 1.25
889 A316 35k "Hreint" 1.25 1.25
890 A316 35k "Endurheimt" 1.25 1.25
891 A316 35k "Eflum" 1.25 1.25
a. Strip of 5, #887-891 6.00 6.00

Reykjavik, European Cultural City for 2000 A317

35k, Facescape, by Erro. 50k, Book, violin, palette, masks, camera, computer.

1999, Oct. 7 Litho. *Perf. 13¼*
892 A317 35k multi 1.10 .90
893 A317 50k multi 1.50 1.50

Souvenir Sheet

View of Skagafjordur, by Carl Emil Baagoe — A318

1999, Oct. 7 *Perf. 13¼x13*
894 A318 200k olive & black 9.00 9.00

Stamp Day. No. 894 sold for 250k.

Children's Art — A319

1999, Nov. 4 Litho. *Perf. 13*

895 A319 35k multi		1.00	1.00

Christmas — A320

No. 896, Elf: a, With walking stick. b, Jumping over rock. c, Waving. d, Licking spoon. e, With hand in cauldron. f, With cup. g, At door. h, With ladle and barrel. i, With sausages. j, At window.

No. 897, Elf: a, Looking up. b, With ham. c, With candles.

1999, Nov. 4

896	Strip of 10	12.50	12.50
a.-j.	A320 35k any single	1.25	1.25
k.	Booklet pane, #896a-896j	12.50	
	Complete booklet, #896k	12.50	
897	Strip of 3	5.25	5.25
a.-c.	A320 50k any single	1.75	1.75

See Nos. 924-926.

Nos. 896a-896k and 897a-897c were also released in a sheet of 15 undenominated labels made available as a gift to buyers of the stamps..

Mushroom Type of 1999

Designs: 40k, Cantharellus cibarius. 50k, Coprinus comatus.

2000, Feb. 4 Litho. *Perf. 13*

898	A314 40k multi	1.25	1.25
a.	Booklet pane of 10	12.50	
	Complete booklet, #898a	12.50	
899	A314 50k multi	1.75	1.75

A321

Christianity in Iceland, 1000th Anniv. — A322

2000, Feb. 4 *Perf. 13¼x13¾*

900 A321 40k multi		1.25	1.25

Souvenir Sheet

Perf. 13¼x13

901 A322 40k multi		1.25	1.25

See Vatican City No. 1151.

Discovery of Vinland, 1000th Anniv. A323

Designs: 40k, Viking with shield, globe. 50k, Viking ship sailing. 75k, Viking ship at shore. 90k, Viking without shield, globe.

Litho. & Engr.

2000, Mar. 16 *Perf. 12½x13*

902	A323 40k multi	1.25	1.25
903	A323 50k multi	1.75	1.75
904	A323 75k multi	2.25	2.25
905	A323 90k multi	2.75	2.75
a.	Souvenir sheet, #902-905	8.00	8.00
	Nos. 902-905 (4)	8.00	8.00

Millennium A324

Designs: 40k, Head, quill pen. 50k, Man, genealogical chart, circuit board.

2000, Apr. 27 Litho. *Perf. 13x13¼*

906	A324 40k multi	1.10	1.10
907	A324 50k multi	1.40	1.40

Locomotive Type of 1999

Perf. 13 on 2 or 3 sides

2000, Apr. 27 Litho.

Booklet Stamps

908	A312 50k Steam roller	1.50	1.50
a.	Booklet pane of 4	6.00	
	Booklet, #908a	6.00	
909	A312 75k Fire pumper	2.25	2.25
a.	Booklet pane of 4	9.00	
	Booklet, #909a	9.00	

Europa, 2000

Common Design Type

2000, May 18 Litho. *Perf. 13¼x13*

910	CD17 50k multi	*1.60*	*1.60*
a.	Booklet pane of 10	*16.00*	
	Booklet, #910a	*16.00*	

Marine Mammals Type of 1999

Designs: 5k, Hyperoodon ampullatus. 40k, Lagenorhynchus acutus. 50k, Megaptera novaeangliae. 75k, Balaenoptera acutorostrata.

2000, May 18 *Perf. 14½*

911	A311 5k multi	.25	.25
912	A311 40k multi	1.40	1.40
913	A311 50k multi	1.75	1.75
914	A311 75k multi	2.50	2.50
	Nos. 911-914 (4)	5.90	5.90

Fish Type of 1998

Designs: 10k, Melanogrammus aeglefinus. 250k, Mallotus villosus.

2000, Sept. 14 Litho. *Perf. 13*

915-916 A301	Set of 2	9.50	9.50

Flowers — A325

Designs: 40k, Viola x wittrockiana. 50k, Petunia x hybrida.

2000, Sept. 14 *Perf. 13*

917-918 A325	Set of 2	2.50	2.50

See Nos. 931-932, 968-969, 982-983, 1005-1006.

Butterflies A326

Designs: 40k, Chloroclysta citrata. 50k, Cerapteryx graminis.

2000, Oct. 9 *Perf. 14x14½*

919-920 A326	Set of 2	2.75	2.75

Souvenir Sheet

Stamp Day — A327

Litho. & Engr.

2000, Oct. 9 *Perf. 13¼*

921 A327 200k multi		9.00	9.00

No. 921 sold for 250k.

Ancient Architecture — A328

Various buildings. Denominations: 45k, 75k.

2000, Nov. 9 Litho. *Perf. 14*

922-923 A328	Set of 2	4.00	4.00

Christmas Type of 1999

Designs: 40k, Elf grasping walking stick. 50k, Female elf carrying bag.

2000, Nov. 9 *Perf. 13*

924	A320 40k multi	1.25	1.00
a.	Perf. 12¾x13¼	1.50	1.00
b.	Booklet pane, 4 #924a	6.00	
c.	Booklet pane, 6 #924a	9.00	
	Booklet, #924b, 924c	15.00	
925	A320 50k multi	1.60	1.25

Souvenir Sheet

926	Sheet of 2	2.90	2.25
a.	A320 40k As #924, 26x40mm	1.25	.95
b.	A320 50k As #925, 26x40mm	1.60	1.25

Coast Guard, 75th Anniv. A329

2001, Jan. 18 Litho. *Perf. 13*

927	A329 (40k) multi	1.50	1.50
a.	Booklet pane of 10	15.00	
	Booklet, #927a	15.00	

Fish Type of 1998

Designs: 55k, Reinhardtius hippoglossoides. 80k, Pollachius virens.

2001, Jan. 18

928-929 A301	Set of 2	4.00	4.00

UN High Commissioner for Refugees, 50th Anniv. — A330

2001, Mar. 8 *Perf. 13¼x13*

930 A330 50k multi		1.50	1.25

Flower Type of 2000

Designs: 55k, Calendula officinalis. 65k, Dorotheanthus bellidiformis.

2001, Mar. 8 *Perf. 13*

931-932 A325	Set of 2	3.75	3.25

Icelandic Sheepdog A331

Dog's coat: 40k, Brown. 80k, Black.

2001, Apr. 18 *Perf. 14¼*

933-934 A331	Set of 2	4.00	3.25

Airplanes A332

Designs: 55k: TF-OGN (biplane). 80k, Klemm TF-SUX (monoplane).

Perf. 13½x12¾ on 2 or 3 Sides

2001, Apr. 18 Booklet Stamps

935	A332 55k multi	1.75	1.40
a.	Booklet pane of 4	7.00	
	Booklet, #935a	7.00	
936	A332 80k multi	2.50	2.25
a.	Booklet pane of 4	10.00	
	Booklet, #936a	10.00	

Europa A333

Designs: 55k, Head, waterfall. 80k, Hand, wave.

2001, May 17 *Perf. 13*

937	A333 55k multi	*1.60*	*1.50*
a.	Booklet pane of 10	*16.00*	
	Booklet, #937a	*17.00*	
938	A333 80k multi	*2.40*	*2.00*
a.	Booklet pane of 10	*24.00*	
	Booklet, #938a	*26.00*	

Horses A334

Designs: 40k, Fet. 50k, Tölt. 55k, Brokk. 60k, Skeidh. 80k, Stökk.

2001, May 17 *Perf. 13x13¼*

939-943 A334	Set of 5	8.75	8.75

No. 873 Surcharged in Red

2001, July 10 Litho. *Perf. 14½*

944 A311 (53k) on 35k multi		1.75	1.75

Marine Mammals Type of 1999

Designs: 5k, Lagenorhynchus albirostris. 40k, Balaenoptera physalus. 80k, Balaenoptera borealis. 100k, Globicephala melas.

2001, Sept. 6 Litho. *Perf. 14½*

945	A311 5k multi	.30	.30
946	A311 40k multi	1.25	1.25
947	A311 80k multi	2.50	2.50
948	A311 100k multi	3.25	3.25
	Nos. 945-948 (4)	7.30	7.30

Islands
A335

Designs: 40k, Grimsey. 55k, Papey.

2001, Oct. 9 Litho. *Perf. 13¼x13*
949-950 A335 Set of 2 2.75 2.50

See Nos. 975-976, 1001-1002, 1033-1034, 1158-1159.

Souvenir Sheet

Esja Mountain — A336

2001, Oct. 9 *Perf. 13¼*
951 A336 250k multi 9.00 9.00

Stamp Day.

Birds — A337

Designs: 42k, Oenanthe oenanthe. 250k, Charadrius hiaticula.

2001, Nov. 8 *Perf. 13¼x13*
952-953 A337 Set of 2 10.00 10.00

Christmas
A338

Churches: (42k), Brautarholt. 55k, Vidhmyri.

2001, Nov. 8
954 A338 (42k) multi 1.25 1.25
a. Booklet pane of 6 7.50 —
Booklet, 4 #954 12.50
955 A338 55k multi 1.60 1.40

First Motorboat in Iceland, Cent.
A339

2002, Jan. 17 Litho. *Perf. 13x13½*
956 A339 60k multi 1.90 1.90

Mushroom Type of 1999

Designs: (40k), Leccinum scabrum. 85k, Hydnum repandum.

2002, Jan. 17 *Perf. 13¼x12¾*
957-958 A314 Set of 2 3.75 3.75
Booklet, 10 #957 12.50

No. 957 is inscribed "Bref 20g."

Intl. Year of Mountains
A340

2002, Mar. 7 Litho. *Perf. 13*
959 A340 (42k) multi 1.50 1.50

Halldór Laxness (1902-98), 1955 Nobel Literature Laureate
A341

2002, Mar. 7 Litho. *Perf. 13x13¼*
960 A341 100k multi 3.50 3.50
a. Souvenir sheet of 1 3.75 3.75

Examples of No. 960a with Nobel Prize medal in margin printed in gold foil and embossed sold for 1700k. Value, $100.

Lighthouses — A342

Perf. 12¾x13¼ on 2 or 3 Sides
2002, Apr. 18 Booklet Stamps
961 A342 60k Gróttа 1.75 1.60
a. Booklet pane of 4 7.00 —
Complete booklet, #961a 7.00
962 A342 85k Kögur 2.50 2.25
a. Booklet pane of 4 10.00 —
Complete booklet, #962a 10.00

Fyssa, by Rúrí — A343

Spenna, by Hafsteinn Austmann
A344

2002, Apr. 18 Litho. *Perf. 14½x14¾*
963 A343 (42k) multi 1.25 1.10
964 A344 60k multi 1.75 1.50

Nordic Council, 50th anniv. (No. 963).

Sesselja Sigmundsdóttir (1902-74), Advocate for Mentally Handicapped
A345

2002, May 9
965 A345 45k multi 1.25 1.10

Europa
A346

Designs: 60k, Acrobats, juggling clown. 85k, Head on stick, lion jumping through ring of fire.

2002, May 9 *Perf. 13*
966 A346 60k multi *1.75 1.25*
a. Booklet pane of 10 *17.50*
Booklet, #966a *19.00*
967 A346 85k multi *2.50 1.50*
a. Booklet pane of 10 *25.00*
Booklet, #967a *26.00*

Flowers Type of 2000

Designs: 10k, Lobelia erinus. 200k, Centaurea cyanus.

2002, Sept. 5 Litho. *Perf. 14¾x14½*
968-969 A325 Set of 2 7.00 7.00

Fish of Lake Thingvallavatn — A347

Designs: (45k), Salvelinus alpinus (Murta). (55k), Salmo trutta, vert. 60k, Salvelinus alpinus (Sílableikja). 90k, Salvelinus alpinus (Kuthungableikja). 200k, Salvelinus alpinus (Dvergbleikja).

Perf. 13¼x12¾, 12¾x13¼ (#971)
2002, Sept. 5
970 A347 (45k) multi 1.50 1.50
a. Perf. 13¼x12½x13¼x13 1.50 1.50
971 A347 (55k) multi 2.50 2.50
a. Perf
13¼x12½:13x13¼x13:12½ 2.50 2.50
972 A347 60k multi 2.00 2.00
a. Perf. 13¼x13 2.00 2.00
973 A347 90k multi 2.75 2.75
a. Perf. 13¼x13 2.75 2.75
974 A347 200k multi 6.00 6.00
a. Perf. 13¼x13 6.00 6.00
b. Booklet pane, #970a-974a 27.50
Complete booklet, #974b 27.50
Nos. 970-974 (5) 14.75 14.75

Nos. 970-974 were issued both in sheet format, perf 13¼x12¾ or 12¾x13¼ (No. 971), and in booklet pane format (Nos. 970a-974a), with small differences in the gauge of the stamps' perforations.

Islands Type of 2001

Designs: 45k, Vigur. 55k, Flatey.

2002, Oct. 9 *Perf. 14*
975-976 A335 Set of 2 2.75 2.75

Souvenir Sheet

Sudurgata, Reykjavik — A348

2002, Oct. 9 *Perf. 14½x14¾*
977 A348 250k multi 9.00 9.00

Stamp Day.

Birds — A349

Designs: 50k, Tringa totanus. 85k, Phalaropus fulicarius.

2002, Nov. 7 *Perf. 13¼x13*
978-979 A349 Set of 2 4.00 4.00

See Nos. 997-998, 1029-1030, 1059-1060.

Christmas — A350

Designs: 45k, Gifts and ornaments. 60k, Gifts.

2002, Nov. 7 *Perf. 13*
980 A350 45k multi 1.25 1.25
a. Booklet pane of 10 12.50
Booklet, #980a 12.50
981 A350 60k multi 1.75 1.75

Flower Type of 2000

Designs: 45k, Phlox drummondii. 60k, Gazania x hybrida.

2003, Jan. 16 *Perf. 13*
982 A325 45k multi 1.25 1.25
a. Booklet pane of 10 12.50
Booklet, #982a 12.50
983 A325 60k multi 1.75 1.75

Icelandic Police Force, Bicent. — A351

Designs: 45k, Police officers, 2003. 55k, Policeman, 1803.

2003, Jan. 16
984-985 A351 Set of 2 2.90 2.90

Icelandic Cattle
A352

Designs: 45k, Bull. 85k, Cow.

2003, Mar. 13 Litho. *Perf. 13x13¼*
986-987 A352 Set of 2 3.75 3.75

Souvenir Sheet

Nordia 2003 Philatelic Exhibition, Reykjavik — A353

Litho. & Engr.
2003, Mar. 13 *Perf. 14*
988 A353 250k multi 9.00 9.00

No. 988 sold for 300k.

Free Church, Reykjavik, Cent. — A354

2003, Apr. 23 Litho. *Perf. 13*
989 A354 200k multi 6.50 6.50

Ferries
A355

No. 990: a, Saefari. b, Saevar.
No. 991: a, Herjólfur. b, Baldur.

Perf. 13 on 2 or 3 Sides
2003, Apr. 23 Booklet Stamps
990 Pair 2.75 2.75
a.-b. A355 45k Either single 1.35 1.35
c. Booklet pane, 2 #990 5.50 —
Complete booklet, #990c 5.50

991 Pair 3.75 3.75
a.-b. A355 60k Either single 1.75 1.75
c. Booklet pane, 2 #991 7.50 —
Complete booklet, #991c 7.50

Icelandic Chickens — A356

2003, May 22 ***Perf. 13¼***
992 A356 45k multi 1.25 1.25

Europa — A357

Poster art.

2003, May 22 ***Perf. 13½***
993 A357 60k red & multi 1.75 *1.25*
a. Booklet pane of 10, perf. 13½ on 3 sides 17.50 —
Complete booklet, #993a 19.00
994 A357 85k green & multi 2.50 *1.75*
a. Booklet pane of 10, perf. 13½ on 3 sides 25.00 —
Complete booklet, #994a 26.00

Friendship A358

2003, Sept. 4 ***Perf. 14¼x14½***
995 A358 45k multi 1.25 1.25

First Census, 300th Anniv. — A359

2003, Sept. 4 ***Perf. 13***
996 A359 60k multi 1.75 1.75

Bird Type of 2002

Designs: 70k, Anthus pratensis. 250k, Numenius phaeopus.

2003, Sept. 4 ***Perf. 13¼x13***
997-998 A349 Set of 2 10.00 10.00

Rangifer Tarandus A360

2003, Oct. 9 **Litho.** ***Perf. 13***
999 A360 45k multi 1.25 1.25

Souvenir Sheet

Quonset Hut — A361

2003, Oct. 9
1000 A361 250k multi 8.25 8.25

Stamp Day.

Islands Type of 2001

Designs: 85k, Heimaey. 200k, Hrísey.

2003, Nov. 6 ***Perf. 13¼x13***
1001-1002 A335 Set of 2 8.50 8.50

Christmas — A362

Designs: 45k, Girl placing ornament on Christmas tree. 60k, Boy lighting candle.

2003, Nov. 6 ***Perf. 14¼***
1003-1004 A362 Set of 2 3.00 3.00
a. Booklet pane of 10, #1003 12.50
Booklet, #1003a 12.50

Flowers Type of 2000

Designs: 50k, Tagetes patula. 55k, Begonia x tuberhybrida.

2004, Jan. 15 **Litho.** ***Perf. 13***
1005-1006 A325 Set of 2 3.25 3.25

Hannes Hafstein (1861-1922), Politician, Poet — A363

2004, Jan. 15 ***Perf. 13¼x13½***
1007 A363 150k multi 4.50 4.50
a. Souvenir sheet of 1 4.50 4.50

Icelandic home rule, cent.

Trawler "Coot," Cent. A364

2004, Mar. 11 **Litho.** ***Perf. 13¼***
1008 A364 50k multi 1.40 1.40

Geothermal Energy — A365

Designs: 50k, Snorralaug hot water pool. 55k, Valve on geodesic dome, steam cloud, vert. (29x47mm). 60k, Steam pipes. 90k, Turbine. 250k, Map of Iceland showing geothermal zones, vert. (29x47mm).

Perf. 13x13¼, 13¼ (55k, 250k)

2004, Mar. 11
1009 A365 50k multi 1.25 1.25
a. Perf. 13¼ *4.00* *4.00*
1010 A365 55k multi 1.40 1.40
1011 A365 60k multi 1.50 1.50
a. Perf. 13¼ *5.00* *5.00*
1012 A365 90k multi 2.75 2.75
a. Perf. 13¼ *7.00* *7.00*
1013 A365 250k multi 6.50 6.50
a. Booklet pane, #1009a, 1010, 1011a, 1012a, 1013 25.00 —
Complete booklet, #1013a 25.00
Nos. 1009-1013 (5) 13.40 13.40

Complete booklet sold for 750k.
Nos. 1009a, 1011a and 1012a only come from the booklet pane No. 1013a.

Souvenir Sheet

Norse Mythology — A366

No. 1014: a, God Odin and bird. b, Odin's horse, Sleipnir, and bird.

2004, Mar. 26 ***Perf. 13***
1014 A366 Sheet of 2 3.50 3.50
a. 50k multi 1.50 1.50
b. 60k multi 2.00 2.00

Automobiles A367

No. 1015: a, 1956 Ford Fairlane Victoria. b, 1954 Pobeta.
No. 1016: a, 1955 Chevrolet Bel Air. b, 1952 Volkswagen.

Perf. 13 on 2 or 3 Sides

2004, Apr. 15 **Booklet Stamps**
1015 Pair 6.50 6.50
a.-b. A367 60k Either single 3.25 3.25
c. Booklet pane, 2 #1015 13.00 —
Complete booklet, #1015c 13.00
1016 Pair 9.50 9.50
a.-b. A367 85k Either single 4.75 4.75
c. Booklet pane, 2 #1016 19.00 —
Complete booklet, #1016c 19.00

Herring Industry, Cent. — A368

2004, May 19 ***Perf. 13¼***
1017 A368 65k multi 2.00 2.00

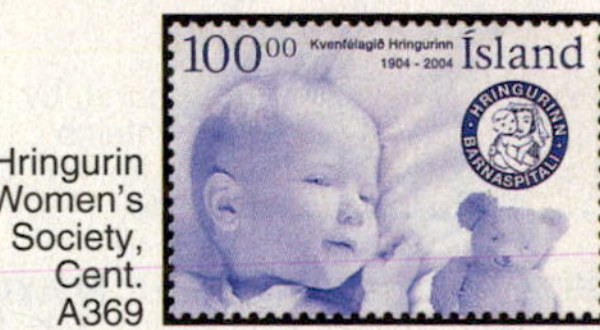

Hringurin Women's Society, Cent. A369

2004, May 19 ***Perf. 13x13¼***
1018 A369 100k violet blue 3.00 3.00

Europa A370

2004, May 19 ***Perf. 13***
1019 A370 65k Cyclists *1.75* *1.75*
a. Booklet pane of 10 *17.50* —
Complete booklet, #1019a *17.50*
1020 A370 90k Cars in snow *2.75* *2.75*
a. Booklet pane of 10 *27.50* —
Complete booklet, #1020a *27.50*

Mushrooms Type of 1999

Designs: 50k, Amanita vaginata. 60k, Camarophyllus pratensis.

2004, Sept. 2 **Litho.** ***Perf. 13***
1021-1022 A314 Set of 2 3.75 3.75

Reykdal Power Station, Cent. — A371

2004, Sept. 2 ***Perf. 13¼***
1023 A371 50k multi 1.50 1.50

First Automobile in Iceland, Cent. A372

2004, Sept. 2
1024 A372 100k multi 3.00 3.00

French Hospital, Fáskrúthsfirthi, Cent. — A373

Litho. & Engr.

2004, Oct. 8 ***Perf. 13¾***
1025 A373 60k multi 1.60 1.60

Souvenir Sheet

Brúarhlöth — A374

2004, Oct. 8 **Litho.** ***Perf. 13***
1026 A374 250k multi 8.00 8.00

Stamp Day.

Insects A375

Designs: 50k, Nebria gyllenhali. 70k, Bombus lucorum.

2004, Oct. 8
1027-1028 A375 Set of 2 4.00 4.00

See Nos. 1043-1044, 1089-1090, 1121-1122, 1161-1161.

Bird Type of 2002

Designs: 55k, Calidris maritima. 75k, Calidris alpina.

2004, Nov. 4 **Litho.** ***Perf. 13¼x13***
1029-1030 A349 Set of 2 4.00 4.00

Christmas — A376

Designs: 45k, Ptarmigan in snow. 65k, Reindeer in snow.

2004, Nov. 4
1031-1032 A376 Set of 2 3.50 3.50
1031a Booklet pane of 10 #1031 14.00 —
Complete booklet, #1031a 14.00

Islands Type of 2001

Designs: 5k, Vithey. 90k, Flatey.

2005, Jan. 13 **Litho.** ***Perf. 14***
1033-1034 A335 Set of 2 3.00 3.00

Organized Forestation, Cent. A377

2005, Jan. 13
1035 A377 45k multi 1.25 1.25

See Nos. 1101-1102, 1154-1155.

Souvenir Sheet

National Museum Artifacts — A378

No. 1036: a, Brooch, 11th cent. b, Statue of Thor, 10th cent.

Litho. & Embossed

2005, Jan. 13 ***Perf. 13½x13***
1036 A378 Sheet of 2 + central label 8.00 8.00
a. 100k multi 3.50 3.50
b. 150k multi 4.50 4.50

Mice A379

Designs: 45k, Apodemus sylvaticus. 125k, Mus musculus.

Perf. 13½x12¾

2005, Mar. 10 **Litho.**
1037-1038 A379 Set of 2 5.00 5.00

Flowers — A380

Designs: No. 1039, 50k, Roses. No. 1040, 50k, African daisies. No. 1041, 50k, Red calla lilies. 70k, Tulip.

2005, Mar. 10 ***Perf. 13¼***
1039-1042 A380 Set of 4 7.50 7.50
1042a Booklet pane, 2 each #1039-1042 15.00 —

Nos. 1039-1042 each printed in sheets of 10, with each stamp in the sheet having a different background swirl pattern. Stamps of the same kind in the booklet pane have the same swirl pattern, which is the same as one found on the sheet.

Insects Type of 2004

Designs: 50k, Araneus diadematus (spider). 70k, Musca domestica.

2005, Apr. 14 ***Perf. 13¼x13***
1043-1044 A375 Set of 2 4.00 4.00

Fishing Boats A381

No. 1045: a, Vörthur ThH4. b, Karl VE47.
No. 1046: a, Saedís IS67. b, Guthbjörg NK74.

Perf. 13 on 2 or 3 Sides

2005, Apr. 14 **Booklet Stamps**
1045 Pair 4.50 4.50
a.-b. A381 70k Either single 2.25 2.25
c. Booklet pane, 2 #1045 9.00 —
Complete booklet, #1045c 9.00
1046 Pair 6.00 6.00
a.-b. A381 95k Either single 3.00 3.00
c. Booklet pane, 2 #1045 12.00 —
Complete booklet, #1045c 12.00

Bridges, Cent. A382

Designs: 50k, Sogith Bridge. 95k, Lagarfljót Bridge. 165k, Jökulsá Bridge.

2005, May 26 **Litho.** ***Perf. 13¼x13½***
1047-1049 A382 Set of 3 10.50 10.50

Europa A383

Fork, knife and: 70k, Fish dish, gutted fish, waterfall. 90k, Meat dish, hanging meat, flowers.

2005, May 26 ***Perf. 13½***
1050 A383 70k multi *2.10 2.10*
a. Booklet pane of 10 *21.00*
Complete booklet, #1050a *21.00*
1051 A383 90k multi *2.75 2.75*
a. Booklet pane of 10 *27.50*
Complete booklet, #1050a *27.50*

Salmon Fishermen and Fishing Flies — A384

Designs; 50k, Fisherman on Laxáí Kjós River, Raud Frances fly. 60k, Fishermen in boat on Laxá i Athaldal River, Laxá Bla fly, vert.

Perf. 13¾x13½, 13½x13¾

2005, Sept. 1 **Litho.**
1052-1053 A384 Set of 2 3.25 3.25

Berries — A385

Designs: 65k, Vaccinium uliginosum. 90k, Fragaria vesca.

2005, Sept. 1 ***Perf. 14***
1054 A385 65k multi 1.75 1.75
a. Tete-beche pair 3.50 3.50
1055 A385 90k multi 2.50 2.50
a. Tete-beche pair 5.00 5.00

See Nos. 1082-1083, 1116-1117.

Motorcycles — A386

2005, Oct. 7 ***Perf. 13¼x13½***
1056 A386 50k multi 1.40 1.40

First motorcycle in Iceland, cent.

Commercial College of Iceland, Cent. A387

2005, Oct. 7 ***Perf. 13½x14¼***
1057 A387 70k multi 2.00 2.00

Souvenir Sheet

Aerial View of Reykjavik Rooftops — A388

2005, Oct. 7 ***Perf. 13¼***
1058 A388 200k multi 6.50 6.50

Stamp Day.

Birds Type of 2002

Designs: 60k, Anser anser. 105k, Sturnus vulgaris.

2005, Nov. 3 ***Perf. 14***
1059-1060 A349 Set of 2 4.50 4.50

Christmas — A389

2005, Nov. 3 ***Perf. 13½***
1061 A389 50k Apple 1.40 1.40
a. White border at top or bottom, perf. 13½ on 2 or 3 sides 1.40 1.40
b. Booklet pane of 10 #1061a 14.00 —
Complete booklet, #1061b 14.00
1062 A389 70k Christmas tree 2.10 2.10

No. 1061 is impregnated with an apple and cinnamon scent; No. 1062 with a pine scent.

National Flower Dryas Octopetala — A390

2006, Feb. 2 **Litho.** ***Perf. 13¾***
1063 A390 50k multi 1.40 1.40

Rock and Roll Music, 50th Anniv. — A391

2006, Feb. 2
1064 A391 60k multi 1.60 1.60

Arrival in Iceland of Refugees of Hungarian Uprising, 50th Anniv. A392

2006, Feb. 2 ***Perf. 13½x13¾***
1065 A392 70k multi 2.00 2.00

Souvenir Sheet

Europa Stamps, 50th Anniv. — A393

No. 1066: a, #407. b, #395.

2006, Feb. 2 ***Perf. 14¼x14***
1066 A393 150k Sheet of 2, #a-b *9.50 9.50*

Motion Pictures in Iceland, Cent. — A394

Designs: 50k, Early theater, projector and program. 95k, Projector reel, actor and actress. 160k, Actor in mask, clapboard, bag of popcorn, cameraman on location.

Perf. 13¾x13½

2006, Mar. 29 **Litho.**
1067-1069 A394 Set of 3 9.00 9.00

Souvenir Sheet

Mythical Beings of Nordic Folklore — A395

2006, Mar. 29 ***Perf. 13¼x13***
1070 A395 95k multi 3.00 3.00

General Purpose Vehicles A396

No. 1071: a, 1951 Land Rover. b, 1946 Willys.
No. 1072: a, 1965 Austin Gypsy. b, 1955 GAZ-69.

Perf. 13 on 2 or 3 Sides

2006, Mar. 29 **Booklet Stamps**
1071 Pair 4.00 4.00
a.-b. A396 70k Either single 2.00 2.00
c. Booklet pane, 2 #1071 8.00 —
Complete booklet, #1071c 8.00
1072 Pair 5.00 5.00
a.-b. A396 90k Either single 2.50 2.50
c. Booklet pane, 2 #1072 10.00 —
Complete booklet, #1072c 10.00

A397

95 ÍSLAND

Europa A398

2006, May 18 ***Perf. 13¼x13¾***
1073 A397 75k blk & red 2.00 2.00

Perf. 13¾x13¼
1074 A398 95k blue & blk 2.75 2.75

Booklet Stamps
Self-Adhesive
Serpentine Die Cut 11¾x12¼
1075 A397 75k blk & red 2.00 2.00
a. Booklet pane of 10 20.00

Serpentine Die Cut 12¼x11¾
1076 A398 95k blue & blk 2.75 2.75
a. Booklet pane of 10 27.50

Waterfalls — A399

Designs: 55k, Faxi. 65k, Oxaráfoss, vert. (29x47mm). 75k, Glymur, vert. (29x47mm). 95k, Hjálparfoss. 220k, Skeifárfoss.

2006, May 18 ***Perf. 13¼***
1077-1081 A399 Set of 5 14.50 14.50
1081a Booklet pane, #1077-1081, perf. 13½ 21.00 —
Complete booklet, #1081a 21.00

Booklet containing No. 1081a sold for 750k.

Berries Type of 2005

Designs: 75k, Empetrum nigrum. 130k, Rubus saxatilis.

2006, Sept. 21 ***Perf. 13¼x13¾***
1082 A385 75k multi 1.90 1.90
a. Tete-beche pair 3.75 3.75
1083 A385 130k multi 3.50 3.50
a. Tete-beche pair 7.00 7.00

Iceland's First Olympic Medal, 50th Anniv. — A400

Litho. & Embossed
2006, Sept. 21 ***Perf. 13¼***
1084 A400 55k multi 1.40 1.40

First Telephone Service in Iceland, Cent. — A401

2006, Sept. 21 **Litho.** ***Perf. 14***
1085 A401 65k multi 1.75 1.75

Souvenir Sheet

Icelandic Wrestling Tournament, Cent. — A402

Litho. & Embossed
2006, Sept. 21 ***Perf. 13¼x14***
1086 A402 200k multi 6.00 6.00

Stamp Day.

Mushrooms Type of 1999

Designs: 70k, Xerocomus subtomentosus. 95k, Kuehneromyces mutabilis.

2006, Nov. 2 **Litho.** ***Perf. 13¾x13¼***
1087-1088 A314 Set of 2 4.50 4.50

Insects Type of 2004

Designs: 65k, Dolichovespula norwegica. 110k, Coccinella undecimpunctata.

2006, Nov. 2 **Litho.** ***Perf. 13¾x14¼***
1089-1090 A375 Set of 2 4.50 4.50

Christmas — A403

Designs: Nos. 1091, 1093, Angel, denomination at LL. 75k, Heart. No. 1094, Angel, denomination at LR.

2006, Nov. 2 ***Perf. 13½x13¾***
1091 A403 55k multi 1.75 1.75
1092 A403 75k multi 1.75 1.75

Self-Adhesive
Booklet Stamps
Serpentine Die Cut 9½x9¾
1093 A403 55k multi 1.75 1.75
1094 A403 55k multi 1.75 1.75
a. Booklet pane, 5 each #1093-1094 20.00 —
Nos. 1091-1094 (4) 7.00 7.00

Women's Rights in Iceland, Cent. — A404

Perf. 13½x13¼
2007, Feb. 15 **Litho.**
1095 A404 60k multi 1.60 1.60

Fishing Trawler Jón Forseti, Cent. A405

2007, Feb. 15 ***Perf. 13¾x13½***
1096 A405 65k multi 1.75 1.75

Geothermal Energy A406

2007, Feb. 15 ***Perf. 14***
1097 A406 75k multi 2.00 2.00

West Nordic Council, 10th anniv.

Souvenir Sheet

Intl. Polar Year — A407

2007, Feb. 15 ***Perf. 14x13½***
1098 A407 Sheet of 2 4.75 4.75
a. 75k Volcano 2.00 2.00
b. 95k Ice cap mapping equipment 2.75 2.75

Youth Organization of Iceland, Cent. — A408

2007, Apr. 20 ***Perf. 14***
1099 A408 70k multi 2.00 2.00

National Archives, 125th Anniv. — A409

2007, Apr. 20 ***Perf. 12½***
1100 A409 80k multi 2.25 2.25
a. Tete-beche pair, with tabs 5.00 5.00

Organized Forestry in Iceland, Cent. — A410

Various tree branches with frame color of: 10k, Olive green. 60k, Rose carmine.

2007, Apr. 20 ***Perf. 14***
1101-1102 A410 Set of 2 3.50 3.50
1101a Perf. 13½x14 *.90 .90*
1102a Perf. 13½x14 *5.25 5.25*

Issued: 1101a, 1102a, 11/6/08.

Cargo Boats A411

No. 1103: a, Hamrafell. b, Tröllafoss.
No. 1104: a, Langjökull. b, Akranes.

Perf. 13 on 2 or 3 Sides
2007, Apr. 20 **Booklet Stamps**
1103 Pair 4.50 4.50
a.-b. A411 80k Either single 2.25 2.25
c. Booklet pane, 2 #1103 9.00 —
Complete booklet, #1103c 9.00
1104 Pair 5.75 5.75
a.-b. A411 105k Either single 2.75 2.75
c. Booklet pane, 2 #1104 11.00 —
Complete booklet, #1104c 11.00

Glaciers A412

Designs: 5k, Breithamerkurjökull. 60k, Eystri Hagafellsjökull and Langjökull, vert. 80k, Mulajökull and Hofsjökull. 110k, Snaefellsjökull. 300k, Hvannadalshnúkur and Oraefajökull (70x30mm).

2007, May 24 ***Perf. 14x13¼***
1105-1109 A412 Set of 5 16.00 16.00
1109a Booklet pane, #1105-1109 25.00 —
Complete booklet, #1109a 25.00

No. 1109a sold for 750k.

Europa — A413

Designs: 80k, Scouting fleur-de-lis. 105k, Scouting clover emblem.

2007, May 24 ***Perf. 13¼***
1110 A413 80k multi 2.25 2.25
1111 A413 105k multi 2.75 2.75

Booklet Stamps
Self-Adhesive
Die Cut
1112 A413 80k multi 2.25 2.25
a. Booklet pane of 10 22.50 22.50
1113 A413 105k multi 2.25 2.25
a. Booklet pane of 10 22.50
Nos. 1110-1113 (4) 9.50 9.50

Scouting, cent.

Soil Conservation Service, Cent. — A414

Perf. 13¾x14¼
2007, May 24 **Photo.**
1114 A414 (60k) multi 1.75 1.75

Self-Adhesive
Serpentine Die Cut 12
1115 A414 (60k) multi 1.75 1.75

No. 1114 was printed in a sheet of 10, No. 1115 was printed in a folded sheet of 50.

Berries Type of 2005

Designs: 120k, Vaccinium myrtillus. 145k, Cornus suecica.

2007, Sept. 20 **Litho.** ***Perf. 14***
1116 A385 120k multi 3.00 3.00
a. Tete-beche pair 6.50 6.50
1117 A385 145k multi 4.00 4.00
a. Tete-beche pair 8.50 8.50

New Bible Translation — A415

Litho. With Foil Application
2007, Sept. 20 ***Perf. 13½***
1118 A415 60k multi 1.75 1.75

Souvenir Sheet

Royal Visit, Cent. — A416

Litho. & Engr.

2007, Sept. 20 ***Perf. 13x13¼***

1119 A416 250k multi 7.00 7.00

Jökulsá Canyon and Selfoss Waterfall — A417

No. 1120: a, Jökulsá Canyon (45x29mm). b, Selfoss Waterfall (30x29mm)

2007, Oct. 1 Litho. ***Perf. 13¼x13¾***

1120 A417 Horiz. pair 5.00 5.00
a. 80k multi 2.25 2.25
b. 105k multi 2.75 2.75

Insects Type of 2004

Designs: 70k, Prionocera turcica. 190k, Euceraphis punctipennis.

2007, Nov. 8 Litho. ***Perf. 14***

1121-1122 A375 Set of 2 6.75 6.75

Jónas Hallgrímsson (1807-45), Poet — A418

2007, Nov. 8 Engr. ***Perf. 12¾x13***

1123 A418 65k brown 1.60 1.60

Kleppur Psychiatric Hospital, Cent. — A419

2007, Nov. 8 Litho. ***Perf. 13¼***

1124 A419 80k multi 2.25 2.25

Christmas A420

Various cut patterns in Icelandic leaf bread: 60k, 80k.

2007, Nov. 8 ***Serpentine Die Cut***

Self-Adhesive

1125 A420 60k red & multi 1.75 1.75
a. Booklet pane of 10 17.50
1126 A420 80k grn & multi 2.25 2.25

Teachers' College of Iceland, Cent. — A421

2008, Feb. 14 Litho. ***Perf. 14x13¼***

1127 A421 85k multi 2.25 2.25

Kisses — A422

Lines from poem by Erla Thorsteindottir and people kissing with photograph colors in: No. 1128, 65k, Blue. No. 1129, 65k, Sepia. 75k, Green. 85k, Red violet.

2008, Feb. 14

1128-1131 A422 Set of 4 6.50 6.50

Agricultural Tools — A423

No. 1132: a, Ferguson tractor. b, International Harvester TD6 bulldozer.
No. 1133: a, Horse-drawn plow. b, Lanz turfkiller.

2008, Mar. 27 Litho. ***Perf. 13¼***

Booklet Stamps

1132 Pair 4.50 4.50
a.-b. A423 85k Either single 2.25 2.25
c. Booklet pane, 2 #1132 9.00
Complete booklet, #1132c 9.00
1133 Pair 6.00 6.00
a.-b. A423 110k Either single 3.00 3.00
c. Booklet pane, 2 #1133 12.00
Complete booklet, #1133c 12.00

Embroidery — A424

Designs: 65k, Refilsaumur. 85k, Augnsaumur. 110k, Krosssaumur.

2008, Mar. 27 ***Perf. 14***

1134-1136 A424 Set of 3 7.50 7.50

Souvenir Sheet

Snaefellsnes — A425

2008, Mar. 27 ***Perf. 14x13¼***

1137 A425 120k multi 3.00 3.00

Personalized Stamp — A426

Serpentine Die Cut 10 Syncopated

2008, May 8 Self-Adhesive Litho.

1138 A426 (75k) multi 2.00 2.00

The vignette of the stamp shown above is the generic image for the issue, which was available at face value. Other images with the stamp frame shown are personalized stamps which sold for 3120k for a sheet of 24 stamps.

Geothermal Space Heating, Cent. — A427

2008, May 8 ***Perf. 14x13½***

1139 A427 75k multi 2.00 2.00

Hafnarfjördhur, Cent. — A428

2008, May 8 ***Perf. 13x12½***

1140 A428 80k multi 2.00 2.00

Icelandic Industrial Design A429

Designs: 65k, Proprio Foot prosthetic foot. 120k, Marel OptiCut volumetric portioning and meat cutting machine. 155k, Wish fly fishing reel. 200k, Gavia submarine.

2008, May 8 ***Perf. 12½x13***

1141-1144 A429 Set of 4 13.50 13.50
1141a Tête-bêche pair 3.25 3.25
1142a Tête-bêche pair 5.75 5.75
1143a Tête-bêche pair 6.75 6.75

Europa — A430

Letter folded into: 85k, Boat. 110k, Airplane.

2008, May 8 ***Perf. 14***

1145 A430 85k multi 2.25 2.25
1146 A430 110k multi 2.75 2.75

Booklet Stamps

Self-Adhesive

Serpentine Die Cut 9½x10

1147 A430 85k multi 2.25 2.25
a. Booklet pane of 10 22.50
1148 A430 110k multi 2.75 2.75
a. Booklet pane of 10 27.50

Knight and Final Position of 1958 Chess Match Between Fridhrik Olafsson and Bobby Fischer — A431

2008, Sept. 18 Litho. ***Perf. 13¼***

1149 A431 80k multi 1.60 1.60

First Cod War, 50th Anniv. A432

2008, Sept. 18 ***Perf. 13¼x13***

1150 A432 90k multi 1.75 1.75

Aegagropila Linnaei — A433

2008, Sept. 18 ***Perf. 13¼x13¾***

1151 A433 140k multi 2.75 2.75

Souvenir Sheet

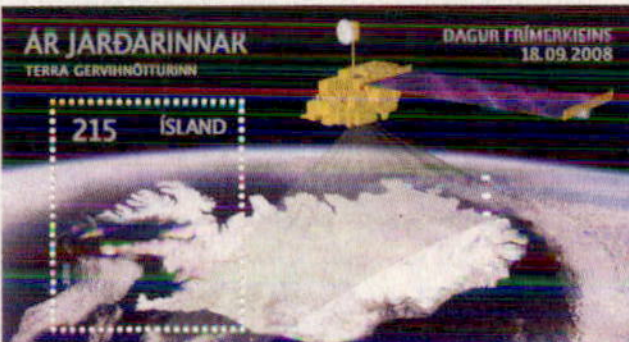

Intl. Year of Planet Earth — A434

2008, Sept. 18

1152 A434 215k multi 4.00 4.00

Stamp Day.

Peace Tower, Videy — A435

2008, Oct. 9 Litho. ***Perf. 13¼***

1153 A435 120k multi + label 2.40 2.40

Parts of the design were printed with a glow-in-the-dark ink.

Forestry Type of 2005 Redrawn and

Forestry in Vaglaskógur, Cent. — A436

2008, Nov. 6 Litho. *Perf. 13½x14*
1154 A436 400k multi 8.00 8.00
1155 Booklet pane of 4, #1101a, 1102a, 1154, 1155a *55.00 55.00*
a. A377 45k multi, denomination as "45" only *14.00 28.00*
Complete booklet, #1155 *55.00 55.00*

No. 1155 sold for 800k.

Christmas A437

Winning designs in children's stamp art contest: 70k, Christmas goblin Stiff-legs, by Heidhar Jökull Hafsteinsson. 90k, Christmas Cat, by Konrádh Kárason Thormar.

Serpentine Die Cut 12½
2008, Nov. 6 Self-Adhesive
1156 A437 70k multi 1.50 1.50
a. Booklet pane of 10 15.00
1157 A437 90k multi 1.75 1.75

Vertical pairs in booklet pane are tete-beche.

Islands Type of 2001

Designs: 75k, Hjörsey. 90k, Málmey.

2009, Jan. 29 Litho. *Perf. 14*
1158-1159 A335 Set of 2 3.25 3.25

Insects Type of 2004

Designs: 80k, Psychodidae. 120k, Gnaphosidae (spider).

2009, Jan. 29
1160-1161 A375 Set of 2 4.00 4.00

Souvenir Sheet

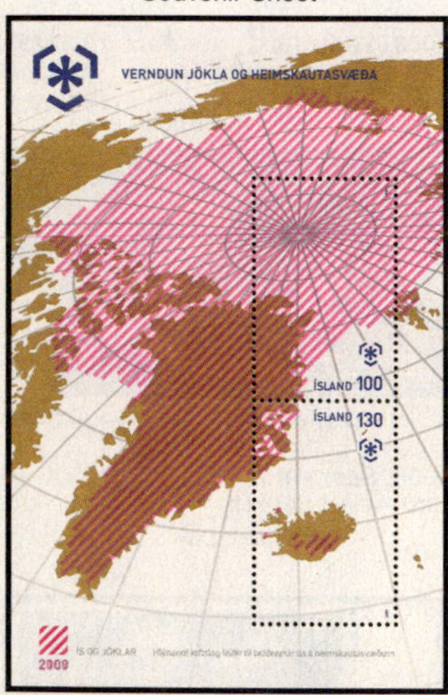

Intl. Polar Year — A438

No. 1162 — Map of ice cover of: a, 100k, North Pole, Northern Greenland. b, 130k, Iceland, Eastern Greenland.

Litho. & Photo.
2009, Jan. 29 *Perf. 13x13½*
1162 A438 Sheet of 2, #a-b 4.50 4.50

Parts of the design were printed with a thermographic ink that disappeared when warmed.

Civil Aviation in Iceland, 90th Anniv. A439

No. 1163: a, Avro 504K. b, Waco ZKS-7.
No. 1164: a, Boeing 757. b, Fokker 50.

Perf. 14¼ Horiz.
2009, Mar. 19 Litho.
Booklet Stamps
1163 Vert. pair 3.75 3.75
a.-b. A439 90k Either single 1.75 1.75
c. Booklet pane, 2 #1163 7.00 —
Complete booklet, #1163c 7.00
1164 Vert. pair 5.75 5.75
a.-b. A439 120k Either single 2.75 2.75
c. Booklet pane, 2 #1164 11.00 —
Complete booklet, #1164c 11.00

Miniature Sheet

Legendary Creatures from Folktales — A440

No. 1165: a, Hrosshvalur. b, Skoffín. c, Múshveli. d, Raudhkembingur. e, Selamódhir. f, Ofuguggi. g, Saeneyti. h, Skeljaskrímsli. i, Urdharkött tur. j, Fjörulalli.

2009, Mar. 19 *Perf. 13¼*
1165 A440 80k Sheet of 10, #a-j 17.00 17.00

Reykjavik Water Works, Cent. — A441

2009, May 7 Litho. *Perf. 12½*
1166 A441 10k multi .25 .25

Iceland Youth Organization National Tournaments, Cent. — A442

2009, May 7 *Perf. 13¼*
1167 A442 105k multi 2.25 2.25

Skrúdhur Garden, Cent. — A443

2009, May 7 *Perf. 12½*
1168 A443 140k multi 3.00 3.00

Europa — A444

Designs: 105k, Sun and shadows at different times. 140k, Observatory.

2009, May 7 *Perf. 13¼*
1169 A444 105k multi 2.25 2.25
1170 A444 140k multi 3.00 3.00

Booklet Stamps
Self-Adhesive
Serpentine Die Cut 9¾x10
1171 A444 105k multi 2.25 2.25
a. Booklet pane of 10 22.50
1172 A444 140k multi 3.00 3.00
a. Booklet pane of 10 30.00

Intl. Year of Astronomy.

Souvenir Sheet

Nordia 2009 Philatelic Exhibition, Hafnarfjördhur — A445

2009, May 7 *Perf. 13*
1173 A445 190k multi 4.50 4.50

Icelandic Sheep A446

Shepherds and sheep in: 95k, Open pasture. 160k, Pen, vert.

Perf. 12½x13, 13x12½
2009, Sept. 16
1174-1175 A446 Set of 2 5.00 5.00

Skaftafell, Vatnajökull National Park — A447

No. 1176 — Denomination at: a, UL (45x30mm). b, UR (30x30mm).

2009, Sept. 16 *Perf. 13½x14*
1176 A447 120k Horiz. pair, #a-b 4.75 4.75

Souvenir Sheet

National Center for Cultural Heritage, Cent. — A448

2009, Sept. 16 *Perf. 13*
1177 A448 150k multi 3.50 3.50

Stamp Day.

Birds — A449

Designs: 110k, Uria lomvia. 130k, Larus hyperboreus.

2009, Nov. 5 *Perf. 13x13¼*
1178-1179 A449 Set of 2 4.75 4.75

Thingvellir Church, 150th Anniv. — A450

2009, Nov. 5
1180 A450 190k multi 4.00 4.00

Christmas A451

Stained-glass windows: (70k), The Sermon on the Mount, by Gudmundur Einarsson. 120k, Holy Mother of God, by Finnur Jónsson.

2009, Nov. 5 *Die Cut Perf. 13½*
Self-Adhesive
1181 A451 (70k) multi 1.75 1.75
a. Booklet pane of 10 17.50
1182 A451 120k multi 2.40 2.40

Seals A452

Designs: 5k, Phoca vitulina. 220k, Phoca groenlandica.

2010, Jan. 28 Litho. *Perf. 13¼x13¾*
1183-1184 A452 Set of 2 3.50 3.50

Home Furnishings — A453

Designs: 75k, Hanger tree, designed by Katrin Olina Pétursdóttir and Michael Young. 140k, Tango chair, designed by Sigurdhur Gústafsson. 155k, MGO 180 dining room table, designed by Gudhrún M. Olafsdóttir and Oddgeir Thórdharson, horiz. 165k, Dimon sofa, designed by Erla Sólveig Oskarsdóttir.

Perf. 13¼x12½, 12½x13¼

2010, Jan. 28

1185-1188	A453	Set of 4	7.50	7.50
1185a		Tête-bêche pair	2.40	2.40
1186a		Tête-bêche pair	4.50	4.50
1187a		Tête-bêche pair	5.00	5.00
1188a		Tête-bêche pair	5.25	5.25

Wood and Bone Carvings A454

Designs: 10k, Door of Valthjófsstadhir. Nos. 1190, 1192, (75k), Judge's drinking horn. 200k, Play in Leaves, sculpture by Sigrídhur Jóna Kristjánsdóttir.

2010, Mar. 18 *Perf. 14x13¼, 13¼x14*

1189-1191 A454 Set of 3 4.50 4.50

Self-Adhesive

Serpentine Die Cut 12

Size: 32x27mm

1192 A454 (75k) multi 1.25 1.25

Fishing Trawlers — A455

No. 1193: a, Bjarni Riddari GK 1. b, Ingólfur Arnarson RE 201.

No. 1194: a, Sólborg IS 260. b, Hardhbakur EA 3.

2010, Mar. 18 *Perf. 14 Horiz.*

Booklet Stamps

1193	Vert. pair	2.50	2.50
a.-b.	A455 75k Either single	1.25	1.25
c.	Booklet pane, 2 #1193	5.00	—
	Complete booklet, #1193c	5.00	
1194	Vert. pair	5.25	5.25
a.-b.	A455 165k Either single	2.60	2.60
c.	Booklet pane, 2 #1194	10.50	—
	Complete booklet, #1194c	10.50	

Souvenir Sheet

Life by the Sea — A456

No. 1195: a, Man rolling herring barrel. b, Women filling herring barrels, fish.

2010, Mar. 18 *Perf. 13¼x14*

1195 A456 75k Sheet of 2, #a-b 2.50 2.50

Europa A457

Illustrations from children's books: 165k, The Fate of the Gods, by Ingunn Asdísardóttir and Kristin Ragna Gunnarsdóttir. 220k, Good Evening, by Aslaug Jónsdóttir.

2010, May 6 **Litho.** *Perf. 13¾x14*

1196 A457 165k multi 2.60 2.60

1197 A457 220k multi 3.50 3.50

Booklet Stamps

Self-Adhesive

Die Cut Perf. 13¼

1198	A457 165k multi	2.60	2.60
a.	Booklet pane of 10	26.00	
1199	A457 220k multi	3.50	3.50
a.	Booklet pane of 10	35.00	

Garden Parks — A458

Designs: 90k, Jónsgardhur, Isafjödhur. 130k, Hellisgerdhi, Hafnarfjödhur. 285k, Skalla-grímsgardhur, Borgarnes, horiz.

Perf. 13¼x13¾, 13¾x13¼

2010, May 6

1200-1202 A458 Set of 3 7.00 7.00

A460

Personalized Stamps — A461

Serpentine Die Cut 10 Syncopated

2010, May 6 **Self-Adhesive**

1203 A460 (165k) silver & blue 2.50 2.50

1204 A461 (220k) bronze & brn 3.00 3.00

The vignettes shown above of Nos. 1203-1204 are generic images. The vignette portion of the stamp could be personalized.

Souvenir Sheet

Iceland Pavilion, Expo 2010, Shanghai — A462

2010, May 6 *Perf. 13x12½x12¾x13*

1205 A462 130k multi 2.25 2.25

A463

A464

2010 Eruption of Eyjafjallajökull Volcano — A465

Litho. & Silk-screened

2010, July 22 *Perf. 13¼*

1206	A463 (75k) multi	1.25	1.25
1207	A464 (165k) multi	2.50	2.50
1208	A465 (220k) multi	3.00	3.00
	Nos. 1206-1208 (3)	6.75	6.75

Volcanic ash from the eruption was added to the ink used on the silk-screened parts of Nos. 1206-1208.

Vífilstadhir Sanatorium, Cent. — A466

Perf. 13½x13¼

2010, Sept. 16 **Litho.**

1209 A466 (90k) multi 2.25 2.25

2010 Youth Olympics, Singapore A467

2010, Sept. 16 *Perf. 13x12½*

1210 A467 165k multi 2.50 2.50

Gas Lighting In Reykjavik, 150th Anniv. — A468

2010, Sept. 16 *Perf. 13*

1211 A468 450k multi 6.25 6.25

Souvenir Sheet

Intl. Year of Biodiversity — A469

No. 1212: a, Hawk, wolf, rodent. b, Fish, duck.

2010, Sept. 16 *Perf. 13¼*

1212 A469 90k Sheet of 2, #a-b 3.00 3.00

Visir Newspaper, Cent. — A470

2010, Nov. 4 **Litho.** *Perf. 13*

1213 A470 140k drab & blk 2.25 2.25

Foss, by Isleifur Konrádhsson — A471

Skeggjadhur Madhur og Blómaflúr, by Sölvi Helgason A472

Breidhfirskur Víkingur, by Sigurlaug Jónasdóttir A473

Fiskar, by Karl Einarsson Dunganon A474

2010, Nov. 4

1214	A471 (75k) multi	1.25	1.25
1215	A472 (90k) multi	1.40	1.40
1216	A473 (165k) multi	2.60	2.60
1217	A474 (220k) multi	3.25	3.25
	Nos. 1214-1217 (4)	8.50	8.50

A booklet containing single stamps of Nos. 1214-1217 in mounts sold for 1,550k.

Wreath and Dove — A475

Wreath and Two Doves — A476

2010, Nov. 4 ***Die Cut Perf. 13¾***

Self-Adhesive

1218 A475 (75k) multi 1.25 .90
a. Booklet pane of 10 12.50
1219 A476 (165k) multi 2.60 2.60

Halichoerus Grypus — A477

Phoca Hispida A478

2011, Jan. 27 **Litho.** ***Perf. 13¼x13¾***
1220 A477 (90k) multi 3.00 3.00
1221 A478 (220k) multi 1.75 1.75

Branta Leucopsis A479

Melanitta Nigra A480

Anser Albifrons A481

Anas Strepera A482

2011, Jan. 27
1222 A479 (75k) multi 1.75 1.75
1223 A480 (75k) multi 1.75 1.75
1224 A481 (165k) multi 2.75 2.75
1225 A482 (165k) multi 2.75 2.75
Nos. 1222-1225 (4) 8.50 8.50

Worldwide Fund for Nature (WWF).

Motor Sports A483

No. 1226 — Inscriptions: a, Mótokross. b, Rally.
No. 1227 — Inscriptions: a, Torfaera. b, Kvartmíla.

2011, Mar. 17 **Litho.** ***Perf. 14 Horiz.***

Booklet Stamps

1226 A483 Vert. pair 2.50 2.50
a.-b. (75k) Either single 1.25 1.25
c. Booklet pane, 2 #1226 5.00 —
Complete booklet, #1226c 5.00 —
1227 A483 Vert. pair 5.50 5.50
a.-b. (165k) Either single 2.75 2.75
c. Booklet pane, 2 #1227 11.00 —
Complete booklet, #1227c 11.00 —

Langanes Lighthouse A484

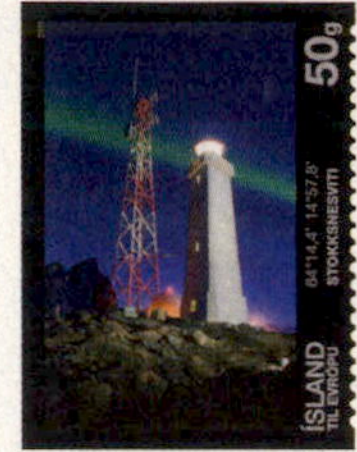

Stokknes Lighthouse A485

Die Cut Perf. 13¼ at Bottom

2011, Mar. 17 **Self-Adhesive**
1228 A484 (75k) multi 1.75 1.75

Die Cut Perf. 13¼ at Right

1229 A485 (165k) multi 2.75 2.75

Tree Rings and Table A486

Leaf and Curved Arrows A487

Litho. With Foil Application

2011, Mar. 17 ***Perf. 13¾x14***
1230 A486 (165k) multi 2.50 2.50
1231 A487 (220k) multi 3.50 3.50

Booklet Stamps Self-Adhesive

Die Cut Perf. 13¼

1232 A486 (165k) multi 2.60 2.60
a. Booklet pane of 10 26.00
1233 A487 (220k) multi 3.50 3.50
a. Booklet pane of 10 35.00

Europa, Intl. Year of Forests.

University of Iceland, Cent. — A488

2011, May 4 **Litho.** ***Perf. 12½x13***
1234 A488 (75k) multi 1.25 1.25

Melavöllur Stadium, Reykjavik, Cent. A489

2011, May 4 ***Perf. 13¼***
1235 A489 (130k) multi 2.25 1.75

Austurvöllur Park, Reykjavik — A490

Parliament Park, Reykjavik — A491

2011, May 4 ***Perf. 13¼x12½***
1236 A490 (90k) multi 1.75 1.75
1237 A491 (285k) multi 4.00 4.00

Miniature Sheet

Opening of Harpa Reykjavik Concert Hall and Conference Center — A492

No. 1238 — Portions of building facade in colors of: a, Black and blue green. b, Black and gray with country name on white area. c, Black and gray with country name on gray area. d, Black and pink. e, Black and yellow green. Stamps are polygonal and various sizes.

2011, May 4 **Litho. & Engr.** ***Die Cut***

Self-Adhesive

1238 A492 Sheet of 5 8.50
a.-e. (75k) Any single 1.75 1.75

Pres. Jón Sigurdhsson (1811-79) A493

Sigurdhsson as: Nos. 1239, 1241a, Young man. No. 1240, Old man.

2011, June 17 **Litho.** ***Perf. 13***
1239 A493 (75k) multi 1.25 1.25
1240 A493 1000k multi, year date 2¼mm wide 14.00 14.00
a. Year date 2½mm wide 14.00 14.00

Souvenir Sheet

1241 Sheet of 2, #1240a, 1241a 17.50 17.50
a. A493 100k multi 1.60 1.60

Wetlands Conservation A494

2011, Sept. 15 ***Perf. 13¼***
1242 A494 (90k) multi 1.25 1.25

Amnesty International, 50th Anniv. — A495

2011, Sept. 15 ***Perf. 13½x14***
1243 A495 (285k) yel & blk 4.00 4.00

Snaefell Glacier National Park — A496

No. 1244: a, Mountain (45x29mm). b, Mountain, diff. (30x29mm).

2011, Sept. 15 ***Perf. 13¼x13¾***
1244 A496 Horiz. pair 4.00 4.00
a.-b. (165k) Either single 2.00 2.00

Souvenir Sheet

Fishing Boat at Húsavik — A497

2011, Sept. 15 ***Perf. 13x13¼***
1245 A497 (165k) multi 2.00 2.00

See Malta No. 1438.

Souvenir Sheet

Saga of Burnt Niall — A498

No. 1246: a, Flying horseman carrying torch. b, Burning of Niall and family. c, Swordsman raising sword, dead swordsman.

2011, Sept. 15 ***Perf. 12½***
1246 A498 Sheet of 3 6.75 6.75
a.-c. (110k) Any single 2.25 2.25

Sólarlag vidh Tjörnina, by Thórarinn B. Thorláksson — A499

Botnssúlur, by Asgrímur Jónsson A500

Utreidharfólk, by Jón Stefánsson — A501

Fornar Slódhir, by Jóhannes Kjarval A502

2011, Nov. 3 Litho. ***Perf. 13x13¼***

1247	A499	(90k) multi	1.75	1.75
1248	A500	(110k) multi	2.25	2.25
1249	A501	(165k) multi	2.75	2.75
1250	A502	(220k) multi	2.75	2.75
	Nos. 1247-1250 (4)		9.50	9.50

A503

Christmas A504

Die Cut Perf. 13¾x13½
2011, Nov. 3 Litho. & Embossed
Self-Adhesive

1251	A503	(90k) multi	1.25	.90
a.	Booklet pane of 10		12.50	
1252	A504	(165k) multi	2.25	2.25

National Olympic and Sports Association, Cent. — A505

2012, Jan. 26 Litho. ***Perf. 13¼x13¾***

1253	A505	(97k) multi	1.25	1.25

Landmannalaugar — A506

Lake Hnausapollur A507

2012, Jan. 26 ***Perf. 13¾***

1254	A506	(175k) multi	2.75	2.75
1255	A507	(230k) multi	2.75	2.75

Silver Chalice, 15th Cent. — A508

Silver Headdress, by Sigurdhar Gudhmundsson — A509

Silver Bowl, by Pétur Tryggvi Hjálmarsson A510

Silver Chalice, 15th Cent. — A511

2012, Jan. 26 ***Perf. 13¼x14, 14x13¼***

1256	A508	(97k) multi	1.25	1.25
1257	A509	(175k) multi	1.25	1.25
1258	A510	(230k) multi	3.00	3.00
	Nos. 1256-1258 (3)		5.50	5.50

Self-Adhesive
Serpentine Die Cut 12

1259	A511	(97k) multi	1.25	1.25

Shoes and Socks Designed by Hugrún Dögg Arnadóttir and Magni Thorsteinsson — A512

Dress Designed by Steinunn Sigurdardottir — A513

Wool Sweater Designed by Bergthora Gudnadottir — A514

Coat Designed by 66 Degrees North — A515

2012, Mar. 22 ***Perf. 12½x13***

1260	A512	(97k) multi	1.25	1.25
1261	A513	(110k) multi	1.75	1.75
1262	A514	(175k) multi	2.75	2.75
1263	A515	(230k) multi	2.75	2.75
	Nos. 1260-1263 (4)		8.50	8.50

Waterfall A516

Aluminum A517

Geothermal Energy A518

Tomatoes A519

Booklet Stamps

Serpentine Die Cut 13¼

2012, Mar. 22 **Self-Adhesive**

1264	A516	(75k) multi	1.25	1.25
1265	A517	(75k) multi	1.25	1.25
a.	Booklet pane of 4, 2 each #1264-1265		5.00	
1266	A518	(175k) multi	2.75	2.75
1267	A519	(175k) multi	2.75	2.75
a.	Booklet pane of 4, 2 each #1266-1267		11.00	
	Nos. 1264-1267 (4)		8.00	8.00

Green energy.

Souvenir Sheet

Sea Rescue — A520

2012, Mar. 22 ***Perf. 14¼x14¾***

1268	A520	(155k) multi	3.50	3.50

Akureyri, 150th Anniv. A521

2012, May 3 ***Perf. 14x13½***

1269	A521	(75k) multi	1.25	1.25
a.	With period after "08"		1.25	1.25

No. 1269 is missing period after "08". Issued: No. 1269a, 7/2.

Scouting in Iceland, Cent. A522

2012, May 3 ***Perf. 13¾***

1270	A522	(75k) multi	1.25	1.25

2012 Summer Olympics, London A523

2012, May 3 ***Perf. 14x13½***

1271	A523	(580k) multi	8.00	8.00

Akureyri Park, Akureyri — A524

Hallargardhur Park, Reykjavik — A525

2012, May 3 ***Perf. 13¼***

1272	A524	(225k) multi	4.00	4.00
1273	A525	(300k) multi	4.00	4.00

Geyser — A526

Aurora Borealis — A527

2012, May 3 ***Serpentine Die Cut 18***
Self-Adhesive

1274 A526 (175k) multi 3.00 3.00
1275 A527 (230k) multi 3.00 3.00

Booklet Stamps
Serpentine Die Cut 18 on 3 Sides

1276 A526 (175k) multi 3.00 3.00
a. Booklet pane of 10 30.00
1277 A527 (230k) multi 3.00 3.00
a. Booklet pane of 10 30.00

Europa.

No. 1150 Surcharged

Method and Perf. As Before
2012, July 2
1278 A432 (103k) on 90k #1150 1.60 1.60

Russula Xerampelina A528

2012, July 2 Litho. ***Perf. 13¼x12¾***
1279 A528 (103k) multi 1.25 1.25

Cystophora Cristata — A529

Odobenus Rosmarus — A530

2012, Sept. 13 ***Perf. 13¼x13¾***
1280 A529 (475k) multi 4.00 4.00
1281 A530 (480k) multi 7.00 7.00

Engey Lighthouse A531

Kálfshamar Lighthouse A532

Die Cut Perf. 13¼ at Bottom
2012, Sept. 13 **Self-Adhesive**
1282 A531 (103k) multi 1.75 1.75
Die Cut Perf. 13¼ at Right
1283 A532 (175k) multi 3.00 3.00

Souvenir Sheet

Archaeological Excavations at Skridhuklaustur — A533

2012, Sept. 13 ***Perf. 14x13¼***
1284 A533 (565k) multi 7.00 7.00

Consecration of Skridhuklaustur Church, 500th anniv.

Boletus Edulis A534

2012, Nov. 1 ***Perf. 13¼x12¾***
1285 A534 (103k) multi 1.25 1.25

Dapri Prinsinn, by Gudhmundur Thorsteinsson — A535

Uppstilling, by Kristín Jónsdóttir A536

Frá Vestmannaeyjum, by Júlíana Sveinsdóttir — A537

Módhurást, Sculpture by Nína Saemundsson A538

2012, Nov. 1 ***Perf. 14x13¼***
1286 A535 (120k) multi 1.75 1.75
1287 A536 (125k) multi 2.25 2.25
1288 A537 (175k) multi 2.75 2.75
Perf. 13¼x14
1289 A538 (230k) multi 2.75 2.75
Nos. 1286-1289 (4) 9.50 9.50

A539

Christmas A540

Self-Adhesive
Litho. With Foil Application
2012, Nov. 1 ***Die Cut Perf. 13½***
1290 A539 (120k) multi 1.25 .90
a. Booklet pane of 10 12.50
1291 A540 (175k) multi 2.25 2.25

Intl. Year of Water Cooperation A541

2013, Jan. 24 Litho. ***Perf. 13¾x13½***
1292 A541 (103k) multi 1.25 1.25

Aldeyjarfoss A542

Hafursey A543

2013, Jan. 24 ***Perf. 13¾***
1293 A542 (175k) multi 2.75 2.75
1294 A543 (230k) multi 2.75 2.75

National Museum, 150th Anniv. — A544

Self-Adhesive
2013, Jan. 24 ***Perf. 13½***
1295 A544 (125k) rose & blue 2.25 2.25

Puffin, by Sigurdur Oddsson — A545

Sofa, by Ragnar Freyr Pálsson — A546

An All Icelandic Hot Dog, by Rán Flygenring A547

Horses, by Sigurdur Eggertsson A548

2013, Mar. 14 ***Perf. 13¼x14***
1296 A545 (120k) multi 1.25 1.25
1297 A546 (155k) multi 2.75 2.75
1298 A547 (300k) multi 4.00 4.00
1299 A548 (475k) multi 4.00 4.00
Nos. 1296-1299 (4) 12.00 12.00

A549

Motor Vehicles A550

Designs: No. 1300, 1931 Ford AA truck. No. 1301, 1942-43 Chevrolet dual purpose vehicle. No. 1302, 1957 Mercedes-Benz bus. No. 1303, 1955, Bedford fire engine.

2013, Mar. 14 ***Die Cut Perf. 13¼***
Booklet Stamps
Self-Adhesive

1300 A549 (103k) multi 1.25 1.25
1301 A549 (103k) multi 1.25 1.25
a. Booklet pane of 4, 2 each #1300-1301 5.00
1302 A550 (175k) multi 2.75 2.75
1303 A550 (175k) multi 2.75 2.75
a. Booklet pane of 4, 2 each #1302-1303 11.00
Nos. 1300-1303 (4) 8.00 8.00

Reykjavik Gay Pride Parade — A551

Never Been South Music Festival, Isafjördhur A552

Great Fish Day — A553

Smelter Music Festival, Borganfjordur Eystri — A554

Vestmannaeyjar National Holiday — A555

2013, May 2 ***Perf. 13¾x14¼***

Self-Adhesive

1304 A551 (103k) multi 1.25 1.25
1305 A552 (103k) multi 1.25 1.25
1306 A553 (120k) multi 1.25 1.25
1307 A554 (120k) multi 1.25 1.25
1308 A555 (120k) multi 1.25 1.25
Nos. 1304-1308 (5) 6.25 6.25

2012 Ford Transit Mail Van A556

2010 Man TGS Mail Truck A557

Serpentine Die Cut 13½

2013, May 2

Self-Adhesive

1309 A556 (175k) multi 2.75 2.75
1310 A557 (230k) multi 2.75 2.75

Booklet Stamps

Serpentine Die Cut 13½ on 3 Sides

1311 A556 (175k) multi 2.75 2.75
a. Booklet pane of 10 27.50
1312 A557 (230k) multi 2.75 2.75
a. Booklet pane of 10 27.50

Europa.

Miniature Sheet

Aurora Borealis — A558

No. 1313 — Various depictions of Aurora Borealis with: a, Brown orange sky over country name. b, White area over "til." c, Brown orange sky over "50g til." d, Light sky over "rópu" and country name.

2013, May 2 ***Die Cut Perf. 14½***

Self-Adhesive

1313 A558 Sheet of 4 11.00
a.-d. (175k) Any single 2.75 2.75

Nordia 2013 Stamp Exhibition, Gardhabaer.

Capra Hircus — A559

2013, Sept. 12 ***Perf. 13¼***

1314 A559 (175k) multi 2.75 2.75

Emergence of Surtsey Island, 50th Anniv. — A560

2013, Sept. 12 ***Perf. 13¼x13***

1315 A560 (565k) multi 7.00 7.00

Vattarnes Lighthouse A561

Skardhsfjara Lighthouse A562

Die Cut Perf. 15 at Bottom

2013, Sept. 12 **Self-Adhesive**

1316 A561 (120k) multi 1.75 1.75

Die Cut Perf. 15 at Right

1317 A562 (300k) multi 4.00 4.00

Souvenir Sheet

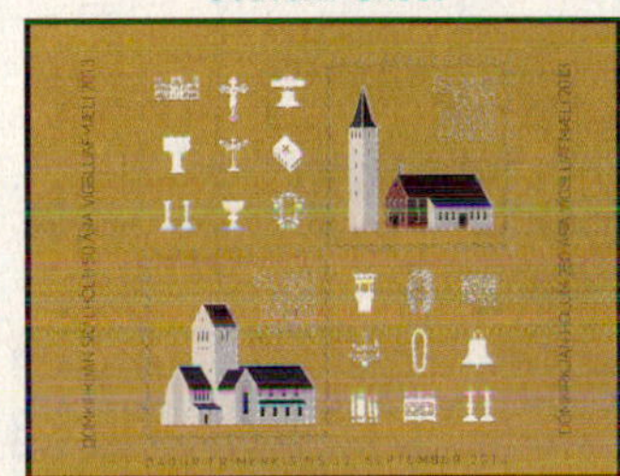
Stamp Day — A563

No. 1318: a, Hólar Cathedral (two separate buildings). b, Skalholt Cathedral (one building).

2013, Sept. 12 ***Die Cut Perf. 9***

Self-Adhesive

1318 A563 Sheet of 2 7.00
a.-b. (225k) Either single 3.50 3.50

Morgunbladhidh Newspaper, Cent. — A564

2013, Oct. 31 **Litho.** ***Perf. 13¾x13½***

1319 A564 (120k) gray & blk 1.50 1.50

Cleft in Thingvellir Lava Fieldi, by Eggert M. Laxdal (1897-1951) — A565

Stjarna's Bones, by Finnur Jónsson (1892-1993) — A566

Sulphur Waves at Landmannlaugar, by Gudhmundur Einarsson from Midhdalur (1895-1963) — A567

Herdhubreidh Mountain, by Sveinn Thórarinsson (1899-1977) — A568

2013, Oct. 31 **Litho.** ***Perf. 13x13½***

1320 A565 (103k) multi 1.40 1.40
1321 A566 (225k) multi 3.50 3.50
1322 A567 (580k) multi 8.00 8.00
1323 A568 (955k) multi 8.00 8.00
Nos. 1320-1323 (4) 20.90 20.90

A569

A570

Details from Stained-Glass Windows, Hallgrimskirkja, Reykjavik — A571

Serpentine Die Cut 9¾ Vert.

2013, Oct. 31 **Litho.**

Self-Adhesive

1324 A569 (103k) multi 1.25 1.25
1325 A570 (120k) multi 1.75 1.25
1326 A571 (175k) multi 3.00 3.00
Nos. 1324-1326 (3) 6.00 5.50

Christmas.

Protection for Haliaeetus Albicilla, Cent. — A572

2014, Jan. 16 **Litho.** ***Die Cut***

Self-Adhesive

1327 A572 (103k) multi 1.50 1.50

Statistics Iceland, Cent. — A573

2014, Jan. 16 **Litho.** ***Perf. 13¼x13***

1328 A573 (120k) multi 1.75 1.25

Icelandic Steamship Company, Cent. A574

2014, Jan. 16 **Litho.** ***Perf. 14xx13¼***

1329 A574 (175k) multi 3.00 3.00

Sjálfberg A575

Kvlár Glacier A576

2014, Jan. 16 **Litho.** ***Perf. 13¼***

1330 A575 (175k) multi 3.00 3.00
1331 A576 (230k) multi 3.00 3.00

Stoneharp, Invented by Páll Gudmundsson — A577

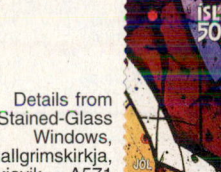

Electromagnetic Harp, Invented by Ulfur Hansson — A578

Serpentine Die Cut 10 Vert.

2014, Mar. 27 **Litho.**

Self-Adhesive

1332 A577 (175k) multi 3.00 3.00
1333 A578 (230k) multi 3.00 3.00

Europa.

Swimming Pool, Hofsós — A579

Akureyri Park Café — A580

Borgarfjördhur High School — A581

Footbridge Over Hringbraut — A582

2014, Mar. 27 Litho. *Perf. 13½*

1334 A579 (112k) multi 1.40 1.40
1335 A580 (130k) multi 1.75 1.75
1336 A581 (155k) multi 2.40 2.40
1337 A582 (175k) multi 3.00 3.00
Nos. 1334-1337 (4) 8.55 8.55

Souvenir Sheet

Container Ship — A583

2014, Mar. 27 Litho. *Perf. 13½*

1338 A583 (155k) multi 3.50 3.50

Pavilion Park, Reykjavik — A584

Klambratún, Reykjavik — A585

2014, May 8 Litho. *Perf. 13¼x13¾*

1339 A584 (130k) multi 1.75 1.75
1340 A585 (135k) multi 2.40 2.40

Lobster Festival, Höfn — A586

Herring Adventure, Siglufjördhur A587

Night of Lights, Reykjanesbaer A588

Danish Days, Stykkisholmur A589

Culture Night, Reykjavik A590

2014, May 8 Litho. *Perf. 13¾x14¼*
Self-Adhesive

1341 A586 (112k) multi 1.50 1.50
1342 A587 (112k) multi 1.75 1.75
1343 A588 (130k) multi 3.00 3.00
1344 A589 (175k) multi 3.00 3.00
1345 A590 (230k) multi 3.00 3.00
Nos. 1341-1345 (5) 12.25 12.25

A591

Fishing Vessels A592

Designs: No. 1346, Bardhi NK 120. No. 1347, Stálvík SI 1. No. 1348, Orvar HU 21. No. 1349, Breki VE 61.

Die Cut Perf. 13¼
2014, May 8 Litho.
Booklet Stamps
Self-Adhesive

1346 A591 (112k) multi 1.50 1.50
1347 A591 (112k) multi 1.50 1.50
a. Booklet pane of 4, 2 each #1346-1347 6.00
1348 A592 (175k) multi 3.00 3.00
1349 A592 (175k) multi 3.00 3.00
a. Booklet pane of 4, 2 each #1348-1349 12.00
Nos. 1346-1349 (4) 9.00 9.00

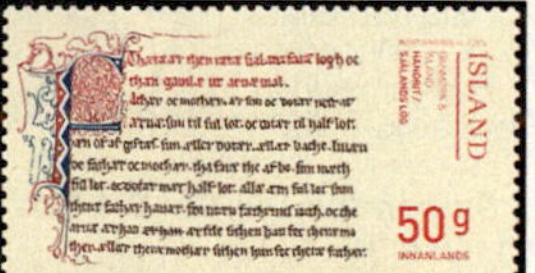

Valdemar's Law of Zealand, 13th Cent. — A593

Njáls Saga, c. 1350 A594

Litho. & Engr.
2014, Aug. 28 *Perf. 13x12¾*

1350 Sheet of 2 5.00 5.00
a. A593 (145k) multi 1.75 1.75
b. A594 (180k) multi 3.00 3.00

Self-Adhesive
Die Cut Perf. 13¼x13½

1351 A593 (145k) multi 1.75 1.75
1352 A594 (180k) multi 3.00 3.00

See Denmark Nos. 1691-1693.

Sturla Thórdharson (1214-84), Chieftain and Poet — A595

2014, Sept. 11 Litho. *Perf. 13¼*

1353 A595 (310k) multi 4.00 4.00

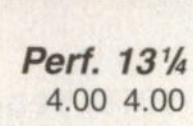

Dyrhólaey Lighthouse A596

Akranes Lighthouse A597

Die Cut Perf. 13¼ at Bottom
2014, Sept. 11 Litho.
Self-Adhesive

1354 A596 (125k) multi 1.75 1.75

Die Cut Perf. 13¼ at Right

1355 A597 (240k) multi 3.00 3.00

Two Girls with a Doll, by Snorri Arinbjarnar (1901-58) A598

Búdhin, by Gunnlaugur Scheving (1904-72) A599

Síldarstúlka, by Gunnlaugur Blöndal (1893-1962) A600

Skip vidh Bryggju, by Thorvaldur Skúlason (1906-84) A601

Perf. 13x13¼, 13¼x13
2014, Nov. 6 Litho.

1356 A598 (125k) multi 1.50 1.50
1357 A599 (145k) multi 1.75 1.75
1358 A600 (180k) multi 3.00 3.00
1359 A601 (630k) multi 9.50 9.50
Nos. 1356-1359 (4) 15.75 15.75

Nativity — A602

Annunciation A603

Adoration of the Magi — A604

Litho. & Thermography
2014, Nov. 6 *Die Cut Perf. 14*
Self-Adhesive

1360 A602 (125k) lilac & blk 1.50 1.25
a. Booklet pane of 10 15.00
1361 A603 (145k) green & blk 1.75 1.25
1362 A604 (180k) sil & blk 3.00 3.00
Nos. 1360-1362 (3) 6.25 5.50

Christmas.

Bicycles in Iceland, 125th Anniv. — A605

Serpentine Die Cut
2015, Feb. 19 Litho.
Self-Adhesive

1363 A605 (125k) multi 1.50 1.25

Iceland Airwaves Music Festival A606

2015, Feb. 19 Litho. *Perf. 13¼*

1364 A606 (180k) multi 2.75 2.75

Gatastakkur A607

Eldhraun Lava Field — A608

2015, Feb. 19 Litho. *Perf. 13¼*

1365 A607 (180k) multi 2.75 2.75
1366 A608 (240k) multi 2.75 2.75

Silver Necklace by Asthór Helgason — A609

Silver Ring by Gudhbjörg K. Ingvarsdóttir A610

Silver Necklace by Helga Osk Einarsdóttir — A611

Brooch by Helga R. Mogensen A612

Perf. 12½x13, 13x12½

2015, Feb. 19 Litho.

1367	A609 (145k) multi	1.75	1.75
1368	A610 (165k) multi	2.50	2.50
1369	A611 (180k) multi	2.75	2.75
1370	A612 (240k) multi	3.00	3.00
	Nos. 1367-1370 (4)	10.00	10.00

Icelandic Bible Society, 200th Anniv. A613

2015, Apr. 30 Litho. *Perf. 13¼x12¾*

1371	A613 (125k) multi	1.50	1.25

Woman Suffrage, Cent. — A614

2015, Apr. 30 Litho. *Perf. 13¼x13¾*

1372	A614 (145k) multi	1.50	1.25

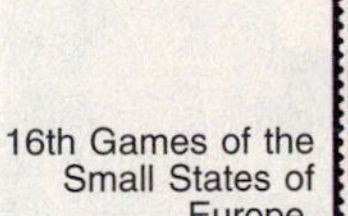

16th Games of the Small States of Europe, Iceland — A615

Die Cut Perf. 15¼x14½

2015, Apr. 30 Litho.

Self-Adhesive

1373	A615 (180k) multi	2.75	2.75

A616

Flag of Iceland, Cent. — A617

2015, Apr. 30 Litho. *Perf. 13¼*

1374	A616 (145k) multi	1.75	1.75

Litho. With Foil Application

Souvenir Sheet

Perf. 13½x13

1375	A617 (630k) multi	9.75	9.75

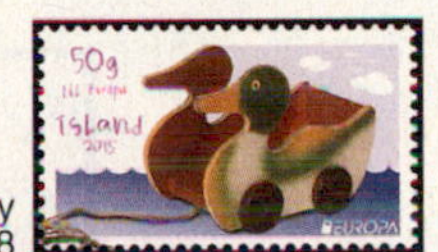

Toy Duck — A618

Toy Truck — A619

2015, Apr. 30 Litho. *Perf. 13½*

1376	A618 (180k) multi	2.75	2.75
1377	A619 (240k) multi	3.75	3.75

Booklet Stamps

Self-Adhesive

Die Cut Perf. 13½

1378	A618 (180k) multi	2.75	2.75
a.	Booklet pane of 10	27.50	
1379	A619 (240k) multi	3.75	3.75
a.	Booklet pane of 10	37.50	

Europa.

Ellidhaey Lighthouse A620

Aedhey Lighthouse A621

Die Cut Perf. 13¼ at Bottom

2015, Sept. 10 Litho.

Self-Adhesive

1380	A620 (153k) multi	2.50	2.50

Die Cut Perf. 13¼ at Right

1381	A621 (180k) multi	3.00	3.00

A622

Old Buildings A623

Designs: No. 1382, Turf shed, Vatnsfjödhur. No. 1383, Flatey Library. No. 1384, Vigur Windmill. No. 1385, Chuch, Hof.

Die Cut Perf. 14½x14¾

2015, Sept. 10 Litho.

Booklet Stamps

Self-Adhesive

1382	A622 (132k) buff & blk	2.10	2.10
1383	A622 (132k) buff & blk	2.10	2.10
a.	Booklet pane of 4, 2 each #1382-1383	8.50	
1384	A623 (180k) buff & blk	3.00	3.00
1385	A623 (180k) buff & blk	3.00	3.00
a.	Booklet pane of 4, 2 each #1384-1385	12.00	
	Nos. 1382-1385 (4)	10.20	10.20

Souvenir Sheet

International Year of Soils — A624

No. 1386: a, Grass. b, Roots.

Perf. 13¾x13¼

2015, Sept. 10 Litho.

1386	A624 Sheet of 2	8.00	8.00
a.-b.	(255k) Either single	4.00	4.00

An Heitis, by Ingibjörg Stein Bjarnason (1901-77) — A625

Orlagateningurínn, by Finnur Jónsson (1892-1993) — A626

Composition, by Baldvin Björnsson (1879-1945) A627

Hvítasunnudagsmorgunn, by Jóhannes Kjarval (1885-1972) — A628

2015, Nov. 5 Litho. *Perf. 13¼x13*

1387	A625 (132k) multi	2.00	2.00
1388	A626 (180k) multi	2.75	2.75
1389	A627 (185k) multi	3.00	3.00

Perf. 13x13¼

1390	A628 (565k) multi	8.50	8.50
	Nos. 1387-1390 (4)	16.25	16.25

Hands, Hot Drinks and Cookies A629

People Walking on Ice — A630

Computer, Cat, Musical Notes A631

Litho. With Foil Application

2015, Nov. 5 *Die Cut Perf. 11¾x12*

Self-Adhesive

1391	A629 (132k) multi	2.00	2.00
a.	Booklet pane of 10	20.00	
1392	A630 (153k) multi	2.40	2.40
1393	A631 (180k) multi	2.75	2.75
	Nos. 1391-1393 (3)	7.15	7.15

Christmas.

Icelandic Federation of Labor Unions, Cent. A632

Perf. 13¼x13½

2016, Feb. 18 Litho.

1394	A632 (137k) multi	2.10	2.10

Isafjördhur, 150th Anniv. A633

Die Cut Perf. 13¼x13½

2016, Feb. 18 Litho.

Self-Adhesive

1395	A633 (159k) multi	2.50	2.50

Icelandic Literary Society, 200th Anniv. — A634

Die Cut Perf. 15x15¾

2016, Feb. 18 **Litho.**

Self-Adhesive

1396 A634 (159k) multi	2.50	2.50

Icelandic Foods A635

Die Cut Perf. 14

2016, Feb. 18 **Litho.**

Self-Adhesive

1397 A635 (180k) multi	2.75	2.75

Sediments, Ceramic Art by Olöf Erla Bjarnadóttir A636

Jökla Dinner Service, Designed by Gudhbjörg Káradóttir and Olöf Jakobina Ernudóttir A637

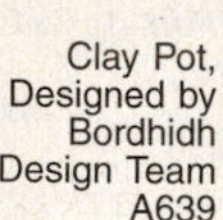

Dialog, Ceramic Art by Hanna Dís Whitehead A638

Clay Pot, Designed by Bordhidh Design Team A639

Die Cut Perf. 13¼

2016, Feb. 18 **Litho.**

Self-Adhesive

1398 A636 (137k) multi	2.10	2.10
1399 A637 (180k) multi	2.75	2.75
1400 A638 (255k) multi	4.00	4.00
1401 A639 (490k) multi	7.50	7.50
Nos. 1398-1401 (4)	16.35	16.35

2014 Eruption of Holuhraun Volcano — A640

Die Cut Perf. 12

2016, Apr. 28 **Litho.**

Self-Adhesive

1402 A640 (159k) multi	2.60	2.60

Thjofafoss Waterfall A641

Jökulsárlón Glacial Lagoon A642

2016, Apr. 28 **Litho.** ***Perf. 13¼***

1403 A641 (180k) multi	3.00	3.00
1404 A642 (240k) multi	4.00	4.00

Spring Flowers — A643

Butterflies in Summer — A644

Snowflakes in Winter — A645

Autumn Leaves — A646

Die Cut Perf. 14

2016, Apr. 28 **Litho.**

Self-Adhesive

1405 A643 (137k) multi	2.25	2.25
1406 A644 (159k) multi	2.60	2.60
1407 A645 (310k) multi	5.25	5.25
1408 A646 (985k) multi	16.00	16.00
Nos. 1405-1408 (4)	26.10	26.10

SEPAC Issue.

A647

Europa A648

2016, Apr. 28 **Litho.** ***Perf. 13¼***

1409 A647 (180k) multi	3.00	3.00
1410 A648 (240k) multi	4.00	4.00

Booklet Stamps
Self-Adhesive

Die Cut Perf. 15½x15

1411 A647 (180k) multi	3.00	3.00
a. Booklet pane of 10	30.00	
1412 A648 (240k) multi	4.00	4.00
a. Booklet pane of 10	40.00	

Think Green Issue.

Icelandic National Television Network, 50th Anniv. A649

2016, Sept. 16 **Litho.** ***Die Cut***

Self-Adhesive

1413 A649 (160k) multi	3.00	3.00

Actinauge Sp. — A650

Gorgonocephalus Sp. — A651

Die Cut Perf. 13½

2016, Sept. 16 **Litho.**

Self-Adhesive

1414 A650 (160k) multi	3.00	3.00
1415 A651 (200k) multi	3.50	3.50

Silene Acaulis — A652

Silene Uniflora — A653

Die Cut Perf. 14x13½

2016, Sept. 16 **Litho.**

Self-Adhesive

1416 A652 (180k) multi	3.25	3.25
1417 A653 (275k) multi	5.00	5.00

Souvenir Sheet

Wreck of the Research Ship Pourquoi-Pas? Off Iceland, 80th Anniv. — A654

Die Cut Perf. 13¼x13

2016, Sept. 16 **Litho.**

Self-Adhesive

1418 A654 (480k) multi	8.50	8.50

Composition, by Karl Kvaran (1924-89) — A655

Abstraction, by Nina Tryggvadóttir (1913-68) — A656

A Svortüm Grunni, by Valtyr Pétursson (1919-88) — A657

Málverk, by Thorvaldur Skúlason (1906-84) A658

2016, Nov. 3 **Litho.** ***Perf. 13¼x13***

1419 A655 (175k) multi	3.25	3.25
1420 A656 (310k) multi	5.75	5.75
1421 A657 (480k) multi	8.75	8.75
1422 A658 (490k) multi	9.00	9.00
Nos. 1419-1422 (4)	26.75	26.75

Star of Bethlehem Sweater Design A659

Candle Sweater Design — A660

Christmas Ornament Sweater Design A661

Die Cut Perf. 13½

2016, Nov. 3 **Litho.**

Self-Adhesive

1423 A659 (160k) multi	3.00	3.00
a. Booklet pane of 10	30.00	
1424 A660 (175k) multi	3.25	3.25
1425 A661 (180k) multi	3.25	3.25
Nos. 1423-1425 (3)	9.50	9.50

A662

Design: Prime Minister Jón Magnússon, Labor Minister Sigurdur Jonsson, Finance Minister Björn Kristjánsson.

Die Cut Perf. 14¾x16

2017, Feb. 16 Litho.

Self-Adhesive

1426 A662 (160k) multi 3.00 3.00

First Icelandic government, cent.

Reykjavik Craftsmen Guild, 150th Anniv. A663

Die Cut Perf. 14

2017, Feb. 16 Litho.

Self-Adhesive

1427 A663 (160k) multi 3.00 3.00

Laekjartorg Kiosk, Reykjavik, Designed by Rögnvaldur Olafsson (1874-1917) — A664

Die Cut Perf. 13x12¼

2017, Feb. 16 Litho.

Self-Adhesive

1428 A664 (175k) multi 3.25 3.25

Scarf by Vík Prjónsdóttir A665

Felt Sound Absorber by Bryndís Bolladóttir A666

Textile Art by Ragna Fródhadóttir A667

Spring/Summer 2016, Textile by Anita Hirlekar A668

Die Cut Perf. 13¼

2017, Feb. 16 Litho.

Self-Adhesive

1429	A665 (160k) multi		3.00	3.00
1430	A666 (175k) multi		3.25	3.25
1431	A667 (480k) multi		9.00	9.00
1432	A668 (565k) multi		11.00	11.00
	Nos. 1429-1432 (4)		26.25	26.25

Icelandic Sweater — A669

Die Cut Perf. 13¼

2017, Apr. 27 Litho.

Self-Adhesive

Flocked Paper

1433 A669 (225k) multi 4.25 4.25

Kid — A670

Kitten — A671

Die Cut Perf. 14

2017, Apr. 27 Litho.

Self-Adhesive

1434	A670 (160k) multi	3.00	3.00
1435	A671 (175k) multi	3.25	3.25

Blue Lagoon A672

Myvatn Nature Baths A673

Die Cut Perf. 14

2017, Apr. 27 Litho.

Self-Adhesive

1436	A672 (200k) multi	3.75	3.75
1437	A673 (250k) multi	4.75	4.75

International Year of Sustainable Tourism for Development.

Horses and Rider — A674

Glacier Tour — A675

2017, Apr. 27 Litho. *Perf. 13*

1438	A674 (225k) multi	4.25	4.25
1439	A675 (285k) multi	5.50	5.50

Tourism.

Castle in the Air — A676

Snow Castle — A677

Die Cut Perf. 16x15

2017, Apr. 27 Litho.

Self-Adhesive

1440	A676 (340k) multi	6.50	6.50
1441	A677 (535k) multi	10.00	10.00

Europa.

Title Page of First Icelandic Translation of the New Testament A678

Die Cut Perf. 13½

2017, Sept. 14 Litho.

Self-Adhesive

1442 A678 (180k) multi 3.50 3.50

Protestant Reformation, 500th anniv.

Iceland Chamber of Commerce, Cent. — A679

Die Cut Perf. 14

2017, Sept. 14 Litho.

Self-Adhesive

1443 A679 (195k) multi 3.75 3.75

Acesta Excavata A680

Madrepora Oculata A681

Die Cut Perf. 13¼x13

2017, Sept. 14 Litho.

Self-Adhesive

1444	A680 (195k) multi	3.75	3.75
1445	A681 (300k) multi	5.75	5.75

Xanthoria Parietina — A682

Placopis Gelida — A683

Die Cut Perf. 14x13½

2017, Sept. 14 Litho.

Self-Adhesive

1446	A682 (180k) multi	3.50	3.50
1447	A683 (470k) multi	9.00	9.00

Souvenir Sheet

Stamp Day — A684

2017, Sept. 14 Litho. *Perf. 13¼*

1448 A684 (630k) black 12.00 12.00

Foriegn expeditions to Iceland, 250th anniv.

Painting, by Kristján Davidhsson (1917-2013) — A685

Untitled Painting by Hafsteinn Austmann A686

Composition, by Eiríkur Smith — A687

Organ Fugue, Sculpture by Gerdur Helgadóttir (1928-75) — A688

Perf. 13x13¼, 13¼x13

2017, Nov. 2 Litho.

1449	A685 (180k) multi	3.50	3.50
1450	A686 (195k) multi	3.75	3.75
1451	A687 (285k) multi	5.50	5.50
1452	A688 (650k) multi	12.50	12.50
	Nos. 1449-1452 (4)	25.25	25.25

Santa Claus Near Window of House — A689

Santa Clauses Watching Children Carrying Christmas Tree — A690

Santa Claus and Children on Sled — A691

Die Cut Perf. 14x14¼

2017, Nov. 2 **Litho.**

Self-Adhesive

1453	A689 (180k) multi		3.50	3.50
1454	A690 (195k) multi		3.75	3.75
1455	A691 (225k) multi		4.25	4.25
	Nos. 1453-1455 (3)		11.50	11.50

Christmas.

National Library of Iceland, 200th Anniv. A692

Die Cut Perf. 14x14½

2018, Feb. 15 **Litho.**

Self-Adhesive

1456	A692 (195k) multi	4.00	4.00

Jón Thoroddsen (1818-68), Writer — A693

Die Cut Perf. 14½x14¼

2018, Feb. 15 **Litho.**

Self-Adhesive

1457	A693 (200k) multi	4.00	4.00

Ellidaár Estuary Footbridge A694

Jökulsá River Suspension Bridge A695

Die Cut Perf. 14

2018, Feb. 15 **Litho.**

Self-Adhesive

1458	A694 (225k) multi	4.50	4.50
1459	A695 (285k) multi	5.75	5.75

Althing and Supreme Court — A696

Cabinet Building A697

Die Cut Perf. 14

2018, Feb. 15 **Litho.**

Self-Adhesive

1460	A696 (180k) shown	3.75	3.75
1461	A697 (195k) shown	4.00	4.00

Souvenir Sheet

Stamps Inscribed "1000 grömm innanlands"

Die Cut Perf. 13½ on 5 Sides

1462	Sheet of 2	19.00	
a.	A696 (480k) multi	9.50	9.50
b.	A697 (480k) multi	9.50	9.50

Icelandic independence, cent.

SEMI-POSTAL STAMPS

Shipwreck and Rescue by Breeches Buoy SP1

Children Gathering Rock Plants SP2

Old Fisherman at Shore SP3

Unwmk.

1933, Apr. 28 **Engr.** ***Perf. 14***

B1	SP1	10a + 10a red brown	1.75	*6.00*
B2	SP2	20a + 20a org red	1.75	*6.00*
B3	SP1	35a + 25a ultra	1.75	*6.00*
B4	SP3	50a + 25a blue grn	1.75	*6.00*
		Nos. B1-B4 (4)	7.00	*24.00*
		Set, never hinged	14.00	

Receipts from the surtax were devoted to a special fund for use in various charitable works especially those indicated on the stamps: "Slysavarnir" (Rescue work), "Barnahaeli" (Asylum for scrofulous children), "Ellhaeli" (Asylum for the Aged).

Souvenir Sheets

King Christian X — SP4

1937, May 15 **Typo.**

B5	SP4	Sheet of 3	45.00	*300.00*
		Never hinged	85.00	
a.		15a violet	10.00	*55.00*
b.		25a red	10.00	*55.00*
c.		50a blue	10.00	*55.00*

Reign of Christian X, 25th anniv. Sheet sold for 2kr.

SP5

Designs: 30a, 40a, Ericsson statue, Reykjavik. 60a, Iceland's position on globe.

1938, Oct. 9 **Photo.** ***Perf. 12***

B6	SP5	Sheet of 3	5.00	*30.00*
		Never hinged	10.00	
a.		30a scarlet	1.25	*12.00*
b.		40a purple	1.25	*12.00*
c.		60a deep green	1.25	*12.00*

Leif Ericsson Day, Oct. 9, 1938.

Catalogue values for unused stamps in this section, from this point to the end of the section, are for Never Hinged items.

Ill Child — SP6

Red Cross Nurse and Patient — SP7

Nurse Covering Patient — SP8

Elderly Couple — SP9

Rescue at Sea — SP10

Unwmk.

1949, June 8 **Engr.** ***Perf. 14***

B7	SP6	10a + 10a olive grn	.85	*1.25*
B8	SP7	35a + 15a carmine	.85	*1.25*
B9	SP8	50a + 25a choc	.85	*1.25*
B10	SP9	60a + 25a brt ultra	.85	*1.25*
B11	SP10	75a + 25a slate gray	.85	*1.25*
		Nos. B7-B11 (5)	4.25	*6.25*

The surtax was for charitable purposes.

Nos. 262 and 265 Surcharged in Black

1953, Feb. 12 **Unwmk.** ***Perf. 13***

B12	A50	75a + 25a red org	1.40	*5.25*
B13	A50	1.25k + 25a red vio	2.40	*5.25*

The surtax was for flood relief in the Netherlands.

St. Thorlacus — SP11

Cathedral at Skalholt SP12

1.75k+1.25k, Bishop Jon Thorkelsson Vidalin.

1956, Jan. 23 ***Perf. 11½***

B14	SP11	75a + 25a car	.25	*.25*
B15	SP12	1.25k + 75a dk brn	.25	*.60*
B16	SP11	1.75k + 1.25k black	1.00	*1.75*
		Nos. B14-B16 (3)	1.50	*2.60*

Bishopric of Skalholt, 900th anniv.

The surtax was for the rebuilding of Skalholt, former cultural center of Iceland.

Ambulance SP13

1963, Nov. 15 **Photo.** **Unwmk.**

B17	SP13	3k + 50a multi	.45	*1.40*
B18	SP13	3.50k + 50a multi	.45	*1.40*

Centenary of International Red Cross.

Rock Ptarmigan in Summer SP14

Design: #B20, Rock ptarmigan in winter.

1965, Jan. 27 **Photo.** ***Perf. 12½***

Granite Paper

B19	SP14	3.50k + 50a multi	.85	*2.40*
B20	SP14	4.50k + 50a multi	.85	*2.40*

Ringed Plover's Nest — SP15

Design: 5k+50a, Rock ptarmigan's nest.

1967, Nov. 22 **Photo.** ***Perf. 11½***

B21	SP15	4k + 50a multi	.85	*1.75*
B22	SP15	5k + 50a multi	.85	*1.75*

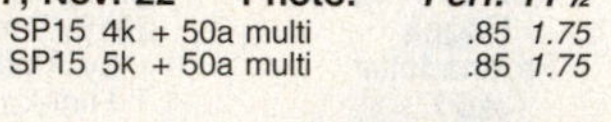

Arctic Terns — SP16

1972, Nov. 22 **Litho.** ***Perf. 13***

B23	SP16	7k + 1k multi	.75	*1.50*
B24	SP16	9k + 1k multi	.75	*1.50*

AIR POST STAMPS

No. 115 Overprinted

Perf. 14x14½

1928, May 31 Wmk. 114

C1 A8 10a red	.85	*12.00*
Never hinged	1.75	

Same Overprint on No. 82

1929, June 29 Wmk. 113 *Perf. 13*

C2 A5 50a gray & violet	60.00	*120.00*
Never hinged	200.00	

Gyrfalcon AP1

Perf. 12½x12

1930, Jan. 1 Litho. Unwmk.

C3 AP1 10a dp ultra & gray blue	25.00	*75.00*
Never hinged	50.00	

Imperfs were privately printed.
For overprint see No. CO1.

Snaefellsjokull, Extinct Volcano — AP2

Parliament Millenary: 20a, Fishing boat. 35a, Iceland pony. 50a, Gullfoss (Golden Falls). 1k, Ingolfour Arnarson Statue.

Wmk. 47

1930, June 1 Typo. *Perf. 14*

C4 AP2 15a org brn & dl bl	30.00	*55.00*
C5 AP2 20a bis brn & sl bl	30.00	*55.00*
C6 AP2 35a olive grn & brn	60.00	*120.00*
C7 AP2 50a dp grn & dp bl	60.00	*120.00*
C8 AP2 1k olive grn & dk red	60.00	*120.00*
Nos. C4-C8 (5)	240.00	*470.00*
Set, never hinged	510.00	

Regular Issue of 1920 Overprinted

Perf. 14x14½

1931, May 25 Wmk. 114

C9 A8 30a red & green	35.00	*160.00*
C10 A8 1k dp bl & dk brn	12.00	*120.00*
C11 A8 2k ol brn & myr grn	50.00	*160.00*
Nos. C9-C11 (3)	97.00	*440.00*
Set, never hinged	215.00	

Nos. 185, 128 and 187 Overprinted in Red

1933, June 16

C12 A8 1k dk bl & lt brn	175.	*650.*
Never hinged	475.	
C13 A8 5k brn & indigo	600.	*1,500.*
Never hinged	1,500.	
C14 A8 10k yel grn & blk	1,300.	*3,000.*
Never hinged	3,250.	

Excellent counterfeit overprints exist.

Visit of the Italian Flying Armada en route from Rome to Chicago; also for the payment of the charges on postal matter sent from Iceland to the US via the Italian seaplanes.

Plane over Thingvalla Lake — AP7

10a-20a, Plane over Thingvalla Lake. 25a-50a, Plane and Aurora Borealis. 1k-2k, Map of Iceland.

Perf. 12½x14

1934, Sept. 1 Engr. Unwmk.

C15 AP7 10a blue	1.75	*3.50*
Revenue cancellation		17.50
C16 AP7 20a emerald	4.75	*8.00*
Revenue cancellation		35.00
a. Perf. 14	30.00	21.00
C17 AP7 25a dk vio, perf. 14	12.00	*19.00*
Revenue cancellation		50.00
a. Perf. 12½x14	30.00	*35.00*
Never hinged	115.00	
C18 AP7 50a red vio, perf. 14	3.50	*8.00*
Revenue cancellation		24.00
C19 AP7 1k dark brown	17.50	*35.00*
Revenue cancellation		25.00
C20 AP7 2k red orange	9.00	*15.00*
Revenue cancellation		24.00
Nos. C15-C20 (6)	48.50	*88.50*
Set, never hinged	150.00	

Catalogue values for unused stamps in this section, from this point to the end of the section, are for Never Hinged items.

Thingvellir, Old Site of the Parliament AP10

Isafjörthur AP11

Eyjafjörthur AP12

Mt. Strandatindur AP13

Mt. Thyrill AP14

Aerial View of Reykjavik AP15

1947, Aug. 18 *Perf. 14*

C21 AP10 15a red orange	.85	*1.50*
C22 AP11 30a gray black	.85	*1.50*
C23 AP12 75a brown red	.85	*1.25*
C24 AP13 1k indigo	.85	*1.25*
C25 AP14 2k chocolate	1.50	*2.50*
C26 AP15 3k dark green	1.50	*2.50*
Nos. C21-C26 (6)	6.40	*10.50*

Snaefellsjokull AP16

Views: 2.50k, Eiriksjokull. 3.30k, Oraefajokull.

1952, May 2 Unwmk. *Perf. 13½x14*

C27 AP16 1.80k slate blue	17.50	15.00
C28 AP16 2.50k green	30.00	1.25
C29 AP16 3.30k deep ultra	7.00	9.50
Nos. C27-C29 (3)	54.50	*25.75*

See Nos. 302-304.

Vickers Viscount and Plane of 1919 AP17

4.05k, Skymaster and plane of 1919.

1959, Sept. 3 Engr. *Perf. 13½*

C30 AP17 3.50k steel blue	1.00	.85
C31 AP17 4.05k green	.85	1.25

40th anniv. of air transportation in Iceland.

AIR POST OFFICIAL STAMPS

No. C3 Overprinted In Red

1930, Jan. 1 Unwmk. *Perf. 12½x12*

CO1 AP1 10a dp ultra & gray blue	25.00	*140.00*

Imperfs were privately printed.

OFFICIAL STAMPS

For Nos. O1-O12, see note on condition before No. 1.

O1

Perf. 14x13½

1873 Typo. Wmk. 112

O1 O1 4s green	*8,500.*	*8,500.*
a. Imperf.	150.	
O2 O1 8s red lilac	650.	*700.*
a. Imperf.	750.	

Perf. 12½

O3 O1 4s green	110.	*400.*
Never hinged	350.00	

The imperforate varieties lack gum.

No. O1 values are for stamps with perfs just touching the design on at least one side.

Fake and favor cancellations are often found on Nos. O1-O37. Values are considerably less than those shown.

O2

1876-95 *Perf. 14x13½*

O4 O2 3a yellow	45.00	*60.00*
O5 O2 5a brown	9.50	*17.50*
a. Imperf.	450.00	
O6 O2 10a blue	85.00	16.00
a. 10a ultramarine	475.00	85.00
O7 O2 16a carmine	35.00	*60.00*
O8 O2 20a yellow green	35.00	*50.00*
O9 O2 50a rose lilac ('95)	90.00	*95.00*
Nos. O4-O9 (6)	299.50	*298.50*
Set, never hinged	975.00	

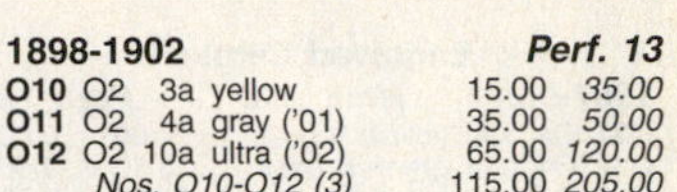

1898-1902 *Perf. 13*

O10 O2 3a yellow	15.00	*35.00*
O11 O2 4a gray ('01)	35.00	*50.00*
O12 O2 10a ultra ('02)	65.00	*120.00*
Nos. O10-O12 (3)	115.00	*205.00*
Set, never hinged	360.00	

A 5a brown and 20a yellow green, both perf. 13 with Wmk. 112, exist. They were not regularly issued.

See note after No. O30.

For overprints see Nos. O20-O30.

O3

1902 Wmk. 113 *Perf. 13*

O13 O3 3a buff & black	5.00	3.00
O14 O3 4a dp grn & blk	5.00	2.50
O15 O3 5a org brn & blk	4.00	*5.00*
O16 O3 10a ultra & black	4.00	*5.00*
O17 O3 16a carmine & blk	4.00	*20.00*
O18 O3 20a green & blk	25.00	8.50
O19 O3 50a violet & blk	8.00	*12.50*
Nos. O13-O19 (7)	55.00	*56.50*
Set, never hinged	200.00	

Stamps of 1876-1901 Overprinted in Black

1902-03 Wmk. 112 *Perf. 13*

O20 O2 3a yellow	1.25	*3.00*
a. "I" before Gildi omitted	175.00	
b. Inverted overprint	42.50	*65.00*
c. As "a," invtd.	200.00	
d. Pair, one without ovpt.	190.00	
e. '03-'03	500.00	
f. 02'-'03	500.00	
O21 O2 4a gray	1.25	*2.75*
a. "I" before Gildi omitted	175.00	
b. Inverted overprint	60.00	*75.00*
e. '03-'03	525.00	
f. 02'-'03	525.00	
g. Pair, one without ovpt.	225.00	
i. "L" only of "I GILDI" inverted	—	
O22 O2 5a brown	1.00	*2.75*
a. Double overprint	225.00	
O23 O2 10a ultramarine	1.00	*2.75*
a. "I" before Gildi omitted	275.00	
b. Inverted overprint	55.00	*75.00*
c. '03-'03	425.00	
d. 02'-'03	425.00	
e. "L" only of "I GILDI"	60.00	90.00
f. As "e," inverted	425.00	
g. "IL" only of "I GILDI"	225.00	275.00
O24 O2 20a yel green	1.00	*25.00*
Nos. O20-O24 (5)	5.50	*36.25*
Set, never hinged	10.00	

Perf. 14x13½

O25 O2 3a yellow	325.00	*1,400.*
a. "02'-'03"	1,100.	
b. '03-'03	1,200.	
O26 O2 5a brown	8.00	*175.00*
a. Inverted overprint	90.00	
b. '03-'03	425.00	
c. 02'-'03	425.00	
d. "L" only of "I GILDI" inverted	—	
O27 O2 10a blue	425.00	*750.00*
a. "I" before Gildi omitted	—	
b. Inverted overprint	825.00	*850.00*
c. '03-'03	950.00	
d. 02'-'03	950.00	
O28 O2 16a carmine	18.00	*75.00*
a. "I" before Gildi omitted	650.00	
c. Dbl. ovpt., one inverted	425.00	
d. Inverted overprint		—
e. '03-'03	700.00	
f. 02'-'03	700.00	
O29 O2 20a yel green	35.00	*95.00*
a. Inverted overprint	175.00	*190.00*
b. '03-'03	500.00	
c. 02'-'03	500.00	
O30 O2 50a red lilac	6.00	*60.00*
a. "I" before Gildi omitted	50.00	110.00
b. Inverted overprint	190.00	
Nos. O25-O30 (6)	817.00	*2,555.*
Set, never hinged	1,800.	

Nos. O10-O12, O20-O24, O28 and O30 were reprinted in 1904. They have the watermark of 1902 (type 113) and are perf. 13. Value $65 each. Without overprint $90 each.

Christian IX, Frederik VIII — O4

Engraved Center

1907-08 Wmk. 113 *Perf. 13*

No.	Type	Value	Description	Unused	Used
O31	O4	3a	yellow & gray	7.00	*8.00*
O32	O4	4a	green & gray	3.50	*9.00*
O33	O4	5a	brn org & gray	11.00	4.50
O34	O4	10a	deep bl & gray	2.50	*3.25*
O35	O4	15a	lt blue & gray	4.75	*9.00*
O36	O4	16a	carmine & gray	4.75	*30.00*
O37	O4	20a	yel grn & gray	20.00	6.00
O38	O4	50a	violet & gray	7.00	*11.00*
			Nos. O31-O38 (8)	60.50	*80.75*
			Set, never hinged	240.00	

1918 Wmk. 114 *Perf. 14x14½*

No.	Type	Value	Description	Unused	Used
O39	O4	15a	lt bl & gray	15.00	*35.00*

Christian X — O5

1920-30 Typo.

No.	Type	Value	Description	Unused	Used
O40	O5	3a	yellow & gray	5.00	*4.25*
			Revenue cancellation		30.00
O41	O5	4a	dp grn & gray	1.25	*3.75*
O42	O5	5a	orange & gray	1.25	1.75
			Revenue cancellation		30.00
O43	O5	10a	dk bl & gray	35.00	1.40
			Revenue cancellation		30.00
O44	O5	15a	lt blue & gray	.65	*1.25*
			Revenue cancellation		30.00
O45	O5	20a	yel grn & gray	50.00	4.50
O46	O5	50a	violet & gray	45.00	2.75
			Revenue cancellation		30.00
O47	O5	1k	car & gray	45.00	2.25
			Revenue cancellation		30.00
O48	O5	2k	bl & blk ('30)	5.00	*21.00*
			Revenue cancellation		35.00
O49	O5	5k	brn & blk ('30)	30.00	*55.00*
			Revenue cancellation		35.00
			Nos. O40-O49 (10)	218.15	97.90
			Set, never hinged	875.00	

See No. O68.

Nos. 97 and 98 Overprinted

1922, May Wmk. 113 *Perf. 13*

No.	Type	Description	Unused	Used
O50	A7	2k rose, larger letters, no period	25.00	*60.00*
a.		Smaller letters, with period	95.00	60.00
O51	A7	5k brown	240.00	*260.00*

No. 115 Surcharged

1923 Wmk. 114 *Perf. 14x14½*

No.	Type	Description	Unused	Used
O52	A8	20a on 10a red	30.00	2.40

Parliament Millenary Issue

#152-166 Overprinted in Red or Blue

1930, Jan. 1 Unwmk. *Perf. 12½x12*

No.	Type	Value	Overprint	Unused	Used
O53	A15	3a	(R)	15.00	*45.00*
O54	A15	5a	(R)	15.00	*45.00*
O55	A15	7a	(R)	15.00	*45.00*
O56	A15	10a	(Bl)	15.00	*45.00*
O57	A15	15a	(R)	15.00	*45.00*
O58	A15	20a	(Bl)	15.00	*45.00*
O59	A15	25a	(Bl)	15.00	*45.00*
O60	A15	30a	(R)	15.00	*45.00*
O61	A15	35a	(R)	15.00	*45.00*
O62	A15	40a	(Bl)	15.00	*45.00*
O63	A15	50a	(Bl)	140.00	*350.00*
O64	A15	1k	(R)	140.00	*350.00*
O65	A15	2k	(R)	175.00	*400.00*
O66	A15	5k	(Bl)	140.00	*350.00*
O67	A15	10k	(Bl)	140.00	*350.00*
			Nos. O53-O67 (15)	885.00	*2,250.*
			Set, never hinged	2,250.	

Type of 1920 Issue Redrawn

1931 Wmk. 114 Typo.

No.	Type	Value	Description	Unused	Used
O68	O5	20a	yel grn & gray	45.00	3.00

For differences in redrawing see note after No. 187.

No. 82 Overprinted in Black

Overprint 15mm long

1936, Dec. 7 Wmk. 113 *Perf. 13*

No.	Type	Value	Description	Unused	Used
O69	A5	50a	gray & vio	25.00	*30.00*

Same Overprint on Nos. 180 and 115

Perf. 14x14½

Wmk. 114

No.	Type	Value	Description	Unused	Used
O70	A8	7a	yellow green	2.40	*24.00*
O71	A8	10a	red	15.00	2.25
			Nos. O69-O71 (3)	42.40	*56.25*

IFNI

'if-nē

LOCATION — An enclave in southern Morocco on the Atlantic coast
GOVT. — Spanish possession
AREA — 580 sq. mi.
POP. — 51,517 (est. 1964)
CAPITAL — Sidi Ifni

Ifni was ceded to Spain by Morocco in 1860, but the Spanish did not occupy it until 1934. Sidi Ifni was also the administrative capital for Spanish West Africa. Spain turned Ifni back to Morocco June 30, 1969.

100 Centimos = 1 Peseta

Catalogue values for unused stamps in this country are for Never Hinged items, beginning with Scott 28 in the regular postage section, Scott B1 in the semi-postal section, and Scott C38 in the airpost section.

Stamps of Spain, 1936-40, Overprinted in Red or Blue

1941-42 Unwmk. *Imperf.*

No.	Type	Value	Description	Unused	Used
1	A159	1c	green	7.50	5.50
			Perf. 10 to 11		
2	A160	2c	org brn (Bl)	7.50	5.50
3	A161	5c	gray brown	1.25	1.10
5	A161	10c	dk car (Bl)	4.50	2.25
a.			Red overprint	17.50	8.25
6	A161	15c	lt green	1.25	1.10
7	A166	20c	brt violet	1.25	1.10
8	A166	25c	deep claret	1.25	1.10
9	A166	30c	blue	1.25	1.10
10	A166	40c	Prus green	1.75	1.10
11	A166	50c	indigo	7.50	2.00
12	A166	70c	blue	7.50	4.50
13	A166	1p	gray black	7.50	4.50
14	A166	2p	dull brown	75.00	110.00
15	A166	4p	dl rose (Bl)	275.00	190.00
16	A166	10p	light brn	775.00	550.00
			Nos. 1-16 (15)	1,175.	880.85
			Set, never hinged	2,000.	

Counterfeit overprints exist.

Nomads — A1

Alcazaba Fortress — A3

Designs: 2c, 20c, 45c, 3p, Marksman.

1943 Litho. *Perf. 12½*

No.	Type	Value	Description	Unused	Used
17	A1	1c	brn & lil rose	.30	.25
18	A1	2c	yel grn & sl lil	.30	.25
19	A3	5c	magenta & vio	.30	.25
20	A1	15c	sl grn & grn	.30	.25
21	A1	20c	vio & red brn	.30	.25
22	A1	40c	rose vio & vio	.35	.30
23	A1	45c	brn vio & red	.40	.35
24	A3	75c	indigo & bl	.40	.35
25	A1	1p	red & brown	2.25	1.75
26	A1	3p	bl vio & sl grn	4.00	2.75
27	A3	10p	blk brn & blk	40.00	27.50
			Nos. 17-27,E1 (12)	51.15	35.85
			Set, never hinged	90.00	

Nos. 17-27 exist imperf. Value, set $150.

Catalogue values for unused stamps in this section, from this point to the end of the section, are for Never Hinged items.

1947, Feb. *Perf. 10*

No.	Type	Value	Description	Unused	Used
28	A1	50c	Nomad family	18.00	.80

No. 28 exists imperf. Value, $50.

Stamps of Spain, 1939-48, Overprinted in Carmine

1948, Aug. 2 *Perf. 9½x10½, 11, 13*

No.	Type	Value	Description	Unused	Used
29	A161	5c	gray brn (#664)	4.50	.75
30	A194	15c	gray green	5.00	.75
31	A167	90c	dk grn (#714a)	20.00	4.25
32	A166	1p	gray black	.70	.30
			Nos. 29-32 (4)	30.20	6.05

See Nos. 36 and 45.

Spain Nos. 769 and 770 Overprinted in Violet Blue or Carmine

1949, Oct. 9 *Perf. 12½x13*

No.	Type	Value	Description	Unused	Used
33	A202	50c	red brown (VB)	2.50	1.25
34	A202	75c	violet blue (C)	2.50	1.25
			Nos. 33-34,C40 (3)	8.00	4.00

75th anniv. of the UPU.

Stamps of Spain, 1938-48, Overprinted in Blue or Carmine like Nos. 29-32

Perf. 13, 13½, 12½x13, 9½x10½

1949 Unwmk.

No.	Type	Value	Description	Unused	Used
35	A160	2c	org brn (Bl)	.30	.25
36	A161	5c	gray brn (#664a)	.30	.25
37	A161	10c	dk car (Bl)	.30	.25
38	A161	15c	dk green (II)	.30	.25
39	A166	25c	brown violet	.30	.25
40	A166	30c	blue	.40	.25
41	A195	40c	red brown	.40	.25
42	A195	45c	car rose (Bl)	.70	.30
43	A166	50c	indigo	.75	.30
44	A195	75c	dk vio bl	.85	.45
45	A167	90c	dk grn (#714)	.95	.60
47	A167	1.35p	purple	5.00	4.50
48	A166	2p	dl brn	4.75	2.75
49	A166	4p	dl rose (Bl)	17.50	8.00
50	A166	10p	lt brn	42.50	24.00
			Nos. 35-50 (15)	75.30	42.65

Gen. Francisco Franco and Desert Scene A4

Perf. 12½x13

1951, July 18 Photo. Unwmk.

No.	Type	Value	Description	Unused	Used
51	A4	50c	dp org	.45	.25
52	A4	1p	chocolate	3.00	1.25
53	A4	5p	bl grn	32.50	12.00
			Nos. 51-53 (3)	35.95	13.50

Visit of Gen. Francisco Franco, 1950.

View of Granada and Globe — A5

1952, Dec. 10 *Perf. 13x12½*

No.	Type	Value	Description	Unused	Used
54	A5	5c	red org	.35	.25
55	A5	35c	dk ol grn	.40	.25
56	A5	60c	brown	.40	.30
			Nos. 54-56 (3)	1.15	.80

400th anniversary of the death of Leo Africanus (c. 1485-c. 1554), Arab traveler and scholar, author of "Descrittione dell' Africa."

Musician A6

Design: 60c, Two musicians.

1953, June 1 *Perf. 12½x13*

No.	Type	Value	Description	Unused	Used
57	A6	15c	olive gray	.30	.25
58	A6	60c	brown	.35	.30
			Nos. 57-58,B13-B14 (4)	1.30	1.10

Issued to promote child welfare.

Fish and Branched Sponges A7

15c, Fish and jellyfish.

1953, Nov. 23

No.	Type	Value	Description	Unused	Used
59	A7	15c	dark green	.30	.25
60	A7	60c	brown	.45	.30
			Nos. 59-60,B15-B16 (4)	1.40	1.10

Colonial Stamp Day, Nov. 23, 1953.

Sea Gull — A8

Cactus — A9

25c, 60c, 2p, 5p, Salsola vermiculata.

1954, Apr. 22 *Perf. 12½x13, 13x12½*

No.	Type	Value	Description	Unused	Used
61	A8	5c	red org	.25	.25
62	A9	10c	olive	.25	.25
63	A9	25c	brn car	.25	.25
64	A8	35c	olive gray	.25	.25

65	A9	40c rose lilac	.25	.25
66	A9	60c dk brn	.25	.25
67	A8	1p brown	7.25	.70
68	A9	1.25p car rose	.30	.25
69	A9	2p darp blue	.35	.25
70	A9	4.50p olive grn	.45	.40
71	A9	5p olive blk	37.50	10.50
		Nos. 61-71 (11)	47.35	13.60

Mother and Child
A10 A11

1954, June 1 ***Perf. 13x12½***

72	A10	15c dk gray grn	.30	.25
73	A11	60c dk brn	.35	.30
		Nos. 72-73,B17-B18 (4)	1.30	1.10

Lobster
A12

Design: 60c, Hammerhead shark.

1954, Nov. 23 ***Perf. 12½x13***

74	A12	15c olive green	.35	.25
75	A12	60c rose brown	.45	.35
		Nos. 74-75,B19-B20 (4)	1.45	1.15

Issued to publicize Colonial Stamp Day.

Farmer Plowing and Statue of "Justice" A13

1955, June 1 **Photo.** **Unwmk.**

76	A13	50c gray olive	.35	.30
		Nos. 76,B21-B22 (3)	1.00	.85

Squirrel
A14

1955, Nov. 23

77	A14	70c yellow green	.35	.30
		Nos. 77,B23-B24 (3)	1.00	.85

Issued to publicize Colonial Stamp Day.

Senecio Antheuphorbium A15

Design: 50c, Limoniastrum Ifniensis.

1956, June 1 ***Perf. 13x12½***

78	A15	20c bluish green	.35	.25
79	A15	50c brown	.40	.35
		Nos. 78-79,B25-B26 (4)	1.40	1.15

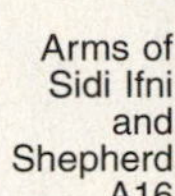

Arms of Sidi Ifni and Shepherd A16

1956, Nov. 23 ***Perf. 12½x13***

80	A16	70c light green	.35	.25

Issued for Colonial Stamp Day.

Rock Doves — A17

1957, June 1 **Photo.** ***Perf. 13x12½***

81	A17	70c yel grn & brn	.40	.35
		Nos. 81,B29-B30 (3)	1.05	.90

See No. 86.

Jackal
A18

Design: 70c, Jackal's head, vert.

Perf. 12½x13, 13x12½

1957, Nov. 23

82	A18	20c emerald & lt grn	.35	.25
83	A18	70c green & brown	.45	.35
		Nos. 82-83,B31-B32 (4)	1.45	1.15

Issued for the Day of the Stamp, 1957. See Nos. 87, B41.

Basketball Players — A19

Design: 70c, Cyclists.

1958, June 1 ***Perf. 13x12½***

84	A19	20c bluish green	.30	.25
85	A19	70c olive green	.45	.35
		Nos. 84-85,B36-B37 (4)	1.40	1.15

Types of 1957 inscribed "Pro-Infancia 1959"

Designs: 20c, Goat. 70c, Ewe and lamb.

1959, June 1 ***Perf. 13x12½, 12½x13***

86	A17	20c dull green	.30	.25
87	A18	70c yellow green	.40	.35
		Nos. 86-87,B41-B42 (4)	1.35	1.15

Issued to promote child welfare.

Red-legged Partridges — A20

1960, June 10 ***Perf. 13x12½***

88	A20	35c shown	.30	.25
89	A20	80c Camels	.40	.35
		Nos. 88-89,B46-B47 (4)	1.35	1.15

White Stork A21

Birds: 50c, 1.50p, 5p, European goldfinches. 75c, 2p, 10p, Skylarks, vert.

1960 **Unwmk.** ***Perf. 12½x13***

90	A21	25c violet	.25	.25
91	A21	50c olive black	.25	.25
92	A21	75c dull purple	.30	.25
93	A21	1p orange ver	.40	.25
94	A21	1.50p brt grnsh bl	.45	.30
95	A21	2p red lilac	.50	.35
96	A21	3p dark blue	.85	.40
97	A21	5p red brown	1.40	.65
98	A21	10p olive	5.25	1.75
		Nos. 90-98 (9)	9.65	4.45

Map of Ifni — A22

General Franco A23

Design: 70c, Government palace.

Perf. 13x12½, 12½x13

1961, Oct. 1 **Photo.**

99	A22	25c gray violet	.25	.25
100	A23	50c olive brown	.30	.25
101	A23	70c brt green	.35	.30
102	A23	1p red orange	.40	.35
		Nos. 99-102 (4)	1.30	1.15

25th anniv. of the nomination of Gen. Francisco Franco as Head of State.

Admiral Jofre Tenoria — A24

Design: 50c, Cesareo Fernandez-Duro (1830-1908), writer.

1962, July 10 ***Perf. 13x12½***

103	A24	25c dull violet	.25	.25
104	A24	50c deep blue grn	.30	.25
105	A24	1p orange brown	.35	.35
		Nos. 103-105 (3)	.90	.85

Mailman — A25

Stamp Day: 35c, Hands, letter and winged wheel.

1962, Nov. 23 **Unwmk.**

106	A25	15c dark blue	.25	.25
107	A25	35c lilac rose	.35	.30
108	A25	1p rose brown	.40	.35
		Nos. 106-108 (3)	1.00	.90

Golden Tower, Seville — A26

1963, Jan. 29 **Photo.**

109	A26	50c green	.30	.25
110	A26	1p brown orange	.40	.35

Issued for flood relief in Seville.

Butterflies — A27

Design: 50c, Butterfly and flower.

1963, July 6 ***Perf. 13x12½***

111	A27	25c deep blue	.30	.25
112	A27	50c light green	.35	.30
113	A27	1p carmine rose	.45	.40
		Nos. 111-113 (3)	1.10	.95

Issued for child welfare.

Child with Flowers and Arms A28

1963, July 12 ***Perf. 12½x13***

114	A28	50c gray olive	.30	.25
115	A28	1p reddish brown	.40	.35

Issued for Barcelona flood relief.

Beetle (Steraspis Speciosa) — A29

Stamp Day: 50c, Grasshopper.

1964, Mar. 6 ***Perf. 13x12½***

116	A29	25c violet blue	.25	.25
117	A29	50c olive green	.35	.30
118	A29	1p red brown	.45	.30
		Nos. 116-118 (3)	1.05	.85

Mountain Gazelle — A30

Design: 50c, Head of roebuck.

1964, June 1 **Photo.**

119	A30	25c brt violet	.25	.25
120	A30	50c slate blk	.35	.25
121	A30	1p orange red	.40	.35
		Nos. 119-121 (3)	1.00	.85

Issued for child welfare.

Bicycle Race A31

Stamp Day: 1p, Motorcycle race.

1964, Nov. 23 ***Perf. 12½x13***

122 A31 50c brown .30 .25
123 A31 1p orange ver .35 .30
124 A31 1.50p Prus green .40 .35
Nos. 122-124 (3) 1.05 .90

Man — A32

Two Boys in School — A33

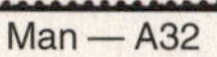

Cable Cars, Sidi Ifni — A34

Perf. 13x12½, 12½x13

1965, Mar. 1 **Photo.** **Unwmk.**

125 A32 50c dark green .30 .25
126 A33 1p orange ver .35 .30
127 A34 1.50p dark blue .40 .35
Nos. 125-127 (3) 1.05 .90

25 years of peace after the Spanish Civil War.

Eugaster Fernandezi A35

Insect: 1p, Halter halteratus.

1965, June 1 **Photo.** **Unwmk.**

128 A35 50c purple .30 .25
129 A35 1p rose red .35 .30
130 A35 1.50p violet blue .40 .35
Nos. 128-130 (3) 1.05 .90

Issued for child welfare.

Eagle — A36

Arms of Sidi Ifni — A37

Perf. 13x12½, 12½x13

1965, Nov. 23 **Photo.**

131 A36 50c dk red brown .25 .25
132 A37 1p orange ver .35 .30
133 A36 1.50p grnsh blue .40 .35
Nos. 131-133 (3) 1.00 .90

Issued for Stamp Day 1965.

Jetliner over Sidi Ifni — A38

Design: 2.50p, Two 1934 biplanes, horiz.

Perf. 13x12½, 12½x13

1966, June 1 **Photo.** **Unwmk.**

134 A38 1p orange brn .30 .30
135 A38 1.50p brt blue .50 .40
136 A38 2.50p dull violet 2.25 2.00
Nos. 134-136 (3) 3.05 2.70

Issued for child welfare.

Syntomis Alicia — A39

40c, 4p, Danais chrysippus (butterfly).

1966, Nov. 23 **Photo.** ***Perf. 13***

137 A39 10c green & red .40 .25
138 A39 40c dk brn & gldn brn .45 .30
139 A39 1.50p violet & yel .55 .35
140 A39 4p dk pur & brt bl .65 .40
Nos. 137-140 (4) 2.05 1.30

Issued for Stamp Day, 1966.

Coconut Palms — A40

Designs: 40c, 4p, Cactus.

1967, June 1 **Photo.** ***Perf. 13***

141 A40 10c dp grn & brn .25 .25
142 A40 40c Prus grn & ocher .25 .25
143 A40 1.50p bl grn & sepia .35 .30
144 A40 4p sepia & ocher .45 .35
Nos. 141-144 (4) 1.30 1.15

Issued for child welfare.

Sidi Ifni Harbor A41

1967, Sept. 28 **Photo.** ***Perf. 12½x13***

145 A41 1.50p grn & red brn .35 .25

Modernization of harbor installations.

Needlefish (Skipper) — A42

Fish: 1.50p, John Dory, vert. 3.50p, Gurnard (Trigla lucerna).

1967, Nov. 23 **Photo.** ***Perf. 13***

146 A42 1p blue & green .30 .25
147 A42 1.50p vio blk & yel .35 .25
148 A42 3.50p brt bl & scar .45 .35
Nos. 146-148 (3) 1.10 .85

Issued for Stamp Day 1967.

Zodiac Issue

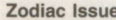

Pisces — A43

Signs of the Zodiac: 1.50p, Capricorn. 2.50p, Sagittarius.

1968, Apr. 25 **Photo.** ***Perf. 13***

149 A43 1p brt mag, *lt yel* .30 .25
150 A43 1.50p brown, *pink* .35 .30
151 A43 2.50p dk vio, *yel* .45 .35
Nos. 149-151 (3) 1.10 .90

Issued for child welfare.

Mailing a Letter A44

Designs: 1.50p, Carrier pigeon carrying letter. 2.50p, Stamp under magnifying glass.

1968, Nov. 23 **Photo.** ***Perf. 12½x13***

152 A44 1p org yel & sl grn .25 .25
153 A44 1.50p brt bl & vio blk .35 .30
154 A44 2.50p emer & vio blk .45 .35
Nos. 152-154 (3) 1.05 .90

Issued for Stamp Day.

SEMI-POSTAL STAMPS

Catalogue values for unused stamps in this section are for Never Hinged items.

Gen. Francisco Franco — SP1

Perf. 13x12½

1950, Oct. 19 **Unwmk.**

B1 SP1 50c + 10c sepia .70 .55
B2 SP1 1p + 25c blue 18.00 7.00
B3 SP1 6.50p + 1.65p dl grn 7.50 3.25
Nos. B1-B3 (3) 26.20 10.80

The surtax was for child welfare.

Fennec — SP2

1951, Nov. 30

B4 SP2 5c + 5c brown .30 .25
B5 SP2 10c + 5c red org .35 .25
B6 SP2 60c + 15c olive brn .55 .30
Nos. B4-B6 (3) 1.20 .80

Colonial Stamp Day, Nov. 23, 1951.

Mother and Child — SP3

1952, June 1

B7 SP3 5c + 5c brn .30 .25
B8 SP3 50c + 10c brn blk .40 .30
B9 SP3 2p + 30c dp bl 2.25 .85
Nos. B7-B9 (3) 2.95 1.40

The surtax was for child welfare.

Common Shag — SP4

1952, Nov. 23

B10 SP4 5c + 5c brn .30 .25
B11 SP4 10c + 5c brn car .30 .25
B12 SP4 60c + 15c dk grn .50 .35
Nos. B10-B12 (3) 1.10 .85

Colonial Stamp Day, Nov. 23, 1952.

Musician Type of Regular Issue

1953, June 1 ***Perf. 12½x13***

B13 A6 5c + 5c as No. 57 .30 .25
B14 A6 10c + 5c as No. 58 .35 .30

The surtax was for child welfare.

Fish Type of Regular Issue

1953, Nov. 23

B15 A7 5c + 5c as No. 59 .30 .25
B16 A7 10c + 5c as No. 60 .35 .30

Colonial Stamp Day, Nov. 23, 1953.

Type of Regular Issue

1954, June 1 ***Perf. 13x12½***

B17 A10 5c + 5c org .30 .25
B18 A11 10c + 5c rose vio .35 .30

The surtax was for child welfare.

Type of Regular Issue

1954, Nov. 23 ***Perf. 12½x13***

B19 A12 5c + 5c as No. 74 .30 .25
B20 A12 10c + 5c as No. 75 .35 .30

"Dama de Elche" Protecting Caravan SP5

1955, June 1 **Photo.** **Unwmk.**

B21 A13 10c + 5c rose lilac .30 .25
B22 SP5 25c + 10c violet .35 .30

The surtax was to help Ifni people.

Squirrel Type of Regular Issue

Design: 15c+5c, Squirrel holding nut.

1955, Nov. 23

B23 A14 5c + 5c red brown .30 .25
B24 A14 15c + 5c olive bister .35 .30

Type of Regular Issue

1956, June 1 ***Perf. 13x12½***

B25 A15 5c + 5c as No. 78 .30 .25
B26 A15 15c + 5c as No. 79 .35 .30

The tax was for child welfare.

Dorcas Gazelles and Arms of Spain — SP6

Design: 15c+5c, Arms of Sidi Ifni, boat and woman with drum.

1956, Nov. 23

B27 SP6 5c + 5c dark brown .30 .25
B28 SP6 15c + 5c golden brn .35 .30

Issued for Colonial Stamp Day.

Dove Type of Regular Issue

1957, June 1 Photo. *Perf. 13x12½*

B29 A17 5c + 5c as No. 81 .30 .25
B30 A17 15c + 5c Stock doves .35 .30

The surtax was for child welfare.

Type of Regular Issue

Perf. 12½x13, 13x12½

1957, Nov. 23 Photo. Unwmk.

B31 A18 10c + 5c as No. 82 .30 .25
B32 A18 15c + 5c as No. 83 .35 .30

Swallows and Arms of Valencia and Sidi Ifni — SP7

1958, Mar. 6 *Perf. 12½x13*

B33 SP7 10c + 5c org brn .30 .25
B34 SP7 15c + 10c bister .35 .25
B35 SP7 50c + 10c brn olive .40 .30
Nos. B33-B35 (3) 1.05 .80

The surtax was to aid the victims of the Valencia flood, Oct. 1957.

Sport Type of Regular Issue, 1958

1958, June 1 Photo. *Perf. 13x12½*

B36 A19 10c + 5c as No. 84 .30 .25
B37 A19 15c + 5c as No. 85 .35 .30

The surtax was for child welfare.

Guitarfish — SP8

Sailboats SP9

Stamp Day: 10c+5c, Spotted dogfish.

Perf. 13x12½, 12½x13

1958, Nov. 23

B38 SP9 10c + 5c brn red .30 .25
B39 SP8 25c + 10c dull vio .35 .25
B40 SP9 50c + 10c olive .40 .30
Nos. B38-B40 (3) 1.05 .80

Type of 1957 and

Donkey and Man — SP10

Design: 10c+5c, Ewe and lamb.

Perf. 12½x13, 13x12½

1959, June 1 Photo. Unwmk.

B41 A18 10c + 5c lt red brn .30 .25
B42 SP10 15c + 5c golden brn .35 .30

The surtax was for child welfare.

Soccer — SP11

Designs: 20c+5c, Soccer players. 50c+20c, Javelin thrower.

1959, Nov. 23 *Perf. 13x12½*

B43 SP11 10c + 5c fawn .30 .25
B44 SP11 20c + 5c slate green .35 .30
B45 SP11 50c + 20c olive gray .40 .35
Nos. B43-B45 (3) 1.05 .90

Issued for the day of the Stamp, 1959.
See Nos. B52-B54.

Type of Regular Issue, 1960

1960, June 10 *Perf. 13x12½*

B46 A20 10c + 5c as No. 89 .30 .25
B47 A20 15c + 5c Wild boars .35 .30

The surtax was for child welfare.

Santa Maria del Mar — SP12

Stamp Day: 20c+5c, 50c+20c, New school building, horiz.

Perf. 13x12½, 12½x13

1960, Dec. 29 Photo.

B48 SP12 10c + 5c org brn .30 .25
B49 SP12 20c + 5c dk sl grn .30 .25
B50 SP12 30c + 10c red brn .35 .30
B51 SP12 50c + 20c sepia .35 .30
Nos. B48-B51 (4) 1.30 1.10

Type of 1959 inscribed: "Pro-Infancia 1961"

Designs: 10c+5c, 80c+20c, Pole vaulting, horiz. 25c+10c, Soccer player.

Perf. 12½x13, 13x12½

1961, June 21 Unwmk.

B52 SP11 10c + 5c rose brn .30 .25
B53 SP11 25c + 10c gray vio .35 .25
B54 SP11 80c + 20c dk green .40 .30
Nos. B52-B54 (3) 1.05 .80

The surtax was for child welfare.

Camel Rider and Truck SP13

Stamp Day: 25c+10c, 1p+10c, Ship in Sidi Ifni harbor.

1961, Nov. 23 *Perf. 12½x13*

B55 SP13 10c + 5c rose brn .30 .25
B56 SP13 25c + 10c dk pur .30 .25
B57 SP13 30c + 10c dk red brn .35 .30
B58 SP13 1p + 10c red org .35 .35
Nos. B55-B58 (4) 1.30 1.15

AIR POST STAMPS

Stamps formerly listed as Nos. C1-C29 were privately overprinted. These include 1936 stamps of Spain overprinted "VIA AEREA" and plane, and 1939 stamps of Spain, type AP30, overprinted "IFNI" or "Territorio de Ifni."

Oasis AP1

The Sanctuary AP2

1943 Unwmk. Litho. *Perf. 12½*

C30 AP2 5c cer & vio brn .35 .25
C31 AP1 25c yel grn & ol grn .35 .25
C32 AP2 50c ind & turq grn .45 .35
C33 AP1 1p pur & grnsh bl .50 .35
C34 AP2 1.40p gray grn & bl .55 .35
C35 AP1 2p mag & org brn 1.50 1.25
C36 AP2 5p brn & pur 2.25 1.75
C37 AP1 6p brt bl & gray grn 35.00 30.00
Nos. C30-C37 (8) 40.95 34.55
Set, never hinged 80.00

Nos. C30-C37 exist imperforate. Value, set $115.

Catalogue values for unused stamps in this section, from this point to the end of the section, are for Never Hinged items.

Type of Spain, 1939-47, Overprinted in Carmine

1947, Nov. 29

C38 AP30 5c dull yellow 2.75 .85
C39 AP30 10c dk bl green 2.75 .85

Spain No. C126 Overprinted in Carmine like Nos. 33-34

1949, Oct. 9 *Perf. 12½x13*

C40 A202 4p dk olive grn 3.00 1.50

75th anniv. of the UPU.

Spain, Nos. C110 and C112 to C116, Overprinted in Blue or Carmine like Nos. 29-32

1949 *Perf. 10*

C41 AP30 25c redsh brn (Bl) .65 .25
C42 AP30 50c brown .75 .25
C43 AP30 1p chalky blue .85 .25
C44 AP30 2p lt gray grn 5.00 .85
C45 AP30 4p gray blue 13.00 4.50
C46 AP30 10p brt purple 17.50 8.75
Nos. C41-C46 (6) 37.75 14.85

Lope Sancho de Valenzuela and Sheik — AP3

1950, Nov. 23 Photo. *Perf. 13x12½*

C47 AP3 5p brown black 3.25 .85

Stamp Day, Nov. 23, 1950.

Woman Holding Dove — AP4

1951, Apr. 22 Engr. *Perf. 10*

C48 AP4 5p red 24.00 8.25

500th anniversary of the birth of Queen Isabella I of Spain.

The majority of this issue are poorly centered. Values are for very fine examples.

Ferdinand the Catholic — AP5

Perf. 13x12½

1952, July 18 Photo. Unwmk.

C49 AP5 5p brown 32.00 8.25

500th anniv. of the birth of Ferdinand the Catholic of Spain.

Plane and Mountain Gazelle — AP6

1953, Apr. 1

C50 AP6 60c light grn .40 .30
C51 AP6 1.20p brn car .45 .30
C52 AP6 1.60p lt brown .50 .35
C53 AP6 2p deep blue 3.50 .50
C54 AP6 4p grnsh blk 2.00 .65
C55 AP6 10p brt red vio 11.00 2.00
Nos. C50-C55 (6) 17.85 4.10

SPECIAL DELIVERY STAMPS

Inscribed: "URGENTE"

1943 *Perf. 12½*

E1 A3 25c slate green & car 2.25 1.60

Spain No. E20 Overprinted in Blue like Nos. 29-32

1949 Unwmk. *Perf. 10*

E2 SD10 25c carmine .35 .25

INDIA

'in-dē-ə

LOCATION — Southern, central Asia
GOVT. — Republic
AREA — 1,266,732 sq. mi.
POP. — 1,000,848,550 (1999 est.)
CAPITAL — New Delhi

On August 15, 1947, India was divided into two self-governing dominions: Pakistan and India. India became a republic in 1950.

The stamps of pre-partition India fall into three groups:

1) Issues inscribed simply "East India" (to 1881) and "India" (from 1882), for use mainly in British India proper, but available and valid throughout the country;

2) Issues as above and overprinted with one of the names of the six "Convention" states (Chamba, Faridkot, Gwalior, Jind, Nabha and Patiala) which had a postal convention with British India, for use in these states.

3) Issues of the feudatory states, over which the British India government exercised little internal control, valid for use only within the states issuing them.

12 Pies = 1 Anna
16 Annas = 1 Rupee
100 Naye Paise = 1 Rupee (1957)
100 Paise = 1 Rupee (1964)

Catalogue values for unused stamps in this country are for Never Hinged items, beginning with Scott 168 in the regular postage section, Scott C7 in the air post section, Scott M44 in the military section, Scott O113 in the official section, Scott RA1 in the postal tax section, Scott 51 in Hyderabad regular issues, Scott O54 in Hyderabad officials, Scott 49 in Jaipur regular issues, Scott O30 in Jaipur officials, Scott 39 in Soruth regular issues and Scott O19 in Soruth official

All of the values are for Never Hinged for all of the items in the sections for the International Commission in Indo-China, Jasdan, Rajasthan, and Travancore-Cochin.

Watermarks

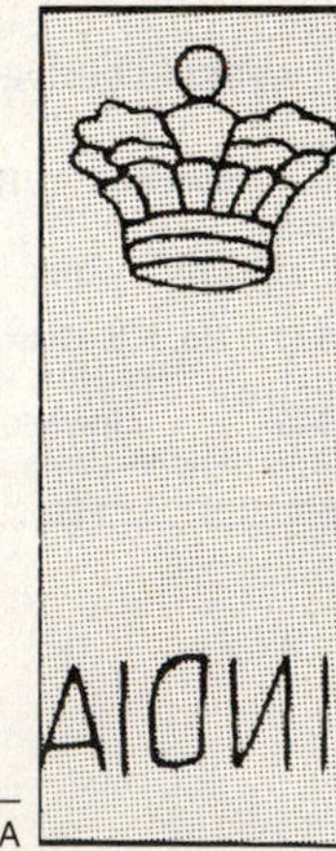

Wmk. 36 — Crown and INDIA

Wmk. 37 — Coat of Arms in Sheet. (Reduced illustration. Watermark covers a large section of the sheet.)

Wmk. 38 — Elephant's Head

Wmk. 39 — Star

Wmk. 40

Wmk. 41 — Small Umbrella

Wmk. 42 — Urdu Characters

Wmk. 43 — Shell

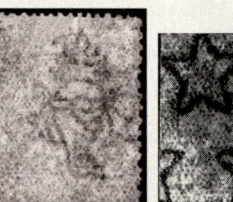

Wmk. 43A — Shell

Wmk. 196 — Multiple Stars

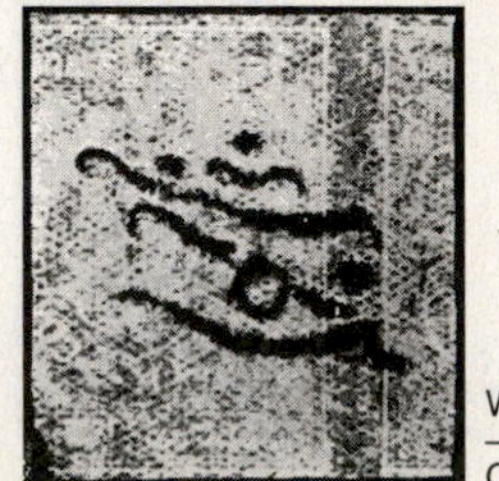

Wmk. 211 — Urdu Characters

Wmk. 294 — Letters and Ornaments in Sheet (size reduced)

Wmk. 324 — Asoka Pillar, Multiple

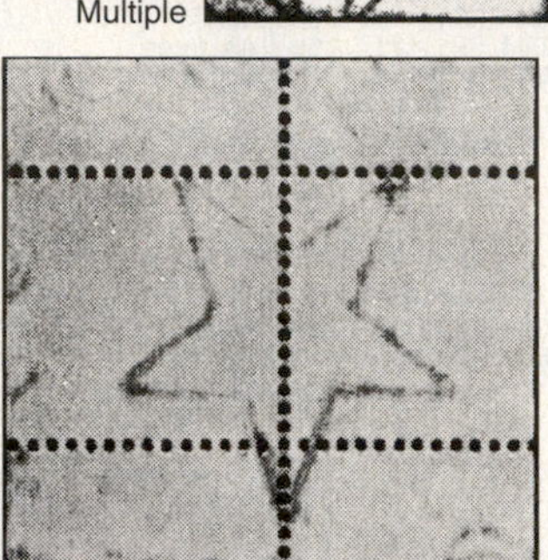

Wmk. 360 — Star and GOVT INDIA

SCINDE DISTRICT POST

A1

1852, July 1	Embossed		*Imperf.*
A1 A1 ½a *white*		21,000.	2,600.
A2 A1 ½a blue		*47,500.*	11,000.
A3 A1 ½a *red*		*165,000.*	40,000.

Obsolete October, 1854.

Nos. A1-A3 were issued without gum. No. A3 is embossed on red wafer. It is usually found with cracks and these examples are worth somewhat less than the values given, depending on the degree of cracking.

GENERAL ISSUES

Unused stamps of India are valued with original gum as defined in the catalogue introduction except for Nos. 1-7 which are valued without gum.

East India Company

A1

A2

A3

A4

A5

Queen Victoria

Litho.; Typo. (#5)

1854	Wmk. 37		*Imperf.*
1	A1 ½a red	3,250.	
2	A2 ½a blue	100.00	35.00
a.	½a deep blue	120.00	37.50
b.	Printed on both sides		*30,000.*
4	A3 1a red	150.00	55.00
a.	1a scarlet	400.00	65.00
5	A4 2a green	250.00	40.00
a.	Half used as 1a on cover		*200,000.*
6	A5 4a red & blue	7,500.	575.00
a.	4a deep red & blue	8,000.	675.00
	Cut to shape		42.50
c.	Head inverted		*225,000.*
	As "c," cut to shape		*165,000.*
e.	Double impression of head		*30,000.*

No. 1 was not placed in use.

Nos. 2, 4, 5 and 6 are known with unofficial perforation.

There are 3 dies of No. 2, and 2 dies of No. 4, showing slight differences.

There are 4 dies of the head and 2 dies of the frame of No. 6.

No. 5 is known with the watermark having the words "One Anna" in place of the lions and shield, with Urdu and Bengali characters. Values: $1,200 unused; $650 used.

Beware of forgeries. Reprints also exist.

A6

1855			
7	A6 1a red	2,000.	225.00

No. 7 was printed from a lithographic transfer made from the original die retouched. The lines of the bust at the lower left are nearly straight and meet in a point.

Beware of forgeries.

Nos. 9-35 are normally found with very heavy cancellations, and values are for stamps so canceled. Lightly canceled stamps are seldom seen. The same holds true for Nos. O1-O26.

Diadem includes Maltese Crosses — A7

1855-64	Unwmk. Typo.		*Perf. 14*
	Blue Glazed Paper		
9	A7 4a black	1,500.	22.50
a.	Imperf., pair	*17,500.*	*17,500.*
b.	Half used as 2a on cover		*20,000.*
10	A7 8a rose	1,150.	22.50
a.	Imperf., pair	9,000.	—
b.	Half used as 4a on cover		*125,000.*

See Nos. 11-18, 20, 22-25, 31. For overprints see Nos. O1-O5, O7-O9, O16-O19, O22-O24.

1855-64			**White Paper**
11	A7 ½a blue	175.00	6.75
a.	Imperf., pair	1,100.	*4,250.*
12	A7 1a brown	95.00	5.00
a.	Imperf., pair	2,000.	*5,500.*
b.	Vert. pair, imperf between		
c.	Half used as ½a on cover		*125,000.*
13	A7 2a dull rose	1,300.	52.50
a.	Imperf., pair	7,500.	*5,000.*
14	A7 2a yellow green	2,000.	*3,500.*
a.	Imperf., pair	24,000.	
15	A7 2a buff	900.00	37.50
a.	2a orange	1,500.	45.00
b.	Imperf., pair	5,000.	*8,000.*
c.	2a yellow ('63)	1,300.	60.00
16	A7 4a black	900.00	10.00
a.	Imperf., pair	*9,000.*	*7,000.*
b.	Diagonal half used as 2a on cover		*50,000.*

17 A7 4a green ('64) 4,000. 50.00
18 A7 8a rose 900.00 30.00
a. Half used as 4a on cover 120,000.

No. 14 was not regularly issued. See note after No. 25.

Many stamps of types A7-A90 are overprinted "Service" or "On H. M. S." For these, see listings of Official stamps.

Crown Colony

Queen Victoria — A8

1860-64	**Unwmk.**		***Perf. 14***
19	A8 8p lilac	95.00	8.00
a.	Diagonal half used as 4p on cover		120,000.
b.	Imperf., pair	15,000.	9,000.
19C	A8 8p lilac, *bluish*	625.00	150.00

See No. 21. For overprint see No. O6 and footnote after No. O4.

1865-67			**Wmk. 38**
20	A7 ½a blue	22.00	1.00
a.	Imperf., pair	950.00	*2,500.*
21	A8 8p lilac	12.00	*15.00*
22	A7 1a brown	11.00	1.25
23	A7 2a brnsh org	42.50	3.00
a.	2a yellow	375.00	7.50
b.	Imperf., pair		6,500.
c.	2a orange	200.00	3.50
24	A7 4a green	*1,300.*	30.00
25	A7 8a rose	*5,000.*	95.00

No. 21 was variously surcharged locally, "NINE" or "NINE PIE," to indicate that it was being sold for 9 pies (the soldier's letter rate had been raised from 8 to 9 pies). These surcharges were made without government authorization.

Stamps of types A7 and A9 overprinted with crown and surcharged with new values were for use in Straits Settlements.

A9

A10

Diadem: Rows of pearls & diamonds — A11

Type I

FOUR ANNAS
Type I — Slanting line at corner of mouth extends downward only. Shading about mouth and chin. Pointed chin.

Type II — Line at corner of mouth extends both up and down. Upper lip and chin are defined by a colored line. Rounded chin.

1866-68			
26	A9 4a green, type I	110.00	4.50
26B	A9 4a bl grn, type II	32.50	3.75
27	A10 6a8p slate	80.00	29.00
a.	Imperf., pair	11,000.	
28	A11 8a rose ('68)	70.00	11.00
	Nos. 26-28 (4)	292.50	48.25

Type A11 is a redrawing of type A7. Type A7 has Maltese crosses in the diadem, while type A11 has shaded lozenges.

For overprints see Nos. O10, O20-O21, O25-O26.

For designs A9-A85 overprinted CHAMBA, FARIDKOT, GWALIOR, JIND (JHIND, JEEND), NABHA, PATIALA (PUTTIALLA), see the various Convention States.

A12

SIX ANNAS
Type I — "POSTAGE" 3½mm high
Type II — "POSTAGE" 2½mm high

Blue Glazed Paper
Green Overprint

Perf. 14 Vert.

1866, June 28			**Wmk. 36**
29	A12 6a vio, type I	1,800.	175.
a.	Inverted overprint		*25,000.*
30	A12 6a vio, type II	3,500.	225.

Nos. 29 and 30 were made from revenue stamps with the labels at top and bottom cut off. Most and sometimes all of the watermark was removed with the labels. Twenty different varieties of this overprint exist.

These stamps are often found with cracked surface or scuffs. Such examples sell for somewhat less.

A13

A14

A15

A16

1873-76	**Wmk. 38**		***Perf. 14***
31	A7 ½a blue, redrawn	8.50	1.25
32	A13 9p lilac ('74)	20.00	16.00
33	A14 6a bister ('76)	10.00	2.25
34	A15 12a red brown ('76)	17.50	*32.50*
35	A16 1r slate ('74)	85.00	37.50
	Nos. 31-35 (5)	141.00	89.50
	Set, never hinged	300.00	

In the redrawn ½ anna the lines of the mouth are more deeply cut, making the lips appear fuller and more open, and the nostril is defined by a curved line.

Victorian and Edwardian stamps overprinted "Postal Service" and new denominations were customs fee due stamps, not postage stamps.

Empire

A17

A18

A19

A20

A21

A22

A23

A24

A25

A26

A27

1882-87			**Wmk. 39**
36	A17 ½a green	8.00	.25
a.	Double impression	*1,750.*	*2,250.*
37	A18 9p rose	1.25	*2.25*
38	A19 1a maroon	8.25	.50
a.	1a violet brown	8.25	.60
39	A20 1a6p bis brn	1.50	*1.75*
40	A21 2a ultra	5.00	.55
a.	Double impression	7,750.	*3,000.*
41	A22 3a brown org	12.00	2.00
a.	3a orange	22.50	8.75
42	A23 4a olive green	20.00	3.00
43	A24 4a6p green	32.50	7.00
44	A25 8a red violet	30.00	2.75
a.	8a rose lilac	27.50	2.75
45	A26 12a violet, *red*	11.00	5.00
46	A27 1r gray	30.00	8.00
	Nos. 36-46 (11)	159.50	33.05
	Set, never hinged	300.00	

A 6a die essay was prepared, but no stamps were printed.

A postal counterfeit exists of No. 46. Examples are scarce.

No. 40a used value is for copy with postal cancellation.

See Nos. 56-58. For surcharges see Nos. 47, 53 and British East Africa No. 59. For overprints see Nos. M2-M4, M6-M9, Gwalior Nos. O1-O5.

Beginning with the 1882-87 issue, higher denomination stamps exist used for telegrams. The telegraph cancellation has concentric circles. These sell for 10-15% of the postally used values.

No. 43 Surcharged

1891, Jan. 1			
47	A24 2½a on 4a6p green	6.75	1.25

A28

A29

1892			
48	A28 2a6p green	7.00	.80
49	A29 1r aniline car & grn	26.00	2.75

See No. 59. For overprints see Nos. M5, M10 and Gwalior No. O6.

Queen Victoria — A30

1895, Sept. 1			
50	A30 2r yel brn & rose	55.00	14.50
a.	Brn & rose	75.00	21.00
51	A30 3r green & brown	50.00	12.00
52	A30 5r violet & ultra	65.00	42.50
	Nos. 50-52 (3)	170.00	69.00
	Set, never hinged	260.00	

Used high values such as Nos. 50-52, 71-76, 95-98, 124-125, as well as similar high value official issues are for postally used examples. Stamps bearing telegraph or revenue cancellations sell for much lower prices. Most telegraph cancellations on issues of Edward VII and George V can be recognized by the appearance of "T," "TEL" or "GTO" or if they contain the concentric circles of a target.

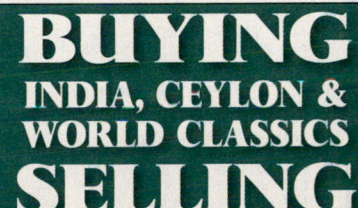

No. 36 Surcharged

1898

53 A17 ¼a on ½a green .25 *.55*
a. Double surcharge 600.00
b. Double impression of stamp 600.00

For Nos. 61, 81 with this overprint see Nos. 77, 105.

Queen Victoria — A31

1899

54 A31 3p carmine rose .45 .25

For overprint see No. M1, Gwalior No. O11.

Type of 1882-1892 Stamps

1900

55 A31 3p gray 1.00 *1.75*
56 A17 ½a light green 2.00 .60
57 A19 1a carmine rose 2.50 .25
58 A21 2a violet 6.00 2.75
59 A28 2a6p ultramarine 7.00 4.50
Nos. 55-59 (5) 18.50 9.85

For overprints see Nos. M11, Gwalior O7-O10.

Edward VII — A32

A33

A34 A35

A36 A37

A38 A39

A40 A41

A42 A43

1902-09

60 A32 3p gray 1.25 .35
61 A33 ½a green 2.25 .25
a. Booklet pane of 6 ('04) 75.00
62 A34 1a carmine rose 2.00 .25
a. Booklet pane of 6 ('04) 175.00
63 A35 2a violet 8.00 .55
64 A36 2a6p ultra 8.50 .75
65 A37 3a brown org 7.00 .75
66 A38 4a olive green 4.50 .90
67 A39 6a bister 13.50 5.50
68 A40 8a red violet 10.00 1.25
69 A41 12a violet, *red* 12.00 2.75
70 A42 1r car rose & grn 9.00 1.00
71 A43 2r brown & rose 62.50 5.00
72 A43 3r grn & brn ('04) 50.00 27.50
73 A43 5r vio & ultra ('04) 100.00 42.50
74 A43 10r car rose & grn ('09) 170.00 50.00
75 A43 15r ol gray & ultra ('09) 250.00 52.50
76 A43 25r ultra & org brn 1,400. 1,550.
Telegraph cancel 300.00
Nos. 60-75 (16) 710.50 191.80

For overprints and surcharge see Nos. M12-M20, O33, O37-O44, O47-O51, O67-O69, O73, Gwalior O12-O18.

No. 61 Surcharged Like No. 53

1905

77 A33 ¼a on ½a green .85 .25
a. Inverted surcharge 925.00

A44 A45

1906

78 A44 ½a green 4.50 .30
a. Booklet pane of 4 *45.00*
79 A45 1a carmine rose 2.50 .30
a. Booklet pane of 4 *75.00*

For overprints see Nos. O45-O46, Gwalior Nos. O19-O20.

A46 A47

A48 A49

A50 A51

A52 A53

A54 A55

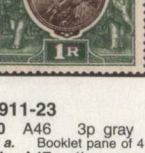

George V — A56

1911-23 **Wmk. 39**

80 A46 3p gray 1.50 .30
a. Booklet pane of 4 *50.00*
81 A47 ½a green 2.75 .25
a. Double impression 175.00
b. Booklet pane of 4 *45.00*
82 A48 1a carmine rose 3.00 .30
a. Printed on both sides
b. Booklet pane of 4 *70.00*
83 A48 1a dk brn ('22) 1.25 .40
a. Booklet pane of 4 80.00
84 A49 2a dull violet 4.75 .70
a. Booklet pane of 4 *80.00*
85 A50 2a6p ultramarine 2.50 *3.25*
86 A51 3a brown org 4.75 .30
87 A51 3a ultra ('23) 17.50 3.50
88 A52 4a olive green 9.00 1.00
89 A53 6a yel bister 5.75 2.50
90 A53 6a bister ('15) 7.00 1.60
91 A54 8a red violet 7.50 1.40
92 A55 12a claret 7.75 2.50
93 A56 1r grn & red brn 20.00 2.50
94 A56 2r brn & car rose 27.50 2.75
95 A56 5r vio & ultra 62.50 9.50
96 A56 10r car rose & grn 90.00 17.50
97 A56 15r ol grn & ultra 120.00 32.50
98 A56 25r ultra & brn org 210.00 45.00
Nos. 80-98 (19) 605.00 127.75
Set, never hinged 800.00

See Nos. 106-108, 110-111, 113-125. For surcharges and overprints see Nos. 104-105, M23-M25, M27, M29-M37, M39-M43, O52-O66, O70-O71, O74, O78-O81, O85, O87-O92, Gwalior O21-O27, O29-O32, O35-O39, O44-O45.

Nos. 93-98 also were used to pay for radio licenses, and stamps so used include "WIRELESS" in the cancel. Used values so canceled are worth 10-15% of the values shown, which are for postally used examples.

A57

1913-26

99 A57 2a6p ultramarine 3.50 .50
100 A57 2a6p brown org ('26) 7.00 5.00

See No. 112. For overprints see Nos. M28, M38.

"One and Half" — A58

1919

101 A58 1½a chocolate 4.00 .55
a. Booklet pane of 4 *60.00*

For overprint and surcharge see Nos. M26, O75.

"One and a Half" — A59

1921-26

102 A59 1½a chocolate 5.50 *6.75*
103 A59 1½a rose ('26) 4.50 .55

See No. 109. For surcharge see No. O76.

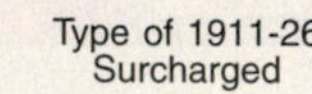

Type of 1911-26 Surcharged

1921

104 A48 9p on 1a rose 1.25 .75
a. Surcharged "NINE-NINE" 95.00 *160.00*
b. Surcharged "PIES-PIES" 95.00 *160.00*
c. Double surcharge 200.00 *225.00*
e. Booklet pane of 4 47.50

Forgeries exist of Nos. 104a-104c.

No. 81 Surcharged Like No. 53

1922

105 A47 ¼a on ½a green .75 .55
a. Inverted surcharge 12.00
b. Pair, one without surcharge 250.00

Types of 1911-26 Issues

1926-36 **Wmk. 196**

106 A46 3p slate .45 .35
107 A47 ½a green 1.75 .25
108 A48 1a dark brown .80 .25
a. Tete beche pair 2.75 *15.00*
b. Booklet pane of 4 *25.00*
109 A59 1½a car rose ('29) 2.75 .25
110 A49 2a dull violet 2.25 .25
a. Booklet pane of 4 *50.00*
111 A49 2a ver ('34) 4.25 .75
a. Small die ('36) 7.00 .55
112 A57 2a6p buff 2.75 .30
113 A51 3a ultramarine 12.50 1.50
114 A51 3a blue ('30) 12.00 .30
115 A51 3a car rose ('32) 9.75 .30
116 A52 4a olive green 1.50 .25
117 A53 6a bister ('35) 17.50 2.25
118 A54 8a red violet 5.75 .30
119 A55 12a claret 7.50 .30
120 A56 1r grn & brn 7.00 .60
121 A56 2r brn org & car rose 22.50 .85
122 A56 5r dk vio & ultra 47.50 1.75
123 A56 10r car & grn 110.00 6.50
124 A56 15r ol grn & ultra 47.50 35.00
125 A56 25r blue & ocher 300.00 47.50
Nos. 106-125 (20) 616.00 99.80
Set, never hinged 975.00

No. 111 measures 19x22½mm, while the small die, No. 111a, measures 18½x22mm.

For overprints see Gwalior Nos. O30-O39, O44-O45.

A60

A61

1926-32 **Typo.**

126 A60 2a dull violet 3.00 .25
a. Tete beche pair 15.00 *55.00*
b. 2a rose violet 17.50 15.00
c. Booklet pane of 4 21.00
127 A60 2a vermilion ('32) 16.00 7.50
128 A61 4a olive green 8.50 .30
Nos. 126-128 (3) 27.50 8.05

For overprints see #O82-O83, O86, Gwalior O33-O34.

Fortress of Purana Qila — A62

George V Flanked by Dominion Columns A67

½a, War Memorial Arch. 1a, Council Building. 2a, Viceroy's House. 3a, Parliament Building.

Wmk. 196 Sideways

1931, Feb. 9 **Litho.** ***Perf. 13½x14***

129 A62 ¼a brown & ol grn 2.50 *5.50*
130 A62 ½a green & violet 1.60 .40
131 A62 1a choc & red vio 1.25 .30
132 A62 2a blue & green 1.60 1.10
133 A62 3a car & choc 4.25 2.50
134 A67 1r violet & green 21.00 *40.00*
Nos. 129-134 (6) 32.20 49.80
Set, never hinged 66.00

Change of the seat of Government from Calcutta to New Delhi.

A68

A69

A70

Wmk. 196

1932, Apr. 22		Litho.	*Perf. 14*	
135	A68	9p dark green	7.50	.25
136	A69	1a3p violet	1.25	.25
137	A70	3a6p deep blue	8.00	.30
		Nos. 135-137 (3)	16.75	.80

No. 135 exists both litho. and typo.

For overprints see Nos. O94, O96, O104 and Gwalior Nos. O41 and O43.

A71

A72

1934			Typo.	
138	A71	½a green	7.50	.25
139	A72	1a dark brown	8.50	.25

For overprints see Nos. O93, O95 and Gwalior Nos. O40 and O42.

Silver Jubilee Issue

Gateway of India, Bombay A73

Designs: 9p, Victoria Memorial, Calcutta. 1a, Rameswaram Temple, Madras. 1¼a, Jain Temple, Calcutta. 2½a, Taj Mahal, Agra. 3½a, Golden Temple, Amritsar. 8a, Pagoda, Mandalay.

Wmk. 196 Sideways

1935		Litho.	*Perf. 13½x14*	
142	A73	½a lt green & black	1.25	.30
143	A73	9p dull green & blk	2.25	.30
144	A73	1a brown & black	4.50	.30
145	A73	1¼a violet & black	1.10	.30
146	A73	2½a brown org & blk	8.50	.80
147	A73	3½a blue & black	5.50	9.00
148	A73	8a rose lilac & blk	5.75	3.00
		Nos. 142-148 (7)	28.85	14.00
		Set, never hinged	45.00	

25th anniv. of the reign of George V.

King George VI

A80 A82

Dak Runner A81

Mail transport: 2a6p, Dak bullock cart. 3a, Dak tonga. 3a6p, Dak camel. 4a, Mail train. 6a, Mail steamer. 8a, Mail truck. 12a, 14a, Mail plane.

Perf. 13½x14 or 14x13½

1937-40		Typo.	Wmk. 196	
150	A80	3p slate	1.25	.25
151	A80	½a brown	6.00	.25
152	A80	9p green	5.00	.55
153	A80	1a carmine	.75	.25
a.		Tete beche pair	3.00	2.75
b.		Booklet pane of 4	*10.00*	
154	A81	2a scarlet	7.75	.35
155	A81	2a6p purple	.90	.30
156	A81	3a yellow green	7.75	.35
157	A81	3a6p ultramarine	6.75	.50
158	A81	4a dark brown	9.00	.30
159	A81	6a pck blue	10.00	1.10
160	A81	8a blue violet	4.50	.50
161	A81	12a car lake	11.00	1.25
161A	A81	14a rose vio ('40)	16.00	2.00
162	A82	1r brn & sl	1.75	.25
163	A82	2r dk brn & dk violet	8.50	.40
164	A82	5r dp ultra & dk grn	29.00	.60
165	A82	10r rose car & dk vio	21.00	1.00
166	A82	15r dk grn & dk brn	100.00	*95.00*
167	A82	25r dk vio & blue vio	160.00	28.00
		Nos. 150-167 (19)	406.90	*133.20*
		Set, never hinged	620.00	

The King's portrait is larger on No. 161A than on other stamps of type A81.

For overprints see Nos. O97-O103, Gwalior Nos. O46-O51.

Catalogue values for unused stamps in this section, from this point to the end of the section, are for Never Hinged items.

A83

A84

A85

Perf. 13½x14

1941-43		Typo.	Wmk. 196	
168	A83	3p slate ('42)	.75	.25
169	A83	½a rose vio ('42)	1.50	.25
170	A83	9p light green	1.25	.25
171	A83	1a car rose ('43)	2.00	.25
172	A84	1a3p bister	1.25	.25
172A	A84	1½a dark pur ('42)	2.50	.25

173 A84 2a scarlet 1.75 .25
174 A84 3a violet 4.00 .25
175 A84 3½a ultramarine 1.50 .90
176 A85 4a chocolate 1.50 .25
177 A85 6a peacock blue 4.50 .25
178 A85 8a blue violet 1.50 .35
179 A85 12a carmine lake 14.00 1.00
Nos. 168-179 (13) 38.00 4.75

Early printings of the 1½a and 3a were lithographed.
For surcharge see No. 199.

For stamps with this overprint, or a smaller type, see Oman (Muscat).

Symbols of Victory A86

1946, Jan. 2 Litho. *Perf. 13*
195 A86 9p green .90 *1.25*
196 A86 1½a dull purple .70 .35
197 A86 3½a ultramarine 1.75 *2.50*
198 A86 12a brown lake 2.25 1.40
Nos. 195-198 (4) 5.60 5.50

Victory of the Allied Nations in WWII.

No. 172 Surcharged With New Value and Bars

1946, Aug. 8 *Perf. 13½x14*
199 A84 3p on 1a3p bister .35 .25

Dominion of India

Asoka Pillar — A87

National Flag A88

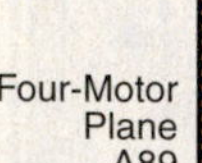

Four-Motor Plane A89

Perf. 14x13½, 13½x14

1947 Litho. Wmk. 196
200 A87 1½a greenish gray 1.00 .30
201 A88 3½a multicolored 3.00 *2.00*
202 A89 12a ultramarine 4.00 *2.50*
Nos. 200-202 (3) 8.00 4.80

Elevation to dominion status, Aug. 15, 1947.

Mahatma Gandhi — A90

Design: 10r, Gandhi profile.

Perf. 11½

1948, Aug. 15 Unwmk. Photo.

Size: 22x32½mm
203 A90 1½a brown *9.50* 1.50
204 A90 3½a violet *19.00* 6.00
205 A90 12a dark gray green *29.00* 10.00

Size: 22x37mm
206 A90 10r rose brn & brn *350.00* *100.00*
Nos. 203-206 (4) 407.50 117.50

Mohandas K. Gandhi, 1869-1948.
Nos. 203-206 exist with "Specimen" overprints in a limited edition presentation booklet. The stamps are affixed to gold foil pages. Value, complete booklet*$13,000*.
For overprints see Nos. O112A-O112D.

Ajanta Panel — A91

Konarak Horse — A92

Bodhisattva A93

Tomb of Muhammad Adil Shah, Bijapur A95

Sanchi Stupa A94

Victory Tower, Chittorgarh A96

Red Fort, Delhi A97

Satrunjaya Temple, Palitana A98

9p, Trimurti. 2a, Nataraja. 3½a, Bodh Gaya Temple. 4a, Bhuvanesvara. 8a, Kandarya Mahadeva Temple. 12a, Golden Temple, Amritsar. 5r, Taj Mahal. 10r, Qutb Minar.

Perf. 13½x14, 14x13½

1949, Aug. 15 Typo. Wmk. 196
207 A91 3p gray violet .40 .25
208 A92 6p red brown .40 .25
209 A93 9p green .60 .25
210 A93 1a turquoise .80 .25
211 A93 2a carmine 1.50 .25
212 A94 3a red orange 2.75 .25
213 A94 3½a ultramarine 2.25 7.00
214 A94 4a brown lake 7.00 .55
215 A95 6a purple 3.00 .60
216 A95 8a blue green 2.50 .25
217 A95 12a blue 10.00 .35

Litho.
218 A96 1r dk green & pur 37.50 1.50
219 A97 2r pur & rose red 27.50 .50
220 A97 5r brn car & dk grn 67.50 2.50
221 A96 10r dp bl & brn car 150.00 18.50

Perf. 13½x13
222 A98 15r dp car & dk brn 25.00 *27.50*
Nos. 207-222 (16) 338.70 60.75

See Nos. 231, 235-236. For overprints see Nos. M44-M46, M48-M55 and Intl. Commission in Indo-china issues for Cambodia, Nos. 1, 3-5, Laos Nos. 1, 3-5 and Vietnam Nos. 1, 3-5.

Symbols of UPU and Asoka Pillar — A99

1949, Oct. Litho. *Perf. 13½x13*
223 A99 9p dull green 4.75 2.00
224 A99 2a carmine rose 4.50 2.00
225 A99 3½a ultramarine 7.00 3.00
226 A99 12a red brown 11.00 3.50
Nos. 223-226 (4) 27.25 10.50

75th anniv. of the formation of the UPU.

Republic of India

Rejoicing Crowds A100

Designs: 3½a, Quill pen, vert. 4a, Plow and wheat. 12a, Charkha and cloth.

Perf. 13½x13

1950, Jan. 26 Wmk. 196
227 A100 2a carmine 5.75 .60
228 A100 3½a ultramarine 8.75 *7.00*
229 A100 4a purple 8.75 1.25
230 A100 12a claret 14.00 2.50
Nos. 227-230 (4) 37.25 11.35

Type of 1949 Redrawn

Bodhisattva — A101

1950, July 15 Typo. *Perf. 13½x14*
231 A101 1a turquoise 4.50 .90

For overprints see No. M47, Intl. Commission in Indo-china issues for Cambodia, No. 2, Laos, No. 2, and Vietnam, No. 2.

Extinct Stegodon Ganesa A102

1951, Jan. 13 *Perf. 13*
232 A102 2a dp car & blk 4.50 1.00

Geological Survey of India, cent.

Torch and Map — A103

1951, Mar. 4 Typo.
233 A103 2a red vio & red org 4.00 1.00
234 A103 12a dk brn & ultra 15.00 2.40

First Asian Games, New Delhi.

Temple Type of 1949

2½a, Bodh Gaya Temple. 4a, Bhuvanesvara.

Perf. 13½x14

1951, Apr. 30 Wmk. 196
235 A94 2½a brown lake 5.50 3.00
236 A94 4a ultramarine 11.00 .35

Kabir — A104

1a, Tulsidas, poet & saint. 2a, Meera, Rajput princess. 4a, Surdas, blind poet and saint. 4½a, Ghalib, Urdu poet. 12a, Rabindranath Tagore.

1952, Oct. 1 Photo. *Perf. 14x13½*
237 A104 9p emerald 3.25 .80
238 A104 1a crimson 3.25 .35
239 A104 2a red orange 4.00 .35
240 A104 4a ultramarine 13.00 1.25
241 A104 4½a red violet 2.50 1.50
242 A104 12a brown 22.50 1.90
Nos. 237-242 (6) 48.50 6.15

First Locomotive and Streamliner A105

1953, Apr. 16 *Perf. 14½x14*
243 A105 2a black 3.50 .45

Centenary of India's railroads.

Mt. Everest A106

1953, Oct. 2
244 A106 2a violet 5.00 .35
245 A106 14a brown 13.50 1.75

Conquest of Mt. Everest, May 29, 1953.

Telegraph Poles of 1851 and 1951 A107

1953, Nov. 1
246 A107 2a blue green 2.75 .35
247 A107 12a blue 19.00 .75

Centenary of the telegraph in India.

Mail Transport, 1854 A108

Designs: 2a and 14a, Pigeon and plane. 4a, Mail transport, 1954.

1954, Oct. 1
248 A108 1a rose lilac .40 .30
249 A108 2a rose pink 1.50 .30
250 A108 4a yellow brown 12.00 1.50
251 A108 14a blue 7.25 .45
Nos. 248-251 (4) 21.15 2.55

Centenary of India's postage stamps.

UN Emblem and Lotus Blossom A109

1954, Oct. 24
252 A109 2a Prussian green 1.25 .40

United Nations Day.

Forest Research Institute, Dehra Dun A110

1954, Dec. 11
253 A110 2a ultramarine 1.25 .30

4th World Forestry Cong., Dehra Dun.

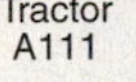
Tractor A111 — Charkha Operator A112

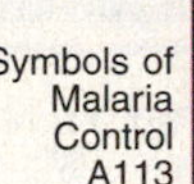
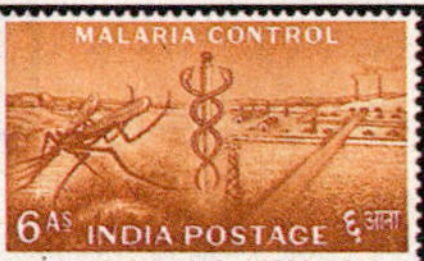
Symbols of Malaria Control A113

Designs: 6p, Power looms. 9p, Bullock irrigation pump. 1a, Damodar Valley dam. 3a, Naga woman at hand loom. 4a, Bullock team. 8a, Chittaranjan Locomotive Works. 10a, Plane over Marine Drive, Bombay. 12a, Hindustan aircraft factory. 14a, Plane over Kashmir valley. 1r, Telephone factory worker. 1r2a, Plane over Cape Comorin. 1r8a, Plane over Kanchenjunga Mountains. 2r, Rare earth factory. 5r, Sindri fertilizer factory. 10r, Steel mill.

Perf. 14x14½, 14½x14

1955, Jan. 26 **Photo.**
254 A111 3p rose lilac .45 .25
255 A111 6p deep violet .45 .25
256 A111 9p org brn .60 .25
257 A111 1a dp bl grn .60 .25
258 A112 2a blue .45 .25
259 A112 3a blue green .90 .25
260 A111 4a rose red .85 .25
261 A113 6a yellow brown 2.25 .25
262 A111 8a deep blue 10.00 .25
263 A113 10a aquamarine 5.00 3.25
264 A111 12a violet blue 5.50 .25
265 A113 14a emerald 7.00 .55
266 A111 1r grnsh blk 6.00 .25
267 A113 1r2a gray 3.00 *6.00*
268 A113 1r8a claret 12.00 7.00
269 A111 2r carmine rose 5.50 .25
270 A111 5r brown 19.00 .70
271 A111 10r orange 20.00 5.00
Nos. 254-271 (18) 99.55 25.50

See Nos. 316-319.

Bodhi Tree — A114

Ornament and Bodhi Tree A115

1956, May 24 **Wmk. 196** ***Perf. 13***
272 A114 2a brown 2.00 .30
273 A115 14a brick red 13.00 3.75

2500th anniv. of the birth of Buddha.

Bal Gangadhar Tilak — A116

1956, July 23 **Wmk. 196** **Photo.**
274 A116 2a orange brown .80 .40

Birth cent. of Bal Gangadhar Tilak, independence leader.

Map of India — A117

1957-58 ***Perf. 14x14½***
275 A117 1np blue green .25 .25
276 A117 2np light brown .25 .25
277 A117 3np brown .25 .25
278 A117 5np emerald 5.25 .25
279 A117 6np gray .40 .25
280 A117 8np brt green ('58) 5.00 1.00
281 A117 10np dark green 5.50 .25
282 A117 13np brt carmine .90 .25
283 A117 15np violet ('58) 5.00 .25
284 A117 20np bright blue .90 .25
285 A117 25np ultramarine .95 .25
286 A117 50np orange 4.75 .25
287 A117 75np plum 2.25 .25
288 A117 90np red lilac ('58) 6.50 2.00
Nos. 275-288 (14) 38.15 6.00

Denominations of the 8np, 15np and 90np are inscribed nP.

See Nos. 302-315. For overprints see No. M60 and Intl. Commission in Indo-China issues for Cambodia, Nos. 6-10, Laos, Nos. 6-10, and Vietnam, Nos. 6-10.

Laxmibai, Rani of Jhansi A118

Banyan Sapling, Arch and Flames — A119

Perf. 14½x14, 13

1957, Aug. 15 **Wmk. 196**
289 A118 15np brown .50 .35
290 A119 90np bright red violet 8.50 1.25

Centenary of the struggle for independence (Indian Mutiny).

Henri Dunant A120

1957, Oct. 28 ***Perf. 13½x13***
291 A120 15np car rose & black .50 .30

19th Intl. Red Cross Conf., New Delhi.

Boy Eating Banana A121

Bankura Horse — A122

Children's Day: 15np, Girl writing on tablet.

1957, Nov. 14 ***Perf. 13½***
292 A121 8np rose lilac .35 .25
293 A121 15np aquamarine .35 .25
294 A122 90np lt orange brown 1.10 .25
Nos. 292-294 (3) 1.80 .75

Madras University A123

University Centenaries: No. 296, Calcutta. No. 297, Bombay, vert.

1957, Dec. 31 **Photo.**

Size: 29½x25mm
295 A123 10np light brown 1.00 *.35*
296 A123 10np gray 1.00 *.35*

Size: 21½x38mm
297 A123 10np violet 1.00 *.35*
Nos. 295-297 (3) 3.00 1.05

J. N. Tata and Steel Works, Jamshedpur — A124

1958, Mar. 1 ***Perf. 14½x14***
298 A124 15np red orange .50 .30

50th anniv. of Indian steel industry.

Dr. Dhondo Keshav Karve — A125

1958, Apr. 18 ***Perf. 14x13½***
299 A125 15np orange brown .60 .30

Cent. of the birth of Karve, educator and pioneer of women's education.

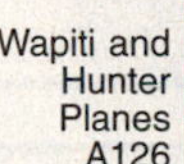

Wapiti and Hunter Planes A126

1958, Apr. 30 ***Perf. 14½x14***
300 A126 15np bright blue 1.50 .30
301 A126 90np ultramarine 2.50 2.00

25th anniv. of the Indian Air Force.

Map Type of 1957-58 and Industrial Type of 1955

1r, Telephone factory worker. 2r, Rare earth factory. 5r, Sindri fertilizer factory. 10r, Steel mill.

Perf. 14x14½

1958-63 **Photo.** **Wmk. 324**
302 A117 1np bl grn ('60) 1.50 .75
a. Imperf., pair 650.00
303 A117 2np light brown .40 .25
304 A117 3np brown .40 .25
305 A117 5np emerald .40 .25
306 A117 6np gray ('63) .55 *3.25*
307 A117 8np bright green 1.00 .25
308 A117 10np dark green .60 .25
a. Imperf., pair *1,000.*
309 A117 13np brt car ('63) 2.50 *3.75*
310 A117 15np violet ('59) 1.00 .25
311 A117 20np bright blue .85 .25
312 A117 25np ultramarine .85 .25
313 A117 50np orange ('59) 1.25 .25
314 A117 75np plum ('59) 2.00 .30
315 A117 90np red lil ('60) 6.00 .30
316 A111 1r dk grn ('59) 5.00 .30
317 A111 2r lil rose ('59) 8.25 .30
318 A111 5r brown ('59) 10.00 .50
319 A111 10r orange ('59) 35.00 7.00
Nos. 302-319 (18) 77.55 18.70

For overprints see Nos. M56-M59, M61, Intl. Commission in Indo-china issues for Cambodia, No. 12, Laos, Nos. 12-16, and Vietnam Nos. 11-16.

Bipin Chandra Pal — A128

1958, Nov. 7 ***Perf. 13½***
320 A128 15np dull green .60 .40

Birth cent. of Pal, early leader of India's freedom movement.

1958, Nov. 30

Portrait: Sir Jagadis Chandra Bose.

321 A128 15np brt greenish blue .60 .40

Bose, physicist, plant physiologist, birth cent.

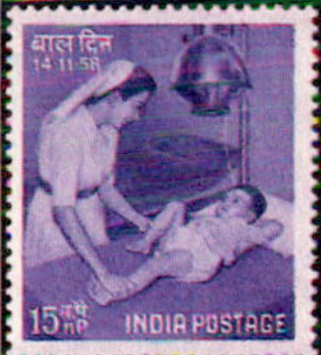
Nurse and Child — A129

1958, Nov. 14 **Wmk. 324**
322 A129 15np violet .60 .40

Children's Day, Nov. 14.

Exhibition Gate A130

1958, Dec. 30 ***Perf. 14½x14***
323 A130 15np claret .60 .30

India 1958 Exhibition at Kampur.

Sir Jamsetjee Jejeebhoy — A131

1959, Apr. 13 ***Perf. 13½***
324 A131 15np brown .60 .30

Cent. of the death of Jejeebhoy, philosopher and philanthropist.

"Triumph of Labor," by D. P. Roy Chowdhary A132

1959, June 15 ***Perf. 14½x14***
325 A132 15np dull green .60 .40

40th anniv. of the ILO.

Children Arriving at Institution — A133

Perf. 14x14½

1959, Nov. 14 Photo. Wmk. 324

326 A133 15np dull green .60 .40
a. Imperf., pair *1,200.*

Children's Day, Nov. 14.

Farmer Plowing with Bullocks A134

1959, Dec. 30 ***Perf. 13***

327 A134 15np gray .50 .30

World Agriculture Fair, New Delhi.

Thiruvalluvar Holding Stylus and Palmyra Leaf — A135

1960, Feb. 15 ***Perf. 14***

328 A135 15np rose lilac .60 .40

Honoring the ancient and saintly Tamil poet, Thiruvalluvar.

Scene from Meghduta — A136

Scene from Sakuntala A137

1960, June 22 ***Perf. 13***

329 A136 15np gray .90 .30
330 A137 1.03r brown & bister 3.75 1.00

Honoring Kalidasa, 5th cent. poet and dramatist.

For surcharge see No. 371.

Subramania Bharati — A138

1960, Sept. 11 Photo. ***Perf. 14x13½***

331 A138 15np bright blue .60 .40

Honoring the poet and statesman Subramania Bharati (1882-1921).

Dr. M. Visvesvaraya A139

1960, Sept. 15 ***Perf. 13x13½***

332 A139 15np car rose & brown .60 .40

Birth cent. of Visvesvaraya, engineer and statesman.

Children Playing and Studying A140

1960, Nov. 14 ***Perf. 13½x13***

333 A140 15np green .60 .40

Children's Day, Nov. 14.

Children and UN Emblem A141

1960, Dec. 11 Wmk. 324

334 A141 15np olive gray & org brn .60 .40

UNICEF Day.

Tyagaraja, Indian Musician — A142

1961, Jan. 6 Photo. ***Perf. 14***

335 A142 15np bright blue .60 .40

114th anniv. of Tyagaraja's death.

First Airmail Postmark — A143

Boeing 707 Jetliner — A144

Design: 1r, Humber-Sommer biplane.

Perf. 14, 13x13½

1961, Feb. 18 Wmk. 324

336 A143 5np olive bister 2.75 .30
337 A144 15np gray & green 2.50 .30
338 A144 1r gray & claret 7.25 2.50
Nos. 336-338 (3) 12.50 3.10

50th anniv. of the world's 1st airmail. The flight was from Allahabad to Naini, Feb. 18, 1911.

Chatrapati Sivaji Maharaj (1627-1680) A145

1961, Apr. 17 ***Perf. 13x13½***

339 A145 15np gray grn & brn 1.50 .50

Leader of the Maharattas in the fight against the Moguls.

Motilal Nehru — A146

1961, May 6 ***Perf. 14x13½***

340 A146 15np orange & ol gray .60 .30

Cent. of the birth of Motilal Nehru, leader in India's fight for freedom.

Rabindranath Tagore — A147

1961, May 7 ***Perf. 13***

341 A147 15np blue grn & org 1.10 .40

Cent. of the birth of Tagore, poet.

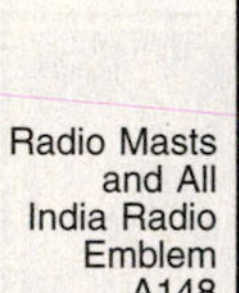

Radio Masts and All India Radio Emblem A148

1961, June 8 Photo. Wmk. 324

342 A148 15np ultramarine .60 .40

25th anniv. of All India Radio.

Prafulla Chandra Ray — A149

1961, Aug. 2 ***Perf. 14x13½***

343 A149 15np gray .60 .30

Cent. of the birth of Ray, scientist.

Vishnu Narayan Bhatkhande A150

1961, Sept. 1 ***Perf. 13***

344 A150 15np olive gray .60 .40

Bhatkhande (1860-1936), musician.

Boy Making Pottery — A151

1961, Nov. 14 ***Perf. 13½***

345 A151 15np brown .60 .40

Children's Day, Nov. 14.

Gate at Fair — A152

1961, Nov. 14 ***Perf. 14x14½***

346 A152 15np blue & carmine .60 .40

Indian Industries Fair at New Delhi.

Forest and Himalayas — A153

1961, Nov. 21 ***Perf. 13***

347 A153 15np brown & green .60 .35

Cent. of the introduction of scientific forestry in India.

Yaksha, God of Fertility — A154

Kalibangan Seal — A155

1961, Dec. 14 Photo. ***Perf. 14***

348 A154 15np orange brown 1.00 .45
349 A155 90np org brn & ol 3.75 .45

Cent. of the Archaeological Survey of India.

Madan Mohan Malaviya — A156

1961, Dec. 25 ***Perf. 14x13½***

350 A156 15np slate .60 .40

Cent. of the birth of Malaviya, Pres. of the Indian Natl. Cong. and Vice Chancellor of Benares University.

Nunmati Refinery, Gauhati — A157

1962, Jan. 1 **Photo.** ***Perf. 13***
351 A157 15np blue .90 .40

1st Indian oil refinery at Gauhati.

Bhikaiji Cama — A158

1962, Jan. 26 ***Perf. 14***
352 A158 15np rose lilac .60 .40

Cent. of the birth of Madame Cama, a leader in India's fight for independence.

Village Council, Banyan Tree, Parliament and Map — A159

1962, Jan. 26 ***Perf. 13***
353 A159 15np red lilac .60 .40

Panchayati Raj, the system of government by village council.

Dayananda Sarasvati — A160

1962, Mar. 4 ***Perf. 14***
354 A160 15np brown orange .60 .40

135th anniv. of the birth of Sarasvati, reformer of the Vedic religion and founder of the Arya Samaj educational institutions.

Ganesh Shankar Vidyarthi — A161

1962, Mar. 25
355 A161 15np reddish brown .60 .40

Vidyarthi (1890-1931), reformer of community life.

Malaria Eradication Emblem — A162

1962, Apr. 7 ***Perf. 13***
356 A162 15np dk car rose & yel .60 .40

WHO drive to eradicate malaria.

Dr. Rajendra Prasad — A163

1962, May 13 ***Perf. 13***
357 A163 15np bright red lilac .60 .40

Prasad, President of India (1950-62).

High Court, Calcutta A164

1962 **Photo.** ***Perf. 13½x14***
358 A164 15np green .80 .30
359 A164 15np Madras .80 .30
360 A164 15np Bombay .80 .30
Nos. 358-360 (3) 2.40 .90

Indian High Courts, cent. Issued: No. 358, July 1; No. 359, Aug. 8; No. 360, Aug. 14.

Ramabai Ranade — A165

1962, Aug. 15 ***Perf. 14***
361 A165 15np brown orange .60 .40

Ramabai Ranade (1862-1924), woman social reformer.

Indian Rhinoceros A166

10np, Gaur. No. 363, Lesser panda, vert. 30np, Elephant, vert. 50np, Tiger. 1r, Lion.

1962-63 **Wmk. 324** ***Perf. 14***

Size: 30x26mm

361A A166 10np yel org & blk ('63) 1.50 *1.75*
362 A166 15np Prus blue & brn .90 .30

Perf. 13x13½, 13½x13

Size: 25x36mm, 36x25mm

363 A166 15np grn & red brn ('63) 2.00 .60
364 A166 30np bis & sl ('63) 5.50 1.50
365 A166 50np dp grn, ocher & brn ('63) 5.75 1.00
366 A166 1r brt bl & pale brn ('63) 5.75 1.00
Nos. 361A-366 (6) 21.40 6.15

Child Reaching for Flag A167

1962, Nov. 14 ***Perf. 13***
367 A167 15np lt bluish grn & ver .60 .40

Children's Day.

Eye within Lotus Blossom A168

1962, Dec. 3 **Photo.**
368 A168 15np olive gray .60 .30

16th Intl. Cong. of Ophthalmology, New Delhi, Dec. 1962.

Srinivasa Ramanujan A169

1962, Dec. 22 ***Perf. 13½x14***
369 A169 15np olive gray 1.00 .45

75th anniv. of the birth of Ramanujan (1887-1920), mathematician.

Swami Vivekananda — A170

1963, Jan. 17 ***Perf. 14x14½***
370 A170 15np ol & org brn .70 .40

Cent. of the birth of Vivekananda (1863-1902), philosopher.

No. 330 Surcharged with New Value and Two Bars

1963, Feb. 2 ***Perf. 13***
371 A137 1r on 1.03r brn & bis 8.75 .70

Hands Reaching for "FAO" Emblem — A171

1963, Mar. 21 **Photo.**
372 A171 15np chalky blue 2.00 .50

UNFAO Freedom from Hunger campaign.

Henri Dunant and Centenary Emblem — A172

1963, May 8 ***Perf. 13***
373 A172 15np gray & red 4.00 .50

Centenary of the International Red Cross.
No. 373 exists with red cross omitted. Value, $25,000.

Field Artillery and Helicopter A173

Design: 1r, Soldier guarding frontier and plane dropping supplies.

1963, Aug. 15 ***Perf. 13½x14***
374 A173 15np dull green 1.25 .30
375 A173 1r red brown 2.25 .90

Honoring the Armed Forces and the 16th anniv. of independence.

Dadabhoy Naoroji — A174

1963, Sept. 4 ***Perf. 13***
376 A174 15np gray green .60 .40

Honoring Dadabhoy Naoroji (1825-1917), mathematician and statesman.

Annie Besant — A175

1963, Oct. 1 **Photo.** ***Perf. 14***
377 A175 15np blue green .60 .40

Besant (1847-1933), an English woman devoted to the cause of India's freedom, theosophist and writer. Stamp gives birth date as 1837.

School Lunch — A176

1963, Nov. 14 **Wmk. 324** ***Perf. 14***
378 A176 15np olive bister .60 .40

Children's Day.

Eleanor Roosevelt at Spinning Wheel A177

1963, Dec. 10 ***Perf. 13***
379 A177 15np rose violet .55 .35

Honoring Eleanor Roosevelt on the 15th anniv. of the Universal Declaration of Human Rights.

Gopabandhu Das (1877-1928) A178

1964, Jan. 4 ***Perf. 13***
380 A178 15np dull purple .70 .40

Gopabandhu Das, social reformer.

Lakshmi, Goddess of Wealth — A179

1964, Jan. 4 **Photo.**
381 A179 15np dull violet blue .60 .40

26th Intl. Cong. of Orientalists, New Delhi, Jan. 4-14.

Purandaradasa Holding Veena and Chipala — A180

1964, Jan. 14
382 A180 15np golden brown .55 .35

400th anniv. of the death of Purandaradasa (1484-1564), musician.

Subhas Chandra Bose and INA Emblem A181

Design: 55np, Bose addressing troops.

1964, Jan. 23 ***Perf. 13***
383 A181 15np olive .55 .35
384 A181 55np red & black 1.25 .40

67th anniv. of the birth of Bose, organizer of the Indian Natl. Army.

Sarojini Naidu (1879-1949) A182

1964, Feb. 13 ***Perf. 14x13½***
385 A182 15np dl lil & sl grn .55 .35

Mrs. Sarojini Naidu, poet, politician, governor of United Provinces.

Kasturba Gandhi — A183

1964, Feb. 22 **Photo.** **Wmk. 324**
386 A183 15np brown orange .55 .35

20th anniv. of the death of Kasturba Gandhi (1869-1944), wife of Mahatma Gandhi.

Dr. Waldemar M. Haffkine (1860-1930) A184

1964, Mar. 16 ***Perf. 13***
387 A184 15np violet brown, *buff* 1.00 .40

Haffkine, bacteriologist, who as director of Haffkine Institute introduced inoculations against cholera and plague.

Jawaharlal Nehru (1889-1964) and People A185

1964, June 12 **Unwmk.** ***Perf. 13***
388 A185 15p grayish blue .55 .35

Prime Minister Jawaharlal Nehru.

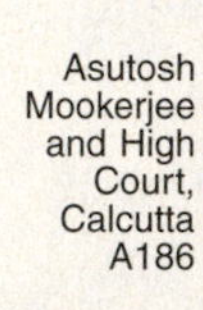

Asutosh Mookerjee and High Court, Calcutta A186

1964, June 29 **Wmk. 324**
389 A186 15p olive green & brn .55 .35

Cent. of the birth of Asutosh Mookerjee (1864-1924), educator, lawyer and judge.

Sri Aurobindo Ghose (1872-1950), Writer and Philosopher A187

1964, Aug. 15 **Photo.**
390 A187 15p violet brown .55 .35

Raja Rammohun Roy — A188

1964, Sept. 27 ***Perf. 13***
391 A188 15p reddish brown .55 .35

Roy (1772-1833), Hindu religious reformer.

Globe, Lotus, and Calipers — A189

1964, Nov. 9 **Unwmk.** **Photo.**
392 A189 15p carmine rose .55 .35

6th gen. assembly of the Intl. Organization for Standardization.

Nehru Medal and Rose — A190

1964, Nov. 14 ***Perf. 13½***
393 A190 15p blue gray .80 .40

Children's Day. For overprints, see Nos. M62, Intl. Commission in Indo-china issues for Laos and Vietnam, No. 1.

St. Thomas Statue, Ortona, Italy — A191

1964, Dec. 2 **Unwmk.** ***Perf. 13½***
394 A191 15p rose violet .45 .35

Visit of Pope Paul VI, Nov. 30-Dec. 2.

Globe and Pickax — A192

1964, Dec. 14 **Wmk. 324**
395 A192 15p bright green .55 .40

22nd Intl. Geological Cong., New Delhi.

Jamsetji N. Tata A193

1965, Jan. 7 **Unwmk.** ***Perf. 13***
396 A193 15p dk brown & orange .45 .35

125th anniv. of the birth of Tata (1839-1904), founder of India's steel industry.

Lala Lajpatrai (1865-1928), a Leader in India's Fight for Independence A194

1965, Jan. 28 **Photo.** ***Perf. 13***
397 A194 15p brown .45 .35

ICC Emblem and Globe A195

1965, Feb. 8 **Litho.**
398 A195 15p dull green & car .45 .35

20th cong. of the Intl. Chamber of Commerce, New Delhi.

Freighter Jalausha at Visakhapatnam — A196

Perf. 14½x14
1965, Apr. 5 **Photo.** **Wmk. 324**
399 A196 15p ultramarine .65 .45

National Maritime Day.

Death Centenary of Abraham Lincoln — A197

1965, Apr. 15 ***Perf. 13***
400 A197 15p yellow & dk brown .70 .40

ITU Emblem, Old and New Communication Equipment — A198

1965, May 17 **Photo.** ***Perf. 14½x14***
401 A198 15p rose violet 1.50 .60

Cent. of the ITU.

Torch and Rose — A199

1965, May 27 **Wmk. 324** ***Perf. 13***
402 A199 15p carmine & blue .40 .35

1st anniv. of the death of Jawaharlal Nehru.

ICY Emblem A200

1965, June 26 **Photo.** **Unwmk.**

403 A200 15p bister & dk green 1.25 .75

International Cooperation Year.

Indians Raising Flag on Everest — A201

1965, Aug. 15 **Unwmk.** ***Perf. 13***

404 A201 15p plum .50 .40

Success of the Indian Mt. Everest Expedition, May 20, 1965.

Elephant from Konarak Temple, Orissa A202

Tea Picking A203

Woman Writing Letter, Chandella Carving, 11th Century — A204

Trombay Atomic Center A205

Designs: 2p, Vase (bidri ware). 3p, Brass lamp. 4p, Coffee berries. 5p, Family (family planning). 8p, Axis deer (chital). 10p, Electric locomotive, 1961. 20p, Gnat plane. 30p, Male and female figurines. 40p, General Post Office, Calcutta, 1868. 50p, Mangoes. 60p, Somnath Temple. 70p, Stone chariot, Hampi, Mysore. 2r, Dal Lake, Kashmir. 5r, Bhakra Dam, Punjab.

Perf. 14½x14, 14x14½

1965-68		**Photo.**	**Wmk. 324**	
405	A202	2p redsh brown ('67)	.25	*.55*
406	A202	3p olive bis ('67)	.40	*2.40*
407	A203	4p orange brn ('68)	.25	*2.10*
408	A202	5p cerise ('67)	.25	.25
409	A202	6p gray ('66)	.25	*3.25*
410	A202	8p red brown ('67)	.40	*4.00*
411	A203	10p brt blue ('66)	.60	.25
412	A203	15p dk yel green	3.50	.25
413	A203	20p plum ('67)	8.00	.25
414	A202	30p brown ('67)	.25	.25
415	A203	40p brown vio ('68)	.25	.25
416	A202	50p green ('67)	.35	.25
417	A202	60p dark gray ('67)	.45	.25
418	A203	70p violet ('67)	.95	.25
419	A204	1r dp clar & red brn ('66)	.95	.25
420	A205	2r vio & brt bl ('67)	3.25	.25
421	A205	5r brn & vio ('67)	3.50	1.60
422	A205	10r green & gray	24.00	1.10
		Nos. 405-422 (18)	47.85	17.75

See Nos. 623, 666-670, 678, 680, 684-685. For overprints see Nos. RA1-RA2, Intl. Commission in Indo-china issues for Laos and Viet-nam, Nos. 2-9.

1975-76 **Wmk. 360** ***Perf. 14½x14***

422A A202 2p redsh brown 1.50 *2.25*
423 A202 5p cerise 1.75 .25

Unwmk.

423A A202 5p cerise ('76) 1.50 .25

A206

1965, Sept. 10 **Unwmk.** ***Perf. 13***

424 A206 15p dk grn & brn .50 .50

Govind Ballabh Pant (1887-1961), Home Minister of India.

A207

1965, Oct. 31 ***Perf. 14***

425 A207 15p gray .50 .50

Vallabhbhai Patel (1875-1950), Deputy Prime Minister of India.

Chittaranjan Das (1870-1925) A208

1965, Nov. 5 **Photo.** ***Perf. 13***

426 A208 15p brown .50 .50

Das, freedom fighter, pres. of Indian Natl. Cong., mayor of Calcutta.

Vidyapati, 15th Cent. Poet — A209

1965, Nov. 17 ***Perf. 14x14½***

427 A209 15p brown .50 .50

Tomb of Akbar the Great, Sikandra A210

1966, Jan. 24 ***Perf. 14***

428 A210 15p dark gray .50 .50

Pacific Area Travel Assoc. Conf., New Delhi.

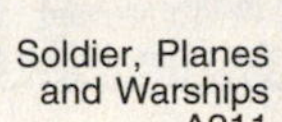

Soldier, Planes and Warships A211

1966, Jan. 26

429 A211 15p bright violet 2.00 .65

Honoring the Indian armed forces.

Lal Bahadur Shastri — A212

1966, Jan. 26 ***Perf. 13***

430 A212 15p gray 1.00 .60

Prime Minister Shastri (1904-66).

Kambar — A213

1966, Apr. 9 ***Perf. 14x14½***

431 A213 15p green .50 .50

Kambar, 9th century Tamil poet.

B. R. Ambedkar — A214

1966, Apr. 14 **Unwmk.** ***Perf. 14***

432 A214 15p violet brown .50 .50

10th anniv. of the death of Dr. Bhimrao R. Ambedkar (1891-1956), lawyer and leader in social reform.

Kunwar Singh — A215

1966, Apr. 23 **Photo.**

433 A215 15p orange brown .50 .50

Kunwar Singh (1777-1858), hero of 1857 War of Independence (1857 Mutiny).

Gopal Krishna Gokhale A216

1966, May 9 **Unwmk.** ***Perf. 13***

434 A216 15p violet brown & yel .50 .50

Cent. of the birth of Gokhale (1866-1915), professor of history and political economy and leader of the opposition party.

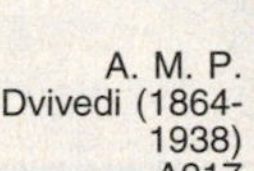

A. M. P. Dvivedi (1864-1938) A217

1966, May 15 ***Perf. 14***

435 A217 15p olive gray .50 .50

Acharya Mahavir Prasad Dvivedi, Hindi writer.

Ranjit Singh (1780-1839) — A218

1966, June 28 **Unwmk.** ***Perf. 14***

436 A218 15p plum .50 .50

Maharaja Ranjit Singh, ruler of Punjab.

Homi Bhabha and Atomic Reactor A219

1966, Aug. 4 ***Perf. 14½x14***

437 A219 15p brown violet 1.00 1.00

Dr. Homi Bhabha (1909-1966), scientist.

Rama Tirtha A220

1966, Nov. 11 **Unwmk.** ***Perf. 13***

438 A220 15p greenish blue .50 .50

60th anniv. of the death of Swami Rama Tirtha (1873-1906).

A221

1966, Nov. 11 **Photo.** ***Perf. 13½***

439 A221 15p dark violet blue .50 .50

Abul Kalam Azad (1888-1958), president of the All-India Congress.

Child and Dove — A222

1966, Nov. 14 ***Perf. 13***

440 A222 15p brt purple 1.10 .70

Children's Day.

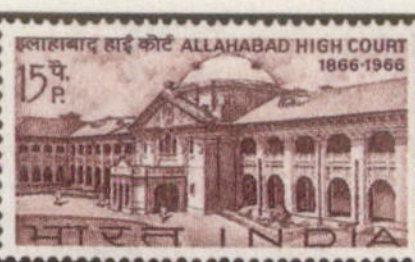

Allahabad High Court, Cent. A223

1966, Nov. 25 ***Perf. 14½x14***
441 A223 15p violet brown .50 .50

Family A224

1966, Dec. 12 ***Perf. 13½x13***
442 A224 15p brown .50 .50

Intl. Conf. for Marriage Guidance, New Delhi, and Family Planning Week.

Hockey A225

1966, Dec. 31 **Unwmk.** ***Perf. 13***
443 A225 15p bright blue 1.50 1.50

Victory of the Indian hockey team at the 5th Asian Games, Bangkok, Dec. 19.

Grain Harvest A226

1967, Jan. 11 ***Perf. 13½***
444 A226 15p yellow green .75 .90

1st anniv. of the death of Prime Minister Lal Bahadur Shastri, who advocated self-sufficiency in food production.

Voters — A227

1967, Jan. 13 **Photo.**
445 A227 15p light red brown .50 .50

General elections, Feb. 1967.

Guru Dwara Shrine, Patna — A228

1967, Jan. 17 ***Perf. 14***
446 A228 15p violet .70 .70

300th anniv. of the birth of Gobind Singh (1666-1708), religious leader.

Taj Mahal A229

1967, Mar. 19 ***Perf. 14½x14***
447 A229 15p brown & orange .60 .60

International Tourist Year.

Nandalal Bose and Garuda — A230

1967, Apr. 16 ***Perf. 13½***
448 A230 15p brown .50 .50

Nandalal Bose (1882-1966), painter.

Survey of India Emblem A231

1967, May 1 **Unwmk.** ***Perf. 13***
449 A231 15p lilac .90 .80

Bicentenary of Survey of India.

Basaveswara, 12th Cent. Statesman and Philosopher, at Work — A232

1967, May 11 ***Perf. 13½x14***
450 A232 15p deep orange .50 .50

Narsinh Mehta — A233

1967, May 30 ***Perf. 13½***
451 A233 15p gray brown .50 .50

Narsinh Mehta, 15th cent. poet.

Maharana Pratap — A234

1967, June 11 ***Perf. 14x14½***
452 A234 15p reddish brown .50 .50

Pratap (1540-1597), Mewar ruler.

Narayana Guru — A235

1967, Aug. 21 **Photo.** ***Perf. 14***
453 A235 15p brown .60 .60

Narayana Guru (1855-1928), religious reformer.

Dr. Sarvepalli Radhakrishnan A236

1967, Sept. 5 **Unwmk.** ***Perf. 13***
454 A236 15p dull claret .80 .40

Radhakrishnan, Pres. of India 1962-67.

Martyrs' Memorial, Patna A237

1967, Oct. 1 **Photo.** ***Perf. 14½x14***
455 A237 15p dark carmine .50 .50

25th anniv. of the "Quit India" revolt led by Gandhi.

Map Showing Indo-European Telegraph A238

1967, Nov. 9 **Photo.** ***Perf. 13½***
456 A238 15p blue & black 1.00 .80

Cent. of the laying of the Indo-European telegraph line.

Wrestlers A239

1967, Nov. 12
457 A239 15p ocher & plum .80 .55

World Wrestling Championships, New Delhi, Nov. 1967.

Nehru and Naga Tribesmen — A240

1967, Dec. 4 **Photo.** ***Perf. 13***
458 A240 15p ultramarine .50 .50

Rashbehari Basu — A241

1967, Dec. 26 ***Perf. 13½***
459 A241 15p dull purple .50 .50

Basu (1886-1945), Bengali leader.

Bugle, Scout Emblem and Scout Sign A242

1967, Dec. 27 ***Perf. 14½x14***
460 A242 15p orange brown 1.50 .60

Boy Scout Movement, 60th anniv.

People Encircling the Globe and Human Rights Flame A243

1968, Jan. 1 ***Perf. 13***
461 A243 15p dark green .80 .75

Intl. Human Rights Year.

Conference Emblem and Gopuram Temple — A244

1968, Jan. 3 **Photo.** **Unwmk.**
462 A244 15p purple .80 .55

2nd Intl. Conf. on Tamil Studies, Madras.

UN Emblem, Plane and Ship A245

1968, Feb. 1 ***Perf. 14½x14***
463 A245 15p greenish blue 1.00 .55

UN Conference on Trade and Development, New Delhi, Feb. 1968.

Symbolic Bow and Quill Pen — A246

1968, Feb. 20 ***Perf. 13½x14***
464 A246 15p ocher & sepia .50 .50

Cent. of the newspaper Amrit Bazar Patrika, Calcutta.

Maxim Gorky (1868-1936), Russian Writer — A247

1968, Mar. 28 Photo. *Perf. 14*
465 A247 15p brown violet .50 .50

Exhibition Emblem — A248

1968, Mar. 31 *Perf. 13*
466 A248 15p dark blue & org .60 .30

First Triennial Exhibition, New Delhi.

Symbolic Mail Box — A249

1968, July 1 Unwmk. *Perf. 13*
467 A249 20p vermilion & blue .60 .45

Opening of 100,000th Indian post office.

Wheat and Indian Agricultural Research Institute A250

1968, July 15 Photo. *Perf. 13*
468 A250 20p brt grn & brn org .60 .35

India's 1968 bumper wheat crop.

Gaganendranath Tagore (1867-1938), Self-portrait A251

1968, Sept. 17 Unwmk. *Perf. 13*
469 A251 20p ocher & deep clar .80 .55

Lakshminath Bezbaruah (1868-1938), Writer — A252

1968, Oct. 5 Photo. *Perf. 13½*
470 A252 20p sepia .50 .40

19th Olympic Games, Mexico City A253

1968, Oct. 12 *Perf. 14½x14*
471 A253 20p blue gray & red brn .40 .40
472 A253 1r olive gray & dk brn .85 .40

Bhagat Singh (1907-1931), Revolutionary — A254

1968, Oct. 19 Photo. *Perf. 13½x13*
473 A254 20p orange brown .80 .80

Bose Reading Proclamation — A255

1968, Oct. 21 *Perf. 14x14½*
474 A255 20p dark blue .60 .60

25th anniv. of the establishment of the Azad Hind (Free India) government by Subhas Chandra Bose (1897-1945), independence leader.

Sister Nivedita — A256

1968, Oct. 27
475 A256 20p blue green .60 .50

Sister Nivedita (Margaret Noble, 1867-1911), Irish-born friend of India.

Marie Curie and Patient Receiving Radiation A257

1968, Nov. 6 *Perf. 14½x14*
476 A257 20p purple 2.50 .70

Marie Sklodowska Curie (1867-1934), discoverer of radium and polonium.

World Map — A258

1968, Dec. 1 *Perf. 13*
477 A258 20p blue .60 .45

21st Intl. Geographical Congress.

Interior of Cochin Synagogue A259

Perf. 13x13½
1968, Dec. 15 Photo. Unwmk.
478 A259 20p vio bl & car rose 1.75 .75

400th anniv. of Cochin Synagogue.

Frigate Nilgiri A260

1968, Dec. 15 *Perf. 13½x13*
479 A260 20p dull violet blue 2.75 .60

Navy Day. The Nilgiri, launched Oct. 23, 1968, was the 1st Indian warship.

Redbilled Blue Magpie A261

Birds: 50p, Brown-fronted pied woodpecker. 1r, Slaty-headed scimitar babbler, vert. 2r, Yellow-backed sunbirds.

1968, Dec. 31 *Perf. 14½x14, 14x14½*
480 A261 20p pink & multi 1.10 .70
481 A261 50p multicolored 1.50 1.75
482 A261 1r multicolored 2.60 1.40
483 A261 2r multicolored 2.25 2.00
Nos. 480-483 (4) 7.45 5.85

Chatterjee (1838-94) — A262

1969, Jan. 1 *Perf. 13½*
484 A262 20p ultramarine .50 .50

Bankim Chandra Chatterjee, writer.

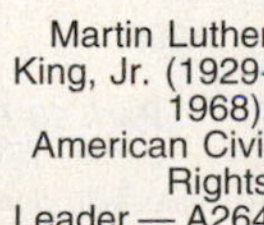
Dr. Bhagavan Das — A263

1969, Jan. 12 Photo. *Perf. 13½*
485 A263 20p red brown .50 .50

Das (1869-1958), philosopher.

Martin Luther King, Jr. (1929-1968), American Civil Rights Leader — A264

1969, Jan. 25
486 A264 20p olive gray .90 .35

Mirza Ghalib A265

1969, Feb. 17 *Perf. 14½x14*
487 A265 20p dk gray & salmon .50 .50

Mirza Ghalib (Asad Ullah Beg Khan 1797-1869), poet who modernized the Urdu language.

Osmania University, Hyderabad, 50th Avviv. A266

1969, Mar. 15 Photo. *Perf. 14½x14*
488 A266 20p green .50 .50

Rafi Ahmed Kidwai A267

1969, Apr. 1 *Perf. 13*
489 A267 20p grayish blue 1.75 .60

Minister of communications and food, introduced around-the-clock airmail service.

ILO Emblems A268

1969, Apr. 11 *Perf. 14½x14*
490 A268 20p orange brown .50 .50

50th anniv. of the ILO.

Memorial Monument and Hands Strewing Flowers — A269

1969, Apr. 13 *Perf. 13½*
491 A269 20p rose carmine .50 .50

50th anniv. of Jallianwala Bagh, Amritsar, massacre.

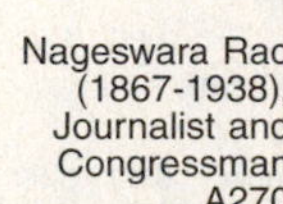

Nageswara Rao (1867-1938), Journalist and Congressman A270

1969, May 1 Photo. *Perf. 13½x14*
492 A270 20p brown .50 .50

Ardaseer Cursetjee Wadia and Ships A271

1969, May 27 Photo. *Perf. 14½x14*
493 A271 20p blue green .80 .75

Wadia (1808-1877), shipbuilder.

Serampore College, 150th Anniv. — A272

1969, June 7 Photo. *Perf. 13½*

494 A272 20p violet brown .50 .50

Dr. Zakir Husain (1897-1969), President of India 1967-1969 A273

1969, June 11 *Perf. 13*

495 A273 20p olive gray .50 .50

Laxmanrao Kirloskar and Plow A274

1969, June 20

496 A274 20p gray .50 .50

Kirloskar (1869-1956), industrialist and social reformer, introduced the iron plow to India.

Mahatma Gandhi (1869-1948) A275

Gandhi on the Dandi March A276

20p, Gandhi and his wife Kasturba, horiz. 5r, Gandhi with spinning wheel, horiz.

1969, Oct. 2 Photo. Unwmk.

Size: 29x25mm

Perf. 13½

497 A275 20p sepia .80 .80

Size: 28x38mm

Perf. 13

498 A275 75p ol gray, sal & brn 1.90 .30

Size: 20x38mm

Perf. 14x14½

499 A276 1r bright blue 1.90 1.60

Size: 35½x25½mm

Perf. 13

500 A275 5r orange & sepia 6.50 5.50

Nos. 497-500 (4) 11.10 8.20

Freighter and IMCO Emblem A277

1969, Oct. 14 *Perf. 13*

501 A277 20p ultramarine 2.75 .70

10th anniv. of the Intergovernmental Maritime Consultative Organization.

Globe and Parliament, New Delhi A278

1969, Oct. 30 Photo. *Perf. 14½x14*

502 A278 20p bright blue .50 .50

57th Interparliamentary Conf., New Delhi.

Astronaut on Moon — A279

1969, Nov. 19 *Perf. 14x14½*

503 A279 20p olive brown 1.00 .60

See note after US No. C76.

Nanak Mausoleum, Talwandi, Punjab — A280

1969, Nov. 23 Photo. *Perf. 13½*

504 A280 20p gray violet .50 .50

500th anniv. of the birth of the Guru Nanak, Sikh leader.

Tiger and Globe A281

1969, Nov. 24 *Perf. 14½x14*

505 A281 20p olive grn & red brn .90 .65

Intl. Union for the Conservation of Nature and Natural Resources.

T. L. Vaswani — A282

1969, Nov. 25 *Perf. 14x14½*

506 A282 20p dark gray .50 .50

T. L. Vaswani (1879-1966), writer and orator.

Thakkar Bapa — A283

1969, Nov. 29 *Perf. 13½*

507 A283 20p dark brown .50 .50

Thakkar Bapa (1869-1951), statesman who worked to help the untouchables.

Globe and Telecommunications Symbols — A284

1970, Jan. 21 *Perf. 13*

508 A284 20p Prussian blue .50 .25

12th Plenary Assembly of the Intl. Radio Consultative Committee.

C. N. Annadurai (1909-1969), Journalist — A285

1970, Feb. 2

509 A285 20p dk blue & magenta .50 .50

Munshi Newal Kishore and Printing Plant — A286

1970, Feb. 19 Photo. *Perf. 13x13½*

510 A286 20p dark carmine .50 .50

Kishore (1836-1895), publisher.

Cent. of Nalanda College A287

1970, Mar. 27 Photo. *Perf. 14½x14*

511 A287 20p light red brown .80 .45

Swami Shraddhanand (1856-1926), Patriot — A288

1970, Mar. 30 *Perf. 13½*

512 A288 20p orange brown 1.00 .50

Lenin A289

1970, Apr. 22 Photo. *Perf. 13*

513 A289 20p multicolored .60 .30

UPU Headquarters, Bern — A290

1970, May 20

514 A290 20p black & green .50 .50

New UPU Headquarters in Bern.

Sher Shah Suri — A291

1970, May 22 Photo. *Perf. 13*

515 A291 20p blue green .50 .50

Suri, 15th cent. ruler of Delhi and postal service reformer.

Vir D. Savarkar and Prison at Port Blair, Andamans A292

1970, May 28

516 A292 20p orange brown .80 .80

V. D. Savarkar (1883-1966), patriot.

"UN" and UN Emblem — A293

1970, June 26 Photo. *Perf. 13*

517 A293 20p blue .60 .35

25th anniv. of the UN.

Harvest, Crane, Factory and Emblem A294

1970, Aug. 18 *Perf. 14½x14*

518 A294 20p violet .50 .40

Asian Productivity Year.

Dr. Maria Montessori and Education Symbol A295

1970, Aug. 31 *Perf. 13½x13*

519 A295 20p dull claret .60 .50

Intl. Education Year and Maria Montessori (1870-1952), Italian educator and physician.

Jatindra Nath Mukherjee A296

1970, Sept. 9 ***Perf. 14½x14***
520 A296 20p dark red brown 1.75 .60

Mukherjee (1879-1915), revolutionary leader.

Srinivasa Sastri (1869-1946) A297

1970, Sept. 22 **Photo.** ***Perf. 13***
521 A297 20p dk brown & ocher .60 .50

V. S. Srinivasa Sastri, statesman.

Iswar Chandra Vidyasagar A298

1970, Sept. 26
522 A298 20p rose lilac & brown .60 .60

Vidyasagar (1820-91), educator and writer.

Maharishi Valmiki (born c. 1400 B.C.), Poet A299

1970, Oct. 14 **Photo.** ***Perf. 13***
523 A299 20p plum .60 .40

Calcutta Harbor A300

1970, Oct. 17
524 A300 20p blue 2.25 1.00

Cent. of Calcutta Port Commissioners.

Jamia Millia Islamia University, 50th Anniv. A301

1970, Oct. 29 ***Perf. 14½x14***
525 A301 20p yellow green .90 .90

Jamnalal Bajaj (1889-1942), Patriot — A302

1970, Nov. 4 **Wmk. 324** ***Perf. 13***
526 A302 20p sepia .50 .40

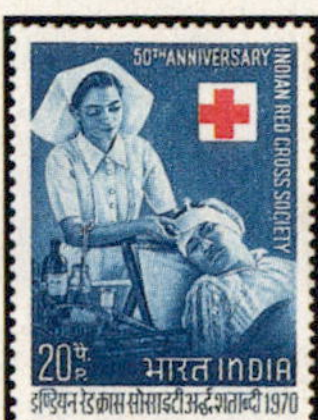

Nurse and Patient — A303

1970, Nov. 5
527 A303 20p Prus. blue & red .90 .65

50th anniv. of the Indian Red Cross Soc.

Sant Namdeo (1270-1350), Holy Man — A304

1970, Nov. 9 **Photo.**
528 A304 20p orange .50 .50

Ludwig van Beethoven A305

1970, Dec. 16 **Unwmk.** ***Perf. 13***
529 A305 20p dk brn & org 3.00 .90

Children with Stamp Album A306

Design: 1r, Hands holding magnifying glass over Gandhi stamp.

1970, Dec. 23 **Photo.** ***Perf. 13***
530 A306 20p dull green & lt brn .75 .35
531 A306 1r ocher & brown 5.00 1.25

INPEX 1970, Indian Natl. Phil. Exhib., New Delhi, Dec. 23, 1970-Jan. 6, 1971.

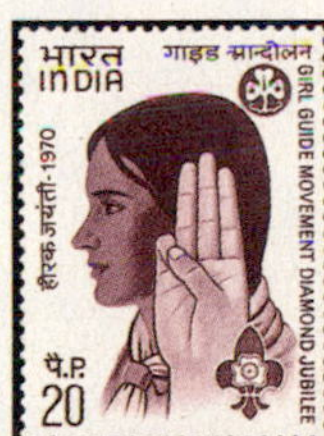

Girl Guide and Sign — A307

1970, Dec. 27
532 A307 20p dark brown violet .80 .40

Girl Guides, 60th anniv.

Hands Shielding Flame — A308

1971, Jan. 11
533 A308 20p bis brn & dp clar .50 .40

Centenary of Indian Life Insurance.

Kashi Vidyapith, 50th Anniv. A309

1971, Feb. 10 ***Perf. 14½x14***
534 A309 20p black brown .50 .40

Kashi Vidyapith University, Benares.

Charles Freer Andrews (1871-1940), British Publicist, Friend of Gandhi — A310

1971, Feb. 12 ***Perf. 13x13½***
535 A310 20p orange brown .60 .45

Ravidas, 15th Cent. Poet and Holy Man A311

1971, Feb. ***Perf. 13***
536 A311 20p rose carmine 1.10 .60

Acharya Narendra Deo (1889-1956), Educator, Patriot, Statesman A312

1971, Feb. 18 **Photo.** ***Perf. 13***
537 A312 20p olive bister .50 .50

Cent. of Indian Census A313

1971, Mar. 10
538 A313 20p ultra & sepia .50 .40

Ramana Maharshi (1879-1950), Holy Man — A314

1971, Apr. 14 **Photo.** ***Perf. 13½x14***
539 A314 20p ol gray & orange .60 .50

Raja Ravi Varma (1848-1906) and His Painting, Damayanti and the Swan — A315

1971, Apr. 29 ***Perf. 13x13½***
540 A315 20p deep yellow green .80 .65

Dadasaheb Phalke, Movie Camera A316

1971, Apr. 30 ***Perf. 13½x13***
541 A316 20p violet brown 1.25 .60

Dadasaheb Phalke (1870-1944), motion picture pioneer.

Abhisarika, by Abanindranath Tagore — A317

1971, Aug. 7 **Unwmk.** ***Perf. 14x14½***
542 A317 20p dark brn & ocher .60 .50

Tagore (1871-1951), painter.

Swami Virjanand — A318

1971, Sept. 14 ***Perf. 14x13½***
543 A318 20p orange brown .60 .50

Virjanand (1778-1868), scholar and sage.

Scuptures and Stairway, Persepolis Palace A319

1971, Oct. 12 ***Perf. 13***
544 A319 20p sepia 1.25 .70

2500th anniv. of the founding of the Persian empire by Cyrus the Great.

World Thrift Day A320

1971, Oct. 31 ***Perf. 14½x14***
545 A320 20p dark violet blue .50 .40

Bodhisatva Padampani, from Ajanta Cave — A321

1971, Nov. 4 *Perf. 13*
546 A321 20p brown 2.50 .90

25th anniv. of UNESCO.

Girls at Work, by Geeta Gupta — A322

1971, Nov. 14 *Perf. 14x14½*
547 A322 20p salmon pink .50 .50

Chidren's Day.

C. V. Raman A323

1971, Nov. 21 *Perf. 13*
548 A323 20p brown & dp org 1.00 .55

Sir Chandrasekhara Venkata Raman (1888-1970), physicist, Nobel Prize winner.

Rabindranath Tagore, Visva-Bharati Building — A324

1971, Dec. 24 *Perf. 14½x14*
549 A324 20p blk brn & org brn 1.00 .80

50th anniv. of Visva-Bharati, center for Eastern cultural studies.

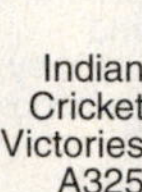

Indian Cricket Victories A325

1971, Dec. 24
550 A325 20p green 3.50 1.10

Intelsat 3 over Map of Eastern Hemisphere A326

1972, Feb. 26 **Photo.** *Perf. 13½*
551 A326 20p dark purple .50 .40

Arvi Satellite Earth Station.

Plumb Line and Symbols — A327

1972, May 29 **Photo.** *Perf. 13*
552 A327 20p bluish gray & black .50 .50

Indian Standards Institution (ISI), 25th anniv.

Signal Panel and Route Diagram — A328

1972, June 30
553 A328 20p black & multi 2.50 1.25

Intl. Railroad Union (UIC), 50th anniv.

Hockey, Olympic Rings A329

20th Olympic Games, Munich, Aug. 26-Sept. 11: 1.45r, "1972," Olympic rings, symbols for running, wrestling, shooting and hockey.

1972, Aug. 10 **Photo.** *Perf. 13*
554 A329 20p dull violet 3.50 .35
555 A329 1.45r bl grn & dk red 4.00 3.00

Marchers with Flag, Parliament A330

1972, Aug. 15
556 A330 20p blue & multi 1.00 .60

25th anniv. of Independence.

Armed Forces' Emblems — A331

1972, Aug. 15
557 A331 20p blue & multi .75 .55

Honoring India's defense forces.

Symbol of Aurobindo and Sun — A332

1972, Aug. 15 *Perf. 14x13½*
558 A332 20p yellow & blue .50 .50

Sri Aurobindo Ghose (1872-1950).

V.O. Chidambaram Pillai and Ship — A333

Perf. 13½x13

1972, Sept. 5 **Unwmk.**
559 A333 20p bl & dk red brn 1.25 .65

V.O. Chidambaram Pillai (1872-1936), founder of steamship company, trade union leader, resistance fighter.

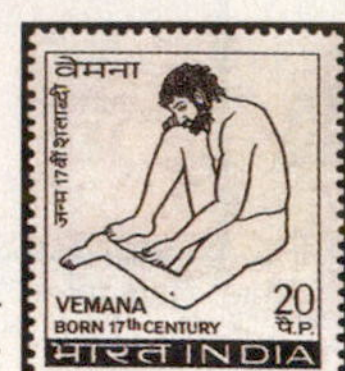

Vemana, 17th-18th Cent. Poet — A334

1972, Oct. 16 **Wmk. 324** *Perf. 14*
560 A334 20p black .50 .50

Bertrand Russell — A335

1972, Oct. 16 **Unwmk.**
561 A335 1.45r black 5.25 4.00

British philosopher and pacifist (1872-1970).

Bhai Vir Singh — A336

1972, Oct. 16 *Perf. 13½*
562 A336 20p dull purple .90 .45

Bhai Vir Singh (1872-1957), poet and scholar.

T. Prakasam — A337

1972, Oct. 16
563 A337 20p yellow brown .50 .40

T. Prakasam (1872-1957), national leader and lawyer.

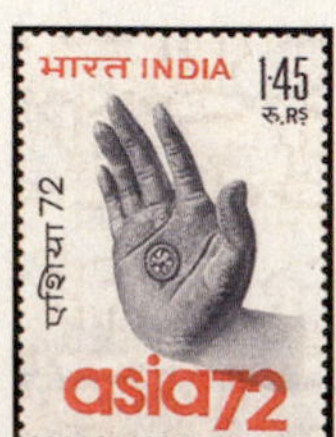

Hand of Buddha, 9th Century Sculpture — A338

20p, Stylized Hand of Buddha as Fair emblem.

1972, Nov. 3 **Wmk. 324** *Perf. 13*
564 A338 20p orange & black .40 .40
565 A338 1.45r orange, blk & ind 1.00 *2.40*

3rd Asian Intl. Trade Fair, ASIA 72, New Delhi.

Vikram Ambalal Sarabhai, Rohini Rocket and Dove A339

1972, Dec. 30 **Unwmk.**
566 A339 20p slate grn & brn .60 .60

1st anniv. of the death of Dr. Vikram Ambalal Sarabhai (1919-1971), chairman of Natl. Committee for Space Research.

Flag of USSR and Spasski Tower A340

1972, Dec. 30 *Perf. 13*
567 A340 20p red & yellow .60 .60

50th anniv. of the Soviet Union.

INDIPEX 73 Emblem — A341

1973, Jan. 8 **Photo.** *Perf. 13*
568 A341 1.45r black, pink & gold .80 *1.40*

Intl. Phil. Exhib., New Delhi, 11/14-23/73. See Nos. 597-599.

Wheel of Asoka, Naga (Serpent) — A342

India Gate, Gnat Planes, India's Colors A343

1973, Jan. 26 *Perf. 13*
569 A342 20p orange & multi .35 .35

Perf. 14½x14

570 A343 1.45r violet & multi 2.00 2.00

Republic Day, 25th year of Independence.

Ramakrishna Paramahamsa (1836-86) — A344

1973, Feb. 18 **Photo.** *Perf. 13*
571 A344 20p yellow brown .60 .50

Hindu spiritual leader; Ramakrishna Mission founded by his followers.

Army Postal Service Corps Emblem — A345

1973, Mar. 1
572 A345 20p violet blue & red .60 .60

1st anniv. of establishment of Army Postal Service Corps.

Flower, Flag, Map — A346

1973, Apr. 10 Unwmk. *Perf. 13*
573 A346 20p blue & multi .60 .60

1st anniv. of Bangladesh independence.

Kumaran Asan — A347

1973, Apr. 12
574 A347 20p brown .50 .50

Kumaran Asan (1873-1924), Kerala social reformer and writer.

Flame and Flag of India — A348

1973, Apr. 13
575 A348 20p deep blue & multi .50 .50

In honor of the martyrs of the massacre of Jallianwala Bagh, Apr. 13, 1919.

B. R. Ambedkar and Parliament Building A349

1973, Apr. 14 *Perf. 14½x14*
576 A349 20p olive & plum .50 .50

Bhimrao R. Ambedkar (1891-1956), lawyer, reformer of Hindu law and one of the writers of India's Constitution.

Radha-Kishangarh, by Nihal Chand, 1778 — A350

Indian Miniatures: 50p, Dancing Couple, late 17th century. 1r, Lovers on a Camel, by Nasir-ud-Din, c. 1605. 2r, Chained Elephant, by Zain-al-Abidin, 16th century.

1973, May 5 Photo. *Perf. 13½x13*

577	A350	20p gold & multi	.55	*.60*
578	A350	50p lilac & multi	1.25	*2.25*
579	A350	1r ocher & multi	1.60	*1.75*
580	A350	2r gold & multi	2.25	*3.75*
		Nos. 577-580 (4)	5.65	8.35

Himalayas A351

1973, May 15 *Perf. 13½x13*
581 A351 20p blue .80 .65

15th anniv. of Indian Mountaineering Foundation.

Air India Jet — A352

1973, June 8 Photo. *Perf. 13*
582 A352 1.45r multicolored 5.50 5.50

Air India, 25 years of intl. service.

Stone Cross on St. Thomas's Mount, Madras — A353

1973, July 3
583 A353 20p gray ol & blue gray .50 .50

1900th anniv. of the death of St. Thomas.

Michael Madhusudan Dutt — A354

1973, July 21 Photo. *Perf. 13*
584 A354 20p ocher & olive 1.00 .80

Dutt (1824-1873), writer and poet.

Vishnu Dingambar Paluskar (1872-1931), Musician — A355

1973, July 21
585 A355 30p red brown 1.75 1.75

Dr. Armauer G. Hansen, Microscope, Petri Dish with Bacilli A356

1973, July 21
586 A356 50p deep brown 2.00 2.00

Cent. of the discovery by Hansen of the Hansen bacillus, the cause of leprosy.

Nicolaus Copernicus, Heliocentric System A357

1973, July 21
587 A357 1r vio blue & red brn 2.00 2.00

500th anniv. of the birth of Nicolaus Copernicus (1473-1543), Polish astronomer.

Allan Octavian Hume (1829-1912) A358

1973, July 31
588 A358 20p gray .50 .50

Hume, British civil servant and friend of India, on the 25th anniv. of independence.

Nehru and Gandhi A359

1973, Aug. 15 Photo. *Perf. 13*
589 A359 20p bl vio & red brn .50 .50

25th anniv. of India's independence.

Romesh Chunder Dutt — A360

Ranjit Sinhji — A361

Vithalbhai Patel (1873-1933), National Leader — A362

1973, Sept. 27 Photo. *Perf. 13*

590	A360	20p brown	.50	.50
591	A361	30p dark green	5.50	5.50
592	A362	50p brown	.50	.50
		Nos. 590-592 (3)	6.50	6.50

Birth anniv.: Dutt (1848-1909), economist and pres. of Natl. Cong. in 1890; Sinhji, Maharaja of Nawanagar (1872-1933), cricketer.

President's Body Guard — A363

1973, Sept. 30
593 A363 20p multicolored 2.00 1.50

Bicentenary of President's Body Guard.

INTERPOL Emblem — A364

1973, Oct. 9 Photo. *Perf. 13*
594 A364 20p brown .70 .70

50th anniv. of Intl. Criminal Police Org.

Syed Ahmad Khan, Aligarh University A365

1973, Oct. 17
595 A365 20p olive gray .50 *1.00*

Khan (1817-1898), founder of Aligarh Muslim Univ.

Child's Drawing A366

1973, Nov. 14 Photo. *Perf. 13*
596 A366 20p multicolored .50 .50

Children's Day.

Elephant with Howdah, and No. 200 — A367

1973, Nov. 14

597	A367	20p Emblem	.30	.30
598	A367	1r shown	1.25	1.25
599	A367	2r Peacock, vert.	1.50	1.50
a.		Souvenir sheet of 4	9.00	9.00
		Nos. 597-599 (3)	3.05	3.05

Intl. Phil. Exhib., INDIPEX 73, New Delhi, Nov. 14-23. No. 599a contains 4 imperf. stamps similar to Nos. 568, 597-599. The imperf. stamps from No. 599a were not valid individually.

NCC Emblem — A368

1973, Nov. 25

600	A368	20p multicolored	.50	.40

National Cadet Corps, 25th anniv.

Rajagopalachari A369

1973, Dec. 25

601	A369	20p gray olive	.50	.50

Chakravarti Rajagopalachari (1878-1972), statesman, governor general (1948-50).

Sun Mask — A370

Narasimha Mask — A371

Designs: Masks.

1974, Apr. 15 Photo. *Perf. 13*

602	A370	20p shown	.40	.40
603	A370	50p Moon	.60	.50
604	A371	1r shown	.95	.80
605	A371	2r Ravana, horiz.	1.25	1.50
a.		Souvenir sheet of 4, #602-605	4.00	4.00
		Nos. 602-605 (4)	3.20	3.20

300th Anniv. of the Coronation of Chatrapati Sivaji Maharaj (1627-1680), Military Leader of the Maharattas and Enlightened Ruler — A372

1974, June 2 Photo. *Perf. 13*

606	A372	25p gold & multi	1.00	.90

Maithili Sharan Gupta — A373

Utkal Gourab Madhusudan Das — A374

Kandukuri Veeresalingam A375

Tipu Sultan — A376

No. 608, Jainarain Vyas. 1r, Max Mueller.

1974 Photo. *Perf. 13*

607	A373	25p red brown	.30	.35
608	A373	25p brown	.30	.35
609	A374	25p olive gray	.30	.35
610	A375	25p red brown	.40	.45
611	A376	50p violet brown	.85	1.10
612	A376	1r brown	.95	1.10
		Nos. 607-612 (6)	3.10	3.70

Gupta (1886-1964), poet and patriot; Vyas (1899-1963), writer and member of parliament; Das (1848-1934), writer and patriot. Veeresalingam (1848-1919), reformer; Sultan (1750-99), military leader and reformer; Mueller (1823-1900), German scholar of Sanskrit and Indian culture.

Issued: Nos. 607-609, 7/3; Nos. 610-612, 7/15.

Kamala Nehru — A377

1974, Aug 1 Photo. *Perf. 14½x14*

613	A377	25p multicolored	1.00	1.00

Kamala Nehru (1899-1936), champion of India's freedom, mother of Indira Gandhi.

WPY Emblem — A378

1974, Aug. 14 Unwmk. *Perf. 13½*

614	A378	25p buff & plum	.50	.40

V. V. Giri — A379

1974, Aug. 24 *Perf. 13x13½*

615	A379	25p green & multi	.50	.50

Vaharagiri Venkata Giri, pres. of India, 1969-74.

Type of 1965-68 and

Tiger — A380

Veena A381

Design: 25p, Axis deer (chital).

1974 Wmk. 324 *Perf. 14½x14*

622	A380	15p dk brn (white "15")	4.50	.75
623	A202	25p brown	1.25	1.00
624	A381	1r black & brown	3.25	.25
		Nos. 622-624 (3)	9.00	2.00

Issue dates: 25p, Aug. 20; 15p, 1r, Oct. 1. See Nos. 671-682.

Madhubani Folk Design, UPU Emblem A384

Designs: 25p, UPU emblem. 2r, Arrows circling globe, UPU emblem, vert.

1974, Oct. 3 Unwmk. *Perf. 13*

634	A384	25p brt blue & gray	.85	.30
635	A384	1r olive & multi	1.25	.85
636	A384	2r ocher & multi	2.00	1.90
a.		Souvenir sheet of 3, #634-636	10.00	10.00
		Nos. 634-636 (3)	4.10	3.05

Cent. of UPU.

Cent. of Mathura Museum — A385

No. 637, Flute player. No. 638, Vidyadhara with garland.

1974, Oct. 9 Photo. *Perf. 13½*

637		25p red brn & mar	.60	.50
638		25p red brn & mar	.60	.50
a.		A385 Pair, #637-638	2.00	2.00

Nicholas Konstantin Roerich, by Henry Dropsy A387

1974, Oct. 9 *Perf. 13*

639	A387	1r dark gray & yellow	.80	.80

Roerich (1874-1947), Russian painter and sponsor of Roerich Peace Pact.

Pavapuri Temple, Bihar A388

1974, Nov. 13 Photo. *Perf. 13*

640	A388	25p slate	.60	.25

2500th anniv. of attainment of Nirvana by Bhagwan Mahavira, leader and preacher of Jainism.

Dancers and Musician (Child's Drawing) A389

1974, Nov. 14 *Perf. 14½x14*

641	A389	25p multicolored	.60	.55

UNICEF in India.

Cat (Child's Drawing) — A390

1974, Nov. 14 *Perf. 13*

642	A390	25p multicolored	1.00	.50

Children's Day.

Territorial Army Emblem — A391

1974, Nov. 16 ***Perf. 13***
643 A391 25p green, yel & black .80 .60

Territorial Army, 25th anniv.

Cows, from Handpainted Rajasthan Cloth — A392

1974, Dec. 2 ***Perf. 14***
644 A392 25p ocher & maroon .60 .35

19th Intl. Dairy Cong., New Delhi, Dec. 2-6.

Symbol of Retardates and Child — A393

1974, Dec. 8 Photo. ***Perf. 13½x13***
645 A393 25p black & vermilion .75 .65

Help the Retardates!

Guglielmo Marconi — A394

1974, Dec. 12 ***Perf. 13x13½***
646 A394 2r slate 4.00 3.00

Marconi (1874-1937), Italian electrical engineer and inventor.

St. Francis Xavier's Tomb and Statue — A395

1974, Dec. 24 ***Perf. 13½x13***
647 A395 25p multicolored .50 .50

Showing of the body of St. Francis Xavier, Apostle to the Indies.

Saraswati, Goddess of Language and Learning, Inscription in Hindi — A396

1975, Jan. 10 Photo. ***Perf. 14x14½***
648 A396 25p dark red & gray .50 .50

World Hindi Convention, Nagpur, Jan. 10-14. See No. 654.

Parliament House — A397

1975, Jan. 26 ***Perf. 13***
649 A397 25p black, blue & silver 1.00 .95

Republic of India, 25th anniv.

Table Tennis Paddle and Ball — A398

1975, Feb. 6 ***Perf. 13½x13***
650 A398 25p black, red & olive 1.50 .55

33rd World Table Tennis Championship, Calcutta.

Woman's Hands Releasing Doves — A399

1975, Feb. 16
651 A399 25p yellow & multi .90 .55

International Women's Year.

Bicentenary of Army Ordnance Corps — A400

1975, Apr. 8 Photo. ***Perf. 13x13½***
652 A400 25p black & vermilion 1.75 1.10

Flame — A401

1975, Apr. 11 ***Perf. 13½x13***
653 A401 25p orange & black .60 .50

Cent. of the founding of Arya Samaj, a movement dedicated to enlightenment and progress and to a revival of Vedic Law and Aryan culture.

Saraswati Type of 1975

25p, Saraswati and inscription in Telugu.

1975, Apr. 12 ***Perf. 14x14½***
654 A396 25p dp grn & dk gray .80 .45

World Telugu Conf., Hyderabad, Apr. 12-18.

Aryabhata Satellite — A402

1975, Apr. 20 ***Perf. 13½x13***
655 A402 25p multicolored .90 .85

Launching of 1st Indian satellite, Apr. 19, 1975.

Bluewinged Pitta — A403

Birds: 50p, Black-headed oriole. 1r, Western tragopan, vert. 2r, Himalayan monal pheasant, vert.

1975, Apr. 28 ***Perf. 13½x13, 13x13½***
656 A403 25p multicolored .95 .30
657 A403 50p multicolored 2.25 2.25
658 A403 1r multicolored 3.25 3.25
659 A403 2r multicolored 4.50 4.50
Nos. 656-659 (4) 10.95 10.30

Quotation from Ram Charit Manas — A404

1975, May 24 Photo. ***Perf. 13½x13***
660 A404 25p red, org & blk 1.00 .25

Ram Charit Manas, Hindi poem by Goswami Tulsidas (1532-1623).

Women and YWCA Emblem — A405

1975, June 20 Photo. ***Perf. 13x13½***
661 A405 25p gray & multi .60 .50

YWCA of India, cent.

Creation of Adam, by Michelangelo — A406

Design: Nos. 664-665, Creation of sun, moon and plants, by Michelangelo.

1975, June 28 ***Perf. 14x13½***
662 50p multicolored .65 .50
663 50p multicolored 1.25 1.00
a. A406 Pair #662-663 2.75 2.75
664 50p multicolored 1.25 1.00
665 50p multicolored 1.25 1.00
b. A406 Pair #664-665 2.75 2.75

Michelangelo Buonarroti (1475-1564), Italian sculptor, painter and architect.

Types of 1965-1974 Without Currency Designation and

Flying Crane — A408

Jawaharlal Nehru — A409

Mahatma Gandhi — A410

Himalayas — A411

Designs: 2p, Bidri vase. 5p, Family. 10p, Electric locomotive. 15p, Tiger. 20p, Wooden toy horse. 30p, Male and female figurines. No. 680, Somnath Temple. 1r, Veena. 5r, Bhakra Dam, Punjab. 10r, Trombay Atomic Center.

Three types of 25p Nehru:
Type I: Size at top, 25mm. Character before NEHRU has 2 lower points.
Type II: Smaller portrait. Size at top, 23mm. Character has 3 points.
Type III: Portrait as in type I. Size at top, 25½mm. Character has 3 points.

Perf. 14½x14, 14x14½, 14 (#674-676), 13 (#681)
Wmk. 324; 360 (# 666A, 667, 668, 670)

1975-88 **Photo.**
666 A202 2(p) redsh brn, wmk. 324 ('76) 1.25 *2.25*
666A A202 2(p) redsh brn, wmk. 360 ('76) 1.25 *2.25*
667 A202 2(p) redsh brn, wmk. 360, litho. ('79) 1.25 *2.25*
668 A202 5(p) cerise ('76) .75 .25
669 A203 10(p) brt blue ('76) .75 .25
670 A203 10(p) brt blue ('79) 4.00 .60
671 A380 15(p) dk brn (brn "15") 2.00 .25
672 A408 20(p) green .40 .25
673 A409 25(p) vio, I ('76) 10.00 .75
674 A409 25(p) vio, II ('76) 6.50 .75
675 A409 25(p) vio, III ('76) 5.00 .75
676 A410 25(p) red brn ('76) (23x29mm) 1.25 .30
677 A410 25(p) red brn ('78) (17x20mm) 8.00 2.25
678 A202 30(p) brown ('79) 4.00 .50
679 A408 50(p) violet blue 6.50 .30
680 A202 60(p) dk gray ('76) 2.00 1.00
681 A410 60(p) black ('88) 1.10 .25
682 A381 1(r) blk & brn 4.25 .25
683 A411 2(r) vio & brn 17.00 .50
684 A205 5(r) brn & vio ('76) 2.50 .90
685 A205 10(r) dl grn & sl ('76) 2.25 1.10
Nos. 666-685 (21) 82.00 17.95

No. 667 has a background of fine horizontal lines.

See Nos. 841-842, 844-845, 846A-846B, 916.

Size of No. 681, 17x20mm.

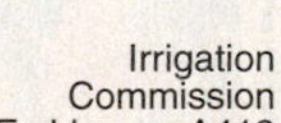

Irrigation Commission Emblem — A412

Unwmk.

1975, July 28 Photo. ***Perf. 14***
686 A412 25p multicolored .65 .30

9th Intl. Cong. on Irrigation and Drainage, Moscow, and 25th anniv. of the Intl. Commission on Irrigation and Drainage.

"Educational Television" — A413

1975, Aug. 1 ***Perf. 13x13½***
687 A413 25p multicolored .65 .45

Inauguration of the Satellite Instructional Television Experiment (SITE).

Arunagirinathar A414

1975, Aug. 14 Photo. ***Perf. 13½***
688 A414 50p rose lilac 1.75 1.25

600th birth anniv. of Arunagirinathar, Advaita philosopher, saint and author of Tiruppugazh, a collection of songs.

A415

1975, Aug. 26 Photo. ***Perf. 13½***
689 A415 25p rose & black .80 .55

Namibia Day. See note after UN No. 241.

A416

1975, Sept. 4
690 A416 25p slate green .50 .50

Mir Anees (1803-1874), Urdu poet.

Chhatri at Maheshwar A417

1975, Sept. 4 ***Perf. 13x13½***
691 A417 25p red brown .50 .50

Queen Ahilyabai Holkar (1725-1795); building shown was place of last rites.

Bharata Natyam Dance — A418

Designs: Indian traditional dances.

1975, Oct. 20 Photo. ***Perf. 13x13½***
692 A418 25p shown .95 .65
693 A418 50p Orissi 1.40 .70
694 A418 75p Kathak 1.90 .90
695 A418 1r Kathakali 2.25 1.10
696 A418 1.50r Kuchipudi 2.75 1.60
697 A418 2r Manipuri 2.75 1.60
Nos. 692-697 (6) 12.00 6.55

Krishna Menon — A419

Ameer Khusrau — A420

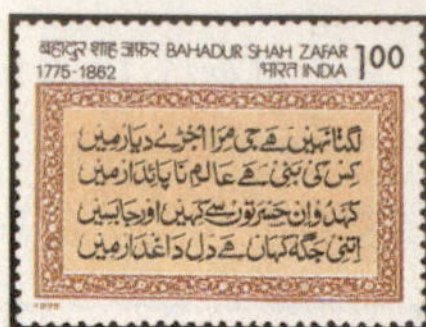
Poem by Bahadur Shah Zafar A421

Design: No. 699, Sardar Vallabhbhai Patel.

1975 ***Perf. 13x13½, 13½x13***
698 A419 25p olive 1.40 .70
699 A419 25p slate .50 .50
700 A420 50p yellow & brown 1.60 .80
701 A421 1r black, brn & buff 2.00 1.00
Nos. 698-701 (4) 5.50 3.00

Men of India: V. K. Krishna Menon (1896-1974), founder of India League and member of Parliament; Patel (1875-1950), statesman who unified India, birth cent.; Khusrau (1253-1325), poet; Zafar (1775-1862), last Mogul emperor and poet.
Issued: Nos. 699, 10/31; others 10/24.

Parliament Annex, New Delhi A422

1975, Oct. 28 ***Perf. 14½x14***
702 A422 2r gray olive 3.25 2.00

21st Commonwealth Parliamentary Conf., New Delhi, Oct. 28-Nov. 4.

Karmavir Nabin Chandra Bardoloi (1875-1936), Writer and Gandhi Associate — A423

1975, Nov. 3 Photo. ***Perf. 13***
703 A423 25p reddish brown .50 .35

Cow, Child's Painting A424

1975, Nov. 14
704 A424 25p multicolored 1.00 .55

Children's Day.

Security Press Building A425

1975, Dec. 13 Photo. ***Perf. 13***
705 A425 25p multicolored .70 .35

India Security Press, 50th anniv.

Gurdwara Sisganj, Chandni Chawk — A426

1975, Dec. 16
706 A426 25p multicolored .80 .50

300th anniv. of martyrdom of Tegh Bahadur (1621-75), 9th Sikh Guru; building shown was place of beheading.

Theosophical Society Emblem — A427

1975, Dec. 20
707 A427 25p multicolored .70 .35

Centenary of Theosophical Society.

Meteorological Instruments A428

1975, Dec. 24 Photo. ***Perf. 13***
708 A428 25p blue vio, blk & grn 1.00 .55

Indian Meteorological Dept., cent.

Early Mail Cart A429

Indian Bishop Mark, 1775 — A430

1975, Dec. 25
709 A429 25p brown & black 1.00 .40
710 A430 2r reddish brn & blk 3.25 1.75

INPEX 75, Indian Natl. Phil. Exhib., Calcutta, Dec. 25-31.

Lalit Narayan Mishra — A431

1976, Jan. 3
711 A431 25p sepia .60 .30

Mishra (1923-75), Minister of Railroads.

Tiger — A432

1976, Jan. 24
712 A432 25p multicolored 1.75 .90

Jim Corbett (1875-1955), conservationist.

Painted Storks A433

1976, Feb. 10 Photo. ***Perf. 13***
713 A433 25p sky blue & multi 1.75 .85

Keoladeo Ghana, Bharatpur Water Bird Sanctuary.

Tank A434

1976, Mar. 4 Photo. ***Perf. 13***
714 A434 25p multicolored 2.25 .55

16th Light Cavalry, senior regiment of Armoured Corps, bicentenary.

Alexander Graham Bell — A435

1976, Mar. 10 Photo. ***Perf. 13x13½***
715 A435 25p yellow & black 1.40 .90

Cent. of 1st telephone call by Bell, Mar. 10, 1876.

Muthuswami Dikshitar — A436

1976, Mar. 18 ***Perf. 14x13½***
716 A436 25p dull violet 1.00 .55

Dikshitar (1775-1835), musician, composer.

Eye and Red Cross A437

1976, Apr. 7 ***Perf. 13½x13***
717 A437 25p dark brown & red 1.40 .55

World Health Day: "Foresight prevents blindness."

"Industries"
A438

Perf. 13x13½

1976, Apr. 30 **Unwmk.**

718 A438 25p multicolored .40 .25

Industrial development and progress.

1 F/I type, Ajmer, 1895
A439

Locomotives: 25p, WDM 2 Diesel Locomotive, 1963. 1r, 1 WP./1, 4-6-2 Pacific type, 1963. 2r, 1 GIP No. 1, 1853.

1976, May 15 ***Perf. 15x14***

719 A439 25p multicolored 1.10 .25
720 A439 50p multicolored 1.75 .80
721 A439 1r multicolored 4.00 1.90
722 A439 2r multicolored 4.75 2.10
Nos. 719-722 (4) 11.60 5.05

Kumaraswamy Kamaraj (1903-1975), Independence Fighter — A440

1976, July 15 **Photo.** ***Perf. 13x13½***

723 A440 25p sepia .50 .50

Target, Olympic Rings — A441

Hockey — A442

1976, July 17 ***Perf. 14***

724 A441 25p dk blue & car .40 .30
725 A441 1r "Team handball" 1.60 .80
726 A442 1.50r black & brt pur 2.75 1.60
727 A441 2.80r "Running" 2.75 2.75
Nos. 724-727 (4) 7.50 5.45

21st Olympic Games, Montreal, Canada, July 17-Aug. 1.

Subhadra Kumari Chauhan — A443

1976, Aug. 6 **Photo.** ***Perf. 13x13½***

728 A443 25p grayish blue .50 .50

Chauhan (1904-1948), Hindi poetess and member of Legislative Assembly.

Param Vir Chakra Medal — A444

1976, Aug. 15

729 A444 25p yellow & multi .50 .50

Medal of Honor awarded for bravery to military men.

Women's University, Bombay
A445

1976, Sept. 3 **Photo.** ***Perf. 13½x14***

730 A445 25p violet .50 .30

Indian Women's Univ., 60th anniv.

Bharatendu Harishchandra
A446

1976, Sept. 9 ***Perf. 13***

731 A446 25p black brown .50 .50

Harishchandra (1850-1885), writer, "Father of Modern Hindi."

Sarat Chandra Chatterji — A447

1976, Sept. 15 **Unwmk.**

732 A447 25p dull purple .50 .50

Chatterji (1876-1938), writer.

Family Planning — A448

1976, Sept. 22 **Photo.** ***Perf. 14x14½***

733 A448 25p multicolored .50 .50

Maharaja Agrasen, Coin and Brick Wall
A449

1976, Sept. 24 ***Perf. 13½x13***

734 A449 25p red brown .50 .50

Maharaja Agrasen, legendary ruler of Agra.

India Blood Donation Day — A450

1976, Oct. 1 ***Perf. 13x13½***

735 A450 25p bister, car & black 1.25 .70

Wildlife Protection
A451

1976, Oct. 1 ***Perf. 14x14½, 14½x14***

736 A451 25p Swamp deer .70 .35
737 A451 50p Lion 1.90 .95
738 A451 1r Leopard, horiz. 2.75 1.25
739 A451 2r Caracal, horiz. 3.00 1.50
Nos. 736-739 (4) 8.35 4.05

Suryakant Tripathi "Nirala" (1896-1961), Hindi poet — A452

1976, Oct. 15 ***Perf. 13***

740 A452 25p dark violet .50 .50

Children's Day — A453

25p, Mongoose and Woman.

1976, Nov. 14 **Unwmk.** ***Perf. 14***

741 A453 25p multicolored .60 .30

Hiralal Shastri — A454

1976, Nov. 24 ***Perf. 13***

742 A454 25p red brown .50 .50

Hiralal Shastri (1899-1974), social worker and political leader.

Hari Singh Gour — A455

1976, Nov. 26

743 A455 25p plum .50 .50

Hari Singh Gour (1870-1949), University administrator, member Indian Legislative and Constituent Assemblies.

Airbus
A456

1976, Dec. 1 ***Perf. 14½x14***

744 A456 2r multicolored 4.00 2.10

Inauguration of Indian Airlines Airbus.

Hybrid Coconut Palm — A457

1976, Dec. 27 **Photo.** ***Perf. 13x13½***

745 A457 25p multicolored .50 .40

75th anniv. of coconut research in India.

Vande Mataram, First Stanza
A458

1976, Dec. 30 ***Perf. 13***

746 A458 25p multicolored .50 .40

Vande Mataram, national song of India, music by Bankim Chandra Chatterjee, 1896, words by Rabindranath Tagore, 1911.

Film and Globe
A459

1977, Jan. 3

747 A459 2r multicolored 2.50 1.25

6th Intl. Film Festival, New Delhi, Jan. 3-16.

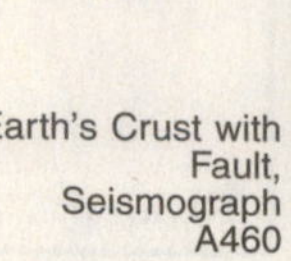

Earth's Crust with Fault, Seismograph A460

1977, Jan. 10

748 A460 2r dull purple 1.75 1.40

6th World Conference on Earthquake Engineering, New Delhi, Jan. 10-14.

Tarun Ram Phookun — A461

1977, Jan. 22 Photo. ***Perf. 13x13½***

749 A461 25p sepia .50 .50

Phookun (1877-1939), lawyer, Assam political leader.

Paramahansa Yogananda A462

1977, Mar. 7 Photo. ***Perf. 13½***

750 A462 25p deep orange 1.50 .80

Yogananda (1893-1952), religious leader, founder of Self-realization Society in America.

Red Cross Conference Emblem — A463

1977, Mar. 9

751 A463 2r multicolored 3.50 2.00

1st Asian Regional Red Cross Conference, New Delhi, Mar. 9-16.

Fakhruddin Ali Ahmed (1905-77) — A464

1977, Mar. 22 Photo. ***Perf. 13½x13***

752 A464 25p multicolored .60 .40

Ahmed, Pres. of India, 1974-77.

Asian-Oceanic Postal Union Emblem — A465

1977, Apr. 1 ***Perf. 13***

753 A465 2r silver & multi 1.50 1.25

Asian-Oceanic Postal Union, 15th anniv.

"Loyalty" and Morarjee A466

1977, Apr. 2 ***Perf. 13½x13***

754 A466 25p blue 1.25 .70

Narottam Morarjee (1877-1929), founder of Scindia Steam Ship Navigation Co.

Makhanlal Chaturvedi A467

1977, Apr. 4 ***Perf. 13***

755 A467 25p orange brown .50 .50

Chaturvedi (1889-1968), Hindi writer.

Mahaprabhu Vallabhacharya A468

1977, Apr. 14

756 A468 1r olive brown .50 .50

Vallabhacharya (1479-1531), philosopher.

Federation Emblem A469

1977, Apr. 23 ***Perf. 13½x13***

757 A469 25p ocher & purple .50 .50

Federation of Indian Chambers of Commerce, 50th anniv.

Protection of Environment A470

1977, June 5 Photo. ***Perf. 13***

758 A470 2r multicolored .80 .55

Council of States Chamber A471

1977, June 21

759 A471 25p multicolored .50 .50

Council of States, Rajya Sabha (Parliament), 25th anniv.

Lotus A472

50p and 1r are vert.

1977, July 1 ***Perf. 15x14, 14x15***

760 A472 25p shown .50 .30
761 A472 50p Rhododendron .85 .50
762 A472 1r Kadamba 1.10 .75
763 A472 2r Gloriosa lily 1.90 1.10
Nos. 760-763 (4) 4.35 2.65

Berliner Gramaphone — A473

1977, July 20 ***Perf. 13½x13***

764 A473 2r black & brown 1.50 .90

Centenary of the phonograph.

Ananda Kentish Coomaraswamy (1877-1947) and Dancing Shiva — A474

1977, Aug. 22 Photo. ***Perf. 13x13½***

765 A474 25p multicolored .60 .30

Coomaraswamy, art historian and critic.

Ganga Ram (1851-1927) and Hospital, New Delhi — A475

1977, Sept. 4 ***Perf. 14½x14***

766 A475 25p rose carmine .50 .35

Ram, social reformer and philanthropist.

Dr. Samuel Hahnemann and Cinchona — A476

1977, Oct. 6 Photo. ***Perf. 13***

767 A476 2r black & green 5.50 2.75

32nd Intl. Homeopathic Cong., New Delhi.

19th Century Postman — A477

Lion and Palm Tree, East India Co. Essay — A478

1977, Oct. 12 ***Perf. 13***

768 A477 25p multicolored 1.00 .50

Perf. 13½

769 A478 2r mag & gray, *buff* 2.75 1.75

INPEX '77 Phil. Exhib., Bangalore, 10/12-16.

Ram Manohar Lohia (1910-67), Founder of Congress Socialist Party, Sec. of Foreign Dept. — A479

1977, Oct. 12 ***Perf. 13x13½***

770 A479 25p red brown 1.25 1.10

Red Scinde Dawks, 1852 A480

Design: 3r, Foreign mail arriving at Ballard Pier, Bombay, 1927.

1977, Oct. 19 ***Perf. 13½x13***

771 A480 1r orange & multi 2.00 1.10
772 A480 3r orange & multi 4.00 2.10

ASIANA 77, First Asian International Philatelic Exhibition, Bangalore, Oct. 19-23.

Statue of Rani Channamma — A481

1977, Oct. 23

773 A481 25p gray green 2.25 1.10

Rani Channamma of Kittue (1778-1829), who fought against British rule.

Mother and Child, Khajuraho Sculpture — A482

1977, Oct. 23 ***Perf. 13x13½***

774 A482 2r gray & sepia 3.50 2.25

15th Intl. Pediatrics Congress.

Sun and National Colors — A483

1977, Nov. 8 Photo. *Perf. 13*
775 A483 25p multicolored .60 .35

Union Public Service Commission, founded 1926.

Stylized Grain — A484

1977, Nov. 13
776 A484 25p green .60 .30

AGRIEXPO '77, Intl. Agriculture Exhib.

Cats A485

1r, Friends. Designs are from children's drawings.

1977, Nov. 14
777 A485 25p multicolored .95 .45
778 A485 1r multicolored 3.00 2.25

Children's Day.

Jotirao Phooley — A486

1977, Nov. 28 Wmk. 324
779 A486 25p gray olive .50 .40

Phooley (1827-1890), social reformer.

Senapati Bapat — A487

1977, Nov. 28
780 A487 25p brown orange .50 .40

Senapati Bapat (Pandurang Mahadev Bapat, 1880-1967), scholar and fighter for India's independence.

Diagram of Population Growth — A488

Perf. 13x13½
1977, Dec. 13 Unwmk.
781 A488 2r carmine & blue grn .80 .55

41st Session of Intl. Statistical Institute, New Delhi, Dec. 5-15.

Kamta Prasad (1875-1947) and Hindi Grammar A489

1977, Dec. 25 Wmk. 324 *Perf. 14*
782 A489 25p sepia .50 .50

Prasad, compiler of Hindi Grammar.

Spasski Tower, Russian Flag — A490

1977, Dec. 30 Unwmk. *Perf. 13*
783 A490 1r multicolored .80 .55

60th anniv. of Russian October revolution.

Climber Crossing Crevasse — A491

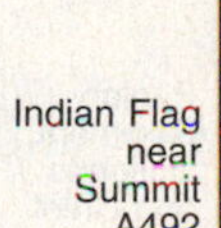

Indian Flag near Summit A492

Perf. 13½x13, 13x13½
1978, Jan. 15 Photo.
784 A491 25p multicolored .30 .30
785 A492 1r multicolored .70 .55

Conquest of Kanchenjunga (Himalayas), by Indian team under Col. N. Kumar, May 31, 1977.

Tourists in Shikara on Dal Lake A493

1978, Jan. 23 *Perf. 13x13½*
786 A493 1r multicolored 3.00 1.75

27th Pacific Area Travel Assoc. Conf., New Delhi, Jan. 23-26.

Children in Library, Fair Emblem A494

1978, Feb. 11 Photo. *Perf. 13*
787 A494 1r rose brown & indigo .65 .40

3rd World Book Fair, New Delhi, Feb. 1978.

Mother of Pondicherry A495

1978, Feb. 21
788 A495 25p dark & light brown .50 .40

Mother of the Sri Aurobindo Ashram, Pondicherry (Mira Richard, 1878-1973, born in Paris).

Wheat, Globe and Genetic Helix — A496

1978, Feb. 23
789 A496 25p yel & blue grn .50 .40

5th Intl. Wheat Genetics Symposium.

Nanalal Dalpatram Kavi — A497

Wmk. 324
1978, Mar. 16 Photo. *Perf. 13*
790 A497 25p rose brown .50 .40

Kavi (1877-1946), Gujarati poet.

Surjya Sen (1894-1934), Patriot — A498

1978, Mar. 22
791 A498 25p ver, black & brown .50 .40

Two Vaishnavas (Vishnu Worshippers) by Jaminy Roy — A499

Modern Indian Paintings: 50p, The Mosque, by Sailoz Mookherjea. 1r, Woman's Head, by Rabindranath Tagore. 2r, Hill Women, by Amrita Sher Gil.

Perf. 13½x14
1978, Mar. 23 Unwmk.
792 A499 25p black & multi .30 .30
793 A499 50p black & multi .60 .60
794 A499 1r black & multi 1.10 1.10
795 A499 2r black & multi 1.25 1.25
Nos. 792-795 (4) 3.25 3.25

Rubens, Self-portrait A500

1978, Apr. 4 Photo. *Perf. 13½x13*
796 A500 2r multicolored 4.00 2.40

"The Little Tramp," Charlie Chaplin — A501

1978, Apr. 16 *Perf. 13*
797 A501 25p gold & indigo 2.75 1.25

Deendayal Upadhyaya (1916-68) — A502

1978, May 5 Photo. *Perf. 13*
798 A502 25p multicolored .50 .40

Upadhyaya, social and political reformer.

Syama Prasad Mookerjee (1901-1953) A503

1978, July 6 Photo. *Perf. 13*
799 A503 25p gray olive .50 .35

Dr. Mookerjee, educator, member of 1st natl. government.

"Airavat," 19th Century Wood Carving — A504

Kushan Gold Coin, 1st Century A505

Designs: 50p, Wish-fulfilling tree, 2nd century B.C. 2r, Dagger and knife.

1978, July 27

800 A504	25p multicolored	.60	.60
801 A504	50p multicolored	.80	.80
802 A505	1r multicolored	1.10	1.10
803 A505	2r multicolored	1.40	1.40
	Nos. 800-803 (4)	3.90	3.90

Treasures from Indian museums.

Krishna and Arjuna on Battlefield, Quotation A506

1978, Aug. 25 Unwmk. *Perf. 13*
804 A506 25p orange red & gold .50 .40

Bhagavad Gita, part of Mahabharata Epic, the Divine Song of the Lord.

Bethune College for Women, Calcutta A507

1978, Sept. 4
805 A507 25p green & brown .50 .40

E. V. Ramasami A508

1978, Sept. 17
806 A508 25p black .50 .40

E. V. Ramasami (1879-1973), founder of Self-respect Movement, fighting caste system and social injustice.

Uday Shankar — A509

1978, Sept. 26
807 A509 25p buff & violet brown .50 .40

Uday Shankar (1900-77), dancer.

Leo Tolstoi — A510

1978, Oct. 2
808 A510 1r multicolored .75 .40

Tolstoi, novelist and philosopher.

Vallathol Narayana Menon — A511

1978, Oct. 15 Photo. *Perf. 13*
809 A511 25p multicolored .50 .50

Menon (1878-1958), poet.

"Two Friends" A512

1978, Nov. 14 Photo. *Perf. 13*
810 A512 25p multicolored .50 .40

Children's Day.

Worker at Lathe — A513

1978, Nov. 17 *Perf. 13½*
811 A513 25p green .50 .40

Small Industries Fair.

Skinner's Horse Soldiers — A514

1978, Nov. 25 *Perf. 13*
812 A514 25p multicolored 1.25 .80

175th anniv. of Skinner's Horse Regiment.

Chakravarti Rajagopalachari A515

1978, Dec. 10 Photo. *Perf. 13*
813 A515 25p maroon .50 .40

Chakravarti Rajagopalachari (1878-1972), first post-independence Governor General.

A516

1978, Dec. 10
814 A516 25p olive green .50 .40

Mohammad Ali Jauhar (1878-1931), writer and patriot.

A517

1978, Dec. 23 *Perf. 13x14*
815 A517 1r ocher & purple 1.25 .40

Wright Brothers, Flyer, 75th anniv. of 1st powered flight.

Ravenshaw College, Orissa, Centenary A518

1978, Dec. 24 *Perf. 14*
816 A518 25p green & maroon .50 .40

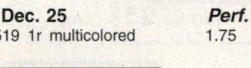

Franz Schubert (1797-1828), Austrian Composer — A519

1978, Dec. 25 *Perf. 13*
817 A519 1r multicolored 1.75 .90

Punjab Regiment, Uniforms and Crest A520

1979, Feb. 20 Photo. Unwmk.
818 A520 25p multicolored 2.00 1.00

Oldest Indian infantry unit.

Bhai Parmanand (1876-1947) A521

1979, Feb. 24
819 A521 25p violet blue .50 .40

Parmanand, writer and educator.

Gandhi and Child — A522

Design: 1r, IYC emblem.

1979, Mar. 5 Photo. *Perf. 13*
820 A522 25p dk brown & red .50 .30
821 A522 1r dp org & dk brn .75 .60

Albert Einstein (1879-1955), Theoretical Physicist — A523

1979, Mar. 14
822 A523 1r black 1.25 .65

Rajarshi Shahu Chhatrapati (1874-1922), Ruler of Kolhapur — A524

1979, May 1 Photo. *Perf. 13x13½*
823 A524 25p dull purple .50 .40

Lotus, India '80 Emblem A525

1979, July 2 Photo. *Perf. 13*
824 A525 30p dp org & grn .50 .40

India '80 Phil. Exhib., New Delhi, Jan. 25-Feb. 3, 1980.

Postal Cards, 1879 and 1979 — A526

1979, July 2
825 A526 50p multicolored .50 .40

Raja Mahendra Pratap (1886-1979), Patriot — A527

1979, Aug. 15 Photo. *Perf. 13*
826 A527 30p olive gray .50 .40

Jatindra Nath Das (1904-1929) A528

1979, Sept. 13
827 A528 30p dark brown .50 .40

Das, political martyr.

Early and Modern Light Bulbs — A529

1979, Oct. 21 Photo. *Perf. 13*
828 A529 1r rose magenta .80 .65

Centenary of invention of electric light.

Buddhist Text A530

1979, Oct. 23 *Perf. 14½x14*
829 A530 30p brown & bister .50 .40

National Archives.

Hirakud Dam A531

Perf. 13½x13
1979, Oct. 29 Wmk. 324
830 A531 30p brown red & dull grn .50 .40

13th Congress (Golden Jubilee) of the Intl. Commission on Large Dams, New Delhi, 10/29-11/2.

Boy and Alphabet Book A532

1979, Nov. 10 Photo. *Perf. 14½x14*
831 A532 30p multicolored .50 .40

Intl. Children's Book Fair, New Delhi, 11/10-19.

Fair Emblem — A533

1979, Nov. 10 *Perf. 13*
832 A533 1r black & orange .50 .40

India Intl. Trade Fair, New Delhi, 11/10-12/9.

Dove, Agency Emblem A534

1979, Dec. 4 *Perf. 13½x13*
833 A534 1r multicolored .60 .45

23rd Intl. Atomic Energy Agency Conf., New Delhi, Dec. 4-10.

Hindustan Pushpak Plane, Rohini-1 Glider A535

1979, Dec. 10 *Perf. 13½x13*
834 A535 30p multicolored 2.25 1.40

Gurdwara Baoli Shrine, Goindwal — A536

1979, Dec. 21 *Perf. 13x13½*
835 A536 30p multicolored .50 .40

Guru Amardas (1469-1574), Sikh spiritual leader.

Types of 1975-79 and

Adult Education — A536a

Fish — A536b

Agriculture Technology — A536c

Child Nutrition — A536d

Chick and Eggs — A536e

Farm, Wheat, Tractor — A536f

Women in Rice Field — A537

Family Planning — A537a

Hybrid Cotton — A537b

Weaver — A537c

Rubber Tapping — A537d

Designs: Nos. 841, 844, 846A, Jawaharlal Nehru. Nos. 842, 845, 846B, Mahatma Gandhi.

Perf. 14x14½, 14½x14, 13 (#840B)
1979-85 Photo. Wmk. 324

836	A536a	2p	violet	.80	.65
837	A536b	5p	blue	.80	.65
838	A536c	15p	blue grn ('80)	.80	.65
839	A536d	20p	hen brn ('81)	.80	.65
840	A536e	25p	brown	.80	.65
840B	A536f	25p	brt grn ('85)	.80	.65
841	A409	30p	violet ('80)	3.00	.80
842	A410	30p	red brn ('80)	2.00	.80
843	A537	30p	yel green	.80	.65
844	A409	35p	violet ('80)	2.00	.80
845	A410	35p	red brn ('80)	1.40	.80
846	A537a	35p	cerise ('80)	.80	.65
846A	A409	50p	violet ('83)	.80	.65
846B	A410	50p	red brn ('83)	2.00	.80
847	A537b	1r	brown ('80)	.80	.65
848	A537c	2r	rose vio ('80)	1.25	.65
849	A537d	5r	multi ('80)	1.75	.80
	Nos. 836-849 (17)			21.40	11.95

Size: Nos. 841-842, 844-845, 846A-846B, 17x20mm.
See Nos. 903, 904, 906.

1979-83 *Perf. 13*

837a	A536b	5p		.25	.25
837b	A536b	5p	Litho. ('82)	.60	.30
838a	A536c	15p		.25	.25
839a	A536d	20p		.40	.25
840a	A536e	25p	brown	.40	.25
843a	A537	30p		.60	.25
844a	A409	35p		.90	.30
845a	A410	35p		.30	.25
846c	A537a	35p		.60	.25
846d	A409	50p		.60	.25
846e	A410	50p		.25	.25

Perf. 12½x13

847a	A537b	1r		.25	.25

Perf. 13x13½, 13½x13

848a	A537c	2r ('83)		.25	.25
849a	A537d	5r ('83)		.50	.35
	Nos. 837a-849a (14)			6.15	3.70

People Holding Hands, UN Emblem — A538

1980, Jan. 21 Photo. *Perf. 13*
851 A538 1r multicolored .50 .40

UN Industrial Development Org. (INIDO), 3rd Gen. Conf., New Delhi, Jan. 21-Feb. 8.

Field Post Office, Cancels — A539

Money Order Centenary — A540

2-Anna Copper Coins, 1774 — A541

Rowland Hill, Birthplace, Kidderminster A542

Wmk. 360, Unwmkd. (1r)
1980, Jan. 25

852	A539	30p	gray olive	.55	.40
853	A540	50p	brown & citron	.85	.85
854	A541	1r	bronze	1.10	1.00
855	A542	2r	dark gray	1.10	1.00
	Nos. 852-855 (4)			3.60	3.25

INDIA '80 Intl. Stamp Exhib., New Delhi, Jan. 25-Feb. 3.

India Institution of Engineers, 60th Anniversary

Perf. 13x13½
1980, Feb. 17 Unwmk.
856 A543 30p dark blue & gold .50 .40

Uniforms, 1780 and 1980, Arms and Ribbon — A544

1980, Feb. 26
857 A544 30p multicolored 1.60 1.00

Madras Sappers bicentennial.

2nd Intl. Apiculture Conf., New Delhi A545

1980, Feb. 29 *Perf. 13½*
858 A545 1r multicolored 1.60 1.00

A546

1980, Feb. 29 **Wmk. 360**
859 A546 30p bright blue .60 .40

4th World Book Fair, New Delhi.

A547

1980, Mar. 18 ***Perf. 13x13½***
860 A547 30p blue gray .50 .35

Welthy Fisher (b. 1879), educator, Literacy House, Lucknow.

Darul Uloom Islamic School, Deoband A548

1980, Mar. 21 ***Perf. 13½***
861 A548 30p gray green .50 .40

Keshub Chunder Sen — A549

Perf. 13x13½

1980, Apr. 15 **Photo.** **Wmk. 360**
862 A549 30p brown .50 .40

Sen (1838-84), scholar, writer, journalist.

Sivaji, Raigad Fort — A550

1980, Apr. 21 **Unwmk.**
863 A550 30p multicolored .50 .40

Sivaji (1627-80), Indian patriot.

Narayan Malhar Joshi — A551

Perf. 13x13½

1980, June 5 **Wmk. 360**
864 A551 30p lilac rose .80 .50

Joshi (1879-1955), trade union pioneer.

Ulloor S. Parameswara Iyer — A552

1980, June 6
865 A552 30p dull purple .80 .50

Iyer (1877-1949), poet and scholar.

Syed Mohammad Zamin Ali — A553

1980, June 25
866 A553 30p dk yellow green .50 .40

Ali (1880-1955), linguist and educator.

Helen Keller (1880-1968) — A554

1980, June 27
867 A554 30p orange & black 1.25 .75

Keller, blind and deaf writer and lecturer.

High Jump, Olympic Rings A555

1980, July 19 **Photo.** ***Perf. 13½x14***
868 A555 1r shown .70 .25
869 A555 2.80r Equestrian 1.75 1.50

22nd Summer Olympic Games, Moscow, July 19-Aug. 3.

Prem Chand (1880-1936) A556

1980, July 31 ***Perf. 13***
870 A556 30p red brown .50 .40

Pen name of Nawab Rai, writer.

Mother Teresa, Nobel Peace Prize Medallion A557

Perf. 13½x13

1980, Aug. 27 **Photo.** **Wmk. 360**
871 A557 30p violet, *grayish* 2.50 1.25

Mother Teresa, founder of Missionaries of Charity, 70th birthday.

Earl Mountbatten of Burma — A558

1980, Aug. 28 ***Perf. 13x13½***
872 A558 2.80r multicolored 4.00 2.00

Mountbatten (1900-79), 1st governor gen. of India.

Asian Table Tennis Championship A559

1980, Sept. **Photo.** ***Perf. 13x13½***
873 A559 30p magenta .80 .55

Scottish Church College, Calcutta, Sesquicentennial — A560

1980, Sept. 27 **Photo.** ***Perf. 13½***
874 A560 35p dull purple .50 .40

Rajah Annamalai Chettiar (1881-1948), Banker, Founder of Annamalai University — A561

1980, Sept. 30 **Unwmk.** ***Perf. 14x15***
875 A561 35p dull purple .50 .40

Gandhi A562

No. 876, Gandhi on Dandi March. No. 877, Gandhi Defying Salt Law.

1980, Oct. 2 ***Perf. 15x14***
876 35p multicolored .60 .50
877 35p multicolored .60 .50
a. A562 Pair, #876-877 2.40 2.40

Jayaprakash Narayan (1902-79), Independence Activist & Social Reformer — A564

1980, Oct. 8 **Wmk. 360** ***Perf. 14x15***
878 A564 35p red brown .80 .55

Intl. Symposium on Bustards, Jaipur — A565

1980, Nov. 1 **Photo.** ***Perf. 13***
879 A565 2.30r Great Indian bustards 2.25 1.75

Hegira (Pilgrimage Year) A566

1980, Nov. 3 ***Perf. 13x13½***
880 A566 35p multicolored .50 .50

Children's Day — A567

Perf. 13½x13

1980, Nov. 14 **Unwmk.**
881 A567 35p multicolored 1.50 .90

Dhyan Chand — A568

1980, Dec. 3 **Wmk. 360** ***Perf. 14x15***
882 A568 35p dark rose brown 1.50 1.00

Chand (1906-1979), field hockey player.

Miner, Molten Gold — A569

Perf. 13x13½

1980, Dec. 20 **Unwmk.**
883 A569 1r multicolored 2.75 .70

Kolar gold fields centenary.

Mukhtar Ahmad Ansari (1880-1936), Surgeon — A570

Perf. 14x15

1980, Dec. 25 Wmk. 360

884 A570 35p olive gray .60 .30

Government Mint, Bombay, Sesquicentennial — A571

Perf. 13½x13

1980, Dec. 27 Unwmk.

885 A571 35p multicolored .40 .25

Regional Bridal Outfits — A572

1980, Dec. 30 ***Perf. 13x13½***

886 A572 1r Kashmir .75 .50
887 A572 1r Bengal .75 .50
888 A572 1r Rajasthan .75 .50
889 A572 1r Tamilnadu .75 .50
Nos. 886-889 (4) 3.00 2.00

Mazharul Haque (1866-1930), Patriot — A573

1981, Jan. 2 Wmk. 360 ***Perf. 14x15***

890 A573 35p violet .50 .40

St. Stephen's College Centenary — A574

1981, Feb. 1 Photo. ***Perf. 14x14½***

891 A574 35p dull red .50 .40

Gommateshwara Statue, Shravanabelgola A575

1981, Feb. 9 Unwmk.

892 A575 1r multicolored .50 .40

Ganesh V. Mavalankar (1888-1956) A576

1981, Feb. 27

893 A576 35p light red brown .50 .40

Mavalankar, 1st speaker of parliament.

Fruit and Nuts — A576a

Trees on Hillside — A576b

Windmill — A576c

Designs: 2.25r, Cashew. 2.80r, Apples. 3.25r, Oranges.

Perf. 14½x14

1981-86 Photo. Wmk. 324

895 A576a 2.25r multi .75 .50
a. Perf. 14x14½ .30 .25
b. Perf. 13 .25 .25
896 A576a 2.80r multi 1.00 .60
a. Perf. 14x14½ .40 .25
897 A576a 3.25r multi ('83) .60 .45
a. Perf. 13½x13 ('85) .30 .25
b. Perf. 13 .30 .25
900 A576b 10r multi ('84) .75 .40
b. Perf. 13x13½ 1.25 .60

Perf. 13½x13

900A A576c 50r multi ('86) 2.00 1.25
Nos. 895-900A (5) 5.10 3.20

Homage to Martyrs — A577

1981, Mar. 23 Unwmk. ***Perf. 14x15***

901 A577 35p multicolored .50 .40

Heinrich von Stephan and UPU Emblem A578

1981, Apr. 8 ***Perf. 15x14***

902 A578 1r red brown & brt blue .50 .40

Types of 1975-79 and

Telecommunications — A578a

Natural Gas — A578b

Irrigation — A578c

Dairy Industry — A578d

Design: 1r, Mahatma Gandhi.

Perf. 14x14½, 14½x14, 13 (40p, 75p), 13x13½ (20r)

Wmk. 324, 360 (2p, 5p, 15p)

1981-90 Photo.

Size: 20x17mm, 17x20mm (1r)

903 A536a 2p violet .25 .25
904 A536b 5p blue .25 .25
905 A578c 10p green .25 .25
a. Perf. 13 .25 .25
906 A536c 15p blue green .25 .25
912 A578a 40p dull red .25 .25
914 A578d 50p dark blue .25 .25
a. Perf. 13 .25 .25
915 A537a 75p vermilion .25 .25
916 A410 1r orange brown .25 .25

Size: 32x19mm

917 A578b 20r sepia & dark blue 1.00 .60
Nos. 903-917 (9) 3.00 2.60

Issued: 10p, 50p, 1/25/82; 40p, 10/15/88; 20r, 11/30/88; 75p, 1990; 1r, 1/30/91; others, 3/25/81.

Intl. Year of the Disabled A579

Perf. 14½x14

1981, Apr. 20 Photo. Unwmk.

919 A579 1r blue & black .60 .40

Tribesman — A580

1981, May 30 ***Perf. 14x14½***

920 A580 1r Khiamngan Naga .70 .50
921 A580 1r Toda .70 .50
922 A580 1r Bhil .70 .50
923 A580 1r Dandami Maria .70 .50
Nos. 920-923 (4) 2.80 2.00

World Environment Day — A581

1981, June 15

924 A581 1r multicolored .50 .40

Nilmoni Phukan (1880-1978), Writer — A582

1981, June 22

925 A582 35p red brown .50 .40

Sanjay Gandhi (1946-1980), Politician — A583

1981, June 23 ***Perf. 13x13½***

926 A583 35p multicolored .75 .60

SLV-3 Take-off — A584

1981, July 18 Photo. ***Perf. 14x15***

927 A584 1r multicolored .60 .40

Launching of India's 1st indigenous satellite, 1st anniv.

Mascot, Field Hockey A585

1981, July 28 ***Perf. 13½x13***

928 A585 1r shown 1.60 .75
929 A585 1r Emblem 1.60 .75

9th Asian Games, New Delhi, 1982.

Flame of the Forest — A586

Designs: Flowering trees.

1981, Sept. 1 Photo. ***Perf. 13***

930 A586 35p shown 1.00 .35
931 A586 50p Crateva .60 .45
932 A586 1r Golden shower 1.40 .75
933 A586 2r Bauhinia 2.00 1.50
Nos. 930-933 (4) 5.00 3.05

World Food Day — A587

1981, Oct. 16 Photo. ***Perf. 14x14½***
934 A587 1r multicolored .60 .45

Cyrestis Achates — A588

35p, Stichophthalma camadeva, horiz. 50p, Cethosia biblis, horiz. 2r, Treinopalpus imperialis.

1981, Oct. 20 ***Perf. 13***
935 A588 35p multicolored 1.50 .50
936 A588 50p multicolored 2.50 1.50
937 A588 1r shown 3.25 1.00
938 A588 2r multicolored 4.00 4.00
Nos. 935-938 (4) 11.25 7.00

Bellary Raghava (1880-1946), Actor — A589

1981, Oct. 31 ***Perf. 14½x14***
939 A589 35p olive gray 1.10 .60

40th Anniv. of Mahar Regiment — A590

1981, Nov. 9 ***Perf. 13***
940 A590 35p multicolored 1.75 .60

Children's Day — A591

1981, Nov. 14 ***Perf. 14x14½***
941 A591 35p multicolored 1.10 .45

Rajghat Stadium — A591a

1981 ***Perf. 13½x13***
942 A591a 1r shown 2.40 .45
943 A591a 1r Nehru Stadium .35 .25

Asian games. Issued: No. 942, 11/19; No. 943, 12/30.

Kashi Prasad Jayaswal (1881-1937), Historian — A592

1981, Nov. 27 ***Perf. 14x14½***
944 A592 35p chalky blue .80 .35

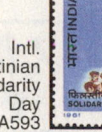

Intl. Palestinian Solidarity Day A593

1981, Nov. 29 ***Perf. 14½x14***
945 A593 1r multicolored 3.50 .70

Naval Ship Taragiri A594

1981, Dec. 4
946 A594 35p multicolored 4.00 2.25

Henry Heras (1888-1955), Historian — A595

1981, Dec. 14 Photo. ***Perf. 14½x14***
947 A595 35p rose violet .60 .35

Indian Ocean Commonwealth Submarine Telephone Cable — A596

1981, Dec. 24 ***Perf. 13½***
948 A596 1r multicolored 3.00 .55

5th World Field Hockey Championship, Bombay — A597

1981, Dec. 29 ***Perf. 13½x13***
949 A597 1r multicolored 2.00 .60

Telephone Service Centenary — A598

Perf. 13x13½
1982, Jan. 28 **Unwmk.**
950 A598 2r multicolored .75 .50

12th Intl. Soil Science Congress, New Delhi, Feb. 8-16 A599

1982, Feb. 8 ***Perf. 13½x13***
951 A599 1r multicolored .40 .25

Sir Jamsetjee Jejeebhoy School of Art, Bombay — A600

1981, Mar. 2 Photo. ***Perf. 14x14½***
952 A600 35p multicolored .40 .30

Three Musicians, by Pablo Picasso (1881-1973) — A601

1982, Mar. 15 Photo. ***Perf. 14***
953 A601 2.85r multicolored 2.50 1.00

Deer, 5th Cent. Bas Relief — A602

Radio Telescope, Ooty A603

Festival of India, England: No. 955, Krishna, 9th cent. bronze sculpture.

1982, Mar. 23 ***Perf. 14x15***
954 A602 2r multicolored .60 .60
955 A602 3.05r multicolored .40 .40

Perf. 13
956 A603 3.05r multicolored .60 .35
Nos. 954-956 (3) 1.60 1.35

TB Bacillus Centenary A604

1982, Mar. 24 ***Perf. 13***
957 A604 35p rose violet 3.00 1.60

Durgabai Deshmukh (1909-1981), Social Worker — A605

1982, May 9 Photo. ***Perf. 14½x14***
958 A605 35p blue .80 .35

Himalayan Flowers — A606

1982, May 29 ***Perf. 14x14½***
959 A606 35p Blue poppies 1.00 .60
960 A606 1r Showy inula 2.50 .60
961 A606 2r Cobra lily 3.00 2.50
962 A606 2.85r Brahma kamal 3.50 4.25
Nos. 959-962 (4) 10.00 7.95

Ariana Passenger Payload Experimental (APPLE) Satellite, First Anniv. — A607

1982, June 19 ***Perf. 13½x13***
963 A607 2r multicolored 1.00 .65

Bidhan Chandra Roy (1882-1962), Physician and Politician — A608

1982, July 1 ***Perf. 14½x14***
964 A608 50p orange brown 1.40 .95

Sagar Samrat Drilling Rig — A609

1982, Aug. 14 Photo. ***Perf. 13***
985 A609 1r multicolored 2.50 1.25

Bindu (Cosmic Spirit), by Raza — A610

Paintings; 3.05r, Between the Spider and the Lamp, 1956, by M.F. Husain.

1982, Sept. 17 ***Perf. 14x14½***
986 A610 2r multicolored .75 .55
987 A610 3.05r multicolored 1.00 1.00

Kashmir Stag — A611

1982, Oct. 1 *Perf. 13x13½*
988 A611 2.85r multicolored 4.00 3.25

50th Anniv. of Indian Air Force A612

1982, Oct. 8 *Perf. 13½x13*
989 A612 1r Wapiti, MiG 25 8.00 2.00

50th Anniv. of Civil Aviation A613

3.25r, J.R.D. Tata and his Puss Moth, 1932.

1982, Oct. 15
990 A613 3.25r multicolored 7.00 3.00

Police Memorial Day — A614

1982, Oct. 21
991 A614 50p Beat patrol .90 .55

Post Office Savings Bank Centenary A615

1982, Oct. 23
992 A615 50p brown .50 .40

9th Asian Games A616

No. 993, Wrestling, by Janaki, 17th cent. No. 993A, Archery.

1982 *Perf. 13½x14*
993 A616 1r multicolored 1.25 .70
993A A616 1r multicolored 2.75 .60

Issued: No. 993, 10/30; No. 993A, 11/6.

India-USSR Troposcatter Communications Link — A617

1982, Nov. 2 *Perf. 13½x13*
994 A617 3.05r multicolored .70 .50

Children's Day — A618

1982, Nov. 14 *Perf. 14x15*
995 A618 50p multicolored .60 .40

9th Asian Games A619

1982 *Perf. 13*
996 A619 50p Cycling .25 .25
997 A619 2r Yachting .40 .30
998 A619 2r Javelin .45 .40
999 A619 2.85r Rowing .65 .45
1000 A619 2.85r Discus 2.00 .45
1001 A619 3.25r Soccer 2.50 .65
Nos. 996-1001 (6) 6.25 2.50

Issued: Nos. 997, 999, 11/25; others 11/19.

50th Anniv. of Indian Military Academy, Dehradun A620

1982, Dec. 10 *Perf. 13½x13*
1002 A620 50p multicolored .70 .50

Purushottamdas Tandon (1882-1962), Politician — A621

1982, Dec. 15 *Perf. 13*
1003 A621 50p bister .50 .40

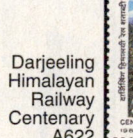

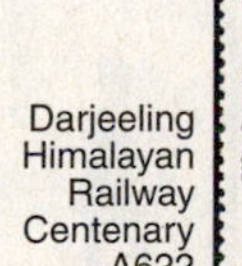
Darjeeling Himalayan Railway Centenary A622

1982, Dec. 18 *Perf. 13½x13*
1004 A622 2.85r multicolored 8.00 7.50

Indian Railway Car — A623

Nos. 2 and 201 — A624

1982, Dec. 30 **Photo.** *Perf. 13, 14*
1005 A623 50p multicolored 1.90 1.10
1006 A624 2r multicolored 3.00 3.00

INPEX '82 Stamp Exhibition.

First Anniv. of Antarctic Expedition A625

1983, Jan. 9 **Photo.** *Perf. 13½x13*
1007 A625 1r multicolored 6.00 3.50

Pres. Franklin D. Roosevelt (1882-1945) — A626

1983, Jan. 30 *Perf. 13*
1008 A626 3.25r brown .90 .75

Siberian Cranes — A627

1983, Feb. 7 *Perf. 13x13½*
1009 A627 2.85r multicolored 4.25 3.25

180th Anniv. of Jat Regiment A628

1983, Feb. 16 *Perf. 13½x13*
1010 A628 50p Soldiers, emblem 2.75 2.10

7th Non-aligned Summit Conference A629

1983, Mar. 7
1011 A629 1r Emblem .35 .35
1012 A629 2r Jawaharlal Nehru .45 .45

Commonwealth Day — A630

1r, Shore Temple, Mahabalipuram. 2r, Mountains, Gomukh.

1983, Mar. 14 *Perf. 13*
1013 A630 1r multicolored .25 .30
1014 A630 2r multicolored .45 .45

86th Session of Intl. Olympic Committee, New Delhi, Mar. 21-28 A631

1983, Mar. 25 **Litho.** *Perf. 13½x13*
1015 A631 1r Acropolis .60 .40

A632

St. Francis of Assisi (1182-1226), by Giovanni Collina.

1983, Apr. 4 **Photo.** *Perf. 13*
1016 A632 1r brown 1.10 .55

A633

1983, May 5 **Photo.** *Perf. 13x12½*
1017 A633 1r brown .70 .50

Karl Marx (1818-1883).

Charles Darwin (1809-1882) — A634

1983, May 18 *Perf. 12½x13*
1018 A634 2r multicolored 4.25 2.50

50th Anniv. of Kanha Natl. Park A635

1983, May 30 *Perf. 13½x13*
1019 A635 1r Barasinga stag 3.50 1.25

World Communications Year — A636

1983, July 18 **Photo.** *Perf. 13*
1020 A636 1r multicolored .60 .30

Simon Bolivar (1783-1830) — A637

1983, July 24
1021 A637 2r multicolored 3.00 2.50

Quit India Resolution, Aug. 8, 1942 — A638

Meera Behn (Madeleine Slade). Disciple of Gandhi, d. 1982 — A639

Design: No. 1024, Mahadev Desai (1892-1942).

1983, Aug. 9 **Photo.** ***Perf. 14***
1022 A638 50p shown 1.40 1.10

Perf. 13½x13

1023 A639 50p shown 1.40 1.10
1024 A639 50p org, green & brn 1.40 1.10
a. Pair, #1023-1024 2.75 2.75

See Nos. 1033, 1035, 1042, 1052-1057, 1077, 1093-1094, 1103, 1107, 1109, 1122, 1137-1139, 1144, 1147-1149, 1163, 1167, 1198, 1202-1205, 1229-1231, 1238, 1243, 1257, 1268-1271, 1277.

Ram Nath Chopra (1882-1973), Pharmacologist — A640

1983, Aug. 17 ***Perf. 13***
1025 A640 50p brown .80 .65

Indian Mountaineering Foundation, 25th Anniv. — A641

2r, Nanda Devi, Himalayas.

1983, Aug. 27 ***Perf. 13½***
1026 A641 2r multicolored 3.25 2.25

Bombay Natural History Soc. — A642

1983, Sept. 15 ***Perf. 13x13½***
1027 A642 1r multicolored 5.00 1.60

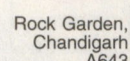

Rock Garden, Chandigarh A643

1983, Sept. 23 ***Perf. 13x13½***
1028 A643 1r multicolored 2.50 1.25

Wildlife A644

1r, Golden langur. 2r, Lion-tailed macaque.

1983, Oct. 1 ***Perf. 13½x13***
1029 A644 1r multicolored 2.75 .75
1030 A644 2r multicolored 4.25 3.75

World Tourism, 5th General Assembly — A645

1983, Oct. 3 **Photo.** ***Perf. 14***
1031 A645 2r Ghats of Varanasi 1.00 .50

Krishna Kanta Handique, Linguist, Sanskritist, Educator and Scholar — A646

1983, Oct. 7 **Litho.** ***Perf. 13***
1032 A646 50p deep gray violet .50 .35

Famous Indians Type of 1983

Design: Hemu Kalani, revolutionary patriot.

1983, Oct. 18 **Photo.** ***Perf. 13½x13***
1033 A639 50p org, grn & red brn .50 .50

Children's Day — A648

Painting: Festival, by Kashyap Premswala

1983, Nov. 14 **Photo.** ***Perf. 13***
1034 A648 50p multicolored .60 .45

Famous Indians Type of 1983

Design: Acharya Vinoba Bhave (1895-1982), freedom fighter.

1983, Nov. 15 **Photo.** ***Perf. 13½x13***
1035 A639 50p org, grn & dull brn .50 .50

Manned Flight Bicent. — A650

1r, 1st Indian Balloon. 2r, Montgolfier Balloon.

1983, Nov. 21 **Photo.** ***Perf. 13***
1036 A650 1r multicolored 1.25 .55
1037 A650 2r multicolored 1.75 1.10

Project Tiger — A651

1983, Nov. 22 **Photo.** ***Perf. 13***
1038 A651 2r multicolored 5.00 4.25

Commonwealth Heads of Government Meeting, New Delhi — A652

Design: 2r, Goanese Couple, 19th century.

1983, Nov. 23 **Photo.** ***Perf. 13***
1039 A652 1r lt brnsh blue & multi .50 .40
1040 A652 2r pink & multi 1.00 .50

Pratiksha — A653

1983, Dec. 5 **Photo.** ***Perf. 13***
1041 A653 1r multi .40 .30

Nanda Lal Bose (1882-1966), artist.

Famous Indians Type of 1983

Design: Surendranath Banerjee, journalist.

1983, Dec. 28 **Photo.** ***Perf. 13½x13***
1042 A639 50p org, green & olive .50 .50

7th Light Cavalry Bicent. — A655

1984, Jan. 7
1043 A655 1r Soldier, banner 4.75 2.25

Deccan Horse Regiment, 194th Anniv. — A656

1984, Jan. 9 ***Perf. 13x13½***
1044 A656 1r multicolored 4.50 2.00

Asiatic Society Bicentenary — A657

Design: Society building, Calcutta; founder William Jones.

1984, Jan. 15 ***Perf. 13***
1045 A657 1r brt green & dp lilac .50 .35

Postal Life Insurance Centenary — A658

1984, Feb. 1 **Photo.** ***Perf. 13x13½***
1046 A658 1r Emblem .50 .35

Presidential Review of Naval Fleet A659

1984, Feb. 3 ***Perf. 13½x13***
1047 A659 1r Jet 2.50 1.50
1048 A659 1r Aircraft carrier 2.50 1.50
1049 A659 1r Submarine 2.50 1.50
1050 A659 1r Missile destroyer 2.50 1.50
a. Block of 4, #1047-1050 14.00 14.00

12th Intl. Leprosy Congress, New Delhi A660

1984, Feb. 10 ***Perf. 13x13½***
1051 A660 1r Globe, emblem .80 .60

Famous Indians Type of 1983

No. 1052, Vasudeo Balvant Phadke (d. 1884), freedom fighter. No. 1053, Baba Kanshi Ram. No. 1054, Begum Hazrat Mahal. No. 1055, Mangal Pandey. No. 1056, Nana Sahib. No. 1057, Tatya Tope.

1984 ***Perf. 13½x13***
1052 A639 50p org, grn & dk ol .55 .55
1053 A639 50p org, grn & brn .55 .55
1054 A639 50p org, grn, red org & gray 1.25 .80
1055 A639 50p org, grn, brn & gray 1.25 .80
1056 A639 50p org, grn, vio & gray 1.25 .80
1057 A639 50p org, grn, dk ol & gray 1.25 .80
Nos. 1052-1057 (6) 6.10 4.30

Issued: No. 1052, 2/23. No. 1053, 4/23. Nos. 1054-1057, 5/10.

Indian-Russian Space Cooperation — A662

1984, Apr. 3 Photo. *Perf. 14*

1058 A662 3r Spacecraft 1.25 .85

G. D. Birla (1894-1983), Industrialist — A663

Birla, Birla Institute of Technology, Pilani.

1984, June 11

1060 A663 50p sepia .80 .45

1984 Summer Olympics — A664

50p, Basketball. 1r, High jump. 2r, Gymnastics, horiz. 2.50r, Weight lifting, horiz.

Perf. 13x12½, 12½x13

1984, July 28 Photo.

1061	A664	50p	multicolored	1.25	.65
1062	A664	1r	multicolored	1.00	.35
1063	A664	2r	multicolored	1.40	.95
1064	A664	2.50r	multicolored	1.00	1.50
			Nos. 1061-1064 (4)	5.25	3.45

Vellore Fort — A665

1984, Aug. 3 *Perf. 13½x13, 13x13½*

1065	A665	50p	Gwalior, horiz.	.85	.55
1066	A665	1r	shown	1.25	.40
1067	A665	1.50r	Simhagad	2.25	1.90
1068	A665	2r	Jodhpur, horiz.	2.60	2.50
			Nos. 1065-1068 (4)	6.95	5.35

B.V. Paradkar, Editor — A665a

1984, Sept. 14 Photo. *Perf. 13x13½*

1068A A665a 50p sepia .80 .55

Dr. D.N. Wadia (1883-1969), Geologist — A665b

1984, Oct. 23 *Perf. 13*

1068B A665b 1r multicolored 2.00 .40

Indira Gandhi — A666

1984, Nov. 19 Photo. *Perf. 15x14*

1069 A666 50p multicolored 3.00 3.00

Children's Day — A667

1984, Nov. 14 Photo. *Perf. 13*

1070 A667 50p Birds in trees 1.10 .70

12th World Mining Congress — A668

1984, Nov. 20 Photo. *Perf. 13*

1071 A668 1r Congress emblem 1.90 .45

Dr. Rajendra Prasad (1884-1963), 1st, Pres. — A669

1984, Dec. 3 Photo. *Perf. 13*

1072 A669 50p multicolored 1.25 .90

Roses — A670

1984, Dec. 23 Litho. *Perf. 13*

1073	A670	1.50r	Mrinalini	3.25	2.25
1074	A670	2r	Sugandha	3.50	2.50

Fergusson College Centenary A671

1985, Jan. 2 Photo. *Perf. 13x13½*

1076 A671 100p multicolored 1.00 .50

Famous Indians Type of 1983

Design: Narhar Vishnu Gadgil (1896-1966), freedom fighter.

1985, Jan. 10 Photo. *Perf. 13½x13*

1077 A639 50p org, grn & brn 6.00 4.00

Artillery Regiment, 50th Anniv. A673

1985, Jan. 15 *Perf. 13½x13*

1078 A673 1r Gunner, howitzer 5.50 2.25

Indira Gandhi (1917-1984) — A674

2r, Addressing UN General Assembly.

1985, Jan. 31 *Perf. 14*

1079 A674 2r multicolored 5.25 4.25

See Nos. 1098-1099.

Minicoy Lighthouse Cent. — A675

1985, Feb. 2 *Perf. 13*

1080 A675 1r multicolored 6.75 1.60

Bengal Medical College, 150th Anniv. A676

1985, Feb. 20 *Perf. 13½x13*

1081 A676 1r multicolored 4.00 .95

Madras Medical College, 150th Anniv. A677

1985, Mar. 8 *Perf. 13½x13*

1082 A677 1r multicolored 4.00 .95

Assam Rifles, North-East Sentinels, 150th Anniv. A679

1985, Mar. 29

1084 A679 1r multicolored 6.00 2.50

Potato Research, 50th Anniv. — A680

1985, Apr. 1 *Perf. 13*

1085 A680 50p brn & pale brn 2.00 1.60

Baba Jassa Singh Ahluwalia, 1718-1783, Sikh Leader — A681

1985, Apr. 4

1086 A681 50p rose violet 2.00 1.60

St. Xavier's College, 125th Anniv. A682

1985, Apr. 12

1087 A682 1r multicolored 2.25 .80

White-winged Wood Duck — A683

1985, May 18 *Perf. 14*

1088 A683 2r multicolored 9.00 5.50

Bougainvillea A684

1985, June 5 *Perf. 13*

1089	A684	50p	multicolored	2.00	1.75
1090	A684	1r	multicolored	2.50	1.50

Statue of Didarganj Yakshi, Indian Deity — A685

Yaudheya Tribal Republic Copper Coin, c. 200 B.C. — A686

1985

1091 A685 1r multicolored 4.00 2.10
1092 A686 2r multicolored 2.25 .50

Festival of India, festival in France and the US for cultural exchange.
Issue dates: 1r, June 7. 2r, June 13.

Famous Indians Type of 1983

Designs: No. 1093, Jairamdas Doulatram (1891-1979), journalist and politician. No. 1094, Nellie (1909-1973) & Jatindra Mohan (d. 1933) Sengupta, political activists, horiz.

1985 ***Perf. 13½x13***
1093 A639 50p org, grn & dl red brn .75 .50

Perf. 13x13½
1094 A639 50p org, green & fawn .75 .50

Issued: No. 1093, 7/21; No. 1094, 7/22.

Swami Haridas (1478-1573), Philosopher A689

1985, Sept. 19 Photo. ***Perf. 13½x13***
1095 A689 1r multicolored 2.50 1.50

Border Roads Org., 25th Anniv. — A690

1985, Oct. 10 ***Perf. 13x14***
1096 A690 2r multicolored 2.75 2.75

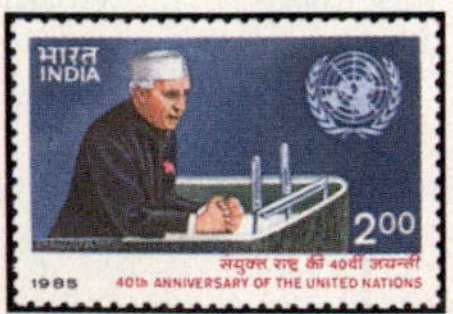

Prime Minister Nehru at Podium A691

1985, Oct. 24 ***Perf. 13x13½***
1097 A691 2r multicolored 1.50 1.10

UN, 40th anniv.

Indira Gandhi Memorial Type of 1985

2r, Gandhi addressing crowd. 3r, Portrait.

1985 ***Perf. 14***
1098 A674 2r multicolored 3.50 3.50
1099 A674 3r multicolored 3.50 3.50

Issued: 2r, 10/31. 3r, 11/19.

Children's Day — A692

1985, Nov. 14 ***Perf. 13½x13***
1100 A692 50p multicolored 1.40 .80

Halley's Comet — A693

1985, Nov. 19 ***Perf. 13x13½***
1101 A693 1r multicolored 2.50 1.60

Intl. Astronomical Union, 19th General Assembly, New Delhi, Nov. 19-28.

St. Stephen's Hospital, Delhi, Cent. A694

1985, Nov. 25 ***Perf. 13***
1102 A694 1r multicolored 1.25 .55

Famous Indians Type of 1983

Design: Kakasaheb Kalelkar (1885-1981), author.

1985, Dec. 2 ***Perf. 13½x13***
1103 A639 50p org, grn & ol brn .75 .50

Map of South Asia A696

Flags of India, Pakistan, Bangladesh, Nepal, Bhutan, Sri Lanka and the Maldive Islands — A697

1985, Dec. 8 ***Perf. 13½x13, 14***
1104 A696 1r multicolored 2.50 .50
1105 A697 3r multicolored 4.00 3.50

South Asian Regional Cooperation, SARC.

Shyama Shastri (1762-1827), Composer — A698

1985, Dec. 21 ***Perf. 13½x13***
1106 A698 1r multicolored 3.50 1.60

Famous Indians Type of 1983

Master Tara Singh (1885-1967), Sikh leader.

1985, Dec. 23 ***Perf. 13½x13***
1107 A639 50p org, green & blue .75 .50

Intl. Youth Year A700

1985, Dec. 24
1108 A700 2r multicolored 3.50 2.25

Famous Indians Type of 1983

Design: Ravishankar Maharaj (1884-1984), freedom fighter, politician.

1985, Dec. 24 ***Perf. 13½x13***
1109 A639 50p org, green & slate .75 .50

Handel and Bach — A702

1985, Dec. 27 ***Perf. 13x13½***
1110 A702 5r multicolored 6.50 4.75

Congress Presidents, 1924-1985 A703

1985, Dec. 28 ***Perf. 14***
1111 Block of 4 13.00 13.00
a.-d. A703 1r any single 2.50 2.25

Indian Natl. Congress, cent. Withdrawn on day of issue for a period of two weeks.

Naval Dockyard, Bombay, 250th Anniv. A704

1986, Jan. 11 Photo. ***Perf. 13½***
1112 A704 2.50r multicolored 6.00 4.50

INPEX '86, Jaipur, Feb. 14-19 A705

Designs: 50p, Hawa Mahal Palace, Jaipur No. 3. 2r, Khar Desert mobile post office.

1986, Feb. 14 ***Perf. 13½x13***
1113 A705 50p multicolored 2.00 .90
1114 A705 2r multicolored 3.00 2.10

Vikrant Aircraft Carrier, 25th Anniv. — A706

1986, Feb. 16 ***Perf. 13x13½***
1115 A706 2r multicolored 9.00 8.00

Inaugural Airmail Flight, 75th Anniv. A707

1986, Feb. 18 ***Perf. 13½x13, 13x13½***
1116 A707 50p Biplane 3.25 2.10

Size: 41x28mm

1117 A707 3r Jet 7.25 5.50

Sixth Triennale of the Arts, Lalit Kala Academy — A708

1986, Feb. 22 ***Perf. 13x13½***
1118 A708 1r multicolored 2.00 1.50

Sri Chaitanya Mahaprabhu A709

1986, Mar. 3 ***Perf. 13***
1119 A709 2r multicolored 3.75 3.25

Mayo College, Ajmer, 111th Anniv. A710

1986, Apr. 12 ***Perf. 13½x13***
1120 A710 1r multicolored 2.25 1.10

1986 World Cup Soccer Championships, Mexico — A711

1986, May 31 Photo. ***Perf. 13***
1121 A711 5r multicolored 6.25 4.25

Famous Indians Type of 1983

Bhim Sen Sachar (1894-1978), freedom fighter.

1986, Aug. 14 Photo. ***Perf. 13½x13***
1122 A639 50p org, green & sepia 2.00 1.00

Swami Sivananda (1887-1963), Religious Author — A713

1986, Sept. 8 Photo. ***Perf. 13½x13***
1123 A713 2r multicolored 4.00 3.00

10th Asian Games — A714

1.50r, Women's volleyball. 3r, Hurdling.

1986, Sept. 16 ***Perf. 13x13½***
1124 A714 1.50r multicolored 3.75 2.50
1125 A714 3r multicolored 4.00 3.50

Madras Post Office, Bicent. A715

1986, Oct. 9 Photo. ***Perf. 13x13½***
1126 A715 5r blk & brn org 6.50 4.50

1st Battalion of Parachutists Regiment, 225th Anniv. — A716

1986, Oct. 17
1127 A716 3r multicolored 7.00 4.50

Indian Police Force, 125th Anniv. — A717

Uniforms, 1861-1986. No. 1129a has a continuous design.

1986, Oct. 21 ***Perf. 13½***
1128 A717 1.50r multicolored 5.00 5.00
1129 A717 2r multicolored 5.00 5.00
a. Pair, #1129, 1128 12.00 12.00

Intl. Peace Year A718

1986, Oct. 24
1130 A718 5r sage grn, blue & rose 4.50 2.75

Children's Day — A719

1986, Nov. 14 Photo. ***Perf. 13x13½***
1131 A719 50p multicolored 3.25 2.10

UN, 40th Anniv. A720

50p, Growth monitoring. 5r, Immunization.

1986, Dec. 11 ***Perf. 13½x13***
1132 A720 50p multicolored 2.75 2.25
1133 A720 5r multicolored 5.50 5.00

Child Survival Campaign.

Miyan Tansen, 17th Cent. Dhrupad Singer, Playing the Surbahar — A721

1986, Dec. 12
1134 A721 1r multicolored 2.75 1.00

Corbett Natl. Park, 50th Anniv. A722

1986, Dec. 15
1135 A722 1r Elephant 5.00 1.75
1136 A722 2r Gavial 6.00 5.25

Famous Indians Type of 1983

Designs: No. 1137, Alluri Seetarama Raju (b. 1897), freedom fighter. No. 1138, Sagarmal Gopa (b. 1900), freedom fighter. No. 1139, Veer Surendra Sai (b. 1809), freedom fighter.

1986 ***Perf. 13½x13***
1137 A639 50p red, grn & sepia 2.00 1.00
1138 A639 50p red, grn & sl blue 2.00 1.00
1139 A639 50p red, grn & dp red brn 2.00 1.00
Nos. 1137-1139 (3) 6.00 3.00

Issued: No. 1137, 12/26; No. 1138, 12/29; No. 1139, 12/30.

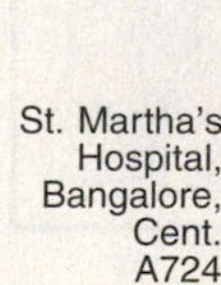

St. Martha's Hospital, Bangalore, Cent. A724

1986, Dec. 30 ***Perf. 13½***
1140 A724 1r multicolored 3.00 2.25

Yacht Trishna A725

1987, Jan. 10
1141 A725 6.50r multicolored 6.25 4.25

1st Indian Army circumnavigation of the world, Sept. 28, 1985 to 1987.

Africa Fund — A726

1987, Jan. 25 Photo. ***Perf. 14x14½***
1142 A726 6.50r black 6.50 4.50

ICC 29th Congress, New Delhi — A727

1987, Feb. 11 ***Perf. 13½***
1143 A727 5r multicolored 4.50 3.00

Famous Indians Type of 1983

Design: Hakim Ajmal Khan (1864-1927), physician, politician.

1987, Feb. 13 ***Perf. 13½x13***
1144 A639 60p org, grn & brn 2.75 .30

A729

Family Planning A730

1987, Feb. 27 ***Perf. 13, 13x13½***
1145 A729 35p dark red .40 .25
1146 A730 60p green & dark red 1.00 .25

Famous Indians Type of 1983

Designs: No. 1147, Lala Har Dayal (1884-1939). No. 1148, Manabendra Nath Roy (1887-1954). No. 1149, T. Ramaswamy Chowdary (1887-1943).

1987 Photo. ***Perf. 13½x13***
1147 A639 60p org, grn & pur .50 .25
1148 A639 60p org, grn & red brn .50 .25
1149 A639 60p org, grn & brt blue .50 .25
Nos. 1147-1149 (3) 1.50 .75

Issued: No. 1147, 3/18; No. 1148, 3/21; No. 1149, 4/25.

SER Emblem, Blast Furnaces — A732

Steam Locomotive No. 691 — A733

Electric Train Crossing Bridge — A734

4r, Steam locomotive, c. 1890.

1987, Mar. 28 ***Perf. 13x13½, 13½x13***
1150 A732 1r shown .25 .25
1151 A733 1.50r shown .65 .35
1152 A734 2r shown 1.10 .45
1153 A733 4r multicolored 1.50 .75
Nos. 1150-1153 (4) 3.50 1.80

Southeastern Railway, cent.

Kalia Bhomora Bridge, Assam A735

1987, Apr. 14 ***Perf. 13½***
1154 A735 2r multicolored .60 .30

Madras Christian College, 150th Anniv. A736

1987, Apr. 16 ***Perf. 13x13½***
1155 A736 1.50r black & rose lake .50 .40

A737

1987, May 1 ***Perf. 13½***
1156 A737 1r dull brown .60 .30

Shree Shree Ma Anandamayee (1896-1982), spiritualist.

A738

1987, May 8 *Perf. 14*
1157 A738 2r multicolored .70 .35

Rabindranath Tagore (1861-1941), 1913 Nobel Laureate for literature.

A739

1987, May 10 *Perf. 13½*
1158 A739 1r multicolored 1.00 .50

Garhwal Rifles and Garhwal Scouts, cent.

A740

1987, May 11
1159 A740 60p black brn & buff 1.10 .90

J. Krishnamurti (1895-1986), mystic.

7th Battalion, Mechanised Infantry Regiment, Cent. A741

1987, June 3 *Perf. 13½x13*
1160 A741 1r multicolored .90 .45

INDIA '89, New Delhi, Jan. 20-29, 1989 A742

50p, Swan emblem. 5r, Hall of Nations, New Delhi.

1987, June 15
1161 A742 50p multicolored .25 .25
a. Bklt. pane of 4+inscribed margin ('89) .50
1162 A742 5r multicolored 1.25 .45
a. Souv. sheet of 2, #1161-1162 3.50 3.50
b. Bklt. pane of 4+inscribed margin ('89) 6.00 6.00

Inscribed 1986. No. 1162a sold for 8r.

Famous Indians Type of 1983

Kailas Nath Katju (1887-1968), Chief Minister.

1987, June 17 *Perf. 13½x13*
1163 A639 60p org, grn & yel brn .35 .25

Sadyah-Snata, Sanghol Sculpture, c. 2000 B.C. A744

1987, July 3
1164 A744 6.50r multicolored 1.45 .55

Festival of India in the USSR, July 3, 1987-88.

Natl. Independence, 40th Anniv. — A745

1987, Aug. 15 **Photo.** *Perf. 13x13½*
1165 A745 60p org, brt bl & dk grn .50 .40

Sant Harchand Singh Longowal (1932-1985), Social Reformer — A746

1987, Aug. 20 *Perf. 13½*
1166 A746 1r multicolored 1.10 .40

Famous Indians Type of 1983

Design: S. Satyamurti (1887-1943), political reformer, martyr.

1987, Aug. 22 *Perf. 13½x13*
1167 A639 60p org, green & brn .50 .25

Guru Ghasidas (1756-1837), Founder of the Saman Sect — A748

1987, Sept. 1
1168 A748 60p henna brown .50 .40

Sri Sri Thakur Anukul Chandra (1888-1969), Guru — A749

1987, Sept. 2 *Perf. 13½*
1169 A749 1r multicolored .60 .60

University of Allahabad, Cent. A750

1987, Sept. 23 *Perf. 13½x13*
1170 A750 2r multicolored .50 .30

Phoolwalon Ki Sair — A751

2r, Pankha (embroidered apron).

1987, Oct. 1 *Perf. 13x13½*
1171 A751 2r multicolored .50 .30

Festival of thanksgiving for fulfilled prayers.

Maharaja Chhatrasal A752

1987, Oct. 2 *Perf. 14*
1172 A752 60p henna brown .50 .35

Chhatrasal (1649-1731), military commander during the war against the Moguls.

Intl. Year of Shelter for the Homeless A753

1987, Oct. 5 *Perf. 13½x13*
1173 A753 5r multicolored .80 .40

Asia Regional Conference of Rotary Intl. — A754

6.50r, Polio immunization.

1987, Oct. 14
1174 A754 60p shown .25 .25
1175 A754 6.50r multicolored 1.10 .50

Service to the Blind, Cent. A755

1987, Oct. 15
1176 A755 1r shown .30 .30
1177 A755 2r Eye donation .50 .35

World White Cane Day.

INDIA '89 — A756

Designs: 60p, The Iron Pillar, Quwwat-ul-Islam Mosque courtyard, 5th cent., Delhi. 1.50r, The India Gate, New Delhi, war memorial by Luytens, 1921. 5r, The Dewan-E-Khas, Hall of Private Audience, Red Fort, Delhi, c. 1648. 6.50r, Purana Qila, Old Fort, Delhi, c. 1540.

1987, Oct. 17
1178 A756 60p multicolored .25 .25
a. Bklt. pane of 4 + inscribed margin ('89) .80
1179 A756 1.50r multicolored .50 .25
a. Bklt. pane of 4 + inscribed margin ('89) 2.10
1180 A756 5r multicolored 1.25 .45
a. Bklt. pane of 4 + inscribed margin ('89) 5.25
1181 A756 6.50r multicolored 2.00 .60
a. Souv. sheet of 4, #1178-1811 4.00 4.00
b. Bklt. pane of 4 + inscribed margin ('89) 7.75
Nos. 1178-1181 (4) 4.00 1.55

No. 1181a sold for 15r.

Tyagmurti Goswami Ganeshdutt (1889-1959), Educator, Social Activist — A757

1987, Nov. 2 *Perf. 13½*
1182 A757 60p terra cotta .50 .40

Children's Day — A758

1987, Nov. 14
1183 A758 60p multicolored .50 .30

Trees A759

1987, Nov. 19 **Photo.** *Perf. 13½*
1184 A759 60p Chinar, vert. .35 .30
1185 A759 1.50r Pipal .40 .30
1186 A759 5r Sal, vert. 1.10 .65
1187 A759 6.50r Banyan 1.50 .90
Nos. 1184-1187 (4) 3.35 2.15

Festival of the USSR in India — A760

Votive coin based on The Worker and the Peasant Woman, by Soviet sculptor Mukhina.

1987, Nov. 21 *Perf. 14*
1188 A760 5r multicolored .80 .50

White Tiger — A761

1987, Nov. 29 Photo. *Perf. 13½*
1189 A761 1r shown .75 .25
1190 A761 5r Snow leopard, horiz. 2.25 .90

Rameshwari Nehru (1886-1966), Human Rights and World Peace Activist — A762

1987, Dec. 10
1191 A762 60p red brown .50 .40

Execution of Veer Narayan Singh (1795-1857), Sikh Uprising Leader — A763

1987, Dec. 10
1192 A763 60p brown .50 .40

Father Kuriakose Elias Chavara (1806-1871), Theologian Beatified by Pope John Paul II Feb. 8, 1986 — A764

1987, Dec. 20
1193 A764 60p dark brown olive .50 .40

Dr. Rajah Sir M.A. Muthiah Chettiar (1905-1984), Politician, Pro-chancellor of Annamalai University — A765

1987, Dec. 21 *Perf. 13*
1194 A765 60p chalky blue black .50 .40

Sri Harmandir Sahib (Gold Temple), Amritsar, 400th Anniv. — A766

1987, Dec. 26 *Perf. 13½*
1195 A766 60p multicolored 1.00 .70

Rukmini Devi (1904-1986), Dancer, Choreographer — A767

1987, Dec. 27
1196 A767 60p dark red .60 .35

Dr. Hiralal (1867-1934), Historian — A768

1987, Dec. 31
1197 A768 60p dark blue .50 .40

Famous Indians Type of 1983

Design: Pandit Hriday Nath Kunzru (1887-1978), human rights activist, statesman.

1987, Dec. 31 *Perf. 13½x13*
1198 A639 60p org, grn & red brn .35 .25

75th Session of the Indian Science Congress Assoc. A770

1988, Jan. 1
1199 A770 4r multicolored .90 .55

Solar Energy — A771

Wmk. 324

1988, Jan. 1 Photo. *Perf. 13*
1200 A771 5r dp orange & sepia .80 .40

13th Asia Pacific Dental Congress, New Delhi, Jan. 28-Feb.2 — A772

1988, Jan. 28 Unwmk. *Perf. 13*
1201 A772 4r multicolored .75 .50

Famous Indians Type of 1983

Designs: No. 1202, Mohan Lal Sukhadia (1916-1982). No. 1203, Dr. S.K. Sinha (1887-1961). No. 1204, Chandra Shekhar Azad (1906-1931). No. 1205, Govind Ballabh Pant (1887-1961).

1988 *Perf. 13½x13*
1202 A639 60p org, grn & bluish blk .75 .60
1203 A639 60p org, grn & org brn .75 .60
1204 A639 60p org, grn & rose red .75 .60
1205 A639 60p org, grn & purple .75 .60
Nos. 1202-1205 (4) 3.00 2.40

Issue dates: Nos. 1202, Feb. 2; No. 1203, Feb. 4; No. 1204, Feb. 27; No. 1205, Mar. 7.

U. Tirot Sing (1800-1833), Patriot — A774

1988, Feb. 3
1206 A774 60p dull brown .50 .40

Kumaon Regiment 4th Battalion, Bicent. — A775

1r, Uniforms of 1788, 1947, 1988.

1988, Feb. 19 *Perf. 14*
1207 A775 1r multicolored .60 .30

Balgandharva (1888-1967), Musician — A776

1988, Feb. 22 *Perf. 13x13½*
1208 A776 60p brown .50 .40

Mechanised Infantry Regiment A777

1988, Feb. 24 *Perf. 13½x13*
1209 A777 1r multicolored .90 .45

A778

1988, Feb. 26 *Perf. 13*
1210 A778 60p bluish black .50 .40

Sir B.N. Rau (1887-1953), constitutional advisor.

A779

1988, Mar. 14 Photo. *Perf. 13x13½*
1211 A779 1r bright rose .50 .40

Mohindra College, Patiala, founded in 1875 by Maharaja Mohinder Singh, is now part of Punjabi University.

Dr. D.V. Gundappa (1887-1975), Journalist, and Gikhala Institute of Public Affairs — A780

1988, Mar. 17 *Perf. 13½x13*
1212 A780 60p slate blue .50 .40

Woman Warrior Riding into Battle — A781

1988, Mar. 20 *Perf. 13x13½*
1213 A781 60p bright rose .50 .40

Rani Avantibai (d. 1858), heroine of the 1857 independence war.

Malayala Manorama Newspaper, Cent. — A782

1988, Mar. 23
1214 A782 1r blue & black .50 .40

Malayala Manorama, published in Kottayam, is the largest circulated daily newspaper in India.

Maharshi Dadhichi, Vedic Period Saint Purported to Have Introduced Fire to Man — A783

1988, Mar. 26
1215 A783 60p deep orange .50 .40

Mohammad Iqbal (1877-1938), Poet — A784

1988, Apr. 21
1216 A784 60p carmine & gold .50 .40

Samarth Ramdas (1608-1682), Philosopher A785

1988, May 1 *Perf. 13*
1217 A785 60p dk yellow green .50 .40

Swati Tirunal Rama Varma (1813-1846), Carnatic Composer — A786

1988, May 2 *Perf. 13x13½*
1218 A786 60p brt violet .50 .40

1st War of Independence, the "Indian Mutiny of 1857" — A787

Painting: Rani Laxmi Bai transformed from a queen into a warrior fighting for justice, by M.F. Husain.

1988, May 9 **Photo.** *Perf. 13x13½*
1219 A787 60p multicolored .50 .40

Bhaurao Patil (b. 1887), Educator A788

1988, May 9 *Perf. 13½x13*
1220 A788 60p red brown .50 .40

Himalayan Peaks A789

1988, May 19

1221 A789 1.50r Broad Peak	1.40	.30
1222 A789 4r Godwin Austen	1.60	.40
1223 A789 5r Kanchenjunga	1.60	.55
1224 A789 6.50r Nandadevi	1.60	.70
Nos. 1221-1224 (4)	6.20	1.95

Care for the Elderly — A790

1988, May 24 *Perf. 13x13½*
1225 A790 60p multicolored .50 .40

Victoria Terminal, Bombay, Cent. A791

1988, May 30 *Perf. 13½x13*
1226 A791 1r multicolored .80 .30

Lawrence School, Lovedale, 130th Anniv. A792

1988, May 31 *Perf. 13*
1227 A792 1r dk grn & red brn .70 .40

World Environment Day — A793

1988, June 5 *Perf. 14*
1228 A793 60p Khejri tree .50 .40

Famous Indians Type of 1983

No. 1229, Dr. Anugrah Narain Singh (1887-1957), statesman. No. 1230, Kuladhor Chaliha (1886-1963), political and social reformer. No. 1231, Shivprasad Gupta (1883-1944), freedom fighter.

1988 *Perf. 13½x13*

1229 A639 60p org, grn & rose vio	.65	.40
1230 A639 60p org, grn & gray blk	.65	.40
1231 A639 60p org, grn & dk vio	.65	.40
Nos. 1229-1231 (3)	1.95	1.20

Issued: No. 1229, 6/18; No. 1230, 6/19; No. 1231, 6/28.

Rani Durgawati (d. 1564), Ruler of Gondwana — A795

1988, June 24
1232 A795 60p red .50 .40

A796

1988, July 28 **Photo.** *Perf. 13x13½*
1233 A796 60p red brown .50 .40

Acharya Shanti Dev (687-765), Sanskrit and Pali scholar.

A797

1988, Aug. 4
1234 A797 60p blue violet .50 .40

Yashwant Singh Parmar (1906-1981), administrator of Himachal Pradesh State.

Painting by M.F. Husain — A798

1988, Aug. 16 **Photo.** *Perf. 13x13½*

1235 60p India at upper left	.60	.60
1236 60p India at lower left	.60	.60
a. A798 Pair, #1235-1236	2.00	2.00

Natl. Independence 40th anniv.

Durgadas Rathore (1638-1718), Guardian of King Ajit Singh — A799

1988, Aug. 26 **Litho.**
1237 A799 60p dark red brown .50 .40

Famous Indians Type of 1983

Design: Sarat Chandra Bose (1889-1950), politician, lawyer, publisher.

1988, Sept. 6 **Photo.** *Perf. 13½x13*
1238 A639 60p org, grn & dk blue grn .50 .40

Gopinath Kaviraj (1887-1976), Scholar — A801

1988, Sept. 7 *Perf. 13x13½*
1239 A801 60p brown olive .50 .40

Hindi Language Day, Sept. 14 — A802

1988, Sept. 14 **Photo.** *Perf. 13x13½*
1240 A802 60p ver & dk olive green .50 .40

Indian Olympic Assoc. Emblem — A803

Glory of Sport, Independence 40th Anniv. — A804

Perf. 13½x13, 13x13½

1988, Sept. 17

1241 A803 60p deep claret	.80	.45
1242 A804 5r multicolored	3.25	1.60

Famous Indians Type of 1983

Baba Kharak (1867-1963), nationalist.

1988, Oct. 6 *Perf. 13½x13*
1243 A639 60p org, green & org brn .50 .40

Jerdon's Courser — A806

1988, Oct. 7 *Perf. 13½*
1244 A806 1r multicolored 4.00 .65

The Times of India, Newspaper, 150th Anniv. — A807

1988, Nov. 3 *Perf. 13½x14*
1245 A807 1.50r black & gold .50 .35

INDIA '89 — A808

Perf. 13½x13

1988, Oct. 9 **Unwmk.** **Photo.**

1246 A808 4r Bangalore P.O.	.75	.30
a. Bklt. pane of 6+inscribed margin ('89)	4.50	
1247 A808 5r Bombay P.O.	1.50	.35
a. Bklt. pane of 6+inscribed margin ('89)	9.00	

Portrait of Azad by K.K. Hebbar — A809

1988, Nov. 11
1248 A809 60p multicolored .50 .40

Maulana Abul Kalam Azad (1888-1958), minister of education, natl. resources and scientific research.

Jawaharlal Nehru — A810

Perf. 13x13½, 13½x13 (1r)

1988, Nov. 14
1249 A810 60p dk gray, dk org & dk grn .65 .35
1250 A810 1r Portrait, vert. .75 .35

Birsa, Munda Leader A811

1988, Nov. 15 *Perf. 13½x13*
1251 A811 60p brown .50 .40

Bhakra Dam, 25th Anniv. — A812

1988, Dec. 15 *Perf. 14*
1252 A812 60p carmine rose .70 .70

INDIA '89 — A813

60p, Dead-letter cancellations, 1886. 6.50r, Traveling p.o. cancellation, 1864-69.

1988, Dec. 20 *Perf. 13½x13*
1253 A813 60p multicolored .75 .40
a. Bklt. pane of 6+inscribed margin ('89) 5.00
1254 A813 6.50r multicolored 2.50 1.40
a. Bklt. pane of 6+inscribed margin ('89) 15.00

K.M. Munshi (1887-1971), Environmentalist, Statesmen — A814

1988, Dec. 30
1255 A814 60p dark olive green .50 .40

Mannathu Padmanabhan (1878-1970), Social Reformer — A815

1989, Jan. 2 *Perf. 13½x13*
1256 A815 60p dull brown .50 .40

Famous Indians Type of 1983

Hare Krushna Mahtab (1899-1987), author.

1989, Jan. 2 *Perf. 13½x13*
1257 A639 60p org, grn & blk .60 .40

Lok Sabha Secretariat, 60th Anniv. A817

1989, Jan. 10 *Perf. 13½x13*
1258 A817 60p dark olive green .50 .40

State Museum, Lucknow, 125th Anniv. — A818

60p, Goddess Durga, lion.

1989, Jan. 11 *Perf. 14*
1259 A818 60p blue & dk blue .50 .40

INDIA '89 — A819

60p, Youth collecting. 1.50r, Postal coach & p.o., 1842. 5r, Travancore #2. 6.50r, Philatelic journal mastheads.

1989, Jan. 20 *Perf. 13½x13*
1260 A819 60p multicolored .25 .25
a. Bklt. pane of 6 + inscribed margin .60
1261 A819 1.50r multicolored .40 .25
a. Bklt. pane of 6 + inscribed margin 2.40
1262 A819 5r multicolored 1.00 .40
a. Bklt. pane of 6 + inscribed margin 6.00
1263 A819 6.50r multicolored 1.50 .50
a. Bklt. pane of 6 + inscribed margin 9.00
Nos. 1260-1263 (4) 3.15 1.40

St. John Bosco (1815-1888), Educator — A820

1989, Jan. 31 *Perf. 13*
1264 A820 60p carmine rose .50 .40

3rd Cavalry, 148th Anniv. A821

1989, Feb. 8 *Perf. 13½x13*
1265 A821 60p multicolored .80 .55

Dargah Sharif Ajmer A822

1989, Feb. 13 Litho. *Perf. 13½x13*
1266 A822 1r multicolored .50 .40

President's Review of the Naval Fleet — A823

1989, Feb. 15 *Perf. 14*
1267 A823 6.50r multicolored 3.00 1.90

Famous Indians Type of 1983

No. 1268, Sheikh Mohammad Abdullah. No. 1269, Balasaheb Gangadhar Kher (1888-1957), politician. No. 1270, Saifuddin Kitchlew (1888-1963), lawyer, diplomat. No. 1271, Rajkumari Amrit Kaur (d. 1964), minister of health and welfare.

1988-89 Photo. *Perf. 13½x13*
1268 A639 60p org, grn & lil rose .50 .40
1269 A639 60p org, grn & dk vio .50 .40
1270 A639 60p org, grn & blk brn .50 .40
1271 A639 60p org, grn & grnsh blk .50 .40
Nos. 1268-1271 (4) 2.00 1.60

Issue dates: No. 1268, 12/5; No. 1269, 3/8/89; Nos. 1270-1271, 4/13/89.

Freedom Fighters — A825

No. 1272, Baldev Ramji Mirdha (1889-1956). No. 1273, Rao Gopal Singh (1899-1939).

1989 *Perf. 13x13½*
1272 A825 60p slate .50 .40
1273 A825 60p dark olive .50 .40

Issue dates: No. 1272, 1/17; No. 1273, 3/30.

Freedom Fighters A826

Designs: No. 1274, Shaheed Laxman Nayak (1899-1943), protest leader. No. 1275, Bishu Ram Medhi (1888-1981), politician.

1989 *Perf. 13½x13*
1274 A826 60p org, sage grn & brn .25 .25

Size: 24x37mm

1275 A826 60p org, sage grn & dp yel grn .35 .25

Issued: No. 1274, 3/29; No. 1275, 4/24.
See Nos. 1292, 1299-1300, 1317, 1429, 1487.

Sydenham College, Bombay A827

1989, Apr. 19 *Perf. 13½*
1276 A827 60p black .50 .40

Famous Indians Type of 1983

Design: Asaf Ali (1888-1953), patriot.

1989, May 11 Photo. *Perf. 13½x13*
1277 A639 60p org, grn & sepia .25 .25

N.S. Hardikar (1889-1975), Freedom Fighter — A829

1989, May 13 *Perf. 13x13½*
1278 A829 60p chestnut brown .50 .40

Sankaracharya (b. 788), Philosopher — A830

1989, May 17 *Perf. 14x13½*
1279 A830 60p multicolored .50 .40

Punjab University, Chandigarh A831

1989, May 19 *Perf. 13½x13*
1280 A831 1r blue green & brn .50 .40

Film Industry, 75th Anniv. — A832

1989, May 30 Photo. *Perf. 14*
1281 A832 60p dk olive bis & blk .60 .45

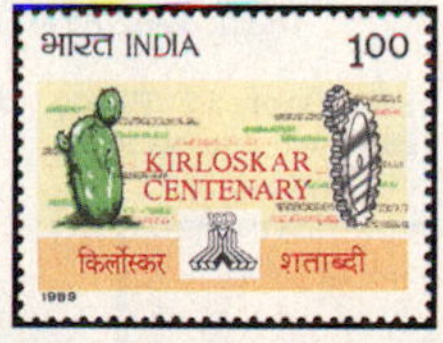

Kirloskar Corporation, Cent. A833

1989, June 20 Photo. *Perf. 13½x13*
1282 A833 1r multicolored .50 .40

DAV Education Movement, Cent. A834

1989, June 27 Photo. *Perf. 13½x13*
1283 A834 1r multicolored .50 .40

Dakshin Gangotri Post Office in the Antarctic, 1988 A835

1989, July 11 *Perf. 14*
1284 A835 1r multicolored 2.00 .50

Allahabad Bank, 125th Anniv. A836

1989, July 19
1285 A836 60p multicolored .50 .40

Central Reserve Police Force, 50th Anniv. A837

1989, July 27 ***Perf. 13½x13***
1286 A837 60p golden brown 2.00 .80

Military Farms, Cent. A838

1989, Aug. 18
1287 A838 1r multicolored 1.20 4.50

Kemal Ataturk (1881-1938), 1st President of Turkey — A839

1989, Aug. 30 ***Perf. 13x13½***
1288 A839 5r multicolored 1.90 .80

Sarvepalli Radhakrishnan, President of India, 1962-67 — A840

1989, Sept. 11 Photo. ***Perf. 13x13½***
1289 A840 60p black .50 .40

P. Subbarayan (1889-1962), Lawyer, Political Reformer — A841

1989, Sept. 30 ***Perf. 13x13½***
1290 A841 60p brown orange .50 .40

Mohun Bagan Soccer Team, Cent. A842

1989, Sept. 23 Photo. ***Perf. 13½x13***
1291 A842 1r multicolored 1.90 1.00

Freedom Fighter Type of 1989

Shyamji Krishna Varma (1857-1930).

1989, Oct. 4 Photo. ***Perf. 13½x13***
1292 A826 60p org, sage grn & dk red brn .50 .40

Sayaji Rao Gaekwad III (1863-1939), Maharaja of the Former State of Baroda — A843

1989, Oct. 6 ***Perf. 13x13½***
1293 A843 60p black .50 .40

Use Pin Code A844

1989, Oct. 14 ***Perf. 14***
1294 A844 60p multicolored .65 .25

Namakkal Kavignar (1888-1972), Poet Laureate — A845

1989, Oct. 19 Photo. ***Perf. 13x13½***
1295 A845 60p black .50 .40

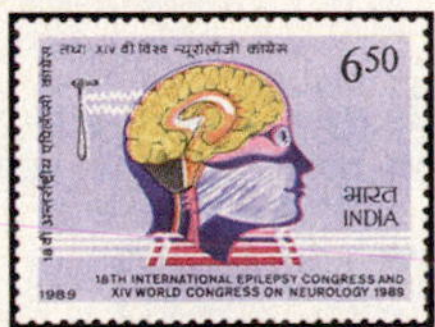

18th Intl. Epilepsy Congress and 14th World Neurology Congress, New Delhi A846

1989, Oct. 21 ***Perf. 13½x13***
1296 A846 6.50r multicolored 3.50 1.10

Ramabai and Sharada Sadan School A847

1989, Oct. 26
1297 A847 60p brown .50 .30

Pandita Ramabai (1858-1920), women's rights activist, founder of mission to help destitute women and children.

Pigeon Post A848

1989, Nov. 3
1298 A848 1r brown orange .90 .35

Freedom Fighter Type of 1989

No. 1299, Acharya Narendra Deo (1889-1956), democratic socialist movement founder. No. 1300, Acharya Kripalani (1888-1982), politician.

1989 ***Perf. 13½x13***
1299 A826 60p org, sage grn & brn .50 .40
1300 A826 60p org, sage grn & dp gray .50 .40

Issue dates: No. 1299, 11/6; No. 1300, 11/11.

Jawaharlal Nehru, Birth Cent. — A849

1989, Nov. 14 ***Perf. 14x15***
1301 A849 1r buff, dk red brn & sepia 1.00 .30

8th Asian Track and Field Meet, Nov. 14-19, New Delhi — A850

1989, Nov. 19 ***Perf. 14x14½***
1302 A850 1r black, org & dp grn .80 .45

A851

1989, Nov. 20 ***Perf. 13x13½***
1303 A851 60p deep brown .60 .45

Gurunath Bewoor (b. 1888), 1st Indian appointed postmaster general.

A852

1989, Dec. 8 Photo. ***Perf. 13x13½***
1304 A852 60p black .60 .45

Balkrishna Sharma Navin (1897-1960), litterateur, politician.

Bombay Art Soc., Cent. A853

1989, Dec. 15 ***Perf. 13½x13***
1305 A853 1r multicolored .60 .45

Likh Florican — A854

1989, Dec. 20 ***Perf. 13x13½***
1306 A854 2r multicolored 2.50 .95

Digboi Oil Field, 1889 — A855

1989, Dec. 29 ***Perf. 14***
1307 A855 60p dark red brown .80 .45

Discovery of oil, Digboi, Assam, cent.

M.G. Ramachandran (1917-1987), Actor, Chief Minister — A856

1990, Jan. 17 ***Perf. 13x13½***
1308 A856 60p dark red brown .80 .30

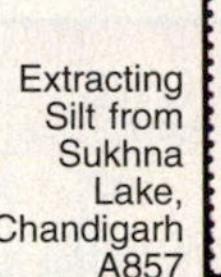

Extracting Silt from Sukhna Lake, Chandigarh A857

1990, Jan. 29 ***Perf. 13½x13***
1309 A857 1r multicolored .60 .45

Sukhna Shramda, society for the preservation of Sukhna Lake.

Presentation of Colors by Pres. Venkataraman to the Bombay Sappers (Corps of Engineers), Feb. 21 — A858

Perf. 15x14x14
1990, Feb. 21 **Photo.**
1310 A858 60p multicolored 1.50 1.25

Asian Development Bank — A859

1990, May 2 Photo. ***Perf. 14***
1311 A859 2r Seashell 1.10 .45

Great Britain No. 1, Simulated Cancel of India, Envelope A860

1990, May 6 ***Perf. 13x13½***
1312 A860 6r multicolored 2.00 .75

Penny Black, 150th anniv.

Residence and Portrait A861

1990, May 17 Photo. ***Perf. 13½x13***
1313 A861 2r red brown & green .60 .40

Ho Chi Minh (1890-1969), Vietnamese Communist Party leader.

A862

1990, May 29
1314 A862 1r orange brown .50 .45

Prime Minister Chaudhary Charan Singh (1902-1987).

A863

1990, July 30 Photo. ***Perf. 13x13½***
1315 A863 2r multicolored .80 .55

Indian peace keeping force in Sri Lanka.

Indian Council of Agricultural Research — A864

1990, July 31 ***Perf. 14***
1316 A864 2r multicolored .60 .40

Freedom Fighter Type of 1989

Design: Khudiram Bose (1889-1908), vert.

1990, Aug. 11 Photo. ***Perf. 13x13½***
Size: 26x35mm
1317 A826 1r org, grn & red brn .60 .45

Russian Child's Drawing of India — A865

6.50r, Indian child's drawing of Red Square.

1990, Aug. 16 Photo. ***Perf. 14***
1318 1r multicolored 2.40 1.60
1319 6.50r multicolored 2.40 1.60
a. A865 Pair, #1318-1319 5.50 5.50

See Russia Nos. 5925-5926.

K. Kelappan (1889-1971), Social Reformer — A866

1990, Aug. 24 ***Perf. 13***
1320 A866 1r lt red brown .60 .45

A867

1990, Sept. 5 ***Perf. 13x13½***
1321 A867 1r multicolored .75 .50

Care for young girls.

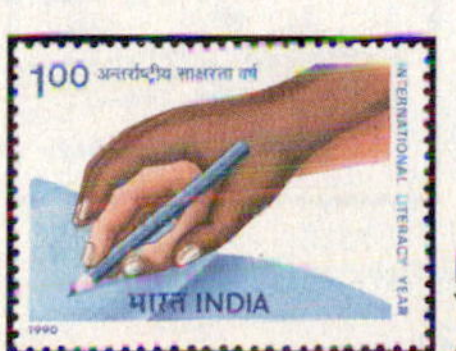
Intl. Literacy Year A868

1990, Sept. 8 ***Perf. 13½x13***
1322 A868 1r blue, brn & tan .75 .50

A869

1990, Sept. 10 ***Perf. 13x14***
1323 A869 4r blue grn & red 2.00 1.60

Safe drinking water.

A870

1990, Sept. 28 Photo. ***Perf. 13x13½***
1324 A870 60p rose lake .75 .50

Sunder Lal Sharma (1881-1940), social reformer.

11th Asian Games, Beijing — A871

1990, Sept. 29
1325 A871 1r Kabbadi .65 .35
1326 A871 4r Sprinting 1.90 1.75
1327 A871 4r Cycling 1.90 1.75
1328 A871 6.50r Archery 2.50 2.25
Nos. 1325-1328 (4) 6.95 6.10

A.K. Gopalan (1904-1977), Political and Social Reformer — A872

1990, Oct. 1
1329 A872 1r red brown .75 .50

5th Gurkha Rifles, 3rd and 5th Battalions — A873

1990, Oct. 1
1330 A873 2r yel brown & dk vio 2.25 1.75

Suryamall Mishran (1815-1868), Poet — A874

1990, Oct. 19
1331 A874 2r brown & yel brown .80 .60

Children's Day — A875

Perf. 13½x13
1990, Nov. 14 Photo. Unwmk.
1332 A875 1r multicolored .90 .60

Border Security Force, 25th Anniv. A876

1990, Nov. 30
1333 A876 5r multicolored 2.50 1.60

Greetings — A877

4r, Two elephants carrying riders, horiz.

Perf. 13x13½, 13½x13
1990, Dec. 17 Photo.
1334 A877 1r multicolored .35 .30
1335 A877 4r multicolored 1.00 .50

Cities of India A878

1990, Dec. 24 Photo. ***Perf. 13½x13***
1336 A878 4r Bikaner .80 .65
1337 A878 5r Hyderabad 1.25 .95
1338 A878 6.50r Cuttack 1.75 1.25
Nos. 1336-1338 (3) 3.80 2.85

Bhakta Kanakadas (1488-1578), Mystic — A879

1990, Dec. 26 ***Perf. 14***
1339 A879 1r red orange .90 .45

Dnyaneshwari, 700th Anniv. — A880

1990, Dec. 31 ***Perf. 13½x13***
1340 A880 2r org red, red brown & blk .60 .40

Calcutta, 300th Anniv. — A881

Designs: 1r, Shaheed Minar. 6r, Sailing ships on Ganges River.

Unwmk.
1990, Dec. 28 Photo. ***Perf. 14***
1341 A881 1r multicolored .50 .30
Size: 44x35mm
1342 A881 6r multicolored 2.00 1.50

Pandit Mohan Malaviya, Banaras Hindu University A882

1991, Jan. 20 ***Perf. 13½x13***
1343 A882 1r dk carmine rose .60 .35

Banaras Hindu University, 75th Anniv.

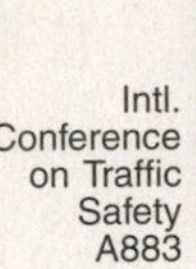

Intl. Conference on Traffic Safety A883

1991, Jan. 30 ***Perf. 13½x13***
1344 A883 6.50r blue, red & blk 1.25 .80

7th Art Triennial — A884

1991, Feb. 12 Photo. ***Perf. 13x13½***
1345 A884 6.50r multicolored 1.00 .60

Jagannath Sunkersett A885

1991, Feb. 15
1346 A885 2r ultra & henna brn .80 .50

Jagannath Sunkersett (1803-1865), educator, reformer.

Tata Memorial Center, 50th Anniv. A886

1991, Feb. 28 ***Perf. 13½x13***
1347 A886 2r brown & buff .60 .35

River Dolphin A887

1991, Mar. 4
1348 A887 4r shown 2.25 1.75
1349 A887 6.50r Sea cow 3.00 2.40

Fight Against Drugs — A888

1991, Mar. 5 ***Perf. 13x13½***
1350 A888 5r dp violet & red 2.50 1.90

World Peace — A889

1991, Mar. 7 Photo. ***Perf. 13x13½***
1351 A889 6.50r black & tan 1.25 .75

Indian Remote Sensing Satellite 1A — A890

1991, Mar. 18 ***Perf. 14***
1352 A890 6.50r blue, red brn & blk 1.00 .60

Babu Jagjivan Ram (1908-1976), Politician — A891

1991, Apr. 5 Photo. ***Perf. 13½***
1353 A891 1r yellow & brown .60 .50

Dr. B.R. Ambedkar (1891-1956), Social Reformer — A892

1991, Apr. 14 ***Perf. 13½x13***
1354 A892 1r red brown & blue .60 .35

Tribal Dances A893

1991, Apr. 30 Photo. ***Perf. 13½x13***
1355 A893 2.50r Valar .70 .50
1356 A893 4r Kayang .90 .60
1357 A893 5r Hozagiri 1.20 .70
1358 A893 6.50r Velakali 1.40 .85
Nos. 1355-1358 (4) 4.20 2.65

Ariyakudi Ramanuja Iyengar (1890-1967), Musician — A894

1991, May 18
1359 A894 2r green & red brown 1.00 .60

Karpoori Thakur (1924-1988), Politician — A895

1991, May 30 ***Perf. 13x13½***
1360 A895 1r red brown .60 .50

Antarctic Treaty, 30th Anniv. A896

1991, June 23 Photo. ***Perf. 13½x13***
1361 A896 5r Penguins 3.00 2.10
1362 A896 6.50r Map, penguins 3.00 2.10
a. Pair, #1361-1362 6.50 6.50

No. 1362a printed in continuous design.

New Delhi, 60th Anniv. A897

Views of New Delhi architecture.

1991, June 25
1363 A897 5r multicolored 3.00 1.60
1364 A897 6.50r multicolored 3.00 1.60
a. Pair, #1363-1364 6.00 6.00

No. 1364a printed in continuous design.

Sri Ram Sharma Acharya (1911-1990), Social Reformer — A898

1991, June 27
1365 A898 1r red & blue green .60 .50

K. Shankar Pillai (1902-1989), Cartoonist — A899

6.50r, The Big Show, vert.

1991, July 31 Photo. ***Perf. 13½x13***
1366 A899 4r shown 1.45 1.25

Perf. 13x13½
1367 A899 6.50r dp purple 2.00 1.90

Sriprakash (1890-1971), Politician — A900

1991, Aug. 3 ***Perf. 13½x13***
1368 A900 2r yellow brown .60 .40

Gopinath Bardoloi (1890-1950), Politician — A901

1991, Aug. 5 ***Perf. 13x13½***
1369 A901 1r violet .60 .50

Rajiv Gandhi (1944-1991), Prime Minister — A902

1991, Aug. 20 ***Perf. 13***
1370 A902 1r multicolored 1.50 1.00

Jain Muni Mishrimalji (1891-1984), Philosopher — A903

1991, Aug. 24 Photo. ***Perf. 13½***
1371 A903 1r brown .60 .35

Mahadevi Verma (1907-1987), Writer and Poet — A904

No. 1373: Jayshankar Prasad (1890-1937), poet and dramatist.

1991, Sept. 16
1372 A904 2r black & blue *10.00* .50
1373 A904 2r black & blue *10.00* .50
a. Pair, #1372-1373 *40.00 27.50*

37th Commonwealth Parliamentary Conference — A905

1991, Sept. 27 Photo. ***Perf. 13½x13***

1374 A905 6.50r dk blue & brown .80 .60

Greetings — A906

1991, Sept. 30 ***Perf. 13x13½***

1375 A906 1r Frog .25 .25
1376 A906 6.50r Bird .90 .45
a. Pair, #1375-1376 1.10 1.00

Orchids — A907

1r, Cymbidium aloifolium. 2.50r, Paphiopedilum venustum. 3r, Aerides crispum. 4r, Cymbidium bicolour. 5r, Vanda spathulata. 6.50r, Cymbidium devonianum.

1991, Oct. 12

1377 A907 1r multicolored .40 .30
1378 A907 2.50r multicolored .75 .40
1379 A907 3r multicolored 1.00 .50
1380 A907 4r multicolored 1.50 .60
1381 A907 5r multicolored 1.75 .85
1382 A907 6.50r multicolored 2.25 1.25
Nos. 1377-1382 (6) 7.65 3.90

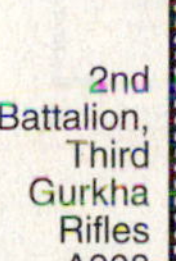

2nd Battalion, Third Gurkha Rifles A908

1991, Oct. 18 ***Perf. 13½x13***

1383 A908 4r multicolored 2.75 2.00

Kamaladevi Chattopadhyaya (1903-1988), Founder of All-India Handicrafts Board — A909

1991, Oct. 29 ***Perf. 13x13½***

1384 A909 1r Horsemen .70 .30
1385 A909 6.50r Puppet 1.90 1.10

Chithira Tirunal Bala Rama Varma (1912-1991), Maharaja of Travancore — A910

1991, Nov. 7 Photo. ***Perf. 13½x13***

1386 A910 2r violet 1.00 .90

Children's Day — A911

1991, Nov. 14 ***Perf. 13x13½***

1387 A911 1r multicolored 1.00 .50

18th Cavalry, Sesquicentennial (in 1992) — A912

1991, Nov. 14 ***Perf. 13½x13***

1388 A912 6.50r multicolored 3.50 2.50

India Tourism Year A913

1991, Nov. 15

1389 A913 6.50r multicolored 1.25 .95

Intl. Conference on Youth Tourism — A914

1991, Nov. 18 Photo. ***Perf. 13x13½***

1390 A914 6.50r multicolored 1.50 1.25

Wolfgang Amadeus Mozart, Death Bicent. — A915

1991, Dec. 5

1391 A915 6.50r multicolored 2.50 1.90

SAARC Year of Shelter A916

1991, Dec. 7 ***Perf. 13½x13***

1392 A916 4r lake & bister 1.00 .75

Run for Your Heart A917

1991, Dec. 11

1393 A917 1r black, red & gray .60 .50

Siddhartha With An Injured Bird — A918

1991, Dec. 28 ***Perf. 13x13½***

1394 A918 2r multicolored .60 .40

Asit Kumar Haldar (1890-1964), Painter

Yoga Exercises A919

2r, Bhujangasana. 5r, Dhanurasana. 6.50r, Ustrasana. 10r, Utthita trikonasana.

1991, Dec. 30 Photo. ***Perf. 13½x13***

1395 A919 2r multicolored .35 .30
1396 A919 5r multicolored .80 .35
1397 A919 6.50r multicolored 1.10 .50
1398 A919 10r multicolored 1.90 .75
Nos. 1395-1398 (4) 4.15 1.90

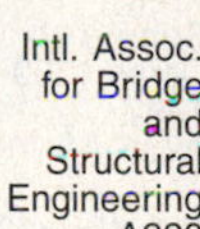

Intl. Assoc. for Bridge and Structural Engineering A920

No. 1399, Hooghly River Bridge, Madurai Temple. No. 1400, Sanchi Stupa gates, Hall of Nations.

1992, Mar. 1 Photo. ***Perf. 13½x13***

1399 A920 2r sal, brn & blue *10.00* .85
1400 A920 2r sal, brn & blue *10.00* .85
a. Pair, #1399-1400 *35.00* *25.00*

Fifth Intl. Conference on Goats — A921

1992, Mar. 2 ***Perf. 13x13½***

1401 A921 6r dk blue & brown 3.75 2.75

Natl. Council of YMCAs, Cent. (in 1991) — A922

1992, Feb. 21

1402 A922 1r blue & vermilion .60 .40

National Archives A923

1992, Apr. 20 Photo. ***Perf. 13½x13***

1403 A923 6r multicolored .80 .55

Krushna Chandra Gajapathi — A924

Vijay Singh Pathik, Writer — A925

1992, Apr. 29 ***Perf. 13x13½***

1404 A924 1r violet .60 .40
1405 A925 1r red brown .60 .40

Adventure Sports A926

1992, Apr. 29 ***Perf. 13½x13***

1406 A926 2r Hang gliding .45 .40
1407 A926 4r Wind surfing 1.25 .65
1408 A926 5r River rafting 1.75 1.10
1409 A926 11r Skiing 2.25 1.75
Nos. 1406-1409 (4) 5.70 3.90

Henry Gidney (1873-1942), Physician and Politician — A927

1992, May 9 ***Perf. 13½x13***

1410 A927 1r blue & black .90 .55

Telecommunication Training Center, Jabalpur, 50th Anniv. — A928

1992, May 30
1411 A928 1r lemon .60 .50

Sardar Udham Singh (1899-1940), freedom fighter. — A929

1992, July 31 ***Perf. 13x13½***
1412 A929 1r black & brown .60 .50

1992 Summer Olympics, Barcelona. A930

1992, Aug. 8

1413	A930	1r Discus	.45	.25
1414	A930	6r Gymnastics	1.25	.85
1415	A930	8r Field hockey	3.00	1.90
1416	A930	11r Boxing	3.00	2.25
		Nos. 1413-1416 (4)	7.70	5.25

Quit India Movement, 50th Anniv. A931

Designs: 1r, Spinning wheel, inscription. 2r, Mahatma Gandhi, inscription.

1992, Aug. 9 ***Perf. 13½x13***

1417	A931	1r pink, blk & pale pink	1.75	.65
1418	A931	2r gray, blk & claret	2.75	3.00

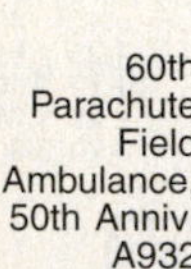

60th Parachute Field Ambulance, 50th Anniv. A932

1992, Aug. 10
1419 A932 1r multicolored 2.25 .90

Indian Air Force, 60th Anniv. — A933

1r, Mikoyan Gurevich Mig-29 Fighter & Ilyushin IL-76 Transport Aircraft. 10r, Mig-27 Fighter & a Westland Wapiti Biplane.

1992, Oct. 8 Photo. ***Perf. 13½x13***

1420		1r multicolored	*10.00*	*.85*
1421		10r multicolored	*10.00*	*1.50*
a.		A933 Pair, #1420-1421	*35.00*	*25.00*

Phad Painting of Dev Narayan A934

1992, Sept. 2 Photo. ***Perf. 13½x14***
1422 A934 5r multicolored 1.00 .95

Sisters of Jesus and Mary, 150th Anniv. — A935

1992, Nov. 13 Photo. ***Perf. 13x13½***
1423 A935 1r gray & blue .60 .35

Children's Day A936

1992, Nov. 14 ***Perf. 13½x13***
1424 A936 1r multicolored .60 .35

Shri Yogiji Maharaj, Religious Leader, Birth Cent. — A937

1992, Dec. 2 Photo. ***Perf. 13x13½***
1425 A937 1r blue 2.25 1.50

Army Service Corps 1760-1992 A938

1992, Dec. 8 Photo. ***Perf. 13½x13***
1426 A938 1r multicolored 3.00 .80

Stephen Smith (1891-1951), Rocket Mail Pioneer — A939

1992, Dec. 19 Photo. ***Perf. 13½x13***
1427 A939 11r multicolored 1.75 1.10

State of Haryana, 25th Anniv. A940

1992, Dec. 20
1428 A940 2r green & orange .60 .60

Freedom Fighter Type of 1989

Design: Madan Lal Dhingra, vert.

1992, Dec. 28 ***Perf. 13x13½***
1429 A826 1r org, grn & brn .60 .35

Dr. Shri Shiyali Ramamrita Ranganathan (1892-1972), Mathematician and Librarian — A941

1992, Aug. 30 Photo. ***Perf. 13½x13***
1430 A941 1r blue 2.00 .65

Hanuman Prasad Poddar — A942

1992, Sept. 19 Photo. ***Perf. 13x13½***
1431 A942 1r green .60 .30

Pandit Ravishankar Shukla — A943

1992, Dec. 31
1432 A943 1r rose lake .60 .30

Birds — A944

2r, Pandion haliaetus. 6r, Falco peregrinus. 8r, Gypaetus barbatus. 11r, Aquila chrysaetos.

1992, Dec. 30

1433	A944	2r multicolored	1.25	.85
1434	A944	6r multicolored	1.75	1.25
1435	A944	8r multicolored	1.90	1.40
1436	A944	11r multicolored	2.10	1.90
		Nos. 1433-1436 (4)	7.00	5.40

William Carey, Baptist Missionary to India, Bicent. of Appointment A945

1993, Jan. 9 Photo. ***Perf. 13½x13***
1437 A945 6r multicolored 2.00 1.10

Fakir Mohan Senapati, Writer — A946

1993, Jan. 14 ***Perf. 13x13½***
1438 A946 1r orange brown .75 .40

Council of Scientific and Industrial Research, 50th Anniv. — A947

1993, Feb. 28 ***Perf. 13½x13***
1439 A947 1r violet brown .90 .45

Squadron No. 1, Indian Air Force, 60th Anniv. A948

No. 1440, Westland Wapiti Biplane. No. 1441, Paratroopers, planes, artillery.

1993, Apr. 1

1440	A948	1r multicolored	1.25	.35
1441	A948	1r multicolored	1.25	.35

Parachute Field Regiment 9, 50th anniv. (No. 1441).

Rahul Sankrityayan (1893-1963), Politician — A949

1993, Apr. 9
1442 A949 1r multicolored .75 .35

Mountain Locomotives A950

1r, Neral Matheran. 6r, DHR (Darjeeling). 8r, Nilgiri Mountain Railway. 11r, Kalka-Simla.

1993, Apr. 16 ***Perf. 13½x13***

1443	A950	1r multicolored	1.00	.30
1444	A950	6r multicolored	2.00	1.00
1445	A950	8r multicolored	2.25	1.25
1446	A950	11r multicolored	3.25	1.60
		Nos. 1443-1446 (4)	8.50	4.15

89th Inter-Parliamentary Union Conference, New Delhi — A951

1993, Apr. 11 Photo. ***Perf. 13x13½***
1447 A951 1r indigo .75 .35

Meerut College, Cent. (in 1992) — A952

1993, Apr. 25 *Perf. 14*
1448 A952 1r indigo & red brown .75 .60

P.C. Mahalanobis (b. 1893), Statistician — A953

1993, June 29 *Perf. 13x13½*
1449 A953 1r olive yellow .60 .35

Dadabhai Naoroji's Election to House of Commons, Cent. — A957

1993, Aug. 26 Photo. *Perf. 14*
1453 A957 6r blue & red brown 1.00 .70

A958

1993, Sept. 11 *Perf. 13x13½*
1454 A958 2r gray, red brn & org 1.00 .55

Swami Vivekananda, Chicago address, cent.

A959

Trees: 1r, Lagerstroemia speciosa. 6r, Cochlospermum religiosum. 8r, Erythrina variegata. 11r, Thespesia populnea.

1993, Oct. 9 Photo. *Perf. 13x13½*
1455 A959 1r multicolored .40 .30
1456 A959 6r multicolored 1.00 .30
1457 A959 8r multicolored 1.50 .65
1458 A959 11r multicolored 2.25 .90
Nos. 1455-1458 (4) 5.15 2.15

Dr. Dwarkanath Kotnis A960

1993, Dec. 9 Photo. *Perf. 13½x13*
1459 A960 1r black & gray .80 .40

A961

1993, Nov. 14 *Perf. 14*
1460 A961 1r multicolored .60 .35

Children's Day.

A962

1993, Nov. 8 *Perf. 13x13½*
1461 A962 2r multicolored .60 .35

College of Military Engineering, Pune, 50th anniv.

A963

Design: Dr. Dwaram Venkataswamy Naidu.

1993, Nov. 8
1462 A963 1r orange brown .60 .35

A964

1993, July 31
1463 A964 2r multicolored .60 .35

Bombay Municipal Corporation Building, cent.

India Tea A965

1993, Dec. 11 *Perf. 13*
1464 A965 6r green & red 1.10 .75

Papal Seminary, Pune, Cent. A966

1993, Dec. 16 *Perf. 13½x13*
1465 A966 6r multicolored 1.25 .85

Natl. Integration A967

1993, Aug. 19
1466 A967 1r orange & green .60 .30

Khan Abdul Ghaffar Khan A968

1993, Aug. 9
1467 A968 1r multicolored .60 .30

Heart Care Festival A969

1993, Dec. 9
1468 A969 6.50r multicolored 1.40 .75

Inpex '93 — A970

1993
1469 A970 1r shown .40 .40
1470 A970 2r Boats, beach 1.00 .40

Issued: 1r, Dec. 25; 2r, Dec. 27.

Meghnad Saha (1893-1956), Astrophysicist A971

1993, Dec. 23 Photo. *Perf. 13x13½*
1471 A971 1r dark blue .75 .45

Dinanath Mangeshkar, Musician — A972

1993, Dec. 29 *Perf. 13½x13*
1472 A972 1r orange brown .60 .30

Nargis Dutt, Actress and Social Worker — A973

1993, Dec. 30 *Perf. 13*
1473 A973 1r orange brown .60 .30

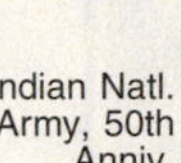

Indian Natl. Army, 50th Anniv. A974

1r, Netaji Subhash Bose inspecting soldiers.

1993, Dec. 31 *Perf. 13½x13*
1474 A974 1r multicolored .80 .50

Satyendra Nath Bose (1894-1974), Mathematician and Physicist — A975

1994, Jan. 1
1475 A975 1r dark rose brown .80 .45

Satyajit Ray (1921-92) A976

6r, Scene from film, Pather Panchali.

1994, Jan. 11 *Perf. 13*
1476 A976 6r multicolored 2.40 1.60
1477 A976 11r multicolored 2.75 1.60
a. Pair, #1476-1477 5.25 5.25

No. 1476 is 68x30mm. No. 1477a is a continuous design.

Dr. Sampurnanand — A977

1994, Jan. 10 Photo. *Perf. 13½x13*
1478 A977 1r multicolored .60 .60

Dr. Shanti Swarup Bhatnagar A978

1994, Feb. 21
1479 A978 1r dark blue .70 .70

Eighth Triennale A979

1994, Mar. 14
1480 A979 6r multicolored 1.00 .50

Prajapita Brahma (1876-1969), Religious Leader — A980

1994, Mar. 7 Photo. *Perf. 13½x13*
1481 A980 1r multicolored .70 .70

Sanchi Stupa A981

Wmk. 324
1994, Apr. 4 Photo. *Perf. 13*
1482 A981 5r blue green & brn .60 .40

ILO, 75th Anniv. A982

1994, May 1 Unwmk. *Perf. 13½x13*
1483 A982 6r multicolored 1.00 .70

United Planters Assoc. of Southern India, Cent. — A983

1994, Mar. 26 Photo. *Perf. 13x13½*
1484 A983 2r multicolored .70 .50

Rani Rashmoni (1793-1861), Philanthropist — A984

1994, Apr. 9 *Perf. 13½x13*
1485 A984 1r brown .70 .55

Jallianwala Bagh Martyrdom, 75th Anniv. A985

1994, Apr. 13
1486 A985 1r red & black .70 .70

Freedom Fighter Type of 1989

1r, Chandra Singh Garhwali (1891-1979).

1994, Apr. 23
1487 A826 1r org, sage grn & grn .70 .70

IPTA — A986

1994, May 25 *Perf. 13*
1488 A986 2r multi .70 .40

Small Families — A987

1r, Family of 3 in front of house.

1994 *Perf. 13x12½*
1489 A987 75p red brn & brn .30 .30
1490 A987 1r green & rose .30 .30

4th Battalion Madras Regiment, Bicent. — A988

1994, Aug. 12
1491 A988 6.50r multicolored 1.25 .85

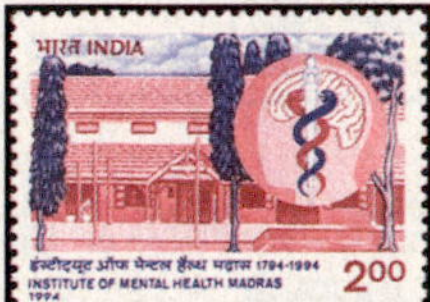
Institute of Mental Health, Madras, Bicent. A989

1994, Sept. 23 Photo. *Perf. 13½x13*
1492 A989 2r multicolored .70 .40

Mahatma Gandhi (1869-1948) A990

Design: 11r, Flag colors, Gandhi walking and at spinning wheel.

1994, Oct. 2 *Perf. 13*
1493 A990 6r multicolored 2.25 1.50
1494 A990 11r multicolored 3.00 2.50
a. Pair, #1493-1494 5.50 5.50

No. 1494 is 68x30mm.

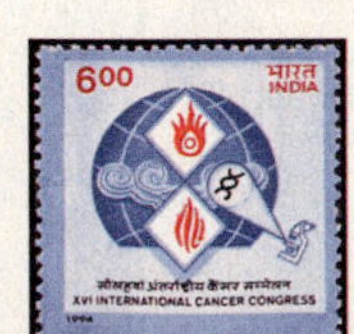
16th Intl. Cancer Congress — A991

1994, Oct. 30 Photo. *Perf. 13½*
1495 A991 6r multicolored 1.25 .70

World Conference on Human Resource Development — A992

1994, Nov. 8 *Perf. 13½x13*
1496 A992 6r multicolored 1.00 .65

Intl. Year of the Family — A993

1994, Nov. 20 *Perf. 13x12½*
1497 A993 2r multicolored .60 .35

Children's Day A994

1994, Nov. 14 *Perf. 13½x13*
1498 A994 1r multicolored .60 .50

J.R.D. Tata (1904-93) — A995

1994, Nov. 29 *Perf. 14*
1499 A995 2r multicolored .60 .40

Calcutta School for the Blind, Cent. A996

1994 Nov. 30 *Perf. 13½x13*
1500 A996 2r brown & carmine .60 .35

Endangered Waterbirds — A996a

Designs: 1r, Andaman teal. 6r, Eastern white stork. 8r, Black-necked crane. 11r, Pink-headed duck.

1994, Nov. 23 *Perf. 13*
1501 1r multicolored 12.50 3.75
1502 6r multicolored 19.00 7.50
1503 8r multicolored 19.00 8.00
1504 11r multicolored 20.00 11.00
a. A996a Block of 4, #1501-1504 75.00 75.00

This set was withdrawn shortly after issue, when it was discovered that it was printed with water soluble ink.

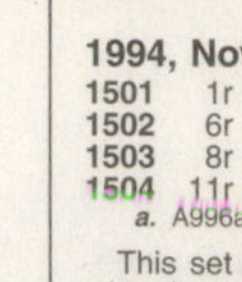

Begum Akhtar A996b

1994, Dec 2 *Perf. 13x13½*
1504B A996b 2r multicolored 15.00 10.00

No. 1504B was withdrawn shortly after issue, when it was discovered that it was printed with water soluble ink.

Remount Veterinary Corps, 215th Anniv. — A998

1994, Dec. 14 Photo. *Perf. 13x13½*
1505 A998 6r multicolored 2.25 1.60

College of Engineering, Guindy, Madras, Bicent. — A999

1994, Dec. 19 *Perf. 14*
1506 A999 2r multicolored .60 .35

Baroda Museum, Vadodara — A1000

Designs: 6r, Ancient artifact. 11r, Ancient artifact, man standing on pedestal.

1994, Dec. 20 *Perf. 14x13½*
1507 6r black & bister 4.50 2.25
1508 11r black & bister 4.50 2.25
a. A1000 Pair, #1507-1508 9.50 9.50

Khuda Bakhsh Oriental Public Library A1001

1994, Nov. 21 Photo. *Perf. 14*
1509 A1001 6r multicolored 6.50 1.60

A1002

1995, Jan. 9 Photo. *Perf. 13x13½*
1510 A1002 1r Chhoturam 1.25 .30

A1003

1995, Jan. 7
1511 A1003 6r multicolored .80 .55

India Natl. Science Academy, 60th Anniv.

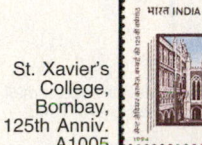

St. Xavier's College, Bombay, 125th Anniv. A1005

1994, Dec. 4 Photo. *Perf. 13½*
1513 A1005 2r multicolored .35 .25

General Post Office, Bombay, Bicent. — A1006

1994, Dec. 28 Litho. *Perf. 13½*
1514 A1006 6r multicolored 8.00 3.00

Motion Pictures, Cent. — A1007

Designs: 6r, Colored film, world map. 11r, Early camera, black & white film.

1995, Jan. 11 Litho. *Perf. 13*
1515 6r multicolored 1.60 1.60
1516 11r multicolored 2.50 2.50
a. A1007 Pair, #1515-1516 4.25 4.25

Oil Conservation A1008

1995, Feb. 18 Photo. *Perf. 13*
1517 A1008 1r red brown & black .25 .25

Rafi Ahmed Kidwai — A1009

1995, Feb. 18
1518 A1009 1r red brown .60 .60

K. L. Saigal A1010

1995, Apr. 4 Photo. *Perf. 13½x13*
1519 A1010 5r black & brown 1.75 1.00

King Rajaraja Chola — A1011

1995, Jan. 5 Photo. *Perf. 13*
1520 A1011 2r multicolored 5.50 1.10

8th Intl. Conference of Tamil Studies.

A1012

1995, Jan. 12 Photo. *Perf. 13½x13*
1521 A1012 2r multicolored .60 .40

SAARC Youth Year.

A1013

1995, Jan. 15
1522 A1013 2r multicolored 5.75 1.10

Prithvi Theater, 50th anniv.

A1014

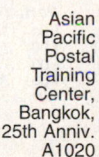

Field Marshall K.M. Cariappa (1900-93).

1995, Jan. 15
1523 A1014 2r multicolored .55 .45

A1015

1995, Jan. 18
1524 A1015 2r multicolored .60 .40

Tex-Styles India '95, National Textile Fair, Bombay.

A1017

UN, 50th Anniv.: 6r, Planting seedling, mother and child, child reading.

1995, June 6 Photo. *Perf. 13*
1526 A1017 1r multicolored .25 .25
1527 A1017 6r multicolored .65 .45

R.S. Ruikar — A1018

1995, May 1 Photo. *Perf. 13½*
1528 A1018 1r brown violet .60 .60

Bharti Bhavan Library, Allahabad A1019

1995, Aug. 30 *Perf. 14*
1529 A1019 6r multicolored .75 .60

Asian Pacific Postal Training Center, Bangkok, 25th Anniv. A1020

1995, Sept. 4 Litho. *Perf. 13½x13*
1530 A1020 10r multicolored 1.75 1.25

Headquarters Delhi Area — A1021

1995, Sept. 26 Photo. *Perf. 13*
1531 A1021 2r multicolored .75 .55

Louis Pasteur (1822-95) A1022

1995, Sept. 28
1532 A1022 5r pale yel & black 3.00 1.50

La Martiniere College, Lucknow, 150th Anniv. A1023

1995, Oct. 1
1533 A1023 2r multicolored .60 .40

Mahatma Gandhi (1869-1948) — A1024

1995, Oct. 2
1534 1r As young man .85 .40
1535 2r As older man .85 .40
a. A1024 Pair, #1534-1535 1.75 1.75
b. Souvenir sheet, #1535a 3.00 3.00

See South Africa Nos. 918-919.

FAO, 50th Anniv. A1025

1995, Oct. 16 *Perf. 13½*
1536 A1025 5r multicolored 1.40 1.00

A1026

1995, Oct. 30 *Perf. 13*
1537 A1026 1r carmine .60 .50

P.M. Thevar (1908-63), politician.

A1027

1995, Nov. 8 Photo. *Perf. 13x13½*
1538 A1027 6r multicolored 2.50 1.90

Wilhelm Roentgen (1845-1923), discovery of the X-Ray, cent.

JAT Regiment, Bicent. A1028

1995, Nov. 20 ***Perf. 13***
1539 A1028 5r multicolored 2.25 1.75

Radio Communication, Cent. — A1029

1995, May 17 Litho. ***Perf. 13½x13***
1540 A1029 5r multicolored 1.75 1.75

Dehli Development Authority — A1030

1995, May 23
1541 A1030 2r multicolored .60 .60

Children's Day — A1031

1995, Nov. 14 Photo. ***Perf. 13x13½***
1542 A1031 1r multicolored .60 .50

Rajputana Rifles, 175th Anniv. A1032

1995, Nov. 28 ***Perf. 13½***
1543 A1032 5r multicolored 2.75 1.75

Communal Harmony — A1033

1995, Nov. 19 Photo. ***Perf. 13***
1544 A1033 2r multicolored 2.50 1.40

Sant Tukdoji Maharaj, Patriot, Social Worker A1034

1995, Dec. 10
1545 A1034 1r brown .70 .55

Dated 1993.

A1035

Design: Yellapragada Subbarow (1895-1948), biochemist.

1995, Dec. 19
1546 A1035 1r yellow brown .70 .55

A1036

Giani Zail Singh (1916-94), Pres. of India.

1995, Dec. 25
1547 A1036 1r multicolored .70 .55

Dome Barelvi's Mausoleum, Dargah — A1037

1995, Dec. 31 **Litho.**
1548 A1037 1r multicolored .70 .55

Ala Hazrat Barelvi (1856-1921), religious scholar.

Cricket Players — A1038

1996, Mar. 13 Photo. ***Perf. 14***
1549 A1038 2r Deodhar 1.00 .75
1550 A1038 2r Vijay Merchant 1.00 .75
1551 A1038 2r Vinoo Mankad 1.00 .75
1552 A1038 2r C.K. Nayudu 1.00 .75
Nos. 1549-1552 (4) 4.00 3.00

Dated 1995.

Homi Bhabha and Tata Institute of Fundamental Research — A1039

1996, Feb. 9 Photo. ***Perf. 13***
1553 A1039 2r multicolored .80 .50

Kasturba Trust — A1040

1996, Feb. 22
1554 A1040 1r multicolored .60 .35

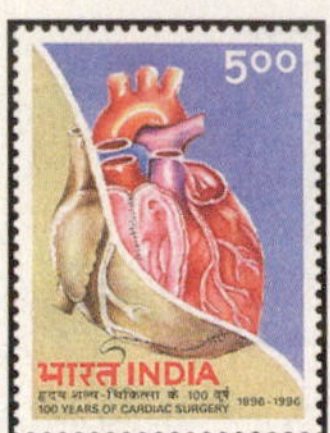

Cardiac Surgery, Cent. — A1041

1996, Feb. 25 **Litho.**
1555 A1041 5r multicolored 2.75 1.25

Miniature Paintings A1042

No. 1556, Two women picking berries from trees. No. 1557, Woman, man embracing. No. 1558, Women looking upward, men, animals. No. 1559, Ceremony, black clouds.

1996, Mar. 13 ***Perf. 13½***
1556 A1042 5r multicolored 2.00 1.00
1557 A1042 5r multicolored 2.00 1.00
1558 A1042 5r multicolored 2.00 1.00
1559 A1042 5r multicolored 2.00 1.00
Nos. 1556-1559 (4) 8.00 4.00

Pt. Kunjilal Dubey — A1043

1996, Mar. 18 Photo. ***Perf. 13***
1560 A1043 1r brown .60 .50

Himalayan Wildlife A1044

No. 1561, Saussurea simpsoniana. No. 1562, Capra falconeri. No. 1563, Ithaginis cruentus. No. 1564, Meconopsis horridula.

1996, May 10 **Litho.**
1561 A1044 5r multicolored 2.25 1.75
1562 A1044 5r multicolored 2.25 1.75
1563 A1044 5r multicolored 2.25 1.75
1564 A1044 5r multicolored 2.25 1.75
a. Souv. sheet of 4, #1561-1564 9.00 9.00
Nos. 1561-1564 (4) 9.00 7.00

No. 1564a sold for 30r. Stamps in No. 1564a do not have "1996."

Morarji Desai — A1045

1996, Apr. 10 Photo. ***Perf. 13x13½***
1565 A1045 1r carmine .60 .35

SKCG College A1047

1996, May 25 **Photo.**
1567 A1047 1r lt brn & dk brn .80 .65

Muhammad Ismail Sahib — A1048

1996, June 5 ***Perf. 13x13½***
1568 A1048 1r claret .80 .80

1996 Summer Olympic Games, Atlanta — A1049

1996, June 25
1569 A1049 5r Olympic stadium .90 .55
1570 A1049 5r Torch .90 .55

A1050

1996, July 19 ***Perf. 13x13½***
1571 A1050 1r blue & black .65 .65

Sister Alphonsa (1910-46).

A1051

1996, Aug. 2 Litho. ***Perf. 14***
1572 A1051 5r multicolored 2.25 1.40

VSNL, 125th anniv.

A1052

1r, Chembai Vaidyanatha Bhagavathar. 2r, Ahilyabai Holkar.

1996 Photo. *Perf. 13x13½*
1573 A1052 1r dk bl grn & brn .80 .55
1574 A1052 2r rose brn & lt brn .80 .65

Issued: 1r, 8/28; 2r, 8/25.

Sir Pherozeshah Mehta — A1053

1996, Aug. 4 Photo. *Perf. 13*
1575 A1053 1r gray blue .80 .80

Poultry Production A1054

1996, Sept. 2
1576 A1054 5r Gallus gallus 4.00 3.00

Rani Gaidinliu — A1055

1996, Sept. 12
1577 A1055 1r dark blue green .80 .80

Barrister Nath Pai — A1056

1996, Sept. 25
1578 A1056 1r blue .80 .80

Indepex '97 World Philatelic Exhibition A1057

1996, Oct. 5 Litho. *Perf. 13x13½*
1579 A1057 2r lake & bister .80 .50

Children's Day A1058

1996, Nov. 14 Photo. *Perf. 13½x13*
1580 A1058 8r multicolored 2.00 1.25

South Asian Assoc. for Regional Cooperation (SAARC), 10th Anniv. A1059

1996, Dec. 8 *Perf. 13*
1581 A1059 11r multicolored 2.40 1.60

Abai Konunbaev (1845-1904), Poet — A1060

1996, Dec. 9 *Perf. 13x13½*
1582 A1060 5r red brown & lake 2.40 1.60

Dated 1995.

2nd Intl. Crop Science Congress A1061

1996, Nov. 17 *Perf. 13*
1583 A1061 2r multicolored 1.10 .70

Sikh Regiment, 150th Anniv. A1062

1996, Oct. 19
1584 A1062 5r multicolored 2.40 1.50

Natl. Rail Museum, 25th Anniv. — A1063

1996, Oct. 7 Litho. *Perf. 13½*
1585 A1063 5r multicolored 3.75 2.10

Jananayak Debeswar Sarmah (1896-1993), Politician — A1064

1996, Oct. 10
1586 A1064 2r lt brn & red brn .80 .50

Dr. Salim Ali, Birth Cent. — A1065

1996, Nov. 12 Photo. *Perf. 13*
1587 8r Dr. Salim Ali 3.75 2.50
1588 11r Water fowl 3.75 2.50
a. A1065 Pair, #1587-1588 9.00 9.00

Second Battalion, The Grenadiers, Bicent. A1066

1996, Dec. 4 *Perf. 14*
1589 A1066 5r multicolored 2.40 1.25

Vijay Divas A1067

1996, Dec. 16
1590 A1067 2r multicolored .35 .25

Vivekananda Rock Memorial, Kanyakumari — A1068

1996, Dec. 26 Litho. *Perf. 13*
1591 A1068 5r multicolored 3.25 1.90

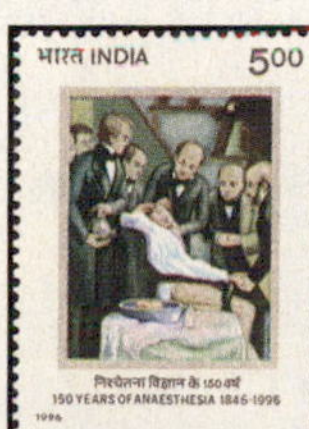

Use of Anesthesia, 150th Anniv. — A1069

1996, Dec. 27 *Perf. 13*
1592 A1069 5r multicolored 2.40 1.40

University of Roorkee, 150th Anniv. A1070

1997, Jan. 1 Photo. *Perf. 13*
1593 A1070 8r multicolored 1.50 1.10

Vrindavan Lal Verma, Writer — A1071

1997, Jan. 9 Photo. *Perf. 13x13½*
1594 A1071 2r red .80 .50

Army Postal Service Corps. (APS), 25th Anniv. A1072

1997, Jan. 22 *Perf. 13½x13*
1595 A1072 5r multicolored 2.75 1.90

Jose Marti (1853-95), Cuban Revolutionary A1073

1997, Jan. 28 *Perf. 13x13½*
1596 A1073 11r multicolored 2.25 1.00

Inter-Parliamentary Specialized Conference, New Dehli — A1074

1997, Feb. 15 Photo. *Perf. 13*
1597 A1074 5r multicolored .80 .40

A1075

1997, Mar. 4 Photo. *Perf. 13*
1598 A1075 1r lake, dk brn, flesh .80 .50

Shyam Lal Gupt (b. 1896), composer of song on natl. flag.

A1076

1997, Mar. 8 *Perf. 13x13½*

1599	5r Parijat Tree	1.25	.75
1600	6r Branch, flower	1.25	.75
a.	A1076 Pair, #1599-1600	2.50	2.50

Rashtriya Indian Military College, Dehra Dun, 75th Anniv. A1077

1997, Mar. 13 *Perf. 13½*

1601 A1077 2r multicolored 1.60 .60

Netaji Subhas Chandra Bose (1897-1945), Nationalist Leader — A1078

1997, Jan. 23 *Perf. 13*

1602 A1078 1r dk brn & lt brn .80 .45

St. Andrews Church — A1079

1997, Feb. 25 Photo. *Perf. 13x13½*

1603 A1079 8r multicolored 1.60 .95

Morarji Desai, Prime Minister, 1977-79 — A1080

1997, Feb. 28 Photo. *Perf. 13*

1604 A1080 1r brown & buff .80 .45

Saint Dnyaneshwar (1274-95), Poet — A1081

1997, Mar. 5 Photo. *Perf. 13*

1605 A1081 5r multicolored 1.10 .65

Ram Manohar Lohia (1910-67), Politician — A1082

1997, Mar. 23 Litho. *Perf. 13x13½*

1606 A1082 1r multicolored .75 .40

CENTIPEX '97 — A1083

Philatelic Society of India, Cent.: No. 1608, #1, Front cover of "The Philatelic Journal of India," 1897.

1997, Mar. 27

1607	2r multicolored	1.25	1.00
1608	2r multicolored	1.25	1.00
a.	Pair, #1607-1608	2.50	2.50

Jnanpith Award Winners — A1084

K.V. Puttappa, D.R. Bendre, Prof. V.K. Gokak, Dr. Masti V. Iyengar, writers.

1997, Mar. 28 Photo. *Perf. 13*

1609 A1084 2r multi .80 .50

Madhu Limaye (1922-95), Politician — A1085

1997, May 1

1610 A1085 2r green .80 .50

Pandit Omkarnath Thakur — A1086

1997, June 24 Photo. *Perf. 13x13½*

1611 A1086 2r black & blue 1.10 .65

A1087

1997, Aug. 6 Photo. *Perf. 13*

1612 A1087 2r brown 1.75 1.25

Thirumathi Rukmini Lakshmipathi (1892-1951), reformer.

Independence, 50th Anniv. — A1088

Officers from Indian Natl. Army, Shah Nawaz Khan, G.S. Dhillon, P.K. Sahgal.

1997, Aug. 15

1613 A1088 2r multicolored .40 .25

Newspaper Swantantra Bharat, 50th Anniv. A1089

1997, Aug. 15 *Perf. 13½x13*

1614 A1089 2r multicolored .60 .40

A1090

1997, Aug. 20 *Perf. 13*

1615 A1090 2r black & gray 1.75 .75

Sir Ronald Ross (1857-1932), physician, medical researcher.

A1091

1997, Sept. 6

1616 A1091 5r red brown 1.75 1.00

Swami Bhaktivedanta (b. 1896), humanitarian.

A1092

1997, Sept. 14

1617 A1092 2r black & gray .60 .40

Swami Brahmanand (1894-1984), social reformer.

A1093

1997, Aug. 8

1618 A1093 2r Sri Basaveswara .60 .40

Maratha Parachute Regiment, Bicent. A1094

1997, Sept. 7 *Perf. 13½x13*

1619 A1094 2r multicolored .90 .45

Hazari Prasad Dwivedi — A1095

1997, Dec. 13 Photo. *Perf. 13x13½*

1620 A1095 2r gray brown .60 .40

Firaq Gorakhpuri A1096

1997, Aug. 28

1621 A1096 2r brown .60 .40

Fossil Plants — A1097

No. 1622, Birbalsahnia divyadarshanii. No. 1623, Glossopteris. 6r, Pentoxylon. 10r, Williamsonia sewardiana.

1997, Sept. 11

1622	A1097	2r multicolored	.50	.35
1623	A1097	2r multicolored	.50	.35
1624	A1097	6r multicolored	1.50	.90
1625	A1097	10r multicolored	2.25	1.50
		Nos. 1622-1625 (4)	4.75	3.10

Sir William Jones, 250th Birth Anniv. — A1098

1997, Sept. 28
1626 A1098 4r multicolored .70 .35

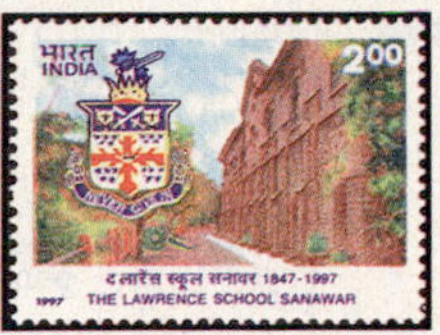

Lawrence School, Sanawar, 150th Anniv. A1099

1997, Oct. 4 ***Perf. 13½x13***
1627 A1099 2r multicolored .90 .55

Indepex '97 A1100

1997, June 6 Photo. ***Perf. 13½x13***

1628	A1100	2r Nalanda	.50	.40
1629	A1100	6r Bodhgaya	.80	.50
1630	A1100	10r Vaishali	1.25	.80
1631	A1100	11r Kushinagar	1.60	.80
a.		Block of 4, #1628-1631	4.50	4.50

66th General Assembly Session of Interpol, 1997 A1101

1997, Oct. 15 ***Perf. 13½***
1632 A1101 4r multicolored 1.25 .80

V.K. Krishna Menon — A1102

1997, Oct. 6 ***Perf. 13***
1633 A1102 2r brown carmine .75 .75

Indepex '97 World Philatelic Exhibition A1103

Rural Indian women: 2r, Arunachal Pradesh. 6r, Gujarat. 10r, Ladakh. 11r, Kerala.

1997, Oct. 15 Photo. ***Perf. 13x13½***

1634	A1103	2r multicolored	.50	.30
1635	A1103	6r multicolored	.95	.50
1636	A1103	10r multicolored	1.25	.70
1637	A1103	11r multicolored	1.50	.95
a.		Block of 4, #1634-1637	4.50	4.50

Scindia School, Cent. — A1104

Designs: No. 1638, Outdoor class. No. 1639, Founder, school building, aerial view.

1997, Oct. 20 ***Perf. 14***

1638	5r multicolored	.70	.35
1639	5r multicolored	.70	.35
a.	A1104 Pair, #1638-1639	1.40	1.40

Medicinal Plants A1105

2r, Ocimum sanctum. 5r, Curcuma longa. 10r, Rauvolfia serpentina. 11r, Aloe barbadensis.

1997, Oct. 28

1640	A1105	2r multicolored	.60	.35
1641	A1105	5r multicolored	1.25	.60
1642	A1105	10r multicolored	1.60	1.10
1643	A1105	11r multicolored	1.90	1.10
a.		Block of 4, #1640-1643	5.50	4.50

A1106

1997, July 2 Litho. ***Perf. 13x13½***
1644 A1106 2r brown & sepia .60 .40

Ram Sewak Yadav (1926-74), politician, social reformer.

A1107

1997, July 11
1645 A1107 2r multicolored .60 .40

Sibnath Banerjee (1897-1982), politician, union leader.

Indepex '97 A1110

Indian beaches: 2r, Gopalpur on Sea, Orissa. 6r, Kovalam Beach, Thiruvananthapuram. 10r, Anjuna Beach, Goa. 11r, Bogmalo Beach, Goa.

1997, Aug. 11 Photo. ***Perf. 13½x13***

1648	A1110	2r multicolored	.60	.30
1649	A1110	6r multicolored	.90	.55
1650	A1110	10r multicolored	1.60	.80
1651	A1110	11r multicolored	2.25	1.00
		Nos. 1648-1651 (4)	5.35	2.65

Sant Kavi Sunderdas (1596-1689) A1111

1997, Nov. 8 Photo. ***Perf. 13x13½***
1652 A1111 2r lt brn & dk brn 1.00 .50

Kotamraju Rama Rao — A1112

1997, Nov. 9
1653 A1112 2r dk brn & yel brn 1.40 .70

Children's Day A1113

1997, Nov. 14 ***Perf. 13½x13***
1654 A1113 2r Nehru with child .70 .40

A1114

1997, Nov. 23 Photo. ***Perf. 13***
1655 A1114 4r multicolored 1.75 1.10

World Convention on Reverence for All Life.

A1115

1997, Dec. 15 Photo. ***Perf. 13x13½***
1656 A1115 2r dk brn & lt brn .60 .40

Sardar Vallabhbhai Patel (1875-1950), politician.

Indepex '97 A1116

Designs: 2r, Post Office Heritage Building. 6r, Indian River Mail. 10r, Cancellations, Jal Cooper. 11r, Mail ship, SS Hindosthan.

1997, Dec, 15 Photo. ***Perf. 13½x13***

1657	A1116	2r multicolored	.60	.50
1657A	A1116	6r multicolored	1.25	.55
1657B	A1116	10r multicolored	1.60	1.10
1657C	A1116	11r multicolored	2.25	1.25
d.		Block of 4, #1657-1657C	5.75	4.75

Souvenir Sheet

Mother Teresa (1910-97) — A1117

1997, Dec. 15 Litho. ***Perf. 13x13½***
1658 A1117 45r multicolored 6.00 6.00

Indian Armed Forces, 50th Anniv. A1118

1997, Dec. 16 Photo. ***Perf. 13½x13***
1659 A1118 2r multicolored .80 .40

Dr. B. Pattabhi Sitaramayya (1880-1959), Author, Politician — A1119

1997, Dec. 17 ***Perf. 13x13½***
1660 A1119 2r dk brn & lt brn .85 .55

Fr. Jerome D'Souza (1897-1977) A1120

1997, Dec. 18 ***Perf. 13½x13***
1661 A1120 2r red brown .60 .40

Ashfaquallah Khan and Ram Prasad Bismil, Revolutionaries A1121

1997, Dec. 19 ***Perf. 13***
1662 A1121 2r dk brn & brn .60 .40

Cellular Jail Natl. Memorial, Port Blair A1122

1997, Dec. 30
1663 A1122 2r multicolored .60 .40

A1123

1998, Jan. 2
1664 A1123 2r red brown .40 .25

Nanak Singh (1897-1971), novelist.

A1124

1998, Jan. 9
1665 A1124 2r plum .40 .25

Nahar Singh, minor leader of Great Mutiny.

Rotary Intl., 1998 Council on Legislation, New Delhi
A1125

1998, Jan. 12 ***Perf. 13½X13***
1666 A1125 8r multicolored 1.25 1.00

A1126

A1127

No. 1667, Maharana Pratap (1540-97), ruler, warrior. No. 1668, Vishnu S. Khandekar (b. 1898), writer.

1998, Jan. 19 ***Perf. 13x13½***
1667 A1126 2r violet brown .80 .50
1668 A1127 2r rose red & dull red .80 .50

A1128

1998, Jan. 25
1669 A1128 10r multicolored 2.25 1.50

Bharat Paryatan Diwas (India Tourism Day).

A1129

1998, Jan. 2 ***Perf. 13½x13***
1670 A1129 4r multicolored 3.00 1.75

11th Gurkha Rifles, 50th anniv.

A1130

Mahatma Gandhi, 50th Anniv. of Death: 2r, Peasants' welfare. 6r, Social upliftment. 10r, Salt Satyagraha. 11r, Communal harmony.

1998, Jan. 30 **Photo.** ***Perf. 14***
1671 2r multicolored .60 .45
1672 6r multicolored .90 .75
1673 10r multicolored 1.10 1.10
1674 11r multicolored 1.75 1.25
a. A1130 Block of 4, #1671-1674 4.75 4.25

A1131

1998, Mar. 8 **Photo.** ***Perf. 13x13½***
1675 A1131 6r multicolored 1.00 .60

Universal Declaration of Human Rights, 50th anniv.

Savitribai Phule (1831-97), Educator, Women's Reformer
A1132

1998, Mar. 10 ***Perf. 13½x13***
1676 A1132 2r dk brn & lt brn .80 .50

Jagdish Chandra Jain
A1133

1998, Jan. 28 **Photo.** ***Perf. 13x13½***
1677 A1133 2r red brown .80 .50

Syed Ahmad Khan (1817-98), Philosopher and Scholar — A1134

1998, Mar. 27
1678 A1134 2r brn & olive brn .80 .50

Sardar A. Vedaratnam
A1135

1998, Feb. 25
1679 A1135 2r violet black .80 .50

Global Environment Facility First Assembly Meeting — A1136

1998, Apr. 1 ***Perf. 13***
1680 A1136 11r multicolored 1.45 1.10

A1137

1998, Apr. 16 **Photo.** ***Perf. 14***
1681 A1137 6r carmine 1.10 .70

Defense Services Staff College.

A1138

Design: Pres. Zakir Husain (1897-1969).

1998, May 3 **Photo.** ***Perf. 13***
1682 A1138 2r sepia .60 .40

A1139

Jnanpith Literary Award winners, year: Shri Bishnu Dey (1909-82), 1971; Shri Tarashankar Bandopadhyay (1898-1971), 1966; Smt. Ashapurna Devi (1909-95), 1976.

1998, June 5
1683 A1139 2r olive brown .60 .40

A1140

Designs: 5r, Parliament Clock Tower, London. 6r, Airplane, mascot, Gateway of India, Bombay.

1998, June 8 **Photo.** ***Perf. 13***
1684 5r multicolored .75 .40

Size: 56x35mm

1685 6r multicolored 1.00 .50
a. A1140 Pair, #1684-1685 1.75 1.75

Air India's 1st intl. flight, 50th anniv.

A1141

Design: Salem C. Vijiaraghavachariar (1852-1944), freedom fighter.

1998, June 18
1686 A1141 2r red brown .60 .35

A1142

1998, May 1
1687 A1142 2r N.G. Goray .60 .35

Sri Ramana Maharshi
A1143

1998, Apr. 14
1688 A1143 2r violet black .60 .40

Konkan Railway — A1143a

1998, May 1 **Photo.** ***Perf. 13***
1689 A1143a 8r multicolored 2.00 .95

A1144

Mohammed Abdurahiman Shahib.

1998, May 15
1690 A1144 2r red brown .60 .40

A1145

1998, May 21 Photo. *Perf. 14*
1691 A1145 2r brown & sepia .60 .40

Lokanayak Omeo Kumar Das, freedom fighter.

Revolutionaries — A1146

Design: Satyendra Chandra Bardhan, Vakkom Abdul Khader, Fouja Singh.

1998, May 25 *Perf. 13*
1692 A1146 2r brn & red brn .60 .40

Natl. Savings Organization, 50th Anniv. — A1147

Design: 6r, Hand dropping coin into bank.

1998, June 30
1693 5r multicolored .80 .30
1694 6r multicolored 1.00 .50
a. A1147 Pair, #1693-1694 1.90 1.25

Bhagwan Gopinathji, Spiritual Leader, Birth Cent. — A1148

1998, July 3 *Perf. 13½*
1695 A1148 3r brown & sepia .60 .40

Ardeshir (1868-1926) & Pirojsha (1882-1972) Godrej, Inventors and Manufacturers — A1149

1998, July 11 *Perf. 13*
1696 A1149 3r green .60 .40

Aruna Asaf Ali, Revolutionay A1150

1998, July 16
1697 A1150 3r brown .60 .40

Vidyasagar College, 125th Anniv. A1151

1998, July 29
1698 A1151 2r dark gray .60 .30

Shivpujan Sahai (1893-1963), Writer — A1152

1998, Aug. 9 Photo. *Perf. 13*
1699 A1152 2r brown .60 .30

Homage to Martyrs A1153

Designs: 3r, Minaret, silhouettes of soldiers standing in fort, flag of India. 8r, Symbols of industrial, scientific and technological developments.

1998, Aug. 15 *Perf. 14*
1700 A1153 3r multicolored .50 .30
1701 A1153 8r multicolored 1.10 .55
a. Pair, #1700-1701 1.60 1.40

Gostha Behari Paul (1896-1976), Soccer Player — A1154

1998, Aug. 20 *Perf. 13*
1702 A1154 3r sepia .60 .40

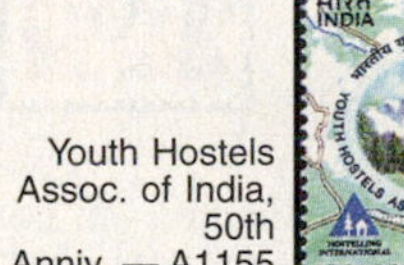

Youth Hostels Assoc. of India, 50th Anniv. — A1155

1998, Aug. 23 *Perf. 14*
1703 A1155 5r multicolored .80 .45

Brigade of the Guards, Fourth Battalion, Bicent. A1156

1998, Sept. 15 Photo. *Perf. 13½*
1704 A1156 6r multicolored 1.10 .55

Bhai Kanhaiyaji A1157

1998, Sept. 18 *Perf. 13*
1705 A1157 2r red .60 .30

20th Intl. Congress of Radiology A1158

1998, Sept. 18 *Perf. 13½x13*
1706 A1158 8r multicolored 1.40 .90

28th IBBY Congress A1159

1998, Sept. 20 *Perf. 13*
1707 A1159 11r multicolored 1.40 .85

Dr. Tristao Braganza Cunha — A1160

1998, Sept. 26
1708 A1160 3r dark brown .60 .40

Jananeta Hijam Irawat Singh — A1161

1998, Sept. 30
1709 A1161 3r brown .60 .40

Acharya Tulsi (1914-97) A1162

1998, Oct. 20 Photo. *Perf. 13½x13*
1710 A1162 3r brown & orange .60 .40

Indian Women in Aviation — A1163

1998, Oct. 15 *Perf. 13*
1711 A1163 8r blue 1.40 .85

Pulse Polio Immunization — A1164

1998, Sept. 21
1712 A1164 3r maroon .25 .25

2nd Battalion of the Rajput Regiment (Kalichindi), Bicent. — A1165

1998, Nov. 30
1713 A1165 3r multicolored .60 .30

David Sassoon Library & Reading Room, Mumbai — A1166

1998, Nov. 30
1714 A1166 3r lt blue & dk blue .60 .40

Army Postal Service Center, Kamptee, 50th Anniv. A1167

1998, Dec. 2
1715 A1167 3r multicolored 1.45 .55

Connemara Public Library, Chennai A1168

1998, Dec. 5 *Perf. 13½x13*
1716 A1168 3r bister & brown .80 .40

A1169

1998, Dec. 10 Litho. *Perf. 13½*
1717 A1169 3r multicolored 1.45 .60

Indian Pharmaceutical Cong. Assoc., 50th anniv.

A1170

Design: Baba Raghav Das (1896-1958), reformer, freedom fighter.

1998, Dec. 12 Photo. *Perf. 13*
1718 A1170 2r deep gray violet .60 .30

Indra Lal Roy (1898-1918), World War I Pilot — A1171

1998, Dec. 19
1719 A1171 3r multicolored 1.45 .40

Sant Gadge Baba (1876-1956), Religious Philosopher — A1172

1998, Dec. 20
1720 A1172 3r multicolored .60 .40

Traditional Musical Instruments A1173

Designs: 2r, Rudra veena (stringed instrument). 6r, Flute (wind insrument). 8r, Pakhawaj (percussion instrument). 10r, Sarod (stringed instrument).

1998, Dec. 29
1721 A1173 2r multicolored .35 .25
1722 A1173 6r multicolored .85 .55
1723 A1173 8r multicolored 1.10 .70
1724 A1173 10r multicolored 1.50 .90
Nos. 1721-1724 (4) 3.80 2.40

Children's Day A1174

1998, Nov. 14 Photo. *Perf. 13½*
1725 A1174 3r multicolored .60 .40

INS Delhi A1175

1998, Nov. 15
1726 A1175 3r multicolored 1.45 .60

President's Bodyguard A1176

1998, Nov. 16
1727 A1176 3r multicolored 1.45 .60

Shells A1177

Designs: No. 1728, Cypraea staphylaea. No. 1729, Cassis cornuta. No. 1730, Chicoreus brunneus. 11r, Lambis lambis.

1998, Dec. 30
1728 A1177 3r multicolored .65 .80
1729 A1177 3r multicolored .90 .80
1730 A1177 3r multicolored 1.60 .80
1731 A1177 11r multicolored 2.25 1.60
Nos. 1728-1731 (4) 5.40 4.00

Indian Police Service, 50th Anniv. A1178

1999, Jan. 13 Litho. *Perf. 13½x13¼*
1732 A1178 3r multicolored 2.00 .55

Defense Research & Development Organization — A1179

1999, Jan. 26 Photo. *Perf. 13*
1733 A1179 10r multicolored 2.00 1.00

Newspapers in Assam, 150th Anniv. — A1180

1999, Jan. 29 *Perf. 13x13½*
1734 A1180 3r multicolored 1.00 .70

Sanskrit College, Calcutta, 175th Anniv. A1181

1999, Feb. 25 *Perf. 13½x13*
1735 A1181 3r brown & yellow 1.00 .45

National Defense Academy, 50th Anniv. A1182

Perf. 13½x13¼
1999, Feb. 19 Litho.
1736 A1182 3r multicolored 1.75 .70

Hindu College, Delhi, Cent. A1183

1999, Feb. 17 Photo. *Perf. 13½x13*
1737 A1183 3r blue .60 .40

Biju Patnaik (1916-97), Politician A1184

1999, Mar. 5
1738 A1184 3r multicolored 1.00 .50

A1185

1999, Mar. 12 *Perf. 13*
1739 A1185 15r multicolored 1.75 1.00

Press Trust of India, 50th anniv.

A1186

1999, Mar. 6
1740 A1186 15r multicolored 1.75 1.00

Temple Complex of Khajuraho, 1000th anniv.

Dr. K.B. Hedgewar (1889-1940) A1187

1999, Mar. 18
1741 A1187 3r multicolored .60 .40

Bethune Collegiate School, 150th Anniv. A1188

1999 Photo. *Perf. 13*
1742 A1188 3r green .70 .50

Creation of the Khalsa, 300th Anniv. A1189

1999, Apr. 14
1743 A1189 3r multicolored 1.75 .55

Maritime Heritage A1190

No. 1744, Boat from 2200 B.C. No. 1745, Ship from 1700.

1999, Apr. 5 Litho. *Perf. 13½x13¼*
1744 A1190 3r multicolored .70 .50
1745 A1190 3r multicolored .70 .50

Technology Day A1191

1999, May 11 Litho. *Perf. 13½x13¼*
1746 A1191 3r multicolored .70 .50

Mumbai Port Trust, 125th Anniv. A1192

1999, June 26 Photo. *Perf. 12¾x13*
1747 A1192 3r blue gray .70 .50

A1193

1999, June 30 Photo. *Perf. 13x12¾*
1748 A1193 3r multicolored .60 .40

Mizoram Accord.

A1194

1999, July 4 Photo. ***Perf. 13¼***
1749 A1194 3r multicolored .60 .40

Gulzari Lal Nanda (b. 1899), interim Prime Minister.

Jijabai, Mother of Shivaji — A1195

1999, July 7 Photo. ***Perf. 14x13½***
1750 A1195 3r claret .60 .40

P. S. Kumaraswamy Raja — A1196

1999, July 8 Photo. ***Perf. 13¼***
1751 A1196 3r sky blue & brown .60 .40

Balai Chand Mukhopadhyay (1879-1979), Writer — A1197

1999, July 19 Photo. ***Perf. 13¼***
1752 A1197 3r slate blue .60 .40

Sindh River Festival A1198

Perf. 13½x13¼
1999, July 28 Photo.
1753 A1198 3r multicolored .60 .40

Geneva Conventions, 50th Anniv. — A1199

1999, Aug. 12 Photo. ***Perf. 13¾***
1754 A1199 15r black & red 2.25 1.60

Freedom Fighters A1200

No. 1755, Swami Ramanand Teerth. No. 1756, Vishwambhar Dayalu Tripathi. No. 1757, Swami Keshawanand. No. 1758, Sardar Ajit Singh.

Perf. 13½x13¼
1999, Aug. 15 Photo.
1755 A1200 3r multicolored .55 .40
1756 A1200 3r multicolored .55 .40
1757 A1200 3r multicolored .55 .40
1758 A1200 3r multicolored .55 .40
Nos. 1755-1758 (4) 2.20 1.60

Kalki Krishnamurthy (1899-1954), Novelist — A1201

1999, Sept. 9 Photo. ***Perf. 13¾***
1759 A1201 3r black .60 .50

Qazi Nazrul Islam (1899-1976), Poet — A1202

Rambriksh Benipuri, Writer A1203

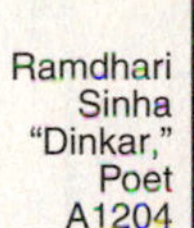

Ramdhari Sinha "Dinkar," Poet A1204

Jhaverchand Kalidas Meghani (b. 1896), Poet — A1205

1999, Sept. 14 Photo. ***Perf. 13x13¼***
1760 A1202 3r multicolored .60 .50

Perf. 13¼
1761 A1203 3r multicolored .60 .50

Perf. 13¼x13
1762 A1204 3r multicolored .60 .50
1763 A1205 3r multicolored .60 .50
Nos. 1760-1763 (4) 2.40 2.00

Arati Gupta, First Asian Woman to Swim Across English Channel A1206

1999, Sept. 29 Photo. ***Perf. 13x13¼***
1764 A1206 3r multi .60 .50

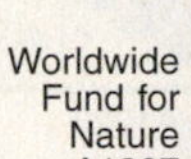

Worldwide Fund for Nature A1207

Asiatic lion: No. 1765, Male atop female. No. 1766, Two lions. No. 1767, Three lions. 15r, Two lions, diff.

1999, Oct. 4 ***Perf. 13¼x13***
1765 A1207 3r multi 2.00 .60
1766 A1207 3r multi 2.00 .60
1767 A1207 3r multi 2.00 .60
1768 A1207 15r multi 3.50 1.75
Nos. 1765-1768 (4) 9.50 3.55

UPU, 125th Anniv. A1208

No. 1769, Muria ritual object. No. 1770, Mask for Chhau dance. No. 1771, Rathva wall painting. 15r, Angami ornament.

1999, Oct. 9 ***Perf. 13¼x13, 13x13¼***
1769 A1208 3r multi .70 .35
1770 A1208 3r multi .70 .35
1771 A1208 3r multi, vert. .70 .35
1772 A1208 15r multi, vert. 2.25 1.40
Nos. 1769-1772 (4) 4.35 2.45

Dr. T. M. A. Pai (1898-1979) — A1209

Chhaganlal K. Parekh (1894-1968) — A1209a

A. B. Walawalkar, Draftsman for Konkar Railway — A1209b

A. D. Shroff — A1209c

1999, Oct. 9 ***Perf. 13x13¼***
1773 A1209 3r yel & brn .60 .60

Perf. 12¾x13¼
1774 A1209a 3r org brn & ind .60 .60

Perf. 13¼
1775 A1209b 3r lilac & maroon .60 .60
1776 A1209c 3r bister & olive .60 .60
Nos. 1773-1776 (4) 2.40 2.40

Veerapandia Kattabomman (1760-99), Freedom Fighter — A1210

1999, Oct. 16 Photo. ***Perf. 13x13¼***
1777 A1210 3r olive green .60 .50

Musicians A1211

No. 1778, Ustad Allauddin Khan Saheb (1870-1972), sarod player. No. 1779, Musiri Subramania Iyer (1899-1975), music teacher.

1999, Oct. 19 Photo. ***Perf. 13¾***
1778 A1211 3r multicolored .75 .60
1779 A1211 3r multicolored .75 .60

A1212

Perf. 13¼x13½
1999, Oct. 27 Photo.
1780 A1212 3r violet brown .70 .50

Brigadier Rajinder Singh (1899-1947).

Children's Day — A1213

1999, Nov. 14 Photo. ***Perf. 14***
1781 A1213 3r multi .60 .40

Sri Sathya Sai Water Supply Project A1214

Perf. 12¾x13¼
1999, Nov. 23 Photo.
1782 A1214 3r multi .90 .50

Supreme Court, 50th Anniv. A1215

Perf. 12¾x13¼
1999, Nov. 26 Photo.
1783 A1215 3r multi .60 .50

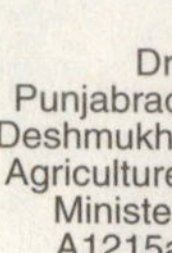

Dr. Punjabrao Deshmukh, Agriculture Minister A1215a

A. Vaidyanatha Iyer (d. 1955), Advocate of Untouchables — A1216

P. Kakkan, Politician A1217

Indulal Kanaiyalal Yagnik, Politician A1218

1999, Dec. 9 *Perf. 13¼*

1784 A1215a 3r brown & grn .35 .25
1785 A1216 3r orange brown .35 .25
1786 A1217 3r green & brn .35 .25
1787 A1218 3r tan & black .35 .25
Nos. 1784-1787 (4) 1.40 1.00

Thermal Power, Cent. A1219

1999, Dec. 14 Photo. *Perf. 13¼x13*

1788 A1219 3r bister & brn .60 .50

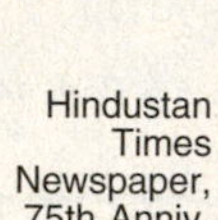

Hindustan Times Newspaper, 75th Anniv. A1220

1999, Dec. 16 Photo. *Perf. 13¼*

1789 A1220 15r multi 2.25 1.60

Family Planning Assoc. of India, 50th Anniv. — A1221

1999, Dec. 18 *Perf. 14x13¾*

1790 A1221 3r multi .60 .50

Birth of Jesus Christ, 2000th Anniv. — A1222

1999, Dec. 25

1791 A1222 3r multi 1.00 .80

Tabo Monastery — A1223

1999, Dec. 31 *Perf. 12¾x13¼*

1792 5r shown .90 .90
1793 10r People 1.00 1.00
a. A1223 Pair, #1792-1793 2.00 2.00

First Sunrise of the Millennium A1224

2000, Jan. 1 *Perf. 13¼x13*

1794 A1224 3r multi 2.00 2.00

Agni II Missile A1225

2000, Jan. 1 Litho. *Perf. 13x13¼*

1795 A1225 3r multi .95 .95

Mahatma Gandhi — A1226

2000, Jan. 27 *Perf. 14x13¾*

1796 A1226 3r red & black .60 .60

Republic of India, 50th anniv.

Gallantry Award Winners A1227

Designs: No. 1797, Karam Singh, regimental crest. No. 1798, Abdul Hamid, jeep-mounted artillery gun. No. 1799, Albert Ekka, grenades, knife. No. 1800, N. J. S. Sekhon, airplane. No. 1801, M. N. Mulla, ship.

2000, Jan. 27 *Perf. 13¼x13*

1797 A1227 3r multi .60 .60
1798 A1227 3r multi .60 .60
1799 A1227 3r multi .60 .60
1800 A1227 3r multi .60 .60
1801 A1227 3r multi .60 .60
a. Strip of 5, #1797-1801 2.50 2.50

Republic of India, 50th anniv.

Millepex 2000 — A1228

Endangered reptiles: No. 1802, Batagur terrapin. No. 1803, Olive ridley turtle.

2000, Jan. 29 *Perf. 13¼*

1802 3r multi .50 .40
1803 3r multi .50 .40
a. A1228 Pair, #1802-1803 2.00 1.75

Famous Men — A1229

Designs: No. 1804, Balwantrai Mehta. No. 1805, Arun Kumar Chanda. No. 1806, Dr. Harekrushna Mahatab, politician.

2000, Feb. 17 Litho. *Perf. 13x13¼*

1804 A1229 3r multi .60 .60
1805 A1229 3r multi .60 .60
1806 A1229 3r multi .60 .60
Nos. 1804-1806 (3) 1.80 1.80

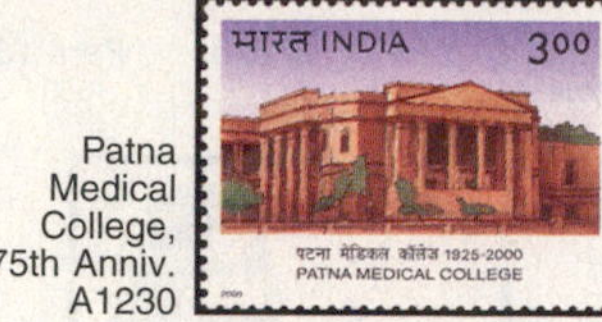

Patna Medical College, 75th Anniv. A1230

2000, Feb. 26 *Perf. 13¼x13*

1807 A1230 3r multi .60 .60

Dr. Burgula Ramakrishna Rao, Politician — A1231

2000, Mar. 13 *Perf. 13x13¾*

1808 A1231 3r brn & ocher .60 .60

Potti Sriramulu (1901-52), Advocate of Untouchables — A1232

2000, Mar. 16 *Perf. 13¼x13*

1809 A1232 3r red .60 .60

Basawon Sinha (1909-89), Socialist Party Leader — A1233

2000, Mar. 23 *Perf. 13x13¼*

1810 A1233 3r multi .60 .60

Indepex Asiana 2000 — A1234

2000, Mar. 31 *Perf. 13x13¼*

1811 A1234 3r Siroi lily .55 .55
1812 A1234 3r Wild guava .55 .55
1813 A1234 3r Sangai deer .55 .55
1814 A1234 15r Slow loris 2.00 2.00
a. Souvenir sheet, #1811-1814 4.50 4.50
Nos. 1811-1814 (4) 3.65 3.65

See Nos. 1831-1834.

Arya Samaj, 125th Anniv. — A1235

Perf. 13x13¼

2000, Apr. 5 Litho. Unwmk.

1815 A1235 3r multi 1.45 1.45

Indigenous Cattle Breeds A1236

Perf. 13¼x13

2000, Apr. 25 Litho. Unwmk.

1816 A1236 3r Gir .60 .50
1817 A1236 3r Kangayam .60 .50
1818 A1236 3r Kankrej .60 .50
1819 A1236 15r Hallikar 2.25 1.60
Nos. 1816-1819 (4) 4.05 3.10

Blackbuck A1237

Patel A1237a

Smooth Indian Otter — A1238

Leopard Cat — A1239

Tiger A1240

Amaltaas — A1241

50p, Nilgiri tahr. 1r, Sarus crane. 2r, Sardar Vallabhbhai Patel (1875-1950), Politician. 15r, Butterfly. 50r, Paradise flycatcher.

Perf. 12¾x13, 13x12¾

2000 Photo. Wmk. 324

1820 A1237 25p olive brn .30 .30
1821 A1237 50p yel brn .30 .30
1822 A1237 1r blue .30 .30
1823 A1237a 2r black .30 .30
1824 A1238 3r gray vio .30 .30
1825 A1239 5r multi .30 .30
1826 A1240 10r multi .70 .70
1827 A1240 15r multi 1.00 1.00
1828 A1241 20r multi 1.50 1.50
1829 A1241 50r multi 4.00 4.00
Nos. 1820-1829 (10) 9.00 9.00

Issued: 25p, 50p, 1r, 3r, 7/20; 2r, 10/31; 5r, 10r, 4/30; 15r, 20r, 11/20; 50r, 10/30.

Railways in Doon Valley, Cent. — A1244

Perf. 13¼

2000, May 6 Litho. Unwmk.
1830 A1244 15r multi 3.00 3.00

Indepex Asiana Type of 2000

Birds: No. 1831, Rosy pastor. No. 1832, Garganey teal. No. 1833, Forest wagtail. No. 1834, White stork.

2000, May 24 *Perf. 13¼x13*
1831 A1234 3r multi, horiz. 1.10 1.10
1832 A1234 3r multi, horiz. 1.10 1.10
1833 A1234 3r multi, horiz. 1.10 1.10
1834 A1234 3r multi, horiz. 1.10 1.10
a. Block of strip of 4, #1831-1834 4.50 4.50
b. Souvenir sheet, #1831-1834 6.00 6.00

Dr. Nandamuri Taraka Rama Rao (1923-96), Actor, Politician A1245

2000, May 28
1835 A1245 3r multi .60 .60

Swami Sahajanand Saraswati (1889-1950), Freedom Fighter — A1246

2000, June 26 *Perf. 13x13¼*
1836 A1246 3r multi .80 .80

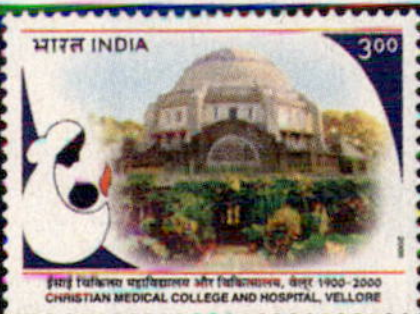

Christian Medical College and Hospital, Vellore, Cent. A1247

2000, Aug. 12 *Perf. 13¼x13*
1837 A1247 3r multi .80 .80

Social and Political Leaders — A1248

Designs: No. 1838, Radha Gobinda Baruah (1900-75), newspaper publisher. No. 1839, Vijaya Lakshmi Pandit (1900-90), President of UN General Assembly. No. 1840, Jaglal Choudhary (1895-1975), politician. No. 1841, R. Srinivasan (1859-1945), advocate of untouchables, newspaper founder.

2000, Aug. 15 *Perf. 13x13¼*
1838 A1248 3r multi .60 .60
1839 A1248 3r multi .60 .60
1840 A1248 3r multi .60 .60
1841 A1248 3r multi .60 .60
Nos. 1838-1841 (4) 2.40 2.40

Kodaikanal Intl. School, Cent. A1249

Perf. 13¼x13

2000, Aug. 26 Litho. Unwmk.
1842 A1249 15r multi 2.25 2.25

2000 Summer Olympics, Sydney A1250

Designs: 3r, Discus. 6r, Tennis. 10r, Field hockey. 15r, Weight lifting.

2000, Sept. 17 *Perf. 13x13¼*
1843-1846 A1250 Set of 4 5.50 5.50

India in Space A1251

No. 1847, Oceansat 1. No. 1848, Insat 3B in orbit.
No. 1849, vert.: a, Astronaut on planet, spacecraft. b, Earth, spacecraft.

Perf. 13¼x13, 13x13¼

2000, Sept. 29
1847-1848 A1251 3r Set of 2 1.50 1.50
1849 Pair 1.50 1.50
a.-b. A1251 3r Any single 1.00 1.00

Madhubani-Mithila Painting — A1252

No. 1850, 3 figures. No. 1851, 2 figures and bird. No. 1852, 2 figures and cow, vert.
No. 1853, vert.: a, Red fish, palanquin. b, Yellow fish, elephant.

2000, Oct. 15 *Perf. 13¼*
1850-1852 A1252 3r Set of 3 1.25 1.25
1853 Pair 2.10 2.10
a. A1252 5r multi .55 .55
b. A1252 10r multi 1.40 1.40

Raj Kumar Shukla (b. 1875), Farmer — A1253

2000, Oct. 16 Litho. *Perf. 13x13¼*
1854 A1253 3r multi *16.00 16.00*

Pres. Shanker Dayal Sharma (1918-99) A1254

2000, Oct. 29 Litho.
1855 A1254 3r multicolored .80 .80

Children's Day — A1255

2000, Nov. 14
1856 A1255 3r multicolored .80 .80

Maharaja Bijli Pasi A1256

2000, Nov. 16 *Perf. 13¼x13*
1857 A1256 3r multicolored .90 .90

Gems and Jewelry — A1257

No. 1858, 3r, Ancient India. No. 1859, 3r, Sarpech. No. 1860, 3r. Taxila. No. 1861, 3r, Navratna. No. 1862, 3r, Temple. No. 1863, 3r, Bridal.

2000, Dec. 7 *Perf. 13¼*
1858-1863 A1257 Set of 6 6.50 6.50
a. Block of 6, #1858-1863 7.50 7.50
b. Souvenir sheet, #1858, 1860-1861, 1863 8.00 8.00

Issued: No. 1863b, 12/11. No. 1863b sold fo 15r.

Warship of Adm. Mohammed Kunjali Marakkar A1258

2000, Dec. 17 *Perf. 13¼x13*
1864 A1258 3r multi 1.45 1.45

Ustad Hafiz Ali Khan (1888-1972), Musician — A1259

2000, Dec. 28
1865 A1259 3r multi 1.00 1.00

Famous Men A1260

No. 1866, Gen. Zorawar Singh (1786-1841). No. 1867, Rajarshi Bhagyachandra (1740-98), King of Manipur, vert. No. 1868, Samrat Prithviraj Chauhan (1162-92), ruler of Delhi, vert. No. 1869, Raja Bhamashah (c. 1542-98), military leader, vert.

2000, Dec. 31 *Perf. 13¼x13, 13x13¼*
1866-1869 A1260 3r Set of 4 2.40 2.40

St. Aloysius College Chapel Paintings, Cent. A1261

Perf. 13¼

2001, Jan. 12 Litho. Unwmk.
1870 A1261 15r multi 2.40 2.40

Subhas Chandra Bose A1262

Dr. B. R. Ambedkar A1263

Perf. 12¾x13

2001 Photo. Wmk. 324
1871 A1262 1r brown .25 .25
1872 A1263 3r blue green .25 .25

Issued: 1r, 1/23; 3r, 4/14.

Famous Men — A1264

Designs: No. 1873, 3r, Sane Guruji (1899-1950), social reformer. No. 1874, 3r, N. G. Ranga (1900-95), politician. No. 1875, 3r, E. M. S. Namboodiripad (1909-98), Marxist leader. No. 1876, 3r, Giani Gurmukh Singh Musafir (1899-1976), politician.

Perf. 13x13¼

2001, Jan. Litho. Unwmk.
1873-1876 A1264 Set of 4 2.40 2.40

Issued: No. 1873, 1/25; others, 1/27.

Famous Men — A1265

Designs: No. 1877, 3r, Sheel Bhadra Yajee (1906-96), freedom figher. No. 1878, 3r, Jubba Sahni (1906-44), revolt leader. No. 1879, 3r,

Yogendra (1896-1966) and Baikunth (1907-34) Shukla, freedom fighters.

2001, Jan.
1877-1879 A1265 Set of 3 1.75 1.75

Issued: No. 1877, 1/28; others, 1/29.

Western Railways Building, Mumbai, Cent. (in 1999) A1266

2001, Feb. 6 ***Perf. 13¼x13***
1880 A1266 15r multi 3.75 3.75

Dated 1999.

2001 Census — A1267

2001, Feb. 10 ***Perf. 13x13¼***
1881 A1267 3r multi .95 .95

President's International Fleet Review — A1268

Designs: No. 1882, 3r, Pal. No. 1883, 3r, Galbat. No. 1884, 3r, Tarangini. 15r, Emblem.

2001, Feb. 18 ***Perf. 13¼x13***
1882-1885 A1268 Set of 4 3.00 3.00

Geological Survey of India, 150th Anniv. A1269

2001, Mar. 4
1886 A1269 3r multi .95 .95

4th Battalion of Maratha Light Infantry, Bicent. — A1270

2001, Mar. 6 ***Perf. 13x13¼***
1887 A1270 3r multi 1.75 1.75

Bhagwan Mahavira, 2600th Anniv. of Birth — A1271

2001, Apr. 6
1888 A1271 3r multi 1.25 1.25

First Manned Space Flight, 40th Anniv. A1272

2001, Apr. 12 ***Perf. 13¼x13***
1889 A1272 15r multi 3.25 3.25

Frederic Chopin (1810-49), Composer A1273

2001, May 4
1890 A1273 15r multi 3.25 3.25

Suraj Narain Singh (1908-73), Politician A1274

2001, May 31 ***Perf. 13x13¼***
1891 A1274 3r multi .80 .80

B. P. Mandal (1918-82), Politician — A1275

2001, June 1
1892 A1275 3r multi .80 .80

Samanta Chandra Sekhar (1835-1904), Astronomer A1276

2001, June 11
1893 A1276 3r multi .80 .80

Sant Ravidas, 15th Cent Religious Leader — A1277

2001, June 24
1894 A1277 3r multi .80 .80

Famous Men — A1278

Designs: No. 1895, 4r, Krishna Nath Sarmah (1887-1947), social reformer. No. 1896, 4r, C. Sankaran Nair (1857-1934), President of Indian National Congress. No. 1897, 4r, Syama Prasad Mookerjee (1901-53), politician. No. 1898, 4r, U Kiang Nongbah (d. 1862), soldier.

2001, July 6 Litho. ***Perf. 13x13¼***
1895-1898 A1278 Set of 4 2.40 2.40

Chandragupta Maurya, Emperor, 3rd Cent. B.C. — A1279

2001, July 21 Litho. ***Perf. 13¼***
1899 A1279 4r multi .80 .80

Jhalkari Bai — A1280

2001, July 22 Litho. ***Perf. 13x13¼***
1900 A1280 4r multi .80 .80

Corals A1281

Designs: No. 1901, 4r, Acropora digitifera. No. 1902, 4r, Fungia horrida. 15r, Montipora acquituberculata. 45r, Acropora formosa.

2001, Aug. 2 ***Perf. 13¼***
1901-1904 A1281 Set of 4 5.50 5.50

Dwarka Prasad Mishra (1901-88), Politician — A1282

2001, Aug. 5 ***Perf. 13x13¼***
1905 A1282 4r multi .80 .80

Chaudhary Brahm Parkash (1918-93), Government Minister — A1283

2001, Aug. 11
1906 A1283 4r multi .80 .80

Ballia Revolution of August 1942 — A1284

2001, Aug. 19
1907 A1284 4r multi .80 .80

Jagdev Prasad (1922-74), Socialist Politician — A1285

2001, Sept. 5
1908 A1285 4r multi .80 .80

Rani Avantibai (d. 1858), Queen of Ramgarh — A1286

2001, Sept. 19
1909 A1286 4r multi .80 .80

Painted Stork — A1287

Perf. 12¾x13
2001, Sept. 20 Photo. Wmk. 324
1910 A1287 4r bister brown 1.45 1.45

Rao Tula Ram (1825-63), Chieftain — A1288

Perf. 13x13¼

2001, Sept. 23 Litho. Unwmk.
1911 A1288 4r multi .80 .80

Chaudhary Devi Lal (1914-2001), Deputy Prime Minister — A1289

2001, Sept. 25
1912 A1289 4r multi .80 .80

Satis Chandra Samanta (1900-83), Politician — A1290

2001, Sept. 29
1913 A1290 4r multi .80 .80

Sivaji Ganesan (1928-2001), Actor — A1291

2001, Oct. 1
1914 A1291 4r multi .80 .80

Mahatma Gandhi, Man of the Millennium — A1292

No. 1915: a, Gandhi and followers, birds. b, Gandhi.

Type A Syncopation (1st stamp No. 1915): On the two longer sides, an oval hole equal in width to 3 holes is located in the center, with an equal number of normal round holes to either side.

Perf. 13x13¼ Syncopated Type A

2001, Oct. 2
1915 A1292 4r Horiz. pair, #a-b 2.50 2.50

Literary and Performing Arts Personalities A1293

Designs: No. 1916, 4r, Lachhu Maharaj (1901-78), choreographer. No. 1917, 4r, Master Mitrasen (1895-1946), playwright, theater founder. No. 1918, 4r, Bharathidasan (1891-1964), Tamil poet.

2001, Oct. 9 ***Perf. 13¼x13***
1916-1918 A1293 Set of 3 2.00 2.00

Jayaprakash Narayan (1902-79), Socialist Politician A1294

2001, Oct. 11
1919 A1294 4r multi .95 .95

Panchatantra Fables — A1295

No. 1920 — The Monkey and the Crocodile, 4r: a, Monkey in tree. b, Monkey on crocodile's back.

No. 1921 — The Lion and the Rabbit, 4r: a, Lion and rabbit. b, Lion and rabbit on bridge.

No. 1922 — The Crows and the Snake, 4r: a, Crows with necklace. b, Villagers pursuing snake.

No. 1923 — The Tortoise and the Geese, 4r: a, Tortoise in pond. b, Tortoise flying with geese.

Sizes: Nos. 1920a-1923a, 58x39mm; Nos. 1920b-1923b, 29x39mm.

2001, Oct. 17 ***Perf. 13x13¼***
Horiz. Pairs, #a-b
1920-1923 A1295 Set of 4 6.00 6.00

Global Iodine Deficiency Disorders Day — A1296

2001, Oct. 21
1924 A1296 4r multi 1.25 1.25

Thangal Kunju Musaliar (1897-1966), Industrialist A1297

2001, Oct. 26
1925 A1297 4r multi .90 .90

Children's Day — A1298

2001, Nov. 14 Litho. ***Perf. 13x13¼***
1926 A1298 4r multi .80 .80

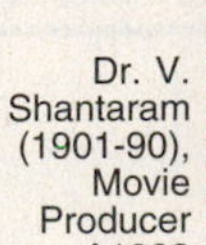

Dr. V. Shantaram (1901-90), Movie Producer A1299

Perf. 13¼x13 Syncopated

2001, Nov. 17
1927 A1299 4r multi .80 .80

Sobha Singh (1901-86), Artist — A1300

2001, Nov. 29 Litho. ***Perf. 13x13¼***
1928 A1300 4r multi 1.25 1.25

Sun Temple, Konark — A1301

No. 1929: a, 4r, Carved wheel. b, 15r, Sun Temple.

Perf. 13¼x13 Syncopated

2001, Dec. 1
1929 A1301 Horiz. pair, #a-b 3.50 3.50

Intl. Volunteers Year A1302

2001, Dec. 5 Litho. ***Perf. 13¼x13***
1930 A1302 4r multi .80 .80

Raj Kapoor (1924-88), Film Actor, Director and Producer A1303

Perf. 13¼x13 Syncopated

2001, Dec. 14 Litho.
1931 A1303 4r multi 1.25 1.25

Greetings — A1304

Flowers and: 3r, Fireworks. 4r, Butterflies.

Perf. 13x13¼ Syncopated

2001, Dec. 18 Litho.
1932-1933 A1304 Set of 2 2.00 2.00

Digboi Refinery, Cent. A1305

2001, Dec. 18 ***Perf. 13¼x13***
1934 A1305 4r multi 1.25 1.25

Vijaye Raje Scindia (1919-2001), Politician — A1306

Perf. 13x13¼ Syncopated

2001, Dec. 20
1935 A1306 4r multi .80 .80

Temples A1307

Designs: No. 1936, 4r, Kedarnath. No. 1937, 4r, Tryambakeshwar. No. 1938, 4r, Aundha Nagnath. 15r, Rameswaram.

2001, Dec. 22 ***Perf. 13¼x13***
1936-1939 A1307 Set of 4 3.75 3.75

Cancer Awareness Day — A1308

2001, Nov. 7 ***Perf. 13x13¼***
1940 A1308 4r multi .80 .80

Maharaja Ranjit Singh (1780-1839), Founder of Sikh Kingdom of the Punjab — A1309

2001, Nov. 9
1941 A1309 4r multi 1.25 1.25

Directorate General of Mine Safety, Cent. — A1310

Perf. 13x13¼ Syncopated

2002, Jan. 7 Litho.
1942 A1310 4r multi 1.00 1.00

May 2001 Ascent of Mt. Everest by Indian Army Mountaineers A1311

2002, Jan. 15 ***Perf. 13x13¼***
1943 A1311 4r multi 1.50 1.50

Bauddha Mahotsav Festival A1312

Designs: No. 1944, 4r, Dhamek Stupa, Sarnath. No. 1945, 4r, Gridhakuta Hills, Rajgir. 8r, Mahaparinirvana Temple, Kushinagar. 15r, Mahabodhi Temple, Bodhgaya.

Perf. 13¼x13 Syncopated

2002, Jan. 21
1944-1947 A1312 Set of 4 4.50 4.50

Book Year A1313

2002, Jan. 28 *Perf. 13¼x13*
1948 A1313 4r multi 1.00 1.00

Swami Ramanand A1314

2002, Feb. 4 *Perf. 13x13¼*
1949 A1314 4r multi 1.00 1.00

Indian Munitions Factories, 50th Anniv. A1315

Perf. 13¼ Syncopated

2002, Mar. 18 **Litho.**
1950 A1315 4r multi 1.00 1.00

Sido and Kanhu Murmu, 1855-57 Revolt Leaders A1316

2002, Apr. 6 *Perf. 13¼*
1951 A1316 4r multi 1.00 1.00

Indian Railways, 150th Anniv. — A1317

2002, Apr. 16 *Perf. 13¼x13*
1952 A1317 15r multi 4.25 4.25
a. Souvenir sheet of 1 4.25 4.25

India — Japan Diplomatic Relations, 50th Anniv. — A1318

No. 1953: a, Kathakali actor, India. b, Kabuki actor, Japan.

2002, Apr. 26 Litho. *Perf. 13x13¼*
1953 A1318 15r Horiz. pair, #a-b 6.00 6.00
c. Souvenir sheet, #1953a-1953b 5.00 5.00

Parliament, 50th Anniv. A1319

Litho. & Embossed

2002, May 13 *Perf. 13¼*
1954 A1319 4r gold 1.00 1.00

Prabodhankar Thackeray (1885-1973), Writer — A1320

Perf. 13x13¼ Syncopated

2002, May 19 **Litho.**
1955 A1320 4r black 1.00 1.00

Cotton College, Guwahati A1321

2002, May 26 Photo. *Perf. 13¼x13*
1956 A1321 4r grn & claret .80 .80

P. L. Deshpande (1919-2000), Actor — A1322

2002, June 16 Litho. *Perf. 13¼*
1957 A1322 4r multi .80 .80

Brajlal Biyani (1896-1968), Politician and Writer — A1323

Perf. 13x13¼ Syncopated

2002, June 22
1958 A1323 4r multi .80 .80

Writers — A1324

Designs: No. 1959, 5r, Babu Gulabrai (1888-1963). No. 1960, 5r, Pandit Suryanarayan Vyas (1902-76).

2002, June 22
1959-1960 A1324 Set of 2 1.60 1.60

Sree Thakur Satyananda (1902-69), Writer — A1325

2002, July 23 Litho. *Perf. 13x13¼*
1961 A1325 5r multi .80 .80

Anna Bhau Sathe (1920-69), Writer — A1326

Perf. 13x13¼ Syncopated

2002, Aug. 1 **Litho.**
1962 A1326 4r gray & black .80 .80

Anand Rishiji Maharaj (1900-92), Humanitarian A1327

2002, Aug. 9 *Perf. 13¼*
1963 A1327 4r multi .80 .80

Vithalrao Vikhe Patil (1901-80), Initiator of Cooperatives A1328

Perf. 13x13¼ Syncopated

2002, Aug. 10
1964 A1328 4r multi .80 .80

Sant Tukaram (1608-50), Poet — A1329

2002, Aug. 10
1965 A1329 4r multi 1.00 1.00

Bhaurao Krishnaroao Gaikwad (1902-71), Politician — A1330

2002, Aug. 26
1966 A1330 4r multi .80 .80

Social Reformers A1331

Designs: No. 1967, 5r, Ayyan Kali (1863-1941), advocate of rights for untouchables. No. 1968, 5r, Chandraprabha Saikiani (1901-72), women's rights advocate. No. 1969, 5r, Gora (1902-75), advocate of atheism.

Perf. 13¼x13 Syncopated

2002, Sept. 12
1967-1969 A1331 Set of 3 2.50 2.50

Ananda Nilayam Vimanam A1332

2002, Oct. 11 *Perf. 13¼x13*
1970 A1332 15r multi 3.25 3.25

Kanika Bandopadhyay (1924-2000), Singer — A1333

2002, Oct. 12 Photo. *Perf. 13x13¼*
1971 A1333 5r multi 1.00 1.00

Arya Vaidya Sala Health Organization, Cent. — A1334

Perf. 13¼x13 Syncopated

2002, Oct. 12 **Litho.**
1972 A1334 5r multi 1.00 1.00

Bhagwan Baba (1896-1965), Religious Leader — A1335

Perf. 13x13¼ Syncopated

2002, Oct. 15
1973 A1335 5r multi .90 .90

Bihar Chamber of Commerce, 75th Anniv. (in 2001) — A1336

2002, Oct. 28
1974 A1336 4r multi 1.10 1.10

UN Climate Change Convention A1337

Mangroves: No. 1975, 5r, Rhizophora mucronata. No. 1976, 5r, Nypa fruticans. No. 1977, 5r, Bruguiera gymnorrhiza. 15r, Sonneratia alba.

Perf. 13¼x13 Syncopated

2002, Oct. 30

1975-1978 A1337	Set of 4	4.00	4.00
1978a	Souvenir sheet, #1975-1978	5.00	5.00

Rose — A1338

Perf. 12¾x13

2002, Aug. 16 Photo. Wmk. 324

1979 A1338	2r multi	.25	.25

Swami Pranavananda (1896-1941), Religious Leader — A1339

Perf. 12¾x13¼

2002, Nov. 3 Litho. Unwmk.

1980 A1339	5r multi	1.50	1.50

Nagpur, 300th Anniv. — A1340

2002, Nov. 11 ***Perf. 13x13¼***

1981 A1340	5r multi	1.40	1.40

Children's Day A1341

2002, Nov. 14 ***Perf. 12¾x13¼***

1982 A1341	5r multi	1.40	1.40

Crafts — A1342

No. 1983: a, Cane and bamboo containers. b, Thewa. c, Patan's Patola. d, Dhokra.

2002, Nov. 15 ***Perf. 13¼***

1983 A1342	5r Block of 4, #a-d	3.00	3.00
e.	Souvenir sheet of 1 #1983	5.25	5.25

Santidev Ghose (1910-99), Dancer and Musician A1343

2002, Dec. 1

1984 A1343	5r multi	1.40	1.40

Formation of Tamralipta Jatiya Sarkar (National Government of Tamluk), 60th Anniv. — A1344

No. 1985: a, Ajoy Kumar Mukherjee (1901-86). b, Matangini Hazra (d. 1942).

2002, Dec. 17 ***Perf. 13¼x13***

1985 A1344	5r Horiz. pair, #a-b	2.25	2.25

Anglo-Bengali Inter College, Allahabad — A1345

Perf. 13¼x13 Syncopated

2002, Dec. 23

1986 A1345	5r multi	.80	.80

Gurukula Kangri Vishwavidyalaya, Hardwar — A1346

Perf. 13x13¼ Syncopated

2002, Dec. 24

1987 A1346	5r multi	1.00	1.00

Dhirubhai H. Ambani (1932-2002), Industrialist A1347

2002, Dec. 28 ***Perf. 13¼***

1988 A1347	5r multi	1.25	1.25

T. T. Krishnamachari (1899-1974), Finance Minister A1348

2002, Dec. 31

1989 A1348	5r multi	1.25	1.25

Forts in Andhra Pradesh — A1349

Designs: No. 1990, 5r, Goloconda Fort. No. 1991, 5r, Palace, Chandragiri Fort.

2002, Dec. 31 ***Perf. 13¼x13***

1990-1991 A1349	Set of 2	1.60	1.60

Aircraft A1350

Designs: No. 1992, 5r, HT-2 airplane. No. 1993, 5r, Marut airplane. No. 1994, 5r, LCA airplane. 15r, Dhruv helicopter.

2003, Feb. 5 ***Perf. 13¼***

1992-1995 A1350	Set of 4	5.00	5.00
1995a	Souvenir sheet, #1992-1995	5.25	5.25

Ghantasala (1922-74), Singer — A1351

2003, Feb. 11

1996 A1351	5r multi	.80	.80

S. L. Kirloskar (1903-94), Industrialist A1352

2003, Feb. 26

1997 A1352	5r multi	.80	.80

Kusumagraj (V. V. Shirwadkar) (1912-99), Poet A1353

2003, Mar. 14

1998 A1353	5r multi	.80	.80

Sant Eknath (1533-99) — A1354

2003, Mar. 23

1999 A1354	5r multi	.80	.80

Frank Anthony (b. 1908), Philantropist A1355

2003, Mar. 28 ***Perf. 13x13¼***

2000 A1355	5r multi	.80	.80

Kakaji Maharaj (1918-86), Yogi — A1356

2003, Mar. 30 ***Perf. 13¼***

2001 A1356	5r multi	.80	.80

Medicinal Plants — A1357

No. 2002: a, Commiphora wightii. b, Bacopa monnieri. c, Withania somnifera. d, Emblica officinalis.

2003, Apr. 7 Litho. ***Perf. 13x13¼***

2002 A1357	5r Block of 4, #a-d	3.50	3.50
e.	Souvenir sheet, #2002a-2002d	4.50	4.50

Durga Das (1900-74), Journalist — A1358

2003, May 2 Photo. ***Perf. 13x13¼***

2003 A1358	5r multi	.80	.80

Singers — A1359

Designs: No. 2004, 5r, Kishore Kumar (1929-87). No. 2005, 5r, Mukesh (1923-76). No. 2006, 5r, Mohammed Rafi (1924-80). No. 2007, 5r, Hemant Kumar (1920-89).

Perf. 13x13¼ Syncopated

2003, May 15 Litho.

2004-2007 A1359	Set of 4	3.25	3.25
2007a	Souvenir sheet, #2004-2007	4.50	4.50

Ascent of Mt. Everest, 50th Anniv. — A1360

2003, May 29 ***Perf. 13x13¼***

2008 A1360	15r multi	2.50	2.50
a.	Souvenir sheet of 1	4.50	4.50

Muktabai (1279-99), Poet Saint — A1361

2003, May 30 ***Perf. 13¼x12½***
2009 A1361 5r multi .80 .80

Government Museum, Chennai — A1362

Designs: No. 2010, 5r, Sculpted medallion, Amravati, c. 150. No. 2011, 5r, Natesa, 12th cent. bronze sculpture. 15r, Museum Theater (58x28mm).

2003, June 19 ***Perf. 13x13¼***
2010-2012 A1362 Set of 3 3.25 3.25
2012a Souvenir sheet, #2010-2012 *4.75 4.75*

V. K. Rajwade (1863-1926), Historian — A1363

2003, June 23 **Photo.**
2013 A1363 5r multi 1.25 1.25

Bade Ghulam Ali Khan (1902-68), Singer — A1364

2003, June 30 **Litho.**
2014 A1364 5r multi 1.25 1.25

Temples — A1365

Designs: No.2015, Vishal Badri Temple, Badrinath. No.2016, Mallikarjunaswamy Temple, Srisailam. No.2017, Tripureswari Temple, Udaipur. No.2018, Jagannath Temple, Puri.

2003, Sept. 15 **Photo.** ***Perf. 13¼x13***
2015 A1365 5r multicolored .85 .85
2016 A1365 5r multicolored .85 .85
2017 A1365 5r multicolored .85 .85
2018 A1365 5r multicolored .85 .85
a. Horiz. strip of 4, #2015-2018 3.50 3.50

Janardan Swami — A1366

2003, Sept. 24 **Photo.** ***Perf. 13x13¼***
2019 A1366 5r brown .80 .80

Intl. Autism Conference, Delhi A1367

2003, Sept. 30 **Litho.** ***Perf. 13¼x13***
2020 A1367 5r multi 1.25 1.25

Waterfalls A1368

Designs: No. 2021, 5r, Kempty Falls, No. 2022, 5r, Athirapalli Falls. No. 2023, 5r, Kakolat Falls. 15r, Jog Falls.

2003, Oct. 3 **Litho.** ***Perf. 13x13¼***
2021-2024 A1368 Set of 4 4.50 4.50
2024a Souvenir sheet, #2021-2024 6.00 6.00

Jnanpith Award Winners for Literature A1369

No. 2025: a, G. Sankara Kurup (1901-78), poet. b, S. K. Pottekkatt (1913-82), novelist. c, Thakazhi Sivasankara Pillai (1912-99), novelist.

2003, Oct. 9 **Photo.** ***Perf. 13¼x13***
2025 Horiz. strip of 3 7.50 7.50
a.-c. A1369 5r Any single 1.00 1.00

Kota Shivarama Karanth (1902-97), Writer and Educator — A1370

2003, Oct. 10 ***Perf. 13x13¼***
2026 A1370 5r multi .80 .80

Narendra Mohan (1934-2002), Journalist A1371

2003, Oct. 14 **Litho.** ***Perf. 13¼***
2027 A1371 5r brown .80 .80

Govindrao Pansare (1913-46), Martyr A1372

2003, Oct. 21 **Photo.** ***Perf. 13¾x14***
2028 A1372 5r multi .80 .80

Greetings A1373

No. 2029: a, Birds. b, Fish and starfish. c, Squirrels. d, Butterflies and flowers.

2003, Oct. 30 **Litho.** ***Perf. 13¼x13***
2029 Horiz. strip of 4 4.50 4.50
a.-b. A1373 4r Either single .95 .95
c.-d. A1373 5r Either single 1.25 1.25

First Telegraph Line in India, 150th Anniv. A1374

2003, Nov. 1 ***Perf. 13¼***
2030 A1374 5r multi 1.45 1.45

Bengal Sappers, Bicent. A1375

2003, Nov. 7 **Photo.** ***Perf. 13¼x13***
2031 A1375 5r multi 1.45 1.45

Kalka-Shimla Railway, Cent. — A1376

2003, Nov. 9 **Litho.**
2032 A1376 5r multi 1.50 1.50

Snakes A1377

Designs: No. 2033, 5r, Python. No. 2034, 5r, Bamboo pit viper. No. 2035, 5r, King cobra. No. 2036, 5r, Gliding snake.

2003, Nov. 12
2033-2036 A1377 Set of 4 3.50 3.50
2036a Souvenir sheet, #2033-2036 6.00 6.00

Children's Day A1378

2003, Nov. 14
2037 A1378 5r multi 1.00 1.00

2nd Guards Batttalion (1st Grenadiers Battalion), 225th Anniv. — A1379

2003, Nov. 22 **Photo.** ***Perf. 13***
2038 A1379 5r multi 1.45 1.45

Harivansh Rai Bachchan (1907-2003), Poet — A1380

2003, Nov. 27 **Litho.** ***Perf. 13x13¼***
2039 A1380 5r sepia & blk .80 .80

French and Indian Artisan's Work — A1381

No. 2040: a, Illumination depicting rooster, France, 15th cent. b, Jewelry design, India, 19th cent.

2003, Nov. 29
2040 A1381 22r Horiz. pair, #a-b 5.75 5.75
c. Souvenir sheet, #2040 10.00 10.00

See France Nos. 2986-2987.

Yashpal (1903-76), Writer A1382

2003, Dec. 3 **Photo.** ***Perf. 13¼***
2041 A1382 5r multi .80 .80

India — South Korea Diplomatic Relations, 30th Anniv. — A1383

No. 2042: a, Cheomsongdae Astronomical Observatory, Gyeongju, Korea. b, Jantar Mantar, Jaipur, India.

2003, Dec. 10 **Litho.**
2042 A1383 15r Pair, #a-b 4.50 4.50

See South Korea No. 2136.

A privately-produced booklet containing two strips of No. 2046 exists.

Rajya Sabha, 200th Session — A1384

2003, Dec. 11
2043 A1384 5r multi .80 .80

Mukut Behari Lal Bhargava (b. 1903), Politician A1385

2003, Dec. 18 **Photo.**
2044 A1385 5r multi .80 .80

Swami Swaroopanandji (1903-74), Religious Leader — A1386

2003, Dec. 20 Litho. ***Perf. 13¼x13***
2045 A1386 5r multi .80 .80

Sangeet Natak Akademi, 50th Anniv. A1387

No. 2046: a, Musicians. b, Actors. c, Dancers.

2003, Dec. 22
2046 Strip of 3, #a-c 4.75 4.75
a.-c. A1387 5r Any single 1.10 1.10
d. Souvenir sheet, #2046 5.00 5.00

Folk Musicians A1388

Designs: No. 2047, 5r, Allah Jilai Bai (1902-92). No. 2048, 5r, Lalan Fakir (1774-1890).

2003, Dec. 29
2047-2048 A1388 Set of 2 2.00 2.00

Siddavanahalli Nijalingappa (1902-2000), Politician A1389

2003, Dec. 31 ***Perf. 13x13¼***
2049 A1389 5r multi 1.00 1.00

Major Somnath Sharma (1923-47), Military Hero — A1390

Perf. 13¼x12¾
2003, Dec. 31 **Photo.**
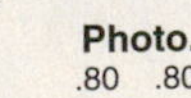
2050 A1390 5r multi .80 .80

Chintaman D. Deshmukh (1896-1982), Finance Minister — A1391

2004, Jan. 14 Litho. ***Perf. 13¼x13***
2051 A1391 5r multi .80 .80

Nani A. Palkhivala (1920-2002), Jurist — A1392

2004, Jan. 16
2052 A1392 5r multi .80 .80

A privately-produced booklet containing six examples of No. 2052 exists.

Dr. Bhalchandra D. Garware, Businessman — A1393

2004, Feb. 6
2053 A1393 5r multi .80 .80

Annamacharya, Mystic Saint — A1394

2004, Mar. 18 Photo. ***Perf. 13¾***
2054 A1394 5r multi .80 .80

9th Battalion of Madras Regiment (Travancore), 300th Anniv. — A1395

2004, Apr. 1 Litho. ***Perf. 13¼x13***
2055 A1395 5r multi 1.50 1.50

V. Lakshminarayana, Violinist — A1396

2004, Apr. 14 **Photo.**
2056 A1396 5r multi 1.50 1.50

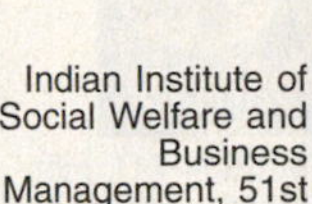

Indian Institute of Social Welfare and Business Management, 51st Anniv. — A1397

2004, Apr. 25 Litho. ***Perf. 13x13¼***
2057 A1397 5r multi 1.00 1.00

Baji Rao Peshwa, General, Statesman A1398

2004, Apr. 25 **Photo.**
2058 A1398 5r multi 1.00 1.00

Circumnavigation of I.N.S. Tarangini — A1399

2004, Apr. 25 Litho. ***Perf. 13¼x13***
2059 A1399 5r multi 1.00 1.00
a. Souvenir sheet of 1 19.00 19.00

Siddhar Swamigal (1904-64), Spiritual Leader — A1400

2004, May 15 ***Perf. 13x13¼***
2060 A1400 5r multi .80 .80

Indra Chandra Shastri (1912-86), Philosopher A1401

2004, May 27 **Photo.**
2061 A1401 5r black & green .80 .80

Woodstock School, Mussoorie, 150th Anniv. A1402

2004, June 2 Litho. ***Perf. 12½x13¼***
2062 A1402 5r multi .80 .80

Jyotiprasad Agarwalla (1903-51), Musician, Cinematographer A1403

2004, June 17 Photo. ***Perf. 13x13¼***
2063 A1403 5r multi 1.00 1.00

P. N. Panicker (1909-95), Educator A1404

2004, June 19
2064 A1404 5r multi .80 .80

Great Trigonometrical Survey — A1405

Designs: No. 2065, 5r, Nain Singh (c. 1826-1882), Himalayan explorer. No. 2066, 5r, Radhanath Sikdar (1813-70), Surveyor who calculated height of Mt. Everest. No. 2067, 5r, Stylized map of India, triangles (38x28mm).

2004, June 27 Litho. ***Perf. 13¼***
2065-2067 A1405 Set of 3 2.50 2.50
2067a Souvenir sheet, #2065-2067 8.00 8.00

A privately-produced booklet containing six examples of No. 2067 exists.

Aacharya Bhikshu, Founder of Jain Swetamber Terapanth Sect — A1406

2004, June 30 **Photo.**
2068 A1406 5r multi .75 .75

2004 Summer Olympics, Athens — A1407

No. 2069: a, 5r, Wrestling. b, 5r, Women's long jump. c, 15r, Shooting. d, 15r, Field hockey.

Perf. 13¾x14¼
2004, Aug. 13 **Photo.**
2069 A1407 Block of 4, #a-d 3.00 3.00

Poets — A1408

No. 2070: a, Kabir (1440-1518), Indian poet. b, Hafiz Shirazi (c. 1325-c. 1389), Persian poet.

2004, Aug. 16 ***Perf. 13¼***
2070 A1408 15r Horiz. pair, #a-b 2.00 2.00

See Iran No. 2894.

Murasoli Maran (1934-2003), Politician, Film Maker, Journalist — A1409

2004, Aug. 17 ***Perf. 12½x13¼***
2071 A1409 5r multi 1.00 1.00

Prime Minister Rajiv Gandhi (1944-91) and Windmills — A1410

2004, Aug. 20 **Litho.** ***Perf. 13¼***
2072 A1410 5r multi 1.00 1.00

Rajiv Gandhi Renewable Energy Day.

S. S. Vasan (1904-69), Film Producer, Magazine Publisher A1411

2004, Aug. 28 **Photo.** ***Perf. 13x13¼***
2073 A1411 5r multi 1.00 1.00

Panini (c. 520 B.C.-c. 460 B.C.), Grammarian — A1412

2004, Aug. 30 ***Perf. 13¼x13***
2074 A1412 5r multi .75 .75

K. Subrahmanyam (1904-71), Film Director and Producer — A1413

2004, Sept. 10
2075 A1413 5r multi .80 .80

M. C. Chagla (1900-81), Judge, Diplomat A1414

2004, Oct. 1
2076 A1414 5r multi .75 .75

Tirupur Kumaran (1904-32), Martyred Protester — A1415

2004, Oct. 4 ***Perf. 13x13¼***
2077 A1415 5r multi .50 .50

India Post, 150th Anniv. A1416

No. 2078: a, Boat, #2, coach, train on bridge. b, Train on bridge, airplane, man with spear, frame of #C1. c, Mail box, building, #201. d, Computer, emblems for postal consumer services.

2004, Oct. 4 ***Perf. 14¼x13¾***
2078 Horiz. strip of 4 2.00 2.00
a.-d. A1416 5r Any single .30 .30
e. Souvenir sheet, #2078, perf. 13¼ 10.00 10.00

Ashoka Chakra Winners — A1417

No. 2079: a, Neerja Bhanot (1963-86), airline purser killed in hijacking. b, Randhir Prasad Verma (1952-91), slain policeman.

2004, Oct. 8 ***Perf. 13¼x13***
2079 A1417 5r Horiz. pair, #a-b 1.00 1.00

Guru Dutt (1925-64), Film Actor, Director A1418

2004, Oct. 10
2080 A1418 5r multi 1.00 1.00

Indian Soldiers in UN Peacekeeping Forces — A1419

2004, Oct. 24 ***Perf. 13¼***
2081 A1419 5r multi .80 .80
a. Souvenir sheet of 1 12.00 12.00

Periya (1748-1801) and Chinna (1753-1801) Marudhu, Rulers of Sivaganga, Rebellion Leaders A1420

2004, Oct. 24 ***Perf. 13¾x14***
2082 A1420 5r multi .80 .80

A privately-produced booklet containing six examples of No. 2082 exists.

Greetings — A1421

No. 2083: a, Kites. b, Dolls.

2004, Oct. 25 ***Perf. 13½x13***
2083 A1421 4r Horiz. pair, #a-b 1.10 1.10

Dr. Svetoslav Roerich (1904-93), Painter A1422

2004, Oct. 27 ***Perf. 13¼x13***
2084 A1422 5r multi .80 .80

Tenneti Viswanatham (1895-1979), Politician — A1423

2004, Nov. 10 **Photo.** ***Perf. 13x13¼***
2085 A1423 5r multi .80 .80

Children's Day — A1424

2004, Nov. 14
2086 A1424 5r multi .75 .75

Walchand Hirachand (1882-1953), Industrialist A1425

2004, Nov. 23 ***Perf. 13¾***
2087 A1425 5r multi .75 .75

Dula Bhaya Kag (1903-77), Poet — A1426

2004, Nov. 25 ***Perf. 13x13¼***
2088 A1426 5r multi .75 .75

Aga Khan Award for Architecture — A1427

No. 2089: a, Khas Mahal (blue panel). b, Agra Fort (orange panel).

2004, Nov. 28 ***Perf. 14x13¾***
2089 Horiz. pair 2.50 2.50
a.-b. A1427 15r Either single .95 .95
c. Souvenir sheet, #2089a, 2089b, perf. 13¼ 15.00 15.00

Bhagat Puran Singh (1904-92), Founder of Home for Poor — A1428

2004, Dec. 10 **Litho.** ***Perf. 13x13¼***
2090 A1428 5r multi .75 .75

Women's Insurrections of 1904 and 1939 — A1429

2004, Dec. 12 **Photo.** ***Perf. 13¼x13***
2091 A1429 5r multi .75 .75

Energy Conservation Day — A1430

2004, Dec. 14
2092 A1430 5r multi .75 .75

Completion of Taj Mahal, 350th Anniv. — A1431

2004, Dec. 16 ***Perf. 14x13¾***
2093 A1431 15r multi 1.25 1.25
a. Souvenir sheet of 1, perf. 13¼ *13.00 13.00*

A privately produced booklet containing 3 No. 2093 exists.

Sahitya Academy, 50th Anniv. A1432

2004, Dec. 21 ***Perf. 13¼x13***
2094 A1432 5r multi .75 .75

Bhaskara Sethupathy (1868-1903), Ramanathapuram Ruler — A1433

2004, Dec. 27 ***Perf. 13x13¼***
2095 A1433 5r multi .75 .75

Dogs A1434

No. 2096: a, Himalayan sheepdog. b, Rampur hound. c, Mudhol hound. d, Rajapalayam.

2005, Jan. 9 ***Perf. 13¼***
2096 Horiz. strip of 4 4.00 4.00
a.-c. A1434 5r Any single .40 .40
d. A1434 15r multi .90 .90

Padampat Singhania (1905-79), Industrialist A1435

2005, Feb. 3
2097 A1435 5r multi .75 .75

Rotary International, Cent. — A1436

2005, Feb. 23 ***Perf. 13¼x13***
2098 A1436 5r multi .90 .90

Vice-President Krishan Kant (1927-2002) — A1437

2005, Feb. 27 **Photo.** ***Perf. 13¼***
2099 A1437 5r multi .75 .75

Madhavrao Scindia (1945-2001), Government Minister — A1438

2005, Mar. 10
2100 A1438 5r multi .75 .75

Flora and Fauna — A1439

No. 2101: a, Clouded leopard. b, Dillenia indica. c, Mishmi takin. d, Pitcher plant.

2005, Mar. 24 **Photo.** ***Perf. 13¼***
2101 A1439 5r Block of 4, #a-d 2.00 2.00
e. Souvenir sheet, #2101 11.00 11.00

Intl. Year of Physics A1440

Perf. 12¾x13
2005, Mar. 31 **Wmk. 324**
2102 A1440 5r multi 1.00 1.00

Salt March to Dandi, 75th Anniv. — A1441

Mohandas Gandhi and: a, Marchers. b, Newspaper. c, Map of march. d, Text by Gandhi.

Perf. 13¼
2005, Apr. 5 **Photo.** **Unwmk.**
2103 A1441 5r Block of 4, #a-d 2.00 2.00
e. Souvenir sheet, #2103 10.00 10.00

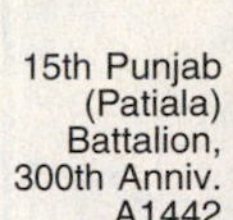

15th Punjab (Patiala) Battalion, 300th Anniv. A1442

2005, Apr. 13
2104 A1442 5r multi .75 .75

Bandung Conference, 50th Anniv. — A1443

2005, Apr. 18
2105 A1443 15r multi 1.25 1.25

Narayan Meghaji Lokhande (1848-1897), Labor Activist A1444

2005, May 3 ***Perf. 13¾***
2106 A1444 5r multi .75 .75

Cooperative Movement in India, Cent. — A1445

2005, May 8 ***Perf. 13¼***
2107 A1445 5r multi .75 .75

World Environment Day — A1446

2005, June 5
2108 A1446 5r multi 1.25 1.25

Guru Granth Sahib A1447

2005, June 16 **Photo.** ***Perf. 14x13¾***
2109 A1447 10r multi *45.00* —
a. Souvenir sheet of 1 *90.00* —

Because of a lack of an agreement with Indian postal officials and Sikh religious representatives, local post offices were alerted that the issuance of Nos. 2109 and 2109a was to be postponed and the stamps were not to be placed on sale on June 16. Examples were sold at several locations that apparently did not receive the message.

Abdul Qaiyum Ansari (1905-73), Nationalist Leader A1448

2005, July 1 **Photo.** ***Perf. 13¼***
2110 A1448 5r brown .75 .75

Dheeran Chinnamalai (1765-1805), Freedom Fighter — A1449

2005, July 31
2111 A1449 5r multi .75 .75

State Bank of India, Bicent. — A1450

2005, Aug. 31
2112 A1450 15r multi 1.25 1.25

Intl. Day of Peace — A1451

2005, Sept. 21 **Photo.** ***Perf. 13x13¼***
2113 A1451 5r multi .75 .75

A. M. M. Murugappa Chettiar (1902-65), Industrialist A1452

2005, Oct. 1
2114 A1452 5r multi .75 .75

Pratap Singh Kairon (1901-65), Government Minister — A1453

2005, Oct. 1 ***Perf. 13¼x13***
2115 A1453 5r multi .75 .75

Dr. T. S. Soundram (1904-84), Founder of Gandhigram Development Program — A1454

2005, Oct. 2
2116 A1454 5r multi .90 .90

Mailboxes A1455

No. 2117: a, Victorian era box, horse-drawn carriage. b, Man inserting letter into Penfold box. c, Two cylindrical boxes. d, Two square letter boxes.

2005, Oct. 18 ***Perf. 13x13¼***
2117 Horiz. strip of 4 3.50 3.50
a.-d. A1455 5r Any single .75 .30
e. Souvenir sheet, #2117a-2117d, perf. 13¾ 15.00 15.00

V. Kalyanasundarnar (1883-1953), Union Leader — A1456

2005, Oct. 21 ***Perf. 13¼***
2118 A1456 5r multi .75 .75

Ayothidhasa Pandithar (1845-1914), Social Reformer A1457

2005, Oct. 21
2119 A1457 5r multi .75 .75

Kavimani Desiga Vinayagam Pillai (1876-1954), Poet — A1458

2005, Oct. 21 ***Perf. 13¼x13***
2120 A1458 5r multi .75 .75

Prabodh Chandra (1911-86), Writer — A1459

2005, Oct. 24 ***Perf. 13x13¼***
2121 A1459 5r multi .75 .75

Children's Day — A1460

2005, Nov. 14
2122 A1460 5r multi .75 .75

Children's Film Society, 50th Anniv. A1461

2005, Nov. 14 ***Perf. 13¾***
2123 A1461 5r multi 1.00 1.00

Progress, Harmony and Development Chamber of Commerce and Industry, Cent. — A1462

2005, Nov. 16
2124 A1462 5r multi .75 .75

World Summit on the Information Society, Tunis A1463

2005, Nov. 17 **Photo.** ***Perf. 13¼x13***
2125 A1463 5r multi .75 .75

Calcutta Police Commissionerate, 150th Anniv. — A1464

2005, Nov. 19 ***Perf. 13¾***
2126 A1464 5r multi .40 .40

Newborn Health — A1465

2005, Nov. 24 ***Perf. 13¼***
2127 A1465 5r blue .40 .40

Jawaharlal Darda, Politician A1466

2005, Dec. 2
2128 A1466 5r multi .25 .25

Navy Ships Delhi, Kora and Udaygiri — A1467

2005, Dec. 4 ***Perf. 13***
2129 A1467 5r multi .60 .60

M. S. Subbulakshmi (1916-2004), Singer — A1468

2005, Dec. 18 ***Perf. 13¼x13***
2130 A1468 5r multi .40 .40

Integral Coach Factory, 50th Anniv. — A1469

2005, Dec. 19 ***Perf. 13¾***
2131 A1469 5r multi .70 .70

Jadavpur University, 50th Anniv. — A1470

2005, Dec. 21
2132 A1470 5r multi .40 .40

16th Air Force Squadron, 55th Anniv. — A1471

2005, Dec. 27 ***Perf. 14x13¾***
2133 A1471 5r multi .40 .40

De Facto Transfer of Pondicherry, 50th Anniv. (in 2006) — A1472

2005, Dec. 30 ***Perf. 13¼x13***
2134 A1472 5r multi .35 .35

Pongal Festival A1473

2006, Jan. 12 ***Perf. 13¾***
2135 A1473 5r multi .70 .70

A. V. Meiyappan (1907-79), Film Producer and Director A1474

2006, Jan. 22 ***Perf. 13¼***
2136 A1474 5r multi .70 .70

N. M. R. Subbaraman, Politician, Cent. of Birth — A1475

2006, Jan. 29 **Photo.**
2137 A1475 5r multi .35 .35

Dated 2005.

Third Battalion of the Sikh Regiment, 150th Anniv. A1476

2006, Feb. 1 ***Perf. 13¼x13***
2138 A1476 5r multi .50 .50

President's Fleet Review, Visakhapatnam — A1477

No. 2139: a, Aircraft carrier and jet. b, Helicopter and two ships. c, Airplane and two ships. d, Two submarines.

2006, Feb. 12 ***Perf. 13¾x13***
2139 A1477 5r Block of 4, #a-d 2.50 2.50

Thirumuruga Kirupananda Variyar (1906-93), Tamil Magazine Publisher A1478

Devaneya Pavanar (1902-81), Tamil Writer — A1479

Dr. U. V. Swaminatha Iyer (1855-1942), Tamil Literature Researcher A1480

Tamilavel Umamaheswarar, Editor of Tamil Literary Magazine A1481

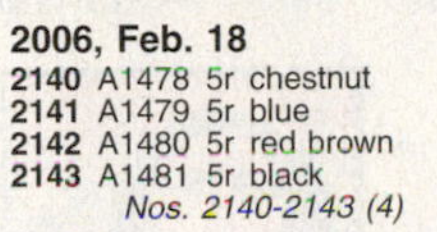

2006, Feb. 18 *Perf. 13¼*
2140 A1478 5r chestnut .35 .35
2141 A1479 5r blue .35 .35
2142 A1480 5r red brown .35 .35
2143 A1481 5r black .35 .35
Nos. 2140-2143 (4) 1.40 1.40

St. Bede's College, Shimla, 102nd Anniv. — A1482

2006, Feb. 24 *Perf. 13x13¼*
2144 A1482 5r multi .35 .35

Gemini Ganesan (1920-2005), Actor A1483

2006, Feb. 25 *Perf. 13¼x13*
2145 A1483 5r black .70 .70

Salesians of Don Bosco in India, Cent. — A1484

2006, Feb. 27 *Perf. 13x13¼*
2146 A1484 5r brown .40 .40

M. Singaravelar (1860-1946), Communist Politician — A1485

2006, Mar. 2
2147 A1485 5r multi .35 .35

World Consumer Rights Day A1486

2006, Mar. 15 *Perf. 13¼x13*
2148 A1486 5r multi .40 .40

Indian Agricultural Research Institute, Delhi, Cent. A1487

2006, Mar. 30
2149 A1487 5r multi .40 .40

62nd Cavalry Armored Regiment, 50th Anniv. A1488

2006, Apr. 1
2150 A1488 5r multi .40 .40

Folk Dances — A1489

No. 2151 — Folk dances from: a, India. b, Cyprus.

2006, Apr. 12 *Perf. 13x13¾*
2151 A1489 15r Horiz. pair, #a-b 2.75 2.75
c. Souvenir sheet, #2151, perf. 13¾x13¼ *8.50 8.50*

See Cyprus No. 1052.

Calcutta Girls' High School, 150th Anniv. A1490

2006, Apr. 21 *Perf. 13¾x13*
2152 A1490 5r multi .40 .40

Pannalal Barupal (1913-83), Politician A1491

2006, Apr. 28 *Perf. 13x13¼*
2153 A1491 5r multi .35 .35

Kurinji Flower A1492

2006, Apr. 29 *Perf. 13x13¾*
2154 A1492 15r multi 2.00 2.00
a. Souvenir sheet of 1 *9.00 9.00*

Rainwater Harvesting A1493

2006, June 5 *Perf. 13¼x13*
2155 A1493 5r multi .70 .70

Sri Pratap College, Srinigar, Cent. — A1494

2006, June 15 *Perf. 13*
2156 A1494 5r multi .40 .40

Indraprastha Girls' School, New Delhi, 102nd Anniv. — A1495

2006, July 8 *Perf. 13¾x13*
2157 A1495 5r multi .40 .40

Voorhees College, Vellore, 111th Anniv. A1496

2006, July 10 *Perf. 13¼*
2158 A1496 5r multi .35 .35

Vellore Mutiny, Bicent. — A1497

2006, July 10 **Litho.** *Perf. 13¼*
2159 A1497 5r multi .70 .70

High Court of Jammu and Kashmir — A1498

Perf. 13¾x13¼
2006, July 29 **Photo.**
2160 A1498 5r multi .40 .40

Pankaj Kumar Mullick (1904-78), Composer A1499

2006, Aug. 4 *Perf. 13¼x13*
2161 A1499 5r multi .50 .50

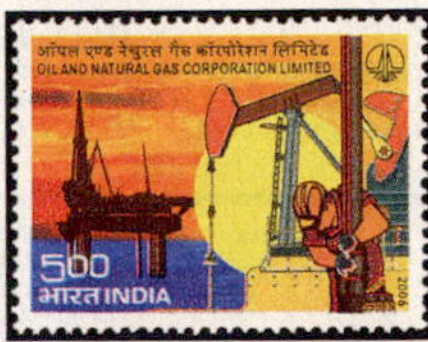
Oil and Natural Gas Corporation, Limited A1500

2006, Aug. 14
2162 A1500 5r multi .60 .60

M. P. Sivagnanam, Tamil Politician, Cent. of Birth — A1501

2006, Aug. 15 **Litho.** *Perf. 13¼*
2163 A1501 5r multi .35 .35

University of Madras A1502

2006, Sept. 4 **Photo.**
2164 A1502 5r multi .40 .40

L. V. Prasad (1908-94), Film Actor and Director A1503

2006, Sept. 5
2165 A1503 5r multi .65 .65

Indian Merchants Chamber — A1504

2006, Sept. 7 *Perf. 13x13¼*
2166 A1504 5r multi .40 .40

Horse Sculptures — A1505

No. 2167: a, Horse and rider. b, Horse only.

2006, Sept. 11 *Perf. 13¼x13¾*
2167 A1505 15r Horiz. pair, #a-b 2.75 2.75
c. Souvenir sheet, #2167 *8.50 8.50*

See Mongolia No. 2621.

Birds
A1506

No. 2168: a, Greater adjutant stork. b, Nilgiri laughing thrush. c, Manipur bush-quail. d, Lesser florican.

2006, Oct. 5 ***Perf. 13***
2168 Vert. strip of 4 1.75 1.75
a.-d. A1506 5r Any single .40 .40
e. Souvenir sheet, #2168a-2168d 7.00 7.00

Madhya Pradesh Chamber of Commerce and Industry, Cent.
A1507

2006, Oct. 12 **Photo.** ***Perf. 13¼***
2169 A1507 5r multi .40 .40

Bishwanath Roy (1906-84), Politician
A1508

2007, Oct. 31 **Litho.** ***Perf. 13¼x13***
2170 A1508 5r multi .40 .40

G. Varadaraj, Industrialist (1936-90)
A1509

2006, Nov. 1
2171 A1509 5r multi .40 .40

Lakes — A1510

No. 2172: a, Roop Kund. b, Chandra Tal, vert. c, Tsomo Riri. d, Sela. e, Tsangu.

2006, Nov. 6 **Photo.** ***Perf. 13***
2172 A1510 5r Block of 5, #a-e 3.00 3.00

Lala Deen Dayal (1844-1905), Photographer
A1511

2006, Nov. 11
2173 A1511 5r multi .40 .40

Children's Day — A1512

No. 2174 — Various children's drawings: a, Denomination at LL. b, Denomination at UL.

2006, Nov. 14 **Litho.** ***Perf. 13***
2174 A1512 5r Horiz. pair, #a-b .60 .60

The Tribune, 125th Anniv.
A1513

2006, Nov. 24 **Photo.** ***Perf. 14***
2175 A1513 5r multi .40 .40

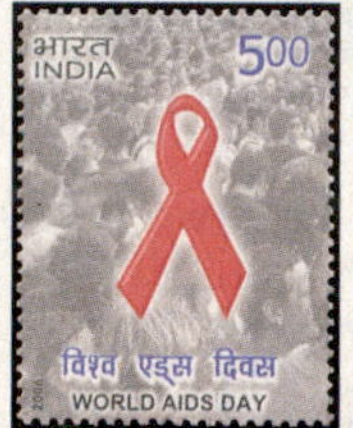
World AIDS Day — A1514

2006, Dec. 1 ***Perf. 13x13¼***
2176 A1514 5r multi .70 .70

Bartholomaeus Ziegenbalg (1682-1719), First Lutheran Missionary to India — A1515

2006, Dec. 8 ***Perf. 13¼***
2177 A1515 5r multi .40 .40

Army Field Post Offices, 150th Anniv. — A1516

No. 2178: a, Soldier, cancel, ship, map of Bushire-Bombay route. b, Soldier writing letter, camel. c, Soldier reading letter, sign. d, Soldier reading letter, helicopter.

2006, Dec. 10 **Litho.** ***Perf. 13x13¼***
2178 Horiz. strip of 4 1.60 1.60
a.-d. A1516 5r Any single .40 .40

Sandalwood Carving
A1517

2006, Dec. 18 **Photo.** ***Perf. 13¼x13***
2179 A1517 15r multi 2.00 2.00
a. Souvenir sheet of 1, perf. 13 *8.50 8.50*

Stamps are impregnated with a sandalwood scent.

Stop Child Labor — A1518

No. 2180: a, Girl on tightrope. b, Boy with hoe. c, Boy pouring tea. d, Boy with large basket.

2006, Dec. 28 ***Perf. 13¼x13***
2180 A1518 5r Block of 4, #a-d 1.40 1.40

Bimal Roy (1909-66), Film Director
A1519

2007, Jan. 8 **Litho.** ***Perf. 13***
2181 A1519 5r multi .40 .40

Tamil Nadu Cricket Association, 70th Anniv. — A1520

2007, Jan. 26 ***Perf. 13x13¼***
2182 A1520 5r multi .40 .40

Rose Varieties — A1521

No. 2183: a, 5r, Bhim. b, 5r, Neelam. c, 15r, Delhi Princess. d, 15r, Jawahar.

2007, Feb. 7 **Photo.** ***Perf. 13x13¼***
2183 A1521 Block of 4, #a-d 1.90 1.90
e. Souvenir sheet, #2183 *5.00 5.00*

Stamps are impregnated with a rose scent.

Manoharbhai Patel (1906-70), Politician
A1522

2007, Feb. 9
2184 A1522 5r multi .40 .40

Fairs — A1523

Designs: No. 2185, 5r, Sonepur Fair. No. 2186, 5r, Pushkar Fair. No. 2187, 5r, Goa Carnival. No. 2188, 5r, Baul Mela.

2007, Feb. 27 **Litho.**
2185-2188 A1523 Set of 4 1.60 1.60
2188a Souvenir sheet, #2185-2188 *3.00 3.00*

Women's Day — A1524

No. 2189: a, Two women. b, Woman, three birds. c, Two women and birds. d, Woman and birds.

2007, Mar. 8 **Photo.** ***Perf. 13x13¼***
2189 Horiz. strip of 4 1.90 1.90
a.-b. A1524 5r Either single .25 .25
c.-d. A1524 15r Either single .70 .70
e. Souvenir sheet, #2189 *3.50 3.50*

Raj Narain (1917-86), Politician
A1525

2007, Mar. 23 **Litho.** ***Perf. 13¼***
2190 A1525 5r multi .40 .40

Mehboob Khan (1907-64), Film Producer and Director — A1526

2007, Mar. 30
2191 A1526 5r multi .40 .40

Dr. R. M. Alagappa Chettiar (1909-57), Industrialist and Philanthropist — A1527

2007, Apr. 6 Photo. ***Perf. 13x13¼***
2192 A1527 5r multi .40 .40

A1528

A1529

A1530

A1531

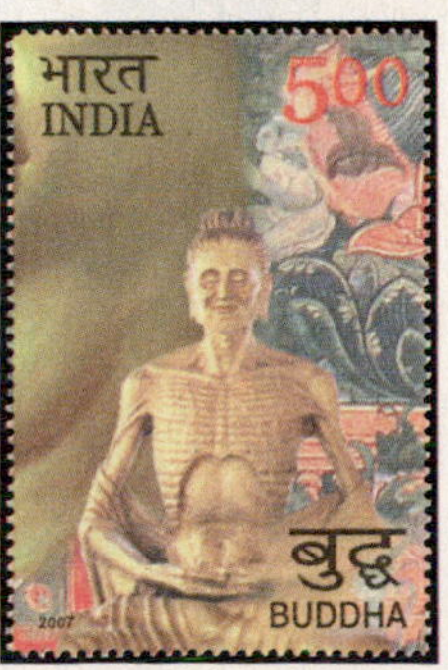

A1532

Mahaparinirvana of Buddha, 2550th Anniv. — A1533

2007, May 2 ***Perf. 13¼***
2193 A1528 5r multi .30 .30
2194 A1529 5r multi .30 .30
2195 A1530 5r multi .30 .30
2196 A1531 5r multi .30 .30
2197 A1532 5r multi .30 .30
2198 A1533 5r multi .30 .30
a. Miniature sheet, #2193-2198 3.50 3.50
Nos. 2193-2198 (6) 1.80 1.80

Natl. Parks — A1534

No. 2199: a, Bandhavgarh Natl. Park. b, Bandipur Natl. Park. c, Kaziranga Natl. Park. d, Mudumalai Natl. Park. e, Periyar Natl. Park.

2007, May 31
2199 Vert. strip of 5 2.00 2.00
a.-e. A1534 5r Any single .40 .40

First War of Independence, 150th Anniv. — A1535

2007, Aug. 9 ***Perf. 13¼x13***
2200 A1535 Vert. pair 1.50 1.50
a. 5r Battle of Lucknow .40 .40
b. 15r Battle of Kanpur 1.10 1.10
c. Souvenir sheet, #2200a-2200b 2.50 2.50

Saint Vallalar (1823-74) — A1536

Maraimalai Adigal (1876-1950), Tamil Scholar — A1537

V. G. Suryanarayana Sastriar (1870-1903), Tamil Writer — A1538

2007, Aug. 18 Litho. ***Perf. 13x13¼***
2201 A1536 5r multi .35 .35
2202 A1537 5r multi .35 .35
2203 A1538 5r multi .35 .35
Nos. 2201-2203 (3) 1.05 1.05

Bridges — A1539

No. 2204: a, Howrah Bridge. b, Mahatma Gandhi Bridge. c, Pamban Bridge. d, Vidyasagar Bridge.

2007, Aug. 17 Photo.
2204 Vert. strip or block of 4 2.00 2.00
a.-d. A1539 5r Any single .50 .50
e. Souvenir sheet, #2204a-2204d 2.50 2.50

J. P. Naik (1907-81), Education Reformer — A1540

2007, Sept. 5 Litho. ***Perf. 13¼x13***
2205 A1540 5r multi .40 .40

53rd Commonwealth Parliamentary Conference, New Delhi — A1541

2007, Sept. 23 Litho. ***Perf. 13¼***
2206 A1541 15r multi 1.00 1.00

Sachin Deb Burman (1906-75), Composer — A1542

2007, Oct. 1 ***Perf. 13¼x13***
2207 A1542 15r multi 1.00 1.00

Satyagraha (Non-Violent Resistance), Cent. — A1543

No. 2208 — Mohandas Gandhi and: a, Train. b, House, newspaper article. c, Crowd, building. d, People marching.

2007, Oct. 2 Photo. ***Perf. 13¼x13***
2208 Horiz. strip of 4 1.60 1.60
a.-d. A1543 5r Any single .40 .40
e. Souvenir sheet, #2208a-2208d 3.00 3.00

Indian Air Force, 75th Anniv. — A1544

Designs: No. 2209, 5r, DHRUV helicopter. No. 2210, 5r, Westland Wapiti biplane. No. 2211, 5r, AWACS airplane (84x32mm). 15r, IL-78 (84x32mm).

2007, Oct. 8 Litho. ***Perf. 13¼x13***
2209-2212 A1544 Set of 4 1.60 1.60
2212a Souvenir sheet, #2209-2212 4.00 4.00

Fourth Military World Games, Hyderabad — A1545

No. 2213: a, Parachutist. b, Soccer player. c, Swimmer.

2007, Oct. 14 ***Perf. 13¼x13***
2213 Vert. strip of 3 .80 .80
a.-c. A1545 5r Any single .25 .25
d. Souvenir sheet, #2213, perf. 13 3.50 3.50

Maharashtra Police Academy — A1546

2007, Nov. 3 Photo. ***Perf. 13¼***
2214 A1546 5r multi .50 .50

Children's Day — A1547

Children's art: No. 2215, 5r, Children and stars. No. 2216, 5r, Fishermen and canoes at night.

2007, Nov. 14 Litho. ***Perf. 13¼x13***
2215-2216 A1547 Set of 2 .80 .80
2216a Souvenir sheet, #2215-2216 2.00 2.00

Renewable Energy — A1548

Designs: No. 2217, 5r, Solar energy. No. 2218, 5r, Wind energy. No. 2219, 5r, Small hydroelectric power, vert. No. 2220, 5r, Biomass energy, vert.

2007, Nov. 22 Photo. ***Perf. 13***
2217-2220 A1548 Set of 4 1.60 1.60
2220a Souvenir sheet, #2217-2220, perf. 13¾x13¼, 13¼x13¾ 3.50 3.50
2220b Miniature sheet, 6 each #2217-2218, 3 each #2219-2220 5.25 5.25

First Battalion of the Fourth Gorkha Rifles, 150th Anniv. A1549

2007, Nov. 27 Litho. *Perf. 13¼*
2221 A1549 5r multi .60 .60

Intl. Day of Disabled Persons — A1550

Photo. & Embossed
2007, Dec. 3 *Perf. 13*
2222 A1550 5r multi .60 .60

Daly College, Indore, 125th Anniv. — A1551

2007, Dec. 8 Litho. *Perf. 13¼*
2223 A1551 5r multi .40 .40

Wilson College, Bombay, 175th Anniv. — A1552

2007, Dec. 11 Photo. *Perf. 13*
2224 A1552 5r multi .40 .40

Greetings A1553

No. 2225: a, Sun, wheat, path. b, Fish, lotus flower. c, Bird. d, Man, flower, butterfly, deer. e, Flowers, stars and text, "Happy New Year," (58x29mm).

2007, Dec. 15 Photo. *Perf. 13*
2225 Horiz. strip of 5 1.50 1.50
a.-e. A1553 5r Any single .30 .30

S. B. Chavan (1920-2004), Politician — A1554

2007, Dec. 17 Litho. *Perf. 13¼x13*
2226 A1554 5r multi .50 .50

Snows Basilica, 425th Anniv. — A1555

2007, Dec. 25 *Perf. 13*
2227 A1555 5r multi .50 .50

Water Year — A1556

2007, Dec. 28
2228 A1556 5r multi .40 .40

Ritwik Ghatak (1925-76), Film Director A1557

2007, Dec. 31 Photo. *Perf. 13¼x13*
2229 A1557 5r brown & black .40 .40

Butterflies Of Andaman and Nicobar Islands — A1558

No. 2230: a, Male Papilio mayo. b, Female Papilio mayo. c, Female Pachliopta rhodifer. d, Male Pachliopta rhodifer.

2008, Jan. 2 *Perf. 13*
2230 A1558 5r Block of 4, #a-d 1.60 1.60
e. Souvenir sheet, #2230 3.00 3.00

Dr. Benjamin Peary Pal (1906-89), Rose Breeder and Plant Scientist A1559

2008, Jan. 5 Litho.
2231 A1559 5r multi .40 .40

Dr. Dhananjaya Ramachandra Gadgil (1901-71), Economist A1560

2008, Feb. 8 Photo.
2232 A1560 5r multi .40 .40

Damodaram Sanjeevaiah (1921-72), Politician — A1561

2008, Feb. 14 Litho.
2233 A1561 5r multi .40 .40

Maharshi Bulusu Sambamurthy (1886-1958), Lawyer — A1562

2008, Mar. 4
2234 A1562 5r multi .40 .40

Madhubala (1933-1969), Film Actress — A1563

2008, Mar. 18 Photo. *Perf. 13*
2235 A1563 5r multi .40 .40
a. Souvenir sheet of 1, perf. 13x13¾ 1.75 1.75

Asrar Ul Haq (Majaaz) (1909-55), Urdu Poet A1564

2008, Mar. 28 Litho. *Perf. 13*
2236 A1564 5r multi .40 .40

Civil Service A1565

Photo. & Embossed
2008, Apr. 21
2237 A1565 5r multi .40 .40

Tata Steel, Cent. — A1566

2008, Apr. 22 Litho.
2238 A1566 5r multi .40 .40

Jasmine Flowers — A1567

2008, Apr. 26 Photo.
2239 A1567 5r shown .40 .40
2240 A1567 15r Flowers, horiz. 1.00 1.00
a. Souvenir sheet, #2239-2240 3.00 3.00

Nos. 2239-2240, 2240a are impregnated with a jasmine scent.

Aga Khan Foundation, 30th Anniv. — A1568

No. 2241: a, 5r, Heritage restoration (46x39mm). b, 15r, Social commitment (70x39mm).

2008, May 17 Photo. *Perf. 13*
2241 A1568 Horiz. pair, #a-b 1.10 1.10
c. Souvenir sheet, #2241a-2241b 3.00 3.00

Shri Shirdi Sai Baba (1835-1918), Hindu Saint — A1569

2008, May 20
2242 A1569 5r multi .40 .40

Rajesh Pilot (1945-2008), Politician A1570

2008, June 12 Litho. *Perf. 13*
2243 A1570 5r multi .40 .40

Henning Holck-Larsen (1907-2003), Engineer and Industrialist A1571

2008, June 12 Litho. *Perf. 13¼x13*
2244 A1571 5r multi .40 .40

Madhav Institute of Technology, Gwalior, 50th Anniv. — A1572

2008, June 30 Litho. *Perf. 13¼*
2245 A1572 5r multi .40 .40

Temples — A1573

No. 2246: a, Maha Bodhi Temple, India. b, White Horse Temple, China.

2008, July 11 Photo. *Perf. 13*
2246 A1573 15r Horiz. pair, #a-b 1.75 1.75
c. Souvenir sheet, #2246 4.00 4.00

See People's Republic of China Nos. 3678-3679.

Punjab Regiment 14th Battalion, 250th Anniv. — A1574

2008, July 21 Litho. *Perf. 13¼*
2247 A1574 5r multi .40 .40

Damodar Dharmananda Kosambi (1907-66), Mathematician — A1575

2008, July 31
2248 A1575 5r multi .40 .40

Aldabra Giant Tortoise A1576

Tortoise facing: 5r, Left. 15r, Forward.

2008, Aug. 2 Photo. *Perf. 13*
2249-2250 A1576 Set of 2 1.40 1.40

2008 Summer Olympics, Beijing — A1577

No. 2251 — 2008 Summer Olympics emblem and: a, 5r, Olympic torch and mascot. b, 5r, Boxing. c, 15r, Shooting. d, 15r, Archery.

2008, Aug. 8
2251 A1577 Block of 4, #a-d 2.50 2.50
e. Souvenir sheet, #2251a-2251d 3.50 3.50

Indian Coast Guard, 30th Anniv. — A1578

No. 2252: a, Airplane. b, Helicopter. c, Hovercraft (large wave at LL). d, Patrol boat (large wave at LR).

2008, Aug. 12 Litho. *Perf. 13¼*
2252 A1578 5r Block of 4, #a-d 1.60 1.60
e. Souvenir sheet, #2252a-2252d 3.00 3.00

Ustad Bismillah Khan (1916-2006), Musician — A1579

2008, Aug. 21
2253 A1579 5r multi .40 .40

Sir Pitti Theagarayar (1853-1925) — A1580

Dr. Taravat Mahadevan Nair (1868-1919) A1581

Dr. C. Natesan (1869-1937) A1582

2008, Sept. 17 *Perf. 13x13¼*
2254 A1580 5r multi .40 .40

Perf. 13¾ Syncopated

2255 A1581 5r multi .40 .40
2256 A1582 5r multi .40 .40
Nos. 2254-2256 (3) 1.20 1.20

Founders of South Indian Welfare Association.

Festivals — A1583

Designs: No. 2257, 5r, Dussehra Festival, Calcutta (Kolkata). No. 2258, 5r, Dussehra Festival, Mysore. No. 2259, 5r, Deepavali Festival, vert.

2008, Oct. 7 Photo. *Perf. 13*
2257-2259 A1583 Set of 3 1.25 1.25
2259a Souvenir sheet, #2257-2259 3.00 3.00

3rd Commonwealth Youth Games, Pune — A1584

No. 2260: a, Tiger mascot. b, Wrestling. c, Badminton. d, Hurdling.

2008, Oct. 12 *Perf. 13x13¼*
2260 Horiz. strip of 4 1.20 1.20
a.-d. A1584 5r Any single .30 .30
e. Souvenir sheet, #2260a-2260d 3.00 3.00

Indian Post Office A1585

Perf. 13¾ Syncopated

2008, Oct. 13 Litho.
2261 A1585 5r multi .40 .40

Philately Day. A souvenir sheet of one sold for 15r.

Food Safety and Quality Year — A1586

2008, Oct. 16
2262 A1586 5r multi .40 .40

19th Commonwealth Games, Delhi — A1587

2008, Oct. 18 Photo. *Perf. 13¼x13*
2263 A1587 5r multi .40 .40

A souvenir sheet of one sold for 15r.

A1588

A1589

Children's Day — A1590

2008, Nov. 14 Litho. *Perf. 13¼*
2264 A1588 5r multi .25 .25
2265 A1589 5r multi .25 .25
2266 A1590 5r multi .25 .25
a. Souvenir sheet of 3, #2264-2266 2.75 2.75
Nos. 2264-2266 (3) .75 .75

Bomireddi N. Reddi (1908-77), Film Director A1591

2008, Nov. 16
2267 A1591 5r multi .40 .40

Canonization of Saint Alphonsa (1910-46) A1592

2008, Nov. 16 Photo. *Perf. 13x13¼*
2268 A1592 5r multi .40 .40

A souvenir sheet of one sold for 15r.

Standard Chartered Bank, 150th Anniv. A1593

2008, Nov. 17 **Litho.** ***Perf. 13¼***
2269 A1593 5r multi .40 .40

Gas Authority of India Limited, 25th Anniv. A1594

2008, Nov. 19 ***Perf. 13***
2270 A1594 5r multi .40 .40

Joachim (1907-79) and Violet (1908-69) Alva, Politicians A1595

Perf. 13¾ Syncopated

2008, Nov. 20
2271 A1595 5r multi .40 .40

Sardar Vallabhbhai Patel Natl. Police Academy, Hyderabad A1596

Building and: 5r, Police cadets training and marching. 20r, Statue, policeman with sword.

2008, Nov. 27
2272-2273 A1596 Set of 2 1.25 1.25
2273a Souvenir sheet, #2272-2273 *3.50 3.50*

St. Joseph's Boys' High School, Bangalore, 150th Anniv. A1597

2008, Nov. 28
2274 A1597 5r multi .40 .40

Buddhadeva Bose (1908-74), Writer — A1598

2008, Nov. 30 ***Perf. 13***
2275 A1598 5r multi .40 .40

Prime Minister Jawaharlal Nehru (1889-1964) A1599

E.V. Ramasami (1879-1973), Politician A1600

Mahatma Gandhi (1869-1948) A1601

Dr. Bhimrao R. Ambedkar (1891-1956), Politician A1602

Satyajit Ray (1921-92), Film Director A1603

Homi Jahangir Bhabha (1909-66), Nuclear Physicist A1604

Prime Minister Indira Gandhi (1917-84) A1605

Prime Minister Rajiv Gandhi (1944-91) A1606

C.V. Raman (1888-1970), 1930 Nobel Physics Laureate A1607

J. R. D. Tata (1904-93), Industrialist A1608

Mother Teresa (1910-97), 1979 Nobel Peace Laureate A1609

Rukmini Devi Arundale (1904-86), Dancer A1610

Perf. 12¾x13¼

2008-09		**Photo.**		**Wmk. 324**
2276	A1599	25p rose lil & blk	.25	.25
2277	A1600	50p blue	.25	.25
2278	A1601	1r olive brown	.25	.25
2279	A1602	2r rose lilac	.25	.25
2280	A1603	3r vio brown	.25	.25
2281	A1604	4r brt blue	.25	.25
2282	A1605	5r gray grn & blk	.25	.25
2283	A1606	5r brown	.25	.25
2284	A1607	10r multi	.45	.45
2285	A1608	15r purple	.60	.60
2286	A1609	20r multi	.80	.80
2287	A1610	50r multi	2.10	2.10
		Nos. 2276-2287 (12)	5.95	5.95

Issued: 25p, Nos. 2282, 2283, 12/1; 1r, 2r, 3r, 4r, 15r, 20r, 3/1/09; 50p, 10r, 5/11/09. 50r, 5/11/09.

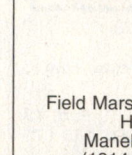

Discovery of Evershed Effect at Kodaikanal Solar Observatory, Cent. — A1611

Perf. 13¾ Syncopated

2008, Dec. 2 **Litho.** **Unwmk.**
2288 A1611 5r multi .40 .40

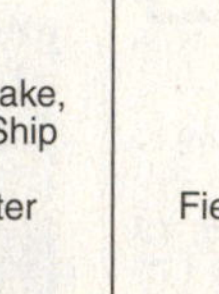

Map, Handshake, Indian Ship and Helicopter A1612

2008, Dec. 4
2289 A1612 5r multi .40 .40

Navy Day.

Dr. Laxmi Mall Singhvi (1931-2007), Jurist — A1613

2008, Dec. 8
2290 A1613 5r multi .40 .40

Christmas — A1614

No. 2291: a, 5r, Lambs. b, 20r, Madonna and Child.

2008, Dec. 8 **Photo.** ***Perf. 13***
2291 A1614 Horiz. pair, #a-b 1.10 1.10

Universal Declaration of Human Rights, 60th Anniv. A1615

2008, Dec. 10
2292 A1615 5r multi .40 .40

Indian Institute of Science, Bangalore, Cent. — A1616

No. 2293: a, 5r, Building. b, 20r, Building and scientists.

2008, Dec. 14
2293 A1616 Horiz. pair, #a-b 1.40 1.40
c. Souvenir sheet, #2293a-2293b *3.50 3.50*

Swami Ranganathananda (1908-2005), Hindu Monk — A1617

Perf. 13¾ Syncopated

2008, Dec. 15 **Litho.**
2294 A1617 5r multi .40 .40

Field Marshal S. H. F. J. Manekshaw (1914-2008) A1618

2008, Dec. 16 **Photo.** ***Perf. 13x13¼***
2295 A1618 5r multi .40 .40

Thazhuvia V. Ramasubbaiyer (1908-84), Founder of Dinamalar Newspaper A1619

Perf. 13¾ Syncopated

2008, Dec. 21 **Litho.**
2296 A1619 5r multi .40 .40

Brahmos Cruise Missile, 10th Anniv. — A1620

Designs: 5r, Missile in flight, airplane. 20r, Missiles, airplane, ship, launch vehicle, horiz.

2008, Dec. 22 **Photo.** ***Perf. 13***
2297-2298 A1620 Set of 2 1.40 1.40
2298a Souvenir sheet, #2297-2298 *3.50 3.50*

Udumalai Narayana Kavi (1899-1981), Lyricist — A1621

2008, Dec. 31 ***Perf. 13x13¼***
2299 A1621 5r multi .40 .40

Thillaiyadi Valliammai (1898-1914), Freedom Fighter — A1622

2008, Dec. 31 *Perf. 13*
2300 A1622 5r multi .40 .40

Sheik Thambi Pavalar (1874-1950), Freedom Fighter — A1623

2008, Dec. 31
2301 A1623 5r multi .40 .40

A. T. Paneerselvam, Politician A1624

2008, Dec. 31 *Perf. 13x13¼*
2302 A1624 5r multi .40 .40

M. Bhakthavatsalam (1897-1987), Politician A1625

2008, Dec. 31 *Perf. 13*
2303 A1625 5r multi .40 .40

Velu Nachchiyar, Tamil Queen A1626

2008, Dec. 31 **Litho.**
2304 A1626 5r multi .40 .40

Louis Braille (1809-52), Educator of the Blind — A1627

Photo. & Embossed

2009, Jan. 4 *Perf. 13¼x13*
2305 A1627 5r multi .50 .50

Vaikom Muhammad Basheer (1908-94), Writer — A1628

2009, Jan. 21 **Litho.** *Perf. 13*
2306 A1628 5r multi .25 .25

St. Paul's Church, Madras A1629

2009, Jan. 25 *Perf. 13¾ Syncopated*
2307 A1629 5r multi .25 .25

Preservation of Heritage Monuments — A1630

No. 2308: a, Jaisalmer Fort, Jaisalmer. b, Mongyu Monastery, Laddakh. c, St. Anne Church, Goa. d, Qila Mubarak, Patiala.

2009, Jan. 28 **Photo.** *Perf. 13*
2308 A1630 5r Block of 4, #a-d 1.25 1.25
e. Souvenir sheet, #2308a-2308d *2.75 2.75*

Bishnu Prasad Rabha (1909-69), Writer, Singer A1631

Perf. 13¾ Syncopated

2009, Jan. 31 **Litho.**
2309 A1631 5r multi .25 .25

Steel Authority of India, 50th Anniv. — A1632

2009, Mar. 3 **Photo.** *Perf. 13*
2310 A1632 5r multi .25 .25

Natl. Girl Child Day — A1633

2009, Feb. 5
2311 A1633 5r multi .25 .25

Santaji Jagnade Maharaj (1624-88), Marathi Saint — A1634

Perf. 13¾ Syncopated

2009, Feb. 9 **Litho.**
2312 A1634 5r multi .25 .25

Mahi Kavi Magh, 8th Cent. Poet — A1635

2009, Feb. 9 **Photo.** *Perf. 13*
2313 A1635 5r multi .25 .25

Postal Life Insurance, 125th Anniv. — A1636

Perf. 13¾ Syncopated

2009, Feb. 11 **Litho.**
2314 A1636 5r multi .25 .25

Vallabh Suri (1870-1954), Jain Religious Leader — A1637

2009, Feb. 21
2315 A1637 5r multi .25 .25

Harakh Chand Nahata (1936-99), Film Financer A1638

2009, Feb. 28
2316 A1638 5r multi .25 .25

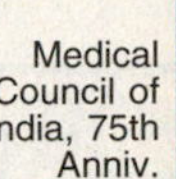
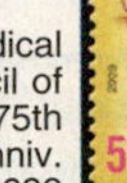

Medical Council of India, 75th Anniv. A1639

2009, Mar. 1 **Photo.** *Perf. 13*
2317 A1639 5r multi .25 .25

Pterospermum Acerifolium Tree and Flower — A1640

2009, Mar. 6 **Litho.**
2318 A1640 5r multi .25 .25

Baburao Puleshwar Shedmake, 19th Cent. Freedom Fighter A1641

2009, Mar. 12
2319 A1641 5r multi .25 .25

Dr. Krishna Kumar Birla (1918-2008), Industrialist — A1642

2009, Mar. 13
2320 A1642 5r multi .25 .25

Spices — A1643

No. 2321: a, Black pepper. b, Cinnamon. c, Cardamom d, Cloves. e, Turmeric, coriander and chili peppers.

2009, Apr. 29 **Photo.**
2321 Strip of 5 1.60 1.60
a.-d. A1643 5r Any single .25 .25
e. A1643 20r multi .80 .80
f. Souvenir sheet of 5, #2321a-2321e *4.75 4.75*

R. Sankar (1909-72), Politician A1644

Perf. 13¾ Syncopated

2009, Apr. 30 **Litho.**
2322 A1644 5r multi .25 .25

Lifeline Express Hospital Train — A1645

2009, May 12 ***Perf. 13***
2323 A1645 5r multi .25 .25

Madras Regiment, 250th Anniv. — A1646

Perf. 13¾ Syncopated

2009, May 28 **Litho.** **Unwmk.**
2324 A1646 5r multi .25 .25

Rev. J.J.M. Nichols Roy (1883-1959), Politician — A1647

2009, June 12 **Photo.** ***Perf. 13***
2325 A1647 5r multi .25 .25

Sacred Heart Church, Pudducherry, Cent. — A1648

Perf. 13¾ Syncopated

2009, June 19
2326 A1648 5r multi .25 .25

Raza Library, Rampur A1649

Ram, Laxman and Jatayu From Valmiki Ramayana, by Sumer Chand — A1650

Madonna Holding Book — A1651

Illustrated Page from Diwan-i-Hafiz of Akbar's Collection A1652

2009, June 19 **Litho.**
2327 A1649 5r multi .25 .25
2328 A1650 5r multi .25 .25
2329 A1651 5r multi .25 .25
2330 A1652 5r multi .25 .25
  a. Souvenir sheet, #2327-2330 *3.00 3.00*
  Nos. 2327-2330 (4) 1.00 1.00

Indian Oil Corporation, 50th Anniv. — A1653

2009, June 30 ***Perf. 13***
2331 A1653 5r multi .25 .25

Lal Bahadur Shastri Natl. Academy of Administration, Mussoorie, 50th Anniv. — A1654

2009, July 4 **Photo.**
2332 A1654 5r multi .25 .25

Ramcharan Agarwal (1919-77), Politician A1655

Perf. 13¾ Syncopated

2009, July 25 **Litho.**
2333 A1655 5r multi .25 .25

A1656

A1657

A1658

A1659

A1660

A1661

A1662

A1663

A1664

A1665

Scenes from Geetagovinda, Poem by Jayadeva — A1666

2009, July 27 **Photo.** ***Perf. 13***
2334 Horiz. strip of 11 2.75 2.75
  a. A1656 5r multi .25 .25
  b. A1657 5r multi .25 .25
  c. A1658 5r multi .25 .25
  d. A1659 5r multi .25 .25
  e. A1660 5r multi .25 .25
  f. A1661 5r multi .25 .25
  g. A1662 5r multi .25 .25
  h. A1663 5r multi .25 .25
  i. A1664 5r multi .25 .25
  j. A1665 5r multi .25 .25
  k. A1666 5r multi .25 .25
  l. Souvenir sheet, #2334a-2334k *5.00 5.00*

St. Joseph's College, Bangalore A1667

Perf. 13¾ Syncopated

2009, Aug. 1 **Litho.**
2335 A1667 5r multi .25 .25

Maharishi Patanjali, Compiler of Yoga Sutras — A1668

2009, Aug. 4 ***Perf. 13***
2336 A1668 5r multi .25 .25

Pingali Venkaiah (1876-1963), Designer of Indian Flag — A1669

2009, Aug. 12 **Photo.** ***Perf. 13¼x13***
2337 A1669 5r multi .25 .25

Railway Stations — A1670

Designs: No. 2338, 5r, Howrah Station, Calcutta. No. 2339, 5r, Chennai Central Station. No. 2340, 5r, Mumbai CST (Chhatrapati Shivaji Terminus). No. 2341, 5r, Old Delhi Station.

2009, Aug. 16 **Litho.** ***Perf. 13***
2338-2341 A1670 Set of 4 1.25 1.25
  2341a Souvenir sheet, #2338-2341 *3.25 3.25*

Uttam Kumar (1926-80), Actor — A1671

Perf. 13¾ Syncopated

2009, Sept. 3 **Litho.**

2342 A1671 5r multi .25 .25

Sacred Heart Matriculation Higher Secondary School, Chennai — A1672

2009, Sept. 9 **Photo.** ***Perf. 13***

2343 A1672 5r multi .25 .25

Holy Cross Church, Mapranam A1673

Perf. 13¾ Syncopated

2009, Sept. 14 **Litho.**

2344 A1673 5r multi .25 .25

Dushyant Kumar (1933-75), Writer A1674

2009, Sept. 27 ***Perf. 13¼x13***

2345 A1674 5r multi .25 .25

Mammals A1675

Designs: No. 2346, 5r, Red panda. No. 2347, 5r, Marbled cat, vert. No. 2348, 5r, Barbe's leaf monkey, vert.

Perf. 13¾ Syncopated

2009, Oct. 1 **Litho.**

2346-2348 A1675 Set of 3 1.00 1.00

2348a Souvenir sheet, #2346-2348 2.50 2.50

Mahatma Gandhi — A1676

Wmk. 324

2009, Oct. 2 **Photo.** ***Perf. 13¼***

2349 A1676 25r multi 1.10 1.10

Bishop Cotton School, Shimla — A1677

Unwmk.

2009, Oct. 6 **Litho.** ***Perf. 13***

2350 A1677 5r multi .25 .25

R.K. Narayan (1906-2001), Writer — A1678

Perf. 13¼

2009, Oct. 10 **Litho.** **Unwmk.**

2351 A1678 5r multi .25 .25

Dineshnandini Dalmia (1928-2007), Writer — A1679

Perf. 13¾ Syncopated

2009, Oct. 11 **Litho.**

2352 A1679 5r multi .25 .25

India Post Airplane A1680

2009, Oct. 12 **Litho.** ***Perf. 13¼x13***

2353 A1680 5r multi .25 .25

Temples — A1681

Designs: No. 2354, 5r, Dilwara Temple. No. 2355, 5r, Ranakpur Temple.

2009, Oct. 14 ***Perf. 13***

2354-2355 A1681 Set of 2 .60 .60

Gulab Singh (1792-1857), First Maharaja of Jammu and Kashmir — A1682

Perf. 13¾ Syncopated

2009, Oct. 21 **Litho.**

2356 A1682 5r multi .25 .25

Major General Dewan Misri Chand (1907-70), Pilot — A1683

2009, Oct. 22

2357 A1683 5r multi .25 .25

Canonization of Jeanne Jugan — A1684

No. 2358: a, 5r, Little Sisters of the Poor Home for the Aged, Bangalore (40x32mm). b, 20r, St. Jeanne Jugan (1792-1879), Founder of Little Sisters of the Poor (29x32mm).

2009, Oct. 29 ***Perf. 13***

2358 A1684 Horiz. pair, #a-b 1.10 1.10

Dr. Rajkumar (1929-2006), Actor — A1685

2009, Nov. 1

2359 A1685 5r multi .25 .25

Dr. Mahendra Lal Sircar (1833-1904), Founder of Indian Association for the Cultivation of Science — A1686

2009, Nov. 2 ***Perf. 13¾***

2360 A1686 5r multi .25 .25

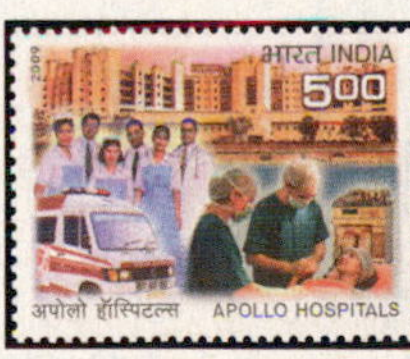

Apollo Hospitals A1687

2009, Nov. 2

2361 A1687 5r multi .25 .25

Danmal Mathur, Scouting Leader — A1688

2009, Nov. 7 **Photo.** ***Perf. 13x13¼***

2362 A1688 5r multi .25 .25

Virchand Raghavji Gandhi (1864-1901), Representative of Jains at 1893 World Parliament of Religions — A1689

2009, Nov. 8 **Litho.** ***Perf. 13***

2363 A1689 5r multi .25 .25

Horse Breeds A1690

Designs: No. 2364, 5r, Kathiawari. No. 2365, 5r, Marwari. No. 2366, 5r, Zanskari. No. 2367, 5r, Manipuri.

2009, Nov. 9 ***Perf. 13¾ Syncopated***

2364-2367 A1690 Set of 4 .90 .90

2367a Souvenir sheet, #2364-2367 2.50 2.50

Rajabhau Khobragade (1925-84), Politician — A1691

2009, Nov. 11

2368 A1691 5r multi .25 .25

Gaurishankar Dalmia (1910-88), Magazine Publisher A1692

2009, Nov. 12 ***Perf. 13¼***

2369 A1692 5r multi .25 .25

British Commonwealth, 60th Anniv. — A1693

2009, Nov. 13 ***Perf. 13***

2370 A1693 5r multi .25 .25

Children's Day A1694

Designs: No. 2371, 5r, Deer at pond. No. 2372, 5r, Tiger.

2009, Nov. 14 ***Perf. 13¼***

2371-2372 A1694 Set of 2 .45 .45

Silent Valley National Park — A1695

2009, Nov. 15 ***Perf. 13***
2373 A1695 5r multi .25 .25
a. Souvenir sheet of 1 *1.40 1.40*

Marine Life — A1696

No. 2374: a, 5r, Gangetic dolphin. b, 20r, Butanding.

2009, Nov. 16
2374 A1696 Horiz. pair, #a-b 1.10 1.10
c. Souvenir sheet, #2374a-2374b *3.00 3.00*

See Philippines Nos. 3246-3247.

Ganpatrao Govindrao Jadhav (1908-87), Newspaper Publisher A1697

2009, Nov. 18 ***Perf. 13¼***
2375 A1697 5r multi .25 .25

Tamil Nadu Police, 150th Anniv. — A1698

2009, Nov. 30 ***Perf. 13***
2376 A1698 5r multi .25 .25

A1699

A1700

A1701

Greetings A1702

2009, Dec. 1
2377 A1699 5r multi .25 .25
2378 A1700 5r multi .25 .25
2379 A1701 5r brown .25 .25
2380 A1702 5r multi .25 .25
a. Souvenir sheet, #2377-2380 *2.50 2.50*
Nos. 2377-2380 (4) 1.00 1.00

Convent of Jesus and Mary, Ambala Cantonment, Cent. — A1703

2009, Dec. 2
2381 A1703 5r multi .25 .25

Second Lancers (Gardiner's Horse) Regiment A1704

2009, Dec. 2 ***Perf. 13¼***
2382 A1704 5r multi .25 .25

Traditional Textiles A1705

Designs: No. 2383, 5r, Kalamkari. No. 2384, 5r, Apa Tani weaves. No. 2385, 5r, Kanchipuram silk. No. 2386, 5r, Banaras silk.

2009, Dec. 10 ***Perf. 13***
2383-2386 A1705 Set of 4 .90 .90
2386a Souvenir sheet, #2383-2386 *2.50 2.50*

Henry Louis Vivian Derozio (1809-31), Poet — A1706

2009, Dec. 15 ***Perf. 13x13¼***
2387 A1706 5r multi .25 .25

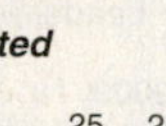
Lal Pratap Singh, Prince of Kalakankar A1707

Perf. 13¾ Syncopated
2009, Dec. 17
2388 A1707 5r multi .25 .25

Preservation of Polar Regions and Glaciers — A1708

Designs: No. 2389, 5r, Penguins. No. 2390, 5r, Polar bear.

2009, Dec. 19 ***Perf. 13***
2389-2390 A1708 Set of 2 .45 .45
2390a Souvenir sheet, #2389-2390 *1.75 1.75*

Indian Mathematical Society, Cent. — A1709

2009, Dec. 27 ***Perf. 13¼***
2391 A1709 5r multi .25 .25

Venkataramana Bhagavathar (1781-1874), Composer A1710

2009, Dec. 27 ***Perf. 13¾***
2392 A1710 5r multi .25 .25

Maharaja Surajmal (1707-63), Ruler of Bharatpur A1711

Perf. 13¾ Syncopated
2009, Dec. 29
2393 A1711 5r multi .25 .25

20th Conference of Speakers and Presiding Officers of the Commonwealth, New Delhi — A1712

2010, Jan. 5 ***Perf. 13¼***
2394 A1712 5r multi .25 .25

Reserve Bank of India, 75th Anniv. — A1713

2010, Jan. 16 ***Perf. 13***
2395 A1713 5r multi .40 .40

Election Commission of India, 60th Anniv. — A1714

2010, Jan. 25 **Litho.**
2396 A1714 5r multi .25 .25

Bible Society of India, Bicent. — A1715

2010, Feb. 21 **Photo.** ***Perf. 13x13¼***
2397 A1715 5r multi .25 .25

P. C. Sorcar (1913-71), Magician A1716

2010, Feb. 23 **Litho.**
2398 A1716 5r multi .25 .25

16th Punjab (2nd Patiala) Regiment A1717

2009, Mar. 19 **Photo.** ***Perf. 13¼x13***
2399 A1717 5r multi .25 .25

Muthuramalinga Sethupathi (1760-1809), King of Ramanathapuram A1718

2010, Mar. 30 ***Perf. 13x13¼***
2400 A1718 5r multi .25 .25

Special Protection Group — A1719

2010, Mar. 30 **Litho.** ***Perf. 13***
2401 A1719 5r multi .25 .25

Vallal Pachaiyappa (1754-94), Philantropist — A1720

2010, Mar. 31 Photo. ***Perf. 13¼x13***
2402 A1720 5r multi .25 .25

Signs of the Zodiac A1721

Designs: No. 2403, 5r, Aries. No. 2404, 5r, Taurus. No. 2405, 5r, Gemini. No. 2406, 5r, Cancer, vert. No. 2407, 5r, Leo, vert. No. 2408, 5r, Virgo, vert. No. 2409, 5r, Libra. No. 2410, 5r, Scorpio. No. 2411, 5r, Sagittarius. No. 2412, 5r, Capricorn, vert. No. 2413, 5r, Aquarius, vert. No. 2414, 5r, Pisces, vert.

Perf. 13¼x13, 13x13¼

2010, Apr. 14 Litho.
2403-2414 A1721 Set of 12 2.75 2.75
2414a Souvenir sheet, #2403-2414, perf. 13 *5.00 5.00*

Chandra Shekhar (1927-2007), Prime Minister — A1722

2010, Apr. 17 Photo. ***Perf. 13x13¼***
2415 A1722 5r multi .25 .25

Kanwar Ram Sahib (1885-1939), Religious Leader — A1723

2010, Apr. 26 Litho.
2416 A1723 5r multi .25 .25

Velu Thampi (1765-1809), Prime Minister of Travancore A1724

2010, May 6 ***Perf. 13x13¼***
2417 A1724 5r multi .25 .25

Robert Caldwell (1814-91), Bishop and Linguist — A1725

2010, May 7 Photo.
2418 A1725 5r multi .25 .25

Dr. Guduru Venkata Chalam (1909-67), Agricultural Scientist — A1726

2010, May 8 Litho.
2419 A1726 5r multi .25 .25

Indian Post Offices — A1727

Post offices in: No. 2420, 5r, Lucknow. No. 2421, 5r, Cooch Behar. No. 2422, 5r, Nagpur. No. 2423, 5r, Udagamandalam. No. 2424, 5r, Delhi. No. 2425, 5r, Shimla.

2010, May 13 Litho. ***Perf. 13***
2420-2425 A1727 Set of 6 1.40 1.40
2425a Souvenir sheet, #2420-2425 *2.50 2.50*

Indipex 2011 World Philatelic Exhibition, New Delhi.

C. V. Raman Pillai (1858-1922), Writer — A1728

2010, May 19 Photo. ***Perf. 13x13¼***
2426 A1728 5r multi .25 .25

Intl. Year of Biodiversity A1729

Designs: 5r, Owl, sunflower, people in rice paddy. 20r, Birds, crab, water lilies.

Perf. 13¾ Syncopated

2010, June 5 Litho.
2427-2428 A1729 Set of 2 1.10 1.10
2428a Souvenir sheet, #2427-2428 *3.00 3.00*

Deshbandhu Gupta (1905-51), Politician and Journalist — A1730

2010, June 14
2429 A1730 5r multi .25 .25

2010 Commonwealth Games, Delhi — A1731

Map and: 5r, Tiger mascot holding torch. 20r, Hand holding torch, mascot running with torch.

2010. June 25 Photo. ***Perf. 13***
2430-2431 A1731 Set of 2 1.10 1.10
2431a Souvenir sheet, #2430-2431 *3.00 3.00*

Kumaraguruparar Swamigal (1625-88), Poet — A1732

Perf. 13¾ Syncopated

2010, June 27 Litho.
2432 A1732 5r multi .25 .25

World Classical Tamil Conference, Kovai — A1733

2010, June 27 Photo. ***Perf. 13x13¼***
2433 A1733 5r multi .25 .25

Indian Naval Air Squadron 300, 50th Anniv. — A1734

Perf. 13¾ Syncopated

2010, July 7 Litho.
2434 A1734 5r multi .25 .25

Birds A1735

Designs: No. 2435, 5r, Pigeons. No. 2436, 5r, Sparrows.

2010, July 9 Litho. ***Perf. 13***
2435-2436 A1735 Set of 2 .45 .45
2436a Souvenir sheet of 2, #2435-2436 *2.00 2.00*

Rath Yatra Festival, Puri A1736

2010, July 12 Photo. ***Perf. 13***
2437 A1736 5r multi .25 .25

Stadia for 2010 Commonwealth Games, Delhi — A1737

Designs: No. 2438, 5r, Jawaharlal Nehru Stadium. No. 2439, 5r, Talkatora Stadium.

2010, Aug. 1 Litho. ***Perf. 13***
2438-2439 A1737 Set of 2 .45 .45
2439a Souvenir sheet, #2438-2439 *2.00 2.00*

Syed Mohammed Ali Shihab Thangal (1936-2009), Politician — A1738

Perf. 13¾ Syncopated

2010, Aug. 2 Litho.
2440 A1738 5r multi .25 .25

Vethathiri (1911-2006), Founder of World Community Service Center — A1739

2010, Aug. 14
2441 A1739 5r multi .25 .25

P. Jeevanandham (1907-63), Tamil Communist Leader — A1740

Perf. 13¾ Syncopated

2010, Aug. 21 Litho.
2442 A1740 5r multi .25 .25

Omanthur P. Ramaswamy Reddiar (1895-1970), Politician A1741

2010, Aug. 25
2443 A1741 5r multi .25 .25

G. K. Moopanar (1931-2001), Politician and Philanthropist A1742

2010, Aug. 30 Photo. *Perf. 13x13¼*
2444 A1742 5r multi .25 .25

Dr. Y. S. Rajasekhara Reddy (1949-2009), Politician A1743

2010, Sept. 2 Litho. *Perf. 13¾x14*
2445 A1743 5r multi .25 .25

Brihadeeswarar Temple, Thanjavur — A1744

Perf. 13¾ Syncopated
2010, Sept. 26
2446 A1744 5r multi .25 .25

Sports of 2010 Commonwealth Games, Delhi — A1745

Designs: No. 2447, 5r, Badminton. No. 2448, 5r, Archery. No. 2449, 5r, Field hockey. No. 2450, 5r, Track.

2010, Oct. 3 *Perf. 13¾ Syncopated*
2447-2450 A1745 Set of 4 .90 .90
2450a Souvenir sheet, #2447-2450 *3.50 3.50*

Feudatory States Stamps A1746

Designs: No. 2451, 5r, Indore #2, type A6, vignette of #1. No. 2452, 5r, Sirmoor #22, 2, 13. No. 2453, 5r, Bamra type A2, revenue stamp. No. 2454, 5r, Cochin #15, type A4.

2010, Oct. 6 *Perf. 13¼x13*
2451-2454 A1746 Set of 4 .90 .90
2454a Souvenir sheet, #2451-2454, perf. 13 *3.50 3.50*

Indipex 2011 World Philatelic Exhibition, New Delhi (No. 2454a).

Doon School, Dehradun, 75th Anniv. A1747

2010, Oct. 22 *Perf. 13¾ Syncopated*
2455 A1747 5r multi .25 .25

Sant Shadaram Sahib (1708-93), Religious Leader — A1748

2010, Oct. 25 *Perf. 13x13¼*
2456 A1748 5r multi .25 .25

Cathedral and John Connon School, Mumbai, 150th Anniv. A1749

2010, Oct. 27 *Perf. 13¼x13*
2457 A1749 5r multi .25 .25

Kranti Trivedi (1930-2009), Writer — A1750

2010, Oct. 29 *Perf. 13x13¼*
2458 A1750 5r multi .25 .25

K. A. P. Viswanatham (1899-1994), Medical Writer — A1751

2010, Nov. 10 *Perf. 13¼x13*
2459 A1751 5r multi .25 .25

Children's Day — A1752

Designs: No. 2460, 5r, Dolls depicting women carrying baskets on heads. No. 2461, 5r, Kite. No. 2462, 5r, Tops. No. 2463, 5r, Dolls depicting women in native costumes (28x38mm).

Perf. 13¼, 13x13¼ (#2463)
2010, Nov. 14
2460-2463 A1752 Set of 4 .90 .90
2463a Souvenir sheet, #2460-2463, perf. 13 *3.00 3.00*

Lakshmipat Singhania (1910-76), Industrialist A1753

Perf. 13¾ Syncopated
2010, Nov. 15
2464 A1753 5r multi .25 .25

Comptroller and Auditor General of India, 150th Anniv. — A1754

2010, Nov. 16 Photo. *Perf. 13x13¼*
2465 A1754 5r multi .25 .25

Chidambaram Subramaniam (1910-2000), Statesman — A1755

Perf. 13¾ Syncopated
2010, Nov. 28 Litho.
2466 A1755 5r multi .25 .25

Kamlapat Singhania (1884-1937), Industrialist A1756

2010, Dec. 1
2467 A1756 5r multi .25 .25

Performing Artists — A1757

Designs: No. 2468, 5r, Thanjavur Balasaraswathi (1918-84), dancer. No. 2469, 5r, T. N. Rajarathinam Pillai (1898-1956), musician. No. 2470, 5r, Veenai Dhanammai (1867-1938), musician, horiz.

2010, Dec. 3
2468-2470 A1757 Set of 3 .70 .70

Sri Sri Borda (1911-94), Philosopher A1758

2010, Dec. 6 Photo. *Perf. 13x13¼*
2471 A1758 5r multi .25 .25

Prafulla Chandra Chaki (1888-1908), Assassin of British Colonialists A1759

2010, Dec. 11
2472 A1759 5r multi .25 .25

Dances A1760

Designs: 5r, Jarabe Tapatío (Mexican Hat dance), Mexico. 20r, Kalbelia dance, India.

2010, Dec. 15 Litho. *Perf. 13*
2473-2474 A1760 Set of 2 1.10 1.10
2474a Souvenir sheet of 2, #2473-2474, perf. 13¼ syncopated *3.00 3.00*

See Mexico No. 2726.

Crafts Museum, New Delhi A1761

Designs: No. 2475, 5r, Tiger. No. 2476, 5r, Figurines of two men and dog.

2010, Dec. 21 Litho. *Perf. 13*
2475-2476 A1761 Set of 2 .45 .45
2476a Souvenir sheet of 2, #2475-2476 *1.75 1.75*

Yashwantrao Balwantrao Chavan (1913-84), Politician A1762

2010, Dec. 22 Photo. *Perf. 13x13¼*
2477 A1762 5r multi .25 .25

Bhausaheb Hiray (1905-61), Social Reformer A1763

2010, Dec. 22 Litho. *Perf. 13¼x13*
2478 A1763 5r multi .25 .25

Central Bank of India, Cent. A1764

Perf. 13¾ Syncopated
2010, Dec. 23
2479 A1764 5r multi .25 .25

Bhai Jeevan Singh (1649-1705), Sikh Warrior — A1765

2010, Dec. 23 ***Perf. 13x13¼***
2480 A1765 5r multi .25 .25

A1766

No. 2481: a, National Council of Education Building (39x29mm). b, Dr. Triguna Sen (1905-98), educator.

2010, Dec. 24 ***Perf. 13¼***
2481 A1766 5r Horiz. pair, #a-b .45 .45

Immanuel Sekaranar (1924-57), Social Reformer A1767

2010, Dec. 31 ***Perf. 13¾***
2482 A1767 5r multi .25 .25

National Academy of Art, New Delhi — A1768

Perf. 13¼ Syncopated
2010, Dec. 31
2483 A1768 5r multi .25 .25

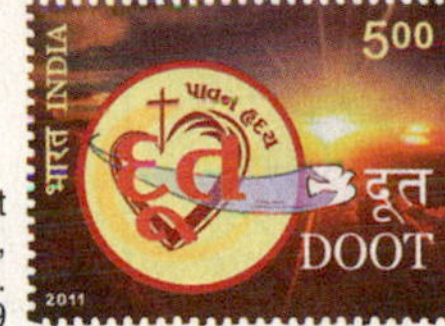

Doot Magazine, Cent. A1769

2011, Jan. 15 ***Perf. 13¼x13***
2484 A1769 5r multi .25 .25

Krishnadevaraya (d. 1529), Vijayanagara Emperor — A1770

2011, Jan. 27 ***Perf. 13¼ Syncopated***
2485 A1770 5r multi .25 .25
a. Souvenir sheet of 1 *1.40 1.40*

Chaudhary Ranbir Singh (1914-2009), Politician — A1771

2011, Feb. 1 ***Perf. 13¾ Syncopated***
2486 A1771 5r multi .25 .25

Mary Ward (1585-1645), Nun and Educational Buildings — A1772

2011, Feb. 2 ***Perf. 13¼ Syncopated***
2487 A1772 5r multi .25 .25

Loreto Institutions founded by Ward, 400th anniv.

Army Corps of Signals, Cent. A1773

2011, Feb. 4 ***Perf. 13***
2488 A1773 5r multi .25 .25

V. Subbiah (1911-93), Communist Leader — A1774

2011, Feb. 7 ***Perf. 13¾ Syncopated***
2489 A1774 5r multi .25 .25

2011 Census A1775

2011, Feb. 8 **Litho.**
2490 A1775 5r multi .25 .25

V. Venkatasubba Reddiar (d. 1981), Politician — A1776

Perf. 13¾ Syncopated
2011, Feb. 11
2491 A1776 5r multi .25 .25

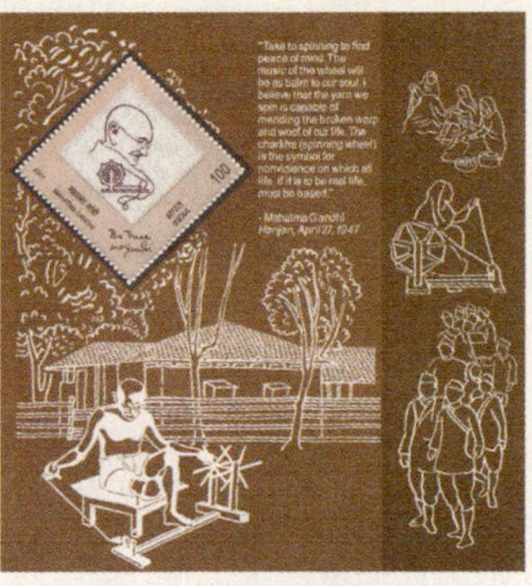

The souvenir sheet above was issued in limited quantities and sold for well above the face value of the stamp.

First Airmail Flight, Cent. A1777

Designs: No. 2492, 5r, Henri Pequet (1888-1974), pilot for first airmail flight, his airplane, newspaper clipping. No. 2493, 5r, Covers and cancels. No. 2494, 5r, Map of first flight, fort, vert. (32x58mm). No. 2495, 5r, Airplane, cancel, boat, vert. (32x58mm).

Perf. 13¼x13, 13 (#2494-2495)
2011, Feb. 12
2492-2495 A1777 Set of 4 .90 .90
2495a Souvenir sheet of 4, #2492-2495 *2.60 2.60*

Taj Mahal — A1778

Aries — A1779

Taurus — A1780

Gemini — A1781

Cancer — A1782

Leo — A1783

Virgo — A1784

Libra — A1785

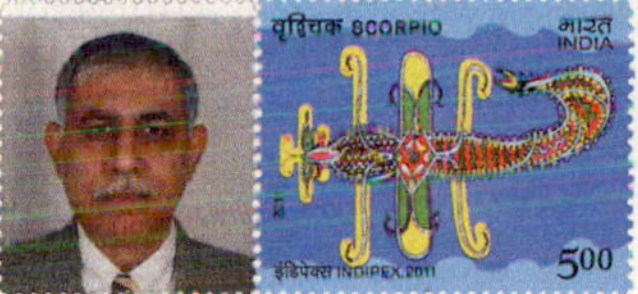

Scorpio — A1786

Sagittarius — A1787

Capricorn — A1788

Aquarius — A1789

Pisces — A1790

Trains — A1791

Aircraft — A1792

Fables — A1793

Wildlife — A1794

No. 2509: a, 1WP/1, 1963. b, 2 WDM 2, 1963. c, 1 GIP NO 1, 1853. d, 1 F/1, 1895.
No. 2510: a, LCA-Tejas airplane. b, Dhruv helicopter with red paint at top of fuselage. c, Dhruv helicopter with camouflage paint. d, HT-2 airplane.
No. 2511: a, The Lion and the Rabbit. b, The Monkey and the Crocodile. c, The Crows and the Snake. d, The Tortoise and the Geese.
No. 2512: a, Indian lion. b, Indian elephant. c, Tiger. d, Rhinoceros.

2011, Feb. 12 ***Perf. 13***

2496	A1778	5r multi + label	.55	.55
2497	A1779	5r multi + label	.55	.55
2498	A1780	5r multi + label	.55	.55
2499	A1781	5r multi + label	.55	.55
2500	A1782	5r multi + label	.55	.55
2501	A1783	5r multi + label	.55	.55
2502	A1784	5r multi + label	.55	.55
2503	A1785	5r multi + label	.55	.55
2504	A1786	5r multi + label	.55	.55
2505	A1787	5r multi + label	.55	.55
2506	A1788	5r multi + label	.55	.55
2507	A1789	5r multi + label	.55	.55
2508	A1790	5r multi + label	.55	.55
2509	A1791	5r Block of 4, #a-d, + 4 labels	2.25	2.25
2510	A1792	5r Block of 4, #a-d, + 4 labels	2.25	2.25
2511	A1793	5r Block of 4, #a-d, + 4 labels	2.25	2.25
2512	A1794	5r Block of 4, #a-d, + 4 labels	2.25	2.25
		Nos. 2496-2512 (17)	16.15	16.15

Indipex 2011, New Delhi. Nos. 2496-2508 were each printed in sheets of 12 + 12 labels. Nos. 2509-2512 were each printed in sheets containing 3 blocks of 4 + 12 labels. Each sheet sold for 150r and labels could be personalized. Compare types A1779-A1790 with type A1727, type A1791 with type A439, and type A1793 with type A1295.

Film Actresses A1795

Designs: No. 2513, 5r, Devika Rani (1908-94). No. 2514, 5r, Nutan (1936-91). No. 2515, 5r, Kanan Devi (1916-92). No. 2516, 5r, Savithri (1935-81). No. 2517, 5r, Meena Kumari (1932-72). No. 2518, 5r, Leela Naidu (1940-2009).

2011, Feb. 13 ***Perf. 13¼x13***
2513-2518 A1795 Set of 6 1.40 1.40
2518a Souvenir sheet of 6, #2513-2518 *3.50 3.50*

La Martiniere Schools, 175th Anniv. A1796

2011, Mar. 1 ***Perf. 13¾ Syncopated***
2519 A1796 5r multi .25 .25

Subhadra Joshi (1919-2003), Politician — A1797

2011, Mar. 23 ***Perf. 13¼x13***
2520 A1797 5r multi .25 .25

Chitralekha Magazine, 61st Anniv. — A1798

2011, Apr. 20 ***Perf. 13¾ Syncopated***
2521 A1798 5r multi .25 .25

Umrao Kunwar Ji Archana (1922-2009), Hospital Founder — A1799

2011, Apr. 30
2522 A1799 5r multi .25 .25

Rabindranath Tagore (1861-1941), Poet — A1800

Designs: No. 2523, 5r, Tagore writing. No. 2524, 5r, Tagore, flower.

2011, May 7 ***Perf. 13***
2523-2524 A1800 Set of 2 .45 .45
2524a Souvenir sheet of 2, #2523-2524 *1.75 1.75*

Second Africa-India Forum Summit, Addis Ababa, Ethiopia — A1801

Designs: 5r, Asian elephants. 25r, African elephants.

2011, May 25 ***Perf. 13¼x13***
2525-2526 A1801 Set of 2 1.40 1.40
2526a Souvenir sheet of 2, #2525-2526 *3.50 3.50*

Dr. Daulat Singh Kothari (1906-93), Physicist A1802

2011, July 6 ***Perf. 13¾ Syncopated***
2527 A1802 5r multi .25 .25

United Theological College, Bangalore, 101st Anniv. — A1803

Perf. 13¼x13 Syncopated
2011, July 8
2528 A1803 5r multi .25 .25

Vitthal Sakharam Page (1910-90), Politician A1804

2011, July 21 ***Perf. 13¼x13***
2529 A1804 5r multi .25 .25

Kasu Brahmananda Reddy (1909-94), Politician A1805

2011, July 28 ***Perf. 13¾ Syncopated***
2530 A1805 5r multi .25 .25

K. M. Mathew (1917-2010), Journalist A1806

2011, Aug. 1 **Litho.**
2531 A1806 5r multi .25 .25

Rashtrapati Bhavan (Presidential Palace), New Delhi — A1807

Designs: No. 2532, 5r, Elephant statues. No. 2533, 5r, Flag over central dome. No. 2534, 5r, Latticed stone screen. No. 2535, 5r, Rashtrapati Bhavan, horiz. (87x35mm).

2011, Aug. 5 ***Perf. 13x13¼***
2532-2535 A1807 Set of 4 .90 .90
2535a Souvenir sheet of 4, #2532-2535, perf. 13 *2.75 2.75*

Pandit K. Santanam (1885-1949), Life Insurance Company Founder — A1808

2011, Aug. 25 **Photo.** ***Perf. 13¼x13***
2536 A1808 5r multi .25 .25

Dr. Madhav Srihari Aney (1880-1968), Politician A1809

2011, Aug. 29 **Litho.** ***Perf. 13x13¼***
2537 A1809 5r multi .25 .25

Surendranath Jauhar (1903-86), Founder of Youth and National Integration Camps — A1810

2011, Sept. 2 ***Perf. 13***
2538 A1810 5r multi .25 .25

Dev Narayan, Rajasthan Folk Deity — A1811

Tejaji Maharaj, Rajasthan Folk Deity — A1812

2011, Sept. 7 ***Perf. 13¾ Syncopated***
2539 A1811 5r multi .25 .25
2540 A1812 5r multi .25 .25

Tripuraneni Gopichand (1910-62), Writer — A1813

2011, Sept. 8 **Litho.**
2541 A1813 5r multi .25 .25

Jaimalji Maharaj (1708-96), Religious Leader — A1814

2011, Sept. 25 Litho. *Perf. 13x13¼*
2542 A1814 5r multi .25 .25

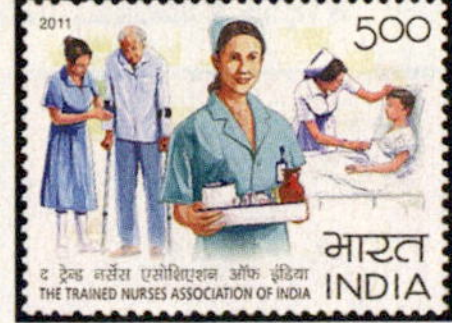

Trained Nurses Association of India, 103rd Anniv. A1815

Perf. 13¾ Syncopated
2011, Sept. 30
2543 A1815 5r multi .25 .25

Chitrapur Math (Community Temple) — A1816

2011, Oct. 9
2544 A1816 5r multi .25 .25

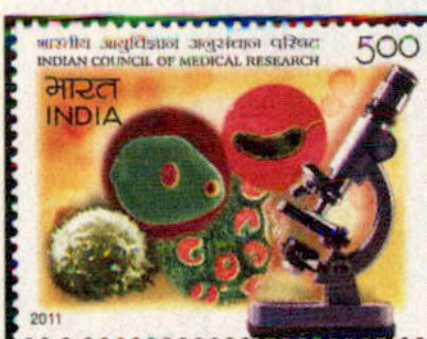

Punjab Regiment — A1817

Perf. 13¼ &13¾ Syncopated x13¼
2011, Oct. 12
2545 A1817 5r multi .25 .25

Indian Council of Medical Research, Cent. A1818

2011, Nov. 8 *Perf. 13¾ Syncopated*
2546 A1818 5r multi .25 .25

Children's Day — A1819

Designs: 5r, Tiger. 20r, Tiger, diff.

2011, Nov. 14 Photo. *Perf. 13x13¼*
2547-2548 A1819 Set of 2 1.00 1.00
2548a Souvenir sheet of 2, #2547-2548 *3.25 3.25*

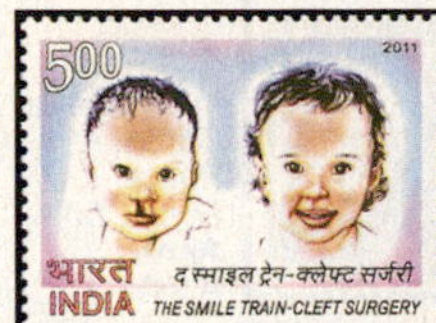

Grand Masonic Lodge of India, New Delhi, 50th Anniv. — A1820

2011, Nov. 25 Litho. *Perf. 13x13¼*
2549 A1820 5r multi .25 .25

Cleft Palate Surgery of Smile Train Charity A1821

2011, Dec. 6 *Perf. 13¼x13*
2550 A1821 5r multi .25 .25

Kavi Pradeep (1915-98), Songwriter A1822

2011, Dec. 14 Photo. *Perf. 13x13¼*
2551 A1822 5r multi .25 .25

President's Fleet Review, Mumbai — A1823

Designs: No. 2552, 5r, Submarine. No. 2553, 5r, Warship. No. 2554, 5r, President's yacht. No. 2555, 5r, Airplane.

Perf. 13¼ & 13¾ Syncopated x13¼
2011, Dec. 19 Litho.
2552-2555 A1823 Set of 4 .75 .75

Liberation of Goa, 50th Anniv. A1824

2011, Dec. 19 *Perf. 13¼x13*
2556 A1824 5r multi .25 .25

Archaeological Survey of India, 150th Anniv. — A1825

Designs: 5r, Zoomorphic figurines. 20r, Archaeological artifacts.

Perf. 13¾ Syncopated
2011, Dec. 20
2557-2558 A1825 Set of 2 .95 .95
2558a Souvenir sheet of 2, #2557-2558 *3.25 3.25*

Chhatrapati Shahuji Maharaj Medical University (King George's Medical College), Lucknow, Cent. — A1826

2011, Dec. 23 *Perf. 13*
2559 A1826 5r multi .25 .25

Srinivasa Ramanujan (1887-1920), Mathematician — A1827

Perf. 13¾ Syncopated
2011, Dec. 26
2560 A1827 5r multi .25 .25

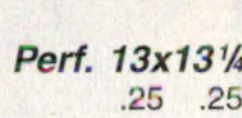

Madan Mohan Malaviya (1861-1946), President of Indian National Congress A1828

2011, Dec. 27 *Perf. 13x13¼*
2561 A1828 5r multi .25 .25

Puran Chandra Gupta (1912-86), Newspaper Publisher A1829

2012, Jan. 2 Photo. *Perf. 13¼x13*
2562 A1829 5r multi .25 .25

Bhai Jagta Ji, 19th Century Sikh Saint — A1830

2012, Jan. 15 *Perf. 13x13¼*
2563 A1830 5r multi .25 .25

Shyam Narayan Singh (1901-68), Politician A1831

2012, Jan. 24
2564 A1831 5r multi .25 .25

Dedication of India International Center, New Delhi, 50th Anniv. — A1832

2012, Feb. 9 Litho. *Perf. 13*
2565 A1832 5r multi .25 .25

Employees' State Insurance Corporation A1833

Perf. 13¾ Syncopated
2012, Feb. 24
2566 A1833 5r multi .25 .25

Vasantdada Patil (1917-89), Politician A1834

2012, Mar. 1
2567 A1834 5r multi .25 .25

Shyama Charan Shukla (1925-2007), Politician A1835

2012, Mar. 9 Photo. *Perf. 13x13¼*
2568 A1835 5r multi .25 .25

Civil Aviation in India, Cent. A1836

Designs: No. 2569, 5r, Helicopter in flight above terminal, airplane on ground. No. 2570, 5r, Terminal, airplanes on ground and in flight, air traffic controllers. No. 2571, 5r, Control tower, airplanes on ground and in flight, members of runway crew. 20r, Early airplane.

2012, Mar. 14 *Perf. 13*
2569-2572 A1836 Set of 4 1.40 1.40
2572a Souvenir sheet of 4, #2569-2572 *4.25 4.25*

Isabella Thoburn College, Lucknow, 125th Anniv. (in 2011) A1837

Perf. 13¾ Syncopated
2012, Apr. 12 Litho.
2573 A1837 5r multi .25 .25

Godiji Temple, Mumbai, 200th Anniv. — A1838

2012, Apr. 17 Photo. ***Perf. 13x13¼***
2574 A1838 5r multi .25 .25

Pres. Ramaswamy Venkataraman (1910-2009) A1839

2012, Apr. 18
2575 A1839 5r multi .25 .25

Karpoor Chandra Kulish (1926-2006), Founder of Rajasthan Patrika Newspaper — A1840

Perf. 13¾ Syncopated
2012, May 16 **Litho.**
2576 A1840 5r multi .25 .25

M. B. Kadadi (1909-92), Founder of Sangameshwar College, Solapur — A1841

2012, May 17
2577 A1841 5r multi .25 .25

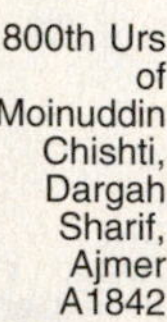

800th Urs of Moinuddin Chishti, Dargah Sharif, Ajmer A1842

Designs: 5r, Muslims seated. 20r, Dargah.

2012, May 27
2578-2579 A1842 Set of 2 .90 .90
2579a Souvenir sheet of 2, #2578-2579 *3.50 3.50*

Warli Painting A1843

Shekhawati Painting — A1844

Perf. 13¼ Syncopated
2012, June 20
2580 A1843 5r red brown .25 .25
2581 A1844 20r multi .75 .75
a. Sheet of 16, 8 each #2580-2581 *16.00 16.00*

2012, Summer Olympics, London — A1845

Designs: No. 2582, 5r, Rowing. No. 2583, 5r, Sailboarding. No. 2584, 20r, Volleyball. No. 2585, 20r, Badminton.

2012, July 25 ***Perf. 13¼x13***
2582-2585 A1845 Set of 4 1.90 1.90
2585a Souvenir sheet of 4, #2582-2585, perf. 13 *5.25 5.25*

Customs Act, 50th Anniv. — A1846

2012, July 26 Photo. ***Perf. 13x13¼***
2586 A1846 5r multi .25 .25

Durga Prasad Chaudhary, Newspaper Publisher — A1847

Perf. 13¾ Syncopated
2012, July 31 **Litho.**
2587 A1847 5r multi .25 .25

Armed Forces Medical College, Pune, 50th Anniv. — A1848

2012, Aug. 4 ***Perf. 13¼***
2588 A1848 5r multi .25 .25

Husain Ahmad Madani (1879-1957), Islamic Scholar — A1849

2012, Aug. 29 ***Perf. 13x13¼***
2589 A1849 5r multi .25 .25

Motilal Nehru (1861-1931), President of Indian National Congress A1850

2012, Sept. 25 **Photo.**
2590 A1850 5r multi .25 .25

Indo-Tibetan Border Police Force, 50th Anniv. A1851

2012, Oct. 1 Litho. ***Perf. 13¼x13***
2591 A1851 5r multi .25 .25

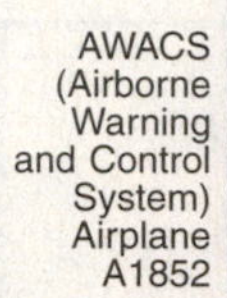

AWACS (Airborne Warning and Control System) Airplane A1852

2012, Oct. 8
2592 A1852 5r multi .25 .25

Souvenir Sheet

India Nos. 6c and 200 — A1853

2012, Oct. 12 ***Perf. 13***
2593 A1853 20r multi .75 .75

Philately Day.

Fauna — A1854

Designs: No. 2594, 5r, Nicobar megapode. No. 2595, 5r, Hoolock gibbon. No. 2596, 5r, Venated gliding frog. 25r, Bugun liocichla.

2012, Oct. 16 ***Perf. 13¾***
2594-2597 A1854 Set of 4 1.50 1.50
2597a Souvenir sheet of 4, #2594-2597 *4.75 4.75*

Flowers — A1855

Designs: No. 2598, 5r, Lilies. No. 2599, 5r, Pansies. No. 2600, 5r, Cinerarias. No. 2601, 5r, Dahlias.

2012, Oct. 19 Litho. ***Perf. 13***
Stamps + Label
2598-2601 A1855 Set of 4 4.00 4.00

Nos. 2598-2601 each were printed in sheets of 12 + 12 labels. Labels could be personalized. Generic labels depict various flowers.

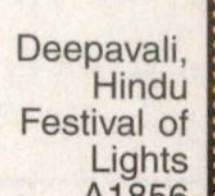

Deepavali, Hindu Festival of Lights A1856

Hanukkah, Jewish Festival of Lights A1857

Perf. 13¾ Syncopated
2012, Nov. 5 **Litho.**
2602 A1856 5r multi .25 .25
2603 A1857 5r multi .25 .25

See Israel Nos. 1956-1957.

T.S. Narayanawami (1911-68), Industrialist A1858

2012, Nov. 11 ***Perf. 13x13¼***
2604 A1858 5r multi .25 .25

Children's Day A1859

Perf. 13¾ Syncopated
2012, Nov. 14
2605 A1859 5r multi .25 .25

Scinde Horse Cavalry Regiment A1860

2012, Nov. 16 ***Perf. 13¼x13***
2606 A1860 5r multi .25 .25

Ramgopal Maheshwari (1911-99), Newspaper Publisher A1861

2012, Nov. 20 ***Perf. 13¼***
2607 A1861 5r multi .25 .25

Consumer Protection Act of 1986 A1862

Perf. 13¾ Syncopated

2012, Nov. 29
2608 A1862 5r multi .25 .25

Sri Shivarathri Shivayogi, 10th Century Saint — A1863

2012, Dec. 21 ***Perf. 13x13¼***
2609 A1863 5r multi .25 .25

Srinivasa Ramanujan (1887-1920), Mathematician — A1864

2012, Dec. 22 ***Perf. 13¼x13***
2610 A1864 5r multi .25 .25

National Mathematics Day.

Lighthouses A1865

Designs: 5r, Mahabalipuram Lighthouse. 20r, Alleppey Lighthouse.

2012, Dec. 23 ***Perf. 13¼x13***
2611-2612 A1865 Set of 2 .95 .95
2612a Souvenir sheet of 2, #2611-2612, perf. 13 syncopated *3.25 3.25*

Indian Science Congress, Cent. A1866

2013, Jan. 3 ***Perf. 13¾ Syncopated***
2613 A1866 5r multi .25 .25

Postgraduate Institute of Medical Education and Research, Chandigarh, 50th Anniv. — A1867

2013, Jan. 7 ***Perf. 13¾x14***
2614 A1867 5r multi .25 .25

Ghadar Movement for Indian Independence, Cent. — A1868

2013, Jan. 8 ***Perf. 13x13¼***
2615 A1868 5r multi .25 .25

Uttar Pradesh Legislature, 125th Anniv. A1869

2013, Jan. 8 ***Perf. 13¼x13***
2616 A1869 5r multi .25 .25

Silk Letter Movement for Indian Independence, Cent. — A1870

2013, Jan. 11 ***Perf. 13x13¼***
2617 A1870 5r multi .25 .25

A1871

A1872

A1873

Swami Vivekananda (1863-1902), Hindu Monk — A1874

2013, Jan. 12 **Litho.** ***Perf. 13***
2618 A1871 5r multi .25 .25
2619 A1872 5r multi .25 .25
2620 A1873 5r multi .25 .25
2621 A1874 20r multi .75 .75
Nos. 2618-2621 (4) 1.50 1.50

Chelat Achyutha Menon (1913-91), Politician — A1875

2013, Jan. 13 ***Perf. 13x13¼***
2622 A1875 5r multi .25 .25

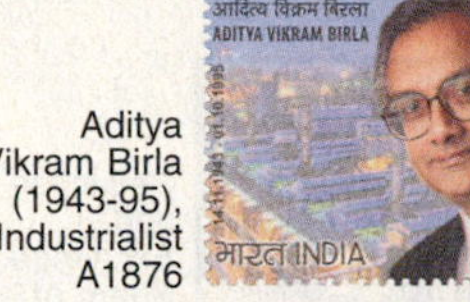

Aditya Vikram Birla (1943-95), Industrialist A1876

2013, Jan. 14 ***Perf. 13¾ Syncopated***
2623 A1876 5r multi .25 .25

Basilica of Our Lady of Good Health, Vailankanni A1877

2013, Jan. 22 ***Perf. 13¾***
2624 A1877 5r multi .25 .25

Third Battalion of Special Forces Parachute Regiment, Bicent. — A1878

2013, Mar. 2 ***Perf. 13¾ Syncopated***
2625 A1878 5r multi .25 .25

Officers Training Academy, Chennai, 50th Anniv. — A1879

2013, Mar. 7 ***Perf. 13x13¼***
2626 A1879 5r multi .25 .25

Sahir Ludhianvi (1921-80), Poet and Lyricist — A1880

2013, Mar. 8 ***Perf. 13¾ Syncopated***
2627 A1880 5r multi .25 .25

Malayala Manorama Newspaper, 125th Anniv. A1881

2013, Mar. 16 **Litho.**
2628 A1881 5r multi .25 .25

Jhulelal Sahib, Sindhi God — A1882

2013, Mar. 17
2629 A1882 5r multi .25 .25

Shiv Ram Hari Rajguru (1908-31), Revolutionist — A1883

2013, Mar. 22 ***Perf. 13¼x13***
2630 A1883 5r multi .25 .25

Architectural Heritage of Srikakulam A1884

Designs: 5r, Srikurmam Temple. 20r, Arasavalli Temple.

2013, Apr. 11 ***Perf. 13¾ Syncopated***
2631-2632 A1884 Set of 2 .95 .95
2632a Souvenir sheet of 2, #2631-2632 *3.25 3.25*

Post Office Centenaries A1885

Designs: No. 2633, 5r, Mumbai General Post Office. No. 2634, 5r, Agra Head Post Office.

2013, Apr. 12 ***Perf. 13¼x13***
2633-2634 A1885 Set of 2 .40 .40
2634a Souvenir sheet of 2, #2633-2634, perf. 13 *1.90 1.90*

Chaitya Bhoomi, Mumbai, and B. R. Ambedkar (1891-1956), Law Minister — A1886

2013, Apr. 14 ***Perf. 13¼x13***
2635 A1886 5r multi .25 .25

Hari Singh Nalwa (1791-1837), General, Governor of Kashmir, Peshawar and Nazara — A1887

2013, Apr. 30 ***Perf. 13¾ Syncopated***

2636 A1887 5r multi .25 .25

Indian Cinema, Cent. — A1888

No. 2637, 5r: a, Allu Ramalingiah (1922-2004), actor. b, Ashok Mehta (1947-2012), cinematographer. c, Balraj Sahni (1913-73), actor. d, Bhanumathi (1925-2005), actress. e, C. V. Sridhar (1933-2008), director. f, Chetan Anand (1921-97), director. g, Kamaal Amrohi (1918-93), director. h, Geeta Dutt (1930-72), singer.

No. 2638, 5r: a, Kannadasan (1927-81), lyricist. b, Madan Mohan (1924-75), music director. c, Mehmood (1932-2004), actor. d, Motilal (1910-65), actor. e, Nagesh (1933-2009), actor. f, O. P. Nayyar (1926-2007), music director. g, Prem Nazir (1926-89), actor. h, R. D. Burman (1939-94), music director.

No. 2639, 5r: a, Raj Khosla (1925-91), director. b, Rajendra Kumar (1929-99), actor. c, Rajesh Khanna (1942-2012), actor. d, S. V. Ranga Rao (1918-74), actor. e, Salil Chowdhury (1922-95), music director. f, Sanjeev Kumar (1938-85), actor. g, Shailendra (1923-66), lyricist. h, Shakeel Badayuni (1916-70), lyricist.

No. 2640, 5r: a, Shammi Kapoor (1930-2011), actor. b, Shankar Singh Raghuvanshi (1922-87), and Jaikishan Dayabhai Panchal (1929-71), composers. c, Smita Patil (1955-86), actress. d, Suraiya (1929-2004), actress. e, Tarachand Barjatya (1914-92), producer. f, T. R. Sundaram (1907-63), actor. g, Utpal Dutt (1929-93), actor. h, Vishnu Vardhan (1950-2009), actor.

No. 2641, 5r: a, Ashok Kumar (1911-2001), actor. b, B. N. Sircar (1901-80), producer. c, B. R. Chopra (1914-2008), director. d, Bhalji Pendharkar (1897-1994), director. e, Bhupen Hazarika (1926-2011), lyricist. f, Dev Anand (1923-2011), actor. g, Dhirendranath Ganguly (1893-1978), director. h, Durga Khote (1905-91), actress. i, Hrishikesh Mukherjee (1922-2006), director.

No. 2642, 5r: a, Majrooh Sultanpuri (1919-2000), lyricist. b, Naushad (1919-2006), music director. c, Nitin Bose (1897-1986), director. d, Prithviraj Kapoor (1901-72), actor. e, Raichand Boral (1903-81), music director. f, Ruby Myers (1907-83), actress. g, Sohrab Modi (1897-1984), actor. h, Tapan Sinha (1924-2009), director. i, Yash Chopra (1932-2012), director.

Perf. 13¾ Syncopated

2013, May 3 **Litho.**

Sheets of 8, #a-h

2637-2640 A1888 Set of 4 6.00 6.00

Sheets of 9, #a-i

2641-2642 A1888 Set of 2 3.50 3.50

Wild Asses A1889

Designs: 5r, Kiang, Ladakh Region. 20r, Ghor Khar, Kutch Region.

Perf. 13¾ Syncopated

2013, May 10 **Litho.**

2643-2644 A1889 Set of 2 .85 .85

2644a Souvenir sheet of 2, #2643-2644 *3.50 3.50*

Securities and Exchange Board of India A1890

2013, May 24 **Litho.** ***Perf. 13¼x13***

2645 A1890 5r multi .25 .25

Peerzada Ghulam Ahmad Mejhoor (1885-1952), Poet — A1891

2013, June 25 **Litho.** ***Perf. 13¼x13***

2646 A1891 5r multi .25 .25

Delhi Gymkhana Club, Cent. A1892

2013, July 3 **Litho.** ***Perf. 13¼x13***

2647 A1892 5r multi .25 .25

Kerala Legislative Assembly A1893

2013, Aug. 7 **Litho.** ***Perf. 13***

2648 A1893 5r multi .25 .25

Raj Bahadur (1912-90), Politician — A1894

2013, Aug. 21 **Litho.** ***Perf. 13x13¼***

2649 A1894 5r multi .25 .25

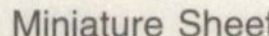

Miniature Sheet

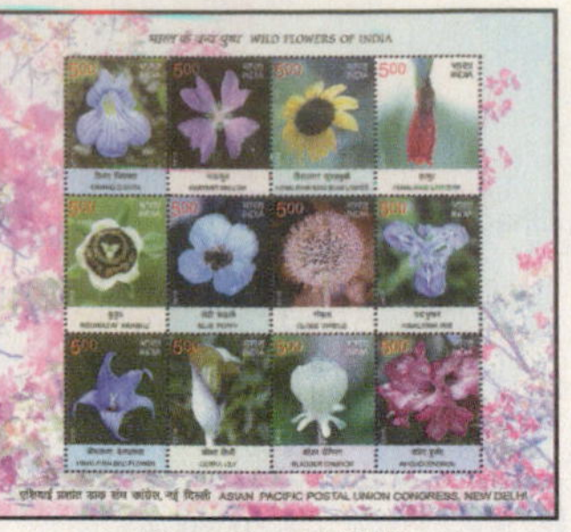

Flowers — A1895

No. 2650: a, Dibang chirita. b, Kashmir mallow. c, Himalayan mini-sunflower. d, Himalayan lantern. e, Roundleaf asiabell. f, Blue poppy. g, Globe thistle. h, Himalayan iris. i, Himalayan bellflower. j, Cobra lily. k, Bladder campion. l, Rhododendron.

2013, Sept. 3 **Litho.** ***Perf. 13***

2650 A1895 5r Sheet of 12, #a-l 1.90 1.90

m. Souvenir sheet of 4, #2650c, 2650f, 2650g, 2650l, perf. 13x13¼ 2.00 2.00

n. Souvenir sheet of 4, #2650d, 2650e, 2650h, 2650i, perf. 13x13¼ 2.00 2.00

o. Souvenir sheet of 4, #2650a, 2650b, 2650j, 2650k, perf. 13x13¼ 2.00 2.00

Asian-Pacific Postal Union Congress, New Delhi.

Lala Jagat Narain (1899-1981), Politician and Newspaper Publisher A1896

2013, Sept. 9 **Litho.** ***Perf. 13x13¼***

2651 A1896 5r multi .25 .25

Acharya Gyansagar (1891-1973), Poet — A1897

Perf. 13¾ Syncopated

2013, Sept. 10 **Litho.**

2652 A1897 5r multi .25 .25

Gurajada Venkata Apparao (c. 1861-1915), Writer — A1898

2013, Sept. 21 **Litho.** ***Perf. 13x13¼***

2653 A1898 5r multi .25 .25

Pratap Narayan Mishra (1856-94), Writer — A1899

2013, Sept. 24 **Litho.** ***Perf. 13x13¼***

2654 A1899 5r multi .25 .25

Joomdev (1921-96), Founder of Social Welfare Organizations A1900

2013, Sept. 30 **Litho.** ***Perf. 13x13¼***

2655 A1900 5r multi .25 .25

Souvenir Sheet

Mahatma Gandhi (1869-1948), India Nos. 205 and 498 — A1901

2013, Oct. 12 **Litho.** ***Perf. 13***

2656 A1901 20r multi .65 .65

Philately Day.

Bhakra Dam, 50th Anniv. A1902

2013, Oct. 22 **Litho.** ***Perf. 13¼x13***

2657 A1902 5r multi .25 .25

Ruchi Ram Sahni (1863-1948), Scientist and Politician — A1903

2013, Oct. 24 **Litho.** ***Perf. 13x13¼***

2658 A1903 5r multi .25 .25

Boys' High School, Allahabad A1904

2013, Nov. 5 **Litho.** ***Perf. 13¼x13***

2659 A1904 5r multi .25 .25

K. M. Munshi (1887-1971), Founder of Bharatiya Vidya Bhavan (Indian Educational Trust) — A1905

2013, Nov. 7 **Litho.** ***Perf. 13***

2660 A1905 5r multi .25 .25

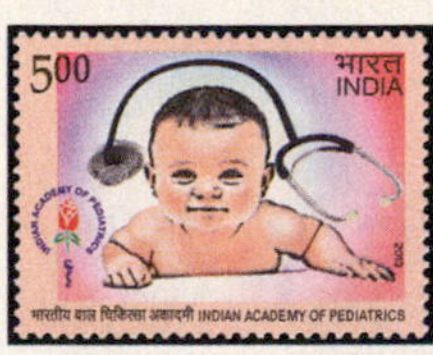

Indian Academy of Pediatrics, 50th Anniv. A1906

2013, Nov. 8 Litho. *Perf. 13¼x13*
2661 A1906 5r multi .25 .25

Central Bureau of Investigation, 50th Anniv. — A1907

2013, Nov. 11 Litho. *Perf. 13¼x13*
2662 A1907 5r multi .25 .25

The Times of India Newspaper, 175th Anniv. — A1908

2013, Nov. 13 Litho. *Perf. 13x13¼*
2663 A1908 5r multi .25 .25

Children's Day A1909

2013, Nov. 14 Litho. *Perf. 13¼x13*
2664 A1909 5r multi .25 .25

A1910

Retirement of Sachin Tendulkar, Cricket Player — A1911

2013, Nov. 14 Litho. *Perf. 13x13¼*
2665 A1910 20r multi .65 .65
2666 A1911 20r multi .65 .65
a. Souvenir sheet of 2, #2665-2666 *4.00 4.00*

Satya Sai Baba (1926-2011), Guru — A1912

2013, Nov. 23 Litho. *Perf. 13x13¼*
2667 A1912 5r multi .25 .25

Intelligence Bureau, 125th Anniv. — A1913

2013, Nov. 23 Litho. *Perf. 13x13¼*
2668 A1913 5r multi .25 .25

Locomotives and Railway Workshops A1914

Locomotive and: 5r, Kanchrapara Workshop. 20r, Jamalpur Workshop.

2013, Nov. 26 Litho. *Perf. 13¼x13*
2669-2670 A1914 Set of 2 .80 .80
2670a Souvenir sheet of 2, #2669-2670 *3.50 3.50*

Railway workshops, 150th anniv. (in 2012).

Sashastra Seema Bal (Armed Border Force), 50th Anniv. A1915

2013, Nov. 29 Litho. *Perf. 13¼x13*
2671 A1915 5r multi .25 .25

Nagaland, 50th Anniv. — A1916

Perf. 13¾ Syncopated
2013, Dec. 1 Litho.
2672 A1916 5r multi .25 .25

Commissioning of Aircraft Carrier INS Vikramaditya — A1917

Perf. 13¾ Syncopated
2013, Dec. 4 Litho.
2673 A1917 5r multi .25 .25

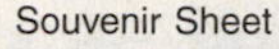

Souvenir Sheet

Qutub Minar, Delhi, and Tokyo Tower, Tokyo — A1918

Perf. 13¼ Syncopated
2013, Dec. 5 Litho.
2674 A1918 20r multi .65 .65

State visit of Japanese Emperor Akihito and Empress Michiko.

Indian Institute of Foreign Trade, 50th Anniv. — A1919

2013, Dec. 10 Litho. *Perf. 13x13¼*
2675 A1919 5r multi .25 .25

Beant Singh (1924-95), Politician — A1920

Perf. 13¾ Syncopated
2013, Dec. 17 Litho.
2676 A1920 5r multi .25 .25

Gulab Singh Lodhi (?-1935), Freedom Fighter — A1921

2013, Dec. 23 Litho. *Perf. 13x13¼*
2677 A1921 5r multi .25 .25

Eklavya, Prince in the Mahabharata A1922

2013, Dec. 27 Litho. *Perf. 13x13¼*
2678 A1922 5r multi .25 .25

Babu Banarsi Das (1912-85), Politician — A1923

2013, Dec. 31 Litho. *Perf. 13x13¼*
2679 A1923 5r multi .25 .25

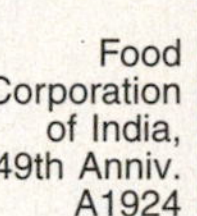

Food Corporation of India, 49th Anniv. A1924

Perf. 13¾ Syncopated
2014, Jan. 14 Litho.
2680 A1924 5r multi .25 .25

International Year of Crystallography — A1925

Perf. 13¾ Syncopated
2014, Jan. 30 Litho.
2681 A1925 20r multi .65 .65

Souvenir Sheet

Indian Museum, Kolkata, 200th Anniv. — A1926

No. 2682: a, 5r, Peacock (29x29mm). b, 20r, Museum (39x29mm). c, 20r, Archer on bull (29x29mm).

Perf. 13¾, 13¾ Syncopated (#2682b)
2014, Feb. 2 Litho.
2682 A1926 Sheet of 3, #a-c 1.50 1.50

Jagjit Singh (1941-2011), Musician — A1927

No. 2683: a, 5r, Singh (29x29mm). b, 20r, Singh with instrument (52x29mm).

2014, Feb. 8 Litho. *Perf. 13*
2683 A1927 Horiz. pair, #a-b .80 .80

Central Vigilance Commission, 50th Anniv. A1928

Perf. 13¾ Syncopated
2014, Feb. 11 Litho.
2684 A1928 5r multi .25 .25

Hasrat Mohani (1875-1951), Writer — A1929

Perf. 13¾ Syncopated

2014, Feb. 25 **Litho.**
2685 A1929 5r multi .25 .25

National Council of Churches, Cent. — A1930

Perf. 13¾ Syncopated

2014, Apr. 25 **Litho.**
2686 A1930 5r multi .25 .25

Chattampiswamikal (1853-1924), Social Reformer — A1931

Perf. 13¾ Syncopated

2014, Apr. 30 **Litho.**
2687 A1931 5r multi .25 .25

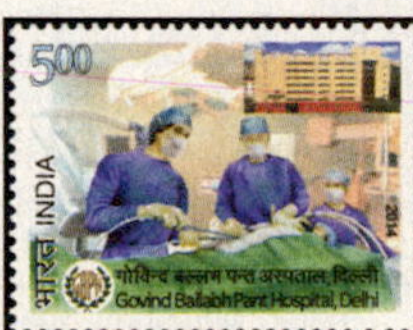
Govind Ballabh Pant Hospital, Delhi, 50th Anniv. A1932

Perf. 13¾ Syncopated

2014, Apr. 30 **Litho.**
2688 A1932 5r multi .25 .25

Drukpa Lineage of Buddhism A1933

Perf. 13¾ Syncopated

2014, May 14 **Litho.**
2689 A1933 5r multi .25 .25

2014 World Cup Soccer Championships, Brazil — A1934

Designs: No. 2690, 5r, Player readying shot on goal. No. 2691, 5r, Goalie diving for ball. No. 2692, 25r, Player making bicycle kick. No. 2693, 25r, Mascot.

2014, June 12 **Litho.** ***Perf. 13¼***
2690-2693 A1934 Set of 4 2.00 2.00
2693a Souvenir sheet of 4, #2690-2693 *7.50 7.50*

Fairy Queen Locomotive — A1934a

Taj Mahal, Agra — A1934b

Red Fort, Delhi — A1934c

St. Francis Church, Goa — A1934d

Hawa Mahal, Jaipur — A1934e

Ajanta Caves, Aurangabad District — A1934f

Qutub Minar, Delhi — A1934h

Butterfly and Flower — A1934i

Mysore Palace at Night — A1934j

Mysore Palace in Daylight — A1934k

2014 **Litho.** ***Perf. 13, 13¾ (#2693I)***

2693B	A1934a	5r multi + label	1.60	1.60
2693C	A1934b	5r multi + label	1.60	1.60
2693D	A1934c	5r multi + label	1.60	1.60
2693E	A1934d	5r multi + label	1.60	1.60
2693F	A1934e	5r multi + label	1.60	1.60
2693G	A1934f	5r multi + label	1.60	1.60
2693I	A1934h	5r multi + label	1.60	1.60
2693J	A1934i	5r multi + label	1.60	1.60
2693K		Horiz. pair + 2 labels	3.25	3.25
l.		A1934j 5r multi + label	1.60	1.60
m.		A1934k 5r multi + label	1.60	1.60
		Nos. 2693B-2693K (9)	16.05	16.05

Issued: No. 2693B, 7/16; Nos. 2693C-2693G, 8/4; Nos. 2693I-2693K, 8/5.

Nos. 2693B-2693G, 2693I-2693J were each printed in sheets of 12 + 12 labels. No. 2693K was printed in sheets of 12 containing 6 each of Nos. 2693l and 2693m + 12 labels. Each sheet sold for 300r. Labels could be personalized.

An additional stamp was issued in this set. The editors would like to examine any example of it.

Gaiety Theater Complex, Shimla, 125th Anniv. — A1935

2014, Aug. 20 **Litho.** ***Perf. 13***
2694 A1935 5r multi .25 .25

Musicians A1936

Designs: No. 2695, 5r, Damal Krishnaswamy Pattammal (1919-2009), singer. No. 2696, 5r, Gangubai Hangal (1913-2009), singer. No. 2697, 5r, Kumar Gandharva (1924-92), singer. No. 2698, 5r, Vilayat Khan (1928-2004), sitar player. No. 2699, 5r, Mallikarjun Mansur (1910-92), singer. No. 2700, 5r, Ali Akbar Khan (1922-2009), sarod player. No. 2701, 25r, Ravi Shankar (1920-2012), sitar player. No. 2702, 25r, Bhimsen Joshi (1922-2011), singer.

Perf. 13¾ Syncopated

2014, Sept. 3 **Litho.**
2695-2702 A1936 Set of 8 2.60 2.60
2702a Sheet of 8, #2695-2702 *9.50 9.50*

Anagarika Dharmapala (1864-1933), Founder of Mahabodhi Society — A1937

Perf. 13¾ Syncopated

2014, Oct. 25 **Litho.**
2703 A1937 5r multi .25 .25

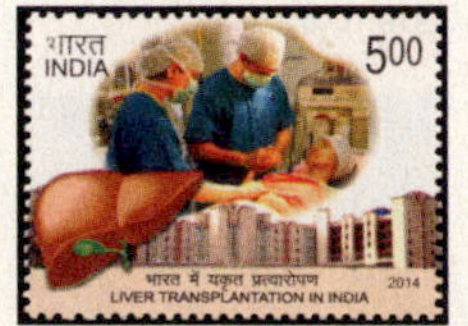
Liver Transplantation in India, 15th Anniv. — A1938

Perf. 13¾ Syncopated

2014, Nov. 4 **Litho.**
2704 A1938 5r multi .25 .25

Unit Trust of India, 50th Anniv. A1939

Perf. 13¾ Syncopated

2014, Nov. 12 **Litho.**
2705 A1939 5r multi .25 .25

Children's Art A1940

Designs: 5r, Dancers, by Sara Zivkovic, Slovenia. 25r, Indian family and house, by Roshan V. Anvekar, India.

Perf. 13¾ Syncopated

2014, Nov. 28 **Litho.**
2706-2707 A1940 Set of 2 1.00 1.00
2707a Souvenir sheet of 2, #2706-2707 *4.25 4.25*

See Slovenia No. 1097.

Sagol Kangjei, 150th Anniv. A1941

Perf. 13¾ Syncopated

2014, Nov. 29 **Litho.**
2708 A1941 5r multi .25 .25

Swami Ekrasanand Saraswati (1866-1938), Founder of Daivia Sampad Mandal — A1942

Perf. 13¾ Syncopated

2014, Dec. 4 **Litho.**
2709 A1942 5r multi .25 .25

Kendriya Vidyalaya Sanghthan, 50th Anniv. (in 2013) A1943

Perf. 13¾ Syncopated

2014, Dec. 15 **Litho.**
2710 A1943 5r multi .25 .25

Kuka Movement A1944

Perf. 13¾ Syncopated

2014, Dec. 24 **Litho.**
2711 A1944 5r multi .25 .25

Baba Amte (1914-2008), Founder of Ashrams for Lepers
A1945

Perf. 13¾ Syncopated

2014, Dec. 30 **Litho.**
2712 A1945 5r multi .25 .25

Return of Mohandas Gandhi to India, Cent.
A1946

Gandhi and: 5r, Cover page of *Souvenir of the Passive Resistance Movement in South Africa 1906-1914*. 25r, Wife, Kasturba and ship.

Perf. 13¼ Syncopated

2015, Jan. 8 **Litho.**
2713-2714 A1946 Set of 2 1.00 1.00
2714a Souvenir sheet of 2, #2713-2714 *4.25 4.25*

Campaign to Eliminate Female Feticide and Increase Education of Girls
A1947

Perf. 13¾ Syncopated

2015, Jan. 22 **Litho.**
2715 A1947 5r multi .25 .25

A1948

A1949

Campaign to Clean India — A1950

Perf. 13¾ Syncopated

2015, Jan. 30 **Litho.**
2716 A1948 5r multi .25 .25
2717 A1949 5r multi .25 .25
2718 A1950 5r multi .25 .25
a. Souvenir sheet of 3, #2716-2718 *3.25 3.25*

Statue of Mahatma Gandhi — A1951

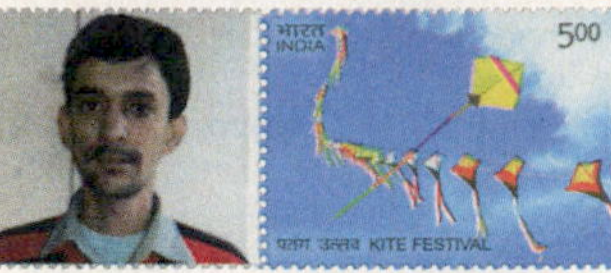

Kite Festival — A1952

Dandiya Dance — A1953

2015, Jan. 7 **Litho.** ***Perf. 13***
2719 A1951 5r multi + label 2.00 2.00
2720 A1952 5r multi + label 2.00 2.00
2721 A1953 5r multi + label 2.00 2.00
Nos. 2719-2721 (3) 6.00 6.00

Nos. 2719-2721 were printed in sheets of 12, containing 4 of each stamp, + 12 labels that could be personalized. Sheets sold for 300r.

Project Rukmani Military Satellite Communications System — A1954

Perf. 13¾ Syncopated

2015, Feb. 14 **Litho.**
2722 A1954 5r multi .25 .25

11th Cent. Emperor Rajendra Chola I and Ship on Indian Ocean
A1955

Perf. 13¾ Syncopated

2015, Mar. 20 **Litho.**
2723 A1955 5r multi .25 .25

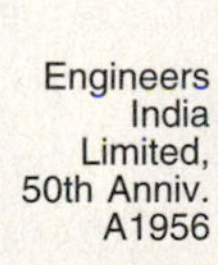

Engineers India Limited, 50th Anniv.
A1956

Perf. 13¾ Syncopated

2015, Mar. 27 **Litho.**
2724 A1956 5r multi .25 .25

French and Indian Cooperation in Space, 50th Anniv.
A1957

Designs: 5r, Megha-Tropiques satellite. 25r, Saral satellite.

Perf. 13¾ Syncopated

2015, Apr. 10 **Litho.**
2725-2726 A1957 Set of 2 .95 .95
2726a Souvenir sheet of 2, #2725-2726 *4.25 4.25*

See France Nos. 4798-4799.

Patna High Court, Cent. — A1958

Perf. 13¼x13 Syncopated

2015, Apr. 18 **Litho.**
2727 A1958 5r multi .25 .25

Old Seminary Theological College, Kottayam, 50th Anniv.
A1959

Perf. 13¾ Syncopated

2015, Apr. 21 **Litho.**
2728 A1959 5r multi .25 .25

International Day of Yoga — A1960

Perf. 13¾ Syncopated

2015, June 21 **Litho.**
2729 A1960 5r multi .25 .25
a. Souvenir sheet of 1 *1.60 1.60*

Godavari Pushkaram — A1961

2015, July 14 **Litho.** ***Perf. 13***
2730 A1961 5r multi + label 1.60 1.60

No. 2730 was printed in sheets of 12 + 12 labels that could be personalized. Sheets sold for 300r.

Nabakalebara Ritual — A1962

Perf. 13¾ Syncopated

2015, July 17 **Litho.**
2731 A1962 5r multi .25 .25

Asoka the Great (304 B.C.-232 B.C.), Maurya Emperor
A1963

2015, Aug. 24 **Litho.** ***Perf. 14½***
2732 A1963 5r multi .25 .25

A1964

Empowerment of Women — A1965

Designs: No. 2733, Mother and child, women in military, legal and medical professions. No. 2734, Women and elephant. No. 2735, Two women using laptop computer. No. 2736, Woman on bicycle, woman astronaut.

Perf. 14x13¼, 13¾ Syncopated (A1965)

2015, Sept. 2 **Litho.**
2733 A1964 5r multi .25 .25
a. Perf. 14x13¾ *.80 .80*
2734 A1965 5r multi .25 .25
2735 A1964 5r multi .25 .25
a. Perf. 14x13¾ *.80 .80*
2736 A1965 5r multi .25 .25
a. Souvenir sheet of 4, #2733a, 2734, 2735a, 2736 *3.25 3.25*
Nos. 2733-2736 (4) 1.00 1.00

10th World Hindi Conference, Bhopal
A1966

Perf. 13¾ Syncopated

2015, Sept. 10 **Litho.**
2737 A1966 5r multi .25 .25

India-Pakistan War, 50th Anniv. — A1967

Designs: No. 2738, 5r, Soldiers. No. 2739, 5r, Indian Navy ship. No. 2740, 5r, Airplane battle.

Perf. 13¾ Syncopated

2015, Sept. 15 **Litho.**
2738-2740 A1967 Set of 3 .50 .50

Dr. Bhimrao R. Ambedkar (1891-1956), Architect of Indian Constitution — A1968

Perf. 13¾ Syncopated

2015, Sept. 30 **Litho.**
2741 A1968 5r multi .25 .25

Mahant Avaidyanath (1919-2014), Politician — A1969

Perf. 13¾ Syncopated

2015, Oct. 1		**Litho.**
2742 A1969 5r multi	.25	.25

Dr. Avul Pakir Jainulabdeen Abdul Kalam (1931-2015), President of India and Space Program Administrator A1970

2015, Oct. 15	**Litho.**	***Perf. 14x13¾***	
2743 A1970 5r multi		.25	.25

Spinning Wheels A1971

Inscriptions: No. 2744, 5r, Bardoli Charkha. No. 2745, 5r, Peti Charkha.

Perf. 13¾ Syncopated

2015, Oct. 15			**Litho.**
2744-2745 A1971	Set of 2	.30	.30
2745a	Souvenir sheet of 2, #2744-2745	*2.25*	*2.25*

Border Security Force, 50th Anniv. A1972

Perf. 13¾ Syncopated

2015, Oct. 21		**Litho.**
2746 A1972 5r multi	.25	.25

Third India-Africa Forum Summit A1973

Designs: No. 2747, 5r, Indian rhinoceros. No. 2748, 5r, African rhinoceros. No. 2749, 5r, Black buck. No. 2750, 5r, Thomson's gazelle. No. 2751, 25r, Indian lion. No. 2752, 25r, African lion.

Perf. 13¾ Syncopated

2015, Oct. 29			**Litho.**
2747-2752 A1973	Set of 6	2.25	2.25
2752a	Souvenir sheet of 6, #2747-2752	*6.00*	*6.00*

A souvenir sheet like No. 2752a with foil application and embossing sold for 200r.

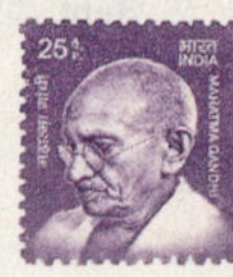

Famous People — A1974

Designs: 25p, Mahatma Gandhi (1869-1948). No. 2757, Shyama Prasad Mukherjee (1901-53), politician. No. 2758, Bhagat Singh (1907-31), revolutionary socialist. No. 2759, Ram Manohar Lohia (1910-67), independence activist. No. 2762, Lal Bahadur Shastri (1904-66), Prime minister. No. 2763, Jayaprakash Narayan (1902-79), political leader.

Perf. 12¾x13

2015-16	**Photo.**	**Wmk. 324**	
2753 A1974 25p slate lilac		.25	.25
2757 A1974 5r dull mauve		.25	.25
2758 A1974 5r lt brown		.25	.25
2759 A1974 5r reddish pur		.25	.25
2762 A1974 5r blue		.25	.25
2763 A1974 5r brn lake		.25	.25
Nos. 2753-2763 (6)		1.50	1.50

Issued: 25p, Jan. 2016; Nos. 2757, 2758, 2759, Oct. 2015; Nos. 2762, 2763, Feb. 2016. Additional stamps were issued in this set. The editors would like to examine any examples.

See Nos. 2792-2794, 2797, 2804.

Famous People Type of 2015-16

Designs: 50p, Subramania Bharati (1882-1921), writer. No. 2755, Deendayal Upadhyaya (1916-68), politician. No. 2756, Rajendra Prasad (1884-1963), first President of India. No. 2760, Swami Vivekananda (1863-1902), Hindu monk. No. 2761, Moulana Abul Kalam Azad (1888-1958), Minister of Education.

Perf. 12¾x13

2015-16	**Photo.**	**Wmk. 324**	
2754 A1974 50p slate vio		.25	.25
2755 A1974 5r reddish lil		.25	.25
2756 A1974 5r chestnut		.25	.25
2760 A1974 5r brown		.25	.25
2761 A1974 5r mauve		.25	.25
Nos. 2754-2761 (5)		1.25	1.25

Issued: 50p, Feb. 2016; Nos. 2755, 2756, 2760, 2761, Oct. 2015.

First Gorkha Rifles, 200th Anniv. A1975

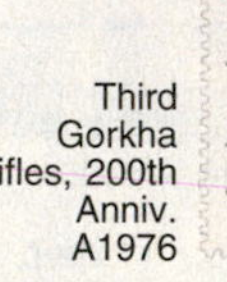

Third Gorkha Rifles, 200th Anniv. A1976

Perf. 13¾ Syncopated

2015, Nov. 2	**Litho.**	**Unwmk.**	
2764 A1975 5r multi		.25	.25
2765 A1976 5r multi		.25	.25

Children's Day A1977

Designs: 5r, Children playing in water. 25r, Children's drawing of children playing under rainbow.

Perf. 13¾ Syncopated

2015, Nov. 14			**Litho.**
2766-2767 A1977	Set of 2	.90	.90
2767a	Souvenir sheet of 2, #2766-2767	*4.25*	*4.25*

Bharat Heavy Electricals Limited, 51st Anniv. A1978

Perf. 13¾ Syncopated

2015, Nov. 16		**Litho.**
2768 A1978 5r multi	.25	.25

Diplomatic Relations Between India and Singapore, 50th Anniv. A1979

Presidential residences: 5r, Istana, Singapore. 25r, Rashtrapati Bhavan, India.

Perf. 13¾ Syncopated

2015, Nov. 24			**Litho.**
2769-2770 A1979	Set of 2	.90	.90

See Singapore Nos.

Engineering Export Promotion Council, 60th Anniv. — A1980

Perf. 13¾x13¼

2015, Nov. 24		**Litho.**
2771 A1980 5r multi	.25	.25

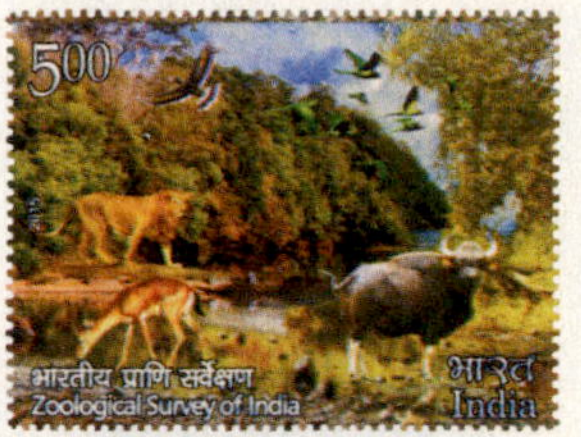

Zoological Survey of India, 99th Anniv. — A1981

Designs: 5r, Lion, birds, antelope, bull. 25r, Elephant, antelope, peacock, tiger, leopard.

2015, Dec. 3	**Litho.**	***Perf. 14½***	
2772-2773 A1981	Set of 2	.90	.90
2773a	Souvenir sheet of 2, #2772-2773	*4.25*	*4.25*

Sumitranandan Pant (1900-77), Poet — A1982

Perf. 13¼x13¾

2015, Dec. 23		**Litho.**
2774 A1982 5r multi	.25	.25

Alagumuthu Kone (1710-59), Freedom Fighter — A1983

Perf. 13¾x13¼

2015, Dec. 26		**Litho.**
2775 A1983 5r multi	.25	.25

Institute for Defense Studies and Analysis, 50th Anniv. A1984

Perf. 13¼x13¾

2015, Dec. 30		**Litho.**
2776 A1984 5r multi	.25	.25

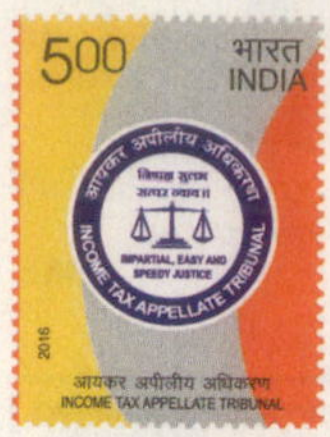

Income Tax Appellate Tribunal, 75th Anniv. — A1985

2016, Jan. 24	**Litho.**	***Perf. 13¾x13¼***	
2777 A1985 5r multi		.25	.25

Souvenir Sheet

Vibrant India — A1986

Perf. 13¾ Syncopated

2016, Jan. 25		**Litho.**
2778 A1986 25r multi	.75	.75

International Fleet Review A1987

2016, Feb. 6	**Litho.**	***Perf. 13¼x13¾***	
2779 A1987 5r multi		.25	.25

Stamps with Attached Labels

Beginning in 2016, Indian postal officials allowed "sponsored" stamps to be created. Such stamps, with attached labels much like earlier personalized stamp issues, could be designed by the sponsor (often a corporation), who would pay a fee for the printing of 5,000 sheets of stamps (60,000 stamps total). While the sponsor may not receive the entire printing of the stamps, and some of these stamps, if not all, may be available from post offices, the sheets were sold at prices well above the face value of the stamps. Because the labels on the sheets were already printed with designs of the sponsor's choosing, it is presumed that any purchaser of a sheet could not have the sponsor-designed labels personalized with another image. Unlike normal commemorative and definitive stamps, information about these sponsored stamps is not provided to the editors by the India postal authorities. Listings for stamps with attached labels will be limited to items the editors believe had labels that could be personalized by the public, such as the items below.

Ellora Caves — A1989

Victoria Memorial — A1990

Ghats of Varanasi — A1991

Ghats of Varanasi — A1992

Perf. 13¼

2016, Feb. 15 Litho. Unwmk.

2781 A1989 5r multi + label 1.60 1.60
2782 A1990 5r multi + label 1.60 1.60

Perf. 13¾ Syncopated

2783 A1991 5r multi + label 1.60 1.60
2784 A1992 5r multi + label 1.60 1.60
a. Horiz. pair, #2783-2784, + 2 labels 3.20 3.20
Nos. 2781-2784 (4) 6.40 6.40

Nos. 2781 and 2782 were each printed in sheets of 12 + 12 labels that could be personalized. Nos. 2783-2784 were printed together in sheets of 12 (6 of each design) + 12 labels that could be personlaized. Sheets sold for 300r.

Gateway of India — A1993

Sun Temple, Konark — A1994

Mahabodhi Temple — A1995

Perf. 13¾ Syncopated

2016, Feb. 29 Litho.

2785 A1993 5r multi + label 1.60 1.60
2786 A1994 5r multi + label 1.60 1.60

Perf. 13¾x13½

2787 A1995 5r multi + label 1.60 1.60
Nos. 2785-2787 (3) 4.80 4.80

Nos. 2785-2787 were each printed in sheets of 12 + 12 labels that could be personalized. Sheets sold for 300r.

Vasantrao Srinivassa Sinai Dempo (1916-2000), Industrialist A1996

Perf. 13¾ Syncopated

2016, Mar. 4 Litho.

2788 A1996 5r multi .25 .25

HeForShe Gender Equality Movement — A1997

No. 2789: a, 5r, Face at right. b, 25r, Face at left.

Perf. 13¾ Syncopated

2016, Mar. 8 Litho.

2789 A1997 Horiz. pair, #a-b .90 .90
c. Souvenir sheet of 2, #2789a-2789b, perf. 13¾x13¼ 3.75 3.75

Intl. Women's Day.

National Archives of India, 125th Anniv. — A1998

Perf. 13¾ Syncopated

2016, Mar. 11 Litho.

2790 A1998 5r multi .25 .25

Famous People Type of 2015-16 and

Yoga — A1999

Designs: 1r, Bal Gangadhar Tilak (1856-1920), independence activist. No. 2793, Madurai S. Subbulakshmi (1916-2004), Carnatic vocalist. No. 2794, Ravi Shankar (1920-2012), composer. 4r, Srinivasa Ramanujan (1887-1920), mathematician. No. 2795, Bismillah Khan (1916-2006), musician. No. 2796, Bhimsen Joshi (1922-2011), singer. No. 2798, Subhas Chandra Bose (1897-1945), nationalist leader. No. 2799, Sardar Vallabhbhai Patel (1875-1950), deputy prime minister. No. 2800, Dr. Bhimrao R. Ambedkar (1891-1956), politician. No. 2801, Jawaharlal Nehru (1889-1964), prime minister. No. 2802, Gopinath Bardoloi (1890-1950), Assamese politician. No. 2804, Chhtarapati Shri Shivaji Maharaj (c.1627-80), king. No. 2805, Maharana Pratap (1540-97), King of Mewar.

Perf. 12¾x13

2016 Photo. Wmk. 324

2791 A1999 25p multi .25 .25
2792 A1974 1r grnish gray .25 .25
2793 A1974 3r chocolate .25 .25
2794 A1974 3r deep claret .25 .25
2795 A1974 3r brn rose .25 .25
2796 A1974 3r dull pur .25 .25
2797 A1974 4r green .25 .25
2798 A1974 5r brown .25 .25
2799 A1974 5r olive brown .25 .25
2800 A1974 5r gray blue .25 .25
2801 A1974 5r slate lil .25 .25
2802 A1974 5r multi .25 .25
2804 A1974 10r red brown .25 .25
2805 A1974 10r dp turq blue .30 .30
Nos. 2791-2805 (14) 3.55 3.55

Issued: 1r, Nos. 2794, 2797, 2804, March. No. 2793, February. No. 2795, March; No. 2796, 6/16; No. 2798, April; No. 2799, 5/19; No. 2800, 5/25; Nos. 2801, 2805, June.

Additional stamps were issued in this set. The editors would like to examine any examples.

High Court of Allahabad, 150th Anniv. — A2000

No. 2808: a, 5r, Court building, Lucknow. b, 15r, Court building, Allahabad.

Perf. 13¾ Syncopated

2016, Mar. 13 Litho. Unwmk.

2808 A2000 Horiz. pair, a-b .60 .60
c. As "a," perf. 13¼x13¾ .85 .85
d. As "b," perf. 13¼x13¾ .85 .85
e. Souvenir sheet of 2, #2808c-2808d 3.25 3.25

Fire Services Day — A2001

Perf. 13¾ Syncopated

2016, Apr. 14 Litho.

2809 A2001 5r multi .25 .25

Govardhanram Tripathi (1855-1907), Writer — A2002

Perf. 13¾ Syncopated

2016, Apr. 27 Litho.

2810 A2002 5r multi .25 .25

Swami Chidananda (1916-2008), Religious Leader — A2003

2016, May 21 Litho. ***Perf. 13¾x13½***

2811 A2003 5r multi .25 .25

Tata Power, Cent. A2004

Perf. 13½x13¾

2016, June 10 Litho.

2812 A2004 5r multi .25 .25

Surya Namaskar A2005

Designs: Nos. 2813, 2824, Pranamasana. Nos. 2814, 2823, Hastauttanasana. Nos. 2815, 2822, Padahastasana. Nos. 2816, 2821, Asvasanchalanasana, horiz. Nos. 2817, 2820, Parvatasana, horiz. No. 2818, Ashtanga Namaskara, horiz. No. 2819, Bhujangasana.

Perf. 13¾x13½, 13½x13¾

2016, June 20 Litho.

2813 A2005 5r multi .25 .25
2814 A2005 5r multi .25 .25
2815 A2005 5r multi .25 .25
2816 A2005 5r multi .25 .25
a. Perf. 13¾ syncopated .55 .55
2817 A2005 5r multi .25 .25
a. Perf. 13¾ syncopated .55 .55
2818 A2005 5r multi .25 .25
a. Perf. 13¾ syncopated .55 .55
2819 A2005 25r multi .75 .75
a. Perf. 13¾ syncopated 2.60 2.60
2820 A2005 25r multi .75 .75
a. Perf. 13¾ syncopated 2.60 2.60
2821 A2005 25r multi .75 .75
a. Perf. 13¾ syncopated 2.60 2.60
2822 A2005 25r multi .75 .75
2823 A2005 25r multi .75 .75
2824 A2005 25r multi .75 .75
a. Souvenir sheet of 12, #2813-2815, 2316a-2321a, 2322-2324 12.50 12.50
Nos. 2813-2324 (12) 6.00 6.00

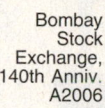

Bombay Stock Exchange, 140th Anniv. A2006

Perf. 13¾ Syncopated

2016, July 9 Litho.

2825 A2006 5r multi .25 .25

Tigers From Tadoba Andhari National Park — A2007

Designs: 5r, Two adults. 25r, Adult and cub, horiz.

Perf. 13¾ Syncopated

2016, July 29 Litho.

2826 A2007 5r multi .25 .25
a. Perf. 13¾x13½ .75 .75
2827 A2007 25r multi .65 .65
a. Perf. 13½x13¾ 3.50 3.50
b. Souvenir sheet of 2, #2826a, 2827a 4.25 4.25

2016 Summer Olympics, Rio de Janeiro — A2008

Designs: No. 2828, 5r, Badminton. No. 2829, 5r, Boxing. No. 2830, 25r, Shooting. No. 2831, 25r, Wrestling.

Perf. 13 Syncopated

2016, Aug. 5 Litho.

2828-2831 A2008 Set of 4 1.90 1.90
2831a Souvenir sheet of 4, #2828-2831 6.75 6.75

Orchids A2009

Designs: No. 2832, 5r, Esmerelda cathcartii. No. 2833, 5r, Paphiopedilum villosum. No. 2834, 15r, Dendrobium gibsonii. No. 2835, 15r, Esmerelda clarkei. No. 2836, 25r, Cypripedium himalacium. No. 2837, 25r, Dendrobium falconeri.

Perf. 13¾ Syncopated

2016, Aug. 8 Litho.

2832-2837 A2009 Set of 6 2.75 2.75
2837a Souvenir sheet of 4, #2832-2837 9.50 9.50

Souvenir Sheet

Tourist Sites in India — A2010

Perf. 13½x13¾

2016, Aug. 15 **Litho.**
2838 A2010 25r multi .75 .75

Independence Day.

Metal Crafts — A2011

Designs: No. 2839, 5r, Iron surahi. No. 2840, 5r, Bronze Nataraja. No. 2841, 15r, Copper pandan. No. 2842, 15r, Brass incense burner. No. 2843, 25r, Silver spouted lota. No. 2844, 25r, Gold Gajalakshmi lamp.

Perf. 13 Syncopated

2016, Aug. 26 **Litho.**
2839-2844 A2011 Set of 6 2.75 2.75
2844a Souvenir sheet of 6, #2839-2844 *9.50 9.50*

Jagadguru Sri Shivarathri Rajendra Swamy (1916-86), Religious Leader — A2012

Perf. 13¾ Syncopated

2016, Aug. 27 **Litho.**
2845 A2012 5r multi .25 .25

Souvenir Sheet

Canonization of St. Teresa of Calcutta (Mother Teresa) — A2013

2016, Sept. 4 **Litho.** *Perf. 13¾x13½*
2846 A2013 50r multi 1.50 1.50

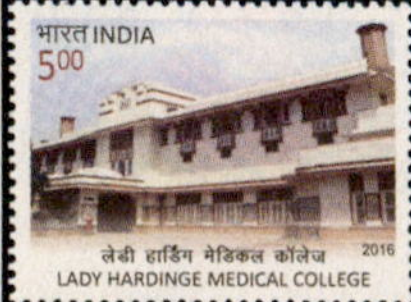

Lady Hardinge Medical College, New Delhi, Cent. A2014

Perf. 13½x13¾

2016, Sept. 23 **Litho.**
2847 A2014 5r multi .25 .25

Swachh Bharat (Campaign to Clean India) — A2015

Winning art in stamp design contest depicting: 5r, People cleaning street. 25r, Sun, flowers, waves, water, hills.

Perf. 13¾ Syncopated

2016, Oct. 2 **Litho.**
2848 A2015 5r multi .25 .25
a. Perf. 13¾x13½ *.65 .65*
2849 A2015 25r multi .65 .65
a. Perf. 13¾x13½ *3.25 3.25*
b. Souvenir sheet of 2, #2848a, 2849a *4.00 4.00*

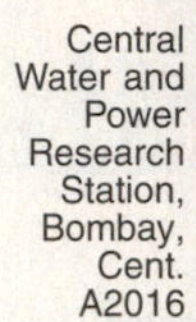

Central Water and Power Research Station, Bombay, Cent. A2016

Perf. 13¾ Syncopated

2016, Oct. 4 **Litho.**
2850 A2016 5r multi .25 .25

Introduction of C-130J Super Hercules Aircraft, 5th Anniv. A2017

Perf. 13¾ Syncopated

2016, Oct. 6 **Litho.**
2851 A2017 5r multi .25 .25

Threatened Birds — A2018

Designs: 5r, Nicobar pigeon. 10r, Nilgiri flycatcher. 15r, Andaman woodpecker. 25r, Black and orange flycatcher.

2016, Oct. 17 **Litho.** *Perf. 13¾x13½*
2852 A2018 5r multi .25 .25
2853 A2018 10r multi .30 .30

Perf. 13¾ Syncopated

2854 A2018 15r multi .45 .45
a. Perf. 13¾x13½ *2.10 2.10*
2855 A2018 25r multi .75 .75
a. Perf. 13¾x13½ *3.50 3.50*
b. Souvenir sheet of 4, #2852-2853, 2854a, 2855a *6.25 6.25*
Nos. 2852-2855 (4) 1.75 1.75

Renaming of Banaras to Varanasi, 60th Anniv. A2019

Perf. 13¾ Syncopated

2016, Oct. 24 **Litho.**
2856 A2019 5r multi .25 .25

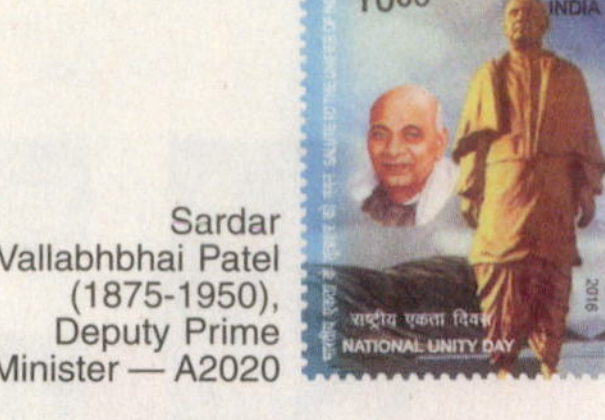

Sardar Vallabhbhai Patel (1875-1950), Deputy Prime Minister — A2020

Perf. 13¾ Syncopated

2016, Oct. 31 **Litho.**
2857 A2020 10r multi .25 .25

National Unity Day.

Haryana State, 50th Anniv. A2021

Perf. 13¾ Syncopated

2016, Nov. 1 **Litho.**
2858 A2021 5r multi .25 .25

Children's Day — A2022

Picnic scenes with "Children's Day" in: No. 2859, Royal blue. No. 2860, Red, horiz.

Perf. 13¾x13½

2016, Nov. 14 **Litho.** **Unwmk.**
2859 A2022 15r multi .45 .45

Perf. 13½x13¾

2860 A2022 15r multi .45 .45
a. Perf. 13¾ Syncopated .70 .70
b. Souvenir sheet of 2, #2859, 2860a 1.50 1.50

Third Battalion of the Garhwal Rifles, Cent. — A2023

Perf. 13¾x13½

2016, Nov. 19 **Litho.**
2861 A2023 5r multi .25 .25

All India Institute of Medical Sciences, 60th Anniv. A2024

Perf. 13¾ Syncopated

2016, Dec. 3 **Litho.**
2862 A2024 5r multi .25 .25

Birds A2025

Designs: No. 2863, 5r, Cape parrot. No. 2864, 5r, Blue-throated macaw, vert. No. 2865, 10r, Hyacinth macaw. No. 2866, 10r, Sun conure, vert. No. 2867, 15r, Lesser sulphur-crested cockatoo. No. 2868, 15r, Magnum Amazon.

Perf. 13¾ Syncopated

2016, Dec. 5 **Litho.**
2863-2868 A2025 Set of 6 1.75 1.75
2867a Souvenir sheet of 3, #2863, 2865, 2867 *3.50 3.50*
2868a Souvenir sheet of 3, #2864, 2866, 2868 *3.50 3.50*

A2026

No. 2869: a, 5r, Pramukh Swami Maharaj (1921-2016), religious leader (39x39mm). b, 15r, Akshardham Temple, New Delhi (52x39mm).

2016, Dec. 7 **Litho.** *Perf. 14¼*
2869 A2026 Horiz. pair, #a-b .60 .60

Acharya Vimal Sagar (1916-94), Jain Monk — A2027

Perf. 13¾ Syncopated

2016, Dec. 14 **Litho.**
2870 A2027 5r multi .25 .25

Samrat Vikramadittya, Legendary Emperor of India — A2028

Perf. 13¾x13½

2016, Dec. 22 **Litho.**
2871 A2028 5r multi .25 .25

Christmas A2029

Designs: 10r, Christmas tree and gifts. 20r, Santa Claus, reindeer and sleigh, horiz.

Perf. 13¾ Syncopated

2016, Dec. 23 **Litho.**
2872 A2029 10r multi .30 .30
a. Perf. 13¾x13¼ *1.50 1.50*
2873 A2029 20r multi .60 .60
a. Perf. 13¼x13¾ *2.75 2.75*
b. Souvenir sheet of 2, #2872a, 2873a *4.25 4.25*

Hardayal Municipal Heritage Public Library A2030

Perf. 13¾ Syncopated

2016, Dec. 26 **Litho.**
2874 A2030 5r multi .25 .25

Sachchidananda Sinha (1871-1950), Politician — A2031

Kunwar Singh (1777-1858), Leader of Rebellion of 1857 — A2032

Dashrath Manjhi (1934-2007), Mountain Path Builder — A2033

Kailashpati Mishra (1923-2012), Politician — A2034

Karpoori Thakur (1920-88), Politician — A2035

Vidyapati (1352-1448), Writer — A2036

Phanishwar Nath Renu (1921-77), Writer — A2037

Sri Krishna Sinha (1887-1961), Politician — A2038

Perf. 13¾ Syncopated

2016, Dec. 26 **Litho.**

2875 A2031 5r multi .25 .25
2876 A2032 5r multi .25 .25
2877 A2033 5r multi .25 .25
2878 A2034 5r multi .25 .25
2879 A2035 5r multi .25 .25
2880 A2036 5r multi .25 .25

Perf. 13¾x13¼

2881 A2037 5r multi .25 .25
2882 A2038 5r multi .25 .25
Nos. 2875-2882 (8) 2.00 2.00

Famous men of Bihar.

Deendayal Upadhyaya (1916-68), Politician — A2039

Perf. 13¾x13½

2016, Dec. 29 **Litho.**

2883 A2039 10r multi .30 .30

Singers — A2040

Designs: No. 2884, Talat Mahmood (1924-98). No. 2885, Manna Dey (1919-2013). No. 2886, Mohammed Rafi (1924-80). No. 2887, Kishore Kumar (1929-87). No. 2888, Mukesh (1923-76). No. 2889, Hemant Kumar (1920-89). No. 2890, Bhupen Hazarika (1926-2011). No. 2891, Geeta Dutt (1930-72). No. 2892, T. M. Soundararajan (1922-2013). No. 2893, Shamshad Begum (1919-2013).

Perf. 13¾ Syncopated

2016, Dec. 30 **Litho.**

2884 A2040 5r multi .25 .25
a. Perf. 13¾x13½ .30 .30
2885 A2040 5r multi .25 .25
a. Perf. 13¾x13½ .30 .30
2886 A2040 5r multi .25 .25
a. Perf. 13¾x13½ .30 .30
2887 A2040 5r multi .25 .25
a. Perf. 13¾x13½ .30 .30
2888 A2040 5r multi .25 .25
a. Perf. 13¾x13½ .30 .30
2889 A2040 5r multi .25 .25
a. Perf. 13¾x13½ .30 .30
2890 A2040 5r multi .25 .25
a. Perf. 13¾x13½ .30 .30
2891 A2040 5r multi .25 .25
a. Perf. 13¾x13½ .00 .30
2892 A2040 5r multi .25 .25
a. Perf. 13¾x13½ .30 .30
2893 A2040 5r multi .25 .25
a. Perf. 13¾x13½ .30 .30
b. Souvenir sheet of 10, #2884a-2893a 3.00 3.00
Nos. 2884-2893 (10) 2.50 2.50

Miniature Sheet

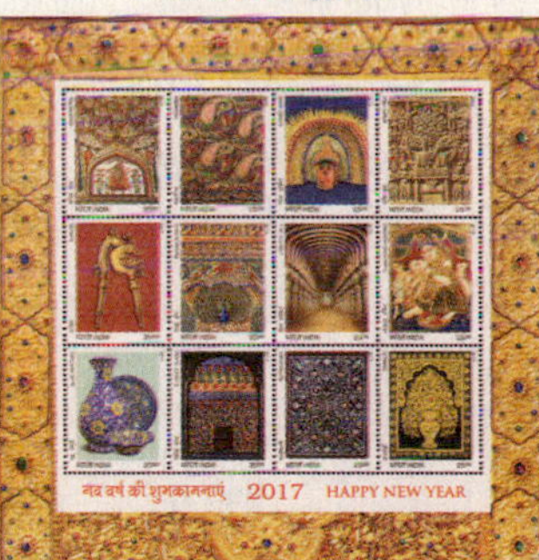

New Year 2017 — A2041

No. 2894: a, Ganesh Pol. b, Pashmina wool shawl. c, Chhau mask. d, Worship of the Bodhi Tree sculpture, Sanchi Stupa Complex. e, Sarota. f, Peacock Gate decoration, Chandra Mahal. g, Chaitya Hall, Karle. h, Thanjavur painting. i, Blue pottery. j, Stained-glass window, Bagore-Ki-Haveli, Udaipur. k, Peitra Dura table top. l, Zardozi carpet.

Perf. 13 Syncopated

2017, Jan. 1 **Litho.**

2894 A2041 25r Sheet of 12, #a-l 12.00 12.00

A calendar with each page bearing one each of Nos. 2894a-2894l in a larger size sold for 1000r.

Sikh Temple A2042

2017, Jan. 5 **Litho.** ***Perf. 14½***

2895 A2042 10r multi .30 .30
a. Souvenir sheet of 1 .70 .70

Guru Gobind Singh (1666-1708), 10th Sikh guru.

Dancers A2043

Designs: 5r, Dandiya dancers, India. 25r, Pauliteiros dancers, Portugal.

2017, Jan. 7 **Litho.** ***Perf. 13½x13¾***

2896 A2043 5r multi .25 .25
a. Perf. 13¾ Syncopated .30 .30
2897 A2043 25r multi .75 .75
a. Perf. 13¾ Syncopated 1.25 1.25
b. Souvenir sheet of 2, #2896a, 2897a 1.60 1.60

Diplomatic Relations between India and Portugal.
See Portugal Nos.

Dr. M. G. Ramachandran (1917-87), Film Actor and Politician — A2044

Perf. 13¾ Syncopated

2017, Jan. 17 **Litho.**

2898 A2044 15r multi .45 .45

Indian Fauna — A2045

Designs: No. 2899, Peacock. No. 2900, Elephants. No. 2901, Cranes. No. 2902, Tiger, horiz. No. 2903, Butterfly, horiz. No. 2904, Deer, horiz.

2017, Jan. 25 **Litho.** ***Perf. 13¾x13½***

2899 A2045 5r multi .25 .25
a. Perf. 13¾ Syncopated .30 .30
2900 A2045 5r multi .25 .25
a. Perf. 13¾ Syncopated .30 .30
2901 A2045 5r multi .25 .25
a. Perf. 13¾ Syncopated .30 .30

Perf. 13½x13¾

2902 A2045 5r multi .25 .25
a. Perf. 13¾ Syncopated .30 .30
2903 A2045 5r multi .25 .25
a. Perf. 13¾ Syncopated .30 .30
2904 A2045 5r multi .25 .25
a. Perf. 13¾ Syncopated .30 .30
b. Souvenir sheet of 6, #2899a-2904a 1.90 1.90
Nos. 2899-2904 (6) 1.50 1.50

India Post Payments Bank — A2046

Perf. 13¾ Syncopated

2017, Jan. 30 **Litho.**

2905 A2046 5r multi .25 .25

Miniature Sheet

Traditional Headcoverings — A2047

No. 2906: a, Haryanvi turban. b, Hornbill warrior cap. c, Gujarati turban. d, Bison horn Maria tribal cap. e, Rajasthani turban. f, Himachali cap. g, Angami tribal cap. h, Japi cap. i, Puneri turban. j, Naga hat. k, Mysore peta. l, Dastar. m, Karakul cap. n, Mithila turban. o, Brokpa tribe tepi. p, Gonda Ladakhi cap.

2017, Feb. 10 **Litho.** ***Perf. 14½***

2906 A2047 10r Sheet of 16, #a-p 6.50 6.50

Poona Horse Regiment, 200th Anniv. — A2048

Perf. 13¾x13½

2017, Feb. 11 **Litho.**

2907 A2048 5r multi .25 .25

Ramjas College, Cent. A2049

Perf. 13¾ Syncopated

2017, Feb. 13 **Litho.**

2908 A2049 5r multi .25 .25

A2050

A2051

A2052

Ladybugs A2053

Perf. 13½x13¾

2017, Feb. 23 **Litho.**

2909 A2050 5r multi .25 .25
a. Perf. 13¾ Syncopated .30 .30
2910 A2051 5r multi .25 .25
a. Perf. 13¾ Syncopated .30 .30
2911 A2052 15r multi .45 .45
a. Perf. 13¾ Syncopated .80 .80
2912 A2053 15r multi .45 .45
a. Perf. 13¾ Syncopated .80 .80
b. Souvenir sheet of 4, #2909a-2912a 2.25 2.25
Nos. 2909-2912 (4) 1.40 1.40

Yogoda Satsanga Society of India, Cent. — A2054

Perf. 13¾x13 Syncopated

2017, Mar. 7 **Litho.**

2913 A2054 5r multi .25 .25

Methods of Transportation — A2055

No. 2914: a, Long palanquin. b, Meeana palanquin. c, Boutcha palanquin. d, Chowpaul palanquin.

No. 2915: a, Bullock cart. b, Rath bullock cart. c, Tonga. d, Horse carriage.

No. 2916: a, Cycle rickshaw. b, Motorcycle rickshaw. c, Hand rickshaw. d, School rickshaw.

No. 2917: a, Tram. b, Metro. c, Double-decker bus. d, Bus.

No. 2918: a, 1909 Rolls-Royce. b, 1926 Austin. c, 1932 Chevrolet. d, 1938 Ford.

2017, Mar. 25 **Litho.** *Perf. 13*

2914 Horiz. strip of 4 3.00 3.00
a. A2055 5r multi .25 .25
b. A2055 10r multi .55 .55
c. A2055 15r multi .80 .80
d. A2055 25r multi 1.40 1.40
2915 Horiz. strip of 4 3.00 3.00
a. A2055 5r multi .25 .25
b. A2055 10r multi .55 .55
c. A2055 15r multi .80 .80
d. A2055 25r multi 1.40 1.40
2916 Horiz. strip of 4 3.00 3.00
a. A2055 5r multi .25 .25
b. A2055 10r multi .55 .55
c. A2055 15r multi .80 .80
d. A2055 25r multi 1.40 1.40
2917 Horiz. strip of 4 3.00 3.00
a. A2055 5r multi .25 .25
b. A2055 10r multi .55 .55
c. A2055 15r multi .80 .80
d. A2055 25r multi 1.40 1.40
2918 Horiz. strip of 4 3.00 3.00
a. A2055 5r multi .25 .25
b. A2055 10r multi .55 .55
c. A2055 15r multi .80 .80
d. A2055 25r multi 1.40 1.40
Nos. 2914-2918 (5) 15.00 15.00

Cub Scouts, Cent. (in 2016) A2056

Perf. 13½x13¾

2017, Mar. 30 **Litho.**

2919 A2056 5r multi .25 .25

Deekshabhoomi — A2057

No. 2920: a, Statue of Buddha, Dr. B. R. Ambedkar (1891-1956), governmental minister (39x39mm). b, Deekshabhoomi Stupa (52x39mm).

2017, Apr. 14 **Litho.** *Perf. 14¼*

2920 A2057 5r Horiz. pair, #a-b .30 .30

Bharat Ratna Bhimrao Ambedkar Institute of Telecom Training, Jabalpur — A2058

Perf. 13¾ Syncopated

2017, Apr. 22 **Litho.**

2921 A2058 15r multi .50 .50
a. Souvenir sheet of 1, perf. 13¾x13½ .90 .90

Souvenir Sheet

Coffee — A2059

Perf. 13¾ Syncopated

2017, Apr. 23 **Litho.**

2922 A2059 100r multi 3.25 3.25

No. 2922 is impregnated with a coffee scent.

Viswanatha Satyanarayana (1895-1976), Writer — A2060

Tarigonda Vengamamba (1730-1817), Poet — A2061

Aatukuri Molla (1440-1530), Poet — A2062

Perf. 13¾ Syncopated

2017, Apr. 26 **Litho.**

2923 A2060 5r multi .25 .25
2924 A2061 5r multi .25 .25
2925 A2062 5r multi .25 .25
Nos. 2923-2925 (3) .75 .75

Ramanujacharya (c. 1017-1137), Philosopher A2063

2017, May 1 **Litho.** *Perf. 13¾x13½*

2926 A2063 25r multi .80 .80

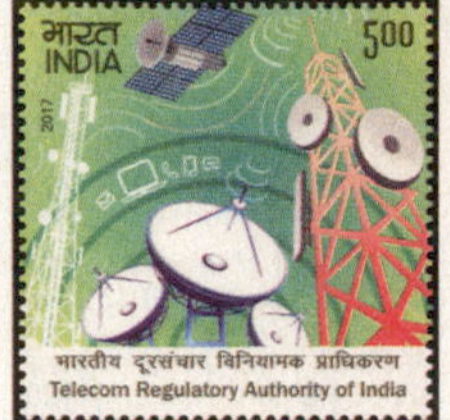

Telecom Regulatory Authority, 20th Anniv. A2064

2017, May 5 **Litho.** *Perf. 14¼*

2927 A2064 5r multi .25 .25

Champaran Satyagraha (First Civil Resistance Inspired by Mahatma Gandhi), Cent. — A2065

Designs: 5r, Gandhi and quotation. 10r, Gandhi's wife, Kasturbai, statue of Gandhi in Champaran (39x39mm). 25r, Gandhi, workers in indigo field (68x39mm).

2017, May 13 **Litho.** *Perf. 13¾x13½*

2928 A2065 5r multi .25 .25
a. Perf. 13¾x13x13¾x14¼ .30 .30

Perf. 14¼

2929 A2065 10r multi .30 .30
a. Perf. 13¾x14¼x13¾x13 .40 .40

Perf. 13x13¾

2930 A2065 25r multi .30 .30
a. Perf. 13¾x14¼ .90 .90
b. Souvenir sheet of 3, #2928a-2930a 1.60 1.60
Nos. 2928-2930 (3) .85 .85

Birth of Shri Hanagal Kumaraswamiji, Religious Leader, 150th Anniv. — A2066

2017, May 19 **Litho.** *Perf. 13¾x13½*

2931 A2066 5r multi .25 .25

Balwant Gargi (1916-2003), Writer — A2067

Shrilal Shukla (1925-2011), Writer — A2068

K. V. Puttappa (1904-94), Writer — A2069

Bhisham Sahni (1915-2003), Writer — A2070

Krishan Chander (1914-77), Writer — A2071

2017, May 31 **Litho.** *Perf. 13¾x13½*

2932 A2067 10r multi .35 .35
2933 A2068 10r multi .35 .35

Perf. 13¾ Syncopated

2934 A2069 10r multi .35 .35
a. Perf. 13¾x13½ .50 .50
2935 A2070 10r multi .35 .35
a. Perf. 13¾x13½ .50 .50
2936 A2071 10r multi .35 .35
a. Perf. 13¾x13½ .50 .50
b. Souvenir sheet of 5, #2932-2933, 2934a-2936a 2.50 2.50
Nos. 2932-2936 (5) 1.75 1.75

Jhala Manna, 16th Cent. Rajput Warrior — A2072

Perf. 13¾ Syncopated

2017, June 18 **Litho.**

2937 A2072 5r multi .25 .25

Survey of India, 250th Anniv. — A2073

Designs: 5r, Emblem. 15r, Theodolite.

Perf. 13¾ Syncopated

2017, June 22 **Litho.**

2938 A2073 5r multi .25 .25
a. Perf. 13¾x13½ .30 .30
2939 A2073 15r multi .50 .50
a. Perf. 13¾x13½ .95 .95
b. Souvenir sheet of 2, #2938a-2939a 1.25 1.25

Passports Act, 50th Anniv. — A2074

2017, June 23 **Litho.** *Perf. 13¾*

2940 A2074 25r multi .80 .80

Banaras Hindu University, Cent. (in 2016) — A2075

No. 2941: a, 5r, Gate (39x32mm). b, 15r, Building (58x32mm).

2017, June 28 Litho. *Perf. 13*
2941 A2075 Horiz. pair, #a-b .70 .70

Shrimad Rajchandraji (1867-1901), Poet A2076

Perf. 13½x13¾
2017, June 29 Litho.
2942 A2076 5r multi .25 .25

A2077

A2078

A2079

A2080

A2081

A2082

A2083

1942 Freedom Movement, 75th Anniv. A2084

2017, Aug. 9 Litho. *Perf. 13¼*
2943 A2077 5r multi .25 .25
a. Perf. 13 .30 .30
2944 A2078 5r multi .25 .25
a. Perf. 13 .30 .30
2945 A2079 5r multi .25 .25
a. Perf. 13 .30 .30
2946 A2080 5r multi .25 .25
a. Perf. 13 .30 .30
2947 A2081 5r multi .25 .25
a. Perf. 13 .30 .30
2948 A2082 5r multi .25 .25
a. Perf. 13 .30 .30
2949 A2083 5r multi .25 .25
a. Perf. 13 .30 .30
2950 A2084 5r multi .25 .25
a. Perf. 13 .30 .30
b. Souvenir sheet of 8, #2943a-2950a 2.40 2.40
Nos. 2943-2950 (8) 2.00 2.00

A2085

Winning Photographs in "Beautiful India" Photography Competition A2086

Perf. 13¾ Syncopated
2017, Aug. 15 Litho.
2951 A2085 15r multi .50 .50
a. Perf. 13½x13¾ .75 .75
2952 A2086 15r multi .50 .50
a. Perf. 13¾x13½ .75 .75
b. Souvenir sheet of 2, #2951a-2952a 1.50 1.50

Caves of Meghalaya A2087

Designs: No. 2953, Krem Blang. No. 2954, Krem Khung, horiz. No. 2955, Krem Syndai, horiz. No. 2956, Krem Lymput.

Perf. 13¾ Syncopated (#2953, 2956), 13½x13¾
2017, Aug. 15 Litho.
2953 A2087 5r multi .25 .25
a. Perf. 13¾x13½ .30 .30
2954 A2087 5r multi .25 .25
2955 A2087 5r multi .25 .25
2956 A2087 5r multi .25 .25
a. Perf. 13¾x13½ .30 .30
b. Souvenir sheet of 4, #2953a, 2954-2955, 2956a 1.25 1.25
Nos. 2953-2956 (4) 1.00 1.00

Diplomatic Relations Between India and Belarus, 25th Anniv. A2088

Perf. 13½x13¾
2017, Sept. 12 Litho.
2957 A2088 25r multi .80 .80
a. Souvenir sheet of 1, perf. 13¾ syncopated 1.25 1.25

See Belarus No. 1058.

Vulnerable Birds A2089

Designs: No. 2958, Nilgiri wood pigeon. No. 2959, Broad-tailed grass warbler. No. 2960, Nilgiri pipit.

Perf. 13½x13¾
2017, Sept. 18 Litho.
2958 A2089 5r multi .25 .25
a. Perf. 13¾ Syncopated .30 .30
2959 A2089 5r multi .25 .25
a. Perf. 13¾ Syncopated .30 .30
2960 A2089 5r multi .25 .25
a. Perf. 13¾ Syncopated .30 .30
b. Souvenir sheet of 3, #2958a-2960a .90 .90
Nos. 2958-2960 (3) .75 .75

Diwali — A2090

Designs: 5r, Diwali lamp. 25r, Diwali lamp, diff.

Perf. 13¾x13½
2017, Sept. 21 Litho.
2961 A2090 5r multi .25 .25
a. Perf. 13¾ Syncopated .30 .30
2962 A2090 25r multi .80 .80
a. Perf. 13¾ Syncopated 1.10 1.10
b. Souvenir sheet of 2, #2961a-2962a 1.50 1.50

See Canada Nos. 3023-3025. A perf. 13¼ version of No. 2962 is found on Canada No. 3023, which was sold by Canada Post.

Rama and Sita Marrying A2091

A2092 (Banishment of Rama)

Banishment of Rama — A2092

Bharata Meeting Rama A2093

Crossing the Ganges A2094

Rama and Jatayu A2095

Rama and Shabari A2096

Hanuman and Sita A2097

Building Bridge Across Sea A2098

Hanuman Flying and Holding Mountain — A2099

Rama Killing Ravana A2100

Rama and His Court — A2101

2017, Sept. 22 Litho. *Perf. 13x13¾*
2963 Sheet of 11 3.00 3.00
a. A2091 5r multi .25 .25
b. A2092 5r multi .25 .25
c. A2093 5r multi .25 .25
d. A2094 5r multi .25 .25
e. A2095 5r multi .25 .25
f. A2096 5r multi .25 .25
g. A2097 5r multi .25 .25
h. A2098 5r multi .25 .25
i. A2099 5r multi .25 .25
j. A2100 5r multi .25 .25
k. A2101 15r multi .50 .50
l. Sheet of 12, #2963a-2963k, green sheet margin 3.00 3.00

Epic poem, Ramayana. Nos. 2963 and 2963l were printed by different printers. No. 2963 has a 187x240mm sheet margin with a brown purple background. No. 2963l has a 236x141mm green and light green sheet margin. The colors on the stamps on No. 2963 are darker than the stamps on No. 2963l, most noticeable with dark blue shades. On No. 2963l, the separation between Nos. 2963b and 2963c and 2963h and 2963i is perf. 13.

Rapid Action Force, 25th Anniv. A2102

2017, Oct. 7 Litho. ***Perf. 13½x13¾***
2964 A2102 5r multi .25 .25

Nanaji Deshmukh (1916-2010), Politician — A2103

2017, Oct. 11 Litho. ***Perf. 13¾x13½***
2965 A2103 5r multi .25 .25

Chhatrapati Shivaji International Airport, Mumbai, 75th Anniv. A2104

Designs: 5r, Interior of terminal. 15r, Airplane and exterior of terminal (58x29mm).

2017, Oct. 15 Litho. ***Perf. 13½x13¾***
2966 A2104 5r multi .25 .25
a. Perf. 13¾ .30 .30

Perf. 13¾

2967 A2104 15r multi .50 .50
a. Souvenir sheet of 2, #2966a, 2967 1.00 1.00

3 Kumaon Rifles Battalion, Cent. — A2105

2017, Oct. 23 Litho. ***Perf. 13¾x13½***
2968 A2105 5r multi .25 .25

Beryozka Dancers, Russia A2106

Bhavai Dancers, India A2107

Perf. 13¾ Syncopated

2017, Oct. 26 **Litho.**
2969 A2106 5r multi .25 .25
a. Perf. 13½x13¾ .30 .30
2970 A2107 25r multi .80 .80
a. Perf. 13½x13¾ 1.10 1.10
b. Souvenir sheet of 2, #2969a, 2970a 1.50 1.50

Diplomatic Relation between India and Russia.

See Russia Nos.

Draksharamam Bhimeswara Temple — A2108

Adikavi Nannaya, 11th Cent. Writer A2109

Kavi Muddana (1870-1901), Poet — A2110

Perf. 13¾ Syncopated

2017, Nov. 1 **Litho.**
2971 A2108 5r multi .25 .25
2972 A2109 5r multi .25 .25
2973 A2110 5r multi .25 .25
Nos. 2971-2973 (3) .75 .75

A2113

A2114

A2115

A2116

A2117

A2118

A2119

A2120

A2121

A2122

A2123

A2124

A2125

A2126

A2127

A2128

A2129

Mahabharat A2130

Perf. 13¼x13 (15r, 25r), 13¾x13 (50r), 13 (100r)

2017, Nov. 27 **Litho.**
2977 Sheet of 18 14.50 14.50
a. A2113 15r multi .50 .50
b. A2114 15r multi .50 .50
c. A2115 15r multi .50 .50
d. A2116 15r multi .50 .50
e. A2117 15r multi .50 .50
f. A2118 15r multi .50 .50
g. A2119 15r multi .50 .50
h. A2120 15r multi .50 .50
i. A2121 15r multi .50 .50
j. A2122 15r multi .50 .50
k. A2123 15r multi .50 .50
l. A2124 15r multi .50 .50
m. A2125 25r multi .80 .80
n. A2126 25r multi .80 .80
o. A2127 25r multi .80 .80
p. A2128 25r multi .80 .80
q. A2129 50r multi 1.60 1.60
r. A2130 100r multi 3.25 3.25
s. Souvenir sheet of 1 #2977q 2.00 2.00
t. Souvenir sheet of 1 #2977r 4.00 4.00

INS Kalvari — A2131

2017, Dec. 7 **Litho.** ***Perf. 13¾***
2978 A2131 5r multi .25 .25
a. Souvenir sheet of 3 1.25 1.25

Cent. of Death of Shri Shirdi Sai Baba, Religious Leader (in 2018) — A2132

Perf. 13¾x13½

2017, Dec. 15			**Litho.**	
2979	A2132	5r multi	.25	.25

Dr. Shambhunath Singh (1916-91), Poet — A2133

Perf. 13¾x13½

2017, Dec. 26			**Litho.**	
2980	A2133	5r multi	.25	.25

Dadabhai Naoroji (1825-1917), Member of British House of Commons — A2135

Perf. 13¼ Syncopated

2017, Dec. 29			**Litho.**	
2982	A2135	5r multi	.25	.25

AIR POST STAMPS

De Havilland Hercules over Lake AP1

Wmk. 196 Sideways

1929-30		**Typo.**	***Perf. 14***	
C1	AP1	2a dull green	1.00	.50
C2	AP1	3a deep blue	1.40	.90
C3	AP1	4a gray olive	4.00	1.90
a.		4a olive green ('30)	5.00	1.90
C4	AP1	6a bister	5.00	1.10
C5	AP1	8a red violet	5.75	5.75
C6	AP1	12a brown red	17.50	17.50
		Nos. C1-C6 (6)	34.65	27.65
		Set, never hinged	60.00	

Catalogue values for unused stamps in this section, from this point to the end of the section, are for Never Hinged items.

Dominion of India

Lockheed Constellation — AP2

Perf. 13½x14

1948, May 29		**Litho.**	**Wmk. 196**	
C7	AP2	12a ultra & slate blk	3.25	3.25

Bombay-London flight of June 8, 1948.

Republic of India

The Spirit of '76, by Archibald M. Willard — AP3

1976, May 29			***Perf. 13x13½***	
C8	AP3	2.80r multicolored	2.00	2.00

American Bicentennial.

INDIA '80 Emblem, De Havilland Puss Moth AP4

1979, Oct. 15		**Photo.**	***Perf. 14½x14***	
C9	AP4	30p shown	.60	.30
C10	AP4	50p Chetak helicopter	.75	.50
C11	AP4	1r Boeing 737	.95	.90
C12	AP4	2r Boeing 747	1.25	1.10
		Nos. C9-C12 (4)	3.55	2.80

INDIA '80 Intl. Stamp Exhib., New Delhi, Jan. 25-Feb. 3, 1980.

MILITARY STAMPS

China Expeditionary Force

Regular Issues of India, 1882-99, Overprinted

1900		**Wmk. 39**	***Perf. 14***	
M1	A31	3p carmine rose	.70	2.10
M2	A17	½a dark green	1.25	.45
M3	A19	1a maroon	7.00	2.50
M4	A21	2a ultra	5.25	15.00
M5	A28	2a6p green	4.75	21.00
M6	A22	3a orange	4.75	27.50
M7	A23	4a olive green	4.75	13.00
M8	A25	8a red violet	4.75	30.00
M9	A26	12a violet, *red*	30.00	30.00
M10	A29	1r car rose & grn	37.50	37.50
a.		Double overprint		
		Nos. M1-M10 (10)	100.70	179.05

The 1a6p of this set was overprinted, but not issued. Value $250.

Overprinted on 1900 Issue of India

1904, Feb. 27				
M11	A19	1a carmine rose	55.00	15.00

Overprinted on 1902-09 Issue of India

1904				
M12	A32	3p gray	8.00	10.00
M13	A34	1a carmine rose	12.00	1.10
M14	A35	2a violet	22.50	3.75
M15	A36	2a6p ultra	5.25	8.00
M16	A37	3a brown org	5.75	6.50
M17	A38	4a olive green	13.50	19.00
M18	A40	8a red violet	13.00	12.00
M19	A41	12a violet, *red*	18.00	30.00
M20	A42	1r car rose & grn	20.00	45.00
		Nos. M12-M20 (9)	118.00	135.35

Overprinted on 1906 Issue of India

1909				
M21	A44	½a green	1.50	1.00
M22	A45	1a carmine rose	1.50	.40

Overprinted on 1911-19 Issues of India

1913-21				
M23	A46	3p gray	8.00	35.00
M24	A47	½a green	6.25	7.50
M25	A48	1a car rose	7.25	4.75
M26	A58	1½a chocolate	40.00	95.00
M27	A49	2a violet	27.50	80.00
M28	A57	2a6p ultra	20.00	30.00
M29	A51	3a brn org	40.00	240.00
M30	A52	4a ol grn	37.50	210.00
M31	A54	8a red violet	40.00	400.00
M32	A55	12a claret	37.50	140.00
M33	A56	1r grn & red brn	110.00	375.00
		Nos. M23-M33 (11)	374.00	1,617.

Issue dates: No. M23, 1913; others, 1921.

Indian Expeditionary Force

Regular Issues of India, 1911-13, Overprinted

1914		**Wmk. 39**	***Perf. 14***	
M34	A46	3p gray	.30	.55
a.		Double overprint	70.00	55.00
M35	A47	½a green	.80	.55
a.		Double overprint	175.00	300.00
M36	A48	1a car rose	2.10	.55
M37	A49	2a violet	2.10	.55
M38	A57	2a6p ultra	2.50	4.00
M39	A51	3a brn org	1.75	2.75
M40	A52	4a olive grn	1.75	2.75
M41	A54	8a red violet	2.10	4.25
M42	A55	12a claret	3.75	10.50
M43	A56	1r grn & red brn	4.50	7.25
		Nos. M34-M43 (10)	21.65	33.70

Catalogue values for unused stamps in this section, from this point to the end of the section, are for Never Hinged items.

Korea Custodial Unit

Regular Issues of India Overprinted in Black

Perf. 13½x14, 14x13½

1953			**Wmk. 196**	
M44	A91	3p gray violet	.35	5.50
M45	A92	6p red brown	.35	5.50
M46	A91	9p green	.35	4.50
M47	A101	1a turquoise	.50	4.50
M48	A93	2a carmine	.80	4.50
M49	A94	2½a brown lake	1.50	4.75
M50	A94	3a red orange	1.75	5.50
M51	A94	4a ultra	2.10	4.75
M52	A95	6a purple	8.00	9.00
M53	A95	8a blue green	5.75	11.00
M54	A95	12a blue	7.75	17.00
M55	A96	1r dk grn & pur	12.50	17.00
		Nos. M44-M55 (12)	41.70	93.50

Hindi overprint reads "Indian Custodial Unit, Korea."

Indian UN Force in Congo

Nos. 302-303, 305, 307, 282 and 313 Overprinted: "U.N. FORCE (INDIA) CONGO"

Wmk. 324, 196 (13np)

1962, Jan. 15		**Photo.**	***Perf. 14x14½***	
M56	A117	1np blue green	.90	.90
M57	A117	2np light brown	.90	.90
M58	A117	5np emerald	.90	.90
M59	A117	8np bright green	.90	.90
M60	A117	13np brt carmine	1.50	1.50
M61	A117	50np orange	2.75	2.75
		Nos. M56-M61 (6)	7.85	7.85

Indian UN Force in Gaza

No. 393 Overprinted in Carmine

1965, Jan. 15		**Unwmk.**	***Perf. 13½***	
M62	A190	15p blue gray	4.00	8.00

Overprint letters stand for "United Nations Emergency Force."

INTERNATIONAL COMMISSION IN INDO-CHINA

Catalogue values for all unused stamps in this section are for Never Hinged items.

Cambodia

India Nos. 207, 231, 211, 216 and 217 Overprinted in Black

Perf. 13½x14

1954, Dec. 1			**Wmk. 196**	
1	A91	3p gray violet	.50	.50
2	A101	1a turquoise	.60	.60
3	A93	2a carmine	1.00	1.00
4	A95	8a blue green	4.00	4.25
5	A95	12a blue	5.50	6.25
		Nos. 1-5 (5)	11.60	12.60

The overprint reads "International Commission Cambodia." Top line is 18mm on Nos. 4-5; 15½mm on Nos. 1-3, 6-12.

Same Overprint on India Nos. 276, 279, 282, 286 and 287

1957, Apr. 1			***Perf. 14x14½***	
6	A117	2np light brown	.40	.40
7	A117	6np gray	.40	.40
8	A117	13np bright carmine	1.00	.70
9	A117	50np orange	4.75	2.50
10	A117	75np plum	5.25	4.75
		Nos. 6-10 (5)	11.80	8.75

Same Overprint on India No. 303

1962			**Wmk. 324**	
12	A117	2np light brown	.65	.65

Laos

India Nos. 207, 231, 211, 216 and 217 Overprinted in Black

Perf. 13½x14

1954, Dec. 1			**Wmk. 196**	
1	A91	3p gray violet	.50	.50
2	A101	1a turquoise	.60	.60
3	A93	2a carmine	1.00	1.00
4	A95	8a blue green	4.00	4.25
5	A95	12a blue	5.50	6.25
		Nos. 1-5 (5)	11.60	12.60

The overprint reads "International Commission Laos." Top line is 18mm on Nos. 4-5; 15½mm on Nos. 1-3, 6-16.

Same Overprint on India Nos. 276, 279, 282, 286 and 287

1957, Apr. 1			***Perf. 14x14½***	
6	A117	2np light brown	.40	.40
7	A117	6np gray	.40	.40
8	A117	13np brt carmine	1.00	.70
9	A117	50np orange	4.75	2.50
10	A117	75np plum	5.25	4.75
		Nos. 6-10 (5)	11.80	8.75

Same Overprint on India Nos. 303-305, 313-314

1962-65			**Wmk. 324**	
12	A117	2np light brown	2.50	3.00
13	A117	3np brown ('63)	.60	.60
14	A117	5np emerald ('63)	.60	.60
15	A117	50np orange ('65)	2.00	2.25
16	A117	75np plum ('65)	4.25	4.75
		Nos. 12-16 (5)	9.95	11.20

Laos and Viet Nam

No. 393 Overprinted in Carmine

1965, Jan. 15 Unwmk. *Perf. 13½*
1 A190 15p blue gray 4.00 4.00

Overprint letters stand for "International Control Commission."

Nos. 406-408, 411-412, 417 and 419-420 Overprinted in Carmine

Perf. 14½x14, 14x14½
1968, Oct. 2 Photo. Wmk. 324
2 A202 2p reddish brown .50 .50
3 A202 3p olive bister .50 .50
4 A202 5p cerise .50 .50
5 A203 10p bright blue 2.50 2.50
6 A203 15p green 1.00 1.00
7 A202 60p dark gray 1.10 1.10
8 A204 1r dp cl & red brn 1.75 *2.25*
9 A205 2r violet & brt blue 4.00 *5.50*
Nos. 2-9 (8) 11.85 *13.85*

The arrangement of the lines of the overprint varies on each denomination.

Viet Nam

India Nos. 207, 231, 211, 216 and 217 Overprinted in Black

Perf. 13½x14
1954, Dec. 1 Wmk. 196
1 A91 3p gray violet .50 .50
2 A101 1a turquoise .60 .60
3 A93 2a carmine 1.00 1.00
4 A95 8a blue green 4.00 *4.25*
5 A95 12a blue 5.50 *6.25*
Nos. 1-5 (5) 11.60 *12.60*

The overprint reads "International Commission Viet Nam." Top line of overprint is 18mm on Nos. 4-5; 15½mm on Nos. 1-3, 6-16.

Same Overprint on India Nos. 276, 279, 282, 286 and 287

1957, Apr. 1 *Perf. 14x14½*
6 A117 2np light brown .40 .40
7 A117 6np gray .40 .40
8 A117 13np bright carmine 1.00 .70
9 A117 50np orange 4.75 2.10
10 A117 75np plum 5.25 4.75
Nos. 6-10 (5) 11.80 8.35

Same Overprint on India Nos. 302-305, 313-314

1961-65 Wmk. 324
11 A117 1np blue green 1.40 *1.40*
12 A117 2np light brown ('62) 2.75 2.75
13 A117 3np brown ('63) 1.00 1.00
14 A117 5np emerald ('63) .65 .80
15 A117 50np orange ('65) 2.25 *2.75*
16 A117 75np plum ('65) 4.25 *4.75*
Nos. 11-16 (6) 12.30 *13.45*

OFFICIAL STAMPS

Nos. O1-O26 are normally found with very heavy cancellations, and values are for stamps so canceled. Lightly canceled stamps are seldom seen.

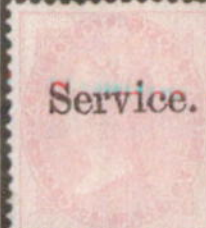

Nos. 11-12, 18, 20-22, 23a, 24, 26 Overprinted in Black

1866, Aug. 1 Unwmk. *Perf. 14*
O1 A7 ½a blue 1,100. 140.00
  a. Inverted overprint
O3 A7 1a brown 140.00
O4 A7 8a rose 22.50 50.00

The 8p lilac unwatermarked (No. 19) with "Service" overprint was not officially issued.

Wmk. 38
O5 A7 ½a blue 300.00 12.50
  a. Inverted overprint
  b. Without period 210.00
O6 A8 8p lilac 20.00 *52.50*
O7 A7 1a brown 300.00 15.00
  a. Inverted overprint
O8 A7 2a yellow 300.00 85.00
  a. Imperf.
  b. Inverted overprint
O9 A7 4a green 200.00 80.00
  a. Inverted overprint
O10 A9 4a green (I) 1,000. 250.00

Reprints were made of Nos. O5, O7, O10 (type II).

Revenue Stamps Surcharged or Overprinted

Queen Victoria — O1

Blue Glazed Paper Black Surcharge

1866 Wmk. 36 *Perf. 14 Vertically*
O11 O1 2a violet 350.00 250.00

The note after No. 30 will apply here also.
No. O11 is often found with cracked surface or scuffs. Such examples sell for somewhat less.
Reprints of No. O11 are surcharged in either black or green, and have the word "SERVICE" 16½x2½mm, instead of 16½x2¾mm and "TWO ANNAS" 18x3mm, instead of 20x3¼mm.

O2

O3

O4

1866 Green Overprint
O12 O2 2a violet 1,000. 325.
O13 O3 4a violet *4,500. 1,250.*
O14 O4 8a violet *5,000. 5,000.*

The note after No. 30 will apply here also.
These stamps are often found with cracked surface or scuffs. Such examples sell for somewhat less.
Reprints of No. O12 have the overprint in sans-serif letters 2¼mm high, instead of Roman letters 2½mm high. On the reprints of No. O13 "SERVICE" measures 16½x2¼mm, instead of 20¼x3mm and "POSTAGE" 18x2¼mm, instead of 22x3mm.
On No. O14 "SERVICE" is 20½mm long, instead of 20mm and "POSTAGE" is 23mm long, instead of 22mm. All three overprints are in a darker green than on the original stamps.

O5

Green Overprint

1866 Wmk. 40 *Perf. 15½x15*
Lilac Paper
O15 O5 ½a violet 425.00 85.00
  a. Double overprint 3,000.

Nos. 20, 31, 22-23, 23a, 26, 28 Overprinted in Black

1866-73 Wmk. 38 *Perf. 14*
O16 A7 ½a blue 30.00 .35
O17 A7 ½a bl, re-engraved 140.00 67.50
  a. Double overprint
O18 A7 1a brown 32.50 .40
O19 A7 2a orange 4.50 2.00
  a. 2a yellow 20.00 2.25
O20 A9 4a green (I) 2.75 1.50
O21 A11 8a rose 3.00 1.50
Nos. O16-O21 (6) 212.75 73.25

The 6a8p with this overprint was not issued. Value $25.

Nos. 31, 22-23, 26, 28 Overprinted in Black

1874-82
O22 A7 ½a blue, re-engraved 8.00 .25
  a. Blue overprint 350.00 45.00
O23 A7 1a brown 12.50 .25
  a. Blue overprint 550.00 120.00
O24 A7 2a orange 40.00 17.50
O25 A9 4a green (I) 12.50 2.75
O26 A11 8a rose 4.25 4.00
Nos. O22-O26 (5) 77.25 24.75

Same Overprint on Nos. 36, 38, 40, 42, 44, 49

1883-97 Wmk. 39
O27 A17 ½a green .40 .25
  a. Pair, one without overprint
  b. Double overprint 1,150.
O28 A19 1a maroon .75 .25
  a. Inverted overprint 350.00 475.00
  b. Double overprint 1,150.
  c. 1a violet brown 2.25 .35
O29 A21 2a ultramarine 4.50 .50
O30 A23 4a olive green 15.00 .40
O31 A25 8a red violet 7.00 .40
O32 A29 1r car rose & grn 11.00 .40
Nos. O27-O32 (6) 38.65 2.20

Same Overprint on No. 54

1899
O33 A31 3p carmine rose .25 .25

Same Overprint on Nos. 56-58

1900
O34 A17 ½a light green 1.25 .30
O35 A19 1a carmine rose 2.50 .25
  a. Double overprint 1,350.
  b. Inverted overprint 1,400.
O36 A21 2a violet 27.50 .50
Nos. O34-O36 (3) 31.25 1.05

Same Overprint on Nos. 60-63, 66-68, 70

1902-09
O37 A32 3p gray .85 .25
O38 A33 ½a green 1.00 .25
O39 A34 1a carmine rose .85 .25
O40 A35 2a violet *2.50* .25
O41 A38 4a olive green *4.25* .25
O42 A39 6a bister *2.25* .25
O43 A40 8a red lilac *5.25* .50
O44 A42 1r car rose & green ('05) *4.50* .25
Nos. O37-O44 (8) *21.45* 2.25

Same Overprint on Nos. 78-79

1906-07
O45 A44 ½a green 1.00 .25
O46 A45 1a carmine rose 1.75 .25
  a. Pair, one without overprint
  b. Overprint on back —

Same Overprint on Nos. 71, 73-76

1909
O47 A43 2r brown & rose *6.50* .90
O48 A43 5r violet & ultra *11.00* 1.00
O49 A43 10r car rose & grn *21.00* 8.50
  a. 10r red & green 52.50 6.00
O50 A43 15r ol gray & ultra 52.50 30.00
O51 A43 25r ultra & org brn 130.00 50.00
Nos. O47-O51 (5) 221.00 90.40

For surcharges see Nos. O67-O69.

Nos. 80-84, 88, 90-91 Overprinted in Black

1912-22
O52 A46 3p gray .25 .25
O53 A47 ½a green .25 .25
  a. Double overprint 110.00
O54 A48 1a carmine rose .75 .25
  a. Double overprint 950.00
O55 A48 1a dk brn ('22) 1.00 .25
  a. Imperf., pair 75.00
O56 A49 2a violet .50 .25
O57 A52 4a olive green .75 .25
O58 A53 6a bister 1.25 *1.75*
O59 A54 8a red violet 1.75 .75

Nos. 93-98 Overprinted in Black

O60 A56 1r green & red brn 2.00 .80
O61 A56 2r yel brn & car rose 2.50 *3.50*
O62 A56 5r violet & ultra 10.50 *13.50*
O63 A56 10r car rose & grn 35.00 32.50
O64 A56 15r ol grn & ultra 80.00 *95.00*
O65 A56 25r ultra & brn org 180.00 150.00
Nos. O52-O65 (14) 316.50 299.30

For surcharge see No. O69b.

O6

1921 Black Surcharge
O66 O6 9p on 1a rose .75 .60

For overprint see Gwalior No. O28.

Nos. O49-O51 Surcharged

1925
O67 A43 1r on 15r ol gray & ultra 4.00 3.00
O68 A43 1r on 25r ultra & org brn 20.00 *60.00*
O69 A43 2r on 10r red & grn 3.50 3.50
  a. 2r on 10r car rose & green 210.00 55.00
  b. Surcharge on #O63 (error) 4,500.

Nos. O64-O65 Surcharged

O70 A56 1r on 15r ol grn & ultra 19.00 *65.00*
a. Inverted surcharge
O71 A56 1r on 25r ultra & brn org 5.00 *9.00*
a. Inverted surcharge 4,000.
Nos. O67-O71 (5) 51.50 *140.50*

O7

1926 Black Surcharge
O73 O7 1a on 6a bister .40 .40

Nos. 83, 101, 102, 99 Surcharged

O74 A48 1a on 1a dk brn (error) 180.00 180.00
O75 A58 1a on 1½a choc .25 .25
O76 A59 1a on 1½a choc 1.75 *4.00*
b. Double surcharge 30.00
O77 A57 1a on 2a6p ultra .50 .50
Nos. O73-O77 (5) 182.90 185.15

Nos. O74, O75 and O76 have short bars over the numerals in the upper corners.

Nos. 106-108, 111, 126-127, 112, 116, 128, 118-119 Overprinted — a

1926-35 Wmk. 196
O78 A46 3p slate ('29) .25 .25
O79 A47 ½a green ('31) 5.00 .40
O80 A48 1a dark brown .25 .25
a. Overprint as on No. O55 100.00 4.75
O81 A49 2a vermilion ('35) 1.00 1.00
a. Small die .85 .25
O82 A60 2a dull violet .25 .25
O83 A60 2a vermilion ('32) .90 2.00
O84 A57 2a6p buff ('32) .25 .25
O85 A52 4a olive green ('35) 1.00 .25
O86 A61 4a olive green .35 .25
O87 A53 6a bister('35) 18.00 9.00
O88 A54 8a red violet .50 .25
O89 A55 12a claret .50 *1.75*

Nos. 120-121, 123 Overprinted - b

O90 A56 1r grn & brn ('30) 2.25 .90
O91 A56 2r brn org & car rose ('30) 6.00 6.00
O92 A56 10r car & grn ('31) 70.00 50.00
Nos. O78-O92 (15) 106.50 72.80

Nos. 138, 135, 139, 136 Overprinted Type "a"

1932-35
O93 A71 ½a green ('35) .60 .25
O94 A68 9p dark green .25 .25
O95 A72 1a dark brown ('35) 1.90 .25
O96 A69 1a3p violet .25 .25
Nos. O93-O96 (4) 3.00 1.00

Nos. 151-153, 162-165 Overprinted Type "a"

1937-39 *Perf. 13½x14*
O97 A80 ½a brown ('38) 22.50 .45
O98 A80 9p green 25.00 .60
O99 A80 1a carmine 4.75 .35

Type "b" Overprint
O100 A82 1r brn & slate ('38) .70 .55
O101 A82 2r dk brn & dk vio ('38) 1.90 *3.25*
O102 A82 5r dp ultra & dk grn ('38) 3.25 *7.50*
O103 A82 10r rose car & dk violet ('39) 19.00 6.75
Nos. O97-O103 (7) 77.10 19.45

No. 136 Surcharged in Black

1939, May Wmk. 196 *Perf. 14*
O104 A69 1a on 1a3p violet *17.00* 3.00

King George VI — O8

1939-43 Typo. *Perf. 13½x14*
O105 O8 3p slate .40 .40
O106 O8 ½a brown 8.00 .40
O106A O8 ½a dk rose vio ('43) .40 .40
O107 O8 9p green .40 .40
O108 O8 1a car rose .40 .40
O108A O8 1a3p bister ('41) *7.00* *1.25*
O108B O8 1½a dull pur ('43) .40 .40
O109 O8 2a scarlet .40 .40
O110 O8 2½a purple .40 .40
O111 O8 4a dark brown .40 .40
O112 O8 8a blue violet .60 .40
Nos. O105-O112 (11) *18.80* *5.25*

For overprints see Gwalior Nos. O52-O61 and Patiala Nos. O63-O73. Stamps overprinted "Postal Service" or "I. P. N." were not used as postage stamps.

Catalogue values for unused stamps in this section, from this point to the end of the section, are for Never Hinged items.

Nos. 203-206 (Gandhi Issue) Overprinted Type "a"

Perf. 11½

1948, Aug. Unwmk. Photo.
O112A A90 1½a brown *65.00* *45.00*
O112B A90 3½a violet *7,500.* *750.00*
O112C A90 12a dk gray green *8,000.* *2,500.*
O112D A90 10r rose brn & brn *225,000.*

Overprint forgeries exist.

Capital of Asoka Pillar
O9 O10

Perf. 13½x14

1950 Wmk. 196 Typo.
O113 O9 3p violet blue .40 .40
O114 O9 6p chocolate .40 .40
O115 O9 9p green .65 .40
O116 O9 1a turquoise .95 .40
O117 O9 2a red .40 .40
O118 O9 3a vermilion 4.75 2.75
O119 O9 4a brown car 7.00 .40
O120 O9 6a purple 5.75 .40
O121 O9 8a orange brn 2.75 .40

Litho.

Perf. 14x13½
O122 O10 1r dark purple 3.75 .40
O123 O10 2r brown red 1.50 .40
O124 O10 5r dark green 2.75 2.25
O125 O10 10r red brown 8.50 *22.50*
Nos. O113-O125 (13) 39.55 *31.50*

Issue dates: 1r-10r, Jan. 2, others, July 1.

1951, Oct. 1 Typo.
O126 O9 4a violet blue .25 .25

Type of 1950 Redrawn, Denomination in Naye Paise

Typo. or Litho.

1957-58 *Perf. 13½x14*
O127 O9 1np slate blue .55 .55
O128 O9 2np blue violet .55 .55
O129 O9 3np chocolate .55 .55
O130 O9 5np yellow green .55 .55
O131 O9 6np turquoise .55 .55
O132 O9 13np red .55 .55
O133 O9 15np dk purple ('58) .55 .55
O134 O9 20np vermilion .55 .55
O135 O9 25np violet blue .55 .55
O136 O9 50np reddish brown 1.00 .55
Nos. O127-O136 (10) 5.95 5.50

Issue dates: 15np, June; others, Apr. 1.

Redrawn Type of 1957-58

Typo. or Litho.

1958-71 Wmk. 324 *Perf. 13½x14*
O137 O9 1np slate blue ('59) .30 .30
O138 O9 2np blue violet ('59) .30 .30
O139 O9 3np chocolate .30 .30
O140 O9 5np yel green .30 .30
O141 O9 6np turquoise ('59) .30 .30
O142 O9 10np dk green ('63) .30 .30
O142A O9 13np red ('63) .30 .30
O143 O9 15np dk purple .30 .30
O144 O9 20np ver ('59) .30 .30
O145 O9 25np vio blue ('59) .30 .30
O146 O9 50np redsh brown ('59) .30 .30

Litho.

Perf. 14
O147 O10 1r rose vio ('59) .30 .30
O148 O10 2r rose red ('60) .50 .30
a. Watermark sideways ('69) .50 *.60*
O149 O10 5r green ('59) 1.00 1.40
a. Watermark sideways ('69) .90 .30
O150 O10 10r rose lake ('59) 1.50 1.10
a. Watermark sideways ('71) 3.75 3.75
Nos. O137-O150 (15) 6.60 6.40

O11

Perf. 14½x14

1967-76 Photo. Wmk. 360

Without Gum
O151 O11 2p violet black .85 .85
O152 O11 3p dk red brown .85 .85
O153 O11 5p bright green .85 .85
O154 O11 6p Prussian blue 3.25 3.25
O155 O11 10p slate green .85 .85
O156 O11 15p purple .85 .85
O157 O11 20p orange ver .85 .85
O158 O11 25p deep car ('76) 26.00 11.00
O159 O11 30p violet blue .85 .85
O160 O11 50p red brown .85 .85
Nos. O151-O160 (10) 36.05 21.05

No. O153 Overprinted

1971, Nov. 15 Wmk. 360

Without Gum
O161 O11 5p green .40 .40

No. O153 Overprinted "Refugee / Relief"
O162 O11 5p green 1.00 1.00

No. O162 was used in Maharashtra state.

Capital of Asoka Pillar — O12

1971, Dec. 1(?) Without Gum
O163 O12 5p green .25 .25

Nos. O161-O163 were obligatory on all official mail as a postal tax to benefit refugees from East Pakistan. The tax was paid out of the various governmental departments' budgets.

Type of 1968

1967-74 Wmk. 324 *Perf. 14½x14*
O164 O11 2p violet .80 *1.00*
O165 O11 5p brt green ('74) .80 .25
O166 O11 10p slate green ('74) 1.25 .25
O167 O11 15p purple ('73) 1.60 .40
O168 O11 20p dp orange ('74) 5.25 5.00
O169 O11 30p ultramarine 3.50 1.00
O170 O11 50p red brown ('73) 2.75 2.00
O171 O11 1r dull purple .55 .25
Nos. O164-O171 (8) 16.50 10.15

O13 O14

Without Currency Designation

Perf. 14½x14

1976-80 Litho. Wmk. 360

Without Gum
O172 O13 2p violet black .35 .35
O173 O13 5p bright green .35 .35
O174 O13 10p slate green .35 .35
O175 O13 15p purple .35 .35
O176 O13 20p brown orange .35 .35
O177 O13 25p carmine rose .80 .80
O178 O13 30p blue ('79) 2.50 2.50
O179 O13 35p violet ('80) .75 .35
O180 O13 50p red brown 3.50 1.75
O181 O13 1r dull purple ('80) 4.00 .90

Wmk. 324
O182 O13 1r dull purple .90 .90

Perf. 14x13½
O183 O14 2r salmon rose 3.50 3.50
O184 O14 5r deep green 3.50 3.50
O185 O14 10r red brown 1.25 1.25
Nos. O172-O185 (14) 22.45 17.20

O15

Perf. 15x14

1981, Feb. Litho. Wmk. 360

Without Gum
O186 O15 2r orange vermilion 1.00 .60
O187 O15 5r dark green 3.00 1.40
O188 O15 10r dark red brown 6.00 3.00
Nos. O186-O188 (3) 10.00 5.00

Unwmk.

1981, Dec. 10 Litho. *Imperf.*

Cream Paper
O189 O13 5p bright green .90 *1.25*
O190 O13 10p slate green 1.00 *1.25*
O191 O13 15p purple 1.00 *1.25*
O192 O13 20p brown orange 1.00 *1.25*
O193 O13 25p carmine rose 2.25 *2.75*
O194 O13 35p violet 1.25 .90
O195 O13 50p brown 2.25 2.25
O196 O13 1r dull purple 2.50 2.25
O197 O15 2r salmon rose 2.50 *5.25*
O198 O15 5r deep green 2.75 *7.25*
O199 O15 10r red brown 3.75 *9.75*
Nos. O189-O199 (11) 21.15 35.40

Perf. 12½x13

1982, Nov. 22 Photo. Wmk. 360

Without Gum
O200 O13 5p bright green .80 *1.10*
O201 O13 10p slate green 1.00 *1.25*
O202 O13 15p purple 1.10 *1.25*
O203 O13 20p fawn 1.25 1.25
O204 O13 25p car rose 1.60 *2.50*
O205 O13 30p dark blue 1.60 *2.50*
O206 O13 35p violet 1.60 .70
O207 O13 50p light brown 2.50 2.50
O208 O13 1r dull purple 2.50 2.50
O209 O15 2r salmon rose 2.75 3.75
O210 O15 5r deep green 3.25 6.50
O211 O15 10r red brown 4.00 9.00
Nos. O200-O211 (12) 23.95 34.80

Perf. 12½x13

1984-99 Photo. Wmk. 324

Without Gum
O212 O13 5p green .25 .25
O213 O13 10p dark green .25 .25
O214 O13 15p rose lake .25 .25
O215 O13 20p fawn .25 .25
O216 O13 25p deep carmine .25 .25

O217 O13 30p blue .25 .25
O218 O13 35p purple .25 .25
O219 O13 40p violet .25 .25
O220 O13 50p brown .25 .25
O221 O13 60p brown .25 .25
O222 O15 1r violet brown .25 .25
O223 O15 2r orange ver .40 .25
O223A O15 3r orange .25 .25
O224 O15 5r gray green 1.00 .50
O225 O15 10r red brown 2.00 1.00
Nos. O213-O225 (14) 6.15 4.50

Issued: 25p, 1986. 60p, 4/15/88; 40p, 10/15/88; 3r, 3/22/99; others, 4/16/84.

This is an expanding set. Numbers may change again.

POSTAL TAX STAMPS

Catalogue values for unused stamps in this section are for Never Hinged items.

No. 408 Overprinted

Perf. 14½x14

1971, Nov. 15 Photo. Wmk. 324
RA1 A202 5p cerise .25 .25

No. 408 Overprinted "Refugee/Relief"

RA2 A202 5p cerise .25 .25

No. RA2 was used in Maharashtra. In order to make the obligatory tax stamps available immediately throughout India postmasters were authorized to overprint locally No. 408. This resulted in a great variety of mostly hand-stamped overprints of various types and sizes.

Refugees — PT1

Perf. 14x14½

1971, Dec. 1 Photo. Wmk. 324
RA3 PT1 5p cerise .25 .25

Nos. RA1-RA3 were obligatory on all mail. The tax was for refugees from East Pakistan.

See Nos. O161-O163.

INDIA - CONVENTION STATES

CONVENTION STATES OF THE BRITISH EMPIRE IN INDIA

Stamps of British India overprinted for use in the States of Chamba, Faridkot, Gwalior, Jhind, Nabha and Patiala.

These stamps had franking power throughout all British India.

Forgeries

Numerous forgeries exist of the high valued Convention States stamps, unused and used. Most cancelled examples of those stamps whose value used is far greater than unused bear favor or counterfeit cancels. Such stamps are worth far less than the values below, which are for postally used examples. More valuable Indian States stamps should be expertized.

CHAMBA

'chəm-bə

LOCATION — A State of India located in the north Punjab, south of Kashmir.

AREA — 3,127 sq. mi.

POP. — 168,908 (1941)

CAPITAL — Chamba

The varieties with small letters in the overprint are not listed as the letters are merely broken and not from another font of type.

Indian Stamps Overprinted in Black

1887-95 Wmk. 39 *Perf. 14*
1 A17 ½a green 1.50 *1.75*
a. "CHMABA" *600.00* *950.00*
c. Double overprint 950.00
2 A19 1a vio brn 3.75 *3.75*
a. "CHMABA" *700.00* 950.00
3 A20 1a6p bis brn ('95) 4.50 *21.00*
4 A21 2a ultra 2.00 *3.25*
a. "CHMABA" *2,750.* *4,000.*
5 A28 2a6p grn ('95) 52.50 *150.00*
6 A22 3a brn org 4.50 *9.00*
a. 3a orange 16.00 *35.00*
b. Inverted overprint
c. "CHMABA" 7,500. *11,000.*
7 A23 4a ol grn 8.25 *14.00*
a. "CHMABA" *2,400.* *4,000.*
8 A25 8a red violet 13.50 *18.00*
a. "CHMABA" 6,000. *6,250.*
9 A26 12a vio, *red* ('90) 10.50 *24.00*
a. "CHMABA" 12,500.
b. 1st "T" of "STATE" invtd. 12,500.
10 A27 1r gray 72.50 *225.00*
a. "CHMABA" 21,000.
11 A29 1r car rose & grn ('95) 14.00 *25.00*
12 A30 2r brn & rose ('95) 150.00 *600.00*
13 A30 3r grn & brn ('95) 175.00 *525.00*
14 A30 5r vio & bl ('95) 190.00 *825.00*

Wmk. 38
15 A14 6a bis ('90) 8.25 *32.50*
Nos. 1-15 (15) 710.75 *2,477.*

1900 Wmk. 39
15B A31 3p carmine rose .90 *1.40*

1902-04
16 A31 3p gray ('04) .90 *3.25*
a. Inverted overprint 120.00
17 A17 ½a light green 1.00 *2.50*
18 A19 1a carmine rose 1.00 .60
19 A21 2a violet ('03) 16.00 *52.50*
Nos. 16-19 (4) 18.90 *58.85*

1903-05
20 A32 3p gray .35 *2.40*
21 A33 ½a green 1.20 .90
22 A34 1a carmine rose 2.40 1.40
23 A35 2a violet 2.75 *5.25*
24 A37 3a brown org ('05) 7.00 *9.00*
25 A38 4a olive green ('04) 10.50 *32.50*
26 A39 6a bister ('05) 6.50 *35.00*
27 A40 8a red violet ('04) 9.00 *35.00*
28 A41 12a violet, *red* 12.00 *47.50*
29 A42 1r car rose & grn ('05) 11.00 *35.00*
Nos. 20-29 (10) 62.70 *203.95*

1907
30 A44 ½a green 3.75 *6.00*
31 A45 1a carmine rose 3.75 *6.00*

1913-24
32 A46 3p gray .60 *1.90*
33 A47 ½a green 1.50 *1.90*
34 A48 1a carmine rose 15.00 *17.50*
35 A48 1a dk brn ('22) 5.25 *8.25*
36 A49 2a violet 6.00 *17.50*
37 A51 3a brown orange 7.00 *13.00*
38 A51 3a ultra ('24) 6.25 *35.00*
39 A52 4a olive green 6.00 *8.25*
40 A53 6a bister 6.50 *11.00*
41 A54 8a red violet 9.00 *24.00*
42 A55 12a claret 8.25 *19.00*
43 A56 1r grn & red brn 27.50 *47.50*
Nos. 32-43 (12) 98.85 *204.80*

India No. 104 Overprinted

1921
44 A48 9p on 1a rose 1.50 *27.50*

India Stamps of 1913-26 Overprinted

1922-27
45 A58 1½a chocolate 40.00 *190.00*
46 A59 1½a chocolate 3.75 *9.50*
47 A59 1½a rose 1.40 *35.00*
48 A57 2a6p ultramarine .90 *6.50*
49 A57 2a6p brown orange 4.00 *35.00*
Nos. 45-49 (5) 50.05 *276.00*

India Stamps of 1926 Overprinted

1927-28 Wmk. 196
50 A46 3p slate .30 *2.50*
51 A47 ½a green .45 *3.75*
52 A48 1a dark brown 2.50 2.25
53 A60 2a dull violet 3.25 6.00
54 A51 3a ultramarine 1.90 *32.50*
55 A61 4a olive green 1.90 *10.00*
57 A54 8a red violet 2.40 *17.50*
58 A55 12a claret 2.40 *24.00*

Overprinted

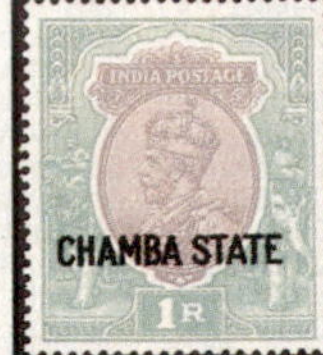

59 A56 1r green & brown 17.50 *45.00*
Nos. 50-55,57-59 (9) 32.60 *143.50*

India Stamps of 1926-35 Overprinted

1932-37
60 A71 ½a green 1.60 *16.00*
61 A68 9p dark green 7.50 *32.50*
62 A72 1a dark brown 2.50 2.25
63 A69 1a3p violet 2.10 *9.50*
64 A59 1½a carmine rose 9.50 *11.00*
65 A49 2a vermilion 1.90 *37.50*
a. Small die 175.00 *210.00*
66 A57 2a6p buff 5.00 *30.00*
67 A51 3a carmine rose 3.25 *17.50*
68 A52 4a ol grn ('36) 8.25 *25.00*
69 A53 6a bister ('37) 45.00 *250.00*
Nos. 60-69 (10) 86.60 *431.25*

Same Overprint on India Stamps of 1937

1938 Wmk. 196 *Perf. 13½x14*
70 A80 3p slate 14.00 *32.50*
71 A80 ½a brown 2.00 21.00
72 A80 9p green 12.50 *57.50*
73 A80 1a carmine 2.50 *5.50*

74 A81 2a scarlet 10.00 *24.00*
75 A81 2a6p purple 11.00 *47.50*
76 A81 3a yellow green 11.50 *42.50*
77 A81 3a6p ultra 11.50 *45.00*
78 A81 4a dark brown 30.00 *45.00*
79 A81 6a peacock blue 32.50 *100.00*
80 A81 8a blue violet 30.00 *97.50*
81 A81 12a carmine lake 22.50 *97.50*

Overprinted

82 A82 1r brown & slate 45.00 *110.00*
83 A82 2r dk brn & dk vio 75.00 *525.00*
84 A82 5r dp ultra & dk green 120.00 *700.00*
85 A82 10r rose car & dk vio 190.00 *1,100.*
86 A82 15r dk grn & dk brown 200.00 *1,500.*
87 A82 25r dk vio & bl vio 290.00 *1,600.*
Nos. 70-87 (18) 1,110. *6,151.*
Set, never hinged 1,300.

India Nos. 151 and 153 Overprinted

1942
87B A80 ½a brown 62.50 *67.50*
Never hinged 75.00
88 A80 1a carmine 95.00 *90.00*
Never hinged 110.00

Same Ovpt. on India Stamps of 1941-42

1942-44
89 A83 3p slate 1.50 *8.25*
90 A83 ½a rose vio ('43) 1.00 *9.50*
91 A83 9p lt green ('43) 1.40 *30.00*
92 A83 1a car rose ('43) 2.50 *8.25*
93 A84 1½a dk purple ('44) 3.00 *21.00*
94 A84 2a scarlet ('43) 11.00 *24.00*
95 A84 3a violet ('43) 26.00 *72.50*
96 A84 3½a ultra ('43) 14.00 *67.50*
97 A85 4a chocolate ('43) 19.00 75.00
98 A85 6a pck blue ('43) 21.00 *62.50*
99 A85 8a blue vio ('43) 22.50 *75.00*
100 A85 12a car lake ('43) 30.00 *97.50*
Nos. 89-100 (12) 152.90 *551.00*
Set, never hinged 200.00

India Nos. 162-167 Overprinted

1943 Wmk. 196 *Perf. 13½x14*
101 A82 1r brown & slate 26.00 *97.50*
102 A82 2r dk brn & dk vio 30.00 *400.00*
103 A82 5r dp ultra & dk grn 55.00 *450.00*
104 A82 10r rose car & dk vio 85.00 *700.00*
105 A82 15r dk grn & dk brn 190.00 *1,250.*
106 A82 25r dk vio & bl vio 175.00 *1,250.*
Nos. 101-106 (6) 561.00 *4,148.*
Set, never hinged 850.00

India No. 161A Ovptd.

1947
107 A81 14a rose violet 17.50 4.50

OFFICIAL STAMPS

Indian Stamps Overprinted in Black

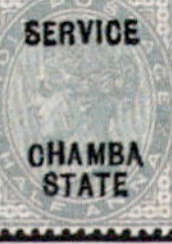

1887-98 Wmk. 39 *Perf. 14*

O1	A17	½a green	.90	.25
a.		"CHMABA"	375.00	375.00
c.		"SERV CE"		
O2	A19	1a vio brn	3.00	2.25
a.		"CHMABA"	600.00	600.00
c.		"SERV CE"	*5,250.*	
d.		"SERVICE" double	*3,000.*	*1,600.*
O3	A21	2a ultra	3.75	3.00
a.		"CHMABA"	*1,500.*	*3,250.*
O4	A22	3a brn org	3.00	*19.00*
a.		3a orange	—	—
b.		"CHMABA"	*4,500.*	*5,250.*
O5	A23	4a ol grn	4.50	*12.00*
a.		"CHMABA"	*1,600.*	*3,250.*
c.		"SERV CE"	6,000.	
O6	A25	8a red violet	4.50	*4.50*
a.		"CHMABA"	*12,000.*	*12,000.*
O7	A26	12a vio, *red* ('90)	12.50	*72.50*
a.		"CHMABA"	*11,000.*	
b.		1st "T" of "STATE" invtd.	*10,000.*	
O8	A27	1r gray ('90)	19.00	*225.00*
a.		"CHMABA"	*7,500.*	
O9	A29	1r car rose & grn ('98)	9.00	*62.50*

Wmk. 38

O10	A14	6a bister	6.25	*22.50*
		Nos. O1-O10 (10)	66.40	423.50

1902-04 Wmk. 39

O11	A31	3p gray ('04)	.75	*1.20*
O12	A17	½a light green	1.50	*6.00*
O13	A19	1a carmine rose	1.90	.90
O14	A21	2a violet ('03)	14.50	*52.50*
		Nos. O11-O14 (4)	18.65	*60.60*

A 2a value, Scott No. O14, was overprinted in Calcutta but never issued.

1903-05

O15	A32	3p gray	.40	.25
O16	A33	½a green	.30	.25
O17	A34	1a carmine rose	1.50	.45
O18	A35	2a violet	1.50	*2.25*
O19	A38	4a olive green ('05)	4.25	*30.00*
O20	A40	8a red violet ('05)	10.00	*30.00*
O21	A42	1r car rose & grn ('05)	2.00	*21.00*
		Nos. O15-O21 (7)	19.95	*84.20*

1907

O22	A44	½a green	.85	*1.10*
a.		Inverted overprint	*6,750.*	*8,250.*
O23	A45	1a carmine rose	4.75	*3.75*

1913

O24	A49	2a violet	22.50	
O25	A52	4a olive green	20.00	

India No. 63 Overprinted

O26	A35	2a violet	60.00	

No. O26 was never placed in use.

India Stamps of 1911-29 Overprinted

a

b

1913-25

O27	A46 (a)	3p gray	.30	*.60*
O28	A47 (a)	½a green	.30	*.90*
O29	A48 (a)	1a carmine rose	.30	.25
O30	A48 (a)	1a dk brn ('25)	6.50	1.00
O31	A49 (a)	2a violet ('14)	1.60	*22.50*
O32	A52 (a)	4a olive green	1.60	*30.00*
O33	A54 (a)	8a red violet	2.50	*30.00*
O34	A56 (b)	1r grn & red brn	8.25	*47.50*
		Nos. O27-O34 (8)	21.35	132.75

India No. O66 Overprinted

1921

O35	O6	9p on 1a rose	.25	*12.50*

India Stamps of 1926-35 Overprinted

1927-39 Wmk. 196

O36	A46	3p slate	.65	.60
O37	A47	½a green	.40	.25
O38	A68	9p dk grn ('32)	5.00	*16.00*
O39	A48	1a dark brown	.25	.25
O40	A69	1a3p violet ('32)	7.50	1.50
O41	A60	2a dull violet	3.25	*.90*
O42	A61	4a olive green	1.90	4.00
O43	A54	8a red violet	10.00	*16.00*
O44	A55	12a claret	6.50	*37.50*

Overprinted

O45	A56	1r grn & brn	19.00	*72.50*
O45A	A56	2r brn org & car rose ('39)	30.00	*375.00*
O45B	A56	5r dk vio & ultra ('39)	52.50	*450.00*
O45C	A56	10r car & grn ('39)	82.50	*450.00*
		Nos. O36-O45C (13)	219.45	1,425.

India Stamps of 1926-35 Overprinted

1935-36

O46	A71	½a green	7.00	*.75*
O47	A72	1a dark brown	6.75	.65
O48	A49	2a vermilion	7.00	1.90
a.		Small die	9.50	*30.00*
O49	A52	4a olive grn ('36)	10.00	9.50
		Nos. O46-O49 (4)	30.75	*12.80*

Same Overprint on India Stamps of 1937

1938 *Perf. 13½x14*

O50	A80	9p green	30.00	*100.00*
		Never hinged	37.50	
O51	A80	1a carmine	37.50	9.00
		Never hinged	45.00	

India Stamps of 1937 Overprinted

1940-41

O51A	A82	1r brn & sl ('41)	300.00	*1,100.*
O52	A82	2r dk brn & dk vio	52.50	*600.00*
O53	A82	5r dp ultra & dk grn	75.00	*650.00*
O54	A82	10r rose car & dk vio	105.00	*1,200.*
		Set, never hinged	625.00	

India Official Stamps of 1939-43 Overprinted

1941-46 Wmk. 196

O55	O8	3p slate ('44)	.85	*1.90*
O56	O8	½a brown	37.50	5.50
O57	O8	½a dk rose vio ('44)	.85	*5.50*
O58	O8	9p green	8.75	*17.50*
O59	O8	1a carmine rose	1.25	*4.50*
O60	O8	1a3p bister ('46)	105.00	32.50
O61	O8	1½a dull pur ('46)	9.50	*12.50*
O62	O8	2a scarlet ('44)	9.50	*12.50*
O63	O8	2½a purple ('44)	5.50	*35.00*
O64	O8	4a dk brn ('44)	9.50	*27.50*
O65	O8	8a blue vio ('41)	21.00	*100.00*
		Nos. O55-O65 (11)	209.20	*254.90*
		Set, never hinged	250.00	

India Nos. 162-165 Overprinted

1944

O66	A82	1r brown & slate	27.50	*325.00*
O67	A82	2r dk brn & dk vio	42.50	*450.00*
O68	A82	5r dp ultra & dk grn	80.00	*650.00*
O69	A82	10r rose car & dk vio	95.00	*1,100.*
		Nos. O66-O69 (4)	245.00	*2,525.*
		Set, never hinged	295.00	

FARIDKOT

fe-'rēd-ˌkōt

LOCATION — A State of India lying northeast of Nabha in the central Punjab.
AREA — 638 sq. mi.
POP. — 164,364
CAPITAL — Faridkot

Previous stamp issues are listed under Feudatory States. Stamps of Faridkot were superseded by those of India in 1901.

The varieties with small letters in the overprint are not listed as the letters are merely broken and not from another font.

India Stamps Overprinted in Black

1887-93 Wmk. 39 *Perf. 14*

4	A17	½a green	3.75	2.50
a.		"ARIDKOT"		
b.		"FAR DKOT"	—	*2,500.*
5	A19	1a violet brown	2.25	*3.75*
6	A21	2a ultramarine	4.75	*10.50*
7	A22	3a orange	5.50	*9.00*
8	A23	4a olive green	12.50	*27.50*
a.		"ARIDKOT"	2,100.	
9	A25	8a red violet	22.50	*67.50*
a.		"ARIDKOT"	4,500.	
10	A27	1r gray	67.50	*550.00*
a.		"ARIDKOT"	*5,250.*	
11	A29	1r car rose & grn ('93)	60.00	*175.00*

Wmk. 38

12	A14	6a bister	3.00	*27.50*
a.		"ARIDKOT"	2,750.	
		Nos. 4-12 (9)	181.75	*873.25*

1900 Wmk. Star. (39)

13	A31	3p car rose	2.25	*67.50*
14	A26	12a violet, *red*	67.50	*625.00*

OFFICIAL STAMPS

India Stamps Overprinted in Black

1886 Wmk. 39 *Perf. 14*

O1	A17	½a green	.90	*1.10*
a.		"SERV CE"	3,750.	
b.		"FAR DKOT"	3,500.	
c.		"ESRVICE"	3,500.	
O2	A19	1a violet brown	1.50	*3.00*
a.		"SERV CE"	5,500.	
O3	A21	2a ultramarine	3.00	*16.00*
a.		"SERV CE"	5,500.	
O4	A22	3a orange	6.00	*57.50*
O5	A23	4a olive green	7.00	*45.00*
a.		"SERV CE"	4,750.	
O6	A25	8a red lilac	15.00	*45.00*
a.		"SERV CE"	4,500.	
O7	A27	1r gray	82.50	*400.00*

Wmk. 38

O8	A14	6a bister	37.50	*42.50*
a.		"ARIDKOT"	2,100.	
b.		"SERVIC"	4,500.	
		Nos. O1-O8 (8)	153.40	*610.10*

1896 Wmk. 39

O9	A29	1r car rose & grn	140.00	*1,000.*

Obsolete March 31, 1901.

GWALIOR

'gwäl-ē-ˌo̦ə̦r

LOCATION — One of the Central Provinces of India
AREA — 26,008 sq. mi.
POP. — 4,006,159 (1941)
CAPITAL — Lashkar

The varieties with small letters in the overprint are not listed as the letters are merely broken and not from another font.

India Stamps Overprinted in Black

Lines Spaced 16-17mm

1885 Wmk. 39 *Perf. 14*

1	A17	½a green	90.00	
2	A19	1a violet brown	97.50	
3	A20	1a6p bister brown	125.00	
4	A21	2a ultramarine	100.00	
5	A25	8a red lilac	110.00	
6	A27	1r gray	110.00	

Wmk. 38

7	A9	4a green	140.00	
8	A14	6a bister	140.00	
		Nos. 1-8 (8)	912.50	

The Hindi overprint measures 13½-14x2mm and 15-15½x2½mm.

The two sizes are found in the same sheet in the proportion of one of the smaller to three of the larger.

The ½a, 1a, 2a, also exist with lines 13mm apart and the short Hindi overprint.

Reprints of the ½a and 1a have the 13mm spacing, the short Hindi overprint and usually carry the overprint "Specimen."

India Stamps Overprinted

Red Overprint

1885 Wmk. 39

9	A17	½a green	1.90	.25
10	A21	2a ultramarine	35.00	*27.50*
11	A27	1r gray	12.50	*37.50*

Wmk. 38

12	A9	4a green	42.50	24.00
		Nos. 9-12 (4)	91.90	89.25

Nos. 9-12 have been reprinted. They have the short Hindi overprint. Most stamps bear the word "Reprint." Those without it cannot be distinguished from the originals.

1885-91 Black Overprint Wmk. 39

13	A17	½a green	.75	.25
a.		"GWALICR"	125.00	*150.00*
b.		Double overprint		1,400.
14	A18	9p rose	47.50	*82.50*
15	A19	1a violet brown	3.00	.25
16	A20	1a6p bister brown	3.25	2.00
17	A21	2a ultramarine	4.00	.25
18	A22	3a orange	7.00	.25
19	A23	4a olive green	8.50	2.00
20	A25	8a red violet	9.00	2.00
21	A26	12a violet, *red*	5.00	1.00
22	A27	1r gray	6.50	5.25

Wmk. 38

23	A14	6a bister	7.50	18.00
		Nos. 13-23 (11)	102.00	*113.75*

The Hindi overprint measures 13½-14x2mm and 15-15½x2½mm as in the preceding issue.

1896 Wmk. 39

24	A28	2a6p green	14.00	*30.00*
a.		"GWALICR"	1,000.	

No.	Type	Description	Unused	Used
25	A29	1r car rose & grn	12.00	8.50
a.		"GWALICR"	1,350	*2,400.*
26	A30	2r bis brn & rose	8.25	4.50
27	A30	3r grn & brn	11.00	5.25
28	A30	5r vio & blue	21.00	9.50
		Nos. 24-28 (5)	66.25	57.75

The Hindi inscription varies from 13 to 15½mm long.

1899

No.	Type	Description	Unused	Used
29	A31	3p carmine rose	.75	.25
a.		Inverted overprint	1,650.	825.00

1901-04

No.	Type	Description	Unused	Used
30	A31	3p gray ('04)	11.00	*90.00*
31	A17	½a light green	2.10	*2.40*
32	A19	1a carmine rose	1.90	.50
33	A21	2a violet	4.00	8.25
34	A28	2a6p ultra ('03)	2.25	9.50
		Nos. 30-34 (5)	21.25	*110.65*

1903-08

No.	Type	Description	Unused	Used
35	A32	3p gray	2.10	.25
36	A33	½a green	2.25	.45
37	A34	1a carmine rose	2.25	.45
38	A35	2a violet	3.00	1.50
39	A36	2a6p ultra ('05)	37.50	*120.00*
40	A37	3a brn org ('04)	3.00	.50
41	A38	4a olive green	3.75	.60
42	A39	6a bister ('06)	9.00	2.10
43	A40	8a red violet	7.50	2.40
44	A41	12a vio, *red* ('05)	4.50	*30.00*
45	A42	1r car rose & grn ('05)	4.50	2.50
46	A43	2r brown & rose	13.50	*16.50*
47	A43	3r grn & brn ('08)	42.50	*75.00*
48	A43	5r vio & bl ('08)	27.50	*40.00*
		Nos. 35-48 (14)	162.85	*292.25*

There are two settings of the overprint on Nos. 35, 37-46. In the first (1903), "GWALIOR" is 14mm long and lines are spaced 1¾mm. In the second (1908), "GWALIOR" is 13mm long and lines are 2¾mm apart. No. 36 exists only with first overprint, Nos. 47-48 only with second.

1907

No.	Type	Description	Unused	Used
49	A44	½a green	.30	*1.00*
50	A45	1a carmine rose	2.25	.25

No. 49 exists with both settings of overprint. See note below No. 48.

1912-23

No.	Type	Description	Unused	Used
51	A46	3p gray	.30	.25
52	A47	½a green	.30	.25
a.		Inverted overprint		*600.00*
53	A48	1a car rose	.35	.25
a.		Double overprint	37.50	
54	A48	1a dk brown ('23)	1.60	.25
55	A49	2a violet	1.20	.25
56	A51	3a brown orange	1.00	.25
57	A52	4a olive grn ('13)	.90	.90
58	A53	6a bister	1.90	2.10
59	A54	8a red vio ('13)	3.25	1.20
60	A55	12a claret ('14)	2.10	*6.00*
61	A56	1r green & red brn	13.50	.65
62	A56	2r brn & car rose	7.50	6.50
63	A56	5r violet & ultra	35.00	9.50
		Nos. 51-63 (13)	68.90	28.35

India No. 104 Overprinted

1921

No.	Type	Description	Unused	Used
64	A48	9p on 1a rose	1.00	*.75*
a.		Inverted overprint	—	

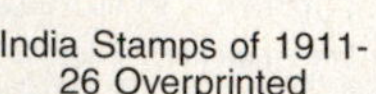

India Stamps of 1911-26 Overprinted

Hindi Overprint 15mm Long

1923-27

No.	Type	Description	Unused	Used
66	A59	1½a choc ('25)	3.25	.75
67	A59	1½a rose ('27)	.30	.25
a.		Inverted overprint	—	—
68	A57	2a6p ultra ('25)	3.25	2.50
69	A57	2a6p brown org ('27)	.50	*.75*
70	A51	3a ultra ('24)	3.75	.90
		Nos. 66-70 (5)	11.05	5.15

Similar Ovpt. on India Stamps of 1926-35
Hindi Overprint 13½mm Long

1928-32 **Wmk. 196**

No.	Type	Description	Unused	Used
71	A46	3p slate ('32)	1.25	.25
72	A47	½a green ('30)	1.90	.25
73	A48	1a dark brown	1.10	.25
74	A60	2a dull violet	.70	.45
75	A51	3a ultramarine	1.25	.60
76	A61	4a olive green	1.60	1.50
77	A54	8a red violet	1.60	1.60
78	A55	12a claret	2.75	*5.25*

Overprinted

No.	Type	Description	Unused	Used
79	A56	1r green & brown	3.75	*6.00*
80	A56	2r brn org & car rose	6.75	6.50
81	A56	5r dk vio & ultra ('29)	24.00	*37.50*
82	A56	10r car & grn ('30)	82.50	62.50
83	A56	15r ol grn & ultra ('30)	130.00	100.00
84	A56	25r bl & ocher ('30)	275.00	250.00
		Nos. 71-84 (14)	534.15	472.65

India Stamps of 1932-35 Overprinted in Black

Hindi Overprint 13½mm Long

1933-36

No.	Type	Description	Unused	Used
85	A71	½a green ('36)	.65	.25
86	A68	9p dk green ('33)	3.75	.45
87	A72	1a dk brown ('36)	.30	.25
88	A69	1a3p violet ('36)	.65	.25
89	A49	2a vermilion ('36)	3.75	5.25
		Nos. 85-89 (5)	9.10	6.45

Same Ovpt. on India Stamps of 1937

1938-40 ***Perf. 13½x14***

No.	Type	Description	Unused	Used
90	A80	3p slate ('40)	10.00	.25
91	A80	½a brown	11.00	.25
92	A80	9p green ('40)	60.00	6.00
93	A80	1a carmine	10.00	.25
94	A81	3a yel green ('39)	35.00	7.50
95	A81	4a dark brown	55.00	5.25
96	A81	6a pck blue ('39)	5.00	*16.50*
		Nos. 90-96 (7)	186.00	36.00
		Set, never hinged	225.00	

Same Overprinted on India Stamps of 1941-43

1942-49

No.	Type	Description	Unused	Used
100	A83	3p slate ('44)	.55	.25
101	A83	½a rose vio ('46)	1.25	.25
102	A83	9p light green	.55	.25
103	A83	1a car rose ('44)	1.25	.25
104	A84	1½a dk purple ('44)	8.75	.25
105	A84	2a scarlet ('44)	1.90	.25
106	A84	3a violet ('44)	20.00	2.50
108	A85	4a choc ('44)	4.00	.25
109	A85	6a pck blue ('48)	17.50	*40.00*
110	A85	8a blue violet	4.75	*4.00*
111	A85	12a carmine lake	7.00	*35.00*

India Nos. 162-167 Overprinted

Perf. 13½x14

No.	Type	Description	Unused	Used
112	A82	1r brn & sl ('45)	15.00	2.50
113	A82	2r dk brn & dk vio ('49)	62.50	14.00
114	A82	5r dp ultra & dk grn ('49)	40.00	60.00
115	A82	10r rose car & dk vio ('49)	40.00	*62.50*
116	A82	15r dk grn & dk brn ('48)	110.00	*250.00*
117	A82	25r dk vio & blue vio ('48)	110.00	*190.00*
		Nos. 100-106,108-117 (17)	445.00	662.25
		Set, never hinged	525.00	

India Stamps of 1941-43 Overprinted

1949

No.	Type	Description	Unused	Used
118	A83	3p slate	2.50	.75
119	A83	½a rose violet	2.50	.75
120	A83	1a carmine rose	2.25	.90
121	A84	2a scarlet	32.50	3.25
122	A84	3a violet	80.00	45.00
123	A85	4a chocolate	9.25	5.00
124	A85	6a pck blue	67.50	*97.50*
125	A85	8a blue violet	140.00	82.50
126	A85	12a carmine lake	525.00	225.00
		Nos. 118-126 (9)	861.50	460.65
		Set, never hinged	1,050.	

OFFICIAL STAMPS

India Stamps Overprinted in Black

1895 **Wmk. 39** ***Perf. 14***

No.	Type	Description	Unused	Used
O1	A17	½a green	.75	.25
a.		Double overprint		1,400.
O2	A19	1a maroon	18.00	2.10
O3	A21	2a ultramarine	5.00	.60
O4	A23	4a olive green	5.25	2.25
O5	A25	8a red violet	6.50	5.00
O6	A29	1r car rose & grn	12.50	4.50
		Nos. O1-O6 (6)	48.00	14.70

Nos. O1 to O6 inclusive are known with the last two characters of the lower word transposed.

1901-04

No.	Type	Description	Unused	Used
O7	A31	3p gray ('04)	3.75	*5.25*
O8	A17	½a light green	1.10	.25
O9	A19	1a carmine rose	9.00	.25
O10	A21	2a violet ('03)	2.50	2.25
		Nos. O7-O10 (4)	16.35	8.00

1902

No.	Type	Description	Unused	Used
O11	A31	3p carmine rose	1.90	.35

1903-05

No.	Type	Description	Unused	Used
O12	A32	3p gray	.90	.25
O13	A33	½a green	4.00	.25
O14	A34	1a carmine rose	1.40	.25
O15	A35	2a violet	2.25	.45
O16	A38	4a olive grn ('05)	22.50	2.50
O17	A40	8a red violet	9.50	1.00
O18	A42	1r car rose & grn ('05)	3.50	3.00
		Nos. O12-O18 (7)	44.05	7.70

1907

No.	Type	Description	Unused	Used
O19	A44	½a green	2.50	.25
O20	A45	1a carmine rose	10.00	.25

Two spacings of the overprint lines, 10mm and 8mm, are found on Nos. O12-O20.

No. O13 with 10mm spacing is known with the two overprint lines transposed. This is due to a shift in the positioning of the overprint, rather than an actual transposition of the overprint.

1913

No.	Type	Description	Unused	Used
O21	A46	3p gray	.35	.25
O22	A47	½a green	.30	.25
O23	A48	1a carmine rose	.45	.25
a.		Double overprint	97.50	
O24	A49	2a violet	2.25	.25
O25	A52	4a olive green	.90	*2.25*
O26	A54	8a red violet	1.90	1.50
O27	A56	1r grn & red brn	40.00	35.00
		Nos. O21-O27 (7)	46.15	39.75

India No. O66 Overprinted

1921

No.	Type	Description	Unused	Used
O28	O6	9p on 1a rose	.25	*.45*

India No. 83 Overprinted

1923

No.	Type	Description	Unused	Used
O29	A481	a dark brown	5.50	.25

Similar Ovpt. on India Stamps of 1926-35

1927-35 **Wmk. 196**

No.	Type	Description	Unused	Used
O30	A46	3p slate	.30	.25
O31	A47	½a green	.30	.25
O32	A48	1a dark brown	.30	.25
O33	A60	2a dull violet	.30	.25
O34	A61	4a olive green	1.00	.45
O35	A54	8a red violet	.90	*1.60*

Overprinted

No.	Type	Description	Unused	Used
O36	A56	1r green & brown	1.50	*2.50*
O37	A56	2r brn org & car rose ('35)	29.00	*30.00*
O38	A56	5r dk vio & ultra ('32)	35.00	*250.00*
O39	A56	10r car & grn ('32)	240.00	*650.00*
		Nos. O30-O39 (10)	308.60	*935.55*

India Stamps of 1926-35 Overprinted

1933-37 ***Perf. 13½x14, 14***

No.	Type	Description	Unused	Used
O40	A71	½a green ('36)	.35	.25
O41	A68	9p dk green ('35)	.30	.25
O42	A72	1a dk brown ('36)	.30	.25
O43	A69	1a3p violet ('33)	.75	.25
O44	A49	2a ver ('36)	.30	*.60*
a.		Small die ('36)	3.75	1.90
O45	A52	4a olive green ('37)	.90	*1.10*
		Nos. O40-O45 (6)	2.90	2.70

For surcharge see No. O62.

Same Overprint on India Stamps

1938 ***Perf. 13½x14***

No.	Type	Description	Unused	Used
O46	A80	½a brown	8.00	.45
		Never hinged	9.50	
O47	A80	1a carmine	2.00	.25
		Never hinged	2.25	

India Nos. 162-165 Overprinted

1945-48 **Wmk. 196** ***Perf. 13½x14***

No.	Type	Description	Unused	Used
O48	A82	1r brown & slate	12.50	*32.50*
O49	A82	2r dk brn & dk vio	22.50	*140.00*
O50	A82	5r dp ultra & dk grn ('46)	37.50	*825.00*
O51	A82	10r rose car & dk vio ('48)	100.00	*1,650.*
		Nos. O48-O51 (4)	172.50	*2,648.*
		Set, never hinged	200.00	

India Official Stamps of 1939-43 Overprinted

1940-44 **Wmk. 196** ***Perf. 13½x14***

No.	Type	Description	Unused	Used
O52	O8	3p slate	.65	.25
O53	O8	½a brown	5.50	.35
O54	O8	½a dk rose vio ('43)	.75	.25
O55	O8	9p green ('43)	.85	*1.00*
O56	O8	1a car rose ('41)	2.75	.25
O57	O8	1a3p bister ('42)	55.00	2.50
O58	O8	1½a dl pur ('43)	1.50	.45
O59	O8	2a scarlet ('41)	1.50	.45
O60	O8	4a dk brn ('44)	1.50	*5.00*
O61	O8	8a blue vio ('44)	6.00	*14.00*
		Nos. O52-O61 (10)	76.00	24.50
		Set, never hinged	95.00	

Gwalior No. O43 with Additional Surcharge in Black

1942

No.	Type	Description	Unused	Used
O62	A69	1a on 1a3p violet	30.00	4.50
		Never hinged	37.50	

JIND

'jind

(Jhind)

LOCATION — A State of India in the north Punjab.
AREA — 1,299 sq. mi.
POP. — 361,812 (1941)
CAPITAL — Sangrur

Previous stamp issues are listed under Feudatory States.

The varieties with small letters are not listed as the letters are merely broken and not from another font.

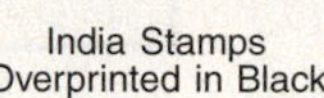

India Stamps Overprinted in Black

1885 Wmk. 39 Perf. 14

No.	Type	Description	Unused	Used
33	A17	½a green	7.00	8.25
a.		Overprint reading down	140.00	160.00
34	A19	1a violet brown	62.50	90.00
a.		Overprint reading down	1,400.	1,500.
35	A21	2a ultra	29.00	32.50
a.		Overprint reading down	1,000.	1,200.
36	A25	8a red lilac	625.00	
a.		Overprint reading down	18,000.	
37	A27	1r gray	700.00	
a.		Overprint reading down	21,000.	

Wmk. 38

No.	Type	Description	Unused	Used
38	A9	4a green	97.50	140.00
		Nos. 33-38 (6)	1,521.	270.75

On the reprints of Nos. 33 to 38 "Jhind" measures 8mm instead of 9mm and "State" 9mm instead of 9½mm.

Examples of "inverted overprints" exist of the ½a, 1a and 2a with the lines much less curved. These are thought to come from a trial printing.

India Stamps Overprinted in Red or Black

1885 Wmk. 39

No.	Type	Description	Unused	Used
39	A17	½a green (R)	210.00	
40	A19	1a violet brown	210.00	
41	A21	2a ultra (R)	210.00	
42	A25	8a red lilac	290.00	
43	A27	1r gray (R)	290.00	

Wmk. 38

No.	Type	Description	Unused	Used
44	A9	4a green (R)	290.00	
		Nos. 39-44 (6)	1,500.	

India Stamps Overprinted

1886 Wmk. 39 Red Overprint

No.	Type	Description	Unused	Used
45	A17	½a green	52.50	
a.		"JEIND"	1,800.	
46	A21	2a ultramarine	57.50	
a.		"JEIND"	1,800.	
47	A27	1r gray	90.00	
a.		"JEIND"	2,750.	

Wmk. 38

No.	Type	Description	Unused	Used
48	A9	4a green	90.00	
		Nos. 45-48 (4)	290.00	

Nos. 46, 47 and 48 were not placed in use.

1886-98 Wmk. 39 Black Overprint

No.	Type	Description	Unused	Used
49	A17	½a green ('88)	1.20	.25
a.		Inverted overprint	300.00	
50	A19	1a vio brn	3.75	.25
a.		"JEIND"	750.00	
51	A20	1a6p bis brn ('97)	3.75	5.50
52	A21	2a ultra	3.75	.60
53	A22	3a orange	5.00	1.00
54	A23	4a olive green	6.00	3.25
55	A25	8a red violet	12.50	30.00
a.		"JEIND"	2,400.	
56	A26	12a vio, *red* ('97)	10.00	37.50
57	A27	1r gray ('91)	17.50	82.50
58	A29	1r car rose & grn ('98)	16.50	90.00
59	A30	2r brn & rose ('97)	525.00	1,500.
60	A30	3r grn & brn ('97)	750.00	1,350.
61	A30	5r vio & bl ('97)	750.00	1,250.

Wmk. 38

No.	Type	Description	Unused	Used
62	A14	6a bister	6.50	21.00
		Nos. 49-62 (14)	2,111.	4,372.

1900 Wmk. 39

No.	Type	Description	Unused	Used
63	A31	3p carmine rose	1.60	2.50

1902-04

No.	Type	Description	Unused	Used
64	A31	3p gray ('04)	.60	6.00
65	A17	½a light green	7.00	10.00
66	A19	1a carmine rose	1.90	10.00
		Nos. 64-66 (3)	9.50	26.00

1903-09

No.	Type	Description	Unused	Used
67	A32	3p gray	.35	.25
68	A33	½a green	2.50	2.50
69	A34	1a car rose ('09)	2.75	2.40
70	A35	2a violet ('06)	4.25	3.25
70A	A36	2a6p ultra ('09)	.85	10.00
71	A37	3a brown orange	3.25	.60
a.		Double overprint	175.00	325.00
72	A38	4a olive green	11.50	14.00
73	A39	6a bister ('05)	9.25	32.50
74	A40	8a red violet	4.00	32.50
75	A41	12a vio, *red* ('05)	4.25	17.50
76	A42	1r car rose & grn ('05)	4.75	32.50
		Nos. 67-76 (11)	47.70	148.00

1907

No.	Type	Description	Unused	Used
77	A44	½a green	.60	.25
78	A45	1a carmine rose	2.25	1.00

1913

No.	Type	Description	Unused	Used
80	A46	3p gray	.30	3.50
81	A47	½a green	.30	1.10
82	A48	1a carmine rose	.30	.65
83	A49	2a violet	.30	6.25
84	A51	3a brown orange	2.25	21.00
85	A53	6a bister	12.50	42.50
		Nos. 80-85 (6)	15.95	75.00

India Stamps of 1911-26 Overprinted

1913-14

No.	Type	Description	Unused	Used
88	A46	3p gray	1.50	.25
89	A47	½a green	3.75	.25
90	A48	1a carmine rose	2.40	.25
91	A49	2a violet	6.50	1.90
92	A51	3a brown orange	.75	6.00
93	A52	4a olive green	3.00	14.00
94	A53	6a bister	6.00	24.00
95	A54	8a red violet	8.25	24.00
96	A55	12a claret	7.50	30.00
97	A56	1r grn & red brn	17.50	35.00
		Nos. 88-97 (10)	57.15	135.65

India No. 104 Overprinted

1921

No.	Type	Description	Unused	Used
98	A48	9p on 1a rose	1.90	22.50

India Stamps of 1913-19 Overprinted

1922

No.	Type	Description	Unused	Used
99	A58	1½a chocolate	5.00	9.00
100	A57	2a6p ultramarine	.75	7.00

Same Overprint on India Stamps of 1911-26

1924

No.	Type	Description	Unused	Used
101	A48	1a dark brown	9.00	4.50
102	A59	1½a chocolate	.75	2.25

Same Overprint on India No. 87

1925

No.	Type	Description	Unused	Used
103	A51	3a ultramarine	3.00	7.50

Same Overprint on India Stamps of 1911-26

1927

No.	Type	Description	Unused	Used
104	A59	1½a rose	.30	2.25
105	A57	2a6p brown orange	1.90	12.00
106	A56	2r yel brn & car rose	9.50	225.00
107	A56	5r violet & ultra	67.50	450.00
		Nos. 104-107 (4)	79.20	689.25

India Stamps of 1926-35 Overprinted

1927-32 Wmk. 196

No.	Type	Description	Unused	Used
108	A46	3p slate	.30	.25
109	A47	½a green	.30	.50
110	A68	9p dk grn ('32)	2.75	.60
111	A48	1a dark brown	.30	.25
112	A69	1a3p violet ('32)	.35	.45
113	A59	1½a carmine rose	.75	5.50
114	A60	2a dull violet	4.25	.60
115	A57	2a6p buff	2.00	16.00
116	A51	3a ultramarine	8.00	27.50
117	A61	4a olive green	2.00	5.25
118	A54	8a red violet	7.50	3.25
119	A55	12a claret	12.00	32.50

Indian Stamps of 1911-23 Overprinted

No.	Type	Description	Unused	Used
120	A56	1r grn & brn	6.50	9.00
121	A56	2r buff & car rose	55.00	225.00
122	A56	5r dk vio & ultra	16.00	62.50
123	A56	10r car rose & grn	19.00	27.50
124	A56	15r ol grn & blue	120.00	1,050.
125	A56	25r blue & ocher	190.00	1,250.
		Nos. 108-125 (18)	447.00	2,717.

India Stamps of 1926-35 Overprinted

1934-37

No.	Type	Description	Unused	Used
126	A71	½a green	.45	.35
127	A72	1a dark brown	2.50	.45
128	A49	2a vermilion	4.75	.90
129	A51	3a carmine rose	4.25	.60
130	A70	3a6p deep blue ('37)	3.25	30.00
131	A52	4a olive green	4.25	2.25
132	A53	6a bister ('37)	.85	32.50
		Nos. 126-132 (7)	20.30	67.05

Same Overprint on India Stamps of 1937

1937-38 Wmk. 196 Perf. 13½x14

No.	Type	Description	Unused	Used
133	A80	3p slate ('38)	11.00	3.75
134	A80	½a brown ('38)	.80	7.50
135	A80	9p green	.80	6.00
136	A80	1a carmine	.80	.90
137	A81	2a scarlet ('38)	1.75	27.50
138	A81	2a6p purple ('38)	1.40	35.00
139	A81	3a yel grn ('38)	6.75	30.00
140	A81	3a6p ultra ('38)	4.25	35.00
141	A81	4a dk brown ('38)	10.00	27.50
142	A81	6a pck blue ('38)	6.50	42.50
143	A81	8a blue vio ('38)	5.25	35.00
144	A81	12a car lake ('38)	3.00	45.00

Indian Stamps of 1937-40 Overprinted

1938

No.	Type	Description	Unused	Used
145	A82	1r brn & slate	13.00	62.50
146	A82	2r dk brn & dk vio	16.00	190.00
147	A82	5r dp ultra & dk grn	25.00	125.00
148	A82	10r rose car & dk violet	50.00	120.00
149	A82	15r dk grn & dk brown	110.00	1,200.
150	A82	25r dk vio & bl vio	575.00	1,400.
		Nos. 133-150 (18)	841.30	3,393.
		Set, never hinged	1,200.	

India Stamps of 1937 Overprinted

1942-43 Wmk. 196 Perf. 13½x14

No.	Type	Description	Unused	Used
155	A80	3p slate	17.50	32.50
156	A80	½a brown	1.25	3.75
157	A80	9p green	16.00	30.00
158	A80	1a carmine	1.25	9.00
159	A82	1r brn & slate	11.00	40.00
160	A82	2r dk brn & dk violet	22.50	52.50
161	A82	5r dp ultra & dk green	50.00	140.00
162	A82	10r rose car & dk vio ('43)	75.00	140.00
163	A82	15r dk grn & dk brn ('43)	160.00	250.00
164	A82	25r dk vio & bl vio	75.00	525.00
		Nos. 155-164 (10)	429.50	1,223.
		Set, never hinged	510.00	

Same Overprint on India Stamps of 1941-43

No.	Type	Description	Unused	Used
165	A83	3p slate	.60	2.10
166	A83	½a rose vio ('43)	.60	3.25
167	A83	9p light green	.95	6.50
168	A83	1a car rose ('43)	1.25	2.25
169	A84	1a3p bister ('43)	1.25	7.50
170	A84	1½a dark purple	10.00	7.50
171	A84	2a scarlet	2.25	7.50
172	A84	3a violet ('43)	30.00	9.00
173	A84	3½a ultramarine	11.00	17.50
174	A85	4a chocolate	7.50	9.00
175	A85	6a pck blue	8.00	25.00
176	A85	8a blue violet	5.25	22.50
177	A85	12a carmine lake	17.50	27.50
		Nos. 165-177 (13)	98.15	147.10
		Set, never hinged	115.00	

OFFICIAL STAMPS

India Stamps Overprinted in Black

1885 Wmk. 39 Perf. 14

No.	Type	Description	Unused	Used
O1	A17	½a green	3.00	.60
a.		"JHIND STATE" reading down	150.00	90.00
O2	A19	1a violet brown	1.00	.25
a.		"JHIND STATE" reading down	17.50	11.00
O3	A21	2a ultra	60.00	72.50
a.		"JHIND STATE" reading down	1,500.	1,750.
		Nos. O1-O3 (3)	64.00	73.35

The reprints may be distinguished by the same measurements as the reprints of the corresponding regular issue.

India Stamps Overprinted in Red or Black

1885

No.	Type	Description	Unused	Used
O4	A17	½a green (R)	150.00	
O5	A19	1a violet brown	125.00	
O6	A21	2a ultra (R)	140.00	
		Nos. O4-O6 (3)	415.00	

India Stamps Overprinted

1886 Red Overprint

No.	Type	Description	Unused	Used
O7	A17	½a green	42.50	
a.		"JEIND"	1,050.	
b.		"ERVICE"	6,000.	

O8 A21 2a ultramarine 47.50
a. "JEIND" 1,750.
b. "ERVICE" 3,750.

No. O8 was not placed in use.

1886-96 Black Overprint

O9 A17 ½a green ('88) 2.50 .25
O10 A19 1a violet brown 16.00 2.25
a. "JEIND" 750.00
b. "ERVICE"
O11 A21 2a ultramarine 4.25 1.50
O12 A23 4a olive green 4.50 3.00
O13 A25 8a red violet 7.00 *12.50*
O14 A29 1r car rose & grn ('96) 8.00 *75.00*
Nos. O9-O14 (6) 42.25 *94.50*

1902

O15 A17 ½a light green 3.75 .45

1903-06

O16 A32 3p gray .85 .25
O17 A33 ½a green 4.50 .25
a. "HIND" 4,500. 450.00
O18 A34 1a carmine rose 3.75 .25
a. "HIND" 5,250. 400.00
O19 A35 2a violet 2.50 .25
O20 A38 4a olive green 2.10 .65
O21 A40 8a red violet 7.50 2.25
O22 A42 1r car rose & grn ('06) 3.25 3.25
Nos. O16-O22 (7) 24.45 7.15

1907

O23 A44 ½a green 1.50 .25
O24 A45 1a carmine rose 2.50 .25

Indian Stamps of 1911-26 Overprinted

a

b

1914-27

O25 A46(a) 3p gray .30 .25
O26 A47(a) ½a green .40 .25
O27 A48(a) 1a car rose 1.00 .25
O28 A49(a) 2a violet .35 *.45*
O29 A52(a) 4a olive green 1.90 .25
O30 A54(a) 8a red violet 1.00 1.50
O31 A56(b) 1r grn & red brn 3.75 2.50
O32 A56(b) 2r yel brn & car rose ('27) 27.50 *100.00*
O33 A56(b) 5r vio & ultra ('27) 35.00 *375.00*
Nos. O25-O33 (9) 71.20 *480.45*

India Nos. 83 and 89 Overprinted Type "a"

1924-27

O34 A48 1a dark brown .90 .25
O35 A53 6a bister ('27) 2.50 *3.25*

India Stamps of 1926-35 Overprinted — c

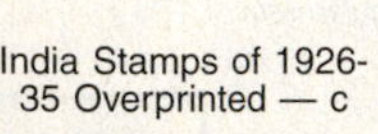

1927-32

O36 A46 3p slate .25 .25
O37 A47 ½a green .25 *1.50*
O38 A68 9p dark green ('32) .90 .25
O39 A48 1a dark brown .25 .25
O40 A69 1a3p violet ('32) .60 .25
O41 A60 2a dull violet .35 .25
O42 A61 4a olive green .50 .35
O43 A54 8a red violet .90 *2.50*
O44 A55 12a claret 3.25 *27.50*

Indian Stamps of 1911-23 Overprinted — d

O45 A56 1r green & brown 7.50 *8.25*
O46 A56 2r buff & car rose 75.00 62.50
O47 A56 5r dk vio & ultra 19.00 *400.00*
O48 A56 10r car rose & grn 57.50 *225.00*
Nos. O36-O48 (13) 166.25 *728.85*

India Stamps of 1926-35 Overprinted Type "c"

1934-37

O49 A71 ½a green .30 .25
O50 A72 1a dark brown .30 .25
O51 A49 2a vermilion .45 .25
O52 A57 2a6p buff ('37) 1.90 *30.00*
O53 A52 4a olive green 9.00 .45
O54 A53 6a bister ('37) 5.50 25.00
Nos. O49-O54 (6) 17.45 56.20

India Nos. 151-153 Overprinted Type "c"

1937-42 Perf. 13½x14

O55 A80 ½a brown ('42) 67.50 .45
O56 A80 9p green 2.50 *24.00*
O57 A80 1a carmine 1.90 .45

India Nos. 162-165 Overprinted Type "d"

O58 A82 1r brn & sl ('40) 45.00 *67.50*
O59 A82 2r dk brn & dk vio ('40) 47.50 *375.00*
O60 A82 5r dp ultra & dk grn ('40) 100.00 *600.00*
O61 A82 10r rose car & dk vio ('40) 450.00 *1,500.*
Nos. O55-O61 (7) 714.40 *2,567.*
Set, never hinged 875.00

India Official Stamps of 1939-43 Overprinted

1940-43

O62 O8 3p slate .65 *3.00*
O63 O8 ½a brown 2.10 1.90
O64 O8 ½a dk rose vio ('43) .65 .45
O65 O8 9p green 3.25 19.00
O66 O8 1a car rose 3.75 .25
O67 O8 1¼a dull pur ('43) 9.25 2.40
O68 O8 2a scarlet 8.50 .45
O69 O8 2½a purple 5.25 *14.00*
O70 O8 4a dark brown 9.50 7.00
O71 O8 8a blue violet 9.50 *12.00*

India Nos. 162-165 Overprinted

1942 Wmk. 196 Perf. 13½x14

O72 A82 1r brown & slate 19.00 *82.50*
O73 A82 2r dk brn & dk vio 45.00 *250.00*
O74 A82 5r dp ultra & dk green 75.00 *625.00*
O75 A82 10r rose car & dk violet 150.00 *825.00*
Nos. O62-O75 (14) 341.40 *1,843.*
Set, never hinged 500.00

NABHA

'näb-hə

LOCATION — A State of India in the eastern and southeastern Punjab
AREA — 966 sq. mi.
POP. — 340,044 (1941)
CAPITAL — Nabha

The varieties with small letters in the overprint are not listed as the letters are merely broken and not from another font.

Indian Stamps Overprinted in Black

1885 Wmk. 39 Perf. 14

1 A17 ½a green 6.25 *9.00*
2 A19 1a violet brown 82.50 *290.00*
3 A21 2a ultramarine 37.50 *97.50*
4 A25 8a red lilac 475.00
5 A27 1r gray 550.00

Wmk. 38

6 A9 4a green 125.00 *375.00*

On the reprints "Nabha" and "State" each measure 9½mm. On the originals they measure 11 and 10mm respectively.

Indian Stamps Overprinted

1885 Wmk. 39 Red Overprint

7 A17 ½a green 1.90 1.50
8 A21 2a ultramarine 3.75 3.25
9 A27 1r gray 190.00 *450.00*

Wmk. 38

10 A9 4a green 67.50 *325.00*

1885-97 Wmk. 39 Black Overprint

11 A17 ½a green .90 .25
12 A18 9p rose ('92) .30 *5.25*
13 A19 1a violet brown 4.50 1.50
14 A20 1a6p bister brn 2.50 *6.00*
a. "ABHA" 450.00
15 A21 2a ultramarine 4.50 3.00
16 A22 3a orange 16.00 *32.50*
17 A23 4a olive green 9.00 5.00
18 A25 8a red lilac 6.00 5.25
19 A26 12a vio, *red* ('89) 7.00 *8.25*
20 A27 1r gray 22.50 *90.00*
21 A29 1r car rose & grn ('93) 21.00 10.50
a. "N BHA" —
22 A30 2r brn & rose ('97) 210.00 *450.00*
23 A30 3r grn & brn ('97) 210.00 *550.00*
24 A30 5r vio & blk ('97) 225.00 *825.00*

Wmk. 38

25 A14 6a bister ('89) 5.50 *6.50*
Nos. 11-25 (15) 744.70 *1,999.*

Nos. 7, 8, 9, 10, 13, and 18 have been reprinted. They usually bear the overprint "Specimen."

1900 Wmk. 39

26 A31 3p carmine rose .45 .25

1903-09

27 A32 3p gray .95 .25
28 A33 ½a green 1.40 1.00
a. "NABH" 1,650.
29 A34 1a car rose 2.10 2.25
30 A35 2a violet 3.25 *5.25*
30A A36 2a6p ultra 24.50 *130.00*
31 A37 3a brn org 2.00 .60
32 A38 4a olive green 6.00 2.50
33 A39 6a bister 5.00 *30.00*
34 A40 8a red violet 13.00 *40.00*
35 A41 12a violet, *red* 5.50 *40.00*
36 A42 1r car rose & grn 12.00 *27.50*
Nos. 27-36 (11) 75.70 *279.35*

1907

37 A44 ½a green 2.25 1.90
38 A45 1a carmine rose 2.25 1.00

1913

40 A46 3p gray .75 .75
41 A47 ½a green .75 .45
42 A48 1a carmine rose 1.60 .25
43 A49 2a violet 1.50 1.50
44 A51 3a brown orange .75 .45
45 A52 4a olive green 1.00 *3.00*
46 A53 6a bister 1.90 *9.50*
47 A54 8a red violet 9.50 9.00
48 A55 12a claret 4.50 *35.00*
49 A56 1r green & red brn 15.00 11.00
Nos. 40-49 (10) 37.25 *70.90*

1924

50 A48 1a dark brown 10.00 6.00

India Stamps of 1926-35 Overprinted

1927-32 Wmk. 196

51 A46 3p slate ('32) 2.50 .25
52 A47 ½a green 1.50 .45
53 A48 1a dark brown 2.25 .25
54 A60 2a dull violet ('32) 3.75 .50
55 A57 2a6p buff ('32) 1.75 *14.00*
56 A51 3a blue ('30) 4.50 2.10
57 A61 4a olive green ('32) 6.75 3.75

Indian Stamps of 1937-40 Overprinted

58 A56 2r brn org & car rose ('32) 47.50 *210.00*
59 A56 5r dk vio & ultra ('32) 110.00 *600.00*
Nos. 51-59 (9) 180.50 *831.30*

India Stamps of 1926-35 Overprinted

1936-37

63 A71 ½a green .75 .60
64 A68 9p dark green ('37) 3.00 1.60
65 A72 1a dark brown .75 .45
66 A69 1a3p violet ('37) 3.50 *11.00*
67 A51 3a car rose ('37) 5.00 *25.00*
68 A52 4a olive green ('37) 7.50 7.50
Nos. 63-68 (6) 20.50 *46.15*
Set, never hinged 25.00

Same Overprint in Black on 1937 Stamps of India

1938-39 Perf. 13½x14

69 A80 3p slate 9.50 2.25
70 A80 ½a brown 7.50 2.50
71 A80 9p green 21.00 7.50
72 A80 1a carmine 3.25 1.50
73 A81 2a scarlet 1.25 *12.00*
74 A81 2a6p purple 1.25 *17.50*
75 A81 3a yel green 1.50 *9.00*
76 A81 3a6p ultramarine 1.75 *37.50*
77 A81 4a dark brown 8.00 *10.50*
78 A81 6a peacock blue 3.50 *40.00*
79 A81 8a blue violet 2.25 *37.50*
80 A81 12a car lake 3.00 *37.50*

Overprinted

81 A82 1r brown & slate 13.00 *52.50*
82 A82 2r dk brn & dk vio 32.50 *175.00*
83 A82 5r dp ultra & dk green 42.50 *300.00*
84 A82 10r rose car & dk vio ('39) 65.00 *600.00*
85 A82 15r dk grn & dk brn ('39) 200.00 *1,250.*
86 A82 25r dk vio & blue vio ('39) 150.00 *1,250.*
Nos. 69-86 (18) 566.75 *3,843.*
Set, never hinged 1,200.

India Stamps of 1937 Overprinted in Black

1942 Perf. 13½x14

87 A80 3p slate 50.00 9.00
88 A80 ½a brown 100.00 10.50
89 A80 9p green 14.00 24.00
90 A80 1a carmine 15.00 6.50
Nos. 87-90 (4) 179.00 50.00
Set, never hinged 210.00

Same on India Nos. 168-179

1942-46 Wmk. 196

100 A83 3p slate 1.25 1.25
101 A83 ½a rose vio ('43) 3.25 2.50
102 A83 9p lt green ('43) 2.50 2.50
103 A83 1a car rose ('46) 1.10 *6.50*
104 A84 1a3p bister ('44) 1.10 *5.50*
105 A84 1½a dark pur ('43) 2.50 *4.50*
106 A84 2a scarlet ('44) 1.20 *6.50*
107 A84 3a violet ('44) 7.00 7.00
108 A84 3½a ultramarine 18.00 *100.00*
109 A85 4a choc ('43) 1.90 1.50

110 A85 6a pck blue ('44) 15.00 *82.50*
111 A85 8a blue vio ('44) 13.50 62.50
112 A85 12a car lake ('44) 12.00 *100.00*
Nos. 100-112 (13) 80.30 *382.75*
Set, never hinged 110.00

OFFICIAL STAMPS

Indian Stamps Overprinted in Black

1885 Wmk. 39 *Perf. 14*
O1 A17 ½a green 7.50 2.25
O2 A19 1a violet brown 1.00 .30
O3 A21 2a ultra 125.00 *250.00*
Nos. O1-O3 (3) 133.50 *252.55*

The reprints have the same measurements as the reprints of the regular issue of the same date.

Indian Stamps Overprinted

1885 Red Overprint
O4 A17 ½a green 11.00 8.25
O5 A21 2a ultramarine 2.40 *.80*

1885-97 Black Overprint
O6 A17 ½a green .60 .25
a. Period after "SERVICE" 190.00 3.25
O7 A19 1a violet brown 3.00 .35
a. "NABHA STATE" double 2,750. *375.00*
b. Period after "SERVICE" 13.50 1.10
O8 A21 2a ultra 5.00 2.50
O9 A22 3a orange 37.50 *140.00*
O10 A23 4a olive green 5.25 2.25
O11 A25 8a red vio ('89) 4.00 2.25
O12 A26 12a vio, *red* ('89) 9.50 *32.50*
O13 A27 1r gray ('89) 62.50 *525.00*
O14 A29 1r car rose & grn ('97) 24.00 *35.00*

Wmk. 38
O15 A14 6a bister ('89) 32.50 *52.50*
Nos. O6-O15 (10) 183.85 *792.60*

Nos. O4, O5, and O7 have been reprinted. They usually bear the overprint "Specimen."

1903-06 Wmk. 39
O16 A32 3p gray ('06) 3.75 25.00
O17 A33 ½a green 1.20 .50
O18 A34 1a carmine rose 1.20 .25
O19 A35 2a violet 5.00 2.10
O20 A38 4a olive green 2.40 .75
O21 A40 8a red violet 2.50 2.25
O22 A42 1r car rose & grn 2.50 *3.75*
Nos. O16-O22 (7) 18.55 34.60

1907
O23 A44 ½a green 2.50 .75
O24 A45 1a carmine rose 1.00 .40

1913
O25 A52 4a olive green 17.50 *100.00*
O26 A56 1r grn & red brn 92.50 *750.00*

Indian Stamps of 1911-26 Overprinted

a

b

1913
O27 A46(a) 3p gray 1.40 *15.00*
O28 A47(a) ½a green .85 .25
O29 A48(a) 1a carmine rose .75 .25
O30 A49(a) 2a violet 1.60 .25
O31 A52(a) 4a olive green 1.25 .90
O32 A54(a) 8a red violet 2.10 *3.00*
O33 A56(b) 1r grn & red brn 8.50 6.50
Nos. O27-O33 (7) 16.45 *26.15*

India Stamps of 1926-35 Overprinted

Perf. 13½x14, 14
1932-45 Wmk. 196
O34 A46 3p slate .30 .25
O35 A72 1a dk brn ('35) .30 .25
O36 A52 4a ol grn ('45) 35.00 3.75
O37 A54 8a red violet ('37) 1.50 *4.00*
Nos. O34-O37 (4) 37.10 8.25

Same Overprint in Black on India Stamps of 1937

1938
O38 A80 9p green 6.00 6.00
Never hinged 7.00
O39 A80 1a carmine 22.50 1.60
Never hinged 27.50

Official Stamps of India 1939-43 Overprinted in Black

1942-44 *Perf. 13½x14*
O40 O8 3p slate 1.25 *3.00*
O41 O8 ½a brown ('43) 1.20 .45
O42 O8 ½a dk rose vio ('44) 4.75 2.25
O43 O8 9p green ('43) 1.25 .45
O44 O8 1a car rose ('43) .65 .25
O45 O8 1½a dull purple ('43) .70 .60
O46 O8 2a scarlet ('43) 2.25 2.25
O47 O8 4a dark brown ('43) 3.50 *5.25*
O48 O8 8a blue violet ('43) 6.75 *30.00*

India Nos. 162-164 Overprinted in Black

O49 A82 1r brown & slate 9.00 *62.50*
O50 A82 2r dk brn & dk vio 32.50 *275.00*
O51 A82 5r dp ultra & dk green 175.00 *825.00*
Nos. O40-O51 (12) 238.80 *1,207.*
Set, never hinged 300.00

PATIALA

,pət-ē-'äl-ə

LOCATION — A State of India in the central Punjab
AREA — 5,942 sq. mi.
POP. — 1,936,259 (1941)
CAPITAL — Patiala

The varieties with small letters in the overprint are not listed as the letters are merely broken and not from another font.

Indian Stamps Overprinted in Red

1884 Wmk. 39 *Perf. 14*
1 A17 ½a green 6.00 *7.00*
a. Double overprint, one horiz. 4,750. 1,200.
2 A19 1a violet brown 75.00 *110.00*
a. Double overprint
b. Double opt., one in black 1,050.
c. Pair, one as "b," one without overprint
3 A21 2a ultra 19.00 *24.00*
4 A25 8a red lilac 650.00 *1,600.*
a. Double opt., one in black 190.00 *650.00*
c. Overprint reversed
d. Pair like "a," one with overprint reversed
5 A27 1r gray 225.00 *950.00*

Wmk. 38
6 A9 4a green 140.00 150.00
Nos. 1-6 (6) 1,115. *2,841.*

Indian Stamps Overprinted in Red

1885 Wmk. 39
7 A17 ½a green 3.25 .45
a. "AUTTIALLA" 24.00 *52.50*
c. "STATE" only
8 A21 2a ultra 9.00 2.50
a. "AUTTIALLA" 62.50
9 A27 1r gray 24.00 *125.00*
a. "AUTTIALLA" 650.00

Wmk. 38
10 A9 4a green 6.00 *6.25*
a. Double overprint, one in black 375.00
b. Pair, one as "a," one with black overprint

Same, Overprinted in Black
Wmk. 39
11 A19 1a violet brown .90 .45
a. "AUTTIALLA" 100.00
c. Double overprint, one in red 17.50 *140.00*
d. Pair, one as "c," one without overprint
12 A25 8a red lilac 35.00 *82.50*
a. "AUTTIALLA" 550.00
Nos. 7-12 (6) 78.15 *217.15*

Nos. 7-12 have been reprinted. Most of them bear the word "Reprint." The few stamps that escaped the overprint cannot be distinguished from the originals.

The error "AUTTIALLA" has been reprinted in entire sheets, in red on the ½, 2, 4a and 1r and in black on the ½, 1, 2, 4, 8a and 1r. "STATE" is 7¾mm long, instead of 8½mm. Most stamps are overprinted "Reprint."

Same, Overprinted in Black

1891-96
13 A17 ½a green .75 .25
14 A18 9p rose 1.50 3.25
15 A19 1a violet brown 2.10 .45
a. "STATE" only 300.00 *625.00*
16 A20 1a6p bister brown 2.10 *3.00*
17 A21 2a ultra 3.25 1.50
18 A22 3a orange 3.75 1.10
19 A23 4a ol grn ('96) 3.75 1.10
a. "STATE" only 750.00 *375.00*
20 A25 8a red vio ('96) 5.50 *24.00*
21 A26 12a violet, *red* 3.75 *24.00*
22 A29 1r car rose & grn ('96) 6.50 *82.50*
23 A30 2r brn & rose ('95) 210.00 *1,250.*
24 A30 3r grn & brn ('95) 290.00 *1,350.*
25 A30 5r vio & bl ('95) 325.00 *1,400.*

Wmk. 38
26 A14 6a bister 3.75 *22.50*
Nos. 13-26 (14) 861.70 4,164.

1899 Wmk. 39
27 A31 3p carmine rose .45 .25
a. Pair, one without overprint 6,000.

1902
28 A17 ½a light green 1.50 .90
29 A19 1a carmine rose 3.75 2.50

1903-06
31 A32 3p gray .50 .25
32 A33 ½a green 1.40 .25
33 A34 1a carmine rose 1.75 .25
a. Pair, one without overprint *1,500.*
34 A35 2a violet 2.00 1.00
35 A37 3a brown orange 2.00 .50
36 A38 4a olive green ('06) 3.50 2.25
37 A39 6a bister ('05) 4.25 *15.00*
38 A40 8a red violet ('06) 4.75 4.50
39 A41 12a vio, *red* ('06) 9.25 *40.00*
40 A42 1r car rose & grn ('05) 5.50 *9.00*
Nos. 31-40 (10) 34.90 *73.00*

1908
41 A44 ½a green .60 .35
42 A45 1a carmine rose 2.50 1.50

1912-14
43 A46 3p gray .35 .25
44 A47 ½a green .85 .25
45 A48 1a carmine rose 2.00 .25
46 A49 2a violet 1.90 2.25
47 A51 3a brown orange 3.25 2.50
48 A52 4a olive green 4.50 5.25
49 A53 6a bister 2.50 *6.50*
50 A54 8a red violet 3.75 3.75
51 A55 12a claret 4.75 *15.00*
52 A56 1r green & red brn 12.00 *22.50*
Nos. 43-52 (10) 35.85 *58.50*

1922-26
53 A48 1a dk brown ('23) 3.50 .75
54 A58 1½a chocolate .35 *.85*
55 A51 3a ultra ('26) 4.25 *14.00*
56 A56 2r yel brn & car rose ('26) 18.00 *225.00*
57 A56 5r vio & ultra ('26) 45.00 *300.00*
Nos. 53-57 (5) 71.10 *540.60*

India Stamps of 1926-35 Overprinted

1928-34 Wmk. 196
60 A46 3p slate 2.50 .25
61 A47 ½a green .35 .25
62 A68 9p dark green 2.75 1.50
63 A48 1a dark brown .95 .35
64 A69 1a3p violet 3.75 .25
65 A60 2a dull violet 2.10 .60
66 A57 2a6p buff 6.00 4.00
67 A51 3a blue 3.75 4.00
68 A61 4a olive green 6.50 3.00
69 A54 8a red violet 10.50 6.00

Indian Stamps of 1911-23 Overprinted

70 A56 1r green & brown 9.00 *15.00*
71 A56 2r buff & car rose 13.50 *82.50*
Nos. 60-71 (12) 61.65 117.70

India Stamps of 1926-35 Overprinted Like Nos. 60-69

1935-37 *Perf. 14*
75 A71 ½a green ('37) 1.00 .45
76 A72 1a dk brown ('36) 1.40 .25
77 A49 2a ver ('36) .50 *2.25*
78 A51 3a car rose ('37) 7.00 *8.00*
79 A52 4a olive green 2.25 3.50
Nos. 75-79 (5) 12.15 *14.45*
Set, never hinged 29.00

Same Overprint in Black on Stamps of India, 1937

1937-38 *Perf. 13½x14*
80 A80 3p slate ('38) 21.00 .50
81 A80 ½a brown ('38) 8.50 .75
82 A80 9p green 5.25 1.50
83 A80 1a carmine 3.00 .25
84 A81 2a scarlet ('38) 1.60 *14.00*
85 A81 2a6p purple ('38) 6.00 *30.00*
86 A81 3a yel green ('38) 6.50 *13.50*
87 A81 3a6p ultra ('38) 6.75 *37.50*
88 A81 4a dk brn ('38) 24.00 25.00
89 A81 6a pck blue ('38) 25.00 *90.00*
90 A81 8a blue violet ('38) 27.50 *62.50*
91 A81 12a car lake ('38) 25.00 *105.00*

Overprinted Like Nos. 70-71

1938
92 A82 1r brown & slate 30.00 *62.50*
93 A82 2r dk brn & dk vio 30.00 *160.00*
94 A82 5r dp ultra & dk green 40.00 *375.00*
95 A82 10r rose car & dk vio 52.50 *600.00*
96 A82 15r dk grn & dk brn 130.00 *950.00*
97 A82 25r dk vio & bl vio 150.00 *950.00*
Nos. 80-97 (18) 592.60 *3,478.*
Set, never hinged 850.00

India Nos. 150-153 Overprinted in Black

1942-43 *Perf. 13½x14*
98 A80 3p slate 11.50 4.00
99 A80 ½a brown ('43) 6.75 3.25
100 A80 9p green ('43) 320.00 12.00
101 A80 1a carmine 25.00 3.75
Nos. 98-101 (4) 363.25 23.00
Set, never hinged 515.00

India Stamps of 1941-43 with same Overprint in Black

1942-47 ***Perf. 13½x14***

102 A83 3p slate 4.25 .25
103 A83 ½a rose vio ('43) 4.25 .25
104 A83 9p lt grn ('43) 1.60 .25
a. Pair, one without overprint 4,750.
105 A83 1a car rose ('46) 1.10 .25
106 A84 1a3p bister ('43) 1.75 *5.25*
107 A84 1½a dk pur ('43) 13.50 5.50
108 A84 2a scar ('46) 9.50 .75
109 A84 3a violet ('46) 8.50 3.75
110 A84 3½a ultra ('46) 20.00 *57.50*
111 A85 4a choc ('46) 9.25 6.50
112 A85 6a pck blue ('46) 3.50 *45.00*
113 A85 8a blue vio ('46) 3.25 *22.50*
114 A85 12a car lake ('45) 30.00 *125.00*

No. 102 India No. 162 Overprinted in Black

115 A82 1r brn & slate ('47) 16.00 *120.00*
Nos. 102-115 (14) 126.45 *392.75*
Set, never hinged 170.00

OFFICIAL STAMPS

Indian Stamps Overprinted in Black and Red

1884 **Wmk. 39** ***Perf. 14***

O1 A17 ½a green 27.50 .60
O2 A19 1a vio brown 1.50 .25
a. "SERVICE" double 3,000. 950.00
b. "SERVICE" inverted 2,500.
c. "PUTTIALLA STATE" dbl. 175.00
d. "PUTTIALLA STATE" invtd. 3,000. 400.00
O3 A21 2a ultra *7,500.* 175.00

Overprinted in Red or Black

a

b

1885-90

O4 A17(a) ½a grn (R & Bk) 2.25 .35
a. "AUTTIALLA" 80.00 25.00
d. "SERVICE" double 1,050.
O5 A17(b) ½a green (Bk) 2.25 .25
O6 A19(a) 1a vio brn (Bk) 2.25 .25
a. "AUTTILLA" 1,050. 72.50
c. "SERVICE" dble., one invtd. 900.00
d. "SERVICE" double 3,000.
O7 A21(b) 2a ultra (R) 1.10 .60
c. "SERVICE" dbl., one invtd. 45.00 *290.00*
Nos. O4-O7 (4) 7.85 1.45

There are reprints of Nos. O4, O6 and O7. That of No. O4 has "SERVICE" overprinted in red in large letters and that of No. O6 has the same overprint in black. The originals have the word in small black letters. The reprints of No. O7, except those overprinted "Reprint," cannot be distinguished from the originals. These three reprints also exist with the error "AUTTIALLA."

Same, Overprinted in Black

1891-1900

O8 A17 ½a green ('95) .75 .25
b. "SERVICE" inverted 90.00
O9 A19 1a vio brn ('00) 9.00 .25
a. "SERVICE" inverted 90.00
O10 A21 2a ultramarine 5.00 3.25
a. "SERVICE" inverted 90.00 *300.00*
O11 A22 3a orange 3.75 5.00
O12 A23 4a olive green 3.00 .45
O13 A25 8a red violet 5.25 2.50
O14 A26 12a violet, *red* 3.50 .80
O15 A27 1r gray 3.75 1.00

Wmk. 38

O16 A14 6a bister 2.40 .50
Nos. O8-O16 (9) 36.40 14.00

1902 **Wmk. 39**

O17 A19 1a carmine rose 1.40 .25

1903

O18 A29 1r car rose & green 9.00 15.00

1903-09

O19 A32 3p gray .60 .25
O20 A33 ½a green 1.50 .25
O21 A34 1a carmine rose .90 .25
O22 A35 2a violet 1.20 .25
O23 A37 3a brown orange 6.00 5.25
O24 A38 4a olive green ('05) 4.00 .25
O25 A40 8a red violet 2.50 1.10
O26 A42 1r car rose & grn ('06) 3.00 1.20
Nos. O19-O26 (8) 19.70 8.80

1907

O27 A44 ½a green .75 .25
O28 A45 1a carmine rose .90 .25

India Stamps of 1911-26 Overprinted

a

b

1913-26

O29 A46(a) 3p gray .30 .25
O30 A47(a) ½a green .25 .25
O31 A48(a) 1a car rose .25 .25
O32 A49(a) 2a violet 1.20 1.10
O33 A52(a) 4a olive green .75 .50
O34 A54(a) 8a red violet .80 *1.00*
O35 A56(b) 1r grn & red brn 1.75 2.10
O36 A56(b) 2r yel brn & car rose ('26) 24.00 *75.00*
O37 A56(b) 5r vio & ultra ('26) 15.00 *35.00*
Nos. O29-O37 (9) 44.30 *115.45*

Same Overprint on India Nos. 83 and 89

1925-26

O38 A48(a) 1a dark brown 9.50 1.50
O39 A53(a) 6a bister ('26) 2.10 *3.75*

India Stamps of 1926-35 Overprinted

1927-36 **Wmk. 196**

O40 A46 3p slate .25 .25
O41 A47 ½a green 1.25 .80
O42 A48 1a dark brown .25 .25
O43 A69 1a3p violet .60 .25
O44 A60 2a dull violet .25 *.45*
O45 A60 2a vermilion .45 .50
O46 A57 2a6p buff 3.75 .50
O47 A61 4a olive green .75 .45
O48 A54 8a red violet 1.60 1.00

Indian Stamps of 1911-23 Overprinted

O49 A56 1r green & brown 6.50 5.00
O50 A56 2r brn org & car rose ('36) 20.00 *62.50*
Nos. O40-O50 (11) 35.65 *71.95*

India Stamps of 1926-34 Overprinted

1935-36

O51 A71 ½a green ('36) .25 .25
O52 A72 1a dark brown ('36) .45 .45
O53 A49 2a vermilion .30 *.45*
a. Small die 21.00 7.50
O54 A52 4a olive green ('36) 3.50 2.50
Nos. O51-O54 (4) 4.50 *3.65*
Set, never hinged 5.00

Same Overprint on India Nos. 151-153

1938-39 ***Perf. 13½x14***

O55 A80 ½a brown ('39) .95 .30
O56 A80 9p green ('39) 16.00 *95.00*
O57 A80 1a carmine .95 .60
Nos. O55-O57 (3) 17.90 *95.90*
Set, never hinged 22.00

India No. 136 Surcharged in Black

1939 ***Perf. 14***

O58 A69 1a on 1a3p violet 15.00 5.25
Never hinged 18.00

"SERVICE" measures 9¼mm.

No. 64 Surcharged in Black

1940

O59 A69 1a on 1a3p violet 12.50 5.00
Never hinged 15.00

"SERVICE" measures 8½mm.

India Nos. 162-164 Overprinted

Perf. 13½x14

O60 A82 1r brown & slate 1.25 *10.50*
O61 A82 2r dk brn & dk vio 7.50 7.50
O62 A82 5r dp ultra & dk grn 21.00 95.00
Set, never hinged 36.00

India Official Stamps of 1939-43 Overprinted

1940-45

O63 O8 3p slate ('41) 1.90 .25
O64 O8 ½a brown 5.25 .25
O65 O8 ½a dk rose vio ('43) 1.10 .25
O66 O8 9p green 1.10 .75
O67 O8 1a carmine rose 3.50 .25
O68 O8 1a3p bister ('41) 1.25 .35
O69 O8 1½a dull purple ('45) 6.75 1.90
O70 O8 2a scarlet ('41) 11.00 .50
O71 O8 2½a purple ('41) 4.00 1.50
O72 O8 4a dk brown ('45) 1.90 *3.75*
O73 O8 8a blue violet ('45) 5.25 *9.00*

India Nos. 162-164 Overprinted in Black

O74 A82 1r brn & slate ('43) 5.25 *16.00*
O75 A82 2r dk brn & dk vio ('45) 13.50 *95.00*
O76 A82 5r dp ultra & dk grn ('45) 22.00 *125.00*
Nos. O63-O76 (14) 83.75 *254.75*
Set, never hinged 145.00

INDIA - FEUDATORY STATES

FEUDATORY STATES

These stamps had franking power solely in the states in which they were issued, except for Cochin and Travancore which had a reciprocal postal agreement.

ALWAR

'əl-wər

LOCATION — A Feudatory State of India, lying southwest of Delhi in the Jaipur Residency.
AREA — 3,158 sq. mi.
POP. — 749,751.
CAPITAL — Alwar

Katar (Indian Dagger) — A1

1877 Unwmk. Litho. *Rouletted*

1 A1 ¼a ultramarine 7.00 1.60
a. ¼a blue 7.00 1.60
2 A1 1a brown 5.25 1.90
a. 1a yellow brown 16.00 8.25
b. 1a red brown 5.00 2.25

Redrawn

1899-1901 *Pin-perf. 12*

3 A1 ¼a sl blue, wide margins 12.50 4.50
a. Horiz. pair, imperf. between 600.00 *750.00*
b. Vert. pair, imperf. between 1,200. *1,250.*
4 A1 ¼a yel grn, narrow margins ('01) 11.00 4.00
a. Horiz. pair, imperf. between 950.00
b. Imperf, pair 950.00
c. ¼a emer, wide margins ('99) 600.00
d. ¼a emer, narrow margins 5.25 4.75
e. As "d," imperf, pair 550.00
f. As "d," vert. pair, imperf horiz. 500.00
g. As "d," horiz. pair, imperf vert. 450.00 *525.00*
h. As "d," vert. pair, imperf horiz. 450.00 *525.00*

Nos. 3 and 4b are printed farther apart in the sheet.
On Nos. 3 and 4, the shading of the left border line is missing.
Nos. 1 to 4 occasionally show portions of the papermaker's watermark, W. T. & Co.
Alwar stamps became obsolete in 1902.

BAMRA

'bäm-rə

LOCATION — A Feudatory State in the Eastern States, Orissa States Agency, Bengal.
AREA — 1,988 sq. mi.
POP. — 151,259
CAPITAL — Deogarh

Stamps of Bamra were issued without gum.

A1

1888 Unwmk. Typeset *Imperf.*

1 A1 ¼a black, *yellow* 700.00
a. "g" inverted *7,000.*
2 A1 ½a black, *rose* 125.00
a. "g" inverted *2,400.*
3 A1 1a black, *blue* 100.00
a. "g" inverted *2,100.*
4 A1 2a black, *green* 140.00 *550.00*
a. "postge" *2,400.*
5 A1 4a black, *yellow* 120.00 *550.00*
a. "postge" *2,250.*
6 A1 8a black, *rose* 72.50
a. "postge" *1,900.*
Nos. 1-6 (6) 1,258.

All values may be found with the scroll inverted, and with the long end of the scroll pointing to the right or left.
On No. 5 the last character on the 3rd line is a vertical line. On No. 1 it is not vertical.
On No. 2 the last character on the 3rd line looks like a backwards "R" with a bent leg. On No. 6 it looks like an apostrophe.
Nos. 1 and 2 have been reprinted in blocks of 8 and Nos. 1-6 in blocks of 20. In the reprints the 4th character of the native inscription often has the curved upper line broken at the left, but in many instances comparison with photographic reproductions of the original settings is the only certain test.

A2

1890

7 A2 ¼a blk, *rose lil* 7.00 *9.00*
a. "Quatrer" 32.50 *57.50*
b. "e" of "Postage" inverted 32.50 *57.50*
c. "Eeudatory" 32.50 *57.50*
8 A2 ½a black, *green* 5.25 5.25
a. "Eeudatory" 90.00 *110.00*
b. "postage" with small "p" 5.25 5.25
9 A2 1a black, *yellow* 6.50 5.00
a. "Eeudatory" 195.00 *225.00*
b. "postage" with small "p" 6.50 5.00
c. "annas" 300.00 *325.00*
10 A2 2a blk, *rose lil* 30.00 *57.50*
a. "Eeudatory" 275.00 *550.00*
11 A2 4a blk, *brt rose* 9.50 *12.50*
a. "Eeudatory" 6,750.
12 A2 8a blk, *rose lil* 40.00 *100.00*
a. "BAMBA" 375.00 *550.00*
b. "Foudatory" & "Postage" 375.00 *550.00*
c. "postage" with small "p" 40.00 *100.00*
13 A2 1r blk, *rose lil* 100.00 *160.00*
a. "BAMBA" 650.00 *825.00*
b. "Eeudatory" 825.00 *1,050.*
c. "postage" with small "p" 100.00 160.00
Nos. 7-13 (7) 198.25 *349.25*

1893

14 A2 ¼a black, *rose* 3.00 *4.50*
a. "postage" with small "p" 3.00 *4.50*
15 A2 ¼a black, *magenta* 3.00 *4.00*
a. "postage" with small "p" 3.00 *4.00*
d. "AMRA" of "BAMRA" inverted 100.00 100.00
e. "M" and 2nd "A" of "BAMRA" inverted 140.00 140.00
f. First "a" of "anna" inverted 72.50 82.50
16 A2 2a black, *rose* 21.00 12.00
a. "postage" with small "p" 21.00 12.00
17 A2 4a black, *rose* 16.00 12.00
a. "postage" with small "p" 16.00 12.00
b. "BAMBA" 1,600. *1,800.*
18 A2 8a black, *rose* 42.50 29.00
a. "postage" with small "p" 42.50 29.00
19 A2 1r black, *rose* 35.00 35.00
a. "postage" with small "p" 35.00 35.00
Nos. 14-19 (6) 120.50 96.50

The central ornament varies in size and may be found in various positions.
Bamra stamps became obsolete Dec. 31, 1894.

BARWANI

bər-'wän-ē

LOCATION — A Feudatory State of Central India, in the Malwa Agency.
AREA — 1,178 sq. mi.
POP. — 141,110
CAPITAL — Barwani

The stamps of Barwani were all typographed and normally issued in booklets containing panes of four. Exceptions are noted (Nos. 14-15, 20-25). The majority were completely perforated, but some of the earlier printings were perforated only between the stamps, leaving one or two sides imperf. Nos. 1-25 were issued without gum. Many shades exist.

Rana Ranjit Singh — A1

1921, April (?) Unwmk. *Pin-Perf 7*
Toned Medium Wove Paper
Clear Impression

1 A1 ¼a dull Prus green 225.00 *625.00*
2 A1 ½a dull blue 500.00 *950.00*

1921 *Coarse Perf. 7 x Imperf.*
White Thin Wove Paper
Blurred Impression

3 A1 ¼a dull green 37.50 *190.00*
4 A1 ½a pale blue 25.00 *275.00*

1921 Toned Laid Paper *Imperf.*

5 A1 ¼a light green 30.00 *125.00*
6 A1 ½a light green 8.25
a. Perf. 11, top or bottom only 7.00

1921 *Coarse Perf. 7, 7 x Imperf.*
Thick Wove Paper
Very Blurred Impression

7 A1 ¼a dull blue 25.00
8 A1 ½a dull green 22.50

In 1927 Nos. 7-8 were printed on thin hard paper.

Rana Ranjit Singh — A2

1922 *Perf. 7 x Imperf.*
Thick Glazed Paper

9 A1 ¼a dull ultra 160.00

Rough Perf. 11 x Imperf.

10 A2 1a vermilion 3.75 *30.00*
11 A2 2a violet 3.25 *37.50*
a. Double impression *450.00*
Nos. 9-11 (3) 167.00 67.50

Shades of No. 11 include purple. No. 11 was also printed on thick dark toned paper.

1923-26 Wove, Laid Paper *Perf.*

12 A1 ¼a grayish ultra, perf. 8½ 2.40 *72.50*
13 A1 ¼a black, perf. 7 x imperf. 110.00 *550.00*
14 A1 ¼a dull rose, perf. 11½-12 3.75 *21.00*
15 A1 ¼a dk bl, perf. 11 ('26) 2.25 *16.00*
16 A1 ½a grn, perf. 11 x imperf. 1.90 *30.00*
Nos. 12-16 (5) 120.30 *689.50*

No. 12 was also printed on pale gray thin toned paper.
No. 14 was printed on horizontally laid paper in horizontal sheets of 12 containing three panes of 4.
No. 15 was printed on vertically laid paper in horizontal sheets of 8.

Rana Ranjit Singh — A3

1927-28 Thin Wove Paper *Perf. 7*

17 A3 4a dull orange 200.00 *675.00*

No. 17 was also printed in light brown on thick paper, pin-perf. 6, and in orange brown on thick paper, rough perf. 7.

1928 *Coarse Perf. 7*
Thick Glazed Paper

18 A1 ¼a bright blue 16.00
19 A1 ½a bright yel green 37.50

1928, Nov. *Rough Perf. 10½*

20 A1 ¼a deep ultra 9.50
a. Tête bêche pair 19.00
21 A1 ½a yellow green 7.00
a. Tête bêche pair 14.00

1929-31 *Perf. 11*

22 A1 ¼a blue 3.25 *21.00*
a. ¼a ultramarine 3.00 *21.00*
23 A1 ½a emerald green 4.00 *24.00*
24 A2 1a car pink ('31) 24.00 *67.50*
25 A3 4a salmon 120.00 *325.00*
Nos. 22-25 (4) 151.25 437.50

Nos. 20-25 were printed in sheets of 8 (4x2).
No. 22 had five printings in various shades (bright to deep blue) in horizontal or vertical format.
No. 23 also printed in dark myrtle green.

Rana Devi Singh — A4

1932-48 Glazed Paper *Perf. 11, 12*

26 A4 ¼a dark gray 3.75 *35.00*
27 A4 ½a blue green 6.00 *35.00*
28 A4 1a brown 6.00 *32.50*
a. 1a chocolate, perf. 8½ ('48) 21.00 75.00
29 A4 2a deep red violet 5.50 *62.50*
a. Perf. 12x11
b. 2a red lilac 12.50
30 A4 4a olive green 9.00 *62.50*
Nos. 26-30 (5) 30.25 *227.50*

Types of 1921-27

1934-48 *Perf. 11*

31 A1 ¼a slate gray 6.00 *47.50*
32 A1 ½a green 6.50 *60.00*
33 A2 1a dark brown 16.00 *29.00*
a. 1a brown, perf. 8½ ('48) 15.00 *75.00*
34 A2 2a brt purple ('38) 125.00 *490.00*
35 A2 2a rose car ('46) 35.00 *190.00*
36 A3 4a olive green 20.00 *67.50*
Nos. 31-36 (6) 208.50 884.00

In the nine printings of Nos. 26-36, several plate settings spaced the cliches from 2 to 9mm apart. Hence the stamps come in different overall sizes. Not all values were in each printing. Values are for the commonest varieties.
No. 36 was also printed in pale sage green.

Rana Devi Singh — A5

1938

37 A5 1a dark brown 50.00 *110.00*
a. Booklet pane of 4 —

Stamps of type A5 in red are revenues.
Barwani stamps became obsolete July 1, 1948.

BHOPAL

bō-'päl

LOCATION — A Feudatory State of Central India, in the Bhopal Agency.
AREA — 6,924 sq. mi.
POP. — 995,745
CAPITAL — Bhopal

Inscription in Urdu in an octagon embossed on Nos. 1-83, in a circle embossed on Nos. 84-90. On designs A1-A3, A7, A11-A12, A14-A15, A19-A21 the embossing makes up the central part of the design.
The embossing may be found inverted or sideways.

Expect irregular perfs on the perforated stamps, Nos. 19-77, due to a combination of imperfect perforating methods and the fragility of the papers.
Nos. 1-90 issued without gum.

A1

Double Lined Frame

1876 Unwmk. Litho. *Imperf.*

1 A1 ¼a black 950.00 *700.00*
a. "EGAM" 2,750. *2,400.*
b. "BFGAM" 2,750. *2,400.*
c. "BEGAN" 1,500. *1,250.*
2 A1 ½a red 30.00 *72.50*
a. "EGAM" 110.00 *250.00*
b. "BFGAM" 110.00 *250.00*
c. "BEGAN" 72.50 *160.00*

A2

1877 Single Lined Frame

3 A2 ¼a black *9,000.*
4 A2 ½a red 52.50 *110.00*
a. "NWAB" 250.00 *490.00*

A3

1878

5 A3 ¼a black 12.00 *24.00*
a. "J" diagonal, plate II 13.50 *27.50*

All stamps of type A3 are lettered "EEGAM" for "BEGAM."

A4

1878

6 A4 ½a pale red 10.50 *24.00*
a. ½a brown red 42.50 67.50
b. "NWAB" 35.00
c. "JAHN" 57.50
d. "EECAM" 57.50

A5

1879-80

7 A5 ¼a green 21.00 *40.00*
8 A5 ½a red 27.50 *35.00*

Perf.

9 A5 ¼a green 16.00 *27.50*
10 A5 ½a red 160.00
Nos. 7-10 (4) 224.50 102.50

Nos. 7 and 9 have the value in parenthesis; Nos. 8 and 10 are without parenthesis.

A6

1881 *Imperf.*

11 A6 ¼a green 13.50
a. "NAWA" 42.50
b. "CHAH" 120.00

Perf.

12 A6 ¼a green 18.00
a. "NAWA" 67.50
b. "CHAH" 160.00

A7

1881-89 *Imperf.*

13 A7 ¼a black 9.00 *35.00*
a. "NWAB" 22.50
14 A7 ½a red 7.50 *25.00*
a. "NWAB" 18.00
15 A7 1a brown 6.50 *29.00*
a. "NWAB" 14.00
16 A7 2a blue 5.00 *29.00*
a. "NWAB" 9.50
17 A7 4a yellow 30.00 *100.00*
a. "NWAB" 82.50
Nos. 13-17 (5) 58.00 *218.00*

A8

A9

1884 *Perf.*

19 A8 ¼a green 225.00 *275.00*
a. "JAN" 225.00 *275.00*
b. "BEGM" 450.00 *625.00*
c. "NWAB" 950.00
d. "SHAHAN" 950.00
f. "JAHA" 450.00
20 A9 ¼a green 8.25 *27.50*

On type A9 there is a dash at the left of "JA" of "JAHAN" instead of a character like a comma as on types A5 and A6.

Imitations of No. 19 were printed about 1904 in black on wove paper and in red on laid paper, both imperf. and pin-perf.

A10

1884 Laid Paper *Imperf.*

21 A10 ¼a blue green 240.00 *275.00*
a. "NWAB" 675.00
b. "NAWAJANAN" 675.00
c. "SAH" 675.00
22 A10 ½a black 3.25 *3.75*
a. "NWAB" 15.00 *18.00*
b. "NAWAJANAN" 15.00 *18.00*
c. "SAH" 15.00 *18.00*

Perf.

23 A10 ¼a blue green 1.50 *6.00*
a. "NWAB" 6.00
b. "NAWAJANAN" 6.00
c. "SAH" 6.00
24 A10 ½a black 1.40 *5.00*
a. "NWAB" 5.50 *12.50*
b. "NAWAJANAN" 5.50 *12.50*
c. "SAH" 5.50 *12.50*
Nos. 21-24 (4) 246.15 289.75

Type Redrawn

1886 Wove Paper *Imperf.*

25 A10 ¼a grayish green .80 *5.00*
a. ¼a green .80 *5.00*
b. "NWAB" 4.50 *13.50*
c. "NAWA" 3.00 *10.50*
d. "NAWAA" 4.50 *13.50*
e. "NAWABABEGAAM" 4.50 *13.50*
f. "NWABA" 4.50 *13.50*
26 A10 ½a red 1.00 *2.50*
a. "SAH" 6.00 *9.50*
b. "NAWABA" 4.50 *7.50*

Perf.

27 A10 ¼a green 3.75 *6.00*
a. "NWAB" 20.00
b. "NAWA" 12.00
c. "NAWAA" 20.00
d. "NAWABABEGAAM" 20.00
e. "NWABA" 20.00
28 A10 ½a red 1.20 *3.00*
a. "SAH" 9.00
b. "NAWABA" 12.00
Nos. 25-28 (4) 6.75 16.50

On Nos. 25-28 the inscriptions are closer to the value than on Nos. 21-24.

A11

A12

1886 *Imperf.*

29 A11 ½a red 4.00 *15.00*
a. "BEGAM" 18.00 *47.50*
b. "NWAB" 18.00

Laid Paper

30 A12 4a yellow 18.00 *57.50*
a. "EEGAM" 24.00
b. Wove paper 1,500.
c. As "a," wove paper *1,900.*

Perf.

31 A12 4a yellow 6.50 *30.00*
a. "EEGAM" 9.50 *42.50*
Nos. 29-31 (3) 28.50

A13

A14

1889 Wove Paper *Imperf.*

32 A13 ¼a green 1.50 *3.00*
a. "SAH" 6.50 *10.50*
b. "NAWA" 6.50 *10.50*
33 A14 ¼a black 3.25 8.25
a. "EEGAN" 27.50 *47.50*

Perf.

34 A13 ¼a green 3.00 *4.00*
a. "SAH" 11.00 *13.50*
b. "NAWA" 11.00 *13.50*
c. Vert. pair, imperf between 325.00
35 A14 ¼a black 2.50 *8.25*
a. "EEGAN" 22.50 *47.50*
b. Horiz. pair, imperf. between 400.00
Nos. 32-35 (4) 10.25 23.50

Type A13 has smaller letters in the upper corners than Type A10.

A15

A16

1890 *Imperf.*

36 A15 ¼a black 3.25 *3.00*
37 A15 1a brown 3.25 *7.00*
a. "EEGAM" 21.00 *40.00*
b. "BBGAM" 21.00 *40.00*
38 A7 2a greenish blue 3.00 *3.25*
a. "BBEGAM" 12.50 *21.00*
b. "NAWAH" 12.50 *21.00*
39 A7 4a yellow 3.75 *5.50*
40 A16 8a blue 100.00 *180.00*
a. "HAH" 110.00 *190.00*
b. "JABAN" 120.00
Nos. 36-40 (5) 113.25 198.75

An imperf. imitation of Nos. 36 and 41 was printed about 1904 in black on wove paper.

Perf.

41 A15 ¼a black 4.50 *6.25*
a. Pair, imperf. between 500.00
42 A15 1a brown 6.50 *11.00*
a. "EECAM" 37.50 *52.50*
b. "BBGAM" 37.50 *52.50*
43 A7 2a greenish blue 3.75 *5.50*
a. "BBEGAM" 14.00 *27.50*
b. "NAWAH" 14.00 *27.50*
44 A7 4a yellow 4.50 *12.00*
45 A16 8a blue 100.00 *180.00*
a. "HAH" 110.00
b. "JABAN" 120.00
Nos. 41-45 (5) 119.25 214.75

Nos. 40 and 45 have a frame line around each stamp.

Imperf

46 A12 ½a red (BECAM) 3.00 *5.50*
47 A13 ½a red (NWAB) 3.00 2.25
a. Inverted "N"
b. "SAH" 9.00

Perf.

48 A12 ½a red (BECAM) 2.50 7.00
a. Without embossing
49 A13 ½a red (NWAB) 1.20 3.00
a. Inverted "N"
b. "SAH" 7.50
Nos. 46-49 (4) 9.70 17.75

1891-93 Laid Paper *Imperf.*

50 A16 8a deep green 110.00 *225.00*
a. "HAH" 125.00
b. "JABAN" 150.00

Perf.

51 A16 8a deep green 110.00 *225.00*
a. "HAH" 125.00
b. "JABAN" 140.00

For overprint, see No. 83.

1894 Redrawn *Imperf.*

53 A10 ¼a green 2.25 *2.50*
a. "NAWAH" 11.00 *12.00*
54 A11 ½a brick red 3.25 3.25
55 A16 8a blue black 32.50 32.50
a. Laid paper 300.00 *450.00*

Perf.

56 A10 ¼a green 4.50 3.25
a. "NAWAH" 19.00 16.00
57 A11 ½a brick red 1.20 *3.00*
58 A16 8a blue black 45.00 *60.00*
Nos. 53-58 (6) 88.70 104.50

The ¼a redrawn has letters in corners larger; value in very small characters.

The 8a redrawn has no frame to each stamp but a frame to the sheet.

1898 *Imperf.*

60 A16 8a black 62.50 *82.50*
b. "E" of "BEGAM" inverted 140.00 150.00

A17

A18

A19

A20

A21

1895 Laid Paper

61 A17 ¼a green 2.25 2.50
62 A18 ¼a red 10.50 5.00
63 A19 ¼a black 5.25 4.50
a. "A" inserted in "NAW B" 12.50 10.00
64 A20 ½a black 2.25 *2.50*
65 A21 ½a red 3.25 3.25

Perf.

66 A17 ¼a green 4.50 3.25
67 A18 ¼a red 1,250.
Nos. 61-67 (7) 28.00 1,271.

On No. 63a, the second "A" in "NAWAB" has been inserted by hand and varies somewhat in size.

Imperf. imitations of No. 65 were printed about 1904 in deep red on laid paper and in black on wove paper.

Stamps of types A16 and A19-A21 with a circular embossed seal and perforated, were prepared but not issued.

A22

A23

1898 *Imperf.*

72 A22 ¼a black .75 .75
a. "SHAN" 5.00 5.00
73 A22 ¼a green 1.10 *1.20*
a. "SHAN" 5.25 5.25
74 A23 ¼a black 2.10 2.10
Nos. 72-74 (3) 3.95 4.05

1899

75 A13 ½a black ("NWAB") 6.50 *9.50*
b. "NWASBAHJAHNJ" 32.50 *42.50*
d. "SBAH" 15.00 *22.50*
e. "SBAN" 32.50 *42.50*
f. "NWIB" 32.50 *42.50*
g. "BEIAM" 32.50 *42.50*

A24

1902

76	A24	¼a red	5.50	*9.00*
77	A24	½a black	6.00	*10.00*
a.		Printed on both sides	1,100.	
78	A24	1a brown	10.00	*25.00*
79	A24	2a blue	12.50	*22.50*
80	A24	4a orange	110.00	*160.00*
81	A24	8a violet	150.00	*290.00*
82	A24	1r rose	400.00	*600.00*
		Nos. 76-82 (7)	694.00	*1,117.*

No. 50 Overprinted in Red

1903

83	A16	8a deep green	210.00	225.00
a.		Inverted overprint	550.00	*600.00*

There are two types of the overprint which is the Arabic S, initial of the Begum.

Inscription in Circle Embossed on Each Stamp

1903 **Wove Paper**

84	A24	¼a red	2.25	*7.50*
85	A24	½a black	1.90	*7.50*
86	A24	1a brown	4.50	*11.00*
87	A24	2a blue	10.00	*37.50*
88	A24	4a orange	27.50	*75.00*
89	A24	8a violet	82.50	*190.00*
90	A24	1r rose	125.00	*290.00*
		Nos. 84-90 (7)	253.65	*618.50*

Laid Paper

84a	A24	¼a red	1.50	*12.00*
85a	A24	½a black	1.50	*12.50*
86a	A24	1a brown	10.00	
87a	A24	2a blue	250.00	*325.00*
88a	A24	4a orange	500.00	500.00
89a	A24	8a violet	2,400.	
90a	A24	1r rose	1,900.	
		Nos. 84a-90a (7)	5,063.	*849.50*

The embossing in a circle, which was first used in 1903, has been applied to many early stamps and impressions from redrawn plates of early issues. So far as is now known, these should be classed as reprints.

Coat of Arms — A25

1908 **Engr.** ***Perf. 13½***

99	A25	1a yellow green	5.50	*6.75*
a.		Printed on both sides	180.00	

OFFICIAL STAMPS

O1

Overprinted

Size: 20½x25mm

1908 **Unwmk.** **Engr.** ***Perf. 13½***

O1	O1	½a yellow green	3.25	.25
a.		Pair, one without ovpt.	950.00	
b.		Inverted overprint	275.00	225.00
c.		Double ovpt., one invtd.	160.00	
O2	O1	1a carmine	6.25	.60
a.		Inverted overprint	180.00	150.00
O3	O1	2a blue	36.00	.25
O4	O1	4a red brown	21.00	.80
		Nos. O1-O4 (4)	66.50	1.90

Overprinted

O5	O1	½a yellow green	11.00	1.90
O6	O1	1a carmine	14.00	1.40
O7	O1	2a blue	6.00	.90
a.		Inverted overprint	37.50	
O8	O1	4a red brown	120.00	2.25
a.		Inverted overprint	30.00	*100.00*
		Nos. O5-O8 (4)	151.00	6.45

The difference in the two overprints is in the shape of the letters, most noticeable in the "R."

Type of 1908 Issue

Overprinted

Size: 25½x30½mm

1930-31 **Litho.** ***Perf. 14***

O9	O1	½a gray green ('31)	18.00	2.50
O10	O1	1a carmine	16.00	.25
O11	O1	2a blue	14.00	.65
O12	O1	4a brown	15.00	1.40
		Nos. O9-O12 (4)	63.00	4.80

½a, 2a, 4a are inscribed "POSTAGE" on the left side; 1a "POSTAGE AND REVENUE."

Similar to Type O1

Size: 21x25mm

"POSTAGE" at left

"BHOPAL STATE" at right

1932-33 ***Perf. 11½, 13, 13½, 14***

O13	O1	¼a orange yellow	3.75	.75
a.		Pair, one without overprint	180.00	
b.		Perf. 13½	16.00	.45
c.		Perf. 14	18.00	.45

"BHOPAL GOVT." at right

Perf. 13½

O14	O1	½a yellow green	11.00	.25
a.		Perf 14 ('34)	24.00	.60
O15	O1	1a brown red	16.00	.25
O16	O1	2a blue	16.00	.65
O17	O1	4a brown	16.00	1.50
a.		Perf 14 ('34)	24.00	16.00
		Nos. O13-O17 (5)	62.75	3.40

No. O14, O16-O17 Surcharged in Red, Violet, Black or Blue

a

b

c

1935-36 ***Perf. 13½***

O18	O1(a)	¼a on ½a (R)	47.50	21.00
a.		Inverted surcharge	300.00	125.00
O19	O1(b)	3p on ½a (R)	5.50	5.25
O20	O1(a)	¼a on 2a (R)	42.50	30.00
a.		Inverted surcharge	300.00	110.00
O21	O1(b)	3p on 2a (R)	6.75	6.75
a.		Inverted surcharge	120.00	60.00
O22	O1(a)	¼a on 4a (R)	1,500.	500.00
O23	O1(a)	¼a on 4a (Bk) ('36)	120.00	40.00
O24	O1(b)	3p on 4a (R)	210.00	100.00
O25	O1(b)	3p on 4a (Bk) ('36)	3.75	*5.00*
O26	O1(c)	1a on ½a (V)	7.50	2.25
a.		Inverted surcharge	100.00	67.50
O27	O1(c)	1a on 2a (R)	3.25	3.00
a.		Inverted surcharge	140.00	140.00
O28	O1(c)	1a on 2a (Bk) ('36)	1.00	*3.75*
O29	O1(c)	1a on 4a (Bl)	10.50	*7.50*
		Nos. O18-O29 (12)	1,958.	724.50

Nos. O18-O25 are arranged in composite sheets of 100. The 2 top horizontal rows of each value are surcharged "a" and the next 5 rows as "b." The next 3 rows as "b" but in a narrower setting.

Various errors of spelling or inverted letters are found on Nos. O18-O29.

Arms of Bhopal — O2

1935 **Litho.**

O30	O2	1a3p claret & blue	5.25	2.25

Inscribed: "Bhopal State Postage" Ovptd. "SERVICE" 11mm long

1937 ***Perf. 12***

O31	O2	1a6p dk clar & bl	3.75	1.50
a.		Overprint omitted	275.00	210.00
b.		Double overprint, one inverted	750.00	750.00
c.		Blue printing double		250.00
d.		Imperf., pair		275.00
e.		Pair, imperf between	300.00	*325.00*

See Nos. O42, O45.

Arms of Bhopal — O3

Brown or Black Overprint

1936-38 **Typo.**

O32	O3	¼a orange (Br)	1.40	.90
a.		Inverted overprint	525.00	400.00
b.		Vert. pair, imperf between	250.00	
c.		Horiz. pair, imperf between		450.00
d.		Black overprint	12.50	1.10
e.		As "d," inverted ovpt.		600.00
f.		As "d," double ovpt.		450.00
O32G	O3	¼a yel (Br) ('38)	5.25	2.25
O33	O3	1a carmine	1.90	.25
a.		Horiz. pair, imperf vert.		250.00
b.		Vert. pair, imperf between		490.00
c.		Horiz. pair, imperf between	200.00	*225.00*
d.		Block of 4, imperf between	625.00	625.00
		Nos. O32-O33 (3)	8.55	3.40

Moti Mahal O4

Overprinted in Black

1936 ***Perf. 11½***

O34	O4	½a grn & choc	.85	*1.20*
a.		Double impression of stamp	150.00	22.50
b.		Double overprint	350.00	250.00
c.		Vert. pair, imperf between		325.00
d.		Horiz. pair, imperf between		325.00

Moti Masjid — O5

4a, Taj Mahal and Be-Nazir Palaces.

Overprinted in Black

1937 ***Perf. 11½***

O35	O5	2a dk blue & brown	2.50	1.40
a.		Inverted overprint	375.00	*550.00*
b.		Vert. pair, imperf between		525.00
c.		Horiz. pair, imperf between		375.00
O36	O5	4a bister brn & blue	4.50	.75
a.		Double overprint		240.00
b.		Center double		600.00
c.		Horiz. pair, imperf between		1,000.
d.		Overprint omitted		490.00

Types of 1937

Overprinted "SERVICE" in Black or Brown

Designs: 4a, Taj Mahal. 8a, Ahmadabad Palace. 1r, Rait-Ghat.

1938-44

O37	O4	½a dp grn & brn	.90	.60
O38	O5	2a vio & dp grn	15.00	.45
O39	O5	4a red brn & brt bl	4.25	.80
a.		Frame double		450.00
O40	O5	8a red vio & blue	7.00	3.25
a.		"SERAICE"	550.00	*825.00*
b.		Overprint omitted		250.00
c.		Double overprint		240.00
d.		Vert. pair, imperf between		625.00
e.		"1" for "I" in "SERVICE"	550.00	*825.00*
O41	O5	1r bl & red vio (Br)	27.50	12.50
a.		Black overprint ('44)	21.00	6.50
b.		"SREVICE"	160.00	*375.00*
c.		Overprint omitted	1,100.	
d.		Vert. pair, imperf horiz.		2,250.
		Nos. O37-O41 (5)	54.65	17.60

No. O39 measures 36½x22½mm, No. O40 39x24mm, No. O41 45½x27¾mm.

Type of 1935

1939 ***Perf. 12***

O42	O2	1a6p dark claret	7.50	2.50
a.		Overprint omitted		625.00
b.		Double overprint		625.00
c.		Double overprint, one inverted		625.00
d.		Pair, imperf between	250.00	*325.00*

Tiger — O6

Design: 1a, Deer.

1940 **Typo.** ***Perf. 11½***

O43	O6	¼a ultramarine	6.00	2.50
O44	O6	1a red violet	35.00	4.50

Type of 1935

Inscribed: "Bhopal State Postage"

1941

O45	O2	1a3p emerald	2.50	3.25
a.		Pair, imperf between	550.00	*700.00*

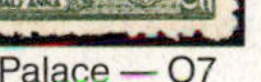

Moti Palace — O7

Coat of Arms — O8

2a, Moti Mosque. 4a, Be-Nazir Palaces.

Perf. 11½, 12

1944-46 **Unwmk.** **Typo.**

O46	O8	3p ultramarine	1.25	1.25
O47	O7	½a light green	1.10	*1.50*
O48	O8	9p org brn ('46)	12.00	5.00
a.		Imperf., pair		290.00
O49	O8	1a brt red vio ('45)	6.25	2.60
O50	O8	1½a deep plum	1.90	1.90
O51	O7	2a red violet ('45)	13.50	6.00
O52	O8	3a yellow ('46)	16.00	*21.00*
a.		Imperf., pair		290.00
O53	O7	4a brown ('45)	8.75	3.25
O54	O8	6a brt rose ('46)	24.00	*75.00*
a.		Imperf., pair		400.00
		Nos. O46-O54 (9)	84.75	*117.50*

For surcharges see Nos. O58-O59.

1946-47 **Unwmk.** ***Perf. 11½***

O55	O8	1a violet	11.00	4.75
O56	O7	2a violet ('47)	13.50	22.50
O57	O8	3a deep orange	125.00	*160.00*
a.		Imperf., pair	—	275.00
		Nos. O55-O57 (3)	149.50	187.25

No. O50 Surcharged "2 As." and Bars

1949 ***Perf. 12***

O58	O8	2a on 1½a dp plum	3.00	*11.00*
c.		Imperf., pair	300.00	*450.00*

Same Surcharged "2 As." and Rosettes

1949 *Imperf.*
O59 O8 2a on 1½a dp plum 1,250. 1,500.
a. Perf 12 1,350. *1,600.*

Three or more types of "2" in surcharge. Bhopal stamps became obsolete in 1950.

BHOR

'bō͵ə͵r

LOCATION — A Feudatory State in the Kolhapur Residency and Deccan States Agency.
AREA — 910 sq. mi.
POP. — 141,546
CAPITAL — Bhor

A1

A2

Handstamped
1879 **Unwmk.** *Imperf.*
Without Gum

1 A1 ½a carmine 5.50 *7.50*
2 A2 1a carmine 8.25 *12.00*

Pant Sachiv Shankarrao — A3

1901 **Without Gum** **Typo.**
3 A3 ½a red 24.00 *60.00*

BIJAWAR

bi-'jä-wər

LOCATION — A Feudatory State in the Bundelkhand Agency of Central India.
AREA — 973 sq. mi.
POP. — 115,852
CAPITAL — Bijawar

Maharaja Sir Sawant Singh — A1

1935-36 **Typo.** **Unwmk.** *Perf. 10½*
1 A1 3p brown 11.00 8.25
a. Imperf., pair 13.50
b. Rouletted 7 ('36) 9.00 *9.00*
2 A1 6p carmine 9.50 8.25
a. Rouletted 7 ('36) 12.00 *32.50*
3 A1 9p purple 12.50 7.50
a. Rouletted 7 ('36) 9.00 *160.00*
4 A1 1a dark blue 14.00 8.25
a. Rouletted 7 ('36) 15.00 *180.00*
5 A1 2a slate green 13.50 7.50
a. Rouletted 7 ('36) 19.00 *190.00*

Maharaja Sir Sawant Singh — A2

1937 *Perf. 9*
6 A2 4a red orange 22.50 *140.00*
7 A2 6a yellow 22.50 *140.00*
8 A2 8a emerald 24.00 *180.00*
9 A2 12a turquoise blue 24.00 *200.00*
10 A2 1r purple 62.50 *250.00*
a. "1Rs" instead of "1R" 75.00 *500.00*
Nos. 1-10 (10) 216.00 *949.75*

Bijawar stamps became obsolete in 1939.

BUNDI

'bün-dē

LOCATION — A Feudatory State in the Rajputana Agency of India.
AREA — 2,220 sq. mi.
POP. — 216,722
CAPITAL — Bundi

Katar (Indian Dagger) — A1

Laid Paper
Without Gum
Gutters between Stamps

1894 **Unwmk.** **Litho.** *Imperf.*
1 A1 ½a slate 19,000. *3,250.*

Redrawn; Blade Does Not Touch Oval
No Gutters between Stamps
Wove Paper

1A A1 ½a slate 67.50 *72.50*
b. Value above, name below 400.00 *525.00*
c. Top right ornament omitted 3,750. *4,000.*

On No. 1A, the dagger is thinner and its point does not touch the oval inner frame.

A2

Without Gum

1896 **Laid Paper**
2 A2 ½a slate 9.00 14.00

A3

1897-98 **Without Gum**
3 A3 1a red 18.00 *27.50*
4 A3 2a yellow green 21.00 *40.00*
5 A3 4a yellow green 100.00 *140.00*
6 A3 8a red 160.00 *450.00*
7 A3 1r yellow, *blue* 500.00 *825.00*
Nos. 3-7 (5) 799.00 *1,483.*

A4

A5

Redrawn; Blade Wider and Diamond-shaped

1898-1900 **Without Gum**
8 A3 ½a slate 7.00 7.00
9 A3 1a red 5.50 5.50
10 A3 2a emerald 19.00 25.00
a. 1st 2 characters of value omitted 3,000. 3,000.
11 A3 4a yel grn 42.50 *100.00*
12 A4 8a red 21.00 *27.50*
13 A5 1r yellow, *blue* 47.50 *82.50*
a. Wove paper 24.00 *40.00*
Nos. 8-13 (6) 142.50 *247.50*

On Nos. 9-10, the blade is wider and nearly diamond-shaped.

Point of Dagger to Left
14 A3 4a green 5.00 5.00

Maharao Rajah with Symbols of Spiritual and Temporal Power — A6

Rouletted 11 to 13 in Color
1915 **Typo.** **Without Gum**
"Bundi" in 3 Characters (word at top right)

15 A6 ¼a blue 2.90 *6.25*
a. Laid paper 6.75 *35.00*
16 A6 ½a black 4.00 *9.00*
17 A6 1a vermilion 5.50 *18.00*
a. Laid paper 15.00 *45.00*
18 A6 2a emerald 11.00 *35.00*
19 A6 2½a yellow 11.00 *40.00*
20 A6 3a brown 12.50 *67.50*
21 A6 4a yel green 5.25 *62.50*
23 A6 6a ultramarine 21.00 *160.00*
a. 6a deep blue 11.00 *180.00*
24 A6 8a orange 11.00 *160.00*
25 A6 10a olive 24.00 *150.00*
26 A6 12a dark green 19.00 *140.00*
27 A6 1r violet 40.00 *250.00*
28 A6 2r car brn & blk 125.00 *325.00*
29 A6 3r blue & brown 210.00 *450.00*
30 A6 4r pale grn & red brn 400.00 *550.00*
31 A6 5r ver & pale grn 400.00 *550.00*
Nos. 15-31 (16) 1,302. *2,973.*

Minor differences in lettering in top and bottom panels may be divided into 8 types, but not all values come in each type. In one subtype the top appears as one word. Nos. 30-31 have an ornamental frame around the design.

For overprints see Nos. O1-O39.

1941 *Perf. 11*
"Bundi" in 4 Characters (word at top right)

32 A6 ¼a light blue 2.25 62.50
33 A6 ½a black 40.00 47.50
34 A6 1a carmine 15.00 *75.00*
35 A6 2a yellow green 20.00 110.00
Nos. 32-35 (4) 77.25 295.00

The 4-character spelling of "Bundi" is found also on stamps rouletted in color: on ½a and 4a in small characters, and on ¼a, ½a, 1a, 4a, 4r and 5r in large characters like those on Nos. 32-35.

For overprints see Nos. O41-O48.

Arms of Bundi — A7

1941-45 **Typo.** *Perf. 11*
36 A7 3p bright ultra 3.50 *7.50*
37 A7 6p indigo 5.25 *12.50*
38 A7 1a red orange 8.00 *15.00*
39 A7 2a fawn 10.50 *27.50*
a. 2a brown ('45) 19.00 *30.00*
40 A7 4a brt yel green 19.00 *82.50*
41 A7 8a dull green 25.00 *300.00*
42 A7 1r royal blue 52.50 *450.00*
Nos. 36-42 (7) 123.75 *895.00*

The 1st printing of Nos. 36-42 was gummed. All later printings were without gum. **Values are for stamps without gum.**

For overprints see Nos. O49-O55.

A8

Maj. Maharao Rajah Bahadur Singh — A9

View of Bundi — A10

1947 *Perf. 11*
43 A8 ¼a deep green 2.75 *57.50*
44 A8 ½a purple 2.50 *47.50*
45 A8 1a yellow green 2.50 *47.50*
46 A9 2a red 2.40 *97.50*
47 A9 4a deep orange 2.75 *140.00*
48 A10 8a violet blue 3.75
49 A10 1r chocolate 19.00
Nos. 43-49 (7) 35.65

For overprints see Rajasthan Nos. 1-14.

OFFICIAL STAMPS

Regular Issue of 1915 Handstamped in Black, Red or Green

a

Rouletted 11 to 13 in Color
1918 **Unwmk.** **Without Gum**
O1 A6 ¼a dark blue 1.90
O2 A6 ½a black 1.10
O3 A6 1a vermilion 1.90
O4 A6 2a emerald 9.50
O5 A6 2½a yellow 6.00
O6 A6 3a brown 5.50
O7 A6 4a yel green 18.00
O8 A6 6a blue 22.50
O9 A6 8a orange 22.50
O10 A6 10a olive green 75.00
O11 A6 12a dark green 75.00
O12 A6 1r violet 90.00
O13 A6 2r car brn & blk 600.00
O14 A6 3r blue & brown 525.00
O15 A6 4r pale grn & red brn 450.00
O16 A6 5r ver & pale grn 490.00
Nos. O1-O16 (16) 2,394.

All values come with black handstamp and most exist in red. The overprint is found in various positions, double, inverted, etc.

Several denominations exist in two or more types. See notes following Nos. 31 and 35.

Regular Issue of 1915 Handstamped in Black, Red or Green

b

1919				Without Gum
O17	A6	¼a	dark blue	2.60
O18	A6	½a	black	4.50
O19	A6	1a	vermilion	16.00
O20	A6	2a	emerald	29.00
O21	A6	2½a	yellow	30.00
O22	A6	3a	brown	35.00
O23	A6	4a	yel green	120.00
O24	A6	6a	blue	45.00
O25	A6	8a	orange	52.50
O26	A6	10a	olive green	140.00
O27	A6	12a	dark green	120.00
O28	A6	1r	violet	82.50
O29	A6	2r	car brn & blk	275.00
O30	A6	3r	blue & brown	325.00
O31	A6	4r	pale grn & red brn	450.00
O32	A6	5r	ver & pale grn	490.00
	Nos. O17-O32 (16)			2,217.

Note following No. O16 applies to this issue.

Regular Issue of 1915 Handstamped in Carmine or Black

c

1919				*Rouletted in Color*
			Without Gum	
O33	A6	¼a	blue	11.00
O34	A6	½a	black	18.00
O35	A6	1a	vermilion	35.00
O36	A6	2a	yel green	140.00
O37	A6	8a	orange	450.00
O38	A6	10a	olive	700.00
O39	A6	12a	dark green	900.00
	Nos. O33-O39 (7)			2,254.

Nos. 33 and 35 Handstamped Type "a" in Black or Carmine

1941				*Perf. 11*
O41	A6	½a	black	24.00
O42	A6	2a	yellow green	825.00

Nos. 32 and 35 Handstamped Type "b" in Black or Carmine

O43	A6	¼a	light blue	90.00
O44	A6	2a	yellow green	210.00

Nos. 32-35 Handstamped Type "c" in Black or Carmine

1941				
O45	A6	¼a	light blue	190.00
O46	A6	½a	black	375.00
O47	A6	1a	carmine	700.00
O48	A6	2a	yellow green	625.00
	Nos. O45-O48 (4)			1,890.

Nos. 36 to 42 Overprinted in Black or Carmine

1941					*Perf. 11*
O49	A7	3p	brt ultra (C)	7.50	*24.00*
O50	A7	6p	indigo (C)	20.00	*24.00*
O51	A7	1a	red orange	19.00	*16.00*
O52	A7	2a	fawn	20.00	*19.00*
O53	A7	4a	brt yel green	72.50	*160.00*
O54	A7	8a	dull green	225.00	*950.00*
O55	A7	1r	royal blue (C)	310.00	*950.00*
	Nos. O49-O55 (7)			674.00	*2,143.*

BUSSAHIR

'bus-ə-ˌhi˛ə˛r

(Bashahr)

LOCATION — A Feudatory State in the Punjab Hill States Agency
AREA — 3,439 sq. mi.
POP. — 100,192
CAPITAL — Bashahr

Tiger
A1 A2

A3

A4

A5

A6

A7

A8

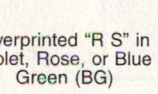

Overprinted "R S" in Violet, Rose, or Blue Green (BG)

Laid Paper

1895	Unwmk.		Litho.		*Imperf.*
1	A1	¼a	pink (V)	3,750.	
2	A2	½a	slate (R)	750.00	*1,000.*
3	A3	1a	red (V)	300.00	
4	A4	2a	yellow (V,R)	110.00	*300.00*
5	A5	4a	violet (V,R)	190.00	
6	A6	8a	brown (V,BG)	210.00	*375.00*
a.			Without overprint	400.00	
7	A7	12a	green (R)	450.00	
8	A8	1r	ultra (R)	190.00	
	Nos. 1-8 (8)			5,950.	
			Perf. 7 to 14		
9	A1	¼a	pink (V,BG)	100.00	*150.00*
10	A2	½a	slate (R)	35.00	*210.00*
11	A3	1a	red (V)	35.00	*140.00*
a.			Pin-perf.	275.00	*300.00*
12	A4	2a	yel (V,R,BG)	47.50	*140.00*
a.			Pin-perf. (V,R)	100.00	*240.00*
13	A5	4a	vio (V,R,BG)	37.50	*140.00*
a.			Pin-perf. (R)	450.00	
14	A6	8a	brown (V,BG)	35.00	*160.00*
15	A7	12a	green (V,R)	120.00	*200.00*
a.			Pin-perf. (R)	650.00	*825.00*
b.			Without overprint	325.00	
16	A8	1r	ultra (V,R)	65.00	*180.00*
a.			Pin-perf. (R)	700.00	
	Nos. 9-16 (8)			475.00	*1,320.*

"R. S." are the initials of Tika Raghunath Singh, son of the Raja.

Overprinted "R S" Like Nos. 1-16

A9

A10

A11

A12

A13

A14

Wove Paper

1896		Engr.		*Pin-perf.*
17	A9	¼a dk gray vio (R)	—	1,500.
18	A10	½a blue gray (R)	1,200.	450.00

1900		Litho.		*Imperf.*
19	A9	¼a red (V,BG)	7.50	*16.00*
20	A9	¼a violet (V,R)	12.50	
21	A10	½a blue (V,R)	15.00	*40.00*
22	A11	1a olive (R)	27.50	*65.00*
23	A11	1a red (V,BG)	7.00	*24.00*
24	A12	2a yellow (V)	75.00	
a.		2a ocher (R)	75.00	
25	A13	2a yellow (V)	90.00	
26	A14	4a brn vio (V,R,BG)	82.50	*180.00*
		Nos. 19-26 (8)	317.00	
		Pin-perf.		
27	A9	¼a red (V,BG)	6.25	*16.00*
28	A9	¼a violet (R)	30.00	27.50
29	A10	½a blue (V,R)	90.00	140.00
30	A11	1a olive (V,R)	40.00	
31	A11	1a red (V)	—	300.00
32	A11	1a vermilion (BG)	11.00	*22.50*
33	A12	2a yellow (BG)	1,250.	*1,300.*
34	A13	2a yellow (V,R)	75.00	*120.00*
a.		2a ocher (V)	100.00	
35	A14	4a brn vio (V,R,BG)	120.00	
		Nos. 27-35 (9)	1,622.	

Obsolete March 31, 1901.

Stamps overprinted with the monogram above (RNS) or with the monogram "PS" were never issued for postal purposes. They are either reprints or remainders to which this overprint has been applied. Many other varieties have appeared since the stamps became obsolete. It is probable that all or nearly all of them are reprints.

CHARKHARI

chər-'kär-ē

LOCATION — A Feudatory State in the Bundelkhand Agency in Central India.
AREA — 880 sq. mi.
POP. — 120,351
CAPITAL — Maharajnagar

A1

Thin White or Blue Wove Paper
Value in the Plural
Without Gum

1894		Unwmk. Typo.		*Imperf.*
1	A1	1a green	2,750.	*3,750.*
2	A1	2a green	3,250.	
3	A1	4a green	2,250.	

Value in the Singular

1897		Without Gum		
3A	A1	¼a rose	1,800.	1,100.
4	A1	¼a purple	5.50	5.50
5	A1	½a purple	3.75	*4.50*
6	A1	1a green	6.50	*9.50*
7	A1	2a green	11.00	*12.50*
8	A1	4a green	17.50	*27.50*
		Nos. 4-8 (5)	44.25	*59.50*

In a later printing, the numerals of Nos. 4-8 are smaller or of different shape.

Proofs are known on paper of various colors.

A2

Size: 19½x23mm

1909		Litho.		*Perf. 11*
9	A2	1p red brown	7.00	*57.50*
10	A2	1p pale blue	.90	.65
11	A2	½a scarlet	1.50	*1.90*
12	A2	1a light green	3.75	2.40
13	A2	2a ultra	4.50	*5.25*
14	A2	4a deep green	6.25	*8.25*
15	A2	8a brick red	11.00	*30.00*
16	A2	1r red brown	19.00	*62.50*
		Nos. 9-16 (8)	53.90	*168.45*

See Nos. 22-27, 39-43. For surcharges see Nos. 37-38A.

A3

1912-17		Handstamped Without Gum		*Imperf.*
21	A3	1p violet ('17)	10.50	7.50
c.		Double frameline	1,050.	125.00

The 1p black, type A3, is a proof.

A3a

Wove Paper
Handstamped

1922		Without Gum		*Imperf.*
21A	A3a	1a violet	120.00	*125.00*
b.		Perf. 11, laid paper	110.00	*210.00*

Type of 1909 Issue Redrawn
Size: 20x23½mm

1930-40		Without Gum		Typo.
22	A2	1p dark blue	.90	*21.00*
23	A2	½a olive green	3.75	*21.00*
23A	A2	½a cop brown ('40)	9.00	*37.50*
24	A2	1a light green	3.75	*24.00*
25	A2	1a chocolate	19.00	*40.00*
25A	A2	1a dull red ('40)	190.00	100.00
26	A2	2a light blue	1.90	*25.00*
a.		Tête bêche pair	14.00	
27	A2	4a carmine	4.50	*30.00*
a.		Tête bêche pair	21.00	
		Nos. 22-27 (8)	232.80	*298.50*

Guesthouse of Raja at Charkhari Reservoir — A4

Imlia Palace — A5

Industrial School — A6

View of City — A7

Maharajnagar Fort, Charkhari City — A8

Guesthouse A9

Palace Gate — A10

Temples at Rampur — A11

Govordhan Temple — A12

1931			*Perf. 11, 11½, 12*	
28	A4	½a dull green	3.25	.25
29	A5	1a black brown	2.40	.25
30	A6	2a purple	2.50	.25
31	A7	4a olive green	2.25	.25
32	A8	8a magenta	3.00	.25
33	A9	1r rose & green	4.00	.30
34	A10	2r brown & red	6.00	.35
35	A11	3r bl grn & choc	22.50	.60
36	A12	5r violet & blue	14.00	.75
		Nos. 28-36 (9)	59.90	3.25

Size range of A4-A12: 30-31x19½-24mm.
Many errors of perforation and printing exist.
Used values are for canceled to order stamps.

Nos. 15-16 Surcharged in Black

1940				*Perf. 11*
37	A2	½a on 8a brick red	52.50	*200.00*
a.		Surcharge inverted	450.00	600.00
b.		"1" of "½" inverted	400.00	
38	A2	1a on 1r red brown	175.00	*625.00*
b.		Surcharge inverted	490.00	
38A	A2	"1 ANNA" on 1r red brown	400.00	*450.00*

Type of 1930

1943		Unwmk. Typo. Size: 20x23½mm		*Imperf.*
39	A2	1p violet	32.50	*240.00*
a.		Tête bêche pair	82.50	
40	A2	1p apple green	90.00	*325.00*
41	A2	½a orange red	30.00	*62.50*
42	A2	½a black	90.00	*290.00*
43	A2	2a grayish green	140.00	*290.00*
a.		Tête bêche pair	180.00	
		Nos. 39-43 (5)	382.50	*1,208.*

COCHIN

kō-'chin

LOCATION — A Feudatory State in the Madras States Agency in Southern India.
AREA — 1,480 sq. mi.
POP. — 1,422,875 (1941)
CAPITAL — Ernakulam

See the United State of Travancore and Cochin.

6 Puttans = 5 Annas
12 Pies = 1 Anna
16 Annas = 1 Rupee

A1

State Seal

1892		Unwmk. Typo.		*Perf. 12*
1	A1	½p yellow	3.75	4.50
a.		Imperf., pair	—	—
b.		Laid paper	800.00	200.00
2	A1	1p red violet	4.50	4.00
a.		Vert. pair, imperf. between		*4,000.*
b.		1p purple (error)	175.00	125.00
3	A1	2p purple	3.00	*3.25*
a.		Imperf.	—	—
		Nos. 1-3 (3)	11.25	11.75

Nos. 1 to 3 sometimes have watermark large umbrella in the sheet.

A1a

Wmk. Coat of Arms and Inscription in Sheet

1896				
4	A1a	1p violet	145.00	*160.00*
		Wmk. 43		
4A	A1a	1p violet	27.50	*47.50*

Originally intended for revenue use, Nos. 4-4A were later authorized for postal use. Beware of fraudulently removed fiscal markings.

1894		Wmk. 41		**Thin Paper**
5	A1	½p orange	4.00	2.25
a.		Imperf., pair		
6	A1	1p magenta	12.00	10.50
7	A1	2p purple	9.00	5.00
a.		Imperf., pair	—	—
b.		Double impression		*2,000.*
c.		Printed on both sides	*2,500.*	
d.		Tete beche pair	*6,250.*	
		Nos. 5-7 (3)	25.00	17.75

A2

A3

A4

A5

1898				**Thin Paper**
8	A2	3p ultra	2.10	1.60
a.		Double impression	950.00	
b.		Horiz. pair, imperf. between	800.00	
c.		Vert. pair, imperf. between	900.00	
9	A3	½p gray green	2.50	2.25
a.		Pair, one sideways		3,750.
b.		Horiz. pair, imperf. between	*1,750.*	*1,700.*

10 A4 1p rose 5.50 2.50
a. Laid paper 2,400.
b. Tete beche pair 5,250. 3,250.
c. As "a," tete beche pair 12,000.
11 A5 2p purple 5.00 3.25
a. Vert. pair, imperf. between 850.00
b. Vert. strip of 3, imperf. between 1,000.
Nos. 8-11 (4) 15.10 9.60

1903 Thick Paper

12 A2 3p ultra 1.80 .25
d. Horiz. pair, imperf. between *1,350.*
i. Double impression 450.00
12A A3 ½p gray green 1.90 .60
e. Double impression 450.00
f. Pair, one sideways 1,350. 1,350.
j. Horiz. pair, imperf. between *1,750.*
12B A4 1p rose 2.50 .25
g. Tete beche pair 5,250.
12C A5 2p purple 3.75 .75
h. Double impression 1,250. 450.00
Nos. 12-12C (4) 9.95 1.85

Beware of fake overprint surcharge varieties, such as double, inverted, etc. This applies also to early Official varieties. Such varieties require expertization.

Type of 1898 Surcharged

1909

13 A2 2p on 3p red violet .25 *.75*
a. Inverted surcharge 160.00 160.00
b. Pair, stamps tete beche 250.00 *300.00*
c. Pair, stamps & surch. tete beche 300.00 *400.00*

The surcharge is also known in a thin "2" measuring 5½x7mm, with curving foot. Values: unused $1,200; used $600.

Sri Rama Varma I — A6

1911-13 Engr. *Perf. 14*

14 A6 2p brown .55 .25
a. Imperf., pair
15 A6 3p blue 3.00 .25
a. Perf. 14x12½ 40.00 3.00
16 A6 4p yel green 3.25 .25
16A A6 4p apple green 4.00 .75
17 A6 9p car rose 2.75 .25
18 A6 1a orange buff 4.50 .25
19 A6 1½a lilac 11.00 .65
20 A6 2a gray 11.00 .60
21 A6 3a vermilion 57.50 57.50
Nos. 14-21 (8) 93.55 60.00

For surcharge and overprints see Nos. 34, O2-O9, O23-O24, O27.

Sri Rama Varma II
A7 A8

1918-23 Engr. *Perf. 14*

23 A7 2p brown 12.00 .25
a. Imperf., pair *750.00*
24 A7 4p green 1.50 .25
25 A7 6p red brown ('22) 3.75 .25
26 A7 8p black brown ('23) 2.50 .25
27 A7 9p carmine rose 32.50 .50
28 A7 10p deep blue 9.00 .25
29 A8 1a brown orange 27.50 5.00
30 A7 1½a red violet ('21) 5.50 .30
31 A7 2a gray 6.25 .25
32 A7 2¼a yel green ('22) 10.50 4.75
33 A7 3a vermilion 17.50 .50
Nos. 23-33 (11) 128.50 12.55

The 2p and 1a are found in two types, the difference lying in the first of the three characters directly above the maharaja's head.

For surcharges and overprints see Nos. 36-40, 52-53, O10-O22, O25-O26, O28-O36, O71A.

No. 15 Surcharged

Type I — Numeral 8mm high. Curved foot. Top begins with a ball. (As illustrated.)
Type II — Numeral 9mm high. Curved foot. Top begins with a curved line.
Type III — Numeral 6mm high. Straight foot. "Two pies" 15mm wide.
Type IV — "2" as in type III. Capital "P" in "Pies." "Two Pies" 13mm wide.
Type V — Heavy gothic numeral. Capital "P" in "Pies."

1922-29

34 A6 2p on 3p blue (Type I) .60 .45
a. Type II 5.00 1.25
b. Type III 10.50 .50
c. Type IV 17.50 20.00
d. Type V 120.00 *225.00*
e. Double surcharge, I 500.00 500.00
f. Double surcharge II 1,100.
g. As "b," perf. 14x12½ 17.50 20.00

Types II and III exist with a capital "P" in "Pies." It occurs once in each sheet of the second and third settings. There are four settings.

Type V is the first stamp, fourth row, of the fourth setting.

No. 32 Surcharged

1928

36 A7 1a on 2¼a yel green 9.00 *18.00*
a. Double surcharge
b. "REVENUF" for "REVENUE" 85.00 125.00

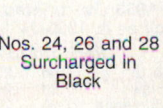

Nos. 24, 26 and 28 Surcharged in Black

1932-33

38 A7 3p on 4p green 1.90 *2.10*
39 A7 3p on 8p black brown 3.25 *4.00*
40 A7 9p on 10p deep blue 2.25 *5.00*
Nos. 38-40 (3) 7.40 11.10

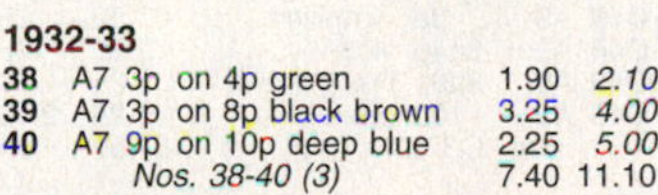

Sri Rama Varma III
A9 A10

1933-38 Engr. *Perf. 13x13½*

41 A9 2p brown ('36) 1.50 .75
42 A9 4p green .90 .25
43 A9 6p red brown 1.00 .25
44 A10 1a brown org ('34) 2.00 .30
45 A9 1a8p rose red 4.50 *9.50*
46 A9 2a gray black ('38) 9.00 2.40
47 A9 2¼a yellow green 2.50 .45
48 A9 3a red org ('38) 8.25 2.40
49 A9 3a4p violet 2.50 2.10
50 A9 6a8p black brown 2.50 22.50
51 A9 10a deep blue 4.50 25.00
Nos. 41-51 (11) 39.15 65.90

See Nos. 55-58. For overprints and surcharges see Nos. 54, 59-62, 73A-74, 76-77, 89, O37-O57, O70-O71, O72-O77A, O89.

Nos. 26 and 28 Surcharged in Red

1934 *Perf. 13½*

52 A7 6p on 8p black brown 1.10 .90
53 A7 6p on 10p dark blue 2.50 *3.00*

No. 44 Overprinted in Black — a

1939 Engr.

54 A10 1a brown orange 10.00 2.50

Types of 1933-38

1938-41 Litho. *Perf. 11*

55 A9 2p dull brown 1.25 .60
56 A9 4p dl grn ('41) 1.25 .50
57 A9 6p red brown 4.50 .25
57A A10 1a brn org 95.00 *140.00*
58 A9 2¼a yellow green 7.50 .35
Nos. 55-58 (5) 109.50 *141.70*

Perf. 13x13½

55B A9 2p dull brown 11.00 1.00
56B A9 4p dl grn ('41) 10.00 20.00
57C A9 6p red brown 5,250.
57D A10 1a brn org 160.00 *200.00*
58B A9 2¼a yellow green 22.50 8.00

Type of 1934 Overprinted in Black Type "a" or — b

1941-42 *Perf. 11 (#59), 13 (#60)*

59 A10(a) 1a brown org 525.00 2.50
a. Perf. 13 525.00
60 A10(b) 1a brn org ('42) 20.00 1.00
a. Perf. 11 1.25 2.50

No. 45 Surcharged in Black — c

1943-44 Engr. *Perf. 13x13½*

61 A9 3p on 1a8p rose red ('44) 12.50 *25.00*
62 A9 1a3p on 1a8p rose red 1.25 .75

Maharaja Sri Kerala Varma
A11 A12

1943 Litho. Wmk. 294 *Perf. 11, 13*

63 A11 2p dull gray brn, wmk. 41 8.00 *9.00*
a. Wmk. 294 42.50 6.25
b. #63, Perf. 11 *3,500.*
c. As 'a,', perf. 11 *4,500.*
64 A11 4p gray green, wmk. 294 8.00 25.00
a. Wmk. 41 1,750. *625.00*
b. #64, perf. 11 4.75 *6.25*
65 A11 6p red brown 7.50 .25
a. Perf. 11 10.00 2.00
66 A11 9p ultramarine 75.00 1.90
a. Horiz. pair, imperf. between 3,500.
67 A12 1a brn org, wmk. 294 27.50 85.00
a. Wmk. 41 150.00 *175.00*
b. Perf. 13x13½ *225.00* *275.00*
68 A11 2¼a lt ol green 35.00 10.00
a. Perf. 13x13½ 40.00 6.00
Nos. 63-68 (6) 161.00 131.15

For surcharges and overprints see Nos. 69-73, 75, 78, 78B, O58-O69.

No. 64 Surcharged Type "c"

69 A11 3p on 4p gray green 9.50 .25
a. Wmk. 41 140.00 35.00

Nos. 64, 64a and 65 Surcharged in Black — d

1944-48 Wmk. 294

70 A11 2p on 6p red brown .95 *6.00*
a. Perf. 11 1.20 3.50
71 A11 3p on 4p gray green 12.50 .25
72 A11 3p on 6p red brown 1.00 1.00
a. Perf. 13x13½ 2.50 .25
73 A11 4p on 6p red brown 8.50 *18.00*
Nos. 70-73 (4) 22.95 25.25

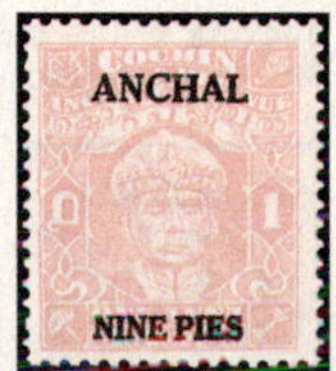

Nos. 57A, 67a Surcharged in Black

1944 Litho. Wmk. 41

73A A10 6p on 1a brn org *250.00* 100.00
b. Perf. 11 450.00 275.00
74 A10 9p on 1a brn org 550.00 60.00
75 A12 9p on 1a brn org 12.00 6.25
Nos. 73A-75 (3) *812.00* 166.25

No. 56 Surcharged Type "c" in Black

76 A9 3p on 4p dull green 8.75 6.00
a. Perf. 13x13½ 25.00 5.00

Nos. 57A, 67a Surcharged in Black

1944

77 A10 9p on 1a brown orange 45.00 12.50
78 A12 9p on 1a brown orange 14.00 5.00

No. 67a Surcharged Type "c"

1944 Wmk. 41

78B A12 1a3p on 1a brn org 7,750.

Maharaja Ravi Varma — A13

1944-46 Wmk. 294 *Perf. 13*

79 A13 9p ultra ('46) 32.50 27.50
a. Perf. 11 27.50 8.00
b. Perf. 13x13½ 62.50 7.00
80 A13 1a3p magenta 12.50 12.50
a. Perf. 13x13½ *500.00* 110.00
81 A13 1a9p ultra ('46) 12.00 24.00
Nos. 79-81 (3) 57.00 64.00

For overprints and surcharges see Nos. O78-O80, Travancore-Cochin Nos. 12, 14, O10.

Maharaja Ravi Varma — A15

1946-50		**Litho.**		***Perf. 13***
82	A15	2p dull brown	4.00	.25
a.		Perf. 11	10.00	.90
b.		Perf. 11x13	*550.00*	210.00
c.		Vert. pair, imperf. horiz.	*4,250.*	*4,250.*
83	A15	3p carmine rose	.60	.45
83A	A15	4p gray grn ('50)	*4,000.*	120.00
84	A15	6p red brn ('47)	30.00	11.00
a.		Perf. 11	250.00	8.25
85	A15	9p ultramarine	3.50	.25
a.		Horiz. pair, imperf. between		*4,000.*
86	A15	1a dp org ('47)	11.00	*47.50*
a.		Perf. 11	750.00	
87	A15	2a gray ('47)	175.00	12.50
a.		Perf. 11	225.00	10.00
88	A15	3a vermilion	110.00	4.00
		Nos. 82-83,84-88 (7)	334.10	75.95

For surcharges and overprints see Nos. 98-99, O81-O88, Travancore-Cochin Nos. 8, 13, 15-15A, O11.

No. 45 Surcharged Type "d"

Perf. 13x13½

1947-48		**Wmk. 41**		**Engr.**
89	A9	6p on 1a8p rose red	6.00	30.00

Maharaja Sri Kerala Varma II — A16

Die I

Die II

Two dies on 2p:
Die I, back of headdress almost touches value tablet.
Die II, back of headdress farther away from value tablet.

Die I

Die II

Two dies on 3a4p:
Die I, white frame line around head is continuous, and two white lines beneath value inscriptions at bottom.
Die II, white frame line around head broken by value tablets at the sides, and single white line beneath value inscriptions at bottom. Die II comes from the first two stamps of the bottom row of the sheet.

1948-49		**Wmk. 294**		***Perf. 11***
90	A16	2p olive brown	2.25	.25
a.		Die II	190.00	4.50
b.		#90, horiz. pair, imperf. vert.		*4,000.*
91	A16	3p car ('49)	4.00	.25
a.		#90, vert. pair, imperf. between		*2,900.*
92	A16	4p gray green	21.00	6.25
a.		Horiz. pair, imperf. vert.	375.00	500.00
93	A16	6p red brown	27.50	.35
94	A16	9p ultra ('49)	3.00	.90
95	A16	2a black	90.00	3.75
96	A16	3a ver ('49)	100.00	1.50
97	A16	3a4p violet ('49)	87.50	525.00
a.		Die II	350.00	
		Nos. 90-97 (8)	335.25	538.25

For overprints see Nos. O90-O97, Travancore-Cochin Nos. 9-11, O8-O9, O24.

No. 86 Surcharged Type "d" in Black

1949				
98	A15	6p on 1a dp orange	90.00	*225.00*
99	A15	9p on 1a dp orange	150.00	*225.00*

A17

Design: 2a, Chinese fishing net. 2¼a, Dutch Palace.

1949		**Unwmk.**		***Perf. 11***
100	A17	2a gray black	9.00	*15.00*
a.		Imperf. vert., horiz. pair	750.00	
101	A17	2¼a dull green	3.50	*15.00*
a.		Imperf. vert., horiz. pair	750.00	600.00

See Travancore-Cochin for succeeding issues.

OFFICIAL STAMPS

See note above No. 13.

Stamps and Type of 1911-14 Overprinted — h

1913-14		**Wmk. 41**	**Engr.**	***Perf. 14***
O2	A6	4p yel green	15.00	.25
a.		Inverted overprint	—	450.00
O3	A6	9p car rose	25.00	.25
O4	A6	1½a red violet	72.50	.25
a.		Double overprint	—	1,100.
O5	A6	2a gray	19.00	.25
O6	A6	3a vermilion	82.50	.65
O7	A6	6a violet	90.00	3.00
O8	A6	12a blue	60.00	10.00
O9	A6	1½r deep green	52.50	*110.00*
		Nos. O2-O9 (8)	416.50	124.65

Values for Nos. O2 and O3 are for the cheaper varieties with watermark sideways.

Stamps and Type of 1918-23 Overprinted — i

1918-34				
O10	A7	4p green	6.25	.25
a.		Double overprint	—	825.00
O11	A7	6p red brn ('22)	22.50	.25
a.		Double overprint	—	750.00
O12	A7	8p blk brn ('26)	16.00	.25
O13	A7	9p carmine rose	97.50	.25
O14	A7	10p dp blue ('23)	22.50	.25
O16	A7	1½a red vio ('21)	8.25	.25
a.		Double overprint		1,100.
O17	A7	2a gray	62.50	.45
O18	A7	2¼a yel grn ('22)	20.00	.25
b.		Double overprint		750.00
O19	A7	3a ver ('22)	27.50	.35
a.		Double overprint		750.00
O20	A7	6a violet ('22)	57.50	.75
O21	A7	12a blue ('29)	25.00	7.50
O22	A7	1½r dk green ('34)	37.50	*175.00*
		Nos. O10-O22 (12)	403.00	*185.80*

On Nos. O2-O22, width of overprint varies from 14¾mm to 16½mm.

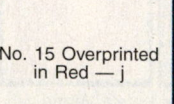

No. 15 Overprinted in Red — j

1921				
O23	A6	3p blue	175.00	.25
a.		Overprint in black		*1,900.*
b.		Double overprint (R)		750.00
c.		Inverted "S" (R)		75.00

Nos. O3 and O13 Surcharged with New Values

1923-29				
O24	A6	8p on 9p car rose	525.00	2.50
a.		Double surcharge		500.00
O25	A7	8p on 9p car rose	150.00	.25
a.		Double surcharge		400.00
O26	A7	10p on 9p car rose ('25)	120.00	1.50
a.		Double surcharge		450.00
b.		Surcharge measures 25mm		450.00
c.		As "b," double surcharge		500.00
O27	A6	10p on 9p car rose ('29)	2,200.	27.50
a.		Double surcharge		900.00
		Nos. O24-O27 (4)	2,995.	31.75

Surcharge measures 27½ mm.

Regular Issue of 1918-23 Overprinted — k

1929-31				
O28	A7	4p green ('31)	32.50	3.00
O29	A7	6p red brown ('30)	21.00	.25
O30	A7	8p black brown ('30)	10.00	.25
O31	A7	10p deep blue	9.00	.25
O32	A7	2a gray ('30)	60.00	.35
O33	A7	3a vermilion ('30)	12.50	.30
O34	A7	6a dk violet ('30)	150.00	4.50
		Nos. O28-O34 (7)	295.00	8.90

Inverted "S" in Overprint

O28a	A7	4p green ('31)	325.00	25.00
O29a	A7	6p red brown ('30)	175.00	5.50
O30a	A7	8p black brown ('30)	85.00	6.00
O31a	A7	10p deep blue	85.00	6.00
O32a	A7	2a gray ('30)	400.00	15.00
O33a	A7	3a vermilion ('30)	150.00	10.00
O34a	A7	6a dk violet ('30)	950.00	125.00
		Nos. O28a-O34a (7)	2,170.	192.50

Same with Additional Surcharge on Type of Regular Issue of 1918-23 in Red

1933				
O35	A7	6p on 8p black brown	3.75	.25
a.		Inverted "S"	32.50	6.00
O36	A7	6p on 10p dk blue	6.00	.25
a.		Inverted "S"	60.00	5.00

Regular Issue of 1933 Overprinted Type "k" in Black as in 1933-34

1933-35				***Perf. 13x13½***
O37	A9	4p green	8.50	.25
O38	A9	6p red brown	7.50	.25
O39	A10	1a brown orange	27.50	.25
O40	A9	1a8p rose red	2.25	.45
O41	A9	2a gray	35.00	.25
O42	A9	2¼a yellow green	12.50	.25
O43	A9	3a vermilion	67.50	.25
O44	A9	3a4p violet	2.25	.25
O45	A9	6a8p black brown	2.25	.30
O46	A9	10a deep blue	2.25	2.00
		Nos. O37-O46 (10)	167.50	4.50

Regular Stamps of 1934-38 Overprinted in Black — m

1937-38				***Perf. 11, 13x13½***
O47	A10	1a brown orange	50.00	.90
O48	A9	2a gray black	27.50	3.00
O49	A9	3a red orange	13.50	3.75
		Nos. O47-O49 (3)	91.00	7.65

Similar Overprint on Types of 1933-36

Perf. 11, 13x13½

1938-44		**Litho.**		**Wmk. 294**
O50	A9	4p dl grn, perf. 13x13½	3.00	1.00
a.		Perf. 11 ('42)	110.00	24.00

Wmk. 41

O51	A9	6p red brown ('41)	18.00	7.00
a.		Wmk. 294	25.00	1.50
b.		As "a," perf. 11	250.00	12.50
c.		Printed both sides		*250.00*
O52	A10	1a brown orange	1.25	.25
a.		Wmk. 294	3.00	*6.50*
b.		As "a," perf. 11	15.00	6.00
c.		Printed both sides		*250.00*
O53	A9	3a orange ('40)	3.75	3.25
b.		Wmk. 294	30.00	12.50
		Nos. O50-O53 (4)	26.00	11.50

Similar Overprint in Narrow Serifed Capitals on No. 57

		Wmk. 41		***Perf. 11***
O53A	A9	6p red brown	1,250.	600.00

Type of 1933-36 Overprinted in Black — o

Perf. 10½, 11, 13x13½

O54	A9	4p dl grn, perf. 13x13½ ('41)	27.50	3.25
a.		Perf. 11	40.00	4.00
b.		Inverted "S"	55.00	4.00
O55	A9	6p red brown ('41)	40.00	.60
a.		Inverted "S"	50.00	3.00
O56	A9	2a gray black	25.00	1.50
a.		Inverted "S"	27.50	2.00
		Nos. O54-O56 (3)	92.50	5.35

Type of 1934 Overprinted in Black — p

1941				***Perf. 11***
O57	A10	1a brown orange	425.00	3.75

Stamps and Types of 1944 Overprinted in Black — q

Perf. 11, 13x13½

1944-48				**Wmk. 294**
O58	A11	4p gray green	75.00	12.50
a.		Perf. 11	200.00	8.25
b.		Perf. 13	750.00	90.00
O59	A11	6p red brn, perf. 11	3.50	.25
a.		Perf. 13x13½	5.50	.25
b.		Perf. 13	10.00	3.50
c.		As "a," double overprint	175.00	8.25
d.		As "b," double overprint		*120.00*
O59E	A11	1a brn org, perf. 13x13½	17,000.	85.00
O60	A11	2a gray black	8.75	1.50
O61	A11	2¼a dl yel grn	5.25	1.60
a.		Additional ovpt. on reverse		200.00
O62	A11	3a red org, perf. 13x13½	13.50	3.75
a.		Perf. 11	16.00	.50
		Nos. O58-O62 (5)	106.00	19.60

Same Overprint with Additional Surcharge

O63	A11	3p on 4p gray grn, perf. 13x13½	5.50	.25
a.		Perf. 11	12.50	.75
b.		As "a," additional overprint on reverse		210.00

O64 A12 3p on 1a brn org 40.00 12.50
O65 A11 9p on 6p red brn 17.00 6.00
a. Additional overprint on reverse 750.00
O66 A12 1a3p on 1a brn org 26.00 5.00
Nos. O63-O66 (4) 88.50 23.75

Same Overprint in Black on Types of 1944 Surcharged Type "c"

O67 A11 3p on 4p gray grn, perf. 13½x13 8.00 .80
a. Perf. 11 600.00 225.00
O68 A11 9p on 6p red brn 7.50 1.00
O69 A12 1a3p on 1a brn org 5.50 .25
Nos. O67-O69 (3) 21.00 2.05

Nos. O52 and O16 Surcharged Type "d"

1944 Wmk. 41 *Perf. 11, 13x13½, 14*
O70 A10 3p on 1a brn org 5.00 *5.00*
O71 A10 9p on 1a brn org 475.00 87.50

Engr.

O71A A7 9p on 1½a red vio 1,000. 40.00

No. O52 Surcharged Type "c"

O72 A10 1a3p on 1a brn org 500.00 150.00

No. 76 Overprinted in Black

Perf. 13x13½

O72A A9 3p on 4p dl grn 250.00 90.00

No. 45 Overprinted Type "k" and Surcharged Type "d"

1944-48 Wmk. 41 *Perf. 13x13½*
O73 A9 9p on 1a8p rose red 200.00 50.00
O74 A9 1a9p on 1a8p rose red 5.00 4.00

No. 45 Overprinted Type "k" and Surcharged Type "c"

O75 A9 3p on 1a8p rose red 8.00 4.50
O76 A9 1a9p on 1a8p rose red 3.50 .60

Type of 1939-41 Overprinted in Black

1946 Wmk. 294 *Perf. 11*
O77 A9 2a gray 110.00 1.20
b. Overprint omitted 2,000.
O77A A9 2¼a yellow green 2,900. 12.00

Same Overprint in Black on Nos. 79-81

1946 Litho. *Perf. 13*
O78 A13 9p ultramarine 4.00 .25
a. Perf. 13x13½ 7.50 .25
b. Additional overprint on reverse 900.00
O79 A13 1a3p magenta 2.00 .25
a. Double overprint 25.00 18.00
b. Additional overprint on reverse 200.00
c. As "b," overprint doubled and inverted 110.00 100.00
O80 A13 1a9p ultramarine .50 *1.50*
a. Double overprint
b. Pair, one without overprint 2,750.
Nos. O78-O80 (3) 6.50 2.00

Types and Stamps of 1946-48 Overprinted Type "h"

1946-48
O81 A15 3p car rose 2.75 .25
a. Additional overprint on reverse *950.00*
O82 A15 4p gray green 40.00 10.00
O83 A15 6p red brown 25.00 4.00
O84 A15 9p ultra 1.00 .25
a. Additional overprint on reverse, inverted
O85 A15 1a3p magenta 7.50 2.10
O86 A15 1a9p ultra 8.50 .60
O87 A15 2a gray black 19.00 4.50
O88 A15 2¼a olive green 35.00 10.00
Nos. O81-O88 (8) 138.75 31.70

No. 56 Overprinted Type "q" and Surcharged Type "d"

1947 Wmk. 41 Engr. *Perf. 13x13½*
O89 A9 3p on 4p dull green 50.00 17.50
a. Double surcharge 650.00 300.00

Stamps and Type of 1948-49 Overprinted Type "o"

1948-49 Wmk. 294 Litho. *Perf. 11*
O90 A16 3p car ('49) 1.50 .25
O91 A16 4p gray green 3.00 .60
b. Additional overprint on reverse 120.00 120.00
c. Horizontal pair, imperf. between 2,500.
d. Vertical pair, imperf. between 2,500.
O92 A16 6p red brown 5.00 .45
b. Vertical pair, imperf. between 3,250.
O93 A16 9p ultramarine 6.00 .25
O94 A16 2a black ('49) 4.50 .25
O95 A16 2¼a lt ol grn ('49) 6.00 *9.50*
O96 A16 3a ver ('49) 1.50 *1.75*
O97 A16 3a4p dp pur ('49) 75.00 70.00
Nos. O90-O97 (8) 102.50 83.05

See Travancore-Cochin for succeeding issues.

DHAR

'där

LOCATION — A Feudatory State in the Malwa Agency in Central India.
AREA — 1,800 sq. mi.
POP. — 243,521
CAPITAL — Dhar

Arms of Dhar — A1

The stamps of type A1 have an oval control mark handstamped in black.

Unwmk.
1897-1900 Typeset Without Gum *Imperf.*
1 A1 ½p black, *red* 4.50 *5.00*
a. Characters for "pice" transposed 100.00
b. Four characters in first word 4.00 *6.00*
c. Without control mark 500.00
2 A1 ¼a blk, *org red* ('00) 5.50 *7.50*
a. Without control mark 375.00
3 A1 ½a black, *lil rose* 6.75 *8.25*
4 A1 1a black, *bl grn* 12.50 *25.00*
5 A1 2a black, *yel* ('00) 42.50 *75.00*
Nos. 1-5 (5) 71.75 *120.75*

Arms of Dhar — A2

1898-1900 Typo. *Perf. 11½*
6 A2 ½a red 7.00 *9.50*
7 A2 ½a rose ('00) 6.25 *9.00*
a. Imperf., pair 60.00
8 A2 1a maroon 6.25 *12.00*
9 A2 1a violet ('00) 6.25 *22.50*
10 A2 1a claret ('00) 6.25 *12.00*
11 A2 2a dark green ('00) 11.00 *37.50*
Nos. 6-11 (6) 43.00 *102.50*

Obsolete Mar. 31, 1901.

DUNGARPUR

'dəŋ-gə-,pər

LOCATION — A princely state in Rajasthan, in northwestern India.
AREA — 1,447 sq. mi.
POP. — 100,103 (1901)
CAPITAL — Dungarpur

Arms of Dungarpur — A1

1933-1947 Unwmk. Litho. *Perf. 11*
1 A1 ¼a bister yellow 2,000. 400.00
a. ¼a lemon yellow ('34) 2,500. 500.00
2 A1 ¼a salmon ('35) 5,000. 1,000.
a. ¼a red brown ('36) 3,750. 750.00
b. ¼a orange red ('38) 6,250. 1,250.
3 A1 1a pale turq bl 1,500. 300.00
a. 1a turquoise blue 2,000. 400.00
4 A1 1a3p dp red vio ('35) 3,000. 600.00
5 A1 2a dp dl grn ('47) 3,750. 750.00
6 A1 4a dull rose red 6,250. 1,250.
a. 4a rose red ('34) 7,000. 1,400.

A2

A3

A4

A5

Maharawal Lakshman Singh

1934-38 Typo. *Perf. 12*
7 A2 ¼a org buff ('36) 1,750. 200.00
8 A3 ½a vermilion, Die I 500.00 125.00
9 A4 1a blue
a. Perf 11½ ('38) 750.00 125.00
10 A5 4a gray brown 2,000. 650.00

There are three dies of the ½ anna: Die I measures 21x25½mm, and width of turban is 7½mm; Die II measures 20x20½mm; Die III measures 21x25½mm, and width of turban is 6½mm. There are 4 distinct cliches of Die III, printed in a block of 4, differing in the space between the top of the turban and the frame: Pos. 1 = 2mm; Pos. 2 = 2.5mm; Pos. 3 = 1mm; Pos. 4 = 1.5mm.

Maharawal Lakshman Singh — A6

1940-41 *Perf. 11, 11½ (#15)*
11 A2 ¼a dull org('41) 1,500. 150.00
12 A3 ½a carmine, Die I 500.00 150.00
13 A4 1a blue 500.00 100.00
14 A6 2a bright green 2,500. 900.00
15 A5 4a gray brown 1,800. 450.00

1943 *Pin-Perf 11½*
16 A6 2a bright green 2,500. 900.00

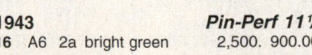

A7

A8

Maharawal Lakshman Singh

1943-44 *Perf. 10½*
17 A2 ¼a dull org('44) 1,500. 150.00
18 A3 ½a ver, Die I ('44) 600.00 175.00
19 A7 ½a ver, Die II ('44) 600.00 175.00
a. Horiz. pair, #18 + #19 1,300. 450.
b. Vert. pair, imperf between 5,000.

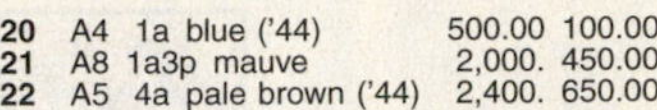
20 A4 1a blue ('44) 500.00 100.00
21 A8 1a3p mauve 2,000. 450.00
22 A5 4a pale brown ('44) 2,400. 650.00

A9

A10

Maharawal Lakshman Singh

1945 *Perf. 10*
23 A2 ¼a orange 2,000. 150.00
24 A9 ½a ver, Die III ('44) 800.00 100.00
25 A4 1a blue 500.00 100.00
26 A8 1a3p bright mauve 2,000. 450.00
27 A10 1½a deep violet 2,000. 450.00
28 A5 4a brown 1,600. 400.00

The stamps of Dungarpur became obsolete in Sept. 1949.

DUTTIA

'dət-ē-ə

(Datia)

LOCATION — A Feudatory State in the Bundelkhand Agency in Central India.
AREA — 912 sq. mi.
POP. — 158,834
CAPITAL — Datia

Ganesh, Elephant-headed God

A1 A2

All Duttia stamps have a circular control mark, about 23mm in diameter, handstamped in blue or black. All were issued without gum.

1893 Typeset Unwmk. *Imperf.*
1 A1 ¼a blk, *org red* 6,250.
2 A1 ½a blk, *grysh grn* 24,000.
3 A2 1a black, *red* 4,750. *7,500.*
4 A1 2a blk, *yel* 5,250.
5 A1 4a black, *rose* 1,900.

Type A2 with Frameline around God, Rosettes in Lower Corners

1896 (?)
5A A2 ½ black, *green* *15,000.*
5C A2 2a dk blue, *lemon* *3,750.*

A 1a in this revised type has been reported.

1897
6 A2 ½a black, *green* 100.00 *675.00*
7 A2 1a black 150.00 *525.00*
a. Laid paper 32.50
8 A2 2a black, *yellow* 42.50 *500.00*
9 A2 4a black, *rose* 40.00 *325.00*
Nos. 6-9 (4) 332.50 *2,025.*

A3

10 A3 ½a black, *green* 150.00 *825.00*
11 A3 1a black 290.00
12 A3 2a black, *yellow* 175.00 *825.00*
13 A3 4a black, *rose* 175.00 *825.00*
Nos. 10-13 (4) 790.00 2,475.

A4

Rouletted in Colored Lines on 2 or 3 Sides

1899-1900

14 A4 ¼a red (shades) 5.00 *32.50*
 b. Tete beche pair 4,900.
15 A4 ½a black, *green* 4.00 *30.00*
16 A4 1a black 4.50 *30.00*
17 A4 2a black, *yellow* 5.25 *35.00*
18 A4 4a black, *rose red* 5.00 *32.50*
 a. Tete beche pair
 Nos. 14-18 (5) 23.75 160.00

1904 ***Imperf.***

22 A4 ¼a carmine 5.50 *47.50*
23 A4 ½a black, *green* 27.50
24 A4 1a black 21.00 *75.00*
 Nos. 22-24 (3) 54.00 122.50

1911 ***Perf. 13½***

25 A4 ¼a carmine 9.50 *75.00*

1916 ***Imperf.***

26 A4 ¼a dull blue 8.25 *40.00*
27 A4 ½a green 8.25 *40.00*
28 A4 1a violet 10.00 *42.50*
 a. Tete beche pair 35.00
29 A4 2a brown 22.50 *52.50*
29A A4 4a brick red 110.00
 Nos. 26-29A (5) 159.00 175.00

1918

31 A4 ½a ultramarine 5.25 *27.50*
32 A4 1a rose 5.25 *27.50*
33 A4 2a violet 11.00 *40.00*

Perf. 12

34 A4 ¼a black 7.50 *37.50*
 Nos. 31-34 (4) 29.00 *132.50*

1920 ***Rouletted***

35 A4 ¼a blue 4.00 *21.00*
36 A4 ½a rose 5.25 *24.00*

Perf. 7

37 A4 ½a dull red 24.00 *62.50*
 Nos. 35-37 (3) 33.25 *107.50*

Duttia stamps became obsolete in 1921.

FARIDKOT

fe-'rēd-ˌkōt

LOCATION — A Feudatory State in the Punjab Agency of India.
AREA — 638 sq. mi.
POP. — 164,364
CAPITAL — Faridkot

4 Folus or Paisas = 1 Anna

A1

A2

A3

Handstamped

1879-86 **Unwmk.** ***Imperf.***
Without Gum

1 A1 1f ultramarine 4.00 *6.00*
 a. Laid paper 21.00 *24.00*
 b. Tete beche pair 400.00
2 A2 1p ultramarine 7.50 *16.00*
 a. Laid paper 125.00 *150.00*
3 A3 1p ultramarine 2.25
 a. Tete beche pair 340.00
 Nos. 1-3 (3) 13.75 22.00

Several other varieties exist, but it is believed that only the stamps listed here were issued for postal use. They became obsolete Dec. 31, 1886. See Faridkot under Convention States for issues of 1887-1900.

HYDERABAD (DECCAN)

'hīd-ˌə-ˌrə-ˌbad

LOCATION — Central India
AREA — 82,313 sq. mi.
POP. — 16,338,534 (1941)
CAPITAL — Hyderabad

This independent princely state was occupied and annexed by India in 1948.

Catalogue values for unused stamps in this State are for Never Hinged items, beginning with Scott 51 in the regular postage section, and Scott O54 in the officials section.

Expect irregular perfs on the Nos. 1-14 and O1-O20 due to the nature of the paper.

A1

A2

1869-71 **Engr.** **Unwmk.** ***Perf. 11½***

1 A1 ½a brown ('71) 6.00 *6.50*
2 A2 1a olive green 27.50 11.00
 a. Imperf. horiz., pair 900.00 175.00
3 A1 2a green ('71) 90.00 72.50
 Nos. 1-3 (3) 123.50 90.00

For overprints see Nos. O1-O3, O11-O13.
The reprints are perforated 12½.

A3

Wove Paper

1871-1909 ***Perf. 12½***

4 A3 ½a org brn 4.00 .25
 a. ½a red brown 4.00 .25
 b. ½a magenta (error) 75.00 12.00
 c. Perf. 11½ 27.50 *30.00*
 d. ½a rose 4.00 .30
 e. ½a bright vermilion 4.00 .25
5 A3 1a dark brown 1.90 .25
 a. Imperf., pair 550.00
 b. Horiz. pair, imperf. vert. 1,350.
 c. Vert. pair, imperf. horiz. 1,350.
 d. Perf. 11½ 180.00 *200.00*
6 A3 1a black ('09) 3.50 .25
7 A3 2a green 5.50 .25
 a. 2a olive green ('09) 5.50 .50
 b. Perf. 11½ 1,900.
8 A3 3a yellow brown 4.50 2.25
 a. Perf. 11½ 60.00 *82.50*
9 A3 4a slate 11.00 5.25
 a. Imperf. horiz., pair 1,350. 1,350.
 b. Perf. 11½ 225.00 225.00
10 A3 4a deep green 8.25 5.00
 a. 4a olive green 9.00 3.75
11 A3 8a bister brown 5.25 *6.50*
 a. Perf. 11½
12 A3 12a blue 7.00 *12.00*
 a. Perf. 11½ 500.00
 b. 12a slate green 7.50 7.50
 Nos. 4-12 (9) 50.90 32.00

For overprints see Nos. 13, O4-O10, O14-O20, O25-O26.

Surcharged

1900

13 A3 ¼a on ½a brt ver .75 *1.25*
 a. Inverted surcharge 57.50 35.00

A4

1900, Sept. 20

14 A4 ¼a blue 8.25 5.25

Seal of the Nizam — A5

Engraved by A. G. Wyon

1905 **Wmk. 42**

17 A5 ¼a blue 3.75 .90
18 A5 ½a red 6.00 .35
19 A5 ½a orange 9.00 .50
 Nos. 17-19 (3) 18.75 1.75

For overprints see Nos. O21-O23.

Perf. 11, 11½, 12½, 13½ and Compound

1908-11

20 A5 ¼a gray 1.50 .25
21 A5 ½a green 7.00 .25
22 A5 1a carmine 5.25 .25
23 A5 2a lilac 2.40 .25
24 A5 3a brn orange ('09) 4.00 1.50
25 A5 4a olive green ('09) 4.50 1.90
26 A5 8a violet ('11) 1.90 1.20
27 A5 12a blue green ('11) 10.50 6.00
 Nos. 20-27 (8) 37.05 11.60

For overprints see Nos. O24, O27-O38.

Engr. by Bradbury, Wilkinson & Co.

1912

28 A5 ¼a brown violet 1.20 .25
29 A5 ½a deep green 2.50 .25
 a. Imperf., pair 550.00

The frame of type A5 differs slightly in each denomination.
Nos. 20-21 measure 19½x20½mm.
Nos. 28-29 measure 20x21½mm.
For overprints see Nos 37, O39-O40, O44.

Seal of the Nizam — A6

1915-16

30 A6 ½a green 1.50 .25
31 A6 1a carmine rose 3.75 .25
32 A6 1a red 2.50 .25
 Nos. 30-32 (3) 7.75 .75

Unless used, imperf. stamps of types A5 and A6 are from plate proof sheets.
See No. 58. For overprints see Nos. 38, O41-O43, O45.

A7

1927 **Wmk. 211** ***Perf. 13½***

36 A7 1r yellow 13.50 *18.00*

Stamps of 1912-16 Surcharged in Red

(4 pies)

(8 pies)

1930

37 A5 4p on ¼a brn vio .45 .25
 a. Perf. 11 675.00
 b. Double surcharge 350.00
38 A6 8p on ½a green .60 .25
 a. Perf. 11 400.00 210.00

For overprints see Nos. O44-O45.

Seal of Nizam — A8

Char Minar — A9

High Court of Justice A10

Reservoir for City of Hyderabad A11

Bidar College — A13

Entrance to Ajanta Caves A12

Victory Tower at Daulatabad A14

Wmk. 211

1931-48 **Engr.** ***Perf. 13½***

39 A8 4p black .45 .25
 a. Laid paper ('47) 3.75 *8.25*
39B A8 6p car lake ('48) 15.00 12.50
40 A8 8p green .75 .25
 a. 8p yel grn, laid paper ('47) 4.50 *6.75*
 b. Imperf., pair 90.00 *180.00*
41 A9 1a dark brown .75 .25
42 A10 2a dark violet 4.50 .25
 a. Imperf., pair 195.00 *400.00*
43 A11 4a ultramarine 2.40 1.00
 a. Imperf., pair 210.00 *500.00*
44 A12 8a deep orange 10.50 6.00
45 A13 12a scarlet 11.00 *18.00*
46 A14 1r yellow 7.50 7.00
 Nos. 39-46 (9) 52.85 45.50

On No. 39B, "POSTAGE" has been moved to ribbon at bottom of design.
Nos. 39a and 40a are printed from worn plates. The background of the design is unshaded.
See No. 59. For overprints see Nos. O46-O53, O56.

Unani General Hospital A15

Osmania General Hospital A16

Osmania University A17

Osmania Jubilee Hall — A18

Perf. 13½x14

1937, Feb. 13 Litho. Unwmk.

47	A15	4p violet & black	.75	*3.25*
48	A16	8p brown & black	1.25	*3.25*
49	A17	1a dull orange & gray	1.75	*2.10*
50	A18	2a dull green & gray	2.25	*6.75*
		Nos. 47-50 (4)	6.00	*15.35*

The Nizam's Silver Jubilee.

Catalogue values for unused stamps in this section, from this point to the end of the section, are for Never Hinged items.

Returning Soldier — A19

1946 Typo. *Perf. 13½*

51	A19	1a dark blue	.25	.25

Wmk. 211

52	A19	1a blue	.25	.25

Wmk. Nizam's Seal in Sheet

Laid Paper

53	A19	1a dark blue	1.00	*1.20*
		Nos. 51-53 (3)	1.50	1.70

Victory of the Allied Nations in WW II.

Town Hall, Hyderabad A20

1947, Feb. 17 Litho. Wove Paper

54	A20	1a black	2.00	*2.90*

Inauguration of the Reformed Legislature, Feb. 17th, 1947.

Power House, Hyderabad A21

Designs: 3a, Kaktyai Arch, Warangal Fort. 6a, Golkunda Fort.

Perf. 13½x14

1947-49 Typo. Wmk. 211

55	A21	1a4p dark green	1.50	*3.25*
56	A21	3a blue	2.50	*6.50*
57	A21	6a olive brown	5.50	*27.50*
a.		6a red brown ('49)	25.00	*47.50*
b.		Imperf., pair	190.00	
		Nos. 55-57 (3)	9.50	37.25

Seal Type of 1915

1947 Engr. *Perf. 13½*

58	A6	½a rose lake	3.75	1.10

For overprint see No. O54.

Seal Type of 1931

1949 Litho.

59	A8	2p brown	3.00	3.50

For overprint see No. O55.

OFFICIAL STAMPS

Regular Issues of 1869-71 Overprinted

1873 Unwmk. *Perf. 11½, 12½*

Red Overprint

O1	A1	½a brown	195.00	125.00
O2	A2	1a olive green	35.00	35.00
O3	A1	2a green	72.50	57.50
O4	A3	½a red brown	27.50	9.00
O5	A3	1a dark brown	195.00	125.00
O6	A3	2a green	72.50	57.50
O7	A3	3a yel brown	250.00	250.00
O8	A3	4a slate	120.00	72.50
O9	A3	8a bister	125.00	*225.00*
O10	A3	12a blue	195.00	*240.00*

Black Overprint

O11	A1	½a brown		52.50
O12	A2	1a olive green	4.50	3.75
O13	A1	2a green	7.50	*9.00*
O14	A3	½a red brown	16.00	5.25
O15	A3	1a dark brown	—	52.50
O16	A3	2a green	7.50	*9.00*
O17	A3	3a yel brown	62.50	52.50
O18	A3	4a slate	32.50	30.00
O19	A3	8a bister	75.00	62.50
O20	A3	12a blue	90.00	*120.00*

The above official stamps became obsolete in August, 1878. Since that date the "Official" overprint has been applied to the reprints and probably to original stamps. Two new varieties of the overprint have also appeared, both on the reprints and on the current stamps. These are overprinted in various colors, positions and combinations.

Same Ovpt. On Regular Issues of 1905-11

1908 Wmk. 42

O21	A5	½a green	30.00	.25
O22	A5	1a carmine	97.50	.25
O23	A5	2a lilac	97.50	.25
		Nos. O21-O23 (3)	225.00	.75

Perf. 11, 11½, 12½, 13½ and Compound

1909-11

O24	A5	½a red	210.00	.25
O25	A3	1a black	140.00	.75
O26	A3	2a olive green	150.00	1.50
O27	A5	3a brown orange	11.00	5.00
O28	A5	4a olive green ('11)	45.00	1.90
O29	A5	8a violet ('11)	19.00	5.25
O30	A5	12a blue green ('11)	15.00	5.00
		Nos. O24-O30 (7)	590.00	19.65

Regular Issue of 1908-11 Overprinted

1911-12

O31	A5	¼a gray	6.75	1.10
O32	A5	½a green	5.25	.25
O33	A5	1a carmine	3.00	.25
O34	A5	2a lilac	2.50	1.90
O35	A5	3a brown orange	27.50	1.10
O36	A5	4a olive green	7.00	.25
O37	A5	8a violet	11.00	.30
O38	A5	12a blue green	36.00	3.75
		Nos. O31-O38 (8)	99.00	8.90

Same Overprint on Regular Issue of 1912

1912

O39	A5	¼a brown violet	5.50	.25
a.		¼a gray violet	5.50	.25
O40	A5	½a deep green	5.25	.25

Same Ovpt. On Regular Issue of 1915-16

1917

O41	A6	½a green	5.25	.25
O42	A6	1a carmine rose	7.00	.25
O43	A6	1a red	4.00	.25
		Nos. O41-O43 (3)	16.25	.75

Same Overprint on Nos. 37 and 38

1930

O44	A5	4p on ¼a brown violet	3.25	.25
O45	A6	8p on ½a green	2.25	.25

Same Overprint on Regular Issue of 1931

1934-47 Wmk. 211 *Perf. 13½*

O46	A8	4p black	4.00	.25
a.		Laid paper ('47)		7.50
b.		Imperf., pair	120.00	
O47	A8	8p green	1.90	.25
a.		8p yel grn, laid paper ('47)	10.00	7.50
b.		Inverted overprint		240.00
O48	A9	1a dark brown	3.00	.25
O49	A10	2a dark violet	11.00	.25
O50	A11	4a ultramarine	6.00	.35
O51	A12	8a deep orange	21.00	.90
O52	A13	12a scarlet	19.00	2.50
O53	A14	1r yellow	30.00	3.75
		Nos. O46-O53 (8)	95.90	8.50

Catalogue values for unused stamps in this section, from this point to the end of the section, are for Never Hinged items.

Same Overprint on Nos. 58-59, 39B

1947-50 *Perf. 13½*

O54	A6	½a rose lake	9.00	*10.50*
O55	A8	2p brown ('49)	9.00	*15.00*
O56	A8	6p car lake ('50)	11.00	*35.00*
		Nos. O54-O56 (3)	29.00	*60.50*

IDAR

'ē-dər

LOCATION — A Feudatory State in the Western India States Agency.
AREA — 1,669 sq. mi.
POP. — 262,660
CAPITAL — Himmatnagar

Stamps of Idar are in booklet panes of four. All stamps have one or two straight edges.

Maharaja Shri Himatsinhji — A1

1939 Unwmk. Typo. *Perf. 11*

1	A1	½a light green	21.00	*37.50*

1941 Same Redrawn

2	A1	½a green	17.50	*40.00*

The panels containing denomination and name of state are shaded.

Maharaja Shri Himatsinhji — A2

1944 Unwmk. *Perf. 12*

3	A2	½a green	4.00	*110.00*
4	A2	1a purple	4.00	*100.00*
a.		Imperf., pair	250.00	
5	A2	2a blue	4.50	*150.00*
6	A2	4a red	4.75	*160.00*
		Nos. 3-6 (4)	17.25	

INDORE

in-'dō̦ə̦r

(Holkar)

LOCATION — A Feudatory State in the Indore Agency in Central India.
AREA — 9,902 sq. mi.
POP. — 1,513,966
CAPITAL — Indore

Maharaja Tukoji Rao II — A1

A2

1886 Unwmk. Litho. *Perf. 15*

1	A1	½a lilac	5.50	3.25

1889 Handstamped *Imperf.*

3	A2	¼a black, *rose*	5.25	*5.50*

No. 3 exists in two types.

The originals of this stamp are printed in water color. The reprints are in oil color and on paper of a deeper shade of rose.

Maharaja Shivaji Rao — A3

1889-92 Engr. *Perf. 15*

4	A3	¼a orange	2.25	1.20
5	A3	½a brown violet	3.75	.25
6	A3	1a green	4.50	1.90
7	A3	2a vermilion	10.50	3.00
		Nos. 4-7 (4)	21.00	6.35

For overprint see No. 14.

Maharaja Tukoji Rao III

A4 A5

1904-08 *Perf. 13½, 14*

8	A4	¼a orange	.90	.25
9	A5	½a lake ('08)	13.50	.25
a.		Imperf., pair	35.00	
10	A5	1a green ('07)	3.75	.25
a.		Imperf., pair	175.00	
11	A5	2a brown ('05)	22.50	1.50
a.		Imperf., pair	120.00	
12	A5	3a violet	35.00	10.50
13	A5	4a ultramarine	7.50	2.10
		Nos. 8-13 (6)	83.15	14.85

For overprints see Nos. O1-O7.

No. 5 Surcharged

1905 *Perf. 15*

14	A3	¼a on ½a brown violet	9.00	*30.00*

Maharaja Yeshwant Rao II

A6 A7

1928-38 Engr. *Perf. 13½*

15	A6	¼a orange	.90	.30
16	A6	½a claret	3.25	.25
17	A6	1a green	4.00	.25
18	A6	1¼a green ('33)	6.00	1.25
19	A6	2a dark brown	19.00	3.25

20 A6 2a Prus blue ('36) 19.00 3.25
a. Imperf., pair 37.50 275.00
21 A6 3a dull violet 3.00 14.00
22 A6 3½a dull violet ('34) 10.50 15.00
a. Imperf., pair 100.00 650.00
23 A6 4a ultramarine 10.50 7.50
24 A6 4a bister ('38) 52.50 2.50
a. Imperf., pair 45.00 500.00
25 A6 8a gray 9.50 6.50
26 A6 8a red orange ('38) 40.00 35.00
27 A6 12a rose red ('34) 7.50 15.00

Perf. 14

28 A7 1r lt blue & black 12.50 22.50
29 A7 2r car lake & black 82.50 90.00
30 A7 5r org brn & black 140.00 140.00
Nos. 15-30 (16) 420.65 356.55

Imperforates of types A6 and A7 were used with official sanction at Indore City during a stamp shortage in 1938. They were from sheets placed by the printers (Perkins, Bacon) on top of packets of 100 perforated sheets as identification.

Stamps of 1929-33 Surcharged in Black

1940 *Perf. 13, 14*

31 A7 ¼a on 5r org brn & blk 19.00 2.50
a. Dbl. surch., black over green 700.00
32 A7 ½a on 2r car lake & blk 32.50 5.00
33 A6 1a on 1¼a green 32.50 1.20
a. Inverted surcharge 110.00
Nos. 31-33 (3) 84.00 8.70

Stamps with green surcharge only are proofs.

A8

1941-47 **Typo.** *Perf. 11*

34 A8 ¼a orange 2.50 .25
35 A8 ½a rose lilac 4.75 .25
36 A8 1a dk olive green 12.50 .25
37 A8 1¼a yellow green 20.00 20.00
a. Imperf., pair 275.00
38 A8 2a turquoise blue 14.00 1.75
39 A8 4a bister ('47) 20.00 20.00

Size: 23x28¼mm

40 A8 2r car lake & blk ('47) 16.00 250.00
41 A8 5r brn org & blk 15.00 325.00
Nos. 34-41 (8) 104.75 617.50

OFFICIAL STAMPS

Stamps and Type of 1904-08 Overprinted

1904-06 *Perf. 13½, 14*

O1 A5 ½a lake 1.10 1.90
a. Inverted overprint 35.00 62.50
b. Double overprint 35.00
c. Imperf., pair 110.00
O2 A5 1a green .25 .25
O3 A5 2a brown ('05) .45 .45
O4 A5 3a violet ('06) 2.50 5.50
a. Imperf., pair 425.00
O5 A5 4a ultra ('05) 7.50 2.25
Nos. O1-O5 (5) 11.80 10.35

No. O1-O5 has an "R" that has a curved foot that is wholly underneath the curve of the "R"

No. 8 Overprinted in Black

1907
O6 A4 ¼a orange 1.10 1.90

No. 9 Overprinted

O7 A5 ½a lake .25 1.75

No. O7 "SERVICE" in slightly thinner letters and the letter "R" has a straight foot which projects at a distinct angle beyond the curve of the "R" than No. O1.

JAIPUR

ˈjī-ˌpu̇ə̇r

LOCATION — A Feudatory State in the Jaipur Residency of India.
AREA — 15,610 sq. mi.
POP. — 3,040,876
CAPITAL — Jaipur

Catalogue values for unused stamps in this State are for Never Hinged items, beginning with Scott 49 in the regular postage section, and Scott O30 in the official section.

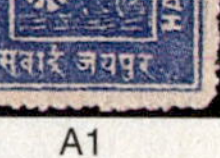
A1

A1a

Chariot of Surya, Sun God

Pin-perf. 14x14½

1904 **Typo.** **Unwmk.**

1 A1 ½a ultramarine 290.00 275.00
a. ½a pale blue 210.00 275.00
b. ½a gray blue 3,250. 300.00
c. As "b," imperf. 525.00 900.00
1D A1a ½a blue 5.00 10.00
e. ½a ultramarine 5.50 10.00
f. Imperf. 5.50 10.00
2 A1 1a dull red 8.25 21.00
a. 1a chestnut 8.25 21.00
3 A1 2a pale green 8.25 21.00
a. 2a emerald 9.00
Nos. 1-3 (4) 311.50 327.00

No. 1 has 36 varieties (on 2 plates), differing in minor details. Nos. 1b and 1c are from plate II. No. 1D has 24 varieties (one plate).

Chariot of Surya — A2

Perf. 12½x12 and 13½

1904-06 **Engr.**

4 A2 ¼a olive green ('06) 1.25 1.60
5 A2 ½a deep blue 2.75 .75
6 A2 1a carmine 3.75 6.75
7 A2 2a dark green 5.25 2.25
8 A2 4a red brown 11.00 3.25
9 A2 8a violet 6.00 4.00
10 A2 1r yellow 35.00 24.00
Nos. 4-10 (7) 65.00 42.60

For overprints see Nos. 21-22.

A3

Without Gum

1911 **Typo.** *Imperf.*

11 A3 ¼a yellow green 3.75 5.00
a. ¼a olive green 3.75 5.00
b. "¼" inverted 9.00
12 A3 ¼a olive yellow .45 1.50
b. ¼a blue (error) —
13 A3 ½a ultramarine .45 1.50
a. ½a dull blue 4.00 4.00
b. "½" for "½" 7.00
14 A3 1a carmine .75 1.50
15 A3 2a deep green 3.00 9.50
a. 2a gray green 4.00 8.25
Nos. 11-15 (5) 8.40 19.00

There are six types for each value and several settings of the ¼a and ½a in the 1911 issue.

A4

Wmk. "Dorling & Co., London" in Sheet

1913-18 *Perf. 11*

16 A4 ¼a olive bister 1.00 2.25
a. Vert. pair, imperf. between 300.00 300.00
b. Horiz. pair, imperf. between — 240.00
17 A4 ½a ultramarine 2.25 1.90
18 A4 1a carmine ('18) 8.25 8.25
a. 1a scarlet 6.00 5.50
b. Vert. pair, imperf. btwn. 1,250. 1,250.
c. Vert. pair, imperf. horiz. 1,250.
19 A4 2a green ('18) 6.00 7.50
20 A4 4a red brown 10.50 15.00
Nos. 16-20 (5) 28.00 34.90

For overprints see Nos. O1-O6, O9-O10.

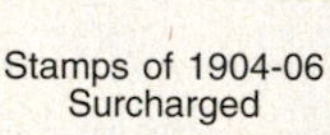

Stamps of 1904-06 Surcharged

1926 **Unwmk.** **Engr.** *Perf. 13½*

21 A2 3a on 8a violet 3.00 5.25
a. Inverted surcharge 275.00 210.00
22 A2 3a on 1r yellow 4.00 9.50
a. Inverted surcharge 825.00 275.00

Wmk. "Overland Bank" in Sheet

1928 **Typo.** *Perf. 12*

17a A4 ½a ultramarine 4.75 6.00
18d A4 1a rose red 40.00 25.00
18e A4 1a scarlet 62.50 17.50
19a A4 2a green 140.00 45.00
20a A4 4a pale brown
23 A4 1r red orange 600.00 825.00

Durbar Commemorative Issue

Chariot of Surya, Sun God — A5

Maharaja Man Singh II — A6

Elephant with Standard — A7

Sowar in Armor — A8

Blue Peafowl — A9

Royal Bullock Carriage — A10

Royal Elephant Carriage — A11

Albert Museum — A12

Sireh-Deorhi Gate — A13

Chandra Palace — A14

Amber Palace — A15

Rajas Jai Singh II and Man Singh II — A16

Perf. 13½x14, 14, 14x13½

1931, Mar. 14 Typo. Unwmk.

24	A5	¼a red brn & blk	4.50	4.00
25	A6	½a dull vio & blk	.75	.30
26	A7	1a blue & black	13.50	*14.00*
27	A8	2a ocher & black	13.50	*14.00*
28	A9	2½a rose & black	47.50	*90.00*
29	A10	3a dk green & blk	27.50	*67.50*
30	A11	4a dull grn & blk	27.50	*82.50*
31	A12	6a dk blue & blk	9.00	*82.50*
32	A13	8a brown & black	30.00	*140.00*
33	A14	1r olive & black	60.00	*500.00*
34	A15	2r lt green & blk	62.50	*550.00*
35	A16	5r violet & black	82.50	*600.00*
		Nos. 24-35 (12)	378.75	*2,145.*

Investiture of the Maharaja Man Singh II with full ruling powers.

Eighteen sets of this issue were overprinted in red "INVESTITURE—MARCH 14, 1931" for presentation to distinguished personages.

For surcharges see Nos. 47, 48, 58. For overprints see Nos. O12-O16, O22-O32, Rajasthan 16.

Man Singh II Type of 1931 and

Raja Man Singh II — A18

1932-46 ***Perf. 14***

36	A6	¼a red brn & blk	.75	.75
36A	A6	¾a brn org & blk ('43)	12.00	6.25
37	A18	1a blue & black	5.00	2.50
37A	A6	1a blue & black	14.00	6.75
38	A18	2a ocher & black	6.75	4.00
38A	A6	2a ocher & blk ('45)	19.00	7.50
39	A6	2½a dk car & blk	6.75	5.00
40	A6	3a green & black	6.00	1.00
41	A18	4a gray grn & blk	6.75	*17.50*
41A	A6	4a gray grn & blk ('45)	72.50	2.40
42	A6	6a blue & black	9.00	*45.00*
43	A18	8a choc & black	9.00	*22.50*
43A	A6	8a choc & blk ('45)	42.50	*190.00*
44	A18	1r bis & gray blk	40.00	*175.00*
44A	A6	1r bis & gray blk ('46)	30.00	*240.00*
45	A18	2r yel grn & blk	140.00	*700.00*
		Nos. 36-45 (16)	420.00	*1,426.*

For overprints see Nos. O17-O30, Rajasthan Nos. 15, 17-25.

Stamps of 1931-32 Surcharged in Red or Black

1936 ***Perf. 14x13½, 13½x14***

46	A18	1r on 2r yel grn & blk (R)	15.00	*160.00*
47	A16	1r on 5r violet & blk	15.00	*125.00*

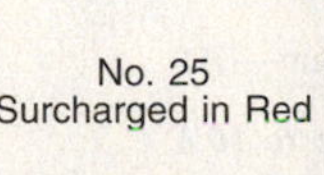

No. 25 Surcharged in Red

1938 ***Perf. 14x13½***

48	A6	¼a on ½a dl vio & blk	17.50	*25.00*

Catalogue values for unused stamps in this section, from this point to the end of the section, are for Never Hinged items.

Amber Palace A19

Designs: ¼a, Palace gate. ¾a, Map of Jaipur. 1a, Observatory. 2a, Palace of the Winds. 3a, Arms of the Raja. 4a, Gate of Amber Fort. 8a, Chariot of the Sun. 1r, Raja Man Singh II.

1947-48 Unwmk. Engr. ***Perf. 14***

49	A19	¼a dk grn & red brn ('48)	2.25	*7.50*
50	A19	½a blue vio & dp grn	.75	*6.75*
51	A19	¾a dk car & blk ('48)	2.25	*9.00*
52	A19	1a dp ultra & choc	1.50	*7.00*
53	A19	2a car & blue vio	1.50	*7.50*
54	A19	3a dk gray & grn ('48)	2.50	*9.50*
55	A19	4a choc & dp ultra	1.50	*7.50*
56	A19	8a dk brown & red	1.50	*9.00*
57	A19	1r dk red vio & bl grn ('48)	4.00	*67.50*
		Nos. 49-57 (9)	17.75	*131.25*

25th anniv. of the enthronement of Raja Man Singh II.

No. 25 Surcharged in Carmine with New Value and Bars

1947

58	A6	3p on ½a	25.00	40.00
a.		"3 PIE"	75.00	*160.00*
b.		Inverted surcharge	72.50	62.50
c.		Double surch., one inverted	110.00	82.50
d.		As "a," inverted surcharge	375.00	325.00

For overprint see No. O31.

OFFICIAL STAMPS

Regular Issue of 1913-22 Overprinted in Black or Red

1929 Unwmk. ***Perf. 12½x12, 11***

O1	A4	¼a olive green	3.75	*4.00*
O2	A4	½a ultramarine	1.90	.30
a.		Inverted overprint		675.00
O3	A4	½a ultra (R)	4.00	.45
O4	A4	1a red	2.25	.45
O5	A4	2a green	2.25	.60
O6	A4	4a red brown	3.00	2.50
O7	A4	8a purple (R)	25.00	*82.50*
O8	A4	1r red orange	57.50	*550.00*
		Nos. O1-O8 (8)	99.65	*640.80*

The 8a and 1r not issued without overprint.
For overprint see No. O11.

Regular Issue of 1913-22 Overprinted in Black or Red — b

1931 ***Perf. 11, 12½x12***

O9	A4	½a ultra	575.00	.25
O10	A4	½a ultra (R)	300.00	.25
O10A	A4	8a purple	800.00	300.00
O10B	A4	1r red orange	975.00	400.00
		Nos. O9-O10B (4)	2,650.	700.50

No. O5 Surcharged

1932

O11	A4	½a on 2a green	225.00	3.00

Regular Issue of 1931 Overprinted in Red

1931-37 ***Perf. 13½x14, 14***

O12	A6	¼a red brn & blk ('36)	.60	.25
O13	A6	½a dull vio & blk	.45	.25
O14	A7	1a blue & black	400.00	4.50
O15	A8	2a ocher & blk ('36)	6.75	*8.25*
O16	A11	4a dl grn & blk ('37)	72.50	60.00

For overprint see No. O32.

Same on Regular Issue of 1932 in Red

1932-37 ***Perf. 14***

O17	A18	1a blue & black	6.75	.30
O18	A18	2a ocher & black	8.25	.30
O19	A18	4a gray grn & blk ('37)	*550.00*	*16.00*
O20	A18	8a choc & black	17.50	1.60
O21	A18	1r bister & gray blk	45.00	40.00
		Nos. O17-O21 (5)	*627.50*	*58.20*

No. 36 Overprinted Type "b" in Black

1939 ***Perf. 14***

O22	A6	¼a red brown & blk	140.00	110.00

Nos. 36A, 38A, 39, 41A, 43A, 44A and Type of 1931 Overprinted in Carmine

1941-46 Unwmk. ***Perf. 13½, 14***

O23	A6	¾a brn org & blk ('43)	2.25	.75
O24	A6	1a blue & blk ('41)	6.75	.45
O25	A6	2a ocher & black	6.00	5.00
O26	A6	2½a dk car & blk ('46)	16.00	*160.00*
O27	A6	4a gray grn & blk ('46)	9.00	*11.00*
O28	A6	8a choc & black	6.00	12.50
O29	A6	1r bis & gray blk	*60.00*	
		Nos. O23-O28 (6)	46.00	*189.70*

Catalogue values for unused stamps in this section, from this point to the end of the section, are for Never Hinged items.

No. O24 Surcharged with New Value and Bars in Carmine

1947 ***Perf. 13½***

O30	A6	9p on 1a blue & blk	5.50	5.50

No. 58 Overprinted in Red "SERVICE"

Perf. 14

O31	A6	3p on ½a	9.00	*21.00*
a.		Inverted surcharge	—	2,250.
b.		Double surch., one inverted	72.50	72.50
c.		"3 PIE"	400.00	*450.00*

No. O13 Surcharged "Three-quarter Anna" in Devanagari, similar to surcharge on No. 48, and Bars in Carmine

1949 ***Perf. 14x13½***

O32	A6	¾a on ½a dl vio & blk	27.50	*30.00*

For later issues see Rajasthan.

JAMMU AND KASHMIR

ˈjəm-ˌü and ˈkash-ˌmiˌəˌr

LOCATION — A Feudatory State in the Kashmir Residency in the extreme north of India.
AREA — 82,258 sq. mi.
POP. — 4,021,616 (1941)
CAPITAL — Srinagar

All stamps of Jammu and Kashmir were issued without gum.

½ Anna — A1

1 Anna — A2

4 Annas (¼ Rupee) — A3

Native Grayish Laid Paper

Handstamped

1866-67 Unwmk. ***Imperf.***

Printed in Water Colors

1	A1	½a gray black	375.00	150.00
		Cut to shape	75.00	30.00
2	A2	1a dull blue	900.00	180.00
a.		1a ultramarine	900.00	180.00
b.		1a royal blue	—	750.00
		Cut to shape	—	150.00
3	A2	1a gray black	2,400.	2,100.
		Cut to shape	475.00	425.00
4	A3	4a dull blue	*4,500.*	*4,500.*
a.		4a ultramarine	*4,500.*	*4,500.*
b.		4a indigo	*4,500.*	*4,500.*
		Cut to shape	900.00	900.00
5	A3	4a gray black	3,000.	
		Cut to shape	1,600.	—
		Nos. 1-5 (5)	11,175.	6,930.

It has now been proved by the leading authorities on Indian stamps that all stamps of ½ anna and 1 anna printed from the so-called Die A are forgeries and that no such die was ever in use.

See Nos. 24-59.

JAMMU

A part of the Feudatory State of Jammu & Kashmir, both being ruled by the same sovereign.

½ Anna — A4

1 Anna — A5

Printed in blocks of four, three types of the ½a and one of the 1a.

Native Grayish Laid Paper

Printed in Water Colors

1867-77 Unwmk. ***Imperf.***

6	A4	½a black	1,800.	625.00
7	A4	½a indigo	625.00	490.00
a.		½a deep ultramarine	490.00	290.00
b.		½a deep violet blue	325.00	160.00
8	A4	½a red	12.50	6.75
a.		½a orange red	375.00	120.00
b.		½a orange	195.00	*225.00*
9	A5	1a black	3,750.	2,600.
10	A5	1a indigo	1,350	625.00
a.		1a deep ultramarine	1,200.	625.00
b.		1a deep violet blue	1,200.	625.00
11	A5	1a red	30.00	19.00
a.		1a orange red	1,250.	525.00
b.		1a orange	4,750.	2,750.

1876

12	A4	½a emerald	3,750.	1,900.
13	A4	½a bright blue	2,400.	550.00
14	A5	1a emerald	5,250.	3,000.
15	A5	1a bright blue	700.00	*750.00*

Native Grayish Laid Paper

1877 Printed in Oil Colors

16	A4	½a red	18.00	13.50
a.		½a brown red	—	67.50
17	A4	½a black		1,800.
18	A5	1a red	57.50	40.00
a.		1a brown red	—	225.00
19	A5	1a black	*3,750.*	*2,750.*

The formerly listed ½a dark blue, ½a dark green, 1a dark blue and 1a dark green are believed to be reprints.

European White Laid Paper

20	A4	½a red	—	*1,600.*
a.		Thin laid bâtonné paper		*2,750.*
21	A5	1a red	—	
a.		Thin laid bâtonné paper	*6,750.*	

European White Wove Paper

22	A4	½a red		*675.00*
23	A5	1a red		

RE-ISSUES

For Jammu Only

Native Grayish Laid Paper

Printed in Water Colors

1869-76 ***Imperf.***

24	A1 ½a deep black	*500.00*	
25	A1 ½a bright blue	550.00	*675.00*
26	A1 ½a orange red	1,000.	1,100.
a.	½a orange to salmon	400.00	
b.	½a red	150.00	*525.00*
27	A1 ½a emerald	175.00	*450.00*
28	A1 ½a yellow	1,100.	*1,400.*
29	A2 1a deep black	500.00	
30	A2 1a bright blue	195.00	*550.00*
31	A2 1a orange red	1,000.	*1,100.*
b.	1a red	300.00	*500.00*
32	A2 1a emerald	195.00	450.00
33	A2 1a yellow	1,400.	
34	A3 4a deep black	450.00	—
35	A3 4a bright blue	325.00	
a.	4a indigo	—	—
36	A3 4a orange red	325.00	*425.00*
a.	4a orange		—
b.	4a red	325.00	*425.00*
37	A3 4a emerald	450.00	*1,000.*
38	A3 4a yellow	900.00	

Native Grayish Laid Paper

1877 **Printed in Oil Colors**

39	A1 ½a red	52.50	*90.00*
40	A1 ½a black	57.50	*97.50*
41	A1 ½a slate blue	240.00	*400.00*
42	A1 ½a sage green	210.00	
43	A2 1a red	72.50	*290.00*
45	A2 1a slate blue	57.50	*450.00*
46	A2 1a sage green	225.00	
47	A3 4a red	475.00	*825.00*
50	A3 4a sage green	225.00	

European White Laid Paper

51	A1 ½a red		1,800.
52	A1 ½a black	47.50	*97.50*
53	A1 ½a slate blue	82.50	*450.00*
54	A1 ½a yellow	*240.00*	
56	A2 1a slate blue	90.00	*600.00*
57	A3 4a red	650.00	*750.00*
58	A3 4a sage green	*2,250.*	

European Brownish Wove Paper

59	A1 ½a red		*1,400.*

It is probable that the issues of 1876, 1877 and the re-issues of the circular stamps were made to supply the demands of philatelists more than for postal needs. They were, however, available for postage.

There exist also reprints, printed in a variety of colors, on native and European thin wove paper. Collectors are warned against official imitations, which are very numerous. They are printed on several kinds of paper and in a great variety of colors.

A5a

Handstamped in Oil Color

1877, Nov.

60	A5a (½a) red		*1,900.*

This provisional, made with a canceling device, was used only in Nov. 1877, at Jammu city.

KASHMIR

A part of the Feudatory State of Jammu & Kashmir, both being ruled by the same sovereign.

½ Anna — A6

Printed in Water Colors

Native Grayish Laid Paper

Printed from a Single Die

1866 **Unwmk.** ***Imperf.***

62	A6 ½a black	*5,250.*	675.00

¼ Anna — A7

½ Anna — A8

1 Anna A9

2 Annas A10

4 Annas — A11

8 Annas — A12

The ¼a, 1a and 2a are printed in strips of five varieties, the ½a in sheets of twenty varieties and the 4a and 8a from single dies.

1866-70

63	A7 ¼a black	6.75	*7.00*
64	A8 ½a black	*2,250.*	*300.00*
65	A8 ½a ultra	7.50	2.50
a.	½a blue	13.50	6.75
66	A9 1a black	4,000.	750.00
67	A9 1a red orange	22.50	17.50
68	A9 1a Venetian red	27.50	19.00
69	A9 1a orange brown	22.50	17.50
70	A9 1a ultra	*6,500.*	*2,500.*
71	A10 2a olive yellow	30.00	*32.50*
72	A11 4a emerald	75.00	72.50
73	A12 8a red	75.00	72.50

All the stamps printed in oil colors are reprints.

As in Jammu, official imitations are numerous and are found in many colors and on various papers.

JAMMU & KASHMIR

¼ Anna — A13

½ Anna — A14

1 Anna — A15

Laid Paper

Printed in Oil Colors

1878 ***Rough Perf. 10-14***

74	A13 ¼a red	—	—
75	A14 ½a red	21.00	*25.00*
a.	Wove paper		*500.00*
76	A14 ½a slate blue	110.00	110.00
77	A15 1a red	1,900.	
78	A15 1a bright violet	—	—

2 Annas — A16

4 Annas — A17

1878-80 ***Imperf.***

79	A13 ¼a red	35.00	30.00
80	A14 ½a red	15.00	*16.00*
81	A14 ½a slate	27.50	24.00
82	A15 1a red	14.00	17.50
83	A15 1a violet	40.00	42.50
a.	1a dull purple	67.50	62.50
84	A16 2a red	140.00	140.00
85	A16 2a bright violet	60.00	57.50
86	A16 2a dull ultra	*175.00*	175.00
87	A17 4a red	340.00	290.00

Thick Wove Paper

88	A14 ½a red	47.50	*90.00*
89	A15 1a red	75.00	37.50
90	A16 2a red	32.50	40.00

8 Annas — A18

1879-80 **Thin Toned Wove Paper**

91	A13 ¼a red	5.50	*6.75*
92	A14 ½a red	1.50	1.50
93	A15 1a red	3.75	*5.25*
94	A16 2a red	5.00	*7.00*
95	A17 4a red	16.00	16.00
96	A18 8a red	17.50	20.00
	Nos. 91-96 (6)	49.25	56.50

Thin Laid Bâtonné Paper

1880 **Printed in Water Color**

97	A13 ¼a ultramarine	1,350.	900.00

Thin Toned Wove Paper

1881 **Printed in Oil Colors**

98	A13 ¼a orange	17.50	*24.00*
99	A14 ½a orange	35.00	25.00
100	A15 1a orange	37.50	21.00
101	A16 2a orange	27.50	21.00
102	A17 4a orange	67.50	*82.50*
103	A18 8a orange	110.00	*120.00*
	Nos. 98-103 (6)	295.00	293.50

⅛ Anna — A19

Thin White or Yellowish Wove Paper

1883-94

104	A19 ⅛a yellow brown	2.25	*3.00*
a.	⅛a yellow	2.25	*3.00*
105	A13 ¼a brown	1.90	1.50
a.	Double impression	1,800.	
106	A14 ½a red	1.90	1.25
a.	½a rose	2.40	1.50
106B	A19 ⅛a bright blue	82.50	
c.	⅛a dull blue	12.00	
107	A15 1a bronze green	1.50	1.50
108	A15 1a yel green	1.50	1.50
109	A15 1a blue green	3.00	
110	A15 1a bister	—	
111	A17 4a green	6.50	6.00
112	A17 4a olive green	6.00	*7.00*
113	A18 8a deep blue	19.00	*22.50*
114	A18 8a dark ultra	18.00	*21.00*
115	A18 8a gray violet	15.00	*32.50*

Printed in Water Color

116	A18 8a gray blue	225.00	225.00

Printed in Oil Colors

Yellow Pelure Paper

117	A16 2a red	4.00	1.90

Yellow Green Pelure Paper

118	A16 2a red	5.50	*6.00*

Deep Green Pelure Paper

119	A16 2a red	27.50	27.50

Coarse Green Pelure Paper

120	A16 2a red	4.00	1.90
	Nos. 104-120 (18)	425.05	360.05

Thin Creamy Laid Paper

1886-94

121	A19 ⅛a yellow	90.00	*100.00*
122	A13 ¼a brown	13.50	*10.00*
123	A14 ½a vermilion	15.00	9.50
124	A14 ½a rose red		110.00
125	A15 1a green	150.00	150.00
126	A17 4a green	—	—

Printed in Water Color

127	A18 8a gray blue	160.00	150.00
	Nos. 121-127 (7)	428.50	529.50

Impressions of types A13 to A19 in colors other than the issued stamps are proofs. Forgeries to defraud the post exist, and some are common.

A fugitive pigment in No. 104 often leaves the stamp a dull yellowish brown.

1/4 Anna

Stamps of the above type, printed in red or black, were never placed in use.

OFFICIAL STAMPS

Same Types as Regular Issues

White Laid Paper

1878 **Unwmk.** ***Rough Perf. 10-14***

O1	A14 ½a black		*3,000.*

Imperf

O3	A14 ½a black	150.00	140.00
O4	A15 1a black	100.00	100.00
O5	A16 2a black	82.50	*90.00*
	Nos. O3-O5 (3)	332.50	330.00

Thin White or Yellowish Wove Paper

1880

O6	A13 ¼a black	2.50	*3.00*
O7	A14 ½a black	.25	*1.10*
O8	A15 1a black	3.00	*1.50*
O9	A16 2a black	.45	*.65*
O10	A17 4a black	1.90	*2.50*
O11	A18 8a black	3.75	1.60
	Nos. O6-O11 (6)	11.85	10.35

Thin Creamy Laid Paper

1890-91

O12	A13 ¼a black	12.50	*13.50*
O13	A14 ½a black	7.00	*7.00*
O14	A15 1a black	4.00	*5.25*
O15	A16 2a black	22.50	
O16	A17 4a black	82.50	*97.50*
O17	A18 8a black	42.50	*75.00*
	Nos. O12-O17 (6)	171.00	

Obsolete October 31, 1894.

JASDAN

jas-dən

LOCATION — A Feudatory State in the Kathiawar Agency in Western India.

AREA — 296 sq. mi.

POP. — 34,056 (1931)

CAPITAL — Jasdan

In 1948 Jasdan was incorporated in the United State of Saurashtra (see Soruth).

Catalogue values for all unused stamps in this state are for Never Hinged items.

Sun — A1

Perf. 8½ to 10½

1942 **Unwmk.** **Typo.**

1	A1 1a green	30.00	240.00

Issued in booklet panes of 4 and 8.

The 1a carmine is a revenue stamp.

Jasdan's stamp became obsolete Feb. 15, 1948.

JHALAWAR

'jäl-ə-,wär

LOCATION — A Feudatory State in the Rajputana Agency of India.
AREA — 813 sq. mi.
POP. — 107,890
CAPITAL — Jhalrapatan

A1

Apsaras, Hindu Nymph — A2

Laid Paper

1887-90 Unwmk. *Imperf.*
Without Gum

1	A1	1p yellow green	7.00	22.50
2	A2	¼a green	1.90	3.75

Obsolete October 31, 1900.

JIND

'jind

(Jhind)

LOCATION — A State of India in the north Punjab.
AREA — 1,299 sq. mi.
POP. — 361,812 (1941)
CAPITAL — Sangrur

A1

A2

A3

A4

A5

1874 Unwmk. Litho. *Imperf.*
Without Gum
Thin White Wove Paper

1	A1	½a blue	10.00	6.25
2	A2	1a lilac	10.00	9.50
3	A3	2a yellow	1.50	6.75
4	A4	4a green	37.50	9.00
5	A5	8a dark violet	340.00	140.00
		Nos. 1-5 (5)	399.00	171.50

Thick Blue Laid Paper

1875 Without Gum

6	A1	½a blue	1.50	7.00
7	A2	1a red violet	4.00	16.00
8	A3	2a brown orange	6.50	22.50
9	A4	4a green	5.50	22.50
10	A5	8a purple	13.50	32.50
		Nos. 6-10 (5)	31.00	100.50

Nos. 3 and 6 were perforated 12 in 1885 for use as fiscal stamps.

A6

A7

A8

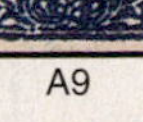

A9

A10

A11

1882-84 Without Gum *Imperf.*
Thin Yellowish Wove Paper

12	A6	¼a buff	.45	2.25
a.		Double impression	75.00	
13	A7	½a yellow	3.75	2.50
14	A8	1a brown	2.50	5.00
15	A9	2a blue	3.00	13.50
16	A10	4a green	2.25	1.50
17	A11	8a red	9.50	6.75
		Nos. 12-17 (6)	21.45	31.50

Perf. 12

18	A6	¼a buff	1.50	4.00
19	A7	½a yellow	240.00	240.00
20	A8	1a brown	3.75	8.25
21	A9	2a blue	5.50	15.00
22	A10	4a green	7.50	16.00
23	A11	8a red	18.00	
a.		Thick white paper	15.00	
		Nos. 18-23 (6)	276.25	283.25

Laid Paper

Imperf

24	A6	¼a buff	1.90	
25	A7	½a yellow	1.90	
26	A8	1a brown	1.90	3.75
27	A9	2a blue	27.50	30.00
28	A11	8a red	3.75	16.00
		Nos. 24-28 (5)	36.95	49.75

Perf. 12

29	A6	¼a buff	12.50	
30	A7	½a yellow	190.00	40.00
31	A8	1a brown	2.25	
32	A11	8a red	3.75	15.00
		Nos. 29-32 (4)	208.50	55.00

As postage stamps these issues became obsolete in July, 1885, but some possibly remained in use as revenue stamps.

For later issues see Jind under Convention States.

KISHANGARH

'kish-ən-,gär

LOCATION — A Feudatory State in the Jaipur Residency of India.
AREA — 858 sq. mi.
POP. — 85,744
CAPITAL — Kishangarh

Kishangarh was incorporated in Rajasthan in 1947-49.

Stamps were issued without gum except Nos. 27-35.

Coat of Arms — A1

1899-1900 Unwmk. Typo. *Imperf.*
Soft Porous Paper

1	A1	1a green	32.50	90.00
2	A1	1a blue ('00)	600.00	

Pin-perf

3	A1	1a green	110.00	

A2

A3

Coat of Arms — A4

Maharaja Sardul Singh — A5

A6

A7

A8

Coat of Arms — A9

Thin Wove Paper

1899-1900 Handstamped *Imperf.*

4	A2	¼a rose pink	1.90	4.00
a.		¼a carmine	12.50	
5	A2	¼a green	825.00	1,200.
6	A3	½a light blue	1.90	2.50
7	A3	½a green	57.50	62.50
8	A3	½a carmine	3,750.	1,900.
9	A3	½a violet	240.00	490.00
10	A4	1a gray violet	1.60	1.50
a.		1a gray	7.50	7.50
11	A4	1a rose	110.00	300.00
11A	A5	2a orange	7.50	6.75
12	A6	4a chocolate	9.00	15.00
a.		Laid paper	125.00	125.00
13	A7	1r dull green	35.00	52.50
13A	A7	1r light brown	30.00	37.50
14	A8	2r brown red	125.00	190.00
a.		Laid paper	100.00	
15	A9	5r violet	120.00	150.00
a.		Laid paper	120.00	

Pin-perf

16	A2	¼a magenta	7.50	10.00
a.		¼a rose	.35	.60
17	A2	¼a green	400.00	700.00
a.		Imperf. vertically, pair	1,900.	
18	A3	½a blue	1.50	.75
a.		½a dark blue	3.75	5.00
19	A3	½a green	27.50	40.00
a.		Imperf. vert., pair	275.00	
20	A4	1a gray violet	1.10	1.50
a.		1a gray	8.25	5.25
b.		1a red lilac	2.25	3.00
d.		As "b," laid paper	62.50	19.00
20E	A4	1a rose	125.00	375.00
21	A5	2a orange	6.00	7.50
21B	A6	4a pale red brn	5.25	9.00
c.		4a chocolate	3.50	9.00
22	A7	1r dull green	16.00	22.50
b.		Laid paper	140.00	
23	A8	2r brown red	52.50	82.50
b.		Laid paper	67.50	
24	A9	5r red violet	52.50	82.50
d.		Laid paper	110.00	

Nos. 4-24 exist tête bêche and sell for a slight premium.

For overprints see Nos. O1-O11, Rajasthan Nos. 26-28, 30-32.

A9a

A9b

1901 Soft Porous Paper Typo.

24A	A9a	½a rose	12.00	9.00
24B	A9b	1a dull violet	72.50	40.00

For overprint see No. O12.

A10

1903 Stout Hard Paper *Imperf.*

25	A10	½a pink	20.00	5.25
a.		Printed on both sides		2,100.

A11

1904 Thin Wove Paper *Pin-perf.*

25B	A11	8a gray	7.50	11.00
c.		tête bêche pair	40.00	

For overprints see Nos. O13, O33, Rajasthan No. 29.

A11a

25D	A11a	1r green	27.50	27.50

For overprint see No. O13A.

Maharaja Sardul Singh — A12

1903 Stout Hard Paper *Imperf.*

26	A12	2a yellow	4.50	9.00

For overprints see Nos. O14, O34.

Maharaja Madan Singh — A13

1904-05 Engr. *Perf. 12½, 13½*

27	A13	¼a carmine	.65	1.10
28	A13	½a chestnut	1.90	.45
29	A13	1a deep blue	3.75	4.00
30	A13	2a orange	22.50	10.00
31	A13	4a dark brown	22.50	25.00
32	A13	8a purple ('05)	19.00	37.50
33	A13	1r dark green	42.50	67.50
34	A13	2r lemon yellow	42.50	250.00
35	A13	5r purple brown	35.00	300.00
		Nos. 27-35 (9)	190.30	695.55

For overprints see Nos. O15-O22, O35-O38, Rajasthan Nos. 33-39.

Maharaja Madan Singh — A14

Thin Wove Paper

1913 Typo. *Rouletted 9½*

37	A14	2 "ANNA" violet	8.25	13.50
a.		tête bêche pair	18.00	60.00

See Nos. 40-50. For overprint see Rajasthan No. 43.

A15

Maharaja Madan Singh — A16

Thick, Chalk-surfaced Paper

1913 *Rouletted 6½, 12*
38 A15 ¼a pale blue .45 *1.40*
a. "Kishangahr" 7.50 *10.00*
b. Imperf., pair 11.00
39 A16 2a purple 12.50 *27.50*
a. "Kishangahr" 75.00 *140.00*

For overprint see No. O23.

1913-16 *Rouletted 12, 14½*
40 A14 ¼a pale blue .30 *.65*
41 A14 ½a green ('15) .30 *1.50*
a. Printed on both sides 350.00
42 A14 1a carmine 1.90 3.75
43 A14 2 "ANNAS" pur 9.00 *12.00*
44 A14 4a ultramarine 9.00 *12.00*
45 A14 8a brown 10.00 *60.00*
46 A14 1r rose lilac 24.00 *190.00*
47 A14 2r dark green 150.00 *525.00*
48 A14 5r brown 60.00 *675.00*
Nos. 40-48 (9) 264.50 *1,480.*

On Nos. 40-48 the halftone screen covers the entire design.

Nos. 41-48 have ornaments on both sides of value in top panel.

For overprints see Nos. O24-O30, O39-O43, Rajasthan Nos. 40-42, 44-48.

Type of 1913-16 Redrawn

1918 *Rouletted*
50 A14 1a rose red 2.25 *8.25*

The redrawn stamp is 24¾mm wide instead of 26mm. There is a white oval around the portrait with only traces of the red line. There is less shading outside the wreath.

For overprint see No. O44.

Maharaja Jagjanarajan Singh
A17 A18

Thick Glazed Paper

1928-29 *Pin-perf. 14½ to 16*
52 A17 ¼a light blue 1.90 *3.00*
53 A17 ½a lt yellow green 6.00 3.50
a. Imperf., pair 180.00 180.00
54 A18 1a carmine rose 1.10 *2.25*
55 A18 2a red violet 5.00 *12.50*
56 A17 4a yellow brown 2.50 2.50
57 A17 8a purple 8.25 *42.50*
58 A17 1r green 30.00 *95.00*
59 A17 2r lemon 42.50 *340.00*
60 A17 5r red brown 67.50 *400.00*
a. Imperf., pair 190.00
Nos. 52-60 (9) 164.75 *901.25*

1945-47

Thick Soft Unglazed Paper

52a A17 ¼a gray blue 6.25 *19.00*
b. ¼a greenish blue ('47) 4.00 *15.00*
53b A17 ½a deep green 2.25 *4.00*
54a A18 1a dull carmine 12.50 6.50
55a A18 2a deep red violet 16.00 *19.00*
b. 2a violet brown, imperf. 125.00 30.00
56a A17 4a brown 35.00 *30.00*
57a A17 8a violet 60.00 *240.00*
58a A17 1r deep green 75.00 *250.00*
59a A17 2r lemon —
60b A17 5r red brown 875.00 *1,100.*

For overprints see Rajasthan Nos. 49-58.
For later issues see Rajasthan.

OFFICIAL STAMPS

Used values are for CTO stamps.

Regular Issues of 1899-1916 Handstamped in Black

On Issue of 1899-1900

1918 **Unwmk.** *Imperf.*
O1 A2 ¼a carmine 12.00
O2 A4 1a gray violet 82.50 8.25
O3 A6 4a chocolate — 190.00

Pin-perf
O4 A2 ¼a carmine 3.25 .90
O4A A2 ¼a green — 175.00
O4B A3 ½a blue 640.00 67.50
O6 A4 1a gray violet 67.50 2.25
O7 A5 2a orange — 225.00
O8 A6 4a chocolate 100.00 24.00
O9 A7 1r dull green 250.00 180.00
O10 A8 2r brown red — 1,400.
O11 A9 5r red violet — 3,000.

See tete beche note after No. 24.

On Issue of 1901
O12 A9b 1a dull violet 75.00 2.25

On Issue of 1904
O13 A11 8a gray 140.00 35.00
O13A A11a 1r green *1,350.*

Imperf.
O14 A12 2a yellow 125.00 7.50

On Issue of 1904-05

Perf. 12½, 13½
O15 A13 ¼a carmine *450.00*
O16 A13 ½a chestnut 1.50 .50
O17 A13 1a deep blue 16.00 6.00
O18 A13 2a orange — 1,500.
O19 A13 4a dk brn 90.00 27.50
O20 A13 8a purple 600.00 375.00
O21 A13 1r dk grn 1,200. 1,100.
O22 A13 5r purple brn

On Issue of 1913

Rouletted
O23 A15 ¼a pale blue 11.00

On Issue of 1913-16
O24 A14 ¼a pale blue .90 .75
O25 A14 ½a green 1.50 1.10
O26 A14 1a carmine 24.00 13.50
O27 A14 2a purple 12.50 6.00
O28 A14 4a ultra 42.50 22.50
O29 A14 8a brown 190.00 67.50
O30 A14 1r rose lilac 525.00 500.00
O31 A14 2r dk grn
O32 A14 5r brown 2,750.

Red Handstamp

On Issue of 1904

Pin-perf
O33 A11 8a gray — 450.00

Imperf
O34 A12 2a yellow 675.00 400.00

On Issue of 1904-05

Perf. 12½, 13½
O35 A13 1a deep blue 35.00 10.00
O36 A13 4a dk brn 140.00 62.50
O37 A13 8a purple — *400.00*
O38 A13 1r dk grn — *1,000.*

On Issue of 1913-16

Rouletted
O39 A14 ¼a pale blue 3.00 2.50
O40 A14 ½a green 6.50 2.40
O41 A14 2a purple 210.00 100.00
O42 A14 4a ultra — 52.50
O43 A14 8a brown — 140.00

On Issue of 1918

Redrawn
O44 A14 1a rose red

The overprint on Nos. O1 to O44 is handstamped and, as usual with that style of overprint, is found inverted, double, etc. In this instance there is evidence that many of the varieties were deliberately made.

KOTAH

kō-tə

LOCATION — A Feudatory State in the Rajputana Agency of India.
AREA — 5714 sq. mi.
POP. — 526,827 (1880)
CAPITAL — Kotah City

All Kotah stamps are only known on cover, including the uncanceled stamps. Values are for covers bearing a single stamp.

A1

A2

A3

Wove Paper

Handstamped

1883 **Unwmk.** *Imperf.*
1 A1 2p green, *yellow* *20,000.* *8,500.*
a. Double impression —
2 A2 2p black, *yellow* *20,000.*
3 A3 2p indigo, *pink* *20,000.*

A4

1886 **Wove Paper**
4 A4 1p green, *yellow* —

The stamps of Kotah became obsolete in 1886.

LAS BELA

ləs 'bāl-ə

LOCATION — A Feudatory State in the Baluchistan District.
AREA — 7,132 sq. mi.
POP. — 63,008
CAPITAL — Bela

A1

1897-98 **Unwmk.** **Typo.** *Perf. 12*
1 A1 ½a black, *white* 45.00 25.00
2 A1 ½a black, *gray* 25.00 16.00
3 A1 ½a black, *blue* ('98) 30.00 16.00
Nos. 1-3 (3) 100.00 57.00

A2

1901
4 A2 1a black, *red orange* 40.00 *75.00*

1904 *Pin-perf*
5 A1 ½a black, *lt blue* 24.00 13.50

Granite Paper
6 A1 ½a black, *greenish gray* 24.00 13.50

Las Bela stamps became obsolete in Mar. 1907.

MORVI

'mor-vē

LOCATION — A Feudatory State in the Kathiawar Agency, Western India.
AREA — 822 sq. mi.
POP. — 113,023
CAPITAL — Morvi

In 1948 Morvi was incorporated in the United State of Saurashtra (see Soruth).

Sir Lakhdhirji Waghji The Thakur Sahib of Morvi — A1

Size: 21½x26½mm

1931 **Unwmk.** **Typo.** *Perf. 12*
1 A1 3p red 4.50 *22.50*
a. 3p deep blue (error) 6.50 *35.00*
2 A1 ½a deep blue 40.00 67.50
3 A1 1a red brown 5.00 *25.00*
4 A1 2a yellow brown 6.00 *60.00*
Nos. 1-4 (4) 55.50 *175.00*

Nos. 1-4 and 1a were printed in two blocks of four, with stamps 5½mm apart, and perforated on four sides. Nos. 1 and 2 were also printed in blocks of four, with stamps 10mm apart, and perforated on two or three sides.

A2

1932 **Size: 21x25½mm** *Perf. 11*
5 A2 3p rose 7.50 *21.00*
6 A2 6p gray green 12.00 *25.00*
7 A2 6p emerald 9.50 *21.00*
8 A2 1a ultramarine 6.50 *21.00*
9 A2 2a violet 16.00 *60.00*
Nos. 5-9 (5) 51.50 *148.00*

A3

1934-48 *Perf. 14, Rough Perf. 11*
10 A3 3p carmine rose 3.75 *5.25*
a. 3p red 2.50 *6.50*
11 A3 6p emerald 2.50 *10.00*
a. 6p green 10.00 *25.00*
12 A3 1a red brown 2.75 *21.00*
a. 1a brown 15.00 *25.00*
13 A3 2a violet 3.75 *30.00*
Nos. 10-13 (4) 12.75 *66.25*

The 1934 London printing of Nos. 10-13 is perf. 14; the later Morvi Press printing is rough perf. 11.

Morvi stamps became obsolete Feb. 15, 1948.

NANDGAON

'nän̦d̦-̦gaun

LOCATION — A Feudatory State in the Chhattisgarh States Agency in Central India.
AREA — 871 sq. mi.
POP. — 182,380
CAPITAL — Rajnandgaon

A1

White Paper

1892, Feb. Unwmk. Typo. *Imperf.*
Without Gum

No.	Type	Description	Unused	Used
1	A1	½a blue	10.00	*275.00*
2	A1	2a rose	40.00	*825.00*

Some authorities claim that No. 2 was a revenue stamp.

For overprints see Nos. O1-O2.

A2

1893 Without Gum

No.	Type	Description	Unused	Used
4	A2	½a green	19.00	*140.00*
5	A2	2a rose	19.00	*140.00*

For overprint see No. O5.

Same Redrawn

1894 Without Gum

No.	Type	Description	Unused	Used
6	A2	½a yellow green	37.50	*140.00*
7	A2	1a rose	82.50	*175.00*
a.		Laid paper	375.00	

The redrawn stamps have smaller value characters and wavy lines between the stamps.

For overprints see Nos. O3-O4.

OFFICIAL STAMPS

Regular Issues Handstamped in Violet

1893-94 Unwmk. *Imperf.*
Without Gum

No.	Type	Description	Unused	Used
O1	A1	½a blue	*550.00*	
O2	A1	2a red	*1,350.*	
O3	A2	½a yellow green	9.50	17.50
O4	A2	1a rose	16.00	*37.50*
a.		Laid paper	16.00	*125.00*
O5	A2	2a rose	3.00	3.00

Some authorities believe that this handstamp was used as a control mark, rather than to indicate a stamp for official mail.

The 1 anna has been reprinted in brown and in blue.

Nandgaon stamps became obsolete in July, 1895.

NOWANUGGUR

ˌnau-ə-ˈnəg-ər

(Navanagar)

LOCATION — A Feudatory State in the Kathiawar Agency, Western India.
AREA — 3,791 sq. mi.
POP. — 402,192
CAPITAL — Navanagar

Stamps of Nowanuggur were superseded by those of India.

6 Dokra = 1 Anna
16 Annas = 1 Rupee

Kandjar (Indian Dagger) — A1

Without Gum
Laid Paper

1877 Unwmk. Typo. *Imperf.*

No.	Type	Description	Unused	Used
1	A1	1d dull blue	1.00	*37.50*
a.		1d ultramarine	1.00	*37.50*
b.		Tete beche pair	1,900.	

Perf. 12½

No.	Type	Description	Unused	Used
2	A1	1d slate	120.00	175.00
a.		Tete beche pair	2,400.	

No. 2 on wove paper is of private origin.

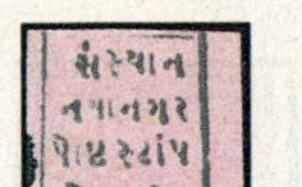

A2

Wove Paper

1877-88 Without Gum *Imperf.*

No.	Type	Description	Unused	Used
3	A2	1d black, *red violet*	5.25	*16.00*
a.		1d black, *rose*	5.25	
b.		Characters at beginning of 3rd line read "4102" instead of "418"		
4	A2	2d black, *green*	8.25	*21.00*
a.		2d black, *blue green*	12.50	
b.		"4102" instead of "418"		
5	A2	3d black, *yellow*	9.00	*30.00*
a.		3d black, *orange yellow*	19.00	
b.		"4102" instead of "418"		
c.		Laid paper	160.00	
d.		2d black, *yellow* (error in sheet of 3d)	600.00	
		Nos. 3-5 (3)	22.50	*67.00*

Nos. 3-5 range in width from 14 to 19mm.

Seal of the State — A3

Without Gum

1893 Thick Paper *Imperf.*

No.	Type	Description	Unused	Used
6	A3	1d black	450.00	

Perf. 12

No.	Type	Description	Unused	Used
7	A3	1d black	6.50	
8	A3	3d orange	7.50	

Imperf
Thin Paper

No.	Type	Description	Unused	Used
9	A3	1d black	350.00	
10	A3	2d dark green	450.00	
11	A3	3d orange	400.00	
		Nos. 9-11 (3)	1,200.	

Perf. 12

No.	Type	Description	Unused	Used
12	A3	1d black	2.50	*9.00*
13	A3	2d green	3.40	*12.00*
14	A3	3d orange	3.40	*17.50*
a.		Imperf. vert., pair		
		Nos. 12-14 (3)	9.30	38.50

Obsolete at end of 1895.

ORCHHA

ˈor-chə

(Orcha)

LOCATION — A Feudatory State in the Bundelkhand Agency in Central India.
AREA — 2,080 sq. mi.
POP. — 314,661
CAPITAL — Tikamgarh

Seal of Orchha — A1

Without Gum

1913-17 Unwmk. Litho. *Imperf.*

No.	Type	Description	Unused	Used
1	A1	¼a ultra ('15)	3.00	*7.50*
2	A1	½a emerald ('14)	.85	*9.50*
a.		Background of arms unshaded	52.50	*150.00*
3	A1	1a carmine ('14)	3.75	*10.00*
a.		Background of arms unshaded	30.00	*275.00*
4	A1	2a brown ('17)	6.75	*35.00*
5	A1	4a orange ('14)	12.00	*57.50*
		Nos. 1-5 (5)	26.35	*119.50*

Essays similar to Nos. 2-5 are in different colors.

A2

Maharaja Singh Dev — A3

1939-40 *Perf. 13½, 13½x14*

No.	Type	Description	Unused	Used
6	A2	¼a chocolate	5.00	*12.00*
7	A2	½a yellow green	4.50	*100.00*
8	A2	¾a ultramarine	7.00	*150.00*
9	A2	1a rose red	4.50	*30.00*
10	A2	1¼a deep blue	5.50	*150.00*
11	A2	1½a lilac	6.00	*190.00*
12	A2	2a vermilion	4.50	*120.00*
13	A2	2½a turq green	7.50	*340.00*
14	A2	3a dull violet	8.00	*180.00*
15	A2	4a blue gray	9.00	*42.50*
16	A2	8a rose lilac	15.00	*340.00*
17	A3	1r sage green	26.00	*750.00*
18	A3	2r lt violet ('40)	60.00	*1,000.*
19	A3	5r yel org ('40)	200.00	*2,750.*
20	A3	10r blue	700.00	*4,500.*
		Nos. 6-20 (15)	1,063.	*10,655.*

POONCH

ˈpünch

LOCATION — A Feudatory State in the Kashmir Residency in India.
AREA — 1,627 sq. mi.
POP. — 287,000 (estimated)
CAPITAL — Poonch

Poonch was feudatory to Jammu and Kashmir. Cancellations of Jammu and Kashmir are found on Poonch stamps, which became obsolete in 1894. The stamps are all printed in watercolor and handstamped from single dies. They may be found on various papers, including wove, laid, wove batonne, laid batonne and ribbed, in various colors and tones. Nearly all Poonch stamps exist tete beche and impressed sideways. Issued without gum.

A1

White Paper

Handstamped

1876 Unwmk. *Imperf.*
Size: 22x21mm

No.	Type	Description	Unused	Used
1	A1	6p red	18,000.	240.

1877 Size: 19x17mm

No.	Type	Description	Unused	Used
1A	A1	½a red	22,500.	*7,500.*

1879 Size: 21x19mm

No.	Type	Description	Unused	Used
1B	A1	½a red	—	7,500.

A2

A3

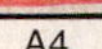

A4

A5

A6

1880-88 White Paper

No.	Type	Description	Unused	Used
2	A2	1p red ('84)	40.00	40.00
3	A3	½a red	4.00	*5.25*
4	A4	1a red	6.75	
5	A5	2a red	16.00	*19.00*
6	A6	4a red	25.00	

Yellow Paper

No.	Type	Description	Unused	Used
7	A2	1p red	5.50	5.50
8	A3	½a red	9.50	9.50
9	A4	1a red	82.50	
10	A5	2a red	15.00	*17.50*
11	A6	4a red	7.50	7.50

Blue Paper

No.	Type	Description	Unused	Used
12	A2	1p red	4.00	3.75
13	A4	1a red	600.00	*625.00*

Orange Paper

No.	Type	Description	Unused	Used
14	A2	1p red	5.50	5.50
15	A3	½a red	42.50	
16	A5	2a red	150.00	
17	A6	4a red	37.50	

Green Paper

No.	Type	Description	Unused	Used
18	A3	½a red	67.50	
19	A4	1a red	5.00	*7.50*
20	A5	2a red	67.50	
21	A6	4a red	100.00	

Lavender Paper

No.	Type	Description	Unused	Used
22	A2	1p red	75.00	*82.50*
23	A4	1a red	125.00	*160.00*
24	A5	2a red	5.00	*5.50*

OFFICIAL STAMPS

White Paper

Handstamped

1888 Unwmk. *Imperf.*

No.	Type	Description	Unused	Used
O1	A2	1p black	4.00	*4.50*
O2	A3	½a black	4.50	*6.00*
O3	A4	1a black	4.00	*4.50*
O4	A5	2a black	7.50	7.50
O5	A6	4a black	12.00	*16.00*
		Nos. O1-O5 (5)	32.00	*38.50*

1890 Yellowish Paper

No.	Type	Description	Unused	Used
O6	A2	1p black	3.75	
O7	A3	½a black	4.50	*5.25*
O8	A4	1a black	22.50	21.00
O9	A5	2a black	9.50	9.50
O10	A6	4a black	15.00	
		Nos. O6-O10 (5)	55.25	35.75

Obsolete since 1894.

RAJASTHAN

ˈrä-jə-ˌstän

(Greater Rajasthan Union)

AREA — 128,424 sq. miles
POP. — 13,085,000

The Rajasthan Union was formed in 1947-49 by 14 Indian States, including the stamp-issuing States of Bundi, Dungarpur, Jaipur and Kishangarh.

Catalogue values for all unused stamps in this state are for Never Hinged items.

Bundi Nos. 43 to 49 Overprinted — a

1948 Unwmk. *Perf. 11*

Handstamped in Black

No.	Type	Description	Unused	Used
1	A8	¼a dp grn	8.25	*50.00*
a.		Pair, one without overprint	550.00	
2	A8	½a purple	8.25	*50.00*
a.		Pair, one without overprint	600.00	
3	A8	1a yel green	7.00	*42.50*
4	A9	2a red	21.00	*125.00*
5	A9	4a dp orange	72.50	*450.00*
6	A10	8a vio blue	13.50	*80.00*
		Nos. 1-6 (6)	130.50	*797.50*

Handstamped in Violet

No.	Type	Description	Unused	Used
1b	A8	¼a dp grn	9.00	*55.00*
2b	A8	½a purple	9.00	*55.00*
c.		Pair, one without overprint	550.00	
3a	A8	1a yel green	24.00	*140.00*
b.		Pair, one without overprint	550.00	
4a	A9	2a red	47.50	*275.00*
5a	A9	4a dp orange	47.50	*275.00*
6a	A10	8a vio blue	14.00	*80.00*
7	A10	1r chocolate	400.00	2,400.
		Nos. 1b-7 (7)	551.00	*3,280.*

Handstamped in Blue

No.	Type	Description	Unused	Used
1c	A8	¼a dp grn	52.50	*300.00*
2d	A8	½a purple	72.50	*450.00*
3c	A8	1a yel green	67.50	*400.00*
5b	A9	4a dp orange	190.00	*1,100.*
6b	A10	8a vio blue	120.00	*725.00*
7a	A10	1r chocolate	140.00	825.00
		Nos. 1c-7a (6)	642.50	*3,800.*

Typo. in Black

No.	Type	Description	Unused	Used
11	A9	2a red	15.00	*100.00*
a.		Inverted overprint	450.00	
12	A9	4a deep orange	6.00	*100.00*
a.		Double overprint	400.00	
13	A10	8a violet blue	27.50	
a.		Inverted overprint	950.00	
b.		Double overprint	600.00	
14	A10	1r chocolate	11.00	
		Nos. 11-14 (4)	59.50	

Stamps of Jaipur, 1931-47, Overprinted in Blue or Carmine

1949 Center in Black *Perf. 14*

No.	Type	Description	Unused	Used
15	A6	¼a red brown (Bl)	12.00	*32.50*
16	A6	½a dull violet	9.50	*35.00*
17	A6	¾a brown org (Bl)	15.00	*40.00*
18	A6	1a blue	11.00	*72.50*
19	A6	2a ocher	12.50	*100.00*
20	A6	2½a rose (Bl)	13.50	*45.00*
21	A6	3a green	16.00	*110.00*
22	A6	4a gray green	14.00	*125.00*
23	A6	6a blue	14.00	*180.00*
24	A6	8a chocolate	24.00	*250.00*
25	A6	1r bister	35.00	*375.00*
		Nos. 15-25 (11)	176.50	*1,365.*

Kishangarh Stamps and Types of 1899-1904 Handstamped Type "a" in Rose

1949 *Pin-perf., Rouletted*

No.	Type	Description	Unused	Used
26	A3	½a blue (#18)	900.00	
27	A4	1a dull lilac (#20)	21.00	*62.50*
28	A6	4a pale red brn (#21B)	125.00	*160.00*
29	A11	8a gray (#25B)	160.00	*275.00*
30	A7	1r dull green (#22)	450.00	*500.00*
31	A8	2r brown red (#23)	550.00	
32	A9	5r red violet (#24)	525.00	525.00
		Nos. 26-32 (7)	2,731.	

Kishangarh Nos. 28, 31-36 Handstamped Type "a" in Rose or Green

1949 Engr. *Perf. 13½, 12½*

No.	Type	Description	Unused	Used
33	A13	½a chestnut (R)		300.00
34	A13	4a dark brown (G)	375.00	
35	A13	4a dark brown (R)	20.00	
36	A13	8a purple (R)	16.00	
37	A13	1r dark green (R)	21.00	
38	A13	2r lemon yellow (R)	27.50	
39	A13	5r purple brown (R)	47.50	
		Nos. 33-39 (7)	507.00	

Kishangarh Nos. 40-42, 37, 43, 46-48 Handstamped Type "a" in Rose

1949 Typo. *Rouletted*

No.	Type	Description	Unused	Used
40	A14	¼a pale blue	8.00	8.00
41	A14	½a green	675.00	375.00
42	A14	1a carmine	—	450.00
43	A14	2 "anna" violet	825.00	
44	A14	2 "annas" purple	4.50	12.50
45	A14	8a brown	7.50	
46	A14	1r rose lilac	15.00	
47	A14	2r dark green	15.00	
48	A14	5r brown	675.00	
		Nos. 40-48 (9)	2,225.	

Kishangarh Stamps and Types of 1928-29 Handstamped Type "a" in Rose

1949 *Pin-perf*

No.	Type	Description	Unused	Used
49	A17	¼a greenish blue	75.00	75.00
50	A17	½a yel green	60.00	60.00
51	A18	1a car rose	110.00	110.00
52	A18	2a red violet	325.00	325.00
53	A17	4a yel brown	4.00	*12.50*
54	A17	8a purple	21.00	*90.00*
55	A17	1r deep green	10.00	
56	A17	2r lemon	140.00	
57	A17	5r red brown	75.00	
		Nos. 49-57 (9)	820.00	

Type of Kishangarh 1928-29, Handstamped Type "a" in Rose

1949 *Pin-perf*

No.	Type	Description	Unused	Used
58	A18	1a dark violet blue	140.00	

No. 58 exists imperf.

Rajasthan stamps became obsolete Apr. 1, 1950.

RAJPEEPLA

räj-ˈpē-plə

(Rajpipla)

LOCATION — A Feudatory State near Bombay in the Gujarat States Agency in India.
AREA — 1,517 sq. mi.
POP. — 206,086
CAPITAL — Nandod

4 Paisas = 1 Anna

Kandjar (Indian Daggers) — A1

A2 A3

Without Gum

1880 Unwmk. Litho. *Perf. 11, 12½*

No.	Type	Description	Unused	Used
1	A1	1pa ultramarine	5.25	*57.50*
2	A2	2a green	45.00	*160.00*
a.		Horiz. pair, imperf. btwn.	900.00	900.00
3	A3	4a red	24.00	*100.00*
		Nos. 1-3 (3)	74.25	*317.50*

The stamps of Rajpeepla have been obsolete since 1886.

SIRMOOR

sir-ˈmu̇ə̦r

(Sirmur)

LOCATION — A Feudatory State in the Punjab District of India.
AREA — 1,046 sq. mi.
POP. — 148,568
CAPITAL — Nahan

A1

Wove Paper

1879 Unwmk. *Perf. 11½*

No.	Type	Description	Unused	Used
1	A1	1p green	24.00	*500.00*
a.		Imperf., pair		

Laid Paper

No.	Type	Description	Unused	Used
2	A1	1p blue	6.75	*250.00*
a.		Imperf., pair		

Raja Sir Shamsher Prakash — A2

1885-88 Litho. *Perf. 14 and 14½.*

No.	Type	Description	Unused	Used
3	A2	3p brown	1.00	.60
4	A2	3p orange	2.50	.45
5	A2	6p green	6.50	6.00
6	A2	1a blue	4.00	*5.50*
7	A2	2a carmine	6.25	*21.00*
		Nos. 3-7 (5)	20.25	*33.55*

There are several printings, dies and minor variations of this issue.

For overprints see Nos. O1-O16.

A3

1893 *Perf. 11½*

No.	Type	Description	Unused	Used
9	A3	1p yellow green	1.60	1.60
a.		1pa dark blue green	1.10	1.10
10	A3	1p ultramarine	1.90	1.20
b.		Imperf., pair	110.00	

Nos. 9 and 10 are re-issues, which were available for postage.

The printed perforation, which is a part of the design, is in addition to the regular perforation.

Elephant — A4

1895-99 Engr. *Perf. 14*

No.	Type	Description	Unused	Used
11	A4	3p orange	5.45	.45
12	A4	6p green	1.10	.45
a.		Vert. pair, imperf between	15,000.	
13	A4	1a dull blue	6.50	5.25
14	A4	2a dull red	5.25	2.25
15	A4	3a yellow green	35.00	*67.50*
16	A4	4a dark green	24.00	*35.00*
17	A4	8a deep blue	27.50	*42.50*
18	A4	1r vermilion	57.50	*110.00*
		Nos. 11-18 (8)	162.30	*263.40*

No. 12a is unique.

Sir Surendar Bikram Prakash — A5

1899

No.	Type	Description	Unused	Used
19	A5	3a yellow green	6.25	*32.50*
20	A5	4a dark green	8.25	*35.00*
21	A5	8a blue	11.00	*30.00*
22	A5	1r vermilion	18.00	*75.00*
		Nos. 19-22 (4)	43.50	*172.50*

OFFICIAL STAMPS

Regular Stamps Overprinted in Black

1890-91 Unwmk. *Perf. 14, 14½*

No.	Type	Description	Unused	Used
O1	A2	3p orange	4.50	*52.50*
O2	A2	6p green	2.25	2.25
a.		Double overprint	275.00	
b.		Double ovpt., one in red	1,250.	
O3	A2	1a blue	600.00	*700.00*
O4	A2	2a carmine	27.50	*100.00*
		Nos. O1-O4 (4)	634.25	

1890-92 Red Overprint

No.	Type	Description	Unused	Used
O5	A2	6p green	42.50	3.50
O6	A2	1a blue	37.50	*47.50*

No.	Type	Description	Unused	Used
O7	A2	6p green	8.25	.75
b.		Inverted overprint	210.00	150.00
O8	A2	1a blue	27.50	6.25
a.		Inverted overprint	500.00	300.00
b.		Double overprint	500.00	

1892 Black Overprint

No.	Type	Description	Unused	Used
O9	A2	3p orange	.90	.75
a.		Inverted overprint	375.00	
O10	A2	6p green	12.00	3.25
O11	A2	1a blue	18.00	1.50
a.		Double overprint	600.00	
O12	A2	2a carmine	10.00	10.00
a.		Inverted overprint	1,350.	1,350.
		Nos. O9-O12 (4)	40.90	15.50

Black Overprint

No.	Type	Description	Unused	Used
O13	A2	3p orange	19.00	1.90
a.		Inverted overprint		
b.		Double overprint		1,000.
O14	A2	6p green	8.25	.90
O15	A2	1a blue	11.00	1.90
O16	A2	2a carmine	25.00	21.00
		Nos. O13-O16 (4)	63.25	25.70

There are several settings of some of these overprints, differing in the sizes and shapes of the letters, the presence or absence of the periods, etc.

The overprints on Nos. O1-O16 are press printed. In addition, nine varieties of handstamped overprints were applied in 1894-96. Most of the handstamps are very similar to the press printed overprints.

Obsolete Mar. 31, 1901.

SORUTH

(Sorath)

(Junagarh)

(Saurashtra)

LOCATION — A Feudatory State near Bombay in the Western India States Agency in India.
AREA — 3,337 sq. mi.
POP. — 670,719
CAPITAL — Junagarh

The United State of Saurashtra (area 31,885 sq. mi.; population 2,900,000) was formed in 1948 by 217 States, including the stamp-issuing States of Jasdan, Morvi, Nowanuggur and Wadhwan.

Nos. 1-27 were issued without gum.

Catalogue values for unused stamps in this State are for Never Hinged items, beginning with Scott 39 in the regular postage section, and Scott O19 in the officials section.

Junagarh

A1

Handstamped in Watercolor

1864 Unwmk. *Imperf.*

Laid Paper

1 A1 (1a) black, *bluish* 950.00 125.00
 a. Wove paper 275.00
1B A1 (1a) black, *gray* 950.00 125.00

Wove Paper

2 A1 (1a) black, *cream* 1,500.

A2

1868 Typo. *Imperf.*

Wove Paper

3 A2 1a black, *yellowish* 37,500.
4 A2 1a red, *green* 16,000.
5 A2 1a red, *blue* 12,500.
6 A2 1a black, *pink* 825.00 110.00
7 A2 2a black, *yellow* 16,000.

Laid Paper

8 A2 1a black, *blue* 140.00 13.50
 a. Left character, 3rd line, omitted
9 A2 1a red 32.50 37.50
 a. Left character, 3rd line, omitted
10 A2 4a black 400.00 *675.00*
 a. Left character, 3rd line, omitted

A 1a black on white laid paper exists in type A2. Value, used $9,500.

In 1890 official imitations of 1a and 4a stamps, type A2, were printed in sheets of 16 and 4. Original sheets have 20 stamps. Four of these imitations are perf. 12, six are imperf.

A3

A4

1877-86 Laid Paper *Imperf.*

11 A3 1a green 1.50 .75
 a. Printed on both sides 750.00 *825.00*
12 A4 4a vermilion 4.00 2.50
 a. Printed on both sides 950.00
13 A4 4a scarlet, *bluish* 5.50 5.00
 Nos. 11-13 (3) 11.00 8.25

Perf. 12

14 A3 1a green .60 .25
 a. 1a blue (error) 900.00 900.00
 c. Wove paper 5.25 2.25
 d. Imperf., pair 120.00 160.00
 e. As "a," wove paper — 900.00
 f. As "c," vert. pair, imperf horiz. 240.00
15 A3 1a green, *bluish* 5.25 *6.75*
 a. Vert. pair, imperf horiz. 525.00
 b. Horiz. pair, imperf vert. 210.00 —
16 A4 4a red 4.00 1.90
 a. 4a carmine 6.50 5.25
 c. Wove paper 7.50 18.00
 d. As "c," imperf., pair 340.00 450.00
17 A4 4a scarlet, *bluish* 16.00 *25.00*
 Nos. 14-17 (4) 25.85 *33.90*

Nos. 14c and 16c Surcharged

1913-14 *Perf. 12*

Wove Paper

18 A3 3p on 1a green .25 .45
 a. Laid paper 110.00 45.00
 b. Inverted surcharge 52.50 30.00
 c. Imperf., pair 52.50
19 A4 1a on 4a red 3.75 10.00
 a. Laid paper 11.00 *82.50*
 b. Imperf., pair 950.00
 c. Double surcharge 1,000.

A5

A6

1914 *Perf. 12*

20 A5 3p green 2.10 .50
 a. Imperf., pair 12.50 *40.00*
21 A6 1a rose carmine 2.25 *3.25*
 a. Imperf., pair 30.00 140.00
 b. Laid paper 375.00 160.00

Nawab Mahabat Khan III
A7 A8

1923-29 Wove Paper *Perf. 12*

22 A7 3p violet .50 .65
 a. Imperf, pair 450.00
 b. Laid paper ('29) 7.50 6.50
 c. As "b," imperf, pair ('29) 5.25 *52.50*
 d. As "b," horiz. pair, imperf btwn. 4.50 *37.50*
23 A8 1a red 4.50 *14.00*
 b. Laid paper 4.50 14.00

Single examples of Nos. 23 and 23b cannot usually be distinguished.

Surcharged with New Value

27 A8 3p on 1a red 7.50 10.00

Two types of surcharge.

Junagarh City and The Girnar
A9

Gir Lion — A10

Nawab Mahabat Khan III — A11

Kathi Horse
A12

1929 *Perf. 14*

30 A9 3p dk green & blk 1.50 .25
31 A10 ½a dk blue & blk 9.00 .25
32 A11 1a claret & blk 7.50 1.50
33 A12 2a org buff & blk 19.00 3.00
34 A9 3a car rose & blk 9.00 *19.00*
35 A10 4a dull vio & blk 19.00 *42.50*
36 A12 8a apple grn & blk 25.00 *35.00*
37 A11 1r dull blue & blk 21.00 *45.00*
 Nos. 30-37 (8) 111.00 *146.50*

For surcharges see Nos. 40-42, O20-O25.
For overprints see Nos. O1-O14.

Type of 1929

Inscribed "Postage and Revenue"

1937

38 A11 1a claret & black 15.00 1.50

For overprint see No. O15.

Catalogue values for unused stamps in this section, from this point to the end of the section, are for Never Hinged items.

United State of Saurashtra

A13

Bhavnagar Court Fee Stamp Overprinted in Black "U.S.S. Revenue & Postage Saurashtra"

1949 Unwmk. Typo. *Perf. 11*

39 A13 1a deep claret 16.00 15.00
 a. "POSTAGE" omitted 525.00 375.00
 b. Double overprint 525.00 *600.00*

Nos. 30, 31 Surcharged in Black or Carmine "POSTAGE & REVENUE ONE ANNA"

1949-50 *Perf. 14*

40 A9 1a on 3p dk grn & blk (bl) ('50) 60.00 *82.50*
 a. "OSTAGE" 750.00 *900.00*
41 A10 1a on ½a dk bl & blk (C) 14.00 7.50
 a. Double surcharge 825.00

For overprint see No. O19.

No. 33 Surcharged in Green "Postage & Revenue ONE ANNA"

1949

42 A12 1a on 2a org buff & blk 24.00 *40.00*
 a. "EVENUE" omitted 1,100.

For overprint see No. O26.

OFFICIAL STAMPS

Regular Issue of 1929 Overprinted in Red

a

1929 Unwmk. *Perf. 14*

O1 A9 3p dk green & black 2.50 .25
O2 A10 ½a dk blue & black 6.00 .25
O3 A11 1a claret & black 6.00 .25
O4 A12 2a org buff & black 3.75 .90
O5 A9 3a car rose & black 1.10 .75
O6 A10 4a dull violet & blk 6.25 .65
O7 A12 8a apple green & blk 5.50 4.50
O8 A11 1r dull blue & blk 5.50 *35.00*
 Nos. O1-O8 (8) 36.60 42.55

For surcharges see Nos. O20-O24.

Regular Issue of 1929 Overprinted in Red

b

1933-49

O9 A9 3p dk grn & blk ('49) 375.00 25.00
O10 A10 ½a dk bl & blk ('49) 900.00 22.50
O11 A9 3a car rose & blk 32.50 27.50
O12 A10 4a dull vio & blk 42.50 24.00
O13 A12 8a apple grn & blk 47.50 27.50
O14 A11 1r dull blue & blk 52.50 140.00

The 3p is also known with ms. "SARKARI" overprint in carmine.

For surcharge see No. O25.

No. 38 Overprinted Type "a" in Red

1938

O15 A11 1a claret & black 21.00 2.25

Catalogue values for unused stamps in this section, from this point to the end of the section, are for Never Hinged items.

United State of Saurashtra No. 41 with Manuscript "Service" in Carmine

1949

O19 A10 1a on ½a dk bl & blk (C) 225.00

Used value for No. O19 is for an example used on piece, cancelled at Gadhda or Una between June and December, 1949.

No. 42 is also known with carmine ms. "Service" overprint in English or Gujarati.

Nos. O4-O8 and O14 Surcharged "ONE ANNA" in Blue or Black

1949 Surcharge 2¼mm high

O20 A12 1a on 2a (Bl) 21,000. 40.00
O21 A9 1a on 3a 5,250. 100.00
O22 A10 1a on 4a 600.00 100.00
O23 A12 1a on 8a 525.00 72.50

Surcharge 4mm High, Handstamped

O24 A11 1a on 1r (#O8) 3,250. 72.50
O25 A11 1a on 1r (#O14) 1,350. 75.00
 Nos. O20-O25 (6) 31,975. 460.00

No. 42 Overprinted Type "b" in Carmine

1949 Unwmk. *Perf. 14*

O26 A12 1a on 2a 125.00 35.00

TONK

ˈtänk

LOCATION — A Feudatory State in the Rajputana Agency of India.
AREA — 2509 sq. mi.
POP. — 307,528 (1900)
CAPITAL — Nimbahera

Three examples of Tonk No. 1 are known. All are on covers dated 1906.

A1

Handstamped with black octagonal control seal

1906 Unwmk. Litho. *Imperf.*

Wove Paper

1 A1 ¼a yellow brown —

The stamps of Tonk became obsolete in 1907.

TRAVANCORE

ˈtrav-ən-ˌkō̇ə̇r

LOCATION — A Feudatory State in the Madras States Agency, on the extreme southwest coast of India.
AREA — 7,662 sq. mi.
POP. — 6,070,018 (1941)
CAPITAL — Trivandrum

16 Cash = 1 Chuckram
2 Chuckrams = 1 Anna

Conch Shell (State Seal) — A1

1888 Unwmk. Typo. *Perf. 12*
Laid Paper

1 A1 1ch ultramarine 5.00 5.00
2 A1 2ch orange red 8.00 *12.00*
3 A1 4ch green 25.00 18.00
Nos. 1-3 (3) 38.00 35.00

The frame and details of the central medallion differ slightly on each denomination of type A1.
Laid paper printings of Nos. 1-3, 5-7 in completely different colors are essays.

1889-99 Wmk. 43 Wove Paper

4 A1 ½ch violet .90 .35
a. Vert. pair, imperf. between 450.00 450.00
b. Double impression 450.00
5 A1 1ch ultramarine 2.25 .25
a. Vert. pair, imperf. between 675.00
b. Horiz. pair, imperf. between 675.00
c. Double impression 600.00
d. Tete beche pair 5,750. 5,000.
6 A1 2ch scarlet 5.00 1.25
a. Horiz. pair, imperf. between 550.00 550.00
b. Vert. pair, imperf. between 250.00
c. Double impression 300.00
7 A1 4ch dark green 5.00 1.00
a. Double impression *650.00*
Nos. 4-7 (4) 13.15 2.85

Shades exist for each denomination.
For surcharges see Nos. 10-11. For type surcharged see No. 20. For overprints see Nos. O1-O2, O4, O6, O18, O24-O25, O27B, O32-O33, O42.

Conch Shell (State Seal) — A2

1901-32 Handmade Wove Paper

8 A2 ¾ch black 3.00 1.50
9 A2 ¾ch brt violet ('32) .50 .25
a. Horizontal pair, imperf. between *275.00*
d. Perf. compound 12x12½ 25.00 10.00

Machine-made Paper
Wmk. 43A

8A A2 ¾ch black ('32) 11.50 .75

For overprints see Nos. O26-O27, O44, O52.

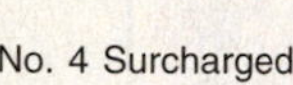
No. 4 Surcharged

1906 Wmk. 43

10 A1 ¼ch on ½ch violet 1.10 .25
a. Inverted surcharge 100.00 55.00
11 A1 ⅜ch on ½ch violet .60 .50
a. Pair, one without surcharge —
b. Inverted surcharge 90.00
c. Double surcharge

A3

A4

1908-11

12 A3 4ca rose .45 .25
a. Vertical pair, imperf. between 450.00 425.00
13 A1 6ca red brown ('10) .45 .25
a. Printed on both sides 75.00
b. Horizontal pair, imperf. between *425.00*
14 A4 3ch purple ('11) 4.00 .30
a. Vertical pair, imperf. between 450.00 *425.00*
b. Vertical strip of 3, imperf. between *500.00*
Nos. 12-14 (3) 4.90 .80

For surcharge & overprints see Nos. 19, O3, O5, O8, O13, O15, O20, O22, O30-O31, O53.

A5

A6

1916

15 A5 7ch red violet 3.50 1.00
a. 7ch carmine-red (error) 60.00
16 A6 14ch orange 4.00 3.75
a. Horizontal strip of 3, imperf. vertically 625.00

For overprints see Nos. O11-O12, O34-O35.

A7

1920-33

17 A7 1 ¼ch claret .80 .80
a. Horiz. pair, imperf. between 500.00 *475.00*
18 A7 1 ½ch light red ('33) 4.00 .25
a. Horizontal strip of 3, imperf. between 325.00
b. Perf. 12½ 25.00 3.25
c. Perf. compound 12x12½ 60.00

For surcharges see Nos. 27-28. For overprints see Nos. O7, O17, O28-O29, O38, O56.

No. 12 and Type of 1888 Surcharged

1921

19 A3 1ca on 4ca rose .25 .25
a. Inverted surcharge 37.50 25.00
20 A1 5ca on 1ch dull bl (R) 1.50 .25
a. Inverted surcharge 19.00 12.50
b. Double surcharge 100.00 75.00
c. Vertical pair, imperf. between *425.00*

A8

1921-32

21 A8 5ca bister 1.20 .25
a. Horizontal pair, imperf. between 75.00 75.00
22 A8 5ca brown ('32) 4.00 .35
a. Horizontal pair, imperf. between 55.00
b. Vertical pair, imperf. between 300.00
23 A8 10ca rose .60 .25
Nos. 21-23 (3) 5.80 .85

For surcharges & overprints see Nos. 29-30, O9-O10, O14, O16, O19, O21, O23, O36-O37.

Sri Padmanabha Shrine at Trivandrum A9

State Chariot — A10

Maharaja Sir Bala Rama Varma — A11

1931, Nov. 6

24 A9 6ca emer & blk 2.40 2.40
a. Horizontal pair, imperf. between 225.00 225.00
25 A10 10ca ultra & black 1.90 1.00
a. Vertical pair, imperf. between *750.00*
26 A11 3ch violet & black 4.00 4.50
Nos. 24-26 (3) 8.30 7.90

Investiture of Sir Bala Rama Varma with full ruling powers.

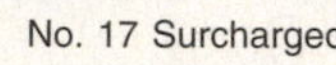
No. 17 Surcharged

1932, Jan. 14

27 A7 1ca on 1 ¼ch claret .25 *.75*
a. Inverted surcharge 6.50 *10.00*
b. Double surcharge 50.00 47.50
c. Horizontal pair, imperf. between 190.00
28 A7 2ca on 1 ¼ch claret .25 .25
a. Inverted surcharge 6.50 *10.00*
b. Double surcharge 42.50
c. Pair, one without surcharge 180.00 190.00
d. Double surcharge, one inverted 80.00
e. Triple surcharge 100.00
f. Triple surcharge, one inverted 85.00 85.00
i. Horizontal pair, imperf. between 180.00
j. Vertical pair, imperf. between 190.00

Type of 1932 and No. 23 Surcharged like Nos. 19-20

1932, Mar. 5

29 A8 1ca on 5ca chocolate .25 .25
a. Inverted surcharge 11.00 *15.00*
b. Double surcharge
c. Pair, one without surcharge 180.00
d. Horizontal pair, imperf. between 190.00
e. Surcharge inverted on reverse only 115.00
30 A8 2ca on 10ca rose .25 .25
a. Inverted surcharge 7.50 *12.00*
b. Double surcharge 32.50 *35.00*
c. Horizontal pair, imperf. between 200.00
d. Double surcharge, one inverted 115.00 110.00
e. Double surcharge, both inverted 65.00
31 A8 1ca on 5ca slate pur 2.25 .50
a. Inverted surcharge 450.00

Untouchables Entering Temple and Maharaja — A12

Designs: Different temples and frames.

1937, Mar. 29 Litho. *Perf. 11½*

32 A12 6ca carmine 4.25 1.50
b. Horizontal strip of 3, imperf. between 750.00
33 A12 12ca ultramarine 5.25 .90
d. Vertical pair, imperf. between 750.00
34 A12 1 ½ch light green 2.25 *3.50*
b. Vertical pair, imperf. between 525.00
35 A12 3ch purple 6.50 3.50
Nos. 32-35 (4) 18.25 9.40

Temple Entry Bill.

Perf. 12½

32A A12 6ca carmine 3.75 3.00
c. Compound perf. 75.00 82.50
33A A12 12ca ultramarine 7.00 1.25
b. Vertical pair, imperf. between 700.00
c. Compound perf. 110.00
34A A12 1 ½ch light green 40.00 11.50
c. Compound perf. 175.00
35A A12 3ch purple 6.50 5.50
Nos. 32A-35A (4) 57.25 21.25

Lake Ashtamudi A13

A14

A15

Sir Bala Rama Varma — A16

Sri Padmanabha Shrine — A17

View of Cape Comerin A18

Pachipara Reservoir A19

1939, May 9 Litho. *Perf. 12½*

36 A13 1ch yellow green 12.00 .25
37 A14 1 ½ch carmine 7.00 *7.00*
d. Perf. 13½ 27.50 *100.00*
38 A15 2ch orange 12.00 4.00
39 A16 3ch chocolate 11.00 .25
40 A17 4ch henna brown 14.00 .60
41 A18 7ch light blue 17.50 *30.00*
42 A19 14ch turq green 10.00 *100.00*
Nos. 36-42 (7) 83.50 142.10

Perf. 11

36A A13 1ch yellow green 17.50 .25
d. Vert. pair, imperf. between —
e. Vertical strip of 3, imperf. between —
37A A14 1 ½ch carmine 8.00 37.50
38A A15 2ch orange 27.50 2.75
39A A16 3ch chocolate 30.00 .50
40A A17 4ch henna brown 62.50 .75
41A A18 7ch light blue 150.00 62.50
42A A19 14ch turq green 18.00 *180.00*

Perf. 12

36B A13 1ch yellow green 37.50 3.75
d. Vert. pair, imperf. between —
e. Vertical strip of 3, imperf. between —
37B A14 1 ½ch carmine 62.50 9.00
38B A15 2ch orange 175.00 10.00
39B A16 3ch chocolate 65.00 7.50
40B A17 4ch henna brown 55.00 14.00

Perf. Compound 11, 12, 12½

36C A13 1ch yellow green 45.00 5.00
d. Vert. pair, imperf. between —
37C A14 1 ½ch carmine 85.00 15.00
38C A15 2ch orange 175.00 10.00
39C A16 3ch chocolate 75.00 1.50
40C A17 4ch henna brown 275.00 200.00
41C A17 7ch light blue 175.00 75.00

27th birthday of Maharaja Sir Bala Rama Varma.
For surcharges and overprints see Nos. 45, O45-O51, Travancore-Cochin 3-7, O3-O7.

Maharaja Sir Bala Rama Varma and Aruvikara Falls A20

Maharaja and Marthanda Varma Bridge, Alwaye A21

1941, Oct. 20 **Typo.** ***Perf. 12½***

43 A20 6ca violet black 11.00 .25
a. Perf. 11 9.00 .25
b. As "a," vertical pair, imperf. between 35.00
c. As "a," vertical pair, imperf. horiz. 80.00 100.00
d. Perf. 12 80.00 100.00
e. As "d," horiz. pair, imperf. between 37.50
f. As "d," vert. pair, imperf. between 90.00
h. Compound perf. 14.50 3.00
44 A21 ¾ch dull brown 12.50 .35
a. Vertical pair, imperf. between *750.00*
b. Perf. 11 12.00 .25
c. As "b," horizontal pair, imperf. between *350.00*
d. As "b," vert. pair, imperf. between 37.50 85.00
g. Perf. 12 80.00 16.00
h. Compound perf. 22.50 1.25

29th birthday of the Maharaja, Oct. 20, 1941.
For overprints & surcharges see Nos. 46-47, 49, O54-O55, O58-O59, Travancore-Cochin Nos. 1, O1.

Stamps and Types of 1939-41 Surcharged in Black

Perf. 11, 12½

1943, Sept. 17 **Wmk. 43**

45 A14 2ca on 1½ch car 2.25 1.90
a. Vertical pair, imperf. between 80.00
e. Perf. 11 .50 .50
h. Compound perf. 1.15 2.40
i. As "h," vertical pair, imperf. between 240.00
46 A21 4ca on ¾ch dl brn 6.00 .45
a. Perf. 11 8.00 1.00
b. Perf. 12 *225.00*
c. Compound perf. 10.00 2.00
47 A20 8ca on 6ca red 7.00 .25
a. Perf. 11 7.00 .25
b. As "a," horiz. pair, imperf between 60.00
c. Perf. 12 125.00
d. Compound perf. 25.00 13.50
Nos. 45-47 (3) 15.25 2.60

For overprints see Nos. O57-O59.

Maharaja Sir Bala Rama Varma — A22

1946, Oct. 24 **Typo.** ***Perf. 11***

48 A22 8ca rose red 3.50 3.00
a. Perf. 12½ 3.50 3.00
b. Perf. 12 50.00 7.00
c. As "b," horizontal pair, imperf. between *100.00* 100.00
d. As "b," horizontal strip of 3, imperf. between *100.00*
e. Compound perf.

For overprint see No. O60. For surcharges see Travancore-Cochin Nos. 2, O2.

No. O54 Overprinted "SPECIAL" Vertically in Orange

1946 ***Perf. 12½***

49 A20 6ca violet black 9.50 5.00
a. Perf. 11 55.00 9.00
b. Compound perf. 10.00 9.00

OFFICIAL STAMPS

Nos. O1-O60 were issued without gum.

Regular Issues of 1889-1911 Overprinted in Red or Black

Perf. 12, 12½

1911, Aug. 16 **Wmk. 43**

O1 A1 1ch indigo (R) 1.65 .25
a. Inverted overprint 10.00 6.50
b. "nO" for "On" 120.00 120.00
c. Double overprint 100.00 75.00
d. Vertical pair, imperf. between *275.00*
O2 A1 2ch scarlet .50 .25
a. Inverted overprint 12.00 12.00
b. Blue overprint 180.00
O3 A4 3ch purple .50 .25
a. Inverted overprint 15.00 15.00
b. Double overprint 120.00 100.00
c. Vertical pair, imperf. between 325.00 *300.00*
d. Horizontal pair, imperf. vertically 225.00
e. Blue overprint 225.00 110.00
O4 A1 4ch dark green .80 .25
a. Inverted overprint 82.50 19.00
b. Double overprint 190.00 140.00
c. Horizontal pair, imperf. between *400.00*
Nos. O1-O4 (4) 3.45 1.00

Same Ovpt. on Regular Issues of 1889-1920

1918-20

O5 A3 4ca rose .25 .25
a. Imperf., pair 450.00 450.00
b. Inverted overprint 120.00
c. Double overprint 180.00 140.00
d. Double impression *425.00*
O6 A1 ½ch violet (R) 3.75 .50
a. Inverted overprint 19.00 6.00
b. "chucrram" 18.50 6.50
c. Double overprint, both inverted 240.00
d. "On" omitted *210.00*
e. Double impression 75.00
f. Horizontal pair, imperf. between 240.00 210.00
g. Vertical pair, imperf. between 100.00 100.00
O7 A7 1¼ch claret .60 .25
a. Inverted overprint 14.00 12.00
b. Double overprint 67.50
d. Double impression *475.00*
e. A7 1¼ch carmine (error of color) 60.00
Nos. O5-O7 (3) 4.60 1.00

Same Ovpt. on Regular Issues of 1909-21

1921

O8 A1 6ca red brown .45 .25
a. Inverted overprint 200.00 18.00
b. Double overprint 200.00 180.00
c. Vertical pair, imperf. between *350.00*
O9 A8 10ca rose 2.00 .25
a. Inverted overprint 27.50
b. Double overprint 100.00 100.00
c. Horizontal pair, imperf. between *225.00*
d. 10ca scarlet ('25) 18.00

Same Overprint on Regular Issue of 1921

1922

O10 A8 5ca bister 2.50 .25
a. Inverted overprint 21.00 13.50

For surcharge see No. O39B.

Same Overprint on Regular Issue of 1916

1925

O11 A5 7ch plum 2.50 .45
O12 A6 14ch orange 3.25 .60

Same Overprint in Blue on Regular Issues of 1889-1921

O13 A3 4ca rose 80.00 *1.00*
O14 A8 5ca bister .90 .25
a. Horizontal pair, imperf. between 375.00 *375.00*
b. Inverted overprint 40.00 22.50
O15 A1 6ca red brown 22.00 2.50
O16 A8 10ca rose 120.00 32.50
O17 A7 1¼ch claret — 120.00
O18 A1 4ch dark green — *150.00*

Some authorities question the authenticity of No. O14.

1930 **Black Overprint**

O19 A8 5ca brown .35 *.90*

Regular Issues of 1889-1932 Overprinted in Black or Red

1930-34

O20 A3 4ca rose 30.00 *95.00*
O21 A8 5ca brown 45.00 14.00
a. Inverted overprint 100.00 110.00
O22 A1 6ca org brown .25 .25
a. Inverted overprint 30.00
b. Double overprint 100.00
d. Vertical pair, imperf. between 100.00 100.00
O23 A8 10ca rose 6.50 4.50
a. Horizontal pair, imperf. between 20.00 *35.00*
b. Vertical pair, imperf. between 15.00 *32.50*
O24 A1 ½ch violet ('34) .85 .25
O25 A1 ½ch purple (R) .25 .25
b. Vertical pair, imperf. between 180.00 *175.00*
O26 A2 ¾ch blk (R) ('32) .60 .25
a. Inverted overprint *375.00*
O27 A2 ¾ch brt vio ('33) .45 .25
a. Double overprint 200.00
c. Vertical pair, imperf. between 240.00
d. Compound perf. (12x12½) 50.00 32.50
O27B A1 1ch gray blue (R) ('33) 1.50 .35
e. Horizontal pair, imperf. between 200.00 200.00
f. Vertical pair, imperf. between 32.50 *47.50*
g. Perf. 12½ 15.00 8.50
h. Compound perf. (12x12½) 37.50 17.50
i. As "h," vertical pair, imperf. between *325.00*
O28 A7 1¼ch claret 2.10 *2.00*
O29 A7 1½ch dl red ('32) .60 .25
a. Double overprint 80.00 80.00
b. Perf. 12½ 70.00 18.00
c. Compound perf. (12x12½) 45.00
d. As "c," double impression 350.00
e. Vertical pair, imperf. between *250.00*
O30 A4 3ch purple ('33) 1.90 .90
a. Double overprint 150.00
O31 A4 3ch purple (R) 1.20 .25
a. Inverted overprint 80.00
b. Horizontal pair, imperf. between 150.00 75.00
c. Vertical pair, imperf. between 110.00 65.00
d. Perf. 12½ 5.00
e. As "d," vertical pair, imperf. between *325.00*
f. Compound perf. (12x12½) — 20.00
O32 A1 4ch dp grn (R) 3.00 .25
O33 A1 4ch deep green 2.75 *7.50*
O34 A5 7ch maroon 1.90 .45
a. Vertical pair, imperf. between 65.00 65.00
b. Perf. 12½ 20.00
c. Compound perf. (12x12½) 75.00 16.00
d. As "c," vertical pair, imperf. between 190.00
O35 A6 14ch orange ('31) 2.50 .60
a. Inverted overprint 500.00 425.00
b. Horizontal pair, imperf. between 60.00 *85.00*
c. Vertical pair, imperf. between 300.00
Nos. O20-O35 (17) 101.35 127.30

The overprint on Nos. O22, O26 and O28 is smaller than the illustration. There are three sizes of the overprint on No. O27.
For surcharges see Nos. O39, O40-O41.

Type of 1921-32 and No. 17 Surcharged and Overprinted

1932

O36 A8 6ca on 5ca dk brn .50 *.50*
b. Inverted surcharge 12.00 12.50
c. Double surcharge 150.00
d. Double surcharge, one inverted 130.00
e. Pair, one without surcharge 500.00
O36A A8 6ca on 5ca bister 2.50 *3.00*
f. Inverted surcharge 110.00
O37 A8 12ca on 10a rose .25 .25
a. New value inverted 9.00 *11.00*
b. Overprint and surcharge inverted 55.00 50.00
c. Double surcharge 160.00
d. Inverted overprint 11.00 11.00
k. Surcharge on front and back 300.00
O38 A7 1ch8ca on 1¼ch cl .50 .30
a. Inverted surcharge *200.00*
b. Double surcharge 75.00
c. Vertical pair, imperf. between 500.00
e. Wrong font "1c" 27.50 22.50
Nos. O36-O38 (4) 3.75 *4.05*

Nos. O21, O10, O23 and O28 Surcharged in Black

O39 A8 6ca on 5ca dk brown .30 .45
a. New value inverted 16.00 *19.00*
c. Pair, one without surcharge 325.00
O39B A8 6ca on 5ca bis *50.00* *20.00*
O40 A8 12ca on 10ca rose 3.00 2.25
a. New value inverted 10.00 10.00
b. "On S S" inverted 24.00 27.50
c. Ovpt. & surch. inverted 60.00 *70.00*
d. Ovpt. & surch. inverted 60.00 *62.50*
O41 A7 1ch8ca on 1¼ch cl 4.50 1.90
a. New value inverted 160.00
Nos. O39-O41 (4) 57.80 24.60

No. O39B can be distinguished from O36A by the letters "S" in the overprint, which are closer together on No. O39B.

Regular Issue of 1889-94 Overprinted

1933

O42 A1 ¾ch violet 5.50 .25
a. Horizontal pair, imperf. between 130.00 100.00
b. Horizontal strip of 3, imperf. between *250.00*
c. Vertical pair, imperf. between *200.00*
d. Double impression *325.00*

Regular Issue of 1901 Overprinted in Red

1933

O44 A2 ¾ch black .50 .40

No. O44 can be distinguished from No. O26 by its overprint, which is significantly smaller than No. O26.

Regular Issue of 1939 Overprinted in Black

a

"SERVICE" 13mm wide, letter "R" with curved tail

1939 **First Overprint** ***Perf. 12½***

O45 A13 1ch yellow green 11.00 .50
O46 A14 1½ch carmine 20.00 2.50
a. "SESVICE" 200.00 45.00
b. Perf. 12 110.00 27.50
c. As "b," "SESVICE" *325.00*
d. As "b," horizontal pair, imperf. between *450.00*
e. Compound perf. (12x12½) 37.50 *5.50*
O47 A15 2ch orange 11.00 11.00
a. "SESVICE" 190.00 *210.00*
b. Compound perf. (12x12½) 200.00 200.00
O48 A16 3ch chocolate 9.50 .30
a. "SESVICE" 150.00 30.00
b. Perf. 12 50.00 .75
c. As "b," "SESVICE" 450.00 65.00
d. Compound perf. (12x12½) 22.50 7.00
O49 A17 4ch henna brown 24.00 8.50
O50 A18 7ch light blue 25.00 6.50
O51 A19 14ch turq green 42.50 12.50
Nos. O45-O51 (7) 143.00 41.80

27th birthday of Maharaja Sir Bala Rama Varma.

Overprinted "SERVICE" 13½mm wide, letter "R" with straight tail

1941-42 *Perf. 12½*

Second Overprint

O45F A13 1ch yel grn 2.00 .25
a. Inverted overprint 60.00
b. Double overprint 30.00
c. Vertical pair, imperf. between 85.00 85.00
O46F A14 1½ch scarlet 6.50 .25
a. Horizontal pair, imperf. between 100.00
O47F A15 2ch orange 5.50 .35
O48F A16 3ch chocolate 4.00 .25
a. Vertical pair, imperf. between 1,000.
O49F A17 4ch hen brn 5.50 1.25
O50F A18 7ch light blue 11.00 .45
O51F A19 14ch turq green 19.00 .85

Perf. 11

O45G A13 1ch yel grn 1.25 .25
a. Double overprint 225.00 210.00
b. Vertical pair, imperf. between 65.00
O46G A14 1½ch scarlet 5.00 .25
a. Vertical pair, imperf. between 240.00 225.00
b. Vertical strip of 3, imperf. between 175.00
c. Horizontal pair, imperf. between 225.00
O47G A15 2ch orange 20.00 4.00
a. Vertical pair, imperf. between 1,000.
O48G A16 3ch chocolate 4.25 .25
O49G A17 4ch hen brn 6.50 .65
O50G A18 7ch light blue 11.00 .45
O51G A19 14ch turq green 24.00 1.75

Perf. 12

O45H A13 1ch yel grn 5.00 .60
a. Inverted overprint 210.00
b. Double overprint 27.50 42.50
c. Double impression 180.00
d. Vertical pair, imperf. between 140.00 135.00
O46H A14 1½ch scarlet 11.00 1.25
a. Vertical strip of 3, imperf. between 350.00
O47H A15 2ch orange 225.00 200.00
a. Vertical pair, imperf. between 1,100. 1,000.
O48H A16 3ch chocolate 10.00 4.00
a. Vertical pair, imperf. between 1,000. 900.00
O49H A17 4ch hen brn 32.50 9.00
O50H A18 7ch light blue 37.50 15.00
O51H A19 14ch turq green 17.50 3.00

Perf. Compound (12x12½)

O45I A13 1ch yel grn 10.00 3.00
O46I A14 1½ch scarlet 5.00 .50
O47I A15 2ch orange 200.00 200.00
O48I A16 3ch chocolate 32.50 1.00
O49I A17 4ch hen brn 80.00 32.50
O50I A18 7ch light blue 25.00 6.00
O51I A19 14ch turq green 125.00 20.00

"SERVICE" Overprint 13mm

No. 9 Overprinted — b

1939 **Wmk. 43** *Perf. 12.*

O52 A2 ¾ch violet 42.50 2.50
a. Perf. 12½ 260.00 125.00
b. Compound perf. (12x12½) 240.00 120.00

"SERVICE" 13½mm

1941 *Perf. 12½*

O52F A2 ¾ch violet 25.00 .25
a. Horizontal pair, imperf. between 220.00 220.00
b. Perf. 11 100.00 1.25
c. Perf. 12 30.00 .25
d. Compound perf. (12x12½) 55.00 1.00

No. 13 Overprinted Type "b"

1941

O53 A1 6ca red brown 1.25 .50
a. Perf. 11 2.00 .90
b. Perf. 12 1.00 .40
c. Compound perf. (12x12½) 1.00 1.25

Nos. 43-44 Overprinted Type "a"

1941 *Perf. 12½*

O54 A20 6ca violet black .90 .75
a. Perf. 11 1.00 .25
b. Perf. 12 110.00 17.50
c. Compound perf. (12x12½) 1.75 1.75
O55 A21 ¾ch dull brown 9.50 .25
a. Vertical pair, imperf. between 750.00
b. Perf. 11 10.00 .25
c. Perf. 12 110.00 5.00
d. Compound perf. (12x12½) 12.50 1.00

29th birthday of the Maharaja, Oct. 20, 1941.
For overprint see No. 49.

No. 18 Overprinted Type "b"

1944 *Perf. 12*

O56 A7 1½ch light red 6.50 1.25
a. Perf. 12½ ('44) 21.00 12.00
b. Compound perf. (12x12½) 28.50 17.50

Nos. 45-48 Overprinted Type "a"

1945-49 *Perf. 11, 12*

O57 A14 2ca on 1½ch car .90 1.50
a. Pair, one without surcharge 500.00
b. Perf. 12½ .75 1.20
c. Compound perf. (12x12½) 1.00 1.50
d. As "c," "2" omitted in surcharge 750.00 750.00
e. Perf. 12
O58 A21 4ca on ¾ch dl brn 6.00 .60
a. Perf. 12½ ('45) 8.00 .75
b. Compound perf. (12x12½) 4.50 1.75
O59 A20 8ca on 6ca red 2.00 .25
a. Inverted surcharge 2,250.
b. Perf. 12½ 4.00 .40
c. Compound perf. (12x12½) 10.00 1.50
O60 A22 8ca rose red ('49) 5.00 1.75
a. Double impression of stamp 47.50
b. Horizontal pair, imperf. between 65.00
c. Vertical pair, imperf. between 375.00
d. Perf. 12½ .75 1.20
e. As "d," double impression 50.00
f. Perf. 12 4.50 1.75
g. As "f," double impression 75.00
Nos. O57-O60 (4) 13.90 4.10

Travancore stamps became obsolete June 30, 1949.

TRAVANCORE-COCHIN

'trav-ən-ˌkō̤ə̣r kō-'chin

LOCATION — Southern India
AREA — 9,155 sq. mi.
POP. — 7,492,000

The United State of Travancore-Cochin was established July 1, 1949.

Catalogue values for all unused stamps in this state are for Never Hinged items.

Travancore Stamps of 1939-47 Surcharged in Red or Black

a

1949, July 1 **Wmk. 43** *Perf. 12*

1 A20 2p on 6ca vio blk (R) .95 .30
a. Horiz. pair, imperf. between 110.00 —
b. Vert. pair, imperf. between 10.00 26.00
c. Inverted surcharge 200.00 —
d. Vert. strip of 3, imperf. between 47.50 —
e. Horiz. strip of 3, imperf. between 110.00 —
f. Block of 4, imperf. between (horiz. & vert.) 100.00 —
2 A22 4p on 8ca rose red 1.85 .40
a. Vert. pair, imperf. between 30.00 —
b. Inverted surcharge 250.00 —
c. Pair, one without surcharge 325.00 —
d. "FOUP" 225.00 125.00
e. "S" inverted 150.00
3 A13 ½a on 1ch yel grn 1.25 .50
a. Horiz. pair, imperf. between 110.00 110.00
b. Vert. pair, imperf. between 8.00 22.50
c. Inverted surcharge 6.25
d. "NANA" 400.00 200.00
e. Block of 4, imperf. between (horiz. & vert.) 80.00 —
4 A15 1a on 2ch orange 6.25 .65
a. Horiz. pair, imperf. between 17.50 —
b. Vert. pair, imperf. between 10.00 25.00
c. Block of 4, imperf. between (horiz. & vert.) 80.00
5 A17 2a on 4ch hen brn 6.25 .70
a. "O" inverted 85.00 27.50
6 A18 3a on 7ch lt blue 16.00 5.00
7 A19 6a on 14ch turq grn 35.00 55.00
a. Accent omitted from Malayalam surcharge 600.00 675.00
Nos. 1-7 (7) 67.55 62.55

For overprints see Nos. O1-O7, O12-O17.
For types overprinted see Nos. O18-O23.

Perf. 11

1g A20 2p on 6ca vio blk (R) 2.75 .50
h. Vert. pair, imperf. between 375.00 375.00
i. Pair, one without surcharge 190.00 —
2g A22 4p on 8ca rose red 3.50 .40
h. Vert. pair, imperf. between 325.00 325.00
i. Pair, one without surcharge 325.00 —
j. Inverted surcharge 200.00 —
k. "FOUP" 310.00 160.00
l. "S" inverted 150.00 62.50
3g A13 ½a on 1ch yel grn 4.25 .25
h. Vert. pair, imperf. between 55.00 —
i. Inverted surcharge — 450.00
j. "NANA" 400.00 185.00
k. Inverted "H" in "HALF" — 175.00
4g A15 1a on 2ch orange 1.85 .40
h. Double surcharge 67.50 —
5g A17 2a on 4ch hen brn 5.25 .75
h. "O" inverted — 27.50
6g A18 3a on 2ch lt blue 8.00 5.50
h. Blue 100.00 6.25
i. "3" omitted — 1,500.
7g A19 6a on 14ch turq grn 30.00 50.00
h. Accent omitted from Malayalam surcharge 550.00 650.00
Nos. 1g-7g (7) 55.60 57.80

Perf. 12½

1m A20 2p on 6ca vio blk (R) 4.25 2.25
n. Inverted surcharge 62.50 —
2m A22 4p on 8ca rose red 2.25 .50
n. Inverted surcharge 92.50 —
o. "S" inverted 150.00 62.50
3m A13 ½a on 1ch yel grn 5.25 .40
n. Vert. pair, imperf. between — 325.00
o. "NANA" 350.00 135.00
p. Inverted "H" in "HALF" — 175.00
4m A15 1a on 2ch orange 5.50 .40
5m A17 2a on 4ch hen brn 6.25 .75
n. Inverted surcharge — 475.00
o. "O" inverted 75.00 25.00
6m A18 3a on 2ch lt blue 16.00 9.00
7m A19 6a on 14ch turq grn 35.00 67.50
n. Accent omitted from Malayalam surcharge 550.00 625.00
Nos. 1m-7m (7) 74.50 80.80

Perf. 14

1q A20 2p on 6ca vio blk (R) — 800.00
3q A13 ½a on 1ch yel grn — 775.00

Perf. 13½

2r A22 4p on 8ca rose red — 1,100.
4r A15 1a on 2ch orange 275.00 2.50

Compound Perforation

1s A20 2p on 6ca vio blk (R) — 62.50
2s A22 4p on 8ca rose red — 67.50
3s A13 ½a on 1ch yel grn — 67.50
4s A15 1a on 2ch orange 75.00 30.00
5s A17 2a on 4ch hen brn 85.00 52.50
6s A18 3a on 7ch lt blue — 125.00
t. Blue — 175.00
7s A19 6a on 14ch turq grn 92.50 110.00
t. Accent omitted from Malayalam surcharge 875.00
Nos. 1s-7s (7) 252.50 515.00

Imperforate Pairs

1u A20 2p on 6ca vio blk (R) 12.00 —
2u A22 4p on 8ca rose red 110.00 —
3u A13 ½a on 1ch yel grn 12.50 30.00
4u A15 1a on 2ch orange 15.00 —
7u A19 6a on 14ch turq grn — —
Nos. 1u-7u (5) 149.50 30.00

Cochin Nos. 80, 91 and Types of 1944-46 Surcharged in Black or Carmine — b

1949-50 **Wmk. 294** *Perf. 11, 13*

8 A15 3p on 9p ultra 15.00 32.50
9 A16 3p on 9p ultra 5.75 3.50
a. Vert. pair, imperf. between 4,000.
b. Double surcharge 975.00
c. Surcharged on both sides 725.00
10 A16 3p on 9p ultra (C) 11.00 3.50
11 A16 6p on 9p ultra (C) 2.75 .60
12 A13 6p on 1a3p mag ('50) 11.50 8.50
13 A15 6p on 1a3p magenta 25.00 23.00
a. Double surcharge 1,100.
14 A13 1a on 1a9p ultra (C) 3.00 1.90
15 A15 1a on 1a9p ultra (C) 7.25 3.25
b. Black surcharge 5,500.
c. Hindi characters 7.5mm long 7,500.
Nos. 8-15 (8) 81.25 76.75

The surcharge exists with line of Hindi characters varying from 16½ to 23mm wide.
For overprints see Nos. O10-O11, O24.

Cochin No. 86 Overprinted

1949

15A A15 1a deep orange 11.00 125.00
d. No period after "S" 110.00 —
e. Raised period after "T" 110.00 —

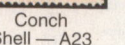

Conch Shell — A23

View of River — A24

Wmk. 196

1950, Oct. **Litho.** *Perf. 14*

16 A23 2p rose red 4.50 5.50
17 A24 4p ultramarine 5.50 22.00

Cochin No. 86 and Type of 1948-50 Overprinted in Black

1950, Apr. 1 **Wmk. 294** *Perf. 13, 11*

18 A15 1a deep orange 11.00 110.00
a. No period after "T" 80.00 450.00
b. Inverted overprint 375.00
c. As No. 18b, raised period after "T" 2,450.

No. 18 Surcharged in Black

20 A15 6p on 1a dp org 6.75 90.00
a. Surcharge on No. 15A 18.00
b. As No. 20a, no period after "S" 275.00
c. As No. 20a, raised period after "T" 275.00
21 A15 9p on 1a dp org 5.50 90.00
a. Surcharge on No. 15A 275.00
b. As No. 21a, no period after "S" 1,150.
c. As No. 21a, raised period after "T" 1,150.

OFFICIAL STAMPS

Travancore Stamps of 1939-46 Surcharged Type "a" in Red or Black and Overprinted

c

1949 **Wmk. 43** *Perf. 12*

O1 A20 2p on 6ca vio blk (R) 1.80 .75
a. Horiz. pair, imperf. between 15.00 35.00
b. Vert. pair, imperf. between 8.00
c. Block of 4, imperf. between (horiz. & vert.) 35.00
O2 A22 4p on 8ca rose red 7.25 1.25
a. "FOUB" 200.00 72.50
b. Pair, one without 4p surcharge 1,350.
O3 A13 ½a on 1ch yel grn 24.50 3.50
a. "NANA" 800.00 300.00
b. Pair, one without surcharge 220.00
c. Inverted surcharge on back only 600.00
O4 A15 1a on 2ch orange — —
O5 A17 2a on 4ch hen brn 12.00 6.75
a. Pair, one without surcharge 1,050.
O6 A18 3a on 7ch lt blue 6.00 9.75
a. Horiz. pair, imperf. between 30.00
b. Vert. pair, imperf. between 11.00
c. Block of 4, imperf. between (horiz. & vert.) 60.00
d. blue 100.00 6.75
e. As "d," horiz. pair, imperf. between 1,000.
O7 A19 6a on 14ch turq grn 80.00 13.50
a. Horiz. pair, imperf. between 40.00
b. Vert. pair, imperf. between 50.00
c. Block of 4, imperf. between (horiz. & vert.) 85.00
Nos. O1-O7 (7) 97.50 6.10

Perf. 11

O1f A20 2p on 6ca vio blk (R) 1.50 .25
g. Vert. pair, imperf. between 375.00 375.00

O2f	A22	4p on 8ca rose red	6.00	.35
g.		"FOUB"	160.00	40.00
O3f	A13	½a on 1ch yel grn	3.75	.30
g.		Inverted surcharge	110.00	—
h.		"NANA"	500.00	160.00
i.		Pair, one without surcharge	300.00	
O4f	A15	1a on 2ch orange	19.50	9.00
g.		Pair, one without surcharge	1,150.	
O5f	A17	2a on 4ch hen brn	8.50	.75
g.		Inverted surcharge	1,700.	
O6f	A18	3a on 2ch lt blue	6.75	1.25
g.		blue	100.00	22.00
O7f	A19	6a on 14ch turq grn	19.50	14.50
		Nos. O1f-O7f (7)	65.50	26.40

Perf. 12½

O1j	A20	2p on 6ca vio blk (R)	2.50	1.00
k.		Vert. pair, imperf. between	375.00	375.00
l.		Pair, one without surcharge	325.00	
O2j	A22	4p on 8ca rose red	8.50	1.50
k.		"FOUB"	400.00	145.00
O3J	A13	½a on 1ch yel grn	2.75	.30
k.		"NANA"	500.00	135.00
l		Pair, one without surcharge	175.00	
m.		Inverted surcharge	50.00	
O4j	A15	1a on 2ch orange	22.00	9.75
k.		Pair, one without surcharge	1,050.	
l.		Inverted surcharge	125.00	
O5j	A17	2a on 4ch hen brn	4.50	1.25
O6j	A18	3a on 2ch lt blue	8.50	4.00
k.		Vert. pair, imperf. between	30.00	
O7j	A19	6a on 14ch turq grn	24.50	16.00
k		Vert. pair, imperf. between	50.00	
		Nos. O1j-O7j (7)	73.25	33.80

Compound Perforation

O1n	A20	2p on 6ca vio blk (R)	100.00	—
O2n	A22	4p on 8ca rose red	35.00	30.00
O3n	A13	½a on 1ch yel grn		50.00
O5n	A17	2a on 4ch hen brn		67.50
		Nos. O1n-O5n (4)	135.00	147.50

Imperforate Pairs

O1o	A20	2p on 6ca vio blk (R)	10.00	35.00
O5o	A17	2a on 4ch hen brn	17.00	
O6o	A18	3a on 7ch lt blue	16.00	—
O7o	A19	6a on 14ch turq grn	20.00	—
		Nos. O1o-O7o (4)	63.00	35.00

Cochin Nos. O90-O91 Surcharged Type "b" in Black

1950 Wmk. 294 ***Perf. 11***

O8	A16	6p on 3p carmine	1.90	1.10
a.		Double surcharge	—	525.00
b.		Vert. pair, imperf. between	—	2,300.
c.		"C" in place of "G"	24.50	12.25
O9	A16	9p on 4p gray grn	1.60	*4.00*
a.		Horiz. pair, imperf. between	1,250.	1,350.
b.		Hindi characters 22mm long	1.35	1.55
c.		As "b," horiz. pair, imperf. between	1,175.	1,175.
d.		"C" in place of "G"	32.50	37.50

Hindi characters in surcharge on No. O9 are 18mm long.

Travancore-Cochin Nos. 14-15 Overprinted "ON C G S"

Perf. 13

O10	A13	1a on 1a9p ultra	.90	1.00
O11	A15	1a on 1a9p ultra	37.50	25.00

Nos. 2-7 Overprinted in Black — d

1949-51 Wmk. 43 ***Perf. 12***

O12	A22	4p on 8ca rose red	.35	.25
O13	A13	½a on 1ch yel green	1.50	.25
a.		"AANA"	170.00	80.00
O14	A15	1a on 2ch orange	.60	.25
O15	A17	2a on 4ch hen brn	18.00	1.35
O16	A18	3a on 7ch lt blue	6.00	2.50
O17	A19	6a on 14ch turq grn	60.00	*8.00*
		Nos. O12-O17 (6)	86.45	12.60

Perf. 11

O12b	A22	4p on 8ca rose red	.60	.25
O13b	A13	½a on 1ch yel green	.60	.25
c.		"AANA"	110.00	50.00
O14b	A15	1a on 2ch orange	4.50	.60
O15b	A17	2a on 4ch hen brn	1.85	1.35
O16b	A18	3a on 7ch lt blue	1.85	1.35
O17b	A19	6a on 14ch turq grn	17.00	8.00
		Nos. O12b-O17b (6)	26.40	11.80

Perf. 12½

O12d	A22	4p on 8ca rose red	1.25	.25
O13d	A13	½a on 1ch yel green	2.75	.25
e.		"AANA"	400.00	90.00
O14d	A15	1a on 2ch orange	.50	.35
O15d	A17	2a on 4ch hen brn	5.25	1.00
O16d	A18	3a on 7ch lt blue	10.50	1.35
O17d	A19	6a on 14ch turq grn	1.85	*5.50*
		Nos. O12d-O17d (6)	22.10	8.70

Compound Perforation

O12f	A22	4p on 8ca rose red	14.50	14.50
O13f	A13	½a on 1ch yel green	57.50	32.00
g.		"AANA"	—	425.00
O14f	A15	1a on 2ch orange	36.50	32.00
O15f	A17	2a on 4ch hen brn	36.50	24.50
O16f	A18	3a on 7ch lt blue	—	100.00
O17f	A19	6a on 14ch turq grn	170.00	*170.00*
		Nos. O12f-O17f (6)	315.00	373.00

Imperforate Pairs

O12h	A22	4p on 8ca rose red	10.00	—
O13h	A13	½a on 1ch yel green	11.00	30.00
O14h	A15	1a on 2ch orange	29.00	—
O16h	A18	3a on 7ch lt blue	67.50	—
		Nos. O12h-O16h (4)	117.50	30.00

Types of 1949 Overprinted Type "d"

1951 Wmk. 294

O18	A13	½a on 1ch yel grn, perf. 12½	5.50	.80
a.		Perf. 11	.50	.50
b.		Perf. 12	28.00	19.50
c.		Compound perf.	21.00	3.75
O19	A15	1a on 2ch org, perf. 12½	2.75	1.25
a.		Perf. 11	.60	.50
b.		Perf. 12	16.00	5.00
c.		Perf. 13½	2.50	1.25
d.		Compound perf.	8.50	3.75

Type of 1949 Overprinted Type "c" Unwmk.

O20	A22	4p on 8ca rose red	1.40	1.10

No. O20 is not from an unwatermarked part of sheet with wmk. 294 but is printed on paper entirely without watermark.

Nos. 1, 3 and 5 Overprinted Type "c"

Wmk. 294

O21	A13	½a on 1ch yel grn	1.10	.50
O22	A20	2p on 6ca vio blk, perf. 12½	.50	*2.75*
a.		"SERVICE" double	22.00	—
b.		Perf. 11	.60	2.75
c.		Perf. 12	1.50	2.10
O23	A17	2a on 4ch hen brn, perf. 12½	4.00	3.25
a.		Perf. 11	1.85	1.35
b.		Vert. pair, imperf. between	525.00	*525.00*
c.		Perf. 12	—	115.00
d.		Compound perf.	90.00	55.00
		Nos. O21-O23 (3)	5.60	6.50

No. 9 Overprinted in Black

1951

O24	A16	3p on 9p ultra	.90	*1.20*
a.		Horiz. pair, imperf. between		*3,500.*

WADHWAN

wə-'dwän

LOCATION — A Feudatory State in Kathiawar Agency, Western India.
AREA — 242 sq. mi.
POP. — 44,259
CAPITAL — Wadhwan

Coat of Arms — A1

1888 Litho. Unwmk. ***Pin-perf.***

Thin Paper

1	A1	½p black	160.00	

Perf. 12½

2	A1	½p black	30.00	*100.00*

1889 ***Perf. 12 and 12½***

Thick Paper

3	A1	½p black	12.50	*14.00*
		Nos. 1-3 (3)	202.50	

INDO-CHINA

ˌin-ˌdō-ˈchī-nə

LOCATION — French possessions on the Cambodian Peninsula in southeastern Asia, bordering on the South China Sea and the Gulf of Siam

GOVT. — French Colony and Protectorate

AREA — 280,849 sq. mi.

POP. — 27,030,000 (estimated 1949)

CAPITAL — Hanoi

In 1949, Indo-China was divided into Cambodia, Laos and Viet Nam each issuing its own stamps.

100 Centimes = 1 Franc

100 Cents = 1 Piaster (1918)

Stamps of French Colonies Surcharged in Black or Red

a

b

1889 Unwmk. Perf. 14x13½

No.	Type	Description	Unused	Used
1	A9(a)	5c on 35c dp vio, *org*	14.00	*12.00*
a.		"89" omitted	275.00	250.00
b.		Pair, #1 and #1a	425.00	425.00
2	A9(b)	5c on 35c dp vio, *org* (R)	110.00	100.00
a.		Date in smaller type	275.00	260.00
b.		Inverted surcharge, #2	2,000.	2,000.
c.		Inverted surcharge, #2a	3,000.	3,000.
d.		Pair, #2 and #2a	575.00	575.00

Issue dates: No. 1, Jan. 8; No. 2, Jan. 10.

"R" is is the Colonial Governor, P. Richaud, "D" is the Saigon P.M. General P. Demars.

For other overprints on designs A3-A27a see various issues of French Offices in China.

Navigation & Commerce — A3

Name of Colony in Blue or Carmine

1892-1900 Typo. Perf. 14x13½

No.	Type	Description	Unused	Used
3	A3	1c blk, *lil bl*	1.25	1.25
a.		"INDO-CHINE" double	*9,000.*	
4	A3	2c brn, *buff*	1.75	1.75
5	A3	4c claret, *lav*	1.75	1.75
6	A3	5c grn, *grnsh*	2.50	2.50
7	A3	5c yel grn ('00)	2.10	1.25
8	A3	10c blk, *lavender*	8.00	2.00
9	A3	10c red ('00)	3.75	2.25
10	A3	15c blue, quadrille paper	42.50	2.25
11	A3	15c gray ('00)	9.00	2.40
12	A3	20c red, *grn*	12.00	7.25
13	A3	25c blk, *rose*	20.00	4.25
a.		"INDO-CHINE" omitted	*7,500.*	*7,500.*
14	A3	25c blue ('00)	24.00	5.00
15	A3	30c brn, *bis*	29.00	8.00
16	A3	40c red, *straw*	29.00	15.00
17	A3	50c car, *rose*	45.00	16.00
18	A3	50c brn, *az* ('00)	30.00	9.50
19	A3	75c dp vio, *org*	24.00	19.00
a.		"INDO-CHINE" inverted	*7,750.*	*7,750.*
b.		As "a", in pair with normal	*10,000.*	
20	A3	1fr brnz grn, *straw*	60.00	40.00
a.		"INDO-CHINE" double	1,200.	*1,400.*
21	A3	5fr red lil, *lav* ('96)	145.00	120.00
		Nos. 3-21 (19)	490.60	261.40

Perf. 13½x14 stamps are counterfeits.

For surcharges and overprints see Nos. 22-23, Q2-Q4.

Nos. 11 and 14 Surcharged in Black

1903

No.	Type	Description	Unused	Used
22	A3	5c on 15c gray	2.00	1.25
23	A3	15c on 25c blue	2.50	1.60

Issue dates: No. 22, Dec. 4; No. 23, Aug. 8.

France — A4

1904-06

No.	Type	Description	Unused	Used
24	A4	1c olive grn	.80	.80
25	A4	2c vio brn, *buff*	1.25	.80
26	A4	4c claret, *bluish*	.80	.80
27	A4	5c deep green	1.25	.50
a.		Double impression	*450.00*	*450.00*
28	A4	10c carmine	1.60	.75
29	A4	15c org brn, *bl*	1.60	1.00
30	A4	20c red, *grn*	3.50	1.60
31	A4	25c deep blue	15.00	1.60
32	A4	30c pale brn	6.00	3.00
33	A4	35c blk, *yel* ('06)	22.00	3.25
34	A4	40c blk, *bluish*	5.75	1.60
35	A4	50c bister brn	11.00	3.00
36	A4	75c red, *org*	45.00	30.00
37	A4	1fr pale grn	22.50	8.50
38	A4	2fr brn, *org*	55.00	42.50
39	A4	5fr dp vio, *lil*	250.00	200.00
40	A4	10fr org brn, *grn*	225.00	190.00
		Nos. 24-40 (17)	668.05	489.70

For surcharges see Nos. 59-64.

Annamite Girl — A5

Cambodian Girl — A6

Cambodian Woman — A7

Annamite Women — A8

Hmong Woman — A9

Laotian Woman — A10

Cambodian Woman — A11

1907 Perf. 14x13½

No.	Type	Description	Unused	Used
41	A5	1c ol brn & blk	.40	.40
42	A5	2c yel brn & blk	.40	.40
43	A5	4c blue & blk	1.25	1.25
44	A5	5c grn & blk	1.60	.80
45	A5	10c red & blk	1.60	.55
46	A5	15c vio & blk	1.40	1.25
47	A6	20c vio & blk	3.75	1.60
48	A6	25c bl & blk	8.50	1.25
49	A6	30c brn & blk	13.00	7.50
50	A6	35c ol grn & blk	2.75	2.25
51	A6	40c yel brn & blk	4.50	2.00
52	A6	45c org & blk	11.00	7.00
53	A6	50c car & blk	16.00	6.00

Perf. 13½x14

No.	Type	Description	Unused	Used
54	A7	75c ver & blk	14.00	9.00
55	A8	1fr car & blk	62.50	22.50
56	A9	2fr grn & blk	18.00	17.50
57	A10	5fr blue & blk	47.50	*55.00*
58	A11	10fr pur & blk	100.00	*110.00*
		Nos. 41-58 (18)	308.15	246.25

For surcharges see Nos. 65-93, B1-B7.

Nos. 41, 47-51, 54-55 exist imperf.

Stamps of 1904-06 Surcharged in Black or Carmine

1912, Nov. Perf. 14x13½

No.	Type	Description	Unused	Used
59	A4	5c on 4c cl, *bluish*	6.00	6.00
60	A4	5c on 15c org brn, *bl* (C)	1.25	1.25
61	A4	5c on 30c pale brn	1.60	1.60
62	A4	10c on 40c blk, *bluish* (C)	1.60	1.60
63	A4	10c on 50c bis brn (C)	2.00	2.00
64	A4	10c on 75c red, *org*	5.25	5.25
		Nos. 59-64 (6)	17.70	17.70

Two spacings between the surcharged numerals are found on Nos. 59-64.

Nos. 41-58 Surcharged in Cents or Piasters in Black, Red or Blue

1919, Jan.

No.	Type	Description	Unused	Used
65	A5	⅖c on 1c	.85	.55
66	A5	⅘c on 2c	1.40	.90
67	A5	1⅗c on 4c (R)	2.00	.80
68	A5	2c on 5c	1.75	.30
a.		Inverted surcharge	160.00	
69	A5	4c on 10c (Bl)	1.60	.55
a.		Closed "4"	32.50	3.25
b.		Double surcharge	160.00	
70	A5	6c on 15c	6.75	1.25
a.		Inverted surcharge	160.00	
71	A6	8c on 20c	5.50	1.90
72	A6	10c on 25c	5.25	1.00
a.		Pair, one without surcharge	*675.00*	
73	A6	12c on 30c	7.00	1.10
74	A6	14c on 35c	3.50	.75
a.		Closed "4"	12.00	5.75
75	A6	16c on 40c	6.75	2.00
76	A6	18c on 45c	8.50	2.75
77	A6	20c on 50c (Bl)	13.00	1.25
78	A7	30c on 75c (Bl)	16.00	2.75
79	A8	40c on 1fr (Bl)	25.00	2.75
80	A9	80c on 2fr (R)	29.00	8.50
a.		Double surcharge	400.00	300.00
81	A10	2pi on 5fr (R)	110.00	110.00
82	A11	4pi on 10fr (R)	150.00	150.00
		Nos. 65-82 (18)	393.85	289.10

Types of 1907 Issue Surcharged with New Values in Black or Red

Nos. 88-92

No. 93

1922

No.	Type	Description	Unused
88	A5	1c on 5c ocher & blk	1.60
89	A5	2c on 10c gray grn & blk	2.40
90	A6	6c on 30c lt red & blk	2.75
91	A6	10c on 50c lt bl & blk	2.75
92	A6	11c on 55c vio & blk, *bluish*	3.00
93	A6	12c on 60c lt bl & blk, *pnksh* (R)	3.00
		Nos. 88-93 (6)	15.50

Nos. 88-93 were sold officially in Paris but were never placed in use in the colony.

Nos. 88-93 exist without surcharge but were not regularly issued in that condition. Value, Nos. 88-89, each $190; Nos. 90-91, each $140; Nos. 92-93, each $100.

A12

A13

Two types of "CENTS" for the 4c, 5c, 10c-12c values: Type 1, thin font (April 1922); type 2, thicker font (Oct. 1922 and later printings). All other denominations are type 2. For more detailed listings, see the *Scott Classic Specialized Catalogue of Stamps and Covers.*

"CENTS" below Numerals

1922-23 Perf. 14x13½

No.	Type	Description	Unused	Used
94	A12	⅒c blk & sal ('23)	.25	.25
a.		Double impression of frame		
95	A12	⅕c blue & blk	.25	.25
96	A12	⅖c ol brn & blk	.25	.25
a.		Head and value doubled	275.00	275.00
97	A12	⅘c rose & blk, *lav*	.40	.35
98	A12	1c yel brn & blk	.25	.25
99	A12	2c gray grn & blk	.75	.55
100	A12	3c vio & blk	.35	.35
101	A12	4c org & blk, type 2	.35	.35
b.		Head and value doubled	225.00	225.00
102	A12	5c car & blk, type 2	.35	.35
b.		Head and value doubled	300.00	300.00
103	A13	6c dl red & blk	.50	.30
104	A13	7c grn & blk	.75	.65
105	A13	8c blk, *lav*	2.00	1.25
106	A13	9c ocher & blk, *grnsh*	1.50	.90
107	A13	10c bl & blk, type 2	.80	.75
108	A13	11c vio & blk, type 2	.75	.75
109	A13	12c brn & blk, type 2	.55	.55
b.		Head and value double (11c+12c)	550.00	550.00
110	A13	15c org & blk	1.10	.80
111	A13	20c bl & blk, *straw*	1.75	.80
112	A13	40c ver & blk, *bluish*	2.75	1.40
113	A13	1pi bl grn & blk, *grnsh*	5.75	5.25
114	A13	2pi vio brn & blk, *pnksh*	13.00	13.00
		Nos. 94-114 (21)	34.40	29.35

For overprints see Nos. O17-O32.

Plowing near Tower of Confucius A14

Ha Long Bay A15

Angkor Wat, Cambodia A16

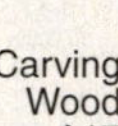

Carving Wood A17

That Luang Temple, Laos A18

Founding of Saigon A19

1927, Sept. 26

No.	Type	Description	Unused	Used
115	A14	⅒c lt olive grn	.25	.25
116	A14	⅕c yellow	.25	.25
117	A14	⅖c light blue	.25	.25
118	A14	⅘c dp brn	.55	.55
119	A14	1c orange	.65	.30
120	A14	2c blue grn	1.10	.50

121 A14 3c indigo .70 .30
122 A14 4c lil rose 1.60 1.25
123 A14 5c dp vio .80 .30
a. Booklet pane of 10 *200.00*
124 A15 6c deep red 2.25 .80
a. Booklet pane of 10 *200.00*
125 A15 7c lt brn 1.50 .80
126 A15 8c gray green 2.10 1.00
127 A15 9c red vio 1.50 1.00
128 A15 10c light blue 2.00 1.25
129 A15 11c orange 2.00 1.25
130 A15 12c myrtle grn 1.50 1.00
131 A16 15c dl rose & ol brn 8.00 7.50
132 A16 20c vio & slate 4.00 2.40
133 A17 25c org brn & lil rose 8.75 6.50
134 A17 30c dp bl & ol gray 4.25 4.00
135 A18 40c ver & lt bl 7.75 3.25
136 A18 50c lt grn & slate 9.50 3.25
137 A19 1pi dk bl, blk & yel 22.50 8.25
a. Yellow omitted 300.00
138 A19 2pi red, dp bl & org 30.00 16.00
Nos. 115-138 (24) 113.75 62.20

Common Design Types pictured following the introduction.

Colonial Exposition Issue
Common Design Types Surcharged

No. 140

No. 141

No. 142

1931, Apr. 13 Engr. *Perf. 12½*
Name of Country in Black
140 CD71 4c on 50c violet 3.50 3.50
141 CD72 6c on 90c red org 3.75 3.50
142 CD73 10c on 1.50fr dl bl 4.75 4.50
Nos. 140-142 (3) 12.00 11.50
Set, never hinged 18.50

Junk — A20

Tower at Ruins of Angkor Thom — A21

Planting Rice — A22

Apsaras, Celestial Dancer A23

1931-41 Photo. *Perf. 13½x13*
143 A20 ⅒c Prus blue .25 .25
144 A20 ⅕c lake .25 .25
145 A20 ⅖c org red .25 .25
146 A20 ½c red brn .25 .25
147 A20 ⅘c dk vio .25 .25
148 A20 1c blk brn .25 .25
149 A20 2c dk grn .25 .25
150 A21 3c dp brn .25 .25
151 A21 3c dk grn ('34) 6.00 1.60
152 A21 4c dk bl 1.25 .50
153 A21 4c dk grn ('38) .80 .55
153A A21 4c yel org ('40) .40 .40
154 A21 5c dp vio .30 .30
154A A21 5c dp grn ('41) .40 .40
155 A21 6c org red .25 .25
a. Bklt. pane 5 + 1 label 100.00
156 A21 7c blk ('38) .30 .30
157 A21 8c rose lake ('38) .40 .40
157A A21 9c blk, *yel* ('41) .75 .75
158 A22 10c dark blue .65 .50
158A A22 10c ultra, *pink* ('41) .55 .55
159 A22 15c dk brn 5.75 1.40
160 A22 15c dk bl ('33) .25 .25
161 A22 18c blue ('38) .75 .50
162 A22 20c rose .30 .25
163 A22 21c olive grn .30 .30
164 A22 22c dk grn ('38) .55 .55
165 A22 25c dp vio 3.50 1.60
165A A22 25c dk bl ('41) .55 .55
166 A22 30c org brn ('32) .50 .30

Perf. 13½
167 A23 50c dk brn .75 .25
168 A23 60c dl vio ('32) .90 .65
168A A23 70c lt bl ('41) .55 .55
169 A23 1pi yel grn .90 .65
170 A23 2pi red 1.10 .75
Nos. 143-170 (34) 30.70 17.05

Nos. 166, 167, 169 and 170 were issued without the letters "RF" in 1943, by the Vichy Government.
For surcharge & overprints see Nos. 214A, O1-O16, Viet Nam, Democratic Republic No. 1L14.

Emperor Bao-Dai A24

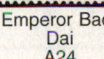

King Sisowath Monivong A25

For Use in Annam
1936, Nov. 20 Engr. *Perf. 13*
171 A24 1c brown 1.00 1.00
172 A24 2c green 1.00 1.00
173 A24 4c violet 1.00 1.00
174 A24 5c red brn 1.50 1.50
175 A24 10c lil rose 2.00 2.00
176 A24 15c ultra 2.75 2.75
177 A24 20c scarlet 2.75 2.75
178 A24 30c plum 3.50 3.50
179 A24 50c slate grn 3.50 3.50
180 A24 1pi rose vio 4.75 4.75
181 A24 2pi black 5.75 5.75
Nos. 171-181 (11) 29.50 29.50

For Use in Cambodia
182 A25 1c brown 1.00 1.00
183 A25 2c green 1.00 1.00
184 A25 4c violet 1.10 1.10
185 A25 5c red brn 1.10 1.10
186 A25 10c lil rose 2.40 2.40
187 A25 15c ultra 3.25 3.25
188 A25 20c scarlet 2.75 2.75
189 A25 30c plum 3.25 3.25
190 A25 50c slate grn 3.25 3.25
191 A25 1pi rose vio 4.25 4.25
192 A25 2pi black 5.75 5.75
Nos. 182-192 (11) 29.10 29.10

Paris International Exposition Issue
Common Design Types
1937, Apr. 15
193 CD74 2c dp vio 1.60 1.60
194 CD75 3c dk grn 1.10 1.10
195 CD76 4c car rose 1.10 1.10
196 CD77 6c dk brn 1.10 1.10
197 CD78 9c red 1.40 1.40
198 CD79 15c ultra 1.40 1.40
Nos. 193-198 (6) 7.70 7.70
Set, never hinged 14.00

Colonial Arts Exhibition Issue
Souvenir Sheet
Common Design Type
1937, Apr. 15 *Imperf.*
199 CD79 30c dull violet 10.00 *12.00*
Never hinged 16.50

Governor-General Paul Doumer — A26

1938, June 8 Photo. *Perf. 13½x13*
200 A26 5c rose car 1.00 .65
201 A26 6c brown 1.10 1.10
202 A26 18c brt bl 1.10 1.10
Nos. 200-202,C18 (4) 3.95 3.10
Set, never hinged 6.50

Trans-Indo-Chinese Railway, 35th anniv.

New York World's Fair Issue
Common Design Type
1939, May 10 Engr. *Perf. 12½x12*
203 CD82 13c car lake .80 .80
Never hinged 1.40
204 CD82 23c ultra 1.25 1.25
Never hinged 2.25

Mot Cot Pagoda, Hanoi — A27

1939, June 12 *Perf. 13*
205 A27 6c blk brn 1.10 1.10
206 A27 9c vermilion 1.10 1.10
207 A27 23c ultra 1.10 1.10
208 A27 39c rose vio 1.50 1.50
Nos. 205-208 (4) 4.80 4.80
Set, never hinged 9.00

Golden Gate International Exposition.

Angkor Wat and Marshal Pétain A27a

1941 Engr. *Perf. 12½x12*
209 A27a 10c dk car .80
209A A27a 25c blue .80

Nos. 209-209A were issued by the Vichy government in France, but were not placed on sale in Indo-China.
For overprints, see Nos. 262-263. For surcharges, see B21A-B21B.

Gum
#210-261 issued without gum.

Imperfs
Many issues between Nos. 209-263, B19A-B26 and C1-C28, plus some postage dues and official stamps, exist imperf.

King Norodom Sihanouk of Cambodia — A28

Pin-perf. 12½
1941, Oct. 15 Unwmk. Litho.
210 A28 1c red org 1.60 1.60
211 A28 6c violet 3.25 3.25
212 A28 25c dp ultra 21.00 21.00
Nos. 210-212 (3) 25.85 25.85

Coronation of Norodom Sihanouk, King of Cambodia, October, 1941.
For surcharges see Viet Nam, Democratic Republic Nos. 1L27-1L29.

Harnessed Elephant on Parade — A29

1942, Mar. 29
213 A29 3c reddish brown 2.00 1.60
214 A29 6c crimson 2.00 1.60

Fête of Nam-Giao in Annam.
For surcharges see Viet Nam, Democratic Republic Nos. 1L32-1L33, 1L53-1L54.

No. 165 Surcharged in Black

1942 *Perf. 13*
214A A22 10c on 25c dp vio, gum .50 .30

View of Saigon Fair — A30

1942, Dec. 20 *Perf. 13½*
215 A30 6c carmine rose .80 .80

Saigon Fair of 1942.
For surcharge see Viet Nam, Democratic Republic No. 1L51.

Nam-Phuong, Empress of Annam — A31

1942, Sept. 1 *Pin-perf. 11½*
216 A31 6c carmine rose 1.25 .80

For surcharge see Viet Nam, Democratic Republic No. 1L55.

Marshal Pétain — A32

Perf. 11½, 12, 13½ and Compound
1942-44
217 A32 1c blk brn .35 .35
218 A32 3c olive brn ('43) .35 .35
219 A32 6c rose red .55 .55
220 A32 10c dull grn ('43) 1.20 1.20
221 A32 40c dk blue ('43) 1.60 1.60
222 A32 40c slate bl ('44) .80 *1.25*
Nos. 217-222 (6) 4.85 5.30

Values are for the lowest-valued perforation varieties.
For overprints see Viet Nam, Democratic Republic Nos. 1L6-1L10, 1L21.

Bao-Dai, Emperor of Annam — A33

1942 *Perf. 13½*
223 A33 ½c brown 1.25 *1.60*
224 A33 6c carmine rose 1.25 1.25

Issue dates: ½c, Nov. 1; 6c, Sept. 1.
For surcharge see Viet Nam, Democratic Republic No. 1L56.

Norodom Sihanouk, King of Cambodia — A34

1943 *Perf. 12*
225 A34 1c brown 1.25 .80
a. Perf. 13¾ 8.00 8.00
226 A34 6c red 1.00 .55
a. Perf. 13¾ 8.00 8.00

Issue dates: 1c, Mar. 10; 6c, May 10.
For surcharge see Viet Nam, Democratic Republic No. 1L30.

Types of 1931-32 Without "RF"

1943 **Photo.** *Perf. 13½x13*
226A A22 30c orange brown 1.60
226B A23 50c dark brown 1.60
226C A23 1pi yellow green 2.75
226D A23 2pi red 3.50
Nos. 226A-226D (4) 9.45

Nos. 226A-226D were issued by the Vichy government in France, but were not placed on sale in Indo-China. Nos. 226A-226D were issued with gum.

Sisavang-Vong, King of Laos — A35

1943 *Perf. 12*
227 A35 1c bister brown .80 *1.25*
a. Perf. 13¾ 10.00 10.00
228 A35 6c carmine rose 1.25 .65
a. Perf. 11½x12 32.50 32.50
b. Perf. 13¾ 32.50 32.50

Issue dates: 1c, Mar. 10; 6c, June 1.
For surcharge see Viet Nam, Democratic Republic No. 1L31.

Family, Country and Labor — A36

1943, Nov. 5 *Perf. 12*
229 A36 6c carmine rose .65 .50
a. Perf. 11½ .80 .80

National revolution, 3rd anniversary.
For surcharge see Viet Nam, Democratic Republic No. 1L52.

Admiral Rigault de Genouilly A37

François Chasseloup-Laubat A38

Admiral André A. P. Courbet A39

1943 *Perf. 11½, 12, 12x11½*
230 A37 6c carmine rose .50 *1.40*
231 A38 6c carmine rose .50 .35
232 A39 6c carmine rose 1.40 .25
Nos. 230-232 (3) 2.40 2.00

Issued: Nos. 230, 232, 9/1; No. 231, 10/5.
A 5c dull brown, type A37, was not regularly issued without the Viet Nam overprint. Value, $10.
For overprints see Viet Nam, Democratic Republic Nos. 1L15-1L16, 1L25-1L26.
A 3c light brown, type A39, was prepared but not issued. Value, $10.

Pigneau de Behaine, Bishop of Adran — A40

1943, June 10 *Perf. 12*
233 A40 20c dull red 1.50 *1.75*

For surcharge see Viet Nam, Democratic Republic No. 1L50.

Alexandre Yersin — A41

1943-45 *Perf. 12x11½*
234 A41 6c carmine rose 1.50 1.50
235 A41 15c vio brn ('44) .55 .55
236 A41 1pi yel grn ('45) .75 .75
Nos. 234-236 (3) 2.80 2.80

Issued to honor Dr. Alexandre Yersin (1863-1943), the Swiss bacteriologist who introduced rubber culture into Indo-China.
Issued: 6c, 10/5; 15c, 12/10; 1pi, 1/10.
For overprint and surcharges see Viet Nam, Democratic Republic Nos. 1L1, 1L49.

Lt. M. J. François Garnier A42

1943, Sept. *Perf. 12*
237 A42 1c dull olive bister .90 *1.25*

A 15c brown violet was prepared but not issued. Value, $16.
For surcharges see Viet Nam, Democratic Republic Nos. 1L41-1L42.

Alexandre de Rhodes A43

1943-45 *Pin-perf., Perf. 12*
238 A43 15c dk vio brn ('45) .40 .40
239 A43 30c org brn .80 .80
a. 30c yellow brown, perf. 13½ .80 .80

Nos. 239, 239a carry the monogram "EF."
Issue dates: 15c, Mar. 10; 30c, June 15.
For overprints see Viet Nam, Democratic Republic Nos. 1L2-1L3.

Athlete Giving Olympic Salute A44

1944, July 10 *Perf. 12*
241 A44 10c dk vio brn & yel 2.40 2.40
242 A44 50c dl red 2.75 2.75

For overprints see Viet Nam, Democratic Republic Nos. 1L4-1L5.

Adm. Pierre de La Grandière A45

1943-45
243 A45 1c dull brn .25 *1.25*
244 A45 5c dark brn ('45) .30 .30

The upper left corner of No. 244 contains the denomination "5c" instead of "EF" monogram.
Issue dates: 1c, Aug.; 5c, Jan. 10.
For surcharges see Viet Nam, Democratic Republic Nos. 1L39-1L40.

Auguste Pavie A46

1944 *Perf. 12*
245 A46 4c org yel .50 .30
246 A46 10c dl grn .30 *.65*

Issue dates: 4c, Feb. 10; 10c, Jan. 5.
A 20c dark red, type A46, was not regularly issued without the Viet Nam overprint. Value without overprint, $10.
For overprints see Viet Nam, Democratic Republic Nos. 1L11-1L13.

Governor-General Pierre Pasquier — A47

1944
247 A47 5c brn vio .65 .65
248 A47 10c dl grn .30 *1.25*

Issue dates: 5c, Nov. 1; 10c, Sept.
For surcharges see Viet Nam, Democratic Republic Nos. 1L34-1L35.

Joost Van Vollenhoven — A48

1944, Oct. 10
249 A48 1c olive brown .35 .35
250 A48 10c green .75 .90

For surcharges see Viet Nam, Democratic Republic Nos. 1L44-1L45.

Governor-General J. M. A. de Lanessan — A49

1944
251 A49 1c dl gray brn .65 .50
252 A49 15c dl rose vio 1.90 1.60

Issued: 1c, 12/10; 15c, 10/16.
For surcharges see Viet Nam, Democratic Republic Nos. 1L43, 1L46.

Governor-General Paul Doumer — A50

1944
253 A50 2c red vio .30 .30
254 A50 4c lt brn .30 .30
255 A50 10c yel grn .30 .30
Nos. 253-255 (3) .90 .90

Issue dates: 2c, 4/15; 4c, 6/15; 10c, 1/5.
For overprints see Viet Nam, Democratic Republic Nos. 1L18-1L20.

Admiral Charner — A51

1944
256 A51 10c green .50 *1.40*
257 A51 20c brn red .65 *1.40*
258 A51 1pi pale yel grn 1.00 1.00
Nos. 256-258 (3) 2.15 3.80

Issue dates: 10c, 20c, 8/10; 1pi, July.
For overprints see Viet Nam, Democratic Republic Nos. 1L22-1L24.

Doudart de Lagrée — A52

1944-45
259 A52 1c dl gray brn ('45) .25 .25
260 A52 15c dl rose vio .50 .55
261 A52 40c brt bl .65 1.00
Nos. 259-261 (3) 1.40 1.80

Issue dates: 1c, 1/10; 15c, 40c, Nov.
For overprint and surcharges see Viet Nam, Democratic Republic Nos. 1L17, 1L37-1L38.

Nos. 209-209A Overprinted in Black

1946 Unwmk. *Perf. 12½x12*
262 A27a 10c dk car 1.10 *1.60*
263 A27a 25c blue 2.75 *3.25*

SEMI-POSTAL STAMPS

No. 45 Surcharged

Perf. 14x13½
1914, Oct. 28 Unwmk.
B1 A5 10c +5c red & blk 1.60 1.60

Nos. 44-46 Surcharged

1915-17
B2 A5 5c + 5c grn & blk ('17) 1.60 1.60
a. Double surcharge 220.00 210.00
B3 A5 10c + 5c red & blk 2.50 2.00
B4 A5 15c + 5c vio & blk ('17) 2.50 2.00
a. Triple surcharge 200.00
b. Quadruple surcharge 200.00
Nos. B2-B4 (3) 6.60 5.60

Nos. B2-B4 Surcharged with New Values in Blue or Black

1918-19
B5 A5 4c on 5c + 5c (Bl) 4.25 4.25
a. Closed "4" 220.00
B6 A5 6c on 10c + 5c 3.75 *4.00*
B7 A5 8c on 15c + 5c ('19) 15.00 15.00
a. Double surcharge 225.00
Nos. B5-B7 (3) 23.00 23.25

France Nos. B5-B10 Surcharged

1919 (?)
B8 SP5 10c on 15c + 10c 1.60 1.60
a. "10 CENTS" double 525.00 525.00
B9 SP5 16c on 25c + 15c 4.00 4.00
B10 SP6 24c on 35c + 25c 7.25 7.25
a. Double surcharge 800.00 800.00
b. CENTS" double 950.00
B11 SP7 40c on 50c + 50c 12.50 12.50
B12 SP8 80c on 1fr + 1fr 27.50 27.50
B13 SP8 4pi on 5fr + 5fr 225.00 225.00
a. PIASTRES" double 6,250. 5,400.
Nos. B8-B13 (6) 277.85 277.85

Curie Issue
Common Design Type
Inscription and Date in Upper Margin
1938, Oct. 24 Engr. *Perf. 13*
B14 CD80 18c + 5c brt ultra 12.00 12.00
Never hinged 20.00

French Revolution Issue
Common Design Type
Name and Value Typo. in Black
1939, July 5 Photo.
B15 CD83 6c + 2c green 12.00 12.00
B16 CD83 7c + 3c brown 12.00 12.00
B17 CD83 9c + 4c red org 12.00 12.00
B18 CD83 13c + 10c rose pink 12.00 12.00
B19 CD83 23c + 20c blue 12.00 12.00
Nos. B15-B19 (5) 60.00 60.00
Set, never hinged 112.50

Common Design Type and

Tonkinese Sharpshooter SP1

Legionary SP2

1941 Photo. *Perf. 13½*
B19A SP1 10c + 10c red 1.60
B19B CD86 15c + 30c maroon 1.60
B19C SP2 25c + 10c blue 1.60
Nos. B19A-B19C (3) 4.80

Nos. B19A-B19C were issued by the Vichy government in France, but were not placed on sale in Indo-China.

Gum
#B20-B31 issued without gum.

Portal and Flags, City University, Hanoi — SP3

Perf. 11½
1942, June 1 Unwmk. Litho.
B20 SP3 6c + 2c car rose 1.25 1.25
a. Perf. 13½ 120.00
B21 SP3 15c + 5c brn vio 1.25 1.25

Nos. 209-209A Srchd. in Black or Red

1944 Engr. *Perf. 12½x12*
B21A 5c + 15c on 25c blue (R) .95
B21B + 25c on 10c dk car 1.00

Colonial Development Fund.
Nos. B21A-B21B were issued by the Vichy government in France, but were not placed on sale in Indo-China.

No. B20 Surcharged in Black

1944, June 10
B22 SP3 10c + 2c on 6c + 2c 1.25 1.25

Coat of Arms and Sword — SP4

1942, Aug. 1 *Perf. 12*
B23 SP4 6c + 2c red & blue .80 .80
B24 SP4 15c + 5c vio blk, red & bl .80 .80

No. B23 Surcharged in Black Like No. B22

1944, Mar. 15
B25 SP4 10c + 2c on 6c + 2c .80 .80

Aviator Do-Huu-Vi SP5

1943, Aug. 1
B26 SP5 6c + 2c car rose .65 1.60

No. B26 Surcharged in Black Like No. B22

1944, Feb. 10
B27 SP5 10c + 2c on 6c + 2c .80 .80

Surcharge arranged to fit size of stamp.

Aviator Roland Garros — SP6

1943, Nov. 15
B28 SP6 6c + 2c rose car .80 .80

No. B28 Surcharged in Black Like No. B22

1944, Feb. 10
B29 SP6 10c + 2c on 6c + 2c .80 .80

Cathedral of Orléans SP7

1944, Dec. 20
B30 SP7 15c + 60c brn vio 1.60 1.60
B31 SP7 40c + 1.10pi blue 1.60 2.75

For surcharges see Viet Nam, Democratic Republic Nos. 1L36, 1L47-1L48.

Type of France, 1945, Surcharged in Black

1945 Unwmk. Engr. *Perf. 13*
B32 A152 50c + 50c on 2fr green .65 .65
B33 A152 1pi + 1pi on 2fr hn brn .65 .65
B34 A152 2pi + 2pi on 2fr Prus grn 1.00 1.00
Nos. B32-B34 (3) 2.30 2.30
Set, never hinged 4.75

AIR POST STAMPS

Airplane AP1

1933-41 Unwmk. Photo. *Perf. 13½*
C1 AP1 1c ol brn .25 .25
C2 AP1 2c dk grn .30 .25
C3 AP1 5c yel grn .30 .25
C4 AP1 10c red brn .65 .30
C5 AP1 11c rose car ('38) .80 .30
C6 AP1 15c dp bl .70 .25
C6A AP1 16c brt pink ('41) .35 .35
C7 AP1 20c grnsh gray .50 .50
C8 AP1 30c org brn .30 .25
C9 AP1 36c car rose 1.90 .35
C10 AP1 37c ol grn ('38) .80 .30
C10A AP1 39c dk ol grn ('41) .35 .35
C11 AP1 60c dk vio 1.90 .35
C12 AP1 66c olive grn .55 .25
C13 AP1 67c brt bl ('38) 1.20 1.00
C13A AP1 69c brt ultra ('41) .65 .65
C14 AP1 1pi black .70 .25
C15 AP1 2pi yel org 1.00 .35
C16 AP1 5pi purple 1.90 .50
C17 AP1 10pi deep red 3.75 .90
Nos. C1-C17 (20) 18.85 7.95

See Nos. C27-C28.
Issue dates: 11c, 37c, June 8; 67c, Oct. 5; 16c, 39c, 69c, Feb. 5; others, June 1, 1933.
See Nos. C18A-C18O, C27-C28.

Trans-Indo-Chinese Railway Type
1938, June 8
C18 A26 37c red orange .75 .25

Type of 1933-38 Without "RF"
1942-44 *Perf. 13½*
C18A AP1 5c yellow green .25
C18B AP1 10c red brown .25
C18C AP1 11c rose carmine .30
C18D AP1 15c deep blue .40
C18E AP1 20c greenish gray .40
C18F AP1 36c carmine rose .40
C18G AP1 37c olive green .70
C18H AP1 60c dark violet .70
C18I AP1 66c brown olive .70
C18J AP1 67c bright blue .80
C18K AP1 69c br ultramarine .90
C18L AP1 1pi black 1.30
C18M AP1 2pi yellow orange 1.30
C18N AP1 5pi purple 1.75
C18O AP1 10pi deep red 3.50
Nos. C18A-C18O (15) 13.65

Nos. C18A-C18O were issued by the Vichy government in France, but were not placed on sale in Indo-China.

Victory Issue
Common Design Type
Perf. 12½
1946, May 8 Unwmk. Engr.
C19 CD92 80c red org 1.00 .55

Chad to Rhine Issue
Common Design Types
1946, June 6
C20 CD93 50c yel grn .90 .90
C21 CD94 1pi violet .90 .90
C22 CD95 1.50pi carmine 1.10 1.10
C23 CD96 2pi vio brn 1.10 1.10
C24 CD97 2.50pi dp bl 1.10 1.10
C25 CD98 5pi org red 1.30 1.30
Nos. C20-C25 (6) 6.40 6.40
Set, never hinged 10.00

UPU Issue
Common Design Type
1949, July 4 *Perf. 13*
C26 CD99 3pi dp bl, dk vio, grn & red 4.75 4.00
Never hinged 8.50

Plane Type of 1933-41
1949, June 13 Photo. *Perf. 13½*
C27 AP1 20pi dk bl grn 11.50 6.50
C28 AP1 30pi brown 13.00 6.50

AIR POST SEMI-POSTAL STAMP

French Revolution Issue
Common Design Type
Unwmk.
1939, July 5 Photo. *Perf. 13*
Name and Value Typo. in Orange
CB1 CD83 39c + 40c brn blk 25.00 25.00
Never hinged 45.00

Poor Family — SPAP1

Orphans SPAP2

Caring for Children — SPAP3

Perf. 13½x12½, 13 (#CB4)
Photo, Engr. (#CB4)

1942, June 22

CB2 SPAP1 15c + 35c green 1.00
CB3 SPAP2 20c + 60c brown 1.00
CB4 SPAP3 30c + 90c car red 1.05
Nos. CB2-CB4 (3) 3.05

Native children's welfare fund.

Nos. CB2-CB4 were issued by the Vichy government in France, but were not placed on sale in Indo-China.

Colonial Education Fund
Common Design Type
Perf. 12½x13½

1942, June 22 **Engr.**
CB5 CD86a 12c + 18c blue & red 1.10

No. CB5 was issued by the Vichy government in France, but was not placed on sale in Indo-China.

POSTAGE DUE STAMPS

French Colonies No. J21 Surcharged

1904, June 26 **Unwmk.** ***Imperf.***
J1 D1 5c on 60c brn, *buff* 14.50 14.50

French Colonies Nos. J10-J11 Surcharged in Carmine

1905, July 22

J2 D1 5c on 40c black 32.00 16.00
J3 D1 10c on 60c black 32.00 20.00
J4 D1 30c on 60c black 32.00 20.00
Nos. J2-J4 (3) 96.00 56.00

Dragon from Steps of Angkor Wat — D1

1908 **Typo.** ***Perf. 14x13½***

J5 D1 2c black 1.40 1.00
J6 D1 4c dp bl 1.40 1.00
J7 D1 5c bl grn 1.75 1.10
J8 D1 10c carmine 3.00 1.10
J9 D1 15c violet 3.75 2.75
J10 D1 20c chocolate 1.90 1.40
J11 D1 30c ol grn 1.90 1.40
J12 D1 40c claret 8.50 7.25
J13 D1 50c grnsh bl 7.25 1.60
J14 D1 60c orange 12.00 11.00
J15 D1 1fr gray 24.00 18.50
J16 D1 2fr yel brn 24.00 18.50
J17 D1 5fr red 40.00 37.50
Nos. J5-J17 (13) 130.85 104.10

Surcharged in Cents or Piasters in Black, Blue or Red

1919

J18 D1 ⅘c on 2c blk 1.75 1.25
J19 D1 1⅗c on 4c dp bl 1.75 1.25
J20 D1 2c on 5c bl grn 3.00 1.60
J21 D1 4c on 10c car 4.25 1.25
J22 D1 6c on 15c vio 9.50 3.00
J23 D1 8c on 20c choc 6.75 2.40
J24 D1 12c on 30c ol grn 9.50 2.40
J25 D1 16c on 40c cl 9.50 2.00
J26 D1 20c on 50c grnsh bl 12.50 6.50
J27 D1 24c on 60c org 3.25 2.00
a. Closed "4" 20.00 16.00
J28 D1 40c on 1fr gray 5.50 1.60
a. Closed "4" 20.00 16.00
J29 D1 80c on 2fr yel brn 42.50 20.00
J30 D1 2pi on 5fr red 62.50 42.50
a. Double surcharge 240.00 190.00
b. Triple surcharge 225.00 180.00
Nos. J18-J30 (13) 172.25 87.75

Dragon from Steps of Angkor Wat — D2

"CENT" below Numerals

1922, Oct.

J31 D2 ⅖c black .25 .25
J32 D2 ⅘c red .30 .30
J33 D2 1c buff .50 .40
J34 D2 2c gray grn .65 .50
J35 D2 3c violet .75 .75
J36 D2 4c orange .75 .40
a. "4 CENTS" omitted 700.00
b. "4 CENTS" double 105.00 105.00
J37 D2 6c ol grn 1.60 .65
J38 D2 8c blk, *lav* 1.25 .65
J39 D2 10c dp bl 2.00 .65
J40 D2 12c ocher, *grnsh* 1.60 1.25
J41 D2 20c dp bl, *straw* 2.00 .90
J42 D2 40c red, *bluish* 2.00 1.10
J43 D2 1pi brn vio, *pnksh* 6.75 3.75
Nos. J31-J43 (13) 20.40 11.55

Pagoda of Mot Cot, Hanoi — D3

Dragon of Annam — D4

Perf. 14x13½, 13½x14

1927, Sept. 26

J44 D3 ⅖c vio brn & org .25 .25
J45 D3 ⅘c vio & blk .25 .25
J46 D3 1c brn red & sl .90 .90
J47 D3 2c grn & brn ol 1.00 1.00
J48 D3 3c red brn & bl 1.60 1.60
J49 D3 4c ind & brn 1.60 1.60
J50 D3 6c dp red & ver 2.00 1.60
J51 D3 8c ol brn & vio 1.60 1.25
J52 D4 10c dp bl 2.50 1.25
J53 D4 12c olive 5.75 4.75
J54 D4 20c rose 4.00 2.00
J55 D4 40c bl grn 4.00 3.50
J56 D4 1pi red org 20.00 20.00
Nos. J44-J56 (13) 45.45 39.95

Surcharged in Black or Blue — D5

1931-41 ***Perf. 13***

J57 D5 ⅕c red, *org* ('38) .25 .25
J58 D5 ⅖c red, *org* .25 .25
J59 D5 ⅘c red, *org* .25 .25
J60 D5 1c red, *org* .25 .25
J61 D5 2c red, *org* .25 .25
J62 D5 2.5c red, *org* ('40) .25 .25
J63 D5 3c red, *org* ('38) .40 .25
J64 D5 4c red, *org* .30 .30
J65 D5 5c red, *org* ('38) .40 .30
J66 D5 6c red, *org* .30 .30
J67 D5 10c red, *org* .30 .30
J68 D5 12c red, *org* .50 .30
J69 D5 14c red, *org* ('38) .50 .30
J70 D5 18c red, *org* ('41) .50 .50
J71 D5 20c red, *org* .50 .50
J72 D5 50c red, *org* .75 .50
J72A D5 1pi red, *org* 10.00 9.50
J73 D5 1pi red, *org* (Bl) 2.25 1.25
Nos. J57-J73 (18) 18.20 15.80

D6

D7

Perf. 12, 13½ and Compound

1943-44 **Litho.** **Unwmk.**

J74 D6 1c red, *org* .25 .25
J75 D6 2c red, *org* .25 .25
J76 D6 3c red, *org* .30 .30
J77 D6 4c red, *org* .30 .30
J78 D6 6c red, *org* .40 .40
J79 D6 10c red, *org* .40 .40
J80 D7 12c blue, *pnksh* .50 .50
J81 D7 20c blue, *pnksh* .50 .50
J82 D7 30c blue, *pnksh* .50 .50
Nos. J74-J82 (9) 3.40 3.40

Issued: 2c, 3c, 7/15/43; 6c-30c, 8/43; 1c, 4c, 6/10/44. Issued without gum.

OFFICIAL STAMPS

Regular Issues of 1931-32 Overprinted in Blue or Red

Perf. 13, 13½

1933, Feb. 27 **Unwmk.**

O1 A20 1c black brown (Bl) .80 .75
O2 A20 2c dark green (Bl) .90 .50

Regular Issues of 1931-32 Overprinted in Blue or Red

O3 A21 3c deep brown (Bl) 1.25 .65
a. Inverted overprint 160.00
O4 A21 4c dark blue (R) 1.50 .90
a. Inverted overprint 160.00
O5 A21 5c deep violet (Bl) 2.40 .90
O6 A21 6c orange red (Bl) 2.40 1.25

Regular Issues of 1931-32 Overprinted in Blue or Red

O7 A22 10c dk blue (R) 1.25 1.00
O8 A22 15c dk brown (Bl) 3.00 1.75
O9 A22 20c rose (Bl) 3.25 .85
O10 A22 21c olive grn (Bl) 3.00 1.75
O11 A22 25c dp violet (Bl) 1.60 .50
O12 A22 30c orange brn (Bl) 3.25 .85

Regular Issues of 1931-32 Overprinted in Blue or Red

O13 A23 50c dark brown (Bl) 12.50 3.50
O14 A23 60c dull violet (Bl) 2.75 2.40
O15 A23 1pi yellow green (Bl) 30.00 11.00
O16 A23 2pi red (Bl) 11.50 9.50
Nos. O1-O16 (16) 81.35 38.05

Type of 1922-23 Issue Overprinted diagonally in Black or Red

1934, Oct. 4 ***Perf. 14x13***

O17 A13 1c olive green 1.25 .75
O18 A13 2c brown orange 1.25 .75
O19 A13 3c yellow green 1.40 .65
O20 A13 4c cerise 2.50 1.30
O21 A13 5c yellow 1.40 .75
O22 A13 6c orange red 6.00 5.25
O23 A13 10c gray grn (R) 3.50 2.25
O24 A13 15c ultra 2.10 1.50
O25 A13 20c gray black (R) 2.00 1.50
O26 A13 21c light violet 11.00 9.25
O27 A13 25c rose lake 13.00 11.00
O28 A13 30c lilac gray 1.75 1.30
O29 A13 50c brt violet 8.00 6.75
O30 A13 60c gray 15.00 11.00
O31 A13 1pi blue (R) 30.00 24.50
O32 A13 2pi deep red 47.50 37.50
Nos. O17-O32 (16) 147.65 116.00

The value tablet has colorless numeral and letters on solid background.

PARCEL POST STAMPS

French Colonies No. 50 Overprinted

1891 **Unwmk.** ***Perf. 14x13½***
Q1 A9 10c black, *lavender* 24.00 10.50

The overprint on No. Q1 was also handstamped in shiny ink. Value unused, $750.

Indo-China No. 8 Overprinted

1898
Q2 A3 10c black, *lavender* 29.00 29.00

Nos. 8 and 9 Overprinted

1902

Q3 A3 10c black, *lavender* 55.00 35.00
a. Inverted overprint 115.00 50.00
Q4 A3 10c red 55.00 24.00
a. Inverted overprint 85.00 50.00
b. Double overprint 85.00 50.00

INDONESIA

ˌin-də-ˈnē-zhə

LOCATION — In the East Indies
GOVT. — Republic
AREA — 741,101 sq. mi.
POP. — 195,280,000 (1995 est.)
CAPITAL — Jakarta

Formerly Netherlands Indies, Indonesia achieved independence late in 1949 as the United States of Indonesia and became the Republic of Indonesia August 15, 1950. See Netherlands Indies for earlier issues.

100 Sen = 1 Rupiah

Catalogue values for all unused stamps in this country are for Never Hinged items.

Watermarks

Wmk. 404

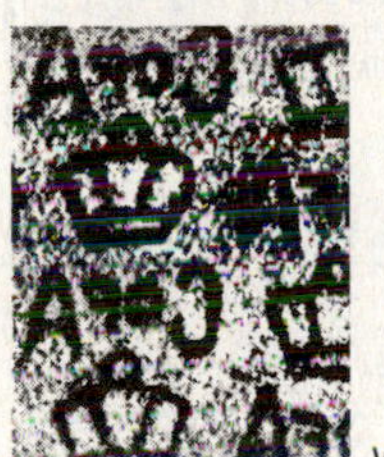

Wmk. 228

REVOLUTIONARY ISSUES

Following the surrender of Japan to the Allies in 1945, Indonesian nationalists declared independence and formed the Republic of Indonesia. On Sept. 27, the Djawan PTT (now PT Pos Indonesia) was established and assumed reponsibility for the postal system. Within days, civil war had broken out between the nationalists and the returning Dutch, who sought to reestablish control over their East Indies colony. During the hostilities, which continued until Dec. 1949, a Dutch blockade of the rebel strongholds in Java and Sumatra made regular communications between the two islands impossible, and the Djawan PTT was forced to organize separate postal services, using locally produced stamps, on Java and Sumatra.

JAVA ISSUES

Netherlands Indies Nos. 168, 200, 201 Ovptd. in Black or Red (R)

1945, Nov. ***Perf. 11½***
1L1 A17 1c lilac gray (R) 2.50 *3.50*
1L2 A17 2c plum 5.50 *7.50*
1L3 A17 3½c dark gray (R) 100.00 100.00
Nos. 1L1-1L3 (3) 108.00 111.00

Forgeries of Nos. 1L1-1L3 exist.

Netherlands Indies Nos. 228-231 Ovptd. in Black or Red (R)

1945, Nov. ***Perf. 12½***
1L4 A23 2½c rose violet 2.00 *3.50*
1L5 A24 3c green (R) 2.00 *3.50*
1L6 A25 4c olive green (R) 2.50 *4.50*
1L7 A26 5c blue (R) 150.00 *175.00*
Nos. 1L4-1L7 (4) 156.50 *186.50*

Forgeries of Nos. 1L4-1L7 exist.

Netherlands Indies Nos. N2, N3 Ovptd. in Black or Red (R)

1945, Nov. ***Perf. 12½***
1L8 OS2 3½s carmine 425.00 375.00
1L9 OS3 5s green (R) 25.00 22.50

Forgeries of Nos. 1L8-1L9 exist.

Netherlands Indies Nos. N5-N11 Ovptd. in Black or Red (R)

1945, Nov. ***Perf. 12½***
1L10 OS5 3½s rose red 50.00 50.00
1L11 OS6 5s yel grn (R) .80 *1.50*
1L12 OS7 10s dk blue (R) .80 *1.50*
a. Perf 12 2.50 2.50
1L13 OS8 20s gray ol (R) .85 *1.50*
1L14 OS9 40s rose lilac (R) .75 *1.50*
1L15 OS10 60s red orange 1.25 *1.50*
1L16 OS11 80s fawn 25.00 25.00
Nos. 1L10-1L16 (7) 79.45 *82.50*

Forgeries of Nos. 1L10-1L16 exist.

Netherlands Indies Nos. 200, 201, 228-230, N38 Overprinted in Red or Brown (Br)

Perf. 12½, 12x12½ (#A18, A19)
1945, Nov.
1L17 A17 1s lilac gray 2.25 *3.50*
1L18 A17 1s lilac gray (Br) 15.00 *17.50*
1L19 OS21 2s carmine 1.50 *2.00*
1L20 A23 2½s rose violet 25.00 25.00
1L21 A24 3s green 4.75 4.75
1L22 A25 4s olive green 4.50 *4.50*
Nos. 1L17-1L22 (6) 53.00 *57.25*

Forgeries of Nos. 1L17-1L22 exist.

A large number of proofs, both perf and imperf, in original and in different colors, exist for Nos. 1L23-1L50. All are scarce.

Bull — A1

Bull & Flag — A2

Perf. 11½
1945, Dec. 1 **Typo.** **Unwmk.**
With Gum
1L23 A1 10s chocolate 10.00 10.00
a. Imperf 110.00 *200.00*
1L24 A2 20s choc & carmine red 8.25 9.50

Issued to celebrate the first half-year of Indonesian independence.

Nos. 1L25-1L49 were issued without gum.

Road & Mountains — A3

Sentry — A4

Boat in Storm — A5

Wayang Puppet — A6

Kris & Flag — A7

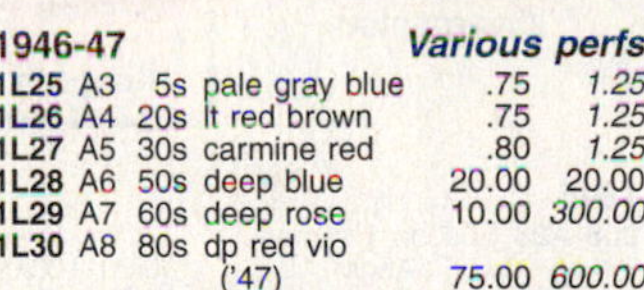

Temple — A8

1946-47 ***Various perfs***
1L25 A3 5s pale gray blue .75 *1.25*
1L26 A4 20s lt red brown .75 *1.25*
1L27 A5 30s carmine red .80 *1.25*
1L28 A6 50s deep blue 20.00 20.00
1L29 A7 60s deep rose 10.00 *300.00*
1L30 A8 80s dp red vio ('47) 75.00 *600.00*
Nos. 1L25-1L30 (6) 107.30 *923.75*

Issued: 5s, 20s, 6/1/46. 30s, 50s, 7/1/46. 60s, 9/1/46. 80s, 7/1/47.

Buffalo Breaking Chains — A9

Bandung, March 1946 — A10

Bombing of Soerabaya, Nov. 1945 — A11

Anti-aircraft Crew — A12

Quai at Tandjong Priok — A13

Pilot — A14

Ambarawa A15

Wonokroma Dam, Soerabaya A16

Meeting, Jakarta — A17

Mounted Soldier — A18

1946-47 ***Various perfs***
1L31 A9 3s dull carmine .35 *1.75*
a. Imperf .25 .25
1L32 A10 5s gray blue .60 *.95*
a. Imperf .35 .50
1L33 A11 10s blue black 11.50 6.25
a. Imperf 11.50 11.50
1L34 A11 15s dark purple .95 *1.25*
a. Imperf .95 .95
1L35 A12 30s green 2.40 *5.75*
a. Imperf 1.75 2.40
1L36 A13 40s dk blue vio .95 *2.40*
a. Imperf 1.00 1.00
1L37 A9 50s violet black 1.75 *2.90*
a. Imperf 1.20 1.20
1L38 A10 60s dp red vio 3.50 *4.50*
a. Imperf 1.75 1.75
1L39 A14 80s br rose red 1.20 *7.00*
a. Imperf *150.00*
1L40 A15 100s dull brn red 1.75 *3.50*
a. Imperf 1.20 1.20
1L41 A16 200s dull lilac 2.90 *3.50*
a. Imperf 1.50 2.40
1L42 A17 500s car red 15.00 *27.50*
a. Imperf 9.00 9.00
1L43 A18 1000s lt blue green 16.50 *30.00*
a. Imperf 7.00 7.00
Nos. 1L31-1L43 (13) 59.35 *97.25*

First anniv. of independence.
Issued: 3s, 10s-200s, 8/17/46. 5s, 500s, 1000s, 2/1/47.

Worker & Ship — A19

1948, Aug. 17 *Imperf.*

1L44 A19 50s dull blue 5.00 *5.00*
a. Perf 11 14.50
1L45 A19 100s dull scarlet 5.00 *7.50*
a. Perf 11 14.50

Nos. 1L44 and 1L45 were printed on paper with papermaker's watermark. Nos. 1L44a and 1L45a were printed on unwatermarked paper.

Flag Over Waves — A20

1949, July 20 *Imperf.*

1L46 A20 100s car rose 8.50 *9.00*
a. Perf 11 200.00 *350.00*
1L47 A20 150s car rose 10.00 *22.00*
a. Perf 11 62.50 *225.00*

Return of the Indonesian government to Jakarta.

Nos. 1L46-1L47 were printed on paper bearing papermaker's watermark "MADE IN U.S.A." once in each sheet, and a few stamps within each sheet bear portions of the watermark.

Nos. 1L46a, 1L47a overprinted in Black — No. A49

1949, Dec. 27 *Perf. 11*

1L48 A20 100s car rose 22.50
1L49 A20 150s car rose 25.00 *100.00*

Return of the Indonesian government to Jakarta.

POSTAGE DUE STAMPS

Netherlands Indies Nos. J29, J32a Overprinted — No. AJ1

1948 *Perf. 12½*

1LJ1 D5 25s on 7½c salmon 50.00 *50.00*
1LJ2 D5 25s on 15c salmon 60.00 *75.00*

MILITARY STAMP

M1

1949, Aug. Without Gum *Imperf.*

1LM1 M1 15r ultramarine *4,250. 5,250.*

No. 1LM1 was issued for provisional use at Surakarta, a Dutch stronghold in central Java, occupied by Indonesian forces in August, 1949.

SUMATRA ISSUES

Netherlands Indies Nos. 231, 201 Overprinted in Black

1946

2L1 A26 15s on 5c blue 1.25 *1.75*
2L2 A17 40s on 2c plum .80 *2.00*

Netherlands Indies Nos. 164//203 Overprinted

Overprint Bar is 5mm's thick.

1946

2L3 A17 20s on 3½c dk gray 32.50 40.00
2L4 A17 30s on 1c lilac gray 16.00 16.00
2L5 A17 40s on 2c plum 1.50 1.50
2L6 A17 60s on 2½c bister 200.00 *250.00*
2L7 A17 80s on 3c yel grn 16.50 *20.00*
Nos. 2L3-2L7 (5) 266.50 327.50

Some examples of Nos. 2L3-2L7 bear handstamps previously applied by local authorities during and after the Japanese occupation. Such multiply-overprinted stamps command prices that may be more or less than the values shown, which are for examples without other overprints.

Netherlands Indies Nos. 234, 236 Overprinted

1946

2L8 A28 50s on 17½c orange 100.00 100.00
2L9 A28 1r on 10c red org 22.50 *25.00*

Nos. 2L10-2L84 were issued without gum.

Farmer & Oxen in Rice Paddy — A23

Sentry & Flag — A24

Airplane over City — A25

1946, May 17 *Perf. 11½x10*

2L10 A23 5s (+25s) yel grn 1.25 2.25
2L11 A24 15s (+35s) deep red 2.50 *4.00*
2L12 A25 40s (+60s) orange 1.25 *2.50*
Nos. 2L10-2L12 (3) 5.00 *8.75*

Nos. 2L10-2L12 were sold at a premium over face value, not indicated on the stamps themselves, to benefit the Freedom Fund ("Fonds Kemerdekkan").

Pres. Soekarno — A26

1946, June 1 *Perf. 10¾*

2L13 A26 40s (+60s) red 1.25 2.00
2L14 A26 40s (+60s) deep red 15.00 15.00

Nos. 2L13-2L14 were sold at a premium over face value, not indicated on the stamps themselves, to benefit the Freedom Fund ("Fonds Kemerdekkan").

As Nos. 2L10-2L12, in different colors on thicker paper

1946, Aug. 17 *Perf. 11½x10*

2L15 A23 5s (+25s) turquoise 1.75 *3.00*
2L16 A24 15s (+35s) purple 1.75 *3.00*
2L17 A25 40s (+60s) deep red 9.00 *9.00*
2L18 A25 40s (+60s) bister 17.50 *30.00*
Nos. 2L15-2L18 (4) 30.00 *45.00*

Nos. 2L15-2L18 were sold at a premium over face value, not indicated on the stamps themselves, to benefit the Freedom Fund ("Fonds Kemerdekkan").

Nos. 2L15-2L17, One- or two-bar Overprint

1946 *Perf. 11½x10¾*

2L19 A23 5s turquoise 80.00 *125.00*
2L20 A24 15s purple 80.00 *125.00*
2L21 A25 40s deep red 75.00 110.00
Nos. 2L19-2L21 (3) 235.00 *360.00*

Farmer & Oxen in Rice Paddy — A26a

Sentry & Flag — A26b

Airplane over City — A26c

First Issue

1946-47 *Perf. 11¾x10½*

2L22 A26a 2s red 1.50 *4.00*
2L23 A26a 3s green 2.25 *10.00*
2L24 A26a 5s turquoise .65 *8.00*
2L25 A26b 15s purple .75 *3.50*
2L26 A26c 40s brown 1.00 *35.00*
Nos. 2L22-2L26 (5) 6.15 *60.50*

Second Issue

2L27 A26a 2s chocolate 5.00 *7.50*
2L28 A26a 3s orange 6.50 *5.00*
2L29 A26b 15s green 7.00 *7.50*
2L30 A26c 40s blue 30.00 *50.00*
Nos. 2L27-2L30 (4) 48.50 70.00

Japanese Occupation of Sumatra Revenue Stamps Overprinted

1947, May 12 *Various Rough Perfs*

2L31 A27 50s light red 50.00 *75.00*
2L32 A27 1f light red 45.00 *60.00*
2L33 A27 2f light red 35.00 *60.00*
2L34 A27 2.50f light red 30.00 *30.00*
Nos. 2L31-2L34 (4) 160.00 225.00

No. 2L13 Surcharged

1947, May 12

2L35 A26 50s on 40s red 10.00 10.00
2L36 A26 1f on 40s red 18.50 15.00
2L37 A26 1.50f on 40s red 12.00 10.00
2L38 A26 2.50f on 40s red 1.75 *5.00*
2L39 A26 3.50f on 40s red 2.50 *6.00*
2L40 A26 5f on 40s red 2.00 *5.00*
Nos. 2L35-2L40 (6) 46.75 *51.00*

Nos. 2L24, 2L26 Srchd. With Small Ornament Covering Original Value

1947

2L41 A26a 50s on 5s turq 15.00 15.00
2L42 A26a 1f on 5s turq 15.00 15.00
2L43 A26a 1.50f on 5s turq 18.00 15.00
2L44 A26c 1r on 40s purple 1.50 *3.00*
2L45 A26a 2r on 5s turq 2.25 *4.00*
Nos. 2L41-2L45 (5) 51.75 52.00

The tail of the surcharged "5" ends in a ball on No. 2L41. Compare with No. 2L65.

Types A26a-A26b Srchd., in Black or Red (R), with Large Ornament covering Original Value

1947

2L46 A26b 1s on 15s vio (R) 1.25 *3.50*
2L47 A26a 5s on 3s sl bl (R) 1.00 *3.00*
2L48 A26b 10s on 15s orange 1.25 *2.50*
2L49 A26a 50s on 3s br red 35.00 *42.50*
Nos. 2L46-2L49 (4) 38.50 51.50

Nos. 2L48 and 2L49 were not issued without ovpt.

No. 2L15 Surcharged

1947

2L50 A25 30s on 40s dp red 1.50 *2.00*
2L51 A25 50s on 40s dp red 25.00 *40.00*
2L52 A25 1f on 40s dp red 5.00 4.00
2L53 A25 1.50f on 40s dp red 7.50 *10.00*
2L54 A25 2.50f on 40s dp red 1.50 *2.50*
Nos. 2L50-2L54 (5) 40.50 58.50

Nos. 2L23-2L26, Srchd. in Black or Red, New Value 2.8mm High

1948

2L55 A26a .50f on 5s turq *1,200. 1,000.*
2L56 A26b .50f on 15s pur *1,200. 1,000.*
2L57 A26a 1f on 5s turq 200.00 175.00
2L58 A26b 1f on 15s pur 400.00 400.00
2L59 A26c 1f on 40s brn 750.00 1,250.
2L60 A26a 2.50f on 5s turq *1,250. 1,250.*
2L61 A26b 2.50f on 15s pur 750.00 675.00
2L62 A26b 5f on 15s pur *1,350. 1,100.*
2L63 A26c 5f on 40s brn 500.00 650.00
2L64 A26a 50s on 5s turq *1,650. 1,750.*
2L65 A26b 50s on 15s pur 525.00 *675.00*
Nos. 2L55-2L65 (11) 9,775. 9,925.

The tail of the surcharged "5" is plain on No. 2L64. Compare with No. 2L41.

New Currency

Values 3.2mm High

1949

2L66 A26a 2.50r on 3s grn 32.50 *40.00*
a. Red overprint 35.00 *50.00*
2L67 A26b 5r on 15s pur 12.50 25.00
a. Red overprint 15.00 *45.00*

2L68 A26a 10r on 3s grn 110.00 *150.00*
 a. Red overprint 125.00 *160.00*
 Nos. 2L66-2L68 (3) 155.00 *215.00*

Emergency provisional issue for Aceh Province.

Nos. 2L22, 2L23, 2L25, 2L26 Srchd. in Black or Red, New Value 4.5mm High

1949

2L69 A26a 2r on 3s grn 50.00 *75.00*
 a. Red overprint 55.00 *80.00*
2L70 A26a 2.50r on 3s grn 30.00 *75.00*
 a. Red overprint 32.50 *80.00*
2L71 A26b 5r on 15s pur 12.50 *20.00*
 a. Red overprint 14.00 *20.00*
2L72 A26a 10r on 3s grn 22.50 *60.00*
 a. Red overprint 25.00 *70.00*
2L73 A26a 20r on 2s red 400.00 *500.00*
 a. Red overprint 475.00 *600.00*
2L74 A26b 50r on 15s pur 525.00 *700.00*
 a. Red overprint 550.00 *750.00*
2L75 A26b 100r on 15s pur 225.00 225.00
 a. Red overprint 250.00 250.00
2L76 A26c 200r on 40s brn 250.00 250.00
 a. Red overprint 300.00 *350.00*
 Nos. 2L69-2L76 (8) 1,515. *1,905.*

Nos. 2L22, 2L25, 2L26 Srchd. in Black, New Value 7.2mm High

1949

2L77 A26b 10s on 15s pur 25.00 25.00
2L78 A26b 20s on 15s pur 25.00 25.00
2L79 A26b 30s on 15s pur 22.50 20.00
2L80 A26a 1r on 2s red 100.00 *200.00*
2L81 A26b 1.50f on 15s pur *1,000.*
2L82 A26b 2.50f on 15s pur 30.00 *75.00*
2L83 A26c 5r on 40s brn 375.00 250.00
 Nos. 2L77-2L83 (7) 577.50 1,595.

Nos. 1L46-1L47 Surcharged

1949

2L84 A20 15r on 100s car rose 40.00 *100.00*
2L85 A20 15r on 150s car rose 45.00 *100.00*

AIR POST STAMPS

Nos. 66, 75 Overprinted

1947

2LC1 A26 10r on 40s br red 5.00 *12.50*
2LC2 A26 20r on 5s turq 4.00 *10.00*

REPUBLIC OF INDONESIA

Nos. 1-119, C1-C61, CE1-CE4, CO1-CO16, E1-E1G, J1-J39 and O1-O24 were authorized by the Indonesia PTT and were produced in Vienna and Philadelphia. Because most were printed by the Austrian State Printing Office (Staatsdruckerei), they are usually described as the "Vienna" issues. The first issue was released in Dec. 1948, but supplies did not reach republican-held areas of Java and Sumatra until mid-Jan., 1949. Through 1949, small supplies of these issues were sent to some 20 post offices in Java and Sumatra, where they were used both for local mail and for foreign destinations, which was carried through the Dutch blockade by overseas (largely Indian) air carriers.

Following independence, the Vienna issues continued to be valid for postage for several years. While most covers on the market are philatelic in nature, commercial covers dated 1949-53 exist.

The Vienna issues were produced and heavily marketed by a U.S. stamp dealer. Proofs, deluxe sheetlets of one, and various overprints exist for these issues, as well as several unissued sets.

Values for the Vienna Issues are for mint never hinged stamps. Hinged examples are generally offered at 50-75% of these values. Used stamps are scarce, though generally not rare, and pricing information on values for used stamps is not presently available.

Map, Indonesian Archipelago A28

Farmer — A29

Red Cross Airplane A30

Balinese Dancer — A31

Military Officer, Flag of Republic A32

Designs: 1s, Map of Indonesian Archipelago. 2s, Republican sentry and Toba Lake, Sumatra. 2½, Military review, Gen. Soedirmari. 3s, Farmer working field with pitchfork. 3½s, Sultan Sjahrir and Thomas Jefferson. 4s, Buffalo Canyon, Sumatra. 5s, Policemen on motorcycles, Sastroamidjojo. 7½s, Red Cross nurse with wounded soldier. 10s, Dr. Maramis, Minister of Finance, and Alexander Hamilton. 15s, Construction of Great Postal Road, Java. 17½s, Hadji Agoes Salim, philosopher, and Benjamin Franklin. 20s, Red Cross Boeing aircraft. 30s, Djanger dancer, Bali. 35s, Planting rice. 40s, Vice Pres. Mohammed Hatta and Abraham Lincoln. 50s, Mountain, Sumatra. 60s, Rice fields, Java. 80s, Boy holding pineapple. 1r, Pres. Soekarno and George Washington. 2r, Mosque, Medan, Sumatra. 2½r, Fish ponds, Tjipanas. 5r, Officer presenting flag. 10r, Vice Pres. Hatta. 25r, Pres. Soekarno.

Perf. 14x13¾, 13¼x14 (#6), 13½x14¼ (#12, 14-16, 19, 20), 14¼x13½ (#13, 17, 17, 21), 12½ (#22-24)

Photo, Engr. (#22-24)

1948, Dec. 15 **Unwmk.**

No.	Type	Value / Color	Unused	Used
1	A28	1s dk turq grn & brn	.50	—
2	A28	2s dp brn & dp blue	.25	—
3	A28	2½s dk brn & org red	.35	—
4	A29	3s dk lil & dp red brn	.25	—
5	A28	3½s dk bl vio & br grn	.25	—
6	A29	4s dk bl vio & dp ol grn	.40	—
7	A28	5s turq & dull blue	.25	—
8	A28	7½s dp brn & dk lil	.35	—
9	A28	10s dp blue & brn rose	.50	—
10	A28	15s brown & dk grn	.75	—
11	A28	17½s ultra & org brn	.30	—
12	A30	20s Prus grn & dp bis brn	.45	—
13	A31	30s dk brn & dull vio	.30	—
14	A30	35s dk lilac & brn	.30	—
15	A30	40s dk brn & blue	.30	—
16	A30	50s dk brn & turq	.30	—
17	A31	60s dk brn & lt red brn	.50	—
18	A31	80s dk lilac & slate	.45	—
19	A30	1r br blue & pur brn	.35	—
20	A30	2r dk brn & dk grn	.55	—
21	A31	2½r dk lilac & blue	.65	—
22	A32	5r yel brn & black	5.00	—
23	A32	10r emerald & black	7.50	—
24	A32	25r rose red & blk	12.50	—
		Nos. 1-24 (24)	33.30	

See Nos. C1-C13.
For overprints, see Nos. 70-90, O1-O6.

A33

Designs: 10s, 25s, Map, ships. 15s, 60s, Dockworkers loading ship, vert. 1r, Ships.

1949, Aug. 17 **Photo.** ***Perf. 12½***

No.	Type	Value / Color	Unused	Used
25	A33	10s gray & green	1.00	—
26	A33	15s gray & maroon	1.00	—
27	A33	25s gray & blue	1.00	—
28	A33	60s maroon & gray	5.00	—
29	A33	1r org & dull blue	14.00	—
		Nos. 25-29 (5)	22.00	

Failure of Dutch blockade.
See Nos. C14-C18.

Sentry — A34

Soekarno Decorating Soldier — A35

Planting Rice — A36

Boy Holding Pineapple — A37

Military Officer, Flag of Republic A38

Designs: 1s, Republican sentry and Toba Lake, Sumatra. 2s, Soekarno decorating soldier. 2½s, Woman weaving batik. 3s, Metalcraft worker. 3½s, Construction of Great Postal Road, Java. 4s, Farmer working field with pitchfork. 5s, Javanese Wajang Wong dancer. 7½s, Planting rice on the sawah. 10s, Red Cross nurse with wounded soldier. 15s, Buffalo Canyon, Sumatra. 17½s, Plowing with oxen. 20s, Planting rice. 30s, Mountain, Sumatra. 35s, Boy holding pineapple. 40s, Fish ponds, Tjipanas. 50s, Djanger dancer, Bali. 60s, Javanese Serimpi court dancer. 80s, Mosque, Medan, Sumatra. 1r, Overcoming illiteracy. 2r, Idol. 2½r, Map of Indonesian Archipelago. 5r, Officer presenting flag. 10r, Vice Pres. Mohammed Hatta. 25r, Pres. Soekarno.

Country name inscription has been changed from "Repoeblik" to "Republik," to make spelling more American and less Dutch. This spelling change also officially changed Pres. Soekarno's name to Sukarno.

Perf. 14x13¾, 13¾x14 (#31-33, 35, 36, 39), 13½x14¼ (#41, 42, 47, 50), 14¼x13½ (#43-46), 12½ (#51-53)

Photo, Engr. (#51-53)

1949, Aug. 17

No.	Type	Value / Color	Unused	Used
30	A34	1s dp brn & dp blue	.30	—
31	A35	2s dk red vio & dp grn	.40	—
32	A35	2½s dk brn & br scarlet	.35	—
33	A35	3s dp turq & org ver	.45	—
34	A34	3½s dp brn & dp grn	.40	—
35	A35	4s turq & dull blue	.50	—
36	A35	5s dull vio & dk yel brn	.35	—
37	A34	7½s dp brn & dk lil	.40	—
38	A34	10s dk brn & dp vio	.50	—
39	A35	15s dk vio & dp dull grn	1.00	—
40	A34	17½s dk brn & red org	.75	—
41	A36	20s dull vio & dp brn	.25	—
42	A36	30s dp brn & dk blue vio	.60	—
43	A37	35s sl vio & blue	.25	—
44	A37	40s dull vio & dk yel brn	.45	—
45	A37	50s dk brn & Prus grn	.40	—
46	A37	60s br blue & dk yel brn	.75	—
47	A36	80s dull vio & dull bl	.75	—
48	A36	1r dp blue & dp choc	.50	—
49	A37	2r dp brn & org ver	.30	—
50	A36	2½r dp brn & br blue	1.50	—
51	A38	5r red vio & black	10.00	—
52	A38	10r green & black	6.00	—
53	A38	25r orange & black	10.00	—
		Nos. 30-53 (24)	37.15	

For overprints, see Nos. 91-111, O7-O12.

A39

A40

Designs: 10s, 25s, Map, ships. 15s, 60s, Dockworkers loading ship, vert. 1r, Ships.

1948, Dec. 15 Photo. *Perf. 14½*

54 A39 10s gray & red 2.00 —
55 A39 15s gray & dp blue 2.00 —
56 A39 25s gray & red brn 1.45 —
57 A39 60s gray & maroon 2.50 —
58 A39 1r gray & maroon 7.50 —
Nos. 54-58 (5) 15.45

Souvenir Sheets

59 A40 10s, 15s, 25s, 60s 100.00 —
a. Imperf 450.00 —
60 A40 30s, 50s, 1r, 2½r 45.00 —
a. Imperf 250.00 —
b. A39 2½r gray & maroon — —
c. As "b," imperf — —
61 A40 1r, 4½r 75.00 —
a. Imperf 100.00 —
b. A39 4½r maroon — —
c. As "b," imperf — —

Failure of Dutch blockade, second issue.
The stamps contained in No. 60 and the 4½r stamp contained in No. 61 are air post stamps and are inscribed "POS UDARA."
See Nos. C32-C36.
For overprints, see Nos. 112-119.

Map, UPU Emblem & *Banteng* (Nationalist Symbol) — A41

Wmk. 404

1949, Dec. 1 Photo. *Perf. 14*

62 A41 10s multicolored .55 —
a. Imperf .60 —
63 A41 20s multicolored .55 —
a. Imperf .60 —
64 A41 50s multicolored .60 —
a. Imperf .70 —
65 A41 1r multicolored .60 —
a. Imperf 1.00 —
b. Souvenir Sheet of 4, #62-65 30.00 —
c. As "b," imperf 35.00 —
Nos. 62-65 (4) 2.30

Unwatermarked

66 A41 10s multicolored .45 —
a. Imperf .45 —
67 A41 20s multicolored .45 —
a. Imperf .45 —
68 A41 50s multicolored .45 —
a. Imperf .45 —
69 A41 1r multicolored .45 —
a. Imperf .45 —
Nos. 66-69 (4) 1.80

Nos. 64, 65, 68 and 69 are air post stamps and are inscribed "POS UDARA."
Souvenir sheets of 4, as No. 65c, without watermark, are proofs.
Most varieties of Nos. 1-69 exist overprinted "RIS," "RIS Merdeka" and "RIS Djakarta." These were not issued in Indonesia.

Liberation of Jakarta

Nos. 1-21 Overprinted

1949, Dec. 7

70 A28 1s dk turq grn & brn .25 —
71 A28 2s dp brn & dp blue 1.25 —
72 A28 2½s dk brn & org red .25 —
73 A29 3s dk lil & dp red brn .45 —
74 A28 3½s dk bl vio & br grn .25 —
75 A29 4s dk bl vio & dp ol grn .75 —
76 A28 5s turq & dull blue .25 —
77 A28 7½s dp brn & dk lil .45 —
78 A28 10s dp blue & brn rose .25 —
79 A28 15s brown & dk grn 1.50 —
80 A28 17½s ultra & org brn 2.50 —
81 A30 20s Prus grn & dp bis brn 1.50 —
82 A31 30s dk brn & dull vio 5.00 —
83 A30 35s dk lilac & brn 7.00 —
84 A30 40s dk brn & blue 1.00 —
85 A30 50s dk brn & turq 7.00 —
86 A31 60s dk brn & lt red brn 8.00 —
87 A31 80s dk lilac & slate 2.50 —
88 A30 1r br blue & pur brn 5.00 —
89 A30 2r dk brn & dk grn 1.50 —
90 A31 2½r dk lilac & blue 12.50 —
Nos. 70-90 (21) 59.15

Nos. 30-50 overprinted

91 A34 1s dp brn & dp blue .25 —
92 A35 2s dk red vio & dp grn 2.00 —
93 A35 2½s dk brn & br scarlet .25 —
94 A35 3s dp turq & org ver .25 —
95 A34 3½s dp brn & dp grn .25 —
96 A35 4s turq & dull blue .25 —
97 A35 5s dull vio & dk yel brn .50 —
98 A34 7½s dp brn & dk lil .75 —
99 A34 10s dk brn & dp vio .75 —
100 A35 15s dk vio & dp dull grn 1.50 —
101 A34 17½s dk brn & red org 1.50 —
102 A36 20s dull vio & dp brn 4.00 —
103 A36 30s dp brn & dk blue vio 3.50 —
104 A37 35s sl vio & blue 3.50 —
105 A37 40s dull vio & dk yel brn 3.50 —
106 A37 50s dk brn & Prus grn 5.50 —
107 A37 60s br blue & dk yel brn 5.50 —
108 A36 80s dull vio & dull bl 6.00 —
109 A36 1r dp blue & dp choc 3.00 —
110 A37 2r dp brn & org ver 3.50 —
111 A36 2½r dp brn & br blue 7.50 —
Nos. 91-111 (21) 53.75

Nos. 54-61 overprinted

112 A39 10s gray & red .40 —
113 A39 15s gray & dp blue .40 —
114 A39 25s gray & red brn 1.40 —
115 A39 60s gray & maroon 1.40 —
116 A39 1r gray & maroon 3.50 —
Nos. 112-116 (5) 7.10

Souvenir Sheets

117 A40 10s, 15s, 25s, 60s 1,000. —
a. Imperf 2,500. —
118 A40 30s, 50s, 1r, 2½r 125.00 —
a. Imperf 250.00 —
b. A39 2½r gray & maroon — —
c. As "b," imperf — —
119 A40 1r, 4½r 50.00 —
a. Imperf 125.00 —
b. A39 4½r maroon — —
c. As "b," imperf — —

The stamps contained in No. 118 and the 4½r stamp contained in No. 119 are air post stamps and are inscribed "POS UDARA."

United States of Indonesia

Mountain, Palms and Flag of Republic — A49

Perf. 12½x12

1950, Jan. 17 Photo. Unwmk.
Size: 20½x26mm

333 A49 15s red 1.25 .30

Exists imperf, without gum. Value $70.

1950, June *Perf. 11½*
Size: 18x23mm

334 A49 15s red 6.25 1.25

Exists imperf, without gum. Value $50.

Netherlands Indies Nos. 307-315 Overprinted in Black

1950 *Perf. 11½, 12½*

335 A42 1s gray 1.00 .80
336 A42 2s claret 1.40 *3.50*
a. Perf 11½ 1.60 *2.00*
337 A42 2½s olive brown 1.00 .75
a. Perf 12½ 1.40 .70
338 A42 3s rose pink 1.00 .60
a. Perf 12½ .90 .45
339 A42 4s green 1.00 .75
a. Perf 12½ 1.60 1.00
340 A42 5s blue 1.00 .75
341 A42 7½s dark green 1.00 .75
342 A42 10s violet 1.00 .75
a. Perf 12½ 1.60 1.60
343 A42 12½s bright red 1.10 .75

Netherlands Indies Nos. 317-330 Overprinted in Black

Perf. 11½, 12½

345 A43 20s gray black 25.00 *32.50*
346 A43 25s ultra .85 .75
a. Perf 12½ 1.40 .75
347 A44 30s bright red 8.50 *20.00*
a. Perf 12½ 45.00 *65.00*
348 A44 40s gray green 1.00 .45
a. Perf 12½ 1.00 .45
349 A44 45s claret 1.80 1.10
350 A45 50s orange brown 1.50 1.00
351 A45 60s brown 7.25 *12.50*
a. Perf 12½ — 35.00
352 A45 80s scarlet 3.50 1.20
a. Perf 12½ 2.90 *1.00*

Perf. 11½, 20s, 45s, 50s. Others, both perfs.

Overprint 12mm High
Perf. 12½

353 A46 1r purple 2.10 .50
354 A46 2r olive green 360.00 100.00
355 A46 3r red violet 130.00 65.00
356 A46 5r dark brown 55.00 19.00
357 A46 10r gray 95.00 45.00
358 A46 25r orange brown 22.50 16.00
Nos. 335-358 (23) 723.50 324.40
Set, hinged 325.00

For overprints see Riau Archipelago Nos. 17-22.

Republic of Indonesia

Arms of the Republic — A50

Perf. 12½x12

1950, Aug. 17 Photo. Unwmk.

359 A50 15s red 1.75 .30
360 A50 25s dull green 2.75 1.60
361 A50 1r sepia 9.00 2.25
Nos. 359-361 (3) 13.50 4.15

5th anniv. of Indonesia's proclamation of independence.

Doves in Flight — A51

1951, Oct. 24 Engr. *Perf. 12*

362 A51 7½s blue green 2.75 1.00
363 A51 10s violet .85 .45
364 A51 20s red 1.75 1.00
365 A51 30s carmine rose 2.75 1.25
366 A51 35s ultra 2.75 1.25
367 A51 1r sepia 17.00 4.00
Nos. 362-367 (6) 27.85 8.95

6th anniv. of the UN and the 1st anniv. of the Republic of Indonesia as a member.

A52

Post Office — A53

Mythological Hero — A54

Pres. Sukarno — A55

1951-53 Photo. *Perf. 12½*

368 A52 1s gray .45 .90
369 A52 2s plum .45 .80
370 A52 2½s brown 6.50 .25
371 A52 5s car rose .45 .25
372 A52 7½s green .45 .25
373 A52 10s blue .50 .25
a. Perf 11½ 8.75 8.75
374 A52 15s purple .50 .25
375 A52 20s rose red .50 .25
376 A52 25s deep green .50 .25
377 A53 30s red orange .25 .25
378 A53 35s purple .40 .25
379 A53 40s dull green .25 .25
380 A53 45s deep claret .25 .30
381 A53 50s brown 2.50 .25
382 A54 60s dark brown .25 .25
383 A54 70s gray .25 .25
384 A54 75s ultra .25 .25
385 A54 80s claret .25 .25
386 A54 90s gray green .25 .25
Nos. 368-386 (19) 15.20 6.00

Perf. 12½x12

387 A55 1r purple .30 .25
388 A55 1.25r dp orange 1.25 .25
389 A55 1.50r brown .30 .25
390 A55 2r green .30 .25
391 A55 2.50r rose brown .30 .25
392 A55 3r blue .30 .25
392A A55 4r apple green .30 .25
393 A55 5r brown .30 .25
394 A55 6r rose lilac .30 .25
395 A55 10r slate .30 .25
396 A55 15r yellow .30 .25
397 A55 20r sepia .30 .25
398 A55 25r scarlet .80 .25
399 A55 40r yellow green .80 2.75
400 A55 50r violet 1.20 .25
Nos. 387-400 (15) 7.35 6.25

Nos. 368-376, 387, 390, 392, 393, 395, 398 were issued in 1951; Nos. 377-386, 388-389, 391, 392A, 394, 396-397, 399-400 in 1953.
Values are for the later Djakarta printings which have thicker numerals and a darker over-all impression. An earlier printing by Joh. Enschede and Sons, Haarlem, Netherlands, sell for more. The Enschede printing is on thicker paper and has more contrast between the portrait and the background.
For surcharge see No. B68. For overprints see Riau Archipelago Nos. 1-16, 32-40.

Melati Flowers — A56

1953, Dec. 22 *Perf. 12½*
401 A56 50s blue green 9.00 .70

25th anniv. of the formation of the Indonesian Women's Congress.

Crowd Releasing Doves — A57

1955, Apr. 18 *Perf. 13x12½*
402 A57 15s gray .40 .75
403 A57 35s brown .65 .75
404 A57 50s deep magenta 1.75 .75
405 A57 75s blue green 1.25 .75
Nos. 402-405 (4) 4.05 3.00

Asian-African Conf., Bandung, April 18-24.

Proclamation of Independence A58

1955, Aug. 17 **Photo.** *Perf. 12½*
406 A58 15s green .75 .90
407 A58 35s ultra .75 .90
408 A58 50s brown 4.50 .55
409 A58 75s magenta .80 .80
Nos. 406-409 (4) 6.80 3.15

Ten years of independence.

Voters — A59

1955, Sept. 29 *Perf. 12*
Without gum
410 A59 15s rose violet .60 .75
411 A59 35s green .60 .75
412 A59 50s carmine rose 2.10 .50
413 A59 75s lt ultra .85 .65
Nos. 410-413 (4) 4.15 2.65

First free elections in Indonesia.

Mas Soeharto Postmaster General — A60

1955, Sept. 27 *Perf. 12½*
414 A60 15s brown .80 .75
415 A60 35s dark carmine .80 .75
416 A60 50s ultra 5.00 2.00
417 A60 75s dull green 2.00 .75
Nos. 414-417 (4) 8.60 4.25

Issued to mark 10 years of Indonesia's Postal, Telegraph and Telephone system.

Helmet, Wreath and Monument — A61

1955, Nov. 10
418 A61 25s bluish green .40 .30
419 A61 50s ultra 1.25 .70
420 A61 1r dk car rose 8.00 .30
Nos. 418-420 (3) 9.65 1.30

Issued in honor of the soldiers killed in the war of liberation from the Netherlands.

Torch, Book and Map — A62

1956, May 26 **Photo.**
421 A62 25s ultra .90 .30
422 A62 50s carmine rose 4.50 1.25
423 A62 1r dark green 1.75 1.25
Nos. 421-423 (3) 7.15 2.80

Asia-Africa Student Conf., Bandung, May, 1956.

Lesser Malay Chevrotain — A63

Animals: 5s, 10s, Lesser Malay chevrotain. 20s, 25s, Otter. 35s, Malayan pangolin. 50s, Banteng. 75s, Asiatic two-horned rhinoceros.

1956 **Unwmk.** *Perf. 12½x13½*
424 A63 5s deep ultra .25 .25
425 A63 10s yellow brown .25 .25
426 A63 15s rose violet .25 .25
427 A63 20s dull green .25 .25
428 A63 25s deep claret .25 .25
429 A63 35s brt violet blue .25 .25
430 A63 50s brown .25 .25
431 A63 75s dark brown .25 .25
Nos. 424-431 (8) 2.00 2.00

See Nos. 450-456. For overprints see Riau Archipelago Nos. 23-31.

Dancing Girl and Gate — A64

1956, Oct. 7 *Perf. 12½x12*
432 A64 15s slate green .50 .60
433 A64 35s brown violet 1.25 .60
434 A64 50s blue black 2.00 1.10
435 A64 75s deep claret 2.50 1.10
Nos. 432-435 (4) 6.25 3.40

Founding of the city of Jogjakarta, 200th anniv.

Telegraph Key — A65

1957, May 10 **Unwmk.**
436 A65 10s lt crimson 2.00 .60
437 A65 15s brt blue .50 .30
438 A65 25s gray .40 .25
439 A65 50s brown red .50 .30
440 A65 75s lt blue green .50 .25
Nos. 436-440 (5) 3.90 1.70

Indonesian telegraph system centenary.

Thrift Symbolism — A66

Design: 15s, 1r, People and hands holding wreath of rice and cotton.

1957, July 12 **Photo.** *Perf. 12½*
441 A66 10s blue .45 .45
442 A66 15s rose carmine .45 .45
443 A66 50s green .90 .75
444 A66 1r brt violet 1.40 .25
Nos. 441-444 (4) 3.20 1.90

Cooperation Day, July 12.

Douglas DC-3 — A67

Aircraft: 15s, Helicopter. 30s, Miles Magister. 50s, Two-motor plane of Indonesian Airways. 75s, De Havilland Vampire.

1958, Apr. 9 *Perf. 12½x12*
445 A67 10s reddish brown .25 .25
446 A67 15s blue .25 .25
447 A67 35s orange .25 .25
448 A67 50s bright green .45 .40
449 A67 75s gray .80 .40
Nos. 445-449 (5) 2.00 1.55

Issued for National Aviation Day, April 9.

Animal Type of 1956

Animals: 30s, Otter. 40s, 45s, Malayan pangolin. 60s, 70s, Banteng. 80s, 90s, Asiatic two-horned rhinoceros.

1958 **Photo.** *Perf. 12½x13½*
450 A63 30s orange .25 .25
451 A63 40s brt yellow grn .25 .25
452 A63 45s rose lilac 1.00 .25
453 A63 60s dark blue .25 .25
454 A63 70s orange ver 1.75 .30
455 A63 80s red .30 .25
456 A63 90s yellow green .30 .25
Nos. 450-456 (7) 4.10 1.80

Thomas Cup A68

1958, Aug. 15 *Perf. 13½x13*
457 A68 25s rose carmine .25 .25
458 A68 50s orange .25 .25
459 A68 1r brown .30 .25
Nos. 457-459 (3) .80 .75

Indonesia's victory in the 1958 Thomas Cup World Badminton Championship.

Satellite Circling Globe — A69

1958, Oct. 15 **Litho.** *Perf. 12½x12*
460 A69 10s dk grn, pink & lt bl .85 .60
461 A69 15s vio, gray & pale blu-ish grn .25 .25
462 A69 35s brown, blue & pink .25 .25
463 A69 50s bl, redsh brn & gray .25 .25
464 A69 75s black, vio & buff .25 .25
Nos. 460-464 (5) 1.85 1.60

International Geophysical Year, 1957-58.

Bicyclist and Map A70

1958, Nov. 15 **Photo.** *Perf. 13½x13*
465 A70 25s bright blue .45 .30
466 A70 50s brown carmine .60 .30
467 A70 1r gray .35 .30
Nos. 465-467 (3) 1.40 .90

Bicycle Tour of Java, Aug. 15-30.

Man Looking into Light — A71

Designs: 15s, Hands and flame. 35s, Woman holding candle. 50s, Family hailing torch. 75s, Torch and "10."

1958, Dec. 10 *Perf. 12½x12*
468 A71 10s gray brown .25 .25
469 A71 15s dull red brn .25 .25
470 A71 35s ultra .25 .25
471 A71 50s pale brown .25 .25
472 A71 75s lt blue grn .25 .25
Nos. 468-472 (5) 1.25 1.25

10th anniv. of the signing of the Universal Declaration of Human Rights.

Wild Boar (Babirusa) — A72

Animals: 15s, Anoa (smallest buffalo). 20s, Orangutan. 50s, Javan rhinoceros. 75s, Komodo dragon (lizard). 1r, Malayan tapir.

1959, June 1 **Photo.** *Perf. 12*
473 A72 10s olive bis & sepia .25 .25
474 A72 15s org brn & sepia .25 .25
475 A72 20s lt ol grn & sepia .30 .30
476 A72 50s bister brn & sepia .45 .45
477 A72 75s dp rose & sepia .45 .25
478 A72 1r blue grn & blk .55 .25
Nos. 473-478 (6) 2.25 1.75

Issued to publicize wildlife preservation.

A73

1959, Aug. 17 **Litho.** *Perf. 12*
479 A73 20s blue & red .25 .25
480 A73 50s rose red & blk .25 .25
481 A73 75s brown & red .25 .25
482 A73 1.50r lt green & blk .25 .25
Nos. 479-482 (4) 1.00 1.00

Introduction of the constitution of 1945 embodying "guided democracy."

Factories — A74

Designs: 20s, 75s, Cogwheel and train. 1.15r, Means of transportation.

1959, Oct. 26 **Photo.** *Perf. 12*
483 A74 15s brt green & blk .25 .25
484 A74 20s dull org & blk .25 .25
485 A74 50s red & black .25 .25
486 A74 75s brt grnsh bl & blk .25 .25
487 A74 1.15r magenta & blk .25 .25
Nos. 483-487 (5) 1.25 1.25

11th Colombo Plan Conference, Jakarta.

Mother & Child, WRY Emblem — A75

15s, 75s, Destroyed town & fleeing family. 20s, 1.15r, World Refugee Year emblem.

1960, Apr. 7 Unwmk. *Perf. 12½x12*

No.	Type	Description	Unused	Used
488	A75	10s claret & blk	.25	.25
489	A75	15s bister & blk	.25	.25
490	A75	20s org brn & blk	.25	.25
491	A75	50s green & blk	.25	.25
492	A75	75s dk blue & blk	.25	.25
493	A75	1.15r scarlet & blk	.25	*1.10*
		Nos. 488-493 (6)	1.50	2.35

World Refugee Year, 7/1/59-6/3/60.

Tea Plantation — A76

5s, Oil palms. 10s, Sugar cane and railroad. 15s, Coffee. 20s, Tobacco. 50s, Coconut palms. 75s, Rubber plantation. 1.15r, Rice.

1960 *Perf. 12x12½*

No.	Type	Description	Unused	Used
494	A76	5s gray	.25	.25
495	A76	10s red brown	.25	.25
496	A76	15s plum	.25	.25
497	A76	20s ocher	.25	.25
498	A76	25s brt blue grn	.25	.25
499	A76	50s deep blue	.25	.25
500	A76	75s scarlet	.25	.25
501	A76	1.15r plum	.25	.25
		Nos. 494-501 (8)	2.00	2.00

For surcharges see Nos. B132-B134.

Anopheles Mosquito — A77

1960, Nov. 12 Photo. *Perf. 12x12½*

No.	Type	Description	Unused	Used
502	A77	25s carmine rose	.25	.25
503	A77	50s orange brown	.25	.25
504	A77	75s brt green	.25	.25
505	A77	3r orange	.30	.30
		Nos. 502-505 (4)	1.05	1.05

World Health Day, Nov. 12, 1960, and to promote malaria control.

Pres. Sukarno with Hoe — A78

1961, Feb. 15 *Perf. 12½x12*

No.	Type	Description	Unused	Used
506	A78	75s gray	.70	.25

Planned National Development.

Dayak Dancer of Borneo A79

Designs: 10s, Ambonese boat. 15s, Tangkubanperahu crater. 20s, Bull races. 50s, Toradja houses. 75s, Balinese temple. 1r, Lake Toba. 1.50r, Balinese dancer and musicians. 2r, Buffalo hole, view. 3r, Borobudur Temple, Java.

1961 *Perf. 13½x13*

No.	Type	Description	Unused	Used
507	A79	10s rose lilac	.50	.55
508	A79	15s gray	.50	.55
509	A79	20s orange	.50	.55
510	A79	25s orange ver	.50	.55
511	A79	50s carmine rose	.50	.55
512	A79	75s red brown	.50	.55
513	A79	1r brt green	.90	.45
514	A79	1.50r bister brn	.90	.45
515	A79	2r grnsh blue	1.40	.45
516	A79	3r gray	1.40	.45
		Set of 4 souvenir sheets	24.00	22.50
		Nos. 507-516 (10)	7.60	5.10

Issued for tourist publicity.

The four souvenir sheets among them contain one each of Nos. 507-516 imperf., with two or three stamps to a sheet and English marginal inscriptions: "Visit Indonesia" and "Visit the Orient Year." Size: 139x105mm or 105x139mm.

Sports Hall and Thomas Cup A80

Perf. 13½x12½

1961, June 1 Photo.

No.	Type	Description	Unused	Used
517	A80	75s pale violet & blue	.25	.25
518	A80	1r citron & dk grn	.25	.25
519	A80	3r salmon pink & dk bl	.30	.25
		Nos. 517-519 (3)	.80	.75

1961 Thomas Cup World Badminton Championship.

New Buildings and Workers A81

1961, July 6 Unwmk.

No.	Type	Description	Unused	Used
520	A81	75s violet & grnsh bl	.25	.25
521	A81	1.50r emerald & buff	.25	.25
522	A81	3r dk red & salmon	.40	.25
		Nos. 520-522 (3)	.90	.75

16th anniversary of independence.

Sultan Hasanuddin — A82

Portraits: 20s, Abdul Muis. 30s, Surjopranoto. 40s, Tengku Tjhik Di Tiro. 50s, Teuku Umar. 60s, K. H. Samanhudi. 75s, Captain Pattimura. 1r, Raden Adjeng Kartini. 1.25r, K. H. Achmad Dahlan. 1.50r, Tuanku Imam Bondjol. 2r, Si Singamangaradja XII. 2.50r, Mohammad Husni Thamrin. 3r, Ki Hadjar Dewantoro. 4r, Djenderal Sudirman. 4.50r, Dr. G. S. S. J. Ratulangie. 5r, Pangeran Diponegoro. 6r, Dr. Setyabudi. 7.50r, H. O. S. Tjokroaminoto. 10r, K. H. Agus Salim. 15r, Dr. Soetomo.

Perf. 13½x12½

1961-62 Unwmk. Photo.

Black Inscriptions; Portraits in Sepia

No.	Type	Description	Unused	Used
523	A82	20s olive	.25	.30
524	A82	25s gray olive	.25	.30
525	A82	30s brt lilac	.25	.30
526	A82	40s brown orange	.25	.30
527	A82	50s bluish green	.25	.30
528	A82	60s green ('62)	.25	.30
529	A82	75s lt red brown	.25	.30
530	A82	1r lt blue	.90	.30
531	A82	1.25r lt ol grn ('62)	.60	.30
532	A82	1.50r emerald	.90	.30
533	A82	2r org red ('62)	.60	.30
534	A82	2.50r rose claret	.90	.30
535	A82	3r gray blue	.75	.30
536	A82	4r olive green	.75	.30
537	A82	4.50r red lilac ('62)	.35	.30
538	A82	5r brick red	.85	.30
539	A82	6r bister ('62)	.75	.30
540	A82	7.50r violet bl ('62)	.85	.30
541	A82	10r green ('62)	1.25	.30
542	A82	15r dp org ('62)	.60	.30
		Nos. 523-542 (20)	11.80	6.00

National heroes. The 25s, 75s, 1.50r, 5r issued on 8/17, Independence Day; 40s, 50s, 4r on 10/5, Army Day; 20s, 30s, 1r, 2.50r, 3r on 11/10, Republic Day; 60s, 2r, 7.50r, 15r on 10/5/62; 1.25r, 4.50r, 6r, 10r on 11/10/62.

Symbols of Census A83

1961, Sept. 15 *Perf. 13½x12½*

No.	Type	Description	Unused	Used
543	A83	75s rose violet	.60	.25

First census in Indonesia.

Djataju — A84

Scenes from Ramayana Ballet: 40s, Hanuman. 1r, Dasamuka. 1.50r, Kidang Kentiana. 3r, Dewi Sinta. 5r, Rama.

Perf. 12x12½

1962, Jan. 15 Unwmk.

No.	Type	Description	Unused	Used
544	A84	30s ocher & red brn	.35	.45
545	A84	40s rose lilac & vio	.35	.45
546	A84	1r green & claret	.45	.45
547	A84	1.50r sal pink & dk grn	.55	.45
548	A84	3r pale grn & dp bl	1.10	.45
549	A84	5r brn org & dk brn	1.40	.45
		Nos. 544-549 (6)	4.20	2.70

Asian Games Emblem — A85

Main Stadium — A86

Designs: 10s, Basketball. 15s, Main Stadium, Jakarta. 20s, Weight lifter. 25s, Hotel Indonesia. 30s, Cloverleaf intersection. 40s, Discus thrower. 50s, Woman diver. 60s, Soccer. 70s, Press House. 75s, Boxers. 1r, Volleyball. 1.25r, 2r, 3r, 5r, Asian Games emblem. 1.50r, Badminton. 1.75r, Wrestlers. 2.50r, Woman rifle shooter. 4.50r, Hockey. 6r, Water polo. 7.50r, Tennis. 10r, Table tennis. 15r, Bicyclist. 20r, Welcome Monument.

1962 Photo. *Perf. 12½*

No.	Type	Description	Unused	Used
550	A85	10s green & yel	.25	.25
551	A86	15s grnsh blk & bis	.25	.25
552	A85	20s red lil & lt grn	.30	.25
553	A86	25s car & lt grn	.25	.25
554	A86	30s bl grn & yel	.35	.25
555	A85	40s ultra & pale bl	.35	.25
556	A85	50s choc & gray	.35	.30
557	A85	60s lil rose & vio gray	.35	.30
558	A85	70s dk brn & rose	.35	.30
559	A85	75s choc & org	.35	.25
560	A85	1r purple & lt bl	.35	.30
561	A85	1.25r dk bl & rose car	.35	.40
562	A85	1.50r red org & lil	1.25	.40
563	A85	1.75r dk car & rose	.80	.40
564	A85	2r brn & yel grn	.55	.40
565	A85	2.50r dp bl & lt grn	.70	.40
566	A85	3r black & dk red	.70	.40
567	A85	4.50r dk grn & red	.70	.40
568	A85	5r gray grn & lem	.70	.40
569	A85	6r brn red & dp yel	.75	.40
570	A85	7.50r red brn & sal	.75	.25
571	A85	10r dk blue & blue	1.00	.55
572	A85	15r dl vio & pale vio	1.25	1.10
573	A85	20r dk grn & ol bis	2.40	1.25
		Nos. 550-573 (24)	15.40	9.70

4th Asian Games, Jakarta.

Malaria Eradication Emblem — A87

1962, Apr. 7 *Perf. 12½x12*

No.	Type	Description	Unused	Used
574	A87	40s dull bl & vio bl	.25	.25
575	A87	1.50r yel org & brn	.25	.25
576	A87	3r green & indigo	.25	.25
577	A87	6r lilac & blk	.25	.25
		Nos. 574-577 (4)	1.00	1.00

WHO drive to eradicate malaria. The 1.50r and 6r have Indonesian inscription on top.

Atom Diagram — A88

1962, Sept. 24 Photo. *Perf. 12x12½*

No.	Type	Description	Unused	Used
578	A88	1.50r dk blue & yel	.25	.25
579	A88	4.50r brick red & yel	.25	.30
580	A88	6r green & yel	.30	.30
		Nos. 578-580 (3)	.80	.85

Development through science.

Pacific Travel Association Emblem — A89

1.50r, Prambanan Temple and Mount Merapi. 6r, Balinese Meru (Buildings), Pura Taman Ajun.

1963, Mar. 14 Unwmk.

No.	Type	Description	Unused	Used
581	A89	1r grn & indigo	.25	.25
582	A89	1.50r olive & indigo	.25	.25
583	A89	3r ocher & indigo	.35	.25
584	A89	6r dp org & indigo	.35	.25
		Nos. 581-584 (4)	1.20	1.00

12th conf. of the Pacific Area Travel Assoc., Bandung.

Mechanized Plow — A90

1r, 3r, Hand holding rice stalks, vert.

1963, Mar. 21 *Perf. 12½x12, 12x12½*

No.	Type	Description	Unused	Used
585	A90	1r blue & yel	.25	.25
586	A90	1.50r brt grn & indigo	.25	.25
587	A90	3r rose car & org	.25	.25
588	A90	6r orange & blk	.25	.25
		Nos. 585-588 (4)	1.00	1.00

FAO "Freedom from Hunger" campaign. English inscription on 3r and 6r.

Long-Armed Lobster — A91

Fish: 1.50r, Little tuna. 3r, River roman. 6r, Chinese pompano.

1963, Apr. 6 *Perf. 12½x12*

No.	Type	Description	Unused	Used
589	A91	1r ver, blk & yel	.25	.25
590	A91	1.50r ultra, blk & yel	.25	.25
591	A91	3r Prus bl, bis & car	.75	.40
592	A91	6r ol grn, blk & ocher	.75	.60
		Nos. 589-592 (4)	2.00	1.50

Pen and Conference Emblem — A92

Designs: 1.50r, Pen, Emblem and map of Africa and Southeast Asia. 3r, Globe, pen and broken chain, vert. 6r, Globe, hand holding pen and broken chain, vert.

Perf. 12½x12, 12x12½

1963, Apr. 24 Photo. Unwmk.

593	A92	1r lt bl & dp org	.25	.25
594	A92	1.50r pale vio & mar	.25	.25
595	A92	3r olive, bl & blk	.30	.25
596	A92	6r brick red & blk	.45	.25
		Nos. 593-596 (4)	1.25	1.00

Asian-African Journalists' Conference.

"Indonesia's Flag from Sabang to Merauke" — A93

4.50r, Parachutist landing in New Guinea. 6r, Bird of paradise & map of New Guinea.

1963, May 1 ***Perf. 12½x12***

597	A93	1.50r org brn, blk & red	.25	.25
598	A93	4.50r multicolored	.25	.25
599	A93	6r multicolored	.65	.65
		Nos. 597-599 (3)	1.15	1.15

Issued to mark the acquisition of Netherlands New Guinea (West Irian).

Centenary Emblem — A94

Design: 1.50r, 6r, Red Cross.

1963, May 8 ***Perf. 12***

600	A94	1r brt grn & red	.25	.25
601	A94	1.50r lt bl & red	.25	.25
602	A94	3r gray & red	.25	.25
603	A94	6r yel bis & red	.25	.25
		Nos. 600-603 (4)	1.00	1.00

Centenary of the International Red Cross.

Bank of Indonesia, Djalan A95

Daneswara, God of Prosperity A96

1963, July 5 Photo. ***Perf. 12***

604	A95	1.75r lt bl & pur	.25	.25
605	A96	4r citron & sl grn	.25	.25
606	A95	6r lt green & brn	.25	.25
607	A96	12r org & dk red brn	.25	.25
		Nos. 604-607 (4)	1.00	1.00

Issued for National Banking Day.

Standard Bearers — A97

Designs: 1.75r, "Pendet" dance. 4r, GANEFO building, Senajan, Jakarta. 6r, Archery. 10r, Badminton. 12r, Javelin. 25r, Sailing. 50r, Torch.

1963, Nov. 10 Unwmk. ***Perf. 12½***

608	A97	1.25r gray vio & dk brn	.25	.25
609	A97	1.75r org & ol grn	.25	.25
610	A97	4r emer & dk brn	.25	.25
611	A97	6r rose brn & blk	.25	.25
612	A97	10r lt ol grn & dk brn	.25	.25
613	A97	12r rose car & grnsh blk	.30	.25
614	A97	25r blue & dk blue	.40	.40
615	A97	50r red & black	.45	.45
		Nos. 608-615 (8)	2.40	2.35

1st Games of the New Emerging Forces, GANEFO, Jakarta, Nov. 10-22.

Pres. Sukarno — A98

1964 Photo. ***Perf. 12½x12***

616	A98	6r brown & dk bl	.25	.25
617	A98	12r bister & plum	.25	.25
618	A98	20r blue & org	.25	.25
619	A98	30r red org & bl	.25	.25
620	A98	40r green & brn	.25	.25
621	A98	50r red & dp grn	.25	.25
622	A98	75r vio & red org	.25	.25
623	A98	100r sil & red brn	.25	.25
624	A98	250r dk blue & sil	.25	.25
625	A98	500r red & gold	.30	.30
		Nos. 616-625 (10)	2.55	2.55

See Nos. B165-B179. For surcharges see Nos. 661, 663-667.

Trailer Truck — A99

Designs: 1r, Oxcart. 1.75r, Freighter. 2r, Lockheed Electra plane. 2.50r, Buginese sailboat, vert. 4r, Mailman with bicycle. 5r, Dakota plane. 7.50r, Teletype operator. 10r, Diesel train. 15r, Passenger ship. 25r, Convair Coronado Plane. 35r, Telephone switchboard operator.

1964 ***Perf. 12x12½, 12½x12***

626	A99	1r dull claret	.25	.25
627	A99	1.25r red brown	.25	.25
628	A99	1.75r Prus blue	.25	.25
629	A99	2r red orange	.25	.25
630	A99	2.50r brt blue	.25	.25
631	A99	4r bluish grn	.25	.25
632	A99	5r olive bister	.25	.25
633	A99	7.50r brt green	.25	.25
634	A99	10r orange	.25	.25
635	A99	15r dark blue	.25	.25
636	A99	25r violet blue	.25	.25
637	A99	35r red brown	.25	.25
		Nos. 626-637 (12)	3.00	3.00

For surcharges see Nos. 659-660, 662.

Ramses II — A100

Design: 6r, 18r, Kiosk of Trajan, Philae.

1964, Mar. 8 ***Perf. 12½x12***

638	A100	4r ol bis & ol grn	.25	.25
639	A100	6r grnsh bl & ol grn	.25	.25
640	A100	12r rose & ol grn	.30	.25
641	A100	18r emer & ol grn	.30	.25
		Nos. 638-641 (4)	1.10	1.00

UNESCO world campaign to save historic monuments in Nubia.

Stamps of Netherlands Indies and Indonesia — A101

1964, Apr. 1 ***Perf. 12½***

642	A101	10r gold, dk bl & red org	1.00	.25

Centenary of postage stamps in Indonesia.

Indonesian Pavilion — A102

1964, May 16 ***Perf. 12½x12***

643	A102	25r sil, blk, red & dk bl	.35	.45
644	A102	50r gold, Prus bl, red & grn	.75	.45

New York World's Fair, 1964-65.

Thomas Cup — A103

1964, Aug. 15 ***Perf. 12½x13½***

645	A103	25r brt grn, gold & red	.25	.30
646	A103	50r ultra, gold & red	.30	.30
647	A103	75r purple, gold & red	.45	.95
		Nos. 645-647 (3)	1.00	1.55

Thomas Cup Badminton World Championship, 1964.

Cruisers and Map of West Irian — A104

30r, Submarine. 40r, Torpedo boat.

Perf. 12½x12

1964, Oct. 5 Photo. Unwmk.

648	A104	20r yellow & brn	.30	.25
649	A104	30r rose & blk	.35	.25
650	A104	40r brt grn & ultra	.65	.95
		Nos. 648-650 (3)	1.30	1.45

Issued to honor the Indonesian Navy.

Map of Africa and Asia and Mosque — A105

15r, 50r, Mosque and clasped hands.

1965, Mar. 6 Photo. ***Perf. 12½***

651	A105	10r lt blue & pur	.25	.25
652	A105	15r org & red brn	.25	.25
653	A105	25r brt grn & brn	.35	.25
654	A105	50r brn red & blk	.45	.70
		Nos. 651-654 (4)	1.30	1.45

Afro-Asian Islamic Conf., Bandung, Mar. 1965.

Hand Holding Scroll — A106

Design: 25r, 75r, Conference emblem (globe, cotton and grain).

1965, Apr. 18 Unwmk. ***Perf. 12½***

655	A106	15r silver & dp car	.25	.25
656	A106	25r aqua, gold & red	.25	.25
657	A106	50r gold & dp ultra	.25	.25
658	A106	75r pale vio, gold & red	.45	.80
		Nos. 655-658 (4)	1.20	1.55

10th anniv. of the First Afro-Asian Conf.

Nos. 618-623 and Nos. 634-636 Surcharged in Orange or Black

1965, Dec. ***Perf. 12x12½, 12½x12***

659	A99	10s on 10r (B)	.25	.25
660	A99	15s on 15r	.25	.25
661	A98	20s on 20r	.25	.25
662	A99	25s on 25r (B)	.25	.25
663	A98	30s on 30r	.25	.25
664	A98	40s on 40r	.25	.25
665	A98	50s on 50r	.25	.25
666	A98	75s on 75r	.25	2.00
667	A98	100s on 100r	.25	.25
		Nos. 659-667 (9)	2.25	4.00

The surcharge on Nos. 659-660 and No. 662 is in two lines and larger.

Pres. Sukarno — A107

1966-67 Photo. ***Perf. 12½x12***

668	A107	1s sep & Prus grn	.25	.25
669	A107	3s sep & lt ol grn	.25	.25
670	A107	5s sep & dp car	.25	.25
671	A107	8s sep & Prus grn	.25	.25
672	A107	10s sep & vio bl	.25	.25
673	A107	15s sep & blk	.25	.25
674	A107	20s sep & dp grn	.25	.25
675	A107	25s sep & dk red brn	.25	.25
676	A107	30s sep & dp bl	.25	.25
677	A107	40s sep & red brn	.25	.25
678	A107	50s sep & brt vio	.25	.25
679	A107	80s sep & org	.25	.25
680	A107	1r sep & emer	.25	.25

681 A107 1.25r sep & dk gray ol .25 .25
682 A107 1.50r sep & emer .25 .25
683 A107 2r sep & mag .25 .25
684 A107 2.50r sep & gray .25 .25
685 A107 5r sep & ocher .25 .30
686 A107 10r sep & ol grn .25 .25
686A A107 12r grn & org ('67) .25 .25
686B A107 25r grn & brt pur ('67) .25 .30
Nos. 668-686B (21) 5.25 5.35

The 12r is inscribed "1967" instead of "1966."

Dockyard Workers — A108

Designs: 40s, Lighthouse. 50s, Fishermen. 1r, Maritime emblem (wheel and eagle). 1.50r, Sailboat. 2r, Loading dock. 2.50r, Diver emerging from water. 3r, Liner at pier.

1966 Photo. ***Perf. 12x12½***
687 A108 20s lt ultra & grn .25 .25
688 A108 40s pink & dk bl .25 .25
689 A108 50s green & brn .25 .25
690 A108 1r salmon, bl & yel .25 .25
691 A108 1.50r dull lil & dl grn .25 .25
692 A108 2r gray & dp org .25 .25
693 A108 2.50r rose lil & dk red .25 .25
694 A108 3r brt green & blk .25 .25
a. Souvenir sheet 10.50 13.50
Nos. 687-694 (8) 2.00 2.00

Maritime Day. Issued: Nos. 687-690, 9/23; Nos. 691-694, 10/23.
No. 694a contains one imperf. stamp similar to No. 694.

Gen. Ahmad Yani — A109

Heroes of the Revolution: No. 696, Lt. Gen. R. Suprapto. No. 697, Lt. General Harjono. No. 698, Lt. Gen. S. Parman. No. 699, Maj. Gen. D. I. Pandjaitan. No. 700, Maj. Gen. Sutojo Siswomihardjo. No. 701, Brig. General Katamso. No. 702, Colonel Soegijono. No. 703, Capt. Pierre Andreas Tendean. No. 704, Adj. Insp. Karel Satsuit Tubun.

1966, Nov. 10 **Deep Blue Frame**
695 A109 5r org brn .25 .25
696 A109 5r brt grn .25 .25
697 A109 5r gray brn .25 .25
698 A109 5r olive .25 .25
699 A109 5r gray .25 .25
700 A109 5r brt purple .25 .25
701 A109 5r red lilac .25 .25
702 A109 5r slate green .25 .25
703 A109 5r dull rose lil .25 .25
704 A109 5r orange .25 .25
Nos. 695-704 (10) 2.50 2.50

Issued to honor military men killed during the Communist uprising, October, 1965.

Tjlempung, Java — A110

Musical Instruments and Maps: 1r, Sasando, Timor. 1.25r, Foi doa, Flores. 1.50r, Kultjapi, Sumatra. 2r, Arababu, Sangihe and Talaud Islands. 2.50r, Drums, West New Guinea. 3r, Katjapi, Celebes. 4r, Hape, Borneo. 5r, Gangsa, Bali. 6r, Serunai, Sumatra. 8r, Rebab, Java. 10r, Trompet, West New Guinea. 12r, Totobuang, Moluccas. 15r, Drums, Nias. 20r, Kulintang, Celebes. 25r, Keledi, Borneo.

1967 Unwmk. Photo. ***Perf. 12½x12***
705 A110 50s red & gray .25 .40
706 A110 1r brn & dp org .25 .40
707 A110 1.25r mar & ultra .25 .40
708 A110 1.50r grn & lt vio .25 .40
709 A110 2r vio bl & yel bis .25 .40
710 A110 2.50r ol grn & dl red .25 .40
711 A110 3r brt grn & dl cl .25 .40
712 A110 4r vio bl & org .35 .40
713 A110 5r dull red & bl .35 .40
714 A110 6r blk & brt pink .35 .45
715 A110 8r red brn & brt grn .40 .45
716 A110 10r lilac & red .45 .40
717 A110 12r ol grn & lil .45 .65
718 A110 15r vio & lt ol grn .45 .40
719 A110 20r gray & sepia .45 .40
720 A110 25r black & green .45 .40
Nos. 705-720 (16) 5.45 6.75

Issued: 1.25r, 10r, 12r, 15r, 20r, 25r, Mar. 1; others Feb. 1.
For surcharges see Nos. J118-J137.

Aviator and MiG-21 — A111

Aviation Day: 4r, Traffic control tower and 990A Convair jetliner. 5r, Hercules transport plane.

1967, Apr. 9 ***Perf. 12½***
721 A111 2.50r multicolored .35 .30
722 A111 4r multicolored .35 .30
723 A111 5r multicolored .55 .30
Nos. 721-723 (3) 1.25 .90

Thomas Cup with Victory Dates — A112

Design: 12r, Thomas Cup and globe.

1967, May 31 ***Perf. 12x12½***
724 A112 5r multicolored .25 .25
725 A112 12r multicolored .50 .25

Issued to commemorate the Thomas Cup Badminton World Championship of 1967.

Balinese Girl in Front of Temple Gate — A113

1967, July 1 Photo. ***Perf. 12½***
726 A113 12r multicolored 1.10 1.00
a. Souv. sheet of 1, imperf. 4.00 5.00

Intl. Tourist Year, 1967. See No. 739.

Heroes of the Revolution Monument, Lubang Buaja — A114

Designs: 5r, Full view of monument, horiz. 7.50r, Shrine at monument.

Perf. 12x12½, 12½x12
1967, Aug. 17 **Photo.**
727 A114 2.50r pale grn & dk brn .25 .25
728 A114 5r brt rose lil & pale brn .40 .30
729 A114 7.50r pink & Prus grn .40 .30
Nos. 727-729 (3) 1.05 .85

Issued to publicize the "Heroes of the Revolution" Monument in Lubang Buaja.

Forest Fire, by Raden Saleh A115

50r, Fight to Death, by Raden Saleh.

1967, Oct. 30 Photo. ***Perf. 12½***
730 A115 25r org & gray grn .30 .50
a. Souvenir sheet of 1 4.50 7.00
731 A115 50r vio brn & org .50 .45

Indonesian painter Raden Saleh (1813-80).

Human Rights Flame — A116

1968, Jan. 1 Photo. ***Perf. 12½***
732 A116 5r grn, lt vio bl & red .30 .25
733 A116 12r grn, ol bis & red .35 .25

International Human Rights Year 1968.

Armed Forces College Emblem — A117

1968, Jan. 29 Litho. ***Perf. 12½***
734 A117 10r lt blue, yel & brn .60 .30

Integration of the Armed Forces College.

WHO Emblem and "20" — A118

20th anniv. of WHO: 20r, WHO emblem.

1968, Apr. 7 Photo. ***Perf. 12½***
735 A118 2r dp yel, pale yel & dk brn .30 .30
736 A118 20r emerald & blk .40 .30

Trains of 1867 and 1967 and Railroad's Emblem — A119

1968, May 15 Photo. ***Perf. 12½x12***
737 A119 20r multicolored .30 .30
738 A119 30r multicolored .50 1.00

Indonesian railroad centenary (in 1967).

Tourist Type of 1967

Tourist Publicity: 30r, Butterfly dancer from West Java.

1968, July 1 ***Perf. 12½***
739 A113 30r gray & multi 1.20 1.60
a. Souv. sheet of 1 + label 4.50 7.50

Bosscha Observatory and Andromeda Nebula — A120

30r, Observatory, globe and sky, vert.

1968, Sept. 20 Photo. ***Perf. 12½x12***
740 A120 15r ultra & yellow .35 .30
741 A120 30r violet & orange .55 .30

Bosscha Observatory, 40th anniversary.

Weight Lifting — A121

Designs: 7.50r+7.50r, Sailing, horiz. 12r, Basketball. 30r, Dove, Olympic flame and emblem, horiz.

1968, Oct. 12 ***Perf. 12½***
742 A121 5r ocher, blk & grn .25 .25
743 A121 Pair .55 .55
a. 7.50r Left half .25 .25
b. 7.50r Right half .25 .25
c. Souvenir sheet 5.00 8.00
744 A121 12r blue & multi .30 .40
745 A121 30r blue grn & multi .50 .25
Nos. 742-745 (4) 1.60 1.45

19th Olympic Games, Mexico City, Oct. 12-27. No. 743 is perforated vertically in the center, dividing it into two separate stamps, each inscribed "Republic Indonesia" and "7.50r." There is no gutter along the center perforation; and the design is continous over the two stamps.
No. 743c contains one No. 743 with track design surrounding the stamps.

Eugenia Aqua Burm. f. — A122

Fruits: 15r, Papaya. 30r, Durian, vert.

Perf. 12½x12, 12x12½
1968, Dec. 20 **Photo.**
746 A122 7.50r multicolored .25 .25
747 A122 15r multicolored .45 .35
a. Souvenir sheet of 1 4.00 6.00

748 A122 30r multicolored .70 .50
a. Souvenir sheet of 1 4.00 6.00
Nos. 746-748 (3) 1.40 1.10

Issued for the 11th Social Day.

Globe, ILO and UN Emblems A123

Designs: 7.50r, 25r, ILO and UN emblems.

1969, Feb. 1 Photo. *Perf. 12½*
749 A123 5r yel grn & scar .25 .25
750 A123 7.50r org & dk grn .25 .25
751 A123 15r lilac & org .25 .25
752 A123 25r bl grn & dull red .25 .25
Nos. 749-752 (4) 1.00 1.00

50th anniv. of the ILO.

R. Dewi Sartika — A124

Heroes of Indonesian Independence: No. 754, Tjoet Nja Din. No. 755, Tjoet Nja Meuthia. No. 756, General Gatot Subroto. No. 757, Sutan Sjahrir. No. 758, Dr. F. L. Tobing. Nos. 753-755 show portraits of women.

1969, Mar. 1 Photo. *Perf. 12½x12*
753 A124 15r green & pur .25 .25
754 A124 15r red lilac & grn .25 .25
755 A124 15r dk blue & ver .25 .25
756 A124 15r lilac & dk blue .25 .25
757 A124 15r lemon & red .25 .25
758 A124 15r pale brn & blue .25 .25
Nos. 753-758 (6) 1.50 1.50

Red Crosses — A125

20r, Red Cross surrounded by arms.

1969, May 5 Photo. *Perf. 12*
759 A125 15r green & dp red .40 .25
760 A125 20r org yel & red .45 .35

50th anniversary of the League of Red Cross Societies.

"Family Planning Leads to National Development and Prosperity" — A126

Design: 10r, Family, birds and factories.

1969, June 2 Photo. *Perf. 12½*
761 A126 10r blue grn & org .25 .25
762 A126 20r gray & magenta .50 .30

Planned Parenthood Conference of Southeast Asia and Oceania, Bandung, June 1-7.

Map of Bali and Mask A127

Designs: 15r, Map of Bali and woman carrying basket with offerings on head. 30r, Map of Bali and cremation ceremony.

1969, July 1 Litho. *Perf. 12½x12*
763 A127 12r gray & multi .45 .35
764 A127 15r lilac & multi .65 .40
765 A127 30r multicolored .65 .40
a. Souvenir sheet of 1 4.00 6.00
Nos. 763-765 (3) 1.75 1.15

Issued for tourist publicity.

Agriculture A128

Designs: 5r, Religious coexistence (roofs of mosques and churches). 10r, Social welfare (house and family). 12r, Import-export (cargo and ship). 15r, Clothing industry (cloth and spindles). 20r, Education (school children). 25r, Research (laboratory). 30r, Health care (people and syringe). 40r, Fishing (fish and net). 50r, Statistics (charts).

1969 Photo. *Perf. 12x12½*
766 A128 5r yel grn & bl .25 .25
767 A128 7.50r rose brn & yel .25 .25
768 A128 10r slate & red .25 .25
769 A128 12r blue & dp org 1.40 .65
770 A128 15r slate grn & org .25 .25
771 A128 20r purple & yel .25 .25
772 A128 25r orange & blk .25 .25
773 A128 30r car rose & gray .40 .25
774 A128 40r green & org .50 .25
775 A128 50r sepia & org .50 .25
Nos. 766-775 (10) 4.30 2.90

Five-year Development Plan.
See No. 968a.

Radar, Djatiluhur Station — A129

30r, Communications satellite and earth.

1969, Sept. 29 *Perf. 12½*
776 A129 15r multicolored .40 .25
777 A129 30r multicolored .60 .55

Vickers Vimy and Borobudur Temple A130

100r, Vickers Vimy and map of Indonesia.

1969, Nov. 1 *Perf. 13½x12½*
778 A130 75r dp org & dull pur .40 .60
779 A130 100r yellow & green .50 .60

50th anniv. of the 1st flight from England to Australia (via Java).

EXPO '70, Indonesian Pavilion — A131

Designs: 15r, Garuda, symbol of Indonesian EXPO '70 committee. 30r, like 5r.

1970, Feb. 15 Photo. *Perf. 12x12½*
780 A131 5r brown, yel & grn .40 .30
781 A131 15r dk bl, yel grn & red .55 .40
782 A131 30r red, yel & dk bl 1.10 .65
Nos. 780-782 (3) 2.05 1.35

Issued to publicize EXPO '70 International Exposition, Osaka, Japan, Mar. 15-Sept. 13.

Upraised Hands, Bars and Scales of Justice — A132

1970, Mar. 15 Photo. *Perf. 12½*
783 A132 10r red orange & pur .65 .40
784 A132 15r brt green & pur .80 .40

Rule of law and justice in Indonesia.

UPU Monument, Bern — A133

Design: 30r, UPU Headquarters, Bern.

1970, May 20 Photo. *Perf. 12x12½*
785 A133 15r emer & copper red .40 .40
786 A133 30r ocher & blue 1.00 .95

Inauguration of the new UPU Headquarters in Bern, Switzerland.

Dancers — A134

1970, July 1 Photo. *Perf. 12*
787 A134 20r Timor dancers .80 .50
788 A134 45r Bali dancers 1.10 .85
a. Souvenir sheet of 1 7.00 9.00

Tourist publicity. No. 788a sold for 60r.

Asian Productivity Year — A135

1970, Aug. 1 Photo. *Perf. 12*
789 A135 5r emerald, org & red .40 .25
790 A135 30r violet, org & red 1.00 .65

Independence Proclamation Monument A136

1970, Aug. 17
791 A136 40r lt ultra & magenta 10.00 4.50

The 25th anniversary of independence.

Post and Telecommunications Emblems — A137

Postal Worker and Telephone Dial — A138

Perf. 12x12½, 12½x12
1970, Sept. 27 Photo.
792 A137 10r green, ocher & yel 2.50 .30
793 A138 25r pink, blk & yel 6.00 .70

25th anniversary of the postal service.

UN Emblem — A139

1970, Oct. 10 Photo. *Perf. 12½*
794 A139 40r pur, red & yel grn 10.00 6.00

25th anniversary of the United Nations.

Education Year and UNESCO Emblems A140

Design: 50r, similar to 25r, but without oval background.

1970, Nov. 16 Photo. *Perf. 12½*
795 A140 25r yel, dk red & brn 5.50 3.75
796 A140 50r lt blue, blk & red 12.00 5.00

International Education Year.

Batik Worker — A141

50r, Woman with bamboo musical instrument (angklung). 75r, Menangkabau house & family in traditional costumes.

1971, May 26 Litho. *Perf. 12½*
797 A141 20r multi 1.75 1.50
798 A141 50r multi, vert. 3.50 4.00
a. Souvenir sheet of 1 40.00 65.00
799 A141 75r multi 5.50 6.00
Nos. 797-799 (3) 10.75 11.50

"Visit ASEAN lands." No. 798a sold for 70r.

Fatahillah Park, Djakarta — A142

30f, City Hall. 65r, Lenong Theater performance. 80r, Ismail Marzuki Cultural Center.

1971, June 19 Photo. *Perf. 12½*
800 A142 15r yel grn, brn & bl 2.00 1.10
801 A142 65r org brn, dk brn & lt grn 4.00 4.50
802 A142 80r olive, bl & mag 8.00 3.50
Nos. 800-802 (3) 14.00 9.10

Souvenir Sheet

803 A142 30r bl, yel & lil rose 18.00 27.50

444th anniv. of Djakarta. No. 803 sold for 60r.

Rama and Sita — A143

Design: 100r, Rama with bow.

1971, Aug. 31
804 A143 30r yellow, grn & blk 1.50 .85
805 A143 100r blue, red & blk 3.50 2.00

International Ramayana Festival.

Carrier Pigeon and Conference Emblem — A144

1971, Sept. 20
806 A144 50r ocher & dp brown 1.60 1.10

5th Asian Regional Postal Conference.

Globes and UPU Monument, Berne — A145

1971, Oct. 4 Photo. *Perf. 13½x13*
807 A145 40r blue & dull vio 1.60 1.10

Universal Postal Union Day.

Boy Writing, UNICEF Emblem — A146

40r, Boy with sheaf of rice, emblem.

1971, Dec. 11 *Perf. 12½*
808 A146 20r orange & multi 1.75 .60
809 A146 40r blue & multi 3.25 1.25

25th anniv. UNICEF.

Lined Tang A147

Fish: 30r, Moorish goddess. 40r, Imperial angelfish.

1971, Dec. 27 Litho. *Perf. 12½*
810 A147 15r lilac & multi 3.50 1.25
811 A147 30r dull grn & multi 7.25 3.50
812 A147 40r blue & multi 11.50 5.00
Nos. 810-812 (3) 22.25 9.75

See Nos. 834-836, 859-861, 926-928, 959-961.

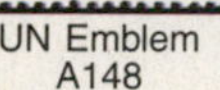

UN Emblem A148 | Radio Tower A149

Design: 100r, Road and dam.

1972, Mar. 28 Photo. *Perf. 12½*
813 A148 40r lt grnsh bl & bl 2.00 1.00
814 A149 75r dk car, yel & grnsh bl 3.25 1.00
815 A148 100r green, yel & blk 3.75 2.25
Nos. 813-815 (3) 9.00 4.25

UN Economic Commission for Asia and the Far East (ECAFE), 25th anniv.

"Your Heart is your Health" — A150

1972, Apr. 7
816 A150 50r multicolored 1.60 .80

World Health Day.

Woman Weaver, Factories A151

1972, Apr. 22
817 A151 35r orange, yel & pur 1.60 .80

Textile Technology Institute, 50th anniv.

Book Readers A152

1972, May 15 *Perf. 13½x12½*
818 A152 75r blue & multi 2.50 1.25

International Book Year 1972.

Weather Satellite — A153

50r, Astronaut on moon. 60r, Indonesian rocket Kartika 1.

1972, July 20 Photo. *Perf. 12½*
819 A153 35r shown 1.50 .65
820 A153 50r multicolored 3.00 3.50
821 A153 60r multicolored 4.50 1.25
Nos. 819-821 (3) 9.00 5.40

Space achievements.

Hotel Indonesia — A154

1972, Aug. 5
822 A154 50r grn, lt bl & car 2.00 1.10

Hotel Indonesia, 10th anniversary.

Silat (Self Defense) — A155

Olympic Emblems and: 35r, Running. 50r, Diving. 75r, Badminton. 100r, Olympic Stadium.

1972, Aug. 26 Photo.
823 A155 20r lt blue & multi 1.25 .25
824 A155 35r multicolored 1.25 .40
825 A155 50r yel grn & multi 2.10 .70
826 A155 75r multicolored 2.10 1.75
827 A155 100r multicolored 3.50 2.75
Nos. 823-827 (5) 10.20 5.85

20th Olympic Games, Munich, 8/26-9/11.

Family, Houses of Worship — A156

Family planning: 75r, Healthy family. 80r, Working family (national prosperity).

1972, Sept. 27 *Perf. 12½x13½*
828 A156 30r lemon & multi 1.25 .70
829 A156 75r lilac & multi 2.50 2.50
830 A156 80r multicolored 4.25 3.25
Nos. 828-830 (3) 8.00 6.45

Moluccas Dancer — A157

60r, Man, woman and Toradja house, Celebes. 100fr, West Irian house, horiz.

Perf. 12½x13½, 13½x12½
1972, Oct. 28 Photo.
831 A157 30r olive pink & brn 1.75 .65
832 A157 60r multicolored 2.50 3.00
833 A157 100r lt bl, brn & dl yel 5.25 3.00
Nos. 831-833 (3) 9.50 6.65

Fish Type of 1971

Fish: 30r, Butterflyfish. 50r, Regal angelfish. 100r, Spotted triggerfish.

1972, Dec. 4 Litho. *Perf. 12½*
834 A147 30r blue & multi 5.50 2.00
835 A147 50r blue & multi 8.75 2.75
836 A147 100r blue & multi 11.50 5.00
Nos. 834-836 (3) 25.75 9.75

Thomas Cup, Shuttlecock — A158

Thomas Cup, Shuttlecock and: 75r, National monument & Istora Sports Hall. 80r, Indonesian flag & badminton player.

1973, Jan. 2 Litho. *Perf. 12½*
837 A158 30r emerald & brt bl 1.00 .30
838 A158 75r dull grn & dk car 1.50 .55
839 A158 80r gold & red 2.25 1.10
Nos. 837-839 (3) 4.75 1.95

Thomas Cup Badminton World Championship 1973.

WMO Emblem, Anemometer, Wayang Figure — A159

Perf. 13½x12½
1973, Feb. 15 Litho.
840 A159 80r blue, grn & claret 1.60 .80

Cent. of intl. meteorological cooperation.

"Health Begins at Home" — A160

1973, Apr. 7 Photo. *Perf. 12½*
841 A160 80r dk grn, org & ultra 1.40 .85

25th anniv. of WHO.

Ceremonial Mask, Java — A161

60r, Mask, Kalimantan. 100r, Mask, Bali.

1973, June 1 Photo. *Perf. 12½*
842 A161 30r shown 2.75 .90
843 A161 60r multi 5.50 4.00
844 A161 100r multi 9.00 2.00
Nos. 842-844 (3) 17.25 6.90

Tourist publicity.

Hand Putting Coin into Bank — A162

30r, Symbolic coin bank and hand, horiz.

1973, July 2 Photo. *Perf. 12½*
845 A162 25r yellow, lt brn & blk 1.00 .55
846 A162 30r green, yel & gold 1.25 .55

National savings movement.

Chess — A163

8th National Sports Week: 60r, Karate. 75r, Hurdling, horiz.

1973, Aug. 4 Photo. *Perf. 12½*
847 A163 30r red, yellow & blk 1.25 1.10
848 A163 60r black, ocher & lt grn 2.00 1.10
849 A163 75r black, lt bl & rose 3.25 .90
Nos. 847-849 (3) 6.50 3.10

INTERPOL Emblem and Policemen A164

Design: 50r, INTERPOL emblem and guard statue from Sewu Prambanan Temple, vert.

1973, Sept. 3
850 A164 30r yellow, grn & blk .90 .35
851 A164 50r yellow, brn & blk 1.60 .65

50th anniv. of Intl. Police Organization.

Batik Worker and Parang Rusak Pattern A165

Batik designs: 80r, Man and Pagi Sore pattern. 100r, Man and Merak Ngigel pattern.

1973, Oct. 9 Photo. *Perf. 12½*
852 A165 60r multicolored 1.90 1.90
853 A165 80r multicolored 3.25 2.25
854 A165 100r multicolored 7.25 4.00
Nos. 852-854 (3) 12.40 8.15

Farmer, Grain, UN and FAO Emblems — A166

1973, Oct. 24 Photo. *Perf. 12½*
855 A166 30r lilac & multi 1.75 .65

World Food Program, 10th anniversary.

Houses of Worship — A167

Family planning: 30r, Classroom. 60r, Family and home.

1973, Nov. 10
856 A167 20r dk bl, lt bl & ver .55 .45
857 A167 30r ocher, blk & yel 1.40 .70
858 A167 60r lt grn, yel & blk 2.75 .60
Nos. 856-858 (3) 4.70 1.75

Fish Type of 1971

Fish: 40r, Acanthurus leucosternon. 65r, Chaetodon trifasciatus. 100r, Pomacanthus annularis.

1973, Dec. 10 Litho. *Perf. 12½*
859 A147 40r multicolored 1.90 .95
860 A147 65r multicolored 7.50 2.00
861 A147 100r multicolored 9.50 3.25
Nos. 859-861 (3) 18.90 6.20

Adm. Sudarso and Battle of Arafuru — A168

1974, Jan. 15
862 A168 40r brt blue & multi 2.00 .85

12th Navy Day.

Bengkulu Costume A169

Designs: Regional Costumes: 7.50r, Kalimantan, Timor. 10r, Kalimantan, Tengah. 15r, Jambi. 20r, Sulawesi, Tenggara. 25r, Nusatenggara, Timor. 27.50r, Maluku. 30r, Lampung. 35r, Sumatra, Barat. 40r, Aceh. 45r, Nusatenggara, Barat. 50r, Riouw. 55r, Kalimantan, Barat. 60r, Sulawesi, Utara. 65r, Sulawesi, Tengah. 70r, Sumatra, Selatan. 75r, Java, Barat. 80r, Sumatra, Utara. 90r, Yogyakarta. 95r, Kalimantan, Selatan. 100r, Java, Timor. 120r, Irian, Jaya. 130r, Jawa Tengah. 135r, Sulawesi, Selatan. 150r, Bali. 160r, Djakarta.

1974, Mar. 28 Litho. *Perf. 12½*
863 A169 5r shown 14.00 1.00
864 A169 7.50r multi 7.00 1.00
865 A169 10r multi 4.00 .80
866 A169 15r multi 1.25 .80
867 A169 20r multi 1.25 .80
868 A169 25r multi 1.40 .80
869 A169 27.50r multi 1.40 *2.50*
870 A169 30r multi 1.40 *1.50*
871 A169 35r multi 1.40 .80
872 A169 40r multi 1.40 .80
873 A169 45r multi 3.00 .80
874 A169 50r multi 1.75 2.00
875 A169 55r multi 2.60 .80
876 A169 60r multi 2.60 .80
877 A169 65r multi 2.60 .80
878 A169 70r multi 2.60 .80
879 A169 75r multi 2.60 .80
880 A169 80r multi 2.60 .80
881 A169 90r multi 3.00 *4.00*
882 A169 95r multi 2.60 .80
883 A169 100r multi 2.60 1.60
884 A169 120r multi 5.00 1.00
885 A169 130r multi 5.00 .80
886 A169 135r multi 6.00 .80
887 A169 150r multi 6.00 .80
888 A169 160r multi 6.00 1.60
Nos. 863-888 (26) 91.05 29.80

Baladewa A170

Designs (Figures from Shadow Plays): 80r, Kresna. 100r, Bima.

1974, June 1 Photo. *Perf. 12½*
889 A170 40r lt violet & multi 1.75 1.25
890 A170 80r salmon & multi 4.50 2.75
891 A170 100r rose 5.50 2.75
Nos. 889-891 (3) 11.75 6.75

Pres. Suharto — A171

1974-76 Photo. *Perf. 12½*
Portrait in Dark Brown
901 A171 40r lt green & blk .70 .25
903 A171 50r ultra & blk 1.50 .25
906 A171 65r brt pink & blk 1.00 .65
908 A171 75r yellow & blk 1.60 .25
912 A171 100r buff & blk 1.60 .25
913 A171 150r citron & blk 1.60 .30
914 A171 200r green & blue 4.25 .25
915 A171 300r brn org & car 1.75 .25
916 A171 400r green & yellow 2.60 .30
917 A171 500r lilac & car 4.00 1.00
Nos. 901-917 (10) 20.60 3.75

Nos. 914-917 have wavy lines in background.
Issued: Nos. 901-913, 8/17/74; Nos. 914-917, 8/17/76.

Family and WPY Emblem — A172

1974, Aug. 19
918 A172 65r ultra, gray & ocher 1.25 .55

World Population Year 1974.

"Welfare" A173

"Development" A174

"Religion" A175

1974, Sept. 9
919 A173 25r green & multi .80 .45
920 A174 40r yellow grn & multi 1.25 .45
921 A175 65r dk vio brn & multi 2.00 .45
Nos. 919-921 (3) 4.05 1.35

Family planning.

Mailmen with Bicycles, UPU Emblem — A176

UPU cent.: 40r, Horse-drawn mail cart. 65r, Mailman on horseback. 100r, Sailing ship, 18th century.

1974, Oct. 9
922 A176 20r dk green & multi 1.75 .45
923 A176 40r dull blue & multi 1.90 .70
924 A176 65r black brn & yel 2.10 .70
925 A176 100r maroon & multi 2.25 1.90
Nos. 922-925 (4) 8.00 3.75

Fish Type of 1971

Fish: 40fr, Zebrasoma veliferum. 80r, Euxiphipops navarchus. 100r, Synchiropus splendidus.

1974, Oct. 30 Photo. *Perf. 12½*
926 A147 40r blue & multi 2.75 .45
927 A147 80r blue & multi 4.00 1.90
928 A147 100r blue & multi 5.75 2.40
Nos. 926-928 (3) 12.50 4.75

Drill Team Searching for Oil — A177

Designs (Pertamina Emblem and): 75r, Oil refinery. 95r, Pertamina telecommunications and computer center. 100r, Gasoline truck and station. 120r, Plane over storage tanks. 130r, Pipes and tanker. 150r, Petro-chemical storage tanks. 200r, Off-shore drilling platform. 95r, 100r, 120r, 130r, vertical.

1974, Dec. 10 *Perf. 13½*
929 A177 40r black & multi .45 .30
930 A177 75r black & multi .50 .30
931 A177 95r black & multi .60 .30
932 A177 100r black & multi .60 .30
933 A177 120r black & multi .70 .30
934 A177 130r black & multi .70 .30
935 A177 150r black & multi .75 .30
936 A177 200r black & multi .85 .30
Nos. 929-936 (8) 5.15 2.40

Pertamina State Oil Enterprise, 17th anniv.

Spittoon, Sumatra A178

Artistic Metalware: 75r, Condiment dish, Sumatra. 100r, Condiment dish, Kalimantan.

1975, Feb. 24 Photo. *Perf. 12½*
937 A178 50r red & black 1.40 1.40
938 A178 75r green & black 2.10 1.40
939 A178 100r brt blue & multi 3.00 1.40
Nos. 937-939 (3) 6.50 4.20

Blood Donors' Emblem — A179

1975, Apr. 7
940 A179 40r yellow, red & grn 1.20 .65

"Give blood, save lives."

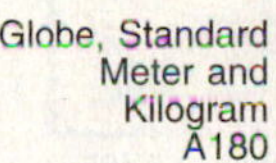

Globe, Standard Meter and Kilogram A180

1975, May 20
941 A180 65r blue, red & yel 1.75 .65

Cent. of Intl. Meter Convention, Paris, 1875.

Farmer, Teacher, Mother, Policewoman and Nurse — A181

IWY Emblem — A182

1975, June 26 Photo. *Perf. 12½*
942 A181 40r multicolored 1.20 .65
943 A182 100r multicolored 2.00 .65

International Women's Year 1975.

Dendrobium Pakarena A183

Orchids: 70r, Aeridachnis bogor. 85r, Vanda genta.

1975, July 21

944	A183	40r multicolored	2.50	1.25
945	A183	70r multicolored	4.25	2.40
946	A183	85r multicolored	5.75	3.50
		Nos. 944-946 (3)	12.50	7.15

See Nos. 1010-1012, 1036-1038.

Stupas and Damaged Temple — A184

Designs (UNESCO Emblem and): 40r, Buddha statues, stupas and damaged wall. 65r, Stupas and damaged wall, horiz. 100r, Buddha statue and stupas, horiz.

1975, Aug. 10 ***Perf. 12½***

947	A184	25r yel, brn & org	2.10	.80
948	A184	40r black, grn & yel	2.60	1.00
949	A184	65r lemon, cl & grn	5.00	4.25
950	A184	100r bis, brn & sl bl	7.50	4.25
		Nos. 947-950 (4)	17.20	10.30

UNESCO campaign to save Borobudur Temple, Java.

Banjarmasin Battle — A185

Battle Scenes: 40r, Batua, 9/8/46. 75r, Margarana, 11/20/46. 100r, Palembang, 1/1/47.

1975, Aug. 17

951	A185	25r yellow & blk	.65	.45
952	A185	40r org ver & red	.85	.45
953	A185	75r vermilion & blk	1.00	1.25
954	A185	100r orange & blk	1.40	.90
		Nos. 951-954 (4)	3.90	3.05

Indonesian independence, 30th anniversary.

"Education" — A186

Family plannings: 25r, "Religion." 40r, "Prosperity."

1975, Oct. 20 **Photo.** ***Perf. 12½***

955	A186	20r blue, salmon & blk	.50	.25
956	A186	25r emerald, sal & blk	.80	.30
957	A186	40r dp org, blue & blk	1.25	.55
		Nos. 955-957 (3)	2.55	1.10

Heroes' Monument, Surabaya — A187

1975, Nov. 10

958	A187	100r maroon & green	1.75	.55

War of independence, 30th anniversary.

Fish Type of 1971

Fish: 40r, Coris angulata. 75r, Chaetodon ephippium. 150r, Platax pinnatus, vert.

1975, Dec. 15 **Litho.** ***Perf. 12½***

959	A147	40r multicolored	1.25	.45
960	A147	75r multicolored	3.75	1.40
961	A147	150r multicolored	5.00	2.75
		Nos. 959-961 (3)	10.00	4.60

Thomas Cup — A188

40r, Uber Cup. 100r, Thomas & Uber Cups.

1976, Jan. 31 **Photo.** ***Perf. 12½***

962	A188	20r blue & multi	.80	.35
963	A188	40r multicolored	.80	.60
964	A188	100r green & multi	1.75	.60
		Nos. 962-964 (3)	3.35	1.55

Indonesia, Badminton World Champions.

Refugees on Truck and New Village — A189

Designs: 50r, Neglected and restored village streets. 100r, Derelict and rebuilt houses.

1976, Feb. 28 **Photo.** ***Perf. 12½***

965	A189	30r yellow & multi	.80	.25
966	A189	50r blue & multi	1.00	.45
967	A189	100r ocher & multi	1.60	.45
		Nos. 965-967 (3)	3.40	1.15

World Human Settlements Day.

Telephones, 1876 and 1976 — A190

1976, Mar. 10 **Photo.** ***Perf. 12½***

968	A190	100r yel, org & brn	1.25	.55
a.		Bklt. pane of 8, 4 #968, 4 #775 + 2 labels ('78)	7.75	

Centenary of first telephone call by Alexander Graham Bell, Mar. 10, 1876.
Stamps from No. 968a have straight edges.

Eye and WHO Emblem — A191

Design: 40r, Blind man, eye and World Health Organization emblem.

1976, Apr. 7 **Photo.** ***Perf. 12½***

969	A191	20r yel, lt grn & blk	.40	.30
970	A191	40r yel, blue & blk	.85	.45

Foresight prevents blindness.

Montreal Stadium — A192

1976, May 17

971	A192	100r ultra	1.25	.65

21st Olympic Games, Montreal, Canada, July 17-Aug. 1.

Lake Tondano, Celebes — A193

Tourist publicity: 40r, Lake Kelimutu, Flores. 75r, Lake Maninjau, Sumatra.

1976, June 1

972	A193	35r lt green & blk	.65	.45
973	A193	40r gray, rose & lt grn	.80	.45
974	A193	75r blue & sl grn	1.00	.55
a.		Bklt. pane of 8 (7 #974, #998, 2 labels) ('78)	7.75	
		Nos. 972-974 (3)	2.45	1.45

Stamps from No. 974a have straight edges.

Radar Station — A194

Designs: 50r, Master control radar station. 100r, Palapa satellite.

1976, July 8 **Photo.** ***Perf. 12½***

975	A194	20r multicolored	.65	.40
976	A194	50r green & blk	.85	.40
977	A194	100r multicolored	1.40	.75
a.		Bklt. pane of 9 (4 #977, 5 #967, label) ('78)	12.50	
		Nos. 975-977 (3)	2.90	1.55

Inauguration of domestic satellite system.
Stamps from No. 977a have straight edges.

Arachnis Flos-aeris — A195

Orchids: 40r, Vanda putri serang. 100r, Coelogyne pandurata.

1976, Sept. 7

978	A195	25r multicolored	1.50	1.10
a.		Souvenir sheet of 1	*50.00*	*72.50*
979	A195	40r multicolored	2.00	1.10
980	A195	100r multicolored	3.50	2.40
		Nos. 978-980 (3)	7.00	4.60

Tree and Mountain — A196

1976, Oct. 4

981	A196	20r green, blue & brn	.85	.40

16th National Reforestation Week.

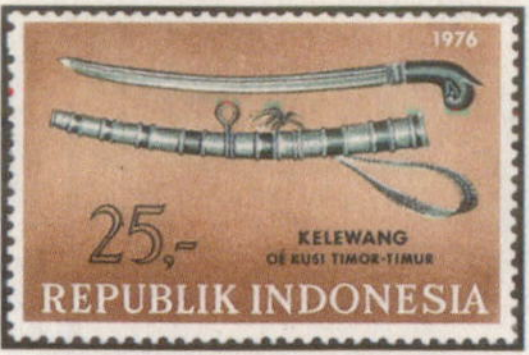

Dagger and Sheath from Timor — A197

Historic Daggers and Sheaths: 40r, from Borneo. 100r, from Aceh.

1976, Nov. 1 ***Perf. 12½***

982	A197	25r multicolored	.80	.45
983	A197	40r multicolored	1.60	.85
a.		Souvenir sheet of 1, imperf	12.50	17.50
984	A197	100r green & multi	2.60	2.60
		Nos. 982-984 (3)	5.00	3.90

No. 983a exists perf. Value $15.

Open Book A198

Children Reading A199

1976, Dec. 8 **Photo.** ***Perf. 12½***

985	A198	20r multicolored	.55	.30
986	A199	40r multicolored	1.10	.45

Better books for children.

UNICEF Emblem — A200

1976, Dec. 11

987	A200	40r multicolored	1.25	.45

UNICEF, 30th anniv.
See No. 977a.

Ballot Box — A201

1977 elections: 75r, Ballot box, grain and factory. 100r, Coat of arms.

1977, Jan. 5 **Photo.** ***Perf. 12½***

988	A201	40r multicolored	1.40	.30
989	A201	75r multicolored	1.75	.45
990	A201	100r multicolored	3.00	1.40
		Nos. 988-990 (3)	6.15	2.15

Camp and Flags Scout Emblems, A202

Designs: 30r, Tent, emblems and trees. 40r, Boy and Girl Scout flags and emblems.

1977, Feb. 28

991	A202	25r multicolored	1.25	.55
992	A202	30r multicolored	1.25	.55
993	A202	40r multicolored	1.40	1.25
		Nos. 991-993 (3)	3.90	2.35

11th National Scout Jamboree.

Letter with "AOPU" — A203

Design: 100r, Stylized bird and letter.

1977, Apr. 1 Photo. *Perf. 12½*
994 A203 65r multicolored .50 .40
995 A203 100r multicolored 1.25 .55

Asian-Oceanic Postal Union, 15th convention.

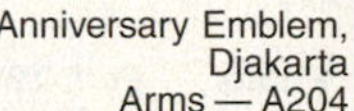
Anniversary Emblem, Djakarta Arms — A204

Designs: Anniversary emblem and arms of Djakarta in different arrangements.

1977, May 23 Photo. *Perf. 12½*
996 A204 20r orange & blue .50 .45
997 A204 40r emerald & blue .75 .45
998 A204 100r slate & blue 1.50 .85
a. Souvenir sheet of 1 7.50 9.00
Nos. 996-998 (3) 2.75 1.75

450th anniversary of Djakarta. No. 998a also issued imperf. Value $17.50.

Rose — A205

1977, May 26 Photo. *Perf. 12½*
999 A205 100r shown 1.25 .45
a. Souvenir sheet 7.00 12.00
1000 A205 100r Envelope 1.25 .45
a. Souvenir sheet of 4 7.00 12.00
b. Pair, Nos. 999-1000 2.75 1.50

Amphilex 77 Phil. Exhib., Amsterdam, May 26-June 5. No. 999a contains one stamp similar to No. 999 with blue background. No. 1000a contains 2 each of Nos. 999-1000.

Nos. 999a, 1000a exist imperf. Values: No. 999a, $6; No. 1000a, $20.

See No. 1013a.

Various Sports Emblems A206

9th Natl. Sports Week: 50r, 100r, Different sports emblems.

1977, June 22
1001 A206 40r silver & multi 2.25 1.75
1002 A206 50r silver & multi 2.75 1.75
1003 A206 100r gold & multi 5.75 4.00
Nos. 1001-1003 (3) 10.75 7.50

Contest Trophy A207

Emblem A208

1977, July 20
1004 A207 40r green & multi 1.75 .55
1005 A208 100r yellow & multi 2.75 1.00

10th Natl. Koran Reading Contest, 7/20-27.

Map of ASEAN Countries, Satellite — A209

35r, Map of ASEAN countries. 50r, Flags of founding members: Indonesia, Malaysia, Philippines, Singapore & Thailand; ship, plane & train.

1977, Aug. 8
1006 A209 25r multicolored .75 .25
1007 A209 35r multicolored 1.75 .70
1008 A209 50r multicolored 2.25 .85
Nos. 1006-1008 (3) 4.75 1.80

Association of South East Asian Nations (ASEAN), 10th anniversary.

Uniform, Jakarta Regiment A210

1977, Aug. 19
1009 A210 25r green, gold & brn .75 .30

Indonesia-Pakistan Economic and Cultural Organization, 1968-1977.

Orchid Type of 1975

Orchids: 25r, Taeniophyllum. 40r, Phalaenopsis violacea. 100r, Dendrobium spectabile.

1977, Oct. 28 Photo. *Perf. 12½*
1010 A183 25r orange & multi 1.25 .80
1011 A183 40r blue & multi 1.75 1.75
1012 A183 100r yel grn & multi 4.00 2.75
a. Souvenir sheet of 1, imperf 9.00 12.00
Nos. 1010-1012 (3) 7.00 5.30

No. 1012a contains one stamp similar to No. 1012 with blue background. No. 1012a exists perf. Value $7.

Child and Mosquito A211

1977, Nov. 7 *Perf. 12½*
1013 A211 40r brt grn, red & blk .75 .35
a. Bklt. pane of 9+label (4 #999, 5 #1013) ('78) 7.75

Natl. Health campaign to eradicate malaria.

Stamps from No. 1013a have straight edges.

Issued: No. 1013a, 9/27/78.

Proboscis Monkey — A212

Designs: 40r, Indian elephant. 100r, Tiger.

1977, Dec. 22
1014 A212 20r multicolored .90 .35
1015 A212 40r multicolored 1.75 .75
1016 A212 100r multicolored 5.50 1.50
a. Souvenir sheet of 1 5.00 10.00
Nos. 1014-1016 (3) 8.15 2.60

Wildlife protection. No. 1016a exists imperf. Value $6.

Conference Emblem — A213

1978, Mar. 27 Photo. *Perf. 12½*
1017 A213 100r lt blue & ultra 1.25 .60

United Nations Conference on Technical Cooperation among Developing Countries.

Mother and Child — A214

75r, Mother and child, symbolic design.

1978, Apr. 7 Photo. *Perf. 12½*
1018 A214 40r lt green & blue .45 .30
1019 A214 75r orange red & brn 1.00 .45

Promotion of breast feeding.

Dome of The Rock, Jerusalem — A215

1978, May 15 Photo. *Perf. 12½*
1020 A215 100r multicolored 1.40 .55

Palestinian fighters and their families.

Argentina '78 Emblem — A216

1978, June 1
1021 A216 40r multicolored .55 .30
1022 A216 100r multicolored 1.10 .70

11th World Cup Soccer Championships, Argentina, June 1-25.

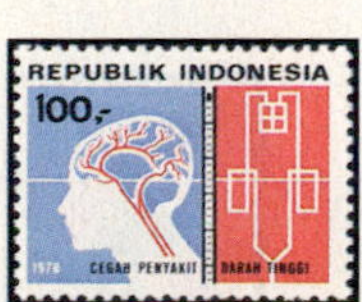

Head and "Blood Circulation" A217

1978, June 17 Photo. *Perf. 12½*
1023 A217 100r black, blue & red 1.00 .55

World Health Day and drive against hypertension.

Leather Puppets — A218

Art from Wayang Museum, Djakarta: 75r, Wooden puppets. 100r, Actors with puppet masks.

1978, July 22 Litho. *Perf. 12½*
1024 A218 40r multicolored 1.75 .70
1025 A218 75r multicolored 2.25 1.40
1026 A218 100r multicolored 5.00 2.40
Nos. 1024-1026 (3) 9.00 4.50

Congress Emblem — A219

1978, Aug. 1
1027 A219 100r slate 1.00 .45

27th Congress of World Confederation of Organizations of Teachers (WCOTP), Djakarta, June 26-Aug. 2.

IAAY Emblem — A220

1978, Aug. 16 Photo. *Perf. 12½*
1028 A220 100r org & dk blue 1.20 .45

International Anti-Apartheid Year.

Congress Emblem — A221

Design: 100r, People and trees.

1978, Oct. 16 Photo. *Perf. 12½*
1029 A221 40r emerald & blue .25 .25
1030 A221 100r emerald & blk 1.00 .55

8th World Forestry Congress, Djakarta.

Youth Pledge Emblem — A222

1978, Oct. 28
1031 A222 40r dk brown & red .55 .30
1032 A222 100r salmon, brn & red .90 .45

50th anniv. of Youth Pledge. See No. 1044b.

Wildlife Protection — A223

40r, Porcupine anteater. 75r, Deer. 100r, Clouded tiger.

1978, Nov. 1
1033 A223 40r multi 1.20 .40
1034 A223 75r multi 2.00 .80
a. Souv. sheet of 5, #1034, 4 #1035 + label 10.00 10.00
1035 A223 100r multi 3.25 1.10
a. Souvenir sheet of 1 4.00 4.00
Nos. 1033-1035 (3) 6.45 2.30

Stamps in No. 1034a are in changed colors. Souvenir sheets inscribed for Essen 2nd Intl. Stamp Fair.

Orchid Type of 1975

Orchids: 40r, Phalaenopsis sri rejeki. 75r, Dendrobium macrophilium. 100r, Cymbidium fynlaysonianum.

1978, Dec. 22 Photo. *Perf. 12½*
1036 A183 40r multicolored 1.20 .45
1037 A183 75r multicolored 1.60 .70
1038 A183 100r multicolored 2.75 1.00
a. Souvenir sheet of 1 4.00 6.00
Nos. 1036-1038 (3) 5.55 2.15

Douglas DC-3, 1949, over Volcano — A224

Designs: 75r, Douglas DC-9 over village. 100r, Douglas DC-10 over temple.

1979, Jan. 26 Photo. *Perf. 12½*
1039 A224 40r multicolored .65 .40
1040 A224 75r multicolored .80 .40
1041 A224 100r multicolored 1.60 1.10
Nos. 1039-1041 (3) 3.05 1.90

Garuda Indonesian Airways, 30th anniv.

A225

40r, Thomas Cup and badminton player. No. 1043, Player hitting ball. No. 1044, Player facing left.

1979, Feb. 24 Photo. *Perf. 12½*
1042 A225 40r red & blue .50 .55
1043 A225 100r red & brown .85 .85
1044 A225 100r red & brown .85 .85
a. Pair, #1043-1044 1.90
b. Bklt. pane, 3 each #1032, 1043-1044 + label 6.00
Nos. 1042-1044 (3) 2.20 2.25

11th Thomas Cup, Djakarta, May 24-June 2. No. 1044a forms a continuous design.
Stamps from No. 1044b have straight edges.

Paphiopedilum Lowii — A227

Orchids: 100r, 300r, Vanda limbata. 125r, Phalaenopsis gigantea. 250r, as 60r.

1979, Mar. 22 Photo. *Perf. 12½*
1045 A227 60r multi .75 .40
1046 A227 100r multi 1.40 .55
1047 A227 125r multi 2.25 .85
a. Souvenir sheet of 1 4.50 4.50
b. Souv. sheet of 2 (250r, 300r) 7.00 7.00
Nos. 1045-1047 (3) 4.40 1.80

No. 1047b, issued for Asian Phil. Exhib., Dortmund, West Germany, May 24-27. Sold for 650r.

Family and Houses — A228

Third Five-year Plan: 12.50r, Plane. 17.50r, Bridge. 60r, Pylon and fields. 100r, School and clinic. 125r, Factories and trucks. 150r, Motorized mail delivery.

1979-82
1047C A228 12.50r rose car, yel ol ('80) .45 .25
1047D A228 17.50r pur brn, grey ol ('82) .50 .25
1048 A228 35r green & olive .25 .25
1049 A228 60r blue & olive .25 .25
1050 A228 100r blue & dk brn .50 .25
1051 A228 125r red brn & ol .75 .25
1052 A228 150r car & yel .90 .45
Nos. 1047C-1052 (7) 3.60 1.95

See No. 1058a.

R. A. Kartini and Girls' School A229

1979, Apr. 21 Photo. *Perf. 12½*
1053 100r Kartini .65 .40
1054 100r School .65 .40
a. A229 Pair, #1053-1054 1.40 2.00

Mrs. R. A. Kartini, educator, birth centenary.

Bureau of Education, UNESCO Emblems — A231

1979, May 25 Photo. *Perf. 12½*
1055 A231 150r multicolored 1.25 .45

50th anniversary of the statutes of the International Bureau of Education.

Self Defense — A232

Designs: 125r, Games' emblem. 150r, Senayan Main Stadium.

1979, June 21 Photo. *Perf. 12½*
1056 A232 60r multicolored .55 .30
1057 A232 125r multicolored .90 .45
1058 A232 150r multicolored 1.10 .70
a. Bklt. pane of 6+4 labels (#1052, 5 #1058) 6.50
Nos. 1056-1058 (3) 2.55 1.45

10th So. East Asia Games, Djakarta, Sept. 21-30.
Stamps from No. 1058a have straight edges.
Issue date: No. 1058a, 9/27.

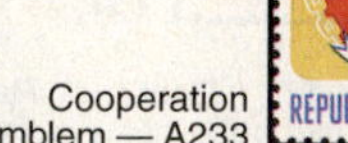
Cooperation Emblem — A233

1979, July 12 Photo. *Perf. 12½*
1059 A233 150r multicolored .90 .40

32nd Indonesian Cooperative Day.

A234

Designs: 60r, IYC and natl. IYC emblems. 150r, IYC emblem.

1979, Aug. 4 Photo. *Perf. 12½*
1060 A234 60r emerald & blk .40 .25
1061 A234 150r blue & blk .75 .45

International Year of the Child.

TELECOM 79 — A235

1979, Sept. 20 Photo. *Perf. 12½*
1062 A235 150r bl, red, grey 1.00 .55

3rd World Telecommunications Exhibition, Geneva, Sept. 20-26.

Fight Drug Abuse — A236

1979, Oct. 17 Photo. *Perf. 12½*
1063 A236 150r deep rose & blk .90 .55

Dolphin — A237

Wildlife Protection: 125r, Freshwater dolphin. 150r, Leatherback turtle.

1979, Nov. 24 Photo. *Perf. 12½*
1064 A237 60r multi .90 .65
1065 A237 125r multi 2.75 .85
1066 A237 150r multi 4.50 1.25
Nos. 1064-1066 (3) 8.15 2.75

Souvenir Sheet
1066A A237 200r like #1066 6.50 8.00

Ship Made of Cloves — A238

Spice Race, Jakarta-Amsterdam (Sailing Ships): 60r, Penisi, vert. 150r, Madurese boat, vert.

1980 Photo. *Perf. 12½*
1067 A238 60r bright blue .40 .25
1068 A238 125r red brown .75 .45
1069 A238 150r red lilac 1.25 .45
Nos. 1067-1069 (3) 2.40 1.15

Souvenir Sheets
1069A A238 300r like #1068 4.00 5.00
1069B A238 500r like #1067 6.50 6.50

Issued: Nos. 1067-1069, 300r, 3/12. 500r, 5/6. No. 1069B for London 1980 Intl. Stamp Exhib.

Rubber Raft in Rapids A239

125r, Mountain climbing, vert. 150r, Hang gliding, vert.

Perf. 13½x13, 13x13½
1980, Mar. 21 Photo.
1070 A239 60r shown .40 .25
1071 A239 125r multicolored .75 .55
1072 A239 150r multicolored 1.40 .85
Nos. 1070-1072 (3) 2.55 1.65

Souvenir Sheet
1072A A239 300r like #1070 4.00 5.00

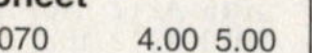

Anti-Smoking Campaign — A240

1980, Apr. 15 *Perf. 12½*
1073 A240 150r multicolored 1.00 .45

A241

1980, Apr. 21 Photo. *Perf. 12½*
1074 A241 125r Flowers In vase .80 .45
1075 A241 150r Bouquet 1.00 .70

2nd Flower Festival, Jakarta, Apr. 19-21.
See No. 1080a-1080b.

Conference Building — A242

1980, Apr. 24 *Perf. 13x13½*
1076 A242 150r gold & lil rose 1.10 .45

Souvenir Sheet
1076A A242 300r multicolored 4.00 5.25

1st Asian-African Conf., 25th anniv.

A243

Designs: 60r, Male figure. 125r, Elephant stone. 150r, Taman Bali Stone Sarcophagus, 2000 B.C.

1980, May 2 *Perf. 12½*
1077 A243 60r multicolored .55 .30
1078 A243 125r multicolored .75 .55
1079 A243 150r multicolored .90 .70
Nos. 1077-1079 (3) 2.20 1.55

Flower and Sculpture Types of 1980
Souvenir Sheet

1980 Photo. *Perf. 12½*
1080 Sheet of 8 16.00 16.00
a. A241 100r like #1074 1.10 1.10
b. A241 100r like #1075 1.10 1.10
c. A243 200r like #1077 2.00 2.00
d. A243 200r like #1079 2.00 2.00

London 1980 Intl. Stamp Exhib., May 6-14. No. 1080 contains 2 stamps of each design (4x2).

Draftsman in Wheelchair A244

1980, May 18 Photo. *Perf. 12½*
1081 A244 100r multicolored .90 .30

Disabled Veterans Corp, 30th anniversary.

Discus Thrower — A245

1980, May 18
1082 A245 75r dp orange & sep .75 .30

Olympics for the Disabled, Arnhem, Netherlands, June 21-July 5.

Pres. Suharto — A246

A246a A246b

Perf. 13½x12½, 12½

1980-83 **Photo.**
1083 A246 12.50r lt grn & grn .35 .25
1084 A246 50r lt grn & bl .35 .30
1084A A246 55r red rose & red lil .50 .25
1085 A246 75r lem & gldn brn .85 .25
1086 A246 100r brt pink & bl 2.25 .40
a. Bklt pane of 8 + 2 labels (6 #1086, 2 #1088, Inscribed 1981) 8.00
1087 A246a 110r dull org & dp red lil .50 .25
1088 A246 200r dl org & brn 6.00 .85
1088A A246a 250r dl org & brn .90 .25
1089 A246a 275r lt ap grn & dk grn 1.25 .25
1090 A246 300r rose lil & gold 1.40 .25
1091 A246 400r multicolored 1.60 .25

Engr.
Perf. 12½x13
1092 A246b 500r dk red brown 3.75 1.00
Nos. 1083-1092 (12) 19.70 4.55

Issued: 12.50r, 50r, 75r, 100r, 200r, 6/8; 300r, 400r, 8/8/81; 250r, 9/82; 500r, 3/11/83; 55r, 7/83; 110r, 275r, 9/27/83.

See Nos. 1257-1261, 1265, 1268. For surcharge see No. 1527.

Map of Indonesia, People — A247

1980, July 17 ***Perf. 12½***
1093 A247 75r blue & pink .45 .25
1094 A247 200r blue & dull yel .90 .40

1980 population census.

Ship Laying Cable — A248

1980, Aug. 8 **Photo.** ***Perf. 12½***
1095 A248 75r multicolored .55 .25
1096 A248 200r multicolored .90 .45

Singapore-Indonesia submarine cable opening.

50s Stamp of 1946 — A249

100r, 15s Battle of Surabaya stamp, 1946, horiz. 200r, 15s Independence Fund stamp, 1946.

1980, Aug. 17
1097 A249 75r dk brn & dp org .40 .40
1098 A249 100r gold & purple .90 .45
1099 A249 200r multicolored 1.10 .70
Nos. 1097-1099 (3) 2.40 1.55

Independence, 35th anniversary.

Asian Oceanic Postal Training School — A250

1980, Sept. 10 **Photo.** ***Perf. 12½***
1100 A250 200r multicolored 1.40 .25

OPEC Anniv. Emblem — A251

1980, Sept. 14
1101 A251 200r multicolored 1.20 .30

Organization of Petroleum Exporting Countries, 20th anniversary.

Armed Forces, 35th Anniversary — A252

200r, Service men and emblem.

1980, Oct. 5 **Photo.** ***Perf. 13½x13***
1102 A252 75r shown .65 .25
1103 A252 200r multicolored 1.00 .40

Vulturine Parrot — A253

Parrots: 100r, Yellow-backed lory. 200r, Red lory.

1980, Nov. 25 **Photo.** ***Perf. 13x12½***
1104 A253 75r shown 2.10 .70
1105 A253 100r multi 2.60 1.40
1106 A253 200r multi 3.50 2.00
Nos. 1104-1106 (3) 8.20 4.10

Souvenir Sheet
Perf. 12½
1106A Sheet of 3 21.00 21.00
b. A253 250r like #1105 7.00 7.00
c. A253 350r like #1104 7.00 7.00
d. A253 400r like #1106 7.00 7.00

One Day Beauty Orchid — A254

Orchids: 100r, Dendrobium discolor. 200r, Dendrobium lasianthera.

1980, Dec. 10 ***Perf. 13x13½***
1107 A254 75r shown .75 .25
1108 A254 100r multicolored 1.10 1.00
1109 A254 200r multicolored 2.60 .70
Nos. 1107-1109 (3) 4.45 1.95

Souvenir Sheet

1980 ***Perf. 13x13½***
1110 Sheet of 2 13.00 15.00
a. A254 250r like #1109 6.50 6.50
b. A254 350r like #1108 6.50 6.50

Heinrich von Stephan (1831-1897), UPU Founder — A255

1981, Jan. 7 ***Perf. 13½x12½***
1111 A255 200r brt bl & dk bl 1.25 .60

6th Asian Pacific Scout Jamboree A256

1981 ***Perf. 13½x12½, 12½x13½***
1112 A256 75r Emblems .40 .40
1113 A256 100r Scouts, vert. 1.10 .40
1114 A256 200r Emblems, diff. 1.20 .85
Nos. 1112-1114 (3) 2.70 1.65

Souvenir Sheet
1115 A256 150r like #1113 5.00 6.00

Issued: Nos. 1112-1114, 2/22; No. 1115, 8/14.

4th Asian-Oceanian Postal Union Congress A257

1981, Mar. 18 ***Perf. 12½***
1116 A257 200r multicolored 1.40 .30

Blood Donor Campaign — A258

75r, Girl holding blood drop. 100r, Hands holding blood drop. 200r, Hands, blood, diff.

1981, Apr. 22
1117 A258 75r multicolored .50 .25
1118 A258 100r multicolored .80 .40
1119 A258 200r multicolored 1.10 .70
Nos. 1117-1119 (3) 2.40 1.35

Intl. Family Planning Conference — A259

1981, Apr. 26
1120 A259 200r multicolored 1.20 .40

Natl. Education Day — A260

Traditional Bali Paintings: Nos. 1121-1122, Song of Sritanjung. No. 1123, Birth of the Eagle.

1981, May 2
1121 100r multicolored .80 .30
1122 200r multicolored 1.20 .65
a. A260 Pair #1121-1122 2.50 1.10

Souvenir Sheet
1123 Sheet of 2 10.00 12.00
a. A260 400r multicolored 3.50 3.50
b. A260 600r multicolored 6.00 6.00

No. 1123 has margin showing WIPA '81 emblem. No. 1123 exists with marginal inscription "Indonesien grusst WIPA." Value, $17.50.

A262

1981, May 9
1124 A262 200r multicolored 1.40 .45

ASEAN Building Jakarta, opening.

A263

1981, May 22
1125 A263 200r multicolored 2.25 .45

Uber Cup '81 Badminton Championship, Tokyo.

World Environment Day — A264

Bas-reliefs, Candhi Merut Buddhist Temple, Central Java: 75r, Tree of Life. 200r, Reclining Buddha.

1981, June 5
1126 A264 75r multicolored .65 .25
1127 A264 200r multicolored .95 .30

12th Koran Reading Competition, June 7-14 — A265

1981, June 7 ***Perf. 13½x12½***
1128 A265 200r multicolored 1.00 .45

Intl. Year of the Disabled
A266

75r, Blind man. 200r, Speech, hearing disabilities.

1981, July 31 *Perf. 12½*
1129 A266 75r multicolored .40 .25
1130 A266 200r multicolored .95 .45

Soekarno-Hatta Independence Monument, Jakarta — A267

1981, Aug. 17
1131 A267 200r multicolored 1.40 .40

Natl. Sports Week, Sept. 19-30 — A268

75r, Skydiving. 100r, Skin diving, horiz. 200r, Equestrian.

1981, Sept. 19
1132 A268 75r multicolored .40 .25
1133 A268 100r multicolored .65 .65
1134 A268 200r multicolored 1.20 .55
Nos. 1132-1134 (3) 2.25 1.45

The horse on No. 1134 is brown black, See Nos. 1374-1375 for souvenir sheets containing No. 1134 in different colors.

World Food Day — A268a

1981, Oct. 16
1135 A268a 200r multicolored 2.10 .70

Provincial Arms — A269

Natl. Arms A270

No. 1136, Aceh. No. 1137, Bali. No. 1138, Bengkulu. No. 1139, Jakarta. No. 1140, West Irian. No. 1141, West Java. No. 1142, Jambi. No. 1143, Central Java. No. 1144, East Java. No. 1145, South Kalimantan. No. 1146, East Kalimantan. No. 1147, West Kalimantan. No. 1148, Lampung. No. 1149, Central Kalimantan. No. 1150, Moluccas. No. 1151, West Nusa Tenggara. No. 1152, East Nusa Tenggara. No. 1153, Southeast Sulawesi. No. 1154, Central Sulawesi. No. 1155, West Sumatra. No. 1156, North Sulawesi. No. 1157, North Sumatra. No. 1158, South Sumatra. No. 1159, Riau. No. 1160, South Sulawesi. No. 1161, Yogyakarta. No. 1161A, Timor.

1981-83
1136 A269 100r multi 2.50 .75
1137 A269 100r multi 2.50 .75
1138 A269 100r multi 2.50 .75
1139 A269 100r multi 3.00 1.50
1140 A269 100r multi 10.00 .85
1141 A269 100r multi 1.00 .45
1142 A269 100r multi 1.00 .45
1143 A269 100r multi 1.00 .45
1144 A269 100r multi 1.00 .45
1145 A269 100r multi 1.00 .45
1146 A269 100r multi 1.00 .45
1147 A269 100r multi 1.00 .45
1148 A269 100r multi 1.10 .45
1149 A269 100r multi 1.00 .45
1150 A269 100r multi .80 .45
1151 A269 100r multi 1.10 .45
1152 A269 100r multi .80 .25
1153 A269 100r multi .80 .25
1154 A269 100r multi .80 .25
1155 A269 100r multi .90 .25
1156 A269 100r multi .90 .25
1157 A269 100r multi .80 .25
1158 A269 100r multi .80 .25
1159 A269 100r multi .80 .25
1160 A269 100r multi .80 .25
1161 A269 100r multi 2.00 .25
1161A A269 100r multi 1.00 .60
1162 A270 250r shown 4.50 1.00
Nos. 1136-1162 (28) 46.40 13.65

Issued: Nos. 1136-1140, 1981; Nos. 1141-1161, 1162, 1982; No. 1161A, 1983.
Barat = West; Timur = East; Utara = North; Selatan = South; Tenggara = Southeast; Tengah = Central.

Pink-crested Cockatoo — A271

100r, Sulphur-crested cockatoo. 200r, King cockatoo.

1981, Dec. 10
1163 A271 75r shown 2.50 .80
1164 A271 100r multi 2.75 .80
1165 A271 200r multi 4.50 2.75
Nos. 1163-1165 (3) 9.75 4.35

Souvenir Sheet

1166 Sheet of 2 17.50 21.00
a. A271 150r like #1164 4.00 4.00
b. A271 350r like #1165 12.50 12.50

Bumiputra Mutual Life Insurance Co., 70th Anniv. — A272

75r, Family. 100r, Family, diff. 200r, Hands holding symbols.

1982, Feb. 12
1167 A272 75r multi .40 .25
1168 A272 100r multi .65 .40
1169 A272 200r multi 1.00 .65
Nos. 1167-1169 (3) 2.05 1.30

Search and Rescue Institute, 10th Anniv. — A273

1982, Feb. 28 *Perf. 12½x13½*
1170 A273 250r multicolored 1.40 .30

General Election — A274

1982, Mar. 1 *Perf. 12½*
1171 A274 75r Ballot, houses .40 .25
1172 A274 100r Farm .55 .30
1173 A274 200r Arms 1.10 .70
Nos. 1171-1173 (3) 2.05 1.25

2nd UN Conference on Exploration and Peaceful Uses of Outer Space, Vienna, Aug. 9-21 — A275

1982, Apr. 19 *Perf. 13x13½*
1174 A275 150r Couple .65 .40
1175 A275 250r Emblem 1.10 .65

12th Thomas Badminton Cup, London, May — A276

1982, May 19
1176 A276 250r multicolored 1.50 .45
a. Souvenir sheet of 2 6.50

No. 1176a also exists overprinted "INDONESIE SALUE PHILEXFRANCE" in red or black. Value, each $45.

1982 World Cup — A277

1982, June 14
1177 A277 250r multi 1.75 .45
a. Souvenir sheet of 2 10.00
b.-c. Souvenir sheets of 2, each 75.00 80.00

No. 1177b overprinted "ITALIA WORLD CHAMPION" in black; No. 1177c overprinted same in red. Fake overprints exist.

60th Anniv. of Taman Siswa Educational System — A278

1982, July 3
1178 A278 250r multicolored 1.25 .50

15th Anniv. of Assoc. of South East Asian Nations (ASEAN) — A279

1982, Aug. 8 **Photo.** *Perf. 12½*
1179 A279 150r Members' flags 1.40 .45

Balinese Starling — A280

250r, King birds of paradise.

1982, Oct. 11 **Photo.** *Perf. 13x13½*
1180 A280 100r shown 2.50 .40
1181 A280 250r multi 4.00 1.10

Souvenir Sheet

1181A A280 500r like 100r 13.00 13.00

3rd World Natl. Park Cong., Denpasar Bali.

Red Birds of Paradise — A281

100r, Lawe's six-wired parotia. 150r, Twelve-wired birds of paradise.

1982, Dec. 20 *Perf. 12½x13½*
1182 A281 100r multi 1.75 .40
1183 A281 150r multi 2.50 .80
1184 A281 250r shown 4.25 1.25
Nos. 1182-1184 (3) 8.50 2.45

Souvenir Sheet

Perf. 12½x13½

1184A Sheet of 2 22.00 22.00
b. A281 200r like 100r 7.75 7.75
c. A281 300r like 250r 12.50 12.50

Scouting Year A282

1983, Feb. 22 **Photo.** *Perf. 13½x13*
1185 A282 250r multi 1.75 .30

Restoration of Borobudur Temple — A283

100r, Scaffolding, crane, vert. 150r, Buddha statue, stupas, vert. 250r, Statue, temple. 500r, Temple.

1983, Feb. 23 *Perf. 12½*
1186 A283 100r multi 1.00 .45
1187 A283 150r multi 1.50 .45
1188 A283 250r multi 4.50 2.75
Nos. 1186-1188 (3) 7.00 3.65

Souvenir Sheet

1189 A283 500r multi 15.00 19.00

Gas Plant — A284

1983, May 16 **Photo.** *Perf. 12½*
1190 A284 275r multi 1.20 .40

7th Intl. Liquefied Natural Gas Conference and Exhibition, Jakarta, May 16-19.

World Communications Year — A285

75r, Dove, ships. 110r, Satellite. 175r, Dish antenna, jet. 275r, Airmail envelope, globe.

1983, May 17 *Perf. 12½x13½*

1191 A285 75r multi .25 .25
1192 A285 110r multi .45 .25
1193 A285 175r multi .80 .40
1194 A285 275r multi 1.20 .65
Nos. 1191-1194 (4) 2.70 1.55

See Nos. 1215-1216.

13th Natl. Koran Reading Competition, Padang, May 23-31 — A286

1983, May 23 *Perf. 13½x13*

1195 A286 275r multi 1.25 .55

Total Solar Eclipse, June 11 — A287

1983, June 11 *Perf. 12½*

1196 A287 110r Map, eclipse .65 .25
1197 A287 275r Map 2.10 .40

Souvenir Sheet

1198 A287 500r like 275r 14.00 17.00

Launch of Palapa B Satellite — A288

1983, June 18 *Perf. 12½x13½*

1199 A288 275r multi 1.40 .55

Agricultural Census — A289

1983, July 1 Photo. *Perf. 12½*

1200 A289 110r Produce .55 .25
1201 A289 275r Farmer 1.00 .25

15th Anniv. of Indonesia-Pakistan Economic and Cultural Cooperation Org. — A290

Weavings: No. 1202, Indonesian, Lombok. No. 1203, Pakistani, Baluchistan.

1983, Aug. 19

1202 A290 275r multicolored 1.25 .85
1203 A290 275r multicolored 1.25 .85

Krakatoa Eruption Centenary A291

1983, Aug. 26

1204 A291 110r Volcano .55 .30
1205 A291 275r Map 1.40 .45

CN-235, Light Air Transport — A292

1983, Sept. 10 Photo. *Perf. 12½*

1206 A292 275r multi 1.25 .55

Tropical Fish — A293

110r, Puntius tetrazona. 175r, Rasbora einthoveni. 275r, Toxotes jaculator.

1983, Oct. 17 Photo. *Perf. 12½*

1207 A293 110r multi 1.75 .65
1208 A293 175r multi 1.75 .65
1209 A293 275r multi 5.50 2.00
Nos. 1207-1209 (3) 9.00 3.30

Canderawasih Birds — A294

110r, Diphyllodes respublica. 175r, Epimachus fastuosus. 275r, Drepanornis albertisi.

1983, Nov. 30 Photo. *Perf. 12½*

1210 A294 110r multi 1.25 .25
1211 A294 175r multi 1.75 .25
1212 A294 275r multi 3.50 .25
1213 A294 500r as #1212 5.00 .40
a. Souvenir sheet of 1 22.50 22.50
Nos. 1210-1213 (4) 11.50 1.15

Inalienable Rights of the Palestinian People A295

1983, Dec. 20 *Perf. 13½x13*

1214 A295 275r multi 1.25 .30

WCY Type of 1983

Souvenir Sheets

1983 Photo. *Perf. 12½x13½*

1215 A285 400r like No. 1192 9.00 8.00
1216 A285 500r like No. 1194 11.00 7.00

Telecom '83 exhib., Geneva, Oct. 26-Nov. 1 (400r). Philatelic Museum opening, Jakarta (500r). Issued: 400r, Oct. 26; 500r, Sept. 29.

Fight Against Polio — A296

1984, Feb. 17 Photo. *Perf. 12½*

1217 A296 110r Emblem .40 .25
1218 A296 275r Stylized person 1.20 .30

4th Five-Year Development Plan — A297

1984, Apr. 1 Photo. *Perf. 12½*

1219 A297 55r Fertilizer industry .25 .25
1220 A297 75r Aviation .25 .25
1221 A297 110r Shipping .45 .25
1222 A297 275r Communications 1.25 .60
Nos. 1219-1222 (4) 2.20 1.35

Forestry Resources A298

75r, Forest, paper mill. 110r, Seedling. 175r, Tree cutting. 275r, Logs.

1984, May 17 Photo. *Perf. 12½*

1223 A298 75r multi 1.10 .25
1224 A298 110r multi 1.10 .25
1225 A298 175r multi 1.10 .40
1226 A298 275r multi 1.10 .55
a. Souv. sheet of 2, #1225-1226 17.00 12.00
Nos. 1223-1226 (4) 4.40 1.45

17th Annual Meeting of ASEAN Foreign Ministers — A299

1984, July 9 Photo. *Perf. 12½*

1227 A299 275r Flags 1.75 .55

1984 Summer Olympics A300

1984, July 28 Photo. *Perf. 12½*

1228 A300 75r Pole vault .35 .25
1229 A300 110r Archery .40 .25
1230 A300 175r Boxing .50 .25
1231 A300 250r Shooting 1.00 .45
1232 A300 275r Weight lifting 1.40 .45
1233 A300 325r Swimming 2.25 .25
Nos. 1228-1233 (6) 5.90 1.90

Horse Dancers, Central Java — A301

Processions: 110r, Reyog Ponorogo, East Java. 275r, Lion Dance, West Java. 325r, Barong of Bali.

1984, Aug. 17 *Perf. 12½x13½*

1234 A301 75r shown .75 .25
1235 A301 110r multi 1.10 .25
1236 A301 275r multi 1.10 .60
1237 A301 325r multi 2.90 .60
Nos. 1234-1237 (4) 5.85 1.70

Natl. Sports Day A302

110r, Thomas Cup victory. 275r, Gymnastics.

1984, Sept. 9 Photo. *Perf. 13½x13*

1238 A302 110r multi .95 .30
1239 A302 275r multi 1.40 .45

Postcode System Inauguration A303

1984, Sept. 27 Photo. *Perf. 12½*

1240 A303 110r multi .40 .30
1241 A303 275r multi .85 .70

Birds of Irian Jaya — A304

75r, Chlamydera lauterbachi. 110r, Sericulus aureus. 275r, Astrapia nigra. 325r, Lophorhina superba.

1984, Oct. 15 *Perf. 12½x13½*

1242 A304 75r multi 2.10 .25
1243 A304 110r multi 3.50 .25
1244 A304 275r multi 3.75 .25
1245 A304 325r multi 4.25 .30
a. Souv. sheet of 2, #1242, 1245 25.00 27.00
Nos. 1242-1245 (4) 13.60 1.05

No. 1245a for PHILAKOREA '84.

Oath of the Youth — A305

1984, Oct. 28 *Perf. 12½*

1246 A305 275r Emblem 1.20 .70

ICAO, 40th Anniversary — A306

275r, Airplane, Emblem.

1984, Dec. 7 Photo. *Perf. 13½x12½*

1247 A306 275r multi 1.25 .70

Indonesia Netherlands Marine Exped., 1984-85 — A307

Survey ship Snellius II and: 50r, Marine geological and geophysical exploration. 100r, Mapping ocean currents. 275r, Studying marine flora and fauna.

1985, Feb. 27 Photo. *Perf. 13x13½*

1248 A307 50r multi .65 .25
1249 A307 100r multi 1.10 .25
1250 A307 275r multi 1.25 .40
Nos. 1248-1250 (3) 3.00 .90

75th Intl. Women's Day — A308

100r, Emblem. 275r, Silhouettes, emblem.

1985, Mar. 8

1251 A308 100r dp mauve & red 2.00 .65
1252 A308 275r brown & red 3.00 2.50

Five Year Plan A309

75r, Mecca pilgrimage program. 140r, Compulsory education. 350r, Cement industry, Padang works.

1985, Apr. 1 *Perf. 13½x13*

1254 A309 75r brn & red .35 .25
1255 A309 140r brn, grey grn .50 .45
1256 A309 350r brn, turq grn 1.00 1.00
Nos. 1254-1256 (3) 1.85 1.70

Suharto Type of 1980-83 and

A310 A310a A310b A310c

Perf. 13½x12½, 12½ (A310, A310a, A310b, A310c)

1983-93 Photo.

1257	A246	10r pale grn & dk grn	1.00	.25
1258	A246	25r pale org & dk cop red	.45	.25
1259	A246	50r beige & dk brn	.25	.25
1260	A246	55r sal rose & rose	.25	.25
1261	A246	100r lt bl grn & ultra	.40	.25
1262	A310	140r rose & dp brn	.60	.25
1263	A310c	150r yel grn & multi	.25	.25
1264	A310b	200r pink, bl & red	.40	.25
1265	A246	300r lt dull grn, bl grn & gold	1.10	.25
1266	A310c	300r multicolored	.35	.25
1267	A310	350r red & brt lil	1.00	.35
1268	A246	400r bl grn, int bl & gold	1.00	.25
1268A	A310b	700r pale grn, rose lil & grn	.90	.25
1268B	A310c	700r red & multi	.65	.25
1269	A310a	1000r multi	.90	.25
		Nos. 1257-1269 (15)	9.50	3.85

Issued: 10r, 25r, 3/11; 140r, 350r, 4/10/85; 50r, 100r, No. 1265, 12/24/86; 55r, 400r, 12/87; 200r, 12/89; 700r, 3/90; 1000r, 8/17/88; 150r, Nos. 1266, 1268B, 8/17/93.

For surcharge see No. 1527.

Asia-Africa Conference, 30th Anniv. — A311

350r, Emblem, inscription.

1985, Apr. 24 *Perf. 12½*

1270 A311 350r multi 1.60 .45

Intl. Youth Year — A312

75r, Three youths, globe. 140r, Youths supporting globe.

1985, July 12 *Perf. 12½x13½*

1271 A312 75r multi .60 .25
1272 A312 140r multi 1.00 .25

UN Decade for Women — A313

55r, Profiles of women, emblem. 140r, Globe, emblem.

1985, July 26

1273 A313 55r multi .55 .25
1274 A313 140r multi .90 .25

Indonesian Trade Fair — A314

140r, Hydro-electric plant. 350r, Farmer, industrial plant.

1985, Aug. 1

1275 A314 140r multi .65 .25
1276 A314 350r multi 1.40 .40

Republic of Indonesia, 40th anniv.

11th Natl. Sports Week, Jakarta, Sept. 9-20 A315

55r, Sky diving. 100r, Combat sports. 140r, High jump. 350r, Wind surfing, vert.

Perf. 13½x12½, 12½x13½

1985, Sept. 9 Photo.

1277 A315 55r multi .35 .25
1278 A315 100r multi .75 .25
1279 A315 140r multi .80 .25
1280 A315 350r multi 1.40 .40
Nos. 1277-1280 (4) 3.30 1.15

Org. of Petroleum Exporting Countries, OPEC, 25th Anniv. — A316

1985, Sept. 14 *Perf. 12½*

1281 A316 140r multi 1.25 .30

Natl. Oil Industry, Cent. A317

1985, Oct. 8 *Perf. 13½x13*

1282 A317 140r Oil tankers .55 .30
1283 A317 250r Refinery 1.00 .45
1284 A317 350r Offshore oil rig 1.40 .90
Nos. 1282-1284 (3) 2.95 1.65

UN, 40th Anniv. — A318

Design: 140r, Doves, 40, emblem. 300r, Bombs transformed into plants.

1985, Oct. 24 *Perf. 12½*

1285 A318 140r multicolored .45 .25
1286 A318 300r multicolored 1.40 .45

Wildlife A318a

75r, Rhinoceros sondaicus. 150r, Anoa depressicornis. 300r, Varanus komodoensis.

1985, Dec. 27 Photo. *Perf. 14½x13*

1286A A318a 75r multi 1.10 .30
1286B A318a 150r multi 1.60 .45
1286C A318a 300r multi 2.75 .70
Nos. 1286A-1286C (3) 5.45 1.45

1986 Industrial Census — A319

1986, Feb. 8 Photo. *Perf. 12½*

1287 A319 Pair 1.40 1.25
a. 175r Census emblem .65 .25
b. 175r Symbols of industry .65 .25

UN Child Survival Campaign A320

1986, Mar. 15 Photo. *Perf. 12½*

1288 A320 75r Breastfeeding .65 .25
1289 A320 140r Immunization .85 .30

UNICEF, 40th anniv.

4th 5-year Development Plan — A321

1986, Apr. 1 Photo. *Perf. 12½*

1290 A321 140r Construction .55 .30
1291 A321 500r Agriculture .75 .40

14th Thomas Cup, 13th Uber Cup, Jakarta — A322

1986, Apr. 22

1292 A322 55r Cup, racket .65 .25
1293 A322 150r Cups, horiz. 1.10 .25

EXPO '86, Vancouver — A323

75r, Pinisi junk. 150r, Kentongan, satellite. 300r, Pavilion emblem.

1986, May 2 *Perf. 12½x14½*

1294 A323 75r multi .50 .25
1295 A323 150r multi 1.00 .30
1296 A323 300r multi 1.50 .40
Nos. 1294-1296 (3) 3.00 .95

Natl. Scout Jamboree, JAMNAS '86, Cibubur Jakarta East A324

Perf. 13½x12½, 12½x13½

1986, June 21 Photo.

1297 A324 100r Saluting flag .35 .25
1298 A324 140r Cookout 1.40 .30
1299 A324 210r Map-reading, vert. 1.60 .40
Nos. 1297-1299 (3) 3.35 .95

Air Show '86, Jakarta, June 22-July 1 A325

1986, June 23 *Perf. 13½x12½*

1300 A325 350r multi 1.75 .50

Folk Dances — A326

1986, July 30 Photo. *Perf. 12½*

1301 A326 140r Legong Kraton	1.10	.25
1302 A326 350r Barong	1.75	.45
1303 A326 500r Kecak	2.60	.60
Nos. 1301-1303 (3)	5.45	1.30

19th Congress of Intl. Society of Sugar Cane Technologists, Jakarta — A327

1986, Aug. 5 *Perf. 12½x13½*

1304 A327 150r Planting	.50	.25
1305 A327 300r Sugar	1.50	.25

Sea-Me-We Submarine Cable Inauguration — A328

1986, Sept. 8 *Perf. 12½*

1306 A328 140r shown	.50	.25
1307 A328 350r Map, diff.	1.50	.45

Southeast Asia, Middle East, Western Europe Submarine Cable.

Intl. Peace Year — A329

500r, Dove circling Earth.

1986, Dec. 17 Photo. *Perf. 12½*

1308 A329 350r shown	1.10	.30
1309 A329 500r multi	1.40	.25

1987 General Election — A330

75r, Tourism, party emblems, industry. 350r, Emblems, natl. eagle, ballot box.

1987, Jan. 19

1310 A330 75r multi	.45	.25
1311 A330 140r multi	.65	.25
1312 A330 350r multi	1.25	.40
Nos. 1310-1312 (3)	2.35	.90

A331

350r, Satellite, horiz.

1987, Mar. 21 Photo. *Perf. 12½*

1313 A331 350r multi	1.00	.40
1314 A331 500r shown	1.50	.25

Launch of Palapa B-2P, Cape Canaveral.

A332

140r, Boy carving figurines, horiz.

1987, Apr. 1

1315 A332 140r multi	.30	.25
1316 A332 350r shown	.80	.35

4th 5-Year Development Plan.

Folk Costumes — A333

140r, Kalimantan Timur. 350r, Daerah Aceh. 400r, Timor Timur.

1987, May 25 *Perf. 13x13½*

1317 A333 140r multi	1.75	.40
1318 A333 350r multi	7.50	4.75
1319 A333 400r multi	9.00	1.10
Nos. 1317-1319 (3)	18.25	6.25

See Nos. 1358-1363, 1412-1417, 1448-1453, 1464-1469.

14th Southeast Asia Games, Jakarata, Sept. 9-20 — A334

1987, June 10 *Perf. 12½*

1320 A334 140r Weight lifting	.45	.25
1321 A334 250r Swimming	.85	.30
1322 A334 350r Running	1.25	.45
Nos. 1320-1322 (3)	2.55	1.00

Anniv. Emblems — A335

1987, June 20

1323 A335 75r multi, horiz.	.75	.25
1324 A335 100r shown	1.25	.25

City of Jakarta, 460th anniv.; Jakarta Fair, 20th anniv.

Children's Day — A336

100r, Education, horiz. 250r, Universal immunization.

1987, July 23

1325 A336 100r multicolored	.60	.25
1326 A336 250r multicolored	1.00	.25

ASEAN Headquarters, Jakarta — A337

1987, Aug. 8

1327 A337 350r multi	1.40	.45

ASEAN, 20th anniv.

Assoc. of Physicians Specializing in Internal Diseases, 30th Anniv. — A338

300r, Stylized man, caduceus.

1987, Aug. 23 Photo.

1328 A338 300r multicolored	1.25	.25

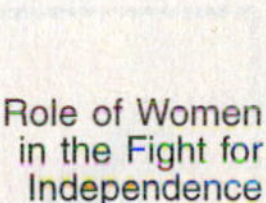

Sand Craters, Mt. Bromo, Timur A339

350r, Bratan (Bedugul) Lake, Bali. 500r, Sea gardens, Bunaken Island.

1987, Oct. 20 *Perf. 13½x12½*

1329 A339 140r shown	.40	.25
1330 A339 350r multi	1.60	.65
1331 A339 500r multi	2.00	.30
Nos. 1329-1331 (3)	4.00	1.20

Tourism. See Nos. 1367-1370A, 1408-1410, 1420-1422.

Role of Women in the Fight for Independence A340

75r, Veteran. 100r, Soldiers, barbed wire (Laskar Wanita).

1987, Nov. 10 *Perf. 12½*

1332 A340 75r multicolored	.40	.25
1333 A340 100r multicolored	.85	.25

Fish — A341

150r, Osphronemus goramy. 200r, Cyprinus carpio. 500r, Clarias batrachus.

1987, Dec. 30

1334 A341 150r multicolored	1.10	.65
1335 A341 200r multicolored	1.75	.30
1336 A341 500r multicolored	3.75	.30
Nos. 1334-1336 (3)	6.60	1.25

Natl. Veteran's League, 31st Anniv. — A342

1988, Jan. 2

1337 A342 250r blue grn & org	1.10	.25

Occupational Health and Safety for Greater Efficiency and Productivity — A343

350r, Worker using safety equipment.

1988, Jan. 12 *Perf. 13½x12½*

1338 A343 350r multicolored	1.25	.45

See No. 1419.

Natl. Craft Council, 8th Anniv. — A344

Crafts: 120r, Carved wood snake and frog. 350r, Cane rocking chair. 500r, Ornate carved bamboo containers and fan.

1988, Mar. 3 Photo. *Perf. 12½*

1339 A344 120r ultra & dark brn	.70	.25
1340 A344 350r lt bl & dk brn	1.00	.45
1341 A344 500r yel grn & dk brn	1.75	.25
Nos. 1339-1341 (3)	3.45	.95

Pelita IV (Five-Year Development Plan) — A345

140r, Oil rig, refinery. 400r, Crayfish, trawler.

1988, Apr. 1

1342 A345 140r multicolored	.30	.25
1343 A345 400r multicolored	.75	.30

World Expo '88, Brisbane, Australia — A346

Designs: 200r, Two children, Borobudur Temple in silhouette. 300r, Boy wearing armor and headdress. 350r, Girl, boy and a Tongkonan house, Toraja, South Sulawesi.

1988, Apr. 30 Photo. *Perf. 12½*

1344 A346 200r multi	.80	.25
1345 A346 300r multi	1.20	.25
1346 A346 350r multi	1.50	.30
a. Souv. sheet of 3, #1344-1346	12.00	12.00
Nos. 1344-1346 (3)	3.50	.80

No. 1346a exists imperf. Value: $30 unused or used.

Intl. Red Cross and Red Crescent Organizations, 125th Annivs. — A347

1988, May 8

1347 A347 350r black & red	1.10	.25

Orchids — A348

400r, Dendrobium none. 500r, Dendrobium abang.

1988, May 17 *Perf. 13x13½*
1348 A348 400r multi 1.60 .45
1349 A348 500r multi 1.60 .30

1988 Summer Olympics, Seoul — A349

1988, June 15 Photo. *Perf. 12½*
1350 A349 75r Running .50 .25
1351 A349 100r Weight lifting .75 .25
1352 A349 200r Archery .90 .25
1353 A349 300r Table tennis .50 .25
1354 A349 400r Swimming .65 .30
a. Souv. sheet of 3 + label, #1351-1352, 1354, imperf 13.00 15.00
1355 A349 500r Tennis 2.25 .35
a. Souv. sheet of 3 + label, #1350, 1353, 1355, imperf 13.00 15.00
Nos. 1350-1355 (6) 5.55 1.65

Sheets exist perf. Value, each $12.

Intl. Council of Women, Cent. — A350

1988, June 26
1356 A350 140r brt blue & blk .85 .25

7th Natl. Farmers' Week — A351

1988, July 9
1357 A351 350r lake & bister 1.25 .55

Folk Costumes Type of 1987

Traditional wedding attire from: 55r, West Sumatra. 75p, Jambi. 100r, Bengkulu. 120r, Lampung. 200r, Moluccas. 250r, East Nusa.

1988, July 15 *Perf. 12½x14½*
1358 A333 55r multicolored .25 .25

Perf. 12½x13½
1359 A333 75r multicolored .25 .25
1360 A333 100r multicolored .55 .25
1361 A333 120r multicolored .80 .25

Perf. 12½x14½
1362 A333 200r multicolored 1.50 .25
1363 A333 250r multicolored 2.00 1.00
Nos. 1358-1363 (6) 5.35 2.25

A352

1988, Sept. 29 Photo. *Perf. 12½*
1364 A352 500r multicolored 1.50 .30

13th Congress of the Non-Aligned News Agencies Pool, Jakarta, Sept. 29-Oct. 1.

A353

1988, Oct. 9
1365 A353 140r multicolored .85 .25

Intl. Letter Writing Week.

Transportion and Communications Decade for Asia and the Pacific (1985-1995) A354

1988, Oct. 24
1366 A354 350r blk & lt blue 1.40 .55

Tourism Type of 1987

Architecture: 250r, Al Mashun Mosque, Medan. 300r, Pagaruyung Palace, Batusangkar. 500r, 1000r, Keong Emas Taman Theater, Jakarta.

1988-89 Photo. *Perf. 13½x13*
1367 A339 250r multi .50 .40
1368 A339 300r multi 1.00 .30
1369 A339 500r multi 2.25 .30
Nos. 1367-1369 (3) 3.75 1.00

Souvenir Sheets

Imperf
1370 A339 1000r multi 7.50 7.50

Perf. 14½x13
1370A Sheet of 2 20.00 15.00
b. A339 1500r like No. 1367 7.25 1.60
c. A339 2500r like No. 1368 11.50 2.75

No. 1370 exists perf 14½x12½. Value $10.

Issue dates: No. 1370A, Nov. 1989; others, Nov. 25, 1988. World Stamp Expo '89, Washington, DC.

Butterflies — A356

400r, Papilio gigon. 500r, Graphium androcles.

1988, Dec. 20 *Perf. 12½x13½*
1371 A356 400r multi 1.50 .45
1372 A356 500r multi 2.50 .65

Souvenir Sheet

Imperf
1373 A356 1000r like 500r 9.00 9.00

No. 1373 exists perf. 12½x14½. Value $26.

Equestrian Type of 1981
Souvenir Sheets

1988 *Imperf.*
1374 Sheet of 4 8.00 8.00
a. A268 200r blk, dark red & grn .50 .25
1375 Sheet of 1 + label, dk bl, dark red & deep org 9.00 9.00

FILACEPT '88, The Hague, Oct. 18-23, 1988. Nos. 1374-1375 exist perf. 12½. Value, as 1374, $8; as 1375, $18.

Flora — A357

200r, Rafflesia. 1000r, Amorphophallus titanum.

1989, Jan. 7 Photo. *Perf. 13½x13*
1376 A357 200r multi 1.00 .40
1377 A357 1000r multi 2.50 .40

Souvenir Sheet
Perf. 13½x14½
Value in Black
1378 A357 1000r like No. 1377 20.00 25.00

Garuda Indonesia Airlines, 40th Anniv. — A358

1989, Jan. 26 *Perf. 12½*
1379 A358 350r bl grn & brt bl 1.60 .65

World Wildlife Fund — A359

Orangutans, Pongo pygmaeus: 75r, Adult and young. 100r, Adult hanging in tree. 140r, Adult, young in tree. 500r, Adult's head.

1989, Mar. 6 Photo. *Perf. 12½*
1380 A359 75r multi 1.75 1.10
1381 A359 100r multi 2.25 .65
a. Souv. sheet of 2, #1380-1381 60.00 60.00
1382 A359 140r multi 2.75 .65
1383 A359 500r multi 7.00 5.00
a. Souv. sheet of 2, #1382-1383 60.00 60.00
Nos. 1380-1383 (4) 13.75 7.40

Use of Postage Stamps in Indonesia, 125th Anniv. — A360

1989, Apr. 1
1384 A360 1000r grn, rose lil & dp blue 2.00 .25

5th Five-year Development Plan — A361

Industries: 55r, Fertilizer. 150r, Cilegon Iron and Steel Mill. 350r, Petroleum.

1989, Apr. 1
1385 A361 55r multi .30 .25
1386 A361 150r multi .30 .25
1387 A361 350r multi .70 .25
Nos. 1385-1387 (3) 1.30 .75

See Nos. 1427-1428, 1461-1462, 1488-1489, 1530-1532.

Natl. Education Day — A362

Ki Hadjar Dewantara (b. 1889), founder of Taman Siswa school and: 140r, Graduate. 300r, Pencil, globe and books.

1989, May 2
1388 A362 140r ver, lake & brt rose lil .60 .25
1389 A362 300r vio & pale grn .90 .30

Terbuka University (140r) and freedom from illiteracy (300r).

Asia-Pacific Telecommunity, 10th Anniv. — A363

1989, July 1 Photo. *Perf. 12½*
1390 A363 350r green & vio 1.25 .85

Sudirman Cup, Flag — A364

1989, July 3
1391 A364 100r scar, gold & dark red brn 1.50 .25

Sudirman Cup world badminton mixed team championships, Jakarta, May 24-28.

Natl. Children's Day — A365

1989, July 23
1392 A365 100r Literacy .50 .25
1393 A365 250r Physical fitness 1.00 .30

CIRDAP, 10th Anniv. — A366

1989, July 29
1394 A366 140r bl & dk red brn 1.00 .25

Center on Integrated Rural Development for Asia and the Pacific.

A367

Paleoanthropological Discoveries in Indonesia: Fossils of *Homo erectus* and *Homo sapiens* men: 100r, Sangiran 17. 150r, Perning 1. 200r, Sangiran 10. 250r, Wajak 1. 300r, Sambungmacan. 350r, Ngandong 7.

1989, Aug. 31
1395 A367 100r multi .50 .25
1396 A367 150r multi .70 .25
1397 A367 200r multi 1.10 .40
1398 A367 250r multi 1.40 .30
1399 A367 300r multi 1.60 .45
1400 A367 350r multi 2.25 .30
Nos. 1395-1400 (6) 7.55 1.95

Nos. 1398-1400 vert.

A368

1989, Sept. 4
1401 A368 350r dp bl & yel grn 1.25 .75

Interparliamentary Union, Cent.

12th Natl. Sports Week — A369

1989, Sept. 18

1402 A369 75r Tae kwando .30 .25
1403 A369 100r Tennis .40 .25
1404 A369 140r Judo .50 .25
1405 A369 350r Volleyball 1.25 .70
1406 A369 500r Boxing 2.25 .35
1407 A369 1000r Archery 3.25 .60
Nos. 1402-1407 (6) 7.95 2.40

Tourism Type of 1987

Structures in Miniature Park: 120r, Taman Burung. 350r, Natl. Philatelic Museum. 500r, Istana Anak-Anak, vert.

Perf. 13½x12½, 12½x13½

1989, Oct. 9

1408 A339 120r multicolored .65 .25
1409 A339 350r multicolored 1.00 .45
1410 A339 500r multicolored 1.75 .40
Nos. 1408-1410 (3) 3.40 1.10

Film Festival — A370

1989, Nov. 11 Photo. *Perf. 12½*

1411 A370 150r yel bister & blk 1.20 .25

Folk Costumes Type of 1987

Traditional wedding attire from: 50r, North Sumatra. 75r, South Sumatra. 100r, Jakarta. 140r, North Sulawesi. 350r, Mid Sulawesi. 500r, South Sulawesi. 1500r, North Sulawesi.

1989, Dec. 11 *Perf. 13x13½*

1412 A333 50r multicolored .35 .25
1413 A333 75r multicolored .35 .25
1414 A333 100r multicolored .35 .25
1415 A333 140r multicolored .80 .25
1416 A333 350r multicolored 1.25 .90
1417 A333 500r multicolored 1.75 .50
Nos. 1412-1417 (6) 4.85 2.40

Souvenir Sheet

Imperf

1418 A333 1500r multicolored 6.50 6.50

No. 1418 exists perf. 12½x13½. Value $11.

Health and Safety Type of 1988

200r, Lineman, power lines.

1990, Jan. 12 *Perf. 13x12½*

Size: 29x21mm

1419 A343 200r blue grn & org brn 1.10 .25

Tourism Type of 1987

Architecture: 200r, Fort Marlborough, Bengkulu. 400r, 1000r, National Museum, Jakarta. 500r, 1500r, Mosque of Baiturrahman, Banda Aceh.

1990, Feb. 1 *Perf. 13½x13*

1420 A339 200r multicolored .75 .25
1421 A339 400r multicolored 1.25 .25
1422 A339 500r multicolored 1.50 .30
Nos. 1420-1422 (3) 3.50 .80

Souvenir Sheet

1423 Sheet of 2 9.00 9.00
a. A339 1000r multicolored 3.25 .50
b. A339 1500r multicolored 5.75 .75

Flora A371

75r, Mammilaria fragilis. 1000r, Gmelina ellipitca.

1990, Mar. 1

1424 A371 75r multi .40 .25
1425 A371 1000r multi 2.10 .45

Souvenir Sheet

1426 A371 1500r like #1425 11.00 11.00

5th Five-year Development Plan Type of 1989

200r, Road construction. 1000r, Lighthouse, ship.

1990, Apr. 1 *Perf. 12½*

1427 A361 200r multi .35 .25
1428 A361 1000r multi 1.25 1.10

Visit Indonesia Year, 1991 A372

Perf. 13½x12½, 12½x13½

1990, May 1

1429 A372 100r shown .40 .25
1430 A372 500r Steps, ruin 1.25 .40

Souvenir Sheet

Perf. 14½x12½

1430A A372 5000r like #1429 16.00 11.00

No. 1430A, Stamp World London '90.

A373

1990, May 18 *Perf. 12½*

1431 A373 1000r gray grn & brn org 1.50 .90

Disabled Veterans Corps, 40th anniv.

A374

1990, June 8 *Perf. 12½*

1432 A374 75r shown .60 .25
1433 A374 150r multi, diff. .90 .25
1434 A374 400r multi, diff. 2.00 .40
Nos. 1432-1434 (3) 3.50 .90

Souvenir Sheet

1435 A374 1500r multi 8.00 8.50

World Cup Soccer Championships, Italy.

Family Planning in Indonesia, 20th Anniv. — A375

1990, June 29

1436 A375 60r brown & red .85 .25

Natl. Census — A376

1990, July 1

1437 A376 90r yel grn & dk grn 1.00 .25

Natl. Children's Day — A377

1990, July 23

1438 A377 500r multicolored 1.40 .40

Souvenir Sheet

Traditional Lampung Wedding Costumes — A378

Perf. 12½x14½

1990, June 10 Photo.

1439 A378 2000r multicolored 7.00 7.00

Natl. Philatelic Exhibition, Stamp World London '90 and New Zealand '90.

Independence, 45th Anniv. — A379

200r, Soldier raising flag. 500r, Skyscraper, highway.

1990, Aug. 17 *Perf. 12½x13½*

1440 A379 200r multicolored .70 .25
1441 A379 500r multicolored 1.00 .45

Souvenir Sheet

1442 A379 1000r like #1441 7.50 7.50

Indonesia-Pakistan Economic & Cultural Cooperation Organization — A380

Designs: 400r, Woman dancing in traditional costume, vert.

Perf. 13½x12½, 12½x13½

1990, Aug. 19 Litho.

1443 A380 75r multicolored .55 .25
1444 A380 400r multicolored 1.25 .45

Asian Pacific Postal Training Center, 20th Anniv. — A381

1990, Sept. 10 Photo. *Perf. 12½*

1445 A381 500r vio bl, bl & ultra 1.40 .25

A382

1990, Sept. 14

1446 A382 200r gray, blk & org 1.25 .25

Organization of Petroleum Exporting Countries (OPEC), 30th anniv.

A383

1990, Oct. 24

1447 A383 1000r multicolored 2.10 .30

Environmental Protection Laws, 40th anniv.

Folk Costumes Type of 1987

Traditional wedding attire from: 75r, West Java. 100r, Central Java. 150r, Yogyakarta. 200r, East Java. 400r, Bali. 500r, West Nusa Tenggara.

1990, Nov. 1 *Perf. 13x13½*

1448 A333 75r multicolored .35 .25
1449 A333 100r multicolored .45 .25
1450 A333 150r multicolored .50 .25
1451 A333 200r multicolored .70 .25
1452 A333 400r multicolored 1.00 .40
1453 A333 500r multicolored 1.10 .55
Nos. 1448-1453 (6) 4.10 1.95

A385

Visit Indonesia Year 1991: Women in traditional costumes.

1991, Jan. 1 Photo. *Perf. 12½x13½*

1454 A385 200r multicolored 1.00 .25
1455 A385 500r multicolored 1.25 .60
1456 A385 1000r multicolored 2.60 .45
Nos. 1454-1456 (3) 4.85 1.30

Souvenir Sheet

1456A A385 1500r As No. 1454 13.00 12.00

A386

1991, Feb. 4 *Perf. 12½*

1457 A386 200r yel, grn & bl grn 1.25 .25

16th natl. Koran reading competition, Jogjakarta.

Palace of Sultan Ternate, the Moluccas A387

Design: 1000r, 2500r, Bari House, Palembang, South Sumatra.

1991, Mar. 1 *Perf. 13½x12½*

1458 A387 500r multicolored 1.10 .30

1459 A387 1000r multicolored 1.75 .35

Souvenir Sheet

1460 A387 2500r multicolored 6.50 6.00

5th Five Year Development Plan Type of 1989

1991, Apr. 1 *Perf. 12½*
1461 A361 75r Steel mill, vert. .35 .25
1462 A361 200r Computers .60 .25

Danger of Smoking — A388

1991, May 31 Photo. *Perf. 12½*
1463 A388 90r multicolored 1.20 .25

Folk Costumes Type of 1987

Traditional wedding attire from: 100r, West Kalimantan. 200r, Mid Kalimantan. 300r, South Kalimantan. 400r, Southeast Sulawesi. 500r, Riau. 1000r, Irian Jaya.

1991, June 15 *Perf. 13x13½*
1464 A333 100r multicolored .30 .25
1465 A333 200r multicolored 1.00 .25
1466 A333 300r multicolored .60 .25
1467 A333 400r multicolored .75 .25
1468 A333 500r multicolored 1.00 .30
1469 A333 1000r multicolored 1.25 .65
Nos. 1464-1469 (6) 4.90 1.95

Natl. Scouting Jamboree, Cibubur — A389

1991, June 15 *Perf. 12½*
1470 A389 200r multicolored 1.25 .25

Monument A390

1991, July 6
1471 A390 200r multicolored 1.25 .25

Natl. Farmers' Week — A391

1991, July 15
1472 A391 500r brt bl, yel & grn 1.50 .25

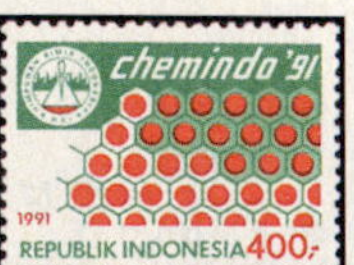

Indonesian Chemical Society, 4th Natl. Congress A392

1991, July 28
1473 A392 400r grn, ver & dull grn 1.50 .25

Chemindo '91.

A393

1991, Aug. 24 Photo. *Perf. 12½*
1474 A393 300r blk, red & gray 1.50 .25

5th Junior Men's and 4th Women's Asian Weightlifting Championships.

A394

1991, Aug. 30
1475 A394 500r lilac & sky blue 1.50 .25

World Cup Parachuting Championships.

A395

1991, Sept. 17
1476 A395 200r multicolored 1.40 .25

Indonesian Red Cross, 46th aAnniv.

A396

1991, Oct. 6
1477 A396 300r yellow & blue 1.40 .25

Intl. Amateur Radio Union, 8th regional conf., Bandung.

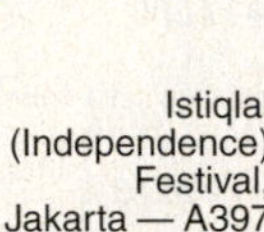

Istiqlal (Independence) Festival, Jakarta — A397

1991, Oct. 15
1478 A397 200r gray, blk & ver 1.40 .25

Intl. Conference on the Great Apes — A398

Pongo pygmaeus: 200r, Sitting in tree. 500r, Walking. 1000r, 2500r, Sitting on ground.

1991, Dec. 18 *Perf. 12½x13½*
1479 A398 200r multicolored 1.00 .25
1480 A398 500r multicolored 1.25 .30
1481 A398 1000r multicolored 2.25 .60
Nos. 1479-1481 (3) 4.50 1.15

Souvenir Sheet

1481A A398 2500r multicolored 8.00 8.00

Intl. Convention on Quality Control Circles, Bali — A399

1991, Oct. 22 *Perf. 12½*
1482 A399 500r multicolored 1.75 .45

Automation of the Post Office — A400

200r, P.O. 500r, Mail sorting equipment.

1992, Jan. 9 Photo. *Perf. 13½x13*
1483 A400 200r multicolored .40 .25
1484 A400 500r multicolored .95 .30

National Elections A401

100r, Ballot boxes, globe. 500r, Hands dropping ballots in ballot boxes.

1992, Feb. 10 *Perf. 12½*
1485 A401 75r shown .25 .25
1486 A401 100r multicolored .45 .25
1487 A401 500r multicolored 1.00 .30
Nos. 1485-1487 (3) 1.70 .80

5th Five-year Development Plan Type of 1989

150r, Construction worker. 300r, Aviation technology.

1992, Apr. 1 Photo. *Perf. 12½*
1488 A361 150r multicolored .30 .25
1489 A361 300r multicolored .60 .25

Visit Asia Year, 1992 A402

300r, Lembah Baliem, Irian Jaya. 500r, Tanah Lot, Bali. 1000r, Lombah Anai, Sumatra Barat.

1992, Mar. 1 *Perf. 13½x13*
1490 A402 300r multicolored .45 .25
1491 A402 500r multicolored .90 .40
1492 A402 1000r multicolored 2.25 .40
Nos. 1490-1492 (3) 3.60 1.05

Souvenir Sheet

1493 A402 3000r like #1491 8.00 8.00

Birds — A403

100r, Garrulax leucolophus. 200r, Dinopium javanense. 400r, Buceros rhinoceros. 500r, Alisterus amboinensis.

1992, July 1 Photo. *Perf. 12½x13½*
1494 A403 100r multi .25 .25
1495 A403 200r multi .50 .25
1496 A403 400r multi .80 .45
1497 A403 500r multi 1.25 .55
Nos. 1494-1497 (4) 2.80 1.50

Souvenir Sheet

1498 A403 3000r like #1494 8.00 8.00

Children's Day — A404

75r, Street scene. 100r, Children with balloons. 200r, Boating scene. 500r, Girl feeding bird.

1992, July 23 *Perf. 12½*
1499 A404 75r multicolored .25 .25
1500 A404 100r multicolored .30 .25
1501 A404 200r multicolored .50 .25
1502 A404 500r multicolored 1.10 .75
Nos. 1499-1502 (4) 2.15 1.50

1992 Summer Olympics, Barcelona — A405

75r, Weight lifting. 200r, Badminton. 300r, Symbols of events. 500r, Women's tennis. 1000r, Archery.

No. 1508a, 2000r, like #1504. b, 3000r, like #1507.

1992, June 1 *Perf. 12½x13½*
1503 A405 75r multi .25 .25
1504 A405 200r multi .35 .25
1505 A405 300r multi .65 .25
1506 A405 500r multi .85 .25
1507 A405 1000r multi 1.75 .40
Nos. 1503-1507 (5) 3.85 1.40

Souvenir Sheet

1508 A405 Sheet of 2, #a.-b. 9.00 9.00

ASEAN, 25th Anniv. A406

1992, Aug. 8 *Perf. 13½x12½*
1509 A406 200r shown .40 .25
1510 A406 500r Flags, map 1.10 .40
1511 A406 1000r Flags on poles 2.10 .45
Nos. 1509-1511 (3) 3.60 1.10

Flowers A407

Designs: 200r, Phalaenopsis ambilis. 500r, Rafflesia arnoldii. 1000r, 2000r, Jasminum sambae.

Perf. 13½x12½

1992, Jan. 20 Photo.
1512 A407 200r multicolored .40 .25
1513 A407 500r multicolored 1.10 .40
1514 A407 1000r multicolored 1.50 .65
Nos. 1512-1514 (3) 3.00 1.30

Souvenir Sheet

Perf. 13½x13

1515 A407 2000r multicolored 8.00 8.00

A408

Perf. 12½x13½

1992, Sept. 6 **Photo.**
1516 A408 200r shown .60 .25
1517 A408 500r Flags, emblem .80 .45

10th Non-Aligned Summit, Jakarta.

A409

1992, Nov. 29 **Photo.** ***Perf. 12½***
1518 A409 200r green & blue 1.00 .25

Intl. Planned Parenthood Federation, 40th anniv.

A410

200r, Globe, satellite. 500r, Palapa satellite. 1000r, Old, new telephones.

Perf. 12½x13½

1992, Aug. 16 **Photo.**
1519 A410 200r multicolored .70 .25
1520 A410 500r multicolored .80 .40
1521 A410 1000r multicolored 2.00 .45
Nos. 1519-1521 (3) 3.50 1.10

Satellite Communications in Indonesia, 16th anniv.

A411

Traditional Dances: 200r, 3000r, Tari Ngremo, Timor. 500r, Tari Gending Sriwijaya, Sumatra.

1992, Oct. 1 ***Perf. 12½x13½***
1522 A411 200r multicolored .35 .25
1523 A411 500r multicolored 1.20 1.20

Souvenir Sheet

1524 A411 3000r like #1522 6.00 6.00

No. 1523 was withdrawn from sale on 10/5.
See Nos. 1564-1567, 1596-1600, 1628-1632, 1688-1692, 1747-1751, 1815-1820.

Antara News Agency, 55th Anniv. — A412

1992, Dec. 13 **Photo.** ***Perf. 12½***
1525 A412 500r blue & black 1.25 .25

Natl. Afforestation Campaign — A413

Perf. 13½x12½

1992, Dec. 24 **Photo.**
1526 A413 500r multicolored 1.25 .25

No. 1260 Surcharged

1993, Feb. 1 **Photo.** ***Perf. 13½x12½***
1527 A246 50r on 55r #1260 .75 .25

1993 General Session of the People's Consultative Assembly — A414

1993, Mar. 1 **Photo.** ***Perf. 13½x12½***
1528 A414 300r Building exterior .50 .25
1529 A414 700r Building interior 1.10 .30

5th Five Year Development Plan Type of 1989

300r, Soldier's silhouettes over city. 700r, Immunizing children. 1000r, Runners.

1993, Apr. 1 ***Perf. 12½***
1530 A361 300r multicolored .35 .30
1531 A361 700r multicolored .80 .75
1532 A361 1000r multicolored 1.10 1.00
Nos. 1530-1532 (3) 2.25 2.05

Ornithoptera Goliath — A415

1993, Apr. 20 **Photo.** ***Perf. 12½***
1533 A415 1000r multicolored 1.75 .30

For overprint see No. 1540.

Surabaya 700th Anniv. A416

Designs: 300r, Siege of Yamato Hotel. 700r, World Habitat Award, Surabaya skyline. 1000r, Candi Bajang Ratu, natl. monument.

Perf. 13½x12½

1993, May 29 **Photo.**
1534 A416 300r multicolored .45 .40
1535 A416 700r multicolored .90 .80
1536 A416 1000r multicolored 1.25 1.25
Nos. 1534-1536 (3) 2.60 2.45

For overprints see Nos. 1538-1539, 1541.

Nos. 1533-1536 Ovptd. in Red

and

Indopex '93 — A417

1993 ***Perfs. as Before***
1538 A416 300r on #1534 .50 .25
1539 A416 700r on #1535 1.40 .40
1540 A415 1000r on #1533 2.00 .80
1541 A416 1000r on #1536 2.00 .60
Nos. 1538-1541 (4) 5.90 2.05

Souvenir Sheet

Perf. 13½x12½

1542 A417 3500r multicolored 4.50 4.50

Location of overprint varies. Issued: No. 1540, Apr. 20; others, May 29.

Environmental Protection — A418

Flowers: Nos. 1543a, 1545a, Jasminum sambac. No. 1543b, Phalaenopsis amabilis. No. 1543c, Rafflesia arnoldi.
Wildlife: Nos. 1544a, 1545b, Varanus komodoensis. No. 1544b, Scleropages formasus. No. 1544c, Spizaetus bartelsi.

Perf. 12½x13½

1993, June 5 **Photo.**
1543 A418 300r Tripytych, #a.-c. 1.40 1.40
1544 A418 700r Tripytych, #a.-c. 4.50 4.50

Souvenir Sheet of 2

1545 A418 1500r #a.-b. 5.00 5.00

1st World Community Development Camp — A419

Designs: 300r, Boy scouts working on road. 700r, Pres. Suharto shaking hands with scout.

Perf. 13½x12½

1993, July 27 **Photo.**
1546 A419 300r multicolored .35 .25
1547 A419 700r multicolored 1.10 .25

Papilio Blumei — A420

Perf. 12½x13½

1993, Aug. 24 **Photo.**
1548 A420 700r multicolored 1.40 .25

Souvenir Sheets

1549 A420 3000r multicolored 6.00 6.00
1550 A420 3000r multicolored 6.00 6.00

Inscription at top of No. 1549 is like that on No. 1548. No. 1550 contains a stamp inscribed "1993," a se-tenant label and Bangkok '93 Philatelic Exhibition inscription in sheet margin.

Armed Forces Day — A421

No. 1551, Soedirman. No. 1552, Oerip Soemohardjo.

1993, Oct. 5 ***Perf. 12½***
1551 A421 300r brown & red .50 .25
1552 A421 300r brown & red .50 .25
a. Pair, #1551-1552 1.00 .75

Tourism — A422

300r, 3000r, Waterfall. 700r, Cave formations. 1000r, Dormant volcanic crater, horiz.

Perf. 12½x13½, 13½x12½

1993, Oct. 4
1553 A422 300r multicolored .45 .40
1554 A422 700r multicolored .85 .85
1555 A422 1000r multicolored 1.25 1.25
Nos. 1553-1555 (3) 2.55 2.50

Souvenir Sheet

1556 A422 3000r multicolored 4.00 4.00

13th Natl. Sports Week — A423

1993, Sept. 9 ***Perf. 12½x13½***
1557 A423 150r Swimming .25 .25
1558 A423 300r Cycling .35 .30
1559 A423 700r Mascot .80 .70
1560 A423 1000r High jump 1.25 1.00
Nos. 1557-1560 (4) 2.65 2.25

Souvenir Sheet

1561 A423 3500r like No. 1560 5.00 5.00

Flora and Fauna — A424

Designs: a, Michelia champaca. b, Cananga odorata. c, Copsychus pyrropygus. d, Gracula religiosa robusta.

1993, Nov. 5 **Photo.** ***Perf. 12½x13½***
1562 A424 300r Block of 4, #a.-d. 3.50 3.50

Migratory Farm Workers — A425

1993, Dec. 4 ***Perf. 12½***
1563 A425 700r Field workers .90 .70

Traditional Dance Type of 1992

Dance and region: 300r, Gending Sriwijaya, South Sumatra. 700r, Tempayan, West Kalimantan. 1000r, 3500r, Tifa, Irian Jaya.

1993, Dec. 22 ***Perf. 12½x13½***
1564 A411 300r multicolored .55 .25
1565 A411 700r multicolored .90 .25
1566 A411 1000r multicolored 1.25 .25
Nos. 1564-1566 (3) 2.70 .75

Souvenir Sheet

1567 A411 3500r multicolored 4.50 4.50

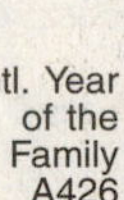

Intl. Year of the Family A426

1994, Mar. 1 **Photo.** ***Perf. 13½x12½***
1568 A426 300r multicolored .75 .25

Indonesian Postage Stamps, 130th Anniv. — A427

Design: 700r, Netherlands Indies #B7, #N7, Indonesia #B214.

1994, Apr. 1 ***Perf. 12½***
1569 A427 700r multicolored 1.25 .55

Souvenir Sheet
Imperf

1569A A427 3500r like #1569 5.50 5.50

PHILAKOREA '94 (No. 1569A).

6th Five Year Development Plan — A428

Buddhist dieties and: 100r, Professional women. 700r, Education. 2000r, Medical care for children.

1994, Apr. 1 ***Perf. 12½***
1570 A428 100r multicolored .30 .25
1571 A428 700r multicolored 1.00 .70
1572 A428 2000r multicolored 2.75 2.00
Nos. 1570-1572 (3) 4.05 2.95

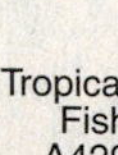

Tropical Fish A429

Designs: 300r, Telmatherina ladigesi. 700r, 3500r, Melanotaenia boesemani.

1994, Apr. 20 **Photo.** ***Perf. 13***
1573 A429 300r multicolored .60 .25
1574 A429 700r multicolored .80 .40

Souvenir Sheet

1575 A429 3500r multicolored 6.00 6.00

No. 1575 has continuous design.

Intl. Federation of Red Cross & Red Crescent Societies, 75th Anniv. — A429a

1994, May 5 ***Perf. 12½x13***
1575A A429a 300r multicolored .80 .25

Second Asian and Pacific Ministerial Conference on Women, Jakarta — A430

1994, June 13 ***Perf. 13½x12½***
1576 A430 700r multicolored 1.00 .25

A431

1994 World Cup Soccer Championships, US: 150r, Player dribbling ball, vert. 300r, Mascot chasing ball, vert. 700r, 1994 Tournament emblem. 1000r, Ball in net. 3500r, Soccer ball in net.

1994, June 17 ***Perf. 12½x13½***
1577 A431 150r multicolored .30 .25
1578 A431 300r multicolored .50 .25

Perf. 13½x12½

1579 A431 700r multicolored .90 .40
1580 A431 1000r multicolored 1.50 .45
Nos. 1577-1580 (4) 3.20 1.35

Souvenir Sheet

1581 A431 3500r multicolored 5.00 5.00

Thomas & Uber Cups — A432

Designs: a, Uber Cup. b, Thomas Cup.

1994, June 22 ***Perf. 12½***
1582 A432 300r Pair, #a.-b. 1.25 .55

Souvenir Sheet of 2

1583 A432 1750r #a.-b. 4.50 4.50

Human Rights Day — A433

Perf. 12½x13½
1994, July 27 **Photo.**
1584 A433 700r multicolored 1.10 .25

A434

300r, Brown pottery vase. 700r, Blue & white vase.

Perf. 13]x13½
1994, Aug. 19 **Photo.**
1585 A434 300r multicolored .55 .25
1586 A434 700r multicolored 1.10 .60

Indonesia-Pakistan Econiomic & Cultural Cooperation Organization.
See Pakistan Nos. 822-823.

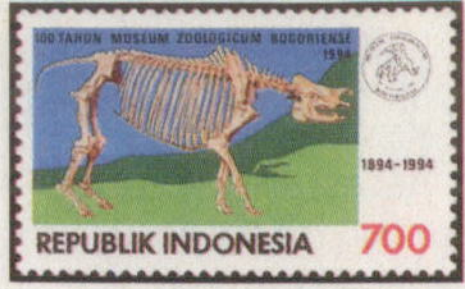

Bogoriense Zoological Museum, Cent. — A435

700r, Skeleton of Javan rhinoceros. 1000r, 3500r, Skeleton of blue whale.

1994, Aug. 20 ***Perf. 13½x13***
1587 A435 700r multicolored 1.25 .55

Size: 80x22mm

1588 A435 1000r multicolored 1.75 .60

Souvenir Sheet
Perf. 13x13½

1588A A435 3500r multicolored 5.50 5.50

12th Asian Games, Hiroshima 1994 A436

1994, Oct. 2 **Litho.** ***Perf. 13½x13***
1589 A436 300r Mascots .50 .25
1590 A436 700r Hurdlers 1.00 .60

Bakosurtanal, 25th Anniv. — A437

1994, Oct. 17 **Litho.** ***Perf. 13½x13***
1591 A437 700r multicolored 1.25 .30

Flora & Fauna — A438

Designs: a, Morus macroura. b, Oncosperma tigillaria. c, Eucalyptus urophylla. d, Phalaenopsis amabilis. e, Pometia pinnata. f, Argusianus argus. g, Loriculus pusillus. h, Philemon buceroides. i, Alisterus amboinensis. j, Seleucidis melanoleuca.
3500r, Philemon buceroides, diff.

1994, Nov. 5 **Photo.** ***Perf. 12½x13½***
1592 A438 150r Block or strip of 10, #a.-j. 6.00 6.00

Souvenir Sheet

1593 A438 3500r multicolored 5.50 5.50
a. With added inscription in blue 12.00

Inscription in sheet margin of No. 1593a contains emblem and "PRIMERA '95." Issued: No. 1593a, 8/21/95.
See Nos. 1622, 1680-1682, 1737-1738, 1812-1814.

Asian-Pacific Economic Cooperation Summit (APEC '94) — A439

Design: 700r, Presidential retreat, Bogor.

1994, Nov. 15 ***Perf. 13½X13***
1594 A439 700r multicolored 1.20 .25

For overprint see No. 1616A.

ICAO, 50th Anniv. A440

1994, Dec. 7
1595 A440 700r multicolored 1.40 .25

Traditional Dance Type of 1992

Dance, region: 150r, Mengaup, Jambi. 300r, Mask, West Java. 700r, Anging Mamiri, South Sulawesi. 1000r, Pisok, North Sulawesi. 2000r, Bidu, East Nusa Tenggara. 3500r, Mask dance, West Java.

1994, Dec. 27 ***Perf. 12½x13½***
1596 A411 150r multicolored .30 .25
1597 A411 300r multicolored .50 .25
1598 A411 700r multicolored 1.00 .30
1599 A411 1000r multicolored 1.40 .25
1600 A411 2000r multicolored 2.75 1.00
a. Bklt. pane, 2 ea #1596-1600 13.00
Complete booklet, #1600a 13.00
Nos. 1596-1600 (5) 5.95 2.05

Souvenir Sheet

1601 A411 3500r multicolored 5.50 5.50

World Tourism Organization, 20th Anniv. — A441

Designs: 300r, Yogyakarta Palace. 700r, Floating market. 1000r, Pasola Sumba ritual.

1995, Jan. 2 ***Perf. 13½x12½***
1602 A441 300r multicolored .25 .25
1603 A441 700r multicolored .75 .65
1604 A441 1000r multicolored 1.00 .85
Nos. 1602-1604 (3) 2.00 1.75

Indonesian Children, First Lady & Pres. Suharto A442

Perf. 13½x12½
1995, Mar. 11 **Photo.**
1605 A442 700r multicolored 1.25 .65

6th Five Year Development Plan — A443

Designs: 300r, Letter from King of Klunglung, 18th-19th cent. 700r, Carrier pigeon mascot of natl. letter writing campaign.

1995, Apr. 1 **Photo.** ***Perf. 12½***
1606 A443 300r multicolored .40 .25
1607 A443 700r multicolored 1.10 .70

4th Intl. Bamboo Conference — A444

Designs: 300r, Schizostachyum brachycladum. 700r, Dendrocalamus asper.

Perf. 12½x13½
1995, June 19 **Photo.**
1608 A444 300r multicolored .40 .25
1609 A444 700r multicolored 1.10 .70

First Flight of N250 Turboprop Commuter Airplane A445

1995, Aug. 10 *Perf. 13½x12½*
1610 A445 700r multicolored 1.20 .65

Independence, 50th Anniv. — A446

300r, Anniv. emblem. 700r, Boy, national flag.

1995, Aug. 17
1611 A446 300r multi .40 .25
1612 A446 700r multi 1.10 .70

Souvenir Sheet

1612A A446 2500r like No. 1612 4.50 4.50

JAKARTA '95, 8th Asian Intl. Philatelic Exhibition A447

Scenes in Jakarta: 300r, Kota Intan Drawbridge. 700r, Fatahillah Historical Museum.

1995, Aug. 19
1613 A447 300r multicolored .40 .25
1614 A447 700r multicolored 1.00 .70

No. 1613 exists in 7 souvenir sheets of 1, each with different color margins. Sold at the 2nd International Stamp Exhibition in Jakarta. Value, set of 7 sheets $75.

Sail Indonesia '95 A448

1995, Aug. 19
1615 A448 700r multicolored 1.00 .60

Souvenir Sheet

1616 A448 2500r multicolored 4.50 4.50

No. 1594 Overprinted "PRIMERA '95" in Blue

1995, Aug. 21 Photo. *Perf. 13½x13*
1616A A439 700r on #1594 2.75 2.75

Istiqlal (Independence) Festival II 1995, Jakarta — A449

1995, Sept. 23 *Perf. 12½x13½*
1617 A449 700r multicolored 1.00 .60

Takeover of Post, Telegraph, & Telephone Headquarters, 50th Anniv. — A450

1995, Sept. 27 *Perf. 13½x12½*
1618 A450 700r multicolored 1.00 .60

FAO, 50th Anniv. — A451

1995, Oct. 16 *Perf. 12½x13½*
1619 A451 700r multicolored 1.00 .60

UN, 50th Anniv. — A452

UN emblem, "50," and: 300r, Flags of nations. 700r, Rainbow over earth.

1995, Oct. 24 *Perf. 12½*
1620 A452 300r multicolored .40 .25
1621 A452 700r multicolored 1.00 .70

Flora and Fauna Type of 1994

Designs: a, Cyrtostachys renda. b, Panthera tigris sumatrae. c, Bouea macrophylla. d, Rhinoceros sondaicus. e, Santalum album. f, Varanus komodoensis. g, Diospyros celebica. h, Macrocephalon maleo. i, Nephleium ramboutan-ake. j, Polyplectron schleiermacheri.
2500r, Panthera tigris sumatrae.

1995, Nov. 5 Photo. *Perf. 12½x13½*
1622 A438 150r Block of 10, #a.-j. 5.00 4.00

Souvenir Sheet

1623 A438 2500r multicolored 9.00 8.00

1995 Aga Khan Award for Architecture — A453

Designs: 300r, Masjid Agung, Kraton Yogyakarta. 700r, Kraton Surakarta.

1995, Nov. 23 *Perf. 13½x13*
1624 A453 300r multicolored .50 .25
1625 A453 700r multicolored 1.10 .70

Sir Rowland Hill (1795-1879) — A454

300r, Hill, letter carriers on motorcycles. 700r, Hill, Indonesian postal service logo.

1995, Dec. 3 *Perf. 13½x12½*
1626 A454 300r multicolored .40 .25
1627 A454 700r multicolored 1.10 .70

Traditional Dance Type of 1992

Dance and region: 150r, Nguri, West Nusa Tenggara. 300r, Muli Betanggai, Lampung. 700r, Mutiara, Maluku. 1000r, Gantar, East Kalimantan. 2500r, Tari Nguri, Nusa Tenggara Barrat.

1995, Dec. 27 *Perf. 12½x13½*
1628 A411 150r multicolored .40 .25
1629 A411 300r multicolored .50 .25
1630 A411 700r multicolored 1.00 .60
1631 A411 1000r multicolored 1.25 .80
Nos. 1628-1631 (4) 3.15 1.90

Souvenir Sheet

1632 A411 2500r multicolored 4.00 3.00

1996 Economic Census — A455

Design: 300r, Economic sectors, vert.

1996, Jan. 2 *Perf. 12½*
1633 A455 300r multicolored .40 .25
1634 A455 700r multicolored 1.00 .70

Greetings Stamps — A456

Various flowers.

1996, Feb. 1 Photo. *Perf. 12½*
1635 A456 150r multicolored .30 .25
1636 A456 300r multicolored .50 .25
1637 A456 700r multicolored .80 .55
Nos. 1635-1637 (3) 1.60 1.05

See Nos. 1657-1659.

PWI Journalists' Assoc., 50th Anniv. — A457

Designs: 300r, RM Soemanang Soeriowinoto. 700r, Djamaluddin Adinegoro.

1996, Feb. 9
1638 A457 300r multicolored .40 .25
1639 A457 700r multicolored 1.10 .55

Australian Spotted Cuscus — A458

Design: Nos. 1640, 1642a, shown. Nos. 1641, 1642b, Indonesian bear cuscus.

1996, Mar.22 Photo. *Perf. 13x13½*
1640 A458 300r multicolored .55 .40
1641 A458 300r multicolored .55 .40
a. Pair, Nos. 1640-1641 1.40 1.40
b. Sheet of 5 #1641a 35.00 17.50

Souvenir Sheet

1642 A458 1250r Sheet of 2, #a.-b. 3.50 3.50
c. #1642 with added inscription, ovpt. 7.00 7.00

Indonesia '96 (No. 1641b).

No. 1642c has black CHINA '96 exhibition emblem in upper right corner. The bottom sheet margin contains gold overprint: "CHINA '96 - 9th Asian International Philatelic Exhibition" in both Chinese and English.

No. 1641b exists folded and affixed to a booklet cover. Value, $15.

See Australia Nos. 1489-1490.

A459

Launching of Palapa C Satellite A460

1996, Jan. 31 *Perf. 13*
1643 A459 300r multicolored .65 .25

Perf. 12½

1644 A460 700r multicolored 1.60 .60

Indonesia '96, World Junior Philatelic Exhibition A461

Designs: 300r, No. 1647a, Building. 700r, No. 1647b, Decorated sun umbrellas.

1996, Mar. 21 *Perf. 13½x13*
1645 A461 300r multicolored .45 .25
1646 A461 700r multicolored 1.25 .55

Souvenir Sheet of 2

1647 A461 1250r #a.-b. 6.50 3.25

No. 1647 exists imperf with different color margins. A souvenir sheet containing No. 1645-1646 and progressive color proofs of No. 1646 exists.

Education Day A462

Children's drawings: 150r, Teachers, students with outstretched arms. 300r, Children carrying books to school. 700r, Classroom instruction.

1996, May 2 Photo. *Perf. 13½x13*
1648 A462 150r multicolored .35 .25
1649 A462 300r multicolored .50 .25
1650 A462 700r multicolored 1.10 .55
Nos. 1648-1650 (3) 1.95 1.05

Natl. Youth Kirab A463

700r, Holding flag, emblem.

1996, June 8
1651 A463 300r shown .40 .25
1652 A463 700r multicolored 1.00 .55

1996 Summer Olympics, Atlanta A464

1996, May 15
1653 A464 300r Archery .50 .30
1654 A464 700r Weight lifting 1.00 .60
1655 A464 1000r Badminton 1.40 1.00
Nos. 1653-1655 (3) 2.90 1.90

Souvenir Sheet

1656 A464 2500r like #1653 3.50 3.00

No. 1656 is a continuous design.

Greetings Type of 1996

150r, Roses. 300r, Orchids. 700r, Chrysanthemums.

1996, Apr. 15 Photo. *Perf. 12½*
1657 A456 150r multicolored .35 .25
1658 A456 300r multicolored .50 .25
1659 A456 700r multicolored 1.00 .55
Nos. 1657-1659 (3) 1.85 1.05

Maritime and Aviation Year — A465

300r, N-2130 aircraft, control tower at Soekarno-Hatta Airport. 700r, Inter-island passenger ship.

1996, June 22
1660 A465 300r multicolored .30 .25
1661 A465 700r multicolored 1.10 .55

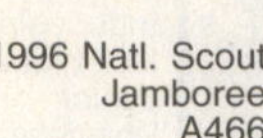

1996 Natl. Scout Jamboree A466

Designs: a, Climbing rope. b, Sliding down rope. c, Girls at bottom of ropes. d, Girls assembling wood and rope ladder. e, Riding unicycle, eagle emblem, boys building scaffolding. f, Girls building scaffolding, campground. g, Two boys with project. h, Woman seated at control center.

No. 1662I, like #1662a-1662d. No. 1662J, like #1662e-1662h.

1996, June 26
1662 A466 150r Block of 8, #a.-h. 2.50 1.75

Souvenir Sheets
1662I A466 1250d multicolored 2.50 2.50
1662J A466 1250d multicolored 2.50 2.50

Istanbul '96 (Nos. 1662I-1662J). Nos. 1662I-1662J each contain one 64x48mm stamp.

Nos. 1662a-1662d, 1663e-1662h are continuous designs.

Bank BNI, 50th Anniv. A467

1996, July 5
1663 A467 300r shown .40 .25
1664 A467 700r Sailing ship 1.10 .55

UNICEF, 50th Anniv. A468

1996, July 23 ***Perf. 13½x13***
1665 A468 300r Child reading .40 .30
1666 A468 700r Two children .80 .60
1667 A468 1000r Three children 1.25 .90
Nos. 1665-1667 (3) 2.45 1.80

Ibu Tien Suharto (1923-96) First Lady — A469

1996, Aug. 5 ***Perf. 12½x13½***
1668 A469 700r multicolored 1.00 .55

Souvenir Sheet
1669 A469 2500r like #1668 3.00 3.00

No. 1669 is a continuous design.

14th Natl. Sports Week, Jakarta A470

Perf. 13½x12½
1996, Sept. 2 **Photo.**
1670 A470 300r Softball .40 .30
1671 A470 700r Field hockey .85 .60
1672 A470 1000r Basketball 1.25 .90
Nos. 1670-1672 (3) 2.50 1.80

World Wildlife Fund A471

Rhinoceros sondaicus: a, Adult. b, Adult with young. Dicerorhinus sumatrensis: c, Up close. d, Adult.

No. 1674: a, Like No. 1673a; b, Like No. 1673d.

1996, Oct. 2 **Photo.** ***Perf. 13½x13***
1673 A471 300r Block of 4, #a.-d. 2.25 2.25
e. Souvenir sheet, 2 #1673 4.50 4.50
f. As "e," ovptd. in sheet margin 5.75 3.75

Souvenir Sheet
1674 A471 1500r Sheet of 2, #a.-b. 4.50 4.50

Overprint in margin of No. 1673f reads: "Bursa Filateli SEA Games XIX / Jakarta, 11-19 Oktober 1997" in gold.

Greetings Stamps — A472

Bouquets of various flowers.

1996, Oct. 15 **Photo.** ***Perf. 12½***
Background Colors
1675 A472 150r yellow & blue .30 .25
1676 A472 300r yellow & green .40 .25
1677 A472 700r pink & blue .85 .55
Nos. 1675-1677 (3) 1.55 1.05

Financial Day, 50th Anniv. A473

1996, Oct. 30 ***Perf. 13½x12½***
1678 A473 700r multicolored 1.40 .55

Flora & Fauna Type of 1994

Fauna: No. 1680: a, Aceros cassidix. b, Orcaella brevirostris. c, Oriolus chinensis. d, Helarctos malayanus. e, Leucopsar rothschildi.

Flora: f, Borassus flabellifer. g, Coelogyne pandurata. h, Michelia alba. i, Amorphophallus titanum. j, Dysoxylum densiflorium.

No. 1681, Like No. 1680e. No. 1682, Like No. 1680g.

1996, Nov. 5 **Litho.** ***Perf. 12½x13½***
1680 A438 300r Block or strip of 10, #a.-j. 4.50 4.50
a.-j. Any single .45 .30

Souvenir Sheets
1681 A438 1250r multicolored 3.50 3.50
1682 A438 1250r multicolored 3.50 3.50

Souvenir Sheet

Aceros Cassidix — A474

Perf. 12½x13½
1996, Dec. 14 **Photo.**
1683 A474 2000r multicolored *10.00 10.00*

ASEANPEX '96.

Scenes from Timor A475

Designs: 300r, Deep sea diving. 700r, Sailing ships entering harbor, 18th cent.

1996-97 ***Perf. 13½x12½***
1684 A475 300r multicolored .50 .30
1685 A475 700r multicolored 1.25 .60

Souvenir Sheet
1685A A475 2000d like #1685 5.50 2.75

Hong Kong '97 (No. 1685A).

Issued: Nos. 1686-1687, 12/18/96; No. 1685A, 2/12/97.

Foster Parents A476

150r, Children at playground, vert. 300r, Children, adult's hand holding picture of girl.

Perf. 12½x13½, 13½x12½
1996, Dec. 20
1686 A476 150r multicolored .30 .25
1687 A476 300r multicolored .45 .25

Traditional Dance Type of 1992

Dance, region: 150r, Tari Baksa Kembang, Kalimantan Selatan. 300r, 2000r, Tari Ngarojeng, Jakarta. 700r, Tari Rampai, Aceh. 1000r, Tari Boituka, Timor.

1996, Dec. 27 ***Perf. 12½x13½***
1688 A411 150r multicolored .30 .25
1689 A411 300r multicolored .40 .25
1690 A411 700r multicolored .75 .55
1691 A411 1000r multicolored 1.25 .80
Nos. 1688-1691 (4) 2.70 1.85

Souvenir Sheet
1692 A411 2000r multicolored 3.00 3.00

Telecommunications Year — A477

Designs: 300r, Satellite dish, men at computers, map. 700r, Telephone keypad, woman using telephone, satellite in earth orbit.

1997, Jan. 1 ***Perf. 13½x12½***
1693 A477 300r multicolored .40 .25
1694 A477 700r multicolored .80 .55

Greetings Stamps — A478

Designs: No. 1695, Heart, ribbon. No. 1696, Children, "Happy Birthday."

1997, Jan. 15 ***Perf. 12½***
1695 A478 600r multicolored .70 .45
1696 A478 600r multicolored .70 .45

1997 General Election A479

Ballot box and: 300r, Means of transportion. 700r, Indonesian Archipelago, House of Representatives Building. 1000r, Map, symbols of development.

1997, Feb. 3 ***Perf. 13½x13***
1697 A479 300r multicolored .45 .30
1698 A479 700r multicolored .80 .60
1699 A479 1000r multicolored 1.40 .90
Nos. 1697-1699 (3) 2.65 1.80

Birth of Indonesia's 200-millionth Citizen — A480

700r, Pres. Suharto, baby.

Perf. 13½x12½
1997, Mar. 24 **Litho.**
1700 A480 700r multicolored 1.00 .55

A481

Indonesian Philatelists Assoc., 75th Anniv.: 300r, Youth examining stamps, #1672. 700r, Magnifying glass, #1660, #1592h, #1580.

1997, Mar. 29 ***Perf. 12½x13½***
1701 A481 300r multicolored .50 .30
1702 A481 700r multicolored .90 .60

A482

Indonesian Artists: 300r, Wage Rudolf Soepratman (1903-38), composer, violinist. 700r, Usmar Ismail (1921-71), film pioneer, director. 1000r, Affandi (1907-90), painter.

1997, Apr. 30 Litho. *Perf. 13x13½*
1703 A482 300r multicolored .40 .30
1704 A482 700r multicolored .80 .60
1705 A482 1000r multicolored 1.40 .90
b. Sheet, 3 each #1703-1705 + label 8.00 7.00
Nos. 1703-1705 (3) 2.60 1.80

Souvenir Sheet

1705A A482 2000r like #1705 2.50 2.50

Indonesia 2000 A483

Gemstones: 300r, Picture jasper. 700r, Chrysocolla. 1000r, Geode. 2000r, Banded agate.

1997, May 20 Litho. *Perf. 13½x13*
1706 A483 300r multicolored .50 .30
1707 A483 700r multicolored .75 .45
1708 A483 1000r multicolored 1.50 .90
a. Sheet, 3 each, #1706-1708 + label 8.50 4.75
b. As "a," control No. in margin *17.50 8.75*
Nos. 1706-1708 (3) 2.75 1.65

Souvenir Sheet

1709 A483 2000r multicolored 4.00 2.50
a. Control No. in margin *4.75 2.50*

Nos. 1708b, 1709a promote INDONESIA 2000, Jakarta, Aug. 15-21, 2000. Nos. 1708a-1709 and 1708b-1709a were issued in presentation packs with certificate of authenticity.

See Nos. 1764-1767A, 1848-1851, 1851A, 1888-1891.

A484

1997, May 31 Photo. *Perf. 12½*
1710 A484 1000r multicolored 1.25 .80

World Day to Stop Smoking.

World Environment Day — A485

Various marine life of the coral reefs.

1997, June 5 Litho. *Perf. 13x13½*
1711 A485 150r multicolored .40 .25
1712 A485 300r multicolored .45 .25
1713 A485 700r multicolored .90 .55
Nos. 1711-1713 (3) 1.75 1.05

Souvenir Sheet

1714 A485 2000r multicolored 4.00 4.00

ASEAN, 30th Anniv. A486

300r, Hands reaching out to each other. 700r, Rice stalks arranged to form number 30, globe.

1997, Aug. 8 Litho. *Perf. 13½x13*
1715 A486 300r multicolored .40 .25
1716 A486 700r multicolored .85 .55

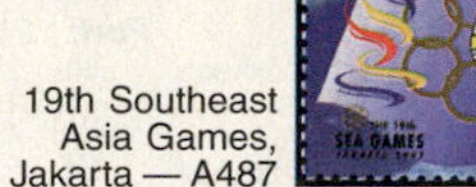

19th Southeast Asia Games, Jakarta — A487

No. 1717, Logo, "Hanoman" mascot. No. 1718, Runner carrying torch, flags of participating nations, logo. No. 1719, Runner, track, discus thrower. No. 1720, Hurdler, runners.

1997, Sept. 9 Litho. *Perf. 12½*
1717 A487 300r multicolored .30 .25
1718 A487 300r multicolored .30 .25
a. Pair, #1717-1718 .75 .75
1719 A487 700r multicolored .75 .50
1720 A487 700r multicolored .75 .50
a. Pair, #1719-1720 2.00 2.00
b. Bklt. pane, 2 ea #1717-1720 5.50
Complete booklet, 1 #1720b 5.50
Nos. 1717-1720 (4) 2.10 1.50

Transportation — A488

1997, Sept. 17
1721 A488 300r Buses, ox cart .45 .25
1722 A488 300r Trains .45 .25
a. Pair, #1721-1722 .90 .50
1723 A488 700r Ships 1.25 .50
1724 A488 700r Airplanes 1.25 .50
a. Pair, #1723-1724 2.50 1.00
Nos. 1721-1724 (4) 3.40 1.50

Souvenir Sheet

Oriolus Chinensis — A489

1997, May 29 *Perf. 12½x13½*
1725 A489 2000r multicolored 6.50 3.25

PACIFIC 97.

Nusantara Royal Palace Festival A490

Royal carriages: 300r, Singa Baraong wooden carriage, 1549, with carving of mythical animal. 700r, Paksi Naga Liman carriage, phoenix-like bird.

1997, July 1 Litho. *Perf. 13½x12½*
1726 A490 300r multicolored .45 .25
1727 A490 700r multicolored .80 .50

18th Natl. Koran Reading Contest — A491

Designs: 300r, Decorated roof peaks, windows. 700r, Al-Ikhsaniah Mosque.

1997, July 9 *Perf. 12½*
1728 A491 300r multicolored .45 .25
1729 A491 700r multicolored .80 .50

Indonesian Membership in UPU, 50th Anniv. — A492

Emblem of UPU and: 300r, Mas Soeharto. 700r, Heinrich von Stephan.

1997, Sept. 27 Litho. *Perf. 13½x13*
1730 A492 300r multicolored .40 .25
1731 A492 700r multicolored .80 .50

1997-98 General Session of People's Consultative Assembly — A493

1997, Oct. 1 *Perf. 12½*
1732 A493 700r multicolored .75 .50

Indonesian Armed Forces Day A494

Designs: a, ABRI Village Program. b, Jalesveva Jayamahe Monument. c, Blue Falcon Flight Demonstration Team. d, Police Fast Reaction Unit.

1997, Oct. 5 *Perf. 13½x12½*
1733 A494 300r Block of 4, #a.-d. 1.50 1.00

Flora and Fauna Type of 1994

Fauna: No. 1737: a, Chitala lopis. b, Haliastur indus. c, Rhinoplax vigil. d, Cervus timorensis. e, Bubalus depressicornis.

Flora: f, Lansium domesticum. g, Salacca zalacca. h, Shorea stenoptera. i, Diospyros macrophylla. j, Diplocaulobium utile.

No. 1738: a, Shorea stenoptera. b, Haliastur indus.

1997, Nov. 5 *Perf. 12½x13½*
1737 A438 300r Block of 10 3.50 2.50
a.-j. Any single .35 .25

Souvenir Sheet

1738 A438 1250r Sheet of 2, #a.-b. 2.50 2.00

A495

Indonesian Cooperatives Day — A496

Designs: No. 1739, Cooperatives Monument, Tasikmalaya. No. 1740, Cooperatives Monument, Jakarta. No. 1741, Adult taking child's hand. No. 1742, Globe, movement towards globalization. No. 1743, Dr. Mohammad Hatta, Pres. Suharto.

1997, July 12 Litho. *Perf. 12½x13½*
1739 A495 150r multicolored .30 .25
1740 A495 150r multicolored .30 .25
a. Pair, #1739-1740 .60 .40
1741 A495 300r multicolored .40 .25
1742 A495 300r multicolored .40 .25
a. Pair, #1741-1742 .80 .50

Perf. 12½

1743 A496 700r multicolored 1.00 .50
Nos. 1739-1743 (5) 2.40 1.50

ASCOPE '97 (Asian Council on Petroleum) A497

a, LNG tanker. b, Petroleum trucks. c, Drilling rig, pumping wells. d, Refinery.

1997, Nov. 24 *Perf. 13½x12½*
1744 A497 300r Block of 4, #a.-d. 1.50 .90

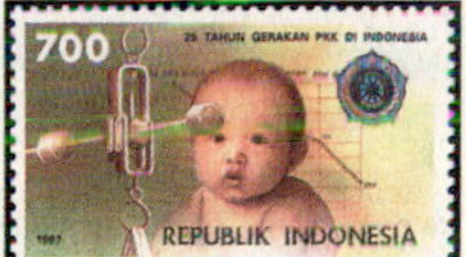

Foster Parents Natl. Movement A498

1997, Dec. 20 Photo.
1745 A498 700r multicolored .80 .40

Family Welfare Movement, 25th Anniv. A499

1997, Dec. 27 Litho.
1746 A499 700r multicolored .80 .45

Traditional Dance Type of 1992

Dance, region: 150r, Mopuputi Cengke (clove picking), Central Sulawesi. 300r, Mandau Talawang Nyai Balau, Central Kalimantan. 600r, 2000r, Gambyong, Central Java. 700r, Cawan (bowl,) North Sumatra. 1000r, Legong Keraton, Bali.

1997, Dec. 27
1747 A411 150r multicolored .30 .25
1748 A411 300r multicolored .40 .25
1749 A411 600r multicolored .60 .40
1750 A411 700r multicolored .75 .45
1751 A411 1000r multicolored .90 .60
Nos. 1747-1751 (5) 2.95 1.95

Souvenir Sheet

Perf. 12½x13½

1752 A411 2000r multicolored 2.50 1.60

No. 1752 is a continuous design.

Souvenir Sheet

Sulawesi Selatan — A500

1997, Oct. 11 Litho. *Perf. 13½x12½*
1753 A500 2000r multicolored 2.50 1.50

Makasser '97 National Philatelic Exhibition.

Year of Art and Culture 1998 — A501

Designs: 300r, Erau Festival, East Kalimantan. 700r, Tabot Festival, Bengkulu.

1998, Jan. 1 Litho. *Perf. 12½*
1754 A501 300r multicolored .40 .30
1755 A501 700r multicolored .60 .30

Indonesian Folktales A502

Folktale, region — No. 1759; a-e, Malin Kundang, West Sumatra. f-j: Sangkuriang, West Java. k-o, Roro Jonggrang, Central Java. p-t: Tengger, East Java. Each horizontal strip of 5 has continuous design.
2500r, Kasodo Ceremony, Tenegger, East Java.

1998, Feb. 2 *Perf. 13½x12½*
1759 Sheet of 20 4.00 3.00
a.-t. A502 300r Any single .30 .25

Souvenir Sheet

1760 A502 2500r like #1759e 1.75 1.00

See Nos. 1828-1829, 1886-1887, 1929-1930.

Presidential Palaces — A503

Designs: a, Jakarta. b, Bogor. c, Cipanas. d, Yogyakarta. e, Tampak Siring.

1998, Apr. 1
1761 A503 300r Strip of 5, #a.-e. 1.10 .60

World Health Organization, 50th Anniv. — A504

Designs: 300r, Pregnant woman, man, vert. 700r, Woman holding baby.

1998, Apr. 7 Litho. *Perf. 12½*
1762 A504 300r multicolored .30 .25
1763 A504 700r multicolored .60 .30

Indonesia 2000 Type of 1997

Gemstones: 300r, Chrysopal. 700r, Tektite. 1000r, Amethyst. No. 1767, Petrified wood. No. 1767A, opal.

1998, May 20 *Perf. 13½x12½*
1764 A483 300r multicolored .40 .25
1765 A483 700r multicolored .40 .25
1766 A483 1000r multicolored .40 .35
a. Sheet, 3 each #1764-1766 + label 5.00 2.50
Nos. 1764-1766 (3) 1.20 .85

Souvenir Sheets

1767 A483 2500r multicolored 1.75 1.00

Perf. 13½x14

1767A A483 2500r multicolored 5.00 3.00
b. Sheet, 2 each, #1764-1766, 1 each #1767, 1767A 15.00 14.00

Nos. 1767A, 1767Ab were issued in presentation packs with control numbers printed in margin and certificate of authenticity.
No. 1767A sold for 10,000r. No. 1767Ab sold for 25,000r.

1998 World Cup Soccer Championships, France — A505

Young boys playing soccer in Indonesia: 300r, Outside school, boy on bicycle. 700r, In neighborhood lot. 1000r, 2500r, In rural area.

1998, June 1
1768 A505 300r multicolored .30 .25
1769 A505 700r multicolored .40 .25
1770 A505 1000r multicolored .80 .35
Nos. 1768-1770 (3) 1.50 .85

Souvenir Sheet

1771 A505 2500r multicolored 1.50 1.00

World Environment Day — A506

Trees along river bank, denomination at: No. 1772, lower right. No. 1773, lower left.

1998, June 5
1772 A506 700r multicolored .60 .25
1773 A506 700r multicolored .60 .25
a. Pair, #1772-1773 1.25 .70

Souvenir Sheet

Juvalux '98, World Philatelic Exhibition, Luxembourg — A507

1998, June 18 *Perf. 12½x13½*
1774 A507 5000r Felis viverrina 4.00 2.50

World Day to Fight Drug Abuse and Illicit Drug Trafficking — A508

Cartoons depicting how to say no to drugs.

1998, June 26
1775 A508 700r red & multi .50 .30
1776 A508 700r yellow & multi .50 .30
a. Pair, #1775-1776 1.25 .70
b. Tete beche pair, #1775-1776 1.25 .70

Tourism — A509

Temples, shrines in Bali: Nos. 1777, 1779, Pura Besakih. No. 1778, Pura Taman Ayun.

1998, July 1 *Perf. 12½*
1777 A509 700r multicolored .50 .25
1778 A509 700r shown .50 .25
a. Pair, #1777-1778 1.00 .60

Souvenir Sheet
Perf. 13½x13

1779 A509 2500r multicolored 1.75 1.00

No. 1777 is 64x24mm. No. 1779 contains one 41x25mm stamp.

Souvenir Sheet

Panthera Tigris — A510

1998, July 23 Litho. *Perf. 13½x12½*
1780 A510 5000r multicolored 3.00 3.00

Singpex '98.

Trains A511

Train going right: a, Cattle, freight cars. b, Freight, box cars. c, Passenger cars. d, Passenger car, tender. e, Locomotive 850.
Train going left: f, Locomotive D52. g, Coal tender. h, Car with 2 doors. i, Dining car with large windows. j, Car with two windows.
2500r, Locomotive.

1998, Aug. 10
1781 A511 300r Block of 10, #a.-j. 3.50 2.50

Souvenir Sheet

1782 A511 2500r multicolored 1.75 1.10

No. 1781 issued in sheets of 20 stamps consisting of two tete-beche blocks of 10. No. 1782 contains one 41x25mm stamp.

Pres. H.B.J. Habibie — A512

1998, Aug. 17 *Perf. 12½x13½*
1783 A512 300r pink & multi .35 .25
1784 A512 700r blue & multi .45 .25
1785 A512 4500r green & multi 1.60 .90
1786 A512 5000r yellow & multi 1.75 1.00
Nos. 1783-1786 (4) 4.15 2.40

13th Asian Games A513

1998, Sept. 9 *Perf. 13½x12½*
1787 A513 300r Fencing .35 .25
1788 A513 700r Taekwondo .45 .25
1789 A513 4000r Wushu 1.50 .85
a. Sovenir sheet, #1787-1789 2.40 1.50
Nos. 1787-1789 (3) 2.30 1.35

Intl. Year of the Ocean A514

Perf. 13½x12½
1998, Sept. 26 Litho.
1790 A514 700r multicolored .75 .25

Souvenir Sheets

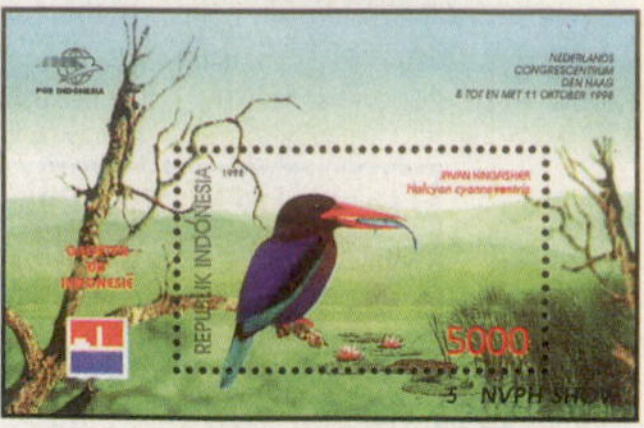

5th NVPH (Netherlands Philatelic Congress) Exhibition, The Hague — A514a

Birds: 5000r, Halcyon cyannoventris. 35,000r, Vannelus macropterus, vert.

1998, Oct. 8 Litho. *Perf. 13½x12½*
1790A A514a 5000r multi 2.00 2.00
1790B A514a 35,000r multi 12.50 12.50

A515

1998, Oct. 9 *Perf. 12½x13½*
1791 A515 700r #922 .50 .25
1792 A515 700r #414 .50 .25
a. Pair, #1791-1792 1.25 .30

World Stamp Day.

A516

Ducks and Geese: 250r, No. 1805, Aythya australis. 500r, Anas superciliosa. 700r, Anas gibberifrons. 1000r, Nettapus coromandelianus. 1500r, Nettapus pulchelus. 2500r, Dendrocygna javanica. 3500r, Dendrocygna arcuata. 4000r, Anseranas semipalmata. No. 1801, Dendrocygna guttata. 10,000r, Anas waigiuensis. 15,000r, Tadorna radjah. 20,000r, Cairina scutulata.

Litho. (#1793-1799, 1805)
1998 *Perf. 12½*
1793 A516 250r multi .25 .25
1794 A516 500r multi .35 .25
1795 A516 700r multi .40 .25
1796 A516 1000r multi .50 .30
1797 A516 1500r multi .65 .40
1798 A516 2500r multi .80 .65
1799 A516 3500r multi 1.25 .85

Litho. With Hologram
Perf. 13½x12½
Size: 42x25mm

1800 A516 4000r horiz. 1.25 .90
1801 A516 5000r horiz. 1.50 1.25
1802 A516 10,000r horiz. 3.25 2.25
1803 A516 15,000r horiz. 4.00 3.25
1804 A516 20,000r horiz. 6.50 4.25
a. Sheet of 5, #1800-1804, + 4 labels 20.00 12.50
Nos. 1793-1804 (12) 20.70 14.85

Souvenir Sheet
Perf. 12½

1805 A516 5000r lt blue sky 3.25 3.25

Soaking in water may affect the hologram on Nos. 1800-1804.
Issued: Nos. 1793-1799, 1805, 12/1; others 10/19.
See Nos. 1918-1919.

Souvenir Sheet

Italia '98 — A516a

5000r, Jakarta Cathedral.

1998, Oct. 23 ***Perf. 12½x13½***
1805A A516a 5000r multi 2.25 2.25

National Flag — A517

Mountains and: No. 1806, Flagpole at right. No. 1807, Flagpole at left.

1998, Oct. 28 Litho. ***Perf. 12½x13½***
1806 A517 700r multicolored .50 .25
1807 A517 700r multicolored .50 .25
a. Pair, #1806-1807 1.10 .40

Reform Movement A518

No. 1809, Dove, national flag. No. 1810, Students, Parliament Building.

1998, Oct. 28 ***Perf. 13½x12½***
1808 A518 700r shown .35 .25
1809 A518 700r multicolored .35 .25
a. Pair, #1808-1809 1.00 .40

Size: 83x25mm

1810 A518 1000r multicolored .75 .30

Flora and Fauna Type of 1994

Flora — No. 1812: a, Stelechocarpus burahol. b, Polianthes tuberosa. c, Mirabilis jalapa. d, Mangifera casturi. e, Ficus minahassae.
Fauna — f, Geopelia striata. g, Gallus varius. h, Elephas maximus. i, Nasalis larvatus. j, Tarsius spectrum.
No. 1813, like #1812b. No. 1814, like #1812i.

1998, Nov. 5 ***Perf. 12½x13½***
1812 A438 500r Block of 10 4.00 2.00
a.-j. Any single .40 .25

Souvenir Sheets

1813 A438 2500r multicolored 1.50 1.50
1814 A438 2500r multicolored 1.50 1.50

Traditional Dance Type of 1992

Dance, region: 300r, Oreng-oreng Gae, Southeast Sulawesi. 500r, Tribute dance, Bengkulu. 700r, Fan dance, Riau. 1000r, Srimpi, Yogyakarta. 2000r, 5000r, Tribute dance, West Sumatra.

1998, Dec. 27
1815 A411 300r multicolored .35 .25
1816 A411 500r multicolored .35 .25
1817 A411 700r multicolored .45 .25
1818 A411 1000r multicolored .55 .25
1819 A411 2000r multicolored 1.00 .40
Nos. 1815-1819 (5) 2.70 1.40

Souvenir Sheet

1820 A411 5000r multicolored 3.00 1.40

Creation and Engineering Year — A519

Designs: 500r, Hydroelectric turbine, power lines. 700r, Plumbing fixture, water pipes.

1999, Jan. 1 Litho. ***Perf. 12½***
1821 A519 500r multicolored .40 .25
1822 A519 700r multicolored .50 .25

7th Far East & South Pacific Games for Disabled — A520

No. 1823, Throwing shotput. No. 1824, Medals, wheelchair.

1999, Jan. 10 ***Perf. 12½x13½***
1823 A520 500r multi .40 .25
1824 A520 500r multi .40 .25
a. Pair, #1823-1824 .80 .25

Garuda Indonesia Airways, 50th Anniv. — A521

500r, Logo. 700r, Aircraft maintenance. 2000r, Pilot, attendant.

1999, Jan. 26 ***Perf. 13x13½***
1825 A521 500r multi .25 .25
1826 A521 700r multi .35 .25
1827 A521 2000r multi .70 .40
Nos. 1825-1827 (3) 1.30 .90

Indonesian Folktales Type of 1998

Folktale, region — No. 1828: a-e, Danau Toba, North Sumatra. f-j, Banjarmasin, South Kalimantan. k-o, Buleleng, Bali. p-t, Woiram, Irian Jaya.
5000r, like #1828e.

1999, Feb. 15 ***Perf. 13½x12½***
1828 Sheet of 20 6.00 4.00
a.-e. A502 500r Strip of 5 1.50 1.00
f.-j. A502 500r Strip of 5 1.50 1.00
k.-o. A502 500r Strip of 5 1.50 1.00
p.-t. A502 500r Strip of 5 1.50 1.00

Souvenir Sheet

1829 A502 5000r multicolored 2.50 1.50

Nos. 1829 is a continuous design.

Souvenir Sheet

Surabaya '99, Natl. Philatelic Exhibition — A522

1999, Mar. 4 Litho. ***Perf. 13½x12½***
1830 A522 5000r Apples 2.75 1.75
a. Ovptd. in sheet margin 4.00 3.00

No. 1830a Overprinted in Gold in Sheet Margin with "APPI SHOW '99 / SURABAYA, 10-18 JULI 1999" and Emblem. Issued, 7/10.

Souvenir Sheet

Australia '99, World Stamp Expo — A523

1999, Mar. 19 ***Perf. 12½x13½***
1831 A523 5000r Tarsius spectrum 2.50 2.50
a. Ovptd. in sheet margin 4.00 4.00

No. 1831a Overprinted in Gold in Sheet Margin with "The 13th / Thaipex / China / Stamp Exhibition / Bangkok '99 / 4 -15. 8. 99" and Emblem. Issued, 8/15.

Mushrooms — A524

No. 1832: a, Mutinus bambusinus. b, Ascosparassis heinricherii. c, Mycena sp.
No. 1833: a, Microporus xanthopus. b, Gloeophyllum imponens. c, Termitomyces eurrhizus.
No. 1834: a, Aseroe rubra. b, Calostoma orirubra. c, Boedijnopeziza insititia.
5000r, Termitomyces eurrhizus.

1999, Apr. 1 ***Perf. 12½***
1832 A524 500r Triptych, #a.-c. 1.25 .70
1833 A524 700r Triptych, #a.-c. 1.50 .75
1834 A524 1000r Triptych, #a.-c. 2.25 1.00
d. Souvenir sheet, #1832-1834 5.00 3.00

Souvenir Sheet

1835 A524 5000r multicolored 2.50 1.75

Booklet Stamps

Size:32x24mm

1836 A524 500r Like #1832a .80 .25
1837 A524 500r Like #1832b .80 .25
1838 A524 500r Like #1832c .80 .25
a. Booklet pane, 3 each #1836-1838, + label 7.50
Complete booklet, #1838a 7.50
Nos. 1836-1838 (3) 2.40 .75

No. 1835 contains one 25x41mm stamp. Numbers have been reserved for additional values in this set.

Public Health Care Insurance A525

1999, Apr. 7 ***Perf. 13½x12½***
1845 A525 700r multicolored .70 .25

Souvenir Sheet

IBRA '99, Intl. Philatelic Exhibition, Nuremberg — A526

5000r, Dendrobium abang betawi.

1999, Apr. 27 ***Perf. 12½x13½***
1846 A526 5000r multi 2.75 2.75

Y2K Millennium Bug — A527

Designs: a, "Bug." b, Circuit, android.

1999, May 2 ***Perf. 13½x12½***
1847 A527 500r Pair, #a.-b. .90 .50

Indonesia 2000 Type of 1997

500r, Chrysoprase.1000r, Smoky quartz. 2000r, Opal blue.
No. 1851, Silicified coral. No. 1851A, Javan jade.

1999, May 20 Litho. ***Perf. 13½x12¾***
1848 A483 500r multi .35 .25
1849 A483 1000r multi .55 .30
1850 A483 2000r multi 1.00 .65
a. Sheet, 3 ea #1848-1850 + label 6.00 6.00
Nos. 1848-1850 (3) 1.90 1.20

Souvenir Sheet

1851 A483 4000r multi 3.50 3.50
1851A A483 4000r multi 12.00 12.00
b. Sheet, #1851-1851A, 2 ea # 1849-1850, 4 #1848 18.00 18.00

Nos. 1851A, 1851Ab were issued in presentation packs with certificate of authenticity. Control numbers and silver overpint "1 Tahun/ Lagi / 1 Year / to Go" printed in margin. No. 1851A sold for 10,000r; No. 1851Ab for 30,000r.

Environmental Care — A528

Winning designs of 1999 Ecophila Stamp Design Contest: 500r, Girl wrapped in blanket, people walking through water. 1000r, 3000r, Boy swimming with duck, plant, cherry. 2000r, Elderly woman drinking water from pitcher, outdoor scene.

1999, June 5
1852 A528 500r multicolored .30 .25
1853 A528 1000r multicolored .60 .45
1854 A528 2000r multicolored 1.25 .80
Nos. 1852-1854 (3) 2.15 1.50

Souvenir Sheet

1855 A528 3000r multicolored 2.00 1.10

1999 General Election — A529

Designs: a, "48," Banner, people standing in line to vote. b, People waiting turn to enter election booth, map.

1999, June 4
1856 A529 1000r Pair, #a.-b. 1.40 .75

Souvenir Sheet

PhilexFrance '99 — A530

1999, July 2 Litho. ***Perf. 12¾x13½***
1858 A530 5000r multi 3.50 3.50

Red Cross / Red Crescent Millennium Year Campaign — A531

Photo. & Litho.

1999, Aug. 12 ***Perf. 12½***
1859 A531 1000r multicolored .80 .40

National Heroes — A532

No. 1860: a, Dr. W. Z. Johannes (1895-1924). b, Martha Christina Tijahahu (1800-18), freedom fighter. c, Frans Kaisiepo (1921-79), politician. d, Maria Walanda Maramis (1872-1924), educator.

Litho. & Engr.

1999, Aug. 17 ***Perf. 12½***
1860 Strip of 4 1.50 .80
a.-d. A532 500r any single .40 .25
e. Booklet pane of 4, #1860a 2.00
f. Booklet pane of 4, #1860b 2.00
g. Booklet pane of 4, #1860c 2.00
h. Booklet pane of 4, #1860d 2.00
Complete bklt., #1860e-1860h 8.00

Complete booklet sold for 10,000r.

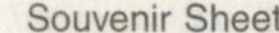
Souvenir Sheet

China 1999 World Philatelic Exhibition — A533

Perf. 13½x12¾

1999, Aug. 21 Litho.
1861 A533 5000r multi 2.50 2.00

Gadjah Mada University, 50th Anniv. — A534

1999, Sept. 19 ***Perf. 12½***
1862 A534 500r shown .50 .25
1863 A534 1000r Building, diff. .60 .25

Intl. Year of Older Persons A535

1999, Oct. 1 ***Perf. 13½x12¾***
1864 A535 500r multi .65 .25

UPU, 125th Anniv. — A536

No. 1865, Postman on horse. No. 1866, Postman on motorcycle.

1999, Oct. 9 ***Perf. 12½***
1865 A536 500r multicolored .50 .25
1866 A536 500r multicolored .50 .25
a. Pair, #1865-1866 + label 1.25 .50
1866B Pair + 2 labels *3.00 2.00*
c. A536 1000r Like #1865, 30x32mm *1.50 1.00*
d. A536 1000r Like #1866, 30x32mm *1.50 1.00*

No. 1866B issued in sheets of 5 pairs. As the labels could be personalized, sheets were available only through special orders with Indonesia Post and sold for 20,000r.

Batik Designs — A537

1999, Oct. 1
1867 A537 500r Cirebon .40 .25
1868 A537 500r Madura .40 .25
1869 A537 500r Jambi .40 .25
1870 A537 500r Yogyakarta .40 .25
Nos. 1867-1870 (4) 1.60 1.00

Domesticated Animals — A538

1999, Nov. 5 ***Perf. 13½x12¾***
1871 A538 500r Dogs .30 .25
1872 A538 500r Chickens .30 .25
a. Pair, #1871-1872 .75 .50
1873 A538 500r Cat .30 .25
1874 A538 500r Rabbits .30 .25
a. Pair, #1873-1874 .75 .50
1875 A538 1000r Pigeon .70 .40
1876 A538 1000r Geese .70 .40
a. Pair, #1875-1876 1.50 .80
b. Sheet of 6, #1871-1876 3.50 2.50
Nos. 1871-1876 (6) 2.60 1.80

Souvenir Sheet

1877 A538 4000r Like #1874 2.50 1.75

Millennium — A539

Designs: No. 1878, 1000r, No. 1880, 20,000r, 1999 agenda book. No. 1879, 1000r, No. 1881, 20,000r, Clock, child.

Litho. & Photo.

1999-2000 ***Perf. 13½x12¾***
1878-1879 A539 Set of 2 1.25 .75
a. Sheet of 20 + 20 labels 25.00 25.00

Souvenir Sheets

1880-1881 A539 Set of 2 20.00 20.00

Labels on No. 1879a could be personalized. The sheet sold for 38,000r.

Issued: Nos. 1878, 1880, 12/31/99; Nos. 1879, 1879a, 1881, 1/1/00.

Visit Indonesia Decade — A540

Designs: 500r, Satellite, fish. 1000r, Hydroponic agriculture.

2000, Jan. 1 ***Perf. 12¾x13½***
1882-1883 A540 Set of 2 1.25 .65

University of Indonesia, 50th Anniv. — A541

Designs: 500r, Salemba campus. 1000r, University building, Depok.

2000, Feb. 2 ***Perf. 12½***
1884-1885 A541 Set of 2 1.25 .65

Indonesian Folktales Type of 1998

Folktale, region — No. 1886: a-e, Tapak Tuan, Aceh. f-j, Batu Ballah, West Kalimantan. k-o, Sawerigading, South Sulawesi. p-t, 7 Putri kahyangan, Moluccas.
5000r, Like #1886e

2000, Feb. 5 ***Perf. 13½x12¾***
1886 Sheet of 20 10.00 10.00
a.-e. 500r Strip of 5 2.50 2.00
f.-j. 500r Strip of 5 2.50 2.00
k.-o. 500r Strip of 5 2.50 2.00
p.-t. 500r Strip of 5 2.50 2.00

Souvenir Sheet

1887 A502 5000r multi 3.00 2.50

Indonesia 2000 Type of 1997

Designs: 500r, Prehnite. 1000r, Chalcedony. 2000r, Volcanic obsidian.

2000, Mar. 1
1888-1890 A483 Set of 3 2.50 1.50
1890a Souvenir sheet, 3 each #1888-1890 + label 7.50 3.50

Souvenir Sheet

1891 A483 5000r Jasperized limestone 3.50 3.50
a. Sheet, #1891, 14 #1888, 2 #1889, 3 #1890 + 20 labels 20.00 —

No. 1891a sold for 41,000r with labels personalized.

Comic Strip Characters — A542

Designs: No. 1892, 500r, I Brewok, by Gungun. No. 1893, 500r, Pak Tuntung, by Basuki. No. 1894, Pak Bei, by Masdi Sunardi. No. 1895, 500r, Mang Ohle, by Didin D. Basuni. No. 1896, 500r, Panji Koming, by Dwi Koendoro.

Perf. 12¾x13½

2000, Mar. 13 Photo.
1892-1896 A542 Set of 5 1.75 1.10
1896a Souvenir sheet, 3 each #1892-1896 + label 6.50 3.50

World Meteorological Organization, 50th Anniv. — A543

Litho. & Photo.

2000, Mar. 23 ***Perf. 12½***
1897 A543 500r multi .80 .30

Souvenir Sheet

Bangkok 2000 Stamp Exhibition — A544

2000, Mar. 23 ***Perf. 13½x12¾***
1898 A544 5000r multi 4.00 2.50

15th Natl. Sports Week A545

Designs: 500r, Cycling. 1000r, Canoeing. 2000r, High jump.

2000, Apr. 1
1899-1901 A545 Set of 3 2.50 1.60

Souvenir Sheet

The Stamp Show 2000, London — A546

2000, May 22

1902 A546 5000r multi 4.00 2.50

Environmental Care — A547

Designs; 500r, Birds in nest. 1000r, Monkeys. 2000r, Fish.

2000, June 5

1903-1905 A547 Set of 3 2.75 1.75

Souvenir Sheet

1906 A547 4000r Like #1904 4.00 2.00

2000 Summer Olympics, Sydney — A548

No. 1907, 500r: a, Boxing. b, Judo.
No. 1908, 1000r: a, Badminton. b, Weight lifting.
No. 1909, 2000r: a, Swimming. b, Running.

2000, July 1

Pairs, #a-b

1907-1909 A548 Set of 3 4.50 3.00

Souvenir Sheet

1910 A548 5000r Like #1908b 4.00 2.25

Worldwide Fund for Nature (WWF) — A549

Komodo dragon: No. 1911, 500r, No. 1915a, 2500r, With tongue extended. No. 1912, 500r, On log. No. 1913, 500r, Pair walking. No. 1914, 500r, No. 1915b, 2500r, Pair fighting.

2000, Aug. 13

1911-1914 A549 Set of 4 2.50 2.00
a. Souvenir sheet, 2 each #1911-1914 9.00 7.50

Souvenir Sheet

1915 A549 2500r Sheet of 2, #a-b 5.50 4.00

Souvenir Sheet

Olymphilex 2000 Stamp Exhibition — A550

2000, Sept. 15 ***Perf. 12¾x13½***

1916 A550 5000r multi 4.00 2.25

A551

No. 1917: a, Pres. Abdurrahman Wahid. b, Vice Pres. Megawati Soekarnoputri

Photo. & Engr.

2000, Sept. 27 ***Perf. 12½***

1917 A551 1000r Pair, #a-b 1.50 1.00

Ducks and Geese Type of 1998

2000, Sept. 27 Photo. ***Perf. 12½***

1918 A516 800r Like #1798 1.25 1.00
1919 A516 900r Like #1793 1.25 1.00

Traditional Costumes A552

Provinces and regions: a, Aceh. b, Jambi. c, Banten. d, Yogyakarta. e, Central Kalimantan (Kalimantan Tengah). f, Southeast Sulawesi (Sulawesi Tenggara). g, East Nusa Tenggara (Nusa Tenggara Timur). h, North Sumatra (Sumatera Utara). i, Bengkulu. j, Jakarta. k, East Java (Jawa Timur). l, East Kalimantan (Kalimantan Timur). m, South Sulawesi (Sulawesi Selatan). n, Maluku. o, West Sumatra (Sumatera Barat). p, South Sumatra (Sumatera Selatan). q, West Java (Jawa Barat). r, West Kalimantan (Kalimantan Barat). s, North Sulawesi (Sulawesi Utara). t, Bali. u, North Maluku (Maluku Utara). v, Riau. w, Lampung. x, Central Java (Jawa Tengah). y, South Kalimantan (Kalimantan Selatan). z, Central Sulawesi (Sulawesi Tengah). aa, West Nusa Tenggara (Nusa Tenggara Barat). ab, Irian Jaya.

Litho. & Photo.

2000, Oct. 28 ***Perf. 12½***

1920 Sheet of 28 + 7 labels 25.00 15.00
a.-ab. A552 900r Any single .55 .50

Artists and Entertainers — A553

No. 1921, horiz.: a, Bing Slamet (1927-74), singer, comedian. b, S. Sudjojono (1913-86), painter. c, I Ketut Maria (1897-1968), dancer. d, Chairil Anwar (1922-49), poet. e, Ibu Sud (1908-93), musician.

2000, Nov. 1 ***Perf. 13½x12¾***

1921 Horiz. strip of 5 3.50 2.00
a.-e. A553 900r Any single .60 .40

Souvenir Sheet

1922 A553 4000r Chairil Anwar 2.50 2.00

Indonesia Post in the 21st Century — A554

Designs: 800r, Philately, vert. 900r, Business communications. 1000r, Business financial services, vert. 4000r, Business logistics, vert.

Litho. & Photo.

2000, Dec. 20 ***Perf. 12½***

1923 A554 800r multi .60 .30
1924 A554 900r multi .60 .40
1925 A554 1000r multi 1.00 .50
1926 A554 4000r multi 3.50 1.75
Nos. 1923-1926 (4) 5.70 2.95

Solar System — A555

No. 1927: a, Sun. b, Mercury. c, Venus. d, Earth. e, Mars. f, Jupiter. g, Saturn. h, Uranus. i, Neptune. j, Pluto.

2001, Jan. 1 Litho. ***Perf. 13½x12¾***

1927 Block of 10 + 5 labels 7.00 3.50
a.-j. A555 900r Any single .60 .30
k. Sheet of 10 + 5 labels 8.00 4.00
l. Sheet of 20 + 20 labels 20.00 20.00

Souvenir Sheet

1928 A555 5000r Sun 3.00 2.00

Labels on No. 1927l could be personalized. The sheet sold for 36,000r.

Indonesian Folktales Type of 1998

Folktale, region — No. 1929: a-e, Batang Tuaka, Riau. f-j, Si Pitung, Jakarta. k-o, Terusan Nusa, Central Kalimantan. p-t, Ile Mauraja, East Nusa Tenggara.
5000r, Like No. 1929h.

Litho. & Photo.

2001, Feb. 2 ***Perf. 13½x12¾***

1929 Sheet of 20 10.00 6.00
a.-e. A502 900r Strip of 5 2.50 1.50
f.-j. A502 900r Strip of 5 2.50 1.50
k.-o. A502 900r Strip of 5 2.50 1.50
p.-t. A502 900r Strip of 5 2.50 1.50

Souvenir Sheet

1930 A502 5000r multi 2.50 1.25

Masks — A556

No. 1931, 500r — Arsa Wijaya, Bali: a, Denomination at L. b, Denomination at R.
No. 1932, 800r — Asmat, Irian Jaya: a, Denomination at L. b, Denomination at R.
No. 1933, 800r — Cirebon, West Java: a, Denomination at L. b, Denomination at R.
No. 1934, 900r — Hudoq, East Kalimantan: a, Denomination at L. b, Denomination at R.
No. 1935, 900r — Wayang Wong, Yogyakarta: a, Denomination at L. b, Denomination at R.
5000r, Like No. 1934b.

2001, Mar. 2 ***Perf. 12¾x13½***

Pairs, #a-b

1931-1935 A556 Set of 5 4.50 2.25
c. Sheet, #1931-1935 +2 labels 5.00

Souvenir Sheet

1936 A556 5000r multi 3.00 2.00
a. Ovptd. in margin in silver 4.50 3.00

Issued: No. 1936a, 10/16/01. No. 1936 overprinted with "HAFNIA '01 / World Philatelic Exhibition / Copenhagen / 16-21 October 2001," show emblem and new price of 7500r.

Traditional Communication Instruments — A557

No. 1937: a, Beduk. b, Bendé. c, Kentongan. d, Nafiri.

2001, Mar. 10 ***Perf. 12½***

1937 Vert. strip of 4 2.00 1.50
a.-d. A557 900r Any single .50 .35
e. Sheet, 2 each #1937a-1937d 8.00 4.00

Greetings — A558

Various flowers. Denominations: 800, 900, 1000, 1500, 2000, 4000, 5000, 10000r

Litho. & Typo.

2001, Apr. 21 ***Perf. 12½***

1938-1945 A558 Set of 8 14.00 8.75

A558a

Greetings — A558b

Perf. 13½x12¾

2001, Apr. 21 Litho. & Typo.
1945A A558a 900r multi + label 3.50 2.50

Perf. 12½

1945B A558b 900r multi + label 3.50 2.50

No. 1945A was issued in sheets of 20 + 20 labels that could be personalized. The sheet sold for 36,000r. No. 1945B was issued in sheets of 10 + 10 labels that could be personalized. The sheet sold for 20,000r.

Environmental Care — A559

Children and: 800r, Fish. 900r, 5000r, Deer. 1000r, Sea turtle.

Litho. & Photo.

2001, June 5 *Perf. 13½x12¾*
1946 A559 800r multi .50 .30
a. Tete-beche pair 1.00 1.00
1947 A559 900r multi .50 .30
a. Tete-beche pair 1.00 1.00
1948 A559 1000r multi .75 .40
a. Tete-beche pair 1.50 1.50
Nos. 1946-1948 (3) 1.75 1.00

Souvenir Sheet

1949 A559 3000r multi 3.50 3.00

No. 1949 exists imperf. Value $3.50.

Pres. Sukarno (1901-70) — A560

Various portraits: 500, 800, 900, 1000r. 5000r, Sukarno at microphone.

2001, June 6 *Perf. 12½*
1950-1953 A560 Set of 4 2.00 1.25
a. Sheet, 2 each #1950-1953 6.50 3.25

Souvenir Sheet

Perf. 13½x12¾

1954 A560 5000r multi 3.00 2.25

No. 1954 contains one 41x25mm stamp

National Police — A561

Police and: a, Children. b, Helicopter.

2001, July 1 Photo. *Perf. 13½x12¾*
1955 A561 1000r Horiz. pair, #a-b 1.25 1.10

National Scouting Jamboree — A562

Scouts: a, Raising flag. b, Pitching tent.

2001, July 3
1956 A562 1000r Horiz. pair, #a-b 1.25 1.10

Children's Games A563

Designs: 800r, Kaki Siapa. 900r, Egrang Bambu. 1000r, Dakon. 2000r, Kuda Pelepah Pisang.

Litho. & Photo.

2001, July 23 *Perf. 13½x12¾*
1957-1960 A563 Set of 4 2.50 1.25
a. Sheet, 2 each #1957-1960 6.00 4.50

Souvenir Sheet

Phila Nippon '01, Japan — A564

2001, Aug. 1 Photo.
1961 A564 10,000r multi 6.00 4.00

Dr. R. Soeharso Orthopedic Hospital, Surakarta, 50th Anniv. A565

Litho. & Photo.

2001, Aug. 28 *Perf. 13½x12¾*
1962 A565 1000r multi .85 .30

Traditional Transportation — A566

Designs: No. 1963, 1000r, Rowboat. No. 1964, 1000r, Trishaw. No. 1965, Horse-drawn carriage.

2001, Sept. 17
1963-1965 A566 Set of 3 1.50 1.00
a. Sheet, 3 each #1963-1965 +label 6.00 6.00

Post Offices A567

Buildings in: 800r, Makassar. 900r, Bandung. 1000r, Balikpapan. 2000r, Padang.

2001, Sept. 27
1966-1969 A567 Set of 4 2.50 1.60

Gemstones — A568

Designs: 800r, Rose quartz. 900r, Brecciated jasper. 1000r, Malachite. 5000r, Diamond.

2001, Oct. 1
1970-1972 A568 Set of 3 1.75 1.10
a. Sheet, 3 each #1970-1972 + label 5.50 4.50

Souvenir Sheet

1973 A568 5000r multi 3.00 2.25

Year of Dialogue Among Civilizations — A569

2001, Oct. 9 Litho. *Perf. 12¾x13½*
1974 A569 1000r multi 1.25 .40

Beetles — A570

Designs: 800r, Agestrata dehaan. 900r, Mormolyce phyllodes. No. 1977, 1000r, Batocera rosenbergi. No. 1978, 1000r, Chrysochroa buqueti. 2000r, 5000r, Chalcosoma caucasus.

2001, Nov. 5 Litho. & Photo.
1975-1979 A570 Set of 5 3.50 2.25
a. Booklet pane, #1975-1979 + label 6.00 —
Booklet, 2 #1979a 12.00

Souvenir Sheet

1980 A570 5000r multi 3.00 2.50

Folktales — A571

No. 1981, 1000r — Pulau Kembara, South Sumatra: a, Four people, lanterns. b, Two men, woman, boat. c, Man and woman standing in boat. d, Man and woman in water. e, Boat, snake, fish.

No. 1982, 1000r — Nyi Koro Kidul, Yogyakarta: a, Woman at tight pointing. b, Woman at foreground with hand at mouth. c, Two men with hats at right. d, Woman in sea. e, Sea and island.

No. 1983, 1000r — Aji Tatin, East Kalimantan: a, Bird in tree, woman, man with hand outstretched. b, Woman, bird boat. c, Sinking boat. d, Woman and tree. e, Bird in tree.

No. 1984, 1000r — Danau Tondano, North Sulawesi: a, Woman with long hair in foreground. b, Man holding spear. c, Man at left with arm to head. d, Man and woman embracing. e, Sea and island.

5000r, Like No. 1981e.

Illustration reduced.

Litho. & Photo.

2002, Feb. 2 *Perf. 13½x12¾*

Blocks of 5, #a-e

1981-1984 A571 Set of 4 8.00 4.00

Souvenir Sheet

1985 A571 5000r multi 3.00 2.00

Nos. 1981-1984 are printed in sheets of four blocks of five. Stamp "e" is always adjacent to the LL stamp in the block of the remaining four stamps, and is found tete beche to both stamps "a" and "e" from adjacent blocks of five.

2002 World Cup Soccer Championships, Japan and Korea — A572

Celebrations: 1000r, Player lifting shirt over face. 1500r, Four players with fists raised, horiz. 2000r, 5000r, Player with arms outstretched.

Perf. 12¾x13½, 13½x12¾

2002, Apr. 1 Litho. & Photo.
1986-1988 A572 Set of 3 2.50 2.00

Souvenir Sheet

1989 A572 5000r multi 3.00 2.00

Indonesian Cancer Foundation, 25th Anniv. — A573

2002, Apr. 17 *Perf. 12¾x13½*
1990 A573 1000r multi .90 .45
a. Tete-beche pair 1.80 1.25

Telecommunications — A574

No. 1991: a, Woman using telephone (2/4). b, Man using cellular phone (1/4). c, Satellite above Earth (4/4). d, Satellite, world map, computer, satellite dish (3/4).

2002, May 17
1991 A574 1000r Block of 4, #a-d 2.50 1.50
e. Sheet, 2 each #1991a-1991d 5.00 4.00
f. Booklet pane, 4 #1991a 2.50
g. Booklet pane, 4 #1991b 2.50
h. Booklet pane, 4 #1991c 2.50
i. Booklet pane, 4 #1991d 2.50
Booklet, #1991f-1991i 10.00

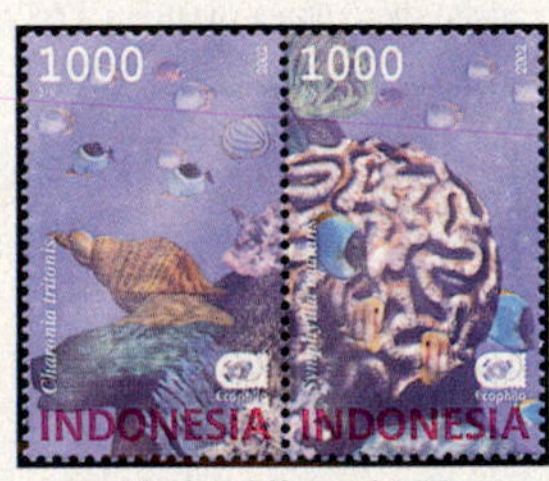

Marine Life — A575

No. 1992, 1000r: a, Charonia tritonis. b, Symphyllia radians.

No. 1993, 1500r: a, Cromileptes altivelis. b, Acanthaster planci.

No. 1994, 2000r, horiz.: a, Paracanthurus hepatus. b, Tridacna gigas.

5000r, Acanthaster planci.

2002, June 5

Horiz. Pairs, #a-b

1992-1994 A575 Set of 3 5.00 3.50
1994c Sheet, #1992, 1993, 1994a, 1994b 7.00 3.50

Souvenir Sheet

1995 A575 5000r multi 3.00 2.00

Aceh Province — A576

Designs: 1500r, Student, Aceh dance, map of Aceh. 3500r, Masjid Raya Banda Aceh, map of Indonesia.

2002, June 15 *Perf. 12½*
1996-1997 A576 Set of 2 2.75 .45

Natl. Family Day A577

Perf. 13½x12¾
2002, June 29 **Litho. & Typo.**
1998 A577 1000r multi .85 .45

33rd Intl. Physics Olympiad, Bali — A578

No. 1999: a, Eclipse (1/2). b, Spectrum colors and Balinese symbols (2/2).

2002, July 14 *Perf. 12¾x13½*
1999 A578 1000r Horiz. pair, #a-b 1.25 1.00

Kites A579

No. 2000: a, Popotengan (bird-shaped) (1/5). b, Barong (dragon head) (2/5). c, Fighting (3/5). d, Behean (4/5). e, Modern (box and wing) (5/5).
5000r, Popotengan.

Litho. & Photo.
2002, July 15 *Perf. 13½x12¾*
2000 Horiz. strip of 5 2.50 2.50
a.-e. A579 1000r Any single .50 .30

Souvenir Sheet
2001 A579 5000r multi 3.00 2.00

Fruit — A580

Designs: 300r, Morinda citrifolia. 500r, Mangifera indica. 1500r, Averrhoa carambola. 3000r, Durio zibethinus.

2002, Aug. 1 **Photo.** *Perf. 13½x12¾*
2002 A580 300r multi .35 .25
2003 A580 500r multi .35 .25
2004 A580 1500r multi .65 .65
2005 A580 3000r multi 1.40 1.10
Nos. 2002-2005 (4) 2.75 2.25

Souvenir Sheet

Philakorea 2002 World Stamp Exhibition, Seoul — A581

2002, Aug. 2 **Litho.** *Perf. 12¾x13½*
2006 A581 7000r multi 4.00 3.00

Mohammad Hatta (1902-80), Prime Minister — A582

No. 2007, 1000r: a, Denomination at left. b, Denomination at right.
No. 2008, 1500r: a, Denomination at left. b, Denomination at right.
5000r, Hatta standing.

Litho. & Photo.
2002, Aug. 12 *Perf. 12½*
Pairs, #a-b
2007-2008 A582 Set of 2 2.50 2.00
2008c Sheet, 2 each #2007-2008 + 2 labels 4.00 4.00

Souvenir Sheet
Perf. 12¾x13½
2009 A582 5000r multi 3.50 3.50

No. 2009 contains one 25x41mm stamp.

President and Vice-President — A583

No. 2010, 1500r: a, Pres. Megawati Soekarnoputri. b, Vice-president Hamzah Haz.

Photo. with Foil Application
2002, Aug. 17 *Perf. 12½*
2010 A583 Horiz. pair, #a-b, + central label 1.75 1.75

Souvenir Sheet

Amphilex 2002 Intl. Stamp Exhibition, Amsterdam — A584

Perf. 13½x12¾
2002, Aug. 30 **Photo.**
2011 A584 7000r multi 5.00 4.00

Souvenir Sheet

Panfila 2002 Philatelic Exhibition, Yogyakarta — A585

2002, Sept. 19 *Perf. 12¾x13½*
2012 A585 6000r multi 3.00 3.00

Paintings — A586

No. 2013, 1000r: a, Seko, Guerrilla Vanguard, by S. Sudjojono. b, Cat, by Popo Iskandar.
No. 2014, 1500r, vert.: a, Catching Lice, by Hendra Gunawan. b, Gatut Kaca with Prigiwa and Prigiwati, by R. Basuki Abdullah.

Litho. & Photo.
2002, Sept. 27 *Perf. 12½*
Pairs, #a-b
2013-2014 A586 Set of 2 2.50 2.50
2014c Sheet, 2 each #2013-2014 6.50 6.50

Souvenir Sheet

España 2002 Youth Philatelic Exhibition, Salamanca — A587

2002, Oct. 4 **Photo.** *Perf. 13½x12¾*
2015 A587 7000r multi 2.50 2.50

Flora and Fauna A588

No. 2016, 1000r: a, Trimeresurus hageni. b, Rafflesia micropylora.
No. 2017, 1500r: a, Panthera pardus. b, Terminalia catappa.
No. 2018, 2000r: a, Papilionanthe hookeriana. b, Varanus salvator.
3500r, Panthera pardus.

Litho. & Photo.
2002, Nov. 5 *Perf. 12¾x13½*
Horiz. Pairs, #a-b
2016-2018 A588 Set of 3 4.50 3.50

Souvenir Sheet
2019 A588 3500r multi 2.00 2.00

No. 2019 exists imperf. Value $2.-

Antara, Indonesian News Agency — A589

Litho. & Typo.
2002, Dec. 13 *Perf. 12½*
2020 A589 1500r multi 1.00 .45

Happy Birthday — A590

No. 2021: a, Food platter. b, Birthday cake.

2003 **Photo.** *Perf. 12½*
2021 Strip of 2 stamps and 2 alternating labels 2.00 1.75
a.-b. A590 1500r Any single .80 .50
c. Sheet of 5 #2021 10.00 10.00

No. 2021 was printed in sheets containing 10 strips with labels that could be personalized. The sheet sold for 45,000r. The labels on No. 2021c could also be personalized, and that sheet sold for 30,000r.

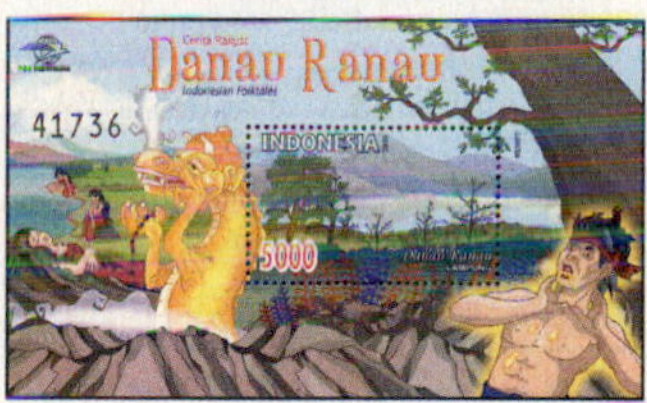

Folklore — A591

No. 2022 — Scenes from Danau Ranau, Lampung (Nos. a.-e.), Kongga Owose, Southeast Sulawesi (Nos. f.-j.), Putri Gading Cempaka, Bengkulu (Nos. k.-o.), Putri Mandalika Nyale, West Nusa Tenggara (Nos. p.-t.) and stamp numbers: a, 01/20. b, 02/20. c, 03/20. d, 04/20. e, 05/20. f, 06/20. g, 07/20. h, 08/20. i, 09/20. j, 10/20. k, 11/20. l, 12/20. m, 13/20. n, 14/20. o, 15/20. p, 16/20. q, 17/20. r, 18/20. s, 19/20. t, 20/20.
5000r, Like #2022e.

Litho. & Photo.
2003, Feb. 2 *Perf. 13½x12¾*
2022 A591 1500r Sheet of 20, #a-t 12.00 12.00

Souvenir Sheet
2023 A591 5000r multi 2.50 2.50

22nd South East Asia Games, Hanoi, Viet Nam A592

Designs: 1000r, Billiards. 1500r, Rowing. 2500r, Rhythmic gymnastics.

Litho. & Photo.

2003, May 12 *Perf. 14*
2024-2026 A592 Set of 3 2.50 2.00

Values are for stamps with surrounding selvage.

Volcanoes — A593

Designs: 500r, Kerinci. No. 2028, 1000r, Krakatoa. No. 2029, 1000r, Merapi. No. 2030, 1000r, Tambora. 2000r, Ruang.

2003, June 5 *Perf. 12½*
2027-2031 A593 Set of 5 3.00 2.00
2031a Sheet, 2 each #2027-2031 + 2 labels 6.00 4.50

Astronomy — A594

No. 2032: a, Andromeda Galaxy (1/5). b, Earth and Mars (2/5). c, Moon (3/5).
No. 2033: a, External view of observatory (4/5). b, Zeiss telescope (5/5).
5000r, Like No. 2033a.

2003, June 7 *Perf. 12½*
2032 Strip of 3 1.40 1.40
a.-c. A594 1000r Any single .40 .30
2033 Pair 1.50 1.50
a.-b. A594 1500r Either single .60 .40
c. Sheet, 2 each #2032a-2032c, 2033a-2033b 5.00 4.00

Souvenir Sheet

Perf. 13½x12¾

2034 A594 5000r multi 3.00 2.50

Stamps in No. 2033c are tete-beche. No. 2034 contains one 41x25mm stamp.

Bank Indonesia, 50th Anniv. — A595

Designs: 1000r, Tower and flowers. 1500r, People at graduation ceremony, books.

Perf. 13½x13¼ Syncopated

2003, July 1
2035-2036 A595 Set of 2 1.50 1.00

Sri Sultan Hamengku Buwono IX and Lord Robert Baden-Powell — A596

Perf. 13½x12¾

2003, Aug. 14 **Photo.**
2037 A596 1500r multi 1.00 .50

Independence Day Games — A597

No. 2038, 1000r: a, Panjat Pinang (1/4). b, Pukul Bantal (2/4).
No. 2039, 1500r, horiz.: a, Balap Kelom (3/4). b, Balap Karung (4/4).

Perf. 12¾x13½, 13½x12¾

2003, Aug. 17 **Litho. & Photo.**

Pairs, #a-b

2038-2039 A597 Set of 2 2.50 1.75
2039c Sheet, 2 each #2038a-2038b, 2039a-2039b 5.00 3.75

Souvenir Sheet

Paintings of Srihadi Soedarsono — A598

No. 2040: a, Pendet, Dinamika Remaja. b, Borobudur-Purnama dalam Keheningan.

2003 ***Perf. 13½ Syncopated***
2040 A598 3000r Sheet of 2, #a-b 1.75 1.75
c. Sheet with margin design in cyan only 1.75 1.75
d. As "c," with magenta added to margin design 3.50 3.00
e. As "d," with yellow added to margin design 3.50 3.00
f. As "e," with black added to margin design, but lacking artist's face and signature 3.50 3.00
g. Sheet, 2 each #2040a-2040b 6.50 6.00

Emmitan-Philex 2003, Surabaya (Nos. 2040, 2040c, 2040d, 2040e, 2040f), 10th ASEAN Postal Business Meeting (No. 2040g).
Issued: No. 2040, 9/4; No. 2040c, 8/29; No. 2040d, 8/30; No. 2040e, 8/31; No. 2040f, 9/1; No. 2040g, 9/3. No. 2040 exists imperf, issued 9/2. Value, $6.

Tourism — A599

No. 2041, 1000r: a, Jou Uci Sabea, North Maluku (1/4). b, Mome'ati, Gorontalo (2/4).
No. 2042, 1500r: a, Muang Jong, Bangka Belitung (3/4). b, Seba Baduy, Banten (4/4).
5000r, Like No. 2042a.

2003, Sept. 27 *Perf. 12½*

Vert. Pairs, #a-b

2041-2042 A599 Set of 2 3.00 1.50

Souvenir Sheet

2043 A599 5000r multi 3.00 2.50

Souvenir Sheet

Bangkok 2003 World Philatelic Exhibition — A600

2003, Oct. 4 ***Perf. 13½x12¾***
2044 A600 8000r multi 3.00 1.75

Handshake — A601

Fish and Water Lily — A602

Birds — A603

Handshake and Flag — A604

Flower — A605

2003, Oct. 27 **Litho.** *Perf. 12½*
2045 A601 1000r multi + label .85 .85
2046 A602 1500r multi + label 1.00 1.00
2047 A603 1500r multi + label 1.00 1.00
2048 A604 1500r multi + label 1.00 1.00
2049 A605 1500r multi + label 1.00 1.00
Nos. 2045-2049 (5) 4.85 4.85

Nos. 2045-2049 were each issued in sheets of 20 stamps + 20 labels that could be personalized. Sheets of No. 2045 sold for 35,000r, while sheets of Nos. 2046-2049 each sold for 45,000r.

Indonesian Youth Pledge, 75th Anniv. — A606

2003, Oct. 28 **Litho.** ***Perf. 12¾x13¼***
2050 A606 1500r Nos. 1031-1032, 1246 1.00 .50

Flowers and Insects — A607

No. 2051: a, Paphiopedilum mastersianum (9/12). b, Platylomia flavida (8/12). c, Osmoxylon palmatum (7/12). d, Apis dorsata (12/12). e, Freycinetia pseudoinsignis (11/12). f, Sia ferox (10/12). g, Aularches miliaris (3/12). h, Butea monosperma (2/12). i, Orthetrum testaceum (1/12). j, Anaphalis javanica (6/12). k, Hierodula vitrea (5/12). l, Saraca declinata (4/12).
No. 2052: a, Like #2051j. b, Like #2051i.

Litho. & Photo.

2003, Nov. 5 *Perf. 12½*
2051 A607 1500r Block of 12, #a-l 8.00 8.00
m. Booklet pane, #2051a, 2051c, 2051e, 2051h, 2051j, 2051l 7.50 —
n. Booklet pane, #2051b, 2051d, 2051f, 2051g, 2051i, 2051k 7.50 —
Complete booklet, #2051m, 2051n 15.00

Souvenir Sheet

2052 A607 3000r Sheet of 2, #a-b, + label 3.00 2.25

Famous Men A608

No. 2053: a, Prof. Roosseno (1908-96) (3/4). b, Prof. Sutami (1928-80) (4/4). c, Nurtanio Pringgoadisuryo (1923-66) (1/4). d, Martinus Putuhena (1901-82) (2/4).

Litho. & Engr.

2003, Nov. 10 ***Perf. 13¼x13***
2053 Strip of 4 3.50 2.25
a.-d. A608 2000r Any single .55 .55

Flowers — A609

No. 2054: a, Styrax benzoin (1/30). b, Kopsia fruticosa (2/30). c, Impatiens tujuhensis (3/30). d, Hoya diversifolia (4/30). e, Etlingera elatior (5/30). f, Dillenia suffruticosa (6/30). g, Papilionanthe hookerianum (7/30). h, Medinilla speciosa (8/30). i, Costus speciosus (9/30). j, Melastoma sylvaticum (10/30). k, Nelumbo nucifera (11/30). l, Begonia robusta (12/30). m, Anaphalis longifolia (13/30). n, Pisonia grandis (14/30). o, Ixora javanica (15/30). p, Plumeria acuminata (16/30). q, Cassia fistula (17/30). r, Calotropis gigantea (18/30). s, Dimorphorchis lowii (19/30). t, Aeschynanthus radicans (20/30). u, Sonneratia caseolaris (21/30). v, Rhododendron orbiculatum (22/30). w, Passiflora edulis (23/30). x, Pterospermum celebicum (24/30). y, Quisqualis indica (25/30). z, Spathiphyllum commutatum (26/30). aa, Lilium longiflorum (27/30). ab, Clitoria ternatea (28/30). ac, Pecteilis susannae (29/30). ad, Grammatophyllum speciosum (30/30).

Litho. & Photo.

2004, Jan. 5 *Perf. 12½*
2054 Sheet of 30 17.00 17.00
a.-ad. A609 1500r Any single .75 .30

Folktales — A610

No. 2055 — Scenes from Putri Selaras Pinang Masak, Jambi (Nos. a.-e.), Tanjung Lesung, Banten (Nos. f.-j.), Patung Palindo, Central Sulawesi (Nos. k.-o.), Danau Tolire, North Maluku (Nos. p.-t.) and stamp number: a, 01/20. b, 02/20. c, 03/20. d, 04/20. e, 05/20. f, 06/20. g, 07/20. h, 08/20. i, 09/20. j, 10/20. k, 11/20. l, 12/20. m, 13/20. n, 14/20. o, 15/20. p, 16/20. q, 17/20. r, 18/20. s, 19/20. t, 20/20.
6000r, Like # 2055j.

Litho. & Photo.

2004, Feb. 20 ***Perf. 13½x12¾***
2055 A610 1500r Sheet of 20, #a-t 12.00 12.00

Souvenir Sheet

2056 A610 6000r multi 3.00 2.50

Museums — A611

No. 2057: a, Sri Baduga Museum, Bandung (3/4). b, Bahari Museum, Jakarta (1/4). c, Telecommunications Museum, Jakarta (4/4). d, Geology Museum, Bandung (2/4).

2004, Feb. 29 ***Perf. 13¼x12¾***

2057 Vert. strip of 4 3.00 1.75
a.-d. A611 1500r Any single .75 .40

General Elections — A612

No. 2058: a, Man and woman pointing at people holding flags (1/2). b, Man and woman casting ballots (2/2).

2004, Apr. 5 Litho. ***Perf. 12¾x13¼***

2058 A612 1500r Horiz. pair, #a-b 1.50 1.10

Famous Women — A613

No. 2059: a, Gedong Bagoes Oka (1921-2002), social worker, religious leader (2/4). b, Ani Idrus (1918-99), journalist (1/4). c, Nyonya Meneer (1895-1978), founder of herbal medicine factory (3/4). d, Sandiah (Ibu Kasur) (1926-2002), composer of children's songs, television personality (4/4).

Perf. 13¼x13½ Syncopated

2004, Apr. 21 **Litho. & Engr.**

2059 Horiz. strip of 4 3.50 2.50
a.-d. A613 2500r Any single .85 .60

2004 Summer Olympics, Athens A614

No. 2060: a, Swimming (1/3). b, Women's high jump (2/3). c, Hurdling (3/3).

Litho. & Photo.

2004, May 5 ***Perf. 14***

2060 Horiz. strip of 3 3.00 2.25
a.-c. A614 2500r Any single 1.10 .65

Environmental Protection — A615

Designs: Nos. 2061a, 2062a, Bird, killer whale (1/2). Nos. 2061b, 2062b, Shark, turtle (2/2).

2004, June 5 ***Perf. 13¼x12¾***

2061 A615 1500r Vert. pair, #a-b 1.50 1.00

Souvenir Sheet

2062 A615 2500r Sheet of 2, #a-b 2.50 2.25

Indonesian Cuisine — A616

No. 2063: a, Gajebo, West Sumatra (1/4). b, Sambal Udang Terung Pipit, West Kalimantan (3/4). c, Kare Rajungan, East Java (2/4). d, Tinotuan, North Sulawesi (4/4).

2004, July 6 Litho. ***Perf. 13¼x12¾***

2063 A616 1500r Block of 4, #a-d 2.00 2.00

Presidential Limousines — A617

No. 2064: a, 1939 Buick with REP-1 license plate (1/2). b, 1942 DeSoto with REP-2 license plate (2/2).

2004, Aug. 17

2064 A617 2500r Vert. pair, #a-b 2.00 2.00
c. Souvenir sheet #2064a-2064b 2.00 2.00

16th National Games — A618

No. 2065: a, Volleyball (1/2). b, Sepak takraw (2/2).

Litho. & Photo.

2004, Sept. 2 ***Perf. 14***

2065 A618 1500r Pair, #a-b 1.50 1.00

Flowers and Insects Type of 2003

No. 2066: a, Gryllotalpa hirsuta (4/6). b, Alstonia scholaris (5/6). c, Scolopendra subspinipes (6/6). d, Cinnamomun sintok (3/6). e, Heterometrus cyaneus (2/6). f, Parkia roxburghii (1/6).

No. 2067: a, Like #2066e. b, Like #2066f.

2004, Nov. 5 ***Perf. 12½***

2066 A607 1500r Block of 6, #a-f 3.50 3.00

Souvenir Sheet

2067 A607 3000r Sheet of 2, #a-b, + label 3.00 2.50

National Teacher's Day — A619

No. 2068: a, Teacher, students with microscope and book (1/2). b, Teacher students with pen and book (2/2).

2004, Nov. 25 ***Perf. 12¾x13¼***

2068 A619 1500r Horiz. pair, #a-b 1.25 1.00

Souvenir Sheet

National Philatelic Exhibition, Surabaya — A620

No. 2069 — Paintings by Sunaryo: a, Setagen Rhythm. b, Sebelum Pentas. c, Bercinta.

2004, Dec. 16 Litho. ***Perf. 12½***

2069 A620 5000r Sheet of 3, #a-c 8.00 6.50
d. Souvenir sheet of 1, #2069a 2.50 2.00
e. Souvenir sheet of 1, #2069b 2.50 2.00
f. Souvenir sheet of 1, #2069c 2.50 2.00
g. Souvenir sheet of 1, #2069a, imperf. 2.50 2.00
h. Souvenir sheet of 1, #2069b, imperf. 2.50 2.00
i. Souvenir sheet of 1, #2069c, imperf. 2.50 2.00

Folktales — A621

No. 2070 — Scenes from Lahilote, Gorontalo (Nos. a.-e.), Kolam Putri, Riau Islands (Nos. f.-j.), Batu Balai, Bangka Belitung (Nos. k.-o.), Bulan & Sagu di Ibuanari, Papua (Nos. p.-t.) and stamp number: a, 1/20. b, 2/20. c, 3/20. d, 4/20. e, 5/20. f, 6/20. g, 7/20. h, 8/20. i, 9/20. j, 10/20. k, 11/20. l, 12/20. m, 13/20. n, 14/20. o, 15/20. p, 16/20. q, 17/20. r, 18/20. s, 19/20. t, 20/20.

6000r, Like #2070j.

2005, Feb. 2 Litho. ***Perf. 13½x12¾***

2070 A621 1500r Sheet of 20, #a-t 10.00 10.00

Souvenir Sheet

2071 A621 6000r multi 2.50 2.00

Asian-African Summit, 50th Anniv. — A622

No. 2072: a, Dove and "50." b, Dove, world map and people.

Perf. 13½x13¼ Syncopated

2005, Apr. 18 **Litho. & Photo.**

2072 Horiz. pair + central label 1.75 1.50
a.-b. A622 2500r Either single .85 .75
c. Souvenir sheet, #2072b 1.50 .75

Mangrove Forest Protection — A623

No. 2073 — Mangroves and: a, Bird. b, Fish.

2005, June 5 Litho. ***Perf. 12¾x13¼***

2073 A623 1500r Horiz. pair, #a-b 1.25 1.00
c. Souvenir sheet, #2073 1.50 1.00

Voyages of Admiral Zheng He, 600th Anniv. A624

Litho. & Photo.

2005, June 28 ***Perf. 13½x12¾***

2074 A624 2500r multi 1.25 .45
a. Souvenir sheet of 1 2.50 1.00

Traditional Food A625

No. 2075: a, Sayur Tauco (North Sumatra) (1/4). b, Soto Banjar (South Kalimantan) (3/4). c, Nasi Timbel (West Java) (2/4). d, Langga Roko (South Sulawesi) (4/4).

2005, July 6 **Litho.**

2075 Vert. strip of 4 2.00 1.40
a.-d. A625 1500r Any single .50 .35

Energy Conservation A626

Designs: 1500r, Bus, electric plug (1/3). 2000r, Electric plugs and outlet (2/3). 2500r, Automobile (3/3).

2005, Aug. 17 ***Perf. 12½***

2076-2078 A626 Set of 3 2.25 1.25

Indonesian Leaders A627

Designs: Nos. 2079a, 2080a, Pres. Susilo Banbang Yudhoyono. Nos. 2079b, 2080b, Vice-president Muhammad Jusuf Kalla.

2005, Aug. 17 **Litho.**

2079 Horiz. pair with central label 1.00 .75
a.-b. A627 1500r Either single .50 .25

Litho. With Foil Application

2080 Horiz. pair with central label 1.50 1.50
a.-b. A627 2500r Either single .75 .75
c. Souvenir sheet, #2080a, 2080b 3.00 1.50

Borobudur Ship Expedition — A628

No. 2081: a, Ship, head of Buddha (2/2). b, Carving of ship (1/2).

2005, Sept. 17

2081 A628 1500r Pair, #a-b 1.50 1.25
c. As "a," with "2/2" removed 2.00 1.00
d. As "b," with "1/2" removed 2.00 1.00
e. Souvenir sheet, #2081c, 2081d + central label 1.50 1.25

Souvenir Sheet

National Philatelic Exhibition, Cilegon — A629

No. 2082 — Paintings by Sudjana Kerton: a, Nyawer. b, Makan Siang. c, Wayang Golek. d, Tanah Air Indonesia.

2005, Sept. 23 ***Perf. 12½***

2082 A629 Sheet of 4 7.00 6.00
a.-c. 5000r Any single 1.50 1.00
d. 8000r multi 2.50 1.50
e. Souvenir sheet, #2082a, imperf. 1.60 .85
f. Souvenir sheet, #2082b, imperf. 1.60 .85
g. Souvenir sheet, #2082c, imperf. 1.60 .85
h. Souvenir sheet, #2082d, imperf. 2.75 1.75

Sea Mammals and Plants — A630

No. 2083: a, Neophocaena phocaenoides (1/4). b, Dugong dugon (2/4). c, Gelidium latifolium (3/4). d, Halimeda opuntia (4/4).

2005, Nov. 5 ***Perf. 12½***

2083 A630 1500r Block of 4, #a-d 2.00 1.50
e. As "a," with "1/4" removed 2.00 1.00
f. As "b," with "3/4" removed 2.00 1.00
g. Souvenir sheet, #2083e, 2083f + central label 1.50 1.00

Folktales — A631

No. 2084: a, Bawang Merah & Bawang Putih (1/4). b, Keong Emas (2/4). c, Si Kancil (3/4). d, Timun Emas (4/4).

2006, Feb. 6 Litho. ***Perf. 12¾x13½***

2084 Block or strip of 4 2.50 1.60
a.-d. A631 1500r Any single .60 .30
e. Souvenir sheet, #2084a-2084d, imperf. 3.00 2.50

Miniature Sheets

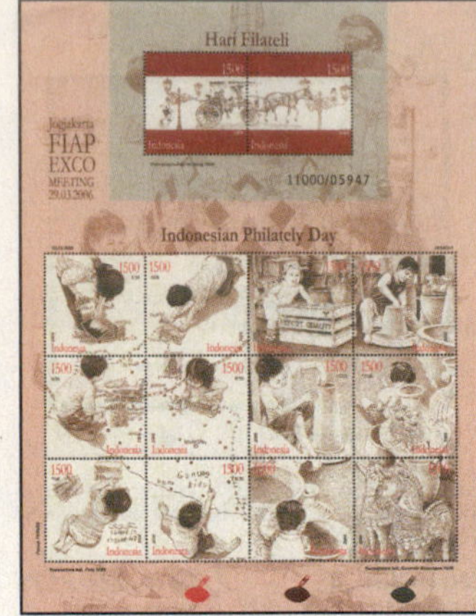

Philately Day — A632

No. 2085, 1500r — Illustrations in brown: a, Family in coach (1/28). b, Horse pulling coach (2/28). c, Girl, standing, with three photographs (3/28). d, Boy with one photograph (4/28). e, Boy with three photographs (5/28). f, Girl, wearing sandals, holding photograph (6/28). g, Barefoot girl touching photograph (7/28). h, Boy drawing map (8/28). i, Boy and crate (9/28). j, Boy at potter's wheel, finished pottery (10/28). k, Boy at potter's wheel (11/28). l, Girl pointing (12/28). m, Boy touching pottery (13/28). n, Caparisoned pottery horses (14/28).

No. 2086, 1500r — Illustrations in color: a, Like #2085a (15/28). b, Like #2085b (16/28). c, Like #2085c (17/28). d, Like #2085d (18/28). e, Like #2085e (19/28). f, Like #2085f (20/28). g, Like #2085g (21/28). h, Like #2085h (22/28). i, Like #2085i (23/28). j, Like #2085j (24/28). k, Like #2085k (25/28). l, Like #2085l (26/28). m, Like #2085m (27/28). n, Like #2085n (28/28).

2006, Mar. 29 Litho. ***Perf. 14***
Sheets of 14, #a-n

2085-2086 A632 Set of 2 16.00 12.00

2006 World Cup Soccer Championships, Germany — A633

No. 2087: a, World Cup emblem, goal, soccer ball (1/4). b, World Cup emblem, soccer ball (2/4). c, World Cup trophy at right, soccer ball at bottom (3/4). d, World Cup trophy at left, soccer ball at right (4/4).

Die Cut, With Perf. 14 Selvage Between Stamps

2006, May 6 Self-Adhesive

2087 A633 2500r Block of 4, #a-d 4.00 2.75
e. Booklet pane, #2087a-2087d, die cut, imperf. selvage between stamps 4.00 —
Complete booklet, #2087e 4.50

Individual stamps have various die cut soccer players in center. Values are for unused stamps with surrounding selvage. Used stamps may or may not have the die cut soccer players.

Environmental Care — A634

No. 2088: a, Village, flowers, butterfly (1/2). b, Girl (2/2).

2006, June 5 Litho. ***Perf. 13¼x12¾***

2088 A634 1500r Pair, #a-b 1.25 .90
c. Souvenir sheet, #2088a-2088b 1.50 .90

Local Foods A635

No. 2089: a, Pempek (South Sumatra, 1/4). b, Gudeg (Yogyakarta, 2/4). c, Ayam Betutu (Bali, 3/4). d, Aunu Senebre (Papua, 4/4).

2006, July 6

2089 Block or strip of 4 2.50 1.25
a.-d. A635 1500r Any single .60 .30

National Scout Jamboree — A636

No. 2090: a, Kak Mashudi and scouts around campfire (1/2). b, Jigsaw puzzle of scouts (2/2).

Litho. & Photo.

2006, July 16 ***Perf. 12½***

2090 A636 1500r Pair, #a-b 1.25 1.00

Sultans A637

No. 2091d Overprinted in Red Foil

No. 2091: a, Sultan Ma'moen Al Rasyid Perkasa Alamsyah Sultan Deli IX (1873-1924) (1/4). b, Sultan Agung Sultan Mataram III (1613-45) (2/4). c, Sultan Adji Mohamad Parikesit Sultan Kutai Kertanegara XX (1920-60) (3/4). d, Sultan Hasanuddin Sultan Gowa XVI (1653-69) (4/4).

Litho., Litho. with Foil Application (#2091e)

Perf. 13½ Syncopated

2006, Aug. 17

2091 Block or strip of 4 2.25 1.50
a.-d. A637 1500r Any single .50 .35
e. As "d," overprinted in red foil 3.00 1.50
f. Block or strip of 4, #2091a-2091c, 2091e 8.00 4.00

Puppets — A638

No. 2092: a, Indonesian puppet (1/2). b, Slovakian marionette (2/2).

Litho. & Photo.

2006, Sept. 27 ***Perf. 13x13¼***

2092 A638 2500r Horiz. pair, #a-b 1.75 1.00
c. Souvenir sheet, #2092 2.00 1.00

See Slovakia Nos. 506-507.

Miniature Sheet

Eid ul-Fitr — A639

No. 2093: a, Man sitting with crossed legs in prayer (1/8). b, Drummer (5/8). c, Older woman hugging young woman (2/8). d, Woman and man with hands in prayer (6/8). e, Mosque (3/8). f, People getting on bus (7/8). g, Geometric design (4/8). h, People and horse cart (8/8).

Nos. 2093lj-2093lq: As Nos. 2039a-2093h, but with Prisma emblem in lower corner of stamp and persoanlized photo above arc.

2006, Oct. 3 Litho. ***Perf. 12½***

2093 A639 1500r Sheet of 8, #a-h 4.50 3.50
2093l A639 1500r Sheet of 8, #j-q 6.00 6.00

No. 2093l sold for 20,000r.

Flora and Fauna — A640

No. 2094: a, Licuala arbuscula (3/4). b, Livistona mamberamoensis (4/4). c, Melipotes carolae (1/4). d, Amblyornis flavifrons (2/4).

2006, Nov. 5 ***Perf. 12½***

2094 A640 1500r Block of 4, #a-d 2.50 1.75
e. As "a," with "3/4" removed 2.00 1.00
f. As "d," with "2/4" removed 2.00 1.00
g. Souvenir sheet, #2094e-2094f + label 3.00 2.00

Souvenir Sheet

Bandung '06 Natl. Philatelic Exhibition — A641

No. 2095: a, Panthera pardus (1/2). b, Bouea macrophylla (2/2).

Perf. 13½x12¾

2006, Nov. 30 **Litho.**

2095 A641 2500r Sheet of 2, #a-b 1.75 1.50
c. Like #2095, with margin illustration in blue and black 1.75 1.50
d. Like #2095, with margin illustration in red and black 1.75 1.50
e. Like #2095, with margin illustration in yellow and black 1.75 1.50
f. Like #2095, with margin illustration in black 1.75 1.50

On No. 2095, the code number at lower left of sheet ends with "5," that of Nos. 2095c-2095f end in "1" to "4" respectively. Margin illustrations show progressive color printing.

Containers — A642

No. 2096: a, Container from Bali (2/2). b, Lidded basket from East Kalimantan (1/2).

2006, Dec. 23 ***Perf. 13½x12¾***

2096 A642 1500r Horiz. pair, #a-b 1.50 .75

New Year 2007 (Year of the Pig) A643

No. 2097: a, Chinese zodiac animals and lanterns (1/2). b, Chinese zodiac animals, people and temple (2/2).

No. 2098: a, Rat (1/13). b, Ox (2/13). c, Tiger (3/13). d, Rabbit (4/13). e, Dragon (5/13). f, Snake (6/13). g, Horse (7/13). h, Goat (8/13). i, Monkey (9/13). j, Rooster (10/13). k, Dog (11/13). l, Pig (12/13). m, Like #2097b (96x64mm, 13/13)

No. 2099, Like #2097b.

Litho., Litho. With Foil Application (#2098m, 2099)

2007, Feb. 1 ***Perf. 12½***

2097 Pair 1.25 .70
a.-b. A643 1500r Either single .60 .30
2098 Sheet of 13 10.00 10.00
a.-l. A643 2000r Any single .60 .30
m. A643 6000r multi 2.00 1.00

Souvenir Sheet

2099 A643 6000r multi 2.00 1.00

Dances — A644

No. 2100: a, Lion dance (1/2). b, Dragon dance (2/2).

Perf. 13¼x13½ Syncopated

2007, Apr. 13 **Litho.**

2100 A644 2500r Pair, #a-b 1.60 .80
c. Souvenir sheet, #2100a-2100b 2.50 1.25

See People's Republic of China Nos. 3581-3582.

Reading and Writing A645

No. 2101: a, Boy writing in book, mother reading (2/2). b, Boy looking at girl writing in book (1/2).

2007, May 2 **Litho.** ***Perf. 13½x12¾***

2101 A645 1500r Pair, #a-b 1.10 .55

A646

Environmental Care — A647

Nos. 2102, 2104: a, Iceberg, top of polar bear's head (1/4). b, Crying polar bear (2/4).

No. 2103: a, Forest fire (3/4). b, Burnt forest (4/4).

2007, June 5

2102 A646 1500r Vert. pair, #a-b 1.10 .55
2103 A647 1500r Vert. pair, #a-b 1.10 .55

Souvenir Sheet

2104 A646 2500r Sheet of 2, #a-b 2.00 1.50

Nos. 2102 and 2103 were each printed in sheets containing 10 pairs with the bottom stamp in the pair tete-beche with the same stamp.

Campaign Against Drug Abuse — A648

No. 2105: a, Guitarist, Indonesian inscription (1/2). b, Basketball player, English inscription (2/2).

2007, June 26 ***Perf. 12¾x13½***

2105 A648 1500r Pair, #a-b 1.75 .85

Traditional Foods A649

No. 2106: a, Roti Cane and Kari Kambing (Aceh, 1/4). b, Gecok (West Nusa Tenggara, 3/4). c, Soto Kudus (Central Java, 2/4). d, Ikan Air Garam (Maluku, 4/4).

2007, July 6 ***Perf. 13½x12¾***

2106 Strip of 4 2.00 1.50
a.-d. A649 1500r Any single .50 .30

A650

A651

A652

Greetings With Hands — A653

2007, June 3 **Litho.** ***Perf. 12½***

2107 A650 1500r multi + label .60 .40
2108 A651 1500r multi + label 1.00 .75
a. Pair, #2107-2108, + 2 labels 1.75 1.50
2109 A652 1500r multi + label 1.00 .75
2110 A653 1500r multi + label 1.00 .75
a. Pair, #2109-2110, + 2 labels 3.00 3.00
Nos. 2107-2110 (4) 3.60 2.65

Nos. 2107-2108 and 2109-2110 were each printed in sheets of 20 stamps + 20 labels, containing ten of each stamp. Sheets sold for 45,000r. Labels could be personalized. A sheet of 20 No. 2107 + 20 non-personalizable labels, issued in 2008, also sold for 45,000r.

Fireworks — A654

Guitar and G Clef A655

Paint Brushes — A656

Film and Reel A657

Perf. 12½x12½x12½x4

2007, July 21 **Litho.**

2111 A654 1500r multi + label .75 .30
2112 A655 1500r multi + label 1.25 1.00
2113 A656 1500r multi + label 1.25 1.00
2114 A657 1500r multi + label 1.25 1.00
Nos. 2111-2114 (4) 4.50 3.30

Nos. 2111-2114 were each printed in sheets of 8 stamps + 8 labels that sold for 15,000r face. No. 2111 also was printed in four different sheets of 12 stamps + 12 labels that each sold for 30,000r. Labels could not be personalized.

Scouting, Cent. — A658

No. 2115, 2500r: a, Centenary emblem, full color background (1/4). b, Scout, full color (2/4).

No. 2116, 1500r: a, Centenary emblem, blue background (3/4). b, Scout in blue (4/4).

2007, Aug. 1 ***Perf. 13½ Syncopated***

2115 A658 Horiz. pair, #a-b 2.25 1.10

Booklet Stamps

2116 A658 Horiz. pair, #a-b 1.10 .55
c. Booklet pane, 5 #2116 5.50 —
Complete booklet, #2116c 5.50

Nepenthes Mirabilis — A659

Nepenthes Ampuliaria — A660

2007, Aug. 3 ***Perf. 13½x12¾***

2117 A659 1500r multi .60 .30

Perf. 12¾x13½

2118 A660 1500r multi .60 .30

Souvenir Sheet

Perf. 13½x12¾

2119 Sheet of 2 2.50 1.25
a. A659 2500r multi 1.25 .60
b. A660 2500r multi 1.25 .60

Bangkok 2007 Intl. Stamp Exhibition.

Association of South East Asian Nations (ASEAN), 40th Anniv. A661

Designs: 1500r, Fatahillah Museum, Jakarta.

No. 2121: a, Secretariat Building, Bandar Seri Begawan, Brunei (1/10). b, National Museum of Cambodia (2/10). c, Fatahillah Museum, Jakarta (3/10). d, Typical house, Laos (4/10). e, Malayan Railway Headquarters Building, Kuala Lumpur, Malaysia (5/10). f, Yangon Post Office, Myanmar (6/10). g, Malacañang Palace, Philippines (7/10). h, National Museum of Singapore (8/10). i, Vimanmek Mansion, Bangkok, Thailand (9/10). j, Presidential Palace, Hanoi, Viet Nam (10/10).

2007, Aug. 8 ***Perf. 13½ Syncopated***

2120	A661 1500r multi	.85	.30
2121	Sheet of 10	9.00	4.50
a.-j.	A661 2500r Any single	.90	.45

See Brunei No. 607, Burma No. 370, Cambodia No. 2339, Laos Nos. 1717-1718, Malaysia No. 1170, Philippines Nos. 3103-3105, Singapore No. 1265, Thailand No. 2315, and Viet Nam Nos. 3302-3311.

Lighthouses — A662

No. 2122: a, Semarang Lighthouse (1/2). b, Cikoneng Lighthouse (2/2).

2007, Aug. 17 ***Perf. 12¾x13½***

2122	A662 1500r Horiz. pair, #a-b	1.25	.60

Padjadjaran University, 50th Anniv. — A663

No. 2123: a, Tiger and ram (1/4). b, Men and dancers (2/4). c, Building (3/4). d, Symbols and globe (4/4).

2007, Sept. 5 ***Perf. 13½x12¾***

2123	Horiz. strip of 4 + central label	2.25	2.00
a.-d.	A663 1500r Any single	.50	.30

Butterflies — A664

No. 2124: a, Delias kristianiae (1/4). b, Ornithoptera aesacus (2/4). c, Ornithoptera croesus (3/4). d, Troides hypolitus (4/4).
No. 2125: a, Like #2124a. b, Like #2124c.

2007, Nov. 5 ***Perf. 12½***

2124	Block of 4	2.25	1.10
a.-d.	A664 1500r Any single	.35	.30

Souvenir Sheet

2125	Sheet of 2 + central label	2.00	1.00
a.-b.	A664 2500r Either single	1.00	.50

No. 2125 Surcharged in Gold

2007, Nov. 21 **Litho.** ***Perf. 12½***

2126	Sheet of 2 + central label	4.00	3.00
a.-b.	A664 5000r on 2500r Either single	1.75	1.50

No. 2126 also is overprinted in gold in margin and label with emblem and text for Bandungfilex 2007 and Jakarta 2008 Intl. Stamp Exhibition.

24th South East Asian Games, Nakhon Ratchasima, Thailand — A665

No. 2127: a, Bowling (1/4). b, Indoor soccer (2/4). c, Kempo (3/4). d, Hammer throw (4/4).

2007, Dec. 6 ***Perf. 14***

2127	Horiz. strip of 4	4.00	2.00
a.-d.	A665 2500r Any single	1.00	.50

Djuanda Declaration, 50th Anniv. — A666

No. 2128: a, Map of Indonesia, children (1/3). b, Prime Minister Djuanda Kartawidjaja, eagle, and procession (2/3). c, Djuanda Kartawidjaja and map of Indonesia (3/3).

2007, Dec. 13 ***Perf. 13½x12¾***

2128	Vert. strip of 3	1.50	1.25
a.-c.	A666 1500r Any single	.80	.40

Miniature Sheet

Jakarta 2008 Intl. Stamp Exhibition — A667

No. 2129: a, Prasasti Tugu (2/7). b, Arca Dewa Visnu (statue of Vishnu) (3/7). c, Prasasti Padrao (4/7). d, Peta Nusantara Zaman Portugis (5/7). e, Naskah Perjanjian Sunda Kelapa (6/7). f, Kapal Bangsa Portugis (7/7). g, Bendera Singa Ali and Fatahillah (1/7). Nos. 2129a-2129f are 41x25mm; No. 2129g, 83x25mm.

2008, Jan. 20 **Litho.** ***Perf. 13½x12¾***

2129	A667 Sheet of 7	7.00	7.00
a.-f.	2500r Any single	.55	.35
g.	10,000r multi	2.75	2.25

A668

New Year 2008 (Year of the Rat) — A669

No. 2130: a, Rat facing right (1/3). b, Rat facing left (2/3). c, Rat on hind legs (3/3).

2008, Jan. 26 ***Perf. 13½x12¾***

2130	Vert. strip of 3 + label	1.60	.80
a.-c.	A668 2000r Any single	.50	.25

Souvenir Sheet

Perf. 12½

2131	A669 5000r black & gray	2.25	1.10

Souvenir Sheet

Flora and Fauna — A670

No. 2132: a, Casuarius casuarius (1/2). b, Crinum asiaticum (2/2).

2008, Mar. 7 ***Perf. 12¾x13½***

2132	A670 5000r Sheet of 2, #a-b	3.00	2.00

Jakarta 2008 Intl. Stamp Exhibition, Taipei 2008 Intl. Stamp Exhibition, Stamp Passion '08 Stamp Exhibition, Netherlands.

2008 Summer Olympics, Beijing — A671

No. 2133: a, Sailboarding (1/4). b, Soccer (2/4). c, Badminton (3/4). d, Weight lifting (4/4).

2008, Mar. 18 ***Perf. 14***

2133	A671 2500r Block of 4, #a-d	3.00	2.00

Miniature Sheet

Jakarta 2008 Intl. Stamp Exhibition — A672

No. 2134: a, Istana Pemerintahan Batavia (2/7). b, Gedung Keuangan (3/7). c, Penyerangan Batavia oleh Sultan Agung, denomination at LR (4/7). d, Penyerangan Batavia oleh Sultan Agung, denomination at LL (5/7). e, Perubahan Batavia Menjadi Jakarta (6/7). f, Penyerahan Kekuasaan Indonesia (7/7). g, Penangkapan Pangeran Jayawikarta oleh Pasukan Banten (1/7). Nos. 2134a-2134f are 41x25mm; No. 2134g, 83x25mm.

Perf. 13½x12¾

2008, Mar. 29 **Litho.**

2134	A672 Sheet of 7	6.50	6.50
a.-f.	2500r Any single	.65	.40
g.	10,000r multi	2.75	2.25

Diplomatic Relations Between Indonesia and Japan, 50th Anniv. — A673

No. 2135, 2500r: a, Kelimutu Volcano, Indonesia (1/10). b, Mt. Fuji, Japan (2/10).
No. 2136, 2500r: a, Borobudur, Indonesia (3/10). b, Toji Temple, Japan (4/10).
No. 2137, 2500r: a, Rafflesia arnoldi (5/10). b, Cherry blossoms (6/10).
No. 2138, 2500r: a, Angklung (7/10). b, Gaku biwa (8/10).
No. 2139, 2500r, horiz: a, Scleropages formosus (9/10). b, Nishiki-goi (10/10).

2008, Apr. 15 ***Perf. 12½***

Horiz. Pairs, #a-b

2135-2139	A673 Set of 5	7.00	7.00
2139c	Miniature sheet, #2135-2139	7.00	7.00

Nos. 2135-2139 were each printed in sheets of 4 pairs. See Japan No. 3018.

indonesia 1500

Special Needs Education A674

No. 2140: a, Boy in wheelchair waving flags (1/3). b, Man in racing wheelchair (2/3). c, Handicapped children playing anklungs (3/3).

Litho. & Embossed

2008, May 2 ***Perf. 13½x12¾***

2140	Strip of 3	1.60	1.00
a.-c.	A674 1500r Any single	.50	.25

National Awakening, Cent. — A675

No. 2141: a, People with fists raised, flag. b, Flag, people, satellite.

2008, May 20 Litho. ***Perf. 12¾x13½***
2141 A675 1500r Horiz. pair, #a-b .80 .40

Environmental Care — A676

Nos. 2142 and 2143: a, Cyclists, motor vehicles (1/2). b, Seedling, forest (2/2). Stamps from No. 2143 lack stamp numbers.

2008, June 5 ***Perf. 13½x12¾***
2142 A676 1500r Pair, #a-b 1.00 .75

Souvenir Sheet

2143 A676 2500r Sheet of 2, #a-b 1.40 1.40

Miniature Sheet

Jakarta 2008 Intl. Stamp Exhibition — A677

No. 2144: a, Jakarta Philatelic Center (Kantor Filateli Jakarta) (2/7). b, National Museum (3/7). c, Dunia Fantasi (4/7). d, Taman Mini Indonesia (5/7). e, Wisana Seni and Budaya (6/7). f, Wisata Bihari (7/7). g, Warna Warni Jakarta (1/7). Nos. 2144a-2144f are 41x25mm; No. 2144g, 83x25mm.

2008, June 22 ***Perf. 13½x12¾***
2144 A677 Sheet of 7 7.00 7.00
a.-f. 2500r Any single .55 .35
g. 10,000r multi 2.75 2.50

17th National Games — A678

No. 2145: a, Mountain biking (1/4). b, Bodybuilding (2/4). c, Steeplechase (3/4). d, Palaran Main Stadium, Samarinda (4/4).

2008, July 5 ***Perf. 14***
2145 A678 1500r Block of 4, #a-d 2.00 1.00

Traditional Foods Type of 2007

No. 2146: a, Nasi Lemak (Riau, 1/4). b, Sate Bandeng (Banten, 2/4). c, Ayem Cincane (East Kalimantan, 3/4). d, Kaledo (Central Sulawesi, 4/4).

2008, July 6 ***Perf. 13½x12¾***
2146 Block of 4 1.60 .80
a.-d. A649 1500r Any single .40 .25

Printed in sheets containing four of each stamp + four labels.

Provincial Arms and Architecture — A679

Arms of: Nos. 2147, 1500r, 2158a, 2500r, Bali (1/33). Nos. 2148, 1500r, 2158b, 2500r, Gorontalo (2/33). Nos. 2149, 1500r, 2158c, 2500r, Jawa Barat (West Java) (3/33). Nos. 2150, 1500r, 2158d, 2500r, Jawa Tengah (Central Java) (4/33). Nos. 2151, 1500r, 2158e, 2500r, Kalimantan Barat (West Kalimantan) (5/33). Nos. 2152, 1500r, 2158f, 2500r, Maluku (Moluccas) (6/33). Nos. 2153, 1500r, 2158g, 2500r, Aceh (7/33). Nos. 2154, 1500r, 2158h, 2500r, Papua (8/33). Nos. 2155, 1500r, 2158i, 2500r, Riau (9/33). Nos. 2156, 1500r, 2158j, 2500r, Sulawesi Barat (West Sulawesi) (10/33). Nos. 2157, 1500r, 2158k, 2500r, Sumatera Barat (West Sumatra) (11/33).

2008, Aug. 17 ***Perf. 12½***
2147-2157 A679 Set of 11 5.50 2.75
2158 Sheet of 11 + label 7.50 4.00
a.-k. A679 2500r Any single .65 .30

Nos. 2147-2157 each were printed in sheets of 10.

See Nos. 2200-2211, 2253-2264.

Great Post Road of Java — A680

No. 2159: a, Lighthouse, map of western part of road (1/4). b, Building, map of central part of road (2/4). c, Lighthouse, map of eastern part of road (3/4). d, Letter from Governor General Herman Daendels (4/4).

10,000r, Map of entire road.

2008, Sept. 27 ***Perf. 13½x12¾***
2159 Horiz. strip of 4 2.75 2.50
a.-d. A680 2500r Any single .65 .35

Souvenir Sheet

2160 A680 10,000r multi 3.00 2.50

No. 2160 contains one 125x25mm stamp.

Souvenir Sheets

A681

A682

A683

A684

A685

Jakarta 2008 Intl. Stamp Exhibition — A686

2008 ***Perf. 13½x12¾***
2161 A681 5000r multi 1.40 1.10
2162 A682 5000r multi 1.40 1.10
2163 A683 5000r multi 1.40 1.10
2164 A684 5000r multi 1.40 1.10
2165 A685 5000r multi 1.40 1.10
2166 A686 5000r multi 1.40 1.10
Nos. 2161-2166 (6) 8.40 6.60

Issued: No. 2161, 10/23; No. 2162, 10/24; No. 2163, 10/25; No. 2164, 10/26; No. 2165, 10/27; No. 2166, 10/28.

Miniature Sheet

Friendship Between Indonesia and Turkey — A687

No. 2167: a, Blue Mosque, Turkey (1/10). b, Istiqlal Mosque, Indonesia (2/10). c, Bosporus Bridge, Turkey (3/10). d, Barelang Bridge, Indonesia (4/10). e, Whirling dervishes (5/10). f, Saman dance (6/10). g, Turkish tulip (7/10). h, Flame of Irian (8/10). i, Turkish Van cat (9/10). j, Flat-headed cat (10/10).

2008, Oct. 24 ***Perf. 13½ Syncopated***
2167 A687 2500r Sheet of 10, #a-j 7.50 7.50

See Turkey No. 3142.

Miniature Sheet

Flora and Fauna of the Provinces — A688

No. 2168: a, Leucopsar rothschildi, Dysoxylum densiflorum, Bali (1/11). b, Liza dussumieri, Vitex cofassus, Gorontalo (2/11). c, Panthera pardus, Bouea macrophylla, Jawa Barat (West Java) (3/11). d, Oriolus chinensis, Michelia alba, Jawa Tengah (Central Java) (4/11). e, Rhinoplax vigil, Shorea stenoptera, Kalimantan Barat (West Kalimantan) (5/11). f, Alisterus amboinensis, Dendrobium phalaenopsis, Maluku (Moluccas) (6/11). g, Copsychus pyrropygus, Michelia champaca, Aceh (7/11). h, Seleucidis melanoleuca, Pometia pinnata, Papua (8/11). i, Loriculus galgulus, Oncosperma tigillarium, Riau (9/11). j, Aramidopsis plateni, Elmerrillia ovalis, Sulawesi Barat (West Sulawesi) (10/11). k, Argusianus argus, Morus macroura, Sumatera Barat (West Sumatra) (11/11).

2008, Nov. 5 ***Perf. 13½x12¾***
2168 A688 2500r Sheet of 11, #a-k, + label 8.00 7.00

See Nos. 2217, 2249-2252.

Cut Nyak Dhien (1848-1908), Leader of Aceh Resistance to Dutch Rule — A689

No. 2169: a, House (1/2). b, Cut Nyak Dhien (2/2).

2008, Nov. 5

2169 A689 1500r Horiz. pair, #a-b 1.00 .75

Islands A690

No. 2170: a, Damar Island (1/4). b, Sebatik Island (2/4). c, Batubawaikang Island (3/4). d, Bras Island (4/4).

2008, Dec. 3

2170 Block or strip of 4 2.00 1.00
a.-d. A690 1500r multi .50 .25
e. Miniature sheet, 4 each #2170a-2170d 8.00 4.00

New Year 2009 (Year of the Ox) A691

Designs: Nos. 2171, 2174a, 2000r, Head of ox (1/3). Nos. 2172, 2174b, 2000r, Ox looking left (2/3). Nos. 2173, 2174c, 2000r, Ox in water (3/3).
10,000r, Ox, diff.

2009, Jan. 10 **Litho.**

2171-2173 A691 Set of 3 1.75 .85

Litho. & Embossed With Foil Application (Chinese Character in Gold)

2174 A691 2000r Vert. strip of 3, #a-c 2.00 1.00

Souvenir Sheet

2175 A691 10,000r multi 3.00 2.50

Nos. 2171-2173 were printed in a sheet of 24 stamps containing 8 of each stamp. No. 2174 was printed in a sheet containing 2 strips.

Bandung Institute of Technology, 50th Anniv. — A692

No. 2176: a, Building, colored triangles (1/4). b, Emblems, crowd of dignitaries (2/4). c, "89 Tahun," text (3/4). d, Emblem dated "1920" (4/4).

2009, Mar. 2 **Litho.**

2176 Horiz. strip of 4 + central label 2.00 2.00
a.-d. A692 1500r Any single .45 .30

A693

A694

A695

General Elections — A696

2009, Mar. 5 ***Perf. 13x13¼***

2177 Strip of 4 1.60 .80
a. A693 1500r multi .40 .25
b. A694 1500r multi .40 .25
c. A695 1500r multi .40 .25
d. A696 1500r multi .40 .25

Souvenir Sheet

Preservation of Polar Regions and Glaciers — A697

No. 2178 — Snowflake emblem and: a, Iceberg, top of polar bear's head. b, Crying polar bear.

2009, Mar. 18 ***Perf. 13½x12¾***

2178 A697 2500r Sheet of 2, #a-b 2.00 1.00

Compare with No. 2104.

Souvenir Sheet

China 2009 World Stamp Exhibition, Luoyang — A698

2009, Apr. 10

2179 A698 10,000r multi 2.75 1.40

Intl. Year of Astronomy A699

Nos. 2180 and 2181: a, Galileo's telescope (1/3). b, Intl. Year of Astronomy emblem (2/3). c, Galileo Galilei (1564-1642) (3/3).

2009, May 2 **Litho.** ***Perf. 13x13¼***

2180 Horiz. strip of 3 2.50 1.25
a.-c. A699 2500r Any single .80 .25

Souvenir Sheet

Litho. With Hologram

2181 Sheet of 3 5.00 2.50
a.-c. A699 5000r Any single 1.60 .80

World Ocean Conference, Manado — A700

No. 2182: a, Blue-ringed angelfish (1/4). b, Anemone shrimp and sea anemone (2/4). c, Goldback anthias (3/4). d, Coral reef (4/4).
5000r, Sea turtle.

2009, May 11 ***Perf. 13½x12¾***

2182 A700 2500r Block or strip of 4, #a-d 3.00 1.50

Souvenir Sheet

2183 A700 5000r multi 1.75 .85

World Environment Day — A701

No. 2184: a, Boy holding plant, parched earth (3/3). b, Factories, people in bubble (2/3). c, Smokestacks, tree, boy near forest (1/3).
5000r, Like 2184c.

2009, June 5

2184 Strip of 3 1.50 1.00
a.-c. A701 1500r Any single .50 .30

Souvenir Sheet

2185 A701 5000r multi 1.50 1.00

Opening of Suramadu Bridge — A702

No. 2186: a, City, statue, end of bridge (1/3). b, Bridge towers (2/3). c, End of bridge, boat, farmer with oxen (3/3).
10,000r, Entire bridge, city, sculpture, boat, farmer with oxen.

2009, June 10

2186 Horiz. strip of 3 1.50 1.00
a.-c. A702 1500r Any single .50 .30

Souvenir Sheet

2187 A702 10,000r multi 3.00 2.50

No. 2187 contains one 126x25mm stamp.

Traditional Foods A703

No. 2188: a, Ihutilinanga (Gorontalo, 1/6). b, Gulai Balak (Lampung, 2/6). c, Sate Tambulinas (Southeast Sulawesi, 3/6). d, Sambal Goreng Papai (Central Kalimantan, 4/6). e, Nasi Uduk (Jakarta, 5/6). f, Ikan Bobara Kuah Asam (West Papua, 6/6).

2009, July 6

2188 Block of 6 3.00 1.50
a.-f. A703 1500r Any single .50 .25

BirdLife International — A704

No. 2189, 2500r: a, Ciconia stormi, with first "0" in denomination below bird (6/6). b, Aceros corrugatus, with first "0" in denomination touching central line of leaf (1/6).
No. 2190, 2500r, horiz.: a, Harpactes kasumba, with "A" of "Indonesia" barely touching bird's tail (41x25mm, 2/6). b, Actenoides concretus, with entire center of "D" in "Indonesia" over tree branch (41x25mm, 3/6).
No. 2191, 2500r, horiz.: a, Cairina scutulata, with farthest extent of white water ripple line running through "5" in denomination (41x25mm, 4/6). b, Argusianus argus, with white water ripple line touching "2" and "5" in denomination (41x25mm, 5/6).
No. 2192, 2500r: a, Like #2189a, with first "0" in denomination touching bird. b, Like #2189b, with first "0" in denomination above central line of leaf. c, Like #2190a, with "A" of "Indonesia" half on bird's tail, and without "2/6." d, Like #2190b, with center of "D" of "Indonesia" partly on tree branch. e, Like #2191a, with farthest extent of white water ripple line to left of "5" in denomination. f, Like #2191b, with white water ripple line below "2" and "5" in denomination.

2009, July 15 ***Perf. 13½x12¾***

Horiz. Pairs, #a-b

"Burung" in Blue

2189-2191 A704 Set of 3 5.00 2.50

Souvenir Sheet

"Burung" in Black

2192 A704 2500r Sheet of 6, #a-f 5.00 2.50

For overprint see No. 2212.

Children's Day — A705

No. 2193 — Children: a, Jumping rope (1/4). b, Flying kites (2/4). c, Playing hide-and-seek (3/4). d, Riding bicycles (4/4).

2009, July 23

2193 A705 1500r Block of 4, #a-d 2.00 1.50

Souvenir Sheet

Philakorea 2009 Intl. Philatelic Exhibition, Seoul — A706

2009, July 30 ***Perf. 14***

2194 A706 10,000r multi 3.00 2.50

A707

A708

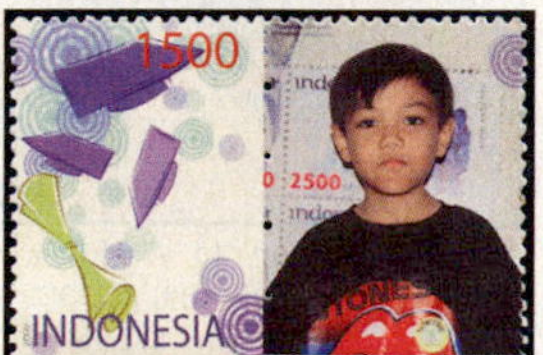

A709

A710

Personalizable Stamps — A711

2009 Litho. *Perf. 12½x4x12½x12½*

2195 A707 1500r multi + label	2.00	2.00
2196 A708 1500r multi + label	2.00	2.00
2197 A709 1500r multi + label	2.00	2.00
2198 A710 1500r multi + label	2.00	2.00
2199 A711 1500r multi + label	2.00	2.00
Nos. 2195-2199 (5)	10.00	10.00

Nos. 2195-2199 each were printed in sheets of 8 stamps + 8 labels that could be personalized. Each sheet sold for 20,000r.

Provincial Arms Type of 2008

Arms of: Nos. 2200, 1500r, 2211a, 2500r, Banten (12/33). Nos. 2201, 1500r, 2211b, 2500r, Jawa Timur (East Java) (13/33). Nos. 2202, 1500r, 2211c, 2500r, Kalimantan Tengah (Central Kalimantan) (14/33). Nos. 2203, 1500r, 2211d, 2500r, Kalimantan Timur (East Kalimantan) (15/33). Nos. 2204, 1500r, 2211e, 2500r, Kepulauan Riau (Riau Archipelago) (16/33). Nos. 2205, 1500r, 2211f, 2500r, Lampung (17/33). Nos. 2206, 1500r, 2211g, 2500r, Nusa Tenggara Timur (East Nusa Tenggara) (18/33). Nos. 2207, 1500r, 2211h, 2500r, Papua Barat (West Papua) (19/33). Nos. 2208, 1500r, 2211i, 2500r, Sulawesi Tengah (Central Sulawesi) (20/33). Nos. 2209, 1500r, 2211j, 2500r, Sulawesi Tenggara (Southeast Sulawesi) (21/33). Nos. 2210, 1500r, 2211k, 2500r, Sumatera Selatan (South Sumatra) (22/33).

2009, Aug. 17 Litho. *Perf. 12½*

2200-2210 A679 Set of 11	5.50	2.75
2211 Sheet of 11 + label	8.00	8.00
a.-k. A679 2500r Any single	.75	.35

No. 2192 Overprinted in Gold With JIPEX 2009 Emblem

Methods and Perfs As Before

2009, Oct. 28

2212 A704 2500r Sheet of 6, #a-f 5.50 4.00

Tourist Sites in Indonesia and Singapore — A712

Designs: 1500r, Sentosa, Singapore (4/4). 2500r, Taman Mini Indonesia Indah (Beautiful Indonesia Miniature Park), Indonesia (3/4). 4000r, Merlion, Singapore (2/4). 7500r, Singaraja Statue, Indonesia (1/4).

2009, Oct. 28 Litho. *Perf. 13½x12¾*

2213-2216 A712 Set of 4	4.50	2.75
2216a Miniature sheet, 2 each #2213-2216	9.00	9.00

See Singapore Nos. 1402-1405.

Flora and Fauna of the Provinces Type of 2008

Miniature Sheet

No. 2217: a, Rhinoceros sondaicus, Vatica bantenensis, Banten (1/11). b, Gallus varius x Gallus gallus, Polyanthes tuberosa, Jawa Timur (East Java) (2/11). c, Polyplectron schleirmacheri, Nephelium ramboutan-ake, Kalimantan Tengah (Central Kalimantan) (3/11). d, Orcaella brevirostris, Coelogyne pandurata, Kalimantan Timur (East Kalimantan) (4/11). e, Lutjanus sanguineus, Piper betle, Kepulauan Riau (Riau Archipelago) (5/11). f, Elephas maximus sumatranus, Magnolia candolili, Lampung (6/11). g, Varanus komodoensis, Santalum album, Nusa Tenggara Timur (East Nusa Tenggara) (7/11). h, Paradisaea rubra, Dendrobium conoideus, Papua Barat (West Papua) (8/11). i, Macrocephalon maleo, Diospyros celebica, Sulawesi Tengah (Central Sulawesi) (9/11). j, Bubalus depressicornis, Diplocaulobium utile, Sulawesi Tenggara (Southeast Sulawesi) (10/11). k, Notopterus chitala, Lansium domesticum, Sumatera Selatan (South Sumatra) (11/11).

2009, Nov. 5

2217 A688 2500r Sheet of 11, #a-k, + label 9.00 9.00

Buildings in Indonesia and Iran — A713

Designs: 1500r, Soltanieh Dome, Iran (2/2). 3000r, Al-Markaz Mosque, Indonesia (1/2).

2009, Dec. 18 *Perf. 13x13¼*

2218 A713 1500r multi	.50	.35
2219 A713 3000r multi	1.00	.70
a. Miniature sheet of 12, 6 each #2218-2219	9.00	9.00

See Iran No. 3013.

New Year 2010 (Year of the Tiger) A714

Tiger: No. 2220, 1500r, Head (1/3). No. 2221, 1500r, Walking (2/3). No. 2222, 1500r, Running (3/3).
5000r, Tiger, sky.

2010, Feb. 6 Litho. *Perf. 13½x12¾*

2220-2222 A714 Set of 3	1.40	.75
2222a Souvenir sheet of 6, 2 each #2220-2222	2.25	2.00

Souvenir Sheet

2223 A714 5000r multi 2.25 2.25

UNESCO Intangible Cultural Heritage A720

Designs: 1000r, Batik in Campuran design (4/6). 1500r, Hanoman puppet, vert. (3/6). 2000r, Arjuna puppet, vert. (1/6). 2500r, Kresna puppet, vert. (2/6). 3000r, Kris, vert. (6/6). No. 2234, 5000r, Batik in Kembangan design (5/6).
No. 2235, 5000r, Hanoman puppet, diff., vert. No. 2236, 5000r, Kris, diff., vert.

Perf. 13½x12¾, 12¾x13½

2010, Mar. 29 Litho.

2229-2234 A720 Set of 6 5.00 3.50

Souvenir Sheets

2235-2236 A720 Set of 2 4.50 4.00

Nos. 2235-2236 exist imperforate.

2010 World Cup Soccer Championships, South Africa — A721

No. 2237: a, Soccer player (1/4). b, Mascot (2/4). c, Emblem (3/4). d, Goalie making save (4/4).

2010, May 1 *Perf. 12¾x13½*

2237 A721 1500r Block or horiz. strip of 4, #a-d	2.00	2.00
e. Booklet pane of 4, #2237a-2237d	2.00	—
Complete booklet, #2237e	2.00	

A722

Environmental Care — A723

Designs: No. 2238, Hands holding seedling (3/3).
No. 2239: a, Bird, sheep, palm tree, child (1/3). b, Earth and hands (2/3).
5000r, Like #2238.

Perf. 12¾x13½, 13½x12¾

2010, June 5

2238 A722 1500r multi	.70	.30
2239 A723 1500r Vert. pair, #a-b	.70	.30

Souvenir Sheet

2240 A722 5000r multi 1.40 1.40

Muhammadiyah Islamic Organization, Cent. — A724

No. 2241: a, Building (1/3). b, Kyai Haji Ahmad Dahlan (1868-1923), founder (2/3). c, Student, graduate, building (3/3).

2010, July 3 *Perf. 12½*

2241 Strip of 3	1.25	1.25
a.-c. A724 1500r Any single	.35	.25
d. Souvenir sheet of 6, 2 each #2241a-2241c	2.50	2.50

Traditional Foods A725

No. 2242: a, Sup Lobster Kelapa Muda, West Sulawesi (1/7). b, Gulai Iga Kemba'ang, Bengkulu (2/7). c, Ayam Cincane, East Kalimantan (3/7). d, Sate Udang Pentuk Asam Manis, Jambi (4/7). e, Lempah Kuning, Bangka Belitung (5/7). f, Asam Padeh Baung, Riau (6/7). g, Lapis Palaro, North Moluccas (7/7).

2010, July 6 *Perf. 13½x12¾*

2242 Block of 7 + label	4.00	4.00
a.-g. A725 1500r Any single	.50	.35

Elected Leaders A726

No. 2243 — Flag and: a, Pres. Susilo Bambang Yudhoyono (1/2). b, Vice-president Boediono (2/2).

2010, Aug. 17 *Perf. 14*

2243 Pair	1.50	1.00
a.-b. A726 2500r Either single	.75	.35
c. Souvenir sheet of 2, #2243a-2243b	1.50	1.50

2010 Youth Olympic Games, Singapore — A727

No. 2244 — Badminton player with denomination at: a, LR. b, LL.

2010, July 15 Litho. *Perf. 13½x12¾*

2244 A727 1500r Pair, #a-b 1.10 1.10

Bandung, 200th Anniv. — A728

No. 2245: a, Soccer player. b, R. Dewi Sartika (1884-1947), advocate for women's education.

No. 2246: a, Pasupati Bridge. b, City street. 5000r, Pasupati Bridge.

2010, Sept. 25 *Perf. 12¾x13½*

2245 A728 1000r Pair, #a-b .75 .75
2246 A728 1500r Pair, #a-b 1.25 1.25

Souvenir Sheet

2247 A728 5000r multi 1.50 1.50

Worldwide Fund for Nature (WWF) — A729

No. 2248 — Sea turtles: a, Lepidochelys olivacea (1/4). b, Chelonia mydas (2/4). c, Dermochelys coriacea (3/4). d, Eretmochelys imbricata (4/4).

2010, Oct. 24 *Perf. 13½x12¾*

2248 Strip or block of 4 2.75 2.75
a.-d. A729 1500r Any single .65 .25

Flora and Fauna of the Provinces Type of 2008

No. 2249: a, Haliastur indus, Salacca zalacca, Jakarta (5/11). b, Geopelia striata, Stelechocarpus burahol, Yogyakarta (6/11).

No. 2250: a, Gracula religiosa robusta, Cananga odorata, Sumatera Utara (North Sumatra) (1/11). b, Panthera tigris sumatrae, Cyrtostachys renda, Jambi (2/11). c, Helarctos malayanus, Amorphophallus titanum, Bengkulu (3/11). d, Tarsius bancanus saltator, Palaquium rostratum, Bangka Belitung (4/11).

2000r, Cervus timorensis, Diospyros macrophylla, Nusa Tenggara Barat (West Nusa Tenggara) (11/11).

No. 2252: a, Nasalis larvatus, Mangifera casturi, Kalimantan Selatan (South Kalimantan) (7/11). b, Aceros cassadix, Borassus flabellifer, Sulawesi Selatan (South Sulawesi) (8/11). c, Tarsius spectrum, Ficus minahassae, Sulawesi Utara (North Sulawesi) (9/11). d, Semioptera wallacii, Syzygium aromaticum, Maluku Utara (North Moluccas (10/11).

2010, Nov. 5 **Litho.**

2249 A688 1000r Pair, #a-b .75 .75
2250 A688 1500r Strip or block of 4, #a-d 2.00 2.00
2251 A688 2000r multi .75 .35
2252 A688 2500r Strip or block of 4, #a-d 3.50 3.50
e. Souvenir sheet, #2249a-2249b, 2250a-2250d, 2251, 2252a-2252d, + label 7.50 7.50
Nos. 2249-2252 (4) 4.55 2.20

Provincial Arms Type of 2008

Arms of: No. 2253, 1500r, Sumatera Utara (North Sumatra) (23/33). No. 2254, 1500r, Jambi (24/33). No. 2255, 1500r, Bengkulu (25/35). No. 2256, 1500r, Kepulauan Bangka Belitung (26/33). No. 2257, 1500r, DKI Jakarta (27/33). No. 2258, 1500r, Yogyakarta (28/33). No. 2259, 1500r, Kalimantan Selatan (South Kalimantan) (29/33). No. 2260, 1500r, Sulawesi Selatan (South Sulawesi) (30/33). No. 2261, 1500r, Sulawesi Utara (North Sulawesi) (31/33). No. 2262, 1500r, Maluku Utara (North Maluku) (32/33). No. 2263, 1500r, Nusa Tenggara Barat (West Nusa Tenggara) (33/33).

No. 2264, Like #2257.

2010, Dec. 13 **Litho.** *Perf. 12½*

2253-2263 A679 Set of 11 5.00 3.00
2263a Sheet of 11, #2253-2263, + label 5.00 5.00

Souvenir Sheet

2264 A679 5000r multi 4.00 2.00

New Year 2011 (Year of the Rabbit) A730

Indonesian flag and: 1500r, Brown rabbit (1/3). 3000r, Gray rabbit (2/3). 4000r, Gray and brown rabbits (3/3).

5000r, Head of brown rabbit.

2011, Jan. 25 **Litho.** *Perf. 13½x12¾*

2265-2267 A730 Set of 3 3.00 .95
2267a Sheet of 6, 2 each #2265-2267, + 2 labels 7.00 7.00

Souvenir Sheet

Litho. with Foil Application

2268 A730 5000r multi 2.00 2.00

Traditional Rituals — A731

No. 2269: a, Grebeg Syawal ritual, Yogyakarta (1/4). b, Ngaben ritual, Bali (2/4). c, Pasola ritual, Sumba, East Nusa Tenggara (3/4). d, Tiwah ritual, Dayak, Central Kalimantan (4/4).

Perf. 13½x12¾

2011, Feb. 24 **Litho.**

2269 A731 1500r Block or horiz. strip of 4, #a-d 2.25 2.25

Intl. Year of Chemistry — A732

Designs: 1500r, Molecular model of Artoindonesianin C. 2500r, International Year of Chemistry emblem, vert.

Perf. 13½x12¾, 12¾x13½

2011, Mar. 1

2270-2271 A732 Set of 2 1.50 .75

Traditional Textiles — A733

No. 2272: a, Ulos Batak, Sulawesi Utara (North Sulawesi) (1/8). b, Tenun Tampan, Lampung (2/8). c, Batik Lasem, Jawa Tengah (Central Java) (3/8). d, Batik Parang Garuda, Yogyakarta (4/8). e, Sasirangan Banjar, Kalimantan Selatan (South Kalimantan) (5/8). f, Tenun Iban, Kalimantan Timur (East Kalimantan) (6/8). g, Tenun Toraja, Sulawesi Selatan (South Sulawesi) (7/8). h, Tenun Sumba, Nusa Tenggara Timur (East Nusa Tenggara) (8/8).

5000r, Woman weaving fabric.

2011, Mar. 30 *Perf. 13½x12¾*

2272 A733 2500r Sheet of 8, #a-h 8.00 8.00
i. As #2272, with Indonesia 2012 emblem overprinted in sheet margin in metallic red 8.00 8.00

Souvenir Sheet

2273 A733 5000r multi 2.00 2.00
a. As #2273, with Indonesia 2012 emblem overprinted in sheet margin in metallic red 2.00 2.00

See Nos. 2281-2282, 2292-2293, 2307-2308.
Nos. 2272i and 2273a exist imperforate.

Spacecraft — A734

No. 2274: a, Rocket on launch pad (1/2). b, TUBSAT (2/2).

2011, Apr. 12 *Perf. 12¾x13½*

2274 A734 2500r Pair, #a-b 1.75 1.50

Internet Safety — A735

No. 2275 — Child in helmet and: a, Plug in outlet in globe (1/2). b, Children using laptop computer (2/2).

2011, Apr. 21 *Perf. 13½x12¾*

2275 A735 2500r Horiz. pair, #a-b 1.75 1.50

No. 2275 was printed in sheets containing eight pairs and four labels.

Environmental Care — A736

No. 2276: a, Pine cone on branch (1/2). b, Squirrel on pine tree (2/2).

2011, June 5 **Litho.**

2276 A736 2500r Vert. pair, #a-b 1.75 1.50
c. Souvenir sheet, #2276a-2276b 1.75 1.75

Fish and Seaweed Production — A737

Designs: 1500r, Fish and vegetables on plate (3/4). 2000r, Fish and vegetables (2/4). 3000r, Man processing seaweed (4/4). 5000r, Fisherman and fish (1/4).

2011, June 22 *Perf. 12½*

2277-2280 A737 Set of 4 3.50 2.00
2280a Souvenir sheet of 4, #2277-2280 3.50 3.50

Traditional Textiles Type of 2011

No. 2281: a, Tenun Aceh Nanggroe, Aceh (1/8). b, Tenun Pandai Sikek, Sumatara Barat (West Sumatra) (2/8). c, Batik Basurek, Bengkulu (3/8). d, Songket Palembang, Sumatera Selatan (South Sumatra) (4/8). e, Batik Madura, Jawa Timur (East Java) (5/8). f, Tenun Sambas, Kalimantan Barat (West Kalimantan) (6/8). g, Tenun Bentenan, Sulawesi Utara (North Sulawesi) (7/8). h, Batik Masambo, Nusa Tenggara Barat (West Nusa Tenggara) (8/8).

5000r, Man behind team of oxen with Karapan Sabi, Jawa Timur (East Java).

2011, July 6 *Perf. 13½x12¾*

2281 A733 2500r Sheet of 8, #a-h 8.00 8.00
i. Like #2281, with gold design in sheet margin 8.00 8.00

Souvenir Sheet

2282 A733 5000r multi 2.00 2.00

Nos. 2281i, 2282 exist imperf.

Souvenir Sheet

PhilaNippon '11 World Stamp Exhibition, Yokohama, Japan — A738

2011, July 28

2283 A738 10,000r multi 3.25 3.25

Friendship Between Malaysia and Indonesia A739

No. 2284: a, Proclamation Monument, Indonesia (1/8). b, 1945 Indonesia 5-sen banknote (2/8). c, Indonesia #1LM1 (3/8). d, Gallus varius (4/8).

No. 2285: a, National Monument, Malaysia (5/8). b, 1959 Malaya and North Borneo $1 banknote (6/8). c, Malaya #84 (7/8). d, Gallus gallus (8/8).

2011, Aug. 8 *Perf. 13¼x13*

2284 Vert strip of 4 4.00 4.00
a.-d. A739 2500r Any single 1.00 .30
2285 Vert strip of 4 4.00 4.00
a.-d. A739 2500r Any single 1.00 .30
e. Sheet of 8, #2284a-2284d, 2285a-2285d 8.00 8.00

See Malaysia No. 1360.

Scouting In Indonesia, 50th Anniv. — A740

Designs: No. 2286, 2500r, Dove, Scout holding Scouting flag (1/3). No. 2287, 2500r, Four Scouts, Scouting and Indonesian flag (2/3). No. 2288, 2500r, Scout leaders teaching Scouts (3/3).

5000r, Like No. 2286.

2011, Apr. 14 *Perf. 13½x12¾*

2286-2288 A740 Set of 3 2.50 .90

Souvenir Sheet

2289 A740 5000r multi 1.75 1.75

Landmarks — A741

No. 2290: a, Lawang Sewu Building, Semarang (2/5). b, Equator Monument, Pontianak (3/5). c, Garuda Wisnu Kencana Cultural Park,

Denpasar (4/5). d, Fort Rotterdam, Makassar (5/5). e, Ampera Bridge, Palembang (1/5).

2011, Sept. 27 ***Perf. 13½x12¾***
2290 Strip of 5 3.50 3.00
a.-e. A741 2500r Any single .70 .30

Famous Men — A742

No. 2291: a, Dr. Mohammed Natsir (1908-93), Prime minister. b, Sutomo (1920-81), politician.

2011, Aug. 17 ***Perf. 13x13¼***
2291 A742 2500r Horiz. pair, #a-b 1.75 1.50

Traditional Textiles Type of 2011

No. 2292: a, Songket Malayu, Riau (1/8). b, Songket Mentok, Bangka Belitung (2/8). c, Batik Mega Mendung, Jawa Barat (West Java) (3/8). d, Tenun Sora Langi, Sulawesi Barat (West Sulawesi) (4/8). e, Tenun Tolaki, Sulawesi Tenggara (Southeast Sulawesi) (5/8). f, Tenun Tanimbar, Maluku (6/8). g, Batik Papua, Papua (7/8). h, Batik Papua Barat, Papua Barat (West Papua) (8/8).
5000r, Masked dancer, Tari Topeng, Jawa Barat (West Java).

2011, Oct. 2 Litho. ***Perf. 13½x12¾***
2292 A733 2500r Sheet of 8, #a-h 8.00 8.00

Souvenir Sheet

2293 A733 5000r multi 2.00 2.00

Operation Trikora, 50th Anniv. A743

Designs: No. 2294, 2500r, Trikora Monument, ships, map of West Papua, helicopter (1/4). No. 2295, 2500r, Soldiers and armored personnel carrier (2/4). No. 2296, 2500r, Navy ships, soldiers in water (3/4). No. 2297, 2500r, Soldiers and jet fighter (4/4).

2011, Oct. 5 ***Perf. 13½x12¾***
2294-2297 A743 Set of 4 3.50 1.50
2297a Souvenir sheet of 8, 2 each #2294-2297 + 2 labels 7.00 6.00

Indonesian Historical Links With South Africa A744

No. 2298: a, Sheikh Yusuf (1626-99), establisher of Islam in South Africa (1/10). b, Balla Lampoa Museum, Sulawesi Selantan (South Sulawesi) (2/10). c, Alat Musik Tifa, Papua (3/10). d, Topi Tilangga, Nusa Tenggara Timur, and Kelom Geulis, Jawa Barat (West Java) (4/10). e, Tari Pakarena, Sulawesi Selatan (South Sulawesi) (5/10).

2011, Oct. 15 ***Perf. 13¼x13***
2298 A744 2500r Vert. strip of 5, #a-e 4.00 4.00

See South Africa No. 1469.

2011 South East Asian Games, Jakarta and Palembang — A745

No. 2299: a, Mascot and tower in Jakarta (1/6). b, Mascot and towers in Palembang (2/6). c, Mascot playing soccer (5/6). d, Mascot in pencak silat outfit (6/6). e, Mascot playing table tennis (3/6). f, Mascot playing badminton (4/6).

2011, Oct. 18 ***Perf. 12¾x13½***
2299 A745 2500r Block of 6, #a-f 5.00 5.00

Flora and Fauna — A746

Nos. 2300 and 2301: a, Leptophryne cruentata. b, Nymphoides indica.

2011, Nov. 5 ***Perf. 13½x12¾***
2300 A746 2500r Horiz. pair, #a-b 1.75 1.50
c. Vert. tete-beche pair 1.75 1.50

Souvenir Sheet

2301 A746 5000r Sheet of 2, #a-b 3.50 3.50

No. 2301 has a curved die-cut slit that encompasses the stamps and text in the sheet margin.

China 2011 International Stamp Exhibition, Wuxi, People's Republic of China — A747

2011 **Litho.**
2302 A747 10,000r multi 3.50 3.50

New Year 2012 (Year of the Dragon) A748

No. 2303 — Various dragons: a, Green and multicolored (1/3). b, Red brown and multicolored (2/3). c, Indigo and multicolored (3/3).
5000r, Dragon, diff.

2012, Jan. 15 ***Perf. 13½x12¾***
2303 Strip of 3 2.50 2.50
a.-c. A748 2500r Any single .75 .30
d. Souvenir sheet of 6, 2 each #2303a-2303c, + 2 labels 5.00 5.00

Souvenir Sheet

2304 A748 5000r multi 2.25 2.25

National Sports Week — A749

No. 2305 — Mascot: a, Parachuting (1/6). b, Shooting (2/6). c, On gymnastic rings (3/6). d, Playing sepak takraw (4/6). e, Sailboarding (5/6). f, Canoeing (6/6).

2012, Feb. 22
2305 A749 2500r Block of 6, #a-f 5.00 4.00

Asian-Pacific Postal Union, 50th Anniv. — A750

2012, Apr. 1
2306 A750 5000r multi 1.60 .80

Traditional Textiles Type of 2011

No. 2307: a, Batik Bongbong, Riau Kepulauan (25/33). b, Batik Angso Duo, Jambi (26/33). c, Tenun Baduy, Banten (27/33). d, Tenun Gringsing, Bali (28/33). e, Kain Benang Bintik, Kalimantan Tengah (Central Kalimantan) (29/33). f, Tenun Donggala, Sulawesi Tengah (Central Sulawesi) (30/33). g, Kain Kerawang, Gorontalo (31/33). h, Batik Ternate, Maluku Utara (North Moluccas) (32/33). i, As "a," numbered 1/8. j, As "b," numbered 2/8. k, As "c," numbered 3/8. l, As "d," numbered 4/8. m, As "e," numbered 5/8. n, As "f," numbered 6/8. o, As "g," numbered 7/8. p, As "h," numbered 8/8.
5000r, Tari Barong, Bali.

2012, Apr. 21
2307 A733 2500r Block of 8, #a-h 7.00 7.00
i.-p. Any single .75 .30
q. Souvenir sheet of 8, #2307i-2307p 7.00 7.00

Souvenir Sheet

2308 A733 5000r multi 1.75 1.75

No. 2307 was printed in a sheet containing three blocks of eight stamps. No. 2308 is dated 2011.

Environmental Care — A751

No. 2309: a, Gasoline pump nozzle (1/2). b, Rhinoceros, Earth in drop of gasoline (2/2).
5000r, Gasoline pump nozzle, rhinoceros, Earth in drop of gasoline, vert.

2012, June 5 ***Perf. 13½x12¾***
2309 A751 2000r Vert. pair, #a-b 1.40 1.20

Souvenir Sheet

2310 A751 5000r multi 1.60 1.20

No. 2310 contains one 42x51mm stamp.

Traditional Foods A752

No. 2311: a, Daging Sei and Jagung Bose, Nusa Tenggara Timur (1/2). b, Gulai Asam Pedas, Kepulauan Riau (2/2).

2012, July 6 **Litho.**
2311 A752 2500r Pair, #a-b 1.75 1.40

No. 2311 was printed in sheets containing 10 pairs and a central label.

Endangered Birds — A753

No. 2312: a, Otus siaoensis (1/4). b, Nisaetus floris (2/4). c, Aethopyga duyvenbodei (3/4). d, Habroptila wallacii (4/4).

2012, July 15 ***Perf. 14***
2312 A753 2500r Block of 4, #a-d 3.00 3.00
e. Souvenir sheet of 4, #2312a-2312d 3.00 3.00

Scouting in Indonesia, Cent. — A763

No. 2324 — Scouts at flag ceremony with denomination at: a, Left (1/2). b, Right (2/2).

Perf. 13½x12¾

2012, Aug. 14 **Litho.**
2324 A763 2500r Horiz. pair, #a-b 1.60 1.25
c. Souvenir sheet of 2, #2324a-2324b 1.60 1.60

Television Broadcasting in Indonesia, 50th Anniv. — A764

No. 2325: a, Black-and-white television (1/2). b, High-definition color television (2/2).

2012, Aug. 24
2325 A764 2500r Pair, #a-b 1.60 1.25

People at Building Site — A765

Various People A766

People Holding Hands — A767

Perf. 12¾x13½, 13½x12¾ (A766)

2012, Oct. 1
2326 Strip of 3 2.50 2.00
a. A765 2500r multi (1/3) .75 .30
b. A766 2500r multi (2/3) .75 .30
c. A767 2500r multi (3/3) .75 .30

Houses of Worship A768

No. 2327: a, Masjid Agung, Palembang (3/5). b, Pura, Besakih (4/5). c, Wihara Dharma Bhakti, Jakarta (5/5). d, Gereja Blenduk, Semarang (1/5). e, Gereja Puhsarang, Kediri (2/5).

2012, Oct. 27 ***Perf. 13½x12¾***
2327 Strip of 5 3.50 3.50
a.-e. A768 2500r Any single .60 .30

Flora and Fauna — A769

Nos. 2328 and 2329: a, Spilocuscus rufoniger (1/2). b, Kandelia candel (2/2). Stamps on No. 2329 lack "1/2" and "2/2."

2012, Nov. 5 ***Perf. 12¾x13½***
2328 A769 2500r Pair, #a-b 1.75 1.25

Souvenir Sheet

2329 A769 5000r Sheet of 2, #a-b 3.50 3.50

New Year 2013 (Year of the Snake) — A770

Various depictions of snakes.

2013, Jan. 22
2330 Strip of 3 5.00 4.00
a. A770 2500r multi (1/3) .75 .30
b. A770 5000r multi (2/3) 1.25 .65
c. A770 7500r multi (3/3) 1.75 1.00
d. Miniature sheet of 6, 2 each #2330a-2330c 6.50 3.25

Souvenir Sheet

2331 A770 10,000r multi 3.25 3.25

Ratu Boko Palace A771

Sumunaring Abhayagiri Dancers — A772

2013, Feb. 20 ***Perf. 13½x12¾***
2332 A771 2500r multi .85 .30
2333 A772 2500r multi .85 .30

Musical Instruments — A773

Designs: No. 2334, 2500r, Gambus, Riau (1/33). No. 2335, 2500r, Celempung, Jawa Barat (West Java) (4/33). No. 2336, 2500r, Kollatung, Kalimantan Barat (West Kalimantan) (6/33). No. 2337, 2500r, Calong, Sulawesi Barat (West Sulawesi) (7/33). No. 2338, 2500r, Tambua, Sumatera Barat (West Sumatra) (8/33). No. 2339, 2500r, Siter, Jawa Tengah (Central Java) (9/33). No. 2340, 3000r, Serune Kalee, NAD (Aceh) (2/33). No. 2341, 3000r, Fu, Maluku (Moluccas) (3/33). No. 2342, 3000r, Cengceng, Bali (5/33). No. 2343, 3000r, Tifa, Papua (10/33). No. 2344, 3000r, Polopalo, Gorontalo (11/33).

2013, Mar. 9 **Litho.**
2334-2344 A773 Set of 11 10.00 5.00
2344a Block of 11, #2334-2344, + label 10.00 10.00

Nos. 2334-2344 were printed in sheets containing two of each stamp and 2 labels in center of sheet. See Nos. 2371-2381, 2402-2412, 2423.

Diplomatic Relations Between Indonesia and Mexico, 60th Anniv. — A774

No. 2345: a, Clouded leopard, Indonesia (1/2). b, Mexican jaguar (2/2).

2013, Apr. 6 ***Perf. 13¼x13***
2345 A774 8000r Horiz. pair, #a-b 5.00 4.00

See Mexico Nos. 2818-2819.

A775

A776

Transfer of Control of West Irian to Indonesia, 50th Anniv. A777

2013, May 1 ***Perf. 13½x12¾***
2346 Strip of 3 2.50 2.00
a. A775 2500r multi (1/3) .75 .30
b. A776 2500r multi (2/3) .75 .30
c. A777 2500r multi (3/3) .75 .30

Publication of Anti-Colonial Writings by Ki Hadjar Dewantara (1889-1959), Cent. — A778

2013, May 2 ***Perf. 13¼x13***
2347 A778 2500r multi .90 .30

Souvenir Sheets

Australia 2013 World Stamp Expo, Melbourne — A779

Designs: No. 2348, 10,000r, Orangutans. No. 2349, 10,000r, Kangaroos.

2013, May 10 ***Perf. 12¾x13½***
2348-2349 A779 Set of 2 3.50 3.50

World Environment Day — A780

No. 2350: a, Fruit in top of hourglass (1/2). b, Garbage in bottom of hourglass (2/2). 5000r, Fruit and garbage in hourglass, vert.

2013, June 5 ***Perf. 13½x12¾***
2350 A780 2500r Vert. pair, #a-b 1.75 1.40

Souvenir Sheet

2351 A780 5000r multi 1.75 1.75

No. 2351 contains one 42x51mm stamp.

Cave Painting, Uhallie A781

Ramayana Epic, Prambanan Temple, Yogyakarta — A782

Buddha Attaining Enlightenment, Borobudur Temple — A783

2013, June 14
2352 A781 2500r multi .85 .30
2353 A782 2500r multi .85 .30

Souvenir Sheet

2354 A783 10,000r multi 3.25 3.25

Indonesian Archaeological Institute, Cent.

SOS Children's Villages A784

No. 2355: a, Building, child on swing (1/2). b, Children and bicycle (2/2).

2013, July 23 **Litho.** ***Perf. 13½x12¾***
2355 A784 2500r Pair, #a-b 1.60 1.25

Souvenir Sheet

2013 Thailand World Stamp Expo, Bangkok — A785

2013, Aug. 2 Litho. *Perf. 12¾x13½*
2356 A785 10,000r multi 3.00 3.00

Postal Services
A786 A787

Designs: 2500r, 4000r, PosPay (online bill paying) service. 3000r, 4500r, WeselPos (money order) service. 3500r, 5000r, PosExpress and Poskilat Khusus (express and document delivery) services.

Perf. 13½x12¾

2013, Aug. 26 Litho.

2357 A786 2500r multi	.70	.25
2358 A786 3000r multi	.85	.40
2359 A786 3500r multi	1.00	.50

Perf. 12¾ Syncopated

2360 A787 4000r multi	1.10	.60
2361 A787 4500r multi	1.10	.60
2362 A787 5000r multi	.90	.45
Nos. 2357-2362 (6)	5.65	2.80

Diplomatic Relations Between Indonesia and South Korea, 40th Anniv. — A788

No. 2363: a, Large lion figure from Korean folk play, small bull figure from Indonesian folk play (1/2). b, Small lion figure, large bull figure (2/2).

2013, Sept. 17 Litho. *Perf. 13¼x13*
2363 A788 7500r Horiz. pair, #a-b 4.50 3.50

See South Korea No. 2415

Souvenir Sheet

2013 National Philatelic Exhibition, Bandung — A789

Perf. 13½x12¾

2013, Sept. 25 Litho.
2364 A789 10,000r multi 3.00 3.00

Garuda Contingent (Indonesian Armed Forces in United Nations Peace-Keeping Missions) — A790

No. 2365: a, Boy and soldier wearing United Nations helmets saluting each other (1/4). b, Soldiers and United Nations vehicle (2/4). c, Ships at sea (3/4). d, Soldier and United Nations Peacekeepers flag (4/4).

2013, Oct. 5 Litho. *Perf. 13¼x13*
2365 A790 2500r Block of 4, #a-d 3.00 2.50

Flora and Fish — A791

Nos. 2366 and 2367: a, Metroxylon sago (2/2). b, Pristis microdon (1/2).

2013, Nov. 5 Litho. *Perf. 13½x12¾*
2366 A791 2500r Pair, #a-b 1.50 1.20

Souvenir Sheet

2367 A791 5000r Sheet of 2, #a-b 3.00 3.00

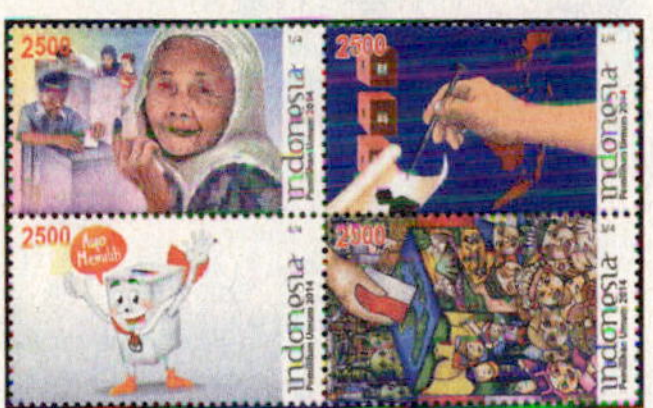

General Elections — A792

No. 2368: a, Voters at polls, woman showing finger mark (1/4). b, Map of Indonesia, hand with stylus, ballot boxes, vert. (2/4). c, Caricature of ballot box (4/4). d, Voters, hand placing Indonesian flag in ballot box, vert. (3/4).

2014, Jan. 9 Litho. *Perf. 13½x12¾*
2368 A792 2500r Block of 4, #a-d 3.00 2.50

New Year 2014 (Year of the Horse) — A793

No. 2369 — Horse and rider with top panel color of: a, Dark gray (1/3). b, Greenish gray (2/3). c, Brown (3/3).
10,000r, Four horses.

2014, Jan. 15 Litho. *Perf. 12¾x13¼*

2369 Strip of 3	2.50	2.00
a.-c. A793 2500r Any single	.75	.30
d. Souvenir sheet of 6, 2 each #2369a-2369c	5.00	5.00

Souvenir Sheet

2370 A793 10,000r multi 3.00 3.00

Musical Instruments Type of 2013

Designs: No. 2371, 3000r, Dogdog Lojor, Banten (12/33). No. 2372, 3000r, Terompet Reog, Jawa Timur (East Java) (13/33). No. 2373, 5000r, Japen, Kalimantan Tengah (Central Kalimantan) (14/33). No. 2374, 5000r, Sampek, Kalimantan Timur (East Kalimantan) (15/33). No. 2375, 5000r, Gendang Panjang, Kepulauan Riau (Riau Islands) (16/33). No. 2376, 5000r, Cetik, Lampung (17/33). No. 2377, 5000r, Lalove, Sulawesi Tengah (Central Sulawesi) (20/33). No. 2378, 5000r, Latatou, Sulawesi Tenggara (Southeast Sulawesi) (21/33). No. 2379, 5000r, Accordion, Sumatra Selatan (South Sumatra (22/33). No. 2380, 8000r, Sasando, Nusa Tenggara Timur (East Nusa Tenggara) (18/33). No. 2381, 8000r, Tambur, Papua Barat (West Papua) (19/33).

2014, Mar. 9 Litho. *Perf. 13½x12¾*

2371-2381 A773 Set of 11	10.00	5.00
2381a Block of 11, #2371-2381, + label	10.00	5.00

Nos. 2371-2381 were printed in sheets containing two of each stamp and 2 labels in center of sheet.

Stamps of Netherlands Indies and Indonesia — A794

No. 2382: a, 5000r, Netherlands Indies #1. b, 8000r, Netherlands Indies #N1. c, 10,000r, Indonesia #1L23.
50,000r, Netherlands Indies #1.

Perf. 13¼x13½ Syncopated

2014, Apr. 1 Litho.
2382 A794 Horiz. strip of 3, #a-c 6.50 5.00

Litho. With Hologram Affixed

Souvenir Sheet

Perf. 14x14½

2383 A794 50,000r multi 15.00 10.00

First Netherlands Indies stamp, 150th anniv. No. 2383 contains one 48x66mm stamp.

Education A795

No. 2384: a, Children and teacher (1/3). b, Children making origami figures (2/3). c, Children and house, vert. (3/3).

2014, May 2 Litho. *Perf. 13½x12¾*

2384 Strip of 3	2.50	2.00
a.-c. A795 3000r Any single	.75	.30

Miniature Sheet

Worldwide Fund for Nature (WWF) — A796

No. 2385 — Panthera pardus melas: a, Head, denomination at UR (1/4). b, Head, denomination at UL (2/4). c, Entire animal, denomination at UR (3/4). d, Entire animal, denomination at UL (4/4).

2014, May 2 Litho. *Perf. 13½x12¾*
2385 A796 5000r Sheet of 4, #a-d 5.00 5.00

2014 Four Nations Stamp Show, Bandung.

Environmental Care — A797

Nos. 2386 and 2387: a, Leptoptilos javanicus (1/2). b, Scylla serrata (2/2).

2014, June 5 Litho. *Perf. 13½x12¾*
2386 A797 3000r Vert. pair, #a-b 1.75 1.40

Souvenir Sheet

2387 A797 5000r Sheet of 2, #a-b 2.75 2.75

Birds — A798

No. 2388: a, Mycteria cinerea (1/4). b, Charadrius javanicus (2/4). c, Gymnocrex rosenbergii (3/4). d, Pseudibis davisoni (4/4).

2014, July 15 Litho. *Perf. 14*

2388 A798 5000r Block of 4, #a-d	3.50	2.75
e. Souvenir sheet of 4, #2388a-2388d	3.50	3.50

Indonesian First Ladies — A799

No. 2389: a, Fatmawati Soekarno (1923-80) (1/5). b, Tien Soeharto (1923-96) (2/5). c, Ainun Habibie (1937-2010) (3/5). d, Sinta Nuriyah Wahid (4/5). e, Ani Yudhoyono (5/5).

2014, July 23 Litho. *Perf. 12½*

2389 Horiz. strip of 5	6.00	5.00
a.-e. A799 5000r Any single	1.00	.40

Indonesian Paleoanthropology, 125th Anniv. — A800

No. 2390: a, Homo erectus family (1/2). b, Maps and Homo sapiens skull (2/2).

Perf. 13½x12¾

2014, Aug. 31 Litho.
2390 A800 3000r Horiz. pair, #a-b 1.50 1.20

Ancient Calendars and Inscriptions — A801

No. 2391: a, Batak calendar (4/4). b, Tanjung Tanah manuscript with post-Pallava inscriptions (1/4). c, Sundanese Inscriptions on tablet (2/4). d, Balinese calendar (3/4).

2014, Sept. 8 Litho. *Perf. 12¾x13½*

2391 Strip of 4	3.00	2.50
a.-d. A801 3000r Any single	.75	.30

Postman With Bicycle — A802

2014, Sept. 27 **Litho.** ***Perf. 12½***
2392 A802 10,000r shown 2.75 1.40
2393 A802 20,000r Post office 5.50 2.75

Armed Forces A803

No. 2394: a, KRI Dewa Ruci and figurehead (1/3). b, Sukhoi jet and eagle (2/3) c, Leopard tank and leopard (3/3).

2014, Oct. 5 **Litho.** ***Perf. 13¼x13***
2394 Strip of 3 2.50 2.00
a.-c. A803 3000r Any single .75 .30

Flora and Fauna — A804

No. 2395: a, Eretmochelys imbricata (1/2). b, Tacca leontopetaloides (2/2).
5000r, Like No. 2395a.

2014, Nov. 5 **Litho.** ***Perf. 13½x12¾***
2395 A804 3000r Pair, #a-b 1.75 1.25

Souvenir Sheet

2396 A804 5000r multi 1.50 1.50

Stamp on No. 2396 is surrounded by turtle-shaped rouletting in sheet margin. No. 2396 exists imperforate without the rouletting in the sheet margin.

National Health Day, 50th Anniv. A805

No. 2397: a, 50th anniversary emblem (1/2). b, President Sukarno spraying insecticide (2/2).

Perf. 13½x12¾

2014, Nov. 12 **Litho.**
2397 A805 3000r Pair, #a-b 1.75 1.25

Souvenir Sheet

Malaysia 2014 World Youth Stamp Exhibition, Kuala Lumpur — A806

2014, Dec. 1 **Litho.** ***Perf. 13½x12¾***
2398 A806 10,000r multi 3.00 3.00

Discovery of Borobudur Temple, 200th anniv.

Bridges — A807

No. 2399: a, Kelok Sembilan Bridge (2/2). b, Bali Mandara Bridge (1/2).

2014, Dec. 3 **Litho.** ***Perf. 13½x12¾***
2399 A807 5000r Pair, #a-b 3.00 2.00

New Year 2015 (Year of the Ram) A808

No. 2400: a, Ram wearing decorations (1/3). b, Ram leaping to right (2/3). c, Ram leaping to left (3/3).
10,000r, Ram wearing decorations, vert.

2015, Feb. 4 **Litho.** ***Perf. 13½x12¾***
2400 Horiz. strip of 3 2.50 2.00
a.-c. A808 3000r Any single .75 .30
d. Souvenir sheet of 6, 2 each #2400a-2400c 5.00 5.00

Souvenir Sheet

Perf. 12¾x13½

2401 A808 10,000r multi 3.00 3.00

Musical Instruments Type of 2013

Designs: No. 2402, 3000r, Dol, Bengkulu (23/33). No. 2403, 3000r, Tehyan, DKI Jakarta (24/33). No. 2404, 3000r, Cangor, Jambi (25/33). No. 2405, 3000r, Panting, Kalimantan Selatan (South Kalimantan) (26/33). No. 2406, 3000r, Kacapi, Sulawesi Selatan (South Sulawesi) (27/33). No. 2407, 3000r, Kendang, DI Yogyakarta (28/33). No. 2408, 3000r, Hasapi, Sumatera Utara (North Sumatra) (29/33). No. 2409, 3000r, Kolintang,Sulawesi Utara (North Sulawesi) (30/33). No. 2410, 3000r, Bambu Hitada, Maluku Utara (North Maluku) (31/33). No. 2411, 3000r, Dambus, Kepulauan Bangka Belitung (32/33). No. 2412, 3000r, Sarone, Nusa Tenggara Barat (West Nusa Tenggara) (33/33).

2015, Mar. 9 **Litho.** ***Perf. 13½x12¾***
2402-2412 A773 Set of 11 8.00 4.00
2412a Block of 11, #2402-2412, + label 8.00 8.00

Nos. 2402-2412 were printed in sheets containing two of each stamp and 2 labels in center of sheet.

United Nations World Conference on Disaster Risk Reduction — A809

No. 2413: a, Erupting volcano, woman adjusting surgical mask over child's face (1/3). b, Rescuers saving flood victims (2/3). c, Rescue workers and victims, horiz. (3/3).
5000r, Eruption of Tambora Volcano, 200th anniv., horiz.

Perf. 12¾x13½, 13½x12¾

2015, Mar. 14 **Litho.**
2413 Vert. strip of 3 2.50 1.75
a.-c. A809 3000r Any single .75 .30

Souvenir Sheet

Perf. 13¼x13

2414 A809 5000r multi 2.00 2.00

No. 2414 contains one 40x30mm stamp.

Orchids and Past Leaders of Indonesia and North Korea — A810

No. 2415: a, Phalaenopsis amabila, Indonesian Pres. Sukarno (1901-70). b, Dendrobium kimilsung, North Korean Pres. Kim Il-sung (1912-94)

2015, Apr. 15 **Litho.** ***Perf. 13x13¼***
2415 Horiz. pair 5.00 3.00
a.-b. A810 8000r Either single 2.50 1.25

Printed in sheets of 11 each Nos. 2415a-2415b + 2 central labels.

Musical Instruments Type of 2013 and

A811

A812

A813

A814

A815

A816

Folklore, Arms, and Food of North Kalimantan Province — A817

Design: No. 2423, Babun (8/8).

2015, Apr. 22 **Litho.** ***Perf. 13½x12¾***
2416 A811 3000r multi .80 .30
2417 A812 3000r multi .80 .30
2418 A813 3000r multi .80 .30
2419 A814 3000r multi .80 .30
2420 A815 3000r multi .80 .30
2421 A816 3000r multi .80 .30
2422 A817 3000r multi .80 .30
2423 A773 3000r multi .80 .30
Nos. 2416-2423 (8) 6.40 2.40

Nos. 2416-2423 were printed in sheets containing three of each stamp + label.

Environmental Care — A819

2015, June 5 **Litho.** ***Perf. 14***
2425 A819 3000r multi .90 .30

Souvenir Sheet

Perf.

2426 A819 5000r multi 2.00 2.00

Value for No. 2425 is for stamp with surrounding selvage.

23rd World Scout Jamboree, Japan — A820

No. 2427: a, Neckerchief and knot slide (1/2). b, Hands and knots (2/2).

2015, July 28 **Litho.** ***Perf. 13¼x13***
2427 A820 5000r Horiz. pair, #a-b 2.50 1.75

Pritned in sheets of 10 pairs + central label.

Flags and Emblem of Association of Southeast Asian Nations A821

2015, Aug. 8 **Litho.** ***Perf. 14***
2428 A821 7000r multi 1.75 1.00

See Brunei No. 656, Burma Nos. 417-418, Cambodia No. , Laos No. , Malaysia No. 1562, Philippines No. 3619, Singapore No. 1742, Thailand No. 2875, Viet Nam No. 3529.

Souvenir Sheet

Singapore 2015 World Stamp Exhibition — A822

2015, Aug. 14 **Litho.** ***Perf. 13x13¼***
2429 A822 5000r multi 1.50 1.50

A823

New President and Vice-President — A824

No. 2430: a, Pres. Joko Widodo (1/2). b, Vice-President Muhammad Jusuf Kalla (2-2).
No. 2431, 8000r, Pres. Widodo. No. 2432, 8000r, Vice-President Kalla.

2015, Aug. 17 Litho. *Perf. 13x13¼*
2430 A823 5000r Pair, #a-b 2.50 1.75

Souvenir Sheets

2431-2432 A824 Set of 2 4.50 4.50

Indonesian House of Representatives, 70th Anniv. — A825

No. 2433 — House of Representatives Building and: a, Silhouettes of people and flagbearer (1/2). b, Map of Asia and Africa, computer keyboard (2/2).

2015, Aug. 29 Litho. *Perf. 13¼x13*
2433 A825 3000r Horiz. pair, #a-b 1.60 1.20

Indonesian Red Cross Society, 70th Anniv. — A826

No. 2434: a, Mohammad Hatta, 1945-46 chairman, Red Cross workers raising Red Cross flag (1/2). b, Ambulances at Red Cross Headquarters, 1959 (2/2).

2015, Sept. 10 Litho. *Perf. 13¼x13*
2434 A826 3000r Horiz. pair, #a-b 1.25 .90

Pancasila Sanctity Day — A827

2015, Oct. 1 Litho. *Perf. 12¾x13½*
2435 A827 3000r multi .90 .30

Defense Industry Products A828

No. 2436: a, KRI Banda Aceh. b, ANOA armored personnel carrier. c, CN 235 airplane.

2015, Oct. 5 Litho. *Perf. 13½x12¾*
2436 Strip of 3 2.00 1.50
a.-c. A828 3000r Any single .65 .30

Miniature Sheet

Surabaya 2015 National Philatelic Exhibition — A829

No. 2437: a, Elephant facing right. b, Elephant facing left. c, Head of elephant. d, Adult and juvenile.

Sheet of 4, #a-d

2015, Nov. 2 Litho. *Perf. 13½x12¾*
2437 A829 5000r Sheet of 4, #a-d 4.50 4.50

Flora and Fauna A830

No. 2438: a, Gracula religiosa robusta. b, Amorphophallus paeoniifolius.
5000r, Like #2438a.

2015, Nov. 5 Litho. *Perf. 13½x12¾*
2438 A830 3000r Pair, #a-b 1.40 1.10

Souvenir Sheet

2439 A830 5000r multi 1.10 1.10

New Year 2016 (Year of the Monkey) — A832

Various monkeys with background color of: a, Red. b, Bright yellow green. c, Pale blue.
10,000r, Monkey, diff.

2016, Jan. 24 Litho. *Perf. 12¾x13½*
2442 A832 3000r Horiz. strip of 3, #a-c 2.00 1.50

Souvenir Sheet

Perf. 13x13¼

2443 A832 10,000r multi 3.00 3.00

March 9, 2016 Solar Eclipse — A833

Nos. 2444 and 2445 — Map of Indonesia showing path of eclipse and: a, Moon at left. b, Total eclipse. c, Moon at right.

Perf. 12¾x12½

2016, Feb. 23 Litho.
2444 A833 3000r Horiz. strip of 3, #a-c 2.00 1.50

Souvenir Sheet

2445 A833 5000r Sheet of 3, #a-c 3.00 3.00

A834

Diplomatic Relations Between Indonesia and Thailand — A835

No. 2446 and 2447 — Scenes from the epic poem *Ramayana*: a, Four characters and tree. b, Characters kneeling.

Serpentine Die Cut 10¼

2016, May 5 Litho.

Self-Adhesive

2446 A834 8000r Pair, #a-b 3.00 2.00

Souvenir Sheet

Litho. With Hologram

2447 A835 18,000r Sheet of 2, #a-b 7.50 7.50

See Thailand No. 2914.

SEMI-POSTAL STAMPS

Symbols of Olympic Games — SP43

Perf. 12½x12

1951, Jan. 2 Photo. Unwmk.

B58	SP43	5s + 3s gray grn	.25	.25
B59	SP43	10s + 5s dk vio bl	.25	.25
B60	SP43	20s + 5s org red	.25	.25
B61	SP43	30s + 10s dk brn	.25	.25
B62	SP43	35s + 10s ultra	2.50	2.10
		Nos. B58-B62 (5)	3.50	3.10

Issued to publicize the Asiatic Olympic Games of 1951 at New Delhi, India.

Wings and Flame — SP44

1951, Oct. 15

B63	SP44	5s + 3s olive green	.30	.30
B64	SP44	10s + 5s dull blue	.30	.30
B65	SP44	20s + 5s red	.30	.30
B66	SP44	30s + 10s brown	.30	.30
B67	SP44	35s + 10s ultra	.30	*1.10*
		Nos. B63-B67 (5)	1.50	2.30

2nd Natl. Games, Djakarta, 10/21-28/51.

No. 378 Surcharged in Black

1953, May 8 *Perf. 12½*
B68 A53 35s + 10s purple .75 .25

The surcharge reads "Natural Disaster." Surtax was for emergency relief following volcanic eruption and floods.

Merapi Erupting — SP45

1954, Apr. 15 Litho. *Perf. 12½x12*

B69	SP45	15s + 10s bl grn	1.50	*1.75*
B70	SP45	35s + 15s pur	1.50	*1.40*
B71	SP45	50s + 25s red	1.50	*1.40*
B72	SP45	75s + 25s vio bl	1.50	*1.40*
B73	SP45	1r + 25s car	1.50	*1.40*
B74	SP45	2r + 50s blk brn	2.50	*1.40*
B75	SP45	3r + 1r gray grn	10.00	8.75
B76	SP45	5r + 2.50r org brn	10.00	12.00
		Nos. B69-B76 (8)	30.00	29.50

The surtax was for victims of the Merapi volcano eruption.

Young Musicians — SP46

15s+10s, Parasol dance. 35s+15s, Girls playing dakon. 50s+15s, Boy on stilts. 75s+25s, Bamboo flute players. 1r+25s, Javanese dancer.

1954, Dec. 22 Photo. *Perf. 12½*

B77	SP46	10s + 10s dk pur	.30	*.70*
B78	SP46	15s + 10s dk grn	.30	*.80*
B79	SP46	35s + 15s car rose	.30	*.80*
B80	SP46	50s + 15s rose brn	.30	*.80*
B81	SP46	75s + 25s ultra	.30	*3.00*
B82	SP46	1r + 25s red org	.30	*5.00*
		Nos. B77-B82 (6)	1.80	*11.10*

The surtax was for child welfare.

Scout Emblem SP47

Scout Signaling SP48

Designs: 50s+25s, Campfire. 75s+25s, Scout feeding fawn. 1r+50s, Scout saluting.

1955, June 27 Unwmk. *Perf. 12½*

B83	SP47	15s + 10s bl grn	.35	*.50*
B84	SP48	35s + 15s ultra	.35	*.50*
B85	SP48	50s + 25s scar	.35	*.50*
B86	SP48	75s + 25s brn	.35	*.50*
B87	SP48	1r + 50s vio	.35	*.50*
		Nos. B83-B87 (5)	1.75	*2.50*

First National Boy Scout Jamboree.

Blind Weaver — SP49

35s+15s, Basket weaver. 50s+25s, Boy studying map. 75s+50s, Woman reading Braille.

1956, Jan. 4

B88	SP49	15s + 10s dp grn	.25	.70
B89	SP49	35s + 15s yel brn	.30	.70
B90	SP49	50s + 25s rose car	2.25	1.50
B91	SP49	75s + 50s ultra	1.25	.70
		Nos. B88-B91 (4)	4.05	3.60

The surtax was for the benefit of the blind.

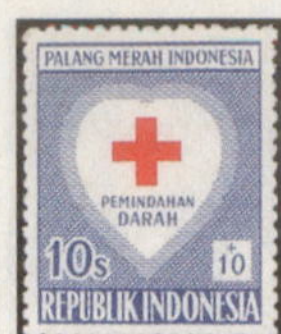

Red Cross and Heart — SP50

Designs: 35s+15s, 50s+15s, Transfusion bottle. 75s+25s, 1r+25s, Outstretched hands.

1956, July 26 Cross in Red Litho.

B92 SP50 10s + 10s ultra .25 .25
B93 SP50 15s + 10s carmine .25 .25
B94 SP50 35s + 15s lt brn .25 .25
B95 SP50 50s + 15s bl grn .25 .25
B96 SP50 75s + 25s orange .40 .30
B97 SP50 1r + 25s brt pur .60 .45
Nos. B92-B97 (6) 2.00 1.75

Surtax for the Indonesian Red Cross.

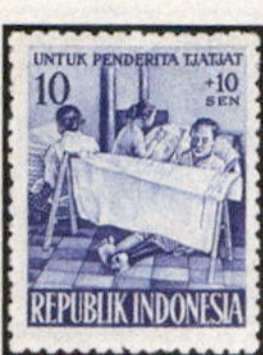

Invalids Doing Batik Work — SP51

Designs: 15s+10s, Amputee painting. 35s+15s, Lathe operator. 50s+15s, Crippled child learning to walk. 75s+25s, Treating amputee. 1r+25s, Painting with artificial hand.

1957, Mar. 26 Photo. *Perf. 12½*

B98 SP51 10s + 10s dp blue .30 .25
B99 SP51 15s + 10s brown .30 .25
B100 SP51 35s + 15s red .30 .25
B101 SP51 50s + 15s dp vio .30 .30
B102 SP51 75s + 25s green .40 .40
B103 SP51 1r + 25s dk car rose .45 *.65*
Nos. B98-B103 (6) 2.05 2.10

The surtax was for rehabilitation of invalids.

Kembodja Flower SP52

Designs: 15s+10s, Michelia. 35s+15s, Sunflower. 50s+15s, Jasmine. 75s+50s, Orchid.

1957, Dec. 23 *Perf. 13½x12½*
Flowers in Natural Colors

B104 SP52 10s + 10s blue 1.40 1.25
B105 SP52 15s + 10s dp yel grn 1.25 1.25
B106 SP52 35s + 15s dk red brn .65 *.95*
B107 SP52 50s + 15s ol & dk brn .40 *.80*
B108 SP52 75s + 50s rose brn .50 *.80*
Nos. B104-B108 (5) 4.20 5.05

Children — SP53

15s+10s, 50s+25s, 1r+50s, Girl and boy.

1958, July 1 Photo. *Perf. 12½x12*

B109 SP53 10s + 10s blue .25 .25
B110 SP53 15s + 10s rose brn .25 .25
B111 SP53 35s + 15s gray green .25 .25
B112 SP53 50s + 25s gray olive .25 .25
B113 SP53 75s + 50s brn car .25 .25
B114 SP53 1r + 50s brown .25 .25
Nos. B109-B114 (6) 1.50 1.50

The surtax was for orphans.

Indonesian Scout Emblem — SP54

Design: 15s + 10s, 50s + 25s, 1r + 50s, Scout emblem and compass.

Emblem in Red

1959, July 17 Photo. Unwmk.

B115 SP54 10s + 5s bister .25 .25
B116 SP54 15s + 10s bluish grn .25 .25
B117 SP54 20s + 10s lilac gray .25 *.30*
B118 SP54 50s + 25s olive .30 *.50*
B119 SP54 75s + 35s yel brn .30 *.50*
B120 SP54 1r + 50s dark gray .30 *.50*
Nos. B115-B120 (6) 1.65 2.30

10th World Scout Jamboree, Makiling National Park near Manila, July 17-26.

Palm-leaf Ribs, Gong and 5 Rings SP55

Young Couple Holding Sharpened Bamboo Weapon SP56

Design: 20s+10s, 75s+35s, Bamboo musical instrument and 5-ring emblem.

1960, Feb. 14 *Perf. 12½x12*

B121 SP55 15s + 5s bis & dk brn .25 .30
B122 SP55 20s + 10s grn & blk .25 .30
B123 SP55 50s + 25s bl & pur .25 .30
B124 SP55 75s + 35s ol & dk grn .25 .30
B125 SP56 1.15r + 50s car & blk .35 .30
Nos. B121-B125 (5) 1.35 1.50

All-Indonesian Youth Cong., Bandung, 2/14-21/60.

Social Emblem — SP57

Designs: 15s+15s, Rice, lotus and cotton. 20s+20s, Lotus blossom and tree. 50s+25s, Girl and boy. 75s+25s, Watering of plant in man's hand. 3r+50s, Woman nursing infant.

Perf. 12½x12
1960, Dec. 20 Photo. Unwmk.
Inscribed: "Hari Sosial Ke III"

B126 SP57 10s + 10s ocher & blk .25 .25
B127 SP57 15s + 15s dp cl & blk .25 .25
B128 SP57 20s + 20s bl & blk .25 .25
B129 SP57 50s + 25s bis brn & blk .25 .30
B130 SP57 75s + 25s emer & blk .25 .30
B131 SP57 3r + 50s red & blk .30 .30
Nos. B126-B131 (6) 1.55 1.65

3rd Social Day, Dec. 20.

Type of 1960 Surcharged: "BENTJANA ALAM 1961"

1961, Feb. 17 *Perf. 12x12½*

B132 A76 15s + 10s plum .25 .25
B133 A76 20s + 15s ocher .25 .25
B134 A76 75s + 25s scarlet .25 .25
Nos. B132-B134 (3) .75 .75

The surtax was for flood relief.

Pineapple — SP58

4th Social Day: 75s+25s, Mangosteen. 3r+1r, Rambutan.

1961, Dec. 20 *Perf. 12½x13½*

B135 SP58 20s + 10s bl, yel & red .40 .50
B136 SP58 75s + 25s gray, grn & dp claret .60 .50
B137 SP58 3r + 1r grn, yel & red 1.00 1.40
Nos. B135-B137 (3) 2.00 2.40

Istiqlal Mosque, Djakarta — SP59

40s+20s, 3r+1r, Different view of mosque.

1962, Feb. 22 *Perf. 12½x12*

B138 SP59 30s + 20s Prus grn & yel .25 .30
B139 SP59 40s + 20s dk red & yel .25 .30
B140 SP59 1.50r + 50s brn & yel .35 .30
B141 SP59 3r + 1r grn & yel .45 .30
Nos. B138-B141 (4) 1.30 1.20

Issued for the benefit of the new Istiqlal Mosque.

National Monument, Djakarta — SP60

1.50r+50s, 6r+1.50r, Aerial view of monument.

1962, May 20 Photo. *Perf. 12x12½*

B142 SP60 1r + 50s org brn & blk .25 .25
B143 SP60 1.50r + 50s ol grn & ultra .25 .25
B144 SP60 3r + 1r lil rose & dk grn .30 .25
B145 SP60 6r + 1.50r vio bl & red .30 .25
Nos. B142-B145 (4) 1.10 1.00

Vanda Tricolor SP61

Orchids: 1.50r+50s, Phalaenopsis amabilis, vert. 3r+1r, Dendrobium phalaenopsis, vert. 6r+1.50r, Paphiopedilum praestans.

Perf. 13½x12½, 12½x13½
1962, Dec. 20 Unwmk.
Orchids in Natural Colors

B146 SP61 1r + 50s ultra & yel .35 .25
B147 SP61 1.50r + 50s grnsh bl & ver .35 .25
B148 SP61 3r + 1r dp bl & ocher .35 .25
B149 SP61 6r + 1.50r org & dl vio .40 .25
Nos. B146-B149 (4) 1.45 1.00

Issued for the 5th Social Day.

West Irian Monument, Djakarta — SP62

1963, Feb. 15 *Perf. 12½x13½*

B150 SP62 1r + 50s rose red & blk .25 .25
B151 SP62 1.50r + 50s mag & dk brn .25 .25
B152 SP62 3r + 1r bl & dk brn .25 .25
B153 SP62 6r + 1.50r grn & brn .25 .25
Nos. B150-B153 (4) 1.00 1.00

The surtax was for the construction of the West Irian Monument in Djakarta.

Erupting Volcano SP63

1963, June 29 Photo. *Perf. 13½x13*

B154 SP63 4r + 2r rose red .25 .25
B155 SP63 6r + 3r grnsh bl .25 .25

The surtax was for victims of national natural disasters.

Papilio Blumei, Celebes — SP64

Butterflies: 4r+1r, Charaxes dehaani, Java. 6r+1.50r, Graphium, West Irian. 12r+3r, Troides amphrysus, Sumatra.

1963, Dec. 20 *Perf. 12x12½*

B156 SP64 1.75r + 50s multi .30 .25
B157 SP64 4r + 1r multi .30 .25
B158 SP64 6r + 1.50r multi .30 .25
B159 SP64 12r + 3r multi .50 .40
Nos. B156-B159 (4) 1.40 1.15

Issued for the 6th Social Day.

Malaysian Fantails — SP65

Birds: 6r+1.50r, Zebra doves. 12r+3r, Black drongos. 20r+5r, Black-naped orioles. 30r+7.50r, Javanese sparrows.

Perf. 12½x13½
1965, Jan. 25 Photo. Unwmk.

B160 SP65 4r + 1r dl yel, lil & blk .25 .25
B161 SP65 6r + 1.50 grn, blk & pink .25 .25
B162 SP65 12r + 3r ol & blk .35 .30
B163 SP65 20r + 5r gray, yel & red .40 .40
B164 SP65 30r + 7.50r car rose, sl bl & blk .65 .40
Nos. B160-B164 (5) 1.90 1.60

Issued for the 7th Social Day.

Type of Regular Issue, 1964, Inscribed Vertically "Conefo"

1965 *Perf. 12½x12*

B165 A98 1r + 1r org red & brn .25 .25
B166 A98 1.25r + 1.25r org red & brn .25 .25
B167 A98 1.75r + 1.75r org, red & brn blk .25 .25
B168 A98 2r + 2r org red & sl grn .25 .25
B169 A98 2.50r + 2.50r org red & red brn .25 .25
B170 A98 4r + 3.50r org red & dp bl .25 .25
B171 A98 6r + 4r org red & emer .25 .25
B172 A98 10r + 5r org red & yel grn .25 .25
B173 A98 12r + 5.50r org red & org .25 .25
B174 A98 15r + 7.50r org red & bl grn .25 .25
B175 A98 20r + 10r org red & dk gray .25 .25

B176 A98 25r + 10r org red & pur .25 .25
B177 A98 40r + 15r ver & plum .25 .25
B178 A98 50r + 15r org red & dp vio .25 .25
B179 A98 100r + 25r org red & dk ol gray .25 .25
Nos. B165-B179 (15) 3.75 3.75

Conference of New Emerging Forces.

Makara Mask and Magic Rays — SP66

1965, July 17 ***Perf. 12***

B180 SP66 20r + 10r red & dk bl .35 .25
B181 SP66 30r + 15r bl & dk red .35 .25

Issued to publicize the fight against cancer.

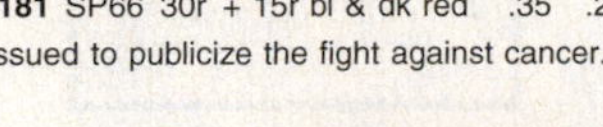

Family and Produce SP67

State Principles: 20r+10r, Humanitarianism; clasped hands, globe, flags and chain. 25r+10r, Nationalism; map of Indonesia and tree. 40r+15r, Democracy; conference and bull's head. 50r+15r, Belief in God; houses of worship and star.

1965, Aug. 17 **Photo.** ***Perf. 12½***

B182 SP67 10r + 5r fawn, yel & blk .35 .25
B183 SP67 20r + 10r dp yel, red & blk .25 .25
B184 SP67 25r + 10r rose red, red, grn & blk .25 .25
B185 SP67 40r + 15r bl, red & blk .40 .25
B186 SP67 50r + 15r lil, yel & blk .40 .25
Nos. B182-B186 (5) 1.65 1.25

Samudra Beach Hotel and Pres. Sukarno — SP68

Designs: 25r+10r, 80r+20r, Ambarrukmo Palace Hotel and Pres. Sukarno.

1965, Dec. 1 **Photo.** ***Perf. 12½***

B187 SP68 10r + 5r dk bl & lt bl grn .25 .25
B188 SP68 25r + 10r vio blk & yel grn .25 .25
B189 SP68 40r + 15r dk brn & vio bl .30 .30
B190 SP68 80r + 20r dk pur & org .35 .30
Nos. B187-B190 (4) 1.15 1.10

Issued for tourist publicity.

Gloriosa — SP69

40r+15r, Magaguabush. 80r+20r, Balsam. 100r+25r, Crape myrtle.

1965, Dec. 20 **Photo.** ***Perf. 12***

Flowers in Natural Colors

B191 SP69 30r + 10r deep blue .30 .95
B192 SP69 40r + 15r deep blue .40 .95
B193 SP69 80r + 20r deep blue .45 .95
B194 SP69 100r + 25r deep blue .50 .95
Nos. B191-B194 (4) 1.65 3.80

Dated "1966"

10s+5s, Senna. 20s+5s, Crested barleria. 30s+10s, Scarlet ixora. 40s+10s, Rose of China (hibiscus).

1966, Feb. 10

Flowers in Natural Colors

B195 SP69 10s + 5s Prus bl .30 .95
B196 SP69 20s + 5s grn .40 .95
B197 SP69 30s + 10s grn .45 .95
B198 SP69 40s + 10s Prus bl .55 .95
Nos. B195-B198 (4) 1.70 3.80

Nos. B191-B198 issued for the 8th Social Day, Dec. 20, 1965. An imperf. souvenir sheet contains one No. B198. Size: 58x78mm. Value, $6.

Type of 1965 Inscribed: "BENTJANA ALAM / NASIONAL 1966"

15s+5s, Gloriosa. 25s+5s, Magaguabush. 30s+10s, Balsam. 80s+20s, Crape myrtle.

1966, May 2

Flowers in Natural Colors

B199 SP69 15s + 5s blue .30 .65
B200 SP69 25s + 5s dk bl .35 .65
B201 SP69 30s + 10s dk bl .45 .65
B202 SP69 80s + 20s lt bl .55 .65
Nos. B199-B202 (4) 1.65 2.60

The surtax was for victims of national natural disasters.

Reticulated Python — SP70

Reptiles: 3r+50s, Bloodsucker. 4r+75s. Saltwater crocodile. 6r+1r, Hawksbill turtle (incorrectly inscribed *chelonia mydas,* "green turtle").

1966, Dec. 20 **Photo.** ***Perf. 12½x12***

B203 SP70 2r + 25s multi .30 .30
B204 SP70 3r + 50s multi .30 .30
B205 SP70 4r + 75s multi .35 .30
B206 SP70 6r + 1r multi .55 .30
Nos. B203-B206 (4) 1.50 1.20

Flooded Village — SP71

2.50r+25s, Landslide. 4r+40s, Fire destroying village. 5r+50s, Erupting volcano.

1967, Dec. 20 **Photo.** ***Perf. 12½***

B207 SP71 1.25r + 10s dl vio bl & yel .30 .40
B208 SP71 2.50r + 25s dl vio bl & yel .30 .40
B209 SP71 4r + 40s dp org & blk .30 .40
B210 SP71 5r + 50s dp org & blk .30 .40
a. Souv. sheet of 2, #B209-B210 30.00 45.00
Nos. B207-B210 (4) 1.20 1.60

Surtax for victims of natl. natural disasters.

Buddha & Stupa, Borobudur Temple — SP72

Designs: No. B211, Musicians. No. B212, Sudhana and Princess Manohara. No. B213, Procession with elephant and horses.

1968, Mar. 1 **Photo.** ***Perf. 12½***

B211 SP72 2.50r + 25s brt grn & gray ol .35 .30
B212 SP72 2.50r + 25s brt grn & gray ol .35 .30
B213 SP72 2.50r + 25s brt grn & gray ol .35 .30
a. Souv. sheet of 3, #B211-B213 30.00 40.00
b. Strip of 3, #B211-B213 1.50 1.50
B214 SP72 7.50r + 75s org & gray ol .55 .30
Nos. B211-B214 (4) 1.60 1.20

The surtax was to help save Borobudur Temple in Central Java, c. 800 A.D.

No. B213b has continuous design showing a frieze from Borobudur.

Scout with Pickax — SP73

Designs: 10r+1r, Bugler. 30r+3r, Scouts singing around campfire, horiz.

1968, June 1 **Photo.** ***Perf. 12½***

Size: 28½x44½mm

B215 SP73 5r + 50 dp org & brn .35 .30
B216 SP73 10r + 1r brn & gray ol .50 .50

Size: 68x28½mm

B217 SP73 30r + 3r ol gray & grn .65 .65
Nos. B215-B217 (3) 1.50 1.45

Surtax for Wirakarya Scout Camp.

Woman with Flower SP74

1969, Apr. 21 ***Perf. 13½x12½***

B218 SP74 20r + 2r emer, red & yel .75 .40

Emancipation of Indonesian women.

Noble Voluta — SP75

Sea shells: 7.50r+50s, Common hairy triton. 10r+1r, Spider conch. 15r+1.50r, Murex ternispina.

1969, Dec. 20 **Photo.** ***Perf. 12½***

B219 SP75 5r + 50s multi .40 .55
B220 SP75 7.50r + 50s multi .45 .55
B221 SP75 10r + 1r multi .75 .80
B222 SP75 15r + 1.50r multi .65 .80
Nos. B219-B222 (4) 2.25 2.70

Issued for the 12th Social Day, Dec. 20.

Chrysocoris Javanus SP76

Insects: 15r+1.50r, Dragonfly. 20r+2r, Carpenter bee.

1970, Dec. 21 **Photo.** ***Perf. 12½***

B223 SP76 7.50r + 50c multi 5.00 1.60
B224 SP76 15r + 1.50r multi 10.50 8.00
B225 SP76 20r + 2r multi 14.50 5.50
Nos. B223-B225 (3) 30.00 15.10

The 13th Social Day, Dec. 20.

Fight Against Cancer — SP77

Patient receiving radiation treatment, Jakarta Hospital.

1983, July 1 **Photo.** ***Perf. 12½***

B226 SP77 55r + 20r multi .70 .50
B227 SP77 75r + 25r multi 1.00 .50

Children's Day SP78

Children's Drawings. Surtax was for Children's Palace building fund.

1984, June 17 **Photo.** ***Perf. 13½x13***

B228 SP78 75r + 25r multi 1.10 .25
B229 SP78 110r + 25r multi .75 .25
B230 SP78 175r + 25r multi 1.75 .40
B231 SP78 275r + 25r multi 1.75 .40
a. Souv. sheet of 2, #B230-B231 45.00 45.00
b. Souv. sheet of 4 + 2 labels 20.00 20.00
Nos. B228-B231 (4) 5.35 1.30

AUSIPEX '84. No. B231b for FILACENTO '84, Netherlands, Sept. 6-9.

SP79

1987, May 12 **Photo.** ***Perf. 12½***

B232 SP79 350r +25r dark ultra & yel 1.50 .50

Yayasan Cancer Medical Assoc., 10th anniv.

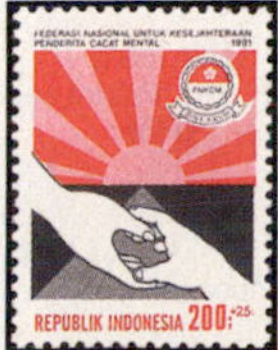

SP80

1991, June 1 **Photo.** ***Perf. 12½***

B233 SP80 200r +25r multi 1.25 .30

Natl. Fed. for Welfare of Mentally Handicapped, 24th anniv.

Yayasan Cancer Medical Assoc., 15th Anniv. — SP81

1992, May 12 Photo. *Perf. 12½*
B234 SP81 200r +25r brn & mag .50 .25
B235 SP81 500r +50r bl & mag 1.00 .30

Natl. Kidney Foundation — SP82

Perf. 13½x12½
1994, Apr. 30 Photo.
B236 SP82 300r +30r multi .60 .30

Rehabilitation Intl., 10th Asia & Pacific Regional Conference — SP83

Design: 700r+100r, Painting, Mother's Love, by disabled artist Patricia Saerang.

Perf. 13½x12½
1995, Sept. 12 Photo.
B238 SP83 700r +100r multi 1.25 .85

March 1, 1949, Day of Total Attack SP84

Designs: No. B239, Natl. flag, tanks, map. No. B240, Soldiers fighting, soldiers standing at attention, natl. flag.

1996, Mar. 1 Photo. *Perf. 13½x12½*
B239 SP84 700r +100r multi 1.25 .65
B240 SP84 700r +100r multi 1.25 .65
a. Pair, #B239-B240 2.75 1.60

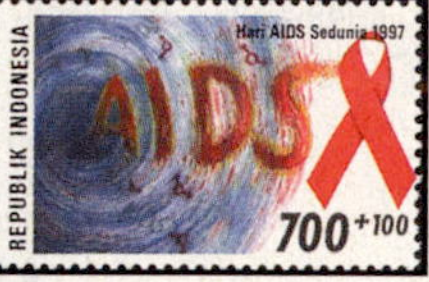

World AIDS Day SP85

1997, Dec. 1 Photo. *Perf. 13½x12½*
B241 SP85 700r +100r multi 1.00 .50

PETA (Pembela Tanah Air) Volunteer Army — SP86

Perf. 12½x13½
1998, Nov. 10 Litho.
B242 SP86 700r Statue, museum .65 .25

National Disaster Fund — SP87

2005, May 20 Litho. *Perf. 12½*
B243 SP87 1500r +300r multi + label 1.00 .65

Surtax for victims of Dec. 26, 2004 tsunami.

International Red Cross, 150th Anniv. — SP88

No. B244: a, Jean Henri Dunant (1828-1910), founder of Red Cross, flags (1/2). b, Helicopter, boat, Red Cross worker carrying man (2/2).

2013, May 8 *Perf. 13½x12¾*
B244 SP88 2500r +500r Pair, #a-b 2.00 1.50

AIR POST STAMPS

Airplane, Marshal Surydarma AP1

Airplane Over Buffalo Canyon AP2

Designs: 10s, Airplane, Air Chief Marshal Suryadi Surydarma. 20s, Sentry and aircraft, Lake Toba, Sumatra. 30s, Pilots. 40c, Indian Red Cross plane, Sumatra. 50s, Red Cross plane. 75s, Airplane over Buffalo Canyon. 1r, Crew studying flight plan. 1½r, Aircraft over Tjipanas Fish Ponds, Java. 4½r, DC-3 over rice fields. 7½r, DC-4 over Indonesian Archipelago.

Nos. C10, C12 and C13 are overprinted ("POS UDARA" and Airplane) on Nos. 22-24.

Perf. 14½, 12½ (#C10, C12, C13)
1948, Dec. 15 Photo.
C1 AP1 10s dk lilac & brn .35 —
C2 AP1 20s Pruss grn & org red .40 —
C3 AP1 30s dp blue & dull lil .45 —
C4 AP1 40s red brn & blue emerald .25 —
C5 AP1 50s dp vio & dull bl .25 —
C6 AP2 75s dp brn & org brn .75 —
C7 AP1 1r dp choc & pur brn .90 —
C8 AP2 1½r dk vio & dp yel brn 3.00 —
C9 AP2 4½r Pruss grn & dl pur 2.25 —
C10 A32 5r yel brn & black 10.00 —
C11 AP1 7½r brn & slate vio 5.00 —
C12 A32 10r emerald & black 12.50 —
C13 A32 25r rose red & black 15.00 —
Nos. C1-C13 (13) 51.10

AP3

Designs: 30s, 1r, Map, ships. 50s, Harbor scene, vert. 2½r, 4½r, Ships.

1949, Aug. 17 Photo. *Perf. 12½*
C14 AP3 30s blue & orange 1.75 —
C15 AP3 50s green & orange 3.00 —
C16 AP3 1r brn & green 1.90 —
C17 AP3 2½r blk & dull grn 7.50 —
C18 AP3 4½r blue & rose red 22.50 —
Nos. C14-C18 (5) 36.65

Failure of Dutch blockade.

Nos. 51-53 Ovptd. "POS UDARA" and airplaine and

Airplane, Indonesian Archipelago — AP4

DC-3 Over Rice Fields — AP5

Designs: 10s, DC-4 over Indonesian Archipelago. 20s, Aircraft mechanics working on plane. 30s, Servicing plane on runway. 40c, Pilots. 50s, Briefing pilots. 75s, Sentry and aircraft, Lake Toba, Sumatra. 1r, Plane, mountain in Sumatra. 4½r, Airplane over Buffalo Canyon. 7½r, Aircraft over Tjipanas Fish Ponds, Java.

Perf. 14½, 12½ (#C10, C12, C13)
1949, Aug. 17 Photo.
C19 AP4 10s pur & lt blue .50 —
C20 AP5 20s brn & sl blue 1.00 —
C21 AP4 30s red brn & bl grn 2.00 —
C22 AP4 40s dk brn & pur 1.50 —
C23 AP4 50s dp bl grn & red brn 3.50 —
C24 AP4 75s bl grn & brn .95 —
C25 AP4 1r pur & dk grn 1.25 —
C26 AP5 1½r blk bl & org 3.00 —
C27 AP5 4½r pur & chestnut 3.50 —
C28 A38 5r On No. 51 3.50 —
C29 AP5 7½r dk grn & vio brn 3.50 —
C30 A38 10r On No. 52 6.00 —
C31 A38 25r On No. 53 17.50 —
Nos. C19-C31 (13) 47.70

AP6

Designs: 50s, Map, airplanes, horiz. 30s, 1r, Harbor scene. 2½r, Airplane on runway, horiz. 4½r, Airplane landing, horiz.

1949 Photo. *Perf. 14½*
C32 AP6 30s multicolored 1.75 —
C33 AP6 50s multicolored 2.00 —
C34 AP6 1r multicolored 1.25 —
C35 A39 2½r multicolored 2.00 —
C36 A39 4½r multicolored 3.50 —
Nos. C32-C36 (5) 10.50

Liberation of Jakarta

Nos. C1-C9, C11 Overprinted

1949, Dec. 7
C37 AP1 10s dk lilac & brn .35 —
C38 AP1 20s Pruss grn & org red .35 —
C39 AP1 30s dp blue & dull lil .35 —
C40 AP1 40s red brn & blue emerald 15.00 —
C41 AP1 50s dp vio & dull bl .55 —
C42 AP2 75s dp brn & org brn .55 —
C43 AP2 1r dp choc & pur brn 1.25 —
C44 AP2 1½r dk vio & dp yel brn 1.40 —
C45 AP2 4½r Pruss grn & dl pur 2.00 —
C46 AP1 7½r brn & slate vio 15.00 —
Nos. C37-C46 (10) 36.80

Nos. C19-C27, C29 Overprinted

C47 AP4 10s pur & lt blue .25 —
C48 AP5 20s brn & sl blue 1.25 —
C49 AP4 30s red brn & bl grn .30 —
C50 AP4 40s dk brn & pur 1.10 —
C51 AP4 50s dp bl grn & red brn .30 —
C52 AP4 75s bl grn & brn .30 —
C53 AP4 1r pur & dk grn 1.50 —
C54 AP4 1½r blk bl & org 2.00 —
C55 AP5 4½r pur & chestnut 2.50 —
C56 AP5 7½r dk grn & vio brn 2.75 —
Nos. C47-C56 (10) 12.25

Nos. C32-C36 Overprinted

C57 AP6 30s multicolored 5.00 —
C58 AP6 50s multicolored 3.00 —
C59 AP6 1r multicolored 3.00 —
C60 A39 2½r multicolored 4.50 —
C61 A39 4½r multicolored 6.50 —
Nos. C57-C61 (5) 22.00

AIR POST SPECIAL DELIVERY STAMPS

Aircraft Over Beach APSD1

Perf. 14½
1948, Dec. 15 Photo. Unwmk.
CE1 APSD1 40s dk brn & blue emerald .80 —

Type APSD1, inscribed "REPUBLIK"

1948, Dec. 15 *Perf. 13½x14*
CE2 APSD1 40s brn & blue emer .75 —

No. CE1, Overprinted "Merdeka Djojakarta 6 Djuli 1949"

1949, Dec. 7
CE3 APSD1 40s brn & blue emer .75 —

No. CE2 Overprinted

1949, Dec. 7
CE4 APSD1 40s brn & blue emer 10.00 —

AIR POST OFFICIAL STAMPS

Nos. C1, C3, C5, C7 Overprinted

1948, Dec. 15
CO1 AP1 10s dk lilac & brown 1.25 —
CO2 AP1 30s dp blue & dull lil 2.00 —
CO3 AP1 50s dp vio & dull blue 2.25 —
CO4 AP1 1r dp choc & pur brn 5.00 —
Nos. CO1-CO4 (4) 10.50

Nos. C19//C25 Overprinted

1949, Aug. 17
CO5 AP4 10s pur & lt blue 3.50 —
CO6 AP4 30s red brn & bl grn 2.00 —
CO7 AP4 50s dp bl grn & red brn 4.50 —
CO8 AP4 1r pur & dk grn 3.25 —
Nos. CO5-CO8 (4) 13.25

Nos. CO1-CO4 Overprinted

1949, Dec. 7
CO9 AP1 10s dk lilac & brown 3.00 —
CO10 AP1 30s dp blue & dull lil 6.50 —
CO11 AP1 50s dp vio & dull bl 3.50 —
CO12 AP1 1r dp choc & pur brn 3.00 —
Nos. CO9-CO12 (4) 16.00

Nos. CO5-CO8 Overprinted

1949, Dec. 7
CO13 AP4 10s pur & lt blue 2.00 —
CO14 AP4 30s red brn & bl grn 10.00 —
CO15 AP4 50s dp bl grn & red brn 1.25 —
CO16 AP4 1r pur & dk grn 3.50 —
Nos. CO13-CO16 (4) 16.75

SPECIAL DELIVERY STAMPS

Train & Minangkabau House — SD1

Perf. 13½x14¼
1948, Dec. 15 Unwmk. Photo.
E1 SD1 10s dp bluish grn & chestnut .35 —
E1A SD1 15s ches & steel bl .50 —

Type SD1, Inscribed "REPUBLIK"
1949, Aug. 17
E1B SD1 10s red brn & dp blue .50 —
E1C SD1 15s turq & dk yel brn .35 —

Nos. E1-E1A Overprinted

1949, Dec. 7
E1D SD1 10s dp bluish grn & chestnut .40 —
E1E SD1 15s ches & steel bl .90 —

Nos. E1B-E1C Overprinted "Merdeka Djojakarta 6 Djuli 1949"
1949, Dec. 7
E1F SD1 10s red brn & dp blue .40 —
E1G SD1 15s urq & dk yel brn .75 —

Garuda SD2

Perf. 13½x12½
1967 Unwmk. Photo.
E1H SD2 10r lt ultra & dl pur .50 .25
E2 SD2 15r org & dl pur .70 .50

1968 Inscribed "1968"
E3 SD2 10r lt ultra & dl pur .60 .25
E4 SD2 15r org & dl pur .70 .25
E5 SD2 20r yel & dl pur .70 .25
E6 SD2 30r brt grn & dl pur 1.10 .60
E7 SD2 40r lil & dl pur .90 .25
Nos. E3-E7 (5) 4.00 1.60

1969 Same Inscribed "1969"
E8 SD2 20r yel & dl pur .50 .25
E9 SD2 30r brt grn & dl pur .50 .25
E10 SD2 40r lil & dl pur .65 .25
Nos. E8-E10 (3) 1.65 .75

POSTAGE DUE STAMPS

D1

Perf. 13¾x14, 14½ (#J8-J13)
1948 Unwmk.
J1 D1 1s blue & brn .30 —
J2 D1 2½s dk brn & dk pur .45 —
J3 D1 3½s pur & lt grn .25 —
J4 D1 5s dk grn & brn .40 —
J5 D1 7½s dk brn & dk grn .50 —
J6 D1 10s dk pur & brn .45 —
J7 D1 20s brn & org yel 1.25 —
J8 D1 25s dk pur & dk brn 1.50 —
J9 D1 30s blue & car red 1.25 —
J10 D1 40s blue & org yel 1.50 —
J11 D1 50s lt brn & pur 2.00 —
J12 D1 75s dk bl & dk grn 3.50 —
J13 D1 1r brn & green 4.00 —
Nos. J1-J13 (13) 17.35

As Type D1, inscribed "REPUBLIK"
Perf. 13¾x14, 14½ (#J8-J13)
1949, Aug. 17 Unwmk.
J14 D1 1s dk blue & brn 35.00 —
J15 D1 2½s brn & pur 35.00 —
J16 D1 3½s pur & grn 35.00 —
J17 D1 5s dk grn & brn 35.00 —
J18 D1 7½s dk brn & dk grn 35.00 —
J19 D1 10s pur & brn 35.00 —
J20 D1 20s dk brn & yel 35.00 —
J21 D1 25s vio & dk pur 35.00 —
J22 D1 30s blue & red 35.00 —
J23 D1 40s blue & yel 35.00 —
J24 D1 50s brn & pur 35.00 —
J25 D1 75s dk bl & dk grn 35.00 —
J26 D1 1r dk brn & green 35.00 —
Nos. J14-J26 (13) 455.00

Nos. J1-J13 Overprinted

1949, Dec. 7
J27 D1 1s blue & brn 1.25 —
J28 D1 2½s dk brn & dk pur .65 —
J29 D1 3½s pur & lt grn .75 —
J30 D1 5s dk grn & brn .75 —
J31 D1 7½s dk brn & dk grn 1.25 —
J32 D1 10s dk pur & brn .35 —
J33 D1 20s brn & org yel 10.00 —
J34 D1 25s dk pur & dk brn 4.60 —
J35 D1 30s blue & car red 15.00 —
J36 D1 40s blue & org yel 20.00 —
J37 D1 50s lt brn & pur 9.00 —
J38 D1 75s dk bl & dk grn 25.00 —
J39 D1 1r brn & green 20.00 —
Nos. J27-J39 (13) 108.50

Netherlands Indies Nos. J57 to J59 Surcharged in Black

1950 Wmk. 228 *Perf. 14½x14*
J60 D7 2½s on 50c yellow 1.10 .50
J61 D7 5s on 100c apple grn 2.60 .75
J62 D7 10s on 75c aqua 7.00 1.75
Nos. J60-J62 (3) 10.70 3.00

D8

Wmk. 228
1951-52 Litho. *Perf. 12½*
J63 D8 2½s vermilion .25 .50
J64 D8 5s vermilion .25 .25
J65 D8 10s vermilion .25 .25
J66 D8 20s blue ('52) .25 .25
J67 D8 25s olive bister ('52) .85 .50
J68 D8 50s vermilion 11.50 1.00
J69 D8 1r citron 1.90 1.75
Nos. J63-J69 (7) 15.25 4.50

1953-55 Unwmk.
J70 D8 15s lt magenta ('55) .25 .25
J71 D8 30s red brown .25 .25
J72 D8 40s green .25 .25
Nos. J70-J72 (3) .75 .75

1958-61 *Perf. 13½x12½*
J73 D8 10s orange .30 .55
J74 D8 15s orange ('59) .30 .55
J74A D8 20s orange ('61) .30 .55
J75 D8 25s orange .30 .55
J76 D8 30s orange ('60) .30 .55
J77 D8 50s orange 1.75 .55
J78 D8 100s orange ('60) 1.00 .55
Nos. J73-J78 (7) 4.25 3.85

1962-65 *Perf. 13½x12½*
J79 D8 50s light bluish green .25 .25
J80 D8 100s bister .25 .25
J81 D8 250s blue .25 .25
J82 D8 500s dull yellow .25 .25
J83 D8 750s pale lilac .25 .25
J84 D8 1000s salmon .25 .25
J85 D8 50r red ('65) .25 .25
J86 D8 100r maroon ('65) .25 .25
Nos. J79-J86 (8) 2.00 2.00

"1966" — D9

1966-67 Unwmk. Photo.
J91 D9 5s dl grn & dl yel .30 .25
J92 D9 10s red & lt bl .30 .25
J93 D9 20s dk bl & pink .30 .25
J94 D9 30s brn & rose .30 .25
J95 D9 40s plum & bis .30 .25
J96 D9 50s ol grn & pale lil .30 .25
J97 D9 100s dk red & yel grn .30 .25
J98 D9 200s brt grn & pink ('67) .30 .25
J99 D9 500s yel & lt bl ('67) .30 .25
J100 D9 1000s rose lil & yel ('67) .30 .30
Nos. J91-J100 (10) 3.00 2.55

1967 Dated "1967"
J101 D9 50s ol grn & pale lil .30 .30
J102 D9 100s dk red & yel grn .30 .30
J103 D9 200s brt grn & pink .30 .30
J104 D9 500s yel & lt bl .60 .40
J105 D9 1000s rose lil & yel .60 .40
J106 D9 15r org & gray 1.25 .60
J107 D9 25r lil & citron 2.00 1.00
Nos. J101-J107 (7) 5.35 3.30

Similar stamps inscribed "Bajar" or "Bayar", year date and "Sumbangan Ongkos Tjetak" or ". . . Cetak" are revenues.

Inscribed "BAYAR PORTO"
1973 Dated "1973"
J108 D9 25r lilac & citron 1.40 .30

Inscribed "BAYAR PORTO"
1974 Dated "1974"
J109 D9 65r olive grn & bister 1.90 .50
J110 D9 125r lil & pale pink 4.00 1.50

Dated "1975"
Inscribed "BAYAR PORTO"
1975 Photo. *Perf. 13½x12½*
J111 D9 25r lilac & citron 1.50 1.00

"1976" — D10

1976
J112 D10 15r vermilion & dull gray 1.50 2.00
J112A D10 25r violet & dl yel .50 .70
J112B D10 65r olive grn & bister 1.00 1.25
J112C D10 125r red lil & pale pink 2.00 5.00

1977 Dated "1977"
J113 D10 100r dp vio & pale pink .75 .30
J114 D10 200r brt bl & lt lil .80 .30
J115 D10 300r choc & lt sal 1.25 .50
J116 D10 400r brt grn & tan 1.50 .60
J117 D10 500r red & tan 1.75 .75
Nos. J113-J117 (5) 6.05 2.45

See Nos. J138, J139, J142.

Nos. 706, 709, 712-713, 716, 718 Surcharged in Red

1978 Photo. Perf. 12½x12

J118	A110	25r on 1r	.40	.40
J119	A110	50r on 2r	.40	.40
J120	A110	100r on 4r	1.00	1.00
J121	A110	200r on 5r	1.50	1.50
J122	A110	300r on 10r	2.25	2.25
J123	A110	400r on 15r	2.50	2.50
		Nos. J118-J123 (6)	8.05	8.05

Surcharged in Black

J124	A110	25r on 1r	.50	.50
J125	A110	50r on 2r	.50	.50
J126	A110	100r on 4r	1.00	1.00
J127	A110	200r on 5r	1.50	1.50
J128	A110	300r on 10r	2.50	2.50
J129	A110	400r on 15r	3.50	3.50
		Nos. J124-J129 (6)	9.50	9.50

Nos. 710, 717 Surcharged

1978 Photo. Perf. 12½x12

J130	A110	40r on 2.50r	1.50	1.50
J131	A110	40r on 12r	1.00	1.00
J132	A110	65r on 2.50r	1.50	1.50
J133	A110	65r on 12r	2.50	2.50
J134	A110	125r on 2.50r	1.50	1.50
J135	A110	125r on 12r	3.50	3.50
J136	A110	150r on 2.50r	3.00	3.00
J137	A110	150r on 12r	1.00	1.00
		Nos. J130-J137 (8)	15.50	15.50

Type of 1976 Dated "1979"

1979 Perf. 13½x12½

J138	D10	25r lilac & citron	1.00	.25

Type of 1976 and

D11

Perf. 13½x12½, 13½x13 (#J144-J148, J150-J153), 14½x13 (#J154-J156A)

1980-90 Photo. Dated "1980"

J139	D10	25r dk lil & beige	.25	.25
J140	D11	50r multi	.50	.50
J141	D11	75r rose lake & rose	.90	.80
J142	D10	125r rose lil & lt pink	1.25	1.00
		Nos. J139-J142 (4)	2.90	2.55

Dated "1981"

J144	D11	25r brt vio & pale yel grn	.30	.30
J145	D11	50r sl grn & lt vio	.45	.45
J146	D11	75r rose vio & pink	.75	.75
J147	D11	125r pur & yel grn	1.25	1.25
		Nos. J144-J147 (4)	2.75	2.75

Dated "1982"

J148	D11	125r dp rose lil & pink	4.00	.50

Dated "1983"

J149	D11	125r dp rose & lil pink	.30	.30
J150	D11	200r dp vio & lt bl	.60	.30
J151	D11	300r dk grn & cit	.75	.30
J152	D11	400r ol grn & brn ol	1.00	.50
J153	D11	500r sepia & beige	1.25	.75
		Nos. J149-J153 (5)	3.90	2.15

Dated "1984"

J154	D11	25r brt vio & pale yel grn	.75	.30
J155	D11	50r sl grn & lt vio	.90	.50
J156	D11	125r rose lil & lt pink	2.00	.30
J156A	D11	500r sepia & beige	7.50	1.25
		Nos. J154-J156A (4)	11.15	2.35

Dated "1988"

J157	D11	1000r dp vio & gray	1.00	.75
J158	D11	2000r red & dp rose lil	1.75	1.25
J159	D11	3000r brn & dl org	2.50	2.00
J160	D11	5000r grn & bl grn	5.00	2.50
		Nos. J157-J160 (4)	10.25	6.50

Dated "1990"

J161	D11	2000r emer & brt yel	3.50	2.50
J162	D11	3000r dk bl grn & rose lil	5.00	3.50
J163	D11	4000r brn vio & brt yel grn	9.00	6.50
		Nos. J161-J163 (3)	17.50	12.50

OFFICIAL STAMPS

Nos. 2//16 Overprinted

1948, Dec. 15

O1	A28	2s dp brn & dp blue	.35	—
O2	A28	5s turq & dull blue	.50	—
O3	A28	10s dp blue & brn rose	.45	—
O4	A28	15s brown & dk grn	.35	—
O5	A31	30s dk brn & dull vio	3.00	—
O6	A30	50s dk brn & turq	.75	—
		Nos. O1-O6 (6)	5.40	

Nos. 31//45 Overprinted

1949, Aug. 17

O7	A35	2s dk red vio & dp grn	.35	—
O8	A35	5s dk yel brn & dull vio	.35	—
O9	A34	10s dk brn & dp vio	1.00	—
O10	A35	15s dk vio & dp dull grn	1.50	—
O11	A36	30s dp brn & dk blue vio	.75	—
O12	A37	50s dk brn & Prus grn	2.50	—
		Nos. O7-O12 (6)	6.45	

Nos. O1-O6 Overprinted

1948, Dec. 15

O13	A28	2s dp brn & dp blue	.75	—
O14	A28	5s turq & dull blue	1.60	—
O15	A28	10s dp blue & brn rose	1.60	—
O16	A28	15s brown & dk grn	1.60	—
O17	A31	30s dk brn & dull vio	4.00	—
O18	A30	50s dk brn & turq	4.00	—
		Nos. O13-O18 (6)	13.55	

Nos. O7-O12 Overprinted

1948, Dec. 15

O19	A35	2s dk red vio & dp grn	1.00	—
O20	A35	5s dk yel brn & dull vio	.45	—
O21	A34	10s dk brn & dp vio	.45	—
O22	A35	15s dk vio & dp dull grn	1.00	—
O23	A36	30s dp brn & dk blue vio	2.50	—
O24	A37	50s dk brn & Pruss grn	4.00	—
		Nos. O19-O24 (6)	9.40	

RIAU ARCHIPELAGO

(Riouw Archipelago)
100 Sen = 1 Rupiah
(1 rupiah = 1 Malayan dollar)

Indonesia Nos. 371-386 Overprinted in Black

a

b

Overprint "a"

1954 Unwmk. Perf. 12½

1	A52	5s car rose	67.50	57.50
2	A52	7½s green	1.50	1.50
3	A52	10s blue	80.00	80.00
4	A52	15s purple	3.00	3.00
5	A52	20s rose red	3.00	3.00
6	A52	25s dp green	150.00	42.50

Overprint "b"

7	A53	30s red orange	6.00	6.00
8	A53	35s purple	1.50	1.50
9	A53	40s dull green	1.50	1.50
10	A53	45s dp claret	1.50	1.50
11	A53	50s brown	525.00	100.00
12	A54	60s dk brown	1.50	1.50
13	A54	70s gray	2.75	2.75
14	A54	75s ultra	12.00	3.25
15	A54	80s claret	2.40	3.50
16	A54	90s gray green	2.40	3.50

Netherlands Indies Nos. 325-330 Overprinted Type "a" in Black

17	A46	1r purple	15.00	5.25
18	A46	2r olive grn	3.25	6.00
19	A46	3r red violet	5.25	6.00
20	A46	5r dk brown	5.25	6.00
21	A46	10r gray	6.75	10.00
22	A46	25r orange brn	6.75	10.00
		Nos. 1-22 (22)	903.80	355.75

Mint values are for stamps with somewhat tropicalized gum (stained brown and cracked). Stamps with clean, clear gum sell for about twice as much.

Indonesia Nos. 424-428, 450 and 430 Overprinted Type "b" or

1957-64 Photo. Perf. 12½x13½

23	A63(b)	5s dp ultra	.90	.90
24	A63	10s yellow brn	13.00	10.00
25	A63(b)	10s yellow brn	.90	.90
26	A63(b)	15s rose vio ('64)	.90	*.90*
27	A63(b)	20s dull grn ('60)	.90	.90
27A	A63	25s dp claret	*40.00*	*40.00*
28	A63(b)	25s dp claret	.90	.90
29	A63(b)	30s orange	.90	.90
30	A63	50s brown	13.00	10.00
31	A63(b)	50s brown	.90	.90

The "b" overprint measures 12mm in this set.

Sukarno Type of Indonesia Overprinted Type "a"

1960 Perf. 12½x12

32	A55	1.25r dp orange	4.50	6.75
33	A55	1.50r brown	4.50	6.75
34	A55	2.50r rose brown	6.75	10.00
35	A55	4r apple green	1.25	*.50*
36	A55	6r rose lilac	1.25	*.50*
37	A55	15r yellow	1.25	*.50*
38	A55	20r sepia	1.25	*.50*
39	A55	40r yellow grn	1.25	*.50*
40	A55	50r violet	2.40	*.50*
		Nos. 23-40 (19)	96.70	92.80

Nos. 26, 35-37, 39-40 are valued CTO with Bandung cancels. Postally used sell for much more.

WEST IRIAN

'west ˌir-ē-'än

(Irian Barat)
(West New Guinea)

LOCATION — Western half of New Guinea, southwest Pacific Ocean
GOVT. — Province of Indonesia
AREA — 162,927 sq. mi.
POP. — 923,440 (1973)
CAPITAL — Djajapura (formerly Hollandia)

The former Netherlands New Guinea became a territory under the administration of the United Nations Temporary Executive Authority on Oct. 1, 1962.

The territory came under Indonesian administration on May 1, 1963.

100 Sen = 1 Rupiah
(1 rupiah = 1 former Netherlands New Guinea gulden)

Catalogue values for all unused stamps in this country are for Never Hinged items.

Netherlands New Guinea Stamps of 1950-60 Overprinted

Type 2 Overprint

Perf. 12½x12, 12½x13½

1962-63 Photo. Unwmk.

1a	A4	1c vermilion & yel	.25	.25
2a	A1	2c deep orange	.25	.25
3a	A4	5c choc & yel	.25	.25
4a	A5	7c org red, bl & brn vio	.25	.25
5a	A4	10c aqua & red brn	.25	.25
6a	A5	12c grn, bl & brn vio	.25	.25
7a	A4	15c dp yel & red brn	.50	.25
8a	A5	17c brn vio & bl	.60	.35
9a	A4	20c lt bl grn & red brn	.60	.35
10a	A6	25c red	.35	.30
11a	A6	30c deep blue	.80	.35
12a	A6	40c deep orange	.80	.35
13a	A6	45c dark olive	1.40	.75
14a	A6	55c slate blue	1.25	.55
15a	A6	80c dl gray vio	8.00	*10.00*
16a	A6	85c dk vio brn	4.00	*5.00*
17a	A6	1g plum	3.50	1.90

Engr.

18a	A3	2g reddish brn	15.00	*20.00*
19a	A3	5g green	7.50	*6.00*
		Nos. 1a-19a (19)	45.80	47.65

The overprint exists in four types:

1) Size 17½mm. Applied locally and sold in 1962 in West New Guinea. Top of "N" is slightly lower than the "U," and the base of the "T" is straight, or nearly so. This set sells for about $20 more than Nos. 1a-19a.

2) Size 17½mm. Applied in the Netherlands and sold in 1963 by the UN in New York. Top of the "N" is slightly higher than the "U," and the base of the "T" is concave. This is the set listed above.

3) Size 14mm. Exists on eight values. Set value, $200.

4) Size 19mm. Exists on 1c and 10c. Set value, $160.

Types 3 and 4 were applied in West New Guinea and it is doubtful whether they were regularly issued.

See the *Scott U.S. Specialized Catalogue* for complete listings and values of the UNTEA overprints.

Indonesia Nos. 454, 456, 494-501, 387, 390, 392 and 393 Surcharged or Overprinted: "IRIAN BARAT"

Perf. 12½x13½

1963, May 1 Photo. Unwmk.

20	A63	1s on 70s org ver	.25	.25
21	A63	2s on 90s yel grn	.25	.25

Perf. 12x12½

22	A76	5s gray	.25	.25
23	A76	6s on 20s ocher	.25	.25
24	A76	7s on 50s dp bl	.25	.25
25	A76	10s red brn	.25	.25
26	A76	15s plum	.25	.25
27	A76	25s brt bl grn	.25	.25
28	A76	30s on 75s scar	.25	*.25*
29	A76	40s on 1.15r plum	.25	*.30*

Perf. 12½x12

30	A55	1r purple	.45	*.55*
31	A55	2r green	.80	*.90*
32	A55	3r dk bl	1.40	*1.50*
33	A55	5r brown	2.25	*3.00*
		Nos. 20-33 (14)	7.40	8.50

"Indonesia's Flag from Sabang to Merauke" — A1

20s, 50s, Parachutist landing in New Guinea. 60s, 75s, Bird of paradise and map of New Guinea.

1963, May 1

34	A1	12s org brn, blk & red	.25	.30
35	A1	17s org brn, blk & red	.25	.40
36	A1	20s multi	.30	.60
37	A1	50s multi	.30	1.00
38	A1	60s multi	.70	1.10
39	A1	75s multi	.90	2.00
		Nos. 34-39 (6)	2.70	5.40

Liberation of West New Guinea.

Maniltoa Gemmipara — A2

15s, Dendrobium lancifolium (orchid). 30s, Gardenia gjellerupii. 40s, Maniltoa flower. 50s, Phalanger. 75s, Cassowary. 1r, Kangaroo. 3r, Crowned pigeons.

1968, Aug. 17 Photo. *Perf. 12½x12*

40	A2	5s dl grn & vio blk	.60	.85
41	A2	15s emer & dk pur	.90	1.75
42	A2	30s org & dp grn	2.00	2.75
43	A2	40s lemon & brt pur	2.10	3.00
44	A2	50s rose car & blk	2.75	3.75
45	A2	75s dl bl & blk	3.00	5.25
46	A2	1r brn org & blk	5.00	8.00
47	A2	3r apple grn & blk	7.75	10.50
		Nos. 40-47 (8)	24.10	35.85

Man, Map of Indonesia and Torches — A3

1968, Aug. 17

48	A3	10s ultra & gold	4.00	2.75
49	A3	25s crimson & gold	6.25	3.50

Issued to publicize the pledge of the people of West Irian to remain unified and integrated with the Republic of Indonesia.

Carving, Mother and Child — A4

West Irian Wood Carvings: 6s, Shield with 3 human figures. 7s, Child atop filigree carving. 10s, Drum. 25s, Seated man. 30s, Drum (3-tiered base). 50s, Carved bamboo. 75s, Man-shaped ornament. 1r, Shield. 2r, Seated man (hands raised).

1970 Photo. *Perf. 12½x12*

50	A4	5s multi	.40	.55
51	A4	6s multi	.40	.55
52	A4	7s multi	.55	1.50
53	A4	10s multi	.55	1.50
54	A4	25s multi	.55	.55
55	A4	30s multi	.65	.80
56	A4	50s multi	.70	.80
57	A4	75s multi	.80	.95
58	A4	1r multi	.90	1.25
59	A4	2r multi	1.25	1.40
		Nos. 50-59 (10)	6.75	9.85

Issued: Nos. 50-54, 4/30; Nos. 55-59, 4/15.

Black-capped Lory — A5

1970, Oct. 26 Photo. *Perf. 12x12½*

60	A5	5r shown	2.50	6.00
61	A5	10r Bird of paradise	2.25	7.50

POSTAGE DUE STAMPS

Type of Indonesia Overprinted: "IRIAN BARAT"

Perf. 13½x12½

1963, May 1 Litho. Unwmk.

J1	D8	1s light brown	.25	.50
J2	D8	5s light gray olive	.30	.55
J3	D8	10s light blue	.30	.55
J4	D8	25s gray	.30	1.00
J5	D8	40s salmon	.50	1.60
J6	D8	100s bister	1.10	3.75
		Nos. J1-J6 (6)	2.75	7.95

Type of Indonesia Dated "1968" and Overprinted: "IRIAN BARAT"

1968 Photo. *Perf. 13½x12½*

J7	D9	1s blue & lt grn	.25	.60
J8	D9	5s grn & pink	.25	.70
J9	D9	10s red & gray	.30	.70
J10	D9	25s grn & yel	.30	1.10
J11	D9	40s vio brn & pale grn	.65	1.75
J12	D9	100s org & bister	1.25	4.75
		Nos. J7-J12 (6)	3.00	9.60

INHAMBANE

ˌin-yəm-ˈban-ə

LOCATION — East Africa
GOVT. — A district of Mozambique, former Portuguese colony
AREA — 21,000 sq. mi. (approx.)
POP. — 248,000 (approx.)
CAPITAL — Inhambane

1000 Reis = 1 Milreis
100 Centavos = 1 Escudo (1913)

Stamps of Mozambique Overprinted

On 1886 Issue

1895, July 1 Unwmk. *Perf. 12½*

Without Gum

1	A2	5r black	37.50	30.00
2	A2	10r green	50.00	25.00
a.		Perf. 13½	80.00	75.00
3	A2	20r rose	60.00	30.00
4	A2	25r lilac	*1,000.*	*250.00*
5	A2	40r chocolate	60.00	40.00
6	A2	50r blue	60.00	32.50
a.		Perf. 13½	50.00	50.00
7	A2	100r yellow brown	*1,000.*	*400.00*
8	A2	200r gray violet	75.00	40.00
9	A2	300r orange	75.00	40.00
		Nos. 1-9 (9)	*2,418.*	*887.50*

On 1894 Issue

Perf. 11½

10	A3	50r lt blue	42.50	35.00
a.		Perf. 12½	55.00	42.50
11	A3	75r rose	55.00	40.00
12	A3	80r yellow green	45.00	37.50
13	A3	100r brown, *buff*	200.00	60.00
14	A3	150r carmine, *rose*	50.00	45.00
		Nos. 10-14 (5)	392.50	217.50

700th anniv. of the birth of St. Anthony of Padua.

The status of Nos. 4 and 7 is questionable. No. 3 is always discolored.

Forged overprints exist. Genuine overprints are 21mm high.

King Carlos — A1

Name and Value in Black except 500r

1903, Jan. 1 Typo. *Perf. 11½*

15	A1	2½r gray	.30	.30
16	A1	5r orange	.30	.30
17	A1	10r lt green	.60	.40
18	A1	15r gray green	1.00	.75
19	A1	20r gray violet	.85	.55
20	A1	25r carmine	.70	.55
21	A1	50r brown	1.75	1.25
22	A1	65r dull blue	25.00	15.00
23	A1	75r lilac	2.00	1.40
24	A1	100r dk blue, *blue*	2.75	1.25
25	A1	115r org brn, *pink*	5.00	5.00
26	A1	130r brown, *straw*	5.00	5.00
27	A1	200r red vio, *pink*	5.00	4.25
28	A1	400r dull bl, *straw*	8.25	7.50
29	A1	500r blk & red, *bl*	18.00	12.00
30	A1	700r gray blk, *straw*	20.00	13.00
		Nos. 15-30 (16)	96.50	68.50

For surcharge & overprints see Nos. 31-47, 88-101.

No. 22 Surcharged in Black

1905

31	A1	50r on 65r dull blue	3.00	2.00

Nos. 15-21, 23-30 Overprinted in Carmine or Green

1911

32	A1	2½r gray	.25	.25
33	A1	5r orange	.25	.25
34	A1	10r lt green	.25	.25
35	A1	15r gray green	.30	.30
36	A1	20r gray violet	.30	.30
37	A1	25r carmine (G)	.70	.50
38	A1	50r brown	.50	.50
39	A1	75r lilac	.50	.50
40	A1	100r dk blue, *bl*	.50	.50
41	A1	115r org brn, *pink*	1.00	.95
42	A1	130r brown, *straw*	1.00	.95
43	A1	200r red vio, *pink*	1.00	.95
44	A1	400r dull bl, *straw*	1.25	1.00
45	A1	500r blk & red, *bl*	1.50	1.00
46	A1	700r gray blk, *straw*	1.75	1.50
		Nos. 32-46 (15)	11.05	9.70

No. 31 Overprinted in Red

1914

47	A1	50r on 65r dull blue	1.75	1.25
a.		"Republica" inverted	25.00	25.00

Vasco da Gama Issue of Various Portuguese Colonies

Common Design Types CD20-CD27 Surcharged

1913 On Stamps of Macao

48	CD20	¼c on ½a bl grn	1.25	1.25
49	CD21	½c on 1a red	1.25	1.25
50	CD22	1c on 2a red vio	1.25	1.25
a.		Inverted surcharge	35.00	35.00
51	CD23	2½c on 4a yel grn	1.25	1.25
52	CD24	5c on 8a dk bl	1.25	1.25
53	CD25	7½c on 12a vio brn	2.25	2.25
54	CD26	10c on 16a bis brn	1.75	1.75
55	CD27	15c on 24a bis	1.75	1.75
		Nos. 48-55 (8)	12.00	12.00

On Stamps of Portuguese Africa

56	CD20	¼c on 2½r bl grn	1.25	1.00
57	CD21	½c on 5r red	1.25	1.00
58	CD22	1c on 10r red vio	1.25	1.00
59	CD23	2½c on 25r yel grn	1.25	1.00
60	CD24	5c on 50r dk bl	1.25	1.00
61	CD25	7½c on 75r vio brn	2.00	2.00
62	CD26	10c on 100r bis brn	1.50	1.50
63	CD27	15c on 150r bis	1.50	1.50
		Nos. 56-63 (8)	11.25	10.00

On Stamps of Timor

64	CD20	¼c on ½a bl grn	1.25	1.25
a.		Inverted surcharge	35.00	35.00
65	CD21	½c on 1a red	1.25	1.25
66	CD22	1c on 2a red vio	1.25	1.25
67	CD23	2½c on 4a yel grn	1.25	1.25
68	CD24	5c on 8a dk bl	1.25	1.25
69	CD25	7½c on 12a vio brn	2.50	2.50
70	CD26	10c on 16a bis brn	1.75	1.75
71	CD27	15c on 24a bis	1.75	1.75
		Nos. 64-71 (8)	12.25	12.25
		Nos. 48-71 (24)	35.50	34.25

Ceres — A2

Name and Value in Black

Chalky Paper

1914 Typo. *Perf. 15x14*

72	A2	¼c olive brown	.50	.50
73	A2	½c black	.50	.50
a.		Imperf.		
74	A2	1c blue green	.50	.50
75	A2	1½c lilac brown	.50	.50
76	A2	2c carmine	.50	.50
77	A2	2½c lt violet	.35	.35
78	A2	5c deep blue	.80	.80
79	A2	7½c yellow brown	1.25	1.25
80	A2	8c slate	1.25	1.25
81	A2	10c orange brown	1.10	1.10
82	A2	15c plum	3.00	1.60
83	A2	20c yellow green	3.00	1.60
84	A2	30c brown, *grn*	4.00	2.50
85	A2	40c brown, *pink*	5.00	3.00
86	A2	50c orange, *sal*	6.00	5.00
87	A2	1e green, *blue*	8.00	6.00
		Nos. 72-87 (16)	36.25	26.95

No. 31 Overprinted in Carmine

1915 *Perf. 11½*

88	A1	50c on 65r dull blue	9.00	6.00

Nos. 15-21, 23-30 Overprinted Locally

1917

89	A1	2½r gray	25.00	25.00
90	A1	5r orange	25.00	25.00
91	A1	15r gray green	4.00	2.50
92	A1	20r gray violet	4.00	2.00
93	A1	50r brown	3.00	2.00
94	A1	75r lilac	3.00	2.00
95	A1	100r blue, *blue*	4.00	2.50
96	A1	115r org brn, *pink*	4.00	2.50
97	A1	130r brn, *straw*	4.00	2.50
98	A1	200r red vio, *pink*	4.00	2.50
99	A1	400r dull bl, *straw*	6.00	3.00
100	A1	500r blk & red, *bl*	7.00	3.00
101	A1	700r gray blk, *straw*	14.00	8.00
		Nos. 89-101 (13)	107.00	82.50

The stamps of Inhambane have been superseded by those of Mozambique.

ININI

ˌē-ni-'nē

LOCATION — In northeastern South America, adjoining French Guiana
GOVT. — Territory of French Guiana
AREA — 30,301 sq. mi.
POP. — 5,024 (1946)
CAPITAL — St. Elie

Inini was separated from French Guiana in 1930 and reunited with it when the colony became an integral part of the Republic, acquiring the same status as the departments of Metropolitan France, under a law effective Jan. 1, 1947.

100 Centimes = 1 Franc

Used values are for canceled-to-order stamps.

Stamps of French Guiana, 1929-40, Overprinted in Black, Red or Blue

Nos. 1-9

Nos. 10-26

Nos. 27-40

1932-40 Unwmk. *Perf. 13½x14*

1	A16	1c gray lil & grnsh bl	.40	*.55*
2	A16	2c dk red & bl grn	.40	*.55*
3	A16	3c gray lil & grnsh bl ('40)	.55	*.70*
4	A16	4c ol brn & red vio ('38)	.55	*.80*
5	A16	5c Prus bl & red org	.55	*.80*
6	A16	10c magenta & brn	.40	*.55*
7	A16	15c yel brn & red org	.40	*.55*
8	A16	20c dk bl & ol grn	.40	*.55*
9	A16	25c dk red & dk brn	.90	*1.25*

Perf. 14x13½

10	A17	30c dl grn & lt grn	2.40	*2.40*
11	A17	30c grn & brn ('40)	.60	*.90*
12	A17	35c Prus grn & ol ('38)	1.20	*1.40*
13	A17	40c org brn & ol gray	.80	*1.20*
14	A17	45c ol grn & lt grn ('40)	1.40	*1.50*
15	A17	50c dk bl & ol gray	.70	*1.05*
16	A17	55c vio bl & car ('38)	5.50	*6.50*
17	A17	60c sal & grn ('40)	.70	*1.05*
18	A17	65c sal & grn ('38)	2.10	*2.25*
19	A17	70c ind & sl bl ('40)	1.00	*1.10*
20	A17	75c ind & sl bl (Bl)	4.25	*3.50*
21	A17	80c blk & vio bl (R) ('38)	1.25	*1.25*
22	A17	90c dk red & ver	3.50	*2.25*
23	A17	90c red vio & brn ('39)	1.75	*1.40*
24	A17	1fr lt vio & brn	21.00	*23.00*
25	A17	1fr car & lt red ('38)	2.75	*1.75*
26	A17	1fr blk & vio bl ('40)	1.00	*1.40*
27	A18	1.25fr blk brn & bl grn ('33)	2.25	*1.60*
28	A18	1.25fr rose & lt red ('39)	1.40	*1.40*
29	A18	1.40fr ol brn & red vio ('40)	1.25	*1.40*
30	A18	1.50fr dk bl & lt bl	1.05	*1.50*
31	A18	1.60fr ol brn & bl grn ('40)	1.00	*1.40*
32	A18	1.75fr brn, red & blk brn ('33)	25.00	24.00
33	A18	1.75fr vio bl ('38)	1.75	*2.40*
34	A18	2fr dk grn & rose red	1.25	*1.75*
35	A18	2.25fr vio bl ('39)	1.10	*1.40*
36	A18	2.50fr cop red & brn ('40)	1.00	*1.40*
37	A18	3fr brn red & red vio	1.50	*1.75*
38	A18	5fr dl vio & yel grn	1.25	*1.75*
39	A18	10fr ol gray & dp ultra (R)	1.75	*2.10*
40	A18	20fr indigo & ver	1.75	*2.10*
		Nos. 1-40 (40)	99.75	*106.15*

Without "RF," see Nos. 46-49.

Common Design Types pictured following the introduction.

Colonial Arts Exhibition Issue
Souvenir Sheet
Common Design Type

1937 ***Imperf.***

41	CD75	3fr red brown	21.00	*27.50*
		Never hinged	29.00	

New York World's Fair Issue
Common Design Type

1939, May 10 Engr. *Perf. 12½x12*

42	CD82	1.25fr car lake	3.75	*4.50*
43	CD82	2.25fr ultra	3.75	*4.50*
		Set, never hinged	11.50	

French Guiana Nos. 170A-170B Overprinted in Green or Red

1941 Engr. *Perf. 12½x12*

44	A21a	1fr deep lilac	1.00
45	A21a	2.50fr blue (R)	1.00

Nos. 44-45 were issued by the Vichy government in France, but were not placed on sale in Inini.

For surcharges, see Nos. B9-B10.

Types of 1932-40 Without "RF" Methods and Perfs as Before

1942

46	A16	20c dk bl & ol grn	2.25
47	A17	1fr black & ultra	2.25
48	A18	10fr ol gr & dp ultra (R)	2.75
49	A18	20fr indigo & ver	5.00
		Nos. 46-49 (4)	12.25

Nos. 46-49 were issued by the Vichy government in France, but were not placed on sale in Inini.

SEMI-POSTAL STAMPS

French Revolution Issue
Common Design Type
Photo.; Name & Value Typo. in Black

1939, July 5 Unwmk. *Perf. 13*

B1	CD83	45c + 25c green	16.00	*20.00*
B2	CD83	70c + 30c brown	16.00	*20.00*
B3	CD83	90c + 35c red org	16.00	*20.00*
B4	CD83	1.25fr + 1fr rose pink	16.00	*20.00*
B5	CD83	2.25fr + 2fr blue	16.00	*20.00*
		Nos. B1-B5 (5)	80.00	100.00

"Defense" Common Design Type and French Guiana Nos. B9 and B11 Ovptd. in Blue or Red

1941 Photo. *Perf. 13½*

B6	SP1	1fr + 1fr red (B)	1.75
B7	CD86	1.50fr + 3fr maroon	1.75
B8	SP2	2.50fr + 1fr blue (R)	1.75
		Nos. B6-B8 (3)	5.25

Nos. B6-B8 were issued by the Vichy government in France, but were not placed on sale in Inini.

Nos. 44-45 Srchd. in Black or Red

1944 Engr. *Perf. 12½x12*

B9	A21a	50c + 1.50fr on 2.50fr blue (R)	1.10
B10	A21a	+ 2.50fr on 1fr dp lilac	1.10

Colonial Development Fund.

Nos. B9-B10 were issued by the Vichy government in France, but were not placed on sale in Inini.

AIR POST SEMI-POSTAL STAMPS

Nurse with Mother & Child — SPAP1

Unwmk.

1942, June 22 Engr. *Perf. 13*

CB1	SPAP1	1.50fr + 50c green	1.25
CB2	SPAP1	2fr + 6fr brn & red	1.25

Native children's welfare fund.

Nos. CB1-CB2 were issued by the Vichy government in France, but were not placed on sale in Inini.

Colonial Education Fund
Common Design Type

1942, June 22

CB3	CD86a	1.20fr + 1.80fr blue & red	1.25

No. CB3 was issued by the Vichy government in France, but was not placed on sale in Inini.

POSTAGE DUE STAMPS

Postage Due Stamps of French Guiana, 1929, Overprinted in Black

1932, Apr. 7 Unwmk. *Perf. 13½x14*

J1	D3	5c indigo & Prus bl	.25	*.40*
J2	D3	10c bis brn & Prus grn	.65	*1.00*
J3	D3	20c grn & rose red	.65	*1.00*
J4	D3	30c ol brn & rose red	.65	*1.00*
J5	D3	50c vio & ol brn	1.00	*1.50*
J6	D3	60c brn red & ol brn	1.10	*1.50*

Overprinted in Black or Red

J7	D4	1fr dp bl & org brn	1.75	*1.75*
J8	D4	2fr brn red & bluish grn	2.50	*2.50*
J9	D4	3fr vio & blk (R)	7.50	7.50
J10	D4	3fr vio & blk	4.25	*5.00*
		Nos. J1-J10 (10)	20.30	*23.15*

IONIAN ISLANDS

ī-'ō-nē-ən 'ī-ləndz

LOCATION — Seven Islands, of which six-Corfu, Paxos, Lefkas (Santa Maura), Cephalonia, Ithaca and Zante-are in the Ionian Sea west of Greece, and a seventh-Cerigo (Kithyra)-is in the Mediterranean south of Greece

GOVT. — Integral part of Kingdom of Greece

AREA — 752 sq. miles

POP. — 231,510 (1938)

These islands were acquired by Great Britain in 1815 but in 1864 were ceded to Greece on request of the inhabitants.

In 1941 the islands were occupied by Italian forces. The Italians withdrew in 1943 and German forces continued the occupation, using current Greek stamps without overprinting, except for Zante.

For stamps of the Italian occupation of Corfu, see Corfu.

10 Oboli = 1 Penny
12 Pence = 1 Shilling
100 Lepta = 1 Drachma
100 Centesimi = 1 Lira

Watermarks

Wmk. 138 — "2"

Wmk. 139 — "1"

ISSUES OF THE BRITISH PROTECTORATE

Queen Victoria — A1

1859 Unwmk. Engr. *Imperf.*

1	A1	(½p) orange	140.00	*750.00*

Wmk. 138

2	A1	(1p) blue	35.00	*300.00*

Wmk. 139

3	A1	(2p) lake	28.00	*300.00*
		Nos. 1-3 (3)	203.00	*1,350.*

Forged cancellations are plentiful.

ISSUED UNDER ITALIAN OCCUPATION

Values of stamps overprinted by letterpress in pairs are for unsevered pairs. Single stamps, unused, sell for one third the price of a pair; used, one half the price of a pair.

Handstamped overprints were also applied to pairs, with "isola" instead of "isole."

Issue for Cephalonia and Ithaca

Stamps of Greece, 1937-38, Overprinted in Pairs Vertically, Reading Down, or Horizontally (H) in Black

Perf. 12½x12, 13½x12, 12x13½

1941 Wmk. 252, Unwmk.

N1	A69	5 l brn red & bl	55.00	*55.00*
N2	A70	10 l bl & red brn (#413) (H)	55.00	*55.00*
a.		On No. 397	400.00	*400.00*
N3	A71	20 l blk & grn (H)	55.00	*55.00*
a.		Overprint inverted	275.00	225.00
N4	A72	40 l grn & blk	55.00	*55.00*
N5	A73	50 l brn & blk	55.00	*55.00*
N6	A74	80 l ind & yel brn (H)	95.00	95.00
a.		Overprint inverted	350.00	275.00
N7	A67	1d green (H)	260.00	200.00
N8	A84	1.50d green (H)	200.00	130.00
a.		Overprint inverted	325.00	240.00
N9	A75	2d ultra	55.00	55.00
N10	A76	5d red	200.00	90.00
N11	A77	6d ol brn	200.00	90.00
N12	A78	7d dk brn	200.00	90.00
N13	A67	8d dp blue (H)	225.00	130.00
N14	A79	10d red brn	200.00	90.00
N15	A80	15d green	275.00	145.00
N16	A81	25d dk blue (H)	300.00	200.00
a.		Overprint inverted	650.00	525.00
N17	A84	30d org brn (H)	1,400.	950.00
a.		Overprint inverted	2,100.	1,050.
		Nos. N1-N17 (17)	3,885.	2,540.

A variety with wrong font "C" in "Cephalonia" is found in several positions in each sheet of all denominations except those overprinted on single stamps. It sells for about three times the price of a normal pair.

Several other minor spelling errors in the overprint occur on several denominations in one of the printings.

Forgeries exist of many of the higher valued stamps and minor varieties of Nos. N1-N17, NC1-NC11 and NRA1-NRA5.

Overprint Reading Up

N1a	A69	5 l	55.00	*55.00*
N4a	A72	40 l	55.00	*55.00*
N5a	A73	50 l	55.00	*55.00*
N9a	A75	2d	72.50	65.00
N10a	A76	5d	200.00	87.50
N11a	A77	6d	200.00	87.50
N12a	A78	7d	200.00	87.50
N14a	A79	10d	200.00	95.00
N15a	A80	15d	275.00	145.00
		Nos. N1a-N15a (9)	1,313.	732.50

General Issue

Stamps of Italy, 1929, Overprinted in Red or Black

1941 Wmk. 140 *Perf. 14*

N18	A90	5c olive brn (R)	.80	*2.75*
N19	A92	10c dk brown (R)	.80	*2.75*
N20	A91	20c rose red	.80	*2.75*
N21	A94	25c deep green	.80	*2.75*
N22	A95	30c olive brn (R)	.80	*2.75*
a.		"SOLE" for "ISOLE"	72.50	
N23	A95	50c purple (R)	.80	*2.75*
N24	A94	75c rose red	.80	*2.75*
N25	A94	1.25 l dp blue (R)	.80	*2.75*
		Nos. N18-N25 (8)	6.40	*22.00*

The stamps overprinted "Isole Jonie" were issued for all the Ionian Islands except Cerigo which used regular postage stamps of Greece.

ISSUED UNDER GERMAN OCCUPATION

Zante Issue

Nos. N21 and N23 with Addtl. Handstamped Ovpt. in Black

1943 Wmk. 140 *Perf. 14*

N26	A94	25c deep green	25.00	*45.00*
a.		Carmine overprint	35.00	*75.00*
N27	A95	50c purple	25.00	*45.00*
a.		Carmine overprint	35.00	*75.00*

No. N19 with this overprint is a proof. Value, black $70; carmine $375.

Nos. N26-N27 were in use 8 days, then were succeeded by stamps of Greece.

Forgeries of Nos. N26-N27, NC13 and their cancellations are plentiful.

Greek stamps with Italian overprints for the islands of Cerigo (Kithyra), Paxos and Lefkas (Santa Maura) are fraudulent.

OCCUPATION AIR POST STAMPS

Issued under Italian Occupation

Issue for Cephalonia and Ithaca

Stamps of Greece Overprinted in Pairs Vertically, Reading Down, or Horizontally (H) in Black Like Nos. N1-N17

Perf. 13x12½, 12½x13

1941 Grayish Paper Unwmk.

On Greece Nos. C22, C23, C25 and C27 to C30

NC1	AP16	1d dp red	145.00	*130.00*
NC1A	AP17	2d dl bl	80.00	*65.00*
NC2	AP19	7d bl vio (H)	160.00	*190.00*
a.		Overprint inverted	350.00	175.00
NC3	AP21	25d rose (H)	650.00	475.00
a.		Overprint inverted	1,050.	525.00
NC4	AP22	30d dk grn	800.00	550.00
a.		Overprint reading up	800.00	550.00
b.		Horizontal overprint on single stamp	—	—
c.		As "b," inverted	—	
NC5	AP23	50d vio (H)	4,500.	3,500.
a.		Overprint inverted	6,500.	4,000.
NC6	AP24	100d brown	2,250.	1,900.
a.		Overprint reading up	2,250.	1,900.

No. NC1A is known only with overprint reading up.

On Greece Nos. C31-C34

Reengraved; White Paper

NC7	AP16	1d red	145.00	*130.00*
NC8	AP17	2d gray bl	120.00	*110.00*
a.		Overprint reading up	120.00	110.00
b.		Horiz. ovpt. on pair	*2,400.*	*1,900.*
c.		Horizontal overprint on single stamp		
NC9	AP18	5d vio (H)	130.00	105.00
a.		Overprint inverted	1,100.	500.00
b.		Vert. ovpt. on single stamp, up or down	1,100.	525.00
NC10	AP19	7d dp ultra (H)	325.00	250.00
a.		Overprint inverted	1,050.	450.00

Overprinted Horizontally on No. C36

Rouletted 13½

NC11	D3	50 l vio brn	2,400.	1,900.
a.		Pair, one without ovpt.	—	
b.		On No. C36a	—	

See footnote following No. N17.

General Issue

Italy No. C13 Overprinted in Red Like Nos. N18-N25

1941 Wmk. 140 *Perf. 14*

NC12	AP3	50c olive brown	.80	*3.25*
a.		"SOLE" for "ISOLE"	65.00	

Used in all the Ionian Islands except Cerigo which used air post stamps of Greece.

No. NC12 with additional overprint "BOLLO" is a revenue stamp.

Issued under German Occupation ZANTE ISSUE

No. NC12 with Additional Handstamped Overprint in Black Like Nos. N26-N27

1943 Wmk. 140 *Perf. 14*

NC13	AP3	50c olive brown	27.50	*55.00*
a.		"SOLE" for "ISOLE"	*450.00*	
b.		Carmine overprint	150.00	*300.00*

See note after No. N27.

OCCUPATION POSTAGE DUE STAMPS

General Issue

Postage Due Stamps of Italy, 1934, Overprinted in Black Like Nos. N18-N25

1941 Wmk. 140 *Perf. 14*

NJ1	D6	10c blue	3.25	*6.50*
NJ2	D6	20c rose red	3.25	*6.50*
NJ3	D6	30c red orange	3.25	*6.50*
NJ4	D7	1 l red orange	3.25	*6.50*
		Nos. NJ1-NJ4 (4)	13.00	*26.00*

See footnote after No. N25.

OCCUPATION POSTAL TAX STAMPS

Issued under Italian Occupation

Issue for Cephalonia and Ithaca

Greece No. RA56 with Additional Overprint on Horizontal Pair in Black Like Nos. N1-N17

Serrate Roulette 13½

1941 Unwmk.

NRA1	D3	10 l car (Bl+Bk)	32.50	*40.00*
a.		Blue overprint double	105.00	105.00
b.		Inverted overprint	300.00	300.00

Same Overprint Reading Down on Vertical Pairs of Nos. RA61-RA63

Perf. 13½x12

NRA2	PT7	10 l brt rose, *pale rose*	35.00	35.00
a.		Overprint on horiz. pair	120.00	75.00
b.		Horizontal overprint on single stamp	*1,100.*	
c.		Overprint reading up	35.00	35.00
NRA3	PT7	50 l gray grn, *pale grn*	32.50	24.00
a.		Overprint reading up	32.50	24.00
b.		Ovpt. on horiz. pair	—	—
c.		Horizontal overprint on single stamp	—	—
NRA4	PT7	1d dl bl, *lt bl*	90.00	72.50
a.		Overprint reading up	105.00	95.00

Same Overprint Reading Down on Vertical Pair of No. RA65

NRA5	PT7	50 l gray grn, *pale grn*	875.00	875.00
a.		Overprint reading up	875.00	875.00

Nos. NRA5 and NRA5a were not placed in use on any compulsory day.

See footnote following No. N17.

IRAN

i-'rän

(Persia)

LOCATION — Western Asia, bordering on the Persian Gulf and the Gulf of Oman
GOVT. — Islamic republic
AREA — 636,000 sq. mi.
POP. — 65,179,752 (1999 est.)
CAPITAL — Tehran

20 Shahis (or Chahis) = 1 Kran
10 Krans = 1 Toman
100 Centimes = 1 Franc = 1 Kran (1881)
100 Dinars = 1 Rial (1933)
100 Rials = 1 Pahlavi
100 Rials = 1 Toman

Catalogue values for unused stamps in this country are for Never Hinged items, beginning with Scott 1054 in the regular postage section, Scott B36 in the semi-postal section, Scott C83 in the airpost section, Scott O72 in the officials section, Scott Q36 in the parcel post section, and Scott RA4 in the postal tax section.

Values of early stamps vary according to condition. Quotations for Nos. 1-20, 33-40 are for fine copies. Very fine to superb specimens sell at much higher prices, and inferior or poor copies sell at reduced prices, depending on the condition of the individual specimen.

Cracked gum on unused stamps does not detract from the value.

Beware of forgeries and/or reprints of most Iran stamps between the years 1870-1925. Scott values are for genuine stamps. Collectors should be aware that forgeries of many issues outnumber genuine examples by factors of 10 or 20 to one. Failing specialized knowledge on the part of the collector, these stamps should be examined or authenticated by acknowledged experts before purchase.

Watermarks

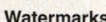

Wmk. 161 — Lion

Wmk. 306 — Arms of Iran

Wmk. 316 — Persian Inscription

Wmk. 349 — Persian Inscription and Crown in Circle

Illustration of Wmk. 349 shown sideways. Circles in Wmk. 349 are 95mm apart.

Wmk. 353 — Persian Inscription and Coat of Arms in Circle

Wmk. 381 — "Islamic Republic of Iran" in Persian (Partial Illustration)

Wmk. 411

Many issues have handstamped surcharges. As usual with such surcharges there are numerous inverted, double and similar varieties.

Coat of Arms — A1

Design A2 has value numeral below lion.

1870 Unwmk. Typo. *Imperf.*

1	A1 1s dull violet	325.00	
2	A1 2s green	275.00	
3	A1 4s greenish blue	225.00	
4	A1 8s red	275.00	
	Nos. 1-4 (4)	1,100.	

Values for used examples of Nos. 1-4 are omitted, since this issue was only pen canceled. After 1875, postmarked remainders were sold to collectors. Values same as unused.

Printed in blocks of 4. Many shades exist. Forgeries exist.

Printed on Both Sides

1a	A1 1s	20,000.
2a	A1 2s	40,000.
3a	A1 4s	
4a	A1 8s	18,000.

Coat of Arms — A2

Vertically Rouletted 10½ on 1 or 2 Sides

1875 Thick Wove Paper

11	A2 1s black	225.00	75.00
a.	Imperf.	*3,500.*	*5,000.*
12	A2 2s blue	225.00	75.00
a.	Tête bêche pair	*30,000.*	
b.	Imperf.	—	—
13	A2 4s vermilion	300.00	100.00
a.	Imperf.	—	—
b.	4s bright red, thin paper, imperf.	750.00	*750.00*
14	A2 8s yellow green	200.00	175.00
b.	Tête bêche pair	*15,000.*	*10,000.*
c.	Imperf.	*2,000.*	*1,250.*
	Nos. 11-14 (4)	950.00	425.00

Four varieties of each.

Nos. 11-14 were printed in horizontal strips of 4 with 3-10mm spacing between stamps. The strips were then cut very close all around (generally touching or cutting the outer framelines). Then they were hand-rouletted between the stamps. Values are for stamps with rouletting on both sides and margins clear at top and bottom. Stamps showing the rouletting on only one side sell for considerably less.

Nos. 11 to 14 also exist pin-perforated and percé en scie.

No. 13b has spacing of 2-3mm.

See Nos. 15-20, 33-40.

Medium to Thin White or Grayish Paper

1876 *Imperf.*

14A	A2 1s black	400.00	*600.00*
15	A2 1s gray black	50.00	*175.00*
a.	Printed on both sides	*1,500.*	
b.	Laid paper	1,000.	1,500.
16	A2 2s gray blue	600.00	*750.00*
a.	Printed on both sides	*7,000.*	
17	A2 2s black	1,000.	
a.	Tête bêche pair	*6,000.*	
18	A2 4s vermilion	500.00	150.00
a.	Printed on both sides	5,000.	5,000.
19	A2 1k rose	1,500.	100.00
a.	Printed on both sides		4,000.
b.	Laid paper	*6,000.*	1,200.
c.	1k yellow (error)	*35,000.*	15,000.
d.	Tête bêche pair		*120,000.*
20	A2 4k yellow	3,000.	300.00
a.	Printed on both sides		*5,000.*
b.	Laid paper	*5,000.*	300.00
c.	Tête bêche pair		*18,000.*

Nos. 15-16, 18-20 were printed in blocks of 4, and Nos. 14A and 17 in vertical strips of 4, with spacing of 2mm or less.

Nos. 14A and 17 are on medium to thick grayish wove paper. Forgeries exist.

Official reprints of the 1s and 4s are on thick coarse white paper without gum. Value, each $350.

1875 and 1876 issues

Various forgeries exist including forgeries printed from the replica cliches of the genuine issues in Paris by the order of Fabius Boital, a French engineer who was a concession-hunter, living in Iran during the 1870s through 1890s. There also are modern forgeries made by laser printers.

Nasser-eddin Shah Qajar — A3

Perf. 10½, 11, 12, 13, and Compounds

1876 Litho.

27	A3 1s lilac & blk	30.00	6.00
28	A3 2s green & blk	35.00	7.50
29	A3 5s rose & blk	30.00	4.00
30	A3 10s blue & blk	45.00	8.00
	Nos. 27-30 (4)	140.00	25.50

Bisects of the 5s and 1s, the latter used with 2s stamps, were used to make up the 2½ shahis postcard rate. Bisects of the 10s were used in the absence of 5s stamps to make up the letter rate.

The 10s was bisected and surcharged "5 Shahi" or "5 Shahy" for local use in Azerbaijan province and Khoy in 1877.

"Imperfs" of the 5s are envelope cutouts.

Forgeries and official reprints exist.

Very fine examples will have perforations cutting the background net on one side. Genuine stamps withs perfs clear of net on all four sides are very scarce.

1878 Typo. *Imperf.*

33	A2 1k car rose	950.00	175.00
34	A2 1k red, *yellow*	*5,000.*	175.00
a.	Tête bêche pair		*10,000.*
35	A2 4k ultramarine	450.00	175.00
a.	Printed on both sides		*4,000.*
36	A2 5k violet	1,500.	350.00
37	A2 5k gold	*8,500.*	750.00
38	A2 5k red bronze	*35,000.*	2,500.
39	A2 5k vio bronze	*65,000.*	4,000.
40	A2 1t bronze, *bl*	*75,000.*	*8,000.*

Four varieties of each except for 4k which has 3.

Nos. 33 and 34 are printed from redrawn clichés. They have wide colorless circles around the corner numerals.

Nasser-eddin Shah Qajar — A6

Perf. 10½, 12, 13, and Compounds

1879 Litho.

41	A6 1k brown & blk	450.00	7.00
a.	Pair, imperf between	—	
b.	Inverted center		*5,000.*
42	A6 5k blue & blk	400.00	5.00
a.	Imperf., pair	3,000.	*600.00*
b.	Inverted center		2,500.
c.	Inverted center, imperf		2,500.

1880

43	A6 1s red & black	50.00	15.00
b.	Pair, imperf between	*4,500.*	
44	A6 2s yellow & blk	85.00	10.00
a.	Imperf., pair		*2,500.*
45	A6 5s green & blk	350.00	2.00
46	A6 10s violet & blk	700.00	30.00
	Nos. 43-46 (4)	1,185.	57.00

Forgeries and official reprints exist.

Imperf examples of No. 46 are proofs on thin yellow paper or thick white card with a cancellation line.

The 2, 5 and 10sh of this issue and the 1 and 5kr of the 1879 issue have been reprinted from a new die which resembles the 5 shahi envelope. The aigrette is shorter than on the original stamps and touches the circle above it.

Sun — A7

1881 Litho. *Perf. 12, 13, 12x13*

47	A7 5c dull violet	50.00	25.00
48	A7 10c rose	50.00	25.00
49	A7 25c green	6,750.	100.00
	Nos. 47-49 (3)	6,850.	150.00

1882 Engr., Border Litho.

No.	Type	Description	Unused	Used
50	A7	5c blue vio & vio	50.00	60.00
51	A7	10c dp pink & rose	50.00	60.00
52	A7	25c deep grn & grn	1,400.	40.00
		Nos. 50-52 (3)	1,500.	160.00

Very fine examples of Nos. 50-52 will have perforations cutting the outer colored border but clear of the inner framelines.

Counterfeits of Nos. 50-52, 53, 53a are plentiful and have been used to create forgeries of Nos. 66, 66a, 70 and 70a. They usually have a strong, complete inner frameline at right. On genuine stamps that line is weak or missing.

A8

Type I

Type II (error)

Shah Nasr-ed-Din
A9 A10

A11

Type I: Three dots at right end of scroll.
Type II: Two dots at right end of scroll.

1882-84 Engr.

No.	Type	Description	Unused	Used
53	A8	5s green, type I	50.00	1.50
a.		5s green, type II	100.00	10.00
54	A9	10s buff, org & blk	85.00	10.00
55	A10	50c buff, org & blk	700.00	80.00
56	A10	50c gray & blk ('84)	150.00	70.00
57	A10	1fr blue & black	150.00	20.00
58	A10	5fr rose red & blk	140.00	20.00
59	A11	10fr buff, red & blk	150.00	30.00
		Nos. 53-59 (7)	1,425.	231.50

Crude forgeries of Nos. 58-59 exist. Halves of the 10s, 50c and 1fr surcharged with Farsi characters in red or black are frauds. The 50c and 1fr surcharged with a large "5" surrounded by rays are also frauds.

No. 59 used is valued for c-t-o.

For overprints and surcharges see Nos 66-72.

Very fine examples of Nos. 53-59 will have perforations cutting the outer colored border but clear of the inner framelines.

A12

Perf. 12-12½, 13

1885, March-May Litho.

No.	Type	Description	Unused	Used
59A	A12	5c blue	1,500.	50.00
a.		5c violet blue	1,500.	75.00
b.		5c ultramarine	1,500.	75.00
c.		5c dp reddish lilac	2,500.	300.00
d.		As "a," imperf	7,500.	

No. 59A was issued because of an urgent need for 5c stamps, pending the arrival of No. 62 in July. No. 59A has 88 sunrays instead of the 124 sunrays on the typographed stamp, No. 62.

A13

1885-86 Typo.

No.	Type	Description	Unused	Used
60	A12	1c green	25.00	2.00
61	A12	2c rose	25.00	2.00
62	A12	5c dull blue	200.00	1.00
63	A13	10c brown	40.00	2.00
64	A13	1k slate	100.00	3.00
65	A13	5k dull vio ('86)	800.00	40.00
		Nos. 60-65 (6)	1,190.	50.00

Nos. 53, 54, 56 and 58 Surcharged in Black

a

b

c

d

e

f

1885

No.	Surch.	Description	Unused	Used
66	(a)	6c on 5s grn, type I	150.00	30.00
a.		6c on 5s green, type II	275.00	100.00
67	(b)	12c on 50c gray & blk	150.00	30.00
68	(c)	18c on 10s buff, org & black	150.00	30.00
69	(d)	1t on 5fr rose red & black	150.00	50.00
		Nos. 66-69 (4)	600.00	140.00

1887

No.	Surch.	Description	Unused	Used
70	(e)	3c on 5s grn, type I	150.00	30.00
a.		3c on 5s green, type II	275.00	100.00
71	(a)	6c on 10s buff, org & blk	150.00	30.00
72	(f)	8c on 50c gray & blk	150.00	30.00
		Nos. 70-72 (3)	450.00	90.00

The word "OFFICIEL" indicated that the surcharged stamps were officially authorized.

Surcharges on the same basic stamps of values other than those listed are believed to be bogus.

Counterfeits of Nos. 66-72 abound.

Very fine examples of Nos. 66-72 will have perforations cutting the outer colored border but clear of the inner framelines.

Beware of forgeries and/or reprints of most Iran stamps between the years 1870-1925. Scott values are for genuine stamps. Collectors should be aware that forgeries of many issues outnumber genuine examples by factors of 10 or 20 to one. Failing specialized knowledge on the part of the collector, these stamps should be examined or authenticated by acknowledged experts before purchase.

A14

A15

1889 Typo. *Perf. 11, 13½, 11x13½*

No.	Type	Description	Unused	Used
73	A14	1c pale rose	2.50	.75
74	A14	2c pale blue	2.50	.75
75	A14	5c lilac	1.50	.50
76	A14	7c brown	7.50	1.50
77	A15	10c black	2.50	.75
78	A15	1k red orange	4.50	.75
79	A15	2k rose	40.00	6.00
80	A15	5k green	25.00	6.00
		Nos. 73-80 (8)	86.00	17.00

All values exist imperforate.

Canceled to order stamps of No. 76 abound.

For surcharges see Nos. 622-625.

Nos. 73-80 with average centering, faded colors and/or toned paper sell for much less.

A16

A17

1891 *Perf. 10½, 11½*

No.	Type	Description	Unused	Used
81	A16	1c black	2.50	1.00
82	A16	2c brown	2.50	1.00
83	A16	5c deep blue	2.50	.25
84	A16	7c gray	350.00	12.00
85	A16	10c rose	2.50	.50
86	A16	14c orange	2.50	1.50
87	A17	1k green	30.00	2.00
88	A17	2k orange	700.00	25.00
89	A17	5k ocher yellow	8.00	30.00
		Nos. 81-89 (9)	1,101.	73.25

For surcharges see Nos. 626-629.

A18

Nasser-eddin Shah Qajar — A19

1894 *Perf. 12½*

No.	Type	Description	Unused	Used
90	A18	1c lilac	1.00	.25
91	A18	2c blue green	1.00	.25
92	A18	5c ultramarine	1.00	.25
93	A18	8c brown	1.00	.25
		Perf. 11½x11		
94	A19	10c orange	1.25	.75
95	A19	16c rose	25.00	75.00
96	A19	1k red & yellow	3.00	.75
97	A19	2k brn org & pale bl	4.00	1.00
98	A19	5k violet & silver	10.00	1.50
99	A19	10k red & gold	20.00	10.00
100	A19	50k green & gold	50.00	15.00
		Nos. 90-100 (11)	117.25	105.00

Canceled to order stamps sell for one-third of listed values.

Reprints exist. They are hard to distinguish from the originals. Value, set $15.

See Nos. 104-112, 136-144. For overprints see Nos. 120-128, 152-167, 173-181. For surcharges see Nos. 101-103, 168, 206, 211.

Nos. 93, 98 With Violet or Magenta Surcharge

a

b

1897 *Perf. 12½, 11½x11*

No.	Type	Description	Unused	Used
101	A18(a)	5c on 8c brn (V)	30.00	5.00
a.		Inverted surcharge	150.00	25.00
102	A19(b)	1k on 5k vio & sil (V)	40.00	20.00
103	A19(b)	2k on 5k vio & sil (M)	60.00	35.00
		Nos. 101-103 (3)	130.00	60.00

Forgeries exist.

Lion Type of 1894 and

Mozaffar-eddin Shah Qajar — A22

1898 Typo. *Perf. 12½*

No.	Type	Description	Unused	Used
104	A18	1c gray	5.00	.35
105	A18	2c pale brown	5.00	.35
106	A18	3c dull violet	10.00	3.00
107	A18	4c vermilion	10.00	3.00
108	A18	5c yellow	5.00	.25
109	A18	8c orange	20.00	7.00
110	A18	10c light blue	5.00	.50
111	A18	12c rose	15.00	1.00
112	A18	16c green	20.00	7.00
113	A22	1k ultramarine	10.00	1.00
114	A22	2k pink	10.00	2.00
115	A22	3k yellow	10.00	3.00
116	A22	4k gray	10.00	5.00
117	A22	5k emerald	10.00	6.00
118	A22	10k orange	40.00	15.00
119	A22	50k bright vio	60.00	25.00
		Nos. 104-119 (16)	245.00	79.45

Unauthorized reprints of Nos. 104-119 were made from original clichés. Paper shows a vertical mesh. These abound unused and canceled to order. Value set, unused, hinged, $20.

See Nos. 145-151. For overprints see Nos. 129-135, 182-188. For surcharges see Nos. 169, 171, 207, 209, 211.

Reprints have been used to make counterfeits of Nos. 120-135, 152-167.

Stamps of 1898 Handstamped in Violet

a

b

c

d

e

f

g

h

1899

No.	Type	Denomination	Unused	Used
120	(a)	1c gray	5.00	5.00
121	(b)	2c pale brown	5.00	8.00
122	(b)	3c dull violet	12.00	15.00
123	(c)	4c vermilion	18.00	30.00
124	(c)	5c yellow	10.00	3.00
125	(d)	8c orange	15.00	40.00
126	(d)	10c light blue	6.50	10.00
a.		Type "b" handstamp	500.00	500.00
127	(d)	12c rose	15.00	8.00
128	(d)	16c green	25.00	30.00
129	(e)	1k ultramarine	25.00	10.00
130	(f)	2k pink	30.00	25.00
131	(f)	3k yellow	80.00	250.00
132	(g)	4k gray	100.00	250.00
133	(g)	5k emerald	30.00	40.00
134	(h)	10k orange	60.00	60.00
135	(h)	50k brt violet	120.00	150.00
		Nos. 120-135 (16)	556.50	934.00

The handstamped control marks on Nos. 120-135 exist sideways, inverted and double. Counterfeits are plentiful.

Types of 1894-98

1899 Typo. Perf. 12½

No.	Type	Denomination	Unused	Used
136	A18	1c gray, *green*	7.50	.75
137	A18	2c brown, *green*	7.50	.75
138	A18	3c violet, *green*	20.00	5.00
139	A18	4c red, *green*	12.00	5.00
140	A18	5c yellow, *green*	5.00	.30
141	A18	8c orange, *green*	15.00	5.00
142	A18	10c pale blue, *grn*	5.00	.50
143	A18	12c lake, *green*	15.00	1.25
144	A18	16c green, *green*	25.00	5.00
145	A22	1k red	30.00	1.25
146	A22	2k deep green	35.00	8.50
147	A22	3k lilac brown	35.00	17.00
148	A22	4k orange red	35.00	17.00
149	A22	5k gray brown	40.00	17.00
150	A22	10k deep blue	400.00	100.00
151	A22	50k brown	75.00	30.00
		Nos. 136-151 (16)	762.00	214.30

Canceled to order stamps abound.

Unauthorized reprints of Nos. 136-151 were made from original clichés. Paper is chalky and has white gum. The design can be seen through the back of the reprints. Value unused, hinged, set, $30.

For surcharges and overprints see Nos. 171, 173-188, 206-207, 209, 211.

Nos. 104-111 Handstamped in Violet

(Struck once on every two stamps.)

1900

No.	Type	Denomination	Unused	Used
152	A18	1c gray	50.00	20.00
153	A18	2c pale brown	60.00	25.00
154	A18	3c dull violet	150.00	70.00
155	A18	4c vermilion	150.00	70.00
156	A18	5c yellow	25.00	10.00
158	A18	10c light blue	2,500.	2,500.
159	A18	12c rose	100.00	50.00
		Nos. 152-159 (7)	3,035.	2,745.

Values are for single authenticated stamps. Pairs sell for much more.

This control mark, in genuine state, was not applied to the 8c orange (Nos. 109, 125).

Same Overprint Handstamped on Nos. 120-127 in Violet

(Struck once on each block of 4.)

No.	Type	Denomination	Unused	Used
160	A18	1c gray	100.00	50.00
163	A18	4c vermilion	300.00	140.00
164	A18	5c yellow	50.00	20.00
166	A18	10c light blue	1,250.	600.00
a.		Type "b" handstamp	500.00	250.00
167	A18	12c rose	150.00	50.00
		Nos. 160-167 (5)	550.00	760.00

Values are for single authenticated stamps. Blocks are rare and worth much more.

Counterfeits exist of Nos. 152-167.

No. 93 Surcharged in Violet

1900

No.	Type	Denomination	Unused	Used
168	A18	5c on 8c brown	50.00	2.50
a.		Inverted surcharge	250.00	25.00

No. 145 Surcharged in Violet

1901

No.	Type	Denomination	Unused	Used
169	A22	12c on 1k red	100.00	100.00
a.		Blue surcharge	125.00	125.00

Counterfeits exist.

Some specialists state that No. 169 with black surcharge was made for collectors.

A23

1902 Violet Surcharge

No.	Type	Denomination	Unused	Used
171	A23	5k on 50k brown	200.00	80.00
a.		Blue surcharge	200.00	90.00

Counterfeits exist. See No. 207.

Nos. 136-151 Overprinted in Black

1902

No.	Type	Denomination	Unused	Used
173	A18	1c gray, *green*	50.00	20.00
174	A18	2c brown, *green*	50.00	20.00
175	A18	3c violet, *green*	300.00	300.00
176	A18	4c red, *green*	400.00	400.00
177	A18	5c yellow, *green*	20.00	5.00
178	A18	8c orange, *green*	400.00	400.00
179	A18	10c pale blue, *grn*	50.00	15.00
180	A18	12c lake, *green*	125.00	50.00
181	A18	16c green, *green*	500.00	400.00
182	A22	1k red	100.00	45.00
183	A22	2k deep green	250.00	100.00
188	A22	50k brown	600.00	250.00

Overprinted on No. 168

No.	Type	Denomination	Unused	Used
206	A18	5c on 8c brown	200.00	100.00

Overprinted on Nos. 171 and 171a

No.	Type	Denomination	Unused	Used
207	A23	5k on 50k brown	200.00	100.00
a.		On #171a	250.00	100.00

Overprinted on Nos. 169 and 169a

No.	Type	Denomination	Unused	Used
209	A22	12c on 1k red	100.00	50.00
a.		On #169a	100.00	50.00

Counterfeits of the overprint of Nos. 173-183, 188, 206-207, 209 are plentiful. Practically all examples with overprint sideways, inverted, double and double with one inverted are frauds.

Nos. 142 Surcharged in Violet

1902

No.	Type	Denomination	Unused	Used
211	A18	5c on 10c pale bl, *grn*	60.00	20.00

Surcharges in different colors were made for collectors.

Initials of Victor Castaigne, Postmaster of Meshed — A24

1902 Typo. Imperf.

No.	Type	Denomination	Unused	Used
222	A24	1c black	1,500.	450.00
a.		Inverted frame		—
b.		Inverted center	—	3,000.
223	A24	2c black	1,250.	450.00
a.		Inverted frame		—
b.		"2" in right upper corner	3,000.	1,750.
224	A24	3c black	3,250.	1,750.
225	A24	5c violet	750.00	200.00
a.		"5" in right upper corner		—
b.		Frame printed on both sides	2,250.	1,000.
c.		Inverted center		—
226	A24	5c black	900.00	350.00
a.		Persian "5" in lower left corner		—
b.		Inverted center		—
227	A24	12c dull blue	4,000.	1,500.
a.		Inverted frame		—
b.		Inverted center		—
228	A24	1k rose	30,000.	3,500.

Used values for Nos. 222-228 canceled to order are about ⅓ to ½ the values shown, which are for postally used stamps.

The design of No. 228, shown, differs slightly from the design of Nos. 222-227.

Nos. 222-228 were printed in three operations. Inverted centers have frames and numerals upright. Inverted frames have centers and numerals upright.

Pin-perforated

No.	Type	Denomination	Unused	Used
234	A24	12c dull blue	4,000.	1,500.

Monsieur Victor Castaigne, the Belgian director of post and customs in the northwestern province of Khorassan, on his own intiiative, prepared a set of provisional stamps to meet the shortage of low-denomination stamps. These stamps were printed individually from two cliches, one for the frame and one for the vignette, reading V.C. (Castaigne's initials taken from his ring). Printed stamps were initialed by the director in red ink for the shahis (ch) denominations and in violet ink for the 1k. Remainders exist posthumously canceled wtih fake MECHED postmarks. Various forgeries exist, including examples printed by two cliches for the frame and vignette, as well as one cliche for both. Values quoted are for examples accompanied by certificates of authenticity.

A25

Black Serpents Head

Hollow Serpents Head

TWO TYPES:

Type I — "CHAHI" or "KRANS" are in capital letters.

Type II — Only "C" of "Chahi" or "K" of "Krans" is a capital. The handstamp appears only on type I stamps and comes in two varieties: black serpent's head and hollow serpent's head.

The 3c and 5c sometimes have a tall narrow figure in the upper left corner. The 5c is also found with the cross at the upper left broken or missing. These varieties are known with many of the overprints.

Stamps of Design A25 have a faint fancy background in the color of the stamp. All issued stamps have handstamped controls as listed.

Type I
Handstamp Overprinted in Black

1902 Typeset Imperf.

No.	Type	Denomination	Unused	Used
235	A25	1c gray & buff	300.00	150.00
236	A25	2c brown & buff	400.00	150.00
237	A25	3c green & buff	400.00	150.00
238	A25	5c red & buff	300.00	100.00
239	A25	12c ultra & buff	500.00	150.00
		Nos. 235-239 (5)	1,900.	700.00

Counterfeits abound. Type II stamps with this overprint are forgeries.

The 3c with violet overprint is believed not to have been regularly issued.

Handstamp Overprinted in Rose

1902 Type I

No.	Type	Denomination	Unused	Used
247	A25	1c gray & buff	25.00	2.00
248	A25	2c brown & buff	25.00	2.00
249	A25	3c dp grn & buff	25.00	2.00
250	A25	5c red & buff	25.00	.75
251	A25	10c ol yel & buff	50.00	3.00
252	A25	12c ultra & buff	75.00	5.00
253	A25	1k violet & bl	60.00	6.00
254	A25	2k ol grn & bl	100.00	12.50
256	A25	10k dk bl & bl	150.00	30.00
257	A25	50k red & blue	1,500.	800.00
		Nos. 247-257 (10)	2,035.	863.25

A 5k exists but its status is doubtful. Value $500.

Stamps with handstamps other than bright red are either fake or were not regularly issued.

Type II

No.	Type	Denomination	Unused	Used
280	A25	1c gray & yellow	250.00	200.00
281	A25	2c brown & yel	200.00	200.00
282	A25	3c dk grn & yel	2,000.	750.00
a.		"Persans"		—
283	A25	5c red & yellow	50.00	15.00
284	A25	10c ol yel & yel	100.00	15.00
285	A25	12c blue & yel	150.00	25.00
290	A25	50k org red & bl	1,250.	600.00

The 3c, inscribed "Persans," was never issued.

Denominations with handstamps other than bright red are either fake or not regularly issued.

Remainders exist with fake control handstamps.

Type II stamps with high denominations of 10t (100k), 20t, 25t, 50t and 100t with blue rosette 1319 handstamps and black control numbers on the front were used on postal money orders. Denominations with control numbers in colors other than black are forgeries.

Beware of forgeries and/or reprints of most Iran stamps between the years 1870-1925. Scott values are for genuine stamps. Collectors should be aware that forgeries of many issues outnumber genuine examples by factors of 10 or 20 to one. Failing specialized knowledge on the part of the collector, these stamps should be examined or authenticated by acknowledged experts before purchase.

Handstamp Surcharged in Black

1902 **Type I**

308 A25 5k on 5k ocher & bl *200.00 50.00*

Counterfeits of No. 308 abound.
This surcharge in rose, violet, blue or green is considered bogus.
This surcharge on 50k orange red and blue, and on 5k ocher and blue, type II, is considered bogus.

Handstamp Overprinted Diagonally in Black

1902 **Type I**

315 A25 2c brown & buff 250.00 125.00
a. Rose overprint *500.00 500.00*

Type II

316 A25 2c brown & yel — —
a. Rose overprint

"P. L." stands for "Poste Locale."
Counterfeits of Nos. 315-316 exist.
Some specialists believe that Type II stamps were not used officially for this overprint.

Handstamp Overprinted in Black or Rose

1902 **Type II**

317 A25 2c brn & yellow 250.00 125.00
318 A25 2c brown & yel (R) *500.00 500.00*

Counterfeits of Nos. 317-318 exist.

Overprinted in Blue

1903 **Type I**

321 A25 1k violet & blue 125.00 125.00

Type II

336 A25 1c gray & yellow 60.00 60.00
337 A25 2c brown & yellow 60.00 60.00
338 A25 5c red & yellow 40.00 40.00
339 A25 10c olive yel & yel 75.00 75.00
340 A25 12c blue & yellow 90.00 90.00
Nos. 321-340 (6) 450.00 450.00

A 3c Type I exists but was not regularly issued. Value $250.
The overprint also exists in violet and black, but it is doubtful whether such items were regularly issued.
Forgeries of Nos. 321, 336-340 abound. Genuine unused examples are seldom found.

Arms of Persia — A26

Mozaffar-eddin Shah Qajar — A27

1902 (Dec.)-1904 **Typo.** ***Perf. 12½***

351 A26 1c violet 2.00 .25
352 A26 2c gray 2.00 .25
353 A26 3c green 2.00 .25
354 A26 5c rose 2.00 .25
355 A26 10c yellow brn 3.00 1.50
356 A26 12c blue 4.00 .50

Engr.

Perf. 11½x11

357 A27 1k violet 15.00 .50
358 A27 2k ultramarine 25.00 1.25
359 A27 5k orange brn 40.00 2.00
360 A27 10k rose red 50.00 4.00
361 A27 20k orange ('04) 45.00 5.00
362 A27 30k green ('04) 70.00 12.50
363 A27 50k green 550.00 100.00
Nos. 351-363 (13) 810.00 128.25

No. 355 exists with blue diagonal surcharge "1 CHAHI"; its status is questioned.
A government decree in November, 1903, required that all picture postcards be censored by the Central Post Office, which would apply a control mark on each card to show that the 2c tax for this service had been paid. No. 352 was overprinted "Controle" in several styles, for this purpose. Value: unused $100; used, from $25.
See Nos. 428-433. For surcharges and overprints see #364-420, 446-447, 464-469, O8-O28, P1.

No. 353 Surcharged in Violet or Blue

1903

364 A26 1c on 3c green (V) 75.00 25.00
365 A26 2c on 3c green (Bl) 75.00 25.00

A 2c surcharge on No. 354 exists, but its status is dubious.

No. 360 Surcharged in Blue

366 A27 12c on 10k rose red 75.00 40.00
a. Black surcharge 150.00 70.00
b. Violet surcharge 150.00 70.00
Nos. 364-366 (3) 225.00 90.00

Nos. 366, 366a and 366b used are valued canceled to order.

No. 363 Surcharged in Blue or Black

1903

368 A27 2t on 50k grn (Bl) 200.00 60.00
a. Rose surcharge 225.00 100.00
b. Black surcharge 225.00 100.00
370 A27 3t on 50k grn (Bk) 200.00 60.00
a. Violet surcharge 225.00 60.00
b. Rose surcharge 250.00 125.00

No. 363 Surcharged in Blue or Black

1904

372 A27 2t on 50k grn (Bl) 200.00 60.00
375 A27 3t on 50k grn (Bk) 200.00 60.00

The 2t on 50k also exists with surcharge in rose, violet, black and magenta; the 3t on 50k in rose, violet and blue. Values about the same unused; about 50 percent higher used.

No. 352 Overprinted in Violet

1904 ***Perf. 12½***

393 A26 2c gray 100.00 25.00
a. Black overprint 150.00 50.00
b. Rose overprint 135.00 35.00

This overprint also exists in blue, violet blue, maroon and gray, but these were not regularly issued.

Stamps of 1903 Surcharged in Black

a

b

c

1904

400 A26(a) 3c on 5c rose 40.00 .75
401 A26(b) 6c on 10c brown 75.00 .75
402 A27(c) 9c on 1k violet 50.00 3.50
Nos. 400-402 (3) 165.00 5.00

Stamps of 1903 Surcharged in Black, Magenta or Violet

1905-06

404 A26 1c on 3c green ('06) 75.00 25.00
405 A27 1c on 1k violet 35.00 15.00
406 A27 2c on 5k orange brn 40.00 25.00
407 A26 1c on 3c grn (M) ('06) 15.00 5.00
408 A27 1c on 1k violet (M) 20.00 10.00
409 A27 2c on 5k org brn (V) 30.00 15.00
Nos. 404-409 (6) 215.00 95.00

Nos. 355 and 358 Surcharged in Violet

1906

419 A26 1c on 10c brown *150.00* —
420 A27 2c on 2k ultra *250.00* —

These stamps were prepared on the initiative of the Tabriz postmaster. Tabriz is the capital of the northeastern province of Azerbaijan.
Forgeries of Nos. 419-420 are common. Forgeries of No. 420, especially, are hard to distinguish since the original handstamp was used. Genuine used stamps may, in some cases, be identified by the cancellation.

A28

Typeset; "Provisoire" Overprint Handstamped in Black

1906 ***Imperf.***

422 A28 1c violet 25.00 1.00
a. Irregular pin perf. or perf. 10½ 75.00 25.00
423 A28 2c gray 150.00 10.00
424 A28 3c green 25.00 1.00
425 A28 6c red 25.00 .75
426 A28 10c brown 70.00 *40.00*
427 A28 13c blue 50.00 10.00
Nos. 422-427 (6) 345.00 62.75

Stamps of type A28 have a faint background pattern of tiny squares within squares, an ornamental frame and open rectangles for the value corners.
The 3c and 6c also exist perforated.
Nos. 422-427 are known without overprint but were probably not issued in that condition. Nearly all values are known with overprint inverted and double.
Forgeries are plentiful.

Lion Type of 1903 and

Mohammed-Ali Shah Qajar
A29 A30

1907-09 **Typo.** ***Perf. 12½***

428 A26 1c vio, *blue* 5.00 .25
429 A26 2c gray, *blue* 5.00 .25
430 A26 3c green, *blue* 5.00 .25
431 A26 6c rose, *blue* 5.00 .25
432 A26 9c org, *blue* 5.00 .30
433 A26 10c brown, *blue* 6.00 1.00

Engr.

Perf. 11, 11½

434 A29 13c dark blue 10.00 2.00
435 A29 1k red 10.00 1.50
436 A29 26c red brown 10.00 2.00
437 A29 2k deep grn 30.00 1.50
438 A29 3k pale blue 30.00 1.00
439 A29 4k brt yellow 500.00 17.50
440 A29 4k bister 30.00 3.00
441 A29 5k dark brown 35.00 3.00
442 A29 10k pink 40.00 3.00
443 A29 20k gray black 40.00 10.00
444 A29 30k dark violet 45.00 15.00
445 A30 50k gold, ver & black ('09) 165.00 30.00
Nos. 428-445 (18) 976.00 91.80

Frame of No. 445 lithographed. Nos. 434-444 were issued in 1908.
Remainders canceled to order abound. Used values for Nos. 437-445 are for c-t-os.

Nos. 428-429 Overprinted in Black

1909 ***Perf. 12½***

446 A26 1c violet, *blue* 90.00 40.00
447 A26 2c gray, *blue* 80.00 30.00

Counterfeits of Nos. 446-447 exist.

Coat of Arms — A31

1909 **Typo.** ***Perf. 12½x12***

448 A31 1c org & maroon *.50* .35
449 A31 2c vio & maroon *.50* .35
450 A31 3c yel grn & mar *.50* .35
451 A31 6c red & maroon *.50* .25
452 A31 9c gray & maroon *.50* .35
453 A31 10c red vio & mar *.50* .35
454 A31 13c dk blue & mar *.50* *2.00*
455 A31 1k sil, vio & bis brn *1.00* *2.00*
456 A31 26c dk grn & mar *1.00* *3.00*
457 A31 2k sil, dk grn & bis brown *1.00* *2.00*
458 A31 3k sil, gray & bis brn *1.00* *3.50*
459 A31 4k sil, bl & bis brn *1.00* *3.50*
460 A31 5k gold, brn & bis brn *2.50* *3.50*
461 A31 10k gold, org & bis brn *5.00* *10.00*
462 A31 20k gold, ol grn & bis brn *7.00* *20.00*

463	A31	30k	gold, car & bis brn	*12.00*	*20.00*
			Nos. 448-463 (16)	35.00	71.50

Unauthorized reprints of Nos. 448-463 abound. Originals have clean, bright colors, centers stand out clearly, and paper is much thinner. Nos. 460-463 originals have gleaming gold margins; reprint margins appear as blackish yellow. Centers of reprints of Nos. 448-454, 456 are brown.

Values above are for unused reprints and for authenticated used stamps. Original unused stamps sell for much higher prices.

For surcharges & overprints see Nos. 516-519, 541-549. 582-585, 588-594, 597, 601-606, 707-722, C1-C16, O31-O40.

> In 1909 two sets of 16 stamps were prepared for the coronation of Ahmad Shad Qajar. The first set with lion and sun high values and gold borders was for postal use, while the second set with city gate high values and silver borders was inscribed "SERVICE". While neither set was placed in use, both were sold to collectors at a later date.

Nos. 428-444, Imperf., Surcharged in Red or Black

1910 — Blue Paper — *Imperf.*

464	A26	1c	on 1c violet	200.00	140.00
465	A26	1c	on 2c gray	200.00	140.00
466	A26	1c	on 3c green	200.00	140.00
467	A26	1c	on 6c rose (Bk)	200.00	140.00
468	A26	1c	on 9c orange	200.00	140.00
469	A26	1c	on 10c brown	200.00	140.00

White Paper

470	A29	2c	on 13c dp bl	200.00	140.00
471	A29	2c	on 26c red brn (Bk)	200.00	140.00
472	A29	2c	on 1k red (Bk)	200.00	140.00
473	A29	2c	on 2k dp grn	200.00	140.00
474	A29	2c	on 3k pale bl	200.00	140.00
475	A29	2c	on 4k brt yel	200.00	140.00
476	A29	2c	on 4k bister	200.00	140.00
477	A29	2c	on 5k dk brn	200.00	140.00
478	A29	2c	on 10k pink (Bk)	200.00	140.00
479	A29	2c	on 20k gray blk	200.00	140.00
480	A29	2c	on 30k dk vio	200.00	140.00
			Nos. 464-480 (17)	3,400.	2,380.

Nos. 464-480 were prepared for use on newspapers, but nearly the entire printing was sold to stamp dealers. The issue is generally considered speculative. Counterfeit surcharges exist on trimmed stamps.

Used values are for c-t-o.

> Early printings of Nos. 481-500 were made by wet printing, while later issues were mostly produced by dry printing. As a result, there are two heights of the central (engraved) vignette, 23mm (dry printing) and 22½ (wet printing), caused by the shrinkage of the paper as it dried after printing.

Ahmad Shah Qajar — A32

Engr. center, Typo. frame

1911-21

Tall Portrait (23mm)

Perf. 11½

481	A32	1c	green & org	.50	1.00
482	A32	2c	red & sepia	.50	1.00
483	A32	3c	gray brn & grn	.50	1.00
483B	A32	3c	3c bister brown & green	.50	1.00
484	A32	5c	brn & car ('13)	.50	
485	A32	6c	gray & car	.50	.30
486	A32	6c	grn & red brn ('13)	.50	.40
487	A32	9c	yel brn & vio	.75	2.00
488	A32	10c	red & org brn	.75	35.00
489	A32	12c	grn & ultra ('13)	.50	.50
490	A32	13c	violet & ultra	1.00	2.00
491	A32	1k	ultra & car	1.00	4.00
492	A32	24c	vio & grn ('13)	.50	.50
493	A32	26c	ultra & green	1.00	5.00
494	A32	2k	grn & red vio	2.00	2.00
495	A32	3k	violet & blk	2.00	4.00
496	A32	4k	ultra & gray ('13)	—	
497	A32	5k	red & ultra	3.00	4.00
498	A32	10k	ol bis & cl	5.00	5.00
499	A32	20k	vio brn & bis	5.00	5.00
500	A32	30k	red & green	7.00	5.00
			Nos. 481-500 (21)	33.00	78.70

Values for Nos. 481-500 unused are for reprints, which cannot be distinguished from the late printings of the stamps.

The reprints include inverted centers for some denominations. Values, each $30-$50.

For surcharges and overprints see Nos. 501-515, 520-540, 586-587, 595, 596, 598, 600, 607-609, 630-634, 646-666.

Perf. 11½x11

481a	A32	1c	green & org	10.00	.25
482a	A32	2c	red & sepia	20.00	.25
483a	A32	3c	gray brn & grn	25.00	.25
483Ba	A32	3c	bister brn & grn ('21)	60.00	3.00
484a	A32	5c	brn & car ('13)	35.00	.40
485a	A32	6c	gray & car	30.00	.30
486a	A32	6c	grn & red brown ('13)	35.00	.40
487a	A32	9c	yel brn & violet	40.00	.25
488a	A32	10c	red & org brn	55.00	.25
489a	A32	12c	grn & ultra ('13)	45.00	.50
490a	A32	13c	violet & ultra	60.00	2.00
492a	A32	24c	ultra & carmine	60.00	.50
494a	A32	2k	green & red vio	115.00	1.00
495a	A32	3k	violet & black	170.00	4.00
497a	A32	5k	red & ultra	150.00	4.00
498a	A32	10k	ol bis & claret	500.00	5.00
499a	A32	20k	vio brn & bister	500.00	5.00
500a	A32	30k	red & green	500.00	5.00
			Nos. 481a-500a (18)	2,410.	31.45

Perf. 11½x12

488b	A32	10c	red & org brn	75.00	25.00
490b	A32	13c	violet & ultra	75.00	2.00
493b	A32	26c	ultra & green	250.00	75.00
496b	A32	4k	ultra & gray ('13)	450.00	100.00
497b	A32	5k	red & ultra	300.00	50.00
			Nos. 488b-497b (5)	1,150.	252.00

No. 496b with inverted center is a reprint. Value, $50.

Short Portrait (22½mm)

Perf. 11½

481c	A32	1c	green & org	50.00	20.00
482c	A32	2c	red & sepia	85.00	20.00
483c	A32	3c	gray brn & grn	70.00	10.00
484c	A32	5c	brn & car ('13)	—	—
485c	A32	6c	gray & car	35.00	5.00
487c	A32	9c	yel brn & violet	30.00	5.00
491c	A32	1k	ultra & carmine	—	
493c	A32	26c	ultra & green	135.00	15.00
494c	A32	2k	green & red vio	300.00	
495c	A32	3k	violet & black	65.00	
496c	A32	4k	violet & black ('13)		—
500c	A32	30k	red & green	800.00	75.00
			Nos. 481c-500c (12)	1,570.	150.00

No. 491c is known only with the "Controlle 1922" overprint. Nos. 494c and 495c were apparently never used.

Perf. 11½x11

481d	A32	1c	green & org	35.00	1.00
482d	A32	2c	red & sepia	85.00	10.00
483d	A32	3c	gray brn & grn	70.00	10.00
485d	A32	6c	gray & car	60.00	3.00
488d	A32	10c	red & org brn	95.00	30.00
490d	A32	13c	violet & ultra	75.00	2.00
491d	A32	1k	ultra & carmine	125.00	2.00
493d	A32	26c	ultra & green	70.00	15.00
494d	A32	2k	green & red vio	150.00	2.00
495d	A32	3k	violet & black	300.00	10.00
497d	A32	5k	red & ultra	350.00	20.00
498d	A32	10k	ol bis & claret	650.00	75.00
			Nos. 481d-498d (12)	2,065.	180.00

Perf. 11½x12

493e	A32	26c	ultra & green	500.00	100.00
494e	A32	2k	green & red vio	400.00	30.00
495e	A32	3k	violet & black	400.00	35.00
496e	A32	4k	violet & black ('13)	600.00	150.00
498e	A32	10k	ol bis & claret	700.00	50.00
499e	A32	20k	vio brn & bister	800.00	75.00

Stamps of 1911 Overprinted in Black

1911 "Officiel" Overprint On Nos. 481/500

1911 — Tall Portrait — *Perf. 11½*

503	A32	3c	gray brn & grn	50.00	8.00
			Never hinged	100.00	
504	A32	6c	gray & car	50.00	8.00
			Never hinged	100.00	
507	A32	13c	vio & ultra	125.00	12.00
			Never hinged	200.00	
509	A32	26c	ultra & green	175.00	15.00
			Never hinged	300.00	
513	A32	10k	ol bis & claret	1,350.	75.00
			Never hinged	2,250.	
			Nos. 503-513 (5)	1,750.	118.00

On Nos. 481a/500a

Perf. 11½x11

501	A32	1c	green & org	50.00	8.00
502	A32	2c	red & sepia	50.00	8.00
503a	A32	3c	gray brn & grn	50.00	8.00
504a	A32	6c	gray & carmine		20.00
506	A32	10c	red & org brn	85.00	12.00
508	A32	1k	ultra & car	*195.00*	*15.00*
510	A32	2k	grn & red vio	225.00	17.00
511	A32	3k	vio & black	300.00	25.00
512	A32	5k	red & ultra	350.00	50.00
513a	A32	10k	ol bis & claret	1,350.	75.00
514	A32	20k	vio brn & bis	1,150.	85.00
515	A32	30k	red & green	1,350.	90.00
			Nos. 501-515 (12)	5,155.	413.00

Short Portrait

On Nos. 481c/500c

Perf. 11½

501c	A32	1c	green & org		20.00
502c	A32	2c	red & sepia		20.00
503c	A32	3c	gray brn & grn		20.00
504c	A32	6c	gray & carmine	70.00	12.00
505	A32	9c	yel brn & vio	70.00	12.00
515c	A32	30k	red & green	1,500.	100.00
			Nos. 501c-515c (6)	1,640.	184.00

On Nos. 481d/514d

Perf. 11½x11

501d	A32	1c	green & org	70.00	12.00
502d	A32	2c	red & sepia	70.00	12.00
503d	A32	3c	gray brn & grn	70.00	12.00
504d	A32	6c	gray & carmine	70.00	12.00
506d	A32	10c	red & org brn	85.00	12.00
507d	A32	13c	violet & ultra	125.00	12.00
508d	A32	1k	ultra & carmine		95.00
509d	A32	26c	ultra & green	175.00	15.00
510d	A32	2k	grn & red violet	225.00	17.00
511d	A32	3k	violet & black	300.00	25.00
512d	A32	5k	red & ultra	350.00	50.00
513d	A32	10k	olive bister & claret	1,500.	85.00
514d	A32	20k	vio brn & bis	1,250.	90.00
			Nos. 501d-514d (13)	4,290.	449.00

The "Officiel" overprint does not signify that the stamps were intended for use on official correspondence but that they were issued by authority. It was applied to the stocks in Tabriz and all post offices in the Tabriz region after a large quantity of stamps had been stolen during the Russian occupation of Tabriz.

The "Officiel" overprint has been counterfeited.

Stamps of 1909-11 Overprinted in Black

1911, Oct. — On #449-451, 454

516	A31	2c	vio & maroon	300.00	150.00
517	A31	3c	yel grn & mar	300.00	150.00
518	A31	6c	red & maroon	300.00	150.00
519	A31	13c	dk blue & mar	300.00	150.00
			Nos. 516-519 (4)	1,200.	600.00

On Nos. 482a/490s

520	A32	2c	red & sepia (on #482a)	300.00	150.00
b.			On #482c	—	—
c.			On #482d	—	—
521	A32	3c	gray brn & grn (on #483d)	—	—
a.			On #483a	300.00	150.00
522	A32	6c	gray & car (on #485)	125.00	75.00
a.			On #485a	—	—
b.			On #485c	—	—
c.			On #485d	—	—
523	A32	13c	violet & ultra (on #490)	200.00	125.00
a.			On #490a	—	—
b.			On #490d	—	—
			Nos. 520-523 (4)	625.00	350.00

Stamps were sold at a 10% discount to stagecoach station keepers on the Tehran-Recht route. To prevent speculation, these stamps were overprinted "Stagecoach Stations" in French and Farsi.

Forgeries exist, usually overprinted on reprints of the 1909 issue and used examples of the 1911 issue. Values are for authenticated stamps.

In 1912 this overprint, reading "Sultan Mohammad Ali Shah Qajar," was handstamped on outgoing mail in the Persian Kurdistan region occupied by the forces of the former Shah Mohammad Ali. It was applied after the stamps were on cover and is found on 8 of the Shah Ahmed stamps of 1911 (1c, 2c, 3c, 6c, 9c, 13c, 1k and 26c). Two covers are known with 10c stamp.

Nos. 490 and 493 Surcharged

a

b

1914

535	A32(a)	1c on 13c (on #490)	30.00	2.00
a.		On #490a	30.00	2.00
b.		On #490b)	30.00	2.00
c.		On #490d	30.00	2.00
536	A32(b)	3c on 26c (on #493)	30.00	4.00
a.		On #493b	30.00	2.00
b.		On #493c	30.00	2.00
c.		on 26c (on #493d)	30.00	2.00
d.		On #493e	30.00	2.00

> In 1914 a set of 19 stamps was prepared as a coronation issue. The 10 lower values each carry a different portrait; the 9 higher values show buildings and scenes. Value $2,500 each set. The same set printed with black centers was overprinted in red "SERVICE."

Nos. 484 and 489 Surcharged in Black or Violet

c

d

1915

537	A32(c)	1c on 5c (on #484a)	20.00	2.00
538	A32(c)	2c on 5c (on #484a)	200.00	40.00
539	A32(c)	2c on 5c (V) (on #484a)	20.00	2.00
540	A32(d)	6c on 12c (on #489a)	30.00	2.00
		Nos. 537-540 (4)	270.00	46.00

Nos. 455, 454 Surcharged

e

f

1915 — *Perf. 12½x12*

541	A31(e)	5c on 1k multi	75.00	5.00
542	A31(f)	12c on 13c multi	110.00	7.00

Counterfeit surcharges on reprints abound.

Nos. 448-453, 455 Overprinted

1915

No.	Type	Description	Unused	Used
543	A31	1c org & maroon	70.00	5.00
544	A31	2c vio & maroon	50.00	5.00
545	A31	3c grn & maroon	60.00	5.00
546	A31	6c red & maroon	60.00	5.00
547	A31	9c gray & maroon	100.00	7.00
548	A31	10c red vio & mar	150.00	10.00
549	A31	1k sil, vio & bis brn	250.00	10.00
		Nos. 543-549 (7)	740.00	47.00

This overprint ("1333") also exists on the 2k, 10k, 20k and 30k, but they were not issued.

Counterfeit overprints, usually on reprints, abound.

Beware of forgeries and/or reprints of most Iran stamps between the years 1870-1925. Scott values are for genuine stamps. Collectors should be aware that forgeries of many issues outnumber genuine examples by factors of 10 or 20 to one. Failing specialized knowledge on the part of the collector, these stamps should be examined or authenticated by acknowledged experts before purchase.

Imperial Crown — A33

King Darius, Farvahar overhead — A34

Ruins of Persepolis — A35

Perf. 11½ or Compound 11x11½

Engr., Typo.

1915, Mar. Wmk. 161

No.	Type	Description	Unused	Used
560	A33	1c car & indigo	.25	2.00
561	A33	2c bl & carmine	.25	2.00
562	A33	3c dark green	.25	2.00
a.		Inverted center	—	
564	A33	5c red	.25	2.50
565	A33	6c olive grn & car	.25	2.00
a.		Inverted center	—	
566	A33	9c yel brn & vio	.25	2.00
567	A33	10c bl grn & yel brn	.25	2.00
568	A33	12c ultramarine	.25	2.00
569	A34	1k sil, yel brn & gray	.65	5.00
570	A33	24c yel brn & dk brn	.25	5.00
571	A34	2k silver, bl & rose	.65	5.00
572	A34	3k sil, vio & brn	.65	5.00
573	A34	5k sil, brn & green	.65	7.00
574	A35	1t gold, pur & blk	.65	10.00
575	A35	2t gold, grn & brn	1.00	10.00
576	A35	3t gold, cl & red brn	1.00	10.00
577	A35	5t gold, blue & ind	1.00	10.00
		Nos. 560-577 (17)	8.50	83.50

Coronation of Shah Ahmed.

Nos. 560-568, 570 are engraved. Nos. 569, 571-573 are engraved except for silver margins. Nos. 574-577 have centers engraved, frames typographed.

The 3c and 6c with inverted centers are considered genuine errors. Unauthorized reprints exist of these varieties and of other denominations with inverted centers. **Values unused for Nos. 560-577 are for reprints.**

For surcharges and overprints see Nos. 610-616, 635-646, O41-O57, Q19-Q35.

Nos. 455, 461-463 Overprinted

1915 Unwmk. Typo. *Perf. 12½x12*

No.	Type	Description	Unused	Used
582	A31	1k sil, vio & bis brn	*2.00*	*20.00*
583	A31	10k multicolored	*5.00*	*30.00*
584	A31	20k multicolored	*10.00*	*100.00*
585	A31	30k multicolored	*12.00*	*60.00*
		Nos. 582-585 (4)	*29.00*	*210.00*

Genuine unused examples are rare. Most unused stamps offered in the marketplace are reprints, and the unused values above are for reprints. Used values for authenticated stamps.

Forgeries abound of Nos. 582-585.

In May 1917, 17 contemporaneous Russian stamps overprinted "Occupation Azerbayedjan" appeared on the philatelic market. These were a bogus production, purportedly prepared by Anglo-Russian forces in occupation of the province of Azerbaijan in Iran. While British and Russian troops were indeed in the province at that time, they were there strictly to support Persian forces against the Turks, and were in no sense occupiers. Covers canceled with the consular handstamp of Tabriz were privately created to lend credence to the issue. Later, other covers were created using a forged October 1917 datestamp of Baku, causing subsequent catalogs to attribute them to the Russian province of Azerbaijan. The issue has been extensively forged.

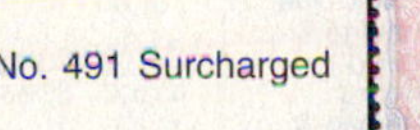

No. 491 Surcharged

1917 *Perf. 11½*

No.	Type	Description	Unused	Used
586	A32	12c on 1k multi (on #491a)	*2,500.*	*3,500.*
587	A32	24c on 1k multi (on #491a)	*1,500.*	*1,750.*

Issued during the Turkish occupation of Kermanshah. Forgeries exist.

Values for unused stamps are for reprints.

No. 448 Overprinted "1335" in Persian Numerals

1917 *Perf. 12½x12*

No.	Type	Description	Unused	Used
588	A31	1c org & maroon	*350.00*	250.00

Overprint on No. 588 is similar to date in "k" and "l" surcharges. Forgeries exist.

Nos. 449, 452-453, 456 Surcharged

k

l

1917

No.	Type	Description	Unused	Used
589	A31(k)	1c on 2c	30.00	3.00
590	A31(k)	1c on 9c	40.00	4.00
591	A31(k)	1c on 10c	30.00	3.00
592	A31(l)	3c on 9c	50.00	4.00
593	A31(l)	3c on 10c	40.00	3.00
594	A31(l)	3c on 26c	40.00	5.00

Same Surcharge on No. 488

No.	Type	Description	Unused	Used
595	A32(k)	1c on 10c (on #488)	75.00	2.00
a.		On #488a	75.00	2.00
b.		On #488d	75.00	2.00
596	A32(l)	3c on 10c (on #488)	75.00	2.00

Nos. 454 & 491 Surcharged Type "e"

No.	Type	Description	Unused	Used
597	A31	5c on 13c	50.00	5.00
598	A32	5c on 1k (on #489a)	75.00	2.00
		Never hinged	125.00	

Counterfeit surcharges on "canceled" reprints of Nos. 449, 452-454, 456 abound.

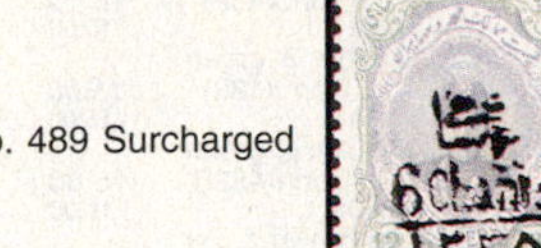

No. 489 Surcharged

No.	Type	Description	Unused	Used
600	A32	6c on 12c grn & ultra (on #489a)	125.00	20.00
		Never hinged	220.00	

No. 457 Overprinted

1918

No.	Type	Description	Unused	Used
601	A31	2k multi	175.00	25.00

Nos. 459-460 Surcharged

1918

No.	Type	Description	Unused	Used
602	A31	24c on 4k multi	150.00	25.00
603	A31	10k on 5k multi	175.00	25.00

The surcharges of Nos. 602-603 have been counterfeited.

Nos. 457-463 Overprinted

1918

No.	Type	Description	Unused	Used
603A	A31	2k multicolored	*3.00*	*65.00*
604	A31	3k multicolored	*3.00*	*15.00*
604A	A31	4k multicolored	*5.00*	*150.00*
604B	A31	5k multicolored	*5.00*	*75.00*
605	A31	10k multicolored	*8.00*	*50.00*
605A	A31	20k multicolored	*20.00*	*200.00*
606	A31	30k multicolored	*15.00*	*100.00*
		Nos. 603A-606 (7)	*59.00*	*655.00*

Genuine unused examples are rare. Most unused stamps offered in the marketplace are reprints, and the unused values above are for reprints. Used values for authenticated stamps.

Forgeries abound of Nos. 603A-606.

Nos. 489, 488 and 491 Surcharged

m

n

No.	Type	Description	Unused	Used
607	A32(m)	3c on 12c (on #489a)	75.00	2.00
608	A32(n)	6c on 10c (on #489a)	100.00	2.00
609	A32(m)	6c on 1k (on #491)	75.00	2.00
		Never hinged	125.00	
a.		On #491a	75.00	2.00
		Nos. 607-609 (3)	250.00	6.00

Nos. 571-577 Overprinted in Black or Red

1918 Wmk. 161

No.	Type	Description	Unused	Used
610	A34	2k sil, blue & rose	15.00	15.00
611	A34	3k sil, vio & brn (R)	15.00	15.00
612	A34	5k sil, brn & grn (R)	15.00	15.00
613	A35	1t gold, pur & black (R)	20.00	20.00
614	A35	2t gold, grn & brn	20.00	20.00
615	A35	3t gold, cl & red brn	20.00	20.00
616	A35	5t gold, bl & ind (R)	25.00	25.00
		Nos. 610-616 (7)	130.00	130.00

The overprint commemorates the end of World War I. Counterfeits of this overprint are plentiful.

A36

Color Litho., Black Typo.

1919 Unwmk. *Perf. 11½*

No.	Type	Description	Unused	Used
617	A36	1c yel & black	25.00	2.00
618	A36	3c green & black	25.00	2.00
619	A36	5c rose & black	65.00	5.00
620	A36	6c vio & black	45.00	2.00
621	A36	12c blue & black	150.00	15.00
		Nos. 617-621 (5)	310.00	26.00

Nos. 617-621 exist imperf.

This issue has been extensively counterfeited, and most examples in the marketplace are forgeries.

Counterfeits having double line over "POSTES" abound.

Nos. 75, 85-86 Surcharged in Various Colors

1919 *Perf. 10½, 11, 11½, 13½*

No.	Type	Description	Unused	Used
622	A14	2k on 5c lilac (Bk)	15.00	15.00
623	A14	3k on 5c lilac (Br)	15.00	15.00
624	A14	4k on 5c lilac (G)	15.00	15.00
625	A14	5k on 5c lilac (V)	15.00	15.00
626	A16	10k on 10c rose (Bl)	25.00	25.00
627	A16	20k on 10c rose (G)	25.00	25.00
628	A16	30k on 10c rose (Br)	25.00	25.00
629	A16	50k on 14c org (V)	30.00	30.00
		Nos. 622-629 (8)	165.00	165.00

Nos. 622-629 exist with inverted and double surcharge. Some specialists consider these fraudulent. Forgeries exist.

Nos. 486, 489 Handstamp Surcharged

1921 ***Perf. 11½, 11½x11***

No.	Type	Description	Unused	Used
630	A32	10c on 6c (on #486)	100.00	25.00
		No gum	50.00	
		No gum	50.00	
631	A32	1k on 12c (on #489)	100.00	25.00
		No gum	50.00	
a.		On #489a	100.00	25.00
		No gum	50.00	

Counterfeits exist.

No. 489 Surcharged

No.	Type	Description	Unused	Used
632	A32	6c on 12c (on #489)	650.00	20.00
		No gum	250.00	
a.		On #489a	650.00	20.00
		No gum	250.00	

Surcharged in Black or Violet

1921

No.	Type	Description	Unused	Used
633	A32	10c on 6c (V) (on #486)	*200.00*	*50.00*
		No gum	*100.00*	
a.		Surcharge handstamped in black	400.00	350.00
		No gum	200.00	
634	A32	1k on 12c (V) (on #489)	200.00	50.00
		No gum	100.00	
a.		On #489	200.00	50.00
		No gum	100.00	
b.		As "a," black surcharge	400.00	50.00
		No gum	200.00	

Counterfeits exist.

Coronation Issue of 1915 Overprinted

1921, May **Wmk. 161** ***Perf. 11, 11½***

No.	Type	Description	Unused	Used
635	A33	3c dark grn	15.00	
a.		Center and overprint inverted	—	
636	A33	5c red	15.00	
637	A33	6c olive grn & car	15.00	
638	A33	10c bl grn & yel brn	15.00	
639	A33	12c ultramarine	15.00	
640	A34	1k sil, yel brn & gray	20.00	
641	A34	2k sil, blue & rose	20.00	
642	A34	5k sil, brn & green	20.00	
643	A35	2t gold, grn & brn	25.00	
644	A35	3t gold, cl & red brn	30.00	
645	A35	5t gold, blue & ind	30.00	
		Nos. 635-645 (11)	220.00	

Counterfeits of this Feb. 21, 1921, overprint are plentiful. Inverted overprints exist on all values; some specialists consider them fraudulent.

Stamps of 1911-13 Overprinted

1922 **Unwmk.** ***Perf. 11½, 11½x11***

No.	Type	Description	Unused	Used
646	A32	1c grn & orange (on #481)	10.00	.35
a.		Inverted overprint	*300.00*	
b.		On #481a	10.00	.35
c.		As "b," pair, one without	300.00	—
d.		On #481c	200.00	.50
647	A32	2c red & sepia (on #482)	10.00	.35
a.		On #482a	15.00	.35
648	A32	3c brn & green (on #483)	*15.00*	.35
a.		On #483a	15.00	.35
648C	A32	3c brn & green (on #483B)	15.00	1.00
a.		On #483Ba	15.00	1.00
649	A32	5c brown & car (on #484a)	150.00	50.00
		Never hinged	300.00	
a.		On #484c	150.00	50.00
650	A32	6c grn & red brn (on #486)	10.00	.35
a.		On #486a	10.00	.35
651	A32	9c yel brn & vio (on #487)	12.00	.35
a.		On #487a	12.00	.35
652	A32	10c red & org brn (on #488)	20.00	.50
a.		Double ovpt., one inverted	*500.00*	
b.		On #488c	20.00	.50
c.		On #488a	30.00	1.00
653	A32	12c green & ultra (on #489)	30.00	.75
a.		Double overprint	500.00	
b.		On #487a	30.00	.75
654	A32	1k ultra & car (on #491)	35.00	1.00
a.		On #491a	35.00	1.00
b.		On #491c	40.00	1.00
655	A32	24c vio & green (on #492)	30.00	1.00
a.		On #492a	30.00	1.00
656	A32	2k grn & red vio (on #494)	95.00	1.00
a.		On #494a	95.00	1.00
657	A32	3k vio & black (on #495)	100.00	2.00
a.		On #495a	100.00	2.00
658	A32	4k ultra & gray (on #496b)	250.00	45.00
		Never hinged	500.00	
a.		On #496c		75.00
b.		On #496e	350.00	60.00
659	A32	5k red & ultra (on #497)	250.00	3.00
660	A32	10k ol bis & cl (on #498)	*1,000.*	7.00
a.		On #498a	1,000.	7.00
661	A32	20k vio brn & bis (on #499)	*1,000.*	8.00
a.		On #499a	1,000.	8.00
b.		On #499c	1,000.	30.00
662	A32	30k red & green (on #500)	*1,000.*	15.00
		Nos. 646-662 (18)	*4,032.*	137.00

The status of inverted overprints on 5c and 12c is dubious. Unlisted inverts on other denominations are generally considered fraudulent. Counterfeits of this overprint exist.

Nos. 653, 655 Surcharged

1922

No.	Type	Description	Unused	Used
663	A32	3c on 12c (on #489)	100.00	2.00
		No gum	50.00	
a.		On #489a	150.00	2.00
		No gum	50.00	
664	A32	6c on 24c (on #492)	150.00	3.00
		No gum	75.00	
a.		On #492a	250.00	3.00
		No gum	75.00	

Nos. 661-662 Surcharged

Type I

Type II

1923

No.	Type	Description	Unused	Used
665	A32	10c on 20k (on #499)	175.00	15.00
		No gum	65.00	
666	A32	1k on 30k (on #500), Ty I	*200.00*	*20.00*
		No gum	*80.00*	
a.		1k on 30k, Ty 2	250.00	25.00

There are two types of 'K' in 'Kran' — Type I: No. 666, one with straight serifs. Type II: No. 666a with a curved serif on the top right bar. Values are the same for either type.

Forgeries exist, generally made by handstamps applied to mint reprints or postally used original stamps.

Ahmed Shah Qajar — A37

Perf. 11½, 11x11½, 11½x11

1924-25 **Engr.**

No.	Type	Description	Unused	Used
667	A37	1c orange	2.50	.25
668	A37	2c magenta	2.50	.25
a.		Imperf. btwn., pair		*3,000.*
669	A37	3c org brn	2.50	.25
670	A37	6c blk brn	2.50	.25
671	A37	9c dark green	2.00	5.00
672	A37	10c dark violet	2.00	.30
673	A37	12c red	2.00	.30
674	A37	1k dark blue	2.00	.35
675	A37	2k indigo & red	5.00	5.00
a.		Center inverted	45,000.	*7,500.*
676	A37	3k dk vio & red brn	17.00	2.00
677	A37	5k red & brn	20.00	*30.00*
678	A37	10k choc & lilac	25.00	25.00
679	A37	20k dk grn & brn	30.00	30.00
680	A37	30k org & blk brn	40.00	40.00
		Nos. 667-680 (14)	155.00	138.95

For overprints see Nos. 703-706.

A38

SIX CHAHIS

Type I

Type II

Dated 1924

Color Litho., Black Typo.

1924 ***Perf. 11***

No.	Type	Description	Unused	Used
681	A38	1c yel brn & blk	20.00	1.00
682	A38	2c gray & blk	20.00	1.00
683	A38	3c dp rose & blk	20.00	1.00
684	A38	6c orange & blk (I)	30.00	1.50
a.		6c orange & blk (II)	35.00	2.00
		Nos. 681-684 (4)	90.00	4.50

The 1c was surcharged "Chahis" by error. Later the "s" was blocked out in black.

Counterfeits having double line over "POSTES" are plentiful.

1925 **Dated 1925**

No.	Type	Description	Unused	Used
686	A38	2c yel grn & blk	10.00	1.00
687	A38	3c red & blk	10.00	1.00
689	A38	6c chalky bl & blk	10.00	1.00
690	A38	9c lt brn & blk	30.00	2.00
691	A38	10c gray & blk	75.00	5.00
694	A38	1k emer & blk	65.00	10.00
695	A38	2k lilac & blk	175.00	40.00
		Nos. 686-695 (7)	375.00	60.00

Counterfeits having double line over "POSTES" are plentiful.

A39

Gold Overprint on Treasury Department Stamps

1925

No.	Type	Description	Unused	Used
697	A39	1c red	20.00	6.00
698	A39	2c yellow	20.00	6.00
699	A39	3c yellow green	20.00	6.00
700	A39	5c dark gray	75.00	30.00
701	A39	10c deep orange	45.00	10.00
702	A39	1k ultramarine	50.00	15.00
		Nos. 697-702 (6)	230.00	73.00

Deposition of Ahmad Shah Qajar and establishment of provisional government of Reza Shah Pahlavi.

Nos. 697-702 have same center (Persian lion in sunburst) with 6 different frames. Overprint reads: "Post / Provisional Government / of Pahlavi / 9th Abanmah / 1304 / 1925."

Nos. 667-670 Overprinted

1926 ***Perf. 11½, 11x11½, 11½x11***

No.	Type	Description	Unused	Used
703	A37	1c orange	5.00	3.00
704	A37	2c magenta	5.00	5.00
705	A37	3c orange brown	5.00	3.00
706	A37	6c black brown	125.00	85.00
		Nos. 703-706 (4)	140.00	96.00

Overprinted to commemorate the Pahlavi dynasty, dated 16 December 1925. Counterfeits exist.

Nos. 448-463 Overprinted

1926 ***Perf. 11½, 12½x12***

No.	Type	Description	Unused	Used
707	A31	1c org & maroon	20.00	.25
a.		Inverted overprint	2,000.	
708	A31	2c vio & maroon	20.00	.25
709	A31	3c yel grn & mar	20.00	.25
a.		Inverted overprint	2,000.	
710	A31	6c red & maroon	20.00	.25
711	A31	9c gray & mar	20.00	.25
712	A31	10c red vio & mar	25.00	.35
713	A31	13c dk bl & mar	30.00	.35
714	A31	1k multi	65.00	.35
715	A31	26c dk grn & mar	30.00	.35
716	A31	2k multi	75.00	1.00
717	A31	3k multi	175.00	2.00
718	A31	4k sil, bl & bis brn	550.00	35.00
719	A31	5k multi	250.00	10.00
720	A31	10k multi	800.00	15.00
721	A31	20k multi	850.00	15.00
722	A31	30k multi	900.00	20.00
		Nos. 707-722 (16)	3,850.	100.65

Overprinted to commemorate the Pahlavi government in 1926.

Values for Nos. 707-722 are for stamps perf. 11½, on thick paper. Stamps perf. 12½x12 on thin paper are worth substantially more.

Forgeries exist perf. 12½x12, with either machine overprints or handstamps. Most of these fakes can be identified by the absence of the top serif of the "1" in "1926."

A40

Reza Shah Pahlavi — A41

1926-29 **Typo.** ***Perf. 11***

723 A40 1c yellow green 6.00 .25
724 A40 2c gray violet 6.00 .25
725 A40 3c emerald 6.00 .25
727 A40 6c magenta 6.00 .25
728 A40 9c rose 12.00 .50
729 A40 10c bister brown 30.00 5.00
730 A40 12c deep orange 30.00 3.00
731 A40 15c pale ultra 35.00 2.00
733 A41 1k dull bl ('27) 60.00 15.00
734 A41 2k brt vio ('29) 180.00 75.00
Nos. 723-734 (10) 371.00 101.50

1928 **Redrawn**

740 A40 1c yellow green 30.00 .25
741 A40 2c gray violet 30.00 .25
742 A40 3c emerald 30.00 .25
743 A40 6c rose 30.00 .50
Nos. 740-743 (4) 120.00 1.25

On the redrawn stamps much of the shading of the face, throat, collar, etc., has been removed.

The letters of "Postes Persanes" and those in the circle at upper right are smaller. The redrawn stamps measure 20¼x25¾mm instead of 19¾x25¼mm.

A42

Reza Shah Pahlavi — A43

Perf. 11½, 12, 12½, Compound

1929 **Photo.**

744 A42 1c yel grn & cer 3.50 .25
745 A42 2c scar & brt blue 3.50 .25
a. Center inverted *45,000. 7,500.*
746 A42 3c mag & myr grn 3.50 .25
747 A42 6c yel brn & ol grn 3.50 .25
748 A42 9c Prus bl & ver 5.00 .25
749 A42 10c bl grn & choc 6.00 .25
750 A42 12c gray blk & pur 8.00 .30
751 A42 15c citron & ultra 10.00 .30
752 A42 1k dull bl & blk 15.00 .50
753 A42 24c ol grn & red brn 12.00 .50

Engr.

Perf. 11½

754 A42 2k brn org & dk vio 125.00 3.00
755 A42 3k dark grn & dp rose 150.00 5.00
756 A42 5k red brn & dp green 100.00 5.00
757 A42 1t ultra & dp rose 125.00 10.00
758 A42 2t carmine & blk 200.00 20.00

Engr. and Typo.

759 A43 3t gold & dp vio 175.00 35.00
Nos. 744-759 (16) 945.00 81.10

For overprints see Nos. 810-817.

Reza Shah Pahlavi — A44

1931-32 **Litho.** ***Perf. 11***

760 A44 1c ol brn & ultra 6.00 .25
761 A44 2c red brn & blk 6.00 .25
762 A44 3c lilac rose & ol 6.00 .25
763 A44 6c red org & vio 6.00 .25
764 A44 9c ultra & red org 12.00 .40
765 A44 10c ver & gray 40.00 1.00
766 A44 11c bl & dull red 37.50 35.00
767 A44 12c turq blue & lil rose 45.00 .70
768 A44 16c black & red 50.00 1.75
769 A44 1k car & turq bl 85.00 1.75
770 A44 27c dk gray & dl bl 90.00 1.75
Nos. 760-770 (11) 383.50 43.35

For overprints see Nos. 818-826.

A45

Reza Shah Pahlavi — A46

1933-34

771 A45 5d olive brown 3.00 .25
772 A45 10d blue 3.00 .25
773 A45 15d gray 3.00 .25
774 A45 30d emerald 3.00 .25
775 A45 45d turq blue 3.00 .50
776 A45 50d magenta 4.00 .50
777 A45 60d green 5.00 .50
778 A45 75d brown 8.00 1.50
779 A45 90d red 10.00 2.50
780 A46 1r dk rose & blk 25.00 2.00
781 A46 1.20r gray blk & rose 30.00 2.00
782 A46 1.50 citron & bl 35.00 2.00
783 A46 2r lt bl & choc 45.00 2.00
784 A46 3r mag & green 60.00 4.00
785 A46 5r dk brn & red org 225.00 50.00
Nos. 771-785 (15) 462.00 68.50

For overprints see Nos. 795-809.

"Justice" A47

"Education" A49

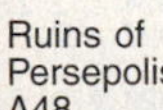
Ruins of Persepolis A48

Tehran Airport A50

Sanatorium at Sakhtessar — A51

Cement Factory, Chah-Abdul-Azim — A52

Gunboat "Palang" A53

Railway Bridge over Karun River A54

Post Office and Customs Building, Tehran A55

1935, Feb. 21 **Photo.** ***Perf. 12½***

786 A47 5d red brn & grn 1.00 .75
787 A48 10d red org & gray black 1.00 .75
788 A49 15d mag & Prus bl 1.50 .75
789 A50 30d black & green 1.50 .75
790 A51 45d ol grn & red brn 2.00 .75
791 A52 75d grn & dark brn 6.00 1.25
792 A53 90d blue & car rose 20.00 5.00
793 A54 1r red brn & pur 60.00 30.00
794 A55 1½r violet & ultra 25.00 10.00
Nos. 786-794 (9) 118.00 50.00

Reign of Reza Shah Pahlavi, 10th anniv.

Stamps of 1933-34 Overprinted in Black

1935 ***Perf. 11***

795 A45 5d olive brown 3.00 .50
796 A45 10d blue 3.00 .50
797 A45 15d gray 3.00 .50
798 A45 30d emerald 3.00 .50
799 A45 45d turq blue 10.00 3.00
800 A45 50d magenta 6.00 .50
801 A45 60d green 6.00 .50
802 A45 75d brown 10.00 10.00
803 A45 90d red 35.00 40.00
804 A46 1r dk rose & blk 125.00 *200.00*
805 A46 1.20r gray blk & rose 15.00 2.00
806 A46 1.50r citron & bl 15.00 2.00
807 A46 2r lt bl & choc 40.00 2.00
808 A46 3r mag & green 75.00 10.00
809 A46 5r dk brn & red org 300.00 *500.00*
Nos. 795-809 (15) 649.00 772.00

Same Overprint on Stamps of 1929

1935 ***Perf. 12, 12x12½***

810 A42 1c yel grn & cerise 500.00 *600.00*
811 A42 2c scar & brt blue 300.00 *400.00*
812 A42 3c mag & myr grn 200.00 *200.00*
813 A42 6c yel brn & ol grn 140.00 *150.00*
814 A42 9c Prus bl & ver 85.00 *100.00*

Perf. 11½

815 A42 1t ultra & dp rose 50.00 *75.00*
816 A42 2t carmine & blk 50.00 40.00
817 A43 3t gold & dp vio 70.00 50.00
Nos. 810-817 (8) 1,395. 1,615.

No. 817 is overprinted vertically.
Forged overprints exist.

Same Ovpt. on Stamps of 1931-32

1935 ***Perf. 11***

818 A44 1c ol brn & ultra 400.00 400.00
819 A44 2c red brn & blk 150.00 150.00
820 A44 3c lil rose & ol 100.00 125.00
821 A44 6c red org & vio 200.00 200.00
822 A44 9c ultra & red org 200.00 *225.00*
823 A44 11c blue & dull red 12.50 3.50
824 A44 12c turq bl & lil rose 600.00 *900.00*
825 A44 16c black & red 15.00 5.00
826 A44 27c dk gray & dull bl 19.00 5.00
Nos. 818-826 (9) 1,697. 2,014.

Forged overprints exist.

Reza Shah Pahlavi — A56

1935 **Photo.** ***Perf. 11***

Size: 19x27mm

827 A56 5d violet 3.00 .25
828 A56 10d lilac rose 3.00 .25
829 A56 15d turquoise bl 3.00 .25
830 A56 30d emerald 3.00 .25
831 A56 45d orange 3.00 .25
832 A56 50d dull lt brn 4.00 .30
833 A56 60d ultramarine 15.00 .65
834 A56 75d red orange 15.00 .75
835 A56 90d rose 15.00 .75

Size: 21½x31mm

836 A56 1r dull lilac 30.00 .50
837 A56 1.50r blue 45.00 2.00
838 A56 2r dk olive grn 45.00 .75
839 A56 3r dark brown 50.00 2.00
840 A56 5r slate black 275.00 15.00
Nos. 827-840 (14) 509.00 23.95

Reza Shah Pahlavi — A57

1936-37 **Litho.** ***Perf. 11***

Size: 20x27mm

841 A57 5d bright vio 4.00 .25
842 A57 10d magenta 4.00 .25
843 A57 15d bright ultra 6.00 .25
844 A57 30d yellow green 25.00 .25
845 A57 45d vermilion 25.00 .25
846 A57 50d blk brn ('37) 30.00 .25
847 A57 60d brown orange 25.00 .25
848 A57 75d rose lake 15.00 .25
849 A57 90d rose red 20.00 .35

Size: 23x31mm

850 A57 1r turq green 20.00 .25
851 A57 1.50r deep blue 20.00 .35
852 A57 2r bright blue 35.00 .35
853 A57 3r violet brown 45.00 .80
854 A57 5r slate green 45.00 1.25
855 A57 10r dk brn & ultra ('37) 225.00 25.00
Nos. 841-855 (15) 544.00 30.35

Reza Shah Pahlavi — A58

1938-39 **Size: 20x27mm** ***Perf. 11***

856 A58 5d light violet 2.00 .25
857 A58 10d magenta 2.00 .25
858 A58 15d violet blue 2.00 .25
859 A58 30d bright green 2.00 .25
860 A58 45d vermilion 3.00 .25
861 A58 50d black brown 3.00 .25
862 A58 60d brown orange 3.00 .25
863 A58 75d rose lake 3.00 .25
864 A58 90d rose red ('39) 5.00 .25

Size: 22½x30mm

865 A58 1r turq green 10.00 .25
866 A58 1.50r deep blue 15.00 .30
867 A58 2r lt blue ('39) 30.00 .30

868	A58	3r	violet brown	30.00	.70
869	A58	5r	gray grn ('39)	50.00	1.25
870	A58	10r	dk brn & ultra ('39)	175.00	10.00
			Nos. 856-870 (15)	335.00	15.05

Reza Shah Pahlavi — A58a

1939, Mar. 15 *Perf. 13*

870A	A58a	5d	gray blue	3.00	3.00
870B	A58a	10d	brown	3.00	3.00
870C	A58a	30d	green	3.00	3.00
870D	A58a	60d	dk brn	3.00	3.00
870E	A58a	90d	red	5.00	5.00
870F	A58a	1.50r	blue	15.00	10.00
870G	A58a	5r	lilac	35.00	30.00
870H	A58a	10r	carmine	50.00	50.00
			Nos. 870A-870H (8)	117.00	107.00

60th birthday of Reza Shah Pahlavi. Printed in sheets of 4, perf. 13 and imperf. The 1r violet and 2r orange were not available to the public. Value, perf. 13 unused $35 each, imperf, 35% more. Value of sheets (including 1r and 2r), perf. 13 $1,100, imperf. $1,500.

Crown Prince and Princess Fawziya A59

1939, Apr. 25 **Photo.** *Perf. 11½*

871	A59	5d	red brown	.50	.50
872	A59	10d	bright violet	.50	.50
873	A59	30d	emerald	1.50	.50
874	A59	90d	red	12.00	2.00
875	A59	1.50r	bright blue	20.00	4.00
			Nos. 871-875 (5)	34.50	7.50

Wedding of Crown Prince Mohammad Reza Pahlavi to Princess Fawziya of Egypt.

Bridge over Karun River A60

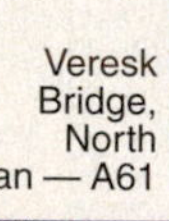

Veresk Bridge, North Iran — A61

Granary, Ahwaz A62

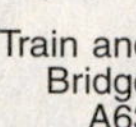

Train and Bridge A63

Museum, Side View A64 A67

Ministry of Justice A65

School Building A66

Mohammad Reza Shah Pahlavi A68 A69

1942-46 **Unwmk.** **Litho.** *Perf. 11*

876	A60	5d	violet	3.50	.25
877	A60	5d	red org ('44)	1.50	.25
878	A61	10d	magenta	3.50	.25
879	A61	10d	pck grn ('44)	1.50	.25
880	A62	20d	lt red violet	6.00	.25
881	A62	20d	mag ('44)	3.50	.25
882	A63	25d	rose carmine	40.00	5.00
883	A63	25d	violet ('44)	10.00	.50
884	A64	35d	emerald	3.00	.30
885	A65	50d	ultramarine	4.50	.30
886	A65	50d	emerald ('44)	3.00	.25
887	A66	70d	dull vio brn	3.00	.35
888	A67	75d	rose lake	20.00	.35
889	A67	75d	rose car ('46)	20.00	.35
890	A68	1r	carmine	20.00	.25
891	A68	1r	maroon ('45)	20.00	.25
892	A68	1.50r	red	20.00	.25
893	A68	2r	light blue	50.00	.25
894	A68	2r	sage grn ('44)	40.00	.30
895	A68	2.50r	dark blue	25.00	.30
896	A68	3r	peacock grn	125.00	1.00
897	A68	3r	brt vio ('44)	55.00	.35
898	A68	5r	sage green	350.00	10.00
899	A68	5r	lt blue ('44)	40.00	.50
900	A69	10r	brn org & blk	70.00	3.00
901	A69	10r	dk org brn & black ('44)	50.00	1.00
902	A69	20r	choc & vio	1,100.	50.00
903	A69	20r	org & blk ('44)	165.00	4.00
904	A69	30r	gray blk & emer	*1,600.*	50.00
905	A69	30r	emer & blk ('44)	70.00	5.00
906	A69	50r	dl bl & brn red	350.00	25.00
907	A69	50r	brt vio & blk ('45)	125.00	10.00
908	A69	100r	rose red & blk ('45)	700.00	60.00
909	A69	200r	bl & blk ('45)	600.00	60.00
			Nos. 876-909 (34)	5,698.	290.35

Sixteen denominations of this issue were handstamped at Tabriz in 1945-46 in Persian characters: "Azerbaijan National Government, Dec. 12, 1945." A rebel group did this overprinting while the Russian army held that area.

Flag of Iran A70

Designs: 50d, Docks at Bandar Shapur. 1.50r, Motor convoy. 2.50r, Gorge and railway viaduct. 5r, Map and Mohammad Reza Shah Pahlavi.

Inscribed: "En souvenir des efforts de l'Iran pour la Victoire"

Engr. & Litho.

1949, Apr. 28 *Perf. 12½*

910	A70	25d	multicolored	15.00	15.00

Engr.

911	A70	50d	purple	5.00	3.00
a.	Imperf.			*650.00*	
912	A70	1.50r	carmine rose	15.00	3.00
913	A70	2.50r	deep blue	20.00	5.00
a.	Imperf.			*700.00*	
914	A70	5r	green	50.00	5.00
a.	Imperf.			*850.00*	
			Nos. 910-914 (5)	105.00	31.00

Iran's contribution toward the victory of the Allied Nations in World War II.

Bank Melli Building, Tehran A71

Post and Customs House, Tehran A72

Former Ministry of P.T.T. — A73

Mohammad Reza Shah Pahlavi — A74

Shah and: 5d, Ramsar Hotel, Caspian Sea. 10d, Bridge over Zaindeh River. 25d, Old Royal Palace, Isfahan. 50d, Chaharbagh Madrassa, Isfahan. 75d, Railway Station. 1r, Ministry of Justice, Tehran. 1.50r, Shah Mosque, Tehran. 2.50r, Parliament, Tehran. 3r, Great Gate, Isfahan. 5r, Building, Isfahan.

1949-50 **Unwmk.** **Litho.** *Perf. 10½*

915	A71	5d	rose & dk grn	2.00	.25
916	A71	10d	ultra & brown	2.00	.25
917	A71	20d	vio & ultra	2.00	.25
918	A71	25d	blk brn & dp blue	2.00	.25
919	A71	50d	grn & ultra	2.00	.25
920	A71	75d	dk brn & red	3.50	.25
921	A72	1r	vio & green	3.50	.25
922	A72	1.50r	dk grn & ver	4.50	.25
923	A72	2r	dp car & blk brn	6.00	.25
924	A72	2.50r	chlky bl & bl	7.00	.25
925	A72	3r	vio bl & red org	8.00	.25
926	A72	5r	dp car & vio	15.00	.25
927	A73	10r	car & bl grn ('50)	45.00	.50
a.	Inverted center			3,500.	
928	A73	20r	brn blk & red ('50)	350.00	20.00
929	A74	30r	choc & dp blue ('50)	120.00	20.00
930	A74	50r	red & dp blue ('50)	125.00	20.00
			Nos. 915-930 (16)	697.50	63.50

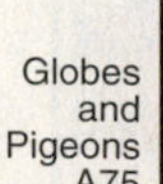

Globes and Pigeons A75

Symbols of UPU — A76

1950, Mar. 16 **Photo.**

931	A75	50d	brn carmine	30.00	25.00
932	A76	2.50r	deep blue	35.00	32.50

UPU, 75th anniv. (in 1949).

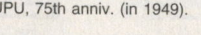

Reza Shah Pahlavi and his Tomb — A77

1950, May 8

933	A77	50d	brown	25.00	15.00
934	A77	2r	sepia	35.00	20.00

Re-burial of Reza Shah Pahlavi, May 12, 1950.

Mohammad Reza Shah Pahlavi, 31st Birthday — A78

Various portraits.

1950, Oct. 26 **Engr.** *Perf. 12½*

Center in Black

935	A78	25d	carmine	10.00	2.00
936	A78	50d	orange	10.00	2.00
937	A78	75d	brown	30.00	12.00
938	A78	1r	green	25.00	10.00
939	A78	2.50r	deep blue	25.00	10.00
940	A78	5r	brown lake	40.00	10.00
			Nos. 935-940 (6)	140.00	46.00

Shah and Queen Soraya A79

A80

1951, Feb. 12 **Litho.** *Perf. 10½*

941	A79	5d	rose violet	3.00	1.00
942	A79	25d	orange red	5.00	1.00
943	A79	50d	emerald	7.50	2.00
944	A80	1r	brown	12.00	2.00
945	A80	1.50r	carmine	17.50	2.00
946	A80	2.50r	blue	35.00	2.50
			Nos. 941-946 (6)	80.00	10.50

Wedding of Mohammad Reza Shah Pahlavi to Soraya Esfandiari.

Farabi — A81

1951, Feb. 20

947	A81	50d red	15.00	2.00
948	A81	2.50r blue	20.00	3.00

Death millenary of Farabi, Persian philosopher.

Mohammad Reza Shah Pahlavi
A82 A83

1951-52 Unwmk. Photo. *Perf. 10½*

950	A82	5d brown orange	1.00	.25
951	A82	10d violet	1.00	.25
952	A82	20d choc ('52)	2.00	.35
953	A82	25d blue ('52)	2.50	.25
954	A82	50d green	3.00	.25
955	A82	75d rose	4.00	.30
956	A83	1r gray green	4.00	.25
957	A83	1.50r cerise	4.00	.45
958	A83	2r chocolate	6.00	.25
959	A83	2.50r deep blue	7.00	.25
960	A83	3r red orange	8.00	.25
961	A83	5r dark green	15.00	.25
962	A83	10r olive ('52)	45.00	.50
963	A83	20r org brn ('52)	35.00	3.00
964	A83	30r vio bl ('52)	35.00	2.00
965	A83	50r blk brn ('52)	75.00	7.50
		Nos. 950-965 (16)	247.50	16.35

See Nos. 975-977.

Oil Well and Mosque — A84

Oil Well, Mosque and Monument A85

1953, Feb. 20 Litho.

966	A84	50d green & yel	4.00	1.00
967	A85	1r lil rose & yel	4.00	1.00
968	A84	2.50r blue & yellow	7.00	2.50
969	A85	5r blk brn & yel	10.00	5.00
		Nos. 966-969 (4)	25.00	9.50

Discovery of oil at Qum.

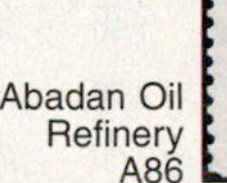

Abadan Oil Refinery A86

Super Fractionators — A87

Designs: 1r, Storage tanks. 5r, Pipe lines. 10r, Abadan refinery.

1953, Mar. 20 Photo.

970	A86	50d blue green	4.00	2.00
971	A86	1r rose	5.00	2.00
972	A87	2.50r bright ultra	8.00	3.50
973	A86	5r red orange	12.00	4.00
974	A86	10r dark violet	17.00	6.00
		Nos. 970-974 (5)	46.00	17.50

Nationalization of oil industry, 2nd anniv.

Shah Types of 1951-52

1953-54 Photo. *Perf. 10½*

975	A82	50d dark gray grn	75.00	.35
976	A83	1r dk blue green	6.00	.25
977	A83	1.50r cerise ('54)	6.00	.25
		Nos. 975-977 (3)	87.00	.85

The background has been highlighted on the 1r and 1.50r.

Gymnast — A88

Archery A89

Designs: 3r, Climbing Mt. Demavend. 5r, Ancient polo. 10r, Lion hunting.

1953, Oct. 26

978	A88	1r deep green	12.00	7.00
979	A89	2.50r brt grnsh bl	20.00	10.00
980	A89	3r gray	25.00	10.00
981	A88	5r bister	25.00	15.00
982	A88	10r rose lilac	75.00	30.00
		Nos. 978-982 (5)	157.00	72.00

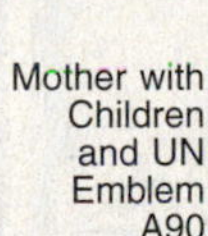

Mother with Children and UN Emblem A90

1953, Oct. 24

983	A90	1r bl grn & dk grn	2.00	1.00
984	A90	2.50r lt bl & indigo	3.00	1.50

United Nations Day, Oct. 24.

Herring A91

Refrigeration Compressor — A92

Processing Equipment, National Fisheries — A93

Designs: 2.50r, Sardines. 10r, Sturgeon.

1954, Jan. 31

985	A91	1r multi	15.00	10.00
986	A91	2.50r multi	45.00	20.00
987	A92	3r vermilion	20.00	10.00
988	A93	5r deep bl grn	20.00	10.00
989	A91	10r multi	75.00	35.00
		Nos. 985-989 (5)	175.00	85.00

Nationalization of fishing industry.

Broken Shackles — A94

3r, Torch flag. 5r, Citizen holding flag of Iran.

1954, Aug. 19 Litho.

990	A94	2r multicolored	15.00	5.00
991	A94	3r multicolored	20.00	10.00
992	A94	5r multicolored	30.00	15.00
		Nos. 990-992 (3)	65.00	30.00

Return of the royalist government, 1st anniv.

Mother Feeding Baby — A95

1954, Oct. 24 Photo.

993	A95	2r red lil & org	2.50	1.00
994	A95	3r vio bl & org	3.50	1.50

Issued to honor the United Nations.

Woodsman Felling Tree — A96

Designs: 2.50r, Laborer carrying firewood. 5r, Worker operating saw. 10r, Wooden galley.

1954, Dec. 11

995	A96	1r brn & grnsh black	40.00	30.00
996	A96	2.50r grnsh blk & bl	50.00	35.00
997	A96	5r lil & dk brn	75.00	60.00
998	A96	10r bl & claret	100.00	80.00
		Nos. 995-998 (4)	265.00	205.00

4th World Forestry Congress, Dehra Dun, India, 1954.

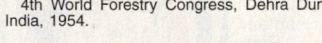

Mohammad Reza Shah Pahlavi
A97 A98

1954-55 Unwmk.

999	A97	5d yellow brn	2.00	.25
1000	A97	10d violet	2.00	.25
1001	A97	25d scarlet	2.00	.25
1002	A97	50d black brn	2.00	.25
1003	A98	1r blue green	2.00	.25
1004	A98	1.50r cerise	2.00	.25
1005	A98	2r ocher	3.50	.25
1006	A98	2.50r blue	4.00	.25
1007	A98	3r olive	10.00	.25
1008	A98	5r dk sl grn	10.00	1.50
1009	A98	10r lilac rose	30.00	1.50
1010	A98	20r indigo	60.00	12.00
1011	A98	30r dp yel brn	200.00	35.00
1012	A98	50r dp orange	75.00	25.00
1013	A98	100r light vio	500.00	125.00
1014	A98	200r yellow	175.00	50.00
		Nos. 999-1014 (16)	1,080.	252.25

See Nos. 1023-1036.

Regional Costume — A99

Regional Costumes: 1r, 2r, Men's costumes. 2.50r, 3r, 5r, Women's costumes.

1955, June 26 Photo. *Perf. 11*

1015	A99	1r bluish gray & multi	15.00	10.00
1016	A99	2r dl rose & multi	15.00	10.00
1017	A99	2.50r buff & multi	35.00	20.00
1018	A99	3r rose lil & multi	20.00	10.00
1019	A99	5r gray brn & multi	40.00	20.00
		Nos. 1015-1019 (5)	125.00	70.00

Parliament Gate — A100

Designs: 3r, Statue of Liberty, vert. 5r, Old Gate of Parliament.

1955, Aug. 6 Wmk. 306 *Perf. 11*

1020	A100	2r red vio & grn	5.00	3.00
1021	A100	3r dk bl & aqua	12.00	4.00
1022	A100	5r Prus grn & red org	15.00	8.00
		Nos. 1020-1022 (3)	32.00	15.00

50th anniversary of constitution.

Shah Types of 1954-55

1955-56 Wmk. 306 *Perf. 11*

1023	A97	5d violet ('56)	5.00	1.50
1024	A97	10d carmine ('56)	2.00	.25
1025	A97	25d brown	2.00	.25
1026	A97	50d dk carmine	2.00	.25
1027	A98	1r dark bl grn	2.00	.25
1028	A98	1.50r red brn ('56)	85.00	3.00
1029	A98	2r ol grn ('56)	40.00	.25
1030	A98	2.50r blue ('56)	7.00	.30
1031	A98	3r bister	10.00	.25
1032	A98	5r red lilac	12.00	.25
1033	A98	10r brt grnsh bl	10.00	.35
1034	A98	20r slate green	50.00	5.00
1035	A98	30r red org ('56)	90.00	30.00
1036	A98	50r red brn ('56)	175.00	40.00
		Nos. 1023-1036 (14)	492.00	81.90

UN Emblem and Globes A101

1955, Oct. 24 *Perf. 11x12½*

1039	A101	1r dp car & org	1.50	.75
1040	A101	2.50r dk bl & grnsh blue	2.00	1.50

UN, 10th anniv., Oct. 24, 1955.

Wrestlers A102

1955, Oct. 26 Wmk. 306 *Perf. 11*

1041	A102 2.50r multi		15.00	7.50

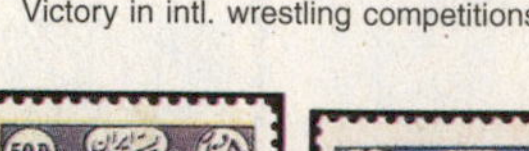

Victory in intl. wrestling competitions.

Garden, Namazi Hospital A103

Immortal Guardsman A105

Namazi Hospital, Shiraz A104

5r, Gate of the Koran. 10r, Ha'fez of Shiraz.

1956, Mar. 21 *Perf. 11x12½*

1042	A103	50d multi	5.00	2.00
1043	A104	1r multi	6.00	2.50
1044	A105	2.50r multi	9.00	7.00
1045	A104	5r multi	15.00	6.00
1046	A105	10r multi	25.00	10.00
	Nos. 1042-1046 (5)		60.00	27.50

Opening of Namazi Hospital, Shiraz.

Arms of Iran and Olympic Rings — A106

1956, May 15 Wmk. 306

1047	A106 5r rose lilac	40.00	30.00

National Olympic Committee, 10th anniv.

Tomb at Maragheh A107

2.50r, Astrolabe. 5r, Nasr-ud-Din of Tus.

1956, May 26 Photo. *Perf. 11x12½*

1048	A107	1r orange	7.50	2.50
1049	A107	2.50r deep ultra	9.50	3.50
1050	A107	5r sepia & pur	15.00	4.00
	Nos. 1048-1050 (3)		32.00	10.00

700th death anniv. of Nasr-up-Din of Tus, mathematician and astronomer.

WHO Emblem — A108

Perf. 11x12½

1956, Sept. 19 Wmk. 306

1051	A108 6r cerise	5.00	2.00

6th Regional Congress of the WHO.

Scout Bugler and Camp A109

5r, Scout badge and Shah in scout uniform.

1956, Aug. 5 *Perf. 12½x11*

1052	A109	2.50r ultra & blue	25.00	10.00
1053	A109	5r lil & red lil	25.00	15.00

National Boy Scout Jamboree.

Catalogue values for unused stamps in this section, from this point to the end of the section, are for Never Hinged items.

Former Telegraph Office, Tehran A110

6r, Telegraph lines & ancient monument.

1956, Oct. 26

1054	A110	2.50r brt bl & grn, *bluish*	20.00	7.00
1055	A110	6r rose car & lil	25.00	8.00

Centenary of Persian telegraph system.

UN Emblem and People of the World A111

Design: 2.50r, UN Emblem and scales.

1956, Oct. 24

1056	A111	1r bluish green	1.50	.40
1057	A111	2.50r blue & green	3.00	.60

United Nations Day, Oct. 24.

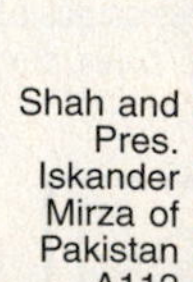

Shah and Pres. Iskander Mirza of Pakistan A112

1956, Oct. 31

1058	A112 1r multicolored	12.00	2.50

Visit of Pres. General Iskander Mirza of Pakistan to Tehran, Oct. 31-Nov. 10.

Mohammad Reza Shah Pahlavi A113 A114

Perf. 13½x11

1956-57 Wmk. 306 Photo.

1058A	A113	5d brt car & red	1.00	*1.00*
1058B	A113	10d vio bl & dl vio	1.00	*1.00*
1059	A113	25d dk brn & brn	1.25	.35
1059A	A113	50d brn & ol brn	1.25	.25
b.		Inverted center	*3,750.*	
1060	A113	1r brn & brt grn	1.50	.25
1061	A113	1.50r brt lil & brn	1.50	.25
1062	A113	2r red vio & red	2.00	.25
1063	A113	2.50r ultra & blue	2.00	.25
1064	A113	3r brn & dk ol bis	2.50	.25
1065	A113	5r ver & mar	3.00	.25
1066	A114	6r dk vio & brn lil	10.00	.25
1067	A114	10r lt blue & grn	17.00	.25
1068	A114	20r green & blue	35.00	3.00
1069	A114	30r rose red & org	60.00	7.50
1070	A114	50r dk grn & ol grn	70.00	17.50
1071	A114	100r lilac & cer	425.00	35.00
1072	A114	200r dp plum & vio bl	275.00	25.00
		Nos. 1058A-1072 (17)	909.00	92.60

Issued: 1.50r, 2r, 3r, 5r, 6r, 1956; others, 1957.

See Nos. 1082-1098.

Lord Baden-Powell A115

1957, Feb. 22 *Perf. 12½*

1073	A115 10r dk grn & brn	15.00	8.50

Birth cent. of Robert Baden-Powell, founder of the Boy Scout movement.

Railroad Tracks — A116

Train and Map A117

Design: 10r, Train and mosque.

1957, May 2 *Perf. 11x12½, 12½x11*

1074	A116	2.50r grnsh blk, bl & ocher	25.00	5.60
1075	A117	5r multi	30.00	7.00
1076	A116	10r blk, yel & bl	40.00	15.00
	Nos. 1074-1076 (3)		95.00	27.60

Opening of the Tehran Meshed-Railway.

Pres. Giovanni Gronchi of Italy and Shah — A118

Design: 6r, Ruins of Persepolis and Colosseum in Rome and flags.

Wmk. 316

1957, Sept. 7 Photo. *Perf. 11*

1077	A118	2r slate bl, grn & red	8.00	3.00
1078	A118	6r slate bl, grn & red	12.00	4.00

Visit of Pres. Giovanni Gronchi of Italy to Iran, Sept. 7.

Queen Soraya and Hospital A119

1957, Sept. 29 Wmk. 316 *Perf. 11*

1079	A119 2r lt bl & grn	15.00	4.00

Sixth Medical Congress, Ramsar.

Globes Showing Location of Iran — A120

1957, Oct. 22 Litho. *Perf. 12½x11*

1080	A120 10r blk, lt bl, yel & red	15.00	4.00

Intl. Cartographic Conference, Tehran.

Shah and King Faisal II — A121

1957, Oct. 18 Photo.

1081	A121 2r slate bl, grn & red	15.00	4.00

Visit of King Faisal of Iraq, Oct. 19.

Shah Types of 1956-57

1957-58 Wmk. 316 *Perf. 11*

1082	A114	5d violet & pur	1.00	*2.00*
1083	A114	10d claret & rose car	1.00	*2.00*
1084	A114	25d rose car & brick red	1.00	.35
1085	A114	50d grn & ol grn	1.25	.25
1086	A114	1r dark green	1.50	.25
1087	A114	1.50r claret & red lil	2.00	.25
1088	A114	2r bl & grnsh blue	3.00	.25
1089	A114	2.50r dk bl & blue	3.00	.25
1090	A114	3r rose car & ver	3.50	.25
1091	A114	5r violet blue	3.50	.25
1092	A113	6r bright blue	5.00	.25
1093	A113	10r deep green	7.50	.30
1094	A113	20r grn & olive grn	45.00	1.00
1095	A113	30r vio bl & dk brn	60.00	15.00
1096	A113	50r dk brn & lt brn	65.00	15.00
1097	A113	100r rose lil & car rose	200.00	35.00

1098 A113 200r vio & yel brn 175.00 40.00
Nos. 1082-1098 (17) 578.25 112.65

Issued: 1.50r, 2r, 3r, 1957; others, 1958.

Weight Lifter — A122

1957, Nov. 8 ***Perf. 11x14½***
1099 A122 10r bl, grn & red 15.00 5.00

Iran's victories in weight lifting.

Modern and Old Houses, Radio Transmitter A123

1958, Feb. 22 **Litho.**
1100 A123 10r brn, ocher & bl 17.50 6.00

30th anniversary of radio in Iran.

Oil Derrick and Symbolic Flame — A124

Wmk. 316

1958, Mar. 10 **Photo.** ***Perf. 11***
1101 A124 2r gray & multi 15.00 3.00
1102 A124 10r multicolored 20.00 5.00

Drilling of Iran's 1st oil well, 50th anniv.

Train on Viaduct — A125

Design: 8r, Train and map.

1958, Apr. 24 **Wmk. 306** ***Perf. 11***
1103 A125 6r dull purple 40.00 10.00
1104 A125 8r green 50.00 15.00

Opening of Tehran-Tabriz railway line.

Exposition Emblem A126

1958, Apr. 17 ***Perf. 12½x11***
1105 A126 2.50r bl & light bl 1.25 .30
1106 A126 6r car & salmon 2.25 .50

World's Fair, Brussels, Apr. 17-Oct. 19.

Mohammad Reza Shah Pahlavi — A127

1958-59 **Wmk. 316** **Photo.** ***Perf. 11***

1107	A127	5d blue violet	1.00	.25
1108	A127	10d lt vermilion	1.00	.25
1109	A127	25d crimson	1.00	.25
1110	A127	50d brt blue	1.00	.25
1111	A127	1r dark green	2.00	.25
1113	A127	2r dark brown	12.50	.25
1115	A127	3r dk red brown	20.00	.25
1117	A127	6r bright blue	10.00	.45
1118	A127	8r magenta	10.00	.35
1120	A127	14r blue violet	17.50	2.00
1121	A127	20r green	35.00	1.00
a.		Wmk. 306	35.00	20.00
1122	A127	30r brt car rose	30.00	5.00
1123	A127	50r rose violet	65.00	15.00
1124	A127	100r red orange	35.00	10.00
1125	A127	200r slate green	125.00	15.00
		Nos. 1107-1125 (15)	366.00	50.55

See Nos. 1138-1151, 1173-1179.

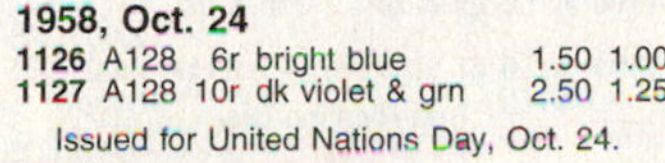

UN Emblem and Map of Iran — A128

1958, Oct. 24
1126 A128 6r bright blue 1.50 1.00
1127 A128 10r dk violet & grn 2.50 1.25

Issued for United Nations Day, Oct. 24.

Globe and Hands A129

1958, Dec. 10
1128 A129 6r dk red brn & brn 1.50 .50
1129 A129 8r dk grn & gray grn 2.50 .75

Universal Declaration of Human Rights, 10th anniv.

Rudaki — A130

Design: 5r, Rudaki, different pose. 10r, Same design as No. 1130.

1958, Dec. 24 **Photo.** **Wmk. 306**
1130 A130 2.50r bluish black 12.50 4.00
1131 A130 5r violet 17.50 6.00
1132 A130 10r dark brown 30.00 10.00
Nos. 1130-1132 (3) 60.00 20.00

1100th birth anniv. of Rudaki, blind Persian poet.

Flag — A130a

Design: 1r & 6r, Red Lion & Sun flag (Iranian Red Cross Organization).

Perf. 14½x11

1959, May 8 **Wmk. 316**
1132A A130a 1r multicolored 5.00 2.00
1132B A130a 6r multicolored 7.00 3.00

Centenary of the Red Cross.

Wrestlers, Flag and Globe — A131

1959 **Litho.** ***Perf. 11x12½***
1133 A131 6r multicolored 27.50 15.00

World Wrestling Championships, Tehran.

Globe, UN Building and Hand Holding Torch of Freedom A132

1959, Oct. 24 **Photo.** ***Perf. 11***
1134 A132 6r gray brn, red & bister 2.00 .60

Issued for United Nations Day, Oct. 24.

Shah and Pres. Ayub Khan of Pakistan — A133

1959, Nov. 9 **Litho.** ***Perf. 11x16***
1135 A133 6r multicolored 12.50 5.00

Visit of Pres. Khan to Iran.

ILO Emblem — A134

1959, Nov. 12 ***Perf. 16***
1136 A134 1r blue 2.00 .50
1137 A134 5r brown 3.00 .75

ILO, 40th anniversary.

Shah Type of 1958-59

1959-63 **Wmk. 316** **Photo.** ***Perf. 11***

1138	A127	5d red brn ('60)	1.00	.30
1139	A127	10d Prus grn ('60)	1.00	.30
a.		10d Prussian blue ('63)	1.50	.50
1140	A127	25d orange	2.00	.25
a.		Perf. 12x11½	100.00	30.00
1141	A127	50d scarlet	2.00	.25
1142	A127	1r deep violet	2.00	.25
1142A	A127	2r brown	12.50	.25
1143	A127	3r olive	5.00	.25
1143A	A127	6r cobalt blue	10.00	.25
1144	A127	8r brown olive	3.00	.25
1145	A127	10r ol blk ('60)	3.00	.25
1146	A127	14r yel green	4.00	.25
a.		14r emerald green	6.50	.50
1147	A127	20r sl grn ('60)	10.00	.35
1148	A127	30r choc ('60)	20.00	4.00
1149	A127	50r dp blue ('60)	20.00	4.00
1150	A127	100r green ('60)	175.00	15.00
1151	A127	200r cer ('60)	275.00	20.00
		Nos. 1138-1151 (16)	545.50	46.20

See Pakistan 274-276, Turkey 1813-1815.

Pahlavi Foundation Bridge, Karun River — A135

Design: 5r, Bridge, different view.

1960, Feb. 29 **Litho.** ***Perf. 16x11***
1152 A135 1r dk brn & brt bl 3.00 1.00
a. Perf. 13½x11 150.00
1153 A135 5r blue & emerald 4.00 1.50

Opening of Pahlavi Foundation Bridge at Khorramshahr on the Karun River.

A136

Uprooted Oak Emblem — A136a

Design: 6r, Arched frame.

1960, Apr. 7 ***Perf. 11***
1154 A136 1r brt ultra 2.25 .50
1155 A136a 6r gray & sage grn 1.00 .75

World Refugee Year, 7/1/59-6/30/60.

Mosquito — A137

Man with Spray Gun — A138

Design: 3r, Mosquito on water.

1960, Apr. 7 **Wmk. 316**
1156 A137 1r blk & red, *yel* 3.00 2.00
1157 A138 2r lt bl, ultra & blk 5.00 2.00
1158 A137 3r blk & red, *yel grn* 7.00 3.00
Nos. 1156-1158 (3) 15.00 7.00

Issued to publicize malaria control.

Polo Player — A139

Design: 6r, Persian archer.

1960, June 9 Litho. Wmk. 316

1159 A139 1r deep claret 4.00 .50
1160 A139 6r dk blue & lt blue 6.00 1.00

17th Olympic Games, Rome, 8/25-9/11.

Shah and King Hussein of Jordan — A140

1960, July 6 ***Perf. 11***

1161 A140 6r multicolored 15.00 5.00

Visit of King Hussein of Jordan to Tehran.

Iranian Scout Emblem in Flower — A141

Tents and Pillars of Persepolis A142

1960, July 18

1162 A141 1r green 1.50 .50
1163 A142 6r brn, brt bl & buff 2.50 .75

3rd National Boy Scout Jamboree.

Shah and Queen Farah — A143

1960, Sept. 9 Litho. ***Perf. 11***

1164 A143 1r green 5.00 1.50
1165 A143 5r blue 10.00 2.00

Marriage of Shah Mohammad Reza Shah Pahlavi and Farah Diba.

UN Emblem and Globe — A144

1960, Oct. 24 Wmk. 316

1166 A144 6r bl, blk & lt brn 2.50 .50

15th anniversary of the United Nations.

Shah and Queen Elizabeth II A145

1961, Mar. 2 Litho. ***Perf. 11***

1167 A145 1r lt red brown 4.00 .45
1168 A145 6r bright ultra 6.00 .90

Visit of Queen Elizabeth II to Tehran, Feb. 1961.

Girl Playing Arganoon — A146

Safiaddin Amavi — A147

1961, Apr. 10 Wmk. 316 ***Perf. 11***

1169 A146 1r dk brown & buff 2.00 .50
1170 A147 6r greenish gray 3.00 .75

International Congress of Music, Tehran.

Shah Type of 1958-59 Redrawn

1961-62 Litho. ***Perf. 11***

1173 A127 25d orange 5.00 .50
1174 A127 50d scarlet 5.00 .40
1175 A127 1r deep violet 8.00 .25
1176 A127 2r chocolate 10.00 .25
1177 A127 3r olive brown 12.00 .50
1178 A127 6r brt blue ('62) 65.00 3.50
1179 A127 8r brown ol ('62) 35.00 2.25
Nos. 1173-1179 (7) 140.00 7.65

On Nos. 1173-1179 (lithographed), a single white line separates the lower panel from the shah's portrait. On Nos. 1107-1125, 1138-1151 (photogravure), two lines, one in color and one in white, separate panel from portrait. Other minor differences exist.

Shah and Queen Farah Holding Crown Prince — A148

1961, June 2 Litho.

1186 A148 1r bright pink 5.00 2.50
1187 A148 6r light blue 10.00 5.00

Birth of Crown Prince Reza Kourosh Pahlavi, Oct. 31, 1960.

Swallows and UN Emblem — A149

1961, Oct. 24 ***Perf. 11***

1188 A149 2r blue & car rose 2.00 .25
1189 A149 6r blue & violet 3.00 .35

Issued for United Nations Day, Oct. 24.

Planting Tree — A150

1962, Jan. 11

1190 A150 2r ol grn, citron & dk bl 2.00 .25
1191 A150 6r ultra, grn & pale bl 3.00 .35

Tree Planting Day.

Worker and Symbols of Labor and Agriculture A151

1962, Mar. 15 Litho.

1192 A151 2r bl grn, brn & blk 2.50 .25
1193 A151 6r lt ultra, brn & blk 3.00 .35

Issued for Workers' Day.

Map, Family and Cogwheel A152

1962, Mar. 20 ***Perf. 11***

1194 A152 2r black, yel & lil 2.00 .30
1195 A152 6r black, bl & ultra 3.00 .65

Social Insurance Week.

Sugar Refinery, Khuzistan — A153

1962, Apr. 14 Wmk. 316

1196 A153 2r dk & lt blue & grn 2.50 .35
1197 A153 6r ultra, buff & blue 3.50 .65

Opening of sugar refinery in Khuzistan.

Karaj Dam — A154

1962, May 15

1198 A154 2r dk brn & gray grn 2.50 .25
1199 A154 6r vio bl & lt blue 2.00 .50

Inauguration of Karaj Dam, renamed Amir Kabir Dam.

Sefid Rud Dam A155

1962, May 19 Litho.

1200 A155 2r dk grn, lt bl & buff 2.00 .35
1201 A155 6r red brn, sl grn & lt blue 3.00 .65

Inauguration of Sefid Rud Dam.

"UNESCO" and UN Emblem — A156

1962, June 2 Wmk. 316 ***Perf. 11***

1202 A156 2r black, emer & red 2.00 .30
1203 A156 6r blue, emer & red 3.00 .50

15th anniv. of UNESCO.

Malaria Eradication Emblem and Sprayer A157

2r, Emblem & arrow piercing mosquito, horiz. 10r, Emblem & globe, horiz. Sizes: 2r, 10r, 40x25mm; 6r, 29 ½x34 ½mm.

1962, June 20

1204 A157 2r black & bluish grn 2.50 .35
1205 A157 6r pink & vio blue 3.00 .50
1206 A157 10r lt blue & ultra 3.50 .75
Nos. 1204-1206 (3) 9.00 1.60

WHO drive to eradicate malaria.

Oil Field and UN Emblem A158

1962, Sept. 1 Photo.

1207 A158 6r grnsh blue & brn 4.00 .50
1208 A158 14r gray & sepia 6.00 1.50

2nd Petroleum Symposium of ECAFE (UN Economic Commission for Asia and the Far East).

Mohammad Reza Shah Pahlavi — A159

Palace of Darius, Persepolis A160

Perf. 11, 10½x11, 11x10½

1962 Photo. Wmk. 316

1209 A159	5d green	1.00	.25
1210 A159	10d chestnut	1.00	.50
1211 A159	25d dark blue	1.00	.35
1212 A159	50d Prus green	1.00	.25
1213 A159	1r orange	3.00	.25
1214 A159	2r violet blue	3.00	.25
1215 A159	5r dark brown	4.00	.25
1216 A160	6r blue	12.00	2.50
1217 A160	8r yellow grn	7.00	1.00
1218 A160	10r grnsh blue	10.00	.50
1219 A160	11r slate green	6.00	.65
1220 A160	14r purple	12.00	.65
1221 A160	20r red brown	15.00	1.50
1222 A160	50r vermilion	17.50	1.50
	Nos. 1209-1222 (14)	93.50	10.40

See Nos. 1331-1344.

No. 1219 perf. 10½x11 is valued unused $9. Otherwise, all perf. varieties have the same values.

Hippocrates and Avicenna — A161

1962, Oct. 7 Litho.

1226 A161	2r brown, buff & ultra	4.00	.50
1227 A161	6r grn, pale grn & ultra	5.00	.75

Near and Middle East Medical Congress.

Hands Laying Bricks A162

Design: 6r, Houses and UN emblem, vert.

1962, Oct. 24

1228 A162	6r dk blue & ultra	3.50	.35
1229 A162	14r dk blue & emer	4.00	.60

Issued for United Nations Day, Oct. 24.

Crown Prince Receiving Flowers — A163

1962, Oct. 31

1230 A163	6r blue gray	6.00	1.00
1231 A163	14r dull green	12.00	1.90

Children's Day, Oct. 31; 2nd birthday of Crown Prince Reza.

Map of Iran and Persian Gulf — A164

1962, Dec. 12 Wmk. 316 *Perf. 11*

1232 A164	6r dk & lt bl, vio bl & rose	3.00	.35
1233 A164	14r dk & lt bl, pink & rose	3.50	.60

The Persian Gulf Seminar.

Hilton Hotel, Tehran — A165

1963, Jan. 21 Photo.

1234 A165	6r deep blue	4.00	.45
1235 A165	14r dark red brown	6.00	.60

Opening of the Royal Tehran Hilton Hotel.

Mohammad Reza Shah Dam A166

1963, Mar. 14 Litho.

Center Multicolored

1236 A166	6r violet blue	5.00	.70
1237 A166	14r dark brown	8.00	1.00

Mohammad Reza Shah Dam inauguration (later Dez Dam).

Worker with Pickax — A167

1963, Mar. 15

1238 A167	2r cream & black	2.00	.25
1239 A167	6r lt blue & blk	4.00	.30

Issued for Labor Day.

Stylized Bird over Globe — A168

Designs: 6r, Stylized globe and "FAO." 14r, Globe in space and wheat emblem.

1963, Mar. 21 *Perf. 11*

1240 A168	2r ultra, lt bl & bis	3.00	.25
1241 A168	6r lt ultra, ocher & blk	5.00	.30
1242 A168	14r slate bl & ocher	7.00	.85
	Nos. 1240-1242 (3)	15.00	1.40

FAO "Freedom from Hunger" campaign.

Shah and List of Bills — A169

1963, Mar. 21 Wmk. 316

1243 A169	6r green & lt blue	10.00	3.00
1244 A169	14r green & dull yel	15.00	4.00

Signing of six socioeconomic bills by Shah, 1st anniv.

Shah and King of Denmark — A170

1963, May 3 Litho. *Perf. 11*

1245 A170	6r indigo & dk ultra	7.00	1.00
1246 A170	14r dk brn & red brn	8.00	1.50

Visit of King Frederik IX of Denmark.

Flags, Shah Mosque, Isfahan, and Taj Mahal, Agra A171

1963, May 19

1247 A171	6r blue, yel grn & red	7.00	1.00
1248 A171	14r multicolored	8.00	1.50

Visit of Dr. Sarvepalli Radhakrishnan, president of India.

Chahnaz Dam — A172

1963, June 8 Wmk. 316 *Perf. 11*

1249 A172	6r ultra, bl & grn	5.00	.75
1250 A172	14r dk grn, bl & buff	7.00	.90

Inauguration of Chahnaz Dam (later Hamadan Dam).

Cent. Emblem with Red Lion and Sun — A173

1963, June 10

1251 A173	6r blue, gray & red	7.00	.65
1252 A173	14r buff, gray & red	8.00	.90

Centenary of International Red Cross.

Shah and Queen Juliana A174

Perf. 11x10½

1963, Oct. 3 Wmk. 349

1253 A174	6r ultra & blue	7.00	.50
1254 A174	14r sl grn & dull grn	8.00	.75

Visit of Queen Juliana of the Netherlands.

Literacy Corps Emblem and Soldier Teaching Village Class — A175

1963, Oct. 15 Litho. *Perf. 10½*

1255 A175	6r multicolored	7.00	1.00
1256 A175	14r multicolored	8.00	1.00

Issued to publicize the Literacy Corps.

Gen. Charles de Gaulle and View of Persepolis — A176

1963, Oct. 16

1257 A176	6r ultra & blue	5.00	1.00
1258 A176	14r brn & pale brn	7.00	1.00

Visit of General de Gaulle of France.

Fertilizer Plant, Oil Company Emblem and Map — A177

Design: 14r, Factory and Iranian Oil Company emblem, horiz.

Perf. 10½x11, 11x10½

1963, Oct. 18 Wmk. 316

1259 A177	6r black, yel & red	12.50	2.00
1260 A177	14r black, bl & yel	17.50	3.00

Opening of Shiraz Chemical Factory.

A178

6r, 14r, Pres. Heinrich Lübke of Germany & Mosque in Isfahan

1963, Oct. 23 Wmk. 349 *Perf. 10½*

1261 A178	6r ultra & dk blue	7.00	.65
1262 A178	14r gray & brown	8.00	1.60

Visit of Pres. Lubke of Germany.

UN Emblem and Iranian Flag A179

1963, Oct. 24
1263 A179 8r multicolored 5.00 .50

Issued for United Nations Day.

UN Emblem and Jets A180

1963, Oct. 24
1264 A180 6r multicolored 6.00 1.00

Iranian jet fighters with UN Force in the Congo.

Crown Prince Reza — A181

1963, Oct. 31
1265 A181 2r brown 3.50 .25
1266 A181 6r blue 6.50 .50

Children's Day; Crown Prince Reza's 3rd birthday.

Pres. Brezhnev of USSR — A182

1963, Nov. 16 Wmk. 349 ***Perf. 10½***
1267 A182 6r dk brn, yel & bl 6.00 .50
1268 A182 11r dk brn, yel & red 9.00 1.00

Visit of Pres. Leonid I. Brezhnev.

Atatürk's Mausoleum, Ankara — A183

1963, Nov. 28 **Litho.**
1269 A183 4r shown 4.50 .30
1270 A183 5r Kemal Ataturk 5.50 .30

25th death anniv. of Kemal Atatürk, president of Turkey.

Scales and Globe — A184

1963, Dec. 10
1271 A184 6r brt yel grn, blk & ultra 4.00 .35
1272 A184 14r org brn, blk & buff 6.00 .45

Universal Declaration of Human Rights, 15th anniv.

Mother and Child — A185

1963, Dec. 16
1273 A185 2r multicolored 4.00 .25
1274 A185 4r multicolored 6.00 .50

Issued for Mother's Day.

Map of Iran, Chamber of Industry and Mines Emblem — A186

1963, Dec. 17 **Litho.**
1275 A186 8r bl grn, buff & dk bl 7.00 .40

Chamber of Industry and Mines.

Factories and Hand Holding Bill — A187

Designs: 4r, Factories and bills on scale. 6r, Man on globe carrying torch of education. 8r, Tractor, map and yardstick. 10r, Forest. 12r, Gate of Parliament and heads of man and woman.

1964, Jan. 26 Wmk. 349 ***Perf. 10½***
1276 A187 2r multicolored 6.00 1.00
1277 A187 4r brown & gray 7.00 1.00
1278 A187 6r multicolored 8.00 1.00
1279 A187 8r multicolored 9.00 1.50
1280 A187 10r multicolored 10.00 1.75
1281 A187 12r red org & brn 15.00 2.00
Nos. 1276-1281 (6) 55.00 8.25

2nd anniv. of six socioeconomic bills: 2r, Shareholding for factory workers. 4r, Sale of shares in government factories. 6r, Creation of Army of Education. 8r, Land reforms. 10r, Nationalization of forests. 12r, Reforms in parliamentary elections.

"ECAFE" and UN Emblem A188

1964, Mar. 2 **Wmk. 349**
1282 A188 14r brt green & blk 5.00 .45

20th session of ECAFE (Economic Commission for Asia and the Far East), Mar. 2-17.

Flowering Branch — A189

1964, Mar. 5 ***Perf. 10½***
1283 A189 50d emerald, blk & org 1.00 .25
1284 A189 1r brt blue, blk & org 1.50 .25

Novrooz, Iranian New Year, Mar. 21.

Anemometer A190

1964, Mar. 23 **Litho.**
1285 A190 6r brt blue & vio bl 4.00 .50

4th World Meteorological Day.

Mosque and Arches, Isfahan — A191

11r, Griffon & winged bull, Persepolis.

1964, Apr. 7 ***Perf. 10½***
1286 A191 6r lilac, grn & blk 5.00 .40
1287 A191 11r orange, brn & blk 7.00 .55

Issued for tourist publicity.

Rudaki and Harp — A192

1964, May 16 Photo. Wmk. 349
1288 A192 6r blue 6.00 .45
1289 A192 8r red brown 8.00 .55

Opening of an institute for the blind. The inscription translates: "Wisdom is better than eye and sight."

Sculpture, Persepolis A193

Designs: 4r, Achaemenian horse-drawn mail cart, map of Iran, horiz. 6r, Vessel with sculptured animals. 10r, Head of King Shapur, sculpture.

1964, June 5 Wmk. 349 Litho.
1290 A193 2r gray & blue 10.00 3.00
1291 A193 4r vio bl, lt bl & bl 15.00 4.00
1292 A193 6r brown & yellow 18.00 5.00
1293 A193 10r yel & ol grn 20.00 7.00
Nos. 1290-1293 (4) 63.00 19.00

Opening of the "7000 Years of Persian Art" exhibition in Washington, D.C.

Shah and Emperor Haile Selassie A194

1964, Sept. 14 Wmk. 349 ***Perf. 10½***
1294 A194 6r ultra & lt blue 7.00 1.00

Visit of Emperor Haile Selassie of Ethiopia.

Tooth and Dentists' Assoc. Emblem A195

"2 I.D.A." A196

1964, Sept. 14 **Litho.**
1295 A195 2r blue, red & dk blue 3.50 .30
1296 A196 4r ultra, bl & pale brn 4.50 .35

Iranian Dentists' Association, 2nd congress.

Research Institute, Microscope, Wheat and Locust — A197

Beetle under Magnifying Glass — A198

1964, Sept. 23 Wmk. 349 ***Perf. 10½***
1297 A197 2r red, orange & brn 7.00 .40
1298 A198 6r blue, brn & indigo 8.00 .60

Fight against plant diseases and damages.

Mithras (Mehr) on Ancient Seal — A199

1964, Oct. 8 **Litho.**
Size: 26x34mm
1299 A199 8r org & brn org 5.00 1.00

Mehragan celebration. See No. 1406.

Eleanor Roosevelt (1884-1962) A200

1964, Oct. 11
1300 A200 10r vio bl & rose vio 7.00 1.00

Exists imperf pair, $75 mint, $50 used.

Clasped Hands and UN Emblem — A201

Symbolic Airplane and UN Emblem — A202

1964, Oct. 24 Wmk. 349 *Perf. 10½*
1301 A201 6r ultra, yel, red & blk 3.50 .40
1302 A202 14r org, ultra & red 4.50 .60

Issued for United Nations Day.

Persian Gymnast — A203

Polo Player A204

1964, Oct. 26
1303 A203 4r tan, sep & Prus bl 3.50 .40
1304 A204 6r red & black 4.50 .60

18th Olympic Games, Tokyo, Oct. 10-25.

Crown Prince Reza — A205

1964, Oct. 31 Litho.
1305 A205 1r dull green & brn 4.00 .30
1306 A205 2r deep rose & ultra 5.00 .50
1307 A205 6r ultra & red 7.00 .65
Nos. 1305-1307 (3) 16.00 1.45

Children's Day; Crown Prince Reza's 4th birthday.

UN Emblem, Flame and Smokestack — A206

1964, Nov. 16 Wmk. 349 *Perf. 10½*
1308 A206 6r black, lt bl & car 4.00 .35
1309 A206 8r black, emer & car 5.00 .40

Petro-Chemical Conference and Gas Seminar, Nov.-Dec. 1964.

Shah and King Baudouin — A207

1964, Nov. 17
1310 A207 6r black, org & yel 3.00 .35
1311 A207 8r black, org & emer 5.00 .75

Visit of King Baudouin of Belgium.

Rhazes A208

1964, Dec. 27 Wmk. 349 *Perf. 10½*
1312 A208 2r multicolored 4.00 .35
1313 A208 6r multicolored 6.00 .60

1100th birth anniv. of Rhazes (abu-Bakr Mohammad Zakariya Razi), Persian physician.

Shah and King Olav V A209

1965, Jan. 7 Litho.
1314 A209 2r dk brown & lilac 3.50 .35
1315 A209 4r brown & green 4.50 .75

Visit of King Olav V of Norway.

Map of Iran and Six-pointed Star — A210

1965, Jan. 26 Wmk. 349 *Perf. 10½*
1316 A210 2r black, brt bl & org 3.00 .25

Shah's six socioeconomic bills, 3rd anniv.

Woman and UN Emblem — A211

1965, Mar. 1 Wmk. 349 *Perf. 10½*
1317 A211 6r black & blue 2.00 .25
1318 A211 8r ultra & red 4.00 .25

18th session of the UN commission on the status of women.

Green Wheat and Tulip — A212

1965, Mar. 6
1319 A212 50d multicolored .50 .25
1320 A212 1r multicolored .70 .25

Novrooz, Iranian New Year, Mar. 21.

Pres. Habib Bourguiba and Minarets of Tunis Mosque — A213

1965, Mar. 14 Litho. *Perf. 10½*
1321 A213 4r multicolored 2.25 .35

Visit of Pres. Habib Bourguiba of Tunisia.

Map of Iran and Trade Mark of Iranian Oil Co. A214

1965, Mar. 20 Litho.
1322 A214 6r multicolored 5.00 .25
1323 A214 14r multicolored 6.00 .55

Oil industry nationalization, 14th anniv.

ITU Emblem, Old and New Communication Equipment — A215

1965, May 17 Wmk. 349 *Perf. 10½*
1324 A215 14r dp car rose & gray 3.00 .60

ITU, centenary.

ICY Emblem A216

1965, June 22 Litho. *Perf. 10½*
1325 A216 10r sl grn & gray bl 4.00 .60

International Cooperation Year, 1965.

Iran Airways Emblem A217

1965, July 17 Wmk. 349 *Perf. 10½*
1326 A217 14r multicolored 5.00 .75

Tenth anniversary of Iran Airways.

Hands Holding Book A218

Map and Flags of Turkey, Iran and Pakistan A219

1965, July 21 Litho.
1327 A218 2r dk brn, org brn & buff 2.00 .25
1328 A219 4r multicolored 3.00 .25

Signing of the Regional Cooperation for Development Pact by Turkey, Iran and Pakistan, 1st anniv.

See Pakistan 217-218, Turkey 1648-1649.

Iranian Scout Emblem and Ornament A220

1965, July 23
1329 A220 2r multicolored 4.00 .25
a. Vert. pair, imperf. horiz. 200.00

Middle East Rover Moot (senior Boy Scout assembly).

Majlis Gate A221

1965, Aug. 5 Wmk. 349 *Perf. 10½*
1330 A221 2r lilac rose & brn 2.50 .25

60th anniversary of Iranian constitution.

Types of Regular Issue, 1962

Wmk. 349

1964-65 Photo. *Perf. 10½*
1331 A159 5d dk sl grn ('65) .50 .30
a. Wmk. 353 .50 .30
1332 A159 10d chestnut .50 .30
1333 A159 25d dk blue ('65) 1.00 .25
1334 A159 50d Prus green 1.00 .25
1335 A159 1r orange 1.00 .25
1336 A159 2r violet blue 1.00 .25
1337 A159 5r dark brown 4.00 .50
1338 A160 6r blue ('65) 12.00 1.00

1339 A160 8r yel grn ('65) 5.00 .25
1340 A160 10r grnsh bl ('65) 5.00 .25
1341 A160 11r sl grn ('65) 12.00 1.50
1342 A160 14r purple ('65) 10.00 1.40
1343 A160 20r red brn ('65) 10.00 2.00
1344 A160 50r org ver ('65) 12.00 2.00
Nos. 1331-1344 (14) 75.00 10.50

Perf. 11x10½

1331b A159 5d Wmk. 353 7.00 1.00
1332a A159 10d 1.00 .50
1333a A159 25d 1.00 .25
1334a A159 50d 4.00 2.00
1335a A159 1r 4.00 2.00
1337a A159 5r 7.00 .50
Nos. 1331b-1337a (6) 24.00 6.25

Dental Congress Emblem — A222

1965, Sept. 7 Litho. *Perf. 10½*
1345 A222 6r gray, ultra, & car 1.00 .25

Iranian Dentists' Association, 3rd congress.

Classroom and Literacy Corps Emblem A223

Alphabets on Globe — A224

Designs: 6r, UNESCO emblem and open book (diamond shape). 8r, UNESCO emblem and inscription, horiz. 14r, Mohammad Reza Shah Pahlavi and inscription in six languages.

1965, Sept. 8
1346 A223 2r multi .60 .25
1347 A224 5r multi .75 .30

Size: 30x30mm

1348 A223 6r multi 1.25 .40

Size: 35x23mm

1349 A223 8r dk bl, car emer & buff 1.50 .45

Size: 34x46mm

1350 A223 14r cit, dk bl & brn 3.00 .75
Nos. 1346-1350 (5) 7.10 2.15

World Congress Against Illiteracy, Tehran, Sept. 8-19.

Mohammad Reza Pahlavi — A225

1965, Sept. 16 Litho. *Perf. 10½*
1351 A225 1r crim, rose red & gray 2.00 .50
1352 A225 2r dk red, rose red & yel 3.00 .75

Reign of Shah, 25th year. (in 1966).

Emblem of Persian Medical Society A226

1965, Sept. 21 Wmk. 349
1353 A226 5r ultra, dp ultra & gold 1.50 .25

14th Medical Congress, Ramsar.

Pres. Jonas of Austria A227

1965, Sept. 30
1354 A227 6r bl, brt bl & gray 2.00 .25

Visit of President Franz Jonas of Austria.

Mithras (Mehr) on Ancient Seal — A228

1965, Oct. 8 Litho. Wmk. 353
1355 A228 4r brt grn, gold, brn & blk 2.50 .25

Mehragan celebration during month of Mehr, Sept. 23-Oct. 22. Persian inscription of watermark vertical on No. 1355.

UN Emblem — A229

1965, Oct. 24 Wmk. 353 *Perf. 10½*
1356 A229 5r bl, grn & rose car 1.00 .25

20th anniversary of the United Nations.

Symbolic Arches A230

1965, Oct. 26
1357 A230 3r vio bl, blk, yel & red 2.00 .25

Exhibition of Iranian Commodities.

Crown Prince Reza A231

1965, Oct. 31
1358 A231 2r brown & yellow 2.00 .45

Children's Day; Crown Prince Reza's 5th birthday.

Weight Lifters — A232

1965, Nov. 1
1359 A232 10r brt bl, vio & brt pink 3.00 .25

World Weight Lifting Championships, Tehran.

Open Book A233

1965, Dec. 1 Wmk. 353 *Perf. 10½*
1360 A233 8r bl, brt pink & blk 3.00 .25

Issued for Book Week.

Shah and King Faisal A234

1965, Dec. 8 Litho.
1361 A234 4r olive bister & brn 3.50 .50

Visit of King Faisal of Saudi Arabia.

Scales and Olive Branch A235

1965, Dec. 12
1362 A235 14r multicolored 2.00 .25

Human Rights Day (Dec. 10).

Tractor, "Land Reform" A236

Symbols of Reform Bills: 2r, Trees, nationalization of forests. 3r, Factory and gear wheel, sale of shares in government factories. 4r, Wheels, shareholding for factory workers. 5r, Parliament gate, women's suffrage. 6r, Children before blackboard, Army of Education. 7r, Caduceus, Army of Hygiene. 8r, Scales, creation of rural courts. 9r, Two girders, creation of Army of Progress.

1966, Jan. 26 Wmk. 353 *Perf. 10½*
1363 A236 1r orange & brown .50 .25
1364 A236 2r dl grn & green .60 .25
1365 A236 3r silver & gray .70 .40
1366 A236 4r light & dk vio 1.00 .50
1367 A236 5r rose & brown 1.50 .55
1368 A236 6r olive & brown 2.00 .65
1369 A236 7r bl & vio blue 2.50 .75
1370 A236 8r ultra & dp ultra 3.00 .85
1371 A236 9r brn org & dk brn 3.50 .90
Nos. 1363-1371 (9) 15.30 5.10

Parliamentary approval of the Shah's reform plan.

Shah — A237

Ruins of Persepolis A238

Wmk. 353

1966-71 Photo. *Perf. 10½*
1372 A237 5d green .50 .25
1373 A237 10d chestnut .50 .25
1374 A237 25d dark blue .50 .25
1375 A237 50d Prussian green .60 .25
a. 50d blue green ('71) .60 .30
b. Printed on reverse *750.00*
1376 A237 1r orange .60 .25
1377 A237 2r violet .60 .25
1377A A237 4r cl brn ('68) 7.50 1.00
1378 A237 5r dark brn 2.00 .25
1379 A238 6r deep blue 2.50 .25
1380 A238 8r yellow grn 2.50 .25
a. 8r dull green ('71) 2.50 .25
1381 A238 10r Prus bl 2.50 .25
1382 A238 11r slate grn 2.50 .25
1383 A238 14r purple 3.00 .25
1384 A238 20r brown 19.00 .50
1385 A238 50r cop red 10.00 1.50
1386 A238 100r brt blue 20.00 2.50
1387 A238 200r chnt brn 20.00 4.50
Nos. 1372-1387 (17) 94.80 13.00

Set, except 4r, issued Feb. 22, 1966.

Student Nurse Taking Oath — A239

1966, Feb. 24 Litho.
1388 A239 5r brt pink & mag 2.00 .50
1389 A239 5r lt bl & brt bl 2.00 .50
a. Se-tenant pair, #1388-1389 5.00 3.00

Nurses' Day. Nos. 1388-1389 printed in sheets of 50 arranged checkerwise.

Narcissus — A240

1966, Mar. 7
1390 A240 50d ultra, yel & emer .60 .25
1391 A240 1r lilac, yel & emer .75 .30

Novrooz, Iranian New Year, Mar. 21.

Oil Derricks in Persian Gulf — A241

1966, Mar. 20 *Perf. 10½*

1392 A241 14r blk, brt bl & brt rose lil 3.50 .75

Formation of six offshore oil companies.

Radio Tower — A242

2r, Radar, horiz. 6r, Emblem & waves. 8r, Compass rose & waves. 10r, Tower & waves.

1966, Apr. 27 **Litho.** **Wmk. 349**

1393 A242 2r dark grn .50 .35
1394 A242 4r ultra & dp org .75 .35
1395 A242 6r gray ol & plum 1.00 .40
1396 A242 8r brt bl & dk bl 2.00 .50
1397 A242 10r brn & bister 2.50 .55
Nos. 1393-1397 (5) 6.75 2.15

Inauguration of the radio telecommunication system of the Central Treaty Organization of the Middle East (CENTO).

WHO Headquarters, Geneva — A243

1966, May 3 **Wmk. 353**

1398 A243 10r brt bl, yel & blk 1.00 .30

Opening of the WHO Headquarters, Geneva.

World Map — A244

1966, May 14 **Litho.**

1399 A244 6r bl & multi 1.00 .30
1400 A244 8r multicolored 2.00 .30

Intl. Council of Women, 18th Conf., Tehran, May 1966.

Globe, Map of Iran and Ruins of Persepolis — A245

1966, Sept. 5 **Wmk. 353** *Perf. 10½*

1401 A245 14r multicolored 2.00 .50

International Iranology Congress, Tehran.

Emblem of Iranian Medical Society A246

1966, Sept. 21

1402 A246 4r ultra, lt bl & bis .75 .30

15th Medical Congress, held at Ramsar.

Gate of Parliament, Mt. Demavend and Congress Emblem — A247

8r, Senate building, Mt. Demavend & emblem.

1966, Oct. 2 **Wmk. 353** *Perf. 10½*

1403 A247 6r brick red, ultra & dk grn 1.00 .30
1404 A247 8r lt lil, ultra & dk grn 1.25 .30

55th Interparliamentary Union Conf., Tehran.

Visit of President Cevdet Sunay of Turkey — A248

1966, Oct. 2 **Litho.**

1405 A248 6r vio & dk brn .75 .25

Mithras Type of 1964

1966, Oct. 8 **Size: 30x40mm**

1406 A199 6r olive bister & brn .75 .30

Mehragan celebration.

Farmers — A249

1966, Oct. 13

1407 A249 5r olive bister & brn 7.50 2.00

Establishment of rural courts of justice.

UN Emblem — A250

1966, Oct. 24 **Wmk. 353** *Perf. 10½*

1408 A250 6r brn org & blk .75 .30

21st anniversary of United Nations.

Crown Prince Reza — A251

1966, Oct. 31 **Litho.**

1409 A251 1r ultramarine 1.50 .75
1410 A251 2r violet 2.00 .75
a. Pair, #1409-1410 4.00 4.00

Children's Day; Crown Prince Reza's 6th birthday.

Symbolic Woman's Face — A252

1966, Nov. 6

1411 A252 5r gold, blk & ultra .60 .25

Founding of the Iranian Women's Org.

Film Strip and Song Bird A253

1966, Nov. 6

1412 A253 4r blk, red lil & vio .75 .25

First Iranian children's film festival.

"Census Count" — A254

1966, Nov. 11

1413 A254 6r dk brn & gray .60 .25

National census.

Book Cover — A255

1966, Nov. 15

1414 A255 8r tan, brn & ultra .60 .25

Issued to publicize Book Week.

Reza Shah Pahlavi A256

Design: 2r, Reza Shah Pahlavi without kepi.

1966, Nov. 16 **Litho.**

1415 A256 1r slate blue 3.50 1.00
1416 A256 1r brown 3.50 1.00
a. Pair, #1415-1416 8.00 3.00
1417 A256 2r gray green 4.00 1.00
1418 A256 2r violet blue 4.00 1.00
a. Pair, #1417-1418 9.00 3.00
Nos. 1415-1418 (4) 15.00 4.00

Reza Shah Pahlavi (1877-1944), founder of modern Iran.

EROPA Emblem and Map of Persia A257

1966, Dec. 4 **Wmk. 353** *Perf. 10½*

1419 A257 8r dk brn & emerald 1.50 .25

4th General Assembly of the Org. of Public Administrators, EROPA.

Shah Giving Deeds to Farmers A258

1967, Jan. 9 **Wmk. 353** *Perf. 10½*

1420 A258 6r ol bis, yel & brn 3.00 .25

Approval of land reform laws, 5th anniv.

Shah and 9-Star Crescent — A259

Design: 2r, Torch and 9-star crescent.

1967, Jan. 26 **Wmk. 353** **Litho.**

1421 A259 2r multicolored 2.00 .50
1422 A259 6r multicolored 3.00 .50

5th anniv. of Shah's reforms, the "White Revolution."

Ancient Sculpture of Bull — A260

Designs: 5r, Sculptured mythical animals. 8r, Pillar from Persepolis.

1967, Feb. 25 Wmk. 353 *Perf. 10½*
1423 A260 3r dk brn & ocher 1.25 .35
1424 A260 5r Prus grn, brn & ocher 1.50 .45
1425 A260 8r vio, blk & sil 2.00 .65
Nos. 1423-1425 (3) 4.75 1.45

Issued to publicize Museum Week.

Planting Tree — A261

1967, Mar. 6
1426 A261 8r brn org & grn .60 .25

Tree Planting Day.

Goldfish — A262

1967, Mar. 11 Size: 26x20mm
1427 A262 1r shown .50 .25

Size: 35x27mm
1428 A262 8r Swallows 2.00 .30

Issued for Novrooz, Iranian New Year.

Microscope, Animals and Emblem — A263

1967, Mar. 11 *Perf. 10½*
1429 A263 5r blk, gray & mag 1.00 .25

Second Iranian Veterinary Congress.

Pres. Arif of Iraq, Mosque — A264

1967, Mar. 14 Litho. Wmk. 353
1430 A264 6r brt bl & grn 1.00 .30

Visit of Pres. Abdul Salam Mohammad Arif.

Fireworks A265

1967, Mar. 17
1431 A265 5r vio bl & multi 3.00 .50

Issued for United Nations Stamp Day.

Map of Iran and Oil Company Emblem — A266

1967, Mar. 20
1432 A266 6r multicolored 3.50 .45

Nationalization of Iranian Oil Industry.

Fencers A267

1967, Mar. 23
1433 A267 5r vio & bister 1.50 .60

Intl. Youth Fencing Championships, Tehran.

Shah and King of Thailand A268

1967, Apr. 23 Wmk. 353 *Perf. 10½*
1434 A268 6r brn org & dk brn 3.00 .45

Visit of King Bhumibol Adulyadej.

Old and Young Couples A269

1967, Apr. 24 Litho.
1435 A269 5r ol bis & vio bl 1.00 .25

15th anniversary of Social Insurance.

Skier and Iranian Olympic Emblem A270

Designs: 6r, Assyrian soldiers, Olympic rings and tablet inscribed "I.O.C." 8r, Wrestlers and Iranian Olympic emblem.

1967, May 5
1436 A270 3r brown & black 1.50 .25
1437 A270 6r multicolored 2.00 .45
1438 A270 8r ultra & brown 2.50 .75
Nos. 1436-1438 (3) 6.00 1.45

65th Intl. Olympic Cong., Tehran, May 2-11.

Lions International — A271

1967, May 11 Size: 41½x30½mm
1439 A271 3r shown 1.25 .50

Size: 36x42mm
1440 A271 7r Emblem, vert. 1.75 .75

50th anniversary of Lions International.

Visit of Pres. Chivu Stoica of Romania — A272

1967, May 13
1441 A272 6r orange & dk bl .75 .25

International Tourist Year Emblem — A273

1967, June 6 Wmk. 353 *Perf. 10½*
1442 A273 3r brick red & ultra .75 .25

Iranian Pavilion and Ornament A274

1967, June 7 Litho.
1443 A274 4r dk brn, red & gold .75 .25
1444 A274 10r red, dk brn & gold 1.25 .30

EXPO '67, Montreal, Apr. 28-Oct. 27.

Stamp of 1870, No. 1 A275

1967, July 23 Wmk. 353 *Perf. 10½*
1445 A275 6r multri .75 .30
1446 A275 8r multi 1.25 .30

Centenary of first Persian postage stamp.

World Map and School Children — A276

1967, Sept. 8 Litho. Wmk. 353
1447 A276 3r ultra & brt & brt bl 1.00 .25
1448 A276 5r brown & yellow 2.00 .35

World campaign against illiteracy.

Globe and Oriental Musician — A277

1967, Sept. 10 *Perf. 10½*
1449 A277 14r brn org & dk brn 1.50 .50

Intl. Conf. on Music Education in Oriental Countries, Sept. 1967.

Child's Hand Holding Adult's — A278

1967, Sept. 14 Litho. Wmk. 353
1450 A278 8r dk brn & yel 12.00 3.00

Introduction of Children's Villages in Iran. (Modelled after Austrian SOS Villages for homeless children).

Winged Wild Goat — A279

1967, Sept. 19
1451 A279 8r dk brn & lemon 1.00 .25

Festival of Arts, Persepolis.

UN Emblem A280

1967, Oct. 17
1452 A280 6r olive bister & vio bl .80 .25

Issued for United Nations Day.

Shah and Empress Farah — A281

1967, Oct. 26 Wmk. 353 *Perf. 10½*
Various Frames
1453 A281 2r sil, bl & brn 2.00 .40
1454 A281 10r sil, bl & vio 3.00 .60
1455 A281 14r lt bl, bl, gold & vio 5.00 1.50
Nos. 1453-1455 (3) 10.00 2.50

Coronation of Shah Mohammad Reza Pahlavi and Empress Farah, Oct. 26, 1967.

Nos. 1453-1455 exist in imperf between pairs, with top sheet margin, value set, $95, and in imperf between blocks of 4, ungummed, value set, $40. Fake imperf between pairs, lacking the top sheet margin, have been manufactured by fraudulently perforating imperf-between blocks.

1967, Oct. 31 **Litho.**

Design: Crown Prince Reza.

1456 A281 2r silver & violet 1.00 .35
1457 A281 8r sil & red brown 1.50 .45

Children's Day; Crown Prince Reza's 7th birthday.

Visit of Pres. Georgi Traikov of Bulgaria — A283

1967, Nov. 20
1458 A283 10r lilac & dk brn .50 .25

Persian Boy Scout Emblem A284

1967, Dec. 3 **Wmk. 353** ***Perf. 10½***
1459 A284 8r olive & red brn 2.00 .50

Cooperation Week of the Iranian Boy Scouts, Dec. 5-12.

Hands Holding Chain Link A285

1967, Dec. 6 **Litho.**
1460 A285 6r multicolored 1.00 .25

Issued to publicize Cooperation Year.

Visit of Sheik Sabah of Kuwait — A286

1968, Jan. 10 **Wmk. 353** ***Perf. 10½***
1461 A286 10r lt bl & slate grn 1.50 .25

List of Shah's 12 Reform Laws 4 — A287

1968, Jan. 27 **Litho.** **Wmk. 353**
1462 A287 2r sl grn, brn & sal 1.00 .30
1463 A287 8r vio, dk grn & lt grn 2.00 .35
1464 A287 14r brn, pink & lt lil 3.00 .50
Nos. 1462-1464 (3) 6.00 1.15

"White Revolution of King and People."

Almond Blossoms A288

Haji Firooz (New Year Singer) A289

Design: 2r, Tulips.

1968, Mar. 12 **Wmk. 353** ***Perf. 10½***
1465 A288 1r multi .50 .25
1466 A288 2r bluish gray & multi .50 .25
1467 A288 2r brt rose lil & multi .50 .25
1468 A289 6r multi 1.50 .45
Nos. 1465-1468 (4) 3.00 1.20

Issued for Novrooz, Iranian New Year.

Oil Worker and Derrick A290

1968, Mar. 20 **Litho.**
1469 A290 14r grn, blk & org yel 2.50 .50

Oil industry nationalization, 17th anniv.

WHO Emblem A291

1968, Apr. 7 **Wmk. 353** ***Perf. 10½***
1470 A291 14r brn, bl & org 1.25 .30

WHO, 20th anniversary.

Marlik Chariot, Ancient Sculpture A292

1968, Apr. 13
1471 A292 8r blue, brn & buff 1.00 .25

Fifth World Congress of Persian Archaeology and Art, Tehran.

Shah and King Hassan II A293

1968, Apr. 16
1472 A293 6r bright vio & buff 1.25 .25

Visit of King Hassan II of Morocco.

Human Rights Flame — A294

Design: 14r, Frameline inscription reads, "International Conference on Human Rights Tehran 1968"; "Iran" at left.

1968, May 5 **Wmk. 353** ***Perf. 10½***
1473 A294 8r red & dk grn 1.00 .25
1474 A294 14r vio bl & bl 1.50 .30

Intl. Human Rights Year. The 8r commemorates the Iranian Human Rights Committee; the 14r, the Intl. Conference on Human Rights, Tehran, 1968.

Soccer Player — A295

1968, May 10 **Litho.**
1475 A295 8r multicolored 1.00 .30
1476 A295 10r multicolored 1.50 .30

Asian Soccer Cup Finals, Tehran.

Tehran Oil Refinery A296

1968, May 21 **Wmk. 353** ***Perf. 10½***
1477 A296 14r brt bl & multi 2.50 .35

Opening of the Tehran Oil Refinery.

Queen Farah as Girl Guide — A297

1968, June 24 **Litho.** ***Perf. 10½***
1478 A297 4r brt rose lil & bl green 3.00 .75
1479 A297 6r car & brn 3.50 1.00

Great Camp of Iranian Girl Guides.

A set of 2 stamps (8r, 14r) were prepared for the International Tennis Congress, Tehran. The stamps were not released when the congress was cancelled. Value, set $2,500.

Anopheles Mosquito, Congress Emblem — A298

1968, Sept. 7 **Wmk. 353** ***Perf. 10½***
1480 A298 6r brt pur & blk .75 .35
1481 A298 14r dk grn & mag 1.25 .40

8th Intl. Congress on Tropical Medicine and Malaria, Tehran, Sept. 7-15.

Winged Figure with Banner, and Globe — A299

1968, Sept. 8 **Litho.**
1482 A299 6r lt vio, bis & bl .75 .25
1483 A299 14r dl yel, sl grn & brn 1.25 .30

World campaign against illiteracy.

Oramental Horse and Flower — A300

1968, Sept. 11
1484 A300 14r sl grn, org & yel grn 1.25 .25

2nd Festival of Arts, Shiraz-Persepolis.

INTERPOL Emblem and Globe — A301

1968, Oct. 6 **Wmk. 353** ***Perf. 10½***
1485 A301 10r dk brn & bl 1.00 .25

37th General Assembly of the Intl. Police Org. (INTERPOL) in Tehran.

Police Emblem on Iran Map in Flag Colors — A302

1968, Oct. 7 **Litho.**
1486 A302 14r multicolored 1.50 .30

Issued for Police Day.

Peace Dove and UN Emblem — A303

1968, Oct. 24
1487 A303 14r bl & vio bl 1.25 .25

Issued for United Nations Day.

Empress Farah — A304

Designs: 8r, Mohammad Reza Shah Pahlavi. 10fr, Shah, Empress and Crown Prince.

1968, Oct. 26
1488 A304 6r multi 8.00 3.75
1489 A304 8r multi 10.00 5.50
1490 A304 10r multi 12.00 6.75
Nos. 1488-1490 (3) 30.00 16.00

Coronation of Mohammad Reza Shah Pahlavi and Empress Farah, 1st anniv.

Shah's Crown and Bull's Head Capital — A305

1968, Oct. 30
1491 A305 14r ultra, gold, sil & red 1.00 .25

Festival of Arts and Culture.

UNICEF Emblem and Child's Drawing — A306

Children's Drawings and UNICEF Emblem: 3r, Boat on lake, house and trees, horiz. 5r, Flowers, horiz.

1968, Oct. 31 **Litho.**
1492 A306 2r dk brn & multi .35 .25
1493 A306 3r dk grn & multi .50 .30
1494 A306 5r multicolored .70 .40
Nos. 1492-1494 (3) 1.55 .95

Issued for Children's Day.

Labor Union Emblem A307

Factory and Insurance Company Emblem A308

Designs: 8r, Members of Army of Hygiene, and Insurance Company emblem. 10r, Map of Persia, Insurance Company emblem, car, train, ship and plane.

1968, Nov. 6 Wmk. 353 *Perf. 10½*
1495 A307 4r sil & vio bl .50 .35
1496 A308 5r multicolored .65 .35
1497 A308 8r ultra, gray & yel .85 .35
1498 A308 10r multicolored .95 .40
Nos. 1495-1498 (4) 2.95 1.45

Issued to publicize Insurance Day.

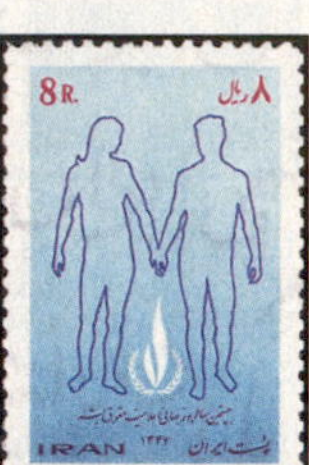
Human Rights Flame, Man and Woman — A309

1968, Dec. 10 Litho. *Perf. 10½*
1499 A309 8r lt bl, vio bl & car .75 .25

International Human Rights Year.

Symbols of Shah's Reform Plan — A310

Design: Each stamp shows symbols of 3 of the Shah's reforms. No. 1503a shows the 12 symbols in a circle with a medallion in the center picturing 3 heads and a torch.

1969, Jan. 26 Wmk. 353 *Perf. 10½*
1500 2r ocher, grn & lil 2.00 .50
1501 4r lil, ocher & grn 2.50 .60
1502 6r lil, ocher & grn 2.50 .75
1503 8r lil, ocher & grn 3.25 1.10
a. A310 Block of 4, #1500-1503 12.50 4.50
Nos. 1500-1503 (4) 10.25 2.95

Declaration of the Shah's Reform Plan.

Shah and Crowd A311

1969, Feb. 1 Litho.
1504 A311 6r red, bl & brn 2.50 .35

10,000th day of the reign of the Shah.

European Goldfinch A312

2r, Ring-necked pheasant. 8r, Roses.

1969, Mar. 6 Wmk. 353 *Perf. 10½*
1505 A312 1r multicolored .35 .25
1506 A312 2r multicolored .50 .25
1507 A312 8r multicolored 1.25 .25
Nos. 1505-1507 (3) 2.10 .75

Issued for Novrooz, Iranian New Year.

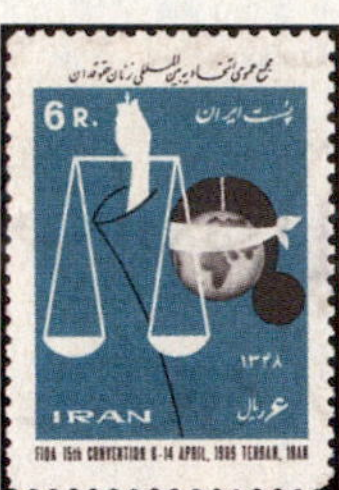
"Woman Lawyer" Holding Scales of Justice — A313

1969, Apr. 8 Litho. *Perf. 10½*
1508 A313 6r blk & brt bl .75 .25

15th General Assembly of Women Lawyers, Tehran, Apr. 8-14.

Workers, ILO and UN Emblems — A314

1969, Apr. 30 Wmk. 353 *Perf. 10½*
1509 A314 10r bl & vio bl .75 .25

ILO, 50th anniversary.

Freestyle Wrestlers and Aryamehr Cup — A315

1969, May 6 Litho.
1510 A315 10r lilac & multi 2.50 .75

Intl. Freestyle Wrestling Championships, 3rd round.

Birds and Flower A316

1969, June 10 Wmk. 353 *Perf. 10½*
1511 A316 10r vio bl & multi 1.00 .25

Issued to publicize Handicrafts Day.

Boy Scout Symbols A317

1969, July 9 Wmk. 353 *Perf. 10½*
1512 A317 6r lt bl & multi 2.00 .30

Philia 1969, an outdoor training course for Boy Scout patrol leaders.

Lady Serving Wine, Safavi Miniature, Iran — A318

No. 1514, Lady on Balcony, Mogul miniature, Pakistan. No. 1515, Sultan Suleiman Receiving Sheik Abdul Latif, 16th cent. miniature, Turkey.

1969, July 21 Litho.
1513 A318 25r multi 3.00 1.00
1514 A318 25r multi 3.00 1.00
1515 A318 25r multi 3.00 1.00
Nos. 1513-1515 (3) 9.00 3.00

Signing of the Regional Cooperation for Development Pact by Turkey, Iran and Pakistan, 5th anniv.

Neil A. Armstrong and Col. Edwin E. Aldrin on Moon — A319

1969, July 26
1516 A319 24r bister, bl & brn 15.00 5.00

See note after Algeria No. 427.

Quotation from Shah's Declaration on Education and Art — A320

1969, Aug. 6 **Wmk. 353** ***Perf. 10½***
1517 A320 10r car, cream & emer 1.00 .25

Anniv. of educational and art reforms.

Offshore Oil Rig in Persian Gulf — A321

1969, Sept. 1 **Litho.**
1518 A321 8r multicolored 2.00 .35

Marine drillings by the Iran-Italia Oil Co., 10th anniv.

Dancers Forming Flower — A322

1969, Sept. 6 **Wmk. 353** ***Perf. 10½***
1519 A322 6r multicolored .75 .25
1520 A322 8r multicolored 1.00 .25

3rd Festival of Arts, Shiraz and Persepolis, Aug. 30-Sept. 9.

Crossed-out Fingerprint, Moon and Rocket — A323

1969, Sept. 8 **Litho.**
1521 A323 4r multicolored .65 .25

World campaign against illiteracy.

Persepolis, Simulated Stamp with UPU Emblem, and Shah — A324

1969, Sept. 28
1522 A324 10r lt bl & multi 4.00 1.00
1523 A324 14r multicolored 6.00 1.50

16th Congress of the UPU, Tokyo.

Fair Emblem — A325

14r, like 8r, inscribed "ASIA 69." 20r, Fair emblem, world map and "ASIA 69," horiz.

1969, Oct. 5 **Wmk. 353** ***Perf. 10½***
1524 A325 8r rose & multi 1.00 .30
1525 A325 14r blue & multi 1.50 .30
1526 A325 20r tan & multi 2.00 .40
Nos. 1524-1526 (3) 4.50 1.00

2nd Asian Trade Fair, Tehran.

Justice — A326

1969, Oct. 13 **Litho.**
1527 A326 8r bl grn & dk brn 1.00 .25

Rural Courts of Justice Day.

UN Emblem A327

1969, Oct. 24
1528 A327 2r lt bl & dp bl .75 .25

25th anniversary of the United Nations.

Emblem and Column Capital, Persepolis — A328

1969, Oct. 28
1529 A328 2r deep blue & multi 1.00 .25

2nd Festival of Arts and Culture.
See Nos. 1577, 1681, 1735.

Child's Drawing and UNICEF Emblem A329

Children's Drawings and UNICEF Emblem: 1r, Boy and birds, vert. 5r, Dinner.

1969, Oct. 31 **Wmk. 353** ***Perf. 10½***
Size: 28x40mm, 40x28mm
1530 A329 1r lt blue & multi .45 .25
1531 A329 2r lt grn & multi .60 .25
1532 A329 5r lt lil & multi .95 .25
Nos. 1530-1532 (3) 2.00 .75

Children's Week. See Nos. 1578-1580.

Globe Emblem A330

1969, Nov. 6
1533 A330 8r dk brn & bl .75 .25

Meeting of the Natl. Society of Parents and Educators, Tehran.

Satellite Communications Station — A331

1969, Nov. 19 **Litho.**
1534 A331 6r blk brn & bis 1.50 .30

1st Iranian Satellite Communications Earth Station, Hamadan.

Mahatma Gandhi (1869-1948) A332

1969, Dec. 29 **Wmk. 353** ***Perf. 10½***
1535 A332 14r gray & dk rose brn 12.00 5.00

Globe, Flags and Emblems A333

Design: 6r, Globe and Red Cross, Red Lion and Sun, and Red Crescent Emblems.

1969, Dec. 31
1536 A333 2r red & multi 1.50 .35
1537 A333 6r red & multi 2.00 .45

League of Red Cross Societies, 50th anniv.

Symbols of Reform Laws and Shah A334

1970, Jan. 26 **Litho.** **Wmk. 353**
1538 A334 1r bister & multi 1.50 .40
1539 A334 2r multicolored 2.00 .60

Declaration of the Shah's Reform Plan.

Pansies A335

New Year's Table A336

1970, Mar. 6 **Wmk. 353** ***Perf. 10½***
1540 A335 1r multicolored .40 .25
1541 A336 8r multicolored 2.10 .30

Issued for the Iranian New Year.

Chemical Plant, Kharg Island, and Iranian Oil Company Emblem — A337

Designs (Iranian Oil Company Emblem and): 2r, Shah's portrait and quotation. 4r, Laying of gas pipe line and tractor. 8r, Tankers at pier of Kharg Island, vert. 10r, Tehran refinery.

1970, Mar. 20 **Wmk. 353** ***Perf. 10½***
1542 A337 2r gray & multi 2.00 .50
1543 A337 4r multicolored 2.50 .75
1544 A337 6r lt bl & multi 3.00 .95
1545 A337 8r multicolored 3.50 1.00
1546 A337 10r multicolored 5.00 1.25
Nos. 1542-1546 (5) 16.00 4.45

Nationalization of the oil industry, 20th anniv.

EXPO '70 Emblem — A338

1970, Mar. 27 **Litho.**
1547 A338 4r brt rose lil & vio bl .50 .25
1548 A338 10r lt bl & pur 1.00 .25

EXPO '70, Osaka, Japan, Mar. 15-Sept. 13.

Radar, Satellite and Congress Emblem — A339

1970, Apr. 20 **Wmk. 353** ***Perf. 10½***
1549 A339 14r multicolored 2.00 .35

Asia-Australia Telecommunications Congress, Tehran.

UPU Headquarters, Bern — A340

1970, May 10
1550 A340 2r gray, brn & lil rose 1.00 .25
1551 A340 4r lil, brn & lil rose 1.00 .25

Inauguration of the new UPU Headquarters, Bern.

Asia Productivity Year Emblem — A341

1970, May 19 Wmk. 353 ***Perf. 10½***
1552 A341 8r gray & multi .75 .25

Asian Productivity Year, 1970.

Bird Bringing Baby A342

1970, June 15 Litho.
1553 A342 8r brn & dk blue .75 .25

Iranian School for Midwives, 50th anniv.

Tomb of Cyrus the Great, Meshed-Morghab in Fars — A343

Designs: 8r, Pillars of Apadana Palace, Persepolis, vert. 10r, Bas-relief from a Mede tomb, Iraq. 14r, Achaemenian officers, bas-relief, Persepolis.

1970, June 21 Photo. ***Perf. 13***
1554 A343 6r gray, red & vio 3.00 .25
1555 A343 8r pale rose, blk & bl grn 3.00 .50
1556 A343 10r yel, red & brn 3.50 .65
1557 A343 14r bl, blk & red brn 4.00 1.00
Nos. 1554-1557 (4) 13.50 2.40

2500th anniversary of the founding of the Persian Empire by Cyrus the Great.
See Nos. 1561-1571, 1589-1596, 1605-1612.

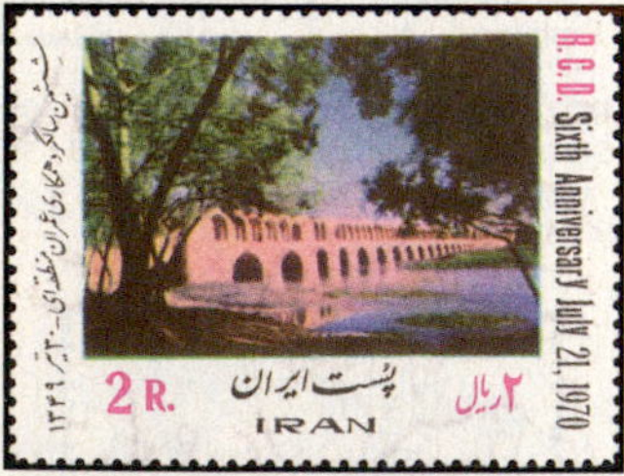

Seeyo-Se-Pol Bridge, Isfahan — A344

No. 1559, Saiful Malook Lake, Pakistan, vert. No. 1560, View of Fethiye, Turkey, vert.

Wmk. 353
1970, July 21 Litho. ***Perf. 10½***
1558 A344 2r multicolored 1.10 .30
1559 A344 2r multicolored 1.10 .30
1560 A344 2r multicolored 1.10 .30
Nos. 1558-1560 (3) 3.30 .90

Signing of the Regional Cooperation for Development Pact by Iran, Turkey and Pakistan, 6th anniv.
See Pakistan 290-292, Turkey 1857-1859.

Queen Buran, Dirhem Coin A345

Wine Goblet with Lion's Head — A346

Designs: No. 1562, Achaemenian eagle amulet. No. 1563, Mithridates I, dirhem coin. No. 1564, Sassanidae art (arch, coin, jugs). No. 1566, Shapur I, dirhem coin. No. 1567, Achaemenian courier. No. 1568, Winged deer. No. 1569, Ardashir I, dirhem coin. No. 1570, Seal of Darius I (chariot, palms, lion). 14r, Achaemenian tapestry.

1970 Wmk. 353 Photo. ***Perf. 13***
1561 A345 1r gold & multi 2.50 .50
1562 A346 2r green & multi 1.60 .40
1563 A345 2r gold & multi 2.50 .50
1564 A346 2r lilac & multi 3.00 .50
1565 A346 6r green & multi 1.90 .40
1566 A345 6r gold & multi 3.00 .60
1567 A345 6r lilac & multi 3.50 .60
1568 A346 8r pink & multi 2.50 .50
1569 A345 8r gold & multi 3.00 .75
1570 A345 8r lilac & multi 4.00 .75
1571 A345 14r lt bl & multi 3.00 1.10
Nos. 1561-1571 (11) 30.50 6.60

2500th anniversary of the founding of the Persian Empire by Cyrus the Great.
Issued: 1r, Nos. 1563, 1566, 1569, 8/22; #1562, 1565, 1568, 14r, 8/6; others, 9/22.

Candle and Globe — A347

1970, Sept. 8 Litho. ***Perf. 10½***
1572 A347 1r lt bl & multi .30 .25
1573 A347 2r pale sal & multi .40 .25

Issued to publicize World Literacy Day.

Persian Decoration A348

1970, Sept. 14
1574 A348 6r multi .75 .25

Isfahan Intl. Cong. of Architects, Sept. 1970.

Emblem — A349

1970, Sept. 28 ***Perf. 10½***
1575 A349 2r lt bl & pur .50 .25

Congress of Election Committees of Persian States and Tehran.

UN Emblem, Dove and Scales — A350

1970, Oct. 24 Litho. Wmk. 353
1576 A350 2r lt bl, mag & dk bl .50 .25

Issued for United Nations Day.

Festival Type of 1969

1970, Oct. 28 ***Perf. 10½***
1577 A328 2r org & multi .50 .25

3rd Festival of Arts and Culture.

UNICEF Type of 1969

Children's Drawings and UNICEF Emblem: 50d, Herdsman and goats. 1r, Family picnic. 2r, Mosque.

1970, Oct. 31 Size: 43½x31mm
1578 A329 50d black & multi .35 .25
1579 A329 1r black & multi .45 .25
1580 A329 2r black & multi .65 .25
Nos. 1578-1580 (3) 1.45 .75

Issued for Children's Week.

Mohammad Reza Shah Pahlavi A351

1971, Jan. 26 Wmk. 353 ***Perf. 10½***
1581 A351 2r lt bl & multi 3.50 1.00

Publicizing the "White Revolution of King and People" and the 12 reform laws.

Sheldrake — A352

2r, Ruddy shelduck. 8r, Flamingo, vert.

1971, Jan. 30 Litho.
1582 A352 1r multicolored 2.00 .50
1583 A352 2r multicolored 2.50 .75
1584 A352 8r multicolored 4.00 1.00
Nos. 1582-1584 (3) 8.50 2.25

Intl. Wetland and Waterfowl Conf., Ramsar.

Reza Shah Pahlavi — A353

1971, Feb. 22 Wmk. 353 ***Perf. 10½***
1585 A353 6r multicolored 8.00 2.75

50th anniversary of the Pahlavi dynasty's accession to power.

Rooster A354

2r, Barn swallow and nest. 6r, Hoopoe.

1971, Mar. 6 Photo. ***Perf. 13½x13***
1586 A354 1r multicolored 1.50 .45
1587 A354 2r multicolored 2.00 .75
1588 A354 6r multicolored 3.50 1.00
Nos. 1586-1588 (3) 7.00 2.20

Novrooz, Iranian New Year.

Shapur II Hunting — A355

Bull's Head, Persepolis A356

1r, Harpist, mosaic. No. 1591, Investiture of Ardashir I, bas-relief. 5r Winged lion ornament. 6r, Persian archer, bas-relief. 8r, Royal audience, bas-relief. 10r, Bronze head of Parthian prince.

1971 Litho. ***Perf. 10½***
1589 A356 1r multicolored 3.00 .45
1590 A355 2r blk & brn org 3.50 .45
1591 A355 2r lil, gldn brn & blk 3.50 .45
1592 A356 4r pur & multi 2.00 .45
1593 A356 5r multicolored 2.25 .55
1594 A356 6r multicolored 2.25 .55
1595 A356 8r lt bl & multi 3.00 .80
1596 A356 10r dp bis, blk & slate 4.00 .90
Nos. 1589-1596 (8) 23.50 4.60

2500th anniversary of the founding of the Persian Empire by Cyrus the Great.
Issued: 4r, 5r, 6r, 8r, 5/15; others, 6/15.

Prisoners Leaving Jail — A357

1971, May 20 Litho. Wmk. 353

1597	A357	6r multicolored	2.00	.25
1598	A357	8r multicolored	3.25	.25

Rehabilitation of Prisoners Week.

Religious School, Chaharbagh, Ispahan A358

No. 1600, Mosque of Selim, Edirne, Turkey. No. 1601, Badshahi Mosque, Lahore, Pakistan, horiz.

1971, July 21 Litho. Perf. 10½

1599	A358	2r multicolored	.75	.25
1600	A358	2r multicolored	.75	.25
1601	A358	2r multicolored	.75	.25
		Nos. 1599-1601 (3)	2.25	.75

7th anniversary of Regional Cooperation among Iran, Pakistan and Turkey.
See Pakistan 305-307, Turkey 1886-1888.

"Fifth Festival of Arts" — A359

1971, Aug. 26 Litho. & Typo.

1602	A359	2r lt & dk grn, red & gold	.90	.30

5th Festival of Arts, Shiraz-Persepolis.

"Fight Against Illiteracy" — A360

1971, Sept. 8 Litho.

1603	A360	2r grn & multi	.65	.30

International Literacy Day, Sept. 8.

Kings Abdullah and Hussein II of Jordan A361

1971, Sept. 11

1604	A361	2r yel grn, blk & red	.75	.35

Hashemite Kingdom of Jordan, 50th anniv.

Shahyad Aryamehr Monument — A362

Designs: 1r, Aryamehr steel mill, near Isfahan. 3r, Senate Building, Tehran. 11r, Shah Abbas Kabir Dam, Zayandeh River.

1971, Sept. 22

1605	A362	1r blue & multi	2.00	.50
1606	A362	2r multicolored	2.50	.50
1607	A362	3r brt pink & multi	3.00	.50
1608	A362	11r org & multi	4.00	1.00
		Nos. 1605-1608 (4)	11.50	2.50

2500th anniversary of the founding of the Persian empire by Cyrus the Great.

Mohammad Reza Shah Pahlavi — A363

Designs: 2r, Reza Shah Pahlavi. 5r, Stone tablet with proclamation of Cyrus the Great, horiz. 10r, Crown of present empire (erroneously inscribed *Le* Couronne).

1971, Oct. 12

1609	A363	1r gold & multi	5.00	2.50
1610	A363	2r gold & multi	5.50	2.50
1611	A363	5r gold & multi	6.50	3.00
1612	A363	10r gold & multi	8.00	3.00
		Nos. 1609-1612 (4)	25.00	11.00

2500th anniversary of the founding of the Persian empire by Cyrus the Great.

Ghatour Railroad Bridge — A364

1971, Oct. 7

1613	A364	2r multicolored	4.00	.85

Iran-Turkey railroad.

Racial Equality Emblem A365

1971, Oct. 24

1614	A365	2r lt blue & multi	.35	.25

Intl. Year Against Racial Discrimination.

Mohammad Reza Shah Pahlavi — A366

Perf. 13½x13
1971, Oct. 26 Photo. Wmk. 353
Size: 20½x28mm

1615	A366	5d lilac	.25	.25
1616	A366	10d henna brown	.25	.25
1617	A366	50d brt bl grn	.25	.25
1618	A366	1r dp yel grn	.30	.25
1619	A366	2r brown	.30	.25

Size: 27x36½mm

1620	A366	6r slate green	1.10	.25
1621	A366	8r violet blue	2.00	1.10
1622	A366	10r red lilac	2.00	.30
1623	A366	11r blue green	6.00	1.10
1624	A366	14r brt blue	9.00	.50
1625	A366	20r car rose	9.50	.65
1626	A366	50r yellow bis	10.00	1.25
		Nos. 1615-1626 (12)	40.95	6.40

See Nos. 1650-1661B, 1768-1772.

Child's Drawing and Emblem — A367

Designs: No. 1631, Ruins of Persepolis, vert. No. 1632, Warrior, mosaic, vert.

1971, Oct. 31 Litho. Perf. 10½

1630	A367	2r multicolored	.50	.25
1631	A367	2r multicolored	.50	.25
1632	A367	2r multicolored	.50	.25
		Nos. 1630-1632 (3)	1.50	.75

Children's Week.

UNESCO Emblem and "25" A368

1971, Nov. 4

1633	A368	6r ultra & rose claret	.60	.25

25th anniversary of UNESCO.

Domestic Animals and Emblem A369

1971, Nov. 22

1634	A369	2r gray, blk & car	.50	.30

4th Iranian Veterinarians' Congress.

ILO Emblem, Cog Wheels and Globe A370

1971, Dec. 4

1635	A370	2r black, org & bl	.50	.25

7th ILO Conference for the Asian Region.

UNICEF Emblem, Bird Feeding Young A371

1971, Dec. 16 Perf. 13x13½

1636	A371	2r lt bl, mag & blk	.60	.30

25th anniversary of UNICEF.

Mohammad Reza Shah Pahlavi A372

1972, Jan. 26 Wmk. 353 Perf. 10½

1637	A372	2r lt green & multi	5.00	2.25
a.		20r Souvenir sheet	17.50	11.50

"White Revolution of King and People" and the 12 reform laws. No. 1637a contains one stamp with simulated perforations.

Pintailed Sandgrouse — A373

No. 1639, Rock ptarmigan. 2r, Yellow-billed waxbill and red-cheeked cordon-bleu.

1972, Mar. 6 Litho. Perf. 13x13½

1638	A373	1r lt green & multi	1.10	.50
1639	A373	1r lt blue & multi	1.10	.50
1640	A373	2r yellow & multi	2.25	.60
		Nos. 1638-1640 (3)	4.45	1.60

Iranian New Year.

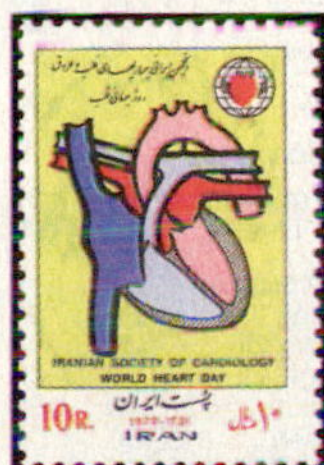

"Your Heart is your Health" — A374

1972, Apr. 4 Perf. 10½

1641	A374	10r lemon & multi	3.00	.30

World Health Day; Iranian Society of Cardiology.

Film Strip and Winged Antelope A375

8r, Film strips and winged antelope.

1972, Apr. 16 Litho. & Engr.

1642	A375	6r ultra & gold	1.50	.30
1643	A375	8r yellow & multi	2.00	.35

Tehran International Film Festival.

Rose and Bud — A376

1972, May 5 **Litho.**

1644	A376	1r shown	.50	.30
1645	A376	2r Yellow roses	.80	.35
1646	A376	5r Red rose	.90	.40
		Nos. 1644-1646 (3)	2.20	1.05

See Nos. 1711-1713.

Persian Woman, by Behzad A377

Paintings: No. 1648, Fisherman, by Cevat Dereli (Turkey). No. 1649, Young Man, by Abdur Rehman Chughtai (Pakistan).

1972, July 21 **Wmk. 353**

1647	A377	5r gray & multi	1.40	.30
1648	A377	5r gray & multi	1.40	.30
1649	A377	5r gray & multi	1.40	.30
		Nos. 1647-1649 (3)	4.20	.90

Regional Cooperation for Development Pact among Iran, Turkey and Pakistan, 8th anniv.

See Pakistan 322-324, Turkey 1912-1914.

Shah Type of 1971

1972-73 **Photo.** ***Perf. 13½x13***

Bister Frame & Crown

Size: 20½x28mm

1650	A366	5d lilac	.25	.25
1651	A366	10d henna brown	.25	.25
1652	A366	50d brt blue grn	.25	.25
1653	A366	1r dp yel grn	.30	.25
a.		Brn frame & crown ('73)	.55	.25
b.		As No. 1653, dp yel grn (Shah) omitted	500.00	
1654	A366	2r brown	.50	.25

Size: 27x36½mm

1655	A366	6r slate grn	1.00	.25
1656	A366	8r violet blue	1.00	.25
a.		Frame omitted	500.00	
b.		Violet blue (Shah) omitted	650.00	
1657	A366	10r red lilac	1.50	.25
a.		Red lilac (Shah) omitted	650.00	
1658	A366	11r blue green	2.00	.80
1659	A366	14r dull blue	6.00	.60
1660	A366	20r car rose	10.00	.50
1661	A366	50r grnsh blue	7.50	1.00
1661A	A366	100r violet ('73)	10.00	2.00
1661B	A366	200r slate ('73)	12.00	3.50
		Nos. 1650-1661B (14)	52.55	10.40

Festival Emblem A378

1972, Aug. 31 **Litho.** ***Perf. 10½***

1662	A378	6r emerald, red & blk	1.25	.25
1663	A378	8r brt mag, blk & grn	1.75	.25

6th Festival of Arts, Shiraz-Persepolis, Aug. 31-Sept. 8.

Pens and Emblem A379

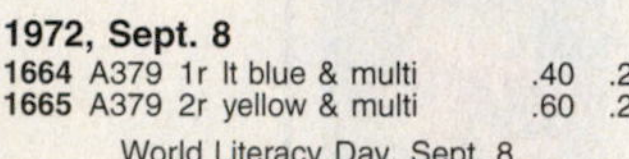

1972, Sept. 8

1664	A379	1r lt blue & multi	.40	.25
1665	A379	2r yellow & multi	.60	.25

World Literacy Day, Sept. 8.

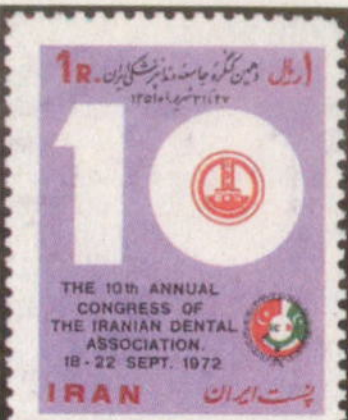

"10" and Emblems A380

1972, Sept. 18

1666	A380	1r lilac & multi	.40	.25
1667	A380	2r dull yel & multi	.60	.25

10th Congress of Iranian Dentists' Assoc., Sept. 18-22.

Asian Broadcasting Union Emblem — A381

1972, Oct. 1

1668	A381	6r lt green & multi	1.00	.25
1669	A381	8r gray & multi	1.75	.25

9th General Assembly of Asian Broadcasting Union, Tehran, Oct. 1972.

No. 450 on Cover — A382

1972, Oct. 9

1670	A382	10r lt blue & multi	3.00	.25

International Stamp Day.

Chess and Olympic Rings — A383

Olympic Rings and: 2r, Hunter. 3r, Archer. 5r, Equestrians. 6r, Polo. 8r, Wrestling.

1972, Oct. 17

1671	A383	1r brown & multi	3.50	1.50
1672	A383	2r blue & multi	3.50	.50
1673	A383	3r lilac & multi	3.50	.50
1674	A383	5r bl grn & multi	4.00	.75
1675	A383	6r red & multi	4.50	.75
1676	A383	8r yel grn & multi	7.00	1.00
a.		Souv. sheet of 6, #1671-1676, imperf.	30.00	15.00
		Nos. 1671-1676 (6)	26.00	5.00

20th Olympic Games, Munich, 8/26-9/11.

Communications Symbol, UN Emblem — A384

1972, Oct. 24

1677	A384	10r multicolored	2.00	.25

United Nations Day.

Children and Flowers — A385

Children's Drawings and Emblem: No. 1679, Puppet show. 6r, Boys cutting wood, horiz.

1972, Oct. 31 **Litho.** **Wmk. 353**

1678	A385	2r gray & multi	.70	.25
1679	A385	2r bister & multi	.70	.25
1680	A385	6r pink & multi	1.60	.25
		Nos. 1678-1680 (3)	3.00	.75

Children's Week.

Festival Type of 1969

Design: 10r, Crown, emblems and column capital, Persepolis.

1972, Nov. 11

1681	A328	10r dp blue & multi	8.00	2.00

10th anniv. of White Revolution; Festival of Culture and Art.

Family Planning Emblem A386

1972, Dec. 5

1682	A386	1r blue & multi	.40	.25
1683	A386	2r brt pink & multi	.60	.25

To promote family planning.

Iranian Scout Organization, 20th anniv. — A387

1972, Dec. 9

1684	A387	2r multicolored	1.00	.25

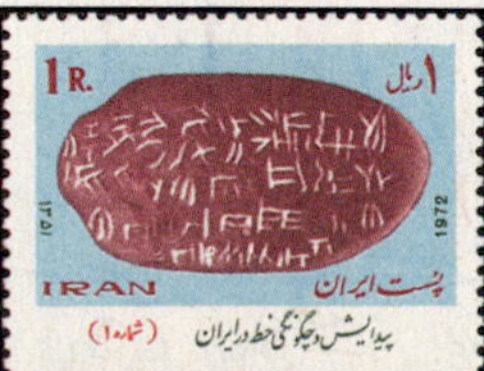

Ancient Seal A388

Designs: Various ancient seals.

1973, Jan. 5 ***Perf. 10½***

1685	A388	1r blue, red & brn	.70	.25
1686	A388	1r yellow & multi	.70	.25
1687	A388	1r pink & multi	.70	.25
1688	A388	2r lt brick red & multi	.80	.25
1689	A388	2r dull org & multi	.80	.25
1690	A388	2r olive & multi	.80	.25
		Nos. 1685-1690 (6)	4.50	1.50

Development of writing.

Books and Book Year Emblem A389

Design: 6r, Illuminated page, 10th century, from Shahnameh, by Firdousi.

1973, Jan. 10

1691	A389	2r black & multi	1.00	.25
1692	A389	6r yellow & multi	1.25	.25

International Book Year.

"12 Improvements by the King" — A390

Designs: 2r, 10r, 12 circles symbolizing 12 improvements. 6r, like 1r.

1973, Jan. 26 **Litho.**

Size: 29x43mm

1693	A390	1r gold, ultra, red & yel	.30	.25
1694	A390	2r sil, plum, ol & yel	.35	.25

Size: 65x84mm

1695	A390	6r gold, ultra, red & yel	2.50	1.50
		Nos. 1693-1695 (3)	3.15	2.00

Souvenir Sheet

Imperf

1696	A390	10r sil, plum, ol & yel	4.25	2.50

Introduction of the King's socioeconomic reforms, 10th anniv.

Blue Surgeonfish A391

Fish: No. 1698, Gilthead. No. 1699, Banded sergeant major. No. 1700, Porkfish. No. 1701, Black-spot snapper.

1973, Mar. 6 **Wmk. 353** ***Perf. 10½***

1697	A391	1r multicolored	1.25	.30
1698	A391	1r multicolored	1.25	.30
1699	A391	2r multicolored	1.75	.45
1700	A391	2r multicolored	1.75	.45
1701	A391	2r multicolored	1.75	.45
		Nos. 1697-1701 (5)	7.75	1.95

Iranian New Year.

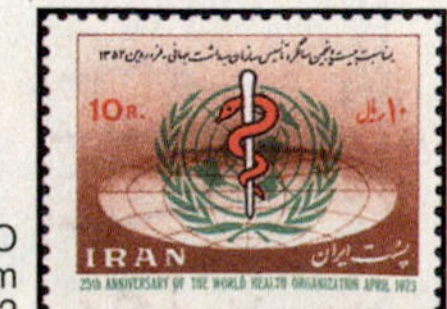

WHO Emblem A392

1973, Apr. 7 **Litho.** **Wmk. 353**

1702	A392	10r brn, grn & red	1.50	.25

25th anniversary of the WHO.

Soccer — A393

1973, Apr. 13
1703 A393 14r orange & multi 2.00 .25

15th Asian Youth Football (soccer) Tournament.

Tracks and Globe — A394

1973, May 10 Wmk. 353 *Perf. 10½*
1704 A394 10r dk grn, lil & vio bl 3.00 .60

13th International Railroad Conference.

Clay Tablet with Aryan Script — A395

Designs: Clay tablets with various scripts.

1973, June 5 *Perf. 10½*
1705 A395 1r shown .50 .25
1706 A395 1r Kharoshthi .50 .25
1707 A395 1r Achaemenian .50 .25
1708 A395 2r Parthian (Mianeh) .90 .25
1709 A395 2r Parthian (Arsacide) .90 .25
1710 A395 2r Gachtak (Dabireh) .90 .25
Nos. 1705-1710 (6) 4.20 1.50

Development of writing.

Flower Type of 1972

1973, June 20
1711 A376 1r Orchid .35 .25
1712 A376 2r Hyacinth .65 .25
1713 A376 6r Columbine 1.75 .25
Nos. 1711-1713 (3) 2.75 .75

Regional Cooperation for Development Pact Among Iran, Turkey and Pakistan, 9th Anniv. — A396

Designs: No. 1714, Head from mausoleum of King Antiochus I (69-34 B.C.), Turkey. No. 1715, Statue, Shahdad Kerman, Persia, 4000 B.C. No. 1716, Street, Mohenjo-Daro, Pakistan.

1973, July 21
1714 A396 2r brown & multi .40 .25
1715 A396 2r green & multi .40 .25
1716 A396 2r blue & multi .40 .25
a. Strip of 3, #1714-1716 1.50 .75

See Pakistan 343-345, Turkey 1941-1943.

Shah, Oil Pump, Refinery and Tanker A397

1973, Aug. 4
1717 A397 5r blue & black 3.00 .75

Nationalization of oil industry.

Soldiers and Rising Sun — A398

1973, Aug. 19 Litho. Wmk. 353
1718 A398 2r ultra & multi .75 .25

20th anniversary of return of monarchy.

Gymnasts and Globe — A399

1973, Aug. 23 *Perf. 10½*
1719 A399 2r olive & multi .40 .25
1720 A399 2r violet bl & multi .40 .25

7th Intl. Congress of Physical Education and Sports for Girls and Women, Tehran, Aug. 19-25.

Shahyad Monument (later Azadi Monument), Rainbow and WMO Emblem — A400

1973, Sept. 4
1721 A400 5r multicolored 1.00 .25

Intl. meteorological cooperation, centenary.

Festival Emblem — A401

1973, Aug. 31
1722 A401 1r silver & multi .40 .25
1723 A401 5r gold & multi .60 .25

7th Festival of Arts, Shiraz-Persepolis.

Wrestlers A402

1973, Sept. 6 Litho. Wmk. 353
1724 A402 6r lt green & multi 2.50 .50

World Wrestling Championships, Tehran, Sept. 6-14.

"Literacy as Light" — A403

1973, Sept. 8
1725 A403 2r multicolored .40 .25

World Literacy Day, Sept. 8.

Audio-Visual Equipment A404

1973, Sept. 11
1726 A404 10r yellow & multi 1.50 .35

Tehran Intl. Audio-Visual Exhib., Sept. 11-24.

Warrior Taming Winged Bull A405

1973, Sept. 16
1727 A405 8r blue gray & multi 1.50 .25

Intl. Council of Military Sports, 25th anniv.

Abu Rayhan Biruni (973-1048), Philosopher and Mathematician A406

1973, Sept. 16
1728 A406 10r brown & black 1.50 .50

Soccer Cup — A407

1973, Oct. 2 Wmk. 353 *Perf. 10½*
1729 A407 2r lilac, blk & buff .50 .25

Soccer Games for the Crown Prince's Cup.

INTERPOL Emblem — A408

1973, Oct. 7
1730 A408 2r multicolored .50 .25

50th anniversary of INTERPOL.

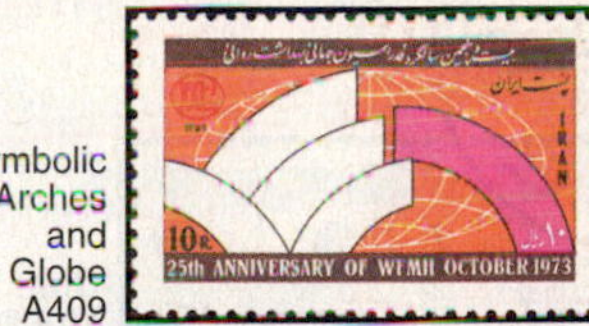

Symbolic Arches and Globe A409

1973, Oct. 8
1731 A409 10r orange & multi .65 .25

World Federation for Mental Health, 25th anniv.

UPU Emblem, Letter, Post Horn — A410

1973, Oct. 9
1732 A410 6r blue & orange .75 .25

World Post Day, Oct. 9.

Honeycomb A411

1973, Oct. 24
1733 A411 2r lt brown & multi .30 .25
1734 A411 2r gray olive & multi .30 .25

UN Volunteer Program, 5th anniv.

Festival Type of 1969

2r, Crown & column capital, Persepolis.

1973, Oct. 26
1735 A328 2r yellow & multi .50 .25

Festival of Culture and Art.

Turkish Bosporus Bridge, Flag A412

8r, Kemal Ataturk & Reza Shah Pahlavi.

1973, Oct. 29 Litho. *Perf. 10½*

1736 A412 2r multicolored .75 .25
1737 A412 8r multicolored 1.25 .25

50th anniversary of the Turkish Republic.

Mother and Child, Emblem — A413

Children's Drawings and Emblem: No. 1739, Wagon, horiz. No. 1740, House and garden with birds.

1973, Oct. 31

1738 A413 2r multicolored .35 .25
1739 A413 2r multicolored .35 .25
1740 A413 2r multicolored .35 .25
Nos. 1738-1740 (3) 1.05 .75

Children's Week.

Cow, Wheat and FAO Emblem A414

1973, Nov. 4

1741 A414 10r multicolored 1.50 .25

10th anniversary of World Food Program.

Proclamation of Cyrus the Great; Red Cross, Lion and Crescent Emblems A415

1973, Nov. 8

1742 A415 6r lt blue & multi 1.25 .25

22nd Intl. Red Cross Conf., Tehran, 1972.

"Film Festival" — A416

1973, Nov. 26 Wmk. 353 *Perf. 10½*

1743 A416 2r black & multi .35 .25

2nd International Tehran Film Festival.

Globe and Travelers — A417

1973, Nov. 26 Litho.

1744 A417 10r orange & multi .60 .25

12th annual Congress of Intl. Assoc. of Tour Managers.

Human Rights Flame A418

1973, Dec. 10

1745 A418 8r lt blue & multi .75 .25

Universal Declaration of Human Rights, 25th anniv.

Score and Emblem — A419

Design: No. 1747, Score and emblem, diff.

1973, Dec. 21

1746 A419 10r yel grn, red & blk 1.00 .25
1747 A419 10r lt bl, ultra & red 1.00 .25

Dedicated to the art of music.

Forestry, Printing, Education — A420

Designs (Symbols of Reforms): No. 1749, Land reform, sales of shares, women's suffrage. No. 1750, Army of progress, irrigation, women's education. No. 1751, Hygiene, rural courts, housing.

1974, Jan. 26 Litho. *Perf. 10½*

1748 1r lt blue & multi .25 .25
1749 1r lt blue & multi .25 .25
1750 2r lt blue & multi .25 .25
1751 2r lt blue & multi .25 .25
a. A420 Block of 4, #1748-1751 2.25 1.50

Imperf

Size: 76½x102mm

1752 A420 20r multicolored 5.00 3.00

"White Revolution of King and People" and 12 reform laws.

Pir Amooz Ketabaty Script — A421

Various Scripts: No. 1754, Mo Eghely Ketabaty. No. 1755, Din Dabireh, Avesta script. No. 1756, Pir Amooz, Naskh style. No. 1757, Pir Amooz, decorative style. No. 1758, Decorative and architectural style.

1974, Feb. 14 Wmk. 353 *Perf. 10½*

1753 A421 1r silver, ocher & multi 1.00 .30
1754 A421 1r gold, gray & multi 1.00 .30
1755 A421 1r silver, yel & multi 1.00 .30
1756 A421 2r gold, gray & multi 1.25 .30
1757 A421 2r gold, slate & multi 1.25 .30
1758 A421 2r gold, claret & multi 1.25 .30
Nos. 1753-1758 (6) 6.75 1.80

Development of writing.

Fowl, Syringe and Emblem A422

1974, Feb. 23

1759 A422 6r red brown & multi .75 .25

5th Iranian Veterinary Congress.

Monarch Butterfly A423

Designs: Various butterflies.

1974, Mar. 6 Litho. *Perf. 10½*

1760 A423 1r rose lilac & multi 1.25 .35
1761 A423 1r brt rose & multi 1.25 .35
1762 A423 2r lt blue & multi 1.75 .45
1763 A423 2r green & multi 1.75 .45
1764 A423 2r bister & multi 1.75 .45
Nos. 1760-1764 (5) 7.75 2.05

Novrooz, Iranian New Year.

Jalaludin Mevlana (1207-1273), Poet — A424

1974, Mar. 12 *Perf. 13*

1765 A424 2r pale violet & multi 1.00 .25

Shah Type of 1971

1974 Photo. *Perf. 13½x13*

Size: 20½x28mm

1768 A366 50d orange & bl 1.00 .25
1769 A366 1r emerald & bl 1.00 .25
1770 A366 2r red & blue 1.00 .25

Size: 27x36½mm

1771 A366 10r lt green & bl 8.50 .25
1772 A366 20r lilac & bl 7.00 .25
Nos. 1768-1772 (5) 18.50 1.25

Palace of the Forty Columns, Hippocrates, Avicenna — A425

1974, Apr. 11 Litho. *Perf. 10½*

1773 A425 10r multicolored 1.00 .25

9th Medical Congress of the Near and Middle East, Isfahan.

Onager — A426

1974, Apr. 13

1774 A426 1r shown 1.00 .25
1775 A426 2r Great bustard 1.25 .25
1776 A426 6r Fawn and deer 2.00 .35
1777 A426 8r Caucasian black grouse 3.00 .40
a. Strip of 4, #1774-1777 9.00 4.50
Nos. 1774-1777 (4) 7.25 1.25

Intl. Council for Game and Wildlife Preservation.

Athlete and Games Emblem — A427

1974, Apr. 30

1778 A427 1r shown .75 .25
1779 A427 1r Table tennis .75 .25
1780 A427 2r Boxing 1.25 .25
1781 A427 2r Hurdles 1.25 .25
1782 A427 6r Weight lifting 2.00 .25
1783 A427 8r Basketball 3.00 .25
Nos. 1778-1783 (6) 9.00 1.50

7th Asian Games, Tehran; first issue.

Lion of Venice — A428

Painting: 8r, Audience with the Doge of Venice.

1974, May 5

1784 A428 6r multicolored .75 .25
1785 A428 8r multicolored 1.25 .35

Safeguarding Venice.

Links and Grain — A429

1974, May 13 Litho. *Perf. 10½*

1786 A429 2r multicolored .30 .25

Cooperation Day.

Military Plane, 1924 A430

1974, June 1

1787 A430 10r shown 2.75 .50
1788 A430 10r Jet, 1974 2.75 .50

50th anniversary of Iranian Air Force.

Swimmer and Games Emblem A431

No. 1790, Tennis, men's doubles. No. 1791, Wrestling. No. 1792, Hockey. No. 1793, Volleyball. No. 1794, Tennis, women's singles.

1974, July 1 Wmk. 353 *Perf. 10½*

1789 A431 1r shown .75 .25
1790 A431 1r multi .75 .25
1791 A431 2r multi 1.00 .25
1792 A431 2r multi 1.00 .25
1793 A431 4r multi 1.50 .40
1794 A431 10r multi 3.00 .50
Nos. 1789-1794 (6) 8.00 1.90

7th Asian Games, Tehran; second issue.

Bicyclists and Games Emblem A432

1974, Aug. 1

1795 A432 2r shown .90 .25
1796 A432 2r Soccer .90 .25
1797 A432 2r Fencing .90 .25
1798 A432 2r Small-bore rifle shooting .90 .25
Nos. 1795-1798 (4) 3.60 1.00

7th Asian Games, Tehran; third issue.

Ghaskai Costume — A433

Regional Costumes: No. 1800, Kurdistan, Kermanshah District. No. 1801, Kurdistan, Sanandaj District. No. 1802, Mazandaran. No. 1803, Bakhtiari. No. 1804, Torkaman.

1974, July 6

1799 A433 2r lt ultra & multi 1.75 .75
1800 A433 2r buff & multi 1.75 .75
1801 A433 2r green & multi 1.75 .75
1802 A433 2r lt blue & multi 1.75 .75
1803 A433 2r gray & multi 1.75 .75
1804 A433 2r dull grn & multi 1.75 .75
a. Block of 6, #1799-1804 8.50 4.50

Gold Winged Lion Cup — A434

1974, July 13

1805 A434 2r dull green & multi .35 .25

Iranian Soccer Cup.

Tabriz Rug, Late 16th Century — A435

Designs: No. 1807, Anatolian rug, 15th century. No. 1808, Kashan rug, Lahore.

1974, July 21

1806 A435 2r brown & multi .45 .25
1807 A435 2r blue & multi .45 .25
1808 A435 2r red & multi .45 .25
a. Strip of 3, #1806-1808 1.40 .30

Regional Cooperation for Development Pact among Iran, Turkey and Pakistan, 10th anniv. See Pakistan 365-367, Turkey 1979-1981

King Carrying Vases, Bas-relief — A436

1974, Aug. 15 Litho. *Perf. 10½*

1809 A436 2r black & multi .35 .25

8th Iranian Arts Festival, Shiraz-Persepolis.

Aryamehr Stadium, Tehran — A437

No. 1811, Games' emblem and inscription. No. 1812, Aerial view of games' site.

1974

1810 A437 6r multicolored 1.25 .25

Souvenir Sheets

1811 A437 10r multicolored *3.50 1.50*
1812 A437 10r multicolored *3.50 1.50*

7th Asian Games, Tehran; fourth and fifth issues. Nos. 1811-1812 contain one imperf 51x38mm stamp each.

Issued: Nos. 1811-1812, 9/1; No. 1810, 9/16.

"Welfare" — A438

"Education" A439

1974, Sept. 11

1813 A438 2r orange & multi .35 .25
1814 A439 2r blue & multi .35 .25

Welfare and free education.

Map of Hasanlu, 1000-800 B.C. — A440

1974, Sept. 24

1815 A440 8r multicolored .70 .25

2nd Intl. Congress of Architecture, Shiraz-Persepolis, Sept. 1974.

Achaemenian Mail Cart and UPU Emblem — A441

Design: 14r, UPU emblem and letters.

1974, Oct. 9 Wmk. 353 *Perf. 10½*

1816 A441 6r orange, grn & blk 1.00 .40
a. Unwatermarked *300.00*
1817 A441 14r multicolored 1.50 .50
a. Unwatermarked *300.00*

Centenary of Universal Postal Union.

Road Through Farahabad Park — A442

1974, Oct. 16

1818 A442 1r shown .30 .25
1819 A442 2r Recreation Bldg. .35 .25

Inauguration of Farahabad Park, Tehran.

Farahnaz Dam and Mohammad Reza Shah Pahlavi — A443

Designs: 5d, Kharg Island petro-chemical plant. 10d, Ghatour Railroad Bridge. 1r, Tehran oil refinery. 2r, Satellite communication station, Hamadan, and Mt. Alvand. 6r, Aryamehr steel mill, Isfahan. 8r, University of Tabriz. 10r, Shah Abbas Kabir Dam. 14r, Rudagi (later Vahdat) Music Hall. 20r, Shayad Monument. 50r, Aryamehr Stadium.

1974-75 Photo. *Perf. 13x13½*

Size: 28x21mm

Frame & Shah in Brown

1820 A443 5d slate green .30 .25
1821 A443 10d orange .30 .25
1822 A443 50d blue green .30 .25
1823 A443 1r ultra .30 .25
1824 A443 2r deep lilac .30 .25

Size: 36x26½mm

Frame & Shah in Dark Blue

1825 A443 6r brown .75 .30
1826 A443 8r grnsh blue 1.50 .40
1827 A443 10r deep lilac 1.00 .30
a. Value in Farsi omitted *40.00 30.00*
1828 A443 14r deep green 17.00 .60
1829 A443 20r magenta 5.00 .50
1830 A443 50r violet 7.00 1.40
Nos. 1820-1830 (11) 33.75 4.75

Issued: 50d, 1r, 2r, 10/16/74; 14r, 11/1974; others 3/6/75.

See Nos. 1831-1841. For overprints see Nos. 2008, 2010.

1975-77 Size: 28x21mm

Frame & Shah in Green

1831 A443 5d orange ('77) .30 .25
1832 A443 10d rose mag ('77) .30 .25
1833 A443 50d lilac .30 .25
1834 A443 1r dark blue .30 .25
1835 A443 2r brown .30 .25

Size: 36x26½mm

Frame & Shah in Brown

1836 A443 6r vio bl ('76) .75 .35
1837 A443 8r deep org ('77) 2.00 .30
1838 A443 10r dp yel grn ('76) 2.25 .25
a. Brown (Shah and frame) omitted *400.00*
1839 A443 14r lilac 10.00 .25
a. Brown (Shah and frame) omitted *300.00*
1840 A443 20r brt green ('76) 5.00 .40
1841 A443 50r dp blue ('76) 7.00 .90
Nos. 1831-1841 (11) 28.50 3.70

Festival Emblem, Crown and Column Capital, Persepolis — A444

1974, Oct. 26 Litho. *Perf. 10½*

1842 A444 2r multicolored .50 .25

Festival of Culture and Art.

Destroyer "Palang" and Flag — A445

1974, Nov. 5

1843 A445 10r multicolored 3.00 .35

Navy Day.

Girl at Spinning Wheel A446

Designs: Children's drawings.

1974, Nov. 7 *Perf. 10½*

1844	A446 2r shown	.35	.25
1845	A446 2r Scarecrow, vert.	.35	.25
1846	A446 2r Picnic	.35	.25
	Nos. 1844-1846 (3)	1.05	.75

Children's Week.

Winged Ibex — A447

1974, Nov. 25 Litho. Wmk. 353

1847	A447 2r vio, org & blk	.45	.25

Third Tehran International Film Festival.

WPY Emblem A448

1974, Dec. 1

1848	A448 8r orange & multi	.60	.25

World Population Year.

Gold Bee A449

Design: 8r, Gold crown, gift of French people to Empress Farah. Bee pin was gift of the Italian people.

1974, Dec. 20

1849	A449 6r multicolored	.75	.30
1850	A449 8r multicolored	1.00	.35

15th wedding anniv. of Shah and Empress Farah.

Angel with Banner — A450

1975, Jan. 7 Litho. *Perf. 10½*

1851	A450 2r org & vio bl	.35	.25

International Women's Year.

Symbols of Agriculture, Industry and the Arts — A451

1975, Jan. 26 Wmk. 353

1852	A451 2r multicolored	.35	.25

"White Revolution of King and People."

Tourism Year 75 Emblem — A452

1975, Feb. 17

1853	A452 6r multicolored	.35	.25

South Asia Tourism Year.

"Farabi" in Shape of Musical Instrument or Alembic — A453

1975, Mar. 1

1854	A453 2r brn red & multi	.35	.25

Abu-Nasr al-Farabi (870?-950), physician, musician and philosopher, 1100th birth anniversary.

Ornament, Rug Pattern — A454

No. 1856, Blossoms and cypress trees. No. 1857, Shah Abbasi flower.

1975, Mar. 6

1855	A454 1r shown	.35	.25
1856	A454 1r multicolored	.35	.25
1857	A454 1r multicolored	.35	.25
a.	Strip of 3, #1855-1857	1.25	.60

Novrooz, Iranian New Year. Nos. 1855-1857 printed in sheets of 45 stamps + 5 labels.

Nasser Khosrov, Poet, Birth Millenary — A455

1975, Mar. 11

1858	A455 2r blk, gold & red	.35	.25

Formula — A456

1975, May 5 Litho. *Perf. 10½*

1859	A456 2r buff & multi	.50	.25

5th Biennial Symposium of Iranian Biochemical Society.

Charioteer, Bas-relief, Persepolis — A457

Design: 2r, Heads of Persian warriors, bas-relief from Persepolis, vert.

1975, May 5

1860	A457 2r lt brn & multi	3.00	.75
1861	A457 10r blue & multi	5.00	1.25

Rotary International, 70th anniversary.

Signal Fire, Persian Castle A458

Design: 8r, Communications satellite.

1975, May 17

1862	A458 6r multicolored	1.25	.45
1863	A458 8r lil & multi	1.75	.55

7th World Telecommunications Day.

Cooperation Day — A459

1975, May 13

1864	A459 2r multicolored	.35	.25

Jet, Shayad Monument, Statue of Liberty — A460

1975, May 29 Litho. Wmk. 353

1865	A460 10r org & multi	1.75	.50

Iran Air's 1st flight to New York, May 1975.

Emblem — A461

1975, June 5

1866	A461 6r blue & multi	.45	.25

World Environment Day.

Dam A462

1975, June 10

1867	A462 10r multicolored	.70	.25

9th Intl. Congress on Irrigation & Drainage.

Resurgence Party Emblem — A463

1975, July 1 Wmk. 353 *Perf. 10½*

1868	A463 2r multicolored	.35	.25

Organization of Resurgence Party.

Girl Scout Symbols A464

1975, July 16

1869	A464 2r multicolored	.50	.25

2nd Natl Girl Scout Camp, Tehran, July 1976.

Festival of Tus — A465

1975, July 17

1870	A465 2r gray, lil & vio	.35	.25

Festival of Tus in honor of Firdausi (940-1020), Persian poet born near Tus in Khorasan.

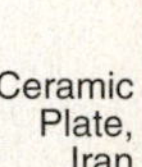

Ceramic Plate, Iran A466

No. 1872, Camel leather vase, Pakistan, vert. No. 1873, Porcelain vase, Turkey, vert.

1975, July 21

1871	A466 2r bister & multi	.35	.25
1872	A466 2r bister & multi	.35	.25
1873	A466 2r bister & multi	.35	.25
	Nos. 1871-1873 (3)	1.05	.75

Regional Cooperation for Development Pact among Iran, Pakistan and Turkey.

See Pakistan 383-385, Turkey 2006-2008.

Majlis Gate A467

1975, Aug. 5 Litho. *Perf. 10½*

1874 A467 10r multi		.75	.25

Iranian Constitution, 70th anniversary.

Column with Stylized Branches — A468

1975, Aug. 21 Litho. Wmk. 353

1875 A468 8r red & multi		.35	.25

9th Iranian Arts Festival, Shiraz-Persepolis.

Flags over Globe — A469

1975, Sept. 8

1876 A469 2r vio bl & multi		.35	.25

Intl. Literacy Symposium, Persepolis.

Stylized Globe — A470

1975, Sept. 13

1877 A470 2r vio & multi		.35	.25

3rd Tehran International Trade Fair.

World Map and Envelope — A471

1975, Oct. 9 Litho. *Perf. 10½*

1878 A471 14r ultra & multi		1.00	.25

World Post Day, Oct. 9.

Crown, Column Capital, Persepolis — A472

1975, Oct. 26 Litho. Wmk. 353

1879 A472 2r ultra & multi		.35	.25

Festival of Culture and Art. See No. 1954.

Face and Film — A473

1975, Nov. 2

1880 A473 6r multicolored		.65	.25

Tehran Intl. Festival of Children's Films.

"Mother's Face" — A474

Girl — A475

Design: No. 1882, 2r, "Our House," horiz. All designs after children's drawings.

1975, Nov. 5

1881 A474 2r multicolored		.35	.25
1882 A475 2r multicolored		.35	.25
1883 A475 2r multicolored		.35	.25
	Nos. 1881-1883 (3)	1.05	.75

Children's Week.

"Film" — A476

1975, Dec. 4 Wmk. 353 *Perf. 10½*

1884 A476 8r multicolored		.60	.25

4th Tehran International Film Festival.

Symbols of Reforms — A477

People — A478

No. 1887, Five reform symbols.

1976, Jan. 26 Litho. *Perf. 10½*

1885 A477 2r shown		.35	.25
1886 A478 2r shown		.35	.25
1887 A477 2r multi		.35	.25
	Nos. 1885-1887 (3)	1.05	.75

"White Revolution of King and People."

Motorcycle Policeman A479

Police Helicopter — A480

1976, Feb. 16

1888 A479 2r multicolored		1.25	.75
1889 A480 6r multicolored		2.00	1.00

Highway Police Day.

Soccer Cup — A481

1976, Feb. 24 Litho. Wmk. 353

1890 A481 2r org & multi		.35	.25

3rd Intl. Youth Soccer Cup, Shiraz and Ahvaz.

Candlestick A482

Designs: No. 1892, Incense burner. No. 1893, Rose water container.

1976, Mar. 6

1891 A482 1r olive & multi		.35	.25
1892 A482 1r claret & multi		.35	.25
1893 A482 1r Prus bl & multi		.35	.25
a.	Strip of 3, #1891-1893	1.25	1.00

Novrooz, Iranian New Year.

Telephones, 1876 and 1976 — A483

1976, Mar. 10

1894 A483 10r multicolored		.75	.25

Centenary of first telephone call by Alexander Graham Bell, Mar. 10, 1876.

Eye Within Square — A484

1976, Apr. 29 Litho. *Perf. 10½*

1895 A484 6r blk & multi		2.00	.25
a.	Perf. 12½	9.50	7.50

World Health Day: "Foresight prevents blindness."

Nurse with Infant A485

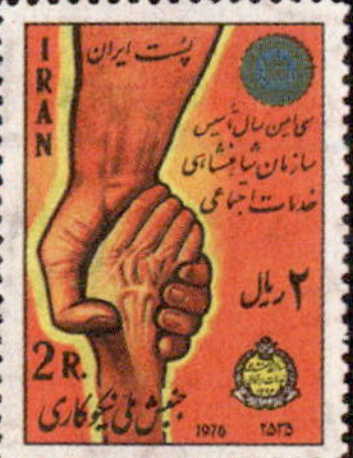

Young Man Holding Old Man's Hand — A486

No. 1897, Engineering apprentices.

1976, May 10

1896 A485 2r shown		.50	.25
1897 A485 2r multi		.50	.25
1898 A486 2r shown		.50	.25
	Nos. 1896-1898 (3)	1.50	.75

Royal Org. of Social Services, 30th anniv.

Map of Iran, Men Linking Hands — A487

1976, May 13 **Wmk. 353**
1899 A487 2r yel & multi .35 .25

Iranian Cooperatives, 10th anniversary.

Waves and Ear Phones — A488

1976, May 17
1900 A488 14r gray & multi .75 .25

World Telecommunications Day.

Emblem, Woman with Flag, Man with Gun — A489

1976, June 6
1901 A489 2r bister & multi .35 .25

To publicize the power of stability.

Map of Iran, Columns of Persepolis, Nasser Khosrow — A490

1976, July 6 **Litho.** ***Perf. 10½***
1902 A490 6r yel & multi .50 .25

Tourist publicity.

Reza Shah Pahlavi — A491

6r, Mohammad Ali Jinnah. 8r, Kemal Ataturk.

1976, July 21 **Litho.** **Wmk. 353**
1903 A491 2r gray & multi .50 .25
1904 A491 6r gray & multi .60 .25
1905 A491 8r gray & multi .75 .25
Nos. 1903-1905 (3) 1.85 .75

Regional Cooperation for Development Pact among Iran, Turkey and Pakistan, 12th anniversary.
See Pakistan 412-414, Turkey 2041-2043.

Torch, Montreal and Iranian Olympic Emblems A492

1976, Aug. 1
1906 A492 14r multicolored 1.00 .25

21st Olympic Games, Montreal, Canada, July 17-Aug. 1.

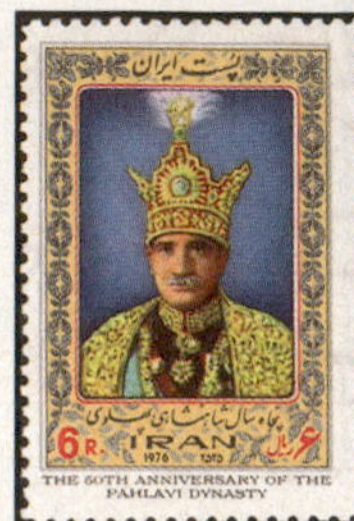
Reza Shah Pahlavi in Coronation Robe — A493

Designs: 2r, Reza Shah and Mohammad Reza Shah Pahlavi, horiz. 14r, 20r, Mohammad Reza Shah Pahlavi in coronation robe and crown.

1976, Aug. 19 **Wmk. 353** ***Perf. 10½***
1907 A493 2r lilac & multi 1.75 .75
1908 A493 6r blue & multi 2.75 1.00
1909 A493 14r grn & multi 4.00 1.50
Nos. 1907-1909 (3) 8.50 3.25

Souvenir Sheet

1976, Oct. 8 ***Imperf.***
1910 A493 20r multi 15.00 7.50

50th anniv. of Pahlavi dynasty; 35th anniv. of reign of Mohammad Reza Shah Pahlavi. No. 1910 contains one stamp 43x62mm.

Festival Emblem — A494

1976, Aug. 29 **Litho.** ***Perf. 10½***
1911 A494 10r multicolored .65 .25

10th Iranian Arts Festival, Shiraz-Persepolis.

Iranian Scout Emblem — A495

1976, Oct. 2 **Litho.** ***Perf. 10½***
1912 A495 2r lt bl & multi .30 .25

10th Asia Pacific Conference, Tehran 1976.

Cancer Radiation Treatment — A496

1976, Oct. 6
1913 A496 2r black & multi .30 .25

Fight against cancer.

Target, Police Woman Receiving Decoration A497

1976, Oct. 7
1914 A497 2r lt bl & multi .30 .25

Police Day.

UPU Emblem, No. 1907 on Cover A498

1976, Oct. 9
1915 A498 10r multicolored 1.00 .25

International Post Day.

Crown Prince Reza with Cup — A499

1976, Oct. 10
1916 A499 6r multicolored .50 .25

Natl. Soc. of Village Culture Houses, anniv.

Reza Shah and Mohammad Reza Shah Pahlavi, Railroad A500

1976, Oct. 15
1917 A500 8r black & multi 5.00 2.00

Railroad Day.

Emblem & Column Capital, Persepolis A501

1976, Oct. 26
1918 A501 14r blue & multi 1.50 .30

Festival of Culture and Art.

Census Emblem — A502

1976, Oct. 30
1919 A502 2r gray & multi .35 .25

Natl. Population & Housing Census, 1976.

Flowers and Birds — A503

Designs: No. 1921, Flowers and bird. No. 1922, Flowers and butterfly. Designs are from covers of children's books.

1976, Oct. 31 ***Perf. 10½***
1920 A503 2r multicolored .35 .25
1921 A503 2r multicolored .35 .25
1922 A503 2r multicolored .35 .25
Nos. 1920-1922 (3) 1.05 .75

Children's Week.

Mohammad Ali Jinnah — A504

1976, Dec. 25 **Litho.** **Wmk. 353**
1923 A504 10r multicolored .60 .25

Jinnah (1876-1948), 1st Governor General of Pakistan.

Development and Agriculture Corps — A505

17-Point Reform Law: 5d, Land reform. 10d, Nationalization of forests. 50d, Sale of shares of state-owned industries. 1r, Profit sharing for factory workers. 2r, Parliament Gate, Woman suffrage. 3r, Education Corps formation. 5r, Health Corps. 8r, Establishment of village courts. 10r, Nationalization of water resources. 12r, Reconstruction program, urban and rural. 14r, Administrative and educational reorganization. 20r, Sale of factory shares. 30r, Commodity pricing. 50r, Free education. 100r, Child care. 200r, Care of the aged (social security).

1977, Jan. 26 **Photo.** ***Perf. 13x13½***

Frame and Shah's Head in Gold

Size: 28x21mm

1924 A505 5d rose & green .35 .25
1925 A505 10d lt grn & brn .35 .25
1926 A505 50d yel & vio bl .35 .25
1927 A505 1r lil & vio bl .35 .25
1928 A505 2r org & green .35 .25
1929 A505 3r lt bl & red .45 .25
1930 A505 5r bl grn & mag .45 .25

Size: 37x27mm

1931 A505 6r brn, mar & black .70 .25
1932 A505 8r ultra, mar & blk .75 .25
1933 A505 10r lt grn, bl & black 1.75 .25
1934 A505 12r vio, mar & black 1.75 .25
1935 A505 14r org, red & blk 1.75 .75

1936 A505 20r gray, ocher & black 3.75 .50
1937 A505 30r bl, grn & blk 4.00 .65
1938 A505 50r yel, brn & blk 6.00 .60
1939 A505 100r multi 7.00 1.25
1940 A505 200r multi 12.00 2.50
Nos. 1924-1940 (17) 42.10 9.00

"White Revolution of King and People" reform laws.

Man in Guilan Costume — A506

2r, Woman in Guilan costume (Northern Iran).

1977, Mar. 6 Wmk. 353 *Perf. 13*
1941 A506 1r multicolored .35 .25
1942 A506 2r multicolored .40 .25

Novrooz, Iranian New Year.

Electronic Tree — A507

1977, May 17 Photo. *Perf. 13*
1943 A507 20r multicolored 1.25 .35

World Telecommunications Day.

Reza Shah Dam A508

1977, May 31 *Perf. 13x13½*
1944 A508 5r multicolored .40 .25

Inauguration of Reza Shah Dam.

Olympic Rings A509

1977, June 23 Litho. *Perf. 10½*
1945 A509 14r multicolored .90 .25

Olympic Day.

Terra-cotta Jug, Iran A510

No. 1947, Terra-cotta bullock cart, Pakistan. No. 1948, Terra-cotta pot with human face, Turkey.

Perf. 13x13½
1977, July 21 Photo. Wmk. 353
1946 A510 5r violet & multi .40 .25
1947 A510 5r emer & multi .40 .25
1948 A510 5r green & multi .40 .25
Nos. 1946-1948 (3) 1.20 .75

Regional Cooperation for Development Pact among Iran, Turkey and Pakistan, 13th anniv.

See Pakistan 431-433, Turkey 2053-2055.

Flowers with Scout Emblems, Map of Asia — A511

1977, Aug. 5 Litho. *Perf. 13*
1949 A511 10r multicolored 1.00 .25

2nd Asia-Pacific Jamboree, Nishapur.

Map of Eastern Hemisphere with Iran — A512

1977, Sept. 20 Photo. Wmk. 353
1950 A512 3r multicolored .35 .25

9th Asian Electronics Conference, Tehran.

Tree of Learning, Symbolic Letters — A513

1977, Oct. 8 Wmk. 353 *Perf. 13*
1951 A513 10r multicolored .60 .25

Honoring the teachers.

Globe, Envelope, UPU Emblem A514

1977, Oct. 9 Photo.
1952 A514 14r multicolored 1.00 .25

Iran's admission to the UPU, cent.

Folk Art — A515

1977, Oct. 16
1953 A515 5r multicolored .40 .25

Festival of Folk Art.

Festival Type of 1975

Design: 20r, similar to 1975 issue, but with small crown within star.

1977, Oct. 26 *Perf. 10½*
1954 A472 20r bis, grn, car & blk 2.00 .25

Festival of Culture and Art.

Joust — A516

No. 1956, Rapunzel. No. 1957, Little princess with attendants.

1977, Oct. 31 Photo.
1955 A516 3r multicolored .35 .25
1956 A516 3r multicolored .35 .25
1957 A516 3r multicolored .35 .25
a. Strip of 3, #1955-1957 1.50 1.00

Children's Week.

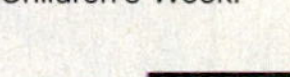

Emblem — A517

1977, Nov. 7 Wmk. 353 *Perf. 13*
1958 A517 5r multicolored .40 .25

First Regional Seminar on the Education and Welfare of the Deaf.

Mohammad Iqbal — A518

1977, Nov. 9 Litho. *Perf. 10½*
1959 A518 5r multicolored .45 .25

Iqbal (1877-1938) of Pakistan, poet and philosopher.

African Sculpture — A519

1977, Dec. 14
1960 A519 20r multicolored 3.25 .55

African art.

Shah Mosque, Isfahan — A520

Designs: 1r, Ruins, Persepolis. 2r, Khajou Bridge, Isfahan. 5r, Imam Reza Shrine, Meshed. 9r, Warrior frieze, Persepolis. 10r, Djameh Mosque, Isfahan. 20r, King on throne, bas-relief. 25r, Sheik Lotfollah Mosque. 30r, Ruins, Persepolis, diff. view. 50r, Ali Ghapou Palace, Isfahan. 100r, Bas-relief, Tagh Bastan. 200r, Horseman and prisoners, bas-relief, Naqsh Rostam.

1977-78 Photo. *Perf. 13x13½*
"Iran" and Head in Gold

Size: 28x21mm

1961 A520 1r deep brn .35 .25
1962 A520 2r emerald .35 .25
1963 A520 3r magenta .60 .25
1964 A520 5r Prus blue .75 .25

Size: 36x27mm

1965 A520 9r sepia ('78) 2.00 .75
1966 A520 10r brt bl ('78) 6.00 .85
1967 A520 20r rose 2.00 .55
1968 A520 25r ultra ('78) 25.00 9.75
1969 A520 30r magenta 3.00 .55
1970 A520 50r deep yel grn ('78) 6.00 3.50
1971 A520 100r dk bl ('78) 15.00 9.75
1972 A520 200r vio bl ('78) 20.00 19.00
Nos. 1961-1972 (12) 81.05 45.70

For overprints see Nos. 2009, 2011-2018.

Persian Rug — A521

Designs: Persian rugs.

1978, Feb. 11 Litho. *Perf. 10½*
1973 A521 3r sil & multi .35 .25
1974 A521 5r sil & multi .45 .25
1975 A521 10r sil & multi .75 .35
Nos. 1973-1975 (3) 1.55 .85

Opening of Carpet Museum.

Mazanderan Man — A522

Design: 5r, Mazanderan woman.

1978, Mar. 6 *Perf. 13*
1976 A522 3r yel & multi .35 .25
1977 A522 5r lt bl & multi .55 .25

Novrooz, Iranian New Year.

Mohammad Reza Shah Pahlavi — A523

1978, Jan. 26
1978 A523 20r multicolored 5.00 1.50

Shah's White Revolution, 15th anniv.

Reza Shah Pahlavi and Crown Prince Inspecting Girls' School — A524

Designs (Reza Shah Pahlavi and Crown Prince Mohammad Reza Shah Pahlavi): 5r, Inauguration of Trans-Iranian railroad. 10r, At stairs of Palace, Persepolis. 14r, Shah handing Crown Prince (later Shah) officer's diploma at Tehran Officers' Academy.

1978, Mar. 15

1979	A524	3r multicolored	1.00	.25
1980	A524	5r multicolored	1.00	.35
1981	A524	10r multicolored	1.50	.40
1982	A524	14r multicolored	2.00	.70
		Nos. 1979-1982 (4)	5.50	1.70

Reza Shah Pahlavi (1877-1944), founder of Pahlavi dynasty.

Communications Satellite over Map of Iran — A525

1978, Apr. 19 Litho. *Perf. 10½*

1983 A525 20r multicolored 1.25 .30

ITU, 7th meeting, Tehran; 10th anniv. of Iran's membership.

Antenna, ITU Emblem A526

1978, May 17 Litho. *Perf. 10½*

1984 A526 15r multicolored .90 .30

10th World Telecommunications Day.

Welfare Legion Emblem — A527

1978, June 13 Photo. *Perf. 13x13½*

1985 A527 10r multicolored .60 .30

Universal Welfare Legion, 10th anniversary.

Pink Roses, Iran — A528

Designs: 10r, Yellow rose, Turkey. 15r, Red roses, Pakistan.

Perf. 13½x13

1978, July 21 Wmk. 353

1986	A528	5r multicolored	.60	.25
1987	A528	10r multicolored	.90	.25
1988	A528	15r multicolored	1.00	.40
		Nos. 1986-1988 (3)	2.50	.90

Regional Cooperation for Development Pact among Iran, Turkey and Pakistan, 14th anniversary.

See Pakistan 449-451, Turkey 2094-2096.

Rhazes, Pharmaceutical Tools — A529

1978, Aug. 26 Wmk. 353 *Perf. 13*

1989 A529 5r multicolored .75 .25

Pharmacists' Day. Rhazes (850-923), chief physician of Great Hospital in Baghdad.

Girl Scouts, Aryamehr Arch A530

1978, Sept. 2 *Perf. 10½*

1990 A530 5r multicolored 1.00 .35

23rd World Girl Scouts Conference, Tehran, Sept. 1978.

Reza Shah Pahlavi A531

Design: 5r, Mohammad Reza Shah Pahlavi.

1978, Sept. 11 Litho. *Perf. 10½*

1991	A531	3r multicolored	2.00	.40
1992	A531	5r multicolored	2.25	.50

Bank Melli Iran, 50th anniversary.

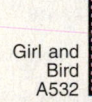

Girl and Bird A532

1978, Oct. 31 Photo. *Perf. 13*

1993 A532 3r multicolored .75 .30

Children's Week.

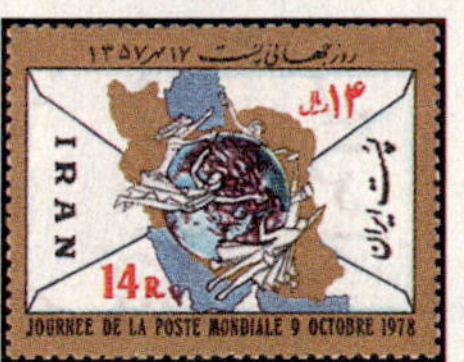

Envelope, Map of Iran, UPU Emblem A533

1978, Nov. 22 *Perf. 13x13½*

1994 A533 14r gold & multi 1.75 .40

World Post Day, Oct. 22.

Communications Symbols and Classroom — A534

1978, Nov. 22 *Perf. 10½*

1995 A534 10r multicolored 1.50 .40

Faculty of Communications, 50th anniv.

Human Rights Flame A535

1978, Dec. 17 Photo. *Perf. 13*

1996 A535 20r bl, blk & gold 4.00 .50

Universal Declaration of Human Rights, 30th anniv.

Kurdistani Man — A536

Design: 5r, Kurdistani woman.

1979, Mar. 17

1997	A536	3r multicolored	.90	.25
1998	A536	5r multicolored	1.25	.25

Rose — A537

1979, Mar. 17

1999 A537 2r multicolored .25 .25

Novrooz, Iranian New Year.

See No. 2310i.

Islamic Republic

Demonstrators — A538

Islamic revolution: 3r, Demonstrators. 5r, Hands holding rose, gun and torch breaking through newspaper. 20r, Hands breaking prison bars, and dove, vert.

1979, Apr. 20 *Perf. 10½*

2000	A538	3r multicolored	2.00	.35
2001	A538	5r multicolored	1.40	.35
2002	A538	10r multicolored	1.40	.65
2003	A538	20r multicolored	3.00	.75
		Nos. 2000-2003 (4)	7.80	2.10

Nos. 1837-1838, 1966, 1970 and Type A520 Overprinted

Designs: 15r, Warriors on horseback, bas-relief, Naqsh-Rostam. 19r, Chehel Sotoon Palace, Isfahan.

1979 Wmk. 353 *Perf. 13x13½*

2008	A443	8r org & brown	*3.00*	1.00
2009	A520	9r gold & dp brn	1.50	1.50
2010	A443	10r dp yel grn	*50.00*	10.00
2011	A520	10r gold & brt bl	1.75	1.00
2012	A520	15r gold & red lil	1.75	1.00
2013	A520	19r gold & slate grn	1.75	1.00
2016	A520	50r gold & dp yel grn	5.00	2.00
2017	A520	100r gold & vio bl	10.00	4.00
2018	A520	200r gold & vio bl	12.50	8.50
		Nos. 2008-2018 (9)	*87.25*	30.00

Overprint means Islamic revolution. Forgeries of No. 2010 exist.

Symbolic Tulip — A539

1979, June 5 Photo. *Perf. 13*

2019 A539 5r multicolored 1.50 .40

Potters, by Kamalel Molk A540

No. 2021, at the Well, by Allah Baksh, Pakistan. No. 2022, Threshing, by Namik Ismail, Turkey.

1979, July 21 Litho. *Perf. 10½*

2020	A540	5r multicolored	3.75	.35
2021	A540	5r multicolored	2.75	.35
2022	A540	5r multicolored	2.75	.35
		Nos. 2020-2022 (3)	9.25	1.05

Regional Cooperation for Development Pact among Iran, Turkey and Pakistan, 15th anniv.

No. 2020 exists imperf. Value, pair $100.

See Pakistan 486-488, Turkey 2112-2114.

"TELECOM 79" — A541

1979, Sept. 20 *Perf. 10½*

2023 A541 20r multicolored *15.00* .30

3rd World Telecommunications Exhibition, Geneva, Sept. 20-26.

Greeting the Sunrise — A542

Children's Drawings and IYC Emblem: 2r, Tulip over wounded man. 2r, Children with banners.

1979, Sept. 23

2024	A542	2r multicolored	3.00	.50
2025	A542	3r multicolored	3.00	.50
2026	A542	5r multicolored	4.00	.50
		Nos. 2024-2026 (3)	10.00	1.50

International Year of the Child.

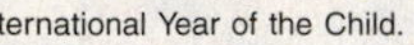

Persian Rug Design — A543

1979-80 Photo. *Perf. 13½x13*

2027	A543	50d brn & pale sal	.25	.25
2028	A543	1r dark & lt bl	.25	.25
2029	A543	2r red & yellow	.25	.25
2030	A543	3r dk bl & lt lil	.25	.25
2031	A543	5r slate grn & lt grn	.25	.25
2032	A543	10r blk & salmon pink ('80)	.30	.25
2033	A543	20r brn & gray ('80)	.55	.25

Size: 27x37½mm

2034	A543	50r dp violet & gray ('80)	1.40	.50
2035	A543	100r blk & slate grn ('80)	5.00	1.40
2036	A543	200r dk bl & cr ('80)	5.50	2.75
		Nos. 2027-2036 (10)	14.00	6.40

Globe in Envelope — A544

1979, Oct. 9 Litho. *Perf. 10½*

2041 A544 10r multicolored *3.00* .40

World Post Day.

Ghyath-al-din Kashani, Astrolabe A545

1979, Dec. 5 Litho. *Perf. 10½*

2042 A545 5r ocher & blk *1.50* .40

Kashani, mathematician, 550th death anniv.

Ka'aba, Flame and Mosque A546

Hegira (Pilgrimage Year): 5r, Koran open over globe, vert. 10r, Salman Farsi (follower of Mohammad), map of Iran.

1980, Jan. 19

2043	A546	3r multicolored	.25	.25
2044	A546	5r multicolored	.25	.25
2045	A546	10r multicolored	.55	.25
		Nos. 2043-2045 (3)	1.05	.75

Reissued in May-June, 1980, with shiny gum and watermark position changed.

People, Map and Flag of Iran — A547

Islamic Revolution, 1st Anniversary: 3r, Blood dripping on broken sword. 5r, Window open on sun of Islam, people.

1980, Feb. 11

2046	A547	1r multicolored	.25	.25
2047	A547	3r multicolored	.35	.25
2048	A547	5r multicolored	.65	.30
		Nos. 2046-2048 (3)	1.25	.80

For similar stamps measuring 24x36mm see Nos. 2310a, 2310b, 2310d.

Dehkhoda, Dictionary Editor, Birth Cent. — A548

1980, Feb. 26

2049 A548 10r multicolored .30 .25

East Azerbaijani Woman — A549

Novrooz (Iranian New Year): 5r, East Azerbaijani man.

1980, Mar. 5

2050	A549	3r multicolored	.25	.25
2051	A549	5r multicolored	.25	.25

Mohammad Mossadegh A550

1980, Mar. 19 Photo. *Perf. 13x13½*

2052 A550 20r multi .60 .25

Oil industry nationalization, 29th anniv.; Mohammad Mossadegh, prime minister who initiated nationalization.

Professor Morteza Motahhari, 1st Death Anniversary — A551

1980, May 1 Litho. *Perf. 10½*

2053 A551 10r black & red .50 .25

World Telecommunications Day — A552

1980, May 17 Photo. *Perf. 13x13½*

2054 A552 20r multicolored .50 .25

Interior of Mosque A553

1r, Demonstration. 3r, Avicenna, al-Biruni, Farabi. 5r, Hegira emblem.

1980, June 11 Litho. *Perf. 10½*

2055	A553	50d shown	.25	.25
2056	A553	1r multicolored	.25	.25
2057	A553	3r multicolored	.40	.25
2058	A553	5r multicolored	.30	.25
		Nos. 2055-2058 (4)	1.20	1.00

Hegira, 1400th anniv.

Ali Sharyati, Educator A554

1980, June 15 Photo. *Perf. 13x13½*

2059 A554 5r multicolored .30 .25

Holy Ka'aba and Hand Waving Banner — A555

1980, June 28

2060 A555 5r multicolored .30 .25

Hazrat Mehdi, 12th Imam's birth anniv.

A556

1980, Sept. 10 *Perf. 13½x13*

2061 A556 5r multicolored .30 .25

Ayatollah Seyed Mahmood Talegani, death anniv. Compare with design A829.

OPEC Emblem — A557

10r, Men holding OPEC emblem.

1980, Sept. 15

2062	A557	5r shown	.30	.25
2063	A557	10r multicolored	.60	.25

20th anniversary of OPEC.

"Let Us Liberate Jerusalem" — A558

1980, Oct. 9 *Perf. 13x13½*

2064	A558	5r multicolored	.25	.25
2065	A558	20r multicolored	.85	.25

Tulip and Fayziyye Seminary, Qum — A559

5r, Blood spilling on tulip. 20r, Tulip, Republic emblem.

1981, Feb. 11 *Perf. 13*

2066	A559	3r shown	.25	.25
2067	A559	5r multicolored	.25	.25
2068	A559	20r multicolored	.50	.25
		Nos. 2066-2068 (3)	1.00	.75

Islamic Revolution, 2nd anniversary.

See Nos. 2310c, 2310e, 2310j, watermark 381 (3r, unserifed "R" in denomination. 5r, bright yellow background; 20r, light blue background behind flower.)

Lorestani Man — A560

Novrooz (Iranian New Year): 10r, Lorestani woman.

1981, Mar. 11

2069	A560	5r multicolored	.25	.25
2070	A560	10r multicolored	.30	.25

Telecommunications Day — A561

Perf. 13½x13

1981, May 17 Photo. Wmk. 353

2071 A561 5r dk grn & org .25 .25

Ayatollah Kashani Birth Centenary — A562

Perf. 13x13½

1981, July 21 Wmk. 381

2072 A562 15r dk grn & dl pur .40 .25

Adult Education A563

50d, Citizens bearing arms. 2r, Irrigation. 3r, Friday prayer service. 5r, Paasdaar emblem and members. 10r, Koran text. 20r, Hejaab (women's veil). 50r, Industrial development. 100r, Religious ceremony, Mecca. 200r, Mosque interior. 5r, 10r, 200r vert.

Perf. 13x13½, 13½x13 (5r, 10r, 200r)

1981, Aug.

2073	A563	50d blk & dp bister	.25	.25
2074	A563	1r dl pur & grn	.25	.25
2075	A563	2r brn & grnsh bl	.25	.25

Size: 38x28mm, 28x38mm

2076	A563	3r brt yel grn & black	.25	.25
2077	A563	5r dk bl & brn org	.25	.25
2078	A563	10r dk bl & grnsh blue	.25	.25
2079	A563	20r red & black	.60	.25
2080	A563	50r lilac & black	1.40	.30
2081	A563	100r org brn & blk	3.00	.60
2082	A563	200r blk & bl grn	5.75	1.25
		Nos. 2073-2082 (10)	12.25	3.90

Islamic Iranian Army A564

1981, Sept. 21 Photo. *Perf. 13*
2087 A564 5r multicolored .65 .30

World Post Day and 12th UPU Day — A565

Perf. 13x13½
1981, Oct. 9 Wmk. 381
2088 A565 20r black & blue .85 .45

Millennium of Nahjul Balaghah (Sacred Book) A566

1981, Oct. 17 *Perf. 13*
2089 A566 25r multicolored .60 .25

Martyrs' Memorial — A567

3r, June 28, 1981 victims. 5r, Pres. Rajai, Prime Minister Bahonar. 10r, Gen. Chamran.

1981, Nov. 9 Photo. *Perf. 13*

2090	A567	3r multicolored	.25	.25
2091	A567	5r multicolored	.25	.25
2092	A567	10r multicolored	.25	.25
		Nos. 2090-2092 (3)	.75	.75

Ayatollah M. H. Tabatabaee, Scholar — A568

1981, Dec. 25 Photo. *Perf. 13*
2093 A568 5r multicolored .25 .25

Literacy Campaign A569

1982, Jan. 20 Photo. *Perf. 13x13½*
2094 A569 5r blue & gold .25 .25

Islamic Revolution, 3rd Anniv. — A570

1982, Feb. 11 Wmk. 381 *Perf. 13*

2095	A570	5r Map	.25	.25
2096	A570	10r Tulip	.25	.25
2097	A570	20r Globe	.50	.25
a.		Strip of 3, #2095-2097	.90	.40

See Nos. 2310f, 2310g, 2310k (5r, orange background, Arabian "5" 6mm above black panel. 10r, dark green background, gray dove with thick black lines around it. 20r, pink background, bright blue globe, faint latitude and longitude lines.)

Unity Week — A571

1982, Feb. 20 Photo. *Perf. 13*
2098 A571 25r multicolored 1.00 .25

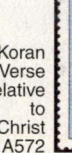

Koran Verse Relative to Christ A572

1982, Mar. 11 Photo. Wmk. 381
2099 A572 20r multicolored .50 .25

Khuzestan Man — A573

5r, Khuzestan woman.

1982, Mar. 13

2100	A573	3r shown	.25	.25
2101	A573	5r multicolored	.25	.25
a.		Pair, #2100-2101	.25	.25

Novrooz (New Year).

3rd Anniv. of Islamic Revolution A574

1982, Apr. 1
2102 A574 30r multicolored .90 .25

Seyed Mohammad Bagher Sadr — A575

1982, Apr. 8 Photo. *Perf. 13½x13*
2103 A575 50r multicolored 1.00 .40

Martyrs of Altar (Ayatollahs Madani and Dastgeyb) — A576

1982, Apr. 21 *Perf. 13*
2104 A576 50r multicolored 1.00 .40

A577

1982, May 1 Photo. *Perf. 13½x13*
2105 A577 100r multi 2.25 .80

Intl. Workers' Solidarity Day.

A578

1982, May 17 *Perf. 13x13½*
2106 A578 100r multi 2.25 .80

14th World Telecommunications Day.

Mab'as Day (Mohammad's Appointment as Prophet) — A579

1982, May 21 *Perf. 13½x13*
2107 A579 32r multicolored .90 .30

1963 Islamic Rising, 19th Anniv. — A580

1982, June 5 Wmk. 381 *Perf. 13*
2108 A580 28r multicolored .60 .30

Lt. Islambuli, Assassin of Anwar Sadat — A581

1982, June 17
2109 A581 2r multicolored .40 .25

1st Death Anniv. of Ayatollah Beheshti — A582

1982, June 28

2110	A582	10r multicolored	.40	.25
a.		Missing dot in Arabic numeral	1.00	1.00

Iran-Iraq War A583

1982, July 7 *Perf. 13x13½*
2111 A583 5r multicolored .25 .25

Universal Jerusalem Day A584

1982, July 15 *Perf. 13*
2112 A584 1r Dome of the Rock .25 .25

Pilgrimage to Mecca — A585

1982, Sept. 28
2113 A585 10r multicolored .30 .25

13th World UPU Day — A586

1982, Oct. 9 *Perf. 13½x13*
2114 A586 30r multicolored .75 .25

4th Anniv. of Islamic Revolution — A587

1983, Feb. 11 **Photo.** *Perf. 13*
2115 A587 30r multicolored .75 .25

See No. 2310n for stamp with orange or orange red crowd and thick sharp lettering in black panels.

4th Anniv. of Islamic Republic — A588

1983, Apr. 1 **Photo.** *Perf. 13*
2116 A588 10r multicolored .30 .25

Teachers' Day — A589

Perf. 13½x13
1983, May 1 **Wmk. 381**
2117 A589 5r multicolored .25 .25

World Communications Year — A590

1983, May 17
2118 A590 20r multicolored .60 .25

First Session of Islamic Consultative Assembly — A591

1983, May 28 *Perf. 13*
2119 A591 5r multicolored .25 .25

20th Anniv. of Islamic Movement — A592

1983, June 5 **Photo.** *Perf. 13*
2120 A592 10r multicolored .30 .25

Iraqi MiG Bombing Now Rooz Oil Well A593

1983, June 11 *Perf. 13x13½*
2121 A593 5r multicolored .50 .25

Ecology week.

Ayatollah Mohammad Sadooghi — A594

1983, July 2 **Photo.** *Perf. 13½*
2122 A594 20r blk & dl red .60 .25

Universal Day of Jerusalem — A595

1983, July 8
2123 A595 5r Dome of the Rock .25 .25

Government Week — A596

1983, Aug. 30 **Wmk. 381** *Perf. 13*
2124 A596 3r multicolored .25 .25

Death of Pres. Rajai and Prime Minister Bahonar, 2nd anniv.

Iran-Iraq War, 3rd Anniv. — A597

1983, Sept. 28 **Photo.** *Perf. 13*
2125 A597 5r rose red & blk .25 .25

Ayatollah Ashrafi Esphahani, Martyr of Altar — A598

1983, Oct. 15 **Photo.** *Perf. 13*
2126 A598 5r multicolored .25 .25

Mirza Kuchik Khan — A599

Religious and Political Figures: 1r, Sheikh Mohammad Khiabani. 3r, Seyd Majtaba Navab Safavi. 5r, Seyd Jamal-ed-Din Assadabadi. 10r, Seyd Hassan Modaress. 20r, Sheikh Fazel Assad Nouri. 30r, Mirza Mohammad Hossein Naiyni. 50r, Sheikh Mohammad Hossein Kashef. 100r, Seyd Hassan Shirazi. 200r, Mirza Reza Kermani.

1983-84 **Photo.** *Perf. 13*

2128	A599	1r black & pink	.25	.25
2129	A599	2r org & black	.25	.25
2130	A599	3r brt bl & blk	.25	.25
2131	A599	5r rose red & blk	.25	.25
2132	A599	10r yel grn & blk	.30	.25
2133	A599	20r lilac & blk	.60	.25
2134	A599	30r gldn brn & blk	.90	.30
2135	A599	50r blk & lt bl	1.50	.50
2136	A599	100r blk & org	3.00	1.00
2137	A599	200r blk & bluish grn	6.00	2.00
		Nos. 2128-2137 (10)	13.30	5.30

Issue dates: 1r, 50r-200r, Feb. 1984. Others, Oct. 23, 1983.

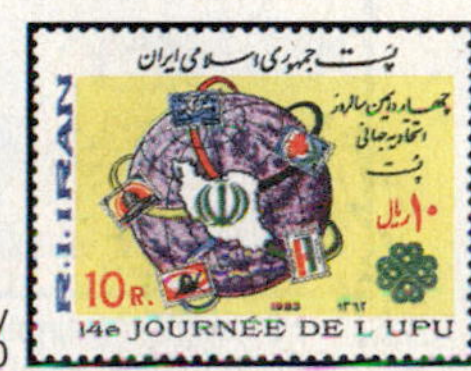

UPU Day A600

1983, Oct. 9 **Photo.** **Wmk. 381**
2138 A600 10r multi .25 .25

Takeover of the US Embassy, 4th Anniv. — A601

1983, Nov. 4 **Photo.** *Perf. 13*
2139 A601 28r multicolored .50 .50

UN Day A602

1983, Oct. 24 *Perf. 13½*
2140 A602 32r multicolored .90 .25

Protest of veto by US, Russia, People's Rep. of China, France and Great Britain.

Intl. Medical Seminar, Tehran — A603

1983, Nov. 20
2141 A603 3r Avicenna .25 .25

People's Forces Preparation Day — A604

1983, Nov. 26 *Perf. 13*
2142 A604 20r multicolored .60 .25

Conference on Crimes of Iraqi Pres. Saddam Hussein — A605

1983, Nov. 28 *Perf. 13½x13*
2143 A605 5r multicolored .25 .25

Mohammad Mofatteh — A606

1983, Dec. 18 **Photo.** *Perf. 13*
2144 A606 10r multicolored .30 .25

Birth Anniversary of the Prophet Mohammad A607

1983, Dec. 22 **Photo.** *Perf. 13*
2145 A607 5r multicolored .45 .25

Approximately 700,000 examples of No. 2145 were issued before a spelling error was discovered, and the remainder of the issue was then withdrawn from sale.

5th Anniv. of Islamic Revolution — A608

1984, Feb. 11 **Photo.** *Perf. 13x13½*
2146 A608 10r multicolored .75 .25

See No. 2310h for stamp with splotchy colors in blue background and denomination, flag colors and darker, thicker black lines around tulips. Background and denominations on No. 2146 have a screened appearance.

Nurses' Day A609

20r, Attending wounded soldiers.

1984, Feb. 24 *Perf. 13*
2147 A609 20r multicolored .45 .25

Invalids' Day — A610

5r, Man in wheelchair.

1984, Feb. 29
2148 A610 5r multicolored .25 .25

Local Flowers — A611

3r, Lotus gebelia. 5r, Tulipa chrysantha. 10r, Glycyrhiza glabra. 20r, Matthiola alyssifolia.

1984, Mar. 10 ***Perf. 13½x13***
2149 A611 3r multicolored .25 .25
2150 A611 5r multicolored .25 .25
2151 A611 10r multicolored .25 .25
2152 A611 20r multicolored .45 .25

Novrooz (New Year).

Islamic Republic, 5th Anniv. — A612

1984, Apr. 1 **Photo.** ***Perf. 13***
2153 A612 5r Flag, globe, map .25 .25

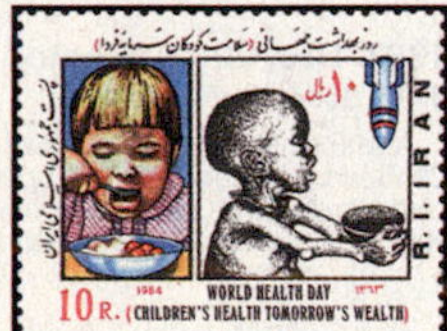
World Health Day A613

1984, Apr. 7
2154 A613 10r Children .30 .25

Sheik Ragheb Harb, Lebanese Religious Leader — A614

1984, Apr. 18
2155 A614 5r multicolored .25 .25

World Red Cross Day — A615

1984, May 8 **Photo.** ***Perf. 13½x13***
2156 A615 5r multicolored .25 .25

16th World Telecommunications Day — A616

1984, May 17
2157 A616 20r multicolored .45 .25

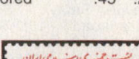

Martyrdom of Seyyed Ghotb — A617

1984, May 28 ***Perf. 13***
2158 A617 10r multicolored .30 .25

Struggle Against Discrimination — A618

1984, Mar. 21 **Photo.** ***Perf. 13***
2159 A618 5r Malcolm X 2.50 .25

Conquest of Mecca Anniv. A619

1984, June 20
2160 A619 5r Holy Ka'aba, idol destruction .25 .25

Universal Day of Jerusalem A620

Id Al-fitr Feast A621

5r, Map, Koran. 10r, Moon, praying crowd, mosque.

1984, June 29
2161 A620 5r multicolored .25 .25
2162 A621 10r multicolored .25 .25
a. Pair, #2161-2162 .40 .25

Tchogha Zanbil Excavation, Susa — A622

Cultural Heritage Preservation: b, Emamzadeh Hossein Shrine, Kazvin. c, Emam Mosque, Isfahan. d, Ark Fortress, Tabriz. e, Mausoleum of Daniel Nabi, Susa.

1984, Aug. 20 ***Perf. 13½***
2163 Strip of 5 .75 .25
a.-e. A622 5r, any single .25 .25

"Eid Ul-Adha" A623

Perf. 13x13½
1984, Sept. 6 **Photo.** **Wmk. 381**
2164 A623 10r Holy Ka'aba .30 .25

Feast of Sacrifices (end of pilgrimage to Mecca).

10th Tehran Intl. Trade Fair — A624

1984, Sept. 11
2165 A624 10r multicolored .30 .25

Iraq-Iran War, 4th Anniv. — A625

1984, Sept. 22 **Photo.** ***Perf. 13x13½***
2166 A625 5r Flower, bullets .25 .25

UPU Day A626

20r, Dove, UPU emblems.

1984, Oct. 9 ***Perf. 13½***
2167 A626 20r multicolored .50 .25

Haj Seyyed Mostafa Khomeini Memorial A627

1984, Oct. 23
2168 A627 5r multicolored .25 .25

Ghazi Tabatabaie Memorial — A628

1984, Nov. 1 ***Perf. 13x13½***
2169 A628 5r Portrait .25 .25

Intl. Saadi Congress A629

10r, Portrait, mausoleum, emblem.

1984, Nov. 25 ***Perf. 13½***
2170 A629 10r multicolored .50 .25

Saadi (c. 1213-1292), Persian poet.

Mohammad's Birthday, Unity Week — A630

1984, Dec. 6 **Photo.** ***Perf. 13x13½***
2171 A630 5r Koran, mosque .25 .25

Islamic Revolution, 6th Anniv. — A631

1985, Feb. 11 ***Perf. 13x13½***
2172 A631 40r multicolored .90 .40

See No. 2310o for stamp with bright pink denomination and dove tail.

Arbor Day — A632

3r, Sapling, deciduous trees. 5r, Maturing trees.

1985, Mar. 6 ***Perf. 13***
2173 A632 3r multicolored .25 .25
2174 A632 5r multicolored .25 .25
a. Pair, #2173-2174 .30 .25

Local Flowers — A633

No. 2175, Fritillaria imperialis. No. 2176, Ranunculus ficarioides. No. 2177, Crocus sativus. No. 2178, Primula heterochroma stapf.

1985, Mar. 9 ***Perf. 13½x13***
2175 A633 5r multicolored .25 .25
2176 A633 5r multicolored .25 .25
2177 A633 5r multicolored .25 .25
2178 A633 5r multicolored .25 .25
a. Block of 4, #2175-2178 .50 .30

Novrooz (New Year).

Women's Day — A634

10r, Procession of women.

1985, Mar. 13 *Perf. 13x13½*
2179 A634 10r multicolored .30 .25

Birth anniv. of Mohammad's daughter, Fatima.

Republic of Iran, 6th Anniv. — A635

20r, Tulip, ballot box.

1985, Apr. 1
2180 A635 20r multicolored .45 .25

Mab'as Festival A636

1985, Apr. 18
2181 A636 10r Holy Koran .30 .25

Religious festival celebrating the recognition of Mohammad as the true prophet.

Day of the Oppressed — A637

1985, May 6
2182 A637 5r Koran, flag, globe .25 .25

Birthday of the 12th Imam.

World Telecommunications Day — A638

1985, May 17 *Perf. 13½x13*
2183 A638 20r ITU emblem .45 .25

Liberation of Khorramshahr, 1st Anniv. — A639

1985, May 24
2184 A639 5r Soldier, bridge .25 .25

Fist, Theological Seminary, Qum — A640

1985, June 5 *Perf. 13x13½*
2185 A640 10r multicolored .50 .25

1963 Uprising, 22nd Anniv.

World Handicrafts Day A641

1985, June 10 *Perf. 13½*
2186 A641 20r Plates, flasks .45 .25

Day of Jerusalem A642

1985, June 14
2187 A642 5r multicolored .25 .25

Id Al-fitr Feast — A643

1985, June 20 *Perf. 13x13½*
2188 A643 5r multicolored .25 .25

Founding of the Islamic Propagation Org. — A644

1985, June 22
2189 A644 5r tan & emerald .25 .25

Ayatollah Sheikh Abdolhossein Amini — A645

1985, July 3 **Photo.** *Perf. 13*
2190 A645 5r multicolored .25 .25

Pilgrimage to Mecca — A646

1985, July 20 **Photo.** *Perf. 13½*
2191 A646 10r multicolored .30 .25

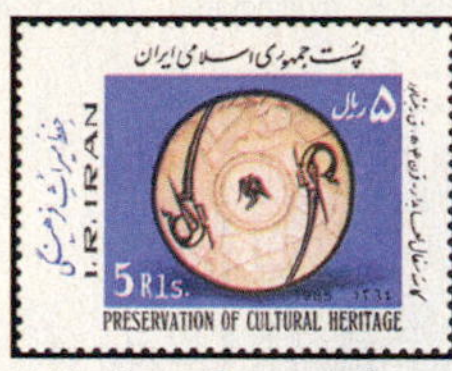
Cultural Heritage Preservation — A647

Ceramic plates from Nishabur: a, Swords. b, Farsi script. c, Peacock. d, Four leaves.

1985, Aug. 20
2192 Block of 4 .60 .25
a.-d. A647 5r, any single .25 .25

Goharshad Mosque Uprising, 50th Anniv. — A648

1985, Aug. 21 *Perf. 13x13½*
2193 A648 10r multicolored .25 .25

Week of Government A649

Designs: a, Industry and communications. b, Industry and agriculture. c, Health care, red crescent. d, Education.

1985, Aug. 30 **Photo.** *Perf. 13x13½*
2194 Block of 4 .60 .25
a.-d. A649 5r, any single .25 .25

Bleeding Tulips — A650

1985, Sept. 8
2195 A650 10r multicolored .30 .25

17th Shahrivar, Bloody Friday memorial.

OPEC, 25th Anniv. — A651

Design: No. 2196b, OPEC emblem and 25.

1985, Sept. 14 *Perf. 13½*
2196 Pair .50 .25
a.-b. A651 5r, any single .25 .25

Iran-Iraq War, 5th Anniv. — A652

Designs: a, Dead militiaman. b, Mosque and Ashura in Persian. c, Rockets descending on doves. d, Palm grove, rifle shot exploding rocket.

1985, Sept. 22
2197 Block of 4 .60 .25
a.-d. A652 5r any single .25 .25

Ashura mourning.

Ash-Sharif Ar-Radi — A653

1985, Sept. 26 **Photo.** *Perf. 13x13½*
2198 A653 20r brt bl, lt bl & gold .60 .25

Ash-Sharif Ar-Radi, writer, death millennium.

UPU Day A654

1985, Oct. 9 *Perf. 13½*
2199 A654 20r multicolored .60 .25

World Standards Day A655

1985, Oct. 14
2200 A655 20r Natl. Standards Office emblem .60 .25

Agricultural Training and Development Year — A656

1985, Oct. 19 *Perf. 13x13½*
2201 A656 5r Hand, wheat .25 .25

Takeover of US Embassy, 6th Anniv. — A657

1985, Nov. 4 ***Perf. 13***
2202 A657 40r multicolored .60 .40

Moslem Unity Week — A658

1985, Nov. 25 ***Perf. 13x13½***
2203 A658 10r Holy Ka'aba .30 .25

Birth of prophet Mohammad, 1015th anniv.

High Council of the Cultural Revolution — A659

1985, Dec. 10
2204 A659 5r Roses .25 .25

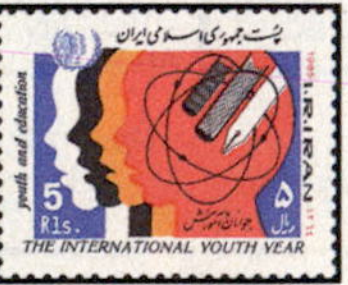

Intl. Youth Year — A660

Designs: a, Education. b, Defense. c, Construction. d, Sports.

1985, Dec. 18 Photo. ***Perf. 13x13½***
2205 Block of 4 .60 .25
a.-d. A660 5r, any single .25 .25

Ezzeddin al-Qassam, 50th Death Anniv. — A661

1985, Dec. 20 ***Perf. 13½***
2206 A661 20r sil, sep & hn brn .60 .25

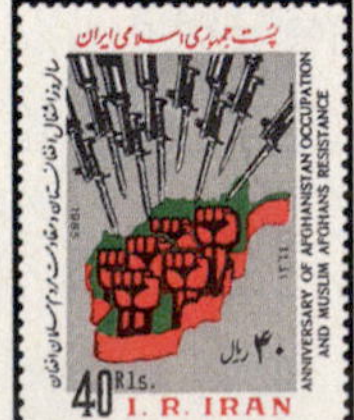

Map, Fists, Bayonets A662

1985, Dec. 25 **Wmk. 381**
2207 A662 40r multicolored 1.25 .40

Occupation of Afghanistan and Moslem resistance, 6th anniv.

Mirza Taqi Khan Amir Kabir (d. 1851) — A663

1986, Jan. 8 Litho. ***Perf. 13***
2208 A663 5r multicolored 1.25 .25

Students Destroying Statue of the Shah, Tulips — A664

1986, Feb. 11 Photo. ***Perf. 13½***
2209 A664 20r multicolored .60 .25

Iranian Revolution, 7th anniv.
See No. 2310l for 24x36mm stamp with yellow Arabic script.

Sulayman Khater, 40th Death Anniv. — A665

1986, Feb. 15 ***Perf. 13***
2210 A665 10r multicolored .30 .25

Women's Day — A666

1986, Mar. 3 ***Perf. 13½***
2211 A666 10r multicolored .30 .25

Birth anniv. of Mohammad's daughter, Fatima.

Flowers — A667

a, Papaver orientale. b, Anemone coronaria. c, Papaver bracteatum. d, Anemone biflora.

1986, Mar. 11 Photo. ***Perf. 13½***
2212 Block of 4 .60 .25
a.-d. A667 5r any single .25 .25

Novrooz (New Year).

2000th Day of Sacred Defense — A668

1986, Mar. 14 Photo. ***Perf. 13x13½***
2213 A668 5r scarlet & grn .25 .25

Intl. Day Against Racial Discrimination A669

1986, Mar. 21
2214 A669 5r multicolored .25 .25

Islamic Republic of Iran, 7th Anniv. — A670

1986, Apr. 1 ***Perf. 13***
2215 A670 10r Flag, map .30 .25

Mab'as Festival A671

1986, Apr. 7
2216 A671 40r multicolored .60 .25

Army Day — A672

1986, Apr. 18 ***Perf. 13½***
2217 A672 5r multicolored .25 .25

Day of the Oppressed — A673

1986, Apr. 25 ***Perf. 13x13½***
2218 A673 10r blk, gold & dk red .25 .25

Helicopter Crash — A674

1986, Apr. 25 **Wmk. 381**
2219 A674 40r multicolored 1.25 .40

US air landing at Tabass Air Base, 6th anniv.

Teacher's Day — A675

1986, May 2 Photo. ***Perf. 13x13½***
2220 A675 5r multicolored .25 .25

World Telecommunications Day — A676

1986, May 17 ***Perf. 13½x13***
2221 A676 20r blk, sil & ultra .60 .25

Universal Day of the Child — A677

No. 2222, Child's war drawing. No. 2223, Hosein Fahmide, Iran-Iraq war hero.

1986, June 1 ***Perf. 13***
2222 A677 15r multicolored .45 .25
2223 A677 15r multicolored .45 .25
a. Pair, #2222-2223 .90 .30

1963 Uprising, 23rd Anniv. — A678

1986, June 5 ***Perf. 13x13½***
2224 A678 10r Qum Theological Seminary .30 .25

Day of Jerusalem — A679

1986, June 6
2225 A679 10r multicolored .30 .25

Id Al-Fitr Feast A680

1986, June 9 ***Perf. 13***
2226 A680 10r Moslems praying .75 .25

World Handicrafts Day A681

a, Baluchi cross-hatched rug. b, Craftsman. c, Qalamkar flower rug. d, Copper repousse vase.

1986, June 10 ***Perf. 13½***
2227 Block of 4 1.25 .40
a.-d. A681 10r, any single .30 .25

Intl. Day for Solidarity with Black So. Africans — A682

1986, June 26
2228 A682 10r multicolored .30 .25

Ayatollah Beheshti — A683

1986, June 28 ***Perf. 13x13½***
2229 A683 10r multicolored .30 .25

Death of Beheshti and Islamic Party workers, Tehran headquarters bombing, 5th anniv.

Ayatollah Mohammad Taqi Shirazi, Map of Iraq — A684

1986, June 30 **Photo.** **Wmk. 381**
2230 A684 20r multicolored .60 .25

Iraqi Moslem uprising against the British.

Shrine of Imam Reza — A685

1986, July 19 ***Perf. 13½***
2231 A685 10r multicolored .30 .25

Eid Ul-Adha, Feast of Sacrifice — A686

1986, Aug. 17 ***Perf. 13x13½***
2232 A686 10r multicolored .30 .25

Cultural Heritage Preservation — A687

Designs: No. 2233, Bam Fortress. No. 2234, Kabud (Blue) Mosque, Tabriz. No. 2235, Mausoleum of Sohel Ben Ali at Astenah, Arak. No. 2236, Soltanieh Mosque, Zendjan Province.

1986, Aug. 20
2233 A687 5r Hilltop .25 .25
2234 A687 5r shown .25 .25
2235 A687 5r Intact roof .25 .25
2236 A687 5r Damaged roof .25 .25
Nos. 2233-2236 (4) 1.00 1.00

Eid Ul-Ghadir Feast — A688

1986, Aug. 25
2237 A688 20r multicolored .60 .25

Population and Housing Census — A689

1986, Sept. 9 ***Perf. 13½x13***
2238 A689 20r multicolored .40 .25

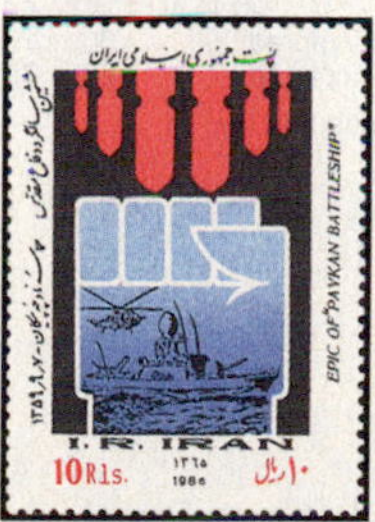

Iran-Iraq War, 6th Year — A690

1986, Sept. 22 ***Perf. 13***
2239 A690 10r Battleship Paykan .30 .25
2240 A690 10r Susangerd .30 .25
2241 A690 10r Khorramshahr .30 .25
2242 A690 10r Howeizeh .30 .25
2243 A690 10r Siege of Abadan .30 .25
Nos. 2239-2243 (5) 1.50 1.25

10th Asian Games, Seoul A691

1986, Oct. 2 **Photo.** **Wmk. 381**
2244 A691 15r Wrestling .40 .25
2245 A691 15r Rifle shooting .40 .25

World Post Day A692

1986, Oct. 9
2246 A692 20r multicolored .60 .25

UNESCO, 40th Anniv. — A693

1986, Nov. 4 **Photo.** ***Perf. 13x13½***
2247 A693 45r blk, sky bl & brt rose 1.25 .45

Ayatollah Tabatabaie (d. 1981) — A694

1986, Nov. 15 **Photo.** ***Perf. 13½x13***
2248 A694 10r multicolored .30 .25

Unity Week — A695

1986, Nov. 20
2249 A695 10r multicolored .30 .25

Birth anniv. of Mohammad.

People's Militia — A696

1986, Nov. 26 ***Perf. 13***
2250 A696 5r multicolored .25 .25

Mobilization of the Oppressed Week.

Afghan Resistance Movement, 7th Anniv. — A697

1986, Dec. 27
2251 A697 40r multicolored 1.25 .40

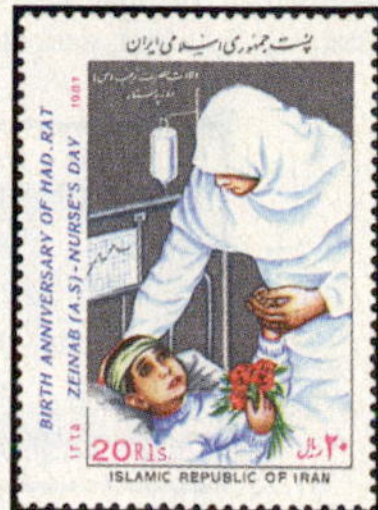

Nurses' Day — A698

1987, Jan. 12 **Photo.** ***Perf. 13***
2252 A698 20r multicolored .60 .25

Hazrat Zainab birth anniv.

Fifth Islamic Theology Conference, Tehran — A699

Wmk. 381

1987, Jan. 29 **Photo.** ***Perf. 13***
2253 A699 20r multicolored .60 .25

Islamic Revolution, 8th Anniv. — A700

1987, Feb. 11
2254 A700 20r multicolored .60 .25

See No. 2310m for 24x36mm stamp.

Islamic Revolutionary Committees, 8th Anniv. — A701

1987, Feb. 12
2255 A701 10r brt bl, scar & yel .30 .25

Women's Day — A702

1987, Feb. 19
2256 A702 10r multicolored .30 .25
Birthday of Fatima, daughter of Mohammad.

Iran Air, 25th Anniv. A703

1987, Feb. 24
2257 A703 30r multicolored .90 .30

Ayatollah Mirza Mohammad Hossein Naeini, 50th Death Anniv. — A704

1987, Mar. 6 Photo. *Perf. 13*
2258 A704 10r multicolored .30 .25

New Year — A705

Flowers: a, Iris persica. b, Rosa damascena. c, Iris paradoxa. d, Tulipa clusiana.

1987, Mar. 11 *Perf. 13½x13*
2259 Block of 4 2.00 .50
a.-d. A705 5r, any single .50 .25

See Nos. 2313, 2361, 2411, 2443.

Mab'as Festival A706

1987, Mar. 28 *Perf. 13*
2260 A706 45r gold, dk grn & grn 1.40 .45

Universal Day of the Oppressed A707

1987, Apr. 14
2261 A707 20r multicolored .60 .25
Savior Mahdi's birthday.

Memorial to Lebanese Hizbollah Martyrs — A708

1987, Apr. 5
2262 A708 10r grn, gray & brt car .30 .25

Revolutionary Guards Day — A709

1987, Apr. 2
2263 A709 5r multi .25 .25
Imam Hossein's birthday.

8th Anniv. of Islamic Republic A710

1987, Apr. 1
2264 A710 20r multicolored .60 .25

World Health Day — A711

Child survival through immunization: 3r, Intravenous. 5r, Oral.

1987, Apr. 7 *Perf. 13x13½*
2265 A711 3r multicolored .25 .25
2266 A711 5r multicolored .30 .25
a. Pair, #2265-2266 .50 .25

Int'l. Labor Day — A712

1987, May 1 Photo. *Perf. 13*
2267 A712 5r multicolored .25 .25

Teachers' Day — A713

1987, May 2 Wmk. 381
2268 A713 5r Ayatollah Mottahari .25 .25

A714

1987, May 17 *Perf. 13½x13*
2269 A714 20r multicolored .70 .25
World Telecommunications Day.

A715

No. 2270, Sassanian silver gilt vase. No. 2271, Bisque pot, Rey, 12th cent.

1987, May 18 *Perf. 13*
2270 A715 20r multicolored .60 .25
2271 A715 20r multicolored .60 .25
Intl. Museum Day.

Universal Day of Jerusalem — A716

1987, May 22 *Perf. 13½x13*
2272 A716 20r multicolored .60 .25

World Crafts Day A717

a, Blown glass tea service. b, Stained glass window. c, Ceramic plate. d, Potter.

1987, June 10 *Perf. 13x13½*
2273 Block of 4 .75 .25
a.-d. A717 5r any single .25 .25

1963 Uprising, 24th Anniv. — A718

1987, June 5 Photo. *Perf. 13½*
2274 A718 20r multicolored .60 .25

Tax Reform Week — A719

1987, July 10 *Perf. 13*
2275 A719 10r black, sil & gold .30 .25

Welfare Week — A720

1987, July 17
2276 A720 15r multicolored .45 .25

Eid Ul-adha, Feast of Sacrifice — A721

1987, Aug. 6
2277 A721 12r sil, blk & Prus grn .45 .25

Eid Ul-Ghadir Festival A722

1987, Aug. 14
2278 A722 18r black, green & gold .55 .25

Banking Week — A723

1987, Aug. 17 ***Perf. 13½x13***
2279 A723 15r red brn, gold & pale grnsh bl .45 .25

1st Cultural and Artistic Congress of Iranian Calligraphers
A724

1987, Aug. 21 Photo. ***Perf. 13x13½***
2280 A724 20r multicolored .60 .25

Memorial to Iranian Pilgrims Killed in Mecca — A725

1987, Aug. 26 Wmk. 381 ***Perf. 13***
2281 A725 8r multicolored .30 .25

Assoc. of Iranian Dentists, 25th Anniv. — A726

1987, Aug. 27 Photo. ***Perf. 13½x13***
2282 A726 10r multicolored .30 .25

Intl. Peace Day — A727

1987, Sept. 1 ***Perf. 13***
2283 A727 20r gold & lt ultra .60 .25

Iran-Iraq War, 7th Anniv. — A728

No. 2285, Soldier, battle scene.

1987, Sept. 22 ***Perf. 13½x13***
2284 A728 25r shown .75 .25
2285 A728 25r multicolored .75 .25
a. Pair, #2284-2285

Police Day — A729

1987, Sept. 28
2286 A729 10r multicolored .30 .25

Intl. Social Security Week, Oct. 4-10 — A730

1987, Oct. 4 **Wmk. 381**
2287 A730 15r blk, gold & brt blue .45 .25

World Post Day — A731

UPU emblem and: No. 2288, M. Ghandi, minister of the Post and Telecommunications Bureau. No. 2289, Globe, dove.

1987, Oct. 9 ***Perf. 13x13½***
2288 A731 15r multicolored .45 .25
2289 A731 15r multicolored .45 .25

> Importation Prohibited
> Importation of stamps was prohibited effective Oct. 29, 1987.

A732

Wmk. 381
1987, Nov. 4 Photo. ***Perf. 13***
2290 A732 40r multicolored 1.25 .25

Takeover of US Embassy, 8th anniv.

A733

1987, Nov. 5
2291 A733 20r multicolored .90 .25

1st Intl. Tehran Book Fair.

Mohammad's Birthday, Unity Week — A734

1987, Nov. 10
2292 A734 25r multicolored .60 .25

Ayatollah Modarres Martyrdom, 50th Anniv. — A735

1987, Dec. 1
2293 A735 10r brn & bister .40 .25

Agricultural Training and Extension Week — A736

1987, Dec. 6
2294 A736 10r multicolored .50 .25

Afghan Resistance, 8th Anniv. — A737

1987, Dec. 27
2295 A737 40r multicolored 1.25 .40

Main Mosques
A738

1987-92 ***Perf. 13x13½, 13½x13***
Silver Background

No.	Type	Value	Unused	Used
2295A	A738	1r Shoushtar	.50	.25
2296	A738	2r Ouroumieh	.50	.25
2296A	A738	3r Kerman	.50	.25
2297	A738	5r Kazvin	.50	.30
2298	A738	10r Varamin	.50	.30
a.		Unwatermarked ('91)	3.00	2.00
2299	A738	20r Saveh	.75	.75
a.		Unwatermarked ('91)	2.00	1.25
2300	A738	30r Natanz, vert.	1.50	1.40
2301	A738	40r Shiraz	2.00	1.75
a.		Unwatermarked ('92)	10.00	5.00
2302	A738	50r Isfahan, vert.	1.50	1.25
a.		Unwatermarked ('91)	3.00	2.00
2303	A738	100r Hamadan	2.00	2.00
a.		Unwatermarked ('91)	5.00	3.00
2304	A738	200r Dezfoul, vert.	4.00	3.50
a.		Unwatermarked ('91)	15.00	5.00
2305	A738	500r Yazd, vert.	13.00	10.00
a.		Unwatermarked ('91)	20.00	15.00
		Nos. 2295A-2305 (12)	27.25	22.00
		Nos. 2298a-2305a (7)	18.00	18.00

Issued: 10r, 12/1; 5r, 12/30; 500r, 1/10/88; 20r, 1/14/88; 2r, 1/24/88; 50r, 1/24/89; 100r, 10/21/89; 200r, 10/28/89; 30r, 40r, 3/17/90; 1r, 3r, 3/92.

For surcharges see Nos. 2750-2751.

Watermarks on this issue can be difficult to discern. The paper of the unwatermarked stamps show fluoresence under long wave ultraviolet light.

Qum Uprising, 10th Anniversary — A739

1988, Jan. 9 ***Perf. 13***
2306 A739 20r multicolored .50 .25

Bombing of Schools by Iraq — A740

1988, Feb. 1 ***Perf. 13x13½***
2307 A740 10r multicolored .80 .25

Gholamreza Takhti, World Wrestling Champion — A741

1988, Feb. 4 ***Perf. 13½***
2308 A741 15r multicolored .50 .50

Women's Day — A742

1988, Feb. 9 ***Perf. 13***
2309 A742 20r multicolored .40 .25

Birth anniv. of Mohammad's daughter, Fatima.

Types of 1979-88 and
Souvenir Sheet

Islamic Revolution, 9th Anniv. — A743

1988, Feb. 11 Wmk. 381 ***Perf. 13***
2310 Sheet of 16 10.00
a. A547 1r like #2046
b. A547 3r like #2047
c. A559 3r like #2066
d. A547 5r like #2048
e. A559 5r like #2067
f. A570 5r like #2095
g. A570 10r like #2096
h. A608 10r like #2146
i. A537 18r like #1999
j. A559 20r like #2068

k. A570 20r like #2097
l. A664 20r like #2209
m. A700 20r like #2254
n. A587 30r like #2115
o. A631 40r like #2172
p. A743 40r shown

Nos. 2310a, 2310b, 2310d, 2310l, 2310m are smaller than the original issues. See original issues for distinguishing features on other stamps.
Exists imperf. Value $15.

Tabriz Uprising, 10th Anniv. — A744

1988, Feb. 18 *Perf. 13*
2311 A744 25r multicolored 1.00 .75

Arbor Day — A745

1988, Mar. 5
2312 A745 15r multicolored .70 .25

New Year Festival Type of 1987

Flowers: a, Anthemis hyalina. b, Malva silvestris. c, Viola odorata. d, Echium amaenum.

1988, Mar. 10 *Perf. 13½x13*
2313 Block of 4 2.00 2.00
a.-d. A705 10r any single

Islamic Republic, 9th Anniv. — A746

1988, Apr. 1 *Perf. 13*
2314 A746 20r multicolored .40 .25

Universal Day of the Oppressed A747

1988, Apr. 3
2314A A747 20r multicolored .30 .25

Savior Mahdi's Birthday.

Cultural Heritage — A748

1988, Apr. 18
2315 A748 10r Mosque .50 .40
2316 A748 10r Courtyard .50 .40
a. Pair, #2315-2316 1.50 1.00
2317 A748 10r Minarets, vert. .50 .40
2318 A748 10r Corridor, vert. .50 .40
a. Pair, #2317-2318 1.50 1.00

Chemical Bombardment of Halabja, Iraq — A749

1988, Apr. 26
2319 A749 20r multicolored .90 .40

A750

A750a

Palestinian Uprising A750b

1988, May 13
2320 Strip of 5 2.50 1.75
a. A750 10r multi
b. A750a 10r multi
c. A750b 10r multi
d. A750b 10r multi, diff.
e. A750b 10r Rock in hand, rioters

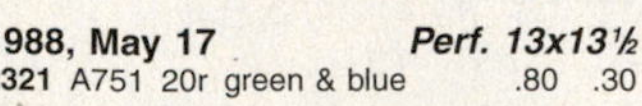
World Telecommunications Day — A751

1988, May 17 *Perf. 13x13½*
2321 A751 20r green & blue .80 .30

Intl. Museum Day — A752

Designs: a, Ceramic vase, 1982. b, Bastan Museum, entranceway. c, Tabriz silk rug, 14th cent. d, Gold ring, 7th cent. B.C.

1988, May 18 *Perf. 13*
2322 Block of 4 1.50 1.50
a.-d. A752 10r any single .30 .25

Mining Day — A753

1988, May 22 **Photo.** **Wmk. 381**
2323 A753 20r multicolored 1.25 .50

Intl. Day of the Child — A754

1988, June 1
2324 A754 10r multicolored .50 .30

June 5th Uprising, 25th Anniv. — A755

1988, June 5
2325 A755 10r multicolored .40 .40

World Crafts Day A756

1988, June 10 *Perf. 13x13½*
2326 A756 10r Straw basket .30 .25
2327 A756 10r Weaver .30 .25
a. Pair, #2326-2327 .80 .60
2328 A756 10r Tapestry, vert. .30 .25
2329 A756 10r Miniature, vert. .30 .25
a. Pair, #2328-2329 .80 .60

Child Health Campaign A757

1988, July 6 *Perf. 13*
2330 A757 20r blk, blue & green .40 .25

Tax Reform Week — A758

1988, July 10
2331 A758 20r multicolored .40 .25

Allameh Balkhi — A759

1988, July 15 *Perf. 13½x13*
2332 A759 20r multicolored .40 .25

A760

No. 2333, Holy Ka'aba, dove, stars.

1988, July 21 *Perf. 13*
2333 A760 10r multicolored .25 .25
2334 A760 10r shown .25 .25

Massacre of Muslim Pilgrims at Mecca.
Nos. 2333-2334 were printed together in one sheet, with alternating placement.

Destruction of Iranian Airliner — A761

1988, Aug. 11
2335 A761 45r multicolored 1.25 1.00

Seyyed Ali Andarzgou A762

1988, Aug. 13
2336 A762 20r multicolored .50 .25

Islamic Banking Week — A763

1988, Sept. 1 *Perf. 13½x13*
2337 A763 20r multicolored .50 .25

Divine Day of 17 Shahrivar, 10th Anniv. — A764

1988, Sept. 8
2338 A764 25r multicolored .70 .25

1988 Summer Olympics, Seoul — A765

Designs: a, Weightlifting. b, Pommel horse. c, Judo. d, Soccer. e, Wrestling.

1988, Sept. 10
2339 Strip of 5 2.00 1.50
a.-e. A765 10r any single .35 .25

Agricultural Census — A766

1988, Sept. 17 *Perf. 13½x13*
2340 A766 30r blk, grn & yel .60 .25

Iran-Iraq War, 8th Anniv. — A767

1988, Sept. 22 *Perf. 13x13½*
2341 A767 20r multicolored .50 .25

World Post Day A768

1988, Oct. 9 *Perf. 13*
2342 A768 20r blk, ultra & grn .80 .30

Parents and Teachers Cooperation Week — A769

1988, Oct. 16
2343 A769 20r multicolored .70 .25

Mohammad's Birthday, Unity Week — A770

1988, Oct. 29
2344 A770 10r multicolored .50 .30

A771

1988, Nov. 4
2345 A771 45r multicolored 1.10 .50

Takeover of US embassy, 9th anniv.

Insurance Day — A772

1988, Nov. 6 *Perf. 13½x13*
2346 A772 10r multicolored .80 .30

Intl. Congress on the Writings of Hafiz — A773

1988, Nov. 19 *Perf. 13x13½*
2347 A773 20r blue, gold & pink .50 .30

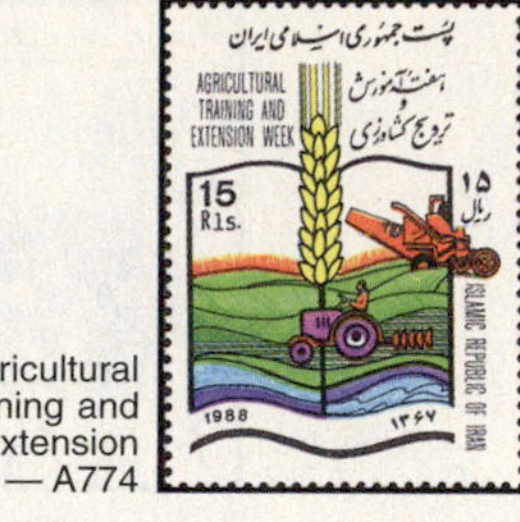

Agricultural Training and Extension Week — A774

1988, Dec. 6 *Perf. 13*
2348 A774 15r multicolored .60 .30

Scientists, Artists and Writers A775

No. 2349, Parvin E'Tessami. No. 2350, Jalal Al-Ahmad. No. 2351, Muhammad Mo'in. No. 2352, Qaem Maqam Farahani. No. 2353, Kamal Al-Molk.

1988, Dec. 18 *Perf. 13x13½*
2349 A775 10r multi .35 .35
2350 A775 10r multi .35 .35
2351 A775 10r multi .35 .35
a. Pair, #2350-2351 .80 .35
2352 A775 10r multi .35 .35
2353 A775 10r multi .35 .35
a. Pair, #2352-2353 .80 .75

See Nos. 2398-2402.

Afghan Resistance, 9th Anniv. — A776

1988, Dec. 27 *Perf. 13*
2354 A776 40r multicolored .45 .40

Transportation and Communication Decade — A777

No. 2355, Satellite, envelopes, microwave dish. No. 2356, Cargo planes. No. 2357, Train, trucks. No. 2358, Ships.

Perf. 13x13½

1989, Jan. 16 **Wmk. 381**
2355 A777 20r multicolored .70 .70
2356 A777 20r multicolored .70 .70
a. Pair, #2355-2356 1.90 1.75
2357 A777 20r multicolored .70 .70
2358 A777 20r multicolored .70 .70
a. Pair, #2357-2358 1.90 1.75

Prophethood of Mohammad A778

1989, Mar. 6 *Perf. 13*
2359 A778 20r multicolored .50 .40

Mab'as festival.

Arbor Day — A779

1989, Mar. 6
2360 A779 20r multicolored .70 .40

New Year Festival Type of 1987

Flowers: a, Cephalanthera kurdica. b, Dactylorhiza romana. c, Comperia comperiana. d, Orchis mascula.

1989, Mar. 11 *Perf. 13½x13*
2361 Block of 4 1.25 1.25
a.-d. A705 10r any single .25 .25

A780

30r, Meteorological devices, ship.

1989, Mar. 23
2362 A780 20r shown .60 .60
2363 A780 30r multicolored .60 .60
a. Pair, #2362-2363 1.50 1.25

World Meteorology Day.

A781

1989, Apr. 1 *Perf. 13*
2364 A781 20r multicolored .40 .40

Islamic Republic, 10th anniv.

Reconstruction of Abadan Refinery A782

1989, Apr. 1
2365 A782 20r multicolored .70 .30

Ayatollah Morteza Motahhari, 10th Death Anniv. — A783

1989, May 2
2366 A783 20r multicolored .40 .30

Teachers' Day.

A784

1989, May 5
2367 A784 30r multicolored .75 .30

Universal Day of Jerusalem.

A785

1989, May 17 ***Perf. 13½x13***
2368 A785 20r multicolored .70 .30

World Telecommunications Day.

A786

Intl. Museum Day: Gurgan pottery, 6th cent.

1989, May 18 ***Perf. 13x13½***
2369 A786 20r Jar .50 .50
2370 A786 20r Bottle .50 .50
a. Pair, #2369-2370 1.25 1.10

Nomads' Day — A787

1989, June 4 ***Perf. 13***
2371 A787 20r multicolored .40 .25

World Crafts Day A788

No. 2372, Engraver. No. 2373, Copper vase. No. 2374, Copper plate, vert. No. 2375, Copper wall hanging, vert.

1989, July 5 ***Perf. 13x13½***
2372 A788 20r multicolored .40 .40
2373 A788 20r multicolored .40 .40
a. Pair, #2372-2373 1.10 1.00
2374 A788 20r multicolored .40 .40
2375 A788 20r multicolored .40 .40
a. Pair, #2374-2375 1.10 1.00

Ayatollah Khomeini (1900-89) A789

1989, July 6 ***Perf. 13***
2376 A789 20r multicolored .50 .30

Pasteur and Avicenna A790

1989, July 7
2377 A790 30r multicolored .70 .70
2378 A790 50r multicolored 1.00 1.00
a. Pair, #2377-2378 3.00 3.00

PHILEXFRANCE.

Asia-Pacific Telecommunity, 10th Anniv. — A791

1989, July 25
2379 A791 30r blk, org brn & bl .80 .40

Mehdi Araghi, 10th Death Anniv. — A792

1989, Aug. 30
2380 A792 20r brn org & org brn .40 .25

M.H. Shahryar, Poet — A793

1989, Sept. 17
2381 A793 20r multicolored .50 .25

Iran-Iraq War, 9th Anniv. — A794

20r, UN Security Council res. 598.

1989, Sept. 22
2382 A794 20r multi .60 .60

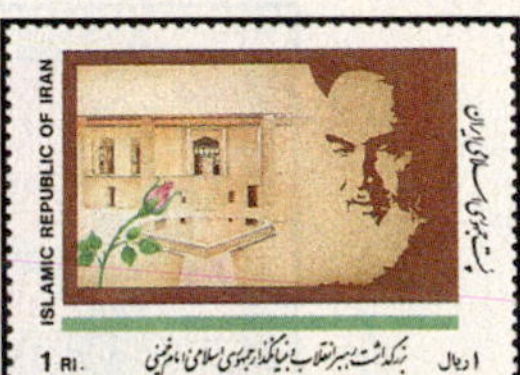

Ayatollah Khomeini — A795

Designs: 1r, Khomeini's birthplace, flower. 2r, Portrait as youth. 3r, Giving speech. 5r, Map, rifles, exile. 10r, Khomeini returns to Iran, Feb. 1, 1979. 20r, Khomeini seated before microphone. 30r, Khomeini with grandson.40r, Other mullahs. 50r, Khomeini gesturing with hands. 70r, On balcony before crowd. 100r, Slogan. 200r, Empty lectern. 500r, Mausoleum. 1000r, Sun rays.

1989-92 Litho. Unwmk. *Perf. 13½*
2382A A795 1r grn & multi .25 .25
2382B A795 2r grn & multi .25 .25
2383 A795 3r grn & multi .25 .25
2384 A795 5r brt vio & multi .25 .25
2385 A795 10r brt bl & multi .35 .25
2386 A795 20r blue & multi .30 .25
2387 A795 30r pink & multi .35 .25
2388 A795 40r red & multi .35 .30
2389 A795 50r gray & multi .40 .30
2390 A795 70r brt grn & multi .55 .35
2391 A795 100r ultra & multi .75 .45
2392 A795 200r red brn & multi 1.50 .75
2393 A795 500r blk & multi 3.50 1.75
2393A A795 1000r multi 7.50 3.50
Nos. 2382A-2393A (14) 16.55 9.15

Issued: 1r, 1/3/91; 3r, 3/16/90; 5r, 12/13; 10r, 10/22; 20r, 30r, 50r, 9/23/90; 40r, 2/9/90; 100, 200r, 9/26/90; 70r, 500r, 6/4/91; 2r, 1000r, 3/16/92.

World Post Day A796

Wmk. 381
1989, Oct. 9 Photo. *Perf. 13*
2394 A796 20r multicolored .85 .50

Mohammad's Birthday, Unity Week — A797

1989, Oct. 18
2395 A797 10r multicolored .80 .50

Takeover of US Embassy, 10th Anniv. — A798

1989, Nov. 4 ***Perf. 13½x13***
2396 A798 40r multicolored .40 .30

Bassij of the Oppressed (Militia), 10th Anniv. — A799

1989, Nov. 27 ***Perf. 13***
2397 A799 10r multicolored .40 .30

Scientists, Artists and Writers Type of 1988

No. 2398, Mehdi Elahi Ghomshei. No. 2399, Dr. Abdulazim Gharib. No. 2400, Seyyed Hossein Mirkhani. No. 2401, Ayatollah Seyyed Hossein Boroujerdi. No. 2402, Ayatollah Sheikh Abdulkarim Haeri.

1989, Dec. 18 ***Perf. 13x13½***
2398 A775 10r gold, red, blk .30 .30
2399 A775 10r gold, grn, blk .30 .30
2400 A775 10r gold, pink, blk .30 .30
a. Pair, #2399-2400 .80 .75
2401 A775 10r gold, bl grn, blk .30 .30
2402 A775 10r gold, buff, blk .30 .30
a. Pair, #2401-2402 .80 .75

Intl. Literacy Year — A800

Wmk. 381
1990, Jan. 1 Photo. *Perf. 13½*
2403 A800 20r multicolored .70 .40

Cultural Heritage A801

Designs: No. 2404, Drinking vessel, 1980. No. 2405, Footed vase, 1979.

1990, Jan. 21 *Perf. 13*

2404	A801 20r blk & deep org	.50	.30
2405	A801 20r blk & yel grn	.50	.30
a.	Pair, #2404-2405	1.25	1.00

New Identification Card System — A802

1990, Feb. 9

2406	A802 10r multicolored	.25	.25

Islamic Revolution, 11th Anniv. — A803

1990, Feb. 11

2407	A803 50r multicolored	1.00	.40

Intl. Koran Recitation Competition A804

1990, Feb. 23

2408	A804 10r blk, bl & grn	.70	.40

Invalids of Islamic Revolution — A805

1990, Mar. 2 *Perf. 13½x13*

2409	A805 10r multicolored	.70	.40

Arbor Day — A806

1990, Mar. 6 *Perf. 13*

2410	A806 20r multicolored	.40	.30

New Year Festival Type of 1987

Flowers: a, Coronilla varia. b, Astragalus cornu-caprae. c, Astragalus obtusifolius. d, Astragalus straussii.

1990, Mar. 11 *Perf. 13½x13*

2411	Block of 4	1.00	.80
a.-d.	A705 10r any single	.25	.25

Islamic Republic, 11th Anniv. — A807

1990, Apr. 1 *Perf. 13*

2412	A807 30r multicolored	.70	.60

World Health Day — A808

1990, Apr. 7

2413	A808 40r multicolored	.90	.50

A809

1990, June 4 Unwmk. *Perf. 11x10½*

2414	A809 50r multicolored	.70	.50

Ayatollah Khomeini, 1st death anniv.

Jerusalem Day — A810

1990, Dec. 15 Litho. *Perf. 10½*

2415	A810 100r multicolored	2.00	.60

World Crafts Day — A811

20r, Turkoman jewelry. 50r, Gilded steel bird.

1990, Oct. 20 *Perf. 13*

2416	A811 20r multicolored	.40	.40
2417	A811 50r multicolored	1.00	1.00
a.	Pair, #2416-2417	1.90	1.75

Intl. Day of the Child — A812

1990, Nov. 17 *Perf. 10½*

2418	A812 20r multicolored	.60	.30

Aid to Earthquake Victims — A813

1990, Nov. 19 *Perf. 13x13½*

2419	A813 100r multicolored	.45	.30

Return and Tribute to Former Prisoners of Iran-Iraq War — A814

1990, Nov. 21 *Perf. 13*

2420	A814 250r multicolored	3.00	.50

Ferdowsi Intl. Congress — A815

No. 2421, Portrait. No. 2422, Statue. No. 2423, Monument. No. 2424, Slogan, diamond cartouche. No. 2425, Rectangular slogan. No. 2426, Slogan, diff. No. 2427, Two riders embracing. No. 2428, Archer, birds. No. 2429, Six men. No. 2430, White elephant. No. 2431, Warrior, genie, horse. No. 2432, Hunting scene. No. 2433, Riding through fire. No. 2434, Four slogan tablets. No. 2435, Man with feet shackled. No. 2436, Palace scene.

1990, Dec. 22 Litho. *Imperf.*
Size: 60x75mm

2421	A815 100r multi	3.50	4.00
2422	A815 100r multi	3.50	4.00
2423	A815 100r multi	3.50	4.00
2424	A815 100r multi	3.50	4.00
2425	A815 100r multi	3.50	4.00
2426	A815 100r multi	3.50	4.00
2427	A815 200r multi	5.50	6.00
2428	A815 200r multi	5.50	6.00
2429	A815 200r multi	5.50	6.00
2430	A815 200r multi	5.50	6.00
2431	A815 200r multi	5.50	6.00
2432	A815 200r multi	5.50	6.00
2433	A815 200r multi	5.50	6.00
2434	A815 200r multi	5.50	6.00
2435	A815 200r multi	5.50	6.00
2436	A815 200r multi	5.50	6.00
	Nos. 2421-2436 (16)	76.00	84.00

Conference on epic poem "Book of Kings" by Ferdowsi.

In 1991 some imperf between blocks of 4 were released. Value, set $250.

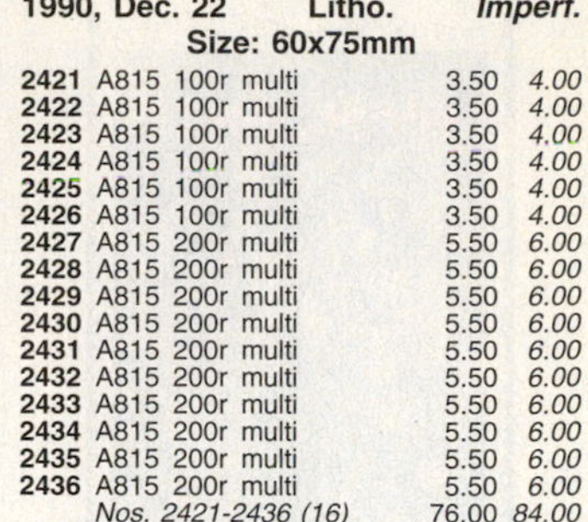

"Victory Over Iraq" — A816

1991, Feb. 25 *Perf. 13*

2437	A816 100r multicolored	1.25	.50

Intl. Museum Day — A817

Designs: No. 2438, Gold jug with Kufric inscription, 10th cent. A.D. No. 2439, Silver-inlaid brass basin, 14th cent. A.D.

1991, Feb. 25

2438	A817 50r multicolored	1.10	.50
2439	A817 50r multicolored	1.10	.50
a.	Pair, #2438-2439	2.25	1.50

A818

1991, Mar. 12 *Perf. 10½*

2440	A818 50r multicolored	1.00	.50

World Telecommunications Day. No. 2440 exists imperf. Value, pair $25.

Opening of Postal Museum A819

1991, Feb. 25 *Perf. 13*

2441	A819 200r org brn & blk	3.00	2.00

Islamic Revolution, 12th Anniv. — A820

1991, Feb. 11 **Photo.** ***Perf. 13***
2442 A820 100r multicolored 2.50 1.00

New Year Festival Type of 1987

Designs: No. 2443a, Iris spuria. b, Iris lycotis. c, Iris demawendica. d, Iris meda.

1991, Mar. 11 ***Perf. 13½x13***
2443 A705 20r Block of 4, #a.-d. 2.00 1.50

Saleh Hosseini, 10th Death Anniv. — A821

1991, Mar. 19 ***Perf. 13½x13***
2444 A821 30r red & black .90 .50

Mab'as Festival A822

1991, Mar. 19 ***Perf. 13x13½***
2445 A822 100r multicolored 1.50 .50

Universal Day of the Oppressed A823

1991, Mar. 25 ***Perf. 13***
2446 A823 50r multicolored 1.00 .50

Savior Mahdi's Birthday.

Revolutionaries, 25th Death Anniv. — A824

1990, June 16
2447 A824 50r maroon & red org .80 .50

Dated 1990.

Islamic Republic, 12th Anniv. — A825

Unwmk.
1991, Apr. 1 **Photo.** ***Perf. 13***
2448 A825 20r blk, slate, grn & red .60 .50

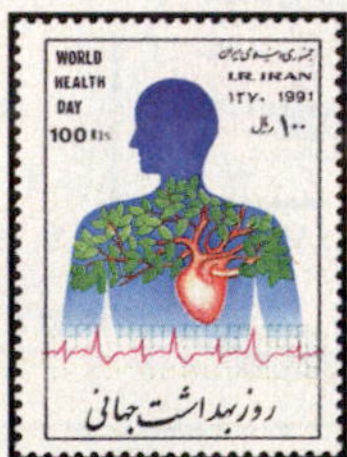

World Health Day — A826

1991, Apr. 7 ***Perf. 13½x13***
2449 A826 100r multicolored 1.50 .50

Day of Jerusalem A827

1991, Apr. 12 ***Perf. 13***
2450 A827 100r bl, blk & brn 1.60 .75

A828

1991, Apr. 12 **Litho.** ***Perf. 10½***
2451 A828 50r multicolored .80 .50

Women's Day. Birth anniv. of Mohammad's daughter, Fatima.

A829

Perf. 13½x13
1991, Apr. 28 **Photo.** **Unwmk.**
2452 A829 200r bl grn & blk 4.00 .50

Ayatollah Borujerdi, 30th death anniv.

Teachers' Day — A830

1991, May 2 ***Perf. 13x13½***
2453 A830 50r multicolored 1.10 .50

Decade for Natural Disaster Reduction A831

1991, May 11 **Litho.** ***Perf. 10½***
2454 A831 100r multicolored 1.75 .50

World Telecommunications Day — A832

Perf. 13½x13
1991, May 17 **Photo.** **Unwmk.**
2455 A832 100r multicolored 1.50 .50

Intl. Museum Day — A833

Ewers, Kashan, 13th cent.: 20r, With spout. 40r, Baluster.

1991, May 18 ***Perf. 13***
2456 A833 20r multicolored .50 .50
2457 A833 40r multicolored 1.00 .50
a. Pair, #2456-2457 2.00 1.10

Flags — A834

1991, May 24 ***Perf. 13x13½***
2458 A834 30r multicolored .85 .50

Liberation of Khorramshahr, 7th anniv.

Abol-Hassan Ali-ebne-Mosa Reza, Birth Anniv. — A835

Views of shrine, Meshed.

1991, May 26 ***Perf. 13***
2459 10r Mausoleum .25 .25
2460 30r Gravestone .75 .50
a. A835 Pair, #2459-2460 1.25 1.10

First Intl. Conf. on Seismology and Earthquake Engineering A836

1991, May 27 ***Perf. 13½x13***
2461 A836 100r multicolored 2.00 .50

World Child Day — A837

1991, June 1 **Photo.** ***Perf. 13½***
2462 A837 50r multicolored 1.00 .50

Holy Shrine at Karbola, Iraq Destroyed by Invasion — A838

Unwmk.
1991, June 3 **Photo.** ***Perf. 13***
2463 A838 70r multicolored 1.10 .50

Ayatollah Khomeini, 2nd Death Anniv. — A839

1991, June 4
2464 A839 100r multicolored 2.50 .75

World Handicrafts Day — A840

Designs: No. 2465, Engraved brass wares. No. 2466, Gilded samovar set.

1991, June 10 ***Perf. 13½x13***

2465 A840 40r multicolored	1.00	.50
2466 A840 40r multicolored	1.00	.50
a. Pair #2465-2466	2.50	1.25

Intl. Congress on Poet Nezami — A841

1991, June 22 ***Perf. 13***

2467 A841 50r multicolored 1.10 .50

A842

1991, July 15 **Photo.** ***Perf. 13***

2468 A842 50r multicolored .80 .50

Ali Ibn Abi Talib, 1330th death anniv.

Blood Transfusion Week — A843

Unwmk.

1991, July 29 **Photo.** ***Perf. 13***

2469 A843 50r multicolored 1.00 .50

Return of Prisoners of War, First Anniv. — A844

1991, Aug. 27 ***Perf. 13x13½***

2470 A844 100r multicolored 1.75 .50

Ayatollah Marashi, Death Anniv. — A845

1991, Aug. 29 ***Perf. 13½x13***

2471 A845 30r multicolored 1.25 .50

Ayatollah-ol-Ozma Seyyed Abdol-Hossein Lary, Revolutionary — A846

Design includes 1909 stamp issued by Lary.

1991, Sept. 9 ***Perf. 13x13½***

2472 A846 30r multicolored .70 .50

Start of Iran-Iraq War, 11th Anniv. — A847

1991, Sept. 22 ***Perf. 13½x13***

2473 A847 20r multicolored .50 .50

Mosque, Kaaba, Unity Week — A848

1991, Sept. 22 ***Perf. 13***

2474 A848 30r multicolored .70 .50

World Tourism Day A849

1991, Sept. 27 **Photo.** ***Perf. 13½***

2475 A849 200r multicolored 4.50 1.00

Dr. Mohammad Gharib, Pediatrician A849a

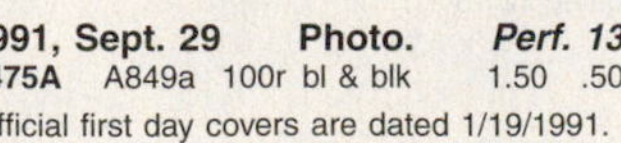

1991, Sept. 29 **Photo.** ***Perf. 13***

2475A A849a 100r bl & blk 1.50 .50

Official first day covers are dated 1/19/1991.

World Post Day A850

Unwmk.

1991, Oct. 9 **Photo.** ***Perf. 13***

2476 A850 70r #2071 on cover 1.00 .50

Khaju-ye Kermani Intl. Congress — A851

1991, Oct. 15

2477 A851 30r multicolored 1.00 .50

World Food Day — A852

1991, Oct. 16

2478 A852 80r multicolored .90 .50

A853

1991, Oct. 19 ***Perf. 13½x13***

2479 A853 40r bl vio & gold .70 .50

Intl. Conference Supporting Palestinians.

Illustrators of Children's Books, 1st Asian Biennial A854

1991, Oct. 25 ***Perf. 13***

2480 A854 100r Hoopoe 1.75 .50

"Children" misspelled.

World Standards Day — A855

1991, Oct. 14 ***Perf. 13½***

2481 A855 100r multicolored 2.00 .50

1st Seminar on Adolescent and Children's Literature A856

1991, Nov. 3 ***Perf. 13***

2482 A856 20r multicolored .70 .50

Roshid Intl. Educational Film Festival A857

1991, Nov. 6

2483 A857 50r multicolored 1.20 .75

7th Ministerial Meeting of the Group of 77 — A858

1991, Nov. 16

2484 A858 30r vio & bl grn .70 .50

Bassij of the Oppressed (Militia), 12th Anniv. — A859

1991, Nov. 25

2485 A859 30r multicolored .65 .50

Ayatollah Aref Hosseini — A860

1991, Dec. 18 ***Perf. 13½***

2486 A860 50r multicolored 1.10 .50

Sadek Ghanji A861

1991, Dec. 20

2487 A861 50r multicolored 1.10 .50

Agricultural Training and Extension Week — A862

1991, Dec. 22 *Perf. 13*
2488 A862 70r multicolored 1.25 .50

World Telecommunications Day — A863

No. 2489: a, 20r, Telegraph key. b, 20r, Phone lines. c, 20r, Early telephones. d, 40r, Satellite dishes. e, 40r, Telecommunications satellite.

1992, May 17 Photo. *Perf. 13*
2489 A863 Strip of 5, #a.-e. 3.50 1.50

New Year — A863a

Flora of Iran: Nos. 2490a, 2490d, 20r. Nos. 2490b, 2490c, 40r.

1992, Apr. 18 *Perf. 13½x13*
2490 A863a Block of 4, #a.-d. 3.00 1.50

Mosque of Jerusalem A864

1992, Mar. 27 *Perf. 13x13½*
2491 A864 200r multicolored 2.50 1.25

Day of Jerusalem and honoring A. Mousavi, the Shiva leader of Lebanon, with Sheikh Ragheb Harb in background.

Reunification of Yemen — A865

1992, May 22 *Perf. 13½x13*
2492 A865 50r multicolored .90 .50

World Child Day A866

1992, June 1 *Perf. 13x13½*
2493 A866 50r multicolored .90 .50

Intl. Conference of Surveying and Mapping A867

1992, May 25 *Perf. 13*
2494 A867 40r multicolored .70 .50

21st FAO Regional Conference A868

1992, May 17 *Perf. 13x13½*
2495 A868 40r blk, bl & grn .50 .35

South and West Asia Postal Union — A869

Mosques: No. 2496, Imam's Mosque, Isfahan. No. 2497, Lahore Mosque, Pakistan. No. 2498, St. Sophia Mosque, Turkey.

1992, Mar. 27 *Perf. 13½x13*
2496 A869 50r multicolored .90 .50
2497 A869 50r multicolored .90 .50
2498 A869 50r multicolored .90 .50

Economic Cooperation Organization Summit — A870

Design: 20r, Flags, emblem, vert.

1992 *Perf. 13½x13, 13x13½*
2499 A870 20r multicolored .75 .50
2500 A870 200r multicolored 4.50 1.00

Issued: 20r, Apr. 25; 200r, Feb. 17.

Natural Resources A871

1992, Apr. 15 Litho. *Perf. 13½x13*
2501 A871 100r multicolored 2.00 1.00

Islamic Republic, 13th Anniv. — A872

1992, Apr. 1 *Perf. 13½x13*
2502 A872 50r multicolored .70 .50

Establishment of Postal Airline — A873

1992, Apr. 1 *Perf. 13x13½*
2503 A873 60r multicolored 1.25 .50

Islamic Revolution, 13th Anniv. — A874

Unwmk.

1992, Feb. 11 Photo. *Perf. 13*
2504 30r multicolored 1.00 .50
2505 50r multicolored 1.25 .50
a. A874 Pair, #2504-2505 2.50 1.25

A875

1992, Mar. 23 Photo. *Perf. 13½x13*
2506 A875 100r multicolored 1.10 .50

World Meteorological Day.

A876

Famous Men: No. 2507, Mohammad Bagher Madjlessi. No. 2508, Hadi Sabzevari, wearing turban. No. 2509, Omman Samani, wearing fez. No. 2510, Chapter of praise from Koran (Arabic script), by Ostad Mir Emad.

1991-92 *Perf. 13x13½*
2507 A876 50r shown .70 .50
2508 A876 50r brown & multi .70 .50
2509 A876 50r multicolored .70 .50
2510 A876 50r multicolored .70 .50

Issued: No. 2510, 12/18/91; others, 5/17/92. First day covers of Nos. 2507-2509 may be dated 12/18/91.

Intl. Museum Day A877

No. 2511, Gray ceramic ware, 1st millennium B.C. No. 2512, Painted ceramic bowl.

1992, May 18
2511 A877 40r multicolored .90 .50
2512 A877 40r multicolored .90 .50

Ayatollah Khomeini, 3rd Anniv. of Death — A878

1992, June 4 *Perf. 13*
2513 A878 100r multicolored 1.40 .50

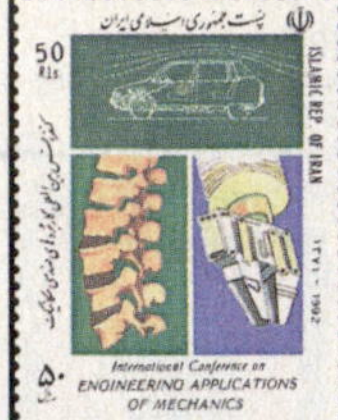
Intl. Conference on Engineering Applications of Mechanics A879

1992, June 9 *Perf. 13½x13*
2514 A879 50r multicolored .80 .50

A880

1992, June 13 *Perf. 13x13½*
2515 A880 20r multicolored .60 .40

In memory of clergy-lady Amini.

Sixth Conference of Nonaligned News Agencies — A881

1992, June 15
2516 A881 100r multicolored 1.10 .50

A882

1992, June 23 *Perf. 13x13½*
2517 A882 100r grn, blk & gold 1.25 .50

Meeting of, Ministers of Industry and Technology.

A883

1992, June 26 *Perf. 13½x13*
2518 A883 100r multicolored 1.75 .60

World Anti-narcotics Day.

Holy Ka'aba — A884

Prayer Calligraphy A885

Designs: No. 2520, Ayatollah Khomeini in prayer. No. 2521, Khomeini holding prayer beads. No. 2522, Khomeini unwrapping turban. Nos. 2523-2524, Islamic prayers.

1992 **Photo.** *Perf. 13½x13*
2519 A884 50r multicolored .70 .50
2520 A884 50r multicolored .70 .50
2521 A884 50r multicolored .70 .50
2522 A884 50r multicolored .70 .50

Perf. 13x13½
2523 A885 50r dk grn & lt grn .70 .50
2524 A885 50r dk blue & lt blue .70 .50

Issue dates: July 27, Aug. 24.

Iran Shipping Line, 25th Anniv. A886

1992, Aug. 24 **Photo.** *Perf. 13x13½*
2525 A886 200r multicolored 2.00 1.00

A887

1992, Sept. 15 *Perf. 13½x13*
2526 A887 40r multicolored .60 .45

Mohammad's Birthday, Unity Week.

A888

Iranian Defense Forces: 20r, Soldiers on patrol. 40r, Soldier seated at water's edge, horiz.

Perf. 13½x13, 13x13½
1992, Sept. 22
2527 A888 20r multicolored .50 .40
2528 A888 40r multicolored .50 .40

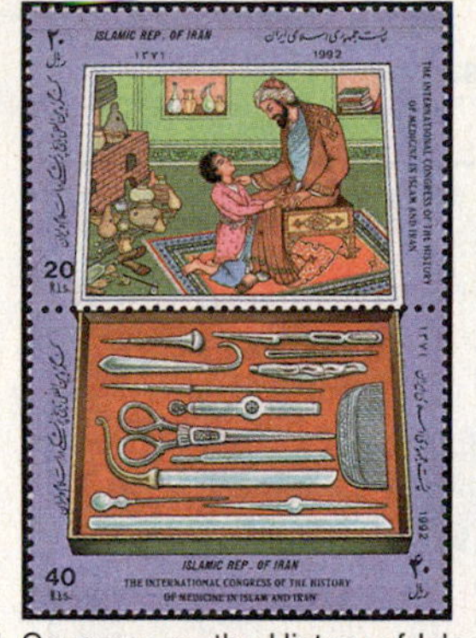
Intl. Congress on the History of Islamic Medicine — A889

20r, Avicenna, child. 40r, Physician's instruments.

1992, Sept. 23 **Litho.** *Perf. 13*
2529 20r multi .60 .50
2530 40r multi .90 .50
a. A889 Pair, #2529-2530 1.75 1.10

Mobarake Steel Plant — A890

1992, Sept. 26 **Photo.** *Perf. 13x13½*
2531 20r Inside plant .40 .50
2532 70r Outside plant .70 .50
a. A890 Pair, #2531-2532 1.40 1.25

Intl. Tourism Day A891

1992, Sept. 27 *Perf. 13x13½*
2533 A891 20r Mazandaran .45 .35
2534 A891 20r Isfahan .45 .35
2535 A891 30r Bushehr (Bushire) .65 .50
2536 A891 30r Hormozgan .65 .50

Intl. Trade Fair — A892

1992, Oct. 2 *Perf. 13½x13*
2537 A892 200r multicolored 2.25 1.00

World Post Day A893

1992, Oct. 9 *Perf. 13x13½*
2538 A893 30r Early post office .80 .50

World Food Day A894

1992, Oct. 16 *Perf. 13*
2539 A894 100r blk, bl & yel 2.50 1.00

Intl. Youth Photo Festival — A895

1992, Nov. 1 **Photo.** *Perf. 13½x13*
2540 A895 40r multicolored 1.00 .50

A896

a, Seizure of US embassy, 12th anniv. b, Student's day (Eagles flying over dead doves). c, Khomeini's exile (Eagles, dove).

1992, Nov. 4 *Perf. 13*
2541 A896 100r Strip of 3, #a.-c. 4.50 1.50

Fighting in Bosnia and Herzegovina A897

1992, Nov. 4 *Perf. 13½x13*
2542 A897 40r multicolored .90 .50

Islamic Development Bank — A898

1992, Nov. 10 **Litho.** *Perf. 13½x13*
2543 A898 20r multicolored .50 .40

Iran-Azerbaijan Telecommunications — A899

1992, Nov. 21 **Photo.** *Perf. 13x13½*
2544 A899 40r multicolored .90 .50

Azad (Open) University, 10th Anniv. — A900

1992, Nov. 23 *Perf. 13½x13*
2545 A900 200r dark grn & emer 1.75 .50

Week of the Basij (Militia) A901

1992, Nov. 26 *Perf. 13x13½*
2546 A901 40r multicolored .60 .50

Seyed Mohammad Hosseyn Shahrian, Poet — A902

1992, Dec. 1
2547 A902 80r multicolored .70 .50

Women's Day — A903

1992, Dec. 15
2548 A903 70r multicolored .70 .50

Birth anniv. of Fatima.

Famous Iranians — A904

Scientists and writers: No. 2551a, Ayatollah Mirza Abolhassan Shar'rani (in turban). b, Prof. Mahmoud Hessabi, U=o formula. c, Mohiyt Tabatabaiy, books on shelves. d, Mehrdad Avesta, calligraphy.

1992, Dec. 18
2549 A904 20r Block of 4, #a.-d. 2.00 1.00

Natl. Iranian Oil Drilling Co. A905

No. 2551, Ocean drilling platform.

1992, Dec. 22

2550 A905 100r shown 1.50 .50
2551 A905 100r multi 1.50 .50

A906

1992, Dec. 28 ***Perf. 13½x13***

2552 A906 80r multicolored .70 .50

Promotion of literacy.

A907

20r, Narcissus. 30r, Iris. 35r, Tulips. 40r, Tuberose. 50r, White jasmine. 60r, Guelder rose. 70r, Pansies. 75r, Snapdragons. 100r, Lily. 120r, Petunia. 150r, Hyacinth. 200r, Damascus rose. 500r, Morning glory. 1000r, Corn rose.

1993-95 **Photo.** ***Perf. 13½x13***

2553 A907 20r multi
2554 A907 30r multi
2555 A907 35r multi
2556 A907 40r multi
2557 A907 50r multi
2558 A907 60r multi
2559 A907 70r multi
2560 A907 75r multi
2561 A907 100r multi
2562 A907 120r multi
2563 A907 150r multi
2564 A907 200r multi
2565 A907 500r multi
2566 A907 1000r multi
Nos. 2553-2566 (14) 25.00 15.00

The 60r exists with inverted flowers. Value $9.

Issued: 20r, 1/12/93; 40r, 2/22/93; 100r, 4/21/93; 200r, 4/29/93; 500r, 6/27/93; 1000r, 7/19/93; 30r, 60r, 10/93; 50r, 8/93; 120r, 5/94; 35r, 75r, 3/95; 70r, 150r, 5/95.

For surcharges see Nos. 2759-2760, 2792-2794.

Prophethood of Mohammad — A908

1993, Jan. 21 **Photo.** ***Perf. 13x13½***

2567 A908 200r multicolored 1.75 .50

Mab'as Festival.

Day of the Disabled — A909

Designs: 40r, Player wearing medal, team members with hands raised.

1993, Jan. 27

2568 20r multicolored .50 .50
2569 40r multicolored .50 .50
a. A909 Pair, #2568-2569 1.25 1.10

Cultural Heritage Preservation A910

1993, Jan. 31 ***Perf. 13½x13***

2570 A910 40r Mosque, exterior 1.00 .50
2571 A910 40r Mosque, interior 1.00 .50
a. Pair, #2570-2571 2.50 1.75

Planning Day — A911

1993, Jan. 31 ***Perf. 13***

2572 A911 100r multicolored 2.00 .50

Universal Day of the Oppressed A912

1993, Feb. 8 **Litho.** ***Perf. 13***

2573 A912 60r multicolored .80 .50

Savior Mahdi's Birthday.

Islamic Revolution, 14th Anniv. — A913

a, Iranian flag. b, Flag, soldiers. c, Soldiers, shellbursts. d, Oil derricks, storage tanks, people harvesting. e, Crowd, car, Ayatollah Khomeini.

1993, Feb. 11 **Photo.** ***Perf. 13x13½***

2574 A913 20r Strip of 5, #a.-e. 5.00 3.00

A914

1st Islamic Women's Games: a, Volleyball. b, Basketball. c, Medal. d, Swimming. e, Running.

1993, Feb. 13 ***Perf. 13***

2575 A914 40r Strip of 5, #a.-e. 6.00 3.00

Morteza Ansari — A915

1993, Feb. 16 ***Perf. 13½***

2576 A915 40r multicolored .80 .50

Arbor Day A916

1993, Mar. 6

2577 A916 70r multicolored 1.10 .50

New Year A917

a, 20r, Butterfly, tulip. b, 20r, Butterfly, lily. c, 40r, Butterfly, flowers. d, 40r, Butterfly, 3 roses.

1993, Mar. 11 ***Perf. 13½x13***

2578 A917 Block of 4, #a.-d. 5.00 2.00

World Jerusalem Day — A918

1993, Mar. 14 ***Perf. 13½x13***

2579 A918 20r multicolored .90 .50

End of Ramadan A919

1993, Mar. 26 ***Perf. 13½x13***

2580 A919 100r multicolored 3.00 1.00

Islamic Republic, 14th Anniv. A920

40r, National anthem.

1993, Apr. 1 ***Perf. 13x13½***

2581 A920 40r multicolored .90 .50

Intl. Congress on the Millennium of Sheik Mofeed — A921

1993, Apr. 17 ***Perf. 13***

2582 A921 80r multicolored 1.10 .50

A922

1993, Apr. 21 ***Perf. 13½x13***

2583 A922 100r multicolored 1.10 .50

13th Conference of Asian and Pacific Labor Ministers.

A924

1993, May 17 ***Perf. 13½x13***

2585 A924 50r multicolored 1.20 .50

Intl. Congress for Advancement of Science and Technology in Islamic World.

Intl. Museum Day — A925

1993, May 1

2586 A925 40r multicolored 1.00 .50

Intl. Child Day — A928

1993, June 1 **Photo.** ***Perf. 13½x13***

2589 A928 50r multicolored 1.00 .50

Ayatollah Khomeini, 4th Death Anniv. — A929

1993, June 4 ***Perf. 13***

2590 A929 20r multicolored .70 .50

World Crafts Day A930

1993, June 10 ***Perf. 13½x13***

2591 A930 70r multicolored 1.50 .60

World Population Day — A931

1993, July 11 ***Perf. 13***

2592 A931 30r multicolored .90 .50

1st Cultural-Athletic Olympiad of Iran University Students — A932

Various sports.

1993, July 22 ***Perf. 13x13½***

Background Colors

2593 A932 20r blue 1.00 .35
2594 A932 40r henna brown 2.50 .75
2595 A932 40r ocher 2.50 .75

Intl. Festival of Films for Children and Young Adults, Isfahan — A935

1993, Sept. 11 **Photo.** ***Perf. 13***

2598 A935 60r multicolored 1.25 .50

World Post Day — A937

1993, Oct. 9 **Photo.** ***Perf. 13***

2600 A937 60r multicolored 1.25 .50

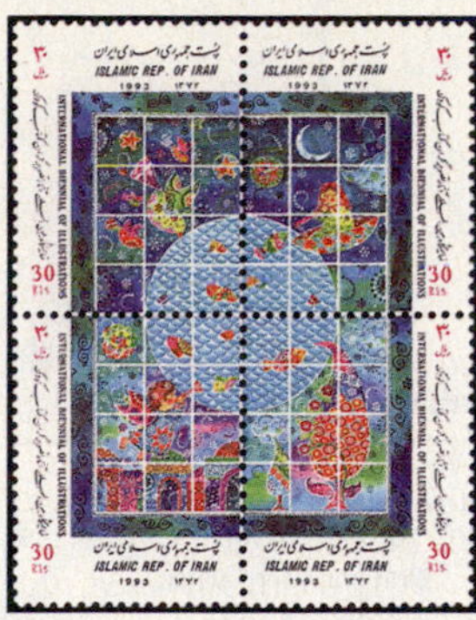

A939

World of water with fish and: a, Birds. b, Girl. c, Angel with trumpet. d, Trees.

1993, Nov. 5 **Photo.** ***Perf. 13½x13***

2602 A939 30r Block of 4, #a.-d. 3.50 2.00

Illustrators of Children's Books, Intl. Biennial.

A940

1993, Nov. 16 **Photo.** ***Perf. 13***

2603 A940 30r multicolored .80 .50

Khaje Nassireddin Tussy, scientist and astronomer.

Week of the Bassij (Militia) A941

Designs: No. 2604, Woman tying bandana around militiman's head. No. 2605, Militiaman facing line of tanks.

1993, Dec. 1 ***Perf. 13x13½***

2604 A941 50r multicolored 1.00 .50
2605 A941 50r multicolored 1.00 .50

Death of Grand Ayatollah Mohammad Reza Golpaigani A942

1993, Dec. 20 ***Perf. 13***

2606 A942 300r multicolored 4.00 2.00

Support for Bosnia and Herzegovina A943

No. 2607, Children playing hopscotch. No. 2608, Soldier, minaret. No. 2609, Woman, mosque.

1993, Dec. 27

2607 A943 40r multicolored 1.00 .50
2608 A943 40r multicolored 1.00 .50
2609 A943 40r multicolored 1.00 .50
a. Strip of 3, #2607-2609 4.00 2.00

Day of Invalids — A944

1994, Jan. 18

2610 A944 80r multicolored .90 .50

Agriculture Week — A945

1994, Jan. 23

2611 A945 60r multicolored .80 .50

Conf. on Islamic Law — A946

1994, Feb. 20

2612 A946 60r multicolored 1.00 .50

Islamic Revolution, 15th Anniv. — A947

Designs: a, Town, farm, telephone lines. b, Flag, Ayatollah Khomeini, revolutionaries. c, Fisherman, bridge. d, Women working.

1994, Feb. 11

2613 A947 40r Block of 4, #a.-d. 3.50 2.25

Youth Welfare A948

1994, Mar. 1

2614 A948 30r multicolored .90 .50

A949

1994, Mar. 28 **Photo.** ***Perf. 13½x13***

2615 A949 30r multicolored .90 .50

25th Iranian Mathematics Conference, Shareef Industrial University.

A950

1994, Mar. 11 ***Perf. 13***

2616 A950 50r multicolored .90 .50

World Jerusalem Day.

New Year — A951

No. 2617, Partridges, horiz. No. 2618, Heron. No. 2619, Bustard. No. 2620, Pheasants, horiz.

1994, Mar. 16 ***Perf. 13x13½, 13½x13***

2617 A951 40r multi 3.50 1.25
2618 A951 40r multi 3.50 1.25
2619 A951 40r multi 3.50 1.25
2620 A951 40r multi 3.50 1.25

Islamic Republic, 15th Anniv. — A952

1994, Apr. 1 **Photo.** ***Perf. 13***

2621 A952 40r multicolored .90 .50

A953

1994, Apr. 7

2622 A953 100r multicolored 1.50 .50

Intl. congress of Dentist's Assoc. and World Health Day.

Re-els Ali Delvary, 80th Anniv. of Death A954

1994, Apr. 9 ***Perf. 13x13½***
2623 A954 50r multicolored 1.00 .50

Intl. Year of the Family — A955

1994, May 10 Photo. ***Perf. 13½x13***
2624 A955 50r multicolored .75 .50

World Telecommunications Day — A956

1994, May 17 ***Perf. 13x13½***
2625 A956 50r multicolored 6.50 2.00

World Museum Day — A957

1994, May 18 ***Perf. 13***
2626 A957 40r Marlik gold cup .90 .50

A958

Cultural Preservation: 40r, Enameled pot with Kufic inscription, 13th cent.

1994, May 21
2627 A958 40r multicolored .80 .25

Ayatollah Khomeini, 5th Death Anniv. — A959

1994, June 4
2628 A959 30r multicolored .50 .25

Ayatollah Motahari, 15th Anniv. of Death — A961

1994, June 10
2630 A961 30r multicolored .60 .25

World Crafts Day — A962

1994, June 10 Photo. ***Perf. 13***
2631 A962 60r Weaver 2.50 1.00
2632 A962 60r Glass pitcher 2.50 1.00

Islamic University Students' Solidarity Games — A963

1994, July 18
2633 A963 60r multicolored .90 .40

Mohammad's Birthday, Unity Week — A964

1994, Aug. 26
2634 A964 30r multicolored .80 .40

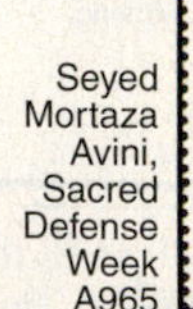

Seyed Mortaza Avini, Sacred Defense Week A965

1994, Sept. 22 ***Perf. 13x13½***
2635 A965 70r multicolored .80 .50

World Post Day A966

1994, Oct. 9
2636 A966 50r multicolored .75 .50

Women's Day — A967

1994, Nov. 24 ***Perf. 13***
2637 A967 70r multicolored .90 .50

Birth anniv. of Fatima.

Week of the Bassij (Militia) — A968

1994, Nov. 26
2638 A968 30r multicolored .45 .25

Book Week — A969

1994, Dec. 10
2639 A969 40r multicolored .60 .50

Support for Moslems of Bosnia & Herzegovina A970

No. 2640, Moslem family. No. 2641, Map, arms, homes.

1994, Dec. 27
2640 A970 80r multicolored 1.25 .50
2641 A970 80r multicolored 1.25 .50

Grand Ayatollah Araky — A971

1995, Jan. 5
2642 A971 100r multicolored 1.25 .50

Universal Day of the Oppressed A972

1995, Jan. 17
2643 A972 50r multicolored .75 .50

Savior Mahdi's birthday.

Major General Mehdi Zin-el-Din A973

Major General Mehdi Bakeri — A974

Major General Hasan Bagheri A975

Martyred commanders: No. 2647, Major General Hosein Kherazi.

1995, Feb. 2
2644 A973 50r multicolored .55 .25
2645 A974 50r multicolored .55 .25
2646 A975 50r multicolored .55 .25
2647 A975 50r multi, diff. .55 .25

A976

1995, Feb. 11
2648 A976 100r multicolored 1.50 .50

Islamic Revolution, 16th anniv.

World Jerusalem Day — A977

1995, Feb. 24
2649 A977 100r multicolored 2.25 .75

Arbor Day — A978

1995, Mar. 6
2650 A978 50r multicolored .70

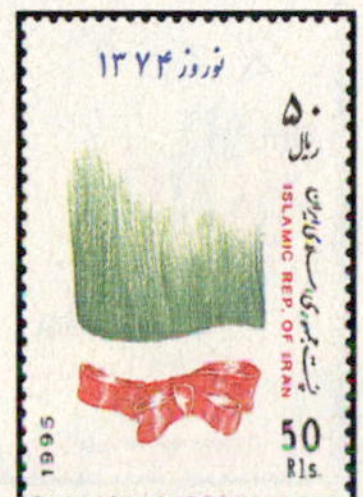
New Year — A979

1995, Mar. 16 ***Perf. 13½x13***
2651 A979 50r shown 1.50 .55
2652 A979 50r Pansies 1.50 .55
2653 A979 50r Hyacinths 1.50 .55
2654 A979 50r Tulips, fish bowl 1.50 .55

Opening of Bafq-Bandar Abbas Railway Line — A980

1995, Mar. 17
2655 A980 100r multicolored 1.75 1.00

Islamic Republic of Iran, 16th Anniv. — A981

1995, Apr. 1 **Photo.** ***Perf. 13***
2656 A981 100r multicolored 1.10 .50

Second Press Fesitval A982

1995, Apr. 26
2657 A982 100r multicolored .90 .50

Ayatollah Ahmad Khomeini A983

1995, Apr. 27
2658 A983 50r multicolored .70 .50

Day of Invalids — A984

1995, June 1
2659 A984 80r Arabic script .80 .50

Ayatollah Ali Vaziri — A985

1995, May 4
2660 A985 100r multicolored .80 .50

World Telecommunications Day — A986

1995, May 17
2661 A986 100r multicolored 1.10 .50

Ayatollah Khomeini, 6th Death Anniv. — A987

1995, June 4
2662 A987 100r multicolored 1.25 .50

UN, 50th Anniv. — A988

a, Infant, hand holding vaccination (WHO). b, Child laughing (UNICEF). c, Shafts of grain, world map (FAO). d, Woman reading (UNESCO).

1995, June 10 ***Perf. 13x13½***
2663 A988 100r Block of 4, #a.-d. 3.50 2.25

Iqbal Ashtiany, Writer — A989

1995, Aug. 14 ***Perf. 13***
2664 A989 100r multicolored 1.10 .50

Government Week — A990

1995, Aug. 28 ***Perf. 13x13½***
2665 A990 100r Workers, dam 1.10 .50

Construction of the Karun dam and hydo-electric power station.

Sacred Defense Week — A991

1995, Sept. 22 ***Perf. 13***
2666 A991 100r Gun, Koran 1.25 .50

World Post Day — A992

100r, Globe, envelopes.

1995, Oct. 9 ***Perf. 13½x13***
2667 A992 100r multicolored 1.25 .50

M.J. Tondgooyan, Oil Minister A993

1995, Dec. 20 ***Perf. 13***
2668 A993 100r multicolored 1.10 .50

Prophet Mohammad A994

100r, Arabic calligraphy.

1995, Dec. 20
2669 A994 100r multicolored 1.25 .50

Fathi Shaghaghi, Islamic Jihad Secretary General A995

1995, Dec. 31
2670 A995 100r multicolored 1.25 .50

Islamic Revolution, 17th Anniv. — A996

1996, Feb. 11
2671 A996 100r multicolored 1.40 .60

World Jerusalem Day — A997

100r, Dome of the Rock.

1996, Feb. 17
2672 A997 100r multicolored 1.25 .60

Birds A998

1996, Mar. 15
2673 A998 100r shown 2.00 .75
2674 A998 100r Crested head 2.00 .75
2675 A998 100r blue & multi 2.00 .75
2676 A998 100r yel, grn & multi 2.00 .75

New year.

Air Force Maj. Gen. Abbas Babai — A999

Major Ali Akbar Shiroody A1000

Maj. Gen. Mahammed Ebrahim Hemmat A1001

Maj. Gen. Mohammad Broujerdi A1002

1996, Mar. 18
2677 A999 100r multicolored 2.25 1.00
2678 A1000 100r multicolored 2.25 1.00
2679 A1001 100r multicolored 2.25 1.00
2680 A1002 100r multicolored 2.25 1.00

See Nos. 2700-2707 for similar stamps dated 1997.

Islamic Republic of Iran, 17th Anniv. — A1003

1996, Mar. 31 **Photo.** ***Perf. 13***
2681 A1003 200r multicolored 2.25 1.00

Intl. Book Fair, Tehran A1004

1996, May 8
2682 A1004 85r multicolored 1.25 .50

For surcharge see No. 2759A.

Mashhad-Sarakhs-Tajan Intl. Railway — A1005

1996, May 13
2683 A1005 200r multicolored 2.00 1.00

Turkmenistan intl. railway link,

Prisoners of War — A1006

1996, May 29
2684 A1006 200r multicolored 2.25 1.00

Captives and Missing Day.

Ayatollah Khomeini, 7th Death Anniv. — A1007

1996, June 3
2685 A1007 200r multicolored 2.00 1.00

World Crafts Day — A1008

1996, June 24 **Photo.** ***Perf. 13***
2686 A1008 200r multicolored 2.00 1.00

Third PTT Ministerial Conference, Tehran A1009

1996, July 8
2687 A1009 200f multicolored 1.60 .50

Prophet Mohammad's Birthday, Unity Week — A1010

Designs: a, Zouqeblateyne Mosque. b, Tomb of Imam Hossein (red flag on top of dome). c, Mohammad's Mosque (dome without flag). d, Tomb of Imam Reza (green flag on top of dome). e, Qaba Mosque (four minarets).

1996, Aug. 3
2688 A1010 200r Strip of 5, #a.-e. 12.50 3.00

Government Week — A1011

Flag colors and: a, Tehran Subway. b, Iron works, Isfahan. c, Merchant fleet. d, Oil refinery, Bandar-e-Imam (clouds in sky). e, Satellite dish, Boumehen.

1996, Aug. 23
2689 A1011 200r Strip of 5, #a.-e. 13.00 3.50

Ayatollah Moqddas Ardebily A1012

1996, Sept. 12 **Photo.** ***Perf. 13***
2690 A1012 200r multicolored 1.60 .75

Sacred Defense Week — A1013

1996, Sept. 21
2691 A1013 200r multicolored 1.60 .60

World Standards Day — A1014

1996, Oct. 13
2692 A1014 200r multicolored 1.60 .50

World Food Day — A1015

1996, Oct. 16
2693 A1015 200r multicolored 1.60 .60

Natl. Census A1016

1996, Oct. 22
2694 A1016 200r multicolored 1.50 .65

2nd World University Wrestling Championships, Tehran — A1017

1996, Dec. 10
2695 A1017 500r multicolored 5.00 2.00

Islamic Revolution, 18th Anniv. — A1018

a, Ayatollah Khomeini holding man to his chest. b, Martyrs. c, Khomeini waving. d, Khomeini, leaders, airplane. e, Soldiers wearing helmets.

1997, Feb. 10
2696 A1018 200r Strip of 5, #a.-e. 16.00 7.50

Arbor Day — A1019

1997, Mar. 5
2697 A1019 200r multicolored 2.00 .80

Islamic Republic, 18th Anniv. — A1020

1997, Apr. 1
2698 A1020 200r multicolored 1.60 .60

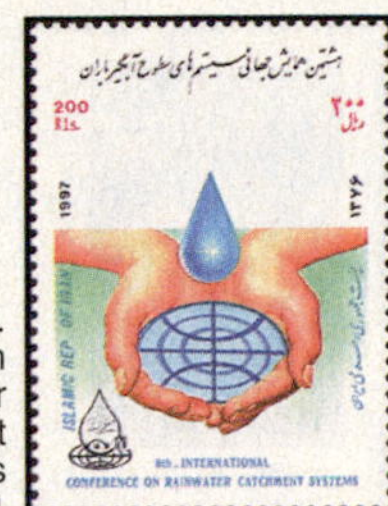

8th Intl. Conference on Rainwater Catchment Systems A1021

1997, Apr. 21
2699 A1021 200r multicolored 1.50 .60

Sheikh Fazlollah Mahallati A1022

Brig. Gen. Abbas Karimi A1023

Brig. Gen. Alireza Movahed Danesh A1024

Sheikh Abdollah Mishmi A1025

Brig. Gen. Naser Kazemi A1026

Gen. Mohammad Reza Vasture A1027

Maj. Gen. Yousef Kolahdooz A1028

Brig. Gen. Yadollah Kalhor A1029

1997, May 4

2700	A1022	100r	multicolored	1.25	.50
2701	A1023	100r	multicolored	1.25	.50
2702	A1024	100r	multicolored	1.25	.50
2703	A1025	100r	multicolored	1.25	.50
2704	A1026	100r	multicolored	1.25	.50
2705	A1027	100r	multicolored	1.25	.50
2706	A1028	100r	multicolored	1.25	.50
2707	A1029	100r	multicolored	1.25	.50

Martyred commanders. See Nos. 2677-2680 for similar stamps.

Post, Telecommunications — A1030

1997, May 22
2708 A1030 200r multicolored 1.75 .50

Ayatollah Khomeini, 8th Death Anniv. — A1031

1997, June 4
2709 A1031 200r multicolored 1.60 .50

Montreal Protocol on Substances that Deplete Ozone Layer, 10th Anniv. — A1032

1997, Sept. 16 Photo. *Perf. 13*
2710 A1032 200r multicolored 1.50 .50

Tehran Subway — A1033

Designs: 50r, Grain elevator. 65r, Medals, Students' Science Olympiad. 70r, Mobarake Steel Plant. 100r, Telecommunications. 130r, Port facilities. 150r, Bandar Abbas Oil Refinery. 200r, Rajai Dam. 350r, Rajai power station. 400r, Front of Foreign Affairs office. 500r, Child receiving oral polio vaccine. 650r, Printing house for Koran. 1000r, Imam Khomeini Intl. Airport. 2000r, Prayer place and tomb of Ayatollah Khomeini, Teheran.

1997 Photo. *Perf. 13½x13*

2711	A1033	40r	multicolored		
2712	A1033	50r	multicolored		
2713	A1033	65r	multicolored		
2714	A1033	70r	multicolored		
2715	A1033	100r	multicolored		
2716	A1033	130r	multicolored		
2717	A1033	150r	multicolored		
2718	A1033	200r	multicolored		
2719	A1033	350r	multicolored		
2720	A1033	400r	multicolored		
2721	A1033	500r	multicolored		
2722	A1033	650r	multicolored		
2723	A1033	1000r	multicolored		
2724	A1033	2000r	multicolored		
	Nos. 2711-2724 (14)			30.00	18.50

Issued: 2000r, 10/22; others, Sept.

Sacred Defense Week — A1034

1997, Sept. 28 Photo. *Perf. 13*
2725 A1034 200r multicolored 1.50 .50

Poets — A1035

No. 2726, Maitre Eqbal Lahouri. No. 2727, Molana Djalaleddin Mohammad Molavi.

1997, Oct. 15

2726	A1035	200r	green & multi	1.50	.50
2727	A1035	200r	salmon & multi	1.50	.50

Compare with Pakistan 870-871.

World Post Day — A1036

1997, Oct. 15
2728 A1036 200r multicolored 1.50 .50

Naim Frasheri (1846-1900), Albanian Moslem Poet — A1037

1997, Nov. 5
2729 A1037 200r multicolored 1.50 .50

Eighth Islamic Summit — A1038

Various ornate designs, Islamic texts: a, Seven ornaments. b, Ornament at bottom. c, Ornament at right. d, Ornament at upper left. e, Ornament above crescent.

1997, Dec. 9
2730 A1038 300r Strip of 5, #a.-e. 20.00 7.50

2nd Islamic Countries Women's Sports Games, Tehran A1039

1997, Dec. 12
2731 A1039 200r multicolored 1.50 .50

Islamic Revolution, 19th Anniv. A1040

a, Natl. flags. b, Harvesting grain, factory. c, Soldiers carrying flags. d, Crowd cheering, picture of Ayatollah Khomeini. e, Ayatollah Khomeini.

1998, Feb. 11
2732 A1040 200r Strip of 5, #a.-e. 12.50 5.00

World Jerusalem Day — A1041

1998, Feb. 17
2733 A1041 250r multicolored 3.00 1.25

New Year — A1042

1998, Mar. 5
2734 A1042 200r Still life 1.60 .60

Arbor Day A1043

1998, Mar. 11
2735 A1043 200r multicolored 1.60 .90

Islamic Republic, 19th Anniv. — A1044

1998, Apr. 1 Photo. ***Perf. 13***
2736 A1044 250r multicolored 4.00 1.50

A1045

1998, May 17 ***Perf. 13½x13***
2737 A1045 200r multicolored 2.25 1.00

World Telecommunications Day.

Election Day — A1046

1998, May 23 Photo. ***Perf. 13***
2738 A1046 200r multicolored 2.25 1.00

War Martyrs

A1047

A1048

A1049

A1050

1998, May 24 Photo. ***Perf. 13***
2739 A1047 100r multicolored 2.50 .90
2740 A1048 100r multicolored 2.50 .90
2741 A1049 100r multicolored 2.50 .90
2742 A1050 100r multicolored 2.50 .90

Shahriyar, Poet — A1051

1998, May 27
2743 A1051 200r multicolored 2.25 1.00

Ayatollah Khomeini, 9th Death Anniv. — A1052

1998, June 4 ***Perf. 13***
2744 A1052 200r multicolored 2.50 1.25

2nd Congress of the South West Asia Postal Union, Tehran A1053

1998, June 8
2745 A1053 250r multicolored 1.75 1.00

1998 World Cup Soccer Championships, France — A1054

1998, June 10
2746 A1054 500r multicolored 3.50 1.00

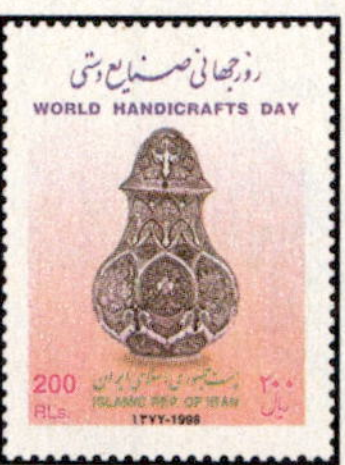

World Handicrafts Day — A1055

1998, June 10
2747 A1055 200r multicolored 2.25 1.25

Union Day — A1056

1998, Sept. 4
2748 A1056 250r multicolored 2.50 1.50

1000th Friday of Public Prayer A1057

1998, Oct. 30 Litho. ***Perf. 13***
2749 A1057 250r multicolored 2.50 1.50

Nos. 2295A & 2296A Surcharged in Black or Green

1998, Nov. 11 ***Perf. 13x13½***
2750 A738 200r on 1r Shoustar 8.00 5.00
2751 A738 200r on 3r Kerman (G) 8.00 5.00

Intl. Year of the Ocean A1058

1998, Nov. 14 ***Perf. 13***
2752 A1058 250r multicolored 3.00 1.75

Sacred Defense Week — A1059

1998, Nov. 23
2753 A1059 250r multicolored 2.50 1.00

World Post Day A1060

1998, Dec. 2
2754 A1060 200r multicolored 2.00 .75

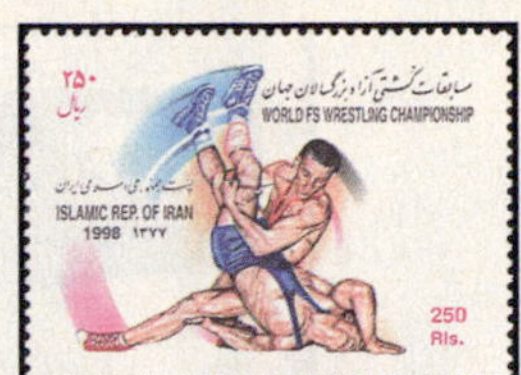

1998 World Wrestling Championships, Tehran — A1061

1998, Dec. 8

2755 A1061 250r multicolored 5.00 2.75

Children and Cancer A1062

1998, Dec. 13

2756 A1062 250r multicolored 2.00 .75

Cultural Development A1063

1998, Dec. 16 Photo. *Perf. 13*

2757 A1063 250r multicolored 2.25 1.00

Islamic Revolution, 20th Anniv. — A1064

1999, Feb. 11 Photo. *Perf. 13*

2758 A1064 250r multicolored 2.00 .75

Nos. 2554, 2682, 2555 Surcharged in Black or Red

Nos. 2759, 2760

No. 2759A

1999, Feb. Photo. *Perf. 13, 13½x13*

2759 A907 200r on 35r (#2555) 15.00 —

2759A A1004 250r on 85r (R, #2682) 35.00 —

2760 A907 900r on 30r (#2554) 25.00 —

Establishment of Islamic Republic, 20th Anniv. — A1065

1999, Apr. 1 Photo. *Perf. 13*

2761 A1065 250r multicolored 2.00 1.00

Ghadir Khom Religious Feast — A1066

1999, Apr. 5 Photo. *Perf. 13*

2762 A1066 250r multicolored 2.00 1.00

Ayatollah Khomieni's Charity Account — A1067

No. 2763, Houses. No. 2764, Village, palm trees.

1999, Apr. 10 Photo. *Perf. 13*

2763 A1067 250r multi 2.25 1.00

2764 A1067 250r multi 2.25 1.00

Army Day A1068

1999, Apr. 18

2765 A1068 250r multicolored 2.50 1.25

Mullah Sadra — A1069

1999, May 22

2766 A1069 250r multicolored 2.00 1.00

Ayatollah Khomeini, 10th Anniv. of Death — A1070

1999, May 25

2767 A1070 250r multicolored 4.00 2.00

Islamic Parliament, 20th Anniv. — A1071

1999, May 28 Photo. *Perf. 13*

2768 A1071 250r multicolored 2.00 1.00

Islamic Inter-parliamentary Conference — A1072

1999, June 15 Photo. *Perf. 13*

2769 A1072 250r multicolored 2.00 1.25

Unity Week A1073

1999, July 1 Photo. *Perf. 13*

2770 A1073 250r multicolored 2.00 1.25

Handicrafts Day — A1074

1999, July 25 Photo. *Perf. 13*

2771 A1074 250r multicolored 3.00 1.25

Total Solar Eclipse, Aug. 11 — A1075

Designs: a, Moon over right portion of sun. b, Baily's beads at top. c, Totality. d, Baily's beads at right. e, Moon over left portion of sun.

1999, Feb. 11 Photo. *Perf. 13*

2772 A1075 250r Strip of 5, #a.-e. 25.00 20.00

Birds — A1076

100r, Hoopoe. 150r, Kingfisher. 200r, Robin. 250r, Lark. 300r, Red-backed shrike. 350r, Eurasian roller. 400r, Blue tit. 500r, Eurasian bee-eater. 1000r, Redwing. 2000r, Twite. 3000r, White throat. 4500r, Turtle dove.

1999-2002 Photo. *Perf. 13x13½*

2773 A1076 100r multi .50

2774 A1076 150r multi .50

2775 A1076 200r multi .50

2776 A1076 250r multi .50

2777 A1076 300r multi .50

2778 A1076 350r multi .50

2779 A1076 400r multi .50

2780 A1076 500r multi .50

2781 A1076 1000r multi 1.00

2782 A1076 2000r multi 1.00

2783 A1076 3000r multi 1.00

2784 A1076 4500r multi 1.00

Nos. 2773-2784 (12) 8.00

Issued: 150r, 8/6; 250r, 8/4; 100r, 6/17/00; 300r, 5/31/00; 500r, 8/30/00; 1000r, 10/30/00; 2000r, 1/13/01; 3000r, 1/23/01. 200r, 4/24/02; 400r, 5/18/02; 4500r, 7/16/02; 350r, 4/17/01.

UPU, 125th Anniv. A1077

1999, Oct. 2 Photo. *Perf. 13*

2787 A1077 250r multicolored 2.25 1.00

Children's Day — A1078

a, Iranian girl. b, Latin American boy. c, Eskimo boy. d, African girl. e, Russian boy. f, French girl. g, Chinese girl. h, Asian Indian girl. i, American Indian girl. j, Arabian boy.

1999, Oct. 8

2788 A1078 150r Strip of 10, #a.-j. 20.00 15.00

Order of stamps in strip varies.

Intl. Exhibition of Children's Book Illustrators A1079

Background colors: a, Blue. b, Yellow. c, Red. d, Green.

1999, Nov. 15

2789 A1079 250r Block of 4, #a.-d. 17.50 10.00

Ayatollah Mohammad Taghi Jafari — A1080

1999, Nov. 16
2790 A1080 250r multicolored 2.00 1.00

Islamic Revolution, 21st Anniv. — A1081

2000, Feb. 11 Photo. *Perf. 13*
2791 A1081 300r multi 2.25 1.25

Nos. 2558, 2560, 2562 Surcharged Like No. 2759

Methods and Perfs. as Before

2000, Feb.
2792 A907 250r on 60r 5.00 3.25
2793 A907 250r on 75r 5.00 3.25
2794 A907 250r on 120r 5.00 3.25

The 60r stamp with the inverted flowers footnoted after No. 2566 is known with the 250r surcharge. Value $35.

New Year — A1082

2000, Mar. 13 Photo. *Perf. 13*
2795 A1082 300r multi 2.75 1.50

Science & Technology University, 70th Anniv. — A1083

2000, July 9 Photo. *Perf. 13*
2796 A1083 300r multi *8.00 5.00*
Dated 1999.

Dr. Mohammad Mofatteh (1928-79), Martyr — A1084

2000, July 22
2797 A1084 300r multi 2.00

A1085

A1086

A1087

A1088

A1089

A1090

A1091

Martyrs A1092

2000

2798	A1085 150r multi		2.00	.50
2799	A1086 150r multi		2.00	.50
2800	A1087 150r multi		2.00	.50
2801	A1088 150r multi		2.00	.50
2802	A1089 150r multi		1.25	.50
2803	A1090 150r multi		1.25	.50
2804	A1091 150r multi		1.25	.50
2805	A1092 150r multi		1.25	.50
	Nos. 2798-2805 (8)		13.00	4.00

Issued: Nos. 2798-2801, 8/6/00; Nos. 2802-2805, 7/30/01.

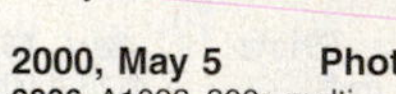
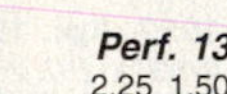
National Archives Day — A1093

2000, May 5 Photo. *Perf. 13*
2806 A1093 300r multi 2.25 1.50

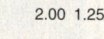

University Jihad Movement A1094

2000, Aug. 6
2807 A1094 300r multi 2.00 1.25

8th Asia-Pacific Postal Union Congress, Tehran — A1095

2000, Sept. 12
2808 A1095 300r multi 2.00 1.25

World Space Week A1096

Satellite and: No. 2809, 500r, Dish at R. No. 2810, 500r, Dish at L.

2000, Oct. 4
2809-2810 A1096 Set of 2 6.00 4.00

World Breastfeeding Week A1097

2000, Oct.
2811 A1097 300r multi 2.00 1.25

Ghadir Khom Festival A1098

2001, Mar. 14
2812 A1098 500r multi 2.25 1.25

Year of H. H. Ali — A1099

2001, Mar. 14
2813 A1099 500r multi 2.25 1.00

New Year — A1100

Birds: No. 2814, 300r, shown. No. 2815, 300r, Bird, diff., vert.

2001, Mar. 18 *Perf. 13x13½, 13½x13*
2814-2815 A1100 Set of 2 6.50 3.00

Palestinian Intifada — A1100a

2001, Apr. 24 Photo. *Perf. 13*
2815A A1100a 350r multi 7.00 5.00

Belgica 2001 Intl Stamp Exhibition, Brussels — A1101

Designs: No. 2816, 350r, Chaffinch (shown). No. 2817, 350r, Waxwing. No. 2818, 350r, National Garden, vert.

2001, June 9 *Perf. 13*
2816-2818 A1101 Set of 3 12.00 8.00

Phila Nippon '01, Japan A1102

Emblem and: No. 2819, 250r, Mount Fuji, Japan. No. 2820, 250r, Mount Damavand, Iran.

2001, Aug. 1 Photo. *Perf. 13*
2819-2820 A1102 Set of 2 4.00 2.50

World Tourism Day — A1103

2001, Sept. 22
2821 A1103 500r multi 2.00 1.25

Police Week — A1104

No. 2822: a, Helicopters, parachutists, police cars, motorcycle police. b, Parachutists, officer saluting flag, motorcycle police, naval patrol.

2001, Sept. 29 *Perf. 13x13½*
2822 A1104 250r Horiz. pair, #a-b 4.00 2.00

Year of Dialogue Among Civilizations A1105

Designs: No. 2823, 250r, Shown. No. 2824, 250r, Cubist and Oriental art, horiz.

2001, Oct. 9 *Perf. 13*
2823-2824 A1105 Set of 2 4.50 2.50

Third Moslem Women's Games, Tehran — A1106

2001, Oct. 24
2825 A1106 250r multi 2.00 1.25

Spring of the Holy Koran — A1107

2001, Nov. 26
2826 A1107 500r multi 2.50 1.50

Honeybee — A1108

2001, Dec. 3
2827 A1108 500r multi 2.75 1.75

UN High Commissioner for Refugees, 50th Anniv. — A1109

2001, Dec. 10
2828 A1109 500r multi 2.00 1.00

Transportation Day — A1110

No. 2829: a, Truck on road. b, Truck on bridge, truck on road, gate.

2001, Dec. 17 *Perf. 13x13½*
2829 A1110 350r Horiz. pair, #a-b 5.00 3.00

Navy Day A1111

No. 2830, 500r: a, Ship heading right. b, Ship heading left.
No. 2831, 500r: a, Helicopter, hovercraft. b, Submarine.

2001, Nov. 28 Photo. *Perf. 13*
Vert. Pairs, #a-b
2830-2831 A1111 Set of 2 8.50 8.50

Tehran Subway A1112

No. 2832: a, Train headed right. b, Train headed left.

2001, Dec. 13
2832 A1112 500r Vert. pair, #a-b 4.00 3.00

Iranian-made Automobiles — A1113

Designs: No. 2833, 500r, shown. No. 2834, 500r, Automobile, vert.

2002, Jan. 15
2833-2834 A1113 Set of 2 4.00 2.50

Arbor Day — A1114

2002, Mar. 6
2835 A1114 500r multi 1.75 1.25

A1115

New Year's Day — A1116

No. 2836: a, Bird with yellow breast. b, Parrot.
No. 2837: a, Stork facing left. b, Hoopoe facing right.

2002, Mar. 16
2836 A1115 500r Horiz. pair, #a-b 3.75 3.00
2837 A1116 500r Horiz. pair, #a-b 3.75 3.00

Imam Hossein — A1117

2002, July 8 Photo. *Imperf.*
2838 A1117 400r multi 1.50 1.50

Butterflies — A1118

No. 2839: a, Danaus sita. b, Polygonia c-album. c, Precis orithya. d, Vanessa cardui. e, Papilio maacki.

2002, July 29 *Perf. 13*
2839 Horiz. strip of 5 6.50 6.50
a.-e. A1118 400r Any single 1.10 .90

A1119

PhilaKorea 2002 World Stamp Exhibition, Seoul — A1120

No. 2840 — Flowers: a, Hyoscyamus muticus. b, Frittillaria. c, Calotropis procera. d, Ranuculus.

No. 2841 — Horse breeds: a, Caspian. b, Kurd. c, Turkoman. d, Arab.

2002, Aug. 2

2840 A1119 400r Block of 4, #a-d, + 2 labels 6.00 6.00
2841 A1120 400r Block of 4, #a-d, + 2 labels 6.00 6.00

Ayatollah Khomeini (1900-89) A1121

2002, Aug. 20

2842 A1121 400r multi 2.00 1.00

No. 2842 exists imperf. Value, pair $25.

Jerusalem Day — A1122

2002, Nov. 29

2843 A1122 400r multi 2.00 1.00

Iran — Brazil Diplomatic Relations, Cent. — A1123

No. 2844: a, Iranian ceramics. b, Brazilian ceramics.

2002, Dec. 15

2844 Horiz. pair + label 5.00 5.00
a.-b. A1123 400r Either single 2.00 1.00

See Brazil Nos. 2868-2869.

2nd Biennial of Contemporary Painting of the Islamic World — A1124

2002, Dec. 25

2845 A1124 400r multi 2.00 1.00

Esco Production Line, 30th Anniv. — A1125

2003, Jan. 13 *Perf. 13x13½*

2846 A1125 400r multi 2.50 1.50

Air Force Day A1126

Various aircraft: 300r, 400r, 500r, 600r, 700r.

2003, Feb. 8 **Photo.** *Perf. 13*

2847-2851 A1126 Set of 5 7.50 7.50

New Year 2003 A1127

Mammals: No. 2852, 1000r, Goitered gazelle without horns. No. 2853, 1000r, Goitered gazelle with horns. No. 2854, 1000r, Red deer. No. 2855, 1000r, Urial.

2003, Mar. 15

2852-2855 A1127 Set of 4 9.00 9.00

Iranian and Chinese Buildings A1128

No. 2856: a, Mosque, Isfahan. b, Bell Tower, Xian, People's Republic of China.

2003, Apr. 15 *Perf. 13x13½*

2856 Horiz. pair + label 6.00 6.00
a.-b. A1128 400r Either single 1.50 1.25

See China (People's Republic) Nos. 3271-3272.

Book, Children and Family — A1129

2003, May 4 **Photo.** *Perf. 13*

2857 A1129 500r multi 1.75 1.25

Butterflies A1130

100r, Zygaena sp. 200r, Issoria lathonia. 250r, Utethesia pulchella. 300r, Argynnis paphia. 500r, Polygonia egea. 600r, Papilio machaon. 650r, Colias aurorina. 1000r, Inachis io. 2000r, Papilio demoleus. 2100r, Papilio domoleus. 3000r, Euphydryas aurinia. 4400r, Danaus melanippus. 5500r, Colias aurorina.

2003-05 **Photo.** *Perf. 13x13½*

2858 A1130 100r multi .25 —
2859 A1130 200r multi .40 —
2859A A1130 250r multi .50 —
2860 A1130 300r multi .60 —
a. Longer "Rls." + label ('04) 1.50 —
2862 A1130 500r multi 1.00 —
2863 A1130 600r multi 1.25 —
a. Longer "Rls." + label ('04) 2.50 —
2864 A1130 650r multi ('04) 1.25 —
2866 A1130 1000r multi ('04) 1.40 —
2867 A1130 2000r multi ('04) 4.00 —
2867A A1130 2100r multi ('05) 2.25 —
2868 A1130 3000r multi ('04) 3.75 —
2868A A1130 4400r multi 4.25 —
2869 A1130 5500r multi 5.50 —

Issued: 100r, 7/14; 200r, 5/12; 300r, 5/14; 500r, 8/25; 600r, 6/10; 250r, 12/17; 1000r, 1/6/04; Nos. 2860a, 2863a, 1/21/04; 1000r, 2/22/04; 3000r, 3/10/04, 650r, 2004. 2100r, 4/18/05; 4400r, 3/15/05; 5500r, 4/13/05.

The period in "Rls." is under the second zero on Nos. 2860a and 2863a. It is under the first zero on Nos. 2860 and 2863. Examples of No. 2860a exist with and without perforations separating the stamp from the label.

Social Security Organization, 50th Anniv. — A1131

2003, Aug. 16 **Photo.** *Perf. 13*

2870 A1131 600r multicolored 1.75 1.00

Government Martyrs — A1132

2003, Aug. 24

2871 A1132 600r multi + label 2.00 2.00

Government Week — A1133

2003, Aug. 25

2872 A1133 600r multicolored 1.50 1.00

Caspian Sea Fauna A1134

No. 2873: a, Caspian seal. b, Beluga.

2003, Sept. 9

2873 Horiz. pair + label 7.50 7.50
a.-b. A1134 600r Either single 1.50 1.50
c. Souvenir sheet, 2 each #2873a-2873b 9.50 9.50

See Russia No. 6795.

World Post Day A1135

No. 2874: a, Computer, UPU emblem, satellite. b, Post office loading dock, mail box, airplanes. c, Postal clerk at desk, truck. d, Post rider, ruins and statues.

2003, Oct. 9

2874 Horiz. strip of 4 8.00 8.00
a.-d. A1135 600r Any single 1.00 .75

Shared Functions of the Police and Post Office — A1136

2003, Oct. 5 **Photo.** *Perf. 13*

2875 A1136 500r multicolored 1.00 .75

Worldwide Fund for Nature (WWF) — A1137

No. 2876 — Cheetah: a, Cub. b, Two adults lying in grass. c, Two adults standing. d, Head of adult.

2003, Nov. 18

2876 A1137 500r Block of 4, #a-d 4.75 4.75

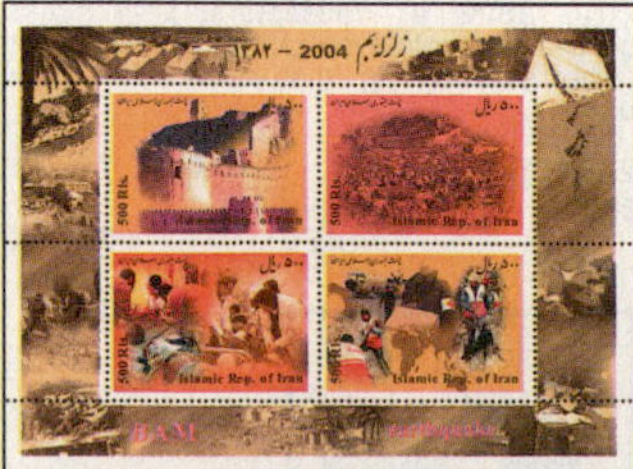

Eid ul-Fitr A1138

2003, Nov. 26

2877 A1138 600r multicolored 1.75 1.25

Miniature Sheet

Bam Earthquake, Dec. 26, 2003 — A1139

No. 2878: a, Landmarks in Bam before earthquake. b, Earthquake devastation. c, Doctors treating injured people. d, Rescue personnel, map of world.

2004, Feb. 4
2878 A1139 500r Sheet of 4, #a-d 3.25 3.25

Islamic Revolution, 25th Anniv. A1140

2004, Feb. 11
2879 A1140 600r multicolored 1.00 1.00

Hossein Rezazadeh, Weightlifter — A1141

2004, Feb. 15
2880 A1141 1200r multicolored 2.00 2.00
Dated 2003.

ISO 9001-2000 Certification A1142

2004, Feb. 29
2881 A1142 600r multicolored 1.00 1.00

Freshwater Fish — A1143

Designs: Nos. 2882, 2888a, 100r, Carassius auratus. Nos. 2883, 2888b, 200r, Carassius auratus, diff. Nos. 2884, 2888c, 300r, Poecilia reticlate. Nos. 2885, 2888d, 400r, Betta splendens. Nos. 2886, 2888e, 500r, Carassius auratus, diff. Nos. 2887, 2888f, 600r, Carassius auratus, diff.

2004, Mar. 6
Stamps With White Frames
2882-2887 A1143 Set of 6 4.00 4.00
Miniature Sheet
Stamps Without White Frames
2888 A1143 Sheet of 6, #a-f 5.00 5.00

FIFA (Fédération Internationale de Football Association), Cent. — A1144

2004, May 21 ***Perf. 13***
2889 A1144 600r multicolored 1.00 1.00

Miniature Sheet

Saltwater Fish — A1145

No. 2890: a, 250r, Balistoides conspicillum. b, 350r, Acanthurus glaucopareius. c, 450r, Pterols volitans. d, 550r, Zebrasoma veliferum. e, 650r, Pygoplites diacanthus. f, 750r, Pseudobalistes fuscus.

2004, May 22 ***Perf. 13***
2890 A1145 Sheet of 6, #a-f 4.25 4.25

España 2004 Intl. Philatelic Exhibition, Riccione Philatelic Exhibition.

Reporter's Day — A1147

2004, Aug. 7
2892 A1147 650r multicolored .80 .80

2004 Summer Olympics, Athens — A1148

No. 2893: a, Taekwondo. b, Weight lifting. c, Wrestling. d, Judo.

2004, Aug. 12
2893 A1148 650r Block of 4, #a-d 3.50 3.50

Poets — A1149

No. 2894: a, Kabir (1440-1518), Indian poet. b, Hafiz Shirazi (c. 1325-c. 1389), Persian poet.

2004, Aug. 16 ***Perf. 13***
2894 A1149 600r Horiz. pair, #a-b 1.50 1.50

See India No. 2070.

International Avicenna Congress — A1150

No. 2895: a, Memorial. b, Avicenna (980-1037), scientist, philosopher.

2004, Aug. 22
2895 A1150 650r Horiz. pair, #a-b 1.60 1.60

Miniature Sheet

Primates — A1151

No. 2896: a, Chacma baboons. b, Chimpanzee. c, Chimpanzees. d, Mandrill.

2004, Aug. 28
2896 A1151 500r Sheet of 4, #a-d 5.00 5.00

World Stamp Championship 2004, Singapore.

Miniature Sheet

Cats — A1152

No. 2897: a, Gray cat, no tail visible. b, Gray cat, tail at right. c, Brown and white cat. d, White cat. e, Gray cat on rock. f, Gray cat, tail at left.

2004, Aug. 31
2897 A1152 500r Sheet of 6, #a-f 6.00 6.00

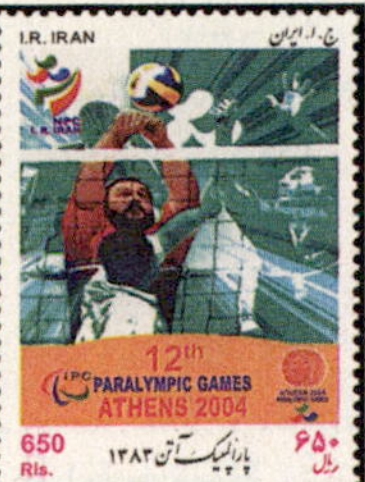
12th Paralympic Games, Athens A1153

2004, Sept. 17
2898 A1153 650r multicolored .80 .50

Iran - Iraq War, 24th Anniv. A1154

2004, Sept. 21
2899 A1154 650r multicolored .80 .50

Tehran University, 70th Anniv. A1155

2004, Oct. 22
2900 A1155 650r multicolored .80 .50

Poets — A1156

No. 2901: a, Dr. Jalal-eddin Ashtiani (wearing turban). b, Mahmoud Farschian (with hand on chin). c, Dr. Jafar Shahidi (looking right). d, Dr. Hosain Mirshamsi (looking left).

2004, Nov. 9 **Photo.** ***Perf. 13***
2901 A1156 500r Block of 4, #a-d 2.50 2.00

Mountains — A1157

No. 2902: a, Damavand Mountain, Iran. b, Bolivar Peak, Venezuela.

2004, Nov. 28 **Photo.** ***Perf. 13***
2902 A1157 650r Horiz. pair, #a-b 1.50 1.00

First Intl. Biennale of Islamic Poster Art — A1158

No. 2903: a, Hand. b, Dove in nest. c, Slingshot. d, Crescent.

2004, Nov. 29
2903 A1158 500r Block of 4, #a-d 2.50 2.00

Imam Reza's Birthday — A1159

No. 2904: a, Corner of mosque. b, Dome. c, Facade. d, Archway.

2004, Dec. 24 Photo. *Perf. 13x13¼*
2904 A1159 500r Block of 4, #a-d 2.50 2.00

Ali Daei, Soccer Player A1160

2005, Feb. 2 Photo. *Perf. 13*
2905 A1160 650r multicolored .75 .50

Iran Film Museum — A1161

No. 2906: a, Scene from *Where is the Friend's Home?* b, Scene from *The Children of Heaven.* c, Museum building. d, Scene from *The Cow.*

2005, Feb. 10
2906 A1161 500r Block of 4, #a-d 2.00 1.00

Airplanes — A1162

No. 2907: a, AN-140. b, IR-140.

2005, Mar. 6 *Perf. 13x13½*
2907 Horiz. pair with central label 2.00 1.00
a.-b. A1162 850r Either single

See Ukraine No. 568.

Souvenir Sheet

Expo 2005, Aichi, Japan — A1163

No. 2908: a, Persepolis. b, Yazd air ventilation towers. c, Iranian flag, typical Iranian desert architecture. d, Clay tablet with inscriptions.

2005, Mar. 24 *Perf. 13*
2908 A1163 650r Sheet of 4, #a-d 2.50 2.00

Tehran University of Medical Sciences, 70th Anniv. — A1164

2005, May 2
2909 A1164 650r multicolored .75 .50

Police Week — A1165

2005, Oct. 29
2910 A1165 650r multicolored .75 .50

Mevlana Jalal ad-Din ar-Rumi (1207-73), Islamic Philosopher A1166

2005, Dec. 3
2911 A1166 650r multicolored 1.50 1.00

See Afghanistan Nos. 1449-1451, Syria No. 1574, Turkey No. 2971.

Gardens — A1167

No. 2912: a, Gardens of Royal Palace of La Granja de San Ildefonso, Segovia, Spain. b, Bagh-e-Shahzadeh, Kerman, Iran.

2005, Dec. 17
2912 A1167 650r Horiz. pair, #a-b 1.50 1.00

See Spain No. 3374.

Self-Sufficiency in Wheat Production A1168

2006, Jan. 4
2913 A1168 650r multicolored .75 .50

Souvenir Sheet

Maps of the Persian Gulf — A1169

No. 2914: a, German map, 16th cent. b, Egyptian Ministry of Culture map, 1966. c, Saudi Arabian map, 1952. d, Map by Scoteri Motthaei, 18th cent.

2006, June 7
2914 A1169 650r Sheet of 4, #a-d 5.00 2.50

2006 World Cup Soccer Championships, Germany — A1170

2006, June 10
2915 A1170 650r multicolored .90 .50

Abbas Shafi — A1171

Alama Mohammed Reza Hakimi A1172

Mohamed Hossein Gandji A1173

Alama Mohammed Hassan Amoli — A1174

2006, Sept. 18 Litho. *Perf. 13*

2916	Block of 4	5.00	*5.00*
a.	A1171 650r multi	1.00	.75
b.	A1172 650r multi	1.00	.75
c.	A1173 650r multi	1.00	.75
d.	A1174 650r multi	1.00	.75

Dated 2005.

Third Meeting of Economic Cooperation Organization Postal Authorities, Tehran — A1175

2006, Sept. 20
2917 A1175 650r multicolored 2.00 1.00

See Kazakhstan No. 526, Pakistan No. 1101 and Turkey No. 3041.

Basij, 27th Anniv. A1176

2006, Nov. 26
2918 A1176 650r multicolored 2.00 1.00

Souvenir Sheet

Isfahan, 2006 Islamic Cultural Capital — A1177

No. 2919: a, Chehel Sotun Palace. b, Emam Mosque. c, Aliqapu Palace. d, Khajo Bridge.

2006, Dec. 30

2919 A1177 650r Sheet of 4, #a-d 5.00 2.50

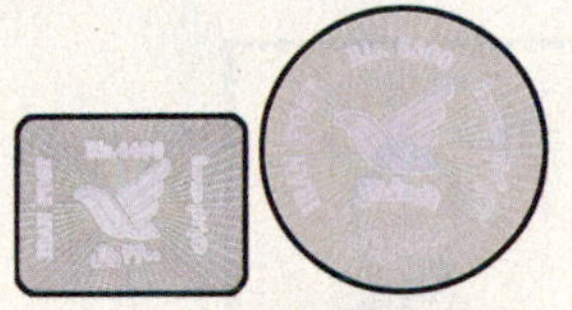

A1177a A1177b

Iran Post Emblem

Hologram on Foil

2006, Dec. Self-Adhesive *Die Cut*

2919E	A1177a	4400r silver	*3.50*	*3.50*
2919F	A1177b	5500r silver	*4.50*	*4.50*

Martyrs — A1178

No. 2920: a, Man and flags. b, Ten men.

2007, Jan. 7

2920 A1178 650r Horiz. pair, #a-b 2.00 1.00

Dated 2006.

Souvenir Sheet

Iranian Constitution, Cent. — A1179

No. 2921: a, Man, gate. b, Parliament. c, Three men, gate. d, Two men, gate.

2006, May 8 Litho. *Perf. 13*

2921 A1179 650r Sheet of 4, #a-d 5.00 3.00

Souvenir Sheet

Seventh General Assembly of Association of Asian Parliaments for Peace, Tehran — A1180

No. 2922: a, Emblem of Association of Asian Parliaments for Peace. b, Dove, colors of Iranian flag. c, Gate and flags. d, Emblem of Islamic Consultative Assembly.

2006, Nov. 14

2922 A1180 650r Sheet of 4, #a-d 5.00 2.50

Peaceful Nuclear Energy — A1181

2007, Feb. 11

2923 A1181 650r multicolored 2.00 1.00

Iranian-built Engine A1182

2007, Feb. 26

2924 A1182 650r multicolored 1.50 .60

Shrine of Fatima, Qom — A1183

2007, Mar. 18

2925 A1183 650r multicolored 1.50 .50

New Year — A1184

No. 2926: a, Flowers, man with drum. b, Trumpeters, fishbowl, Koran, apples, grass.

2007, Mar. 19

2926 A1184 650r Horiz. pair, #a-b 2.00 1.00

Map of Persian Gulf — A1185

2007 Litho. *Perf. 13x13½*

Side Panel Color

2927	A1185	200r brown	1.00	.50
2928	A1185	300r yellow	1.00	.50
a.		Taller Arabic "Rls." + label	3.00	3.00
2929	A1185	650r orange	1.00	.50
a.		Wider "650" + label	3.00	3.00
2930	A1185	2100r blue	4.00	2.00
2931	A1185	4400r blue	8.00	3.00

Issued: 200r, 9/9; 300r, 5/23; 4400r, 7/25. 650r, 10/30; 2100r, 11/24; No. 2929a, 1/27/09.

See Nos. 2943-2945, 2956-2960.

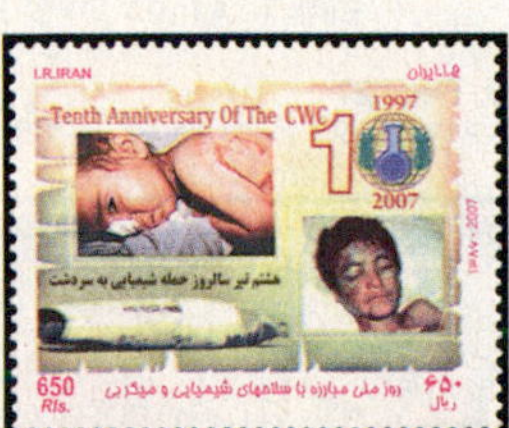

Chemical Weapons Convention, 10th Anniv. — A1186

2007, June 29 *Perf. 13*

2932 A1186 650r multicolored 1.50 .50

38th Intl. Physics Olympiad, Isfahan — A1187

2007, July 3

2933 A1187 650r multicolored 1.50 .50

K. K. Sarughy A1188

2007, Aug. 22

2934 A1188 650r multicolored 1.50 .50

Imam Moussa Sadr, Shiite Leader Who Disappeared in 1978 — A1189

2007, Aug. 31

2935 A1189 650r multicolored 1.50 .50

Worldwide Fund for Nature (WWF) — A1190

No. 2936 — Grus leucogranus: a, Pair, one with head raised, other with head lowered. b, Pair, facing each other. c, Pair, both standing on one leg. d, Running with wings extended.

2007, Sept. 9

2936 A1190 650r Block of 4, #a-d 4.00 2.50

Miniature Sheet

Great Messenger Year — A1191

No. 2937 — Arabic text and: a, Arch. b, Arabic text in diamond. c, Roman Colosseum. d, Pyramids.

2007, Jan. 6 Litho. *Perf. 13*

2937 A1191 650r Sheet of 4, #a-d 5.00 2.50

Communications and Public Relations Day — A1192

2007, May 17

2938 A1192 650r multicolored 1.50 .50

Miniature Sheet

Return of Prisoners of War — A1193

No. 2939 — Flowers and: a, Geese. b, Iranian man, hand symbol. c, Prisoners of war on bus. d, People on motorcycles greeting prisoners of war.

2007, Aug. 17

2939 A1193 650r Sheet of 4, #a-d 5.00 2.50

Jamkaran Mosque A1194

2007, Aug. 29
2940 A1194 650r multicolored 1.50 .50

World Post Day — A1195

2007, Sept. 10
2941 A1195 650r multicolored 2.00 1.00

Mevlana Jalal ad-Din ar-Rumi (1207-73), Islamic Philosopher A1196

2007, Oct. 28
2942 A1196 650r multicolored 2.00 1.00

Map of Persian Gulf Type of 2007

2008 ***Perf. 13x13½***

Side Panel Color

2943 A1185 1000r green 2.00 1.00
2944 A1185 2000r lilac 4.00 2.00
2945 A1185 5500r red 10.00 4.00

Issued: 1000r, 1/16; 2000r, 2/5; 5500r, 1/5.

Information Technology Infrastructure Development A1197

2008, Jan. 16 ***Perf. 13***
2946 A1197 650r multicolored 2.00 .75

Navvab Safavi (1924-55), Founder of Islamic Fedayeen A1198

2008, Jan. 17
2947 A1198 650r multicolored 1.50 .75

Falsafi, Preacher, 100th Anniv. of Birth — A1199

2008, Feb. 27
2948 A1199 650r multicolored 1.50 .75

Death of Emad Moghnie, Hezbollah Leader — A1200

2008, Mar. 10
2949 A1200 650r multicolored 2.00 1.00

New Year A1201

2008, Mar. 15
2950 A1201 650r multicolored 1.50 .75

Abdulazim Shrine — A1202

2008, Apr. 11 ***Perf. 13x13½***
2951 A1202 650r multicolored 1.50 .75

Children and Youth Water Festival A1203

2008, Apr. 21 ***Perf. 13***
2952 A1203 650r multicolored 1.50 .75

Islamic City Councils, 10th Anniv. — A1204

2008, Apr. 28
2953 A1204 650r multicolored 1.50 .75

Thiqat al-Islam Kulayni, Islamic Legal Scholar, 1100th Anniv. of Death — A1205

2008, May 8
2954 A1205 650r multicolored 1.50 .75

Buildings in Morocco and Iran — A1206

No. 2955: a, Kasbah, Oudayas, Morocco. b, Falak-Ol-Aflak Castle, Iran.

2008, May 12 **Litho.** ***Perf. 13***
2955 A1206 650r Horiz. pair, #a-b, + label 2.50 1.50

See Morocco No. 1061.

Map of Persian Gulf Type of 2007

2008-09 **Litho.** ***Perf. 13x13½***

Side Panel Color

2956 A1185 100r blue .50 .50
2957 A1185 250r pale orange .50 .50
2958 A1185 400r red .50 .50
2959 A1185 500r dark green .50 .50
2960 A1185 3000r pink *3.00 3.00*
Nos. 2956-2960 (5) 5.00 5.00

Issued: 100r, 9/8; 250r, 10/20; 400r, 9/13; 500r, 5/28; 3000r, 2/15/09.

Handicrafts Day — A1207

No. 2961: a, Engraved copper cup. b, Mina vase.

2008, June 10 **Litho.** ***Perf. 13***
2961 A1207 650r Horiz. pair, #a-b 2.50 1.50

Miniature Sheet

Trenchless Trench Makers — A1207a

No. 2962 — Men and: a, Construction equipment with extendable arm. b, Bulldozer under roof. c, Utility vehicle. d, Ship on truck's flat-bed trailer.

2008, June 16 **Litho.** ***Perf. 13***
2962 A1207a 650r Sheet of 4, #a-d 3.00 .60

Javid-al-Asar Haj Ahmed Motevasselian, Diplomat A1208

2008, July 3
2963 A1208 650r multicolored 1.50 .75

Mountains in Kyrgyzstan and Iran — A1209

No. 2964: a, Khan-Tengri, Kyrgyzstan. b, Sabalan Peak, Iran.

2008, Aug. 15
2964 A1209 650r Horiz. pair, #a-b, + central label 2.50 1.50

See Kyrgyzstan No. 313.

Ancient Jewelry From Iran and Kazakhstan — A1210

No. 2965: a, Gold medal depicting lions, 7th cent. B.C., Iran. b, Buckle depicting snow leopard and mountains, 4th-5th cent. B.C., Kazakhstan.

2008, Sept. 7
2965 A1210 650r Horiz. pair, #a-b 2.50 1.50

See Kazakhstan No. 578.

Iran Post Corporation, 20th Anniv. — A1211

2008, Oct. 8 ***Perf. 13x13½***
2966 A1211 1200r multicolored 2.00 1.00

Consumer Rights Day — A1212

2008, Feb. 28 *Perf. 13*
2967 A1212 650r multicolored 2.00 1.00

Ayatollah Sheikh Hashem Ghazvini A1213

2008, May 5
2968 A1213 650r multicolored

Bank Melli Iran, 80th Anniv. A1214

2008, Sept. 10
2969 A1214 650r multicolored 2.00 1.00

World Jerusalem Day — A1215

2008, Sept. 26
2970 A1215 650r multicolored 2.00 1.00

Statue of Sheikh Abulhassan Kharaghani A1216

2008, Nov. 6
2971 A1216 650r multicolored 2.00 1.00

Commander M. R. Pourkian and Tank — A1217

2008, Nov. 13
2972 A1217 650r multicolored 2.00 1.00

28-Year Achievements of Security Services A1218

2008, Nov. 19
2973 A1218 650r multicolored 2.50 1.25

Zabol Burnt City Archaeological Site — A1219

2008, Dec. 21
2974 A1219 650r multicolored 2.50 1.25

National Day of Exports A1220

2008, Oct. 21 *Perf. 13*
2975 A1220 650r multicolored 2.50 1.25

Musical Instruments — A1221

No. 2976: a, Gijak of Badahshon. b, Khorasan local dotaar.

2008, Dec. 15
2976 A1221 650r Horiz. pair, #a-b 4.50 2.25

See Tajikistan No. 340.

Support for Gaza Palestinians — A1222

2009, Jan. 27
2977 A1222 1200r multicolored 3.00 1.50

Ayatollah Khomeini (1900-89) — A1223

2009, Feb. 10
2978 A1223 650r multicolored 3.00 1.50

Islamic Revolution, 30th anniv.

Abbas, Karimi, Reza Cheraghi, and Mohammad Hemat — A1224

2009, Mar. 3
2979 A1224 650r multicolored

Safir Omid, First Iranian Satellite — A1225

No. 2980: a, Iranian flag, rocket on launch pad, emblem. b, Satellite, Earth.

2009, Mar. 7
2980 A1225 1300r Horiz. pair, #a-b 4.00 4.00

10th Economic Cooperation Organization Summit, Tehran — A1226

2009, Mar. 11
2981 A1226 1300r multicolored 3.00 1.50

See Azerbaijan 895, compare with Pakistan 1111.

New Year 2009 A1227

2009, Mar. 25
2982 A1227 1300r multicolored 3.50 1.75

Nurse's Day — A1228

2009, Apr. 28
2983 A1228 1300r multicolored 3.00 1.50

Fish — A1229

Designs: 100r, Chaetodon mesoleucos. 200r, Holacanthus ciliaris. 250r, Euxiphipops xanthomelapon. 300r, Pomacanthus maculosus. 350r, Pomacanthus annularis. 400r, Chaetodon rafflesi. 500r, Centropyge bicolor. 1000r, Chaetodontoplus septentrionalis. 2000r, Chaetodon larvatus. 3000r, Chaetodon auriga. 3100r, Chaetodon semilarvatus. 4000r, Pomacanthus chrysurus. 5000r, Pomacanthus navarchus. 6400r, Paracanthurus hepatus. 7500r, Premnas biaculeatus.

2009-11 Litho. *Perf. 13x13½*
Size: 32x25mm

2984	A1229	100r multi	.25	.25
2985	A1229	200r multi	.25	.25
2986	A1229	250r multi	.25	.25
2987	A1229	300r multi	.25	.25
2988	A1229	350r multi	.25	.25
2989	A1229	400r multi	.25	.25
2990	A1229	500r multi	.25	.25
2993	A1229	1000r multi	1.00	.25
2994	A1229	2000r multi	2.00	.40
2994A	A1229	3000r multi	3.00	.60
2995	A1229	3100r multi	3.00	.65

2996 A1229 4000r multi *4.00 .80*
2997 A1229 5000r multi *5.00 1.00*
2998 A1229 6400r multi *5.50 1.40*
2999 A1229 7500r multi *6.00 1.50*
Nos. 2984-2999 (15) *31.25 8.35*

Issued: 100r, 9/25/10; 200r, 10/26; 250r, 4/7/10; 300r, 4/12/10; 350r, 2/26/11. 400r, 12/27/10. 500r, 12/21; 1000r, 6/22; 2000r, 8/1/10; 3000r, 5/8/11; 3100r, 1/19/10; 4000r, 7/18/10; 5000r, 6/15/10; 6400r, 11/10; 7500r, 10/12.

See Nos. 3055A-3055I.

Epic of Presence A1230

2009, June 12 **Litho.** ***Perf. 13***
3000 A1230 1300r multicolored *2.50 1.00*

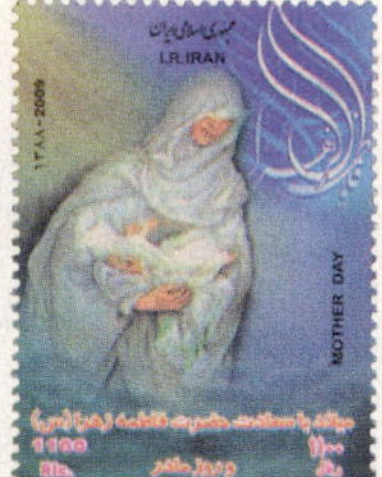

Mother's Day — A1231

2009, June 14
3001 A1231 1100r multicolored *2.50 1.50*

Birds — A1232

No. 3002: a, White-tailed eagle. b, Osprey.

2009, June 24
3002 A1232 2000r Horiz. pair, #a-b *6.00 6.00*

See Portugal Nos. 3155-3156.

Left Part of Stamp

Center Part of Stamp

Birds (Right Part of Stamp) — A1233

The illustration of No. 3003 is broken into the three sections shown on the stamp.

2009, July 11 ***Perf. 13x13½***
3003 A1233 1500r multicolored *6.00 6.00*

See Cuba No. 4835.

Marwa El-Sherbini (1977-2009), Woman Murdered in German Courtroom A1234

2009, July 19 ***Perf. 13***
3004 A1234 1300r multicolored *2.00 1.00*

Islamic Human Rights and Human Dignity Day A1235

2009, Aug. 5
3005 A1235 1200r multicolored *2.00 1.00*

Rural Information and Communication Technologies in Iran — A1236

2009, Aug. 11
3006 A1236 1000r multicolored *2.00 1.00*

Miniature Sheet

Conservation of Marine Turtles — A1237

No. 3007: a, 650r, Eretmochelys imbricata. b, 1000r, Eretmochelys imbricata, diff. c, 1500r, Chelonia mydas. d, 1850r, Chelonia mydas, diff.

2009, Aug. 26
3007 A1237 Sheet of 4, #a-d *4.50 4.50*

A1238

No. 3008: a, World Post Day. b, World Child Day.

2009, Oct. 9
3008 A1238 1200r Horiz. pair, #a-b *3.50 3.50*

17th Book Week — A1239

2009, Nov. 14
3009 A1239 1200r multicolored *3.00 1.50*

Rob'e Rashidi University Endowment Document — A1240

2009, Dec. 1 **Litho.**
3010 A1240 1200r multicolored *3.00 1.50*

Ghadir Khom Festival — A1240a

2009, Dec. 6 **Litho.** ***Perf. 13¾x14¼***
3010A A1240a 1200r multicolored *3.00 1.50*

Universal Declaration of Human Rights, 60th Anniv. — A1241

2009, Dec. 13 ***Perf. 13***
3011 A1241 1200r multicolored *3.00 1.50*

Ayatollah Mohammad Mofatteh (1928-79) A1242

2009, Dec. 18 ***Perf. 13¾x14¼***
3012 A1242 1200r multicolored *3.00 1.50*

Buildings in Indonesia and Iran — A1243

No. 3013: a, Soltanieh Dome, Iran. b, Al-Markaz Mosque, Indonesia.

2009, Dec. 23 ***Perf. 13***
3013 A1243 2000r Horiz. pair, #a-b, + central label *4.50 4.50*

See Indonesia Nos. 2218-2219.

Intl. Year of Astronomy — A1244

No. 3014: a, 1000r, Artificial plan of Maragheh Observatory. b, 1200r, Al-Tafhim, by Abu Ryehan Biruni. c, 1300r, Armillary sphere. d, 1500r, Taqi al-Din and astronomers, 16th cent.

2010, Feb. 24 ***Perf. 13¾x14¼***
3014 A1244 Block of 4, #a-d *4.50 4.50*

Mullah Sadra (c. 1571-1641) A1245

2010, May 18
3015 A1245 1300r multicolored *3.00 1.50*

Khaje Abdullah Ansari (1006-88), Religious Commentator — A1246

2010, July 25 ***Perf. 13¾***
3016 A1246 2000r multicolored *3.50 1.50*

See Afghanistan No. , Tajikistan No. 366.

Destroyer Jamaran — A1247

2010, Sept. 1 *Perf. 14¼x13¾*
3017 A1247 2000r multicolored *3.00 1.50*

Martyred Engineers of the Sacred Defense A1248

2010, Oct. 20 *Perf. 13¾x14¼*
3018 A1248 2000r multicolored *3.00 1.50*

Shah-e-Cheragh Holy Shrine, Shiraz — A1249

No. 3019: a, 1200r, Mosque dome and minaret. b, 1300r, Shrine.

2010, Nov. 14 *Perf. 13¾*
3019 A1249 Horiz. pair, #a-b *4.50 4.50*

A1250

New Year — A1251

No. 3021: a, Flowers and ribbon. b, Candle and Iranian inscription. c, Goldfish in bowl and apples. d, Koran on bookstand and oranges.

Perf. 13¾x14¼

2010, Mar. 27 **Litho.**
3020 A1250 2000r multicolored *2.00 1.00*

Perf. 14¼x13¾

3021 A1251 1250r Sheet of 4, #a-d *4.00 4.00*

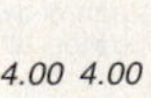

Nature Day — A1252

No. 3022 — Trees in: a, Spring. b, Summer. c, Autumn. d, Winter.

2010, Apr. 2 *Perf. 13¾x14¼*
3022 Horiz. strip of 4 *3.00 3.00*
a. A1252 1100r pink & multi .50 .25
b. A1252 1200r green & multi .50 .25
c. A1252 1300r orange & multi .50 .25
d. A1252 1400r blue & multi .50 .30

Towers in Pakistan and Iran — A1253

No. 3023: a, Minar-e-Pakistan, Lahore. b, Milad Tower, Tehran.

2010, July 28
3023 A1253 2000r Horiz. pair, #a-b, + flanking label *3.50 3.50*

See Pakistan No. 1149.

Miniature Sheet

Products of Iranian Military Industries — A1254

No. 3024: a, 1000r, Sedjil missile. b, 1500r, Saegheh airplane. c, 2000r, Mersad radar system. d, 2500r, Ghadir submarine.

2010, Aug. 22 *Perf. 14¼x13¾*
3024 A1254 Sheet of 4, #a-d *3.50 3.50*

Martyrs of Holy Defense A1255

2010, Sept. 27 *Perf. 13¾x14¼*
3025 A1255 2000r multicolored *3.00 1.50*

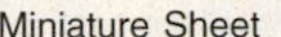

Miniature Sheet

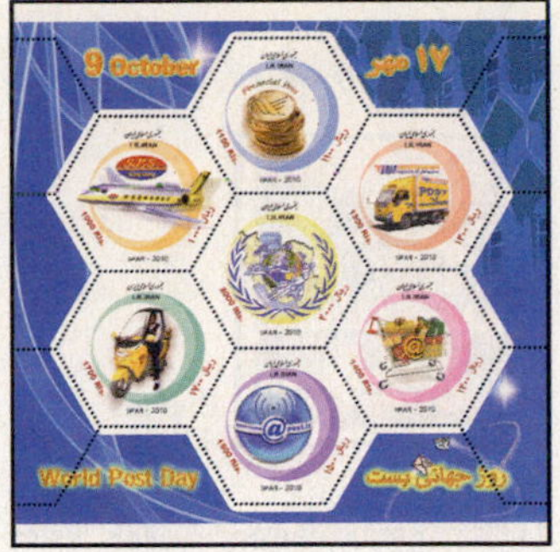

World Post Day — A1256

No. 3026: a, 1000r, Airplane and S.P.S. emblem. b, 1100r, Financial Post emblem. c, 1300r, Mail truck and EMS emblem. d, 1400r, Shopping cart and "@" symbol. e, 1500r, Iran Post e-mail emblem. f, 1700r, Mailman on motorcycle. g, 2000r, UPU emblem, map of Iran.

2010, Oct. 9 *Perf. 14¼*
3026 A1256 Sheet of 7, #a-g *6.50 6.50*

Embroidery — A1257

No. 3027: a, Jazygian embroidery designs, Hungary. b, Termeh embroidery designs, Yazd, Iran.

2010, Nov. 10 *Perf. 14¼x13¾*
3027 A1257 2000r Horiz. pair, #a-b *3.00 3.00*

See Hungary Nos. 4178-4179.

18th Book Week — A1258

2010, Nov. 14 *Perf. 13¾x14¼*
3028 A1258 2000r multicolored *3.00 1.50*

Sheikh Abbas Qummi (1877-1940), Historian A1259

2010, Dec. 2
3029 A1259 2000r multicolored *2.50 1.25*

A1259a

A1259b

Personalized Stamps — A1259c

No. 3029E: f, 300r, Rainbow, denomination on green and blue stripes. g, 700r, Rainbos, denomination on orange, yellow and green stripes. h, 900r, Rainbow and tree, denomination on tree and grass. i, 1200r, Clouds, butterfly and city, denomination on city.

2010-11 **Litho.** *Perf. 13¾x14¼*

Denomination on One Line Country Name at Center

3029A A1259a 300r multi + label *3.00 3.00*
3029B A1259a 650r multi + label *6.00 6.00*
3029C A1259a 1000r multi + label *9.50 9.50*

Country Name at Left Above Denomination on Two Lines

3029D A1259b 650r multi + label *6.00 6.00*

Souvenir Sheet Country Name Not Shown in English

Perf. 14¼x13¾ on 3 Sides

3029E A1259c Sheet of 4, #f-i + 4 labels *6.00 6.00*

Issued: No. 3029A, 2010, others, 2011. Labels on Nos. 3029A-3029E are separated from the stamps by a line of simulated perforations. Other labels exist for No. 3029A. Other labels may exist for Nos. 3029B-3029E.

Space — A1259d

No. 3029J — Inscriptions: k, Space Technology Day. l, Kavoshgar 2. m, Tolou National Satellite. n, Mesbah 2 National Satellite. o, Satellite Ground Stations.

2010, Dec. 6 **Litho.** *Perf. 13¾x14¼*
3029J Horiz. strip of 5 *4.00 4.00*
k.-l. A1259d 1200r Either single .50 .25
m. A1259d 1400r multi .50 .25
n. A1259d 1600r multi .50 .30
o. A1259d 1800r multi .50 .35

Bank Maskan Mehr Housing Project, 73rd Anniv. — A1260

2011, Jan. 15
3030 A1260 2000r multicolored *2.00 1.00*

Electronic Communication Between People and Government
A1261

2011, Jan. 17
3031 A1261 2000r multicolored 2.50 1.75

Islamic Revolution, 32nd Anniv. — A1262

No. 3032 — Ayatollah Khomeini and: a, Red flowers at LR. b, Candle at UL. c, White flowers and three candles at top. d, Birds and white flowers.

2011, Feb. 11
3032 Horiz. strip of 4 3.50 3.50
a.-d. A1262 1000r Any single .50 .25

Convergence of Montheistic Religions — A1263

2011, Feb. 15 ***Perf. 14¼x13¾***
3033 A1263 2000r multicolored 3.00 1.50

Ayatollah Mahmoud Taleghani (1911-79)
A1264

2011, Mar. 5 ***Perf. 13¾x14¼***
3034 A1264 2500r multicolored 3.00 1.50

Miniature Sheet

New Year — A1265

No. 3035: a, 1000r, Bowl of coins. b, 1100r, Grass and painted eggs in bowl. c, 1300r, Bowl of sumac. d, 1400r, Apples in bowl. e, 1500r, Garlic bulbs in bowl. f, 1700r, Oleaster in bowl. g, 2000r, Hyacinth and Koran.

2011, Mar. 26 ***Perf. 14¼***
3035 A1265 Sheet of 7, #a-g 4.00 4.00

Bridges A1266

Designs: 10,000r, Jahanara Bridge. 14,800r, Khajoo Bridge. 20,000r, Veresk Bridge. 20,700r, Javadieh Bridge.

2011 Litho. *Perf. 14*
3036 A1266 10,000r multi 6.00 1.90
3037 A1266 14,800r multi 7.00 2.75
3038 A1266 20,000r multi 8.00 3.50
3039 A1266 20,700r multi 12.00 4.00
Nos. 3036-3039 (4) 33.00 12.15

Issued: 10,000r, 6/15; 14,800r, 7/20; 20,000r, 5/22; 20,700r, 7/6.

World Crafts Day — A1267

No. 3040: a, Vase. b, Lidded container.

2011, June 10 ***Perf. 13¾x14¼***
3040 A1267 2000r Horiz. pair, #a-b 3.50 1.75

Ayatollah Muhammad Fazel Lankarani (1931-2007)
A1268

2011, June 15
3041 A1268 2000r multicolored 2.50 1.25

Souvenir Sheet

Green Pheasants — A1269

2011, July 26 ***Perf. 14¼x13¾***
3042 A1269 5000r multicolored 3.50 3.50

PhilaNippon '11 Intl. Philatelic Exhibition, Yokohama, Japan.

Souvenir Sheet

Iranian Men's Volleyball Team, Champions of 16th Asian Tournament — A1269a

2011, Sept. 29 ***Perf. 14***
3042A A1269a 3400r multi 3.50 3.50

National Veterinary Day — A1270

2011, Oct. 6 ***Perf. 14¼x13¾***
3043 A1270 2200r multicolored 2.00 1.00

2011 Population and Housing Census
A1271

2011, Oct. 23 ***Perf. 13¾x14¼***
3044 A1271 2200r multi 2.00 1.00

Shams Tabrizi (1185-c.1248), Teacher of Poet Mevlana
A1272

2011, Oct. 30
3045 A1272 2200r multi 2.00 1.00

Souvenir Sheet

Buildings in Belarus and Iran — A1273

No. 3046: a, Mir Castle, Mir, Belarus. b, Karimkhani Citadel, Shiraz, Iran.

Perf. 14¼x13¾
2011, Sept. 28 Litho.
3046 A1273 2200r Sheet of 2, #a-b 3.50 3.50

See Belarus No. 783.

World Post Day — A1274

2011, Oct. 9 ***Perf. 13¾***
3047 A1274 2000r multi 2.50 1.25

19th Book Week — A1275

2011, Nov. 13 ***Perf. 13¾x14¼***
3048 A1275 2200r multi 2.00 1.00

Souvenir Sheet

Revival Week — A1276

2011, Nov. 27 ***Perf. 14¼x13¾***
3049 A1276 2200r multi 3.00 3.00

Personalized Stamp — A1276a

2011, Dec. 6 Litho. *Perf. 13¾*
3049A A1276a 2600r multi + label 2.00 2.00

Label on No. 3049A separated from the stamp by a line of simulated perforations. Another label exists for No. 3049A.

Worldwide Fund for Nature (WWF) — A1277

Designs: Nos. 3050, 3054a, 600r, Long-eared owl. Nos. 3051, 3054b, 1100r, Spotted owlet. Nos. 3052, 3054c, 1600r, Pallid scops owl. Nos. 3053, 3054d, 2200r, Brown fish owl.

2011, Dec. 14 Litho.
Stamps With White Frames
3050-3053 A1277 Set of 4 3.00 3.00
Souvenir Sheet
Stamps Without White Frame
3054 A1277 Sheet of 4, #a-d 4.00 4.00

No. 3054 exists imperf. Value, $125.

Islamic Awakening
A1278

2011, Dec. 22 *Perf. 13¾x14¼*
3055 A1278 2200r multi 2.00 1.00

Fish Type of 2009-11

Designs as before.

2011 Litho. *Perf. 14*
Size: 30x23mm

3055A	A1229	300r multi	1.00	.50
3055B	A1229	400r multi	1.00	.50
3055C	A1229	500r multi	1.00	.50
3055D	A1229	1000r multi	1.00	.50
3055E	A1229	2000r multi	2.00	1.00
3055F	A1229	4000r multi	4.00	2.00
3055G	A1229	5000r multi	5.00	2.25
3055H	A1229	6400r multi	6.00	2.50
3055I	A1229	7500r multi	7.00	3.00

No. 3055G exists imperf. Value, pair $50.

Islamic and Iranian Culture and Civilization — A1279

2012, Feb. 1 *Perf. 14¼x13¾*
3056 A1279 2200r multi 2.00 1.00

Souvenir Sheet

Islamic Revolution, 33rd Anniv. — A1280

No. 3057: a, Toppled statue of Shah of Iran, flames. b, Ayatollah Khomeini, tulips.

2012, Feb. 11 *Perf. 13¾x14¼*
3057 A1280 2200r Sheet of 2, #a-b 2.50 2.50

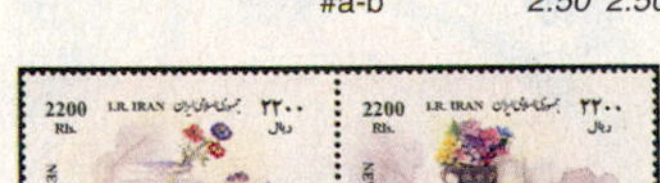

New Year 2012 — A1281

No. 3058 — Flowers and: a, Pen, goldfish in bowl. b, Apples, oil lamp.

2012, Mar. 26 *Perf. 14¼x13¾*
3058 A1281 2200r Horiz. pair, #a-b 2.50 2.50

A souvenir sheet containing Nos. 3058a-3058b was printed in limited quantities. Value $12.

Grand Ayatollah Mohammed Taghi Bahjat (1913-2009)
A1282

2012, May 17 *Perf. 13¾x14¼*
3059 A1282 2200r multi 2.00 .75

A1283

Bridges
A1284

Designs: 200r, Broken Bridge. 1000r, Khosro Abad Bridge. 3000r, Khatoon Bridge. 5000r, Martyr Kalantari Bridge. 8000r, Qishlaq Bridge. 9000r, Mardogh Bridge. 20,000r, Veresk Bridge.

Perf. 14 (A1283), 13x13½ (A1284)
2012-13

3060	A1283	200r multi	.25	.25
3061	A1284	1000r multi	.25	.25
3062	A1284	3000r multi	.50	.50
3063	A1284	5000r multi	.85	.85
3064	A1283	8000r multi	2.00	1.40
3065	A1283	9000r multi	3.00	1.60
3066	A1283	20,000r multi	7.00	3.25
		Nos. 3060-3066 (5)	6.20	6.20

Issued: 200r, Dec. 2012; 1000r, 5000r, Jan. 2013; 3000r, 1/13/13; 8000r, 10/30; 9000r, 2/9. 20,000r, 2012.

See Nos. 3075-3080, 3106-3108, 3110-3112.

Islamic Republic of Iran Day — A1285

2012, Mar. 30 Litho. *Perf. 13¾x14*
3067 A1285 2200r multi 2.00 1.50

25th Tehran Intl. Book Fair — A1286

2012, May 5
3068 A1286 2200r multi 1.25 .50

Ramadan
A1287

2012, July 21
3069 A1287 2200r multi 1.25 .50

Souvenir Sheet

Dedication and Sacrifice — A1288

No. 3070: a, Mohammad Hussein Fahmideh (1967-80), war hero. b, Riz Ali Khajavi, farmer who prevented 1962 train crash.

2012, Dec. 11 ***Perf. 14 Syncopated***
3070 A1288 2200r Sheet of 2, #a-b 2.75 2.75

Miniature Sheet

World Crafts Day — A1289

No. 3071 — Various textile crafts with: a, Green panel, denomination at LL. b, Green panel, denomination at LR. c, Red panel, denomination at UL. d, Red panel, denomination at UR.

Perf. 14x13¾ Syncopated
2012, Dec. 11
3071 A1289 2000r Sheet of 4, #a-d 3.50 3.50

A1290

Personalized Stamps — A1291

2012 *Perf. 13¾x14*
3072 A1290 2200r multi + label 1.25 .50

Perf. 13¾
3073 A1291 2500r multi + label 1.50 .50

Labels on Nos. 3072-3073 are separated from the stamps by a line of simulated perforations. Another label exists for No. 3073. Other labels may exist for No. 3072.

Non-Aligned Movement, 16th Summit, Tehran — A1292

2012, Aug. 28
3074 A1292 2200r multicolored 1.75 .50

Bridge Types of 2012-13

Designs: 100r, Earthen Bridge. 500r, Zamankhan Bridge. 800r, Yaqubie Bridge. 2000r, Tinoj Bridge. 4000r, Ghotoor Bridge. 15,700r, Bahrami Bridge.

Perf. 14 (A1283), 13x13½ (A1284)
2012-13

3075	A1284	100r multi	.25	.25
3076	A1284	500r multi	.25	.25
3077	A1284	800r multi	.25	.25
3078	A1284	2000r multi	.35	.35
3079	A1284	4000r multi	.65	.65
3080	A1283	15,700r multi	2.60	2.60
		Nos. 3075-3080 (6)	4.35	4.35

Issued: 100r, 2/19/13; 500r, 2/13/13; 800r, 3/6/13; 2000r, 3/27/13; 4000r, 3/13/13; 15,700r, 9/5.

Souvenir Sheet

Sacred Defense Week and World Post Day — A1293

2012, Oct. 8 *Perf. 14*
3081 A1293 3400r multi 2.25 2.25

20th Book Week — A1294

2012, Nov. 15 *Perf. 13¾x14*
3082 A1294 2200r multi 1.50 .50

The Canon of Medicine, by Avicenna, 1000th Anniv. of Completion
A1295

2013, Mar. 5
3083 A1295 3000r multi 1.75 .50

Arbor Day — A1297

2013, Mar. 5 Litho. ***Perf. 13¾x14¼***
3084 A1297 3000r multi 1.75 .50

Miniature Sheet

Fish — A1298

No. 3085: a, 3000r, Cyprinus carpio. b, 3600r, Rutilus frisii kutum. c, 3900r, Stizostedion lucioperca. d, 4600r, Salmon trutta caspius.

Perf. 14¼x13¾
2013, Mar. 20 Litho.
3085 A1298 Sheet of 4, #a-d *4.50 4.50*

Souvenir Sheet

New Year — A1299

2013, Mar. 25 Litho. ***Perf. 14x13¾***
3086 A1299 15,000r multi *4.00 4.00*

A1300

Personalized Stamps A1301

2013 Litho. ***Perf. 13¾***
3087 A1300 650r multi + label *10.00 10.00*

Perf. 13¾x14¼
3088 A1301 4500r multi + label *5.00 5.00*

Labels on Nos. 3087-3088 are separated from the stamps by a line of simulate perforations. issued: No. 3087, 7/8; No. 3088, 4/7.

Souvenir Sheet

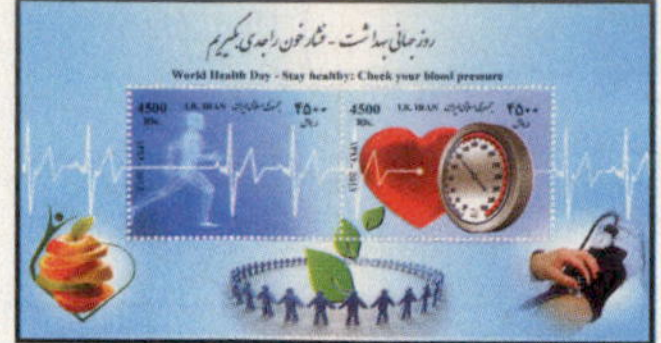

World Health Day — A1302

No. 3089 — Electrocardiogram waves and: a, Running skeleton. b, Heart and sphygmomanometer dial.

2013, Apr. 7 Litho. ***Perf. 14¼x13¾***
3089 A1302 4500r Sheet of 2, #a-b *3.50 3.50*

Souvenir Sheet

Ebrat Museum, Tehran — A1303

2013, May 6 Litho. ***Perf. 14¼x13¾***
3090 A1303 6000r multi *3.50 3.50*

Miniature Sheet

Martyrs — A1304

No. 3091: a, 3000r, Dr. Mostafa Chamran (1932-81), Minister of Defense. b, 3600r, Javad Fakori (1939-81), Minister of Defense. c, 3900r, Mousa Namjoo (1938-81), Minister of Defense. d, 4600r, Mohsen Safavi, combat engineer.

2013, May 9 Litho. ***Perf. 14¼x13¾***
3091 A1304 Sheet of 4, #a-d *4.00 4.00*

World Crafts Day — A1305

No. 3092 — Chalice with background color of: a, 4500r, Red. b, 5400r, Purple. c, 5800r, Red violet. d, 6900r, Brown orange.

Perf. 13¾x14¼
2013, June 10 Litho. Wmk. 411
3092 A1305 Block of 4, #a-d *6.00 6.00*

Unknown Soldiers of Imam Zaman — A1306

Perf. 13¾
2013, June 23 Litho. Unwmk.
3093 A1306 3000r multi *2.50* 1.00

World Children's Day — A1307

Wmk. 411
2013, Nov. 8 Litho. ***Perf. 13¾***
3094 A1307 4500r multi *2.00* .50

Economic Cooperation Organization A1308

Perf. 13¾x14¼
2013, Nov. 25 Litho. Wmk. 411
3095 A1308 4500r multi *2.00* .50

A1309

A1310

A1311

A1312

A1313

A1314

A1315

A1316

A1317

Persian Alphabet A1318

2014 Litho. Wmk. 411 ***Perf. 14***
3096 A1309 500r multi .25 .25
3097 A1310 1000r multi .25 .25
3098 A1311 2000r multi .25 .25
3099 A1312 3000r multi .25 .25
3100 A1313 4000r multi *1.50 1.50*
3101 A1314 5000r multi *1.75 1.75*
3102 A1315 8000r multi *2.50 2.50*
3103 A1316 9000r multi .70 .70
3104 A1317 10,000r multi *3.50 3.50*
3105 A1318 30,000r multi *7.50 7.50*
Nos. 3096-3105 (10) 18.45 18.45

Issued; 500r, 5/7; 1000r, 5/5; 2000r, 5/29; 3000r, 3/1; 4000r, 9/6; 5000r, 3/12; 8000r, 3/10; 9000r, 7/5; 10,000r, 5/15; 30,000r, 2/16.

Bridges Type of 2012-13

Designs: 250r, Latidan Bridge. 300r, Doab Bridge. 400r, Mirbaha Bridge.

2014 Litho. Wmk. 411 ***Perf. 14***
3106 A1283 250r multi .90 .35
3107 A1283 300r multi .90 .35
3108 A1283 400r multi .90 .35
Nos. 3106-3108 (3) 2.70 1.05

Issued: 250r, 2/19; 300r, 400r, 2/23.

World Telecommunications Day — A1319

Wmk. 411
2014, May 17 Litho. ***Perf. 13¾***
3109 A1319 4500r multi *2.00* 1.00

Bridges Type of 2012-13

Designs: 9000r, Mardogh Bridge. 10,000r, Martyr Jahanara Bridge. 20,000r, Veresk Bridge.

2014 Litho. Unwmk. ***Perf. 13x13½***
3110 A1284 9000r multi .70 .70
3111 A1284 10,000r multi .75 .75
3112 A1284 20,000r multi 1.50 1.50
Nos. 3110-3112 (3) 2.95 2.95

A1323

A1325

A1326

A1328

A1329

Persian Alphabet A1330

2014 Litho. Wmk. 411 *Perf. 14*

3116	A1323	3000r multi	.25	.25
3118	A1325	6000r multi	.45	.45
3119	A1326	7000r multi	.55	.55
3121	A1328	10,000r multi	.75	.75
3122	A1329	20,000r multi	1.50	1.50
3123	A1330	30,000r multi	2.25	2.25
		Nos. 3116-3123 (6)	5.75	5.75

Issued: 6000r, 10/18; 7000r, 9/16; 20,000r, 8/12; others, 2014.

World Post Day A1331

Perf. 14x13¾

2014, July 9 Litho. Wmk. 411
3124 A1331 4500r multi 3.00 2.00

Dated 2013.

27th Tehran International Book Fair — A1332

2014, July 9 Litho. *Perf. 13¾x14*
3125 A1332 4500r multi 2.00 1.00

Martyr's Day A1333

Perf. 14x13¾

2014, July 9 Litho. Wmk. 411
3126 A1333 10,000r multi 3.50 2.25

Souvenir Sheet

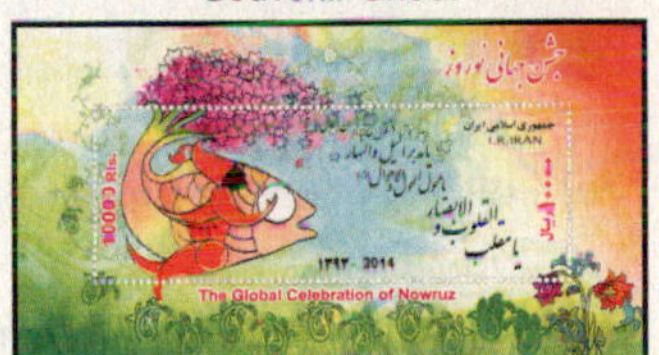
New Year — A1334

Perf. 14¼x13¾

2014, Aug. 10 Litho. Unwmk.
3127 A1334 10,000r multi 2.75 2.00

Souvenir Sheet

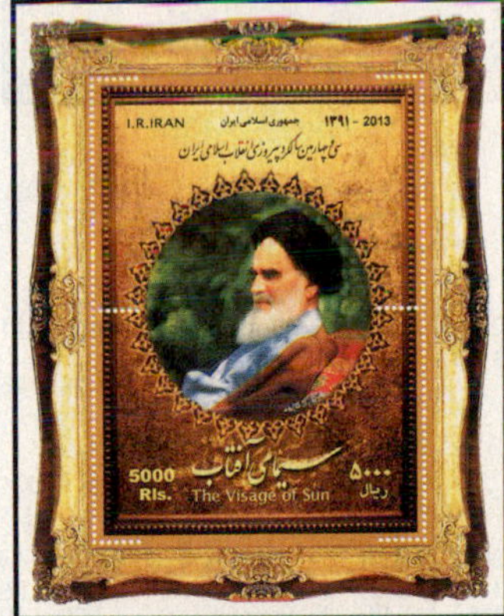
Ayatollah Khomeini (1900-89) — A1335

Perf. 13¾ (Partial)

2014, Aug. 18 Litho. Wmk. 411
3128 A1335 5000r multi 2.75 2.25

Dated 2013.

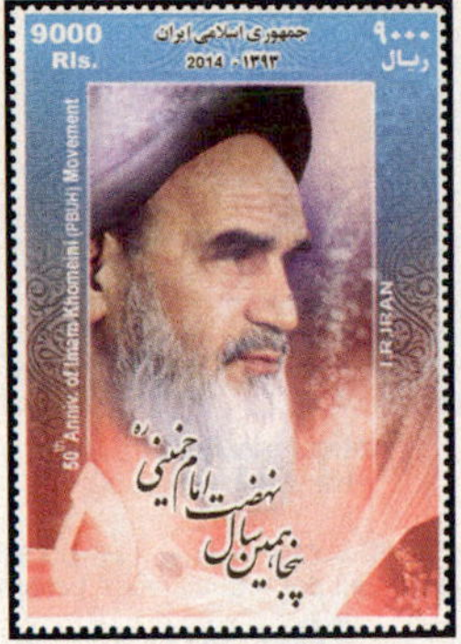
Ayatollah Khomeini Movement, 50th Anniv. — A1336

Unwmk.

2014, Sept. 17 Litho. *Perf. 14*
3129 A1336 9000r multi 3.50 2.00

World Post Day A1337

Perf. 14¼x13¾

2014, Nov. 16 Litho. Wmk. 411
3130 A1337 6000r multi 2.60 1.25

Diplomatic Relations Between Iran and Mexico, 50th Anniv. — A1338

Wmk. 411

2014, Nov. 16 Litho. *Perf. 14*
3131 A1338 8000r multi 2.00 1.25

See Mexico No. 2923.

Souvenir Sheet

Samarkand Observatory — A1339

No. 3132: a, Observatory. b, Open almanac.

Perf. 14x13¾

2014, July 1 Litho. Wmk. 411
3132 A1339 6000r Sheet of 2, #a-b 3.00 1.25

Miniature Sheet

Worldwide Fund for Nature (WWF) — A1340

No. 3133 — Lesser white-fronted goose: a, 5000r, Standing. b, 6000r, In flight. c, 7000r, On water. d, 8000r, Standing, flock flying in background.

Perf. 14x13¾

2014, Dec. 15 Litho. Unwmk.
3133 A1340 Sheet of 4, #a-d 5.00 4.00

Miniature Sheet

Schools and Their Emblems — A1341

No. 3134: a, School of Charbagh, Isfahan. b, Emblem of University of Jondishapour. c, Emblem of University of Tehran. d, School of Darol Fonoun.

Perf. 14x13¾

2015, Feb. 3 Litho. Wmk. 411
3134 A1341 6000r Sheet of 4, #a-d 5.75 4.75

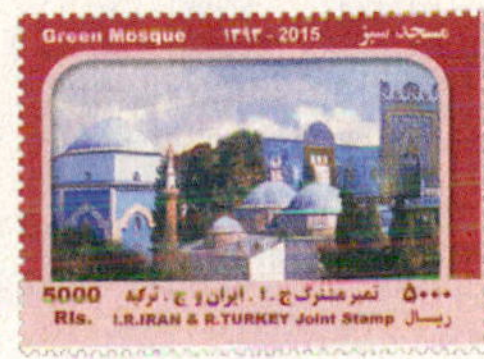
Mosques A1342

No. 3135: a, Green Mosque, Bursa, Turkey. b, Kabood Mosque, Tabriz, Iran.

Perf. 14x13¾

2015, Feb. 18 Litho. Unwmk.
3135 Horiz. pair + central label 3.50 3.50
a.-b. A1342 5000r Either single .60 .40

See Turkey No. 3425.

New Year — A1343

Perf. 14x13¾

2015, Mar. 25 Litho. Unwmk.
3136 A1343 9000r multi 2.75 2.00

World Telecommunications Day — A1344

Perf. 14x13¾

2015, May 10 Litho. Wmk. 411
3137 A1344 9000r multi 2.75 1.50

A1345

Flowers — A1346

Designs: 500r, Origanum majorana. No. 3140, Viola tricolor. No. 3141, Viola tricolor. 2000r, Orchis simia. 3000r, Rheum rhaponticum. No. 3145, Matricaria chamomilla. No. 3146, Matricaria chamomilla. 7000r, Ricinus communis. 10,000r, Glycyrrhiza glabra. No. 3150, Echium amoenum. 30,000r, Crocus sativus.

2015-16 Litho. Wmk. 411 *Perf. 14*

3138	A1345	500r	multi	.25	.25
3139	A1346	500r	multi	.25	.25
3140	A1345	1000r	multi	.25	.25
3141	A1346	1000r	multi	.25	.25
3142	A1346	2000r	multi	.25	.25
3143	A1345	2000r	multi	.25	.25
3144	A1346	3000r	multi	.25	.25
3145	A1345	5000r	multi	.35	.35
3146	A1346	5000r	multi	.35	.35
3147	A1346	7000r	multi	.50	.50
3148	A1345	10,000r	multi	.70	.70
3149	A1346	10,000r	multi	.70	.70
3150	A1346	20,000r	multi	1.40	1.40
3152	A1346	30,000r	multi	2.00	2.00
	Nos. 3138-3152 (14)			7.75	7.75

Issued: No. 3138, 8/23; No. 3140, 7/5; No. 3142, 9/26; No. 3145, 10/5; No. 3148, 10/10. 30,000r, 1/5/16. See Nos. 3164-3165.

Return to Iran of Bodies of 175 Divers Killed in 1986 Operation Karbala-4 — A1348

Perf. 14x13¾

2015, Aug. 11 Litho. Wmk. 411
3153 A1348 9000r multi 2.75 2.00

Miniature Sheet

Expo 2015, Milan — A1349

No. 3154: a, Folio of Iran Miniature. b, Iran Pavilion. c, Saffron and crocus. d, Persian garden carpet.

Perf. 14x13¾

2015, Aug. 23 Litho. Wmk. 411
3154 A1349 9000r Sheet of 4, #a-d 6.50 5.00

Antiquities From Sialk-Kashan — A1350

No. 3155 — Clay pots: a, Left pot with bull design. b, Left pot with diamond pattern.

Perf. 14x13¾

2015, Sept. 15 Litho. Wmk. 411
3155 A1350 9000r Vert. pair, #a-b 3.00 1.50

Alam-al-Hoda (c. 965-1009), Islamic Scholar — A1351

Perf. 13¾x14

2015 Litho. Wmk. 411
3156 A1351 9000r multi 3.00 1.50

World Children's Day — A1352

Perf. 13¾x14

2016 Litho. Wmk. 411
3157 A1352 9000r multi .60 .60

Dated 2015.

Birth Anniversary of Prophet Mohammad A1353

Perf. 13¾x14

2016 Litho. Wmk. 411
3158 A1353 9000r multi .60 .60

Dated 2015.

Cinema Day A1354

Perf. 14x13¾

2016 Litho. Wmk. 411
3159 A1354 9000r multi 3.00 1.50

Navvab Safavi (c. 1924-56), Cleric — A1355

Perf. 13¾x14

2016, Jan. 17 Litho. Wmk. 411
3160 A1355 9000r multi .60 .60

Souvenir Sheet

New Year 2016 — A1356

Perf. 14x13¾

2016 Litho. Wmk. 411
3161 A1356 9000r multi .60 .60

Eurasian Lynx — A1357

No. 3162: a, Lynx facing right. b, Head of lynx.

Perf. 14x13¾

2016 Litho. Wmk. 411
3162 A1357 9000r Horiz. pair, #a-b 1.25 1.25

Poets — A1358

No. 3163: a, Awhadi Maraghei (1271-1338). b, Mir Sayyid Ali Hamadani (1314-84). c, Sheikh Ahmad Jami (1048-1141).

Perf. 13¾x14

2016, Aug. 5 Litho. Wmk. 411
3163 A1358 9000r Horiz. strip of 3, #a-c 1.75 1.75

Flower Types of 2015-16

Designs: 8000r, Salix aegyptiaca. 9000r, Carum carvi.

2016 Litho. Wmk. 411 *Perf. 14*

3164	A1346	8000r	multi	.55	.55
3165	A1346	9000r	multi	.60	.60

Naser Khosrow (1004-1088), Poet — A1359

Perf. 13¾x14

2016 Litho. Wmk. 411
3167 A1359 9000r multi .60 .60

Dated 2015.

International Tourism Day — A1360

Perf. 14x13¾

2016 Litho. Wmk. 411
3168 A1360 15,000r multi 1.00 1.00

Nationalization of Postal Service — A1361

Perf. 14x13¾

2016, Aug. 18 Litho. Unwmk.
3169 A1361 9000r multi .60 .60

World Children's Day — A1362

Perf. 13¾x14

2016, Sept. 7 Litho. Wmk. 411
3170 A1362 9000r multi .60 .60

2015 Pilgrimage Stampede at Mena, Saudi Arabia — A1363

Perf. 13¾x14

2016, Sept. 12 Litho. Unwmk.
3171 A1363 15,000r multi .95 .95

Islamic Revolution, 38th Anniv. — A1364

Perf. 13¾x14

2017, Feb. 10 Litho. Unwmk.

3172 A1364 9000r multi .55 .55

Souvenir Sheet

Pres. Akbar Hashemi Rafsanjani (1934-2017) — A1365

Perf. 14x13¾

2017, Feb. 16 Litho. Unwmk.

3173 A1365 9000r multi .55 .55

Fatimah (c. 616-33), Daughter of Mohammed — A1366

2017 Litho. Unwmk. ***Perf. 13¾x14***

3174 A1366 15,000r multi .95 .95

International Woman's Day.

New Year 2017 A1367

Perf. 13¾x14

2017, Mar. 25 Litho. Unwmk.

3175 A1367 9000r multi .55 .55

Firefighters — A1368

2017 Litho. Unwmk. ***Perf. 13¾x14***

3176 A1368 9000r multi .55 .55

2017 Asia Pacific Postal Union Congress, Tehran — A1369

2017 Litho. Unwmk. ***Perf. 14x13¾***

3177 A1369 9000r multi .55 .55

Souvenir Sheet

Houses of Worship — A1370

No. 3178: a, Blue Mosque, Yerevan, Armenia. b, Holy Savior Cathedral, Isfahan, Iran.

Perf. 14x13¾ on 3 Sides

2017, Oct. 25 Litho. Unwmk.

3178 A1370 15,000r Sheet of 2, #a-b 1.75 1.75

Diplomatic Relations between Iran & Armenia.

See Armenia No.

Martyrs of Terror — A1371

2017 Litho. Unwmk. ***Perf. 13¾x14***

3179 A1371 9000r multi .50 .50

Personalized Stamp — A1372

2017 Litho. Unwmk. ***Perf. 13¾x14***

3180 A1372 10,000r multi .55 .55

Label on No. 3180 separated from the stamp by a line of simulated perforations.

Iran Bastan Museum and Malek National Library and Museum, 80th Anniv. — A1373

2017 Litho. Unwmk. ***Perf. 13¾x14***

3181 A1373 12,000r multi .70 .70

Historic City of Yazd UNESCO World Heritage Site — A1374

2017 Litho. Unwmk. ***Perf. 14x13¾***

3182 A1374 12,000r multi .70 .70

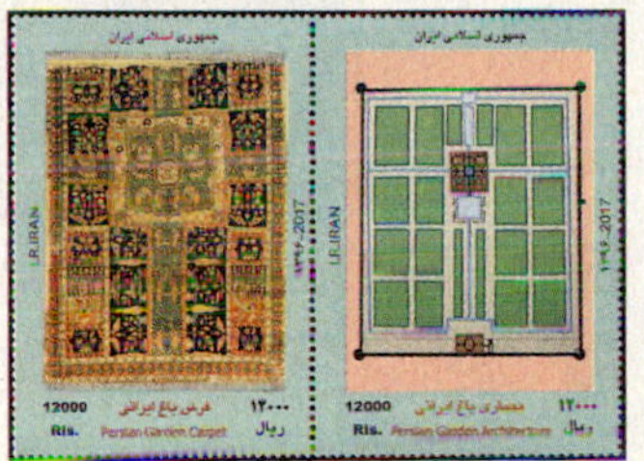
A1375

No. 3183: a, Persian Garden carpet. b, Persian Garden architecture.

2017 Litho. Unwmk. ***Perf. 13¾x14***

3183 A1375 12,000r Horiz. pair, #a-b 1.40 1.40

SEMI-POSTAL STAMPS

Lion and Bull, Persepolis SP1

Persian Soldier, Persepolis — SP2

Palace of Darius the Great — SP3

Tomb of Cyrus the Great, Pasargadae SP4

King Darius on his Throne — SP5

Perf. 13x13½, 13½x13

1948, Jan. 30 Engr. Unwmk.

B1	SP1	50d + 25d emer	2.50	2.50
B2	SP2	1r + 50d red	2.50	2.50
B3	SP3	2½r + 1¼r blue	2.50	2.50
B4	SP4	5r + 2½r pur	3.50	3.50
B5	SP5	10r + 5r vio brn	4.50	4.50
		Nos. B1-B5 (5)	15.50	15.50

The surtax was for reconstruction of the tomb of Avicenna (980-1037), Persian physician and philosopher, at Hamadan.

Ardashir II — SP6

Shapur I and Valerian SP7

Designs: 1r+50d, King Narses, Naqsh-i-Rustam. 5r+2½r, Taq-i-Kisra, Ctesiphon. 10r+5r, Ardashir I and Ahura Mazda.

1949, June 11

B6	SP6	50d + 25d green	2.50	2.50
B7	SP6	1r + 50d ver	2.50	2.50
B8	SP7	2½r + 1½r blue	2.50	2.50
B9	SP7	5r + 2½r magenta	3.50	3.50
B10	SP7	10r + 5r grnsh gray	4.50	4.50
		Nos. B6-B10 (5)	15.50	15.50

The surtax was for reconstruction of Avicenna's tomb at Hamadan.

Gunbad-i-Ali — SP8

Alaviyan, Hamadan SP9

Seldjukide Coin — SP10

Designs: 1r+½r, Masjid-i-Jami, Isfahan. 5r+2½r, Masjid-i-Jami, Ardistan.

1949, Dec. 22

B11	SP8	50d + 25d bl grn	2.00	2.00
B12	SP8	1r + ½r dk brn	2.00	2.00
B13	SP9	2½r + 1¼r blue	2.00	2.00
B14	SP9	5r + 2½r red	3.00	3.00
B15	SP10	10r + 5r olive gray	3.50	3.50
		Nos. B11-B15 (5)	12.50	12.50

The surtax was for reconstruction of Avicenna's tomb at Hamadan.

Koran, Crescent and Flag — SP11

1950, Oct. 2 **Litho.** ***Perf. 11***

B16	SP11	1.50r + 1r multi	40.00	25.00

Economic Conference of the Islamic States.

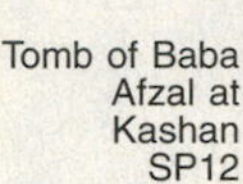

Tomb of Baba Afzal at Kashan SP12

Gorgan Vase — SP13

Designs: 2½r+1¼r, Tower of Ghazan. 5r+2½r, Masjid-i Gawhar. 10r+5r, Mihrab of the Mosque at Rezaieh.

Perf. 13x13½, 13½x13

1950, Aug. 23 **Engr.**

B17	SP12	50d + 25d dk grn	2.00	2.00
B18	SP13	1r + ½r blue	2.00	2.00
B19	SP13	2½r + 1¼r choc	2.00	2.00
B20	SP12	5r + 2½r red	3.00	3.00
B21	SP12	10r + 5r gray	3.50	3.50
		Nos. B17-B21 (5)	12.50	12.50

The surtax was for reconstruction of Avicenna's tomb at Hamadan.

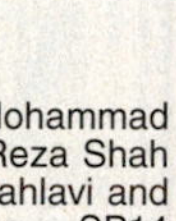

Mohammad Reza Shah Pahlavi and Map — SP14

Monument to Fallen Liberators of Azerbaijan SP15

Designs: 1r+50d, Marching troops. 1.50r+75d, Running advance with flag. 2.50r+1.25r, Mohammad Reza ShahPahlavi. 3r+1.50r, Parade of victors.

1950, Dec. 12 **Litho.**

B22	SP14	10d + 5d blk brn	17.50	10.00
B23	SP15	50d + 25d blk brn	17.50	10.00
B24	SP15	1r + 50d brn lake	25.00	12.00
B25	SP14	1.50r + 75d org ver	25.00	12.00
B26	SP14	2.50r + 1.25r blue	40.00	25.00
B27	SP15	3r + 1.50r ultra	45.00	25.00
		Nos. B22-B27 (6)	170.00	94.00

Liberation of Azerbaijan Province from communists, 4th anniv.

The surtax was for families of Persian soldiers who died in the struggle.

Koran Gate at Shiraz SP16

Saadi — SP17

Design: 50d+50d, Tomb of Saadi, Shiraz.

Perf. 11x10½, 10½x11

1952, Apr. 30 **Photo.** **Unwmk.**

B28	SP16	25d + 25d dl bl grn	5.00	3.00
B29	SP16	50d + 50d brn ol	5.00	3.00
B30	SP17	1.50r + 50d vio bl	30.00	9.00
		Nos. B28-B30 (3)	40.00	15.00

770th birthday of Saadi, Persian poet. The surtax was to help complete Saadi's tomb at Shiraz.

Three stamps of same denominations and colors, with values enclosed in tablets, were prepared but not officially issued.

View of Hamadan SP18

Avicenna — SP19

Designs: 2½r+1¼r, Gonbad Qabus (tower of tomb). 5r+2½r, Old tomb of Avicenna. 10r+5r, New tomb.

Perf. 13x13½, 13½x13

1954, Apr. 21 **Engr.** **Unwmk.**

B31	SP18	50d + 25d dp grn	2.00	2.00
B32	SP19	1r + ½r vio brn	2.00	2.00
B33	SP19	2½r + 1¼r blue	2.00	2.00
B34	SP18	5r + 2½r ver	3.00	3.00
B35	SP18	10r + 5r ol gray	4.00	4.00
		Nos. B31-B35 (5)	13.00	13.00

The surtax was for reconstruction of Avicenna's tomb at Hamadan.

Catalogue values for unused stamps in this section, from this point to the end of the section, are for Never Hinged items.

Mother with Children and Ruins — SP20

Wmk. 316

1963, Feb. 4 **Litho.** ***Perf. 10½***

B36	SP20	14r + 6r dk bl grn & lt brn	3.00	1.00

The surtax was for the benefit of survivors of the Kazvin earthquake.

For overprints see Nos. C86-C88.

AIR POST STAMPS

Type of 1909 Overprinted

1927 **Unwmk.** **Typo.** ***Perf. 11½***

C1	A31	1c org & maroon	3.50	1.50
C2	A31	2c vio & maroon	3.50	1.50
C3	A31	3c grn & maroon	3.50	1.50
C4	A31	6c red & maroon	3.50	1.50
C5	A31	9c gray & maroon	5.00	2.00
C6	A31	10c red vio & mar	7.00	2.50
C7	A31	13c dk bl & mar	8.00	3.00
C8	A31	1k sil, vio & bis brn	8.00	3.00
C9	A31	26c dk grn & mar	8.00	4.00
C10	A31	2k sil, dk grn & bis brown	15.00	5.00
C11	A31	3k sil, gray & bis brn	25.00	7.50
C12	A31	4k sil, bl & bis brn	45.00	17.50
C13	A31	5k gold, brn & bis brown	45.00	15.00
C14	A31	10k gold, org & bis brown	275.00	300.00
C15	A31	20k gold, ol grn & bis brn	275.00	300.00
C16	A31	30k gold, car & bis brown	275.00	300.00
		Nos. C1-C16 (16)	1,005.	965.50

Counterfeit overprints are plentiful. They are found on Nos. 448-463, perf. 12½x12 instead of 11½.

Exist without overprint. Value, set $4,000.

AP1

AP2

AP3

AP4

AP5

Airplane, Value and "Poste aérièn" Surcharged on Revenue Stamps

1928 ***Perf. 11***

C17	AP1	3k yellow brn	125.00	40.00
C18	AP2	5k dark brown	30.00	20.00
C19	AP3	1t gray vio	40.00	30.00
C20	AP4	2t olive bister	40.00	30.00
C21	AP5	3t deep green	55.00	40.00
		Nos. C17-C21 (5)	290.00	160.00

AP6

AP7

1928-29 **"Poste aerienne"**

C22	AP6	1c emerald	2.50	.50
a.		1c yellow green	2.50	.50
b.		Double overprint	35.00	
C23	AP6	2c light blue	2.50	.25
a.		Rosette in place of "2"	*150.00*	*100.00*
C24	AP6	3c bright rose	2.50	.25
C25	AP6	5c olive brn	1.25	.25
a.		"5" omitted	3,000.	*2,250.*
b.		Horiz. pair, imperf. btwn.	*300.00*	
C26	AP6	10c dark green	2.00	.25
a.		"10" omitted	40.00	
b.		"1" inverted	75.00	
C27	AP7	1k dull vio	3.00	1.00
a.		"1" inverted	100.00	
C28	AP7	2k orange	10.00	3.50
a.		"S" for "s" in "Krs"	300.00	*175.00*
		Nos. C22-C28 (7)	23.75	6.00

Counterfeits exist.

Revenue Stamps Similar to Nos. C17 to C21, Overprinted like Nos. C22 to C28: "Poste aerienne"

1929

C29	AP1	3k yellow brn	100.00	25.00
C30	AP2	5k dark brn	25.00	10.00
C31	AP3	10k violet	40.00	30.00
C32	AP4	20k olive grn	45.00	35.00
C33	AP5	30k deep grn	55.00	45.00
a.		"80" instead of "30"		*4,000.*
		Nos. C29-C33 (5)	265.00	145.00

Reza Shah Pahlavi and Eagle — AP8

1930, July 6 **Photo.** ***Perf. 12½x11½***

C34	AP8	1c ol bis & brt bl	1.00	1.00
C35	AP8	2c bl & gray blk	1.00	1.00
C36	AP8	3c ol grn & dk vio	1.00	1.00
C37	AP8	4c dk vio & pck bl	1.00	1.00
C38	AP8	5c lt grn & mag	1.00	1.00
C39	AP8	6c mag & bl grn	1.00	1.00
C40	AP8	8c dk gray & dp vio	1.00	1.00
C41	AP8	10c dp ultra & ver	1.00	1.00
C42	AP8	12c slate & org	1.00	1.00
C43	AP8	15c org brn & ol grn	1.00	1.00
C44	AP8	1k Prus bl & scar	8.00	4.00
		Engr.		
C45	AP8	2k black & ultra	10.00	5.00
C46	AP8	3k dk brn & gray grn	20.00	6.00
C47	AP8	5k dp red & gray black	15.00	5.00
C48	AP8	1t orange & vio	52.00	12.00
C49	AP8	2t dk grn & red brown	50.00	40.00
C50	AP8	3t brn vio & sl bl	250.00	85.00
		Nos. C34-C50 (17)	415.00	167.00

Nos. C34-C50 Overprinted in Black

1935 **Photo.**

C51	AP8	1c ol bis & brt bl	1.00	1.00
C52	AP8	2c blue & gray blk	1.00	1.00
C53	AP8	3c ol grn & dk vio	1.00	1.00
C54	AP8	4c dk vio & pck bl	1.00	1.00
C55	AP8	5c lt grn & mag	1.00	1.00
C56	AP8	6c mag & bl grn	1.00	1.00
C57	AP8	8c dk gray & dp violet	1.00	1.00
C58	AP8	10c dp ultra & ver	1.00	1.00
C59	AP8	12c slate & org	1.00	1.00
C60	AP8	15c org brn & ol green	1.00	1.00
C61	AP8	1k Prus bl & scar	75.00	*100.00*
		Engr.		
C62	AP8	2k blk & ultra	50.00	*65.00*
C63	AP8	3k dk brn & gray green	25.00	15.00
C64	AP8	5k dp red & gray black	10.00	10.00
C65	AP8	1t orange & vio	225.00	175.00
C66	AP8	2t dk grn & red brown	45.00	40.00
C67	AP8	3t brn vio & sl bl	75.00	50.00
		Nos. C51-C67 (17)	515.00	465.00

Plane Over Mt. Demavend AP9

Plane above Mosque AP10

Unwmk.

1953, Jan. 21 Photo. *Perf. 11*

No.	Type	Denomination	Unused	Used
C68	AP9	50d bl green	1.50	.25
C69	AP10	1r car rose	1.50	.25
C70	AP10	2r dark blue	1.50	.25
C71	AP10	3r dark brn	2.50	.25
C72	AP10	5r purple	4.50	.25
C73	AP10	10r org ver	5.00	.30
C74	AP10	20r vio blue	8.00	.50
C75	AP10	30r olive	15.00	7.00
C76	AP10	50r brown	30.00	4.00
C77	AP10	100r black brn	85.00	15.00
C78	AP10	200r dk bl grn	75.00	20.00
		Nos. C68-C78 (11)	229.50	48.05

AP11

Golden Dome Mosque and Oil Well AP12

1953, May 4 Litho. *Perf. 10½*

Mosque in Deep Yellow

No.	Type	Denomination	Unused	Used
C79	AP11	3r violet	15.00	15.00
C80	AP12	5r chocolate	20.00	20.00
C81	AP11	10r bl green	55.00	40.00
C82	AP12	20r red vio	110.00	70.00
		Nos. C79-C82 (4)	200.00	145.00

Discovery of oil at Qum.

Catalogue values for unused stamps in this section, from this point to the end of the section, are for Never Hinged items.

Globe and UN Emblem AP13

Perf. 10½x12½

1957, Oct. 24 Photo. Wmk. 316

No.	Type	Denomination	Unused	Used
C83	AP13	10r brt red lil & rose	3.00	.90
C84	AP13	20r dl vio & rose vio	6.00	1.25

United Nations Day, Oct. 24, 1957.

UNESCO Emblem AP14

Wmk. 353

1966, June 20 Litho. *Perf. 10½*

No.	Type	Denomination	Unused	Used
C85	AP14	14r multicolored	2.00	.50

20th anniversary of UNESCO.

No. B36 Surcharged in Maroon, Brown or Red

1969, Dec. 4 Wmk. 316 *Perf. 10½*

No.	Type	Denomination	Unused	Used
C86	SP20	4r on 14r + 6r (M)	4.00	2.00
C87	SP20	10r on 14r + 6r (B)	5.00	3.00
C88	SP20	14r on 14r + 6r (R)	6.00	4.00
		Nos. C86-C88 (3)	15.00	9.00

1st England-Australia flight, via Iran, made by Capt. Ross Smith and Lt. Keith Smith, 50th anniv.

IATA Emblem and Persepolis AP15

Perf. 13x13½

1970, Oct. 27 Photo. Wmk. 353

No.	Type	Denomination	Unused	Used
C89	AP15	14r multicolored	10.00	3.00

26th meeting of the Intl. Air Transport Assoc. (IATA), Tehran.

"UIT" AP16

1972, May 17 Litho. *Perf. 10½*

No.	Type	Denomination	Unused	Used
C90	AP16	14r multicolored	3.25	.75

4th World Telecommunications Day.

Shah and Jet AP17

1974, June 1 Photo. *Perf. 13*

No.	Type	Denomination	Unused	Used
C91	AP17	4r org & black	1.00	.25
C92	AP17	10r blue & black	2.00	.25
C93	AP17	12r dull yel & blk	2.00	.40
C94	AP17	14r lt green & blk	2.50	.40
C95	AP17	20r red lilac & blk	3.00	.65
C96	AP17	50r dull bl & blk	7.50	1.60
		Nos. C91-C96 (6)	18.00	3.55

Crown Prince at Controls of Light Aircraft — AP18

1974, Oct. 31 Litho. *Perf. 10½*

No.	Type	Denomination	Unused	Used
C97	AP18	14r gold & multi	2.00	.65

Crown Prince Reza's 14th birthday.

Importation Prohibited
Importation of stamps was prohibited effective Oct. 29, 1987.

Islamic Revolution, 10th Anniv. — AP19

1989, Feb. 11 *Perf. 13x13½*

No.	Type	Denomination	Unused	Used
C98	AP19	40r red vio, blk & gold	.75	.50
C99	AP19	50r bl vio, blk & gold	.75	.50
a.		Pair, #C98-C99	1.75	1.50

Ayatollah Khomeini — AP20

1989, July 11 *Perf. 13*

No.	Type	Denomination	Unused	Used
C100	AP20	70r multicolored	1.00	.50

OFFICIAL STAMPS

Four bicolored stamps of this design (1s, 2s, 5s, 10s), with centers embossed, exist, but were never issued or used in Iran. Value $40. They are known imperforate and in many trial colors.

Shah Muzaffar-ed-Din O1

No. 145 Surcharged in Black

1902 *Perf. 12½*

No.	Type	Denomination	Unused	Used
O5	O1	5c on 1k red	30.00	30.00
O6	O1	10c on 1k red	30.00	30.00
O7	O1	12c on 1k red	40.00	40.00
		Nos. O5-O7 (3)	100.00	100.00

Nos. 351-363 Overprinted in Black

1903-06

No.	Type	Denomination	Unused	Used
O8	A26	1c violet	5.00	.75
O9	A26	2c gray	5.00	.75
O10	A26	3c green	5.00	.75
O11	A26	5c rose	5.00	.75
O12	A26	10c yel brown	8.00	.75
O13	A26	12c blue	12.00	.75

Perf. 11½x11

No.	Type	Denomination	Unused	Used
O14	A27	1k violet	14.00	7.50
O15	A27	2k ultra	25.00	12.50
a.		Violet overprint	75.00	
O16	A27	5k org brown	40.00	20.00
O17	A27	10k rose red	50.00	19.00
a.		Violet overprint		75.00
O18	A27	20k orange ('06)	200.00	40.00
O19	A27	30k green ('06)	250.00	90.00
O20	A27	50k green	250.00	125.00
		Nos. O8-O20 (13)	869.00	318.50

Overprinted on Nos. 368, 370a

No.	Type	Denomination	Unused	Used
O21	A27	2t on 50k grn (Bl)	175.00	75.00
O22	A27	3t on 50k grn (V)	175.00	75.00

Overprinted on Nos. 372, 375, New Value Surcharged in Blue or Black

1905

No.	Type	Denomination	Unused	Used
O23	A27	2t on 50k grn (Bl)	200.00	75.00
O28	A27	3t on 50k grn (Bk)	200.00	75.00

The 2t on 50k also exists with surcharge in black and magenta; the 3t on 50k in violet and magenta. Values about the same.

Regular Issue of 1909 Overprinted

There is a space between the word "Service" and the Persian characters.

1911 *Perf. 12½x12*

No.	Type	Denomination	Unused	Used
O31	A31	1c org & maroon	15.00	7.50
O32	A31	2c vio & maroon	15.00	7.50
O33	A31	3c yel grn & mar	15.00	7.50
O34	A31	6c red & maroon	15.00	7.50
O35	A31	9c gray & maroon	25.00	13.00
O36	A31	10c multicolored	30.00	13.00
O38	A31	1k multicolored	60.00	45.00
O40	A31	2k multicolored	150.00	90.00
		Nos. O31-O40 (8)	325.00	191.00

The 13c, 26c and 3k to 30k denominations were not regularly issued with this overprint.

Dangerous counterfeits exist, usually on reprints.

Regular Issue of 1915 Overprinted

1915 Wmk. 161 *Perf. 11, 11½*

No.	Type	Denomination	Unused	Used
O41	A33	1c car & indigo	2.50	*4.00*
O42	A33	2c bl & carmine	2.50	*4.00*
O43	A33	3c dark green	2.50	*4.00*
O44	A33	5c red	2.50	*4.00*
O45	A33	6c ol grn & car	2.50	*4.00*
O46	A33	9c yel brn & vio	2.50	*4.00*
O47	A33	10c multicolored	2.50	*4.50*
O48	A33	12c ultramarine	3.00	*5.00*
O49	A34	1k multicolored	7.00	*10.00*
O50	A33	24c multicolored	3.50	*10.00*
O51	A34	2k sil, bl & rose	7.00	*15.00*
O52	A34	3k sil, vio & brn	7.00	*15.00*
O53	A34	5k multicolored	7.50	*15.00*
O54	A35	1t gold, pur & blk	10.00	*20.00*
O55	A35	2t gold, grn & brn	10.00	*27.50*
O56	A35	3t multicolored	12.50	*27.50*
O57	A35	5t gold, bl & ind	15.00	*30.00*
		Nos. O41-O57 (17)	100.00	*203.50*

Coronation of Shah Ahmed.

Reprints have dull rather than shiny overprint. Value, set, $17.50.

Coat of Arms — O2

1941 Unwmk. Litho. *Perf. 11*

For Internal Postage

O58	O2	5d violet	15.00	.25
O59	O2	10d magenta	15.00	.25
O60	O2	25d carmine	15.00	.25
a.		Printed on both sides	*12,000.*	
O61	O2	50d brown black	20.00	.25
O62	O2	75d claret	25.00	.45

Size: 22½x30mm

O63	O2	1r peacock grn	40.00	.45
O64	O2	1½r deep blue	40.00	1.50
O65	O2	2r light blue	60.00	1.50
O66	O2	3r vio brown	75.00	1.50
O67	O2	5r gray green	150.00	2.00
O68	O2	10r dk brn & bl	550.00	5.00
O69	O2	20r chlky bl & brt pink	700.00	65.00
O70	O2	30r vio & brt grn	900.00	150.00
O71	O2	50r turq grn & dk brown	1,900.	350.00
		Nos. O58-O71 (14)	4,505.	578.40

Catalogue values for unused stamps in this section, from this point to the end of the section, are for Never Hinged items.

Coat of Arms — O3

Perf. 13½x13

1974, Feb. 25 Photo. Wmk. 353

Size: 20x28mm

O72	O3	5d vio & lilac	.35	.30
O73	O3	10d mag & grnsh bl	.35	.30
O74	O3	50d org & lt green	.35	.30
O75	O3	1r green & gold	.45	.30
O76	O3	2r emerald & org	.75	.30

Perf. 13

Size: 23x37mm

O77	O3	6r slate grn & org	1.00	.50
O78	O3	8r ultra & yellow	1.25	.50
O79	O3	10r dk bl & lilac	4.50	.50
O80	O3	11r pur & light bl	2.50	1.25
O81	O3	14r red & lt ultra	2.50	1.25
O82	O3	20r vio blue & org	4.00	2.00
O83	O3	50r dk brn & brt grn	10.00	4.00
		Nos. O72-O83 (12)	28.00	11.50

1977-79 Wmk. 353 *Perf. 13½x13*

Size: 20x28mm

O87	O3	1r black & lt grn	.40	.30
O88	O3	2r brown & gray	.45	.30
O89	O3	3r ultra & orange	.60	.30
O90	O3	5r green & rose	.75	.30

Perf. 13

Size: 23x37mm

O91	O3	6r dk bl & lt bl ('78)	1.00	.30
O92	O3	8r red & bl grn ('78)	1.25	.30
O93	O3	10r dk grn & yel grn	2.00	.50
O94	O3	11r dk blue & brt yellow ('79)	2.50	.50
O95	O3	14r dl grn & gray	2.50	1.25
O96	O3	15r bl & rose lil ('78)	4.00	1.25
O97	O3	20r purple & yel	5.75	2.00
O98	O3	30r brn & ocher ('78)	12.00	4.00
O99	O3	50r blk & gold ('78)	10.00	7.00
		Nos. O87-O99 (13)	43.20	18.30

NEWSPAPER STAMP

No. 429 Overprinted

1909 Typo. Unwmk. *Perf. 12½*

P1	A26	2c gray, *blue*	60.00	30.00

PARCEL POST STAMPS

Regular issues of 1907-08 (types A26, A29) with the handstamp above in blue, black or green are of questionable status as issued stamps. The handstamp probably is a cancellation.

No. 436 Overprinted in Black

1909 Engr. *Perf. 11½*

Q18	A29	26c red brown	20.00	15.00

The overprint is printed.

Regular Issue of 1915 Overprinted in Black

1915 Wmk. 161 *Perf. 11, 11½*

Q19	A33	1c car & indigo	*2.50*	*3.50*
Q20	A33	2c bl & carmine	*2.50*	*3.50*
Q21	A33	3c dark green	*2.50*	*3.50*
Q22	A33	5c red	*2.50*	*3.50*
Q23	A33	6c ol green & car	*2.50*	*3.50*
Q24	A33	9c yel brn & vio	*2.50*	*3.50*
Q25	A33	10c bl grn & yel brn	*2.50*	*3.50*
Q26	A33	12c ultramarine	*3.00*	*5.00*
Q27	A34	1k multicolored	*7.00*	*9.00*
Q28	A34	24c multicolored	*3.50*	*5.00*
Q29	A34	2k multicolored	*7.00*	*9.00*
Q30	A34	3k multicolored	*7.00*	*10.00*
Q31	A34	5k multicolored	*7.50*	*10.00*
Q32	A35	1t multicolored	*10.00*	*15.00*
Q33	A35	2t gold, grn & brn	*10.00*	*15.00*
Q34	A35	3t multicolored	*12.50*	*17.50*
Q35	A35	5t multicolored	*15.00*	*20.00*
		Nos. Q19-Q35 (17)	*100.00*	*140.00*

Coronation of Shah Ahmed.

Reprints have dull rather than shiny overprint.Value, set, $16.

Catalogue values for unused stamps in this section, from this point to the end of the section, are for Never Hinged items.

Post Horn — PP1

Black frame and "IRAN" (reversed) are printed on back of Nos. Q36-Q65, to show through when stamp is attached to parcel.

1958 Wmk. 306 Typo. *Perf. 12½*

Q36	PP1	50d olive bis	.75	.25
Q37	PP1	1r carmine	1.00	.25
Q38	PP1	2r blue	1.00	.25
a.		Imperf., pair	100.00	
Q39	PP1	3r green	1.00	.25
Q40	PP1	5r purple	1.00	.25
Q41	PP1	10r orange brn	3.75	.25
Q42	PP1	20r dp orange	10.00	.35
Q43	PP1	30r lilac	12.50	1.60
Q44	PP1	50r dk carmine	19.00	2.50
Q45	PP1	100r yellow	40.00	5.00
Q46	PP1	200r light grn	60.00	9.00
		Nos. Q36-Q46 (11)	150.00	19.95

1961-66 Wmk. 316

Q51	PP1	5r purple ('66)	12.50	5.00
Q52	PP1	10r org brn ('62)	12.50	5.00
Q53	PP1	20r orange	17.50	7.00
Q54	PP1	30r red lil ('63)	17.50	8.00
Q55	PP1	50r dk car ('63)	25.00	10.00
Q56	PP1	100r yellow ('64)	65.00	30.00
Q57	PP1	200r emer ('64)	80.00	30.00
		Nos. Q51-Q57 (7)	230.00	95.00

1967-74 Wmk. 353 Shiny Gum

Q58	PP1	2r blue ('74)	5.00	—
Q59	PP1	5r dk pur ('69)	5.00	—
Q60	PP1	10r orange brn	5.00	—
Q61	PP1	20r orange ('69)	10.00	—
Q62	PP1	30r red lilac	12.00	—
Q63	PP1	50r red brn ('68)	15.00	—
Q64	PP1	100r yellow	50.00	—
Q65	PP1	200r emerald ('69)	80.00	—
		Nos. Q58-Q65 (8)	182.00	

1977 Wmk. 353 White Dry Gum

Q58a	PP1	2r blue	1.00	.25
Q59a	PP1	5r dk pur	1.00	.25
Q60a	PP1	10r orange brn	1.00	.25
Q61a	PP1	20r orange	1.50	.25
Q62a	PP1	30r pink	2.00	.25
Q63a	PP1	50r red brn	2.50	.50
Q64a	PP1	100r yellow	3.50	1.00
Q65a	PP1	200r emerald	6.00	3.00
		Nos. Q58a-Q65a (8)	18.50	5.75

Without Black Frame and IRAN on Back

Perf. 13½x13, 10½ (#100r)

1981 Typo. Wmk. 353

Q67	PP1	50r orange brown	45.00	25.00
Q68	PP1	100r yellow	400.00	100.00
a.		100r dull orange		
Q69	PP1	200r green	*50.00*	25.00

Nos. Q67, Q69 printed from new dies. Numerals are larger and higher in the value tablet on No. Q67. Numerals read down from upper left to lower right in value tablet on No. Q69.

POSTAL TAX STAMPS

Iranian Red Cross Lion and Sun Emblem PT1

1950 Unwmk. Litho. *Perf. 11*

RA1	PT1	50d grn & car rose	20.00	.90
RA2	PT1	2r vio & lil rose	10.00	1.50

1955 Wmk. 306

RA3	PT1	50d emer & car rose	*300.00*	5.00

Catalogue values for unused stamps in this section, from this point to the end of the section, are for Never Hinged items.

1957-58 Wmk. 316

RA4	PT1	50d emer & rose lil	7.50	.90
RA5	PT1	2r vio & car rose ('58)	3.00	1.00

1965 Wmk. 349 *Perf. 10½*

RA6	PT1	50d emer & car rose	3.00	.50
RA7	PT1	2r vio & lil rose	8.00	.65

1965-66 Wmk. 353

RA8	PT1	50d emer & car rose (I)	2.00	.25
a.		Type II	4.00	.25
RA9	PT1	2r vio & car rose ('66)	3.00	.50

No. RA8 was printed in two types: I. Without diagonal line before Persian "50." II. With line.

1976, Sept.-78 Photo. *Perf. 13x13½*

RA10	PT1	50d emerald & red	3.00	.30
RA11	PT1	2r slate & red ('78)	3.00	2.50

Nos. RA10-RA11 are redrawn and have vertical watermark.

Nos. RA1-RA11 were obligatory on all mail. 50d stamps were for registered mail, 2r stamps for parcel post. The tax was for hospitals.

The 2.25r and 2.50r of type PT1 were used only on telegrams.

IRAQ

i-räk

LOCATION — In western Asia, bounded on the north by Syria and Turkey, on the east by Iran, on the south by Saudi Arabia and Kuwait, and on the west by Jordan
GOVT. — Republic
AREA — 167,925 sq. mi.
POP. — 22,427,150 (1999 est.)
CAPITAL — Baghdad

Iraq, formerly Mesopotamia, a province of Turkey, was mandated to Great Britain in 1920. The mandate was terminated in 1932. For earlier issues, see Mesopotamia.

16 Annas = 1 Rupee
1000 Fils = 1 Dinar (1932)

Catalogue values for unused stamps in this country are for Never Hinged items, beginning with Scott 79 in the regular postage section, Scott C1 in the air post section, Scott CO1 in the air post official section, Scott O90 in the officials section, Scott RA1 in the postal tax section, and Scott RAC1 in the air post postal tax section.

Issues under British Mandate

Sunni Mosque — A1

Gufas on the Tigris — A2

Assyrian Winged Bull — A4

Ctesiphon Arch — A5

Motif of Assyrian Origin — A3

Colors of the Dulaim Camel Corps — A6

Golden Shiah Mosque of Kadhimain — A7

Conventionalized Date Palm or "Tree of Life" — A8

1923-25 Engr. Wmk. 4 *Perf. 12*

1	A1	½a olive grn	1.00	.25
2	A2	1a brown	1.75	.25
3	A3	1½a car lake	1.00	.25
4	A4	2a brown org	1.00	.25
5	A5	3a dp blue	2.00	.25
6	A6	4a dull vio	4.50	.35
7	A7	6a blue grn	2.75	.35
8	A6	8a olive bis	4.00	.75
9	A8	1r grn & brn	6.50	.90
10	A1	2r black	22.50	8.50
11	A1	2r bister ('25)	60.00	4.00
12	A6	5r orange	55.00	17.50
13	A7	10r carmine	67.50	25.00
		Nos. 1-13 (13)	229.50	58.60

For overprints see Nos. O1-O24, O42, O47, O51-O53.

King Faisal I — A9

1927

14	A9	1r red brown	15.00	2.00

See No. 27. For overprint and surcharges see Nos. 43, O25, O54.

King Faisal I
A10 A11

1931

15	A10	½a green	1.00	.30
16	A10	1a chestnut	1.00	.30
17	A10	1½a carmine	1.50	.45
18	A10	2a orange	1.25	.25
19	A10	3a light blue	1.50	.25
20	A10	4a pur brown	2.00	*1.75*
21	A10	6a Prus blue	2.50	.80
22	A10	8a dark green	3.00	2.00
23	A11	1r dark brown	5.50	1.75
24	A11	2r yel brown	7.75	5.00
25	A11	5r dp orange	27.50	*35.00*
26	A11	10r red	82.50	*85.00*
27	A9	25r violet	700.00	*800.00*
		Nos. 15-27 (13)	837.00	*932.85*

See Nos. 44-60. For overprints see Nos. O26-O41, O43-O46, O48-O50, O54-O71.

Issues of the Kingdom

Nos. 6, 15-27 Surcharged in "Fils" or "Dinars" in Red, Black or Green

a

b

c

d

1932, Apr. 1

28	A10(a)	2f on ½a (R)	.50	.25
29	A10(a)	3f on ½a	.50	.25
a.		Double surcharge	*160.00*	
b.		Inverted surcharge	*160.00*	
30	A10(a)	4f on 1a (G)	1.75	.35
31	A10(a)	5f on 1a	.65	.25
a.		Double surcharge	275.00	
b.		Inverted Arabic "5"	*35.00*	*40.00*
32	A10(a)	8f on 1½a	.75	.50
a.		Inverted surcharge	*160.00*	
33	A10(a)	10f on 2a	.80	.25
34	A10(a)	15f on 3a	1.75	1.50
35	A10(a)	20f on 4a	2.75	1.50
36	A6(b)	25f on 4a	4.50	3.75
a.		"Flis" for "Fils"	*350.00*	*425.00*
b.		Inverted Arabic "5"	*425.00*	*550.00*
37	A10(a)	30f on 6a	5.00	.75
38	A10(a)	40f on 8a	4.25	2.75
39	A11(c)	75f on 1r	4.50	4.50
40	A11(c)	100f on 2r	10.00	4.75
41	A11(c)	200f on 5r	42.50	*42.50*
42	A11(d)	½d on 10r	125.00	95.00
a.		Bar in "½" omitted	*1,200.*	*1,200.*
43	A9(d)	1d on 25r	250.00	250.00
		Nos. 28-43 (16)	455.20	*408.85*

King Faisal I
A12 A13

A14

Values in "Fils" and "Dinars"

1932, May 9 Engr.

44	A12	2f ultra	.50	.25
45	A12	3f green	.50	.25
46	A12	4f vio brown	.50	.25
47	A12	5f gray green	.60	.25
48	A12	8f deep red	2.00	.25
49	A12	10f yellow	1.75	.25
50	A12	15f deep blue	1.90	.25
51	A12	20f orange	3.10	.55
52	A12	25f rose lilac	1.75	.55
53	A12	30f olive grn	5.00	.25
54	A12	40f dark violet	2.25	1.00
55	A13	50f deep brown	3.00	.30
56	A13	75f lt ultra	4.00	2.00
57	A13	100f deep green	10.00	1.25
58	A13	200f dark red	25.00	7.00
59	A14	½d gray blue	90.00	40.00
60	A14	1d claret	175.00	*100.00*
		Nos. 44-60 (17)	326.85	154.65

For overprints see Nos. O55-O71.

A15

A16

King Ghazi — A17

1934-38 Unwmk.

61	A15	1f purple ('38)	.75	.25
62	A15	2f ultra	.45	.25
63	A15	3f green	.45	.25
64	A15	4f pur brown	.45	.25
65	A15	5f gray green	.45	.25
66	A15	8f deep red	.75	.25
67	A15	10f yellow	.95	.25
68	A15	15f deep blue	.95	.25
69	A15	20f orange	.95	.25
70	A15	25f brown vio	1.75	.35
71	A15	30f olive grn	1.50	.25
72	A15	40f dark vio	1.75	.25
73	A16	50f deep brown	3.50	.25
74	A16	75f ultra	4.00	.40
75	A16	100f deep green	5.00	.50
76	A16	200f dark red	7.50	3.00
77	A17	½d gray blue	27.50	20.00
78	A17	1d claret	85.00	30.00
		Nos. 61-78 (18)	143.65	57.25

For overprints see Nos. 226, O72-O89.

Catalogue values for unused stamps in this section, from this point to the end of the section, are for Never Hinged items.

Sitt Zubaidah Mausoleum — A18

Mausoleum of King Faisal I — A19

Lion of Babylon — A20

Malwiye of Samarra (Spiral Tower) — A21

Oil Wells — A22

Shrine of the Golden Dome, Samarra — A23

Perf. 14, 13½, 12½, 12x13½, 13½x12, 14x13½

1941-42 Engr.

79	A18	1f dk vio ('42)	.40	.25
80	A18	2f chocolate ('42)	.40	.25
81	A19	3f brt green ('42)	.40	.25
82	A19	4f purple ('42)	.40	.25
83	A19	5f dk car rose ('42)	.40	.25
84	A20	8f carmine	.70	.25
85	A20	8f ocher ('42)	.55	.25
86	A20	10f ocher	16.00	3.25
87	A20	10f carmine ('42)	1.25	.25
88	A20	15f dull blue	2.10	.25
89	A20	15f black ('42)	2.50	.25
90	A20	20f black	4.25	.60
91	A20	20f dull blue ('42)	1.00	.25
92	A21	25f dark violet	.45	.30
93	A21	30f deep orange	.45	.30
94	A21	40f brn orange	1.75	.50
95	A21	40f chestnut ('42)	1.75	.45
96	A21	50f ultra	3.00	.60
97	A21	75f rose violet	2.50	.60
98	A22	100f ol grn ('42)	3.00	1.00
99	A22	200f dp org ('42)	10.00	1.00
100	A23	½d lt bl, perf. 12x13½ ('42)	40.00	6.50
a.		Perf. 14	50.00	9.00
101	A23	1d grnsh bl ('42)	65.00	14.00
		Nos. 79-101 (23)	158.25	31.85

Nos. 92-95 measure 17¾x21½mm, Nos. 96-97 measure 21x24mm.

For overprints see Nos. O90-O114, O165, RA5.

King Faisal II — A24

Photo.; Frame Litho.

1942 *Perf. 13 x 13½*

102	A24	1f violet & brown	.50	.50
103	A24	2f dk blue & brown	.50	.50
104	A24	3f lt green & brown	.50	.50
105	A24	4f dull brown & brn	.50	.50
106	A24	5f sage green & brn	.50	.50
107	A24	6f red orange & brn	.50	.50

No.	Type	Description	Unused	Used
108	A24	10f dl rose red & lt brn	.50	.50
109	A24	12f yel green & brown	.50	.50
		Nos. 102-109 (8)	4.00	4.00

For overprints see Nos. O115-O122.

King Faisal II — A25

Perf. 11½x12

1948, Jan. 15 Engr. Unwmk.

Size: 17¾x20½mm

No.	Type	Description	Unused	Used
110	A25	1f slate	.60	.25
111	A25	2f sepia	.35	.25
112	A25	3f emerald	.35	.25
113	A25	4f purple	.35	.25
114	A25	5f rose lake	.35	.25
115	A25	6f plum	2.00	.25
116	A25	8f ocher	4.50	.75
117	A25	10f rose red	.45	.25
118	A25	12f dark olive	.45	.25
119	A25	15f black	8.00	2.00
120	A25	20f blue	1.00	.25
121	A25	25f rose violet	1.10	.25
122	A25	30f red orange	1.10	.25
123	A25	40f orange brn	2.25	.75

Perf. 12x11½

Size: 22x27½mm

No.	Type	Description	Unused	Used
124	A25	60f deep blue	1.50	.70
125	A25	75f lilac rose	1.50	.70
126	A25	100f olive green	7.00	1.50
127	A25	200f deep orange	5.75	1.50
128	A25	½d blue	15.00	5.00
129	A25	1d green	50.00	17.50
		Nos. 110-129 (20)	103.60	33.15

Sheets of 6 exist, perforated and imperforate, containing Nos. 112, 117, 120 and 125-127, with arms and Arabic inscription in blue green in upper and lower margins. Value perf or imperf, unused $100 each, used $160 each.

See Nos. 133-138. For overprints see Nos. 188-194, O123-O142, O166-O177, O257, O258, O272-O282, RA1-RA4, RA6.

Post Rider and King Ghazi — A26

Designs: 40f, Equestrian statue & Faisal I. 50f, UPU symbols & Faisal II.

1949, Nov. 1 *Perf. 13x13½*

No.	Type	Description	Unused	Used
130	A26	20f blue	2.50	2.00
131	A26	40f red orange	3.50	2.00
132	A26	50f purple	10.00	7.00
		Nos. 130-132 (3)	16.00	11.00

75th anniv. of the UPU.

Type of 1948

1950-51 Unwmk. *Perf. 11½x12*

Size: 17¾x20½mm

No.	Type	Description	Unused	Used
133	A25	3f rose lake	8.00	2.00
134	A25	5f emerald	8.50	4.00
135	A25	14f dk olive ('50)	2.10	.75
136	A25	16f rose red	2.00	.75
137	A25	28f blue	2.10	.45

Perf. 12x11½

Size: 22x27½mm

No.	Type	Description	Unused	Used
138	A25	50f deep blue ('50)	6.50	1.50
		Nos. 133-138 (6)	29.20	9.45

For overprints see Nos. 160, O143-O148, O258, O273, O275-O276.

King Faisal II — A27

1953, May 2 Engr. *Perf. 12*

No.	Type	Description	Unused	Used
139	A27	3f deep rose car	1.25	1.25
140	A27	14f olive	2.50	1.25
141	A27	28f blue	7.00	1.75
b.		Souv. sheet of 3, #139-141	110.00	*200.00*
		Nos. 139-141 (3)	10.75	4.25

Coronation of King Faisal II, May 2, 1953.

King Faisal II — A28

1954-57 *Perf. 11½x12*

Size: 18x20½mm

No.	Type	Description	Unused	Used
141A	A28	1f blue ('56)	.65	.25
142	A28	2f chocolate	.25	.25
143	A28	3f rose lake	.25	.25
144	A28	4f violet	.25	.25
145	A28	5f emerald	.30	.25
146	A28	6f plum	.30	.25
147	A28	8f ocher	.30	.25
148	A28	10f blue	.30	.25
149	A28	15f black	1.75	1.25
149A	A28	16f brt rose ('57)	2.75	2.25
150	A28	20f olive	1.25	.30
151	A28	25f rose vio ('55)	1.25	.25
152	A28	30f ver ('55)	1.25	.25
153	A28	40f orange brn	1.50	.45

Size: 22x27½mm

No.	Type	Description	Unused	Used
154	A28	50f blue	2.00	.70
155	A28	75f pink	3.00	.75
156	A28	100f olive green	6.00	.80
157	A28	200f orange	10.00	1.75
		Nos. 141A-157 (18)	33.35	10.75

For overprints see Nos. 158-159, 195-209, 674, 676, 678, O148A-O161A, O178-O191, O259-O260, O263, O266, O268, O270, O283-O291.

No. 143, 148 and 137 Overprinted in Black

1955, Apr. 6 *Perf. 11½x12*

No.	Type	Description	Unused	Used
158	A28	3f rose lake	1.10	.45
159	A28	10f blue	1.25	.45
160	A25	28f blue	2.10	1.00
		Nos. 158-160 (3)	4.45	1.90

Abrogation of Anglo-Iraq treaty of 1930.

King Faisal II — A29

1955, Nov. 26 *Perf. 13½x13*

No.	Type	Description	Unused	Used
161	A29	3f rose lake	.90	.40
162	A29	10f light ultra	1.60	.60
163	A29	28f blue	2.25	1.50
		Nos. 161-163 (3)	4.75	2.50

6th Arab Engineers' Conf., Baghdad, 1955.
For surcharge see No. 227.

Faisal II and Globe — A30

1956, Mar. 3 *Perf. 13x13½*

No.	Type	Description	Unused	Used
164	A30	3f rose lake	1.25	.60
165	A30	10f light ultra	1.60	.60
166	A30	28f blue	2.25	1.25
		Nos. 164-166 (3)	5.10	2.45

Arab Postal Conf., Baghdad, Mar. 3.
For overprint see No. 173. For surcharge see No. 251.

Mechanical Loom A31

Designs: 3f, Dam. 5f, Modern city development. 10f, Pipeline. 40f, Tigris Bridge.

1957, Apr. 8 Photo. *Perf. 11½*

Granite Paper

No.	Type	Description	Unused	Used
167	A31	1f Prus bl & org yel	.50	.25
168	A31	3f multicolored	.50	.25
169	A31	5f multicolored	.60	.25
170	A31	10f lt bl, ocher & red	1.00	.25
171	A31	40f lt bl, blk & ocher	2.00	.70
		Nos. 167-171 (5)	4.60	1.70

Development Week, 1957. See Nos. 185-187.

Fair Emblem — A32

1957, June 1 Unwmk.

Granite Paper

No.	Type	Description	Unused	Used
172	A32	10f brown & buff	1.00	1.00

Agricultural and Industrial Exhibition, Baghdad, June 1.

No. 166 Overprinted in Red

1957, Nov. 14 *Perf. 13x13½*

No.	Type	Description	Unused	Used
173	A30	28f blue	5.00	2.25
a.		Double overprint	250.00	*275.00*

Iraqi Red Crescent Soc., 25th anniv.

King Faisal II — A33

Perf. 11½x12

1957-58 Unwmk. Engr.

No.	Type	Description	Unused	Used
174	A33	1f blue	.40	.40
175	A33	2f chocolate	.40	.40
176	A33	3f dark car ('57)	.40	.40
177	A33	4f dull violet	.40	.40
177A	A33	5f emerald	1.00	1.00
178	A33	6f plum	1.00	1.00
179	A33	8f ocher	2.00	1.25
180	A33	10f blue	2.00	1.25
		Nos. 174-180 (8)	7.60	*6.10*

Higher denominations exist without Republic overprint. They were probably not regularly issued.

See note below No. 225.

For overprints see Nos. 210-225, 675, O162-O164, O192-O199, O269, O292-O294. For types overprinted see Nos. 677, 679, O261, O264, O267, O271, O295.

Tanks — A34

King Faisal II — A35

Army Day, Jan. 6: 10f, Marching soldiers. 20f, Artillery and planes.

1958, Jan. 6 *Perf. 13x13½*

No.	Type	Description	Unused	Used
181	A34	8f green & black	1.00	.85
182	A34	10f brown & black	1.25	1.10
183	A34	20f blue & red brown	1.25	1.10
184	A35	30f car & purple	2.00	1.50
		Nos. 181-184 (4)	5.50	4.55

Type of 1957

3f, Sugar beet, bag & refining machinery, vert. 5f, Farm. 10f, Dervendi Khan dam.

1958, Apr. 26 Photo. *Perf. 11½*

Granite Paper

No.	Type	Description	Unused	Used
185	A31	3f gray vio, grn & lt gray	.60	.35
186	A31	5f multicolored	.90	.55
187	A31	10f multicolored	2.25	1.10
		Nos. 185-187 (3)	3.75	2.00

Development Week, 1958.

Republic

Stamps of 1948-51 Overprinted

Perf. 11½x12, 12x11½

1958 Engr. Unwmk.

Size: 17¾x20½mm

No.	Type	Description	Unused	Used
188	A25	12f dark olive	.80	.25
189	A25	14f olive	1.00	.25
190	A25	16f rose red	15.00	4.50
191	A25	28f blue	1.25	.65

Size: 22x27½mm

No.	Type	Description	Unused	Used
192	A25	60f deep blue	4.00	.75
193	A25	½d blue	25.00	6.00
194	A25	1d green	50.00	22.00
		Nos. 188-194 (7)	97.05	34.40

Other denominations of type A25 exist with this overprint, but these were probably not regularly issued.

Same Overprint on Stamps of 1954-57

Size: 18x20½mm

No.	Type	Description	Unused	Used
195	A28	1f blue	.85	.30
196	A28	2f chocolate	.85	.30
196A	A28	4f violet	.85	.30
196B	A28	5f emerald	.85	.30
197	A28	6f plum	.85	.30
198	A28	8f ocher	.85	.30
199	A28	10f blue	1.00	.30
200	A28	15f black	1.25	.30
201	A28	16f bright rose	3.25	.50
202	A28	20f olive	1.50	.65
203	A28	25f rose violet	1.00	.65
204	A28	30f vermilion	1.75	.35
205	A28	40f orange brn	1.75	.35

Size: 22½x27½mm

No.	Type	Description	Unused	Used
206	A28	50f blue	8.00	4.00
207	A28	75f pink	6.50	1.50
208	A28	100f olive green	7.00	4.00
209	A28	200f orange	20.00	7.50
		Nos. 195-209 (17)	58.10	21.90

The lines of this overprint are found transposed on Nos. 195, 196 and 199.

Same Overprint on Stamps and Type of 1957-58

Size: 18x20mm

No.	Type	Description	Unused	Used
210	A33	1f blue	3.50	.75
211	A33	2f chocolate	.75	.30
212	A33	3f dark carmine	.75	.30
213	A33	4f dull violet	.80	.30
214	A33	5f emerald	.75	.30
215	A33	6f plum	.75	.30
216	A33	8f ocher	.75	.50
217	A33	10f blue	.75	.30
218	A33	20f olive	.75	.30
219	A33	25f rose violet	1.60	.80
220	A33	30f vermilion	1.75	.30
221	A33	40f orange brn	4.50	1.60

Size: 22x27½mm

No.	Type	Description	Unused	Used
222	A33	50f rose violet	3.50	.75
223	A33	75f olive	3.50	1.50
224	A33	100f orange	4.50	1.50
225	A33	200f blue	12.50	2.50
		Nos. 210-225 (16)	41.40	12.30

Nos. 218-225 were not issued without overprint.

The lines of this overprint are found transposed on Nos. 210 and 214.

Many errors of overprint exist of Nos. 188-226.

For overprint see No. O198.

Same Overprint on No. 78

Perf. 12

No.	Type	Description	Unused	Used
226	A17	1d claret	37.50	35.00

No. 163 Surcharged in Red

1958, Nov. 26 ***Perf. 13x13½***

227	A29	10f on 28f blue	2.00	1.00

Arab Lawyers' Conf., Baghdad, Nov. 26.

Soldier and Flag A36

1959, Jan. 6 **Photo.** ***Perf. 11½***

228	A36	3f bright blue	.40	.25
229	A36	10f olive green	.75	.35
230	A36	40f purple	1.40	.70
		Nos. 228-230 (3)	2.55	1.30

Issued for Army Day, Jan. 6.

Orange Tree — A37

1959, Mar. 21 **Unwmk.** ***Perf. 11½***

231	A37	10f green, dk grn & org	.90	.25

Issued for Arbor Day.

Emblem of Republic — A38

Emblem in Gold, Red and Blue; Blue Inscriptions

1959-60 **Litho. & Photo.** ***Perf. 11½***

Granite Paper

232	A38	1f gray	.25	.25
233	A38	2f salmon	.25	.25
234	A38	3f pale violet	.25	.25
235	A38	4f bright yel	.25	.25
236	A38	5f light blue	.25	.25
237	A38	10f bright pink	.25	.25
238	A38	15f light green	.75	.25
239	A38	20f bister brn	.75	.25
240	A38	30f light gray	.75	.25
241	A38	40f orange yel	1.40	.35
242	A38	50f yel green	5.50	.90
243	A38	75f pale grn ('60)	2.25	.45
244	A38	100f orange ('60)	4.00	.90
245	A38	200f lilac ('60)	6.50	1.00
246	A38	500f bister ('60)	10.00	3.50
247	A38	1d brt grn ('60)	22.00	9.00
		Nos. 232-247 (16)	55.40	18.35

See Nos. 305A-305B. For overprints see Nos. 252, 293-295, O200-O221.

Worker and Buildings — A39

Victorious Fighters A40

Perf. 12½x13, 13x12½

1959, July 14 **Photo.**

248	A39	10f ocher & blue	.60	.55
249	A40	30f ocher & emerald	1.10	.70

1st anniv. of the Revolution of July 14 (1958), which overthrew the kingdom.

Harvest — A41

1959, July 14 ***Perf. 11½***

250	A41	10f lt grn & dk grn	.65	.25

No. 166 Surcharged in Dark Red

1959, June 1 **Engr.** ***Perf. 13x13½***

251	A30	10f on 28f blue	1.75	.75

Issued for Children's Day, 1959.

No. 237 Overprinted

Litho. and Photo.

1959, Oct. 23 ***Perf. 11½***

252	A38	10f multicolored	1.10	.55

Health and Sanitation Week.

Abdul Karim Kassem and Army Band — A42

Abdul Karim Kassem and: 16f, Field maneuvers, horiz. 30f, Antiaircraft. 40f, Troops at attention, flag and bugler. 60f, Fighters and flag, horiz.

1960, Jan. 6 **Photo.** ***Perf. 11½***

253	A42	10f blue, grn & mar	.90	.55
254	A42	16f brt blue & red	1.40	.70
255	A42	30f ol grn, yel & brn	1.40	.70
256	A42	40f deep vio & buff	2.00	.90
257	A42	60f dk brown & buff	2.75	1.00
		Nos. 253-257 (5)	8.45	3.85

Issued for Army Day, Jan. 6.

Prime Minister Abdul Karim Kassem — A43

1960, Feb. 1 **Engr.** ***Perf. 12½***

258	A43	10f lilac	1.00	.45
259	A43	30f emerald	1.75	.65

Issued to honor Prime Minister Kassem on his recovery from an assassination attempt.

Maroof el Rasafi — A44

1960, May 10 **Photo.** ***Perf. 13½x13***

260	A44	10f maroon & blk	4.00	1.40
a.		Inverted overprint	150.00	150.00
b.		Without overprint ('66)	11.00	11.00

No. 260b was released for postal use in 1966.

Symbol of the Army — A45

Unknown Soldier's Tomb and Kassem with Freedom Torch — A46

1960, July 14 ***Perf. 11½***

261	A45	6f ol grn, red & gold	1.00	.55
262	A46	10f green, blue & red	1.10	.55
263	A46	16f vio, blue & red	1.25	.80
264	A45	18f ultra, red & gold	1.25	.80
265	A45	30f brown, red & gold	1.75	1.00
266	A46	60f dk brn, bl & red	2.75	1.50
		Nos. 261-266 (6)	9.10	5.20

2nd anniv. of the July 14, 1958 revolution.

Gen. Kassem and Marching Troops — A47

Gen. Kassem and Arch — A48

1961, Jan. 6 ***Perf. 11½***

Granite Paper

267	A47	3f gray ol, emer, yel & gold	.85	.25
268	A47	6f pur, emer, yel & gold	.95	.25
269	A47	10f sl, emer, yel & gold	1.10	.25
270	A48	20f bl grn, blk & buff	1.40	.25
271	A48	30f bis brn, blk & buff	1.75	.35
272	A48	40f ultra, black & buff	2.00	.65
		Nos. 267-272 (6)	8.05	2.00

Issued for Army Day, Jan. 6.

Gen. Kassem and Children A49

1961, June 1 **Photo.** **Unwmk.**

Granite Paper

273	A49	3f yellow & brown	1.00	.45
274	A49	6f blue & brown	1.25	.45
275	A49	10f pink & brown	1.75	.45
276	A49	30f yellow & brown	2.00	.45
277	A49	50f lt grn & brown	3.00	.70
		Nos. 273-277 (5)	9.00	2.50

Issued for World Children's Day.

Gen. Kassem and Flag — A50

5f, 30f, 40f, Gen. Kassem saluting and flags.

1961, July 14 ***Perf. 11½***

Granite Paper

278	A50	1f multicolored	.65	.25
279	A50	3f multicolored	.65	.25
280	A50	5f multicolored	.65	.25
281	A50	6f multicolored	.65	.25
282	A50	10f multicolored	.65	.25
283	A50	30f multicolored	1.00	.55
284	A50	40f multicolored	1.25	.55
285	A50	50f multicolored	2.00	1.00
286	A50	100f multicolored	5.00	1.75
		Nos. 278-286 (9)	12.50	5.10

3rd anniv. of the July 14, 1958 revolution.

Gen. Kassem and Flag — A51

Gen. Kassem and Symbol of the Army A52

Perf. 11½

1962, Jan. 6 **Unwmk.** **Photo.**

Granite Paper

287	A51	1f multicolored	.70	.25
288	A51	3f multicolored	.75	.25
289	A51	6f multicolored	.85	.25
290	A52	10f blk, lilac & gold	1.40	.25
291	A52	30f black, org & gold	1.60	.30
292	A52	50f blk, pale grn & gold	2.50	.50
		Nos. 287-292 (6)	7.80	1.80

Issued for Army Day, Jan. 6.

Nos. 234, 237 and 240 Overprinted

Litho. & Photo.

1962, May 29 ***Perf. 11½***

293	A38	3f multicolored	.70	.25
294	A38	10f multicolored	.70	.25
295	A38	30f multicolored	1.50	.35
		Nos. 293-295 (3)	2.90	.85

Fifth Islamic Congress.

Hands Across Map of Arabia and North Africa — A53

1962, July 14 **Photo.**

296 A53 1f brn, org, grn & gold .70 .25
297 A53 3f brn, yel grn, grn & gold .75 .25
298 A53 6f blk, lt brn, grn & gold .85 .25
299 A53 10f brn, lil, grn & gold 1.10 .25
300 A53 30f brn, rose, grn & gold 1.40 .30
301 A53 50f brn, gray, grn & gold 2.25 .45
Nos. 296-301 (6) 7.05 1.75

Revolution of July 14, 1958, 4th anniv.

al-Kindi — A54

Designs: 3f, Horsemen with standards and trumpets. 10f, Old map of Baghdad and Tigris. 40f, Gen. Kassem, modern building and flag.

Perf. 14x13½

1962, Dec. 1 **Litho.** **Unwmk.**

302 A54 3f multicolored .70 .25
303 A54 6f multicolored .75 .25
304 A54 10f multicolored .85 .35
305 A54 40f multicolored 2.25 1.00
Nos. 302-305 (4) 4.55 1.85

9th century Arab philosopher al-Kindi; millenary of the Round City of Baghdad.

Emblem of Republic — A54a

1962, Dec. 20 ***Perf. 13½x14***

305A A54a 14f brt green & blk 2.25 .50
305B A54a 35f ver & black 2.75 .75

Nos. 305A-305B were originally sold affixed to air letter sheets, obliterating the portrait of King Faisal II. They were issued in sheets for general use in 1966.

For overprints see Nos. RA15-RA16.

Tanks on Parade and Gen. Kassem — A55

1963, Jan. 6 **Photo.** ***Perf. 11½***

306 A55 3f black & yellow .70 .25
307 A55 5f brown & plum .75 .25
308 A55 6f blk & lt green .80 .25
309 A55 10f blk & lt blue .85 .25
310 A55 10f black & pink .90 .25
311 A55 20f black & ultra 1.10 .25
312 A55 40f blk & rose lilac 1.40 .25
313 A55 50f brn & brt ultra 2.00 .40
Nos. 306-313 (8) 8.50 2.15

Issued for Army Day, Jan. 6.

Malaria Eradication Emblem — A56

1962, Dec. 31 ***Perf. 14***

Republic Emblem in Red, Blue & Gold

314 A56 3f yel grn, blk & dk grn .50 .25
315 A56 10f org, blk & dark blue .75 .25
316 A56 40f lilac, black & blue 1.00 .30
Nos. 314-316 (3) 2.25 .80

WHO drive to eradicate malaria.

Gufas on the Tigris — A57

Designs: 2f, 500f, Spiral tower, Samarra. 4f, 15f, Ram's head harp, Ur. 5f, 75f, Map and Republic emblem. 10f, 50f, Lion of Babylon. 20f, 40f, Baghdad University. 30f, 200f, Kadhimain mosque. 100f, 1d, Winged bull, Khorsabad.

Engr.; Engr. and Photo. (bicolored)

1963, Feb. 16 **Unwmk.** ***Perf. 12x11***

317 A57 1f green .65 .25
318 A57 2f purple .65 .25
319 A57 3f black .65 .25
320 A57 4f black & yel .65 .25
321 A57 5f lilac & lt grn .70 .25
322 A57 10f rose red 1.00 .25
323 A57 15f brn & buff 1.50 .25
324 A57 20f violet blue 1.60 .25
325 A57 30f orange 1.00 .35
326 A57 40f brt green 1.75 .25
327 A57 50f dark brown 7.50 .65
328 A57 75f blk & lt grn 3.75 .45
329 A57 100f brt lilac 4.00 .25
330 A57 200f brown 7.50 .55
331 A57 500f blue 10.00 2.25
332 A57 1d deep claret 13.50 4.50
Nos. 317-332 (16) 56.40 11.25

For overprints see Nos. O314-O317, RA7-RA12.

Shepherd and Sheep A58

10f, Man holding sheaf. 20f, Date palm grove.

1963, Mar. 21 **Litho.** ***Perf. 13½x14***

333 A58 3f emerald & gray .40 .25
334 A58 10f dp brn & lil rose .65 .25
335 A58 20f dk bl & red brn 1.10 .35
a. Souv. sheet of 3, #333-335 8.00 8.00
Nos. 333-335 (3) 2.15 .85

FAO "Freedom from Hunger" campaign. No. 335a sold for 50f.

No. 335a was overprinted in 1970 in black to commemorate the UN 25th anniv. Denominations on the 3 stamps were obliterated, leaving "Price 50 Fils" in the margin. Value $7.50.

Cent. Emblem — A59

Design: 30f, Iraqi Red Crescent Society Headquarters, horiz.

Perf. 11x11½, 11½x11

1963, Dec. 30 **Photo.**

336 A59 3f violet & red .40 .30
337 A59 10f gray & red .60 .30
338 A59 30f blue & red 1.25 .65
Nos. 336-338 (3) 2.25 1.25

Centenary of International Red Cross.

Rifle, Helmet and Flag — A60

1964, Jan. 6 **Unwmk.** ***Perf. 11½***

Granite Paper

339 A60 3f brn, blue & emer .40 .30
340 A60 10f brn, pink & emer .60 .30
341 A60 30f brown, yel & emer 1.25 .70
Nos. 339-341 (3) 2.25 1.30

Issued for Army Day, Jan. 6.

Flag and Soldiers Storming Ministry of Defense A61

1964, Feb. 8 ***Perf. 11½***

Granite Paper

342 A61 10f pur, red, grn & blk .65 .30
343 A61 30f red brn, red, grn & blk 1.10 .65
a. Souv. sheet of 2, imperf 7.00 2.75
b. Souv. sheet of 2 (4th anniv.) ('67) 9.00 2.75

Revolution of Ramadan 14, 1st anniv. No. 343a contains stamps similar to Nos. 342-343 in changed colors (10f olive, red, green & black; 30f ultra, red, green & black). Sold for 50f.

No. 343b consists of various block-outs and overprints on No. 343a. It commemorates the 4th anniv. of the Revolution of Ramadan 14. Sold for 70f. Issued 2/8/67.

Hammurabi and a God from Stele in Louvre — A62

Design: 10f, UN emblem and scales.

1964, June 10 **Litho.** ***Perf. 13½***

344 A62 6f lilac & pale grn .60 .50
345 A62 10f org & vio blue 1.10 .50
346 A62 30f blue & pale grn 1.80 .75
Nos. 344-346 (3) 3.50 1.75

15th anniv. (in 1963) of the Universal Declaration of Human Rights.

"Industrialization of Iraq" — A63

Soldier Planting New Flag — A64

1964, July 14 ***Perf. 11***

347 A63 3f gray, org & black .40 .30
348 A64 10f rose red, blk & emer .40 .30
349 A64 20f rose red, blk & emer .60 .30
350 A63 30f gray, org & black 1.25 .60
Nos. 347-350 (4) 2.65 1.50

6th anniv. of the July 14, 1958 revolution.

Star and Fighters A65

1964, Nov. 18 **Photo.** ***Perf. 11½***

351 A65 5f sepia & orange .40 .30
352 A65 10f lt bl & orange 1.25 .30
353 A65 50f vio & red orange 1.25 .60
Nos. 351-353 (3) 2.90 1.20

Revolution of Nov. 18, 1963, 1st anniv.

Musician with Lute — A66

Perf. 13x13½

1964, Nov. 28 **Litho.** **Unwmk.**

354 A66 3f bister & multi 1.00 .30
355 A66 10f dl grn & multi 1.00 .30
356 A66 30f dl rose & multi 1.50 .90
Nos. 354-356 (3) 3.50 1.50

International Arab Music Conference.

Map of Arab Countries and Emblem A67

1964, Dec. 13 ***Perf. 12½x14***

357 A67 10f lt grn & rose lilac 1.00 .30

9th Arab Engineers' Conference, Baghdad.

Arab Postal Union Emblem — A67a

1964, Dec. 21 **Photo.** ***Perf. 11***

358 A67a 3f sal pink & blue .40 .25
359 A67a 10f brt red lil & brn .50 .25
360 A67a 30f orange & blue 1.40 .50
Nos. 358-360 (3) 2.30 1.00

10th anniv. of Permanent Office of APU

For overprint see No. 707.

Soldier, Flag and Rising Sun — A68

Perf. 14x12½

1965, Jan. 6 **Litho.** **Unwmk.**

361 A68 5f dull green & multi .40 .25
362 A68 15f henna brn & multi .40 .30
363 A68 30f black brn & multi 1.40 .65
Nos. 361-363 (3) 2.20 1.20

Issued for Army Day, Jan. 6.

An imperf. souvenir sheet carries a revised No. 363 with "30 FILS" omitted, and a portrait of Pres. Abdul Salam Arif. Violet inscriptions including "PRICE 60 FILS." Value $10.

Symbols of Agriculture and Industry A69

1965, Jan. 8 ***Perf. 12½x14***
364 A69 10f ultra, brn & blk .60 .30

Arab Labor Ministers' Conference.

Tanker A70

1965, Jan. 30 ***Perf. 14***
365 A70 10f multicolored 1.00 .45

Inauguration (in 1962) of the deep sea terminal for oil tankers.

Soldier with Flag and Rifle — A71

1965, Feb. 8 **Litho.** ***Perf. 13½***
366 A71 10f multicolored .75 .25

Revolution of Ramadan 14, 2nd anniv.

Tree Week — A72

1965, Mar. 6 **Unwmk.** ***Perf. 13***
367 A72 6f multicolored .40 .30
368 A72 20f multicolored 1.25 .30

Federation Emblem — A73

1965, Mar. 24 **Unwmk.** ***Perf. 14***
369 A73 3f lt bl, vio bl & gold .40 .30
370 A73 10f gray, black & gold .40 .30
371 A73 30f rose, car & gold 1.00 .75
Nos. 369-371 (3) 1.80 1.35

Arab Federation of Insurance.

Dagger in Map of Palestine — A74

1965, Apr. 9 **Litho.** ***Perf. 14x12½***
372 A74 10f gray & black 3.50 .35
373 A74 20f lt brn & dk blue 6.50 .55

Deir Yassin massacre, Apr. 9, 1948.

See Jordan No. 499 and Kuwait Nos. 281-282.

Smallpox Attacking People — A75

1965, Apr. 30 **Litho.** ***Perf. 14***
374 A75 3f multicolored .60 .30
375 A75 10f multicolored .75 .30
376 A75 20f multicolored 1.75 .80
Nos. 374-376 (3) 3.10 1.40

WHO's fight against smallpox. Exist imperf. Value $6.25.

ITU Emblem, Old and New Telecommunication Equipment — A76

1965, May 17 ***Perf. 14, Imperf.***
377 A76 10f multicolored .75 .25
378 A76 20f multicolored 2.00 .55
a. Souv. sheet of 2, #377-378 20.00 15.00

ITU, centenary. No. 378a sold for 40f and exists imperf. Value same.

Map of Arab Countries and Banner — A77

1965, May 26 **Litho.** ***Perf. 14x12½***
379 A77 10f multicolored .50 .25

Anniversary of the treaty with the UAR.

Library Aflame and Lamp A78

1965, June **Photo.** ***Perf. 11***
380 A78 5f black, grn & red .50 .30
381 A78 10f blk, green & red .75 .30

Burning of the Library of Algiers, 6/7/62.

Revolutionist with Club, Cannon, Sun and Flames — A79

1965, June 30 **Litho.** ***Perf. 13***
382 A79 5f multicolored .40 .25
383 A79 10f multicolored .45 .25

45th anniversary, Revolution of 1920.

Mosque — A80

1965, July 12 **Photo.** ***Perf. 12***
384 A80 10f multicolored 1.25 .60

Prophet Mohammed's birthday. A souvenir sheet contains one imperf. stamp similar to No. 384. Sold for 50f. Value $8.

Factories and Grain — A81

1965, July 14 **Litho.** ***Perf. 13***
385 A81 10f multicolored .55 .55

7th anniv. of the July 14, 1958 Revolution.

Arab Fair Emblem — A82

1965, Oct. 22 **Unwmk.** ***Perf. 13***
386 A82 10f multicolored .55 .25

Second Arab Fair, Baghdad.

Pres. Abdul Salam Mohammed Arif — A83

1965, Nov. 18 **Photo.** ***Perf. 11½***
Granite Paper
387 A83 5f org, buff & dk blue .65 .25
388 A83 10f lt ultra, gray & dk brn .90 .25
389 A83 50f lil, pale pink & sl blk 2.50 .90
Nos. 387-389 (3) 4.05 1.40

Revolution of Nov. 18, 1963, 2nd anniv.

Date Palms — A85

Census Chart and Adding Machine — A84

1965, Nov. 29 **Litho.** ***Perf. 13***
390 A84 3f gray & plum .50 .25
391 A84 5f brown red & brn .60 .25
392 A84 15f olive bis & dl bl 1.50 .60
Nos. 390-392 (3) 2.60 1.10

Issued to publicize the 1965 census.

1965, Dec. 27 **Litho.** ***Perf. 13½x14***
393 A85 3f olive bis & multi .40 .25
394 A85 10f car rose & multi .90 .25
395 A85 15f blue & multi 2.40 .90
Nos. 393-395 (3) 3.70 1.40

2nd FAO Intl. Dates Conference, Baghdad, Dec. 1965.

For surcharges see Nos. 694-695.

Soldiers' Monument A86

1966, Jan. 6 **Photo.** ***Perf. 12***
396 A86 2f car rose & multi .45 .25
397 A86 5f multicolored .45 .25
398 A86 40f yel grn & multi 1.75 .75
Nos. 396-398 (3) 2.65 1.25

Issued for Army Day.

Eagle and Flag of Iraq — A87

Perf. 12½
1966, Feb. 8 **Photo.** **Unwmk.**
399 A87 5f dl bl & multi .40 .25
400 A87 10f orange & multi .75 .25

3rd anniv. of the Revolution of Ramadan 14, which overthrew the Kassem government.

Arab League Emblem — A88

1966, Mar. 22 ***Perf. 11x11½***
401 A88 5f org, brn & brt grn .50 .25
402 A88 15f ol, rose lil & ultra .50 .25

Arab Publicity Week.

Soccer Players — A89

5f, Player and goal post. 15f, As 2f. 50f, Legs of player, ball and emblem, horiz.

1966, Apr. 1 ***Perf. 12***

403 A89 2f multicolored .75 .25
404 A89 5f multicolored .50 .25
405 A89 15f multicolored 1.50 .45
Nos. 403-405 (3) 2.75 .95

Miniature Sheet

Imperf

406 A89 50f vio & multi 7.50 *10.50*

3rd Arab Soccer Cup, Baghdad, Apr. 1-10.
For overprint, see No. O296.

Steam Shovel Within Cogwheel A90

1966, May 1 **Litho.** ***Perf. 13½***

407 A90 15f multicolored .40 .25
408 A90 25f red, blk, & sil .50 .25

Issued for Labor Day, May 1, 1966.

Queen Nefertari — A91

Facade of Abu Simbel A92

Perf. 12½x13, 13½

1966, May 20 **Litho.**

409 A91 5f olive, yel & blk .40 .25
410 A91 15f blue, yel & brn .40 .25
411 A92 40f bis brn, red & blk 2.00 1.50
Nos. 409-411 (3) 2.80 2.00

UNESCO world campaign to save historic monuments in Nubia.

President Arif and Flag — A93

1966, July 14 **Photo.** ***Perf. 11½***

412 A93 5f multicolored .40 .25
413 A93 15f multicolored .50 .25
414 A93 50f multicolored 1.75 1.00
Nos. 412-414 (3) 2.65 1.50

8th anniv. of the July 14, 1958 revolution.

A94

1966, July 22 **Litho.** ***Perf. 12***

Multicolored Vignette

415 A94 5f lt olive green .40 .25
416 A94 15f lt greenish blue .40 .25
417 A94 30f lt yellow green 1.00 .75
Nos. 415-417 (3) 1.80 1.25

Mohammed's 1,396th birthday.

Iraqi Museum, Baghdad A95

Designs: 50f, Golden headdress, Ur. 80f, Carved Sumerian head, vert.

1966, Nov. 9 **Litho.** ***Perf. 14***

418 A95 15f multicolored .50 .25
419 A95 50f lt bl, blk, gold & pink 1.50 .80
420 A95 80f crim, blk, bl & gold 3.25 1.00
Nos. 418-420 (3) 5.25 2.05

Opening of New Iraqi Museum, Baghdad.

UNESCO Emblem — A96

1966, Dec. ***Perf. 13½***

421 A96 5f blue, black & tan .40 .25
422 A96 15f brt org brn, blk & gray .40 .30

20th anniv. of UNESCO.

Iraqi Citizens — A97

1966, Nov. 18 ***Perf. 13½x13***

423 A97 15f multicolored .60 .50
424 A97 25f multicolored 1.10 1.10

3rd anniv. of the Revolution of 11/18/63.

Rocket Launchers and Soldier A98

1967, Jan. 6 **Photo.** ***Perf. 11½***

425 A98 15f citron, dk brn & dp bis .45 .25
426 A98 20f brt lil, dk brn & dp bis .60 .25

Issued for Army Day, Jan. 6.

Oil Derrick, Pipeline, Emblem — A99

15f, 50f, Refinery and emblem, horiz.

1967, Mar. 6 **Litho.** ***Perf. 14***

427 A99 5f ol grn, pale yel & blk .40 .25
428 A99 15f multicolored .40 .25
429 A99 40f vio, yel & blk .80 .70
430 A99 50f multicolored 1.75 1.00
Nos. 427-430 (4) 3.35 2.20

6th Arab Petroleum Cong., Baghdad, Mar. 1967.

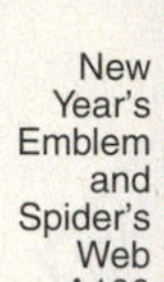

New Year's Emblem and Spider's Web A100

1967, Apr. 11 **Litho.** ***Perf. 13½***

431 A100 5f multicolored .40 .25
432 A100 15f multicolored .40 .25

Issued for Hegira (Pilgrimage) Year.

Worker Holding Cogwheel and Map of Arab Countries — A101

1967, May 1 ***Perf. 12½x13***

433 A101 10f gray & multi .40 .25
434 A101 15f lt ultra & multi .40 .25

Issued for Labor Day.

A102

1967, June 20 **Litho.** ***Perf. 14***

435 A102 5f multicolored .45 .25
436 A102 15f blue & multi .55 .25

Mohammed's 1,397th birthday.

Flag, Hands with Clubs — A103

1967, July 7 ***Perf. 13x13½***

437 A103 5f multicolored .40 .25
438 A103 15f multicolored .50 .25

47th anniversary of Revolution of 1920.

Um Qasr Harbor A104

10f, 15f, Freighter loading in Um Qasr harbor.

1967, July 14 **Litho.** ***Perf. 14x13½***

439 A104 5f multicolored .40 .25
440 A104 10f multicolored .60 .30
441 A104 15f multicolored 1.10 .30
442 A104 40f multicolored 2.00 1.00
Nos. 439-442 (4) 4.10 1.85

9th anniv. of the July 14, 1958 revolution and the inauguration of the port of Um Qasr.

Iraqi Man — A105

Iraqi Costumes: 5f, 15f, 25f, Women's costumes. 10f, 20f, 30f, Men's costumes.

1967, Nov. 10 **Litho.** ***Perf. 13***

443 A105 2f pale brn & multi .40 .25
444 A105 5f ver & multi .40 .25
445 A105 10f multicolored .70 .25
446 A105 15f ultra & multi .95 .50
447 A105 20f lilac & multi 1.25 .50
448 A105 25f lemon & multi 1.25 .60
449 A105 30f fawn & multi 1.50 .60
Nos. 443-449,C19-C21 (10) 17.95 6.85

For overprints see Nos. 597-599, O228-O231, RA17.

President Arif — A106

15f, Pres. Arif and map of Iraq, horiz.

Perf. 11x11½, 11½x11

1967, Nov. 18

450 A106 5f bl, vio blk & yel .40 .25
451 A106 15f rose & multi .75 .40

4th anniversary of Nov. 18th revolution.

Ziggurat of Ur — A107

Designs: 5f, Gate with Nimrod statues. 10f, Gate, Babylon. 15f, Minaret of Mosul, vert. 25f, Arch and ruins of Ctesiphon.

1967, Dec. 1 **Litho.** ***Perf. 13***

452 A107 2f orange & multi .40 .25
453 A107 5f lilac & multi .40 .25
454 A107 10f orange & multi .40 .25
455 A107 15f rose red & multi .60 .25
456 A107 25f vio bl & multi .80 .25
Nos. 452-456,C22-C26 (10) 58.85 24.35

International Tourist Year.
For overprints see Nos. 593, 680, O225-O227, O308, RA18.

Iraqi Girl Scout Emblem and Sign — A108

5f, Girl Scouts at campfire & Girl Scout emblem. 10f, Boy Scout emblem & Boy Scout sign. 15f, Boy Scouts pitching tent & Boy Scout sign.

1967, Dec. 15

457 A108 2f orange & multi 1.40 .40
458 A108 5f blue & multi 1.60 .40
459 A108 10f green & multi 1.75 .65
460 A108 15f blue & multi 1.75 .80
a. Souv. sheet of 4 12.00 9.00
Nos. 457-460 (4) 6.50 2.25

Issued to honor the Scout movement.
No. 460a contains 4 stamps similar to Nos. 457-460 with simulated perforations. Sold for 50f.
For overprint see No. RA19.

Soldiers on Maneuvers A109

1968, Jan. 6 Photo. *Perf. 11½*

461 A109 5f lt bl, brn & brt grn .40 .25
462 A109 15f lt bl, ind & olive .65 .25

Issued for Army Day 1968.

White-cheeked Bulbul — A110

Birds: 10f, Hoopoe. 15f, Eurasian jay. 25f, Peregrine falcon. 30f, White stork. 40f, Black partridge. 50f, Marbled teal.

1968, Jan. Litho. *Perf. 14*

463 A110 5f org & black 1.00 .25
464 A110 10f blue, blk & brn 1.10 .25
465 A110 15f pink & multi 1.60 .25
466 A110 25f dl org & multi 2.50 .50
467 A110 30f emer, blk & brn 2.75 .50
468 A110 40f rose lil & multi 3.50 .75
469 A110 50f multicolored 5.50 1.25
Nos. 463-469 (7) 17.95 3.75

For overprint, see No. O311.

Fighting Soldiers A111

1968, Feb. 8 *Perf. 11½*

470 A111 15f blk, org & brt bl 3.50 .90

Revolution of Ramadan 14, 5th anniv.

Factories, Tractor and Grain — A112

1968, May 1 Litho. *Perf. 13*

471 A112 15f lt bl & multi .40 .25
472 A112 25f multicolored .60 .25

Issued for Labor Day.

Soccer A113

5f, 25f, Goalkeeper holding ball, vert.

1968, June 14 *Perf. 13½*

473 A113 2f multicolored .40 .25
474 A113 5f multicolored .40 .25
475 A113 15f multicolored .50 .25
476 A113 25f multicolored 2.25 .75
a. Souv. sheet, 70f, imperf. 9.00 *10.00*
Nos. 473-476 (4) 3.55 1.50

23rd C.I.S.M. (Conseil Internationale du Sports Militaire) Soccer Championships.
No. 476a shows badge of Military Soccer League.

Soldier, Flag, Chain and Rising Sun — A114

1968, July 14 Photo. *Perf. 13½x14*

478 A114 15f multicolored .50 .25

10th anniv. of the July 14, 1958 revolution.

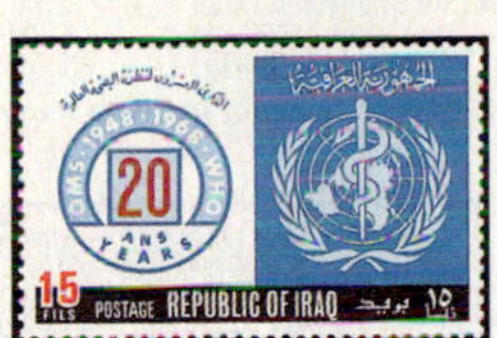

World Health Organization Emblem — A115

5f, 10f, Staff of Aesculapius over emblem, vert.

1968, Nov. 29 Litho. *Perf. 13½*

479 A115 5f multicolored .40 .25
480 A115 10f multicolored .40 .25
481 A115 15f blue, red & black .50 .25
482 A115 25f yel grn, red & blk .75 .30
Nos. 479-482 (4) 2.05 1.05

WHO, 20th anniv. Exist imperf. Value $5.
For overprints, see Nos. O222-O224.

Human Rights Flame — A116

1968, Dec. 22 Litho. *Perf. 13½*

483 A116 10f lt bl, yel & car .40 .25
484 A116 25f lt yel grn, yel & car .50 .25
a. Souv. sheet, 100f, imperf. 5.00 5.00

International Human Rights Year.
For overprint, see No. O232.

Mother and Children — A117

1968, Dec. 31 Litho. *Perf. 13½*

485 A117 15f multi .50 .25
486 A117 25f bl & multi 1.25 .35
a. Souv. sheet, 100f, imperf 8.00 5.25

UNICEF. For overprints see Nos. 624-625, O234-O235.

Tanks A118

1969, Jan. 6 Photo.

487 A118 25f vio, car & brn 3.50 2.00

Issued for Army Day, Jan. 6.
For overprint, see No. O244.

Harvester A119

1969, Feb. Photo. *Perf. 13½*

488 A119 15f yel brn & multi .50 .25

6th anniv. of the Revolution of Ramadan 14.

Mosque A119a

1969, Mar. 19 Photo. *Perf. 13x13½*

488A A119a 15f multicolored 1.00 .75

Issued for Hegira (Pilgrimage) Year.

Emblem A120

1969, Apr. 12 Litho. *Perf. 12½x12*

489 A120 10f yel grn & multi .60 .30
490 A120 15f orange & multi 1.00 .30

1st conference of the Arab Veterinary Union, Baghdad, Apr. 1969.

Barbus Grypus A121

Fish: 3f, Barbus puntius sharpeyi. 10f, Pampus argenteus. 100f, Barbus esocinus.

1969, May 9 *Perf. 14*

491 A121 2f multicolored 1.75 .45
492 A121 3f multicolored 1.90 .45
493 A121 10f multicolored 2.00 .45
494 A121 100f multicolored 6.00 3.75
Nos. 491-494 (4) 11.65 5.10

For overprints, see Nos. O312-O313.

Holy Kaaba, Mecca A122

1969, May 28 Photo. *Perf. 12*

495 A122 15f blue & multi 1.00 .50

Mohammed's 1,399th birthday.

ILO Emblem A123

1969, June 6 Litho. *Perf. 13x12½*

496 A123 5f lt vio, yel & blk .25 .25
497 A123 15f grnsh gray, yel & black .25 .25
498 A123 50f rose, yel & blk 1.25 .80
a. Souv. sheet, 100f, imperf. 6.00 *7.00*
Nos. 496-498 (3) 1.75 1.30

ILO, 50th anniv.
For overprint, see No. O297.

Weight Lifting — A124

Design: 5f, 35f, High jump.

1969, June 20 *Perf. 13½x13*

500 A124 3f org yel & multi .55 .25
501 A124 5f blue & multi .55 .25
502 A124 10f rose pink & multi .65 .30
503 A124 35f yellow & multi 1.25 1.00
a. Souv. sheet of 4, #500-503, imperf. 12.00 12.00
Nos. 500-503 (4) 3.00 1.80

19th Olympic Games, Mexico City, Oct. 12-27, 1968. No. 503a sold for 100f.

Coat of Arms, Symbols of Industry — A125

1969, July 14 Photo. *Perf. 13*

504 A125 10f brn org & multi .40 .25
505 A125 15f multicolored .60 .25

11th anniv. of the July 14, 1958 revolution.

Street Paving A126

Pres. Ahmed Hassan al-Bakr — A127

Design: 20f, Baghdad International Airport.

1969, July 17 *Perf. 13½*

506 A126 10f yel & multi .50 .30
507 A126 15f blue & multi .50 .30
508 A126 20f blue & multi 1.60 .45
509 A127 200f gold & multi 20.00 9.00
Nos. 506-509 (4) 22.60 10.05

Coup of July 17, 1968, 1st anniv. No. 508 also for the inauguration of Baghdad Intl. Airport.

No. 509 exists imperf. Value $25.

Wheat and Fair Emblem — A128

1969, Oct. 1 **Photo.** *Perf. 13½*

510 A128 10f brt grn, gold & dl red .65 .25
511 A128 15f ultra, gold & red .80 .35

6th International Fair, Baghdad.
For overprints see Nos. 567A-567B.

Motor Ship Al-Waleed A129

Designs: 15f, Floating crane Antara. 30f, Pilot ship Al-Rasheed. 35f, Suction dredge Hillah. 50f, Survey ship Al-Fao.

1969, Oct. 8 **Litho.** *Perf. 12½*

512 A129 15f black & multi .50 .25
513 A129 20f black & multi .70 .45
514 A129 30f black & multi 1.10 .55
515 A129 35f black & multi 1.75 1.00
516 A129 50f black & multi 5.25 2.25
Nos. 512-516 (5) 9.30 4.50

50th anniversary of Basrah Harbor.

Radio Tower and Map of Palestine — A130

1969, Nov. 9 **Litho.** *Perf. 12½x13*

517 A130 15f multicolored 3.50 .35
518 A130 50f multicolored 6.50 .80

10th anniversary of Iraqi News Agency.
For overprints see Nos. 698-699.

"Search for Knowledge" — A131

1969, Nov. 21 **Photo.** *Perf. 13*

519 A131 15f blue & multi .35 .25
520 A131 20f green & multi .50 .30

Campaign against illiteracy.

Front Page of First Baghdad Newspaper A132

1969, Dec. 26 **Litho.** *Perf. 13½*

521 A132 15f yel, org & black .70 .30

Centenary of the Iraqi press.
For overprint see No. 552.

Soldier, Map of Iraq and Plane — A133

1970, Jan. 6 **Photo.** *Perf. 13*

522 A133 15f lt vio & multi .70 .30
523 A133 20f yellow & multi 1.40 .65

Issued for Army Day 1970.

Soldier, Farmer and Worker Shoring up Wall in Iraqi Colors — A134

1970, Feb. 8 **Photo.** *Perf. 13*

524 A134 10f multicolored .25 .25
525 A134 15f brick red & multi .40 .25

7th anniv. of the Revolution of Ramadan 14.

Poppies — A135

Flowers: 3f, Poet's narcissus. 5f, Tulip. 10f, 50f, Carnations. 15f, Rose.

1970, June 12 **Litho.** *Perf. 13*

526 A135 2f emer & multi .40 .25
527 A135 3f blue & multi .40 .25
528 A135 5f multicolored .40 .25
529 A135 10f lt grn & multi .60 .35
530 A135 15f pale sal & multi 1.10 .55
531 A135 50f lt grn & multi 3.25 1.25
Nos. 526-531 (6) 6.15 2.90

The overprinted sets Nos. 532-543 were released before Nos. 526-531.

For overprints see Nos. 621-623, RA20. For surcharge see No. 726.

Nos. 526-531 Overprinted in Ultramarine

1970, Mar. 21

532 A135 2f emer & multi .60 .50
533 A135 3f lt bl & multi .60 .50
534 A135 5f multicolored .60 .50
535 A135 10f lt grn & multi .60 .50
536 A135 15f pale sal & multi 1.20 .80
537 A135 50f lt grn & multi 3.50 1.25
Nos. 532-537 (6) 7.10 4.05

Issued for Novrooz (New Year).

Nos. 526-531 Overprinted in Black

1970, Apr. 18

538 A135 2f emer & multi .50 .50
539 A135 3f lt bl & multi .50 .50
540 A135 5f multicolored .50 .50
541 A135 10f lt grn & multi .50 .70
542 A135 15f pale sal & multi 1.40 .90
543 A135 50f lt grn & multi 3.00 1.10
Nos. 538-543 (6) 6.40 4.00

Issued for the Spring Festival, Mosul.

Map of Arab Countries, Slogans — A136

50f, 150f, People, flag, sun and map of Palestine.

1970, Apr. 7 *Perf. 13x12½*

544 A136 15f gold & multi .40 .25
545 A136 35f sil & multi .60 .55
546 A136 50f red & multi 2.00 .70
a. Souv. sheet, 150f, imperf. 11.00 11.00
Nos. 544-546 (3) 3.00 1.50

23rd anniversary of Al-Baath Party.

Workers and Cogwheel — A137

1970, May 1

547 A137 10f silver & multi .40 .25
548 A137 15f silver & multi .50 .35
549 A137 35f silver & multi 1.50 .75
Nos. 547-549 (3) 2.40 1.35

Issued for Labor Day.

Kaaba, Mecca, and Koran A138

1970, May 17 **Photo.** *Perf. 13*

550 A138 15f brt bl & multi .40 .25
551 A138 20f orange & multi .40 .25

Mohammed's 1,400th birthday.

No. 521 Overprinted "1970" and Arabic Inscription in Prussian Blue

1970, June 15 **Litho.** *Perf. 13½*

552 A132 15f yel, org & black .55 .55

Day of Iraqi press.

Revolutionists and Guns — A139

Designs: 35f, Revolutionist and rising sun.

1970, June 30 **Litho.** *Perf. 13*

553 A139 10f blk & apple grn .25 .25
554 A139 15f black & gold .40 .25
555 A139 35f blk & red org .90 .45
a. Souv. sheet, 100f, imperf. 5.50 5.50
Nos. 553-555 (3) 1.55 .95

50th anniversary, Revolution of 1920.

Broken Chain and New Dawn — A140

1970, July 14 *Perf. 13x13½*

557 A140 15f multicolored .35 .25
558 A140 20f multicolored .50 .25

12th anniv. of the July 14, 1958 revolution.

Map of Arab Countries and Hands — A141

1970, July 17 *Perf. 13*

559 A141 15f gold & multi .30 .25
560 A141 25f gold & multi .55 .25

2nd anniversary of coup of July 17, 1968.

Pomegranates A142

1970, Aug. 21 *Perf. 14*

561 A142 3f shown .40 .25
562 A142 5f Grapefruit .40 .25
563 A142 10f Grapes .40 .25
564 A142 15f Oranges 1.10 .35
565 A142 35f Dates 3.50 1.90
Nos. 561-565 (5) 5.80 3.00

The Latin inscriptions on the 5f and 10f have been erroneously transposed.

For overprints & surcharge see Nos. 613-615, 725, O240-O245.

Kaaba, Mecca, Moon over Mountain and Spider Web — A143

1970, Sept. 4 **Photo.** *Perf. 13*

566 A143 15f multicolored .40 .25
567 A143 25f multicolored .55 .25

Issued for Hajeer (Pilgrimage) Year.

Nos. 510-511 Overprinted in Red

1970, Sept. Photo. *Perf. 13½*

567A A128 10f multi 3.50 2.00
567B A128 15f multi 3.50 2.00

7th International Fair, Baghdad.

Intl. Education Year Emblem A144

1970, Nov. 13 Photo. *Perf. 13*

568 A144 5f yel green & multi .35 .25
569 A144 15f brick red & multi .50 .25

Flag and Map of Arab League Countries A145

1970 *Perf. 11*

570 A145 15f olive & multi .40 .25
571 A145 35f gray & multi .50 .40

25th anniversary of the Arab League.

Baghdad Hospital and Emblem A146

1970, Dec. 7 Litho. *Perf. 12*

572 A146 15f yellow & multi .40 .25
573 A146 40f lt green & multi 1.10 .60

Iraqi Medical Society, 50th anniv.

Sugar Beet — A147

15f, Sugar factory, horiz. 30f, like 5f.

Perf. 13x13½, 13½x13

1970, Dec. 25 Photo.

574 A147 5f ocher, grn & blk .30 .25
575 A147 15f black & multi .50 .25
576 A147 30f org ver, grn & blk 1.50 .75
Nos. 574-576 (3) 2.30 1.25

Publicity for Mosul sugar factory.

OPEC Emblem A148

1970, Dec. 30 Litho. *Perf. 13x13½*

577 A148 10f rose claret, bis & bl .75 .40
578 A148 40f emer, bis & blue 3.25 1.25

OPEC, 10th anniversary.

Soldiers — A149

Soldiers, Maps of Arab Countries and Israel — A150

Perf. 13½x14, 11½x12½

1971, Jan. 6

579 A149 15f multicolored 1.00 .40
580 A150 40f red org & multi 4.00 1.50
a. Souv. sheet of 2, #579-580, imperf. 12.00 *12.00*

Army Day, 50th anniversary. No. 580a sold for 100f.

Marchers and Map of Arab Countries — A151

1971, Feb. 8 Litho. *Perf. 11½x12½*

581 A151 15f yellow & multi .45 .25
582 A151 40f pink & multi 1.25 .50

Revolution of Ramadan 14, 8th anniversary.

Spider Web, Pilgrims A152

1971, Feb. 26 Photo. *Perf. 13*

583 A152 10f pink & multi .25 .25
584 A152 15f buff & multi .45 .25

Hajeer (New) Year.

President al-Bakr A153

1971, Mar. 11 Litho. *Perf. 14*

585 A153 15f orange & multi .70 .40
586 A153 100f emer & multi 3.25 1.50

First anniversary of Mar. 11th Manifesto.

Marshland A154

Tourist Publicity: 10f, Stork flying over Baghdad. 15f, "Summer Resorts." 100f, Return of Sindbad the Sailor.

1971, Mar. 15 *Perf. 13*

587 A154 5f multicolored .45 .25
588 A154 10f lt grn & multi .80 .25
589 A154 15f pink & multi 1.00 .50
590 A154 100f multicolored 5.25 3.00
Nos. 587-590 (4) 7.50 4.00

Blacksmith Taming Serpent — A155

1971, Mar. 21 *Perf. 11½x12*

591 A155 15f multicolored .85 .35
592 A155 25f yel & multi 1.75 .70

Novrooz Festival.

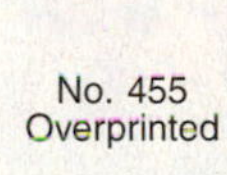

No. 455 Overprinted

1971, Mar. 23 Litho. *Perf. 13*

593 A107 15f rose red & multi 3.25 1.25

World Meteorological Day. See No. C39.

Workers, Soldier, Map of Arab Countries — A156

1971, Apr. 7

594 A156 15f yel & multi .80 .45
595 A156 35f multicolored 1.60 .75
596 A156 250f multicolored 12.00 12.00
Nos. 594-596 (3) 14.40 13.20

24th anniv. of the Al Baath Party. No. 596 has circular perforation around vignette set within a white square of paper, perforated on 4 sides. The design of No. 596 is similar to Nos. 594-595, but with denomination within the circle and no inscriptions in margin.

Nos. 443-444, 448 Overprinted

1971, Apr. 14

597 A105 2f pale brn & multi .50 .25
598 A105 5f ver & multi .70 .25
599 A105 25f lemon & multi 2.25 1.00
Nos. 597-599 (3) 3.45 1.50

Mosul Festival.

Worker, Farm Woman with Torch A157

1971, May 1 Litho. *Perf. 13*

600 A157 15f ocher & multi .35 .25
601 A157 40f olive & multi 1.25 .30

Labor Day.

Muslim Praying in Mecca A158

1971, May 7

602 A158 15f yellow & multi .55 .25
603 A158 100f pink & multi 2.75 1.25

Mohammed's 1,401st birthday.

People, Fists, Map of Iraq A159

1971, July 14 Photo. *Perf. 14*

604 A159 25f green & multi .55 .25
605 A159 50f lt bl & multi 1.75 .60

13th anniv. of the July 14, 1958 revolution.

Surveyor, Preacher, Rising Sun A160

1971, July 17 *Perf. 13*

606 A160 25f multicolored .60 .30
607 A160 70f orange & multi 1.90 .75

3rd anniversary of July 17, 1968, coup.

Rafidain Bank Emblem A161

1971, Sept. 24 Photo. *Perf. 13½*

Diameter: 27mm

608 A161 10f multicolored .55 *.55*
609 A161 15f multicolored .90 *.90*
610 A161 25f multicolored 1.75 *1.75*

Diameter: 32mm

611 A161 65f multicolored 8.50 6.50
612 A161 250f multicolored 22.50 21.00
Nos. 608-612 (5) 34.20 30.70

30th anniversary of Rafidain Bank. Nos. 608-612 have circular perforation around design within a white square of paper, perforated on 4 sides.

Nos. 561, 564-565 Overprinted

1971, Oct. 15 Litho. *Perf. 14*

613	A142	3f bl grn & multi	2.75	2.75
614	A142	15f red & multi	2.75	2.75
615	A142	35f orange & multi	2.75	2.75
		Nos. 613-615 (3)	8.25	8.25

Agricultural census, Oct. 15, 1971.

Soccer A162

Designs: 25f, Track and field. 35f, Table tennis. 75f, Gymnastics. 95f, Volleyball and basketball.

1971, Nov. 17 Litho. *Perf. 13½*

616	A162	15f green & multi	.30	.30
617	A162	25f pink & multi	.80	.40
618	A162	35f lt bl & multi	1.00	.90
619	A162	70f lt grn & multi	4.25	1.50
620	A162	95f yel grn & multi	7.50	2.50
a.		Souvenir sheet of 5	24.00	24.00
		Nos. 616-620 (5)	13.85	5.60

4th Pan-Arab Schoolboys Sports Games, Baghdad. No. 620a contains 5 stamps similar to Nos. 616-620 with simulated perforations. Sold for 200f.

Nos. 527-528, 530 Overprinted and Surcharged

1971, Nov. 23 Litho. *Perf. 13*

621	A135	15f multicolored	1.75	.40
622	A135	25f on 5f multi	2.50	1.25
623	A135	70f on 3f multi	9.50	3.00
		Nos. 621-623 (3)	13.75	4.65

Students' Day. The 15f has only first 3 lines of Arabic overprint.

Nos. 485-486 Overprinted

1971, Dec. 11 Litho. *Perf. 13½*

624	A117	15f multicolored	2.75	1.00
625	A117	25f blue & multi	7.25	3.25

25th anniv. of UNICEF.

Children Crossing Street — A162a

1971, Dec. 17 Litho. *Perf. 13x12½*

625A	A162a	15f yel & multi	2.50	.80
625B	A162a	25f brt rose & multi	4.50	2.50

2nd Traffic Week. For overprints see Nos. 668-669.

Arab Postal Union Emblem A163

1971, Dec. 24 Photo. *Perf. 11½*

626	A163	25f emer, yel & brn	.45	.25
627	A163	70f vio bl, yel & red	1.75	.65

25th anniv. of the Conf. of Sofar, Lebanon, establishing Arab Postal Union.

Racial Equality Emblem — A164

1971, Dec. 31 *Perf. 13½x14*

628	A164	25f brt grn & multi	.25	.25
629	A164	70f orange & multi	1.00	.90

Intl. Year Against Racial Discrimination.

Soldiers with Flag and Torch — A165

1972, Jan. 6 Photo. *Perf. 14x13½*

630	A165	25f blue & multi	1.20	.65
631	A165	70f brt grn & multi	4.00	2.50

Army Day, Jan. 6.

Workers A166

1972, Feb. 8

632	A166	25f brt grn & multi	2.50	.60
633	A166	95f lilac & multi	4.50	2.50

Revolution of Ramadan 14, 9th anniv.

Mosque, Minaret, Crescent and Caravan A167

1972, Feb. 26 Litho. *Perf. 12½x13*

634	A167	25f bl grn & multi	.35	.25
635	A167	35f purple & multi	.70	.40

Hegira (Pilgrimage) Year.

Peace Symbols and "11" — A168

1972, Mar. 11 Photo. *Perf. 11x12½*

636	A168	25f lt blue & blk	1.50	.30
637	A168	70f brt lilac & blk	4.25	1.25

2nd anniversary of Mar. 11 Manifesto.

Mountain Range and Flowers — A169

1972, Mar. 21 *Perf. 11½x11*

638	A169	25f vio blue & multi	1.25	.25
639	A169	70f vio blue & multi	4.25	1.50

Novrooz, New Year Festival.

Party Emblem A170

Symbolic Design — A171

Perf. 14 (A170), 13 (A171)

1972 Litho.

640	A170	10f brn org & multi	.35	.25
641	A171	25f bister & multi	.80	.40
642	A170	35f brn org & multi	.90	.50
643	A171	70f red & multi	2.75	2.10
		Nos. 640-643 (4)	4.80	3.25

Iraqi Arab Baath Socialist Party, 25th anniv. Issued: 25f, 70f, Mar. 23; 10f, 35f, Apr. 7.

Emblem, Map, Weather Balloons and Chart — A172

1972, Mar. 23 Photo. *Perf. 14x13½*

644	A172	25f multicolored	1.90	.50
645	A172	35f yel & multi	3.25	1.50

12th World Meteorological Day.

Cogwheel and Ship — A173

1972, Mar. 25 *Perf. 11x11½*

646	A173	25f ocher & multi	.50	.25
647	A173	35f pink & multi	1.00	.40

Arab Chamber of Commerce.

Derrick and Flame — A174

1972, Apr. 7 *Perf. 13x13½*

648	A174	25f multicolored	1.40	.30
649	A174	35f multicolored	1.90	1.00

Opening of North Rumaila (INOC, North Iraq Oil Fields).

Quill Pens, Map of Arab Countries — A175

1972, Apr. 17 Photo. *Perf. 11x11½*

650	A175	25f orange & multi	.55	.25
651	A175	35f blue & multi	1.75	1.00

3rd Congress of Arab Journalists.

Women's Federation Emblem A176

1972, Apr. 22 Litho. *Perf. 13½*

652	A176	25f green & multi	.55	.30
653	A176	35f lilac & multi	1.75	1.20

Iraqi Women's Federation, 4th anniversary.

Hand Holding Globe-shaped Wrench — A177

1972, May 1 Photo. *Perf. 11½*

654	A177	25f yel grn & multi	.45	.25
655	A177	35f orange & multi	.80	.40

Labor Day.

Kaaba, Mecca, and Crescent — A178

1972, May 26

656 A178 25f green & multi .55 .25
657 A178 35f purple & multi 1.75 1.10

Mohammed's 1,402nd birthday.

Soldier, Civilian and Guns — A179

1972, July 14 Photo. ***Perf. 13½x14***

658 A179 35f multicolored .90 .40
659 A179 70f lilac & multi 3.00 1.20

14th anniv. of July 14, 1958, revolution.

Dome of the Rock, Arab Countries' Map, Fists A180

1972, July 17 ***Perf. 13***

660 A180 25f citron & multi 1.20 .70
661 A180 95f blue & multi 3.25 3.00

4th anniv. of July 17, 1968 coup.

Congress Emblem, Scout Saluting Iraqi Flag — A182

1972, Aug. 12 Photo. ***Perf. 13½x14***

664 A182 20f multicolored 2.25 1.00
665 A182 25f lilac & multi 3.25 1.10

10th Arab Boy Scouts Jamboree and Conference, Mosul, Aug. 10-19.

1972, Aug. 24

Congress emblem and Girl Guide in camp.

666 A182 10f yellow & multi 1.50 .65
667 A182 45f multicolored 4.75 1.40

4th Arab Guides Camp & Conf., Mosul, Aug. 24-30.

No. 625B Ovptd.

No. 625A Ovptd. and Srchd.

1972, Oct. 4 Photo. ***Perf. 13x12½***

668 A162a 25f brt rose & multi 6.75 3.00
669 A162a 70f on 15f multi 8.50 7.00

Third Traffic Week.

Central Bank of Iraq A183

1972, Nov. 16 Photo. ***Perf. 13***

670 A183 25f lt blue & multi .80 .40
671 A183 70f lt green & multi 2.25 .90

25th anniversary, Central Bank of Iraq.

UIC Emblem A184

1972, Dec. 29

672 A184 25f dp rose & multi 1.75 .70
673 A184 45f brt vio & multi 5.00 3.00

50th anniv., Intl. Railroad Union (UIC).

Nos. 148-149, 151, 180 and Type of 1957-58 Overprinted with 3 Bars

1973, Jan. 29 Engr. ***Perf. 11½x12***

674 A28 10f blue 3.50 1.25
675 A33 10f blue 3.50 1.25
676 A28 15f black 3.50 1.25
677 A33 15f black 3.50 1.25
678 A28 25f rose violet 3.50 1.25
679 A33 25f rose violet 3.50 1.25
Nos. 674-679 (6) 21.00 7.50

The size and position of the bottom bar of overprint differs; the bar can be same size as 2 top bars, short and centered or moved to the right.

No. 455 Overprinted

1973, Mar. 25 Litho. ***Perf. 13***

680 A107 15f rose red & multi 10.00 4.00

Intl. History Cong. See Nos. C52-C53.

Workers and Oil Wells A185

1973, June 1 Litho. ***Perf. 13***

681 A185 25f yel & multi 2.00 .90
682 A185 70f rose & multi 9.50 3.00

1st anniv. of nationalization of oil industry. For overprint, see No. O298.

Ram's-head Harp — A186

Designs: 25f, 35f, 45f, Minaret, Mosul, 50f, 70f, 95f, Statue of goddess. 10f, 20f, like 5f.

1973, June Litho. ***Perf. 13x12½***

683 A186 5f orange & blk .25 .25
684 A186 10f bister & blk .35 .25
685 A186 20f brt rose & blk .35 .25
686 A186 25f ultra & blk .35 .25
687 A186 35f emer & blk .60 .30
688 A186 45f blue & black .70 .30
689 A186 50f olive & yel .95 .30
690 A186 70f violet & yel 1.25 .50
691 A186 95f brown & yel 2.25 .75
Nos. 683-691 (9) 7.05 3.15

For overprints see Nos. O299-O307, RA21.

People with Flags, Grain A187

1973, July 14

692 A187 25f multicolored .70 .30
693 A187 35f multicolored 1.40 .40

July Festivals.

Nos. 393 and 395 Surcharged

1973 Litho. ***Perf. 13½x14***

694 A85 25f on 3f multi 4.00 2.25
695 A85 70f on 15f multi 10.00 5.00

Festival of Date Trees.

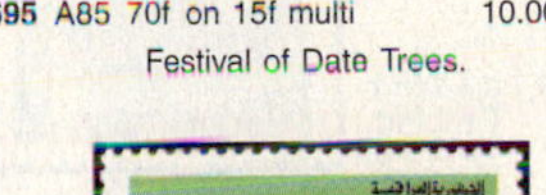

INTERPOL Headquarters — A188

1973, Sept. 20 Litho. ***Perf. 12***

696 A188 25f multicolored 1.00 .60
697 A188 70f brt bl & multi 5.50 3.75

50th anniv. of Intl. Criminal Police Org.

Nos. 517-518 Overprinted in Silver

1973, Sept. 29 Litho. ***Perf. 12½x13***

698 A130 15f multicolored 6.50 2.50
699 A130 50f multicolored 12.00 3.50

Meeting of Intl. Org. of Journalists' Executive Committee, Sept. 26-29.

Flags and Fair Emblem — A189

1973, Oct. 10 Photo. ***Perf. 11***

700 A189 10f brt grn & dk brn .45 .25
701 A189 20f ocher & multi .80 .30
702 A189 65f blue & multi 1.75 .90
Nos. 700-702 (3) 3.00 1.45

10th International Baghdad Fair, Oct. 1-21.

WMO Emblem — A190

1973, Nov. 15 Litho. ***Perf. 12***

703 A190 25f org, blk & green .70 .25
704 A190 35f brt rose, blk & grn 2.25 1.00

Intl. meteorological cooperation, cent.

Flags of Arab League and Iraq, Maghreb Emblem A191

1973, Dec. 1 Photo. ***Perf. 14***

705 A191 20f dl org & multi .40 .25
706 A191 35f blue & multi 1.40 .90

11th session of Civil Aviation Council of Arab States, Baghdad, Dec. 1973.

No. 360 Overprinted

1973, Dec. 12 Photo. ***Perf. 11***

707 A67a 30f orange & blue 5.00 2.75

6th Executive Council Meeting of APU, Baghdad.

Human Rights Flame — A192

1973, Dec. 25 ***Perf. 11½***

708 A192 25f multicolored .25 .25
709 A192 70f ultra & multi .90 .50

Universal Declaration of Human Rights, 25th anniv.

Military College Crest and Cadets
A193

1974, Jan. 6 ***Perf. 12x11½***

710 A193 25f ocher & multi .45 .25
711 A193 35f ultra & multi 1.60 1.00

50th anniversary of the Military College.

UPU and Arab Postal Union Emblems
A194

1974, May 28 Photo. ***Perf. 11½x12***

712 A194 25f gold & multi .90 .25
713 A194 35f gold & multi .90 .40
714 A194 70f gold & multi 1.60 .90
Nos. 712-714 (3) 3.40 1.55

Centenary of the Universal Postal Union.

Symbols of Ancient Mesopotamia and Oil Industry — A195

1974, June 1 Litho. ***Perf. 12½***

715 A195 10f blue & multi .40 .25
716 A195 25f ocher & multi .85 .25
717 A195 70f rose & multi 2.75 2.00
Nos. 715-717 (3) 4.00 2.50

Nationalization of the oil industry, 2nd anniv.

Festival
A196

1974, July 17 ***Perf. 11½x12***

718 A196 20f lilac & multi .35 .25
719 A196 35f dull org & multi 1.00 .50

July Festivals.

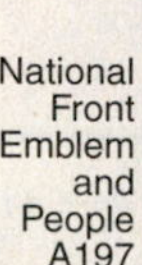

National Front Emblem and People
A197

1974, July 17 ***Perf. 12x11½***

720 A197 25f blue & multi .65 .25
721 A197 70f brt grn & multi 1.50 .75

1st anniv. of Progressive National Front.

Cement Plant and Brick Wall — A198

1974, Oct. 19 ***Perf. 11½x12***

722 A198 20f gray bl & multi .45 .25
723 A198 25f red & multi .65 .30
724 A198 70f emerald & multi 1.40 1.00
Nos. 722-724 (3) 2.50 1.55

25th anniversary of Iraqi Cement Plant.

Nos. 561 and 527 Surcharged

a

b

1975, Jan. 9 Litho. ***Perf. 13, 14***

725 A142 (a) 10f on 3f multi 3.50 2.50
726 A135 (b) 25f on 3f multi 11.00 7.25

Globe and WPY Emblem
A199

1975, Jan. 30 ***Perf. 11½x12***

727 A199 25f dull bl & blk .60 .25
728 A199 35f brt pink & ind 1.25 .65
729 A199 70f yel grn & vio 3.50 1.40
Nos. 727-729 (3) 5.35 2.30

World Population Year 1974.

Festival Symbols — A200

1975, July 17 Litho. ***Perf. 12x11½***

730 A200 5f lt brn & multi .25 .25
731 A200 10f lt brn & multi .25 .25
732 A200 35f lt brn & multi 1.75 .75
Nos. 730-732 (3) 2.25 1.25

Festivals, July 1975.

Map of Arab Countries
A201

1975, Aug. 5 Photo. ***Perf. 13***

733 A201 25f rose & multi .50 .25
734 A201 35f multicolored .90 .60
735 A201 45f multicolored 1.00 .65
Nos. 733-735 (3) 2.40 1.50

Arab Working Org., 10th anniv.

Symbols of Women, Oil Industry and Agriculture
A202

1975, Aug. 15 ***Perf. 14***

736 A202 10f lilac & multi .50 .30
737 A202 35f multicolored 1.00 .85
738 A202 70f bl & multi 4.25 1.50
a. Souv. sheet, 100f, imperf. 10.00 *10.00*
Nos. 736-738 (3) 5.75 2.65

International Women's Year.

Euphrates Dam and Causeway — A203

1975, Sept. 5 Litho. ***Perf. 12x11½***

739 A203 3f orange & multi .25 .25
740 A203 25f purple & multi .70 .25
741 A203 70f rose red & multi 2.75 1.25
Nos. 739-741 (3) 3.70 1.75

Intl. Commission on Irrigation and Drainage, 25th anniv.

National Insurance Co. Seal
A204

1975, Oct. 11 Photo. ***Perf. 13***

742 A204 20f brt bl & multi .80 .25
743 A204 25f crim & multi 1.00 .40
a. Souv. sheet, 100f, imperf. 7.00 *8.50*

Natl. Insurance Co., Baghdad, 25th anniv.

Musician Entertaining King — A205

1975, Nov. 21 ***Perf. 14***

744 A205 25f silver & multi .65 .25
745 A205 45f gold & multi 1.50 .90

Baghdad Intl. Music Conf., Nov. 1975.

Telecommunications Center — A206

1975, Dec. 22 Litho. ***Perf. 12½***

746 A206 5f lil rose & multi .25 .25
747 A206 10f blue & multi .30 .25
748 A206 60f green & multi 1.90 1.20
Nos. 746-748 (3) 2.45 1.70

Inauguration of Telecommunications Center Building during July 1975 Festival.

Diesel Locomotive — A207

Conference Emblem and: 30f, Diesel passenger locomotive #511. 35f, 0-3-0 steam tank locomotive with passenger train. 50f, 2-3-0 German steam locomotive, c. 1914.

1975, Dec. 22 Photo. ***Perf. 14***

749 A207 25f tan & multi 5.50 1.00
750 A207 30f tan & multi 8.50 2.00
751 A207 35f yel grn & multi 11.00 3.50
752 A207 50f yel grn & multi 16.00 9.50
Nos. 749-752 (4) 41.00 16.00

15th Taurus Railway Conference, Baghdad.

A208

Design: Soldier on guard.

1976, Jan. 6 ***Perf. 13***

753 A208 5f silver & multi .25 .25
754 A208 25f silver & multi .55 .25
755 A208 50f gold & multi 1.60 .60
Nos. 753-755 (3) 2.40 1.10

55th Army Day.

Arab Day Eliminate Illiteracy — A209

Fingerprint crossed out, Arab world.

1976, Jan. 8 Photo. ***Perf. 13½x13***

756 A209 5f violet & multi .25 .25
757 A209 15f blue & multi .45 .25
758 A209 35f green & multi 1.60 1.00
Nos. 756-758 (3) 2.30 1.50

Statue of Goddess — A210

20f-30f, Two female figures forming column. 35f-75f, Head of bearded man.

1976, Jan. 1 Litho. *Perf. 13x12½*

No.	Type	Description	Mint	Used
759	A210	5f lilac & multi	.25	.25
760	A210	10f rose & multi	.25	.25
761	A210	15f yellow & multi	.30	.25
762	A210	20f bister & multi	.30	.25
763	A210	25f lt grn & multi	.45	.25
764	A210	30f blue & multi	.70	.25
765	A210	35f lil rose & multi	.80	.30
766	A210	50f citron & multi	1.20	.30
767	A210	75f violet & multi	1.75	.70
		Nos. 759-767 (9)	6.00	2.80

Iraq Earth Station A211

1976, Feb. 8 *Perf. 13x13½*

No.	Type	Description	Mint	Used
768	A211	10f silver & multi	.40	.25
769	A211	25f silver & multi	1.25	.45
770	A211	75f gold & multi	4.50	2.00
		Nos. 768-770 (3)	6.15	2.70

Revolution of Ramadan 14, 13th anniv.

Telephones 1876 and 1976 — A212

1976, Mar. 17 Litho. *Perf. 12x12½*

No.	Type	Description	Mint	Used
771	A212	35f multicolored	1.25	.45
772	A212	50f multicolored	2.50	.70
773	A212	75f multicolored	4.00	1.00
		Nos. 771-773 (3)	7.75	2.15

Centenary of first telephone call by Alexander Graham Bell, Mar. 10, 1876.

Map of Maghreb, ICATU Emblem — A213

1976, Mar. 24 Photo. *Perf. 13½*

No.	Type	Description	Mint	Used
774	A213	5f green & multi	.35	.25
775	A213	10f multicolored	.35	.25
		Nos. 774-775,C54 (3)	5.20	2.50

20th Intl. Conf. of Arab Workers Syndicates.

Map of Iraq, Family, Torch and Wreath — A214

1976, Apr. 1 *Perf. 12½*

No.	Type	Description	Mint	Used
776	A214	5f multicolored	.25	.25
777	A214	15f lilac & multi	.45	.25
778	A214	35f multicolored	2.25	.90
		Nos. 776-778 (3)	2.95	1.40

Police Day.

Pipeline, Map of Iraq — A215

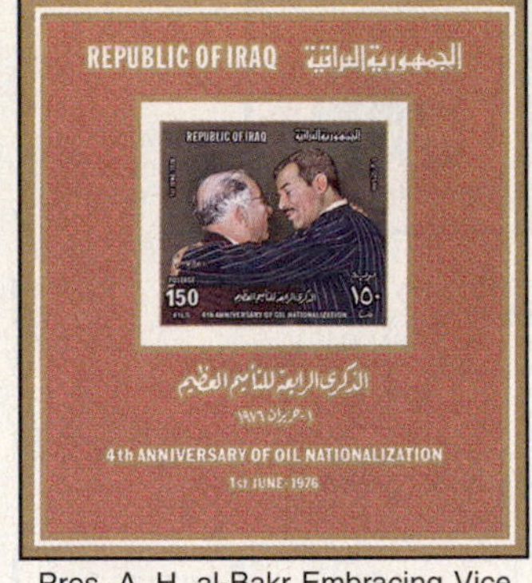

Pres. A. H. al-Bakr Embracing Vice Pres. Saddam Hussein — A216

1976, June 1 Photo. *Perf. 13*

No.	Type	Description	Mint	Used
779	A215	25f multicolored	1.50	.25
780	A215	75f multicolored	4.50	2.00

Souvenir Sheet

Imperf

No.	Type	Description	Mint	Used
781	A216	150f multicolored	32.50	32.50

4th anniversary of oil nationalization.

"Festival" — A217

1976, July 17 *Perf. 14*

No.	Type	Description	Mint	Used
782	A217	15f orange & multi	.35	.25
783	A217	35f orange & multi	1.00	.70

Festivals, July 1976.

Archbishop Capucci, Map of Palestine A218

1976, Aug. 18 Litho. *Perf. 12*

No.	Type	Description	Mint	Used
784	A218	25f multicolored	.80	.25
785	A218	35f multicolored	1.25	.45
786	A218	75f multicolored	3.50	1.50
		Nos. 784-786 (3)	5.55	2.20

Detention of Archbishop Hilarion Capucci in Israel, Aug. 18, 1974.

Common Kingfisher — A219

10f, Turtle dove. 15f, Pin-tailed sandgrouse. 25f, Blue rock thrush. 50f, Purple and gray herons.

1976, Sept. 15 Litho. *Perf. 13½x14*

No.	Type	Description	Mint	Used
787	A219	5f multicolored	2.75	.85
788	A219	10f multicolored	2.75	.85
789	A219	15f multicolored	3.75	.85
790	A219	25f multicolored	7.25	1.10
791	A219	50f multicolored	11.00	1.50
		Nos. 787-791 (5)	27.50	5.15

For overprints see Nos. O327-O331.

"15" — A220

1976, Nov. 23 Photo. *Perf. 13½*

No.	Type	Description	Mint	Used
792	A220	30f multicolored	.75	.25
793	A220	70f multicolored	2.50	.75

15th anniv. of National Students Union.

Oil Tanker and Emblems A221

25f, 50f, Pier, refinery, pipeline.

1976, Dec. 25 *Perf. 12½x12*

No.	Type	Description	Mint	Used
794	A221	10f multicolored	.70	.25
795	A221	15f multicolored	.90	.40
796	A221	25f multicolored	2.10	.75
797	A221	50f multicolored	3.00	1.25
		Nos. 794-797 (4)	6.70	2.65

1st Iraqi oil tanker (10f, 15f) and Nationalization of Basrah Petroleum Co. Ltd., 1st anniv. (25f, 50f).

Happy Children — A222

UNESCO Emblem and: 25f, Children with flowers and butterflies. 75f, Children planting flowers around flagpole.

1976, Dec. 25 *Perf. 12x12½*

No.	Type	Description	Mint	Used
798	A222	10f multicolored	.25	.25
799	A222	25f multicolored	2.00	.40
800	A222	75f multicolored	3.50	1.10
		Nos. 798-800 (3)	5.75	1.75

30th anniv. of UNESCO, and Books for Children Campaign.

Ornament A223

1977, Mar. 2 Photo. *Perf. 13½*

No.	Type	Description	Mint	Used
801	A223	25f gold & multi	.70	.25
802	A223	35f gold & multi	1.00	.30

Birthday of Mohammed (570-632).

Peace Day — A224

25f, 30f, Peace Dove.

1977, Mar. 11 *Perf. 14x13½*

No.	Type	Description	Mint	Used
803	A224	25f lt bl & multi	.35	.25
804	A224	30f buff & multi	.65	.30

Dahlia — A225

Flowers: 10f, Sweet peas. 35f, Chrysanthemums. 50f, Verbena.

1977, Mar. 21 Litho. *Perf. 12½*

No.	Type	Description	Mint	Used
805	A225	5f multicolored	.25	.25
806	A225	10f multicolored	.45	.25
807	A225	35f multicolored	1.10	.30
808	A225	50f multicolored	2.25	.65
		Nos. 805-808 (4)	4.05	1.45

Spring Festivals, Baghdad.

Emblem with Doves A226

Designs: 75f, Emblematic Hindu "7" with flame. 100f, Dove with olive branch.

1977, Apr. 7 Photo. *Perf. 13*

No.	Type	Description	Mint	Used
809	A226	25f yel & multi	.60	.25
810	A226	75f yel & multi	2.25	1.00

Souvenir Sheet

Imperf

No.	Type	Description	Mint	Used
811	A226	100f multicolored	6.00	6.00

Al Baath Party, 30th anniversary. No. 811 contains one 49x35mm stamp.

APU Emblem, Members' Flags A227

1977, Apr. 12 Litho. *Perf. 14*

No.	Type	Description	Mint	Used
812	A227	25f orange & multi	.35	.25
813	A227	35f gray & multi	.70	.40

25th anniversary of Arab Postal Union.

Cogwheel, Globe and "1" — A228

1977, May 1 Litho. *Perf. 14½x14*

No.	Type	Description	Mint	Used
814	A228	10f multicolored	.25	.25
815	A228	30f multicolored	.55	.25
816	A228	35f multicolored	.70	.60
		Nos. 814-816 (3)	1.50	1.10

Labor Day.

Weight Lifting A229

75f, Weight lifter, standing up. 100f, Symbolic weight lifter with Iraqi flag, laurel wreath.

1977, May 8 **Photo.** ***Perf. 14***
817 A229 25f multicolored .90 .60
818 A229 75f multicolored 2.50 1.10

Souvenir Sheet

Imperf

819 A229 100f multicolored 8.50 *8.50*

8th Asian Weight Lifting Championship, Baghdad, May 1977. No. 819 contains one 42x52mm stamp.

Arabian Garden A230

Arab Tourist Year: 10f, View of town with minarets, horiz. 30f, Landscape with bridge and waterfall. 50f, Hosts welcoming tourists, and drum, horiz.

Perf. 11½x12, 12x11½

1977, June 15 **Litho.**
820 A230 5f multicolored .25 .25
821 A230 10f multicolored .25 .25
822 A230 30f multicolored .95 .25
823 A230 50f multicolored 2.75 1.75
Nos. 820-823 (4) 4.20 2.50

Grain and Dove — A231

1977, July 17 **Photo.** ***Perf. 14***
824 A231 25f multicolored .55 .25
825 A231 30f multicolored .70 .30

Festivals, July 1977.

Map of Arab Countries A232

1977, Sept. 9 **Photo.** ***Perf. 13½x14***
826 A232 30f multicolored .80 .45
827 A232 70f multicolored 2.40 .90

UN Conference on Desertification, Nairobi, Kenya, Aug. 29-Sept. 9.

Census Emblem — A233

1977, Oct. 17 **Litho.** ***Perf. 14x14½***
828 A233 20f ultra & multi .30 .25
829 A233 30f brown & multi .70 .25
830 A233 70f gray & multi 1.40 .80
Nos. 828-830 (3) 2.40 1.30

Population Census Day, Oct. 17.

Festival Emblem — A234

1977, Nov. 1 **Photo.** ***Perf. 14***
831 A234 25f silver & multi .30 .25
832 A234 50f gold & multi .65 .40

Al Mutanabby Festival, Nov. 1977.

A235

Jumblatt, caricatures of Britain, US, Israel.

1977, Nov. 16 **Photo.** ***Perf. 14***
833 A235 20f multicolored .40 .25
834 A235 30f multicolored .55 .25
835 A235 70f multicolored 1.25 .60
Nos. 833-835 (3) 2.20 1.10

Kemal Junblatt, Druse leader, killed in Lebanese war.

A236

1977, Dec. 12 **Photo.** ***Perf. 14***
836 A236 30f gold & multi .40 .25
837 A236 35f silver & multi .50 .25

Hegira (Pilgrimage) Year.

Young People and Flags — A237

1978, Apr. 7 **Photo.** ***Perf. 11½x11***
838 A237 10f multicolored .25 .25
839 A237 15f multicolored .25 .25
840 A237 35f multicolored .55 .35
Nos. 838-840 (3) 1.05 .85

Youth Day.

Coins and Coin Bank — A238

1978, Apr. 15
841 A238 15f multicolored .30 .25
842 A238 25f multicolored .50 .25
843 A238 35f multicolored 1.00 .40
Nos. 841-843 (3) 1.80 .90

6th anniversary of postal savings law.

Microwave Transmission and Receiving A239

1978, May 17 **Photo.** ***Perf. 14***
844 A239 25f org & multi .40 .25
845 A239 35f lilac & multi .40 .25
846 A239 75f emer & multi 1.00 .60
Nos. 844-846 (3) 1.80 1.10

10th World Telecommunications Day and 1st anniversary of commissioning of national microwave network.

Emblems and Flags of Participants — A240

Perf. 12½x11½

1978, June 19 **Litho.**
847 A240 25f multicolored .55 .25
848 A240 35f multicolored .85 .50

Conference of Postal Ministers of Arabian Gulf Countries, Baghdad (Saudi Arabia, United Arab Emirates, Qatar, Bahrain, Kuwait, Oman, People's Republic of Yemen).

Ancient Coin — A241

Designs: Ancient Iraqi coins. 75f vertical.

Perf. 11½x12½

1978, June 25 **Photo.**
849 A241 1f citron & multi .25 .25
850 A241 2f lt blue & multi .25 .25
851 A241 3f salmon & multi .25 .25
852 A241 4f yel grn & multi .25 .25
853 A241 75f bl grn & multi 2.40 2.40
Nos. 849-853 (5) 3.40 3.40

Festival Emblem — A242

Festival Poster — A243

1978, July 17 ***Perf. 13½x13***
854 A242 25f multicolored .35 .25
855 A242 35f multicolored .55 .25

Souvenir Sheet

Perf. 13x13½

856 A243 100f multicolored 6.50 6.50

Festivals, July 1978.

WHO Emblem, Nurse, Hospital, Sick Child A244

1978, Aug. 18 **Photo.** ***Perf. 14***
857 A244 25f multicolored .25 .25
858 A244 35f multicolored .65 .25
859 A244 75f multicolored 1.75 .95
Nos. 857-859 (3) 2.65 1.45

Eradication of smallpox.

Maritime Union Emblem A245

1978, Aug. 30 **Photo.** ***Perf. 11½x12***
860 A245 25f multicolored .55 .30
861 A245 75f multicolored 1.40 .55

1st World Maritime Day.

Workers A246

1978, Sept. 12 ***Perf. 14***
862 A246 10f multicolored .25 .25
863 A246 25f multicolored .55 .25
864 A246 35f multicolored 1.00 .65
Nos. 862-864 (3) 1.80 1.15

10th anniv. of People's Work Groups.

Fair Emblem with Atom Symbol — A247

1978, Oct. 1
865 A247 25f multicolored .25 .25
866 A247 35f multicolored .30 .25
867 A247 75f multicolored 1.40 .85
Nos. 865-867 (3) 1.95 1.35

15th International Fair, Baghdad, Oct. 1-15.

Map of Iraq, Ruler and Globe — A248

1978, Oct. 14
868 A248 25f multicolored .25 .25
869 A248 35f multicolored .30 .25
870 A248 75f multicolored 1.40 .85
Nos. 868-870 (3) 1.95 1.35

World Standards Day.

Altharthar-Euphrates Dam — A249

1978 **Photo.** ***Perf. 11½***
871 A249 5f multicolored .25 .25
872 A249 10f multicolored .25 .25
873 A249 15f multicolored .25 .25
874 A249 25f multicolored .30 .25
875 A249 35f multicolored .40 .25
876 A249 50f multicolored .65 .30
Nos. 871-876 (6) 2.10 1.55

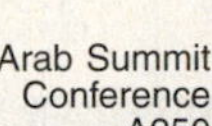
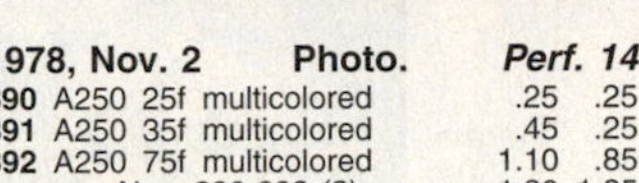

Arab Summit Conference A250

1978, Nov. 2 Photo. *Perf. 14*

890	A250	25f multicolored	.25	.25
891	A250	35f multicolored	.45	.25
892	A250	75f multicolored	1.10	.85
		Nos. 890-892 (3)	1.80	1.35

9th Arab Summit Conference, Baghdad, Nov. 2-5.

Surgeons' Conference Emblem — A251

1978, Nov. 8 Litho. *Perf. 12x11½*

893	A251	25f multicolored	.35	.25
894	A251	75f multicolored	1.00	.65

4th Cong. of the Assoc. of Thoracic & Cardiovascular Surgeons of Asia, Baghdad, Nov. 6-10.

Pilgrims at Mt. Arafat and Holy Ka'aba A252

1978, Nov. 9 Photo. *Perf. 14*

895	A252	25f multicolored	.35	.25
896	A252	35f multicolored	.55	.25

Pilgrimage to Mecca.

Atom Symbol, Map of South America, Africa, Arabia A253

1978, Nov. 11 *Perf. 13½*

897	A253	25f multicolored	.25	.25
898	A253	50f multicolored	.55	.25
899	A253	75f multicolored	.90	.55
		Nos. 897-899 (3)	1.70	1.05

Technical Cooperation Among Developing Countries Conf., Buenos Aires, Argentina, Sept. 1978.

Hands Holding Emblem — A254

1978, Nov. 30 Litho. *Perf. 13½x13*

900	A254	25f multicolored	.40	.25
901	A254	50f multicolored	.70	.30
902	A254	75f multicolored	2.00	.65
		Nos. 900-902 (3)	3.10	1.20

Anti-Apartheid Year.

Globe and Flame Emblem — A255

1978, Dec. 20 *Perf. 14*

903	A255	25f multicolored	.50	.25
904	A255	75f multicolored	1.50	1.00

Declaration of Human Rights, 30th anniv.

Candle and Emblem — A256

1979, Jan. 9 Photo. *Perf. 14*

905	A256	10f multicolored	.35	.25
906	A256	25f multicolored	.35	.25
907	A256	35f multicolored	.65	.25
		Nos. 905-907 (3)	1.35	.75

Police Day.

Book, Pencil and Flame — A257

1979, Feb. 15 Photo. *Perf. 14*

908	A257	15f multicolored	.25	.25
909	A257	25f multicolored	.35	.25
910	A257	35f multicolored	.90	.25
		Nos. 908-910 (3)	1.50	.75

Application of Compulsory Education Law, anniversary.

Pupils, School and Teacher A258

1979, Mar. 1 *Perf. 13*

911	A258	10f multicolored	.25	.25
912	A258	15f multicolored	.25	.25
913	A258	50f multicolored	.80	.50
		Nos. 911-913 (3)	1.30	1.00

Teacher's Day.

Pupils, Flag, Pencil — A259

1979, Mar. 10 *Perf. 13½x13*

914	A259	15f multicolored	.25	.25
915	A259	25f multicolored	.45	.25
916	A259	35f multicolored	.70	.25
		Nos. 914-916 (3)	1.40	.75

National Comprehensive Compulsory Literacy Campaign.

Book, World Map, Arab Achievements A260

1979, Mar. 22 *Perf. 13*

917	A260	35f multicolored	.50	.25
918	A260	75f multicolored	1.50	.65

Achievements of the Arabs.

Girl Playing Flute — A261

1979, Apr. 15 Litho. *Perf. 13½*

919	A261	15f multicolored	.35	.25
920	A261	25f multicolored	.55	.25
921	A261	35f multicolored	1.00	.45
		Nos. 919-921 (3)	1.90	.95

Mosul Spring Festival.

Iraqi Flag, Globe, UPU Emblem A262

1979, Apr. 22 Photo. *Perf. 13x13½*

922	A262	25f multicolored	.60	.25
923	A262	35f multicolored	.60	.25
924	A262	75f multicolored	1.50	.65
		Nos. 922-924 (3)	2.70	1.15

50th anniv. of Iraq's admission to the UPU.

Soccer Tournament Emblem A263

1979, May 4 Photo. *Perf. 13*

925	A263	10f multicolored	.25	.25
926	A263	15f multicolored	.30	.25
927	A263	50f multicolored	1.00	.50
		Nos. 925-927 (3)	1.55	1.00

5th Arabian Gulf Soccer Championship.

Child With Globe and Candle A264

Design: 100f, IYC emblem, boy and girl reaching for UN emblem, vert.

1979, June 1 Photo. *Perf. 13x13½*

928	A264	25f multicolored	.70	.30
929	A264	75f multicolored	1.75	1.00

Souvenir Sheet

930	A264	100f multicolored	30.00	27.50

International Year of the Child.
No. 930 contains one 30x42mm stamp.

Leaf and Flower — A265

1979, July 17 Litho. *Perf. 12½*

931	A265	15f multicolored	.25	.25
932	A265	25f multicolored	.35	.25
933	A265	35f multicolored	.35	.25
		Nos. 931-933 (3)	.95	.75

July festivals.

Students Holding Globe, UNESCO Emblem A266

1979, July 25

934	A266	25f multicolored	.50	.25
935	A266	40f multicolored	.90	.45
936	A266	100f multicolored	2.00	.90
		Nos. 934-936 (3)	3.40	1.60

Intl. Bureau of Education, Geneva, 50th anniv.

S. al Hosari, Philosopher A267

Designs: No. 938, Mustapha Jawad, historian. No. 939, Jawad Selim, sculptor.

1979, Oct. 15 Litho. *Perf. 12½*

937	A267	25f multicolored	.45	.25
938	A267	25f multicolored	.45	.25
939	A267	25f multicolored	.45	.25
		Nos. 937-939 (3)	1.35	.75

Pilgrimage to Mecca A268

1979, Oct. 25 Litho. *Perf. 12½*

940	A268	25f multicolored	.60	.25
941	A268	50f multicolored	1.25	.40

Iraqi News Agency, 20th Anniversary A269

1979, Nov. 9 Photo. *Perf. 11½*

942	A269	25f multicolored	.45	.25
943	A269	50f multicolored	1.00	.25
944	A269	75f multicolored	1.25	.40
		Nos. 942-944 (3)	2.70	.90

Telecom 79 — A270

1979, Nov. 20 Litho. *Perf. 11½*

945 A270 25f multicolored .45 .25
946 A270 50f multicolored .70 .30
947 A270 75f multicolored 1.25 .65
Nos. 945-947 (3) 2.40 1.20

3rd World Telecommunications Exhibition, Geneva, Sept. 20-26.

International Palestinian Solidarity Day — A271

1979, Nov. 29 Photo. *Perf. 11½x12*

948 A271 25f multicolored 1.25 .25
949 A271 50f multicolored 2.25 .45
950 A271 75f multicolored 3.50 .85
Nos. 948-950 (3) 7.00 1.55

A272

Designs: 25f, 75f, Ahmad Hassan Al-Bakr. 35f, 100f, Pres. Saddam Hussein.

1979, Dec. 1 Photo. *Perf. 13x13½*

951 A272 25f multicolored .35 .25
952 A272 35f multicolored .50 .25
953 A272 75f multicolored 1.00 .40
954 A272 100f multicolored 4.00 2.25
Nos. 951-954 (4) 5.85 3.15

A273

Vanguard Emblem and: 10f, Boy and violin. 15f, Children, map of Iraq. 25f, Youths. 35f, Vanguard emblem alone.

1979, Dec. 10 *Perf. 14*

955 A273 10f multicolored .25 .25
956 A273 15f multicolored .25 .25
957 A273 25f multicolored .40 .25
958 A273 35f multicolored .50 .25
Nos. 955-958 (4) 1.40 1.00

World Meteorological Day — A274

1980, Mar. 23 Photo. *Perf. 14*

959 A274 15f multicolored .25 .25
960 A274 25f multicolored .30 .25
961 A274 35f multicolored .70 .25
Nos. 959-961 (3) 1.25 .75

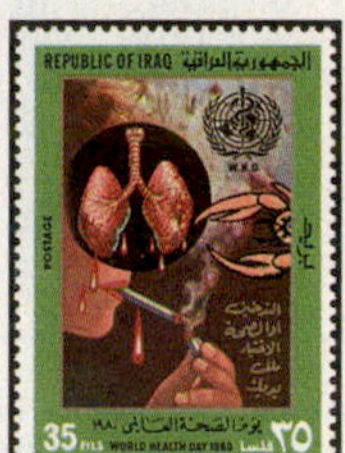

World Health Day — A275

1980, Apr. 7 Photo. *Perf. 14*

962 A275 25f multicolored .35 .25
963 A275 35f multicolored .50 .25
964 A275 75f multicolored 1.90 .50
Nos. 962-964 (3) 2.75 1.00

Festivals Emblem — A276

Pres. Hussein — A277

1980, July 17 Photo. *Perf. 13½x13*

965 A276 25f multicolored .50 .30
966 A276 35f multicolored .75 .35

Souvenir Sheet

Perf. 13½

967 A277 100f multicolored 14.00 12.00

July Festivals.

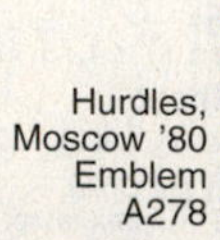

Hurdles, Moscow '80 Emblem A278

20f, Weight lifting, vert. 30f, Boxing. 35f, Soccer, vert.
100f, Wrestling.

1980, July 30 Photo. *Perf. 14*

968 A278 15f shown .25 .25
969 A278 20f multi .45 .35
970 A278 30f multi .85 .40
971 A278 35f multi 1.75 .75
Nos. 968-971 (4) 3.30 1.75

Souvenir Sheet

972 A278 100f multi 10.50 10.50

22nd Summer Olympic Games, Moscow, July 19-Aug. 3.

Fruits — A279

1980, Aug. 15

973 A279 5f Blackberries .25 .25
974 A279 15f Apricots .50 .25
975 A279 20f Pears .70 .25
976 A279 25f Apples .85 .25
977 A279 35f Plums 1.10 .35
Nos. 973-977 (5) 3.40 1.35

World Tourism Conference, Manila, Sept. 27 — A279a

1980, Aug. 30 Litho. *Perf. 12½*

978 A279a 25f multicolored .35 .25
979 A279a 50f multicolored .85 .25
980 A279a 100f multicolored 1.75 .85
Nos. 978-980 (3) 2.95 1.35

Postal Union Emblem, Posthorn, Map of Arab States — A280

1980, Sept. 8 *Perf. 12*

981 A280 10f multicolored .25 .25
982 A280 30f multicolored .35 .25
983 A280 35f multicolored .70 .25
Nos. 981-983 (3) 1.30 .75

Arab Postal Union, 11th Congress, Baghdad.

20th Anniversary of OPEC — A281

1980, Sept. 30

984 A281 30f multicolored 1.00 .25
985 A281 75f multicolored 1.60 .75

Papilio Machaon A282

15f, Danaus chrysippus. 20f, Vanessa atalanta. 30f, Colias croceus.

1980, Oct. 20 Photo. *Perf. 13½x14*

987 A282 10f shown 2.00 .35
988 A282 15f multicolored 2.25 .65
989 A282 20f multicolored 3.25 .80
990 A282 30f multicolored 5.25 1.25
Nos. 987-990 (4) 12.75 3.05

Hegira, 1,500th Anniv. A283

1980, Nov. 9 Litho. *Perf. 11½x12*

991 A283 15f multicolored .40 .25
992 A283 25f multicolored .75 .25
993 A283 35f multicolored 1.00 .35
Nos. 991-993 (3) 2.15 .85

International Palestinian Solidarity Day — A284

1980, Nov. 29

994 A284 25f multicolored 1.25 .50
995 A284 35f multicolored 1.75 .50
996 A284 75f multicolored 3.50 2.00
Nos. 994-996 (3) 6.50 3.00

Army Day — A285

1981, Jan. 6 Photo. *Perf. 14x13½*

997 A285 5f multicolored .30 .25
998 A285 30f multicolored .55 .25
999 A285 75f multicolored 1.60 .70
Nos. 997-999 (3) 2.45 1.20

February Revolution, 18th Anniversary A286

1981, Feb. 8 *Perf. 12*

1000 A286 15f multicolored .25 .25
1001 A286 30f multicolored .45 .25
1002 A286 35f multicolored .70 .25
Nos. 1000-1002 (3) 1.40 .75

Map of Arab Countries A287

1981, Mar. 22 Litho. *Perf. 12½*

1003 A287 5f multicolored .25 .25
1004 A287 25f multicolored .50 .25
1005 A287 35f multicolored .70 .25
Nos. 1003-1005 (3) 1.45 .75

Battle of Qadisiya — A288

1981, Apr. 7 Photo. *Perf. 13½x13*

1006 A288 30f multicolored .45 .25
1007 A288 35f multicolored .60 .25
1008 A288 75f multicolored 1.10 .50
Nos. 1006-1008 (3) 2.15 1.00

Souvenir Sheet

1009 A288 100f multicolored 6.50 *6.50*

No. 1009 contains one horiz. stamp.

Helicopters and Tank A289

1981, June 1 Photo.

1010 A289 5f shown .25 .25
1011 A289 10f Plane .35 .25
1012 A289 15f Rocket .50 .25
Nos. 1010-1012,C66 (4) 5.10 3.25

Air Force, 50th anniv.

Natl. Assembly Election, First Anniv. — A290

1981, June 20 *Perf. 12½*

1013 A290 30f multicolored .45 .25
1014 A290 35f multicolored .60 .25
1015 A290 45f multicolored .95 .35
Nos. 1013-1015 (3) 2.00 .85

July Festivals A291

1981, July 17 Photo.

1016 A291 15f multicolored .25 .25
1017 A291 25f multicolored .40 .25
1018 A291 35f multicolored .70 .25
Nos. 1016-1018 (3) 1.35 .75

Pottery Maker — A292

Designs: Popular industries.

1981, Aug. 15 *Perf. 14*

1019 A292 5f Straw weaver .25 .25
1020 A292 30f Metal worker .55 .25
1021 A292 35f shown .75 .25
1022 A292 50f Rug maker, horiz. 1.00 .35
Nos. 1019-1022 (4) 2.55 1.10

Islamic Pilgrimage — A293

1981, Oct. 7 Photo. *Perf. 12x11½*

1023 A293 25f multicolored .55 .25
1024 A293 45f multicolored 1.00 .30
1025 A293 50f multicolored 1.00 .30
Nos. 1023-1025 (3) 2.55 .85

World Food Day A294

1981, Oct. 16 Photo. *Perf. 14*

1026 A294 30f multicolored .55 .25
1027 A294 45f multicolored 1.00 .40
1028 A294 75f multicolored 1.50 .75
Nos. 1026-1028 (3) 3.05 1.40

Intl. Year of the Disabled — A295

1981, Nov. 15

1029 A295 30f multicolored .45 .25
1030 A295 45f multicolored .75 .30
1031 A295 75f multicolored 1.10 .60
Nos. 1029-1031 (3) 2.30 1.15

5th Anniv. of United Arab Shipping Co. A296

1981, Dec. 2 *Perf. 13x13½*

1032 A296 50f multicolored 1.40 .60
1033 A296 120f multicolored 4.00 1.75

Saddam Hussein Gymnasium A297

50f, Palace of Conferences.

1981, Sept. 26 Litho. *Perf. 12x12½*

1034 A297 45f shown .70 .25
1035 A297 50f multicolored .70 .30
1036 A297 120f like #1035 2.10 1.25
1037 A297 150f like #1034 2.75 1.50
Nos. 1034-1037 (4) 6.25 3.30

For surcharges see Nos. 1097-1099.

35th Anniv. of Al Baath Party — A298

25f, 45f, Pres. Hussein, flowers. 30f, 50f, Iraq Flag as rainbow and "7 7 7". 150f, Pres. Hussein, globe, arabic "7".

1982, Apr. 7 Photo. *Perf. 13½x13*

1038 A298 25f peach & multi .55 .25
1039 A298 30f cream & multi .55 .25
1040 A298 45f gray blue & multi .90 .40
1041 A298 50f white & multi .90 .40
Nos. 1038-1041 (4) 2.90 1.30

Souvenir Sheet

Imperf

1042 A298 150f emer & multi 6.75 6.75

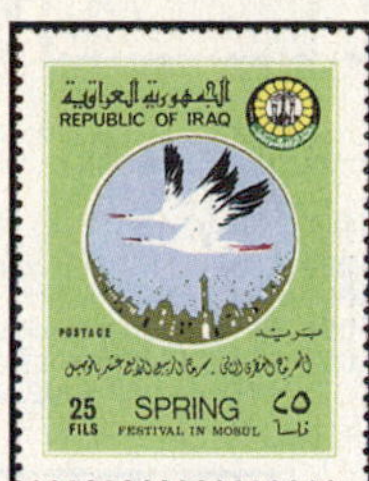

Mosul Spring Festival — A299

1982, Apr. 15 Litho. *Perf. 11½x12*

1043 A299 25f Birds 1.10 .25
1044 A299 30f Girl .70 .25
1045 A299 45f like 25f 1.10 .50
1046 A299 50f like 30f 1.10 .40
Nos. 1043-1046 (4) 4.00 1.40

Intl. Workers' Day A300

1982, May 1 *Perf. 12½*

1047 A300 25f multicolored .45 .25
1048 A300 45f multicolored .70 .30
1049 A300 50f multicolored .75 .40
Nos. 1047-1049 (3) 1.90 .95

14th World Telecommunications Day — A301

1982, May 17 Photo. *Perf. 13x13½*

1050 A301 5f multicolored .25 .25
1051 A301 45f multicolored .70 .35
1052 A301 100f multicolored 1.60 .90
Nos. 1050-1052 (3) 2.55 1.50

10th Anniv. of Oil Nationalization A302

1982, June 1 Litho. *Perf. 12½*

1053 A302 5f Oil gusher .25 .25
1054 A302 25f like 5f .60 .25
1055 A302 45f Statue 1.25 .25
1056 A302 50f like 45f 1.50 .35
Nos. 1053-1056 (4) 3.60 1.10

Martyrs' Day — A303

1981, Dec. 1 Photo. *Perf. 14*

1057 A303 45f multicolored .45 .35
1058 A303 50f multicolored .55 .45
1059 A303 120f multicolored 1.50 1.00
Nos. 1057-1059,O339A-O339C (6) 8.50 3.80

Women's Day — A304

1982, Mar. 4 Litho. *Perf. 12½x13*

1060 A304 25f multicolored .55 .25
1061 A304 45f multicolored .90 .40
1062 A304 50f multicolored .90 .50
Nos. 1060-1062 (3) 2.35 1.15

A305

1982, Apr. 12 *Perf. 12½*

1063 A305 25f multicolored .55 .25
1064 A305 45f multicolored .90 .30
1065 A305 50f multicolored .90 .30
Nos. 1063-1065 (3) 2.35 .85

Arab Postal Union, 30th anniv.

A305a

30f, 50f, Nuclear power emblem, lion. 45f, 120f, Bomb aimed at egg.

1982, June 7 Photo. *Perf. 14*

1065A A305a 30f ol grn & multi .60 .30
1065B A305a 45f rose & multi 1.00 .35
1065C A305a 50f yel & multi 1.10 .50
1065D A305a 120f pur & multi 2.40 1.50
Nos. 1065A-1065D (4) 5.10 2.65

First anniv. of attack on nuclear power reactor.

July Festivals — A306

1982, July 17 Photo. *Perf. 14½x14*

1066 A306 25f multicolored .50 .25
1067 A306 45f multicolored .70 .25
1068 A306 50f multicolored .80 .30
Nos. 1066-1068 (3) 2.00 .80

Lacerta Viridis A307

30f, Vipera aspis. 45f, Lacerta virdis, diff. 50f, Natrix tessellata.

1982, Aug. 20 Litho. *Perf. 12½*

No.	Type	Description	Unused	Used
1069	A307	25f shown	2.25	.75
1070	A307	30f multi	2.25	.75
1071	A307	45f multi	3.00	1.10
1072	A307	50f multi	3.50	1.50
		Nos. 1069-1072 (4)	11.00	4.10

7th Non-aligned Countries Conference, Baghdad, Sept. — A308

No. 1073, Tito. No. 1074, Nehru. No. 1075, Nasser. No. 1076, Kwame Nkrumah. No. 1077, Hussein.

1982, Sept. 6 Photo. *Perf. 13x13½*

No.	Type	Description	Unused	Used
1073	A308	50f multicolored	.85	.40
1074	A308	50f multicolored	.85	.40
1075	A308	50f multicolored	.85	.40
1076	A308	50f multicolored	.85	.40
1077	A308	100f multicolored	1.90	.55
		Nos. 1073-1077 (5)	5.30	2.15

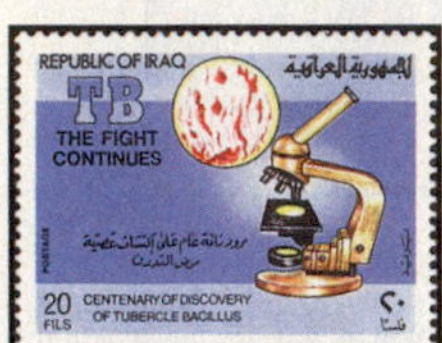

TB Bacillus Centenary A309

1982, Oct. 1 *Perf. 14x14½*

No.	Type	Description	Unused	Used
1078	A309	20f multicolored	.65	.25
1079	A309	50f multicolored	1.10	.30
1080	A309	100f multicolored	2.10	.85
		Nos. 1078-1080 (3)	3.85	1.40

1982 World Cup — A310

Designs: Various soccer players. 150f horiz.

1982, July 1 Litho. *Perf. 11½x12*

No.	Type	Description	Unused	Used
1081	A310	5f multicolored	.50	.25
1082	A310	45f multicolored	1.00	.45
1083	A310	50f multicolored	1.10	.50
1084	A310	100f multicolored	2.00	1.00
		Nos. 1081-1084 (4)	4.60	2.20

Souvenir Sheet

Perf. 12½

No.	Type	Description	Unused	Used
1085	A310	150f multicolored	4.00	4.00

13th UPU Day A311

1982, Oct. 9 *Perf. 12x11½*

No.	Type	Description	Unused	Used
1086	A311	5f multicolored	.25	.25
1087	A311	45f multicolored	.70	.30
1088	A311	100f multicolored	1.60	.85
		Nos. 1086-1088 (3)	2.55	1.40

Musical Instruments A312

5f, Drums. 10f, Zither. 35f, Stringed instrument. 100f, Lute.

1982, Nov. 15 *Perf. 12½x13*

No.	Type	Description	Unused	Used
1089	A312	5f multicolored	.25	.25
1090	A312	10f multicolored	.25	.25
1091	A312	35f multicolored	.85	.35
1092	A312	100f multicolored	2.75	.95
		Nos. 1089-1092 (4)	4.10	1.80

Birth Anniv. of Mohammed — A313

Baghdad and Medina Mosque views.

1982, Dec. 27 Litho. *Perf. 12x11½*

No.	Type	Description	Unused	Used
1093	A313	25f multicolored	.25	.25
1094	A313	30f multicolored	.40	.25
1095	A313	45f multicolored	.55	.25
1096	A313	50f multicolored	.70	.35
		Nos. 1093-1096 (4)	1.90	1.10

Nos. 1034-1036 Surcharged

1983, May 15 Litho. *Perf. 12x12½*

No.	Type	Description	Unused	Used
1097	A297	60f on 50f multi	1.25	.50
1098	A297	70f on 45f multi	1.75	.60
1099	A297	160f on 120f multi	4.50	2.00
		Nos. 1097-1099 (3)	7.50	3.10

July Festivals A314

1983, July 17 Litho. *Perf. 14½x14*

No.	Type	Description	Unused	Used
1100	A314	30f multicolored	.45	.25
1101	A314	60f multicolored	1.00	.35
1102	A314	70f multicolored	1.40	.45
		Nos. 1100-1102 (3)	2.85	1.05

Local Flowers — A315

1983, June 15 Photo. *Perf. 15x14*

Border Color

No.	Type	Description	Unused	Used
1103	A315	10f shown, light blue	.25	.25
1104	A315	20f Flowers, diff., pale yellow	.45	.25
1105	A315	30f like 10f, yellow	.55	.25
1106	A315	40f like 20f, gray	.95	.40
1107	A315	50f like 10f, pale green	1.10	.50
1108	A315	100f like 20f, pink	2.25	1.00
a.		Bklt. pane of 6, #1103-1108	9.75	
		Nos. 1103-1108 (6)	5.55	2.65

Nos. 1103-1108 issued in booklets only. For surcharges see Nos. 1501-1506.

A316

Battle of Thi Qar — A317

1983, Oct. 30 Photo. *Perf. 12½x13*

No.	Type	Description	Unused	Used
1109	A316	20f silver & multi	.25	.25
1110	A317	50f silver & multi	.75	.30
1111	A316	60f gold & multi	1.00	.35
1112	A317	70f gold & multi	1.10	.40
		Nos. 1109-1112 (4)	3.10	1.30

World Communications Year — A318

25f, 70f show emblem and hexagons.

1983, Oct. 20 Photo. *Perf. 11½x12*

No.	Type	Description	Unused	Used
1113	A318	5f brt yel grn & multi	.25	.25
1114	A318	25f rose lil & multi	.30	.25
1115	A318	60f brt org yel & multi	.90	.35
1116	A318	70f brt bl vio & multi	1.10	.40
		Nos. 1113-1116 (4)	2.55	1.25

Souvenir Sheet

No.	Type	Description	Unused	Used
1117	A318	200f apple grn & multi	4.25	4.25

Baghdad Intl. Fair — A319

1983, Nov. 1 Photo. *Perf. 12½*

No.	Type	Description	Unused	Used
1118	A319	60f multicolored	.75	.40
1119	A319	70f multicolored	.95	.50
1120	A319	160f multicolored	2.10	1.25
		Nos. 1118-1120 (3)	3.80	2.15

Symbolic "9" — A320

9th Natl. Congress of Arab Baath Socialist Party: 30f, 70f, Symbols of development. 60f, 100f, Torch, eagle, globe, open book.

1983, Nov. 10 Photo. *Perf. 14*

No.	Type	Description	Unused	Used
1121	A320	30f multicolored	.35	.25
1122	A320	60f multicolored	.75	.40
1123	A320	70f multicolored	.95	.50
1124	A320	100f multicolored	1.40	.70
		Nos. 1121-1124 (4)	3.45	1.85

Festival Crowd — A321

Various Paintings: No. 1126, Men hauling boat, vert. No. 1127,

1983, Nov. 20 Litho. *Perf. 12½*

No.	Type	Description	Unused	Used
1125	A321	60f shown	1.50	.60
1126	A321	60f multicolored	1.50	.60
1127	A321	60f Decorations	1.50	.60
1128	A321	70f Village	2.00	.85
1129	A321	70f Crowd	2.00	.85
		Nos. 1125-1129 (5)	8.50	3.50

Sabra and Shattela Palestinian Refugee Camp Massacre A322

Various Victims.

1983, Nov. 29 *Perf. 11½x12*

No.	Type	Description	Unused	Used
1130	A322	10f multicolored	.25	.25
1131	A322	60f multicolored	1.00	.40
1132	A322	70f multicolored	1.25	.50
1133	A322	160f multicolored	2.75	1.25
		Nos. 1130-1133 (4)	5.25	2.40

Pres. Hussein, Map — A323

1983 Photo. *Perf. 13½x13*

No.	Type	Description	Unused	Used
1134	A323	60f multicolored	.75	.30
1135	A323	70f multicolored	1.00	.50
1136	A323	250f multicolored	3.50	2.00
		Nos. 1134-1136 (3)	5.25	2.80

Hussein as head of Al Baath Party, 4th anniv.

Modern Building — A324

Various buildings.

1983, Dec. 31 Litho. *Perf. 14*

No.	Type	Description	Unused	Used
1137	A324	60f multicolored	.70	.40
1138	A324	70f multicolored	.90	.50
1139	A324	160f multicolored	2.25	1.10
1140	A324	200f multicolored	2.75	1.40
		Nos. 1137-1140,O340-O341 (6)	8.50	4.55

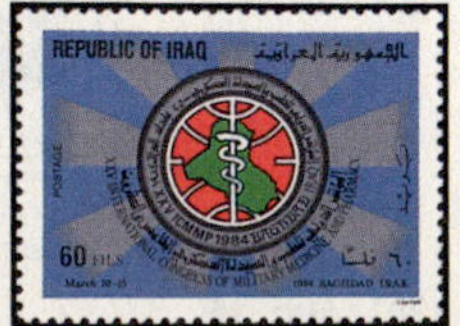

Medical Congress Emblem A325

1984, Mar. 10 *Perf. 13x12½*

No.	Type	Description	Unused	Used
1141	A325	60f multicolored	.80	.40
1142	A325	70f multicolored	1.00	.50
1143	A325	200f multicolored	3.00	1.40
		Nos. 1141-1143 (3)	4.80	2.30

25th Intl. Congress of Military Medicine and Pharmacy, Baghdad, Mar. 10-15.

Pres. Hussein's Birthday — A326

Various portraits of Hussein.

1984, Apr. 28 Litho. *Perf. 12½x13*
1144 A326 60f multicolored .65 .30
1145 A326 70f multicolored .70 .40
1146 A326 160f multicolored 2.10 1.25
1147 A326 200f multicolored 2.50 1.60
Nos. 1144-1147 (4) 5.95 3.55

Souvenir Sheet

Imperf

1148 A326 250f multicolored 6.50 6.50

Gold ink on Nos. 1144-1147 and dark green ink in "margin" of No. 1148 was applied by a thermographic process, producing a raised effect. No. 1148 has perf. 12½x13 label picturing Pres. Hussein.

1984 Summer Olympics, Los Angeles — A327

1984, Aug. 12 Litho. *Perf. 12x11½*
1149 A327 50f Boxing .70 .50
1150 A327 60f Weight lifting .90 .50
1151 A327 70f like 50f 1.10 .60
1152 A327 100f like 60f 1.60 .90

Size: 80x60mm

Imperf

1153 A327 200f Soccer 5.00 5.00
Nos. 1149-1153 (5) 9.30 7.50

Nos. 1153 contains one 32x41mm perf. 12½ label within the stamp.

A328

50f, 70f, Pres. Hussein, flaming horses heads, map. 60f, 100f, Abstract of woman, sapling, rifle. 200f, Shield, heraldic eagle.

1984, Sept. 22 *Perf. 11½x12*
1154 A328 50f multicolored .55 .30
1155 A328 60f multicolored .70 .40
1156 A328 70f multicolored .85 .50
1157 A328 100f multicolored 1.25 .65

Size: 80x60mm

Imperf

1158 A328 200f multicolored 3.50 3.50
Nos. 1154-1158 (5) 6.85 5.35

Battle of Qadisiya. No. 1158 contains one 32x41mm perf. 12½ label within the stamp.

A329

Martyrs' Day: 50f, 70f, Natl. flag as flame. 60f, 100f, Woman holding rifle, medal.

1984, Dec. 1 *Perf. 13½*
1159 A329 50f multicolored .45 .35
1160 A329 60f multicolored .65 .35
1161 A329 70f multicolored .75 .40
1162 A329 100f multicolored 1.00 .65
Nos. 1159-1162 (4) 2.85 1.75

For overprints see Nos. O342-O345

Pres. Hussein's Visit to Al-Mustansiriyah University, 5th Anniv. — A330

1985, Apr. 2 Photo. *Perf. 12x11½*
1163 A330 60f dk bl gray & dk pink .55 .35
1164 A330 70f myr grn & dk pink .65 .40
1165 A330 250f blk & dk pink 2.50 1.40
Nos. 1163-1165 (3) 3.70 2.15

Iraqi Air Force, 54th Anniv. — A331

10f, 160f, Pres. Hussein, fighter planes, pilot's wings. 60f, 70f, 200f, Planes, flag, "54," horiz.

Perf. 13x12½, 13½ (60f, 70f)

1985, Apr. 22 Litho.
1166 A331 10f multicolored .30 .25
1167 A331 60f multicolored 1.50 .75
1168 A331 70f multicolored 1.60 .75
1169 A331 160f multicolored 4.00 2.00
Nos. 1166-1169 (4) 7.40 3.75

Souvenir Sheet

Perf. 12½

1170 A331 200f multicolored 6.75 6.75

Pres. Hussein, 48th Birthday — A332

30f, 70f, Pres. Hussein, sunflower. 60f, 100f, Pres., candle & flowers. 200f, Flowers & text.

1985, Apr. 28 *Perf. 13½*
1171 A332 30f multicolored .35 .25
1172 A332 60f multicolored .65 .30
1173 A332 70f multicolored .75 .40
1174 A332 100f multicolored 1.10 .60
Nos. 1171-1174 (4) 2.85 1.55

Souvenir Sheet

Perf. 13x12½

1175 A332 200f multicolored 4.50 4.50

Posts and Telecommunications Development Program — A333

Designs: 20f, 60f, Graph, woman in modern office. 50f, 70f, Satellite dish and graphs.

1985, June 30 *Perf. 12½*
1176 A333 20f multicolored .35 .25
1177 A333 50f multicolored .70 .30
1178 A333 60f multicolored .70 .30
1179 A333 70f multicolored .95 .50
Nos. 1176-1179 (4) 2.70 1.35

Battle of Qadisiya A334

Designs: 10f, 60f, Shown. 20f, 70f, Pres. Hussein, Al-Baath Party emblem. 200f, Dove, natl. flag as shield, soldier.

1985, Sept. 4 *Perf. 11½x12*
1180 A334 10f multicolored .25 .25
1181 A334 20f multicolored .25 .25
1182 A334 60f multicolored .90 .40
1183 A334 70f multicolored 1.10 .65
Nos. 1180-1183 (4) 2.50 1.55

Souvenir Sheet

Perf. 12x12½

1184 A334 200f multicolored 3.25 3.25

No. 1184 contains one stamp 30x45mm.

Solar Energy Research Center A335

1985, Sept. 19 *Perf. 13½*
1185 A335 10f multicolored .25 .25
1186 A335 50f multicolored .95 .40
1187 A335 100f multicolored 1.90 .95
Nos. 1185-1187 (3) 3.10 1.60

UN Child Survival Campaign A336

Designs: 10f, 50f, Stop Polio Campaign. 15f, 100f, Girl, infant.

1985, Oct. 10
1188 A336 10f multicolored .25 .25
1189 A336 15f multicolored .25 .25
1190 A336 50f multicolored .75 .30
1191 A336 100f multicolored 1.50 .85
Nos. 1188-1191 (4) 2.75 1.65

Al Sharif, Poet, Death Millennium A337

1985, Oct. 20
1192 A337 10f multicolored .25 .25
1193 A337 50f multicolored .55 .30
1194 A337 100f multicolored 1.25 .80
Nos. 1192-1194 (3) 2.05 1.35

UN, 40th Anniv. A338

1985, Oct. 24
1195 A338 10f multicolored .25 .25
1196 A338 40f multicolored .55 .25
1197 A338 100f multicolored 1.40 .75
Nos. 1195-1197 (3) 2.20 1.25

Death of Iraqi Prisoners of War in Iran — A339

30f, 100f, Knife, Geneva Convention declaration, red crescent, red cross. 70f, 200f, POWs, gun shell, natl. flag, cherub & dove.

1985, Nov. 10 *Perf. 14*
1198 A339 30f multicolored .35 .25
1199 A339 70f multicolored .75 .40
1200 A339 100f multicolored 1.10 .65
1201 A339 200f multicolored 2.50 1.25

Size: 110x80mm

Imperf

1202 A339 250f multicolored 5.00 5.00
Nos. 1198-1202 (5) 9.70 7.55

No. 1202 contains 2 perf. 14 labels similar to 100f and 200f designs within the stamp.

Intl. Palestinian Solidarity Day A341

1985, Nov. 29 Litho. *Perf. 13½*
1207 A341 10f multicolored .25 .25
1208 A341 50f multicolored .95 .40
1209 A341 100f multicolored 2.10 .95
Nos. 1207-1209 (3) 3.30 1.60

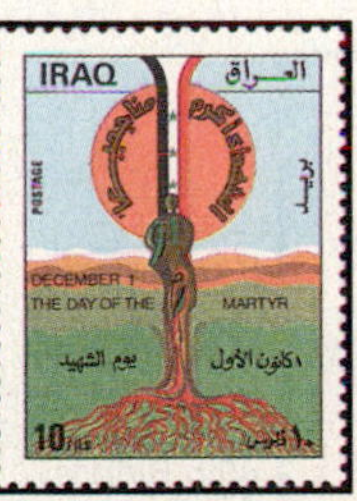

Martyrs' Day — A342

1985, Dec. 1 *Perf. 11½x12*
1210 A342 10f multicolored .25 .25
1211 A342 40f multicolored .45 .25
1212 A342 100f multicolored 1.40 .75
Nos. 1210-1212 (3) 2.10 1.25

Intl. Youth Year — A343

IYY emblem and: 40f, 100f, Soldier holding flag. 50f, 200f, Youths, flag. 250f, Flag, cogwheel, rifle muzzle, symbols of industry.

1985, Dec. 12 Litho. *Perf. 11½x12*

1213 A343 40f multicolored .45 .25
1214 A343 50f multicolored .65 .30
1215 A343 100f multicolored 1.40 .75
1216 A343 200f multicolored 2.75 2.00
Nos. 1213-1216 (4) 5.25 3.30

Souvenir Sheet

Perf. 12x12½

1217 A343 250f multicolored 5.00 5.00

No. 1217 contains one stamp 30x45mm. Exists imperf.

Army Day A344

Pres. Hussein, "6" and: 10f, 50f, Soldier, flowers, vert. 40f, 100f, Flag, cogwheel, rockets. 200f, Al-Baath Party emblem, rifle, waves.

1986, Jan. 6 *Perf. 11½x12, 12x11½*

1218 A344 10f multicolored .25 .25
1219 A344 40f multicolored .65 .25
1220 A344 50f multicolored .85 .30
1221 A344 100f multicolored 1.75 .95
Nos. 1218-1221 (4) 3.50 1.75

Miniature Sheet

Perf. 12½x11½

1222 A344 200f multicolored 5.00 5.00

No. 1222 contains one stamp 52x37mm.

Women's Day A345

Designs: 30f, 100f, Women in traditional and modern occupations, vert. 50f, 150f, Emblem, green flag, battle scene, grapes.

Perf. 11½x12, 12x11½

1986, Mar. 8 Litho.

1223 A345 30f multicolored .45 .25
1224 A345 50f multicolored .65 .30
1225 A345 100f multicolored 1.40 .75
1226 A345 150f multicolored 2.25 1.00
Nos. 1223-1226 (4) 4.75 2.30

Pres. Hussein, 49th Birthday A346

Designs: 30f, 100f, Children greeting Pres. 50f, 150f, Portrait. 250f, Portrait, flag, flowers.

1986, Apr. 28 Litho. *Perf. 11½x12*

1227 A346 30f multicolored .45 .25
1228 A346 50f multicolored .75 .25
1229 A346 100f multicolored 1.50 .45
1230 A346 150f multicolored 2.10 .65

Size: 80x60mm

Imperf

1231 A346 250f multicolored 5.00 5.00
Nos. 1227-1231 (5) 9.80 6.60

Oil Nationalization Day, June 1 — A347

Designs: 10f, 100f, Symbols of industry, horiz. 40f, 150f, Oil well, pipeline to refinery.

Perf. 12x11½, 11½x12

1986, July 25 Litho.

1232 A347 10f multicolored .25 .25
1233 A347 40f multicolored .55 .25
1234 A347 100f multicolored 1.50 .75
1235 A347 150f multicolored 2.10 1.25
Nos. 1232-1235 (4) 4.40 2.50

Labor Day — A348

Designs: 10f, 100f, Laborer, cog wheel. 40f, 150f, May Day emblem.

1986, July 28 *Perf. 11½x12*

1236 A348 10f multicolored .25 .25
1237 A348 40f multicolored .75 .25
1238 A348 100f multicolored 1.40 .65
1239 A348 150f multicolored 2.10 .95
Nos. 1236-1239 (4) 4.50 2.10

Iraqi Air Force, 55th Anniv. A349

Designs: 30f, 100f, Fighter plane, pilot's wings, natl. flag. 50f, 150f, Fighter planes. 250f, Medal, aircraft in flight.

1986, July 28 *Perf. 12x11½*

1240 A349 30f multicolored .70 .25
1241 A349 50f multicolored 1.40 .30
1242 A349 100f multicolored 2.75 1.40
1243 A349 150f multicolored 4.25 1.90

Size: 81x61mm

Imperf

1244 A349 250f multicolored 5.00 5.00
Nos. 1240-1244 (5) 14.10 8.85

No. 1244 also exists perf.

July Festivals A350

Pres. Hussein and: 20f, 100f, Flag. 30f, 150f, "17." 250f, Inscription, portrait inside medal of honor.

1986, July 29 *Perf. 11½x12*

1245 A350 20f multicolored .30 .25
1246 A350 30f multicolored .40 .25
1247 A350 100f multicolored 1.50 .75
1248 A350 150f multicolored 2.25 1.25

Size: 81x61mm

Imperf

1249 A350 250f multicolored 4.00 4.00
Nos. 1245-1249 (5) 8.45 6.50

1st Qadisiya Battle — A351

Designs: 20f, 70f, Warrior, shield, vert. 60f, 100f, Pres. Hussein, star, battle scene.

Perf. 13x13½, 13½x13

1986, Sept. 4 Litho.

1250 A351 20f multicolored .35 .25
1251 A351 60f multicolored .80 .40
1252 A351 70f multicolored .95 .50
1253 A351 100f multicolored 1.60 .65
Nos. 1250-1253 (4) 3.70 1.80

Battle between the Arabs and Persian Empire.

Hussein's Battle of Qadisiya — A352

30f, 100f, Pres. Hussein, soldiers saluting peace, vert. 40f, 150f, Pres., armed forces. 250f, Pres., soldiers, flags, military scenes.

Perf. 11½x12½, 12½x11½

1986, Sept. 4

1254 A352 30f multicolored .90 .25
1255 A352 40f multicolored 1.25 .25
1256 A352 100f multicolored 2.50 .50
1257 A352 150f multicolored 4.25 .70

Size: 80x60mm

Imperf

1258 A352 250f multicolored 4.75 4.75
Nos. 1254-1258 (5) 13.65 6.45

Intl. Peace Year — A353

50f, 150f, Dove, flag, G clef. 100f, Globe, dove, rifle. 200f, Emblem, flag, map, fist.

1986, Nov. 15 Litho. *Perf. 11½x12*

1259 A353 50f lt blue & multi .65 .25
1260 A353 100f grn & multi 1.10 .60
1261 A353 150f yel & multi 1.75 1.00
1262 A353 250f org & multi 2.50 1.40

Size: 80x69mm

Imperf

1263 A353 200f multi 2.75 2.75
Nos. 1259-1263 (5) 8.75 6.00

Pres. Hussein
A354 A355

1264 A354 30f multicolored .70 .25
1265 A355 30f multicolored .70 .25
1266 A354 50f multicolored .90 .25
1267 A355 50f multicolored .90 .25
1268 A354 100f multicolored 1.90 .65
1269 A355 100f multicolored 1.90 .65
1270 A354 150f multicolored 2.40 .85
1271 A355 150f multicolored 2.60 .85
1272 A354 250f multicolored 4.75 1.40
1273 A354 350f multicolored 6.25 1.90
Nos. 1264-1273 (10) 23.00 7.30

For overprints & surcharges see Nos. 1347-1348, 1455, 1480-1481, 1484, 1499-1500, 1518-1519.

Army Day — A356

40f, Hussein, armed forces.

1987, Jan. 6 Litho. *Perf. 12x12½*

1274 A356 20f shown .25 .25
1275 A356 40f multicolored .35 .30
1276 A356 90f like 20f .95 .90
1277 A356 100f like 40f 1.00 1.00
Nos. 1274-1277 (4) 2.55 2.45

United Arab Shipping Co., 10th Anniv. (in 1986) A357

50f, Cargo ship. 100f, Container ship Chaleb Ibn Al Waleeb. 200f, Loading cargo aboard the Waleeb.

1987, Apr. 3 Litho. *Perf. 12½*

1278 A357 50f multi .55 .25
1279 A357 100f multi 1.10 .60
1280 A357 150f like 50f 1.75 .85
1281 A357 250f like 100f 3.00 1.40

Size: 102x91mm

Imperf

1282 A357 200f multi 3.75 3.75
Nos. 1278-1282 (5) 10.15 6.85

Arab Baath Socialist Party, 40th Anniv. — A358

40f, Hussein, "7," map.

1987, Apr. 7 Litho. *Perf. 12x12½*

1283 A358 20f shown .25 .25
1284 A358 40f multicolored .35 .30
1285 A358 90f like 20f .95 .90
1286 A358 100f like 40f 1.00 1.00
Nos. 1283-1286 (4) 2.55 2.45

Pres. Hussein's 50th Birthday A359

1987, Apr. 28 *Perf. 12½x12*

1287 A359 20f shown .25 .25
1288 A359 40f Portrait .35 .30
1289 A359 90f like 20f .95 .90
1290 A359 100f like 40f 1.10 1.00
Nos. 1287-1290 (4) 2.65 2.45

July Festivals — A360

20f, Hussein, star, flag, horiz.

1987, July 17 ***Perf. 12½x12, 12x12½***
1291 A360 20f multi .25 .25
1292 A360 40f shown .35 .30
1293 A360 90f like 20f, horiz. .95 .90
1294 A360 100f like 40f 1.00 1.00
Nos. 1291-1294 (4) 2.55 2.45

UNICEF, 40th Anniv. — A361

1987, Oct. 4 ***Perf. 12x12½, 12½x12***
1295 A361 20f shown .25 .25
1296 A361 40f "40," horiz. .35 .30
1297 A361 90f like 20f .95 .90
1298 A361 100f like 40f, horiz. 1.00 1.00
Nos. 1295-1298 (4) 2.55 2.45

Census Day A362

30f, Graph, Arabs, diff.

1987, Nov. 1 ***Perf. 12x11½***
1299 A362 20f shown .25 .25
1300 A362 30f multicolored .35 .25
1301 A362 50f like 30f .55 .35
1302 A362 500f like 20f 5.25 4.00
Nos. 1299-1302 (4) 6.40 4.85

Army Day A363

20f, "6," Hussein, troops, vert.

Perf. 11½x12, 12x11½
1988, Jan. 6 **Litho.**
1303 A363 20f multicolored .25 .25
1304 A363 30f shown .25 .25
1305 A363 50f like 20f, vert. .55 .25
1306 A363 150f like 30f 1.60 .60
Nos. 1303-1306 (4) 2.65 1.35

Art Day — A364

30f, Hussein, rainbow, gun barrel, music. 150f, Notes, instruments, floral ornament.

1988, Jan. 8 **Litho.** ***Perf. 11½x12***
1307 A364 20f shown .35 .25
1308 A364 30f multicolored .50 .30
1309 A364 50f like 20f .70 .35
1310 A364 100f like 30f 1.25 .40

Size: 60x80mm

Imperf

1311 A364 150f multicolored 2.50 2.50
Nos. 1307-1311 (5) 5.30 3.80

A365

20f, "8," troops, Hussein, horiz. 30f, "8," Hussein, eagle.

1988, Feb. 8 ***Perf. 11½x12, 12x11½***
1312 A365 20f multicolored .35 .25
1313 A365 30f multicolored .45 .25
1314 A365 50f like 20f, horiz. .65 .35
1315 A365 150f like 30f 2.10 .65
Nos. 1312-1315 (4) 3.55 1.50

Popular Army, 18th anniv. (20f, 50f); Feb. 8th Revolution, 25th anniv. (30f, 150f).

Al-Baath Arab Socialist Party, 50th Anniv. — A366

20f, Flag, grain, convention, horiz.

1988, Apr. 7 ***Perf. 12x12½, 12½x12***
1316 A366 20f multicolored .35 .25
1317 A366 30f shown .45 .30
1318 A366 50f like 20f, horiz. .65 .30
1319 A366 150f like 30f 2.10 .60
Nos. 1316-1319 (4) 3.55 1.45

President Hussein, 51st Birthday — A367

30f, Hussein, 3 hands, flowers. 150f, Sun, Hussein, heart, flowers.

1988, Apr. 28 ***Perf. 12x12½***
1320 A367 20f shown .40 .30
1321 A367 30f multicolored .50 .40
1322 A367 50f like 20f .75 .40
1323 A367 100f like 50f 1.50 .60

Size: 90x99mm

Imperf

1324 A367 150f multicolored 4.25 4.25
Nos. 1320-1324 (5) 7.40 5.95

World Health Organization, 40th Anniv. — A368

20f, WHO anniv. emblem, horiz.

1988, June 1 ***Perf. 12½x12, 12x12½***
1325 A368 20f multicolored .35 .25
1326 A368 40f shown .45 .30
1327 A368 90f like 20f, horiz. 1.25 .40
1328 A368 100f like 40f 1.40 .40
Nos. 1325-1328 (4) 3.45 1.35

Regional Marine Environment Day, Apr. 4 — A369

40f, Flag in map, fish, horiz.

1988, Apr. 24 ***Perf. 12x12½, 12½x12***
1329 A369 20f shown .45 .25
1330 A369 40f multicolored .45 .30
1331 A369 90f like 20f 1.25 .40
1332 A369 100f like 40f, horiz. 1.25 .40
Nos. 1329-1332 (4) 3.40 1.35

Shuhada School Victims Memorial A370

A371

40f, Girl caught in explosion, horiz.

1988, June 1 ***Perf. 11½x12, 12x11½***
1333 A370 20f shown .35 .25
1334 A370 40f multicolored .45 .30
1335 A370 90f like 20f 1.25 .40
1336 A370 100f like 40f, horiz. 1.40 .40
Nos. 1333-1336 (4) 3.45 1.35

Souvenir Sheet

Perf. 12½

1337 A371 150f red, blk & brt grn 3.00 3.00

Pilgrimage to Mecca — A372

1988, July 24 **Litho.** ***Perf. 13½***
1338 A372 90f multicolored 1.25 .40
1339 A372 100f multicolored 1.50 .60
1340 A372 150f multicolored 2.25 .70
Nos. 1338-1340 (3) 5.00 1.70

Basra, 1350th Anniv. A373

1988, Oct. 22 ***Perf. 12x11½***
1341 A373 100f multicolored 1.40 .60

Natl. Flag, Grip on Lightning — A374

Pres. Hussein, Natl. Flag — A375

90f, Map, Hussein, desert.

1988, July 17 ***Perf. 12x12½***
1342 A374 50f shown .75 .40
1343 A374 90f multicolored 1.40 .50
1344 A374 100f like 50f 1.50 .50
1345 A374 150f like 90f 2.00 .60

Size: 90x70mm

Imperf

1346 A375 250f shown 6.00 4.50
Nos. 1342-1346 (5) 11.65 6.50

July Festivals and 9th anniv. of Pres. Hussein's assumption of office.

Nos. 1272-1273 Overprinted

1988, Aug. 7 **Litho.** ***Perf. 12½x12***
1347 A354 250f multicolored 6.00 2.00
1348 A354 350f multicolored 8.50 4.00

Victory.

Navy Day — A376

90f, Map, boats. 250f, Emblem, Pres. Hussein decorating officers.

1988, Aug. 12 ***Perf. 12x12½***
1349 A376 50f shown 1.10 .40
1350 A376 90f multi 2.00 .60
1351 A376 100f like 50f 2.25 .85
1352 A376 150f like 90f 3.50 1.00

Size: 91x70mm

Imperf

1353 A376 250f multi 9.00 9.00
Nos. 1349-1353 (5) 17.85 11.85

1988 Summer Olympics, Seoul — A377

100f, Boxing, character trademark. 150f, Flag, emblems. 500f, Emblem, trademark, Hussein, trophy.

1988, Sept. 19 *Perf. 12x12½*
1354 A377 100f multi 2.25 .80
1355 A377 150f multi 3.50 1.10

Size: 101x91mm

Imperf

1356 A377 500f multi 17.00 17.00
Nos. 1354-1356 (3) 22.75 18.90

Liberation of Fao — A378

500f, Hussein, text.

1988, Sept. 1 *Perf. 12x11½*
1357 A378 100f multicolored 2.00 .60
1358 A378 150f multicolored 3.00 .95

Size: 60x80mm

Imperf

1359 A378 500f multicolored 16.50 16.50
Nos. 1357-1359 (3) 21.50 18.05

Mosul
A379

Baghdad
A380

Ancient cities: 50f, Fortress. 150f, Astrolabe, modern architecture.

1988, Oct. 22 *Perf. 12x11½, 11½x12*
1360 A379 50f multicolored .95 .25
1361 A380 150f multicolored 3.00 .95

Al-Hussein
Missile — A381

500f, Hussein, map, missile.

1988, Sept. 10 *Perf. 11½x12*
1362 A381 100f multicolored 1.40 .50
1363 A381 150f multicolored 2.25 .70

Size: 80x60mm

Imperf

1364 A381 500f multicolored 10.00 10.00
Nos. 1362-1364 (3) 13.65 11.20

2nd Intl.
Festival,
Babylon
A382

1988, Sept. 30 *Perf. 11½x12*
1365 A382 100f multicolored 1.40 .60
1366 A382 150f multicolored 2.00 .70

Size: 60x80mm

Imperf

1367 A382 500f Medallions 8.50 8.50
Nos. 1365-1367 (3) 11.90 9.80

Victorious
Iraq
A383

1988, Aug. 8 **Litho.** *Perf. 12x11½*
1368 A383 50f multicolored 6.00 6.00
1369 A383 100f multicolored 10.00 10.00
1370 A383 150f multicolored 14.50 14.50
Nos. 1368-1370 (3) 30.50 30.50

Birthday of
Mohammed
A384

1988, Oct. 23 **Litho.** *Perf. 11½x12*
1371 A384 100f multicolored 1.50 .60
1372 A384 150f multicolored 2.00 .90
1373 A384 1d multicolored 14.00 5.25
Nos. 1371-1373 (3) 17.50 6.75

Martyrs'
Day
A385

1988, Dec. 1 **Litho.** *Perf. 13½*
1374 A385 100f multicolored 1.00 .40
1375 A385 150f multicolored 1.90 .75
1376 A385 500f multicolored 6.50 2.00
Nos. 1374-1376 (3) 9.40 3.15

Police
Day
A386

1989, Jan. 9 **Litho.** *Perf. 12x11½*
1377 A386 50f multicolored .60 .40
1378 A386 100f multicolored 1.40 .45
1379 A386 150f multicolored 2.00 .90
Nos. 1377-1379 (3) 4.00 1.75

Postal Savings
Bank — A387

a

1988 **Litho.** *Perf. 11½x12*
1380 A387 50f shown 1.60 .80

Size: 23½x25mm

Perf. 13½x13

1381 A387(a) 100f multi 6.25 3.00
1382 A387(a) 150f multi 6.75 3.25
Nos. 1380-1382 (3) 14.60 7.05

Nos. 1381-1382 have a line of Arabic at the top.

Nos. 1381-1382 without overprint are postal savings stamps.

For surcharges see Nos. 1507-1510, 1512-1514.

Arab Cooperation Council — A388

1989, Feb. 12 **Litho.** *Perf. 12x11½*
1383 A388 100f shown 1.40 .40
1384 A388 150f Statesmen, diff. 2.00 .70

52nd
Birthday
of Pres.
Hussein
A392

1989, Apr. 28 **Litho.** *Perf. 12x11½*
1392 A392 100f multicolored 1.25 .50
1393 A392 150f multicolored 1.75 .50

Size: 60x81mm

Imperf

1394 A392 250f Hussein, diff. 6.00 6.00
Nos. 1392-1394 (3) 9.00 7.00

Fao Liberation, 1st Anniv. — A393

1989, Apr. 18 *Perf. 12x11½*
1395 A393 100f multi 1.25 .50
1396 A393 150f multi 2.00 .50

Size: 60x81mm

Imperf

1397 A393 250f Calendar 3.00 3.00
Nos. 1395-1397 (3) 6.25 4.00

Gen. Adnan
Khairalla — A394

1989, May 6 **Litho.** *Perf. 13½*
1398 A394 50f gold & multi .80 .30
1399 A394 100f copper & multi 1.60 .40
1400 A394 150f silver & multi 2.40 .75
Nos. 1398-1400 (3) 4.80 1.45

Gen. Adnan Khairalla (1940-1989), deputy commander-in-chief of the armed forces and minister of defense.

Reconstruction of
Basra — A395

1989, June 14
1401 A395 100f multi 1.60 .40
1402 A395 150f multi 2.40 .75

Reconstruction of
Fao — A396

1989, June 25
1403 A396 100f multi 1.60 .40
1404 A396 150f multi 2.40 .75

Women — A397

1989, June 25 **Litho.** *Perf. 11½x12*
1405 A397 100f yel & multi 1.25 .35
1406 A397 150f brt pink & multi 1.40 .55
1407 A397 1d brt blue & multi 12.00 3.75
1408 A397 5d white & multi 50.00 16.00
Nos. 1405-1408 (4) 64.65 20.65

For surcharges see Nos. 1485-1486, 1511, 1522.

July
Festivals — A398

1989, July 17 **Litho.** *Perf. 12x12½*
1409 A398 50f multicolored .65 .30
1410 A398 100f multicolored 1.25 .40
1411 A398 150f multicolored 2.10 .65
Nos. 1409-1411 (3) 4.00 1.35

Election of Pres. Hussein, 10th anniv.

Family
A399

1989, July 19 *Perf. 13½*
1412 A399 50f multicolored 1.00 .45
1413 A399 100f multicolored 1.75 .75
1414 A399 150f multicolored 4.75 1.25
Nos. 1412-1414 (3) 7.50 2.45

A400

Victory Day — A401

1989, Aug. 8 ***Perf. 12x12½***

1415 A400 100f multicolored 1.25 .40
1416 A400 150f multicolored 2.10 .65

Size: 71x91mm

Imperf

1417 A401 250f multicolored 4.25 4.25
Nos. 1415-1417 (3) 7.60 5.30

Interparliamentary Union, Cent. — A402

1989, Sept. 15 ***Perf. 12½x12***

1418 A402 25f multicolored .35 .25
1419 A402 100f multicolored 1.25 .40
1420 A402 150f multicolored 2.10 .65
Nos. 1418-1420 (3) 3.70 1.30

Ancient Cities A403

1989, Oct. 15 ***Perf. 11½x12½***

1421 A403 100f Dhi Qar-ur 1.75 .55
1422 A403 100f Erbil 1.75 .55
1423 A403 100f An Najaf 1.75 .55
Nos. 1421-1423 (3) 5.25 1.65

5th Session of the Arab Ministers of Transport Council, Baghdad, Oct. 21 A404

Designs: 100f, Land, air and sea transport, diff. 150f, Modes of transport, flags, vert.

1989, Oct. 21 ***Perf. 12x11½, 11½x12***

1424 A404 50f shown 1.25 .55
1425 A404 100f multicolored 2.60 .75
1426 A404 150f multicolored 4.00 1.10
Nos. 1424-1426 (3) 7.85 2.40

Iraqi News Agency, 30th Anniv. A405

1989, Nov. 9 ***Perf. 13½***

1427 A405 50f multicolored .55 .30
1428 A405 100f multicolored 1.10 .40
1429 A405 150f multicolored 1.75 .65
Nos. 1427-1429 (3) 3.40 1.35

Declaration of Palestinian State, 1st Anniv. — A406

50f, Palestinian uprising.

1989, Nov. 15 ***Perf. 12x12½***

1430 A406 25f shown .25 .25
1431 A406 50f multicolored .65 .30
1432 A406 100f like 25f 1.25 .40
1433 A406 150f like 50f 2.10 .60
Nos. 1430-1433 (4) 4.25 1.55

Flowers — A407

25f, Viola sp. 50f, Antirrhinum majus. 100f, Hibiscus trionum. 150f, Mesembryanthemum sparkles.

1989, Nov. 20 ***Perf. 13½x13***

1434 A407 25f multi .35 .35
1435 A407 50f multi .75 .35
1436 A407 100f multi 1.50 .45
1437 A407 150f multi 2.40 .45
Nos. 1434-1437 (4) 5.00 1.60

Miniature Sheet

Perf. 12½x11½

1438 Sheet of 4 9.25 9.25
a. A407 25f like No. 1434 2.10 2.10
b. A407 50f like No. 1435 2.10 2.10
c. A407 100f like No. 1436 2.10 2.10
d. A407 150f like No. 1437 2.10 2.10

No. 1438 has a continuous design. No. 1438 sold for 500f.

For overprints and surcharges see Nos. 1450-1451, 1456, 1516, 1524.

A408

1989, Oct. 25 **Litho.** ***Perf. 13½***

1439 A408 100f multicolored 1.40 .40
1440 A408 150f multicolored 2.10 .65

Reconstruction of Fao.

A409

1989, Dec. 4 **Litho.** ***Perf. 13½***

1441 A409 50f multicolored .65 .30
1442 A409 100f multicolored 1.25 .40
1443 A409 150f multicolored 1.75 .65
Nos. 1441-1443 (3) 3.65 1.35

Martyrs' Day.

Iraqi Red Crescent Soc. — A410

1989, Dec. 10 **Litho.** ***Perf. 13½***

1444 A410 100f multicolored .70 .35
1445 A410 150f multicolored 2.00 .80
1446 A410 500f multicolored 6.75 2.50
Nos. 1444-1446 (3) 9.45 3.65

Arab Cooperation Council, 1st Anniv. — A411

1990, Feb. 16 **Litho.** ***Perf. 13x13½***

1447 A411 50f yellow & multi 1.00 .50
1448 A411 100f orange & multi 2.75 .90

Size: 80x62mm

Imperf

1449 A411 250f blue & multi 7.50 7.50
Nos. 1447-1449 (3) 11.25 8.90

For surcharge see No. 1523.

Nos. 1435, 1437 Ovptd.

1990, May 28 **Litho.** ***Perf. 13½x13***

1450 A407 50f multicolored 1.10 .85
1451 A407 150f multicolored 3.75 2.50

Arab League Summit Conf., Baghdad.

End of Iran-Iraq War, 2nd Anniv. — A412

1990, Aug. 30 ***Perf. 13½x13***

1452 A412 50f purple & multi .75
1453 A412 100f blue & multi 1.50

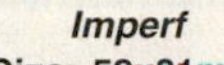

Imperf

Size: 59x81mm

1454 A412 250f Saddam Hussein, dove 5.00

For surcharge see No. 1525.

The surcharged issues of 1992-97 have been extensively forged. Collectors are urged to purchase these stamps with certificates of authenticity or from expert sellers who can attest to their authenticity.

No. 1269 Surcharged

1992(?) **Litho.** ***Perf. 12½x12***

1455 A355 1d on 100f #1269 *8.50*

No. 1434 Surcharged

Type I

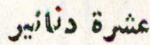

Type II

1993, Aug. 1 **Litho.** ***Perf. 13½x13***

1456 A407 10d on 25f Type I *30.00*
a. Type II *40.00*

No. RA23 Surcharged

1992 **Photo.** ***Perf. 14***

1457 PT3 100f on 5f multi *3.00*

Reconstruction of Iraq — A413

Designs: 250f, Satellite dish. 500f, Bridges. 750f, Power plant, horiz. 1d, Factory.

1993, Sept. **Photo.** ***Perf. 14***

1459 A413 250f red & multi *.85*
1460 A413 500f blue & multi *1.50*
1461 A413 750f yellow & multi *2.25*
1462 A413 1d multicolored *3.00*
Nos. 1459-1462 (4) 7.60

Stamps of this issue may be poorly centered or have perforations running through the design.

For surcharge see No. 1526.

Peace Ship
A414

1993 **Photo.** *Perf. 14*

1463	A414 2d red & multi	*2.50*
1464	A414 5d green & multi	*6.50*

No. RA23 Surcharged

b c d e f g h i j k l m n o

p q

r

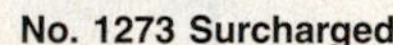

s

t

1994, Feb. 5 **Photo.** *Perf. 14*

1465	PT3(b) 500f on 5f multi, ovpt. 17mm wide	*15.00*
a.	Overprint 14½mm wide	*40.00*
1466	PT3(c) 1d on 5f multi	*2.00*
1467	PT3(d) 1d on 5f multi	*3.50*
a.	PT3(e) 1d on 5f multi	*6.00*
b.	PT3(f) 1d on 5f multi	*3.00*
c.	PT3(g) 1d on 5f multi	*3.00*
1468	PT3(h) 2d on 5f multi	*7.00*
1469	PT3(i) 2d on 5f multi	*3.50*
1470	PT3(j) 3d on 5f multi	*2.00*
1471	PT3(k) 3d on 5f multi	*2.00*
1472	PT3(l) 5d on 5f multi	*3.00*
a.	PT3(m) 5d on 5f multi	*2.00*
b.	PT3(n) 5d on 5f multi	*4.50*
1473	PT3(o) 5d on 5f multi	*4.25*
1474	PT3(p) 10d on 5f multi	*4.25*
1475	PT3(q) 25d on 5f multi	*8.50*
a.	PT3(r) 25d on 5f multi	*14.00*
1476	PT3(s) 25d on 10d on 5f	*5.00*
1477	PT3(t) 50d on 5f multi	*28.00*

No. 1273 Surcharged

u

v

1994, Apr. 28 **Litho.** *Perf. 12½x12*

1480	A354(u) 5d on 350f #1273	*7.00*
1481	A354(v) 5d on 350f #1273	*7.00*
a.	Pair, #1480-1481	*22.50*

Alqa'id Two-Deck Bridge
A415

1994, July 17 *Perf. 14*

1482	A415 1d pink & multi	*3.50*
1483	A415 3d blue & multi	*3.50*
a.	Pair, #1482-1483	*8.50*

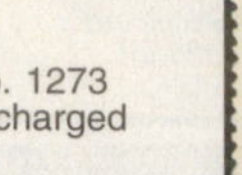

No. 1273 Surcharged

1994, Aug. 8 *Perf. 12½x12*

1484	A354 5d on 350f #1273	*4.75*

No. 1406 Surcharged

w

x

1995, Jan. 2 *Perf. 11½x12*

1485	A397(w) 5d on 150f #1406	*5.00*
1486	A397(x) 5d on 150f #1406	*5.00*
a.	Pair	*20.00*

Baghdad Clock — A416

1995, Feb. 28 *Perf. 11*

1487	A416 7d blue & black	*2.50*

Size: 76x98mm

Imperf

1488	A416 25d multicolored	*14.00*

Saddam Tower — A417

1995, Mar. 12 *Perf. 14*

1489	A417 2d multicolored	*1.00*
1490	A417 5d multicolored	*3.25*
a.	Vert. pair, #1489-1490	*4.50*

Honoring Dead From Battle of Um Almariq (Mother of All Battles) — A418

1995 ***Imperf.***

1491	A418 100d multicolored	*14.00*

Saddam Hussein, 58th Birthday — A419

Design: No. 1492, Saddam seated, flowers & flag behind him, vert.

1995, Apr. 28 ***Imperf.***

1492	A419 25d multicolored	*16.00*
1493	A419 25d multicolored	*16.00*

Saddam River Canal Project
A420

1995, July 17 *Perf. 11*

1494	A420 4d ol yel & blue	*4.00*
1495	A420 4d red & blue	*4.00*

Size: 97x57mm

Imperf

1496	A420 25d multi, denom. in black	*13.50*
a.	Denomination in red	*13.50*

Embargo of Iraq — A421

1995, Aug. 6 *Perf. 11*

1497	A421 10d bl grn & rose lil	*3.00*

Size: 77x100mm

Imperf

1498	A421 25d multicolored	*14.00*

No. 1273 Surcharged

y

z

1995, Oct. 15 **Litho.** *Perf. 12½x12*

1499	A354(y) 25d on 350f #1273	*3.00*
1500	A354(z) 25d on 350f #1273	*3.00*
a.	Pair	*20.00*

Nos. 1103-1108 Surcharged

aa

ab

1995(?) **Photo.** *Perf. 15x14*

1501	A315(aa) 25d on 10f #1103	*2.00*
1502	A315(ab) 100d on 20f #1104	*8.00*
1503	A315(aa) 25d on 30f #1105	*2.00*
1504	A315(ab) 100d on 40f #1106	*8.00*
1505	A315(aa) 25d on 50f #1107	*2.00*

1506 A315(ab) 100d on 100f #1108 8.00
a. Bklt. pane of 6, #1501-1506 32.00

No. 1380, Postal Savings Stamps Similar to Type A387 Surcharged in Red or Black

٢٥ دينار
ac

خمسون دينار
ad

ae

1995(?) Litho. *Perf. 11½x12*
Size: 23½x25mm

1507 A387(ac) 25d on 100f multi 2.00
1508 A387(ac) 25d on 150f blue & multi 2.00
1509 A387(ad) 50d on 250f yel & multi (R) 4.00
1510 A387(ae) 50d on 50f #1380 4.00

The 250f postal savings stamp was also overprinted in denominations of 500f, 2500f and 5000f. These were not issued and were demonitized Feb. 1, 1996. They were subsequently surcharged with new values and with a bar obliterating the original overprint. See Nos. 1512-1514.

No. 1406 Surcharged

1995(?)
1511 A397 100d on 150f multi 5.00

Postal Savings Stamps Similar to Type A387 Surcharged in Red

af

ag

ah

1996 Litho. *Perf. 11½x12*
Size: 23½x25mm
On 250f Yellow & Multi

1512 A387(af) 25d on 500d 6.00
1513 A387(ag) 25d on 5000d 5.00
1514 A387(ah) 50d on 2500d 10.00
Nos. 1512-1514 (3) 21.00

A421a

A421b

Children, Bank — A421c

1996 Litho. *Perf. 13½*
1514A A421a 25d on 10f grn & multi 35.00
1514B A421b 25d on 25f bl & multi 2.00
1514C A421c 50d on 10f grn & multi 110.00

Children, Bank — A422

1996 Litho. *Perf. 13½*
1515 A422 50d on 50f multi 3.00

No. 1515 without surcharge is a postal savings stamp.

No. 1435 Surcharged

1996 *Perf. 13½x13*
1516 A407 100d on 50f multi 6.50

No. O341 Surcharged

1996 *Perf. 14*
1517 A324 100d on 70f #O341 5.00

No. 1273 Surcharged

ak

al

1996 Litho. *Perf. 12½x12*
1517A A354(ak) 25d on 350f 1.25
1519A A354(al) 1000d on 350f 42.50

No. 1273 Surcharged in Blue or Black

ai

aj

1996 *Perf. 12½x12*
1518 A354(ai) 250d on 350f (Bl) 7.50
1519 A354(aj) 350d on 350f 18.00

No. O345 Surcharged

1996 Litho. *Perf. 13½*
1519B A329 100d on 60f 5.00

Battle of Um Al Maarik — A423

1997, Feb. 13 Photo. *Perf. 11*
1520 A423 25d blk, red & green 1.00
1521 A423 100d blue, red & grn 5.00
a. Arabic word at right center reversed 20.00

No. 1406 Surcharged

1997, Apr. 22 Litho. *Perf. 11½x12*
1522 A397 25d on 150f #1406 4.25

Post Day.

No. 1448 Surcharged

1997 *Perf. 13x13½*
1523 A411 25d on 100f #1448 2.00

Baath Party, 50th anniv.

No. 1450 Surcharged like No. 1516

1997 Litho. *Perf. 13½*
1524 A407 100d on 50f multi 45.00

No. 1452 Surcharged

1997 *Perf. 13½x13*
1525 A412 100d on 50f multi 8.00

No. 1459 Surcharged

1997 *Perf. 14*
1526 A413 25d on 250f multi 1.25

Science Day.

A424

Referendum Day: 250d, Saddam Hussein, map of Arab nations.

1997 *Perf. 14*
1527 A424 25d shown 1.50
1527A A424 100d multicolored 6.00

Imperf
Size: 91x77mm

1528 A424 250d multicolored 10.00

A425

Saddam Hussein and: 25d, 100d, No. 1531, Water irrigating trees, grain. No. 1532, Water pipeline, flowers, grain.

1997, Dec. 19 *Perf. 14*
Self-Adhesive (#1530)

1529 A425 25d multicolored 1.00
1530 A425 100d multicolored 3.00

Imperf
Size: 68x81mm

1531 A425 250d multicolored 6.00

Size: 64x82mm

1532 A425 250d multicolored 6.00

Wafa'a Alqa'id project.

Saladin (1169-1250), Founder of Ayyubid Dynasty, Saddam Hussein — A426

1998, Feb. Litho. *Perf. 14*
Self-Adhesive

1533 A426 25d multicolored 1.00
1534 A426 100d multicolored 3.00

Size: 79x67mm
Imperf

1535 A426 250d multicolored 18.00

Nos. 1533-1534 exist imperf. No. 1535 has water-activated gum.

New Year — A427

1998, Mar. 21 *Imperf.*
1536 A427 250d Zinnias 9.00
1537 A427 250d Irises 9.00

1998 World Cup Soccer Championship, France — A428

1998, June *Imperf.*
1538 A428 250d shown 7.00

Size: 63x76mm

1539 A428 250d Two players, vert. 6.00

Souvenir Sheet

Arab Police & Security Leaders Conf., 25th Anniv. — A429

1998, July 12 **Litho.** *Imperf.*
1540 A429 250d multicolored 6.00

A430

"Zad" Day (Arabic Alphabet) — A431

1998, Oct. 25 *Perf. 14*
1541 A430 25d multicolored .50
1542 A431 100d multicolored 2.00

Flowers — A432

Designs: 25d, Chamomilla recutita. 50d, Helianthus annuus. 1000d, Carduus nutans.

1998, Oct. 27
1543 A432 25d multicolored .40
1544 A432 50d brown leaves .75
1545 A432 50d green leaves —
1546 A432 1000d multicolored 8.50

Self-Adhesive

1547 A432 25d like #1543 7.50

No. 1547 is printed on glossy paper.

A433

Martyr's Day — A434

1998, Dec. 1
1548 A433 25d multicolored .50
1549 A434 100d multicolored 1.75

Nos. 1548-1549 exist imperf.

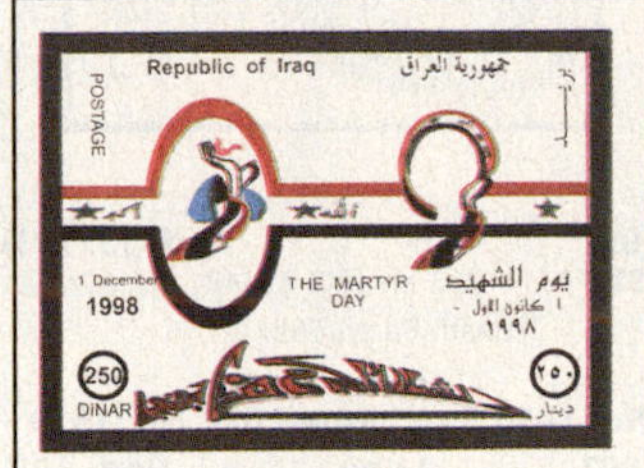

Martyr's Day — A434a

1998, Dec. 1 **Litho.** *Imperf.*
1550 A434a 250d multicolored 4.50

Anthocharis Euphome — A435

1998, Dec. 20
1551 A435 100d Precis orithya 3.00
1552 A435 150d shown 4.50

Exist imperf. Value, set $15.

Intl. Conference on Tower of Babel and Ziggurat of Borsippa — A436

1999, Jan. 23 **Litho.** *Perf. 14*
1553 A436 25d multicolored 1.00
1554 A436 50d multicolored 2.00

Imperf

Size: 71x89mm

1555 A436 250d multicolored 9.00

Great Dam — A437

25d, Dam. 100d, Dam, Saddam Hussein.

1999, Apr. 28 *Perf. 14*
1556 A437 25d multicolored 1.00
1557 A437 100d multicolored 2.50

Imperf

Size: 70x92mm

1558 A437 250d Like #1557 9.00

Saddamiya, Ath-therthar City A438

25d, Saddam Hussein, emblem. 100d, Al-Saddamiyah City. 250d, Clock tower.

1999, May 7 *Perf. 14*
1559 A438 25d multicolored 1.00
1560 A438 100d multicolored 2.00

Imperf

Size: 92x70mm

1561 A438 250d multicolored 9.00

Saddam Hussein, 62nd Birthday — A439

1999, May 17 *Perf. 14*
1562 A439 25d multicolored .25
1563 A439 50d multicolored .50
1564 A439 150d multicolored 1.75
1565 A439 500d multicolored 6.00
1566 A439 1000d multicolored 14.00
1567 A439 5000d multi, horiz. 55.00
Nos. 1562-1567 (6) *77.50*

1998 World Cup, France — A440

1999, July 17
1568 A440 25d Two players 1.75
1569 A440 100d Goalie save, horiz. 4.00

Honey Bees — A441

1999, Sept. 18
1570 A441 25d brown & multi 2.00
1571 A441 50d black & multi 3.00

Al Fat'h Day A442

Saddam Hussein and: 25d, Eagle, flowers. 50d, People. 250d, Eagle, flag.

1999, Dec. 12 **Litho.** *Perf. 14*
1572-1573 A442 Set of 2 2.00

Imperf

Size: 93x71mm

1574 A442 250d multi 6.75

A443

A444

A445

Jerusalem Day A446

2000, Feb. *Perf. 14*
1575 A443 25d multi 1.00
1576 A444 50d multi 1.25
1577 A445 100d multi 2.50
1578 A446 150d multi 3.50
Nos. 1575-1578 (4) *8.25*

Imperf

Size: 93x71mm

1579 A446 250d multi 10.00

A447

Saddam Hussein's Birthday A448

500d, Saddam Hussein, stars.

2000, May 17 *Perf. 14*
1580 A447 25d multi .50
1581 A448 50d multi .75

Imperf
Size: 92x71mm

1582 A448 500d multi *9.00*

Sculpture A449

Text "July Festivals 2000": a, At right. b, At left. c, At bottom center on two lines. d, At lower left. e, At bottom center on 3 lines.

2000, July 12 *Perf. 14*
1583 Horiz. strip of 5 *2.00*
a.-e. A449 25d Any single *.35*

Exists imperf. Value, strip $10.

Victory Day — A450

Designs: 25d, 250d, Saddam Hussein. 50d, Saddam Hussein, flag.

2000, Aug. 8 *Perf. 14*
1584-1585 A450 Set of 2 *2.50*

Imperf
Size: 71x91mm

1586 A450 250d multi *4.50*

Birds A451

Designs: 25d, Anas platyrhynchos. 50d, Passer domesticus. 150d, Porphyrio poliocephalus. 500d, Carduelis carduelis.

2000, Aug. 28 *Perf. 14*
1587-1589 A451 Set of 3 *5.00*

Imperf
Size: 93x71mm

1590 A451 500d multi *10.00*

Prophet Mohammad's Birthday — A452

Designs: 25d, Green background. 50d, Tan background.

2000, Oct. 11 *Perf. 14*
1591-1592 A452 Set of 2 *2.00*

A453

Referendum Day — A454

250d, Saddam Hussein, crowd.

2000, Oct. 15 *Perf. 14*
1593 A453 25d multi .35
1594 A454 50d multi .75

Imperf
Size: 93x72mm

1595 A453 250d multi *4.50*

Baytol Hikma, 1200th Anniv. — A455

2001, Jan. *Perf. 14*
1596-1597 A455 Set of 2 *1.50*
1597a Pair *4.50*

A456

A457

Writing, 5th Millennium A458

2001, Mar. **Litho.** *Perf. 14*
1598 A456 25d multi .30
1599 A457 50d multi .55
1600 A456 75d multi .80
1601 A457 100d multi 1.10
1602 A458 150d multi 1.75
1603 A458 250d multi 2.75
Nos. 1598-1603 (6) 7.25

Bombing of Al Amiriya Shelter, 10th Anniv. A459

Designs: 25d, 150d, Mother, injured child, rescue workers. 50d, Doves, wreath, picture frames, vert.

2001, Mar. *Perf. 14*
1604-1605 A459 Set of 2 *1.50*

Imperf
Size: 91x71mm
Without Gum

1606 A459 150d multi *4.00*

Al Baath Party, 54th Anniv. A460

Designs: 25d, People, torch. 50d, Al Baath Party founder Michel Aflaq, Saddam Hussein. 100d, Map of Middle East.

2001, Apr. 7 *Perf. 14*
1607-1609 A460 Set of 3 *2.00*

Saddam Hussein's 64th Birthday A461

Saddam Hussein: 25d, Seated, with flowers, vert. 50d, Seated. 100d, Seated, with people. 250d, Standing, with crowd.

2001, Apr. 28 *Perf. 14*
1610-1612 A461 Set of 3 *1.50*

Imperf
Size: 89x69mm
Without Gum

1613 A461 250d multi *4.50*

Fish A462

Designs: 25d, Barbus sharpeyi. 50d, Barbus esocinus. 100d, Barbus xanthopterus. 150d, Pampus argenteus.

2001, Aug. 4 *Perf. 14*
1614-1617 A462 Set of 4 *5.00*

Battle of Um Al Maarik, 10th Anniv. — A463

Frame color: 25d, Red. 100d, Black.

2001, Aug.
1618-1619 A463 Set of 2 *1.25*

Mammals A464

Designs: 100d, Gazella subgutturosa. 250d, Lepus europaeus. 500d, Camelus dromedarius. 1000d, Various mammals.

2001, Aug. *Perf. 14*
1620-1622 A464 Set of 3 *7.50*

Imperf
Size: 92x70mm
Without Gum

1623 A464 1000d multi *9.00*

Nationalization of Oil Industries, 29th Anniv. — A465

Designs: 25d, Oil rig, workers, soldier, Iraqi flag. 50d, Oil rig, refinery, pipeline.

2001, Sept. 15 **Litho.** *Perf. 14*
1624-1625 A465 Set of 2 *1.00*

Support for Palestinians A466

Designs: No. 1626, 25d, Saddam Hussein, map of Israel and Iraq. No. 1627, 25d, Dome of the Rock, Palestinian flag, gunman, vert. 50d, Dome of the Rock, Palestinian flag, gunman with arms raised, vert.
No. 1629, 250d, Dome of the Rock, Israeli tank and Palestinian rock-thrower. No. 1630, 250d, Dome of the Rock, doves, Palestinian flag and Mohammad J. Durra and father.

2001, Sept. 20
1626-1628 A466 Set of 3 *1.25*

Imperf
Size: 88x67mm
Without Gum

1629-1630 A466 Set of 2 *5.00*

2001 Youth Soccer World Cup A467

Designs: 25d, Players, map of world. 50d, Map of Asia, player, trophy, vert.

2001, Oct. 7 *Perf. 14*
1631-1632 A467 Set of 2 *1.00*

Iraqi Claim of Depleted Uranium US Bombs Dropped on Iraqi Citizens — A468

Falling bombs and: No. 1633, 25d, Woman and children. No. 1634, 25d, No. 1636, 250d, Disfigured people. 50d, People, Iraqi flag, horiz.

2001, Nov.

1633-1635	A468	Set of 3	*4.00*

Imperf
Size: 70x91mm
Without Gum

1636	A468	250d multi	*7.00*

Army Day — A469

Designs: 25d, Iraqi flag, soldiers, airplanes, ship and tank. No. 1638, 50d, No. 1640, 250d, Monument, vert. 100d, Soldier, Iraqi flag, tank, vert.

2002, Jan. 6 ***Perf. 14***

1637-1639	A469	Set of 3	*3.50*

Imperf
Size: 73x91mm
Without Gum

1640	A469	250d multi	*3.50*

Liberation of Fao — A470

Saddam Hussein and: 25d, Mosque. 100d, Soldier, map of Iraq, horiz.

2002, Apr. 17 ***Perf. 14***

1641-1642	A470	Set of 2	*1.50*

February 8 Revolution, 39th Anniv. — A470a

February 8 Revolution, 39th Anniv. — A470b

2002, Feb. 8 **Litho.** ***Perf. 14***

1642A	A470a	50d multi	8.00	—
1642B	A470b	100d multi	12.00	—

Jerusalem Day — A471

Frame color: 25d, Blue. 50d, Yellow. 100d, Pink.

2002, Apr.

1643-1645	A471	Set of 3	*2.00*

Hegira, Year 1423 A472

Designs: 25d, Mosques, Holy Kaaba. 50d, Minaret and mosque, vert. 75d, Bird, spider web.

2002, Apr.

1646-1648	A472	Set of 3	*1.75*

Bombardment of Al Amirya Shelter, 11th Anniv. — A473

Frame color: 25d, Black. 50d, Red.

2002, Apr.

1649-1650	A473	Set of 2	*1.00*

War Against Iraq, 11th Anniv. — A474

2002, Apr.

1651	A474	100d multi	*1.75*

Flowers — A475

Designs: 25d, Roses. 50d, Roses, diff. 150d, Poppies, carnations.
250d, Roses, diff.

2002, Apr. ***Perf. 14***

1652-1654	A475	Set of 3	*3.50*

Imperf
Size: 73x91mm
Without Gum

1655	A475	250d multi	*5.00*

Saddam Hussein's 65th Birthday — A476

Color of vignette frame and country name: 25d, Red. 50d, Purple. 75d, Green. 100d, Dark blue.

No. 1660, 250d, Saddam Huseein, hearts and flowers. No. 1661, 250d, Saddam Hussein with headdress.

2002, Apr. 28 ***Perf. 14***

1656-1659	A476	Set of 4	*2.75*

Imperf
Size: 74x91mm
Without Gum

1660-1661	A476	Set of 2	*6.00*

Palestinian Unity — A477

2002 **Litho.** ***Perf. 14***

1662	A477	5000d multi	*35.00*

Mosques — A478

Designs: 25d, Sheikh Maroof Mosque. 50d, Al-Mouiz Mosque. 75d, Um Al Marik Mosque.

2002

1663-1665	A478	Set of 3	*2.00*

Post Day — A479

Air mail envelope and: 50d, Stamp with dove. 100d, Airplane, ship, train, map of world.
250d, Globe and dove.

2002

1666-1667	A479	Set of 2	*2.00*

Imperf
Size: 70x91mm
Without Gum

1668	A479	250d multi	*4.50*

2002 World Cup Soccer Championships, Japan and Korea — A480

World Cup, various players and background color of: 50d, Blue. 100d, Yellow. 150d, Red violet.
250d, Purple.

2002 ***Perf. 14***

1669-1671	A480	Set of 3	*3.00*

Imperf
Size: 70x92mm
Without Gum

1672	A480	250d multi	*4.00*

Ancient Ships A481

Various ships: 150d, 250d, 500d.

2002 ***Perf. 14***

1673-1675	A481	Set of 3	*9.00*

Victory Day — A482

Frame color: 25d, Blue. 50d, Pink.
150d, Eagle, vert.

2002 ***Perf. 14***

1676-1677	A482	Set of 2	*1.75*

Imperf
Size: 71x90mm
Without Gum

1678	A482	150d multi	*4.00*

A483

A484

A485

A486

Poets — A487

2002 Litho. *Perf. 14*

1679	A483	25d multi	.35
1680	A484	50d multi	.50
1681	A485	75d multi	1.00
1682	A486	100d multi	1.25
		Nos. 1679-1682 (4)	*3.10*

Imperf

Size: 70x92mm

Without Gum

1683 A487 150d multi *4.00*

A488

A489

A490

Baghdad Day — A491

2002 *Perf. 14*

1684	A488	25d multi	.35
1685	A489	50d multi	.50
1686	A490	75d multi	1.00
		Nos. 1684-1686 (3)	*1.85*

Imperf

Size: 91x70mm

Without Gum

1687 A491 250d multi *5.00*

Referendum Day — A492

Designs: 100d, 250d, Saddam Hussein, people, hands, heart and flowers. 150d, Fist, ballot box.

2002 *Perf. 14*

1688-1689 A492 Set of 2 *2.50*

Imperf

Size: 71x92mm

Without Gum

1690 A492 250d multi *2.75*

Mammals A493

Designs: 25d, Oryx leucoryx. 50d, Acionyx jubatus, vert. 75d, 250d, Panthera leo persica, vert. 100d, Castor fiber. 150d, Equus hemionus hemippus.

2002 *Perf. 14*

1691-1695 A493 Set of 5 *7.00*

Imperf

Size: 70x93mm

Without Gum

1696 A493 250d multi *8.00*

Saddam University A494

Background colors: 50d, Brown. 100d, Blue.

2002 *Perf. 14*

1697-1698 A494 Set of 2 *2.00*

Iraqi Coalition Provisional Authority postal officials have declared as illegal 13 Iraqi stamps of the Saddam Hussein regime with various overprints and surcharges that read "Iraq / In Coalition / Occupation."

Issues of the Coalition Provisional Authority

Transportation — A495

Designs: 50d, Raft. 100d, Horse-drawn carriage. 250d, Horse-drawn rail car. 500d, Boat. 5000d, Camel caravan.

2004, Jan. 15 Litho. *Perf. 14*

1699-1703 A495 Set of 5 *9.75 9.75*

Dated 2003.

New Year — A496

2006, Mar. 16 Litho. *Perf. 13*

1704 A496 250d multi 1.00 1.00

A497

June 30, 2004 Installation of Iraqi Interim Government A498

2006, Sept. 7 Litho. *Perf. 14½*

1705	A497	100d multi	.35	.35
1706	A498	250d multi	.90	.90

Iraq Civilization A499

Designs: 100d, Mannequin with headdress. 150d, Golden bull. 200d, Stone carving. 250d, Paintings of horses on walls.

2006, Sept. 11 Litho. *Perf. 14½*

1707-1709 A499 Set of 3 1.75 1.75

Imperf

Size: 80x61mm

1710 A499 250d multi 2.00 2.00

2004 Summer Olympics, Athens — A500

Designs: 100d, Soccer players. 150d, Runners. 500d, Various athletes.

2006, Sept. 24 *Perf. 14¼*

1711-1712 A500 Set of 2 1.50 1.50

Imperf

Size: 100x70mm

1713 A500 500d multi 2.75 2.75

Paintings — A501

Unnamed paintings by: 100d, Akram Shukri. 150d, Hafidh Al Duroubi. 200d, Faiq Hassan. 250d, Atheer M. G.

2006, Oct. 9 *Perf. 14¼*

1714-1716 A501 Set of 3 2.00 2.00

Imperf

Size: 88x70mm

1717 A501 250d multi 2.25 2.25

The items shown above were prepared in 2006 but not issued.

Flowers — A502

Designs: 250d, Anemone. 750d, Viola mammola. 1000d, Atropa belladonna.

2007 Litho. *Die Cut*

Self-Adhesive

1718-1720 A502 Set of 3 3.50 3.50

1720a Souvenir sheet, #1718-1720 3.75 3.75

Issued: Nos. 1718-1720, 4/11; No. 1720a, 5/7.

Street Vendor A502a

Two Women A502b

2007, Apr. 23 Litho. ***Perf. 13½x13¼***
1720B A502a 100d multi .30 .30
1720C A502b 250d multi .75 .75

Singers and Cat — A503

2007, Apr. 23 ***Perf. 13½x13¼***
1721 A503 5000d multi 15.00 15.00

Dated 2006.

Butterflies A504

Designs: 100d, Papilio demodocus. 250d, Precis orithua. 500d, Coitas croceus. 1000d, Papilio demodocus, diff.

2007, Apr. 23 ***Perf. 13½x13¼***
1722-1724 A504 Set of 3 2.50 2.50

Size: 80x61mm

Imperf

1725 A504 1000d multi 2.75 2.75

Artisans — A505

Designs: 250d, Rug maker. 350d, Blanket maker. 500d, Basket maker.

2007, May 22 Litho. ***Die Cut***

Self-Adhesive

1726-1728 A505 Set of 3 3.50 3.50
1728a Miniature sheet, #1726-1728 4.00

Folklore — A506

2007, June 7 ***Imperf.***
1729 A506 1000d multi 2.75 2.75

Dated 2006.

Rafidain Bank, 65th Anniv. (in 2006) — A507

Background colors: 100d, Light blue. 150d, Orange red. 250d, Brown. 500d, Lilac.

2007, July 10 ***Perf. 14***
1730-1733 A507 Set of 4 2.75 2.75

Dated 2006.

Birds A508

Designs: 150d, Anser anser. 250d, Merops superciliosus. 500d, Pterocles alchata. 1500d, Ducks in flight.

2007, Sept. ***Perf. 14***
1734-1736 A508 Set of 3 2.25 2.25

Imperf

Size: 80x80mm

1737 A508 1500d multi 3.75 3.75

A509

Musicians and Actors A510

Designs: 250d, Mohammad al-Qubanchi, singer. 500d, Haqi al-Shibly, actor, horiz. 750d, Nazem al-Ghazaly, singer, horiz. 1000d, Munir Bashir, musician.

2007, Oct. 1 ***Die Cut***

Self-Adhesive

1738 A509 250d multi 1.25 1.25
1739 A509 500d multi 2.25 2.25
1740 A509 750d multi 3.25 3.25
1741 A510 1000d multi 4.50 4.50
a. Miniature sheet, #1738-1741 12.00
Nos. 1738-1741 (4) 11.25 11.25

A511

A512

National Reconciliation — A513

2008, Oct. 27 Litho. ***Perf. 12¾x13¼***
1742 A511 250d multi .75 .75

Perf. 13

1743 A512 500d multi 1.50 1.50
1744 A513 750d multi 2.25 2.25
Nos. 1742-1744 (3) 4.50 4.50

Diplomatic Relations Between Iraq and People's Republic of China, 50th Anniv. — A514

2008, Oct. 28 ***Perf. 12***
1745 A514 500d multi 1.75 1.75

A three-dimensional souvenir sheet of one 500d stamp without white borders was presented as a gift to Chinese and Iraqi officials.

Wasit Poetry Festival — A515

2008, Nov. 24 ***Perf. 13¼x13***
1746 A515 5000d multi 12.00 12.00

Collective Cemeteries — A516

Rose and: 250d, Corpses and mourners. 500d, Skeletal remains.

2008, Dec. 14
1747-1748 A516 Set of 2 2.10 2.10

Campaign to Regain Stolen Antiquities A517

Buildings and various antiquities: 250d, 500d, 750d.

2009, Mar. 17 ***Perf. 13x13¼***
1749-1751 A517 Set of 3 3.75 3.75

Environmental Protection — A518

2009, Mar. 29
1752 A518 1000d multi 3.00 3.00

Campaign to Restore Marshes A519

2009, Apr. 22
1753 A519 10,000d multi 32.50 32.50

Intl. Children's Day — A520

Children's art: No. 1754, 50d, Shown. No. 1755, 50d, Two women wearing traditional clothing. No. 1756, 50d, Three men, palm trees. No. 1757, 50d, Woman hugging daughter. No. 1758, 50d, Three women. 500d, Woman holding baby, horiz.

2009, June 1 Litho. ***Perf. 13¼x13***
1754-1758 A520 Set of 5 2.50 2.50

Imperf

Size:80x60mm

1759 A520 500d multi *3.00 3.00*

2009 FIFA Confederations Cup Soccer Tournament — A521

Emblem and: 100d, Goalie. 250d, Player dribbling ball. 500d, Player kicking ball. 750d, Emblem only.

2009, June 13 ***Perf. 13x13¼***
1760-1762 A521 Set of 3 2.50 2.50

Imperf

Size: 80x80mm

1763 A521 750d multi 2.00 2.00

Iraqi Tourism Week (in 2008) — A522

No. 1764, 250d — "Iraqi Tourism Week" in white, with denomination at: a, Right (5-1). b, Left (5-2).
No. 1765, 250d — "Iraqi Tourism Week" in black, with denomination at: a, Right (5-3). b, Left (5-4).
500d, Horsemen (5-5).

2009, July 14 ***Perf. 13¼x13***

Horiz. Pairs, #a-b

1764-1765 A522 Set of 2 3.00 3.00

Imperf

Size: 90x60mm

1766 A522 500d multi 1.50 1.50

Dated 2009.

Jerusalem, Capital of Arab Culture — A523

2009, Aug. 2 ***Perf. 13¼x13***
1767 A523 250d lt org & multi .80 .80

Imperf

Size: 60x80mm

1768 A523 750d ol grn & multi 2.10 2.10

Emmanuel Baba Dawud (1934-2009), Soccer Player and Coach — A524

Dawud and: 250d, Pink frame. 500d, Green frame.

2009, Dec. 30 Litho. ***Perf. 13x13¼***
1769-1770 A524 Set of 2 1.75 1.75

Iraqi Republic Railways — A525

Designs: 250d, Steam locomotive. 500d, Diesel locomotive. 750d, Steam locomotive, diff.
1000d, Diesel locomotive, building.

2010, Jan. 25 Litho. ***Perf. 13¼x13***
1772-1774 A525 Set of 3 3.75 3.75

Size: 80x80mm

Imperf

1775 A525 1000d multi 2.50 2.50

Elections — A526

Color of stylized people: 250d, Purple. 500d, Green. 1000d, Red.

2010, Mar. 7 ***Perf. 13¼x13***
1776-1778 A526 Set of 3 4.25 4.25

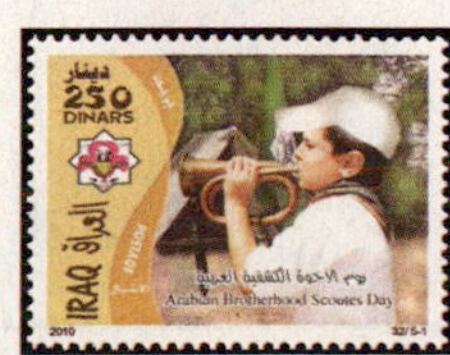

Arabian Brotherhood Scouts Day — A527

Designs: No. 1779, 250d, Bugler. No. 1780, 250d, Girls in field. No. 1781, 250d, Boys saluting flag. No. 1782, 250d, Girls standing at attention.
1000d, Scouts carrying flags.

2010, Mar. 23 ***Perf. 13x13¼***
1779-1782 A527 Set of 4 2.50 2.50

Size: 80x60mm

Imperf

1783 A527 1000d multi 2.50 2.50

Iraqi Post Day — A528

Designs: 250d, Envelope in mail slot. 500d, Dove, envelope, clay tablet.

2010, Apr. 27 ***Perf. 13¼x13***
1784-1785 A528 Set of 2 1.90 1.90

A529

Prehistoric Animals — A530

No. 1786 — Various prehistoric animals with stamps numbered: a, 10-1. b, 10-2. c, 10-3. d, 10-4. e, 10-5. f, 10-6. g, 10-7. h, 10-8.
No. 1787, 500d, 10-9. No. 1788, 500d, 10-10.

2010, June 28 ***Perf. 13¼x13***
1786 Block of 8 7.25 7.25
a.-h. A529 250d Any single .90 .90

Imperf

1787-1788 A530 Set of 2 2.50 2.50

2010 World Cup Soccer Championships, South Africa — A531

Emblem and various soccer players with frame in: 250d, Maroon. 500d, Brown. 750d, Purple. No. 1792, 1000d, Red.
No. 1793, Emblem and two soccer players.

2010, July 13 ***Perf. 13¼x13***
1789-1792 A531 Set of 4 6.25 6.25

Size: 125x70mm

Imperf

1793 A531 1000d multi 2.50 2.50

Koran — A532

2010, Aug. 11 Litho. ***Perf. 13¼x13***
1794 A532 250d multi .65 .65

Size:90x70mm

Imperf

1795 A532 500d multi 1.25 1.25

Intl. Youth Year — A533

"2010," Arabic text and: No. 1796, 250d, Youths, candle, olive branch. No. 1797, 250d, Young woman and man, leaves.

2010, Sept. 8 ***Perf. 13¼x13***
1796-1797 A533 Set of 2 1.25 1.25

Organization of Petroleum Exporting Countries, 50th Anniv. — A534

Sites in Iraq, OPEC 50th anniversary emblem and: 250d, Map of Iraq. 500d, World map.

2010, Sept. 14 ***Perf. 13x13¼***
1798-1799 A534 Set of 2 1.90 1.90

Kirkuk, City of Iraqi Culture — A535

2010, Oct. 4 Litho. ***Perf. 13¼x13***
1800 A535 1000d multi 2.50 2.50

Convention on the Rights of the Child, 20th Anniv. — A536

Stylized faces in oval and: 500d, Child holding adult's hand. 750d, Child solving math problem on blackboard. 1000d, Children on carousel.

2010, Nov.
1801-1803 A536 Set of 3 5.50 5.50

Intl. Year of Biodiversity A537

Designs: 250d, Coccinella septempunctata. 500d, Egretta alba. 750d, Persian gazelle, horiz. No. 1807, 1000d, Ophisops elegans, horiz.
No. 1808, 1000d, Butterfly, dragonfly, ladybug, frog, various birds, horiz.

Perf. 13x13¼, 13¼x13

2011, Jan. 11 Litho.
1804-1807 A537 Set of 4 6.25 6.25

Size: 150x75mm

Imperf

1808 A537 1000d multi 2.60 2.60

2011 Asian Cup Soccer Tournament, Qatar — A538

Designs: 250d, Goalie. 500d, Player. 750d, Player, diff. No. 1812, 1000d, Player scissor kicking ball.
No. 1813, 1000d, Silhouettes of players, vert.

2011, Jan. 27 ***Perf. 13¼x13***
1809-1812 A538 Set of 4 6.25 6.25

Size: 60x60mm

Imperf

1813 A538 1000d multi 2.60 2.60

Biodiversity of Shatt al-Arab and Persian Gulf — A539

Designs: 250d, Metapenaeus affinis. 500d, Torpedo panthera. 750d, Hermit crab. No. 1817, 1000d, Carp.
No. 1818, 1000d, Lionfish.

2011, Feb. 13 ***Perf. 13¼x13***
1814-1817 A539 Set of 4 6.25 6.25

Size: 80x61mm

Imperf

1818 A539 1000d multi 2.60 2.60

Desertification Control Day — A540

Desert and: 750d, Boy examining seedling. 1000d, Hands holding seedling.

2011, Apr. 19 *Perf. 13x13¼*
1819-1820 A540 Set of 2 4.25 4.25

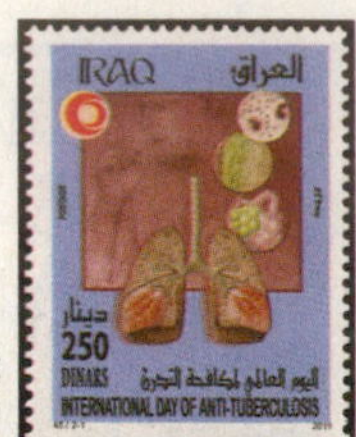

Intl. Day Against Tuberculosis A541

Frame color: 250d, Blue. 500d, Green.

2011, June 21 *Perf. 13¼x13*
1821-1822 A541 Set of 2 1.90 1.90

Archaeological Sites — A542

Designs: 250d, Babylon. 500d, Hatra. 750d, Ziggurat of Ur. No. 1826, 1000d, Nineveh. No. 1827, 1000d, Spiral Minaret, vert.

2011, June 29 *Perf. 13x13¼*
1823-1826 A542 Set of 4 6.50 6.50

Size: 60x80mm

Imperf

1827 A542 1000d multi 2.60 2.60

Poets — A543

Designs: 250d, Abdul al-Wahhab al-Bayati (1926-99). 500d, Muhammad Mahdi al-Jawahiri (1899-1997). 750d, Nazek al-Malaeka (1923-2007).

2011, July 7 *Perf. 13¼x13*
1828-1830 A543 Set of 3 3.75 3.75

Musical Instruments A544

Designs: 250d, Zarna. 500d, Rababa. 750d, Ud. 1000d, Qanun.

2011, July 31
1831-1834 A544 Set of 4 6.50 6.50

Arabian Horses — A545

Designs: 250d, Two black horses. 500d, Two white horses. 750d, Gray and brown horses. No. 1838, 1000d, Gray and white horses. No. 1839, 100d, Five horses.

2011
1835-1838 A545 Set of 4 8.00 8.00

Imperf

Size: 105x85mm

1839 A545 1000d multi 3.00 3.00

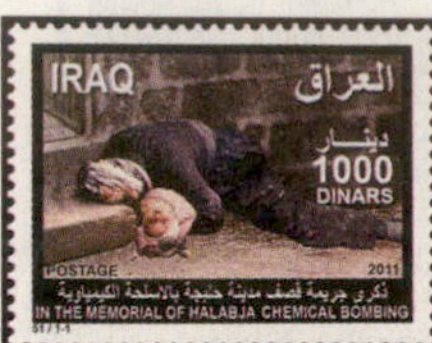

Halabja Chemical Attack, 23rd Anniv. A546

2011, Oct. 24 *Perf. 13x13¼*
1840 A546 1000d multi 2.75 2.75

Iraqi Philatelic and Numismatic Society, 60th Anniv. A547

Designs: 250d, Emblem, stamps and coins. 500d, Coins, emblem and stamps, horiz.

2011, Nov. 3 *Perf. 13x13¼, 13¼x13*
1841-1842 A547 Set of 2 2.00 2.00

Traditional Iraqi Costumes A548

Various men and women in costumes with frame color of: No. 1843, 500d, Brown (6-1). No. 1844, 500d, Purple (6-2). No. 1845, 500d, Gray green (6-3). No. 1846, 500d, Bister (6-4). No. 1847, 500d, Pink (6-5).
No. 1848, 500d, Orange brown (6-6).

2011, Nov. 3 *Perf. 13¼x13*
1843-1847 A548 Set of 5 6.75 6.75

Size: 80x80mm

Imperf

1848 A548 500d multi 1.40 1.40

Ramsar Convention, 40th Anniv. A549

Various birds: 500d, 750d, 1000d. 1000d is vert.

Perf. 13x13¼, 13¼x13

2011, Nov. 3 **Litho.**
1849-1851 A549 Set of 3 6.00 6.00

Discovery of AIDS, 30th Anniv. A550

2012, Jan. 3 *Perf. 13x13¼*
1852 A550 10,000d multi 26.00 26.00

Dated 2011.

Battle of Al-Taaf (Karbala), 680 — A551

Revolution of Imam Hussain — A552

No. 1853: a, Camel caravan. b, Riderless horse. c, Battle scene. d, Birds over battle camp, rider heading to battle.

Litho. With Foil Application

2012, Jan. 11 *Perf. 13¼x13*
1853 Horiz. strip of 4 6.75 6.75
a. A551 250d multi .65 .65
b. A551 500d multi 1.40 1.40
c. A551 750d multi 2.00 2.00
d. A551 1000d multi 2.60 2.60

Imperf

1854 A552 1000d multi 2.60 2.60

No. 1854 is dated 2011.

Martyr's Day A553

Emblem, doves and: 750d, Protesters with flag, coffins, two mourning women. 1000d, Coffins, mourning man.

2012, Mar. 4 **Litho.** *Perf. 13x13¼*
1855-1856 A553 Set of 2 4.75 4.75

Arab Summit Conference, Baghdad — A554

Emblem with background color of: 250d, Pink. 500d, Blue. 750d, Orange.

2012, May 3 *Perf. 13¼x13*
1857-1859 A554 Set of 3 5.75 5.75

Flowers — A555

Designs: No. 1860, 250d, Sunflowers. No. 1861, 500d, Gardenias. No. 1862, 750d, Weasel's snouts. No. 1863, 1000d, Carnations.
No. 1864, 1000d, Various flowers
No. 1865, 250d, Zinnias. No. 1866, 500d, Anemones. No. 1867, 750d, Roses. No. 1868, 1000d, Chrysanthemums.

2012, May 6 *Perf. 13¼x13*
1860-1863 A555 Set of 4 6.75 6.75

Size: 80x80mm (#1864)

Imperf

1864 A555 1000d multi 2.75 2.75

Self-Adhesive

Die Cut

1865-1868 A555 Set of 4 6.75 6.75

Al-Kadhimiya Mosque, Baghdad — A556

Various views of mosque numbered: No. 1869, 250d, 4-1. No. 1870, 250d, 4-2. No. 1871, 250d, 4-3.
500d, Mosque, doves, scroll, horiz (4-4).

2012, June 12 *Perf. 13¼x13*
1869-1871 A556 Set of 3 2.25 2.25

Size: 100x70mm

Imperf

1872 A556 500d multi 1.50 1.50

Genocide of Kurdish Faylees — A557

Map of Iraq and various Kurdish refugees: 750d, 1000d.

2012, June 19 *Perf. 13¼x13*
1873-1874 A557 Set of 2 4.75 4.75

National Commission on Education, Culture and Science — A558

2012, July 27
1875 A558 5000d multi 14.00 14.00

2012 Summer Olympics, London
A559

Designs: 250d, Archery. 500d, Gymnastics. 750d, Fencing. No. 1879, 1000d, Hurdles.
No. 1880, 1000d, Olympic rings, torch bearer, runner, high jump, equestrian, kayaker, swimmer. No. 1881. 1000d, Olympic rings, torch, mascots, stadiums, flags, javelin.

2012, Sept. 9 ***Perf. 13x13¼***
1876-1879 A559 Set of 4 7.00 7.00

Size: 120x70mm

Imperf

1880-1881 A559 Set of 2 5.50 5.50

Kings of Iraq
A560

Designs: 500d, King Faisal II (1935-1958). 750d, King Ghazi (1912-1939). No. 1884, 1000d, King Faisal I (1885-1933).
No. 1885, Kings Faisal I, Ghazi and Faisal II, equestrian statue, arms.

2012, Oct. 2 ***Perf. 14¼***
1882-1884 A560 Set of 3 6.25 6.25

Size: 90x70mm
On Thin Card Stock Without Gum

Imperf

1885 A560 1000d multi 2.75 2.75

Arab Post Day
A561

2012, Nov. 26 ***Perf. 13x13¼***
1886 A561 250d multi .70 .70

Kirkuk Castle — A562

2012, Nov. 26 ***Perf. 13¼x13***
1887 A562 500d multi 1.40 1.40

Water Wheel — A563

2012, Dec. 4 ***Perf. 13¼***
1888 A563 10,000d multi 27.50 27.50

Evacuation of Coalition Troops, 1st Anniv. — A564

Frame color: 250d, Silver. 1000d, Gold.

2012, Dec. 13 ***Perf. 13¼x13***
1889-1890 A564 Set of 2 3.50 3.50

Falcons
A565

Designs: 250d, Gyrfalcons. 500d, Lanner falcons. 750d, Saker falcons (cherrug). No. 1894, 1000d, Peregrine falcons.
No. 1895, 1000d, Falcon on perch.

2012, Dec. 20 ***Perf. 13x13¼***
1891-1894 A565 Set of 4 7.00 7.00

Size: 90x70mm

Imperf

1895 A565 1000d multi 2.75 2.75

Landmarks
A566

Map of Iraq and various landmarks, with stamps numbered: No. 1896, 250d, (8-1). No. 1897, 250d, (8-2). No. 1898, 250d, (8-3). No. 1899. 250d, (8-4). 500d, (8-5), horiz. 750d, (8-6), horiz. No. 1902, 1000d, (8-7), horiz.
No. 1903, 1000d, Map of Iraq, frame, various landmarks (8-8), horiz.

2013, Jan. 28 ***Perf. 13x13¼, 13¼x13***
1896-1902 A566 Set of 7 9.00 9.00

Size: 100x80mm

Imperf

1903 A566 1000d multi 2.75 2.75

Baghdad, Capital of Arab Culture — A567

Emblem and: 250d, Man (5-1). 500d, Woman (5-2). 750d, Man, diff. (5-3). No. 1907, 1000d, Man, diff. (5-4).
No. 1908, 1000d, Round City of Baghdad (5-5).

2013, Apr. 25 ***Perf. 13¼x13***
1904-1907 A567 Set of 4 7.00 7.00

Size: 80x60mm

Imperf

1908 A567 1000d multi 2.75 2.75

World Telecommunications Day — A568

Telecommunications satellites, map of Iraq, flags and: 250d, Globe. 1000d, Binary code, horiz.

Perf. 13¼x13, 13x13¼

2013, Sept. 1 **Litho.**
1909-1910 A568 Set of 2 3.75 3.75

Butterflies
A569

Designs: 200d, Anthocharis cardamines. 250d, Precis orithya. 500d, White glider. 750d, Colias croceus. 1000d, Papilio machaon. 5000d, Vanessa atalanta. 10,000d, Danaus chrysippus.

2013, Sept. 4 **Litho.** ***Perf. 13¼x13½***
1911-1917 A569 Set of 7 52.50 52.50

Camels
A570

Designs: 250d, Two camels in foreground facing left, two camels in background (6-1). 500d, One camel facing right (6-2). 750d, Two camels facing right (6-3). No. 1921, 1000d, One camel standing, three camels resting on ground (6-4).
No. 1922, 1000d, Four camels in foreground facing right, group of camels on sand dune in background, horiz. (6-5). No. 1923, 1000d, Two camels in foreground facing left, two camels on sand dune in background facing left, horiz. (6-6).

2013, Sept. 9 **Litho.** ***Perf. 13½***
1918-1921 A570 Set of 4 6.00 6.00

Size: 110x75mm

Imperf

1922-1923 A570 Set of 2 *16.50 16.50*

Clock Towers — A571

Various clock towers with background color of: 250d, Greenish gray (4-1). 500d, Blue gray (4-2). 750d, Tan (4-3). 1000d, Lilac (4-4).

2013, Sept. 13 **Litho.** ***Perf. 13¼x13***
1924-1927 A571 Set of 4 7.50 7.50

Iraqi Women's Day — A572

2013, Dec. 4 **Litho.** ***Perf. 13¼x13***
1928 A572 1500d multi 4.50 4.50

World Arab Language Day
A573

Background color: 500d, Light blue. 1000d, Yellow green.

2013, Dec. 18 **Litho.** ***Perf. 13x13¼***
1929-1930 A573 Set of 2 4.50 4.50

Intl. Civil Aviation Organization, 70th Anniv. — A574

ICAO emblem, jet and: 500d, Control tower. 1000d, Terminal building. 1500d, World map.

2014, Jan. 28 **Litho.** ***Perf. 13x13¼***
1931-1933 A574 Set of 3 8.75 8.75

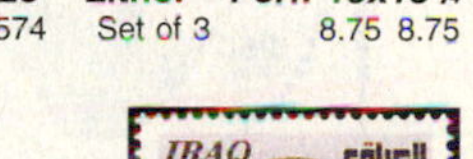

Environmental Year — A575

Background color: 250d, Purple. 500d, Green. 750d, Red.

2014, Apr. 16 **Litho.** ***Perf. 13¼x13***
1934-1936 A575 Set of 3 4.50 4.50

Parliamentary Elections — A576

Stylized voters, map of Iraq, and: 500d, Iraqi tourist attractions. 1000d, Dove and flag. 1500d, Flag, horiz.

Perf. 13¼x13, 13x13¼

2014, Apr. 30 **Litho.**
1937-1939 A576 Set of 3 8.75 8.75

Army Day — A577

Designs: 250d, Ship. 500d, Tank. 750d, Soldiers. 1000d, Airplane.

2015, Jan. 14 Litho. *Perf. 13¼*
1940-1943 A577 Set of 4 7.50 7.50

Diplomatic Relations Between Iraq and Japan, 75th Anniv. — A578

Background colors: 250d, Green. 500d, Yellow green. No. 1946, 1000d, Blue.
No. 1947, 1000d, 75th anniversary emblem, vignettes of Nos. 1944-1946 decreased in size.

2015, Jan. 15 Litho. *Perf. 13½x13*
1944 A578 250d multi .90 .90
1945 A578 500d multi 1.75 1.75
a. With top line of Arabic text under flags extending to left and right frame lines 1.75 1.75
1946 A578 1000d multi 3.50 3.50
Nos. 1944-1946 (3) 6.15 6.15

Size: 90x62mm

Imperf

1947 A578 1000d multi 3.50 3.50

Dated 2014. First day covers are dated 11/1/14, but stamps were not made available until 2015. On No. 1945a, the lines of Arabic text under the flags are nonsensical.

2014 World Cup Soccer Championships, Brazil — A579

Designs: 250d, World Cup, flags of participating nations, soccer field. 500d, World Cup, flags, soccer player and ball. 650d, Flags, mascot with ball. No. 1951, 1000d, World Cup, various players, soccer ball in net.
No. 1952, 1000d, Flags, emblem of 2014 World Cup.

2015, Jan. 18 Litho. *Perf. 13¾*
1948-1951 A579 Set of 4 7.50 7.50

Imperf

Size: 70x70mm

1952 A579 1000d multi 10.50 10.50

Dated 2014. First day cancels are dated 6/12/14 but stamps were not made available until 2015. Values for Nos. 1948-1951 are for stamps with surrounding selvage.

Birds — A580

Designs: 250d, Tree sparrow. 500d, Blue-cheeked bee-eater. 750d, Robin. No. 1956, 1000d, Goldfinch. No. 1957, 1000d, Common kingfisher.
1500d, Tree sparrow, blue-cheeked bee-eater, robin, goldfinch, common kingfisher, horiz.

2015, Jan. 21 Litho. *Perf. 13¼*
1953-1957 A580 Set of 5 10.50 10.50

Imperf

Size: 136x102mm

1958 A580 1500d multi + 3 labels *11.50 11.50*

Dated 2014.

Craftsmen — A581

Designs: 250d, Potter. 500d, Coppersmith. 750d, Weaver. 1000d, Knife sharpener.

2015, Jan. 25 Litho. *Perf. 14¼x14*
1959-1962 A581 Set of 4 7.50 7.50

Fruit — A582

Designs: 250d, Apricots. 500d, Pomegranates. 750d, Figs. No. 1966, 1000d, Apples. No. 1967, 1000d, Grapes.

2015, Jan. 26 Litho. *Perf. 13¼x13*
1963-1967 A582 Set of 5 10.50 10.50

Dated 2014. First day cancels are dated 1/26/14, but stamps were not made available until 2015.

Cars Owned by Royalty A583

Car in: 250d, Black. 500d, Red. 750d, Silver. 1000d, Dark red.

2015, Jan. 26 Litho. *Perf. 13¼*
1968-1971 A583 Set of 4 7.50 7.50

Dated 2014. First day cancels are dated 1/26/14 but stamps were not made available until 2015.

Scenes From Southern Iraq Marshes A584

Designs: 250d, Man standing in small boat. 500d, Cattle.

2015, Feb. 8 Litho. *Perf. 13x13¼*
1972-1973 A584 Set of 2 3.00 3.00

Mosques — A585

Various mosques with side panel in: 250d, Brown ochre. 500d, Blue. 750d, Purple. 1000d, Yellow brown.

2015, Feb. 9 Litho. *Perf. 13½*
1974-1977 A585 Set of 4 7.50 7.50

Dated 2014.

National Day of the Disabled A586

Designs: 250d, Hexagons showing disabilities. 500d, Stylized people helping person in wheelchair, rectangles showing disabilities. 1000d, Umbrella, rectangles and flower petals showing disabilities.

2015, Sept. 17 Litho. *Perf. 14¼x14*
1978-1980 A586 Set of 3 5.00 5.00

A587

A588

War Campaign Against Islamic State of Iraq and the Levant — A589

2015, Oct. 26 Litho. *Perf. 14¼x14*
1981 A587 500d multi 1.50 1.50
1982 A588 750d multi 2.25 2.25
1983 A589 1000d multi 3.00 3.00
Nos. 1981-1983 (3) 6.75 6.75

Destruction of Iraqi Antiquities by Islamic State of Iraq and the Levant — A590

Designs: 500d, Toppled statue. 1000d, Cracked statues, vert.
1500d, Toppled statue and sledgehammer.

2015, Nov. 23 Litho. *Perf. 14¼*
1984-1985 A590 Set of 2 3.25 3.25

Imperf

Size: 64x64mm

1986 A590 1500d multi 3.25 3.25

No. 1986 have simulated perforations.

Farm Pets A591

Designs: 250d, Rabbits. 500d, Pigeons. 750d, Cat and dog, vert. 1000d, Chickens, vert.
1500d, Ducks, cat, dog, rabbits, pigeons and chickens.

Perf. 14x14¼, 14¼x14

2016, Mar. 23 Litho.
1987-1990 A591 Set of 4 7.50 7.50

Size: 103x84mm

Imperf

1991 A591 1500d multi 4.50 4.50

No. 1991 has simulated perfs around details of Nos. 1987-1990.

International Year of Light (in 2015) — A592

2016, Apr. 3 Litho. *Perf. 14x14¼*
1992 A592 10,000d multi 29.00 29.00

UNESCO, 70th anniv. (in 2015).

Children at Play — A593

Designs: 250d, Girls playing hop scotch. 500d, Boys playing marbles, horiz. 750d, Boys playing game, horiz. 1000d, Girls skipping rope.

2016, Apr. 14 Litho. *Perf. 14*
1993-1996 A593 Set of 4 7.25 7.25

Zaha Hadid (1950-2016), Architect — A594

Mohammad Makeyah (1914-2015), Architect — A595

2016, June 16 Litho. *Perf. 14*
1997 A594 750d multi 2.25 2.25
1998 A595 1000d multi 3.00 3.00

Flowers — A596

Various flower arrangements: 250d, 500d, 750d, 1000d, 1500d. 750d is horiz.

2016, July 13 Litho. *Perf. 14*
1999-2003 A596 Set of 5 11.50 11.50

Arab Postal Day — A597

No. 2004 — Background color: a, 500d, Green. b, 1000d, Blue and purple.

2016, Sept. 5 Litho. *Perf. 14x14¼*
2004 A597 Horiz. pair, #a-b 4.50 4.50

Health Organizations — A598

No. 2005: a, 250d, Syndicate of Iraqi Pharmacists. b, 250d, Iraqi Medical Association. c, 500d, Iraqi Red Crescent Society. d, 500d, Anti-tuberculosis and Chest Diseases Society in Iraq.

2016, Sept. 21 Litho. *Perf. 14*
2005 A598 Block of 4, #a-d 4.50 4.50

Liberation of Anbar Province A599

2016, Oct. 5 Litho. *Perf. 14*
2006 A599 1000d multi 3.00 3.00

2016 Summer Olympics, Rio de Janeiro — A600

No. 2007: a, 250d, Track. b, 250d, Soccer. c, 500d, High jump. d, 500d, Handball. e, 750d, Equestrian show jumping. f, 750d, Javelin. g, 1000d, Boxing. h, 1000d, Fencing.
No. 2008, 1000d, Pole vault, gymnastics, basketball, long jump.

2016, Oct. 23 Litho. *Perf. 14*
2007 A600 Sheet of 8, #a-h 15.50 15.50
Size: 140x70mm
Imperf
2008 A600 1000d multi 3.00 3.00

Sheikh Ahmed Al-Waili (1928-2003), Islamic Cleric and Poet — A601

2016, Nov. 13 Litho. *Perf. 14*
2009 A601 1000d multi 3.00 3.00

Addition of South Iraq Marshes to UNESCO World Heritage List — A602

UNESCO and World Heritage Site emblem and: 250d, Gilgamesh. 500d, Statue. 750d, Ziggurat of Ur, horiz. No. 2013, 1000d, Boat in marsh waterway, horiz.
No. 2014, 1000d, Scroll, Gilgamesh, statue, Ziggurat of Ur, boat in marsh waterway.

2016, Dec. 1 Litho. *Perf. 14*
2010-2013 A602 Set of 4 7.25 7.25
Size: 99x92mm
Imperf
2014 A602 1000d multi 3.00 3.00

Diplomatic Relations Between Iraq and Spain, 70th Anniv. — A603

2017, Feb. 5 Litho. *Perf. 14*
2015 A603 1000d multi 3.25 3.25

Brothers Meeting Festival for Hobbies and Miscellaneous Crafts — A604

Emblem and: 500d, Rugs, stringed instrument, books, lantern, cup and coffee pot. 1000d, Rugs, large stringed instrument, plate, musical notes, artist's palette.

2017, Mar. 1 Litho. *Perf. 14*
2016 A604 500d multi 1.60 1.60
Size: 84x84mm
Imperf
2017 A604 1000d multi 3.25 3.25

Al Rasheed Street, Baghdad, Cent. (in 2016) — A605

2017, Mar. 30 Litho. *Perf. 14*
2018 A605 1000d multi 3.25 3.25

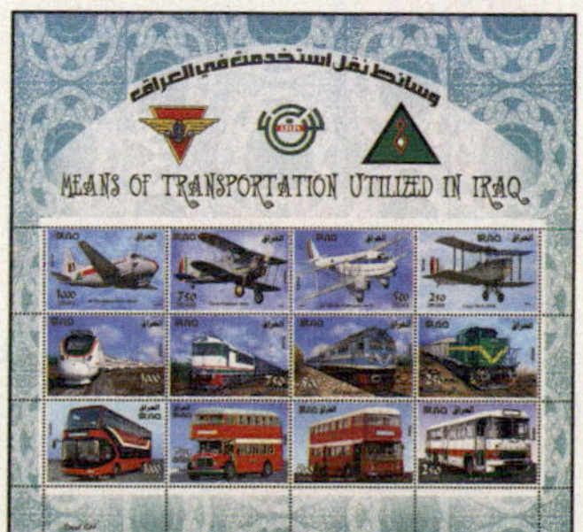
Airplanes, Trains and Buses — A606

No. 2019: a, 250d, Gipsy Moth biplane, 1931. b, 250d, DHL136 train, 2004. c, 250d, Ikarus bus, 1971. d, 500d, De Havilland Dragon biplane, 1933. e, 500d, DEM2745 train, 2001. f, 500d, Leyland bus, 1976. g, 750d, Gloster Gladiator biplane, 1937. h, 750d, DEM2006 train, 1964. i, 750d, AC bus, 1956. j, 1000d, De Havilland Dove airplane, 1948. k, 1000d, DMU train, 2014. l, 1000d, Albs bus, 2013.
No. 2020, Steam train, airplane and bus.

2017, July 5 Litho. *Perf. 14x14¼*
2019 A606 Sheet of 12, #a-l 24.00 24.00
Size:120x90mm
Imperf
2020 A606 1000d multi 3.00 3.00

Liberation of Mosul — A607

Designs: 500d, Troops, tanks, airplanes, damaged mosque. 1000d, Woman holding Iraqi flag, soldiers, horiz.

2017, July 18 Litho. *Perf. 14*
2021 A607 500d multi 1.60 1.60
Size: 100x68mm
Imperf
2022 A607 1000d multi 3.25 3.25

"Baghdad" Overprinted Stamps of Mesopotamia, Cent. — A608

Designs: 250d, Mesopotamia #N1. 500d, Mesopotamia #N5, horiz. 1000d, Mesopotamia #N7, horiz.
1500d, Magnifying glass, canceler, covers bearing various stamps of Mesopotamia, horiz.

2017, Oct. 21 Litho. *Perf. 14*
2023-2025 A608 Set of 3 6.00 6.00
Size: 94x70mm
Imperf
2026 A608 1500d multi 5.25 5.25

Al-Abbas Holy Shrine, Karbala A609

Designs: 250d, Sepulcher of Al-Abbas ibn Ali. 1000d, Worshiper.
1500d, Mosque dome and minarets.

2017, Dec. 3 Litho. *Perf. 14*
2027-2028 A609 Set of 2 4.25 4.25
Size: 100x70mm
Imperf
2029 A609 1500d multi 5.00 5.00

AIR POST STAMPS

Catalogue values for unused stamps in this section are for Never Hinged items.

Basra Airport — AP1

Diyala Railway Bridge — AP2

Vickers Viking over: 4f, 20f, Kut Dam. 5f, 35f, Faisal II Bridge.

Perf. 11½, 11½x12
1949, Feb. 1 Engr. Unwmk.
C1 AP1 3f blue green 1.00 .25
C2 AP1 4f red violet 1.00 .25
C3 AP1 5f red brown 1.00 .25
C4 AP1 10f carmine 5.50 1.50
C5 AP1 20f blue 3.75 .65
C6 AP1 35f red orange 3.75 .65
C7 AP2 50f olive 5.00 1.10
C8 AP2 100f violet 9.75 2.25
Nos. C1-C8 (8) 30.75 6.90

Sheets exist, perf. and imperf., containing one each of Nos. C1-C8, with arms and Arabic inscription in blue green in upper and lower margin. Value (2 sheets), each $80.

Republic

ICY Emblem — AP3

1965, Aug. 13 Litho. *Perf. 13½*
C9 AP3 5f brn org & black 1.00 .25
C10 AP3 10f citron & dk brn 1.50 .25
C11 AP3 30f ultra & black 3.50 1.10
Nos. C9-C11 (3) 6.00 1.60

International Cooperation Year.

Trident 1E Jet Plane AP4

1965, Dec. 1 Photo. *Perf. 11½*
Granite Paper
C12 AP4 5f multicolored .90 .55
C13 AP4 10f multicolored .90 .55
C14 AP4 40f multicolored 6.00 4.75
Nos. C12-C14 (3) 7.80 5.85

Introduction by Iraqi Airways of Trident 1E jet planes.

Arab International Tourist Union Emblem — AP5

Travelers on Magic Carpet AP6

1966, Dec. 3 Litho. *Perf. 13½, 14*
C15 AP5 2f multicolored 1.00 .30
C16 AP6 5f yellow & multi 1.50 .30
C17 AP5 15f blue & multi 1.75 .50
C18 AP6 50f multicolored 3.00 .80
Nos. C15-C18 (4) 7.25 1.90

Meeting of the Arab Intl. Tourist Union, Baghdad.
For overprint see No. RAC1.

Costume Type of Regular Issue

Iraqi Costumes: 40f, Woman's head. 50f, Woman's costume. 80f, Man's costume.

1967, Nov. 10 Litho. *Perf. 13*

C19 A105 40f multicolored 2.50 .90
C20 A105 50f blue & multi 3.50 1.25
C21 A105 80f green & multi 5.50 1.75
Nos. C19-C21 (3) 11.50 3.90

For overprints, see CO1-CO3.

International Tourist Year Type of Regular Issue

Designs: 50f, Female statue, Temples of Hatra. 80f, Spiral Tower (Malwiye of Samarra). 100f, Adam's Tree. 200f, Aladdin's Cave. 500f, Golden Shiah Mosque of Kadhimain. 50f, 80f, 100f and 200f are vert.

1967, Dec. 1 Litho.

C22 A107 50f multicolored 4.00 .40
C23 A107 80f multicolored 4.25 .65
C24 A107 100f multicolored 4.25 .80
C25 A107 200f ver & multi 8.75 3.25
C26 A107 500f brn & multi 35.00 18.00
Nos. C22-C26 (5) 51.50 23.10

For overprints see Nos. C39, C52, C53, CO4.

Arabian AP7

Animals: 2f, Striped hyena. 3f, Leopard. 5f, Mountain gazelle. 200f, Arabian stallion.

1969, Sept. 1 Litho. *Perf. 14*

C27 AP7 2f multicolored .85 .25
C28 AP7 3f multicolored .85 .25
C29 AP7 5f multicolored .85 .25
C30 AP7 10f multicolored 1.10 .30
C31 AP7 200f multicolored 13.50 6.00
Nos. C27-C31 (5) 17.15 7.05

For overprints, see Nos. CO5-CO7.

Ross Smith's Vickers Vimy AP8

1969, Dec. 4 Litho. *Perf. 14*

C32 AP8 15f dk bl & multi 3.50 1.20
C33 AP8 35f multicolored 5.00 2.75
a. Souv. sheet of 2, #C32-C33, imperf. 15.00 13.00

50th anniv. of the first England to Australia flight of Capt. Ross Smith and Lt. Keith Smith. No. C33a sold for 100f.

View Across Euphrates — AP9

Iraqi Banknotes and Pres. Hassan al-Bakr AP10

1970, Oct. 30 Litho. *Perf. 13*

C34 AP9 10f brt bl & multi 2.25 .50
C35 AP9 15f multicolored 3.50 1.10
C36 AP10 1d multicolored 70.00 24.00
Nos. C34-C36 (3) 75.75 25.60

National Development Plan.
For overprints see Nos. C42-C43.

Telecommunications Emblem — AP11

1970, Dec. 15 Litho. *Perf. 14x13½*

C37 AP11 15f gray & multi .90 .25
C38 AP11 25f lt bl & multi 1.10 .50

10th Conf. of Arab Telecommunications Union.

No. C23 Overprinted

1971, Apr. 23 *Perf. 13*

C39 A107 80f multicolored 10.00 5.50

World Meteorological Day.

Iraqi Philatelic Society Emblem — AP12

1972, Feb. 25 Litho. *Perf. 13*

C40 AP12 25f multicolored 1.25 .95
C41 AP12 70f pink & multi 4.00 2.40

Iraqi Philatelic Society, 20th anniversary.

Nos. C34-C35 Overprinted

1972, Feb. 25

C42 AP9 10f brt bl & multi 2.50 2.40
C43 AP9 15f multicolored 2.50 2.40
a. Overprint inverted 150.00

9th Cong. of Natl. Union of Iraqi Students.

Soccer and C.I.S.M. Emblem AP13

20f, 35f, Players, soccer ball, C.I.S.M. emblem. 100f, Winged lion, Olympic & C.I.S.M. emblems.

1972, June 9 Litho. *Perf. 13½*

C46 AP13 10f lt bl & multi .75 .30
C47 AP13 20f dp bl & multi 1.75 .30
C48 AP13 25f green & multi 1.75 .30
C49 AP13 35f brt bl & multi 4.75 .80
a. Souv. sheet, 100f, imperf. 22.50 22.50
Nos. C46-C49 (4) 9.00 1.70

25th Military Soccer Championships (C.I.S.M.), Baghdad, June 9-19.

Statue of Athlete — AP14

Design: 70f, Mesopotamian archer on horseback, ancient and modern athletes.

1972, Nov. 15 Photo. *Perf. 14x13½*

C50 AP14 25f multicolored 1.50 .65
C51 AP14 70f multicolored 3.75 2.10

Cong. of Asian and World Body Building Championships, Baghdad, Nov. 15-23, 1972.

Nos. C23, C26 Overprinted

1973, Mar. 25 Litho. *Perf. 13*

C52 A107 80f multi 21.00 7.25
C53 A107 500f multi 75.00 *75.00*

International History Congress.

ICATU Type of 1976

1976, Mar. 24 Photo. *Perf. 13½*

C54 A213 75f blue & multi 4.50 2.00

Symbolic Eye — AP15

1976, June 20 Photo. *Perf. 14*

C55 AP15 25f ultra & dk brn .40 .25
C56 AP15 35f brt grn & dk brn .60 .25
C57 AP15 50f orange & multi 1.25 .60
Nos. C55-C57 (3) 2.25 1.10

World Health Day: Foresight prevents blindness.

Basketball — AP16

Montreal Olympic Games Emblem and: 35f, Volleyball. 50f, Wrestling. 75f, Boxing. 100f, Target shooting, horiz.

1976, July 30 Litho. *Perf. 12x12½*

C58 AP16 25f yel & multi .75 .25
C59 AP16 35f blue & multi 1.00 .50
C60 AP16 50f ver & multi 1.25 .95
C61 AP16 75f yel grn & multi 2.25 1.25
Nos. C58-C61 (4) 5.25 2.95

Souvenir Sheet

Imperf

C62 AP16 100f grn & multi 7.00 7.00

21st Olympic Games, Montreal, Canada, July 17-Aug. 1.

13th World Telecommunications Day — AP17

1981, May 17 Photo. *Perf. 12½*

C63 AP17 25f multicolored .50 .25
C64 AP17 50f multicolored 1.00 .40
C65 AP17 75f multicolored 1.75 .85
Nos. C63-C65 (3) 3.25 1.50

Air Force Type of 1981

1981, June 1 Photo. *Perf. 14x13½*

C66 A289 120f Planes, vert. 4.00 2.50

AIR POST OFFICIAL STAMP

Catalogue values for all unused stamps in this section are for Never Hinged items.

Nos. C19-C22 Overprinted

1971 Litho. *Perf. 13*

CO1 A105 40f multicolored 4.75 1.40
CO2 A105 50f multicolored 6.00 1.40
CO3 A105 80f multicolored 5.50 1.40

"Official" Reading Down

CO4 A107 50f multicolored 5.25 3.25
Nos. CO1-CO4 (4) 21.50 7.45

Nos. C27-C28, C30 Overprinted or Surcharged

1971 *Perf. 14*

CO5 AP7 10f multicolored 7.50 5.00
CO6 AP7 15f on 3f multi 7.50 5.00
CO7 AP7 25f on 2f multi 7.50 5.00
Nos. CO5-CO7 (3) 22.50 15.00

No bar and surcharge on No. CO5.

OFFICIAL STAMPS

British Mandate

Regular Issue of 1923 Overprinted

k l

1923 Wmk. 4 *Perf. 12*

O1 A1(k) ½a olive grn 1.25 .50
O2 A2(k) 1a brown 1.50 .25
O3 A3(l) 1½a car lake 3.25 .75

O4 A4(k) 2a brown org 2.25 .30
O5 A5(k) 3a deep blue 4.00 .75
O6 A6(l) 4a dull violet 4.25 .50
O7 A7(k) 6a blue green 6.00 1.40
O8 A6(l) 8a olive bister 6.50 1.30
O9 A8(l) 1r grn & brn 7.50 1.40
O10 A1(k) 2r black (R) 22.50 9.00
O11 A6(l) 5r orange 65.00 27.50
O12 A7(k) 10r carmine 95.00 60.00
Nos. O1-O12 (12) 219.00 103.65

Regular Issue of 1923-25 Overprinted

m

n

1924-25

O13 A1(m) ½a olive green 1.75 .30
O14 A2(m) 1a brown 1.50 .30
O15 A3(n) 1½a car lake 1.50 .30
O16 A4(m) 2a brown org 2.25 .30
O17 A5(m) 3a deep blue 2.75 .30
O18 A6(n) 4a dull violet 5.75 .30
O19 A7(m) 6a blue green 2.75 .30
O20 A6(n) 8a olive bister 5.75 .40
O21 A8(n) 1r grn & brn 13.00 1.00
O22 A1(m) 2r bister ('25) 42.50 4.50
O23 A6(n) 5r orange 70.00 50.00
O24 A7(m) 10r brown red 100.00 52.50
Nos. O13-O24 (12) 249.50 110.50

For overprint see Nos. O42, O47, O51-O53.

No. 14 Overprinted Type "n"

1927

O25 A9 1r red brown 10.00 2.00

Regular Issue of 1931 Overprinted Vertically

o

1931

O26 A10 ½a green .35 *3.00*
O27 A10 1a chestnut .35 .25
O28 A10 1½a carmine 8.75 *16.00*
O29 A10 2a orange .85 .25
O30 A10 3a light blue 1.50 .70
O31 A10 4a purple brown 1.75 .90
O32 A10 6a Pruss blue 5.75 *12.50*
O33 A10 8a dark green 5.75 12.50

Overprinted Horizontally

p

O34 A11 1r dark brown 11.00 *12.50*
O35 A11 2r yellow brown 22.50 *45.00*
O36 A11 5r deep orange 52.50 *85.00*
O37 A11 10r red 95.00 *140.00*
Nos. O26-O37 (12) 206.05 328.60

Overprinted Vertically Reading Up

O38 A9(p) 25r violet 925.00 *1,200.*

For overprints see Nos. O39-O41, O43-O46, O48-O50, O54.

Kingdom

Nos. O15, O19, O22-O24, O26-O31, O33-O35, O38 Surcharged with New Values in Fils and Dinars, like Nos. 28-43

1932, Apr. 1

O39 A10 3f on ½a 4.25 4.00
O40 A10 4f on 1a (G) 3.00 .25
O41 A10 5f on 1a 3.00 .25
a. Inverted Arabic "5" *52.50* *35.00*
O42 A3 8f on 1½a 6.75 .60
O43 A10 10f on 2a 4.00 .25
O44 A10 15f on 3a 5.25 2.75
O45 A10 20f on 4a 5.25 2.75
O46 A10 25f on 4a 5.50 2.25
O47 A7 30f on 6a 5.75 2.00
O48 A10 40f on 8a 5.00 4.00
a. "Flis" for "Fils" *300.00* *450.00*
O49 A11 50f on 1r 6.75 4.00
O50 A11 75f on 1r 7.50 7.00
O51 A1 100f on 2r 22.00 4.00
O52 A6 200f on 5r 29.00 26.00
O53 A7 ½d on 10r 8.00 *100.00*
a. Bar in "½" omitted *850.00* *975.00*
O54 A9 1d on 25r 150.00 *210.00*
Nos. O39-O54 (16) 271.00 370.10

Regular Issue of 1932 Overprinted Vertically like Nos. O26-O33

1932, May 9

O55 A12 2f ultramarine 1.10 .30
O56 A12 3f green 1.10 .30
O57 A12 4f violet brn 1.40 .30
O58 A12 5f gray 1.40 .30
O59 A12 8f deep red 1.40 .30
O60 A12 10f yellow 2.50 .30
O61 A12 15f deep blue 3.00 .30
O62 A12 20f orange 3.00 .30
O63 A12 25f rose lilac 3.00 .45
O64 A12 30f olive grn 4.25 .45
O65 A12 40f dark violet 6.50 .45

Overprinted Horizontally Like Nos. O34 to O37

O66 A13 50f deep brown 4.00 .55
O67 A13 75f lt ultra 3.00 1.10
O68 A13 100f deep green 13.50 1.75
O69 A13 200f dark red 25.00 10.00

Overprinted Vertically like No. O38

O70 A14 ½d gray blue 17.50 25.00
O71 A14 1d claret 80.00 *125.00*
Nos. O55-O71 (17) 171.65 *167.15*

Regular Issue of 1934-38 Overprinted Type "o" Vertically Reading up in Black

1934-38 **Unwmk.**

O72 A15 1f purple ('38) 1.25 .75
O73 A15 2f ultramarine 1.25 .30
O74 A15 3f green .75 .30
O75 A15 4f purple brn 1.25 .30
O76 A15 5f gray green 1.10 .30
O77 A15 8f deep red 5.00 .30
O78 A15 10f yellow .55 .30
O79 A15 15f deep blue 11.00 2.00
O80 A15 20f orange 1.25 .30
O81 A15 25f brown violet 22.50 7.00
O82 A15 30f olive green 5.25 .30
O83 A15 40f dark violet 6.25 .45

Overprinted Type "p"

O84 A16 50f deep brown 1.25 .75
O85 A16 75f ultramarine 7.25 1.10
O86 A16 100f deep green 2.00 1.25
O87 A16 200f dark red 5.00 3.50

Overprinted Type "p" Vertically Reading Up

O88 A17 ½d gray blue 12.50 *20.00*
O89 A17 1d claret 50.00 *60.00*
Nos. O72-O89 (18) 135.40 99.20

Catalogue values for unused stamps in this section, from this point to the end of the section, are for Never Hinged items.

Stamps of 1941-42 Overprinted in Black or Red

r

s

Perf. 11½x13½, 13 to 14 and Compound

1941-42

O90 A18(r) 1f dk vio ('42) .75 .30
O91 A18(r) 2f choc ('42) .75 .30
O92 A19(r) 3f brt grn ('42) .75 .30
O93 A19(r) 4f pur (R) ('42) .75 .30
O94 A19(r) 5f dk car rose ('42) .75 .30
O95 A20(s) 8f carmine 2.00 .30
O96 A20(s) 8f ocher ('42) .75 .30
O97 A20(s) 10f ocher 14.00 .90
O98 A20(s) 10f car ('42) 1.75 .30
O99 A20(s) 15f dull blue 14.00 1.75
O100 A20(s) 15f blk (R) ('42) 2.75 .70
O101 A20(s) 20f black (R) 4.25 .70
O102 A20(s) 20f dl bl ('42) 1.50 .30
O103 A21(s) 25f dark vio 2.25 .70
O104 A21(r) 25f dk vio ('42) 2.50 .70
O105 A21(s) 30f dp org 2.25 .70
O106 A21(r) 30f dk org ('42) 2.25 .70
O107 A21(s) 40f brn org 1.25 .30
O108 A21(r) 40f chnt ('42) 2.25 .70
O109 A21(r) 50f ultra 3.75 .30
O110 A21(r) 75f rose vio 2.50 .90
O111 A22(s) 100f ol grn ('42) 5.00 .70
O112 A22(s) 200f dp org ('42) 7.00 2.00
O113 A23(r) ½d blue ('42) 22.50 20.00
O114 A23(r) 1d grnsh bl ('42) 40.00 29.00
Nos. O90-O114 (25) 138.25 63.45

The space between the English and Arabic on overprints "r" and "s" varies with the size of the stamps.

For overprints see Nos. O165, RA5.

Stamps of 1942 Overprinted in Black

1942 **Unwmk.** ***Perf. 13x13½***

O115 A24 1f violet & brown .75 .70
O116 A24 2f dark blue & brn .75 .70
O117 A24 3f lt green & brn .75 .70
O118 A24 4f dl brown & brn .75 .70
O119 A24 5f sage grn & brn 1.00 .90
O120 A24 6f red org & brn 1.00 .90
O121 A24 10f dl rose red & brn 1.25 1.15
O122 A24 12f yel green & brn 1.75 1.60
Nos. O115-O122 (8) 8.00 7.35

Stamps of 1948 Overprinted in Black

1948, Jan. 15 ***Perf. 11½x12***

Size: 17¾x20½mm

O123 A25 1f slate .35 .35
O124 A25 2f sepia .35 .45
O125 A25 3f emerald .35 .45
O126 A25 4f purple .35 .35
O127 A25 5f rose lake .35 .25
O128 A25 6f plum .35 .45
O129 A25 8f ocher .35 .45
O130 A25 10f rose red .35 .35
O131 A25 12f dark olive .35 .35
O132 A25 15f black 4.50 *6.75*
O133 A25 20f blue .35 .25
O134 A25 25f rose violet .35 .25
O135 A25 30f red org .35 .25
O136 A25 40f org brn .65 .45

Perf. 12x11½

Size: 22x27½mm

O137 A25 60f deep blue .90 .25
O138 A25 75f lilac rose 1.75 .40
O139 A25 100f olive grn 1.75 1.00
O140 A25 200f dp orange 2.75 1.00
O141 A25 ½d blue 22.50 16.00
O142 A25 1d green 32.50 35.00
Nos. O123-O142 (20) 71.50 65.05

For overprints see Nos. O166-O177, O257, O272, O274, O277, O282, RA1, RA3, RA4.

Same Overprint on Nos. 133-138

1949-51 ***Perf. 11½x12***

Size: 17¾x20½mm

O143 A25 3f rose lake ('51) 3.25 1.00
O144 A25 5f emerald ('51) 3.50 1.00
O145 A25 14f dk olive ('50) 1.75 .35
O146 A25 16f rose red ('51) 3.25 .35
O147 A25 28f blue ('51) 1.00 .35

Perf. 12x11½

Size: 22x27½mm

O148 A25 50f deep blue 1.25 .50
Nos. O143-O148 (6) 14.00 3.55

For overprints see #O258, O273, O275, O276.

Same Overprint in Black on Stamps and Type of 1954-57

1955-59 ***Perf. 11½x12***

O148A A28 1f blue ('56) .25 .25
O149 A28 2f chocolate .25 .25
O150 A28 3f rose lake .25 .25
O151 A28 4f violet .25 .25
O152 A28 5f emerald .25 .25
O153 A28 6f plum ('56) .25 .25
O154 A28 8f ocher ('56) .25 .25
O155 A28 10f blue .25 .25
O155A A28 16f brt rose ('57) 22.50 22.50
O156 A28 20f olive .45 .25
O157 A28 25f rose violet 2.25 1.00
O158 A28 30f vermilion 1.00 .25
O159 A28 40f orange brn .45 .25

Size: 22½x27½mm

O160 A28 50f blue 2.25 .75
O161 A28 60f pale pur 14.00 5.75
O161A A28 100f ol grn ('59) 32.50 16.00
Nos. O148A-O161A (16) 77.40 48.75

Dates of issue for Nos. O155A and O161A are suppositional.

For overprints see Nos. O178-O191, O259-O260, O283-O291.

Same Ovpt. on Stamps of 1957-58

O162 A33 1f blue 4.25 1.75
O162A A33 2f chocolate 5.00 3.75
O162B A33 3f dk carmine 6.50 2.75
O162C A33 4f dull violet 7.75 1.75
O162D A33 5f emerald 4.25 1.75
O163 A33 6f plum 4.25 2.75
O164 A33 10f blue 4.25 1.40
Nos. O162-O164 (7) 36.25 15.90

For overprints see #O192-O199, O292-O293.

Republic

Official Stamps of 1942-51 with Additional Overprint

Perf. 13½x14

1958-59 **Engr.** **Unwmk.**

O165 A22 200f dp orange 10.00 5.75

Perf. 11½x12, 12x11½

O166 A25 12f dk olive 1.00 .75
O167 A25 14f olive 1.10 .95
O168 A25 15f black .95 .50
O169 A25 16f rose red 3.75 2.10
O170 A25 25f rose vio 3.50 2.00
O171 A25 28f blue 2.00 1.60
O172 A25 40f orange brn 1.25 .95
O173 A25 60f deep blue 5.00 2.50
O174 A25 75f lilac rose 2.25 1.90
O175 A25 200f dp orange 2.75 2.40
O176 A25 ½d blue 17.00 6.25
O177 A25 1d green 27.50 12.50
Nos. O166-O177 (12) 68.05 34.40

Other denominations of types A22 and A25 exist with this overprint, but these were probably not regularly issued.

Same Ovpt. on Nos. O148A-O161A

O178 A28 1f blue .60 .25
O179 A28 2f chocolate .60 .25
O180 A28 3f rose lake .60 .25
O181 A28 4f violet .60 .25
O181A A28 5f emerald .65 .40
O182 A28 6f plum .60 .25
O183 A28 8f ocher .55 .25
O183A A28 10f blue .80 .25
O184 A28 16f bright rose 7.50 7.00
O185 A28 20f olive .65 .25
O186 A28 25f rose violet .65 .25
O187 A28 30f vermilion .70 .40
O188 A28 40f orange brn 1.00 .40
O189 A28 50f blue 1.00 .50
O190 A28 60f pale purple 1.00 .60
O191 A28 100f olive grn 2.10 .60
Nos. O178-O191 (16) 19.60 12.15

Same Ovpts. on #O162-O164, 216

O192 A33 1f blue .25 .25
O193 A33 2f chocolate .25 .25
O194 A33 3f dark carmine .45 .25
O195 A33 4f dull violet .25 .25
O196 A33 5f emerald .25 .25
O197 A33 6f plum .25 .25
O198 A33 8f ocher .65 .25
O199 A33 10f blue .70 .25
Nos. O192-O199 (8) 3.05 2.00

Nos. 232-233, 235-237, 242 Overprinted

Litho. & Photo.

1961, Apr. 1 **Unwmk.** ***Perf. 11½***

O200 A38 1f multi .40 .30
O201 A38 2f multi .40 .30
O202 A38 4f multi .40 .30

No.	Type	Description	Unused	Used
O203	A38	5f multi	.50	.30
O204	A38	10f multi	.80	.60
O205	A38	50f multi	13.50	10.50
		Nos. O200-O205 (6)	16.00	12.30

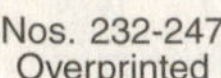

Nos. 232-247 Overprinted

Emblem in Gold, Red and Blue; Blue Inscriptions

1961

No.	Type	Description	Unused	Used
O206	A38	1f gray	.40	.30
O207	A38	2f salmon	.40	.30
O208	A38	3f pale violet	.40	.30
O209	A38	4f bright yel	.40	.30
O210	A38	5f light blue	.40	.30
O211	A38	10f bright pink	.40	.30
O212	A38	15f lt green	.40	.30
O213	A38	20f bister brn	.40	.30
O214	A38	30f light gray	.50	.30
O215	A38	40f orange yel	.50	.30
O216	A38	50f yel green	.60	.30
O217	A38	75f pale green	.80	.40
O218	A38	100f orange	.90	.65
O219	A38	200f lilac	3.25	1.40
O220	A38	500f bister	11.50	5.50
O221	A38	1d brt green	22.50	11.50
		Nos. O206-O221 (16)	43.75	22.75

Nos. 480-482 Overprinted

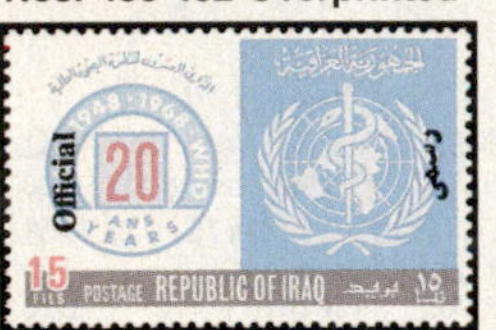

1971 **Litho.** ***Perf. 13½***

No.	Type	Description	Unused	Used
O222	A115	10f multicolored	.80	1.50
O223	A115	15f blue & multi	8.00	1.50
O224	A115	25f multicolored	8.00	3.00
		Nos. O222-O224 (3)	16.80	6.00

Overprint lines are spaced 16mm on No. O222, 32½mm on Nos. O223-O224.

Same Overprint on Nos. 453, 455-456

1971 ***Perf. 13***

No.	Type	Description	Unused	Used
O225	A107	5f lilac & multi	6.00	.30
O226	A107	15f rose red & multi	6.00	.50
O227	A107	25f vio bl & multi	8.50	1.50
		Nos. O225-O227 (3)	20.50	2.30

Overprint horizontal on Nos. O225 and O227; vertical, reading down on No. O226. Distance between English and Arabic words: 8mm.

See No. O308 for 15f stamp with horizontal overprint.

Nos. 446, 448-449 Overprinted

1971 **Litho.** ***Perf. 13***

No.	Type	Description	Unused	Used
O228	A105	15f multicolored	1.50	.65
O229	A105	15f multi, wide ovpt. setting	62.50	7.50
a.		Narrow setting		47.50
O230	A105	25f multicolored	10.50	3.00
O231	A105	30f multicolored	10.50	3.00
		Nos. O228-O231 (4)	85.00	14.15

No. O229 overprinted "Official" horizontally. Two overprint settings on O229: wide, 6.5mm between English and Arab inscriptions; narrow, 2mm between inscriptions.

Same Overprint on Nos. 483-486

1972 ***Perf. 13½***

No.	Type	Description	Unused	Used
O232	A116	10f multicolored	5.00	.50
O233	A116	25f multicolored	5.00	1.00

1972

No.	Type	Description	Unused	Used
O234	A117	15f multicolored	5.00	.50
O235	A117	25f multicolored	5.00	1.00

Same Overprint, "Official" Reading Down on Nos. 562-565

1972

No.	Type	Description	Unused	Used
O240	A142	5f multicolored	5.00	3.75
O241	A142	10f multicolored	5.00	3.75
O242	A142	15f multicolored	5.00	3.75
O243	A142	35f multicolored	5.00	3.75
		Nos. O240-O243 (4)	20.00	15.00

Latin inscription on Nos. O240-O241 obliterated with heavy bar.

No. 487 Overprinted "Official" like No. CO5

1972 **Photo.** ***Perf. 13½***

No.	Type	Description	Unused	Used
O244	A118	25f multicolored	10.50	3.00

Nos. O134, O148 Ovptd. with 3 Bars

Perf. 11½x12, 12x11½

1973, Jan. 29 **Engr.**

No.	Type	Description	Unused	Used
O257	A25	25f rose violet	6.00	1.50
O258	A25	50f deep blue	6.00	5.50

Same on Nos. O157 and O160

No.	Type	Description	Unused	Used
O259	A28	25f rose violet	6.00	1.50
O260	A28	50f blue	6.00	1.50

Type of 1957 Overprinted

Size: 22x27½mm

No.	Type	Description	Unused	Used
O261	A33	50f rose violet	6.00	1.50
		Nos. O257-O261 (5)	30.00	11.50

See note after No. 679. No. O261 not issued without overprints.

King Faisal Issues Overprinted

Two sizes of overprint: Arabic 6½mm or 9mm.

1973

No.	Type	Description	Unused	Used
O263	A28	15f black (#149)	4.00	3.75
O264	A33	15f black	4.00	1.00
O265	A25	25f rose vio (#121)	15.00	6.00
O266	A28	25f rose vio (#151)	4.00	1.00
O267	A33	25f rose violet	4.00	1.00

Same Overprint on Nos. 674-677

No.	Type	Description	Unused	Used
O268	A28	10f blue	3.75	3.75
O269	A33	10f blue	52.50	60.00
O270	A28	15f black	67.50	75.00
O271	A33	15f black	2.50	2.00
		Nos. O263-O271 (9)	157.25	153.50

Official Stamps of 1948-51 Overprinted

Overprint design faces left or right.

1973

No.	Type	Description	Unused	Used
O272	A25	12f (#O131)	1.75	.30
O273	A25	14f (#O145)	1.75	.50
O274	A25	15f (#O132)	1.75	.50
O275	A25	16f (#O146)	3.25	.85
O276	A25	28f (#O147)	6.75	1.10
O277	A25	30f (#O135)	6.75	.95
O278	A25	40f (#O136)	6.75	1.40
O279	A25	60f (#O137)	6.75	5.25
O280	A25	100f (#O139)	22.50	8.50
O281	A25	½d (#O141)	57.50	22.50
O282	A25	1d (#O142)	110.00	110.00
		Nos. O272-O282 (11)	225.50	151.85

Same Overprint on Official Stamps of 1955-59

No.	Type	Description	Unused	Used
O283	A28	3f (#O150)	1.75	.60
O284	A28	6f (#O153)	1.75	.60
O285	A28	8f (#O154)	1.75	.60
O286	A28	16f (#O155A)	*15.00*	*15.00*
O287	A28	20f (#O156)	1.75	.60
O288	A28	30f (#O158)	1.75	.95
O289	A28	40f (#O159)	1.75	1.60
O290	A28	60f (#O161)	8.75	2.00
O291	A28	100f (#O161A)	*27.50*	*8.00*
		Nos. O283-O291 (9)	*61.75*	*29.95*

Same Overprint on 1957-58 Issues

No.	Type	Description	Unused	Used
O292	A33	3f dk car (#O162B)	5.00	1.25
O293	A33	6f plum (#O163)	5.00	1.25
O294	A33	8f ocher (#179)	5.00	1.25
O295	A33	30f red orange	5.00	1.25
		Nos. O292-O295 (4)	20.00	5.00

The overprint on Nos. O294-O295 includes the "On State Service" overprint; No. O295 was not issued without overprints. The overprint leaf design faces left or right and varies in size.

Nos. 403, 497, 681 Overprinted

Perf. 12½, 13x12½, 13½

1974 (?) **Photo., Litho.**

No.	Type	Description	Unused	Used
O296	A89	2f multicolored	5.00	
O297	A123	15f multicolored	6.00	.50
O298	A185	25f multicolored	3.75	1.00
		Nos. O296-O298 (3)	14.75	

Size of "Official" on Nos. O297-O298 9mm.

Nos. 683-691 Overprinted

1974 **Litho.** ***Perf. 13x12½***

No.	Type	Description	Unused	Used
O299	A186	5f orange & blk	.30	.30
O300	A186	10f bister & blk	.30	.30
O301	A186	20f brt rose & blk	.65	.30
O302	A186	25f ultra & blk	1.25	1.25
O303	A186	35f emerald & blk	1.25	.50
O304	A186	45f blue & black	1.25	.60
O305	A186	50f olive & yel	1.75	.65
O306	A186	70f violet & yel	1.75	.95
O307	A186	95f brown & yel	2.50	1.10
		Nos. O299-O307 (9)	11.00	5.95

Nos. 455 and 467 Overprinted

1975 **Litho.** ***Perf. 13, 14***

No.	Type	Description	Unused	Used
O308	A107	15f multicolored	3.50	3.50
O311	A110	30f multicolored	6.25	4.25

Space between Arabic and English lines of overprint is 4mm on No. O308, 13mm on No. O311.

See No. O226 for 15d stamp with vertical overprint.

Nos. 491-493 Overprinted or Surcharged like Nos. CO5-CO7

1975 ***Perf. 14***

No.	Type	Description	Unused	Used
O312	A121	10f multicolored	6.50	4.00
O312A	A121	15f on 3f multi	6.50	4.00
O313	A121	25f on 2f multi	6.50	4.00
		Nos. O312-O313 (3)	19.50	12.00

Nos. 322-325 Overprinted

Engr.; Engr. & Photo.

1975 ***Perf. 12x11***

No.	Type	Description	Unused	Used
O314	A57	10f rose red	8.00	.60
O315	A57	15f brown & buff	8.00	.75
O316	A57	20f violet blue	8.00	.75
O317	A57	30f orange	15.00	.80
		Nos. O314-O317 (4)	39.00	2.90

Arms of Iraq — O1

1975 **Photo.** ***Perf. 14***

No.	Type	Description	Unused	Used
O318	O1	5f multicolored	.30	.30
O319	O1	10f blue & multi	.30	.30
O320	O1	15f yel & multi	.40	.40
O321	O1	20f ultra & multi	.65	.65
O322	O1	25f org & multi	.90	.90
O323	O1	30f rose & multi	1.00	1.00
O324	O1	50f multicolored	1.75	1.75
O325	O1	100f multicolored	3.25	3.25
		Nos. O318-O325 (8)	8.55	8.55

Nos. 787-791 Overprinted "OFFICIAL" in English and Arabic

1976, Sept. 15 **Litho.** ***Perf. 13½x14***

No.	Type	Description	Unused	Used
O327	A219	5f multicolored	1.25	.75
O328	A219	10f multicolored	1.25	.95
O329	A219	15f multicolored	1.40	.95
O330	A219	25f multicolored	3.75	1.25
O331	A219	50f multicolored	6.25	2.25
		Nos. O327-O331 (5)	13.90	6.15

Altharthar - Euphrates Canal — O2

1978 **Photo.** ***Perf. 11½***

No.	Type	Description	Unused	Used
O332	O2	5f multicolored	.30	.30
O333	O2	10f multicolored	.30	.30
O334	O2	15f multicolored	.45	.30
O335	O2	25f multicolored	.90	.30
		Nos. O332-O335 (4)	1.95	1.20

Baghdad University Entrance — O3

1981, Oct. 21 **Litho.** ***Perf. 12x12½***

No.	Type	Description	Unused	Used
O336	O3	45f multicolored	.65	.40
O337	O3	50f multicolored	.70	.50

Nos. O336-O337 Surcharged

1983, May 15 **Litho.** ***Perf. 12x12½***

No.	Type	Description	Unused	Used
O338	O3	60f on 45f multi	2.50	.50
O339	O3	70f on 50f multi	3.00	.75

Martyrs Type of 1981 Inscribed "OFFICIAL" in English and Arabic

1981 **Photo.** ***Perf. 14***

No.	Type	Description	Unused	Used
O339A	A303	45f silver border	1.25	.40
O339B	A303	50f gold border	1.25	.50
O339C	A303	120f metallic bl border	3.50	1.10
		Nos. O339A-O339C (3)	6.00	2.00

Building Type of 1983 Inscribed "OFFICIAL" in English and Arabic

1982, Dec. 31 **Litho.** ***Perf. 14***

No.	Type	Description	Unused	Used
O340	A324	60f multicolored	.90	.50
O341	A324	70f multicolored	1.00	.65

For surcharge see No. 1517.

Martyr Type of 1984 Inscribed "OFFICIAL" in English and Arabic

1984, Dec. 1 ***Perf. 13½***

No.	Type	Description	Unused	Used
O342	A329	20f multicolored	.30	.30
O343	A329	30f multicolored	.30	.30
O344	A329	50f multicolored	.55	.40
O345	A329	60f multicolored	.70	.40
		Nos. O342-O345 (4)	1.85	1.40

No. RA22 Overprinted

1985 (?) **Litho.** ***Perf. 13x12½***

No.	Type	Description	Unused	Used
O346	PT2	5f bister, blk & yel	3.25	1.00

POSTAL TAX STAMPS

Catalogue values for unused stamps in this section are for Never Hinged items.

Nos. O125 and 115 Surcharged in Carmine or Black

1949 Unwmk. *Perf. 11½x12*
RA1 A25 2f on 3f emer (C) *25.00* *15.00*
RA2 A25 2f on 6f plum *32.50* *14.00*

Similar Overprint in Carmine or Black on Nos. O124, O127 and O94, Middle Arabic Line Omitted
Perf. 11½x12
RA3 A25 2f sepia (C) *20.00* *9.00*
RA4 A25 5f rose lake *40.00* *20.00*
Perf. 12x13½, 14
RA5 A19 5f dark car rose *20.00* *10.50*

Larger overprint on #RA5, 20½mm wide. Value $22.50.

No. 115 Surcharged in Black

Perf. 11½x12
RA6 A25 5f on 6f plum *45.00* *17.00*

The tax on Nos. RA1-RA6 was to aid the war in Palestine.

Nos. 317, 322-326 Surcharged

Engr.; Engr. & Photo.
1963 *Perf. 12x11*
RA7 A57 5f on 1f green 3.75 4.50
RA8 A57 5f on 10f rose red 3.75 4.50
RA9 A57 5f on 15f brn & buff 3.75 4.50
RA10 A57 5f on 20f vio blue 3.75 4.50
RA11 A57 5f on 30f orange 3.75 4.50
RA12 A57 5f on 40f brt green 3.75 4.50
Nos. RA7-RA12 (6) 22.50 27.00

Surtax was for the Defense Fund.

PT1

1967, Aug. Photo. *Perf. 13½*
RA13 PT1 5f brown .45 .25

Surtax was for flood victims.

No. RA13 Overprinted

1967, Nov.
RA14 PT1 5f brown .45 .45

Surtax was for Defense Fund.

Nos. 305A-305B with Surcharge Similar to Nos. RA7-RA12

1972 Litho. *Perf. 13½x14*
RA15 A54a 5f on 14f 7.00 7.00
RA16 A54a 5f on 35f 7.00 7.00

Surtax was for the Defense Fund. The 2 disks obliterating old denominations are on one line at the bottom. Size of Arabic inscription: 17x12mm.

No. 452 with Surcharge Similar to Nos. RA7-RA12, and Nos. 443, 457 and 526 Srchd.

1973 Litho. *Perf. 13*
RA17 A105 5f on 2f multi 8.50 8.50
RA18 A107 5f on 2f multi 8.50 8.50
RA19 A108 5f on 2f multi 8.50 8.50
RA20 A135 5f on 2f multi 8.50 8.50
Nos. RA17-RA20 (4) 34.00 34.00

Surtax was for the Defense Fund. Surcharges on Nos. RA17-RA20 are adjusted to fit shape of stamps and to obliterate old denominations.

No 683 Overprinted

1974 Litho. *Perf. 13x12½*
RA21 A186 5f orange & blk 6.00 4.00

Soldier — PT2

1974
RA22 PT2 5f bister, blk & yel 2.50 *3.00*

Surtax of Nos. RA21-RA22 was for the Defense Fund.
For overprint see No. O346.

Dome of the Rock, Jerusalem — PT3

1977 Photo. *Perf. 14*
RA23 PT3 5f multicolored 2.75 1.50

Surtax was for families of Palestinians.
For surcharges see Nos. 1457, 1465-1477.

AIR POST POSTAL TAX STAMPS

Catalogue values for unused stamps in this section are for Never Hinged items.

No. C15 Surcharged Like Nos. RA17-RA20

1973 Litho. *Perf. 13½*
RAC1 AP5 5f on 2f multi 8.50 8.50

Surtax was for the Defense Fund.

IRELAND

'ir-lənd

(Eire)

LOCATION — Comprises the entire island of Ireland, except 5,237 square miles at the extreme north
GOVT. — Republic
AREA — 27,136 sq. mi.
POP. — 3,626,087 (1996)
CAPITAL — Dublin

12 Pence = 1 Shilling
100 Pence = 1 Pound (Punt) (1971)
100 Cents = 1 Euro (2002)

Catalogue values for unused stamps in this country are for Never Hinged items, beginning with Scott 99 in the regular postage section, Scott C1 in the air post section, and Scott J5 in the postage due section.

Watermarks

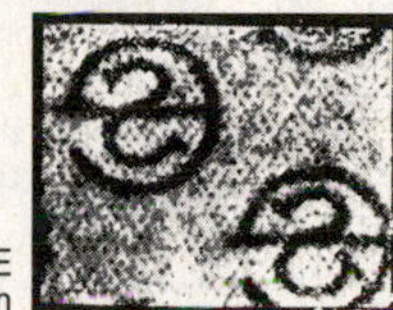
Wmk. 44 — SE in Monogram

The letters "SE" are the initials of "Saorstat Eireann" (Irish Free State).

Wmk. 262 — Multiple "e"

Overprinted by Dollard, Ltd.

Great Britain Nos. 159-167, 170-172, 179-181 Overprinted

Overprint means "Provisional Government of Ireland."

Overprint measures 15x17½mm
Black or Gray Black Overprint

1922, Feb. 17 Wmk. 33 *Perf. 15x14*
1 A82 ½p green 2.00 1.35
Never hinged 3.40
a. Inverted overprint 450.00 *625.00*
Never hinged *750.00*
b. Date omitted 110.00 *90.00*
2 A83 1p scarlet 3.40 1.35
Never hinged 5.00
a. Inverted overprint 300.00 *500.00*
Never hinged *450.00*
b. Double overprint *1,600.*
3 A86 2½p ultra 3.40 *14.50*
Never hinged 13.50
4 A87 3p violet 9.00 *12.00*
Never hinged 16.00
5 A88 4p slate green 9.00 *22.50*
Never hinged 15.00
6 A89 5p yel brown 9.00 *20.00*
Never hinged 16.00
7 A90 9p black brown 26.00 *40.00*
Never hinged 47.50
8 A90 10p light blue 16.00 *32.50*
Never hinged 27.00
Nos. 1-8 (8) 77.80 *144.20*

The ½p with red overprint is a proof. Value, $150.

Red or Carmine Overprint

1922, Apr.-July
9 A86 2½p ultra (R) 2.75 *8.50*
Never hinged 5.50
10 A88 4p sl grn (R) 16.00 *27.00*
Never hinged 32.50
10A A88 4p sl grn (C) 80.00 *130.00*
Never hinged 135.00
11 A90 9p blk brn (R) 32.50 *35.00*
Never hinged 55.00
11A A90 9p blk brn (C) 135.00 *160.00*
Never hinged 200.00
Nos. 9-11A (5) 266.25 *360.50*

Overprinted in Black

There is a variation that is 21x14mm. The "h" and "é" are 1mm apart. See Nos. 36-38.

Overprint measures 21½x14mm

1922, Feb. 17 Wmk. 34 *Perf. 11x12*
12 A91 2sh6p brown 55.00 *100.00*
Never hinged 145.00
a. Double overprint, one albino 1,200. —
13 A91 5sh car rose 90.00 *190.00*
Never hinged 210.00
a. Double overprint, one albino 1,200. —
14 A91 10sh gray blue 225.00 *400.00*
Never hinged 450.00
Nos. 12-14 (3) 370.00 *690.00*

Overprinted by Alex. Thom & Co.

Overprinted in Black

TWO PENCE
Die I — Four horizontal lines above the head. Heavy colored lines above and below the bottom tablet. The inner frame line is closer to the central design than it is to the outer frame line.
Die II — Three lines above the head. Thinner lines above and below the bottom tablet. The inner frame line is midway between the central design and the outer frame line.

Overprint measures 14½x16mm

1922, Feb. 17 Wmk. 33 *Perf. 15x14*
15 A84 1½p red brown 3.25 *2.75*
Never hinged 4.50
a. "PENCF" 540.00 *475.00*
16 A85 2p orange (II) 5.50 2.00
Never hinged 6.50
a. Inverted overprint (II) 375.00 *450.00*
b. 2p orange (I) 5.00 1.75
As "b," never hinged 6.50
c. Inverted overprint (I) 200.00 *300.00*
17 A89 6p red violet 20.00 *27.50*
Never hinged 27.50
18 A90 1sh bister 22.50 20.00
Never hinged 42.50
Nos. 15-18 (4) 51.25 52.25

Important: see Nos. 25-26, 31, 35.

Overprinted by Harrison & Sons

Overprinted in Black in Glossy Black Ink

Overprint measures 15¼x17mm

1922, June Coil Stamps
19 A82 ½p green 5.50 *22.50*
Never hinged 7.00
20 A83 1p scarlet 4.50 *18.00*
Never hinged 6.75
21 A84 1½p red brown 7.25 *52.50*
Never hinged 11.00
22 A85 2p orange (I) 27.00 *45.00*
Never hinged 42.50
a. 2p orange (II) 27.00 *42.50*
Never hinged 45.00
Nos. 19-22 (4) 44.25 *138.00*

In Harrison overprint, "i" of "Rialtas" extends below the base of the other letters.

The Harrison stamps were issued in coils, either horizontal or vertical. The paper is double where the ends of the strips were overlapped. Mint pairs with the overlap sell for about three times the price of a single. The perforations are often clipped.

Overprinted by Alex. Thom & Co.
Stamps of Great Britain, 1912-22 Overprinted as Nos. 15 to 18, in Shiny to Dull Blue Black, or Red

Note: The blue black overprints can best be distinguished from the black by use of 50-power magnification with a light source behind the stamp.

Overprint measures 14½x16mm

1922, July-Nov. *Perf. 15x14*

No.	Type	Description	Unused	Used
23	A82	½p green	3.50	1.80
		Never hinged	5.00	
24	A83	1p scarlet	3.00	2.00
		Never hinged	3.50	
25	A84	1½p red brown	6.00	*9.00*
		Never hinged	13.50	
26	A85	2p orange (II)	5.50	2.00
		Never hinged	6.50	
a.		Inverted overprint (II)	375.00	*500.00*
b.		2p orange (I)	32.50	3.75
		Never hinged	45.00	
27	A86	2½p ultra (R)	9.00	*32.50*
		Never hinged	18.00	
28	A87	3p violet	10.00	*6.50*
		Never hinged	12.50	
29	A88	4p sl grn (R)	4.50	*11.00*
		Never hinged	11.00	
30	A89	5p yellow brown	9.00	*16.00*
		Never hinged	18.00	
31	A89	6p red violet	15.00	6.75
		Never hinged	18.00	
32	A90	9p blk brn (R)	20.00	*26.00*
		Never hinged	35.00	
33	A90	9p ol grn (R)	11.00	*45.00*
		Never hinged	20.00	
34	A90	10p light blue	27.50	*67.50*
		Never hinged	60.00	
35	A90	1sh bister	15.00	*15.00*
		Never hinged	32.50	
		Nos. 23-35 (13)	139.00	*241.05*

Nos. 23, 24, 28, 34 overprinted in dull black, rather than the normal blue-black, are believed to be proofs, pressed into use when supplies of the issued values ran low.

Overprinted as Nos. 12 to 14 in Blue Black (Shiny to Dull)

The "h" and "é" are ½mm apart.

Overprint measures 21x13½mm

1922 **Wmk. 34** *Perf. 11x12*

No.	Type	Description	Unused	Used
36	A91	2sh6p gray brn	290.	*400.*
		Never hinged	500.	
37	A91	5sh car rose	300.	*450.*
		Never hinged	525.	
38	A91	10sh gray blue	1,700.	*2,000.*
		Never hinged	2,400.	
		Nos. 36-38 (3)	2,290.	*2,850.*

Overprinted in Blue Black

Overprint measures 15¾x16mm

1922, Dec. **Wmk. 33** *Perf. 15x14*

No.	Type	Description	Unused	Used
39	A82	½p green	1.35	*2.50*
		Never hinged	2.50	
40	A83	1p scarlet	5.50	*4.50*
		Never hinged	8.00	
41	A84	1½p red brown	3.25	*16.00*
		Never hinged	7.25	
42	A85	2p orange (II)	13.50	13.50
		Never hinged	22.50	
43	A90	1sh bister	45.00	*72.50*
		Never hinged	60.00	
		Nos. 39-43 (5)	68.60	*109.00*

Stamps of Great Britain, 1912-22, Overprinted in Shiny to Dull Blue Black or Red

This overprint means "Irish Free State"

The inner loop of the "9" is an upright oval.

The measurement of "1922" is made across the bottom of the numerals and does not include the serif at the top of the "1."

There were 5 plates for printing the overprint on Nos. 44-55. In the impressions from plate I the 12th stamp in the 15th row has no accent on the 2nd "A" of "SAORSTAT." To correct this an accent was inserted by hand, sometimes this was in a reversed position.

On Nos. 56-58 the accent was omitted on the 2nd stamp in the 3rd and 8th rows. Damage to the plate makes the accent look reversed on the 4th stamp in the 7th row. The top of the "t" slants down in a line with the so-called accent.

Overprint measures 15x8½mm
"1922" is 6¼mm long

1922-23 **Wmk. 33** *Perf. 15x14*

No.	Type	Description	Unused	Used
44	A82	½p green	1.80	1.35
		Never hinged	2.50	
a.		Accent omitted	1,275.	*900.00*
b.		Accent added	115.00	*135.00*
45	A83	1p scarlet	2.25	1.35
		Never hinged	2.50	
a.		Accent omitted	*15,250.*	*9,000.*
b.		Accent added	145.00	*165.00*
c.		Accent and final "t" omitted	*13,500.*	*7,250.*
d.		Accent and final "t" added	225.00	*270.00*
46	A84	1½p red brn	3.25	*16.00*
		Never hinged	9.00	
47	A85	2p org (II)	2.75	*4.50*
		Never hinged	7.50	
48	A86	2½p ultra (R)	6.75	*13.00*
		Never hinged	9.00	
a.		Accent omitted	145.00	*180.00*
49	A87	3p violet	9.00	*11.50*
		Never hinged	20.00	
a.		Accent omitted	300.00	*390.00*
50	A88	4p sl grn (R)	5.50	*12.50*
		Never hinged	10.00	
a.		Accent omitted	200.00	*270.00*
51	A89	5p yel brn	5.25	*5.25*
		Never hinged	9.50	
52	A89	6p dull vio	3.50	2.75
		Never hinged	6.50	
a.		Accent added	*825.00*	*825.00*
53	A90	9p ol grn (R)	10.00	*11.00*
		Never hinged	12.50	
a.		Accent omitted	250.00	*315.00*
54	A90	10p lt blue	18.00	*52.50*
		Never hinged	45.00	
55	A90	1sh bister	13.50	*13.50*
		Never hinged	35.00	
a.		Accent omitted	*11,000.*	*11,000.*
b.		Accent added	*750.00*	*825.00*

Perf. 11x12

Wmk. 34

No.	Type	Description	Unused	Used
56	A91	2sh6p lt brown	57.50	*90.00*
		Never hinged	125.00	
a.		Accent omitted	410.00	*540.00*
57	A91	5sh car rose	90.00	*180.00*
		Never hinged	225.00	
a.		Accent omitted	550.00	*825.00*
58	A91	10sh gray blue	200.00	*450.00*
		Never hinged	500.00	
a.		Accent omitted	*2,750.*	*3,600.*
		Nos. 44-58 (15)	429.05	*865.20*

Overprinted by Harrison & Sons

Coil Stamps

Same Ovpt. in Black or Blue Black

1923 **Wmk. 33** *Perf. 15x14*

No.	Type	Description	Unused	Used
59	A82	½p green	3.00	*13.50*
		Never hinged	6.50	
a.		Tall "1"	18.00	50.00
		Never hinged	27.50	
60	A83	1p scarlet	7.75	*21.00*
		Never hinged	15.00	
a.		Tall "1"	72.50	145.00
		Never hinged	95.00	
61	A84	1½p red brown	7.75	*50.00*
		Never hinged	22.50	
a.		Tall "1"	90.00	225.00
		Never hinged	170.00	
62	A85	2p orange (II)	11.00	*18.00*
		Never hinged	17.00	
a.		Tall "1"	32.50	*55.00*
		Never hinged	40.00	
		Nos. 59-62 (4)	29.50	*102.50*

These stamps were issued in coils, made by joining horizontal or vertical strips of the stamps. See 2nd paragraph after No. 22. In some strips there were two stamps with the "1" of "1922" 2½mm high and with serif at foot.

In this setting the middle "e" of "eireann" is a trifle above the line of the other letters, making the word appear slightly curved. The lower end of the "1" of "1922" is rounded on Nos. 59-62 instead of flat as on Nos. 44-47.

The inner loop of the "9" is round.

See Nos. 77b, 78b and 79b.

Booklet Panes

For very fine, the perforation holes at top or bottom of the pane should be visible, though not necessarily perfect half circles.

"Sword of Light" — A1

Map of Ireland — A2

Coat of Arms — A3

Celtic Cross — A4

Perf. 15x14

1922-23 **Typo.** **Wmk. 44**

No.	Type	Description	Unused	Used
65	A1	½p emerald	2.75	1.50
		Never hinged	4.50	
a.		Booklet pane of 6	*350.00*	
66	A2	1p car rose	2.25	1.50
		Never hinged	4.50	
a.		Booklet pane of 6	*350.00*	
b.		Booklet pane of 3 + 3 labels	*400.00*	
67	A2	1½p claret	3.75	3.00
		Never hinged	8.50	
68	A2	2p deep green	2.25	.75
		Never hinged	3.50	
a.		Booklet pane of 6	*350.00*	
b.		Perf. 15 horiz. ('35)	*12,500.*	*2,000.*

No. 68b is valued in the grade of fine.

No.	Type	Description	Unused	Used
69	A3	2½p chocolate	5.50	*8.50*
		Never hinged	11.00	
70	A4	3p ultra	3.50	3.00
		Never hinged	7.25	
71	A3	4p slate	6.25	*6.25*
		Never hinged	12.50	
72	A1	5p deep violet	22.50	15.00
		Never hinged	57.50	
73	A1	6p red violet	7.25	5.75
		Never hinged	14.50	
74	A3	9p violet	35.00	25.00
		Never hinged	125.00	
75	A4	10p brown	17.00	*35.00*
		Never hinged	57.50	
76	A1	1sh light blue	35.00	17.00
		Never hinged	110.00	
		Nos. 65-76 (12)	143.00	122.25

The 2p was issued in 1922; other denominations in 1923.

No. 68b is a vertical coil stamp.

See Nos. 87, 91-92, 105-117, 137-138, 225-226, 326. For types overprinted see Nos. 118-119.

Overprinted by the Government Printing Office, Dublin Castle and British Board of Inland Revenue at Somerset House, London

Great Britain Nos. 179-181 Ovptd. in Black or Gray Black

The measurement of "1922" is made across the bottom of the numerals and does not include the serif at the top of the "1."

"1922" is 5½mm long

1925 **Wmk. 34** *Perf. 11x12*

No.	Type	Description	Unused	Used
77	A91	2sh6p gray brown	70.00	*175.00*
		Never hinged	125.00	
78	A91	5sh rose red	95.00	*275.00*
		Never hinged	160.00	
79	A91	10sh gray blue	225.00	*575.00*
		Never hinged	425.00	
		Nos. 77-79 (3)	390.00	*1,025.*

In 1927 the 2sh6p, 5sh and 10sh stamps were overprinted from a plate in which the Thom and Castle clichés were combined, thus including wide and narrow "1922" in the same setting.

Overprinted by British Board of Inland Revenue at Somerset House, London

Pair with "1922" Wide and Narrow

1927

No.	Type	Description	Unused	Used
77a	A91	2sh6p	400.	
		Never hinged	775.	
78a	A91	5sh	700.	
		Never hinged	1,350.	
79a	A91	10sh	1,700.	
		Never hinged	3,750.	
		Nos. 77a-79a (3)	2,800.	

Wide "1922"
"1922" is 6¼mm long

1927-28

No.	Type	Description	Unused	Used
77b	A91	2sh6p	60.00	*60.00*
		Never hinged	110.00	
78b	A91	5sh ('28)	90.00	*140.00*
		Never hinged	225.00	
79b	A91	10sh ('28)	250.00	*425.00*
		Never hinged	550.00	
		Nos. 77b-79b (3)	400.00	625.00

Daniel O'Connell — A5

Perf. 15x14

1929, June 22 **Wmk. 44**

No.	Type	Description	Unused	Used
80	A5	2p dark green	.75	.55
		Never hinged	1.25	
81	A5	3p dark blue	4.25	*14.00*
		Never hinged	15.00	
82	A5	9p dark violet	4.75	*13.50*
		Never hinged	16.00	
		Nos. 80-82 (3)	9.75	*28.05*

Catholic Emancipation in Ireland, centenary.

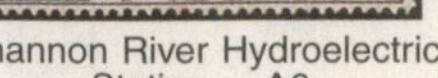

Shannon River Hydroelectric Station — A6

1930, Oct. 15

No.	Type	Description	Unused	Used
83	A6	2p black brown	1.25	*2.75*
		Never hinged	4.25	

Opening of the hydroelectric development of the River Shannon.

Farmer with Scythe — A7

1931, June 12

No.	Type	Description	Unused	Used
84	A7	2p pale blue	1.00	*1.50*
		Never hinged	2.50	

Bicentenary of Royal Dublin Society.

Cross of Cong and Chalice — A8

1932, May 12

No.	Type	Description	Unused	Used
85	A8	2p dark green	2.50	.85
		Never hinged	3.50	
86	A8	3p bright blue	4.50	*8.00*
		Never hinged	7.00	

International Eucharistic Congress.

Type of 1922-23 Issue
Coil Stamp

1933-34 *Perf. 15 Horizontally*

No.	Type	Description	Unused	Used
87	A2	1p rose ('34)	27.50	*60.00*
		Never hinged	45.00	
a.		1p carmine rose	125.00	*300.00*
		Never hinged	200.00	

No. 87a has a single perforation at each side near the top, while No. 87 is perforated top and bottom only.

See No. 68b.

Adoration of the Cross — A9

1933, Sept. 18 *Perf. 15x14*

No.	Type	Description	Unused	Used
88	A9	2p slate green	1.25	.55
		Never hinged	2.50	
89	A9	3p deep blue	3.00	*6.00*
		Never hinged	8.75	

Holy Year.

Hurling — A10

1934, July 27

No.	Type	Description	Unused	Used
90	A10	2p green	1.00	1.50
		Never hinged	2.50	

50th anniv. of the Gaelic Athletic Assoc.

Types of 1922-23
Coil Stamps
Wmk. 44 Sideways

1934 *Perf. 14 Vertically*

No.	Type	Description	Unused	Used
91	A1	½p green	30.00	*75.00*
		Never hinged	45.00	
92	A2	2p gray green	50.00	*125.00*
		Never hinged	85.00	

Overprinted by Harrison & Sons
Great Britain Nos. 222-224
Overprinted in Black

1935 Wmk. 34 *Perf. 11x12*

93 A91 2sh6p brown 52.50 70.00
Never hinged 100.00
94 A91 5sh carmine 200.00 225.00
Never hinged 350.00
95 A91 10sh dark blue 400.00 *650.00*
Never hinged 1,100.
Nos. 93-95 (3) 652.50 945.00

Waterlow printing can be distinguished by the crossed lines in the background of portrait. Previous issues have horizontal lines only.

St. Patrick and Paschal Fire — A11

1937, Sept. 8 Wmk. 44 *Perf. 14x15*

96 A11 2sh6p bright green 90.00 90.00
Never hinged 225.00
97 A11 5sh brown violet 110.00 110.00
Never hinged 250.00
98 A11 10sh dark blue 90.00 90.00
Never hinged 225.00
Nos. 96-98 (3) 290.00 290.00

See Nos. 121-123.

Catalogue values for unused stamps in this section, from this point to the end of the section, are for Never Hinged items.

Allegory of Ireland and Constitution A12

1937, Dec. 29 *Perf. 15x14*

99 A12 2p plum 2.00 .30
100 A12 3p deep blue 7.00 5.50

Constitution Day.
See Nos. 169-170.

Father Theobald Mathew A13

1938, July 1

101 A13 2p black brown 2.50 .50
102 A13 3p ultramarine 9.00 8.50

Temperance Crusade by Father Mathew, centenary.

Washington, US Eagle and Harp — A14

1939, Mar. 1

103 A14 2p bright carmine 1.50 .50
104 A14 3p deep blue 10.00 9.00

US Constitution, 150th anniv.

Type of 1922-23
Coil Stamp

1940-46 Wmk. 262 *Perf. 15 Horiz.*

105 A2 1p car rose ('46) 40.00 32.50
a. Perf. 14 horiz. 60.00 60.00

Types of 1922-23

1940-42 *Perf. 15x14*

Size: 18x22mm

106 A1 ½p emerald ('41) 2.75 1.40
a. Booklet pane of 6 *500.00*
107 A2 1p car rose ('41) 2.00 1.40
a. Booklet pane of 6 6.00
b. Bklt. pane of 3 + 3 labels *9,500.*
108 A2 1½p claret ('41) 17.00 1.40
a. Booklet pane of 6 140.00
109 A2 2p deep green 2.50 1.40
a. Booklet pane of 6 12.50
110 A3 2½p choc ('41) 17.00 3.50
a. Booklet pane of 6 95.00
111 A4 3p dull blue ('41) 2.75 1.40
a. Booklet pane of 6 40.00
112 A3 4p slate 2.75 1.40
a. Booklet pane of 6 65.00
113 A1 5p deep violet 2.75 1.40
114 A1 6p red violet ('42) 2.75 1.40
115 A3 9p violet 2.75 1.40
116 A4 10p olive brown 2.75 1.40
117 A1 1sh blue 175.00 42.50
Nos. 106-117 (12) 232.75 60.00

Types of 1922-23 Overprinted in Green or Violet

Overprint reads: "In memory of the Rebellion of 1916."

1941, Apr. 12 *Perf. 15x14*

118 A2 2p yellow orange 3.00 .70
119 A4 3p blue (V) 35.00 19.00

Volunteer Soldier and Dublin Post Office A15

1941, Oct. 27

120 A15 2½p bluish black 2.00 1.25

Nos. 118-120 commemorate the 25th anniv. of the Easter Rebellion.

St. Patrick Type of 1937

1943-45 Wmk. 262 *Perf. 14x15*

121 A11 2sh6p bright green 7.00 2.75
122 A11 5sh brown violet 9.75 4.00
123 A11 10sh dark blue ('45) 16.00 8.75
Nos. 121-123 (3) 32.75 15.50

Nos. 121-123 exist on chalky paper. Value, set $30.

Dr. Douglas Hyde — A16

1943, July 31 *Perf. 15x14*

124 A16 ½p green .75 1.00
125 A16 2½p red lilac 1.75 1.00

50th anniv. of the Gaelic League.

Sir Rowan Hamilton — A17

1943, Nov. 13 Typo. Wmk. 262

126 A17 ½p deep green .75 1.00
127 A17 2½p dk red brown 1.60 1.00

Centenary of discovery of the mathematical formula of Quaternions by William Rowan Hamilton.

Brother Michael O'Clery — A18

1944, June 30 *Perf. 14x15*

128 A18 ½p emerald .35 .25
a. Booklet pane of 6 25.00
129 A18 1sh reddish brown 1.40 1.25

300th anniv. of the death of Michael O'Clery, Irish historian.

Edmund Rice — A19

1944, Aug. 29 *Perf. 15x14*

130 A19 2½p slate 1.50 1.00

Death centenary of Edmund Ignatius Rice, founder of the Christian Brothers of Ireland.

Sower — A20

1945, Sept. 15

131 A20 2½p ultramarine 1.00 .25
132 A20 6p red violet 9.00 6.75

Commemorates the work of the Young Irelanders and the death centenary of Thomas Davis, Sept. 16, 1845.

Plowman A21

1946, Sept. 16 Typo.

133 A21 2½p red 1.50 .25
134 A21 3p dark blue 5.00 5.00

Birth centenary of Charles Stewart Parnell and Michael Davitt, leaders in the struggle for Irish political independence.

Theobald Wolfe Tone A22

Perf. 15x14

1948, Nov. 19 Wmk. 262

135 A22 2½p deep plum 1.40 .25
136 A22 3p deep violet 6.25 6.25

Insurrection of 1798, 150th anniversary.

Types of 1922-23

1949

137 A1 8p bright red 2.50 1.50
138 A4 11p carmine rose 2.50 1.50

Leinster House, Dublin A23

1949, Nov. 21

139 A23 2½p red brown 1.50 .60
140 A23 3p violet blue 7.50 4.75

International recognition of the Republic, Easter Monday, 1949.

James Clarence Mangan — A24

1949, Dec. 5

141 A24 1p dark green 2.90 1.00

Mangan (1803-1849), poet.

Statue of St. Peter — A25

Wmk. 262

1950, Sept. 11 Engr. *Perf. 12½*

142 A25 2½p violet 1.25 .50
143 A25 3p blue 10.00 11.00
144 A25 9p brown 10.00 12.50
Nos. 142-144 (3) 21.25 24.00

Holy Year, 1950.

Thomas Moore — A26

1952, Nov. 10 *Perf. 13*

145 A26 2½p deep plum .25 .25
146 A26 3½p dk olive green 3.50 3.50

Death centenary of Thomas Moore (1779-1852), poet.

Irish Harp — A27

1953, Feb. 9 Typo. *Perf. 14x15*

147 A27 2½p bright green 2.25 .25
148 A27 1sh4p bright blue 25.00 *26.00*

Ireland's National festival "An Tostal."

Robert Emmet — A28

1953, Sept. 21 Engr. *Perf. 12½x13*

149 A28 3p deep green 3.00 .35
150 A28 1sh3p carmine rose 37.50 16.50

150th anniv. of the execution of Robert Emmet (1778-1803), Irish nationalist.

Madonna by della Robbia — A29

1954, May 24 *Perf. 15*
151 A29 3p blue 1.00 .25
152 A29 5p deep green 7.00 6.25

Marian Year, 1953-54.

John Henry Cardinal Newman — A30

1954, July 19 Typo. *Perf. 15x14*
153 A30 2p rose lilac 2.25 .25
154 A30 1sh3p blue 17.50 8.00

Opening of the Catholic University of Ireland, centenary.

Statue of John Barry — A31

1956, Sept. 16 Engr. *Perf. 15*
155 A31 3p dull purple .75 .25
156 A31 1sh3p blue 11.00 9.75

John Barry (1745-1803), "Father of the American Navy," on the occasion of the unveiling of a statue in Wexford, Ireland, his birthplace.

Redmond — A32

Perf. 14x15
1957, June 11 Wmk. 262
157 A32 3p dark blue 1.25 .25
158 A32 1sh3p rose lake 14.50 14.50

Birth cent. of John Edward Redmond (1856-1918), Irish political leader.

O'Crohan — A33

1957, July 1
159 A33 2p dull purple 1.75 .25
160 A33 5p violet 7.25 6.50

Birth cent. of Thomas O'Crohan (Tomas O'Criomhthain) (1856-1937), fisherman and author.

Brown — A34

1957, Sept. 23 Typo. *Perf. 15x14*
161 A34 3p blue 3.00 .75
162 A34 1sh3p carmine rose 37.50 24.00

Adm. William (Guillermo) Brown (1777-1857), founder of the Argentine Navy.

Father Luke Wadding — A35

1957, Nov. 25 Engr. *Perf. 15*
163 A35 3p dark blue 1.75 .60
164 A35 1sh3p deep claret 19.50 10.00

Luke Wadding (1588-1657), Irish Franciscan friar and historian.

Clarke — A36

1958, July 28 Wmk. 262
165 A36 3p deep green .80 .25
166 A36 1sh3p red brown 13.00 12.50

Thomas J. Clarke (1858-1916), patriot.

Aikenhead — A37

1958, Oct. 20 *Perf. 15x14*
167 A37 3p blue 1.25 .25
168 A37 1sh3p carmine 18.50 11.50

Mother Mary Aikenhead (1787-1858), founder of the Irish Sisters of Charity.

Constitution Type of 1937

1958, Dec. 29 Typo. Wmk. 262
169 A12 3p brown 1.00 .25
170 A12 5p bright green 5.25 5.25

21st anniv. of the constitution.

Arthur Guinness — A38

1959, July 20 Engr. *Perf. 15*
171 A38 3p rose lake 2.75 .25
172 A38 1sh3p dark blue 17.50 9.25

Bicentenary of Guinness Brewery.

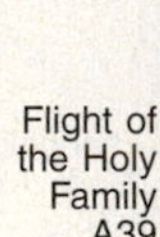

Flight of the Holy Family A39

1960, June 20 *Perf. 15*
173 A39 3p rose violet .30 .25
174 A39 1sh3p sepia 1.15 *2.50*

World Refugee Year, 7/1/59-6/30/60.

Europa Issue

Symbolic Wheel CD3

1960, Sept. 19 Engr. *Perf. 15*
175 CD3 6p orange brown *15.00 7.50*
176 CD3 1sh3p violet *32.50 20.00*
Nos. 175-176 (2) 47.50 27.50

No. 176 has fugitive ink.

De Havilland Dragon, Boeing 707 Jet and Dublin Airport A41

1961, June 26 *Perf. 15*
177 A41 6p dull blue 1.75 2.50
178 A41 1sh3p green 4.75 4.75

25th anniv. of the founding of Aer Lingus, Irish International Airlines.

St. Patrick — A42

1961, Sept. 25 *Perf. 14½*
179 A42 3p blue .75 .25
180 A42 8p pale purple 1.90 *5.00*
181 A42 1sh3p green 2.10 1.50
Nos. 179-181 (3) 4.75 6.75

1,500th anniv. of St. Patrick's death.

John O'Donovan and Eugene O'Curry A43

1962, Mar. 26 *Perf. 15*
182 A43 3p crimson .50 .25
183 A43 1sh3p purple 4.50 4.00

Death centenaries of John O'Donovan (1806-1861) and Eugene O'Curry (1794-1862), Gaelic scholars and translators.

Europa Issue

19 Leaves on Young Tree CD5

1962, Sept. 17 Engr. Wmk. 262
184 CD5 6p pink & dark red *.50 .25*
185 CD5 1sh3p bluish grn & dk blue grn *1.50 .25*

Wheat Emblem and Globe A45

1963, Mar. 21 Wmk. 262
186 A45 4p violet .50 .25
187 A45 1sh3p red 3.00 *3.00*

FAO "Freedom from Hunger" campaign.

Europa Issue

Stylized Links, Symbolizing Unity CD6

1963, Sept. 16 *Perf. 15*
188 CD6 6p rose carmine *1.25 1.25*
189 CD6 1sh3p dark blue *3.50 2.00*

Centenary Emblem A47

1963, Dec. 2 Photo. *Perf. 14½x14*
190 A47 4p gray & red .50 .25
191 A47 1sh3p brt green, gray & red 1.30 *2.25*

Centenary of the International Red Cross.

Wolfe Tone A48

1964, Apr. 13 Engr. *Perf. 15*
192 A48 4p black .40 .25
193 A48 1sh3p dark blue 5.25 5.50

Birth bicentenary of Theobald Wolfe Tone (1763-1798), Irish revolutionist.

Irish Pavilion A49

1964, July 20 Photo. *Perf. 14½x14*
194 A49 5p multicolored .75 .25
a. Brown omitted 5,500.
195 A49 1sh5p multicolored 4.25 4.25

New York World's Fair, 1964-65.

Europa Issue

CEPT Daisy (22 Petals) — CD7

Perf. 14x14½
1964, Sept. 14 Litho. Wmk. 262
196 CD7 8p dull grn & ultra *3.00 1.25*
197 CD7 1sh5p red brown & org *14.00 3.00*

ITU Emblem, Globe and Communication Waves — A51

1965, May 17 Photo. *Perf. 14½x14*
198 A51 3p dp blue & emerald .40 .25
199 A51 8p black & emerald 3.50 *3.50*

ITU, cent.

William Butler Yeats — A52

1965, June 14 *Perf. 15*
200 A52 5p orange brn & blk .50 .25
201 A52 1sh5p gray grn, brn & blk 4.50 3.75

Birth centenary of William Butler Yeats (1865-1939), poet and dramatist.

ICY Emblem A53

1965, Aug. 16 Photo. *Perf. 15*
202 A53 3p brt blue & vio bl .50 .45
203 A53 10p redsh brn & dk brn 3.50 *4.50*

International Cooperation Year.

Europa Issue

Leaves and Fruit — CD8

1965, Sept. 27 *Perf. 15*

No.	Type	Denom.	Color	Unused	Used
204	CD8	8p	brick red & blk	4.50	*.60*
205	CD8	1sh5p	lt blue & claret	11.50	2.75

James Connolly A55

Designs: No. 207, Thomas J. Clarke. No. 208, Patrick Henry Pearse. No. 209, Symbolic of lives lost in fight for independence, and of Ireland marching into freedom. No. 210, Eamonn Ceannt. No. 211, Sean MacDiarmada. No. 212, Thomas MacDonagh. No. 213, Joseph Plunkett.

1966, Apr. 12 **Wmk. 262** *Perf. 15*

No.	Type	Denom.	Color	Unused	Used
206	A55	3p	blue & black	1.60	.55
207	A55	3p	olive green	1.60	.55
a.			Pair, #206-207	4.00	*2.25*
208	A55	5p	olive & black	2.00	.55
209	A55	5p	brt grn, blk & orange	2.00	.55
a.			Pair, #208-209	5.00	*2.50*
210	A55	7p	dull org & blk	2.00	*4.00*
211	A55	7p	blue grn & blk	2.00	*4.00*
a.			Pair, #210-211	5.25	*12.00*
212	A55	1sh5p	grnsh bl & blk	2.00	*3.50*
213	A55	1sh5p	emerald & blk	2.00	*3.50*
a.			Pair, #212-213	7.00	*17.50*
			Nos. 206-213 (8)	15.20	17.20

50th anniv. of the Easter Week Rebellion, and to honor the signers of the Proclamation of the Irish Republic.

Roger Casement — A56

1966, Aug. 3 *Perf. 15*

No.	Type	Denom.	Color	Unused	Used
214	A56	5p	black	.25	.25
215	A56	1sh	dark red brown	1.60	1.35

50th death anniv. of Roger Casement (1864-1916), British consular agent and Irish rebel who was executed for treason.

Europa Issue

Symbolic Sailboat — CD9

1966, Sept. 26 **Photo.** *Perf. 15*

No.	Type	Denom.	Color	Unused	Used
216	CD9	7p	orange & green	2.00	*.40*
217	CD9	1sh5p	gray & green	4.75	*1.60*

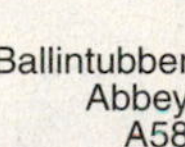

Ballintubber Abbey A58

1966, Nov. 8 *Perf. 15*

No.	Type	Denom.	Color	Unused	Used
218	A58	5p	red brown	.25	.25
219	A58	1sh	black	.55	.55

750th anniversary of Ballintubber Abbey.

Cross and Sword Types of 1922

1966-67 **Photo.** *Perf. 15*

Size: 17x20½mm

No.	Type	Denom.	Color	Unused	Used
225	A4	3p	blue ('67)	.55	.30
226	A1	5p	brt vio, type II ('68)	.65	.30
a.			Booklet pane of 6, No. 226b	62.50	
b.			Type I ('66)	8.25	8.25

Type I has irregularly spaced lines in shading behind sword.

Europa Issue

Cogwheels — CD10

1967, May 2

No.	Type	Denom.	Color	Unused	Used
232	CD10	7p	green & gold	*1.90*	*.80*
233	CD10	1sh5p	dk red & gold	*4.00*	*1.50*

Maple Leaves A60

1967, Aug. 28 **Photo.**

No.	Type	Denom.	Color	Unused	Used
234	A60	5p	multicolored	.25	.25
235	A60	1sh5p	multicolored	.55	.55

Centenary of the Canadian Confederation.

Rock of Cashel A61

1967, Sept. 25 **Wmk. 262** *Perf. 15*

No.	Type	Denom.	Color	Unused	Used
236	A61	7p	sepia	.25	.25
237	A61	10p	Prussian blue	.55	.55

International Tourist Year.

One Cent Fenian Fantasy — A62

Design: 1sh, 24c Fenian fantasy.

1967, Oct. 23 **Photo.** *Perf. 15*

No.	Type	Denom.	Color	Unused	Used
238	A62	5p	lt green & slate grn	.25	.25
239	A62	1sh	pale pink & gray	.70	.70

Fenian Rising, centenary. The Fenian fantasy was created by S. Allan Taylor.

Swift's Bust and St. Patrick's Cathedral, Dublin — A63

Design: 1sh5p, Gulliver, Lilliputian army.

1967, Nov. 30 *Perf. 15*

No.	Type	Denom.	Color	Unused	Used
240	A63	3p	gray & sepia	.25	.25
241	A63	1sh5p	lt blue & sepia	.55	.55

Birth tercentenary of Jonathan Swift (1667-1745), author of Gulliver's Travels.

Europa Issue

Golden Key with CEPT Emblem CD11

1968, Apr. 29 **Photo.** **Wmk. 262**

No.	Type	Denom.	Color	Unused	Used
242	CD11	7p	multicolored	*.90*	*.75*
243	CD11	1sh5p	multicolored	*2.40*	*1.50*

St. Mary's Cathedral, Limerick A65

1968, Aug. 26 **Engr.** *Perf. 15*

No.	Type	Denom.	Color	Unused	Used
244	A65	5p	dull blue	.25	*.35*
245	A65	10p	olive	.60	*1.40*

800th anniv. of the founding of St. Mary's Cathedral by Donal Mor O'Brien, last King of Munster.

Countess Markievicz A66

1968, Sept. 23 **Photo.** **Wmk. 262**

No.	Type	Denom.	Color	Unused	Used
246	A66	3p	black	.25	.25
247	A66	1sh5p	dark blue	.75	.75

Birth centenary of Countess Constance Markievicz (1868-1927), champion of Irish Independence and first Minister of Labor.

James Connolly — A67

1968, Sept. 23 *Perf. 15*

No.	Type	Denom.	Color	Unused	Used
248	A67	6p	brown, dk brn & blk	.35	.35
249	A67	1sh	dull grn, grn & blk	.50	.35

Birth centenary of James Connolly (1868-1916), founder of the Irish Socialist Party, editor of "Workers' Republic" and Commander of the Irish Citizen Army.

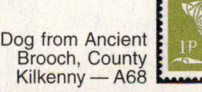

Dog from Ancient Brooch, County Kilkenny — A68

Winged Ox from Lichfield Gospel Book A69

Designs: ½p, 1p, 2p, 3p, 4p, 5p, 6p, Dog. 7p, 8p, 9p, 10p, 1sh, 1sh9p, Stag from ancient bowl, Kent. 2sh6p, 5sh, Winged ox. 10sh, Eagle, from ancient manuscript.

1968-70 **Photo.** **Wmk. 262** *Perf. 15*

No.	Type	Denom.	Color	Unused	Used
250	A68	½p	orange	.25	*.25*
251	A68	1p	yellow green	.25	*.25*
252	A68	2p	ocher	.50	*.25*
253	A68	3p	bright blue	.35	*.25*
254	A68	4p	dark red	.30	*.25*
255	A68	5p	deep green	1.25	*.85*
256	A68	6p	brown	.30	.25
a.			Booklet pane of 6 ('70)	27.50	
257	A68	7p	yel & brown	.45	*3.25*
258	A68	8p	red org & blk	.45	*2.75*
259	A68	9p	ol grn & dk bl	.50	*.25*
260	A68	10p	violet & dk brn	1.50	*2.75*
261	A68	1sh	dk red brn & brown	.40	*.25*
262	A68	1sh9p	grnsh bl & dk brown	4.00	*2.50*
263	A69	2sh6p	red org, bl, ol & dull yel	1.75	.25
264	A69	5sh	ol, gray, bis & yel	3.00	3.50
265	A69	10sh	dk red brn, yel & dp org	4.75	4.75
			Nos. 250-265 (16)	20.00	22.60

Issued: 2p, 8p, 2sh6p, 10sh, 10/14/68; 6p, 9p, 1sh9p, 5sh, 2/24/69; 4p, 5p, 10p, 1sh, 3/31/69; ½p, 1p, 3p, 7p, 6/9/69.

See Nos. 290-304, 343-359, 395-402, 466-475.

1970 **Coil Stamps** *Perf. 14x15*

No.	Type	Denom.	Color	Unused	Used
251a	A68	1p	yellow green	1.75	*5.50*
252a	A68	2p	ocher	1.75	*6.50*
253a	A68	3p	bright blue	1.75	*3.75*
			Nos. 251a-253a (3)	5.25	*15.75*

Human Rights Flame — A70

1968, Nov. 4 **Wmk. 262** *Perf. 15*

No.	Type	Denom.	Color	Unused	Used
266	A70	5p	black, ocher & gold	.25	.25
267	A70	7p	crim, ocher & gold	.50	.50

International Human Rights Year.

First Meeting of Irish Parliament A71

1969, Jan. 21 *Perf. 15x14½*

No.	Type	Denom.	Color	Unused	Used
268	A71	6p	dark slate green	.25	.25
269	A71	9p	dark blue gray	.50	.50

50th anniv. of the first meeting of the Dail Eireann at the Mansion House, Dublin, Jan. 21, 1919.

"EUROPA" and "CEPT" CD12

1969, Apr. 28 **Photo.** *Perf. 15*

No.	Type	Denom.	Color	Unused	Used
270	CD12	9p	ultra, gray & ocher	*1.25*	*.75*
271	CD12	1sh9p	car, gray & gold	*2.25*	*1.25*

Europa and CEPT, 10th anniv.

ILO Emblem — A73

1969, July 14 *Perf. 15*

No.	Type	Denom.	Color	Unused	Used
272	A73	6p	gray & black	.25	.25
273	A73	9p	yellow & black	.50	.50

ILO, 50th anniv.

Last Supper and Crucifixion, by Evie Hone — A74

Perf. 15x14½

1969, Sept. 1 Photo. Wmk. 262

274 A74 1sh multicolored .75 *1.50*

The design is after a stained-glass window by Evie Hone (1894-1955) in the Eton College Chapel.

Mahatma Gandhi A75

1969, Oct. 2 ***Perf. 15***

275 A75 6p dk yel grn & blk .40 .40
276 A75 1sh9p yel, grn & black 1.25 1.25

Mohandas K. Gandhi (1869-1948), leader in India's fight for independence.

Stylized Bird, Tree and Shamrock A76

1970, Feb. 23 ***Perf. 15***

277 A76 6p olive bister & black .25 *.25*
278 A76 9p violet & black .55 .55

Nature Conservation Year.

Europa Issue

Interwoven Threads CD13

1970, May 4 Photo. ***Perf. 15***

279 CD13 6p purple & silver *1.60* .25
280 CD13 9p yel brn & silver *2.40 1.00*
281 CD13 1sh9p dk gray & sil *3.50 1.25*
Nos. 279-281 (3) 7.50 2.50

Sailing Boats, by Peter Monamy (1670-1749) A78

1970, July 13 ***Perf. 15***

282 A78 4p gold & multi .55 .45

250th anniv. of the Royal Cork Yacht Club.

Madonna of Eire, by Mainie Jellett (1896-1943) — A79

1970, Sept. 1 Photo. ***Perf. 15***

283 A79 1sh violet blue & multi .55 .55

Tomás MacCurtain — A80

Nos. 285, 287, Terence MacSwiney.

1970, Oct. 26 ***Perf. 15***

284 A80 9p violet & black 1.00 .50
285 A80 9p violet & black 1.00 .50
a. Pair, #284-285 3.50 *4.00*
286 A80 2sh9p brt blue & blk 2.50 1.25
287 A80 2sh9p brt blue & blk 2.50 1.25
a. Pair, #286-287 8.25 *9.75*

50th anniv. of the deaths of Tomás MacCurtain (1884-1920) and Terence MacSwiney (1879-1920), lord mayors of Cork, who died during the Irish war of independence.

Kevin Barry A81

1970, Nov. 2

288 A81 6p olive green .30 .25
289 A81 1sh2p violet blue .95 .75

50th anniv. of the death of Kevin Barry (1902-1920), who was hanged during the Irish war of independence.

Decimal Currency Issue

Types of 1968-69 (Numerals only)

Designs: ½p, 1p, 1½p, 2p, 2½p, 3p, 3½p, 4p, No. 298A, Dog. No. 298, 6p, 7p, 7½p, 9p, Stag. 10p, 12p, 20p, Winged ox. 50p, Eagle.

Two types of 10p:
I — Ox outlined in lilac
II — Outlined in brown

1971-75 Wmk. 262 Photo. ***Perf. 15***

290 A68 ½p yellow green .25 .25
a. Booklet pane of 6 30.00 40.00
291 A68 1p bright blue .90 .25
a. Booklet pane of 6 5.75 7.00
c. Bklt. pane of 5 + label ('74) 1.75
292 A68 1½p brown red .25 .25
293 A68 2p dark green .25 .25
b. Booklet pane of 5 + label ('75) 1.75
294 A68 2½p sepia .35 .25
a. Booklet pane of 6 15.00
295 A68 3p yel orange .30 .25
296 A68 3½p deep orange .30 .25
297 A68 4p violet .25 .25
298 A68 5p ap grn & brn 1.25 .35
298A A68 5p apple grn ('74) 1.35 1.25
c. Booklet pane of 6 ('74) 12.00
d. Bklt. pane of 5 + label ('74) 2.50
299 A68 6p bl gray & dk brn 1.75 .90
299A A68 7p ol grn & ind ('74) 2.25 1.75
300 A68 7½p rose vio & dk brn .55 *.45*
301 A68 9p bl grn & blk 1.35 .90
302 A69 10p lil & multi (I) 8.00 .50
b. Type II 20.00 6.50
302A A69 12p multi ('74) .90 .45
303 A69 20p slate & multi 4.00 .45
304 A69 50p rose brn & multi 8.00 1.25
Nos. 290-304 (18) 32.25 10.25

Booklet panes have watermark sideways.
Issued: No. 298A, 7p, 12p, 1/29/74; others, 2/15/71.
See Nos. 343-359, 395-402, 466-475.

1971-74 Coil Stamps ***Perf. 14x15***

291b A68 1p bright blue .70 *1.45*
292a A68 1½p brown red .40 .40
293a A68 2p dark green ('72) .40 .40
294b A68 2½p sepia .40 .40
c. Strip of 3 (1p, 1½p, 2½p) 2.00 *4.00*
297a A68 4p violet ('72) .80 *1.75*
b. Strip of 4 (1½p, 2p, 2½p, 4p) ('72) 2.00 *4.00*
298b A68 5p apple green ('74) 1.35 *1.45*
e. Strip of 4 (2x1½p, 2p, 5p) ('74) 2.00 *4.00*

Common Design Type

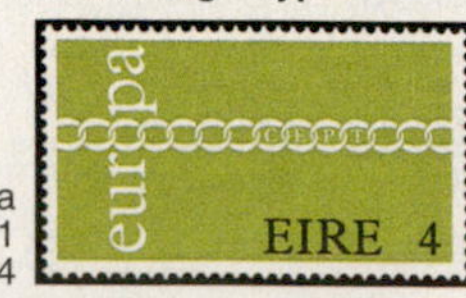

Europa Issue, 1971 — CD14

1971, May 3 Wmk. 262 ***Perf. 15***

305 CD14 4p apple green & blk *.75* .25
306 CD14 6p blue & black *3.75 1.25*

John M. Synge — A82

1971, July 19 Photo. ***Perf. 15***

307 A82 4p gray, black & gold .25 .25
308 A82 10p org, black & gold .75 .75

Birth cent. of John Millington Synge (1871-1909), poet and dramatist.

An Island Man, by Jack B. Yeats — A83

1971, Aug. 30 ***Perf. 15***

309 A83 6p multicolored .75 .75

Jack Butler Yeats (1871-1957), painter.

Racial Equality Emblem — A84

Perf. 14x14½

1971, Oct. 18 Litho. Unwmk.

310 A84 4p red .25 .25
311 A84 10p black .40 .40

Intl. Year Against Racial Discrimination.

Madonna, by John Hughes, Loughrea Cathedral — A85

1971, Nov. 15 Photo. ***Perf. 15***

312 A85 2½p dp bl grn, gold & slate .25 .25
313 A85 6p ultra, gold & slate .50 .50

Christmas.

"Your Heart is your Health" A86

1972, Apr. 7 Photo. Wmk. 262

314 A86 2½p gold & brown .35 .35
315 A86 12p silver & black 1.50 1.50

World Health Day.

Europa Issue

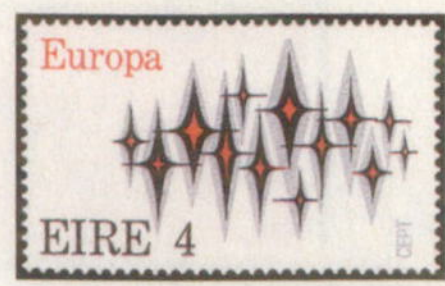

Sparkles, Symbolic of Communications — CD15

1972, May 1 ***Perf. 15***

316 CD15 4p red, black & sil *3.50 .50*
317 CD15 6p blue, black & sil *9.50 4.00*

Dove Soaring Past Rising Moon — A88

1972, June 1 Photo.

318 A88 4p gray blue, org & dk bl .25 .25
319 A88 6p olive, yel & dk green .70 .35

The patriot dead of 1922-23.

Black Lake, by Gerard Dillon A89

1972, July 10 ***Perf. 15***

320 A89 3p indigo & multi .75 .75

Rider from Clonmacnoise Slab and Olympic Rings — A90

1972, Aug. 28 Photo. Wmk. 262

321 A90 3p yellow, black & gold .25 .25
322 A90 6p salmon, black & gold .70 .60

20th Olympic Games, Munich, Aug. 26-Sept. 11, and 50th anniversary of the Olympic Council of Ireland.

Madonna and Child — A91

1972, Oct. 16 Unwmk. ***Perf. 15***

323 A91 2½p dk green & multi .25 .25
324 A91 4p tan & multi .40 .25
325 A91 12p multicolored .90 .50
Nos. 323-325 (3) 1.55 1.00

Christmas. The design is after a miniature in the Book of Kells, 9th century.

Ireland No. 68 — A92

1972, Dec. 6 **Photo.**
326 A92 6p blue gray & dp grn .65 *.65*
a. Souvenir sheet of 4 6.75 *8.50*

50th anniv. of 1st Irish postage stamp.

Recurrent Celtic Head Motif — A93

1973, Jan. 1 **Unwmk.**
327 A93 6p orange & multi .50 *.60*
328 A93 12p green & multi 1.00 1.40

Ireland's entry into the European Community.

Europa Issue

Post Horn of Arrows CD16

1973, Apr. 30
329 CD16 4p bright ultra *1.25* .25
330 CD16 6p black *4.00* *1.75*

"Berlin Blues I," by William Scott A95

Perf. 15x14½
1973, Aug. 9 **Photo.** **Unwmk.**
331 A95 5p lt blue, blue & dk brn .50 .30

Weather Map of Northwest Europe — A96

1973, Sept. 4 ***Perf. 14½x15***
332 A96 3½p ultra & multi .30 .30
333 A96 12p lilac & multi 1.30 *1.60*

Intl. meteorological cooperation, cent.

Tractor Plowing and Birds A97

1973, Oct. 5 ***Perf. 15x14½***
334 A97 5p emerald & multi .25 .25
335 A97 7p emerald & multi .85 .45

World Plowing Championships, Wellington Bridge, County Wexford, Oct. 1-7.

Flight into Egypt, by Jan de Cock — A98

1973, Nov. 1 ***Perf. 15***
336 A98 3½p black & multi .25 .25
337 A98 12p gold & multi 1.00 1.00

Christmas.

Rescue, by Bernard Gribble A99

Design: Ballycotton lifeboat rescuing crew of Daunt Rock Lightship, 1936.

1974, Mar. 28 **Photo.** **Wmk. 262**
338 A99 5p multicolored .50 .40

Sesquicentennial of the founding of the Royal National Lifeboat Institution.

Europa Issue

Edmund Burke, by John Henry Foley — A100

Perf. 14½x15
1974, Apr. 29 **Unwmk.**
339 A100 5p lt ultra & black *1.75* .25
340 A100 7p lt green & black *9.50* *1.25*

Oliver Goldsmith, by John Henry Foley — A101

1974, June 24 **Photo.**
341 A101 3½p brt citron & blk .40 .25
342 A101 12p emerald & black 1.25 1.25

Oliver Goldsmith (1728-1774), writer.

Types of 1968-69

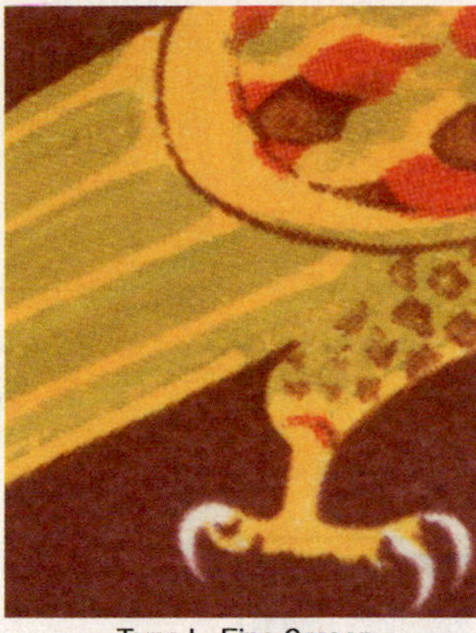

Type I - Fine Screen

Type II - Coarse Screen

½p, 1p, 2p, 3p, 3½p, 5p, Nos. 350, 352, Dog. Nos. 349, 351, 8p, 9p, Stag. 10p, 15p, 20p, Winged ox. 50p, £1, Eagle.

1974-78 **Unwmk.** ***Perf. 15***
343 A68 ½p yel green ('78) .25 .25
344 A68 1p brt blue ('75) .25 .25
345 A68 2p dark green ('76) .25 .25
346 A68 3p ocher ('75) .25 .25
347 A68 3½p deep orange 1.60 *2.75*
348 A68 5p apple green .25 .25
349 A68 6p bl gray & dk brn 1.40 *1.60*
350 A68 6p blue gray ('75) .25 .25
351 A68 7p lt ol grn & indigo 2.00 1.00
352 A68 7p olive green ('75) .25 .25
a. Bklt. pane of 5 + label ('77) 14.00 *16.00*
353 A68 8p brn & dk brn ('75) 2.00 .80
354 A68 9p lt bl grn & blk ('75) 2.00 .40
355 A69 10p lil & multi ('75) 2.00 .40
356 A69 15p multi ('75) 1.40 .80
357 A69 20p slate & multi 1.10 .25
358 A69 50p rose brn & multi, type I ('74) 2.00 .65
a. Type II ('83) 2.90 2.25
359 A69 £1 multi ('75) 4.00 1.00
Nos. 343-359 (17) 21.25 11.40

Coil Stamps

1977, Mar. 21 ***Perf. 14x15***
344b A68 1p bright blue .55 *.65*
345b A68 2p dark green .40 *.50*
348b A68 5p apple green .90 *1.00*
c. Strip of 4 (1p, 2x2p, 5p) 2.50 *2.75*

Kitchen Table, by Norah McGuinness A102

1974, Aug. 19 **Photo.** ***Perf. 14x15***
360 A102 5p multicolored .75 .75

Rugby A103

1974, Sept. 2 **Engr.** ***Perf. 15x14***
361 A103 3½p slate green .50 .50
a. 3½ deep slate green 8.00 *8.25*
362 A103 12p multicolored 2.50 2.50

Centenary of Irish Rugby Union.

No. 361a was printed from a reengraved plate with more deeply engraved lines. The original printing (No. 361) was considered to be of unsatisfactory quality.

UPU "Postmark" A104

1974, Oct. 9 **Photo.** ***Perf. 14½x15***
363 A104 5p emerald & black .25 .25
364 A104 7p ultra & black .70 .70

Centenary of Universal Postal Union.

Virgin and Child, by Bellini — A105

1974, Nov. 14
365 A105 5p multicolored .30 .30
366 A105 15p multicolored .95 .95

Christmas.

"Peace" — A106

1975, Mar. 25 **Photo.** ***Perf. 14½x15***
367 A106 8p dp rose lil & ultra .25 .25
368 A106 15p ultra & emerald .95 .95

International Women's Year.

Europa Issue

Castletown Hunt (detail), by Robert Healy A107

1975, Apr. 28 **Photo.** ***Perf. 15x14½***
369 A107 7p black *3.00* .25
370 A107 9p green *7.00* *2.00*

Chipping from the Fringe A108

1975, June 26 Photo. ***Perf. 15x14½***

371 A108 6p shown .45 .25
372 A108 9p Putting 2.40 1.40

9th European Amateur Golf Team Championships, Killarney.

Bird of Prey, by Oisín Kelly A109

1975, July 28

373 A109 15p ocher .90 *1.10*

Nano Nagle and Pupils, Engraving by Charles Turner — A110

1975, Sept. 1 Photo. ***Perf. 14½x15***

374 A110 5p light blue & black .25 .25
375 A110 7p buff & black .65 .65

Presentation Order of Nuns, bicentenary.

Clock Tower, St. Ann's Church, Shandon — A111

Designs: 7p, 9p, Holycross Abbey.

1975, Oct. 6 Photo. ***Perf. 12½***

376 A111 5p sepia .35 .25
377 A111 6p ultra & multi .50 *.90*
378 A111 7p sapphire .50 .30
379 A111 9p multicolored .70 .60
Nos. 376-379 (4) 2.05 2.05

European Architectural Heritage Year.

St. Oliver Plunkett, by Imogen Stuart — A112

1975, Oct. 13 Engr. ***Perf. 14x14½***

380 A112 7p black .30 .25
381 A112 15p dull red .85 *.90*

Canonization of Oliver Plunkett (1625-1681), Primate of Ireland.

Madonna and Child, by Fra Filippo Lippi — A113

1975, Nov. 13 Photo. ***Perf. 15***

382 A113 5p multicolored .25 .25
383 A113 7p multicolored .30 .25
384 A113 10p gold & multi .65 .75
Nos. 382-384 (3) 1.20 1.25

Christmas.

James Larkin — A114

1976 Jan. 21 Photo. ***Perf. 14½x15***

385 A114 7p gray & slate grn .25 .25
386 A114 11p ocher & brown .90 .90

James Larkin (1876-1947), trade union leader.

Bell Making First Call — A115

1976, Mar. 10 Photo. ***Perf. 14½x15***

387 A115 9p multicolored .25 .25
388 A115 15p multicolored .90 .90

Centenary of first telephone call by Alexander Graham Bell, March 10, 1876.

13 Stars and Stripes A116

Designs: 8p, 50 stars, and stripes. 9p, 15p, Benjamin Franklin on Albany essay of 1847.

1976, May 17 Litho. ***Perf. 15x14***

389 A116 7p ultra, sil & red .25 .25
a. Silver (inscription) omitted *2,000.* *1,200.*
390 A116 8p ultra, sil & red .30 *.60*
a. Silver (inscription) omitted *2,000.* *1,200.*
391 A116 9p bl, sil & ocher .35 .25
a. Silver (inscription) omitted *2,000.* *1,200.*
392 A116 15p red, sil & bl .65 .60
a. Silver (inscription) omitted *950.00* *1,200.*
b. Souvenir sheet of 4, #389-392 5.00 *6.00*
Nos. 389-392 (4) 1.55 1.70

American Bicentennial. No. 392b exists with silver omitted.

Irish Delft Spirit Barrel — A117

Europa: 11p, Bowl, Irish Delft. Designs show mark of Henry Delamain's Factory, Dublin, both pieces c. 1756.

1976, July 1 Photo. ***Perf. 15x14½***

393 A117 9p gray & magenta *2.40* .25
394 A117 11p gray & blue *4.25* *1.00*

Types of 1968

Designs: 8p, 9p, 9½p, No. 399, Dog. No. 398, 11p, 12p, Stag. 17p, Winged ox.

1976-79 Photo. Unwmk. ***Perf. 15***

395 A68 8p brown .30 .25
396 A68 9p blue green .35 .25
397 A68 9½p red ('79) .35 .25
398 A68 10p lilac & black 1.60 .55
399 A68 10p purple ('77) .35 .25
400 A68 11p carmine & black .85 .65
401 A68 12p emer & black ('77) 1.10 .40
402 A69 17p ol, bl & ocher ('77) 1.40 1.00
Nos. 395-402 (8) 6.30 3.60

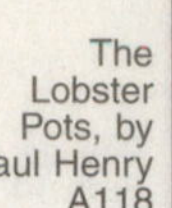

The Lobster Pots, by Paul Henry A118

1976, Aug. 30 Photo. ***Perf. 15***

405 A118 15p gold & multi .95 .95

Paul Henry (1876-1958), birth centenary.

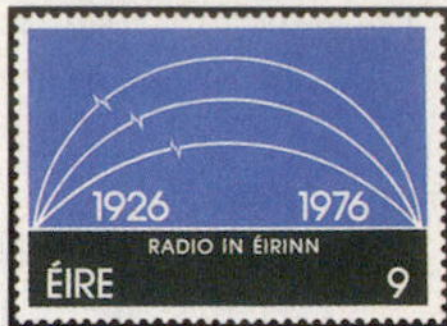

Radio Waves A119

Radio Tower and Waves, Globe — A120

Perf. 14½x14, 14x14½

1976, Oct. 5 Litho.

406 A119 9p brt blue & black .25 .25
407 A120 11p black & multi .80 .80

Irish broadcasting, 50th anniversary.

Nativity, by Lorenzo Monaco A121

1976, Nov. 11 ***Perf. 15x14½***

408 A121 7p multicolored .30 .25
409 A121 9p multicolored .40 .30
410 A121 15p multicolored .75 .65
Nos. 408-410 (3) 1.45 1.20

Christmas.

Irish Manuscript, 16th Century A122

Stone from Newgrange Burial Mound A123

1977, May 9 Photo. ***Perf. 15x14½***

411 A122 8p multicolored .30 .25
412 A123 10p multicolored .70 .65

Centenaries of National Library (8p) and National Museum (10p).

Europa Issue

View of Ballynahinch A124

Lugalla Lake — A125

1977, June 27 Litho. ***Perf. 14x14½***

413 A124 10p multicolored *2.25* *.25*
414 A125 12p multicolored *8.00* *1.40*

Head, by Louis le Brocquy, 1973 — A126

1977, Aug. 8 ***Perf. 14x14½***

415 A126 17p multicolored .75 .75

Girl Guide and Tents A127

Design: 17p, Boy Scout and tents.

1977, Aug. 22 Photo. ***Perf. 15x14½***

416 A127 8p multicolored .40 .25
417 A127 17p multicolored 1.10 *1.25*

European Scout and Guide Conference, Ireland, and 50th anniversary of Catholic Boy Scouts of Ireland.

The Shanachie, by Jack B. Yeats — A128

Eriugena A129

Perf. 14x14½, 14½x14

1977, Sept. 12 Litho.

418 A128 10p black .30 *.35*
419 A129 12p black .45 *.90*

Folklore of Ireland Society, 50th anniv. and 1100th death anniv. of Johannes Scottus Eriugena, philospher, poet and mystic.

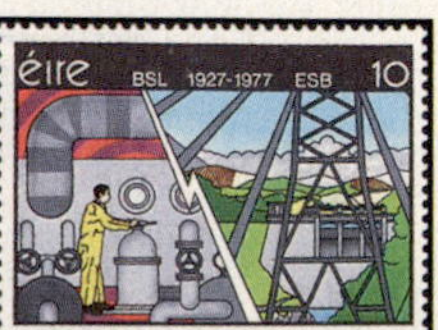

"Electricity," Mural by Robert Ballagh — A130

Bulls, from Contemporary Coin — A131

Greyhound A132

Litho. (10p, 17p); Photo. (12p)
Perf. 14½x14; 15x14½ (12p)

1977, Oct. 10

420	A130	10p multicolored	.25	.25
421	A131	12p multicolored	.50	*.80*
422	A132	17p multicolored	.65	.65
		Nos. 420-422 (3)	1.40	1.70

50th anniversaries of: Electricity Supply Board (10p); Agricultural Credit Act (12p); introduction of greyhound racing (17p).

Holy Family, by Giorgione — A133

1977, Nov. 3 Photo. *Perf. 14½x15*

423	A133	8p multicolored	.25	.25
424	A133	10p multicolored	.40	.40
425	A133	17p multicolored	.60	.55
		Nos. 423-425 (3)	1.25	1.20

Christmas.

Bremen, Junkers Monoplane A134

1978, Apr. 13 Litho. *Perf. 14*

426	A134	10p ultra & black	.25	.25
427	A134	17p lt brown & black	.80	.90

50th anniversary of first East-West transatlantic flight from Baldonnel, County Dublin, to Greenly Island, Gulf of St. Lawrence.

Spring Gentian — A135

Wild flowers: 10p, Strawberry tree. 11p, Large-flowered butterwort. 17p, St. Daboec's heath.

1978, June 12 Litho. *Perf. 14x14½*

428	A135	8p multicolored	.30	.30
429	A135	10p multicolored	.45	.50
430	A135	11p multicolored	.60	*.90*
431	A135	17p multicolored	.75	*1.05*
		Nos. 428-431 (4)	2.10	*2.75*

Catherine McAuley — A136

Vaccination, lithograph by Manigaud — A137

William Orpen, Self-portrait A138

1978, Sept. 18 Litho. *Perf. 14*

432	A136	10p multicolored	.30	.25
433	A137	11p multicolored	.40	.45
434	A138	17p multicolored	.70	.70
		Nos. 432-434 (3)	1.40	1.40

Catherine McAuley (1778-1841), founder of Sisters of Mercy (10p); eradication of smallpox (11p); William Orpen (1878-1931), painter (17p).

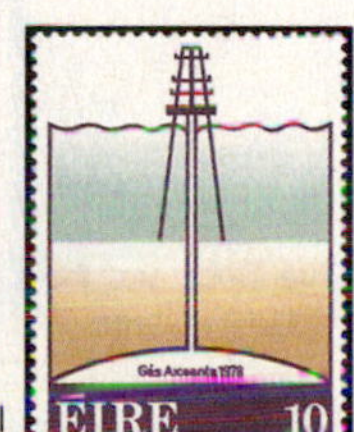

Offshore Oil Well — A139

1978, Oct. 18 Litho. *Perf. 14*

435	A139	10p multicolored	.55	.35

First natural gas coming in off the Irish Coast at Kinsale.

Woodcock on Farthing A140

Coins: 10p, Salmon on florin. 11p, Hen and chicks on penny. 17p, Horse on half crown.

1978, Oct. 26 Photo. *Perf. 15x14½*

436	A140	8p multicolored	.40	.40
437	A140	10p multicolored	.40	.30
438	A140	11p multicolored	.60	*.70*
439	A140	17p multicolored	.75	.70
		Nos. 436-439 (4)	2.15	2.10

Irish currency, 50th anniversary.

Virgin and Child, by Guercino — A141

1978, Nov. 16 Photo. *Perf. 14½x15*

440	A141	8p multicolored	.25	.25
441	A141	10p multicolored	.30	.25
442	A141	17p multicolored	.55	.50
		Nos. 440-442 (3)	1.10	1.00

Christmas.

Conolly Folly, Castletown A142

Europa: 11p, Belvedere on Tower Hill at Dromoland.

1978, Dec. 6 *Perf. 15x14½*

443	A142	10p brown	*1.50*	*.25*
444	A142	11p dull green	*7.00*	*1.00*

Cross-country Runners — A143

1979, Aug. 20 Litho. *Perf. 14½x14*

445	A143	8p multicolored	.30	.30

7th World Cross-country Championships, Greenpark Racecourse, Limerick, March 25.

Rowland Hill, Bronze Statue — A144

1979, Aug. 20 *Perf. 14x14½*

446	A144	17p multicolored	.35	*.45*

Sir Rowland Hill (1795-1879), originator of penny postage.

"European Communities" (7 Languages) A145

1979, Aug. 20 Photo. *Perf. 14½x15*

447	A145	10p lt greenish gray	.25	*.35*
448	A145	11p rose lilac	.35	*.45*

European Parliament, first direct elections, June 7-10.

Wren A146

Birds: 10p, Great crested grebe. 11p, Greenland white-fronted geese. 17p, Peregrine falcon.

1979, Aug. 30 Litho. *Perf. 14½x14*

449	A146	8p multicolored	.65	.60
450	A146	10p multicolored	.70	.65
451	A146	11p multicolored	.80	1.15
452	A146	17p multicolored	1.00	1.60
		Nos. 449-452 (4)	3.15	4.00

A Happy Flower A147

Children's Drawings: 11p, "Me and my skipping rope," vert. 17p, "Swans on a lake."

Perf. 14½x14, 14x14½

1979, Sept. 13 Litho.

453	A147	10p multicolored	.30	.25
454	A147	11p multicolored	.40	*.80*
455	A147	17p multicolored	.80	*.95*
		Nos. 453-455 (3)	1.50	*2.00*

International Year of the Child.

Pope John Paul II A148

1979, Sept. 29 Litho. *Perf. 14½x14*

456	A148	12p multicolored	.50	.35

Visit of Pope John Paul II to Ireland.

Hospitaller Brother Teaching Child A149

1979, Oct. 4

457	A149	9½p rose & black	.45	.25

Hospitaller Order of St. John of God, centenary in Ireland.

Windmill and Sun — A150

1979, Oct. 4 Photo. *Perf. 14½x15*

458	A150	11p multicolored	.45	.35

Energy conservation.

"Seated Figure," by F.E. McWilliam A151

1979, Oct. 4 Litho. *Perf. 14½x14*

459	A151	20p multicolored	1.00	1.00

Patrick Pearse A152

1979, Nov. 10 Photo. *Perf. 15x14½*

460	A152	12p multicolored	.45	.35

Patrick Henry Pearse (1879-1916), Irish writer and leader of Easter Rebellion.

Mother and Child, Panel, Domnach Argid Shrine — A153

1979, Nov. 15 Photo. ***Perf. 14½x15***

461 A153 9½p multicolored .30 .25
462 A153 20p multicolored .65 .45

Christmas.

Europa Issue

Bianconi Long Car, 1836 A154

Laying Transatlantic Cable, Steamer William Cory, 1866 — A155

1979, Dec. 6 Litho. ***Perf. 15x14***

463 A154 12p multicolored *1.50* .40
464 A155 13p multicolored *5.50* .85

Type of 1968

Designs: 13p, 16p, Stag; others, Dog.

1980-82 Photo. ***Perf. 15***

466 A68 12p green .50 .25
467 A68 13p red brn & dk brn .80 1.25
468 A68 15p ultra .40 .25
469 A68 16p olive green & blk .80 1.50

Litho.

Perf. 14x15

470 A68 18p dull red brn ('81) 1.10 .25
471 A68 19p dull blue ('81) 1.10 *1.50*
472 A68 22p gray blue ('81) 1.10 .25
473 A68 24p brown olive ('81) 1.10 *2.00*
474 A68 26p bluish green ('82) 1.10 .25
475 A68 29p dp rose lilac ('82) 1.10 *2.00*
Nos. 466-475 (10) 9.10 9.50

Issued: 12p, 13p, 3/26/80; 15p, 16p, 7/10/80; 18p, 19p, 4/27/81; 22p, 9/1/81; 24p, 10/29/81; 26p, 29p, 4/1/82.

St. Jean Baptiste de la Salle — A156

1980, Mar. 19 Litho. ***Perf. 14x15***

477 A156 12p multicolored .45 .35

The Brothers of the Christian School (founded by St. Jean Baptiste), centenary in Ireland.

Europa Issue

George Bernard Shaw, by Alick Ritchie A157

Oscar Wilde, by Toulouse-Lautrec A158

1980, May 7 Litho. ***Perf. 14x15***

478 A157 12p multicolored *2.50* *.30*
479 A158 13p multicolored *2.50* *.65*

Irish Ermine — A159

1980, July 30 Litho. ***Perf. 14x15***

480 A159 12p shown .35 .30
481 A159 15p Irish hare .40 .35
482 A159 16p Fox .40 .30
483 A159 25p Red deer .85 .75
a. Miniature sheet of 4, #480-483 2.50 *3.00*
Nos. 480-483 (4) 2.00 1.70

Bodhran Drum and Whistle Players — A160

15p, Piper, Uilleann pipes. 25p, Irish jig.

1980, Sept. 25 Photo. ***Perf. 14x15***

484 A160 12p shown .35 .25
485 A160 15p multicolored .50 .55
486 A160 25p multicolored .60 *.65*
Nos. 484-486 (3) 1.45 1.45

Sean O'Casey (1880-1964), Playwright A161

1980, Oct. 23 Litho. ***Perf. 14x14½***

487 A161 12p multicolored .30 .25

Gold Painting No. 57, by Patrick Scott — A162

1980, Oct. 23 ***Perf. 14x15***

488 A162 25p multicolored .65 .45

A163

1980, Dec. 4 Photo. ***Perf. 15x14½***

489 A163 12p multicolored .25 .25
490 A163 15p multicolored .45 .40
491 A163 25p multicolored .75 .70
Nos. 489-491 (3) 1.45 1.35

Christmas.

A164

Scientists and Inventions: 12p, Robert Boyle (1627-1691), and Air Pump, 1659. 15p, Harry Ferguson (1884-1960), hydraulic tractor, 1936. 16p, Charles Parsons (1854-1931), Parsons' turbine, 1884. 25p, John Holland (1841-1914), Holland submarine, 1878.

1981, Mar. 12 Litho. ***Perf. 14x14½***

492 A164 12p multicolored .25 .25
493 A164 15p multicolored .30 .25
494 A164 16p multicolored .40 .35
495 A164 25p multicolored .80 .65
Nos. 492-495 (4) 1.75 1.50

The Cock and the Pot, Rubbing, 1841 — A165

Europa: 19p, The Scales of Judgment, rubbing, 1827.

1981, May 4 Litho. ***Perf. 14½x15***

496 A165 18p multicolored *2.00* *.30*
497 A165 19p multicolored *3.50* *.50*

Hiking A166

15p, Bicycling, vert. 19p, Mountain climbing. 30p, Rock climbing, vert.

Perf. 14x15, 15x14

1981, June 24 Litho.

498 A166 15p multicolored .25 .25
499 A166 18p shown .40 .40
500 A166 19p multicolored .45 .45
501 A166 30p multicolored .75 .75
Nos. 498-501 (4) 1.85 1.85

Youth Hostel Assn., 50th anniv.

Jeremiah O'Donovan Rossa (1831-1915), Journalist — A167

Railway Embankment, by William John Leech (1881-1968) — A168

Perf. 14½x15, 15x14½

1981, Aug. 31

502 A167 15p multicolored .45 .45
503 A168 30p multicolored .90 .90

James Hoban (1762-1831), White House Architect — A169

1981, Sept. 29 ***Perf. 15x14***

504 A169 18p multicolored .65 .40

See US Nos. 1935-1936.

Draft Horse King of Diamonds A170

Famous Horses: No. 505, Show-jumper Boomerang. No. 506, Steeplechaser Arkle. 24p, Flat racer Ballymoss. 36p, Connemara pony Coosheen Finn.

1981, Oct. 23 Litho. ***Perf. 15x14***

505 A170 18p multicolored .60 .50
506 A170 18p multicolored .60 .50
a. Pair, #505-506 1.40 2.50
507 A170 22p multicolored .85 .85
508 A170 24p multicolored .70 *.85*
509 A170 36p multicolored 1.40 1.40
Nos. 505-509 (5) 4.15 4.10

Nativity, by Federico Barocci — A171

1981, Nov. 19 Litho. ***Perf. 14x15***

510 A171 18p multicolored .35 .25
511 A171 22p multicolored .50 .40
512 A171 36p multicolored .90 .80
Nos. 510-512 (3) 1.75 1.45

Christmas 1981.

Land Law Act Cent. — A172

1981, Dec. 10 Litho. ***Perf. 14x14½***

513 A172 18p multicolored .65 .55

Land Law Act centenary.

250th Anniv. of Royal Dublin Society
A173

1981, Dec. 10 *Perf. 14½x14*
514 A173 22p multicolored .75 .60

50th Anniv. of Killarney Natl. Park
A174

1982, Feb. 26 Litho. *Perf. 14½x14*
515 A174 18p Upper Lake .55 .35
516 A174 36p Eagle's Nest .95 1.25

The Stigmatization of St. Francis, by Sassetta — A175

Francis Makemie, Old Presbyterian Church, Ramelton — A176

1982, Apr. 2 *Perf. 14x15, 15x14*
517 A175 22p multicolored .60 .50
518 A176 24p brown .90 .90

800th birth anniv. of St. Francis of Assisi; 300th anniv. of Francis Makemie's ordination (father of American Presbyterianism).

Europa Issue

Great Famine of 1845-50 — A177

Conversion of Ireland to Christianity (St. Patrick and his Followers, by Vincenzo Valdre)
A178

1982, May 4
519 A177 26p tan & brown *5.50* .75
520 A178 29p multicolored *7.50* 4.00

Padraic O'Connaire (1882-1928), Writer — A179

Designs: 26p, James Joyce (1882-1941), writer and poet, by Brancusi. 29p, John Field (1782-1837), Composer and pianist, Nocturne score. 44p, Charles Joseph Kickham (1828-1882), journalist and writer. 29p, 44p by Colin Harrison.

1982, June 16 Litho. *Perf. 14x15*
521 A179 22p blue & black .45 .45
522 A179 26p black & brown .70 .70
523 A179 29p black & blue 1.00 1.00
524 A179 44p gray green & black 1.50 1.50
Nos. 521-524 (4) 3.65 3.65

Porbeagle Shark
A180

No. 526, Oyster. No. 527, Salmon. No. 528, Dublin Bay prawn.

1982, July 29 *Perf. 15x14*
525 A180 22p shown .55 .55
526 A180 22p multicolored .55 .55
527 A180 26p multicolored .85 .55
528 A180 29p multicolored 1.10 1.10
Nos. 525-528 (4) 3.05 2.75

Currach
A181

No. 530, Galway hooker, vert. No. 531, Asgard II training ship. No. 532, Howth 17-footer, vert.

1982, Sept. 21 *Perf. 15x14, 14x15*
529 A181 22p shown .55 .45
530 A181 22p multicolored .55 .45
531 A181 26p multicolored .85 .75
532 A181 29p multicolored 1.20 1.20
Nos. 529-532 (4) 3.15 2.85

The Irish House of Commons, by Francis Wheatley
A182

1982, Oct. 14 Litho. *Perf. 14½x14*
533 A182 22p multicolored .40 .40

Bicentenary of Grattan's Parliament.

Portrait of Eamon de Valera (1882-1975), President, by Robert Ballagh — A183

1982, Oct. 14 *Perf. 14x14½*
534 A183 26p multicolored .60 .60

A183a — 535

Madonna and Child, by Andrea della Robbia (1435-1525)

1982, Nov. 11 Litho. *Perf. 14½x15*
535 A183a 22p lt violet & multi .45 .45
536 A183a 26p gray & multi .55 .55

Christmas.

A184

A185

Killarney Cathedral, 1855 — A186

Designs: 1p-5p, Central Pavilion, Dublin Botanical Gardens. 6p, 7p, 10p, 12p, Dr. Steeven's Hospital, Dublin. 15p, 20p, 22p, Aughnanure Castle, Oughterard, 16th cent. 23p, 26p, Cormac's Chapel, 1134. 29p, 30p, St. Mac Dara's Church. 50p, Casino, Marino. £1, Cahir Castle, 15th century. £5 Central Bus Station, Dublin, 1953.
50p, £1, £5 horiz.

1982-90 Litho. *Perf. 14x15, 15x14*
537 A184 1p dull blue .30 .25
538 A184 2p gray green .30 .25
539 A184 3p black .30 .25
540 A184 4p rose lake .30 .25
a. Perf. 13½ on 3 or 4 sides .95 .25
541 A184 5p brown .45 .30
542 A184 6p dull blue .45 .30
543 A184 7p gray green .85 .45
544 A184 10p black .85 .45
545 A184 12p rose lake .85 .45
546 A185 15p gray green 1.20 .55
547 A185 20p rose lake 1.20 .55
548 A185 22p dull blue 1.20 .55
a. Bklt. pane of 7+label (3 4p, 4 22p) ('83) 9.00
549 A185 23p gray green 1.50 1.00
550 A185 26p black 1.90 1.00
a. Bklt. pane, 2 ea 2p, 22p, 26p 10.50
b. Bklt. pane, 4 ea 2p, 22p, 26p 21.00
c. Bklt. pane, 3 4p, 5 22p, 4 26p ('88) 32.50
d. Perf. 13½ on 3 sides 4.50 2.00
551 A184 29p gray green 2.25 1.25
552 A184 30p black 1.40 .60
a. Perf. 13½ on 3 or 4 sides 2.50 .60

Perf. 14x15, 15x14

553 A186 44p gray & black 2.25 1.25
554 A186 50p gray & dull blue 2.25 .75
555 A186 £1 gray & brown 7.50 2.50
556 A186 £5 gray & rose lake 20.00 9.50
Nos. 537-556 (20) 47.30 22.45

Stamps from No. 550c imprinted "Booklet Stamp" in green on reverse side. No. 550c sold for £2.

Issued: 4p, 6p-7p, 20p, 23p, 30p, 50p, 3/16/83; 1p-3p, 5p, 10p-15p, 7/6/83; Nos. 540a, 550d, 552a, 5/3/90; others, 12/15/82.

See Nos. 638-645, 803a, 804b.

Dublin Chamber of Commerce Bicentenary
A187

Bank of Ireland Bicentenary — A188

22p, Ouzel Galley goblet. 26p, Bank.

1983, Feb. 23 **Litho.**
557 A187 22p blue & black .40 .40
558 A188 26p multicolored .60 .60

Padraig Siochfhradha (1883-1964), Writer — A189

Boys' Brigade Centenary
A190

1983, Apr. 7 Litho. *Perf. 14x14½*
559 A189 26p multicolored .60 .45
560 A190 29p multicolored 1.00 .75

Europa
A191

Design: 26p, Newgrange Winter Solstice, Neolithic Pattern Drawing by Louis le Brocquy. 29p, Quaternion formula, by William Rowan Hamilton (1805-1865).

1983, May 4 Litho. *Perf. 14½x14*
561 A191 26p dk gray & gold *3.50* .65
562 A191 29p multicolored *9.00* *6.00*

Kerry Blue Terrier
A192

Drawings of dogs by Wendy Walsh: No. 564, Irish wolfhound. No. 565, Irish water spaniel. No. 566, Irish terrier. No. 567, Irish setters.

1983, June 23
563 A192 22p shown .70 .70
564 A192 26p multicolored .85 .85
565 A192 26p multicolored .85 .85
566 A192 29p multicolored 1.00 1.00
567 A192 44p multicolored 1.50 1.50
a. Miniature sheet of 5, #563-567 6.00 6.00
Nos. 563-567 (5) 4.90 4.90

Sean Mac Diarmada (1883-1916), Nationalist
A193

Society for the Prevention of Cruelty to Animals A194

Society of St. Vincent de Paul Sesquicentennial A195

Industrial Credit Co., 50th Anniv. A196

US Pres. Andrew Jackson (1767-1845) A197

Perf. 14x14½, 14½x14

1983, Aug. 11

568	A193 22p multicolored	.60	.50
569	A194 22p multicolored	.60	.50
570	A195 26p multicolored	.75	.70
571	A196 26p multicolored	.75	.70
572	A197 44p gray	1.75	1.50
	Nos. 568-572 (5)	4.45	3.90

WCY — A198

1983, Sept. 15 Litho. ***Perf. 14x15***

573	A198 22p Mailman	1.00	1.00
574	A198 29p Dish antenna	1.25	1.25

Handicrafts A199

1983, Oct. 13 Litho. ***Perf. 14x15***

575	A199 22p Weaving	.80	.40
576	A199 26p Basketweaving	.90	.40
577	A199 29p Irish crochet	1.00	1.20
578	A199 44p Harpmaking	1.40	1.60
	Nos. 575-578 (4)	4.10	3.60

La Natividad by Rogier van der Weyden — A200

1983, Nov. 30 Litho. ***Perf. 14x14½***

579	A200 22p multicolored	.40	.25
580	A200 26p multicolored	.90	.60

Christmas.

Irish Railways Sesquicentenary — A201

Locomotives: 23p, Princess, Dublin and Kingstown Railway. 26p, Macha, Great Southern Railways. 29p, Kestrel, Great Northern Railway. 44p, Link-Hoffman railcar, Coras Iompair Eireann.

1984, Jan. 30 ***Perf. 14½x14***

581	A201 23p multicolored	.95	.95
582	A201 26p multicolored	.55	.55
583	A201 29p multicolored	1.10	1.10
584	A201 44p multicolored	1.90	1.90
a.	Souvenir sheet of 4, #581-584	5.50	*6.00*
	Nos. 581-584 (4)	4.50	4.50

Private Overprints

Nos. 584a, 684a, 708a, 708b, 803a, 804a, 811a, 826a, 847a, 855a, 876b, and others, exist with privately applied show overprints.

Local Trees A202

1984, Mar. 1 Litho. ***Perf. 15x14***

585	A202 22p Irish whitebeam	.75	.50
586	A202 26p Irish yew	.80	.50
587	A202 29p Irish willow	1.25	1.50
588	A202 44p Birch	1.50	1.75
	Nos. 585-588 (4)	4.30	4.25

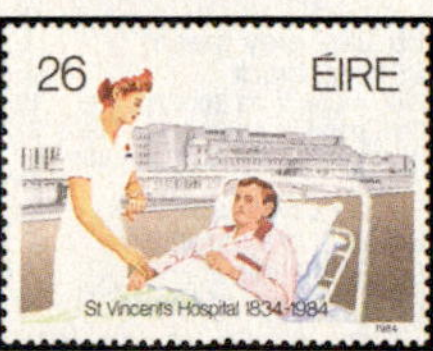

St. Vincent's Hospital, Dublin, Sesquicentenary — A203

Royal College of Surgeons in Ireland Bicentenary — A204

1984, Apr. 12 **Litho.**

589	A203 26p multicolored	.80	.70
590	A204 44p multicolored	1.50	1.40

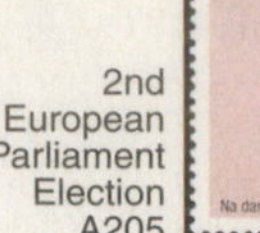

2nd European Parliament Election A205

1984, May 10 Litho. ***Perf. 15x14***

591	A205 26p multicolored	1.25	1.10

Europa (1959-84) A206

1984, May 10

592	A206 26p multicolored	*4.25*	*3.00*
593	A206 29p multicolored	*9.00*	*3.75*

John McCormack (1884-1945), Singer — A207

1984, June 6 Litho. ***Perf. 14x14½***

594	A207 22p multicolored	.85	.85

See US No. 2090.

1984 Summer Olympics A208

1984, June 21 Litho. ***Perf. 14½x14***

595	A208 22p Hammer throw	.60	.50
596	A208 26p Hurdles	.70	.40
597	A208 29p Running	.80	*1.20*
	Nos. 595-597 (3)	2.10	2.10

Gaelic Athletic Assoc. Centenary A209

1984, Aug. 23 Litho. ***Perf. 14x15***

598	A209 22p Hurlers	.65	*.75*
599	A209 26p Soccer, vert.	.90	.75

Mayoral City of Galway, 500th Anniv. — A210

St. Brendan (484-577) A211

26p, Medal. 44p, Portrait, manuscript.

1984, Sept. 18 ***Perf. 14x15, 15x14***

600	A210 26p multicolored	.60	.60
601	A211 44p multicolored	1.25	1.25

Post Office Bicentenary — A212

26p, Handing sealed letter.

1984, Oct. 19 ***Perf. 15x14***

602	A212 26p multicolored	.85	.85

A213

Virgin And Child by Sassoferrato A214

Perf. 14½x14, 14x14½

1984, Nov. 26 **Litho.**

603	A213 17p multicolored	.50	.50
604	A214 22p multicolored	.60	*.65*
605	A214 26p multicolored	.70	.65
	Nos. 603-605 (3)	1.80	1.80

Christmas.

Love A215

A216

22p, Heart-shaped balloon. 26p, Bouquet of hearts.

1985, Jan. 31 Litho. ***Perf. 15x14***

606	A215 22p multicolored	.50	.50
607	A216 26p multicolored	1.10	1.10

Dunsink Observatory, 200th Anniv. — A217

Cork City Charter, 800th Anniv. A218

Royal Irish Academy, 200th Anniv. — A219

1st Manned Flight in Ireland, 200th Anniv. — A220

1985, Mar. 14 **Litho.**

608	A217 22p black	.55	.40
609	A218 26p multicolored	.65	.40
610	A219 37p multicolored	.95	*1.30*
611	A220 44p multicolored	1.60	1.60
	Nos. 608-611 (4)	3.75	3.70

Butterflies A221

1985, Apr. 4 **Litho.** ***Perf. 14x15***

612	A221 22p Common blue	.90	.65
613	A221 26p Red admiral	1.00	.65
614	A221 28p Brimstone	1.50	*2.10*
615	A221 44p Marsh fritillary	2.50	*2.60*
	Nos. 612-615 (4)	5.90	*6.00*

Europa A222

26p, Charles Villiers Stanford (1852-1924), composer. 37p, Turlough O'Carolan (1670-1738), Composer.

1985, May 16 **Litho.** ***Perf. 15x14***

616	A222 26p multicolored	*3.50*	*.75*
617	A222 37p multicolored	*8.50*	*6.50*

European Music Year — A223

Composers: No. 618, Giuseppe Domenico Scarlatti (1685-1757). No. 619, George Frideric Handel (1685-1759). No. 620, Johann Sebastian Bach (1685-1750).

1985, May 16 **Litho.** ***Perf. 14x15***

618	A223 22p multicolored	1.25	*1.50*
619	A223 22p multicolored	1.25	*1.50*
a.	Pair, #618-619	4.00	4.50
620	A223 26p multicolored	1.25	*1.50*
	Nos. 618-620 (3)	3.75	4.50

Irish UN Defense Forces in the Congo, 1960 A224

Thomas Ashe (1885-1917), Patriot and Educator — A225

Bishop George Berkeley (1685-1753), Philosopher and Educator — A226

Perf. 15x14, 14x15

1985, June 20 **Litho.**

621	A224 22p multicolored	.75	.75
622	A225 26p multicolored	.85	.85
623	A226 44p multicolored	1.40	1.40
	Nos. 621-623 (3)	3.00	3.00

Irish forces as part of the UN Defense Forces, 25th anniv. (22p).

Intl. Youth Year — A227

1985, Aug. 1 **Litho.**

624	A227 22p multi, horiz.	.70	.70
625	A227 26p multicolored	.85	.85

Architecture Type of 1982

Designs: 24p, 39p, Cormac's Chapel. 28p, 32p, 37p, St. Mac Dara's Church. 46p, Cahir Castle. £1, Killarney Cathedral. £2, Casino, Marino. 46p, £2, horiz.

Perf. 15x14, 14x15 (A184, No. 644)

1985-88 **Litho.**

638	A185 24p brown	1.30	.70
639	A184 28p rose lake	1.60	.40
a.	Bklt. pane, 4 2p, 2 24p, 1 4p, 5 28p ('88)	8.00	
c.	Bklt. pane, 2 2p, 3 4p, 3 24p, 4 28p ('88)	8.50	
640	A184 32p brown	1.90	1.00
641	A184 37p dull blue	3.25	3.25
642	A185 39p rose lake	3.25	2.25
643	A186 46p gray & gray grn	3.50	2.50
644	A186 £1 gray & dull bl	6.00	2.00
645	A186 £2 gray & gray grn	10.00	6.00
	Nos. 638-645 (8)	30.80	18.10

Issued: 24p, 28p, 37p, £1, June 27, 1985; 32p, 39p, 46p, May 1, 1986; £2, July 26, 1988.

Industrial Innovations A228

Institution of Engineers, 150th Anniv. A229

22p, Computer technology. 26p, Peat production. 44p, The Key Man, by Sean Keating.

1985, Oct. 3 **Litho.** ***Perf. 15x14***

646	A228 22p multicolored	.60	.45
647	A228 26p multicolored	.85	.85
648	A229 44p multicolored	1.50	1.25
	Nos. 646-648 (3)	2.95	2.55

Candle, Holly — A230

Virgin and Child in a Landscape, by Adrian van Ijsenbrandt A231

Christmas: No. 651, The Holy Family, by Murillo. 26p, Adoration of the Shepherds, by Louis Le Nain, horiz.

Perf. 14x15, 15x14

1985, Nov. 26 **Litho.**

649	A230 22p shown	.85	.85
650	A231 22p shown	.85	.85
651	A231 22p multicolored	.85	.85
a.	Pair, #650-651	2.75	2.75
652	A231 26p multicolored	1.25	1.25
	Nos. 649-652 (4)	3.80	3.80

No. 649 was issued in discount sheets of 16 that sold for £3. Value $12.50.

Love — A232

26p, Heart-shaped mailbox.

1986, Jan. 30 ***Perf. 14x15***

653	A232 22p shown	1.10	.80
654	A232 26p multicolored	1.10	1.00

Ferns — A233

1986, Mar. 20 **Litho.** ***Perf. 14½x15***

655	A233 24p Hart's tongue	.75	.35
656	A233 28p Rusty-back	1.00	.90
657	A233 46p Killarney	1.75	1.75
	Nos. 655-657 (3)	3.50	3.00

Europa — A234

28p, Industry and nature. 39p, Hedgerows, horiz.

1986, May 1 ***Perf. 14x15, 15x14***

658	A234 28p multicolored	*7.50*	*1.25*
659	A234 39p multicolored	*25.00*	*6.00*

Aer Lingus, 50th Anniv. A235

28p, Jet, 1986. 46p, The Eagle, 1936.

1986, May 27 ***Perf. 15x14***

660	A235 28p multicolored	1.40	1.40
661	A235 46p multicolored	2.00	2.00

Inland Waterways A236

24p, Robertstown Grand Canal. 28p, Fishing, County Mayo, vert. 30p, Yachting, River Shannon.

1986, May 27 ***Perf. 15x14, 14x15***

662	A236 24p multicolored	1.10	*1.20*
663	A236 28p multicolored	1.30	1.05
664	A236 30p multicolored	1.60	*1.75*
	Nos. 662-664 (3)	4.00	*4.00*

British & Irish Steam Packet Co., 150th Anniv. A237

24p, Steamer Severn, 1836. 28p, M.V. Leinster, 1986.

1986, July 10 ***Perf. 15x14***

665	A237 24p multicolored	1.25	1.25
666	A237 28p multicolored	1.75	1.75

Lighthouses A238

1986, July 10 ***Perf. 14½x15***

667	A238 24p Kish, helicopter	1.40	1.40
668	A238 30p Fastnet	1.75	1.75

Dublin Council of Trade Unions, Cent. — A239

Arthur Griffith (1871-1922), Statesman
A240

Women in Society, Construction Surveyor — A241

A242

Intl. Peace Year
A242a

Perf. 14½x15, 14x15 (#670, 672), 15x14½, 15x14

1986, Aug. 21

669 A239 24p multicolored .60 .60
670 A240 28p multicolored .70 .50
671 A241 28p multicolored .70 .50
672 A242 30p multi, vert. .75 *1.05*
673 A242a 46p shown 1.00 *1.30*
Nos. 669-673 (5) 3.75 3.95

See Nos. 699, 711, 749, 807, 836.

William Mulready (1786-1863), Letter Sheet Designer — A243

Carriages by Charles Bianconi (1786-1875) — A244

Perf. 15x14, 14x15

1986, Oct. 2 **Litho.**

674 A243 24p multicolored .80 .50
675 A244 28p multi, vert. .95 .40
676 A244 39p shown 1.25 1.15
Nos. 674-676 (3) 3.00 2.05

Adoration of the Shepherds, by Francesco Pascucci
A245

Adoration of the Magi, by Frans Francken III (1542-1616)
A246

1986, Nov. 20 ***Perf. 15x14, 14½x15***

677 A245 21p multicolored .75 .75
678 A246 28p multicolored 1.10 1.10

Christmas. No. 677 was issued in discount sheets of 12 that sold for £2.50. Value $20.

Love
A247

Perf. 15x14, 14x15

1987, Jan. 27 **Litho.**

679 A247 24p Flowers, butterfly .85 .85
680 A247 28p Postman, vert. 1.25 1.25

Trolleys
A248

1987, Mar. 4 **Litho.** ***Perf. 15x14***

681 A248 24p Cork Electric .70 .70
682 A248 28p Dublin Standard .85 .85
683 A248 30p Howth (G.N.R.) 1.00 1.00
684 A248 46p Galway Horse 1.50 1.50
a. Miniature sheet of 4, #681-684 5.50 5.50
Nos. 681-684 (4) 4.05 4.05

See note following No. 584.

Waterford Chamber of Commerce, 200th Anniv.
A249

Muintir Na Tire, 50th Anniv.
A250

Trinity College Botanical Gardens, Dublin, 300th Anniv. — A251

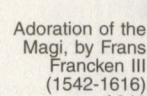

Medical Missionaries of Mary, 50th Anniv. — A252

Anniversaries and events: 24p, Three ships, Chamber crest. 28p, Canon Hayes (1887-1957), founder, and symbols of Muintir Na Tire activities. 30p, College crest, Calceolaria burbidgei. 39p, Intl. Missionary Training Hospital, Drogheda, and Mother Mary Martin.

Perf. 15x14, 14x15

1987, Apr. 9 **Litho.**

685 A249 24p vio bl, blk & dk grn .65 .65
686 A250 28p multicolored .80 .80
687 A251 30p multicolored .90 .90
688 A252 39p multicolored 1.15 1.15
Nos. 685-688 (4) 3.50 3.50

Europa
A253

Modern architecture, art: 28p, Borda na Mona headquarters, Dublin, and The Turf Cutter, by sculptor John Behan. 39p, St. Mary's Church and ruins of Romanesque monastery at Cong.

1987, May 14 ***Perf. 15x14***

689 A253 28p multicolored *5.00* *2.00*
690 A253 39p multicolored *8.00* *5.00*

Cattle
A254

1987, July 2

691 A254 24p Kerry .85 .60
692 A254 28p Friesian 1.10 1.10
693 A254 30p Hereford 1.10 1.10
694 A254 39p Shorthorn 1.50 1.50
Nos. 691-694 (4) 4.55 4.30

Festivals
A255

24p, Fleadh Nua, Ennis. 28p, Festival Queen, Tralee. 30p, Wexford opera festival. 46p, Ballinasloe horse fair.

1987, Aug. 27 ***Perf. 14x15***

695 A255 24p multicolored .85 .75
696 A255 28p multicolored 1.00 .75
697 A255 30p multicolored 1.25 1.25
698 A255 46p multicolored 1.50 1.90
Nos. 695-698 (4) 4.60 4.65

Nos. 695-696 vert.

Statesmen Type of 1986 and

Ewer and Chalice, Company Crest
A256

Harp in Shield, Preamble Excerpt
A257

Woman Leading Board Meeting — A258

Design: No. 699, Cathal Brugha, vert.

Perf. 14x15, 15x14

1987, Oct. 1 **Litho.**

699 A240 24p black .80 .80
700 A256 24p multicolored .80 .80
701 A257 28p multicolored .90 .90
702 A258 46p multicolored 1.40 1.40
Nos. 699-702 (4) 3.90 3.90

Company of Goldsmiths of Dublin, 350th anniv. (No. 700); Irish Constitution, 50th anniv. (28p); Women in Society, (46p).

A259

Christmas
A260

21p, 12 Days of Christmas (1st 3 days). 24p, Embroidery (detail), Waterford Vestments, 15th cent. 28p, Neapolitan creche (detail), 1850.

Perf. 15x14, 14x15

1987, Nov. 17 **Litho.**

703 A259 21p multicolored .65 .40
704 A260 24p multicolored .80 .80
705 A260 28p multicolored 1.00 1.00
Nos. 703-705 (3) 2.45 2.20

No. 703 issued in discount sheets of 14 + center label; sheet sold for £2.90. Value $17.50.

Love
A261

Perf. 15x14½, 14½x15

1988, Jan. 27 **Litho.**

706 A261 24p shown .90 .90
707 A261 28p Pillar box, vert. 1.10 1.10

Dublin Millennium
A262

1988, Mar. 1 ***Perf. 15x14***

708 A262 28p multicolored 1.50 1.00
a. Booklet pane of 4, Gaelic 6.00
b. Booklet pane of 4, English 6.00

Nos. 708a, 708b consist of two vert. pairs separated by a history in Gaelic or English.

See note following No. 584.

A263

Impact of the Irish Abroad A264

Designs: No. 709, Robert O'Hara Burke (1820-1861), by Sir Sidney Nolan; 19th cent. map of Australia with Burke & Wills expedition route. 46p, Mural (detail) of the Eureka Stockade by Nolan.

1988, Mar. 1
709 A263 24p multicolored 1.00 1.00
710 A264 46p multicolored 2.00 2.00

Statesmen Type of 1986 and

1988 Summer Olympics, Seoul A265

Order of Malta Ambulance Corps, 50th Anniv. A266

Barry Fitzgerald (1888-1961), Actor — A267

Designs: 24p, William T. Cosgrave (1880-1965), president of the United Ireland and Fine Gael party. No. 713, Cycling.

Perf. 14x15, 15x14
1988, Apr. 7 **Litho.**
711 A240 24p black .70 .70
712 A265 28p multicolored .75 .60
713 A265 28p multicolored .75 .60
a. Pair, #712-713 3.00 3.00
714 A266 30p multicolored 1.10 1.30
715 A267 50p multicolored 1.25 1.30
Nos. 711-715 (5) 4.55 4.50

Nos. 712-713 printed in sheets of 5 each plus two labels. Value, $16.50.

Sirius Sailing from Passage West, County Cork A268

1988, May 12 **Litho.** ***Perf. 15x14***
716 A268 24p multicolored 1.50 1.50

1st scheduled transatlantic crossing by steamship, sesquicentennial.

Europa A269

28p, Air traffic controllers and A320 Airbus. 39p, Europe on globe, letters.

1988, May 12 **Litho.** ***Perf. 15x14***
717 A269 28p multicolored *3.50* 1.00
718 A269 39p multicolored *6.00* 3.00

Maia and Mercury Flying Boats in Foynes Harbor A269a

1988, May 12 **Litho.** ***Perf. 15x14***
719 A269a 46p multicolored 2.50 2.50

1st east-west transatlantic crossing by seaplane, 50th anniv.

Conservation of Flora — A270

24p, Otanthus maritimus. 28p, Saxifraga hartii. 46p, Astragalus danicus.

1988, June 21 **Litho.** ***Perf. 14x15***
720 A270 24p multicolored .90 .65
721 A270 28p multicolored 1.00 .65
722 A270 46p multicolored 1.90 *2.50*
Nos. 720-722 (3) 3.80 3.80

Irish Security Forces A271

No. 723, Garda Siochana (police). No. 724, Army. No. 725, Navy, air corps. No. 726, FCA, Slua Muiri.

1988, Aug. 23 **Litho.** ***Perf. 15x14***
723 A271 28p multicolored 1.50 1.00
724 A271 28p multicolored 1.50 1.00
725 A271 28p multicolored 1.50 1.00
726 A271 28p multicolored 1.50 1.00
a. Strip of 4, #723-726 6.00 6.00

Institute of Chartered Accountants, Cent. — A272

Defeat of the Spanish Armada, 400th Anniv. A273

46p, Duquesa Santa Ana off Donegal Coast.

Perf. 14x15, 15x14
1988, Oct. 6 **Litho.**
727 A272 24p multicolored .90 .90
728 A273 46p multicolored 1.50 1.50

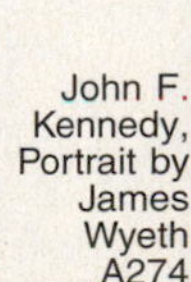

John F. Kennedy, Portrait by James Wyeth A274

1988, Nov. 24 **Litho.** ***Perf. 15x14***
729 A274 28p multicolored 1.60 1.00

A275

Christmas A276

21p, St. Kevin's Church, Glendalough. 24p, Adoration of the Magi. 28p, Flight into Egypt. 46p, Holy Family.

1988, Nov. 24 ***Perf. 14x15***
730 A275 21p multicolored .90 .40
731 A276 24p multicolored .80 .50
732 A276 28p multicolored 1.00 .50
733 A276 46p multicolored 1.50 1.75
Nos. 730-733 (4) 4.20 3.15

No. 730 issued only in discount sheets of 14. Sheet sold for £2.90. Value $15.50.

Love A277

The Sonnet, by William Mulready (1786-1863) A278

Perf. 15x14, 14x15
1989, Jan. 24 **Litho.**
734 A277 24p multicolored 1.00 .80
735 A278 28p multicolored 1.00 .80

Mulready, designer of Rowland Hill's first stamped envelope.

Classic Automobiles — A279

1989, Apr. 11 **Litho.** ***Perf. 15x14***
736 A279 24p Silver Stream .85 .60
737 A279 28p Benz Comfortable 1.00 .60
a. Booklet pane, 2 each 24p, 28p 4.00
738 A279 39p Thomond Car 1.25 *1.50*
739 A279 46p Chambers Car 1.40 1.90
a. Booklet pane of 4, #736-739 6.00
Nos. 736-739 (4) 4.50 4.60

Parks and Gardens A280

24p, Garinish Island. 28p, Glenveagh. 32p, Connemara Natl. Park. 50p, St. Stephen's Green.

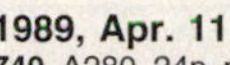

1989, Apr. 11
740 A280 24p multicolored .85 .60
741 A280 28p multicolored .85 .50
742 A280 32p multicolored 1.10 .75
743 A280 50p multicolored 1.75 *2.10*
Nos. 740-743 (4) 4.55 3.95

Europa A281

28p, Ring-a-ring-a-rosie. 39p, Hopscotch.

1989, May 11
744 A281 28p multicolored *1.00* *.90*
745 A281 39p multicolored *1.50* *1.50*

Irish Red Cross Soc., 50th Anniv. — A282

1989, May 11 ***Perf. 14x15***
746 A282 24p multicolored 1.00 1.00

European Parliament 3rd Elections — A283

1989, May 11
747 A283 28p Stars from flag 1.00 1.00

Sts. Kilian, Colman and Totnan (d. 689), Martyred Missionaries, and Shamrock — A284

1989, June 15 **Litho.** ***Perf. 13½***
748 A284 28p multicolored 1.25 1.25
a. Booklet pane of 4, English 5.00
b. Booklet pane of 4, Gaelic 5.00
c. Booklet pane of 4, German 5.00
d. Booklet pane of 4, Latin 5.00

See Federal Republic of Germany No. 1580.

Statesmen Type of 1986 and

RIAI Emblem — A285

Dublin-Cork Coach, 1789 — A286

Singer, Scene from La Boheme A287

Nehru — A288

Design: 24p, Sean Thomas O'Kelly (1883-1966), 2nd president.

Perf. 14x15, 15x14

1989, July 25 **Litho.**

749 A240 24p black .75 .40
750 A285 28p multicolored .80 .50
751 A286 28p multicolored 1.25 1.00
752 A287 30p multicolored .90 *1.15*
753 A288 46p red brown 1.35 *2.00*
Nos. 749-753 (5) 5.05 5.05

Royal Institute of Architects, 150th anniv.; Mail coach in Ireland, bicent.; Margaret Burke Sheridan (1889-1958), soprano; Jawaharlal Nehru, 1st prime minister of independent India.

Flags and Sail Ireland Yacht Rounding Cape Horn, by Des Fallon A289

1989, Aug. 31 **Litho.** ***Perf. 15x14***

754 A289 28p multicolored 1.75 1.35

Whitbread round of the World Yacht Race 1989-90.

Wildlife: Game Birds — A290

24p, Lagopus lagopus. 28p, Vanellus vanellus. 39p, Scolopax rusticola. 46p, Phasianus colchicus.

1989, Oct. 5 **Litho.** ***Perf. 13½***

755 A290 24p multicolored 1.15 .95
756 A290 28p multicolored 1.15 .95
757 A290 39p multicolored 2.00 2.40
758 A290 46p multicolored 2.25 *2.75*
a. Miniature sheet of 4, #755-758 8.00 *8.50*
Nos. 755-758 (4) 6.55 7.05

Children and Creche — A291

Miniatures from a Flemish Psalter, 13th Cent. — A292

24p, Annunciation. 28p, Nativity. 46p, Adoration of the Magi.

1989, Nov. 14 **Litho.** ***Perf. 14x15***

759 A291 21p multicolored .70 .70
760 A292 24p multicolored .70 .70
761 A292 28p multicolored 1.00 1.00
762 A292 46p multicolored 1.50 1.50
Nos. 759-762 (4) 3.90 3.90

No. 759 issued only in discount sheets of 14. Sheet sold for £2.90. Value $15.

Ireland's Presidency of the European Communities — A293

European Tourism Year A294

1990, Jan. 9 **Litho.** ***Perf. 15x14***

763 A293 30p multicolored 1.10 1.10
764 A294 50p multicolored 1.90 1.90

A295

Love Issue — A296

26p, Heart Hot Air Balloon with Love underneath. 30p, "Love!".

1990, Jan. 30 **Litho.** ***Perf. 14x15***

765 A295 26p multicolored 1.30 1.30
766 A296 30p multicolored 1.35 1.35

Enamel Latchet Brooch — A297

Ardagh Chalice A298

Art treasures of Ireland: 1p, 2p, Silver Kite Brooch, vert. 4p, 5p, Dunamase Food Vessel, vert. 10p, Derrinboy Armlets. 20p, Gold Dress Fastener. 26p, 28p, Lismore Crosier, vert. 32p, Broighter Collar. 34p, 37p, 38p, 40p, Gleninsheen Collar, vert. 41p, 44p, 45p, Silver thistle brooch, vert. 50p, 52p, Broighter boat, vert. £2, Tara Brooch. £5, St. Patrick's Bell Shrine, vert.

1990-95 **Litho.** ***Perf. 15x14, 14x15***

767 A297 1p blue & blk .40 .25
768 A297 2p orange & blk .40 .25
770 A297 4p violet & blk .45 .25
a. Perf. 13x13½ .45 *.60*
b. Photo. .60 *.80*
771 A297 5p green & blk .45 .25
774 A297 10p orange & blk .60 .25
777 A297 20p yel & blk (I) 1.15 .40
778 A297 26p violet & blk .95 .40
a. Perf. 13½ on 3 or 4 sides 3.75 *4.00*
779 A297 28p org & blk (I) 1.15 .40
a. Bklt. pane, 3 #770, 4 #779 + label 4.25
b. Photo. 1.90 *2.75*
780 A297 30p brt blue & blk .95 .40
a. Perf. 13½ 3.75 *4.00*
b. Bklt. pane, 3 #540a, 1 #550d, 2 #778a, 2 #780a 8.50
c. Bklt. pane, #768, 3 #770, #778, 2 #780 + label 5.50
781 A297 32p green & blk .95 .40
a. Bklt. pane, 2 #770b, #779b, 2 #781d 4.50
b. Perf. 13½x13 1.00 1.25
c. Bklt. pane, #770a, 3 #781b 6.50
d. Photo. 1.90 2.00
e. Booklet pane, 1 #770, 3 #781 6.50
782 A297 34p yellow & blk 2.75 *3.00*
783 A297 37p green & blk 3.25 3.00
784 A297 38p purple & blk 3.25 3.25
785 A297 40p blue & black 3.50 *3.75*
786 A297 41p orange & blk 2.75 *3.00*
787 A297 44p yellow & blk 2.00 1.90
788 A297 45p violet & black 3.25 3.75
789 A297 50p yellow & blk 2.00 .75
790 A297 52p blue & blk (I) 1.60 1.90
791 A298 £1 yellow & blk (III) 3.50 1.50
792 A298 £2 green & blk (III) 6.25 3.00
793 A298 £5 blue & blk (III) 14.00 9.00

Self-Adhesive

Die cut perf 11

Size: 27x21mm

794 A297 32p like #781 2.00 1.15
a. Die cut perf. 11½ 3.50 3.50
b. Die cut perf. 9½x9 2.00 1.15
Nos. 767-794 (23) 57.55 42.20

Issued: 26p, 30p, 32p, 41p, 50p, £1, 3/8; No. 780b, 5/3; 1p, 2p, 4p, 10p, 34p, £2, 7/26; No. 780c, 11/15; 5p, 20p, £5, 1/26/91; No. 781a, 5/14/91; 28p, 37p, 38p, 44p, 52p, 4/3/91; No. 779a, 10/17/91; No. 794, 10/31/91; 40p, 45p, 5/14/92; Nos. 770a, 781b, 9/24/93; No. 781e, 11/16/95; No. 794b, 6/8/95.

No. 794 was printed on phosphored paper; No. 794a on normal paper.

#777, 779, 790, Type I - Coarse Dot Structure

#777a, 779c, 790a, Type II - Fine Dot Structure

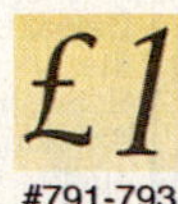

#791-793, Type III

#791a-793a, Type IV

Perf. 14x15, 15x14

1995, Nov. 15 **Litho.**

777a A297 20p Type II 1.25 .90
779c A297 28p Type II 1.75 1.35
790a A297 52p Type II 2.75 *3.00*
791a A298 £1 Type IV 4.75 4.00
792a A298 £2 Type IV 8.50 *9.75*
793a A298 £5 Type IV 22.50 *23.00*
Nos. 777a-793a (6) 41.50 *42.00*

A299

1990, Mar. 22 **Litho.** ***Perf. 14x15***

Booklet Stamps

795 A299 26p Gift boxes 2.25 2.25
796 A299 26p Nosegay 2.25 2.25
797 A299 30p Horseshoe 2.25 2.25
798 A299 30p Balloons 2.25 2.25
a. Bklt. pane of 4, #795-798 English labels 10.00
b. As "a," 4 English, 4 Gaelic labels 10.00

Greetings. Available only in discount booklets containing Nos. 798a, 798b. Bklts. sold for £1.98.

A300

1990, Apr. 5 **Litho.** ***Perf. 14x15***

799 A300 30p Tackle 1.90 1.90
800 A300 30p Heading the ball 1.90 1.90
a. Pair, #799-800 4.00 4.00

1990 World Cup Soccer Championships, Italy.

Printed in sheets of 4 No. 800a plus label. Value, $25.

Williamite Wars, 300th Anniv. — A301

No. 801, Siege of Limerick. No. 802, Battle of the Boyne.

1990, Apr. 5 **Litho.** ***Perf. 13½***

801 A301 30p multicolored 1.60 1.60
802 A301 30p multicolored 1.60 1.60
a. Pair, #801-802 3.50 3.50

Penny Black, 150th Anniv. A302

1990, May 3 **Litho.** ***Perf. 15x14***

803 A302 30p #780 1.25 1.25
a. Bklt. pane, #803, 2 each #552a, 780a 8.00
804 A302 50p #68, 255, 550, 780 1.75 1.75
a. Bklt. pane, 2 ea #803-804 9.50
b. Bklt. pane of 4, #552a, 780a, 803-804 8.00
Complete bklt., #803a, 804a, 804b, 780b 25.00

See note following No. 584.

Europa 1990 — A303

Post offices: 30p, GPO, Dublin. 41p, Westport P.O., County Mayo.

1990, May 3 ***Perf. 14x15***

805 A303 30p multicolored *1.50* *1.25*
806 A303 41p multicolored *1.75* *1.50*

Printed in sheets of 10+2 labels. Value $27.50.

Statesman Type of 1986

1990, June 21 **Litho.** ***Perf. 14x15***

807 A240 30p Michael Collins 3.25 2.50

Irish Missionaries — A304

Design: 50p, Working at water pump.

1990, June 21 ***Perf. 15x14***

808 A304 26p multicolored 1.00 1.00
809 A304 50p multicolored 2.00 2.00

Garden Flowers — A305

1990, Aug. 30 **Litho.** ***Perf. 14x15***

810 A305 26p Narcissus .65 .65
811 A305 30p Rosa x hibernica .85 .85
a. Bklt. pane, 2 each #810-811 7.25
812 A305 41p Primula 1.30 1.30
813 A305 50p Erica erigena 1.40 1.40
a. Booklet pane of 4, #810-813 8.00
Nos. 810-813 (4) 4.20 4.20

See note following No. 584.

Theater A306

Designs: No. 814, Playboy of the Western World. No. 815, Juno and the Paycock. No. 816, The Field. No. 817, Waiting for Godot.

1990, Oct. 18 **Litho.** ***Perf. 13½***

814 A306 30p multicolored 1.25 1.25
815 A306 30p multicolored 1.25 1.25
816 A306 30p multicolored 1.25 1.25
817 A306 30p multicolored 1.25 1.25
a. Block or strip of 4, #814-817 5.50 5.50

A307

Christmas A308

No. 818, Child praying. No. 819, Nativity scene. No. 820, Madonna and Child. No. 821, Adoration of the Magi.

1990, Nov. 15 **Litho.** ***Perf. 14x15***

818 A307 26p multicolored .70 .70
819 A308 26p multicolored .70 .70
820 A308 30p multicolored .90 .90
821 A308 50p multicolored 1.50 1.50
Nos. 818-821 (4) 3.80 3.80

No. 818 sold only in discount sheets of 12 for £2.86. Value $15.

Love — A309

1991, Jan. 29 **Litho.** ***Perf. 14x15***

822 A309 26p shown .90 .75
823 A309 30p Boy, girl kissing 1.10 .90

Irish Cycles — A310

26p, Starley rover. 30p, Child's horse tricycle. 50p, Penny farthing.

1991, Mar. 5

824 A310 26p multicolored .95 .95
825 A310 30p multicolored 1.20 1.20
826 A310 50p multicolored 1.75 1.75
a. Souvenir sheet of 3, #824-826 4.75 *4.75*
Nos. 824-826 (3) 3.90 3.90

See note following No. 584.

1916 Rising, 75th Anniv. A311

Design: Statue of Cuchulainn by Oliver Sheppard, 1916 Proclamation.

1991, Apr. 3 **Litho.** ***Perf. 15x14***

827 A311 32p multicolored 2.25 1.50

Dublin, European City of Culture A312

Designs: 28p, La Traviata, performed by Dublin Grand Opera Society. 32p, Dublin City Hall. 44p, St. Patrick's Cathedral, 800th anniv. 52p, Custom House, 200th anniv.

1991, Apr. 11 ***Perf. 15x14***

828 A312 28p multicolored .65 .65
829 A312 32p multicolored .75 .75
830 A312 44p multicolored 1.00 1.00
a. Booklet pane of 3, #828-830 4.50 4.50

Size: 41x25mm

Perf. 13½

831 A312 52p multicolored 1.40 1.40
a. Booklet pane of 4, #828-831 6.00
Complete booklet, #830a, 831a 11.00
Nos. 828-831 (4) 3.80 3.80

50th anniv. of Dublin Grand Opera Soc. (No. 828).

Europa A313

1991, May 14 **Litho.** ***Perf. 15x14***

832 A313 32p Giotto probe *1.00* *.75*
833 A313 44p Hubble telescope *1.75* *1.75*

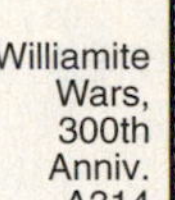

Williamite Wars, 300th Anniv. A314

1991, May 14

834 A314 28p Siege of Athlone 1.50 1.50
835 A314 28p Treaty of Limerick 1.50 1.50
a. Pair, #834-835 3.00 3.00

Statesman Type of 1986 and

Charles Stewart Parnell (1846-1891), Politician — A315

Society of United Irishmen, Bicent. A316

28p, John A. Costello (1891-1976), politician.

Perf. 14x15, 15x14

1991, July 2 **Litho.**

836 A240 28p black .90 .90
837 A315 32p multicolored 1.25 1.25
838 A316 52p multicolored 1.90 1.90
Nos. 836-838 (3) 4.05 4.05

A317

28p, Golfer putting, horiz.

Perf. 15x14, 14x15

1991, Sept. 3 **Litho.**

839 A317 28p multicolored 1.25 1.25
840 A317 32p shown 1.75 1.75

Walker Cup Competition, Portmarnock Golf Club (No. 839).

Irish Sheep — A318

1991, Sept. 3 ***Perf. 14x15, 15x14***

841 A318 32p Wicklow Cheviot 1.00 1.00
842 A318 38p Donegal Blackface 1.50 1.50
843 A318 52p Galway, horiz. 2.10 2.10
Nos. 841-843 (3) 4.60 4.60

Fishing Fleet A319

1991, Oct. 17 **Litho.** ***Perf. 15x14***

844 A319 28p Boatyard .80 .80
845 A319 32p Inshore trawler .90 .90
a. Bklt. pane of 5, #845, 2 each #768, 783 5.00
b. Bklt. pane, 2 each #844, 845 5.75
846 A319 44p Inshore potter 1.30 1.30
847 A319 52p Factory ship 2.00 2.00
a. Booklet pane of 4, #844-847 8.00
Nos. 844-847 (4) 5.00 5.00

See note following No. 584.

A320

Christmas A321

1991, Nov. 14 **Litho.** ***Perf. 14x15***

848 A320 28p Wise men, star .80 .80
849 A321 28p Annunciation 1.10 1.10
850 A321 32p Nativity 1.25 1.25
851 A321 52p Adoration of the Magi 1.75 1.75
Nos. 848-851 (4) 4.90 4.90

No. 848 issued only in discount sheets of 13+2 labels which sold for £3.36. Value $14.50.

Love A322

Design: 32p, Rainbow over meadow, love etched in stone, vert.

Perf. 15x14, 14x15

1992, Jan. 28 **Litho.**

852 A322 28p shown 1.00 1.00
853 A322 32p multicolored 1.50 1.50

1992 Summer Olympics, Barcelona A323

1992, Feb. 25 **Litho.** ***Perf. 15x14***

854 A323 32p Boxing 1.15 1.15
855 A323 44p Sailing 1.40 1.40
a. Sheet of 4, 2 each #854-855 6.00 *6.25*

See note following No. 584.

Healthy Lifestyle — A324

1992, Feb. 25 ***Perf. 14x15***

856 A324 28p multicolored 1.35 1.35

Galway Chamber of Commerce and Industry, Bicent. A325

1992, Apr. 2 Litho. *Perf. 15x14*
857 A325 28p multicolored 1.25 1.25

Intl. Maritime Heritage Year A326

Perf. 15x14, 14x15
1992, Apr. 2 Litho.
858 A326 32p Mari Cog 1.40 1.40
859 A326 52p Ovoca, vert. 1.75 1.75

Greetings — A327

1992, Apr. 2 *Perf. 14x15*
860 A327 28p Coastline 1.60 1.60
861 A327 28p Mountain 1.60 1.60
862 A327 32p Flowers 1.60 1.60
863 A327 32p Pond 1.60 1.60
a. Bklt. pane of 4, #860-863, 8 English labels 7.00
b. Bklt. pane of 4, #860-863, 4 English labels + 4 Gaelic labels 7.00
Nos. 860-863 (4) 6.40 6.40

No. 863a contains Nos. 860-863 in order. No. 863b contains Nos. 862, 863, 860 and 861 in order.

Discovery of America, 500th Anniv. A328

Europa: 44p, Landing in New World.

1992, May 14 Litho. *Perf. 15x14*
864 A328 32p multicolored *1.25 1.00*
865 A328 44p multicolored *1.50 1.25*

Irish in the Americas — A329

Design: No. 867, The White House, bridge, railroad workers, musicians, workers.

1992, May 14 *Perf. 13½*
866 A329 52p multicolored 1.90 1.90
867 A329 52p multicolored 1.90 1.90
a. Pair, #866-867 4.00 4.00

Pine Marten A330

1992, July 9 Litho. *Perf. 15x14*
868 A330 28p shown 1.15 1.15
869 A330 32p In tree 1.40 1.40
870 A330 44p With young 2.00 2.00
871 A330 52p Holding bird 2.40 2.40
Nos. 868-871 (4) 6.95 6.95

World Wildlife Fund.

Trinity College, Dublin, 400th Anniv. — A331

1992, Sept. 2 Litho. *Perf. 13½*
872 A331 32p Library 1.20 1.20
873 A331 52p Main entrance 1.90 1.90

Views of Dublin by James Malton, Bicent. A332

28p, Rotunda, Assembly rooms. 44p, Charlemont House.

1992, Sept. 2 *Perf. 15x14*
874 A332 28p multicolored 1.00 1.00
875 A332 44p multicolored 1.25 1.25

Single European Market A333

1992, Oct. 15 Litho. *Perf. 15x14*
876 A333 32p multicolored 1.30 1.30
a. Bklt. pane of 3 4.00 4.00
b. Bklt. pane of 4 5.50 5.50

No. 876b comes with stamps in three formats: four singles, two pairs, and block of four.
See note following No. 584.

Food and Farming — A334

No. 877, Fresh food. No. 878, Cattle. No. 879, Combine harvesting grain. No. 880, Growing vegetables.

1992, Oct. 15 *Perf. 14x15*
877 A334 32p multicolored 1.50 1.50
878 A334 32p multicolored 1.50 1.50
879 A334 32p multicolored 1.50 1.50
880 A334 32p multicolored 1.50 1.50
a. Strip of 4, #877-880 6.00 6.00

A335

Christmas A336

Designs: No. 881, Rural churchyard. No. 882, The Annunciation, manuscript illustration, Chester Beatty Library, Dublin. 32p, Adoration of the Shepherds, by Jocopo da Empoli. 52p, Adoration of the Magi, by Johann Rottenhammer.

1992, Nov. 19
881 A335 28p multicolored .95 .95
882 A336 28p multicolored 1.10 1.10
883 A336 32p multicolored 1.10 1.10
884 A336 52p multicolored 1.40 1.40
Nos. 881-884 (4) 4.55 4.55

No. 881 issued only in discount sheets of 13+2 labels which sold for £3.36. Value $14.

Love A337

Design: 28p, Queen of Hearts, vert.

Perf. 14x15, 15x14
1993, Jan. 26 Litho.
885 A337 28p multicolored 1.00 1.00
886 A337 32p multicolored 1.10 1.10

Irish Impressionist Paintings — A338

Designs: 28p, Evening at Tangier, by Sir John Lavery. 32p, The Goose Girl, by William J. Leech. 44p, La Jeune Bretonne, by Roderic O'Conor, vert. 52p, Lustre Jug, by Walter Osborne, vert.

1993, Mar. 4 *Perf. 13*
887 A338 28p multicolored .90 .90
888 A338 32p multicolored 1.10 1.10
a. Booklet pane of 2, #887-888 2.75
889 A338 44p multicolored 1.25 1.25
890 A338 52p multicolored 1.75 1.75
a. Booklet pane of 2, #889-890 3.50
b. Booklet pane of 4, #887-890 5.50
Nos. 887-890 (4) 5.00 5.00

No. 890b exists in two formats with different margin inscriptions.

Orchids — A339

28p, Bee orchid. 32p, O'Kelly's orchid. 38p, Dark red helleborine. 52p, Irish lady's tresses.

1993, Apr. 20 Litho. *Perf. 14x15*
891 A339 28p multi .85 .85
892 A339 32p multi 1.00 1.00
893 A339 38p multi 1.50 1.50

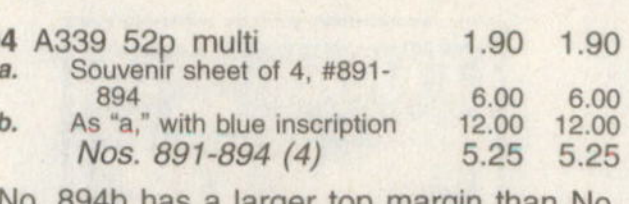
894 A339 52p multi 1.90 1.90
a. Souvenir sheet of 4, #891-894 6.00 6.00
b. As "a," with blue inscription 12.00 12.00
Nos. 891-894 (4) 5.25 5.25

No. 894b has a larger top margin than No. 894a. Added Inscription includes text and flags of Ireland and Thailand.

Contemporary Paintings — A340

Europa: 32p, Pears in a Copper Pan, by Hilda van Stockum. 44p, Arrieta Orzola, by Tony O'Malley.

1993, May 18 Litho. *Perf. 13x13½*
895 A340 32p multicolored *1.25 1.25*
896 A340 44p multicolored *1.75 1.75*

Issued in sheets of 10 + 2 labels. Value for sheet $28.

Gaelic League, Cent. A341

Design: 52p, Illuminated manuscript presented to founder Douglas Hyde, vert.

Perf. 15x14, 14x15
1993, July 8 Litho.
897 A341 32p multicolored 1.25 1.25
898 A341 52p multicolored 1.60 1.60

Irish Amateur Swimming Assoc., Cent. A342

Designs: No. 899, Swimmer diving into water. No. 900, Woman swimming.

1993, July 8 *Perf. 15x14*
899 A342 32p multicolored 1.50 1.50
900 A342 32p multicolored 1.50 1.50
a. Pair, #899-900 3.00 3.00

Royal Hospital Donnybrook, 250th Anniv. — A343

Carlow College, Bicent. — A344

Ceide Fields, County Mayo A345

Edward Bunting (1773-1843), Composer — A346

Perf. 15x14, 14x15, 13½ (52p)

1993, Sept. 2 **Litho.**

901	A343 28p multicolored	.90	.90
902	A344 32p multicolored	1.10	1.10
903	A345 44p multicolored	1.40	1.40
904	A346 52p multicolored	1.60	1.60
	Nos. 901-904 (4)	5.00	5.00

Irish Buses A347

Designs: 28p, Great Northern Railways Gardner. 32p, CIE Leyland Titan. No. 907, Horse-drawn omnibus. No. 908, Char-a-banc.

1993, Oct. 12 **Litho.** ***Perf. 15x14***

905	A347 28p multicolored	1.25	1.25
906	A347 32p multicolored	1.25	1.25
a.	Booklet pane, 2 each #905-906	5.25	
907	A347 52p multicolored	1.60	1.60
908	A347 52p multicolored	1.60	1.60
a.	Pair, #907-908	3.25	3.25
b.	Booklet pane of 4, #905-908	5.75	
	Nos. 905-908 (4)	5.70	5.70

A348

Christmas A349

Designs: 32p, Mary placing infant Jesus in manger. 52p, Adoration of the shepherds.

Perf. 14x15, 15x14

1993, Nov. 16 **Litho.**

909	A348 28p multicolored	.80	.80
910	A349 28p multicolored	1.00	1.00
911	A349 32p multicolored	1.00	1.00
912	A349 52p multicolored	1.60	1.60
	Nos. 909-912 (4)	4.40	4.40

No. 909 issued only in discount sheets of 13+2 labels which sold for £3.36. Value $12.50.

Love A350

32p, Man, woman in shape of heart, vert.

Perf. 15x14, 14x15

1994, Jan. 27 **Litho.**

913	A350 28p multicolored	.90	.90
914	A350 32p multicolored	1.15	1.15

Greetings Stamps — A351

1994, Jan. 27 ***Perf. 14x15***

915	A351 32p Face in sun	1.60	1.60
916	A351 32p Face in flower	1.60	1.60
917	A351 32p Face in heart	1.60	1.60
a.	Souv. sheet of 3, #915-917	7.50	7.50
918	A351 32p Face in rose	1.60	1.60
a.	Booklet pane of 4, #915-918, 4 English + 4 Gaelic labels	8.50	
b.	As "a," 8 English labels	8.50	
	Nos. 915-918 (4)	6.40	6.40

New Year 1994 (Year of the Dog), Hong Kong '94 (No. 917a).

No. 918a contains Nos. 915-918 in order. No. 918b contains Nos. 917, 918, 915, 916 in order.

Macra na Feirme, 50th Anniv. A352

The Taking of Christ, by Caravaggio A353

Irish Co-operative Organization Society, Cent. — A354

Irish Congress of Trade Unions, Cent. A355

1994, Mar. 2 **Litho.** ***Perf. 15x14***

919	A352 28p blue & gold	.95	.95
920	A353 32p multicolored	1.10	1.10
921	A354 38p multicolored	1.40	1.40
922	A355 52p blue, blk & lt blue	1.60	1.60
	Nos. 919-922 (4)	5.05	5.05

Voyages of St. Brendan (484-577) A356

Europa: 32p, St. Brendan, Irish monks sailing past volcano. 44p, St. Brendan on island with sheep, monks in boat.

1994, Apr. 18 **Litho.** ***Perf. 15x14***

923	A356 32p multicolored	*1.25*	*1.25*
924	A356 44p multicolored	*1.75*	*1.75*
a.	Miniature sheet of 2, #923-924	*3.00*	*3.00*

See Faroe Islands Nos. 264-265; Iceland Nos. 780-781.

Parliamentary Anniversaries — A357

No. 925, 1st meeting of the Dail, 1919. No. 926, 4th direct elections to European Parliament.

1994, Apr. 27

925	A357 32p multicolored	1.10	1.10
926	A357 32p multicolored	1.10	1.10
a.	Booklet pane, 1 each #925-926	2.75	
b.	Booklet pane, 2 each #925-926	5.50	
	Complete booklet, #926a, 926b	8.25	

1994 World Cup Soccer Championships, US — A358

Players from: No. 927, Argentina in striped shirt, Ireland in green. No. 928, Ireland, Germany.

1994, May 31 ***Perf. 14x15***

927	A358 32p multicolored	2.25	2.25
928	A358 32p multicolored	2.25	2.25
a.	Pair, #927-928	4.50	4.50

Printed in sheets of 4 No. 928a plus label. Value, $17.50.

Women's Hockey A359

32p, 1994 Women's Hockey World Cup, Dublin. 52p, Irish Ladies' Hockey Union, cent.

1994, May 31 ***Perf. 13x13½***

929	A359 32p multicolored	1.50	1.50
930	A359 52p multicolored	2.00	2.00

Moths A360

28p, Garden tiger. 32p, Burren green. 38p, Emperor. 52p, Elephant hawkmoth.

1994, July 12 **Litho.** ***Perf. 14½x14***

931	A360 28p multi	1.00	1.00
932	A360 32p multi	1.15	1.15
933	A360 38p multi	1.35	1.35
934	A360 52p multi	1.50	1.50
a.	Souvenir sheet of 4, #931-934	6.00	6.00
b.	As "a," overprinted	8.00	8.00
	Nos. 931-934 (4)	5.00	5.00

Size: 34x23mm

Self-Adhesive

Die Cut Perf. 11½

935	A360 32p like #932	2.50	2.50
936	A360 32p like #931	2.50	2.50
937	A360 32p like #934	2.50	2.50
938	A360 32p like #933	2.50	2.50
a.	Strip of 4, #935-938	10.00	10.00

Overprint on No. 934b shows PHILAKOREA '94 exhibition emblem and Korean inscription.

A361

A362

A363

Anniversaries and Events — A364

28p, Medieval view of Drogheda. No. 940, Edmund Ignatius Rice (1762-1844), philantropist. No. 941, Edmund Burke (1729-97), political commentator. No. 942, Eamonn Andrews (1922-87), broadcaster. No. 943, Vickers Vimy aircraft.

1994, Sept. 6 **Litho.** ***Perf. 13½***

939	A361 28p multicolored	.90	.90
	Perf. 14x14½		
940	A362 32p multicolored	1.10	1.10
	Perf. 14x13½		
941	A363 32p multicolored	.90	.90
942	A363 52p multicolored	1.45	1.45
	Perf. 15x14		
943	A364 52p multicolored	1.90	1.90
	Nos. 939-943 (5)	6.25	6.25

Drogheda, 800th anniv. (No. 939). First Newfoundland-Ireland transatlantic flight, 75th anniv. (No. 943).

Nobel Prize Winners A365

No. 944, George Bernard Shaw (1856-1950), dramatist, essayist. No. 945, Samuel Beckett (1906-89), playwright. 32p, Sean McBride (1904-88), statesman. 52p, William Butler Yeats (1865-1939), poet.

1994, Oct. 18 **Litho.** ***Perf. 15x14***

944	A365 28p multicolored	.85	.85
945	A365 28p multicolored	.85	.85
a.	Pair, #944-945	1.75	1.75
946	A365 32p multicolored	.95	.95
a.	Booklet pane of 3, #944-946	2.50	
b.	Bklt. pane, #944-945, 2 #946	3.50	
947	A365 52p multicolored	1.40	1.40
a.	Booklet pane, 1 #946, 2 #947	4.00	
b.	Booklet pane of 4, #944-947	4.50	
	Complete bklt., #946a-946b, 947a-947b	17.50	
	Nos. 944-947 (4)	4.05	4.05

A366

Christmas A367

No. 948, Stained glass nativity scene. No. 949, Annunciation, detail, 11th cent. ivory plaque. 32p, Flight Into Egypt, 15th cent. wood carving. 52p, Nativity, detail, 11th cent. ivory plaque.

1994, Nov. 17 Litho. *Perf. 14x15*

948 A366 28p multicolored .95 .95
949 A367 28p multicolored .75 .75
950 A367 32p multicolored .95 .95
951 A367 52p multicolored 1.60 1.60
Nos. 948-951 (4) 4.25 4.25

No. 948 issued only in discount sheets of 13 plus 2 labels which sold for £3.36. Value $13.

Greetings Stamps — A368

No. 952, Tree of hearts. No. 953, Teddy bear, balloon. No. 954, Clown juggling hearts. No. 955, Bouquet of flowers.

1995, Jan. 24 Litho. *Perf. 14x15*

952 A368 32p multicolored 2.25 2.25

Booklet Stamps

953 A368 32p multicolored 2.25 2.25
954 A368 32p multicolored 2.25 2.25
955 A368 32p multicolored 2.25 2.25
a. Booklet pane, #952-955 + 4 English, 4 Gaelic labels 9.50
b. As "a," 8 English labels 9.50
Complete booklet, #955a-955b 19.00
c. Souvenir sheet, #952, 954-955 + 3 English, 3 Gaelic labels 8.50 8.50

New Year 1995 (Year of the Boar) (No. 955c).

No. 955a contains Nos. 953-954, 952, 955 in order. No. 955b contains Nos. 952, 955, 953-954 in order.

The falling heart on No. 952 has a black outline. The falling heart without an outline comes from Nos. 955a-955c.

Narrow Gauge Railways A369

28p, West Clare. 32p, Co. Donegal. 38p, Cork & Muskerry. 52p, Cavan & Leitrim.

1995, Feb. 28 Litho. *Perf. 15x14*

956 A369 28p multi .60 .60
957 A369 32p multi .65 .65
958 A369 38p multi .80 .80
959 A369 52p multi 3.00 3.00
a. Souvenir sheet of 4, #956-959 6.00 6.00
Nos. 956-959 (4) 5.05 5.05

No. 959a exists with Singapore '95 overprint in sheet margin. Value $10.

Peace & Freedom A370

Europa: Nos. 960, 962, Stylized dove, reconstructed city. 44p, No. 963, Stylized dove, map of Europe.

1995, Apr. 6 Litho. *Perf. 15x14*

960 A370 32p multicolored .90 .90
961 A370 44p multicolored 1.40 1.40

Size: 34½x23mm

Self-Adhesive Coil Stamps

Die Cut Perf. 11½

962 A370 32p multicolored 2.00 2.00
963 A370 32p multicolored 2.00 2.00

Nos. 962-963 are coil stamps, printed in horizontal rolls of 100, with 50 of each design alternating.

1995 Rugby World Cup A371

52p, Player being tackled.

1995, Apr. 6 *Perf. 14*

964 A371 32p shown 1.00 1.00
965 A371 52p multicolored 1.75 1.75

Souvenir Sheet

966 A371 £1 like #964 4.75 *5.50*

No. 966 has a continuous design.

A372

32p, Irish soldiers, Cross of Fontenoy.

1995, May 15 Photo. *Perf. 11½*

967 A372 32p multicolored 1.40 1.40

Battle of Fontenoy, 250th Anniv. See Belgium No. 1583.

A373

Military uniforms: 28p, Irish Brigade, French Army, 1745. No. 969, Tercio Irlanda, Army of Flanders, 1605. No. 970, Royal Dublin Fusiliers, 1914. 38p, St. Patrick's Battalion, Papal Army, 1860. 52p, The Fighting 69th, Army of Potomac, 1861.

1995, May 15 Litho. *Perf. 14x15*

968 A373 28p multicolored .95 .95
969 A373 32p multicolored 1.10 1.10
a. Bklt. pane, 2 ea #968-969 4.25
970 A373 32p multicolored 1.10 1.10
971 A373 38p multicolored 1.25 1.25
a. Bklt. pane of 3, #968-969, #971 3.50
972 A373 52p multicolored 1.40 1.40
a. Bklt. pane of 3, #968-969, 972 3.50
b. Bklt. pane of 4, #968-969, 971-972 4.75
Complete booklet, #969a, 971a, 972a, 972b 16.50
Nos. 968-972 (5) 5.80 5.80

Radio, Cent. A374

Designs: No. 973, Guglielmo Marconi, transmitting equipment. No. 974, Radio channel dial.

1995, June 8 Litho. *Perf. 13½*

973 A374 32p multicolored *11.00 8.75*
974 A374 32p multicolored *11.00 8.75*
a. Pair, #973-974 *24.00 24.00*

See Germany No. 1900, Italy Nos. 2038-2039, San Marino No. 1336-1337, Vatican City No. 978-979.

A375

A376

A377

Anniversaries & Events A378

Designs: 28p, Dr. Bartholomew Mosse, Rotunda Hospital. No. 976, Piper, laurel wreath over map of Europe. No. 977, St. Patrick's College. 52p, Geological map of Ireland.

1995, July 27 Litho. *Perf. 14½x14*

975 A375 28p multicolored .75 .75
976 A376 32p multicolored .90 .90

Perf. 14½

977 A377 32p multicolored .90 .90

Perf. 13½

978 A378 52p multicolored 1.45 1.45
Nos. 975-978 (4) 4.00 4.00

Rotunda Hospital, 250th anniv. (No. 975). End of World War II, 50th anniv. (No. 976). St. Patrick's College, Maynooth, bicent. (No. 977). Geological survey of Ireland, 150th anniv. (No. 978).

Reptiles & Amphibians — A379

No. 979, Natterjack toad. No. 980, Common lizard. No. 981, Smooth newt. No. 982, Common frog.

1995, Sept. 1 Litho. *Perf. 15x14*

979 A379 32p multi 1.25 1.25
980 A379 32p multi 1.25 1.25
981 A379 32p multi 1.25 1.25
982 A379 32p multi 1.25 1.25
a. Strip of 4, #979-982 7.00 7.00

Die Cut Perf. 9¼

Size: 34½x22½mm

Self-Adhesive

982B A379 32p like No. 979 2.75 2.75
982C A379 32p like No. 980 2.75 2.75
982D A379 32p like No. 981 2.75 2.75
982E A379 32p like No. 982 2.75 2.75
f. Strip of 4, Nos. 982B-982E 11.00 11.00

Natl. Botanic Gardens, Bicent. — A380

Designs: 32p, Crinum moorei. 38p, Sarracenia x moorei. 44p, Solanum crispum "glasnevin."

1995, Oct. 9 Litho. *Perf. 14x15*

983 A380 32p multicolored .95 .95
984 A380 38p multicolored 1.05 1.05
985 A380 44p multicolored 1.25 1.25
a. Booklet pane of 3, #983-985 4.00 4.00
b. Bklt. pane of 4, #984-985, 2 #983 5.00
Complete booklet, #985a-985b 9.00
Nos. 983-985 (3) 3.25 3.25

UN, 50th Anniv. A381

1995, Oct. 19 *Perf. 13x13½*

986 A381 32p shown 1.00 1.00
987 A381 52p UN, "50" emblem 1.75 1.75

A382

Christmas A383

Designs: No. 988, Adoration of the Magi. No. 989, Adoration of the Shepherds. 32p, Adoration of the Magi. 52p, Nativity.

1995, Nov. 16 Litho. *Perf. 14½x14*

988 A382 28p multicolored .90 .90
989 A383 28p multicolored .90 .90
990 A383 32p multicolored 1.00 1.00
991 A383 52p multicolored 1.75 1.75
Nos. 988-991 (4) 4.55 4.55

No. 988 issued only in discount sheets of 13+2 labels, which sold for £3.36. Value $12.50.

Greetings/Love Stamps — A384

Television cartoon characters from "Zog, Zig and Zag:" No. 992, With hearts. No. 993, Waving hands. No. 994, In car, wearing space helmets. No. 995, Holding out hands, wearing hats.

1996, Jan. 23 Litho. *Perf. 14x15*
992 A384 32p multicolored 2.50 2.50

Booklet Stamps

993 A384 32p multicolored 2.50 2.50
994 A384 32p multicolored 2.50 2.50
995 A384 32p multicolored 2.50 2.50
a. Booklet pane, Nos. 992-995, 5 English, 3 Gaelic labels 10.00
b. As "a," 7 English, 1 Gaelic label 10.00
Complete booklet, #995a-995b 22.00
c. Souvenir sheet, Nos. 992, 994-995 + 4 English, 2 Gaelic labels, 1 large label with Chinese inscription 7.00 7.00

No. 995a contains Nos. 993-995, 992 in order. No. 995b contains Nos. 995, 992-994 in order.
New Year 1996 (Year of the Rat) (No. 995c).

A385

1996 Summer/Paralympic Games, Atlanta — A386

1996, Feb. 1
996 A385 28p shown 1.00 1.00
997 A386 32p Discus 1.00 1.00
998 A386 32p Canoeing 1.00 1.00
999 A386 32p Running 1.00 1.00
a. Strip of 3, Nos. 997-999 4.50 4.50

No. 999a printed in sheets of 9 stamps. Value $14.

L'Imaginaire Irlandais — A387

1996, Mar. 12 Litho. *Perf. 15x14*
1000 A387 32p multicolored 1.75 1.75

Irish Horse Racing A388

1996, Mar. 12 Litho. *Perf. 15x14*
1001 A388 28p Fairyhouse .75 .75
1002 A388 32p Punchestown .80 .80
1003 A388 32p The Curragh .80 .80
a. Pair, #1002-1003 1.75 1.75
b. Booklet pane, 2 #1001, 1 each #1002-1003 3.00 3.00
c. Souv. sheet, #1002-1003 16.00 16.00
1004 A388 38p Galway 1.15 1.15
a. Booklet pane, 2 #1002, 1 #1004 3.00
1005 A388 52p Leopardstown 1.50 1.50
a. Bklt. pane, #1005, 2 #1003 3.25
b. Bklt. pane, 1 ea #1002-1005 4.50
Complete bklt., Nos. 1003b, 1004a, 1005a, 1005b 14.00
Nos. 1001-1005 (5) 5.00 5.00

No. 1003c for China '96.

UNESCO World Heritage Site A389

UNICEF, 50th Anniv. A390

Designs: 28p, Passage tombs, Bru na Bóinne National Monument, Boyne Valley. 32p, Children.

1996, Apr. 2 Litho. *Perf. 14*
1006 A389 28p sepia & black .90 .90
1007 A390 32p multicolored 1.40 1.40

Europa A391

32p, Louie Bennett (1870-1956), Suffragette, trade unionist. 44p, Lady Augusta Gregory (1852-1932), playwright, co-founder of Abbey Theatre.

1996, Apr. 2 *Perf. 15x14*
1008 A391 32p violet .90 .90
1009 A391 44p green 1.40 1.40

Die Cut Perf. 9¼
Self-Adhesive Coil Stamps

1009A A391 32p like #1008 2.50 2.50
1009B A391 32p like #1009 2.50 2.50

Nos. 962-963 are coil stamps, printed in horizontal rolls with each value alternating.

Irish Winners of Tourist Trophy Motorcycle Races — A392

32p, Stanley Woods. 44p, Artie Bell. No. 1012, Alec Bennett. 52p, No. 1014, Robert & Joey Dunlop.

1996, May 30 *Perf. 14*
1010 A392 32p multicolored 1.00 1.00
1011 A392 44p multicolored 1.25 1.25
1012 A392 50p multicolored 1.50 1.50
1013 A392 52p multicolored 1.60 1.60
Nos. 1010-1013 (4) 5.35 5.35

Souvenir Sheet

1014 A392 50p multicolored 2.50 2.50

See Isle of Man Nos. 701-705.

Michael Davitt (1846-1906), Nationalist Leader — A393

1996, July 4 Litho. *Perf. 13½x13*
1015 A393 28p multicolored .95 .95

Ireland's Presidency of the European Union A394

1996, July 4 *Perf. 13x13½*
1016 A394 32p multicolored 1.00 1.00

Thomas A. McLaughlin (1896-1971), Designer of Ardnacrushna Hydro-electric Power Station — A395

1996, July 4
1017 A395 38p multicolored 1.25 1.25

Bord na Móna (Irish Peat Corp.), 50th Anniv. A396

1996, July 4
1018 A396 52p multicolored 1.30 1.30

Irish Naval Service, 50th Anniv. A397

Designs: 32p, Coastal patrol vessel. 44p, Corvette. 52p, Motor torpedo boat, vert.

1996, July 18 *Perf. 15x14*
1019 A397 32p multicolored .90 .90
a. Booklet pane, 3 #1019 3.25
1020 A397 44p multicolored 1.40 1.40
1021 A397 52p multicolored 1.60 1.60
a. Booklet pane of 3, #1019-1021 6.00
Complete booklet, #1019a, 1021a 9.25
Nos. 1019-1021 (3) 3.90 3.90

People with Disabilities A398

No. 1022, Man in wheelchair. No. 1023, Blind woman, child.

1996, Sept. 3 Litho. *Perf. 14x15*
1022 A398 28p multicolored 1.25 1.25
1023 A398 28p multicolored 1.25 1.25
a. Pair, #1022-1023 2.75 2.75

Freshwater Ducks A399

Designs: 32p, Anas crecca. 38p, Anas clypeata. 44p, Anas penelope. 52p, Anas platyrhynchos.

1996, Sept. 24 *Perf. 15x14*
1024 A399 32p multicolored 1.00 1.00
1025 A399 38p multicolored 1.25 1.25
1026 A399 44p multicolored 1.40 1.40
1027 A399 52p multicolored 1.75 1.75
a. Souvenir sheet, #1024-1027 6.00 6.00
Nos. 1024-1027 (4) 5.40 5.40

No. 1027a is a continuous design.

Motion Pictures, Cent. A400

No. 1028, Man of Aran. No. 1029, My Left Foot. No. 1030, The Commitments. No. 1031, The Field.

1996, Oct. 17 Litho. *Perf. 13½*
1028 A400 32p multicolored 1.30 1.30
1029 A400 32p multicolored 1.30 1.30
1030 A400 32p multicolored 1.30 1.30
1031 A400 32p multicolored 1.30 1.30
a. Strip of 4, #1028-1031 6.00 6.00

A401

Christmas A402

No. 1032, Stained glass scene of Holy Family. No. 1033, Adoration of the Magi. 32p, The Annunciation. 52p, Shepherds receive news of Christ's birth.

1996, Nov. 19 *Perf. 14*
1032 A401 28p multicolored .85 .85
1033 A402 28p multicolored .75 .75
1034 A402 32p multicolored .95 .95
1035 A402 52p multicolored 1.90 1.90
Nos. 1032-1035 (4) 4.45 4.45

No. 1032 sold only in discount sheets of 15 for £3.92. Value $15.

Spideog Robin — A403

Greenland White-fronted Goose — A404

28p, Blue tit. horiz. 44p, Puffin. 52p, Barn owl.

Perf. 15x14, 14x15
1997, Jan. 16 Litho.
1036 A403 28p multi 2.00 2.00
1037 A403 32p shown 2.50 2.50
b. Perf. 14 4.50 4.50
1038 A403 44p multi 3.50 3.50
1039 A403 52p multi 4.00 4.00
1040 A404 £1 shown 5.00 5.00

Booklet Stamp
Size: 18x21mm, 21x18mm

1040A A403 32p Like #1037 4.25 4.25
b. Booklet pane, 3 #1040A, 1 #770 14.00
Complete booklet, #1040b 14.00

Size: 20x23mm

Perf. 14x15

1040C A403 32p Like #1037, "Eire" 8½mm wide ('99) 4.75 4.75
d. Bklt. pane of 5 + 5 labels 24.00
Complete booklet 24.00
Nos. 1036-1040C (7) 26.00 26.00

On Nos. 1037,1037b "Eire" is 9mm wide, and size of design is 21x24mm.

See Nos. 1053-1054C, 1067, 1076-1081A, 1094, 1105-1115C, 1314-1319B, 1340-1343.

Compare with Nos. 1353-1373.

Issued: No. 1040C, 6/30/99

Greetings Stamps — A405

Designs: No. 1041, Doves on tree limb. No. 1042, Cow jumping over moon. No. 1043, Pig going to market. No. 1044, Rooster on fence.

1997, Jan. 28 Litho. *Perf. 14x15*
1041 A405 32p multicolored 1.50 1.50

Booklet Stamps

1042 A405 32p multicolored 1.75 1.75
1043 A405 32p multicolored 1.75 1.75
1044 A405 32p multicolored 1.75 1.75
a. Booklet pane, #1041-1044, 5 English, 3 Gaelic labels 7.00
b. As "a," #1041-1044, 7 English, 1 Gaelic label 7.00
Complete booklet, #1044a, 1044b 14.00
c. Souvenir sheet, 1042-1044, 3 English, 3 Gaelic labels + 1 large label with "Year of the Ox," Hong Kong '97 7.50 7.50

No. 1044a contains Nos. 1042, 1041, 1043-1044 in order. No. 1044b contains Nos. 1043-1044, 1041-1042 in order.

Irish State, 75th Anniv. A406

Designs: No. 1045, Dáil, national flag, constitution. No. 1046, Defense forces, badges, UN flag. No. 1047, Four Courts, scales of justice. No. 1048, Garda badge, Garda Siochána.

1997, Feb. 18 *Perf. 15x14*
1045 A406 32p multicolored 1.10 1.10
1046 A406 32p multicolored 1.10 1.10
a. Pair, #1045-1046 2.25 2.25
1047 A406 52p multicolored 1.75 1.75
1048 A406 52p multicolored 1.75 1.75
a. Pair, #1047-1048 3.50 3.50

See Nos. 1055-1058, 1082-1084, 1095-1096.

Marine Mammals A407

Designs: 28p, Halichoerus grypus, vert. 32p, Tursiops truncatus, vert. 44p, Phocaena phocaena. 52p, Orcinus orca.

Perf. 14x15, 15x14

1997, Mar. 6 Litho.
1049 A407 28p multicolored .75 .75
1050 A407 32p multicolored .90 .90
1051 A407 44p multicolored 1.40 1.40
1052 A407 52p multicolored 1.60 1.60
a. Souvenir sheet, #1049-1052 6.50 6.50
Nos. 1049-1052 (4) 4.65 4.65

Bird Type of 1997

Die Cut Perf. 9x9½

1997, Mar. 6 Litho.

Self-Adhesive Coil Stamps

1053 A403 32p Peregrine falcon 7.50 7.50
1054 A403 32p like #1037 7.50 7.50
a. Pair, #1053-1054 17.50

Die Cut Perf. 11x11¼

1054B A403 32p Like #1053 *20.00 20.00*
1054C A403 32p Like #1054 *20.00 20.00*
d. Pair, #1054B-1054C *40.00*
Nos. 1053-1054C (4) 55.00 55.00

Issued: Nos. 1053-1054, 3/6/97; Nos. 1054B-1054C, 4/97.

Irish State, 75th Anniv. Type of 1997

No. 1055, Singer, violinist, bodhran player. No. 1056, Athlete, soccer and hurling players. No. 1057, Irish currency, blueprint, food processing plant. No. 1058, Abbey Theatre emblem, books, palette, paintbrushes, Séamus Heaney manuscript.

1997, Apr. 3 *Perf. 15x14*
1055 A406 32p multicolored 1.25 1.25
1056 A406 32p multicolored 1.25 1.25
a. Pair, #1055-1056 2.50 2.50
1057 A406 52p multicolored 1.60 1.60
1058 A406 52p multicolored 1.60 1.60
a. Pair, #1057-1058 3.25 3.25

Irish Coinage, Millennium A408

1997, Apr. 3 *Perf. 15x14*
1059 A408 32p First Irish coin 1.60 1.60

Stories and Legends A409

Europa: 32p, "The Children of Lir" flying as swans. 44p, "Oisin & Niamh" on horse.

1997, May 14 Litho. *Perf. 14*
1060 A409 32p multicolored *1.00 1.00*
1061 A409 44p multicolored *1.50 1.50*

Die Cut Perf. 9x9½

Self-Adhesive Coil Stamps

1062 A409 32p like #1060 *2.25 2.25*
1063 A409 32p like #1061 *2.25 2.25*
a. Pair, #1062-1063 *4.50*

The Great Famine, 150th Anniv. A410

Designs: 28p, Passengers waiting to board emigrant ship. 32p, Family group attending dying child. 52p, Irish Society of Friends soup kitchen.

1997, May 14 Litho. *Perf. 15x14*
1064 A410 28p multicolored 1.20 1.20
1065 A410 32p multicolored 1.25 1.25
1066 A410 52p multicolored 2.10 2.10
Nos. 1064-1066 (3) 4.55 4.55

Bird Type of 1997

Souvenir Sheet

1997, May 29 *Perf. 14*
1067 A404 £2 Pintail, horiz. 10.00 10.00

PACIFIC 97.

No. 1067 shows the duck's head in brown. See No. 1111 for stamp with duck's head in black.

Kate O'Brien (1897-1974), Novelist — A411

1997, July 1 Litho. *Perf. 14*
1068 A411 28p multicolored 1.15 1.15

St. Columba (521-97), Irish Patron Saint — A412

1997, July 1 *Perf. 14x15*
1069 A412 28p multicolored 1.15 1.15

A413

A414

Designs: 32p, Daniel O'Connell (1775-1847), politician. 52p, John Wesley (1703-91), founder of Methodism, first visit to Ireland, 250th anniv.

1997, July 1 *Perf. 14x14½*
1070 A413 32p multicolored 1.40 1.40
1071 A414 52p multicolored 1.60 1.60

Lighthouses — A415

Designs: No. 1072, Baily. No. 1073, Tarbert. 38p, Hook Head, vert. 50p, Fastnet, vert.

1997, July 1 *Perf. 15x14, 14x15*
1072 A415 32p multicolored 1.15 1.15
1073 A415 32p multicolored 1.15 1.15
a. Pair, #1072-1073 2.25 2.25
b. Bklt. pane, #1073, 2 #1072 3.00
c. Bklt. pane, 2 ea #1072-1073 4.00
1074 A415 38p multicolored 1.15 1.15
1075 A415 50p multicolored 1.50 1.05
a. Booklet pane, #1074-1075 3.00
b. Bklt. pane of 4, #1073a, 1074-1075 5.00
Complete booklet, #1073b, 1073c, 1075a, 1075b 16.00

Bird Type of 1997

Perf. 14x15, 15x14

1997, Aug. 27 Litho.
1076 A403 1p Magpie .75 .75
1077 A403 2p Gannet .75 .75
1078 A403 4p Corncrake .75 .75
1079 A403 10p Kingfisher 1.00 1.00
1080 A403 20p Lapwing 1.75 1.00
1081 A404 £5 Shelduck 25.00 19.00

Booklet Stamp

Size: 18x21mm

1081A A403 4p Like #1078 4.00 4.00
Nos. 1076-1081A (7) 34.00 27.25

Irish State, 75th Anniv. Type of 1997

28p, Quill, page from Annals of Four Masters, No. 128. 32p, Stained glass window, No. 82. 52p, Aer Lingus airplane, letter, No. C7.

1997, Aug. 27 *Perf. 15x14*
1082 A406 28p multicolored 1.10 1.10
1083 A406 32p multicolored 1.25 1.25
1084 A406 52p multicolored 2.25 2.25
Nos. 1082-1084 (3) 4.60 4.60

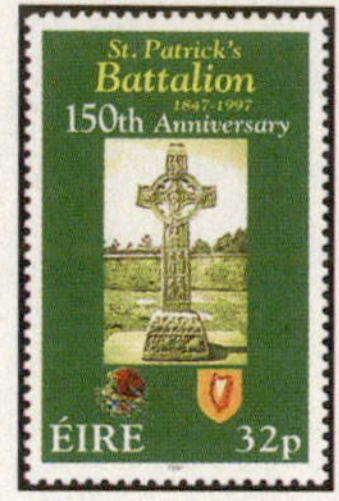

St. Patrick's Battalion, 150th Anniv. — A416

1997, Sept. 12 Litho. *Perf. 14x13½*
1085 A416 32p multicolored 1.60 1.60

See Mexico No. 2049.

Bram Stoker's "Dracula" A417

Scenes of Dracula: 28p, Being transformed into a bat, vert. 32p, With potential victim, vert. 38p, Emerging from coffin. 52p, With wolf.

1997, Oct. 1 *Perf. 14x15, 15x14*
1086 A417 28p multicolored .90 .90
1087 A417 32p multicolored 1.00 1.00
a. Souvenir sheet of 1 3.50 3.50
1088 A417 38p multicolored 1.35 1.35
1089 A417 52p multicolored 1.75 1.75
a. Souv. sheet of 4, #1086-1089 5.75 5.75
Nos. 1086-1089 (4) 5.00 5.00

Stamps from Nos. 1087a, 1089a have souvenir sheet background framing vignette.

A418

Christmas — A419

Nos. 1090-1092: Different images of Holy Family in stained glass. No. 1093, Christmas tree.

1997, Nov. 18 Litho. *Perf. 14x15*
1090 A418 28p multicolored .85 .85
1091 A418 32p multicolored 1.00 1.00
1092 A418 52p multicolored 1.75 1.75
Nos. 1090-1092 (3) 3.60 3.60

Self-Adhesive

Serpentine Die Cut 9x9½

1093 A419 28p multicolored 1.25 1.25
a. Booklet pane, 20 #1093 25.00

By its nature, No. 1093a is a complete booklet. The peelable paper backing serves as a booklet cover.

No. 1093 sold only in discount booklets for £5.32.

Bird Type of 1997

Perf. 15x14 (on 3 Sides)

1997, Dec. 6 **Litho.**

Booklet Stamp

1094 A403 32p like #1053 2.75 2.75
a. Bklt. pane, #1081A, 3 #1094 12.50
Complete booklet, #1094a 13.50

Irish State, 75th Anniv. Type of 1997

No. 1095, General Post Office, No. 68.

No. 1096: a, like No. 1048. b, like No. 1047. c, like No. 1057. d, like No. 1058. e, like No. 1082. f, like No. 1084.

1997, Dec. 6 **Litho.** ***Perf. 15x14***
1095 A406 32p multicolored 2.00 2.00

Sheet of 12

1096 A406 32p #a.-f. + #1045-1046, 1055-1056, 1083, 1095 15.00 15.00

Greetings Stamps — A420

Love is: No. 1097, "...from my heart." No. 1098, "...a birthday wish." No. 1099, "...thinking of you." No. 1100, "...keeping in touch."

1998, Jan. 26 **Litho.** ***Perf. 14x15***
1097 A420 32p multicolored 1.90 1.90
1098 A420 32p multicolored 1.90 1.90
1099 A420 32p multicolored 1.90 1.90
1100 A420 32p multicolored 1.90 1.90
a. Bklt. pane, #1097-1100 + 8 labels 7.50
Complete booklet, 2 #1100a 15.00
b. Souv. sheet, #1098-1100 + 7 labels 7.50 7.50

No. 1100a exists with stamps in two different orders. No. 1100b has 1 English, 4 Chinese, 1 Gaelic labels + 1 large label with "Year of the Tiger," in English and Chinese. Same value.

See Nos. 1120-1123.

Aviation Pioneers A421

28p, Lady Mary Heath (Sophie Catherine Pierce), 1st solo flight, Capetown-Croydon via Cairo, 1928. 32p, Col. James Fitzmaurice, navigator on "Bremen," 1st east-west Atlantic flight, 1928. 44p, Capt. J.P. (Paddy) Saul, navigator aboard Southern Cross, Dublin-Newfoundland, 1930. 52p, Capt. Charles Blair, 1st non-stop commercial flight Foynes-NYC, 1942.

1998, Feb. 24 ***Perf. 15x14***
1101 A421 28p multicolored 1.00 1.00
1102 A421 32p multicolored 1.20 1.20
a. Bklt. pane, 2 ea #1101-1102 4.50
1103 A421 44p multicolored 1.50 1.50
a. Bklt. pane, #1103, 2 #1102 4.00
1104 A421 52p multicolored 1.90 1.90
a. Bklt. pane, #1102, 2 #1104 5.00
b. Bklt. pane of 4, #1101-1104 5.75
Complete booklet, #1102a, 1103a, 1104a, 1104b 20.00
Nos. 1101-1104 (4) 5.60 5.60

Bird Types of 1997

No. 1105, Woodpigeon, horiz. No. 1106, Blackbird. No. 1106B, Goldcrest, bklt. stamp. No. 1107, Stonechat. No. 1108, Ringed plover, horiz. No. 1109, Song thrush. No. 1110, Sparrowhawk, horiz. No. 1111, Pintail.

No. 1111A: b, Like No. 1107. c, Like No. 1080. d, Like No. 1077. e, Like No. 1078. f, Like No. 1076. g, Like No. 1106B, "Eire" 8½mm wide. h, Like No. 1079. i, Like No. 1053. j, Like No. 1039. k, Like No. 1037. l, Like No. 1109. m, Like No. 1106, "Eire" 8½mm wide. n, Wren. o, Pied wagtail. p, Like No. 1038.

1998-99 **Litho.** ***Perf. 15x14, 14x15***
1105 A403 5p multi .90 .75
1106 A403 30p multi 1.50 1.10
d. Perf. 14 1.90 1.10
1106B A403 30p multi 1.90 1.90
c. Booklet pane, 5 each #1106, 1106B 18.00
Complete booklet, #1106Bc 18.00
1107 A403 35p multi 1.90 1.90
a. Perf. 14 2.25 2.25
1108 A403 40p multi 2.25 2.25
a. Perf. 14 2.75 2.75
1109 A403 45p multi 3.50 3.50
a. Perf. 14 3.75 3.75
1110 A403 50p multi 3.75 3.75
a. Perf. 14 4.25 4.25
1111 A404 £2 multi 9.00 9.00

Sheet of 15

1111A A403 30p #b.-p. 25.00 25.00

See note under No. 1067.

Booklet Stamps

Size: 18x21mm, 21x18mm

1112 A403 5p Like #1105 1.50 1.50
1113 A403 30p Like #1106 1.90 1.90
a. Booklet pane, 2 #1112, 3 #1113 9.00
Complete booklet, #1113a 9.00
1113B A403 30p like #1106B 1.10 1.10
c. Bklt. pane, 2 #1112, 3 #1113B + label 4.50
Complete booklet, #1113c 4.50

Size: 20x23mm

1113D A403 45p Like #1109, "Eire" 8½mm wide 3.00 3.00
e. Booklet pane of 4 + 4 labels 12.00
Complete booklet 12.00

Size: 21x24mm

Perf. 10¾x13 on 3 sides

1113F A403 30p Like #1106, "Eire" 8½mm wide 2.00 2.00
i. Like #1113F, perf. 14¼x14¾ on 3 sides ('99) 2.00 2.00
1113G A403 30p Like #1106B, "Eire" 8½mm wide 2.00 2.00
h. Booklet pane, 5 each #1113F-1113G 20.00 —
Booklet, #1113Gh 20.00
j. Like #1113G, perf. 14¼x14¾ on 3 sides ('99) 2.00 2.00
k. Pair, #1113F-1113G 4.00 4.00

Die Cut Perf. 9x9½

Self-Adhesive

1114 A403 30p like #1106 7.00 7.00
1115 A403 30p like #1106B 7.00 7.00
a. Pair, #1114-1115 14.00 14.00

Litho.

Die Cut Perf. 11x11¼

Self-Adhesive Coil Stamps

1115B A403 30p Like #1114 7.00 7.00
1115C A403 30p Like #1115 7.00 7.00
d. Pair, #1115B-1115C 14.00 14.00

Issued: No. 1115B-1115C, 5/98; No. 1106B, 1113B, 9/4/98; No. 1111A, 2/16/99; No. 1113D, 6/30/99; No. 1113F, 1113G, 5/3/01.

Equestrian Sports A422

30p, Show jumping. 32p, Three-day event. 40p, Gymkhana. 45p, Dressage, vert.

1998, Apr. 2
1116 A422 30p multicolored 1.00 1.00
1117 A422 32p multicolored 1.25 1.25
1118 A422 40p multicolored 1.50 1.50
1119 A422 45p multicolored 1.75 1.75
a. Souvenir sheet, #1116-1119 6.75 6.75
Nos. 1116-1119 (4) 5.50 5.50

Greetings Type of 1998

1998, May 6 **Litho.** ***Perf. 14x15***

Booklet Stamps

1120 A420 30p like #1098 1.75 1.75
1121 A420 30p like #1099 1.75 1.75
1122 A420 30p like #1100 1.75 1.75
1123 A420 30p like #1097 1.75 1.75
a. Bklt. pane, #1120-1123 + 8 labels 7.25 7.25
Complete booklet, 2 #1123a 14.50

No. 1123a exists with stamps in different order. Complete booklet contains two different panes.

Festivals A423

Europa: 30p, Crinniú na mBáid, Kinvara (sailboats). 40p, Puck Fair, Killorglin.

1998, May 6 ***Perf. 15x14***
1124 A423 30p multicolored *1.25 1.25*
1125 A423 40p multicolored *1.75 1.75*

Serpentine Die Cut Perf 9x9½

Self-Adhesive

1126 A423 30p like #1124 *2.00 2.00*
1127 A423 30p like #1125 *2.00 2.00*
a. Pair, #1126-1127 *4.00 4.00*
Nos. 1124-1127 (4) 7.00 7.00

1798 Rebellion, Bicent. A424

Battle scene and: No. 1128, "Liberty." No. 1129, Pikeman. No. 1130, French soldier. No. 1131, Wolfe Tone. No. 1132, Henry Joy McCracken.

1998, May 6
1128 A424 30p multicolored 1.00 1.00
1129 A424 30p multicolored 1.00 1.00
1130 A424 30p multicolored 1.00 1.00
a. Strip of 3, #1128-1130 3.00 3.00
1131 A424 45p multicolored 1.40 1.40
1132 A424 45p multicolored 1.40 1.40
a. Pair, #1131-1132 3.00 3.00

Tour de France Bicycle Race A425

No. 1133, 4 cyclists. No. 1134, 2 cyclists, 1 wearing dark glasses. No. 1135, 2 cyclists, 1 wearing hat. No. 1136, Leading rider in yellow jersey.

1998, June 2 **Litho.** ***Perf. 15x14***
1133 A425 30p multicolored 1.10 1.10
1134 A425 30p multicolored 1.10 1.10
1135 A425 30p multicolored 1.10 1.10
1136 A425 30p multicolored 1.10 1.10
a. Strip of 4, #1133-1136 4.50 4.50

Democracy Stamps A426

Designs: 30p, Local government (Ireland Act), cent. 32p, Entrance into European Union, 25th anniv. 35p, Women's vote in local elections, cent. 45c, Republic of Ireland Act, 50th anniv.

1998, June 2
1137 A426 30p multicolored .85 .85
1138 A426 32p multicolored .85 .85
1139 A426 35p multicolored 1.00 1.00
1140 A426 45p multicolored 1.25 1.25
Nos. 1137-1140 (4) 3.95 3.95

1998 Tall Ships Race — A427

No. 1141, Asgard II. No. 1142, Eagle. No. 1143, Boa Esperanza, horiz. No. 1144, T.S. Royalist, horiz.

Perf. 14x15, 15x14

1998, July 20 **Litho.**
1141 A427 30p multi .70 .70
a. Perf. 15 2.75 2.00
1142 A427 30p multi 1.00 1.00
a. Pair, #1141-1142 1.75 1.75
b. Perf. 15 2.75 2.00
c. Bklt. pane, #1142b, 2 #1141a 5.50
1143 A427 45p multi 1.25 1.25
a. Perf. 15 2.75 2.00
1144 A427 £1 multi 2.75 2.75
a. Perf. 15 2.75 2.00
b. Bklt. pane of 3, #1142b, 1143a, 1144a 9.00
Complete booklet, #1142c, 1144b 14.50
Nos. 1141-1144 (4) 5.70 5.70

Souvenir Sheet

1145 A427 £2 like #1143 9.25 9.25

Die Cut Perf. 9x9½, 9½x9

Self-Adhesive

1145A A427 30p like #1143 2.00 2.00
1145B A427 30p like #1141 2.00 2.00
1145C A427 30p like #1142 2.00 2.00
1145D A427 30p like #1144 2.00 2.00
e. Strip of 4, #1145A-1145D 8.00 8.00

Portugal '98 (No. 1145).
Issued: £2, 9/4; others, 7/20.

Postboxes — A428

No. 1146, Ashworth, 1856. No. 1147, Wallbox, 1922. No. 1148, Double Pillarbox, 1899. No. 1149, Penfold, 1866.

1998, Sept. 3
1146 A428 30p multicolored 1.10 1.10
1147 A428 30p multicolored 1.10 1.10
1148 A428 30p multicolored 1.10 1.10
1149 A428 30p multicolored 1.10 1.10
a. Strip of 4, #1146-1149 4.50 4.50

Mary Immaculate College, Limerick, Cent. — A429

Newton School, Waterford, Bicent. — A430

1998, Sept. 3 ***Perf. 15x14, 14x15***
1150 A429 30p multicolored 1.00 1.00
1151 A430 40p multicolored 1.40 1.40

Universal Declaration of Human Rights, 50th Anniv. A431

1998, Sept. 3 ***Perf. 15x14***
1152 A431 45p multicolored 1.25 1.25

Endangered Animals — A432

No. 1153, Cheetah. No. 1154, Scimitar-horned oryx. 40p, Golden lion tamarin. 45p, Tiger.

1998, Oct. 8 Litho. *Perf. 14*

1153 A432 30p multi 1.10 1.10
1154 A432 30p multi 1.10 1.10
a. Pair, #1153-1154 2.25 2.25
1155 A432 40p multi, vert. 1.35 1.35
1156 A432 45p multi, vert. 1.75 1.75
a. Souvenir sheet, #1153-1156, perf. 15 6.50 6.50
b. As "a," inscription on extended margin 10.00 10.00
Nos. 1153-1156 (4) 5.30 5.30

Stamps on Nos. 1156a, 1156b have a white border. No. 1156b contains exhibition logo and "National Stamp Exhibition RDS-Dublin-6-8 November 1998" in sheet margin.

A433

Christmas — A434

No. 1157, Holy family. 32p, Adoration of the Shepherds. 45p, Adoration of the Magi. No. 1160, Choir singers.

1998, Nov. 17 Litho. *Perf. 14x15*

1157 A433 30p multicolored 1.00 1.00
1158 A433 32p multicolored 1.15 1.15
1159 A433 45p multicolored 1.60 1.60
Nos. 1157-1159 (3) 3.75 3.75

Booklet Stamp

Self-Adhesive

Serpentine Die Cut Perf. 11x11½

1160 A434 30p multicolored 1.15 1.15
a. Booklet pane of 20 25.00

No. 1160a is a complete booklet. The peelable paper backing serves as a booklet cover. No. 1160 sold only in discount booklets at £5.40.

A435

Pets greetings stamps.

1999, Jan. 26 Litho. *Perf. 14x15*

1161 A435 30p Dog 1.30 1.30

Booklet Stamps

1162 A435 30p Cat 1.30 1.30
1163 A435 30p Fish 1.30 1.30
1164 A435 30p Rabbit 1.30 1.30
a. Booklet pane, #1161-1164 + 5 English, 3 Gaelic labels 5.75
b. Booklet pane, #1161-1164 + 7 English, 1 Gaelic label 5.75
Complete booklet, #1164a-1164b 12.00
c. Souvenir sheet, #1162-1164 (see footnote) 6.00 6.00

No. 1164a contains Nos. 1161-1164 in order. No. 1164b contains stamps in reverse order. No. 1164c has 1 English, 2 Chinese, 3 Gaelic labels + 1 large label with "Year of the Rabbit" in English and Chinese.

New Year 1999 (Year of the Rabbit) (No. 1164c).

A436

Irish Actors: 30p, Micheál Mac Liammóir (1899-1978). 45p, Siobhán McKenna (1923-86). 50p, Noel Purcell (1900-85).

1999, Feb. 16 Litho. *Perf. 14x15*

1165 A436 30p brown .70 .70
1166 A436 45p green 1.25 1.25
1167 A436 50p blue 1.50 1.50
Nos. 1165-1167 (3) 3.45 3.45

Irish Emigration A437

1999, Feb. 26 Litho. *Perf. 15x14*

1168 A437 45p multicolored 1.75 1.75

See US No. 3286.

Maritime Heritage A438

30p, Polly Woodside. 35p, Ilen. 45p, Royal Natl. Lifeboat Institution. £1, Titanic.

1999, Mar. 19 Litho. *Perf. 14*

1169 A438 30p multi, vert. .85 .85
1170 A438 35p multi, vert. .95 .95
1171 A438 45p multi 1.40 1.40
1172 A438 £1 multi 2.75 2.75
a. Souvenir sheet of 2 6.75 6.75
b. As "a" ovptd. in sheet margin 10.00 10.00
Nos. 1169-1172 (4) 5.95 5.95

Souvenir Sheet

Perf. 14x14½

1173 Sheet of 2, #1173a, Australia #1729 4.00 4.00
a. A438 30p like #1169 1.90 .80

Australia '99, World Stamp Expo. (No. 1172b, No. 1173). See Australia No. 1729a. No. 1172b is overprinted in gold in sheet margin with Australia '99, World Stamp Expo exhibition emblem.

Sky is gray blue, country and denomination are 3mm high on No. 1169. Sky is blue, country and denomination are 4mm high on No. 1173a.

Natl. Parks A438a

Europa: Nos. 1174, 1176, Whooping swans, Kilcolman Nature Reserve. 40p, No. 1177, Fallow deer, Wellington Memorial Obelisk, Phoenix Park.

1999, Apr. 29 Litho. *Perf. 15x14*

1174 A438a 30p multicolored *1.00 1.00*
1175 A438a 40p multicolored *1.25 1.25*

Die Cut Perf. 9x9½

Self-adhesive

1176 A438a 30p Like #1174 *2.25 2.25*
1177 A438a 30p Like #1175 *2.25 2.25*
a. Pair, #1176-1177 *4.50 4.50*

A439

1999, Apr. 29 Litho. *Perf. 14x15*

1178 A439 30p green & black 1.30 1.30

Prime Minister Sean Lemass (1899-1971).

A440

1999, Apr. 29 *Perf. 15x14*

1179 A440 30p multicolored 1.40 1.40

Introduction of the Euro. No. 1179 is denominated in both pence and euros.

A441

1999, Apr. 29 *Perf. 14x15*

1180 A441 45p multicolored 2.25 2.25

Council of Europe, 50th anniv.

Intl. Year of Older Persons A442

1999, June 15 *Perf. 15x14*

1181 A442 30p multicolored 1.30 1.30

UPU, 125th Anniv. A443

No. 1182, Modern mail truck. No. 1183, Early mail truck.

1999, June 15

1182 A443 30p multicolored 1.60 1.60
1183 A443 30p multicolored 1.60 1.60
a. Pair, #1182-1183 3.25 3.25

Pioneer Total Abstinence Assoc., Cent. — A444

1999, June 15 *Perf. 14x15*

1184 A444 32p Fr. James Cullen 1.25 1.25

Gaelic Football Team of the Millennium A445

No. 1185: a, Danno Keeffe. b, Enda Colleran. c, Joe Keohane. d, Seán Flanagan. e, Seán Murphy. f, John Joe Reilly. g, Martin O'Connell. h, Mick O'Connell. i, Tommy Murphy. j, Seán O'Neill. k, Seán Purcell. l, Pat Spillane. m. Mikey Sheehy. n, Tom Langan. o, Kevin Heffernan.

Perf. 14¾x14¼

1999, Aug. 17 Litho.

1185 Sheet of 15 + label 20.00 20.00
a.-o. A445 30p any single 1.25 1.25

Booklet Stamps

Size: 33x22mm

Self-Adhesive

Serpentine Die Cut Perf. 11¼x11½

1186 A445 30p like #1185a 1.75 1.75
1187 A445 30p like #1185c 1.75 1.75
1188 A445 30p like #1185e 1.75 1.75
1189 A445 30p like #1185h 1.75 1.75
1190 A445 30p like #1185l 1.75 1.75
1191 A445 30p like #1185m 1.75 1.75
a. Bklt. pane, #1186-1189, 2 each #1190-1191 17.50
1192 A445 30p like #1185d 1.75 1.75
1193 A445 30p like #1185b 1.75 1.75
1194 A445 30p like #1185n 1.75 1.75
1195 A445 30p like #1185k 1.75 1.75
a. Bklt. pane, 2 ea #1192-1195 17.50
1196 A445 30p like #1185o 1.75 1.75
1197 A445 30p like #1185g 1.75 1.75
1198 A445 30p like #1185i 1.75 1.75
a. Bklt. pane, 3 ea #1196-1197, 2 #1198 17.50
1199 A445 30p like #1185f 1.75 1.75
1200 A445 30p like #1185j 1.75 1.75
a. Bklt. pane, 4 ea #1199-1200 17.50

Nos. 1191a, 1195a, 1198a, 1200a are each complete booklets. The peelable paper backing serves as a booklet cover. No. 1185 exists imperf.

See Nos. 1246-1261.

Airplanes A446

Designs: 30p, Douglas DC-3. 32p, Britten Norman Islander. 40p, Boeing 707. 45p, Lockheed Constellation.

1999, Sept. 9 Litho. *Perf. 14¾x14¼*

1201 A446 30p multicolored .90 .90
a. Booklet pane of 4 3.75
1202 A446 32p multicolored 1.00 1.00
a. Bklt. pane, 2 ea #1201, 1202 4.00
1203 A446 40p multicolored 1.25 1.25
a. Bklt. pane, #1203, 2 #1201 5.00
1204 A446 45p multicolored 1.30 1.30
a. Booklet pane, #1201-1204 4.50
Complete bkt., #1201a-1204a 17.50
Nos. 1201-1204 (4) 4.45 4.45

Extinct Irish Animals A447

Perf. 14¼x14¾, 14¾x14¼

1999, Oct. 11 Litho.

1205 A447 30p Mammoth, vert. 1.10 1.10
1206 A447 30p Giant deer, vert. 1.10 1.10
a. Pair, #1205-1206 2.25 2.25
1207 A447 45p Wolf 1.75 1.75
1208 A447 45p Brown bear 1.75 1.75
a. Pair, #1207-1208 3.50 3.50
b. Souvenir sheet, #1205-1208, perf. 14¾ 5.75 5.75

Stamps from No. 1208b do not have white border.

Die Cut Perf. 9¼x9½, 9½x9¼

1999, Oct. 11 Litho.

Self-Adhesive

1209 A447 30p Like #1208 1.75 1.75
1210 A447 30p Like #1205 1.75 1.75
1211 A447 30p Like #1207 1.75 1.75
1212 A447 30p Like #1206 1.75 1.75
a. Strip, #1209-1212 7.25

Christmas A448

1999, Nov. 4 Litho. *Perf. 14¾x14¼*
1213 A448 30p Holy Family .90 .90
1214 A448 32p Shepherds 1.25 1.25
1215 A448 45p Magi 1.90 1.90
Nos. 1213-1215 (3) 4.05 4.05

Self-Adhesive Booklet Stamp
Size: 19x27mm
Die Cut 11x11¼
1216 A448 30p Angel, vert. 1.10 1.10
a. Booklet pane of 20 22.50 22.50

No. 1216a sold for £5.40 and is a complete booklet.

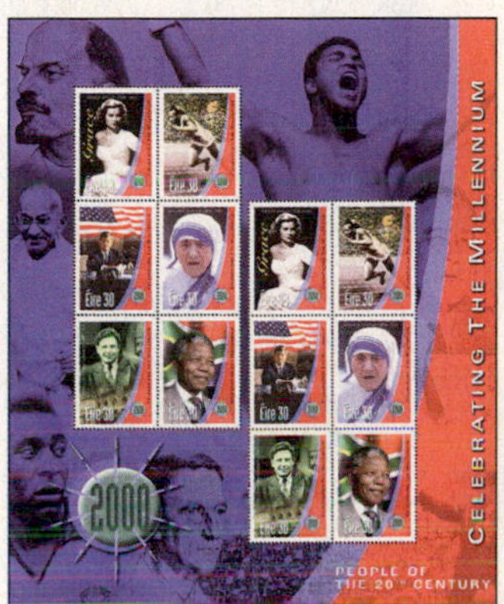

Millennium — A449

People of the 20th Century — No. 1217: a, Grace Kelly. b, Jesse Owens. c, John F. Kennedy. d, Mother Teresa. e, John McCormack. f, Nelson Mandela.

Irish Historic Events — No. 1218, horiz.: a, Norman invasion, 1169. b, Flight of the Earls, 1607. c, Irish Parliament, 1782. d, Land league. e, Irish independence. f, UN peacekeeping.

Discoveries — No. 1219: a, Rev. Nicholas Callan, electrical scientist. b, Birr Telescope. c, Thomas Edison. d, Albert Einstein. e, Marie Curie. f, Galileo.

The Arts — No. 1220: a, Ludwig van Beethoven. b, Dame Ninette de Valois, ballet director. c, James Joyce. d, Mona Lisa, by Leonardo da Vinci. e, Painting by Sir John Lavery. f, William Shakespeare.

World Events — No. 1221, horiz.: a, French Revolution, 1789. b, Industrial Revolution. c, Peace, 1945. d, Women's liberation. e, Fall of the Berlin Wall, 1989. f, Modern communications.

Epic Journeys — No. 1222, horiz.: a, Marco Polo. b, Capt. James Cook. c, Australian explorers Robert O'Hara Burke and William Wills. d, Antarctic explorer Ernest Shackleton. e, Charles Lindbergh. f, Astronaut on moon.

Perf. 14¼x14¾, 14¾x14¼
1999-2001 Litho.
1217 Sheet of 12, 2 ea #a.-f. 20.00 20.00
a.-f. A449 30p Any single 1.60 1.60
1218 Sheet of 12, 2 ea #a.-f. 20.00 20.00
a.-f. A449 30p Any single 1.60 1.60
1219 Sheet of 12, 2 each #a.-f. 20.00 20.00
a.-f. A449 30p Any single 1.60 1.60
1220 Sheet of 12, 2 each #a.-f. 20.00 20.00
a.-f. A449 30p Any single 1.60 1.60
1221 A449 Sheet of 12, 2 each #a-f 20.00 20.00
a.-f. 30p Any single 1.60 1.60
1222 A449 Sheet of 12, 2 each #a-f 20.00 20.00
a.-f. 30p Any single 1.60 1.60

Issued: No. 1217, 12/31; No. 1218, 1/1/00; No. 1219, 2/29/00; No. 1220, 6/16/00; No. 1221, 12/31/00; No. 1222, 1/1/01.

Mythical Creatures — A450

2000, Jan. 26 Litho. *Perf. 14¼x14¾*
1223 A450 30p Frog Prince 1.50 1.50
1224 A450 30p Pegasus 1.50 1.50
1225 A450 30p Unicorn 1.50 1.50
1226 A450 30p Dragon 1.50 1.50
a. Booklet pane, #1223-1226, + 3 Gaelic, 5 English labels 6.00
b. Booklet pane, #1223-1226, + 2 Gaelic, 6 English labels 6.00
c. Booklet pane, #1223, 1226, + 14 labels 3.00
Complete booklet, #1226a-1226c 15.00
d. Souvenir sheet, #1224-1226, + 7 labels 7.00 7.00
Nos. 1223-1226 (4) 6.00 6.00

New Year 2000 (Year of the Dragon), No. 1226d.

Emigrant Ship Jeanie Johnston A451

2000, Mar. 9 Litho. *Perf. 14¾x14¼*
1227 A451 30p multi 1.60 1.60

Common Design Type

Europa, 2000 — CD17

2000, May 9 Litho. *Perf. 14¼x14¾*
1230 CD17 32p multi *1.75 1.75*

Die Cut Perf 9¾x9¼
Self-Adhesive
Size: 22x34mm
1231 CD17 30p multi *2.60 2.60*

Oscar Wilde (1854-1900), Playwright A453

No. 1232, Portrait. No. 1233, The Happy Prince. No. 1234, The Importance of Being Earnest. No. 1235, The Picture of Dorian Gray. No. 1236, £2, Like No. 1232, signature at left.

Perf. 14¼x14¾, 14¼x14 (#1236)
2000, May 22 Litho.
1232 A453 30p multi 1.40 1.40
1233 A453 30p multi 1.40 1.40
1234 A453 30p multi 1.40 1.40
1235 A453 30p multi 1.40 1.40
a. Block, #1232-1235 5.50 5.50

Size: 27x27mm
1236 A453 30p multi + label 10.00 10.00
Sheet of 20 110.00
Nos. 1232-1236 (5) 15.60 15.60

Souvenir Sheet
1237 A453 £2 multi 6.50 6.50
a. With Stamp Show 2000 emblem in margin 10.00 10.00

No. 1237 contains one 30x40mm stamp.

No. 1236 was printed in sheets of 20 stamps and 20 labels for £10. These sheets were not available at Irish post offices, but were sold at the Irish Post booths at The Stamp Show 2000 in London and World Stamp Expo in Ahaheim, California. Labels were blank, but purchasers could provide Irish Post with photographic images or other artwork that would be reproduced on the labels.

2000 Summer Olympics, Sydney A454

2000, July 7 Litho. *Perf. 13¼*
1238 A454 30p Running .90 .90
1239 A454 30p Javelin 1.60 1.60
a. Pair, #1238-1239 2.50 2.50
1240 A454 50p Long jump 1.25 1.25
1241 A454 50p High jump 1.25 1.25
a. Pair, #1240-1241 2.50 2.50

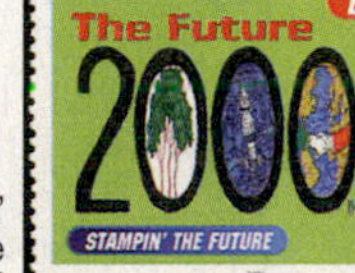

Stampin' the Future A455

Children's Stamp Design Contest Winners: 30p, Marguerite Nyhan (rocket and flowers), vert. 32p, Kyle Staunton (2000). No. 1244, Jennifer Branagan (Earth, sun and moon). No. 1245, Diarmuid O'Ceochain (rocket, building on moon).

Perf. 14¼x14¾, 14¾x14¼
2000, July 7
1242 A455 30p multi .85 .85
1243 A455 32p multi .95 .95
1244 A455 45p multi 1.35 1.35
1245 A455 45p multi 1.40 1.40
a. Pair, #1244-1245 2.75 2.75
Nos. 1242-1245 (4) 4.55 4.55

Team of the Millennium Type of 1999

Hurling — No. 1246: a, Tony Reddin. b, Bobby Rackard. c, Nick O'Donnell. d, John Doyle. e, Brian Whelahan. f, John Keane. g, Paddy Phelan. h, Lory Meagher. i, Jack Lynch. j, Jim Langton. k, Mick Mackey. l, Christy Ring. m, Jimmy Doyle. n, Ray Cummins. o, Eddie Keher.

2000, Aug. 2 Litho. *Perf. 14¾x14¼*
1246 Sheet of 15 + label 10.50 10.50
a.-o. A445 30p Any single 2.10 2.10

No. 1246 exists imperf. Value, $125.

Booklet Stamps
Self-Adhesive
Size: 33x22mm
Serpentine Die Cut 11¼x11½
1247 A445 30p Like #1246a 2.10 2.10
1248 A445 30p Like #1246m 2.10 2.10
1249 A445 30p Like #1246d 2.10 2.10
a. Booklet, 3 each #1247-1248, 4 #1249 21.00
1250 A445 30p Like #1246b 2.10 2.10
1251 A445 30p Like #1246c 2.10 2.10
a. Booklet, 5 each #1250-1251 21.00
1252 A445 30p Like #1246k 2.10 2.10
1253 A445 30p Like #1246e 2.10 2.10
1254 A445 30p Like #1246f 2.10 2.10
a. Booklet, 4 #1252, 3 each #1253-1254 21.00
1255 A445 30p Like #1246g 2.10 2.10
1256 A445 30p Like #1246j 2.10 2.10
1257 A445 30p Like #1246h 2.10 2.10
1258 A445 30p Like #1246o 2.10 2.10
a. Booklet, 2 each #1255-1256, 3 each #1257-1258 21.00
1259 A445 30p Like #1246i 2.10 2.10
1260 A445 30p Like #1246n 2.10 2.10
1261 A445 30p Like #1246l 2.10 2.10
a. Booklet, 3 each #1259-1260, 4 #1261 21.00
Nos. 1247-1261 (15) 31.50 31.50

No. 1246 exists imperf.

Butterflies A456

Designs: 30p, Peacock. 32p, Small tortoiseshell. 45p, Silver-washed fritillary. 50p, Orange-tip.

2000, Sept. 6 *Perf. 13¼x12¾*
1262 A456 30p multi .70 .70
1263 A456 32p multi 1.00 1.00
1264 A456 45p multi 1.50 1.50
1265 A456 50p multi 1.75 1.75
a. Souvenir sheet, #1262-1265 9.00 9.00

Stamps from No. 1265a lack year date.

Military Aircraft A457

Designs: No. 1266, Bristol F.2b Mk II fighter. No. 1267, Hawker Hurricane Mk IIc. No. 1268, Alouette III helicopter. No. 1269, De Havilland DH.115 Vampire T.55.

2000, Oct. 9 Litho. *Perf. 14¾x14¼*
1266 A457 30p multi .80 .80
1267 A457 30p multi .80 .80
a. Pair, #1266-1267 1.75 1.75
b. Booklet pane, 2 each #1266-1267 3.50
1268 A457 45p multi 1.75 1.75
a. Booklet pane, #1266-1268 3.50
1269 A457 45p multi 1.75 1.75
a. Pair, #1268-1269 3.50 3.50
b. Booklet pane, 2 each #1268-1269 7.00
c. Booklet pane, #1266-1269 5.00
Booklet, #1267b, 1268a, 1269b, 1269c 20.00
Nos. 1266-1269 (4) 5.10 5.10

Coil Stamps
Self-Adhesive
Die Cut Perf. 9¾x9½
1270 A457 30p Like #1266 2.00 2.00
1271 A457 30p Like #1267 2.00 2.00
1272 A457 30p Like #1269 2.00 2.00
1273 A457 30p Like #1268 2.00 2.00
a. Strip, #1270-1273 8.50

Dept. of Agriculture, Cent. — A458

2000, Nov. 14 Litho. *Perf. 13½*
1274 A458 50p multi 1.90 1.90

Christmas A459

Designs: No. 1275, Nativity. 32p, Adoration of the Magi. 45p, Adoration of the Shepherds. No. 1278, Flight to Egypt.

2000, Nov. 14 *Perf. 14¼x14¾*
1275 A459 30p multi .85 .85
1276 A459 32p multi 1.40 1.40
1277 A459 45p multi 2.10 2.10

Booklet Stamp
Self-Adhesive
Size: 21x26mm
Serpentine Die Cut 11¼

1278 A459 30p multi 1.30 1.30
a. Booklet of 24 32.50
Nos. 1275-1278 (4) 5.65 5.65

No. 1278 sold for £6.60.

Pets — A460

Designs: Nos. 1279, 1283, Goldfish, hearts. Nos. 1280a, 1284, Snake. Nos. 1280b, 1282, Frog, four-leaf clover. Nos. 1280c, 1285, Turtle, stars. No. 1281, Lizard, daisy.

2001, Jan. 24 Litho. ***Perf. 14¼x14¾***
1279 A460 30p multi 1.50 1.50

Souvenir Sheet

1280 Sheet of 3 5.50 5.50
a.-c. A460 30p Any single 1.75 1.75

Booklet Stamps
Size: 25x30mm
Self-Adhesive
Serpentine Die Cut 12

1281 A460 30p multi 1.40 1.40
1282 A460 30p multi 1.40 1.40
1283 A460 30p multi 1.40 1.40
1284 A460 30p multi 1.40 1.40
1285 A460 30p multi 1.40 1.40
a. Booklet, 2 each #1281-1285 + 10 labels 14.00
Nos. 1281-1285 (5) 7.00 7.00

New Year 2001 (Year of the Snake), No. 1280.

Broadcasting in Ireland — A461

Designs: 30p, Camera, audience, man. 32p, Microphone, announcers. 45p, People listening to radio. 50p, Television.

2001, Feb. 27 ***Perf. 14¾x14¼***
1286 A461 30p multi .85 .85
1287 A461 32p multi 1.00 1.00
1288 A461 45p multi 1.25 1.25
1289 A461 50p multi 1.40 1.40
Nos. 1286-1289 (4) 4.50 4.50

Literary Anniversaries A462

Designs: 30p, Marsh's Library, first public library in Ireland, 300th anniv. 32p, Book of Common Prayer, first book printed in Ireland, 450th anniv.

2001, Mar. 14 ***Perf. 14¼x14¾***
1290 A462 30p multi 1.00 1.00
1291 A462 32p multi 1.75 1.75

Comhaltas Ceoltóirí Eirann, 50th Anniv. — A463

Musician with: No. 1292, Bagpipes. No. 1293, Tambourine. No. 1294, Flute, horiz. No. 1295, Violin, horiz.

Perf. 14¼x14¾, 14¾x14¼
2001, Mar. 14
1292 A463 30p multi .90 .90
1293 A463 30p multi .90 .90
a. Pair, #1292-1293 1.90 1.90
1294 A463 45p multi 1.40 1.40
1295 A463 45p multi 1.40 1.40
a. Pair, #1294-1295 3.00 3.00
Nos. 1292-1295 (4) 4.60 4.60

Race Cars A464

Designs: Nos. 1296, 1300, 1301, Jordan Grand Prix Formula 1. Nos. 1297, 1304, Hillman Imp, Tulip Rally. Nos. 1298, 1303, Mini Cooper S, Monte Carlo Rally. Nos. 1299, 1302, Mercedes SSK, Irish Grand Prix.

2001, Apr. 26 ***Perf. 13¾x14¼***
1296 A464 30p multi .65 .65
1297 A464 32p multi .90 .90
1298 A464 45p multi 1.40 1.40
1299 A464 £1 multi 3.00 3.00
Nos. 1296-1299 (4) 5.95 5.95

Souvenir Sheet

1300 A464 £2 multi 7.00 7.00
a. With Belgica show emblem in margin 8.50 8.50

Booklet Stamps
Size: 36x24mm
Self-Adhesive
Serpentine Die Cut 11¾

1301 A464 30p multi 2.40 2.40
1302 A464 30p multi 2.40 2.40
1303 A464 30p multi 2.40 2.40
1304 A464 30p multi 2.40 2.40
a. Booklet, 4 #1301, 2 each #1302-1304 24.00
Nos. 1301-1304 (4) 9.60 9.60

Issued: No. 1300a, 6/9/01.

Irish Heritage in Australia A465

2001, May 3 ***Perf. 14¾x14¼***
1305 A465 30p Ned Kelly 1.10 1.10
1306 A465 30p Peter Lalor 1.10 1.10
a. Pair, #1305-1306 2.25 2.25
1307 A465 45p Settlers 1.40 1.40
1308 A465 45p Emigrants 1.40 1.40
a. Pair, #1307-1308 3.00 3.00
Nos. 1305-1308 (4) 5.00 5.00

Souvenir Sheet

1309 A465 £1 Like #1305 3.75 3.75

Europa A466

2001, May 16 Litho. ***Perf. 14¾x14¼***
1310 A466 30p Wading *.75 .75*
1311 A466 32p Fishing *1.25 1.25*

Coil Stamps
Self-Adhesive
Die Cut Perf. 9¼x9½

1312 A466 30p Wading *2.00 2.00*
1313 A466 30p Fishing *2.00 2.00*
a. Strip, #1312-1313 *4.00*

Bird Types of 1997 With Added Euro Denominations

Designs: Nos. 1314, 1319A, Blackbird. 1319B, Goldcrest. 32p, Robin. 35p, Puffin. 40p, Wren. 45p, Song thrush. £1, Greenland white-fronted goose.

Perf. 14¼x14¾
2001, June 11 Litho.
1314 A403 30p multi 2.25 2.25
1315 A403 32p multi 2.75 2.75
1316 A403 35p multi 2.75 2.75
1317 A403 40p multi 3.25 3.25
1318 A403 45p multi 4.00 4.00

Perf. 14¾x14¼
1319 A404 £1 multi 7.50 7.50
Nos. 1314-1319 (6) 22.50 22.50

Self-Adhesive
Coil Stamps
Die Cut Perf. 11¼
Size: 21x26mm

1319A A403 30p multi 4.75 4.75
1319B A403 30p multi 4.75 4.75
c. Pair, #1319A-1319B 9.50

Battle of Kinsale, 400th Anniv. A467

Designs: No. 1320, Soldiers on horseback. No. 1321, Soldiers in stream. 32p, Soldiers and ramparts. 45p, View of Kinsale.

2001, July 10 ***Perf. 13½***
1320 A467 30p multi .90 .90
1321 A467 30p multi .90 .90
a. Pair, #1320-1321 1.90 1.90
1322 A467 32p multi 1.75 1.75
1323 A467 45p multi 2.00 2.00
Nos. 1320-1323 (4) 5.55 5.55

Hall of Fame Athletes A468

Designs: Nos. 1324, 1328, Padraic Carney, soccer player. Nos. 1325, 1329, Frank Cummins, hurler. Nos. 1326, 1330, Jack O'Shea, soccer player. Nos. 1327, 1331, Nicky Rackard, hurler.

2001, Sept. 5 Litho. ***Perf. 14¾x14***
1324 A468 30p multi 1.10 1.10
1325 A468 30p multi 1.10 1.10
1326 A468 30p multi 1.10 1.10
1327 A468 30p multi 1.10 1.10
a. Horiz. strip, #1324-1327 4.50 4.50

Booklet Stamps
Size: 33x22mm
Self-Adhesive
Serpentine Die Cut 11x11½

1328 A468 30p multi 2.00 2.00
1329 A468 30p multi 2.00 2.00
1330 A468 30p multi 2.00 2.00
1331 A468 30p multi 2.00 2.00
a. Booklet, 2 each #1328, 1331, 3 each #1329-1330 20.00
Nos. 1324-1331 (8) 12.40 12.40

See Nos. 1429-1432.

Sailboats — A469

Designs: No. 1332, Ruffian 23. No. 1333, Howth 17. No. 1334, 1720 Sportsboat. No. 1335, The Glen. No. 1336, Ruffian 23. No. 1337, Howth 17. No. 1338, The Glen. No. 1339, 1720 Sportsboat.

2001, Sept. 5 ***Perf. 14x14¾***
1332 A469 30p multi 1.25 1.25
1333 A469 32p multi 1.25 1.25
1334 A469 45p multi 1.75 1.75
1335 A469 45p multi 1.75 1.75
a. Horiz. pair, #1334-1335 3.50 3.50
Nos. 1332-1335 (4) 6.00 6.00

Coil Stamps
Self-Adhesive
Serpentine Die Cut 9½x9¼

1336 A469 30p multi 2.50 2.50
1337 A469 30p multi 2.50 2.50
1338 A469 30p multi 2.50 2.50
1339 A469 30p multi 2.50 2.50
a. Strip of 4, #1336-1339 10.00

Bird Type of 1997
Serpentine Die Cut 11¼
2001, Oct. 9 Litho.
Booklet Stamps
Self-Adhesive

1340 A403 N Blackbird 1.75 1.75
1341 A403 N Goldcrest 1.75 1.75
a. Booklet, 5 each #1340-1341 17.50 17.50
1342 A403 E Robin 1.90 1.90
a. Booklet of 10 + 10 etiquettes 19.00
1343 A403 W Song thrush 3.00 3.00
a. Booklet of 10 + 10 etiquettes 30.00
Nos. 1340-1343 (4) 8.40 8.40

Fish A470

Designs: 30p, Perch. No. 1345, Arctic char. No. 1346, Pike. 45p, Common bream.

2001, Oct. 9 ***Perf. 14¾x14***
1344 A470 30p multi 1.25 1.25
1345 A470 32p multi 1.75 1.75
1346 A470 32p multi 1.75 1.75
a. Horiz. pair, #1345-1346 3.50 3.50
1347 A470 45p multi 2.50 2.50
a. Booklet pane, #1344-1347 6.25 —
b. Booklet pane, #1345, 1346, 2 #1347 8.75 —
c. Booklet pane, 2 each #1344, 1347 7.50 —
Booklet, #1347b, 1347c, 2 #1347a 29.00

No. 1347a exists with stamps in different order. The booklet contains the two different panes.

Governmental Support of Arts, 50th Anniv. — A471

2001, Nov. 5 ***Perf. 14x14¾***
1348 A471 50p multi 2.50 2.50

Christmas A472

Designs: No. 1349, Nativity. 32p, Annunciation. 45p, Presentation in the Temple. No. 1352, Madonna and Child.

2001, Nov. 5 *Perf. 14x14¾*
1349 A472 30p multi 1.00 1.00
1350 A472 32p multi 1.40 1.40
1351 A472 45p multi 2.50 2.50

Booklet Stamp
Size: 21x27mm
Self-Adhesive
Serpentine Die Cut 11x11¼

1352 A472 30p multi 1.50 1.50
a. Booklet of 24 35.00
Nos. 1349-1352 (4) 6.40 6.40

No. 1352a sold for £6.60.

100 Cents = 1 Euro (€)

A473

Birds (With Euro Denominations Only) — A474

Designs: 1c, Magpie. 2c, Gannet. 3c, Blue tit, horiz. 4c, Corncrake. 5c, Wood pigeon, horiz. Nos. 1358, 1370, 10c, Kingfisher. 20c, Lapwing. Nos. 1360, 1371, 1372, 38c, Blackbird. No. 1373, 38c, Goldcrest. 41c, Chaffinch. 44c, Robin. 50c, Gray heron, horiz. 51c, Roseate tern, horiz. 57c, Curlew. €1, Barnacle goose. €2, Greenland white-fronted goose, vert. €5, Pintail. €10, Shelduck, vert.

Perf. 14x14¾, 14¾x14

2002, Jan. 1 **Litho.**
1353 A473 1c multi .25 .25
1354 A473 2c multi .25 .25
1355 A473 3c multi .25 .25
1356 A473 4c multi .25 .25
1357 A473 5c multi .25 .25
1358 A473 10c multi .40 .30
1359 A473 20c multi .75 .65
1360 A473 38c multi 1.40 1.25
1361 A473 41c multi 1.60 1.40
1362 A473 44c multi 1.75 1.60
1363 A473 50c multi 1.90 1.75
1364 A473 51c multi 1.90 1.75
1365 A473 57c multi 2.25 1.90
1366 A474 €1 multi 3.75 3.50
1367 A474 €2 multi 7.50 7.00
1368 A474 €5 multi 19.00 17.50
1369 A474 €10 multi 37.50 35.00

Booklet Stamps
Size: 18x20mm
Perf. 14¾x14¼ on 3 Sides

1370 A473 10c multi 1.25 1.25
1371 A473 38c multi 2.75 2.75
a. Booklet pane, #1370, 5 #1371 14.00 —
Booklet, #1371a 14.00

Coil Stamps
Size: 21x26mm
Self-Adhesive
Serpentine Die Cut 11x11¼

1372 A473 38c multi 5.75 5.75
1373 A473 38c multi 5.75 5.75
a. Pair, #1372-1373 14.00 14.00
Nos. 1353-1373 (21) 96.45 90.35

See Nos. 1392-1398, 1421-1423, 1433-1434, 1447-1449, 1492-1495, 1511-1515, 1523-1526.

Introduction of the Euro — A475

Designs: 38c, 1 euro coin introduced in 2002. 41c, 50p coin used from 1971-2001. 57c, 1p coin used from 1928-71.

2002, Jan. 1 **Litho.** *Perf. 14¾x14¼*
1374 A475 38c multi 1.10 1.10
1375 A475 41c multi 1.25 1.25
1376 A475 57c multi 1.75 1.75
Nos. 1374-1376 (3) 4.10 4.10

Toys — A476

Designs: Nos. 1377, 1379, Teddy bear. Nos. 1378a, 1381, Rocking horse. Nos. 1378b, 1382, Wooden locomotive. Nos. 1378c, 1380, Doll. No. 1383, Blocks.

2002, Jan. 22 *Perf. 14¼x14¾*
1377 A476 38c multi 2.00 2.00

Souvenir Sheet
Perf. 14¼x14¾ on 3 or 4 Sides

1378 Sheet of 3 9.00 9.00
a.-c. A476 38c Any single 3.00 3.00

Booklet Stamps
Self-Adhesive
Size: 21x27mm
Serpentine Die Cut 11¼

1379 A476 38c multi 1.75 1.75
1380 A476 38c multi 1.75 1.75
1381 A476 38c multi 1.75 1.75
1382 A476 38c multi 1.75 1.75
1383 A476 38c multi 1.75 1.75
a. Booklet of 10, 2 each #1379-1383, + 10 labels 17.50
Nos. 1379-1383 (5) 8.75 8.75

New Year 2002 (Year of the Horse), No. 1378.

Steeplechasing in Ireland, 250th Anniv. — A477

2002, Mar. 12 *Perf. 14¾x14¼*
1384 A477 38c Arkle 1.25 1.25
1385 A477 38c L'Escargot 1.25 1.25
1386 A477 38c Dawn Run 1.25 1.25
1387 A477 38c Istabraq 1.25 1.25
a. Horiz. strip of 4, #1384-1387 5.00 5.00

Scouting A478

Designs: No. 1388, Scout with peg and mallet. No. 1389, Scouts and leader around camp fire. No. 1390, Scouts on hike. No. 1391, Scouts kayaking.

2002, Mar. 12
1388 A478 41c multi 1.25 1.25
1389 A478 41c multi 1.25 1.25
a. Horiz. pair, #1388-1389 2.50 2.50
1390 A478 57c multi 2.00 2.00
1391 A478 57c multi 2.00 2.00
a. Horiz. pair, #1390-1391 4.00 4.00
Nos. 1388-1391 (4) 6.50 6.50

Bird Type of 2002

Designs: No. 1395, Chaffinch. No. 1396, Goldcrest. 44c, Robin. 47c, Kestrel, horiz. 55c, Oystercatcher, horiz. 57c, Song thrush. 60c, Jay, horiz.

2002 **Litho.** *Perf. 14¾x14*
1392 A473 47c multi 4.25 4.25
1393 A473 55c multi 4.75 4.75
1394 A473 60c multi 6.00 6.00

Self-Adhesive
Serpentine Die Cut 11x11¼
Size: 21x26mm

1395 A473 41c multi 3.75 3.75
1396 A473 41c multi 3.75 3.75
a. Coil pair, #1395-1396 7.50
b. Booklet of 10, 5 each #1395-1396 37.50

Booklet Stamps

1397 A473 44c multi 2.50 2.50
a. Booklet of 10 25.00
1398 A473 57c multi 2.75 2.75
a. Booklet of 10 27.50
Nos. 1392-1398 (7) 27.75 27.75

Issued: Nos. 1395-1398, 4/2. Nos. 1392-1394, 6/17.

Compare Nos. 1395-1396 with Nos. 1433-1434.

Mammals A479

Designs: 41c, Meles meles. 50c, €5, Lutra lutra. 57c, Sciurus vulgaris, vert. €1, Erinaceus europaeus, vert.

Perf. 14¾x14¼, 14¼x14¾
2002, Apr. 23 **Litho.**
1399 A479 41c multi 1.00 1.00
1400 A479 50c multi 1.25 1.25
1401 A479 57c multi 1.40 1.40
1402 A479 €1 multi 2.50 2.50
Nos. 1399-1402 (4) 6.15 6.15

Souvenir Sheet

1403 A479 €5 multi 21.00 21.00

Europa A480

Designs: Nos. 1404, 1406, Clown. Nos. 1405, 1407, Equestrian act.

2002, May 14 **Litho.** *Perf. 14¾x14*
1404 A480 41c multi 1.25 1.25
1405 A480 44c multi 1.40 1.40

Coil Stamps
Size: 34x23mm
Self-Adhesive
Die Cut Perf. 9¼x9½

1406 A480 41c multi 1.25 1.25
1407 A480 41c multi 1.25 1.25
a. Horiz. pair, #1406-1407 2.50 2.50
Nos. 1404-1407 (4) 5.15 5.15

Soccer Stars A481

Designs: Nos. 1408, 1415, Packie Bonner. Nos. 1409, 1412, Roy Keane, vert. Nos. 1410, 1413, Paul McGrath, vert. Nos. 1411, 1414, David O'Leary, vert.

2002, May 14 *Perf. 14¾x14, 14x14¾*
1408 A481 41c multi 1.25 1.25
1409 A481 41c multi 1.25 1.25
1410 A481 41c multi 1.25 1.25
1411 A481 41c multi 1.25 1.25
a. Vert. strip of 3, #1409-1411 5.00 5.00

Booklet Stamps
Sizes: 23x34, 34x23mm
Self-Adhesive
Serpentine Die Cut 11½x11¾, 11¾x11½

1412 A481 41c multi 3.00 3.00
1413 A481 41c multi 3.00 3.00
1414 A481 41c multi 3.00 3.00
1415 A481 41c multi 3.00 3.00
a. Booklet, 3 #1412-1413, 2 #1414-1415 30.00

Canonization of St. Pio of Pietrelcina (1887-1968) A482

2002, June 17 **Litho.** *Perf. 14x14¾*
1416 A482 41c multi 2.00 2.00

Brian Ború, 1000th Anniv of High Kingship A483

Designs: 41c, Leading troops into battle. 44c, Commanding ships. 57c, On throne. €1, Decreeing Armagh as the primacy of the Irish church.

2002, July 9 *Perf. 14¾x14*
1417 A483 41c multi 1.00 1.00
1418 A483 44c multi 1.25 1.25
1419 A483 57c multi 1.40 1.40
1420 A483 €1 multi 2.50 2.50
Nos. 1417-1420 (4) 6.15 6.15

Bird Type of 2002

Designs: No. 1421, Goldcrest. No. 1422, 36c, Wren. No. 1423, Chaffinch.

Perf. 14x14¾ on 3 Sides
2002, Aug. 6 **Litho.**
Booklet Stamps

1421 A473 41c multi 2.25 2.25
a. Booklet pane of 10, 5 each #1361, 1421 22.50 —
Booklet, #1421a 22.50

Size: 18x21mm
Perf. 14¾x14¼ on 3 Sides

1422 A473 36c multi 2.25 2.25
1423 A473 41c multi 2.75 2.75
a. Booklet pane of 5, #1422, 4 #1423 + label 21.00 —
Booklet, #1423a 21.00

Paintings in National Gallery A484

Designs: No. 1424, Before the Start, by Jack B. Yeats. No. 1425, The Conjuror, by Nathaniel Hone. No. 1426, The Colosseum and Arch of Constantine, Rome, by Giovanni Paolo Panini. No. 1427, The Gleaners, by Jules Breton.

2002, Aug. 29 *Perf. 14¾x14*
1424 A484 41c multi 1.25 1.25
a. Booklet pane of 4 5.00 —
1425 A484 41c multi 1.25 1.25
a. Booklet pane of 4 5.00 —
1426 A484 41c multi 1.25 1.25
a. Booklet pane of 4 5.00 —
1427 A484 41c multi 1.25 1.25
a. Horiz. strip, #1424-1427 5.00 5.00
b. Booklet pane of 4 5.00 —
Booklet, #1424a, 1425a, 1426a, 1427b 20.00

See Nos. 1496-1499, 1572-1575.

Archbishop Thomas Croke (1823-1902) A485

2002, Sept. 17 *Perf. 14x14¾*

1428 A485 44c multi 2.00 2.00

Hall of Fame Athletes Type of 2001

Designs: No. 1429, Peter McDermott, soccer player. No. 1430, Jimmy Smyth, hurler. No. 1431, Matt Connor, soccer player. No. 1432, Seanie Duggan, hurler.

2002, Sept. 17 *Perf. 14¾x14*

1429 A468 41c multi 1.25 1.25
1430 A468 41c multi 1.25 1.25
1431 A468 41c multi 1.25 1.25
1432 A468 41c multi 1.25 1.25
a. Horiz. strip, #1429-1432 5.00 5.00

Bird Type of 2002 Redrawn

Designs: No. 1433, Chaffinch. No. 1434, Goldcrest

Serpentine Die Cut 11x11¼
2002, Oct. 17 Coil Stamps Photo.
Self-Adhesive

1433 A473 41c multi 5.00 5.00
1434 A473 41c multi 5.00 5.00
a. Coil pair, #1433-1434 10.00

Text appears grayer on Nos. 1433-1434 than on Nos. 1395-1396. On No. 1433, the second "h" of "Chaffinch" touches the branch, while it does not touch on No. 1395. On No. 1434, the points of the pine needles at the bottom of the stamp are shown, while they are cut off on No. 1396.

Irish Rock Musicians A486

Designs: Nos. 1435, 1439, U2. Nos. 1436, 1440, Phil Lynott. Nos. 1437, 1441, Van Morrison. Nos. 1438, 1442, Rory Gallagher.

2002, Oct. 17 Litho. *Perf. 13¼x12¾*

1435 A486 41c multi 1.25 1.25
1436 A486 41c multi 1.25 1.25
a. Horiz. pair, #1435-1436 2.50 2.50
1437 A486 57c multi 1.75 1.75
1438 A486 57c multi 1.75 1.75
a. Horiz. pair, #1437-1438 3.50 3.50
Nos. 1435-1438 (4) 6.00 6.00

Souvenir Sheets
Perf. 12¾x13¼

1439 A486 €2 multi 12.00 12.00
1440 A486 €2 multi 12.00 12.00
1441 A486 €2 multi 12.00 12.00
1442 A486 €2 multi 12.00 12.00

Christmas — A487

Scenes from *Les Très Riches Heures du Duc de Berry*: No. 1443, Adoration of the Magi. 44c, The Annunciation. 57c, Angels Announcing Birth to Shepherds.
No. 1446, Adoration of the Shepherds.

2002, Nov. 7 Litho. *Perf. 14¼x14¾*

1443 A487 41c multi .95 .95
1444 A487 44c multi 1.10 1.10
1445 A487 57c multi 1.50 1.50

Booklet Stamp
Self-Adhesive
Size: 21x27mm
Serpentine Die Cut 11x11¼

1446 A487 41c multi 1.50 1.50
a. Booklet pane of 24 37.50
Nos. 1443-1446 (4) 5.05 5.05

No. 1446a sold for €9.43.

Bird Type of 2002

Designs: 50c, Puffin. 75c, Ringed plover, horiz.. 95c, Sparrowhawk, horiz.

2003, Jan. 6 Litho. *Perf. 14¾x14*

1447 A473 75c multi 2.50 2.50
1448 A473 95c multi 3.50 3.50

Booklet Stamp
Self-Adhesive
Size: 21x27mm
Serpentine Die Cut 11x11¼

1449 A473 50c multi 2.00 2.00
a. Booklet pane of 10 + 10 etiquettes 20.00

Baby Animals — A488

Designs: Nos. 1450, 1452, Puppies. Nos. 1451a, 1454, Goats. Nos. 1451b, 1453, Chicks. Nos. 1451c, 1455, Kittens. No. 1456, Rabbits.

2003, Jan. 28 *Perf. 14x14¾*

1450 A488 41c multi 2.00 2.00

Souvenir Sheet
Perf. 14x14¾ on 3 or 4 Sides

1451 Sheet of 3 7.00 7.00
a.-c. A488 50c Any single 2.25 2.25

Booklet Stamps
Size: 22x28mm
Self-Adhesive
Serpentine Die Cut 11x11¼

1452 A488 41c multi 1.75 1.75
1453 A488 41c multi 1.75 1.75
1454 A488 41c multi 1.75 1.75
1455 A488 41c multi 1.75 1.75
1456 A488 41c multi 1.75 1.75
a. Booklet pane of 10, 2 each #1452-1456 + 10 labels 17.50
Nos. 1452-1456 (5) 8.75 8.75

New Year 2003 (Year of the Goat), No. 1451.

St. Patrick's Day — A489

Designs: Nos. 1457, 1460, St. Patrick. Nos. 1458, 1461, St. Patrick's Day Parade, Dublin. Nos. 1459, 1462, St. Patrick's Day Parade, New York.

2003, Feb. 28 *Perf. 14x14¾*

1457 A489 41c multi 1.00 1.00
a. Booklet pane of 4 4.00
1458 A489 50c multi 1.25 1.25
a. Booklet pane of 4 5.00
1459 A489 57c multi 1.50 1.50
a. Booklet pane of 4 6.00
b. Booklet pane of 3, #1457-1459 3.75
Complete booklet, #1457a, 1458a, 1459a, 1459b 19.00
Nos. 1457-1459 (3) 3.75 3.75

Booklet Stamps
Self-Adhesive
Size: 22x32mm
Serpentine Die Cut 11¼

1460 A489 41c multi 3.50 3.50
a. Booklet pane of 10 35.00
1461 A489 50c multi 4.25 4.25
a. Booklet pane of 10 42.50
1462 A489 57c multi 4.75 4.75
a. Booklet pane of 10 47.50
Nos. 1460-1462 (3) 12.50 12.50

Beetles A490

Designs: 41c, €2, Seven-spotted ladybug. 50c, Great diving beetle. 57c, Leaf beetle. €1, Green tiger beetle.

2003, Apr. 1 *Perf. 13¾x14*

1463 A490 41c multi 1.00 1.00
1464 A490 50c multi 1.25 1.25
1465 A490 57c multi 1.40 1.40
1466 A490 €1 multi 2.50 2.50
Nos. 1463-1466 (4) 6.15 6.15

Souvenir Sheet

1467 A490 €2 multi 7.50 7.50

European Year of People With Disabilities A491

2003, May 9 *Perf. 14¾x14*

1468 A491 41c multi 1.75 1.75

Europa — A492

Posters by Paul Henry: 41c, Dingle Peninsula (Ireland for Holidays). 57c, Connemara (Ireland This Year).

2003, May 9 *Perf. 14x14¾*

1469 A492 41c multi 1.00 1.00
1470 A492 57c multi 1.50 1.50

11th Special Olympics World Summer Games A493

Designs: 41c, Competitors waving. 50c, Swimmer. 57c, Sprinter. €1, Shot put.

2003, May 20 *Perf. 13¾x14*

1471 A493 41c multi 1.00 1.00
1472 A493 50c multi 1.25 1.25
1473 A493 57c multi 1.40 1.40
1474 A493 €1 multi 2.50 2.50
Nos. 1471-1474 (4) 6.15 6.15

Ford Motor Company, Cent. A494

2003, June 30 Litho. *Perf. 14¼x14*

1475 A494 41c multi 2.00 2.00

Gordon Bennett Race in Ireland, Cent. A495

Race map and 1903 automobiles: Nos. 1476, 1483, Napier. Nos. 1477, 1482, Mercedes. Nos. 1478, 1481, Mors. Nos. 1479, 1480, Winton.

2003, June 30 *Perf. 14¼x14*

1476 A495 41c multi 1.25 1.25
1477 A495 41c multi 1.25 1.25
1478 A495 41c multi 1.25 1.25
1479 A495 41c multi 1.25 1.25
a. Horiz. strip of 4, #1476-1479 5.00 5.00

Coil Stamps
Size: 33x22mm
Self-Adhesive
Serpentine Die Cut 11¼

1480 A495 41c multi 2.25 2.25
1481 A495 41c multi 2.25 2.25
1482 A495 41c multi 2.25 2.25
1483 A495 41c multi 2.25 2.25
a. Strip of 4, #1480-1483 9.00

Rebellion of 1803, Bicent. A496

Designs: 41c, Robert Emmet (1778-1803), rebellion leader. 50c, Thomas Russell (1767-1803), rebellion leader. 57c, Anne Devlin (1780-1851), assistant to Emmet.

2003, July 29 Litho. *Perf. 14¾x14*

1484 A496 41c multi 1.50 1.50
1485 A496 50c multi 1.75 1.75
1486 A496 57c multi 2.25 2.25
Nos. 1484-1486 (3) 5.50 5.50

Powered Flight, Cent. A497

Designs: 41c, First Irish-built monoplane, built by Harry Ferguson, 1909. 50c, John Alcock & Arthur Brown's non-stop transatlantic flight, 1919. No. 1489, Lillian Bland, first female aircraft designer, 1910. Nos. 1490, 1491, Wright Flyer.

2003, July 29

1487 A497 41c multi 1.50 1.50
1488 A497 50c multi 1.75 1.75
1489 A497 57c multi 2.00 2.00
1490 A497 57c multi 2.00 2.00
a. Horiz. pair, #1489-1490 4.00 4.00

Souvenir Sheet

1491 A497 €5 multi 15.00 15.00

Bird Type of 2002

Designs: 7c, Stonechat. 48c, No. 1494, Peregrine falcon. No. 1495, Pied wagtail.

2003, Aug. 25 Litho. *Perf. 14x14¾*

1492 A473 7c multi .40 .40
1493 A473 48c multi 3.00 3.00

Self-Adhesive
Serpentine Die Cut 11x11¼

1494 A473 N multi 2.00 2.00
1495 A473 N multi 2.00 2.00
a. Coil pair, #1494-1495 4.00
b. Booklet pane, 5 each #1494-1495 20.00

Nos. 1494-1495 each sold for 48c on day of issue.

National Gallery Paintings Type of 2002

Designs: No. 1496, Self-portrait as Timanthes, by James Barry. No. 1497, Man Writing a Letter, by Gabriel Metsu. No. 1498, Woman Reading a Letter, by Metsu. No. 1499, Woman Seen From the Back, by Antoine Watteau.

2003, Sept. 9 *Perf. 14x14¾*

1496 A484 48c multi 1.25 1.25
a. Booklet pane of 4 5.00 —
1497 A484 48c multi 1.25 1.25
1498 A484 48c multi 1.25 1.25
a. Booklet pane, 2 each #1497-1498 5.00 —
1499 A484 48c multi 1.25 1.25
a. Horiz. strip, #1496-1499 5.00 5.00
b. Booklet pane of 4 5.00 —
Complete booklet, #1496a, 1499b, 2 #1498a 28.00

Frank O'Connor (1903-66), Writer — A498

2003, Sept. 16 Litho. *Perf. 14x14¼*
1500 A498 50c multi 2.25 2.25

Ernest Thomas Sinton Walton (1903-95), 1951 Nobel Laureate in Physics — A499

2003, Sept. 16
1501 A499 57c multi 2.50 2.50

Mariners A500

Designs: Nos. 1502, 1507, Argentine Admiral William (Guillermo) Brown (1777-1857). Nos. 1503, 1506, 1510, American Commodore John Barry (1745-1803). Nos. 1504, 1508, Captain Robert Halpin (1836-94). Nos. 1505, 1509, Captain Richard Roberts (1803-41).

Perf. 14¼x14 (#1502-1505, 1510)
2003, Sept. 30
1502 A500 48c multi 1.25 1.25
1503 A500 48c multi 1.25 1.25
a. Horiz. pair, #1502-1503 2.50 2.50
1504 A500 57c multi 1.50 1.50
1505 A500 57c multi 1.50 1.50
a. Horiz. pair, #1504-1505 3.00 3.00

Coil Stamps
Self-Adhesive (#1506-1509)
Size: 33x22mm (#1506-1509)
Serpentine Die Cut 11x11¼ (#1506-1509)
1506 A500 48c multi 2.50 2.50
1507 A500 48c multi 2.50 2.50
1508 A500 48c multi 2.50 2.50
1509 A500 48c multi 2.50 2.50
a. Horiz. strip, #1506-1509 10.00 10.00
Nos. 1502-1509 (8) 15.50 15.50

Souvenir Sheet
1510 A500 €5 multi 15.00 15.00

Bird Type of 2002

Designs: 4c, Corncrake. Nos. 1511, 1515, Pied wagtail. Nos. 1513, 1514, Peregrine falcon.

Perf. 14x14¾ on 3 Sides
2003, Sept. 30 Litho.
Booklet Stamps (#1511-1513)
1511 A473 48c multi 2.00 2.00
a. Booklet pane, 5 each #1493, 1511 20.00 —
Complete booklet, #1511a 20.00

Size: 18x20mm
Perf. 15x14 on 3 Sides
1512 A473 4c multi .30 .30
1513 A473 48c multi 2.50 2.50
a. Booklet pane, 2 #1512, 4 #1513 10.50 —
Complete booklet, #1513a 10.50
Nos. 1511-1513 (3) 4.80 4.80

Self-Adhesive
Size: 20x25mm
Serpentine Die Cut 11x11¼
1514 A473 48c multi 2.00 2.00
1515 A473 48c multi 2.00 2.00
a. Coil pair, #1514-1515 4.00
b. Booklet pane, 5 each #1514-1515 20.00

Examples of Nos. 1514-1515 from booklets are on a heavy, opaque paper, while those from coils are on a thinner, semi-transparent paper.

Election of Pope John Paul II, 25th Anniv. — A501

Pope John Paul II: 48c, In Ireland, 1979. 50c, At Vatican. 57c, At United Nations.

2003, Oct. 16 *Perf. 14x14¾*
1516 A501 48c multi 1.25 1.25
1517 A501 50c multi 1.25 1.25
1518 A501 57c multi 1.40 1.40
Nos. 1516-1518 (3) 3.90 3.90

Christmas A502

Designs: No. 1519, Flight into Egypt. 50c, Angel. 57c, Three Kings. No. 1522, Nativity.

2003, Nov. 10 *Perf. 13¼*
1519 A502 48c multi 1.50 1.50

Size: 37x27mm
Perf. 14¾x14
1520 A502 50c multi 1.50 1.50
1521 A502 57c multi 1.75 1.75
Nos. 1519-1521 (3) 4.75 4.75

Booklet Stamp
Self-Adhesive
Size: 26x21mm
Serpentine Die Cut 11¼
1522 A502 48c multi 2.00 2.00
a. Booklet pane of 24 27.50

No. 1522a sold for €11.04.

Bird Type of 2002

Designs: Nos. 1523, 1525, Puffin. Nos. 1524, 1526, Song thrush.

2004, Jan. 5 Litho. *Perf. 14x14¾*
1523 A473 60c multi 2.50 2.50
1524 A473 65c multi 2.50 2.50

Booklet Stamps
Self-Adhesive
Size: 21x26mm
Serpentine Die Cut 11x11¼
1525 A473 60c multi 2.50 2.50
a. Booklet pane of 10 25.00
1526 A473 65c multi 2.75 2.75
a. Booklet pane of 10 27.50

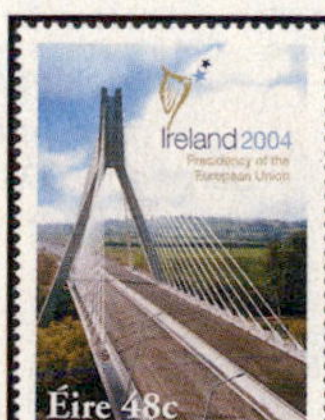
Irish Presidency of the European Union — A503

2004, Jan. 15 *Perf. 14x14¾*
1527 A503 48c multi 1.75 1.75

Love — A504

Designs: Nos. 1528, 1529a, 1530, Chimpanzees. Nos. 1529b, 1531, Panda. Nos. 1529c, 1532, Koala. No. 1533, Hippopotamus.

2004, Jan. 30 *Perf. 14x14¾*
1528 A504 48c multi 2.00 2.00

Souvenir Sheet
Perf. 14x14¾ on 3 or 4 Sides
1529 Sheet of 3 6.00 6.00
a.-c. A504 60c Any single 2.00 2.00

Booklet Stamps
Self-Adhesive
Size: 21x26mm
Serpentine Die Cut 11x11¼
1530 A504 48c multi 2.50 2.50
1531 A504 48c multi 2.50 2.50
1532 A504 48c multi 2.50 2.50
1533 A504 48c multi 2.50 2.50
a. Booklet pane, 3 each #1530-1531, 2 each #1532-1533 + 10 labels 25.00
Nos. 1530-1533 (4) 10.00 10.00

New Year 2004 (Year of the Monkey), No. 1529.

Abbey Theater, Dublin, Cent. — A505

2004, Feb. 27 *Perf. 14x14¾*
1534 A505 48c multi 1.75 1.75

St. Patrick's Day — A506

2004, Feb. 27
1535 A506 65c multi 2.00 2.00

Antarctic Expedition of Ernest Shackleton, 90th Anniv. A507

Designs: No. 1536, Ship's stern, expedition members, dogs. No. 1537, Ship's bow, expedition members, dogs. Nos. 1538, 1540a, Man emerging from tent. Nos. 1539, 1540b, Tents, expedition members.

2004, Mar. 19 *Perf. 13½*
1536 A507 48c multi 1.50 1.50
1537 A507 48c multi 1.50 1.50
a. Horiz. pair, #1536-1537 3.00 3.00
b. Booklet pane, 2 #1537a 6.00 —
1538 A507 65c multi 2.00 2.00
1539 A507 65c multi 2.00 2.00
a. Horiz. pair, #1538-1539 4.00 4.00
b. Booklet pane, 2 #1539a 8.00 —
c. Booklet pane, #1537a, 1539a 7.00 —
Complete booklet, #1537b, 1539b, 2 #1539c 28.00
Nos. 1536-1539 (4) 7.00 7.00

Souvenir Sheet
Perf. 13½ on 2 or 3 Sides
1540 Sheet of 2 7.00 7.00
a.-b A507 €1 Either single 3.50 3.50

No. 1539c exists with two different margins, both of which are in complete booklet.

FIFA (Fédération Internationale de Football Association), Cent. — A508

2004, Mar. 31 *Perf. 13½x13*
1541 A508 60c multi 2.00 2.00

Expansion of the European Union A509

2004, May 1 Litho. *Perf. 14¾x14*
1542 A509 65c multi 4.00 4.00

Europa — A510

Designs: 48c, Ross Castle. 65c, Cliffs of Moher .

2004, May 11 *Perf. 14x13¾*
1543 A510 48c multi 1.25 1.25
1544 A510 65c multi 1.75 1.75

Ducks A511

Designs: 48c, Tufted duck. 60c, Red-breasted merganser. 65c, Gadwall. €1, Garganey.

2004, May 11 *Perf. 13x13¼*
1545 A511 48c multi 1.25 1.25
1546 A511 60c multi 1.50 1.50
1547 A511 65c multi 1.75 1.75
1548 A511 €1 multi 2.50 2.50
a. Souvenir sheet, #1545-1548 7.00 7.00
Nos. 1545-1548 (4) 7.00 7.00

Intl. Year of the Family, 10th Anniv. — A512

2004, May 15 Litho. *Perf. 13¼x13*
1549 A512 65c multi 2.00 2.00

Winning Artwork in Texaco Children's Art Competition A513

Designs: 48c, Untitled work (Frog), by Daire Lee. 60c, Marmalade Cat, by Cian Colman.

65c, Ralleshin Dipditch, by Daire O'Rourke. €1, Fish on a Dish, by Ailish Fitzpatrick, horiz.

2004, May 19 ***Perf. 14x14¾***

1550 A513 48c multi 1.15 1.15
1551 A513 60c multi 1.50 1.50
1552 A513 65c multi 1.60 1.60

Perf. 14¾x14

1553 A513 €1 multi 2.50 2.50
Nos. 1550-1553 (4) 6.75 6.75

Publication of *Ulysses*, by James Joyce, Cent. — A514

Designs: 48c, Caricature of Joyce, by Tullio Percoli. 65c, Photograph of Joyce.

2004, June 16 **Litho.** ***Perf. 13¼***

1554 A514 48c multi 1.25 1.25
1555 A514 65c multi 1.50 1.50

Irish College, Paris, France — A515

2004, June 26 ***Perf. 14x14¾***

1556 A515 65c multi 2.00 2.00

Inauguration of LUAS Tram System, Dublin A516

2004, June 30 ***Perf. 13¼***

1557 A516 48c Environment 1.50 1.50
1558 A516 48c Accessibility 1.50 1.50
a. Horiz. pair, #1557-1558 3.00 3.00

2004 Summer Olympics, Athens A517

Olympic flame, rings and: 48c, Javelin thrower. 60c, Myron's Discobolus.

2004, July 22 ***Perf. 13¾x14***

1559 A517 48c multi 1.25 1.25
1560 A517 60c multi 1.75 1.75

Camogie, Cent. A518

Camogie players and: No. 1561, Camogie Association emblem. No. 1562, Cup.

2004, July 22 ***Perf. 14¾x14***

1561 A518 48c multi 1.25 1.25
1562 A518 48c multi 1.25 1.25
a. Horiz. pair, #1561-1562 2.50 2.50

Flowers — A519

Designs: 4c, Common dog-violet. 5c, Dandelion. Nos. 1565, 1571, Primrose. Nos. 1569A, 1570, Daisy. 60c, Hawthorn. 65c, Bluebell. €2, Lords-and-ladies. €5, Dog-rose, horiz.

Perf. 14x14¾, 14¾x14

2004, Sept. 9 **Litho.**

1563 A519 4c multi .25 .25
1564 A519 5c multi .25 .25
1565 A519 48c multi 1.50 1.50
1566 A519 60c multi 1.90 1.90
1567 A519 65c multi 2.00 2.00

Size: 23x44mm

1568 A519 €2 multi 6.00 6.00

Size: 44x23mm

1569 A519 €5 multi 15.00 15.00
Nos. 1563-1569 (7) 26.90 26.90

Booklet Stamp

Perf. 14x14¾ on 3 Sides

1569A A519 48c multi 1.50 1.50
b. Booklet pane 5 each #1565, 1569A 15.00 —
Complete booklet, #1569Ab 15.00

Self-Adhesive

Size: 20x25mm

Serpentine Die Cut 11x11¼

1570 A519 48c multi 1.50 1.50
1571 A519 48c multi 1.50 1.50
a. Vert. coil pair, #1570-1571 3.00 3.00
b. Booklet pane, 5 each #1570-1571 15.00

No. 1571 is on the left side of No. 1571b.

See Nos. 1606-1610, 1650-1655, 1708-1713, 1723-1729, 1770-1773, 1814, 1852, 1865.

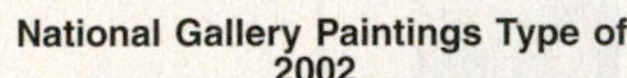

National Gallery Paintings Type of 2002

Designs: No. 1572, The House Builders, by Walter Osborne. No. 1573, Kitchen Maid with the Supper at Emmaus, by Diego Velázquez. No. 1574, The Lamentation Over the Dead Christ, by Nicolas Poussin. No. 1575, The Taking of Christ, by Caravaggio.

2004, Sept. 16 ***Perf. 14¾x14***

1572 A484 48c multi 1.25 1.25
a. Booklet pane of 4 5.00 —
1573 A484 48c multi 1.25 1.25
a. Booklet pane of 4 5.00 —
1574 A484 48c multi 1.25 1.25
a. Booklet pane of 4 5.00 —
1575 A484 48c multi 1.25 1.25
a. Horiz. strip of 4, #1572-1575 5.00 5.00
b. Booklet pane of 4 5.00 —
Complete booklet, #1572a, 1573a, 1574a, 1575b 30.00

Complete booklet sold for €8.

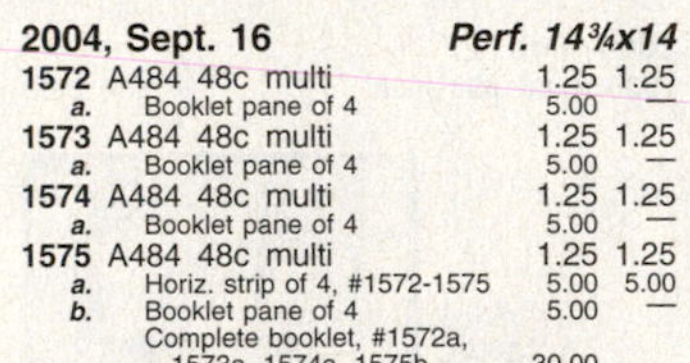

Nobel Prize Winners for Literature — A520

Designs: No. 1576, William Butler Yeats (1865-1939), 1923 winner. No. 1577, George Bernard Shaw (1856-1950), 1925 winner. No. 1578, Samuel Beckett (1906-89), 1969 winner. No. 1579, Seamus Heaney (b. 1939), 1995 winner.

Perf. 12½x13½

2004, Oct. 1 **Litho. & Engr.**

1576 A520 N multi 1.50 1.50
1577 A520 N multi 1.50 1.50
1578 A520 N multi 1.50 1.50
1579 A520 N multi 1.50 1.50
b. Booklet pane of 4, #1576-1579 6.00 —
Complete booklet, #1579b 6.00

Nos. 1576-1579 each sold for 48c on day of issue. See Sweden No. 2492.

Patrick Kavanagh (1904-67), Poet A521

2004, Oct. 21 **Litho.** ***Perf. 13x13¼***

1580 A521 48c green & black 1.50 1.50

Quakerism in Ireland, 350th Anniv. A522

2004, Oct. 21

1581 A522 60c multi 1.90 1.90

Christmas A523

Designs: 48c, Holy Family. 60c, Flight into Egypt. 65c, Adoration of the Magi.

2004, Nov. 10 **Litho.** ***Perf. 14x14¾***

1582 A523 48c multi 1.50 1.50
1583 A523 60c multi 1.90 1.90
1584 A523 65c multi 2.00 2.00
Nos. 1582-1584 (3) 5.40 5.40

Booklet Stamp

Self-Adhesive

Serpentine Die Cut 11x11¼

Size: 21x27mm

1585 A523 48c multi 1.50 1.50
a. Booklet pane of 24 36.00

No. 1585a sold for €11.04.

Love A524

Birds: Nos. 1586, 1587b, 1590, Parrots. Nos. 1587a, 1588, Rooster. Nos. 1587c, 1591, Owl. No. 1589, Storks.

2005, Jan. 28 ***Perf. 14¾x14***

1586 A524 48c multi 4.25 4.25
1587 Sheet of 3 7.50 7.50
a.-c. A524 60c Any single 2.50 2.50

Booklet Stamps

Self-Adhesive

Serpentine Die Cut 11¼x11

Size: 27x21mm

1588 A524 48c multi 1.75 1.75
1589 A524 48c multi 1.75 1.75
1590 A524 48c multi 1.75 1.75
1591 A524 48c multi 1.75 1.75
a. Booklet pane, 3 each #1588, 1590, 2 each #1589, 1591 + 10 labels 17.50

New Year 2005 (Year of the Rooster).

St. Patrick's Day — A525

2005, Feb. 17 **Litho.** ***Perf. 14x14¾***

1592 A525 65c multi 2.00 2.00

Works of Women Artists A526

Designs: No. 1593, Landscape, Co. Wicklow, by Evie Hone (1894-1955). No. 1594, Seabird and Landmarks, by Nano Reid (1905-81). No. 1595, Threshing, by Mildred Anne Butler (1858-1941), vert. No. 1596, Three Graces, by Gabriel Hayes (1909-78), vert.

2005, Feb. 24 ***Perf. 14¾x14, 14x14¾***

1593 A526 48c multi 1.25 1.25
1594 A526 48c multi 1.25 1.25
a. Horiz. pair, #1593-1594 2.50 2.50
1595 A526 65c multi 1.75 1.75
1596 A526 65c multi 1.75 1.75
a. Horiz. pair, #1595-1596 3.50 3.50

Cork, 2005 European Cultural Capital A527

2005, Mar. 7 **Litho.** ***Perf. 13¼***

1597 A527 48c shown 1.75 1.75
1598 A527 48c Buildings, bridge 1.75 1.75
a. Horiz. pair, #1597-1598 3.50 3.50

Intl. Year of Physics — A528

Designs: 48c, William Rowan Hamilton (1805-65), mathematician and astronomer. 60c, UNESCO Headquarters, Paris. 65c, Albert Einstein (1879-1955), physicist.

2005, Mar. 14

1599 A528 48c multi 1.10 1.10
1600 A528 60c multi 1.40 1.40
1601 A528 65c multi 1.50 1.50
Nos. 1599-1601 (3) 4.00 4.00

Dublin-Belfast Railway, 150th Anniv. — A529

Designs: No. 1602, Modern train. No. 1603, Steam locomotive at Connolly Station, Dublin. 60c, Steam locomotive on Boyne Valley Viaduct. 65c, Modern train at station platform.

2005, Apr. 5 **Litho.** ***Perf. 14¾x14***

1602 A529 48c multi 1.50 1.50
a. Booklet pane of 4 6.00 —
1603 A529 48c multi 1.50 1.50
a. Booklet pane of 4 6.00 —
b. Horiz. pair, #1602-1603 3.00 3.00
1604 A529 60c multi 1.90 1.90
a. Booklet pane of 4 7.75 —

1605 A529 65c multi 2.00 2.00
a. Booklet pane of 4 8.00 —
Complete booklet, #1602a, 1603a, 1604a, 1605a 27.75
b. Souvenir sheet, #1602-1605 8.50 8.50
Nos. 1602-1605 (4) 6.90 6.90

Complete booklet sold for €9.

Flowers Type of 2004

Designs: 1c, Bloody crane's-bill. 2c, Irish orchid. 7c, Fly orchid. 10c, Mountain avens. €10, Spring gentian, horiz.

2005, Apr. 12 ***Perf. 14x14¾***
1606 A519 1c multi .25 .25
1607 A519 2c multi .25 .25
1608 A519 7c multi .25 .25
1609 A519 10c multi .30 .30

Size: 44x23mm

1610 A519 €10 multi 20.00 20.00
Nos. 1606-1610 (5) 21.05 21.05

Biosphere Reserves in Ireland and Canada — A530

Designs: 48c, Deer, Killarney National Park, Ireland. 65c, Saskatoon berries, Waterton Lakes National Park, Canada.

2005, Apr. 22 ***Perf. 13¼x13***
1611 A530 48c multi 1.25 1.25
1612 A530 65c multi 1.75 1.75
a. Souvenir sheet, #1611-1612 5.00 5.00

See Canada Nos. 2105-2106.

Europa A531

2005, May 9 **Litho.** ***Perf. 14¼x14***
1613 A531 48c Irish stew 1.50 1.50
1614 A531 65c Oysters 2.00 2.00

Worldwide Fund for Nature (WWF) A532

Butterflies: 48c, Small copper. 60c, Green hairstreak. 65c, €5, Painted lady. €1, Pearl-bordered fritillary.

2005, May 24 ***Perf. 13¼***
1615 A532 48c multi 1.25 1.25
1616 A532 60c multi 1.60 1.60
1617 A532 65c multi 1.75 1.75
1618 A532 €1 multi 2.50 2.50
Nos. 1615-1618 (4) 7.10 7.10

Souvenir Sheet

1619 A532 €5 multi 14.00 14.00

Tall Ships A533

2005, July 4 **Litho.** ***Perf. 13½***
1620 A533 48c Dunbrody 1.25 1.25
1621 A533 60c Tenacious 1.60 1.60
1622 A533 65c Eagle 1.75 1.75
Nos. 1620-1622 (3) 4.60 4.60

Round Towers — A534

2005, July 27 **Litho.** ***Perf. 13¼***
1623 A534 48c Glendalough 1.25 1.25
1624 A534 48c Ardmore 1.25 1.25
1625 A534 48c Clones 1.25 1.25
1626 A534 48c Kilmacduagh 1.25 1.25
a. Horiz. strip of 4, #1623-1626 5.00 5.00

Apimondia 2005 Apriarists Congress, Dublin — A535

2005, Aug. 19 ***Perf. 13½x13***
1627 A535 65c multi 2.25 2.25

2006 Ryder Cup Golf Tournament, K Club, Straffan — A536

Designs: No. 1628, Golfers Darren Clark, Paul McGinley, and Pádraig Harrington. No. 1629, Golfers Eamonn Darcy, Christy O'Connor, Jr., and Philip Walton. 60c, Golfers Harry Bradshaw, Ronan Rafferty, and Christy O'Connor, Sr. 65c, K Club.

2005, Sept. 27 **Litho.** ***Perf. 14¾x14***
1628 A536 48c multi 1.50 1.50
a. Booklet pane of 4 6.00 —
1629 A536 48c multi 1.50 1.50
a. Pair, #1628-1629 3.00 3.00
b. Booklet pane of 4 6.00 —
1630 A536 60c multi 2.00 2.00
a. Booklet pane of 4 8.00 —
b. Booklet pane, 2 each #1628-1630 ('06) 10.00 —
1631 A536 65c multi 2.00 2.00
a. Booklet pane of 4 8.00 —
b. Booklet pane, 2 #1631 ('06) 4.00 —
Complete booklet, #1628a, 1629b, 1630a, 1631a 28.00
Nos. 1628-1631 (4) 7.00 7.00

Nos. 1630b, 1631b issued 9/14/06.

Pres. Erskine Childers (1905-74) A537

2005, Oct. 10 ***Perf. 14x14¾***
1632 A537 48c multi 3.50 3.50

Ireland in the United Nations A538

Designs: No. 1633, Irish Defense Force member assisting man in East Timor. No. 1634, Medical worker aiding child in East Timor. 60c, F. H. Boland, Ireland's signer of United Nations Charter. 65c, Irish Defense Force member in classroom in Lebanon.

2005, Oct. 14 ***Perf. 14¾x14***
1633 A538 48c multi 1.50 1.50
1634 A538 48c multi 1.50 1.50
a. Horiz. pair, #1633-1634 3.00 3.00
1635 A538 60c multi 1.90 1.90
1636 A538 65c multi 2.00 2.00
Nos. 1633-1636 (4) 6.90 6.90

Arthur Griffith's Policy Establishing Sinn Féin, Cent. — A539

2005, Nov. 10 ***Perf. 13½***
1637 A539 48c multi 2.00 2.00

Christmas A540

Designs: 48c, Nativity. 60c, Choir of angels. 65c, Choir of angels, diff.

2005, Nov. 10 ***Perf. 14x14¾***
1638 A540 48c multi 1.50 1.50
1639 A540 60c multi 1.90 1.90
1640 A540 65c multi 2.00 2.00
Nos. 1638-1640 (3) 5.40 5.40

Booklet Stamp
Self-Adhesive
Size: 21x27mm
Serpentine Die Cut 11x11¼

1641 A540 48c multi 1.50 1.50
a. Booklet pane of 26 35.00 35.00

No. 1641a sold for €12.

Patrick Gallagher and Templecrone Cooperative Store — A541

2006, Jan. 16 **Litho.** ***Perf. 14¾x14***
1642 A541 48c sepia 1.75 1.75

Templecrone Cooperative Agricultural Society, cent.

New Year 2006 (Year of the Dog) A542

Designs: Nos. 1643, 1644b, 1647, Dog, man and woman. Nos. 1644a, 1645, Two dogs, man. No. 1644c, 1646, Dog on leash, woman. No. 1648, Dog biting sneaker.

2006, Jan. 16 ***Perf. 14¾x14***
1643 A542 48c multi 1.75 1.75

Souvenir Sheet

1644 Sheet of 3 7.50 7.50
a.-c. A542 65c Any single 2.50 2.50

Booklet Stamps
Self-Adhesive
Size: 26x21mm
Serpentine Die Cut 11¼x11

1645 A542 48c multi 1.75 1.75
1646 A542 48c multi 1.75 1.75
1647 A542 48c multi 1.75 1.75
1648 A542 48c multi 1.75 1.75
a. Booklet pane, 3 each #1645-1646, 2 each #1647-1648, + 10 labels 17.50
Nos. 1645-1648 (4) 7.00 7.00

St. Patrick Lights the Paschal Fire at Slane, by Sean Keating A543

2006, Feb. 16 ***Perf. 14¾x14***
1649 A543 65c multi 2.25 2.25

St. Patrick's Day.

Flowers Type of 2004

Designs: 12c, Autumn gorse. 25c, Common knapweed. 75c, Navelwort. 90c, Viper's bugloss. €1, Foxglove.

2006, Feb. 20 ***Perf. 14x14¾***
1650 A519 12c multi .30 .30
1651 A519 25c multi .60 .60
1652 A519 75c multi 1.90 1.90
1653 A519 90c multi 2.25 2.25

Size: 23x44mm

1654 A519 €1 multi 2.50 2.50
Nos. 1650-1654 (5) 7.55 7.55

Booklet Stamp
Self-Adhesive
Size: 21x27mm
Serpentine Die Cut 11x11¼

1655 A519 75c multi 2.25 2.25
a. Booklet pane of 10 22.50

Trees A544

2006, Mar. 7 ***Perf. 13¼***
1656 A544 48c Sessile oak 1.25 1.25
1657 A544 60c Yew 1.60 1.60
1658 A544 75c Ash 2.00 2.00
1659 A544 €1 Strawberry tree 2.50 2.50
a. Souvenir sheet, #1656-1659 8.00 8.00
b. As "a," with Washington 2006 World Philatelic Exhibition emblem in margin 9.00 9.00
Nos. 1656-1659 (4) 7.35 7.35

No. 1659b issued in June. No. 1659b sold for €3.

St. Hubert, Stained Glass Window by Harry Clarke (1889-1931) A545

2006, Mar. 21 ***Perf. 13¼***
1660 A545 48c multi 1.40 1.40

Easter Rebellion, 90th Anniv. — A546

2006, Apr. 12 *Perf. 13½*

1661	A546 48c multi		1.40	1.40

Adoption of European Union Flag, 20th Anniv. A547

2006, May 9 *Perf. 14¼x14*

1662	A547 48c multi		1.40	1.40

Europa — A548

Winning art in children's stamp design contest: 48c, People holding Irish and European Union flags, by Katie McMillan. 75c, Flowers with flags, by Sarah Naughter.

2006, May 9 *Perf. 14x14¼*

1663	A548 48c multi		1.40	1.40
1664	A548 75c multi		1.90	1.90

University Church, Dublin, 150th Anniv. — A549

2006, May 25 Litho. *Perf. 14x14¾*

1665	A549 48c multi		1.75	1.75

Department of the Gaeltacht, 50th Anniv. — A550

2006, June 6 *Perf. 13¼*

1666	A550 48c multi		1.75	1.75

TG4 Television Channel, 10th Anniv. A551

2006, June 6

1667	A551 48c multi		1.75	1.75

Celtic Scholars — A552

Designs: No. 1668, Máirtín O Cadhain (1906-70), writer. No. 1669, Johann Caspar Zeuss (1806-56), philologist.

2006, June 6 *Perf. 14x14¾*

1668	A552 48c multi		1.50	1.50
1669	A552 48c multi		1.50	1.50
	a.	Pair, #1668-1669	3.00	3.00

Rosslare-Fishguard Ferry Service, Cent. — A553

Designs: No. 1670, Steam ferry. No. 1671, Modern ferry.

2006, June 20 *Perf. 14¾x14*

1670	A553 48c multi		1.50	1.50
1671	A553 48c multi		1.50	1.50
	a.	Pair, #1670-1671	3.00	3.00
	b.	Souvenir sheet, #1670-1671	3.50	3.50

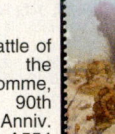

Battle of the Somme, 90th Anniv. A554

2006, June 26 *Perf. 13½x13¾*

1672	A554 75c multi		2.50	2.50

Guide Dog — A555

Litho. & Embossed

2006, July 7 *Perf. 13¼x13*

1673	A555 48c multi		1.75	1.75

A556

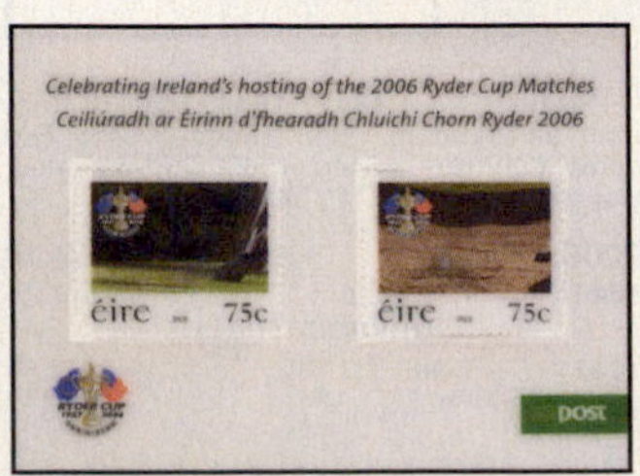

2006 Ryder Cup Golf Tournament, K Club, Straffan — A557

Golf ball: Nos. 1674, 1678, On tee. Nos. 1675, 1679, In rough. Nos. 1676, 1680, In sand trap. Nos. 1677, 1681, Near green.
No. 1682: a, Tee shot. b, Sand trap shot.

2006 Litho. *Perf. 14x14¾*

1674	A556 48c multi		1.25	1.25
1675	A556 48c multi		1.25	1.25
1676	A556 48c multi		1.25	1.25
1677	A556 48c multi		1.25	1.25
	a.	Horiz. strip, #1674-1677	5.00	5.00
	b.	Souvenir sheet #1674-1677	5.50	5.50
	c.	Booklet pane, 2 each #1674-1677	10.00	—
	d.	Booklet pane, #1674-1677	5.00	—

Coil Stamps
Self-Adhesive
Size: 21x27mm
Serpentine Die Cut 11x11¼

1678	A556 48c multi		1.25	1.25
1679	A556 48c multi		1.25	1.25
1680	A556 48c multi		1.25	1.25
1681	A556 48c multi		1.25	1.25
	a.	Vert. strip, #1678-1681	5.00	

Souvenir Sheet
Self-Adhesive
Litho. With Three-Dimensional Plastic Affixed
Serpentine Die Cut 9¼

1682	A557	Sheet of 2	6.50	
	a.-b.	75c Either single	3.25	3.25
		Complete booklet, #1630b, 1631b, 1677c, 1677d, and unbound #1682	40.00	

Issued: Nos. 1674-1678, 7/25; No. 1682, 9/14. Complete booklet sold for €12. No. 1677b has Ryder Cup emblem in margin while No. 1677d does not.

Winning of Olympic 1500-Meter Running Gold Medal by Ronnie Delany, 50th Anniv. — A558

Perf. 13¾x13½

2006, Aug. 16 **Litho.**

1683	A558 48c multi		1.25	1.25

Michael Cusack (1847-1906), Sports Journalist A559

2006, Aug. 23 *Perf. 14x14¾*

1684	A559 48c multi		1.25	1.25

Michael Davitt (1846-1906), Founder of National Land League — A560

2006, Sept. 5

1685	A560 48c multi		1.25	1.25

National Concert Hall, Dublin, 25th Anniv. — A561

2006, Sept. 8

1686	A561 48c multi		1.25	1.25

Inland Waterways — A562

Designs: No. 1687, Barrow River at Graiguenamanagh. No. 1688, Belturbet Marina, Erne River. No. 1689, Grand Canal at Cornalaur. No. 1690, Meelick Pier, Shannon River.

2006, Oct. 20 Litho. *Perf. 13½x13¾*

1687	A562 75c multi		1.75	1.75
	a.	Booklet pane of 4	7.00	—
1688	A562 75c multi		1.75	1.75
	a.	Booklet pane of 4	7.00	—
1689	A562 75c multi		1.75	1.75
	a.	Booklet pane of 4	7.00	—
1690	A562 75c multi		1.75	1.75
	a.	Booklet pane of 4	7.00	—
		Complete booklet, #1687a-1690a	28.00	

Traditional Irish Music Groups — A563

Designs: No. 1691, The Chieftains. No. 1692, The Dubliners. No. 1693, The Clancy Brothers and Tommy Makem. No. 1694, Altan.

2006, Nov. 7 Litho. *Perf. 13½x13¾*

1691	A563 48c multi		1.75	1.75
	a.	Booklet pane of 4	7.00	—
1692	A563 48c multi		1.75	1.75
	a.	Booklet pane of 4	7.00	—
1693	A563 75c multi		2.50	2.50
	a.	Booklet pane of 4	10.00	—
1694	A563 75c multi		2.50	2.50
	a.	Booklet pane of 4	10.00	—
		Complete booklet, #1691a, 1692a, 1693a, 1694a	34.00	
	b.	Souvenir sheet, #1691-1694	7.00	7.00
	c.	As "b," with Belgica '06 emblem added in margin	7.00	7.00
	d.	As "b," with MonacoPhil 2006 emblem added in margin	7.00	7.00

Complete booklet sold for €10.
No. 1694c issued 11/16; No. 1694d, 12/1.

Christmas
A564 A565

Designs: No. 1695, Madonna and Child. 75c, Shepherd and lamb. No. 1697, Nativity.

2006, Nov. 9 *Perf. 14x14¾*

1695	A564 48c multi		1.50	1.50
1696	A564 75c multi		2.25	2.25

Booklet Stamp
Self-Adhesive
Serpentine Die Cut 11x11¼

1697	A565 48c multi		1.50	1.50
	a.	Booklet pane of 26	39.00	
		Nos. 1695-1697 (3)	5.25	5.25

No. 1697a sold for €12.

Father Luke Wadding (1588-1657)
A566

Irish Franciscan College, Louvain, 400th Anniv. — A567

2007, Jan. 24 Litho. *Perf. 14x14¾*

1698 A566 75c multi 2.25 2.25
1699 A567 75c multi 2.25 2.25

Hands With Wedding Rings
A568

Greetings
A569

Designs: No. 1701, Stamp with hat, heart balloon. No. 1702, Birthday cake.

Serpentine Die Cut 11¼

2007, Jan. 26 Booklet Stamps

Self-Adhesive

1700 A568 N multi 1.50 1.50
a. Booklet pane of 10 15.00
1701 A569 N multi 1.50 1.50
1702 A569 N multi 1.50 1.50
a. Booklet pane of 10, 5 each #1701-1702 15.00
Nos. 1700-1702 (3) 4.50 4.50

Nos. 1700-1702 each sold for 48c on day of issue.

New Year 2007 (Year of the Pig)
A570

2007, Feb. 9 Litho. *Perf. 14¾x14*

1703 A570 75c grn & multi 2.00 2.00

Souvenir Sheet

1704 Sheet of 3, #1704a, 2 #1703 7.50 7.50
a. A570 75c red & multi 2.50 2.50

St. Patrick's Day — A571

2007, Feb. 9 *Perf. 13½*

1705 A571 75c multi 2.00 2.00

Flight of the Earls, 400th Anniv. — A572

Designs: No. 1706, Hugh O'Neill, Earl of Tyrone, and ship at right. No. 1707, Rory O'Donnell, Earl of Tyrconnell, and rowboat at left.

2007, Feb. 23 *Perf. 14x14¾*

1706 A572 48c multi 1.50 1.50
1707 A572 48c multi 1.50 1.50
a. Horiz. pair, #1706-1707 3.00 3.00
b. Souvenir sheet, #1707a 3.00 3.00

Flowers Type of 2004

Designs: 3c, Yellow flag. 55c, No. 1712, Large-flowered butterwort. 78c, Black bog-rush. 95c, Purple loosestrife. No. 1713, Blue-eyed grass.

2007, Mar. 1 Litho. *Perf. 14x14¾*

1708 A519 3c multi .25 .25
1709 A519 55c multi 1.50 1.50
1710 A519 78c multi 2.10 2.10
1711 A519 95c multi 2.50 2.50
Nos. 1708-1711 (4) 6.35 6.35

Self-Adhesive

Size: 21x26mm

Serpentine Die Cut 11x11¼

1712 A519 N multi 1.50 1.50
1713 A519 N multi 1.50 1.50
a. Booklet pane, 5 each #1712-1713 15.00
b. Vert. coil pair, #1712-1713 3.00

Nos. 1712-1713 each sold for 55c on day of issue.

Castles
A573

Designs: No. 1714, Trim Castle. No. 1715, Dunluce Castle. No. 1716, Lismore Castle. No. 1717, Portumna Castle.

2007, Mar. 9 *Perf. 14¾x14*

1714 A573 55c multi 1.50 1.50
1715 A573 55c multi 1.50 1.50
1716 A573 55c multi 1.50 1.50
1717 A573 55c multi 1.50 1.50
b. Souvenir sheet, #1714-1717 6.00 6.00

Treaty of Rome, 50th Anniv. — A574

2007, Mar. 28 *Perf. 14x14¾*

1718 A574 55c multi 1.50 1.50

Planets — A575

Earth and: No. 1719, Jupiter. No. 1720, Neptune. No. 1721, Saturn. No. 1722, Uranus.

2007, Apr. 20 Litho. *Perf. 13¼*

1719 A575 55c multi 1.50 1.50
1720 A575 55c multi 1.50 1.50
a. Horiz. pair, #1719-1720 3.00 3.00
1721 A575 78c multi 2.25 2.25
1722 A575 78c multi 2.25 2.25
a. Horiz. pair, #1721-1722 4.50 4.50
b. Souvenir sheet, #1719-1722 7.50 7.50
c. Booklet pane, #1719-1722 7.50 —
Complete booklet, 4 #1722c 30.00
Nos. 1719-1722 (4) 7.50 7.50

No. 1722c has stamps with straight edges at right. Complete booklet contains four examples of No. 1722c with different margins.

Flower Type of 2004

Designs: 5c, Dandelion. 25c, Common knapweed. 55c, Large-flowered butterwort. 78c, Black bog-rush.

Die Cut Perf. 12¾

2007, Apr. 20 Coil Stamp Litho.

Self-Adhesive (#1723, 1728-1729)

Size: 21x26mm

1723 A519 55c multi 1.50 1.50

Booklet Stamps

Size: 17x20mm

Perf. 14¾x14 on 3 Sides

1724 A519 5c multi .25 .25
1725 A519 25c multi .70 .70
1726 A519 55c multi 1.50 1.50
a. Booklet pane of 6, #1725, 2 #1724, 3 #1726 5.75 —
Complete booklet, #1726a 5.75

Size: 20x23mm

Perf. 14x14¾ on 3 Sides

1727 A519 55c multi 1.50 1.50
a. Booklet pane of 10 15.00 —
Complete booklet, #1727a 15.00

Size: 21x26mm

Serpentine Die Cut 11x11¼

1728 A519 55c multi 1.50 1.50
a. Booklet pane of 10 15.00
1729 A519 78c multi 2.25 2.25
a. Booklet pane of 10 22.50
Nos. 1723-1729 (7) 9.20 9.20

Europa
A576

2007, May 9 *Perf. 14¼x14*

1730 A576 55c Female Scout 1.50 1.50
1731 A576 78c Male Scout 2.10 2.10

Scouting, cent.

Canonization of St. Charles of Mount Argus (1821-93)
A577

2007, June 5 *Perf. 13¼*

1732 A577 55c multi 1.50 1.50

Institute of Public Administration, 50th Anniv. — A578

2007, June 13

1733 A578 55c multi 1.50 1.50

RTE Performing Groups
A579

Designs: Nos. 1734, 1742, National Symphony Orchestra (Ceolfhoireann Shiansach Náisiúnta). Nos. 1735, 1740, Concert Orchestra (Ceolfhoireann Cheolchoirme). Nos. 1736, 1743, Vanbrugh Quartet (Ceathairéad Vanbrugh). Nos. 1737, 1741, Philharmonic Choir (Cór Fiolarmónach). Nos. 1738, 1739, Children's Choir (Cór na nOg).

2007, June 19 *Perf. 13¼x13½*

1734 A579 55c multi 1.50 1.50
1735 A579 55c multi 1.50 1.50
1736 A579 55c multi 1.50 1.50
a. Booklet pane, 2 each #1734-1736 9.00 —
1737 A579 55c multi 1.50 1.50
1738 A579 55c multi 1.50 1.50
a. Horiz. strip of 5, #1734-1738 7.50 7.50
b. Booklet pane, 2 each #1737-1738 6.00 —
Complete booklet, 2 each #1736a, 1738b 30.00

Booklet Stamps

Self-Adhesive

Serpentine Die Cut 11¼x11½

1739 A579 55c multi 1.50 1.50
1740 A579 55c multi 1.50 1.50
1741 A579 55c multi 1.50 1.50
1742 A579 55c multi 1.50 1.50
1743 A579 55c multi 1.50 1.50
a. Booklet pane of 10, 2 each #1739-1743 15.00
Nos. 1734-1743 (10) 15.00 15.00

Revival of Honorable Society of King's Inns, 400th Anniv. — A580

2007, July 10 *Perf. 13¼*

1744 A580 55c multi 1.50 1.50

Registry of Deeds Act, 300th Anniv.
A581

2007, July 10 *Perf. 14¾x14*

1745 A581 78c multi 2.25 2.25

National Anthem, Cent.
A582

2007, July 17 Litho. *Perf. 13½*

1746 A582 55c multi 1.50 1.50

Weddings Type of 2007

Serpentine Die Cut 11¼

2007, July 25 Self-Adhesive

Booklet Stamp

1747 A568 55c multi 1.50 1.50
a. Booklet pane of 10 15.00

Viking Ship Skuldelev 2 — A583

Designs: 55c, Ship. €3, Ship on water.

2007, Aug. 7 Litho. *Perf. 14¾x14*

1748 A583 55c multi 1.50 1.50

Souvenir Sheet

1749 A583 €3 multi 7.50 7.50

2007 Rugby World Cup, France — A584

Designs: 55c, Player carrying ball. 78c, Player catching ball.

2007, Aug. 20 ***Perf. 13¼***

1750 A584 55c multi 1.50 1.50
a. Souvenir sheet of 1 1.50 1.50
1751 A584 78c multi 2.25 2.25
a. Souvenir sheet of 1 2.25 2.25

Cat Caricatures by Martyn Turner — A585

Designs: Nos. 1752, 1756a, Fat Cat. Nos. 1753, 1756b, Celtic Tigress. Nos. 1754, 1756c, Cool Cats. Nos. 1755, 1756d, Kilkenny Cat.

2007, Sept. 6 ***Perf. 14x14¾***

1752 A585 55c multi 1.50 1.50
1753 A585 55c multi 1.50 1.50
a. Horiz. pair, #1752-1753 3.00 3.00
1754 A585 78c multi 2.25 2.25
1755 A585 78c multi 2.25 2.25
a. Horiz. pair, #1754-1755 4.50 4.50

Souvenir Sheet

Perf. 13¼

1756 Sheet of 4 7.50 7.50
a.-b. A585 55c Either single, 16x16mm 1.50 1.50
c.-d. A585 78c Either single, 16x16mm 2.25 2.25

Excavations of San Clemente Basilica, Rome, 150th Anniv. — A586

2007, Sept. 12 ***Perf. 14¾x14***

1757 A586 55c multi 1.60 1.60

James Fintan Lalor (1807-49), Political Writer — A587

2007, Sept. 18 ***Perf. 14x14¾***

1758 A587 55c multi 1.60 1.60

Natural History Museum, Dublin, 150th Anniv. — A588

2007, Oct. 25 **Litho.** ***Perf. 13¼***

1759 A588 55c multi 1.60 1.60

Christmas A589

Designs: No. 1760, Presentation in the Temple. No. 1761, Three Magi. No. 1762, Adoration of the Shepherds.

2007, Nov. 8 ***Perf. 14¾x14***

1760 A589 55c multi 1.60 1.60
1761 A589 78c multi 2.40 2.40

Self-Adhesive

Booklet Stamp

Size: 21x27mm

Serpentine Die Cut 11x11¼

1762 A589 55c multi 1.60 1.60
a. Booklet pane of 26 42.50

No. 1762a sold for €13.75.

Charles Wesley (1707-88), Hymn Writer — A590

2007, Nov. 15 ***Perf. 14x14¾***

1763 A590 78c multi 2.40 2.40

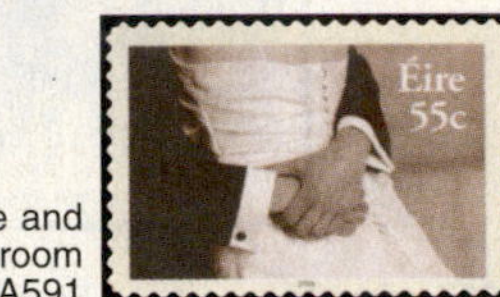

Bride and Groom A591

Serpentine Die Cut 11¼

2008, Jan. 16 **Litho.**

Booklet Stamp

Self-Adhesive

1764 A591 55c multi 1.60 1.60
a. Booklet pane of 10 16.00

Greetings — A592

Serpentine Die Cut 11¼

2008, Jan. 16 **Self-Adhesive**

Booklet Stamps

1765 A592 55c Frog 1.60 1.60
1766 A592 55c Elephant 1.60 1.60
a. Booklet pane of 10, 5 each #1765-1766 16.00

New Year 2008 (Year of the Rat) A593

2008, Jan. 23 ***Perf. 14¾x14***

1767 A593 78c multi 2.40 2.40
a. Souvenir sheet of 3 7.25 7.25

Liam Whelan (1935-58), Soccer Player Killed in Airplane Crash — A594

2008, Feb. 4 ***Perf. 13½x13¾***

1768 A594 55c multi 2.00 2.00

St. Patrick's Day — A595

2008, Feb. 11 ***Perf. 13¼x13***

1769 A595 78c multi 2.40 2.40

Flower Type of 2004

Designs: 20c, Thrift. 50c, Biting stonecrop. 82c, Sea aster.

2008, Mar. 3 **Litho.** ***Perf. 14x14¾***

Size: 20x23mm

1770 A519 20c multi .65 .65
1771 A519 50c multi 1.60 1.60
1772 A519 82c multi 2.50 2.50
a. Booklet pane of 10 25.00 —
Complete booklet, #1772a 25.00
Nos. 1770-1772 (3) 4.75 4.75

Booklet Stamp

Self-Adhesive

Size: 21x25mm

Serpentine Die Cut 11x11¼

1773 A519 82c multi 2.50 2.50
a. Booklet pane of 10 25.00

European Year of Intercultural Dialogue — A596

2008, Mar. 7 ***Perf. 13¼***

1774 A596 55c multi 1.75 1.75

Hugh Lane, by Antonio Mancini — A597

2008, Mar. 28 **Litho.** ***Perf. 13½***

1775 A597 55c multi 1.75 1.75

Dublin City Gallery, cent. (founded by Lane).

Paintings by Paul Henry (1876-1958) A598

Designs: No. 1776, A Connemara Village (left half, "Paul Henry" in blue). No. 1777, A Connemara Village (right half, "Paul Henry" in white). No. 1778, West of Ireland Landscape (left half, "Paul Henry" in gray at left). No. 1779, West of Ireland Landscape (right half, "Paul Henry" in gray at right).

2008, Apr. 17 ***Perf. 13¼***

1776 A598 55c multi 1.75 1.75
1777 A598 55c multi 1.75 1.75
1778 A598 55c multi 1.75 1.75
1779 A598 55c multi 1.75 1.75
a. Horiz. strip of 4, #1776-1779 7.00 7.00
b. Booklet pane of 4, #1776-1779 7.00 —
Complete booklet, 4 #1779b 28.00

No. 1779b has example of No. 1779 with straight edge at right. The four examples of No. 1779b in the complete booklet have different margins. The complete booklet sold for €9.

Credit Union Movement, 50th Anniv. A599

2008, Apr. 23 ***Perf. 14¾x14***

1780 A599 55c multi 1.75 1.75

Intl. Year of Planet Earth A600

Plasticine sculptures of Earth created by children: No. 1781, Africa and Europe, by Mohammed Rahman. No. 1782, South and North America, by Conor Reid.

2008, Apr. 28 ***Die Cut Perf.***

Self-Adhesive

1781 A600 55c red & multi 1.75 1.75
1782 A600 55c blue & multi 1.75 1.75
a. Horiz. pair, #1781-1782, on backing paper without back printing 3.50
b. Booklet pane of 10, 5 each #1781-1782 17.50

Institute of Creative Advertising and Design, 50th Anniv. A601

2008, May 23 ***Perf. 13¼***

1783 A601 55c multi 1.75 1.75

R. M. S. Leinster, 90th Anniv. of Sinking A602

2008, May 30 ***Perf. 14¾x14***

1784 A602 55c multi 1.75 1.75

Europa — A603

Designs: 55c, Boy writing letter. 82c, Girl writing letter.

2008, June 9 *Perf. 14x14¾*

1785 A603 55c multi 1.75 1.75
1786 A603 82c multi 2.50 2.50

Tidy Towns Competition, 50th Anniv. — A604

2008, June 19

1787 A604 55c multi 1.75 1.75

Participation of Irish Defense Forces in UN Missions, 50th Anniv. — A605

2008, June 26 *Perf. 14¾x14*

1788 A605 55c multi 1.75 1.75

Movies Filmed in Ireland — A606

Designs: No. 1789, Kings. No. 1790, Cré na Cille. No. 1791, The Wind that Shakes the Barley. No. 1792, Garage.

2008, July 8 **Litho.** *Perf. 14¾x14*

1789 A606 55c multi 1.75 1.75
1790 A606 55c multi 1.75 1.75
1791 A606 82c multi 2.60 2.60
1792 A606 82c multi 2.60 2.60
a. Booklet pane of 4, #1789-1792 9.25 —
Complete booklet, 4 #1792a 37.50
b. Souvenir sheet of 4, #1789-1792 8.75 8.75
Nos. 1789-1792 (4) 8.70 8.70

No. 1792b has a printed margin. The complete booklet, which sold for €12, contains 4 examples of No. 1792a, each with a different order of stamps and without a printed margin.

2008 Summer Olympics, Beijing A607

Designs: 52c, Rowing. 82c, Shot put.

2008, July 15

1793 A607 55c multi 1.75 1.75
1794 A607 82c multi 2.60 2.60

Souvenir Sheet

Stamps Inscribed "Olympex 2008"

1795 Sheet of 2 4.50 4.50
a. A607 55c multi 1.75 1.75
b. A607 82c multi 2.60 2.60

Mushrooms A608

Designs: No. 1796, Parasol. No. 1797, Orange birch bolete. 82c, Pink waxcap. 95c, Scarlet elfcup.

2008, Aug. 1 **Litho.** *Perf. 14x14¾*

1796 A608 55c multi 1.75 1.75
1797 A608 55c multi 1.75 1.75
a. Horiz. pair, #1796-1797 3.50 3.50
1798 A608 82c multi 2.60 2.60
Nos. 1796-1798 (3) 6.10 6.10

Souvenir Sheet

1799 A608 95c multi 3.00 3.00

First Transatlantic Cable Message From Europe to US, 150th Anniv. — A609

2008, Aug. 15 *Perf. 13¼*

1800 A609 82c multi 2.40 2.40

Old Age Pensions Act, Cent. — A610

2008, Sept. 19 **Litho.** *Perf. 13¼*

1801 A610 55c multi 1.50 1.50

National University of Ireland, Cent. — A611

2008, Sept. 19 *Perf. 13½*

1802 A611 55c multi 1.50 1.50

Patrick Pearse (1879-1916), Patriot, and Founder of St. Enda's School — A612

Pearse and school buildings: No. 1803, Cullenswood House. No. 1804, The Hermitage.

2008, Sept. 25 *Perf. 14¾x14¼*

1803 A612 55c multi 1.50 1.50
1804 A612 55c multi 1.50 1.50

Irish Bands A613

2008, Oct. 10 **Litho.** *Perf. 13½*

1805 A613 55c Planxty 1.50 1.50
1806 A613 55c De Danann 1.50 1.50
1807 A613 82c Tulla Ceili Band 2.25 2.25
1808 A613 82c Bothy Band 2.25 2.25
a. Souvenir sheet, #1805-1808 7.50 7.50
Nos. 1805-1808 (4) 7.50 7.50

Dancers — A614

2008, Nov. 7 **Litho.** *Perf. 13½*

1809 A614 55c Irish dancer 1.40 1.40

Souvenir Sheet

1810 Sheet of 2, #1809, 1810a 3.50 3.50
a. A614 82c Flamenco dancer 2.10 2.10

See Spain No. 3609.

A615

Christmas — A616

Creche figures. No. 1811, Flight into Egypt. 82c, Annunciation. No. 1813, Infant Jesus.

2008, Nov. 7 *Perf. 14¾x14*

1811 A615 55c multi 1.40 1.40
1812 A615 82c multi 2.10 2.10

Booklet Stamp

Self-Adhesive

Serpentine Die Cut 11x11¼

1813 A616 55c multi 1.40 1.40
a. Booklet pane of 26 37.50

No. 1813a sold for €13.75.

Flowers Type of 2004

Design: N, Yellow horned poppy.

Booklet Stamp

Self-Adhesive

Size: 17x21mm

Serpentine Die Cut 14

2008, Dec. 5 **Litho.**

1814 A519 N multi 1.40 1.40
a. Booklet pane of 10 14.00

No. 1814 sold for 55c on day of issue.

Eye — A617

Litho. & Embossed

2009, Jan. 23 *Perf. 14¼*

1815 A617 55c black 1.50 1.50

Louis Braille (1809-52), educator of the blind.

Love A618

Die Cut Perf. 13¼

2009, Jan. 23 **Litho.**

Self-Adhesive

1816 A618 55c multi 1.50 1.50
a. Vert. pair on backing paper without back printing 3.00
b. Booklet pane of 10 15.00

All pairs from booklet pane are on backing paper with printing.

New Year 2009 (Year of the Ox) A619

2009, Jan. 23 *Perf. 14¾x14*

1817 A619 82c multi 2.25 2.25
a. Souvenir sheet of 3 6.75 6.75

St. Patrick Climbs Croagh Patrick, by Margaret Clarke — A620

2009, Feb. 19 *Perf. 14x14¾*

1818 A620 82c multi 2.10 2.10

St. Patrick's Day.

Greetings — A621

Designs: No. 1819, Man lifting girl with letter to mailbox slot. No. 1820, Woman with letter, dog.

2009, Mar. 6 ***Die Cut Perf. 12¾x13¼***

Self-Adhesive

1819 A621 55c multi 1.40 1.40
1820 A621 55c multi 1.40 1.40
a. Horiz. pair, #1819-1820, on backing paper withour back printing 2.80
b. Booklet pane of 10, 5 each #1819-1820, + 10 stickers 14.00

All pairs from booklet pane are on backing paper with printing.

Charles Darwin (1809-82), Naturalist — A622

2009, Mar. 20 *Perf. 13½*

1821 A622 82c multi 2.25 2.25

Scene from "The Playboy of the Western World" — A623

2009, Mar. 24 *Perf. 14x14¾*

1822 A623 55c multi 1.50 1.50

John Millington Synge (1871-1909), writer.

Irish Times Newspaper, Cent. — A624

2009, Mar. 27 *Perf. 13¼*

1823 A624 55c multi 1.50 1.50

A625

A626

A627

A628

A629

A630

A631

A632

An Post, 25th Anniv.

A633 A634

Serpentine Die Cut 11x11¼

2009, Apr. 3 **Litho.**

Coil Stamps

Self-Adhesive

Size: 25x30mm

1824 A625 55c multi 1.50 1.50
1825 A626 55c multi 1.50 1.50
1826 A627 55c multi 1.50 1.50
1827 A628 55c multi 1.50 1.50
1828 A629 55c multi 1.50 1.50
a. Vert. strip of 5, #1824-1828 7.50
1829 A630 55c multi 1.50 1.50
1830 A631 55c multi 1.50 1.50
1831 A632 55c multi 1.50 1.50
1832 A633 55c multi 1.50 1.50
1833 A634 55c multi 1.50 1.50
a. Vert. strip of 5, #1829-1833 7.50
b. Vert. strip of 10, #1824-1833 15.00
Nos. 1824-1833 (10) 15.00 15.00

Serpentine Die Cut 14

1834 Booklet pane of 10 15.00
a. A625 55c multi, 20x24mm 1.50 1.50
b. A626 55c multi, 20x24mm 1.50 1.50
c. A627 55c multi, 20x24mm 1.50 1.50
d. A628 55c multi, 20x24mm 1.50 1.50
e. A629 55c multi, 20x24mm 1.50 1.50
f. A630 55c multi, 20x24mm 1.50 1.50
g. A631 55c multi, 20x24mm 1.50 1.50
h. A632 55c multi, 20x24mm 1.50 1.50
i. A633 55c multi, 20x24mm 1.50 1.50
j. A634 55c multi, 20x24mm 1.50 1.50

No. 1833b was only available in a full roll of 100 stamps. The philatelic bureau sold Nos. 1828a and 1833a as a convenience to collectors rather than No. 1833b.

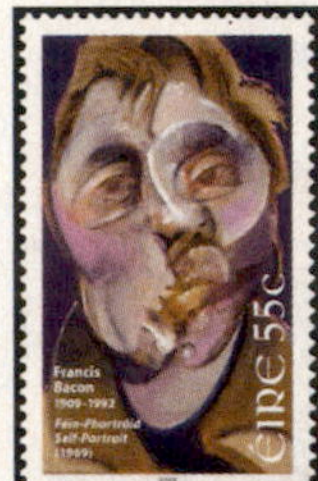

Paintings by Francis Bacon (1909-92) — A635

Designs: 55c, Self-portrait. 82c, Artist's Studio.

2009, Apr. 24 *Perf. 13½*

1835 A635 55c multi 1.50 1.50

Souvenir Sheet

1836 A635 82c multi 2.25 2.25

James Larkin (1875-1947), Union Organizer A636

2009, Apr. 30 *Perf. 13¼*

1837 A636 55c multi 1.50 1.50

Irish Transport and General Workers' Union, cent.

Volvo Ocean Race Stopover in Galway A637

Designs: 55c, Green Dragon yacht. €3, Green Dragon and another yacht, vert.

2009, May 8 *Perf. 13¾x14*

1838 A637 55c multi 1.60 1.60

Souvenir Sheet

1839 A637 €3 multi 8.50 8.50

No. 1839 contains one 27x48mm stamp.

European Conference of Postal and Telecommunications Administrations, 50th Anniv. — A638

2009, May 15 *Perf. 13¼*

1840 A638 82c multi 2.40 2.40

Europa A639

Designs: 55c, Crab Nebula. 82c, Jets from a brown dwarf.

2009, May 15

1841 A639 55c multi 1.60 1.60
1842 A639 82c multi 2.40 2.40

Intl. Year of Astronomy.

European Dog Show, Dublin — A640

2009, May 21 ***Die Cut Perf. 13x13¼***

Self-Adhesive

1843 A640 55c multi 1.60 1.60
a. Horiz. pair on backing paper without back printing 3.25
b. Booklet pane of 10 #1843 16.00

City Status of Kilkenny, 400th Anniv. — A641

2009, June 16 *Perf. 13½*

1844 A641 55c multi 1.60 1.60

Anthony Trollope (1815-82), Writer — A642

2009, June 26 *Perf. 14x14¾*

1845 A642 82c multi 2.40 2.40

Birrell Land Act, Cent. — A643

2009, July 15 *Perf. 13¼*

1846 A643 82c multi 2.40 2.40

Composers — A644

Designs: No. 1847, Wolfgang Amadeus Mozart (1756-91). No. 1848, George Frideric Handel (1685-1759). No. 1849, Joseph Haydn (1732-1809). No. 1850, Frédéric Chopin (1810-49).

2009, Aug. 14 *Perf. 13¼x13*

1847 A644 55c multi 1.60 1.60
1848 A644 55c multi 1.60 1.60
a. Horiz. pair, #1847-1848 3.25 3.25
1849 A644 82c multi 2.40 2.40
1850 A644 82c multi 2.40 2.40
a. Horiz. pair, #1849-1850 5.00 5.00
b. Souvenir sheet of 4, #1847-1850 8.25 8.25
c. Booklet pane of 4, #1847-1850 8.50 —
Complete booklet, 4 #1850c 34.00
Nos. 1847-1850 (4) 8.00 8.00

On No. 1850b, stamps are at upper left with No. 1847 having straight edges at top and left, No. 1848 having straight edge at top and No. 1849 having straight edge at left. On No. 1850c, stamps are at right with Nos. 1848 and 1850 having straight edges at right. Complete booklet sold for €12 and contains four examples of No. 1850c, each with different margins.

Arthur Guinness (1725-1803), Founder of Guinness Brewery — A645

2009, Aug. 28 *Perf. 14x14¾*

1851 A645 82c multi 2.40 2.40

Guinness Brewery, 250th anniv.

Flower Type of 2004

Design: 82c, Sea aster.

2009, Aug. 7 ***Serpentine Die Cut 14***

Booklet Stamp

Self-Adhesive

Size: 17x20mm

1852 A519 82c multi 2.40 2.40
a. Booklet pane of 10 24.00

Compare No. 1852 with No. 1773.

Plantation of Ulster, 400th Anniv. A646

Designs: No. 1853, English text. No. 1854, Gaelic text.

2009, Sept. 4 *Perf. 14¾x14*
1853 A646 55c multi 1.60 1.60
1854 A646 55c multi 1.60 1.60
a. Horiz. pair, #1853-1854 3.20 3.20

Playwrights — A647

Designs: No. 1855, Brian Friel. No. 1856, Tom Murphy. No. 1857, Frank McGuinness.

2009, Sept. 18
1855 A647 55c multi 1.60 1.60
1856 A647 55c multi 1.60 1.60
1857 A647 55c multi 1.60 1.60
Nos. 1855-1857 (3) 4.80 4.80

Dragonflies A648

Designs: No. 1858, Large red damselfly. No. 1859, Irish bluet. 82c, Four-spotted chaser, horiz.
95c, Banded demoiselle, horiz.

2009, Oct. 16 **Litho.** *Perf. 14x14¾*
1858 A648 55c multi 1.75 1.75
1859 A648 55c multi 1.75 1.75
a. Horiz. pair, #1858-1859 3.50 3.50

Perf. 14¾x14
1860 A648 82c multi 2.50 2.50
Nos. 1858-1860 (3) 6.00 6.00

Souvenir Sheet
Perf. 13¼
1861 A648 95c multi 3.00 3.00

No. 1861 contains one 60x25mm stamp.

Illustrations From Gospel Book, Monastery of Gamaghiel, Armenia — A649

Virgin and Child, by Simon Bening — A650

Christmas: No. 1862, Nativity. 82c, Annunciation.

2009, Nov. 6 *Perf. 14¾x14*
1862 A649 55c multi 1.75 1.75
1863 A649 82c multi 2.50 2.50

Booklet Stamp
Self-Adhesive
Serpentine Die Cut 11x11¼
1864 A650 55c multi 1.75 1.75
a. Booklet pane of 26 46.00

No. 1864a sold for €13.75.

Flowers Type of 2004

Design: Large-flowered butterwort.

Serpentine Die Cut 14
2009, Oct. 16 **Litho.**
Booklet Stamp
Self-Adhesive
Size:17x21mm
1865 A519 55c multi 1.75 1.75
a. Booklet pane of 10 17.50

Compare with No. 1728.

Douglas Hyde (1860-1949), First President of Ireland — A651

2010, Jan. 21 **Litho.** *Perf. 14x14¾*
1866 A651 55c multi 1.60 1.60

Lovebirds A652

2010, Jan. 21 *Die Cut Perf. 13¼*
Self-Adhesive
1867 A652 55c multi 1.60 1.60
a. Vert. pair on backing paper without back printing 3.20
b. Booklet pane of 10 16.00

Greetings A653

Designs: No. 1868, Girl astronaut in spaceship, birthday cake. No. 1869, Boy astronaut, heart.

Die Cut Perf. 13¼x12¾
2010, Jan. 28 **Self-Adhesive**
1868 A653 55c multi 1.60 1.60
1869 A653 55c multi 1.60 1.60
a. Vert. pair, #1868-1869, on backing paper without back printing 3.20
b. Booklet pane of 10, 5 each #1868-1869 16.00

New Year 2010 (Year of the Tiger) A654

2010, Feb. 11 *Perf. 13¼*
1870 A654 82c multi 2.25 2.25
a. Souvenir sheet of 3 6.75 6.75

St. Patrick's Day — A655

2010, Feb. 18 *Perf. 14x14¾*
1871 A655 82c multi 2.25 2.25

President's Award, 25th Anniv. A656

2010, Mar. 11 **Litho.** *Perf. 13¼*
1872 A656 55c multi 1.50 1.50

Irish Countrywoman's Association, Cent. — A657

2010, Mar. 25
1873 A657 55c multi 1.50 1.50

Crosses — A658

Designs: No. 1874, Monasterboice Cross, County Louth. No. 1875, Carndonagh Cross, County Donegal. No. 1876, Drumcliffe Cross, County Sligo. No. 1877, Ahenny Cross, County Tipperary.

2010, Apr. 8
1874 A658 55c black 1.50 1.50
1875 A658 55c black 1.50 1.50
1876 A658 55c black 1.50 1.50
1877 A658 55c black 1.50 1.50
a. Horiz. strip of 4, #1874-1877 6.00 6.00
Nos. 1874-1877 (4) 6.00 6.00

Europa — A659

Scenes from children's books: 55c, The Happy Prince, by Oscar Wilde. 82c, Gulliver's Travels, by Jonathan Swift.

2010, May 6
1878 A659 55c multi 1.40 1.40
1879 A659 82c multi 2.10 2.10

Máirtín O Direáin (1910-88), Poet A660

2010, May 27 *Perf. 14¾x14*
1880 A660 55c multi 1.40 1.40

Paintings by Roderic O'Conor (1860-1940) — A661

Designs: No. 1881, The Breton Girl (shown). No. 1882, Self-portrait.

2010, May 27 *Perf. 13¼*
1881 A661 55c multi 1.40 1.40
1882 A661 55c multi 1.40 1.40

Humanitarians — A662

Designs: No. 1883, Mother Teresa (1910-97), 1979 Nobel Laureate for Peace. No. 1884, Henry Dunant (1828-1910), founder of the Red Cross, 1901 Nobel Laureate for Peace.

2010, June 17
1883 A662 55c multi 1.40 1.40
1884 A662 55c multi 1.40 1.40
a. Horiz. pair, #1883-1884 2.80 2.80

Fashion Designers A663

Work of Irish designers: No. 1885, Paul Costelloe. No. 1886, Louise Kennedy. No. 1887, Lainey Keogh. No. 1888, John Rocha. No. 1889, Philip Treacy. No. 1890, Orla Kiely.

Litho. & Embossed
2010, July 15 *Perf. 13¼*
1885 A663 55c multi 1.50 1.50
a. Booklet pane of 3 4.50 —
1886 A663 55c multi 1.50 1.50
a. Booklet pane of 3 4.50 —
1887 A663 55c multi 1.50 1.50
a. Horiz. strip of 3, #1885-1887 4.50 4.50
b. Booklet pane of 3 4.50 —
1888 A663 82c multi 2.25 2.25
a. Booklet pane of 3 6.75 —
1889 A663 82c multi 2.25 2.25
a. Booklet pane of 3 6.75 —
1890 A663 82c multi 2.25 2.25
a. Horiz. strip of 3, #1888-1890 6.75 6.75
b. Booklet pane of 3 6.75 —
c. Complete booklet, #1885a, 1886a, 1887b, 1888a, 1889a, 1890b 34.00
Nos. 1885-1890 (6) 11.25 11.25

Complete booklet sold for €13.

Birds — A664

2010, July 29 **Litho.** *Perf. 13¼*
1891 A664 55c Buzzard 1.50 1.50
1892 A664 55c Golden eagle 1.50 1.50
a. Horiz. pair, #1891-1892 3.00 3.00
1893 A664 82c Peregrine falcon 2.25 2.25
1894 A664 95c Merlin 2.50 2.50
a. Souvenir sheet, #1891-1894 7.75 7.75
Nos. 1891-1894 (4) 7.75 7.75

Romeo and Juliet (Vignette of Sweden No. 1141) — A665

Litho. & Engr.

2010, Aug. 26 *Perf. 12¾*

1895 A665 55c multi 1.40 1.40

Stamp engraving work of Czeslaw Slania. See Sweden No. 2642.

Irish Wheelchair Association, 50th Anniv. — A666

2010, Sept. 8 Litho. *Perf. 14¾x14*

1896 A666 55c multi 1.40 1.40

Showbands — A667

Designs: No. 1897, The Miami Showband. No. 1898, The Drifters Showband. No. 1899, The Royal Showband. No. 1900, The Freshmen.

2010, Sept. 23 *Perf. 13½*

1897 A667 55c multi 1.50 1.50
1898 A667 55c multi 1.50 1.50
1899 A667 82c multi 2.25 2.25
1900 A667 82c multi 2.25 2.25
a. Souvenir sheet of 4, #1897-1900 7.50 7.50
b. Booklet pane of 4, #1897-1900 8.25 —
Complete booklet, 4 #1900b 33.00
Nos. 1897-1900 (4) 7.50 7.50

On No. 1900a, stamps are not near the edge of the sheet and stamps have perforations on all four sides. On No. 1900b, Nos, 1898 and 1900 are at the right side of the sheet and have a straight edge at right. The complete booklet sold for €12 and contains four examples of No. 1900b, each with different margins.

Ireland Automobile Association, Cent. — A668

2010, Oct. 14 *Perf. 14¾x14*

1901 A668 55c multi 1.60 1.60

Irishmen Involved With Chilean Independence A669

Designs: No. 1902, Commander General John Mackenna (1771-1814). No. 1903, Supreme Director Bernardo O'Higgins (1778-1842).

2010, Oct. 28 *Perf. 13¼*

1902 A669 82c multi 2.40 2.40
1903 A669 82c multi 2.40 2.40
a. Horiz. pair, #1902-1903 4.80 4.80

See Chile No. 1562.

A670

Christmas A671

Stained-glass windows from churches in Roscommon: No. 1904, Holy Family. 82c, Joseph and Mary.

2010, Nov. 4 *Perf. 13½*

1904 A670 55c multi 1.60 1.60
1905 A670 82c multi 2.40 2.40

Self-Adhesive

Serpentine Die Cut 11¼x11

1906 A671 55c multi 1.60 1.60
a. Vert. pair on backing paper without printing on back 3.25
b. Booklet pane of 26 #1906 42.00

No. 1906b sold for €13.75 and all stamps have printing on the back of the backing paper.

Bride and Groom — A672

2011, Jan. 20 *Die Cut Perf. 13¼*

Self-Adhesive

1907 A672 55c multi 1.50 1.50
a. Horiz. pair on backing paper without printing on back 3.00
b. Booklet pane of 10 15.00

Tulips — A673

Balloons — A674

2011, Jan. 27 *Die Cut Perf. 13¼x13*

Self-Adhesive

1908 A673 55c multi 1.50 1.50
1909 A674 55c multi 1.50 1.50
a. Vert. pair, #1908-1909 on backing paper without printing on back 3.00
b. Booklet pane of 10, 5 each #1908-1909, + 10 stickers 15.00

American Chamber of Commerce, Ireland, 50th Anniv. — A675

2011, Feb. 3 *Perf. 14x14¾*

1910 A675 55c multi 1.50 1.50

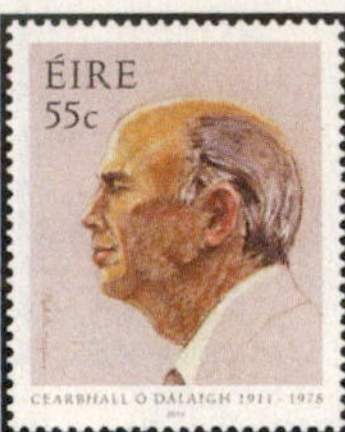

Pres. Cearbhall O Dáleaigh (Carroll O'Daly) (1911-78) A676

2011, Feb. 10 *Perf. 13¾*

1911 A676 55c multi 1.50 1.50

St. Patrick's Day — A677

2011, Feb. 17 *Perf. 14¼x14¾*

1912 A677 82c multi 2.40 2.40

A678

Women's Rights A679

2011, Mar. 3 *Perf. 13¼*

1913 A678 55c multi 1.60 1.60
1914 A679 82c multi 2.40 2.40

Irish Amateur Boxing Association, Cent. — A680

2011, Apr. 14 Litho. *Perf. 14¾x14*

1915 A680 55c multi 1.60 1.60

Europa A681

Designs: 55c, Girl under tulip tree, Knockabbey Gardens. 82c, River Walk, Avondale Forest Park.

2011, May 5

1916 A681 55c multi 1.60 1.60
1917 A681 82c multi 2.40 2.40

Intl. Year of Forests.

Year of Craft — A682

Craft object made of: No. 1918, Ceramics, by Deirdre McLoughlin. No. 1919, Glass, by Róisín de Buitléar. No. 1920, Metal, by Inga Reed. No. 1921, Textiles, by Helen McAllister. No. 1922, Wood, by Liam Flynn.

2011, May 12 *Perf. 13¼*

Booklet Stamps

1918 A682 55c multi 1.60 1.60
a. Booklet pane of 3 5.00 —
1919 A682 55c multi 1.60 1.60
a. Booklet pane of 3 5.00 —
1920 A682 55c multi 1.60 1.60
a. Booklet pane of 3 5.00 —
1921 A682 55c multi 1.60 1.60
a. Booklet pane of 3 5.00 —
1922 A682 55c multi 1.60 1.60
a. Booklet pane of 3 5.00 —
Complete booklet, #1918a, 1919a, 1920a, 1921a, 1922a 25.00
b. Booklet pane of 5, #1918-1922 8.00 —
Complete booklet, #1922b 8.00 8.00
Nos. 1918-1922 (5) 8.00 8.00

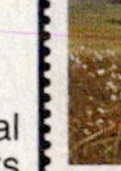

National Parks A683

Designs: No. 1923, Ballycroy National Park. No. 1924, The Burren National Park. No. 1925, Connemara National Park. No. 1926, Glenveagh National Park. No. 1927, Killarney National Park. No. 1928, Wicklow Mountains National Park.

2011, June 6 *Perf. 14¾x14*

1923 A683 55c multi 1.60 1.60
a. Booklet pane of 3 5.00 —
1924 A683 55c multi 1.60 1.60
a. Booklet pane of 3 5.00 —
1925 A683 55c multi 1.60 1.60
a. Booklet pane of 3 5.00 —
b. Horiz. strip of 3, #1923-1925 4.80 4.80
c. Souvenir sheet of 3, #1923-1925 4.80 4.80
1926 A683 82c multi 2.40 2.40
a. Booklet pane of 3 7.50 —
1927 A683 82c multi 2.40 2.40
a. Booklet pane of 3 7.50 —
1928 A683 82c multi 2.40 2.40
a. Booklet pane of 3 7.50 —
Complete booklet, #1923a, 1924a, 1925a, 1926a, 1927a, 1928a 37.50
b. Horiz. strip of 3, #1926-1928 7.25 7.25
c. Souvenir sheet of 3, #1926-1928 7.25 7.25
Nos. 1923-1928 (6) 12.00 12.00

Complete booklet sold for €13.

Amnesty International, 50th Anniv. A684

2011, June 30 *Perf. 13½*
1929 A684 55c multi 1.60 1.60

Hermit Crab — A685

Serpentine Die Cut 14
2011, June 22 **Litho.**
Booklet Stamp
Self-Adhesive

1930 A685 55c multi 1.60 1.60
  a. Booklet pane of 10 16.00
  b. Die cut perf. 14 1.50 1.50
  c. Booklet pane of 10 #1930b 15.00

Issued: No. 1930b, 5/1/12.

Renewable Energy A686

Designs: No. 1931, House with solar panels. No. 1932, Ardnacrusha Hydroelectric Station. No. 1933, Wind turbines. No. 1934, Ocean Energy Development Unit. No. 1935, Field of rape flowers for biofuel.

Die Cut Perf. 13¼x13
2011, Aug. 5 **Litho.**
Self-Adhesive

1931 A686 55c multi 1.60 1.60
  a. Booklet pane of 3 5.25
1932 A686 55c multi 1.60 1.60
  a. Booklet pane of 3 5.25
1933 A686 55c multi 1.60 1.60
  a. Booklet pane of 3 5.25
1934 A686 55c multi 1.60 1.60
  a. Booklet pane of 3 5.25
1935 A686 55c multi 1.60 1.60
  a. Booklet pane of 3 5.25
    Complete booklet, #1931a, 1932a, 1933a, 1934a, 1935a 27.00
  b. Booklet pane of 10, 2 each #1931-1935 16.00
  c. Horiz. strip of 5, #1931-1935, on backing paper without back printing 8.00
  Nos. 1931-1935 (5) 8.00 8.00

Complete booklet sold for €9.

Horses A687

Designs: No. 1936, Colored horse. No. 1937, Irish draft horse. No. 1938, Thoroughbred. No. 1939, Connemara pony.

2011, Sept. 1 **Litho.** *Perf. 13¼*
1936 A687 55c multi 1.50 1.50
1937 A687 55c multi 1.50 1.50
1938 A687 55c multi 1.50 1.50
1939 A687 55c multi 1.50 1.50
  a. Block of 4, #1936-1939 6.00 6.00
  b. Souvenir sheet of 4, #1936-1939 6.00 6.00
  Nos. 1936-1939 (4) 6.00 6.00

2011 Solheim Cup Women's Golf Tournament, Killeen Castle Golf Course, Dunsany — A688

2011, Sept. 15 *Perf. 14¾x14¼*
1940 A688 55c multi 1.50 1.50

Wildlife — A689

Coil Stamps
Serpentine Die Cut 11x11¼
2011, Sept. 29 **Self-Adhesive**

1941 A689 55c Red squirrel 1.50 1.50
1942 A689 55c Bottlenose dolphin 1.50 1.50
  a. Vert. pair, #1941-1942 3.00 3.00

Brian O'Nolan (1911-66), Writer — A690

2011, Oct. 6 *Perf. 13¾*
1943 A690 55c multi 1.50 1.50

Christmas — A691

Serpentine Die Cut 11x11¼
2011, Nov. 10
Self-Adhesive

1944 A691 55c multi 1.50 1.50
  a. Horiz. pair on backing paper without back printing 3.00
  b. Booklet pane of 26 39.00

No. 1944b sold for €13.75.

Television Broadcasting in Ireland, 50th Anniv. — A692

Designs: No. 1945, Gay Byrne hosting *The Late Late Show*. No. 1946, Emma O'Driscoll and puppet on children's show *Hubble*. No. 1947, Newscaster Anne Doyle.

2011, Nov. 24 *Perf. 14¾x14*
1945 A692 55c multi 1.50 1.50
1946 A692 55c multi 1.50 1.50
1947 A692 55c multi 1.50 1.50
  a. Horiz. strip of 3, #1945-1947 4.50 4.50
  Nos. 1945-1947 (3) 4.50 4.50

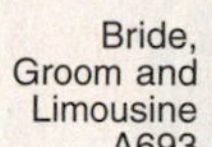

Bride, Groom and Limousine A693

2012, Jan. 19 *Die Cut Perf. 13¼*
Self-Adhesive

1948 A693 55c multi 1.50 1.50
  a. Vert. pair on backing paper without printing on back 3.00
  b. Booklet pane of 10 15.00

Gift — A694

Birthday Candles — A695

Die Cut Perf. 12¾x13½
2012, Jan. 26 **Self-Adhesive**

1949 A694 55c multi 1.50 1.50
1950 A695 55c multi 1.50 1.50
  a. Horiz. pair, #1949-1950, on backing paper without printing on back 3.00
  b. Booklet pane of 10, 5 each #1949-1950 + 10 stickers 15.00

Ireland's Chairmanship of Organization for Security and Cooperation in Europe A696

2012, Feb. 2 *Perf. 13½x13¼*
1951 A696 55c multi 1.50 1.50

St. Patrick's Day — A697

2012, Feb. 9 *Perf. 14x14¾*
1952 A697 82c multi 2.25 2.25

Dancer From Fabulous Beast Dance Theater — A698

Dancers From Dance Theater of Ireland — A699

Dancer From Irish Modern Dance Theater — A700

Dancer from CoisCéim Dance Theater — A701

Die Cut Perf. 13¼
2012, Mar. 22 **Litho.**
Booklet Stamps
Self-Adhesive

1953 A698 55c multi 1.50 1.50
1954 A699 55c multi 1.50 1.50
1955 A700 55c multi 1.50 1.50
1956 A701 55c multi 1.50 1.50
  a. Block of 4, #1953-1956 6.00
  b. Booklet pane of 8, 2 each #1953-1956 12.00
  Nos. 1953-1956 (4) 6.00 6.00

Sinking of the Titanic, Cent. — A702

Designs: No. 1957, Thomas Andrews, shipbuilder in charge of construction of the Titanic, and Titanic under construction. No. 1958, Father Frank Browne, amateur photographer and passenger on Titanic from Southampton to Cork, and Titanic off Cobh. No. 1959, Edward John Smith, ship's captain, and Titanic. No. 1960, Molly Brown, passenger, and Titanic's staircase.

2012, Apr. 12 *Perf. 13¼*
1957 A702 55c multi 1.50 1.50
1958 A702 55c multi 1.50 1.50
  a. Horiz. pair, #1957-1958 3.00 3.00
1959 A702 82c multi 2.25 2.25
1960 A702 82c multi 2.25 2.25
  a. Horiz. pair, #1959-1960 4.50 4.50
  b. Booklet pane of 4, #1957-1960 8.00 —
    Complete booklet, 4 #1960b 32.00
  Nos. 1957-1960 (4) 7.50 7.50

On No. 1960b, Nos. 1958 and 1960 are at the right side of the pane and have a straight edge at right. The complete booklet sold for €12 and contains four examples of No. 1960b, each with different pane margins.

Bram Stoker (1847-1912), Writer — A703

Designs: No. 1961, Stoker. No. 1962, Count Dracula biting woman's neck.

2012, Apr. 19 ***Perf. 14x14¾***

1961 A703 55c multi 1.50 1.50
1962 A703 55c multi 1.50 1.50
a. Horiz. pair, #1961-1962 3.00 3.00
b. Souvenir sheet of 2, #1961-1962 3.00 3.00

Europa A704

Designs: 55c, Little Skellig Island. 82c, Ha'penny Bridge, Dublin.

2012, May 3 ***Perf. 13½***

1963 A704 55c multi 1.50 1.50
1964 A704 82c multi 2.25 2.25

50th Intl. Eucharistic Congress, Dublin — A705

Designs: 55c, Chalice and host. 82c, Monstrance and host.

2012, June 7 ***Perf. 14x14¾***

1965 A705 55c multi 1.40 1.40
1966 A705 82c multi 2.00 2.00

Volvo Ocean Race A706

Designs: 55c, Sailboats. €3, Sailboats, diff., vert.

2012, June 14 ***Perf. 14¾x14¼***

1967 A706 55c multi 1.40 1.40

Souvenir Sheet

1968 A706 €3 multi 7.50 7.50

No. 1968 contains one 28x48mm stamp.

Common Frog — A707

2012, May 1 ***Die Cut Perf. 14x14¼***

Booklet Stamp
Self-Adhesive

1969 A707 82c multi 2.25 2.25
a. Booklet pane of 10 22.50

Dublin Fire Brigade, 150th Anniv. — A708

Designs: No. 1970, Firefighter carrying baby. No. 1971, Firefighters in chemical suits. No. 1972, Firefighters at car accident. No. 1973, Firefighter rescuing drowning man.

2012, June 28 ***Perf. 13¼***

1970 A708 55c multi 1.40 1.40
a. Booklet pane of 4 6.25 6.25
1971 A708 55c multi 1.40 1.40
a. Booklet pane of 4 6.25 6.25
1972 A708 55c multi 1.40 1.40
a. Booklet pane of 4 6.25 6.25
1973 A708 55c multi 1.40 1.40
a. Booklet pane of 4 6.25 6.25
Complete booklet, #1970a, 1971a, 1972a, 1973a 25.00
b. Horiz. strip of 4, #1970-1973 5.60 5.60
Nos. 1970-1973 (4) 5.60 5.60

Nos. 1970a-1973a each have straight edge at right. Complete booklet sold for €10.

Science — A709

Designs: No. 1974, Conference Center, Dublin, molecular structure of DNA. No. 1975, Robert Boyle (1627-91), chemist and physicist, formula and graph of Boyle's Law.

2012, July 5

1974 A709 55c multi 1.40 1.40
1975 A709 55c multi 1.40 1.40
a. Horiz. pair, #1974-1975 2.80 2.80
b. Souvenir sheet of 2, #1974-1975 2.80 2.80

2012 City of Science Festival, Dublin (No. 1974); Boyle's Law, 350th anniv. (No. 1975).

2012 Summer Olympics, London — A710

Emblem of 2012 Summer Olympics and: 55c, Stylized winner's platform. 82c, Vertical bars.

2012, July 19 ***Perf. 14x14¾***

1976 A710 55c multi 1.40 1.40
1977 A710 82c multi 2.10 2.10

Myths and Legends A711

Designs: No. 1978, The Children of Lir (swans in flight). No. 1979, Deirdre of the Sorrows (couple embracing). No. 1980, Fionn Mac Cumhaill (man in water, fish). No. 1981, Setanta (Setanta swinging hurling stick at dog).

Perf. 14¾x14¼

2012, Sept. 13 **Litho.**

1978 A711 55c multi 1.50 1.50
1979 A711 55c multi 1.50 1.50
a. Horiz. pair, #1978-1979 3.00 3.00
1980 A711 82c multi 2.10 2.10
1981 A711 82c multi 2.10 2.10
a. Horiz. pair, #1980-1981 4.20 4.20
Nos. 1978-1981 (4) 7.20 7.20

Barnardos Ireland Children's Charity, 50th Anniv. A712

2012, Oct. 11 ***Perf. 13¼***

1982 A712 55c multi 1.40 1.40

Christmas — A713

Serpentine Die Cut 11x11¼

2012, Nov. 8 **Self-Adhesive**

1983 A713 55c multi 1.40 1.40
a. Horiz. pair on backing paper without back printing 2.80
b. Booklet pane of 26 36.50

No. 1983b sold for €13.75.

Irish Presidency of Council of the European Union — A714

2013, Jan. 17 ***Perf. 14x14¾***

1984 A714 55c multi 1.50 1.50

The Gathering Ireland 2013 Tourism Initiative A715

2013, Jan. 24 ***Perf. 13¼***

1985 A715 82c multi 2.25 2.25

St. Patrick's Day A716

2013, Feb. 7 ***Perf. 14¾x14***

1986 A716 82c multi 2.25 2.25

Bride and Groom Lighting Candles A717

2013, Feb. 14 ***Die Cut Perf. 13¼***

Self-Adhesive

1987 A717 N multi 1.50 1.50
a. Vert. pair on backing paper without back printing 3.00
b. Booklet pane of 10 15.00

No. 1987 sold for 55c on day of issue.

Greetings
A718 A719

2013, Mar. 7 ***Die Cut Perf. 12¾x13½***

Booklet Stamps
Self-Adhesive

1988 A718 N multi 1.50 1.50
1989 A719 N multi 1.50 1.50
a. Booklet pane of 10, 5 each #1988-1989, + 10 stickers 15.00

On day of issue, Nos. 1988-1989 each sold for 55c.

Daffodil A720

2013, Mar. 21 ***Perf. 14¾x14***

1990 A720 N multi 1.40 1.40

Irish Cancer Society, 50th anniv. No. 1990 sold for 55c on day of issue.

Wildlife
A721 A722

Designs: No. 1991, Golden eagle. No. 1992, Red deer. No. 1993, Goldfinch. 90c, Beadlet anemone, horiz.

Serpentine Die Cut 11x11¼

2013, Apr. 2

Coil Stamps
Self-Adhesive

1991 A721 60c multi 1.60 1.60
1992 A721 60c multi 1.60 1.60
a. Vert. pair, #1991-1992 3.20

Booklet Stamps
Serpentine Die Cut 14

1993 A722 60c multi 1.60 1.60
a. Booklet pane of 10 16.00
1994 A722 90c multi 2.40 2.40
a. Booklet pane of 10 24.00
Nos. 1991-1994 (4) 7.20 7.20

Contemporary Arts — A723

No. 1995: a, Doors and Sunlight, painting by Stephen McKenna. b, Ghost Ship, painting by Dorothy Cross. c, The Fall, performance art by Amanda Coogan. d, Smoke Tree, virtual sculpture by John Gerrard.

2013, Apr. 25 ***Perf. 14¼***

1995 Booklet pane of 4 6.50 —
a.-d. A723 60c Any single 1.60 1.60
Complete booklet, #1995 6.50

See No. 2027.

Europa A724

Designs: 60c, Postman pushing cart, postman on bicycle. 90c, Postman and van.

2013, May 2 *Perf. 14¾x14*

1996 A724 60c multi 1.60 1.60
1997 A724 90c multi 2.40 2.40

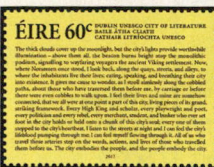

Description of Dublin by Eoin Moore
A725

2013, May 16 **Litho.**

1998 A725 60c yel & blk 1.60 1.60

Selection of Dublin in 2010 as UNESCO City of World Literature.

State Visit to Ireland of Pres. John F. Kennedy, 50th Anniv.
A726

Photographs of Pres. Kennedy: 60c, With distant relative at Kennedy ancestral home in Dunganstown. 90c, Placing wreath on graves of victims of Easter Rising.

2013, June 6 *Perf. 13½x13¼*

1999 A726 60c multi 1.60 1.60
2000 A726 90c multi 2.40 2.40

Port of Cork
A727

Designs: No. 2001, Container ship and tugboat. No. 2002, Sailboats. 90c, Cruise liner.

2013, July 17 *Perf. 14¾x14*

2001 A727 60c multi 1.60 1.60
2002 A727 60c multi 1.60 1.60
a. Horiz. pair, #2001-2002 3.20 3.20
2003 A727 90c multi 2.40 2.40
a. Souvenir sheet of 3, #2001-2003 5.75 5.75
Nos. 2001-2003 (3) 5.60 5.60

General Lockout, Cent. — A728

Photographs of lockout and: No. 2004, Jim Larkin (1876-1947), trade union leader. No. 2005, James Connolly (1868-1916), founder of Irish Socialist Party. No. 2006, Countess Constance Markievicz (1868-1927), socialist leader.

2013, Aug. 22 *Perf. 13¼*

2004 A728 60c multi 1.60 1.60
a. Booklet pane of 3 5.25 —
2005 A728 60c multi 1.60 1.60
a. Booklet pane of 3 5.25 —
2006 A728 60c multi 1.60 1.60
a. Horiz. strip of 3, #2004-2006 4.80 4.80
b. Booklet pane of 3 #2006 5.25 —
c. Booklet pane of 3, #2004-2006 5.25 —
Complete booklet, #2004a, 2005a, 2006b, 2 #2006c 26.50
Nos. 2004-2006 (3) 4.80 4.80

Complete booklet sold for €10 and contains two examples of No. 2006c with different margins.

Irish Defense Forces — A729

Designs: No. 2007, Helicopter. No. 2008, Troops and helicopter. No. 2009, Ships. No. 2010, Soldier and United Nations tank.

2013, Sept. 12

2007 A729 60c multi 1.60 1.60
a. Booklet pane of 4 6.75 —
2008 A729 60c multi 1.60 1.60
a. Booklet pane of 4 6.75 —
2009 A729 60c multi 1.60 1.60
a. Booklet pane of 4 6.75 —
2010 A729 60c multi 1.60 1.60
a. Block of 4, #2007-2010 6.40 6.40
b. Booklet pane of 4 #2010 6.75 —
Complete booklet, #2007a, 2008a, 2009a, 2010b 27.00

Complete booklet sold for €10. The bottom two stamps in each booklet pane have straight edges at bottom.

Integrated Ireland
A730

Designs: No. 2011, Oriental woman in police uniform. No. 2012, Black transit employee and tram. No. 2013, Young black and white hurlers. No. 2014, White woman near window.

2013, Sept. 26 *Perf. 14¾x14*

2011 A730 60c multi 1.60 1.60
2012 A730 60c multi 1.60 1.60
a. Horiz. pair, #2011-2012 3.20 3.20
2013 A730 90c multi 2.50 2.50
2014 A730 90c multi 2.50 2.50
a. Horiz. pair, #2013-2014 5.00 5.00
Nos. 2011-2014 (4) 8.20 8.20

Irish Volunteer Force, Cent. — A731

2013, Oct. 3 *Perf. 13¼*

2015 A731 60c black & green 1.60 1.60

Contemporary Architecture — A732

Designs: No. 2016, Lewis Glucksman Gallery, Cork. No. 2017, Cork Institute of Technology. No. 2018, Fingal County Hall, Swords. No. 2019, Croke Park, Dublin.

2013, Oct. 17 **Litho.** *Perf. 13¼x13½*

2016 A732 60c multi 1.60 1.60
2017 A732 60c multi 1.60 1.60
a. Horiz. pair, #2016-2017 3.20 3.20
2018 A732 90c multi 2.50 2.50
2019 A732 90c multi 2.50 2.50
a. Horiz. pair, #2018-2019 5.00 5.00
b. Souvenir sheet of 4, #2016-2019 8.25 8.25
Nos. 2016-2019 (4) 8.20 8.20

Christmas — A733

Serpentine Die Cut 11x11¼

2013, Nov. 7 **Litho.**

Self-Adhesive

2020 A733 60c multi 1.60 1.60
a. Horiz. pair on backing paper without back printing 3.20
b. Booklet pane of 26 42.00

No. 2020b sold for €15.

Irish Citizen Army, Cent. — A734

2014, Jan. 23 **Litho.** *Perf. 13¼*

2021 A734 60c multi *900.00 900.00*

No. 2021 was quickly withdrawn from sale on day of issue after questions were raised as to whether the correct image of Captain Jack White was actually shown on the stamp.

Greetings — A735

Designs: No. 2022, Robot and alien creature shaking hands. No. 2033, Robots and birthday cake.

Die Cut Perf. 13¼x13

2014, Jan. 30 **Litho.**

Booklet Stamps
Self-Adhesive

2022 A735 60c multi 1.60 1.60
2023 A735 60c multi 1.60 1.60
a. Booklet pane of 10, 5 each #2022-2023, + 10 stickers 16.00

Rose — A736

Die Cut Perf. 13¼x13

2014, Feb. 13 **Litho.**

Booklet Stamp
Self-Adhesive

2024 A736 60c multi 1.60 1.60
a. Vert. pair on backing paper without back printing 3.20
b. Booklet pane of 10 16.00

See No. 2039.

St. Patrick's Day — A737

2014, Feb. 20 **Litho.** *Perf. 14x14¾*

2025 A737 90c multi 2.50 2.50

Brendan Behan (1923-64), Writer — A738

Perf. 14¼x14¾

2014, Mar. 20 **Litho.**

2026 A738 60c multi 1.75 1.75

Contemporary Arts Type of 2013

No. 2027: a, Maesta, painting by Sean Scully. b, Light Receiver, sculpture by Eilis O'Connell. c, Patterned Behavior, painting by Diana Copperwhite. d, Chaplet, photograph by Alice Maher.

2014, Mar. 27 **Litho.** *Perf. 14¼*

2027 Booklet pane of 4 7.00 —
a.-d. A723 60c Any single 1.75 1.75
Complete booklet, #2027 7.00

Cumann na mBan (Auxiliary of Irish Volunteers), Cent. — A739

2014, Apr. 3 **Litho.** *Perf. 14¼*

2028 A739 60c sepia 1.75 1.75

Irish Citizen Army, Cent. — A740

2014, Apr. 17 **Litho.** *Perf. 13¼*

2029 A740 60c sepia 1.75 1.75

See note under No. 2021.

Viking Heritage
A741

Designs: No. 2030, Waterford Kite brooch. No. 2031, Sword.

2014, Apr. 24 **Litho.** *Perf. 13¼*

2030 A741 60c multi 1.75 1.75
2031 A741 60c multi 1.75 1.75
a. Horiz. pair, #2030-2031 3.50 3.50

Europa
A742

Musical instruments: 60c, Bodhrán (drum). 90c, Harp.

2014, May 8 **Litho.** *Perf. 13¼*

2032 A742 60c multi 1.75 1.75
2033 A742 90c multi 2.50 2.50

Home Rule Act, Cent. — A743

2014, May 22 **Litho.** *Perf. 13¼*

2034 A743 60c multi 1.75 1.75

Bloom Garden Festival, Dublin — A744

Designs: No. 2035, Garden. No. 2036, Woman holding box of vegetables.

2014, May 22 Litho. *Perf. 13¼*

2035 A744 60c multi 1.75 1.75
2036 A744 60c multi 1.75 1.75
a. Horiz. pair, #2035-2036 3.50 3.50
b. Souvenir sheet of 2, #2035-2036 3.50 3.50

World Flower Show, Dublin A745

X-ray photograph of Phalaenopsis orchid with denomination at: No. 2037, LR. No. 2038, UR.

2014, June 12 Litho. *Perf. 13¼*

2037 A745 60c multi 1.75 1.75
2038 A745 60c multi 1.75 1.75
a. Horiz. pair, #2037-2038 3.50 3.50
b. Souvenir sheet of 2, #2037-2038 3.50 3.50

Rose Type of 2014

Die Cut Perf. 13¼x13

2014, July 21 Litho.

Self-Adhesive With White Frame

2039 A736 68c multi 1.90 1.90
a. Vert. pair on backing paper without back printing 3.80
b. Booklet pane of 10 19.00

Wildlife
A746 A747

Designs: No. 2040, Black-legged kittiwake. No. 2041, Green crab. No. 2042, Cushion star. €1, Fireworks anemone.

Serpentine Die Cut 11x11¼

2014, July 21 Litho.

Coil Stamps Self-Adhesive

2040 A746 68c multi 1.90 1.90
2041 A746 68c multi 1.90 1.90
a. Vert. pair, #2040-2041 3.80

Booklet Stamps

Serpentine Die Cut 14

2042 A747 68c multi 1.90 1.90
a. Booklet pane of 10 19.00
2043 A747 €1 multi 2.75 2.75
a. Booklet pane of 10 27.50

World War I, Cent. — A748

Recruiting posters with slogan at bottom: 68c, "Join an Irish Regiment Today." €1, "The Real Irish Spirit."

2014, July 24 Litho. *Perf. 13¼*

2044 A748 68c multi 1.90 1.90
2045 A748 €1 multi 2.75 2.75

Irish Prison Service — A749

Designs: No. 2046, Prison guards on patrol. No. 2047, Prisoner polishing bowl. No. 2048, Prisoner cleaning graffiti. No. 2049, Teacher with prisoners.

2014, Aug. 7 Litho. *Perf. 13¼*

2046 A749 68c multi 1.75 1.75
2047 A749 68c multi 1.75 1.75
2048 A749 68c multi 1.75 1.75
2049 A749 68c multi 1.75 1.75
a. Block of 4, #2046-2049 7.00 7.00
Nos. 2046-2049 (4) 7.00 7.00

Seamus Heaney (1939-2013), 1995 Nobel Laureate in Literature A750

2014, Aug. 28 Litho. *Perf. 13¾*

2050 A750 68c multi 1.75 1.75

Cats — A751

Designs: No. 2051, Maine Coon cat. No. 2052, Burmese cat. No. 2053, British Shorthair cat. No. 2054, Persian cat.

2014, Sept. 4 Litho. *Perf. 13¼*

2051 A751 68c multi 1.75 1.75
a. Booklet pane of 4 7.50 —
2052 A751 68c multi 1.75 1.75
a. Booklet pane of 4 7.50 —
2053 A751 68c multi 1.75 1.75
a. Booklet pane of 4 7.50 —
2054 A751 68c multi 1.75 1.75
a. Block of 4, #2051-2054 7.00 7.00
b. Booklet pane of 4 7.50 —
Complete booklet, #2051a, 2052a, 2053a, 2054b 30.00

Complete booklet sold for €12. The stamps on the right side of each booklet pane have a straight edge at the right.

Thomas Davis (1814-45), Poet and Newspaper Publisher — A752

2014, Oct. 9 Litho. *Perf. 14¼x14¾*

2055 A752 68c blk & bl grn 1.75 1.75

Electronic Game Screens and Characters A753

Designs: No. 2056, Pac-Man. b, Space Invaders. c, Sonic the Hedgehog. d, Mario.

2014, Oct. 16 Litho. *Perf. 13¾x13½*

2056 A753 68c multi 1.75 1.75
2057 A753 68c multi 1.75 1.75
2058 A753 68c multi 1.75 1.75
2059 A753 68c multi 1.75 1.75
a. Block of 4, #2056-2059 7.00 7.00
Nos. 2056-2059 (4) 7.00 7.00

Christmas — A754

Serpentine Die Cut 11x11¼

2014, Nov. 6 Litho.

Self-Adhesive

2060 A754 68c multi 1.75 1.75
a. Horiz. pair on backing paper without printing on back 3.50
b. Booklet pane of 26 46.00

No. 2060b sold for €17.

Circles and Squares in Dots — A755

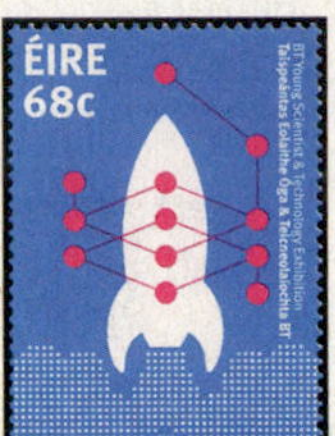
Rocket — A756

2015, Jan. 7 Litho. *Perf. 14¼x14¾*

2061 A755 68c multi 1.60 1.60
2062 A756 68c multi 1.60 1.60
a. Horiz. pair, #2061-2062 3.20 3.20

Trinity College Science Gallery, Dublin (No. 2061), BT Young Scientist Exhibition (No. 2062).

Northern Ireland Peace Talks Between Seán Lemass (1899-1971) and Terence O'Neill (1914-90), 50th Anniv. — A757

2015, Jan. 22 Litho. *Perf. 13¼x13½*

2063 A757 68c black 1.60 1.60

Love — A758

Serpentine Die Cut 9x10¾

2015, Feb. 12 Litho.

Self-Adhesive

2064 A758 N multi 1.60 1.60
a. Vert. pair on backing paper without printing on back 3.20
b. Booklet pane of 10 16.00

No. 2064 sold for 68c on day of issue.

St. Patrick's Day — A759

Perf. 13½x13¼

2015, Feb. 26 Litho.

2065 A759 €1 org & grn 2.25 2.25

Animation Production in Ireland — A760

No. 2066: a, Roy. b, Give Upu Yer Aul Sins. c, The Secret of Kells. d, Nelly and Nora.

2015, Mar. 19 Litho. *Perf. 13¼x13*

2066 A760 Sheet of 4 6.00 6.00
a.-d. 68c Any single 1.50 1.50
e. Booklet pane of 4, #2066a-2066d 6.75 —
Complete booklet, 4 #2066e 27.00

The complete booklet sold for €12 and contains four examples of No. 2066e with different margins.

Battle of Gallipoli, Cent. — A761

Designs: 68c, Irish soldiers in trench. €1, Troop ship SS River Clyde.

2015, Apr. 23 Litho. *Perf. 13¼*

2067 A761 68c multi 1.60 1.60
2068 A761 €1 multi 2.25 2.25

Sinking of the RMS Lusitania, Cent. A762

Designs: 68c, Torpedo approaching RMS Lusitania. €1, RMS Lusitania listing.

2015, May 7 Litho. *Perf. 14¼x14*

2069 A762 68c multi 1.50 1.50
2070 A762 €1 multi 2.25 2.25
a. Souvenir sheet of 2, #2069-2070 3.75 3.75

Europa — A763

2015, May 14 Litho. *Perf. 14x14¼*

2071 A763 68c Toy truck 1.50 1.50
2072 A763 €1 Teddy bear 2.25 2.25

Mountain Rescue Ireland, 50th Anniv. — A764

Designs: No. 2073, Resucers hanging on rock face with litter. No. 2074, Rescuers carrying litter.

2015, June 4 Litho. *Perf. 14x14¼*

2073	A764 68c multi		1.50	1.50
2074	A764 68c multi		1.50	1.50
a.	Horiz. pair, #2073-2074		3.00	3.00

William Butler Yeats (1865-1939), Poet — A765

2015, June 11 Litho. *Perf. 14x14¼*

2075	A765 68c black	1.50	1.50

Wildlife

A766 A767

Designs: No. 2076, Mute swan. No. 2077, Great spotted woodpecker. No. 2078, Red fox. €1.05, Otter.

Serpentine Die Cut 11x11¼

2015, July 1 Litho.

Coil Stamps

Self-Adhesive

2076	A766 70c multi	1.60	1.60
2077	A766 70c multi	1.60	1.60
a.	Vert. pair, #2076-2077	3.20	

Booklet Stamps

Serpentine Die Cut 14

2078	A767 70c multi	1.60	1.60
a.	Booklet pane of 10	16.00	
2079	A767 €1.05 multi	2.40	2.40
a.	Booklet pane of 10 + 10 etiquettes	24.00	

Food Production — A768

Designs: No. 2080, Rancher and steaks. No. 2081, Cheese maker and cheese. No. 2082, Fisherman, lobsters and fish. No. 2083, Farmer, bowl of cereal and fruit.

2015, July 16 Litho. *Perf. 13¼x13½*

2080	A768 70c multi	1.60	1.60
2081	A768 70c multi	1.60	1.60
a.	Horiz. pair, #2080-2081	3.20	3.20
2082	A768 €1.05 multi	2.40	2.40
2083	A768 €1.05 multi	2.40	2.40
a.	Horiz. pair, #2082-2083	4.80	4.80
b.	Souvenir sheet of 4, #2080-2083	8.00	8.00
	Nos. 2080-2083 (4)	8.00	8.00

Speech of Patrick Pearse at Gravesite of Jeremiah O'Donovan Rossa, Cent. — A769

2015, July 30 Litho. *Perf. 13¼x13½*

2084	A769 70c black	1.60	1.60

Toiletry Cabinet and Screen A770

Transat Chair — A771

Adjustable Table — A772

Cabinet With Pivoting Drawers A773

2015, Aug. 13 Litho. *Perf. 13¼*

2085	A770 70c multi	1.60	1.60
2086	A771 70c multi	1.60	1.60
2087	A772 70c multi	1.60	1.60
2088	A773 70c multi	1.60	1.60
a.	Block of 4, #2085-2088	6.40	6.40
b.	Booklet pane of 4, #2085-2088	6.75	—
	Complete booklet, 4 #2088b	27.00	
	Nos. 2085-2088 (4)	6.40	6.40

Furniture designed by Eileen Gray (1878-1976). The complete booklet sold for €12 and contains four examples of No. 2088b with different margins.

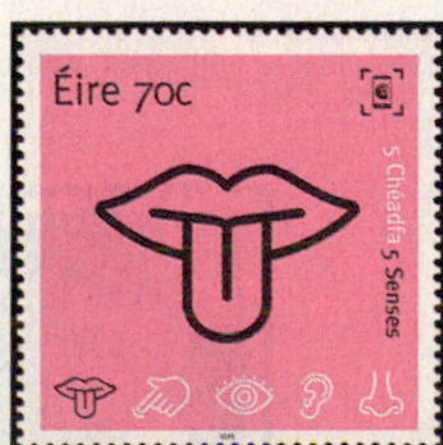

Five Senses A774

Senses: 70c, Taste. €1.05, Touch. €1.25, Vision. €1.70, Hearing. €2.80, Smell.

Litho., Litho. & Thermography (€1.70)

2015, Sept. 10 *Perf. 13½*

2089	A774 70c pink & blk	1.60	1.60
2090	A774 €1.05 org & blk	2.40	2.40
2091	A774 €1.70 blue & blk	4.00	4.00
2092	A774 €2.80 bl grn & blk	6.25	6.25

Self-Adhesive

On Plastic Film

Serpentine Die Cut 11

2093	A774 €1.25 white & blk	3.00	3.00
	Nos. 2089-2093 (5)	17.25	17.25

No. 2089 has strawberry-flavored gum. Portions of the design on No. 2090 was printed with thermochromic ink, which changes color when warmed. Gritty crystals are embedded in the film covering the ear on No. 2091. No. 2092 is impregnated with a mint scent.

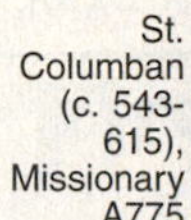

St. Columban (c. 543-615), Missionary A775

2015, Oct. 22 Litho. *Perf. 14¼x14*

2094	A775 €1.05 multi	2.40	2.40

Madonna and Child, by Marco Palmezzano — A776

Serpentine Die Cut 11x11¼

2015, Nov. 5 Litho.

Self-Adhesive

2095	A776 70c multi	1.50	1.50
a.	Horiz. pair on backing paper without back printing	3.00	
b.	Booklet pane of 26	39.00	

Christmas. No. 2095b sold for €17.50.

Irish Republic Flag — A777

Proclamation of the Irish Republic — A778

Easter Rising at General Post Office, Sackville Street, Dublin — A779

Roger Casement (1864-1916), Rebellion Leader — A780

Serpentine Die Cut 11¼x11

2016, Jan. 21 Litho.

Coil Stamps

Self-Adhesive

2096	A777 70c multi	1.60	1.60
2097	A778 70c multi	1.60	1.60
a.	Horiz. pair, #2096-2097	3.20	

Booklet Stamps

Serpentine Die Cut 14

2098	A779 70c multi	1.60	1.60
a.	Booklet pane of 10	16.00	
2099	A780 €1.05 multi	2.40	2.40
a.	Booklet pane of 10 + 10 etiquettes	24.00	

Easter Rising, Cent.

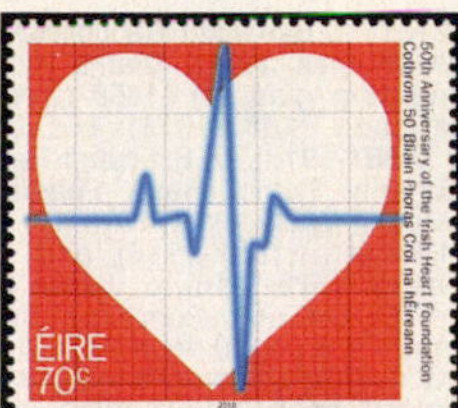

Irish Heart Foundation, 50th Anniv. — A781

2016, Jan. 28 Litho. *Perf. 13¼x13½*

2100	A781 70c multi	1.60	1.60

Love — A782

Serpentine Die Cut 9x10¾

2016, Feb. 11 Litho.

Self-Adhesive

2101	A782 N multi	1.50	1.50
a.	Vert. pair on paper without back printing	3.00	
b.	Booklet pane of 10	15.00	

No. 2101 sold for 70c on day of issue.

St. Patrick's Day A783

2016, Feb. 25 Litho. *Perf. 14¼*

2102	A783 €1.05 multi	2.25	2.25

Dogs — A784

Designs: No. 2103, Irish wolfhound. No. 2104, Irish red setter. No. 2105, Sheepdog. No. 2106, Kerry Blue terrier.

2016, Mar. 10 Litho. *Perf. 14x14¼*

2103	A784 70c multi	1.60	1.60
2104	A784 70c multi	1.60	1.60
2105	A784 70c multi	1.60	1.60
2106	A784 70c multi	1.60	1.60
a.	Block of 4, #2103-2106	6.40	6.40
b.	Souvenir sheet of 4, #2103-2106	6.50	6.50
	Nos. 2103-2106 (4)	6.40	6.40

Miniature Sheet

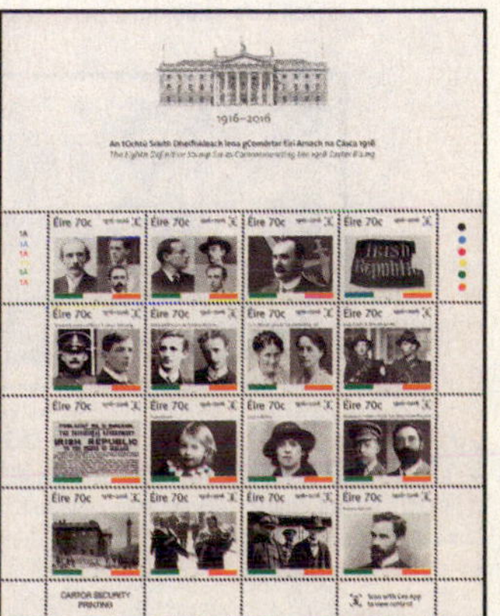

Easter Rising, Cent. — A785

No. 2107: a, Executed Republican revolutionaries Thomas James Clarke (facing forward, wearing glasses) (1858-1916), Seán MacDiarmada (1883-1916) and Eammon Ceannt (1881-1916). b, Executed Republican revolutionaries Patrick Henry Pearse (facing right, without glasses) (1879-1916), Joseph Mary Plunkett (1887-1916) and Thomas MacDonagh (1878-1916). c, James Connolly (1869-1916), executed Republican revolutionary, Starry Plow flag. d, Irish Republic flag. e, Police Constable James O'Brien (1868-1916) and Sean Connolly, (1883-1916) rebel, first casualties of Easter Rising. f, Michael Malone (1888-1916) participant in Battle of Mount Street Bridge and brother, William Malone, soldier killed at Battle of Ypres. g, Dr. Kathleen Lynn (1874-1955) and Elizabeth O'Farrell (1894-1957), nurse. h, Rebels Jack Doyle and Tom McGrath. i, Proclamation of the Irish Republic. j, Seán Foster (1914-16), youngest child killed in Eater Rising. k, Louisa Nolan, recipient of British Military Medal for tending to wounded. l, Sir Francis Fletcher-Vane (1861-1934), British officer who exposed murders of unarmed civilians, and Francis Sheehy-Skeffington (1878-1916), civilian summarily executed by British. m, Easter Rising at General Post Office, Sackville Street. n, Children gathering firewood. o, Two prisoners at Richmond Barracks and British soldier. p, Roger Casement (1864-1916), rebellion leader.

2016, Mar. 24 Litho. *Perf. 13½*

2107 A785 Sheet of 16 26.00 26.00
a.-p. 70c Any single 1.60 1.60
q. Souvenir sheet of 4, #2107a-2107d 8.50 8.50
r. Souvenir sheet of 4, #2107e-2107h 8.50 8.50
s. Souvenir sheet of 4, #2107i-2107l 8.50 8.50
t. Souvenir sheet of 4, #2107m-2107p 8.50 8.50

Nos. 2107q-2107t were sold together as a set in a folder for €15.

Charles Gavan Duffy (1816-1903), Writer, Prime Minister of Victoria — A786

2016, Apr. 7 Litho. *Perf. 14x14¼*

2108 A786 70c multi 1.60 1.60

A787

Europa A788

2016, May 12 Litho. *Perf. 13½*

2109 A787 70c multi 1.60 1.60
2110 A788 €1.05 multi 2.40 2.40

Think Green Issue.

Battle of the Somme, Cent. A789

2016, June 23 Litho. *Perf. 13½*

2111 A789 W multi 2.40 2.40

No. 2111 sold for €1.05 on day of issue.

Police Constable James O'Brien (1868-1916) and Sean Connolly (1883-1916) A790

Michael and William Malone — A791

Dr. Kathleen Lynn (1874-1955) and Elizabeth O'Farrell (1894-1957), Nurse — A792

Rebels Jack Doyle and Tom McGrath — A793

Serpentine Die Cut 11¼x11

2016, July 21 Litho.

Coil Stamps

Self-Adhesive

2112 A790 72c multi 1.60 1.60
2113 A791 72c multi 1.60 1.60
a. Horiz. pair, #2112-2113 3.20

Booklet Stamps

Serpentine Die Cut 14

2114 A792 72c multi 1.60 1.60
a. Booklet pane of 10 16.00
2115 A793 €1.10 multi 2.50 2.50
a. Booklet pane of 10 + 10 etiquettes 25.00

Easter Rising, cent.

Wild Atlantic Way — A794

Designs: No. 2116, Horse riding at Grange. No. 2117, Fly fishing at Glenbeg Lough. No. 2118, Cycling on the Aran Islands. No. 2119, Surfing at Inch.

2016, July 28 Litho. *Perf. 13¼*

2116 A794 72c multi 1.60 1.60
a. Booklet pane of 4 6.75 —
2117 A794 72c multi 1.60 1.60
a. Horiz. pair, #2116-2117 3.20 3.20
b. Booklet pane of 4 6.75 —
2118 A794 €1.10 multi 2.50 2.50
a. Booklet pane of 4 10.50 —
2119 A794 €1.10 multi 2.50 2.50
a. Horiz. pair, #2118-2119 5.00 5.00
b. Booklet pane of 4 10.50 —
Complete booklet, #2116a, 2117b, 2118a, 2119b 35.00
Nos. 2116-2119 (4) 8.20 8.20

Complete booklet sold for €15.

Store Fronts A795

Designs: No. 2120, Vibes & Scribes Arts and Hobby Shop, Cork. No. 2121, The Winding Stair Bookstore, Dublin. No. 2122, Clerke Grocery Store, Skibbereen. No. 2123, Thomas Moran Souvenir Shop, Westport.

2016, Aug. 18 Litho. *Perf. 12x12¼*

2120 A795 72c multi 1.60 1.60
2121 A795 72c multi 1.60 1.60
a. Horiz. pair, #2120-2121 3.20 3.20
2122 A795 €1.10 multi 2.50 2.50
2123 A795 €1.10 multi 2.50 2.50
a. Horiz. pair, #2122-2123 5.00 5.00
Nos. 2120-2123 (4) 8.20 8.20

A796

A797

A798

Cycling A799

2016, Sept. 15 Litho. *Perf. 13¼*

2124 A796 72c multi 1.60 1.60
2125 A797 72c multi 1.60 1.60
2126 A798 72c multi 1.60 1.60
2127 A799 72c multi 1.60 1.60
a. Block of 4, #2124-2127 6.40 6.40
b. Souvenir sheet of 4, #2124-2127 6.40 6.40
Nos. 2124-2127 (4) 6.40 6.40

Commissioners of Irish Lights — A800

Designs: No. 2128, Crane moving buoy. No. 2129, Helicopter and Fanad lighthouse. No. 2130, Computerized navigational technology. No. 2131, ILV Granuaile near lighthouse.

2016, Oct. 6 Litho. *Perf. 13¼x13½*

2128 A800 72c multi 1.60 1.60
2129 A800 72c multi 1.60 1.60
2130 A800 72c multi 1.60 1.60
2131 A800 72c multi 1.60 1.60
a. Block of 4, #2128-2131 6.40 6.40
b. Booklet pane of 4, #2128-2131 7.25 —
Complete booklet, 4 #2131b 29.00
Nos. 2128-2131 (4) 6.40 6.40

Complete booklet sold for €13, and contains four examples of No. 2131b, each with a different pane margin.

Christmas — A801

Serpentine Die Cut 11x11¼

2016, Nov. 3 Litho.

Self-Adhesive

2132 A801 72c multi 1.60 1.60
a. Horiz. pair on backing paper without back printing 3.20
b. Booklet pane of 26 42.00

No. 2132b sold for €18.

Artifacts
A802 A803

Designs: No. 2133, Castlederg bronze cauldron, 700-600 B.C. No. 2134, Armlet, 362-175 B.C. No. 2135, Gold disc, 2200-2000 B.C. No. 2136, Gleninsheen gold gorget, c. 800-700 B.C.

Serpentine Die Cut 11¼

2017, Jan. 12 Litho.

Coil Stamps

Self-Adhesive

2133 A802 N multi 1.60 1.60
2134 A802 N multi 1.60 1.60
a. Vert. pair, #2133-2134 3.20 3.20

Booklet Stamps

Serpentine Die Cut 14

2135 A803 N multi 1.60 1.60
a. Horiz. pair on paper without back printing 3.20
b. Booklet pane of 10 16.00
2136 A803 W multi 2.40 2.40
a. Horiz. pair on paper without back printing 4.80
b. Booklet pane of 10 + 10 etiquettes 24.00

On day of issue, Nos. 2133-2135 each sold for 72c, and No. 2136 sold for €1.10.

Love — A804

Serpentine Die Cut 9x10¾

2017, Feb. 2 Litho.

Self-Adhesive

2137 A804 N gold 1.60 1.60
a. Horiz. pair on paper without back printing 3.20
b. Booklet pane of 10 16.00

No. 2137 sold for 72c on day of issue.

Japanese Noh Mask and Signature of William Butler Yeats (1865-1939), Writer — A805

2017, Feb. 9 Litho. *Perf. 13¼*

2138 A805 W blk, red, gold 2.40 2.40
a. Souvenir sheet of 2 4.80 4.80

No. 2138 sold for €1.10 on day of issue.

St. Patrick's Day — A806

2017, Feb. 23 Litho. *Perf. 13¼*

2139 A806 W emerald 2.40 2.40

No. 2139 sold for €1.10 on day of issue.

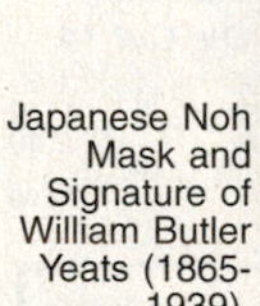

Emojis and "Don't Worry" A807

Emojis and "Be Happy" A808

2017, Mar. 16 Litho. *Perf. 13¼*

2140	A807 N multi		1.60	1.60
2141	A808 N multi		1.60	1.60
a.	Horiz. pair, #2140-2141		3.20	3.20

On day of issue Nos. 2140-2141 each sold for 72c.

Royal Sites in Ireland — A809

Designs: No. 2142, Hill of Tara, County Meath. No. 2143, Eamhain Mhacha (Navan Fort), County Armagh. No. 2144, Rathcroghan, County Roscommon. No. 2145, Rock of Cashel, County Tipperary.

2017, Apr. 20 Litho. *Perf. 13¼*

2142	A809 N multi	2.25	2.25
2143	A809 N multi	2.25	2.25
2144	A809 N multi	2.25	2.25
2145	A809 N multi	2.25	2.25
a.	Block of 4, #2142-2145	9.00	9.00
	Nos. 2142-2145 (4)	9.00	9.00

On day of issue, Nos. 2142-2145 each sold for €1.

Europa A810

Castles: €1, Dublin Castle. €1.35, King John's Castle, Limerick.

2017, May 4 Litho. *Perf. 13¼x13½*

2146	A810 €1 multi	2.25	2.25
2147	A810 €1.35 multi	3.00	3.00

Lions Clubs International, Cent. — A811

2017, June 1 Litho. *Perf. 13¼*

2148	A811 €1.35 multi	3.00	3.00

Battle of Messines Ridge, Cent. — A812

2017, June 8 Litho. *Perf. 13¼*

2149	A812 €1.35 multi	3.25	3.25

Thomas Francis Meagher (1823-67), American Civil War Brigadier General and Acting Territorial Governor of Montana — A813

2017, June 29 Litho. *Perf. 14x14¼*

2150	A813 €1 multi	2.25	2.25

2017 Women's Rugby World Cup, Dublin and Belfast, Northern Ireland — A814

2017, July 13 Litho. *Perf. 13¼*

2151	A814 €1 multi	2.40	2.40

Railroad Stations — A815

Designs: No. 2152, Heuston Station. No. 2153, Clarke Station. No. 2154, Kent Station. No. 2155, Bagenalstown Station.

2017, July 20 Litho. *Perf. 13¼*

2152	A815 €1 multi	2.40	2.40
2153	A815 €1 multi	2.40	2.40
2154	A815 €1 multi	2.40	2.40
2155	A815 €1 multi	2.40	2.40
a.	Block of 4, #2152-2155	9.60	9.60
b.	Souvenir sheet of 4, #2152-2155	9.75	9.75
	Nos. 2152-2155 (4)	9.60	9.60

Francis Ledwidge (1887-1917), Poet — A816

2017, July 27 Litho. *Perf. 14x14¼*

2156	A816 €1 multi	2.40	2.40

John Mary "Jack" Lynch (1917-99), Hurler and Taoiseach of Ireland — A817

2017, Aug. 10 Litho. *Perf. 14x14¼*

2157	A817 €1 multi	2.40	2.40

Free Secondary School Education, 50th Anniv. A818

2017, Sept. 7 Litho. *Perf. 13¼*

2158	A818 €1 multi	2.40	2.40

National Plowing Championships — A819

Designs: No. 2159, Tractor plowing field. No. 2160, Horse-drawn plow.

2017, Sept. 14 Litho. *Perf. 13¼*

2159	A819 €1 multi	2.40	2.40
2160	A819 €1 multi	2.40	2.40
a.	Horiz. pair, #2159-2160	4.80	4.80
b.	Souvenir sheet of 2, #2159-2160	4.80	4.80

Urban Street Art — A820

Art by: No. 2161, Conor Harrington. No. 2162, Fin DAC. No. 2163, James Earley. No. 2164, Maser.

2017, Sept. 21 Litho. *Perf. 14x14¼*

2161	A820 €1 multi	2.40	2.40
2162	A820 €1 multi	2.40	2.40
2163	A820 €1 multi	2.40	2.40
2164	A820 €1 multi	2.40	2.40
a.	Horiz. strip of 4, #2161-2164	9.60	9.60
b.	Booklet pane of 4, #2161-2164	9.75	—
	Complete booklet 4 #2164b	39.00	
	Nos. 2161-2164 (4)	9.60	9.60

Complete booklet contains four examples of No. 2164b, each with a different pane margin.

Ernesto "Che" Guevara (1928-67), Cuban Revolutionary and Government Minister — A821

2017, Oct. 5 Litho. *Perf. 14x14¼*

2165	A821 €1 red & black	*2.40*	*2.40*

Postcrossing — A822

2017, Oct. 5 Litho. *Perf. 13¼*

2166	A822 €1.35 multi	3.25	3.25

Apparition of the Virgin Mary at Fatima, Portugal, Cent. — A823

2017, Oct. 12 Litho. *Perf. 13¼*

2167	A823 €1.35 multi	3.25	3.25

Christmas — A824

Serpentine Die Cut 11x11¼

2017, Nov. 2 Litho.

Self-Adhesive

2168	A824 €1 multi	2.40	2.40
a.	Horiz. pair on paper without back printing	4.80	
b.	Booklet pane of 26	62.50	

No. 2168b sold for €25.

General Post Office, Dublin, 200th Anniv. A825

2018, Jan. 11 Litho. *Perf. 13¼x13½*

2169	A825 €1 multi	2.50	2.50

Sir Alfred Chester Beatty (1875-1968), Philantropist and Art Collector — A826

Birth of the Virgin, by Simon Bening — A827

Shah Jahan, by Bichitr — A828

Allusions to the Seven Lucky Gods, by Yashima Gakutei — A829

2018, Jan. 18 Litho. *Perf. 13¼*

2170 A826 €1 multi 2.50 2.50
2171 A827 €1 multi 2.50 2.50
2172 A828 €1 multi 2.50 2.50
2173 A829 €1 multi 2.50 2.50
a. Horiz. strip of 4, #2170-2173 10.00 10.00
b. Souvenir sheet of 4, #2170-2173 10.00 10.00
Nos. 2170-2173 (4) 10.00 10.00

Artifacts
A830 A831

Designs: N, Paten, 8th-9th cent. W, Donore handle, 700-720.

Serpentine Die Cut 14
2018, Jan. 25 Litho.
Booklet Stamps Self-Adhesive

2174 A830 N multi 2.50 2.50
a. Horiz. pair on paper without back printing 5.00
b. Booket pane of 10 25.00
2175 A831 W multi 3.50 3.50
a. Horiz. pair on paper without back printing 7.00
b. Booket pane of 10 + 10 etiquettes 35.00

On day of issue, No. 2174 sold for €1; No. 2175, for €1.35.

AIR POST STAMPS

Catalogue values for unused stamps in this section are for Never Hinged items.

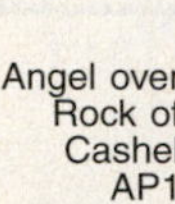

Angel over Rock of Cashel AP1

Designs: 1p, 1sh3p, 1sh5p, Rock of Cashel. 3p, 8p, Lough Derg. 6p, Croagh Patrick. 1sh, Glendalough.

Perf. 15x14
1948-65 Wmk. 262 Engr.

C1 AP1 1p dk brown ('49) 6.50 6.50
C2 AP1 3p blue 11.00 9.50
C3 AP1 6p rose lilac 1.10 .90
C4 AP1 8p red brown ('54) 4.50 3.50
C5 AP1 1sh green ('49) 2.25 1.15
C6 AP1 1sh3p ver ('54) 5.50 1.15

Perf. 15

C7 AP1 1sh5p dark blue ('65) 4.50 .90
Nos. C1-C7 (7) 35.35 23.60

POSTAGE DUE STAMPS

D1

1925 Typo. Wmk. 44 *Perf. 14x15*

J1 D1 ½p emerald 27.50 42.50
Never hinged 140.00
J2 D1 1p carmine 17.00 12.50
Never hinged 60.00
J3 D1 2p dark green 32.50 15.00
Never hinged 125.00
J4 D1 6p plum 10.50 14.00
Never hinged 45.00
Nos. J1-J4 (4) 87.50 84.00

Catalogue values for unused stamps in this section, from this point to the end of the section, are for Never Hinged items.

1940-70 Wmk. 262

J5 D1 ½p emerald ('43) 27.50 22.50
J6 D1 1p brt carmine ('41) 1.10 .50
J7 D1 1½p vermilion ('52) 2.25 *5.00*
J8 D1 2p dark green 1.25 .55
J9 D1 3p blue ('52) 2.25 2.00
J10 D1 5p royal purple ('43) 3.50 *7.50*
J11 D1 6p plum ('60) 4.00 1.75
J12 D1 8p orange ('62) 7.50 7.50
J13 D1 10p red lilac ('65) 8.50 7.00
J14 D1 1sh lt yel grn ('69) 25.00 9.00
Nos. J5-J14 (10) 82.85 63.30

1971, Feb. 15 Typo. Wmk. 262

J15 D1 1p sepia 2.50 *3.50*
J16 D1 1½p bright green 2.50 *3.50*
J17 D1 3p gray green 2.50 *3.50*
J18 D1 4p orange 2.50 *3.50*
J19 D1 5p bright blue 2.50 *3.50*
J20 D1 7p yellow 2.50 *3.50*
J21 D1 8p scarlet 2.50 *3.50*
Nos. J15-J21 (7) 17.50 24.50

1978 Unwmk.

J25 D1 3p gray green 3.50 *3.50*
J26 D1 4p orange 5.00 *10.50*
J27 D1 5p bright blue 3.50 *3.50*
Nos. J25-J27 (3) 12.00 *17.50*

Celtic Knot — D2

1980-85 Photo. *Perf. 15*

J28 D2 1p brt yel green .75 *1.25*
J29 D2 2p ultramarine .75 *1.25*
J30 D2 4p dark green .75 *1.25*
J31 D2 6p yel orange .75 *1.25*
J32 D2 8p violet blue 1.00 *2.00*
J33 D2 18p green 1.60 *2.00*
J33A D2 20p org brown ('85) 3.50 *6.50*
J34 D2 24p emerald 2.25 1.90
J35 D2 30p violet blue ('85) 7.00 *9.00*
J36 D2 50p rose pink ('85) 4.00 4.00
Nos. J28-J36 (10) 22.35 30.40

Issue dates: 1p, 2p, 4p, 6p, 8p, 18p, 24p, June 11; 20p, 30p, 50p, Aug. 22.

D3

1988, Oct. 6 Litho. *Perf. 14x15*

J37 D3 1p blk, dp yel & brt red .80 *1.25*
J38 D3 2p blk, vio brn & brt red .80 *1.25*
J39 D3 3p blk, dull vio & brt red .80 *1.25*
J40 D3 4p blk, vio & brt red .80 *1.25*
J41 D3 5p blk, vio bl & brt red .80 *1.25*
J42 D3 17p blk, brt ol grn & brt red 1.60 *2.40*
J43 D3 20p blk, bluish gray & brt red 2.10 *2.75*
J44 D3 24p blk, bl grn & brt red 2.40 *3.25*
J45 D3 30p blk & brt red 2.40 *3.25*
J46 D3 50p blk, gray & brt red 3.25 *4.25*
J47 D3 £1 blk, dk ol brn & brt red 6.75 *8.25*
Nos. J37-J47 (11) 22.50 30.40

ISRAEL

ˈiz-rē-əl

LOCATION — Western Asia, bordering on the Mediterranean Sea
GOVT. — Republic
AREA — 8,017 sq. mi.
POP. — 5,749,760 (1999 est.)
CAPITAL — Jerusalem

When the British mandate of Palestine ended in May 1948, the Jewish state of Israel was proclaimed by the Jewish National Council in Palestine.

1000 Mils = 1 Pound
1000 Prutot = 1 Pound (1949)
100 Agorot = 1 Pound (1960)
100 Agorot = 1 Shekel (1980)

Catalogue values for all unused stamps in this country are for Never Hinged items.

Tabs

Stamps of Israel are printed in sheets with tabs (labels) usually attached below the bottom row, sometimes at the sides.

Tabs of the following numbers are in two parts, perforated between: 9, 15, 23-37, 44, 46-47, 50, 55, 62-65, 70-72, 74-77, 86-91, 94-99, 104-118, 123-126, 133-136B, 138-141, 143-151, 160-161, 165-167, 178-179, 182, 187-189, 203, 211-213, 222-223, 228-237, 243-244, 246-250, 256-258, 269-270, 272-273, 275, 294-295, 312, 337-339, 341-344, 346-347, 353-354, C1-C13, C22-C30. Both parts must be present to qualify for with tab value. Stamps with only one part sell for about one-quarter to one-third of full tab prices.

Watermarks

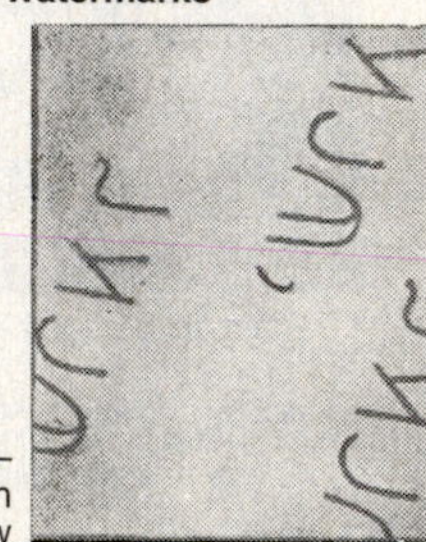

Wmk. 301 — ISRAEL in Hebrew

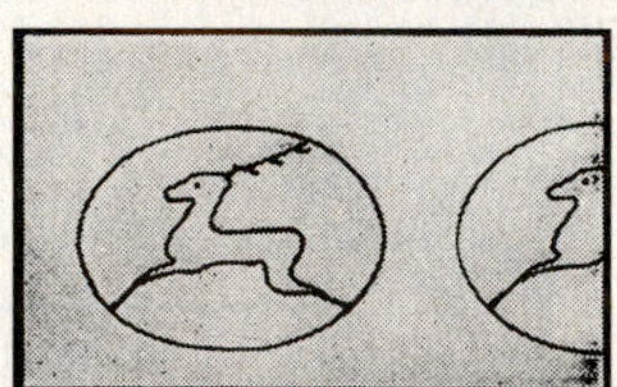

Wmk. 302 — Multiple Stag

Ancient Judean Coins
A1 A2

Designs: Nos. 1-6, Various coins.

Perf. 10, 11 and Compound
1948, May 16 Typo. Unwmk.

1 A1 3m orange .30 .25
2 A1 5m yellow grn .30 .25
3 A1 10m red violet .45 .25
4 A1 15m red .70 .25
5 A1 20m bright ultra 2.00 .30
6 A1 50m orange brown 8.00 .70
Nos. 1-6 (6) 11.75 2.00
Nos. 1-6 (6) with tabs 200.00
Set, with tabs, hinged 85.00

Size: 34½x22mm

7 A2 250m dark sl grn 27.50 9.00
8 A2 500m red brn, *cr* 100.00 45.00

Size: 36½x24mm

9 A2 1000m blk bl, *pale bl* 175.00 90.00
Nos. 7-9 (3) 302.50 144.00
Nos. 7-9 with tabs *5,250.*
Set, hinged 125.00

Nos. 1-9 exist imperf. Value: singles set *$3,000*; tab set *$13,000.*

See design A6. For overprints see Nos. J1-J5.

Rouletted

1a A1 3m .45 .25
2b A1 5m .60 .25
3b A1 10m 10.00 .90
Nos. 1a-3b (3) 11.05 1.40
Set, with tabs 225.00
Set with tabs, hinged 75.00

Flying Scroll — A3

1948, Sept. 26 Litho. *Perf. 11½*

10 A3 3m brn red & ultra .35 .25
11 A3 5m dl grn & ultra .35 .25
12 A3 10m dp car & ultra .35 .25
13 A3 20m dp ultra & ultra 1.75 .70
14 A3 65m brown & red 8.00 3.00
Nos. 10-14 (5) 10.80 4.45
With tabs 225.00
With tabs, hinged 90.00

Jewish New Year, 5709.

Flag of Israel — A4

1949, Mar. 31

15 A4 20m bright blue .50 .25
With tab 42.50

Appointment of the government by the Knesset.

Souvenir Sheet

A5

1949, May 1 *Imperf.*

16 A5 Sheet of 4 55.00 22.50
a. 10m dark carmine rose 12.50 4.00

1st anniv. of Israeli postage stamps.
The sheet was sold at "TABUL," First National Stamp Exhibition, in Tel Aviv, May 1-6, 1949. Tickets, costing 100 mils, covered the entrance fee and one sheet.

Bronze Half-Shekel of 67 A.D. — A6

Approach to Jerusalem — A8

Hebrew University, Jerusalem A7

"The Negev" by Reuven Rubin — A9

1949-50 Unwmk. *Perf. 11½, 14*

17 A6 3p gray black .25 .25
18 A6 5p purple .25 .25
19 A6 10p green .25 .25
20 A6 15p deep rose .25 .25
21 A6 30p dark blue .25 .25
22 A6 50p brown .90 .25
23 A7 100p Prus grn .35 .25
With tab 17.50
24 A8 250p org brn & gray .80 .55
With tab 32.50
25 A9 500p dp org & brown 6.00 5.00
With tab 200.00
Nos. 17-25 (9) 9.30 7.30
Nos. 17-22 with tabs (6) 65.00
Tete beche pairs, Nos. 18-21 75.00 75.00

Each of Nos. 17-22 portrays a different coin.

25th anniv. of the Hebrew University in Jerusalem (No. 23).

Issued: 250p, 2/16; 3p-50p, 12/18; 100p, 5/9/50; 500p, 12/26/50.

See Nos. 38-43, 56-61, 80-83, and design A1. For overprints see Nos. O1-O4.

Well at Petah Tikva — A10

1949, Aug. 10 *Perf. 11*

27 A10 40p dk grn & brn 6.00 .30
With tab 80.00

70th anniv. of Petah Tikva.

Arms and Service Insignia A11

1949, Sept. 20 *Perf. 11½*

28 A11 5p Air Force .30 .25
29 A11 10p Navy .85 .25
30 A11 35p Army 3.00 2.00
Nos. 28-30 (3) 4.15 2.50
With tabs 575.00

Jewish New Year, 5710.

Running Stag — A12

1950, Mar. 26

31 A12 40p purple .50 .30
a. Booklet pane of 4 3.50

32 A12 80p rose red .60 .35
a. Booklet pane of 4 7.00
Complete booklet, 1 ea. #31a, 32a 25.00
b. Nos. 31 and 32 tête bêche 42.50 22.50
With tabs 55.00

75th anniv. (in 1949) of the UPU.

Struggle for Free Immigration A13

Arrival of Immigrants A14

1950, Apr. 23

33 A13 20p dull brown 2.00 1.25
34 A14 40p dull green 4.00 3.00
With tabs 500.00

Independence Day, Apr. 22, 1950.

Fruit and Star of David — A15

1950, Aug. 31 Litho. *Perf. 14*

35 A15 5p vio blue & org .25 .25
36 A15 15p red brn & grn .25 .25
With tabs 42.50

Jewish New Year, 5711.

Runner and Track A16

1950, Oct. 1

37 A16 80p olive & sl blk 1.00 .55
With tab 57.50

3rd Maccabiah, Ramat Gan, Sept. 27, 1950.

Coin Type of 1949 Redrawn

Designs: Various coins.

1950

38 A6 3p gray black .25 .25
39 A6 5p purple .25 .25
a. Tête bêche pair 3.00 3.00
40 A6 10p green .25 .25
a. Tête bêche pair 1.25 1.00
41 A6 15p deep rose .25 .25
a. Tête bêche pair 2.00 1.75
42 A6 30p dark blue .25 .25
a. Tête bêche pair 4.00 4.00
43 A6 50p brown .25 .25
Nos. 38-43 (6) 1.50 1.50
With tabs 2.90

Inscription at left measures 11mm on Nos. 38-43; 9mm on Nos. 17-22.

Detail from Tablet, "Founding of Tel Aviv" A17

1951, Mar. 22

44 A17 40p dark brown .25 .25
With tab 17.50

40th anniversary of Tel Aviv.

Young Man Holding Outline Map of Israel — A18

1951, Apr. 30 Litho.

45 A18 80p red brown .25 .25
With tab 3.25

Issued to promote the sale of Independence Bonds.

Metsudat Yesha A19

Hakastel A20

1951, May 9 Unwmk.

46 A19 15p red brown .25 .25
47 A20 40p deep blue .40 .25
With tabs 40.00

Proclamation of State of Israel, 3rd anniv.

Tractor and Wheat — A21

Tree — A22

Plower and National Fund Stamp of 1902 — A23

1951, June 24 *Perf. 14*

48 A21 15p red brown .25 .25
49 A22 25p Prussian green .25 .25
50 A23 80p dull blue .30 .25
Nos. 48-50 (3) .80 .75
With tabs 80.00

Jewish National Fund, 50th anniversary.

Theodor Zeev Herzl — A24

1951, Aug. 14

51 A24 80p gray green .25 .25
With tab 3.50

23rd Zionist Congress, Jerusalem.

Carrier Pigeons — A25

Designs: 15p, Girl holding dove and fruit. 40p, Scrolls of the law.

1951, Sept. 16

52 A25 5p blue .25 .25
53 A25 15p cerise .25 .25
54 A25 40p rose violet .25 .25
Nos. 52-54 (3) .75 .75
With tabs 3.00

Jewish New Year, 5712.

Menorah and Emblems of Twelve Tribes — A26

1952, Feb. 27

55 A26 1000p dk bl & gray 10.00 4.50
With tab 225.00

Redrawn Coin Type of 1950

Designs: Various coins.

1952, Mar. 30

56 A6 20p orange .25 .25
a. Tête bêche pair 2.25 2.25
57 A6 35p olive green .25 .25
58 A6 40p orange brown .25 .25

59 A6 45p red violet .25 .25
a. Tête bêche pair 4.00 4.00
60 A6 60p carmine .25 .25
61 A6 85p aquamarine .25 .25
Nos. 56-61 (6) 1.50 1.50
With tabs 11.00

Thistle and Yad Mordecai Battlefield A27

Battlefields: 60p, Cornflower and Deganya. 110p, Anemone and Safed.

1952, Apr. 29

62 A27 30p lil rose & vio brn .25 .25
63 A27 60p ultra & gray blk .25 .25
64 A27 110p crimson & gray .35 .25
Nos. 62-64 (3) .85 .75
With tabs 18.00

Proclamation of State of Israel, 4th anniv.

Manhattan Skyline and American Zionists' House A28

1952, May 13

65 A28 220p dark blue & gray .30 .25
With tab 10.00

Opening of American Zionists' House, Tel Aviv.

Figs — A29

Unwmk.

1952, Sept. 3 Litho. *Perf. 14*

66 A29 15p shown .25 .25
67 A29 40p Lily .25 .25
68 A29 110p Dove .25 .25
69 A29 220p Nut cluster .40 .25
Nos. 66-69 (4) 1.15 1.00
With tabs 20.00

Jewish New Year, 5713.

Pres. Chaim Weizmann (1874-1952) and Presidential Standard — A30

1952, Dec. 9

70 A30 30p slate .25 .25
71 A30 110p black .25 .25
With tabs 8.00

Weizmann, president of Israel 1948-52.

Numeral Incorporating Agricultural Scenes — A31

1952, Dec. 31

72 A31 110p brown, buff & emer .25 .25
With tab 8.00

70th anniversary of B.I.L.U. (Bet Yaakov Lechu Venelcha) immigration.

Five Anemones and State Emblem — A32

1953, Apr. 19

73 A32 110p grnsh bl, bl blk & red .25 .25
With tab 2.50

5th anniversary of State of Israel.

Rabbi Moshe ben Maimon (Maimonides) — A33

1953, Aug. 3 Wmk. 301 *Perf. 14x13*

74 A33 110p brown .30 .25
With tab 3.00

7th International Congress of History of Science, Jerusalem, Aug. 4-11.

Holy Ark, Jerusalem — A34

Holy Arks: 45p, Petah Tikva. 200p, Safed.

1953, Aug. 11

75 A34 20p sapphire .25 .25
76 A34 45p brown red .25 .25
77 A34 200p purple .25 .25
Nos. 75-77 (3) .75 .75
With tabs 6.50

Jewish New Year, 5714.

Combined Ball-Globe — A35

Unwmk.

1953, Sept. 20 Litho. *Perf. 14*

78 A35 110p blue & dark brn .25 .25
With tab 2.75

4th Maccabiah, Sept. 20-29, 1953.

Desert Rose — A36

1953, Sept. 22

79 A36 200p multicolored .25 .25
With tab 3.00

Conquest of the Desert Exhib., 9/22-10/14.

Redrawn Type of 1950

Designs: Various coins.

1954, Jan. 5

80 A6 80p olive bister .25 .25
81 A6 95p blue green .25 .25
82 A6 100p fawn .25 .25
83 A6 125p violet blue .25 .25
Nos. 80-83 (4) 1.00 1.00
With tabs 2.00

Marigold and Ruins at Yehiam — A37

350p, Narcissus and bridge at Gesher.

1954, May 5 Litho.

84 A37 60p dk bl, mag & ol gray .25 .25
85 A37 350p dk brn, grn & yel .25 .25
With tabs 1.75

Memorial Day and 6th anniversary of proclamation of State of Israel.

Theodor Zeev Herzl (1860-1904), Founder of Zionist Movement — A38

1954, July 21 Wmk. 302

86 A38 160p dk bl, dk brn & cr .25 .25
With tab .60

Bearers with Grape Cluster A39

1954, Sept. 8 *Perf. 13x14*

87 A39 25p dark brown .25 .25
With tab .25

Jewish New Year, 5715.

19th Century Mail Coach and Jerusalem Post Office A40

200p, Mail truck & present G.P.O., Jerusalem.

1954, Oct. 13 *Perf. 14*

88 A40 60p blue, blk & yel .25 .25
89 A40 200p dk grn, blk & red .25 .25
With tabs 1.75

TABIM, National Stamp Exhibition, Jerusalem, Oct. 13-18.

Baron Edmond de Rothschild (1845-1934) and Grape Cluster — A41

1954, Nov. 23 *Perf. 13x14*

90 A41 300p dark blue green .25 .25
With tab .50

Lighted Oil Lamp A42

1955, Jan. 13 *Perf. 13x14*

91 A42 250p dark blue .25 .25
With tab .50

Teachers' Association, 50th anniversary.

Parachutist and Barbed Wire — A43

1955, Mar. 31 Litho. *Perf. 14*

92 A43 120p dk Prus green .25 .25
With tab .35

Jewish volunteers from Palestine who served in British army in World War II.

Lighted Menorah A44

1955, Apr. 26

93 A44 150p dk grn, blk & org .25 .25
With tab .30

Proclamation of State of Israel, 7th anniv.

Immigration by Ship — A45

Designs: 10p, Immigration by plane. 25p, Agricultural training. 30p, Gardening. 60p, Vocational training. 750p, Scientific education.

1955, May 10 Unwmk. *Perf. 14*

94 A45 5p brt blue & black .25 .25
95 A45 10p red & black .25 .25
96 A45 25p deep grn & black .25 .25
97 A45 30p orange & black .25 .25
98 A45 60p lilac rose & blk .25 .25
99 A45 750p olive bis & blk .25 .25
Nos. 94-99 (6) 1.50 1.50
With tabs 1.25

Israel's Youth Immigration Institution, 20th anniv.

Musicians with Tambourine and Cymbals — A46

Musician with: 60p, Ram's Horn. 120p, Loud Trumpet. 250p, Harp.

1955, Aug. 25 Photo. Wmk. 302

100 A46 25p dark green & org .25 .25

Unwmk.

101 A46 60p dk gray & orange .25 .25
102 A46 120p dark blue & yel .25 .25
103 A46 250p red brn & org .25 .25
#100-103, with tabs .45

Jewish New Year, 5716.

See Nos. 121-123.

Ambulance A47

1955, Nov. 1 Wmk. 301 *Perf. 14*
104 A47 160p grn, red & blk .25 .25
With tab .25

Magen David Adom (Israeli Red Cross), 25th anniv.

Mandrake, Reuben — A48

Twelve Tribes: 20p, Gates of Sechem, Simeon. 30p, Ephod, Levi. 40p, Lion, Judah. 50p, Scales, Dan. 60p, Stag, Naphtali. 80p, Tents, Gad. 100p, Tree, Asher. 120p, Sun and stars, Issachar. 180p, Ship, Zebulon. 200p, Sheaf of wheat, Joseph. 250p, Wolf, Benjamin.

1955-57 Wmk. 302 *Perf. 13x14*

105	A48	10p bright green	.25	.25
106	A48	20p red lilac ('56)	.25	.25
107	A48	30p bright ultra	.25	.25
108	A48	40p brown ('56)	.25	.25
109	A48	50p grnsh bl ('56)	.25	.25
110	A48	60p lemon	.25	.25
111	A48	80p deep vio ('56)	.25	.25
112	A48	100p vermilion	.25	.25
113	A48	120p olive ('56)	.25	.25
114	A48	180p lil rose ('56)	.25	.25
115	A48	200p green ('56)	.25	.25
116	A48	250p gray ('56)	.25	.25
		#105-116, with tabs	2.00	

See Nos. 133-136B.

Albert Einstein (1879-1955) and Equation of his Relativity Theory — A49

1956, Jan. 3 *Perf. 13x14*
117 A49 350p brown .25 .25
With tab .40

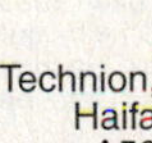

Technion, Haifa A50

1956, Jan. 3 Wmk. 302
118 A50 350p lt ol grn & blk .25 .25
With tab .25

Israel Institute of Technology, 30th anniv.

"Eight Years of Israel" — A51

1956, Apr. 12 Litho. *Perf. 14*
119 A51 150p multicolored .25 .25
With tab .25

Proclamation of State of Israel, 8th anniv.

Jaffa Oranges — A52

1956, May 20 Wmk. 302 *Perf. 14*
120 A52 300p bl grn & orange .25 .25
With tab .25

4th Intl. Congress of Mediterranean Citrus Growers.

New Year Type of 1955

Musician with: 30p, Lyre. 50p, Cymbals. 150p, Double oboe, horiz.

1956, Aug. 14 Photo. *Perf. 14x13*
121 A46 30p brown & brt blue .25 .25

Perf. 14
122 A46 50p purple & orange .25 .25
123 A46 150p dk bl grn & org .25 .25
#121-123, with tabs .25

Jewish New Year, 5717.

Haganah Insignia — A54

1957, Jan. 1 *Perf. 13x14*
124 A54 20p + 80p brt grn .25 .25
125 A54 50p + 150p car rose .25 .25
126 A54 50p + 350p ultra .25 .25
#124-126, with tabs .25

Defense issue. Divided denomination used to show increased postal rate.

Bezalel Museum and Antique Lamp — A55

1957, Apr. 29 Litho. *Perf. 14*
127 A55 400p multicolored .25 .25
With tab .25

Bezalel Natl. Museum, Jerusalem, 50th anniv.

Jet Plane and "9" — A56

1957, Apr. 29
128 A56 250p deep bl & blk .25 .25
With tab .25

Proclamation of State of Israel, 9th anniv.

Horse and Seal — A57

Ancient Seals: 160p, Lion. 300p, Gazelle.

1957, Sept. 4 Wmk. 302 *Perf. 14*
129 A57 50p ocher & blk, *lt bl* .25 .25

Perf. 14x13
Photo. Unwmk.
130 A57 160p grn & blk, *bis brn* .25 .25
131 A57 300p dp car & blk, *pink* .25 .25
#130-131, with tabs .25

Jewish New Year, 5718.

TABIL
Souvenir Sheet

Bet Alpha Synagogue Mosaic — A58

1957, Sept. 17 Litho. *Roulette 13*
132 A58 Sheet of 4 .30 .30
a. 100p multicolored .25 .25
b. 200p multicolored .25 .25
c. 300p multicolored .25 .25
d. 400p multicolored .25 .25

1st Intl. stamp exhib. in Israel, Tel Aviv, 9/17-23.

Tribes Type of 1955-57
Perf. 13x14

1957-59 Unwmk. Photo.

133	A48	10p brt grn ('58)	.25	.25
133A	A48	20p red lilac	.25	.25
133C	A48	40p brown ('59)	.55	.45
134	A48	50p greenish blue	.25	.25
135	A48	60p lemon	.25	.25
136	A48	100p vermilion	.25	.25
136B	A48	120p olive ('58)	.25	.25
		Nos. 133-136B (7)	2.05	1.95
		With tabs	25.00	

Hammer Thrower — A59

1958, Jan. 20 *Perf. 14x13*
137 A59 500p bister & car .25 .25
With tab .25

Maccabiah Games, 25th anniversary.

Ancient Ship — A60

Ships: 20p, Three-master used for "illegal immigration." 30p, Cargo ship "Shomron." 1000p, Passenger ship "Zion."

Wmk. 302
1958, Jan. 27 Litho. *Perf. 14*
Size: 36½x22½mm
138 A60 10p ocher, red & blk .25 .25

Perf. 13x14
Photo.
139 A60 20p brt grn, blk & brn .25 .25
140 A60 30p red, blk & grnsh bl .25 .25

Size: 56½x22½mm
141 A60 1000p brt bl, blk & grn .25 .25
#138-141, with tabs .35

Issued to honor Israel's merchant fleet.

Menorah and Olive Branch — A61

Unwmk.
1958, Apr. 21 Litho. *Perf. 14*
142 A61 400p gold, blk & grn .25 .25
With tab .25

Memorial Day and 10th anniversary of proclamation of State of Israel.

Dancing Youths Forming "10" — A62

1958, July 2
143 A62 200p dk org & dk grn .25 .25
With tab .25

First World Conference of Jewish Youth, Jerusalem, July 28-Aug. 1.

Convention Center, Jerusalem A63

1958, July 2
144 A63 400p vio & org, *yellow* .25 .25
With tab .25

10th Anniversary of Independence Exhibition, Jerusalem, June 5-Aug. 21.

Wheat — A64

1958, Aug. 27 Photo. *Perf. 14x13*
145 A64 50p shown .25 .25
146 A64 60p Barley .25 .25
147 A64 160p Grapes .25 .25
148 A64 300p Figs .25 .25
#145-148, with tabs .30

Jewish New Year, 5719.

"Love Thy Neighbor . . ." — A65

1958, Dec. 10 Litho. *Perf. 14*
149 A65 750p yel, gray & grn .25 .25
With tab .60

Universal Declaration of Human Rights, 10th anniversary.

Designing and Printing Stamps A66

Radio and Telephone — A67

120p, Mobile post office. 500p, Teletype.

1959, Feb. 25 Wmk. 302 *Perf. 14*

150 A66 60p olive, blk & red .25 .25
151 A66 120p olive, blk & red .25 .25
152 A67 250p olive, blk & red .25 .25
153 A67 500p olive, blk & red .25 .25
#150-153, with tabs .45

Decade of postal activities in Israel.

Shalom Aleichem — A68

Portraits: No. 155, Chaim Nachman Bialik. No. 156, Eliezer Ben-Yehuda.

1959 Unwmk. Photo. *Perf. 14x13*

154 A68 250p yel grn & red brn .25 .25
155 A68 250p ocher & ol gray .25 .25
#154-155, with tabs .35

Perf. 14

Litho.

156 A68 250p bl & vio bl .25 .25
With tab .35

Birth cent. of Aleichem (Solomon Rabinowitz), Yiddish writer (No. 154); 25th death anniv. of Bialik, Hebrew poet (No. 155); birth cent. of Ben-Yehuda, father of modern Hebrew (No. 156).

Issued: No. 154, 3/30; No. 155, 7/22; No. 156, 11/25.

Cyclamen — A69

Flowers: 60p, Anemone. 300p, Narcissus.

1959, May 11 Wmk. 302 *Perf. 14*

Flowers in Natural Colors

157 A69 60p deep green .25 .25
158 A69 120p brt purple .25 .25
159 A69 300p blue .25 .25
#157-159, with tabs .35

Memorial Day and 11th anniversary of proclamation of State of Israel.

Buildings, Tel Aviv — A70

1959, May 4

160 A70 120p multicolored .25 .25
With tab .25

50th anniversary of Tel Aviv.

Bristol Britannia and Windsock A71

1959, July 22

161 A71 500p multicolored .25 .25
With tab .30

Civil Aviation in Israel, 10th anniversary.

Pomegranates A72

Perf. 14x13

1959, Sept. 9 Photo. Unwmk.

162 A72 60p shown .25 .25
163 A72 200p Olives .25 .25
164 A72 350p Dates .25 .25
Nos. 162-164 (3) .75 .75
With tabs 1.00

Jewish New Year, 5720.

Merhavya A73

Settlements: 120p, Yesud Ha-Maala. 180p, Deganya.

1959, Nov. 25 Photo. *Perf. 13x14*

165 A73 60p citron & dk grn .25 .25
166 A73 120p red brn & ocher .25 .25
167 A73 180p blue & dk grn .25 .25
Nos. 165-167 (3) .75 .75
With tabs 1.25

Settlements of Merhavya and Deganya, 50th anniv.; Yesud Ha-Maala, 75th anniv.

Judean Coin (66-70 A.D.) — A74

1960 Unwmk. *Perf. 13x14*

Denominations in Black

168 A74 1a brn, *pinkish* .25 .25
a. On surface colored paper .25 .25
As "a," with tab .75
b. Black overprint omitted
169 A74 3a brt red, *pinkish* .25 .25
170 A74 5a gray, *pinkish* .25 .25
171 A74 6a brt grn, *lt bl* .25 .25
171A A74 7a gray, *bluish* .25 .25
172 A74 8a mag, *lt blue* .25 .25
173 A74 12a grnsh bl, *lt bl* .25 .25
a. Black overprint omitted
174 A74 18a orange .25 .25
175 A74 25a blue .25 .25
176 A74 30a carmine .25 .25
177 A74 50a bright lilac .25 .25
#168-177, with tabs 1.50

Issue dates: 7a, July 6; others, Jan. 6.

Operation "Magic Carpet" A75

Design: 50a, Resettled family in front of house, grapes and figs.

1960, Apr. 7 Unwmk. *Perf. 13x14*

178 A75 25a red brown .25 .25
179 A75 50a green .25 .25
#178-179, with tabs .30

World Refugee Year, July 1, 1959-June 30, 1960.

Sand Lily — A76

Design: 32a, Evening primrose.

1960, Apr. 27 Litho. *Perf. 14*

180 A76 12a multicolored .25 .25
181 A76 32a brn, yel & grn .25 .25
#180-181, with tabs .45

Memorial Day; proclamation of State of Israel, 12th anniv. See Nos. 204-206, 238-240.

Atom Diagram and Atomic Reactor A77

1960, July 6 Wmk. 302 *Perf. 14*

182 A77 50a blue, red & blk .25 .25
With tab .45

Installation of Israel's first atomic reactor.

Theodor Herzl and Rhine at Basel — A78

1960, Aug. 31 Litho. *Perf. 14*

183 A78 25a gray brown .25 .25
With tab .40

King Saul — A79

Designs: 25a, King David. 40a, King Solomon.

Kings in Multicolor

1960, Aug. 31 Wmk. 302

184 A79 7a emerald .25 .25

Unwmk.

185 A79 25a brown .25 .25
186 A79 40a blue .25 .25
Nos. 184-186 (3) .75 .75
With tabs .90

Jewish New Year, 5721. See Nos. 208-210.

Jewish Postal Courier, Prague, 18th Century A80

Perf. 13x14

1960, Oct. 9 Photo. Unwmk.

187 A80 25a olive blk, *gray* .25 .25
With tab 1.50
a. Souvenir sheet 9.00 7.00

TAVIV Natl. Stamp Exhib., Tel Aviv, Oct. 9-19.

No. 187a sold only at Exhibition for 50a.

Henrietta Szold and Hadassah Medical Center A81

1960, Dec. 14 *Perf. 13x14*

188 A81 25a turq bl & vio gray .25 .25
With tab .30

Birth cent. of Henrietta Szold, founder of Hadassah, American Jewish women's organization.

Shields of Jerusalem and First Zionist Congress A82

1960, Dec. 14 Unwmk. *Perf. 14*

189 A82 50a vio bl & turq blue .25 .25
With tab .60

25th Zionist Congress, Jerusalem, 1960.

Ram — A83

Signs of Zodiac — A84

1961, Feb. 27 Photo. *Perf. 13x14*

190 A83 1a Ram .25 .25
191 A83 2a Bull .25 .25
192 A83 6a Twins .25 .25
193 A83 7a Crab .25 .25
194 A83 8a Lion .25 .25
a. Booklet pane of 6 ('65) .45
195 A83 10a Virgin .25 .25
196 A83 12a Scales .25 .25
a. Booklet pane of 6 ('65) .45
197 A83 18a Scorpion .25 .25
198 A83 20a Archer .25 .25
199 A83 25a Goat .25 .25
200 A83 32a Water bearer .25 .25
201 A83 50a Fishes .25 .25

Perf. 14

Litho.

202 A84 £1 dk bl, gold & lt bl .25 .25
Nos. 190-202 (13) 3.25 3.25
With tabs 4.00

Booklet pane sheets (Nos. 194a, 196a) of 36 (9x4) contain 6 panes of 6, with gutters dividing the sheet in four sections. Each sheet yields 4 tete beche pairs and 4 tete beche gutter pairs, or strips.

For surcharges see Nos. 215-217.

Vertical strips of 6 of the 1a, 10a and No. 216 (5a) are from larger sheets from which coils were produced. Regular sheets of 50 are arranged 10x5.

Javelin Thrower and "7" — A85

1961, Apr. 18 Litho. *Perf. 14*

203 A85 25a multicolored .25 .25
With tab .40

7th Intl. Congress of the Hapoel Sports Org., Ramat Gan, May 1961.

Flower Type of 1960

7a, Myrtle. 12a, Sea onion. 32a, Oleander.

1961, Apr. 18 Unwmk.
Flowers in Natural Colors

204 A76 7a green .25 .25
205 A76 12a rose carmine .25 .25
206 A76 32a brt greenish bl .25 .25
Nos. 204-206 (3) .75 .75
With tabs .80

Memorial Day; proclamation of State of Israel, 13th anniv.

Scaffold Around "10" and Sapling — A86

1961, June 14 Photo. *Perf. 14*

207 A86 50a Prussian blue .25 .25
With tab .40

Israel bond issue 10th anniv.

Type of 1960

Designs: 7a, Samson. 25a, Judas Maccabaeus. 40a, Bar Cocheba.

1961, Aug. 21 Litho. *Perf. 14*
Multicolored Designs

208 A79 7a red orange .25 .25
209 A79 25a gray .25 .25
210 A79 40a lilac .25 .25
Nos. 208-210 (3) .75 .75
With tabs 1.25

Jewish New Year, 5722.

Bet Hamidrash Synagogue, Medzibozh — A87

1961, Aug. 21 Photo. *Perf. 13x14*

211 A87 25a dk brn & yel .25 .25
With tab .40

Bicentenary of death of Rabbi Israel Baal-Shem-Tov, founder of Hasidism.

Pine Cone — A88

Design: 30a, Symbolic trees.

1961, Dec. 26 Unwmk. *Perf. 13x14*

212 A88 25a green, yel & blk .25 .25
213 A88 30a org, green & ind .25 .25
#212-213, with tabs 1.50

Achievements of afforestation program.

Cello, Harp, French Horn and Kettle Drum — A89

1961, Dec. 26 Litho. *Perf. 14*

214 A89 50a multicolored .25 .25
With tab 1.50

Israel Philharmonic Orchestra, 25th anniv.

Zodiac Type of 1961 Surcharged with New Value

1962, Mar. 18 Photo. *Perf. 13x14*

215 A83 3a on 1a lt lilac .25 .25
a. Without overprint 60.00
216 A83 5a on 7a gray .25 .25
217 A83 30a on 32a emerald .25 .25
a. Without overprint 50.00
#215-217, with tabs .40
#215a and 217a, with tabs 400.00

See note after No. 202.

Anopheles Maculipennis and Chart Showing Decline of Malaria in Israel — A90

1962, Apr. 30 *Perf. 14x13*

218 A90 25a ocher, red & blk .25 .25
With tab .40

WHO drive to eradicate malaria.

View of Rosh Pinna — A91

1962, Apr. 30 Unwmk.

219 A91 20a yel, green & brn .25 .25
With tab .35

Rosh Pinna agricultural settlement, 80th anniv.

Flame ("Hear, O Israel . . .") A92

Yellow Star of David and Six Candles A93

1962, Apr. 30 Photo.

220 A92 12a black, org & red .25 .25

Perf. 14

221 A93 55a multicolored .25 .25
#220-221, with tabs 1.25

Heroes and Martyrs Day, in memory of the 6,000,000 Jewish victims of Nazi persecution.

Vautour Fighter-Bomber — A94

Design: 30a, Fighter-Bombers in formation.

1962, Apr. 30 *Perf. 13x14*

222 A94 12a blue .25 .25
223 A94 30a olive green .25 .25
#222-223, with tabs 1.50

Memorial Day; proclamation of the state of Israel, 14th anniv.

Symbolic Flags — A95

1962, June 5 *Perf. 14*

224 A95 55a multicolored .25 .25
With tab .75

Near East Intl. Fair, Tel Aviv, June 5-July 5.

Wolf and Lamb, Isaiah 11:6 — A96

Designs: 28a, Leopard and kid, Isaiah 11:6. 43a, Child and asp, Isaiah 11:8.

1962, Sept. 5

225 A96 8a buff, red & black .25 .25
226 A96 28a buff, lilac & black .25 .25
227 A96 43a buff, org & black .25 .25
Nos. 225-227 (3) .75 .75
With tabs 2.25

Jewish New Year, 5723.

Boeing 707 — A97

1962, Nov. 7 *Perf. 13x14*

228 A97 55a bl, dk bl & rose lil .30 .25
With tab .95
a. Souvenir sheet 2.00 1.75

El Al Airlines; El Al Philatelic Exhibition, Tel Aviv, Nov. 7-14. Issued in sheets of 15.

No. 228a contains one stamp in greenish blue, dark blue & rose lilac with greenish blue color continuing into margin design (No. 228 has white perforations). Sold for £1 for one day at philatelic counters in Jerusalem, Haifa and Tel Aviv and for one week at the El Al Exhibition.

Cogwheel Symbols of UJA Activities A98

1962, Dec. 26 Unwmk. *Perf. 13x14*

229 A98 20a org red, sil & bl .25 .25
With tab .35

25th anniv. of the United Jewish Appeal (United States) and its support of immigration, settlement, agriculture and care of the aged and sick.

Janusz Korczak A99

1962, Dec. 26 Photo.

230 A99 30a olive grn & blk .25 .25
With tab .35

Dr. Janusz Korczak (Henryk Goldszmit, 1879-1942), physician, teacher and writer, killed in Treblinka concentration camp.

Orange butterflyfish A100

Red Sea fish: 3a, Pennant Coral Fish. 8a, Lionfish. 12a, Zebra-striped angelfish.

1962, Dec. 26 Litho. *Perf. 14*
Fish in Natural Colors

231 A100 3a green .25 .25
232 A100 6a purple .25 .25
233 A100 8a brown .25 .25
234 A100 12a dark blue .25 .25
#231-234, with tabs .60

See Nos. 246-249.

Stockade at Dawn A101

Design: 30a, Completed stockade at night.

1963, Mar. 21 Unwmk. *Perf. 14*

235 A101 12a yel brn, blk & yel .25 .25
236 A101 30a dp plum, blk & lt bl .25 .25
#235-236, with tabs .75

25th anniv. of the "Stockade and Tower" villages.

Hand Offering Food to Bird A102

1963, Mar. 21 Photo. *Perf. 13x14*

237 A102 55a gray & black .25 .25
With tab .70
a. Booklet pane of 4 27.50

FAO "Freedom from Hunger" campaign.

Issued in sheets of 15 (5x3) with 5 tabs. The booklet pane sheet of 16 (4x4) is divided into 2 panes of 8 (4x2) by horizontal gutter. The 4 stamps at left in each pane are inverted in relation to the 4 at right, making 4 horizontal tete beche pairs down the center of the sheet.

Flower Type of 1960

8a, White lily. 30a, Hollyhock. 37a, Tulips.

1963, Apr. 25 Litho. *Perf. 14*
Flowers in Natural Colors

238 A76 8a slate .25 .25
239 A76 30a yellow green .25 .25
240 A76 37a sepia .25 .25
Nos. 238-240 (3) .75 .75
With tabs 2.00

Memorial Day; proclamation of the State of Israel, 15th anniv.

Typesetter, 19th Century — A103

1963, June 19 Photo. *Perf. 14x13*

241 A103 12a tan & vio brn .35 .35
With tab 1.10
a. Sheet of 16 30.00 30.00

Hebrew press in Palestine, cent. The background of the sheet shows page of 1st issue of "Halbanon" newspaper, giving each stamp a different background.

"The Sun Beat upon the Head of Jonah" — A104

Designs: 30a, "There was a mighty tempest in the sea." 55a, "Jonah was in the belly of the fish." 30a, 55a horiz.

1963, Aug. 21 *Perf. 14x13, 13x14*

242 A104 8a org, lil & blk .25 .25
243 A104 30a multicolored .25 .25
244 A104 55a multicolored .25 .25
Nos. 242-244 (3) .75 .75
With tabs 2.75

Jewish New Year, 5724.

Hoe Clearing Thistles — A105

1963, Aug. 21 *Perf. 14*

245 A105 37a multicolored .25 .25
With tab .65

80 years of agricultural settlements in Israel; "Year of the Pioneers."

Fish Type of 1962

Red Sea Fish: 2a, Undulate triggerfish. 6a, Radiate turkeyfish. 8a, Bigeye. 12a, Imperial angelfish.

1963, Dec. 16 **Litho.** *Perf. 14*

Fish in Natural Colors

246 A100 2a violet blue .25 .25
247 A100 6a green .25 .25
248 A100 8a orange .25 .25
249 A100 12a olive green .25 .25
Nos. 246-249 (4) 1.00 1.00
With tabs .90

S.S. Shalom, Sailing Vessel and Ancient Map of Coast Line — A106

1963, Dec. 16 **Photo.** *Perf. 13x14*

250 A106 £1 ultra, brt grn & lil .70 .40
With tab 5.50

Maiden voyage of S.S. Shalom.

"Old Age and Survivors Insurance" — A107

Designs (Insurance): 25a, Maternity. 37a, Large family. 50a, Workers' compensation.

1964, Feb. 24 **Litho.** *Perf. 14*

251 A107 12a multicolored .25 .25
252 A107 25a multicolored .25 .25
253 A107 37a multicolored .25 .25
254 A107 50a multicolored .25 .25
Nos. 251-254 (4) 1.00 1.00
With tabs 4.00

Natl. Insurance Institute 10th anniv.

Pres. Izhak Ben-Zvi (1884-1963) — A108

1964, Apr. 13 **Photo.** *Perf. 14x13*

255 A108 12a dark brown .25 .25
With tab .25

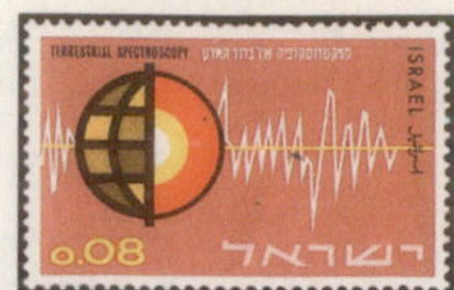

Terrestrial Spectroscopy — A109

Designs: 35a, Macromolecules of the living cell. 70a, Electronic computer.

1964, Apr. 13 *Perf. 14*

256 A109 8a multicolored .25 .25
257 A109 35a multicolored .25 .25
258 A109 70a multicolored .25 .25
Nos. 256-258 (3) .75 .75
With tabs 2.50

Proclamation of the State of Israel, 16th anniv.; Israel's contribution to science.

Basketball Players — A110

8a, Runner. 12a, Discus thrower. 50a, Soccer.

1964, June 24 *Perf. 14x13*

259 A110 8a brt brick red & dk brown .25 .25
260 A110 12a rose lil & dk brn .25 .25
261 A110 30a bl, car & dk brn .25 .25
262 A110 50a yel grn, org red & dk brown .25 .25
Nos. 259-262 (4) 1.00 1.00
With tabs .90

Israel's participation in the 18th Olympic Games, Tokyo, Oct. 10-25.

Serpent of Aesculapius and Menorah — A111

1964, Aug. 5 **Unwmk.**

263 A111 £1 ol bis & slate grn .30 .25
With tab .65

6th World Congress of the Israel Medical Association, Haifa, Aug. 3-13.

Ancient Glass Vase — A112

Different glass vessels, 1st-3rd centuries.

1964, Aug. 5 **Litho.**

264 A112 8a vio, brn & org .25 .25
265 A112 35a ol, grn & bl grn .25 .25
266 A112 70a brt car rose, blue & violet blue .25 .25
Nos. 264-266 (3) .75 .75
With tabs .60

Jewish New Year, 5725.

Steamer Bringing Immigrants — A113

1964, Nov. 2 **Litho.** *Perf. 14*

267 A113 25a slate bl, bl grn & blk .25 .25
With tab .30

30th anniv. of the blockade runners bringing immigrants to Israel.

Eleanor Roosevelt (1884-1962) — A114

1964, Nov. 2 **Photo.** *Perf. 14x13*

268 A114 70a dull purple .25 .25
With tab .40

Chess Board, Knight and Emblem of Chess Olympics — A115

1964, Nov. 2 *Perf. 13x14*

269 A115 12a shown .25 .25
270 A115 70a Rook .35 .30
With tabs 1.75

16th Chess Olympics, Tel Aviv, Nov. 1964.

"Africa-Israel Friendship" — A116

1964, Nov. 30 **Photo.** *Perf. 14x13*

271 A116 57a ol, blk, gold & red brown .35 .25
With tab 1.75
a. Souvenir sheet 1.50 1.50

TABAI, Natl. Stamp Exhibition, dedicated to African-Israel friendship, Haifa, Nov. 30-Dec. 6. No. 271a contains one imperf. stamp. Sold for £1.

View of Masada from West A117

Designs: 36a, Northern Palace, lower terrace. £1, View of Northern Palace, vert.

1965, Feb. 3 **Photo.** *Perf. 13x14*

272 A117 25a dull green .25 .25
273 A117 36a bright blue .25 .25
274 A117 £1 dark red brn .25 .25
Nos. 272-274 (3) .75 .75
With tabs 1.40

Ruins of Masada, the last stronghold in the war against the Romans, 66-73 A.D.

Book Fair Emblem A118

1965, Mar. 24 **Photo.** *Perf. 13x14*

275 A118 70a gray ol, brt bl & blk .25 .25
With tab .25

2nd Intl. Book Fair, Jerusalem, April.

Arms of Ashdod — A119

Town Emblems: 1a, Lydda (Lod). 2a, Qiryat Shemona. 5a, Petah Tikva. 6a, Nazareth. 8a, Beersheba. 10a Bet Shean. 12a, Tiberias. 20a, Elat. 25a, Acre (Akko). 35a, Dimona. 37a, Zefat. 50a, Rishon Leziyyon. 70a, Jerusalem. £1, Tel Aviv-Jaffa. £3, Haifa.

Size: 17x22½mm

1965-66 *Perf. 13x14*

276 A119 1a brown .25 .25
277 A119 2a lilac rose .25 .25
278 A119 5a gray .25 .25
279 A119 6a violet .25 .25
280 A119 8a orange .25 .25
a. Booklet pane of 6 .45
281 A119 10a emerald .25 .25
282 A119 12a dark purple .25 .25
a. Booklet pane of 6 .50
283 A119 15a green .25 .25
284 A119 20a rose red .25 .25
285 A119 25a ultramarine .25 .25
286 A119 35a magenta .25 .25
287 A119 37a olive .25 .25
288 A119 50a greenish bl .25 .25

Perf. 14x13

Size: 22x27mm

289 A119 70a dark brown .25 .25
290 A119 £1 dark green .25 .25
291 A119 £3 dk carmine rose .55 .25
Nos. 276-291 (16) 4.30 4.00
With tabs 8.00

Issued: Nos. 283-286, 3/24/65; No. 290, 11/24/65; No. 291, 3/14/66; others, 2/2/66.

The uncut booklet pane sheets of 36 are divided into 4 panes (2 of 6 stamps, 2 of 12) by horizontal and vertical gutters. alf of the stamps in the 2 panes of 12 are inverted, causing 4 horizontal tête bêche pairs and 4 horizontal tête bêche gutter pairs.

Vertical strips of 6 of the 1a, 5a and 10a are from larger sheets, released Jan. 10, 1967, from which coils were produced. Regular sheets of 50 are arranged 10x5.

No. 290 also comes tagged (1975).

See Nos. 334-336, 386-393.

Hands Reaching for Hope, and Star of David — A120

1965, Apr. 27 **Unwmk.** *Perf. 14x13*

292 A120 25a gray, black & yel .25 .25
With tab .40

Liberation of Nazi concentration camps, 20th anniv.

"Irrigation of the Desert" — A121

1965, Apr. 27 **Photo.**

293 A121 37a olive bister & blue .25 .25

With tab .25

Memorial Day; proclamation of the state of Israel, 17th anniv.

Telegraph Pole and Syncom Satellite A122

1965, July 21 **Unwmk.** ***Perf. 13x14***

294 A122 70a vio, blk & grnsh bl .25 .25

With tab .30

ITU, centenary.

Symbol of Cooperation and UN Emblem A123

1965, July 21 **Litho.** ***Perf. 14***

295 A123 36a gray, dp claret, bl, red & bis .25 .25

With tab .30

International Cooperation Year.

Dead Sea Extraction Plant — A124

1965, July 21

296 A124 12a Crane .25 .25

297 A124 50a shown .25 .25

#296-297, with tabs .60

Dead Sea chemical industry.

"Let There be Light . . ." — A125

Genesis 1, The Creation: 8a, Firmament and Waters. 12a, Dry land and vegetation. 25a, Heavenly lights. 35a, Fish and fowl. 70a, Man.

1965, Sept. 7 **Photo.** ***Perf. 13x14***

298 A125 6a dk pur, lil & gold .25 .25

299 A125 8a brt grn, dk bl & gold .25 .25

300 A125 12a red brn, blk & gold .25 .25

301 A125 25a dk pur, pink & gold .25 .25

302 A125 35a lt & dk bl & gold .25 .25

303 A125 70a dp cl, car & gold .25 .25

Nos. 298-303 (6) 1.50 1.50

With tabs 1.10

Jewish New Year, 5726. Sheets of 20 (10x2).

Charaxes Jasius — A126

Butterflies & Moths: 6a, Papilio alexanor maccabaeus. 8a, Daphnis nerii. 12a, Zegris eupheme uarda.

1965, Dec. 15 **Litho.** ***Perf. 14***

Butterflies in Natural Colors

304 A126 2a lt olive green .25 .25

305 A126 6a lilac .25 .25

306 A126 8a ocher .25 .25

307 A126 12a blue .25 .25

#304-307, with tabs .50

Flags over Rooftops — A127

Designs: 30a, Fireworks over Tel Aviv. 80a, Warships and Super Mirage jets, Haifa.

1966, Apr. 20 **Litho.** ***Perf. 14***

308 A127 12a multi .25 .25

309 A127 30a multi .25 .25

310 A127 80a multi .25 .25

#308-310, with tabs .40

Proclamation of state of Israel, 18th anniv.

Memorial, Upper Galilee — A128

1966, Apr. 20 **Photo.** ***Perf. 14x13***

311 A128 40a olive gray .25 .25

With tab .25

Issued for Memorial Day.

Knesset Building, Jerusalem — A129

1966, June 22 **Photo.** ***Perf. 13x14***

312 A129 £1 deep blue .25 .25

With tab .35

Inauguration of the Knesset Building (Parliament). Sheets of 12.

Road Sign and Motorcyclist — A130

Road Signs and: 5a, Bicyclist. 10a, Pedestrian. 12a, Child playing ball. 15a, Automobile.

1966, June 22 ***Perf. 14***

313 A130 2a sl, red brn & lil rose .25 .25

314 A130 5a ol bis, sl & lil rose .25 .25

315 A130 10a vio, lt bl & lil rose .25 .25

316 A130 12a bl, grn & lil rose .25 .25

317 A130 15a grn, red & lil rose .25 .25

#313-317, with tabs .25

Issued to publicize traffic safety.

Spice Box — A131

Ritual Art Objects: 15a, Candlesticks. 35a, Kiddush cup. 40a, Torah pointer. 80a, Hanging lamp.

1966, Aug. 24 **Photo.** ***Perf. 13x14***

318 A131 12a sil, gold, blk & bl .25 .25

319 A131 15a sil, gold, blk & lil .25 .25

320 A131 35a sil, gold, blk & emer .25 .25

321 A131 40a sil, gold, blk & vio bl .25 .25

322 A131 80a sil, gold, blk & red .25 .25

#318-322, with tabs .65

Jewish New Year, 5727.

Bronze Panther, Avdat, 1st Century, B.C. — A132

30a, Stone menorah, Tiberias, 2nd Cent. 40a, Phoenician ivory sphinx, 9th cent., B.C. 55a, Gold earring (calf's head), Ashdod, 6th-4th cents. B.C. 80a, Miniature gold capital, Persia, 5th cent., B.C. £1.15, Gold drinking horn (ram's head), Persia, 5th cent., B.C., vert.

1966, Oct. 26 **Litho.** ***Perf. 14***

323 A132 15a dp bl & yel brn .25 .25

324 A132 30a vio brn & bister .25 .25

325 A132 40a sepia & yel bis .30 .25

326 A132 55a Prus grn, dp yel & brown .30 .25

327 A132 80a lake, dp yel & brown .50 .25

Perf. 13x14

328 A132 £1.15 vio, gold & brn 1.00 .60

Nos. 323-328 (6) 2.60 1.85

With tabs 5.50

Israel Museum, Jerusalem. Sheets of 12.

Coach and Mailman of Austrian Levant — A133

Designs: 15a, Turkish mailman and caravan. 40a, Palestinian mailman and locomotive. £1, Israeli mailman and jet liner.

1966, Dec. 14 **Photo.** ***Perf. 14***

329 A133 12a ocher & green .25 .25

330 A133 15a lt grn, brn & dp car .25 .25

331 A133 40a brt rose & dk blue .25 .25

332 A133 £1 grnsh bl & brown .25 .25

Nos. 329-332 (4) 1.00 1.00

With tabs .65

Issued for Stamp Day.

Microscope and Cells — A134

1966, Dec. 14 ***Perf. 14x13***

333 A134 15a red & dark slate grn .25 .25

With tab .25

Campaign against cancer.

Arms Type of 1965-66

Town Emblems: 40a, Mizpe Ramon. 55a, Ashkelon. 80a, Rosh Pinna.

1967, Feb. 8 **Unwmk.** ***Perf. 13x14***

334 A119 40a dark olive .25 .25

335 A119 55a dk carmine rose .25 .25

336 A119 80a red brown .25 .25

Nos. 334-336 (3) .75 .75

With tabs 1.25

Port of Acre A135

Ancient Ports: 40a, Caesarea. 80a, Jaffa.

1967, Mar. 22 **Photo.** ***Perf. 13x14***

337 A135 15a purple brown .25 .25

338 A135 40a dark blue grn .25 .25

339 A135 80a deep blue .25 .25

Nos. 337-339 (3) .75 .75

With tabs .80

Page of Shulhan Aruk and Crowns — A136

1967, Mar. 22 ***Perf. 13½x13***

340 A136 40a dk & lt bl, gray & gold .25 .25

With tab .25

400th anniv. of the publication (in 1565) of the Shulhan Aruk, a compendium of Jewish religious and civil law, by Joseph Karo (1488-1575).

War of Independence Memorial — A137

1967, May 10 **Unwmk.** ***Perf. 13x14***

341 A137 55a lt bl, indigo & sil .25 .25

With tab .30

Issued for Memorial Day, 1967.

Auster Plane over Convoy on Jerusalem Road A138

Military Aircraft: 30a, Mystère IV jet fighter over Dead Sea area. 80a, Mirage jet fighters over Masada.

1967, May 10 **Photo.**

342 A138 15a lt ol grn & dk bl grn .25 .25

343 A138 30a ocher & dark brn .25 .25

344 A138 80a grnsh bl & vio bl .25 .25

Nos. 342-344 (3) .75 .75

With tabs .60

Issued for Independence Day, 1967.

Israeli Ships in Straits of Tiran A139

15a, Star of David, sword & olive branch, vert. 80a, Wailing (Western) Wall, Jerusalem.

1967, Aug. 16 ***Perf. 14x13, 13x14***

345 A139 15a dk red, blk & yel .25 .25
346 A139 40a Prussian green .25 .25
347 A139 80a deep violet .25 .25
#345-347, with tabs .25

Victory of the Israeli forces, June, 1967.

Torah, Scroll of the Law — A140

Various ancient, decorated Scrolls of the Law.

1967, Sept. 13 ***Perf. 13x14***

348 A140 12a gold & multi .25 .25
349 A140 15a silver & multi .25 .25
350 A140 35a gold & multi .25 .25
351 A140 40a silver & multi .25 .25
352 A140 80a gold & multi .25 .25
#348-352, with tabs .70

Jewish New Year, 5728. Sheets of 20 (10x2).

Chaim Weizmann A141

Design: 40a, Lord Balfour.

1967, Nov. 2 **Photo.** ***Perf. 13x14***

353 A141 15a dark green .25 .25
354 A141 40a brown .25 .25
#353-354, with tabs .25

50th anniv. of the Balfour Declaration, which established the right to a Jewish natl. home in Palestine. Issued in sheets of 15.

Emblem and Doll — A142

Inscriptions: 30a, Hebrew. 40a, French.

1967, Nov. 2 **Litho.** ***Perf. 14***

355 A142 30a yellow & multi .25 .25
356 A142 40a brt bl & multi .25 .25
357 A142 80a brt grn & multi .25 .25
#355-357, with tabs .40

Intl. Tourist Year. Issued in sheets of 15.

Nubian Ibex — A143

18a, Caracal lynx. 60a, Dorcas gazelles.

1967, Dec. 27 **Litho.** ***Perf. 13***
Animal in Ocher & Brown

358 A143 12a dull purple .25 .25
359 A143 18a bright green .25 .25
360 A143 60a bright blue .25 .25
#358-360, with tabs .40

Flags Forming Soccer Ball — A144

1968, Mar. 11 **Photo.** ***Perf. 13***

361 A144 80a ocher & multi .25 .25
With tab .25

Pre-Olympic soccer tournament.

Welcoming Immigrants — A145

Design: 80a, Happy farm family.

1968, Apr. 24 **Litho.** ***Perf. 14***

362 A145 15a lt green & multi .25 .25
363 A145 80a cream & multi .25 .25
#362-363, with tabs .25

Issued for Independence Day, 1968.

Resistance Fighter — A146

1968, Apr. 24 **Photo.** ***Perf. 14x13***

364 A146 60a brown olive .25 .25
With tab .25

Warsaw Ghetto Uprising, 25th anniv. Design from Warsaw Ghetto Memorial.

Sword and Laurel A147

Rifles and Helmet A148

1968, Apr. 24 **Litho.** ***Perf. 14***

365 A147 40a gold & multi .25 .25
366 A148 55a black & multi .25 .25
#365-366, with tabs .25

Zahal defense army, Independence Day (No. 365); Memorial Day (No. 366).

Candle and Prison Window — A149

1968, June 5 **Photo.** ***Perf. 14x13***

367 A149 80a blk, gray & sepia .25 .25
With tab .25

Issued to honor those who died for freedom.

Prime Minister Moshe Sharett (1894-1965) — A150

1968, June 5 **Unwmk.**

368 A150 £1 deep brown .25 .25
With tab .25

27th Zionist Congress.

Knot Forming Star of David — A151

1968, Aug. 21 **Litho.** ***Perf. 13***

369 A151 30a multi .25 .25
With tab .25

50 years of Jewish Scouting. Sheets of 15.

Dome of the Rock and Absalom's Tomb — A152

Views of Jerusalem: 15a, Church of the Resurrection. 35a, Tower of David and City Wall. 40a, Yemin Moshe District and Mount of Olives. 60a, Israel Museum and "Shrine of the Book."

1968, Aug. 21 **Photo.** ***Perf. 14x13***

370 A152 12a gold & multi .25 .25
371 A152 15a gold & multi .25 .25
372 A152 35a gold & multi .25 .25
373 A152 40a gold & multi .25 .25
374 A152 60a gold & multi .25 .25
#370-374, with tabs .40

Jewish New Year, 5729. Sheets of 15.

Detail from Lions' Gate, Jerusalem (St. Stephen's Gate) A153

1968, Oct. 8 **Unwmk.** ***Perf. 13x14***

375 A153 £1 brown org .25 .25
With tab .25
a. Souvenir sheet .35 .30

TABIRA Natl. Philatelic Exhibition. No. 375a contains one imperf. stamp. Sold only at exhibition for £1.50. No. 375 Issued in sheets of 15.

Abraham Mapu — A154

1968, Oct. 8 **Photo.** ***Perf. 14x13***

376 A154 30a dark olive grn .25 .25
With tab .25

Mapu (1808-1867), novelist and historian.

Wheelchair Basketball — A155

1968, Nov. 6 **Photo.** ***Perf. 14x13***

377 A155 40a green & yel grn .25 .25
With tab .25

17th Stoke-Mandeville Games for the Paralyzed, Nov. 4-13. Sheets of 15.

Port of Elat — A156

Ports of Israel: 60a, Ashdod. £1, Haifa.

1969, Feb. 19 **Unwmk.** ***Perf. 13x14***

378 A156 30a deep magenta .25 .25
379 A156 60a brown .25 .25
380 A156 £1 dull green .25 .25
Nos. 378-380 (3) .75 .75
With tabs 1.75

Tank A157

1969, Apr. 16 **Photo.** ***Perf. 13x14***

381 A157 15a shown .25 .25
382 A157 80a Destroyer .25 .25
#381-382, with tabs .40

Issued for Independence Day 1969.

Israel's Flag at Half-mast — A158

1969, Apr. 16

383 A158 55a vio, gold & bl .25 .25
With tab .25

Issued for Memorial Day.

Worker and ILO Emblem A159

1969, Apr. 16

384 A159 80a dark blue grn .25 .25
With tab .25

ILO, 50th anniversary.

Hand Holding Torch — A160

1969, July 9 Photo. *Perf. 14x13*

385 A160 60a gold & multi .25 .25
With tab .40

Issued to publicize the 8th Maccabiah.

Arms of Hadera — A161

Town Emblems: 3a, Hertseliya. 5a, Holon. 15a, Bat Yam. 18a, Ramla. 20a, Kefar Sava. 25a, Giv'atayim. 30a, Rehovot. 40a, Netanya. 50a, Bene Beraq. 60a, Nahariyya. 80a, Ramat Gan.

1969-73 *Perf. 13x14*

386 A161 2a green .25 .25
387 A161 3a deep magenta .25 .25
388 A161 5a orange .25 .25
389 A161 15a bright rose .25 .25
c. Bklt. pane of 6 (2 #389 + 4 #389A) ('71) .65
389A A161 18a ultra ('70) .25 .25
d. Bklt. pane of 6 ('71) .70
e. Bklt. pane of 6 (1 #281 + 5 #389A) ('73) .65
389B A161 20a brown ('70) .25 .25
f. Bklt. pane of 5 + label ('73) .90
390 A161 25a dark blue .25 .25
390A A161 30a brt pink ('70) .25 .25
391 A161 40a purple .25 .25
392 A161 50a greenish bl .25 .25
392A A161 60a olive ('70) .25 .25
393 A161 80a dark green .25 .25
Nos. 386-393 (12) 3.00 3.00
With tabs 3.00

Nos. 389c and 389d were also sold in uncut sheets of 36, No. 389e in uncut sheet of 18. See note after No. 291 about similar sheets.

Noah Building the Ark — A162

The Story of the Flood: 15a, Animals boarding the Ark. 35a, The Ark during the flood. 40a, Noah sending out the dove. 60a, Noah and the rainbow.

1969, Aug. 13 Unwmk. *Perf. 14*

394 A162 12a multicolored .25 .25
395 A162 15a multicolored .25 .25
396 A162 35a multicolored .25 .25
397 A162 40a multicolored .25 .25
398 A162 60a multicolored .25 .25
#394-398, with tabs .70

Jewish New Year, 5730. Sheets of 15.

King David by Marc Chagall A163

1969, Sept. 24 Photo. *Perf. 14*

399 A163 £3 multicolored .65 .55
With tab 1.00

Atom Diagram and Test Tube — A164

1969, Nov. 3 *Perf. 14x13*

400 A164 £1.15 vio bl & multi .55 .40
With tab 1.25

Weizmann Institute of Science, 25th anniv.

Joseph Trumpeldor — A165

1970, Jan. 21 Photo. *Perf. 14x13*

401 A165 £1 dark purple .25 .25
With tab .60

50th anniv. of the defense of Tel Hay under the leadership of Joseph Trumpeldor.

Dum Palms, Emeq Ha-Arava — A166

Views: 3a, Tahana Waterfall. 5a, Nahal Baraq Canyon, Negev. 6a, Cedars in Judean Hills. 30a, Soreq Cave, Judean Hills.

1970, Jan. 21

402 A166 2a olive .25 .25
403 A166 3a deep blue .25 .25
404 A166 5a orange red .25 .25
405 A166 6a slate green .25 .25
406 A166 30a brt purple .25 .25
#402-406, with tabs .35

Issued to publicize nature reserves.

Magic Carpet Shaped as Airplane — A167

1970, Jan. 21 Litho. *Perf. 13*

407 A167 30a multicolored .25 .25
With tab .25

20th anniv. of "Operation Magic Carpet" which airlifted the Yemeni Jews to Israel.

Prime Minister Levi Eshkol (1895-1969) — A168

1970, Mar. 11 Litho. *Perf. 14*

408 A168 15a bl & multi .25 .25
With tab .25

Mania Shochat — A169

Portrait: 80a, Ze'ev Jabotinsky (1880-1940), writer and Zionist leader.

1970, Mar. 11 Photo. *Perf. 14x13*

409 A169 40a dp plum & buff .25 .25
410 A169 80a green & cream .25 .25
#409-410, with tabs .90

Ha-Shomer (Watchmen defense organization), 60th anniv. (No. 409); defense of Jerusalem, 50th anniv. (No. 410)

Camel and Train — A170

1970, Mar. 11 Litho. *Perf. 13*

411 A170 80a orange & multi .40 .25
With tab .50

Opening of Dimona-Oron Railroad.

Scene from "The Dibbuk" — A171

1970, Mar. 11 Photo. *Perf. 14x13*

412 A171 £1 multicolored .25 .25
With tab .50

Habimah Natl. Theater, 50th anniv.

Memorial Flame — A172

1970, May 6 Photo. *Perf. 13x14*

413 A172 55a vio, pink & blk .25 .25
With tab .25

Issued for Memorial Day, 1970.

Orchis Laxiflorus — A173

Flowers: 15a, Iris mariae. 80a, Lupinus pilosus.

1970, May 6 Litho. *Perf. 14*

414 A173 12a pale gray, plum & grn .25 .25
415 A173 15a multicolored .25 .25
416 A173 80a pale bl & multi .25 .25
Nos. 414-416 (3) .75 .75
With tabs .80

Issued for Independence Day, 1970.

Charles Netter — A174

80a, Agricultural College (Mikwe Israel) & garden.

1970, May 6 Photo. *Perf. 14x13*

417 A174 40a lt grn, dk brn & gold .25 .25
418 A174 80a gold & multi .25 .25
With tabs .80

Centenary of first agricultural college in Israel; its founder, Charles Netter.

420 Class Yachts — A175

Designs: Various 420 Class yachts.

1970, July 8 Photo. *Perf. 14x13*

419 A175 15a grnsh bl, blk & sil .25 .25
420 A175 30a ol, red, blk & sil .25 .25
421 A175 80a ultra, blk & silver .25 .25
Nos. 419-421 (3) .75 .75
With tabs .90

World "420" Class Sailing Championships.

Hebrew Letters Shaped Like Ship and Buildings A176

1970, July 8 *Perf. 13x14*

422 A176 40a gold & multi .25 .25
With tab .25

Keren Hayesod, a Zionist Fund to maintain schools and hospitals in Palestine, 50th anniv.

Arava Plane A177

1970, July 8

423 A177 £1 brt blue, blk & sil .25 .25
With tab .30

First Israeli designed and built aircraft.

Bird (Exiles) and Sun (Israel) A178

1970, Sept. 7 Litho. *Perf. 14*

424 A178 80a yel & multi .25 .25
With tab .25

"Operation Ezra and Nehemiah," the exodus of Iraqi Jews.

Old Synagogue, Cracow — A179

Historic Synagogues: 15a, Great Synagogue, Tunis. 35a, Portuguese Synagogue, Amsterdam. 40a, Great Synagogue, Moscow. 60a, Shearith Israel Synagogue, New York.

Perf. 14, 13 (15a)

1970, Sept. 7 **Photo.**

425	A179	12a gold & multi	.25	.25
426	A179	15a gold & multi	.25	.25
427	A179	35a gold & multi	.25	.25
428	A179	40a gold & multi	.25	.25
429	A179	60a gold & multi	.25	.25
		#425-429, with tabs	.40	

Jewish New Year, 5731.

Tel Aviv Post Office, 1920 — A180

1970, Oct. 18 **Photo.** ***Perf. 14***

430	A180	£1 multicolored	.25	.25
		With tab	.25	
a.		Souvenir sheet	1.50	1.50

TABIT Natl. Stamp Exhibition, Tel Aviv, Oct. 18-29. No. 430a contains an imperf. stamp similar to No. 430. Sold for £1.50.

Mother and Child A181

1970, Oct. 18 ***Perf. 13x14***

431	A181	80a dp grn, yel & gray	.25	.25
		With tab	.30	

WIZO, Women's Intl. Zionist Org., 50th anniv.

Paris Quai, by Camille Pissarro — A182

Paintings from Tel Aviv Museum: 85a, The Jewish Wedding, by Josef Israels. £2, Flowers in a Vase, by Fernand Leger.

1970, Dec. 22 **Litho.** ***Perf. 14***

432	A182	85a black & multi	.25	.25
433	A182	£1 black & multi	.25	.25
434	A182	£2 black & multi	.25	.25
		Nos. 432-434 (3)	.75	.75
		With tabs	1.40	

Hammer and Menorah Emblem — A183

1970, Dec. 22

435	A183	35a gold & multi	.25	.25
		With tab	.25	

General Federation of Labor in Israel (Histadrut), 50th anniversary.

Persian Fallow Deer — A184

Animals of the Bible: 3a, Asiatic wild ass. 5a, White oryx. 78a, Cheetah.

1971, Feb. 16 **Litho.** ***Perf. 13***

436	A184	2a multicolored	.25	.25
437	A184	3a multicolored	.25	.25
438	A184	5a multicolored	.25	.25
439	A184	78a multicolored	.25	.25
		#436-439, with tabs	.45	

"Samson and Dalila," Israel National Opera — A185

Theater Art in Israel: No. 441, Inn of the Ghosts, Cameri Theater. No. 442, A Psalm of David, Inbal Dance Theater.

1971, Feb. 16 ***Perf. 14x13***

440	A185	50a bister & multi	.25	.25
441	A185	50a lt grn & multi	.25	.25
442	A185	50a blue & multi	.25	.25
		Nos. 440-442 (3)	.75	.75
		With tabs	.50	

Basketball — A186

No. 444, Runner. No. 445, Athlete on rings.

1971, Apr. 13 **Litho.** ***Perf. 14***

443	A186	50a green & multi	.25	.25
444	A186	50a ocher & multi	.25	.25
445	A186	50a lt vio & multi	.25	.25
		#443-445, with tabs	.45	

9th Hapoel Games.

Defense Forces Emblem — A187

1971, Apr. 13 **Photo.** ***Perf. 14x13***

446	A187	78a multicolored	.25	.25
		With tab	.25	

Memorial Day, 1971, and the war dead.

Jaffa Gate, Jerusalem — A188

Gates of Jerusalem: 18c, New Gate. 35c, Damascus Gate. 85c, Herod's Gate.

1971, Apr. 13 ***Perf. 14***

Size: 41x41mm

447	A188	15a gold & multi	.25	.25
448	A188	18a gold & multi	.25	.25
449	A188	35a gold & multi	.25	.25
450	A188	85a gold & multi	.60	.40
a.		Souvenir sheet of 4	2.75	2.75
		Nos. 447-450 (4)	1.35	1.15
		With tabs	1.75	

Independence Day, 1971. No. 450a contains 4 stamps similar to Nos. 447-450, but smaller (27x27mm). Sold at the Jerusalem Exhibition for £2.

See Nos. 488-491.

"He Wrote . . . Words of the Covenant" — A189

85a, "First Fruits . . ." Exodus 23:19. £1.50, ". . . Feast of Weeks" Exodus 34:22. The quotation on 50a is from Exodus 34:28. The quotations are in English on the tabs.

1971, May 25 **Photo.** ***Perf. 14x13***

451	A189	50a yellow & multi	.25	.25
452	A189	85a yellow & multi	.25	.25
453	A189	£1.50 yellow & multi	.25	.25
		Nos. 451-453 (3)	.75	.75
		With tabs	1.35	

For the Feast of Weeks (Shabuoth).

"You shall rejoice in your feast" — A190

Designs: 18a, "You shall dwell in booths for seven days . . ." Leviticus 23:42. 20a, "That I made the people of Israel dwell in booths . . ." Lev. 23:43. 40a, ". . . when you have gathered in the produce of the land" Lev. 23:39. 65a, ". . . then I will give you your rains in their season" Lev. 26:4. The quotation on 15a is from Deuteronomy 16:14. The quotations are in English on tabs.

1971, Aug. 24 **Photo.** ***Perf. 14x13***

454	A190	15a yellow & multi	.25	.25
455	A190	18a yellow & multi	.25	.25
456	A190	20a yellow & multi	.25	.25
457	A190	40a yellow & multi	.25	.25
458	A190	65a yellow & multi	.25	.25
		#454-458, with tabs	.60	

For the Feast of Tabernacles (Sukkoth).

Sun Shining on Fields A191

1971, Aug. 24 ***Perf. 14***

459	A191	40a gold & multi	.25	.25
		With tab	.25	

1st cooperative settlement in Israel, at Emeq (Valley of Israel), 50th anniv.

Retort and Grain — A192

1971, Oct. 25 **Litho.** ***Perf. 14***

460	A192	£1 green & multi	.25	.25
		With tab	.25	

50th anniversary of Volcani Institute of Agricultural Research.

Tagging

Starting in 1975, vertical luminescent bands were overprinted on various regular and commemorative stamps.

In the 1971-75 regular series, values issued both untagged and tagged are: 20a, 25a, 30a, 35a, 45a, 50a, 65a, £1.10, £1.30, £2 and £3. Also No. 290 was re-issued with tagging in 1975.

Regular issues from 1975 onward, including the £1.70, are tagged unless otherwise noted.

Tagged commemoratives include Nos. 562-563 and all from Nos. 567-569 onward unless otherwise noted.

Negev — A193

Landscapes: 3a, Judean desert. 5a, Gan Ha-Shelosha. 18a, Kinneret. 20a, Tel Dan. 22a, Fishermen, Yafo. 25a, Arava. 30a, En Avedat. 35a, Brekhat Ram, Golan Heights. 45a, Grazing sheep, Mt. Hermon. 50a, Rosh Pinna. 55a, Beach and park, Netanya. 65a, Plain of Zebulun. 70a, Shore, Engedi. 80a, Beach at Elat. 88a, Boats in Akko harbor. 95a, Hamifratz Hane'elam. £1.10, Aqueduct near Akko. £1.30, Zefat. £1.70, Upper Nazareth. £2, Coral Island. £3, Haifa.

1971-75 **Photo.** ***Perf. 13x14***

461	A193	3a deep blue	.25	.25
462	A193	5a green	.25	.25
463	A193	15a deep org	.25	.25
464	A193	18a bright mag	.65	.25
464A	A193	20a dark green	.25	.25
465	A193	22a brt blue	1.25	.25
465A	A193	25a orange red	.25	.25
466	A193	30a brt rose	.25	.25
466A	A193	35a plum	.25	.25
467	A193	45a dull vio blue	.25	.25
468	A193	50a green	.25	.25
469	A193	55a olive	.25	.25
469A	A193	65a black	.25	.25
470	A193	70a deep car	.25	.25
470A	A193	80a deep ultra	.25	.25
471	A193	88a greenish blue	1.25	.25
472	A193	95a org ver	.80	.25
472A	A193	£1.10 olive	.25	.25
472B	A193	£1.30 deep blue	.25	.25
472C	A193	£1.70 dark brown	.40	.25
473	A193	£2 brown	.40	.25
474	A193	£3 deep violet	.55	.25
		Nos. 461-474 (22)	9.05	5.50
		With tabs	11.00	

Issued: 15a, 18a, 50a, 88a, 10/25; 22a, 55a, 70a, 1/4/72; 3a, 5a, 30a, £3, 11/7/72; 45a, 95a, £2, 1/16/73; 20a, 65a, 10/23/73; 35a, £1.10, 12/20/73; 25a, 80a, £1.30, 11/5/74; £1.70, 6/17/75.

See No. 592.

"Get Wisdom" Proverbs 4:7 — A194

Abstract Designs: 18a, Mathematical and scientific formula. 20a, Tools and engineering symbols. 40a, Abbreviations of various college degrees.

1972, Jan. 4 **Litho.** ***Perf. 14***

475	A194	15a brt grn & multi	.25	.25
476	A194	18a multicolored	.25	.25
477	A194	20a multicolored	.25	.25
478	A194	40a red, blk & gold	.25	.25
		#475-478, with tabs	.30	

The Scribe, Sculpture by Boris Schatz
A195

Works by Israeli Artists: 55a, Young Girl (Sarah), by Abel Pann. 70a, Zefat (landscape), by Menahem Shemi, horiz. 85a, Old Jerusalem, by Jacob Steinhardt. £1, Resurrection (abstract), by Aharon Kahana.

Perf. 13x14 (40a, 85a), 14

1972, Mar. 7

No.	Type	Denom.	Color	Unused	Used
479	A195	40a	black & tan	.25	.25
480	A195	55a	red brn & multi	.25	.25
481	A195	70a	lt grn & multi	.25	.25
482	A195	85a	blk & yellow	.25	.25
483	A195	£1	blk & multi	.25	.25
			Nos. 479-483 (5)	1.25	1.25
			With tabs	1.00	

Exodus — A196

Passover: 45a, Baking unleavened bread. 95a, Seder.

1972, Mar. 7 Litho. *Perf. 13*

No.	Type	Denom.	Color	Unused	Used
484	A196	18a	buff & multi	.25	.25
485	A196	45a	buff & multi	.25	.25
486	A196	95a	buff & multi	.25	.25
			Nos. 484-486 (3)	.75	.75
			With tabs	1.10	

"Let My People Go" — A197

1972, Mar. 7 *Perf. 14*

No.	Type	Denom.	Color	Unused	Used
487	A197	55a	blk, bl & yel grn	.40	.30
			With tab	2.00	

No. 487 inscribed in Hebrew, Arabic, Russian and English.

Gate Type of 1971

Gates of Jerusalem: 15a, Lions' Gate. 18a, Golden Gate. 45a, Dung Gate. 55a, Zion Gate.

1972, Apr. 17 Photo. *Perf. 14*

Size: 40x40mm

No.	Type	Denom.	Color	Unused	Used
488	A188	15a	gold & multi	.25	.25
489	A188	18a	gold & multi	.25	.25
490	A188	45a	gold & multi	.25	.25
491	A188	55a	gold & multi	.25	.25
a.			Souvenir sheet of 4	2.50	2.50
			Nos. 488-491 (4)	1.00	1.00
			With tabs	1.75	

Independence Day. No. 491a contains 4 27x27mm stamps similar to Nos. 488-491. Sold for £2.

Jethro's Tomb — A198

1972, Apr. 17 Litho. *Perf. 13*

No.	Type	Denom.	Color	Unused	Used
492	A198	55a	multicolored	.25	.25
			With tab	.25	

Memorial Day — A199

1972, Apr. 17 *Perf. 14*

No.	Type	Denom.	Color	Unused	Used
493	A199	55a	Flowers	.25	.25
			With tab	.25	

Hebrew Words Emerging from Opened Ghetto — A200

1972, June 6 *Perf. 13*

No.	Type	Denom.	Color	Unused	Used
494	A200	70a	blue & multi	.35	.30
			With tab	1.50	

Rabbi Isaac ben Solomon Ashkenazi Luria ("Ari") (1534-72), Palestinian cabalist.

International Book Year — A201

1972, June 6 *Perf. 14x13*

No.	Type	Denom.	Color	Unused	Used
495	A201	95a	Printed page	.25	.25
			With tab	.30	

Satellite Earth Station, Satellite and Rainbow — A202

1972, June 6 *Perf. 13*

No.	Type	Denom.	Color	Unused	Used
496	A202	£1	tan & multi	.25	.25
			With tab	.30	

Opening of satellite earth station in Israel.

17th Cent. Ark, Ancona — A203

Holy Arks from: 45a, Padua, 1729. 70a, Parma, 17th century. 95a, Reggio Emilia, 1756. Arks moved to Israel from Italian synagogues.

1972, Aug. 8 Photo. *Perf. 14x13*

No.	Type	Denom.	Color	Unused	Used
497	A203	15a	deep brn & yel	.25	.25
498	A203	45a	dp grn, yel grn & gold	.25	.25
499	A203	70a	brn red, yel & bl	.25	.25
500	A203	95a	magenta & gold	.25	.25
			Nos. 497-500 (4)	1.00	1.00
			With tabs	1.00	

Jewish New Year, 5733.

Menorah and "25" — A204

1972, Aug. 8

No.	Type	Denom.	Color	Unused	Used
501	A204	£1	silver, bl & mag	.25	.25
			With tab	.25	

25th anniversary of the State of Israel.

Brass Menorah, Morocco, 18th-19th Century
A205

Menorahs: 25a, Brass, Poland, 18th century. 70a, Silver, Germany, 17th century.

1972, Nov. 7 Litho. *Perf. 14x13*

No.	Type	Denom.	Color	Unused	Used
502	A205	12a	emer, blk & bl grn	.25	.25
503	A205	25a	lil rose, blk & org	.25	.25
504	A205	70a	blue, blk & vio	.25	.25
			#502-504, with tabs	.50	

Hanukkah (Festival of Lights), 1972.

Child's Drawing — A206

Designs: Children's drawings.

Sizes: 22½x37mm (2a, 55a); 17x48mm (3a)

1973, Jan. 16 Litho. *Perf. 14*

No.	Type	Denom.	Color	Unused	Used
505	A206	2a	blk & multi	.25	.25
506	A206	3a	multicolored	.25	.25
507	A206	55a	multicolored	.25	.25
			#505-507, with tabs	.30	

Youth Wing of Israel Museum, Jerusalem (2a, 3a) and Youth Workshops, Tel Aviv Museum (55a).

Pendant — A207

1973, Jan. 16 Photo. *Perf. 14x13*

No.	Type	Denom.	Color	Unused	Used
508	A207	18a	silver & multi	.25	.25
			With tab	.25	

Immigration of North African Jews.

Levi, by Marc Chagall
A208

Tribes of Israel: No. 510, Simeon. No. 511, Reuben. No. 512, Issachar. No. 513, Zebulun. No. 514, Judah. No. 515, Dan. No. 516, Gad. No. 517, Asher. No. 518, Naphtali. No. 519, Joseph. No. 520, Benjamin.

1973 Litho. *Perf. 14*

No.	Type	Denom.	Color	Unused	Used
509	A208	£1	multicolored	.35	.35
510	A208	£1	gray grn & multi	.35	.35
511	A208	£1	olive & multi	.35	.35
512	A208	£1	gray bl & multi	.35	.35
513	A208	£1	lemon & multi	.35	.35
514	A208	£1	gray & multi	.35	.35
515	A208	£1	bl grn & multi	.35	.35
516	A208	£1	gray & multi	.35	.35
517	A208	£1	yel grn & multi	.35	.35
518	A208	£1	sepia & multi	.35	.35
519	A208	£1	olive & multi	.35	.35
520	A208	£1	tan & multi	.35	.35
			Nos. 509-520 (12)	4.20	4.20
			With tabs	7.00	

Designs from stained glass windows by Marc Chagall, Hadassah-Hebrew University Medical Center Synagogue, Jerusalem.

Issued: Nos. 509-514, 3/26; Nos. 515-520, 8/21.

Israel's Declaration of Independence — A209

1973, May 3 Photo. *Perf. 14*

No.	Type	Denom.	Color	Unused	Used
521	A209	£1	ocher & multi	.25	.25
			With tab	.25	
a.			Souvenir sheet	.60	.60

25 years of Independence. No. 521a sold for £1.50.

Star of David and Runners
A210

1973, May 3 Litho.

No.	Type	Denom.	Color	Unused	Used
522	A210	£1.10	multicolored	.25	.25
			With tab	.25	

9th Maccabiah.

Prison-cloth Hand — A211

1973, May 3 Photo.

No.	Type	Denom.	Color	Unused	Used
523	A211	55a	blue black	.25	.25
			With tab	.25	

Heroes and martyrs of the Holocaust, 1933-1945.

Flame — A212

1973, May 3 Litho.

No.	Type	Denom.	Color	Unused	Used
524	A212	65a	multicolored	.25	.25
			With tab	.25	

Memorial Day.

Prophets — A213

1973, Aug. 21 Photo. *Perf. 13x14*

525 A213	18a Isaiah	.25	.25
526 A213	65a Jeremiah	.25	.25
527 A213	£1.10 Ezekiel	.25	.25
	#525-527, with tabs	.25	

Jewish New Year, 5734.

Torch of Learning, Cogwheel — A214

1973, Oct. 23 *Perf. 14x13*

528 A214 £1.25 slate & multi .25 .25
With tab .25

50th anniversary of the Technion, Israel Institute of Technology.

Rescue Boat and Danish Flag — A215

1973, Oct. 23 *Perf. 13x14*

529 A215 £5 bister, red & blk .30 .25
With tab .50

30th anniversary of the rescue by the Danes of the Jews in Denmark.

Spectators at Stamp Show — A216

Design: £1, Spectators, different design.

1973, Dec. 20 Litho. *Perf. 13*

530 A216	20a brown & multi	.25	.25
531 A216	£1 brown & multi	.25	.25
	#530-531, with tabs	.25	

JERUSALEM '73 Philatelic Exhibition, Mar. 25-Apr. 2, 1974.

Souvenir Sheets

Israel No. 7 — A217

Designs: £2, No. 8. £3, No. 9.

1974, Mar. 25 Photo. *Perf. 14x13*

532 A217	£1 silver & dk slate grn	.25	.25
533 A217	£2 silver & red brn	.25	.25
534 A217	£3 silver & blk blue	.25	.25
	Nos. 532-534 (3)	.75	.75

Jerusalem '73 Philatelic Exhibition, Mar. 25-Apr. 2, 1974 (postponed from Dec. 1973), 25th anniv. of State of Israel. Each sheet was sold with a 50 per cent surcharge.

Soldier with Prayer Shawl — A218

1974, Apr. 23 *Perf. 13x14*

535 A218 £1 blk & light bl .25 .25
With tab .25

Memorial Day.

Quill and Inkwell with Hebrew Letters — A219

1974, Apr. 23 *Perf. 14x13*

536 A219 £2 gold & black .25 .25
With tab .25

50th anniversary of Hebrew Writers Assn.

Lady in Blue, by Moshe Kisling A220

Designs: £2, Mother and Child, Sculpture by Chana Orloff. £3, Girl in Blue, by Chaim Soutine.

1974, June 11 Litho. *Perf. 14*

537 A220	£1.25 multicolored	.25	.25
538 A220	£2 multicolored	.25	.25
539 A220	£3 multicolored	.25	.25
	#537-539, with tabs	.90	

Art works from Tel Aviv, En Harod and Jerusalem Museums.

Wrench A221

1974, June 11

540 A221 25a multicolored .25 .25
With tab .25

50th anniv. of Working Youth Movement.

Istanbuli Synagogue, Jerusalem — A222

Designs: Interiors of restored synagogues in Jerusalem's Old City: 70a, Emtzai Synagogue. £1, Rabbi Yohanan Synagogue.

1974, Aug. 6 Photo. *Perf. 13x14*

541 A222	25a shown	.25	.25
542 A222	70a multicolored	.25	.25
543 A222	£1 multicolored	.25	.25
	#541-543, with tabs	.25	

Jewish New Year, 5735.

Lady Davis Technical Center "AMAL," Tel Aviv — A223

60a, Elias Sourasky Library, Tel Aviv University. £1.45, Mivtahim Rest Home, Zikhron Yaaqov.

1974, Aug. 6 *Perf. 13½x14*

544 A223	25a violet black	.25	.25
545 A223	60a dark blue	.25	.25
546 A223	£1.45 maroon	.25	.25
	#544-546, with tabs	.25	

Modern Israeli architecture.

David Ben-Gurion — A224

1974, Nov. 5 *Perf. 14*

547 A224	25a brown	.25	.25
548 A224	£1.30 slate green	.25	.25
	#547-549, with tabs	.25	

David Ben-Gurion (1886-1973), first Prime Minister and Minister of Defense of Israel.

Arrows on Globe — A225

Dove Delivering Letter — A226

1974, Nov. 5 Litho. *Perf. 14*

549 A225 25a black & multi .25 .25

Photo.

550 A226 £1.30 gold & multi .25 .25
#549-550, with tabs .25

Centenary of Universal Postal Union.

Hebrew University, Mount Scopus, Jerusalem — A227

1975, Jan. 14 Litho. *Perf. 13*

551 A227 £2.50 multicolored .25 .25
With tab .25

Hebrew University, 50th anniv.

Girl Carrying Plant — A228

Arbor Day: 35a, Bird singing in tree. £2, Boy carrying potted plant.

1975, Jan. 14 *Perf. 14*

552 A228	1a multicolored	.25	.25
553 A228	35a multicolored	.25	.25
554 A228	£2 multicolored	.25	.25
	#552-554, with tabs	.25	

Welder — A229

80a, Tractor driver. £1.20, Electrical lineman.

1975, Jan. 14 Photo. *Perf. 14x13*

555 A229	30a multicolored	.25	.25
556 A229	80a multicolored	.25	.25
557 A229	£1.20 ultra & multi	.25	.25
	#555-557, with tabs	.25	

Occupational safety and publicity for the Institute for Safety and Hygiene.

Hebrew University Synagogue, Jerusalem — A230

Modern Israeli architecture: £1.30, Yad Mordecai Museum. £1.70, Bat Yam City Hall.

Perf. 14, 13½x14 (#559)

1975, Mar. 4 Photo.

558 A230	80a brown	.25	.25
559 A230	£1.30 slate green	.25	.25
560 A230	£1.70 brown olive	.25	.25
	#558-560, with tabs	.35	

US President Harry S Truman (1884-1972) — A231

1975, Mar. 4 Engr. *Perf. 14*

561 A231 £5 dark brown .25 .25
With tab .30

Eternal Flame over Soldier's Grave — A232

1975, Apr. 10 Photo. *Perf. 14x13*

562 A232 £1.45 black & multi .25 .25
With tab .25

Memorial Day.

Memorial Tablet — A233

1975, Apr. 10

563 A233 £1.45 blk, red & gray .25 .25
With tab .25

In memory of soldiers missing in action.

Hurdling A234

1975, Apr. 10 *Perf. 13x14*

564 A234 25a shown .25 .25
565 A234 £1.70 Bicycling .25 .25
566 A234 £3 Volleyball .25 .25
#564-566, with tabs .35

10th Hapoel Games; 50th anniv. of Hapoel Org.

Yom Kippur, by Maurycy Gottlieb A235

Paintings of religious holidays: £1.00 Hanukkah, by Mortiz D. Oppenheim. 1.40, The Purim Players, by Jankel Adler, horiz.

1975, June 17 Litho. *Perf. 14*

567 A235 £1 multicolored .25 .25
568 A235 £1.40 multicolored .25 .25
569 A235 £4 multicolored .25 .25
#567-569, with tabs .50

Old Couple A236

1975, June 17 Photo. *Perf. 13x14*

570 A236 £1.85 multicolored .25 .25
With tab .25

International Gerontological Association, 10th triennial conference, Jerusalem.

Pres. Zalman Shazar (1889-1974) — A237

1975, Aug. 5 Photo. *Perf. 14x13*

571 A237 35a silver & blk .25 .25
With tab .25

Pioneer Women, 50th Anniv. — A238

1975, Aug. 5 *Perf. 14½*

572 A238 £5 Emblem .30 .25
With tab .35

Judges of Israel — A239

1975, Aug. 5 *Perf. 13x14*

573 A239 35a Gideon .25 .25
574 A239 £1 Deborah .25 .25
575 A239 £1.40 Jephthah .25 .25
#573-575, with tabs .35

Jewish New Year, 5736.

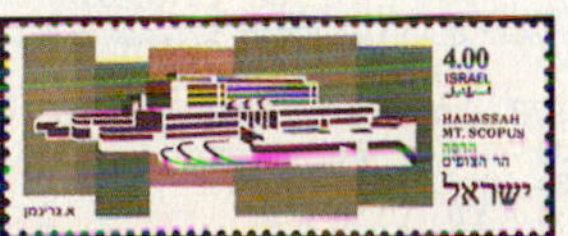

Hebrew University, Mt. Scopus — A240

1975, Oct. 14 Photo. *Perf. 14x13*

576 A240 £4 multicolored .25 .25
With tab .25

Return of Hadassah to Mt. Scopus, Jerusalem.

Collared Pratincoles A241

Protected Birds: £1.70, Spur-winged plover. £2, Black-winged stilts.

1975, Oct. 14 Litho. *Perf. 13*

577 A241 £1.10 pink & multi .25 .25
578 A241 £1.70 lemon & multi .25 .25
579 A241 £2 multicolored .25 .25
#577-579, with tabs .40

Butterfly and Factory (Air Pollution) — A242

Designs: 80a, Fish and tanker (water pollution). £1.70, Ear and jet (noise pollution).

1975, Dec. 9 Photo. *Perf. 14*

580 A242 50a car & multi .25 .25
581 A242 80a green & multi .25 .25
582 A242 £1.70 orange & multi .25 .25
With tabs .40

Environmental protection.

Star of David — A243

1975-80 *Perf. 13x14*

583 A243 75a vio bl & car .25 .25
584 A243 £1.80 violet bl & gray .25 .25
585 A243 £1.85 vio bl & lt brn .25 .25
586 A243 £2.45 vio bl & brt green .25 .25
587 A243 £2.70 vio bl & purple .25 .25
588 A243 £4.30 ultra & red .25 .25
589 A243 £5.40 vio bl & ol .25 .25
590 A243 £8 vio bl & bl .25 .25
Nos. 583-590 (8) 2.00 2.00
With tabs 2.50

Issued: £1.85, 12/9; £2.45, 6/22/76; 75a, 12/77; £5.40, 5/23/78; £1.80, £8, 5/22/79; £2.70, 12/25/79; £4.30, 5/26/80.

Landscape Type of 1971-75

Design: £10, View of Elat and harbor.

1976, Aug. 17 Photo. *Perf. 14x14½*

592 A193 £10 Prussian blue .50 .25
With tab 1.00

No. 592 issued both tagged and untagged.

"In the days of Ahasuerus." — A247

Designs (from Book of Esther): 80a, "He set the royal crown on her head." £1.60, "Thus shall it be done to the man whom the king delights to honor."

1976, Feb. 17 Photo. *Perf. 14*

593 A247 40a multicolored .25 .25
594 A247 80a multicolored .25 .25
595 A247 £1.60 multicolored .25 .25
a. Souv. sheet of 3, #593-595, perf 13x14 .35 .35
#593-595, with tabs .30

Purim Festival. No. 595a sold for £4.

Border Settlement, Barbed Wire — A248

1976, Feb. 17

596 A248 £1.50 olive & multi .25 .25
With tab .25

Border settlements, part of Jewish colonization of Holy Land.

Symbolic Key — A249

1976, Feb. 17

597 A249 £1.85 multicolored .25 .25
With tab .25

Bezalel Academy of Arts and Design, Jerusalem, 70th anniv.

"200" US Flag A250

1976, Apr. 25 Photo. *Perf. 13x14*

598 A250 £4 gold & multi .25 .25
With tab .30

American Bicentennial.

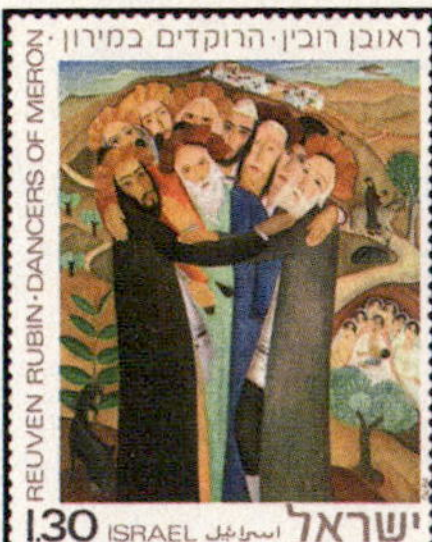

Dancers of Meron, by Reuven Rubin A251

1976, Apr. 25 Litho. *Perf. 14*

599 A251 £1.30 multicolored .25 .25
With tab .25

Lag Ba-Omer festival.

8th Brigade Monument, Ben-Gurion Airport — A252

1976, Apr. 25 Photo. *Perf. 14x13*

600 A252 £1.85 multicolored .25 .25
With tab .25

Memorial Day.

Souvenir Sheet

Tourism, Sport and Industry — A253

1976, Apr. 25

601 A253 Sheet of 3 .50 .50
a. £1 multicolored .25 .25
b. £2 multicolored .25 .25
c. £4 multicolored .25 .25

No. 601 sold for £10.

High Jump A254

1976, June 22 *Perf. 13x14*

602 A254 £1.60 shown .25 .25
603 A254 £2.40 Diving .25 .25
604 A254 £4.40 Gymnastics .25 .25
#602-604, with tabs .50

21st Olympic Games, Montreal, Canada, July 17-Aug. 1.

Tents and Suns — A255

1976, June 22 ***Perf. 14***
605 A255 £1.50 green & multi .25 .25
With tab .25

Israel Camping Union.

"Truth" — A256

Design: £1.50, "Judgment" (scales). £1.90, "Peace" (dove and olive branch).

1976, Aug. 17 Photo. ***Perf. 14x13***
Tagged
606 A256 45a gold & multi .25 .25
607 A256 £1.50 gold & multi .25 .25
608 A256 £1.90 gold & multi .25 .25
#606-608, with tabs .30

Festivals 5737.

Pawn — A257

1976, Oct. 19 Litho. ***Perf. 14***
609 A257 £1.30 shown .25 .25
610 A257 £1.60 Rook .25 .25
#609-610, with tabs .35

22nd Men's and 7th Women's Chess Olympiad, Haifa, Oct. 24-Nov. 11.

Byzantine Building, 6th Century A258

70a, City wall, 7th cent. B.C. £2.40, Robinson's Arch. £2.80, Steps to Gate of Hulda. Both from area leading to 2nd Temple, 1st cent. B.C. £5, Wall, Omayyad Palace, 8th cent. A.D.

1976 Litho. ***Perf. 14***
611 A258 70a multicolored .25 .25
612 A258 £1.30 multicolored .25 .25
613 A258 £2.40 multicolored .25 .25
614 A258 £2.80 multicolored .25 .25
615 A258 £5 multicolored .25 .25
Nos. 611-615 (5) 1.25 1.25
With tabs 1.25

Excavations in Old Jerusalem.

Issued: Nos. 612-614, 10/19; Nos. 611, 615, 12/23.

Clearing the Land, 1890 A259

Designs: 10a, Building harbor wall. 60a, Road building, vert. £1.40, Plower and horse-drawn plow. £1.80, Planting trees.

1976, Dec. 23 Photo. ***Perf. 13***
616 A259 5a brown & gold .25 .25
617 A259 10a purple & gold .25 .25
618 A259 60a gold & car .25 .25
619 A259 £1.40 gold & blue .25 .25
620 A259 £1.80 green & gold .25 .25
#616-620, with tabs .40

Work of the pioneers.

"Let's Pull up Grandfather's Carrot" — A260

1977, Feb. 15 Litho. ***Perf. 14***
621 A260 £2.60 multicolored .25 .25
With tab .30

Voluntary service.

Doves, Jew and Arab Shaking Hands A261

£1.40, Arab & Jew holding hands, and flowers. £2.70, Peace dove, Arab and Jew dancing. Illustrations for the book "My Shalom-My Peace."

1977, Feb. 15
622 A261 50a multicolored .25 .25
623 A261 £1.40 multicolored .25 .25
624 A261 £2.70 multicolored .25 .25
622-#624, with tabs .45

Children's drawings for peace.

"By the Rivers of Babylon . . ." — A262

Drawings by Efraim Moshe Lilien: £1.80, Abraham, vert. £2.10, "May our eyes behold thee when thou returnest to Zion in compassion."

Perf. 14x13, 13x14
1977, Feb. 15 Photo.
625 A262 £1.70 gray, brn & blk .25 .25
626 A262 £1.80 yel, blk & brn .25 .25
627 A262 £2.10 lt grn & dk grn .25 .25
Nos. 625-627 (3) .75 .75
With tabs .60

Souvenirs for 5th Zionist Congress, 1902.

Trumpet — A263

1977, Apr. 19 Litho. ***Perf. 14***
628 A263 £1.50 shown .25 .25
629 A263 £2 Lyre .25 .25
630 A263 £5 Cymbals .25 .25
#628-630, with tabs .50

Ancient musical instruments, Haifa Music Museum and Amli Library.

Embroidered Sabbath Cloth — A264

1977, Apr. 19 ***Perf. 13x14***
631 A264 £3 buff & multi .25 .25
With tab .30

Importance of Sabbath observation in Jewish life.

Parachutists' Memorial, Bilu-Gedera, Tel Aviv — A265

1977, Apr. 19 ***Perf. 13x14***
632 A265 £3.30 gray, blk & grn .25 .25
With tab .40

Memorial Day.

10th Maccabiah — A266

1977, June 23 Photo. ***Perf. 14x13***
633 A266 £1 Fencing .25 .25
634 A266 £2.50 Shot put .25 .25
635 A266 £3.50 Judo .25 .25
Nos. 633-635 (3) .75 .75
With tabs .55

ZOA Convention Emblem — A267

1977, June 23 ***Perf. 14***
636 A267 £4 silver & multi .25 .25
With tab .35

Convention of Zionist Organization of America (ZOA), Jerusalem, June 1977.

Petah Tikva Centenary — A268

1977, June 23 ***Perf. 14x13***
637 A268 £1.50 multicolored .25 .25
With tab .25

Matriarchs of the Bible — A269

1977, Aug. 16 Photo. ***Perf. 14***
638 A269 70a Sarah .25 .25
639 A269 £1.50 Rebekah .25 .25
640 A269 £2 Rachel .25 .25
641 A269 £3 Leah .25 .25
#638-641, with tabs .65

Jewish New Year, 5738.

Frontier Guards — A270

1977, Aug. 16 Litho. ***Perf. 14***
642 A270 £1 shown .25 .25
643 A270 £1 Police .25 .25
644 A270 £1 Civil Guard .25 .25
#642-644, with tabs .35

Israel Police Force, established Mar. 26, 1948.

Illuminated Page — A271

1977, July 21 Photo. ***Perf. 14x13***
645 A271 £4 blk, gold & red .25 .25
With tab .25

4th cent. of Hebrew printing at Safad.

Farm Growing from Steel Helmet — A272

1977, Oct. 18 Litho. ***Perf. 14***
646 A272 £3.50 multicolored .25 .25
With tab .25

Fighting Pioneer Youth (NAHAL), established 1949.

Koffler Accelerator — A273

1977, Oct. 18 Photo. ***Perf. 14x13***
647 A273 £8 black & blue .35 .35
With tab .50

Inauguration of Koffler accelerator at Weizmann Institute of Science, Rehovot. Untagged.

Caesarea — A274

Scenes: £1, Arava on the Dead Sea. £20, Rosh Pinna.

1977-78 ***Perf. 13½x14***

Size: 27x22mm

649 A274 10a violet blue .25 .25
664 A274 £1 olive bister .25 .25

Perf. 14½x14

Size: 27½x26½mm

672 A274 £20 org & dk grn ('78) .65 .25
#649-672, with tabs 1.40

The 10a is untagged. The £1, £20 issued tagged and untagged.
Issued: 10a, £1, 10/18/77; £20, 7/4/78.

First Holy Land Locomotive A276

Locomotives: £1.50, Jezreel Valley train. £2, British Mandate period. £2.50, Israel Railways.

1977, Dec. 13 **Photo.** ***Perf. 13x14***

674 A276 65a multicolored .25 .25
675 A276 £1.50 multicolored .25 .25
676 A276 £2 multicolored .25 .25
677 A276 £2.50 multicolored .25 .25
a. Souvenir sheet of 4, #674-677 1.25 1.10
#674-677, with tabs .90

Railways in the Holy Land. No. 677a sold for £10.

Cypraea Isabella — A277

Red Sea shells: No. 679, Lioconcha castrensis. No. 680, Gloripallium pallium. No. 681, Malea pomum.

1977, Dec. 13 **Litho.** ***Perf. 14***

678 A277 £2 shown .25 .25
679 A277 £2 multicolored .25 .25
680 A277 £2 multicolored .25 .25
681 A277 £2 multicolored .25 .25
#678-681, with tabs .50

Street in Jerusalem, by Haim Glicksberg (1904-1970) A278

Paintings: £3.80, Thistles, by Leopold Krakauer (1890-1954). £4.40, An Alley in Zefat, by Mordekhai Levanon (1901-1968).

1978, Feb. 14

682 A278 £3 multicolored .25 .25
683 A278 £3.80 multicolored .25 .25
684 A278 £4.40 multicolored .25 .25
Nos. 682-684 (3) .75 .75
With tabs .65

Marriage Contract, Netherlands, 1648 — A279

Marriage Contracts (Ketubah): £3.90, Morocco, 1897. £6, Jerusalem, 1846.

1978, Feb. 14

685 A279 75a multicolored .25 .25
686 A279 £3.90 multicolored .25 .25
687 A279 £6 multicolored .25 .25
#685-687, with tabs .50

Eliyahu Golomb — A280

Designs: Portraits.

1978, Apr. 23 **Photo.** ***Perf. 14x13***

688 A280 £2 shown .25 .25
689 A280 £2 Dr. Moshe Sneh .25 .25
690 A280 £2 David Raziel .25 .25
691 A280 £2 Yitzhak Sadeh .25 .25
692 A280 £2 Abraham Stern .25 .25
#688-692, with tabs .60

Heroes of underground movement. Nos. 688-692 issued in sheets of 15.
See Nos. 695-696, 699-700, 705-706, 712-714, 740-742.

Souvenir Sheet

Jerusalem, Mosaic, from Madaba Map — A281

1978, Apr. 23 **Litho.** ***Perf. 14***

693 A281 Sheet of 4 1.25 1.25
a. £1 multicolored .25 .25
b. £2 multicolored .25 .25
c. £3 multicolored .30 .30
d. £4 multicolored .35 .35

Tabir '78 National Stamp Exhibition, Jerusalem, Apr. 23. No. 693 sold for £15.

Flowers A282

Design: Flowers, after children's paintings on Memorial Wall in Yad-Lebanim Museum, Petah Tikva. Each stamp shows different flowers.

1978, Apr. 23 ***Perf. 14***

694 Sheet of 15 1.25 1.25
a.-o. A282 £1.50 single stamp .25 .25

Memorial Day.

Heroes Type

Designs: No. 695, Theodor Herzl. No. 696, Chaim Weizmann.

1978, July 5 **Photo.** ***Perf. 14x13***

695 A280 £2 gray & gray ol .25 .25
696 A280 £2 buff & vio bl .25 .25
#695-696, with tabs .25

Herzl, founder of Zionism; Weizmann, 1st President of Israel.

Hatiqwa, 1st Verse — A285

1978, July 4 ***Perf. 13x14***

697 A285 £8.40 multicolored .30 .30
With tab .40

Centenary of Israeli National Anthem, Hatiqwa, by poet Naftali Herz Imber.

YMCA Building, Jerusalem A286

1978, July 4 **Litho.** ***Perf. 13***

698 A286 £5.40 multicolored .25 .25
With tab .30

Centenary of YMCA in Jerusalem.

Heroes Type

Designs: No. 699, Rabbi Kook (1865-1935). No. 700, Rabbi Ouziel (1880-1963).

1978, Aug. 22 **Photo.** ***Perf. 14x13***

699 A280 £2 pale gray & slate grn .25 .25
700 A280 £2 pale gray & dk pur .25 .25
#699-700, with tabs .25

Patriarchs A288

1978, Aug. 22 ***Perf. 14***

701 A288 £1.10 Abraham & Isaac .25 .25
702 A288 £5.20 Isaac .25 .25
703 A288 £6.60 Jacob .25 .25
#701-703, with tabs .55

Festivals 5739.

Families and Houses A289

1978, Aug. 22 ***Perf. 13x14***

704 A289 £5.10 multicolored .25 .25
With tab .30

Social welfare.

Heroes Type

Designs: No. 705, David Ben-Gurion. No. 706, Ze'ev Jabotinsky.

1978, Oct. 31 **Photo.** ***Perf. 14x13***

705 A280 £2 buff & vio brn .25 .25
706 A280 £2 gray & indigo .25 .25
#705-706, with tabs .25

30 years of independence. Ben-Gurion, first Prime Minister, and Ze'ev Vladimir Jabotinsky (1880-1940), leader of World Union of Zionist Revisionists.

Star of David and Growing Tree — A291

1978, Oct. 31 **Litho.** ***Perf. 14***

707 A291 £8.40 multicolored .35 .30
With tab .45

United Jewish Appeal, established 1939 in US to help Israel.

Old and New Hospital Buildings A292

1978, Oct. 31

708 A292 £5.40 multicolored .25 .25
With tab .30

Opening of new Shaare Zedek Medical Center, Jerusalem.

Silver and Enamel Vase, India — A293

£3, Elephant with howdah, Persia, 13th cent. £4, Mosque lamp, glass and enamel, Syria, 14th cent.

1978, Oct. 31

709 A293 £2.40 multicolored .25 .25
710 A293 £3 multicolored .25 .25
711 A293 £4 multicolored .25 .25
Nos. 709-711 (3) .75 .75
With tabs .55

Leo Arie Mayer Memorial Museum for Islamic Art, Jerusalem.

Heroes Type

No. 712, Menachem Ussishkin (1863-1941). No. 713, Berl Katzenelson (1878-1944). No. 714, Max Nordau (1849-1923).

1978, Dec. 26 **Photo.** ***Perf. 14x13***

712 A280 £2 citron & sl grn .25 .25
713 A280 £2 gray & vio blue .25 .25
714 A280 £2 buff & black .25 .25
#712-714, with tabs .40

30th anniversary of independence.

Iris Lortetii — A295

Protected Wild Flowers: £5.40, Iris haynei. £8.40, Iris nazarena.

1978, Dec. 26 **Litho.** ***Perf. 14***

715 A295 £1.10 multicolored .25 .25
716 A295 £5.40 multicolored .25 .25
717 A295 £8.40 multicolored .25 .25
Nos. 715-717 (3) .75 .75
With tabs .80

Agricultural Mechanization A296

Symbolic Designs: £2.40, Seawater desalination. £4.30, Electronics. £5, Chemical fertilizers.

1979, Feb. 13 **Litho.** ***Perf. 13***

718	A296	£1.10	multicolored	.25	.25
719	A296	£2.40	multicolored	.25	.25
720	A296	£4.30	multicolored	.25	.25
721	A296	£5	multicolored	.25	.25
		#718-721, with tabs		.60	

Technological Achievements.

"Hope from Darkness" A297

1979, Feb. 13

722	A297	£5.40	multicolored	.30	.25
		With tab		.35	

Salute to "the Righteous among Nations," an award to those who helped during Nazi period.

Jewish Brigade Flag — A298

1979, Feb. 13 **Photo.** ***Perf. 14***

723	A298	£5.10	blue, yel & blk	.25	.25
		With tab		.30	

Jewish Brigade served with British Armed Forces during WWII.

Paper (Prayer for Peace) in Crevice of Western Wall — A299

1979, Mar. 26 **Photo.** ***Perf. 14x13***

724	A299	£10	multicolored	.25	.25
		With tab		.35	
a.		Souv. sheet of 1, imperf.		.40	.40

Signing of peace treaty between Israel and Egypt, Mar. 26.

11th Hapoel Games — A300

1979, Apr. 23 **Litho.** ***Perf. 13***

725	A300	£1.50	Weightlifting	.25	.25
726	A300	£6	Tennis	.25	.25
727	A300	£11	Gymnastics	.30	.25
		Nos. 725-727 (3)		.80	.75
		With tabs		.90	

"50" and Rotary Emblem — A301

1979, Apr. 23 **Photo.** ***Perf. 14x13***

728	A301	£7	multicolored	.25	.25
		With tab		.35	

Rotary Intl. in Israel, 50th anniv.

Navy Memorial, Ashdod A302

1979, Apr. 23

729	A302	£5.10	multicolored	.25	.25
		With tab		.30	

Memorial Day.

Rabbi Yehoshua ben Hananya — A303

Craftsmen-Sages: £8.50, Rabbi Meir Baal Ha-Ness, scribe. £13, Rabbi Johanan, sandal maker.

1979, Sept. 4 **Photo.** ***Perf. 14x13***

730	A303	£1.80	multicolored	.25	.25
731	A303	£8.50	multicolored	.25	.25
732	A303	£13	multicolored	.25	.25
		Nos. 730-732 (3)		.75	.75
		With tabs		.70	

Jewish New Year 5740.

Flag Colors as Search Light — A304

1979, Sept. 4

733	A304	£10	multicolored	.25	.25
		With tab		.30	

Jewish Agency, 50th anniversary.

Hot Springs, Tiberias — A305

Design: £12, Dead Sea health resorts.

1979, Sept. 4 **Litho.** ***Perf. 14***

734	A305	£8	multicolored	.25	.25
735	A305	£12	multicolored	.25	.25
		#734-735, with tabs		.55	

Boy Riding Rainbow — A306

1979, Nov. 13 **Photo.** ***Perf. 13x14***

736	A306	£8.50	multicolored	.25	.25
		With tab		.25	

International Year of the Child.

Jerusalem — A307

Children's Drawings of Jerusalem: £4, People of different nationalities, horiz. £5, Praying at the Western Wall, horiz.

1979, Nov. 13 ***Perf. 14***

737	A307	£1.80	multicolored	.25	.25
738	A307	£4	multicolored	.25	.25
739	A307	£5	multicolored	.25	.25
		#737-739, with tabs		.30	

Heroes Type

Designs: £7, Arthur Ruppin (1876-1943). £9, Joseph Trumpeldor (1880-1920). £13, Aaron Aaronsohn (1876-1919).

1979, Nov. 13 **Photo.** ***Perf. 14x13***

740	A280	£7	gray & magenta	.25	.25
741	A280	£9	pale grn & Prus bl	.25	.25
742	A280	£13	pale yel & dk ol	.25	.25
		Nos. 740-742 (3)		.75	.75
		With tabs		1.00	

Sorek Cave — A308

1980, Jan. 15 **Litho.** ***Perf. 13x14***

743	A308	£50	multicolored	.75	.40
		With tab		1.10	

Star of David in Cogwheel — A309

1980, Jan. 15 ***Perf. 14***

744	A309	£13	multicolored	.30	.25
		With tab		.40	

Organization for Rehabilitation through Training (ORT), centenary.

Scolymus Maculatus — A310

Thistles: £5.50, Echinops viscosus. £8.50, Cynara syriaca.

1980, Jan. 15

745	A310	50a	multicolored	.25	.25
746	A310	£5.50	multicolored	.25	.25
747	A310	£8.50	multicolored	.25	.25
		#745-747, with tabs		.45	

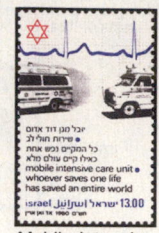

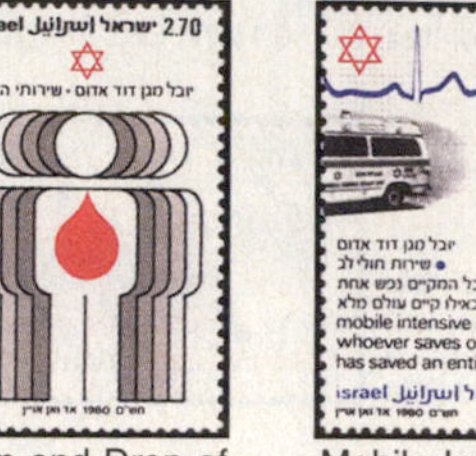

Men and Drop of Blood — A311

Mobile Intensive Care Unit — A312

1980, Apr. 15 **Photo.** ***Perf. 14x13***

748	A311	£2.70	multicolored	.25	.25
749	A312	£13	multicolored	.25	.25
a.		Souv. sheet, 2 each #748-749		1.00	1.00
		#748-749, with tabs		.40	

Magen David Adom (Red Star of David), 50th anniv.

Road of Courage Monument — A313

1980, Apr. 15 **Litho.** ***Perf. 14***

750	A313	£12	multicolored	.25	.25
		With tab		.35	

Memorial Day.

Sabbath Lamp, Netherlands, 18th Century — A314

Sabbath Lamps: £20, Germany, 18th century. £30, Morocco, 19th century.

1980, Aug. 5 **Photo.** ***Perf. 13x14***

751	A314	£4.30	multicolored	.25	.25
752	A314	£20	multicolored	.25	.25
753	A314	£30	multicolored	.25	.25
		Nos. 751-753 (3)		.75	.75
		With tabs		.80	

Yizhak Gruenbaum — A315

1980, Aug. 5 *Perf. 14x13*
754 A315 £32 sepia .60 .60
With tab .85

Yizhak Gruenbaum (1879-1970), first minister of the interior.

Renewal of Jewish Settlement in Gush Etzion — A316

1980, Aug. 5
755 A316 £19 multicolored .25 .25
With tab .35

View of Haifa and Mt. Carmel, 17th Century — A317

1980, Sept. 28 Litho. *Perf. 14x13*
756 A317 Sheet of 2 1.75 *1.75*
a. 2s multicolored .60 *.50*
b. 3s multicolored .80 *.75*

Haifa 80 National Stamp Exhibition, Haifa, Sept. 28-Oct. 7.

A318

1980-81 Photo. *Perf. 13x14*

No.	Type	Value	Description	Unused	Used
757	A318	5a	brt yel grn & green	.25	.25
758	A318	10a	red & brt mag	.25	.25
759	A318	20a	grnsh bl & dk blue	.25	.25
760	A318	30a	lil & dp vio	.25	.25
761	A318	50a	red org & red brown	.25	.25
762	A318	60a	brt yel grn & dk brown	.25	.25
762A	A318	70a	Prus bl & black	.25	.25
763	A318	1s	brt mag & dk green	.25	.25
764	A318	2s	dk bl grn & brn red	.25	.25
765	A318	2.80s	brown & grn	.25	.25
766	A318	3.20s	gray & red	.25	.25
767	A318	4.20s	ultra & dk pur	.30	.25
768	A318	5s	green & blk	.35	.25
769	A318	10s	brn org & brn	.50	.25
			#757-769, with tabs	5.00	

Issued: 70a, 5/5/81; others, 12/16/80.
See Nos. 784-786, 807-808

Prime Minister Golda Meir (1898-1978) — A319

1981, Feb. 10 Photo. *Perf. 14x13*
770 A319 2.60s rose violet .25 .25
With tab .40

View of Jerusalem, by Mordechai Ardon — A320

Paintings of Jerusalem by: 50a, Anna Ticho. 1.50s, Joseph Zaritsky, vert.

1981, Feb. 10 Litho. *Perf. 14*
771 A320 50a multicolored .25 .25
772 A320 1.50s multicolored .25 .25
773 A320 2.50s multicolored .25 .25
Nos. 771-773 (3) .75 .75
With tabs .95

Hand Putting Coin in Light Bulb — A321

1981, Mar. 17 Photo. *Perf. 14*
774 A321 2.60s shown .25 .25
775 A321 4.20s Hand squeezing solar energy .30 .25
#774-775, with tabs .70

Shmuel Yosef Agnon (1880-1970), Writer — A322

Designs: 2.80s, Moses Montefiore (1784-1885), first knighted English Jew. 3.20s, Abba Hillel Silver (1893-1963), statesman.

Perf. 14x13, 14 (3.20s)

1981, Mar. 17
776 A322 2s dk blue & blk .25 .25
777 A322 2.80s dk bl grn & blk .25 .25
778 A322 3.20s deep bis & blk .30 .30
Nos. 776-778 (3) .80 .80
With tabs 1.00

Wind Surfing — A323

1981, May 5 *Perf. 14x13*
779 A323 80a shown .25 .25
780 A323 4s Basketball .30 .30
781 A323 6s High jump .40 .40
Nos. 779-781 (3) .95 .95
With tabs 1.40

11th Maccabiah Games, July 8-16.

Biq'at Hayarden Memorial — A324

1981, May 5 *Perf. 13x14*
782 A324 1s red & black .25 .25
With tab .25

Jewish Family Heritage — A325

1981, May 5 Litho. *Perf. 14*
783 A325 3s multicolored .30 .25
With tab .45

Type of 1980

1981, Aug. 25 Photo. *Perf. 13x14*
784 A318 90a dp vio & brn org .25 .25
785 A318 3s red & dk blue .35 .25
786 A318 4s dk brn vio & dp lil rose .40 .25
Nos. 784-786 (3) 1.00 .75
With tabs 1.40

The Burning Bush — A326

Festivals 5742 (Book of Exodus): 1s "Let my people go . . ." 3s, Crossing of the Red Sea. 4s, Moses with Tablets.

1981, Aug. 25
787 A326 70a multicolored .25 .25
788 A326 1s multicolored .25 .25
789 A326 3s multicolored .30 .25
790 A326 4s multicolored .35 .25
Nos. 787-790 (4) 1.15 1.00
With tabs 1.25

Roses — A327

90a, Rosa damascena. 3.50s, Rosa phoenicia. 4.50s, Rosa hybrida.

1981, Oct. 22 Litho. *Perf. 14*
791 A327 90a multicolored .25 .25
792 A327 3.50s multicolored .30 .25
793 A327 4.50s multicolored .35 .25
Nos. 791-793 (3) .90 .75
With tabs 1.25

Ha-Shiv'a Interchange, Morasha-Ashod Highway — A328

1981, Oct. 22 Photo. *Perf. 14x13*
794 A328 8s multicolored .50 .50
With tab .75

Elat Stone — A329

1981, Dec. 29 Litho. *Perf. 14*
795 A329 2.50s shown .25 .25
796 A329 5.50s Star sapphire .40 .40
797 A329 7s Emerald .55 .55
Nos. 795-797 (3) 1.20 1.20
With tabs 1.75

Arbutus Andrachne — A330

No. 799, Cercis siliquastrum. No. 800, Quercus ithaburensis.

1981, Dec. 29
798 A330 3s shown .25 .25
799 A330 3s multicolored .25 .25
800 A330 3s multicolored .25 .25
a. Vert. or horiz. strip of 3, #798-800 .80 .80
#800a, horiz. strip of 3 with tabs 1.50

Nos. 798-800 issued in sheets of 9.

Road Safety — A331

1982, Mar. 2 Photo. *Perf. 14x13*
801 A331 7s multicolored .60 .60
With tab .90
a. Souvenir sheet 1.25 1.25

No. 801a sold for 10s.

Joseph Gedalyah Klausner (1874-1958), Historian and Philosopher — A331a

7s, Perez Bernstein (1890-1971), writer and editor. 8s, Rabbi Arys Levin (1885-1969).

1982, Mar. 2
802 A331a 7s multi .30 .25
803 A331a 8s multi .35 .25
804 A331a 9s cream & dk bl .40 .25
Nos. 802-804 (3) 1.05 .75
With tabs 1.75

Type of 1980 and

Produce — A332

1982-83 Photo. *Perf. 13 x 14*

No.	Type	Value	Description	Unused	Used
805	A332	40a	Prus bl & grn	.25	.25
806	A332	80a	lt bl & pur	.25	.25
807	A318	1.10s	ol & red	.25	.25
808	A318	1.20s	bl & red	.25	.25
809	A332	1.40s	ol grn & red	.25	.25
810	A332	6s	red vio & brn org	.25	.25
811	A332	7s	brn org & ol	.25	.25
812	A332	8s	brt grn & red brn	.25	.25

813 A332 9s ol & brn .25 .25
814 A332 15s ver & brt grn .25 .25
Nos. 805-814 (10) 2.50 2.50
With tabs 5.00

Issued: 1.10s, 2/11; 1.20s, 3/16; 1.40s, 6/22/82; 40a, 80a, 6s, 1/11/83; 7s-15s, 10/11/83.
See Nos. 876-879.

Tel Aviv Landscape, by Aryeh Lubin (d. 1980) — A333

Landscapes by: 8s, Sionah Tagger, vert. 15s, Israel Paldi (1892-1979).

1982, Apr. 22 Litho. *Perf. 14*
815 A333 7s multicolored .30 .25
816 A333 8s multicolored .30 .25
817 A333 15s multicolored .60 .45
Nos. 815-817 (3) 1.20 .95
With tabs 2.25

Gedudei Nouar Youth Corps — A334

1982, Apr. 22 Photo. *Perf. 14x13*
818 A334 5s multicolored .30 .25
With tab .50

Armour Memorial, En Zetim — A335

1982, Apr. 22 Litho. *Perf. 14*
819 A335 1.50s multicolored .25 .25
With tab .25

Memorial Day.

Joshua Addressing Crowd — A336

Festivals 5743 (Book of Joshua): 5.50s, Crossing River Jordan. 7.50s, Blowing down walls of Jericho. 9.50s, Battle with five kings of Amorites.

1982, Aug. 10 *Perf. 14*
820 A336 1.50s multicolored .25 .25
821 A336 5.50s multicolored .25 .25
822 A336 7.50s multicolored .30 .25
823 A336 9.50s multicolored .30 .25
Nos. 820-823 (4) 1.10 1.00
With tabs 1.25

Hadassah, 70th Anniv. — A337

1982, Aug. 10 Litho.
824 A337 12s multicolored .85 .70
With tab 1.25

Rosh Pinna Settlement Centenary A338

1982 Photo. *Perf. 13x14*
825 A338 2.50s shown .25 .25
826 A338 3.50s Rishon Leziyyon .25 .25
827 A338 6s Zikhron Yaaqov .25 .25
828 A338 9s Mazkeret Batya .25 .25
Nos. 825-828 (4) 1.00 1.00
With tabs 1.25

Issued: 2.50s, 3.50s, Aug. 10; others, Oct. 5.
See Nos. 849-850.

Olive Branch — A339

1982, Sept. 12
829 A339 multicolored .25 .25
With tab .40
a. Booklet pane of 8 + 8 ('84) 3.00

Sold at various values.

Emblem of Council for a Beautiful Israel — A340

1982, Oct. 5 Litho. *Perf. 14*
830 A340 17s multicolored .60 .30
With tab .80
a. Souv. sheet of 1, imperf. 2.00 2.00

No. 830a was for Beer Sheva '82 National Stamp Exhibition. Sold for 25s.

Eliahu Bet Tzuri — A341

Independence Martyrs: b, Hannah Szenes. c, Shlomo Ben Yosef. d, Yosef Lishanski. e, Naaman Belkind. f, Eliezer Kashani. g, Yechiel Dresner. h, Dov Gruner. i, Mordechai Alkachi. j, Eliahu Hakim. k, Meir Nakar. l, Avshalom Haviv. m, Yaakov Weiss. n, Meir Feinstein. o, Moshe Barazani. p, Eli Cohen. q, Samuel Azaar. r, Moshe Marzouk. s, Shalom Salih. t, Yosef Basri.

1982, Dec. *Perf. 14x13½*
831 Sheet of 20 5.50 5.50
a.-t. A341 3s multicolored .25 .25

Anti-Smoking Campaign A342

1983, Feb. 15 Litho. *Perf. 13*
832 A342 7s Candy in ash tray .30 .25
With tab .50

Beekeeping A343

1983, Feb. 15 Photo. *Perf. 13x14*
833 A343 30s multi 1.00 .75
With tab 1.50

A343a

8s, Golan. 15s, Galil. 20s, Yehuda and Shomeron.

1983, Feb. 15 Litho. *Perf. 14*
834 A343a 8s multicolored .25 .25
835 A343a 15s multicolored .50 .35
836 A343a 20s multicolored .75 .45
Nos. 834-836 (3) 1.50 1.05
With tabs 2.40

Memorial Day (Apr. 17) — A344

3s, Division of Steel Memorial, Besor Region.

1983, Apr. 12 *Perf. 13*
837 A344 3s multicolored .25 .25
With tab .25

Independence Day — A345

1983, Apr. 12 *Perf. 14*
838 A345 25s multicolored .65 .50
With tab .95
a. Souvenir sheet, imperf. 2.25 2.25

No. 838a sold for 35s.

12th Hapoel Games — A346

1983, Apr. 12 *Perf. 14x13*
839 A346 6s multicolored .25 .25
With tab .35

50th Anniv. of Israel Military Industries — A347

1983, Apr. 12
840 A347 12s multicolored .40 .35
With tab .50

Souvenir Sheet

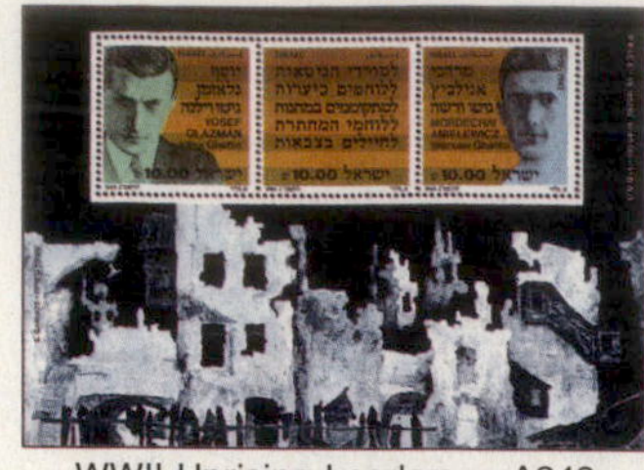

WWII Uprising Leaders — A348

Designs: a, Yosef Glazman (1908-1943), Founder of United Partisans Org. b, Text.1 c, Mordechai Anilewicz (1919-1943), leader of Warsaw Ghetto revolt. No. 841 sold for 45s.

1983, June 7 *Perf. 14*
841 A348 Sheet of 3 2.50 2.50
a. 10s multicolored .60 .40
b. 10s multicolored .60 .40
c. 10s multicolored .60 .40

Raoul Wallenberg (1912-1945), Swedish Diplomat — A349

1983, June 7 *Perf. 14x13*
842 A349 14s multicolored .55 .40
With tab .90

The Last Way, by Yosef Kuzkovski — A350

1983, June 7 *Perf. 14*
843 A350 35s multicolored .75 .60
With tab 1.10

Ohel Moed Synagogue, Tel Aviv A351

12s, Yeshurun Society, Jerusalem. 16s, Ohel Aharon, Haifa. 20s, Eliyahu Khakascni, Beer Sheva.

1983, Aug. 23
844 A351 3s shown .25 .25
845 A351 12s multicolored .25 .25
846 A351 16s multicolored .30 .25
847 A351 20s multicolored .30 .25
Nos. 844-847 (4) 1.10 1.00
With tabs 1.50

View of Afula, Jezreel Valley — A352

1983, Aug. 23
848 A352 15s multicolored .35 .35
With tab .50

Settlement Type of 1982

1983, Aug. 23

849 A338 11s Yesud Ha-Maala .25 .25
850 A338 13s Nes Ziyyona .40 .30
#849-850, with tabs .90

Souvenir Sheet

Tel Aviv Seashore Promenade — A353

1983, Sept. 25 ***Perf. 14x13***

851 A353 Sheet of 2 8.00 8.00
a. 30s multicolored 2.00 2.00
b. 50s multicolored 3.75 3.50

Tel Aviv '83, 13th Natl. Stamp Show, Sept. Sold for 120s.

KFIR-C2 Tactical Fighter — A354

18s, Reshef class missile boat. 30s, Merkava-MK1 battle tank.

1983, Dec. 13 **Photo.** ***Perf. 14***

852 A354 8s shown .25 .25
853 A354 18s multicolored .25 .25
854 A354 30s multicolored .25 .25
Nos. 852-854 (3) .75 .75
With tabs .85

Rabbi Meir Bar-Ilan (1880-1949), Founder of Mizrachi Movement — A355

1983, Dec. 13 **Photo.** ***Perf. 14x13***

855 A355 9s multicolored .25 .25
With tab .25

Jewish Immigration from Germany, 50th Anniv. A356

1983, Dec. 13 **Photo.** ***Perf. 13x14***

856 A356 14s multicolored .35 .30
With tab .45

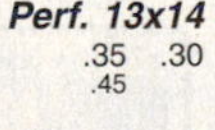

Michael Halperin (1860-1919), Zionist — A357

Uri Zvi Grinberg (1896-1981), Poet — A358

15s, Yigal Allon (1918-1980), military commander, founder of Israel Labor Party.

1984, Mar. 15 **Photo.** ***Perf. 14x13***

857 A357 7s multicolored .25 .25

Litho.

Perf. 14

858 A357 15s multicolored .30 .30

Perf. 13

859 A358 16s multicolored .25 .25
Nos. 857-859 (3) .80 .80
With tabs 1.00

Hevel Ha-Besor Settlement — A359

1984, Mar. 15 ***Perf. 14***

860 A359 12s shown .25 .25
861 A359 17s Arava .30 .25
862 A359 40s Gaza Strip .40 .40
Nos. 860-862 (3) .95 .90
With tabs 1.40

Monument of Alexander Zaid, by David Polus A360

Monuments: No. 864, Tel Hay Defenders (seated lion), by Abraham Melnikov (1892-1960). No. 865, Dov Gruner, by Chana Orloff (1888-1968).

1984, Mar. 15 ***Perf. 13x14***

863 A360 15s multicolored .30 .25
864 A360 15s multicolored .30 .25
865 A360 15s multicolored .30 .25
Nos. 863-865 (3) .90 .75
With tabs 1.25

Memorial Day — A361

Design: Oliphant House (Druse military memorial), Dalyat Al Karmil.

1984, Apr. 26 **Photo.** ***Perf. 14x13***

866 A361 10s multicolored .25 .25
With tab .25

Natl. Labor Fed., 50th Anniv. — A362

1984, Apr. 26

867 A362 35s multicolored .25 .25
With tab .35

Produce Type of 1982-83

1984 **Photo.** ***Perf. 13x14***

876 A332 30s vio brn & red .25 .25
877 A332 50s dp bis & rose mag .30 .30
878 A332 100s gray & green .80 .50
879 A332 500s dp org & bl blk 1.50 .75
Nos. 876-879 (4) 2.85 1.80
With tabs 4.50

Issued: 500s, 11/27; others 4/26.

Leon Pinsker (1821-91), A363

Gen. Charles O. Wingate (1903-44) A364

No. 880, Hovevei Zion founder. No. 881, British soldier.

1984, July 3 ***Perf. 14x13***

880 A363 20s lilac and purple .25 .25
881 A364 20s blk, grn & gray .25 .25
#880-881, with tabs .45

Hearts, Stars — A365

1984, July 3

882 A365 30s multicolored .25 .25
With tab .30

70th anniv. of American Jewish Joint Distribution Committee (philanthropic org. created during World War I).

1984 Summer Olympics A366

1984, July 3 **Litho.** ***Perf. 14***

883 A366 80s Dove .55 .55
With tab .80

Souvenir Sheet

Perf. 14x13

884 A366 240s like 80s 5.00 4.50

No. 884 contains one 23x32mm stamp. Sold for 350s.

Biblical Women — A367

1984, Sept. 4 **Photo.** ***Perf. 13x14***

885 A367 15s Hannah .25 .25
886 A367 70s Ruth .30 .25
887 A367 100s Huldah .35 .25
Nos. 885-887 (3) .90 .75
With tabs 1.20

David Wolffsohn (1856-1914), Jewish Colonial Trust Founder — A368

1984, Sept. 4 ***Perf. 14x14½***

888 A368 150s multicolored .90 .60
With tab 1.25

Nahalal Settlement (Founded 1921) A369

1984, Sept. 4 ***Perf. 14***

889 A369 80s multicolored .35 .25
With tab .45

World Food Day, Oct. 16 — A370

1984, Nov. 27 **Litho.**

891 A370 200s Bread, wheat .55 .55
With tab .80

Rabbi Isaac Herzog (1888-1959), Statesman, Scholar — A371

1984, Nov. 27 **Photo.** ***Perf. 14½***

892 A371 400s multicolored 1.00 1.00
With tab 1.60

A372

Children's Book Illustrations (Authors and their books): 20s, Apartment to Let, by Leah Goldberg (1911-70). 30s, Why is the Zebra Wearing Pajamas, by Omer Hillel (b. 1926) (30x30mm). 50s, Across the Sea, by Haim Nahman Bialik (1873-1934).

Perf. 14, 13 (30s)

1984, Nov. 27 **Litho.**

893 A372 20s multicolored .25 .25
894 A372 30s multicolored .25 .25
895 A372 50s multicolored .25 .25
Nos. 893-895 (3) .75 .75
With tabs .75

Birds of Prey — A373

100s, Lappet faced vulture. 200s, Bonelli's eagle. 300s, Sooty falcon. 500s, Griffon vulture.

1985, Feb. 5 Litho. *Perf. 14*

896	A373 100s multi		.30	.30
897	A373 200s multi		.45	.40
898	A373 300s multi		.70	.65
899	A373 500s multi		1.00	.90
	Nos. 896-899 (4)		2.45	2.25
	With tabs		5.50	

Souvenir Sheet

899A	Sheet of 4	5.00	5.00
b.	A373 100s like #896	.35	.30
c.	A373 200s like #897	.45	.40
d.	A373 300s like #898	.75	.65
e.	A373 500s like #899	1.25	1.00

No. 899A sold for 1650s. Nos. 899Ab-899Ad do not have inscriptions below the design.

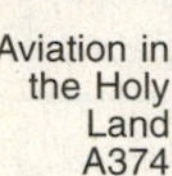

Aviation in the Holy Land A374

50s, Bleriot XI, 1913. 150s, Scipio-Short S-17 Kent, 1931. 250s, Tiger Moth DH-82, 1934. 300s, Scion-Short S-16, 1937.

1985, Apr. 2 Litho. *Perf. 14*

900	A374 50s multi	.25	.25
901	A374 150s multi	.35	.25
902	A374 250s multi	.50	.25
903	A374 300s multi	.45	.40
	Nos. 900-903 (4)	1.55	1.15
	With tabs	2.25	

Natl. Assoc. of Nurses — A375

1985, Apr. 2 Litho. *Perf. 14*

904	A375 400s multicolored	.85	.80
	With tab	1.25	

Golani Brigade Memorial and Museum — A376

1985, Apr. 2 Photo. *Perf. 14x13*

905	A376 50s multicolored	.25	.25
	With tab	.40	

Zivia (1914-1978) and Yitzhak (1915-1981) Zuckerman, Resistance Heroes, Warsaw Ghetto — A377

1985, Apr. 2 Photo. *Perf. 13x14*

906	A377 200s multicolored	.50	.50
	With tab	.80	

Souvenir Sheets

A378

World Stamp Exhibition, Tel Aviv — A379

Adam, Eve and the Serpent (detail) — A380

No. 907: a, Dome of the Rock. b, The Western Wall. c, Church of the Holy Sepulchre.

No. 908: a, 16th Cent. Bas-relief, Ottoman period. b, Hand, 18th cent. bas-relief, Jewish Quarter. c, Rosette carving, 12th-13th cent. Crusader capital.

No. 909, Frontispiece and detail, Schocken Bible, South Germany, ca. 1290.

1985, May 14 Litho. *Perf. 13x14*

907	A378 Sheet of 3	2.75	2.75
a.-c.	200s any single	.60	.60

Sold for 900s.

Perf. 14x13

908	A379 Sheet of 3	3.50	3.50
a.-c.	350s any single	.90	.90

Sold for 1500s.

Perf. 14

909	A380 800s multi	3.25	3.25
	Nos. 907-909 (3)	9.50	9.50

Sold for 1200s.

The Israeli postal administration authorized the Intl. Philatelic Federation (FIP) to overprint a limited number of these souvenir sheets for sale exclusively at ISRAPHIL '85 to raise funds. The FIP overprints have control numbers and are inscribed "Under the Patronage of the Philatelic Federation" in the sheet margin. The sheets remained valid for postage but were not sold by the post office. Value for set of sheets $45.

12th Maccabiah Games — A381

1985, July 16 Litho. *Perf. 14*

910	A381 400s Basketball	.50	.35
911	A381 500s Tennis	.70	.45
912	A381 600s Windsurfing	.90	.55
	Nos. 910-912 (3)	2.10	1.35
	With tabs	3.00	

1985 Festivals — A382

Tabernacle utensils: 100sh, Ark of the Covenant. 150sh, Acacia showbread table. 200sh, Menora. 300sh, Incense altar.

1985, July 16 Litho. *Perf. 14*

913	A382 100s multi	.25	.25
914	A382 150s multi	.30	.30
915	A382 200s multi	.35	.35
916	A382 300s multi	.55	.55
	Nos. 913-916 (4)	1.45	1.45
	With tabs	2.25	

A383

1985, July 16 Litho. *Perf. 14*

917	A383 150s Emblem, badges	.30	.25
	With tab	.50	

Intl. Youth Year.

A384

1985, Nov. 5 Litho. *Perf. 14*

918	A384 200s multi	.70	.25
	With tab	.95	

Leon Yehuda Recanati (1890-1945), financier and philanthropist.

Meir Dizengoff (1861-1936), Founder and Mayor of Tel Aviv — A385

1985, Nov. 5

919	A385 500s multi	1.00	.65
	With tab	2.00	

Gedera Settlement, Cent. A386

1985, Nov. 5 Photo. *Perf. 13x14*

920	A386 600s multi	.85	.75
	With tab	1.40	

The Kibbutz — A387

1985, Nov. 5 Litho. *Perf. 14*

921	A387 900s multi	1.00	.80
	With tab	1.50	

Theodor Herzl A388

Capital, Second Temple, Jerusalem A389

Designs: 1s, Corinthian, A.D. 1st cent. 3s, Ionic, 1st cent. B.C.

1986, Jan. 1 Photo. *Perf. 13x14*

922	A388	1a red & ultra	.25	.25
923	A388	2a green & ultra	.25	.25
924	A388	3a brown & ultra	.25	.25
925	A388	5a blue & ultra	.25	.25
926	A388	10a org & ultra	.25	.25
927	A388	20a pink & ultra	.25	.25
928	A388	30a lemon & ultra	.25	.25
929	A388	50a pur & ultra	.25	.25
930	A389	1s multi	.75	.50
931	A389	3s multi	1.50	1.00
		Nos. 922-931 (10)	4.25	3.50
		With tabs	5.75	

1s and 3s designs with 1000a and 1500a values were not issued.

See Nos. 1014-1020, 1699.

Red Sea Coral A390

1986, Mar. 4 Litho. *Perf. 14*

932	A390 30a Balanophyllia	.30	.25
933	A390 40a Goniopora	.45	.25
934	A390 50a Dendronephthya	.60	.25
	Nos. 932-934 (3)	1.35	.75
	With tabs	2.00	

Arthur Rubinstein (1887-1982), Pianist — A391

1986, Mar. 4 Photo. *Perf. 13x14*

935	A391 60a Picasso portraits	.50	.30
	With tab	1.25	

Broadcasting from Jerusalem, 50th Anniv. — A392

70a, Map and microphone, 1936.

1986, Mar. 4 Litho. *Perf. 14*

936	A392 70a multicolored	.65	.50
	With tab	.85	

Negev Brigade Memorial, Beer Sheva — A393

1986, May 4 **Litho.** ***Perf. 13***
937 A393 20a multicolored .25 .25
With tab .30

Memorial Day.

Al Jazzar Mosque, Akko — A394

1986, May 4 **Photo.** ***Perf. 14x13***
938 A394 30a multicolored .25 .25
With tab .35

Id Al-Fitr Feast.

Institutes of Higher Learning in the US — A395

Designs: No. 939, 942a, Hebrew Union College, Jewish Institute of Religion, 1875, Cincinnati. No. 940, 942b, Yeshiva University, 1886, NYC. No. 941, 942c, Jewish Theological Seminary of America, 1886, NYC.

1986, May 4 **Litho.** ***Perf. 14***
939 A395 50a multicolored .45 .25
940 A395 50a multicolored .45 .25
941 A395 50a multicolored .45 .25
Nos. 939-941 (3) 1.35 .75
With tabs 2.00

Souvenir Sheet

942 Sheet of 3 + label 3.00 2.50
a.-c. A395 75a any single .75 .60

AMERIPEX '86. Size of Nos. 942a-942c: 36x23mm. No. 942 sold for 3s.

Ben Gurion Airport, 50th Anniv. A396

90a, Terminal from aircraft.

1986, July 22 ***Perf. 14x13***
943 A396 90a multicolored 1.00 .50
With tab 1.25

"No to Racism" in Graffiti — A397

1986, July 22 ***Perf. 14***
944 A397 60a multicolored .65 .40
With tab .80

Druze Feast of Prophet Nabi Sabalan A398

1986, July 22 **Photo.** ***Perf. 14***
945 A398 40a Tomb, Hurfeish .30 .25
With tab .45

Joseph Sprinzak (1885-1959), 1st Speaker of Knesset — A399

1986, July 22 **Litho.** ***Perf. 13***
946 A399 80a multicolored .65 .30
With tab .85

Worms Illuminated Mahzor, 13th Cent. — A400

20a, Gates of Heaven. 40a, Sheqalim, prayer. 90a, Rose flower prayer introduction.

1986, Sept. 23 **Litho.** ***Perf. 13x14***
947 A400 20a multicolored .25 .25
948 A400 40a multicolored .25 .25
949 A400 90a multicolored .40 .40
Nos. 947-949 (3) .90 .90
With tabs 1.75

David Ben-Gurion (1886-1973) — A401

1986, Oct. 19 **Litho.** ***Perf. 14x13***
950 A401 1s multicolored .80 .80
With tab 1.10

Souvenir Sheet

Map of the Holyland, by Gerard de Jode, 1578 — A402

1986, Oct. 19 ***Perf. 14½***
951 A402 2s multicolored 4.00 3.50

NATANYA '86 Stamp Exhibition; Organized philately in Natanya, 50th anniv. Sold for 3s.

Israel Meteorological Service, 50th Anniv. — A403

1986, Dec. 18 **Litho.** ***Perf. 13***
952 A403 50a multicolored .40 .30
With tab .60

Basilica of the Annunciation, Nazareth — A404

1986, Dec. 18 **Litho.** ***Perf. 14***
953 A404 70a multicolored .55 .30
With tab .75

Israel Philharmonic Orchestra, 50th Anniv. — A405

No. 9.54, Bronislaw Huberman, violinist. No. 955, Arturo Toscanini, conductor.

1986, Dec. 18
954 A405 1.50s multicolored 1.50 .75
955 A405 1.50s multicolored 1.50 .75
a. Pair, #954-955 3.50 3.25
With tabs 5.00

Owls A406

1987, Feb. 24 **Litho.** ***Perf. 14x13***
956 A406 30a Bubo bubo .50 .30
957 A406 40a Otus brucei .60 .40
958 A406 50a Tyto alba .75 .50
959 A406 80a Strix butleri 1.10 .70
Nos. 956-959 (4) 2.95 1.90
With tabs 6.50

Souvenir Sheet

960 Sheet of 4 8.00 5.00
a. A406 30a like #956 .70 .50
b. A406 40a like #957 1.25 1.00
c. A406 50a like #958 1.75 1.25
d. A406 80a like #959 2.25 1.50

Sold for 3s. Nos. 960a-960d do not have inscriptions below the design.

Ammunition Hill Memorial, Jerusalem A407

1987, Apr. 16 **Litho.** ***Perf. 14***
961 A407 30a multicolored .30 .30
With tab .45

Memorial Day.

13th Hapoel Games A408

1987, Apr. 16
962 A408 90a multicolored .50 .50
With tab .80

Souvenir Sheet

HAIFA '87 Stamp Exhibition — A409

1987, Apr. 16 ***Perf. 14x13***
963 A409 2.70s No. C8 6.00 6.00

Sold for 4s.

Amateur Radio Operators — A410

1987, June 14 **Litho.** ***Perf. 14***
964 A410 2.50s multi 2.25 2.25
With tab 3.50

World Dog Show, June 23-27 — A411

1987, June 14
965 A411 40a Saluki .40 .35
966 A411 50a Sloughi .55 .45
967 A411 2s Canaan 2.25 2.00
Nos. 965-967 (3) 3.20 2.80
With tabs 8.00

Clean Environment A412

1987, June 14 ***Perf. 13***
968 A412 40a multicolored .40 .40
With tab .60

Rabbi Moshe Avigdor Amiel (1883-1945), Founder of Yeshivas — A413

1987, Sept. 10 **Litho.** ***Perf. 14***
969 A413 1.40s multi 1.00 1.00
With tab 1.30

Synagogue Models, Nahum Goldmann Museum, Tel Aviv — A414

30a, Altneuschul, Prague, 13th cent. 50a, Aleppo, Syria, 9th cent. 60a, Florence, Italy, 19th cent.

1987, Sept. 10 ***Perf. 13x14***
970 A414 30a multicolored .30 .25
971 A414 50a multicolored .35 .30
972 A414 60a multicolored .40 .35
Nos. 970-972 (3) 1.05 .90
With tabs 1.40

See Nos. 996-998.

Kupat Holim Health Insurance Institute, 75th Anniv. — A415

1987, Sept. 10 *Perf. 14*

973 A415 1.50s multi .90 .90
With tab 1.25

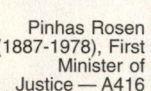

Pinhas Rosen (1887-1978), First Minister of Justice — A416

1987, Nov. 24 **Litho.** *Perf. 13*

974 A416 80a multicolored .45 .45
With tab .70

A417

Exploration of the Holy Land, 19th cent.: 30a, Thomas Howard Molyneux (1847) and Christopher Costigan (1835). 50a, William Francis Lynch (1848). 60a, John MacGregor (1868-1869).

1987, Nov. 24 *Perf. 14*

975 A417 30a multi .30 .30
976 A417 50a multi .40 .40
977 A417 60a multi .50 .50
Nos. 975-977 (3) 1.20 1.20
With tabs 2.00

Souvenir Sheet

978 Sheet of 3 3.50 3.50
a. A417 40a like #975 .50 .50
b. A417 50a like #976 1.00 1.00
c. A417 80a like #977 1.25 1.25

No. 978 sold for 2.50s.

A418

10a, Computer technology. 80a, Genetic engineering. 1.40s, Medical engineering.

1988, Jan. 26

979 A418 10a multicolored .25 .25
980 A418 80a multicolored .40 .35
981 A418 1.40s multicolored .75 .50
Nos. 979-981 (3) 1.40 1.10
With tabs 2.00

Industrialization of Israel, cent.

Water Conservation A419

1988, Jan. 26

982 A419 40a multicolored .25 .25
With tab .40

Australia Bicentennial — A420

1988, Jan. 26 *Perf. 14*

983 A420 1s multi 1.25 1.25
With tab 1.25

Sunflower — A421

1988, Mar. 9 **Photo.** *Perf. 13x14*

984 A421 (30a) dk yel grn & yel .25 .25
With tab .30

A422

Design: Anne Frank (1929-45), Amsterdam house where she hid.

1988, Apr. 19 **Litho.**

985 A422 60a multicolored .50 .50
With tab .60

Independence 40 Stamp Exhibition, Jerusalem A423

Design: Modern Jerusalem.

1988, Apr. 19

986 A423 1s shown .50 .40
With tab .65

Souvenir Sheet

987 A423 2s detail from 1s 3.25 3.00

No. 987 sold for 3s.

Memorial Day A424

1988, Apr. 19 *Perf. 14x13*

988 A424 40a multicolored .25 .25
With tab .30
a. Souvenir sheet of 1 1.00 1.00

Natl. independence, 40th anniv. No. 988a contains one stamp like No. 988 but without copyright inscription LR. Sold for 60a.

Souvenir Sheet

Israel's 40th Anniv. Exhibition, Tel Aviv — A425

Stamps on stamps: a, No. 245. b, No. 297. c, No. 120. d, No. 96. e, Like No. 794. f, No. 252. g, No. 333. h, No. 478.

1988, June 9 **Litho.** *Perf. 14*

989 A425 Sheet of 8 + label 3.00 3.00
a.-h. 20a any single .30 .30

Sold for 2.40s. Center label pictures Israel 40 emblem.

B'nai B'rith in Jerusalem, Cent. — A426

1988, June 27 *Perf. 14*

990 A426 70a multicolored .35 .35
With tab .45

Nature Reserves in the Negev A427

1988, June 27

991 A427 40a Ein Zin .25 .25
992 A427 60a She'Zaf .40 .30
993 A427 70a Ramon .50 .35
Nos. 991-993 (3) 1.15 .90
With tabs 1.60

See Nos. 1052-1054, 1154-1156.

Agents Executed During World War II — A428

Portraits: 40a, Havivah Reik (1914-1944). 1.65s, Enzo Hayyim Sereni (1905-1944).

1988, Sept. 1 **Litho.**

994 A428 40a multicolored .35 .35
995 A428 1.65s multicolored 1.00 1.00
#994-995, with tabs 1.75

Synagogue Models Type of 1987

Models in the Nahum Goldmann Museum, Tel Aviv: 35a, Kai-Feng Fu Synagogue, 12th cent., China. 60a, Zabludow Synagogue, 17th cent., Poland. 70a, Touro Synagogue, 1763, Newport, Rhode Island, designed by Peter Harrison.

1988, Sept. 1 *Perf. 13x14*

996 A414 35a multicolored .25 .25
997 A414 60a multicolored .30 .30
998 A414 70a multicolored .50 .30
Nos. 996-998 (3) 1.05 .85
With tabs 1.50

A429

1988, Nov. 9 *Perf. 14*

999 A429 80a multicolored .60 .60
With tab .80

Kristallnacht, Nazi pogrom in Germany, 50th anniv.

Moshe Dayan (1915-1981), Foreign Minister, Minister of Defense — A430

1988, Nov. 9 *Perf. 13*

1000 A430 40a multicolored .25 .25
With tab .45

Jewish Legion, 70th Anniv. A431

1988, Nov. 9 *Perf. 14*

1001 A431 2s yel brn, sepia & lem 1.00 .75
With tab 1.30

Agricultural Achievements — A433

50a, Avocado (fruit-growing). 60a, Lilium longiflorum (horticulture). 90a, Irrigation.

1988, Dec. 22 *Perf. 14*

1004 A433 50a multicolored .30 .30
1005 A433 60a multicolored .40 .40
1006 A433 90a multicolored .50 .50
Nos. 1004-1006 (3) 1.20 1.20
With tabs 1.75

Natl. Tourism — A434

40a, Red Sea. 60a, Dead Sea. 70a, Mediterranean Sea. 1.70s, Sea of Galilee.

1989, Mar. 12 **Litho.** *Perf. 13*

1007 A434 40a multicolored .25 .25
1008 A434 60a multicolored .30 .30
1009 A434 70a multicolored .40 .40
1010 A434 1.70s multicolored .60 .60
Nos. 1007-1010 (4) 1.55 1.55
With tabs 2.75

Rabbi Judah Leib Maimon (1875-1962) — A435

1989, Mar. 12 *Perf. 14*
1011 A435 1.70s multi 1.00 1.00
With tab 1.50

Rashi, Rabbi Solomon Ben Isaac (b. 1039), Talmudic Commentator — A436

1989, Mar. 12
1012 A436 4s buff & black 2.50 1.50
With tab 3.00

Memorial Day — A437

Fallen Airmen's Memorial at Har Tayassim.

1989, Apr. 30 **Litho.** *Perf. 14*
1013 A437 50a multi .40 .40
With tab .50

Archaeology Type of 1986

Gates of Huldah, Temple Compound, Mt. Moriah: 40a, Rosettes and rhomboids, frieze and columns, facade of the eastern gate, 1st cent. B.C. 60a, Corinthian capital, 6th cent. 70a, Bas-relief from the Palace of Umayade Caliphs, 8th cent. 80a, Corinthian capital from the Church of Ascension on the Mount of Olives, 12-13th cent. 90a, Star of David, limestone relief, northern wall, near the new gate, Suleiman's Wall. 2s, Mamluk relief, 14th century. 10s, Carved frieze from a sepulcher entrance, end of the Second Temple Period.

1988-90 **Litho.** *Perf. 14*

1014	A389 40a multi	.25	.25
1015	A389 60a multi	.30	.25
1016	A389 70a multi	.40	.25
1017	A389 80a multi	.40	.25
1018	A389 90a multi	.90	.25
1019	A389 2s multi	1.00	.75
1020	A389 10s multi	4.50	3.00
	Nos. 1014-1020 (7)	7.75	5.00
	With tabs	12.00	

Issued: 40a, 60a, 12/22/88; 70a, 80a, 6/11/89; 10s, 4/30/89; 90a, 10/17/89; 2s, 6/12/90.

UNICEF — A438

1989, Apr. 30 *Perf. 14*
1022 A438 90a multicolored .60 .50
With tab .75

Moshe Smoira (1888-1961), 1st Pres. of Israeli Supreme Court — A439

1989, June 11 **Litho.** *Perf. 13*
1023 A439 90a deep blue .60 .60
With tab .75

13th Maccabiah Games, July 3-13 — A440

1989, June 11 *Perf. 13x14*
1024 A440 80a multi .60 .60
With tab .70

Ducks — A441

Designs: a, Garganey. b, Mallard. c, Teal. d, Shelduck.

1989, July 18 **Litho.** *Perf. 14*
1025 Strip of 4 3.00 3.00
With tabs 4.00
a.-d. A441 80a any single 1.25 .85

Souvenir Sheet

1025E Sheet of 4 6.00 5.50
f. A441 80a like No. 1025d 1.00 1.00
g. A441 80a like No. 1025b 1.00 1.00
h. A441 80a like No. 1025a 1.00 1.00
i. A441 80a like No. 1025c 1.00 1.00

World Stamp Expo '89. No. 1025E contains four 29x33mm stamps. Sold for 5s.

Graphic Design Industry — A442

1989, July 18
1026 A442 1s multi .60 .35
With tab .80

Souvenir Sheet

French Revolution, Bicent. — A443

1989, July 7
1027 A443 3.50s multi 5.50 4.00
Sold for 5s.

Hebrew Language Council, Cent. — A444

1989, Sept. 3 **Litho.** *Perf. 13x14*
1028 A444 1s multi .60 .35
With tab .75

Rabbi Yehuda Hai Alkalai (1798-1878), Zionist — A445

1989, Sept. 3 *Perf. 14*
1029 A445 2.50s multi 2.00 1.00
With tab 4.50

Mizrah Festival — A446

Paper cutouts: 50a, Menorah and lions, by Gadoliahu Neminsky, Holbenisk, Ukraine, 1921. 70a, Menorah and hands, Morocco, 19th-20th cent. 80a, "Misrah," hunting scene and deer, Germany, 1818.

1989, Sept. 3 *Perf. 14x13*

1030	A446 50a multi	.30	.25
1031	A446 70a multi	.40	.30
1032	A446 80a multi	.60	.30
	Nos. 1030-1032 (3)	1.30	.85
	With tabs	1.75	

Tevel '89 Youth Stamp Exhibition, Oct. 15-21 — A447

1989, Oct. 12 **Photo.** *Perf. 13x14*
1033 A447 50a multi .35 .30
With tab .45

1st Israeli Stamp Day — A448

1989, Oct. 17 **Litho.** *Perf. 14*
1034 A448 1s multi .50 .35
With tab .70

Special Occasions — A449

1989, Nov. 17 **Photo.** *Perf. 13½x14*

1035	A449 (50a) Good luck	.45	.35
1036	A449 (50a) With love	.45	.35
a.	Booklet pane of 10	5.00	
1037	A449 (50a) See you again	.45	.35
a.	Booklet pane of 10 + 2 labels	5.75	
b.	Sheet of 20 + 5 labels	11.50	
	Nos. 1035-1037 (3)	1.35	1.05
	With tabs	1.75	

Nos. 1036a, 1037a contain 5 tete-beche pairs, No. 1037b contains 10 tete-beche pairs.
Nos. 1037a-1037b had value of 80a when released.
Issued: No. 1036a, 8/7/90. Nos. 1037a-1037b, 6/22/93.
See Nos. 1059-1061, 1073-1075.

A450

Design: Tapestry and Rebab, a Stringed Instrument, from the Museum of Bedouin Culture.

1990, Feb. 13 **Litho.** *Perf. 13*
1038 A450 1.50s multicolored .80 .80
With tab 1.10

The Circassians in Israel — A451

Designs: Circassian folk dancers.

1990, Feb. 13 **Photo.** *Perf. 14x13*
1039 A451 1.50s multicolored .75 .75
With tab 1.00

Rehovot City, Cent. — A452

1990, Feb. 13 *Perf. 14*
1040 A452 2s multicolored 1.20 1.00
With tab 1.60

Souvenir Sheet

Isaiah's Vision of Eternal Peace, by Mordecai Ardon — A453

Series of 3 stained-glass windows, The Hall of Eternal Jewishness and Humanism, Hebrew University Library, Jerusalem: a, "Roads to Jerusalem" (inscription at L). b, Isaiah's prophecy of broken guns beaten into ploughshares (inscription at R).

1990, Apr. 17 **Litho.** *Perf. 14*
1041 A453 Sheet of 2 5.50 5.50
a.-b. 1.50s any single 1.50 1.00

Stamp World London '90. Sold for 4.50s.
Also exists imperf. Value $47.50.

Architecture — A454

Design: 75a, School, Deganya Kibbutz, 1930. 1.10s, Dining hall, Kibbutz Tel Yosef by Leopold Krakauer, 1933. 1.20s, Engel House by Ze'ev Rechter, 1933. 1.40s, Home of Dr. Chaim Weizmann, Rehovot by Erich Mendelsohn, 1936. 1.60s, Jewish Agency for Palestine, Jerusalem, by Yohanan Ratner, 1932.

1990-92 **Photo.** *Perf. 14x13½*

1044	A454 75a blk, pale grn & buff	.50	.35
1045	A454 1.10s blk, yel & grn	.60	.35
1046	A454 1.20s blk, bl & yel	.60	.35
1047	A454 1.40s blk, lt lil & buff	.70	.35
1048	A454 1.60s multicolored	.75	.35
a.	Dotted rose lilac background	.75	.35
	Nos. 1044-1048 (5)	3.15	1.75
	With tabs	5.25	

No. 1048 has a solid bluish lilac background.

Issued: 75a, 4/17; 1.10s, 1.20s, 12/12; 1.40s, 4/9/91; 1.60s, 4/26/92; No. 1048a, 7/14/96.

Nature Reserves Type of 1988

60a, Gamla, Yehudiyya. 80a, Huleh. 90a, Mt. Meron.

1990, Apr. 17 Litho. *Perf. 14*

1052 A427 60a multicolored	.30	.25
1053 A427 80a multicolored	.50	.25
1054 A427 90a multicolored	.70	.25
Nos. 1052-1054 (3)	1.50	.75
With tabs	2.25	

Memorial Day A456

60a, Artillery Corps Memorial.

1990, Apr. 17 Photo. *Perf. 13x14*

1055 A456 60a multi	.45	.25
With tab	.60	

Intl. Folklore Festival, Haifa — A457

1990, June 12 Litho. *Perf. 14*

1056 1.90s Denom at UL	1.75	1.75
1057 1.90s Denom at UR	1.75	1.75
a. A457 Pair, #1056-1057	4.00	4.00
With tabs	5.00	

Hagana, 70th Anniv. — A459

1990, June 12

1058 A459 1.50s multicolored	1.40	1.40
With tab	1.50	

Special Occasions Type of 1989

1990, June 12 *Perf. 13½x14*

1059 A449 55a Good luck	.30	.30
1060 A449 80a See you again	.40	.30
1061 A449 1s With love	.50	.30
Nos. 1059-1061 (3)	1.20	.90
With tabs	2.00	

Spice Boxes — A460

55a, Austro-Hungarian spice box, 19th cent. 80a, Italian, 19th cent. 1s, German, 18th cent.

1990, Sept. 4 Litho. *Perf. 13x14*

1062 A460 55a sil, gray & blk	.30	.25
1063 A460 80a sil, gray & blk	.50	.30
1064 A460 1s multicolored	.60	.35
a. Bklt. pane of 6 (3 #1062, 2 #1063, #1064)	7.50	7.50
Nos. 1062-1064 (3)	1.40	.90
With tabs	1.50	

A461

1990, Sept. 4 *Perf. 13*

1065 A461 1.10s Aliya absorption	.75	.75
With tab	.90	

Electronic Mail — A462

1990, Sept. 4 *Perf. 14x13*

1066 A462 1.20s black & grn	.80	.80
With tab	1.00	

Souvenir Sheet

Beersheba '90 Stamp Exhibition — A463

1990, Sept. 4 *Perf. 13x14*

1067 A463 3s multicolored	4.25	4.00

Sold for 4s.

Computer Games — A464

1990, Dec. 12 Litho. *Perf. 13x14*

1068 A464 60a Basketball	.30	.30
1069 A464 60a Chess	.30	.30
1070 A464 60a Auto racing	.30	.30
Nos. 1068-1070 (3)	.90	.90
With tabs	1.25	

Ze'ev Jabotinsky (1880-1940), Zionist Leader — A465

1990, Dec. 12 Litho. *Perf. 13x14*

1071 A465 1.90s multicolored	1.00	1.00
With tab	1.30	

Philately Day — A466

1990, Dec. 12 *Perf. 14*

1072 A466 1.20s P.O., Yafo, #5	.80	.80
With tab	1.15	

Special Occasions Type of 1989

1991, Feb. 19 Photo. *Perf. 13½x14*

1073 A449 (60a) Happy birthday	.40	.30
1074 A449 (60a) Keep in touch	.40	.30
a. Booklet pane of 10 + 2 labels	5.75	
b. Sheet of 20 + 5 labels	11.50	
1075 A449 (60a) Greetings	.40	.30
Nos. 1073-1075 (3)	1.20	.90
With tabs	1.50	

No. 1074a contains 5 tete-beche pairs. No. 1074b contains 10 tete-beche pairs.

Nos. 1074a-1074b had value of 85a when released.

Issued: Nos. 1074a-1074b, 4/18/94.

Famous Women A467

Designs: No. 1076, Sarah Aaronsohn (1890-1917), World War I heroine. No. 1077, Rahel Bluwstein (1890-1931), poet. No. 1078, Lea Goldberg (1911-1970), poet.

1991, Feb. 19 *Perf. 14*

1076 A467 1.30s multicolored	.75	.75
1077 A467 1.30s multicolored	.75	.75
1078 A467 1.30s multicolored	.75	.75
Nos. 1076-1078 (3)	2.25	2.25
With tabs	2.75	

See Nos. 1096-1097, 1102-1103.

Hadera, Cent. — A468

1991, Feb. 19 *Perf. 13*

1079 A468 2.50s multicolored	1.40	1.00
With tab	2.00	

Intelligence Services Memorial, G'lilot A469

1991, Apr. 9 Litho. *Perf. 14*

1080 A469 65a multicolored	.50	.30
With tab	.60	

14th Hapoel Games A470

1991, Apr. 9

1081 A470 60a multicolored	.40	.30
1082 A470 90a multicolored	.50	.40
1083 A470 1.10s multicolored	.60	.50
Nos. 1081-1083 (3)	1.50	1.20
With tabs	2.00	

Electrification A471

Designs: 70a, First power station, Tel Aviv, 1923. 90a, Yarden Power Station, Naharayim, 1932. 1.20s, Rutenberg Power Station, Ashqelon, 1991.

1991, June 11 Litho. *Perf. 13*

1084 A471 70a multicolored	.35	.35
1085 A471 90a multicolored	.60	.45
1086 A471 1.20s multicolored	.75	.55
Nos. 1084-1086 (3)	1.70	1.35
With tabs	2.25	

Rabbi Shimon Hakham (1843-1910) A472

1991, June 11

1087 A472 2.10s multicolored	1.20	1.20
With tab	1.80	

Souvenir Sheet

Postal and Philatelic Museum, Tel Aviv — A473

Israel #5, Palestine #70, Turkey #133.

1991, June 11 *Perf. 14x13*

1088 A473 3.40s multicolored	5.50	5.50

No. 1088 sold for 5s. Exists imperf. Value $40.

A474

Jewish Festivals: 65a, Man blowing ram's horn, Rosh Hashanah. 1s, Father blessing children, Yom Kippur. 1.20s, Family seated at harvest table, Sukkoth.

1991, Aug. 27 Litho. *Perf. 14*

1089 A474 65a multicolored	.35	.30
1090 A474 1s multicolored	.55	.30
1091 A474 1.20s multicolored	.75	.30
Nos. 1089-1091 (3)	1.65	.90
With tabs	2.00	

Jewish Chronicle, 150th Anniv. — A475

1991, Aug. 27

1092 A475 1.50s multicolored	.80	.80
With tab	1.10	

Baron Maurice De Hirsch (1831-1896), Founder of Jewish Colonization Assoc. — A476

1991, Aug. 27 *Perf. 14*

1093 A476 1.60s multicolored .80 .80
With tab 1.00

Souvenir Sheet

Haifa, by Gustav Bauernfeind — A477

1991, Aug. 27 *Perf. 14x13*

1094 A477 3s multicolored 5.00 4.00

Haifa '91, Israeli-Polish Philatelic Exhibition. Sold for 4s.

Philately Day — A478

1991, Dec. 2 **Litho.** *Perf. 13*

1095 A478 70a #2 on piece .40 .40
With tab .50

Famous Women Type of 1991

Designs: 1s, Rahel Yanait Ben-Zvi (1886-1979), politician. 1.10s, Dona Gracia (Nasi, 1510?-1569), philanthropist.

1991, Dec. 2 **Litho.** *Perf. 14*

1096 A467 1s multicolored .40 .40
1097 A467 1.10s multicolored .50 .50
#1096-1097, with tabs 1.30

1992 Summer Olympics, Barcelona — A479

1991, Dec. 2

1098 A479 1.10s multicolored .80 .50
With tab 1.10

Lehi — A480

1991, Dec. 2 *Perf. 14*

1099 A480 1.50s multicolored .60 .60
With tab 1.00

Etzel — A481

1991, Dec. 2

1100 A481 1.50s blk & red .60 .60
With tab 1.00

Wolfgang Amadeus Mozart, Death Bicent. — A482

1991, Dec. 2 *Perf. 13*

1101 A482 2s multicolored 1.75 1.50
With tab 3.25
a. Booklet pane of 4 13.00

One pair in No. 1101a is tete beche.

Famous Women Type of 1991

80a, Hanna Rovina (1889-1980), actress. 1.30s, Rivka Guber (1902-81), educator.

1992, Feb. 18 **Litho.** *Perf. 14*

1102 A467 80a multicolored .40 .40
1103 A467 1.30s multicolored .60 .60
#1102-1103, with tabs 1.40

Sea of Galilee — A483

1992, Feb. 18

1104 A483 85a Trees 1.00 .65
1105 A483 85a Sailboat 1.00 .65
1106 A483 85a Fish 1.00 .65
a. Strip of 3, #1104-1106 3.25 2.00
With tabs 5.00

Anemone — A483a

1992, Feb. 18 **Photo.** *Perf. 13x14*

1107 A483a (75a) multi .30 .25
With tab .40

PALMAH, 50th Anniv. — A484

1992, Feb. 18 **Litho.** *Perf. 14*

1108 A484 1.50s multicolored .60 .60
With tab 1.00

The Samaritans — A485

1992, Feb. 18

1109 A485 2.60s multicolored 1.00 1.00
With tab 1.40

Rabbi Hayyim Joseph David Azulai (1724-1806) A486

Rabbi Joseph Hayyim Ben Elijah (1834-1909) A487

1992, Apr. 26 *Perf. 13*

1110 A486 85a multicolored .35 .35

Perf. 14

1111 A487 1.20s multicolored .50 .50
#1110-1111, with tabs 1.40

Discovery of America, 500th Anniv. A488

1992, Apr. 26 *Perf. 14*

1112 A488 1.60s multicolored .75 .75
With tab 1.00

Memorial Day — A488a

1992, Apr. 26 **Litho.** *Perf. 13*

1113 A488a 85a multicolored .40 .40
With tab .55

Souvenir Sheet

Expulsion of Jews from Spain, 500th Anniv. — A489

Designs: No. 1114a, 80a, Map of Palestine. b, 1.10s, Map of Italy, Sicily, Greece and central Mediterranean. c, 1.40s, Map of Spain and Portugal.

1992, Apr. 26 *Perf. 14*

1114 A489 Sheet of 3, #a.-c. 3.50 3.50

Jaffa-Jerusalem Railway, Cent. — A490

Different train and four scenes on each stamp showing railroad equipment and memorabilia.

1992

1115 A490 85a multicolored .40 .30
1116 A490 1s multicolored .50 .40
1117 A490 1.30s multicolored .70 .50
1118 A490 1.60s multicolored .90 .60
#1115-1118, with tabs 3.25
a. Bklt. pane of 4, #1115-1118 3.50

Souvenir Sheet

1118B Sheet of 4 + 4 labels 4.50 4.50
c. A490 50a like #1118 .85 .75
d. A490 50a like #1117 .85 .75
e. A490 50a like #1115 .85 .75
f. A490 50a like #1116 .85 .75

Nos. 1115 and 1118, 1116 and 1117 are tete beche in No. 1118a. Nos. 1118c and 1118f, 1118d and 1118e are tete beche in No. 1118B.

Issued: No. 1118B, 9/17; others 6/16.

Rabbi Hayyim Benatar (1696-1743) A491

Rabbi Shalom Sharabi (1720-1777) A492

1992, June 16 *Perf. 13*

1119 A491 1.30s multicolored .55 .55
1120 A492 3s multicolored 1.25 1.25
#1119-1120, with tabs 2.25

Jewish Natl. & University Library, Jerusalem, Cent. — A493

85a, Parables, 1491. 1s, Italian manuscript, 15th cent. 1.20s, Bible translation by Martin Buber.

1992, Sept. 17 **Litho.** *Perf. 13x14*

1121 A493 85a multicolored .30 .30
1122 A493 1s multicolored .50 .50
1123 A493 1.20s multicolored .70 .70
Nos. 1121-1123 (3) 1.50 1.50
With tabs 2.00

Supreme Court A494

1992, Sept. 17 *Perf. 14*

1124 A494 3.60s multicolored 1.60 .75
With tab 2.00

Wild Animals A495

No. 1125, Panthera pardus saxicolor. No. 1126, Elephas maximus. No. 1127, Pan troglodytes. No.1128, Panthera leo persica.

1992, Sept. 17

1125 A495 50a multicolored .40 .35
1126 A495 50a multicolored .40 .35
1127 A495 50a multicolored .40 .35
1128 A495 50a multicolored .40 .35
a. Strip of 4, #1125-1128 1.75 1.75
With tabs 2.75

European Unification
A496

1992, Dec. 8 Litho. *Perf. 13*

1129 A496 1.50s multicolored	.55	.55
With tab	.90	

Stamp Day.

First Hebrew Film, 75th Anniv. — A497

Films: 80a, Liberation of the Jews, 1918. 2.70s, Oded, the Vagabond, 1932, first Hebrew feature film. 3.50s, The Promised Land, 1935, first Hebrew talkie.

1992, Dec. 8

1130 A497 80a multicolored	.50	.30
1131 A497 2.70s multicolored	1.00	.45
1132 A497 3.50s multicolored	1.25	.70
Nos. 1130-1132 (3)	2.75	1.45
With tabs	4.75	

Birds — A498

10a, Wallcreeper. 20a, Tristram's grackle. 30a, White wagtail. 50a, Palestine sunbird. 85a, Sinai rosefinch. 90a, Swallow. 1s, Trumpeter finch. 1.30s, Graceful warbler. 1.50s, Black-eared wheatear. 1.70s, Common bulbul.

1992-98 Photo. *Perf. 13x14*

1133	A498	10a multi	.25	.25
1134	A498	20a multi	.25	.25
1135	A498	30a multi	.25	.25
1137	A498	50a multi	.25	.25
1141	A498	85a multi	.30	.25
1142	A498	90a multi	.25	.25
1142A	A498	1s multi	.30	.25
b.		Violet background	.55	.55
1143	A498	1.30s multi	.60	.45
1144	A498	1.50s multi	.50	.40
1146	A498	1.70s multi	.65	.55
		Nos. 1133-1146 (10)	3.60	3.15
		With tabs	5.25	

No. 1142A has a gray background.

Souvenir Sheet

Designs: a, like #1133. b, like #1137. c, like #1135. d, like #1134. e, like #1141. f, like #1144. g, like #1146. h, like #1142A. i, like #1143. j, like #1142.

Litho. *Perf. 14*

1152 Sheet of 10	3.75	3.75
a.-j. A498 30a Any single	.30	.25

Nos. 1152a-1152j, issued for China '96, 9th Asian Intl. Philatelic Exhibition, have color variations and a gray border.

Issued: 10a, 20a, 30a, 90a, 12/8; 1.30s, 1.70s, 12/9/93; 50a, 1.50s, 2/16/93; 85a, 2/8/94; 1s, 6/7/95; No. 1152, 4/17/96; No. 1142Ab, 11/22/98.

Menachem Begin (1913-92), Prime Minister 1977-83 — A499

1993, Feb. 16 Litho. *Perf. 13*

1153 A499 80a multicolored	.30	.25
With tab	.45	

Nature Reserves Type of 1988

1993, Feb. 16 *Perf. 14*

1154 A427 1.20s Hof Dor	.45	.45
1155 A427 1.50s Nahal Ammud	.55	.55
1156 A427 1.70s Nahal Ayun	.65	.65
Nos. 1154-1156 (3)	1.65	1.65
With tabs	2.00	

Baha'i World Center, Haifa — A500

1993, Feb. 16 *Perf. 13*

1157 A500 3.50s multicolored	2.00	1.00
With tab	3.25	

Medical Corps Memorial — A501

1993, Apr. 18 Litho. *Perf. 13*

1158 A501 80a multicolored	.30	.30
With tab	.50	

Scientific Concepts — A502

1993, Apr. 18 *Perf. 14*

1159 A502 80a Principle of lift	.40	.35
1160 A502 80a Waves	.40	.35
1161 A502 80a Color mixing	.40	.35
1162 A502 80a Eye's memory	.40	.35
a. Strip of 4, #1159-1162	1.75	1.75
With tabs	2.75	

Warsaw Ghetto Uprising, 50th Anniv. — A503

1993, Apr. 18 *Perf. 14*

1163 A503 1.20s gray, black & yel	.50	.35
With tab	.75	

See Poland No. 3151.

Independence, 45th Anniv. — A504

1993, Apr. 18 *Perf. 14*

1164 A504 3.60s multicolored	1.60	1.60
With tab	2.00	

Giulio Racah (1909-1965), Physicist — A505

1.20s, Aharon Katchalsky-Katzir (1913-72), chemist.

1993, June 29 Photo. *Perf. 13x14*

1165 A505 80a mag, bis & blue	.35	.35
1166 A505 1.20s mag, bis & blue	.45	.45
#1165-1166, with tabs	1.10	

Traffic Safety — A506

Children's drawings: 80a, Family crossing street. 1.20s, Traffic signs. 1.50s, Traffic director with hand as face.

1993, June 29 Litho. *Perf. 14*

1167 A506 80a multicolored	.40	.30
1168 A506 1.20s multicolored	.45	.30
1169 A506 1.50s multicolored	.60	.30
Nos. 1167-1169 (3)	1.45	.90
With tabs	2.00	

Fight Against Drugs — A507

1993, June 29 *Perf. 14*

1170 A507 2.80s multicolored	1.10	1.10
With tab	1.50	

14th Maccabiah Games A508

1993, June 29 *Perf. 14*

1171 A508 3.60s multicolored	1.60	1.10
With tab	2.00	

Respect for the Elderly — A509

1993, Aug. 22 Litho. *Perf. 14*

1172 A509 80a multicolored	.30	.25
With tab	.50	

Festivals — A510

1993, Aug. 22 *Perf. 14*

1173 A510 80a Wheat	.35	.25
1174 A510 1.20s Grapes	.40	.25
1175 A510 1.50s Olives	.50	.25
Nos. 1173-1175 (3)	1.25	.75
With tabs	1.75	

Environmental Protection — A511

1993, Aug. 22

1176 A511 1.20s multicolored	.45	.45
With tab	.60	

B'nai B'rith, 150th Anniv. — A512

1993, Aug. 22 *Perf. 13*

1177 A512 1.50s multicolored	.60	.60
With tab	.75	

Souvenir Sheet

Telafila '93, Israel-Romania Philatelic Exhibition — A513

3.60s, Immigrant Ship, by Marcel Janco.

1993, Aug. 21 Litho. *Perf. 14x13*

1178 A513 3.60s multicolored	2.75	2.75

Hebrew Magazines for Children, Cent. A514

1993, Dec. 9 Litho. *Perf. 14*

1179 A514 1.50s multicolored	.60	.40
With tab	.75	

Philately Day.

Hanukkah A515

Hanukkah lamp with candles lit and: 90a, Oil lamp, Talmudic Period. 1.30s, Hanukkah Lamp, Eretz Israel carved stone, 20th cent. 2s, Lighting the Hanukkah Lamp, Rothschild Miscellany illuminated manuscript, c. 1470. No. 1183, Moroccan lamp, Mazagan. No. 1184: Folding Hanukkah Lamp, Lodz Ghetto, 1944. 2.10s, Coin of the Bar-Kokhba War. 1.80s, Cubic copper savivon (dreidel). 2.15s, Hanukkah lamp "Mattathias the Hasmonean," by Boris Schatz.

1993-99

1180 A515 90a multicolored	.40	.40
1181 A515 1.30s multicolored	.50	.50
1182 A515 2s multicolored	.60	.60
1183 A515 1.50s multicolored	.40	*.80*

1184 A515 1.50s multicolored .50 .50
1185 A515 2.10s multicolored .65 .35
1186 A515 1.80s multicolored .55 .35
1187 A515 2.15s multicolored .60 .50
Nos. 1180-1187 (8) 4.20 4.00
With tabs 8.75

The numbering of this set reflects the lighting of the candles on the Menorah.

Issued: 90a, 1.30s, 2s, 12/9/93; No. 1183, 11/27/94; No. 1184, 12/14/95; Nos. 1185-1186, 12/23/97; 2.15s, 1/5/99.

Beetles — A516

No. 1189, Graphopterus serrator. No. 1190, Potosia cuprea. No. 1191, Coccinella septempunctata. No. 1192, Chlorophorus varius.

1994, Feb. 8 Litho. *Perf. 14*
1189 A516 85a multicolored .35 .35
1190 A516 85a multicolored .35 .35
1191 A516 85a multicolored .35 .35
1192 A516 85a multicolored .35 .35
a. Bklt. pane, 2 each #1189-1192 5.50
Nos. 1189-1192 (4) 1.40 1.40
With tabs 1.75

Health — A517

1994, Feb. 8 *Perf. 13*
1193 A517 85a Exercise .35 .35
1194 A517 1.30s Don't smoke .45 .45
1195 A517 1.60s Eat sensibly .55 .55
Nos. 1193-1195 (3) 1.35 1.35
With tabs 1.75

Mordecai Haffkine (1860-1930), Developer of Cholera Vaccine — A518

1994, Feb. 8 *Perf. 14*
1196 A518 3.85s multicolored 1.50 1.50
With tab 1.75

Intl. Style Architecture in Tel Aviv, 1930-39 — A519

No. 1197, Citrus House, by Karl Rubin, 1936-38. No. 1198, Assuta Hospital, by Yosef Neufeld, 1934-35. No. 1199, Cooperative Workers' Housing, by Arieh Sharon, 1934-36.

1994, Apr. 5 Litho. *Perf. 14*
1197 A519 85a multicolored .40 .40
1198 A519 85a multicolored .40 .40
1199 A519 85a multicolored .40 .40
Nos. 1197-1199 (3) 1.20 1.20
With tabs 1.90

Memorial Day — A520

85a, Monument to fallen soldiers of Communications, Electronics & Computer Corps, Yehud.

1994, Apr. 5 Litho. *Perf. 14*
1200 A520 85a multicolored .35 .35
With tab .45

Prevent Violence — A521

1994, Apr. 5 *Perf. 13*
1201 A521 3.85s black & red 1.60 1.60
With tab 2.00

Saul Adler (1895-1966), Scientist — A522

1994, Apr. 5 *Perf. 14*
1202 A522 4.50s multicolored 1.75 1.75
With tab 2.25

Hot Air Ballooning — A523

No. 1203, Filling balloon. No. 1204, Balloons in flight. No. 1205, Marking target.

1994, June 21 Litho. *Perf. 14*
1203 A523 85a multicolored .30 .30
1204 A523 85a multicolored .30 .30
1205 A523 85a multicolored .30 .30
Nos. 1203-1205 (3) .90 .90
With tabs 1.25

Tarbut Elementary Schools, 75th Anniv. — A524

1994, June 21
1206 A524 1.30s multicolored .50 .50
With tab .70

Antoine de St. Exupery (1900-44) — A525

1994, June 21
1207 A525 5s multicolored 2.75 2.75
With tab 4.00

Intl. Olympic Committee, Cent. — A526

1994, June 21
1208 A526 2.25s multicolored .85 .85
With tab 1.10

Peace — A527

1994, Aug. 23 Litho. *Perf. 14*
1209 A527 90a multicolored .50 .50
With tab .70

Peace Between Arabs and Israelis.

Children's Drawings of Bible Stories — A528

Designs: 85a, Adam and Eve. 1.30s, Jacob's Dream. 1.60s, Moses in the Bulrushes. 4s, Parting of the Red Sea.

1994, Aug. 23
1210 A528 85a multicolored .40 .25
1211 A528 1.30s multicolored .50 .25
1212 A528 1.60s multicolored .65 .25
Nos. 1210-1212 (3) 1.55 .75
With tabs 2.00

Souvenir Sheet

Perf. 13x14

1213 A528 4s multicolored 3.00 3.00

No. 1213 contains one 40x51mm stamp.

Immigration to Israel — A529

1994, Aug. 23 *Perf. 13*
1214 A529 1.40s Third Aliya .50 .25
1215 A529 1.70s Fourth Aliya .70 .25
#1214-1215, with tabs 1.60

Israel-Jordan Peace Treaty — A530

1994, Oct. 26 Litho. *Perf. 14*
1216 A530 3.50s multicolored 1.35 .50
With tab 1.75

Public Transportation — A531

Designs: 90a, Ford Model T's, 1920's. 1.40s, White Super buses, 1940's. 1.70s, Leyland Royal Tiger buses, 1960's.

1994, Nov. 27
1217 A531 90a multicolored .35 .25
1218 A531 1.40s multicolored .50 .35
1219 A531 1.70s multicolored .75 .55
Nos. 1217-1219 (3) 1.60 1.15
With tabs 2.00

Computerization of Post Offices — A532

1994, Nov. 27
1220 A532 3s multicolored 1.25 .90
With tab 1.60

Dreyfus Affair, Cent. — A533

1994, Nov. 27
1221 A533 4.10s multicolored 1.75 1.75
With tab 2.75

Outdoor Sculpture — A534

Designs: 90a, Serpentine, by Itzhak Danziger (1916-77), Yarkon Park, Tel Aviv. 1.40s, Stabile, by Alexander Calder (1898-1976), Mount Herzl, Jerusalem. 1.70s, Gate to the Hall of Remembrance, by David Palombo (1920-66), Yad Vashem, Jerusalem.

1995, Feb. 7 Litho. *Perf. 14x13*
1222 A534 90a multicolored .50 .50
1223 A534 1.40s multicolored .80 .80
1224 A534 1.70s multicolored .90 .90
Nos. 1222-1224 (3) 2.20 2.20
With tabs 2.50

Jewish Composers — A535

Title of work, composer: No. 1225, Schelomo, by Ernest Bloch (1880-1959). No. 1226, Symphony No. 1 - Jeremiah, by Leonard Bernstein (1918-90).

1995, Feb. 7
1225 A535 4.10s multicolored 2.40 2.40
1226 A535 4.10s multicolored 2.40 2.40
#1225-1226, with tabs 5.25

See Nos. 1231-1232, 1274-1275.

Ordnance Corps Monument, Netanya — A536

1995, Apr. 25 Litho. *Perf. 13*
1227 A536 1s multicolored .60 .60
With tab .65

End of World War II, Liberation of Concentration Camps, 50th Anniv. — A537

1995, Apr. 25 *Perf. 14x13*

1228 A537 1s multicolored 1.40 1.40
With tab 1.60

Souvenir Sheet

1229 A537 2.50s like #1228 3.50 3.50

No. 1229 contains one 51x40mm stamp.

UN, 50th Anniv. A538

1995, Apr. 25 *Perf. 14*

1230 A538 1.50s multicolored .80 .80
With tab .90

Composer Type of 1995

No. 1231, Arnold Schoenberg (1874-1951). No. 1232, Darius Milhaud (1892-1974).

1995, Apr. 25

1231 A535 2.40s multicolored 1.25 1.25
1232 A535 2.40s multicolored 1.25 1.25
#1231-1232, with tabs 2.75

Souvenir Sheet

Jewish Volunteers to British Army in World War II — A539

1995, Apr. 25

1233 A539 2.50s multicolored 3.25 3.25
With tab 3.50 3.50

15th Hapoel Games, Ramat Gan A540

1995, June 7 **Litho.** *Perf. 14*

1234 A540 1s Kayak .65 .65
With tab .70

Kites — A541

Designs: No. 1235, Hexagonal "Tiara" kite, bird-shaped kite, rhombic Eddy kite. No. 1236, Drawing of kite glider, "Cody War Kite," box kite. No. 1237, Rhombic aerobatic kites, aerobatic "Delta" kite, drawing by Otto Lilienthal.

1995, June 7

1235 1s multicolored .50 .50
1236 1s multicolored .50 .50
1237 1s multicolored .50 .50
a. A541 Strip of 3, #1235-1237 1.50 1.50
With tabs 1.75

Children's Books A542

Designs: 1s, Stars in a Bucket, by Anda Amir-Pinkerfeld. 1.50s, Hurry, Run, Dwarfs, by Miriam Yallan-Stekelis. 1.80s, Daddy's Big Umbrella, by Levin Kipnis.

1995, June 7

1238 A542 1s multicolored .45 .45
1239 A542 1.50s multicolored .70 .70
1240 A542 1.80s multicolored .85 .85
Nos. 1238-1240 (3) 2.00 2.00
With tabs 2.25

Zim Israel Navigation Co. Ltd., 50th Anniv. A543

1995, June 7

1241 A543 4.40s multicolored 2.40 2.40
With tab 2.60

Festivals A544

Designs: 1s, Elijah's Chair for circumcision, linen cloth. 1.50s, Tallit bag, usually a Bar-Mitzvah gift. 1.80s, Marriage Stone for breaking glass at wedding, cloth.

1995, Sept. 4 **Litho.** *Perf. 14*

1242 A544 1s multicolored .45 .45
1243 A544 1.50s multicolored .70 .70
1244 A544 1.80s multicolored .85 .85
Nos. 1242-1244 (3) 2.00 2.00
With tabs 2.25

Jerusalem, 3000th Anniv. A545

Designs: 1s, 6th Cent. mosaic pavement, Gaza Synagogue. 1.50s, 19th Cent. illustration of city from map of Eretz Israel, by Rabbi Pinie of Safed. 1.80s, Aerial photograph of Knesset, Supreme Court.

1995, Sept. 4

1245 A545 1s multicolored .45 .45
1246 A545 1.50s multicolored .70 .70
1247 A545 1.80s multicolored .85 .85
Nos. 1245-1247 (3) 2.00 2.00
With tabs 2.25

See Nos. 1862-1863.

Veterinary Services, 75th Anniv. A546

1995, Sept. 4

1248 A546 4.40s multicolored 2.50 2.50
With tab 2.75

Yitzhak Rabin (1922-95), Prime Minister A547

1995, Dec. 5

1249 A547 5s multicolored 2.50 2.50
With tab 2.75

Fire Fighting and Rescue Service, 70th Anniv. A548

Designs: No. 1250, Fighting fire. No. 1251, Rescue vehicle, fireman beside car.

1995, Dec. 14

1250 A548 1s multicolored .60 .60
1251 A548 1s multicolored .60 .60
#1250-1251, with tabs 1.40

Model Planes A549

1995, Dec. 14

1252 A549 1.80s multicolored .80 .80
With tab .90

Philately Day.

Motion Pictures, Cent. A550

Silhouettes of people in theater viewing: 4.40s, Marx Brothers, Simone Signoret, Peter Sellers, Danny Kaye, Al Jolson.

1995, Dec. 14

1253 A550 4.40s multicolored 2.25 2.25
With tab 2.40

Souvenir Sheet

Jerusalem, City of David, 3000th Anniv. — A551

Designs: a, Mosaic pavement of King David playing harp, Gaza Synagogue, 6th cent. CE. b, Map of Eretz Israel drawn by Rabbi Pinie, 19th cent. c, Present day aerial view of Knesset and Supreme Court.

1995, Dec. 16

1254 A551 Sheet of 3 3.00 3.00
a. 1s multicolored .65 .65
b. 1.50s multicolored .95 .95
c. 1.80s multicolored 1.40 1.40

Sports — A552

1.05s, Mountain cycling. 1.10s, Horseback riding. 1.80s, Water skiing. 1.90s, Paragliding. 2s, Women's volleyball. 2.20s, Whitewater rafting. 3s, Beach bat & ball. 5s, Archery. 10s, Rappelling.

1996-98 **Photo.** *Perf. 13x14*

1256 A552 1.05s multi .60 .60
1257 A552 1.10s multi .80 .80
a. Booklet pane of 20 16.00
Complete booklet, #1257a 16.00
1258 A552 1.80s multi .90 .90
1259 A552 1.90s multi 1.10 1.10
1260 A552 2s multi 1.10 1.10
1261 A552 2.20s multi 1.10 1.10
1262 A552 3s multi 1.60 1.60
1263 A552 5s multi 2.75 2.75
1264 A552 10s multi 5.25 5.25
Nos. 1256-1264 (9) 15.20 15.20
With tabs 17.00

Issued: 1.05s, 1.90s, 2s, 2/20/96; 1.10s, 5s, 2/13/97; 10s, 7/8/97; 3s, 9/23/97; 1258, 1261, 2/17/98.

Souvenir Sheet

Synagogue, Dura-Europos, Syria, 3rd Century A.D. — A553

Murals from synagogue walls: a, Temple, walls of Jerusalem. b, Torah Ark niche. c, Anointing of David as king by Prophet Samuel.

1996, Feb. 20 **Litho.** *Perf. 14x13*

1266 A553 Sheet of 3 2.50 2.50
a. 1.05s multicolored .55 .55
b. 1.60s multicolored .85 .85
c. 1.90s multicolored 1.10 1.10

Jerusalem, 3000th anniv.

Israel Cattle Breeders' Assoc., 70th Anniv. A554

1996, Feb. 20 *Perf. 14*

1267 A554 4.65s multicolored 3.00 3.00
With tab 3.50

Hebrew Writers' Assoc., 75th Anniv. — A555

No. 1269: a, M.J. Berdyczewski. b, Yehuda Burla. c, Devorah Baron. d, Haim Hazaz. e, J.L. Gordon. f, Joseph Hayyim Brenner. g, Abraham Shlonsky. h, Yaakov Shabtai. i, I.L. Peretz. j, Nathan Alterman. k, Saul Tchernichowsky. l, Amir Gilboa. m, Yokheved Bat-Miriam. n, Mendele Mokher Sefarim.

1996, Apr. 17 **Litho.** *Perf. 14*

1269 Pane of 14 4.00 4.00
a.-n. A555 40a Any single .25 .25

Manufacturers Assoc. of Israel, 75th Anniv. — A556

1996, Apr. 17

1271 A556 1.05s multicolored .65 .65
With tab .75

Monument to the Fallen Israel Police A557

1996, Apr. 17

1272 A557 1.05s multicolored .65 .65
With tab .75

Settlement of Metulla, Cent. — A558

1996, Apr. 17

1273 A558 1.90s multicolored .95 .95
With tab 1.10

Composer Type of 1995

Designs: No. 1274, Felix Mendelssohn (1809-47). No. 1275, Gustav Mahler (1860-1911).

1996 **Litho.** ***Perf. 14***

1274	A535 4.65s multicolored		3.75	3.75
1275	A535 4.65s multicolored		3.75	3.75
	#1274-1275, with tabs		8.00	

Issued: No. 1275, 4/17/96; No. 1274, 6/25/96.

A559

1996, June 25

1276 A559 1.05s multicolored	.40	.40
With tab	.50	

Eleven Jewish settlements in Negev Desert, 50th Anniv.

A560

1996, June 25

1277 A560 1.05s Fencing	.40	.40
1278 A560 1.60s Pole vault	.60	.60
1279 A560 1.90s Wrestling	.75	.75
a. Booklet pane of 6, 1 #1277, 2 #1278, 3 #1279	12.00	
Complete booklet, #1279a	12.00	
Nos. 1277-1279 (3)	1.75	1.75
With tabs	2.00	

1996 Summer Olympics, Atlanta.

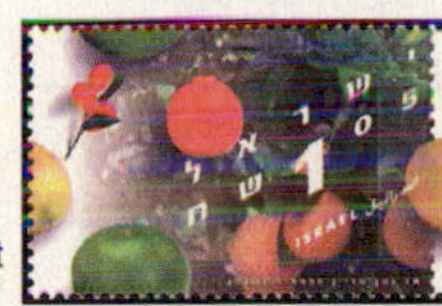

Fruit A561

1.05s, Orange, "sweety", kumquat, lemon. 1.60s, Avocado, persimmon, date, mango, grapes. 1.90s, Carambola, lychee, papaya.

1996, June 25

1280 A561 1.05s multicolored	.45	.45
1281 A561 1.60s multicolored	.70	.70
1282 A561 1.90s multicolored	.85	.85
Nos. 1280-1282 (3)	2.00	2.00
With tabs	2.25	

Public Works Department, 75th Anniv. — A562

1996, Sept. 3 **Litho.** ***Perf. 14***

1283 A562 1.05s multicolored	.65	.65
With tab	.75	

Festivals A563

Stylized designs: 1.05s, Bowl of honey, two lighted candles, Rosh Hashanah. 1.60s, Sukka booth, Sukkot. 1.90s, Inside of synagogue during Torah reading, Simchat Torah.

1996, Sept. 3

1284 A563 1.05s multicolored	.45	.45
1285 A563 1.60s multicolored	.70	.70
1286 A563 1.90s multicolored	.85	.85
Nos. 1284-1286 (3)	2.00	2.00
With tabs	2.25	

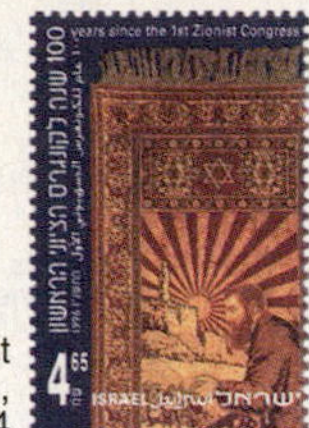

1st Zionist Congress, Cent. — A564

Designs: 4.65s, Tapestry of Theodore Herzl, David's Tower, shining sun. 5s, Casino building, Basel, site of first congress.

1996, Sept. 3

1287 A564 4.65s multicolored	2.25	2.25
With tab	2.50	

Souvenir Sheet

1288 A564 5s multicolored	3.00	3.00

No. 1288 contains one 40x51mm stamp. See No. 1067.

Hanukkah A565

Serpentine Die Cut 11

1996, Oct. 22 **Photo.**

1289 A565 2.50s multicolored	1.15	1.15
With tab	1.25	

See US No. 3118.

Ha-Shilo'ah, Cent., edited by Ahad Ha'am (1856-1927) — A566

1996, Dec. 5 **Litho.** ***Perf. 14***

1290 A566 1.15s multicolored	.60	.60
With tab	.70	

Coexistence: Man and Animals — A567

1996, Dec. 5

1291 A567 1.10s Birds, aircraft	.50	.50
1292 A567 1.75s Pets	.90	.90
1293 A567 2s Dolphins	1.00	1.00
Nos. 1291-1293 (3)	2.40	2.40
With tabs	2.60	

Space Research in Israel A568

1996, Dec. 5

1294 A568 2.05s multicolored	1.05	1.05
With tab	1.20	

Philately Day.

UOAD (Umbrella Organization of Associations for the Disabled) — A569

1996, Dec. 5

1295 A569 5s multicolored	2.50	2.50
With tab	2.75	

Souvenir Sheet

Inventors — A570

Designs: a, 1.50s, Alexander Graham Bell (1847-1922). b, 2s, Thomas Alva Edison (1847-1931).

1997, Feb. 13 **Litho.** ***Perf. 13***

1296 A570 Sheet of 2, #a.-b.	3.50	3.50

Hong Kong '97.

Ethnic Costumes A571

1.10s, Ethiopia. 1.70s, Kurdistan. 2s, Salonica.

1997, Feb. 13 ***Perf. 14***

1297 A571 1.10s multicolored	.55	.55
1298 A571 1.70s multicolored	.85	.85
1299 A571 2s multicolored	1.05	1.05
Nos. 1297-1299 (3)	2.45	2.45
With tabs	2.75	

Miguel de Cervantes (1547-1616), Writer — A572

1997, Feb. 13

1300 A572 3s multicolored	1.75	1.75
With tab	2.00	

Mounument to the Fallen Soldiers of the Logistics Corps A573

1997, Apr. 30 **Litho.** ***Perf. 14***

1301 A573 1.10s multicolored	.45	.45
With tab	.65	

A574

Jewish monuments in Prague: No. 1302, Tombstone of Rabbi Judah Loew MaHaRal. No. 1303, Altneuschul Synagogue.

1997, Apr. 30

1302 A574 1.70s blue & multi	1.00	1.00
1303 A574 1.70s red & multi	1.00	1.00
a. Sheet, 4 each, #1302-1303	17.00	17.00
#1302-1303, with tabs	2.25	

Stamps in No. 1303a do not have tabs. See Czech Republic Nos. 3009-3010.

A575

Design: "The Vilna Gaon," Rabbi Elijah Ben Solomon Zalman (1720-97).

1997, Apr. 30

1304 A575 2s multicolored	.90	.90
With tab	1.00	

Organized Clandestine Immigration (1934-48) — A576

1997, Apr. 30

1305 A576 5s multicolored	2.25	2.25
With tab	2.50	

Souvenir Sheet

Discovery of the Cairo Geniza, Cent., Discovery of Dead Sea Scrolls, 50th Anniv. — A577

Designs: a, 2s, Ben Ezra Synagogue, Cairo. b, 3s, Cliffs, Dead Sea, Prof. Sukenik examining scrolls.

1997, May 29 **Litho.** ***Perf. 13***

1306 A577 Sheet of 2, #a.-b.	4.25	4.25

Pacific '97.

Hello First Grade A578

1997, July 8 **Litho.** ***Perf. 14***

1307 A578 1.10s multicolored	.50	.50
With tab	.60	

Road Safety — A579

No. 1308, "Keep in Lane," car sinking into lake, fish. No. 1309, "Keep Your Distance," car with bird on front grille. No. 1310, "Don't Drink and Drive," man holding drink, car balanced on edge of cliff.

1997, July 8 ***Perf. 13***

1308 A579 1.10s multicolored .45 .45
1309 A579 1.10s multicolored .45 .45
1310 A579 1.10s multicolored .45 .45
Nos. 1308-1310 (3) 1.35 1.35
With tabs 1.60

15th Maccabiah Games A580

1997, July 8 ***Perf. 14***

1311 A580 5s Ice skating 2.25 2.25
With tab 2.50

Festival Stamps — A581

The Visiting Patriarchs, Sukkot: 1.10s, Abraham. 1.70s, Isaac. 2s, Jacob.

1997, Sept. 23 **Litho.** ***Perf. 14***

1312 A581 1.10s multicolored .55 .55
1313 A581 1.70s multicolored .90 .90
1314 A581 2s multicolored 1.00 1.00
a. Booklet pane, 1 #1312, 2 #1313, 3 #1314 9.00
Complete booklet, #1314a 9.00
Nos. 1312-1314 (3) 2.45 2.45
With tabs 2.75

Compare with Nos. 1375-1378.

Music and Dance in Israel — A582

Designs: 1.10s, Zimriya, World assembly of choirs. 2s, Karmiel Dance Festival. 3s, Festival of Klezmers (musical instruments).

1997, Sept. 23 ***Perf. 13***

1315 A582 1.10s multicolored .50 .50
1316 A582 2s multicolored .90 .90
1317 A582 3s multicolored 1.40 1.40
Nos. 1315-1317 (3) 2.80 2.80
With tabs 3.00

UN Resolution on Creation of Jewish State, 50th Anniv. — A583

1997, Sept. 23 ***Perf. 13x14***

1318 A583 5s multicolored 2.25 2.25
With tab 2.60

Souvenir Sheet

Pushkin's "Eugene Onegin," Translated by Abraham Shlonsky — A584

1997, Nov. 19 ***Perf. 14x13***

1319 A584 5s multicolored 3.00 3.00

See Russia No. 6418.

State of Israel, 50th Anniv. in 1998 — A585

1997, Dec. 23 ***Perf. 14***

1320 A585 (1.10s) multicolored .60 .60
With tab 1.00
a. Size: 17x22mm .60 .60
With tab 1.00
b. Booklet pane, 20 #1320a 20.00
Complete booklet, #1320b 18.00
c. As "a," perf. 13x14, photo. — —
With tab —

No. 1320b consists of two blocks of 10 stamps, tete-beche in relationship to each other. No. 1320 is 18x23mm. No. 1320a has brighter blue stripes in flag.

Issued: No. 1320a, 2/17/98; No. 1320c, 5/3/98.

"MACHAL," Overseas Volunteers A586

Designs: 1.80s, "GACHAL," recruitment in the Diaspora.

1997, Dec. 23

1321 A586 1.15s multicolored .50 .50
1322 A586 1.80s multicolored .75 .75
#1321-1322, with tabs 1.50

Chabad's Children of Chernobyl A587

1997, Dec. 23

1323 A587 2.10s multicolored .85 .85
With tab 1.00

A588

1997, Dec. 23

1324 A588 2.50s Julia Set Fractal 1.10 1.10
With tab 1.25

Philately Day.

A589

Three battle fronts during war: Nos. 1325, 1328a (1.50s), Northern Front, photograph of people, Zefat, 1948. Nos. 1326, 1328b (2.50s), Central Front, drawing over photograph of vehicles coming down mountain, outskirts of Jerusalem, 1948. Nos. 1327, 1328c (3s), Southern Front, raising Israeli flag, Elat, 1949.

1998, Feb. 17 **Litho.** ***Perf. 14x13***

1325 A589 1.15s multicolored .65 .65
1326 A589 1.15s multicolored .65 .65
1327 A589 1.15s multicolored .65 .65
Nos. 1325-1327 (3) 1.95 1.95
With tabs 2.25

Souvenir Sheet

1328 A589 Sheet of 3, #a.-c. 4.25 4.25

War of Independence, 1947-49. No. 1328b is 51x40mm.

See No. 1861.

Chaim Herzog (1918-97), President of Israel A590

1998, Feb. 17 ***Perf. 14***

1329 A590 5.35s multicolored 2.25 2.25
With tab 2.50

A591

Jewish Contributions to Modern World Culture: a, Franz Kafka (1883-1924), writer. b, George Gershwin. c, Lev Davidovich Landau (1908-68), physicist. d, Albert Einstein. e, Leon Blum (1872-1950), statesman. f, Elizabeth Rachel Felix (1821-58), actress.

1998, Apr. 27 **Litho.** ***Perf. 14***

1330 Sheet of 6 + 6 labels 4.50 4.50
a.-f. A591 90a Any single .75 .75

See No. 1362.

A592

1998, Apr. 27

1331 A592 1.15s multicolored .50 .50
With tab .60

Memorial Day.

A593

1998, Apr. 27

1332 A593 1.15s multicolored .50 .50
With tab .75

Declaration of the Establishment of the State of Israel, 50th anniv.

A594

1998, Apr. 27

1333 A594 5.35s multicolored 2.10 2.10
With tab 2.50

Israel Defense Forces, 50th anniv.

Holocaust Memorial Day — A595

Non-Jews who risked their lives to save Jews during Holocaust: Giorgio Perlasca, Aristides de Sousa Mendes, Carl Lutz, Sempo Sugihara, Selahattin Ulkumen.

1998, Apr. 27 ***Perf. 13***

1334 A595 6s multicolored 2.50 2.50
With tab 3.00

Children's Pets — A596

Israel '98: a, Cat. b, Dog. c, Bird. d, Goldfish. e, Hamster. f, Rabbit.

1998, May 13

1335 Sheet of 6 4.00 4.00
a.-f. A596 60a Any single .35 .35

No. 1335 contains diagonal perforations so that lower left corner of each stamp can be removed leaving denominated portion in shape of a pentagon.

Postal and Philatelic Museum A597

Illustrations by Kariel Gardosh featuring cartoon character, "Srulik:" a, At post office counter. b, Looking at stamp with magnifying glass. c, Putting mail into post box.

1998, May 13 ***Perf. 14***

1336 Sheet of 3 4.25 4.25
a. A597 1.50s multicolored .90 .90
b. A597 2.50s multicolored 1.40 1.40
c. A597 3s multicolored 1.75 1.75

Aircraft Used in War of Independence, 1948 — A598

No. 1337, Dragon Rapide. No. 1338, Spitfire. No. 1339, B-17 Flying Fortress.

1998, May 3 **Litho.** ***Perf. 14***

1337 A598 2.20s multi 1.25 1.25
1338 A598 2.20s multi 1.25 1.25
1339 A598 2.20s multi 1.25 1.25
a. Strip of 3, #1337-1339 3.75 3.75
With tabs 4.00 4.00

Israel '98.

No. 1339a was issued in sheets containing 2 strips printed tete beche separated by strip of three labels.

A limited-edition booklet exists. It contains the following panes: 1 each Nos. 1305, 1318, 1320, 1320b, 1321-1322, 1325-1327, 1332, 1333, 1339a. Value, $92.50.

Souvenir Sheet

Mosaic of a Young Woman, Zippori — A599

1998, May 13

1340	A599 5s multicolored	3.25	3.25

Israel '98. Sold for 6s.

Souvenir Sheet

King Solomon's Temple — A600

a, Drawing of the temple. b, Inscribed ivory pomegranate.

1998, May 13

1341	A600 Sheet of 2	3.75	3.75
a.	2s multicolored	1.50	1.50
b.	3s multicolored	2.25	2.25

Israel '98. Sold for 7s.

Israel Jubilee Exhibition A601

1998, Aug. 3 Litho. *Perf. 14x13*

1342	A601 5.35s multicolored	2.00	2.00
	With tab	2.25	2.25

Child's Drawing "Living in a World of Mutual Respect" A602

1998, Sept. 8 *Perf. 14*

1343	A602 1.15s multicolored	.45	.45
	With tab	.50	

Holy Cities A603

1998, Sept. 8

1344	A603 1.80s Hebron	.80	.80
1345	A603 2.20s Jerusalem	.95	.95
	#1344-1345, with tabs	2.00	
1346	A603 1.15s Zefat	.60	.60
1347	A603 5.35s Tiberias	2.75	2.75
	#1346-1347, with tabs	3.75	

See No. 1864.

Festival Stamps A604

Holy ark curtains: 1.15s, Peacocks on both sides of menorah, text, Star of David. 1.80s, Menorah, text, two lions. 2.20s, Text surrounded by ornate floral pattern.

1998, Sept. 8

1348	A604 1.15s multicolored	.55	.55
1349	A604 1.80s multicolored	.80	.80
1350	A604 2.20s multicolored	.90	.80
	Nos. 1348-1350 (3)	2.25	2.15
	With tabs	2.75	

Natl. Flag — A605

1998, Dec. 17 Litho. *Die Cut*
Self-Adhesive

1351	A605 1.15s dk bl & bl	.95	.95
1352	A605 2.15s dk bl & grn	1.75	1.75
1353	A605 3.25s dk bl & rose red	2.75	2.75
1354	A605 5.35s dk bl & yel org	4.75	4.75
	Nos. 1351-1354 (4)	10.20	10.20

Hyacinth — A606

1999, Feb. 1 Photo. *Perf. 15*

1355	A606 (1.15s) multicolored	.60	.60
	With tab	.65	

See Nos, 1492A, 1539D-1540.

Knesset, 50th Anniv. A607

1999, Feb. 1 Litho. *Perf. 14*

1356	A607 1.80s multicolored	.60	.60
	With tab	.75	

Manuscript of Rabbi Shalem Shabazi (1619-80), Poet — A608

1999, Feb. 1

1357	A608 2.20s multicolored	1.10	1.10
	With tab	1.25	

Jewish Colonial Trust, Cent. A609

Drawings from one pound sterling share.

1999, Feb. 16

1358	A609 1.80s multicolored	.60	.60
	With tab	.75	

Ethnic Costumes A610

Designs: 2.15s, Yemenite Jewry, Yemen. 3.25s, Bene Israel Community, India.

1999, Feb. 16

1359	A610 2.15s multicolored	.80	.80
1360	A610 3.25s multicolored	1.20	1.20
	#1359-1360, with tabs	2.25	

See Nos. 1373-1374.

Souvenir Sheet

Ancient Boat from Sea of Galilee — A611

a, 3s, Reconstructed boat. b, 5s, Ancient boat.

1999, Mar. 19 Litho. *Perf. 13*

1361	A611 Sheet of 2, #a.-b.	4.50	4.50

Australia '99, World Stamp Expo.

Jewish Contributions to Modern World Culture Type of 1998

Designs: a, Emile Durkheim (1858-1917), social scientist. b, Paul Ehrlich (1854-1915), medical researcher. c, Rosa Luxemburg (1870-1919), politician. d, Norbert Wiener (1894-1964), mathematician, developer of computer science. e, Sigmund Freud (1856-1939), psychologist, founder of psychoanalysis. f, Martin Buber (1878-1965), religious philosopher.

1999, Apr. 18 Litho. *Perf. 14*

1362	Sheet of 6 + 6 labels	3.75	3.75
a.-f.	A591 90a Any single	.60	.60

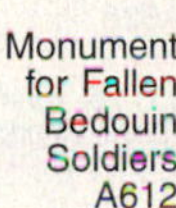

Monument for Fallen Bedouin Soldiers A612

1999, Apr. 18

1363	A612 1.20s multicolored	.45	.45
	With tab	.50	

Israel's Admission to UN, 50th Anniv. A613

1999, Apr. 18

1364	A613 2.30s multicolored	.85	.85
	With tab	1.00	

Simcha Holtzberg (1924-94), Holocaust Survivor, "Father of Wounded Soldiers" A614

1999, Apr. 18

1365	A614 2.50s multicolored	.85	.85
	With tab	1.00	

Painting, "My Favorite Room," by James Ensor (1860-1949) — A614a

1999, May 16 Photo. *Perf. 11½*

1365A	A614a 2.30s multi	1.30	1.30
	With tab	1.50	1.50

See Belgium No. 1738.

"Lovely Butterfly," Children's Television Show A615

Puppets: No. 1366, Ouza, the goose. No. 1367, Nooly, the chick & Shabi, the snail. No. 1368, Batz, the tortoise, and Pingi, the penguin.

1999, June 22 Litho. *Perf. 14*

1366	A615 1.20s multicolored	.65	.65
1367	A615 1.20s multicolored	.65	.65
1368	A615 1.20s multicolored	.65	.65
a.	Strip of 3, #1366-1368	2.00	2.00
	With tabs	2.25	

Pilgrimage to the Holy Land A616

1999, June 22 *Perf. 14x13*

1369	A616 3s Nazareth	1.50	1.50
1370	A616 3s River Jordan	1.50	1.50
1371	A616 3s Jerusalem	1.50	1.50
	Nos. 1369-1371 (3)	4.50	4.50
	With tabs	5.00	

Rabbi Or Sharga (?-1794) — A617

Illustration from Musa-Nameh manuscript, by Shahin, depicting battle of Isreal over Amalek.

1999, June 22 *Perf. 14*

1372	A617 5.60s multicolored	2.00	2.00
	With tab	2.25	2.25

Ethnic Costumes Type of 1999

Designs: 2.30s, Jewish woman in traditional Moroccan costume. 3.40s, Jewish man in traditional costume of Bukhara.

1999, Sept. 1 Litho. *Perf. 14*

1373	A610 2.30s multicolored	.70	.70
1374	A610 3.40s multicolored	1.00	1.00
	#1373-1374, with tab	2.00	

"Ushpizin," Guests in the Sukkah, Festival of Sukkoth — A619

1999, Sept. 1

1375	A619 1.20s Joseph	.60	.60
1376	A619 1.90s Moses	.90	.90
1377	A619 2.30s Aaron	1.00	1.00
1378	A619 5.60s David	2.50	2.50
a.	Bklt. pane, #1376-1378, 3 #1375	11.00	11.00
	Complete booklet, #1378a	11.00	
	Nos. 1375-1378 (4)	5.00	5.00
	With tabs	5.50	

Stamp Day A620

1999, Sept. 1

1379	A620 5.35s multicolored	2.10	2.10
	With tab	2.40	

Ceramic Urns, Museum of Jewish Culture, Bratislava, Slovakia — A621

Designs: No. 1380, Urn from 1776 showing man on sick bed, denomination at UL. No. 1381, Urn from 1734 showing funeral procession, denomination at UR.

1999, Nov. 23 Litho. *Perf. 14*

1380	A621 1.90s multi	.80	.80
1381	A621 1.90s multi	.80	.80
	#1380-1381, with tabs	1.90	

See Slovakia Nos. 344-345.

Kiryat Shemona, 50th Anniv. A622

1999, Dec. 7

1382	A622 1.20s multicolored	.45	.45
	With tab	.55	

Proclamation of Jerusalem as Israel's Capital, 50th Anniv. — A623

1999, Dec. 7 *Perf. 13x14*

1383	A623 3.40s multicolored	1.25	1.25
	With tab	1.40	

Sidna "Baba Sali" The Admor, Israel Abihssira (1890-1984) A624

1999, Dec. 7 *Perf. 13*

1384	A624 4.40s multi	1.50	1.50
	With tab	1.75	

Millennium A625

Designs: 1.40s, Joggers in park. 1.90s, Researcher with flask. 2.30s, Man at computer. 2.80s, Astronaut in space.

2000, Jan. 1

1385	A625 1.40s multi	.70	.70
1386	A625 1.90s multi	.95	.95
1387	A625 2.30s multi	1.10	1.10
1388	A625 2.80s multi	1.40	1.40
	Nos. 1385-1388 (4)	4.15	4.15
	With tabs	4.75	

Stampin' the Future Children's Stamp Design Contest Winners A626

Various children's drawings.

2000, Jan. 1 *Perf. 13x13½*

Background Colors

1389	A626 1.20s blue	.60	.60
1390	A626 1.90s yel org	.95	.95
1391	A626 2.30s red	1.10	1.10
1392	A626 3.40s green	1.60	1.60
	Nos. 1389-1392 (4)	4.25	4.25
	With tabs	4.75	

Fairy Tales of Hans Christian Andersen (1805-75) A627

1.20s, The Little Mermaid. 1.90s, The Emperor's New Clothes. 2.30s, The Ugly Duckling.

2000, Feb. 15 Litho. *Perf. 13x14*

1393	A627 1.20s multi	.60	.60
1394	A627 1.90s multi	.95	.95
1395	A627 2.30s multi	1.10	1.10
	Nos. 1393-1395 (3)	2.65	2.65
	With tabs	3.00	

Pilgrimage to the Holy Land A628

Churches: 1.40s, All Apostles, Capernaum. 1.90s, St. Andrew's, Jerusalem. 2.30s, Church of the Visitation, Ein Kerem.

2000, Feb. 15 *Perf. 14x13*

1396	A628 1.40s multi	.70	.70
1397	A628 1.90s multi	.95	.95
1398	A628 2.30s multi	1.10	1.10
	Nos. 1396-1398 (3)	2.75	2.75
	With tabs	3.00	

King Hussein of Jordan (1935-99) — A629

2000, Feb. 15 Litho. *Perf. 14*

1399	A629 4.40s multi	2.25	2.25
	With tab	2.50	

Shuni Historic Site — A630

Perf. 14 Syncopated

2000, Feb. 15 Photo.

1400	A630 2.30s multi	1.10	1.10
	With tab	1.25	

See Nos. 1409, 1427-1428, 1442, 1478, 1492, 1601.

A631

Worldwide Fund for Nature: Various depictions of Blanford's fox.

2000, May 3 Litho. *Perf. 14*

Denomination Color

1401	A631 1.20s red violet	.65	.65
1402	A631 1.20s green	.65	.65
1403	A631 1.20s blue	.65	.65
1404	A631 1.20s yellow	.65	.65
a.	Strip, #1401-1404 + central label	3.00	3.00
	With tabs	3.75	

See Nos. 1435-1438.

Memorial Day — A632

2000, May 3

1405	A632 1.20s multi	.50	.50
	With tab	.60	

Intl. Communications Day — A633

2000, May 3 *Perf. 13*

1406	A633 2.30s multi	.90	.90
	With tab	1.10	

Land of Three Religions A634

2000, May 3

1407	A634 3.40s multi	1.30	1.30
	With tab	1.50	

See No. 1866.

Johann Sebastian Bach (1685-1750) A635

2000, May 3

1408	A635 5.60s multi	2.25	2.25
	With tab	2.60	

Historic Site Type of 2000

Perf. 14 Syncopated

2000, July 25 Photo.

1409	A630 1.20s Juara	.50	.50
	With tab	.75	
a.	Perf. 14¾x15 Syncopated	*6.00*	*6.00*
	With tab	*7.00*	

The line containing the country name in English and Arabic is 10mm long on No. 1409, 11 mm long on No. 1409a.

Issued: No. 1409a, 2001.

2000 Summer Olympics, Sydney — A636

2000, July 25 Litho. *Perf. 13*

1410	A636 2.80s multi	1.00	1.00
	With tab	1.10	

A637

2000, July 25 *Perf. 14*

1411	A637 4.40s multi	1.50	1.50
	With tab	1.75	

King Hassan II of Morocco (1929-99).

Israeli Food — A638

2000, June 25 *Perf. 13½x13*

1412	A638 1.40s Couscous	.65	.65
1413	A638 1.90s Gefilte fish	.85	.85
1414	A638 2.30s Falafel	1.00	1.00
a.	Booklet pane, #1412, 2 #1413, 3 #1414	8.75	
	Booklet, #1414a	8.75	
	Nos. 1412-1414 (3)	2.50	2.50
	With tabs	2.75	

Dental Health A639

2000, Sept. 19 Litho. *Perf. 14*

1415	A639 2.20s multi	.90	.90
	With tab	1.10	

Dohany Synagogue, Budapest A640

2000, Sept. 19 *Perf. 13x14*

1416	A640 5.60s multi	2.75	2.75
	With tab	3.00	

See Hungary No. 3710.

Jewish New Year Cards — A641

Designs: 1.20s, Boy giving girl a gift. 1.90s, Girl holding Zionist flag. 2.30s, Man giving flowers and greetings to woman.

2000, Sept. 19 *Perf. 14*

1417	A641 1.20s multi	.45	.45
1418	A641 1.90s multi	.70	.70
1419	A641 2.30s multi	.85	.85
	Nos. 1417-1419 (3)	2.00	2.00
	With tabs	2.25	

See Nos. 1455-1457.

Aleppo Codex — A642

2000, Dec. 5 *Perf. 13*
1420 A642 4.40s multi 1.75 1.75
With tab 2.00

Dinosaurs A643

Designs: No. 1421, Struthiomimuses on beach. No. 1422, Struthiomimuses in forest. No. 1423, Struthiomimus on hill.

2000, Dec. 5 Litho. *Perf. 13*
1421 A643 2.20s multi .85 .85
1422 A643 2.20s multi .85 .85
1423 A643 2.20s multi .85 .85
a. Strip of 3, #1421-1423 2.60 2.60
With tabs 2.75

Science Fiction A644

Designs: 2.80s, Robot. 3.40s, Time travel. 5.60s, Space flight.

2000, Dec. 5 *Perf. 14*
1424 A644 2.80s multi 1.10 1.10
1425 A644 3.40s multi 1.35 1.35
1426 A644 5.60s multi 2.10 2.10
Nos. 1424-1426 (3) 4.55 4.55
With tabs 5.00

Historic Sites Type of 2000
Perf. 14 Syncopated

2000-2001 Photo.
1427 A630 2.20s Mitzpe Revivim 1.10 1.10
With tab 1.25
1428 A630 3.40s Ilaniyya 1.60 1.60
With tab 1.75

Issued: 2.20s, 12/5; 3.40s, 2/13/01.

Settlements, Cent. — A645

2001, Feb. 13 Litho. *Perf. 14*
1429 A645 2.50s Yavne'el 1.10 1.10
1430 A645 4.70s Menahamia 2.00 2.00
1431 A645 5.90s Kefar Tavor 2.60 2.60
Nos. 1429-1431 (3) 5.70 5.70
With tabs 6.25

Hebrew Letters Aleph and Beth — A646

No. 1432: a, Aleph. b, Beth. c, Gimel. d, Daleth. e, He. f, Waw. g, Zayin. h, Heth. i, Teth. j, Yod. k, Kaph. l, Lamed. m, Mem. n, Nun. o, Samekh. p, Ayin. q, Pe. r, Sadhe. s, Qoph. t, Resh. u, Sin. v, Taw.

No. 1433 — End-of-word letters: a, Kaph. b, Mem. c, Nun. d, Pe. e, Sadhe.

2001, Feb. 13 Photo. *Perf. 15*
1432 Sheet of 22 2.00 2.00
a.-v. A646 10a Any single .25 .25

Litho.
Perf. 14

1433 Horiz. strip of 5 1.10 1.10
a.-e. A646 10a Any single .25 .25
1434 A646 1s shown .45 .45
With tab .55

No. 1433 issued in sheets of two tete-beche strips. The horizontal strips of stamps in No. 1432 are printed tete-beche.

Worldwide Fund for Nature Type of 2000 Without WWF Emblem

Designs: 1.20s, Lesser kestrel. 1.70s, Kuhl's pipistrelle. 2.10s, Roe deer. 2.50s, Greek tortoise.

2001, Mar. 18 Litho. *Perf. 14*
1435 A631 1.20s multi .55 .55
1436 A631 1.70s multi .70 .70
1437 A631 2.10s multi .90 .90
1438 A631 2.50s multi 1.15 1.15
a. Booklet pane, 2 each #1435-1438 8.00
Nos. 1435-1438 (4) 3.30 3.30
With tabs 3.50

Flowers — A647

No. 1439: a, Prairie gentian (purple). b, Barberton daisy (yellow) c, Star of Bethlehem (orange). d, Calla lily (white).

2001, Mar. 18
1439 Horiz. strip of 4 + 6 labels 3.00 3.00
a.-d. A647 1.20s Any single .60 .60

No. 1439 was printed in sheets of four strips. The second and fourth strips in the sheet have the stamps in reverse order. Sheets sold at the Jerusalem 2001 Stamp Exhibition could have their labels personalized by the purchaser.

See No. 1463.

Souvenir Sheet

Jerusalem 2001 Stamp Exhibition — A648

2001, Mar. 18
1440 A648 10s multi 4.25 4.25

Monument to Fallen Nahal Soldiers — A649

2001, Apr. 18 Litho. *Perf. 13*
1441 A649 1.20s multi .50 .50
With tab .60

Memorial Day.

Historic Sites Type of 2000
Perf. 14 Syncopated

2001, May 23 Photo.
1442 A630 2s Sha'ar HaGay Inn .95 .95
With tab 1.10

Shrine of the Báb Terraces, Haifa — A650

2001, May 23 *Perf. 13x13¼*
1443 A650 3s multi 1.75 1.75
With tab 2.00

Karaite Jews — A651

2001, May 23 Litho. *Perf. 14*
1444 A651 5.60s multi 2.50 2.50
With tab 2.75

Souvenir Sheet

Belgica 2001 Intl. Stamp Exhibition, Brussels — A652

Cut diamonds: a, 1.40s, Marquise. b, 1.70s, Round. c, 4.70s, Square.

2001, May 23 *Perf. 14¾x14½*
1445 A652 Sheet of 3 4.25 4.25
a. 1.40s multi .75 .75
b. 1.70s multi .90 .90
c. 4.70s multi 2.50 2.50

No. 1445 sold for 10s.

Youth Movements A653

2001, July 17 *Perf. 14*
1446 A653 5.60s multi 2.50 2.50
With tab 2.75

Bezalel School of Art Ceramic Facade Tiles — A654

Landscapes of: 1.20s, Hebron. 1.40s, Jaffa. 1.90s, Haifa. 2.30s, Tiberias.

2001, July 17 *Perf. 13x14*
1447 A654 1.20s multi .55 .55
1448 A654 1.40s multi .65 .65
1449 A654 1.90s multi .90 .90
1450 A654 2.30s multi 1.10 1.10
Nos. 1447-1450 (4) 3.20 3.20
With tabs 3.50

Souvenir Sheet

Phila Nippon '01, Japan — A655

Children's stamp design contest winners: a, 1.20s, Balloons. b, 1.40s, Cat. c, 2.50s, Veterinarian with dog. d, 4.70s, Dolphins.

2001, July 17 *Perf. 14¾*
1451 A655 Sheet of 4 4.25 4.25
a. 1.20s multi .50 .50
b. 1.40s multi .60 .60
c. 2.50s multi 1.10 1.10
d. 4.70s multi 2.00 2.00

No. 1451 sold for 10s.

Shota Rustaveli (c. 1172-c. 1216), Georgian Poet — A656

2001, Sept. 3 Litho. *Perf. 13x14*
1452 A656 3.40s multi 1.45 1.45
With tab 1.60

Yehuda Amichai (1924-2000), Poet — A657

2001, Sept. 3
1453 A657 5.60s multi 2.25 2.25
With tab 2.50

Jewish National Fund, Cent A658

2001, Sept. 3 *Perf. 14*
1454 A658 5.60s multi 2.50 2.50
With tab 2.75

Jewish New Year Cards Type of 2000

Designs: 1.20s, Soldier, dove with olive branch. 1.90s, Two women. 2.30s, Boy with flowers.

2001, Sept. 3
1455 A641 1.20s multi .50 .50
1456 A641 1.90s multi .80 .80
1457 A641 2.30s multi 1.00 1.00
Nos. 1455-1457 (3) 2.30 2.30
With tabs 2.50

Selection of Col. Ilan Ramon as Israel's First Astronaut A659

2001, Dec. 11 Litho. *Perf. 13*
1458 A659 1.20s multi .65 .65
With tab .80

Akim Association for the Rehabilitation of the Mentally Handicapped, 50th Anniv. — A660

2001, Dec. 11 *Perf. 13x14*
1459 A660 2.20s multi 1.00 1.00
With tab 1.10

Heinrich Heine (1797-1856), Poet — A661

2001, Dec. 11
1460 A661 4.40s multi 2.00 2.00
With tab 2.25

Institute for the Blind, Jerusalem, Cent. A662

Litho. & Embossed

2001, Dec. 11 *Perf. 14¾*
1461 A662 5.60s multi 2.10 2.10
With tab 2.50

Coastal Conservation A663

2001, Dec. 11 **Litho.** *Perf. 13*
1462 A663 10s multi 4.50 4.50
With tab 5.00

Flower Type of 2001

2002, Feb. 24 **Litho.** *Perf. 14*
1463 A647 1.20s Yellow lily .60 .60
With tab .70

No. 1463 has small picture of flower at left, while No. 1439b has small picture of flower at right.

Languages A664

2002, Feb. 24 *Perf. 13x14*
1464 A664 2.10s Yiddish .90 .90
1465 A664 2.10s Ladino .90 .90
With tabs 2.00

Mushrooms A665

Designs: 1.90s, Agaricus campester. 2.20s, Amanita muscaria. 2.80s, Suillus granulatus.

2002, Feb. 24
1466 A665 1.90s multi .80 .80
1467 A665 2.20s multi .95 .95
1468 A665 2.80s multi 1.25 1.25
Nos. 1466-1468 (3) 3.00 3.00
With tabs 3.50

Months of the Year — A666

Designs: a, Tishrei (shofar, pomegranates). b, Heshvan (dried leaves). c, Kislev (dreidel, Hanukkah candles). d, Tevet (orange, flowers). e, Shevat (seedling, flowers, seeds). f, Adar (party hat, noisemaker, hamentashen). g, Nisan (cup, matzoh, flowers). h, Iyyar (bow and arrows, seeds). i, Sivan (wheat, sickle). j, Tammuz (flower, shells). k, Av (bride, groom, grapes). l, Elul, (cotton, dates, prayer book).

2002, Feb. 24 **Photo.** *Perf. 14x14¼*
1469 A666 Sheet of 12 6.75 6.75
a.-l. 1.20s Any single .55 .55

Self-Adhesive

Serpentine Die Cut 16

1470 A666 Booklet of 12 *11.50*
a.-l. 1.20s Any single *.95* *.95*

Monument to Fallen Military Police A667

2002, Apr. 10 **Litho.** *Perf. 14*
1471 A667 1.20s multi .50 .50
With tab .60

Hakhel Le Yisrael — A668

2002, Apr. 10 *Perf. 13x14*
1472 A668 4.70s multi 2.00 2.00
With tab 2.25
a. Perf. 13¾x13 (1830a) — —

Issued: No. 1472a, 11/21/10.

Israel Foundation for Handicapped Children, 50th Anniv. — A669

2002, Apr. 10
1473 A669 5.90s multi 2.25 2.25
With tab 2.50

Historians — A670

Designs: No. 1474, Heinrich Graetz (1817-91). No. 1475, Simon Dubnow (1860-1941). No. 1476, Benzion Dinur (1884-1973). No. 1477, Yitzhak Baer (1888-1980).

2002, Apr. 10 *Perf. 14*
1474 A670 2.20s multi .90 .90
1475 A670 2.20s multi .90 .90
1476 A670 2.20s multi .90 .90
1477 A670 2.20s multi .90 .90
Nos. 1474-1477 (4) 3.60 3.60
With tabs 4.00

See Nos. 1553-1555.

Historic Sites Type of 2000

Perf. 14 Syncopated

2002, June 18 **Photo.**
1478 A630 3.30s Hatsar Kinneret 1.40 1.40
With tab 1.60

Cable Cars — A671

2002, June 18 **Litho.** *Perf. 14*
1479 A671 2.20s Haifa .95 .95
1480 A671 2.20s Massada .95 .95
1481 A671 2.20s Menara .95 .95
1482 A671 2.20s Rosh Haniqra .95 .95
Nos. 1479-1482 (4) 3.80 3.80
With tabs 4.25

Souvenir Sheet

Geology — A672

2002, June 18
1483 A672 Sheet of 3 5.00 5.00
a. 2.20s Fish fossil 1.10 1.10
b. 3.40s Copper minerals 1.75 1.75
c. 4.40s Ammonite 2.10 2.10

No. 1483 sold for 12s.

Rechavam Ze'evy (1926-2001), Assassinated Tourism Minister — A673

2002, Aug. 27 **Litho.** *Perf. 14*
1484 A673 1.20s multi .50 .50
With tab .60

Baruch Spinoza (1632-77), Philosopher A674

2002, Aug. 27 *Perf. 13x14*
1485 A674 5.90s multi 2.25 2.25
With tab 2.50 2.50

Wine — A675

Designs: 1.20s, Clippers, bunch of grapes. 1.90s, Corkscrew, cork. 2.30s, Wine glass, bottle.

2002, Aug. 27 *Perf. 14*
1486 A675 1.20s multi .45 .45
1487 A675 1.90s multi .75 .75
1488 A675 2.30s multi .90 .90
Nos. 1486-1488 (3) 2.10 2.10
With tabs 2.40

Birds of the Jordan Valley A676

2002, Aug. 27 *Perf. 14½x14*
1489 A676 2.20s Golden eagle .90 .90
1490 A676 2.20s Black stork .90 .90
1491 A676 2.20s Common crane .90 .90
Nos. 1489-1491 (3) 2.70 2.70
With tabs 3.00

Historic Sites Type of 2000

Perf. 14 Syncopated

2002, Aug. 27 **Photo.**
1492 A630 4.60s Kadoorie School 2.00 2.00
With tab 2.25

Hyacinth Type of 1999

Perf. 14 Syncopated

2002, Oct. 21 **Photo.**
1492A A606 (1.20s) multi *7.50* *7.50*
With tab *8.00*

Political Journalists A677

Designs: 1.20s, Abba Ahimeir (1897-1962). 3.30s, Israel Eldad (1910-96). 4.70s, Moshe Beilinson (1890-1936). 5.90s, Rabbi Binyamin (1880-1957).

2002, Nov. 26 **Litho.** *Perf. 14*
1493 A677 1.20s multi .45 .45
1494 A677 3.30s multi 1.30 1.30
1495 A677 4.70s multi 1.90 1.90
1496 A677 5.90s multi 2.25 2.25
Nos. 1493-1496 (4) 5.90 5.90
With tabs 6.75

Toys — A678

2002, Nov. 26
1497 A678 2.20s Five Stones .95 .95
1498 A678 2.20s Marbles .95 .95
1499 A678 2.20s Spinning top .95 .95
1500 A678 2.20s Yo-yo .95 .95
Nos. 1497-1500 (4) 3.80 3.80
With tabs 4.25

Menorah — A679

2002-03 Photo. *Perf. 15x14¾*

1501 A679 20a red .25 .25

1502 A679 30a gray olive .25 .25

1503 A679 40a gray green .25 .25

1504 A679 50a gray brown .25 .25

1505 A679 1s purple .40 .40

1506 A679 1.30s blue .50 .50

Nos. 1501-1506 (6) 1.90 1.90

With tabs 2.75

Issued: 30a, 1s, 11/26/02; 20a, 40a, 50a, 1.30s, 2/11/03.

See Nos. 1758-1760.

Yeshivot Hahesder, 50th Anniv. (in 2004) A680

2003, Feb. 11 Litho. *Perf. 14*

1507 A680 1.20s multi .50 .50

With tab .60

11 September 2001, by Michael Gross — A681

2003, Feb. 11 *Perf. 13x14*

1508 A681 2.30s multi 1.10 1.10

With tab 1.25 1.25

Monument for the Victims of Hostile Acts, Jerusalem A682

2003, Feb. 11 *Perf. 14x13*

1509 A682 4.70s multi 1.75 1.75

With tab 2.00

Powered Flight, Cent. A683

Designs: 2.30s, Wright Flyer in flight. 3.30s, Engine, propellor, Wright brothers. 5.90s, Orville Wright piloting Wright Flyer.

2003, Feb. 11 *Perf. 14*

1510 A683 2.30s multi .95 .95

1511 A683 3.30s multi .90 .90

1512 A683 5.90s multi 1.35 1.35

Nos. 1510-1512 (3) 3.20 3.20

With tabs 5.00

Memorial Day A684

2003, Apr. 27 Litho. *Perf. 14*

1513 A684 1.20s multi .50 .50

With tab .60

Holocaust Memorial Day — A685

2003, Apr. 27 *Perf. 13*

1514 A685 2.20s multi 1.00 1.00

With tab 1.10

Yemeni Jewish Immigration A686

2003, Apr. 27 *Perf. 14*

1515 A686 3.30s multi 1.25 1.25

With tab 1.40

Israeli Aircraft Industries, 50th Anniv. A687

2003, Apr. 27

1516 A687 3.30s multi 1.40 1.40

With tab 1.50

Independence, 55th Anniv. — A688

2002, Apr. 27

1517 A688 5.90s multi 2.25 2.25

With tab 2.50 2.50

Famous Men — A689

Designs: 1.90s, Ya'akov Meridor (1913-95), government minister. 2.20s, Ya'akov Dori (1899-1973), first chief of staff of the Israel Defense Forces. 2.80s, Sheikh Ameen Tarif (1898-1993), President of Druse Religious Court.

2003, Apr. 27 *Perf. 13*

1518 A689 1.90s multi .85 .85

1519 A689 2.20s multi 1.00 1.00

1520 A689 2.80s multi 1.25 1.25

Nos. 1518-1520 (3) 3.10 3.10

With tabs 3.50

Greetings — A690

Designs: No. 1521, Open box, Hebrew letters. No. 1522, Bride and groom. No. 1523, Heart as flower.No. 1524, Hot air balloon, flowers. No. 1525, Flowers and ladybug. No. 1526, Boy and teddy bear.

2003 *Perf. 14*

1521 A690 (1.20s) multi .70 .70

a. Sheet of 12 + 12 labels 13.50 13.50

1522 A690 (1.20s) multi .70 .70

a. Sheet of 12 + 12 labels 13.50 13.50

1523 A690 (1.20s) multi .70 .70

a. Sheet of 12 + 12 labels 13.50 13.50

Nos. 1521-1523 (3) 2.10 2.10

With tabs 2.50

1524 A690 (1.20s) multi .70 .70

a. Sheet of 12 + 12 labels 13.50 13.50

1525 A690 (1.20s) multi .70 .70

a. Sheet of 12 + 12 labels 13.50 13.50

1526 A690 (1.20s) multi .70 .70

a. Sheet of 12 + 12 labels 13.50 13.50

Nos. 1524-1526 (3) 2.10 2.10

With tabs 2.50

Issued: Nos. 1521-1523, 4/27; Nos. 1524-1526, 6/24; Nos. 1521a-1523a, 1524a-1526a, 10/19. Nos. 1521a-1526a each sold for 21.20s. Labels could be personalized.

A sheet containing three No. 1524 + three labels that could not be personalized was issued in 2011 and sold for 15s.

Self-adhesive examples of Nos. 1521, 1523, 1524-1526 come from sheets issued in 1999 that sold for much more than face value.

Village Centenaries — A691

2003, June 24 Litho. *Perf. 14*

1527 A691 3.30s Atlit 1.50 1.50

1528 A691 3.30s Givat-Ada 1.50 1.50

1529 A691 3.30s Kfar-Saba 1.50 1.50

Nos. 1527-1529 (3) 4.50 4.50

With tabs 5.00

Evolution of the Israeli Flag A692

Designs: 1.90s, Flag of the Prague Jewish community, 15th cent. 2.30s, Ness Ziona flag, 1891. 4.70s, Theodor Herzl's "Der Judenstaat" flag design, 1896. 5.90s, Israeli flag, 1948.

2003, June 24

1530 A692 1.90s multi .85 .85

1531 A692 2.30s multi 1.00 1.00

1532 A692 4.70s multi 1.90 1.90

1533 A692 5.90s multi 2.50 2.50

Nos. 1530-1533 (4) 6.25 6.25

With tabs 7.00

Yad Vashem, 50th Anniv. — A693

Stars of David and: No. 1534, List of Jewish forced laborers. No. 1535, Teddy bear, page of testimony.

2003, Sept. 9 Litho. *Perf. 14*

1534 A693 2.20s multi 1.00 1.00

1535 A693 2.20s multi 1.00 1.00

a. Pair, #1534-1535 2.00 2.00

Pair with tabs 2.25

b. Miniature sheet, 3 #1535a 6.00 6.00

No. 1535b issued 2004.

Olive Oil — A694

Designs: 1.30s, Olives. 1.90s, Olive press. 2.30s, Jars of oil.

2003, Sept. 9

1536 A694 1.30s multi .60 .60

1537 A694 1.90s multi .90 .90

1538 A694 2.30s multi 1.10 1.10

a. Booklet pane, #1536, 2 #1537, 3 #1538 5.75 —

Complete booklet, #1538a 5.75

Nos. 1536-1538 (3) 2.60 2.60

With tabs 3.00

Souvenir Sheet

Armenian Ceramics in Jerusalem — A695

No. 1539: a, Deer, by Karakashian-Balian Studio, 1930s-1940s. b, Bird, by Stepan Karakashian, 1980s. c, Tree of Life, by Marie Balian, 1990s.

2003, Sept. 9 *Perf.*

1539 A695 Sheet of 3 6.75 6.75

a. 2.30s multi 1.50 1.50

b. 3.30s multi 2.25 2.25

c. 4.70s multi 3.00 3.00

No. 1539 contains three 31mm diameter stamps and sold for 15s.

Hyacinth Type of 1999

2003 Photo. *Perf. 15 Syncopated*

1539D A606 (1.20s) multi *8.00 8.00*

Booklet Stamp

Self-Adhesive

Serpentine Die Cut 13½x14

1540 A606 (1.30s) multi *1.50 1.50*

a. Booklet pane of 20 *30.00*

Issued: 1.20s, 10/8; 1.30s, 12/4.

Immigrants to Israel — A696

Designs: 2.10s, Leibowitch family, clerical house, Zikhron Ya'acov. 6.20s, Second Aliya immigrants, Rothschild Ave., Tel Aviv.

2003, Dec. 9 Litho. *Perf. 13*

1541 A696 2.10s multi .75 .75

1542 A696 6.20s multi 2.25 2.25

With tabs 3.50

Famous Men — A697

Designs: 3.30s, Aharon David Gordon (1856-1922), laborer. 4.90s, Emile Habiby (1921-96), journalist, politician. 6.20s, Yehoshua Hankin (1865-1945), land developer.

2003, Dec. 9 *Perf. 14*

1543 A697 3.30s multi 1.00 1.00

1544 A697 4.90s multi 1.50 1.50

1545 A697 6.20s multi 2.00 2.00

Nos. 1543-1545 (3) 4.50 4.50

With tabs 5.00

Children on Wheels — A698

No. 1546: a, Boy on bicycle. b, Girl on roller blades. c, Girl on scooter. d, Boy on skateboard.

2003, Dec. 9 *Perf. 13¾*

1546 Horiz. strip of 4 2.10 2.10

a.-d. A698 1.30s Any single .50 .50

Strip with tabs 2.25

Philately Day.

Red Sea Fish A699

Designs: No. 1547, Amphiprion bicinctus. No. 1548, Pseudanthias squamipinnis. No. 1549, Pseudochromis fridmani. No. 1550, Chaetodon paucifasciatus.

2004, Jan. 30 Litho. *Perf. 14*

1547	A699 1.30s multi		.50	.50
1548	A699 1.30s multi		.50	.50
1549	A699 1.30s multi		.50	.50
1550	A699 1.30s multi		.50	.50
a.	Souvenir sheet, #1547-1550		3.00	3.00
	Nos. 1547-1550 (4)		2.00	2.00
	With tabs		2.25	

2004 Hong Kong Stamp Expo (No. 1550a). No. 1550a sold for 7.50s.

Menachem Begin Heritage Center, Jerusalem A700

2004, Feb. 24 *Perf. 13*

1551	A700 2.50s multi	1.10	1.10
	With tab	1.25	

Col. Ilan Ramon (1954-2003), First Israeli Astronaut A701

2004, Feb. 24

1552	A701 2.60s multi	1.25	1.25
	With tab	1.40	

Historians Type of 2002

Designs: 2.40s, Emanuel Ringelblum (1900-44). 3.70s, Jacob Talmon (1916-80). 6.20s, Jacob Herzog (1921-72).

2004, Feb. 24 *Perf. 14*

1553	A670 2.40s multi	1.00	1.00
1554	A670 3.70s multi	1.45	1.45
1555	A670 6.20s multi, Type I	2.50	2.50
a.	Type II	—	—
	Nos. 1553-1555 (3)	4.95	4.95
	With tabs	5.50	

Type II has thicker shadows behind the Hebrew characters and numerals, with the shadow at the top of the "6" with a projection, the shadow is visible below, to the right, and above the horizontal line of the "2," and a shadow all around the "0." The background and face are greener, and the width of the color band at the bottom is wider.

Type I has thin shadows behind the Hebrew characters and numerals, with the shadow at the top of the "6" without a projection, the shadow visible below and to the right only of the horizontal line of the "2," and a partial shadow around the "0." The background and face have a lighter shade. The width of the color band at the bottom is narrower.

Memorial Day A702

2004, Apr. 20 Litho. *Perf. 14*

1556	A702 1.30s multi	.60	.60
	With tab	.65	

FIFA (Fédération Internationale de Football Association), Cent. — A703

2004, May 3 *Perf. 13*

1557	A703 2.10s multi	.85	.85
	With tab	1.00	

Printed in sheets of 12 + 4 central labels.

UEFA (European Football Union), 50th Anniv. A704

2004, May 3 *Perf. 14*

1558	A704 6.20s multi	2.50	2.50
	With tab	2.75	

Ottoman Clock Towers — A705

2004, May 3 *Perf. 13x14*

1559	A705 1.30s Acre	.65	.65
1560	A705 1.30s Safed	.65	.65
1561	A705 1.30s Jaffa	.65	.65
1562	A705 1.30s Jerusalem	.65	.65
1563	A705 1.30s Haifa	.65	.65
	Nos. 1559-1563 (5)	3.25	3.25
	With tabs	3.50	

Booklet Stamps

1563A	A705 3.10s Safed	2.75	2.75
f.	Booklet pane of 1	2.75	—
1563B	A705 3.70s Acre	3.25	3.25
g.	Booklet pane of 1	3.25	—
1563C	A705 5.20s Haifa	4.50	4.50
h.	Booklet pane of 1	4.50	—
1563D	A705 5.50s Jerusalem	4.75	4.75
i.	Booklet pane of 1	4.75	—
1563E	A705 7s Jaffa	6.00	6.00
j.	Booklet pane of 1	6.50	—
k.	Booklet pane, #1563A-1563E	21.50	—
	Complete booklet, #1563Af, 1563Bg, 1563Ch, 1563Di, 1563Ej, 1563Ek	45.00	
	Nos. 1563A-1563E (5)	21.25	21.25

A706

Great Synagogue of Rome — A707

2004, May 20 Litho. *Perf. 13x14*

1564	A706 2.10s multi	.85	.85
1565	A707 2.10s multi	.85	.85
	With tabs	2.00	

See Italy Nos. 2607-2608.

Theodor Herzl (1860-1904), Zionist Leader — A708

2004, July 6 *Perf. 13*

1566	A708 2.50s multi	1.10	1.10
	With tab	1.25	

See Austria No. 1960, Hungary No. 3903.

National Insurance Institute, 50th Anniv. — A709

2004, July 6

1567	A709 7s multi	2.75	2.75
	With tab	3.25	3.25

2004 Summer Olympics, Athens A710

Medals won by Israeli athletes in previous Olympics: 1.50s, 1992 Silver medal, Judo. 2.40s, 1996 Bronze medal, Men's Mistral (windsurfing). 6.90s, 2000 Bronze medal, Kayaking.

2004, July 6 *Perf. 14*

1568	A710 1.50s multi	.55	.55
1569	A710 2.40s multi	.95	.95
1570	A710 6.90s multi	3.00	3.00
	Nos. 1568-1570 (3)	4.50	4.50
	With tabs	5.00	

Founding of Herzliya Hebrew High School, Tel Aviv, Cent. (in 2005) — A711

2004, Aug. 31 Litho. *Perf. 13x14*

1571	A711 2.20s multi	1.00	1.00
	With tab	1.10	

Ben-Gurion Heritage Institute — A712

2004, Aug. 31 *Perf. 13*

1572	A712 2.50s multi	1.10	1.10
	With tab	1.25	

Adventure Stories — A713

Designs: 2.20s, Eight on the Trail of One, by Yemima Avidar-Tchernovitz (parachutist). 2.50s, The "Hasamba" Series, by Igal Mossinsohn (children, donkey). 2.60s, Our Gang, by Pucho (four people).

2004, Aug. 31

1573	A713 2.20s multi	.80	.80
1574	A713 2.50s multi	.90	.90
1575	A713 2.60s multi	1.00	1.00
	Nos. 1573-1575 (3)	2.70	2.70
	With tabs	3.00	

Festivals A714

Bread making: 1.50s, Wheat ears, sickle. 2.40s, Mill, wooden fork. 2.70s, Oven, bread shovel.

2004, Aug. 31 *Perf. 14x13*

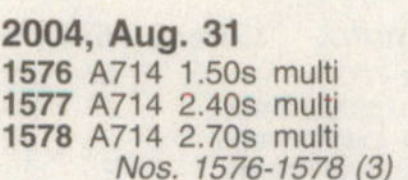

1576	A714 1.50s multi	.60	.60
1577	A714 2.40s multi	1.00	1.00
1578	A714 2.70s multi	1.15	1.15
	Nos. 1576-1578 (3)	2.75	2.75
	With tabs	3.00	

Opening of Third Terminal at Ben-Gurion Airport A715

2004, Nov. 2 Litho. *Perf. 14x13*

1579	A715 2.70s multi	1.10	1.10
	With tab	1.25	

Winning Design of Telabul 2004 Stamp Designing Contest A716

2004, Dec. 14

1580	A716 1.30s multi	.65	.65
	With tab	.75	

Bank of Israel, 50th Anniv. A717

2004, Dec. 14

1581	A717 6.20s multi	2.75	2.75
	With tab	3.00	

Philately Day A718

Designs: 2.10s, Mailbox of Austrian Postal Services, Jerusalem Post Office. 2.20s, Mailbox of British Mandate era, Lilienblum St. Post Office, Tel Aviv. 3.30s, Modern mailbox, Main Post Office, Tel Aviv.

2004, Dec. 14

1582	A718 2.10s multi	.85	.85
1583	A718 2.20s multi	.90	.90
1584	A718 3.30s multi	1.40	1.40
	Nos. 1582-1584 (3)	3.15	3.15
	With tabs	3.50	

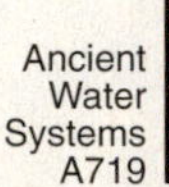

Ancient Water Systems A719

Designs: 2.10s, Hazor water tunnel and ivory cosmetics spoon. 2.20s, Megiddo water system and seal. 3.30s, Caesarea Aqueduct, coin from Caesarea. 6.20s, Hezekiah's tunnel, pool of Siloam, Jerusalem, and imprinted piece of clay.

2005, Feb. 22 Litho. *Perf. 14x13*

1585	A719 2.10s multi	.80	.80
1586	A719 2.20s multi	.85	.85
1587	A719 3.30s multi	1.30	1.30
1588	A719 6.20s multi	2.60	2.60
	Nos. 1585-1588 (4)	5.55	5.55
	With tabs	6.25	

Animals in the Bible
A720

Designs: Nos. 1589, 1593a, Ostrich. Nos. 1590, 1593b, Brown bear. Nos. 1591, 1593c, Wolf. Nos. 1592, 1592d, Nile crocodile.

2005, Feb. 22 ***Perf. 14x13***
1589 A720 1.30s yel & multi .60 .60
1590 A720 1.30s blue & multi .60 .60
1591 A720 2.20s org & multi 1.00 1.00
1592 A720 2.20s pink & multi 1.00 1.00
Nos. 1589-1592 (4) 3.20 3.20
With tabs 3.50

Souvenir Sheet
Perf. 14

1593 Sheet of 4 5.00 5.00
a. A720 1.30s yel & multi .75 .75
b. A720 2.10s blue & multi 1.25 1.25
c. A720 2.30s org & multi 1.35 1.35
d. A720 2.80s pink & multi 1.60 1.60

No. 1593 sold for 12s and contains four 40x25mm stamps.

Memorial Day
A721

2005, May 3 **Litho.** ***Perf. 14x13½***
1594 A721 1.50s multi .60 .60
With tab .70

Reserve Force
A722

2005, May 3
1595 A722 2.20s multi .90 .90
With tab 1.00

Bar-Ilan University, 50th Anniv.
A723

2005, May 3
1596 A723 2.20s multi .90 .90
With tab 1.00

End of World War II, 60th Anniv. — A724

No. 1597: a, Jewish partisan and underground fighters. b, Jewish soldiers in Allied forces.

2005, May 3
1597 A724 Horiz. pair 3.00 3.00
a.-b. 3.30s Either single 1.50 1.50
With tab 3.25

Schools — A725

Designs: 2.10s, Hebrew kindergarden, Rishon Le-Zion. 6.20s, Lemel Elementary School, Jerusalem.

2005, May 3 ***Perf. 13½x14***
1598 A725 2.10s multi .85 .85
1599 A725 6.20s multi 2.50 2.50
With tabs 3.75

Pope John Paul II (1920-2005)
A726

2005, May 18 **Litho.** ***Perf. 13¾x14***
1600 A726 3.30s multi 1.50 1.50
With tab 1.75

See No. 1865.

Historic Sites Type of 2000
Serpentine Die Cut 11¼x11

2005, June 7 **Litho.**

Booklet Stamp
Self-Adhesive

1601 A630 2.20s Mitzpe Revimim 1.15 1.15
a. Booklet pane of 12 14.00

2005 Maccabiah Games — A727

2005, July 11 ***Perf. 13¾x14***
1602 A727 3.30s multi 1.25 1.25
With tab 1.50

Gagea Commutate — A728

Perf. 14 Syncopated

2005, July 26 **Photo.**
1603 A728 (1.30s) multi .60 .60
With tab .70

See Nos. 1618, 1656D.

Maimonides (1138-1204), Rabbi, Philosopher
A729

2005, July 26 **Litho.** ***Perf. 13¾x14***
1604 A729 8.20s multi 3.25 3.25
With tab 3.75

Paintings — A730

Designs: 2.20s, Agrippas Street, by Arie Aroch. 4.90s, Tablets of the Covenant, by Moshe Castel. 6.20s, The Rift in Time, No. 7, by Moshe Kupferman.

2005, July 26 ***Perf. 13¾x14***
1605 A730 2.20s multi .90 .90
1606 A730 4.90s multi 2.00 2.00
1607 A730 6.20s multi 2.40 2.40
Nos. 1605-1607 (3) 5.30 5.30
With tabs 6.00

Prime Minister Yitzhak Rabin (1922-95) and Yitzhak Rabin Center, Tel Aviv — A731

2005, Sept. 27 **Litho.** ***Perf. 13***
1608 A731 2.20s multi .85 .85
With tab 1.00

Albert Einstein (1879-1955), Physicist — A732

2005, Sept. 27
1609 A732 3.30s multi 1.50 1.50
With tab 1.60

Intl. Year of Physics.
See No. 1620.

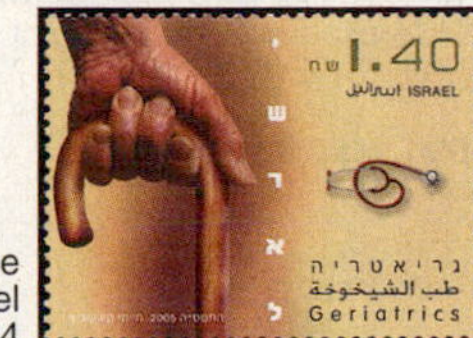

Priestly Blessing at Western Wall — A733

2005, Sept. 27 ***Perf. 13½x14***
1610 A733 6.20s multi 2.50 2.50
With tab 2.75
a. Perf. 13½ (1866a) — —

Issued: No. 1610a, 11/21/10.

Medicine in Israel
A734

2005, Sept. 27 ***Perf. 14x13½***
1611 A734 1.40s Geriatrics .55 .55
1612 A734 2.20s Pediatrics .80 .80
1613 A734 2.20s Rehabilitation .80 .80
1614 A734 6.20s Mental Health 2.40 2.40
Nos. 1611-1614 (4) 4.55 4.55
With tabs 5.25

Orders of the Mishnah
A735

2005, Sept. 27
1615 A735 1.30s Zeraim .55 .55
1616 A735 2.10s Moed .80 .80
1617 A735 2.30s Nashim .90 .90
Nos. 1615-1617 (3) 2.25 2.25
With tabs 2.50

See Nos. 1653-1655.

Gagea Commutate Type of 2005
Serpentine Die Cut 13½x14

2005, Nov. 3 **Photo.**
1618 A728 (1.30s) multi .85 .85
a. Booklet pane of 20 17.00

Diplomatic Relations With Germany, 40th Anniv. — A736

2005, Nov. 3 **Litho.** ***Perf. 13***
1619 A736 2.10s multi .90 .90
With tab 1.00

See Germany No. 2350.

Einstein Type of 2005
Souvenir Sheet

2005, Dec. 27
1620 A732 8.20s multi 5.00 5.00

Philately Day, Jerusalem 2006 National Stamp Exhibition. No. 1620 sold for 12s.

Children's Rights — A737

Inscriptions: No. 1621, Childhood is happiness. No. 1622, Indifference hurts. No. 1623, A warm home.

2005, Dec. 27 ***Perf. 13½x14***
1621 A737 1.30s multi .50 .50
1622 A737 1.30s multi .50 .50
1623 A737 1.30s multi .50 .50
Nos. 1621-1623 (3) 1.50 1.50
With tabs 1.75

Theater Personalities
A738

Designs: No. 1624, Joseph Millo (1916-97), director. No. 1625, Moshe Halevy (1895-1974), director. No. 1626, Shai K. Ophir (1928-87), actor. No. 1627, Nissim Aloni (1926-88), playwright.

2005, Dec. 27
1624 A738 2.20s multi .80 .80
1625 A738 2.20s multi .80 .80
1626 A738 6.20s multi 2.40 2.40
1627 A738 6.20s multi 2.40 2.40
Nos. 1624-1627 (4) 6.40 6.40
With tabs 7.25

Manufacturers Association of Israel, 85th Anniv. — A739

2005, Dec. 29 Litho. ***Perf. 13¾x14***

1628 A739 1.50s multi .55 .55
With tab .65

Emblem of Israel Post A740

2006 ***Perf. 14x13¾***

1629 A740 1.50s multi .55 .55
With tab .65

Souvenir Sheet

Imperf

1630 A740 5.90s multi 3.25 3.25

Issued: 1.50s, 2/28; 5.90s, 5/8. Jerusalem 2006 National Stamp Exhibition (No. 1630). No. 1630 sold for 7.50s.

Embossed and numbered examples of No. 1630 were given as gifts and were not available for sale. Value, $40.

Headquarters of Chabad Lubavitch Hasidism, Brooklyn, NY — A741

2006, Feb. 28 ***Perf. 14x13¾***

1631 A741 2.50s multi .95 .95
With tab 1.10

Pres. Ezer Weizman (1924-2005) A742

2005, Feb. 28 ***Perf. 13¾x14***

1632 A742 7.40s multi 3.00 3.00
With tab 3.25

Children's Art A743

Contest-winning art by Jewish children in US: Nos. 1633, 1637a, Desert Bloom, by Yael Bildner. Nos. 1634, 1637c, Harmony, by Michela T. Janower. Nos. 1635, 1637d, Together in Israel, by Jessica Deutsch. Nos. 1636, 1637b, Colors of Israel, by Marissa Galin.

2006 ***Perf. 14x13¾***

1633 A743 1.50s multi .60 .60
1634 A743 2.40s multi .90 .90
1635 A743 3.60s multi 1.50 1.50
1636 A743 7.40s multi 3.00 3.00
Nos. 1633-1636 (4) 6.00 6.00
With tabs 6.75

Souvenir Sheet

Perf. 14

1637 Sheet of 4 5.75 5.75
a. A743 2.20s multi .95 .95
b. A743 2.40s multi 1.05 1.05
c. A743 3.60s multi 1.50 1.50
d. A743 5.10s multi 2.25 2.25

Issued: Nos. 1633-1636, 2/28; No. 1637, 5/28. Washington 2006 World Philatelic Exhibition (No. 1637). No. 1637 sold for 15s and contains four 40x35mm stamps.

Yad Lashiron Armored Corps Memorial, Latrun A744

2006, Apr. 11 ***Perf. 14x13¾***

1638 A744 1.50s multi .70 .70
With tab .80

Memorial Day.

Tel Aviv University, 50th Anniv. A745

2006, May 8

1639 A745 3.60s multi 1.35 1.35
With tab 1.50

Tulips — A746

2006, May 8 ***Perf. 14x14¼***

1640 A746 1.50s shown .70 .70
a. Sheet of 12 + 12 labels 30.00 30.00
1641 A746 1.50s Columbines .70 .70
With tabs 1.60
a. Sheet of 12 + 12 labels 30.00 30.00

Nos. 1640a and 1641a each sold for 27s. Labels could be personalized. Compare with type A647.

Souvenir Sheet

Jerusalem 2006 National Stamp Exhibition — A747

2006, May 8 ***Perf. 14***

1642 A747 10s multi 6.25 6.25

The Solar System — A748

Designs: Nos. 1643a, 1644d, Sun, Mercury and Venus. Nos. 1643b, 1644c, Earth, Moon and Mars. Nos. 1643c, 1644e, Neptune, Pluto, and moons. Nos. 1643d, 1644b, Jupiter, moons and asteroids. Nos. 1643e, 1644f, Saturn, moon, Sun and asteroids. Nos. 1643f, 1644a, Uranus, moons, asteroids, part of Saturn.

2006, May 8 ***Perf. 13***

1643 A748 Sheet of 6 7.75 7.75
a.-f. 2.50s Any single 1.25 1.25

Self-Adhesive

Serpentine Die Cut 11

1644 A748 Booklet pane of 6 10.00
a.-f. 2.50s Any single 1.60 1.60

Jerusalem 2006 National Stamp Exhibition. The six individual stamps, when separated, could be rearranged to produce a Star of David over the planets.

Religious Zionist Education, Cent. — A749

2006, July 25 ***Perf. 13¾x14***

1645 A749 3.60s multi 1.35 1.35
With tab 1.50

Rabbis of Jerusalem A750

Rabbis: 1.50s, Jacob Saul Eliachar (1817-1906). 2.20s, Samuel Salant (1816-1909). 2.40s, Jacob Meir (1856-1939).

2006, July 25

1646 A750 1.50s multi .65 .65
1647 A750 2.20s multi .90 .90
1648 A750 2.40s multi 1.00 1.00
Nos. 1646-1648 (3) 2.55 2.55
With tabs 2.75

Silver Khamsas A751

Khamsa from: 1.50s, Morocco, 1920. 2.50s, Tunisia, 1930. 7.40s, Iran, 1925.

2006, July 26

1649 A751 1.50s multi .60 .60
1650 A751 2.50s multi .95 .95
1651 A751 7.40s multi 3.00 3.00
Nos. 1649-1651 (3) 4.55 4.55
With tabs 5.00

Abba Eban (1915-2002), Foreign Minister — A752

2006, Sept. 12 ***Perf. 14x13¾***

1652 A752 7.30s multi 2.60 2.60
With tab 3.00

Orders of the Mishnah Type of 2005

2006, Sept. 12

1653 A735 1.50s Nezikin .70 .70
1654 A735 2.20s Kodashim 1.00 1.00
1655 A735 2.40s Tohorot 1.10 1.10
Nos. 1653-1655 (3) 2.80 2.80
With tabs 3.00

Bezalel Academy of Arts and Design, Cent. — A753

2006, Sept. 12 ***Perf. 13***

1656 Horiz. strip of 3 2.75 2.75
a. A753 2.50s green .85 .85
b. A753 2.50s blue .85 .85
c. A753 2.50s orange .85 .85
Strip with tabs 3.25

Gagea Commutate Type of 2005 Redrawn With Two Leaves at Right

2006, Sept. 20 Litho. ***Perf. 14***

1656D A728 (1.50s) multi — —

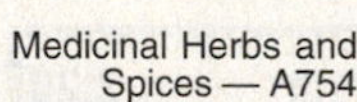

Medicinal Herbs and Spices — A754

Designs: 1.50s, Coriandrum sativum. 2.50s, Micromeria fruticosa. 3.30s, Mentha piperita.

2006, Dec. 17 Litho. ***Perf. 14¼x14***

1657 A754 1.50s multi .60 .60
1658 A754 2.50s multi 1.10 1.10
1659 A754 3.30s multi 1.40 1.40
Nos. 1657-1659 (3) 3.10 3.10
With tabs 3.50

See Nos. 1700-1701, 1747.

Creation of Esperanto Language, 120th Anniv. A755

2006, Dec. 17 ***Perf. 14x13¾***

1660 A755 3.30s multi 1.60 1.60
With tab 1.75

Israeli Fashions A756

Women's fashions from: 1.50s, 1882-1948. 2.50s, 1948-73. 3.30s, 1973-90. 7.30s, 1990-2005.

2006, Dec. 17 ***Perf. 13***
1661 A756 1.50s multi .60 .60
1662 A756 2.50s multi 1.10 1.10
1663 A756 3.30s multi 1.40 1.40
1664 A756 7.30s multi 3.00 3.00
Nos. 1661-1664 (4) 6.10 6.10
With tabs 6.75

Crusader Sites in Israel
A757

2006, Dec. 17 Litho. ***Perf. 14x13¾***
1665 A757 2.50s Atlit 1.10 1.10
1666 A757 2.50s Caesarea 1.10 1.10
1667 A757 2.50s Montfort 1.10 1.10
1668 A757 2.50s Belvoir 1.10 1.10
Nos. 1665-1668 (4) 4.40 4.40
With tabs 4.75

Development — A758

Development of the: 2.50s, Negev. 3.30s, Galilee.

2007, Feb. 20 Litho. ***Perf. 14x13¾***
1669 A758 2.50s multi 1.15 1.15
1670 A758 3.30s multi 1.45 1.45
With tabs 3.00

Sports and Physical Education
A759

Inscriptions: 2.90s, Physical education in schools. 3s, Wingate Institute. 7.30s, Sport for all.

2007, Feb. 20
1671 A759 2.90s multi 1.15 1.15
1672 A759 3s multi 1.25 1.25
1673 A759 7.30s multi 3.00 3.00
Nos. 1671-1673 (3) 5.40 5.40
With tabs 6.00

Educational Television
A760

Designs: Nos. 1674a, 1675, Ma Pit'om (green panel). Nos. 1674b, 1676, Krovim Krovim (blue panel). Nos. 1674c, 1677, No Secrets (orange panel).

2007, Feb. 20 ***Perf. 13¾x14***
1674 Strip of 3 3.25 3.25
a.-c. A760 2.50s Any single 1.05 1.05
Strip with tabs 3.75

Booklet Stamps
Self-Adhesive
Serpentine Die Cut 10¾x11

1675 A760 2.50s multi 1.75 1.75
1676 A760 2.50s multi 1.75 1.75
1677 A760 2.50s multi 1.75 1.75
a. Booklet pane, 2 each #1675-1677 10.50

Memorial Day
A761

2007, Apr. 17 Litho. ***Perf. 14x13¾***
1678 A761 1.50s multi .60 .60
With tab .70

Scouting, Cent.
A762

2007, Apr. 17
1679 A762 2.50s multi 1.10 1.10
With tab 1.25

Regional Development Towns — A763

Towns in: 2.50s, Northern region. 3.30s, Central region. 7.30s, Southern region.

2007, Apr. 17
1680 A763 2.50s multi 1.00 1.00
1681 A763 3.30s multi 1.40 1.40
1682 A763 7.30s multi 3.00 3.00
Nos. 1680-1682 (3) 5.40 5.40
With tabs 6.00

Souvenir Sheet

Neve-Tzedek Neighborhood of Tel Aviv, 120th Anniv. — A764

2007, Apr. 17 ***Perf. 13¾x14***
1683 A764 Sheet of 3 6.50 6.50
a. 2.20s Founders 1.30 1.30
b. 3.30s Neve-Tzedek 1.90 1.90
c. 5.80s Intellectuals 3.25 3.25

No. 1683 sold for 15s.

Reunification of Jerusalem, 40th Anniv. — A765

2007, May 16
1684 A765 1.50s multi .75 .75
With tab .85

Volunteer Organizations
A766

2007, June 20 ***Perf. 13***
1685 A766 1.50s multi .75 .75
With tab .85

Israel Prison Service — A767

2007, June 20 ***Perf. 13¾x14***
1686 A767 2.50s multi 1.10 1.10
With tab 1.25

Dance — A768

No. 1687: a, Ballet. b, Ethnic dance. c, Israeli folk dance. d, Modern dance.

2007, June 20
1687 Horiz. strip of 4 3.75 3.75
a.-d. A768 2.20s Any single .90 .90
Strip with tabs 4.25

UNESCO World Heritage Sites
A769

Designs: 3.30s, Akko (Acre). 5s, 10s, Tel Aviv. 5.80s, Masada.

2007 ***Perf. 14x13¾***
1688 A769 3.30s multi 1.40 1.40
1689 A769 5s multi 2.00 2.00
1690 A769 5.80s multi 2.25 2.25
Nos. 1688-1690 (3) 5.65 5.65
With tabs 6.50

Souvenir Sheet

1691 A769 10s multi 6.50 6.50

Issued: 3.30s, 5s, 5.80s, 6/20; 10s, 8/27. Tel Aviv, cent. (No. 1691). No. 1691 sold for 15s.

Beach — A770

2007, Aug. 27 ***Perf. 14***
1692 A770 (1.50s) multi .75 .75
With tab .85
a. Miniature sheet of 12 + 12 labels 20.00 20.00

No. 1692a sold for 27s. Labels could be personalized. Self-adhesive examples of No. 1692 come from sheets issued in 1999 that sold for much more than face value.

Hashomer
A771

2007, Aug. 27 ***Perf. 14x13¾***
1693 A771 3.30s multi 1.35 1.35
With tab 1.50

Israel Reserve Forces — A772

2007, Aug. 27 ***Perf. 13¾x14***
1694 A772 7.30s multi 3.00 3.00
With tab 3.50

Chalom Messas (1909-2003), Chief Rabbi of Morocco and Jerusalem
A773

2007, Aug. 27
1695 A773 7.30s multi 3.00 3.00
With tab 3.50

Women of the Bible — A774

2007, Aug. 27
1696 A774 1.50s Jael .65 .65
1697 A774 2.20s Esther .95 .95
1698 A774 2.40s Miriam 1.05 1.05
Nos. 1696-1698 (3) 2.65 2.65
With tabs 3.00

Theodor Herzl Type of 1986
Serpentine Die Cut 13½x13¾
2007, Nov. 1 **Litho.**
Self-Adhesive

1699 A388 5a blue & ultra .60 .60

Medicinal Herbs and Spices Type of 2006

Designs: 1.55s, Laurus nobilis. 2.25s, Coridothymus capitatus.

2007, Nov. 5 ***Perf. 14***
1700 A754 1.55s multi .70 .70
1701 A754 2.25s multi 1.10 1.10
With tabs 2.00

Rabbi Itzhak Kaduri (1902-2006)
A775

2007, Dec. 5 ***Perf. 13½x14***
1702 A775 8.15s multi 3.25 3.25
With tab 3.75

Tel Aviv Movie Theaters
A776

Designs: 4.50s, Eden Cinema. 4.60s, Mograbi Cinema.

2007, Dec. 5 *Perf. 14x13½*

1703 A776 4.50s multi 2.10 2.10
1704 A776 4.60s multi 2.10 2.10
With tabs 4.75

Family Love — A777

Designs: 1.55s, Boy giving flower to mother. 2.25s, Girl with baby brother. 3.55s. Father and son.

2007, Dec. 5 *Perf. 13½x14*

1705 A777 1.55s multi .70 .70
1706 A777 2.25s multi 1.05 1.05
1707 A777 3.55s multi 1.60 1.60
Nos. 1705-1707 (3) 3.35 3.35
With tabs 3.75

Hula Nature Reserve A778

Designs: Nos. 1708a, 1710, Pelicans, Caspian terrapins, iris (denomination in yellow). Nos. 1708b, 1709, Water buffalos, marbled duck, reed warbler, wildcat, wild raspberry (denomination in red violet). Nos. 1708c, 1711, Otter, catfish, cranes, willow herb (denomination in orange).

2007, Dec. 5 *Perf. 14x13½*

1708 Strip of 3 3.00 3.00
a.-c. A778 2.25s Any single .95 .95
Strip with tabs 3.50

Booklet Stamps
Self-Adhesive
Serpentine Die Cut 11x10¼

1709 A778 2.25s multi 1.25 1.25
1710 A778 2.25s multi 1.25 1.25
1711 A778 2.25s multi 1.25 1.25
a. Booklet pane, 2 each #1709-1711 7.50
Nos. 1709-1711 (3) 3.75 3.75

Miniature Sheet

Noah's Ark — A779

No. 1712: a, Dove and olive branch. b, Noah and family, animals, leaving ark. c, Camels, giraffes, zebra, elephants, whale. d, Peafowl, bears, tiger. e, Lions, wolf. f, Wolf, leopards, goats, kangaroos.

2007, Dec. 5 *Perf. 14*

1712 A779 Sheet of 6 8.50 8.50
a.-f. 2.25s Any single 1.40 1.40

World Stamp Championship Israel 2008. No. 1712 sold for 16s.

A limited edition booklet containing two self-adhesive examples of Nos. 1712a-1712f sold at the Israel 2008 World Stamp Championship Philatelic Exhibition, Tel Aviv. Value, $25.

Israel Rokach (1896-1959), Mayor of Tel Aviv — A780

2008, Jan. 27 **Litho.** *Perf. 14x13¾*

1713 A780 2.25s multi 1.10 1.10
With tab 1.25

Tel Aviv Land Lottery, Cent. (in 2009) — A781

2008, Jan. 27 *Perf. 13*

1714 A781 4.50s multi 2.00 2.00
With tab 2.25

Intl. Holocaust Remembrance Day — A782

2008, Jan. 27 *Perf. 14*

1715 A782 4.60s multi 2.10 2.10
With tab 2.50

See United Nations No.948, United Nations Offices in Geneva No.479, United Nations Offices in Vienna No. 412.

Mekorot, National Water System, 70th Anniv. — A783

2008, Jan. 27 *Perf. 13¾x14*

1716 A783 5.80s multi 2.75 2.75
With tab 3.25

Akiva Aryeh Weiss (1868-1947), Tel Aviv Builder and Developer — A784

2008, Jan. 27 *Perf. 14x13¾*

1717 A784 8.15s multi 3.50 3.50
With tab 4.00

UNESCO World Heritage Sites A785

Designs: 2.25s, Biblical Tels. 3.40s, Incense Route.

2008, Jan. 27

1718 A785 2.25s multi 1.05 1.05
1719 A785 3.40s multi 1.60 1.60
With tabs 3.00

Israeli Boy and Flag — A786

2008, Apr. 28 **Litho.** *Perf. 14*

1720 A786 (1.55s) multi .70 .70
With tab .80

Booklet Stamp
Self-Adhesive
Serpentine Die Cut 13½x14

1721 A786 (1.55s) multi .90 .90
a. Booklet pane of 20 18.00

Flowers — A787

No. 1722, White roses. No. 1723, Cyclamen persicum.

2008, Apr. 28 *Perf. 14*

1722 A787 (1.55s) multi .90 .90
1723 A787 (1.55s) multi .90 .90
With tabs 2.00

Self-adhesive examples of Nos. 1722-1723 come from sheets issued in 1999 that sold for much more than face value.

Independence, 60th Anniv. — A788

2008, Apr. 28 *Perf. 14x13¾*

1724 A788 1.55s multi .80 .80
With tab .90

Memorial Day — A789

2008, Apr. 28 *Perf. 13¾x14*

1725 A789 1.55s multi .80 .80
With tab .90

Israel Export Institute, 50th Anniv. A790

2008, Apr. 28 *Perf. 14x13¾*

1726 A790 2.80s multi 1.25 1.25
With tab 1.40

Souvenir Sheet

Hatikva (National Anthem), 120th Anniv. — A791

2008, Apr. 28 *Perf. 13¾*

1727 A791 10s multi 7.50 7.50

No. 1727 sold for 15s.

Miniature Sheet

Independence Day Posters — A792

No. 1728 — Poster from: a, 1981 (green panel). b, 1991 (brown panel). c, 2006 (blue panel). d, 1971 (purple panel). e, 1965 (dark red panel). f, 1952 (orange panel).

2008, Apr. 28 *Perf. 13¾x14*

1728 A792 Sheet of 6 6.75 6.75
a.-f. 2.25s Any single 1.05 1.05

Children's Art — A793

Designs: No. 1729, I Love Israel (numbers, symbols, Hebrew and Roman letters), by Etai Epstein. No. 1730, Israel is My Home (Hebrew letters, house and map of Israel), by Yuval Sulema and Eden Vilker. No. 1731, Israel's 60th, (girl, telescope, cat, butterflies, flowers and "60"), by Daniel Hazan.

2008, May 14 **Litho.** *Perf. 13½x14*

1729 A793 2.25s multi 1.20 1.20
1730 A793 2.25s multi 1.20 1.20
1731 A793 2.25s multi 1.20 1.20
Nos. 1729-1731 (3) 3.60 3.60
With tabs 4.00

Souvenir Sheet

Jerusalem of Gold — A794

Litho. & Embossed With Foil Application

2008, May 14 *Perf. 14½x14¼*

1732 A794 18s multi 12.00 12.00

No. 1732 sold for 22.50s.
No. 1732 exists imperf. Value, $80.

Souvenir Sheet

Tel Aviv, Cent. (in 2009) — A795

No. 1733 — Sketches of Tel Aviv life by Nahum Gutman: a, The First Concert. b, The First Lamp Post. c, Dr. Hisin.

2008, May 14 Litho. *Perf. 14x13¾*

1733	A795 Sheet of 3		9.00	9.00
	a.	3.50s multi	2.25	2.25
	b.	4.50s multi	3.00	3.00
	c.	5.50s multi	3.75	3.75

2008 World Stamp Championships, Israel. No. 1733 sold for 18s.

Gush Katif, 1970-2005 Gaza Strip Settlement A796

2008, July 14 Litho. *Perf. 14x13*

1734 A796 1.55s multi .80 .80
With tab .90

Promenades — A797

Designs: 4.50s, Tabgha Promenade (on Sea of Galilee), Capernaum. 4.60s, Armon Hanatziv Promenade, Jerusalem. 8.15s, Rishonim Promenade, Netanya.

2008, July 14

1735 A797 4.50s multi 2.10 2.10
1736 A797 4.60s multi 2.25 2.25
1737 A797 8.15s multi 3.75 3.75
Nos. 1735-1737 (3) 8.10 8.10
With tabs 8.75

2008 Summer Olympics, Beijing A798

2008, July 14

1738 A798 1.55s Swimming .80 .80
1739 A798 1.55s Gymnastics .80 .80
1740 A798 2.25s Sailing 1.25 1.25
1741 A798 2.25s Tennis 1.25 1.25
Nos. 1738-1741 (4) 4.10 4.10
With tabs 4.50

Rabbis A799

Designs: 2.30s, Rabbi Samuel Mohilewer (1824-98). 8.50s, Rabbi Zvi Hirsch Kalischer (1795-1874).

2008, Sept. 17 *Perf. 12½x13*

1742 A799 2.30s multi 1.20 1.20
1743 A799 8.50s multi 4.25 4.25
With tabs 6.00

Torah Crowns A800

Torah crown from: 1.60s, Aden, late 19th cent. No. 1745, Turkey, 19th cent. No. 1746, Poland, 1729.

2008, Sept. 17 *Perf. 14x13*

1744 A800 1.60s multi .80 .80
1745 A800 3.80s multi 1.90 1.90
1746 A800 3.80s multi 1.90 1.90
Nos. 1744-1746 (3) 4.60 4.60
With tabs 5.00

Herbs and Spices Type of 2006 and

Salvia Fruticosa — A801

Design: 1.60s, Artemisia arborescens.

2008-09 *Perf. 13*

1747 A754 1.60s multi .80 .80
1748 A801 (2.90s) multi 1.45 1.45
With tabs 2.50

Self-Adhesive

Booklet Stamps

Serpentine Die Cut 11x10¾

1749 A801 (2.90s) multi 2.00 2.00
a. Booklet pane of 10 + 10 etiquettes 20.00

With Different Arabic Inscription and Dash Before "24"

1749B A801 (2.90s) multi 2.00 2.00
c. Booklet pane of 10 + 10 etiquettes 20.00

Issued: Nos. 1747-1749, 9/17/08. No. 1749B, 1/25/09.

Landmarks of France and Israel — A802

Airplane, stamped first flight cover and: 1.60s, Haifa waterfront, Israel. 3.80s, Eiffel Tower, Paris.

2008, Nov. 6 Litho. *Perf. 14*

1750 A802 1.60s multi .80 .80
1751 A802 3.80s multi 1.90 1.90
With tabs 3.00

First flight between France and Israel, 60th anniv. See France Nos. 3533-3534.

2008 Census A803

2008, Dec. 17 *Perf. 14x13*

1752 A803 1.60s multi .75 .75
With tab .85

Israeli Defense Forces Radio A804

2008, Dec. 17 *Perf. 14x13¾*

1753 A804 2.30s multi 1.10 1.10
With tab 1.25 1.25

Taglit-Birthright Israel — A805

2008, Dec. 17 *Perf. 14x13*

1754 A805 5.60s multi 3.00 3.00
With tab 3.25

Ancient Letters A806

Designs: 1.60s, Bar Kokhba letters, A.D. 134. 2.30s, Lachish letters, 589 B.C. 8.50s, Letter from Ugarit, 1230 B.C.

2008, Dec. 17

1755 A806 1.60s multi .70 .70
1756 A806 2.30s multi 1.05 1.05
1757 A806 8.50s multi 4.00 4.00
Nos. 1755-1757 (3) 5.75 5.75
With tabs 6.25

Menorah Type of 2002-03

2009 *Serpentine Die Cut 13½x13¾*

Self-Adhesive

1758 A679 30a gray olive .30 .30
1758A A679 40a gray green .40 .40
1759 A679 50a gray brown .40 .40
1760 A679 1s purple .50 .50
Nos. 1758-1760 (3) 1.20 1.20

Issued: 30a, 50a, 1s, 2/17; 40a, 9/8.

Tel Aviv, Cent. A807

People and: 1.60s, Boardwalk and beaches. 2.30s, Buildings with different architectural styles. 3.80s, Parks.

2009 *Perf. 14x13¾*

1761 A807 1.60s multi .70 .70
1762 A807 2.30s multi .95 .95
1763 A807 3.80s multi 1.60 1.60
Nos. 1761-1763 (3) 3.25 3.25
With tabs 3.75

Extreme Sports A808

2009, Feb. 17

1764 A808 4.40s Mountain biking 1.90 1.90
1765 A808 5.40s Skydiving 2.40 2.40
1766 A808 5.60s Surfing 2.50 2.50
Nos. 1764-1766 (3) 6.80 6.80
With tabs 7.50

Fruit — A809

No. 1767: a, Grapes. b, Lemons. c, Avocados. d, Oranges. e, Pomegranates.

2009, Feb. 17 *Perf. 14*

1767 Vert. strip of 5 4.00 4.00
a.-e. A809 (1.60s) Any single .80 .80
Strip with tabs 4.50

See Nos. 1792-1796.

Memorial Day A810

2009, Apr. 22 *Perf. 14x13¾*

1768 A810 1.60s multi .70 .70
With tab .80

Intl. Year of Astronomy A811

Designs: 2.30s, Gersonides using Jacob's staff. 3.80s, Gravitational lensing. 8.50s, Laser Interferometer Space Antenna.

2009, Apr. 22

1769 A811 2.30s multi 1.00 1.00
1770 A811 3.80s multi 1.75 1.75
1771 A811 8.50s multi 3.50 3.50
Nos. 1769-1771 (3) 6.25 6.25
With tabs 7.00

Souvenir Sheet

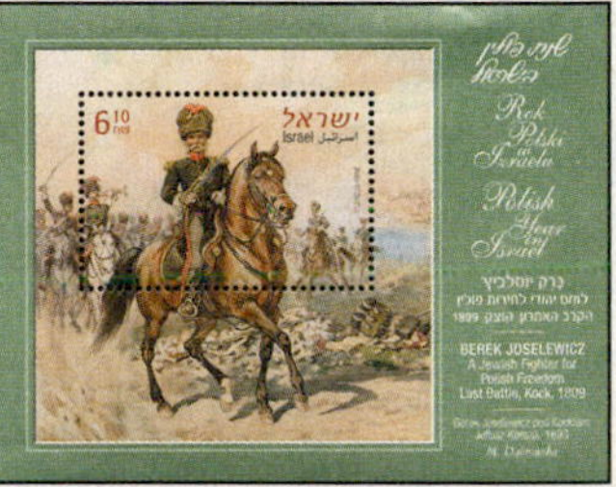

Berek Joselewicz, A Jewish Fighter for Polish Freedom's Last Battle, Kock, by Juliusz Kossak — A812

2009, Apr. 22 *Perf. 14*

1772 A812 6.10s multi 3.00 3.00

See Poland No. 3935.

Miniature Sheet

Israeli Musicians — A813

No. 1773: a, Zohar Argov (1955-87). b, Sasha Argov (1914-95). c, Meir Ariel (1942-99). d, Yossi Banai (1932-2006). e, Naomi Shemer (1930-2004). f, Shoshana Damari (1923-2006). g, Yair Rosenblum (1944-96). h, Moshe Wilensky (1910-97). i, Ehud Manor (1941-2005). j, Arik Lavie (1927-2004). k, Uzi Hitman (1952-2004). l, Ofra Haza (1957-2000).

2009, Apr. 22 *Perf. 13*

1773 A813 Sheet of 12 + 4 labels *15.00 15.00*
a.-l. 1.60s Any single *1.25 1.25*

Love — A814

2009, June 30 *Perf. 14*

1774 A814 (1.60s) multi .85 .85
With tab .95

Dead Sea — A815

2009, June 30 *Perf. 13¾x14*
1775 A815 2.30s multi 1.10 1.10
With tab 1.25

18th Maccabiah Games — A816

2009, June 30
1776 A816 5.60s multi 2.50 2.50
With tab 2.75

Intl. Harp Contest, 50th Anniv. — A817

2009, June 30
1777 A817 8.50s multi 3.75 3.75
With tab 4.25

Environmental Quality — A818

No. 1778: a, Geothermal energy (Earth as teakettle, 31x31mm). b, Global warming (Earth melting in frying pan, 62x31mm). c, Solar energy (house with solar panels on Earth, 31x31mm).

2009, June 30 *Perf. 13*
1778 Horiz. strip of 3 3.25 3.25
a.-c. A818 2.30s Any single 1.05 1.05
Strip with tabs 3.75

Leumit Health Fund, 75th Anniv. A819

2009, Sept. 8 *Perf. 14x13¾*
1779 A819 8.80s multi 4.00 4.00
With tab 4.50

Honey A820

Honeycomb and: 1.60s, Bee on flower. 4.60s, Honeycomb on plate. 6.70s, Honey dripping on apple slice.

2009, Sept. 8
1780 A820 1.60s multi .70 .70
1781 A820 4.60s multi 2.10 2.10
1782 A820 6.70s multi 3.25 3.25
Nos. 1780-1782 (3) 6.05 6.05
With tabs 6.75

Virtual Communications — A821

Designs: 2.40s, Instant messaging software. 5.30s, USB flash drive. 6.50s, Voice over Internet protocol.

2009, Sept. 8
1783 A821 2.40s multi 1.05 1.05
1784 A821 5.30s multi 2.50 2.50
1785 A821 6.50s multi 3.00 3.00
Nos. 1783-1785 (3) 6.55 6.55
With tabs 7.25

Animal Assisted Therapy A822

Designs: Nos. 1786, 1789, Woman and dog. Nos. 1787, 1790, Girl and horse. Nos. 1788, 1791, Girl and dolphin.

2009, Sept. 8 *Perf. 14x13¾*
1786 A822 2.40s multi 1.10 1.10
1787 A822 2.40s multi 1.10 1.10
1788 A822 2.40s multi 1.10 1.10
Nos. 1786-1788 (3) 3.30 3.30
With tabs 3.75

Booklet Stamps
Self-Adhesive
Serpentine Die Cut 11x10¼

1789 A822 2.40s multi 1.50 1.50
1790 A822 2.40s multi 1.50 1.50
1791 A822 2.40s multi 1.50 1.50
a. Booklet pane of 6, 2 each #1789-1791 9.00
Nos. 1789-1791 (3) 4.50 4.50

Fruit Type of 2009
Serpentine Die Cut 14¼x13
2009, Nov. 26 **Litho.**
Booklet Stamps
Self-Adhesive

1792 A809 (1.60s) Lemons 1.00 1.00
1793 A809 (1.60s) Grapes 1.00 1.00
1794 A809 (1.60s) Pomegranates 1.00 1.00
1795 A809 (1.60s) Oranges 1.00 1.00
1796 A809 (1.60s) Avocados 1.00 1.00
a. Booklet pane of 20, 4 each #1792-1796 20.00
Nos. 1792-1796 (5) 5.00 5.00

Yiddish Theater, Iasi, Romania A823

2009, Nov. 26 **Litho.** *Perf. 14*
1797 A823 4.60s multi 2.25 2.25
With tab 2.50

See Romania No. 5142.

Lighthouses — A824

Lighthouses at: 4.60s, Jaffa. 6.70s, Tel Aviv. 8.80s, Ashdod.

2009, Nov. 26 *Perf. 14x13¾*
1798 A824 4.60s multi 2.10 2.10
1799 A824 6.70s multi 3.00 3.00
1800 A824 8.80s multi 4.00 4.00
Nos. 1798-1800 (3) 9.10 9.10
With tabs 10.00

Maritime Archaeology — A825

Diver and: No. 1801, Earthenware jugs. No. 1802, Figurines. 3.60s, Weapons. 5s, Anchors.

2009, Nov. 26
1801 A825 2.40s multi 1.05 1.05
1802 A825 2.40s multi 1.05 1.05
1803 A825 3.60s multi 1.60 1.60
1804 A825 5s multi 2.40 2.40
Nos. 1801-1804 (4) 6.10 6.10
With tabs 6.75

Arava Valley Settlements, 50th Anniv. — A826

2010, Jan. 27 **Litho.** *Perf. 14x13¾*
1805 A826 1.60s multi .75 .75
With tab .85

Lions Club of Israel, 50th Anniv. A827

2010, Jan. 27
1806 A827 4.60s multi 2.00 2.00
With tab 2.25

Intl. Holocaust Remembrance Day — A828

2010, Jan. 27 *Perf. 14*
1807 A828 6.70s multi 3.50 3.50
With tab 4.00

Alliance Israelite Universelle, 150th Anniv. — A829

2010, Jan. 27 *Perf. 14x13¾*
1808 A829 8.80s multi 4.00 4.00
With tab 4.50

Birds — A830

No. 1809: a, Carduelis carduelis. b, Upupa epops. c, Prinia gracilis.

2010, Jan. 27 *Perf. 13¾x14*
1809 Strip of 3, #a-c 4.00 4.00
a.-c. A830 2.40s Any single 1.25 1.25
Strip with tabs 4.50

Memorial Day — A831

2010, Apr. 14 **Litho.** *Perf. 13¾x14*
1810 A831 1.60s multi .80 .80
With tab .90

Tribute to World Trade Center Victims, by Eliezer Weishoff, Jerusalem A832

2010, Apr. 14
1811 A832 2.40s multi 1.20 1.20
With tab 1.40 1.40

Friendship Between Israel and Canada, 60th Anniv. A833

2010, Apr. 14 *Perf. 14x13¾*
1812 A833 4.60s multi 2.00 2.00
With tab 2.25

See Canada No. 2379.

Israeli Innovations A834

Designs: No. 1813, Drip irrigation dripper and farm field. No. 1814, Computer chip and computer. No. 1815, Gastrointestinal camera and intestines.

2010, Apr. 14 *Perf. 14x13¼*
1813 A834 2.40s multi 1.10 1.10
1814 A834 2.40s multi 1.10 1.10
1815 A834 2.40s multi 1.10 1.10
Nos. 1813-1815 (3) 3.30 3.30
With tabs 3.75

Expo 2010, Shanghai.

Souvenir Sheet

Children's Books — A835

No. 1816: a, Alice's Adventures in Wonderland, by Lewis Carroll. b, Peter Pan, by Sir James M. Barrie. c, Gulliver's Travels, by Jonathan Swift.

2010, Apr. 14 *Perf. 14¾x14*
1816 A835 Sheet of 3 6.50 6.50
a.-c. 4.60s Any single 2.10 2.10

London 2010 International Stamp Exhibition.

Souvenir Sheet

Theodor Herzl (1860-1904), Zionist Leader — A836

No. 1817: a, Herzl leaning on railing, settlers. b, Settlers at settlement. c, Boy waving Israeli flag, adults, city skyline.

2010, Apr. 14
1817 A836 Sheet of 3 7.00 7.00
a. 3.70s multi 1.75 1.75
b. 4.60s multi 2.00 2.00
c. 6.70s multi 3.25 3.25

Kibbutzim, Cent. A837

2010, June 14 Litho. *Perf. 14x13½*
1818 A837 2.50s multi 1.15 1.15
With tab 1.30

Rabbi Nachman of Breslev (1772-1810), Philosopher — A838

2010, June 14 *Perf. 13½x14*
1819 A838 3.70s multi 1.75 1.75
With tab 1.90

Simon Wiesenthal (1908-2005), Hunter of Nazi War Criminals — A839

2010, June 14 *Perf. 12½*
1820 A839 5s multi 2.10 2.10
With tab 2.50

The Star of David is made up of tiny holes made by a laser. See Austria No. 2264.

World 420 Sailing Championships, Haifa — A840

2010, June 14 *Perf. 14x15*
1821 A840 9s multi 3.75 3.75
With tab 4.25

Story Gardens, Holon A841

Sculptures based on children's stories: No. 1822, Where is Pluto? (Dog). No. 1823, Shmuel the Hedgehog. No. 1824, Soul Bird.

2010, June 14 *Perf. 14x13½*
1822 A841 2.50s multi 1.20 1.20
1823 A841 2.50s multi 1.20 1.20
1824 A841 2.50s multi 1.20 1.20
Nos. 1822-1824 (3) 3.60 3.60
With tabs 4.00

Musical Instruments A842

No. 1825: a, Zoma and oboe. b, Rebab and violin. c, Darbouka and drum. d, Qanun and piano. e, Oud and guitar.

2010, June 14 *Perf. 13½x14*
1825 Horiz. strip of 5 3.75 3.75
a.-e. A842 1.70s Any single .75 .75
Strip with tabs 4.25

Tzevet (Israel Defense Forces Veterans Association), 50th Anniv. — A843

2010, Aug. 25 Litho. *Perf. 13¼x13*
1826 A843 2.50s multi 1.15 1.15
With tab 1.35

Settlements Outside of Jerusalem's Old City Walls, 150th Anniv. — A844

2010, Aug. 25 *Perf. 13¼*
1827 A844 3.70s multi 1.60 1.60
With tab 1.90
a. Booklet pane of 2 5.00 —

Issued: No. 1827a, 11/21/10.

Urban Renaissance — A845

2010, Aug. 25 *Perf. 13x13¼*
1828 A845 8.90s multi 4.00 4.00
With tab 4.50

Shofars — A846

Shofar blower and shofar made of: 1.70s, Ram's horn. 4.20s, Kudu horn. 6.10s, Ram's horn, diff.

2010, Aug. 25 *Perf. 13¼x13*
1829 A846 1.70s multi .75 .75
1830 A846 4.20s multi 1.90 1.90
a. Booklet pane of 2, #1472a, 1830 — —
1831 A846 6.10s multi 2.75 2.75
Nos. 1829-1831 (3) 5.40 5.40
With tabs 6.00

Issued: No. 1830a, 11/21/10.

Greetings
A847 A848

2010, Aug. 25 *Perf. 13¾x14*
1832 A847 (1.70s) multi .90 .90
With tab 1.00
a. Sheet of 12 + 12 labels 15.00 15.00
1833 A848 (1.70s) multi .90 .90
With tab 1.00
a. Sheet of 12 + 12 labels 15.00 15.00

Booklet Stamps
Self-Adhesive
Serpentine Die Cut 12½x12¾

1834 A847 (1.70s) multi .90 .90
1835 A848 (1.70s) multi .90 .90
a. Booklet pane of 12, 6 each #1834-1835 11.00

Nos. 1832a and 1833a each sold for 28s. Labels could be personalized.

Miniature Sheet

Animals and Their Young — A849

No. 1836: a, Chicks. b, Hen. c, Kitten with ball of yarn. d, Cat. e, Rabbit kit, flower, carrot. f, Rabbit.

2010, Aug. 25 *Perf. 13x13¼*
1836 A849 Sheet of 6 + 3 labels 4.75 4.75
a.-f. 1.70s Any single .75 .75

Garden of Gethsemane, Jerusalem — A850

2010, Nov. 15 Litho. *Perf. 13x13¼*
1837 A850 4.20s multi 2.00 2.00
With tab 2.40

Printed in sheets of 4. See Vatican City No. 1456.

Flag of Israel — A851

2010, Nov. 21 *Perf. 13¾x14*
1838 A851 (1.70s) multi .95 .95
With tab 1.10
a. Sheet of 12 + 12 labels 15.50 15.50

No. 1838a sold for 28s. Labels could be personalized.
See No. 1877.

Movie Theaters A852

Designs: 4.20s, Armon Cinema, Haifa. 9s, Zion Cinema, Jerusalem.

2010, Nov. 21 *Perf. 13x13¼*
1839 A852 4.20s multi 1.90 1.90
1840 A852 9s multi 4.00 4.00
With tabs 6.75

Bible Stories — A853

Designs: No. 1841, Adam and Eve. No. 1842, Samson and the Lion. No. 1843, Jonah and the Fish.
6s, Moses parting the Red Sea, vert.

2010, Nov. 21 *Perf. 14½x14¼*
1841 A853 1.70s multi .95 .95
a. Miniature sheet of 6 8.00 8.00
1842 A853 1.70s multi .95 .95
a. Miniature sheet of 6 8.00 8.00
1843 A853 1.70s multi .95 .95
a. Miniature sheet of 6 8.00 8.00
Nos. 1841-1843 (3) 2.85 2.85
With tabs 3.25

Souvenir Sheet
Perf. 13½x13

1844 A853 6s multi 4.00 4.00

Jerusalem 2010 Intl. Philatelic Exhibition (No. 1844). No. 1844 contains one 30x40mm stamp.

A854

A855

A856

A857

A858

A859

A860

A861

A862

A863

A864

A865

A866

A867

Animation
A868

2010, Nov. 21 Litho. *Perf. 13x13¼*

1845		Sheet of 15	12.00	12.00
a.	A854	1.70s multi	.80	.80
b.	A855	1.70s multi	.80	.80
c.	A856	1.70s multi	.80	.80
d.	A857	1.70s multi	.80	.80
e.	A858	1.70s multi	.80	.80
f.	A859	1.70s multi	.80	.80
g.	A860	1.70s multi	.80	.80
h.	A861	1.70s multi	.80	.80
i.	A862	1.70s multi	.80	.80
j.	A863	1.70s multi	.80	.80
k.	A864	1.70s multi	.80	.80
l.	A865	1.70s multi	.80	.80
m.	A866	1.70s multi	.80	.80
n.	A867	1.70s multi	.80	.80
o.	A868	1.70s multi	.80	.80

Booklet Panes of 1
Self-Adhesive
Serpentine Die Cut 6¼

1846	A854	1.70s multi	.80	.80
1847	A855	1.70s multi	.80	.80
1848	A856	1.70s multi	.80	.80
1849	A857	1.70s multi	.80	.80
1850	A858	1.70s multi	.80	.80
1851	A859	1.70s multi	.80	.80
1852	A860	1.70s multi	.80	.80
1853	A861	1.70s multi	.80	.80
1854	A862	1.70s multi	.80	.80
1855	A863	1.70s multi	.80	.80
1856	A864	1.70s multi	.80	.80
1857	A865	1.70s multi	.80	.80
1858	A866	1.70s multi	.80	.80
1859	A867	1.70s multi	.80	.80
1860	A868	1.70s multi	.80	.80
		Complete booklet, #1846-1860	12.00	
		Nos. 1846-1860 (15)	12.00	12.00

Types of 1995-2010 Redrawn or In Different Sizes

2010, Nov. 21 Litho. *Perf. 13½x13*
Booklet Stamps

1861 A589 1.15s Like #1326, 30x40mm (1863a) .75 .75

Perf. 13x13½

1862 A545 1.50s Like #1246, 40x30mm (1866a) 1.00 1.00
1863 A545 1.80s Like #1247, 40x30mm (1863a) 1.25 1.25
a. Booklet pane of 2, #1861, 1863 2.00 —
1864 A603 2.20s Like #1345, 40x30mm (1867a) 1.50 1.50

Perf. 13½

1865 A726 3.30s Like #1600, redrawn, 30x40mm (1866a) 2.25 2.25

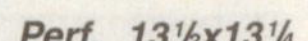
Perf. 13½x13¼

1866 A634 3.40s Like #1407, redrawn, 30x30mm (1866a) 2.25 2.25
a. Booklet pane of 4, #1610a, 1862, 1865, 1866 9.75 —

Perf. 13½

1867 A564 4.65s Like #1287, 30x40mm (1867a) 3.25 3.25
a. Booklet pane of 2, #1864, 1867 4.75 —
Complete booklet, #1827a, 1830a, 1863a, 1866a, 1867a *35.00*
Nos. 1861-1867 (7) 12.25 12.25

Complete booklet sold for 49s.

Intl. Year of Chemistry
A869

Chemical models of: 4.20s, Ubiquitin, protein destroyer. 6.10s, Ribosome, protein constructor.

2011, Jan. 4 Litho. *Perf. 14x13½*

1868	A869	4.20s multi	2.00	2.00
1869	A869	6.10s multi	3.00	3.00
		With tabs	5.50	

Roots of the Hebrew Language
A870

2011, Feb. 7 *Perf. 13½x14*

1870 A870 3.70s multi 1.75 1.75
With tab 2.00

Clalit Health Services, Cent.
A871

2011, Feb. 7 *Perf. 14x13½*

1871 A871 9s multi 4.25 4.25
With tab 4.75

Building Projects of King Herod — A872

2011, Feb. 7 *Perf. 13½x14*

1872	A872	1.70s Masada	.80	.80
1873	A872	1.70s Caesarea	.80	.80
1874	A872	2.50s Jerusalem	1.20	1.20
1875	A872	2.50s Herodian	1.20	1.20
		Nos. 1872-1875 (4)	4.00	4.00
		With tabs	4.50	

Worldwide Fund for Nature (WWF) — A873

No. 1876 — Panthera pardus saxicolor: a, Leaping. b, Standing on hill with rams. c, Drinking. d, With cub.

2011, Feb. 7 *Perf. 14x13½*

1876 A873 Block of 4 3.25 3.25
a.-d. 1.70s Any single .80 .80
Nos. 1876a-1876d, with tabs 3.75

Flag of Israel Type of 2010
Serpentine Die Cut 13x14¼
2011, Apr. 12 Litho.
Booklet Stamp
Self-Adhesive

1877 A851 (1.70s) multi 1.10 1.10
a. Booklet pane of 20 22.00

Memorial Day — A874

2011, Apr. 12 *Perf. 13½x13*

1878 A874 1.70s multi 1.00 1.00
With tab 1.10

Aliyah of Ethiopian Jews — A875

2011, Apr. 12 *Perf. 14¼*

1879 A875 2.50s multi 1.50 1.50
With tab 1.75

Mount Carmel Training Center, 50th Anniv.
A876

2011, Apr. 12 *Perf. 13x13½*

1880 A876 5s multi 2.50 2.50
With tab 3.00

Pres. Ephraim Katzir (1916-2009) — A877

2011, Apr. 12 ***Perf. 13x13½***

1881 A877 9s multi 4.75 4.75
With tab 5.25

Tourism A878

Designs: 4.20s, Sea of Galilee. 6s, Tower of David and Old City Wall, Jerusalem. 6.10s, Red Sea clownfish near Eilat.

2011, Apr. 12 ***Perf. 14x13½***

1882 A878 4.20s multi 2.25 2.25
1883 A878 6s multi 3.25 3.25
1884 A878 6.10s multi 3.50 3.50
Nos. 1882-1884 (3) 9.00 9.00
With tabs 10.00

Miniature Sheet

Butterflies — A879

Designs: Nos. 1885a, 1888, Anaphaeis aurota. Nos. 1885b, 1887, Vanessa atalanta. Nos. 1885c, 1886, Papilio machaon syracus. Nos. 1885d, 1889, Apharitis acamas. Nos. 1885e, 1890, Danaus chrysippus. Nos. 1885f, 1891, Polyommatus icarus zelleri.

2011 ***Perf. 13¾x14***

1885 A879 Sheet of 6 5.50 5.50
a.-f. (1.70s) Any single .90 .90

Booklet Stamps
Self-Adhesive

Serpentine Die Cut 13x14¼

1886 A879 (1.70s) multi 1.00 1.00
1887 A879 (1.70s) multi 1.00 1.00
1888 A879 (1.70s) multi 1.00 1.00
1889 A879 (1.70s) multi 1.00 1.00
1890 A879 (1.70s) multi 1.00 1.00
1891 A879 (1.70s) multi 1.00 1.00
a. Booklet pane of 20, 4 each #1886-1889, 2 each #1890-1891 20.00
Nos. 1886-1891 (6) 6.00 6.00

Issued: No. 1885, 4/12; Nos. 1886-1891, 6/27.

Rabbi Shlomo Goren (1917-94), Chief Rabbi of Israel A880

2011, June 27 ***Perf. 13x13½***

1892 A880 1.70s multi .90 .90
With tab 1.00

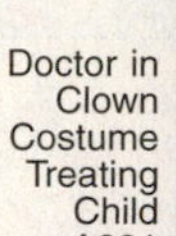

Doctor in Clown Costume Treating Child A881

2011, June 27 **Litho.**

1893 A881 9s multi 4.75 4.75
With tab 5.25

Israeli Agricultural Achievements — A882

Designs: No. 1894, Medjool date trees nourished by saline water in pots. No. 1895, Tomatoes growing in hothouse. No. 1896, Water purification pool, Dan Region Wastewater Treatment Facility.

2011, June 27

1894 A882 2.50s multi 1.35 1.35
1895 A882 2.50s multi 1.35 1.35
1896 A882 2.50s multi 1.35 1.35
Nos. 1894-1896 (3) 4.05 4.05
With tabs 4.25

Miniature Sheet

Beaches — A883

No. 1897: a, Sea of Galilee Beach, hot air balloons. b, Sea of Galilee Beach, no balloons. c, Caesarea Beach, no kites. d, Caesarea Beach, kites. e, Tel Aviv Beach, sailboats. f, Tel Aviv Beach, jetty. g, Dead Sea Beach, no airplane. h, Dead Sea Beach, airplane. i, Eilat Beach, speedboats. j, Eilat Beach, no speedboats.

2011, June 27 ***Perf. 14x13½***

1897 A883 Sheet of 10 10.00 10.00
a.-j. 1.70s Any single 1.00 1.00

Admission of Israel to Organization for Economic Cooperation and Development — A884

2011, Sept. 13

1898 A884 9.30s multi 5.00 5.00
With tab 5.50

Items at Rosh Hashanah Feast A885

Designs: 1.70s, Apples and honey. 4s, Fish head. 5.90s, Pomegranates.

2011, Sept. 13

1899 A885 1.70s multi .80 .80
1900 A885 4s multi 1.90 1.90
1901 A885 5.90s multi 2.75 2.75
Nos. 1899-1901 (3) 5.45 5.45
With tabs 6.25

Children's Games A886

Designs: Nos. 1902, 1905, Hopscotch. Nos. 1903, 1906, Hide and seek. Nos. 1904, 1907, Tag.

2011, Sept. 13 ***Perf. 14x13½***

1902 A886 2.60s multi 1.40 1.40
1903 A886 2.60s multi 1.40 1.40
1904 A886 2.60s multi 1.40 1.40
Nos. 1902-1904 (3) 4.20 4.20
With tabs 4.75

Booklet Stamps
Self-Adhesive

Serpentine Die Cut 12½

1905 A886 2.60s multi 1.40 1.40
1906 A886 2.60s multi 1.40 1.40
1907 A886 2.60s multi 1.40 1.40
a. Booklet pane of 6, 2 each #1905-1907 8.60
Nos. 1905-1907 (3) 4.20 4.20

Miniature Sheet

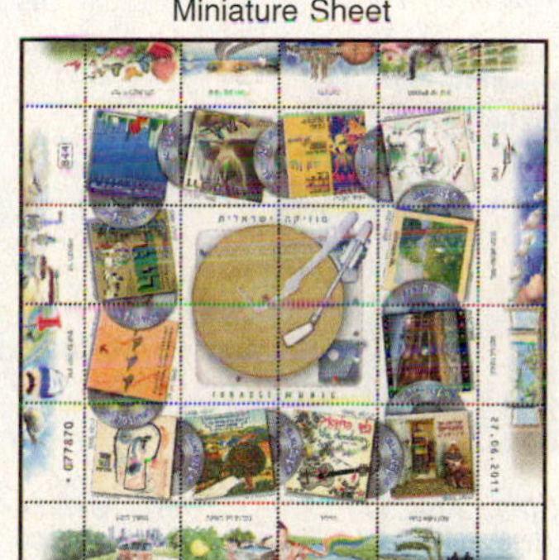

Israeli Record Albums — A887

No. 1908: a, *Why Should I Take it to Heart*, by Arik Einstein and Shalom Hanoch, 1979. b, *Ways*, by Shlomo Artzi, 1979. c, *Barcelona*, by Israel Andalusian Orchestra and Jo Amar, 2000. d, *Poogy Tales*, by Kaveret, 1973. e, *To the Candle and the Spices*, by Lehakat Tsliley Ha'Ud, 1975. f, *HaKeves HaShisha Asar*, by HaKeves Ha Shisha Asar (tree in field with white calf), 1978. g, *Antarctica*, by Corinne Allal, 1989. h, *Ashes and Dust*, by Yehuda Poliker (boy watching train pass), 1988. i, *Continuing to Ride*, by Ehud Banai and the Refugees (abstract head), 1987. j, *The Middle of the Road*, by Yehoram Gaon, 1984. k, *The Flute*, by the Doodaim, 1959. l, *Out of the Depths*, by The Idan Raichel Project (woman sitting by door), 2005.

2011, Sept. 13 ***Perf. 13¼x14***

1908 A887 Sheet of 12 + 4 central labels 11.50 11.50
a.-l. 1.70s Any single .95 .95

Valley Railroad A888

2011, Dec. 6 ***Perf. 14x13¼***

1909 A888 2.60s multi 1.10 1.10
With tab 1.30

Tribute to Rescue Forces — A889

2011, Dec. 6 ***Perf. 13¼x14***

1910 A889 3.80s red & yel grn 1.75 1.75
With tab 2.00

Israel Philharmonic Orchestra, 75th Anniv. — A890

2011, Dec. 6

1911 A890 4s multi 1.75 1.75
With tab 2.10

Miniature Sheet

Israeli Soccer Legends — A891

No. 1912: a, Avi Cohen (1956-2010). b, Menachem Ashkenazi (1934-2000). c, Nahum Stelmach (1936-99). d, Jerry Beit Halevi (1912-97). e, Eli Fuchs (1924-92). f, Shmuel Ben-Dror (1924-2009). g, Natan Panz (1917-48). h, Ya'akov Grundman (1939-2004). i, Avi Ran (1963-87). j, Ya'akov Hodorov (1927-2006). English translations of names are on tabs adjacent to stamps.

2011, Dec. 6 ***Perf. 14x13¼***

1912 A891 Sheet of 10 8.50 8.50
a.-j. 1.70s Any single .85 .85

Memorial Candle — A892

2012, Feb. 7 ***Perf. 13¾***

1913 A892 (1.70s) multi .90 .90
With tab 1.00
a. Sheet of 12 + 12 labels 15.00 15.00

No. 1913a sold for 28s. Labels could be personalized.

Rabbi Shneur Zalman of Lidai (1745-1812), Founder of Chabad Hasidism — A893

2012, Feb. 7 *Perf. 13x13¼*

1914 A893 1.70s multi	.90	.90
With tab	1.00	

Technion (Israel Institute of Technology), Cent. — A894

2012, Feb. 7

1915 A894 2.60s multi	1.40	1.40
With tab	1.60	

Trial, Sentencing and Execution of Nazi War Criminal Adolf Eichmann, 50th Anniv. — A895

2012, Feb. 7 *Perf. 13¼x13*

1916 A895 9.30s multi	5.00	5.00
With tab	5.50	

Famous Women A896

Designs: 4s, Bracha Zefira (1910-90), singer. 5.90s, Batia Makov (1841-1912), business entrepreneur.

2012, Feb. 7 *Perf. 13x13¼*

1917 A896 4s multi	1.90	1.90
1918 A896 5.90s multi	3.00	3.00
With tabs	5.50	

Gemstones From High Priest's Breastplate — A897

Gemstones and inscribed tribe: No. 1919, Carnelian, Reuven. No. 1920, Topaz, Shimon. No. 1921, Emerald, Levi. No. 1922, Turquoise, Yehuda.

2012, Feb. 7 **Litho.** *Perf. 13x13¼*

1919 A897 2.60s multi	1.30	1.30
1920 A897 2.60s multi	1.30	1.30
1921 A897 2.60s multi	1.30	1.30
1922 A897 2.60s multi	1.30	1.30
Nos. 1919-1922 (4)	5.20	5.20
With tabs	5.75	

See Nos. 1925-1928, 1935-1938.

Diplomatic Relations Between Israel and People's Republic of China, 20th Anniv. — A898

Designs: 2s, Waxwing, five-pointed star. 3s, White dove, Star of David.

2012, Mar. 20 **Litho.** *Perf. 13¼x14*

1923 A898 2s multi	1.10	1.10
1924 A898 3s multi	1.60	1.60
With tabs	3.00	

See People's Republic of China Nos. 3986-3987.

Gemstones From High Priest's Breastplate Type of 2012

Gemstones and inscribed tribe: No. 1925, Lazurite, Issachar. No. 1926, Quartz, Zevulun. No. 1927, Zircon, Dan. No. 1928, Amethyst, Naftali.

2012, Apr. 17 *Perf. 14x13¼*

1925 A897 3s multi	1.40	1.40
1926 A897 3s multi	1.40	1.40
1927 A897 3s multi	1.40	1.40
1928 A897 3s multi	1.40	1.40
Nos. 1925-1928 (4)	5.60	5.60
With tabs	6.25	

Memorial Day A899

2012, Apr. 17

1929 A899 1.70s multi	.95	.95
With tab	1.10	

Chain of Generations Center, Western Wall Plaza, Jerusalem A900

2012, Apr. 17 *Perf. 13¼x14*

1930 A900 9.30s multi	5.00	5.00
With tab	5.50	

Jewish Seamanship — A901

Designs: No. 1931, Hehalutz in Jaffa Harbor, 1919. No. 1932, Sara A in Haifa Harbor, 1935, and Jeremiah Helpern. No. 1933, Har Zion in Tel-Aviv Harbor, 1935, and Captain Erich Hirschfeld.

2012, Apr. 17 *Perf. 14x13¼*

1931 A901 3s multi	1.60	1.60
1932 A901 3s multi	1.60	1.60
1933 A901 3s multi	1.60	1.60
Nos. 1931-1933 (3)	4.80	4.80
With tabs	5.25	

Nos. 1931-1933 exist imperf. Value, set with tabs, $50.

Miniature Sheet

Children's Books — A902

No. 1934 — Books and illustrations: a, A Tale of Five Balloons, by Miriam Roth (girl holding blue balloon). b, Raspberry Juice, by Haya Shenhav (lion and giraffe). c, Caspion the Little Fish, by Paul Kor (fish). d, The Absent-minded Guy from Kefar Azar, by Leah Goldberg (man with glasses holding umbrellas). e, Itamar Walks on Walls, by David Grossman (Itamar walking on wall). f, Hot Sweet Corn, by Miriam Roth (five children eating corn on the cob). g, The Lion that Loved Strawberries, by Tirtza Atar (lion and strawberries). h, Come to Me, Nice Butterfly, by Fania Bergstein (child reaching for butterfly in fenced garden).

2012, Apr. 17

1934 A902 Sheet of 8	9.00	9.00
a.-h. 2s Any single	1.10	1.10

Gemstones From High Priest's Breastplate Type of 2012

Gemstone and inscribed tribe: No. 1935, Agate, Gad. No. 1936, Aquamarine, Asher. No. 1937, Onyx, Yosef. No. 1938, Jasper, Binyamin.

2012, June 26 *Perf. 13x13¼*

1935 A897 3s multi	1.60	1.60
1936 A897 3s multi	1.60	1.60
1937 A897 3s multi	1.60	1.60
1938 A897 3s multi	1.60	1.60
Nos. 1935-1938 (4)	6.40	6.40
With tabs	7.25	

Teddy Kollek (1911-2007), Mayor of Jerusalem A903

2012, June 26 *Perf. 13¼x13*

1939 A903 9.40s multi	5.25	5.25
With tab	5.75	

2012 Summer Olympics, London A904

London landmarks, 2012 Olympic Games emblem and: No. 1940, High jump. No. 1941, Artistic gymnastics. 4.50s, Taekwondo.

2012, June 26 *Perf. 13x13¼*

1940 A904 2s multi	1.05	1.05
1941 A904 2s multi	1.05	1.05
1942 A904 4.50s multi	2.50	2.50
Nos. 1940-1942 (3)	4.60	4.60
With tabs	5.25	

Israeli Membership in Intl. Police Association, 50th Anniv. — A905

2012, Sept. 4

1943 A905 4.20s multi	2.00	2.00
With tab	2.25	

Dead Sea, Mt. Everest, Flags of Israel and Nepal — A906

2012, Sept. 4 *Perf. 13¼x13*

1944 A906 5s multi	2.60	2.60
With tab	3.00	

See Nepal Nos. 874-875.

Hadassah (Women's Zionist Organization of America), Cent. — A907

2012, Sept. 4

1945 A907 6.20s multi	3.00	3.00
With tab	3.50	

Contribution of Senior Citizens — A908

2012, Sept. 4 *Perf. 13x13¼*

1946 A908 9.40s multi	4.25	4.25
With tab	4.75	

Worshipers Casting Away Sins at Water's Edge on Rosh Hashanah A909

Synagogue Members Reciting Kol Nidrei Prayer on Yom Kippur A910

Worshipers Holding Palm Fronds on Succoth A911

2012, Sept. 4

1947 A909 2s multi	.90	.90
1948 A910 4.20s multi	2.00	2.00
1949 A911 6.20s multi	3.00	3.00
Nos. 1947-1949 (3)	5.90	5.90
With tabs	6.50	

Tourist Attractions A912

Designs: Nos. 1950, 1953, Grotto, Rosh Hanikra. Nos. 1951, 1954, Jaffa. Nos. 1952, 1955, Solomon's Pillars, Timna Park.

2012, Sept. 4 *Perf. 13x13¼*

1950 A912 3s multi 1.50 1.50
1951 A912 3s multi 1.50 1.50
1952 A912 3s multi 1.50 1.50
Nos. 1950-1952 (3) 4.50 4.50
With tabs 5.00

Nos. 1950-1953 exist imperf. Value, set with tabs $32.50.

Booklet Stamps
Self-Adhesive
Serpentine Die Cut 12½

1953 A912 3s multi 1.75 1.75
1954 A912 3s multi 1.75 1.75
1955 A912 3s multi 1.75 1.75
a. Booklet pane of 6, 2 each #1953-1955 10.50
Nos. 1953-1955 (3) 5.25 5.25

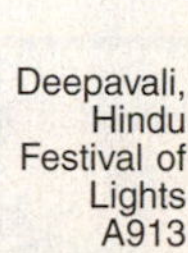

Deepavali, Hindu Festival of Lights A913

Hanukkah, Jewish Festival of Lights A914

2012, Nov. 5 *Perf. 13x13¼*

1956 A913 2s multi 1.10 1.10
1957 A914 2s multi 1.10 1.10
With tabs 2.50

See India Nos. 2602-2603.

Offshore Gas Drilling Platform A915

2012, Dec. 12

1958 A915 4.20s multi 2.25 2.25
With tab 2.50

Philately Day.

Koren Jerusalem Bible, 50th Anniv. — A916

2012, Dec. 12 *Perf. 13¼x13*

1959 A916 9.50s multi 4.25 4.25
With tab 4.75

Wildlife Conservation — A917

No. 1960 — Hands, bandage and: a, Mediterranean spur-thighed tortoise. b, Mountain gazelle fawn. c, Imperial eagle.

2012, Dec. 12 *Perf. 13x13¼*

1960 Horiz. strip of 3 4.50 4.50
a.-c. A917 3s Any single 1.45 1.45
Strip with tabs 5.00

No. 1960 was printed in sheets containing two strips of three stamps.

Souvenir Sheet

High Priest Wearing Breastplate — A918

2012, Dec. 12 *Perf. 13¼x13*

1961 A918 5s multi 3.50 3.50

Tel Aviv 2013 Intl. Stamp Exhibition. No. 1961 sold for 7s.

Arad, 50th Anniv. A919

2013, Feb. 5 *Perf. 13x13¼*

1962 A919 2s multi 1.30 1.30
With tab 1.50

Water, The Source of Life — A920

2013, Feb. 5 *Perf. 14½*

1963 A920 3s multi 1.90 1.90
With tab 2.10

Hebrew Reali School, Haifa, Cent. A921

2013, Feb. 5 *Perf. 13x13¼*

1964 A921 4.20s multi 2.40 2.40
With tab 2.60

Israel Customs Directorate A922

2013, Feb. 5 *Perf. 13¼x13*

1965 A922 9.50s multi 5.25 5.25
With tab 5.75

Gerbera Daisy — A923

No. 1966 — Color of flower: a, Pink. b, Orange and yellow. c, White. d, Yellow. e, Red and white.

2013, Feb. 5 *Perf. 13¾*

1966 Horiz. strip of 5 1.60 1.60
a. A923 20a multi .25 .25
b. A923 30a multi .25 .25
c. A923 40a multi .25 .25
d. A923 50a multi .30 .30
e. A923 1s multi .55 .55
Strip with tabs 1.75

No. 1966 was printed in sheets containing two tete-beche strips of 5 stamps.
See No. 2001.

Memorial Day — A924

2013, Apr. 2 *Perf. 13¼x13*

1967 A924 2s multi 1.10 1.10
With tab 1.25

Pawel Frenkel (1920-43), Commander of Jewish Military Organization in Warsaw Ghetto — A925

2013, Apr. 2 *Perf. 13x13¼*

1968 A925 9.50s multi 5.25 5.25
With tab 5.75

Warsaw Ghetto Uprising, 70th anniv.

Vultures A926

Designs: No. 1969, Torgos tracheliotus negevensis, Neophron percnopterus. No. 1970, Gypaetus barbatus. No. 1971, Gyps fulvus.

2013, Apr. 2 **Litho.**

1969 A926 3s multi 1.75 1.75
1970 A926 3s multi 1.75 1.75
1971 A926 3s multi 1.75 1.75
Nos. 1969-1971 (3) 5.25 5.25
With tabs 5.75

Nos. 1969-1971 exist imperf. Value, set with tabs $40.

Israeli Cardiological Achievements — A927

Designs: 3s, Percutaneous heart valve. 4.20s, Stent. 5s, Implantable defibrillator.

2013, Apr. 2

1972 A927 3s multi 1.75 1.75
1973 A927 4.20s multi 2.40 2.40
1974 A927 5s multi 2.75 2.75
Nos. 1972-1974 (3) 6.90 6.90
With tabs 7.75

Battle of Beersheba, 96th Anniv. A928

Designs: 2s, Statue of Australian Light Horseman, by Peter Corlett, Beersheva, Israel. 6.10s, Australian Light Horsemen, photograph of battle re-enactment.

2013, May 10 *Perf. 13x13¼*

1975 A928 2s multi 1.00 1.00
1976 A928 6.10s multi 3.00 3.00
With tabs 4.50

See Australia Nos. 3914-3915.

19th Maccabiah Games A929

2013, May 26 *Perf. 14x13¼*

1977 A929 3s multi 1.60 1.60
With tab 1.75

Hashomer Hatzair Movement, Cent. — A930

2013, May 26 *Perf. 13¼x14*

1978 A930 3s multi 1.60 1.60
With tab 1.75

Yitzhak Shamir (1915-2012), Prime Minister — A931

2013, May 26

1979 A931 9.50s multi 5.25 5.25
With tab 5.75

Souvenir Sheet

Postal Vehicles — A932

No. 1980: a, Austrian Post horse-drawn mail carriage, Jaffa Gate, Jerusalem. b, Mail train, clerk sorting mail in train car. c, Mail van, airplane.

2013, May 26 *Perf. 14x13¼*

1980 A932 Sheet of 3 8.50 8.50
a. 2s multi 1.75 1.75
b. 3s multi 2.50 2.50
c. 5s multi 4.25 4.25

Tel Aviv 2013 Intl. Stamp Exhibition. No. 1980 sold for 15s.
No. 1980 exists imperf. Value, $37.50.

Miniature Sheet

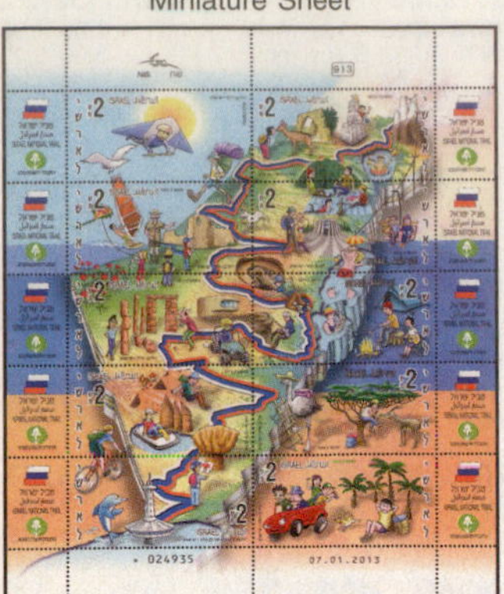

National Trail — A933

No. 1981: a, Sun, hang glider, bird, hiker with backpack. b, Hiker looking at antelope, arch, hiker and statue, mountains, swimmer with pool toy. c, Kite flyer, windsurfer, guide, children, Antipatris Fortress. d, Picnickers, hiker and child, John F. Kennedy Memorial, people on ski lift, man under umbrella. e, Hikers at archaeological site, man in dune buggy. f, Woman climbing rocks, hiker at Beit Guvrin Cave, woman reading newspaper in Dead Sea, campers at campfire. g, Hiker near Solomon's Pillars and Mushroom rock formation, woman in small boat. h, Ostrich, ladder, hiker in tree looking at gazelle. i, Bicycle, dolphin, Underwater Observatory, Eilat, hiker looking at picture of mushroom. j, Tourists in automobile, hiker resting under palm tree.

2013, May 26
1981 A933 Sheet of 10 11.00 11.00
a.-j. 2s Any single 1.10 1.10

Betar (Zionist Youth Movement), 90th Anniv. A934

2013, Aug. 26 Litho. ***Perf. 14x13½***
1982 A934 3.10s multi 1.75 1.75
With tab 1.90

Israel Military Industries, 80th Anniv. A935

2013, Aug. 26 Litho. ***Perf. 14x13½***
1983 A935 9.60s multi 5.50 5.50
With tab 6.00

Etrog Boxes A936

Etrog box made in: 2s, Jerusalem, 20th cent. 3.90s, Austria, 19th cent. 5.70s, Iraq, 19th cent.

2013, Aug. 26 Litho. ***Perf. 14x13½***
1984 A936 2s multi 1.15 1.15
1985 A936 3.90s multi 2.40 2.40
1986 A936 5.70s multi 3.50 3.50
Nos. 1984-1986 (3) 7.05 7.05
With tabs 7.75

Souvenir Sheet

Dorcas Gazelles — A937

2013, Aug. 26 Litho. ***Perf. 14x13½***
1987 A937 7s multi 4.50 4.50

See Greenland No. 646.

Miniature Sheet

Children's Songs — A938

No. 1988: a, A Brave Clock (Clock with eyes and mouth, child with clock's head). b, What Do the Does Do? (doe, elephants and balls). c, I Wanted You to Know (angel, girl in pajamas holding pillow). d, Buba Zehava (doll and teddy bear). e, I Am Always Me (boys with beach balls). f, Why Does the Zebra Wear Pajamas? (zebra wearing cap, pajamas on clothesline). g, Merry Choir (singing birds). h, The Prettiest Girl in Kindergarten (girl and block towers). i, Brave Danny (crying boy, boy and girl holding hands). j, Horse Rider (horse). k, My Dad (boy on father's shoulders, ladder and house). l, The Post Van (Post van with canceled cover).

Perf. 13¼x14, 14x13¼
2013, Aug. 26 Litho.
1988 A938 Sheet of 12 + 4 central labels 14.50 14.50
a.-l. 2s Any single 1.20 1.20

The Annunciation of Sarah, Painting by José Gurvich — A939

2013, Oct. 28 Litho. ***Perf. 13x13¼***
1989 A939 2s multi 1.25 1.25
With tab 1.40

Diplomatic relations between Israel and Uruguay, 65th anniv. See Uruguay No. 2445.

Rachel's Tomb, Gilo — A940

2013, Oct. 28 Litho. ***Perf. 13¼x13***
1990 A940 5s multi 3.00 3.00
With tab 3.25

Haifa Holiday of Holidays Festival, 20th Anniv. — A941

2013, Dec. 3 Litho. ***Perf. 13¼x13***
1991 A941 3.10s multi 1.90 1.90
With tab 2.10

Israeli Opera Production at Masada Opera Festival, and Giuseppe Verdi (1813-1901), Composer — A942

2013, Dec. 3 Litho. ***Perf. 13x13¼***
1992 A942 3.90s multi 2.50 2.50
With tab 2.75

Quasi-periodic Crystals of Aluminum-Managanese Alloy — A943

2013, Dec. 3 Litho. ***Perf. 13x13¼***
1993 A943 10s multi 5.75 5.75
With tab 6.50

Intl. Year of Crystallography, Philately Day.

Aviation in Israel, Cent. A944

Designs: Nos. 1994, 1997, Bleriot XI, 1913 (first plane in Israel). Nos. 1995, 1998, Fouga Magister Air Force training plane, 1960. Nos. 1996, 1999, Heron I drone, 1994.

2013, Dec. 3 Litho. ***Perf. 13x13¼***
1994 A944 3.10s multi 1.90 1.90
1995 A944 3.10s multi 1.90 1.90
1996 A944 3.10s multi 1.90 1.90
Nos. 1994-1996 (3) 5.70 5.70
With tabs 6.25

Nos. 1994-1996 exist imperf. Value, set with tabs $42.50.

Booklet Stamps
Self-Adhesive
Die Cut Perf. 12½

1997 A944 3.10s multi 1.90 1.90
1998 A944 3.10s multi 1.90 1.90
1999 A944 3.10s multi 1.90 1.90
a. Booklet pane of 6, 2 each #1997-1999 11.50 11.50
Nos. 1997-1999 (3) 5.70 5.70

Halls of the Knights Hospitallers, Acre, Israel and Valletta, Malta — A945

2014, Jan. 28 Litho. ***Perf. 13x13½***
2000 A945 3.90s multi 2.50 2.50
With tab 2.75

See Malta No. 1506.

Gerbera Daisy Type of 2013

10a, Red Gerbera daisy.

2014, Feb. 11 Litho. ***Perf. 13¾***
2001 A923 10a multicolored .50 .50
With tab .75

Resistance Radio Broadcasts, 75th Anniv. — A946

2014, Feb. 11 Litho. ***Perf. 13½x13***
2002 A946 9.60s multi 5.50 5.50
With tab 6.00

Ancient Erosion Craters A947

Designs: No. 2003, Makhtesh Gadol, vehicle caravan. No. 2004, Makhtesh Katan, bicyclists. No. 2005, Makhtesh Ramon, rock climber.

2014, Feb. 11 Litho. ***Perf. 13x13½***
2003 A947 3.10s multi 1.75 1.75
2004 A947 3.10s multi 1.75 1.75
2005 A947 3.10s multi 1.75 1.75
Nos. 2003-2005 (3) 5.25 5.25
With tabs 5.75

Nos. 2003-2005 exist imperf. Value, set with tabs $37.50.

Landmarks A948

No. 2006: a, Independence Hall, Tel Aviv. b, Detention Camp, Atlit. c, Synagogue, Peki'in. d, Ein Keshatot, Golan. e, City of David, Jerusalem.

2014, Feb. 11 Litho. ***Perf. 13x13½***
2006 Horiz. strip of 5 6.25 6.25
a.-e. A948 2s Any single 1.25 1.25
Strip with tabs 7.00

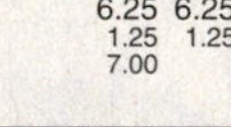

Wedding Rings — A949

2014, Apr. 8 Litho. ***Perf. 14***
2007 A949 (2s) multi 1.35 1.35
With tab 1.50

Memorial Day A950

2014, Apr. 8 Litho. ***Perf. 14x13½***
2008 A950 2s multi 1.35 1.35
With tab 1.50

Mateh Yehuda Regional Council, 50th Anniv. A951

2014, Apr. 8 Litho. *Perf. 14x13½*
2009 A951 3.10s multi 1.90 1.90
With tab 2.10

Violin and Auschwitz Concentration Camp — A952

2014, Apr. 8 Litho. *Perf. 13½x14*
2010 A952 9.60s multi 5.25 5.25
With tab 5.75

Violins that survived the Holocaust.

Non-Olympic Sports — A953

Designs: 3.90s, Water skiing. 5s, Wushu. 5.70s, Paragliding.

2014, Apr. 8 Litho. *Perf. 13½x14*
2011 A953 3.90s multi 1.75 1.75
2012 A953 5s multi 2.75 2.75
2013 A953 5.70s multi 3.00 3.00
Nos. 2011-2013 (3) 7.50 7.50
With tabs 8.00

Israeli Sign Language — A954

Signs for: Nos. 2014a, 2015, Thanks. Nos. 2014b, 2016, Kiss. Nos. 2014c, 2017, Friendship. Nos. 2014d, 2018, Love. Nos. 2014e, 2019, Goodbye.

2014, Apr. 8 Litho. *Perf. 14*
2014 Horiz. strip of 5 5.75 5.75
a.-e. A954 (2s) Any single 1.15 1.15
Strip with tabs 6.50

Booklet Stamps Self-Adhesive

Serpentine Die Cut 13½x14¼

2015 A954 (2s) multi 1.25 1.25
2016 A954 (2s) multi 1.25 1.25
2017 A954 (2s) multi 1.25 1.25
2018 A954 (2s) multi 1.25 1.25
2019 A954 (2s) multi 1.25 1.25
a. Booklet pane of 20, 4 each #2015-2019 25.00
Nos. 2015-2019 (5) 6.25 6.25

No. 2014 was printed in sheets containing two tete-beche strips.

Pomegranates, Mangosteens, Flags of Israel and Thailand — A955

2014, June 5 Litho. *Perf. 14x13½*
2020 A955 3.10s multi 1.90 1.90
With tab 2.10

Diplomatic relations between Israel and Thailand, 60th anniv. See Thailand No. 2811.

Palmer Gate Street, Haifa A956

2014, June 23 Litho. *Perf. 14x13½*
2021 A956 9.60s multi 5.50 5.50
With tab 6.00

Famous Women A957

Designs: 6s, Sara Levi-Tanai (1910-2005), choreographer. 10s, Esther Raab (1894-1981), poet.

2014, June 23 Litho. *Perf. 14x13½*
2022 A957 6s multi 3.50 3.50
2023 A957 10s multi 6.00 6.00
With tabs 10.50

Amphibians A958

No. 2024: a, Pelobates syriacus. b, Salamandra infraimmaculata. c, Ommatotriton vittatus. d, Latonia nigriventer.

2014, June 23 Litho. *Perf. 14xx13½*
2024 Block of 4 5.00 5.00
a.-d. A958 2s Any single 1.25 1.25
Nos. 2024a-2024b pair with tabs 2.75
Nos. 2024c-2024d pair with tabs 2.75

Global City of Tel Aviv A959

2014, Sept. 9 Litho. *Perf. 13x13½*
2025 A959 4.50s multi 2.50 2.50
With tab 2.75

Wolfgang von Weisl (1896-1974), Journalist and Zionist Leader — A960

2014, Sept. 9 Litho. *Perf. 13x13½*
2026 A960 9.70s multi 5.50 5.50
With tab 6.00

Simchat Torah Flags A961

Flag from: 2s, 1930s. 3.80s, 1950s. 5.60s, 1960s.

2014, Sept. 9 Litho. *Perf. 13x13½*
2027 A961 2s multi 1.05 1.05
2028 A961 3.80s multi 1.90 1.90
2029 A961 5.60s multi 3.00 3.00
Nos. 2027-2029 (3) 5.95 5.95
With tabs 6.75

Broadway Premiere of *Fiddler on the Roof*, 50th Anniv. A962

Inscriptions: Nos. 2030, 2033, Fiddler on the Roof. Nos. 2031, 2034, Tevye the Dairyman. Nos. 2032, 2035, Do you love me?

2014, Sept. 9 Litho. *Perf. 13x13½*
2030 A962 3.10s multi 1.75 1.75
2031 A962 3.10s multi 1.75 1.75
2032 A962 3.10s multi 1.75 1.75
Nos. 2030-2032 (3) 5.25 5.25
With tabs 5.75

Nos. 2030-2032 exist imperf. Value, set with tabs $40.

Booklet Stamps Self-Adhesive

Serpentine Die Cut 12½x12¼

2033 A962 3.10s multi 1.90 1.90
2034 A962 3.10s multi 1.90 1.90
2035 A962 3.10s multi 1.90 1.90
a. Booklet pane of 6, 2 each #2033-2035 11.50
Nos. 2033-2035 (3) 5.70 5.70

Ovadia Yosef (1920-2013), Chief Rabbi of Tel Aviv-Jaffa — A963

2014, Sept. 28 Litho. *Perf. 13¼*
2036 A963 2s multi 1.10 1.10
With tab 1.25

Arik Einstein (1939-2013), Singer — A964

2014, Dec. 16 Litho. *Perf. 13¼*
2037 A964 1.80s multi .95 .95
With tab 1.10

Ophrys Fuciflora, Dracula Simia, Flags of Israel and Ecuador — A965

2014, Dec. 16 Litho. *Perf. 13½x13*
2038 A965 5s multi 2.75 2.75
With tab 3.25

Friendship between Israel and Ecuador.

Hanukkah A966

2014, Dec. 16 Litho. *Perf. 13x13½*
2039 A966 9.70s multi 5.00 5.00
With tab 5.50

Sundials A967

Sundial from: 2.70s, Jewish Quarter, Jerusalem. 3.80s, Jezzar Pasha Mosque, Acre. 5.60s, Zoharei Chama Synagogue, Jerusalem.

2014, Dec. 16 Litho. *Perf. 13x13½*
2040 A967 2.70s multi 1.40 1.40
2041 A967 3.80s multi 2.00 2.00
2042 A967 5.60s multi 3.00 3.00
Nos. 2040-2042 (3) 6.40 6.40
With tabs 7.00

Automobiles Made in Israel — A968

Designs: 3.80s, 1936 Standard Carmel. 4s, 1961, Sabra Sport. 4.10s, 1951 Kaiser Manhattan. 8.30s, 1992 Sufa Jeep.

2014, Dec. 16 Litho. *Perf. 13x13½*
2043 A968 3.80s multi 2.00 2.00
2044 A968 4s multi 2.10 2.10
2045 A968 4.10s multi 2.10 2.10
2046 A968 8.30s multi 4.25 4.25
Nos. 2043-2046 (4) 10.45 10.45
With tabs 11.50

Ariel Sharon (1928-2014), Prime Minister — A969

2015, Jan. 27 Litho. *Perf. 13¼*
2047 A969 2.10s multi 1.10 1.10
With tab 1.25

Open Doors Monument, Rishon LeZion, Flags of Israel and the Philippines A970

2015, Jan. 27 Litho. *Perf. 13½x13*
2048 A970 4.50s multi 2.25 2.25
With tab 2.50

See Philippines No. 3567.

2015 European Individual Chess Championships, Jerusalem — A971

2015, Feb. 10 Litho. *Perf. 13x13½*
2049 A971 4.10s multi 2.10 2.10
With tab 2.40

International Year of Light — A972

2015, Feb. 10 Litho. *Perf. 13x13½*

2050 A972 11.80s multi 6.00 6.00
With tab 6.75

Awarding of 2013 Nobel Prize in Chemistry to Martin Karplus, Michael Levitt and Arieh Warshel.

Flowers — A973

Designs: 1.80s, Anthemis leucanthemifolia. 2.10s, Alkanna tinctoria. 2.70s, Anemone coronaria.

2015, Feb. 10 Litho. *Perf. 13½x13*

2051 A973 1.80s multi .95 .95
2052 A973 2.10s multi 1.10 1.10
2053 A973 2.70s multi 1.40 1.40
Nos. 2051-2053 (3) 3.45 3.45
With tabs 3.75

Memorial Day — A974

2015, Apr. 14 Litho. *Perf. 13½x13*

2054 A974 2.20s multi 1.10 1.10
With tab 1.25

Port of Ashdod, 50th Anniv. A975

2015, Apr. 14 Litho. *Perf. 13x13½*

2055 A975 4.30s multi 2.25 2.25
With tab 2.50

Expo 2015, Milan — A976

2015, Apr. 14 Litho. *Perf. 13½x13*

2056 A976 6.50s multi 3.50 3.50
With tab 3.50

Cyrus Declaration A977

2015, Apr. 14 Litho. *Perf. 13x13½*

2057 A977 8.30s multi 4.25 4.25
With tab 4.75

Zion Mule Corps, Cent. A978

2015, Apr. 14 Litho. *Perf. 13x13½*

2058 A978 11.80s multi 6.25 6.25
With tab 7.00

Eastern European Synagogue Hanukkah Lamp, 18th Cent. A979

Dome of Shrine of the Book A980

Turning the World Upside Down, Sculpture by Anish Kapoor A981

2015, Apr. 14 Litho. *Perf. 13x13½*

2059 A979 4.10s multi 2.10 2.10
2060 A980 4.10s multi 2.10 2.10
2061 A981 4.10s multi 2.10 2.10
Nos. 2059-2061 (3) 6.30 6.30
With tabs 7.25

Israel Museum, Jerusalem, 50th anniv.

Diplomatic Relations Between Israel and Germany, 50th Anniv. A982

2015, May 7 Litho. *Perf. 13x13½*

2062 A982 7.40s multi 4.00 4.00
With tab 4.50

See Germany No. 2846.

Bell AH-1 Cobra Attack Helicopter A983

2015, June 16 Litho. *Perf. 13x13½*

2063 A983 2.20s multi 1.25 1.25
With tab 1.40

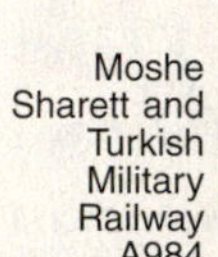

Moshe Sharett and Turkish Military Railway A984

2015, June 16 Litho. *Perf. 13x13½*

2064 A984 11.80s multi 6.25 6.25
With tab 7.00

World War I, cent.

Jewish Bridal Jewelry — A985

Designs: No. 2065, Bridal Necklace, Yemen, 1930s. No. 2066, Wedding ring, Italy, 17th cent. No. 2067, Bridal Head ornament, Bukhara, 19th cent.

2015, June 16 Litho. *Perf. 13½x13*

2065 A985 4.10s multi 2.25 2.25
2066 A985 4.10s multi 2.25 2.25
2067 A985 4.10s multi 2.25 2.25
Nos. 2065-2067 (3) 6.75 6.75
With tabs 7.50

Vegetables — A986

Designs: Nos. 2068a, 2069, Carrots. Nos. 2068b, 2070, Purple cabbage. Nos. 2068c, 2071, Lettuce. Nos. 2068d, 2072, Onions. Nos. 2068e, 2073, Tomatoes.

2015, June 16 Litho. *Perf. 14*

2068 Horiz. strip of 5 6.25 6.25
a.-e. A986 (2.20s) Any single 1.25 1.25
Strip with tabs 7.00

Booklet Stamps Self-Adhesive

Serpentine Die Cut 13¼x14¼

2069 A986 (2.20s) multi 1.25 1.25
2070 A986 (2.20s) multi 1.25 1.25
2071 A986 (2.20s) multi 1.25 1.25
2072 A986 (2.20s) multi 1.25 1.25
2073 A986 (2.20s) multi 1.25 1.25
a. Booklet pane of 20, 4 each #2069-2073 25.00
Nos. 2069-2073 (5) 6.25 6.25

Jewish Resistance Monument, Ramat Gan A987

2015, Sept. 2 Litho. *Perf. 14x13½*

2074 A987 11.80s multi 6.00 6.00
With tab 6.75

Jewish Resistance Movement, 70th Anniv.

Souvenir Sheet

Church of the Holy Sepulchre, Jerusalem — A988

2015, Sept. 2 Litho. *Perf. 14x13½*

2075 A988 7s multi 3.75 3.75

Visit of Pope Francis to Israel. See Vatican City No. 1602.

Children Celebrating Jewish Holidays A989

Children celebrating: 2.20s, Rosh Hashanah. 7.40s, Yom Kippur. 8.30s, Sukkot.

2015, Sept. 2 Litho. *Perf. 14x13½*

2076 A989 2.20s multi 1.10 1.10
2077 A989 7.40s multi 3.75 3.75
2078 A989 8.30s multi 4.25 4.25
Nos. 2076-2078 (3) 9.10 9.10
With tabs 10.00

Rivers A990

Designs: Nos. 2079, 2082, Kziv River. Nos. 2080, 2083, Taninim River. Nos. 2081, 2084, Zin River.

2015, Sept. 2 Litho. *Perf. 14x13½*

2079 A990 4.10s multi 2.10 2.10
2080 A990 4.10s multi 2.10 2.10
2081 A990 4.10s multi 2.10 2.10
Nos. 2079-2081 (3) 6.30 6.30
With tabs 7.00

Booklet Stamps Self-Adhesive

Serpentine Die Cut 12½

2082 A990 4.10s multi 2.10 2.10
2083 A990 4.10s multi 2.10 2.10
2084 A990 4.10s multi 2.10 2.10
a. Booklet pane of 6, 2 each #2082-2084 13.00
Nos. 2082-2084 (3) 6.30 6.30

Nili Resistance Movement, Cent. A991

2015, Dec. 8 Litho. *Perf. 13x13¼*

2085 A991 5s multi 2.60 2.60
With tab 3.00

Mamluk Postal Road A992

2015, Dec. 8 Litho. *Perf. 13x13¼*

2086 A992 10s multi 5.25 5.25
With tab 5.75

Philately Day.

Pension Savings A993

2015, Dec. 8 Litho. *Perf. 13x13¼*

2087 A993 11.70s multi 6.00 6.00
With tab 6.75

Entertainers A994

Designs: 2.30s, Sefi Rivlin (1947-2013), comedian. 4.10s, Channa Marron (1923-2014), actress.

2015, Dec. 8 Litho. *Perf. 13¼x13*

2088 A994 2.30s multi 1.25 1.25
2089 A994 4.10s multi 2.10 2.10
With tabs 3.75

Nostalgia
A995

No. 2090: a, Soda siphon. b, Tembel hat. c, Sussita automobile.

2015, Dec. 8 Litho. *Perf. 13x13¼*
2090 Horiz. strip of 3 3.75 3.75
a.-c. A995 2.30s Any single 1.25 1.25
Strip with tabs 4.25

Full Diplomatic Relations Between Israel and Greece, 25th Anniv.
A996

2016, Feb. 9 Litho. *Perf. 14x13½*
2091 A996 4.10s multi 2.10 2.10
With tab 2.40

See Greece No. 2719.

Winter
A997

2016, Feb. 9 Litho. *Perf. 14x13½*
2092 A997 4.10s multi 2.10 2.10
With tab 2.40

Ephraim Kishon (1924-2005), Writer — A998

2016, Feb. 9 Litho. *Perf. 13½x14*
2093 A998 11.70s multi 6.00 6.00
With tab 6.75

Famous Women
A999

Designs: 2.30s, Nehama Pohatchevsky (1869-1934), writer. 5s, Zelda Schneerson-Mishkovsky (1914-84), poet.

2016, Feb. 9 Litho. *Perf. 14x13½*
2094 A999 2.30s multi 1.25 1.25
2095 A999 5s multi 2.60 2.60
With tabs 4.25

Turtles — A1000

No. 2096: a, Chelonia mydas. b, Caretta caretta. c, Eretmochelys imbricata. d, Dermochelys coriacea.

2016, Feb. 9 Litho. *Perf. 14x13½*
2096 A1000 Block of 4 5.00 5.00
a.-d. 2.30s Any single 1.25 1.25
Nos. 2096a-2096d with tabs 5.50

Memorial Day
A1001

2016, Apr. 19 Litho. *Perf. 13x13¼*
2097 A1001 2.30s multi 1.25 1.25
With tab 1.40

Knesset Building, Jerusalem, 50th Anniv.
A1002

2016, Apr. 19 Litho. *Perf. 13x13¼*
2098 A1002 2.30s multi 1.25 1.25
With tab 1.40

Spring
A1003

2016 Litho. *Perf. 13x13¼*
2099 A1003 4.10s multi 2.25 2.25
With tab 2.50
a. Perf. 14x13½ (#2114a) 2.40 2.40

Issued: No. 2099, 4/19; No. 2099a, 9/13.

Chords Bridge, Jerusalem
A1004

2016, Apr. 19 Litho. *Perf. 13x13¼*
2100 A1004 7.40s multi 4.00 4.00
With tab 4.50

Diplomatic relations between Israel and Spain, 30th anniv. See Spain No. 4120.

Israeli Achievements in Printing — A1005

Designs: 2.30s, Digital prepress. 8.30s, Digital printing.

2016, Apr. 19 Litho. *Perf. 13x13¼*
2101 A1005 2.30s multi 1.25 1.25
2102 A1005 8.30s multi 4.50 4.50
With tabs 6.50

Markets
A1006

Designs: No. 2103, Mahana Yehuda Market, Jerusalem. No. 2104, Old Acre Market. No. 2105, Flea Market, Jaffa.

2016, Apr. 19 Litho. *Perf. 13x13¼*
2103 A1006 4.10s multi 2.25 2.25
2104 A1006 4.10s multi 2.25 2.25
2105 A1006 4.10s multi 2.25 2.25
Nos. 2103-2105 (3) 6.75 6.75
With tabs 7.50

Summer
A1007

2016 Litho. *Perf. 13x13¼*
2106 A1007 4.10s multi 2.25 2.25
With tab 2.50
a. Perf. 14x13½ (#2114a) 2.40 2.40

Issued: No. 2106, 6/21; No. 2106a, 9/13.

German World War I Pilot and Airplane
A1008

2016, June 21 Litho. *Perf. 13x13¼*
2107 A1008 11.70s multi 6.25 6.25
With tab 7.00

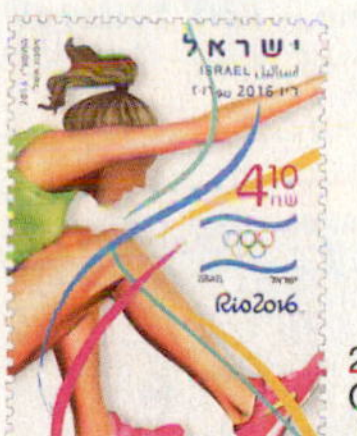
Service Dogs
A1009

Designs: 2.30s, Guide dogs. 10s, Search and rescue dogs.

2016, June 21 Litho. *Perf. 13x13¼*
2108 A1009 2.30s multi 1.25 1.25
2109 A1009 10s multi 5.25 5.25
With tabs 7.25

2016 Summer Olympics, Rio de Janeiro — A1010

Designs: No. 2110, Triple jump. No. 2111, Judo. No. 2112, Windsurfing.

2016, June 21 Litho. *Perf. 13¼x13*
2110 A1010 4.10s multi 2.25 2.25
2111 A1010 4.10s multi 2.25 2.25
2112 A1010 4.10s multi 2.25 2.25
Nos. 2110-2112 (3) 6.75 6.75
With tabs 7.50

Casualties of War and Terror Appreciation Day — A1011

2016, Sept. 13 Litho. *Perf. 14x13½*
2113 A1011 2.30s multi 1.25 1.25
With tab 1.40

Autumn
A1012

2016, Sept. 13 Litho. *Perf. 14x13½*
2114 A1012 4.10s multi 2.25 2.25
With tab 2.50
a. Souvenir sheet of 4, #2092, 2099a, 2106a, 2114 9.75 9.75

Jerusalem 2016 Stamp Exhibition (No. 2114a). No. 2114a sold for 18s.

White Storks, Flags of Israel and Bulgaria
A1013

2016, Sept. 13 Litho. *Perf. 14x13½*
2115 A1013 5s multi 2.75 2.75
With tab 3.00

Israel-Bulgaria Joint Issue, Bird Migration. See Bulgaria No. 4772.

Hands of Artisans in Yom Kippur Poem, "As the Clay in the Hand of the Potter"
A1014

Designs: 2.40s, Potter. 7.40s, Glazier, 8.30s, Silversmith.

2016, Sept. 13 Litho. *Perf. 14x13½*
2116 A1014 2.30s multi 1.25 1.25
2117 A1014 7.40s multi 4.00 4.00
2118 A1014 8.30s multi 4.50 4.50
Nos. 2116-2118 (3) 9.75 9.75
With tabs 10.50

Parables of the Sages
A1015

Designs: Nos. 2119, 2122, The Lion and the Heron. Nos. 2120, 2123, The Reed and the Cedar. Nos. 2121, 2124, The Fox in the Vineyard.

2016, Sept. 13 Litho. *Perf. 14x13½*
2119 A1015 4.10s multi 2.25 2.25
2120 A1015 4.10s multi 2.25 2.25
2121 A1015 4.10s multi 2.25 2.25
Nos. 2119-2121 (3) 6.75 6.75
With tabs 7.50

Booklet Stamps
Self-Adhesive
Die Cut Perf. 12½

2122 A1015 4.10s multi 2.25 2.25
2123 A1015 4.10s multi 2.25 2.25
2124 A1015 4.10s multi 2.25 2.25
a. Booklet pane of 6, 2 each #2122-2124 13.50
Nos. 2122-2124 (3) 6.75 6.75

Yitzhak Navon (1921-2015), President of Israel — A1016

2016, Nov. 13 Litho. *Perf. 13¼x13*
2125 A1016 11.70s multi 6.25 6.25
With tab 7.00

Mosaics
A1017

No. 2126 — Mosaic depicting: a, Leaping tiger, from 6th cent. synagogue, Gaza. b, Fish, from 3rd cent. villa, Lod. c, Peacock, from 6th cent. synagogue, Maon.

2016, Nov. 13 Litho. *Perf. 13x13¼*

2126 Horiz. strip of 3 6.75 6.75
a.-c. A1017 4.10s Any single 2.25 2.25
Strip with tabs 7.50

Tourist Attractions in Jerusalem A1018

No. 2127: a, Biblical Zoo. b, First train station. c, Via Dolorosa. d, Jaffa Road. e, Ramparts Promenade.

2016, Nov. 13 Litho. *Perf. 13x13¼*

2127 Horiz. strip of 5 6.25 6.25
a.-e. A1018 2.40s Any single 1.25 1.25
f. Booklet pane of 10, 2 each #2127a-2127e, + 2 central labels 12.50 —
Complete booklet, #2127f 12.50
Strip with tabs 7.00

Souvenir Sheet

King Solomon's Ships — A1019

2016, Nov. 13 Litho. *Perf. 13¼x13*

2128 A1019 5s multi 2.60 2.60

Jerusalem 2016 Stamp Exhibition.

Etsel Combat Soldiers and Emblem of Brit Hayyale Ha'Etsel — A1020

2017, Feb. 7 Litho. *Perf. 13¼x13*

2129 A1020 2.40s multi 1.40 1.40
With tab 1.60

Zionist Organization of America, 120th Anniv. — A1021

2017, Feb. 7 Litho. *Perf. 13¼x13*

2130 A1021 8.30s multi 4.75 4.75
With tab 5.25

Krav Maga A1022

2017, Feb. 7 Litho. *Perf. 13x13¼*

2131 A1022 11.70s multi 6.50 6.50
With tab 7.25

Aromatic Plants A1023

Designs: No. 2132, Frankincense. No. 2133, Myrrh. No. 2134, Balsam.

2017, Feb. 7 Litho. *Perf. 13x13¼*

2132 A1023 4.10s multi 2.25 2.25
2133 A1023 4.10s multi 2.25 2.25
2134 A1023 4.10s multi 2.25 2.25
Nos. 2132-2134 (3) 6.75 6.75
With tabs 7.50

See Nos. 2151-2153.

UNESCO World Heritage Sites A1024

Designs: 2.40s, Nahal Me'arot Caves. 5s, Bet She'arim Necropolis. 10s, Maresha and Bet-Guvrin Caves.

2017, Feb. 7 Litho. *Perf. 13x13¼*

2135 A1024 2.40s multi 1.40 1.40
2136 A1024 5s multi 2.75 2.75
2137 A1024 10s multi 5.50 5.50
Nos. 2135-2137 (3) 9.65 9.65
With tabs 11.00

National Memorial Hall, Jerusalem — A1025

2017, Apr. 4 Litho. *Perf. 14½x14¼*

2138 A1025 2.40s multi 1.40 1.40
With tab 1.60

Memorial Day.

Dolphin Research A1026

2017, Apr. 4 Litho. *Perf. 13x13¼*

2139 A1026 7.40s multi 4.25 4.25
With tab 4.75

See Portugal No.

Illustrations From Modern Passover Haggadahs A1027

Designs: No. 2140, Jews returning to Israel on boat. No. 2141, Haganah soldiers. No. 2142, Kibbutz members on hill.

2017, Apr. 4 Litho. *Perf. 13x13¼*

2140 A1027 4s multi 2.25 2.25
2141 A1027 4s multi 2.25 2.25
2142 A1027 4s multi 2.25 2.25
Nos. 2140-2142 (3) 6.75 6.75
With tabs 7.50

Settlements, 50th Anniv. — A1028

Settlement in: No. 2143, Golan (apples and Sa'ar River Waterfall). No. 2144, Jordan Valley (dates, date grove near Samaria Mountains). No. 2145, Judea and Samaria (olive branch, youths at Sebastia train station).

2017, Apr. 4 Litho. *Perf. 13¼x13*

2143 A1028 2.40s multi 1.40 1.40
2144 A1028 2.40s multi 1.40 1.40
2145 A1028 2.40s multi 1.40 1.40
Nos. 2143-2145 (3) 4.20 4.20
With tabs 4.75

Souvenir Sheet

Reunification of Jerusalem, 50th Anniv. — A1029

No. 2146: a, Water tower of Hebrew University of Jerusalem. b, Jews at Western Wall.

2017, Apr. 4 Litho. *Perf. 13¼x13*

2146 A1029 Sheet of 2 5.50 5.50
a.-b. 4.10s Either single 2.75 2.75

No. 2146 sold for 10s.

20th Maccabiah Games — A1030

2017, June 13 Litho. *Perf. 13¼x13*

2147 A1030 2.40s multi 1.40 1.40
With tab 1.60

Entry of Field Marshal Edmund Allenby into Jerusalem, Cent. A1031

2017, June 13 Litho. *Perf. 13x13¼*

2148 A1031 11.60s multi 6.75 6.75
With tab 7.50

World War I, end of Turkish rule in Jerusalem, cent.

A1032

A1033

A1034

A1035

A1036

A1037

A1038

A1039

A1040

A1041

A1042

Love Songs — A1043

Litho., Labels Litho. With Foil Application

2017, June 13 ***Perf. 13¼***

2149	Sheet of 12 + 4 central labels	17.00	17.00
a.	A1032 2.40s red & multi	1.40	1.40
b.	A1033 2.40s beige & multi	1.40	1.40
c.	A1034 2.40s blue gray & multi	1.40	1.40
d.	A1035 2.40s black, pink & multi	1.40	1.40
e.	A1036 2.40s sage grn, red & multi	1.40	1.40
f.	A1037 2.40s gray & multi	1.40	1.40
g.	A1038 2.40s azure & multi	1.40	1.40
h.	A1039 2.40s blk, yel ochre & multi	1.40	1.40
i.	A1040 2.40s lt brown & multi	1.40	1.40
j.	A1041 2.40s gray grn, pink & multi	1.40	1.40
k.	A1042 2.40s blk, pale blue & multi	1.40	1.40
l.	A1043 2.40s orange & multi	1.40	1.40

Anemone Coronaria and Iris Croatica Prodán A1044

2017, Sept. 4 **Litho.** ***Perf. 13x13¼***

2150	A1044 6.50s multi	3.75	3.75
	With tab	4.25	

Diplomatic relations between Israel and Croatia, 20th anniv. See Croatia No. 1045.

Aromatic Plants Type of 2017

Designs: No. 2151, Frankincense. No. 2152, Myrrh. No. 2153, Balsam.

Die Cut Perf. 12½x12¼

2017, Sept. 12 **Photo.**

Booklet Stamps Self-Adhesive

2151	A1023 4.10s multi	2.40	2.40
2152	A1023 4.10s multi	2.40	2.40
2153	A1023 4.10s multi	2.40	2.40
a.	Booklet pane of 6, 2 each #2151-2153	14.50	
	Nos. 2151-2153 (3)	7.20	7.20

Shimon Peres (1923-2016), Prime Minister and Ninth President of Israel — A1045

2017, Sept. 12 **Litho.** ***Perf. 13¼***

2154	A1045 2.40s multi	1.40	1.40
	With tab	1.60	

Habimah National Theater, Cent. A1046

2017, Sept. 12 **Litho.** ***Perf. 13x13¼***

2155	A1046 2.40s multi	1.40	1.40
	With tab	1.60	

Balfour Declaration, Cent. — A1047

Perf. 14½x14¼

2017, Sept. 12 **Litho.**

2156	A1047 5s multi	3.00	3.00
	With tab	3.50	

Activities of Jewish Festivals of the Month of Tishrei A1048

Designs: 2.40s, Selichot prayers. 7.40s, Building a sukkah. 8.30s, Second Hakafot.

2017, Sept. 12 **Litho.** ***Perf. 13x13¼***

2157	A1048 2.40s multi	1.40	1.40
2158	A1048 7.40s multi	4.25	4.25
2159	A1048 8.30s multi	4.75	4.75
	Nos. 2157-2159 (3)	10.40	10.40
	With tabs	11.50	

Gorny Convent, Eni Karem A1049

2017, Nov. 14 **Litho.** ***Perf. 14x13½***

2160	A1049 6s multi	3.50	3.50
	With tab	4.00	

Diplomatic Relations between Israel and Russia.
See Russia No.

Integration of the Handicapped into Society — A1050

2017, Dec. 19 **Litho.** ***Perf. 14x13½***

2161	A1050 11.60s multi	6.75	6.75
	With tab	7.50	

Submarines A1051

Designs: No. 2162, S Class submarine, 1959. No. 2163, T Class submarine, 1967. No. 2164, Gal Class submarine, 1976.

2017, Dec. 19 **Litho.** ***Perf. 14x13½***

2162	A1051 2.50s multi	1.50	1.50
2163	A1051 2.50s multi	1.50	1.50
2164	A1051 2.50s multi	1.50	1.50
	Nos. 2162-2164 (3)	4.50	4.50
	With tabs	5.00	

Ancient Roman Arenas A1052

Designs: No. 2165, Amphitheater, Beit Guvrin. No. 2166, Theater, Beit She'an. No. 2167, Hippodrome, Caesarea.

2017, Dec. 19 **Litho.** ***Perf. 14x13½***

2165	A1052 4.10s multi	2.40	2.40
2166	A1052 4.10s multi	2.40	2.40
2167	A1052 4.10s multi	2.40	2.40
	Nos. 2165-2167 (3)	7.20	7.20
	With tabs	8.00	

Snakes — A1053

No. 2168: a, Dolichophis jugularis. b, Psammophis schokari. c, Daboia palaestinae.

2017, Dec. 19 **Litho.** ***Perf. 13½x14***

2168	Horiz. strip of 3	7.20	7.20
a.-c.	A1053 4.10s Any single	2.40	2.40
	Strip with tabs	8.00	

Indian Cavalry in Haifa, 1918 A1054

2018, Feb. 6 **Litho.** ***Perf. 13x13¼***

2169	A1054 2.50s multi	1.50	1.50
	With tab	1.75	

Israel Television, 50th Anniv. A1055

2018, Feb. 6 **Litho.** ***Perf. 13x13¼***

2170	A1055 4.20s multi	2.40	2.40
	With tab	2.60	

Ha'Chizbatron Musical Troupe, 70th Anniv. — A1056

2018, Feb. 6 **Litho.** ***Perf. 13x13¼***

2171	A1056 7.40s multi	4.25	4.25
	With tab	4.75	

Gevatron Chorus, 70th Anniv. — A1057

2018, Feb. 6 **Litho.** ***Perf. 13¼x13***

2172	A1057 10s multi	5.75	5.75
	With tab	6.50	

Wildlife Repopulated by Yotvata Hai-Bar — A1058

No. 2173: a, Equus hemionus. b, Oryx leucoryx. c, Gazella gazella acacia.

2018, Feb. 6 **Litho.** ***Perf. 13x13¼***

2173	Horiz. strip of 3	4.50	4.50
a.-c.	A1058 2.50s Any single	1.50	1.50
	Strip with tabs	5.00	

Yotvata Hai-Bar, 50th anniv.

AIR POST STAMPS

Doves Pecking at Grapes — AP1

Marisa Eagle — AP2

Designs: 30p, Beth Shearim eagle. 40p, Mosaic bird. 50p, Stylized dove. 250p, Mosaic dove and olive branch.

Perf. 11½

1950, June 25 **Unwmk.** **Litho.**

C1	AP1	5p	brt grnsh bl	.65	.25
C2	AP1	30p	gray	.35	.25
C3	AP1	40p	dark green	.35	.25
C4	AP1	50p	henna brown	.35	.25

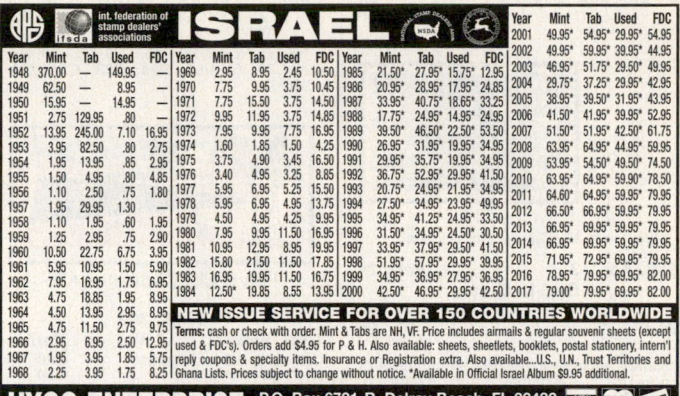

C5 AP2 100p rose car 13.00 12.00
C6 AP2 250p dk gray bl 1.75 .60
Nos. C1-C6 (6) 16.45 13.60
With tabs 250.00

Haifa Bay and City Seal AP3

120p, Haifa, Mt. Carmel and city seal.

1952, Apr. 13 *Perf. 14*
Seal in Gray

C7 AP3 100p ultramarine .30 .25
C8 AP3 120p purple .30 .25
#C7-C8, with tabs 20.00

Stamps were available only on purchase of a ticket to the National Stamp Exhibition, Haifa. Price, including ticket, 340p.

Olive Tree — AP4

Tanur Cascade AP5

Coast at Tel Aviv-Jaffa AP6

70p, En Gev, Sea of Galilee. 100p, Road to Jerusalem. 150p, Lion Rock. 350p, Bay of Elat, Red Sea. 750p, Lake Hule. 3000p, Tomb of Rabbi Meir Baal Haness, Tiberias.

1953-56 **Litho.**

C9 AP4 10p olive grn .25 .25
C10 AP4 70p violet .25 .25
C11 AP4 100p green .25 .25
C12 AP4 150p orange brn .25 .25
C13 AP4 350p car rose .25 .25
C14 AP5 500p dull & dk bl .25 .25
C15 AP6 750p brown .30 .25
C16 AP6 1000p deep bl grn 4.50 1.00
With tab 85.00
C17 AP6 3000p claret .25 .25
Nos. C9-C17 (9) 6.55 3.00
Nos. C9-C15, C17 with tabs 7.50

Issued: 1000p, 3/16/53; 10p, 100p, 500p, 3/2/54; 70p, 150p, 350p, 4/6/54; 750p, 8/21/56; 3000p, 11/13/56.

Old Town, Zefat — AP7

Designs: 20a, Ashkelon, Afridar Center. 25a, Acre, tower and boats. 30a, Haifa, view from Mt. Carmel. 35a, Capernaum, ancient synagogue, horiz. 40a, Jethro's tomb, horiz. 50a, Jerusalem, horiz. 65a, Tiberias, tower and lake, horiz. £1, Jaffa, horiz.

1960-61 **Photo.** *Perf. 13x14, 14x13*

C18 AP7 15a light lil & blk .25 .25
C19 AP7 20a brt yel grn & blk .25 .25
C20 AP7 25a orange & blk ('61) .25 .25
C21 AP7 30a grnsh bl & blk ('61) .25 .25
C22 AP7 35a yel grn & blk ('61) .25 .25
C23 AP7 40a lt vio & blk ('61) .25 .25
C24 AP7 50a olive & blk ('61) .25 .25
C25 AP7 65a lt ultra & black .25 .25
C26 AP7 £1 pink & blk ('61) .40 .30
Nos. C18-C26 (9) 2.40 2.30
With tabs 12.00

Issued: Nos. C18, C19, C25, 2/24/60; Nos. C20-C22, 6/14/61; Nos. C23, C24, C26, 10/26/61.

Port of Elat ('Aqaba) — AP8

Wmk. 302
1962, Feb. 21 **Litho.** *Perf. 14*
C27 AP8 £3 multicolored 1.60 1.00
With tab 10.00

Houbara Bustard — AP9

Birds: 5a, Sinai rose finch, horiz. 20a, White-breasted kingfisher, horiz. 28a, Mourning wheatear, horiz. 30a, Blue-cheeked bee eater. 40a, Graceful prinia. 45a, Palestine sunbird. 70a, Scops owl. £1, Purple heron. £3, White-tailed Sea eagle.

Perf. 13x14, 14x13
1963 **Unwmk.** **Photo.**

C28 AP9 5a dp vio & multi .25 .25
C29 AP9 20a red & multi .25 .25
C30 AP9 28a emerald & multi .25 .25
C31 AP9 30a orange & multi .25 .25
C32 AP9 40a multicolored .25 .25
C33 AP9 45a yellow & multi .25 .25
C34 AP9 55a multicolored .25 .25
C35 AP9 70a black & multi .25 .25
C36 AP9 £1 multicolored .30 .30
C37 AP9 £3 ultra & multi .75 .60
Nos. C28-C37 (10) 3.05 2.90
With tabs 7.50

Issue dates: Nos. C28-C30, 4/15; Nos. C31-C33, 6/19; Nos. C34-C36, 2/13; No. C37, 10/23.

Diamond and Boeing 707 AP10

Boeing 707 and: 10a, Textiles. 30a, Symbolic stamps. 40a, Vase, jewelry. 50a, Chick, egg. 55a, Melon, avocado, strawberries. 60a, Gladioli. 80a, Electronic equipment, chart. £1, Heavy oxygen isotopes (chemical apparatus). £1.50, Women's fashions.

1968 **Photo.** *Perf. 13x14*

C38 AP10 10a ultra & multi .25 .25
C39 AP10 30a gray & multi .25 .25
C40 AP10 40a multicolored .25 .25
C41 AP10 50a multicolored .25 .25
C42 AP10 55a multicolored .25 .25
C43 AP10 60a sl grn, lt grn & red .25 .25
C44 AP10 80a yel, brn & lt bl .25 .25
C45 AP10 £1 dark bl & org .25 .25
C46 AP10 £1.50 multicolored .25 .25
C47 AP10 £3 pur & lt bl .30 .25
Nos. C38-C47 (10) 2.55 2.50
With tabs 4.25

Israeli exports. Sheets of 15 (5x3).
Issued: Nos. C38-C41, 3/11; No. C47, 2/7; Nos. C42-C43, C45, 11/6; Nos. C44, C46, 12/23.

POSTAGE DUE STAMPS

Types of Regular Issue Overprinted in Black

Various coins, as on postage denominations.

Unwmk.
1948, May 28 **Typo.** *Perf. 11*
Yellow Paper

J1 A1 3m orange 3.00 1.25
J2 A1 5m yellow green 4.00 1.75
J3 A1 10m red violet 7.00 4.00
J4 A1 20m ultramarine 13.00 8.00
J5 A1 50m orange brown 55.00 55.00
Nos. J1-J5 (5) 82.00 70.00
With tabs (blank) *2,750.*

The 3m, 20m and 50m are known with overprint omitted.
Nos. J1-J5 exist imperf.

D1

1949, Dec. 18 **Litho.** *Perf. 11½*

J6 D1 2p orange .25 .25
J7 D1 5p purple .40 .25
J8 D1 10p yellow green .40 .25
J9 D1 20p vermilion .50 .25
J10 D1 30p violet blue .65 .30
J11 D1 50p orange brown 1.10 .95
Nos. J6-J11 (6) 3.30 2.25
With tabs (blank) 150.00

Running Stag — D2

1952, Nov. 30 **Unwmk.** *Perf. 14*

J12 D2 5p orange brown .25 .25
J13 D2 10p Prussian blue .25 .25
J14 D2 20p magenta .25 .25
J15 D2 30p gray black .25 .25
J16 D2 40p green .25 .25
J17 D2 50p brown .25 .25
J18 D2 60p purple .25 .25
J19 D2 100p red .25 .25
J20 D2 250p blue .25 .25
Nos. J12-J20 (9) 2.25 2.25
With tabs (blank) 10.00

OFFICIAL STAMPS

Redrawn Type of 1950 Overprinted in Black

1951, Feb. 1 **Unwmk.** *Perf. 14*

O1 A6 5p bright red violet .25 .25
O2 A6 15p vermilion .25 .25
O3 A6 30p ultramarine .25 .25
O4 A6 40p orange brown .25 .25
Nos. O1-O4 (4) 1.00 1.00
With tabs 18.00

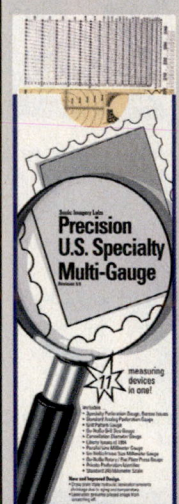

ITALIAN COLONIES

ə-'tal-yən 'kä-lə-nēz

General Issues for all Colonies

100 Centesimi = 1 Lira

Used values in italics are for postaly used stamps. Cancelled-to-order examples sell for about the same as unused, hinged stamps.

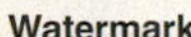

Watermark

Wmk. 140

Type of Italy, Dante Alighieri Society Issue, in New Colors

Overprinted in Red or Black

1932, July 11 Wmk. 140 *Perf. 14*

No.	Type	Denom.	Color	Unused	Used
1	A126	10c	gray blk	1.00	*3.50*
2	A126	15c	olive brn	1.00	*3.50*
3	A126	20c	slate grn	1.00	2.00
4	A126	25c	dk grn	1.00	2.00
5	A126	30c	red brn (Bk)	1.00	2.00
6	A126	50c	bl blk	1.00	1.35
7	A126	75c	car rose (Bk)	1.75	5.75
8	A126	1.25 l	dk bl	1.75	*8.00*
9	A126	1.75 l	violet	1.75	*13.00*
10	A126	2.75 l	org (Bk)	1.75	*22.00*
11	A126	5 l	+ 2 l ol grn	2.25	*25.00*
12	A126	10 l	+ 2.50 l dp bl	2.25	*40.00*
			Nos. 1-12,C1-C6 (18)	32.50	*234.10*

Types of Italy, Garibaldi Issue, in New Colors and Inscribed: "POSTE COLONIALI ITALIANE"

1932, July 1 Photo.

No.	Type	Denom.	Color	Unused	Used
13	A138	10c	green	3.25	*15.00*
14	A138	20c	car rose	3.25	*10.00*
15	A138	25c	green	3.25	*10.00*
16	A138	30c	green	3.25	*16.00*
17	A138	50c	car rose	3.25	*10.00*
18	A141	75c	car rose	4.00	*17.00*
19	A141	1.25 l	deep blue	4.00	*17.00*
20	A141	1.75 l	+ 25c dp bl	9.00	*22.50*
21	A144	2.55 l	+ 50c ol brn	9.00	*40.00*
22	A145	5 l	+ 1 l dp bl	9.00	*50.00*
			Nos. 13-22,C8-C12 (15)	85.25	*306.50*

See Nos. CE1-CE2.

Plowing with Oxen — A1

Pack Camel — A2

Lioness — A3

1933, Mar. 27 Wmk. 140

No.	Type	Denom.	Color	Unused	Used
23	A1	10c	ol brn	11.00	*20.00*
24	A2	20c	dl vio	11.00	*20.00*
25	A3	25c	green	11.00	*20.00*
26	A1	50c	purple	11.00	*20.00*
27	A2	75c	carmine	11.00	*24.00*
28	A3	1.25 l	blue	11.00	*24.00*
29	A1	2.75 l	red orange	22.50	42.50
30	A2	5 l	+ 2 l gray grn	45.00	*85.00*
31	A3	10 l	+ 2.50 l org brn	45.00	*130.00*
			Nos. 23-31,C13-C19 (16)	379.00	*775.50*

Annexation of Eritrea by Italy, 50th anniv.

Agricultural Implements A4

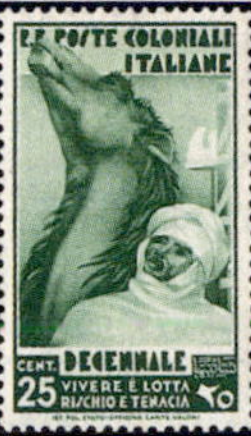

Arab and Camel — A5

"Eager with New Life" — A7

Steam Roller — A6

1933 Photo. *Perf. 14*

No.	Type	Denom.	Color	Unused	Used
32	A4	5c	orange	6.00	*12.50*
33	A5	25c	green	6.00	*12.50*
34	A6	50c	purple	6.00	11.00
35	A4	75c	carmine	6.00	*22.00*
36	A5	1.25 l	deep blue	6.00	*22.00*
37	A6	1.75 l	rose red	6.00	*22.00*
38	A4	2.75 l	dark blue	6.00	*32.00*
39	A5	5 l	brnsh blk	15.00	*42.50*
40	A6	10 l	bluish blk	15.00	*55.00*
41	A7	25 l	gray black	18.00	*85.00*
			Nos. 32-41,C20-C27 (18)	191.50	*631.00*

10th anniversary of Fascism. Each denomination bears a different inscription.

Issue dates: 25 l, Dec. 26; others, Oct. 5.

Mercury and Fasces — A8

1934, Apr. 18

No.	Type	Denom.	Color	Unused	Used
42	A8	20c	red orange	1.25	*7.25*
43	A8	30c	slate green	1.25	*7.25*
44	A8	50c	indigo	1.25	*7.25*
45	A8	1.25 l	blue	1.25	*14.50*
			Nos. 42-45 (4)	5.00	*36.25*

15th annual Trade Fair, Milan.

Scoring a Goal — A9

Soccer Kickoff — A10

1934, June 5

No.	Type	Denom.	Color	Unused	Used
46	A9	10c	olive green	35.00	*47.50*
47	A9	50c	purple	52.50	32.00
48	A9	1.25 l	blue	52.50	*110.00*
49	A10	5 l	brown	70.00	*360.00*
50	A10	10 l	gray blue	70.00	*360.00*
			Nos. 46-50,C29-C35 (12)	586.50	*1,835.*

2nd World Soccer Championship.

SEMI-POSTAL STAMPS

Many issues of Italy and Italian Colonies include one or more semi-postal denominations. To avoid splitting sets, these issues are generally listed as regular postage, airmail, etc., unless all values carry a surtax.

AIR POST STAMPS

Italian Air Post Stamps for Dante Alighieri Society Issue in New Colors and Overprinted in Red or Black Like #1-12

1932, July 11 Wmk. 140 *Perf. 14*

No.	Type	Denom.	Color	Unused	Used
C1	AP10	50c	gray blk (R)	1.50	*7.25*
C2	AP11	1 l	indigo (R)	1.50	*7.25*
C3	AP11	3 l	gray (R)	3.00	*11.00*
C4	AP11	5 l	ol brn (R)	3.00	*16.00*
C5	AP10	7.70 l	+ 2 l car rose	3.00	*22.00*
C6	AP11	10 l	+ 2.50 l org	3.00	*42.50*
			Nos. C1-C6 (6)	15.00	*106.00*

Leonardo da Vinci — AP1

1932, Sept. 7 Photo. *Perf. 14½*

No.	Type	Denom.	Color	Unused	Used
C7	AP1	100 l	dp grn & brn	14.50	*125.00*

Types of Italian Air Post Stamps, Garibaldi Issue, in New Colors and Inscribed: "POSTE AEREA COLONIALE ITALIANA"

1932, July 1

No.	Type	Denom.	Color	Unused	Used
C8	AP13	50c	car rose	4.25	*11.00*
C9	AP14	80c	green	4.25	*11.00*
C10	AP13	1 l	+ 25c ol brn	8.50	*21.00*
C11	AP13	2 l	+ 50c ol brn	8.50	*21.00*
C12	AP14	5 l	+ 1 l ol brn	8.50	*35.00*
			Nos. C8-C12 (5)	34.00	*99.00*

Eagle AP2

Savoia Marchetti 55 — AP3

Savoia Marchetti 55 Over Map of Eritrea AP4

1933 *Perf. 14*

No.	Type	Denom.	Color	Unused	Used
C13	AP2	50c	org brn	16.00	*20.00*
C14	AP2	1 l	blk vio	16.00	*20.00*
C15	AP3	3 l	carmine	23.00	*40.00*
C16	AP3	5 l	olive brn	23.00	*40.00*
C17	AP2	7.70 l	+ 2 l slate	40.00	*90.00*
C18	AP3	10 l	+ 2.50 l dp bl	40.00	*90.00*
C19	AP4	50 l	dk vio	42.50	*90.00*
			Nos. C13-C19 (7)	200.50	*390.00*

50th anniv. of Italian Government of Eritrea.

Issue dates: 50 l, June 1; others, Mar. 27.

Macchi-Costoldi Seaplane — AP5

Savoia S73 — AP6

Winding Propeller AP7

"More Efficient Machinery" AP8

1933-34

No.	Type	Denom.	Color	Unused	Used
C20	AP5	50c	org brn	8.00	19.00
C21	AP6	75c	red vio	8.00	19.00
C22	AP5	1 l	bis brn	8.00	19.00
C23	AP6	3 l	olive gray	8.00	*37.50*
C24	AP5	10 l	dp vio	8.00	*37.50*
C25	AP6	12 l	bl grn	8.00	*57.50*
C26	AP7	20 l	gray blk	21.00	*65.00*
C27	AP8	50 l	blue ('34)	32.50	*60.00*
			Nos. C20-C27 (8)	101.50	*314.50*

Tenth anniversary of Fascism.

Issue dates: 50 l, Dec. 26; others, Oct. 5.

Natives Hailing Dornier Wal — AP9

1934, Apr. 24

No.	Type	Denom.	Color	Unused	Used
C28	AP9	25 l	brown olive	35.00	*215.00*

Issued in honor of Luigi Amadeo, Duke of the Abruzzi (1873-1933).

Airplane over Stadium AP10

Goalkeeper Leaping — AP11

Seaplane and Soccer Ball AP12

1934, June

No.	Type	Denom.	Color	Unused	Used
C29	AP10	50c	yel brn	9.50	*47.50*
C30	AP10	75c	dp vio	9.50	*47.50*
C31	AP11	5 l	brn blk	57.50	*110.00*
C32	AP11	10 l	red org	57.50	*110.00*
C33	AP10	15 l	car rose	57.50	*110.00*

C34 AP11 25 l green 57.50 250.00
C35 AP12 50 l bl grn 57.50 250.00
Nos. C29-C35 (7) 306.50 *925.00*

World Soccer Championship Games, Rome. Issued: 50 l, June 21; others, June 5.

AIR POST SPECIAL DELIVERY STAMPS

Garibaldi Type of Italy

Wmk. 140

1932, Oct. 6 Photo. ***Perf. 14***
CE1 APSD1 2.25 l + 1 l dk vio & sl 10.00 *21.00*
CE2 APSD1 4.50 l + 1.50 l dk brn & grn 10.00 *35.00*

ITALIAN EAST AFRICA

ə-ˈtal-yən ˈēst ˈa-fri-kə

LOCATION — In eastern Africa, bordering on the Red Sea and Indian Ocean
GOVT. — Italian Colony
AREA — 665,977 sq. mi. (estimated)
POP. — 12,100,000 (estimated)
CAPITAL — Asmara

This colony was formed in 1936 and included Ethiopia and the former colonies of Eritrea and Italian Somaliland. For previous issues see listings under these headings.

100 Centesimi = 1 Lira

Used values in italics are for postaly used stamps. Cancelled-to-order examples sell for about the same as unused, hinged stamps.

Grant's Gazelle — A1

Eagle and Lion — A2

Victor Emmanuel III — A3

Fascist Legionary — A5

Statue of the Nile — A4

Desert Road — A6

Wmk. 140

1938, Feb. 7 Photo. ***Perf. 14***
1 A1 2c red orange 2.25 *1.00*
2 A2 5c brown 2.25 .25
3 A3 7½c dk violet 3.00 *4.25*
4 A4 10c olive brown 3.00 .25
5 A5 15c slate green 2.25 .35
6 A3 20c crimson 2.25 .25
7 A6 25c green 3.00 .25
8 A1 30c olive brown 2.25 .70
9 A2 35c sapphire 3.00 *11.00*
10 A3 50c purple 2.25 .25

Engr.

11 A5 75c carmine lake 3.00 .35
12 A6 1 l olive green 1.90 .25
13 A3 1.25 l deep blue 3.00 .35
14 A4 1.75 l orange 15.50 .25
15 A2 2 l cerise 3.00 .35
16 A6 2.55 l dark brown 18.00 *29.00*
17 A1 3.70 l purple 57.50 *85.00*
18 A5 5 l blue 18.00 4.25
19 A2 10 l henna brown 25.00 18.00
20 A4 20 l dull green 36.00 *42.50*
Nos. 1-20,C1-C11,CE1-CE2 (33) 381.30 343.30

Augustus Caesar (Octavianus) A7

Goddess Abundantia A8

1938, Apr. 25 Photo. ***Perf. 14***
21 A7 5c bister brn .75 *1.80*
22 A8 10c copper red .75 1.20
23 A7 25c deep green 1.45 1.10
24 A8 50c purple 1.45 .75
25 A7 75c crimson 1.45 2.75
26 A8 1.25 l deep blue 1.45 7.75
Nos. 21-26,C12-C13 (8) 9.10 *22.85*

Bimillenary of the birth of Augustus Caesar (Octavianus), first Roman emperor.

Rome-Berlin Axis.
Four stamps of type AP8, without "Posta Aerea," were prepared in 1941, but not issued. Value, each $2,400.

Native Boat — A9

Native Soldier — A10

Statue Suggesting Italy's Conquest of Ethiopia — A11

1940, May 11 Wmk. 140
27 A9 5c olive brown .75 *1.10*
28 A10 10c red orange .75 *1.10*
29 A11 25c green 2.25 1.80
30 A9 50c purple 2.25 1.10
31 A10 75c rose red 2.25 *7.00*
32 A11 1.25 l dark blue 2.25 5.50
33 A10 2 l + 75c carmine 2.25 *20.00*
Nos. 27-33,C14-C17 (11) 23.25 *52.10*

Issued in connection with the first Triennial Overseas Exposition held at Naples.

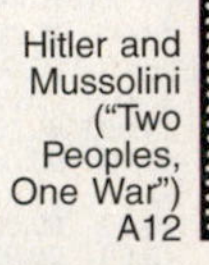

Hitler and Mussolini ("Two Peoples, One War") A12

1941, June 19
34 A12 5c ocher 2.25
35 A12 10c chestnut 2.25
36 A12 20c black 4.25
37 A12 25c turquoise grn 4.25
38 A12 50c rose lilac 4.25
39 A12 75c rose car 4.25
40 A12 1.25 l brt ultra 4.25
Nos. 34-40,C18-C19 (9) 174.75

SEMI-POSTAL STAMPS

Many issues of Italy and Italian Colonies include one or more semi-postal denominations. To avoid splitting sets, these issues are generally listed as regular postage, airmail, etc., unless all values carry a surtax.

AIR POST STAMPS

Plane Flying over Mountains AP1

Mussolini Carved in Stone Cliff — AP2

Airplane over Lake Tsana AP3

Bataleur Eagle — AP4

Wmk. Crowns (140)

1938, Feb. 7 Photo. ***Perf. 14***
C1 AP1 25c slate green 3.50 *4.25*
C2 AP2 50c olive brown 57.50 .25
C3 AP3 60c red orange 2.25 *13.00*
C4 AP1 75c orange brn 3.50 2.25
C5 AP4 1 l slate blue 1.40 .25

Engr.

C6 AP2 1.50 l violet 1.75 .35
C7 AP3 2 l slate blue 1.75 1.60
C8 AP1 3 l carmine lake 2.75 6.00
C9 AP4 5 l red brown 52.50 42.50
C10 AP2 10 l violet brn 10.50 13.00
C11 AP1 25 l slate blue 25.00 32.00
Nos. C1-C11 (11) 162.40 115.45

Eagle Attacking Serpent — AP5

1938, Apr. 25 Photo.
C12 AP5 50c bister brown .90 *2.75*
C13 AP5 1 l purple .90 *4.75*

Bimillenary of the birth of Augustus Caesar (Octavianus), first Roman emperor.

Triennial Overseas Exposition Type

#C14, C16, Tractor. #C15, C17, Plane over city.

1940, May 11
C14 A10 50c olive gray 2.25 *7.25*
C15 A9 1 l purple 2.25 *7.25*
C16 A10 2 l + 75c gray blue 3.00 —
C17 A9 5 l + 2.50 l red brn 3.00 —
Nos. C14-C17 (4) 10.50 *14.50*

Hitler and Mussolini ("Two Peoples, One War") AP8

AP9

1941, Apr. 24
C18 AP8 1 l slate blue 140.00
C19 AP9 1 l slate blue 9.00

Rome-Berlin Axis.

AIR POST SPECIAL DELIVERY STAMPS

Plow and Airplane — APSD1

Wmk. 140

1938, Feb. 7 Engr. ***Perf. 14***
CE1 APSD1 2 l slate blue 7.00 *11.00*
CE2 APSD1 2.50 l dk brn 5.50 *18.00*

SPECIAL DELIVERY STAMPS

Victor Emmanuel III — SD1

Wmk. 140

1938, Apr. 16 Engr. ***Perf. 14***
E1 SD1 1.25 l dark green 11.00 11.00
E2 SD1 2.50 l dark carmine 11.00 *32.00*

POSTAGE DUE STAMPS

Italy, Nos. J28 to J40, Overprinted in Black

1941 Wmk. 140 ***Perf. 14***
J1 D6 5c brown 1.60
J2 D6 10c blue 1.60
J3 D6 20c rose red 3.25
J4 D6 25c green 3.25
J5 D6 30c red orange 8.00
J6 D6 40c black brown 8.00
J7 D6 50c violet 8.00
J8 D6 60c slate black 11.00
J9 D7 1 l red orange 22.50
J10 D7 2 l green 22.50
J11 D7 5 l violet 35.00
J12 D7 10 l blue 22.50
J13 D7 20 l carmine rose 22.50
Nos. J1-J13 (13) 169.70

In 1943 a set of 11 "Segnatasse" stamps, picturing a horse and rider and inscribed "A. O. I.," was prepared but not issued. Value, $17.50.

ITALIAN STATES

ə-'tal-yən 'stāts

Watermarks

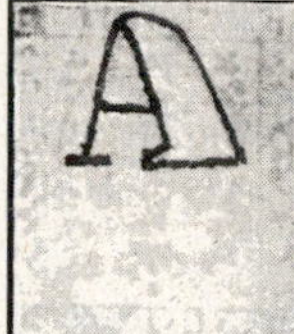
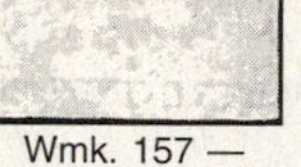

Wmk. 157 — Large Letter "A"

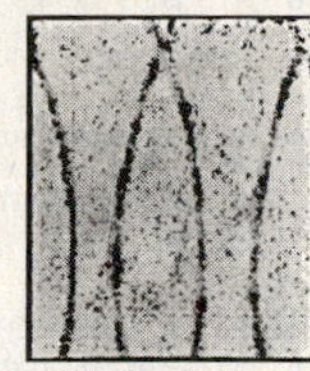

Wmk. 184 — Interlaced Wavy Lines

Wmk. 184 has double lined letters diagonally across the sheet readiing: "II R R POSTE TOSCANE."

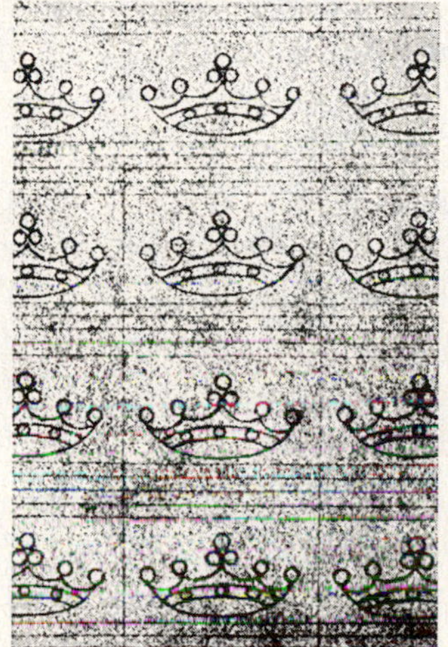

Wmk. 185 — Crowns in the sheet

The watermark consists of twelve crowns, arranged in four rows of three, with horizontal and vertical lines between them. Only parts of the watermark appear on each stamp.

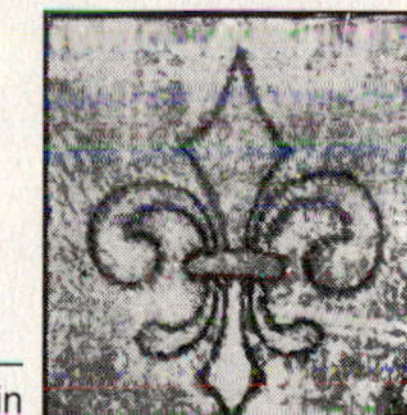

Wmk. 186 — Fleurs-de-Lis in Sheet

MODENA

LOCATION — In northern Italy
GOVT. — Duchy
AREA — 1,003 sq. mi.
POP. — 448,000 (approx.)
CAPITAL — Modena

In 1852, when the first postage stamps were issued, Modena was under the rule of Duke Francis V of the House of Este-Lorraine. In June, 1859, he was overthrown and the Duchy was annexed to the Kingdom of Sardinia which on March 17, 1861, became the Kingdom of Italy.

100 Centesimi = 1 Lira

Values of Modena stamps vary tremendously according to condition. Values are for very fine examples, and values for unused stamps are for examples with original gum as defined in the catalogue introduction. Extremely fine or superb examples sell at much higher prices, and fine or poor examples sell at greatly reduced prices.

Coat of Arms — A1

1852-57 Unwmk. Typo. *Imperf.*

Without Period After Figures of Value

1	A1	5c blk, *green*	2,300.	115.00
2	A1	10c blk, *rose*	690.00	72.50
a.		"EENT. 10"	*9,500.*	*2,875.*
b.		"1" of "10" inverted	*9,500.*	*2,875.*
c.		"CNET"	*1,575.*	*1,600.*
d.		No period after "CENT"	*2,150.*	750.00
3	A1	15c blk, *yellow*	70.00	29.00
a.		"CETN 15."	*9,500.*	*950.00*
b.		No period after "CENT"	345.00	*500.00*
4	A1	25c blk, *buff*	145.00	42.50
a.		No period after "CENT"	690.00	*950.00*
b.		"ENT.25" omitted	*1,000.*	—
c.		25c black, *green* (error)	4,400.	2,875.
d.		"N" of "CENT" omitted	750.00	1,575.
5	A1	40c blk, *blue*	460.00	100.00
a.		40c black, *pale blue*	*20,000.*	2,000.
b.		No period after "CENT"	*2,000.*	*1,600.*
c.		As "a," no period after "CENT"	—	—

Unused examples of No. 5a lack gum.

Used examples of No. 4c have a green administrative cancellation.

See Nos. PR3-PR4.

With Period After Figures of Value

6	A1	5c blk, *green*	40.00	*40.00*
a.		5c black, *olive green* ('55)	525.00	160.00
b.		"ENT"	—	*2,850.*
c.		"CNET"	*4,350.*	*3,500.*
d.		As "a," "CNET"	*2,300.*	*1,850.*
e.		"E" of "CENT" sideways	—	*5,150.*
f.		As "a," "CEN1"	*2,875.*	*2,150.*
g.		As "a," no period after "5"	750.00	475.00
h.		Double impression, no gum	*1,275.*	—
i.		As "a," double impression	*1,275.*	—
j.		Pair, #6a, 6g	1,275.	*2,300.*
7	A1	10c blk, *rose* ('57)	475.00	340.00
a.		"CENE"	1,600.	*1,575.*
b.		"CNET"	700.00	*750.00*
c.		"CE6T"	1,600.	*1,600.*
d.		"N" of "CENT" sideways	*12,750.*	*4,300.*
e.		Double impression	1,275.	*1,275.*
f.		Raised period after "10"	1,600.	1,600.
8	A1	40c blk, *blue* ('54)	52.50	*100.00*
a.		"CNET"	290.00	*750.00*
b.		"CENE"	700.00	*1,600.*
c.		"CE6T"	700.00	*1,600.*
d.		"49"	290.00	*750.00*
e.		"4C"	700.00	*1,600.*
f.		"CEN.T"	*37,500.*	—
g.		Space between "T" and period	290.00	*750.00*
h.		Pair, one with no period after value, on cover		*2,300.*

Wmk. 157

9	A1	1 l black ('53)	52.50	*2,450.*
a.		With period after "LIRA"	135.00	*4,600.*
b.		No period after "1"	130.00	*4,000.*

Provisional Government

Coat of Arms — A2

1859 Unwmk.

10	A2	5c green	1,375.	*630.00*
a.		5c emerald	1,425.	*690.00*
b.		5c dark green	1,425.	690.00
11	A2	15c brown	2,175.	*3,700.*
11A	A2	15c gray	350.00	
b.		15c black brown	2,450.	5,175.
c.		No period after "15"	*3,450.*	*4,600.*
d.		Period before "CENT"	*4,300.*	*6,900.*
e.		Double impression (#11a)	*1,725.*	
12	A2	20c lilac	87.50	*1,300.*
a.		20c violet	3,750.	190.00
b.		20c blue violet	2,575.	190.00
c.		As #12, no period after "20"	100.00	*1,425.*
d.		As #12, "ECNT"	230.00	*3,150.*
e.		As #12, "N" inverted	190.00	*2,150.*
f.		Double impression (#12b)		*6,900.*
13	A2	40c carmine	170.00	*1,300.*
a.		40c brown rose	175.00	*1,300.*
b.		No period after "40"	350.00	*2,150.*
c.		Period before "CENT"	345.00	*2,150.*
d.		Inverted "5" before the "C", no gum	*40,000.*	*48,000.*
e.		Large period after "40"	345.00	*2,150.*
14	A2	80c buff	175.00	*20,000.*
a.		80c brown orange	175.00	*20,000.*
b.		"CENT 8"	345.00	—
c.		"CENT 0"	1,250.	—
d.		No period after "80"	345.00	—
e.		"N" inverted	345.00	—

NEWSPAPER TAX STAMPS

NT1

Type I

Type II

1853 Unwmk. Typo. *Imperf.*

PR1	NT1	9c blk, *violet* (I)	—	*2,875.*
PR2	NT1	9c blk, *violet* (II)	690.00	70.00
a.		No period after "9"	1,000.	215.00

All known unused examples of #PR1 lack gum.

1855-57

PR3	A1	9c blk, *violet*	3.00	
a.		No period after "9"	5.75	
b.		No period after "CENT"	8.75	
PR4	A1	10c blk, *gray vio* ('57)	70.00	*230.00*
a.		"CEN1"	290.00	*1,150.*

No. PR3 was never placed in use.

NT2

1859

PR5	NT2	10c black	1,000.	*1,875.*
a.		Double impression	*15,000.*	*18,750.*
b.		Vert. guidelines between stamps	1,000.	

Values for unused pairs

PR5	NT2	10c black	2,150.

PARMA

LOCATION — Comprising the present provinces of Parma and Piacenza in northern Italy.
GOVT. — Independent Duchy
AREA — 2,750 sq. mi. (1860)
POP. — 500,000 (1860)
CAPITAL — Parma

Parma was annexed to Sardinia in 1860.

100 Centesimi = 1 Lira

Values of Parma stamps vary tremendously according to condition. Values are for very fine examples, and values for unused stamps are for examples with original gum as defined in the catalogue introduction except for No. 8 which is known only without gum. Extremely fine or superb copies sell at much higher prices, and fine or poor stamps sell at greatly reduced prices. In addition, very fine unused stamps without gum sell for about 20% of the values shown.

Crown and Fleur-de-lis — A1

1852 Unwmk. Typo. *Imperf.*

1	A1	5c blk, *yellow*	125.00	*135.00*
2	A1	10c blk, *white*	120.00	*120.00*
3	A1	15c blk, *pink*	5,250.	75.00
a.		Tête bêche pair, horiz.		*85,000.*
b.		Double impression		*4,100.*
4	A1	25c blk, *violet*	*18,000.*	195.00
5	A1	40c blk, *blue*	3,850.	440.00
a.		40c black, *pale blue*	*6,750.*	650.00

1854-55

6	A1	5c org yel	*11,500.*	625.00
a.		5c lemon yellow	*13,250.*	800.00
b.		Double impression		*15,750.*
7	A1	15c red	*13,250.*	240.00
8	A1	25c red brn ('55)	*12,000.*	*365.00*
a.		Double impression		*32,000.*

No. 8 unused is without gum.

Crown and Fleur-de-lis — A2

1857-59

9	A2	15c red ('59)	350.00	300.00
10	A2	25c red brown	650.00	175.00
11	A2	40c bl, wide "0" ('58)	72.50	*440.00*
a.		Narrow "0" in "40"	77.50	*550.00*

Provisional Government

A3

1859

12	A3	5c yel grn	500.00	*29,000.*
a.		5c blue green	2,900.	*4,250.*
13	A3	10c brown	1,000.	*525.00*
a.		10c deep brown	1,000.	*525.00*
b.		"1" of "10" inverted	2,000.	*4,250.*
c.		Thick "0" in "10"	1,450.	*675.00*
14	A3	20c pale blue	1,000.	215.00
a.		20c deep blue	1,000.	240.00
b.		Thick "0" in "20"	1,450.	240.00
15	A3	40c red	525.00	*8,000.*
a.		40c brown red	*22,000.*	*12,500.*
b.		Thick "0" in "40" (#15)	775.00	*10,000.*
c.		Thick "0" in "40," (#15a)	*24,000.*	*13,750.*
16	A3	80c ol yel	7,250.	*200,000.*
a.		80c orange yellow	10,000.	—
b.		80c bister	8,000.	
c.		80c orange bister	8,750.	

Nos. 12-16 exist in two other varieties: with spelling "CFNTESIMI" and with small "A" in "STATI." These are valued about 50 per cent more than normal stamps.

See Nos. PR1-PR2.

NEWSPAPER TAX STAMPS

Type of 1859
Normal Paper ('53)

1853-57	**Unwmk.**	**Typo.**	***Imperf.***
PR1 A3	6c blk, *dp rose*	2,400.	300.00
PR2 A3	9c black, *blue*	875.00	*5,000.*

Thin, Semitransparent Paper ('57)

PR1a A3	6c black, *rose* ('57)	135.00	
PR2a A3	9c black, *blue*	77.50	

These stamps belong to the same class as the Newspaper Tax Stamps of Modena, Austria, etc.

Note following #16 also applies to #PR1-PR2.

Nos. PR1a-PR2a were not issued.

The stamps of Parma were superseded by those of Sardinia in 1860.

ROMAGNA

LOCATION — Comprised the present Italian provinces of Forli, Ravenna, Ferrara and Bologna.
GOVT. — One of the Roman States
AREA — 5,626 sq. mi.
POP. — 1,341,091 (1853)
CAPITAL — Ravenna

Postage stamps were issued when a provisional government was formed pending the unification of Italy. In 1860 Romagna was annexed to Sardinia and since 1862 the postage stamps of Italy have been used.

100 Bajocchi = 1 Scudo

Values of Romagna stamps vary tremendously according to condition. Values are for very fine examples, and values for unused stamps are for examples with original gum as defined in the catalogue introduction. Extremely fine or superb stamps sell at much higher prices, and fine or poor stamps sell at greatly reduced prices. In addition, very fine unused stamps without gum sell for about 20% of the values shown.

A1

1859	**Unwmk.**	**Typo.**	***Imperf.***
1 A1	½b blk, *straw*	42.50	*360.00*
a.	Half used as ¼b on cover		*16,250.*
2 A1	1b blk, *drab*	42.50	*180.00*
3 A1	2b blk, *buff*	55.00	*210.00*
a.	Half used as 1b on cover		6,250.
4 A1	3b blk, *dk grn*	60.00	*360.00*
5 A1	4b blk, *fawn*	650.00	165.00
a.	Half used as 2b on cover		*30,000.*
6 A1	5b blk, *gray vio*	72.50	*400.00*
7 A1	6b blk, *yel grn*	500.00	*9,000.*
a.	Half used as 3b on cover		*150,000.*
8 A1	8b blk, *rose*	210.00	*1,800.*
a.	Half used as 4b on cover		*150,000.*
9 A1	20b blk, *gray grn*	200.00	*2,400.*

Forged cancellations are plentiful.
Bisects used Oct. 12, 1859 to Mar. 1, 1860.

These stamps have been reprinted several times. The reprints usually resemble the originals in the color of the paper but there are impressions on incorrect colors and also in colors on white paper. They often show broken letters and other injuries. The Y shaped ornaments between the small circles in the corners are broken and blurred and the dots outside the circles are often missing or joined to the circles.

The stamps of Romagna were superseded by those of Sardinia in February, 1860.

ROMAN STATES

LOCATION — Comprised most of the central Italian Peninsula, bounded by the former Kingdom of Lombardy-Venetia and Modena on the north, Tuscany on the west, and the Kingdom of Naples on the southeast.
GOVT. — Under the direct government of the See of Rome.
AREA — 16,000 sq. mi.
POP. — 3,124,758 (1853)
CAPITAL — Rome

Upon the formation of the Kingdom of Italy, the area of the Roman States was greatly reduced and in 1870 they disappeared from the political map of Europe. Postage stamps of Italy have been used since that time.

100 Bajocchi = 1 Scudo
100 Centesimi = 1 Lira (1867)

Values of Roman States stamps vary tremendously according to condition. Values are for very fine examples, and values for unused stamps are for examples with original gum as defined in the catalogue introduction. Extremely fine or superb stamps sell at much higher prices, and fine or poor stamps sell at greatly reduced prices. In addition, very fine unused stamps without gum sell for about 20% of the values shown.

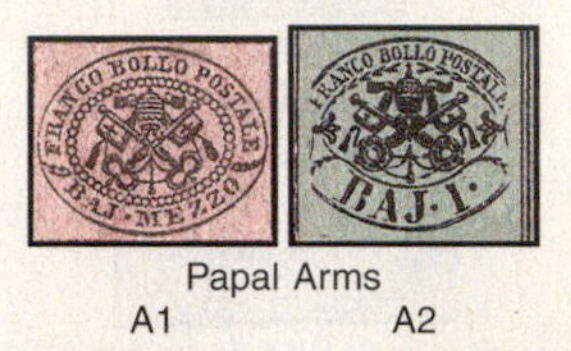
Papal Arms
A1 A2

A3

A4

A5

A6

A7

A8

A9

A10

No. 10a A11

1852	**Unwmk.**	**Typo.**	***Imperf.***
1 A1	½b blk, *dl vio*	55.00	*135.00*
a.	½b black, *gray blue*	675.00	90.00
b.	½b black, *gray lilac*	675.00	360.00
c.	½b black, *gray*	675.00	90.00
d.	½b black, *reddish vio*	3,500.	2,700.
e.	½b black, *dark violet*	295.00	315.00
f.	Vertical pair, tête bêche	—	*30,000.*
h.	As "a," half used as ¼b on wrapper		*54,000.*
	As "h," pen canceled		*9,000.*
i.	As #1, double impression	—	*6,000.*
j.	Impression on both sides	—	*13,000.*
2 A2	1b blk, *gray grn*	390.00	9.00
a.	1b black, *blue green*	800.00	50.00
b.	As "a," half used as ½b on cover		425.00
c.	Grayish oily ink	1,100.	27.50
d.	Double impression		*5,750.*
e.	Impression on both sides	—	*12,750.*
3 A3	2b blk, *grnsh white*	16.00	*65.00*
a.	2b black, *yel grn*	240.00	16.00
b.	As #3, half used as 1b on cover		*5,400.*
c.	As "a," half used as 1b on cover		360.00
d.	Grayish oily ink	1,275.	32.50
e.	No period after "BAJ"	145.00	32.50
f.	As "a" and "e"	500.00	32.50
g.	Double impression		*5,750.*
4 A4	3b blk, *brn*	275.00	55.00
a.	3b black, *light brown*	5,250.	160.00
b.	3b black, *yel brn*	2,500.	40.00
c.	3b black, *yellow buff*	2,500.	*40.00*
d.	3b black, *chrome yel*	42.50	*160.00*
e.	One-third used as 1b on circular		*3,250.*
f.	Two-thirds used as 2b on circular		*10,500.*
g.	Grayish oily ink	7,000.	210.00
h.	Impression on both sides	—	*11,000.*
i.	Double impression	—	*6,000.*
j.	Half used as 1½b on cover		*11,500.*
5 A5	4b blk, *lem*	240.00	70.00
a.	4b black, *yellow*	240.00	72.50
b.	4b black, *rose brown*	13,500.	120.00
c.	4b black, *gray brown*	11,500.	72.50
d.	Half used as 2b on cover		2,250.
e.	One-quarter used as 1b on cover		*20,000.*
f.	Impression on both sides	—	*11,000.*
g.	Ribbed paper	325.00	90.00
h.	Grayish oily ink	23,500.	325.00
i.	As "a," half used as 2b on cover		3,750.
j.	As "a," one-quarter used as 1b on cover		*21,500.*
6 A6	5b black, *rose*	225.00	14.00
a.	5b black, *pale rose*	225.00	16.00
c.	Impression on both sides		*11,000.*
d.	Double impression		*5,500.*
e.	Grayish oily ink	1,400.	32.50
f.	Half used as 2½b on cover		*54,000.*
7 A7	6b blk, *grnsh gray*	975.00	67.50
a.	6b black, *gray*	1,500.	72.50
b.	6b black, *grayish lil*	1,700.	210.00
c.	Grayish oily ink	3,750.	250.00
d.	Double impression	—	*6,000.*
e.	Half used as 3b on cover		4,250.
f.	One-third used as 2b on cover		*16,000.*
8 A8	7b black, *blue*	1,425.	72.50
a.	Half used as 3¼b on cover		*30,000.*
b.	Double impression	—	5,750.
c.	Grayish oily ink	5,000.	135.00
9 A9	8b black	550.00	40.00
a.	Half used as 4b on cover		8,000.
b.	Quarter used as 2b on cover		*80,000.*
c.	Double impression	—	—
d.	Grayish oily ink	2,250.	210.00
10 A10	50b dull blue	*15,000.*	1,650.
a.	50b deep blue (worn impression)	*21,500.*	2,950.
11 A11	1sc rose	*4,000.*	*3,250.*

Counterfeits exist of Nos. 10-11. Fraudulent cancellations are found on No. 11.

A12

A13

A14

A15

A16

A17

A18

1867	**Glazed Paper**		***Imperf.***
12 A12	2c blk, *grn*	90.00	*315.00*
a.	No period after "Cent"	110.00	*350.00*
13 A13	3c blk, *gray*	1,300.	*8,000.*
a.	3c black, *lilac gray*	3,250.	*2,150.*
14 A14	5c blk, *lt bl*	190.00	*215.00*
a.	No period after "5"	375.00	*450.00*
15 A15	10c blk, *ver*	1,900.	95.00
a.	Double impression		5,750.
16 A16	20c blk, *cop red* (unglazed)	190.00	120.00
a.	No period after "20"	540.00	360.00
b.	No period after "CENT"	540.00	360.00
17 A17	40c blk, *yel*	200.00	*160.00*
a.	No period after "40"	260.00	200.00
18 A18	80c blk, *lil rose*	180.00	*450.00*
a.	No period after "80"	250.00	*675.00*

Imperforate stamps on unglazed paper, or in colors other than listed, are unfinished remainders of the 1868 issue.

Fraudulent cancellations are found on Nos. 13, 14, 17, 18.

1868	**Glazed Paper**		***Perf. 13***
19 A12	2c blk, *grn*	9.00	*90.00*
a.	No period after "CENT"	11.00	*110.00*
20 A13	3c blk, *gray*	55.00	*3,250.*
a.	3c black, *lilac gray*	*10,000.*	*18,000.*
21 A14	5c blk, *lt blue*	60.00	*60.00*
a.	No period after "5"	75.00	*72.50*
b.	No period after "Cent"	150.00	*350.00*
c.	5c black, *lt bl* (unglazed, imperf., without gum)	120.00	—
22 A15	10c blk, *org ver*	3.00	*15.00*
a.	10c black, *vermilion*	60.00	15.00
b.	10c black, *ver* (unglazed)	1.25	—
c.	10c black, *ver* (unglazed, imperf., without gum)	1.25	—
23 A16	20c blk, *dp crim*	4.75	*30.00*
a.	20c black, *magenta*	6.00	*42.50*
b.	20c blk, *mag* (unglazed)	300.00	*35.00*
c.	20c blk, *mag* (imperf., without gum)	2.50	—
d.	20c blk, *cop red* (unglazed)	1,950.	42.50
e.	20c blk, *dp crim* (imperf., without gum)	2.50	—
f.	No period after "20" *(copper red)*	*2,800.*	350.00
g.	No period after "20" *(mag)*	24.00	*180.00*
h.	No period after "20" *(deep crimson)*	25.00	*180.00*
i.	No period after "CENT" *(cop red)*	*2,800.*	375.00
j.	No period after "CENT" *(mag)*	24.00	*180.00*
k.	No period after "CENT" *(dp crim)*	24.00	*180.00*
24 A17	40c blk, *grnsh yel*	11.00	*125.00*
a.	40c black, *yellow*	210.00	*75.00*
b.	40c black, *org yel*	90.00	*750.00*
c.	No period after "40"	15.00	*95.00*
25 A18	80c blk, *rose lil*	210.00	*415.00*
a.	80c blk, *brt rose*	*6,250.*	*60,000.*
b.	80c black, *rose* (unglazed)	65.00	—
c.	No period after "80" *(rose lilac)*	110.00	—
d.	80c black, *pale rose lilac* (unglazed)	77.50	—
e.	80c black, *pale rose*	55.00	425.00
f.	As "e," no period after "80"	65.00	650.00
g.	As "a," no period after "80"	7,000.	—
h.	As "e," double impression	—	—
	Nos. 19-25 (7)	352.75	3,985.

All values except the 3c are known imperforate vertically or horizontally. and in vertical and horizontal pairs, imperf between. See the *Scott Specialized Catalogue of Stamps and Covers* for detailed listings.

Double impressions are known of the 5c, 10c, 20c (all three colors), 40c and 80c.

Fraudulent cancellations are found on Nos. 20, 24 and 25.

The stamps of the 1867 and 1868 issues have been privately reprinted; many of these reprints are well executed and it is difficult to distinguish them from the originals. Most reprints show more or less pronounced defects of the design. On the originals the horizontal lines between stamps are unbroken, while on most of the reprints these lines are broken. Most of the perforated reprints gauge 11½.

Roman States stamps were replaced by those of Italy in 1870.

SARDINIA

LOCATION — An island in the Mediterranean Sea off the west coast of Italy and a large area in northwestern Italy, including the cities of Genoa, Turin and Nice.
GOVT. — Kingdom

As a result of war and revolution, most of the former independent Italian States were joined to the Kingdom of

Sardinia in 1859 and 1860. On March 17, 1861, the name was changed to the Kingdom of Italy.

100 Centesimi = 1 Lira

Values of Sardinia stamps vary tremendously according to condition. Values are for very fine examples, and values for unused stamps are for examples with original gum as defined in the catalogue introduction. Extremely fine or superb stamps sell at much higher prices, and fine or poor stamps sell at greatly reduced prices.

King Victor Emmanuel II — A1

1851 Unwmk. Litho. *Imperf.*

No.	Type	Description	Unused	Used
1	A1	5c gray black	13,000.	2,000.
a.		5c black	13,000.	2,000.
2	A1	20c blue	9,500.	235.00
a.		20c deep blue	9,500.	235.00
b.		20c pale blue	9,500.	235.00
3	A1	40c rose	17,750.	*4,000.*
a.		40c violet rose	17,750.	*5,250.*

King Victor Emmanuel II — A2

Vignette & Inscriptions Embossed

1853

No.	Type	Description	Unused	Used
4	A2	5c *blue green*	*17,500.*	1,100.
a.		Double embossing		*3,000.*
5	A2	20c *dull blue*	*18,500.*	200.00
a.		Double embossing		*1,250.*
6	A2	40c *pale rose*	*11,250.*	800.00
b.		Double embossing		*2,250.*

King Victor Emmanuel II — A3

Lithographed Frame in Color, Colorless Embossed Vignette

1854

No.	Type	Description	Unused	Used
7	A3	5c yellow green	30,000.	575.00
a.		Double embossing		1,250.
b.		5c grayish green	3,600.	
8	A3	20c blue	16,000.	175.00
a.		Double embossing		525.00
b.		20c indigo	700.00	
9	A3	40c rose	*82,500.*	2,750.
a.		Double embossing		5,500.
b.		40c brown rose	180.00	—

Nos. 7b, 8b and 9b, differing in shade from the original stamps, were prepared but not issued.

King Victor Emmanuel II — A4

Stamps of this issue vary greatly in color, paper and sharpness of embossing as between the early (1855-59) printings and the later (1860-63) ones. Year dates after each color name indicate whether the stamp falls into the Early or Late printing group.

As a rule, early printings are on smooth thick paper with sharp embossing, while later printings are usually on paper varying from thick to thin and of inferior quality with embossing less distinct and printing blurred. The outer frame shows a distinct design on the early printings, while this design is more or less blurred or even a solid line on the later printings.

Typographed Frame in Color, Colorless Embossed Vignette

1855-63 Unwmk. *Imperf.*

No.	Type	Description	Unused	Used
10	A4	5c grn ('62-63)	4.50	*11.00*
a.		5c yel grn ('62-63)	95.00	17.00
b.		5c olive green ('60-61)	435.00	67.50
c.		5c yel grn ('55-59)	900.00	160.00
d.		5c myrtle green ('57)	7,500.	475.00
e.		5c emerald ('55-57)	3,900.	375.00
f.		Head inverted	—	3,700.
g.		Double head, one inverted	—	*3,500.*
11	A4	10c bister ('63)	4.50	*24.00*
a.		10c ocher ('62)	90.00	22.00
b.		10c olive bister ('62)	190.00	22.00
c.		10c olive brown ('61)	190.00	29.00
d.		10c reddish brn ('61)	1,800.	160.00
e.		10c gray brown ('61)	150.00	40.00
f.		10c olive gray ('60-61)	370.00	55.00
g.		10c gray ('60)	1,350.	180.00
h.		10c grayish brown ('59)	130.00	210.00
i.		10c violet brown ('59)	525.00	300.00
j.		10c dark brown ('58)	*775.00*	360.00
k.		Head inverted	—	4,000.
l.		Double head, one inverted	—	4,000.
m.		Pair, one without embossing	*2,000.*	—
n.		Half used as 5c on cover (15c rate)		*125,000.*
12	A4	20c indigo ('62)	85.00	40.00
a.		20c blue ('61)	165.00	16.00
b.		20c light blue ('60-61)	165.00	16.00
c.		20c Prus bl ('59-60)	775.00	27.50
d.		20c indigo ('57-58)	460.00	40.00
e.		20c sky blue ('55-56)	7,100.	170.00
f.		20c cobalt ('55)	3,600.	100.00
g.		Head inverted	3,100.	1,600.
h.		Double head, one inverted	—	—
i.		Pair, one without embossing	1,100.	—
j.		Half used as 10c on cover		*160,000.*
k.		As "c", one without embossing	1,250.	—
13	A4	40c red ('63)	17.00	*40.00*
a.		40c rose ('61-62)	135.00	60.00
b.		40c carmine ('60)	775.00	350.00
c.		40c light red ('57)	3,800.	110.00
d.		40c vermilion ('55-57)	7,250.	325.00
e.		Head inverted	—	6,250.
f.		Double head, one inverted	—	*6,250.*
g.		Pair, one without embossing	1,625.	—
h.		Half used as 20c on cover		*67,500.*
14	A4	80c org yel ('62)	22.00	*390.00*
a.		80c yellow ('60-61)	25.00	*360.00*
b.		80c yellow ocher ('59)	900.00	690.00
c.		80c ocher ('58)	200.00	*540.00*
d.		80c brown orange ('58)	220.00	*600.00*
e.		Head inverted	—	*22,500.*
f.		Half used as 40c on cover		85,000.
15	A4	3 l bronze, thin paper ('61)	400.00	*3,650.*
		Nos. 10-15 (6)	533.00	4,155.

Forgeries of the inverted and double head varieties have been made by applying a faked head embossing to printer's waste without head. These forgeries are plentiful.

Fraudulent cancellations are found on #13-15.

The 5c, 20c and 40c have been reprinted; the embossing of the reprints is not as sharp as that of the originals, the colors are dull and blurred.

NEWSPAPER STAMPS

N1

Typographed and Embossed

1861 Unwmk. *Imperf.*

No.	Type	Description	Unused	Used
P1	N1	1c black	6.75	*15.00*
a.		Numeral "2"	600.00	*2,500.*
b.		Figure of value inverted	2,400.	*34,000.*
c.		Double impression	2,750.	—
P2	N1	2c black	175.00	105.00
a.		Numeral "1"	*13,000.*	*32,500.*
b.		Figure of value inverted	*2,400.*	*34,000.*

Forgeries of the varieties of the embossed numerals have been made from printer's waste without numerals.

See Italy No. P1 for 2c buff.

The stamps of Sardinia were superseded in 1862 by those of Italy, which were identical with the 1855 issue of Sardinia, but perforated. Until 1863, imperforate and perforated stamps were issued simultaneously.

TUSCANY

LOCATION — In the north central part of the Apennine Peninsula.
GOVT. — Grand Duchy
AREA — 8,890 sq. mi.
POP. — 2,892,000 (approx.)
CAPITAL — Florence

Tuscany was annexed to Sardinia in 1860.

60 Quattrini = 20 Soldi = 12 Crazie = 1 Lira
100 Centesimi = 1 Lira (1860)

Values of Tuscany stamps vary tremendously according to condition. Values are for very fine examples, and values for unused stamps are for examples with original gum as defined in the catalogue introduction. Extremely fine or superb stamps sell at much higher prices, and fine or poor stamps sell at greatly reduced prices.

Dangerous counterfeits exist of #1-PR1c.

Lion of Tuscany — A1

1851-52 Typo. Wmk. 185 *Imperf.*
Blue, Grayish Blue or Gray Paper

No.	Type	Description	Unused	Used
1	A1	1q black, *grayish* ('52)	15,000.	2,250.
2	A1	1s ocher, *grayish*	17,250.	2,100.
a.		1s orange, *grayish*	19,250.	2,100.
b.		1s yellow, *bluish*	20,750.	2,350.
3	A1	2s scarlet	*57,500.*	9,600.
4	A1	1cr carmine	8,800.	145.00
a.		1cr brown carmine	11,600.	145.00
5	A1	2cr blue	5,250.	160.00
a.		2cr greenish blue	5,600.	160.00
6	A1	4cr green	8,800.	125.00
a.		4cr bluish green	9,600.	325.00
7	A1	6cr slate blue	9,600.	275.00
a.		6cr blue	8,800.	275.00
b.		6cr indigo	9,600.	300.00
8	A1	9cr gray lilac	21,000.	300.00
a.		9cr deep violet	21,000.	300.00
9	A1	60cr red ('52)	*95,000.*	*27,500.*

The first paper was blue, later paper more and more grayish. Stamps on distinctly blue paper sell about 20 percent higher, except Nos. 3 and 9 which were issued on blue paper only. Examples without watermark are proofs.

Reprints of Nos. 3 and 9 have re-engraved value labels, color is too brown and impressions blurred and heavy. Paper same as originals.

No. 14a

1857-59 White Paper Wmk. 184

No.	Type	Description	Unused	Used
10	A1	1q black	1,750.	920.00
11	A1	1s yellow	*52,000.*	*6,250.*
12	A1	1cr carmine	11,600.	900.00
13	A1	2cr blue	3,850.	160.00
14	A1	4cr green	8,800.	175.00
a.		Inverted value tablet		*1,100,000.*
15	A1	6cr deep blue	*12,500.*	300.00
16	A1	9cr gray lil ('59)	*52,000.*	*6,250.*

Provisional Government

Coat of Arms — A2

1860

No.	Type	Description	Unused	Used
17	A2	1c brn lilac	3,800.	960.00
a.		1c red lilac	4,400.	1,075.
b.		1c gray lilac	3,800.	960.00
18	A2	5c green	14,000.	260.00
a.		5c olive green	15,200.	275.00
b.		5c yellow green	17,600.	360.00
19	A2	10c dp brn	4,800.	62.50
a.		10c gray brown	4,800.	62.50
b.		10c purple brown	4,125.	62.50
20	A2	20c blue	12,400.	180.00
a.		20c deep blue	12,400.	220.00
b.		20c gray blue	14,000.	220.00
21	A2	40c rose	18,000.	350.00
a.		40c carmine	18,000.	350.00
b.		Half used as 20c on cover		*175,000.*
22	A2	80c pale red brn	*32,000.*	1,500.
a.		80c brown orange	*32,000.*	1,525.
23	A2	3 l ocher	*260,000.*	*125,000.*

NEWSPAPER TAX STAMPS

NT1

1854 Unwmk. Typo. *Imperf.*
Yellowish Pelure Paper

No.	Type	Description	Unused
PR1	NT1	2s black	80.00
a.		Tête bêche pair	750.00
b.		As "a," one stamp on back	750.00
c.		Double impression	560.00
d.		Gummed on the front side	225.00

This stamp represented a fiscal tax on newspapers coming from foreign countries. It was not canceled when used.

The stamps of Tuscany were superseded by those of Sardinia in 1861.

TWO SICILIES

LOCATION — Formerly comprised the island of Sicily and the lower half of the Apennine Peninsula.
GOVT. — Independent Kingdom
CAPITAL — Naples

The Kingdom was annexed to Sardinia in 1860.

200 Tornesi = 100 Grana = 1 Ducat

Values of Two Sicilies stamps vary tremendously according to condition. Values are for very fine examples, and values for unused stamps are for examples with original gum as defined in the catalogue introduction. Extremely fine or superb copies sell at much higher prices, and fine or poor copies sell at greatly reduced prices. In addition, very fine unused stamps without gum sell for about 20%-30% of the values shown.

Naples

Coat of Arms

A1 A2

A3

A4

A5

A6

A7

1858 Engr. Wmk. 186 *Imperf.*

No.	Type	Description	Unused	Used
1	A1	½g pale lake	2,200.	325.00
a.		½g rose lake	2,200.	325.00
b.		½g lake	2,740.	550.00
c.		½g carmine lake	3,300.	700.00
d.		Half used as ¼g on newspaper		*225,000.*
2	A2	1g pale lake	950.00	37.50
a.		1g rose lake	660.00	37.50
b.		1g brown lake	1,600.	82.50
c.		1g carmine lake	1,000.	65.00

d.	Printed on both sides		1,750.
e.	Printed on both sides, one inverted		900.00
3	A3 2g pale lake	660.00	14.00
a.	2g rose lake	660.00	14.00
b.	2g lake	900.00	22.50
c.	2g carmine lake	1,100.	22.50
d.	Impression of 1g on reverse		*1,650.*
e.	Double impression		*9,000.*
f.	Printed on both sides		1,775.
4	A4 5g brown lake	3,300.	67.50
a.	5g rose lake	2,750.	67.50
b.	5g carmine lake	4,000.	67.50
d.	Printed on both sides		*5,000.*
e.	5g rose carmine	6,000.	165.00
f.	5g bright carmine	6,600.	275.00
g.	5g dark carmine	7,600.	300.00
5	A5 10g rose lake	6,600.	190.00
a.	10g lake	7,400.	350.00
b.	10g carmine lake	7,250.	350.00
c.	Printed on both sides		15,000.
d.	Double impression		*15,000.*
6	A6 20g rose lake	6,000.	675.00
a.	20g lake	6,000.	800.00
b.	Double impression	*55,000.*	
c.	20g pale rose	*9,000.*	1,350.
d.	20g pale car rose	*9,500.*	1,600.
7	A7 50g rose lake	*11,000.*	2,400.
a.	50g lake	*11,000.*	2,400.

Nos. 1-2, 4-7 have been reprinted in bright rose and Nos. 1, 7 in dull brown. The reprints are on thick unwatermarked paper. Value $8 each.

Provisional Government

A8

A9

1860

8	A8 ½t deep blue	250,000.	11,000.
9	A9 ½t blue	50,000.	3,250.
a.	½t deep blue	50,000.	3,500.

100 varieties of each.

No. 8 was made from the plate of No. 1, which was altered by changing the "G" to "T."

No. 9 was made from the same plate after a second alteration erasing the coat of arms and inserting the Cross of Savoy. Dangerous counterfeits exist of Nos. 8-9.

Sicily

Ferdinand II — A10

1859 Unwmk. Engr. *Imperf.*
Soft Porous Paper, Brownish Gum
(Naples consignment)

10g	A10	½g orange	700.00	*5,000.*
c.		Printed on both sides	—	*44,000.*
11	A10	1g dk brn	20,000.	875.00
12h	A10	1g pale ol grn (III)	275.00	*240.00*
c.		Double impression	5,250.	4,750.
13g	A10	2g blue	200.00	120.00
b.		Printed on both sides	—	26,000.
14	A10	5g deep rose	950.00	700.00
15	A10	5g vermilion	875.00	*2,350.*
16	A10	10g dark blue	975.00	440.00
17	A10	20g dk gray vio	975.00	775.00
18	A10	50g dk brn red	975.00	*5,850.*

There were three plates each for the 1g and 2g, two each for the ½g and 5g and one plate each for the other values.

Nos. 10a, 10b, 11, 11a, 14, 14a, 14b and 15 are printed from Plate I on which the stamps are 2 to 2½mm apart. On almost all stamps from Plate I, the S and T of POSTA touch.

Nos. 12a, and 15a are from Plate II and No. 12 is from Plate III. On both Plates II and III stamps are spaced 1½mm apart. Most stamps from Plate II have a white line about 1mm long below the beard.

Nos. 10-18 are on soft, porous paper with brownish gum, while Nos. 10, 12 and 13 exist also on hard white paper, with white gum. Color shades exist, some on both types of paper. For detailed listings, see the *Scott Classic Specialized Catalogue of Stamps and Covers.*

The ½g blue is stated to be a proof of which two examples are known. Both originated on the same cover. One stamp is sound and still on its original partial cover. This item was sold at auction in 2011, where it realized $2.6 million. The second stamp is a faulty, loose single.

Fraudulent cancellations are known on Nos. 10, 15, 15a and 18.

Neapolitan Provinces

King Victor Emmanuel II — A11

Lithographed, Center Embossed
1861 Unwmk. *Imperf.*

19	A11 ½t green	14.00	*250.00*
a.	½t yellow green	425.00	340.00
b.	½t emerald	7,850.	1,350.
c.	½t black (error)	*135,000.*	*160,000.*
d.	Head inverted (green)	200.00	
e.	Head inverted (yel grn)		11,250.
f.	Printed on both sides		32,250.
20	A11 ½g bister	200.00	*225.00*
a.	½g brown	200.00	*310.00*
b.	½g gray brown	225.00	*225.00*
c.	Head inverted	1,950.	—
21	A11 1g black	310.00	32.50
a.	Head inverted		*1,675.*
22	A11 2g blue	125.00	14.00
a.	2g deep blue	125.00	14.00
b.	Head inverted	*400.00*	*1,000.*
c.	2g black (error)		*160,000.*
23	A11 5g car rose	225.00	125.00
a.	5g vermilion	225.00	160.00
b.	5g lilac rose	250.00	250.00
c.	Head inverted	1,250.	*8,400.*
e.	Printed on both sides		21,000.
25	A11 10g orange	100.00	*275.00*
a.	10g ocher	*1,250.*	625.00
b.	10g bister	110.00	*275.00*
26	A11 20g yellow	425.00	*3,350.*
a.	Head inverted		42,000.
27	A11 50g gray	32.50	*8,500.*
a.	50g slate	40.00	*8,500.*
b.	50g slate blue	45.00	*11,250.*
	Nos. 19-27 (8)	1,432.	12,772.

Counterfeits of the inverted head varieties of this issue are plentiful. See note on forgeries after Sardinia No. 15.

Fraudulent cancellations are found on Nos. 19-20, 23-27.

Stamps similar to those of Sardinia 1855-61, type A4 but with inscriptions in larger, clearer lettering, were prepared in 1861 for the Neapolitan Provinces. They were not officially issued although a few are known postally used. Denominations: 5c, 10c, 20c, 40c and 80c.

Stamps of Two Sicilies were replaced by those of Italy in 1862.

ITALY

'i-tᵊl-ē

LOCATION — Southern Europe
GOVT. — Republic
AREA — 119,764 sq. mi.
POP. — 56,735,130 (1999 est.)
CAPITAL — Rome

Formerly a kingdom, Italy became a republic in June 1946

100 Centesimi = 1 Lira
100 Cents = 1 Euro (2002)

Catalogue values for unused stamps in this country are for Never Hinged items, beginning with Scott 691 in the regular postage section, Scott B47 in the semi-postal section, Scott C129 in the airpost section, Scott D21 in the pneumatic post section, Scott E32 in the special delivery section, Scott EY11 in the authorized delivery section, Scott J83 in the postage due section, Scott Q77 in the parcel post section, Scott QY5 in the parcel post authorized delivery section, Scott 1N1 in the A.M.G. section, Scott 1LN1 in the Venezia Giulia section, 1LNC1 in the occupation air post section, 1LNE1 in the occupation special delivery section, and all of the items in the Italian Social Republic area.

Watermarks

Wmk. 87 — Honeycomb

Wmk. 140 — Crown

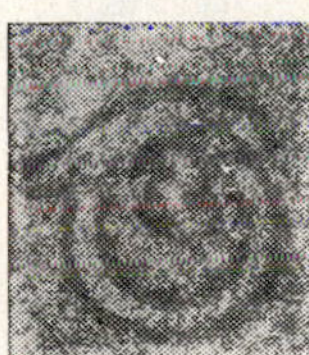
Wmk. 277 — Winged Wheel

Wmk. 303 — Multiple Stars

Values of Italy stamps vary tremendously according to condition. Quotations are for very fine examples, and values for unused stamps are for examples with original gum as defined in the catalogue introduction. Extremely fine or superb copies sell at much higher prices, and fine or poor examples sell at greatly reduced prices. In addition, unused examples without gum are discounted severely.

Very fine examples of Nos. 17-21, 24-75, J2-J27, O1-O8 and Q1-Q6 will have perforations barely clear of the frameline or design due to the narrow spacing of the stamps on the plates.

King Victor Emmanuel II — A4

Typographed; Head Embossed

1862 Unwmk. *Perf. 11½x12*

17	A4 10c bister		*8,000.*	325.00
g.	Vert. half used as 5c on cover			*125,000.*
19	A4 20c dark blue		20.00	*32.50*
f.	Vert. half used as 10c on cover			*170,000.*
20	A4 40c red		250.00	175.00
21	A4 80c orange		50.00	*1,900.*

The outer frame shows a distinct design on the early printings, while this design is more or less blurred, or even a solid line, on the later printings.

Numerous shades of Nos. 17-21 exist. Some are very expensive. For listings, see the *Scott Classic Catalogue.*

The 20c and 40c exist perf. 11½. These are remainders of Sardinia with forged perforations.

Counterfeit cancellations are often found on No. 21.

Lithographed; Head Embossed

1863 *Imperf.*

22	A4 15c blue	57.50	45.00
a.	Head inverted		*70,000.*
b.	Double head	115.00	70.00
c.	Head omitted	575.00	*40,000.*
j.	Triple head	265.00	*475.00*

See note after Sardinia No. 15.
No. 22c is valued with original gum only.

King Victor Emmanuel II — A5

Type I — First "C" in bottom line nearly closed.
Type II — "C" open. Line broken below "Q."

1863 Litho.

23	A5 15c blue, Type II	7.00	*11.50*
a.	Type I	300.00	24.00
	No gum	35.00	
c.	As "a," double impression		*3,800.*
f.	As "a," printed on both sides		17,500.

One example of No. 23f is known used, cancelled "Milano, 25-VII-1863." Unused examples always lack gum and are from printer's waste. They are of little value.

A6

A7

A8

A13

1863-77 Typo. Wmk. 140 *Perf. 14*

24	A6	1c gray grn	6.00	3.00
25	A7	2c org brn ('65)	24.00	2.00
a.		Imperf., pair	210.00	*300.00*
26	A8	5c slate grn	1,825.	3.25
27	A8	10c buff	3,100.	4.25
28	A8	10c blue ('77)	5,850.	4.75
29	A8	15c blue	2,350.	3.00
30	A8	30c brown	9.00	9.00
a.		Imperf., single		—
31	A8	40c carmine	6,500.	5.75
a.		40c rose	8,750.	8.00
32	A8	60c lilac	9.00	*14.00*
33	A13	2 l vermilion	24.00	*90.00*

Nos. 26 to 32 have the head of type A8 but with different corner designs for each value.

Early printings of Nos. 24-27, 29-33 were made in London by De La Rue, later printings in Turin. Used examples can be determined by cancellation date. Unused singles cannot be distinguished.

For overprints see Italian Offices Abroad Nos. 1-5, 8-11.

No. 29 Surcharged in Brown

Type I — Dots flanking stars in oval, and dot in eight check-mark ornaments in corners.
Type II — Dots in oval, none in corners.
Type III — No dots.

1865

34	A8 20c on 15c bl (I)	645.00	4.00
a.	Type II	8,750.	15.00
b.	Type III	1,750.	6.00
c.	Inverted surcharge (I)		*65,000.*
d.	Double surcharge, on cover (I)		*60,000.*
e.	Double surcharge (III)		*25,000.*

A15

1867-77 Typo.

35	A15 20c sky blue (London)	1,600.	3.00
36	A15 20c orange ('77)	4,400.	3.00

For overprints see Italian Offices Abroad Nos. 9-10.

Official Stamps Surcharged in Blue

1878

37	O1	2c on 2c lake	180.00	25.00
38	O1	2c on 5c lake	225.00	30.00
39	O1	2c on 20c lake	800.00	3.50
40	O1	2c on 30c lake	700.00	12.50
41	O1	2c on 1 l lake	550.00	4.00
42	O1	2c on 2 l lake	550.00	10.00
43	O1	2c on 5 l lake	800.00	13.00
44	O1	2c on 10 l lake	550.00	16.50
		Nos. 37-44 (8)	4,355.	114.50

Inverted Surcharge

37a	O1	2c on 2c		1,625.
38a	O1	2c on 5c		1,300.
39a	O1	2c on 20c	*38,000.*	875.
40a	O1	2c on 30c		1,300.
41a	O1	2c on 1 l	*44,000.*	1,200.
42a	O1	2c on 2 l	*44,000.*	1,300.
43a	O1	2c on 5 l		1,300.
44a	O1	2c on 10 l		1,300.

King Humbert I — A17

1879 Typo. *Perf. 14*

45	A17	5c blue green	8.00	1.45
46	A17	10c claret	450.00	1.50
47	A17	20c orange	425.00	1.45
48	A17	25c blue	800.00	7.25
49	A17	30c brown	150.00	*2,650.*
50	A17	50c violet	20.00	22.00
51	A17	2 l vermilion	52.50	*350.00*

Nos. 45-51 have the head of type A17 with different corner designs for each value.

Beware of forged cancellations on No. 49, on or off cover.

For surcharges and overprints see Nos. 64-66, Italian Offices Abroad 12-17.

Arms of Savoy — A24

Humbert I — A25

A26

A27

A28

A29

1889

52	A24	5c dark green	775.00	3.00
53	A25	40c brown	13.00	17.50
a.		Horiz. pair, imperf. between		*17,500.*
54	A26	45c gray green	2,350.	8.50
55	A27	60c violet	17.00	*42.50*
56	A28	1 l brown & yel	17.00	22.00
a.		1 l brown & orange	19.00	27.00
57	A29	5 l grn & claret	35.00	*1,075.*

Forged cancellations exist on Nos. 51, 57.

Parcel Post Stamps of 1884-86 Surcharged in Black

1890

No.	Type	Description	Unused	Used
58	PP1	2c on 10c ol gray	5.40	*7.00*
a.		Inverted surcharge	500.00	*3,250.*
59	PP1	2c on 20c blue	5.40	*7.00*
60	PP1	2c on 50c claret	57.50	42.50
a.		Inverted surcharge		*45,000.*
61	PP1	2c on 75c blue grn	5.40	*7.00*
62	PP1	2c on 1.25 l org	50.00	37.50
a.		Inverted surcharge	*85,000.*	*42,500.*
63	PP1	2c on 1.75 l brn	22.00	*55.00*
		Nos. 58-63 (6)	145.70	156.00

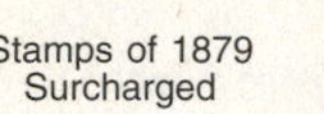

Stamps of 1879 Surcharged

1890-91

No.	Type	Description	Unused	Used
64	A17	2c on 5c bl grn ('91)	20.00	50.00
a.		"2" with thin tail	125.00	290.00
65	A17	20c on 30c brn	425.00	11.00
66	A17	20c on 50c violet	500.00	42.50
		Nos. 64-66 (3)	945.00	103.50

Arms of Savoy — A33

Humbert I — A34

A35

A36

A37

A38

1891-96 Typo.

No.	Type	Description	Unused	Used
67	A33	5c green	500.00	2.25
68	A34	10c claret ('96)	8.50	2.25
69	A35	20c orange ('95)	8.50	2.25
70	A36	25c blue	8.50	9.00
71	A37	45c ol grn ('95)	8.50	9.00
72	A38	5 l blue & rose	85.00	*230.00*

Arms of Savoy — A39

A40

A41

1896-97

No.	Type	Description	Unused	Used
73	A39	1c brown	9.00	7.00
a.		Half used as ½c on cover		*1,450.*
74	A40	2c orange brown	10.00	1.80
75	A41	5c green ('97)	36.00	1.80
		Nos. 73-75 (3)	55.00	10.60

A42

Coat of Arms
A43 A44

Victor Emmanuel III
A45 A46

1901-26

No.	Type	Description	Unused	Used
76	A42	1c brown	1.45	.35
a.		Imperf, single	400.00	*650.00*
b.		Vert. pair, lower stamp imperf.		*3,000.*
77	A43	2c org brn	1.45	.35
a.		Double impression	110.00	*200.00*
b.		Imperf, single	115.00	*160.00*
78	A44	5c blue grn	80.00	.55
a.		Imperf, single	1,800.	
79	A45	10c claret	110.00	1.10
a.		Imperf, single	—	*10,000.*
80	A45	20c orange	22.00	1.10
81	A45	25c ultra	250.00	3.75
82	A46	25c grn & pale grn ('26)	1.45	.30
a.		Frame & vignette double	75.00	3.60
b.		Floral design double	42.50	50.00
c.		Floral design omitted	12.00	6.00
d.		"POSTE ITALIANE" omitted	1,150.	
e.		Imperf., single	75.00	75.00
f.		Vert. pair, lower stamp imperf.	1,900.	
83	A45	40c brown	720.00	8.75
84	A45	45c olive grn	11.00	.35
a.		Imperf, single	145.00	*190.00*
85	A45	50c violet	850.00	16.00
86	A46	75c dk red & rose ('26)	4.25	.30
a.		Floral design omitted	115.00	
b.		Imperf., single	100.00	100.00
87	A46	1 l brn & grn	4.25	.35
a.		Imperf, single	72.50	*110.00*
b.		Floral design (green) omitted	145.00	
c.		Double impression of vignette (brown)	72.50	*100.00*
d.		"POSTE ITALIANE" omitted	550.00	
88	A46	1.25 l bl & ultra ('26)	11.00	.30
89	A46	2 l dk grn & org ('23)	22.00	7.25
90	A46	2.50 l dk grn & org ('26)	57.50	7.25
91	A46	5 l blue & rose	30.00	5.75
		Nos. 76-91 (16)	2,176.	53.80

Nos. 83, 85, unused, are valued in fine condition.

The borders of Nos. 79-81, 83-85, 87, 89 and 91 differ slightly for each denomination.

On Nos. 82, 86, 88 and 90, the value is expressed as "Cent. 25," etc.

See No. 87d in set following No. 174G.

For surcharges and overprints see Nos. 148-149, 152, 158, 174F-174G, B16; Austria N20-N21, N27, N30, N52-N53, N58, N60, N64-N65, N71, N74; Dalmatia 1, 6-7.

Overprints & Surcharges

See Castellorizo, Italian Offices in China, Crete, Africa, Turkish Empire (Albania to Valona) and Aegean Islands for types A36-A58 overprinted or surcharged.

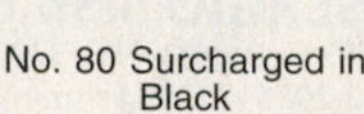

No. 80 Surcharged in Black

1905

No.	Type	Description	Unused	Used
92	A45	15c on 20c org	70.00	1.80
a.		Double surcharge		*5,000.*

A47

No. 93

No. 111

No. 123

1906 Unwmk. Engr. *Perf. 12*

No.	Type	Description	Unused	Used
93	A47	15c slate	70.00	.90
a.		Vert. pair, imperf horiz.	180.00	180.00
b.		Horiz. pair, imperf vert.	180.00	180.00
c.		Booklet pane of 6	*3,300.*	
		Complete bklt., 4 #93c	*14,500.*	
d.		On thin paper	92.50	3.00

A48

1906-19 Wmk. 140 Typo. *Perf. 14*

No.	Type	Description	Unused	Used
94	A48	5c green	1.45	.35
a.		Imperf, single	36.00	36.00
b.		Printed on both sides	225.00	
95	A48	10c claret	3.00	.30
a.		Imperf, single	32.50	37.50
b.		Printed on both sides	225.00	
96	A48	15c slate ('19)	2.90	.30
a.		Imperf, single	125.00	*200.00*
		Nos. 94-96 (3)	7.35	.95

The frame of No. 95 differs in several details.

See Nos. 96b-96d following No. 174G.

For overprints and surcharge see Nos. 142A-142B, 150, 174A, B5, B9-B10; Austria N22-N23, N31, N54-N55, N61-N62, N66-N67; Dalmatia 2-5.

A49

1908-27

No.	Type	Description	Unused	Used
97	A49	20c brn org ('25)	1.45	.90
98	A49	20c green ('25)	.35	.75
99	A49	20c lil brn ('26)	2.75	.30
100	A49	25c blue	2.25	.30
a.		Imperf., pair	105.00	105.00
b.		Printed on both sides	200.00	*325.00*
101	A49	25c lt grn ('27)	7.25	*18.00*
102	A49	30c org brn ('22)	3.00	.70
a.		Imperf, single	240.00	—
103	A49	30c gray ('25)	4.25	.25
a.		Imperf., single	115.00	145.00
104	A49	40c brown	3.75	.30
a.		Imperf., pair	160.00	175.00
105	A49	50c violet	1.45	.30
a.		Imperf., pair	150.00	150.00
106	A49	55c dl vio ('20)	17.00	*37.50*
107	A49	60c car ('17)	2.25	.35
108	A49	60c blue ('23)	8.50	*80.00*
109	A49	60c brn org ('26)	11.50	.55
110	A49	85c red brn ('20)	22.00	30.00
		Nos. 97-110 (14)	87.75	*170.20*

A50

Redrawn

Perf. 13x13½, 13½x14

1909-17 Typo. Unwmk.

No.	Type	Description	Unused	Used
111	A50	15c slate black	270.00	2.25
112	A50	20c brn org ('16)	57.50	4.25

No. 111 is similar to No. 93, but the design has been redrawn and the stamp is 23mm high instead of 25mm. There is a star at each side of the coat collar, but one is not distinct. See illustrations next to A47.

For overprints and surcharges see Nos. B6, B11; Austria N24, N32, N56, N63, N68.

Wmk. 140 ***Perf. 14***

No.	Type	Description	Unused	Used
113	A50	20c brn org ('17)	7.25	.35
a.		Imperf., pair	50.00	

Stamps overprinted "Prestito Nazionale, 1917," or later dates, are Thrift or Postal Savings Stamps.

A51

1910, Nov. 1

No.	Type	Description	Unused	Used
114	A51	10 l gray grn & red	72.50	32.00
a.		Red inverted		*6,600.*

For surcharge see Dalmatia No. 8.

A52

Perf. 14x13½

1910, Apr. 15 Unwmk.

No.	Type	Description	Unused	Used
115	A52	5c green	29.00	25.00
116	A52	15c claret	50.00	50.00

50th anniversary of freedom of Sicily.

Giuseppe Garibaldi — A53

1910, Dec. 1

No.	Type	Description	Unused	Used
117	A53	5c claret	125.00	125.00
118	A53	15c green	225.00	180.00

50th anniversary of the plebiscite of the southern Italian provinces in 1860.

Nos. 115-118 sold for 5c above face value to benefit the anniversary committee. The stamps were valid only on mail to addresses within the Kingdom of Italy. Nos. 115-116 were valid to June 30, 1910; Nos. 117-118 were valid to Jan. 31, 1911.

Used values in italics are for postally used stamps. CTO's sell for about the same as unused, hinged stamps.

Symbols of Rome and Turin — A54

Symbol of Valor — A55

Genius of Italy — A56

Glory of Rome — A57

1911, May 1 Engr. *Perf. 14x13½*

No.	Type	Description	Unused	Used
119	A54	2c brown	2.90	*5.75*
a.		Vert. pair, imperf horiz.	85.00	87.50
b.		Horiz. pair, imperf vert.	85.00	87.50
120	A55	5c deep green	40.00	36.00
121	A56	10c carmine	29.00	*55.00*
a.		Vert. pair, imperf horiz.	—	—
b.		Horiz. pair, imperf vert.	180.00	180.00
122	A57	15c slate	37.50	*72.50*
		Nos. 119-122 (4)	109.40	*169.25*

50th anniv. of the union of Italian States to form the Kingdom of Italy.

Nos. 119 to 122 were sold at a premium over their face value to benefit the anniversary committee. They were valid to Dec. 31, 1911. The stamps were valid only for mail to addresses within the Kingdom of Italy. They were used by military post offices in Libya. After 1913, No. 119 was sold without the premium.

For surcharges see Nos. 126-128.

Victor Emmanuel III — A58

1911, Oct. Re-engraved *Perf. 13½*

No.	Type	Description	Unused	Used
123	A58	15c slate	29.00	1.10
a.		Imperf., single	87.50	*110.00*
b.		Printed on both sides	360.00	*475.00*
c.		Bklt. pane of 6	*1,500.*	
		Cplt. bklt., 4 #123c	*3,250.*	

The re-engraved stamp is 24mm high. The stars at each side of the coat collar show plainly and the "C" of "Cent" is nearer the frame than in No. 93. See illustrations next to A47.

For surcharge see No. 129.

Campanile, Venice — A59

1912, Apr. 25 *Perf. 14x13½*

No.	Type	Description	Unused	Used
124	A59	5c indigo	8.50	*13.00*
125	A59	15c dk brn	47.50	*60.00*

Re-erection of the Campanile at Venice.

Nos. 124-125 were sold only in Venice and were valid to Dec. 31, 1912. The stamps were valid only for mail within Italy.

Nos. 120-121 Surcharged in Black

1913, Mar. 1

No.	Type	Description	Unused	Used
126	A55	2c on 5c dp grn	2.25	*6.00*
127	A56	2c on 10c car	2.25	*6.00*

No. 122 Surcharged in Violet

No.	Type	Description	Unused	Used
128	A57	2c on 15c slate	2.25	*6.00*
		Nos. 126-128 (3)	6.75	*18.00*
		Set, never hinged	16.50	

No. 123 Surcharged

1916, Jan. 8

No.	Type	Description	Unused	Used
129	A58	20c on 15c slate	16.00	1.10
		Never hinged	40.00	
a.		Bklt. pane of 6	*675.00*	
		Cplt. bklt., 4 #129a	*2,700.*	
b.		Inverted surcharge	315.00	315.00
c.		Double surcharge	200.00	200.00
e.		Vert. pair, one without surcharge	1,600.	
g.		Imperf, single	145.00	*180.00*

Old Seal of Republic of Trieste — A60

Wmk. 140

1921, June 5 Litho. *Perf. 14*

No.	Type	Description	Unused	Used
130	A60	15c blk & rose	6.50	*50.00*
a.		Horiz. pair, imperf btwn.	850.00	
131	A60	25c bl & rose	6.50	*50.00*
132	A60	40c brn & rose	6.50	*50.00*
		Nos. 130-132 (3)	19.50	*150.00*
		Set, never hinged	50.00	

Reunion of Venezia Giulia with Italy.

Allegory of Dante's Divine Comedy — A61

Italy Holding Laurels for Dante — A62

Dante Alighieri — A63

1921, Sept. 28 Typo.

No.	Type	Description	Unused	Used
133	A61	15c vio brn	6.50	*32.00*
a.		Imperf, single	36.00	36.00
134	A62	25c gray grn	6.50	*32.00*
a.		Imperf, single	36.00	36.00
135	A63	40c brown	6.50	*32.00*
a.		Imperf, single	36.00	36.00
		Nos. 133-135 (3)	19.50	*96.00*
		Set, never hinged	48.00	

600th anniversary of the death of Dante.

A 15c gray was not issued. Value: hinged $145, never hinged $360, canceled $425; block of 4, hinged $600, never hinged $1,275; imperf., single, hinged $400, canceled $6,100. A 15c gray violet, never issued: hinged $700, never hinged $1,400.

Nos. 133-135 exist in part perforate pairs.

"Victory" — A64

1921, Nov. 1 Engr. *Perf. 14*

No.	Type	Description	Unused	Used
136	A64	5c olive green	1.45	*1.80*
b.		Imperf, single	225.00	250.00
137	A64	10c red	2.10	2.25
c.		Imperf, single	225.00	475.00
138	A64	15c slate green	3.75	*8.50*
139	A64	25c ultra	2.10	*5.75*
c.		Imperf, single	145.00	145.00
d.		As "c," double impression	500.00	—
		Nos. 136-139 (4)	9.40	*18.30*
		Set, never hinged	23.50	

3rd anniv. of the victory on the Piave.

For surcharges see Nos. 171-174.

Flame of Patriotism Tempering Sword of Justice — A65

Giuseppe Mazzini — A66

Mazzini's Tomb A67

1922, Sept. 20 Typo. *Perf. 14*

No.	Type	Description	Unused	Used
140	A65	25c maroon	11.50	*32.00*
141	A66	40c vio brn	22.50	*40.00*
142	A67	80c dk bl	11.50	*50.00*
		Nos. 140-142 (3)	45.50	*122.00*
		Set, never hinged	145.00	

Mazzini (1805-1872), patriot and writer.

Nos. 95, 96, 100 and 104 Overprinted in Black

1922, June 4 Wmk. 140 *Perf. 14*

No.	Type	Description	Unused	Used
142A	A48	10c claret	425.00	425.00
142B	A48	15c slate	225.00	225.00
142C	A49	25c blue	225.00	225.00
142D	A49	40c brown	360.00	360.00
		Nos. 142A-142D (4)	1,235.	1,235.
		Set, never hinged	3,125.	

9th Italian Philatelic Congress, Trieste. Nos. 142A-142D were on sale to Sept. 30, 1922. Counterfeits exist.

Christ Preaching The Gospel — A68

Portrait at upper right and badge at lower right differ on each value. Portrait at upper left is of Pope Gregory XV. Others: 20c, St. Theresa. 30c, St. Dominic. 50c, St. Francis of Assisi. 1 l, St. Francis Xavier.

1923, June 11

No.	Type	Description	Unused	Used
143	A68	20c ol grn & brn org	5.75	*175.00*
a.		Imperf, single	500.00	650.00
b.		Vert. pair, imperf btwn.	1,100.	1,500.
144	A68	30c clar & brn org	5.75	*175.00*
a.		Imperf, single	500.00	650.00
c.		Horiz. pair, imperf btwn.	1,100.	1,500.
145	A68	50c vio & brn org	5.75	*175.00*
a.		Imperf, single	500.00	650.00
c.		Horiz. pair, imperf btwn.	1,750.	2,150.
d.		Vert. pair, imperf btwn.	1,100.	1,500.
146	A68	1 l bl & brn org	5.75	*175.00*
a.			500.00	650.00
c.		Horiz. pair, imperf btwn.	1,100.	1,500.
d.		Vert. pair, imperf btwn.	1,100.	1,500.
		Nos. 143-146 (4)	23.00	*700.00*
		Set, never hinged	58.00	

300th anniv. of the Propagation of the Faith. Practically the entire issue was delivered to speculators.

Forged cancellations exist on Nos. 143-146.

Stamps of Previous Issues, Surcharged

a

b

c

d

e

1923-25

No.	Type	Description	Unused	Used
147	A49(a)	7½c on 85c	.35	*1.20*
a.		Double surcharge	—	*1,450.*
148	A42(b)	10c on 1c	.35	.35
a.		Inverted surcharge	22.00	*36.00*
149	A43(b)	10c on 2c	.35	.30
a.		Inverted surcharge	55.00	*85.00*
150	A48(c)	10c on 15c	.35	.30
a.		Vert. pair, one without surcharge	*1,000.*	—
b.		Surcharge on reverse only	200.00	
151	A49(a)	20c on 25c	.35	.30
152	A45(d)	25c on 45c	1.45	*14.50*
a.		Vert. pair, one without surcharge	*1,000.*	—
153	A49(a)	25c on 60c	3.00	.90
a.		Vert. pair, one without surcharge	*1,000.*	—

154	A49(a)	30c on 50c	.35	.30
155	A49(a)	30c on 55c	1.45	.30
156	A49(a)	50c on 40c	4.00	.35
a.		Inverted surcharge	215.00	*325.00*
b.		Double surcharge	115.00	*135.00*
157	A49(a)	50c on 55c	20.00	14.50
a.		Inverted surcharge	1,100.	*2,000.*
158	A51(e)	1.75 l on 10 l	14.50	*32.00*
a.		Vert. pair, one without surcharge	*1,600.*	
		Nos. 147-158 (12)	46.50	65.30
		Set, never hinged	120.00	

Years of issue: Nos. 148-149, 156-157, 1923; Nos. 147, 152-153, 1924; others, 1925.

Emblem of the New Government A69

Wreath of Victory, Eagle and Fasces A70

Symbolical of Fascism and Italy — A71

Unwmk.

1923, Oct. 24 Engr. *Perf. 14*

159	A69	10c dark green	4.25	*10.00*
a.		Imperf, single	725.00	*850.00*
160	A69	30c dark violet	4.25	*10.00*
161	A69	50c brn car	8.50	*18.00*

Wmk. 140 Typo.

162	A70	1 l blue	14.50	*18.00*
163	A70	2 l brown	17.00	*22.00*
164	A71	5 l blk & bl	29.00	*57.50*
a.		Imperf, single	290.00	—
		Nos. 159-164 (6)	77.50	*135.50*
		Set, never hinged	195.00	

Anniv. of the March of the Fascisti on Rome.

Fishing Scene A72

Designs: 15c, Mt. Resegone. 30c, Fugitives bidding farewell to native mountains. 50c, Part of Lake Como. 1 l, Manzoni's home, Milan. 5 l, Alessandro Manzoni. The first four designs show scenes from Manzoni's work "I Promessi Sposi."

1923, Dec. 29 *Perf. 14*

165	A72	10c brn red & blk	22.00	*180.00*
166	A72	15c bl grn & blk	22.00	*180.00*
167	A72	30c blk & slate	22.00	*180.00*
a.		Imperf, single	*2,700.*	
		Imperf, pair	—	
168	A72	50c org brn & blk	22.00	*180.00*
169	A72	1 l blue & blk	145.00	*700.00*
a.		Imperf, single, no gum	290.00	—
170	A72	5 l vio & blk	725.00	*3,950.*
a.		Imperf, single	850.00	
		Imperf, pair	—	
		Nos. 165-170 (6)	958.00	*5,370.*
		Set, never hinged	2,375.	

50th anniv. of the death of Alessandro Manzoni.

Nos. 136-139 Surcharged

1924, Feb.

171	A64	1 l on 5c ol grn	22.50	*225.00*
172	A64	1 l on 10c red	14.50	*225.00*
173	A64	1 l on 15c slate grn	22.50	*225.00*
174	A64	1 l on 25c ultra	14.50	*225.00*
		Nos. 171-174 (4)	74.00	*900.00*
		Set, never hinged	180.00	

Surcharge forgeries exist.

Perf. 14x13½

171a	A64	1 l on 5c	32.00	*300.00*
172a	A64	1 l on 10c	18.00	*300.00*
173a	A64	1 l on 15c	32.00	*300.00*
174h	A64	1 l on 25c	18.00	*300.00*
		Nos. 171a-174h (4)	100.00	*1,200.*
		Set, never hinged	195.00	

Nos. 95, 102, 105, 108, 110, 87 and 89 Overprinted in Black or Red

1924, Feb. 16

174A	A48	10c claret	2.25	*42.50*
174B	A49	30c org brn	2.25	*42.50*
174C	A49	50c violet	2.25	*42.50*
174D	A49	60c bl (R)	14.50	*125.00*
174E	A49	85c choc (R)	7.25	*125.00*
174F	A46	1 l brn & grn	42.50	*425.00*
174G	A46	2 l dk grn & org	32.00	*425.00*
		Nos. 174A-174G (7)	103.00	*1,228.*
		Set, never hinged	260.00	

These stamps were sold on an Italian merchant ship which made a cruise to South American ports in 1924.

Overprint forgeries exist of Nos. 174D-174G.

Stamps of 1901-22 with Advertising Labels Attached

Perf. 14 all around, Imperf. between

1924-25

96b	A48	15c + Bitter Campari	3.75	*25.00*
96c	A48	15c + Cordial Campari	3.75	*22.00*
96d	A48	15c + Columbia	57.50	50.00
100c	A49	25c + Abrador	100.00	125.00
100d	A49	25c + Coen	215.00	65.00
100e	A49	25c + Piperno	1,450.	1,100.
100f	A49	25c + Reinach	100.00	85.00
100g	A49	25c + Tagliacozzo	850.00	1,150.
102b	A49	30c + Columbia	29.00	*40.00*
105b	A49	50c + Coen	1,450.	85.00
105c	A49	50c + Columbia	22.00	16.00
105d	A49	50c + De Montel	3.75	*16.00*
105e	A49	50c + Piperno	2,000.	315.00
105f	A49	50c + Reinach	215.00	65.00
105g	A49	50c + Siero Casali	22.00	*47.50*
105h	A49	50c + Singer	3.75	*11.00*
105i	A49	50c + Tagliacozzo	*2,175.*	600.00
105j	A49	50c + Tantal	360.00	200.00
87d	A46	1 l + Columbia	850.00	950.00
		Nos. 96b-87d (19)	9,911.	4,968.
		Set, never hinged	20,000.	

No. 97 with Columbia label and No. E3 with Cioccolato Perugina label were prepared but not issued. Values: Columbia, unused $50, never hinged $125; Cioccolato, unused $18, never hinged $42.50.

King Victor Emmanuel III — A78

1925-26 Engr. Unwmk. *Perf. 11*

175	A78	60c brn car	1.45	.70
a.		Perf. 13½	7.25	2.25
b.		Imperf., pair	235.00	260.00
176	A78	1 l dk bl	1.45	.70
a.		Perf. 13½	14.50	14.50
b.		Imperf., pair	235.00	—

Perf. 13½

177	A78	1.25 l dk bl ('26)	4.25	2.25
a.		Perf. 11	100.00	125.00
b.		Imperf., pair	550.00	—
		Nos. 175-177 (3)	7.15	3.65
		Set, never hinged	18.00	

25th year of the reign of Victor Emmanuel III.

Nos. 175 to 177 exist with sideways watermark of fragments of letters or a crown, which are normally on the sheet margin.

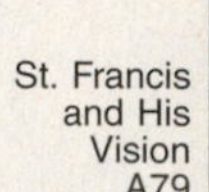

St. Francis and His Vision A79

Monastery of St. Damien A80

Assisi Monastery A81

St. Francis' Death A82

St. Francis — A83

1926, Jan. 30 Wmk. 140 *Perf. 14*

178	A79	20c gray grn	.70	*.90*
a.		Imperf single	1,100.	1,100.
179	A80	40c dk vio	.70	*.90*
180	A81	60c red brn	.90	*.90*
a.		Imperf single	500.00	500.00

Unwmk. *Perf. 11*

181	A83	30c slate blk	.75	*.90*
a.		Perf. 13½	11.00	*20.00*
		Never hinged	27.00	
182	A82	1.25 l dark blue	3.75	.90
a.		Perf. 13½	425.00	40.00
		Never hinged	1,100.	

Perf. 13½

183	A83	5 l + 2.50 l dk brn	10.00	*125.00*
		Nos. 178-183 (6)	16.80	*129.50*
		Set, never hinged	40.00	

700th anniv. of the death of St. Francis of Assisi.

Alessandro Volta — A84

1927 Wmk. 140 Typo. *Perf. 14*

188	A84	20c dk car	3.00	1.10
189	A84	50c grnsh blk	3.00	.75
a.		Vert. pair, imperf. between		2,750.
190	A84	60c chocolate	4.25	4.50
191	A84	1.25 l ultra	14.50	7.25
		Nos. 188-191 (4)	24.75	13.60
		Set, never hinged	50.00	

Cent. of the death of Alessandro Volta.

The 20c in purple is Cyrenaica No. 25 with overprint omitted. Values: $4,000 unused; $6,000 never hinged.

A85

1927-29 Size: 17½x22mm *Perf. 14*

192	A85	50c brn & slate	3.00	.35
a.		Imperf, pair	—	—
b.		Double frame	400.00	325.00

Unwmk.

Engr. *Perf. 11*

Size: 19x23mm

193	A85	1.75 l dp brn	3.75	.30
a.		Perf. 13½ ('29)	*37,500.*	*3,150.*
		Never hinged	*57,500.*	
b.		Perf. 11x13½ ('29)	—	3,150.
c.		Perf. 13½x11 ('29)	—	3,150.
d.		Imperf, single	*4,750.*	
194	A85	1.85 l black	3.00	.65
195	A85	2.55 l brn car	3.75	*8.50*

196	A85	2.65 l dp vio	5.75	*72.50*
a.		Imperf, single	3,150.	—
		Nos. 192-196 (5)	19.25	*82.30*
		Set, never hinged	45.00	

A86

1928-29 Wmk. 140 Typo. *Perf. 14*

197	A86	7½c lt brown	3.00	*11.00*
198	A86	15c brn org ('29)	3.00	.30
199	A86	35c gray blk ('29)	8.00	14.50
200	A86	50c dull violet	17.00	.30
a.		Imperf single	225.00	
		Nos. 197-200 (4)	31.00	*26.10*
		Set, never hinged	75.00	

Emmanuel Philibert, Duke of Savoy — A87

Statue of Philibert, Turin — A88

Philibert and Italian Soldier of 1918 — A89

1928 *Perf. 11*

201	A87	20c red brn & ultra	9.50	*16.00*
a.		Perf. 13½	240.00	240.00
202	A87	25c dp red & bl grn	9.50	*16.00*
a.		Perf. 13½	47.50	*52.50*
203	A87	30c bl grn & red brn	16.00	*32.00*
a.		Center inverted	*67,500.*	*9,200.*
b.		Perf. 13½	35.00	35.00

Perf. 14

204	A89	50c org brn & bl	4.00	1.25
205	A89	75c dp red	4.75	4.00
206	A88	1.25 l bl & blk	4.75	4.00
207	A89	1.75 l bl grn	32.50	*40.00*
208	A87	5 l vio & bl grn (Perf. 11)	29.00	*110.00*
209	A89	10 l blk & pink	35.00	*225.00*
210	A88	20 l vio & blk	70.00	*725.00*
		Nos. 201-210 (10)	215.00	*1,173.*
		Set, never hinged	535.00	

400th anniv. of the birth of Emmanuel Philibert, Duke of Savoy; 10th anniv. of the victory of 1918; Turin Exhibition.

She-wolf Suckling Romulus and Remus

A90 A95a

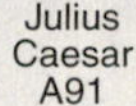
Julius Caesar A91

Augustus Caesar A92

"Italia" — A93

A94

A95

1929-42 Wmk. 140 Photo. *Perf. 14*

213	A90	5c olive brn	.25	.25
214	A91	7½c deep vio	1.60	.25
215	A92	10c dk brn	.25	.25
216	A93	15c slate grn	.25	.25
217	A91	20c rose red	.25	.25
218	A94	25c dp green	.25	.25
219	A95	30c olive brn	.25	.25
a.		Imperf., pair	1,100.	
220	A93	35c dp blue	.25	.25
221	A95	50c purple	.25	.25
a.		Imperf., pair	725.00	*875.00*
222	A94	75c rose red	.25	.25
222A	A91	1 l dk pur ('42)	.25	.25
223	A94	1.25 l dp blue	.25	.25
224	A92	1.75 l red org	.25	.25
225	A93	2 l car lake	.25	.25
226	A95a	2.55 l slate grn	.25	.80
226A	A95a	3.70 l pur ('30)	.25	.80
227	A95a	5 l rose red	.25	.25
228	A93	10 l purple	4.00	4.00
229	A91	20 l lt green	4.75	*12.00*
230	A92	25 l bluish sl	11.00	*35.00*
231	A94	50 l dp violet	13.00	*40.00*
		Nos. 213-231 (21)	38.35	*96.35*
		Set, never hinged	94.00	

Stamps of the 1929-42 issue overprinted "G.N.R." are 1943 local issues of the Guardia Nazionale Repubblicana.

See Nos. 427-438, 441-459.

For surcharge and overprints see Nos. 460, M1-M13, 1N10-1N13, 1LN1-1LN1A, 1LN10; Italian Social Republic 1-5A; Yugoslavia-Ljubljana N36-N54.

Courtyard of Monte Cassino A96

Monks Laying Cornerstone — A98

St. Benedict of Nursia — A100

Designs: 25c, Fresco, "Death of St. Benedict." 75c+15c, 5 l+1 l, Monte Cassino Abbey.

1929, Aug. 1 Photo. Wmk. 140

232	A96	20c red orange	1.60	1.60
233	A96	25c dk green	1.60	1.60
234	A98	50c + 10c ol brn	4.00	*30.00*
235	A98	75c + 15c crim	4.75	*40.00*
236	A96	1.25 l + 25c saph	6.50	*45.00*
237	A98	5 l + 1 l dk vio	9.50	*175.00*

Unwmk.

Engr.

238	A100	10 l + 2 l slate grn	14.50	*325.00*
		Nos. 232-238 (7)	42.45	*618.20*
		Set, never hinged	105.00	

14th cent. of the founding of the Abbey of Monte Cassino by St. Benedict in 529 A.D. The premium on some of the stamps was given to the committee for the celebration of the centenary.

Prince Humbert and Princess Marie José A101

1930, Jan. 8 Photo. Wmk. 140

239	A101	20c orange red	.80	.60
240	A101	50c + 10c ol brn	2.40	*4.00*
241	A101	1.25 l + 25c dp bl	5.50	*13.00*
		Nos. 239-241 (3)	8.70	*17.60*
		Set, never hinged	22.00	

Marriage of Prince Humbert of Savoy with Princess Marie José of Belgium.

The surtax on Nos. 240 and 241 was for the benefit of the Italian Red Cross Society.

The 20c in green is Cyrenaica No. 35 with overprint omitted. Values: $35,000 unused; $52,500 never hinged.

Ferrucci Leading His Army A102

Fabrizio Maramaldo Killing Ferrucci A103

Francesco Ferrucci — A104

1930, July 10

242	A102	20c rose red	.80	.80
243	A103	25c deep green	1.40	.80
244	A103	50c purple	.80	.40
245	A103	1.25 l deep blue	11.00	4.75
246	A104	5 l + 2 l org red	22.50	*140.00*
		Nos. 242-246 (5)	36.50	*146.75*
		Set, never hinged	90.00	
		Nos. 242-246,C20-C22 (8)	60.50	*314.75*
		Set, never hinged	150.00	

4th cent. of the death of Francesco Ferrucci, Tuscan warrior.

Overprints

See Castellorizo and Aegean Islands for types A103-A145 Overprinted.

Helenus and Aeneas A106

Designs: 20c, Anchises and Aeneas watch passing of Roman Legions. 25c, Aeneas feasting in shade of Albunea. 30c, Ceres and her children with fruits of Earth. 50c, Harvesters at work. 75c, Woman at loom, children and calf. 1.25 l, Anchises and his sailors in sight of Italy. 5 l+1.50 l, Shepherd piping by fireside. 10 l+2.50 l, Aeneas leading his army.

1930, Oct. 21 Photo. *Perf. 14*

248	A106	15c olive brn	2.40	2.40
249	A106	20c orange	2.40	1.60
250	A106	25c green	3.20	1.60
251	A106	30c dull vio	9.50	4.00
252	A106	50c violet	16.00	.80
253	A106	75c rose red	4.00	*12.00*
254	A106	1.25 l blue	4.00	*12.00*

Unwmk. Engr.

255	A106	5 l +1.50 l red brn	60.00	*525.00*
256	A106	10 l +2.50 l gray grn	60.00	*725.00*
		Nos. 248-256 (9)	161.50	*1,284.*
		Set, never hinged	405.00	
		Nos. 248-256,C23-C26 (13)	332.00	*2,019.*
		Set, never hinged	835.00	

Bimillenary of the birth of Virgil. Surtax on Nos. 255-256 was for the National Institute Figli del Littorio.

Arms of Italy (Fascist Emblems Support House of Savoy Arms) — A115

1930, Dec. 16 Photo. Wmk. 140

257	A115	2c deep orange	1.60	.25
		Never hinged	4.00	

St. Anthony being Installed as a Franciscan A116

Olivares Hermitage, Portugal A118

St. Anthony Freeing Prisoners A120

St. Anthony's Death A121

St. Anthony Succoring the Poor — A122

Designs: 25c, St. Anthony preaching to the fishes. 50c, Basilica of St. Anthony, Padua.

Wmk. 140

1931, Mar. 9 Photo. *Perf. 14*

258	A116	20c dull violet	4.00	1.25
259	A116	25c gray green	2.40	1.25
260	A118	30c brown	6.50	2.40
261	A118	50c violet	2.00	.80
262	A120	1.25 l blue	20.00	9.50

Unwmk. Engr.

263	A121	75c brown red	9.50	*16.00*
a.		Perf. 12	100.00	*375.00*
		Never hinged	240.00	
264	A122	5 l + 2.50 l ol grn	40.00	*325.00*
		Nos. 258-264 (7)	84.40	*356.20*
		Set, never hinged	210.00	

7th centenary of the death of Saint Anthony of Padua.

Tower of Meloria — A123

Training Ship "Amerigo Vespucci" A124

Cruiser "Trento" A125

1931, Nov. 29 Photo. Wmk. 140

265	A123	20c rose red	8.75	2.00
266	A124	50c purple	8.75	1.60
267	A125	1.25 l dk bl	24.00	4.75
		Nos. 265-267 (3)	41.50	8.35
		Set, never hinged	165.00	

Royal Naval Academy at Leghorn (Livorno), 50th anniv.

Giovanni Boccaccio A126

Designs: 15c, Niccolo Machiavelli. 20c, Paolo Sarpi. 25c, Count Vittorio Alfieri. 30c, Ugo Foscolo. 50c, Count Giacomo Leopardi. 75c, Giosue Carducci. 1.25 l, Carlo Giuseppe Botta. 1.75 l, Torquato Tasso. 2.75 l, Francesco Petrarca. 5 l+2 l, Ludovico Ariosto. 10 l+2.50 l, Dante Alighieri.

1932, Mar. 14 *Perf. 14*

268	A126	10c olive brn	3.25	1.60
269	A126	15c slate grn	3.25	2.00
270	A126	20c rose red	3.25	1.60
271	A126	25c dp green	3.25	1.25
272	A126	30c olive brn	4.00	1.60
273	A126	50c violet	2.40	.80
274	A126	75c car rose	16.00	8.00
275	A126	1.25 l dp blue	4.75	4.00
276	A126	1.75 l orange	12.00	8.00
277	A126	2.75 l gray	24.00	*40.00*
278	A126	5 l + 2 l car rose	29.00	*300.00*
279	A126	10 l + 2.50 l ol grn	35.00	*450.00*
		Nos. 268-279 (12)	140.15	*818.85*
		Set, never hinged	350.00	
		Nos. 268-279,C28-C33,C34 (19)	237.90	*2,427.*
		Set, never hinged	600.00	

Dante Alighieri Society, a natl. literary association founded to promote development of the Italian language and culture. The surtax was added to the Society funds to help in its work.

View of Caprera A138

Garibaldi Carrying His Dying Wife A141

Garibaldi Memorial A144

Giuseppe Garibaldi A145

Designs: 20c, 30c, Garibaldi meeting Victor Emmanuel II. 25c, 50c, Garibaldi at Battle of Calatafimi. 1.25 l, Garibaldi's tomb. 1.75 l+25c, Rock of Quarto.

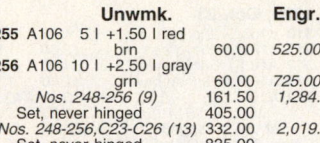

1932, Apr. 6

280 A138 10c gray blk 2.40 1.60
281 A138 20c olive brn 2.40 1.25
282 A138 25c dull grn 3.25 1.60
283 A138 30c orange 3.25 2.40
284 A138 50c violet 1.60 .40
285 A141 75c rose red 16.00 9.50
286 A141 1.25 l dp blue 32.50 4.00
287 A141 1.75 l + 25c bl gray 40.00 *87.50*
288 A144 2.55 l + 50c red brn 32.50 *125.00*
289 A145 5 l + 1 l cop red 32.50 *130.00*
Nos. 280-289 (10) 166.40 *363.25*
Set, never hinged 410.00
Nos. 280-289,C35-C39,CE1-CE2 (17) 242.40 *619.25*
Set, never hinged 600.00

50th anniv. of the death of Giuseppe Garibaldi, patriot.

Plowing with Oxen and Tractor A146

10c, Soldier guarding mountain pass. 15c, Marine, battleship & seaplane. 20c, Head of Fascist youth. 25c, Hands of workers & tools. 30c, Flags, Bible & altar. 35c, "New roads for the new Legions." 50c, Mussolini statue, Bologna. 60c, Hands with spades. 75c, Excavating ruins. 1 l, Steamers & galleons. 1.25 l, Italian flag, map & points of compass. 1.75 l, Flag, athlete & stadium. 2.55 l, Mother & child. 2.75 l, Emblems of drama, music, art & sport. 5 l+2.50 l, Roman emperor.

1932, Oct. 27 **Photo.**

290 A146 5c dk brown 2.40 1.25
291 A146 10c dk brown 2.40 .80
292 A146 15c dk gray grn 2.40 1.25
293 A146 20c car rose 2.40 .60
294 A146 25c dp green 2.40 .40
295 A146 30c dk brown 3.25 2.40
296 A146 35c dk blue 8.00 *9.50*
297 A146 50c purple 1.60 .40
298 A146 60c orange brn 12.00 8.00
299 A146 75c car rose 4.00 4.00
300 A146 1 l black vio 16.00 6.50
301 A146 1.25 l dp blue 4.00 1.60
302 A146 1.75 l orange 24.00 2.00
303 A146 2.55 l dk gray 29.00 *40.00*
304 A146 2.75 l slate grn 29.00 *40.00*
305 A146 5 l + 2.50 l car rose 40.00 *450.00*
Nos. 290-305 (16) 182.85 *568.70*
Set, never hinged 455.00
Nos. 290-305,C40-C41,E16-E17 (20) 202.75 *769.80*
Set, never hinged 520.00

10th anniv. of the Fascist government and the March on Rome.

Statue of Athlete — A162

1933, Aug. 16 ***Perf. 14***

306 A162 10c dk brown .80 .80
307 A162 20c rose red .80 .80
308 A162 50c purple .80 .40
309 A162 1.25 l blue 4.75 *6.50*
Nos. 306-309 (4) 7.15 8.50
Set, never hinged 18.00

Intl. University Games at Turin, Sept., 1933.

Cross in Halo, St. Peter's Dome — A163

Designs: 25c, 50c, Angel with cross. 1.25 l, as 20c. 2.55 l, + 2.50 l, Cross with doves.

1933, Oct. 23

310 A163 20c rose red 4.75 1.25
311 A163 25c green 12.00 1.60
312 A163 50c purple 4.75 .40
313 A163 1.25 l dp blue 12.00 4.75
314 A163 2.55 l + 2.50 l blk 8.00 *240.00*
Nos. 310-314 (5) 41.50 *248.00*
Set, never hinged 105.00
Nos. 310-314,CB1-CB2 (7) 47.90 *435.50*
Set, never hinged 121.00

Issued at the solicitation of the Order of the Holy Sepulchre of Jerusalem to mark the Holy Year.

Anchor of the "Emanuele Filiberto" — A166

Designs: 20c, Anchor. 50c, Gabriele d'Annunzio. 1.25 l, St. Vito's Tower. 1.75 l, Symbolizing Fiume's annexation. 2.55 l+2 l, Victor Emmanuel III arriving aboard "Brindisi." 2.75 l+2.50 l, Galley, gondola and battleship.

1934, Mar. 12

315 A166 10c dk brown 8.00 4.00
316 A166 20c rose red 1.60 1.60
317 A166 50c purple 1.60 1.60
318 A166 1.25 l blue 1.60 *6.50*
319 A166 1.75 l + 1 l indigo 1.60 *35.00*
320 A166 2.55 l + 2 l dull vio 1.60 *55.00*
321 A166 2.75 l + 2.50 l ol grn 1.60 *55.00*
Nos. 315-321 (7) 17.60 *158.70*
Set, never hinged 44.00
Nos. 315-321,C56-C61,CE5-CE7 (16) 29.95 *308.60*
Set, never hinged 66.50

10th anniversary of annexation of Fiume.

Antonio Pacinotti — A172

1934, May 23

322 A172 50c purple .80 .40
323 A172 1.25 l sapphire 1.25 *2.75*
Set, never hinged 5.00

75th anniv. of invention of the dynamo by Antonio Pacinotti (1841-1912), scientist.

Guarding the Goal — A173

Players — A175

Soccer Players A174

1934, May 23

324 A173 20c red orange 6.50 *8.00*
325 A174 25c green 6.50 2.40
326 A174 50c purple 6.50 1.25
327 A174 1.25 l blue 16.00 16.00
328 A175 5 l + 2.50 l brn 95.00 *700.00*
Nos. 324-328 (5) 130.50 *727.65*
Set, never hinged 330.00
Nos. 324-328,C62-C65 (9) 264.00 *1,465.*
Set, never hinged 625.00

2nd World Soccer Championship.

For overprints see Aegean Islands Nos. 31-35.

Luigi Galvani — A176

1934, Aug. 16

329 A176 30c brown, *buff* 1.00 .80
330 A176 75c carmine, *rose* 1.40 3.25
Set, never hinged 6.00

Intl. Congress of Electro-Radio-Biology.

Carabinieri Emblem — A177

Cutting Barbed Wire A178

Designs: 20c, Sardinian Grenadier and soldier throwing grenade. 25c, Alpine Infantry. 30c, Military courage. 75c, Artillery. 1.25 l, Acclaiming the Service. 1.75 l+1 l, Cavalry. 2.55 l+2 l, Sapping Detail. 2.75 l+2 l, First aid.

1934, Sept. 6 **Photo.** **Wmk. 140**

331 A177 10c dk brown 2.40 2.40
332 A178 15c olive grn 2.40 *4.00*
333 A178 20c rose red 2.40 1.60
334 A177 25c green 4.00 1.60
335 A178 30c dk brown 4.00 *8.00*
336 A178 50c purple 2.40 .80
337 A178 75c car rose 40.00 12.00
338 A178 1.25 l dk blue 40.00 8.00
339 A177 1.75 l + 1 l red org 17.50 *60.00*
340 A178 2.55 l + 2 l dp cl 17.50 *80.00*
341 A178 2.75 l + 2 l vio 21.00 *80.00*
Nos. 331-341 (11) 153.60 *258.40*
Set, never hinged 385.00
Nos. 331-341,C66-C72 (18) 202.10 *421.40*
Set, never hinged 505.00

Centenary of Military Medal of Valor.

For overprints see Aegean Islands Nos. 36-46.

Man Holding Fasces A187

Standard Bearer, Bayonet Attack A188

Design: 30c, Eagle and soldier.

1935, Apr. 23 ***Perf. 14***

342 A187 20c rose red .80 .80
343 A187 30c dk brown 6.50 16.00
344 A188 50c purple .80 .40
Nos. 342-344 (3) 8.10 17.20
Set, never hinged 20.00

Issued in honor of the University Contests.

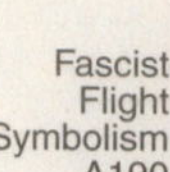

Fascist Flight Symbolism A190

Leonardo da Vinci — A191

1935, Oct. 1

345 A190 20c rose red 20.00 2.00
346 A190 30c brown 35.00 6.50
347 A191 50c purple 72.50 1.25
348 A191 1.25 l dk blue 80.00 7.25
Nos. 345-348 (4) 207.50 17.00
Set, never hinged 830.00

International Aeronautical Salon, Milan.

Vincenzo Bellini — A192

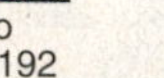

Bellini's Villa — A194

Bellini's Piano A193

1935, Oct. 15

349 A192 20c rose red 16.00 4.00
350 A192 30c brown 24.00 14.50
351 A192 50c violet 24.00 1.60
352 A192 1.25 l dk blue 40.00 20.00
353 A193 1.75 l + 1 l red org 35.00 *325.00*
354 A194 2.75 l + 2 l ol blk 65.00 *340.00*
Nos. 349-354 (6) 204.00 *705.10*
Set, never hinged 510.00
Nos. 349-354,C79-C83 (11) 287.00 *1,022.*
Set, never hinged 710.00

Bellini (1801-35), operatic composer.

Map of Italian Industries A195

Designs: 20c, 1.25 l, Map of Italian Industries. 30c, 50c, Cogwheel and plow.

1936, Mar. 23

355 A195 20c red .80 .40
356 A195 30c brown .80 1.25
357 A195 50c purple .80 .35
358 A195 1.25 l blue 4.75 3.25
Nos. 355-358 (4) 7.15 5.25
Set, never hinged 18.00

The 17th Milan Trade Fair.

Flock of Sheep A197

Ajax Defying the Lightning A199

Bust of Horace A200

Designs: 20c, 1.25 l+1 l, Countryside in Spring. 75c, Capitol. 1.75 l+1 l, Pan piping. 2.55 l+1 l, Dying warrior.

Wmk. Crowns (140)

1936, July 1 Photo. *Perf. 14*

No.	Type	Value / Color	Unused	Used
359	A197	10c dp green	6.50	1.25
360	A197	20c rose red	4.75	.80
361	A199	30c olive brn	6.50	2.40
362	A200	50c purple	6.50	.40
363	A197	75c rose red	16.00	12.00
364	A197	1.25 l + 1 l dk bl	27.50	*160.00*
365	A199	1.75 l + 1 l car rose	32.50	*300.00*
366	A197	2.55 l + 1 l sl blk	40.00	*350.00*
		Nos. 359-366 (8)	140.25	*826.85*
		Set, never hinged	350.00	
		Nos. 359-366,C84-C88 (13)	202.00	*1,153.*
		Set, never hinged	500.00	

2000th anniv. of the birth of Quintus Horatius Flaccus (Horace), Roman poet.

Child Holding Wheat — A204

Child Giving Salute — A205

"Il Bambino" by della Robbia — A207

Child and Fasces — A206

1937, June 28

No.	Type	Value / Color	Unused	Used
367	A204	10c yellow brn	3.25	1.60
368	A205	20c car rose	3.25	1.25
369	A204	25c green	3.25	2.00
370	A206	30c dk brown	4.75	4.00
371	A205	50c purple	3.25	.40
372	A207	75c rose red	16.00	*17.50*
373	A205	1.25 l dk blue	20.00	17.50
374	A206	1.75 l + 75c org	40.00	*250.00*
375	A207	2.75 l + 1.25 l dk bl grn	32.50	*275.00*
376	A205	5 l + 3 l bl gray	40.00	*375.00*
		Nos. 367-376 (10)	166.25	*944.25*
		Set, never hinged	415.00	
		Nos. 367-376,C89-C94 (16)	262.25	*1,378.*
		Set, never hinged	655.00	

Summer Exhibition for Child Welfare. The surtax on Nos. 374-376 was used to support summer camps for children.

Rostral Column — A208

15c, Army Trophies. 20c, Augustus Caesar (Octavianus) offering sacrifice. 25c, Cross Roman Standards. 30c, Julius Caesar and Julian Star. 50c, Augustus receiving acclaim. 75c, Augustus Caesar. 1.25 l, Symbolizing maritime glory of Rome. 1.75 l+1 l, Sacrificial Altar. 2.55 l+2 l, Capitol.

1937, Sept. 23

No.	Type	Value / Color	Unused	Used
377	A208	10c myrtle grn	3.25	.80
378	A208	15c olive grn	3.25	1.25
379	A208	20c red	3.25	.60
380	A208	25c green	3.25	.60
381	A208	30c olive bis	4.00	.80
382	A208	50c purple	3.25	.35
383	A208	75c scarlet	3.25	4.75
384	A208	1.25 l dk blue	8.00	5.50
385	A208	1.75 l + 1 l plum	40.00	*225.00*
386	A208	2.55 l + 2 l sl blk	52.50	*300.00*
		Nos. 377-386 (10)	124.00	*539.65*
		Set, never hinged	300.00	
		Nos. 377-386,C95-C99 (15)	259.00	*812.65*
		Set, never hinged	625.00	

Bimillenary of the birth of Emperor Augustus Caesar (Octavianus) on the occasion of the exhibition opened in Rome by Mussolini, Sept. 22, 1937.

No. 378 exists in violet (error).

For overprints see Aegean Islands Nos. 47-56.

Gaspare Luigi Pacifico Spontini A218

Antonius Stradivarius A219

Count Giacomo Leopardi A220

Giovanni Battista Pergolesi A221

Giotto di Bondone — A222

1937, Oct. 25

No.	Type	Value / Color	Unused	Used
387	A218	10c dk brown	1.60	.80
388	A219	20c rose red	1.60	.80
389	A220	25c dk green	1.60	.80
390	A221	30c dk brown	1.60	1.60
391	A220	50c purple	1.60	.80
392	A221	75c crimson	2.25	*4.75*
393	A222	1.25 l dp blue	3.25	*4.75*
394	A218	1.75 l dp orange	3.25	*4.75*
395	A219	2.55 l + 2 l gray grn	16.00	*260.00*
396	A222	2.75 l + 2 l red brn	16.00	*300.00*
		Nos. 387-396 (10)	48.75	*579.05*
		Set, never hinged	125.00	

Centennials of Spontini, Stradivarius, Leopardi, Pergolesi and Giotto.

For overprints see Aegean Islands Nos. 57-58.

Guglielmo Marconi — A223

1938, Jan. 24

No.	Type	Value / Color	Unused	Used
397	A223	20c rose pink	3.25	.80
398	A223	50c purple	.80	.40
399	A223	1.25 l blue	3.25	6.75
		Nos. 397-399 (3)	7.30	7.95
		Set, never hinged	18.00	

Guglielmo Marconi (1874-1937), electrical engineer, inventor of wireless telegraphy.

Augustus Caesar (Octavianus) A224

10c, Romulus Plowing. 25c, Dante. 30c, Columbus. 50c, Leonardo da Vinci. 75c, Victor Emmanuel II and Garibaldi. 1.25 l, Tomb of Unknown Soldier, Rome. 1.75 l, Blackshirts' March on Rome, 1922. 2.75 l, Map of Italian East Africa and Iron Crown of Monza. 5 l, Victor Emmanuel III.

1938, Oct. 28

No.	Type	Value / Color	Unused	Used
400	A224	10c brown	2.40	.80
401	A224	20c car rose	2.40	.80
402	A224	25c dk green	2.40	.80
403	A224	30c olive brn	2.40	2.00
404	A224	50c lt violet	2.40	.80
405	A224	75c rose red	3.25	3.25
406	A224	1.25 l dp blue	6.50	3.25
407	A224	1.75 l vio blk	8.00	4.00
408	A224	2.75 l slate grn	27.50	*47.50*
409	A224	5 l lt red brn	32.50	*52.50*
		Nos. 400-409 (10)	89.75	*115.70*
		Set, never hinged	220.00	
		Nos. 400-409,C100-C105 (16)	143.25	*284.20*
		Set, never hinged	350.00	

Proclamation of the Empire.

Wood-burning Engine and Streamlined Electric Engine — A234

1939, Dec. 15 Photo. *Perf. 14*

No.	Type	Value / Color	Unused	Used
410	A234	20c rose red	.80	.60
411	A234	50c brt violet	1.60	.80
412	A234	1.25 l dp blue	4.00	4.00
		Nos. 410-412 (3)	6.40	5.40
		Set, never hinged	16.00	

Centenary of Italian railroads.

Adolf Hitler and Benito Mussolini A235

Hitler and Mussolini A236

1941 Wmk. 140

No.	Type	Value / Color	Unused	Used
413	A235	10c dp brown	2.00	2.10
414	A235	20c red orange	2.00	2.10
415	A235	25c dp green	6.50	2.10
416	A236	50c violet	5.00	2.10
417	A236	75c rose red	6.50	5.50
418	A236	1.25 l deep blue	8.00	7.00
		Nos. 413-418 (6)	30.00	20.90
		Set, never hinged	65.00	

Rome-Berlin Axis.

Stamps of type A236 in the denominations and colors of Nos. 413-415 were prepared but not issued. They were sold for charitable purposes in 1948. Value $35 each.

Galileo Teaching Mathematics at Padua — A237

Designs: 25c, Galileo presenting telescope to Doge of Venice. 50c, Galileo Galilei (1564-1642). 1.25 l, Galileo studying at Arcetri.

1942, Sept. 28

No.	Type	Value / Color	Unused	Used
419	A237	10c dk org & lake	.65	.90
420	A237	25c gray grn & grn	.65	.90
421	A237	50c brn vio & vio	.65	.90
a.		Frame missing	*1,750.*	
422	A237	1.25 l Prus bl & ultra	.65	2.50
		Nos. 419-422 (4)	2.60	5.20
		Set, never hinged	5.00	

Statue of Rossini — A241

Gioacchino Rossini — A242

1942, Nov. 23 Photo.

No.	Type	Value / Color	Unused	Used
423	A241	25c deep green	.70	.45
424	A241	30c brown	.70	.45
425	A242	50c violet	.70	.45
426	A242	1 l blue	1.00	1.40
		Nos. 423-426 (4)	3.10	2.75
		Set, never hinged	5.00	

Gioacchino Antonio Rossini (1792-1868), operatic composer.

"Victory for the Axis" A243

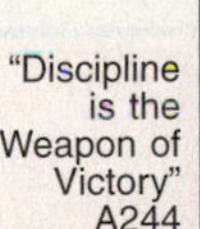

"Discipline is the Weapon of Victory" A244

"Everything and Everyone for Victory" A245

"Arms and Hearts Must Be Stretched Out Towards the Goal" A246

Perf. 14 all around, Imperf. between

1942 Photo. Wmk. 140

No.	Type	Value / Color	Unused	Used
427	A243	25c deep green	.35	*.85*
428	A244	25c deep green	.35	*.85*
429	A245	25c deep green	.35	*.85*
430	A246	25c deep green	.35	*.85*

431 A243 30c olive brown .35 *3.50*
432 A244 30c olive brown .35 *3.50*
433 A245 30c olive brown .35 *3.50*
434 A246 30c olive brown .35 *3.50*
435 A243 50c purple .35 *.90*
436 A244 50c purple .35 *.90*
437 A245 50c purple .35 *.90*
438 A246 50c purple .35 *.90*
Nos. 427-438 (12) 4.20 *21.00*
Set, never hinged 10.00

Issued in honor of the Italian Army.
The left halves of Nos. 431-438 are type A95.
For overprints see Italian Social Republic Nos. 6-17.

She-Wolf Suckling Romulus and Remus — A247

Perf. 10½x11½, 11x11½, 11½, 14
1944, Jan. Litho. Wmk. 87
Without Gum
439 A247 50c rose vio & bis rose 2.00 *3.25*
Unwmk.
440 A247 50c rose vio & pale rose .30 *1.40*

Nos. 439-440 exist imperf., part perf.
No. 440 exists with triple impression. Value, $500.

Types of 1929
1945, May Unwmk. *Perf. 14*
441 A93 15c slate green .25 .25
442 A93 35c deep blue .25 .25
443 A91 1 l deep violet .35 .25
Nos. 441-443 (3) .85 .75
Set, never hinged 2.00

Types of 1929 Redrawn
Fasces Removed

Victor Emmanuel III A248

Julius Caesar A249

Augustus Caesar A250

"Italia" A251

A252

1944-45 Wmk. 140 Photo. *Perf. 14*
444 A248 30c dk brown .35 .25
445 A248 50c purple 2.50 *2.10*
446 A248 60c slate grn ('45) .35 .70
447 A249 1 l dp violet ('45) .35 .25
Nos. 444-447 (4) 3.55 3.30
Set, never hinged 6.50

1945 Unwmk. *Perf. 14*
448 A250 10c dk brown .50 *.70*
448A A249 20c rose red .25 .35
449 A251 50c dk violet .25 .25
450 A248 60c slate grn .25 .25
451 A251 60c red org .25 .35
452 A249 1 l dp violet .25 .25
452A A249 1 l dp vio, redrawn .25 .25
452B A251 2 l dp car 1.25 .75
452C A251 10 l purple 4.00 *7.50*
Nos. 448-452C (9) 7.25 *10.65*
Set, never hinged 15.00

1945 Wmk. 277
453 A249 20c rose red .25 *.60*
454 A248 60c slate grn .25 *.60*
455 A249 1 l dp violet .25 *.60*
456 A251 1.20 l dk brown .25 *.60*

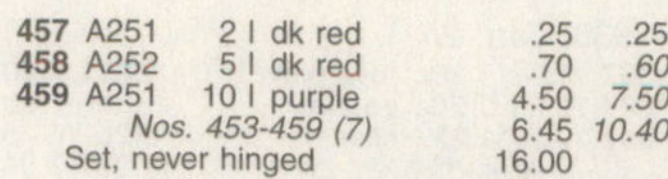

457 A251 2 l dk red .25 .25
458 A252 5 l dk red .70 *.60*
459 A251 10 l purple 4.50 *7.50*
Nos. 453-459 (7) 6.45 *10.40*
Set, never hinged 16.00

Nos. 452A and 457 are redrawings of types A249 and A251. In the redrawn 1 l, the "L" of "LIRE" extends under the "IRE" and the letters of "POSTE ITALIANE" are larger. In the original the "L" extends only under the "I."
In the redrawn 2 l, the "2" is smaller and thinner, and the design is less distinct.
For overprints see Nos. 1LN2-1LN8.

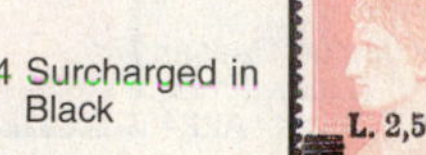

No. 224 Surcharged in Black

1945, Mar. Wmk. 140
460 A92 2.50 l on 1.75 l red org .25 *.50*
Never hinged .30
a. Six bars at left 2.50 3.75

Italian Social Republic Nos. 18-19 Surcharged in Black

No. 18

No. 19

1945, May 2 Photo. *Perf. 14*
461 A1 1.20 l on 20c crim .25 .25
462 A2 2 l on 25c green .25 .25
a. 2½ mm between "2" and "LIRE" 2.75 5.50
Set, never hinged .75

Breaking Chain A255

United Family and Scales A256

Planting Tree — A257

Tying Tree — A258

Torch A259

"Italia" and Sprouting Oak Stump A260

1945-47 Wmk. 277 Photo. *Perf. 14*
463 A255 10c rose brown .25 .25
464 A256 20c dk brown .25 .25
464A A259 25c brt bl grn ('46) .25 .25
465 A257 40c slate .25 .25
465A A255 50c dp vio ('46) .25 .25
466 A258 60c dk green .25 *.40*
467 A255 80c car rose .25 .25
468 A257 1 l dk green .25 .25
469 A259 1.20 l chestnut .25 *.90*
470 A258 2 l dk claret brn .25 .30
471 A259 3 l red .25 .25
471A A259 4 l red org ('46) .25 .25
472 A256 5 l deep blue .35 .25

472A A257 6 l dp vio ('47) 7.50 .25
473 A255 10 l slate 1.20 .25
473A A257 15 l dp bl ('46) 8.00 .25
474 A259 20 l dk red vio 3.00 .25
475 A260 25 l dk grn 20.00 .25
476 A260 50 l dk vio brn 8.50 .25
Nos. 463-476 (19) 51.55 5.60
Set, never hinged 175.00

See Nos. 486-488.
For overprints see Nos. 1LN11-1LN12, 1LN14-1LN19, Trieste 1-13, 15-17, 30-32, 58-68, 82-83.

United Family and Scales A261

1946, July 29 Engr. *Perf. 14*
477 A261 100 l car lake 160.00 1.75
Never hinged 400.00
a. Perf. 14x13½ 350.00 2.50
Never hinged 500.00

For overprints see No. 1LN13, Trieste Nos. 14, 69.
Forgeries exist perf. 11¼ and perf. 11½ on unwatermarked paper.

Cathedral of St. Andrea, Amalfi — A262

Church of St. Michael, Lucca — A263

"Peace" from Fresco at Siena A264

Signoria Palace, Florence A265

View of Cathedral Domes, Pisa A266

Republic of Genoa A267

"Venice Crowned by Glory," by Paolo Veronese A268

Oath of Pontida A269

1946, Oct. 30
478 A262 1 l brown .25 .25
479 A263 2 l dk blue .25 .25
480 A264 3 l dk bl grn .25 .25
481 A265 4 l dp org .25 .25
482 A266 5 l dp violet .25 .25
483 A267 10 l car rose .25 .25
484 A268 15 l dp ultra 1.25 1.00
485 A269 20 l red brown .25 .25
Nos. 478-485 (8) 3.00 2.75
Set, never hinged 2.75

Proclamation of the Republic.

Types of 1945
1947-48 Wmk. 277 Photo. *Perf. 14*
486 A255 8 l dk green ('48) 4.00 .25
487 A256 10 l red orange 24.00 .25
488 A259 30 l dk blue ('48) 150.00 .25
Nos. 486-488 (3) 178.00 .75
Set, never hinged 450.00

St. Catherine Giving Mantle to Beggar — A270

5 l, St. Catherine carrying cross. 10 l, St. Catherine, arms outstretched. 30 l, St. Catherine & scribe.

1948, Mar. 1 Photo.
489 A270 3 l yel grn & gray grn .25 .35
490 A270 5 l vio & bl .25 .35
491 A270 10 l red brn & vio 1.25 *3.25*
492 A270 30 l bis & gray brn 9.00 *22.50*
Nos. 489-492 (4) 10.75 *26.45*
Set, never hinged 25.00
Nos. 489-492,C127-C128 (6) 83.25 90.45
Set, never hinged 140.00

600th anniv. of the birth of St. Catherine of Siena, Patroness of Italy.

"Constitutional Government" — A271

1948, Apr. 12
493 A271 10 l rose vio .70 *.85*
494 A271 30 l blue 1.50 *2.50*
Set, never hinged 6.00

Proclamation of the constitution of 1/1/48.

Uprising at Palermo, Jan. 12, 1848 A272

Designs (Revolutionary scenes): 4 l, Rebellion at Padua. 5 l, Proclamation of statute, Turin. 6 l, "Five Days of Milan." 8 l, Daniele Manin proclaming the Republic of Venice. 10 l, Defense of Vicenza. 12 l, Battle of Curtatone. 15 l, Battle of Gioto. 20 l, Insurrection at Bologna. 30 l, "Ten Days of Brescia." 50 l, Garibaldi in Rome fighting. 100 l, Death of Goffredo Mameli.

1948, May 3
495 A272 3 l dk brown .65 *1.00*
496 A272 4 l red violet .65 *1.00*
497 A272 5 l dp blue 3.25 1.00
498 A272 6 l dp yel grn 1.00 1.00
499 A272 8 l brown 1.00 1.15
500 A272 10 l orange red 1.25 1.00
501 A272 12 l dk gray grn 3.75 3.00
502 A272 15 l gray blk 9.00 2.00
503 A272 20 l car rose 20.00 10.00
504 A272 30 l brt ultra 6.25 2.50
505 A272 50 l violet 45.00 6.00
506 A272 100 l blue blk 55.00 22.50
Nos. 495-506 (12) 146.80 *52.15*
Set, never hinged 405.00
Nos. 495-506,E26 (13) 191.80 74.65
Set, never hinged 540.00

Centenary of the Risorgimento, uprisings of 1848-49 which led to Italian unification.
For overprints see Trieste Nos. 18-29, E5.

Alpine Soldier and Bassano Bridge A273

1948, Oct. 1 Wmk. 277 *Perf. 14*

507 A273 15 l dark green	1.50	*1.75*
Never hinged	3.00	

Bridge of Bassano, re-opening, Oct. 3, 1948.
For overprint see Trieste No. 33.

Gaetano Donizetti — A274

1948, Oct. 23 Photo.

508 A274 15 l dark brown	1.15	*2.10*
Never hinged	2.25	

Death cent. of Gaetano Donizetti, composer.
For overprint see Trieste No. 34.

Fair Buildings A275

1949, Apr. 12

509 A275 20 l dark brown	3.00	*3.75*
Never hinged	8.00	

27th Milan Trade Fair, April 1949.
For overprint see Trieste No. 35.

Standard of Doges of Venice — A276

15 l, Clock strikers, Lion Tower and Campanile of St. Mark's. 20 l, Lion standard and Venetian galley. 50 l, Lion tower and gulls.

1949, Apr. 12 Buff Background

510 A276 5 l red brown	.55	.25
511 A276 15 l dk green	2.00	2.25
512 A276 20 l dp red brn	4.25	.25
513 A276 50 l dk blue	20.00	2.50
Nos. 510-513 (4)	26.80	5.25
Set, never hinged	65.00	

Biennial Art Exhibition of Venice, 50th anniv.
For overprints see Trieste Nos. 36-39.

"Transportation" and Globes — A277

1949, May 2 Wmk. 277 *Perf. 14*

514 A277 50 l brt ultra	20.00	7.50
Never hinged	45.00	

75th anniv. of the UPU.
For overprint see Trieste No. 40.

Workman and Ship — A278

1949, May 30 Photo.

515 A278 5 l dk green	6.00	*6.50*
516 A278 15 l violet	11.50	*17.50*
517 A278 20 l brown	21.00	17.50
Nos. 515-517 (3)	38.50	*41.50*
Set, never hinged	80.00	

European Recovery Program.
For overprints see Trieste Nos. 42-44.

The Vascello, Rome A279

1949, May 18

518 A279 100 l brown	110.00	100.00
Never hinged	225.00	

Centenary of Roman Republic.
For overprint see Trieste No. 41.

Giuseppe Mazzini — A280

1949, June 1

519 A280 20 l gray	3.75	4.50
Never hinged	11.50	

Erection of a monument to Giuseppe Mazzini (1805-72), Italian patriot and revolutionary.
For overprint see Trieste No. 45.

Vittorio Alfieri — A281

1949, June 4 Photo.

520 A281 20 l brown	3.00	3.50
Never hinged	8.00	

200th anniv. of the birth of Vittorio Alfieri, tragic dramatist.
For overprint see Trieste No. 46.

Basilica of St. Just, Trieste A282

1949, June 8

521 A282 20 l brown red	8.00	*17.00*
Never hinged	12.00	

Trieste election, June 12, 1949.
For overprint see Trieste No. 47.

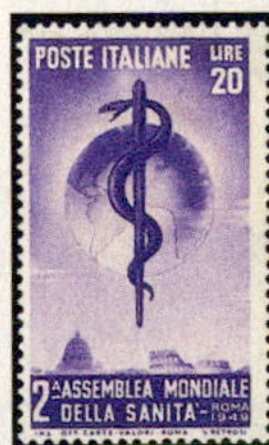

Staff of Aesculapius, Globe — A283

1949, June 13 Wmk. 277 *Perf. 14*

522 A283 20 l violet	12.50	12.50
Never hinged	32.50	

2nd World Health Cong., Rome, 1949.
For overprint see Trieste No. 49.

Lorenzo de Medici — A284

1949, Aug. 4

523 A284 20 l violet blue	3.25	3.75
Never hinged	10.00	

Birth of Lorenzo de Medici, 500th anniv.
For overprint see Trieste No. 50.

Andrea Palladio — A285

1949, Aug. 4

524 A285 20 l violet	5.00	*8.00*
Never hinged	12.50	

Andrea Palladio (1518-1580), architect.
For overprint see Trieste No. 51.

Tartan and Fair Buildings A286

1949, Aug. 16

525 A286 20 l red	2.60	*3.00*
Never hinged	7.00	

133th Levant Fair, Bari, September, 1949.
For overprint see Trieste No. 52.

Voltaic Pile — A287

Alessandro Volta — A288

1949, Sept. 14 Engr. *Perf. 14*

526 A287 20 l rose car	3.00	2.00
a. Perf. 13x14	12.00	9.50
527 A288 50 l deep blue	30.00	27.50
a. Perf. 13x14	300.00	75.00
Set, never hinged	97.50	

Invention of the Voltaic Pile, 150th anniv.
For overprints see Trieste Nos. 53-54.

Holy Trinity Bridge — A289

1949, Sept. 19 Photo.

528 A289 20 l deep green	3.25	3.25
Never hinged	7.50	

Issued to publicize plans to reconstruct Holy Trinity Bridge, Florence.
For overprint see Trieste No. 55.

Gaius Valerius Catullus — A290

1949, Sept. 19 Wmk. 277 *Perf. 14*

529 A290 20 l brt blue	4.00	3.50
Never hinged	10.00	

2000th anniversary of the death of Gaius Valerius Catullus, Lyric poet.
For overprint see Trieste No. 56.

Domenico Cimarosa — A291

1949, Dec. 28

530 A291 20 l violet blk	3.25	2.75
Never hinged	9.00	

Bicentenary of the birth of Domenico Cimarosa, composer.
For overprint see Trieste No. 57.

Milan Fair Scene A292

1950, Apr. 12 Photo.

531 A292 20 l brown	2.00	3.00
Never hinged	3.50	

The 28th Milan Trade Fair.
For overprint see Trieste No. 70.

Flags and Italian Automobile A293

1950, Apr. 29

532 A293 20 l vio gray	3.50	2.50
Never hinged	10.00	

32nd Intl. Auto Show, Turin, May 4-14, 1950.
For overprint see Trieste No. 71.

Pitti Palace, Florence A294

"Perseus" by Cellini — A295

1950, May 22

533 A294 20 l olive grn	3.00	3.00
534 A295 55 l blue	25.00	16.50
Set, never hinged	70.00	

5th General Conf. of UNESCO.
For overprints see Trieste Nos. 72-73.

Composite of Italian Cathedrals and Churches — A296

1950, May 29

535 A296 20 l violet	5.00	.75
536 A296 55 l blue	27.50	3.00
Set, never hinged	85.00	

Holy Year, 1950.

For overprints see Trieste Nos. 74-75.

Gaudenzio Ferrari — A297

1950, July 1 Wmk. 277 *Perf. 14*
537 A297 20 l gray grn 6.50 3.25
Never hinged 17.50

Issued to honor Gaudenzio Ferrari.
For overprint see Trieste No. 76.

Radio Mast and Tower of Florence — A298

1950, July 15 Photo.
538 A298 20 l purple 9.00 5.00
539 A298 55 l blue 70.00 *80.00*
Set, never hinged 175.00

Intl. Shortwave Radio Conf., Florence, 1950.
For overprints Trieste see Nos. 77-78.

Ludovico A. Muratori — A299

1950, July 22
540 A299 20 l brown 2.25 2.60
Never hinged 6.75

200th anniv. of the death of Ludovico A. Muratori, writer.
For overprint see Trieste No. 79.

Guido d'Arezzo — A300

1950, July 29
541 A300 20 l dark green 6.50 3.00
Never hinged 20.00

900th anniv. of the death of Guido d'Arezzo, music teacher and composer.
For overprint see Trieste No. 80.

Tartan and Fair Buildings A301

1950, Aug. 21
542 A301 20 l chestnut brown 3.75 2.60
Never hinged 12.50

Levant Fair, Bari, September, 1950.
For overprint see Trieste No. 81.

G. Marzotto and A. Rossi — A302

1950, Sept. 11
543 A302 20 l indigo 2.00 2.00
Never hinged 3.50

Pioneers of the Italian wool industry.
For overprint see Trieste No. 84.

Tobacco Plant — A303

Designs: 20 l, Mature plant, different background. 55 l, Girl holding tobacco plant.

1950, Sept. 11
544 A303 5 l dp claret & grn 2.00 *3.00*
545 A303 20 l brown & grn 2.75 1.00
546 A303 55 l dp ultra & brn 32.50 25.00
Nos. 544-546 (3) 37.25 29.00
Set, never hinged 80.00

Issued to publicize the European Tobacco Conference, Rome, 1950.
For overprints see Trieste Nos. 85-87.

Arms of the Academy of Fine Arts — A304

1950, Sept. 16
547 A304 20 l ol brn & red brn 2.00 2.60
Never hinged 5.00

200th anniv. of the founding of the Academy of Fine Arts, Venice.
For overprint see Trieste No. 88.

Augusto Righi — A305

1950, Sept. 16
548 A305 20 l cream & gray blk 2.00 2.75
Never hinged 5.00

Centenary of the birth of Augusto Righi, physicist.
For overprint see Trieste No. 89.

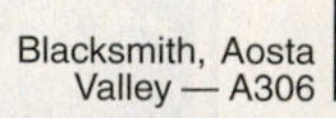
Blacksmith, Aosta Valley — A306

Designs: 1 l, Auto mechanic. 2 l, Mason. 5 l, Potter. 6 l, Lace-making. 10 l, Weaving, 12 l, Sailor steering boat. 15 l, Shipbuilding. 20 l, Fisherman. 25 l, Sorting oranges. 30 l, Woman carrying grapes. 35 l, Olive picking. 40 l, Wine cart. 50 l, Shepherd and flock. 55 l, Plowing. 60 l, Grain cart. 65 l, Girl worker in hemp field. 100 l, Husking corn. 200 l, Woodcutter.

1950, Oct. 20 Wmk. 277 *Perf. 14*
549 A306 50c vio blue .25 .25
550 A306 1 l dk bl vio .25 .25
551 A306 2 l sepia .25 .25
552 A306 5 l dk gray .25 .25
553 A306 6 l chocolate .25 .25
554 A306 10 l dp green 3.25 .25
555 A306 12 l dp blue grn 1.75 .25
556 A306 15 l dk gray bl 1.50 .25
557 A306 20 l blue vio 9.00 .25
558 A306 25 l brn org 1.25 .25
559 A306 30 l magenta 1.25 .25
560 A306 35 l crimson 6.50 1.00
561 A306 40 l brown .50 .25
562 A306 50 l violet 12.00 .25
563 A306 55 l dp blue .75 .25
564 A306 60 l red 2.10 .25
565 A306 65 l dk grn 1.00 .25

Perf. 13x14, 14x13
Engr.
566 A306 100 l brn org 27.50 .35
a. Perf. 13 27.50 .25
b. Perf. 14 30.00 .25
567 A306 200 l ol brn 8.00 3.00
a. Perf. 14 8.00 3.00
Nos. 549-567 (19) 77.60 8.35
Set, never hinged 190.00

See Nos. 668-673A. For overprints see Trieste Nos. 90-108, 122-124, 178-180.

1851 Stamp of Tuscany — A307

Design: 55 l, Tuscany 6cr.

1951, Mar. 27 Photo. *Perf. 14*
568 A307 20 l red vio & red 1.50 .95
569 A307 55 l ultra & blue 18.00 37.50
Set, never hinged 45.00

Centenary of Tuscany's first stamps.
For overprints see Trieste Nos. 109-110.

Italian Automobile A308

1951, Apr. 2
570 A308 20 l dk green 4.50 3.50
Never hinged 12.50

33rd Intl. Automobile Exhib., Turin, Apr. 4-15, 1951.
For overprint see Trieste No. 111.

Altar of Peace, Medea A309

1951, Apr. 11
571 A309 20 l blue vio 2.50 3.00
Never hinged 8.00

Consecration of the Altar of Peace at Redipuglia Cemetery, Medea.
For overprint see Trieste No. 112.

Helicopter over Leonardo da Vinci Heliport — A310

P. T. T. Building, Milan Fair — A311

1951, Apr. 12 Photo.
572 A310 20 l brown 8.00 1.90
573 A311 55 l dp blue 27.50 *55.00*
Set, never hinged 85.00

29th Milan Trade Fair.
For overprints see Trieste Nos. 113-114.

Symbols of the International Gymnastic Festival — A312

Wmk. 277
1951, May 18 Photo. *Perf. 14*
Fleur-de-lis in Red
574 A312 5 l dk brown 20.00 *500.00*
575 A312 10 l Prus green 20.00 *500.00*
576 A312 15 l vio blue 20.00 *500.00*
Nos. 574-576 (3) 60.00 *1,500.*
Set, never hinged 80.00

International Gymnastic Festival and Meet, Florence, 1951.
Fake cancellations exist on Nos. 574-576.
For overprints see Trieste Nos. 115-117.

Statue of Diana, Spindle and Turin Tower — A313

1951, Apr. 26
577 A313 20 l purple 9.50 4.25
Never hinged 24.00

Tenth International Exhibition of Textile Art and Fashion, Turin, May 2-16.
For overprint see Trieste No. 118.

Landing of Columbus A314

1951, May 5
578 A314 20 l Prus green 5.00 4.00
Never hinged 15.00

500th anniversary of birth of Columbus.
For overprint see Trieste No. 119.

Reconstructed Abbey of Montecassino — A315

Design: 55 l, Montecassino Ruins.

1951, June 18
579 A315 20 l violet 3.00 1.90
580 A315 55 l brt blue 30.00 50.00
Set, never hinged 82.50

Issued to commemorate the reconstruction of the Abbey of Montecassino.
For overprints see Trieste Nos. 120-121.

Pietro Vannucci (Il Perugino) — A316

1951, July 23
581 A316 20 l brn & red brn 3.00 *2.50*
Never hinged 4.00

500th anniversary (in 1950) of the birth of Pietro Vannucci, painter.
For overprint see Trieste No. 125.

Stylized Vase — A317

Cartouche of Amenhotep III and Pitcher A318

1951, July 23
582 A317 20 l grnsh gray & blk 7.00 3.75
583 A318 55 l vio bl & pale sal 24.00 40.00
Set, never hinged 40.00

Triennial Art Exhibition, Milan, 1951.
For overprints see Trieste Nos. 126-127.

Cyclist — A319

1951, Aug. 23
584 A319 25 l gray black 4.50 4.50
Never hinged 9.00

World Bicycle Championship Races, Milan, Aug.-Sept. 1951.
For overprint see Trieste No. 128.

Tartan and Globes A320

1951, Sept. 8 **Photo.**
585 A320 25 l deep blue 2.50 3.00
Never hinged 6.50

15th Levant Fair, Bari, September 1951.
For overprint see Trieste No. 129.

"La Figlia di Jorio" by Michetti A321

1951, Sept. 15 **Wmk. 277** ***Perf. 14***
586 A321 25 l dk brown 3.00 3.00
Never hinged 7.50

Centenary of the birth of Francesco Paolo Michetti, painter.
For overprint see Trieste No. 130.

Sardinia Stamps of 1851 A322

1951, Oct. 5
587 A322 10 l shown 2.00 3.00
588 A322 25 l 20c stamp 1.60 1.50
589 A322 60 l 40c stamp 8.50 *10.00*
Nos. 587-589 (3) 12.10 14.50
Set, never hinged 16.00

Centenary of Sardinia's 1st postage stamp.
For overprints see Trieste Nos. 131-133.

Mercury — A323

Roman Census A324

1951, Oct. 31
590 A323 10 l green 1.00 1.50
591 A324 25 l vio gray 1.00 1.50
Set, never hinged 6.00

3rd Industrial and the 9th General Italian Census.
For overprints see Trieste Nos. 134-135.

Winter Scene — A325

Trees A326

1951, Nov. 21
592 A325 10 l ol & dl grn 2.00 *3.00*
593 A326 25 l dull grn 4.50 2.00
Set, never hinged 8.00

Issued to publicize the Festival of Trees.
For overprints see Trieste Nos. 136-137.

Giuseppe Verdi A327

Portraits of Verdi, various backgrounds.

1951, Nov. 19 **Engr.**
594 A327 10 l vio brn & dk grn 2.00 *3.75*
595 A327 25 l red brn & dk brn 5.00 1.50
596 A327 60 l dp grn & indigo 20.00 19.00
Nos. 594-596 (3) 27.00 24.25
Set, never hinged 50.00

50th anniversary of the death of Giuseppe Verdi, composer.
For overprints see Trieste Nos. 138-140.

Vincenzo Bellini — A328

Wmk. 277
1952, Jan. 28 **Photo.** ***Perf. 14***
597 A328 25 l gray & gray blk 1.60 1.50
Never hinged 5.00

150th anniversary of the birth of Vincenzo Bellini, composer.
For overprint see Trieste No. 141.

Palace of Caserta and Statuary A329

1952, Feb. 1
598 A329 25 l dl grn & ol bis 1.25 1.15
Never hinged 4.00

Issued to honor Luigi Vanvitelli, architect.
For overprint see Trieste No. 142.

Statues of Athlete and River God Tiber — A330

1952, Mar. 22
599 A330 25 l brn & sl blk .75 1.05
Never hinged 1.75

Issued on the occasion of the first International Exhibition of Sports Stamps.
For overprint see Trieste No. 143.

Milan Fair Buildings A331

1952, Apr. 12 **Engr.**
600 A331 60 l ultra 22.50 20.00
Never hinged 45.00

30th Milan Trade Fair.
For overprint see Trieste No. 144.

Leonardo da Vinci — A332

Virgin of the Rocks — A332a

1952 **Wmk. 277** **Photo.** ***Perf. 14***
601 A332 25 l deep orange .25 .25

Unwmk.
Engr. ***Perf. 13***
601A A332a 60 l ultra 2.25 *8.75*

Wmk. 277
601B A332 80 l brn car 11.50 .40
c. Perf. 14x13 25.00 .40
Set, never hinged 35.00

Leonardo da Vinci, 500th birth anniv.
For overprints see Trieste Nos. 145, 163-164.

First Stamps and Cathedral Bell Towers of Modena and Parma A333

1952, May 29 ***Perf. 14***
602 A333 25 l blk & red brn 1.00 1.00
603 A333 60 l blk & ultra 4.00 *12.00*
Set, never hinged 8.50

Cent. of the 1st postage stamps of Modena and Parma.
For overprints see Trieste Nos. 146-147.

Globe and Torch — A334

1952, June 7
604 A334 25 l bright blue .85 1.00
Never hinged 2.00

Issued to honor the Overseas Fair at Naples and Italian labor throughout the world.
For overprint see Trieste No. 148.

Lion of St. Mark — A335

1952, June 14
605 A335 25 l black & yellow 1.00 .90
Never hinged 2.50

26th Biennial Art Exhibition, Venice.
For overprint see Trieste No. 149.

"P" and Basilica of St. Anthony — A336

1952, June 19
606 A336 25 l bl gray, red & dk bl 1.75 1.00
Never hinged 5.00

30th International Sample Fair of Padua.
For overprint see Trieste No. 150.

Flag and Basilica of St. Just — A337

1952, June 28
607 A337 25 l dp grn, dk brn & red 1.20 1.20
Never hinged 2.75

4th International Sample Fair of Trieste.
For overprint see Trieste No. 151.

Fair Entrance and Tartan A338

1952, Sept. 6 **Wmk. 277** ***Perf. 14***
608 A338 25 l dark green .75 .70
Never hinged 1.75

16th Levant Fair, Bari, Sept. 1952.
For overprint see Trieste No. 152.

Girolamo Savonarola — A339

1952, Sept. 20

609 A339 25 l purple 1.50 .95
Never hinged 3.25

500th anniversary of the birth of Girolamo Savonarola.
For overprint see Trieste No. 153.

Mountain Peak and Climbing Equipment — A340

1952, Oct. 4

610 A340 25 l gray .55 .55
Never hinged 1.00

Issued to publicize the National Exhibition of the Alpine troops, Oct. 4, 1952.
For overprint see Trieste No. 154.

Colosseum and Plane A341

1952, Sept. 29

611 A341 60 l vio bl & dk bl 3.00 *10.00*
Never hinged 5.50

Issued to publicize the first International Civil Aviation Conference, Rome, Sept. 1952.
For overprint see Trieste No. 155.

Guglielmo Cardinal Massaia and Map A342

1952, Nov. 21 Engr. *Perf. 13*

612 A342 25 l brn & dk brn .80 *.80*
Never hinged 1.75

Centenary of the establishment of the first Catholic mission in Ethiopia.
For overprint see Trieste No. 156.

Symbols of Army, Navy and Air Force A343

Sailor, Soldier and Aviator A344

Design: 60 l, Boat, plane and tank.

1952, Nov. 3 Photo. *Perf. 14*

613 A343 10 l dk green .25 .25
614 A344 25 l blk & dk brn .40 .25
615 A344 60 l black & blue 3.50 *5.50*
Nos. 613-615 (3) 4.15 6.00
Set, never hinged 8.00

Armed Forces Day, Nov. 4, 1952.
For overprints see Trieste Nos. 157-159.

Antonio Mancini — A345

Vincenzo Gemito — A346

1952, Dec. 6

616 A345 25 l dark green .45 *.75*
617 A346 25 l brown .45 *.75*
Set, never hinged 1.75

Birth centenaries of Antonio Mancini, painter, and Vincenzo Gemito, sculptor.
For overprints see Trieste Nos. 160-161.

Martyrs, Jailer and Artist Boldini A347

1952, Dec. 31

618 A347 25 l gray blk & dk blue .75 .75
Never hinged 2.25

Centenary of the deaths of the five Martyrs of Belfiore.
For overprint see Trieste No. 162.

Antonello da Messina — A349

1953, Feb. 21 Photo. *Perf. 14*

621 A349 25 l car lake .75 .75
Never hinged 2.00

Messina Exhibition of the paintings of Antonello and his 15th cent. contemporaries.
For overprint see Trieste No. 165.

Racing Cars A350

1953, Apr. 24

622 A350 25 l violet .50 .50
Never hinged 1.00

20th 1,000-mile auto race.
For overprint see Trieste No. 166.

Decoration "Knights of Labor" Bee and Honeycomb — A351

1953, Apr. 30

623 A351 25 l violet .50 *.50*
Never hinged .90

For overprint see Trieste No. 167.

Arcangelo Corelli — A352

1953, May 30

624 A352 25 l dark brown .50 *.50*
Never hinged 1.00

300th anniv. of the birth of Arcangelo Corelli, composer.
For overprint see Trieste No. 168.

St. Clare of Assisi and Convent of St. Damien — A353

1953, June 27

625 A353 25 l brown & dull red .35 *.45*
Never hinged .65

St. Clare of Assisi, 700th death anniv.
For overprint see Trieste No. 169.

"Italia" after Syracusean Coin — A354

Size: 17x21mm

1953-54 Wmk. 277 *Perf. 14*

626 A354 5 l gray .25 .25
627 A354 10 l org ver .25 .25
628 A354 12 l dull green .25 .25
628A A354 13 l brt lil rose ('54) .25 .25
629 A354 20 l brown 2.00 .25
630 A354 25 l purple 2.00 .25
631 A354 35 l rose car .60 .25
632 A354 60 l blue 15.00 5.00
633 A354 80 l orange brn 32.50 .25
Nos. 626-633 (9) 53.10 7.00
Set, never hinged 100.00

See Nos. 661-662, 673B-689, 785-788, 998A-998W, 1288-1290. For overprints see Trieste Nos. 170-177.

Mountain Peaks — A355

1953, July 11

634 A355 25 l grnsh blue .45 .45
Never hinged 1.25

Festival of the Mountain.
For overprint see Trieste No. 181.

Tyche, Goddess of Fortune — A356

1953, July 16

635 A356 25 l dark brown .45 .25
636 A356 60 l deep blue 2.25 *3.25*
Set, never hinged 6.00

Intl. Exposition of Agriculture, Rome, 1953.
For overprints see Trieste Nos. 182-183.

Continents Joined by Rainbow A357

1953, Aug. 6

637 A357 25 l org & Prus bl 1.25 .25
638 A357 60 l lil rose & dk vio bl 3.50 3.50
Set, never hinged 12.00

Signing of the North Atlantic Treaty, 4th anniv.
For overprints see Trieste Nos. 184-185.

Luca Signorelli — A358

1953, Aug. 13

639 A358 25 l dk brn & dull grn .40 .40
Never hinged .90

Issued to publicize the opening of an exhibition of the works of Luca Signorelli, painter.
For overprint see Trieste No. 186.

Agostino Bassi — A359

1953, Sept. 5

640 A359 25 l dk gray & brown .35 .35
Never hinged .60 —

6th International Microbiology Congress, Rome, Sept. 6-12, 1953.
For overprint see Trieste No. 187.

Siena — A360

Rapallo A361

Views: 20 l, Seaside at Gardone. 25 l, Mountain, Cortina d'Ampezzo. 35 l, Roman ruins, Taormina. 60 l, Rocks and sea, Capri.

1953, Dec. 31 *Perf. 14*

641 A360 10 l dk brn & red brn .25 .25
642 A361 12 l lt blue & gray .25 .25
643 A361 20 l brn org & dk brn .25 .25
644 A360 25 l dk grn & pale bl .40 .25
645 A361 35 l cream & brn .60 .40
646 A361 60 l bl grn & ind 1.15 1.75
Nos. 641-646 (6) 2.90 3.15
Set, never hinged 6.50

For overprints see Trieste Nos. 188-193, 204-205.

Lateran Palace, Rome — A362

1954, Feb. 11
647 A362 25 l dk brown & choc .35 .25
648 A362 60 l blue & ultra 1.75 *2.50*
Set, never hinged 4.00

Signing of the Lateran Pacts, 25th anniv.
For overprints see Trieste Nos. 194-195.

Television Screen and Aerial — A363

1954, Feb. 25
649 A363 25 l purple .75 .25
650 A363 60 l dp blue grn 3.25 *4.50*
Set, never hinged 7.50

Introduction of regular natl. television service.
For overprints see Trieste Nos. 196-197.

"Italia" and Quotation from Constitution A364

1954, Mar. 20
651 A364 25 l purple .45 .25
Never hinged 1.75

Propaganda for the payment of taxes.
For overprint see Trieste No. 198.

Vertical Flight Trophy — A365

1954, Apr. 24
652 A365 25 l gray black .45 *.70*
Never hinged .80

Issued to publicize the experimental transportation of mail by helicopter, April 1954.
For overprint see Trieste No. 199.

Eagle Perched on Ruins — A366

1954, June 1
653 A366 25 l gray, org brn & blk .35 *.35*
Never hinged .45

10th anniv. of Italy's resistance movement.
For overprint see Trieste No. 200.

Alfredo Catalani, Composer, Birth Centenary — A367

1954, June 19 ***Perf. 14***
654 A367 25 l dk grnsh gray .35 *.30*
Never hinged .45

For overprint see Trieste No. 201.

Marco Polo, Lion of St. Mark and Dragon A368

1954, July 8 **Engr.** ***Perf. 14***
655 A368 25 l red brown .35 .25

Perf. 13
656 A368 60 l gray green 2.60 *5.25*
a. Perf. 13x12 5.75 5.75
Set, never hinged 5.25

700th anniv. of the birth of Marco Polo.
For overprints see Trieste Nos. 202-203.

Automobile and Cyclist A369

1954, Sept. 6 **Photo.** ***Perf. 14***
657 A369 25 l dp green & red .30 .30
Never hinged .60

Italian Touring Club, 60th anniv.
For overprint see Trieste No. 206.

St. Michael Overpowering the Devil — A370

1954, Oct. 9
658 A370 25 l rose red .25 .25
659 A370 60 l blue .90 .90
Set, never hinged 1.50

23rd general assembly of the International Criminal Police, Rome 1954.
For overprints see Trieste Nos. 207-208.

Pinocchio and Group of Children — A371

1954, Oct. 26
660 A371 25 l rose red .40 .30
Never hinged 1.00

Carlo Lorenzini, creator of Pinocchio.

Italia Type of 1953-54

1954, Dec. 28 **Engr.** ***Perf. 13***
Size: 22½x27½mm
661 A354 100 l brown 55.00 .30
662 A354 200 l dp blue 3.00 .50
Set, never hinged 125.00

Madonna, Perugino — A372

60 l, Madonna of the Pieta, Michelangelo.

1954, Dec. 31 **Photo.** ***Perf. 14***
663 A372 25 l brown & bister .25 .25
664 A372 60 l black & cream .75 *.50*
Set, never hinged 2.00

Issued to mark the end of the Marian Year.

Amerigo Vespucci and Map — A373

1954, Dec. 31 **Engr.** ***Perf. 13***
665 A373 25 l dp plum .25 .25
a. Perf. 13x14 6.00 .75
666 A373 60 l blue blk 1.00 *1.00*
a. Perf. 13x14 3.00 *2.75*
Set, never hinged 2.75

500th anniv. of the birth of Amerigo Vespucci, explorer, 1454-1512.

Silvio Pellico (1789-1854), Dramatist — A374

Wmk. 277

1955, Jan. 24 **Photo.** ***Perf. 14***
667 A374 25 l brt blue & vio .30 .25
Never hinged .60

Italy at Work Type of 1950

1955-57 **Wmk. 303**

668	A306	50c vio bl	.25	.25
669	A306	1 l dk bl vio	.25	.25
670	A306	2 l sepia	.25	.25
671	A306	15 l dk gray bl	.30	.25
672	A306	30 l magenta	25.00	.25
673	A306	50 l violet	10.00	.25
673A	A306	65 l dk grn ('57)	14.00	*35.00*
		Nos. 668-673A (7)	50.05	36.50
		Set, never hinged	125.00	

Italia Type of 1953-54 and

St. George, by Donatello — A374a

1955-58 **Wmk. 303** **Photo.** ***Perf. 14***
Size: 17x21mm

673B	A354	1 l gray ('58)	.25	.25
674	A354	5 l slate	.25	.25
675	A354	6 l ocher ('57)	.25	.25
676	A354	10 l org ver	.25	.25
677	A354	12 l dull green	.25	.25
678	A354	13 l brt lil rose	.25	.25
679	A354	15 l gray vio ('56)	.25	.25
680	A354	20 l brown	.25	.25
681	A354	25 l purple	.25	.25
682	A354	35 l rose car	.25	.25
683	A354	50 l olive ('58)	.25	.25
685	A354	60 l blue	.25	.25
686	A354	80 l brown org	.25	.25
687	A354	90 l lt red brn ('58)	.25	.25

Size: 22½x28mm

Engr. ***Perf. 13½***

688	A354	100 l brn ('56)	4.25	.25
a.		Perf. 13½x12	7.50	.25
b.		Perf. 13½x14	*1,225.*	22.50
689	A354	200 l gray bl ('57)	3.00	.25
690	A374a	500 l grn ('57)	1.00	.25
b.		Perf. 14x13½	75.00	2.50
690A	A374a	1000 l rose car ('57)	1.50	.60
c.		Perf. 14x13½	5.00	.50
		Nos. 673B-690A (18)	13.25	4.85
		Set, never hinged	30.00	

Nos. 690-690A were printed on ordinary and fluorescent paper.
See Nos. 785-788. See Nos. 998A-998W for small-size set.

Catalogue values for unused stamps in this section, from this point to the end of the section, are for Never Hinged items.

"Italia" — A375

1955, Mar. 15 **Photo.** ***Perf. 14***
691 A375 25 l rose vio 1.75 .25

Issued as propaganda for the payment of taxes.

Oil Derrick and Old Roman Aqueduct — A376

60 l, Marble columns and oil field on globe.

1955, June 6
692 A376 25 l olive green .35 .25
693 A376 60 l henna brown 1.10 *1.10*

4th World Petroleum Cong., Rome, June 6-15, 1955.

Antonio Rosmini, Philosopher, Death Centenary — A377

1955, July 1 **Wmk. 303** ***Perf. 14***
694 A377 25 l sepia .65 .25

Girolamo Fracastoro and Stadium at Verona A378

1955, Sept. 1
695 A378 25 l gray blk & brn .50 .25

Intl. Medical Congress, Verona, Sept. 1-4.

Basilica of St. Francis, Assisi A379

1955, Oct. 4
696 A379 25 l black & cream .40 .25

Issued in honor of St. Francis and for the 7th centenary (in 1953) of the Basilica in Assisi.

Young Man at Drawing Board — A380

1955, Oct. 15
697 A380 25 l Prus green .40 .25

Centenary of technical education in Italy.

Harvester — A381

FAO Headquarters, Rome — A382

1955, Nov. 3

698 A381 25 l rose red & brn .40 .25
699 A382 60 l blk & brt pur 1.25 1.00

Intl. Institute of Agriculture, 50th anniv. and FAO, successor to the Institute, 10th anniv.

A383

1955, Nov. 10

700 A383 25 l rose brown .65 .25

70th anniversary of the birth of Giacomo Matteotti, Italian socialist leader.

A384

1955, Nov. 19

701 A384 25 l dark green .35 .25

Death of Battista Grassi, zoologist, 30th anniv.

"St. Stephen Giving Alms" — A385

"St. Lorenzo Giving Alms" A386

1955, Nov. 26

702 A385 10 l black & cream .25 .25
703 A386 25 l ultra & cream .40 .25

Death of Fra Angelico, painter, 500th anniv.

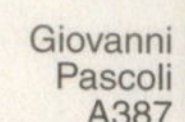

Giovanni Pascoli A387

1955, Dec. 31

704 A387 25 l gray black .30 .25

Centenary of the birth of Giovanni Pascoli, poet.

Ski Jump "Italia" A388

Stadiums at Cortina: 12 l, Skiing. 25 l, Ice skating. 60 l, Ice racing, Lake Misurina.

1956, Jan. 26 **Photo.**

705 A388 10 l blue grn & org .25 .25
706 A388 12 l yellow & blk .25 .25
707 A388 25 l vio blk & org brn .35 .25
708 A388 60 l sapphire & org 1.60 2.25
Nos. 705-708 (4) 2.45 3.00

VII Winter Olympic Games at Cortina d'Ampezzo, Jan. 26-Feb. 5, 1956.

Mail Coach and Tunnel Exit A389

1956, May 19 **Wmk. 303** ***Perf. 14***

709 A389 25 l dk blue grn 4.00 .65

50th anniv. of the Simplon Tunnel.

Arms of Republic and Symbols of Industry A390

1956, June 2

710 A390 10 l gray & slate bl .40 .25
711 A390 25 l pink & rose red .40 .25
712 A390 60 l lt bl & brt bl 4.50 *5.25*
713 A390 80 l orange & brn 7.00 .25
Nos. 710-713 (4) 12.30 6.00

Tenth anniversary of the Republic.

Amedeo Avogadro A391

1956, Sept. 8

714 A391 25 l black vio .25 .25

Centenary of the death of Amedeo Avogadro, physicist.

Europa Issue

"Rebuilding Europe" — A392

1956, Sept. 15

715 A392 25 l dark green *1.25* .25
716 A392 60 l blue *8.00* *1.00*

Issued to symbolize the cooperation among the six countries comprising the Coal and Steel Community.

Globe and Satellites A393

1956, Sept. 22

717 A393 25 l intense blue .25 .25

7th Intl. Astronautical Cong., Rome, Sept. 17-22.

Globe — A394

1956, Dec. 29 **Litho.** **Unwmk.**

718 A394 25 l red & bl grn, *pink* .30 .25
719 A394 60 l bl grn & red, *pale bl grn* .40 .25

Italy's admission to the United Nations. The design, viewed through red and green glasses, becomes three-dimensional.

Postal Savings Bank and Notes A395

1956, Dec. 31 **Photo.** **Wmk. 303**

720 A395 25 l sl bl & dp ultra .25 .25

80th anniversary of Postal Savings.

Ovid — A396

1957, June 10 ***Perf. 14***

721 A396 25 l ol grn & blk .30 .25

2000th anniversary of the birth of the poet Ovid (Publius Ovidius Naso).

Antonio Canova — A397

Paulina Borghese as Venus A398

60 l, Sculpture: Hercules and Lichas.

1957, July 15 **Engr.**

722 A397 25 l brown .25 .25
723 A397 60 l gray .25 .55
724 A398 80 l vio blue .25 .25
Nos. 722-724 (3) .75 1.05

Birth of Antonio Canova, sculptor, 200th anniv.

Traffic Light — A399

Wmk. 303

1957, Aug. 7 **Photo.** ***Perf. 14***

725 A399 25 l green, blk & red .35 .25

Campaign for careful driving.

"United Europe" — A400

1957, Sept. 16 **Litho.** ***Perf. 14***

Flags in Original Colors

726 A400 25 l light blue *.75* .25

Perf. 13

727 A400 60 l violet blue *3.50* *.60*

United Europe for peace and prosperity.

Giosue Carducci — A401

1957, Oct. 14 **Engr.** ***Perf. 14***

728 A401 25 l brown .30 .25

Death of the poet Giosue Carducci, 50th anniv.

Filippino Lippi — A402

1957, Nov. 25 **Wmk. 303** ***Perf. 14***

729 A402 25 l reddish brown .30 .25

Birth of Filippino Lippi, painter, 500th anniv.

2000th Anniv. of the Death of Marcus Tullius Cicero, Roman Statesman and Writer — A403

1957, Nov. 30 **Photo.**

730 A403 25 l brown red .25 .25

St. Domenico Savio and Students of Various Races A404

1957, Dec. 14
731 A404 15 l brt lil & blk .25 .25

Cent. of the death of St. Domenico Savio.

St. Francis of Paola — A405

1957, Dec. 21 **Engr.**
732 A405 25 l black .25 .25

450th anniv. of the death of St. Francis of Paola, patron saint of seafaring men.

Giuseppe Garibaldi — A406

Design: 110 l, Garibaldi monument, horiz.

1957, Dec. 14 ***Perf. 14x13, 13x14***
733 A406 15 l slate green .25 .25
734 A406 110 l dull purple .35 .25

150th anniv. of the birth of Giuseppe Garibaldi.

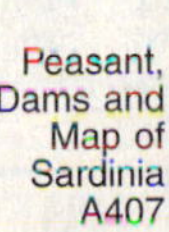

Peasant, Dams and Map of Sardinia A407

1958, Feb. 1 **Engr.** ***Perf. 14***
738 A407 25 l bluish grn .25 .25

Completion of the Flumendosa-Mulargia irrigation system.

Immaculate Conception Statue, Rome, and Lourdes Basilica — A408

1958, Apr. 16 **Wmk. 303** ***Perf. 14***
739 A408 15 l rose claret .25 .25
740 A408 60 l blue .25 .25

Apparition of the Virgin Mary at Lourdes, cent.

Book and Symbols of Labor Industry and Agriculture A409

Designs: 60 l, "Tree of Freedom," vert. 110 l, Montecitorio Palace.

1958, May 9 **Photo.** ***Perf. 14***
741 A409 25 l bl grn & ocher .25 .25
742 A409 60 l blk brn & bl .25 .25
743 A409 110 l ol bis & blk brn .25 .25
Nos. 741-743 (3) .75 .75

10th anniversary of the constitution.

Brussels Fair Emblem — A410

1958, June 12
744 A410 60 l blue & yellow .25 .25

Intl. and Universal Exposition at Brussels.

Prologue from Pagliacci — A411

1958, July 10
745 A411 25 l dk bl & dk red .25 .25

Birth of Ruggiero Leoncavallo, composer, cent.

Scene from La Bohème A412

1958, July 10 **Engr.** **Unwmk.**
746 A412 25 l dark blue .25 .25

Birth of Giacomo Puccini, composer, cent.

Giovanni Fattori, Self-portrait A413

1958, Aug. 7 **Wmk. 303** ***Perf. 13x14***
747 A413 110 l redsh brown .60 .30

Death of Giovanni Fattori, painter, 50th anniv.

"Ave Maria on the Lake" by Giovanni Segantini — A414

1958, Aug. 7 ***Perf. 14***
748 A414 110 l slate, *buff* .60 .25

Birth of Giovanni Segantini, painter, cent.

Map of Brazil, Plane and Arch of Titus A415

1958, Aug. 23 **Photo.** ***Perf. 14***
749 A415 175 l Prus green .75 .75

Italo-Brazilian friendship on the occasion of Pres. Giovanni Gronchi's visit to Brazil.

Common Design Types pictured following the introduction.

Europa Issue, 1958
Common Design Type

1958, Sept. 13 **Size: 20½x35½mm**
750 CD1 25 l red & blue .25 .25
751 CD1 60 l blue & red .80 .35

Issued to show the European Postal Union at the service of European integration.

½g Stamp of Naples — A416

Design: 60 l, 1g Stamp of Naples.

Perf. 14x13½, 13½
1958, Oct. 4 **Engr.** **Unwmk.**
752 A416 25 l brown red .25 .25
753 A416 60 l blk & red brn .25 .25

Centenary of the stamps of Naples.

Evangelista Torricelli — A417

1958, Oct. 20 **Wmk. 303** ***Perf. 14***
754 A417 25 l rose claret .55 .35

350th anniv. of the birth of Evangelista Torricelli, mathematician and physicist.

"The Triumph of Caesar," Montegna — A418

25 l, Coats of Arms of Trieste, Rome & Trento, horiz. 60 l, War memorial bell of Rovereto.

1958, Nov. 3 **Engr.** ***Perf. 14x13½***
755 A418 15 l green .25 .25
756 A418 25 l gray .25 .25
757 A418 60 l rose claret .25 .25
Nos. 755-757 (3) .75 .75

40th anniv. of Italy's victory in World War I.

Persian Style Bas-relief, Sorrento — A419

1958, Nov. 27 **Photo.**
758 A419 25 l sepia, *bluish* .25 .25
759 A419 60 l vio bl, *bluish* .45 .45

Visit of the Shah of Iran to Italy.

Eleonora Duse — A420

Unwmk.
1958, Dec. 11 **Engr.** ***Perf. 14***
760 A420 25 l brt ultra .25 .25

Cent. of the birth of Eleonora Duse, actress.

Dancers and Antenna — A421

Design: 60 l, Piano, dove and antenna.

1958, Dec. 29 **Photo.** **Wmk. 303**
761 A421 25 l red, bl & blk .25 .25
762 A421 60 l ultra & blk .25 .25

10th anniv. of the Prix Italia (International Radio and Television Competitions).

Stamp of Sicily — A422

Design: 60 l, Stamp of Sicily, 5g.

Perf. 14x13½
1959, Jan. 2 **Engr.** **Unwmk.**
763 A422 25 l Prus green .25 .25
764 A422 60 l dp orange .25 .25

Centenary of the stamps of Sicily.

Dome of St. Peter's and Tower of Lateran Palace A423

Wmk. 303
1959, Feb. 11 **Photo.** ***Perf. 14***
765 A423 25 l ultra .25 .25

30th anniversary of the Lateran Pacts.

Map of North Atlantic and NATO Emblem A424

1959, Apr. 4
766 A424 25 l dk bl & ocher .25 .25
767 A424 60 l dk bl & green .25 .25

10th anniv. of NATO.

Arms of Paris and Rome A425

1959, Apr. 9

768	A425	15 l	blue & red	.25	.25
769	A425	25 l	blue & red	.25	.25

Cultural ties between Rome and Paris.

"A Gentle Peace Has Come" — A426

1959, Apr. 13 Engr. Unwmk.

770	A426	25 l	olive green	.25	.25

International War Veterans Association convention, Rome.

Statue of Lord Byron — A427

1959, Apr. 21

771	A427	15 l	black	.25	.25

Unveiling in Rome of a statue of Lord Byron by Bertel Thorvaldson, Danish sculptor.

Camillo Prampolini — A428

1959, Apr. 27 Unwmk. *Perf. 14*

772	A428	15 l	car rose	8.00	.40

Camillo Prampolini, socialist leader and reformer, birth centenary.

Fountain of Dioscuri and Olympic Rings — A429

Baths of Carcalla A430

Designs: 25 l, Capitoline tower. 60 l, Arch of Constantine. 110 l, Ruins of Basilica of Massentius.

1959, June 23 Photo. Wmk. 303

Designs in Dark Sepia

773	A429	15 l	red orange	.25	.25
774	A429	25 l	blue	.25	.25
775	A430	35 l	bister	.25	.25
776	A430	60 l	rose lilac	.25	.30
777	A430	110 l	yellow	.30	.25
			Nos. 773-777 (5)	1.30	1.30

1960 Olympic Games in Rome.

Victor Emanuel II, Garibaldi, Cavour, Mazzini A431

Battle of San Fermo A432

25 l, "After the Battle of Magenta" by Fattori and Red Cross, vert. 60 l, Battle of Palestro. 110 l, "Battle of Magenta" by Induno, vert.

Engr., Cross Photo. on 25 l

1959, June 27 Unwmk.

778	A431	15 l	gray	.25	.25
779	A431	25 l	brn & red	.25	.25
780	A432	35 l	dk violet	.25	.25
781	A432	60 l	ultra	.25	.25
782	A432	110 l	magenta	.25	.25
			Nos. 778-782 (5)	1.25	1.25

Cent. of the war of independence. No. 779 for the centenary of the Red Cross idea.

Labor Monument, Geneva — A433

1959, July 20 *Perf. 14x13, 14*

783	A433	25 l	violet	.25	.25
784	A433	60 l	brown	.30	.25

40th anniv. of the ILO.

Italia Type of 1953-54

Photo.; Engr. (100 l, 200 l)

1959-66 Wmk. 303 *Perf. 14*

Size: 17x21mm

785	A354	30 l	bis brn ('60)	.25	.25
786	A354	40 l	lil rose ('60)	1.25	.25
786A	A354	70 l	Prus grn ('60)	.35	.25
787	A354	100 l	brown	.65	.25
787A	A354	130 l	gray & dl red ('66)	.25	.25
788	A354	200 l	dp blue	.65	.25
			Nos. 785-788 (6)	3.40	1.50

Stamp of Romagna — A434

Design: 60 l, Stamp of Romagna, 20b.

1959, Sept. 1 Photo.

789	A434	25 l	pale brn & blk	.25	.25
790	A434	60 l	gray grn & blk	.25	.25

Centenary of the stamps of Romagna.

Europa Issue, 1959

Common Design Type

1959, Sept. 19 Size: 22x27½mm

791	CD2	25 l	olive green	*.40*	.25
792	CD2	60 l	blue	*.40*	.25

Stamp of 1953 with Facsimile Cancellation A435

1959, Dec. 20 Wmk. 303 *Perf. 14*

793	A435	15 l	gray, rose car & blk	.25	.25

Italy's first Stamp Day, Dec. 20, 1959.

Aeneas Fleeing with Father and Son, by Raphael — A436

1960, Apr. 7 Engr. Unwmk.

794	A436	25 l	lake	.25	.25
795	A436	60 l	gray violet	.25	.25

World Refugee Year, 7/1/59-6/30/60. Design is detail from "The Fire in the Borgo."

Garibaldi's Proclamation to the Sicilians — A437

King Victor Emmanuel and Garibaldi Meeting at Teano — A438

60 l, Volunteers embarking, Quarto, Genoa.

Wmk. 303

1960, May 5 Photo. *Perf. 14*

796	A437	15 l	brown	.25	.25

Perf. 13x14, 14x13

Engr. Unwmk.

797	A438	25 l	rose claret	.25	.25
798	A437	60 l	ultramarine	.25	.25

Cent. of the liberation of Southern Italy (Kingdom of the Two Sicilies) by Garibaldi.

Emblem of 17th Olympic Games — A439

Olympic Stadium A440

Statues: 15 l, Roman Consul on way to the games. 35 l, Myron's Discobolus. 110 l, Seated boxer. 200 l, Apoxyomenos by Lysippus.

Stadia: 25 l, Velodrome. 60 l, Sports palace. 150 l, Small sports palace.

Photogravure, Engraved

Perf. 14x13½, 13½x14

1960 Wmk. 303, Unwmk.

799	A439	5 l	yellow brn	.25	.25
800	A440	10 l	dp org & dk bl	.25	.25
801	A439	15 l	ultra	.25	.25
802	A440	25 l	lt vio & brn	.25	.25
803	A439	35 l	rose cl	.25	.25
804	A440	60 l	bluish grn & brn	.25	.25
805	A439	110 l	plum	.25	.25
806	A440	150 l	blue & brn	1.50	*1.50*
807	A439	200 l	green	.75	.25
			Nos. 799-807 (9)	4.00	3.50

17th Olympic Games, Rome, 8/25-9/11.

The photo. denominations (5-10, 25, 60, 150 l) are wmkd.; the engraved (15, 35, 110, 200 l) are unwmkd.

Bottego Statue, Parma — A441

1960 Unwmk. Engr. *Perf. 14*

808	A441	30 l	brown	.25	.25

Birth cent. of Vittorio Bottego, explorer.

Europa Issue, 1960

Common Design Type

1960 Photo. Wmk. 303

Size: 37x27mm

809	CD3	30 l	dk grn & bis brn	*.25*	.25
810	CD3	70 l	dk bl & salmon	*.25*	.25

Michelangelo da Caravaggio A442

1960 Unwmk. Engr. *Perf. 13x13½*

811	A442	25 l	orange brn	.25	.25

350th anniv. of the death of Michelangelo da Caravaggio (Merisi), painter.

Mail Coach and Post Horn A443

1960 Wmk. 303 Photo. *Perf. 14*

812	A443	15 l	blk brn & org brn	.25	.25

Issued for Stamp Day, Dec. 20.

Slave, by Michelangelo — A444

Designs from Sistine Chapel by Michelangelo: 5 l, 10 l, 115 l, 150 l, Heads of various "slaves." 15 l, Joel. 20 l, Libyan Sybil. 25 l, Isaiah. 30 l, Eritrean Sybil. 40 l, Daniel. 50 l, Delphic Sybil. 55 l, Cumaean Sybil. 70 l, Zachariah. 85 l, Jonah. 90 l, Jeremiah. 100 l, Ezekiel. 200 l, Self-portrait. 500 l, Adam. 1000 l, Eve.

Wmk. 303

1961, Mar. 6 Photo. *Perf. 14*

Size: 17x21mm

813	A444	1 l	gray	.25	.25
814	A444	5 l	brown org	.25	.25
815	A444	10 l	red org	.25	.25
816	A444	15 l	brt lil	.25	.25
817	A444	20 l	Prus grn	.25	.25
818	A444	25 l	brown	.30	.25
819	A444	30 l	purple	.25	.25
820	A444	40 l	rose red	.25	.25
821	A444	50 l	olive	.25	.25
822	A444	55 l	red brn	.25	.25
823	A444	70 l	blue	.25	.25
824	A444	85 l	slate grn	.25	.25
825	A444	90 l	lil rose	.40	.25
826	A444	100 l	vio gray	.40	.25
827	A444	115 l	ultra	.40	.25

Engr.

828	A444	150 l	chocolate	.75	.25
829	A444	200 l	dark blue	1.25	.35
a.			Perf. 13½	1.50	.25

Perf. 13½

Size: 22x27mm

830	A444	500 l	blue grn	3.75	.35
831	A444	1000 l	brown red	3.50	*6.00*
			Nos. 813-831 (19)	13.50	10.70

Map Showing Flight from Italy to Argentina A445

185 l, Italy to Uruguay. 205 l, Italy to Peru.

1961, Apr. **Photo.** ***Perf. 14***

832	A445 170 l ultra	4.50	4.50
833	A445 185 l dull green	4.50	4.50
834	A445 205 l violet blk	15.00	14.00
a.	205 l rose lilac	1,250.	*2,000.*
	Nos. 832-834 (3)	24.00	23.00

Visit of Pres. Gronchi to South America, 4/61.

Nos. 832-833 and 834a were issued Apr. 4, to become valid on Apr. 6. The map of Peru on No. 834a was drawn incorrectly and the stamp was therefore withdrawn on Apr. 4. A corrected design in new color (No. 834) was issued Apr. 6. Forgeries of No. 834a exist.

Statue of Pliny, Como Cathedral — A446

1961, May 27

835	A446 30 l brown	.25	.25

1900th anniversary of the birth of Pliny the Younger, Roman consul and writer.

Ippolito Nievo (1831-61), Writer — A447

1961, June 8 **Wmk. 303** ***Perf. 14***

836	A447 30 l multi	.25	.25

St. Paul Aboard Ship A448

1961, June 28

837	A448 30 l multi	.25	.25
838	A448 70 l multi	.30	.30

1,900th anniversary of St. Paul's arrival in Rome. The design is after a miniature from the Bible of Borso D'Este.

Cavalli Gun and Gaeta Fortress A449

Cent. of Italian unity: 30 l, Carignano palace, Turin. 40 l, Montecitorio palace, Rome. 70 l, Palazzo Vecchio, Florence. 115 l, Villa Madama, Rome. 300 l, Steel construction, Italia '61 Exhibition, Turin.

1961, Aug. 12 **Photo.**

839	A449 15 l dk bl & redsh brn	.25	.25
840	A449 30 l dk bl & red brn	.25	.25
841	A449 40 l bl & brn	.35	.25
842	A449 70 l brn & pink	.35	.25
843	A449 115 l org brn & dk bl	1.75	.25
844	A449 300 l brt grn & red	6.00	8.25
	Nos. 839-844 (6)	8.95	9.50

Europa Issue, 1961
Common Design Type

1961, Sept. 18 **Wmk. 303** ***Perf. 14***
Size: 36½x21mm

845	CD4 30 l carmine	.25	.25
846	CD4 70 l yel grn	.25	.25

Giandomenico Romagnosi — A450

Perf. 13½
1961, Nov. 28 **Unwmk.** **Engr.**

847	A450 30 l green	.25	.25

Bicentenary of the birth of Giandomenico Romagnosi, jurist and philosopher.

Design from 1820 Sardinia Letter Sheet A451

Wmk. 303
1961, Dec. 3 **Photo.** ***Perf. 14***

848	A451 15 l lil rose & blk	.25	.25

Issued for Stamp Day 1961.

Family Scene "I am the Lamp that Glows so Gently . . ." A452

1962, Apr. 6 **Wmk. 303** ***Perf. 14***

849	A452 30 l red	.25	.25
850	A452 70 l blue	.25	.30

Death of Giovanni Pascoli, poet, 50th anniv.

Pacinotti's Dynamo A453

1962, June 12

851	A453 30 l rose & blk	.25	.25
852	A453 70 l ultra & blk	.25	.30

Antonio Pacinotti (1841-1912), physicist and inventor of the ring winding dynamo.

St. Catherine of Siena, by Andrea Vanni — A454

70 l, St. Catherine, 15th century woodcut.

1962, June 26 **Photo.**

853	A454 30 l black	.25	.25

Engraved and Photogravure

854	A454 70 l red & blk	.25	.40

500th anniversary of the canonization of St. Catherine of Siena, Patroness of Italy.

Lion of St. Mark — A455

Design: 30 l, Stylized camera eye.

1962, Aug. 25 **Photo.**

855	A455 30 l bl & blk	.25	.25
856	A455 70 l red org & blk	.25	.25

Intl. Film Festival in Venice, 30th anniv.

Motorcyclist and Bicyclist A456

70 l, Group of cyclists. 300 l, Bicyclist.

1962, Aug. 30

857	A456 30 l grn & blk	.25	.25
858	A456 70 l bl & blk	.25	.25
859	A456 300 l dp org & blk	3.50	3.50
	Nos. 857-859 (3)	4.00	4.00

World Bicycle Championship Races.

Europa Issue, 1962
Common Design Type

1962, Sept. 17 **Size: 37x21mm**

860	CD5 30 l carmine	.25	.25
861	CD5 70 l blue	.75	.30

A457

Design: Swiss and Italian Flags, Eugenio and Angela Lina Balzan Medal.

1962, Oct. 25 **Wmk. 303** ***Perf. 14***

862	A457 70 l rose red, grn & brn	.55	.35

1st distribution of the Balzan Prize by the Intl. Balzan Foundation for Italian-Swiss Cooperation.

Malaria Eradication Emblem — A458

1962, Oct. 31 **Photo.**

863	A458 30 l light violet	.25	.25
864	A458 70 l light blue	.25	.25

WHO drive to eradicate malaria.

Stamps of 1862 and 1961 — A459

1962, Dec. 2

865	A459 15 l pur, buff & bister	.25	.25

Stamp Day and cent. of Italian postage stamps.

A460

30 l, 70 l, Descent of the Holy Spirit on the twelve apostles.

1962, Dec. 8

866	A460 30 l org & dk bl grn, *buff*	.25	.25
867	A460 70 l dk bl grn & org, *buff*	.25	.30

21st Ecumenical Council of the Roman Catholic Church, Vatican II. The design is an illumination from the Codex Syriacus.

A461

Statue of Count Camillo Bensi di Cavour.

1962, Dec. 10 **Engr.** **Unwmk.**

868	A461 30 l dk grn	.25	.25

Centenary of Court of Accounts.

Count Giovanni Pico della Mirandola — A462

Wmk. 303
1963, Feb. 25 **Photo.** ***Perf. 14***

869	A462 30 l gray blk	.25	.25

Mirandola (1463-94), Renaissance scholar.

Gabriele D'Annunzio — A463

1963, Mar. 12 **Engr.** **Unwmk.**

870	A463 30 l dk grn	.25	.25

Issued to commemorate the centenary of the birth of Gabriele d'Annunzio, author and soldier.

Sower — A464

Design: 70 l, Harvester tying sheaf, sculpture from Maggiore Fountain, Perugia.

1963, Mar. 21 **Photo.** **Wmk. 303**

871	A464 30 l rose car & brn	.25	.25
872	A464 70 l bl & brn	.25	.25

FAO "Freedom from Hunger" campaign.

Mt. Viso, Alpine Club Emblem, Ax and Rope — A465

1963, Mar. 30 Wmk. 303 *Perf. 14*
873 A465 115 l dk brn & brt bl .25 .25

Italian Alpine Club founding, cent.

Map of Italy and "INA" Initials — A466

1963, Apr. 4
874 A466 30 l grn & blk .25 .25

50th anniv. of the Natl. Insurance Institute.

Globe and Stamp A467

1963, May 7 Photo. *Perf. 14*
875 A467 70 l bl & grn .25 .25

1st Intl. Postal Conf., Paris, 1863.

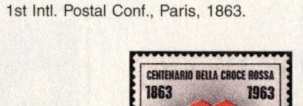

Crosses and Centenary Emblem on Globe — A468

1963, June 8 Wmk. 303 *Perf. 14*
876 A468 30 l dk gray & red .25 .25
877 A468 70 l dl bl & red .25 .25

International Red Cross founding, cent.

Roman Column, Globe and Highways A469

1963, Aug. 21 Wmk. 303 *Perf. 14*
878 A469 15 l gray ol & dk bl .25 .25
879 A469 70 l dl bl & brn .25 .25

UN Tourist Conf., Rome, Aug. 21-Sept. 5.

Europa Issue, 1963
Common Design Type

1963, Sept. 16 Size: 27½x23mm
880 CD6 30 l rose & brn *.25* .25
881 CD6 70 l brn & grn *.25* .25

Bay of Naples, Vesuvius and Sailboats A470

Athlete on Greek Vase A471

1963, Sept. 21 Wmk. 303 *Perf. 14*
882 A470 15 l bl & org .25 .25
883 A471 70 l dk grn & org brn .25 .30

4th Mediterranean Games, Naples, Sept. 21-29.

Giuseppe Gioachino Belli (1791-1863), Poet — A472

1963, Nov. 14 Wmk. 303 *Perf. 14*
884 A472 30 l red brn .25 .25

Stamps Forming Flower — A473

1963, Dec. 1
885 A473 15 l bl & car .25 .25

Issued for Stamp Day.

Pietro Mascagni and Old Costanzi Theater, Rome — A474

No. 886, Giuseppe Verdi & La Scala, Milan.

1963 Photo.
886 A474 30 l gray grn & yel brn .25 .25
887 A474 30 l yel brn & gray grn .25 .25

Verdi (1813-1901), and Mascagni (1863-1945), composers. Issued: No. 886, 10/10; No. 887, 12/7.

Galileo Galilei — A475

1964, Feb. 15 Wmk. 303 *Perf. 14*
888 A475 30 l org brn .25 .25
889 A475 70 l black .25 .25

Galilei (1564-1642), astronomer & physicist.

Nicodemus by Michelangelo A476

1964, Feb. 18 Photo.
890 A476 30 l brown .25 .25

Michelangelo Buonarroti (1475-1564), artist. Head of Nicodemus (self-portrait?) from the Pieta, Florence Cathedral. See No. C137.

Carabinieri A477

70 l, Charge of Pastrengo, 1848, by De Albertis.

1964, June 5 Wmk. 303 *Perf. 14*
891 A477 30 l vio bl & red .25 .25
892 A477 70 l brown .25 .25

150th anniv. of the Carabinieri (police corps).

Giambattista Bodoni — A478

Perf. 14x13
1964, July 30 Engr. Unwmk.
893 A478 30 l carmine .25 .25
a. Perf. 13 .25 .25

Death of Giambattista Bodoni (1740-1813), printer & type designer (Bodoni type), 150th anniv.

Europa Issue, 1964
Common Design Type
Wmk. 303

1964, Sept. 14 Photo. *Perf. 14*
Size: 21x37mm
894 CD7 30 l brt rose lilac *.25* .25
895 CD7 70 l blue green *.25* .25

Walled City — A479

1964, Oct. 15 Photo. *Perf. 14*
896 A479 30 l emer & dk brn .25 .25
897 A479 70 l bl & dk brn .25 .25

Unwmk. Engr.
898 A479 500 l red 1.50 1.75
Nos. 896-898 (3) 2.00 2.25

7th Congress of European Towns. The buildings in design are: Big Ben, London; Campodoglio, Rome; Town Hall, Bruges; Römer, Frankfurt; Town Hall, Paris; Belfry, Zurich; Gate, Kampen (Holland).

Left Arch of Victor Emmanuel Monument, Rome — A480

1964, Nov. 4 Photo. Wmk. 303
899 A480 30 l dk red brn .25 .25
900 A480 70 l blue .25 .25

Pilgrimage to Rome of veterans living abroad.

Giovanni da Verrazano and Verrazano-Narrows Bridge, New York Bay — A481

1964, Nov. 21 Wmk. 303 *Perf. 14*
901 A481 30 l blk & brn .25 .25

Opening of the Verrazano-Narrows Bridge connecting Staten Island and Brooklyn, NY, and to honor Giovanni da Verrazano (1485-1528), discoverer of New York Bay. See No. C138.

Italian Sports Stamps, 1934-63 — A482

1964, Dec. 6 Photo. *Perf. 14*
902 A482 15 l gldn brn & dk brn .25 .25

Issued for Stamp Day.

Italian Soldiers in Concentration Camp — A483

Victims Trapped by Swastika A484

15 l, Italian soldier, sailor and airman fighting for the Allies. 70 l, Guerrilla fighters in the mountains. 115 l, Marchers with Italian flag. 130 l, Ruins of city and torn Italian flag.

1965, Apr. 24 Photo. Wmk. 303
903 A483 10 l black .25 .25
904 A483 15 l grn & rose car .25 .25
905 A484 30 l plum .25 .25
906 A483 70 l deep blue .25 .25
907 A484 115 l rose car .25 .25
908 A484 130 l grn, sepia & red .25 .25
Nos. 903-908 (6) 1.50 1.50

Italian resistance movement during World War II, 20th anniv.

Antonio Meucci, Guglielmo Marconi and ITU Emblem A485

1965, May 17 *Perf. 14*
909 A485 70 l red & dk grn .25 .25

Cent. of the ITU.

Sailboats of Flying Dutchman Class A486

Designs: 70 l, Sailboats of 5.5-meter class, vert. 500 l, Sailboats, Lightning class.

1965, May 31 Photo. Wmk. 303
910 A486 30 l blk & dl rose .25 .25
911 A486 70 l blk & ultra .25 .25
912 A486 500 l blk & gray bl .55 .35
Nos. 910-912 (3) 1.05 .85

Issued to publicize the World Yachting Championships, Naples and Alassio.

Mont Blanc and Tunnel A487

1965, June 16 Wmk. 303 *Perf. 14*

913 A487 30 l black .25 .25

Opening of the Mont Blanc Tunnel connecting Entrayes, Italy, and Le Pelerins, France.

Alessandro Tassoni and Scene from "Seccia Rapita" — A488

Unwmk.

1965, Sept. 20 Photo. *Perf. 14*

914 A488 40 l blk & multi .25 .25

Tassoni (1565-1635), poet. Design is from 1744 engraving by Bartolomeo Soliani.

Europa Issue, 1965

Common Design Type

1965, Sept. 27 Wmk. 303

Size: 36½x27mm

915 CD8 40 l ocher & ol grn .25 .25
916 CD8 90 l ultra & ol grn .25 .25

Dante, 15th Century Bust — A489

Designs (from old Manuscripts): 40 l, Dante in Hell. 90 l, Dante in Purgatory led by Angel of Chastity. 130 l, Dante in Paradise interrogated by St. Peter on faith, horiz.

Perf. 13½x14, 14x13½

1965, Oct. 21 Photo. Unwmk.

917 A489 40 l multi .25 .25
918 A489 90 l multi .25 .25
919 A489 130 l multi .25 .25

Wmk. 303 *Perf. 14*

920 A489 500 l slate grn .55 .35
Nos. 917-920 (4) 1.30 1.10

Dante Alighieri (1265-1321), poet.

House under Construction — A490

1965, Oct. 31 Wmk. 303 *Perf. 14*

921 A490 40 l buff, blk & org brn .25 .25

Issued for Savings Day.

Jet Plane, Moon and Airletter Border A491

Design: 40 l, Control tower and plane.

1965, Nov. 3

922 A491 40 l dk Prus bl & red .25 .25

Unwmk.

923 A491 90 l red, grn, dp bl & buff .25 .25

Night air postal network.

Map of Italy with Milan-Rome Highway — A492

1965, Dec. 5 Photo. *Perf. 13x14*

924 A492 20 l bl, blk, ocher & gray .25 .25

Issued for Stamp Day.

Two-Man Bobsled — A493

Design: 90 l, Four-man bobsled.

1966, Jan. 24 Wmk. 303 *Perf. 14*

925 A493 40 l dl bl, gray & red .25 .25
926 A493 90 l vio & bl .25 .25

Intl. Bobsled Championships, Cortina d'Ampezzo.

Woman Skater — A494

Winter University Games: 40 l, Skier holding torch, horiz. 500 l, Ice hockey.

1966, Feb. 5 Photo.

927 A494 40 l blk & red .25 .25
928 A494 90 l vio & red .25 .25
929 A494 500 l brn & red .55 .35
Nos. 927-929 (3) 1.05 .85

Benedetto Croce — A495

1966, Feb. 25 Wmk. 303 *Perf. 14*

930 A495 40 l brown .25 .25

Benedetto Croce (1866-1952), philosopher, statesman and historian.

Arms of Venice and Other Cities in Venezia — A496

1966, Mar. 22 Photo. Unwmk.

932 A496 40 l gray & multi .25 .25

Centenary of Venezia's union with Italy.

Battle of Bezzecca — A497

1966, July 21 Wmk. 303 *Perf. 14*

933 A497 90 l ol grn .25 .25

Centenary of the unification of Italy and of the Battle of Bezzecca.

Umbrella Pine — A498

Carnations62 A499

25 l, Apples. 50 l, Florentine iris. 55 l, Cypresses. 90 l, Daisies. 170 l, Olive tree. 180 l, Juniper.

1966-68 Unwmk. *Perf. 13½x14*

934 A498 20 l multi .25 .25
934A A498 25 l multi ('67) .25 .25
935 A499 40 l multi .25 .25
935A A498 50 l multi ('67) .25 .25
935B A498 55 l multi ('68) .25 .25
936 A499 90 l multi .25 .25
937 A498 170 l multi .25 .25
937A A498 180 l multi ('68) .25 .25
Nos. 934-937A (8) 2.00 2.00

Tourist Attractions A500

1966, May 28 Wmk. 303 *Perf. 14*

938 A500 20 l yel, org & blk .25 .25

Issued for tourist publicity and in connection with the National Conference on Tourism, Rome.

"I" in Flag Colors — A501

Perf. 13½x14

1966, June 2 Photo. Unwmk.

939 A501 40 l multi .25 .25
940 A501 90 l multi .25 .25

20th anniversary of the Republic of Italy.

Singing Angels, by Donatello — A502

Perf. 13½x14

1966, Sept. 24 Photo. Unwmk.

941 A502 40 l multi .25 .25

Donatello (1386-1466), sculptor.

Europa Issue, 1966

Common Design Type

1966, Sept. 26 Wmk. 303 *Perf. 14*

Size: 22x38mm

942 CD9 40 l brt pur .25 .25
943 CD9 90 l brt bl .25 .25

Madonna, by Giotto — A503

Perf. 13½x14

1966, Oct. 20 Photo. Unwmk.

944 A503 40 l multi .25 .25

700th anniversary of the birth of Giotto di Bondone (1266?-1337), Florentine painter.

Italian Patriots A504

1966, Nov. 3 Wmk. 303 *Perf. 14*

945 A504 40 l gray & dl grn .25 .25

50th anniv. of the execution by Austrians of 4 Italian patriots: Fabio Filzi, Cesare Battisti, Damiano Chiesa and Nazario Sauro.

Postrider — A505

Perf. 14x13½

1966, Dec. 4 Photo. Unwmk.

946 A505 20 l multi .25 .25

Issued for Stamp Day.

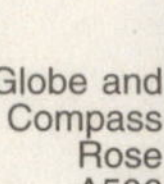

Globe and Compass Rose
A506

1967, Mar. 20 Photo. Wmk. 303
947 A506 40 l dull blue .25 .25

Centenary of Italian Geographical Society.

Arturo Toscanini (1867-1957), Conductor — A507

1967, Mar. 25 ***Perf. 14***
948 A507 40 l dp vio & cream .25 .25

Seat of Parliament on Capitoline Hill, Rome
A508

1967, Mar. 25 ***Perf. 14***
949 A508 40 l sepia .25 .25
950 A508 90 l rose lil & blk .25 .25

10th anniv. of the Treaty of Rome, establishing the European Common Market.

Europa Issue, 1967
Common Design Type
1967, Apr. 10 Wmk. 303 ***Perf. 14***
Size: 22x28mm
951 CD10 40 l plum & pink .25 .25
952 CD10 90 l ultra & pale gray .35 .25

Alpine Ibex, Grand Paradiso Park — A509

National Parks: 40 l, Brown bear, Abruzzi Apennines, horiz. 90 l, Red deer, Stelvio Pass, Ortler Mountains, horiz. 170 l, Oak and deer, Circeo.

Perf. 13½x14, 14x13½
1967, Apr. 22 Photo.
953 A509 20 l multi .25 .25
954 A509 40 l multi .25 .25
955 A509 90 l multi .25 .25
956 A509 170 l multi .25 .25
Nos. 953-956 (4) 1.00 1.00

Claudio Monteverdi and Characters from "Orfeo"
A510

1967, May 15 ***Perf. 14***
957 A510 40 l bis brn & brn .25 .25

Monteverdi (1567-1643), composer.

Bicyclists and Mountains
A511

50th Bicycle Tour of Italy: 90 l. Three bicyclists on the road. 500 l, Group of bicyclists.

Perf. 14x13½
1967, May 15 Photo. Unwmk.
958 A511 40 l multi .25 .25
959 A511 90 l brt bl & multi .25 .25
960 A511 500 l yel grn & multi 1.50 .85
Nos. 958-960 (3) 2.00 1.35

Luigi Pirandello and Stage
A512

1967, June 28 ***Perf. 14x13***
961 A512 40 l blk & multi .25 .25

Pirandello (1867-1936), novelist & dramatist.

Stylized Mask
A513

1967, June 30 Wmk. 303 ***Perf. 14***
962 A513 20 l grn & blk .25 .25
963 A513 40 l car rose & blk .25 .25

10th "Festival of Two Worlds," Spoleto.

Postal Card with Postal Zone Number
A514

Design: 40 l, 50 l, Letter addressed with postal zone number.

Wmk. 303, Unwmkd, (20 l, 40 l)
1967-68
964 A514 20 l multi .25 .25
965 A514 25 l multi ('68) .25 .25
966 A514 40 l multi .25 .25
967 A514 50 l multi ('68) .25 .25
Nos. 964-967 (4) 1.00 1.00

Introduction of postal zone numbers, 7/1/67.

Pomilio PC-1 Biplane and 1917 Airmail Postmark
A515

1967, July 18 Photo. Wmk. 303
968 A515 40 l blk & lt bl .25 .25

1st airmail stamp, Italy No. C1, 50th anniv.

St. Ivo Church, Rome — A516

1967, Aug. 2 Unwmk. ***Perf. 14***
969 A516 90 l multi .25 .25

Francesco Borromini (1599-1667), architect.

Umberto Giordano and "Improvisation" from Opera Andrea Chenier — A517

1967, Aug. 28 Wmk. 303
970 A517 20 l blk & org brn .25 .25

Umberto Giordano (1867-1948), composer.

Oath of Pontida, by Adolfo Cao — A518

1967, Sept. 2
971 A518 20 l dk brn .25 .25

800th anniv. of the Oath of Pontida, which united the Lombard League against Emperor Frederick I.

ITY Emblem — A519

Perf. 13½x14
1967, Oct. 23 Photo. Unwmk.
972 A519 20 l blk, cit & brt bl .25 .25
973 A519 50 l blk, org & brt bl .25 .25

Issued for International Tourist Year, 1967.

Lions Emblem — A520

1967, Oct. 30 ***Perf. 14x13½***
974 A520 50 l multi .25 .25

50th anniversary of Lions International.

Soldier at the Piave — A521

1967, Nov. 9 ***Perf. 13x14***
975 A521 50 l multi .25 .25

50th anniversary of Battle of the Piave.

Enrico Fermi at Los Alamos and Model of 1st Atomic Reactor — A522

Wmk. 303
1967, Dec. 2 Photo. ***Perf. 14***
976 A522 50 l org brn & blk .25 .25

25th anniv. of the 1st atomic chain reaction under Enrico Fermi (1901-54), Chicago, IL.

"Day and Night" and Pigeon Carrying Italy No. 924 — A523

1967, Dec. 3 Unwmk. ***Perf. 13½x14***
977 A523 25 l multi .25 .25

Issued for Stamp Day, 1967.

Scouts at Campfire — A524

1968, Apr. 23 ***Perf. 13x14***
978 A524 50 l multi .25 .25

Issued to honor the Boy Scouts.

Europa Issue, 1968
Common Design Type
Perf. 14x13
1968, Apr. 29 Wmk. 303
Size: 36½x26mm
979 CD11 50 l blk, rose & sl grn .25 .25
980 CD11 90 l blk, bl & brn .25 .25

St. Aloysius Gonzaga, by Pierre Legros — A525

Perf. 13½x14
1968, May 28 Photo. Wmk. 303
981 A525 25 l red brn & dl vio .25 .25

Aloysius Gonzaga (1568-1591), Jesuit priest who ministered to victims of the plague.

Arrigo Boito and Mephistopheles — A526

1968, June 10 Unwmk. ***Perf. 14***
982 A526 50 l multi .25 .25

Boito (1842-1918), composer and librettist.

Francesco Baracca and "Planes," by Giacomo Balla
A527

1968, June 19
983 A527 25 l multi .25 .25

Major Francesco Baracca (1888-1918), World War I aviator.

Giambattista Vico — A528

Designs: No. 985, Tommaso Campanella. No. 986, Gioacchino Rossini.

Perf. 14x13½

1968 Engr. Wmk. 303

984 A528 50 l ultra .25 .25
985 A528 50 l black .25 .25
a. Perf. 13½ .80 .25
986 A528 50 l car rose .25 .25
Nos. 984-986 (3) .75 .75

Vico (1668-1744), philosopher; Campanella (1568-1639), Dominican monk, philosopher poet and teacher; Rossini (1792-1868), composer.

Issued: No. 984, 6/24; No. 985, 9/5; No. 986, 10/25.

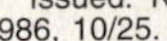

Bicycle Wheel and Velodrome, Rome — A529

90 l, Bicycle and Sforza Castle, Imola.

Perf. 13x14

1968, Aug. 26 Photo. Unwmk.

987 A529 25 l slate, rose & brown .25 .25
988 A529 90 l slate, blue & ver .25 .25

Bicycling World Championships: 25 l for the track championships at the Velodrome in Rome; 90 l, the road championships at Imola.

"The Small St. Mark's Place," by Canaletto — A531

1968, Sept. 30 Unwmk. *Perf. 14*

989 A531 50 l pink & multi .25 .25

Canaletto (Antonio Canale, 1697-1768), Venetian painter.

"Mobilization" — A533

Symbolic Designs: 25 l, Trench war. 40 l, The Navy. 50 l, The Air Force. 90 l, The Battle of Vittorio Veneto. 180 l, The Unknown Soldier.

1968, Nov. 2 Photo. Unwmk.

990 A533 20 l brn & multi .25 .25
991 A533 25 l bl & multi .25 .25
992 A533 40 l multi .25 .25
993 A533 50 l multi .25 .25
994 A533 90 l grn & multi .25 .25
995 A533 180 l bl & multi .25 .25
Nos. 990-995 (6) 1.50 1.50

50th anniv. of the Allies' Victory in WW I.

Emblem — A534

1968, Nov. 20 *Perf. 14x13½*

996 A534 50 l blk, bl grn & red .25 .25

50th anniv. of the Postal Checking Service.

Parabolic Antenna, Fucino A535

1968, Nov. 25 Photo. *Perf. 14*

997 A535 50 l multi .25 .25

Issued to publicize the expansion of the space communications center at Fucino.

Development of Postal Service — A536

1968, Dec. 1 Wmk. 303

998 A536 25 l car & yel .25 .25

Issued for the 10th Stamp Day.

Fluorescent Paper

was introduced in 1968 for regular and special delivery issues. These stamps are about 1mm. smaller each way than the non-fluorescent ones they replaced, except Nos. 690-690A which remained the same size.

Commemorative or nonregular stamps issued only on fluorescent paper are Nos. 935B, 937A, 965, 967 and from 981 onward unless otherwise noted.

Italia Type of 1953-54

Small Size: 16x19½-20mm

Photo.; Engr. (100, 150, 200-400 l)

1968-76 Wmk. 303 *Perf. 14*

998A A354 1 l dk gray .25 .25
998B A354 5 l slate .25 .25
998C A354 6 l ocher .25 .25
998D A354 10 l org ver .25 .25
998E A354 15 l gray vio .25 .25
998F A354 20 l brown .25 .25
998G A354 25 l purple .25 .25
998H A354 30 l bis brn .25 .25
998I A354 40 l lil rose .25 .25
998J A354 50 l olive .25 .25
998K A354 55 l vio ('69) .25 .25
998L A354 60 l blue .25 .25
998M A354 70 l Prus grn .25 .25
998N A354 80 l brn org .25 .25
998O A354 90 l lt red brn .25 .25
998P A354 100 l redsh brn .25 .25
998Q A354 125 l ocher & lil ('74) .25 .25
998R A354 130 l gray & dl red .25 .25
998S A354 150 l vio ('76) .25 .25
998T A354 180 l gray & vio brn ('71) .30 .25
998U A354 200 l slate blue .30 .25
998V A354 300 l Prus grn ('72) .30 .25
998W A354 400 l dull red ('76) .50 .25
Nos. 998A-998W (23) 6.15 5.75

Memorial Medal — A537

Unwmk.

1969, Apr. 22 Photo. *Perf. 14*

999 A537 50 l pink & blk .25 .25

Centenary of the State Audit Bureau.

Europa Issue, 1969

Common Design Type

1969, Apr. 28 *Perf. 14x13*

Size: 35½x25½mm

1000 CD12 50 l mag & multi .25 .25
1001 CD12 90 l bl & multi .25 .25

Niccolo Machiavelli — A538

1969, May 3 *Perf. 14x13½*

1002 A538 50 l blue & multi .25 .25

Niccolo Machiavelli (1469-1527), statesman and political philosopher.

ILO Emblem — A539

Wmk. 303

1969, June 7 Photo. *Perf. 14*

1003 A539 50 l grn & blk .25 .25
1004 A539 90 l car & blk .25 .25

50th anniv. of the ILO.

Federation Emblem, Tower of Superga Basilica and Matterhorn A540

1969, June 26 Unwmk. *Perf. 14*

1005 A540 50 l gold, bl & car .25 .25

Federation of Italian Philatelic Societies, 50th anniv.

Sondrio-Tirano Stagecoach, 1903 — A541

1969, Dec. 7 Engr. Wmk. 303

1006 A541 25 l violet blue .25 .25

Issued for the 11th Stamp Day.

Downhill Skier — A542

90 l, Sassolungo & Sella Group, Dolomite Alps.

Perf. 13x14

1970, Feb. 6 Unwmk. Photo.

1007 A542 50 l blue & multi .25 .25
1008 A542 90 l blue & multi .25 .25

World Alpine Ski Championships, Val Gardena, Bolzano Province, Feb. 6-15.

Galatea, by Raphael A543

Painting: 50 l, Madonna with the Goldfinch (detail), by Raphael, 1483-1520.

1970, Apr. 6 Photo. *Perf. 14x13*

1009 A543 20 l multi .25 .25
1010 A543 50 l multi .25 .25

Symbol of Flight, Colors of Italy and Japan A544

1970, May 2 Unwmk. *Perf. 14*

1011 A544 50 l multi .25 .25
1012 A544 90 l multi .25 .25

50th anniv. of Arturo Ferrarin's flight from Rome to Tokyo, Feb. 14-May 31, 1920.

Europa Issue, 1970

Common Design Type

1970, May 4 Wmk. 303

Size: 36x20mm

1013 CD13 50 l red & org .25 .25
1014 CD13 90 l bl grn & org .25 .25

Gattamelata, Bust by Donatello — A545

1970, May 30 Engr. *Perf. 14x13*

1015 A545 50 l slate green .25 .25

Erasmo de' Narni, called Il Gattamelata (1370-1443), condottiere.

Runner A546

Unwmk.

1970, Aug. 26 Photo. *Perf. 14*

1016 A546 20 l shown .25 .25
1017 A546 180 l Swimmer .30 .25

1970 World University Games, Turin, 8/26-9/6.

Dr. Maria Montessori and Children
A547

1970, Aug. 31 *Perf. 14x13*
1018 A547 50 l multi .25 .25

Montessori (1870-1952), educator & physician.

Map of Italy and Quotation of Count Camillo Cavour — A548

1970, Sept. 19 **Unwmk.** *Perf. 14*
1019 A548 50 l multi .25 .25

Union of the Roman States with Italy, cent.

Loggia of St. Mark's Campanile, Venice
A549

Perf. 14x13½
1970, Sept. 26 **Engr.** **Wmk. 303**
1020 A549 50 l red brown .25 .25

Iacopo Tatti "Il Sansovino" (1486-1570), architect.

Garibaldi at Battle of Dijon
A550

1970, Oct. 15 **Photo.** *Perf. 14*
1021 A550 20 l gray & dk bl .25 .25
1022 A550 50 l brt rose lil & dk bl .25 .25

Cent. of Garibaldi's participation in the Franco-Prussian War during Battle of Dijon.

Tree and UN Emblem — A551

1970, Oct. 24 **Unwmk.** *Perf. 13x14*
1023 A551 25 l blk, sep & grn .25 .25
1024 A551 90 l blk, brt bl & yel grn .25 .25

25th anniversary of the United Nations.

Rotary Emblem
A552

1970, Nov. 12 **Wmk. 303** *Perf. 14*
1025 A552 25 l bluish vio & org .25 .25
1026 A552 90 l bluish vio & org .25 .25

Rotary International, 65th anniversary.

Telephone Dial and Trunk Lines
A553

1970, Nov. 24
1027 A553 25 l yel grn & dk red .25 .25
1028 A553 90 l ultra & dk red .25 .25

Issued to publicize the completion of the automatic trunk telephone dialing system.

"Man Damaging Nature" — A554

1970, Nov. 28 **Wmk. 303** *Perf. 14*
1029 A554 20 l car lake & grn .25 .25
1030 A554 25 l dk bl & emer .25 .25

For European Nature Conservation Year.

Mail Train
A555

1970, Dec. 6 **Engr.**
1031 A555 25 l black .25 .25

For the 12th Stamp Day.

Virgin and Child, by Fra Filippo Lippi — A556

1970, Dec. 12 **Photo.** **Unwmk.**
1032 A556 25 l multi .25 .25

Christmas 1970. See No. C139.

Saverio Mercadante (1795-1870), Composer — A557

1970, Dec. 17 **Wmk. 303**
1033 A557 25 l vio & gray .25 .25

Mercury, by Benvenuto Cellini — A558

1971, Mar. 20 **Photo.** *Perf. 14*
1034 A558 50 l Prussian blue .25 .25

Benvenuto Cellini (1500-1571), sculptor.

Bramante's Temple, St. Peter in Montorio — A559

Photogravure and Engraved
1971, Apr. 8 *Perf. 13x14*
1035 A559 50 l ocher & blk .25 .25

Honoring Bramante (Donato di Angelo di Antonio, 1444-1514), architect.

Adenauer, Schuman, De Gasperi
A560

Perf. 14x13½
1971, Apr. 28 **Photo.** **Wmk. 303**
1036 A560 50 l blk & lt grnsh bl .25 .25
1037 A560 90 l blk & lil rose .25 .25

European Coal & Steel Community, 20th anniv.

Europa Issue, 1971
Common Design Type

1971, May 3 *Perf. 14*
1038 CD14 50 l ver & dk red .25 .25
1039 CD14 90 l brt rose lil & dk lil .40 .25

Giuseppe Mazzini, Italian Flag — A561

Perf. 14x13½
1971, June 12 **Unwmk.**
1040 A561 50 l multi .25 .25
1041 A561 90 l multi .25 .25

25th anniversary of the Italian Republic.

Kayak Passing Between Poles
A562

Design: 90 l, Kayak in free descent.

1971, June 16 **Photo.** *Perf. 14*
1042 A562 25 l multi .25 .25
1043 A562 90 l multi .25 .25

Canoe Slalom World Championships, Merano.

Skiing, Basketball, Volleyball — A563

50 l, Gymnastics, cycling, track and swimming.

Perf. 13½x14
1971, June 26 **Photo.** **Unwmk.**
1044 A563 20 l emer, ocher & blk .25 .25
1045 A563 50 l dl bl, org & blk .25 .25

Youth Games.

Plane Circling Globe and "A" — A564

Designs: 50 l, Ornamental "A." 150 l, Tail of B747 in shape of "A."

1971, Sept. 16 *Perf. 14x13½*
1046 A564 50 l multi .25 .25
1047 A564 90 l multi .25 .25
1048 A564 150 l multi .25 .25
Nos. 1046-1048 (3) .75 .75

ALITALIA, Italian airlines founding, 25th anniv.

Grazia Deledda (1871-1936), Novelist — A565

Photogravure and Engraved
Perf. 13½x14
1971, Sept. 28 **Wmk. 303**
1049 A565 50 l blk & salmon .25 .25

Child in Barrel Made of Banknote — A566

Perf. 13x14
1971, Oct. 27 **Photo.** **Unwmk.**
1050 A566 25 l blk & multi .25 .25
1051 A566 50 l multi .25 .25

Publicity for postal savings bank.

UNICEF Emblem and Children
A567

90 l, Children hailing UNICEF emblem.

1971, Nov. 26 *Perf. 14x13*
1052 A567 25 l pink & multi .25 .25
1053 A567 90 l multi .25 .25

25th anniv. of UNICEF.

Packet Tirrenia and Postal Ensign A568

1971, Dec. 5 Wmk. 303 *Perf. 14*

1054 A568 25 l slate green	.25	.25

Stamp Day.

Nativity A569

Christmas: 90 l, Adoration of the Kings. Both designs are from miniatures in Evangelistary of Matilda in Nonantola Abbey, 12th-13th centuries.

Perf. 14x13

1971, Dec. 10 Photo. Unwmk.

1055 A569 25 l gray & multi	.25	.25
1056 A569 90 l gray & multi	.25	.25

Giovanni Verga and Sicilian Cart A570

1972, Jan. 27

1057 A570 25 l org & multi	.25	.25
1058 A570 50 l multi	.25	.25

Verga (1840-1922), writer & playwright.

Giuseppe Mazzini (1805-1872), Patriot and Writer — A571

Wmk. 303

1972, Mar. 10 Engr. *Perf. 13*

1059 A571 25 l blk & Prus grn	.25	.25
1060 A571 90 l black	.25	.25
1061 A571 150 l blk & rose red	.25	.25
Nos. 1059-1061 (3)	.75	.75

Flags, Milan Fair A572

Designs: 50 l, 90 l, Different abstract views.

Perf. 14x13½

1972, Apr. 14 Photo. Unwmk.

1062 A572 25 l emer & blk	.25	.25
1063 A572 50 l dp org & blk	.25	.25
1064 A572 90 l bl & blk	.25	.25
Nos. 1062-1064 (3)	.75	.75

50th anniversary of the Milan Sample Fair.

Europa Issue 1972

Common Design Type

1972, May 2 *Perf. 13x14*

Size: 26x36mm

1065 CD15 50 l multi	.25	.25
1066 CD15 90 l multi	.30	.25

Alpine Soldier and Pack Mule A573

50 l, Mountains, Alpinist's hat, pick & laurel. 90 l, Alpine soldier & mountains.

1972, May 10 *Perf. 14x13*

1067 A573 25 l ol & multi	.25	.25
1068 A573 50 l bl & multi	.25	.25
1069 A573 90 l grn & multi	.25	.25
Nos. 1067-1069 (3)	.75	.75

Centenary of the Alpine Corps.

Brenta Mountains, Society Emblem A574

Emblem and: 50 l, Mountain climber & Brenta Mountains. 180 l, Sunset over Mt. Crozzon.

Perf. 14x13

1972, Sept. 2 Photo. Unwmk.

1070 A574 25 l multi	.25	.25
1071 A574 50 l multi	.25	.25
1072 A574 180 l multi	.30	.25
Nos. 1070-1072 (3)	.80	.75

Tridentine Alpinist Society centenary.

Conference Emblem, Seating Diagram A575

1972, Sept. 21

1073 A575 50 l multi	.25	.25
1074 A575 90 l multi	.25	.25

60th Conference of the Inter-Parliamentary Union, Montecitorio Hall, Rome.

St. Peter Damian, by Giovanni di Paoli, c. 1445 A576

1972, Sept. 21 Photo.

1075 A576 50 l multi	.25	.25

St. Peter Damian (1007-72), church reformer, cardinal, papal legate.

The Three Graces, by Antonio Canova (1757-1822), Sculptor — A577

1972, Oct. 13 Engr. Wmk. 303

1076 A577 50 l black	.25	.25

Page from Divine Comedy, Foligno Edition A578

Designs (Illuminated First Pages): 90 l, Mantua edition, vert. 180 l, Jesina edition.

Perf. 14x13½, 13½x14

1972, Nov. 23 Photo. Unwmk.

1077 A578 50 l ocher & multi	.25	.25
1078 A578 90 l multi	.25	.25
1079 A578 180 l multi	.25	.25
Nos. 1077-1079 (3)	.75	.75

500th anniversary of three illuminated editions of Dante's Divine Comedy.

Angel — A579

Christmas: 25 l, Christ Child in cradle, horiz. 150 l, Angel. All designs from 18th century Neapolitan crèche.

Perf. 13x14, 14x13

1972, Dec. 6 Photo.

1080 A579 20 l multi	.25	.25
1081 A579 25 l multi	.25	.25
1082 A579 150 l multi	.25	.25
Nos. 1080-1082 (3)	.75	.75

Passenger and Mail Autobus A580

1972, Dec. 16 Engr. Wmk. 303

1083 A580 25 l magenta	.25	.25

Stamp Day.

Leòn Battista Alberti — A581

1972, Dec. 16 *Perf. 14*

1084 A581 50 l ultra & ocher	.25	.25

Leòn Battista Alberti (1404-1472), architect, painter, organist and writer.

Lorenzo Perosi — A582

1972, Dec. 20 Photo. Unwmk.

1085 A582 50 l dk vio brn & org	.25	.25
1086 A582 90 l blk & yel grn	.25	.25

Lorenzo Perosi (1872-1956), priest & composer.

Luigi Orione and Boys — A583

1972, Dec. 30

1087 A583 50 l lt bl & dk bl	.25	.25
1088 A583 90 l ocher & slate grn	.25	.25

Orione (1872-1940), founder of CARITAS; Catholic Welfare Organization.

Ship Exploring Ocean Floor — A584

1973, Feb. 15 Photo. *Perf. 13x14*

1089 A584 50 l multi	.25	.25

Cent. of the Naval Hydrographic Institute.

Palace Staircase, Caserta A585

1973, Mar. 1 Engr. *Perf. 14x13½*

1090 A585 25 l gray olive	.25	.25

Luigi Vanvitelli (1700-1773), architect.

Schiavoni Shore — A586

The Tetrarchs, 4th Century Sculpture — A587

50 l, "Triumph of Venice," by Vittore Carpaccio. 90 l, Bronze horses from St. Mark's. 300 l, St. Mark's Square covered by flood.

1973 Photo. *Perf. 14*

1091 A586 20 l ultra & multi	.25	.25
1092 A587 25 l ultra & multi	.25	.25
1093 A586 50 l ultra & multi	.25	.25
1094 A587 90 l ultra & multi	.25	.25
1095 A586 300 l ultra & multi	.70	.45
Nos. 1091-1095 (5)	1.70	1.45

Save Venice campaign. Issued: No. 1091, 3/5; others 4/10.

Verona Fair Emblem — A588

1973, Mar. 10 *Perf. 13x14*

1096 A588 50 l multi	.25	.25

75th International Fair, Verona.

Title Page for Book about Rosa — A589

1973, Mar. 15 *Perf. 14*
1097 A589 25 l org & blk .25 .25

Salvator Rosa (1615-1673), painter & poet.

G-91 Jet Fighters A590

Designs: 25 l, Formation of S-55 seaplanes. 50 l, G-91Y fighters. 90 l, Fiat CR-32's flying figure 8. 180 l, Camprini-Caproni jet, 1940.

1973, Mar. 28 *Perf. 14x13½*
1098 A590 20 l multi .25 .25
1099 A590 25 l multi .25 .25
1100 A590 50 l multi .25 .25
1101 A590 90 l multi .25 .25
1102 A590 180 l multi .25 .25
Nos. 1098-1102,C140 (6) 1.55 1.50

50th anniversary of military aviation.

Soccer Field and Ball A591

Design: 90 l, Soccer players and goal.

1973, May 19 Photo. *Perf. 14x13½*
1103 A591 25 l ol, blk & lt grn .25 .25
1104 A591 90 l grn & multi .40 .40

75th anniv. of Italian Soccer Federation.

Alessandro Manzoni, by Francisco Hayez — A592

1973, May 22 **Engr.**
1105 A592 25 l blk & brn .25 .25

Manzoni (1785-1873), novelist and poet.

Villa Rotunda, by Andrea Palladio (1508-80), Architect. — A593

1973, May 30 Photo. Unwmk.
Perf. 13x14
1106 A593 90 l blk, yel & lem .25 .25

Spiral and Cogwheels A594

1973, June 20 *Perf. 14x13*
1107 A594 50 l gold & multi .25 .25

50th anniversary of the State Supply Office.

Europa Issue 1973
Common Design Type

1973, June 30 Litho. *Perf. 14*
Size: 36x20mm
1108 CD16 50 l lil, gold & yel .25 .25
1109 CD16 90 l lt bl grn, gold & yel .25 .25
Nos. 1108-1109 (2) .50 .50

Catcher and Diamond A595

Design: 90 l, Diamond and batter.

1973, July 21 Photo. *Perf. 14x13½*
1110 A595 25 l multi .25 .25
1111 A595 90 l multi .25 .25

International Baseball Cup.

Viareggio by Night — A596

1973, Aug. 10 Photo. *Perf. 13x14*
1112 A596 25 l blk & multi .25 .25

Viareggio Carnival.

Assassination of Giovanni Minzoni — A597

1973, Aug. 23 *Perf. 14x13*
1113 A597 50 l multi .25 .25

Minzoni (1885-1923), priest & social worker.

Gaetano Salvemini (1873-1957), Historian, Anti-Fascist — A598

1973, Sept. 8 *Perf. 14x13½*
1114 A598 50 l pink & multi .25 .25

Palazzo Farnese, Caprarola, by Vignola A599

1973, Sept. 21 Engr. *Perf. 14x13½*
1115 A599 90 l choc & yel .25 .25

Giacomo da Vignola (real name, Giacomo Barocchio), 1507-1573, architect.

St. John the Baptist, by Caravaggio A600

Lithographed & Engraved
1973, Sept. 28 *Perf. 14*
1116 A600 25 l blk & dl yel .25 .25

400th anniversary of the birth of Michelangelo da Caravaggio (1573-1610?), painter.

Tower of Pisa — A601

1973, Oct. 8 **Photo.**
1117 A601 50 l multi .25 .25

8th century of Leaning Tower of Pisa.

Famous Men — A602

Designs: No. 1118, Sandro Botticelli. No. 1119, Giambattista Piranesi. No. 1120, Paolo Veronese. No. 1121, Andrea del Verrocchio. No. 1122, Giovanni Battista Tiepolo. No. 1123, Francesco Borromini. No. 1124, Rosalba Carriera. No. 1125, Giovanni Bellini (Giambellino). No. 1126, Andrea Mantegna. No. 1127, Raphael (Raffaello).

1973-74 Photo. *Perf. 14x13½*
1118 A602 50 l multi .25 .25
1119 A602 50 l multi .25 .25
1120 A602 50 l multi .25 .25
1121 A602 50 l multi .25 .25
1122 A602 50 l multi .25 .25
1123 A602 50 l multi .25 .25
1124 A602 50 l multi .25 .25
1125 A602 50 l multi .25 .25
1126 A602 50 l multi .25 .25
1127 A602 50 l multi .25 .25
Nos. 1118-1127 (10) 2.50 2.50

Famous artists.

Issued: Nos. 1118-1122, 11/5; Nos. 1123-1127, 5/25/74.

See Nos. 1204-1209, 1243-1247, 1266-1270.

Trevi Fountain, Rome — A603

Designs: No. 1129, Immacolatella Fountain, Naples. No. 1130, Pretoria Fountain, Palermo.

Photogravure and Engraved
1973, Nov. 10 *Perf. 13½x14*
1128 A603 25 l blk & multi .25 .25
1129 A603 25 l blk & multi .25 .25
1130 A603 25 l blk & multi .25 .25
Nos. 1128-1130 (3) .75 .75

See Nos. 1166-1168, 1201-1203, 1251-1253, 1277-1279, 1341-1343, 1379-1381.

Angels, by Agostino di Duccio — A604

Sculptures by Agostino di Duccio: 25 l, Virgin and Child. 150 l, Angels with flute and trumpet.

1973, Nov. 26
1131 A604 20 l yel grn & blk .25 .25
1132 A604 25 l lt bl & blk .25 .25
1133 A604 150 l yel & blk .25 .25
Nos. 1131-1133 (3) .75 .75

Christmas 1973.

Map of Italy, Rotary Emblems — A605

1973, Nov. 28 **Photo.**
1134 A605 50 l red, grn & dk bl .25 .25

50th anniv. of Rotary International of Italy.

Caravelle A606

Wmk. 303
1973, Dec. 2 Engr. *Perf. 14*
1135 A606 25 l Prussian blue .25 .25

15th Stamp Day.

Gold Medal of Valor, 50th Anniv. — A607

Perf. 13½x14
1973, Dec. 10 Photo. Unwmk.
1136 A607 50 l gold & multi .25 .25

Enrico Caruso (1873-1921), Operatic Tenor — A608

Design: 50 l, Caruso as Duke in Rigoletto.

1973, Dec. 15 **Engr.**
1137 A608 50 l magenta .25 .25

Christ Crowning King Roger — A609

Norman art in Sicily: 50 l, King William II offering model of church to the Virgin, mosaic from Monreale Cathedral. The design of 20 l, is from a mosaic in Martorana Church, Palermo.

Lithographed and Engraved
1974, Mar. 4 ***Perf. 13½x14***
1138 A609 20 l ind & buff .25 .25
1139 A609 50 l red & lt grn .25 .25

Luigi Einaudi (1874-1961), Pres. of Italy — A610

1974, Mar. 23 **Engr.** ***Perf. 14x13½***
1140 A610 50 l green .25 .25

Guglielmo Marconi (1874-1937), Italian Inventor and Physicist — A611

Design: 90 l, Marconi and world map.

1974, Apr. 24 **Photo.** ***Perf. 14x13½***
1141 A611 50 l bl grn & gray .25 .25
1142 A611 90 l vio & multi .25 .25

David, by Giovanni L. Bernini — A612

Europa: 90 l, David, by Michelangelo.

1974, Apr. 29 **Photo.** ***Perf. 13½x14***
1143 A612 50 l sal, ultra & gray .25 .25
1144 A612 90 l grn, ultra & buff .25 .25

Customs Frontier Guards, 1774, 1795, 1817 — A613

Uniforms of Customs Service: 50 l, Lombardy Venetia, 1848, Sardinia, 1815, Tebro Battalion, 1849. 90 l, Customs Guards, 1866, 1880 and Naval Marshal, 1892. 180 l, Helicopter pilot, Naval and Alpine Guards, 1974. All bordered with Italian flag colors.

1974, June 21 **Photo.** ***Perf. 14***
1145 A613 40 l multi .25 .25
1146 A613 50 l multi .25 .25
1147 A613 90 l multi .25 .25
1148 A613 180 l multi .40 .25
Nos. 1145-1148 (4) 1.15 1.00

Customs Frontier Guards bicentenary.

Sprinter — A614

1974, June 28 **Photo.** ***Perf. 14x13***
1149 A614 40 l shown .25 .25
1150 A614 50 l Pole vault .25 .25

European Athletic Championships, Rome.

Sharpshooter — A615

Design: 50 l, Bersaglieri emblem.

1974, June 27
1151 A615 40 l multi .25 .25
1152 A615 50 l grn & multi .25 .25

Bersaglieri Veterans Association, 50th anniv.

View of Portofino — A616

1974, July 10 ***Perf. 14***
1153 A616 40 l shown .25 .25
1154 A616 40 l View of Gradara .25 .25

Tourist publicity.

See Nos. 1190-1192, 1221-1223, 1261-1265, 1314-1316, 1357-1360, 1402-1405, 1466-1469, 1520-1523, 1563A-1563D, 1599-1602, 1630-1633, 1708-1711, 1737-1740, 1776-1779, 1803-1806, 1830-1833, 1901-1904.

Petrarch (1304-74), Poet — A617

50 l, Petrarch at his desk (from medieval manuscript).

Lithographed and Engraved
1974, July 19 ***Perf. 13½x14***
1155 A617 40 l ocher & multi .25 .25
1156 A617 50 l ocher, yel & bl .25 .25

Niccolo Tommaseo (1802-1874), Writer, Venetian Education Minister — A618

Tommaseo Statue, by Ettore Ximenes, Shibenik.

1974, July 19
1157 A618 50 l grn & pink .25 .25

Giacomo Puccini (1858-1924), Composer — A619

1974, Aug. 16 **Photo.**
1158 A619 40 l multi .25 .25

Lodovico Ariosto (1474-1533), Poet — A620

50 l, King Roland, woodcut.

1974, Sept. 9 **Engr.** ***Perf. 14x13½***
1159 A620 50 l blue & red .25 .25

The design is from a contemporary illustration of Ariosto's poem "Orlando Furioso."

Quotation from Menippean Satire by Varro — A621

1974, Sept. 21
1160 A621 50 l ocher & dk red .25 .25

Marcus Terentius Varro (116-27 BC), Roman scholar and writer.

"October," 15th Century Mural — A622

1974, Sept. 28 **Photo.** ***Perf. 14***
1161 A622 50 l multi .25 .25

14th International Wine Congress, Trento.

"UPU" and Emblem — A623

Design: 90 l, Letters, "UPU" and emblem.

1974, Oct. 19 **Photo.** ***Perf. 14***
1162 A623 50 l multi .25 .25
1163 A623 90 l multi .25 .25

Centenary of Universal Postal Union.

St. Thomas Aquinas, by Francesco Traini — A624

1974, Oct. 25 ***Perf. 13x14***
1164 A624 50 l multi .25 .25

St. Thomas Aquinas (1225-1274), scholastic philosopher, 700th death anniversary.

Bas-relief from Ara Pacis — A625

1974, Oct. 26
1165 A625 50 l multi .25 .25

Centenary of the Ordini Forensi (Bar Association).

Fountain Type of 1973

Designs: No. 1166, Oceanus Fountain, Florence. No. 1167, Neptune Fountain, Bologna. No. 1168, Fontana Maggiore, Perugia.

Photogravure and Engraved
1974, Nov. 9 ***Perf. 13x14***
1166 A603 40 l blk & multi .25 .25
1167 A603 40 l blk & multi .25 .25
1168 A603 40 l blk & multi .25 .25
Nos. 1166-1168 (3) .75 .75

St. Francis Adoring Christ Child, Anonymous — A626

Photogravure and Engraved
1974, Nov. 26 ***Perf. 14x13½***
1169 A626 40 l multi .25 .25

Christmas 1974.

Masked Dancers — A627

1974, Dec. 1 Photo. *Perf. 13½x14*

1170	A627	40 l Pulcinella	.25	.25
1171	A627	50 l shown	.25	.25
1172	A627	90 l Pantaloon	.25	.25
		Nos. 1170-1172 (3)	.75	.75

16th Stamp Day 1974.

God Admonishing Adam, by Jacopo della Quercia — A628

Courtyard, Uffizi Gallery, Florence, by Giorgio Vasari A629

1974, Dec. 20 Engr. *Perf. 14*

1173	A628	90 l dk vio bl	.25	.25

Lithographed and Engraved

1174	A629	90 l multi	.25	.25

Italian artists: Jacopo della Quercia (1374-c. 1438), sculptor, and Giorgio Vasari (1511-1574), architect, painter and writer.

Angel with Tablet — A630

Angel with Cross — A632

Angels' Bridge, Rome — A631

Holy Year 1975: 50 l, Angel holding column. 150 l, Angel holding Crown of Thorns. The angels are statues by Giovanni Bernini on the Angels' Bridge (San Angelo).

1975, Mar. 25 Photo. *Perf. 14*

1175	A630	40 l multi	.25	.25
1176	A630	50 l bl & multi	.25	.25
1177	A631	90 l bl & multi	.25	.25
1178	A630	150 l vio & multi	.25	.25
1179	A632	180 l multi	.25	.25
		Nos. 1175-1179 (5)	1.25	1.25

Pitti Madonna, by Michelangelo A633

Works of Michelangelo: 50 l, Niche in Vatican Palace. 90 l, The Flood, detail from Sistine Chapel.

1975, Apr. 18 Engr. *Perf. 13½x14*

1180	A633	40 l dl grn	.25	.25
1181	A633	50 l sepia	.25	.25
1182	A633	90 l red brn	.25	.25
		Nos. 1180-1182 (3)	.75	.75

Michelangelo Buonarroti (1475-1564), sculptor, painter and architect.

Flagellation of Jesus, by Caravaggio A634

Europa: 150 l, Apparition of Angel to Hagar and Ishmael, by Tiepolo (detail).

1975, Apr. 29 Photo. *Perf. 13x14*

1183	A634	100 l multi	.25	.25
1184	A634	150 l multi	.30	.25

Four Days of Naples, by Marino Mazzacurati A635

Resistance Fighters of Cuneo, by Umberto Mastroianni A636

Design: 100 l, Martyrs of Ardeatine Caves, by Francesco Coccia.

1975, Apr. 23

1185	A635	70 l multi	.25	.25
1186	A636	100 l ol & multi	.25	.25
1187	A636	150 l multi	.25	.25
		Nos. 1185-1187 (3)	.75	.75

Resistance movement victory, 30th anniv.

Globe and IWY Emblem A637

1975, May *Perf. 14x13½*

1188	A637	70 l multi	.25	.25

International Women's Year 1975.

Satellite, San Rita Launching Platform — A638

1975, May 28 *Perf. 13½x14*

1189	A638	70 l multi	.25	.25

San Marco satellite project.

Tourist Type of 1974

Paintings: No. 1190, View of Isola Bella. No. 1191, Baths of Montecatini. No. 1192, View of Cefalù.

1975, June 16 Photo. *Perf. 14*

1190	A616	150 l grn & multi	.25	.25
1191	A616	150 l bl grn & multi	.25	.25
1192	A616	150 l red brn & multi	.25	.25
		Nos. 1190-1192 (3)	.75	.75

Artist and Model, Armando Spadini A640

Painting: No. 1194, Flora, by Guido Reni.

1975, June 20 Engr. *Perf. 14*

1193	A640	90 l blk & multi	.25	.25
1194	A640	90 l multi	.25	.25

50th death anniv. of Armando Spadini and 400th birth anniv. of Guido Reni.

Giovanni Pierluigi da Palestrina (1525-94), Composer of Sacred Music — A641

1975, June 27 Engr. *Perf. 13½x14*

1195	A641	100 l magenta & tan	.25	.25

Emmigrants and Ship A642

1975, June 30 Photo. *Perf. 14x13½*

1196	A642	70 l multi	.25	.25

Italian emigration centenary.

Emblem of United Legal Groups A643

1975, July 25 Photo. *Perf. 14x13½*

1197	A643	100 l yel, grn & red	.25	.25

Unification of Italian legal organizations, cent.

Locomotive Wheels A644

1975, Sept. 15 Photo. *Perf. 14x13½*

1198	A644	70 l multi	.25	.25

Intl. Railroad Union, 21st cong., Bologna.

Salvo D'Acquisto, by Vittorio Pisano A645

1975, Sept. 23

1199	A645	100 l multi	.25	.25

D'Acquisto died in 1943 saving 22 people.

Stylized Syracusean Italia — A646

1975, Sept. 26 Photo. *Perf. 13½x14*

1200	A646	100 l org & multi	.25	.25

Cent. of unification of the State Archives.

Fountain Type of 1973

Designs: No. 1201, Rosello Fountain, Sassari. No. 1202, Fountain of the 99 Faucets, Aquila. No. 1203, Piazza Fontana, Milan.

Photogravure and Engraved

1975, Oct. 30 *Perf. 13x14*

1201	A603	70 l blk & multi	.25	.25
1202	A603	70 l blk & multi	.25	.25
1203	A603	70 l blk & multi	.25	.25
		Nos. 1201-1203 (3)	.75	.75

Famous Men Type of 1973-74

Designs: No. 1204, Alessandro Scarlatti. No. 1205, Antonio Vivaldi. No. 1206, Gaspare Spontini. No. 1207, Ferruccio Busoni. No. 1208, Francesco Cilea. No. 1209, Franco Alfano.

1975, Nov. 14 Photo. *Perf. 14x13½*

1204	A602	100 l multi	.25	.25
1205	A602	100 l multi	.25	.25
1206	A602	100 l multi	.25	.25
1207	A602	100 l multi	.25	.25
1208	A602	100 l multi	.25	.25
1209	A602	100 l multi	.25	.25
		Nos. 1204-1209 (6)	1.50	1.50

Famous musicians.

Annunciation to the Shepherds A648

Christmas: 100 l, Nativity. 150 l, Annunciation to the Kings. Designs from painted wood panels, portal of Alatri Cathedral, 14th century.

Lithographed and Engraved

1975, Nov. 25 *Perf. 13½x14*

1210	A648	70 l grn & multi	.25	.25
1211	A648	100 l ultra & multi	.25	.25
1212	A648	150 l brn & multi	.25	.25
		Nos. 1210-1212 (3)	.75	.75

"The Magic Orchard" — A649

Children's Drawings: 70 l, Children on Horseback, horiz. 150 l, Village and procession, horiz.

Perf. 14x13½, 13½x14

1975, Dec. 7 **Photo.**
1213 A649 70 l multi .25 .25
1214 A649 100 l multi .25 .25
1215 A649 150 l multi .25 .25
Nos. 1213-1215 (3) .75 .75

17th Stamp Day.

Boccaccio, by Andrea del Castagno — A650

Design: 150 l, Frontispiece for "Fiammetta," 15th century woodcut.

Engraved and Lithographed

1975, Dec. 22 ***Perf. 13½x14***
1216 A650 100 l yel grn & blk .25 .25
1217 A650 150 l buff & multi .25 .25

Giovanni Boccaccio (1313-1375), writer.

State Advocate's Office, Rome — A651

1976, Jan. 30 **Photo.** ***Perf. 13½x14***
1218 A651 150 l multi .25 .25

State Advocate's Office, centenary.

ITALIA 76 Emblem — A652

Design: 180 l, Milan Fair pavilion.

1976, Mar. 27 **Photo.** ***Perf. 13½x14***
1219 A652 150 l blk, red & grn .25 .25
1220 A652 180 l blk, red, grn & bl .25 .25

ITALIA 76 International Philatelic Exhibition, Milan, Oct. 14-24.

Tourist Type of 1974

Tourist publicity: No. 1221, Fenis Castle. No. 1222, View of Ischia. No. 1223, Itria Valley.

1976, May 21 **Photo.** ***Perf. 14***
1221 A616 150 l grn & multi .25 .25
1222 A616 150 l plum & multi .25 .25
1223 A616 150 l yel & multi .25 .25
Nos. 1221-1223 (3) .75 .75

Majolica Plate, Deruta — A653

Europa: 180 l, Ceramic vase in shape of woman's head, Caltagirone.

1976, May 22 ***Perf. 13½x14***
1224 A653 150 l multi .25 .25
1225 A653 180 l brn & multi .30 .25

Italian Flags — A654

Italian Presidents A655

1976, June 1
1226 A654 100 l multi .25 .25
1227 A655 150 l multi .25 .25

30th anniversary of Italian Republic.

Fortitude, by Giacomo Serpotta, 1656-1732 A656

Paintings: No. 1229, Woman at Table, by Umberto Boccioni, 1882-1916. No. 1230, The Gunner's Letter, by F. T. Marinetti, 1876-1944.

1976, July 26 **Engr.** ***Perf. 14***
1228 A656 150 l blue .25 .25

Lithographed and Engraved

1229 A656 150 l multi .25 .25
1230 A656 150 l blk & red .25 .25
Nos. 1228-1230 (3) .75 .75

Italian art.

Paintings by Vittore Carpaccio (1460-1526), Venetian Painter — A657

Designs: No. 1231, St. George. No. 1232, Dragon, after painting in Church of St. George Schiavoni, Venice.

1976, July 30 **Engr.** ***Perf. 14x13½***
1231 A657 150 l rose lake .25 .25
1232 A657 150 l rose lake .25 .25
a. Pair, #1231-1232 + label .50 .25

Flora, by Titian A658

1976, Sept. 15 **Engr.** ***Perf. 14***
1233 A658 150 l carmine .25 .25

Titian (1477-1576), Venetian painter.

St. Francis, 13th Century Fresco — A659

1976, Oct. 2 **Engr.** ***Perf. 14***
1234 A659 150 l brown .25 .25

St. Francis of Assisi, 750th death anniv.

Cart, from Trajan's Column A660

100 l, Emblem of Kingdom of Sardinia. 150 l, Marble mask, 19th cent. mail box. 200 l, Hand canceler, 19th cent. 400 l, Automatic letter sorting machine.

1976, Oct. 14 **Photo.** ***Perf. 14x13½***
1235 A660 70 l multi .25 .25
1236 A660 100 l multi .25 .25
1237 A660 150 l multi .25 .25
1238 A660 200 l multi .25 .25
1239 A660 400 l multi .45 .25
Nos. 1235-1239 (5) 1.45 1.25

ITALIA 76 International Philatelic Exhibition, Milan, Oct. 14-24.

Girl and Animals — A661

Designs (Children' Drawings): 100 l, Trees, rabbit and flowers. 150 l, Boy healing tree.

1976, Oct. 17 ***Perf. 13½x14***
1240 A661 40 l multi .25 .25
1241 A661 100 l multi .25 .25
1242 A661 150 l multi .25 .25
Nos. 1240-1242 (3) .75 .75

18th Stamp Day and nature protection.

Famous Men Type of 1973-74

Designs: No. 1243, Lorenzo Ghiberti. No. 1244, Domenico Ghirlandaio. No. 1245, Sassoferrato. No. 1246, Carlo Dolci. No. 1247, Giovanni Piazzetta.

1976, Nov. 22 **Photo.** ***Perf. 14x13½***
1243 A602 170 l multi .25 .25
1244 A602 170 l multi .25 .25
1245 A602 170 l multi .25 .25
1246 A602 170 l multi .25 .25
1247 A602 170 l multi .25 .25
Nos. 1243-1247 (5) 1.25 1.25

Famous painters.

The Visit, by Silvestro Lega A662

1976, Dec. 7 **Photo.** ***Perf. 14x13½***
1248 A662 170 l multi .25 .25

Silvestro Lega (1826-1895), painter.

Adoration of the Kings, by Bartolo di Fredi — A663

Christmas: 120 l, Nativity, by Taddeo Gaddi.

1976, Dec. 11 ***Perf. 13½x14***
1249 A663 70 l multi .25 .25
1250 A663 120 l multi .25 .25

Fountain Type of 1973

Designs: No. 1251, Antique Fountain, Gallipoli. No. 1252, Madonna Fountain, Verona. No. 1253, Silvio Cosini Fountain, Palazzo Doria, Genoa.

Lithographed and Engraved

1976, Dec. 21 ***Perf. 13½x14***
1251 A603 170 l blk & multi .25 .25
1252 A603 170 l blk & multi .25 .25
1253 A603 170 l blk & multi .25 .25
Nos. 1251-1253 (3) .75 .75

Snakes Forming Net A664

Design: 170 l, Drug addict and poppy.

1977, Feb. 28 **Photo.** ***Perf. 14x13½***
1254 A664 120 l multi .25 .25
1255 A664 170 l multi .25 .25

Fight against drug abuse.

Micca Setting Fire A665

1977, Mar. 5
1256 A665 170 l multi .25 .25

Pietro Micca (1677-1706), patriot who set fire to the powder magazine of Turin Citadel.

Globe with Cross in Center — A666

Design: 120 l, People of the World united as brothers by St. John Bosco.

1977, Mar. 29 **Photo.** ***Perf. 13x13½***
1257 A666 70 l multi .25 .25
1258 A666 120 l multi .25 .25

Honoring the Salesian missionaries.

Italian Constitution, Article 53 — A667

1977, Apr. 14 **Photo.** ***Perf. 14***
1259 A667 120 l bis, brn & blk .25 .25
1260 A667 170 l lt grn, grn & blk .25 .25

"Pay your taxes."

Tourist Type of 1974

Europa (Europa Emblem and): 170 l, Taormina. 200 l, Castle del Monte.

1977, May 2

1261	A616	170 l multi	.65	.25
1262	A616	200 l multi	.85	.25

Tourist Type of 1974

Paintings: No. 1263, Canossa Castle. No. 1264, Fermo. No. 1265, Castellana Caves.

1977, May 30 Photo. *Perf. 14*

1263	A616	170 l brn & multi	.25	.25
1264	A616	170 l vio & multi	.25	.25
1265	A616	170 l gray & multi	.25	.25
		Nos. 1263-1265 (3)	.75	.75

Famous Men Type of 1973-74

Designs: No. 1266, Filippo Brunelleschi. No. 1267, Pietro Aretino. No. 1268, Carlo Goldoni. No. 1269, Luigi Cherubini. No. 1270, Eduardo Bassini.

1977, June 27 *Perf. 14x13½*

1266	A602	70 l multi	.25	.25
1267	A602	70 l multi	.25	.25
1268	A602	70 l multi	.25	.25
1269	A602	70 l multi	.25	.25
1270	A602	70 l multi	.25	.25
		Nos. 1266-1270 (5)	1.25	1.25

Famous artists, writers and scientists.

Justice, by Andrea Delitio A669

Painting: No. 1272, Winter, by Giuseppe Arcimboldi, 1527-c.1593.

Engraved and Lithographed

1977, Sept. 5 *Perf. 14*

1271	A669	170 l multi	.25	.25
1272	A669	170 l multi	.25	.25

Italian Ships — A670

No. 1273, Corvette Caracciolo. No. 1274, Hydrofoil gunboat Sparviero. No. 1275, Paddle steamer Ferdinando Primo. No. 1276, Passenger liner Saturnia.

Photogravure and Engraved

1977, Sept. 23 *Perf. 14x13½*

1273		170 l multi	.25	.25
1274		170 l multi	.25	.25
1275		170 l multi	.25	.25
1276		170 l multi	.25	.25
a.		A670 Block or strip of 4, #1273-1276 + 2 labels	1.00	.50

See Nos. 1323-1326, 1382-1385, 1435-1438.

Fountain Type of 1973

Designs: No. 1277, Pacassi Fountain, Gorizia. No. 1278, Fraterna Fountain, Isernia. No. 1279, Palm Fountain, Palmi.

Lithographed and Engraved

1977, Oct. 18 *Perf. 13x14*

1277	A603	120 l blk & multi	.25	.25
1278	A603	120 l blk & multi	.25	.25
1279	A603	120 l blk & multi	.25	.25
		Nos. 1277-1279 (3)	.75	.75

Volleyball — A671

Designs (Children's Drawings): No. 1281, Butterflies and net. No. 1282, Flying kites.

1977, Oct. 23 Photo. *Perf. 13x14*

1280	A671	120 l multi	.25	.25
1281	A671	120 l multi	.25	.25
1282	A671	120 l multi	.25	.25
a.		Block of 3, #1280-1282 + label	.50	.30

19th Stamp Day.

Symbolic Blood Donation A672

Design: 70 l, Blood donation symbolized.

1977, Oct. 26 *Perf. 14x13½*

1283	A672	70 l multi	.30	.25
1284	A672	120 l multi	.40	.25

Blood donors.

Quintino Sella and Italy No. 24 — A673

1977, Oct. 23 *Perf. 13½x14*

1285	A673	170 l olive & blk brn	.30	.25

Quintino Sella (1827-1884), statesman, engineer, mineralogist, birth sesquicentenary.

Italia Type of 1953-54 and

Italia — A674

1977-87 Wmk. 303 *Perf. 14*

Size: 16x20mm

Photo.

1288	A354	120 l dk bl & emer	.25	.25

Photo. & Engr.

1289	A354	170 l grn & ocher	.25	.25

Litho. & Engr.

1290	A354	350 l red, ocher & pur	.30	.25

Perf. 14x13½

Engr. Unwmk.

1291	A674	1500 l multi	2.25	.25
1292	A674	2000 l multi	3.00	.25
1293	A674	3000 l multi	4.00	.25
1294	A674	4000 l multi	8.00	.25
1295	A674	5000 l multi	.60	.35
1296	A674	10,000 l multi	12.50	.50
1297	A674	20,000 l multi	25.00	4.00
		Nos. 1288-1297 (10)	56.15	6.60

Issued: 120 l, 170 l, 350l, 11/22/77; 5,000 l, 12/4/78; 4,000 l, 2/12/79; 3,000 l, 3/12/79; 2,000 l, 4/12/79; 1,500 l, 5/14/79; 10,000 l, 6/27/83; 20,000 l, 1/5/87.

Dina Galli (1877-1951), Actress — A675

Perf. 13½x14

1977, Dec. 2 Photo. Unwmk.

1309	A675	170 l multi	.25	.25

Adoration of the Shepherds, by Pietro Testa — A676

Christmas: 120 l, Adoration of the Shepherds, by Gian Jacopo Caraglio.

Lithographed and Engraved

1977, Dec. 13 *Perf. 14*

1310	A676	70 l blk & ol	.25	.25
1311	A676	120 l blk & bl grn	.25	.25

La Scala Opera House, Milan, Bicent. — A677

Designs: 170 l, Facade. 200 l, Auditorium.

1978, Mar. 15 Litho. *Perf. 13½x14*

1312	A677	170 l multi	.25	.25
1313	A677	200 l multi	.40	.25

Tourist Type of 1974

Paintings: 70 l, Gubbio. 200 l, Udine. 600 l, Paestum.

1978, Mar. 30 Photo. *Perf. 14*

1314	A616	70 l multi	.25	.25
1315	A616	200 l multi	.30	.25
1316	A616	600 l multi	.75	.45
		Nos. 1314-1316 (3)	1.30	.95

Giant Grouper A678

Designs (outline of "Amerigo Vespucci" in background): No. 1318, Leatherback turtle. No. 1319, Mediterranean monk seal. No. 1320, Audouin's gull.

1978, Apr. 3 *Perf. 14x13*

1317	A678	170 l multi	.40	.25
1318	A678	170 l multi	.40	.25
1319	A678	170 l multi	.40	.25
1320	A678	170 l multi	.40	.25
a.		Strip of 4, #1317-1320 + label	1.60	1.00

Endangered species in Mediterranean.

Castel Nuovo, Angevin Fortifications, Naples — A679

Europa: 200 l, Pantheon, Rome.

1978, Apr. 29 Litho. *Perf. 14x13½*

1321	A679	170 l multi	.30	.25
1322	A679	200 l multi	.40	.25

Ship Type of 1977

Designs: No. 1323, Cruiser Benedetto Brin. No. 1324, Frigate Lupo. No. 1325, Ligurian brigantine Fortuna. No. 1326, Container ship Africa.

1978, May 8 Litho. & Engr.

1323		170 l multi	.35	.25
1324		170 l multi	.35	.25
1325		170 l multi	.35	.25
1326		170 l multi	.35	.25
a.		A670 Block of 4, #1323-1326 + 2 labels	1.50	1.40

Matilde Serao — A680

Portraits of famous Italians: No. 1328, Vittorino da Feltre. No. 1329, Victor Emmanuel II. No. 1330, Pope Pius IX. No. 1331, Marcello Malpighi. No. 1332, Antonio Meucci.

1978, May 10 Engr. *Perf. 14x13½*

1327	A680	170 l pink & black	.25	.25
1328	A680	170 l blue & black	.25	.25
1329	A680	170 l blue & dk blue	.25	.25
1330	A680	170 l green & black	.25	.25
1331	A680	170 l green & brown	.25	.25
1332	A680	170 l pink & blue	.25	.25
a.		Block of 6, #1327-1332	1.50	.75

Constitution, 30th Anniv. — A681

1978, June 2 Litho. *Perf. 13½x14*

1333	A681	170 l multi	.25	.25

Telegraph Wires and Lens — A682

1978, June 30 Photo.

1334	A682	120 l lt bl & gray	.25	.25

Photographic information.

The Lovers, by Tranquillo Cremona (1837-1878) — A683

Design: 520 l, The Cook (woman with goose), by Bernardo Strozzi (1581-1644).

Engraved and Lithographed

1978, July 12 ***Perf. 14***
1335 A683 170 l multi .50 .25
1336 A683 520 l multi 1.75 .70

Holy Shroud of Turin, by Giovanni Testa, 1578 — A684

1978, Sept. 8 **Photo.** ***Perf. 14***
1337 A684 220 l yel, red & blk .45 .25

400th anniversary of the transfer of the Holy Shroud from Savoy to Turin.

Volleyball — A685

Design: 120 l, Volleyball, diff.

1978, Sept. 20
1338 A685 80 l multi .25 .25
1339 A685 120 l multi .30 .25

Men's Volleyball World Championship.

Mother and Child, by Masaccio — A686

1978, Oct. 18 **Engr.** ***Perf. 13½x14***
1340 A686 170 l indigo .25 .25

Masaccio (real name Tommaso Guidi; 1401-28), painter.

Fountain Type of 1973

Designs: No 1341, Neptune Fountain, Trent. No. 1342, Fortuna Fountain, Fano. No. 1343, Cavallina Fountain, Genzano di Lucania.

1978, Oct. 25 **Litho. & Engr.**
1341 A603 120 l blk & multi .25 .25
1342 A603 120 l blk & multi .25 .25
1343 A603 120 l blk & multi .25 .25
Nos. 1341-1343 (3) .75 .75

Virgin and Child, by Giorgione — A687

Adoration of the Kings, by Giorgione — A688

1978, Nov. 8 **Engr.** ***Perf. 13x14***
1344 A687 80 l dark red .25 .25

Photo. ***Perf. 14x13½***
1345 A688 120 l multi .25 .25

Christmas 1978.

Flags as Flowers — A689

Designs: No. 1347, European flags. No. 1348, "People hailing Europe."

1978, Nov. 26 **Photo.** ***Perf. 13x14***
1346 A689 120 l multi .25 .25
1347 A689 120 l multi .25 .25
1348 A689 120 l multi .25 .25
Nos. 1346-1348 (3) .75 .75

20th Stamp Day on theme "United Europe."

State Printing Office, Stamps A690

Design: 220 l, Printing press and stamps.

1979, Jan. 6 **Photo.** ***Perf. 14x13½***
1349 A690 170 l multi .25 .25
1350 A690 220 l multi .35 .25

1st stamps printed by State Printing Office, 50 anniv.

St. Francis Washing Lepers, 13th Century Painting A691

1979, Jan. 22
1351 A691 80 l multi .25 .25

Leprosy relief.

Bicyclist Carrying Bike — A692

1979, Jan. 27 ***Perf. 13½x14***
1352 A692 170 l multi .25 .25
1353 A692 220 l multi .35 .25

World Crosscountry Bicycle Championships.

Virgin Mary, by Antonello da Messina A693

Painting: 520 l, Haystack, by Ardengo Soffici (1879-1964).

1979, Feb. 15 **Engr.** ***Perf. 14***
1354 A693 170 l multi .30 .25
1355 A693 520 l multi .70 .50

Albert Einstein (1879-1955), Theoretical Physicist and His Equation. — A694

Lithographed and Engraved

1979, Mar. 14 ***Perf. 13x14***
1356 A694 120 l multi .25 .25

Tourist Type of 1974

Paintings: 70 l, Asiago. 90 l, Castelsardo. 170 l, Orvieto. 220 l, Scilla.

1979, Mar. 30 **Photo.** ***Perf. 14***
1357 A616 70 l grn & multi .25 .25
1358 A616 90 l car & multi .25 .25
1359 A616 170 l ultra & multi .25 .25
1360 A616 220 l gray & multi .35 .25
Nos. 1357-1360 (4) 1.10 1.00

Famous Italians — A695

No. 1361, Carlo Maderno (1556-1629), architect. No. 1362, Lazzaro Spallanzani (1729-1799), physiologist. No. 1363, Ugo Foscolo (1778-1827), writer. No. 1364 Massimo Bontempelli (1878-1960), journalist. No. 1365, Francesco Severi (1879-1961), mathematician.

1979, Apr. 23 **Engr.** ***Perf. 14x13½***
1361 A695 170 l multi .25 .25
1362 A695 170 l multi .25 .25
1363 A695 170 l multi .25 .25
1364 A695 170 l multi .25 .25
1365 A695 170 l multi .25 .25
Nos. 1361-1365 (5) 1.25 1.25

Telegraph A696

Europa: 220 l, Carrier pigeons.

1979, Apr. 30 **Photo.** ***Perf. 14***
1366 A696 170 l multi .65 .25
1367 A696 220 l multi .65 .30

Flags and "E" — A697

1979, May 5 ***Perf. 14x13½***
1368 A697 170 l multi .25 .25
1369 A697 220 l multi .30 .25

European Parliament, first direct elections, June 7-10.

Exhibition Emblem, Dome of Milan A698

1979, June 22 **Photo.** ***Perf. 14***
1370 A698 170 l multi .25 .25
1371 A698 220 l multi .30 .25

3rd World Machine Tool Exhib., Milan, Oct. 10-18.

Aeneas and Rotary Emblem — A699

1979, June 9 ***Perf. 13½x14***
1372 A699 220 l multi .30 .25

70th World Rotary Cong., Rome, June 1979.

Basket — A700

120 l, Basketball players.

1979, June 13 ***Perf. 14***
1373 A700 80 l shown .25 .25
1374 A700 120 l multicolored .25 .25

21st European Basketball Championship, June 9-20.

A701

Patient & Physician, 16th cent. woodcut.

1979, June 16 **Photo. & Engr.**
1375 A701 120 l multi .25 .25

Digestive Ailments Study Week.

A702

Design: Ottorino Respighi (1879-1936), composer, Roman landscape.

Lithographed and Engraved

1979, July 9 *Perf. 13x14*
1376 A702 120 l multi .25 .25

Woman Making Phone Call A703

200 l, Woman with old-fashioned phone.

1979, Sept. 20 **Photo.** *Perf. 14*
1377 A703 170 l red & gray .25 .25
1378 A703 220 l grn & slate .30 .25

3rd World Telecommunications Exhibition, Geneva, Sept. 20-26.

Fountain Type of 1973

Designs: No. 1379, Great Fountain, Viterbo. No. 1380, Hot Springs, Acqui Terme. No. 1381, Pomegranate Fountain, Issogne Castle.

Lithographed and Engraved

1979, Sept. 22 *Perf. 13x14*
1379 A603 120 l multi .35 .25
1380 A603 120 l multi .35 .25
1381 A603 120 l multi .35 .25
Nos. 1379-1381 (3) 1.05 .75

Ship Type of 1977

Designs: No. 1382, Cruiser Enrico Dandolo. No. 1383, Submarine Carlo Fecia. No. 1384, Freighter Cosmos. No. 1385, Ferry Deledda.

1979, Oct. 12 *Perf. 14x13½*
1382 170 l multi .35 .25
1383 170 l multi .35 .25
1384 170 l multi .35 .25
1385 170 l multi .35 .25
a. A670 Block of 4, #1382-1385 + 2 labels 1.60 1.40

Penny Black, Rowland Hill A704

1979, Oct. 25 **Photo.**
1386 A704 220 l multi .30 .25

Minstrels and Church A705

1979, Nov. 7 **Photo.** *Perf. 14x13½*
1387 A705 120 l multi .25 .25

Christmas 1979.

Black and White Boys Holding Hands A706

Children's Drawings: 120 l, Children of various races under umbrella map, vert. 150 l, Children and red balloons.

Perf. 14x13½, 13½x14

1979, Nov. 25 **Photo.**
1388 A706 70 l multi .25 .25
1389 A706 120 l multi .25 .25
1390 A706 150 l multi .25 .25
Nos. 1388-1390 (3) .75 .75

21st Stamp Day.

Solar Energy Panels A707

Energy Conservation: 170 l, Sun & pylon.

1980, Feb. 25 **Photo.** *Perf. 14x13½*
1391 A707 120 l multi .25 .25
1392 A707 170 l multi .25 .25

St. Benedict of Nursia, 1500th Birth Anniv. — A708

1980, Mar. 21 **Engr.** *Perf. 13½x14*
1393 A708 220 l dark blue .30 .25

Royal Palace, Naples — A709

Lithographed and Engraved

1980, Apr. 16 *Perf. 13½x14*
1394 A709 220 l multi .30 .25

20th International Philatelic Exhibition, Europa '80, Naples, Apr. 26-May 4.

Antonio Pigafetta, Caravel A710

Europa: 220 l, Antonio Lo Surdo (1880-1949) geophysicist.

1980, Apr. 28 **Litho.** *Perf. 14x13½*
1395 A710 170 l multi .40 .25
1396 A710 220 l multi *.70* .30

St. Catherine, Reliquary Bust — A711

1980, Apr. 29 **Photo.**
1397 A711 170 l multi .25 .25

St. Catherine of Siena (1347-1380).

Italian Red Cross A712

1980, May 15 **Photo.** *Perf. 14x13½*
1398 A712 70 l multi .25 .25
1399 A712 80 l multi .25 .25

Temples of Philae, Egypt — A713

1980, May 20
1400 Pair + label .70 .25
a. A713 220 l shown .35 .25
b. A713 220 l Temple of Philae, diff. .35 .25

Italian civil engineering achievements (Temples of Philae saved from ruin by Italian engineers).

Soccer Player A714

1980, June 11
1401 A714 80 l multi 1.50 1.10

European Soccer Championships, Milan, Turin, Rome, Naples, June 9-22.

Tourist Type of 1974

Paintings: 80 l, Erice. 150 l, Villa Rufolo, Ravello. 200 l, Roseto degli Abruzzi. 670 l, Public Baths, Salsomaggiore Terme.

1980, June 28 *Perf. 14*
1402 A616 80 l multi .25 .25
1403 A616 150 l multi .25 .25
1404 A616 200 l multi .30 .25
1405 A616 670 l multi .90 .75
Nos. 1402-1405 (4) 1.70 1.50

Cosimo I with his Artists, by Giorgio Vasari, and Armillary sphere — A715

1980, July 2 *Perf. 13½x14*
1406 A715 Pair + label .50 .50
a. 170 l Cosimo I .25 .25
b. 170 l Armillary sphere .25 .25

The Medici in Europe of the 16th Century Exhibition, Florence.

Fonte Avellana Monastery Millennium A716

1980, Sept. 3 **Engr.** *Perf. 14x13½*
1407 A716 200 l grn & brn .30 .25

Castles — A717

Designs: No. 1408, St. Angelo Castle, Rome. No. 1409, Sforzesco, Milan. No. 1410, Del Monte, Andria. No. 1411, Ursino, Catania. No. 1412, Rocca di Calascio. No. 1413, Norman Tower, St. Mauro Fort. No. 1414, Isola Capo Rizzuto. No. 1415, Aragonese, Ischia. No. 1416, Estense, Ferrarra. No. 1417, Miramare, Trieste. No. 1418, Ostia, Rome. No. 1419, Gavarone, Savona. No. 1420, Cerro al Volturno, Isernia. No. 1421, Rocca di Mondavio. No. 1422, Svevo, Bari. No. 1423, Mussomelli, Caltanissetta. No. 1424, Imperatore-Prato, Florence. No. 1425, Bosa, Nuoro. No. 1426, Rovereto, Trento. No. 1427, Scaligero, Sirmione. No. 1428, Ivrea, Turin. No. 1429, Rocca Maggiore, Assisi. No. 1430, St. Pierre, Aosta. No. 1431 Montagnana, Padua. No. 1432, St. Severna, Rome. No. 1433, Lombardia, Enna. No. 1434, Serralunga d'Alba, Cuneo.

Photo. (#1408-1417), Litho. and Engr. (#1418-1422, 1425, 1427-1428), Engr. (#1423-1424, 1426, 1429-1434)

Perf. 14x13½

1980, Sept. 22 **Wmk. 303**
1408 A717 5 l multi .25 .25
1409 A717 10 l multi .25 .25
1410 A717 20 l multi .25 .25
1411 A717 40 l multi .25 .25
1412 A717 50 l multi .25 .25
1413 A717 60 l multi .25 .25
1414 A717 90 l multi .25 .25
1415 A717 100 l multi .25 .25
1416 A717 120 l multi .25 .25
1417 A717 150 l multi .25 .25
1418 A717 170 l multi .70 .25
1419 A717 180 l multi 1.20 *1.00*
1420 A717 200 l multi .75 .25
1421 A717 250 l multi .70 .25
1422 A717 300 l multi .80 .25
1423 A717 350 l multi .80 .25
1424 A717 400 l multi .80 .25
1425 A717 450 l multi 1.00 .25
1426 A717 500 l multi .80 .25
1427 A717 600 l multi .90 .25
1428 A717 700 l multi 1.00 .25
1429 A717 800 l multi 1.10 .25
1430 A717 900 l multi 1.25 .25
1431 A717 1000 l multi 1.25 .25
Nos. 1408-1431 (24) 15.55 6.75

Coil Stamps
Perf. 14 Vert.

Size: 16x21mm

1432 A717 30 l multi .25 .25
1433 A717 120 l multi .25 .25
a. Pair, Nos. 1432-1433 .40 .25
1434 A717 170 l multi .30 .25
a. Pair, Nos. 1432, 1434 .75 .75
Nos. 1432-1434 (3) .80 .75

No. 1412 exists dated "1980."

See Nos. 1475-1484, 1657-1666, 1862-1866.

Ship Type of 1977

No. 1435, Corvette Gabbiano. No. 1436, Torpedo boat Audace. No. 1437, Sailing ship Italia. No. 1438, Floating dock Castoro Sei.

Lithographed and Engraved

1980, Oct. 11 *Perf. 14x13½*
1435 200 l multi .60 .40
1436 200 l multi .60 .40
1437 200 l multi .60 .40
1438 200 l multi .60 .40
a. A670 Block of 4, #1435-1438 + 2 labels *6.00* 6.00

Philip Mazzei (1730-1816), Political Writer in US — A718

1980, Oct. 18 Photo. *Perf. 13½x14*
1439 A718 320 l multi .50 .30

Villa Foscari Malcontenta, Venezia — A719

Villas: 150 l, Barbaro Maser, Treviso. 170 l, Godi Valmarana, Vicenza.

Lithographed and Engraved

1980, Oct. 31 *Perf. 14x13½*
1440 A719 80 l multi .30 .30
1441 A719 150 l multi .50 .25
1442 A719 170 l multi .60 .25
Nos. 1440-1442 (3) 1.40 .80

See Nos. 1493-1495, 1528-1530, 1565-1568, 1606-1609, 1646-1649, 1691-1695.

St. Barbara, by Palma the Elder (1480-1528) — A720

Design: No. 1444, Apollo and Daphne, by Gian Lorenzo Bernini (1598-1680).

1980, Nov. 20 *Perf. 14*
1443 A720 520 l multi .75 .55
1444 A720 520 l multi .75 .55

Nativity Sculpture by Federico Brandini, 16th Cent. — A721

1980, Nov. 22 Engr.
1445 A721 120 l brn org & blk .25 .25

Christmas 1980.

View of Verona A722

22nd Stamp Day: Views of Verona drawings by school children.

1980, Nov. 30 Photo. *Perf. 14x13½*
1446 A722 70 l multi .25 .25
1447 A722 120 l multi .25 .25
1448 A722 170 l multi .25 .25
Nos. 1446-1448 (3) .75 .75

Daniele Comboni (1831-1881), Savior of the Africans — A723

1981, Mar. 14 Engr.
1449 A723 80 l multi .25 .25

Alcide de Gasperi (1881-1954), Statesman A724

1981, Apr. 3 *Perf. 13½x14*
1450 A724 200 l olive green .30 .25

International Year of the Disabled — A725

1981, Apr. 11 Photo.
1451 A725 300 l multi .40 .35

A726

1981, Apr. 27 Photo. *Perf. 13½x14*
1452 A726 200 l Roses .30 .25
1453 A726 200 l Anemones .30 .25
1454 A726 200 l Oleanders .30 .25
Nos. 1452-1454 (3) .90 .75

See Nos. 1510-1512, 1555-1557.

Europa — A727

Designs: No. 1455, Chess game with human pieces, Marostica. No. 1456, Horse race, Siena.

1981, May 4
1455 A727 300 l shown 1.00 .25
1456 A727 300 l multicolored 1.00 .25

St. Rita Offering Thorn — A728

1981, May 22
1457 A728 600 l multi .80 .40

St. Rita of Cascia, 600th birth anniversary.

Ciro Menotti (1798-1831), Patriot — A729

1981, May 26 Engr. *Perf. 14x13½*
1458 A729 80 l brn & blk .25 .25

Italian Aircraft — A730

No. 1459, G-222 Aeritalia transport. No. 1460, MB-339 Aermacchi jet. No. 1461, A-109 Agusta helicopter. No. 1462, P-68 Partenavia transport.

1981, June 1 Photo.
1459 200 l multicolored .30 .25
1460 200 l multicolored .30 .25
1461 200 l multicolored .30 .25
1462 200 l multicolored .30 .25
a. A730 Block of 4, #1459-1462 + 2 labels 1.40 1.40

See Nos. 1505-1508, 1550-1553.

Hydro-geological Research — A731

1981, June 8 *Perf. 13½x14*
1463 A731 80 l multi .25 .25

Sao Simao Dam and Power Station, Brazil — A732

Civil Engineering Works Abroad: No. 1465, High Island Reservoir, Hong Kong.

1981, June 26 Engr. *Perf. 14x13½*
1464 A732 300 l dark blue .45 .25
1465 A732 300 l red .45 .25
a. Pair, #1464-1465 + label 1.00 .80

See Nos. 1516-1517, 1538-1539.

Tourist Type of 1974

80 l, View of Matera. 150 l, Lake Garda. 300 l, St. Teresa di Gallura beach. 900 l, Tarquinia.

1981, July 4 Photo. *Perf. 14*
1466 A616 80 l multi .25 .25
1467 A616 150 l multi .35 1.10
1468 A616 300 l multi .50 .45
1469 A616 900 l multi 1.40 .55
Nos. 1466-1469 (4) 2.50 2.35

Naval Academy, Livorno and Navy Emblem A735

Naval Academy of Livorno Centenary: 150 l, View. 200 l, Cadet with sextant, training ship Amerigo Vespucci.

1981, July 24 *Perf. 14x13½*
1472 A735 80 l multi .25 .25
1473 A735 150 l multi .25 .25
1474 A735 200 l multi .35 .25
Nos. 1472-1474 (3) .85 .75

Castle Type of 1980

30 l, Aquila. 70 l, Aragonese, Reggio Calabria. 80 l, Sabbionara, Avio. 550 l, Rocca Sinibalda. 1400 l, Caldoresco, Vasto.

Perf. 14x13½

1981-84 Photo. Wmk. 303
1475 A717 30 l multicolored .25 .25
1476 A717 70 l multicolored .25 .25
1477 A717 80 l multicolored .25 .25

Perf. 13½
1478 A717 550 l multicolored .70 .25

Engr.
1479 A717 1400 l multicolored 1.60 .50
Nos. 1475-1479 (5) 3.05 1.50

Issue dates: Nos. 1475-1477, Aug. 20, 1981; Nos. 1478-1479, Feb. 14, 1984.

Coil Stamps

50 l, Scilla. 200 l, Angioina, Lucera. 300 l, Norman Castle, Melfi. 400 l, Venafro. 450 l, Piobbico Pesaro.

1981-88 Engr. *Perf. 14 Vert.*
Size: 16x21mm
1480 A717 50 l blue .25 .25
1481 A717 200 l blue & pur 1.00 1.00
1482 A717 300 l bl grn & grn .30 .25
1483 A717 400 l ol grn & red brn .60 .25
1484 A717 450 l green .50 .25
a. Pair, #1480, 1484 1.00 .75
Nos. 1480-1484 (5) 2.65 2.00

Issued: Nos. 1481-1482, 9/30; No. 1483, 6/25/83; Nos. 1480, 1484, 7/25/85; No. 1484a, 3/1/88.

Palazzo Spada, Rome (Council Seat) A736

1981, Aug. 31 Engr. Unwmk.
1485 A736 200 l multi .30 .25

State Council sesquicentennial.

World Cup Races — A737

1981, Sept. 4 Photo. *Perf. 13½x14*
1486 A737 300 l multi .40 .25

Harbor View, by Carlo Carra (1881-1966) — A738

No. 1488, Castle, by Guiseppe Ugonia (1881-1944).

Lithographed and Engraved

1981, Sept. 7 *Perf. 14*
1487 A738 200 l multi .30 .25
1488 A738 200 l multi .30 .25

See Nos. 1532-1533, 1638-1639, 1697-1698, 1732.

Riace Bronze, 4th Cent. B.C. — A739

1981, Sept. 9 Photo. *Perf. 13½x14*
1489 200 l Statue .30 .25
1490 200 l Statue, diff. .30 .25
a. A739 Pair, #1489-1490 .70 .60

Greek statues found in 1972 in sea near Reggio di Calabria.

Virgil, Mosaic, Treviri A740

1981, Sept. 19 *Perf. 14*
1491 A740 600 l multi .75 .40

Virgil's death bimillennium.

Food and Wine, by Gregorio Sciltian A741

1981, Oct. 16 Litho. *Perf. 14*
1492 A741 150 l multi .40 .25

World Food Day.

Villa Type of 1980

100 l, Villa Campolieto, Ercolano. 200 l, Cimbrone, Ravello. 300 l, Pignatelli, Naples.

Lithographed and Engraved

1981, Oct. 17 *Perf. 14x13½*
1493 A719 100 l multicolored .25 .25
1494 A719 200 l multicolored .30 .25
1495 A719 300 l multicolored .50 .50
Nos. 1493-1495 (3) 1.05 1.00

Adoration of the Magi, by Giovanni de Campione d'Italia (Christmas 1981) — A743

1981, Nov. 21 Engr. *Perf. 14*
1496 A743 200 l multi .30 .25

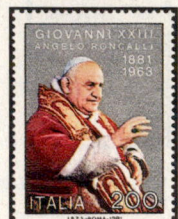

Pope John XXIII (1881-1963) A744

1981, Nov. 25 Photo. *Perf. 13½x14*
1497 A744 200 l multi .65 .25

Stamp Day — A745

120 l, Letters, horiz. 200 l, Angel, letter chest. 300 l, Letter seal.

Photogravure, Photogravure and Engraved (200 l)
Perf. 14x13½, 13½x14

1981, Nov. 29
1498 A745 120 l multicolored .25 .25
1499 A745 200 l multicolored .40 .55
1500 A745 300 l multicolored .60 .25
Nos. 1498-1500 (3) 1.25 1.05

St. Francis of Assisi, 800th Birth Anniv. — A746

Design: St. Francis Receiving the Stigmata, by Pietro Cavaro.

1982, Jan. 6 *Perf. 13½x14*
1501 A746 300 l dk bl & brn .40 .25

Niccolo Paganini (1782-1840), Composer, Violinist — A748

1982, Feb. 19 Photo. *Perf. 13½x14*
1503 A748 900 l multi 1.25 1.00

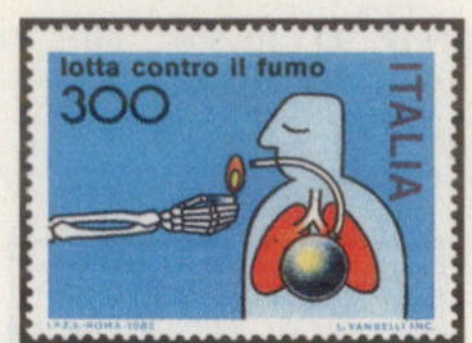

Anti-smoking Campaign — A749

1982, Mar. 2 Photo. *Perf. 14x13½*
1504 A749 300 l multi .40 .25

Aircraft Type of 1981

No. 1505, Aeritalia MRCA. No. 1506, SIAI 260 Turbo. No. 1507, Piaggio 166-dl3 Turbo. No. 1508, Nardi NH-500.

1982, Mar. 27 Litho. *Perf. 14x13½*
1505 300 l multicolored .55 .55
1506 300 l multicolored .55 .55
1507 300 l multicolored .55 .55
1508 300 l multicolored .55 .55
a. A730 Block of 4, #1505-1508 + 2 labels 3.50 3.00

Sicilian Vespers, 700th Anniv. — A750

1982, Mar. 31 Engr. *Perf. 13½x14*
1509 A750 120 l multi .25 .25

Flower Type of 1981

1982, Apr. 10 **Photo.**
1510 A726 300 l Cyclamens .50 .50
1511 A726 300 l Camellias .50 .50
1512 A726 300 l Carnations .50 .50
Nos. 1510-1512 (3) 1.50 1.50

Europa — A751

200 l, Coronation of Charlemagne, 799. 450 l, Treaty of Rome signatures, 1957.

Photogravure and Engraved

1982, May 3 *Perf. 13½x14*
1513 A751 200 l multicolored .70 .70
1514 A751 450 l multicolored 1.10 .55

Engineering Type of 1981

No. 1516, Microwaves across Red Sea. No. 1517, Automatic letter sorting.

1982, May 29 Photo. *Perf. 14x13½*
1516 A732 450 l multicolored .60 .25
1517 A732 450 l multicolored .60 .25
a. Pair, #1516-1517 + label 1.50 1.50

Giuseppe Garibaldi (1807-82) A753

1982, June 2 *Perf. 13½x14*
1518 A753 200 l multicolored .60 .60

Game of the Bridge, Pisa — A754

1982, June 5
1519 A754 200 l multi .35 .35

See Nos. 1562, 1603, 1628-1629, 1655, 1717, 1749, 1775, 1807.

Tourist Type of 1974

No. 1520, Frasassi Caves. No. 1521, Paganella Valley. No. 1522, Temple of Agrigento. No. 1523, Rodi Garganico Beach.

1982, June 28 *Perf. 14*
1520 A616 200 l multicolored .50 .60
1521 A616 200 l multicolored .50 .60
1522 A616 450 l multicolored .75 .40
1523 A616 450 l multicolored .75 .40
Nos. 1520-1523 (4) 2.50 2.00

World Junior Canoeing Championship — A755

1982, Aug. 4 Photo. *Perf. 14*
1524 A755 200 l multi .40 .35

Duke Federico da Montefeltro (1422-1482) — A756

200 l, Urbino Palace, Gubbio Council House.

Photogravure and Engraved

1982, Sept. 10 *Perf. 14x13½*
1525 A756 200 l multicolored .30 .30

Italy's Victory in 1982 World Cup A757

1982, Sept. 12 Photo. *Perf. 14*
1526 A757 1000 l World Cup 1.75 1.50

69th Inter-Parliamentary Conference, Rome — A758

1982, Sept. 14 *Perf. 14x13½*
1527 A758 450 l multi .55 .25

Villa Type of 1980

Designs: 150 l, Temple of Aesculapius, Villa Borghese, Rome. 250 l, Villa D'Este, Tivoli, Rome. 350 l, Villa Lante, Bagnaia, Viterbo.

Photogravure and Engraved

1982, Oct. 1 *Perf. 14x13½*

1528 A719 150 l multi .45 .45
1529 A719 250 l multi .65 .25
1530 A719 350 l multi 1.00 1.10
Nos. 1528-1530 (3) 2.10 1.80

Thurn and Taxis Family Postal Service — A759

300 l, Franz von Taxis (1450-1517).

1982, Oct. 23 **Engr.** *Perf. 13½x14*

1531 A759 300 l multicolored .40 .25

Art Type of 1981

Paintings: No. 1532, The Fortune Teller by G.B. Piazzetta (1682-1754). No. 1533, Antonietta Negroni Prati Morosini as a Little Girl by Francesco Hayez (1791-1882).

Lithographed and Engraved

1982, Nov. 3 *Perf. 14*

1532 A738 300 l multi .55 .50
1533 A738 300 l multi .55 .50

24th Stamp Day A761

Children's Drawings.

1982, Nov. 28 **Photo.** *Perf. 14x13½*

1534 A761 150 l multi .25 .25
1535 A761 250 l multi .50 .30
1536 A761 350 l multi .65 .55
Nos. 1534-1536 (3) 1.40 1.10

Cancer Research — A762

1983, Jan. 14 **Photo.** *Perf. 13½x14*

1537 A762 400 l multi .55 .35

Engineering Type of 1981

No. 1538, Globe, factories. No. 1539, Automated assembly line.

1983, Jan. 20 *Perf. 13½*

1538 A732 400 l multicolored .55 .35
1539 A732 400 l multicolored .55 .35
a. Pair, #1538-1539 1.30 1.30

Crusca Academy, 400th Anniv. — A763

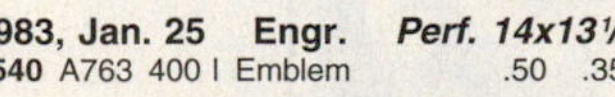

1983, Jan. 25 **Engr.** *Perf. 14x13½*

1540 A763 400 l Emblem .50 .35

World Biathlon Championship — A764

1983, Feb. 5 **Photo.** *Perf. 14*

1541 A764 200 l multi .40 .40

Gabriele Rossetti (1783-1854), Writer — A765

1983, Feb. 28 **Engr.** *Perf. 14x13½*

1542 A765 300 l dk brn & dk bl .40 .30

Francesco Guicciardini (1483-1540), Historian — A766

1983, Mar. 5 **Engr.** *Perf. 13½x14*

1543 A766 450 l sepia .60 .35

Umberto Saba (1883-1957), Poet — A767

1983, Mar. 9 **Photo.** *Perf. 14x13½*

1544 A767 600 l multi .75 .45

Pope Pius XII (1876-1958) A768

1983, Mar. 21 **Engr.** *Perf. 13½x14*

1545 A768 1400 l dark blue 2.00 .95

Holy Year — A769

250 l, St. Paul's Basilica. 300 l, St. Maria Maggiore Church. 400 l, San Giovanni Church. 500 l, St. Peter's Church.

1983, Mar. 25 **Photo.** *Perf. 14*

1546 A769 250 l multicolored .35 .35
1547 A769 300 l multicolored .50 .25
1548 A769 400 l multicolored .55 .25
1549 A769 500 l multicolored .70 .25
Nos. 1546-1549 (4) 2.10 1.10

Aircraft Type of 1981

No. 1550, Caproni C22J glider. No. 1551, Aeritalia Macchi jet fighter. No. 1552, SIAI-211 jet trainer. No. 1553, A-129 Agusta helicopter.

1983, Mar. 28 **Litho.** *Perf. 14x13½*

1550 400 l multicolored .50 .50
1551 400 l multicolored .50 .50
1552 400 l multicolored .50 .50
1553 400 l multicolored .50 .50
a. A730 Block or strip of 4, #1550-1553 + 2 labels 2.50 2.50

Intl. Workers' Day (May 1) — A770

1983, Apr. 29 **Engr.** *Perf. 14x13½*

1554 A770 1200 l blue 1.40 .90

Flower Type of 1981

1983, Apr. 30 **Photo.** *Perf. 13½x14*

1555 A726 200 l Mimosa .50 .50
1556 A726 200 l Rhododendron .50 .50
1557 A726 200 l Gladiolus .50 .50
Nos. 1555-1557 (3) 1.50 1.50

Europa 1983 A771

400 l, Galileo, telescope, 160l. 500 l, Archimedes and his screw.

Litho. & Engr.

1983, May 2 *Perf. 14x13½*

1558 A771 400 l multicolored *1.50* 1.00
1559 A771 500 l multicolored *2.00* .90

Ernesto T. Moneta (1833-1918), Nobel Peace Prize Winner, 1907 — A772

1983, May 5 **Engr.** *Perf. 14x13½*

1560 A772 500 l multi .65 .30

Monument, Globe, Computer Screen — A773

1983, May 9 **Photo.** *Perf. 13½x14*

1561 A773 500 l multi .65 .30

3rd Intl. Congress of Jurisdicial Information.

Folk Celebration Type of 1982

No. 1562, La Corsa Dei Ceri Procession, Gubbio.

1983, May 13 *Perf. 13½*

1562 A754 300 l multi .55 .30

20th Natl. Eucharistic Congress — A775

1983, May 14 *Perf. 14*

1563 A775 300 l multi .40 .30

Tourist Type of 1974

1983, July 30 **Photo.** *Perf. 14*

1563A A616 250 l Alghero .75 1.40
1563B A616 300 l Bardonecchia .75 .75
1563C A616 400 l Riccione .60 .65
1563D A616 500 l Taranto .70 .40
Nos. 1563A-1563D (4) 2.80 3.20

Girolamo Frescobaldi (1583-1643), Composer A776

1983, Sept. 15 **Engr.** *Perf. 13½x14*

1564 A776 400 l brn & grn .50 .30

Villa Type of 1980

Designs: 250 l, Fidelia, Spello. 300 l, Imperiale, Pesaro. 400 l, Michetti Convent, Francavilla al Mare. 500 l, Riccia.

Photogravure and Engraved

1983, Oct. 10 *Perf. 14x13½*

1565 A719 250 l multi .70 1.75
1566 A719 300 l multi .70 .25
1567 A719 400 l multi .80 .25
1568 A719 500 l multi .80 .25
Nos. 1565-1568 (4) 3.00 2.50

Francesco de Sanctis (1817-1883), Writer — A777

1983, Oct. 28 **Photo.**

1569 A777 300 l multi .45 .30

Christmas 1983 — A778

Raphael Paintings: 250 l, Madonna of the Chair. 400 l, Sistine Madonna. 500 l, Madonna of the Candelabra.

1983, Nov. 10 *Perf. 13½x14*

1570 A778 250 l multi .50 .30
1571 A778 400 l multi .65 .25
1572 A778 500 l multi .75 .25
Nos. 1570-1572 (3) 1.90 .80

25th Stamp Day, World Communications Year — A779

Children's Drawings. 200 l, Letters holding hands, horiz. 300 l, Spaceman. 400 l, Flag train, globe, horiz.

Perf. 14x13½, 13½x14

1983, Nov. 27

1573 A779 200 l multicolored .35 .35
1574 A779 300 l multicolored .50 .25
1575 A779 400 l multicolored .75 .30
Nos. 1573-1575 (3) 1.60 .90

Road Safety A780

300 l, Bent road sign, vert. 400 l, Accident.

Perf. 13½x14, 14x13½

1984, Jan. 20 **Photo.**

1576 A780 300 l multicolored .50 .50
1577 A780 400 l multicolored .60 .50

Promenade in Bois de Boulogne, by Giuseppe de Nittis (1846-1884) — A781

Design: 400 l, Portrait of Paul Guillaume, 1916, by Amedeo Modigliani (1884-1920).

Lithographed and Engraved

1984, Jan. 25 ***Perf. 14***

1578 A781 300 l multicolored .55 .45
1579 A781 400 l multicolored .75 .65

Galaxy-Same Tractor — A782

Italian-made vehicles: No. 1581, Alfa-33 car. No. 1582, Maserati Biturbo car. No. 1583, Iveco 190-38 truck.

1984, Mar. 10 **Photo.** ***Perf. 14x13½***

1580 A782 450 l shown .65 .55
1581 A782 450 l multicolored .65 .55
1582 A782 450 l multicolored .65 .55
1583 A782 450 l multicolored .65 .55
a. Block of 4, #1580-1583 + 2 labels 5.00 5.00

See Nos. 1620-1623, 1681-1684.

A783

1984, Apr. 10

1584 A783 300 l Mosaic, furnace .40 .25
1585 A783 300 l Glass Blower .40 .25
a. Pair, #1584-1585 + label 1.10 1.10

2nd European Parliament Elections — A784

400 l, Parliament Strasbourg.

1984, Apr. 16

1586 A784 400 l multicolored .65 .65

Forest Preservation — A785

No. 1587, Helicopter fire patrol. No. 1588, Hedgehog, squirrel, badger. No. 1589, Riverside waste dump. No. 1590, Plant life, animals.

1984, Apr. 24 **Photo.** ***Perf. 14x13½***

1587 A785 450 l multi .55 .55
1588 A785 450 l multi .55 .55
1589 A785 450 l multi .55 .55
1590 A785 450 l multi .55 .55
a. Block of 4, #1587-1590 7.00 7.00

Italia '85 A786

450 l, Ministry of Posts, Rome. 550 l, Via Appia Antiqua, Rome.

1984, Apr. 26 ***Perf. 14***

1591 A786 450 l multi .75 .25
1592 A786 550 l multi .90 .25

Rome Pacts, 40th Anniv. A787

Trade Unionists: Giuseppe di Vittorio, Bruno Buozzi, Achille Grandi.

1984, Apr. 30 ***Perf. 14x13½***

1593 A787 450 l multi .75 .70

Europa (1959-84) A788

1984, May 5

1594 A788 450 l multi *2.50* .90
1595 A788 550 l multi *7.00* 2.50

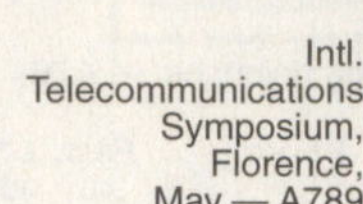

Intl. Telecommunications Symposium, Florence, May — A789

1984, May 7 ***Perf. 14***

1596 A789 550 l multi 1.00 .65

Italian Derby Centenary A790

Lithographed and Engraved

1984, May 12 ***Perf. 14x13½***

1597 A790 250 l Racing .75 *1.50*
1598 A790 400 l Racing, diff. 1.25 .65

Tourist Type of 1974

350 l, Campione d'Italia. 400 l, Chianciano Terme baths. 450 l, Padula. 550 l, Greek ampitheater, Syracuse.

1984, May 19 **Photo.** ***Perf. 14***

1599 A616 350 l multi 1.75 *1.60*
1600 A616 400 l multi .90 .80
1601 A616 450 l multi .90 .80
1602 A616 550 l multi 1.00 .90
Nos. 1599-1602 (4) 4.55 4.10

Folk Celebration Type of 1982

Design: La Macchina Di Santa Rosa.

1984, Sept. 3 **Photo.** ***Perf. 13½x14***

1603 A754 400 l multi .60 .35

Peasant Farming A792

250 l, Grain harvester, thresher. 350 l, Cart, hand press.

1984, Oct. 1 **Photo.** ***Perf. 14x13½***

1604 A792 250 l multicolored .45 .40
1605 A792 350 l multicolored .55 .40

Villa Type of 1980

Designs: 250 l, Villa Caristo, Stignano. 350 l, Villa Doria Pamphili, Genoa. 400 l, Villa Reale, Stupinigi. 450 l, Villa Mellone, Lecce.

Lithographed and Engraved

1984, Oct. 6 ***Perf. 14x13½***

1606 A719 250 l multi 1.05 1.25
1607 A719 350 l multi .90 .90
1608 A719 400 l multi .90 .50
1609 A719 450 l multi 1.00 .50
Nos. 1606-1609 (4) 3.85 3.15

Italia '85 — A793

No. 1610, Etruscan bronze statue. No. 1611, Italia '85 emblem. No. 1612, Etruscan silver mirror.

1984, Nov. 9 ***Perf. 13½x14***

1610 A793 550 l multicolored .55 .30
1611 A793 550 l multicolored .55 .30
1612 A793 550 l multicolored .55 .30
a. Strip of 3, #1610-1612 3.25 3.00

Journalistic Information A794

350 l, Globe, paper tape, microwave dish.

1985, Jan. 15 **Photo.** ***Perf. 13½x14***

1613 A794 350 l multicolored .60 .35

Modern Problems — A795

1985, Jan. 23 **Photo.** ***Perf. 13½x14***

1614 A795 250 l Aging .45 .45

A796

Italia '85. No. 1615, The Hunt, by Raphael (1483-1520). No. 1616, Emblem. No. 1617, Detail from fresco by Baldassare Peruzzi (1481-1536) in Bishop's Palace, Ostia Antica.

Photo. and Engr., Photo. (#1616)

1985, Feb. 13 ***Perf. 13½x14***

1615 A796 600 l multi .80 .30
1616 A796 600 l multi .80 .30
1617 A796 600 l multi .80 .30
a. Strip of 3, #1615-1617 3.25 3.00

Faience Tiles, Plate, Flask and Covered Bowl — A797

Italian ceramics: No. 1619, Tile mural, gladiators in combat.

1985, Mar. 2 **Photo.** ***Perf. 14x13½***

1618 A797 600 l multi .60 .30
1619 A797 600 l multi .60 .30
a. Pair, #1618-1619 + label 2.25 1.75

Italian Vehicle Type of 1984

1985, Mar. 21

1620 A782 450 l Lancia Thema .70 .55
1621 A782 450 l Fiat Abarth .70 .55
1622 A782 450 l Fiat Uno .70 .55
1623 A782 450 l Lamborghini .70 .55
a. Block of 4, #1620-1623 + 2 labels 9.00 9.00

A799

Italia '85: No. 1624, Church of St. Mary of Peace, Rome, by Pietro de Cortona (1596-1669). No. 1625, Exhibition emblem. No. 1626, Church of St. Agnes, Rome, fountain and obelisk.

Photo. and Engr., Photo. (#1625)

1985, Mar. 30 *Perf. 13½x14*

1624	A799 250 l multi	.30	.30
1625	A799 250 l multi	.30	.30
1626	A799 250 l multi	.30	.30
a.	Strip of 3, #1624-1626	2.00	1.50

Pope Sixtus V, (1520-1590), 400th Anniv. of Papacy — A800

Sixtus V, dome of St. Peter's Basilica, Rome.

1985, Apr. 24 **Litho. and Engr.**

1627 A800 1500 l multi 2.25 1.10

Folk Celebration Type of 1982

Folktales: No. 1628, The March of the Turks, Potenza. No. 1629, San Marino Republican Regatta, Amalti.

1985, May 29 **Photo.**

1628	A754 250 l multi	.70	.60
1629	A754 350 l multi	1.00	.60

Tourist Type of 1974

Scenic views: 350 l, Bormio town center. 400 l, Mt. Vesuvius from Castellamare di Stabia. 450 l, Stromboli Volcano from the sea. 600 l, Beach, old town at Termoli.

1985, June 1 *Perf. 14*

1630	A616 350 l multi	.85	1.50
1631	A616 400 l multi	.80	.35
1632	A616 450 l multi	.90	.35
1633	A616 600 l multi	1.25	.70
	Nos. 1630-1633 (4)	3.80	2.90

Nature Conservation A803

No. 1634, European beaver. No. 1635, Primula. No. 1636, Nebrodi pine. No. 1637, Italian sandpiper.

1985, June 5 *Perf. 13½x14*

1634	A803 500 l multicolored	.60	.45
1635	A803 500 l multicolored	.60	.45
1636	A803 500 l multicolored	.60	.45
1637	A803 500 l multicolored	.60	.45
a.	Block of 4, #1634-1637	10.00	10.00

Art Type of 1981

Designs: No. 1638, Madonna bu Il Sassoferrato, G.B. Salvi, 1609-1685. No. 1639, Pride of the Work by Mario Sironi, 1885-1961.

Lithographed and Engraved

1985, June 15 *Perf. 14*

1638	A738 350 l multi	1.00	1.00
1639	A738 400 l multi	1.20	.95

Europa — A805

Tenors and Composers: 500 l, Aureliano Pertile (1885-1969) and Giovanni Martinelli (1885-1962). 600 l, Johann Sebastian Bach (1685-1750) and Vincenzo Bellini (1801-1835).

1985, June 20 **Photo.** *Perf. 13½x14*

1640	A805 500 l multi	*3.50*	.80
1641	A805 600 l multi	*5.00*	*1.10*

San Salvatore Abbey, Monte Amiata, 950th Anniv. A806

Lithographed and Engraved

1985, Aug. 1 *Perf. 14x13½*

1642 A806 450 l multi .60 .30

World Cycling Championships — A807

1985, Aug. 21 **Photo.**

1643 A807 400 l multi 1.00 .35

7th Intl. Congress for Crime Prevention, Milan, Aug. 26-Sept. 6 — A808

1985, Aug. 26

1644 A808 600 l multi 1.25 .45

Intl. Youth Year A809

1985, Sept. 3

1645 A809 600 l multi 1.25 .45

Villa Type of 1980

Designs: 300 l, Nitti, Maratea. 400 l, Aldrovandi Mazzacorati, Bologna. 500 l, Santa Maria, Pula. 600 l, De Mersi, Villazzano.

Lithographed and Engraved

1985, Oct. 1 *Perf. 14x13½*

1646	A719 300 l multi	1.00	.35
1647	A719 400 l multi	1.50	.35
1648	A719 500 l multi	1.50	.30
1649	A719 600 l multi	2.25	.35
	Nos. 1646-1649 (4)	6.25	1.35

Natl. and Papal Arms, Treaty Document A810

1985, Oct. 15 **Photo.**

1650 A810 400 l multi .75 .35

Ratification of new Concordat with the Vatican.

Souvenir Sheets

Parma #10, View of Parma — A812

A813

Sardinia #1, Great Britain #1 — A814

No. 1651: b, Two Sicilies #3, Naples. c, Two Sicilies #10, Palermo. d, Modena #3, Modena. e, Roman States #8, Rome. f, Tuscany #5, Florence. g, Sardinia #15, Turin. h, Romagna #7, Bologna. i, Lombardy-Venetia #4, Milan.

No. 1652a, Switzerland #3L1. b, Japan #1. c, US #2. d, Western Australia #1. e, Mauritius #4.

Lithographed and Engraved

1985, Oct. 25 *Perf. 14*

1651	A812 Sheet of 9	5.00	5.00
a.-i.	300 l, any single	.40	.40

Perf. 14x13½

1652	A813 Sheet of 5 + label	5.00	5.00
a.-e.	500 l, any single	.85	.45

Imperf

1653 A814 4000 l multi 5.50 4.00

Italia '85, Rome, Oct. 25-Nov. 3.

Long-distance Skiing — A815

1986, Jan. 25 **Photo.** *Perf. 14x13½*

1654 A815 450 l multi .80 .45

Folk Celebration Type of 1982

Design: Procession of St. Agnes, Le Candelore Folk Festival, Catania.

1986, Feb. 3 *Perf. 13½x14*

1655 A754 450 l multi .75 .25

Amilcare Ponchielli (1834-1886), Composer — A816

2000 l, Scene from La Giaconda.

Photogravure and Engraved

1986, Mar. 8 *Perf. 14x13½*

1656 A816 2000 l multicolored 3.00 .55

Castle Type of 1980

Designs: 380 l, Vignola, Modena. 650 l, Montecchio Castle, Castiglion Fiorentino. 750 l, Rocca di Urbisaglia.

Perf. 14x13½

1986-90 **Photo.** **Wmk. 303**

1657	A717 380 l multi ('87)	.55	.25
1658	A717 650 l multi	.90	.25

Engr.

1659	A717 750 l multi ('90)	1.10	.25
	Nos. 1657-1659 (3)	2.55	.75

Issue date: 750 l, Sept. 20.

Coil Stamps

100 l, St. Severa. 500 l, Norman Castle, Melfi. 600 l, Scaligero, Sirmione. 650 l, Serralunga D'Alba. 750 l, Venafro. 800 l, Rocca Maggiore, Assisi.

Perf. 14 Vert.

1988-91 **Engr.** **Wmk. 303**

Size: 16x21mm

1661	A717 100 l brown	.25	.25
1662	A717 500 l blue	.80	.40
1663	A717 600 l green	.95	.55
1664	A717 650 l bright mauve	.90	.60
1665	A717 750 l violet	1.10	.65
1666	A717 800 l red	1.25	.65
	Nos. 1661-1666 (6)	5.25	3.10

Issued: 600 l, 800 l, 2/20/91; others, 3/1/88.

Giovanni Battista Pergolesi (1710-1736), Musician — A817

Perf. 13½x14

1986, Mar. 15 **Photo.** **Unwmk.**

1667 A817 2000 l multi 3.25 1.00

The Bay, Acitrezza — A818

450 l, Piazetta, Capri. 550 l, Kursaal, Merano. 650 l, Lighthouse, San Benedetto del Tronto.

1986, Mar. 24 *Perf. 14*

1668	A818 350 l shown	.65	.50
1669	A818 450 l multicolored	.85	.50
1670	A818 550 l multicolored	1.00	.35
1671	A818 650 l multicolored	1.25	.50
	Nos. 1668-1671 (4)	3.75	1.85

Europa 1986 — A819

Trees in special shapes: a, Heart (life). b, Star (poetry). c, Butterfly (color). d, Sun (energy).

1986, Apr. 28 **Photo.** *Perf. 13x14*

1672	Block of 4	*10.00*	*10.00*
a.-d.	A819 650 l, any single	*1.10*	*.45*

25th Intl. Opthalmological Congress, Rome, May 4-10 — A820

1986, May 3 Photo. *Perf. 14*

1673 A820 550 l multi .80 .25

Police in Uniform — A821

1986, May 10

1674 A821 550 l multi 1.25 .55

1675 A821 650 l multi 1.50 .90

European Police Conference, Chianciano Terme, May 10-12. Nos. 1674-1675 printed se-tenant with labels picturing male or female police.

Battle of Bezzecca, 120th Anniv. A822

1986, May 31 *Perf. 14x13½*

1676 A822 550 l multi .85 .35

Memorial Day for Independence Martyrs — A823

1986, May 31 *Perf. 14*

1677 A823 2000 l multi 3.25 .90

Bersaglieri Corps of Mountain Troops, 150th Anniv. — A824

1986, June 1 *Perf. 13½x14*

1678 A824 450 l multi 1.10 .35

Telecommunications — A825

1986, June 16 *Perf. 14x13½*

1679 A825 350 l multi .55 .35

Sacro Monte di Varallo Monastery — A826

1986, June 28 Engr. *Perf. 14*

1680 A826 2000 l Prus bl & sage grn 3.25 1.00

Italian Vehicle Type of 1984

No. 1681, Alfa Romeo AR8 Turbo. No. 1682, Innocenti 650 SE. No. 1683, Ferrari Testarossa. No. 1684, Fiatallis FR 10B.

1986, July 4 Photo. *Perf. 14x13½*

1681 A782 450 l multi .65 .50

1682 A782 450 l multi .65 .50

1683 A782 450 l multi .65 .50

1684 A782 450 l multi .65 .50

a. Block of 4, #1681-1684 + 2 labels *9.00* 9.00

Ladies' Fashions — A827

Breda Heavy Industry — A828

Olivetti Computer Technology — A829

1986, July 14

1685 A827 450 l shown 1.20 .45

1686 A827 450 l Men's fashions 1.20 .45

a. Pair, #1685-1686 + label *7.50* 7.50

1687 A828 650 l shown *2.00* .45

1688 A829 650 l shown *2.00* .45

Nos. 1685-1688 (4) *6.40* 1.80

Alitalia, Italian Airlines, 40th Anniv. A830

550 l, Anniv. emblem. 650 l, Jet, runway lights.

1986, Sept. 16 Photo. *Perf. 14x13½*

1689 A830 550 l multi 1.00 .40

1690 A830 650 l multi 1.25 .40

Villa Type of 1980

No. 1691, Necker, Trieste. No. 1692, Borromeo, Cassano D'Adda. No. 1693, Palagonia, Bagheria. No. 1694, Medicea, Poggio a Caiano. No. 1695, Castello d'Issogne, Issogne.

1986, Oct. 1 Photo. & Engr.

1691 A719 350 l multi .60 .45

1692 A719 350 l multi .60 .45

1693 A719 450 l multi .85 .30

1694 A719 550 l multi .85 .30

1695 A719 650 l multi 1.15 .50

Nos. 1691-1695 (5) 4.05 2.00

Christmas — A831

Madonna and Child, bronze sculpture by Donatello, Basilica del Santo, Padua.

1986, Oct. 10 Engr. *Perf. 14*

1696 A831 450 l brown olive .70 .25

Art Type of 1981

Designs: 450 l, Seated Woman Holding a Book, drawing by Andrea del Sarto, Uffizi, Florence, vert. 550 l, Daphne at Pavarola, painting by Felice Casorati, Museum of Modern Art, Turin, vert.

1986, Oct. 11 Litho. & Engr.

1697 A738 450 l blk & pale org 1.50 .35

1698 A738 550 l multi 1.75 .40

Memorial, Globe, Plane — A832

Plane, Cross, Men — A833

1986, Nov. 11 Photo. *Perf. 13½x14*

1699 A832 550 l multi .95 .40

1700 A833 650 l multi 1.10 .40

Intl. Peace Year, memorial to Italian airmen who died at Kindu, Zaire, while on a peace mission.

Stamp Day A834

1986, Nov. 29 *Perf. 14x13½*

1701 A834 550 l Die of Sardinia No. 2 1.10 .25

Francesco Matraire, printer of first Sardinian stamps.

A835

Industries — A836

No. 1702, Marzotto Textile, 1836. No. 1703, Italgas Energy Corp., 1837.

Perf. 14½x13½

1987, Feb. 27 Photo.

1702 A835 700 l multi 1.00 .55

1703 A836 700 l multicolored 1.00 .55

Environmental Protection — A837

Designs: a, Volturno River. b, Garda Lake. c, Trasimeno Lake. d, Tirso River.

1987, Mar. 6 Litho. *Perf. 14x13½*

1704 A837 Block of 4 7.50 7.50

a.-d. 500 l, any single .85 .40

Antonio Gramsci (1891-1937), Author and Artist — A838

1987, Apr. 27 Litho. *Perf. 14x13½*

1705 A838 600 l scar & gray black 1.00 .40

Europa 1987 A839

Modern architecture: 600 l, Church of Sun Motorway, Florence, designed by Michelucci. 700 l, Railway station, Rome, designed by Nervi.

1987, May 4 Photo.

1706 A839 600 l multi *2.00* .60

1707 A839 700 l multi *2.75* .60

Tourist Type of 1974

380 l, Verbania Pallanza. 400 l, Palmi. 500 l, Vasto. 600 l, Villacidro.

1987, May 9 *Perf. 14*

1708 A616 380 l multi .75 .60

1709 A616 400 l multi .85 .60

1710 A616 500 l multi 1.00 .50

1711 A616 600 l multi 1.25 .50

Nos. 1708-1711 (4) 3.85 2.20

Naples Soccer Club, Nat'l. Champions A840

1987, May 18 Litho. *Perf. 13½x14*

1712 A840 500 l multi 2.00 1.60

The Absinthe Drinkers, by Degas — A841

1987, May 29

1713 A841 380 l multi .90 .45

Fight against alcoholism.

St. Alfonso M. de Liguori (1696-1787) and Gulf of Naples — A842

1987, Aug. 1 ***Perf. 14x13½***

1714 A842 400 l multi .70 .40

Events A843

Emblems and natl. landmarks: No. 1715, OLYMPHILEX '87, Intl. Olympic Committee Building, Foro Italico, Rome. No. 1716, World Athletics Championships, Olympic Stadium, Rome.

1987, Aug. 29 Photo. ***Perf. 14x14½***

1715 A843 700 l multi 1.10 .30
1716 A843 700 l multi 1.10 .30

Folk Celebration Type of 1982

Design: Quintana Joust, Foligno.

Perf. 13½x14½

1987, Sept. 12 **Photo.**

1717 A754 380 l multi .75 .35

Piazzas A844

380 l, Piazza del Popolo, Ascoli Piceno. 500 l, Piazza Giuseppe Verdi, Palermo. 600 l, Piazza San Carlo, Turin. 700 l, Piazza dei Signori, Verona.

Litho. & Engr.

1987, Oct. 10 ***Perf. 14x13½***

1718 A844 380 l multi .75 .45
1719 A844 500 l multi 1.00 .30
1720 A844 600 l multi 1.00 .30
1721 A844 700 l multi 1.00 .50
Nos. 1718-1721 (4) 3.75 1.55

See Nos. 1747-1748, 1765-1766.

Christmas A845

Paintings by Giotto: 500 l, Adoration in the Manger, Basilica of St. Francis, Assisi. 600 l, The Epiphany, Scrovegni Chapel, Padua.

1987, Oct. 15 Photo. ***Perf. 13½x14***

1722 A845 500 l multi 1.00 .30
1723 A845 600 l multi 1.25 .30

Battle of Mentana, 120th Anniv. A846

Litho. & Engr.

1987, Nov. 3 ***Perf. 14x13½***

1724 A846 380 l multi .90 .35

Il Pantocrator (Christ), Mosaic, Monreale Cathedral — A847

Coat of Arms and San Carlo Theater, Naples, from an 18th Cent. Engraving — A848

1987, Nov. 4 ***Perf. 14***

1725 A847 500 l multi 1.25 .50
1726 A848 500 l multi 1.25 .50

Artistic heritage. See Nos. 1768-1769.

Nunziatella Military School, 200th Anniv. A849

1987, Nov. 14 ***Perf. 14x13½***

1727 A849 600 l multi 1.05 .40

Stamp Day — A850

Philatelist Marco DeMarchi (d. 1936) holding magnifying glass and stamp album, Milan Cathedral.

1987, Nov. 20 Photo. ***Perf. 13½x14***

1728 A850 500 l multi 1.40 .45

Homo Aeserniensis (Flint Knapper) — A851

Photo. & Engr.

1988, Feb. 6 ***Perf. 13½x14***

1729 A851 500 l multi .90 .55

Remains of Isernia Man, c. 736,000 years-old, discovered near Isernia.

E. Quirino Visconti School, Rome A852

Litho. & Engr.

1988, Mar. 1 Unwmk. ***Perf. 14x13½***

1730 A852 500 l multi .75 .40

See Nos. 1764, 1824, 1842.

St. John Bosco (1815-1888), Educator — A853

1988, Apr. 2 Photo. ***Perf. 13½x14***

1731 A853 500 l multi .75 .55

Art Type of 1981

Painting: *The Archaeologists*, by Giorgio de Chirico (1888-1978).

1988, Apr. 7 Engr. ***Perf. 14***

1732 A738 650 l multi, vert. 1.75 .65

1st Printed Hebrew Bible, 500th Anniv. A854

Soncino Bible excerpt, 15th cent.

1988, Apr. 22 Photo. ***Perf. 14x13½***

1733 A854 550 l multi .80 .45

Epilepsy Foundation A855

Design: St. Valentine, electroencephalograph readout, epileptic in seizure and medieval crest.

1988, Apr. 23

1734 A855 500 l multi .85 .50

Europa 1988 A856

Transport and communication: 650 l, ETR 450 locomotive. 750 l, Electronic mail, map of Italy.

1988, May 2

1735 A856 650 l multi *1.75 .60*
1736 A856 750 l multi *2.25 .85*

Tourist Type of 1974

Scenic views: 400 l, Castiglione della Pescaia. 500 l, Lignano Sabbiadoro. 650 l, Noto. 750 l, Vieste.

1988, May 7 Photo. ***Perf. 14***

1737 A616 400 l multi .60 .85
1738 A616 500 l multi .80 .65
1739 A616 650 l multi 1.00 .75
1740 A616 750 l multi 1.25 1.10
Nos. 1737-1740 (4) 3.65 3.35

A858

1988, May 16

1741 A858 500 l Golf .80 .45

1990 World Cup Soccer Championships — A859

1988, May 16 Litho. ***Perf. 14x13½***

1742 A859 3150 l blk, grn & dark red 3.75 2.75

1988 Natl. Soccer Championships, Milan — A860

1988, May 23 ***Perf. 13½x14***

1743	A860	650 l multi	.75	.55

Bronze Sculpture, Pergola — A861

1988, June 4 **Engr.** ***Perf. 14***

1744	A861	500 l Horse	.85	.75
1745	A861	650 l Woman	.95	.75

Bologna University, 900th Anniv. — A862

1988, June 10 **Engr.** ***Perf. 13½x14***

1746	A862	500 l violet	.75	.50

Piazza Type of 1987

Designs: 400 l, Piazza del Duomo, Pistoia. 550 l, Piazza del Unita d'Italia, Trieste.

Litho. & Engr.

1988, July 2 ***Perf. 14x13½***

1747	A844	400 l multi	.70	.55
1748	A844	550 l multi	.95	.50

Folk Celebration Type of 1982

Discesa Dei Candelieri, Sassari: Man wearing period costume, column and bearers.

1988, Aug. 13 **Photo.** ***Perf. 13½x14***

1749	A754	550 l multi	1.30	.40

Intl. Gastroenterology and Digestive Endoscopy Congress, Rome — A863

1988, Sept. 5

1750	A863	750 l multi	1.10	.55

Neorealistic Films — A864

Italian films amd directors: 500 l, *Ossessione,* 1942, by Luchino Visconti. 650 l, *Ladri di Biciclette,* 1948, by Vittorio DeSica. 2400 l, *Roma Citta Aperta,* 1945, by Roberto Rossellini. 3050 l, *Riso Amaro,* 1949, by Giuseppe DeSantis.

1988, Oct. 13 **Litho.** ***Perf. 14x13½***

1751	A864	500 l multi	.85	1.10
1752	A864	650 l multi	1.00	1.30
1753	A864	2400 l multi	4.00	1.50
1754	A864	3050 l multi	5.50	2.25
		Nos. 1751-1754 (4)	11.35	6.15

Elsag — A865

Aluminia — A866

State Mint and Polygraphic Insitute — A867

Italian Industries.

1988, Oct. 19 **Photo.**

1755	A865	750 l multi	1.00	.60
1756	A866	750 l multi	1.00	.60

Photo. & Engr.

1757	A867	750 l multi	1.00	.60
		Nos. 1755-1757 (3)	3.00	1.80

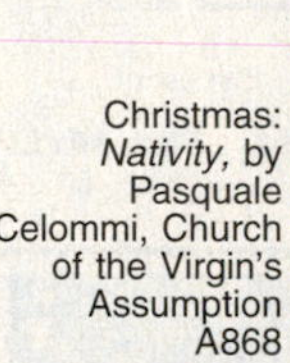
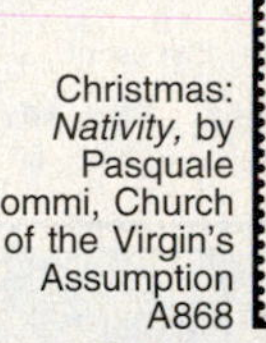

Christmas: *Nativity,* by Pasquale Celommi, Church of the Virgin's Assumption A868

1988, Oct. 29 **Photo.** ***Perf. 13½x14***

1758	A868	650 l multi	1.40	.25

Christmas A869

Photo. & Engr.

1988, Nov. 12 ***Perf. 14x13½***

1759	A869	500 l dark blue grn & chest brn	1.25	.45

St. Charles Borromeo (1538-1584), Ecclesiastical Reformer — A870

1988, Nov. 4 **Litho. & Engr.**

1760	A870	2400 l multi	3.50	1.25

Stamp Day — A871

Japan #69 & stamp designer Edoardo Chiossone.

1988, Dec. 9 **Photo.** ***Perf. 13½x14***

1761	A871	500 l multi	.80	.40

Campaign Against AIDS — A872

1989, Jan. 13

1762	A872	650 l multi	1.00	.35

Paris-Peking Rally — A873

3150 l, Map, Itala race car.

1989, Jan. 21 ***Perf. 14½x13½***

1763	A873	3150 l multicolored	4.25	4.25

School Type of 1988

1989 **Photo. & Engr.** ***Perf. 14x13½***

1764	A852	650 l multi	.85	.40

Piazza Type of 1987

No. 1765, Piazza Del Duomo, Catanzaro. No. 1766, Piazza Di Spagna, Rome.

Litho. & Engr.

1989, Apr. 10 ***Perf. 14x13½***

1765	A844	400 l multi	.65	.65
1766	A844	400 l multi	.65	.65

Velo World Yachting Championships A875

1989, Apr. 8 **Photo.** ***Perf. 14***

1767	A875	3050 l multi	4.25	1.00

Artistic Heritage Type of 1987

Art and architecture: 500 l, King with scepter and orb, Palazzo Della Ragione, Padova, vert. 650 l, Crypt of St. Nicolas, St. Nicolas Basilica, Bari, vert.

1989, Apr. 8 **Litho. & Engr., Engr.**

1768	A847	500 l multi	.85	.75
1769	A847	650 l indigo	1.10	.75

Europa 1989 — A876

Children's games: 500 l, Leapfrog, horiz. 650 l, Playing dress-up. 750 l, Sack race, horiz.

Perf. 14x13½, 13½x14

1989, May 8 **Photo.**

1770	A876	500 l multicolored	*1.10*	*.50*
1771	A876	650 l shown	*1.40*	*.50*
1772	A876	750 l multicolored	*1.60*	*.50*
		Nos. 1770-1772 (3)	4.10	1.50

European Parliament 3rd Elections — A877

1989, June 3 ***Perf. 13½x14***

1773	A877	500 l multi	1.00	.55

No. 1773 also inscribed in European Currency Units "ECU 0,31."

Pisa University — A878

1989, May 29 **Engr.** ***Perf. 14x13½***

1774	A878	500 l violet	.80	.40

Folk Celebration Type of 1982

Priest and Flower Feast street scene.

1989, May 27 **Photo.** ***Perf. 13½x14***

1775	A754	400 l multi	.65	.55

Tourist Type of 1974

1989, June 10 **Photo.** ***Perf. 14***

1776	A616	500 l Naxos Gardens	1.00	.65
1777	A616	500 l Spotorno	1.00	.65
1778	A616	500 l Pompei	1.00	.65
1779	A616	500 l Grottammare	1.00	.65
		Nos. 1776-1779 (4)	4.00	2.60

Ministry of Posts, Cent. A879

500 l, Posthorn, No. 52. 2400 l, Posthorn, Earth.

1989, June 24 ***Perf. 14x13½***

1780	A879	500 l multicolored	.80	1.25
1781	A879	2400 l multicolored	3.25	1.00

INTER Soccer Championships — A880

1989, June 26

1782	A880	650 l multi	.85	.55

Interparliamentary Union, Cent. — A881

1989, June 28
1783 A881 750 l multi .90 .65

French Revolution, Bicent. — A882

1989, July 7 Photo. Perf. 14
1784 A882 3150 l multi 4.25 4.25

Fortified Walls of Corinaldo, by Francesco di Giorgio Martini (1439-1502) — A883

Litho. & Engr.

1989, Sept. 2 Perf. 14
1785 A883 500 l multi .90 .45

Charlie Chaplin (1889-1977) — A884

1989, Sept. 23 Engr. Perf. 14x13½
1786 A884 750 l black & sepia 1.10 .50

Naples-Portici Railway, 150th Anniv. — A885

1989, Oct. 3 Litho. & Engr.

1787	550 l Denom at UL	.55	.25
1788	550 l Denom at UR	.55	.25
a.	A885 Pair, #1787-1788	1.60	1.60

Adoration of the Kings, by Correggio — A887

1989, Oct. 21 Photo. Perf. 13½x14

1789	500 l multicolored	.65	.45
1790	500 l multicolored	.65	.45
a.	A887 Pair, #1789-1790	1.50	1.25

Christmas.

Fidardo Castle, the Stradella, Accordion — A889

Industries: No. 1791, Music. No. 1792, Arnoldo World Publishing.

1989, Oct. 14 Photo. Perf. 14x13½

1791	A889 450 l multicolored	.65	.50
1792	A889 450 l multicolored	.65	.50

Stamp Day — A890

1989, Nov. 24 Perf. 13½x14
1793 A890 500 l Emilio Diena .90 .45

1990 World Soccer Championships, Italy — A891

1989, Dec. 9 Engr. Perf. 13½x14
1794 A891 450 l multicolored .65 .40

Columbus's First Voyage, 1474-1484 — A892

1990, Feb. 24 Photo.

1795	700 l Denom at UL	.90	.30
1796	700 l Denom at UR	.90	.30
a.	A892 Pair, #1795-1796	2.00	1.75

Souvenir Sheets

1990 World Cup Soccer Championships, Italy — A894

Soccer club emblems and stadiums in Italy.
No. 1797: a, Italy. b, US. c, Olympic Stadium, Rome. d, Municipal Stadium, Florence. e, Austria. f, Czechoslovakia.
No. 1798: a, Argentina. b, Russia. c, St. Paul Stadium, Naples. d, New Stadium, Bari. e, Cameroun. f, Romania.
No. 1799: a, Brazil. b, Costa Rica. c, Alps Stadium, Turin. d, Ferraris Stadium, Genoa. e, Sweden. f, Scotland.
No. 1800: a, UAE. b, West Germany. c, Dall'ara Stadium, Bologna. d, Meazza Stadium, Milan. e, Colombia. f, Yugoslavia.
No. 1801: a, Belgium. b, Uruguay. c, Bentegodi Stadium, Verona. d, Friuli Stadium, Udine. e, South Korea. f, Spain.
No. 1802: a, England. b, Netherlands. c, Sant'elia Stadium, Cagliari. d, La Favorita Stadium, Palermo. e, Ireland. f, Egypt.

1990, Mar. 24 Perf. 14x13½

1797	A894 Sheet of 6	3.00	3.00
a.-f.	450 l any single	.45	.85
1798	A894 Sheet of 6	4.00	4.00
a.-f.	600 l any single	.65	.85
1799	A894 Sheet of 6	4.50	4.50
a.-f.	650 l any single	.80	.65
1800	A894 Sheet of 6	5.00	5.00
a.-f.	700 l any single	.85	.65
1801	A894 Sheet of 6	5.50	5.50
a.-f.	800 l any single	1.00	.65
1802	A894 Sheet of 6	8.00	8.00
a.-f.	1200 l any single	1.40	1.25
	Nos. 1797-1802 (6)	30.00	30.00

See No. 1819.

Tourist Type of 1974

No. 1803, Sabbioneta. No. 1804, Montepulciano. No. 1805, Castellammare del Golfo. No. 1806, San Felice Circeo.

1990, Mar. 30 Photo. Perf. 14

1803	A616 600 l multicolored	.75	.45
1804	A616 600 l multicolored	.75	.45
1805	A616 600 l multicolored	.75	.45
1806	A616 600 l multicolored	.75	.45
	Nos. 1803-1806 (4)	3.00	1.80

Folk Celebration Type of 1982

Design: Horse race, Merano.

1990, Apr. 9 Perf. 13½x14
1807 A754 600 l multicolored .80 .45

Aurelio Saffi, Death Cent. A895

1990, Apr. 10 Perf. 14
1808 A895 700 l multicolored .85 .45

Giovanni Giorgi (1871-1950) — A896

1990, Apr. 23 Perf. 14x13½
1809 A896 600 l multicolored .75 .45

Metric System in Italy, 55th. anniv.

Labor Day, Cent. — A897

1990, Apr. 28 Photo. Perf. 13½x14
1810 A897 600 l multicolored .75 .40

Naples Soccer Club, Italian Champions A898

1990, Apr. 30 Perf. 13½x14
1811 A898 700 l multicolored 1.25 .75

Europa A899

Post Offices: 700 l, San Silvestro Piazza, Rome. 800 l, Fondaco Tedeschi, Venice.

1990, May 7 Perf. 14x13½

1812	A899 700 l multicolored	*1.25*	.45
1813	A899 800 l multicolored	*2.25*	.45

Giovanni Paisiello (1740-1816), Composer A900

1990, May 9 Perf. 14x13½
1814 A900 450 l multicolored .65 .65

Dante Alighieri (1265-1321), Poet — A901

1990, May 12 Perf. 14x13½
1815 A901 700 l multicolored .85 .45

Dante Alighieri Soc., cent.

Mosaic (Detail) — A902

Sculpture — A903

Photo. (#1816), Litho. & Engr. (#1817)

1990, May 19 Perf. 13½x14

1816	A902 450 l multicolored	.55	.85
1817	A903 700 l multicolored	.85	.55

Malatestiana Music Festival, Rimini, 40th Anniv. — A904

1990, June 15 Photo. *Perf. 14*
1818 A904 600 l multicolored .75 .45

World Cup Soccer Type of 1990 Inscribed "Campione Del Mondo"
1990, July 9 Litho. *Perf. 14x13½*
1819 A894 600 l like No. 1800b .90 .90

Still Life, by Giorgio Morandi (1890-1964) — A905

1990, July 20 Engr. *Perf. 14*
1820 A905 750 l black 1.00 .65

Greco-Roman Wrestling, World Championships — A906

1990, Oct. 11 Litho. *Perf. 14x13½*
1821 A906 3200 l multicolored 4.00 1.10

Christmas — A907

Paintings of the Nativity by: 600 l, Emidio Vangelli. 750 l, Pellegrino.

1990, Oct. 26 *Perf. 14*
1822 A907 600 l multicolored .70 .35
1823 A907 750 l multicolored 1.00 .45

School Type of 1988 and

Italian Schools — A908

Designs: 600 l, Bernardino Telesio gymnasium, Cosenza. 750 l, University of Catania.

Litho. & Engr.
1990, Nov. 5 *Perf. 14x13½*
1824 A852 600 l multicolored .70 .35

Engr.
1825 A908 750 l multicolored .90 .45

Stamp Day — A909

Self-portrait, Corrado Mezzana (1890-1952).

1990, Nov. 16 Litho. *Perf. 13½x14*
1826 A909 600 l multicolored .80 .45

The Nativity — A910

1991, Jan. 5 Litho. *Perf. 13½x14*
1827 A910 600 l multicolored .75 .45

Genoa Flower Show — A911

1991, Jan. 10 *Perf. 14*
1828 A911 750 l multicolored .95 .45

Seal of the Univ. of Siena — A912

1991, Jan. 15 Photo. *Perf. 13½x14*
1829 A912 750 l multicolored .90 .45

Tourist Type of 1974

1991 Photo.
1830 A616 600 l San Remo .80 .45
1831 A616 600 l Roccaraso .80 .45
1832 A616 600 l La Maddalena .80 .45
1833 A616 600 l Calgi .80 .45
Nos. 1830-1833 (4) 3.20 1.80

United Europe — A913

Perf. 14x13½
1991, Mar. 12 Photo. Unwmk.
1834 A913 750 l multi .95 .25

No. 1834 also carries .48 ECU denomination.

Discovery of America, 500th Anniv. (in 1992) — A914

1991, Mar. 22 Litho.
1835 750 l Ships leaving port 1.00 .45
1836 750 l Columbus, Queen's court 1.00 .45
a. A914 Pair, #1835-1836 2.00 2.00

Giuseppe Gioachino Belli (1791-1863), Poet — A916

1991, Apr. 15 Litho. *Perf. 14x13½*
1837 A916 600 l bl & gray blk .70 .45

Church of St. Gregory, Rome — A917

1991, Apr. 20 Photo. *Perf. 14x13½*
1838 A917 3200 l multicolored 3.75 1.40

Europa A918

750 l, DRS satellite. 800 l, Hermes space shuttle.

1991, Apr. 29 Photo. *Perf. 14x13½*
1839 A918 750 l multi *1.60 .70*
1840 A918 800 l multi *1.60 .70*

Santa Maria Maggiore Church, Lanciano — A919

1991, May 2 Engr. *Perf. 13½x14*
1841 A919 600 l brown .70 .45

Schools Type of 1988

Design: D. A. Azuni school, Sassari.

Litho. & Engr.
1991, May 3 *Perf. 14x13½*
1842 A852 600 l multicolored .70 .45

Team Genoa, Italian Soccer Champions, 1990-91 — A920

1991, May 27 Photo. *Perf. 13½x14*
1843 A920 3000 l multicolored 3.00 2.25

Basketball, Cent. — A921

1991, June 5
1844 A921 500 l multicolored .75 .50

No. 1844 exists with blue in place of purple at the bottom of the design. Value, $15,000.

Children's Rights — A922

750 l, Man, child with balloon.

1991, June 14
1845 A922 600 l shown .70 .25
1846 A922 750 l multicolored .90 .45

Art and Culture A923

Designs: 600 l, Sculpture by Pericle Fazzini (b. 1913). 3200 l, Exhibition Hall, Turin, designed by Pier Luigi Nervi (1891-1979).

Litho. & Engr.
1991, June 21 *Perf. 14*
1847 A923 600 l multicolored .70 .70
1848 A923 3200 l multicolored 3.75 .90

Egyptian Museum, Turin — A924

1991, Aug. 31 Litho. *Perf. 13½x14*
1849 A924 750 l grn, yel & gold .95 .45

Luigi Galvani (1737-1798), Electrophysicist — A925

1991, Sept. 24 *Perf. 14x13½*
1850 A925 750 l multicolored .95 .30

Radio, cent. (in 1995). See Nos. 1873, 1928, 1964.

Nature Protection A926

No. 1851, Marevivo posidonia. No. 1852, Falco pellegrino. No. 1853, Cervo sardo. No. 1854, Orso marsicano.

1991, Oct. 10 Photo. *Perf. 14x13½*

1851	A926 500 l multicolored	.65	.60
1852	A926 500 l multicolored	.65	.60
1853	A926 500 l multicolored	.95	.60
1854	A926 500 l multicolored	.65	.60
	Nos. 1851-1854 (4)	2.90	2.40

World Wildlife Fund.

Wolfgang Amadeus Mozart, Death Bicent. — A927

1991, Oct. 7 *Perf. 13½x14*
1855 A927 800 l multicolored 1.00 .50

Christmas A928

1991, Oct. 18
1856 A928 600 l multicolored .75 .40

Giulio and Alberto Bolaffi, Philatelists — A929

1991, Oct. 25 *Perf. 14*
1857 A929 750 l multicolored .95 .50

Stamp Day.

Pietro Nenni (1891-1980), Politician — A930

1991, Oct. 30
1858 A930 750 l multicolored .95 .40

Fountain of Neptune, Florence, by Bartolomeo Ammannati (1511-1592) A931

1992, Feb. 6 Photo. *Perf. 13½x14*
1859 A931 750 l multicolored .95 .50

22nd European Indoor Track Championships — A932

1992, Jan. 30 *Perf. 14x13½*
1860 A932 600 l multicolored .85 .40

University of Ferrara, 600th Anniv. — A933

1992, Mar. 4 Photo. *Perf. 13½x14*
1861 A933 750 l multicolored .90 .50

Castle Type of 1980

200 l, Cerro al Volturno. 250 l, Mondavio. 300 l, Bari. 450 l, Bosa. 850 l, Arechi, Salerno.

Perf. 14x13½
1992-94 Photo. Wmk. 303

1862	A717 200 l multicolored	.25	.25
1863	A717 250 l multicolored	.40	.25
1864	A717 300 l multicolored	.40	.25
1865	A717 450 l multicolored	.60	.25
1866	A717 850 l multicolored	.95	.40
	Nos. 1862-1866 (5)	2.60	1.40

Issued: 200 l, 250 l, 300 l, 450 l, 2/24/94; 850 l, 3/7/92.

This is an expanding set. Numbers will change if necessary.

University of Naples — A934

1992, Mar. 9 Unwmk. *Perf. 14x13½*
1872 A934 750 l multicolored .95 .50

Radio Cent. Type of 1991

Alessandro Volta (1745-1827), Italian physicist.

1992, Mar. 26
1873 A925 750 l multicolored 1.10 .40

Radio, cent. (in 1995).

Genoa '92 Intl. Philatelic Exhibition — A935

1992, Mar. 27 *Perf. 13½x14*
1874 A935 750 l multicolored .90 .25

Lorenzo de Medici (1449-1492) A936

1992, Apr. 8 *Perf. 14*
1875 A936 750 l bl & org brn .90 .50

Filippini Institute, 300th Anniv. — A937

1992, May 2 Photo. *Perf. 13½x14*
1876 A937 750 l multicolored .90 .45

Discovery of America, 500th Anniv. A938

No. 1877, Columbus seeking Queen Isabella's support. No. 1878, Columbus' fleet. No. 1879, Sighting land. No. 1880, Landing in New World.

1992, Apr. 24 Photo. *Perf. 14x13½*

1877	A938 500 l multicolored	.75	.60
1878	A938 500 l multicolored	.75	.60
1879	A938 500 l multicolored	.75	.60
1880	A938 500 l multicolored	.75	.60
a.	Block of 4, #1877-1880	3.25	3.00

See US Nos. 2620-2623.

Discovery of America, 500th Anniv. — A939

Designs: 750 l, Monument to Columbus, Genoa. 850 l, Globe, Genoa '92 Exhibition emblem.

1992, May 2 *Perf. 13½x14*

1881	A939 750 l multicolored	*1.40*	*.65*
1882	A939 850 l multicolored	*1.75*	*.75*

Europa.

Miniature Sheets

Voyages of Columbus — A940

Columbus: No. 1883: a, Presenting natives. b, Announcing his discovery. c, In chains.

No. 1884: a, Welcomed at Barcelona. b, Restored to favor. c, Describing his 3rd voyage.

No. 1885: a, In sight of land. b, Fleet. c, Queen Isabella pledging her jewels.

No. 1886: a, Soliciting aid from Isabella. b, At La Rabida. c, Recall.

No. 1887: a, Landing. b, Santa Maria. c, Queen Isabella and Columbus. No. 1888, Columbus.

Nos. 1883-1888 are similar in design to US Nos. 230-245.

1992, May 22 Engr. *Perf. 10½*

1883	A940 Sheet of 3	6.50	5.50
a.	50 l olive black	.25	.25
b.	300 l dark blue green	.35	.25
c.	4000 l red violet	5.00	3.25
1884	A940 Sheet of 3	5.00	5.00
a.	100 l brown violet	.25	.25
b.	800 l magenta	.80	.60
c.	3000 l green	3.50	3.25
1885	A940 Sheet of 3	3.50	3.50
a.	200 l dark blue	.25	.25
b.	900 l ultra	1.10	.70
c.	1500 l orange	1.75	1.60
1886	A940 Sheet of 3	2.75	2.75
a.	400 l chocolate	.50	.50
b.	700 l vermillion	.90	.60
c.	1000 l slate blue	2.40	1.30
1887	A940 Sheet of 3	4.00	4.00
a.	500 l brown violet	.60	.50
b.	600 l dark green	.70	.60
c.	2000 l crimson lake	2.40	2.25
1888	A940 5000 l Sheet of 1	6.50	6.50
	Nos. 1883-1888 (6)	28.25	27.25

See US Nos. 2624-2629, Portugal Nos. 1918-1923 and Spain Nos. 2677-2682.

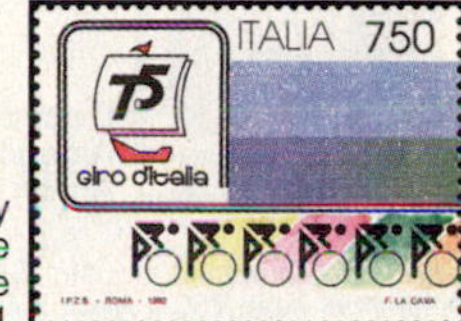
Tour of Italy Bicycle Race A941

1992, May 23 Photo. *Perf. 14x13½*

1889	A941 750 l Ocean	.90	.35
1890	A941 750 l Mountains	.90	.35
a.	Pair, #1889-1890	2.00	1.75

No. 1890a printed in continuous design.

Milan, Italian Soccer Champions A942

1992, May 25 *Perf. 13½x14*
1891 A942 750 l black, red & grn 1.00 .50

Beach Resorts A943

1992 *Perf. 14x13½*

1892	A943 750 l Viareggio	.80	.45
1893	A943 750 l Rimini	.80	.45

Issued: No. 1892, 5/30; No. 1893, 6/13.

Tazio Nuvolari (1892-1953), Race Car Driver — A944

1992, June 5 *Perf. 14x13½*
1900 A944 3200 l multicolored 4.00 1.40

Tourism Type of 1974

1992, June 30 *Perf. 14*

1901 A616 600 l Arcevia	.70	.55
1902 A616 600 l Maratea	.70	.55
1903 A616 600 l Braies	.70	.55
1904 A616 600 l Pantelleria	.70	.55
Nos. 1901-1904 (4)	2.80	2.20

The Shepherds, by Jacopo da Ponte — A945

Litho. & Engr.

1992, Sept. 5 *Perf. 14*

1905 A945 750 l multicolored .85 .45

Discovery of America, 500th Anniv. — A946

500 l, Columbus' house, Genoa. 600 l, Columbus' fleet. 750 l, Map. 850 l, Columbus pointing to land. 1200 l, Coming ashore. 3200 l, Columbus, art by Michelangelo.

1992, Sept. 18 Photo. *Perf. 13½x14*

1906 A946	500 l multicolored	.55	.50
1907 A946	600 l multicolored	.70	.30
1908 A946	750 l multicolored	.85	.40
1909 A946	850 l multicolored	.95	.60
1910 A946	1200 l multicolored	1.40	.90
1911 A946	3200 l multicolored	3.75	1.25
Nos. 1906-1911 (6)		8.20	3.95

Genoa '92.

Stamp Day — A947

1992, Sept. 22 *Perf. 14*

1912 A947 750 l multicolored .95 .30

Self-Adhesive

Perf. 13½

1913 A947 750 l multicolored 2.00 1.50

Lions Intl., 75th Anniv. A948

1992, Sept. 24 *Perf. 14x13½*

1914 A948 3000 l multicolored 3.25 1.50

Single European Market A949

1992, Oct. 5 Photo. *Perf. 14x13½*

1915 A949 600 l multicolored .70 .50

Intl. Conference on Nutrition, Rome A950

1992, Oct. 16 Photo. *Perf. 14x13½*

1916 A950 500 l multicolored .65 .40

Christmas A951

1992, Oct. 31

1917 A951 600 l multicolored .80 .40

Miniature Sheet

United Europe — A952

Buildings on natl. flags, inscriptions in native language: a, Italy (Benvenuta). b, Belgium (Bienvenue, Welkom). c, Denmark (Velkommen). d, France (Bienvenue L'Europe). e, Germany (Willkommen). f, Greece. g, Ireland (Failte). h, Luxembourg (Bienvenue Europe). i, Netherlands (Welkom). j, Portugal (Bem-Vinda). k, United Kingdom (Welcome). l, Spain (Bienvenida).

1993, Jan. 20 Photo. *Perf. 13½x14*

Sheet of 12

1918 A952 750 l #a.-l. 13.00 9.00

Meeting of Veterans of 1943 Battle of Nikolajewka, Russia — A953

1993, Jan. 23 Litho. *Perf. 14x13½*

1919 A953 600 l multicolored 1.25 .50

Carlo Goldoni (1707-93), Playwright A954

Paintings depicting scenes from plays: No. 1920, Man in harlequin costume leaning on picture. No. 1921, Woman seated in front of harlequins.

1993, Feb. 6 Photo. *Perf. 13½x14*

1920 A954 500 l multicolored	.70	.55
1921 A954 500 l multicolored	.70	.55

Mosaic from the Piazza Armerina A955

Photo. & Engr.

1993, Feb. 20 *Perf. 14*

1922 A955 750 l multicolored .95 .50

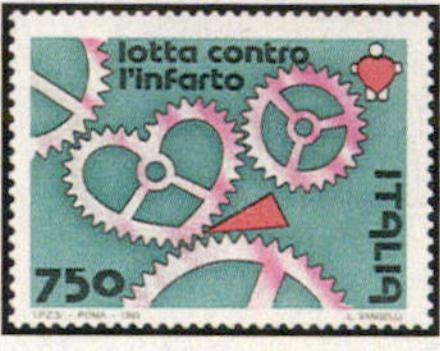

Natl. Health Day Promoting a Healthy Heart A956

1993, Mar. 5 Photo. *Perf. 14x13½*

1923 A956 750 l multicolored .95 .50

Cats A957

No. 1924, European. No. 1925, Maine coon, vert. No. 1926, Devon Rex, vert. No. 1927, White Persian.

1993, Mar. 6 *Perf. 14x13½,13½x14*

1924 A957 600 l multicolored	.75	.50
1925 A957 600 l multicolored	.75	.50
1926 A957 600 l multicolored	.75	.50
1927 A957 600 l multicolored	.75	.50
Nos. 1924-1927 (4)	3.00	2.00

Radio Cent. Type of 1991

Design: 750 l, Temistocle Calzecchi Onesti.

1993, Mar. 26 Litho. *Perf. 14x13½*

1928 A925 750 l multicolored .95 .30

Radio cent. (in 1995).

City Scene, by Francesco Guardi (1712-1793) — A958

Photo. & Engr.

1993, Apr. 6 *Perf. 14*

1929 A958 3200 l multicolored 4.00 2.00

Horace (Quintus Horatius Flaccus), Poet and Satirist, 2000th Anniv. of Death — A959

1993, Apr. 19 Photo. *Perf. 13½x14*

1930 A959 600 l multicolored .75 .40

Contemporary Paintings — A960

Europa: 750 l, Carousel Animals, by Lino Bianchi Barriviera. 850 l, Abstract, by Gino Severini.

1993, May 3

1931 A960 750 l multicolored	*.90*	*.60*
1932 A960 850 l multicolored	*1.10*	*.50*

Natl. Soccer Champions, Milan — A961

1993, May 24

1933 A961 750 l multicolored .95 .40

Natl. Academy of St. Luke, 400th Anniv. — A962

1993, May 31 **Photo.**

1934 A962 750 l multicolored .95 .40

St. Giuseppe Benedetto Cottolengo (1786-1842) A963

1993, May **Photo. & Engr.**

1935 A963 750 l multicolored .95 .30

Family Fest '93 — A964

1993, June 5 Photo. *Perf. 14x13½*

1936 A964 750 l multicolored 1.00 .50

Tourism A965

No. 1937, Palmanova. No. 1938, Senigallia. No. 1939, Carloforte. No. 1940, Sorrento.

1993, June 28 Photo. *Perf. 14x13½*

1937	A965 600 l multicolored	.75	.45
1938	A965 600 l multicolored	.75	.45
1939	A965 600 l multicolored	.75	.45
1940	A965 600 l multicolored	.75	.45
	Nos. 1937-1940 (4)	3.00	1.80

See Nos. 1972-1975, 2032-2035.

1993 World Kayaking Championships, Trentino — A966

1993, July 1 *Perf. 13½x14*

1941	A966 750 l multicolored	.95	.40

Regina Margherita Observatory, Cent. — A967

1993, Sept. 4 Photo. *Perf. 14x13½*

1942	A967 500 l multicolored	.75	.40

Museum Treasures A968

Designs: No. 1943, Concert, by Bartolomeo Manfredi. No. 1944, Ancient map of Foggia. 750 l, Illuminated page with "S," vert. 850 l, The Death of Adonis, by Sebastiano Del Piombo.

Perf. 14x13½, 13½x14

1993, Nov. 27 Litho.

1943	A968 600 l multicolored	.75	.40
1944	A968 600 l multicolored	.75	.45
1945	A968 750 l multicolored	1.00	.25
1946	A968 850 l multicolored	1.00	.45
	Nos. 1943-1946 (4)	3.50	1.55

Holy Stairway, Veroli — A969

1993, Sept. 25 Photo. *Perf. 13½x14*

1947	A969 750 l multicolored	.95	.30

World War II — A970

Events of 1943: No. 1948, Deportation of Jews from Italy, Oct. 16, 1943. No. 1949, Soldiers, helmet (Battle of Naples). No. 1950, Execution of the Cervi Brothers.

1993, Sept. 25

1948	A970 750 l multicolored	1.00	.30
1949	A970 750 l multicolored	1.00	.30
1950	A970 750 l multicolored	1.00	.30
	Nos. 1948-1950 (3)	3.00	.90

See Nos. 1984-1986.

Thurn and Taxis Postal History A971

No. 1951, Coach. No. 1952, Coat of arms. No. 1953, Cart. No. 1954, Post rider on galloping horse. No. 1955, Post rider on walking horse.

1993, Oct. 2 *Perf. 14x13½*

1951	A971 750 l multicolored	.90	.25
1952	A971 750 l multicolored	.90	.25
1953	A971 750 l multicolored	.90	.25
1954	A971 750 l multicolored	.90	.25
1955	A971 750 l multicolored	.90	.25
	Nos. 1951-1955 (5)	4.50	1.25

Perf. 14 Horiz.

1951a	A971 750 l	.85	.65
1952a	A971 750 l	.85	.65
1953a	A971 750 l	.85	.65
1954a	A971 750 l	.85	.65
1955a	A971 750 l	.85	.65
b.	Booklet pane of 5, #1951a-1955a	5.00	4.00

Bank Exterior A972

1000 Lire Note — A972a

1993, Oct. 15 *Perf. 14x13½*

1956	A972 750 l multi	1.00	.30
1957	A972a 1000 l multi	2.00	.75

Bank of Italy, Cent. Nos. 1956-1957 were printed with se-tenant labels. Values, set of two with labels: $5.50 unused, $2.75 used.

Christmas A973

Designs: 600 l, Living Creche in the town of Corchiano. 750 l, Detail of The Annunciation, by Piero Della Francesca.

1993, Oct. 26 Litho. *Perf. 13½x14*

1958	A973 600 l multicolored	.70	.40
1959	A973 750 l multicolored	.95	.50

Stamp Day A974

1993, Nov. 12 Photo. *Perf. 14*

1960	A974 600 l blue & red	.70	.40

First Italian colonial postage stamps, cent.

Circus — A975

600 l, Acrobat, horses. 750 l, Clown performing.

1994, Jan. 8 Litho. *Perf. 13½x14*

1961	A975 600 l multi	.75	.40
1962	A975 750 l multi	.90	.50

Presence of Women in the Home A976

1994, Feb. 14 Photo. *Perf. 14*

1963	A976 750 l multicolored	.95	.25

Radio Cent. Type of 1991

750 l, Augusto Righi (1850-1920), physicist.

Perf. 14x13½

1994, Mar. 11 Photo. Unwmk.

1964	A925 750 l multicolored	.95	.30

Radio cent. (in 1995).

Dogs A977

No. 1965, German shepherd. No. 1966, Abruzzi sheepdog. No. 1967, Boxer. No. 1968, Dalmatian.

1994, Mar. 12 *Perf. 14x13*

1965	A977 600 l multi	.75	.45
1966	A977 600 l multi	.75	.45
1967	A977 600 l multi	.75	.45
1968	A977 600 l multi	.75	.45
	Nos. 1965-1968 (4)	3.00	1.80

Italian Cuisine — A978

1994, Mar. 24 *Perf. 13x14*

1969	A978 500 l Breads	.65	.45
1970	A978 600 l Pasta	.90	.40

Procession Honoring Apparition of Christ, Tarquinia — A979

1994, Apr. 2 *Perf. 13½*

1971	A979 750 l multicolored	1.00	.30

Tourism Type of 1993

No. 1972, Orta San Giulio. No. 1973, Santa Marinella. No. 1974, Messina. No. 1975, Monticchio, Potenza.

1994, Apr. 23 Photo. *Perf. 14x13½*

1972	A965 600 l multi	.75	.30
1973	A965 600 l multi	.75	.30
1974	A965 600 l multi	.75	.30
1975	A965 600 l multi	.75	.30
	Nos. 1972-1975 (4)	3.00	1.20

A981

Nobel Prize Winners: 750 l, Camillo Golgi (1844-1926), Physician, Medicine, 1906. 850 l, Guilio Natta (1903-), Chemistry, 1963.

1994, May 2 Photo. *Perf. 13½x14*

1976	A981 750 l multicolored	*1.00*	*.40*
1977	A981 850 l multicolored	*1.40*	*.50*

Publication of "Summa de Arithemtica, Geometria, Proportioni et Proportionalita," 500th Anniv. — A982

Fra Luca Pacioli (c. 1445-1514), mathematician.

1994, May 2 Photo. *Perf. 14x13*

1978	A982 750 l multicolored	1.00	.30

Lajos Kossuth (1802-94) — A983

1994, Apr. 30 Photo. *Perf. 13½x14*

1979	A983 3750 l multicolored	4.75	1.75

Milan, Winners of 1993-94 Italian Soccer Championships — A984

1994, May 2 *Perf. 14x13½*

1980	A984 750 l multicolored	1.25	.50

World Swimming Championships A985

1994, May 2 Photo. *Perf. 13½x14*

1981	A985 600 l Diving	.75	.45
1982	A985 750 l Water polo	1.00	.30

Archaeology Exhibition, Rimini — A986

1994, May 6

1983 A986 750 l multicolored .95 .30

World War II Type of 1993

Events of 1944: No. 1984, Destruction of Monte Cassino. No. 1985, Massacre of the Ardeatine Caves. No. 1986, Massacre at Marzabotto.

1994, May 18

1984 A970 750 l multicolored .95 .25
1985 A970 750 l multicolored .95 .25
1986 A970 750 l multicolored .95 .25
Nos. 1984-1986 (3) 2.85 .75

22nd Natl. Eucharistic Congress, Siena — A987

1994, May 28 Photo. *Perf. 13½x14*

1987 A987 600 l multicolored .70 .40

Ariadne, Venus and Bacchus, by Tintoretto (1518-94) — A988

1994, May 31 *Perf. 14*

1988 A988 750 l multicolored 1.00 .40

Brotherhood of Mercy, Florence, 700th Anniv. — A989

1994, June 4 *Perf. 14x13½*

1989 A989 750 l multicolored .95 .25

European Parliamentary Elections — A990

1994, June 11 Photo. *Perf. 13½x14*

1990 A990 600 l multicolored .95 .30

Natl. Museums — A991

No. 1991, Attic Krater, Natl. Archaeological Museum. No. 1992, Ancient drawing, Natl. Archives. 750 l, Statue, Natl. Roman Museum. 850 l, Medallion, Natl. Archives.

1994, June 16

1991 A991 600 l multicolored .75 .40
1992 A991 600 l multicolored .75 .40
1993 A991 750 l multicolored .90 .40
1994 A991 850 l multicolored .90 .40
Nos. 1991-1994 (4) 3.30 1.60

Intl. Olympic Committee, Cent. — A992

1994, June 23

1995 A992 850 l multicolored 1.25 .40

G-7 Summit, Naples — A993

1994, July 8

1996 A993 600 l multicolored .85 .40

A 750 l in this design was printed in error but not issued. Value, *$17,000.*

A995

1994, Sept. 8 Photo. *Perf. 14*

1998 A995 500 l multicolored .95 .40

Basilica of Loreto, 500th anniv.

A996

1994, Sept. 19

1999 A996 750 l multicolored 1.00 .25

Frederick II (1194-1250), Holy Roman Emperor.

Stamp Day — A998

Designs: 600 l, Pietro Miliani (1744-1817), paper manufacturer. 750 l, Convent of San Domenico.

1994, Sept. 16 Photo. *Perf. 13½x14*

2001 A998 600 l multicolored .70 .45
2002 A998 750 l multicolored .90 .30

Basilica of St. Mark, 900th Anniv. A999

1994, Oct. 8 Photo. *Perf. 13½x13*

2003 A999 750 l multicolored 1.00 .75
a. Souvenir sheet of 2, tete beche 2.25 2.25

No. 2003 printed with se-tenant label. No. 2003a contains one each No. 2003 and San Marino No. 1314. Only No. 2003 was valid for postage in Italy. See San Marino No. 1314.

Christmas A1000

600 l, The Annunciation, by Melozzo da Forli. 750 l, Madonna and Child, by Lattanzio da Rimini.

1994, Nov. 5 Photo. *Perf. 13½x14*

2004 A1000 600 l multicolored .80 .40
2005 A1000 750 l multicolored 1.10 .30

Italian Touring Club, Cent. — A1001

1994, Nov. 8

2006 A1001 600 l multicolored .85 .40

CREDIOP, 75th Anniv. — A1002

1994, Nov. 11

2007 A1002 750 l multicolored .85 .30

No. 2007 was printed with a se-tenant label. Value with label attached: $2.

Giovanni Gentile (1875-1944), Philosopher A1003

1994, Nov. 21

2008 A1003 750 l multicolored 1.15 .40

Querini Dubois Palace, Venice — A1004

1994 *Perf. 13½x14*

2009 A1004 600 l red & silver .90 .40

New Italian Postal Emblem A1005

1994 *Perf. 14x13½*

2010 A1005 750 l red, blk & grn 1.40 .25
2011 A1005 750 l red brown 1.40 .25
a. Pair, #2010-2011 3.50 2.00

See Nos. 2059-2060.

World Speed Skating Championships — A1006

1995, Feb. 6 Photo. *Perf. 14x13½*

2012 A1006 750 l multicolored 1.10 .30

Achille Beltrame (1871-1945) A1007

Design: 500 l, Cover of first issue of LA DOMENICA DEL CORRIERE.

1995, Feb. 18 Photo. *Perf. 13½x14*

2013 A1007 500 l multicolored 1.10 .40

Italian Food — A1008

1995, Mar. 4

2014 A1008 500 l Rice 1.00 .55
2015 A1008 750 l Olives, olive oil 1.25 .40

See Nos. 2068-2069.

Birds
A1009

1995, Mar. 11 Photo. ***Perf. 14x13½***

2016 A1009 600 l Heron .75 .45
2017 A1009 600 l Vulture .75 .45
2018 A1009 600 l Royal eagle .75 .45
2019 A1009 600 l Alpine chaffinch .75 .45
Nos. 2016-2019 (4) 3.00 1.80

UN, 50th Anniv.
A1010

1995, Mar. 24 Photo. ***Perf. 14x13½***

2020 A1010 850 l multicolored 1.00 .40

Fifth Day of Milan War Memorial, by Giuseppe Grandi, Cent.
A1011

1995, Mar. 25 Photo. ***Perf. 14x13½***

2021 A1011 750 l gold, black & blue 1.00 .30

Miniature Sheet

End of World War II, 50th Anniv. — A1012

Designs: a, Mafalda de Savoy, concentration camp, barbed wire. b, Allied DUKW, Battles of Anzio and Nettuno. c, Women in World War II, Teresa Gullace. d, Gold Medal of Valor, Palazzo Vecchio, Florence. e, Gold Medal of Valor, building, Vittorio Veneto. f, Gold Medal of Valor, Cathedral, Cagliari. g. Mountain Battalion. h, Air dropping supplies, Balkans. i, Atlantic fleet.

1995, Mar. 31 Photo. ***Perf. 14x13½***

2022 A1012 750 l Sheet of 9, #a.-i. 9.50 9.50

Natl. Treasures
A1013

Designs: No. 2023, Illuminated manuscript with "P," State Archives, Rome. No. 2024, Painting of Port of Naples, by Tavola Strozzi, Natl. Museum of San Martino, horiz. No. 2025, Illuminated manuscript with "I," Christ, State Archives, Mantua. No. 2026, Painting, Sacred and Profane Love, by Titian, Borghese Gallery and Museum, Rome, horiz.

Perf. 13½x14, 14x13½

1995, Apr. 28 **Photo.**

2023 A1013 500 l multicolored .65 .50
2024 A1013 500 l multicolored .65 .45
2025 A1013 750 l multicolored .90 .30
2026 A1013 850 l multicolored 1.00 .45
Nos. 2023-2026 (4) 3.20 1.70

Venice Biennial, Cent. — A1014

1995, Apr. 29 ***Perf. 13½x14***

2027 A1014 750 l multicolored 1.00 .30

Basilica of Santa Croce, Florence
A1015

1995, May 3 **Engr.**

2028 A1015 750 l deep brn blk 1.00 .30

Peace & Freedom
A1016

Europa: 750 l, Family, liberating soldiers, Italian flag. 850 l, Stars of European flag, church, mosque.

1995, May 5 Photo. ***Perf. 13½x14***

2029 A1016 750 l multicolored 1.10 .30
2030 A1016 850 l multicolored 1.40 .45

Volleyball, Cent. — A1017

1995, May 8

2031 A1017 750 l multicolored 1.00 .30

Tourism Type of 1993

1995, May 12 Photo. ***Perf. 14x13½***

2032 A965 750 l Nuoro 1.00 .30
2033 A965 750 l Susa 1.00 .30
2034 A965 750 l Alatri 1.00 .30
2035 A965 750 l Venosa 1.00 .30
Nos. 2032-2035 (4) 4.00 1.20

Discovery of the X-Ray, Cent.
A1018

1995, June 2

2036 A1018 750 l multicolored 1.00 .30

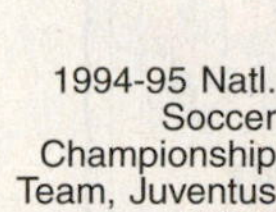

1994-95 Natl. Soccer Championship Team, Juventus
A1019

1995, June 5 ***Perf. 13½x14***

2037 A1019 750 l multicolored 1.25 .40

Radio, Cent.
A1020

Designs: 750 l, Griffone House. 850 l, Guglielmo Marconi, transmitting equipment.

1995, June 8 ***Perf. 14x13½***

2038 A1020 750 multicolored 1.00 .30

Perf. 14

2039 A1020 850 l multicolored 1.25 .40

No. 2039 is 36x21mm. See Germany No. 1900, Ireland No. 974a, San Marino Nos. 1336-1337, Vatican City Nos. 978-979.

A1021

St. Anthony of Padua (1195-1231) — A1022

Perf. 13½x14, 14x13½

1995, June 13

2040 A1021 750 l multicolored 1.10 .30
2041 A1022 850 l multicolored 1.25 .45

See Brazil No. 2539 and Portugal Nos. 2054-2057.

Historical Public Gardens
A1023

Designs: No. 2042, Durazzo Pallavicini, Pegli. No. 2043, Boboli, Firenze. No. 2044, Ninfa, Cisterna di Latina. No. 2045, Royal Park, Caserta.

Litho. & Engr.

1995, June 24 ***Perf. 14x13½***

2042 A1023 750 l multicolored 1.00 .25
2043 A1023 750 l multicolored 1.00 .25
2044 A1023 750 l multicolored 1.00 .25
2045 A1023 750 l multicolored 1.00 .25
Nos. 2042-2045 (4) 4.00 1.00

Congress of European Society of Ophthalmology
A1024

1995, June 24 Litho. ***Perf. 13½x14***

2046 A1024 750 l multicolored 1.00 .30

The Sailors' Wives, by Massimo Campigli (1895-1971) — A1025

1995, July 4 Photo. ***Perf. 14***

2047 A1025 750 l multicolored 1.40 .30

14th World Conference on Relativity, Florence
A1026

750 l, Galileo, Einstein.

1995, Aug. 7 Litho. ***Perf. 14x13***

2048 A1026 750 l dk blue & org brn 1.00 .30

Motion Pictures, Cent. — A1027

No. 2049, Son of the Shiek, Rudolph Valentino. No. 2050, L'oro Di Napoli, Toto. No. 2051, Le Notti Di Cabiria, F. Fellini. No. 2052, Cinecitta '95.

Litho. & Engr.

1995, Aug. 29 ***Perf. 13½x14***

2049 A1027 750 l multicolored 1.00 .45
2050 A1027 750 l multicolored 1.00 .45
2051 A1027 750 l multicolored 1.00 .45
2052 A1027 750 l multicolored 1.00 .45
Nos. 2049-2052 (4) 4.00 1.80

See Nos. 2099-2101, 2170-2172, 2269-2271.

FAO, 50th Anniv.
A1028

1995, Sept. 1 Photo. ***Perf. 14x13½***

2053 A1028 850 l multicolored 1.25 .40

Basilica of Pontida & Death of St. Albert of Prezzate, 900th Anniv.
A1029

1995, Sept. 2 **Engr.**
2054 A1029 1000 l blue & brown 1.40 .50

ROMA '95, First World Military Games — A1030

1995, Sept. 6 **Photo.** ***Perf. 13½x14***
2055 A1030 850 l multicolored 1.10 .40

Italian News Agency (ANSA), 50th Anniv.
A1031

1995, Oct. 27 **Photo.** ***Perf. 14x13½***
2056 A1031 750 l multicolored 1.25 .30

Christmas
A1032

Designs: 750 l, Nativity figurines, Cathedral of Polignano a Mare, by Stefano da Putignano. 850 l, Adoration of the Magi, by Fra Angelico.

1995, Nov. 18
2057 A1032 750 l multicolored 1.75 .30
2058 A1032 850 l multicolored 2.25 .40

New Italian Postal Emblem Type of 1994

1995, Dec. 9 **Photo.** ***Perf. 13½x14***
Size: 26x18mm
2059 A1005 750 l like No. 2011 1.00 .25
a. Booklet pane of 8 8.50
Complete booklet, #2059a 10.00
2060 A1005 850 l like No. 2010 1.25 .25
a. Booklet pane of 8 10.00
Complete booklet, #2060a 11.50

Renato Mondolfo
A1033

1995, Dec. 9 **Photo.** ***Perf. 14x13½***
2061 A1033 750 l multicolored 1.00 .30

Philately Day.

F.T. Marinetti (1876-1944), Poet and Ideologue — A1034

1996, Jan. 19 **Photo.** ***Perf. 14***
2062 A1034 750 l multicolored 1.25 .30

Collections from Natl. Museum and Archives
A1035

No. 2063, Arms of the Academy of Georgofili, Florence. No. 2064, Illuminated manuscript from Lucca (1372), vert. No. 2065, Manuscript of Gabriele D'Annunzio (1863-1938), author, soldier, political leader. No. 2066, French miniature, c. 1486.

1996, Feb. 26 ***Perf. 14x13½, 13½x14***
2063 A1035 750 l multicolored 1.00 .30
2064 A1035 750 l multicolored 1.00 .30
2065 A1035 850 l multicolored 1.40 .45
2066 A1035 850 l multicolored 1.40 .45
Nos. 2063-2066 (4) 4.80 1.50

Sarah and the Angel, by Tiepolo (1696-1770) — A1036

1996, Mar. 5 ***Perf. 14***
2067 A1036 1000 l multicolored 2.00 .50

Italian Food Type of 1995

500 l, White wine, grapes. 750 l, Red wine, grapes.

1996, Mar. 20 ***Perf. 13½x14***
2068 A1008 500 l multi 1.20 .40
2069 A1008 750 l multi 1.75 .30

CHINA '96, 9th Asian Intl. Philatelic Exhibition
A1037

1996, Mar. 22 ***Perf. 14x13½***
2070 A1037 1250 l multicolored 2.25 1.00

Marco Polo's return from China, 700th anniv. (in 1995).
See San Marino No. 1350.

Cathedral of Milan — A1038

No. 2071, Front entrance. No. 2072, Corner, side view.

1996, Mar. 23 ***Perf. 13½x14***
2071 A1038 750 l multicolored .75 .30
2072 A1038 750 l multicolored .75 .30
a. Pair, #2071-2072 2.00 1.50
b. Booklet pane, 4 #2072a 10.00
Complete booklet, #2072b 10.00

No. 2072a is a continuous design.
ITALIA '98, Intl. Philatelic Exhibition, Milan.

A1039

1996, Apr. 3 ***Perf. 13½x14, 14x13½***
2073 A1039 750 l shown 1.25 .40
2074 A1039 750 l Globe, "100" 1.40 .40

Natl. Press Federation, 50th anniv. (No. 2073). "La Gazzetta dello Sport," cent. (No. 2074), horiz.

Intl. Museum of Postal Images, Belvedere Ostrense
A1040

1996, Apr. 13 **Photo.** ***Perf. 13½x14***
2075 A1040 500 l multicolored 1.25 .30

Academy of Finance Police, Cent. — A1040a

1996, Apr. 13
2076 A1040a 750 l multicolored 1.00 .60

RAMOGE Agreement Between France, Italy, Monaco, 20th Anniv.
A1041

Photo. & Engr.
1996, May 14 ***Perf. 14x13½***
2077 A1041 750 l multicolored 1.25 .40

See France No. 2524, Monaco No. 1998.

Rome-New York Trans-Continental Drive — A1042

1996, Apr. 13 **Photo.** ***Perf. 13½x14***
2078 A1042 4650 l multicolored 8.00 4.00

Europa (Famous Women)
A1043

750 l, Carina Negrone, pilot. 850 l, Adelaide Ristori, actress.

1996, Apr. 29 **Photo.** ***Perf. 13½x14***
2079 A1043 750 l multicolored *1.10* *.50*
2080 A1043 850 l multicolored *1.40* *.50*

St. Celestine V (1215-96)
A1044

Litho. & Engr.
1996, May 18 ***Perf. 14x13½***
2081 A1044 750 l multicolored 1.25 .40

Tourism
A1045

No. 2082, Pienza Cathedral. No. 2083, St. Anthony's Church, Diano Marina. No. 2084, Belltower of Church of St. Michael the Archangel, Monte Sant'Angelo. No. 2085, Prehistoric stone dwelling, Lampedusa.

1996, May 18 **Photo.** ***Perf. 14x13½***
2082 A1045 750 l multicolored 1.25 .40
2083 A1045 750 l multicolored 1.25 .40
2084 A1045 750 l multicolored 1.25 .40
2085 A1045 750 l multicolored 1.25 .40
Nos. 2082-2085 (4) 5.00 1.60

Consecration of Reconstructed Farfa Abbey, 500th Anniv. — A1046

1996, May 18 **Photo.** ***Perf. 13½x14***
2086 A1046 1000 l multicolored 1.50 .60

Mediterranean Fair, Palermo — A1047

1996, May 25 ***Perf. 14x13½***
2087 A1047 750 l multicolored 1.10 .30

Italian Republic, 50th Anniv. — A1048

1996, June 1 ***Perf. 13½x14***
2088 A1048 750 l multicolored 1.10 .30

Production of Vespa Motor Scooters, 50th Anniv. — A1049

1996, June 20
2089 A1049 750 l multicolored 1.75 .40

First Meeting of European Economic Community, Messina and Venice, 40th Anniv. — A1050

1996, June 21 ***Perf. 14***
2090 A1050 750 l multicolored 1.25 .40

Modern Olympic Games, Cent. A1051

Designs: 500 l, Runners, 1896. 750 l, Discus, Atlanta skyline, vert. 850 l, Gymnast on rings, basketball, Atlanta stadium. 1250 l, 1896 stadium, Athens, 1996 stadium, Atlanta, vert.

Perf. 14x13½, 13½x14

1996, July 1 **Photo.**

2091	A1051	500 l	multicolored	.60	.35
2092	A1051	750 l	multicolored	1.00	.50
2093	A1051	850 l	multicolored	1.00	.45
2094	A1051	1250 l	multicolored	1.75	.80
	Nos. 2091-2094 (4)			4.35	2.10

Butterflies A1052

No. 2095, Melanargia arge. No. 2096, Papilio hospiton. No. 2097, Zygaena rubicundus. No. 2098, Acanthobrahmaea europaea.

1996, Aug. 26 ***Perf. 14x13½***

2095	A1052	750 l	multicolored	1.10	.30
2096	A1052	750 l	multicolored	1.10	.30
2097	A1052	750 l	multicolored	1.10	.30
2098	A1052	750 l	multicolored	1.10	.30
	Nos. 2095-2098 (4)			4.40	1.20

Motion Picture Type of 1995

No. 2099, Massimo Troisi in "Scusate Il Ritardo." No. 2100, Aldo Fabrizi in "Prima Comunione." No. 2101, Bartolomeo Pagano as Maciste in "Cabiria."

Photo. & Engr.

1996, Aug. 30 ***Perf. 13½x14***

2099	A1027	750 l	multicolored	1.25	.45
2100	A1027	750 l	multicolored	1.25	.45
2101	A1027	750 l	multicolored	1.25	.45
	Nos. 2099-2101 (3)			3.75	1.35

A1054

1996, Sept. 7 **Photo.** ***Perf. 13½x14***
2102 A1054 750 l multicolored 2.00 .30

Milan, 1995-96 national soccer champions.

The Duomo, Cathedral of Santa Maria del Fiore, Florence, 700th Anniv. A1055

1996, Sept. 7 **Engr.** ***Perf. 14x13½***
2103 A1055 750 l dark blue 1.25 .30

13th Intl. Congress of Prehistoric Science — A1056

1996, Sept. 9 **Photo.** ***Perf. 13½x14***
2104 A1056 850 l multicolored 1.25 .35

Levant Fair, Bari A1057

1996, Sept. 13 **Photo.** ***Perf. 14x13½***
2105 A1057 750 l multicolored 1.25 .30

1997 Mediterranean Games, Bari — A1058

1996, Sept. 13 ***Perf. 13½x14***
2106 A1058 750 l multicolored 1.25 .30

Juventus, 1995-96 European Soccer Champions A1059

1996, Sept. 14
2107 A1059 750 l multicolored 2.00 .40

Alessandro Pertini (1896-1990), Former President A1060

1996, Sept. 25 **Photo.** ***Perf. 13½x14***
2108 A1060 750 l multicolored 1.25 .30

Eugenio Montale (1896-1981), Poet — A1061

1996, Oct. 12 **Litho. & Engr.**
2109 A1061 750 l blue & brown 1.25 .30

Annunciation, by Pietro da Cortona (1596-1669) A1062

1996, Oct. 31 **Photo.**
2110 A1062 500 l multicolored .95 .35

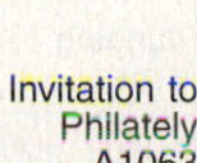
Invitation to Philately A1063

Designs: 750 l, Tex Willer, western scene. 850 l, Seagulls, gondola, city, Corto Maltese.

Litho. & Engr.

1996, Oct. 31 ***Perf. 14x13½***
2111 A1063 750 l multicolored 1.75 .30
2112 A1063 850 l multicolored 1.75 .45

Stamp Day — A1064

1996, Nov. 8 **Photo.** ***Perf. 13½x14***
2113 A1064 750 l multicolored 1.25 .30

Universities of Italy — A1065

Designs: No. 2114, Agrarian School, cent., University of Perugia. No. 2115, University of Sassari (1562-1996), horiz. No. 2116, University of Salerno

Perf. 13½x14, 14x13½

1996, Nov. 9 **Engr.**

2114	A1065	750 l	brown	1.25	.30
2115	A1065	750 l	green	1.25	.30
2116	A1065	750 l	blue	1.25	.30
	Nos. 2114-2116 (3)			3.75	.90

World Food Summit, Rome — A1066

1996, Nov. 13 **Photo.** ***Perf. 14x13½***
2117 A1066 850 l green & black 1.40 .40

Christmas A1067

Designs: 750 l, Madonna and Child, by Pisanello. 850 l, Santa, toys, horiz.

Perf. 13½x14, 14x13½

1996, Nov. 15
2118 A1067 750 l multicolored 1.50 .30
2119 A1067 850 l multicolored 1.60 .45

UNESCO, 50th Anniv. — A1068

850 l, UNICEF 50th Anniv., baby, globe, emblem.

1996, Nov. 20 ***Perf. 13½x14***
2120 A1068 750 l multicolored 1.25 .30
2121 A1068 850 l multicolored 1.25 .45

Natl. Institute of Statistics, 70th Anniv. — A1069

1996, Nov. 26
2122 A1069 750 l multicolored 1.00 .30

"Strega" Literary Award 50th Anniv. — A1070

1996, Nov. 29
2123 A1070 3400 l multicolored 4.75 2.50

First Natl. Flag, Bicent. — A1071

1997, Jan. 7 Photo. ***Perf. 13½x14***
2124 A1071 750 l multicolored 1.00 .25

Sestrieres '97, World Alpine Skiing Championships A1072

1997, Feb. 1 Photo. ***Perf. 13½x14***
2125 A1072 750 l shown 1.00 .35
2126 A1072 850 l Ski of colors 1.25 .45

Galileo Ferraris (1847-97), Physicist, Electrical Engineer A1073

1997, Feb. 7 ***Perf. 14x13½***
2127 A1073 750 l multicolored 1.00 .35

Emanuela Loi (1967-92), Police Woman Killed by Mafia A1074

1997, Mar. 8
2128 A1074 750 l multicolored 1.00 .40

Italia '98, World Philatelic Exhibition, Milan — A1075

Designs: a, Airmail philately. b, Topical philately. c, Postal history. d, Philatelic literature.

1997, Mar. 21 Litho. ***Perf. 13½x14***
2129 Sheet of 4 4.00 3.00
a.-d. A1075 750 l any single .90 .65

Statue of Marcus Aurelius (121-180), Roman Emperor A1076

1997, Mar. 25 Photo.
2130 A1076 750 l multicolored 1.00 .40

Treaty of Rome, 40th anniv.

St. Ambrose (339-397), Bishop of Milan — A1077

Litho. & Engr.
1997, Apr. 4 ***Perf. 14***
2131 A1077 1000 l multicolored 1.50 .45

St. Geminian, 1600th Death Anniv. — A1078

1997, Apr. 4 Photo. ***Perf. 13½x14***
2132 A1078 750 l multicolored 1.00 .40

University of Rome A1079

Design: No. 2134, University of Padua.

1997, Apr. 14 Engr. ***Perf. 14x13½***
2133 A1079 750 l claret 1.00 .30
2134 A1079 750 l blue 1.00 .30

Founding of Rome, 2750th Anniv. A1080

1997, Apr. 21 Photo. ***Perf. 14x13½***
2135 A1080 850 l multicolored 1.25 .40

Timoleontee Wall, Gela — A1081

1997, Apr. 24
2136 A1081 750 l multicolored 1.00 .30

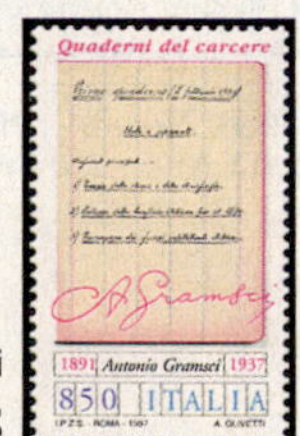

Antonio Gramsci (1891-1937), Politician — A1082

1997, Apr. 26 Photo. ***Perf. 14***
2137 A1082 850 l multicolored 1.25 .40

Monastery Church, Pavia, 500th Anniv. — A1083

1997, May 3 ***Perf. 13½x14***
2138 A1083 1000 l multicolored 1.50 .45

Stories and Legends A1084

Europa: 800 l, Cobbler's workshop. 900 l, Street singer, vert.

Perf. 14x13, 13x14
1997, May 5 Photo.
2139 A1084 800 l multicolored 1.00 .30
2140 A1084 900 l multicolored 1.50 .30

Massimo Theatre, Palermo, Cent. — A1085

1997, May 16 Photo. ***Perf. 13½x14***
2141 A1085 800 l multicolored 1.25 .25

Tourism A1086

Designs: No. 2142, St. Vitalian Basilica, Ravenna. No. 2143, Tomb of Marcus Tullius Cicero (106-43BC), Formia. No. 2144, College of Assumption of the Holy Mary, Positano. No. 2145, St. Sebastian Church, Acireale.

1997, May 17 Photo. ***Perf. 14x13***
2142 A1086 800 l multicolored 1.00 .25
2143 A1086 800 l multicolored 1.00 .25
2144 A1086 800 l multicolored 1.00 .25
2145 A1086 800 l multicolored 1.00 .25
Nos. 2142-2145 (4) 4.00 1.00

Book Fair, Turin — A1087

1997, May 22 ***Perf. 13½x14***
2146 A1087 800 l multicolored 1.40 .40

Queen Paola of Belgium, 60th Birthday A1088

750 l, San Angelo Castle.

1997, May 23 Photo. ***Perf. 14x13½***
2147 A1088 750 l multi 1.25 .30

See Belgium No. 1652.

Rome Fair A1089

1997, May 24 Photo. ***Perf. 14x13½***
2148 A1089 800 l multicolored 1.25 .30

Cathedral of Orvieto — A1090

1997, May 31 Engr. ***Perf. 13x14***
2149 A1090 450 l deep violet .75 .40

Fr. Giuseppe Morosini (1913-44) A1091

1997, June 4 Photo.
2150 A1091 800 l multicolored 1.25 .30

Bologna Fair A1092

1997, June 7 ***Perf. 14x13***
2151 A1092 800 l multicolored 1.25 .30

Juventus, 1996-97 Italian Soccer Champions A1093

1997, June 7 ***Perf. 13½x14***
2152 A1093 800 l multicolored 1.50 .35

Abruzzo Natl. Park, 75th Anniv. — A1094

1997, June 7 Photo. ***Perf. 13½x14***
2153 A1094 800 l multicolored 1.25 .30

Italian Naval League, Cent. — A1095

1997, June 10 Photo. *Perf. 13½x14*
2154 A1095 800 l multicolored 1.25 .30

13th Mediterranean Games, Bari — A1096

1997, June 13 *Perf. 14x13½*
2155 A1096 900 l multicolored 1.25 .40

Public Gardens A1097

Designs: No. 2156, Miramare-Trieste Park. No. 2157, Cavour-Santena. No. 2158, Villa Sciarra, Rome. No. 2159, Orto Botanical Gardens, Palermo.

Photo. & Engr.

1997, June 14 *Perf. 14x13½*
2156 A1097 800 l multicolored 1.00 .30
2157 A1097 800 l multicolored 1.00 .30
2158 A1097 800 l multicolored 1.00 .30
2159 A1097 800 l multicolored 1.00 .30
Nos. 2156-2159 (4) 4.00 1.20

Italian Labor Force — A1098

800 l, Industry. 900 l, Agriculture, horiz.

Perf. 13½x14, 14x13½
1997, June 20
2160 A1098 800 l multi 1.00 .30
2161 A1098 900 l multi 1.25 .40

John Cabot's Voyage to Canada, 500th Anniv. A1099

1997, June 24 Litho. *Perf. 14*
2162 A1099 1300 l multicolored 2.00 2.00

See Canada No. 1649.

Pietro Verri (1728-97), Economist, Journalist A1100

1997, June 28 *Perf. 13½x14*
2163 A1100 3600 l multicolored 4.75 2.50

Madonna of the Rosary by Pomarancio il Vecchio (Niccolo Cercignani)(d. 1597) — A1101

650 l, The Miracle of Ostia, by Paolo de Dono Uccello (1397-1475).

1997, July 19 Photo. *Perf. 13½x14*
2164 A1101 450 l multicolored .75 .30

Size: 26x37mm

2165 A1101 650 l multicolored 1.25 .60

Varia di Palmi Festival — A1102

1997, Aug. 2 *Perf. 13½x14*
2166 A1102 800 l multicolored 1.25 .40

Universiade 97, Sicily A1103

1997, Aug. 19 Photo. *Perf. 14x13½*
2167 A1103 450 l Basketball .75 .35
2168 A1103 800 l High jump 1.25 .30

Antonio Rosmini (1797-1855), Priest, Philosopher — A1104

1997, Aug. 26
2169 A1104 800 l multicolored 1.25 .25

Motion Picture Type of 1995

No. 2170, Pietro Germi in "The Railway Man." No. 2171, Anna Magnani in "Mamma Roma." No. 2172, Ugo Tognazzi in "My Dear Friends."

Photo. & Engr.

1997, Aug. 27 *Perf. 13½x14*
2170 A1027 800 l multicolored 1.25 .40
2171 A1027 800 l multicolored 1.25 .40
2172 A1027 800 l multicolored 1.25 .40
Nos. 2170-2172 (3) 3.75 1.20

Viareggio Literary Prize A1106

1997, Aug. 30 Photo. *Perf. 14x13½*
2173 A1106 4000 l multicolored 4.75 2.00

Intl. Fair, Bolzano A1107

1997, Sept. 1
2174 A1107 800 l multicolored 1.25 .30

A1108

Artifacts and Paintings from Natl. Museums and Galleries: 450 l, Bronze head, 500BC, National Museum, Reggio Calabria. 650 l, Madonna and Child with Two Vases of Roses, by Ercole di Roberti, Natl. Picture Gallery, Ferrara. 800 l, Miniature of troubadour, Sordello da Goito, Arco Palace Museum, Manta. 900 l, St. George and the Dragon, Vitale da Bologna, Natl. Picture Gallery, Bologna.

1997, Sept. 13 Photo. *Perf. 13½x14*
2175 A1108 450 l multicolored .75 .30
2176 A1108 650 l multicolored 1.00 .50
2177 A1108 800 l multicolored 1.25 .30
2178 A1108 900 l multicolored 1.25 .40
Nos. 2175-2178 (4) 4.25 1.50

Pope Paul VI (1897-1978) A1109

1997, Sept. 26 Engr. *Perf. 13x14*
2179 A1109 4000 l dark blue 5.75 2.50

Milan Fair A1110

1997, Sept. 30 Photo. *Perf. 14x13*
2180 A1110 800 l multicolored 1.25 .40

Marshall Plan, 50th Anniv. — A1111

1997, Oct. 17
2181 A1111 800 l multicolored 1.25 .25

Christmas A1112

Nativity scenes: 800 l, Molded polychrome, from Church of St. Francis, Leonessa. 900 l, Fresco, from Baglioni Chapel, St. Mother Mary Church, Spello.

1997, Oct. 18
2183 A1112 800 l multicolored 1.50 .30
2184 A1112 900 l multicolored 1.50 .40

Aristide Merloni (1897-1970) A1113

1997, Oct. 24 *Perf. 13x14*
2185 A1113 800 l multicolored 1.25 .30

Giovanni Battista Cavalcaselle (1819-97), Art Historian A1114

Litho. & Engr.

1997, Oct. 31 *Perf. 13½x14*
2186 A1114 800 l multicolored 1.25 .30

Philately Day — A1115

1997, Dec. 5 Photo.
2187 A1115 800 l multicolored 1.25 .30

Emigration of Italian Population of Dalmatia, Istria & Fiume, 50th Anniv. A1116

1997, Dec. 6 *Perf. 14x13½*
2188 A1116 800 l multicolored 1.25 .30

State Highway Police, 50th Anniv. A1117

1997, Dec. 12
2189 A1117 800 l multicolored 1.25 .30

Constitution, 50th Anniv. — A1118

1998, Jan. 2 Photo. *Perf. 13½x14*
2190 A1118 800 l multicolored 1.25 .30

Hercules and the Hydra, by Antonio Del Pollaiolo (1429-98) A1119

1998, Jan. 3 *Perf. 14*
2191 A1119 800 l multicolored 1.25 .30

See Nos. 2278, 2319.

Famous Writers A1120

450 l, Bertolt Brecht (1898-1956), playwright. 650 l, Federico Garcia Lorca (1898-1936), poet, dramatist. 800 l, Curzio Malaparte (Kurt Suckert) (1898-1957), journalist, writer. 900 l, Leonida Repaci (1898-1985), writer.

1998, Feb. 2 *Perf. 14x13½*
2192 A1120 450 l multi .75 .40
2193 A1120 650 l multi 1.00 .40
2194 A1120 800 l multi 1.25 .25
2195 A1120 900 l multi, vert. 1.50 .25
Nos. 2192-2195 (4) 4.50 1.30

Verona Fair, Cent. A1121

1998, Feb. 11 Photo. *Perf. 14x13½*
2196 A1121 800 l multicolored 1.40 .40

Jewish Emancipation, 150th Anniv. — A1122

1998, Mar. 28 *Perf. 14*
2197 A1122 800 l multicolored 1.25 .40

National Festivals A1123

1998, Apr. 3 Litho. *Perf. 13½x14*
2198 A1123 800 l Umbria Jazz *1.00 .30*
2199 A1123 900 l Giffoni Film *1.50 .40*

Europa.

Completion of "The Last Supper," by Leonardo da Vinci (1452-1519), 500th Anniv. — A1124

1998, Apr. 4 Engr. *Perf. 14x13½*
2200 A1124 800 l red brown 1.50 .40

Gaetano Donizetti (1797-1848), Composer — A1125

1998, Apr. 8 Photo.
2201 A1125 800 l multicolored 1.10 .30

Italian Opera, 400th Anniv. — A1126

1998, Apr. 8 *Perf. 13½x14*
2202 A1126 800 l multicolored 1.10 .30

Cathedral of Turin, 500th anniv., and Shroud of Turin — A1127

1998, Apr. 18 Photo. *Perf. 13½x14*
2203 A1127 800 l multicolored 1.25 .30

Tourism A1128

No. 2204, Castle, Otranto. No. 2205, Mori Fountain and Castle, Marino. No. 2206, Village and chapel, Livigno. No. 2207, Marciana Marina, Elba Island.

1998, Apr. 18 Litho. *Perf. 14x13½*
2204 A1128 800 l multicolored 1.00 .30
2205 A1128 800 l multicolored 1.00 .30
2206 A1128 800 l multicolored 1.00 .30
2207 A1128 800 l multicolored 1.00 .30
Nos. 2204-2207 (4) 4.00 1.20

See Nos. 2283-2286.

Sardinia Intl. Fair A1129

1998, Apr. 23 Photo. *Perf. 14x13½*
2208 A1129 800 l multicolored 1.25 .30

The Charge of Carabinieri at Pastrengo, by Sebastiano de Albertis (1828-97) A1130

1998, Apr. 30 *Perf. 13½x14*
2209 A1130 800 l multicolored 1.25 .30

A1131

1998, May 11 Photo. *Perf. 13½x14*
2210 A1131 800 l Padua Fair 1.25 .30

Juventus, 1997-98 Italian Soccer Champions A1132

1998, May 18
2211 A1132 800 l multicolored 1.25 .40

Polytechnical School, Turin — A1133

1998, May 18 Engr. *Perf. 14x13½*
2212 A1133 800 l dark blue 1.25 .30

World Food Program — A1134

1998, May 22 Photo.
2213 A1134 900 l multicolored 1.50 .40

4th Intl. Convention on Fossils, Evolution, and Environment, Pergola — A1135

1998, May 30 Photo. *Perf. 14x13½*
2214 A1135 800 l multicolored 1.25 .30

Carthusian Monastery of Santa Maria di Pesio, 825th Anniv. A1136

1998, May 30
2215 A1136 800 l multicolored 1.25 .30

A1137

1998, June 2 *Perf. 13½x14*
2216 A1137 800 l multicolored 1.25 .30

Honoring the fallen of the Italian police corps.

6th World Congress of Endoscopic Surgery — A1138

1998, June 3
2217 A1138 900 l multicolored 1.25 .30

Italian Museums A1139

No. 2218, Regional Archeological Museum, Agrigento. No. 2219, Natl. Museum of the Risorgimento, Turin. No. 2220, Peggy Guggenheim Collection, Venier Dei Leoni Palace, Venice.

1998, June 6 *Perf. 13½x14, 14x13½*
2218 A1139 800 l multi 1.00 .30
2219 A1139 800 l multi, horiz. 1.00 .30
2220 A1139 800 l multi, horiz. 1.00 .30
Nos. 2218-2220 (3) 3.00 .90

Vicenza Fair — A1140

1998, June 13 ***Perf. 13½x14***
2221 A1140 800 l multi 1.25 .30

Giacomo Leopardi (1798-1837), Poet — A1141

1998, June 29 **Photo.** ***Perf. 14x13½***
2222 A1141 800 l dark brn & sep 1.25 .30

Women in Art — A1142

Paintings: 100 l, "Young Velca," Etruscan tomb. 450 l, Detail from, "Herod's Feast," by Filippo Lippi. 650 l, Woman in profile, by Fra Benci. 800 l, "Lady with the Unicorn," by Raphael. 1000 l, sculpture of Constanza Buonarelli, by Gian Lorenzo Bernini.

1998, July 8 **Photo.** ***Perf. 14x13½***
2223 A1142 100 l blk & multi .30 .25
2224 A1142 450 l vio & multi .75 .25
2225 A1142 650 l gray grn & multi 1.50 .25

Engr.
Wmk. 303

2226 A1142 800 l red brn & multi 2.50 .25
2227 A1142 1000 l grn bl & multi 2.75 .25
Nos. 2223-2227 (5) 7.80 1.25

Denominated in Lira and Euros

1999, Jan. 28 **Photo.** ***Perf. 14x13½***
2228 A1142 100 l blk & multi .40 .25
2229 A1142 450 l vio & multi 1.00 .25
2230 A1142 650 l gray grn & multi 1.40 .25

Engr.
Wmk. 303

2231 A1142 800 l red brn & multi 1.75 .25
2232 A1142 1000 l grn bl & multi 2.00 .25
Nos. 2228-2232 (5) 6.55 1.25

See Nos. 2436-2453.

33rd World Baseball Cup A1143

Perf. 14x13½
1998, July 21 **Photo.** **Unwmk.**
2251 A1143 900 l multicolored 1.25 .40

Columbus' Landing in Venezuela and Exploration of Amerigo Vespucci, 500th Anniv. A1144

1998, Aug. 12
2252 A1144 1300 l multicolored 2.00 1.00

See Venezuela No. 1595.

Riccione Intl. Stamp Fair, 50th Anniv. — A1145

1998, Aug. 28 ***Perf. 13½x14***
2253 A1145 800 l multicolored 1.25 .40

Mother Teresa (1910-97) A1146

1998, Sept. 5 ***Perf. 14x13½, 13½x14***
2254 A1146 800 l shown 1.25 .30
2255 A1146 900 l Portrait, vert. 1.75 .40

See Albania Nos. 2578-2579.

Father Pio da Pietrelcina (1887-1968) — A1147

1998, Sept. 23 **Engr.** ***Perf. 14x13½***
2256 A1147 800 l deep blue 1.25 .30

1998 World Equestrian Championships, Rome — A1148

1998, Oct. 2 **Photo.** ***Perf. 14x13½***
2257 A1148 4000 l multicolored 5.00 1.75

School of Higher Education in Telecommunications, Rome — A1149

1998, Oct. 9 **Engr.** ***Perf. 14x13½***
2258 A1149 800 l deep blue 1.25 .30

Italia '98, Intl. Philatelic Exhibition — A1150

800 l, Pope John Paul II.

1998, Oct. 23 **Photo.** ***Perf. 14***
2259 A1150 800 l multi 2.50 .30

See San Marino No. 1430 and Vatican City No. 1085.

Armed Forces Day A1151

Emblem from branch of the military and: No. 2260, Aircraft carrier "Giuseppe Garibaldi," Navy. No. 2261, Eurofighter 2000, Air Force. No. 2262, Officer, Carabinieri (police force), vert. No. 2263, Italian monument, El Alamein battlefield, vert.

Perf. 14x13½, 13½x14
1998, Oct. 24 **Photo.**
2260 A1151 800 l multicolored 1.00 .35
2261 A1151 800 l multicolored 1.00 .35
2262 A1151 800 l multicolored 1.00 .35
2263 A1151 800 l multicolored 1.00 .35
Nos. 2260-2263 (4) 4.00 1.40

Air Force, 75th anniv. (No. 2261).

Nos. 2260-2263 were printed se-tenant with Italia '98 label. Values, set with labels: $5 unused, $3 used.

Art Day — A1152

1998, Oct. 25 ***Perf. 13½x14***
2264 A1152 800 l Dionysus 1.25 .35

Italia '98.

Enzo Ferrari (1898-1988) Automobile Manufacturer — A1153

a, 1931 Bobbio-Passo del Penice. b, 1952 Ferrari F1. c, 1963 Ferrari GTO. d, 1998 Ferrari F1.

1998, Oct. 26 **Litho.** ***Perf. 13½***
2265 A1153 800 l Sheet of 4, #a.-d. 7.00 6.00

Italia '98.

Universal Declaration of Human Rights, 50th Anniv. — A1154

1998, Oct. 27 **Photo.** ***Perf. 14x13½***
2266 A1154 1400 l multicolored 2.50 .80

Italia '98.

Printed se-tenant with a label. Value with label, $2.

Europe Day — A1155

1998, Oct. 28 ***Perf. 13½x14***
2267 A1155 800 l multicolored 1.25 .25

Die Cut Perf. 11
Self-Adhesive
Booklet Stamp

2268 A1155 800 l multicolored 1.25 .40
a. Booklet pane of 6 8.00 *7.00*
Complete booklet, #2268a 8.25

Motion Picture Type of 1995

Motion pictures, stars: 450 l, "Ti Conosco Mascherina," Eduardo de Filippo. 800 l, "Fantasmi a Roma," Antonio Pietrangeli. 900 l, "Il Signor Max," Mario Camerini.

1998, Oct. 29 **Litho. & Engr.**
2269 A1027 450 l multicolored .45 .30
2270 A1027 800 l multicolored .80 .35
2271 A1027 900 l multicolored .90 .35
Nos. 2269-2271 (3) 2.15 1.00

Italia '98.

Nos. 2269-2271 each printed se-tenant with label. Value, set with labels $3.25.

Communications Day — A1156

1998, Oct. 31 **Photo.**
2272 A1156 800 l multicolored 1.25 .30

Souvenir Sheet

Stamp Day — A1157

1998, Nov. 1 **Litho.**
2273 A1157 4000 l multicolored 6.00 5.00

Italia '98.

Christmas A1158

800 l, Sculpture, "The Epiphany," Church of St. Mark, Seminara, vert. 900 l, Adoration of the shepherds, drawing by Giulio Romano.

Perf. 13½x14, 14x13½

1998, Nov. 28 **Engr.**

2274 A1158 800 l deep blue 1.25 .30
2275 A1158 900 l brown 1.25 .40

The Ecstasy of St. Teresa, Sculpture by Gian Lorenzo Bernini — A1159

1998, Dec. 1 **Photo.** ***Perf. 13½x14***

2276 A1159 900 l multicolored 1.40 .30

Emancipation of Valdesi, 150th Anniv. — A1160

1998, Dec. 4 ***Perf. 14***

2277 A1160 800 l multicolored 1.25 .30

Art Type of 1998

Conception of Space, by Lucio Fontana (1899-1968).

1999, Feb. 19 **Photo.** ***Perf. 14***

2278 A1119 450 l multicolored 1.00 .40

National Parks A1162

Europa: 800 l, Wolf, Calabria, vert. 900 l, Birds, Tuscan Archipelago.

Perf. 13¼x14, 14x13¼

1999, Mar. 12 **Photo.**

2279 A1162 800 l multicolored *1.10* *.35*
2280 A1162 900 l multicolored *1.50* *.40*

Holy Year 2000 — A1163

1999, Mar. 13 ***Perf. 13¼x13¾***

2281 A1163 1400 l Holy Door 2.00 .45

St. Egidio Church, Cellere A1164

1999, Apr. 10 **Engr.** ***Perf. 13¾x13½***

2282 A1164 800 l brown lake 1.25 .35

Tourism Type of 1998

No. 2283, Earthen pyramids, Segonzano. No. 2284, Waterfalls, river, Terni. No. 2285, Buildings, Lecce. No. 2286, Walls around Lipari.

1999, Apr. 17 **Photo.** ***Perf. 14x13¼***

2283 A1128 800 l multicolored 1.10 .40
2284 A1128 800 l multicolored 1.10 .40
2285 A1128 800 l multicolored 1.10 .40
2286 A1128 800 l multicolored 1.10 .40
Nos. 2283-2286 (4) 4.40 1.60

Museums A1165

No. 2287, Swan on Lake, Casina della Civette, Rome. No. 2288, "Iulia Bela," International Ceramics Museaum, Faenza, vert. No. 2289, Bells, Marinelli Historic Bell Museum, Agnone.

Perf. 14x13¼, 13¼x14

1999, Apr. 17 **Photo.**

2287 A1165 800 l multicolored 1.10 .40
2288 A1165 800 l multicolored 1.10 .40
2289 A1165 800 l multicolored 1.10 .40
Nos. 2287-2289 (3) 3.30 1.20

Constitutional Court — A1166

Perf. 13¾x13¼

1999, Apr. 23 **Photo.**

2290 A1166 800 l multicolored 1.25 .30

Natl. Firefighting Service A1167

1999, Apr. 29

2291 A1167 800 l multicolored 1.40 .40

Military Academy of Modena — A1168

1999, May 3 **Photo.** ***Perf. 13¼x14***

2292 A1168 800 l multicolored 1.25 .40

50th Anniv. of Death of Grande Torino Soccer Team in Airplane Crash A1169

800 l, Plane, team members. 900 l, Superga Basilica, names.

1999, May 4 **Photo.** ***Perf. 14x13¼***

2293 A1169 800 l multi 1.50 .30
2294 A1169 900 l multi 1.90 .40

Council of Europe, 50th Anniv. A1170

1999, May 5 **Photo.** ***Perf. 14x13¼***

2295 A1170 800 l multicolored 1.25 .30

Milan, 1998-99 Italian Soccer Champions A1171

1999, June 7 **Photo.** ***Perf. 13¼x14***

2296 A1171 800 l multicolored 1.50 .35

Elections for European Parliament, 20th Anniv. A1172

1999, June 10 **Photo.** ***Perf. 14x13¼***

2297 A1172 800 l multicolored 1.25 .30

Priority Mail A1173

Typo. & Silk-screened

1999, June 14 ***Die Cut 11¼***

Self-Adhesive

2298 A1173 1200 l multicolored 1.25 .30
Se-tenant with etiquette 2.00 1.50
a. Bklt. pane of 4 + 4 etiquettes 9.00
Complete booklet, #2298a 9.50
b. Bklt. pane of 8, no etiquettes 18.00
Complete booklet, #2298b 18.00

No. 2298 was intended for Priority Mail service. Self-adhesive blue etiquettes to be used with each stamp on mail were provided on the sheets and in booklets of 4 stamps.

The backing paper from the sheet stamps is rouletted, while the backing paper in the booklets is not.

See No. 2324.

Fausto Coppi (1919-60), Cyclist A1174

1999, June 12 **Photo.** ***Perf. 14x13¼***

2299 A1174 800 l multi 1.25 .35

Fiat Automobile Co., Cent. — A1175

1999, July 10 **Photo.** ***Perf. 13¼x14***

2300 A1175 4800 l multi 6.00 2.50

Statue of Our Lady of the Snows, Mt. Rocciamelone, Cent. — A1176

1999, July 19

2301 A1176 800 l multi 1.25 .35

Eleonora de Fonseca Pimentel (1752-1799), Writer — A1177

1999, Aug. 20 ***Perf. 14x13¼***

2302 A1177 800 l multi 1.25 .30

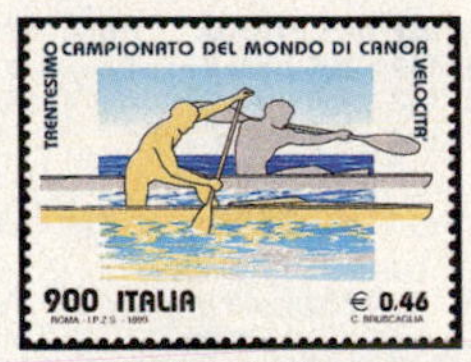

30th World Canoe Championships — A1178

1999, Aug. 26

2303 A1178 900 l multi 1.25 .30

Johann Wolfgang von Goethe (1749-1832), German Poet — A1179

1999, Aug. 28

2304 A1179 4000 l multi 5.00 2.00

World Cycling Championships A1180

1999, Sept. 15 **Photo.** ***Perf. 13¼x14***

2305 A1180 1400 l multi 2.00 .70

Stamp Day — A1181

1999, Sept. 25 Photo. *Perf. 13¼x14*
2306 A1181 800 l multi 1.25 .35

Basilica of St. Francis, Assisi — A1182

Litho. & Engr.
1999, Sept. 25 *Perf. 14x13¼*
2307 A1182 800 l multi 1.25 .35

Giuseppe Parini (1729-99), Poet — A1183

1999, Oct. 2 Engr. *Perf. 13¼x14*
2308 A1183 800 l blue gray 1.25 .30

Alessandro Volta's Pile, Bicent. — A1184

1999, Oct. 11 Photo.
2309 A1184 3000 l multi 4.00 1.75

UPU, 125th Anniv. A1185

1999, Oct. 18 *Perf. 14x13¼*
2310 A1185 900 l multi 1.25 .30

Goffredo Mameli (1827-49), Lyricist of Natl. Anthem, Nos. 506, 518 — A1186

1999, Oct. 22 *Perf. 14*
2311 A1186 1500 l multi 2.00 1.50

"Stamps, Our Friends" — A1187

Various abstract designs: a, 450 l. b, 650 l. c, 800 l. d, 1000 l.

1999, Oct. 23 *Perf. 13¼x14*
2312 A1187 Sheet of 4, #a.-d. 4.50 4.00

First World War Soliders — A1188

1999, Nov. 4
2313 A1188 900 l multi 1.25 .35

Christmas A1189

Designs: 800 l, Santa Claus, reindeer and sleigh. 1000 l, Nativity, By Dosso Dossi.

1999, Nov. 5 Photo.
2314 A1189 800 l multi 1.25 .30
2315 A1189 1000 l multi 1.75 .40

See Finland Nos. 1117-1119.

Holy Year 2000 A1190

No. 2316, Map by Conrad Peutinger, 1507. No. 2317, 18th cent. print of pilgrims in Rome. No. 2318, Bas-relief, facade of Fidenza Duomo.

1999, Nov. 24 Photo. *Perf. 14x13¼*
2316 A1190 1000 l multi 1.50 .50
2317 A1190 1000 l multi 1.50 .50
2318 A1190 1000 l multi 1.50 .50
Nos. 2316-2318 (3) 4.50 1.50

Art Type of 1998

Design: Restless Leopard, by Antonio Ligabue (1899-1965), horiz.

1999, Nov. 27 Photo. *Perf. 14*
2319 A1119 1000 l multi 1.50 .50

Schools A1191

Designs: 450 l, State Institute of Art, Urbino. 650 l, Normal Superior School, Pisa.

1999, Nov. 27 Engr. *Perf. 14x13¼*
2320 A1191 450 l black .50 .30
2321 A1191 650 l brown 1.00 .40

Year 2000 A1192

1999, Nov. 27 Photo.
2322 A1192 4800 l multi 6.00 2.50

Souvenir Sheet

Millennium — A1193

Designs: a, The past. b, The future.

2000, Jan. 1 Litho. *Perf. 14x13¼*
2323 A1193 Sheet of 2 5.50 5.00
a.-b. 2000 l Any single 2.40 .70

See Nos. 2330-2332, 2365-2366.

Priority Mail Type of 1999 Redrawn With Yellow Rectangle at Center
Typo. & Silk-Screened
2000, Jan. 10 *Die Cut 11¼*
Self-Adhesive
2324 A1173 1200 l multi 5.00 .40

No. 2324 was intended for Priority Mail service. A self-adhesive blue etiquette is adjacent to the stamp. No. 2324 is valued with etiquette adjacent. See No. 2393 for similar stamp with Posta Prioritaria in lower case letters.

First Performance of Opera "Tosca," Cent. — A1194

Litho. & Engr.
2000, Jan. 14 *Perf. 14x13¼*
2325 A1194 800 l multi 1.25 .35

Basilica of St. Paul — A1195

2000, Jan. 18 Photo. *Perf. 13¼x14*
2326 A1195 1000 l multi 1.50 .40

Holy Year 2000.

Six Nation Rugby Tournament — A1196

2000, Feb. 5 *Perf. 14x13¼*
2327 A1196 800 l multi 1.25 .35

5th Symposium on Breast Diseases A1197

1000 l, Woman holding rose.

2000, Feb. 12 *Perf. 13¼x14*
2328 A1197 800 l shown 1.25 .40
2329 A1197 1000 l multi 1.60 .50

Millennium Type of 2000
Souvenir Sheet

No. 2330: a, Art. b, Science.
No. 2331: a, Nature. b, The city.
No. 2332: a, Generations. b, Space.

2000 Litho. *Perf. 14x13¼*
2330 A1193 Sheet of 2 2.75 2.75
a.-b. 800 l Any single 1.25 .40
2331 A1193 Sheet of 2 2.75 2.75
a.-b. 800 l Any single 1.25 .40
2332 A1193 Sheet of 2 2.75 2.75
a.-b. 800 l Any single 1.25 .40

Issued: No. 2330, 3/4; No. 2331, 5/4; No. 2332, 7/4.

Skiing World Cup — A1198

2000, Mar. 7 Photo. *Perf. 13¼x14*
2333 A1198 4800 l multi 6.50 2.50

Souvenir Sheet

Italian Design — A1199

Household furnishings designed by: a, Achille & Pier Giacomo Castiglioni, Ettore Sottsass, Jr. Carlo Bartoli, Aldo Rossi. b, Mario Bellini, Alessandro Mendini, Vico Magistretti, Alberto Meda & Paolo Rizzatto. c, Gio Ponti, Gatti Paolini Teodoro, Massimo Morozzi, Tobia Scarpa. d, Pietro Chiesa, Joe Colombo, Cini Boeri & Tomu Katayanagi, Lodovico Acerbis & Giotto Stoppino. e, Gaetano Pesce, Antonio Citterio & Oliver Loew, Enzo Mari, De Pas D'Urbino Lomazzi. f, Marco Zanuso, Anna Castelli Ferrieri, Michele de Lucchi & Giancarlo Fassina, Bruno Munari.

2000, Mar. 9 Litho. *Perf. 13¼*
2334 A1199 Sheet of 6 7.50 7.50
a.-f. 800 l Any single 1.25 .60

Holy Year 2000 A1200

Paintings depicting the life of Jesus: 450 l, The Adoration of the Shepherds, by Ghirlandaio. 650 l, The Baptism and Temptation of Christ, by Veronese, vert. 800 l, The Last Supper, by Ghirlandaio, vert. 1000 l, Fresco from Episodes of the Life of the Virgin

Mary and Christ, by Giotto. 1200 l, The Resurrection of Christ, by Piero della Francesca, vert.

Perf. 14x13¼, 13¼x14

2000, Mar. 10 **Litho.**

2335	A1200	450 l	multi	.50	.30
2336	A1200	650 l	multi	.75	.30
2337	A1200	800 l	multi	1.00	.35
2338	A1200	1000 l	multi	1.75	.50
2339	A1200	1200 l	multi	2.25	.55
	Nos. 2335-2339 (5)			6.25	2.00

La Civiltá Cattolica, 150th Anniv. A1201

2000, Apr. 6 **Photo.** *Perf. 14x13¼*

2340	A1201	800 l	multi	1.25	.40

San Giuseppe de Merode College, Rome, 150th Anniv. A1202

2000, Apr. 8

2341	A1202	800 l	multi	1.25	.40

Intl. Cycling Union, Cent. — A1203

2000, Apr. 14 **Photo.** *Perf. 13¼x14*

2342	A1203	1500 l	multi	2.00	.60

Tourism — A1204

Designs: No. 2343, Terre di Franciacorta, Brescia. No. 2344, Dunarobba Petrified Forest, Avigliano Umbro. No. 2345, Ercolano. No. 2346, Bella di Taormina Island.

2000, Apr. 14 *Perf. 14x13¼*

2343	A1204	800 l	multi	1.00	.40
2344	A1204	800 l	multi	1.00	.40
2345	A1204	800 l	multi	1.00	.40
2346	A1204	800 l	multi	1.00	.40
	Nos. 2343-2346 (4)			4.00	1.60

Little Holy Society, Caltanissetta — A1205

2000, Apr. 19

2347	A1205	800 l	multi	1.25	.40

Niccolò Piccinni (1728-1800), Opera Composer A1206

2000, May 6 *Perf. 13¼x14*

2348	A1206	4000 l	multi	5.75	2.50

Europa, 2000

Common Design Type

2000, May 9

2349	CD17	800 l	multi	1.50	.40

Post and Telecommunications Historical Museum — A1207

No. 2350, Ship, telecommunications equipment. No. 2351, #19, 20.

2000, May 9 **Litho.** *Perf. 14x13¼*

2350	A1207	800 l	multi	1.25	.40
2351	A1207	800 l	multi	1.25	.40

Lazio, 1999-2000 Soccer Champions A1208

2000, May 20 **Photo.** *Perf. 13¼x14*

2352	A1208	800 l	multi	1.25	.40

Monza Cathedral A1209

2000, May 31

2353	A1209	800 l	multi	1.25	.40

Rome, Headquarters of UN Food and Agriculture Agencies A1210

2000, June 17 **Photo.** *Perf. 13¼x14*

2354	A1210	1000 l	multi	1.50	.50

Jesus the Redeemer Monument, Nuoro, Cent. — A1211

2000, June 24

2355	A1211	800 l	multi	1.25	.40

Società Italiana per Condotte d'Acqua, Construction Company, 120th Anniv. — A1212

2000, June 28 *Perf. 14x13¼*

2356	A1212	800 l	multi	1.25	.40

Stampin' the Future Children's Stamp Design Contest Winner — A1213

2000, July 7 *Perf. 13¼x14*

2357	A1213	1000 l	multi	1.50	.55

Archery World Championships, Campagna A1214

2000, July 8

2358	A1214	1500 l	multi	2.25	.75

World Cycling Championships A1215

2000, July 31 **Photo.** *Perf. 13¼x14*

2359	A1215	800 l	multi	1.40	.40

Madonna and Child, by Carlo Crivelli A1216

Litho. & Engr.

2000, Aug. 8 *Perf. 14*

2360	A1216	800 l	multi	1.25	.40

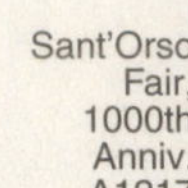

Sant'Orso Fair, 1000th Anniv. A1217

2000, Aug. 8 **Photo.** *Perf. 14x13¼*

2361	A1217	1000 l	multi	1.50	.45

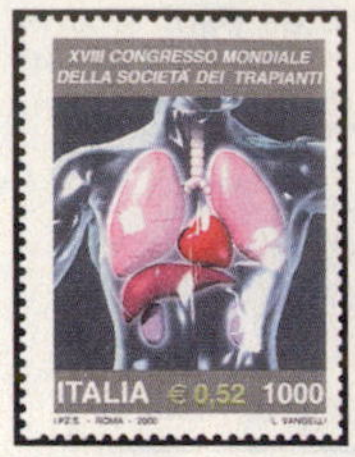

18th World Congress of Transplantation Society — A1218

2000, Aug. 26 **Photo.** *Perf. 13¼x14*

2362	A1218	1000 l	multi	1.50	.50

2000 Summer Olympics, Sydney — A1219

Designs: 800 l, Celebrating athlete, Olympic stadium, Sydney. 1000 l, Myron's Discobolus, Sydney skyline.

2000, Sept. 1

2363	A1219	800 l	multi	1.25	.30
2364	A1219	1000 l	multi	1.50	.30

Millennium Type of 2000

Souvenir Sheets

No. 2365, vert.: a, War. b, Peace.
No. 2366: a, Meditation. b, Expression.

2000 **Litho.** *Perf. 13¼x14, 14x13¼*

2365	A1193 Sheet of 2		2.75	2.00
a.-b.		800 l Any single	1.25	.40
2366	A1193 Sheet of 2		2.75	2.00
a.-b.		800 l Any single	1.25	.40

Issued: No. 2365, 9/4. No. 2366, 11/4.

Battle of Marengo, Bicent. — A1220

2000, Sept. 8 **Photo.** *Perf. 13¼x14*

2367	A1220	800 l	multi	1.25	.40

Fellini Film Year — A1221

2000, Sept. 20 **Photo.** *Perf. 13¼x14*

2368	A1221	800 l	multi	1.25	.40

Philately Day A1222

2000, Sept. 23 Photo. ***Perf. 14x13¼***
2369 A1222 800 l multi 1.25 .40

Father Luigi Maria Monti (1825-1900) — A1223

2000, Sept. 30 Photo. ***Perf. 14x13¼***
2370 A1223 800 l multi 1.25 .40

Antonio Salieri (1750-1825), Composer A1224

2000, Sept. 30 ***Perf. 13¼x14***
2371 A1224 4800 l multi 6.50 3.00

2000 Paralympics, Sydney — A1225

2000, Oct. 2 Photo. ***Perf. 13¼x14***
2372 A1225 1500 l multi 2.25 .75

World Mathematics Year — A1226

2000, Oct. 14 Photo. ***Perf. 14x13¼***
2373 A1226 800 l multi 1.25 .40

Voluntarism A1227

2000, Oct. 18 ***Perf. 13¼x14***
2374 A1227 800 l multi 1.25 .40

Giordano Bruno (1548-1600), Philosopher — A1228

2000, Oct. 20 ***Perf. 14x13¼***
2375 A1228 800 l multi 1.25 .40

Madonna and Child, by Luca Della Robbia A1229

Litho. & Engr.
2000, Oct. 25 ***Perf. 14***
2376 A1229 800 l multi 1.25 .40

Accademia Roveretana Degli Agiati, 250th Anniv. — A1230

2000, Oct. 26 Photo. ***Perf. 13¼x14***
2377 A1230 800 l multi 1.25 .40

Gaetano Martino (1900-67), Statesman — A1231

2000, Nov. 3 Photo. ***Perf. 14***
2378 A1231 800 l multi 1.25 .40

Perseus, by Benvenuto Cellini (1500-71), Sculptor — A1232

Litho. & Engr.
2000, Nov. 3 ***Perf. 14***
2379 A1232 1200 l multi 2.00 1.40

Schools A1233

Designs: 800 l, Camerino University. 1000 l, Calabria University, Cosenza.

2000, Nov. 6 Engr. ***Perf. 14x13¼***
2380 A1233 800 l blue 1.25 .40
2381 A1233 1000 l blue 1.75 .50

Christmas A1234

Designs: 800 l, Snowflakes. 1000 l, Creche, Matera Cathedral, horiz.

Perf. 13¼x14, 14x13¼
2000, Nov. 6 Photo.
2382 A1234 800 l multi 1.40 .30
2383 A1234 1000 l multi 1.75 .50

World Snowboarding Championships A1235

2001, Jan. 15 Photo. ***Perf. 13¼x14***
2384 A1235 1000 l multi 1.50 .50

The Annunciation, by Botticelli — A1236

2001, Jan. 18 ***Perf. 14***
2385 A1236 1000 l multi 1.50 .50

Exhibit of Italian art at Natl. Museum of Western Art, Tokyo.

Souvenir Sheet

Opera Composers — A1237

No. 2386: a, Vincenzo Bellini (1801-35). b, Domenico Cimarosa (1749-1801). c, Gaspare Luigi Pacifico Spontini (1774-1851). d, Giuseppe Verdi (1813-1901).

2001, Jan. 27 Litho. ***Perf. 13¼x14***
2386 A1237 Sheet of 4 5.00 4.50
a.-d. 800 l Any single 1.25 .40

St. Rose of Viterbo (1235-1252) A1238

2001, Mar. 6 Photo. ***Perf. 13¼x14***
2387 A1238 800 l multi 1.25 1.25

Souvenir Sheet

Ferrari, 2000 Formula 1 World Champions — A1239

2001, Mar. 9 Litho. ***Perf. 14x13¼***
2388 A1239 5000 l multi 7.50 7.00

Santa Maria Abbey, Sylvis — A1240

2001, Mar. 10 Engr. ***Perf. 14***
2389 A1240 800 l blue 1.25 .40

Postage Stamp Sesquicentennials A1241

Designs: No. 2390, Tuscany #1. No. 2391, Sardinia #1. No. 2392, Lombardy-Venetia #1.

2001, Mar. 31 Photo. ***Perf. 13¼x14***
2390 A1241 800 l multi 1.50 .40
2391 A1241 800 l multi 1.50 .40
2392 A1241 800 l multi 1.50 .40
Nos. 2390-2392 (3) 4.50 1.20

Priority Mail A1242

Serpentine Die Cut 11
Typo & Silk Screened

2001, Apr. 10 Self-Adhesive
2393 A1242 1200 l multi 2.50 *1.00*
a. Booklet pane of 4 + 4 etiquettes 12.00
Booklet, #2393a 12.00

Compare with No. 2324. No. 2393 was intended for Priority Mail service. A self-adhesive blue etiquette is adjacent to the stamp. No. 2393 is valued with etiquette adjacent.
See Nos. 2466-2471, 2582-2585B, 2613A-2615, 2691A-2691B.

Tourism A1243

2001, Apr. 14 Photo. *Perf. 14x13¼*
2394 A1243 800 l Stintino 1.00 .40
2395 A1243 800 l Comacchio 1.00 .40
2396 A1243 800 l Diamante 1.00 .40
2397 A1243 800 l Pioraco 1.00 .40
Nos. 2394-2397 (4) 4.00 1.60

Nature and the Environment A1244

Designs: 450 l, Campanula. 650 l, Marmots. 800 l, Storks. 1000 l, World Day Against Desertification.

2001, Apr. 21 *Perf. 13¼x14*
2398 A1244 450 l multi .50 .40
2399 A1244 650 l multi .75 .50
2400 A1244 800 l multi 1.25 .40
2401 A1244 1000 l multi 1.50 .60
Nos. 2398-2401 (4) 4.00 1.90

General Agricultural Confederation A1245

2001, Apr. 24 Photo. *Perf. 13¼x14*
2402 A1245 800 l multi 1.10 .40

Gorizia, 1000th Anniv. A1246

2001, Apr. 28 *Perf. 14x13¼*
2403 A1246 800 l multi 1.10 .40

Europa A1247

2001, May 4 Photo. *Perf. 14x13¼*
2404 A1247 800 l multi 1.50 .40

European Union's Charter of Fundamental Rights — A1248

2001, May 9 Photo. *Perf. 14x13¼*
2405 A1248 800 l multi 1.25 .40

Order of the Knights of Labor, Cent. — A1249

2001, May 9 Photo. *Perf. 13¼x14*
2406 A1249 800 l multi 1.10 .40

Workplace Injury Memorial Day — A1250

2001, May 19
2407 A1250 800 l multi 1.10 .40

Art and Student Creativity Day A1251

Children's art by: No. 2408, People staning on rainbow, by Lucia Catena. No. 2409, Painting with eye, by Luigi Di Cristo. No. 2410, Colors and Persons Profile, by Barbara Grilli. No. 2411, Child looking thru magnifying glass at stamp, by Rita Vergari, vert.

2001, May 26 *Perf. 13¼x14, 14x13¼*
2408 A1251 800 l multi 1.10 .40
2409 A1251 800 l multi 1.10 .40
2410 A1251 800 l multi 1.10 .40
2411 A1251 800 l multi 1.10 .40
Nos. 2408-2411 (4) 4.40 1.60

Masaccio (1401-28), Painter — A1252

2001, June 1 *Perf. 13¼x14*
2412 A1252 800 l multi 1.10 .40

Madonna of Senigallia, by Piero della Francesca A1253

Litho. & Engr.

2001, June 9 *Perf. 14*
2413 A1253 800 l multi 1.10 .40

Panathlon International, 50th Anniv. — A1254

2001, June 12 Photo. *Perf. 13¼x14*
2414 A1254 800 l multi 1.10 .40

Republic of San Marino, 1700th Anniv. — A1255

2001, June 23
2415 A1255 800 l multi 1.25 .40

Rome, 2000-2001 Soccer Champions A1256

2001, June 23 Photo. *Perf. 13¼x14*
2416 A1256 800 l multi 1.40 .40

Harbormaster's Corps and Coast Guard — A1257

2001, July 20 Photo. *Perf. 14x13¼*
2417 A1257 800 l multi 1.25 .40

Salvatore Quasimodo (1901-68), Writer — A1258

2001, Aug. 20 *Perf. 13¼x14*
2418 A1258 1500 l multi 2.25 .60

Octagonal Room, Domus Aurea (Golden House of Nero), Rome — A1259

2001, Aug. 31 Engr. *Perf. 14*
2419 A1259 1000 l multi 1.50 .50

Italian Design — A1260

Household furnishings designed by: a, Piero Lissoni, Patricia Urquiola and Anna Bartoli. b, Monica Graffeo and Rodolfo Dordoni. c, Ferruccio Laviani and Massimo Iosa Ghini. d, Anna Gili and Miki Astori. e, Marco Ferreri, M. Cananzi and R. Semprini. f, Stefano Giovannoni and Massimiliano Datti.

2001, Sept. 1 Litho. *Perf. 13¼*
2420 Sheet of 6 8.00 8.00
a.-f. A1260 800 l Any single 1.25 .40

Cent. of Il Quarto Stato, Painting by Giuseppe Pellizza da Volpedo — A1261

2001, Sept. 15 Engr. *Perf. 14x13¼*
2421 A1261 1000 l brown 1.60 .50

Discovery of Mummified Man "Otzi" in Melting Glacier, 10th Anniv. — A1262

2001, Sept. 19 Photo. *Perf. 13¼x14*
2422 A1262 800 l multi 1.25 .40

Stamp Day A1263

2001, Sept. 22 *Perf. 14x13¼*
2423 A1263 800 l multi 1.10 .40

Enrico Fermi (1901-54), Physicist
A1264

2001, Sept. 29 ***Perf. 13¼x14***
2424 A1264 800 l multi 1.10 .40

Schools
A1265

Designs: No. 2425, Pavia University. No. 2426, Bari University, vert. No. 2427, Camilo Cavour State Science High School, Rome.

Perf. 14x13¼, 13¼x14

2001, Sept. 29 **Engr.**
2425 A1265 800 l blue 1.10 .40
2426 A1265 800 l red brown 1.10 .40
2427 A1265 800 l Prus blue 1.10 .40
Nos. 2425-2427 (3) 3.30 1.20

Latin Union
A1266

2001, Oct. 12 **Photo.** ***Perf. 14x13¼***
2428 A1266 800 l multi 1.50 .45

Natl. Archaeological Museum, Taranto — A1267

2001, Oct. 12 **Photo.** ***Perf. 14x13¼***
2429 A1267 1000 l multi 1.25 .40

Intl. Food and Agriculture Organizations
A1268

Wheat and emblem of: a, Intl. Fund for Agricultural Development. b, Food and Agriculture Organization and farmer (49x27mm). c, World Food Program.

2001, Oct. 16 **Photo.** ***Perf. 14x13¼***
2430 Horiz. strip of 3 3.50 2.75
a.-c. A1268 800 l Any single 1.00 .40

Enthroned Christ and Angels, Sancta Sanctorum, St. John Lateran Basilica
A1269

Litho. & Engr.

2001, Oct. 19 ***Perf. 14***
2431 A1269 800 l multi 1.10 .40

Madonna and Child, by Macrino d'Alba
A1270

2001, Oct. 20
2432 A1270 800 l multi 1.20 .40

A1271

Christmas
A1272

2001, Oct. 30 **Photo.** ***Perf. 14x13¼***
2433 A1271 800 l multi 1.00 .40
2434 A1272 1000 l multi 1.25 .50

Souvenir Sheet

Italian Silk Industry — A1273

Silk-screened on Silk

2001, Nov. 29 ***Imperf.***
2435 A1273 5000 l multi 6.50 4.50

100 Cents = 1 Euro (€)

Women in Art Type of 1998 With Denominations in Euros Only

Designs: 1c, Hebe, sculpture by Antonio Canova. 2c, Profile of woman from Syracuse tetradrachm. 3c, Queen of Sheba from "The Meeting of King Solomon and the Queen of Sheba," painting by Piero della Francesa. 5c, "Young Velca," Etruscan tomb. 10c, Head of terra cotta statue, 3rd cent. BC. 20c, Danae, painting by Correggio. 23c, Detail from "Herod's Feast," by Fra Filippo Lippi. 41c, "Lady with the Unicorn," by Raphael. 45c, "Venus of Urbina," by Titian. 50c, "Antea," by Parmigianino. 65c, "Princess of Trebizonde," by Antonio Pisano. 70c, "Neptune Gives to Venice," by Giovanni Battista Tiepolo. 77c, "Primavera," by Botticelli. 85c, "Courtesan," by Vittore Carpaccio. 90c, "Venus and Mars bound by Love", the detail of the face of Venus, by Antonio Ciaburro.

Perf. 14x13¼, 13¼x13½ (#2447, 2449, 2450, 2452, 2453)

2002-04 **Photo.**
2436 A1142 1c multi .25 .25
a. Perf. 13¼x13½ .25 .25
2437 A1142 2c multi .25 .25
a. Perf. 13¼x13½ .25 .25
2438 A1142 3c multi .25 .25
a. Perf. 13¼x13½ .25 .25
2440 A1142 5c multi .25 .25
a. Perf. 13¼x13½ .25 .25
2441 A1142 10c multi .25 .25
a. Perf. 13¼x13½ ('04) .30 .25
2443 A1142 20c multi .50 .25
a. Perf. 13¼x13½ .50 .25
2444 A1142 23c multi .60 .25

Engr.

Wmk. 303

2446 A1142 41c multi 1.00 .45
a. Perf. 13¼x13½ 1.00 .35
2447 A1142 45c multi 1.10 .50
2448 A1142 50c multi 1.25 .55
a. Perf. 13¼x13½ 1.25 .55
2449 A1142 65c multi 1.75 .70
2450 A1142 70c multi 2.00 .75
2451 A1142 77c multi 2.10 .80
a. Perf. 13¼x13½ 2.10 .80
2452 A1142 85c multi 2.25 .90
2453 A1142 90c multi 2.50 1.00
Nos. 2436-2453 (15) 16.30 7.40

Issued: 2c, 5c, 10c, 23c, 41c, 50c, No. 2451, 1/1. 1c, 3c, 20c, 3/1; Nos. 2437a, 2438a, 2004; No. 2446a, 2003. No. 2451a, 2004 (?); Nos. 2436a, 2440a, 2448a, 2004; 45c, 1/27/04; 65c, 3/20/04; 85c, 2/17/04; No. 2443a, 2004; 70c, 7/31/04; 90c, 6/26/04; No. 2441a, 2004.

No. 2446 was reprinted in 2003 with imprint "I.P.Z.S. S.p.A.-Roma."

Italia — A1274

Perf. 14x13¼, 13¼x13½ (#2460, 2461A, 2462)

2002-04 **Engr.** **Unwmk.**
2454 A1274 €1 multi 3.00 .60
2455 A1274 €1.24 multi 4.00 1.00
2457 A1274 €1.55 multi 4.50 1.00
2459 A1274 €2.17 multi 6.00 1.40
2460 A1274 €2.35 multi 6.50 1.00
2461 A1274 €2.58 multi 7.00 1.40
2461A A1274 €2.80 multi 7.50 1.75
2462 A1274 €3 multi 8.00 1.75
2463 A1274 €3.62 multi 10.00 2.50
2465 A1274 €6.20 multi 17.00 5.50
Nos. 2454-2465 (10) 73.50 17.90

Issued: €1, €1.24, €1.55, €2.17, €2.58, €3.62, 1/2. €6.20, 3/1. €2.35, 5/7/04; €2.80, 2/3/04; €3, 5/22/04.

Compare Type A1274 with Type A1407.

Priority Mail Type of 2001 with Euro Denominations Only

Typo. & Silk Screened

2002, Jan. 2 ***Serpentine Die Cut 11***

Self-Adhesive

Background Color

2466 A1242 62c yellow 2.00 .30
Booklet, 4 #2466 9.00
2467 A1242 77c blue green 2.75 .75
2468 A1242 €1 blue 4.50 .50
2469 A1242 €1.24 yel green 5.00 1.50
2470 A1242 €1.86 rose 8.00 2.00
2471 A1242 €4.13 lilac 15.00 4.50
Nos. 2466-2471 (6) 37.25 9.55

A self-adhesive etiquette is adjacent to each stamp. Nos. 2466-2471 are valued with etiquette adjacent.

No. 2466-2471 were reprinted in 2003 with imprint "I.P.Z.S. S.p.A.-Roma-2003." Values, same. No. 2468 was reprinted in 2004 with imprint "I.P.Z.S. S.p.A. - Roma - 2004."

Introduction of the Euro — A1275

No. 2472: a, 1285 Venetian ducat. b, 1252 Genoan genovino and Florentine florin.

No. 2473: a, Euro symbol and flags. b, 1946 Italian 1-lira coin and new 1-euro coin.

2002, Jan. 2 **Photo.** ***Perf. 14x13¼***
2472 A1275 Horiz. pair 2.50 1.25
a.-b. 41c Either single 1.00 .40
2473 A1275 Horiz. pair 2.50 1.25
a.-b. 41c Either single 1.00 .40

Blessed Josemaría Escrivá (1902-75), Founder of Opus Dei
A1276

2002, Jan. 9
2474 A1276 41c multi 1.10 .40

Luigi Bocconi and Luigi Bocconi Commercial University, Milan — A1277

2002, Jan. 24
2475 A1277 41c multi 1.10 .40

Parma Stamps, 150th Anniv. — A1278

2002, Jan. 26 ***Perf. 13¼x14***
2476 A1278 41c No. 1 1.10 .40

Intl. Year of Mountains
A1279

2002, Feb. 1
2477 A1279 41c multi 1.10 .40

2006 Winter Olympics, Turin — A1280

2002, Feb. 23
2478 A1280 41c multi 1.10 .40

Malato Alla Fonte, Sculpture by Arnolfo de Cambio — A1281

2002, Mar. 8 **Engr.** ***Perf. 14***
2479 A1281 41c red lilac 1.25 .40

Tourism
A1282

Designs: No. 2480, Venaria Reale. No. 2481, San Gimignano. No. 2482, Sannicandro di Bari. No. 2483, Capo d'Orlando.

2002, Mar. 23 Photo. ***Perf. 14x13¼***
2480 A1282 41c multi 1.10 .40
2481 A1282 41c multi 1.10 .40
2482 A1282 41c multi 1.10 .40
2483 A1282 41c multi 1.10 .40
Nos. 2480-2483 (4) 4.40 1.60

See Nos. 2542-2544, 2598-2600.

Santa Maria Della Grazie Sanctuary, Spezzano Albanese — A1283

2002, Apr. 3 Engr. ***Perf. 14***
2484 A1283 41c red brown 1.10 .40

State Police, 150th Anniv. A1284

2002, Apr. 12 Photo. ***Perf. 14x13¼***
2485 A1284 41c multi 1.40 .45

Fr. Matteo Ricci (1552-1610), Missionary in China, Geographer — A1285

2002, Apr. 20
2486 A1285 41c multi 1.10 .40

Europa
A1286

2002, May 4 Photo. ***Perf. 14x13¼***
2487 A1286 41c multi 1.25 .45

Francesco Morosini Naval School, Venice A1287

2002, May 4
2488 A1287 41c multi 1.40 .40

Italian Cinema — A1288

Designs: No. 2489, Umberto D., directed by Vittorio De Sica. No. 2490, Miracle in Milan, written by Cesare Zavattini.

Litho. & Engr.
2002, May 10 ***Perf. 13¼x14***
2489 A1288 41c multi 1.10 .40
2490 A1288 41c multi 1.10 .40

Juventus, 2001-02 Italian Soccer Champions A1289

2002, May 18 Photo.
2491 A1289 41c multi 1.10 .40

Giovanni Falcone (1939-92) and Paolo Borsellino (1940-92), Judges Assassinated by Mafia — A1290

2002, May 23 ***Perf. 14x13¼***
2492 A1290 62c multi 1.50 .60

NATO-Russia Summit Meeting, Rome — A1291

2002, May 28 Photo. ***Perf. 14x13¼***
2493 A1291 41c multi 1.00 .40

World Kayak Championships, Valsesia — A1292

2002, May 30 ***Perf. 13¼x14***
2494 A1292 52c multi 1.50 .50

Italian Military Forces in Peace Missions — A1293

2002, June 1
2495 A1293 41c multi 1.00 .40

Modena Stamps, 150th Anniv. — A1294

2002, June 1 Photo. ***Perf. 13¼x14***
2496 A1294 41c multi 1.10 .40

Alfredo Binda (1902-86), Cyclist — A1295

2002, June 14 Photo. ***Perf. 13¼x14***
2497 A1295 41c multi 1.25 .40

St. Pio of Pietrelcina (1887-1968) — A1296

2002, June 16 ***Perf. 14***
2498 A1296 41c multi 1.10 .40

Monument to the Massacre of the Acqui Division — A1297

2002, June 21 ***Perf. 13¼x14***
2499 A1297 41c multi 1.10 .40

The Crucifixion, by Cimabue A1298

Litho. & Engr.
2002, June 22 ***Perf. 14***
2500 A1298 €2.58 multi 7.00 2.50

Prefectural Institute, Bicent. A1299

2002, June 24 Photo. ***Perf. 14x13¼***
2501 A1299 41c multi 1.10 .40

St. Maria Goretti (1890-1902) A1300

2002, July 6 ***Perf. 13¼x14***
2502 A1300 41c multi 1.10 .40

Jules Cardinal Mazarin (1602-61), and Birthplace A1301

2002, July 13 Photo. ***Perf. 14x13¼***
2503 A1301 41c multi 1.10 .40

Italians Around the World — A1302

2002, Aug. 8 ***Perf. 13¼x14***
2504 A1302 52c multi 1.50 .50

Monument to Sant'Anna di Stazzema Massacre A1303

2002, Aug. 17
2505 A1303 41c multi 1.10 .40

UNESCO World Heritage Sites — A1304

Designs: 41c, Pisa. 52c, Aeolian Islands.

2002, Aug. 30 ***Perf. 14***
2506 A1304 41c multi + label 1.25 .40
2507 A1304 52c multi + label 1.50 .50

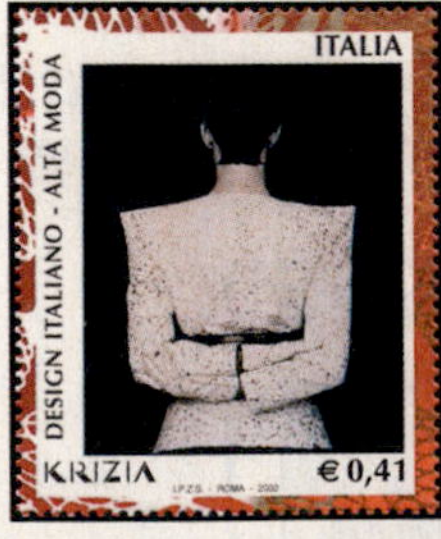

Italian Design A1305

Apparel by: a, Krizia. b, Dolce e Gabbana. c, Gianfranco Ferre. d, Giorgio Armani. e, Laura Biagiotti. f, Prada.

2002, Aug. 30 **Litho.**
2508 Sheet of 6 7.50 6.50
a.-f. A1305 41c Any single 1.25 .40

Carlo Alberto Dalla Chiesa (1920-82), Prefect of Palermo Assassinated by Mafia — A1306

2002, Sept. 3 **Photo.** ***Perf. 13¼x14***
2509 A1306 41c multi 1.25 .40

Concordia Theater, Monte Castello de Vibio — A1307

Litho. & Engr.

2002, Sept. 7 ***Perf. 14***
2510 A1307 41c multi 1.25 .40

Sailboat Gathering, Imperia A1308

2002, Sept. 11 **Photo.** ***Perf. 14x13¼***
2511 A1308 41c multi 1.25 .45

Santa Giulia Museum, Brescia — A1309

Palazzo Altemps, Roman Natl. Museum A1310

Perf. 13¼x14, 14x13¼

2002, Oct. 4 **Photo.**
2512 A1309 41c multi 1.25 .40
2513 A1310 41c multi 1.25 .40

Roman States Postage Stamps, 150th Anniv. — A1311

2002, Oct. 4 **Photo.** ***Perf. 13¼x14***
2514 A1311 41c Roman States #6 1.10 .40

Flora and Fauna — A1312

2002, Oct. 11
2515 A1312 23c Orchid .70 .40
2516 A1312 52c Lynx 1.50 .50
2517 A1312 77c Stag beetle 2.25 .75
Nos. 2515-2517 (3) 4.45 1.65

World Food Day — A1313

2002, Oct. 16 **Photo.** ***Perf. 13¼x14***
2518 A1313 41c multi 1.10 .40

Forestry Corps — A1314

2002, Oct. 22
2519 A1314 41c multi 1.10 .40

Father Carlo Gnocchi (1902-56), Founder of Fondazione Pro Juventute A1315

2002, Oct. 25
2520 A1315 41c multi 1.10 .40

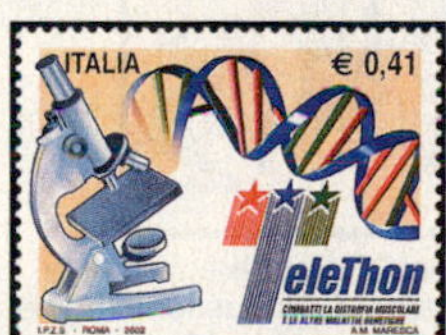

2002 Muscular Dystrophy Telethon A1316

2002, Oct. 31 ***Perf. 14x13¼***
2521 A1316 41c multi 1.00 .40

Christmas A1317

Designs: 41c, Nativity. 62c, Child with candle, Christmas tree, vert.

Perf. 14x13¼, 13¼x14

2002, Oct. 31 **Photo.**
2522 A1317 41c multi 1.25 .40
2523 A1317 62c multi 1.75 .55

Women's Sports — A1318

2002, Nov. 20 **Photo.** ***Perf. 13¼x14***
2524 A1318 41c multi 1.10 .40

Stamp Day A1319

2002, Nov. 29 ***Perf. 14x13¼***
2525 A1319 62c multi 1.75 .50

2002 World Cup Soccer Championships, Japan and Korea — A1320

No. 2526: a, Flags, soccer ball and field (33mm diameter). b, Soccer player, years of Italian championships.

2002, Nov. 29 **Litho.** ***Perf. 14***
2526 A1320 Horiz. pair 3.50 2.50
a.-b. 52c Either single 1.25 .50

See Argentina No. 2184, Brazil No. 2840, France No. 2891, Germany No. 2163 and Uruguay No. 1946.

Vittorio Emanuele Orlando (1860-1952), Politician A1321

2002, Dec. 4 **Photo.** ***Perf. 13¼x14***
2527 A1321 41c multi 1.10 .40

2003 Winter Universiade Games, Tarvisio — A1322

2003, Jan. 16 **Photo.** ***Perf. 13½x14***
2528 A1322 52c multi 1.25 .45

"La Repubblica Italiana" Philatelic Exhibition, Rome A1323

2003, Jan. 16 ***Perf. 14***
2529 A1323 62c multi 2.00 .55
a. Booklet pane of 5 *100.00 100.00*
Complete booklet, #2529a *100.00*

World Cyclocross Championships, Monopoli A1324

2003, Feb. 1 **Photo.** ***Perf. 13¼x14***
2530 A1324 41c multi 1.25 .50

Alinari Brothers Photographic Studio, 150th Anniv. — A1325

2003, Feb. 1 ***Perf. 14x13¼***
2531 A1325 77c multi + label 2.50 1.00

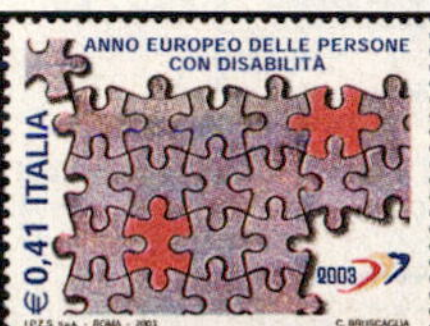

European Year of the Disabled A1326

2003, Feb. 14
2532 A1326 41c multi 1.10 .40

World Nordic Skiing Championships, Val di Fiemme — A1327

2003, Feb. 18 **Photo.** ***Perf. 14x13¼***
2533 A1327 41c multi 1.10 .40

National Civil Service — A1328

2003, Feb. 25 **Photo.** ***Perf. 14x13¼***
2534 A1328 62c multi + label 2.00 .65

Duel of Barletta, 500th Anniv. A1329

2003, Mar. 6
2535 A1329 41c multi 1.25 .40

Torquato Tasso High School, Rome — A1330

2003, Mar. 11 **Photo.** ***Perf. 14***
2536 A1330 41c multi 1.10 .40

Encounter at the Golden Door, by Giotto A1331

2003, Mar. 20 **Litho. & Engr.**
2537 A1331 41c multi 1.10 .40

Gian Rinaldo Carli High School, Pisino d'Istria — A1332

2003, Mar. 24 **Photo.**
2538 A1332 41c multi 1.10 .40

Lincei Academy, 400th Anniv. — A1333

Litho. & Engr.
2003, Mar. 26 ***Perf. 13¼x14***
2539 A1333 41c multi 1.00 .40

World Junior Fencing Championships, Trapani — A1334

2003, Apr. 4 **Photo.** ***Perf. 14x13¼***
2540 A1334 41c multi 1.25 .40

Acquasanta Golf Club, Rome, Cent. — A1335

2003, Apr. 5
2541 A1335 77c multi 2.25 .75

Tourism Type of 2002

2003, Apr. 5
2542 A1282 41c Sestri Levante 1.25 .40
2543 A1282 41c Lanciano 1.25 .40
2544 A1282 41c Procida 1.25 .40
Nos. 2542-2544 (3) 3.75 1.20

La Sapienza University, Rome, 700th Anniv. — A1336

2003, Apr. 10 **Photo.** ***Perf. 14***
2545 A1336 41c multi 1.10 .40

Natl. Pasta Museum, Rome — A1337

2003, Apr. 17 ***Perf. 13¼x14***
2546 A1337 41c multi 1.10 .40

Guido Carli Free Intl. University for Social Studies — A1338

2003, Apr. 23 **Photo.** ***Perf. 14***
2547 A1338 €2.58 multi 6.50 2.50

Europa — A1339

Poster art by Marcello Dudovich: 41c, Woman in blue dress. 52c, Women in white dresses.

2003, May 5 **Photo.** ***Perf. 13¼x14***
2548 A1339 41c multi 1.25 .30
2549 A1339 52c multi 1.50 .40

Central State Archives, 50th Anniv. A1340

2003, May 8 ***Perf. 14x13¼***
2550 A1340 41c multi 1.00 .40

Veronafil Philatelic Exhibition, Verona A1341

2003, May 9
2551 A1341 41c multi 1.10 .40

Aldo Moro (1916-78), Premier — A1342

2003, May 9 ***Perf. 13¼x14***
2552 A1342 62c multi 1.60 .40

Souvenir Sheet

Antonio Meucci (1808-96), Telephone Pioneer — A1343

2003, May 28 **Litho.**
2553 A1343 52c multi 1.75 1.75

Father Eugenio Barsanti and Felice Matteucci, Internal Combustion Engine Pioneers — A1344

2003, May 31 **Photo.** ***Perf. 14x13¼***
2554 A1344 52c multi 1.50 .50

Post Office, Latina A1345

2003, June 30 **Engr.** ***Perf. 14***
2555 A1345 41c blue 1.25 .40

City of Latina, 70th anniv.

Italian Presidency of the Council of the European Union A1346

2003, July 1 **Photo.** ***Perf. 14x13¼***
2556 A1346 41c multi 1.10 .40

Ezio Vanoni (1903-56), Economist A1347

2003, July 1 ***Perf. 13¼x14***
2557 A1347 €2.58 multi 7.00 3.00

The Assumption, by Corrado Giaquinto (c. 1694-1765) — A1348

2003, July 2 ***Perf. 14***
2558 A1348 77c multi 2.50 .70

Eugenio Balzan (1874-1953), Journalist — A1349

2003, July 15 **Photo.** ***Perf. 14x13¼***
2559 A1349 41c multi 1.10 .40

Francesco Mazzola "Il Parmigianino," (1503-40), Painter — A1350

2003, Aug. 23 **Photo.** ***Perf. 14x14¼***
2560 A1350 41c multi 1.25 .50

Juventus, 2002-03 Italian Soccer Champions A1351

2003, Aug. 30 ***Perf. 13¼x14***
2561 A1351 41c multi 1.50 .40

Abbey of St. Sylvester I, Nonantola — A1352

Litho. & Engr.

2003, Sept. 6 ***Perf. 14***
2562 A1352 41c multi 1.25 .40

Italian Aviation Pioneers A1353

2003, Sept. 12 **Photo.** ***Perf. 13x13¼***
2563 A1353 52c Mario Calderara 1.40 .50
2564 A1353 52c Mario Cobianchi 1.40 .50
2565 A1353 52c Gianni Caproni 1.40 .50
2566 A1353 52c Alessandro Marchetti 1.40 .50
a. Souvenir sheet, #2563-2566 6.50 6.50
Nos. 2563-2566 (4) 5.60 2.00

Giovanni Giolitti (1842-1928), Premier — A1354

2003, Sept. 13 **Photo.** ***Perf. 14x13¼***
2567 A1354 41c multi 1.10 .40

Europalia Italia Festival, Belgium A1355

Designs: 41c, Still Life, by Giorgio Morandi. 52c, 1947 Cisitalia 202, designed by Battista Pininfarina.

2003, Sept. 13
2568 A1355 41c multi 1.10 .45
2569 A1355 52c multi 1.50 .55

See Belgium Nos. 1980-1981.

Cent. of First Publication of Leonardo Magazine, by Attilio Vallecchi (1880-1946) — A1356

2003, Sept. 27 **Photo.** ***Perf. 13x13¼***
2570 A1356 41c multi 1.10 .40

The Family — A1357

2003, Oct. 3 ***Perf. 13¼x13***
2571 A1357 77c multi 2.25 .75

Maestà, by Duccio di Buoninsegna A1358

2003, Oct. 4
2572 A1358 41c multi 1.10 .40

Exhibition of paintings by Duccio di Buoninsegna, Siena.

Vittorio Alfieri (1749-1803), Poet — A1359

2003, Oct. 8 ***Perf. 13x13¼***
2573 A1359 41c multi 1.10 .40

Ugo La Malfa (1903-79), Government Minister — A1360

2003, Oct. 13 ***Perf. 13¼x13***
2574 A1360 62c multi 1.75 .60

Bernardino Ramazzini (1633-1714), Physician — A1361

2003, Oct. 15 ***Perf. 13x13¼***
2575 A1361 41c multi 1.25 .40

Confedilizia Property Owner's Organization, 120th Anniv. — A1362

2003, Oct. 15 ***Perf. 13¼x13***
2576 A1362 €2.58 multi 7.00 3.00

Nativity, by Gian Paolo Cavagna A1363

Poinsettia A1364

2003, Oct. 24
2577 A1363 41c multi 1.25 .35
2578 A1364 62c multi 1.75 .55

Christmas.

Futurist Art by Giacomo Balla A1365

Designs: 41c, Forme Grido Viva L'Italia. 52c, Linee-Forza del Pugno di Boccioni.

2003, Nov. 26 **Photo.** ***Perf. 13x13¼***
2579 A1365 41c multi 1.25 .35
2580 A1365 52c multi 1.50 .45

Philately Day A1366

2003, Nov. 28 **Photo.** ***Perf. 13x13¼***
2581 A1366 41c multi 1.10 .40

Priority Mail Type of 2001 With Euro Denominations Only

Self-Adhesive

Typo. & Silk Screened

2004 ***Serpentine Die Cut 11***

Background Color

2582 A1242 60c org (gold frame) 2.00 .65
2583 A1242 80c yel brn 2.60 .80
2584 A1242 €1.40 green 5.50 1.00
2585 A1242 €1.50 gray 4.50 1.00

Photo.

2585A A1242 60c dl org (bronze frame) 1.75 .85
2585B A1242 80c dl brn (bronze frame) 2.40 1.25
Nos. 2582-2585B (6) 18.75 5.55

Issued: 60c, 1/2; €1.40, 1/10; 80c, €1.50, No. 2585A, 3/19/04. A self-adhesive etiquette is adjacent to each stamp. Values are for stamps with adjacent etiquette.

The frame has a splotchy appearance on Nos. 2585A and 2585B.

No. 2585A exists dated 2005. Undated examples of No. 2585B were issued in 2008.

See No. 2613A.

A1367

Television Transmissions in Italy, 50th Anniv. — A1368

2004, Jan. 3 **Photo.** ***Perf. 13x13¼***
2586 A1367 41c multi 1.10 .40
2587 A1368 62c multi 1.50 .50

Giorgio La Pira (1904-77), Judge A1369

2004, Jan. 9 **Photo.** ***Perf. 13x13¼***
2588 A1369 41c multi 1.00 .40

Genoa, 2004 European Cultural Capital — A1370

2004, Feb. 12 **Photo.** ***Perf. 13¼x13***
2589 A1370 45c multi 1.25 .40

2006 Winter Olympics, Turin — A1371

Designs: 23c, Santa Maria Assunta Church, Pragelato. 45c, San Pietro Apostolo Church, Bardonecchia. 62c, Mole Antonelliana, Turin. 65c, Fountain, Sauze d'Oulx.

2004, Mar. 9
2590 A1371 23c multi .60 .25
2591 A1371 45c multi 1.25 .35
2592 A1371 62c multi 1.60 .45
2593 A1371 65c multi 1.75 .45
Nos. 2590-2593 (4) 5.20 1.50

Petrarch (1304-74), Poet — A1372

2004, Mar. 18
2594 A1372 45c multi 1.25 .40

Giorgio Amarelli Licorice Museum, Rossano — A1373

2004, Apr. 3 *Perf. 14*
2595 A1373 45c multi 1.25 .40

Road Safety A1374

Designs: 60c, Car dashboard, traffic signs. 62c, Seat belt, map of Italy, vert.

2004, Apr. 7 *Perf. 13x13¼, 13¼x13*
2596 A1374 60c multi 1.50 .45
2597 A1374 62c multi 1.60 .45

Tourism Type of 2002

2004, Apr. 10 Photo. *Perf. 13x13¼*
2598 A1282 45c Vignola 1.25 .35
2599 A1282 45c Viterbo 1.25 .35
2600 A1282 45c Isole Egadi 1.25 .35
Nos. 2598-2600 (3) 3.75 1.05

Casa del Fascio, Como, Designed by Giuseppe Terragni (1904-43), Architect A1375

2004, Apr. 17 *Perf. 13x13¼*
2601 A1375 85c multi 2.50 .50

Souvenir Sheet

Rome-Bangkok Foundation — A1376

No. 2602: a, Wat Saket, Bangkok. b, Colosseum, Rome.

2004, Apr. 21 Litho. *Perf. 14x13¼*
2602 A1376 Sheet of 2 3.75 3.75
a.-b. 65c Either single 1.50 .95

See Thailand No. 2125.

Martyrdom of St. George, 1700th Anniv. — A1377

2004, Apr. 23 Photo. *Perf. 14*
2603 A1377 €2.80 multi 7.00 3.00

Europa A1378

Map of Europe and: 45c, Closed suitcase. 62c, Open suitcase.

2004, May 7 *Perf. 13x13¼*
2604 A1378 45c multi 1.25 .45
2605 A1378 62c multi 1.50 .55

Souvenir Sheet

L'Aquila - Foggia Livestock Trail — A1379

2004, May 8 Litho. *Perf. 14x13¼*
2606 A1379 45c multi 1.50 1.50

Great Synagogue, Rome — A1380

2004, May 20 Photo. *Perf. 13¼x14*
2607 A1380 60c shown 1.60 .40
2608 A1380 62c Synagogue, diff. 1.75 .40

See Israel Nos. 1564-1565.

Milan, 2003-04 Italian Soccer Champions A1381

2004, May 22 *Perf. 13x13¼*
2609 A1381 45c multi 1.50 .40

50th Puccini Festival — A1382

2004, May 28 Photo. *Perf. 13¼x13*
2610 A1382 60c multi 1.75 .40

University of Turin, 600th Anniv. — A1383

2004, June 3 Engr. *Perf. 14*
2611 A1383 45c brown 1.25 .40

Achille Varzi (1904-48), Automobile and Motorcycle Racer A1384

2004, June 5 Photo. *Perf. 13x13¼*
2612 A1384 45c multi 1.25 .40

Penitentiary Police Corps A1385

2004, June 16 Photo. *Perf. 13x13¼*
2613 A1385 45c multi 1.25 .40

Priority Mail Type of 2001 With Euro Denominations Only Self-Adhesive

Serpentine Die Cut 11

2004, June 16 **Photo.**

Background Color

2613A A1242 €1.40 bl grn 5.00 1.00
2614 A1242 €2 sl grn (brnz frame) 5.50 1.50
2615 A1242 €2.20 rose 6.00 2.25
Nos. 2613A-2615 (3) 16.50 4.75

Issued: €2, 6/16; €1.40, July; €2.20, 6/26.

A self-adhesive etiquette is adjacent to each stamp. Values are for stamps with adjacent etiquette.

No. 2613A has a less obvious coating over the circled "P" that shines most when viewed from an oblique angle. No. 2613A exists dated 2006. Undated examples of No. 2613A were issued in 2007. Undated examples of Nos. 2614 and 2615 were issued in 2008.

Ascent of K2 By Italian Mountaineers, 50th Anniv. — A1386

2004, July 31 Photo. *Perf. 13¼x13*
2616 A1386 65c multi 1.75 .40

Italian Regions A1387

2004, Aug. 27 *Perf. 14x13¼*
2617 A1387 45c Liguria 1.50 .40
2618 A1387 45c Emilia Romagna 1.50 .40
2619 A1387 45c Abruzzo 1.50 .40
2620 A1387 45c Basilicata 1.50 .40
Nos. 2617-2620 (4) 6.00 1.60

See Nos. 2654-2657, 2746-2749, 2796-2799, 2876-2879.

Apparition of Madonna of Tirano, 500th Anniv. — A1388

2004, Sept. 4 *Perf. 13¼x13*
2621 A1388 45c multi 1.25 .40

St. Nilus of Rossano (c. 905-1005), Abbot — A1389

2004, Sept. 25 Photo. *Perf. 14¼x14*
2622 A1389 45c multi 1.25 .40

State Archives, Florence — A1390

2004, Sept. 30 Photo. *Perf. 14¼x14*
2623 A1390 45c multi 1.25 .40

Lacemaking — A1391

2004, Oct. 8 Embroidered *Imperf.*
Self-Adhesive
2624 A1391 €2.80 blue & gray 8.25 *4.00*

Filo d'Oro Society — A1392

2004, Oct. 9 Photo. *Perf. 13¼x13*
2625 A1392 45c multi 1.25 .40

Victor Emmanuel III State Technical Institute, Lucera
A1393

2004, Oct. 16 *Perf. 14x14¼*
2626 A1393 45c multi 1.25 .40

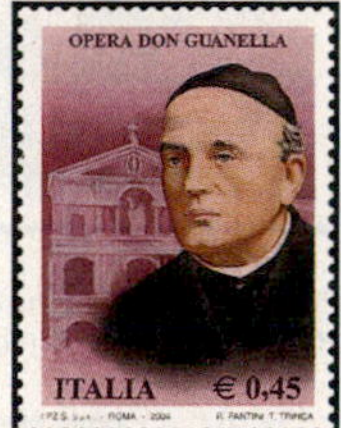

Father Luigi Guanella (1842-1915)
A1394

2004, Oct. 19 Photo. *Perf. 13¼x13*
2627 A1394 45c multi 1.25 .40

Return of Trieste to Italy, 50th Anniv.
A1395

2004, Oct. 26 *Perf. 13x13¼*
2628 A1395 45c multi 1.50 .60
a. Booklet pane of 4 6.00 —
Complete booklet, #2628a 6.00

Military Information and Security Service
A1396

2004, Oct. 27 Photo. *Perf. 13x13¼*
2629 A1396 60c multi 1.50 .40

European Constitution
A1397

2004, Oct. 29
2630 A1397 62c multi 1.75 .40

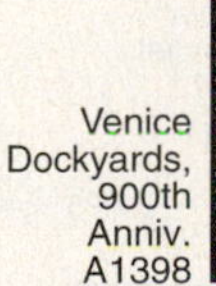

Venice Dockyards, 900th Anniv.
A1398

2004, Oct. 30 Photo. *Perf. 13x13¼*
2631 A1398 €2.80 multi 7.00 2.00

Live Nativity Scene, Tricase
A1399

Christmas Tree — A1400

2004, Oct. 30 Photo. *Perf. 13x13¼*
2632 A1399 45c multi 1.25 .40

Photo. & Embossed
Perf. 13¼x13
2633 A1400 62c multi 1.75 .40

Hands and Braille Book
A1401

Photo. & Embossed
2004, Nov. 6 *Perf. 14*
2634 A1401 45c multi 1.25 .40

Martyrdom of St. Lucy, 1700th Anniv. — A1402

2004, Nov. 6 Photo. *Perf. 13¼x13*
2635 A1402 45c multi 1.25 .40

Philately Day — A1403

2004, Nov. 12 *Perf. 13¼x14*
2636 A1403 45c multi 1.25 .45

Tenth "Sport For All" World Congress
A1404

2004, Nov. 12 Photo. *Perf. 13¼x13*
2637 A1404 65c multi 1.75 .50

Maria Santissima Assunta Free University, Rome — A1405

2004, Nov. 15 *Perf. 14*
2638 A1405 45c multi 1.25 .40

Souvenir Sheet

Italian-made Footwear — A1406

No. 2639: a, Woman's shoe by Casadei. b, Men's shoes by Moreschi. c, Men's shoe by Fratelli Rosetti. d, Athletic shoe by Superga.

2004, Nov. 27 Photo. *Perf. 13¼x13*
2639 A1406 Sheet of 4 5.75 5.00
a.-d. 45c Any single 1.25 .40

Italia With Large Numerals — A1407

Perf. 13¼x13½
2005, Jan. 21 Engr. Unwmk.
2640 A1407 €1 multi 2.75 .50

Compare type A1407 with type A1274.

Italian Auto Club, Cent. — A1408

2005, Jan. 21 Photo. *Perf. 13¼x13*
2648 A1408 45c multi 1.25 .40

Luigi Calabresi (1937-72), Assassinated Police Commissioner
A1409

2005, Jan. 26
2649 A1409 45c multi 1.25 .40

Exodus of Italians From Istria, Fiume and Dalmatia, 60th Anniv.
A1410

2005, Feb. 10 Photo. *Perf. 14x13¼*
2650 A1410 45c multi 1.25 .40

Rotary International, Cent. — A1411

2005, Feb. 23 *Perf. 13¼x14*
2651 A1411 65c multi 1.75 .45

Sassari Brigade
A1412

2005, Mar. 1 *Perf. 14x13¼*
2652 A1412 45c multi 1.25 .40

14th Art Quadrennial, Rome — A1413

2005, Mar. 4
2653 A1413 45c multi 1.25 .40

Italian Regions Type of 2004

No. 2654, Lombardy. No. 2655, Friuli-Venezia Giulia. No. 2656, Campania. No. 2657, Calabria.

2005, Mar. 18 *Perf. 13x13¼*
2654 A1387 45c multi 1.50 .35
2655 A1387 45c multi 1.50 .35
2656 A1387 45c multi 1.50 .35
2657 A1387 45c multi 1.50 .35
Nos. 2654-2657 (4) 6.00 1.40

2006 Winter Olympics, Turin — A1414

Turin Olympics emblem and: 23c, Pinerolo. 45c, Cesana Torinese. 60c, Mascots Neve and Gliz. 62c, Sestriere.

2005, Mar. 21 *Perf. 13¼x13*
2658 A1414 23c multi .75 .25
2659 A1414 45c multi 1.40 .35
2660 A1414 60c multi 1.75 .40
2661 A1414 62c multi 1.75 .40
Nos. 2658-2661 (4) 5.65 1.40

Intl. Year of Physics A1415

2005, Mar. 29 ***Perf. 14x13¼***
2662 A1415 85c multi 2.50 .75

Opening of New Milan Fair Complex A1416

2005, Mar. 31
2663 A1416 45c multi 1.25 .40

State Railways, Cent. A1417

2005, Apr. 22 **Photo.** ***Perf. 13x13¼***
2664 A1417 45c multi 1.25 .40

Italian Army — A1418

2005, Apr. 29 ***Perf. 13¼x13***
2665 A1418 45c multi 1.25 .40

Europa — A1419

2005, May 9 **Photo.** ***Perf. 13¼x13***
2666 A1419 45c Wheat 1.00 .40
2667 A1419 62c Grapes 1.50 .40

St. Ignatius of Làconi (1701-81) A1420

2005, May 11 **Photo.** ***Perf. 13¼x13***
2668 A1420 45c multi 1.25 .40

Commercial Confederation, 60th Anniv. — A1421

2005, May 18
2669 A1421 60c multi 1.75 .50

Tommaso Campanella High School, Reggio Calabria A1422

2005, May 20 **Photo.** ***Perf. 13x13¼***
2670 A1422 45c multi 1.25 .40

San Giuseppe da Copertino Basilica A1423

2005, May 21 **Engr.** ***Perf. 14***
2671 A1423 45c blue gray 1.25 .40

Tourism — A1424

No. 2672, Asolo. No. 2673, Rocchetta a Volturno. No. 2674, Amalfi.

2005, May 26 **Photo.**
2672 A1424 45c multicolored 1.25 .40
2673 A1424 45c multicolored 1.25 .40
2674 A1424 45c multicolored 1.25 .40
Nos. 2672-2674 (3) 3.75 1.20

See Nos. 2734-2736, 2803-2806, 2887-2890, 2948-2951, 3080-3083, 3126-3129.

St. Gerardo Maiella (1726-55) A1425

2005, May 28 ***Perf. 13x13¼***
2675 A1425 45c multi 1.25 .40

Juventus, 2004-05 Italian Soccer Champions A1426

2005, June 6 ***Perf. 13¼x13***
2676 A1426 45c multi 1.25 .40

Ratification of Modifications to Italy-Vatican Concordat, 20th Anniv. — A1427

Arms of Vatican City and Italy and: 45c, Map. €2.80, Pen.

2005, June 9 ***Perf. 13x13¼***
2677 A1427 45c multi 1.25 .40
2678 A1427 €2.80 multi 7.75 2.25

See Vatican City Nos. 1301-1302.

First Italian Dirigible Flight by Almerico da Schio, Cent. A1428

2005, June 17 **Photo.** ***Perf. 13x13¼***
2679 A1428 €3 multi 7.50 2.75

European Youth Olympic Festival, Lignano Sabbiadoro — A1429

2005, June 20 **Photo.** ***Perf. 13¼x13***
2680 A1429 62c multi 1.75 .50

Intl. Day Against Illegal Drugs A1430

2005, June 25 **Photo.** ***Perf. 13x13¼***
2681 A1430 45c multi 1.25 .40

Institute for Maritime Trades Social Insurance A1431

2005, June 28
2682 A1431 45c multi 1.25 .40

Leo Longanesi (1905-57), Writer — A1432

2005, Aug. 26 **Engr.** ***Perf. 13¼x14***
2683 A1432 45c dark blue 1.25 .40

Alberto Ascari (1918-55), Race Car Driver A1433

2005, Sept. 2 **Photo.** ***Perf. 13x13¼***
2684 A1433 €2.80 multi 7.50 3.00

A1434

National Military Aerobatic Team A1435

2005, Sept. 3 **Photo.** ***Perf. 13x13¼***
2685 A1434 45c multi 1.25 .40
2686 A1435 60c multi 1.75 .55

Pietro Savorgnan di Brazzà (1852-1905), Explorer of Africa — A1436

2005, Sept. 14 **Photo.** ***Perf. 13¼x13***
2687 A1436 45c multi 1.25 .40

Guido Gonella (1905-82), Politician, Journalist A1437

2005, Sept. 17
2688 A1437 45c multi 1.25 .40

Italian Participation in Exploration of Mars — A1438

Photo. With Hologram Applied
2005, Sept. 21 ***Die Cut***
Self-Adhesive
2689 A1438 80c multi 2.25 1.25

Printed in sheets of 4.

Intercultura, 50th Anniv. A1439

2005, Sept. 23 Photo. ***Perf. 13x13¼***
2690 A1439 60c multi 1.75 .50

Souvenir Sheet

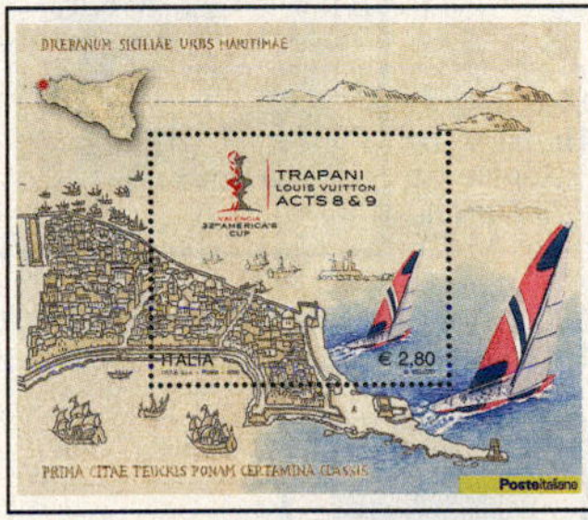

Louis Vuitton Cup Acts 8 & 9 (Races to Determine America's Cup Challenger), Trapani — A1440

2005, Sept. 28 Photo. ***Perf. 13¼x13***
2691 A1440 €2.80 multi 7.00 7.00

Priority Mail Type of 2001 With Euro Denominations Only Inscribed "I. P. Z. S. S. p. A. - ROMA 2005" at Bottom

2005 Photo. ***Serpentine Die Cut 11***
Self-Adhesive
Background Color

2691A A1242 62c yellow 4.00 .55
2691B A1242 €1.50 gray 9.00 1.00

Issued: 62c, Oct.; €1.50, Dec.

Nos. 2466 and 2585 have different printer's inscriptions and have a more easily seen coating over the circled "P" than on Nos. 2691A and 2691B. The coating over the circled "P" on Nos. 2691A and 2691B shines most when viewed from an oblique angle. A self-adhesive etiquette is adjacent to each stamp. Values are for stamps with adjacent etiquette.

Nos. 2691A and 2691B have self-adhesive selvage surrounding the stamp and etiquette. This selvage is not found on Nos. 2466 and 2585.

No. 2691B exists without year date and without etiquette, issued in 2007.

Stamp Day — A1441

2005, Oct. 7 Photo. ***Perf. 13¼x13***
2692 A1441 45c multi 1.25 .40

Italian Organ Donation Association A1442

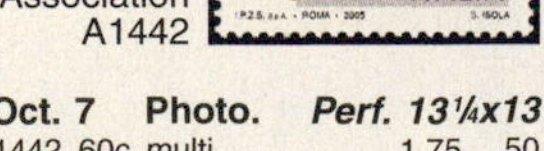
2005, Oct. 7 Photo. ***Perf. 13¼x13***
2693 A1442 60c multi 1.75 .50

National Association of Communities A1443

2005, Oct. 19
2694 A1443 45c multi 1.25 .40

Story of Sts. Stephan and John The Baptist, by Fra Filippo Lippi A1444

2005, Oct. 25 ***Perf. 13x13¼***
2695 A1444 45c shown 1.25 .40
2696 A1444 €1.50 Four men 4.25 1.25

A1445

Christmas A1446

2005, Oct. 31 Photo. ***Perf. 13x13¼***
2697 A1445 45c multi 1.25 .40

Perf. 13¼x13
2698 A1446 62c multi 1.75 .50

Alcide De Gasperi (1881-1954), Prime Minister — A1447

2005, Nov. 9 Photo. ***Perf. 13¼x13***
2699 A1447 62c multi 1.75 .50

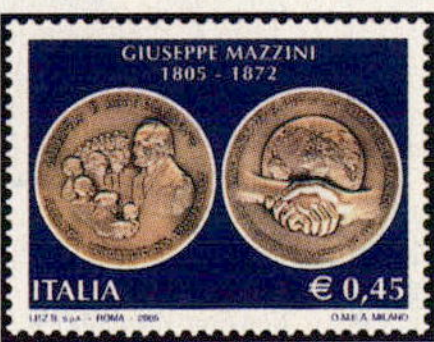

Giuseppe Mazzini (1805-72), Revolution Leader A1448

2005, Nov. 10 Photo. ***Perf. 13x13¼***
2700 A1448 45c multi 1.25 .40

National Civil Protection A1449

2005, Nov. 16 Photo. ***Perf. 13¼x13***
2701 A1449 45c multi 1.25 .40

Italian Red Cross — A1450

2005, Nov. 16
2702 A1450 45c multi 1.25 .40

Admission to United Nations, 50th Anniv. A1451

2005, Nov. 23 ***Perf. 13x13¼***
2703 A1451 70c multi 2.00 .50

Popes Reigning in 2005 A1452

Designs: 45c, Pope John Paul II (1920-2005). 65c, Pope Benedict XVI.

2005, Nov. 26 Photo. ***Perf. 13x13¼***
2704 A1452 45c multi 1.40 .45
2705 A1452 65c multi 1.75 .60

Reconstitution of Caserta Province, 60th Anniv. — A1453

2005, Dec. 5 Photo. ***Perf. 13x13¼***
2706 A1453 45c multi 1.25 .40

Opening of Enrico Toti Submarine Exhibit at Natl. Museum of Science and Technology, Milan A1454

2005, Dec. 7
2707 A1454 82c multi 1.75 .60

Eighteenth Birthday Greetings A1455

2006, Jan. 1 Photo. ***Perf. 13½x13***
2708 A1455 45c blue & multi 1.50 .40
2709 A1455 45c pink & multi 1.50 .40

Souvenir sheets of 1 of redrawn stamps similar to Nos. 2708-2709 exist from a limited printing. Value, set of two sheets *$1,300.*

Panini, Soccer Card and Sticker Creators A1456

2006, Jan. 30 Photo. ***Perf. 13x13¼***
2710 A1456 €2.80 multi 8.00 3.00

Quattroruote Magazine, 50th Anniv. — A1457

2006, Feb. 1 ***Perf. 13¼x13***
2711 A1457 62c multi 1.75 .50

Carlo Bo University, Urbino, 500th Anniv. — A1458

Ernesto Cairoli State High School, Varese — A1459

Alessandron Tassoni State Science High School, Modena — A1460

Agostino Nifo State High School, Sessa Aurunca — A1461

2006, Feb. 6

2712	A1458	45c multi	1.25	.40
2713	A1459	45c multi	1.25	.40
2714	A1460	45c multi	1.25	.40
2715	A1461	45c multi	1.25	.40
		Nos. 2712-2715 (4)	5.00	1.60

2006 Winter Olympics, Turin A1462

2006, Feb. 8 ***Perf. 13x13¼***

2716	A1462	23c	Biathlon	.60	.25
2717	A1462	45c	Figure skating	1.25	.40
2718	A1462	65c	Ice hockey	1.60	.50
2719	A1462	70c	Curling	1.75	.60
2720	A1462	85c	Bobsled	2.10	.65
2721	A1462	90c	Alpine skiing	2.25	.75
2722	A1462	€1	Torch	2.50	.80
2723	A1462	€1.30	Luge	3.25	.90
2724	A1462	€1.70	Medals	4.50	1.25
a.			Souvenir sheet, #2716-2724	20.00	20.00
			Nos. 2716-2724 (9)	19.80	6.10

Nos. 23, 45, 79 and 239 A1463

2006, Feb. 9 **Photo.** ***Perf. 13¼x13***

2725	A1463	60c multi	1.75	.85
a.		Booklet pane of 4	7.00	—
		Complete booklet, #2725a	7.50	

Kingdom of Italy Stamp Show, Rome.

Dalmatian Historical Society, 80th Anniv. A1464

2006, Feb. 10 **Engr.** ***Perf. 13x13¼***

2726	A1464	45c red vio & dk bl	1.25	.40

Detail of Fresco From Mantua Castle Bridal Chamber, by Andrea Mantegna (1431-1506) — A1465

2006, Feb. 25 **Photo.** ***Perf. 13x13¼***

2727	A1465	45c multi	1.25	.40

2006 Winter Paralympics, Turin — A1466

2006, Mar. 9 ***Perf. 13¼x13***

2728	A1466	60c multi	1.75	.40

Items Made in Italy A1467

60c, Gelato. €2.80, Carrara marble.

2006, Mar. 11 ***Perf. 13x13¼***

2729	A1467	60c multi	1.50	.50
2730	A1467	€2.80 multi	7.50	3.00

National Singers Association, 25th Anniv. — A1468

2006, Mar. 17

2731	A1468	45c multi	1.25	.40

Aircraft Carrier "Cavour" A1469

2006, Mar. 17

2732	A1469	60c multi	1.50	.50

Centenary of Sempione Tunnel — A1470

2006, Mar. 18 ***Perf. 13¼x13***

2733	A1470	62c multi	1.50	.45

Tourism Type of 2005

No. 2734, Lago di Como. No. 2735, Marina di Pietrasanta. No. 2736, Pozzuoli.

2006, Mar. 24

2734	A1424	45c multi	1.25	.40
2735	A1424	45c multi	1.25	.40
2736	A1424	45c multi	1.25	.40
		Nos. 2734-2736 (3)	3.75	1.20

Intl. Day of Mountains A1471

2006, Mar. 30 ***Perf. 13x13¼***

2737	A1471	60c multi	1.60	.40

Madonna and Child Icon, Mondragone Basilica — A1472

2006, Apr. 1

2738	A1472	45c multi	1.25	.40

First Vote for Italian Citizens Abroad — A1473

2006, Apr. 3 ***Perf. 13¼x13***

2739	A1473	62c multi	1.60	.40

"Two Republics" Philatelic Exhibition A1474

2006, Apr. 5 **Photo.** ***Perf. 13x13¼***

2740	A1474	62c multi	1.60	.50
a.		Souvenir sheet, #2740, San Marino #1676a	3.50	3.50

See San Marino No. 1676. On No. 2740a, the Italian stamp is on the left. On San Marino No. 1676, the Italian stamp is on the right. Both stamps in No. 2740a have text printed on reverse.

Matterhorn Ski School, 70th Anniv. — A1475

2006, Apr. 13 **Photo.** ***Perf. 13¼x13***

2741	A1475	45c multi	1.25	.40

Madonna of Humility, by Gentile da Fabriano A1476

2006, Apr. 20 **Photo.** ***Perf. 13x13¼***

2742	A1476	€2.80 multi	7.00	2.50

Il Giorno Newspaper, 50th Anniv. — A1477

2006, Apr. 21 ***Perf. 13¼x13***

2743	A1477	45c multi	1.25	.40

Constitutional Court, 50th Anniv. — A1478

2006, Apr. 22 **Engr.**

2744	A1478	45c blue	1.25	.40

Enrico Mattei (1906-62), Public Administrator A1479

2006, Apr. 29 **Photo.** ***Perf. 13¼x13***

2745	A1479	45c multi	1.25	.40

Italian Regions Type of 2004

2006, Apr. 29 ***Perf. 13x13¼***

2746	A1387	45c	Piedmont	1.25	.40
2747	A1387	45c	Tuscany	1.25	.40
2748	A1387	45c	Lazio	1.25	.40
2749	A1387	45c	Puglia	1.25	.40
			Nos. 2746-2749 (4)	5.00	1.60

Targa Floria Automobile Race Track, Cent. — A1480

2006, May 6 Photo. ***Perf. 13¼x13***
2750 A1480 60c multi 1.75 .50

Christopher Columbus (1451-1506), Explorer — A1481

2006, May 6 Photo. ***Perf. 13x13¼***
2751 A1481 62c multi 1.75 .50

Europa A1482

People sitting on wall: 45c, View of faces. 62c, View of backs.

2006, May 8
2752 A1482 45c multi 1.10 .40
2753 A1482 62c multi 1.50 .50

General Assembly of Intl. Military Sport Council, Rome A1483

2006, May 9
2754 A1483 45c multi 1.25 .40

2006 World Team Chess Championships, Turin — A1484

2006, May 20 Photo. ***Perf. 13¼x13***
2755 A1484 62c multi 1.60 .45

Constituent Assembly, 60th Anniv. A1485

2006, June 1 ***Perf. 13x13¼***
2756 A1485 60c multi 1.60 .40

Woman Suffrage, 60th Anniv. — A1486

2006, June 1 ***Perf. 13¼x13***
2757 A1486 60c multi 1.60 .40

2006 World Bridge Championships, Verona — A1487

2006, June 9 ***Perf. 13x13¼***
2758 A1487 65c multi 1.75 .45

Salto di Quirra Proving Grounds, 50th Anniv. — A1488

2006, June 13 ***Perf. 13¼x13***
2759 A1488 60c multi 1.75 .40

Customs Department General Headquarters, Cent. — A1489

Customs Cadet Legion, Cent. A1490

2006, June 21 ***Perf. 13¼x13***
2760 A1489 60c multi 1.60 .40

Perf. 13x13¼
2761 A1490 60c multi 1.60 .40

Reopening of Greek Theater, Tindari, 50th Anniv. — A1491

2006, July 6 ***Perf. 13¼x13***
2762 A1491 €1.50 multi 4.25 1.25

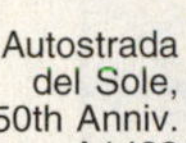

Autostrada del Sole, 50th Anniv. A1492

2006, July 10 ***Perf. 13x13¼***
2763 A1492 60c multi 1.75 .40

Terrorist Bombing in Bologna, 26th Anniv. — A1493

2006, Aug. 2 ***Perf. 13¼x13***
2764 A1493 60c multi 1.75 .40

Italian Philatelic Union, 40th Anniv. — A1494

2006, Sept. 1 ***Perf. 13x13¼***
2765 A1494 60c multi + label 1.60 1.25

St. Gregory the Great (540-604) A1495

2006, Sept. 2 ***Perf. 13¼x13***
2766 A1495 60c multi 1.75 .40

Victory of Italian 2006 World Cup Soccer Team A1496

2006, Sept. 9 Photo. ***Perf. 13x13¼***
2767 A1496 €1 multi 2.75 .70

Victims of Terrorism A1497

2006, Sept. 16
2768 A1497 60c multi 1.60 .40

Ettore Majorana (1906-38?), Physicist A1498

2006, Sept. 18 ***Perf. 13¼x13***
2769 A1498 60c multi 1.75 .40

Saints A1499

Designs: No. 2770, St. Ignatius of Loyola (1491-1556). No. 2771, St. Francis Xavier (1506-52).

2006, Sept. 27 ***Perf. 13x13¼***
2770 A1499 60c multi 1.60 .40
2771 A1499 60c multi 1.60 .40

World Fencing Championships, Turin — A1500

2006, Sept. 29
2772 A1500 65c org, blk, white 1.75 .50

Lottery, 500th Anniv. A1501

2006, Oct. 6 Photo. ***Perf. 13x13¼***
2773 A1501 60c multi 1.60 .40

Philately Day A1502

2006, Oct. 6
2774 A1502 60c multi 1.60 .40

Land and Marine Area Protection System A1503

2006, Oct. 6
2775 A1503 65c multi 1.75 .40

Luchino Visconti (1906-76), Film Director — A1504

2006, Oct. 13 ***Perf. 13¼x13***
2776 A1504 60c multi 1.60 .40

Dino Buzzati (1906-72), Writer A1505

2006, Oct. 16 ***Perf. 13x13¼***
2777 A1505 60c multi 1.60 .40

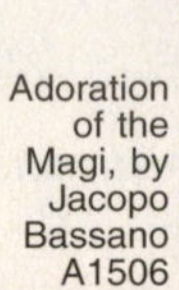

Adoration of the Magi, by Jacopo Bassano A1506

Christmas Tree — A1507

2006, Oct. 28 **Engr.** ***Perf. 13x13¼***
2778 A1506 60c rose 1.60 .40

Photo.
Perf. 13¼x13
2779 A1507 65c multi 1.75 .50

Vittoriano Building, Tomb of the Unknown Soldier, Rome A1508

2006, Nov. 11 **Photo.** ***Perf. 13x13¼***
2780 A1508 60c multi 1.75 .40

Cathedral of St. Evasius, Casale Monteferrato — A1509

2007, Jan. 4 **Engr.** ***Perf. 13x13¼***
2781 A1509 60c rose 1.60 .40

First Montessori School, Cent. — A1510

2007, Jan. 5 **Photo.** ***Perf. 13¼x13***
2782 A1510 60c multi 1.60 .40

School for Public Administration, 50th Anniv. — A1511

2007, Jan. 10 **Photo.** ***Perf. 13x13¼***
2783 A1511 65c multi 1.75 .45

Parma Cathedral — A1512

2007, Jan. 13 **Engr.** ***Perf. 13¼x13***
2784 A1512 60c green 1.60 .40

Arturo Toscanini (1867-1957), Conductor A1513

2007, Jan. 16 **Photo.**
2785 A1513 60c multi 1.60 .40

St. Francis of Paola (1416-1507) — A1514

2007, Jan. 27 ***Perf. 13x13¼***
2786 A1514 60c multi 1.60 .40

Ferrante Gonzaga (1507-57), Soldier A1515

2007, Jan. 27
2787 A1515 €1 multi 2.75 .65

Antonio Genovesi Salerno Foundation, 20th Anniv. A1516

2007, Jan. 29 **Photo.** ***Perf. 13x13¼***
2788 A1516 60c multi 1.60 .40

Relocation of Istrian Area Refugees to Giuliana di Fertilia District, Sardinia, 60th Anniv. A1517

2007, Feb. 10 **Photo.** ***Perf. 13x13¼***
2789 A1517 60c multi 1.60 .40

Father Lodovico Acernese (1835-1916) A1518

2007, Feb. 16 **Photo.** ***Perf. 13¼x13***
2790 A1518 23c multi .70 .25

Giosuè Carducci (1835-1907), 1906 Nobel Laureate in Literature — A1519

2007, Feb. 16 **Photo.** ***Perf. 13x13¼***
2791 A1519 60c multi 1.60 .40

University of Brescia — A1520

2007, Feb. 26 ***Perf. 13¼x13***
2792 A1520 60c multi 1.60 .40

European Equal Opportunity Year — A1521

2007, Mar. 1 **Photo.** ***Perf. 13¼x13***
2793 A1521 60c multi 1.60 .40

Scipione Maffei State High School, Verona — A1522

2007, Mar. 14 **Photo.** ***Perf. 13¼x13***
2794 A1522 60c multi 1.60 .40

Nicolò Carosio (1907-84), Radio Sportscaster — A1523

2007, Mar. 15 ***Perf. 13x13¼***
2795 A1523 65c multi 2.00 .50

Italian Regions Type of 2004

No. 2796, Trentino-Alto Adige. No. 2797, Marche. No. 2798, Umbria. No. 2799, Sardinia.

2007, Mar. 16 **Photo.** ***Perf. 13x13¼***
2796 A1387 60c multi 1.75 .40
2797 A1387 60c multi 1.75 .40
2798 A1387 60c multi 1.75 .40
2799 A1387 60c multi 1.75 .40
Nos. 2796-2799 (4) 7.00 1.60

Venice, UNESCO World Heritage Site — A1524

2007, Mar. 16 **Engr.** ***Perf. 13¼x13***
2800 A1524 60c black 1.60 .40

Intl. Electrotechnical Commission — A1525

2007, Mar. 16 **Photo.** ***Perf. 13x13¼***
2801 A1525 €1.50 multi 3.75 1.00

Souvenir Sheet

Treaty of Rome, 50th Anniv. — A1526

2007, Mar. 25 **Photo.** ***Perf. 13x13¼***
2802 A1526 Sheet of 2 3.50 3.50
a. 60c Stars and "50" 1.50 .40
b. 65c "Insieme dal 1957" 1.60 .50

Tourism Type of 2005

No. 2803, Brunico-Bruneck. No. 2804, Gaeta. No. 2805, Massafra. No. 2806, Cattolica Eraclea.

2005, Apr. 13 ***Perf. 13¼x13***
2803 A1424 60c multi 1.60 .40
2804 A1424 60c multi 1.60 .40
2805 A1424 60c multi 1.60 .40
2806 A1424 60c multi 1.60 .40
Nos. 2803-2806 (4) 6.40 1.60

Giuseppe Tomasi di Lampedusa (1896-1957), Writer — A1527

2007, Apr. 14 Photo. ***Perf. 13¼x13***

2807 A1527 60c multi 1.60 .40

Forum, Rome A1528

2007, Apr. 21 ***Perf. 13x13¼***

2808 A1528 60c multi 1.60 .40

Europa — A1529

Scouts: 60c, In canoe. 65c, At campfire.

2007, Apr. 23 ***Perf. 13¼x13***

2809 A1529 60c multi 1.75 .45

2810 A1529 65c multi 2.00 .55

a. Souvenir sheet, #2809-2810 5.00 5.00

Duccio Galamberti (1906-44), World War II Resistance Leader — A1530

2007, Apr. 24

2811 A1530 60c multi 1.60 .40

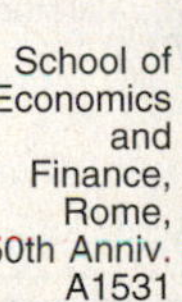

School of Economics and Finance, Rome, 50th Anniv. A1531

2007, Apr. 27 ***Perf. 13x13¼***

2812 A1531 €2.80 multi 7.00 2.25

Cinecittà Film Studios, Rome, 70th Anniv. A1532

2007, Apr. 28

2813 A1532 65c multi 1.75 .50

Polirone Monastery, San Benedetto Po, 1000th Anniv. — A1533

2007, May 5 Engr. ***Perf. 13¼x13***

2814 A1533 60c blue & dark blue 1.60 .40

Malatesta Castle, Montefiore Conca — A1534

2007, May 12

2815 A1534 60c brown 1.60 .40

Bancarella Musica Folk Music Project — A1535

2007, May 23 Photo.

2816 A1535 60c multi 1.60 .40

Emblem of Lamborghini Automobiles A1536

2007, May 23

2817 A1536 85c multi 2.50 .75

F. C. Internazionale, 2006-07 Italian Soccer Champions A1537

2007, June 4 Photo. ***Perf. 13¼***

2818 A1537 60c multi 1.75 .40

Chianca Dolmen — A1538

2007, June 9 Engr. ***Perf. 13¼x13***

2819 A1538 60c brown 1.60 .40

Luigi Ganna, (1883-1957), Cyclist — A1539

2007, June 9 Photo. ***Perf. 13¼x13***

2820 A1539 60c multi 1.60 .40

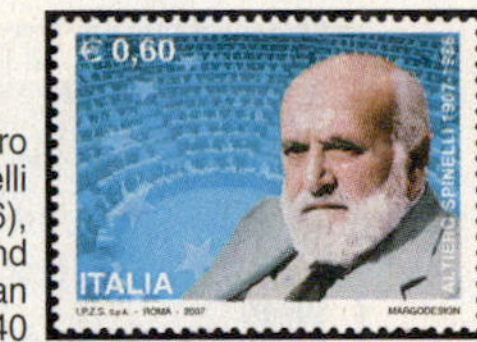

Altiero Spinelli (1907-86), Writer and Politician A1540

2007, June 21 ***Perf. 13x13¼***

2821 A1540 60c multi 1.60 .40

Two Worlds Festival, 50th Anniv. A1541

2007, June 29 Photo. ***Perf. 13x13¼***

2822 A1541 60c multi 1.60 .40

San Vincenzo Basilica, Galliano — A1542

On Wood Veneer
Self-Adhesive

2007, July 2 Litho. ***Rouletted 7***

2823 A1542 €2.80 black 7.50 2.75

Fiat 500 Automobile A1543

2007, July 4 Photo. ***Perf. 13x13¼***

2824 A1543 60c multi 1.75 .40

Giuseppe Garibaldi (1807-82), Patriot A1544

2007, July 4

2825 A1544 65c multi 1.75 .50

Capt. Maurizio Poggiali (1965-97), Pilot A1545

2007, July 6

2826 A1545 60c multi 1.60 .40

Roman Speleology Club A1546

2007, July 9

2827 A1546 €1.40 multi 3.75 1.25

Primo Carnera (1906-67), Boxer A1547

2007, July 13

2828 A1547 60c multi 1.60 .40

Marco Foscarini School, Venice — A1548

St. Pius V Institute for Political Studies, Rome — A1549

Salerno Medical College — A1550

2007, Sept. 17 Photo. ***Perf. 13¼x13***

2829 A1548 60c multi 1.60 .40

2830 A1549 60c multi 1.60 .40

2831 A1550 60c multi 1.60 .40

Nos. 2829-2831 (3) 4.80 1.20

Protected Donkey Breeds A1551

2007, Sept. 22 ***Perf. 13x13¼***
2832 A1551 60c multi 1.60 .40

31st European Women's Basketball Championships A1552

2007, Sept. 22 ***Perf. 13¼x13***
2833 A1552 65c multi 1.75 .45

Sacra di San Michele Abbey, Sant'Ambroglio di Torino — A1553

2007, Sept. 29 **Engr.**
2834 A1553 60c red brown 1.60 .40

Concetto Marchesi (1878-1957), Historian A1554

2007, Oct. 1 **Photo.**
2835 A1554 60c multi 1.60 .40

Jacopo Barozzi (Il Vignola) (1507-73), Architect A1555

2007, Oct. 1 ***Perf. 13x13¼***
2836 A1555 €2.80 multi 7.50 2.00

Grandparent's Day — A1556

2007, Oct. 2
2837 A1556 60c multi 1.60 .40

Philately Day — A1557

2007, Oct. 12 ***Perf. 13¼x13***
2838 A1557 60c multi 1.60 .40

Cupid and Psyche, Sculpture by Antonio Canova (1757-1822) — A1558

2007, Oct. 12 **Engr.** ***Perf. 13x13¼***
2839 A1558 €1.50 black 4.00 1.40

Miniature Sheet

Entertainers — A1559

No. 2840: a, Beniamino Gigli (1890-1957), opera singer. b, Maria Callas (1923-77), opera singer. c, Amedeo Nazzari (1907-79), actor.

2007, Oct. 18 **Photo.** ***Perf. 13¼x13***
2840 A1559 Sheet of 3 5.00 4.50
a.-c. 60c Any single 1.60 .40

Giuseppe Di Vittorio (1892-1957), Union Leader — A1560

2007, Nov. 3 ***Perf. 13x13¼***
2841 A1560 60c multi 1.60 .40

Mondadori Publishing House, Cent. A1561

2007, Nov. 12
2842 A1561 60c multi 1.60 .40

Madonna and Child, by Giovan Battista Cima da Conegliano A1562

Snow-covered House and Trees — A1563

2007, Nov. 20 **Engr.** ***Perf. 13¼x13***
2843 A1562 60c green 1.50 .40

Photo.

2844 A1563 65c multi 1.60 .45

Christmas.

Italian 2007-08 Term on UN Security Council A1564

2007, Dec. 1 **Photo.** ***Perf. 13x13¼***
2845 A1564 85c multi 2.25 .80

Governor's Palace, Fiume (Rijeka, Croatia) A1565

2007, Dec. 10
2846 A1565 65c multi 1.75 .50

Italian Constitution, 60th Anniv. — A1566

2008, Jan. 2 ***Perf. 13¼x13***
2847 A1566 60c multi 1.60 .40

Italian Red Cross Volunteer Nursing Corps, Cent. — A1567

2008, Jan. 29
2848 A1567 60c multi 1.60 .40

Amintore Fanfani (1908-99), Politician A1568

2008, Feb. 6 ***Perf. 13x13¼***
2849 A1568 €1 multi 2.50 .75

Italian Stock Exchange, Bicent. — A1569

2008, Feb. 8 ***Perf. 13¼x13***
2850 A1569 65c multi 1.75 .50

Olivetti Typewriter and First Olivetti Factory A1570

2008, Feb. 12 ***Perf. 13x13¼***
2851 A1570 60c multi 1.60 .40

Olivetti Corporation, Cent.

Villa Reale, Monza, Designed by Giuseppe Piermarini A1571

2008, Feb. 18 **Engr.** ***Perf. 13x13¼***
2852 A1571 €1.40 black & blue 3.50 1.00

Natl. Council of Economics and Labor, 50th Anniv. A1572

2008, Feb. 20 **Photo.**
2853 A1572 €1.50 multi 4.00 1.00

Dorando Pietri (1885-1942), Marathon Runner — A1573

2008, Feb. 23
2854 A1573 60c multi 1.60 .40

Souvenir Sheet

Song, "Nel Blu, Dipinto di Blu," 50th Anniv. — A1574

2008, Feb. 25 ***Perf. 13¼x13***
2855 A1574 60c multi 2.00 2.00

Anna Magnani (1908-73), Actress — A1575

2008, Mar. 7
2856 A1575 60c multi 1.60 .40

Emblem of Ricordi Publishing House and La Scala Theater, Milan A1576

2008, Mar. 7 Photo. *Perf. 13x13¼*
2857 A1576 60c indigo & gray 1.60 .40

Ricordi Music Publishing House, bicent.

Italia 2009 Intl. Philatelic Exhibition, Rome — A1577

Exhibition emblem and: 60c, Congress Center. 65c, Colosseum.

2008, Mar. 7 Photo. *Perf. 13¼x13*
2858 A1577 60c multi 1.75 .40
2859 A1577 65c multi 2.00 .50

Carlo Combi High School, Capodistria — A1578

2008, Mar. 8
2860 A1578 60c multi 1.60 .40

Edmondo de Amicis (1846-1908), Writer — A1579

2008, Mar. 11 Photo. *Perf. 13¼x13*
2861 A1579 60c multi 1.60 .40

Self-portrait, by Bernardino di Betto (Pintoricchio, c. 1454-1513) — A1580

2008, Mar. 14 *Perf. 13x13¼*
2862 A1580 60c multi 1.75 .40

Running of the Madonna, Sulmona — A1581

2008, Mar. 15 *Perf. 13¼x13*
2863 A1581 60c multi 1.60 .40

Italian Rowing Federation, 120th Anniv. A1582

2008, Mar. 31 Photo. *Perf. 13x13¼*
2864 A1582 65c multi 1.75 .50

Confirmation of the Rule, by Giotto — A1583

2008, Apr. 16 Photo. *Perf. 13x13¼*
2865 A1583 60c multi 1.60 .40

Rule of life of St. Francis of Assisi, 700th anniv.

Imperial Forum, Rome A1584

2008, Apr. 21
2866 A1584 60c multi 1.60 .40

Italian National Press Federation, Cent. — A1585

2008, Apr. 23 *Perf. 13¼x13*
2867 A1585 60c multi 1.60 .40

Flight, Sculpture by Pasquale Basile A1586

2008, Apr. 23 *Perf. 13x13¼*
2868 A1586 €1.40 multi 3.50 1.00

Intl. Decade of Education for Sustainable Development.

Giovannino Guareschi (1908-68), Journalist A1587

2008, May 1 Photo. *Perf. 13¼x13*
2869 A1587 60c multi 1.60 .40

Ludovico Geymonat (1908-91), Philosopher — A1588

2008, May 8 *Perf. 13x13¼*
2870 A1588 60c multi 1.60 .40

Europa — A1589

Designs: 60c, Red mailbox. 65c, Brown mailbox.

2008, May 9 Photo. *Perf. 13¼x13*
2871 A1589 60c multi 1.40 .45
2872 A1589 65c multi 1.60 .55

Works of Andrea Palladio (1508-80), Architect A1590

Designs: 60c, Alpini Bridge, Bassano. 65c, Palladian Basilica, Vicenza.

2008, May 10 Engr. *Perf. 13x13¼*
2873 A1590 60c multi 1.50 .40
2874 A1590 65c multi 1.75 .50

St. Francis Caracciolo (1563-1608) — A1591

2008, May 23 Photo. *Perf. 13x13¼*
2875 A1591 60c multi 1.60 .40

Italian Regions Type of 2004

2008, May 23 Photo. *Perf. 13x13¼*
2876 A1387 60c Valle d'Aosta 1.60 .40
2877 A1387 60c Veneto 1.60 .40
2878 A1387 60c Molise 1.60 .40
2879 A1387 60c Sicily 1.60 .40
Nos. 2876-2879 (4) 6.40 1.60

Guastalla School, Monza — A1592

2008, May 24 Photo. *Perf. 13¼x13*
2880 A1592 60c dk & lt blue 1.60 .40

Ducati Desmosedici GP7 Motorcycle — A1593

2008, May 31 *Perf. 13x13¼*
2881 A1593 60c multi 2.00 .40

Giacomo Puccini (1858-1924), Composer A1594

2008, June 21 Photo. *Perf. 13¼x13*
2882 A1594 €1.50 multi 4.00 1.25

F. C. Internazionale, 2007-08 Italian Soccer Champions — A1595

2008, July 4 Photo. *Perf. 13x13¼*
2883 A1595 60c multi 1.75 .40

2008 Summer Olympics, Beijing A1596

Olympic rings and: 60c, Torch bearer and map. 85c, Greek and Chinese athletes.

2008, July 7 Photo. *Perf. 13x13¼*

2884 A1596 60c multi 1.60 .40
2885 A1596 85c multi 2.25 .75

Tommaso Landolfi (1908-79), Writer A1597

2008, July 19 Photo. *Perf. 13x13¼*

2886 A1597 60c multi 1.60 .40

Tourism Type of 2005

No. 2887, Tre Cime di Lavaredo. No. 2888, Introdacqua. No. 2889, Casamicciola Terme. No. 2890, Mamoiada.

2008, July 24 Photo. *Perf. 13¼x13*

2887 A1424 60c multi 1.50 .40
2888 A1424 60c multi 1.50 .40
2889 A1424 60c multi 1.50 .40
2890 A1424 60c multi 1.50 .40
Nos. 2887-2890 (4) 6.00 1.60

Bowl of Saffron and Crocuses — A1598

Ingredients for Spaghetti all'Amatriciana — A1599

2008 Photo. *Perf. 13¼x13*

2891 A1598 60c multi 1.60 .40

Perf. 13x13¼

2892 A1599 60c multi 1.60 .40

Issued: No. 2891, 7/26; No. 2892, 8/29.

Bell Tower, Treviglio A1600

2008, Aug. 30 Engr. *Perf. 13x13¼*

2893 A1600 60c multi 1.60 .40

Dante Alighieri High School, Gorizia — A1601

Seal of the University of Perugia — A1602

2008, Sept. 8 Photo. *Perf. 13¼x13*

2894 A1601 60c multi 1.50 .40
2895 A1602 60c multi 1.50 .40

Cesare Pavese (1908-50), Writer — A1603

2008, Sept. 9

2896 A1603 65c multi 1.75 .50

Alberico Gentili (1552-1608), Jurist — A1604

2008, Sept. 13 *Perf. 13x13¼*

2897 A1604 65c multi 1.75 .50

Malatestiana Library, Cesena — A1605

2008, Sept. 19 Engr. *Perf. 13¼x13*

2898 A1605 60c black 1.60 .40

World Road Cycling Championships, Varese — A1606

2008, Sept. 22 Photo. *Perf. 13x13¼*

2899 A1606 60c multi 1.60 .40

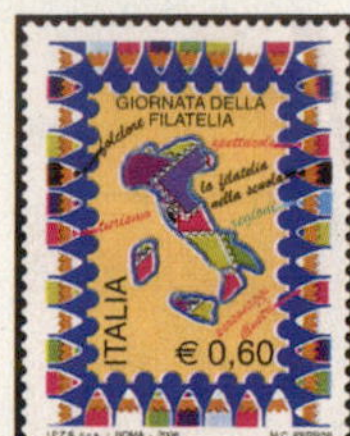

Philately Day — A1607

2008, Oct. 10 *Perf. 13¼x13*

2900 A1607 60c multi 1.60 .40

Italia 2009 Intl. Philatelic Exhibition, Rome A1608

2008, Oct. 10 Photo. *Perf. 13x13¼*

2901 A1608 85c multi 2.25 .60

Litho. on Gold Foil
Self-Adhesive
Rouletted 8

2902 A1608 €2.80 multi 8.00 5.00

Local Police — A1609

2008, Oct. 23 Photo. *Perf. 13¼x13*

2903 A1609 60c multi 1.60 .40

Oath of the Plebian Tribune, 2500th Anniv. A1610

2008, Oct. 24 *Perf. 13x13¼*

2904 A1610 60c multi 1.60 .40

Madonna and Child Enthroned with Two Angels, by Lorenzo di Credi — A1611

Wreath — A1612

2008, Oct. 30 Photo. *Perf. 13¼x13*

2905 A1611 60c multi 1.60 .40

Litho. on Gold Foil
Self-Adhesive
Rouletted 8

2906 A1612 €2.80 multi 8.00 5.00

Christmas.

UNESCO World Heritage Sites — A1613

Designs: 60c, Val d'Orcia. €2.80, Historic Center of Urbino.

2008, Oct. 31 Engr. *Perf. 13¼x13*

2907 A1613 60c multi 1.50 .40
2908 A1613 €2.80 blue & black 7.00 2.00

Messina Earthquake, Cent. — A1614

2008, Nov. 3 Photo. *Perf. 13x13¼*

2909 A1614 60c multi 1.60 .40

Corriere dei Piccoli Comic Strips, Cent. A1615

2008, Nov. 8

2910 A1615 60c multi 1.60 .40

Charles Darwin (1809-82), Naturalist A1616

2009, Feb. 12

2911 A1616 65c multi 1.75 .50

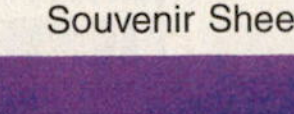

Souvenir Sheet

Song, "Tintarella di Luna," 50th Anniv. — A1617

2009, Feb. 17 ***Perf. 13¼x13***
2912 A1617 60c multi 1.75 1.75

5th Natl. Conference on Drugs, Trieste — A1618

2009, Mar. 12
2913 A1618 60c multi 1.60 .40

Valle Camonica Rock Drawing UNESCO World Heritage Site — A1619

2009, Mar. 27 **Engr.**
2914 A1619 €2.80 brown 7.00 2.00

Italia 2009 Intl. Philatelic Exhibition, Rome — A1620

People and: 60c, Italian stamps. €1, Map of Europe.

2009, Mar. 27 **Photo.**
2915 A1620 60c multi 1.75 .50
2916 A1620 €1 multi 2.75 .80

Father Primo Mazzolari (1890-1959), Writer on Social and Religious Issues — A1621

2009, Apr. 14 ***Perf. 13x13¼***
2917 A1621 60c multi 1.60 .40

Sardinia Grenadier Corps, 350th Anniv. A1622

2009, Apr. 16
2918 A1622 60c multi 1.60 .40

Piazza di Spagna, Spanish Steps, Fontana della Barcaccia, Rome A1623

2009, Apr. 21
2919 A1623 60c multi 1.60 .40

Indro Montanelli (1909-2001), Journalist A1624

2009, Apr. 22 ***Perf. 13¼x13***
2920 A1624 60c multi 1.60 .40

Bulgari Jewelers, 125th Anniv. — A1625

2009, Apr. 24
2921 A1625 60c multi 1.60 .50

Italy-Switzerland Chamber of Commerce, Cent. — A1626

2009, May 2 ***Perf. 13x13¼***
2922 A1626 60c multi 1.60 .40

Carabinieri Command for Cultural Heritage Protection A1627

2009, May 4
2923 A1627 60c multi 1.60 .40

16th Mediterranean Games, Pescara — A1628

2009, May 5
2924 A1628 60c multi 1.60 .40

European Parliament Elections A1629

2009, May 7
2925 A1629 60c multi 1.60 .40

Europa A1630

Designs: 60c, Galileo National Telescope, La Palma, Canary Islands. 65c, AGILE astronomical satellite.

2009, May 7
2926 A1630 60c multi 1.60 .45
2927 A1630 65c multi 1.75 .55

Intl. Year of Astronomy.

Giro d'Italia Bicycle Race, Cent. — A1631

2009, May 9 ***Perf. 13¼x13***
2928 A1631 60c multi 1.60 .55

Academy of Italian-German Studies, Merano, 50th Anniv. — A1632

2009, May 9 ***Perf. 13x13¼***
2929 A1632 60c multi 1.60 .40

Mille Miglia Auto Race A1633

2009, May 14 ***Perf. 13x13¼***
2930 A1633 60c multi 1.60 .55

Festival of Mysteries, Campobasso A1634

2009, May 22 ***Perf. 13¼***
2931 A1634 60c multi 1.60 .55

See Nos. 3041, 3160, 3162-3163, 3262, 3283-3284, 3324.

Cathedral of Santa Maria Madre di Dio, Rieti — A1635

2009, May 27 **Engr.** ***Perf. 13¼x13***
2932 A1635 60c black 1.60 .55

Giovanni Palatucci (1909-45), Police Official Who Saved Jews From Deportation A1636

2009, May 29 **Photo.**
2933 A1636 60c multi 1.60 .55

Gilera Motorbikes, Cent. — A1637

2009, June 6 ***Perf. 13x13¼***
2934 A1637 60c multi 1.60 .55

Postage Stamps of Sicily, 150th Anniv. A1638

2009, June 18 **Photo.** ***Perf. 13x13¼***
2935 A1638 60c multi 1.60 .55

Souvenir Sheet

2009 Baseball World Cup Tournament — A1639

2009, June 20 Photo. ***Perf. 13x13¼***
2936 A1639 60c multi 1.75 1.75

St. Giovanni Leonardi (1541-1609) A1640

2009, June 23 ***Perf. 13¼x13***
2937 A1640 60c multi 1.60 .55

F. C. Internazionale, 2008-09 Italian Soccer Champions A1641

2009, June 25
2938 A1641 60c multi 1.60 .55

San Daniele Prosciutto, 500th Anniv. of Historical Documentation of Production — A1642

2009, June 26 ***Perf. 13x13¼***
2939 A1642 60c multi 1.60 .55

St. Mark's Square, Venice A1643

2009, July 2
2940 A1643 60c multi 1.60 .55

Envelope A1644

2009 Engr. ***Serpentine Die Cut 11***
Self-Adhesive
Denomination Color

2941 A1644	60c blue	1.60	.40
2942 A1644	€1.40 red	4.00	1.00
2943 A1644	€1.50 green	4.00	1.00
2944 A1644	€2 brown	5.25	1.50
2945 A1644	€3.30 black	8.50	2.50
Nos. 2941-2945 (5)		23.35	6.40

Issued: Nos. 2941-2944, 7/7. No. 2945, 10/31. See Nos. 3074, 3166-3168A, 3273-3274, 3331.

Insurrection of the Women of Carrara, 65th Anniv. — A1645

2009, July 7 Photo. ***Perf. 13x13¼***
2946 A1645 €1.50 multi 4.00 1.25

G8 Summit, L'Aquila — A1646

2009, July 8 Photo. ***Perf. 13¼x13***
2947 A1646 65c multi 1.75 .80

Tourism Type of 2005

No. 2948, Verezzi. No. 2949, Isola del Giglio. No. 2950, Costa degli Dei, Capo Vaticano. No. 2951, Gole dell'Alcantara.

2009, July 10 Photo. ***Perf. 13¼x13***

2948 A1424 60c multi	1.60	.40
2949 A1424 60c multi	1.60	.40
2950 A1424 60c multi	1.60	.40
2951 A1424 60c multi	1.60	.40
Nos. 2948-2951 (4)	6.40	1.60

La Nazione Newspaper, Florence, 150th Anniv. — A1647

2009, July 14
2952 A1647 60c multi 1.60 .55

13th World Aquatics Championships, Rome — A1648

2009, July 18 Engr. & Embossed
2953 A1648 €1.50 blue 4.00 1.25

Forest Fire Prevention A1649

2009, Aug. 1 Photo.
2954 A1649 60c multi 1.60 .50

30th Rimini Meeting A1650

2009, Aug. 25
2955 A1650 60c green & black 1.60 .50

Montebello Lancers Cavalry Regiment, 150th Anniv. — A1651

2009, Sept. 4
2956 A1651 60c multi 1.60 .50

Painting by Francesco Solimena A1652

2009, Sept. 17 Photo. ***Perf. 13x13¼***
2957 A1652 60c multi 1.60 .50

Portrait of a Woman, by Giovanni Ambrogio de Predis, and Ambrosian Academy Library and Gallery, Milan — A1653

2009, Sept. 21 Engr. ***Perf. 13¼x13***
2958 A1653 €1.40 black 3.75 1.25

Emilio Alessandrini (1942-79), Magistrate Killed by Terrorists A1654

2009, Sept. 26 Photo. ***Perf. 13¼x13***
2959 A1654 60c multi 1.60 .40

Souvenir Sheet

Christian Roots of Europe — A1655

No. 2960: a, Green cross, yellow brown map. b, Yellow brown cross, green map.

2009, Oct. 7 ***Perf. 13x13¼***

2960 A1655	Sheet of 2	3.50	3.50
a.	60c multi	1.60	.40
b.	65c multi	1.75	.45

L'Unione Sarda Newspaper, 120th Anniv. — A1656

2009, Oct. 13 ***Perf. 13¼x13***
2961 A1656 60c multi 1.60 .40

Father Luigi Sturzo (1871-1959), Politician A1657

2009, Oct. 14
2962 A1657 €1.50 multi 4.00 1.00

Norberto Bobbio (1909-2004), Historian A1658

2009, Oct. 16
2963 A1658 65c multi 1.75 .50

Fathers Giovanni Minozzi (1884-1959) and Giovanni Semeria (1867-1931), Founders of Natl. Institute of Southern Italy — A1659

2009, Oct. 19
2964 A1659 60c multi 1.60 .50

Philately Day A1660

2009, Oct. 21 ***Perf. 13x13¼***
2965 A1660 60c multi 1.60 .50

Italian Language Day — A1661

2009, Oct. 21 Photo. ***Perf. 13¼x13***
2966 A1661 60c multi + label 1.60 .40

Printed in sheets of 5 + 5 labels. Value, sheet $12.

See San Marino No. 1801; Vatican City No. 1426.

Sports Day at Italia 2009 Intl. Philatelic Exhibition, Rome — A1662

Sports figures: 60c, Gino Bartali (1914-2000), cyclist. 65c, Valentino Mazzola (1919-49), soccer player. €1.40, Michele Alboreto (1956-2001), race car driver.

2009, Oct. 22 Photo. ***Perf. 13¼x13***
2967 A1662 60c multi 1.60 .50
2968 A1662 65c multi 1.75 .55
2969 A1662 €1.40 multi 4.00 1.10
Nos. 2967-2969 (3) 7.35 2.15

Souvenir Sheet

Diplomatic Relations Between Italy and Bulgaria, 130th Anniv. — A1663

2009, Oct. 22 ***Perf. 13¼***
2970 A1663 65c multi 2.00 2.00

See Bulgaria No. 4525.

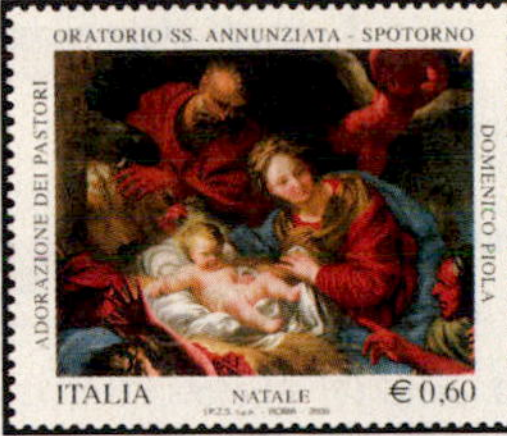

Adoration of the Shepherds, by Domenico Piola (1627-1703) — A1664

Ornaments — A1665

2009, Oct. 23 ***Perf. 13¼x13***
2971 A1664 60c multi 1.60 .40

Self-Adhesive
Serpentine Die Cut 11
2972 A1665 60c multi 2.50 .55

Christmas.

Souvenir Sheet

Comic Strips — A1666

No. 2973: a, Cocco Bill, by Benito Jacovitti. b, Diabolik, by Angela and Luciana Giussani. c, Lupo Alberto, by Silver.

2009, Oct. 23 ***Perf. 13x13¼***
2973 A1666 Sheet of 3 7.50 7.50
a.-c. €1 Any single 2.25 .90

Collector's Day at Italia 2009 Intl. Philatelic Exhibition, Rome.

Music Day at Italia 2009 Intl. Philatelic Exhibition, Rome — A1667

Designs: 65c, Luciano Pavarotti (1935-2007), singer. €1, Mino Reitano (1944-2009), singer. €1.50, Nino Rota (1911-79), composer.

2009, Oct. 24 ***Perf. 13¼***
2974 A1667 65c multi 1.75 .55
2975 A1667 €1 multi 2.50 .75
2976 A1667 €1.50 multi 4.00 1.25
Nos. 2974-2976 (3) 8.25 2.55

Europe Day at Italia 2009 Intl. Philatelic Exhibition, Rome A1668

No. 2977 — Roman architectural works: a, Pont du Gard, France. b, Hadrian's Wall, Great Britain. c, Odeon of Petras, Greece. d, Porta Nigra, Trier, Germany. e, Segovia Aqueduct, Spain.

2009, Oct. 25 ***Serpentine Die Cut 11***
Self-Adhesive
2977 Booklet pane of 5 + label 9.50 *9.50*
a.-e. A1668 65c Any single 1.75 .50
Complete booklet, #2977 10.00

Art of the 20th Century — A1669

Designs: 60c, Guantanamera, sculpture by Giacomo Manzù (1908-91). 65c, Danza dell'Orzo (The Bear Dance), by Gino Severini (1883-1966). 85c, Donna e Ambiente, by Federico de Pistoris (1898-1975).

2009, Oct. 30 ***Perf. 13¼x13***
2978 A1669 60c multi 1.75 .55
2979 A1669 65c multi 1.75 .60
2980 A1669 85c multi 2.50 .80
Nos. 2978-2980 (3) 6.00 1.95

Giorgio Perlasca (1910-92), Rescuer of Jews in World War II — A1670

2010, Jan. 31 Photo. ***Perf. 13x13¼***
2981 A1670 60c multi 1.60 .50

Souvenir Sheet

Santa Maria de Collemaggio Basilica, L'Aquila — A1671

2010, Feb. 10 Photo. ***Perf. 13¼x13***
2982 A1671 60c multi 1.60 1.60

Folk Festivals Type of 2009

Designs: No. 2983, Acireale Carnival. No. 2984, Jousting tournament, Sa Sartiglia, Oristano.

2010, Feb. 12 Photo. ***Perf. 13½***
2983 A1634 60c multi 1.60 .50
2984 A1634 60c multi 1.60 .50

2010 Winter Olympics, Vancouver A1672

Serpentine Die Cut 11
2010, Feb. 12 **Self-Adhesive**
2985 A1672 85c multi 2.25 .75

2010 Youth Olympics, Singapore — A1673

2010, Feb. 12 **Photo.**
Self-Adhesive
2986 A1673 85c multi 2.25 .75

Mario Pannunzio (1910-68), Journalist A1674

2010, Mar. 5 ***Perf. 13x13¼***
2987 A1674 60c multi 1.60 .50

Ennio Flaiano (1910-72), Screenwriter A1675

2010, Mar. 5 Photo. ***Perf. 13¼x13***
2988 A1675 60c multi 1.60 .50

Madonna dei Miracoli Basilica, Motta di Livenza — A1676

2010, Mar. 9
2989 A1676 60c black 1.60 .50

Massimo D'Azeglio, First President of Province of Milan, and Isimbardi Palace A1677

2010, Mar. 19 ***Perf. 13x13¼***
2990 A1677 60c multi 1.60 .50

Province of Milan, 150th anniv.

Alfa Romeo Automobiles, Cent. — A1678

No. 2991: a, 1910 24HP. b, 2010 Giulietta.

2010, Mar. 20
2991 Horiz. pair + central label 3.50 3.00
a.-b. A1678 60c Either single 1.60 .50

Burial of Christ with Three Angels Holding the Shroud, by Gerolamo della Rovere — A1679

2010, Mar. 22 ***Perf. 13¼x13***

2992 A1679 60c multi 1.60 .50

Confindustria (Federation of Employers), Cent. — A1680

2010, May 5 ***Perf. 13x13¼***

2993 A1680 €1.40 multi 3.75 1.40

Miniature Sheet

Expedition of the Thousand, 150th Anniv. — A1681

No. 2994 — Paintings: a, Garibaldi Sets Sail From Quarto, by V. Azzola. b, Landing at Marsala, by unknown artist. c, Battle of Calatafimi, by Remigio Legat. d, Encounter in Teano of Garibaldi and Victor Emmanuel II, by Pietro Aldi.

2010, May 5

2994 A1681	Sheet of 4	8.00	7.00
a.	60c multi	1.60	.50
b.	65c multi	1.75	.55
c.	85c multi	2.25	.80
d.	€1 multi	2.50	.80

Rhaetian Railway in the Albula - Bernina Landscapes UNESCO World Heritage Site — A1682

2010, May 6 ***Perf. 13¼x13***

2995 A1682 65c multi 1.75 .60

Pinocchio, by Carlo Collodi — A1683

Geronimo Stilton, by Elisabetta Dami — A1684

2010, May 7

2996 A1683 60c multi 1.40 .60

2997 A1684 65c multi 1.60 .75

Europa.

Sister Maria Domenica Brun Barbentini (1789-1868), Founder of the Congregation of the Sister Servants of the Sick of St. Camillus — A1685

2010, May 22 ***Perf. 13x13¼***

2998 A1685 60c multi 1.60 .50

Hanbury Botanic Gardens, Ventimiglia A1686

2010, May 29

2999 A1686 60c multi 1.60 .50

Tourism Type of 2005 and

1955 Tourism Poster — A1687

2010, June 4 ***Perf. 13¼x13***

3000 A1424 60c Courmayeur		1.60	.50
3001 A1424 60c Todi		1.60	.50
3002 A1424 60c Viggiano		1.60	.50
3003 A1424 60c Isole Tremiti		1.60	.50
	Nos. 3000-3003 (4)	6.40	2.00

Self-Adhesive

Serpentine Die Cut 11

3004 A1687 60c multi 1.60 .50

Camilo Benso, Count of Cavour (1810-61), Statesman A1688

2010, June 6 ***Perf. 13¼x13***

3005 A1688 60c multi 1.60 .50

Association of Italian Joint Stock Companies, Cent. A1689

2010, June 17 **Photo.** ***Perf. 13x13¼***

3006 A1689 60c multi 1.60 .50

F.C. Internazionale, 2009-10 Italian Soccer Champions A1690

2010, June 24 ***Perf. 13¼x13***

3007 A1690 60c multi 1.60 .50

Federacciai Iron and Steel Plant, Bagnoli, Cent. — A1691

Litho. & Silk-Screened

2010, June 28 ***Perf. 13¼x14***

3008 A1691 €3.30 black 8.50 3.00

No. 3008 is coated with a varnish producing a rough surface, and is printed with a special ink that allows the stamp to be lifted by a magnet.

Envelope A1692

Serpentine Die Cut 11x11¼

2010, July 1 **Photo.**

Self-Adhesive

Color of Denomination

3009 A1692 5c dark blue		.25	.25
3010 A1692 10c black		.30	.25
3011 A1692 20c blue green		.60	.25
	Nos. 3009-3011 (3)	1.15	.75

See Nos. 3165, 3330.

Giovanni Virginio Schiaparelli (1835-1910), Astronomer — A1693

2010, July 2 ***Perf. 13x13¼***

3012 A1693 65c multi 1.75 .50

Pope Benedict XVI, Statue of Pope Celestine V — A1694

2010, July 4 ***Perf. 13¼x13***

3013 A1694 60c multi 1.60 .50

Celestinian Jubliee Year.

David with the Head of Goliath, by Caravaggio (1571-1610) — A1695

2010, July 16 ***Perf. 13x13¼***

3014 A1695 60c multi 1.75 .50

Ettore Paratore (1907-2000), Latin Scholar, Mosaic and Theater Mask — A1696

2010, July 17 ***Perf. 13¼x13***

3015 A1696 65c multi 1.75 .55

50th Plautus Festival, Sarsina.

Samnite Theater, Pietrabbondante — A1697

2010, July 31 **Engr.**

3016 A1697 60c brown 1.60 .50

Joe Petrosino (1860-1909), New York City Policeman, Statue of Liberty, Brooklyn Bridge — A1698

2010, Aug. 30 **Photo.** ***Perf. 13x13¼***

3017 A1698 85c multi 2.25 .75

1960 Summer Olympics, Rome, 50th Anniv. A1699

2010, Sept. 7
3018 A1699 60c multi 1.60 .50

First National Gathering of Fire Brigades, Cortina d'Ampezzo A1700

2010, Sept. 10 ***Perf. 13x13¼***
3019 A1700 60c multi 1.60 .50

National Aerobatic Team, 50th Anniv. A1701

2010, Sept. 11
3020 A1701 60c multi 1.60 .50

Piazzale di Porta Pia, Rome A1702

2010, Sept. 20
3021 A1702 60c multi 1.60 .50

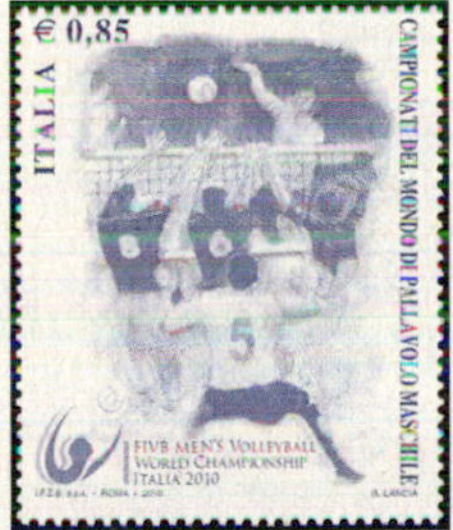
Men's Volleyball World Championships, Italy — A1703

Engr. & Embossed

2010, Sept. 24 ***Perf. 13x13¼***
3022 A1703 85c blue 2.25 .75

Torre Del Greco Coral — A1704

2010, Sept. 30 Photo. ***Perf. 13¼x13***
3023 A1704 60c multi 1.60 .55

Souvenir Sheet

Turin-Salerno High Speed Rail Line — A1705

2010, Oct. 2 ***Perf. 13x13¼***
3024 A1705 60c multi 1.60 1.60

Corriere Adriatico Newspaper, Ancona, 150th Anniv. — A1706

2010, Oct. 5 ***Perf. 13¼x13***
3025 A1706 60c multi 1.60 .50

National Anti-trust Authority, 20th Anniv. A1707

2010, Oct. 10 ***Perf. 13x13¼***
3026 A1707 €1.40 multi 3.75 1.20

School of Oenology, Conegliano A1708

2010, Oct. 21 ***Perf. 13x13¼***
3027 A1708 60c multi 1.60 .50

Leonardo Sciascia (1921-89), Writer A1709

2010, Oct. 23 **Engr.**
3028 A1709 60c black 1.60 .50

Italian Tennis Federation, Cent. A1710

2010, Oct. 25 **Photo.**
3029 A1710 60c multi 1.60 .50

Self-Portrait of Pietro Annigoni (1910-88) — A1711

2010, Oct. 27 ***Perf. 13¼x13***
3030 A1711 60c multi 1.75 .50

Souvenir Sheet

Italian Film Personalities — A1712

No. 3031: a, Federico Fellini (1920-93), director. b, Vittorio Gassman (1922-2000), actor, director. c, Alberto Sordi (1920-2003), actor, director.

2010, Oct. 28
3031 A1712 Sheet of 3 5.00 5.00
a.-c. 60c Any single 1.60 .50

Philately Day — A1713

2010, Oct. 29
3032 A1713 60c multi 1.60 .50

Frette Textiles, 150th Anniv. — A1714

2010, Oct. 29
3033 A1714 60c multi 1.60 .50

Adoration of the Magi, by Sandro Botticelli — A1715

Toy Train A1716

2010, Oct. 29 ***Perf. 13¼x13***
3034 A1715 60c multi 1.60 .50

Perf. 13x13¼
3035 A1716 65c multi 1.75 .60

Christmas.

Mario Mazzuca (1910-83), Rugby Player A1717

2010, Oct. 30 ***Perf. 13x13¼***
3036 A1717 60c multi 1.60 .50

Gentilini Cookies, 120th Anniv. — A1718

2010, Oct. 31 ***Perf. 13¼x13***
3037 A1718 60c multi 1.60 .50

Berlucchi Wines, 50th Anniv. (in 2011) — A1719

2010, Nov. 5
3038 A1719 60c multi 1.60 .50

A1720

Italian Flag, 150th Anniv. — A1721

2011, Jan. 7 Photo. ***Perf. 13x13¼***

Souvenir Sheet

3039 A1720 60c multi 1.60 .50

Self-Adhesive

Serpentine Die Cut 11

3040 A1721 60c multi 2.25 .60

Unification of Italy, 150th anniv.

Folk Festivals Type of 2009

Design: No. 3041, Battle of the Oranges, Carnival of Ivrea.

2011, Feb. 20 **Photo.** ***Perf. 13½***

3041 A1634 60c multi 1.60 .50

Antonio Fogazzaro (1842-1911), Writer — A1722

2011, Mar. 7 ***Perf. 13x13¼***

3042 A1722 60c multi 1.60 .50

Intl. Women's Day A1723

2011, Mar. 8

3043 A1723 75c multi 1.75 .60

Miniature Sheet

Taxation Agencies, 10th Anniv. — A1724

No. 3044: a, Territorio (Land Registry). b, Dogane (Customs). c, Demanio (State Property). d, Entrate (Revenue).

2011, Mar. 10

3044 A1724 Sheet of 4 6.00 6.00
a.-d. 60c Any single 1.60 .50

Souvenir Sheet

Proclamation of the Kingdom of Italy, 150th Anniv. — A1725

2011, Mar. 17 **Photo.** ***Perf. 13x13¼***

3045 A1725 60c multi 1.75 1.75

Souvenir Sheet

Piazza del Popolo, Rome — A1726

2011, Mar. 21 ***Perf. 13¼x13***

3046 A1726 €1.50 multi 4.50 4.50

Unification of Italy, 150th anniv. See Vatican City No. 1470.

Cheeses Made in Italy — A1727

Designs: No. 3047, Gorgonzola. No. 3048, Parmigiano Reggiano. No. 3049, Mozzarella di Bufala Campana (buffalo milk mozzarella). No. 3050, Ragusano.

2011, Mar. 25

3047 A1727 60c multi 1.60 .50
3048 A1727 60c multi 1.60 .50
3049 A1727 60c multi 1.60 .50
3050 A1727 60c multi 1.60 .50
Nos. 3047-3050 (4) 6.40 2.00

World Theater Day — A1728

Serpentine Die Cut 11

2011, Mar. 27 **Self-Adhesive**

3051 A1728 60c multi 1.60 .50

Italy No. 22 — A1729

Serpentine Die Cut 11¼

2011, Mar. 29 **Photo.**

Self-Adhesive

3052 A1729 60c aqua &dk blue 1.60 .50
a. Booklet pane of 10 16.00
Complete booklet, #3052a 17.50

First Man in Space, 50th Anniv. A1730

Serpentine Die Cut 11

2011, Apr. 12 **Photo.**

Self-Adhesive

3054 A1730 75c multi 2.10 .75

Quadriga on King Victor Emmanuel II Monument, Rome — A1731

2011, Apr. 21 ***Perf. 13¼x13***

3055 A1731 60c multi 1.60 .50

Emilion Salgari (1862-1911), Writer — A1732

2011, Apr. 23 ***Perf. 13x13¼***

3056 A1732 60c multi 1.60 .50

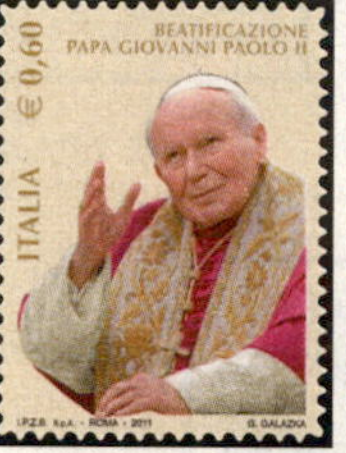

Beatification of Pope John Paul II — A1733

Serpentine Die Cut 11

2011, Apr. 29 **Self-Adhesive**

3057 A1733 60c multi 1.60 .50

Europa — A1734

Forest and: 60c, Mushrooms, squirrel. 75c, Bird, flowers.

2011, May 9 ***Perf. 13¼x13***

3058 A1734 60c multi 1.60 .50
3059 A1734 75c multi 2.00 1.00

Intl. Year of Forests.

Amnesty International, 50th Anniv. — A1735

Serpentine Die Cut 11¼

2011, May 28 **Photo.**

Self-Adhesive

3060 A1735 60c multi 1.60 .50

National Emigration Museum, Rome A1736

2011, June 1 ***Perf. 13x13¼***

3061 A1736 60c multi 1.60 .55

Souvenir Sheets

Unification of Italy, 150th Anniv. — A1737

Famous people and artwork: No. 3062, Camillo Benso, Conte di Cavour (1810-61), statesman, scene from 1856 Congress of Paris. No. 3063, Carlo Cattaneo (1801-69), writer, scene from 1848 Milan Revolt. No. 3064, Giuseppe Garibaldi (1807-82), military leader, scene of Garibaldi entering Naples, Sept. 7, 1860. No. 3065, Vincenzo Gioberti (1801-52), politician, scene of people celebrating in Naples. No. 3066, Clara Maffei (1814-86), Cristina Trivulzio Belgiojoso (1808-71), advocates of independence, scene of soldiers carrying injured Luciano Manara at Villa Spada, 1850. No. 3067, Giuseppe Mazzini (1805-72), politician, cover page of Giovine Italia, and Unione, Forza e Liberta flag. No. 3068, Carlo Pisacane (1818-57), patriot, and depiction of his murder. No. 3069, King Victor Emmanuel II (1820-78), and depiction of him on horseback

2011, June 2

3062 A1737 60c multi 1.75 1.75
3063 A1737 60c multi 1.75 1.75
3064 A1737 60c multi 1.75 1.75
3065 A1737 60c multi 1.75 1.75
3066 A1737 60c multi 1.75 1.75
3067 A1737 60c multi 1.75 1.75
3068 A1737 60c multi 1.75 1.75
3069 A1737 60c multi 1.75 1.75
Nos. 3062-3069 (8) 14.00 14.00

Souvenir Sheet

Anita and Giuseppe Garibaldi, First Tower of San Marino — A1738

2011, June 4

3070 A1738 €1.50 multi 4.00 4.00

Granting of San Marino citizenship to Garibaldis. See San Marino No. 1851.

Miniature Sheet

Italian Navy, 150th Anniv. — A1739

No. 3071: a, Arms of the Savoia family, Navy arms and pennant. b, Naval Academy, Livorno. c, Training ship Amerigo Vespucci. d, Emblems of Italian Sailor's Union and National Association of Italian Sailors

2011, June 10

3071	A1739	Sheet of 4	6.00	6.00
a.-d.		60c Any single	1.60	.55

Italian Referees Association, Cent. — A1740

2011, June 18

3072 A1740 60c multi 1.60 .55

Carlo Dapporto (1911-89), Actor — A1741

2011, June 25 ***Perf. 13¼x13***

3073 A1741 60c multi 1.60 .55

Envelope Type of 2009

Self-Adhesive

Serpentine Die Cut 11

2011, June 28 **Engr.**

Denomination Color

3074 A1644 75c lilac 2.00 .75

Parks and Gardens — A1742

Designs: No. 3075, Flower Garden, Appennnica di Capracotta. No. 3076, Padua Botanical Gardens.

2011, July 4 **Photo.** ***Perf. 13¼x13***

3075 A1742 60c multi 1.60 .55
3076 A1742 60c multi 1.60 .55

Holy Trinity Benedictine Abbey, Cava de'Tirreni, 1000th Anniv. — A1743

2011, July 7 **Engr.** ***Perf. 13¼x13***

3077 A1743 60c black 1.60 .55

Compasso d'Oro Award for Industrial Design — A1744

2011, July 12 **Photo.** ***Perf. 13½***

3078 A1744 60c multi 1.60 .55

Hadrian's Villa, Tivoli — A1745

2011, July 14 ***Perf. 13¼x13***

3079 A1745 60c multi 1.60 .55

Tourism Type of 2005 and

1955 Tourism Poster — A1746

No. 3080, Tarvisio. No. 3081, Riviera del Conero, Sirolo. No. 3082, Sepino. No. 3083, Bosa.

2011, July 23 **Photo.** ***Perf. 13¼x13***

3080	A1424	60c multi	1.60	.55
3081	A1424	60c multi	1.60	.55
3082	A1424	60c multi	1.60	.55
3083	A1424	60c multi	1.60	.55
		Nos. 3080-3083 (4)	6.40	2.20

Self-Adhesive

Serpentine Die Cut 11

3084 A1746 60c multi 1.60 .55

Souvenir Sheet

St. Luke Painting the Virgin, by Giorgio Vasari (1511-74) — A1747

2011, July 30 ***Perf. 13x13¼***

3085 A1747 €1.40 multi 3.50 3.50

Folk Festivals Type of 2009

Design: Mastrogiurato Festival, Lanciano.

2011, Aug. 26 ***Perf. 13½***

3086 A1634 60c multi 1.60 .75

Milan, 2010-11 Italian Soccer Champions A1748

F. C. Internazionale, 2010-11 Italy Cup Soccer Champions — A1749

2011, Aug. 27 ***Perf. 13¼x13***

3087 A1748 60c multi 1.60 .55

Perf. 13x13¼

3088 A1749 60c multi 1.60 .55

World Sports Fishing Championships, Italy — A1750

Serpentine Die Cut 11

2011, Aug. 27 **Self-Adhesive**

3089 A1750 60c multi 1.60 .55

2011 European Field Archery Championships, Montevarchi — A1751

Serpentine Die Cut 11

2011, Aug. 27 **Self-Adhesive**

3090 A1751 75c multi 2.00 .75

25th National Eucharistic Congress — A1752

2011, Sept. 3 **Photo.**

Self-Adhesive

3091 A1752 60c multi 1.60 .55

Arch of Trajan, Benevento A1753

2011, Sept. 9 **Engr.** ***Perf. 13x13¼***

3092 A1753 60c black 1.60 .55

Intl. Year of Chemistry A1754

Serpentine Die Cut 11

2011, Sept. 11 **Photo.**

Self-Adhesive

3093 A1754 €1.40 multi 3.50 1.25

Council of State, 180th Anniv. — A1755

Serpentine Die Cut 11

2011, Sept. 13 **Engr.**

Self-Adhesive

3094 A1755 60c black 1.60 .55

Organization for Economic Cooperation and Development, 50th Anniv. — A1756

2011, Sept. 30 **Photo.**

Self-Adhesive

3095 A1756 60c multi 1.60 .55

European Year of Volunteers A1757

Self-Adhesive

2011, Oct. 4 ***Serpentine Die Cut 11***
3096 A1757 75c multi 2.00 .75

Marzotto Textiles, 175th Anniv. A1758

2011, Oct. 14 **Photo.**
Self-Adhesive
3097 A1758 60c multi 1.60 .55

Italo Svevo (1861-1928), Writer — A1759

Self-Adhesive

2011, Oct. 28 ***Serpentine Die Cut 11***
3098 A1759 60c multi 1.60 .55

Equestrian Order of the Holy Sepulchre of Jerusalem A1760

2011, Nov. 3 **Photo.**
Self-Adhesive
3099 A1760 60c multi 1.60 .55

Souvenir Sheets

Battles — A1761

No. 3100: a, Battle of Pastrengo, 1848. b, Battle of Solferino, 1859. c, Battle of Volturno, 1860.

No. 3101: a, Battle of Bezzecca, 1866. b, Breach of Porta Pia, 1870. c, Battles of the Isonzo, 1915-17.

2011, Nov. 4 ***Perf. 13x13¼***
3100 A1761 Sheet of 3 4.50 4.50
a.-c. 60c Any single 1.60 .75
3101 A1761 Sheet of 3 4.50 4.50
a.-c. 60c Any single 1.60 .75

Italian Military Missions in Foreign Countries A1762

Serpentine Die Cut 11
2011, Nov. 12 **Self-Adhesive**
3102 A1762 75c multi 2.00 .75

Philately Day — A1763

Self-Adhesive

2011, Nov. 18 **Photo.**
3103 A1763 60c multi 1.60 .80

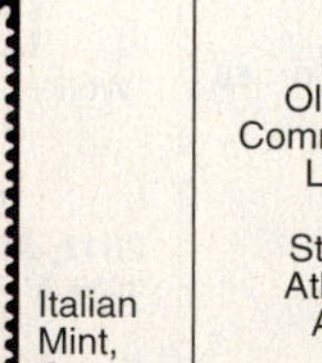

Italian Mint, Cent. A1764

2011, Nov. 18 **Self-Adhesive**
3104 A1764 60c multi 1.60 .55

Postal Savings Booklets A1765

Designs: 60c, Old postal savings booklets. 75c, Modern postal savings booklets.

2011, Nov. 18 **Self-Adhesive**
3105 A1765 60c multi 1.60 .55
3106 A1765 75c multi 2.00 .75

Fratelli Carli Olive Oil, Cent. A1766

2011, Nov. 19 **Self-Adhesive**
3107 A1766 60c multi 1.60 .55

Madonna and Child with Pomegranate, by Unknown Artist — A1767

Flying Reindeer — A1768

2011, Nov. 19 **Self-Adhesive**
3108 A1767 60c multi 1.60 .55
3109 A1768 60c multi 1.60 .55

Christmas.

Russian-Italian Year of Culture — A1769

2011, Dec. 10 **Self-Adhesive**
3110 A1769 75c multi 2.00 .75

See Russia No. 7326.

Italian Olympic Committee Library and Stylized Athletes A1770

Self-Adhesive

2012, Jan. 4 ***Serpentine Die Cut 11***
3111 A1770 60c multi 1.60 1.60

Giulio Onesti (1912-81), Member of Italian Olympic Committee and collector of books on sports.

Souvenir Sheet

Introduction of the Italian Lira, 150th Anniv. — A1771

No. 3112: a, Italia holding lira coin. b, "150" with coin as zero. c, Coin.

2012, Mar. 23 ***Perf. 13x13¼***
3112 A1771 Sheet of 3 4.50 4.50
a.-c. 60c Any single 1.60 .55

Italian Regional Wine Grapes and Vineyards A1772

No. 3113 — Grapes and vineyards for wines guaranteed to be from specific regions: a, Aglianico del Vulture Superiore. b, Cannellino di Frascati. c, Barolo. d, Greco di Tufo. e, Brunello di Montalcino. f, Montepulciano d'Abruzzo Colline Teramane. g, Colli Orientali del Fruili Picolit. h, Montefalco Sagrantino. i, Prosecco Conegliano Valdobbiadene Superiore. j, Vernaccia di Serrapetrona. k, Cerasuolo di Vittoria. l, Vermentino di Gallura. m, Moscato di Scanzo. n, Romagna Albana. o, Primitivo di Manduria Dolce Naturale.

Serpentine Die Cut 11
2012, Mar. 24 **Self-Adhesive**
3113 Sheet of 15 30.00 30.00
a.-o. A1772 60c Any single 1.60 .55

Milanofil 2012 Intl. Philatelic Exhibition, Milan. See Nos. 3196, 3270, 3337, 3373.

Le Fracchie di San Marco — A1773

2012, Mar. 31 ***Perf. 13¼***
3114 A1773 60c multi 1.60 .55

Giovanni Pascoli (1855-1912), Poet — A1774

Self-Adhesive

2012, Apr. 6 ***Serpentine Die Cut 11***
3115 A1774 60c multi 1.60 .80

Savings Banks Association (ACRI), Cent. — A1775

2012, Apr. 11 **Self-Adhesive**
3116 A1775 60c multi 1.60 .80

Publication of Lunario Barbanera (Almanac), 250th Anniv. A1776

2012, Apr. 11 **Self-Adhesive**
3117 A1776 60c multi 1.60 .80

Balsamic Vinegar From Modena A1777

2012, Apr. 17 **Self-Adhesive**
3118 A1777 60c multi 1.60 .80

Miniature Sheet

Italian Post Office, 150th Anniv. — A1778

No. 3119: a, Men and women in office with pillars and machinery. b, Postman on camel. c, Airplane ground crew handling mail sacks. d, Mail vehicles in arc. e, Man handling mail sack on streetcar. f, Woman and computer. g, Postman on scooter. h, Customers at postal bank. i, Postal workers in office with computers.

2012, May 5 **Self-Adhesive**
3119 A1778 Sheet of 9 17.50 17.50
a.-i. 60c Any single 1.50 .75

Europa A1779

Woman and: 60c, Field of sunflowers, building, building pillars. 75c, Dancer, coastal village.

2012, May 9 **Self-Adhesive**
3120 A1779 60c multi 1.50 .75
3121 A1779 75c multi 2.00 .95

Santa Maria Novella Perfumes and Pharmaceuticals Shop, Florence, 400th Anniv. — A1780

Self-Adhesive

2012, May 10 ***Serpentine Die Cut 11***
3122 A1780 75c multi 2.00 1.25

Trani Cathedral A1781

2012, June 1 **Engr.** ***Perf. 13x13¼***
3123 A1781 60c black 1.50 .75

Pres. Luigi Einaudi (1874-1961) A1782

Serpentine Die Cut 11
2012, July 2 **Photo.**
Self-Adhesive
3124 A1782 60c multi 1.50 .75

Horse Battle, by Aligi Sassu (1912-2000) — A1783

2012, July 17 ***Perf. 13¼x13***
3125 A1783 60c multi 1.50 .75

Tourism Type of 2005 and

Travel Poster — A1784

Serpentine Die Cut 11
2012, July 19 **Self-Adhesive**

3126	A1424	60c Baveno		1.50	.75
3127	A1424	60c Maiori		1.50	.75
3128	A1424	60c Monte Cassino		1.50	.75
3129	A1424	60c Ustica		1.50	.75
3130	A1784	60c multi		1.50	.75
		Nos. 3126-3130 (5)		7.50	3.75

Juventus, 2011-12 Italian Soccer Champions A1785

2012, July 21 **Photo.**
Self-Adhesive
3131 A1785 60c multi 1.50 .75

Expo 2015, Milan A1786

2012, Aug. 1 ***Serpentine Die Cut 11***
Self-Adhesive
3132 A1786 60c multi 1.50 .75

Boniface VIII Baths, Fiuggi — A1787

2012, Aug. 4 **Engr.**
Self-Adhesive
3133 A1787 €1.50 black 4.00 4.00

Fermo Cathedral A1788

2012, Aug. 14 ***Perf. 13x13¼***
3134 A1788 60c black 1.50 .55

Roma Newspaper, 150th Anniv. A1789

Serpentine Die Cut 11
2012, Sept. 10 **Photo.**
Self-Adhesive
3135 A1789 60c multi 1.50 .75

Souvenir Sheet

Battle of the Milvian Bridge, 1700th Anniv. — A1790

2012, Sept. 13 ***Perf. 13x13¼***
3136 A1790 €1.40 multi 3.75 3.75

See Vatican City No. 1507.

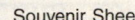

Anti-Mafia Investigation Department A1791

Serpentine Die Cut 11
2012, Sept. 21 **Self-Adhesive**
3137 A1791 60c multi 1.50 .80

Italian Surgery Congress, Rome — A1792

2012, Sept. 23 **Photo.**
Self-Adhesive
3138 A1792 60c red & green 1.50 .80

Botanical Gardens — A1793

Botanical Gardens in: No. 3139, Rome. No. 3140, Catania.

Serpentine Die Cut 11
2012, Sept. 28 **Self-Adhesive**
3139 A1793 75c multi 2.00 1.00
3140 A1793 75c multi 2.00 1.00

See Nos. 3175-3177, 3235-3237.

Court of Auditors, 150th Anniv. A1794

2012, Oct. 1 **Engr.**
Self-Adhesive
3141 A1794 60c green & black 1.50 .80

Cusano Milanino, Cent. A1795

2012, Oct. 6 **Photo.**
Self-Adhesive
3142 A1795 60c multi 1.50 .80

Second Vatican Council (Vatican II), 50th Anniv. — A1796

2012, Oct. 11 ***Serpentine Die Cut 11***
Self-Adhesive
3143 A1796 60c multi 1.75 .80

National Corps of Scouts and Guides, Cent. A1797

2012, Oct. 12 **Photo.**
Self-Adhesive
3144 A1797 60c multi 1.50 .80

Philately Day — A1798

No. 3145 — Steps in the creation of an Italian stamp: a, Philatelic consultation group (Consulta filatelica). b, Signing of decree (Decretazione). c, Graphic design (Ideazione grafica). d, Philatelic commision inspecting designs (Commissione filatelica). e, Printing of stamps (Produzione carte valori).

2012, Oct. 12 ***Perf. 13¼x13***
3145 Horiz. strip of 5 8.00 7.00
a.-e. A1798 60c Any single 1.60 .55

See Nos. 3197, 3277.

Manger with Saints John the Baptist and Bartholomew, by Antonio del Massaro — A1799

Christmas Tree — A1800

2012, Oct. 12 ***Serpentine Die Cut 11***
Self-Adhesive
3146 A1799 60c multi 1.50 .80
3147 A1800 60c multi 1.50 .80

Christmas.

Guzzini Housewares — A1801

2012, Oct. 13 **Photo.**
Self-Adhesive
3148 A1801 60c multi 1.50 .80

Ceramics A1802

No. 3149: a, Castelli ceramic plate. b, Caltagirone ceramic tiles. c, Ceramic tiles with inscription "Arte della ceramica" in square. d, Castellamonte ceramic stoves. e, Squillace ceramic plate.

2012, Oct. 14 ***Perf. 13¼x13***
3149 Horiz. strip of 5 7.50 7.50
a.-e. A1802 60c Any single 1.60 .55

Pope John Paul I (1912-78) — A1803

2012, Oct. 17 ***Serpentine Die Cut 11***
Self-Adhesive
3150 A1803 60c multi 1.50 1.50

Astronomical Observatories — A1804

Galaxy and: No. 3151, Brera Observatory, Milan. No. 3152, Capodimonte Observatory, Naples.

2012, Oct. 22 **Self-Adhesive**
3151 A1804 60c multi 1.50 .80
3152 A1804 60c multi 1.50 .80

Luigi Carlo Farini (1812-66), Prime Minister — A1805

2012, Oct. 22 **Self-Adhesive**
3153 A1805 60c multi 1.50 .80

Italian El Alamein War Memorial, Italian Base Q33, Emblem of Folgore Parachute Brigade A1806

2012, Oct. 23 ***Serpentine Die Cut 11***
Self-Adhesive
3154 A1806 €1.40 multi 3.75 3.75

Battle of El Alamein, 70th anniv.

81st General Assembly of Interpol, Rome A1807

2012, Nov. 3 **Photo.**
Self-Adhesive
3155 A1807 60c multi 1.50 .80

Italian National Electricity Company, 50th Anniv. — A1808

2012, Nov. 5 ***Serpentine Die Cut 11***
Self-Adhesive
3156 A1808 60c multi 1.50 .80

Elimination of Architectural Barriers to the Handicapped — A1809

2012, Nov. 9 **Photo.**
Self-Adhesive
3157 A1809 60c multi 1.50 .80

Primo Levi (1919-87), Writer A1810

Serpentine Die Cut 11
2012, Nov. 10 **Self-Adhesive**
3158 A1810 75c multi 2.00 1.00

Emblem of Health and Anti-Adulteration Center, 50th Anniv. — A1811

2012, Nov. 29 **Photo.**
Self-Adhesive
3159 A1811 60c multi 1.50 .80

Folk Festival Type of 2009

Design: Ndocciata Christmas Festival, Agnone.

2012, Dec. 7 ***Perf. 13¼***
3160 A1634 60c multi 1.50 .80

Awarding of 2012 Nobel Peace Prize to the European Union — A1812

2012, Dec. 10 ***Perf. 13¼x13***
3161 A1812 75c multi 2.00 .75

Folk Festival Type of 2009

Designs: 60c, Carnival, Fano. 70c, Canival, Termini Imerese.

2013 **Photo.** ***Perf. 13¼***
3162 A1634 60c multi 1.50 .55
3163 A1634 70c multi 1.75 .65

Issued: 60c, 1/12; 70c, 2/4.

Nordic Skiing World Championships, Val di Fiemme — A1813

2013, Feb. 1 ***Serpentine Die Cut 11***
Self-Adhesive
3164 A1813 85c multi 2.25 1.25

Envelope Types of 2009-10
Serpentine Die Cut 11x11¼
2013 **Photo.**
Self-Adhesive
Denomination Color

3165 A1692 25c pale org .65 .30

Engr.
Serpentine Die Cut 11

3166 A1644 70c black 1.75 .90
3167 A1644 85c orange 2.25 1.10
3168 A1644 €1.90 green 4.75 2.50
3168A A1644 €3.60 brown 9.00 5.00
Nos. 3165-3168A (5) 18.40 9.80

Issued: 25c, 2/13; 70c, 3/1. 85c, €1.90, 8/10; €3.60, 9/21.

Portrait of Anna Maria Luisa de'Medici (1667-1743), Patron of the Arts, by Antonio Franchi — A1814

Serpentine Die Cut 11

2013, Feb. 18 **Photo.**

Self-Adhesive

3169 A1814 €3.60 multi 9.50 6.50

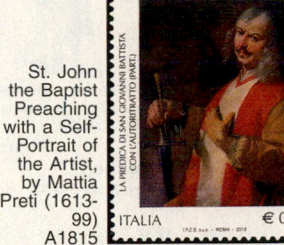

St. John the Baptist Preaching with a Self-Portrait of the Artist, by Mattia Preti (1613-99) A1815

Serpentine Die Cut 11

2013, Feb. 23 **Self-Adhesive**

3170 A1815 70c multi 1.75 .95

Sketches for Italian State Emblem and Stamp Designs, by Paolo Paschetto (1885-1963) — A1816

2013, Mar. 9 **Photo.**

Self-Adhesive

3171 A1816 70c multi 1.75 .95

Gabriele d'Annunzio (1863-1938), Writer — A1817

Serpentine Die Cut 11

2013, Mar. 12 **Self-Adhesive**

3172 A1817 70c multi 1.75 .95

Souvenir Sheet

Verona Opera Festival, Cent. — A1818

2013, Mar. 15 *Perf. 13¼x13*

3173 A1818 €1.90 multi 5.00 5.00

Italian Air Force, 90th Anniv. — A1819

Serpentine Die Cut 11x11¼

2013, Mar. 28 **Self-Adhesive**

3174 A1819 70c multi 1.75 .95

Botanical Gardens Type of 2012

Designs: No. 3175, Gardens of Castel Trauttmansdorff, Merano. No. 3176, Cinque Terre National Park. No. 3177, Botanical Garden Museum, Bari.

2013, Apr. 5 *Serpentine Die Cut 11*

Self-Adhesive

3175 A1793 70c multi 1.75 .95
3176 A1793 70c multi 1.75 .95
3177 A1793 70c multi 1.75 .95
Nos. 3175-3177 (3) 5.25 2.85

Souvenir Sheet

Edict of Milan, 1700th Anniv. — A1820

2013, Apr. 5 *Perf. 13x13¼*

3178 A1820 €1.90 multi 5.00 5.00

See Vatican City Nos. 1532-1535.

Election of Pope Francis — A1821

2013, May 2 *Serpentine Die Cut 11*

Self-Adhesive

3179 A1821 70c multi 2.00 .95

See Argentina No. 2682, Vatican City Nos. 1523-1526.

Polytechnic University of Milan, 150th Anniv. A1822

2013, May 7 **Self-Adhesive**

3180 A1822 70c multi 1.75 .95

Europa A1823

Postal vehicles: 70c, Motorcycles. 85c, Vans.

2013, May 9 **Photo.**

Self-Adhesive

3181 A1823 70c multi 1.75 .95
3182 A1823 85c multi 2.10 1.10

Municipal Theater of Bologna, 250th Anniv. — A1824

2013, May 14 **Engr.** *Perf. 13¼x13*

3183 A1824 70c black 1.75 .95

State Police Headquarters — A1825

Serpentine Die Cut 11

2013, May 16 **Photo.**

Self-Adhesive

3184 A1825 70c multi 1.75 .95

Gold Items Made in Italy A1826

No. 3185: a, Etruscan earrings with amphora pendants, 3rd-2nd cent. B.C. (black background). b, Salt cellars depicting Neptune and Earth, by Benvenuto Cellini, 16th cent. (red background). c, Star-shaped buckle, 14th cent. (green background). d, Golden Sphere monstrance, by Leonardo Montalbano, 1640 (red background). e, Brooch depicting Venus, engraved by Antonio Bernini, 19th cent. (blue background).

2013, May 18 **Photo.** *Perf. 13x13¾*

3185 Horiz. strip of 5 9.50 6.50
a.-e. A1826 70c Any single 1.90 .95

Twelve-Foot Dinghy, Cent. A1827

Serpentine Die Cut 11

2013, May 22 **Photo.**

Self-Adhesive

3186 A1827 70c multi 1.75 .95

50th Intl. Submariner Association Congress, Catania — A1828

Serpentine Die Cut 11

2013, May 23 **Photo.**

Self-Adhesive

3187 A1828 70c multi 1.75 .95

Italian Alpine Club, 150th Anniv. A1829

2013, May 25 **Photo.**

Self-Adhesive

3188 A1829 70c multi 1.75 .95

Italian Medicines Agency A1830

2013, June 3 *Serpentine Die Cut 11*

Self-Adhesive

3189 A1830 70c multi 1.75 .95

Giovanni Boccaccio (1313-75), Poet — A1831

2013, June 5 **Engr.**

Self-Adhesive

3190 A1831 70c blue 1.75 .95

Miniature Sheet

Determination of San Marino Borders, 550th Anniv. — A1832

No. 3191 — Map of various border areas of San Marino and: a, Bird and flower (Monte Lupo and Serravalle area). b, Insect. c, Bird and flower (Penna Rossa, Fiorentino, Torricella and Valle Sant'Anastasio area). d, Bird.

2013, June 7 **Photo.** *Perf. 13x13¼*

3191 A1832 Sheet of 4 7.50 7.50
a.-d. 70c Any single 1.90 .95

See San Marino No. 1891.

Sacred Hermitage, Camaldoli — A1833

2013, July 11 Photo. *Perf. 13¼x13*

3192 A1833 70c multi 1.75 .95

2013 Road Cycling World Championships, Tuscany — A1834

Serpentine Die Cut 11

2013, Sept. 21 Photo.

Self-Adhesive

3193 A1834 70c multi 1.75 .95

Giuseppe Verdi (1813-1901), Composer A1835

Serpentine Die Cut 11

2013, Oct. 10 Photo.

Self-Adhesive

3194 A1835 70c multi 1.75 .95

Olympic Victory, Sculpture by Emilio Greco (1913-95) — A1836

2013, Oct. 11 Engr. *Perf. 13¼x13*

3195 A1836 70c black 1.75 .95

Italian Regional Wine Grapes and Vineyards Type of 2012

No. 3196 — Grapes and vineyards for wines guaranteed to be from specific regions: a, Aglianico del Taburno. b, Alta Langa. c, Amarone della Valpolicella. d, Barbera d'Asti. e, Bardolino Superiore. f, Castel del Monte Bombino Nero. g, Cesanese del Piglio. h, Colli Bolognesi Classico Pignoletto. i, Morellino di Scansano. j, Oltrepò Pavese Metodo Classico. k, Ramandolo. l, Sfursat di Valtellina. m, Torgiano Rosso Riserva. n, Castelli di Jesi Verdicchio Riserva. o, Vino Nobile di Montepulciano.

Serpentine Die Cut 11

2013, Oct. 18 Photo.

Self-Adhesive

3196 Sheet of 15 28.50 28.50
a.-o. A1772 70c Any single 1.90 .95

Philately Day Type of 2013

No. 3197: a, Two Sicilies #9, Tuscany #23 on cover to Paris (blue background). b, First Italian postal card (pink background). c, Italy #116, 118 (green background). d, Italy #C49 on cover to Chicago, Italy #C48 (yellow brown background). e, Italian stamp catalog (dull rose background).

2013, Oct. 18 Photo. *Perf. 13¼x13*

3197 Horiz. strip of 5 9.50 7.50
a.-e. A1798 70c Any single 1.90 .95

Juventus, 2012-13 Italian Soccer Champions A1837

Serpentine Die Cut 11

2013, Oct. 19 Photo.

Self-Adhesive

3198 A1837 70c multi 1.75 .95

Archimedean Year — A1838

Serpentine Die Cut 11

2013, Oct. 19 Photo.

Self-Adhesive

3199 A1838 70c multi 1.75 .95

St. Joseph with the Child, by Guido Reni A1839

Envelope, Card, Pen, Ribbon and Ornaments A1840

Serpentine Die Cut 11

2013, Oct. 20 Photo.

Self-Adhesive

3200 A1839 70c multi 1.75 .95
3201 A1840 85c multi 2.10 1.10

Christmas.

Social Theater of Como, 200th Anniv. — A1841

2013, Oct. 28 Engr. *Perf. 13¼x13*

3202 A1841 70c black 1.75 .95

La Fenice Theater, Venice — A1842

Serpentine Die Cut 11

2013, Nov. 9 Photo.

Self-Adhesive

3203 A1842 70c multi 1.90 .95

Civita Association, 25th Anniv. — A1843

2013, Nov. 15 Photo. *Perf. 13¼*

3204 A1843 70c multi 1.75 .75

Tourism — A1844

1935 Italian Tourism Poster — A1845

Designs: No. 3205, San Leo. No. 3206, Scanno. No. 3207, Ponza. No. 3208, Tropea.

Serpentine Die Cut 11

2013, Nov. 16 Photo.

Self-Adhesive

3205 A1844 70c multi 1.75 .95
3206 A1844 70c multi 1.75 .95
3207 A1844 70c multi 1.75 .95
3208 A1844 70c multi 1.75 .95
3209 A1845 70c multi 1.75 .95
Nos. 3205-3209 (5) 8.75 4.75

See Nos. 3251-3254, 3291-3294, 3401-3404.

Rita Levi-Montalcini (1909-2012), 1986 Nobel Laureate in Physiology or Medicine A1846

Serpentine Die Cut 11

2013, Nov. 16 Photo.

Self-Adhesive

3210 A1846 70c multi 1.75 .95

Cola di Rienzo (1313-54), Roman Tribune — A1847

Serpentine Die Cut 11

2013, Nov. 23 Photo.

Self-Adhesive

3211 A1847 70c Prus grn & blk 1.75 .95

Giuseppe Gioachino Belli (1791-1863), Poet — A1848

Serpentine Die Cut 11

2013, Nov. 23 Photo.

Self-Adhesive

3212 A1848 85c multi 2.10 1.10

Mole Antonelliana, Turin — A1849

Nardo Cathedral A1850

Alba Fucens Archaeological Site — A1851

Santa Sofia Monument Complex, Benevento — A1852

Renaissance Era City Walls of Lucca — A1853

Serpentine Die Cut 11
2013, Nov. 13 Engr.
Self-Adhesive

3213 A1849 70c black 1.75 .95
3214 A1850 70c black 1.75 .95

Photo.

3215 A1851 70c multi 1.75 .95
3216 A1852 70c multi 1.75 .95
3217 A1853 70c black 1.75 .95
Nos. 3213-3217 (5) 8.75 4.75

Adnkronos News Agency, 50th Anniv. — A1854

2013, Dec. 4 Photo. *Perf. 13¼*
3218 A1854 70c multi 1.75 .75

Birds of the Alps A1855

No. 3219: a, Rock ptarmigan (Pernice bianca). b, Gray-headed woodpecker (Picchio cenerino). c, Bearded vulture (Gipeto). d, Boreal owl (Civetta capogrosso). e, Western capercaillie (Gallo cedrone).

2013, Dec. 4 Photo. *Perf. 13x13¼*
3219 Horiz. strip of 5 10.00 7.50
a.-e. A1855 70c Any single 2.00 1.00

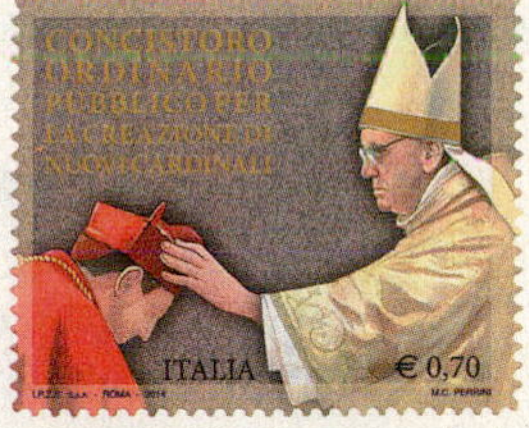
Ordinary Public Consistory for the Creation of New Cardinals — A1856

Serpentine Die Cut 11
2014, Feb. 22 Photo.
Self-Adhesive

3220 A1856 70c multi 1.75 .95

Father Martino Martini (1614-61), Missionary to China and Cartographer A1857

Serpentine Die Cut 11
2014, Mar. 8 Photo.
Self-Adhesive

3221 A1857 85c multi 2.10 1.10

Miniature Sheet

Renewable Energy — A1858

No. 3222: a, Solar energy, b, Hydroelectric energy. c, Geothermal energy. d, Wind energy. e, Wave energy. f, Biomass energy.

Serpentine Die Cut 11
2014, Mar. 21 Photo.
Self-Adhesive

3222 A1858 Sheet of 6 12.00 12.00
a.-f. 70c Any single 2.00 1.00

Christ Bound at the Column, by Donato Bramante (1444-1514) — A1859

Serpentine Die Cut 11
2014, Mar. 22 Photo.
Self-Adhesive

3223 A1859 70c multi 1.75 .95

David, by Michelangelo (1475-1564) — A1860

2014, Mar. 23 Engr. *Perf. 13x13¼*
3224 A1860 70c black 1.75 .75

Institute for International Political Studies, 80th Anniv. — A1861

Serpentine Die Cut 11
2014, Mar. 27 Photo.
Self-Adhesive

3225 A1861 70c multi 1.75 .95

Galileo Galilei (1564-1642), Astronomer A1862

2014, Apr. 5 Engr. *Perf. 13¼*
3226 A1862 70c black 1.75 .75

New Town of Bari — A1863

Serpentine Die Cut 11
2014, Apr. 23 Photo.
Self-Adhesive

3227 A1863 70c multi 1.75 .95

Canonization of Popes — A1864

Designs: No. 3228, Pope John XXIII. No. 3229, Pope John Paul II.

Serpentine Die Cut 11
2014, Apr. 24 Photo.
Self-Adhesive

3228 A1864 70c multi 1.75 .95
3229 A1864 70c multi 1.75 .95

See Vatican City No. 1557.

Bridge on Ancient Roman Road, Via Claudia Augusta — A1865

Serpentine Die Cut 11
2014, May 2 Photo.
Self-Adhesive

3230 A1865 70c multi 1.75 .95

Tiberio Bridge, Rimini — A1866

2014, May 2 Engr. *Perf. 13¼x13*
3231 A1866 €1.90 black 4.75 2.50

Europa — A1867

Musicians: 70c, Zampogna player. 85c, Launeddas player.

Serpentine Die Cut 11
2014, May 9 Photo.
Self-Adhesive

3232 A1867 70c multi 1.75 .95
3233 A1867 85c multi 2.10 1.10

Nutella Chocolate-Hazelnut Spread, 50th Anniv. — A1868

Serpentine Die Cut 11
2014, May 14 Photo.
Self-Adhesive

3234 A1868 70c multi 1.75 .95

Botanical Gardens Type of 2012

Designs: No. 3235, Minerva Garden, Salerno. No. 3236, Etna Park. No. 3237, Gola del Furlo State Nature Reserve.

Serpentine Die Cut 11
2014, May 23 Photo.
Self-Adhesive

3235 A1793 70c multi 1.75 .95
3236 A1793 70c multi 1.75 .95
3237 A1793 70c multi 1.75 .95
Nos. 3235-3237 (3) 5.25 2.85

Bombing of Piazza della Loggia, Brescia, 40th Anniv. — A1869

Serpentine Die Cut 11
2014, May 28 Photo.
Self-Adhesive

3238 A1869 70c brn red & blk 1.75 .95

Libraries and Colleges A1870

Designs: No. 3239, Oliveriana Library, Pesaro. No. 3240, Braidense National Library, Milan. No. 3241, Tulliano College, Arpino.

Serpentine Die Cut 11
2014, May 31 Photo.
Self-Adhesive

3239 A1870 70c multi 1.75 .95
3240 A1870 70c multi 1.75 .95
3241 A1870 70c multi 1.75 .95
Nos. 3239-3241 (3) 5.25 2.85

See Nos. 3288-3290, 3345-3347, 3420.

Italian Red Cross, 150th Anniv. — A1871

Serpentine Die Cut 11

2014, June 4 **Photo.**

Self-Adhesive

3242 A1871 70c multi 1.75 .95

Convention of Friendship With San Marino, 75th Anniv. A1872

Serpentine Die Cut 11

2014, June 5 **Photo.**

Self-Adhesive

3243 A1872 70c multi 1.75 .95

See San Marino No. 1910.

Italian Olympic Committee, Cent. — A1873

Serpentine Die Cut 11

2014, June 7 **Photo.**

Self-Adhesive

3244 A1873 70c multi 1.75 .95

Enrico Berlinguer (1922-84), Communist Politician — A1874

Serpentine Die Cut 11

2014, June 11 **Photo.**

Self-Adhesive

3245 A1874 70c red & black 1.75 .95

Silvano Arieti (1914-81), Psychiatrist A1875

Serpentine Die Cut 11

2014, June 28 **Photo.**

Self-Adhesive

3246 A1875 70c multi 1.75 .95

Italian Presidency of the Council of the European Union A1876

Serpentine Die Cut 11

2014, July 1 **Photo.**

Self-Adhesive

3247 A1876 70c multi 1.75 .95

Agostino Gemelli Teaching Hospital, Rome, 50th Anniv. A1877

Serpentine Die Cut 11

2014, July 7 **Photo.**

Self-Adhesive

3248 A1877 70c multi 1.75 .95

St. Camillus de Lellis (1550-1614) A1878

Serpentine Die Cut 11

2014, July 14 **Photo.**

Self-Adhesive

3249 A1878 70c multi 1.75 .95

Miniature Sheet

Carabinieri Force, 200th Anniv. — A1879

No. 3250: a, Statue of Carabinier, by Edoardo Rubino. b, Bergia Carabinieri Barracks, Turin. c, Emblem of Carabinieri Force. d, Sculpture depicting two Carabinieri, by Antonio Berti.

2014, July 16 **Photo.** ***Perf. 13x13¼***

3250 A1879 Sheet of 4 7.00 7.00
a.-d. 70c Any single 1.75 .65

Tourism Type of 2013 and

1963 Italian Tourism Poster — A1880

Designs: No. 3251, Margherita di Savoia. No. 3252, Monsummano Terme. No. 3253, Lovere. No. 3254, Olbia.

Serpentine Die Cut 11

2014, July 19 **Photo.**

Self-Adhesive

3251 A1844 70c multi 1.75 .95
3252 A1844 70c multi 1.75 .95
3253 A1844 70c multi 1.75 .95
3254 A1844 70c multi 1.75 .95
3255 A1880 70c multi 1.75 .95
Nos. 3251-3255 (5) 8.75 4.75

Election of Pope Hormisdas, 1500th Anniv. — A1881

2014, July 20 **Engr.** ***Perf. 13¼x13***

3256 A1881 70c black 1.75 .95

Juventus, 2013-14 Italian Soccer Champions A1882

Serpentine Die Cut 11

2014, Aug. 1 **Photo.**

Self-Adhesive

3257 A1882 70c multi 1.75 .95

Italian Catholic Guides and Scouts Association, 40th Anniv. — A1883

Serpentine Die Cut 11

2014, Aug. 7 **Photo.**

Self-Adhesive

3258 A1883 70c multi 1.75 .95

Emperor Augustus (63 B.C.-14 A.D.) — A1884

Serpentine Die Cut 11

2014, Aug. 19 **Photo. & Engr.**

Self-Adhesive

3259 A1884 70c pale yel & blk 1.75 .95

St. Pius X (1835-1914) A1885

Serpentine Die Cut 11

2014, Aug. 20 **Photo.**

Self-Adhesive

3260 A1885 70c multi 1.75 .95

Gazzetta di Mantova Newspaper, 350th Anniv, A1886

Serpentine Die Cut 11

2014, Sept. 1 **Photo.**

Self-Adhesive

3261 A1886 70c multi 1.75 .95

Folk Festivals Type of 2009

Design: 70c, Giro della Rua, Vicenza.

2014, Sept. 6 **Photo.** ***Perf. 13¼***

3262 A1634 70c multi 1.75 .90

National Nuclear Physics Laboratories A1887

No. 3263: a, KLOE kaon experiment equipment, Frascati National Laboratory. b, Borexino neutrino detection equipment, Gran Sasso National Laboratory. c, AGATA gamma ray detector, Legnaro National Laboratory. d, K800 Cyclotron, National Laboratory of the South.

Serpentine Die Cut 11

2014, Sept. 16 **Photo.**

Self-Adhesive

3263 Horiz. strip of 4 7.00 7.00
a.-d. A1887 70c Any single 1.75 .90

2015 Women's World Volleyball Championships, Italy — A1888

Serpentine Die Cut 11

2014, Sept. 23 **Photo.**

Self-Adhesive

3264 A1888 70c multi 1.75 .90

Vajont Dam and Basin and Church, Pirago — A1889

Serpentine Die Cut 11

2014, Oct. 9 **Photo.**

Self-Adhesive

3265 A1889 70c multi 1.75 .85

Vajont Foundation, and 51st anniv. of Vajont Dam disaster.

Real Ferdinando Bridge — A1890

Celtic Huts, Fiumalbo — A1891

Trabocchi Coast — A1892

Villa Nobel, Sanremo — A1893

2014, Oct. 25 Engr. *Perf. 13¼x13*
3266 A1890 70c black 1.75 .85
3267 A1891 70c blue & black 1.75 .85

Photo.
Serpentine Die Cut 11
Self-Adhesive

3268 A1892 70c multi 1.75 .85
3269 A1893 70c multi 1.75 .85
Nos. 3266-3269 (4) 7.00 3.40

Italian Regional Wine Grapes and Vineyards Type of 2012

No. 3270 — Grapes and vineyards for wines guaranteed to be from specific regions: a, Barbaresco. b, Castel del Monte Nero di Troia Riserva. c, Chianti. d, Fior d'Arancio Colli Euganei. e, Franciacorta. f, Frascati Superiore. g, Gattinara. h, Malanotte del Piave. i, Offida. j, Recioto di Soave. k, Rosazzo. l, Ruche di Castagnole Monferrato. m, Taurasi. n, Val di Cornia Rosso. o, Vernaccia di San Gimignano.

Serpentine Die Cut 11
2014, Nov. 22 Photo.
Self-Adhesive

3270 Sheet of 15 30.00 30.00
a.-o. A1772 80c Any single 2.00 1.00

Callipo Canned Fish, 101st Anniv. — A1894

Serpentine Die Cut 11
2014, Nov. 29 Photo.
Self-Adhesive

3271 A1894 80c multi 2.00 1.00

Straw Hat Industry of Florence — A1895

Serpentine Die Cut 11
2014, Nov. 29 Photo.
Self-Adhesive

3272 A1895 80c multi 2.00 1.00

Envelopes Type of 2009

Serpentine Die Cut 11
2014, Dec. 1 Engr.
Self-Adhesive
Denomination Color

3273 A1644 80c red 2.00 1.00
3274 A1644 95c dark blue 2.40 1.25

Madonna With Child and Saints, by Agostino Carracci A1896

Child Looking at Christmas Presents A1897

Serpentine Die Cut 11
2014, Dec. 1 Photo.
Self-Adhesive

3275 A1896 80c multi 2.00 1.00
3276 A1897 95c multi 2.40 1.25

Christmas.

Philately Day Type of 2012

No. 3277 — Journey of a letter: a, Person writing letter. b, Person placing letter in mailbox. c, Letter sorting. d, Delivery of letter. e, Opening of letter.

2014, Dec. 15 Photo. *Perf. 13¼x13*
3277 Horiz. strip of 5 10.00 10.00
a.-e. A1798 80c Any single 2.00 1.00

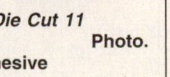

Giuseppe Mercalli (1850-1914), Vulcanologist A1898

Serpentine Die Cut 11
2014, Dec. 15 Photo.
Self-Adhesive

3278 A1898 80c multi 1.75 1.00

Launch of San Marco 1 Satellite, 50th Anniv. A1899

Serpentine Die Cut 11
2014, Dec. 15 Photo.
Self-Adhesive

3279 A1899 80c multi 2.00 1.00

Marsica Earthquake, Cent. — A1900

Serpentine Die Cut 11
2015, Jan. 13 Photo.
Self-Adhesive

3280 A1900 80c multi 1.90 .95

International Year of Light — A1901

Serpentine Die Cut 11
2015, Jan. 26 Photo.
Self-Adhesive

3281 A1901 80c multi 1.90 .95

Turin, 2015 European Capital of Sports — A1902

Serpentine Die Cut 11
2015, Jan. 30 Photo.
Self-Adhesive

3282 A1902 80c multi 1.90 .95

Folk Festivals Type of 2009

Designs: No. 3283, Sciacca Carnival. No. 3284, Putignano Carnival.

2015, Feb. 5 Photo. *Perf. 13¼*
3283 A1634 80c multi 1.90 .75
3284 A1634 80c multi 1.90 .75

Aldo Manuzio (1449-1515), Printer — A1903

Serpentine Die Cut 11
2015, Feb. 6 Engr.
Self-Adhesive

3285 A1903 80c black 1.90 .90

Floranga 2015 Flower Competition — A1904

Serpentine Die Cut 11
2015, Feb. 19 Photo.
Self-Adhesive

3286 A1904 80c multi 1.90 .90

SZ 1, by Alberto Burri — A1905

Serpentine Die Cut 11
2015, Mar. 12 Photo.
Self-Adhesive

3287 A1905 80c multi 1.90 .90

Libraries and Colleges Type of 2014

Designs: No. 3288, Lucchesiana Library, Agrigento. No. 3289, Guglielmo Tagliacarne Institute, Rome. No. 3290, Victor Emmanuel III National Library, Naples.

Serpentine Die Cut 11
2015, Mar. 21 Photo.
Self-Adhesive

3288 A1870 80c multi 1.90 .90
3289 A1870 80c multi 1.90 .90
3290 A1870 80c multi 1.90 .90
Nos. 3288-3290 (3) 5.70 2.70

Tourism Type of 2013 and

1963 Travel Poster — A1906

Designs: No. 3291, Bressanone. No. 3292, Valnerina. No. 3293, Tricarico. No. 3294, Isola di Burano.

Serpentine Die Cut 11
2015, Apr. 10 Photo.
Self-Adhesive

3291 A1844 80c multi 1.90 .95
3292 A1844 80c multi 1.90 .95
3293 A1844 80c multi 1.90 .95
3294 A1844 80c multi 1.90 .95
3295 A1906 80c multi 1.90 .95
Nos. 3291-3295 (5) 9.50 4.75

Banco Popolare, Milan, 150th Anniv. A1907

Serpentine Die Cut 11
2015, Apr. 11 Photo.
Self-Adhesive

3296 A1907 80c multi 1.90 .95

Fernet Branca Liqueur, 170th Anniv. — A1908

Gianduiotto Chocolates, 150th Anniv. A1909

Lavazza Coffee, 120th Anniv. — A1910

Serpentine Die Cut 11

2015, Apr. 24 **Photo.**

Self-Adhesive

3297 A1908 80c multi 1.90 .95
3298 A1909 80c multi 1.90 .95
3299 A1910 80c multi 1.90 .95
Nos. 3297-3299 (3) 5.70 2.85

World War II Liberation, 70th Anniv. — A1911

Serpentine Die Cut 11

2015, Apr. 25 **Photo.**

Self-Adhesive

3300 A1911 80c multi 1.90 .95

Giorgio Armani Fashions, 40th Anniv. A1912

Serpentine Die Cut 11

2015, Apr. 30 **Photo.**

Self-Adhesive

3301 A1912 80c multi 1.90 .95

Europa A1913

Old toys: 80c, Pinocchio on tricycle, 1940. 95c, Biplane W, 1938, horiz.

Serpentine Die Cut 11

2015, May 9 **Photo.**

Self-Adhesive

3302 A1913 80c multi 1.90 .90
3303 A1913 95c multi 2.25 1.10

St. John Bosco (1815-88) — A1914

Serpentine Die Cut 11

2015, May 19 **Photo.**

Self-Adhesive

3304 A1914 80c multi 1.90 .90

See Vatican City No. 1589.

Miniature Sheet

World War I, Cent. — A1915

No. 3305: a, Pilot Francesco Barraca and airplane. b, Machine gun emplacement on mountain. c, Anti-submarine boat. d, Soldiers in trench with machine guns.

2015, May 24 **Photo.** ***Perf. 13x13½***

3305 A1915 Sheet of 4 8.00 8.00
a.-d. 80c Any single 1.90 .90

Teatro Stabile, Turin — A1916

Teatro Petrarca, Arezzo — A1917

Malatesta Castle, Longiano — A1918

Colombaia Castle, Trapani — A1919

National Archaeological Museum of Sybaris — A1920

Fenestrelle Fort — A1921

Santa Maria della Consolazione Church, Todi — A1922

Serpentine Die Cut 11

2015, May 27 **Engr.**

Self-Adhesive

3306 A1916 80c black 1.90 .90
3307 A1917 80c black 1.90 .90
3308 A1918 80c black 1.90 .90
3309 A1919 80c black 1.90 .90

Photo.

3310 A1920 80c multi 1.90 .90
3311 A1921 80c multi 1.90 .90
3312 A1922 80c multi 1.90 .90
Nos. 3306-3312 (7) 13.30 6.30

Vignola and Local Cherries A1923

Serpentine Die Cut 11

2015, June 6 **Photo.**

Self-Adhesive

3313 A1923 80c multi 1.90 .90

Juventus, 2015 Italian Soccer Champions A1924

Serpentine Die Cut 11

2015, June 11 **Photo.**

Self-Adhesive

3314 A1924 80c multi 1.90 .90

Souvenir Sheet

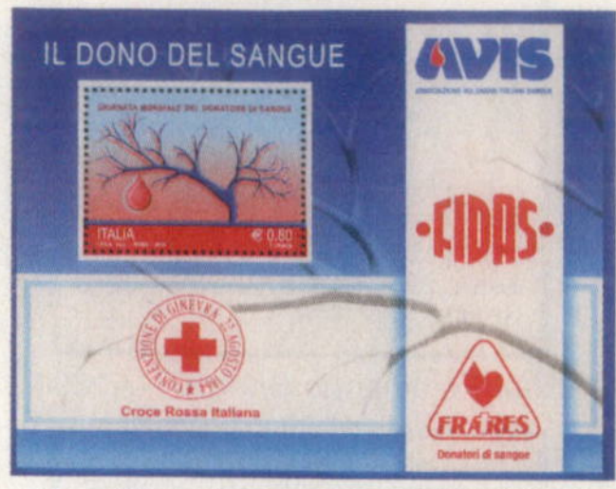

Blood Donation — A1925

2015, June 14 **Photo.** ***Perf. 13x13½***

3315 A1925 80c multi 1.90 .90

Daughters of St. Paul, Cent. A1926

Serpentine Die Cut 11

2015, June 15 **Photo.**

Self-Adhesive

3316 A1926 80c multi 1.90 .90

Souvenir Sheet

Selection of Florence as Capital of Italy, 150th Anniv. — A1927

2015, June 19 **Photo.** ***Perf. 13½x13***

3317 A1927 80c multi 1.90 .90

Pesaro Film Festival, 50th Anniv. A1928

Serpentine Die Cut 11

2015, June 22 **Photo.**

Self-Adhesive

3318 A1928 80c multi 1.90 .90

Mascot of Expo 2015, Milan — A1929

Serpentine Die Cut 11

2015, July 3 **Photo.**

Self-Adhesive

3319 A1929 80c multi 1.90 .90

Miniature Sheet

Expo 2015, Milan — A1930

No. 3320: a, Beet. b, Fish. c, Cabbage. d, Plums. e, Wheat. f, Artichoke. g, Bees. h, Carrots. i, Peppers. j, Acorn. k, Parsley. l, Peach. m, Oranges. n, Beans. o, Deer.

Serpentine Die Cut 11

2015, July 3 Photo.

Self-Adhesive

3320 A1930 Sheet of 15 30.00 30.00
a.-o. 80c Any single 1.90 .90

Italian Coast Guard, 150th Anniv. A1931

Serpentine Die Cut 11

2015, July 20 Photo.

Self-Adhesive

3321 A1931 80c multi 1.90 .90

St. Philip Neri (1515-95) A1932

Serpentine Die Cut 11

2015, July 22 Photo.

Self-Adhesive

3322 A1932 80c multi 1.90 .90

Dolomites — A1933

Serpentine Die Cut 11

2015, July 25 Photo.

Self-Adhesive

3323 A1933 95c multi 2.25 1.10

Folk Festivals Type of 2009

Design: Gulf of La Spezia boat race.

2015, Aug. 1 Photo. *Perf. 13¼*

3324 A1634 95c multi 2.25 1.10

Botanical Gardens Type of 2012

Designs: No. 3325, Municipal Botanical Garden of Trieste. No. 3326, Asinara National Park. No. 3327, Vulci Archaeological Park. No. 3328, Alpine Botanical Garden of Campo Imperatore.

Serpentine Die Cut 11

2015, Aug. 12 Photo.

Self-Adhesive

3325 A1793 95c multi 2.25 1.10
3326 A1793 95c multi 2.25 1.10
3327 A1793 95c multi 2.25 1.10
3328 A1793 95c multi 2.25 1.10
Nos. 3325-3328 (4) 9.00 4.40

2015 Canoe Sprint World Championships, Milan — A1934

Serpentine Die Cut 11

2015, Aug. 19 Photo.

Self-Adhesive

3329 A1934 95c multi 2.25 1.10

Envelope Types of 2009-10

Serpentine Die Cut 11x11¼

2015, Sept. 19 Photo.

Self-Adhesive

Denomination Color

3330 A1692 15c cerise .35 .25

Engr.

Serpentine Die Cut 11

3331 A1644 €1 black 2.25 1.10

Vitruvian Man, by Leonardo da Vinci A1935

Aerial Screw, by Leonardo da Vinci A1936

Mechanical Wing, by Leonardo da Vinci A1937

Giant Crossbow, by Leonardo da Vinci A1938

Serpentine Die Cut 11

2015, Oct. 1 Engr.

Self-Adhesive

3332 A1935 (€2.80) multi 6.50 3.25
3333 A1936 (€3.50) multi 8.25 4.00
3334 A1937 (€4.50) multi 10.50 5.00
3335 A1938 (€5.50) multi 13.00 6.25
Nos. 3332-3335 (4) 38.25 18.50

150th anniv. of the Unification of Italy.

Italian Banking Association, 70th Anniv. — A1939

Serpentine Die Cut 11

2015, Oct. 7 Photo.

Self-Adhesive

3336 A1939 95c multi 2.25 1.10

Italian Regional Wine Grapes and Vineyards Type of 2012

No. 3337 — Grapes and vineyards for wines guaranteed to be from specific regions: a, Elba Aleatico Passito. b, Asti. c, Friularo di Bagnoli. d, Castel del Monte Rosso Riserva. e, Chianti Classico. f, Asolo Prosecco superiore. g, Dolcetto di Diano d'Alba. h, Fiano di Avellino. i, Gavi. j, Ghemme. k, Lison. l, Ovada. m, Recioto della Valpolicella. n, Valtellina Superiore. o, Verdicchio di Matelica Riserva.

Serpentine Die Cut 11

2015, Oct. 10 Photo.

Self-Adhesive

3337 Sheet of 15 32.50 32.50
a.-o. A1772 95c Any single 2.25 1.10

End of World War I Postcard Illustration by Antonio Marchisio A1940

Serpentine Die Cut 11

2015, Oct. 15 Photo.

Self-Adhesive

3338 A1940 95c multi 2.25 1.10

10th Mediterranean and Black Sea Regional Sea Power Symposium, Venice — A1941

Serpentine Die Cut 11

2015, Oct. 21 Photo.

Self-Adhesive

3339 A1941 95c multi 2.25 1.10

San Marino-Italy Techno Science Park A1942

Designs: No. 3340, Balloon, flags of Italy and San Marino, stylized lightbulb, drone. No. 3341, Lightbulb in head.

2015, Oct. 23 Photo. *Perf. 13x13¼*

3340 A1942 95c multi 2.25 1.10
3341 A1942 95c multi 2.25 1.10

See San Marino Nos. 1946-1947.

Stamp Day — A1943

Designs: No. 3342, Bird on wall (stamp collecting in prison). No. 3343, Hot air balloon (stamp collecting in schools). No. 3344, Penny Black, 175th anniv.

Serpentine Die Cut 11

2015, Oct. 24 Photo.

Self-Adhesive

3342 A1943 95c multi 2.25 1.10
3343 A1943 95c multi 2.25 1.10
3344 A1943 95c multi 2.25 1.10
Nos. 3342-3344 (3) 6.75 3.30

Libraries and Colleges Type of 2014

Designs: No. 3345, Library of the Italian Encyclopedia Institute, Rome. No. 3346, National Library, Rome. No. 3347, Polytechnic University, Bari.

2015, Oct. 31 Photo. *Perf. 13x13¼*

Souvenir Sheet

3345 A1870 95c multi 2.25 1.10

Self-Adhesive

Serpentine Die Cut 11

3346 A1870 95c multi 2.25 1.10
3347 A1870 95c multi 2.25 1.10

Truffles and Forest A1944

Serpentine Die Cut 11

2015, Oct. 31 Photo.

Self-Adhesive

3348 A1944 95c multi 2.25 1.10

Pier Paolo Pasolini (1922-75), Writer — A1945

Serpentine Die Cut 11

2015, Nov. 2 Engr.

Self-Adhesive

3349 A1945 95c black 2.25 1.10

International Affairs Institute, 50th Anniv. — A1946

Serpentine Die Cut 11

2015, Nov. 13 Photo.

Self-Adhesive

3350 A1946 95c multi 2.25 1.00

Madonna and Child with Saints Joseph and Catherine of Alexandria, by Polidoro da Lanciano (1515-65) — A1947

Stylized Christmas Tree — A1948

Serpentine Die Cut 11

2015, Nov. 21 Photo.

Self-Adhesive

3351 A1947 95c multi 2.25 1.10
3352 A1948 95c gold & multi 2.25 1.10

Christmas.

Souvenir Sheet

San Giovanni Battista Hospital, Rome — A1949

No. 3353: a, Exterior of old hospital entrance, tree. b, Exterior of modern hospital, bushes.

2015, Nov. 27 Photo. ***Perf. 13x13¼***

3353 A1949 Sheet of 2 4.50 4.50
a.-b. 95c Either single 2.25 1.10

Women's Shoes by Salvatore Ferragamo, S.p.A. — A1950

Serpentine Die Cut 11

2015, Nov. 30 Photo.

Self-Adhesive

3354 A1950 95c multi 2.25 1.10

Gaetano Perusini (1879-1915), Physician A1951

Serpentine Die Cut 11

2015, Dec. 7 Engr.

Self-Adhesive

3355 A1951 95c black 2.25 1.10

Extraordinary Jubilee of Mercy — A1952

Pope Francis and holy door of: 95c, St. Peter's Basilica. €1, Basilica of St. Mary Major. €2.20, Basilica of St. John Lateran. €2.90, Basilica of St. Paul Outside the Walls.

Serpentine Die Cut 11

2015, Dec. 7 Engr.

Self-Adhesive

3356 A1952 95c black 2.25 1.10

Photo.

3357 A1952 €1 multi 2.25 1.10
3358 A1952 €2.20 multi 5.00 2.40
3359 A1952 €2.90 multi 7.00 3.25
Nos. 3356-3359 (4) 16.50 7.85

School of Barbiana and Students A1953

Serpentine Die Cut 11

2015, Dec. 9 Photo.

Self-Adhesive

3360 A1953 95c multi 2.25 1.10

La Repubblica Newspaper, 40th Anniv. — A1954

Serpentine Die Cut 11

2016, Jan. 14 Photo.

Self-Adhesive

3361 A1954 95c lav gray & blk 2.25 1.10

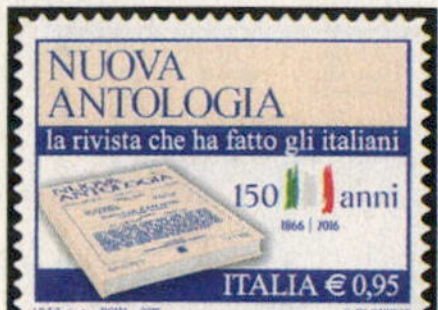

Nuova Antologia Magazine, 150th Anniv. A1955

Serpentine Die Cut 11

2016, Jan. 31 Photo.

Self-Adhesive

3362 A1955 95c multi 2.25 1.10

Elio Vittorini (1908-66), Writer A1956

Serpentine Die Cut 11

2016, Feb. 12 Photo.

Self-Adhesive

3363 A1956 95c multi 2.25 1.10

Carnival of Viareggio A1957

Serpentine Die Cut 11

2016, Feb. 13 Photo.

Self-Adhesive

3364 A1957 95c multi 2.25 1.10

Terni Basilica Stained-Glass Window Depicting St. Valentine A1958

2016, Feb. 14 Photo. ***Perf. 13¼***

3365 A1958 95c multi 2.25 1.10

Meyer Pediatric Hospital, Florence, 125th Anniv. A1959

Serpentine Die Cut 11

2016, Feb. 19 Photo.

Self-Adhesive

3366 A1959 95c multi 2.25 1.10

Benedetto Croce (1866-1952), Philosopher and Politician — A1960

Serpentine Die Cut 11

2016, Feb. 25 Photo.

Self-Adhesive

3367 A1960 95c multi 2.25 1.10

Father Carlo Gnocchi (1902-56), Educator A1961

Serpentine Die Cut 11

2016, Feb. 27 Photo.

Self-Adhesive

3368 A1961 95c multi 2.25 1.10

Italian Boxing Federation, Cent. — A1962

Serpentine Die Cut 11

2016, Mar. 2 Photo.

Self-Adhesive

3369 A1962 95c multi 2.25 1.10

Corriere Della Sera Newspaper, 140th Anniv. — A1963

Serpentine Die Cut 11

2016, Mar. 5 Photo.

Self-Adhesive

3370 A1963 95c multi 2.25 1.10

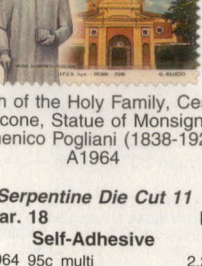

Church of the Holy Family, Cesano Boscone, Statue of Monsignor Domenico Pogliani (1838-1921) A1964

Serpentine Die Cut 11

2016, Mar. 18 Photo.

Self-Adhesive

3371 A1964 95c multi 2.25 1.10

Holy Family Institute Foundation, 120th anniv.

Holy Thorn of Andria A1965

Serpentine Die Cut 11

2016, Mar. 25 Photo.

Self-Adhesive

3372 A1965 95c multi 2.25 1.10

Italian Regional Wine Grapes and Vineyards Type of 2012

No. 3373 — Grapes and vineyards for wines guaranteed to be from specific regions: a, Barbera del Monferrate Superiore. b, Brachetto d' Acqui. c, Carmignano. d, Colli di Conegliano. e, Conero Riserva. f, Dogliani. g, Erbaluce di Caluso. h, Montecucco Sangiovese. i, Montello. j, Recioto di Gambellara. k, Roero. l, Soave Superiore. m, Suvereto.

Serpentine Die Cut 11

2016, Apr. 11 Photo.

Self-Adhesive

3373 Sheet of 13 29.50 29.50
a.-m. A1772 95c Any single 2.25 1.10

Vinitaly Wine Competition Emblem — A1966

Vinitaly Wine Competition 50th Anniv. Emblem — A1967

Serpentine Die Cut 11

2016, Apr. 11 Photo.

Self-Adhesive

3374 A1966 95c multi 2.25 1.10
3375 A1967 95c multi 2.25 1.10

Women's Health Day — A1968

Serpentine Die Cut 11
2016, Apr. 22 Photo.
Self-Adhesive
3376 A1968 95c multi 2.25 1.10

Italian Worldwide Fund for Nature (WWF), 50th Anniv. A1969

Serpentine Die Cut 11
2016, Apr. 22 Photo.
Self-Adhesive
3377 A1969 95c multi 2.25 1.10

Totocalcio Soccer Pool, 70th Anniv. — A1970

Serpentine Die Cut 11
2016, May 5 Photo.
Self-Adhesive
3378 A1970 95c multi 2.25 1.10

Italian Sports Center, Rome, 110th Anniv. A1971

Serpentine Die Cut 11
2016, May 6 Photo.
Self-Adhesive
3379 A1971 95c multi 2.25 1.10

100th Targa Florio Road Race A1972

Serpentine Die Cut 11
2016, May 7 Photo.
Self-Adhesive
3380 A1972 95c multi 2.25 1.10

Judge Francesco Coco (1908-76) and Magistrate Vittorio Occorsio (1929-76), Victims of Terrorism — A1973

Serpentine Die Cut 11
2016, May 9 Photo.
Self-Adhesive
3381 A1973 95c multi 2.25 1.10

A1974

Europa A1975

Serpentine Die Cut 11
2016, May 9 Photo.
Self-Adhesive
3382 A1974 95c multi 2.25 1.10
3383 A1975 €1 multi 2.25 1.10

Think Green Issue.

Red Coral of Alghero and Alghero Buildings A1976

Serpentine Die Cut 11
2016, May 14 Photo.
Self-Adhesive
3384 A1976 95c multi 2.25 1.10

Military Corps of Italian Red Cross, 150th Anniv. A1977

Serpentine Die Cut 11
2016, June 1 Photo.
Self-Adhesive
3385 A1977 95c multi 2.25 1.10

Italian Republic, 70th Anniv. A1978

Serpentine Die Cut 11
2016, June 2 Photo.
Self-Adhesive
3386 A1978 95c multi 2.25 1.10

Woman Suffrage in Italy, 70th Anniv. — A1979

Serpentine Die Cut 11
2016, June 2 Photo.
Self-Adhesive
3387 A1979 95c multi 2.25 1.10

Appointment of First Female Government Minister, 40th Anniv. — A1980

Serpentine Die Cut 11
2016, June 2 Photo.
Self-Adhesive
3388 A1980 95c multi 2.25 1.10

Juventus, 2012-16 Italian Soccer Champions A1981

Serpentine Die Cut 11
2016, June 27 Photo.
Self-Adhesive
3389 A1981 95c multi 2.25 1.10

No. 3389 was printed in sheets of 5.

Piazza della Republica, Rome A1982

Piazza del Plebiscito, Naples A1983

Piazza Ruggiero Settimo, Palermo A1984

Piazza del Duomo, Milan A1985

Piazza San Carlo, Turin A1986

Piazza Maggiore, Bologna A1987

Piazza de Ferrari, Genoa A1988

Piazza della Signoria, Florence A1989

Serpentine Die Cut 11
2016, July 2 Engr.
Self-Adhesive

3390 A1982	(95c) multi	2.25	1.10
3391 A1983	(€1) multi	2.40	1.10
3392 A1984	(€2.20) multi	5.25	2.50
3393 A1985	(€2.55) multi	6.00	2.75
3394 A1986	(€2.70) multi	6.50	3.00
3395 A1987	(€2.90) multi	7.00	3.25
3396 A1988	(€3.70) multi	8.75	4.00
3397 A1989	(€4.60) multi	11.00	5.25
Nos. 3390-3397 (8)		49.15	22.95

Italian Shooting Federation, 90th Anniv. A1990

Serpentine Die Cut 11
2016, July 5 Photo.
Self-Adhesive
3398 A1990 95c multi 2.25 1.10

Canonization of St. Frances Xavier Cabrini (1850-1917), 70th Anniv. — A1991

Serpentine Die Cut 11
2016, July 7 Photo.
Self-Adhesive
3399 A1991 95c multi 2.25 1.10

Slow Food Organization, 30th Anniv. — A1992

Serpentine Die Cut 11
2016, July 26 Photo.
Self-Adhesive
3400 A1992 95c multi 2.25 1.10

Tourism Type of 2013

Designs: No. 3401, Albenga. No. 3402, Camerino. No. 3403, Carovilli. No. 3404, Sperlinga.

Serpentine Die Cut 11
2016, Aug. 6 Photo.
Self-Adhesive

3401 A1844	95c multi	2.25	1.10
3402 A1844	95c multi	2.25	1.10
3403 A1844	95c multi	2.25	1.10
3404 A1844	95c multi	2.25	1.10
Nos. 3401-3404 (4)		9.00	4.40

Dynamism of a Man's Head, by Umberto Boccioni (1882-1916) A1993

Serpentine Die Cut 11

2016, Aug. 17 **Photo.**

Self-Adhesive

3405 A1993 95c multi 2.25 1.10

Anna Magnani (1908-73), Actress — A1994

Serpentine Die Cut 11

2016, Aug. 31 **Photo.**

Self-Adhesive

3406 A1994 95c multi 2.25 1.10

Luchino Visconti (1906-76), Theater and Film Director — A1995

Serpentine Die Cut 11

2016, Aug. 31 **Photo.**

Self-Adhesive

3407 A1995 95c multi 2.25 1.10

Aldo Moro (1916-78), Prime Minister — A1996

Serpentine Die Cut 11

2016, Sept. 23 **Photo.**

Self-Adhesive

3408 A1996 95c multi 2.25 1.10

Grand Duke Cosimo III of Tuscany (1642-1723) and Map of Tuscany — A1997

Serpentine Die Cut 11

2016, Sept. 24 **Photo.**

Self-Adhesive

3409 A1997 95c multi 2.25 1.10

Declaration of boundaries of Chianti, Pomino Carmignano and Vald'Arno di Sopra, 300th anniv.

Salini Impreglio Group, 110th Anniv. A1998

Serpentine Die Cut 11

2016, Sept. 27 **Photo.**

Self-Adhesive

3410 A1998 95c multi 2.25 1.10

Piero Calamandrei (1889-1956), Politician and Writer — A1999

Serpentine Die Cut 11

2016, Sept. 27 **Photo.**

Self-Adhesive

3411 A1999 95c multi 2.25 1.10

Antonio Mattei Biscotti — A2000

Serpentine Die Cut 11

2016, Sept. 29 **Photo.**

Self-Adhesive

3412 A2000 95c multi 2.25 1.10

Il Secolo XIX Newspaper, 130th Anniv. — A2001

Serpentine Die Cut 11

2016, Sept. 30 **Photo.**

Self-Adhesive

3413 A2001 95c multi 2.25 1.10

Alto Adige Speck A2002

Serpentine Die Cut 11

2016, Oct. 1 **Photo.**

Self-Adhesive

3414 A2002 95c multi 2.25 1.10

Gallo Rice A2003

Serpentine Die Cut 11

2016, Oct. 3 **Photo.**

Self-Adhesive

3415 A2003 95c multi 2.25 1.10

Statue of Virgil, Mantua — A2004

Serpentine Die Cut 11

2016, Oct. 15 **Photo.**

Self-Adhesive

3416 A2004 95c red 2.25 1.10

Mantua, 2016 Italian Capital of Culture.

Teresio Olivelli (1916-45), Beatified Soldier of World War II Resistance Movement A2005

Serpentine Die Cut 11

2016, Oct. 15 **Photo.**

Self-Adhesive

3417 A2005 95c multi 2.25 1.10

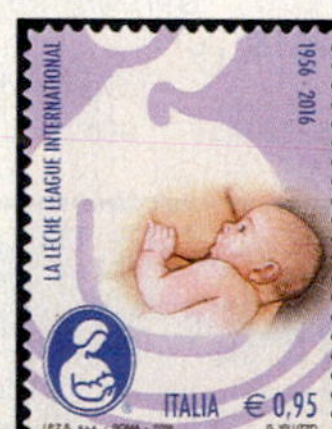

La Leche League International, 60th Anniv. — A2006

Serpentine Die Cut 11

2016, Oct. 17 **Photo.**

Self-Adhesive

3418 A2006 95c multi 2.25 1.10

Santa Cecilia National Academy A2007

Serpentine Die Cut 11

2016, Oct. 20 **Photo.**

Self-Adhesive

3419 A2007 95c black & red 2.25 1.10

Libraries and Colleges Type of 2014

Design: 95c, Biblioteca Nazionale Marciana (St. Mark's National Library), Venice.

Serpentine Die Cut 11

2016, Oct. 20 **Photo.**

Self-Adhesive

3420 A1870 95c multi 2.25 1.10

Philately Day — A2008

Serpentine Die Cut 11

2016, Oct. 21 **Photo.**

Self-Adhesive

3421 A2008 95c multi 2.25 1.10

50th Comics and Games Convention, Lucca — A2009

Serpentine Die Cut 11

2016, Oct. 28 **Photo.**

Self-Adhesive

3422 A2009 95c multi 2.25 1.10

A2010

Design: 95c, Children's Drawing Depicting Rescue of Art Treasures in 1967 Flood in Florence.

Serpentine Die Cut 11

2016, Nov. 4 **Photo.**

Self-Adhesive

3423 A2010 95c multi 2.25 1.10

International Bicycle and Motorcycle Exhibition, Milan — A2011

Serpentine Die Cut 11

2016, Nov. 8 **Photo.**

Self-Adhesive

3424 A2011 95c multi 2.25 1.10

DeCecco Pasta, 130th Anniv. — A2012

Serpentine Die Cut 11

2016, Nov. 18 **Photo.**

Self-Adhesive

3425 A2012 95c multi 2.25 1.10

UNICEF, 70th Anniv. — A2013

Serpentine Die Cut 11

2016, Nov. 20 **Photo.**

Self-Adhesive

3426 A2013 €1 blue	2.25	1.10

Victorious Youth Sculpture A2014

Villa Grock, Imperia — A2015

Fort Bard A2016

Santa Maria della Croce Church, Casarano — A2017

Alessandro Bonci Theater, Cesena — A2018

Santa Maria della Quercia Sanctuary and Bell Tower, Viterbo — A2019

Serpentine Die Cut 11

2016, Nov. 25 **Photo.**

Self-Adhesive

3427 A2014 95c multi	2.25	1.10
3428 A2015 95c multi	2.25	1.10
3429 A2016 95c multi	2.25	1.10
3430 A2017 95c multi	2.25	1.10
3431 A2018 95c multi	2.25	1.10
3432 A2019 95c multi	2.25	1.10
Nos. 3427-3432 (6)	13.50	6.60

French Academy in Rome, 350th Anniv. A2020

Serpentine Die Cut 11

2016, Nov. 30 **Photo.**

Self-Adhesive

3433 A2020 95c multi	2.25	1.10

See France No. 5149.

Sister Cities Agreement Between Rome and Paris, France, 60th Anniv. A2021

Serpentine Die Cut 11

2016, Nov. 30 **Photo.**

Self-Adhesive

3434 A2021 95c multi	2.25	1.10

Tommaso Maestrelli (1922-76), Soccer Player and Coach A2022

Serpentine Die Cut 11

2016, Dec. 2 **Photo.**

Self-Adhesive

3435 A2022 95c multi	2.25	1.10

Leonardo Ximenes (1716-86), Astronomer and Hydraulic Engineer A2023

Serpentine Die Cut 11

2016, Dec. 5 **Photo.**

Self-Adhesive

3436 A2023 95c multi	2.25	1.00

Italian Victory in Davis Cup Tennis Tournament, 40th Anniv. — A2024

Serpentine Die Cut 11

2016, Dec. 6 **Photo.**

Self-Adhesive

3437 A2024 95c multi	2.25	1.00

Madonna and Child, by Niccolò di Segna A2025

Reindeer A2026

Serpentine Die Cut 11

2016, Dec. 7 **Photo.**

Self-Adhesive

3438 A2025 95c multi	2.25	1.00
3439 A2026 €1 multi	2.40	1.10

Christmas.

Luigi Tenco (1938-67), Singer — A2027

Serpentine Die Cut 11

2017, Jan. 27 **Photo.**

Self-Adhesive

3440 A2027 95c multi	2.25	1.10

La Stampa Newspaper, 150th Anniv. — A2028

Serpentine Die Cut 11

2017, Feb. 9 **Photo.**

Self-Adhesive

3441 A2028 95c multi	2.25	1.00

Baccalà alla Vicentina — A2029

Serpentine Die Cut 11

2017, Mar. 1 **Photo.**

Self-Adhesive

3442 A2029 95c multi	2.25	1.00

Penitentiary Police Corps, 200th Anniv. A2030

Serpentine Die Cut 11

2017, Mar. 18 **Photo.**

Self-Adhesive

3443 A2030 95c multi	2.25	1.10

Padua Astronomical Observatory, 250th Anniv. — A2031

Serpentine Die Cut 11

2017, Mar. 21 **Photo.**

Self-Adhesive

3444 A2031 95c multi	2.25	1.10

Auricchio Cheese Company, 140th Anniv. A2032

Serpentine Die Cut 11

2017, Mar. 22 **Photo.**

Self-Adhesive

3445 A2032 95c multi	2.25	1.10

Treaty of Rome, 60th Anniv. A2033

Serpentine Die Cut 11

2017, Mar. 25 **Photo.**

Self-Adhesive

3446 A2033 95c multi	2.10	1.10

Borsalino Hats, 160th Anniv. — A2034

Serpentine Die Cut 11

2017, Apr. 4 **Photo.**

Self-Adhesive

3447 A2034 95c multi	2.10	1.10

Christ as Savior with Martin Luther, by Lucas Cranach, the Elder (1472-1553) A2035

Serpentine Die Cut 11

2017, Apr. 24 **Photo.**

Self-Adhesive

3448 A2035 95c multi 2.10 1.10

Protestant Reformation and Lutheran Church, 500th anniv.

Pio La Torre (1927-82), and Rosario di Salvo (1946-82), Politicians Killed by the Mafia — A2036

Serpentine Die Cut 11

2017, Apr. 28 **Photo.**

Self-Adhesive

3449 A2036 95c multi 2.10 1.10

Livy (59 B.C.-17 A.D.), Historian — A2037

Serpentine Die Cut 11

2017, May 2 **Photo.**

Self-Adhesive

3450 A2037 95c multi 2.10 1.10

Europa A2038

Designs: 95c, Doria Castle, Dolceacqua. €1, Scaligero Castle, Malcesine.

Serpentine Die Cut 11

2017, May 9 **Photo.**

Self-Adhesive

3451 A2038 95c multi 2.10 1.10
3452 A2038 €1 multi 2.25 1.10

Piccolo Theater, Milan — A2039

People's Theater, Castelfiorentino — A2040

Serpentine Die Cut 11

2017, May 19 **Photo.**

Self-Adhesive

3453 A2039 95c multi 2.10 1.10
3454 A2040 95c multi 2.10 1.10

G7 Summit, Taormina — A2041

Serpentine Die Cut 11

2017, May 26 **Photo.**

Self-Adhesive

3455 A2041 95c multi 2.10 1.10

Pistoia, 2017 Italian Capital of Culture A2042

Serpentine Die Cut 11

2017, May 19 **Photo.**

Self-Adhesive

3456 A2042 95c multi 2.10 1.10

Lambretta Motor Scooters, 70th Anniv. A2043

Serpentine Die Cut 11

2017, June 3 **Photo.**

Self-Adhesive

3457 A2043 95c multi 2.25 1.10

15th World Paragliding Championships, Monte Avena — A2044

Serpentine Die Cut 11

2017, June 1 **Photo.**

Self-Adhesive

3458 A2044 95c multi 2.10 1.10

Historical Museum of the Carabinieri, 80th Anniv. — A2045

Serpentine Die Cut 11

2017, June 6 **Photo.**

Self-Adhesive

3459 A2045 95c multi 2.25 1.10

Banca Popolare dell'Emilia Romagna, 150th Anniv. A2046

Serpentine Die Cut 11

2017, June 12 **Photo.**

Self-Adhesive

3460 A2046 95c multi 2.25 1.10

Montelupo Fiorentino Ceramics — A2047

Serpentine Die Cut 11

2017, June 17 **Photo.**

Self-Adhesive

3461 A2047 95c multi 2.25 1.10

Sixth Consecutive Championship of Juventus Soccer Team — A2048

Serpentine Die Cut 11

2017, July 1 **Photo.**

Self-Adhesive

3462 A2048 95c multi 2.25 1.10

Fiat Nuova 500, 60th Anniv. A2049

Serpentine Die Cut 11

2017, July 4 **Photo.**

Self-Adhesive

3463 A2049 95c multi 2.25 1.10

Vittorio Valletta (1883-1967), President of Fiat Automobiles A2050

Giuseppe di Vittorio (1892-1957), Politician — A2051

Serpentine Die Cut 11

2017, July 4 **Photo.**

Self-Adhesive

3464 A2050 95c multi 2.25 1.10
3465 A2051 95c multi 2.25 1.10

British Institute of Florence, Cent. A2052

Serpentine Die Cut 11

2017, July 22 **Photo.**

Self-Adhesive

3466 A2052 95c multi 2.25 1.10

SEMI-POSTAL STAMPS

Many issues of Italy and Italian Colonies include one or more semi-postal denominations. To avoid splitting sets, these issues are generally listed as regular postage, airmail, etc., unless all values carry a surtax.

Italian Flag — SP1

Italian Eagle Bearing Arms of Savoy — SP2

1915-16 **Typo.** ***Perf. 14***

B1 SP1 10c + 5c rose 8.50 12.00
B2 SP2 15c + 5c slate 6.75 9.50
B3 SP2 20c + 5c orange 32.50 65.00
Nos. B1-B3 (3) 47.75 *86.50*
Set, never hinged 125.00

No. B2 Surcharged

1916

B4 SP2 20c on 15c + 5c 20.00 55.00
Never hinged 50.00
a. Double overprint 800.00 —
Never hinged —
b. Inverted overprint 800.00 1,400.
Never hinged —
c. Pair, one without surcharge 1,800.
Never hinged 2,600.

Regular Issues of 1906-16 Overprinted in Blue or Red

1921

No.	Type	Description	Unused	Used
B5	A48	10c claret (Bl)	900.00	1,450.
a.		Double overprint	1,300.	
B6	A50	20c brn org (Bl)	1,250.	425.00
B7	A49	25c blue (R)	220.00	180.00
a.		Double overprint	360.00	
B8	A49	40c brn (Bl)	85.00	18.00
a.		Inverted overprint	425.00	700.00
		Nos. B5-B8 (4)	2,455.	2,073.
		Set, never hinged	5,000.	

Regular Issues of 1901-22 Overprinted in Black, Blue, Brown or Red

1922-23

No.	Type	Description	Unused	Used
B9	A48	10c cl ('23) (Bk)	110.00	100.00
a.		Blue ovpt.	85.00	80.00
		Never hinged	215.00	
b.		Brown ovpt.	85.00	80.00
		Never hinged	215.00	
d.		Blk ovpt. double	160.00	
e.		As "b," ovpt. double	160.00	
B10	A48	15c slate (Org)	290.00	*475.00*
a.		Blue ovpt.	900.00	725.00
		Never hinged	1,900.	
b.		Red overprint	360.00	575.00
		Never hinged	900.00	
B11	A50	20c brn org (Bk)	360.00	*475.00*
a.		Blue ovpt.	800.00	325.00
		Never hinged	1,575.	
B12	A49	25c blue (BK; '23)	100.00	87.50
b.		Red overprint	200.00	475.00
		Never hinged	725.00	
c.		Orange overprint	325.00	540.00
		Never hinged	800.00	
B12A	A49	30c org brn (Bk)	220.00	200.00
		Never hinged	540.00	
B13	A49	40c brn (Bl)	170.00	87.50
a.		Black ovpt.	190.00	87.50
		Never hinged	425.00	
b.		As "a," invtd. ovpt.	210.00	—
B14	A49	50c vio ('23) (Bk)	725.00	500.00
a.		Blue overprint		—
B15	A49	60c car (Bk)	2,200.	1,900.
		Never hinged	4,000.	
B15A	A49	85c choc (Bk)	290.00	*475.00*
		Never hinged	725.00	
B16	A46	1 l brn & grn ('23) (Bk)	3,250.	2,200.
a.		Inverted overprint	*5,000.*	
		Never hinged	*6,250.*	
		Set, never hinged	21,060.	

The stamps overprinted "B. L. P." were sold by the Government below face value to the National Federation for Assisting War Invalids. Most of them were affixed to special envelopes (Buste Lettere Postali) which bore advertisements. The Federation was permitted to sell these envelopes at a reduction of 5c from the face value of each stamp. The profits for the war invalids were derived from the advertisements.

Values of Nos. B5-B16 unused are for stamps with original gum. Most copies without gum or with part gum sell for about a quarter of values quoted. Uncanceled stamps affixed to the special envelopes usually sell for about half value.

The overprint on Nos. B9-B16 is wider (13½mm) than that on Nos. B5-B8 (11mm). The 1922-23 overprint exists both typo. and litho. on 10c, 15c, 20c and 25c; only litho. on 40c, 50c, 60c and 1 l; and only typo. on 30c and 85c.

Counterfeits of the B.L.P. overprints exist.

Administering Fascist Oath — SP3

1923, Oct. 29 — ***Perf. 14x14½***

No.	Type	Description	Unused	Used
B17	SP3	30c + 30c brown	32.50	*160.00*
B18	SP3	50c + 50c violet	32.50	*160.00*
a.		Horiz. pair, imperf between	1,900.	
B19	SP3	1 l + 1 l gray	32.50	*160.00*
		Nos. B17-B19 (3)	97.50	*480.00*
		Set, never hinged	250.00	

The surtax was given to the Benevolent Fund of the Black Shirts (the Italian National Militia).

Anniv. of the March of the Fascisti on Rome.

St. Maria Maggiore SP4

Pope Opening Holy Door SP8

Designs: 30c+15c, St. John Lateran. 50c+25c, St. Paul's Church. 60c+30c, St. Peter's Basilica. 5 l+2.50 l, Pope closing Holy Door.

1924, Dec. 24 — ***Perf. 12***

No.	Type	Description	Unused	Used
B20	SP4	20c + 10c dk grn & brn	4.50	*12.50*
B21	SP4	30c + 15c dk brn & brn	4.50	*12.50*
B22	SP4	50c + 25c vio & brn	4.50	*12.50*
B23	SP4	60c + 30c dp rose & brn	4.50	*40.00*
B24	SP8	1 l + 50c dp bl & vio	7.50	*40.00*
B25	SP8	5 l + 2.50 l org brn & vio	9.50	*80.00*
		Nos. B20-B25 (6)	35.00	*197.50*
		Set, never hinged	82.00	

The surtax was contributed toward the Holy Year expenses.

Castle of St. Angelo SP10

Designs: 50c+20c, 60c+30c, Aqueduct of Claudius. 1.25 l+50c, 1.25 l+60c, Capitol, Roman Forum. 5 l+2 l, 5 l+2.50 l, People's Gate.

Unwmk.

1926, Oct. 26 — **Engr.** — ***Perf. 11***

No.	Type	Description	Unused	Used
B26	SP10	40c + 20c dk brn & blk	3.25	*24.00*
B27	SP10	60c + 30c brn red & ol brn	3.25	*24.00*
B28	SP10	1.25 l + 60c bl grn & blk	3.25	*72.50*
B29	SP10	5 l + 2.50 l dk bl & blk	6.50	*225.00*
		Nos. B26-B29 (4)	16.25	*345.50*
		Set, never hinged	40.00	

Stamps inscribed "Poste Italiane" and "Fiere Campionaria di Tripoli" are listed in Libya.

1928, Mar. 1

No.	Type	Description	Unused	Used
B30	SP10	30c + 10c dl vio & blk	12.50	*65.00*
B31	SP10	50c + 20c ol grn & sl	21.00	*65.00*
B32	SP10	1.25 l + 50c dp bl & blk	25.00	*140.00*
B33	SP10	5 l + 2 l brn red & blk	55.00	*450.00*
		Nos. B30-B33 (4)	113.50	*720.00*
		Set, never hinged	275.00	

The tax on Nos. B26 to B33 was devoted to the charitable work of the Voluntary Militia for National Defense.

See Nos. B35-B38.

Victor Emmanuel II — SP14

1929, Jan. 4 — **Photo.** — ***Perf. 14***

No.	Type	Description	Unused	Used
B34	SP14	50c + 10c ol grn	4.75	*12.00*
		Never hinged	12.00	

50th anniv. of the death of King Victor Emmanuel II. The surtax was for veterans.

Type of 1926 Issue

Designs in same order.

1930, July 1 — **Engr.**

No.	Type	Description	Unused	Used
B35	SP10	30c + 10c dk grn & vio	2.40	*40.00*
B36	SP10	50c + 10c dk grn & bl grn	3.25	*30.00*
B37	SP10	1.25 l + 30c ind & grn	8.00	*95.00*
B38	SP10	5 l + 1.50 l blk brn & ol brn	16.00	*450.00*
		Nos. B35-B38 (4)	29.65	*615.00*
		Set, never hinged	74.00	

The surtax was for the charitable work of the Voluntary Militia for National Defense.

Militiamen at Ceremonial Fire with Quotation from Leonardo da Vinci — SP15

Symbolical of Pride for Militia — SP16

Symbolical of Militia Guarding Immortality of Italy SP17

Militia Passing Through Arch of Constantine SP18

1935, July 1 — **Photo.** — **Wmk. 140**

No.	Type	Description	Unused	Used
B39	SP15	20c + 10c rose red	9.50	*12.50*
B40	SP16	25c + 15c grn	9.50	*20.00*
B41	SP17	50c + 30c pur	9.50	*28.00*
B42	SP18	1.25 l + 75c blue	9.50	*42.50*
		Nos. B39-B42 (4)	38.00	*103.00*
		Set, never hinged	96.00	
		Nos. B39-B42,CB3 (5)	47.50	*143.00*
		Set, never hinged	117.50	

The surtax was for the Militia.

Roman Battle SP19

Roman Warriors SP20

1941, Dec. 13

No.	Type	Description	Unused	Used
B43	SP19	20c + 10c rose red	.75	*1.50*
B44	SP19	30c + 15c brown	.75	*1.90*
B45	SP20	50c + 25c violet	.75	*1.90*
B46	SP20	1.25 l + 1 l blue	1.50	*3.00*
		Nos. B43-B46 (4)	3.75	*8.30*
		Set, never hinged	7.50	

2,000th anniv. of the birth of Livy (59 B.C.-17 A.D.), Roman historian.

Catalogue values for unused stamps in this section, from this point to the end of the section, are for Never Hinged items.

Aid for Flood Victims — SP21

1995, Jan. 2 — **Photo.** — ***Perf. 13½x14***

No.	Type	Description	Unused	Used
B47	SP21	750 l +2250 l multi	5.00	5.00

Queen Helen (1873-1952) SP22

2002, Mar. 2 — **Photo.** — ***Perf. 13¼x14***

No.	Type	Description	Unused	Used
B48	SP22	41c + 21c multi	2.00	.85

Surtax for breast cancer research and prevention.

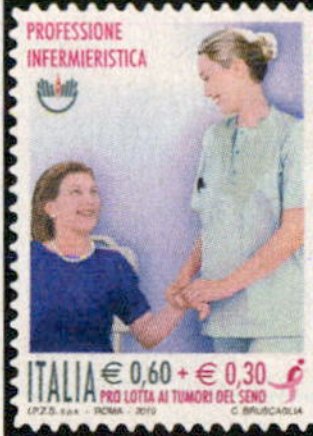

Intl. Commission on Occupational Health, 28th Congress — SP23

2006, Mar. 8 — **Photo.** — ***Perf. 13x13¼***

No.	Type	Description	Unused	Used
B49	SP23	60c +30c multi	2.50	1.75

Surtax for breast cancer research.

Nursing — SP24

Serpentine Die Cut 11

2010, May 16 — **Photo.**

Self-Adhesive

No.	Type	Description	Unused	Used
B50	SP24	60c +30c multi	2.25	2.25

Surtax for breast cancer research.

AIR POST STAMPS

Used values for Nos. C1-C105 are for postally used stamps with legible cancellations. Forged cancels on these issues abound, and expertization is srongly recommended.

Special Delivery No. E1 Ovptd.

1917, May **Wmk. 140** ***Perf. 14***

C1	SD1 25c rose red	24.00	*40.00*
	Never hinged	60.00	

Type of SD3 Surcharged in Black

1917, June 27

C2	SD3 25c on 40c violet	24.00	*47.50*
	Never hinged	60.00	

Type SD3 was not issued without surcharge.

AP2

1926-28 **Typo.**

C3	AP2	50c rose red ('28)	19.00	12.00
C4	AP2	60c gray	4.75	*12.00*
C5	AP2	80c brn vio & brn ('28)	35.00	*120.00*
C6	AP2	1 l blue	12.00	*12.00*
C7	AP2	1.20 l brn ('27)	24.00	*120.00*
C8	AP2	1.50 l buff	19.00	32.50
C9	AP2	5 l gray grn	40.00	*105.00*
		Nos. C3-C9 (7)	*153.75*	*413.50*
		Set, never hinged	385.00	

Nos. C4 and C6 Surcharged

1927, Sept. 16

C10	AP2 50c on 60c gray	24.00	*95.00*
a.	Pair, one without surcharge	2,250.	
C11	AP2 80c on 1 l blue	60.00	*450.00*
	Set, never hinged	200.00	

Pegasus AP3

Wings AP4

Spirit of Flight — AP5

Arrows AP6

1930-32 **Photo.** **Wmk. 140**

C12	AP4	25c dk grn ('32)	.25	.25
C13	AP3	50c olive brn	.25	.25
C14	AP5	75c org brn ('32)	.40	.25
C15	AP4	80c org red	.25	*.70*
C16	AP5	1 l purple	.25	.25
C17	AP6	2 l deep blue	.40	.25
C18	AP3	5 l dk green	.80	*1.60*
C19	AP3	10 l dp car	1.60	*6.50*
		Nos. C12-C19 (8)	*4.20*	10.05
		Set, never hinged	10.00	

The 50c, 1 l and 2 l were reprinted in 1942 with labels similar to those of Nos. 427-438, but were not issued. Value, set of 3: unused $550; never hinged $1,400.

For overprints see Nos. MC1-MC5. For overprints and surcharges on design AP6 see Nos. C52-C55; Yugoslavia-Ljubljana NB9-NB20, NC11-NC17.

Ferrucci Type of Postage

Statue of Ferrucci.

1930, July 10

C20	A104	50c purple	4.00	*17.50*
C21	A104	1 l orange brn	4.00	*20.00*
C22	A104	5 l + 2 l brn vio	16.00	*130.00*
		Nos. C20-C22 (3)	*24.00*	*167.50*
		Set, never hinged	60.00	

For overprinted types see Aegean Islands Nos. C1-C3.

Virgil Type of Postage

Jupiter sending forth his eagle.

1930, Oct. 21 **Photo.** **Wmk. 140**

C23	A106	50c lt brown	24.00	*40.00*
C24	A106	1 l orange	24.00	*45.00*

Engr.
Unwmk.

C25	A106	7.70 l + 1.30 l vio brn	55.00	*520.00*
C26	A106	9 l + 2 l indigo	65.00	*600.00*
		Nos. C23-C26 (4)	*168.00*	*1,205.*
		Set, never hinged	430.00	

The surtax on Nos. C25-C26 was for the National Institute Figli del Littorio.

For overprinted types see Aegean Islands Nos. C4-C7.

Trans-Atlantic Squadron — AP9

1930, Dec. 15 **Photo.** **Wmk. 140**

C27	AP9 7.70 l Prus bl & gray	450.00	*1,600.*
	Never hinged	900.00	
a.	Seven stars instead of six	2,000.	—
	Never hinged	4,000.	

Flight by Italian aviators from Rome to Rio de Janeiro, Dec. 1930-Jan. 12, 1931.

Leonardo da Vinci's Flying Machine AP10

Leonardo da Vinci AP11

Leonardo da Vinci — AP12

1932

C28	AP10	50c olive brn	4.75	*14.50*
C29	AP11	1 l violet	6.50	*16.00*
C30	AP11	3 l brown red	8.00	*40.00*
C31	AP11	5 l dp green	13.00	*47.50*
C32	AP10	7.70 l + 2 l dk bl	9.50	*200.00*
C33	AP11	10 l + 2.50 l blk brn	11.00	*340.00*
		Nos. C28-C33 (6)	*52.75*	*658.00*
		Set, never hinged	132.00	

Engr.
Unwmk.

C34	AP12 100 l brt bl & grnsh blk	45.00	*950.00*
	Never hinged	110.00	
a.	Thin paper	260.00	*1,800.*

Dante Alighieri Soc. and especially Leonardo da Vinci, to whom the invention of a flying machine has been attributed. Surtax was for the benefit of the Society.

Inscription on No. C34: "Man with his large wings by beating against the air will be able to dominate it and lift himself above it."

Issued: Nos. C28-C33, 3/14; No. C34, 8/6.

For overprinted types see Aegean Islands Nos. C8-C13.

Garibaldi's Home at Caprera AP13

Farmhouse where Anita Garibaldi Died AP14

50c, 1 l+25c, Garibaldi's home, Caprera. 2 l+50c, Anita Garibaldi. 5 l+1 l, Giuseppe Garibaldi.

1932, Apr. 6 **Photo.** **Wmk. 140**

C35	AP13	50c copper red	4.75	*8.00*
C36	AP14	80c deep green	5.00	*13.00*
C37	AP13	1 l + 25c red brn	8.00	*32.50*
C38	AP13	2 l + 50c dp bl	13.00	*45.00*
C39	AP14	5 l + 1 l dp grn	13.00	*52.50*
		Nos. C35-C39 (5)	*43.75*	*151.00*
		Set, never hinged	110.00	

50th anniv. of the death of Giuseppe Garibaldi, patriot. The surtax was for the benefit of the Garibaldi Volunteers.

For overprinted types see Aegean Islands Nos. C15-C19.

March on Rome Type of Postage

50c, Eagle sculpture and airplane. 75c, Italian buildings from the air.

1932, Oct. 27 ***Perf. 14***

C40	A146	50c dark brown	3.25	*9.50*
C41	A146	75c orange brn	9.50	*32.50*
		Set, never hinged	32.00	

Graf Zeppelin Issue

Zeppelin over Pyramid of Caius Cestius AP19

5 l, Tomb of Cecilia Metlella. 10 l, Stadium of Mussolini. 12 l, St. Angelo Castle and Bridge. 15 l, Roman Forum. 20 l, Imperial Avenue.

1933, Apr. 24

C42	AP19	3 l blk & grn	22.50	*125.00*
C43	AP19	5 l grn & brn	22.50	*140.00*
C44	AP19	10 l car & dl bl	22.50	*325.00*
C45	AP19	12 l dk bl & red org	22.50	*575.00*
C46	AP19	15 l dk brn & gray	22.50	*725.00*
C47	AP19	20 l org brn & bl	22.50	*800.00*
a.		Vertical pair, imperf. between	10,000.	
		Never hinged	15,000.	
		Nos. C42-C47 (6)	*135.00*	*2,690.*
		Set, never hinged	330.00	

Balbo's Trans-Atlantic Flight Issue

Italian Flag

King Victor Emmanuel III

Allegory "Flight" — AP25

No. C49, Colosseum at Rome, Chicago skyline. Nos. C48-C49 consist of 3 parts; Italian flag, Victor Emmanuel III, & scene arranged horizontally.

1933, May 20

C48	AP25	5.25 l + 19.75 l red, grn & ultra	125.00	*2,000.*
		Never hinged	250.00	
a.		Left stamp without ovpt.	*37,500.*	
		Never hinged	*57,500.*	
C49	AP25	5.25 l + 44.75 l grn, red & ultra	160.00	*2,000.*
		Never hinged	325.00	

Transatlantic Flight, Rome-Chicago, of 24-seaplane squadron led by Gen. Italo Balbo. Center and right sections paid postage. At left is registered air express label overprinted "APPARECCHIO" and abbreviated pilot's name. Twenty triptychs of each value differ in name overprint.

No. C49 overprinted "VOLO DI RITORNO/ NEW YORK-ROMA" was not issued; flight canceled. Value: unused $36,000; never hinged $54,000.

Nos. C48-C49 exist imperf. at bottom. Value, set $112,000.

For overprints see Nos. CO1, Aegean Islands C26-C27.

Type of Air Post Stamp of 1930 Surcharged in Black

1934, Jan. 18

C52	AP6	2 l on 2 l yel	10.50	*95.00*
C53	AP6	3 l on 2 l yel grn	10.50	*140.00*
C54	AP6	5 l on 2 l rose	10.50	*275.00*
C55	AP6	10 l on 2 l vio	10.50	*400.00*
		Nos. C52-C55 (4)	42.00	*910.00*
		Set, never hinged	104.00	

For use on mail carried on a special flight from Rome to Buenos Aires.

Annexation of Fiume Type

25c, 75c, View of Fiume Harbor. 50c, 1 l+50c, Monument to the Dead. 2 l+1.50 l, Venetian Lions. 3 l+2 l, Julian wall.

1934, Mar. 12

C56	A166	25c green	.95	*4.00*
C57	A166	50c brown	.95	*2.40*
C58	A166	75c org brn	.95	*9.50*
C59	A166	1 l + 50c dl vio	.95	*16.00*
C60	A166	2 l + 1.50 l dl bl	.95	*21.00*
C61	A166	3 l + 2 l blk brn	.95	*23.00*
		Nos. C56-C61 (6)	4.80	*76.40*
		Set, never hinged	14.40	

Airplane and View of Stadium AP32

Soccer Player and Plane AP33

Airplane and Stadium Entrance AP35

Airplane over Stadium AP34

1934, May 24

C62	AP32	50c car rose	11.00	*52.50*
C63	AP33	75c gray blue	17.50	*65.00*
C64	AP34	5 l + 2.50 l ol grn	52.50	*425.00*
C65	AP35	10 l + 5 l brn blk	52.50	*650.00*
		Nos. C62-C65 (4)	133.50	*1,193.*
		Set, never hinged	332.50	

2nd World Soccer Championships.

For overprinted types see Aegean Islands Nos. C28-C31.

Zeppelin under Fire AP36

Air Force Memorial — AP40

Designs: 25c, 80c, Zeppelin under fire. 50c, 75c, Motorboat patrol. 1 l+50c, Desert infantry. 2 l+1 l, Plane attacking troops.

1934, Apr. 24

C66	AP36	25c dk green	3.25	*8.00*
C67	AP36	50c gray	3.25	*9.50*
C68	AP36	75c dk brown	3.25	*11.00*
C69	AP36	80c slate blue	3.25	*14.50*
C70	AP36	1 l + 50c red brn	8.00	*32.50*
C71	AP36	2 l + 1 l brt bl	11.50	*40.00*
C72	AP40	3 l + 2 l brn blk	16.00	*47.50*
		Nos. C66-C72 (7)	48.50	*149.00*
		Set, never hinged	120.00	

Cent. of the institution of the Military Medal of Valor.

For overprinted types see Aegean Islands Nos. C32-C38.

King Victor Emmanuel III — AP41

1934, Nov. 5

C73	AP41	1 l purple	3.25	*95.00*
C74	AP41	2 l brt blue	3.25	*105.00*
C75	AP41	4 l red brown	7.50	*325.00*
C76	AP41	5 l dull green	7.50	*425.00*
C77	AP41	8 l rose red	23.00	*525.00*
C78	AP41	10 l brown	25.00	*800.00*
		Nos. C73-C78 (6)	69.50	*2,275.*
		Set, never hinged	160.00	

65th birthday of King Victor Emmanuel III and the nonstop flight from Rome to Mogadiscio.

For overprint see No. CO2.

Muse Playing Harp AP42

Angelic Dirge for Bellini AP43

Scene from Bellini Opera, La Sonnambula — AP44

1935, Sept. 24

C79	AP42	25c dull yellow	4.75	*13.00*
C80	AP42	50c brown	4.75	*11.00*
C81	AP42	60c rose carmine	16.00	*32.50*
C82	AP43	1 l + 1 l purple	24.00	*240.00*
C83	AP44	5 l + 2 l green	32.50	*325.00*
		Nos. C79-C83 (5)	82.00	*621.50*
		Set, never hinged	204.00	

Vincenzo Bellini, (1801-35), operatic composer.

Quintus Horatius Flaccus Type

25c, Seaplane in Flight. 50c, 1 l+1 l, Monoplane over valley. 60c, Oak and eagle. 5 l+2 l, Ruins of ancient Rome.

1936, July 1

C84	A197	25c dp green	3.25	*12.00*
C85	A197	50c dk brown	5.00	*12.00*
C86	A197	60c scarlet	8.50	*20.00*
C87	A197	1 l + 1 l vio	19.00	*240.00*
C88	A197	5 l + 2 l slate bl	24.00	*350.00*
		Nos. C84-C88 (5)	59.75	*634.00*
		Set, never hinged	150.00	

Child of the Balilla AP49

Heads of Children AP50

1937, June 28

C89	AP49	25c dk bl grn	8.00	*27.50*
C90	AP50	50c brown	16.00	17.50
C91	AP49	1 l purple	12.00	*35.00*
C92	AP50	2 l + 1 l dk bl	16.00	*200.00*
C93	AP49	3 l + 2 l org	20.00	*275.00*
C94	AP50	5 l + 3 l rose lake	24.00	*340.00*
		Nos. C89-C94 (6)	96.00	*895.00*
		Set, never hinged	240.00	

Summer Exhibition for Child Welfare. The surtax on Nos. C92-C94 was used to support summer camps for poor children.

Prosperous Italy AP51

50c, Prolific Italy. 80c, Apollo's steeds. 1 l+1 l, Map & Roman Standard. 5 l+1 l, Augustus Caesar.

1937, Sept. 23

C95	AP51	25c red vio	8.00	*16.00*
C96	AP51	50c olive brn	8.00	*12.00*
C97	AP51	80c orange brn	24.00	*22.50*
C98	AP51	1 l + 1 l dk bl	30.00	*175.00*
C99	AP51	5 l + 1 l dl vio	65.00	*340.00*
		Nos. C95-C99 (5)	135.00	*565.50*
		Set, never hinged	335.00	

Bimillenary of the birth of Augustus Caesar (Octavianus) on the occasion of the exhibition opened in Rome by Mussolini on Sept. 22nd, 1937.

For overprinted types see Aegean Islands Nos. C39-C43.

King Victor Emmanuel III — AP56

25c, 3 l, King Victor Emmanuel III. 50c, 1 l, Dante Alighieri. 2 l, 5 l, Leonardo da Vinci.

1938, Oct. 28

C100	AP56	25c dull green	4.75	6.50
C101	AP56	50c dk yel brn	4.75	6.50
C102	AP56	1 l violet	8.00	*9.50*
C103	AP56	2 l royal blue	8.00	*36.00*
C104	AP56	3 l brown car	13.00	*45.00*
C105	AP56	5 l dp green	15.00	*65.00*
		Nos. C100-C105 (6)	54.00	*170.50*
		Set, never hinged	134.00	

Proclamation of the Empire.

Plane and Clasped Hands AP59

Swallows in Flight AP60

1945-47 Wmk. 277 Photo. *Perf. 14*

C106	AP59	1 l slate bl	.25	.25
C107	AP60	2 l dk blue	.25	.25
C108	AP59	3.20 l red org	.30	.25
C109	AP60	5 l dk green	.25	.25
C110	AP59	10 l car rose	.25	.25
C111	AP60	25 l dk bl ('46)	6.50	13.00
C112	AP60	25 l brown ('47)	.25	.25
C113	AP59	50 l dk grn ('46)	12.00	20.00
C114	AP59	50 l violet ('47)	.25	.25
		Nos. C106-C114 (9)	20.30	34.75
		Set, never hinged	40.00	

Issued: Nos. C111, C113, 7/13/46; NOs. C112, C114, 4/21/47.

See Nos. C130-C131. For surcharges and overprints see Nos. C115, C136, 1LNC1-1LNC7, Trieste C1-C6, C17-C22.

No. C108 Surcharged in Black

1947, July 1

C115	AP59	6 l on 3.20 l	.25	.25
		Never hinged	.25	
a.		Horiz. pair, one without surcharge	*2,000.*	
b.		Inverted surcharge		*26,000.*

Radio on Land — AP61

Designs: 6 l, 25 l, Radio on land. 10 l, 35 l, Radio at sea. 20 l, 50 l, Radio in the skies.

1947, Aug. 1 Photo. *Perf. 14*

C116	AP61	6 l dp violet	.25	.25
C117	AP61	10 l dk car rose	.25	.25
C118	AP61	20 l dp orange	.40	1.00
C119	AP61	25 l aqua	.90	1.50
C120	AP61	35 l brt blue	1.50	2.40
C121	AP61	50 l lilac rose	2.00	3.00
		Nos. C116-C121 (6)	5.30	8.40
		Set, never hinged	6.50	

50th anniv. of radio.

For overprints see Trieste Nos. C7-C12.

Plane over Capitol Bell Tower — AP65

1948

C123	AP65	100 l green	.90	.25
C124	AP65	300 l lilac rose	.25	.60
C125	AP65	500 l ultra	.65	.75

Engr.

C126	AP65	1000 l dk brown	.65	2.50
a.		Vert. pair, imperf. btwn.	*275.00*	*275.00*
b.		Perf. 14x13	2.00	2.40
		Nos. C123-C126 (4)	2.45	4.10
		Set, never hinged	6.50	

See No. C132-C135. For overprints see Trieste Nos. C13-C16, C23-C26.

St. Catherine Carrying Cross AP66

200 l, St. Catherine with outstretched arms.

1948, Mar. 1 **Photo.**

C127 AP66 100 l bl vio & brn org 45.00 40.00
C128 AP66 200 l dp blue & bis 27.50 24.00
Set, never hinged 130.00

600th anniversary of the birth of St. Catherine of Siena, patroness of Italy.

Catalogue values for unused stamps in this section, from this point to the end of the section, are for Never Hinged items.

Giuseppe Mazzini (1805-1872), Patriot — AP67

1955, Dec. 31 **Wmk. 303** ***Perf. 14***

C129 AP67 100 l Prus green 1.50 1.00

Types of 1945-46, 1948

1955-62 **Wmk. 303** ***Perf. 14***

C130 AP60 5 l green ('62) .25 .25
C131 AP59 50 l vio ('57) .25 .25
C132 AP65 100 l green .60 .25
C133 AP65 300 l lil rose .70 .55
C134 AP65 500 l ultra ('56) 1.00 .90

Engr.

Perf. 13½

C135 AP65 1000 l maroon ('59) 1.75 2.00
Nos. C130-C135 (6) 4.55 4.20

Fluorescent Paper

See note below No. 998.

No. C132 was issued on both ordinary and fluorescent paper. The design of the fluorescent stamp is smaller.

Airmail stamps issued only on fluorescent paper are Nos. C139-C140.

Type of 1945-46 Surcharged in Ultramarine

1956, Feb. 24

C136 AP59 120 l on 50 l mag 1.00 *1.25*

Visit of Pres. Giovanni Gronchi to the US and Canada.

Madonna of Bruges, by Michelangelo AP68

Wmk. 303

1964, Feb. 18 **Photo.** ***Perf. 14***

C137 AP68 185 l black .30 .25

Michelangelo Buonarroti (1475-1564), artist.

Verrazano Type of Regular Issue

1964, Nov. 21 **Wmk. 303** ***Perf. 14***

C138 A481 130 l blk & dull grn .30 .25

See note after No. 901.

Adoration of the Kings, by Gentile da Fabriano — AP69

1970, Dec. 12 **Photo.** **Unwmk.**

C139 AP69 150 l multicolored .25 .25

Christmas 1970.

Aviation Type of Regular Issue

Design: F-104S Starfighter over Aeronautical Academy, Pozzuoli.

1973, Mar. 28 **Photo.** ***Perf. 14x13½***

C140 A590 150 l multicolored .30 .25

AIR POST SEMI-POSTAL STAMPS

Holy Year Type of Postage

Dome of St. Peter's, dove with olive branch, Church of the Holy Sepulcher.

Wmk. 140

1933, Oct. 23 **Photo.** ***Perf. 14***

CB1 A163 50c + 25c org brn 2.40 *27.50*
CB2 A163 75c + 50c brn vio 4.00 *160.00*
Set, never hinged 16.00

Symbolical of Military Air Force — SPAP2

1935, July 1

CB3 SPAP2 50c + 50c brown 9.50 *40.00*

The surtax was for the Militia.

AIR POST SPECIAL DELIVERY STAMPS

Garibaldi, Anita Garibaldi, Plane APSD1

Wmk. 140

1932, June 2 **Photo.** ***Perf. 14***

CE1 APSD1 2.25 l + 1 l 16.00 *52.50*
CE2 APSD1 4.50 l + 1.50 l 16.00 *52.50*
Set, never hinged 80.00

Death of Giuseppe Garibaldi, 50th anniv.

For overprinted types see Aegean Islands Nos. CE1-CE2.

Airplane and Sunburst APSD2

1933-34

CE3 APSD2 2 l gray blk ('34) .25 *3.25*
CE4 APSD2 2.25 l gray blk 4.75 *200.00*
Set, never hinged 12.50

For overprint and surcharge see Nos. MCE1, Yugoslavia-Ljubljana NCE1.

Annexation of Fiume Type

Flag raising before Fascist headquarters.

1934, Mar. 12

CE5 A166 2 l + 1.25 l 4.75 *27.50*
CE6 A166 2.25 l + 1.25 l .95 *22.50*
CE7 A166 4.50 l + 2 l .95 *24.00*
Nos. CE5-CE7 (3) 5.60 *77.00*
Set, never hinged 17.00

Triumphal Arch in Rome APSD4

1934, Aug. 31

CE8 APSD4 2 l + 1.25 l brown 16.00 *45.00*
CE9 APSD4 4.50 l + 2 l cop red 20.00 *45.00*
Set, never hinged 90.00

Centenary of the institution of the Military Medal of Valor.

For overprinted types see Aegean Islands Nos. CE3-CE4.

AIR POST OFFICIAL STAMPS

Balbo Flight Type of Air Post Stamp of 1933 Overprinted

1933 **Wmk. 140** ***Perf. 14***

CO1 AP25 5.25 l + 44.75 l red, grn & red vio 3,300. *14,000.*
Never hinged 5,000.

Air Post Stamp of 1934 Overprinted in Gold

1934

CO2 AP41 10 l blue blk 875.00 *14,000.*
Never hinged 1,750.

65th birthday of King Victor Emmanuel III and the non-stop flight from Rome to Mogadiscio.

PNEUMATIC POST STAMPS

PN1

1913-28 **Wmk. 140** **Typo.** ***Perf. 14***

D1 PN1 10c brown 2.40 *32.50*
D2 PN1 15c brn vio ('28) 3.25 *16.00*
a. 15c dull violet ('21) 3.25 *45.00*
D3 PN1 15c rose red ('28) 16.00 *40.00*
D4 PN1 15c claret ('28) 4.75 *16.00*
D5 PN1 20c brn vio ('25) 24.00 *65.00*
D6 PN1 30c blue ('23) 8.00 *225.00*
D7 PN1 35c rose red ('27) 25.00 *475.00*
D8 PN1 40c dp red ('26) 27.50 *450.00*
Nos. D1-D8 (8) 110.90 *1,320.*

Nos. D1, D2a, D5-D6, D8 Surcharged Like Nos. C10-C11

1924-27

D9 PN1 15c on 10c 4.75 *40.00*
D10 PN1 15c on 20c ('27) 9.50 *72.50*
D11 PN1 20c on 10c ('25) 9.50 *80.00*
D12 PN1 20c on 15c ('25) 12.50 *47.50*
D13 PN1 35c on 40c ('27) 21.00 *400.00*
D14 PN1 40c on 30c ('25) 12.50 *425.00*
Nos. D9-D14 (6) 69.75 *1,065.*

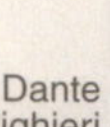

Dante Alighieri PN2

Galileo Galilei PN3

1933, Mar. 29 **Photo.**

D15 PN2 15c dark violet .45 *1.60*
D16 PN3 35c rose red .45 *7.25*

Similar to Types of 1933, Without "REGNO"

1945, Oct. 22 **Wmk. 277**

D17 PN2 60c dull brown .25 *3.25*
D18 PN3 1.40 l dull blue .25 *3.25*

Minerva — PN6

1947, Nov. 15

D19 PN6 3 l rose lilac 4.50 *9.50*
D20 PN6 5 l aqua .25 .25
Set, never hinged 7.00

Catalogue values for unused stamps in this section, from this point to the end of the section, are for Never Hinged items.

1958-66 **Wmk. 303**

D21 PN6 10 l rose red .25 .25
D22 PN6 20 l sapphire ('66) .25 .25

SPECIAL DELIVERY STAMPS

Victor Emmanuel III — SD1

1903-26 **Typo.** **Wmk. 140** ***Perf. 14***

E1 SD1 25c rose red 47.50 1.20
a. Imperf., pair 475.00 600.00
E2 SD1 50c dl red ('20) 4.75 1.60
E3 SD1 60c dl red ('22) 9.50 1.20
E4 SD1 70c dl red ('25) 1.60 .35
E5 SD1 1.25 l dp bl ('26) .80 .25
Nos. E1-E5 (5) 64.15 4.60

No. E1 is almost always found poorly centered, and it is valued thus.

For overprints and surcharges see Nos. C1, E11, E13, Austria NE1-NE2, Dalmatia E1, Offices in Crete, Offices in Africa, Offices in Turkish Empire.

Victor Emmanuel III — SD2

1908-26

E6 SD2 30c blue & rose 2.25 *4.00*
E7 SD2 2 l bl & red ('25) 8.00 *160.00*
E8 SD2 2.50 l bl & red ('26) 3.25 *10.50*
Nos. E6-E8 (3) 13.50 *174.50*

The 1.20 lire blue and red (see No. E12) was prepared in 1922, but not issued. Value: unused $200; never hinged $400.

For surcharges and overprints see Nos. E10, E12, Austria NE3, Dalmatia E2, Offices in China, Offices in Africa, Offices in Turkish Empire.

SD3

1917, Nov.

E9 SD3 25c on 40c violet 40.00 *125.00*

Type SD3 not issued without surcharge. For surcharge see No. C2.

No. E6 Surcharged

1921, Oct.

E10 SD2 1.20 l on 30c 2.40 *27.50*
a. Comma in value omitted 12.50 *55.00*
b. Double surcharge 350.00

No. E2 Surcharged

1922, Jan. 9

E11 SD1 60c on 50c dull red 47.50 1.60
a. Inverted surcharge 275.00 275.00
b. Double surcharge 2,000.
c. Imperf., pair 475.00 *600.00*

Type of 1908 Surcharged

1924, May

E12 SD2 1.60 l on 1.20 l bl & red 3.25 *135.00*
a. Double surch., one inverted 350.00

No. E3 Surcharged like No. E11

1925, Apr. 11

E13 SD1 70c on 60c dull red 1.60 1.20
a. Inverted surcharge 340.00 *400.00*

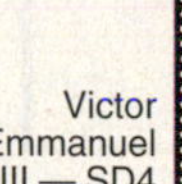

Victor Emmanuel III — SD4

1932-33 **Photo.**

E14 SD4 1.25 l green .30 .25
E15 SD4 2.50 l dp org ('33) .30 *6.50*

For overprints and surcharges see Italian Social Republic Nos. E1-E2; Yugoslavia-Ljubljana NB5-NB8, NE1.

March on Rome Type of Postage

1.25 l Ancient Pillars and Entrenchments. 2.50 l, Head of Mussolini, trophies of flags, etc.

1932, Oct. 27

E16 A146 1.25 l deep green 2.40 1.60
E17 A146 2.50 l deep orange 8.00 *160.00*
Set, never hinged 26.00

"Italia" SD7

1945, Aug. **Wmk. 277** ***Perf. 14***

E18 SD7 5 l rose carmine .25 1.00

Winged Foot SD8

Rearing Horse and Torch-Bearer — SD9

1945-51

E19 SD8 5 l henna brn .25 .25
E20 SD9 10 l deep blue .25 .25
E21 SD9 15 l dk car rose ('47) 1.60 .25
E22 SD8 25 l brt red org ('47) 15.00 .25
E23 SD8 30 l dp vio ('46) 3.00 3.25
E24 SD8 50 l lil rose ('51) 17.50 .25
E25 SD9 60 l car rose ('48) 25.00 .25
Nos. E19-E25 (7) 62.60 4.75
Set, never hinged 140.00

See No. E32. For overprints see Nos. 1LNE1-1LNE2, Trieste E1-E4, E6-E7.

Type of Regular Issue of 1948 Inscribed: "Espresso"

1948, Sept. 18 **Photo.** ***Perf. 14***

E26 A272 35 l violet *(Naples)* 45.00 22.50
Never hinged 120.00

Catalogue values for unused stamps in this section, from this point to the end of the section, are for Never Hinged items.

Type of 1945-51

1955, July 7 **Wmk. 303** ***Perf. 14***

E32 SD8 50 l lilac rose 4.50 .25

Etruscan Winged Horses SD10

1958-76 **Photo.**

Size: 36 ½x20 ¼mm

E33 SD10 75 l magenta .25 .25

Size: 36x20mm

E34 SD10 150 l dl bl grn ('68) .25 .25
a. Size: 36 ½x20 ¼mm ('66) .50 .25
E35 SD10 250 l blue ('74) .30 .25
E36 SD10 300 l brown ('76) .40 .25
Nos. E33-E36 (4) 1.20 1.00

Nos. E34-E36 are fluorescent.

AUTHORIZED DELIVERY STAMPS

For the payment of a special tax for the authorized delivery of correspondence privately instead of through the post office.

AD1

1928 **Wmk. 140** **Typo.** ***Perf. 14***

EY1 AD1 10c dull blue 9.50 .60
a. Perf. 11 37.50 4.75

Coat of Arms — AD2

1930 **Photo.** ***Perf. 14***

EY2 AD2 10c dark brown .25 .25

For surcharge and overprint see Nos. EY3, Italian Social Republic EY1.

No. EY2 Surcharged in Black

1945

EY3 AD2 40c on 10c dark brown .50 1.50

Coat of Arms — AD3

1945-46 **Photo.** **Wmk. 277**

EY4 AD3 40c dark brown .25 1.00
EY5 AD3 1 l dk brown ('46) 3.25 5.00

For overprint see Trieste No. EY1.

"Italia" — AD4

1947-52 **Size: 27 ½x22 ½mm**

EY6 AD4 1 l brt grnsh bl .25 .35
EY7 AD4 8 l brt red ('48) 12.00 .35

Size: 20 ½x16 ½mm

EY8 AD4 15 l violet ('49) 31.00 .30
EY9 AD4 20 l rose vio ('52) 2.00 .25
Nos. EY6-EY9 (4) 45.25 1.25
Set, never hinged 125.00

For overprints see Trieste Nos. EY2-EY5.

Catalogue values for unused stamps in this section, from this point to the end of the section, are for Never Hinged items.

Italia Type of 1947

1955-90 **Wmk. 303** **Photo.** ***Perf. 14***

Size: 20 ½x16 ½mm

EY11 AD4 20 l rose vio .25 .25
EY12 AD4 30 l Prus grn ('65) .25 .25
EY13 AD4 35 l ocher ('74) .25 .25
EY14 AD4 110 l lt ultra ('77) .25 .25
EY15 AD4 270 l brt pink ('84) .75 .25

Size: 19 ½x16 ½mm

EY16 AD4 300 l rose & grn ('87) .60 .40
EY17 AD4 370 l tan & brn vio .65 .40
Nos. EY11-EY17 (7) 3.00 2.05

Issue date: 370 l, Sept. 24, 1990.

POSTAGE DUE STAMPS

Unused values for Postage Due stamps are for examples with full original gum. Stamps with part gum or privately gummed sell for much less.

D1

1863 **Unwmk.** **Litho.** ***Imperf.***

J1 D1 10c yellow 2,000. 240.00
No gum 80.00
a. 10c yellow orange 2,250. 260.00
No gum 90.00

D2

1869 **Wmk. 140** **Typo.** ***Perf. 14***

J2 D2 10c buff 9,000. 80.00

D3

1870-1925

J3 D3 1c buff & mag 4.00 12.00
J4 D3 2c buff & mag 8.00 24.00
J5 D3 5c buff & mag .80 .80
J6 D3 10c buff & mag ('71) .80 .80
b. Imperf, single *2,200.*
J7 D3 20c buff & mag ('94) 8.00 .80
a. Imperf., pair 240.00 *240.00*
J8 D3 30c buff & mag 2.40 1.20
b. Imperf, pair *6,000.* 3,600.
J9 D3 40c buff & mag 2.40 2.40
J10 D3 50c buff & mag 2.40 1.20
b. Imperf, single *2,000.*
J11 D3 60c buff & mag 120.00 4.75
J12 D3 60c buff & brn ('25) 40.00 16.00
J13 D3 1 l lt bl & brn 8,000. 20.00
J14 D3 1 l bl & mag ('94) 45.00 1.25
a. Imperf., pair 400.00 350.00
J15 D3 2 l lt bl & brn 7,250. 32.50
J16 D3 2 l bl & mag ('03) 65.00 9.50
J17 D3 5 l bl & brn ('74) 500.00 35.00
J18 D3 5 l bl & mag ('03) 250.00 55.00
J19 D3 10 l bl & brn ('74) *9,500.* 35.00
J20 D3 10 l bl & mag ('94) 225.00 8.00

Early printings of 5c, 10c, 30c, 40c, 50c and 60c were in buff and magenta, later ones (1890-94) in stronger shades. The earlier, paler shades and their inverted-numeral varieties sell for considerably more than those of the later shades. Values are for the later shades.

For surcharges and overprints see Nos. J25-J27, Offices in China, Offices in Turkish Empire; Austria Nos. NJ1-NJ16.

Numeral Inverted

J3a	D3	1c	4,750.	3,000.
J4a	D3	2c	*12,000.*	4,500.
J5a	D3	5c	6.50	12.00
J6a	D3	10c	8.00	16.00
J7b	D3	20c	65.00	60.00
J8a	D3	30c	12.00	*24.00*
J9a	D3	40c	550.00	*650.00*
J10a	D3	50c	60.00	80.00
J11a	D3	60c	550.00	400.00
J13a	D3	1 l		—
J14b	D3	1 l	5,200.	4,500.
J15a	D3	2 l		*3,000.*
J16a	D3	2 l	*4,500.*	*4,500.*
J17a	D3	5 l		1,400.
J19a	D3	10 l	*2,700.*	450.00

D4

1884-1903

J21 D4 50 l green 87.50 95.00
J22 D4 50 l yellow ('03) 95.00 47.50
J23 D4 100 l claret 87.50 47.50
J24 D4 100 l blue ('03) 72.50 20.00
Nos. J21-J24 (4) 342.50 210.00

Nos. J3 & J4 Surcharged in Black

1890-91

J25 D3 10c on 2c 130.00 35.00
J26 D3 20c on 1c 525.00 27.50
a. Inverted surcharge *10,000.*
J27 D3 30c on 2c 2,000. 12.00
a. Inverted surcharge *2,750.*
Nos. J25-J27 (3) 2,655. 74.50

Coat of Arms
D6 D7

1934 Photo.
J28 D6 5c brown .80 .40
J29 D6 10c blue .80 .40
J30 D6 20c rose red .80 .40
J31 D6 25c green .80 .40
J32 D6 30c red org .80 .40
J33 D6 40c blk brn .80 4.75
J34 D6 50c violet .80 .40
J35 D6 60c slate blk .80 14.00
J36 D7 1 l red org .80 .40
J37 D7 2 l green .80 .40
J38 D7 5 l violet 1.60 .80
J39 D7 10 l blue 6.50 12.00
J40 D7 20 l car rose 12.50 40.00
Nos. J28-J40 (13) 28.60 74.75

For overprints and surcharges see Italian Social Republic #J1-J13, Yugoslavia-Ljubljana NJ14-NJ22.

D8 D9

1945-46 Unwmk. *Perf. 14*
J41 D8 5c brn, *grayish* ('46) 2.00 6.00
J42 D8 10c blue .40 1.25
J43 D8 20c rose red, *grayish* ('46) 2.00 1.25
J44 D8 25c dk grn .40 1.25
J45 D8 30c red org .40 1.25
J46 D8 40c blk brn .40 1.25
J47 D8 50c violet .40 1.25
J48 D8 60c black .40 6.00
J49 D9 1 l red org .40 1.25
J50 D9 2 l green .40 1.25
J51 D9 5 l violet .40 1.25
J52 D9 10 l blue .40 1.25
J53 D9 20 l car rose .45 5.00
Nos. J41-J53 (13) 8.45 29.50

Nos. J41 and J43 have yellow gum.

Wmk. 277
J54 D8 10c dark blue .40 4.50
J55 D8 25c dk grn 1.00 5.00
J56 D8 30c red org 1.00 9.00
J57 D8 40c blk brn .40 .45
J58 D8 50c vio ('46) 5.75 7.00
J59 D8 60c bl blk ('46) 7.50 20.00
J60 D9 1 l red org .40 .45
J61 D9 2 l dk grn .40 .45
J62 D9 5 l violet 12.00 9.00
J63 D9 10 l dark blue 18.00 9.00
J64 D9 20 l car rose 29.00 25.00
Nos. J54-J64 (11) 75.85 89.85
Set, never hinged 175.00

For overprints see Trieste Nos. J1, J3-J5.

D10

1947-54 Photo. *Perf. 14*
J65 D10 1 l red orange .25 .25
J66 D10 2 l dk green .40 .25
J67 D10 3 l carmine 1.10 2.00
J68 D10 4 l brown .50 1.25
J69 D10 5 l violet .80 .25
J70 D10 6 l vio blue 2.00 3.00
J71 D10 8 l rose vio 10.00 3.00
J72 D10 10 l deep blue .75 .25
J73 D10 12 l golden brn 3.00 2.00
J74 D10 20 l lil rose 30.00 .25
J75 D10 25 l dk red ('54) 30.00 .80
J76 D10 50 l aqua 25.00 .25
J77 D10 100 l org yel ('52) 8.00 .25

Engr.
Perf. 13½x14
J78 D10 500 l dp bl & dk car ('52) 10.00 .45
a. Perf. 11x13 10.00 .45
b. Perf. 13 10.00 .45
Nos. J65-J78 (14) 121.80 14.25
Set, never hinged 290.00

For overprints see Trieste Nos. J2, J6-J29.

Catalogue values for unused stamps in this section, from this point to the end of the section, are for Never Hinged items.

1955-91 Wmk. 303 Photo. *Perf. 14*
J83 D10 5 l violet .25 .25
J85 D10 8 l rose vio 175.00 175.00
J86 D10 10 l deep blue .25 .25
J87 D10 20 l lil rose .25 .25
J88 D10 25 l dk red .25 .25
J89 D10 30 l gray brn ('61) .25 .25
J90 D10 40 l dl brn ('66) .25 .25
J91 D10 50 l aqua .25 .25
a. Type II .30 .25
J92 D10 100 l org yel ('58) .25 .25

Engr.
J93 D10 500 l dp bl & dk car ('61) 2.90 .25
J94 D10 900 l dp car & gray grn ('84) 1.20 .25
J95 D10 1500 l brn & org 2.50 .50
Nos. J83,J86-J95 (11) 8.60 3.00

Type I imprint on No. J91 reads: "1ST POL. STATO OFF. CARET VALORI". Type II imprint reads: "I.P.Z.S. OFF. CARTE VALORI" (1992). No. J91 has lighter background with more distinguishable lettering and design.
No. J92 exists with both Type I & Type II imprints.
Nos. J92 and J93 exist with "I. P. Z. S. ROMA" imprint.
Issue date: 1500 l, Feb. 20, 1991.

MILITARY STAMPS

Regular Stamps, 1929-42, Overprinted

1943 Wmk. 140 *Perf. 14*
M1 A90 5c ol brn .40 2.50
M2 A92 10c dk brn .40 2.50
M3 A93 15c slate grn .40 2.50
M4 A91 20c rose red .40 2.50
M5 A94 25c dp grn .40 2.50
M6 A95 30c ol brn .40 2.50
M7 A95 50c purple .40 2.50
M8 A91 1 l dk pur 3.75 20.00
M9 A94 1.25 l deep blue .40 4.00
M10 A92 1.75 l red org .40 4.00
M11 A93 2 l car lake .40 4.00
M12 A95a 5 l rose red .40 4.00
M13 A93 10 l purple 3.00 29.00
Nos. M1-M13 (13) 11.15 82.50
Set, never hinged 27.50

Due to a shortage of regular postage stamps during 1944-45, this issue was used for ordinary mail. "P. M." stands for "Posta Militare."

MILITARY AIR POST STAMPS

Air Post Stamps, 1930 Overprinted Like Nos. M1-M13 in Black

1943 Wmk. 140 *Perf. 14*
MC1 AP3 50c olive brown .45 3.00
MC2 AP5 1 l purple .45 3.00
MC3 AP6 2 l deep blue .45 15.00
MC4 AP3 5 l dark green 3.75 25.00
MC5 AP3 10 l deep carmine 3.75 32.50
Nos. MC1-MC5 (5) 8.85 78.50
Set, never hinged 25.00

MILITARY AIR POST SPECIAL DELIVERY STAMPS

No. CE3 Overprinted Like Nos. M1-M13

1943 Wmk. 140 *Perf. 14*
MCE1 APSD2 2 l gray black 3.50 29.00

MILITARY SPECIAL DELIVERY STAMPS

No. E14 Overprinted Like Nos. M1-M13

1943 Wmk. 140 *Perf. 14*
ME1 SD4 1.25 l green .45 10.00

OFFICIAL STAMPS

O1

1875 Wmk. 140 Typo. *Perf. 14*
O1 O1 2c lake 3.25 4.75
O2 O1 5c lake 3.25 4.75
O3 O1 20c lake 1.60 1.60
O4 O1 30c lake 1.60 3.25
O5 O1 1 l lake 4.75 20.00
O6 O1 2 l lake 12.50 60.00
O7 O1 5 l lake 55.00 225.00
O8 O1 10 l lake 95.00 160.00
Nos. O1-O8 (8) 176.95 479.35

For surcharges see Nos. 37-44.
Stamps inscribed "Servizio Commissioni" were used in connection with the postal service but not for the payment of postage.

NEWSPAPER STAMP

N1

Typographed, Numeral Embossed
1862 Unwmk. *Imperf.*
P1 N1 2c buff 52.50 110.00
a. Numeral double 475.00 1,650.
b. Printed on gummed side 500.00

Black 1c and 2c stamps of similar type are listed under Sardinia.

PARCEL POST STAMPS

King Humbert I — PP1

1884-86 Wmk. 140 Typo. *Perf. 14*
Various Frames
Q1 PP1 10c olive gray 125.00 120.00
Q2 PP1 20c blue 260.00 175.00
Q3 PP1 50c claret 9.50 14.50
Q4 PP1 75c blue grn 9.50 14.50
Q5 PP1 1.25 l orange 20.00 32.50
Q6 PP1 1.75 l brown 24.00 120.00
Nos. Q1-Q6 (6) 448.00 476.50

For surcharges see Nos. 58-63.

Parcel Post stamps from No. Q7 onward were used by affixing them to the waybill so that one half remained on it following the parcel, the other half staying on the receipt given the sender. Most used halves are right halves. Complete stamps were and are obtainable canceled, probably to order.
Both unused and used values are for complete stamps.

PP2

1914-22 Wmk. 140 *Perf. 13*
Q7 PP2 5c brown 4.75 20.00
Q8 PP2 10c deep blue 4.75 20.00
Q9 PP2 20c black ('17) 17.50 20.00
Q10 PP2 25c red 24.00 20.00
Q11 PP2 50c orange 35.00 40.00
Q12 PP2 1 l violet 40.00 16.00
Q13 PP2 2 l green 40.00 20.00
Q14 PP2 3 l bister 47.50 55.00
Q15 PP2 4 l slate 60.00 72.50
Q16 PP2 10 l lilac ('22) 95.00 72.50
Q17 PP2 12 l red brn ('22) 160.00 450.00
Q18 PP2 15 l ol grn ('22) 140.00 450.00
Q19 PP2 20 l brn vio ('22) 120.00 450.00
Nos. Q7-Q19 (13) 788.50 1,706.

Halves Used
Q7-Q14, each .40
Q15 .80
Q16 1.60
Q17 4.00
Q18 4.00
Q19 6.50

Imperfs exist. Value per pair: 20c, 25c, 50c, 2 l, 3l, 4 l: $50 each; 10l $225.

No. Q7 Surcharged

Q20 PP2 30c on 5c brown 1.60 24.00
Half stamp 3.25
Q21 PP2 60c on 5c brown 1.60 24.00
Half stamp 3.25
Q22 PP2 1.50 l on 5c brown 6.50 190.00
Half stamp 6.50
a. Double surcharge 250.00

No. Q16 Surcharged

Q23 PP2 3 l on 10 l rose lil 6.50 80.00
Half stamp 3.25
Nos. Q20-Q23 (4) 16.20 318.00

PP3

1927-39 Wmk. 140
Q24 PP3 5c brn ('38) .80 3.25
Q25 PP3 10c dp bl ('39) .80 3.25
Q26 PP3 25c red ('32) .80 3.25
Q27 PP3 30c ultra .80 4.00
Q28 PP3 50c org ('32) .80 3.25
Q29 PP3 60c red .80 4.00
Q30 PP3 1 l lilac ('31) .80 3.25
Q31 PP3 1 l brn vio ('36) 24.00 87.50
Q32 PP3 2 l grn ('32) .80 4.00
Q33 PP3 3 l yel bister .80 9.50
a. Printed on both sides 65.00
Q34 PP3 4 l gray .80 9.50
Q35 PP3 10 l rose lil ('34) 2.40 55.00
Q36 PP3 20 l lil brn ('33) 3.25 80.00
Nos. Q24-Q36 (13) 37.65 269.75

Value of used halves: Nos. Q24-Q34, each 40c; Q35 80c; Q36 $4.
For overprints see Italian Social Republic Nos. Q1-Q12.

Nos. Q24-Q30, Q32-Q36 Overprinted Between Halves in Black

1945 Wmk. 140 *Perf. 13*
Q37 PP3 5c brown 1.50 8.00
Q38 PP3 10c dp blue 1.50 8.00
Q39 PP3 25c red 1.50 8.00
Q40 PP3 30c ultra 15.00 20.00
Q41 PP3 50c orange 1.50 6.50
Q42 PP3 60c red 1.50 6.50
Q43 PP3 1 l lilac 1.50 6.50
Q44 PP3 2 l green 1.50 6.50
Q45 PP3 3 l yel bister 1.50 6.50
Q46 PP3 4 l gray 1.50 6.50
Q47 PP3 10 l rose lilac 17.50 65.00
Q48 PP3 20 l lilac brn 35.00 125.00
Nos. Q37-Q48 (12) 81.00 273.00
Set, never hinged 150.00

Halves Used
Q37-48, each .25

Type of 1927
With Fasces Removed

1946 Typo.
Q55 PP3 1 l lilac 2.25 5.00
Q56 PP3 2 l green 1.50 5.00
Q57 PP3 3 l yellow org 2.25 8.50
Q58 PP3 4 l gray 4.50 8.50
Q59 PP3 10 l rose lilac 40.00 75.00
Q60 PP3 20 l lilac brn 50.00 250.00
Nos. Q55-Q60 (6) 100.50 352.00
Set, never hinged 200.00

Halves Used

Q55-Q58, each	.25
Q59	.80
Q60	1.25

PP4

PP5

Perf. 13¼, 13¼x14, 12¼x13x13¼

1946-54 Photo. Wmk. 277

No.	Type	Description	Unused	Used
Q61	PP4	25c dl vio bl ('48)	.25	.25
Q62	PP4	50c brn ('47)	.40	.25
Q63	PP4	1 l gldn brn ('47)	.50	.25
Q64	PP4	2 l lt bl grn ('47)	.80	.75
Q65	PP4	3 l red org ('47)	.40	.25
Q66	PP4	4 l gray blk ('47)	6.00	*9.00*
Q67	PP4	5 l lil rose ('47)	.40	.25
a.		Perf. 13¼	.60	.25
Q68	PP4	10 l violet	6.00	.55
a.		Perf. 13¼	6.00	.55
Q69	PP4	20 l lilac brn	2.75	.60
a.		Perf. 13¼	6.50	.80
Q70	PP4	30 l plum ('52)	3.00	5.00
a.		Perf. 13¼	3.00	*5.00*
Q71	PP4	50 l rose red	12.00	2.00
a.		Perf. 13¼	12.00	2.00
Q72	PP4	100 l sapphire	30.00	30.00
a.		Perf. 13¼	30.00	30.00
Q73	PP4	200 l grn ('48)	45.00	75.00
a.		Perf. 13¼	45.00	80.00
Q74	PP4	300 l brn car ('48), perf 13¼	550.00	900.00
Q75	PP4	500 l brn ('48)	50.00	100.00
a.		Perf. 12¼x13¼	50.00	100.00

Engr.

Perf. 13

No.	Type	Description	Unused	Used
Q76	PP5	1000 l ultra ('54)	2,000.	2,750.
		Nos. Q61-Q76 (16)	2,708.	3,874.
		Set, never hinged	5,000.	

Halves Used

Q61-Q73, each	.25
Q74	8.00
Q75	3.25
Q76	22.50

For overprints see Trieste Nos. Q1-Q26.

Catalogue values for unused stamps in this section, from this point to the end of the section, are for Never Hinged items.

Perf. 12½x13

1955-59 Wmk. 303 Photo.

Without Imprint

No.	Type	Description	Unused	Used
Q77	PP4	25c vio bl	.25	.25
Q77A	PP4	50c brn ('56)	3.50	*4.00*
Q78	PP4	5 l lil rose ('59)	.25	.25
Q79	PP4	10 l violet	.25	.25
Q80	PP4	20 l lil brn	.25	.25
Q81	PP4	30 l plum ('56)	.25	.25
Q82	PP4	40 l dl vio ('57)	.25	.25
Q83	PP4	50 l rose red	.25	.25
Q84	PP4	100 l sapphire	.25	.25
Q85	PP4	150 l org brn ('57)	.25	.25
Q86	PP4	200 l grn ('56)	.30	.25
Q87	PP4	300 l brn car ('58)	.60	.25
Q88	PP4	400 l gray blk ('57)	.55	.45
Q89	PP4	500 l brn ('57)	1.25	.50

Engr.

Perf. 13

No.	Type	Description	Unused	Used
Q90	PP5	1000 l ultra ('57)	1.25	.75
Q91	PP5	2000 l red brn & car ('57)	4.50	4.00
		Nos. Q77-Q91 (16)	14.20	*12.45*

Halves Used

Q77-Q89, each	.25
Q90-Q91, each	.40

1960-66 Photo. *Perf. 12½x13*

No.	Type	Description	Unused	Used
Q92	PP4	60 l bright lilac	.25	.25
Q93	PP4	140 l dull red	.30	.25
Q94	PP4	280 l yellow	.60	.45
Q95	PP4	600 l olive bister	1.00	.50
Q96	PP4	700 l blue ('66)	2.00	.95
Q97	PP4	800 l dp org ('66)	2.40	.95
		Nos. Q92-Q97 (6)	6.55	3.35

Halves Used

Q92-Q93, each	.25
Q94	.25
Q95	.40
Q96-Q97, each	.25

Imprint: "I.P.S.-Off. Carte Valori-Roma"

1973, Mar. Photo. Wmk. 303

No.	Type	Description	Unused	Used
Q98	PP4	20 l lilac brown	.25	.25
Q99	PP4	30 l plum	.25	.25

PARCEL POST AUTHORIZED DELIVERY STAMPS

For the payment of a special tax for the authorized delivery of parcels privately instead of through the post office.

PAD1

1953 Wmk. 277 Photo. *Perf. 13*

No.	Type	Description	Unused	Used
QY1	PAD1	40 l org red	12.00	*13.00*
QY2	PAD1	50 l ultra	140.00	*140.00*
QY3	PAD1	75 l brown	80.00	*80.00*
QY4	PAD1	110 l lil rose	90.00	*100.00*
		Nos. QY1-QY4 (4)	322.00	*333.00*
		Set, never hinged	400.00	

Halves Used

QY1	.35
QY2	1.25
QY3	3.25
QY4	3.25

For overprints see Trieste Nos. QY1-QY4.

Catalogue values for unused stamps in this section, from this point to the end of the section, are for Never Hinged items.

1956-58 Wmk. 303 *Perf. 12½x13*

No.	Type	Description	Unused	Used
QY5	PAD1	40 l org red	2.25	2.25
QY6	PAD1	50 l ultra	2.50	2.50
QY7	PAD1	60 l brt vio bl ('58)	7.00	4.00
QY8	PAD1	75 l brown	325.00	140.00
QY9	PAD1	90 l lil ('58)	.35	*.40*
QY10	PAD1	110 l lil rose	325.00	200.00
QY11	PAD1	120 l grnsh bl ('58)	.35	*.40*
		Nos. QY5-QY11 (7)	662.45	349.55

Halves Used

QY5-QY6, each	.25
QY7	.90
QY8,QY10	8.00
QY9	.30
QY11	.25

1960-81

No.	Type	Description	Unused	Used
QY12	PAD1	70 l green ('66)	9.00	9.00
QY13	PAD1	80 l brown	.30	.30
QY14	PAD1	110 l org yel	.30	.30
QY15	PAD1	140 l black	.30	.30
QY16	PAD1	150 l car rose ('68)	.30	.30
QY17	PAD1	180 l red ('66)	.50	.50
QY18	PAD1	240 l dk bl ('66)	1.00	.70

Engr. *Perf. 13½*

No.	Type	Description	Unused	Used
QY19	PAD1	500 l ocher ('76)	1.40	1.40
QY20	PAD1	600 l bl grn ('79)	1.50	1.50
QY21	PAD1	900 l ultra ('81)	1.60	1.60
		Nos. QY12-QY21 (10)	16.20	15.90

Halves Used

QY12	4.00
QY13-QY15, QY18, QY21, each	.25
QY16, QY17, QY19, each	.25
QY20	.35

PAD2

Perf. 14x13½

1984 Photo. Wmk. 303

No.	Type	Description	Unused	Used
QY22	PAD2	3000 l multi	3.50	3.50

OCCUPATION STAMPS

Issued under Austrian Occupation

Austria Nos. M49-M64 Surcharged in Black

Austria Nos. M65-M67 Surcharged in Black

1918 Unwmk. *Perf. 12½*

No.	Type	Description	Unused	Used
N1	M3	2c on 1h grnsh bl	.25	*.45*
N2	M3	3c on 2h red org	.25	*.40*
N3	M3	4c on 3h ol gray	.25	*.45*
N4	M3	6c on 5h ol grn	.25	*.40*
N5	M3	7c on 6h vio	.25	*.45*
a.		Perf. 12½x11½	16.00	*95.00*
N6	M3	11c on 10h org brn	.25	*.45*
N7	M3	13c on 12h blue	.25	*.45*
N8	M3	16c on 15h brt rose	.25	*.40*
N9	M3	22c on 20h red brn	.25	*.45*
a.		Perf. 11½	24.00	*80.00*
N10	M3	27c on 25h ultra	.65	*1.60*
N11	M3	32c on 30h slate	.65	*1.60*
N12	M3	43c on 40h ol bis	.65	*1.60*
a.		Perf. 11½	16.00	*72.50*
N13	M3	53c on 50h dp grn	.65	*1.60*
N14	M3	64c on 60h rose	.65	*1.60*
N15	M3	85c on 80h dl bl	.65	*1.20*
N16	M3	95c on 90h dk vio	.65	*1.20*
N17	M4	2 l 11c on 2k rose, *straw*	.65	2.40
N18	M4	3 l 16c on 3k grn, *bl*	1.20	3.25
N19	M4	4 l 22c on 4k rose, *grn*	2.40	5.50
		Nos. N1-N19 (19)	11.05	*25.45*

Exist imperf. Values: unused, $160; never hinged, $325. See No. N33.

Austria Nos. M60-M82 Surcharged in Black

1918

No.	Type	Description	Unused
N20	M5	2c on 1h grnsh bl	6.00
N21	M5	3c on 2h orange	6.00
N22	M5	4c on 3h ol gray	6.00
N23	M5	6c on 5h yel grn	6.00
N24	M5	11c on 10h dk brn	6.00
N25	M5	22c on 20h red	6.00
N26	M5	27c on 25h blue	6.00
N27	M5	32c on 30h bister	6.00
N28	M5	48c on 45h dk sl	6.00
N29	M5	53c on 50h dp grn	6.00
N30	M5	64c on 60h violet	6.00
N31	M5	85c on 80h rose	6.00
N32	M5	95c on 90h brn vio	6.00
N33	M4	1 l 6c on 1k ol bister, *blue*	6.00
		Nos. N20-N33 (14)	84.00

Nos. N20 to N33 inclusive were never placed in use in the occupied territory. They were, however, on sale at the Post Office in Vienna for a few days before the Armistice.

Exist imperf. Values unused, $325; never hinged, $800.

OCCUPATION SPECIAL DELIVERY STAMPS

Bosnia Nos. QE1-QE2 Surcharged

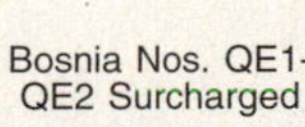

1918 Unwmk. *Perf. 12½*

No.	Type	Description	Unused	Used
NE1	SH1	3c on 2h ver	12.00	*24.00*
NE2	SH1	6c on 5h dp grn	12.00	*24.00*

Nos. NE1-NE2 are on yellowish paper. Reprints on white paper sell for about $1.25 a set.

OCCUPATION POSTAGE DUE STAMPS

Bosnia Nos. J16, J18-J19, J21-J24 Surcharged Like Nos. NE1-NE2

1918 Unwmk. *Perf. 12½*

No.	Type	Description	Unused	Used
NJ1	D2	6c on 5h red	3.25	*6.50*
a.		Perf. 11½	8.00	*12.00*
NJ2	D2	11c on 10h red	2.40	*8.00*
a.		Perf. 11½	8.00	*12.00*
NJ3	D2	16c on 15h red	.80	*3.25*
NJ4	D2	27c on 25h red	.80	*3.25*
NJ5	D2	32c on 30h red	.80	*4.00*
NJ6	D2	43c on 40h red	.80	*4.00*
NJ7	D2	53c on 50h red	.80	*4.00*
		Nos. NJ1-NJ7 (7)	9.65	*33.00*

OCCUPATION NEWSPAPER STAMPS

Austrian Nos. MP1-MP4 Surcharged

1918 Unwmk. *Perf. 12½*

No.	Type	Description	Unused	Used
NP1	MN1	3c on 2h blue	.80	*1.20*
a.		Perf. 11½	12.00	*40.00*
NP2	MN1	7c on 6h org	1.10	*2.40*
NP3	MN1	11c on 10h car	1.10	*2.40*
NP4	MN1	22c on 20h brn	1.10	*2.75*
a.		Perf. 11½	125.00	*250.00*
		Nos. NP1-NP4 (4)	4.10	*8.75*

A.M.G.

Issued jointly by the Allied Military Government of the United States and Great Britain, for civilian use in areas under Allied occupation.

Catalogue values for unused stamps in this section are for Never Hinged items.

OS4

Offset Printing

"Italy Centesimi" (or "Lira") in Black

1943 Unwmk. *Perf. 11*

No.	Type	Description	Unused	Used
1N1	OS4	15c pale orange	1.00	1.50
1N2	OS4	25c pale citron	1.00	1.50
1N3	OS4	30c light gray	1.50	1.50
1N4	OS4	50c light violet	1.50	1.50
1N5	OS4	60c orange yellow	1.50	1.50
1N6	OS4	1 l lt yel green	1.50	1.50
1N7	OS4	2 l deep rose	1.50	4.00
1N8	OS4	5 l light blue	3.00	*7.50*
1N9	OS4	10 l buff	3.00	*7.50*
		Nos. 1N1-1N9 (9)	15.50	*28.00*

Italy Nos. 217, 220 and 221 Overprinted in Blue, Vermilion, Carmine or Orange

1943, Dec. 10 Wmk. 140 *Perf. 14*

No.	Type	Description	Unused	Used
1N10	A91	20c rose red (Bl)	2.00	*4.00*
1N11	A93	35c dp blue (C)	17.50	*25.00*
a.		35c deep blue (V)	35.00	*35.00*

1N13	A95 50c purple (C)		1.00	*2.00*
a.	50c purple (O)		1.00	*2.00*
	Nos. 1N10-1N13 (3)		20.50	*31.00*

Nos. 1N1-1N9 were for use in Sicily, Nos. 1N10-1N13 for use in Naples.

VENEZIA GIULIA

Catalogue values for unused stamps in this section are for Never Hinged items.

Stamps of Italy, 1929 to 1945 Overprinted in Black

a

On Stamps of 1929

1945-47 Wmk. 140 *Perf. 14*

1LN1	A92 (a) 10c dk brown	.30	*.35*
1LN1A	A91 (a) 20c rose red ('47)	.40	*.50*

b

On Stamps of 1945

1945 Wmk. 277 *Perf. 14*

1LN2	A249 (a) 20c rose red	.35	*.50*
1LN3	A248 (a) 60c sl grn	.45	.35
1LN4	A249 (a) 1 l dp vio	.30	.35
1LN5	A251 (a) 2 l dk red	.35	.35
1LN6	A252 (b) 5 l dk red	.65	.50
1LN7	A251 (a) 10 l purple	.90	*1.25*
	Nos. 1LN2-1LN7 (6)	3.00	*3.30*

On Stamps of 1945

1945-46 Unwmk.

1LN7A	A250(a) 10c dk brn ('46)	.30	.25
1LN7B	A249(a) 20c rose red ('46)	.25	*.50*
1LN8	A251(a) 60c red org	.25	.25
	Nos. 1LN7A-1LN8 (3)	.80	*1.00*

On Air Post Stamp of 1930

1945 Wmk. 140 *Perf. 14*

1LN9	AP3 (a) 50c olive brn	.25	*.50*

1946 On Stamp of 1929

1LN10	A91 (a) 20 l lt green	2.25	*6.50*

On Stamps of 1945

Wmk. 277

1LN11	A260 (a) 25 l dk green	8.00	*9.00*
1LN12	A260 (a) 50 l dk vio brn	8.00	*15.00*

Italy No. 477 Overprinted in Black

1LN13	A261 100 l car lake	29.00	*90.00*
	Nos. 1LN10-1LN13 (4)	47.25	*120.50*

Stamps of Italy, 1945-47 Overprinted Type "a" in Black

1947

1LN14	A259 25c brt bl grn	.25	1.00
1LN15	A258 2 l dk claret brn	.60	*.35*
1LN16	A259 3 l red	.45	.25
1LN17	A259 4 l red org	.70	.25
1LN18	A257 6 l deep violet	2.00	*1.90*
1LN19	A259 20 l dk red vio	*55.00*	7.50
	Nos. 1LN14-1LN19 (6)	*59.00*	*11.25*

Some denominations of the Venezia Giulia A.M.G. issues exist with inverted overprint; several values exist in horizontal and vertical pairs, one stamp without overprint.

OCCUPATION AIR POST STAMPS

Catalogue values for unused stamps in this section are for Never Hinged items.

Italy Nos. C106-C107 and C109-C113 Overprinted in Black

1946-47 Wmk. 277 *Perf. 14*

1LNC1	AP59 1 l sl blue ('47)	.40	*5.00*
1LNC2	AP60 2 l dk blue ('47)	.40	*2.50*
1LNC3	AP60 5 l dk grn ('47)	3.00	*1.50*
1LNC4	AP59 10 l car rose ('47)	3.00	*1.50*
1LNC5	AP60 25 l dk blue	3.00	*1.50*
1LNC6	AP60 25 l brown ('47)	35.00	*47.50*
1LNC7	AP59 50 l dk green	6.50	*11.00*
	Nos. 1LNC1-1LNC7 (7)	51.30	*70.50*

Nos. 1LNC5 and 1LNC7 exist with inverted overprint; No. 1LNC5 with double overprint, one inverted.

OCCUPATION SPECIAL DELIVERY STAMPS

Catalogue values for unused stamps in this section are for Never Hinged items.

Italy Nos. E20 and E23 Overprinted in Black

1946 Wmk. 277 *Perf. 14*

1LNE1	SD9 10 l deep blue	4.00	*1.60*
1LNE2	SD8 30 l deep violet	8.75	*19.00*

ITALIAN SOCIAL REPUBLIC

On Sept. 15, 1943, Mussolini proclaimed the establishment of a Republican fascist party and a new fascist government. This government's authority covered only the Northern Italy area occupied by the Germans.

Catalogue values for unused stamps in this section are for hinged stamps. Never hinged examples are valued at 2-2.5 times the values shown.

Italy Nos. 218, 219, 221 to 223 and 231 Overprinted in Black or Red

a

b

c

1944 Wmk. 140 *Perf. 14*

1	A94(a) 25c deep grn	.35	*2.00*
2	A95(b) 30c ol brn (R)	.35	*2.00*
3	A95(c) 50c pur (R)	.35	*2.00*
4	A94(a) 75c rose red	.35	*2.40*
5	A94(b) 1.25 l dp bl (R)	.35	*2.40*
5A	A94(b) 50 l dp vio (R)	200.00	*4,000.*
	Nos. 1-5 (5)	1.75	10.80

Nos. 1 to 5 exist with overprint inverted. Value, each: unused $30; used $37.50.

No. 1 exists with overprint "b." Value: unused, $60; used $800.

Counterfeits of No. 5A exist.

Italy Nos. 427 to 438 Overprinted Same in Black or Red

6	A243(a) 25c deep green	.45	*3.50*
7	A244(a) 25c deep green	.45	*3.50*
8	A245(a) 25c deep green	.45	*3.50*
9	A246(a) 25c deep green	.45	*3.50*
10	A243(b) 30c ol brn (R)	.45	*30.00*
11	A244(b) 30c ol brn (R)	.45	*30.00*
12	A245(b) 30c ol brn (R)	.45	*30.00*
13	A246(b) 30c ol brn (R)	.45	*30.00*
14	A243(c) 50c purple (R)	.45	*3.50*
15	A244(c) 50c purple (R)	.45	*3.50*
16	A245(c) 50c purple (R)	.45	*3.50*
17	A246(c) 50c purple (R)	.45	*3.50*
	Nos. 6-17 (12)	5.40	*148.00*

Loggia dei Mercanti, Bologna — A1

Basilica of San Lorenzo, Rome — A2

Drummer Boy — A3

1944 Photo. *Perf. 14*

18	A1 20c crimson	.25	*.75*
19	A2 25c green	.25	*.75*
20	A3 30c brown	.25	*.75*
21	A3 75c dark red	.25	*1.75*
	Nos. 18-21 (4)	1.00	4.00

For surcharges see Italy Nos. 461-462.

Church of St. Ciriaco, Ancona A4

Monte Cassino Abbey A5

Loggia dei Mercanti, Bologna A6

Basilica of San Lorenzo, Rome A7

Statue of "Rome" A8

Basilica of St. Maria delle Grazie, Milan A9

1944 Unwmk.

22	A4 5c brown	.25	*.30*
23	A5 10c brown	.25	.25
24	A6 20c rose red	.25	.25
25	A7 25c deep green	.25	.25
26	A3 30c brown	.25	.25
27	A8 50c purple	.25	.25
28	A3 75c dark red	1.00	*21.00*
29	A5 1 l purple	.25	.25

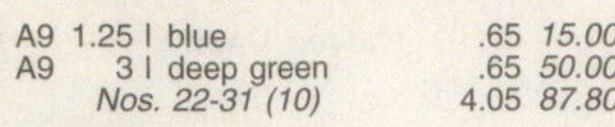

30	A9 1.25 l blue	.65	*15.00*
31	A9 3 l deep green	.65	*50.00*
	Nos. 22-31 (10)	4.05	*87.80*

Bandiera Brothers — A10

1944, Dec. 6

32	A10 25c deep green	.25	*1.00*
33	A10 1 l purple	.25	*1.00*
34	A10 2.50 l rose red	.25	*7.50*
	Nos. 32-34 (3)	.75	*9.50*

Cent. of the execution of Attilio (1811-44) and Emilio Bandiera (1819-44), revolutionary patriots who were shot at Cosenza, July 23, 1844, by Neapolitan authorities after an unsuccessful raid.

This set was overprinted in 1945 by the committee of the National Philatelic Convention to publicize that gathering at Venice.

SPECIAL DELIVERY STAMPS

Italy Nos. E14 and E15 Overprinted in Red or Black

1944 Wmk. 140 *Perf. 14*

E1	SD4 1.25 l green (R)	.35	*.80*
E2	SD4 2.50 l deep orange	.35	*20.00*

Cathedral, Palermo SD1

1944 Photo.

E3	SD1 1.25 l green	.25	*1.00*

AUTHORIZED DELIVERY STAMP

Catalogue values for unused stamps in this section are for Never Hinged items.

Italy No. EY2 Overprinted

1944 Wmk. 140 *Perf. 14*

EY1	AD2 10c dark brown	.25	*.80*

Italy No. EY2 with overprint type a and type b were prepared but not issued. Values: type a, unused $135, never hinged $425; type b, unused $250, never hinged $800.

POSTAGE DUE STAMPS

Italy #J28-J40 Overprinted Like #EY1

1944 Wmk. 140 *Perf. 14*

J1	D6 5c brown	4.00	*5.00*
J2	D6 10c blue	4.00	*5.00*
J3	D6 20c rose red	4.00	*5.00*
J4	D6 25c green	4.00	*5.00*
J5	D6 30c red org	4.00	*10.00*
J6	D6 40c blk brn	4.00	*15.00*
J7	D6 50c violet	4.00	*5.00*

No.	Type	Description	Unused	Used
J8	D6	60c slate blk	20.00	*50.00*
J9	D7	1 l red org	7.00	*5.00*
J10	D7	2 l green	14.00	*32.50*
J11	D7	5 l violet	40.00	*225.00*
J12	D7	10 l blue	65.00	*550.00*
J13	D7	20 l car rose	65.00	*850.00*
		Nos. J1-J13 (13)	239.00	*1,763.*

PARCEL POST STAMPS

Both unused and used values are for complete stamps.

Italian Parcel Post Stamps and Types of 1927-39 Overprinted

1944 Wmk. 140 *Perf. 13*

No.	Type	Description	Unused	Used
Q1	PP3	5c brown	5.00	*65.00*
Q2	PP3	10c deep blue	5.00	*65.00*
Q3	PP3	25c carmine	5.00	*65.00*
Q4	PP3	30c ultra	5.00	*65.00*
Q5	PP3	50c orange	5.00	*65.00*
Q6	PP3	60c red	5.00	*450.00*
Q7	PP3	1 l lilac	5.00	*65.00*
Q8	PP3	2 l green	300.00	*2,000.*
Q9	PP3	3 l yel bister	45.00	*750.00*
Q10	PP3	4 l gray	75.00	*850.00*
Q11	PP3	10 l rose lilac	160.00	*3,000.*
Q12	PP3	20 l lilac brn	450.00	*4,250.*
		Nos. Q1-Q12 (12)	1,065.	11,690.

No parcel post service existed in 1944. Nos. Q1-Q12 were used undivided, for regular postage.

ITALY OFFICES ABROAD

Stamps listed under this heading were issued for use in the Italian Post Offices which, for various reasons, were maintained from time to time in foreign countries.

100 Centesimi = 1 Lira

GENERAL ISSUE

Values of Italian Offices Abroad stamps vary tremendously according to condition. Quotations are for very fine examples, and values for unused stamps are for examples with original gum as defined in the catalogue introduction. Extremely fine or superb examples sell at much higher prices, and fine or poor examples sell at greatly reduced prices. In addition, unused examples without gum are discounted severely.

Very fine examples of Nos. 1-17 will have perforations barely clear of the frameline or design due to the narrow spacing of the stamps on the plates.

Italian Stamps with Corner Designs Slightly Altered and Overprinted

1874-78 Wmk. 140 *Perf. 14*

No.	Type	Description	Unused	Used
1	A6	1c ol grn	47.50	*47.50*
a.		Inverted overprint	*40,000.*	
c.		2 dots in lower right corner	87.50	*275.00*
d.		Three dots in upper right corner	400.00	*1,750.*
e.		Without overprint	75,000.	
2	A7	2c org brn	52.50	*55.00*
a.		Without overprint	75,000.	
3	A8	5c slate grn	1,200.	55.00
a.		Lower right corner not altered	*24,000.*	2,600.
4	A8	10c buff	3,600.	120.00
a.		Upper left corner not altered	*30,000.*	1,800.
b.		None of the corners altered	—	*75,000.*
c.		Lower corners not altered		*12,000.*
5	A8	10c blue ('78)	725.00	35.00
6	A15	20c blue	2,800.	55.00
7	A15	20c org ('78)	13,000.	32.50
8	A8	30c brown	8.00	*32.50*
a.		None of the corners altered		*55,000.*
b.		Right lower corner not altered	—	—
c.		Double overprint		—
9	A8	40c rose	8.00	*32.50*
10	A8	60c lilac	27.50	*350.00*
11	A13	2 l vermilion	350.00	*1,100.*

1881

No.	Type	Description	Unused	Used
12	A17	5c green	47.50	20.00
13	A17	10c claret	9.50	*16.00*
14	A17	20c orange	9.50	*9.50*
a.		Double overprint, on piece		—
15	A17	25c blue	9.50	*24.00*
16	A17	50c violet	24.00	*80.00*
17	A17	2 l vermilion	47.50	—
		Nos. 12-17 (6)	147.50	
		Nos. 12-16 (5)		149.50

The "Estero" stamps were used in various parts of the world, South America, Africa, Turkey, etc.

Forged cancellations exist on Nos. 1-2, 9-11, 16.

OFFICES IN CHINA

100 Cents = 1 Dollar

PEKING

Italian Stamps of 1901-16 Handstamped

Wmk. 140, Unwmk.

1917 *Perf. 12, 13½, 14*

No.	Type	Description	Unused	Used
1	A48	2c on 5c green	450.00	300.00
a.		Inverted surcharge	400.00	275.00
b.		Double surcharge, one inverted	1,100.	875.00
c.		4c on 5c green	*9,500.*	
3	A48	4c on 10c claret (No. 95)	800.00	475.00
a.		Inverted surcharge	725.00	450.00
b.		Double surcharge, one inverted	1,750.	1,200.
c.		4c on 10c claret (No. 70)		—
5	A58	6c on 15c slate	1,600.	1,100.
b.		8c on 15c slate	5,500.	5,200.
c.		Pair, one without surcharge		—
7	A58	8c on 20c on 15c slate	6,000.	4,500.
a.		Inverted surcharge	5,500.	4,000.
8	A50	8c on 20c brn org (No. 112)	*12,000.*	4,500.
a.		Inverted surcharge	*10,500.*	*4,200.*
9	A49	20c on 50c vio	*30,000.*	*25,000.*
a.		Inverted surcharge	*40,000.*	*27,000.*
b.		40c on 50c violet	*24,000.*	*24,000.*
c.		As "b," inverted surcharge	*22,000.*	*22,000.*
11	A46	40c on 1 l brn & grn	*350,000.*	*60,000.*
a.		Inverted surcharge	300,000.	52,000.

Excellent forgeries exist of the higher valued stamps of Offices in China.

Italian Stamps of 1901-16 Overprinted

1917-18

No.	Type	Description	Unused	Used
12	A42	1c brown	40.00	*80.00*
13	A43	2c orange brown	40.00	*80.00*
a.		Double overprint	450.00	—
14	A48	5c green	12.00	*27.50*
a.		Double overprint	275.00	—
15	A48	10c claret	12.00	*27.50*
16	A50	20c brn org (No. 112)	300.00	*350.00*
17	A49	25c blue	12.00	*35.00*
18	A49	50c violet	12.00	*35.00*
19	A46	1 l brown & grn	27.50	*72.50*
20	A46	5 l blue & rose	55.00	*120.00*
21	A51	10 l gray grn & red	400.00	*675.00*
		Nos. 12-21 (10)	910.50	*1,503.*

Italy No. 113, the watermarked 20c brown orange, was also overprinted "Pechino," but not issued. Value: hinged $32.50; never hinged $80.

Italian Stamps of 1901-16 Surcharged

Type I

Type II

TWO DOLLARS:
Type I — Surcharged "2 dollari Pechino"
Type II — Surcharged "2 DOLLARI."
Type III — Surcharged "2 dollari." "Pechino" measures 11½mm wide, instead of 13mm.

1918-19 *Perf. 14*

No.	Type	Description	Unused	Used
22	A42	½c on 1c brown	350.00	*350.00*
a.		Surcharged "1 cents"	1,100.	1,200.
23	A43	1c on 2c org brn	12.00	*24.00*
a.		Surcharged "1 cents"	550.00	650.00
24	A48	2c on 5c green	12.00	*24.00*
25	A48	4c on 10c clar	12.00	*24.00*
26	A50	8c on 20c brn org (No. 112)	65.00	*47.50*
a.		"8 CENTS" doubled	525.00	525.00
27	A49	10c on 25c blue	24.00	*47.50*
a.		"10 CENTS" doubled	525.00	525.00
28	A49	20c on 50c vio	32.50	*47.50*
29	A46	40c on 1 l brn & grn	350.00	*450.00*
30	A46	$2 on 5 l bl & rose (type I)	650.00	*1,050.*
a.		Type II	*70,000.*	*60,000.*
b.		Type III	*20,000.*	*16,000.*
		Nos. 22-30 (9)	1,508.	*2,065.*

Italy No. 100 Surcharged

1919

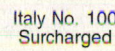

No.	Type	Description	Unused	Used
32	A49	10c on 25c blue	11.00	*27.50*

Imperf. examples of No. 32 are proofs.

PEKING SPECIAL DELIVERY STAMPS

Italian Special Delivery Stamp 1908 Ovptd.

1917 Wmk. 140 *Perf. 14*

No.	Type	Description	Unused	Used
E1	SD2	30c blue & rose	16.00	*60.00*

No. E1 Surcharged

1918

No.	Type	Description	Unused	Used
E2	SD2	12c on 30c bl & rose	125.00	*450.00*

PEKING POSTAGE DUE STAMPS

Italian Postage Due Stamps Overprinted Like Nos. 12-21

1917 Wmk. 140 *Perf. 14*

No.	Type	Description	Unused	Used
J1	D3	10c buff & magenta	5.50	*14.00*
a.		Double overprint	400.00	
J2	D3	20c buff & magenta	5.50	*14.00*
J3	D3	30c buff & magenta	5.50	*14.00*
J4	D3	40c buff & magenta	11.00	*14.00*
		Nos. J1-J4 (4)	27.50	*56.00*

Nos. J1-J4 Surcharged Like No. E2

1918

No.	Type	Description	Unused	Used
J5	D3	4c on 10c	*125,000.*	*100,000.*
J6	D3	8c on 20c	55.00	*110.00*
a.		Pair, one without surcharge	2,000.	
J7	D3	12c on 30c	125.00	*275.00*
J8	D3	16c on 40c	550.00	*950.00*

In 1919, the same new values were surcharged on Italy Nos. J6-J9 in a different style: four lines to cancel the denomination, and "-PECHINO- 4 CENTS." These were not issued. Value $17.50 each, never hinged $42.50 each.

TIENTSIN

Italian Stamps of 1906 Handstamped

Wmk. 140, Unwmk.

1917 *Perf. 12, 13½, 14*

No.	Type	Description	Unused	Used
1	A48	2c on 5c green	575.00	575.00
a.		Surcharge inverted	575.00	475.00
b.		Double surcharge	1,200.	875.00
c.		4c on 5c green	*16,000.*	
d.		Double surcharge, one inverted	1,250.	950.00
2	A48	4c on 10c claret	875.00	475.00
a.		Surcharge inverted	875.00	425.00
b.		Double surcharge	1,900.	1,100.
c.		Double surcharge, one inverted	2,000.	1,200.
4	A58	6c on 15c slate	1,750.	1,500.
a.		Surcharge inverted	1,750.	1,100.
b.		4c on 15c slate	8,750.	8,000.
		Nos. 1-4 (3)	3,200.	2,550.

Italian Stamps of 1901-16 Overprinted

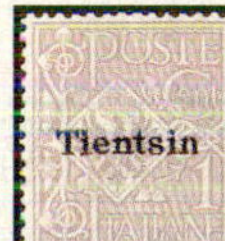

1917-18

No.	Type	Description	Unused	Used
5	A42	1c brown	30.00	*45.00*
a.		Inverted overprint	400.00	400.00
6	A43	2c orange brn	30.00	*45.00*
7	A48	5c green	10.00	*18.00*
8	A48	10c claret	10.00	*18.00*
a.		Double overprint	425.00	
9	A50	20c brn org (#112)	200.00	*180.00*
10	A49	25c blue	10.00	*18.00*
11	A49	50c violet	10.00	*18.00*
12	A46	1 l brown & grn	24.00	*65.00*
13	A46	5 l blue & rose	36.00	*55.00*
14	A51	10 l gray grn & red	240.00	*550.00*
		Nos. 5-14 (10)	600.00	*1,012.*

Italy No. 113, the watermarked 20c brown orange was also overprinted "Tientsin," but not issued. Value: hinged $32.50; never hinged $80.

Italian Stamps of 1901-16 Surcharged

Type I

TWO DOLLARS:
Type I — Surcharged "2 Dollari Tientsin"
Type II — Surcharged "2 dollari."
Type III — Surcharged "2 Dollari." "Tientsin" measures 10mm wide instead of 13mm.

1918-21 *Perf. 14*

15	A42	½c on 1c brn	350.00	*350.00*
a.		Inverted surcharge	650.00	650.00
b.		Surcharged "1 cents"	1,100.	1,200.
16	A43	1c on 2c org brn	12.00	*24.00*
a.		Surcharged "1 cents"	550.00	650.00
b.		Inverted surcharge	650.00	650.00
17	A48	2c on 5c grn	12.00	*24.00*
18	A48	4c on 10c clar	12.00	*24.00*
19	A50	8c on 20c brn org (#112)	65.00	55.00
20	A49	10c on 25c blue	24.00	*47.50*
21	A49	20c on 50c vio	32.50	*47.50*
22	A46	40c on 1 l brn & grn	350.00	*450.00*
23	A46	$2 on 5 l bl & rose (type I)	650.00	*1,050.*
a.		Type II	*20,000.*	*20,000.*
b.		Type III ('21)	*17,500.*	*16,000.*
		Nos. 15-23 (9)	1,508.	*2,072.*

SPECIAL DELIVERY STAMPS

Italian Special Delivery Stamp of 1908 Overprinted

1917 **Wmk. 140** *Perf. 14*

E1 SD2 30c blue & rose 16.00 *60.00*

No. E1 Surcharged

1918

E2 SD2 12c on 30c bl & rose 125.00 *450.00*

POSTAGE DUE STAMPS

Italian Postage Due Stamps Overprinted

1917 **Wmk. 140** *Perf. 14*

J1	D3	10c buff & magenta	5.50	*14.00*
a.		Double overprint	400.00	
J2	D3	20c buff & magenta	5.50	*14.00*
J3	D3	30c buff & magenta	5.50	*14.00*
a.		Double overprint	400.00	
J4	D3	40c buff & magenta	11.00	*14.00*
		Nos. J1-J4 (4)	27.50	*56.00*

Nos. J1-J4 Surcharged

1918

J5	D3	4c on 10c	*9,500.*	*9,500.*
J6	D3	8c on 20c	55.00	*110.00*
a.		"8 CENTS" double	2,750.	
J7	D3	12c on 30c	120.00	*275.00*
J8	D3	16c on 40c	550.00	*950.00*

In 1919, the same new values were surcharged on Italy Nos. J6-J9 in a different style: four lines to cancel the denomination, and "-TIENTSIN- 4 CENTS." These were not issued. Value $17 each, never hinged $42.50 each.

OFFICES IN CRETE

40 Paras = 1 Piaster
100 Centesimi = 1 Lira (1906)

Italy Nos. 70 and 81 Surcharged in Red or Black

a

b

1900-01 **Wmk. 140** *Perf. 14*

1	A36(a)	1pi on 25c blue	8.00	*80.00*
2	A45(b)	1pi on 25c dp bl (Bk) ('01)	4.50	*10.00*

Italian Stamps Overprinted

1906

On Nos. 76-79, 92, 81, 83-85, 87, 91

3	A42	1c brown	2.75	*6.00*
a.		Pair, one without ovpt.	*1,325.*	
b.		Double overprint	375.00	
4	A43	2c org brn	2.75	*6.00*
a.		Imperf., pair	*2,400.*	
b.		Double overprint	375.00	
5	A44	5c bl grn	5.00	*7.00*
6	A45	10c claret	300.00	250.00
7	A45	15c on 20c org	5.00	*7.00*
8	A45	25c blue	11.50	*23.00*
9	A45	40c brown	11.50	*23.00*
10	A45	45c ol grn	11.50	*23.00*
11	A45	50c violet	11.50	*23.00*
12	A46	1 l brn & grn	45.00	*85.00*
13	A46	5 l bl & rose	375.00	*500.00*
		Nos. 3-13 (11)	781.50	*953.00*

On Nos. 94-95, 100, 104-105

1907-10

14	A48	5c green	1.90	2.00
a.		Inverted overprint	300.00	
15	A48	10c claret	1.90	2.00
a.		Double overprint	—	
16	A49	25c blue	2.75	*14.50*
17	A49	40c brown	30.00	*45.00*
18	A49	50c violet	2.75	*14.50*
		Nos. 14-18 (5)	39.30	*78.00*

On No. 111 in Violet

1912 **Unwmk.** *Perf. 13x13½*

19 A50 15c slate black 3.00 *4.00*

SPECIAL DELIVERY STAMPS

Special Delivery Stamp of Italy Overprinted

1906 **Wmk. 140** *Perf. 14*

E1 SD1 25c rose red 12.00 *24.00*

OFFICES IN AFRICA

40 Paras = 1 Piaster
100 Centesimi = 1 Lira (1910)

BENGASI

Italy No. 81 Surcharged in Black

1901 **Wmk. 140** *Perf. 14*

1 A45 1pi on 25c dp bl 65.00 *160.00*

Same Surcharge on Italy No. 100

1911

1A A49 1pi on 25c blue 65.00 *160.00*

TRIPOLI

Italian Stamps of 1901-09 Overprinted in Black or Violet

1909 **Wmk. 140**

2	A42	1c brown	4.75	3.25
a.		Inverted overprint	275.00	
3	A43	2c orange brn	2.40	*3.25*
4	A48	5c green	175.00	9.50
a.		Double overprint	325.00	
5	A48	10c claret	3.25	3.25
a.		Double overprint	225.00	*225.00*
6	A49	25c blue	2.40	*3.25*
7	A49	40c brown	8.00	8.00
8	A49	50c violet	9.50	9.50

Perf. 13½x14
Unwmk.

9	A50	15c slate blk (V)	4.75	4.75
		Nos. 2-9 (8)	210.05	*44.75*

Italian Stamps of 1901 Overprinted

1909 **Wmk. 140** *Perf. 14*

10	A46	1 l brown & grn	140.00	100.00
11	A46	5 l blue & rose	47.50	300.00

Same Overprint on Italy Nos. 76-77

1915

12	A42	1c brown	3.50
13	A43	2c orange brown	3.50

Nos. 12-13 were prepared but not issued. No. 12 exists as a pair, one without overprint, value $2,400 hinged, $3,600 never hinged. No. 12 also exists with inverted overprint. Value, $1,600.

SPECIAL DELIVERY STAMPS

Italy Nos. E1, E6 Ovptd. Like Nos. 10-11

1909 **Wmk. 140** *Perf. 14*

E1	SD1	25c rose red	19.00	12.00
E2	SD2	30c blue & rose	6.50	*16.00*

Tripoli was ceded by Turkey to Italy in Oct., 1912, and became known as the Colony of Libia. Later issues will be found under Libya.

OFFICES IN TURKISH EMPIRE

40 Paras = 1 Piaster

Various powers maintained post offices in the Turkish Empire before World War I by authority of treaties which ended with the signing of the Treaty of Lausanne in 1923. The foreign post offices were closed Oct. 27, 1923.

GENERAL ISSUE

Italian Stamps of 1906-08 Surcharged

Printed at Turin

1908 **Wmk. 140**

1	A48	10pa on 5c green	8.00	4.75
2	A48	20pa on 10c claret	8.00	4.75
3	A49	40pa on 25c blue	3.25	3.25
4	A49	80pa on 50c violet	6.50	4.75

See Janina Nos. 1-4.

Surcharged in Violet

Unwmk.

5	A47	30pa on 15c slate	2.40	2.40
		Nos. 1-5 (5)	28.15	19.90

Nos. 1, 2, 3 and 5 were first issued in Janina, Albania, and subsequently for general use. They can only be distinguished by the cancellations.

Italian Stamps of 1901-08 Surcharged

Nos. 6-8

No. 9

Nos. 10-12

Printed at Constantinople

1908 **First Printing**

6	A48	10pa on 5c grn	400.00	475.
a.		Vert. pair, one without surcharge	4,000.	
7	A48	20pa on 10c claret	400.00	475.
8	A47	30pa on 15c slate	1,200.	*1,400.*
9	A49	1pi on 25c blue	1,200.	*1,400.*
a.		"PIASTRE"	2,000.	2,000.
10	A49	2pi on 50c vio	3,250.	*4,000.*
11	A46	4pi on 1 l brn & grn	*17,500.*	*12,000.*
12	A46	20pi on 5 l bl & rose	*40,000.*	*35,000.*

On Nos. 8, 9 and 10 the surcharge is at the top of the stamp. No. 11 has the "4" closed at the top. No. 12 has the "20" wide.

Second Printing

Italian Stamps of 1901-08 Surcharged

Nos. 13-15

No. 16

Nos. 17-19

13	A48	10pa on 5c green	40.00	*52.50*
14	A48	20pa on 10c claret	40.00	*52.50*
15	A47	30pa on 15c slate	160.00	*120.00*
a.		Double surcharge	350.00	350.00
b.		Triple surcharge	800.00	800.00
16	A49	1pi on 25c blue	40.00	*52.50*
a.		"PIPSTRA"	250.00	250.00
b.		"1" omitted	250.00	250.00
17	A49	2pi on 50c violet	240.00	240.00
a.		Surcharged "20 PIASTRE"	2,400.	2,400.
b.		"20" with "0" scratched out	800.00	800.00
c.		"2" 5mm from "PIASTRE"	650.00	650.00
18	A46	4pi on 1 l brn & grn	1,600.	1,600.
19	A46	20pi on 5 l bl & rose	9,500.	5,200.
		Nos. 13-19 (7)	11,620.	7,318.

On No. 18 the "4" is open at the top.

Third Printing

Surcharged in Red

20	A47	30pa	on 15c slate	9.50	*9.50*
a.			Double surcharge	240.00	240.00

Fourth Printing

20B	A46	4pi	on 1 l brn & grn	65.00	95.00
c.			Inverted "S"	200.00	200.00
20D	A46	20pi	on 5 l bl & rose	210.00	*240.00*
i.			Inverted "S"	550.00	550.00

Fifth Printing

20E	A46	4pi	on 1 l brn & grn	55.00	72.50
f.			Surch. "20 PIASTRE"	2,750.	
20G	A46	20pi	on 5 l bl & rose	55.00	72.50
h.			Double surcharge	1,600.	1,600.

Italian Stamps of 1906-19 Surcharged

1921

21	A48	1pi	on 5c green	350.00	*475.00*
22	A48	2pi	on 15c slate	8.00	*12.00*
23	A50	4pi	on 20c brn org (No. 113)	80.00	*95.00*
24	A49	5pi	on 25c blue	80.00	*95.00*
a.			Double surcharge	350.00	
25	A49	10pi	on 60c carmine	4.75	*8.00*
			Nos. 21-25 (5)	522.75	*685.00*

No. 21 is almost always found poorly centered, and it is valued thus.

On No. 25 the "10" is placed above "PIASTRE."

Italian Stamps of 1901-19 Surcharged

n

o

1922

26	A42(n)	10pa	on 1c brn	2.40	*2.75*
27	A43(n)	20pa	on 2c org brn	2.40	*2.75*
28	A48(n)	30pa	on 5c grn	6.50	*6.50*
29	A48(o)	1pi20pa	on 15c slate	7.25	*2.75*
30	A50(n)	3pi	on 20c brn org (#113)	9.50	*17.50*
31	A49(o)	3pi30pa	on 25c blue	4.75	*2.75*
32	A49(o)	7pi20pa	on 60c carmine	9.50	*6.50*
33	A46(n)	15pi	on 1 l brn & grn	27.50	*47.50*
			Nos. 26-33 (8)	69.80	*89.00*

On No. 32, the distance between the two lines is 2mm. See note after No. 58A.

Italy No. 100 Surcharged

34	A49	3.75pi	on 25c blue	2.40	2.75

Italian Stamps of 1901-20 Surcharged

q

r

1922

35	A48	30pi	on 5c grn	4.00	*17.50*
36	A49	1.50pi	on 25c blue	2.40	*9.50*
37	A49	3.75pi	on 40c brn	3.25	*11.00*
a.			Double surcharge	325.00	
38	A49	4.50pi	on 50c vio	8.00	*24.00*
39	A49	7.50pi	on 60c car	6.50	*17.50*
a.			Double surcharge	400.00	
b.			Pair, one without surcharge	1,750.	
40	A49	15pi	on 85c red brn	12.00	*40.00*
41	A46	18.75pi	on 1 l brn & grn	5.50	*32.50*

On No. 40 the numerals of the surcharge are above "PIASTRE."

Italian Stamps of 1901-20 Surcharged

42	A46	45pi	on 5 l bl & rose	450.00	*725.00*
43	A51	90pi	on 10 l gray grn & red	475.00	*875.00*

On No. 42 the figure "4" is open at top. See note after No. 61.

On No. 43 the figure "9" has a curved or arched bottom. See note after No. 62.

Italian Stamps of 1901-17 Surcharged Type "q" or:

44	A43	30pa	on 2c org brn	2.40	*6.50*
45	A50	1.50pi	on 20c brn org (#113)	2.40	*6.50*
			Nos. 35-45 (11)	971.45	*1,765.*

Italian Stamps of 1901-20 Surcharged in Black or Red

46	A48	30pa	on 5c green	2.40	*4.00*
47	A48	1½pi	on 10c claret	2.40	*4.00*
48	A49	3pi	on 25c blue	20.00	8.00
49	A49	3¾pi	on 40c brown	4.00	*4.00*
50	A49	4½pi	on 50c violet	47.50	45.00
51	A49	7½pi	on 85c red brn	9.50	*12.00*
a.			"PIASIRE"	47.50	*47.50*
52	A46	7½pi	on 1 l brn & grn (R)	12.00	*14.00*
a.			Double surcharge	175.00	
b.			"PIASIRE"	55.00	*55.00*
53	A46	15pi	on 1 l brn & grn	72.50	*175.00*
54	A46	45pi	on 5 l blue & rose	110.00	*110.00*
55	A51	90pi	on 10 l gray grn & red	87.50	*200.00*
			Nos. 46-55 (10)	367.80	*576.00*

Italian Stamps of 1901-20 Surcharged Type "o" or

No. 58

No. 59

Nos. 61-62

1923

56	A49	1pi20pa	on 25c blue	14.00
57	A49	3pi30pa	on 40c brn	14.00
58	A49	4pi20pa	on 50c vio	14.00
58A	A49	7pi20pa	on 60c car	40.00
59	A49	15pi	on 85c red brn	14.00
60	A46	18pi30pa	on 1 l brn & grn	14.00
a.			Double surcharge	*325.00*
61	A46	45pi	on 5 l bl & rose	40.00
62	A51	90pi	on 10 l gray grn & red	35.00
			Nos. 56-62 (8)	185.00

On No. 58A the distance between the lines is 1.5mm. On No. 61 the figure "4" is closed at top. On No. 62 the figure "9" is nearly rectilinear at bottom.

Nos. 56-62 were not issued.

SPECIAL DELIVERY STAMPS

Italian Special Delivery Stamps Surcharged

1908 **Wmk. 140** ***Perf. 14***

E1	SD1	1pi	on 25c rose red	3.25	*4.75*

Surcharged

1910

E2	SD2	60pa	on 30c blue & rose	6.50	*8.00*

Surcharged

1922

E3	SD2	15pi	on 1.20 l on 30c bl & rose	35.00	*87.50*

On No. E3, lines obliterate the first two denominations.

Surcharged

1922

E4	SD2	15pi	on 30c bl & rose	525.00	*1,050.*

Surcharged

1923

E5	SD2	15pi	on 1.20 l blue & red	16.00

No. E5 was not regularly issued.

ALBANIA

Stamps of Italy Surcharged in Black

1902 **Wmk. 140** ***Perf. 14***

1	A44	10pa	on 5c green	4.75	2.40
2	A45	35pa	on 20c orange	7.25	8.00
3	A45	40pa	on 25c blue	14.00	8.00
			Nos. 1-3 (3)	26.00	18.40

Nos. 1-3 with red surcharges are proofs.

1907

4	A48	10pa	on 5c green	55.00	*65.00*
5	A48	20pa	on 10c claret	35.00	*27.50*
6	A45	80pa	on 50c violet	35.00	*27.50*
			Nos. 4-6 (3)	125.00	*120.00*

No. 5 is almost always found poorly centered, and it is valued thus.

CONSTANTINOPLE

Stamps of Italy Surcharged in Black or Violet

Wmk. 140, Unwmk. (#3)

1909-11 ***Perf. 14, 12***

1	A48	10pa	on 5c green	2.40	*2.40*
2	A48	20pa	on 10c claret	2.40	*2.40*
3	A47	30pa	on 15c slate (V)	2.40	*2.40*
4	A49	1pi	on 25c blue	2.40	*2.40*
a.			Double surcharge	210.00	*210.00*
5	A49	2pi	on 50c violet	4.75	*3.25*

Surcharged

6	A46	4pi	on 1 l brn & grn	4.75	4.00
7	A46	20pi	on 5 l bl & rose	72.50	72.50
8	A51	40pi	on 10 l gray grn & red	8.00	*32.50*
			Nos. 1-8 (8)	99.60	*121.85*

Italian Stamps of 1901-19 Surcharged

Nos. 10, 12-13

Nos. 9, 11

1922

9	A48	20pa	on 5c green	20.00	*32.50*
10	A48	1pi20pa	on 15c slate	2.40	2.40
11	A49	3pi	on 30c org brn	2.40	2.40
12	A49	3pi30pa	on 40c brown	2.40	2.40
13	A46	7pi20pa	on 1 l brn & grn	2.40	2.40
			Nos. 9-13 (5)	29.60	42.10

Italian Stamps of 1901-20 Surcharged

1923

14 A48 30pa on 5c grn 3.25 2.40
15 A49 1pi20pa on 25c blue 3.25 2.40
16 A49 3pi30pa on 40c brn 3.25 2.00
17 A49 4pi20pa on 50c vio 3.25 2.00
18 A49 7pi20pa on 60c car 3.25 2.00
19 A49 15pi on 85c red brn 3.25 3.25
20 A46 18pi30pa on 1 l brn & grn 3.25 3.25
21 A46 45pi on 5 l bl & rose 3.25 *7.25*
22 A51 90pi on 10 l gray grn & red 3.25 *8.00*
Nos. 14-22 (9) 29.25 32.55

CONSTANTINOPLE SPECIAL DELIVERY STAMP

Unissued Italian Special Delivery Stamp of 1922 Surcharged in Black

1923 **Wmk. 140** ***Perf. 14***

E1 SD2 15pi on 1.20 l bl & red 8.00 *45.00*

CONSTANTINOPLE POSTAGE DUE STAMPS

Italian Postage Due Stamps of 1870-1903 Overprinted

1922 **Wmk. 140** ***Perf. 14***

J1 D3 10c buff & mag 80.00 *110.00*
J2 D3 30c buff & mag 80.00 *110.00*
J3 D3 60c buff & mag 80.00 *110.00*
J4 D3 1 l blue & mag 80.00 *110.00*
J5 D3 2 l blue & mag 1,900. *3,400.*
J6 D3 5 l blue & mag 875.00 *1,200.*
Nos. J1-J6 (6) 3,095. *5,040.*

A circular control mark with the inscription "Poste Italiane Constantinopoli" and with the arms of the Kingdom of Italy (Savoy Cross) in the center was applied to each block of four of these stamps in black. Value, set of 6 blocks of four with control marks: unused $20,000; used $28,000.

DURAZZO

Stamps of Italy Surcharged in Black or Violet

Wmk. 140, Unwmk. (#3)

1909-11 ***Perf. 14, 12***

1 A48 10pa on 5c green 1.60 *3.25*
2 A48 20pa on 10c claret 1.60 *3.25*
3 A47 30pa on 15c slate (V) 80.00 4.00
4 A49 1pi on 25c blue 2.40 *4.00*
5 A49 2pi on 50c violet 2.40 *4.00*

Surcharged

6 A46 4pi on 1 l brn & grn 4.00 *4.75*
7 A46 20pi on 5 l bl & rose 325.00 275.00
8 A51 40pi on 10 l gray grn & red 20.00 *140.00*
Nos. 1-8 (8) 437.00 438.25

No. 3 Surcharged

1916 **Unwmk.** ***Perf. 12***

9 A47 20c on 30pa on 15c slate 4.75 *20.00*

JANINA

Stamps of Italy Surcharged

1902-07 **Wmk. 140** ***Perf. 14***

1 A44 10pa on 5c green 9.50 3.75
2 A45 35pa on 20c orange 7.00 *4.00*
3 A45 40pa on 25c blue 35.00 11.50
4 A45 80pa on 50c vio ('07) 62.50 *47.50*
Nos. 1-4 (4) 114.00 *66.75*

Surcharged in Black or Violet

Wmk. 140, Unwmk. (#7)

1909-11 ***Perf. 14, 12***

5 A48 10pa on 5c green 1.25 *2.50*
6 A48 20pa on 10c claret 1.25 *2.50*
7 A47 30pa on 15c slate (V) 1.25 *2.50*
8 A49 1pi on 25c blue 1.25 *2.50*
9 A49 2pi on 50c violet 1.25 *3.25*

Surcharged

10 A46 4pi on 1 l brn & grn 4.00 *4.75*
11 A46 20pi on 5 l bl & rose *275.00* *350.00*
12 A51 40pi on 10 l gray grn & red 17.50 *100.00*
Nos. 5-12 (8) 302.75 468.00

JERUSALEM

Stamps of Italy Surcharged in Black or Violet

Wmk. 140, Unwmk. (#3)

1909-11 ***Perf. 14, 12***

1 A48 10pa on 5c green 8.00 *20.00*
2 A48 20pa on 10c claret 8.00 *20.00*
3 A47 30pa on 15c slate (V) 8.00 *27.50*
4 A49 1pi on 25c blue 8.00 *20.00*
5 A49 2pi on 50c violet 27.50 *65.00*

Surcharged

6 A46 4pi on 1 l brn & grn 35.00 *87.50*
7 A46 20pi on 5 l bl & rose 1,250. *1,400.*
8 A51 40pi on 10 l gray grn & red 47.50 *600.00*
Nos. 1-8 (8) 1,392. *2,240.*

Forged cancellations exist on Nos. 1-8.

SALONIKA

Stamps of Italy Surcharged in Black or Violet

Wmk. 140, Unwmk. (#3)

1909-11 ***Perf. 14, 12***

1 A48 10pa on 5c green 1.50 *3.25*
2 A48 20pa on 10c claret 1.50 *3.25*
3 A47 30pa on 15c slate (V) 1.75 *3.50*
4 A49 1pi on 25c blue 1.75 *3.50*
5 A49 2pi on 50c violet 2.40 *4.25*

Surcharged

6 A46 4pi on 1 l brn & grn 3.50 *4.75*
7 A46 20pi on 5 l bl & rose *475.00* *600.00*
8 A51 40pi on 10 l gray grn & red 16.50 *95.00*
Nos. 1-8 (8) 503.90 717.50

SCUTARI

Stamps of Italy Surcharged in Black or Violet

Wmk. 140, Unwmk. (#3)

1909-11 ***Perf. 14, 12***

1 A48 10pa on 5c green 1.60 *3.25*
2 A48 20pa on 10c claret 1.60 *3.25*
3 A47 30pa on 15c slate (V) 27.50 6.50
4 A49 1pi on 25c blue 1.60 *3.25*
5 A49 2pi on 50c violet 1.60 *4.75*

Surcharged

6 A46 4pi on 1 l brn & grn 3.25 *4.75*
7 A46 20pi on 5 l bl & rose 35.00 *55.00*
8 A51 40pi on 10 l gray grn & red 75.00 *175.00*
Nos. 1-8 (8) 147.15 *255.75*

Surcharged like Nos. 1-5

1915

9 A43 4pa on 2c org brn 2.40 *5.50*

No. 3 Surcharged

1916 **Unwmk.** ***Perf. 12***

10 A47 20c on 30pa on 15c slate 6.50 *27.50*

SMYRNA

Stamps of Italy Surcharged in Black or Violet

Wmk. 140, Unwmk. (#3)

1909-11 ***Perf. 14, 12***

1 A48 10pa on 5c green 1.60 1.60
2 A48 20pa on 10c claret 1.60 1.60
3 A47 30pa on 15c slate (V) 3.25 *4.75*
4 A49 1pi on 25c blue 3.25 *4.75*
5 A49 2pi on 50c violet 4.00 *6.50*

Surcharged

6 A46 4pi on 1 l brn & grn 4.75 *8.00*
7 A46 20pi on 5 l bl & rose 190.00 240.00
8 A51 40pi on 10 l gray grn & red 20.00 *120.00*
Nos. 1-8 (8) 228.45 *387.20*

Italian Stamps of 1901-22 Surcharged

Nos. 10, 12-13

Nos. 9, 11

1922

9 A48 20pa on 5c green 32.50
10 A48 1pi20pa on 15c slate 1.60
11 A49 3pi on 30c org brn 1.60
12 A49 3pi30pa on 40c brn 4.00
13 A46 7pi20pa on 1 l brn & grn 4.00
Nos. 9-13 (5) 43.70

Nos. 9-13 were not issued.

VALONA

Stamps of Italy Surcharged in Black or Violet

Wmk. 140, Unwmk. (#3)

1909-11 ***Perf. 14, 12***

1 A48 10pa on 5c green 1.60 *3.25*
2 A48 20pa on 10c claret 1.60 *3.25*
3 A47 30pa on 15c slate (V) 20.00 6.50
4 A49 1pi on 25c blue 2.40 *3.25*
5 A49 2pi on 50c violet 2.40 *4.00*

Surcharged

6 A46 4pi on 1 l brn & grn 2.40 4.00
7 A46 20pi on 5 l bl & rose 55.00 65.00
8 A51 40pi on 10 l gray grn & red 65.00 175.00
Nos. 1-8 (8) 150.40 *264.25*

Italy No. 123 Surcharged in Violet or Red Violet

1916
9 A58 30pa on 15c slate (V) 4.75 *14.00*
a. Red violet surcharge 11.00 *32.50*

No. 9 Surcharged

10 A58 20c on 30pa on 15c slate 2.40 *20.00*

AEGEAN ISLANDS

(Dodecanese)

A group of islands in the Aegean Sea off the coast of Turkey. They were occupied by Italy during the Tripoli War and were ceded to Italy by Turkey in 1924 by the Treaty of Lausanne. Stamps of Italy overprinted with the name of the island were in use at the post offices maintained in the various islands.

Rhodes, on the island of the same name, was capital of the entire group.

100 Centesimi = 1 Lira

GENERAL ISSUE

Italian Stamps of 1907-08 Overprinted

1912 Wmk. 140 *Perf. 14*
1 A49 25c blue 55.00 *35.00*
a. Inverted overprint 300.00 *300.00*
2 A49 50c violet 55.00 *35.00*
a. Inverted overprint 300.00 *300.00*

Virgil Issue

Italian Stamps of 1930 Ovptd. in Red or Blue

1930 Photo. Wmk. 140 *Perf. 14*
3 A106 15c vio blk 1.60 *21.00*
4 A106 20c org brn 1.60 *21.00*
5 A106 25c dk green 1.60 *9.50*
6 A106 30c lt brown 1.60 *9.50*
7 A106 50c dull vio 1.60 *9.50*
8 A106 75c rose red 1.60 *21.00*
9 A106 1.25 l gray bl 1.60 *27.50*

Engr.
Unwmk.
10 A106 5 l + 1.50 l dk vio 4.75 *52.50*
11 A106 10 l + 2.50 l ol brn 4.75 *52.50*
Nos. 3-11,C4-C7 (13) 35.00 436.50

St. Anthony of Padua Issue

Italian Stamps of 1931 Ovptd. in Blue or Red

1932 Photo. Wmk. 140 *Perf. 14*
12 A116 20c black brn 32.50 27.50
13 A116 25c dull grn 32.50 27.50
14 A118 30c brown org 32.50 32.50
15 A118 50c dull vio 32.50 24.00
16 A120 1.25 l gray bl 32.50 47.50

Engr.
Unwmk.
17 A121 75c lt red 32.50 *35.00*
18 A122 5 l + 2.50 l dp org 32.50 *175.00*
Nos. 12-18 (7) 227.50 *369.00*

Dante Alighieri Society Issue

Italian Stamps of 1932 Overprinted

1932 Photo. Wmk. 140
19 A126 10c grnsh gray 1.60 *8.00*
20 A126 15c black vio 1.60 *8.00*
21 A126 20c brown org 1.60 *8.00*
22 A126 25c dp green 1.60 8.00
23 A126 30c dp org 1.60 *8.00*
24 A126 50c dull vio 1.60 4.00
25 A126 75c rose red 1.60 *11.00*
26 A126 1.25 l blue 1.60 *9.50*
27 A126 1.75 l ol brn 3.25 *11.00*
28 A126 2.75 l car rose 3.25 *11.00*
29 A126 5 l + 2 l dp vio 3.25 *25.00*
30 A126 10 l + 2.50 l dk brn 3.25 *45.00*
Nos. 19-30 (12) 25.80 *156.50*

See Nos. C8-C14.

Soccer Issue

Types of Italy, "Soccer" Issue, Overprinted in Black or Red

1934
31 A173 20c brn rose (Bk) 87.50 100.00
32 A174 25c green (R) 87.50 100.00
33 A174 50c violet (R) 340.00 80.00
34 A174 1.25 l gray bl (R) 87.50 *190.00*
35 A175 5 l +2.50 l bl (R) 87.50 *450.00*
Nos. 31-35 (5) 690.00 *920.00*

See Nos. C28-C31.

Same Overprint on Types of Medal of Valor Issue of Italy, in Red or Black

1935
36 A177 10c sl gray (R) 47.50 *95.00*
37 A178 15c brn (Bk) 47.50 *95.00*
38 A178 20c red org (Bk) 47.50 *95.00*
39 A177 25c dp grn (R) 47.50 *95.00*
40 A178 30c lake (Bk) 47.50 *95.00*
41 A178 50c ol grn (Bk) 47.50 *95.00*
42 A178 75c rose red (Bk) 47.50 *95.00*
43 A178 1.25 l dp bl (R) 47.50 *95.00*
44 A177 1.75 l + 1 l pur (R) 47.50 *95.00*
45 A178 2.55 l + 2 l dk car (Bk) 47.50 *95.00*
46 A178 2.75 l + 2 l org brn (Bk) 47.50 *95.00*
Nos. 36-46 (11) 522.50 *1,045.*

See Nos. C32-C38, CE3-CE4.

Types of Italy, 1937, Overprinted in Blue or Red

1938 Wmk. 140 *Perf. 14*
47 A208 10c dk brn (Bl) 4.00 9.50
48 A208 15c pur (R) 4.00 9.50
49 A208 20c chestnut (Bl) 4.00 9.50
50 A208 25c myr grn (R) 4.00 9.50
51 A208 30c dp cl (Bl) 4.00 9.50
52 A208 50c sl grn (R) 4.00 16.00
53 A208 75c rose red (Bl) 4.00 16.00
54 A208 1.25 l dk bl (R) 4.00 16.00
55 A208 1.75 l + 1 l dp org (Bl) 6.50 *30.00*
56 A208 2.55 l + 2 l ol brn (R) 6.50 *30.00*
Nos. 47-56 (10) 45.00 155.50

Bimillenary of birth of Augustus Caesar (Octavianus), first Roman emperor.
See Nos. C39-C43.

Same Overprint of Type of Italy, 1937, in Red

1938
57 A222 1.25 l deep blue 1.60 *2.40*
58 A222 2.75 l + 2 l brown 1.75 *9.50*

600th anniversary of the death of Giotto di Bondone, Italian painter.

Statue of Roman Wolf — A1

Arms of Rhodes — A2

Dante's House, Rhodes A3

1940 Photo.
59 A1 5c lt brown .80 1.20
60 A2 10c pale org .80 1.20
61 A3 25c blue grn 1.60 2.00
62 A1 50c rose vio 1.60 2.00
63 A2 75c dull ver 1.60 4.00
64 A3 1.25 l dull blue 1.60 4.00
65 A2 2 l + 75c rose 1.60 27.50
Nos. 59-65,C44-C47 (11) 18.60 81.40

Triennial Overseas Exposition, Naples.

AIR POST STAMPS

Ferrucci Issue

Types of Italian Air Post Stamps of 1930 Overprinted in Blue or Red Like Nos. 12-18

1930 Wmk. 140 *Perf. 14*
C1 A104 50c brn vio (Bl) 11.00 *24.00*
C2 A104 1 l dk bl (R) 11.00 *24.00*
C3 A104 5 l + 2 l dp car (Bl) 21.00 *67.50*
Nos. C1-C3 (3) 43.00 *115.50*

Nos. C1-C3 were sold at Rhodes only.

Virgil Issue

Types of Italian Air Post Stamps of 1930 Overprinted in Red or Blue Like Nos. 3-11

1930 Photo.
C4 A106 50c dp grn (R) 2.40 *40.00*
C5 A106 1 l rose red (Bl) 2.40 *40.00*

Engr.
Unwmk.
C6 A106 7.70 l + 1.30 l dk brn (R) 4.75 *52.50*
C7 A106 9 l + 2 l gray (R) 4.75 *80.00*
Nos. C4-C7 (4) 14.30 *212.50*

Dante Alighieri Society Issue

Types of Italian Air Post Stamps of 1932 Overprinted Like Nos. 19-30

1932 Wmk. 140
C8 AP10 50c car rose 1.60 *6.50*
C9 AP11 1 l dp grn 1.60 *6.50*
C10 AP11 3 l dl vio 1.60 *9.50*
C11 AP11 5 l dp org 1.60 *9.50*
C12 AP10 7.70 l + 2 l ol brn 4.75 *22.50*
C13 AP11 10 l + 2.50 l dk bl 4.75 *30.00*
Nos. C8-C13 (6) 15.90 *84.50*

Leonardo da Vinci — AP12

1932 Photo. *Perf. 14½*
C14 AP12 100 l dp bl & grnsh gray 21.00 *140.00*

Garibaldi Types of Italian Air Post Stamps of 1932 Overprinted in Red or Blue

1932
C15 AP13 50c deep green 60.00 *140.00*
C16 AP14 80c copper red 60.00 *140.00*
C17 AP13 1 l + 25c dl bl 60.00 *140.00*
C18 AP13 2 l + 50c red brn 60.00 *140.00*
C19 AP14 5 l + 1 l bluish sl 60.00 *140.00*
Nos. C15-C19 (5) 300.00 *700.00*

See Nos. CE1-CE2.

Graf Zeppelin over Rhodes AP17

1933 *Perf. 14*
C20 AP17 3 l olive brn 95.00 *240.00*
C21 AP17 5 l dp vio 95.00 *275.00*
C22 AP17 10 l dk green 95.00 *450.00*
C23 AP17 12 l dk blue 95.00 *500.00*
C24 AP17 15 l car rose 95.00 *500.00*
C25 AP17 20 l gray blk 95.00 *500.00*
Nos. C20-C25 (6) 570.00 *2,465.*

Balbo Flight Issue

Italian Air Post Stamps of 1933 Ovptd.

1933 Wmk. 140 *Perf. 14*
C26 AP25 5.25 l + 19.75 l grn, red & bl gray 60.00 *165.00*
C27 AP25 5.25 l + 44.75 l red, grn & bl gray 60.00 *165.00*

Soccer Issue

Types of Italian Air Post Stamps of 1934 Overprinted in Black or Red Like #31-35

1934
C28 AP32 50c brown (R) 20.00 *80.00*
C29 AP33 75c rose red) 20.00 *80.00*
C30 AP34 5 l + 2.50 l red org 32.50 *160.00*
C31 AP35 10 l + 5 l grn (R) 32.50 *190.00*
Nos. C28-C31 (4) 105.00 *510.00*

Types of Medal of Valor Issue of Italy Overprinted in Red or Black Like Nos. 31-35

1935
C32 AP36 25c dp grn 67.50 *110.00*
C33 AP36 50c blk brn (R) 67.50 *110.00*
C34 AP36 75c rose 67.50 *110.00*
C35 AP36 80c dk brn 67.50 *110.00*
C36 AP36 1 l + 50c ol grn 47.50 *110.00*
C37 AP36 2 l + 1 l dp bl (R) 47.50 *110.00*
C38 AP40 3 l + 2 l vio (R) 47.50 *110.00*
Nos. C32-C38 (7) 412.50 *770.00*

Types of Italy Air Post Stamps, 1937, Overprinted in Blue or Red Like Nos. 47-56

1938 Wmk. 140 *Perf. 14*
C39 AP51 25c dl gray vio (R) 4.75 9.50
C40 AP51 50c grn (R) 4.75 9.50
C41 AP51 80c brt bl (R) 4.75 30.00
C42 AP51 1 l + 1 l rose lake 9.50 30.00
C43 AP51 5 l + 1 l rose red 12.50 *60.00*
Nos. C39-C43 (5) 36.25 139.00

Bimillenary of the birth of Augustus Caesar (Octavianus).

Statues of Stag and Roman Wolf AP18

Plane over Government Palace, Rhodes — AP19

1940 Photo.
C44 AP18 50c olive blk 2.40 4.00
C45 AP19 1 l dk vio 2.40 4.00
C46 AP18 2 l + 75c dk bl 2.40 12.00
C47 AP19 5 l + 2.50 l cop brn 2.40 22.50
Nos. C44-C47 (4) 9.60 42.50

Triennial Overseas Exposition, Naples.

AIR POST SPECIAL DELIVERY STAMPS

Type of Italian Garibaldi Air Post Special Delivery Stamps Overprinted in Blue or Ocher Like Nos. 12-18

1932 Wmk. 140 *Perf. 14*
CE1 APSD1 2.25 l + 1 l bl & rose & (Bl) 95.00 *260.00*
CE2 APSD1 4.50 l + 1.50 l ocher & gray (O) 95.00 *260.00*

Type of Medal of Valor Issue of Italy, Ovptd. in Black

1935
CE3 APSD4 2 l + 1.25 l dp bl 47.50 *110.00*
CE4 APSD4 4.50 l + 2 l grn 47.50 *110.00*

ISSUES FOR THE INDIVIDUAL ISLANDS

Italian Stamps of 1901-20 Overprinted with Names of Various Islands as

a

b

c

The 1912-22 issues of each island have type "a" overprint in black on all values except 15c (type A58) and 20c on 15c, which have type "b" overprint in violet.

The 1930-32 Ferruci and Garibaldi issues are types of the Italian issues overprinted type "c." Stamps with type "c" overprints are also listed in Castellorizo.

CALCHI

Overprinted "Karki" in Black or Violet

1912-22 Wmk. 140 *Perf. 13½, 14*
1 A43 2c orange brn 8.00 9.50
a. Double overprint 400.00 *600.00*
2 A48 5c green 4.75 *9.50*
3 A48 10c claret 1.60 *9.50*
4 A48 15c slate ('22) 4.75 *47.50*
a. Double overprint 400.00
5 A50 20c brn org ('21) 4.75 *45.00*
6 A49 25c blue 1.60 *9.50*
7 A49 40c brown 1.60 *9.50*
8 A49 50c violet 1.60 *19.00*

Unwmk.
9 A58 15c slate (V) 47.50 19.00
10 A50 20c brn org ('17) 140.00 *175.00*
Nos. 1-10 (10) 216.15 *353.00*

No. 9 Surcharged

1916 *Perf. 13½*
11 A58 20c on 15c slate 2.40 *27.50*

Ferrucci Issue
Types of Italy
Overprinted in Red or Blue

1930 Wmk. 140 *Perf. 14*
12 A102 20c vio (R) 4.00 *9.50*
13 A103 25c dk grn (R) 4.00 *9.50*
14 A103 50c blk (R) 4.75 *16.00*
15 A103 1.25 l dp bl (R) 4.75 *16.00*
16 A104 5 l + 2 l dp car (Bl) 11.00 *27.50*
Nos. 12-16 (5) 28.50 *78.50*

Garibaldi Issue
Types of Italy
Overprinted "CARCHI" in Red or Blue

1932
17 A138 10c brown 19.00 *36.00*
18 A138 20c red brn (Bl) 19.00 *36.00*
19 A138 25c dp grn 19.00 *36.00*
20 A138 30c bluish sl 19.00 *36.00*
21 A138 50c red vio (Bl) 19.00 *36.00*
22 A141 75c cop red (Bl) 19.00 *36.00*
23 A141 1.25 l dl bl 19.00 *36.00*
24 A141 1.75 l + 25c brn 19.00 *36.00*
25 A144 2.55 l + 50c org (Bl) 19.00 *36.00*
26 A145 5 l + 1 l dl vio 19.00 *36.00*
Nos. 17-26 (10) 190.00 *360.00*

CALINO

Overprinted "Calimno" in Black or Violet

1912-21 Wmk. 140 *Perf. 13½, 14*
1 A43 2c orange brn 9.50 9.50
2 A48 5c green 3.25 *9.50*
3 A48 10c claret 1.60 *9.50*
4 A48 15c slate ('21) 4.75 *55.00*
5 A50 20c brn org ('21) 4.75 *55.00*
6 A49 25c blue 9.50 *9.50*
7 A49 40c brown 1.60 *9.50*
8 A49 50c violet 1.60 *19.00*

Unwmk.
9 A58 15c slate (V) 40.00 19.00
10 A50 20c brn org ('17) 95.00 *225.00*
Nos. 1-10 (10) 171.55 *420.50*

No. 9 Surcharged Like Calchi No. 11

1916 *Perf. 13½*
11 A58 20c on 15c slate 17.50 *40.00*

Ferrucci Issue
Types of Italy
Overprinted in Red or Blue

1930 Wmk. 140 *Perf. 14*
12 A102 20c violet (R) 4.00 *9.50*
13 A103 25c dk grn (R) 4.00 *9.50*
14 A103 50c black (R) 4.75 *16.00*
15 A103 1.25 l dp bl (R) 4.75 *16.00*
16 A104 5 l + 2 l dp car (Bl) 11.00 *27.50*
Nos. 12-16 (5) 28.50 *78.50*

Garibaldi Issue
Types of Italy
Overprinted in Red or Blue

1932
17 A138 10c brown 19.00 *35.00*
18 A138 20c red brn (Bl) 19.00 *35.00*
19 A138 25c dp grn 19.00 *35.00*
20 A138 30c bluish sl 19.00 *35.00*
21 A138 50c red vio (Bl) 19.00 *35.00*
22 A141 75c cop red (Bl) 19.00 *35.00*
23 A141 1.25 l dull blue 19.00 *35.00*
24 A141 1.75 l + 25c brn 19.00 *35.00*
25 A144 2.55 l + 50c org (Bl) 19.00 *35.00*
26 A145 5 l + 1 l dl vio 19.00 *35.00*
Nos. 17-26 (10) 190.00 *350.00*

CASO

Overprinted "Caso" in Black or Violet

1912-21 Wmk. 140 *Perf. 13½, 14*
1 A43 2c orange brn 8.00 9.50
2 A48 5c green 4.75 *9.50*
3 A48 10c claret 1.60 *9.50*
4 A48 15c slate ('21) 4.75 *47.50*
5 A50 20c brn org ('20) 4.00 *35.00*
6 A49 25c blue 1.60 *9.50*
7 A49 40c brown 1.60 *9.50*
8 A49 50c violet 1.60 *19.00*

Unwmk.
9 A58 15c slate (V) 47.50 *19.00*
10 A50 20c brn org ('17) 140.00 *225.00*
Nos. 1-10 (10) 215.40 *393.00*

No. 9 Surcharged Like Calchi No. 11

1916 *Perf. 13½*
11 A58 20c on 15c slate 1.60 *40.00*

Ferrucci Issue
Types of Italy
Overprinted in Red or Blue

1930 Wmk. 140 *Perf. 14*
12 A102 20c violet (R) 4.00 *9.50*
13 A103 25c dk green (R) 4.00 *9.50*
14 A103 50c black (R) 4.00 *16.00*
15 A103 1.25 l dp bl (R) 4.00 *16.00*
16 A104 5 l + 2 l dp car (Bl) 11.00 *27.50*
Nos. 12-16 (5) 27.00 *78.50*

Garibaldi Issue
Types of Italy
Overprinted in Red or Blue

1932
17 A138 10c brown 19.00 *35.00*
18 A138 20c red brn (Bl) 19.00 *35.00*
19 A138 25c dp grn 19.00 *35.00*
20 A138 30c bluish sl 19.00 *35.00*
21 A138 50c red vio (Bl) 19.00 *35.00*
22 A141 75c cop red (Bl) 19.00 *35.00*
23 A141 1.25 l dull blue 19.00 *35.00*
24 A141 1.75 l + 25c brn 19.00 *35.00*
25 A144 2.55 l + 50c org (Bl) 19.00 *35.00*
26 A145 5 l + 1 l dl vio 19.00 *35.00*
Nos. 17-26 (10) 190.00 *350.00*

COO

(Cos, Kos)
Overprinted "Cos" in Black or Violet

1912-22 Wmk. 140 *Perf. 13½, 14*
1 A43 2c orange brn 8.00 9.50
2 A48 5c green 100.00 9.50
3 A48 10c claret 4.75 *9.50*
4 A48 15c slate ('22) 4.75 *55.00*
5 A50 20c brn org ('21) 4.00 *35.00*
6 A49 25c blue 40.00 9.50
7 A49 40c brown 1.60 *9.50*
8 A49 50c violet 1.60 *19.00*

Unwmk.
9 A58 15c slate (V) 60.00 19.00
10 A50 20c brn org ('17) 65.00 *225.00*
Nos. 1-10 (10) 289.70 *400.50*

No. 9 Surcharged Like Calchi No. 11

1916 *Perf. 13½*
11 A58 20c on 15c slate 19.00 *40.00*

Ferrucci Issue
Types of Italy
Overprinted in Red or Blue

1930 Wmk. 140 *Perf. 14*
12 A102 20c violet (R) 4.00 *9.50*
13 A103 25c dk green (R) 4.00 *9.50*
14 A103 50c black (R) 4.00 *16.00*
15 A103 1.25 l dp bl (R) 4.00 *16.00*
16 A104 5 l + 2 l dp car (Bl) 11.00 27.50
Nos. 12-16 (5) 27.00 *78.50*

Garibaldi Issue
Types of Italy
Overprinted in Red or Blue

1932
17 A138 10c brown 19.00 *35.00*
18 A138 20c red brn (Bl) 19.00 *35.00*
19 A138 25c dp grn 19.00 *35.00*
20 A138 30c bluish sl 19.00 *35.00*
21 A138 50c red vio (Bl) 19.00 *35.00*
22 A141 75c cop red (Bl) 19.00 *35.00*
23 A141 1.25 l dull blue 19.00 *35.00*
24 A141 1.75 l + 25c brn 19.00 *35.00*
25 A144 2.55 l + 50c org (Bl) 19.00 *35.00*
26 A145 5 l + 1 l dl vio 19.00 *35.00*
Nos. 17-26 (10) 190.00 *350.00*

LERO

Overprinted "Leros" in Black or Violet

1912-22 Wmk. 140 *Perf. 13½, 14*
1 A43 2c orange brn 9.50 9.50
2 A48 5c green 8.00 9.50
3 A48 10c claret 3.25 *9.50*
4 A48 15c slate ('22) 4.75 *40.00*
5 A50 20c brn org ('21) 175.00 125.00
6 A49 25c blue 72.50 9.50
7 A49 40c brown 4.75 *9.50*
8 A49 50c violet 1.60 *19.00*

Unwmk.
9 A58 15c slate (V) 87.50 19.00
10 A50 20c brn org ('17) 65.00 *225.00*
Nos. 1-10 (10) 431.85 *475.50*

No. 9 Surcharged Like Calchi No. 11

1916 *Perf. 13½*
11 A58 20c on 15c slate 19.00 *40.00*

Ferrucci Issue
Types of Italy
Overprinted in Red or Blue

1930 *Perf. 14*
12 A102 20c violet (R) 4.00 *9.50*
13 A103 25c dk green (R) 4.00 *9.50*
14 A103 50c black (R) 4.00 *16.00*
15 A103 1.25 l dp bl (R) 4.00 *16.00*
16 A104 5 l + 2 l dp car (Bl) 11.00 *27.50*
Nos. 12-16 (5) 27.00 *78.50*

Garibaldi Issue
Types of Italy
Overprinted in Red or Blue

1932
17 A138 10c brown 19.00 *35.00*
18 A138 20c red brn (Bl) 19.00 *35.00*
19 A138 25c dp grn 19.00 *35.00*
20 A138 30c bluish sl 19.00 *35.00*
21 A138 50c red vio (Bl) 19.00 *35.00*
22 A141 75c cop red (Bl) 19.00 *35.00*
23 A141 1.25 l dull blue 19.00 *35.00*
24 A141 1.75 l + 25c brn 19.00 *35.00*
25 A144 2.55 l + 50c org (Bl) 19.00 *35.00*
26 A145 5 l + 1 l dl vio 19.00 *35.00*
Nos. 17-26 (10) 190.00 *350.00*

LISSO

Overprinted "Lipso" in Black or Violet

1912-22 Wmk. 140 *Perf. 13½, 14*
1 A43 2c orange brn 8.00 9.50
2 A48 5c green 4.75 *9.50*
3 A48 10c claret 3.25 *9.50*
4 A48 15c slate ('22) 4.75 *40.00*
5 A50 20c brn org ('21) 4.75 *47.50*
6 A49 25c blue 1.60 *9.50*

7 A49 40c brown 3.25 9.50
8 A49 50c violet 1.60 19.00

Unwmk.

9 A58 15c slate (V) 47.50 19.00
10 A50 20c brn org ('17) 95.00 225.00
Nos. 1-10 (10) 174.45 398.00

No. 9 Surcharged Like Calchi No. 11

1916 *Perf. 13½*
11 A58 20c on 15c slate 1.60 40.00

Ferrucci Issue
Types of Italy
Overprinted in Red or Blue

1930 Wmk. 140 *Perf. 14*
12 A102 20c violet (R) 4.00 9.50
13 A103 25c dk green (R) 4.00 9.50
14 A103 50c black (R) 4.00 16.00
15 A103 1.25 l dp bl (R) 4.00 16.00
16 A104 5 l + 2 l dp car (Bl) 11.00 29.00
Nos. 12-16 (5) 27.00 80.00

Garibaldi Issue
Types of Italy
Overprinted "LIPSO" in Red or Blue

1932
17 A138 10c brown 19.00 35.00
18 A138 20c red brn (Bl) 19.00 35.00
19 A138 25c dp grn 19.00 35.00
20 A138 30c bluish sl 19.00 35.00
21 A138 50c red vio (Bl) 19.00 35.00
22 A141 75c cop red (Bl) 19.00 35.00
23 A141 1.25 l dull blue 19.00 35.00
24 A141 1.75 l + 25c brn 19.00 35.00
25 A144 2.55 l + 50c org (Bl) 19.00 35.00
26 A145 5 l + 1 l dl vio 19.00 35.00
Nos. 17-26 (10) 190.00 350.00

NISIRO

Overprinted "Nisiros" in Black or Violet

1912-22 Wmk. 140 *Perf. 13½, 14*
1 A43 2c orange brn 8.00 9.50
2 A48 5c green 4.75 9.50
3 A48 10c claret 1.60 9.50
4 A48 15c slate ('22) 32.50 55.00
5 A50 20c brn org ('21) 110.00 125.00
6 A49 25c blue 3.25 9.50
7 A49 40c brown 1.60 9.50
8 A49 50c violet 4.00 19.00

Unwmk.

9 A58 15c slate (V) 47.50 19.00
10 A50 20c brn org ('17) 140.00 225.00
Nos. 1-10 (10) 353.20 490.50

No. 9 Surcharged Like Calchi No. 11

1916 *Perf. 13½*
11 A58 20c on 15c slate 1.60 40.00

Ferrucci Issue
Types of Italy
Overprinted in Red or Blue

1930 Wmk. 140 *Perf. 14*
12 A102 20c violet (R) 4.00 9.50
13 A103 25c dk grn (R) 4.00 9.50
14 A103 50c black (R) 4.00 16.00
15 A103 1.25 l dp bl (R) 4.00 16.00
16 A104 5 l + 2 l dp car (Bl) 11.00 27.50
Nos. 12-16 (5) 27.00 78.50

Garibaldi Issue
Types of Italy
Overprinted in Red or Blue

1932
17 A138 10c brown 19.00 35.00
18 A138 20c red brn (Bl) 19.00 35.00
19 A138 25c dp grn 19.00 35.00
20 A138 30c bluish sl 19.00 35.00
21 A138 50c red vio (Bl) 19.00 35.00
22 A141 75c cop red (Bl) 19.00 35.00
23 A141 1.25 l dull blue 19.00 35.00
24 A141 1.75 l + 25c brn 19.00 35.00
25 A144 2.55 l + 50c org (Bl) 19.00 35.00
26 A145 5 l + 1 l dl vio 19.00 35.00
Nos. 17-26 (10) 190.00 350.00

PATMO

Overprinted "Patmos" in Black or Violet

1912-22 Wmk. 140 *Perf. 13½, 14*
1 A43 2c orange brn 8.00 9.50
2 A48 5c green 4.75 9.50
3 A48 10c claret 3.25 9.50
4 A48 15c slate ('22) 4.75 52.50
5 A50 20c brn org ('21) 175.00 225.00
6 A49 25c blue 1.60 9.50
7 A49 40c brown 4.00 9.50
8 A49 50c violet 1.60 19.00

Unwmk.

9 A58 15c slate (V) 47.50 19.00
10 A50 20c brn org ('17) 95.00 225.00
Nos. 1-10 (10) 345.45 588.00

No. 9 Surcharged Like Calchi No. 11

1916 *Perf. 13½*
11 A58 20c on 15c slate 19.00 40.00

Ferrucci Issue
Types of Italy
Overprinted in Red or Blue

1930 Wmk. 140 *Perf. 14*
12 A102 20c violet (R) 4.00 9.50
13 A103 25c dk green (R) 4.00 9.50
14 A103 50c black (R) 4.00 16.00
15 A103 1.25 l dp bl (R) 4.00 16.00
16 A104 5 l + 2 l dp car (Bl) 11.00 29.00
Nos. 12-16 (5) 27.00 80.00

Garibaldi Issue
Types of Italy
Overprinted in Red or Blue

1932
17 A138 10c brown 19.00 35.00
18 A138 20c red brn (Bl) 19.00 35.00
19 A138 25c dp grn 19.00 35.00
20 A138 30c bluish sl 19.00 35.00
21 A138 50c red vio (Bl) 19.00 35.00
22 A141 75c cop red (Bl) 19.00 35.00
23 A141 1.25 l dull blue 19.00 35.00
24 A141 1.75 l + 25c brn 19.00 35.00
25 A144 2.55 l + 50c org (Bl) 19.00 35.00
26 A145 5 l + 1 l dl vio 19.00 35.00
Nos. 17-26 (10) 190.00 350.00

PISCOPI

Overprinted "Piscopi" in Black or Violet

1912-21 Wmk. 140 *Perf. 13½, 14*
1 A43 2c orange brn 8.00 9.50
2 A48 5c green 4.75 9.50
3 A48 10c claret 1.60 9.50
4 A48 15c slate ('21) 19.00 52.50
5 A50 20c brn org ('21) 65.00 72.50
6 A49 25c blue 1.60 9.50
7 A49 40c brown 1.60 9.50
8 A49 50c violet 1.60 19.00

Unwmk.

9 A58 15c slate (V) 47.50 19.00
10 A50 20c brn org ('17) 95.00 225.00
Nos. 1-10 (10) 245.65 435.50

No. 9 Surcharged Like Calchi No. 11

1916 *Perf. 13½*
11 A58 20c on 15c slate 1.60 40.00

Ferrucci Issue
Types of Italy
Overprinted in Red or Blue

1930 Wmk. 140 *Perf. 14*
12 A102 20c violet (R) 4.00 9.50
13 A103 25c dk green (R) 4.00 9.50
14 A103 50c black (R) 4.00 16.00
15 A103 1.25 l dp bl (R) 4.00 16.00
16 A104 5 l + 2 l dp car (Bl) 11.00 29.00
Nos. 12-16 (5) 27.00 80.00

Garibaldi Issue
Types of Italy
Overprinted in Red or Blue

1932
17 A138 10c brown 19.00 35.00
18 A138 20c red brn (Bl) 19.00 35.00
19 A138 25c dp grn 19.00 35.00
20 A138 30c bluish sl 19.00 35.00
21 A138 50c red vio (Bl) 19.00 35.00
22 A141 75c cop red (Bl) 19.00 35.00
23 A141 1.25 l dull blue 19.00 35.00
24 A141 1.75 l + 25c brn 19.00 35.00
25 A144 2.55 l + 50c org (Bl) 19.00 35.00
26 A145 5 l + 1 l dl vio 19.00 35.00
Nos. 17-26 (10) 190.00 350.00

RHODES

(Rodi)

Overprinted "Rodi" in Black or Violet

1912-24 Wmk. 140 *Perf. 13½, 14*
1 A43 2c org brn 1.60 9.50
2 A48 5c green 4.75 9.50
a. Double overprint 400.00 600.00
3 A48 10c claret 1.60 9.50
4 A48 15c slate ('21) 175.00 72.50
5 A45 20c org ('16) 3.25 8.00
6 A50 20c brn org ('19) 6.50 20.00
a. Double overprint 87.50
7 A49 25c blue 4.75 9.50
8 A49 40c brown 6.50 9.50
9 A49 50c violet 1.60 19.00
10 A49 85c red brn ('22) 87.50 125.00
11 A46 1 l brn & grn ('24) 3.25

No. 11 was not regularly issued.

Unwmk.

12 A58 15c slate (V) 47.50 19.00
13 A50 20c brn org ('17) 240.00 225.00
Nos. 1-13 (13) 583.80 536.00

No. 12 Surcharged Like Calchi No. 11

1916 *Perf. 13½*
14 A58 20c on 15c slate 140.00 175.00

Windmill, Rhodes — A1

Medieval Galley — A2

Christian Knight — A3

Crusader Kneeling in Prayer — A4

Crusader's Tomb — A5

No Imprint

1929 Unwmk. Litho. *Perf. 11*
15 A1 5c magenta 11.00 2.40
16 A2 10c olive brn 11.00 1.60
17 A3 20c rose red 11.00 .80
18 A3 25c green 11.00 .80
19 A4 30c dk blue 72.50 2.40
20 A5 50c dk brown 11.00 .80
21 A5 1.25 l dk blue 11.00 2.40
22 A4 5 l magenta 80.00 140.00
23 A4 10 l olive brn 240.00 340.00
Nos. 15-23 (9) 458.50 491.20

Visit of the King and Queen of Italy to the Aegean Islands. The stamps are inscribed "Rodi" but were available for use in all the Aegean Islands.

Nos. 15-23 and C1-C4 were used in eastern Crete in 1941-42 with Greek postmarks.

See Nos. 55-63. For surcharges and overprints see Nos. 29-44, B1-B18, E3-E4.

Ferrucci Issue
Overprinted in Red or Blue

1930 Wmk. 140 *Perf. 14*
24 A102 20c violet (R) 4.00 9.50
25 A103 25c dk green (R) 4.00 9.50
26 A103 50c black (R) 4.00 16.00
27 A103 1.25 l dp blue (R) 4.00 16.00
28 A104 5 l + 2 l dp car (Bl) 11.00 29.00
Nos. 24-28 (5) 27.00 80.00

Hydrological Congress Issue

Rhodes Issue of 1929 Overprinted

1930 Unwmk. *Perf. 11*
29 A1 5c magenta 65.00 55.00
30 A2 10c olive brn 65.00 55.00
31 A3 20c rose red 72.50 55.00
32 A3 25c green 80.00 55.00
33 A4 30c dk blue 65.00 55.00
34 A5 50c dk brown 600.00 95.00
35 A5 1.25 l dk blue 450.00 140.00
36 A4 5 l magenta 400.00 600.00
37 A4 10 l olive grn 400.00 650.00
Nos. 29-37 (9) 2,198. 1,760.

Rhodes Issue of 1929 Overprinted in Blue or Red

1931
38 A1 5c mag (Bl) 9.50 22.50
39 A2 10c ol brn (R) 9.50 22.50
40 A3 20c rose red (Bl) 9.50 37.50
41 A3 25c green (R) 9.50 37.50
42 A4 30c dk blue (R) 9.50 37.50
43 A5 50c dk brown (R) 65.00 87.50
44 A5 1.25 l dk bl (R) 55.00 125.00
Nos. 38-44 (7) 167.50 370.00

Italian Eucharistic Congress, 1931.

Garibaldi Issue
Types of Italy
Overprinted in Red or Blue

1932 Wmk. 140 *Perf. 14*
45 A138 10c brown 19.00 35.00
46 A138 20c red brn (Bl) 19.00 35.00
47 A138 25c dp grn 19.00 35.00
48 A138 30c bluish sl 19.00 35.00
49 A138 50c red vio (Bl) 19.00 35.00
50 A141 75c cop red (Bl) 19.00 35.00
51 A141 1.25 l dl bl 19.00 35.00
52 A141 1.75 l + 25c brn 19.00 35.00
53 A144 2.55 l + 50c org (Bl) 19.00 35.00
54 A145 5 l + 1 l dl vio 19.00 35.00
Nos. 45-54 (10) 190.00 350.00

Types of Rhodes Issue of 1929 Imprint: "Officina Carte-Valori Roma"

1932
55 A1 5c rose lake 1.60 .25
56 A2 10c dk brn 1.60 .25
57 A3 20c red 1.60 .25
58 A3 25c dl grn 1.60 .25
59 A4 30c dl bl 1.60 .25
60 A5 50c blk brn 1.60 .25
61 A5 1.25 l dp bl 1.60 .25
62 A4 5 l rose lake 1.60 2.25
63 A4 10 l ol brn 4.00 4.75
Nos. 55-63 (9) 16.80 8.75

Aerial View of Rhodes A6

Map of Rhodes — A7

1932 Wmk. 140 Litho. *Perf. 11*
Shield in Red
64 A6 5c blk & grn 9.50 24.00
65 A6 10c blk & vio bl 9.50 20.00
66 A6 20c blk & dl yel 9.50 20.00
67 A6 25c lil & blk 9.50 20.00
68 A6 30c blk & pink 9.50 20.00

Shield and Map Dots in Red

69	A7	50c blk & gray	9.50	*20.00*
70	A7	1.25 l red brn & gray	9.50	*40.00*
71	A7	5 l dk bl & gray	24.00	*100.00*
72	A7	10 l dk grn & gray	65.00	*180.00*
73	A7	25 l choc & gray	250.00	*1,200.*
		Nos. 64-73 (10)	405.50	*1,644.*

20th anniv. of the Italian occupation and 10th anniv. of Fascist rule.

Deer and Palm — A8

1935, Apr. Photo. Wmk. 140

74	A8	5c orange	27.50	*35.00*
75	A8	10c brown	27.50	*35.00*
76	A8	20c car rose	27.50	*45.00*
77	A8	25c green	27.50	*45.00*
78	A8	30c purple	27.50	*52.50*
79	A8	50c red brn	27.50	*52.50*
80	A8	1.25l blue	27.50	*120.00*
81	A8	5 l yellow	240.00	*450.00*
		Nos. 74-81 (8)	432.50	*835.00*

Holy Year.

The above overprints on No. 55 are stated to have been prepared locally for use on German military correspondence, but banned by postal authorities in Berlin.

RHODES SEMI-POSTAL STAMPS

Rhodes Nos. 55-62 Surcharged in Black or Red

1943 Wmk. 140 *Perf. 14*

B1	A1	5c + 5c rose lake	3.75	4.50
B2	A2	10c + 10c dk brn	3.75	4.50
B3	A3	20c + 20c red	3.75	4.50
B4	A3	25c + 25c dl grn	3.75	4.50
B5	A4	30c + 30c dl bl (R)	6.00	7.50
B6	A5	50c + 50c blk brn	6.00	7.50
B7	A5	1.25 l + 1.25 l dp bl (R)	7.50	11.00
B8	A4	5 l + 5 l rose lake	150.00	250.00
		Nos. B1-B8 (8)	184.50	294.00

The surtax was for general relief.

Rhodes Nos. 55-58, 60 and 61 Surcharged in Black or Red

1944

B9	A1	5c + 3 l rose lake	4.50	*10.50*
B10	A2	10c + 3 l dk brn (R)	4.50	*10.50*
B11	A3	20c + 3 l red	4.50	*10.50*
B12	A3	25c +3 l dl grn (R)	4.50	*10.50*
B13	A5	50c + 3 l blk brn (R)	4.50	*10.50*
B14	A5	1.25 l + 5 l dp bl (R)	37.50	*70.00*
		Nos. B9-B14 (6)	60.00	*122.50*

The surtax was for war victims.

Rhodes Nos. 62 and 63 Surcharged in Red

1945

B17	A4	5 l + 10 l rose lake	15.00	*34.00*
B18	A4	10 l + 10 l ol brn	15.00	*34.00*

The surtax was for the Red Cross.

RHODES AIR POST STAMPS

Symbolical of Flight — AP18

Wmk. 140 Upright (No. C1), Sideways (No. C2a-C4a)

1937-38 Typo. *Perf. 14*

C1	AP18	50c blk & yel	.80	.40
C2a	AP18	80c blk & mag	.80	*2.40*
C3a	AP18	1 l blk & grn	.80	.40
C4a	AP18	5 l blk & red vio	1.60	*4.75*
		Nos. C1-C4a (4)	4.25	8.30

Nos. C2a-C4a were issued in 1937-38, on paper with sideways watermark. The 1935 first printing, which includes C1, is on paper within which the watermark is upright. For detailed listings, see the *Scott Classic Specialized Catalogue.*

RHODES AIR POST SEMI-POSTAL STAMPS

Rhodes Nos. C1-C4 Surcharged in Silver

1944 Wmk. 140 *Perf. 14*

CB1	AP18	50c + 2 l	12.00	3.75
CB2	AP18	80c + 2 l	12.00	7.50
CB3	AP18	1 l + 2 l	16.00	9.00
CB4	AP18	5 l + 2 l	100.00	*110.00*
		Nos. CB1-CB4 (4)	140.00	*130.25*

The surtax was for war victims.

RHODES SPECIAL DELIVERY STAMPS

Stag — SD1

1936 Photo. Wmk. 140 *Perf. 14*

E1	SD1	1.25 l green	4.75	4.75
E2	SD1	2.50 l vermilion	8.00	8.00

Nos. 58 and 57 Surcharged in Black

1943

E3	A3	1.25 l on 25c dl grn	1.50	*3.75*
E4	A3	2.50 l on 20c red	1.50	*3.75*

RHODES SEMI-POSTAL SPECIAL DELIVERY STAMPS

Rhodes Nos. E1 and E2 Srchd. in Red or Black

1943 Wmk. 140 *Perf. 14*

EB1	SD1	1.25 l + 1.25 l (R)	82.50	92.50
EB2	SD1	2.50 l + 2.50 l	97.50	150.00

The surtax was for general relief.

RHODES POSTAGE DUE STAMPS

Maltese Cross PD1

Immortelle PD2

1934 Photo. Wmk. 140 *Perf. 13*

J1	PD1	5c vermilion	4.75	8.00
J2	PD1	10c carmine	4.75	8.00
J3	PD1	20c dk grn	4.75	6.50
J4	PD1	30c purple	4.75	6.50
J5	PD1	40c dk bl	4.75	12.50
J6	PD2	50c vermilion	4.75	6.50
J7	PD2	60c carmine	4.75	24.00
J8	PD2	1 l dk grn	4.75	24.00
J9	PD2	2 l purple	4.75	12.50
		Nos. J1-J9 (9)	42.75	108.50

RHODES PARCEL POST STAMPS

Both unused and used values are for complete stamps.

PP1

PP2

1934 Photo. Wmk. 140 *Perf. 13*

Q1	PP1	5c vermilion	6.50	12.00
Q2	PP1	10c carmine	6.50	12.00
Q3	PP1	20c dk green	6.50	12.00
Q4	PP1	25c purple	6.50	12.00
Q5	PP1	50c dk blue	6.50	12.00
Q6	PP1	60c black	6.50	12.00
Q7	PP2	1 l vermilion	6.50	12.00
Q8	PP2	2 l carmine	6.50	12.00
Q9	PP2	3 l dk green	6.50	12.00
Q10	PP2	4 l purple	6.50	12.00
Q11	PP2	10 l dk blue	6.50	12.00
		Nos. Q1-Q11 (11)	71.50	132.00

Value of used halves, Nos. Q1-Q11, each 80 cents.

See note preceding No. Q7 of Italy.

SCARPANTO

Overprinted "Scarpanto" in Black or Violet

1912-22 Wmk. 140 *Perf. 13½, 14*

1	A43	2c org brn	9.50	9.50
2	A48	5c green	3.25	*9.50*
3	A48	10c claret	1.60	*9.50*
4	A48	15c slate ('22)	19.00	*40.00*
5	A50	20c brn org ('21)	65.00	65.00
6	A49	25c blue	9.50	9.50
7	A49	40c brown	1.60	*9.50*
8	A49	50c violet	3.25	*19.00*

Unwmk.

9	A58	15c slate (V)	40.00	19.00
10	A50	20c brn org ('17)	140.00	*225.00*
		Nos. 1-10 (10)	292.70	*415.50*

No 9 Surcharged Like Calchi No. 11

1916 *Perf. 13½*

11	A58	20c on 15c slate	1.60	*40.00*

Ferrucci Issue

Types of Italy

Overprinted in Red or Blue

1930 Wmk. 140 *Perf. 14*

12	A102	20c violet (R)	4.00	*9.50*
13	A103	25c dk green (R)	4.00	*9.50*
14	A103	50c black (R)	4.00	*16.00*
15	A103	1.25 l dp bl (R)	4.00	*16.00*
16	A104	5 l + 2 l dp car (Bl)	11.00	*27.50*
		Nos. 12-16 (5)	27.00	*78.50*

Garibaldi Issue

Types of Italy

Overprinted in Red or Blue

1932

17	A138	10c brown	19.00	*35.00*
18	A138	20c red brn (Bl)	19.00	*35.00*
19	A138	25c dp grn	19.00	*35.00*
20	A138	30c bluish sl	19.00	*35.00*
21	A138	50c red vio (Bl)	19.00	*35.00*
22	A141	75c cop red (Bl)	19.00	*35.00*
23	A141	1.25 l dull blue	19.00	*35.00*
24	A141	1.75 l + 25c brn	19.00	*35.00*
25	A144	2.55 l + 50c org (Bl)	19.00	*35.00*
26	A145	5 l + 1 l dl vio	19.00	*35.00*
		Nos. 17-26 (10)	190.00	*350.00*

SIMI

Overprinted "Simi" in Black or Violet

1912-21 Wmk. 140 *Perf. 13½, 14*

1	A43	2c org brn	16.00	9.50
2	A48	5c green	40.00	9.50
3	A48	10c claret	1.60	*9.50*
4	A48	15c slate ('21)	140.00	72.50
5	A50	20c brn org ('21)	72.50	40.00
6	A49	25c blue	9.50	*9.50*
7	A49	40c brown	1.60	*9.50*
8	A49	50c violet	1.60	*19.00*

Unwmk.

9	A58	15c slate (V)	72.00	19.00
10	A50	20c brn org ('17)	72.50	*125.00*
		Nos. 1-10 (10)	427.30	*323.00*

No. 9 Surcharged Like Calchi No. 11

1916 *Perf. 13½*

11	A58	20c on 15c slate	9.50	*40.00*

Ferrucci Issue

Types of Italy

Overprinted in Red or Blue

1930 Wmk. 140 *Perf. 14*

12	A102	20c violet (R)	4.75	*9.50*
13	A103	25c dk green (R)	4.75	*9.50*
14	A103	50c black (R)	4.75	*16.00*
15	A103	1.25 l dp bl (R)	4.75	*16.00*
16	A104	5 l + 2 l dp car (Bl)	11.00	*27.50*
		Nos. 12-16 (5)	30.00	*78.50*

Garibaldi Issue

Types of Italy

Overprinted in Red or Blue

1932

17	A138	10c brown	19.00	*35.00*
18	A138	20c red brn (Bl)	19.00	*35.00*
19	A138	25c dp grn	19.00	*35.00*
20	A138	30c bluish sl	19.00	*35.00*
21	A138	50c red vio (Bl)	19.00	*35.00*
22	A141	75c cop red (Bl)	19.00	*35.00*
23	A141	1.25 l dull blue	19.00	*35.00*
24	A141	1.75 l + 25c brn	19.00	*35.00*
25	A144	2.55 l + 50c org (Bl)	19.00	*35.00*
26	A145	5 l + 1 l dl vio	19.00	*35.00*
		Nos. 17-26 (10)	190.00	*350.00*

STAMPALIA

Overprinted "Stampalia" in Black or Violet

1912-21 Wmk. 140 *Perf. 13½, 14*

1	A43	2c org brn	9.50	9.50
2	A48	5c green	1.60	*9.50*
3	A48	10c claret	1.60	*9.50*
4	A48	15c slate ('21)	11.00	*40.00*
5	A50	20c brn org ('21)	55.00	*72.50*
6	A49	25c blue	1.60	*9.50*

7 A49 40c brown 4.75 *9.50*
8 A49 50c violet 1.60 *19.00*

Unwmk.

9 A58 15c slate (V) 47.50 19.00
10 A50 20c brn org ('17) 95.00 *125.00*
Nos. 1-10 (10) 229.15 *323.00*

No. 9 Surcharged Like Calchi No. 11

1916 ***Perf. 13½***
11 A58 20c on 15c slate 1.60 *40.00*

Ferrucci Issue
Types of Italy
Overprinted in Red or Blue

1930 **Wmk. 140** ***Perf. 14***
12 A102 20c violet (R) 4.00 *9.50*
13 A103 25c dk green (R) 4.00 *9.50*
14 A103 50c black (R) 4.00 *16.00*
15 A103 1.25 l dp bl (R) 4.00 *16.00*
16 A104 5 l + 2 l dp car (Bl) 11.00 *27.50*
Nos. 12-16 (5) 27.00 *78.50*

Garibaldi Issue
Types of Italy
Overprinted in Red or Blue

1932
17 A138 10c brown 19.00 *35.00*
18 A138 20c red brn (Bl) 19.00 *35.00*
19 A138 25c dp grn 19.00 *35.00*
20 A138 30c bluish sl 19.00 *35.00*
21 A138 50c red vio (Bl) 19.00 *35.00*
22 A141 75c cop red (Bl) 19.00 *35.00*
23 A141 1.25 l dull blue 19.00 *35.00*
24 A141 1.75 l + 25c brn 19.00 *35.00*
25 A144 2.55 l + 50c org (Bl) 19.00 *35.00*
26 A145 5 l + 1 l dl vio 19.00 *35.00*
Nos. 17-26 (10) 190.00 *350.00*

TRIESTE

A free territory (1947-1954) on the Adriatic Sea between Italy and Yugoslavia. In 1954 the territory was divided, Italy acquiring the northern section and seaport, Yugoslavia the southern section (Zone B).

Catalogue values for all unused stamps in this country are for Never Hinged items.

ZONE A

Issued jointly by the Allied Military Government of the United States and Great Britain
Stamps of Italy 1945-47 Overprinted

a

b

c

1947, Oct. 1 **Wmk. 277** ***Perf. 14***
1 A259(a) 25c brt bl grn .30 *1.60*
2 A255(a) 50c dp vio .30 *1.60*
3 A257(a) 1 l dk grn .30 .25
4 A258(a) 2 l dk cl brn .30 .25
5 A259(a) 3 l red .30 .25
6 A259(a) 4 l red org .30 .25
7 A256(a) 5 l deep blue .30 .25
8 A257(a) 6 l dp vio .30 .25
9 A255(a) 10 l slate .30 .25
10 A257(a) 15 l deep blue 2.75 .25
11 A259(a) 20 l dk red vio 4.50 .25
12 A260(b) 25 l dk grn 6.50 *13.00*
13 A260(b) 50 l dk vio brn 7.00 *8.00*

Perf. 14x13½
14 A261(c) 100 l car lake 55.00 45.00
Nos. 1-14 (14) 78.45 *71.45*

The letters "F. T. T." are the initials of "Free Territory of Trieste."

Italy Nos. 486-488 Ovptd. Type "a"

1948, Mar. 1 ***Perf. 14***
15 A255 8 l dk green 6.50 *11.00*
16 A256 10 l red org 20.00 .30
17 A259 30 l dk blue 275.00 19.00
Nos. 15-17 (3) 301.50 30.30

Italy Nos. 495 to 506 Overprinted — d

1948, July 1
18 A272 3 l dk brn .45 .45
19 A272 4 l red vio .45 .45
20 A272 5 l deep blue .45 .45
21 A272 6 l dp yel grn .90 .45
22 A272 8 l brown .45 .45
23 A272 10 l org red .90 .45
24 A272 12 l dk gray grn .90 *1.40*
25 A272 15 l gray blk 20.00 17.50
26 A272 20 l car rose 35.00 17.50
27 A272 30 l brt ultra 2.75 2.75
28 A272 50 l violet 24.00 *32.50*
29 A272 100 l bl blk 52.50 *80.00*
Nos. 18-29 (12) 138.75 *154.35*

Italy Nos. 486-488 Overprinted in Carmine

1948, Sept. 8
30 A255 8 l dk green .30 .25
31 A256 10 l red org .30 .25
32 A259 30 l dk blue 2.75 2.75
Nos. 30-32,C17-C19 (6) 6.55 6.45

The overprint is embossed.

Italy No. 507 Overprinted in Carmine

1948, Oct. 15
33 A273 15 l dk green 6.00 6.00

Italy No. 508 Overprinted in Green — e

1948, Nov. 15
34 A274 15 l dk brown 20.00 4.00

Italy No. 509 Overprinted in Red

1949, May 2 **Wmk. 277** ***Perf. 14***
35 A275 20 l dk brown 16.00 8.00

Italy Nos. 510-513 Overprinted — f

1949, May 2 **Buff Background**
36 A276 5 l red brown .80 *1.60*
37 A276 15 l dk green 13.00 *24.00*
38 A276 20 l dp red brn 7.25 1.60
39 A276 50 l dk blue 16.00 12.00
Nos. 36-39 (4) 37.05 *39.20*

Italy No. 514 Overprinted in Red

1949, May 2
40 A277 50 l brt ultra 5.50 5.50

Italy No. 518 Overprinted in Red

1949, May 30
41 A279 100 l brown 72.50 *120.00*

Italy Nos. 515-517 Overprinted in Black

1949, June 15
42 A278 5 l dk green 14.50 9.50
43 A278 15 l violet 14.50 *17.50*
44 A278 20 l brown 14.50 14.50
Nos. 42-44 (3) 43.50 41.50

Italy Nos. 519 and 520 Overprinted in Carmine

1949, July 16
45 A280 20 l gray 14.50 8.00
46 A281 20 l brown 14.50 8.00

Italy, No. 521 Ovptd. in Green — g

1949, June 8
47 A282 20 l brown red 8.00 8.00

Italy No. 522 Overprinted in Carmine

1949, July 8
49 A283 20 l violet 22.50 16.00

Italy No. 523 Overprinted in Black, Without Periods

1949, Aug. 27
50 A284 20 l violet blue 16.00 8.00

Italy No. 524 Overprinted

1949, Aug. 27
51 A285 20 l violet 24.00 24.00

Italy No. 525 Overprinted in Green

1949, Sept. 10
52 A286 20 l red 14.50 8.00

Italy Nos. 526 and 527 Overprinted — h

Wmk. 277
1949, Nov. 7 **Photo.** ***Perf. 14***
53 A287 20 l rose car 6.50 6.50
54 A288 50 l deep blue 24.00 *26.00*

No. 528 Overprinted

1949, Nov. 7
55 A289 20 l dp grn 8.75 6.50

No. 529 Overprinted

1949, Nov. 7
56 A290 20 l brt blue 5.50 4.75

No. 530 Overprint in Red

1949, Dec. 28

57 A291 20 l violet blk 7.25 4.00

Italian Stamps of 1945-48 Overprinted in Black

1949-50				**Photo.**
58	A257	1 l dk green	.25	*1.00*
59	A258	2 l dk cl brn	.25	.25
60	A259	3 l red	.25	.25
61	A256	5 l deep blue	.25	.25
62	A257	6 l dp violet	.25	.25
63	A255	8 l dk green	55.00	47.50
64	A256	10 l red org	.25	.25
65	A257	15 l deep blue	4.00	.80
66	A259	20 l dk red vio	2.40	.25
67	A260	25 l dk grn ('50)	40.00	4.75
68	A260	50 l dk vio brn ('50)	60.00	4.00
		Engr.		
69	A261	100 l car lake	120.00	32.50
		Nos. 58-69 (12)	282.90	92.05

Issued: 3 l, 20 l, 10/21; 5 l, 11/5; 10 l, 11/7; 100 l, 11/23; 15 l, 11/28; 1 l, 2 l, 6 l, 8 l, 12/28; 50 l, 1/19; 25 l, 2/25.

Italy No. 531 Overprinted in Carmine

1950, Apr. 12

70 A292 20 l brown 7.25 4.00

Italy No. 532 Overprinted in Carmine

1950, Apr. 29

71 A293 20 l vio gray 5.50 5.50

Italy Nos. 533-534 Overprinted in Carmine

1950, May 22

72 A294 20 l olive green 5.50 5.50
73 A295 55 l blue 20.00 20.00

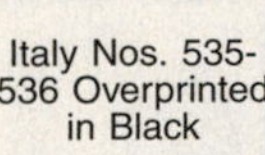

Italy Nos. 535-536 Overprinted in Black

1950, May 29

74 A296 20 l violet 9.00 4.75
75 A296 55 l blue 35.00 27.50

Italy No. 537 Overprinted in Carmine

1950, July 10

76 A297 20 l gray grn 5.50 5.50

Italy Nos. 538-539 Overprint in Carmine

1950, July 15

77 A298 20 l purple 9.50 5.50
78 A298 55 l blue 35.00 *40.00*

Italy No. 540 Overprinted

1950, July 22

79 A299 20 l brown 9.50 8.00

Italy, No. 541 Overprinted in Carmine — i

1950, July 29

80 A300 20 l dk grn 9.00 7.25

Italy No. 542 Overprinted

1950, Aug. 21

81 A301 20 l chnt brn 4.75 4.75

Italy Nos. 473A-474 Overprinted

1950, Aug. 27

82 A257 15 l blue 8.00 4.75
83 A259 20 l dk red vio 8.00 7.25

Trieste Fair.

Italy No. 543 Overprinted in Carmine

1950, Sept. 11

84 A302 20 l indigo 4.75 4.00

Italy Nos. 544-546 Overprinted

1950, Sept. 16		**Wmk. 277**		***Perf. 14***
85	A303	5 l dp cl & grn	2.00	*4.75*
86	A303	20 l brn & grn	4.75	4.75
87	A303	55 l dp ultra & brn	40.00	*40.00*
		Nos. 85-87 (3)	46.75	*49.50*

Italy No. 547 Overprinted in Black

1950, Sept. 16

88 A304 20 l ol brn & red brn 5.50 4.75

Italy No. 548 Overprinted in Black

1950, Sept. 16

89 A305 20 l cream & gray blk 9.00 7.25

Italy Nos. 549 to 565 Overprinted in Black

1950, Oct. 20				
90	A306	50c violet blue	.25	.25
91	A306	1 l dk blue vio	.25	.25
92	A306	2 l sepia	.25	.25
93	A306	5 l dk gray	.25	.25
94	A306	6 l chocolate	.25	.25
95	A306	10 l deep green	.80	.25
96	A306	12 l dp blue grn	2.40	.80
97	A306	15 l dk gray bl	2.40	.25
98	A306	20 l blue vio	2.40	.25
99	A306	25 l brown org	4.00	.25
100	A306	30 l magenta	1.60	.80
101	A306	35 l crimson	4.00	1.60
102	A306	40 l brown	1.75	1.60
103	A306	50 l violet	.80	.80
104	A306	55 l deep blue	.80	.80
105	A306	60 l red	12.00	*14.50*
106	A306	65 l dk green	.80	.80

Italy Nos. 566 and 567 Overprinted — k

		Perf. 14, 14x13½		
		Engr.		
107	A306	100 l brown org	9.00	.25
108	A306	200 l olive brn	8.00	*9.00*
		Nos. 90-108 (19)	52.00	*33.20*

Italy Nos. 568-569 Overprinted in Black

1951, Mar. 27		**Photo.**		***Perf. 14***
109	A307	20 l red vio & red	8.00	8.00
110	A307	55 l ultra & bl	65.00	65.00

Italy No. 570 Overprinted

1951, Apr. 2

111 A308 20 l dk grn 4.00 4.00

Italy No. 571 Overprinted

1951, Apr. 11

112 A309 20 l bl vio 4.75 4.75

Italy Nos. 572-573 Overprinted

1951, Apr. 12

113 A310(h) 20 l brown 4.75 4.75
114 A311(g) 55 l deep blue 7.25 7.25

Italy Nos. 574-576 Overprinted in Black

1951, May 18		**Fleur-de-Lis in Red**		
115	A312	5 l dk brown	11.00	*75.00*
116	A312	10 l Prus grn	11.00	*75.00*
117	A312	15 l vio bl	11.00	*75.00*
		Nos. 115-117 (3)	33.00	*225.00*

Italy No. 577 Overprinted — m

1951, Apr. 26
118 A313 20 l violet 4.75 4.75

Italy No. 578 Overprinted

1951, May 5
119 A314 20 l Prus green 4.25 4.75

Italy Nos. 579-580 Ovptd. Type "g"

1951, June 18
120 A315 20 l violet 2.00 2.00
121 A315 55 l brt blue 4.75 4.75

Nos. 94, 98 and 104 Overprinted

1951, June 24
122 A306 6 l chocolate .80 *2.00*
123 A306 20 l blue violet 2.00 .80
124 A306 55 l deep blue 2.00 2.00
Nos. 122-124 (3) 4.80 4.80

Issued to publicize the Trieste Fair, 1951.

Italy No. 581 Overprinted — n

1951, July 23
125 A316 20 l brn & red brn 4.00 4.00

Italy Nos. 582 and 583 Overprinted in Red

1951, July 23
126 A317(n) 20 l grnsh gray & blk 2.75 2.75
127 A318(h) 55 l vio bl & pale sal 5.25 5.25

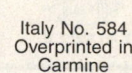

Italy No. 584 Overprinted in Carmine

1951, Aug. 23
128 A319 25 l gray blk 17.50 8.00

Italy No. 585 Overprinted in Black

1951, Sept. 8
129 A320 25 l deep blue 4.00 4.00

Italy No. 586 Ovptd. in Red

1951, Sept. 15
130 A321 25 l dk brn 4.00 4.00

Italy Nos. 587-589 Ovptd. in Blue — o

1951, Oct. 11
131 A322 10 l dk brn & gray 2.00 2.00
132 A322 25 l rose red & grnsh bl 2.00 2.00
133 A322 60 l vio bl & red org 4.00 4.00
Nos. 131-133 (3) 8.00 8.00

Italy Nos. 590-591 Overprinted — p

Overprint Spaced to Fit Design

1951, Oct. 31 **Photo.**
134 A323 10 l green 2.50 2.50
135 A324 25 l vio gray 2.50 2.50

Italy Nos. 592-593 Ovprinted in Black

1951, Nov. 21
136 A325 10 l ol & dull grn 2.50 2.50
137 A326 25 l dull green 2.50 2.50

Italy Nos. 594-596 Overprinted in Black

No. 138

No. 139

Overprint "p" Spaced to Fit Design

1951, Nov. 23
138 A327(p) 10 l vio brn & dk grn 2.00 *2.50*
139 A327(k) 25 l red brn & dk brn 2.00 1.60
140 A327(p) 60 l dp grn & ind 4.00 4.00
Nos. 138-140 (3) 8.00 8.10

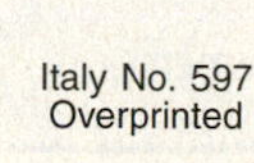

Italy No. 597 Overprinted

Overprint Spaced to Fit Design

1952, Jan. 28 **Wmk. 277** ***Perf. 14***
141 A328 25 l gray & gray blk 4.00 3.25

Italy No. 598 Ovptd. in Black

1952, Feb. 2
142 A329 25 l dl grn & ol bis 4.00 3.25

Italy No. 599 Overprinted in Black

1952, Mar. 26
143 A330 25 l brn & sl blk 4.00 3.25

Italy No. 600 Overprinted in Blue

1952, Apr. 12
144 A331 60 l ultra 4.00 *4.75*

Italy No. 601 Overprinted in Black

1952, Apr. 16
145 A332 25 l dp orange .80 .40

Stamps of Italy Overprinted in Various Sizes and Arrangements

No. 146

On Nos. 602-603

1952, June 14 **Wmk. 277** ***Perf. 14***
146 A333 25 l blk & red brn 2.00 2.00
147 A333 60 l blk & ultra 2.75 2.75

1952, June 7 **On No. 604**
148 A334 25 l bright blue 4.00 4.00

Italy No. 605 Overprinted in Black

1952, June 14
149 A335 25 l black & yellow 4.00 4.00

1952, June 19 **On No. 606**
150 A336 25 l bl gray, red & dk bl (R) 4.00 4.00

1952, June 28 **On No. 607**
151 A337 25 l dp grn, dk brn & red 4.00 4.00

1952, Sept. 6 **On No. 608**
152 A338 25 l dark green 4.00 4.00

On No. 609 in Gold

1952, Sept. 20
153 A339 25 l purple 4.00 4.00

1952, Oct. 4 **On No. 610**
154 A340 25 l gray 4.00 4.00

1952, Oct. 1 **On No. 611**
155 A341 60 l vio bl & dk bl 4.75 4.75

Italy No. 612 Overprinted in Black

1952, Nov. 21 ***Perf. 13***
156 A342 25 l brn & dk brn 3.25 2.40

Italy Nos. 613-615 Overprinted in Black

1952, Nov. 3 ***Perf. 14***
157 A343 10 l dk green .80 .80
158 A344 25 l blk & dk brn 1.60 .80
159 A344 60 l blk & blue 2.25 *2.25*
Nos. 157-159 (3) 4.65 *3.85*

1952, Dec. 6 **On Nos. 616-617**
160 A345 25 l dk green 4.00 4.00
161 A346 25 l brown 4.00 4.00

1953, Jan. 5 **On No. 618**
162 A347 25 l gray blk & dk bl (Bl) 4.00 4.00

On Nos. 601A-601B

1952, Dec. 31
163 A332a 60 l ultra (G) 3.25 *3.25*
164 A332 80 l brown car 4.00 *4.50*

1953, Feb. 21 **On No. 621**
165 A349 25 l car lake 4.00 4.00

1953, Apr. 24 **On No. 622**
166 A350 25 l violet 4.00 4.00

1953, Apr. 30 **On No. 623**
167 A351 25 l violet 4.00 4.00

1953, May 30 **On No. 624**
168 A352 25 l dark brown 4.00 4.00

1953, June 27 **On No. 625**
169 A353 25 l brn & dull red 4.00 4.00

1953-54 On Nos. 626-633

170 A354 5 l gray .25 *.35*
171 A354 10 l org ver .25 .25
172 A354 12 l dull grn .25 .25
172A A354 13 l brt lil rose ('54) .25 .25
173 A354 20 l brown .80 .80
174 A354 25 l purple .80 .90
175 A354 35 l rose car 4.00 4.00
176 A354 60 l blue 6.50 6.50
177 A354 80 l org brn 20.00 20.00
Nos. 170-177 (9) 33.10 33.30

Issue dates: 13 l, Feb. 1. Others, June 16.

Italy, Nos. 554, 558 and 564 Overprinted in Red or Green

1953, June 27

178 A306 10 l dp green (R) .80 1.25
179 A306 25 l brown org .80 .80
180 A306 60 l red 3.25 2.75
Nos. 178-180 (3) 4.85 4.80

5th International Sample Fair of Trieste.

Italy No. 634 Overprinted in Black

1953, July 11

181 A355 25 l grnsh blue 4.00 4.00

1953, July 16 On Nos. 635-636

182 A356 25 l dark brown 2.00 *.80*
183 A356 60 l deep blue 2.75 *4.00*

1953, Aug. 6 On Nos. 637-638

184 A357 25 l org & Prus bl 2.50 2.50
185 A357 60 l lil rose & dk vio bl 4.00 4.00

1953, Aug. 13 On No. 639

186 A358 25 l dk brn & dl grn 4.00 4.00

1953, Sept. 5 On No. 640

187 A359 25 l dk gray & brn 4.00 4.00

1954, Jan. 26 On Nos. 641-646

188 A360 10 l dk brn & red brn .40 .40
189 A361 12 l lt bl & gray .40 .40
190 A361 20 l brn org & dk brn .40 .40
191 A360 25 l dk grn & pale bl .40 .40
192 A361 35 l cream & brn 3.25 3.25
193 A361 60 l bl grn & ind 3.25 3.25
Nos. 188-193 (6) 8.10 8.10

1954, Feb. 11 On Nos. 647-648

194 A362 25 l dk brn & choc 1.60 .80
195 A362 60 l bl & ultra 3.25 *4.00*

1954, Feb. 25 On Nos. 649-650

196 A363 25 l purple 1.60 .80
197 A363 60 l dp bl grn 3.25 *4.00*

1954, Mar. 20 On No. 651

198 A364 25 l purple 4.00 4.00

1954, Apr. 24 On No. 652

199 A365 25 l gray blk 4.00 4.00

1954, June 1 On No. 653

200 A366 25 l gray, org brn & blk 4.00 4.00

1954, June 19 On No. 654

201 A367 25 l dk grnsh gray 4.00 4.00

1954, July 8 On Nos. 655-656

202 A368 25 l red brown 1.60 1.60
203 A368 60 l gray green 3.25 3.25

Nos. 644, 646 With Additional Overprint

1954, June 17

204 A360 25 l dk grn & pale bl 1.60 1.60
205 A361 60 l bl grn & indigo 3.25 3.25

International Sample Fair of Trieste.

Italy No. 657 Overprinted in Black

1954, Sept. 6

206 A369 25 l dp grn & red 4.00 4.00

1954, Oct. 30 On Nos. 658-659

207 A370 25 l rose red 1.60 1.60
208 A370 60 l blue 3.25 3.25

OCCUPATION AIR POST STAMPS

Air Post Stamps of Italy 1945-47 Overprinted in Black

1947, Oct. 1 Wmk. 277 *Perf. 14*

C1 AP59 1 l slate bl .25 .25
C2 AP60 2 l dk blue .25 .25
C3 AP60 5 l dk green 9.00 8.75
C4 AP59 10 l car rose 9.00 8.75
C5 AP60 25 l brown 27.50 17.50
C6 AP59 50 l violet 120.00 25.00
Nos. C1-C6 (6) 166.00 60.50

Italy Nos. C116-C121 Overprinted in Black

1947, Nov. 19

C7 AP61 6 l dp violet 2.40 *4.00*
C8 AP61 10 l dk car rose 2.40 *4.00*
C9 AP61 20 l dp org 21.00 16.00
C10 AP61 25 l aqua 3.25 *4.75*
C11 AP61 35 l brt blue 3.25 *6.50*
C12 AP61 50 l lilac rose 21.00 12.50
Nos. C7-C12 (6) 53.30 *47.75*

Italy Nos. C123-C126 Overprinted in Black

1948

C13 AP65 100 l green 127.50 9.00
C14 AP65 300 l lil rose 27.50 *40.00*
C15 AP65 500 l ultra 50.00 *55.00*
C16 AP65 1000 l dk brown 275.00 *360.00*
Nos. C13-C16 (4) 480.00 *464.00*

Issue date: Nos. C13-C15, Mar. 1.

Italy, No. C110, C113 and C114, Ovptd. in Black

1948, Sept. 8

C17 AP59 10 l carmine rose .40 .40
C18 AP60 25 l brown .80 .80
C19 AP59 50 l violet 2.00 2.00
Nos. C17-C19 (3) 3.20 3.20

The overprint is embossed.

Italy Air Post Stamps of 1945-48 Overprinted in Black

1949-52

C20 AP59 10 l car rose .25 .25
C21 AP60 25 l brown ('50) .25 .25
C22 AP59 50 l violet .25 .25
C23 AP65 100 l green 1.60 .25
C24 AP65 300 l lil rose ('50) 22.50 *40.00*
C25 AP65 500 l ultra ('50) 47.50 47.50
C26 AP65 1000 l dk brn ('52) 75.00 *110.00*
Nos. C20-C26 (7) 147.35 *198.50*

No. C26 is found in two perforations: 14 and 14x13.

Issued: 100 l, 11/7; 50 l, 12/5; 10 l, 12/28; 25 l, 1/23; 300 l, 500 l, 11/25; 1000 l, 2/18.

OCCUPATION SPECIAL DELIVERY STAMPS

Special Delivery Stamps of Italy 1946-48 Overprinted in Black

1947-48 Wmk. 277 *Perf. 14*

E1 SD9 15 l dk car rose .25 .30
E2 SD8 25 l brt red org ('48) 95.00 32.50
E3 SD8 30 l dp vio .60 .60
E4 SD9 60 l car rose ('48) 95.00 45.00
Nos. E1-E4 (4) 190.85 78.40

Issue dates: Oct. 1, 1947. Mar. 1, 1948.

Italy No. E26 Overprinted in Black

1948, Sept. 24

E5 A272 35 l violet 4.00 4.00

Italy No. E25 Overprinted in Black

1950, Sept. 27

E6 SD9 60 l car rose 9.00 3.25

Italy No. E32 Overprinted in Black

1952, Feb. 4

E7 SD8 50 l lilac rose 9.00 3.25

OCCUPATION AUTHORIZED DELIVERY STAMPS

Italy No. EY5 Overprinted in Black

1947, Oct. 1 Wmk. 277 *Perf. 14*

EY1 AD3 1 l dark brown .80 *1.60*

Italy, No. EY7 Overprinted in Black

1947, Oct. 29

EY2 AD4 8 l bright red 14.50 4.75

Italy No. EY8 Overprinted in Black

1949, July 30

EY3 AD4 15 l violet 80.00 40.00

Italy No. EY8 Overprinted in Black

1949, Nov. 7

EY4 AD4 15 l violet 1.60 *2.00*

Italy No. EY9 Overprinted in Black

1952, Feb. 4

EY5 AD4 20 l rose violet 14.50 2.40

OCCUPATION POSTAGE DUE STAMPS

Postage Due Stamps of Italy, 1945-47, Overprinted Type "a"

1947, Oct. 1 Wmk. 277 *Perf. 14*

J1 D9 1 l red orange .80 .80
J2 D10 2 l dk green .40 .80
J3 D9 5 l violet 8.00 2.50
J4 D9 10 l dk blue 16.00 9.00
J5 D9 20 l car rose 32.50 12.00
J6 D10 50 l aqua 2.40 1.60
Nos. J1-J6 (6) 60.10 26.70

Italy Nos. J65, J67-J74 Overprinted in Black

1949

J7	D10	1 l red orange	.40	*.80*
J8	D10	3 l carmine	.80	*3.25*
J9	D10	4 l brown	22.50	*40.00*
J10	D10	5 l violet	175.00	52.50
J11	D10	6 l vio blue	65.00	*80.00*
J12	D10	8 l rose vio	110.00	*190.00*
J13	D10	10 l deep blue	250.00	52.50
J14	D10	12 l golden brn	40.00	*55.00*
J15	D10	20 l lilac rose	40.00	17.50
		Nos. J7-J15 (9)	703.70	491.55

Issued: 3 l, 4 l, 6 l, 8 l, 12 l, 1/24; others, 4/15.

Italy Nos. J65-J78 Overprinted in Black

1949-54

J16	D10	1 l red orange	.25	.25
J17	D10	2 l dk green	.25	.25
J18	D10	3 l car ('54)	.25	.50
J20	D10	5 l violet	1.25	.25
J21	D10	6 l vio bl ('50)	.25	.25
J22	D10	8 l rose vio ('50)	.25	*1.00*
J23	D10	10 l deep blue	.35	*1.00*
J24	D10	12 l gldn brn ('50)	1.60	1.00
J25	D10	20 l lilac rose	4.00	.25
J26	D10	25 l dk red ('54)	5.50	3.25
J27	D10	50 l aqua ('50)	6.50	.25
J28	D10	100 l org yel ('52)	10.00	1.75
J29	D10	500 l dp bl & dk car ('52)	120.00	110.00
		Nos. J16-J29 (13)	150.45	120.00

Issued: 5 l, 10 l, 11/7; 1 l, 11/22; 2 l, 20 l, 12/28; 6 l, 8 l, 12 l, 5/16; 50 l, 11/25; 100 l, 11/11; 500 l, 6/19; 3 l, 1/24; 25 l, 2/1.

OCCUPATION PARCEL POST STAMPS

See note preceding Italy No. Q7.

Parcel Post Stamps of Italy, 1946-48, Overprinted

1947-48 Wmk. 277 *Perf. 13½*

Q1	PP4	1 l golden brn	.80	*2.40*
Q2	PP4	2 l lt bl grn	1.00	*4.00*
Q3	PP4	3 l red org	.80	*4.00*
Q4	PP4	4 l gray blk	1.25	*4.75*
Q5	PP4	5 l lil rose ('48)	27.50	*35.00*
Q6	PP4	10 l violet	8.00	*20.00*
Q7	PP4	20 l lilac brn	8.00	*20.00*
Q8	PP4	50 l rose red	12.00	*37.50*
Q9	PP4	100 l sapphire	17.50	*47.50*
Q10	PP4	200 l grn ('48)	575.00	*1,000.*
Q11	PP4	300 l brn car ('48)	350.00	*525.00*
Q12	PP4	500 l brn ('48)	200.00	*300.00*
		Nos. Q1-Q12 (12)	1,202.	*2,000.*

Halves Used

Q1-Q4	.40
Q5	.40
Q6-Q7	.40
Q8	.40
Q9	.40
Q10	.80
Q11	.60
Q12	.60

Issued: Nos. Q1-Q4, Q6-Q9, Oct. 1; others, Mar. 1.

Parcel Post Stamps of Italy, 1946-54, Overprinted

1949-54

Q13	PP4	1 l gldn brn ('50)	1.75	1.60
Q14	PP4	2 l lt bl grn ('51)	.85	*1.00*
Q15	PP4	3 l red org ('51)	.85	*1.00*
Q16	PP4	4 l gray blk ('51)	.85	1.00
Q17	PP4	5 l lilac rose	.85	*1.00*
Q18	PP4	10 l violet	2.25	2.25
Q19	PP4	20 l lil brn	2.25	2.25
Q20	PP4	30 l plum ('52)	.85	*1.00*
Q21	PP4	50 l rose red ('50)	1.75	*2.00*
Q22	PP4	100 l saph ('50)	4.00	*7.00*
Q23	PP4	200 l green	27.50	*72.50*
Q24	PP4	300 l brn car ('50)	140.00	*225.00*
Q25	PP4	500 l brn ('51)	77.50	*135.00*

Perf. 13x13½

Q26	PP5	1000 l ultra ('54)	200.00	*600.00*
		Nos. Q13-Q26 (14)	461.25	*1,053.*

Halves Used

Q13-Q18, Q20	.40
Q19, Q22	.40
Q21	.40
Q23	.80
Q24	.80
Q25	.80
Q26	2.00

Pairs of Q18 exist with 5mm between overprints instead of 11mm. Value $1,000.

Issued: 20 l, 200 l, 11/22; 5 l, 10 l, 11/28; 300 l, 1/19; 50 l, 3/10; 1 l, 10/7; 100 l, 11/9; 500 l, 11/25; 2 l, 3 l, 4 l, 8/1; 30 l, 3/6; 1000 l, 8/12.

PARCEL POST AUTHORIZED DELIVERY STAMPS

For the payment of a special tax for the authorized delivery of parcels privately instead of through the post office. Both unused and used values are for complete stamps.

Italy Nos. QY1-QY4 Overprinted in Black

1953, July 8 Wmk. 277

QY1	PAD1	40 l org red	21.00	*7.00*
QY2	PAD1	50 l ultra	21.00	*7.00*
QY3	PAD1	75 l brown	21.00	*13.00*
QY4	PAD1	110 l lilac rose	21.00	*13.00*
		Nos. QY1-QY4 (4)	84.00	*40.00*

Halves Used

QY1	.25
QY2	.25
QY3-QY4, each	.35

IVORY COAST

'iv-rē 'kōst

LOCATION — West coast of Africa, bordering on Gulf of Guinea
GOVT. — Republic
AREA — 127,520 sq. mi.
POP. — 15,818,068 (1999 est.)
CAPITAL — Yamoussoukro

The former French colony of Ivory Coast became part of French West Africa and used its stamps, starting in 1945. On December 4, 1958, Ivory Coast became a republic, with full independence on August 7, 1960.

100 Centimes = 1 Franc

Catalogue values for unused stamps in this country are for Never Hinged items, beginning with Scott 165 in the regular postage section, Scott B8 in the semi-postal section, Scott C6 in the air-post section, Scott J19 in the postage due section, Scott M1 in the military section, and Scott O1 in the official section.

Navigation and Commerce — A1

Perf. 14x13½

1892-1900 Typo. Unwmk.

Colony Name in Blue or Carmine

1	A1	1c black, *lil bl*	2.25	2.25
2	A1	2c brown, *buff*	3.75	3.00
3	A1	4c claret, *lav*	5.25	4.50
4	A1	5c green, *grnsh*	15.00	11.00
5	A1	10c black, *lavender*	20.00	15.00
6	A1	10c red ('00)	130.00	110.00
7	A1	15c blue, quadrille paper	32.50	13.50
8	A1	15c gray ('00)	22.00	4.75
9	A1	20c red, *green*	21.00	16.00
10	A1	25c black, *rose*	24.00	7.50
11	A1	25c blue ('00)	40.00	37.50
12	A1	30c brown, *bister*	35.00	27.50
13	A1	40c red, *straw*	30.00	16.00
14	A1	50c car, *rose*	75.00	65.00
15	A1	50c brn, *azure* ('00)	40.00	25.00
16	A1	75c deep vio, *org*	32.50	32.50
17	A1	1fr brnz grn, *straw*	52.50	45.00
		Nos. 1-17 (17)	580.75	436.00

Perf. 13½x14 stamps are counterfeits.
For surcharges see Nos. 18-20, 37-41.

Nos. 12, 16-17 Surcharged in Black

1904

18	A1	0,05c on 30c brn, *bis*	87.50	87.50
19	A1	0,10c on 75c vio, *org*	18.00	18.00
20	A1	0,15c on 1fr brnz grn, *straw*	26.00	26.00
		Nos. 18-20 (3)	131.50	131.50

Gen. Louis Faidherbe A2

Oil Palm — A3

Dr. N. Eugène Ballay A4

1906-07

Name of Colony in Red or Blue

21	A2	1c slate	2.00	2.00
a.		"CÔTE D'IVOIRE" omitted	225.00	225.00
22	A2	2c chocolate	2.00	2.00
23	A2	4c choc, *gray bl*	2.40	2.40
a.		"CÔTE D'IVOIRE" double	250.00	
b.		"CÔTE D'IVOIRE" omitted	275.00	
24	A2	5c green	4.00	2.75
a.		"CÔTE D'IVOIRE" omitted	175.00	140.00
25	A2	10c carmine (B)	9.50	6.50
a.		"CÔTE D'IVOIRE" double	210.00	400.00
b.		"CÔTE D'IVOIRE" omitted		400.00
26	A3	20c black, *azure*	11.00	9.50
27	A3	25c bl, *pinkish*	9.50	6.00
28	A3	30c choc, *pnksh*	15.00	8.75
30	A3	35c black, *yel*	15.00	5.75
a.		"CÔTE D'IVOIRE" omitted	300.00	
31	A3	45c choc, *grnsh*	18.00	12.50
32	A3	50c deep violet	16.00	12.50
33	A3	75c blue, *org*	16.00	12.50
34	A4	1fr black, *azure*	40.00	35.00
35	A4	2fr blue, *pink*	52.50	50.00
36	A4	5fr car, *straw* (B)	100.00	95.00
		Nos. 21-36 (15)	312.90	263.15

Stamps of 1892-1900 Surcharged in Carmine or Black

1912

37	A1	5c on 15c gray (C)	1.60	1.60
38	A1	5c on 30c brn, *bis* (C)	2.40	2.75
39	A1	10c on 40c red, *straw*	2.40	2.75
a.		Pair, one without surcharge	75.00	75.00
40	A1	10c on 50c brn, *az* (C)	4.00	4.75
41	A1	10c on 75c dp vio, *org*	9.00	10.00
		Nos. 37-41 (5)	19.40	21.85

Two spacings between the surcharged numerals are found on Nos. 37 to 41. For detailed listings, see the *Scott Classic Specialized Catalogue of Stamps and Covers.*

River Scene A5

1913-35

42	A5	1c vio brn & vio	.25	.25
43	A5	2c brown & blk	.30	.25
44	A5	4c vio & vio brn	.35	.30
45	A5	5c yel grn & bl grn	1.10	.50
46	A5	5c choc & ol brn ('22)	.35	.35
47	A5	10c red org & rose	2.00	.95
48	A5	10c yel grn & bl grn ('22)	.70	.70
49	A5	10c car rose, *bluish* ('26)	.35	.35
50	A5	15c org & rose ('17)	1.10	.75
51	A5	20c black & gray	.80	.55
52	A5	25c ultra & bl	11.00	6.50
53	A5	25c blk & vio ('22)	.75	.75
54	A5	30c choc & brn	2.40	2.00
55	A5	30c red org & rose ('22)	2.75	2.75
56	A5	30c lt bl & rose red ('26)	.40	.40
57	A5	30c dl grn & grn ('27)	.80	.80
58	A5	35c vio & org	1.10	.80
59	A5	40c gray & bl grn	1.60	.80
60	A5	45c red org & choc	1.10	.80
61	A5	45c dp rose & mar ('34)	5.25	4.50
62	A5	50c black & vio	5.00	3.50
63	A5	50c ultra & bl ('22)	2.25	2.25
64	A5	50c ol grn & bl ('25)	.80	.80
65	A5	60c vio, *pnksh* ('25)	.80	.80
66	A5	65c car rose & ol grn ('26)	1.60	1.60
67	A5	75c brn & rose	1.10	.80
68	A5	75c ind & ultra ('34)	3.75	3.75
69	A5	85c red vio & blk ('26)	1.60	1.60
70	A5	90c brn red & rose ('30)	11.00	11.00
71	A5	1fr org & black	1.10	1.00
72	A5	1.10fr dl grn & dk brn ('28)	7.50	7.50
73	A5	1.50fr lt bl & dp bl ('30)	7.50	7.50
74	A5	1.75fr lt ultra & mag ('35)	15.00	9.00
75	A5	2fr brn & blue	5.25	2.60
76	A5	3fr red vio ('30)	7.50	7.50
77	A5	5fr dk bl & choc	7.50	5.25
		Nos. 42-77 (36)	113.70	91.50

Nos. 45, 47, 50, 52, 56 and 58 exist on both ordinary and chalky paper. See the *Scott Classic Specialized Catalogue of Stamps & Covers 1840-1940* for listings.

For surcharges see Nos. 78-91, B1.

Nos. 45, 47 and 52, pasted on cardboard and overprinted "Valeur d'echange" and value of basic stamp, were used as emergency currency in 1920.

Stamps and Type of 1913-34 Srchd.

1922-34

78	A5	50c on 45c dp rose & mar ('34)	4.00	2.75
79	A5	50c on 75c indigo & ultra ('34)	3.00	2.00
80	A5	50c on 90c brn red & rose ('34)	3.00	2.25
81	A5	60c on 75c vio, *pnksh*	.75	.75
a.		Surcharge omitted	160.00	*175.00*
82	A5	65c on 15c org & rose ('25)	1.25	1.25
83	A5	85c on 75c brn & rose ('25)	1.40	1.10
		Nos. 78-83 (6)	13.40	10.10

Stamps and Type of 1913 Surcharged with New Value and Bars

1924-27

84 A5 25c on 2fr (R) .35 1.00
85 A5 25c on 5fr .35 1.00
86 A5 90c on 75c brn red & cer ('27) 2.00 1.60
a. Surcharge omitted 240.00
87 A5 1.25fr on 1fr dk bl & ultra (R) ('26) 1.25 1.25
88 A5 1.50fr on 1fr lt bl & dk blue ('27) 1.90 1.90
89 A5 3fr on 5fr brn red & bl grn ('27) 6.00 6.00
a. Double surcharge 160.00
90 A5 10fr on 5fr dl red & rose lil ('27) 19.00 16.00
91 A5 20fr on 5fr bl grn & ver ('27) 19.00 18.00
Nos. 84-91 (8) 49.85 46.75

Common Design Types pictured following the introduction.

Colonial Exposition Issue

Common Design Types
Name of Country in Black

1931 **Engr.** ***Perf. 12½***

92 CD70 40c deep green 4.50 4.50
93 CD71 50c violet 6.00 6.00
94 CD72 90c red orange 6.00 6.00
95 CD73 1.50fr dull blue 6.00 6.00
Nos. 92-95 (4) 22.50 22.50

Stamps of Upper Volta 1928, Overprinted

1933 ***Perf. 13½x14***

96 A5 2c brown & lilac .25 .25
a. Inverted overprint 27.50
b. Double overprint 40.00 47.50
97 A5 4c blk & yellow .25 .30
a. Inverted overprint 100.00
b. Double overprint 65.00 72.50
98 A5 5c ind & gray bl .35 .45
a. Inverted overprint 47.50
b. Double overprint 65.00
99 A5 10c indigo & pink .35 .45
100 A5 15c brown & blue 1.10 .90
101 A5 20c brown & green 1.10 .90
102 A6 25c brn & yellow 2.25 1.90
103 A6 30c dp grn & grn 2.75 1.75
a. Double overprint 75.00
104 A6 45c brown & blue 8.25 6.00
a. Inverted overprint 80.00
b. Double overprint 120.00
105 A6 65c indigo & bl 3.00 2.60
a. Double overprint 95.00
106 A6 75c black & lilac 3.75 2.25
a. Double overprint 95.00
107 A6 90c brn red & lil 3.00 2.60

Burkina Faso Nos. 58 & 60 Ovptd.

108 A7 1fr brn & grn 3.75 3.00
a. Inverted overprint 150.00 160.00
109 A7 1.50fr ultra & grysh 3.75 3.00
a. Inverted overprint 150.00
b. Double overprint 95.00

Burkina Faso Nos. 52 & 54 Surcharged

110 A6 1.25fr on 40c blk & pink 2.25 2.25
a. Double overprint 100.00
111 A6 1.75fr on 50c blk & green 3.75 3.00
a. Double overprint 100.00
Nos. 96-111 (16) 39.90 31.60

Baoulé Woman — A6

Rapids on Comoe River — A9

Mosque at Bobo-Dioulasso — A7

Coastal Scene A8

1936-44 ***Perf. 13***

112 A6 1c carmine rose .25 .25
113 A6 2c ultramarine .25 .25
114 A6 3c dp grn ('40) .25 .25
115 A6 4c chocolate .25 .25
116 A6 5c violet .25 .25
117 A6 10c Prussian bl .25 .25
118 A6 15c copper red .25 .25
119 A7 20c ultramarine .25 .25
120 A7 25c copper red .25 .25
121 A7 30c blue green .25 .25
122 A7 30c brown ('40) .25 .25
123 A6 35c dp grn ('38) .75 .75
124 A7 40c carmine rose .25 .25
125 A7 45c brown .35 .35
126 A7 45c blue grn ('40) .25 .25
127 A7 50c plum .35 .35
128 A7 55c dark vio ('38) .40 .75
129 A8 60c car rose ('40) .25 .25
130 A8 65c red brown .40 .40
131 A8 70c red brn ('40) .40 .25
132 A8 75c dark violet 1.10 .75
133 A8 80c blk brn ('38) 1.20 .75
134 A8 90c carmine rose 8.25 5.25
135 A8 90c dk grn ('39) .75 .75
136 A8 1fr dark green 3.75 2.75
137 A8 1fr car rose ('38) 1.50 .75
138 A8 1fr dk vio ('40) .35 .35
139 A8 1.25fr copper red .35 .35
140 A8 1.40fr ultra ('40) .35 .35
141 A8 1.50fr ultramarine .35 .35
141A A8 1.50fr grnsh blk ('42) 1.90 1.50
142 A8 1.60fr blk brn ('40) .75 .75
143 A9 1.75fr carmine rose .35 .35
144 A9 1.75fr dull bl ('38) 1.50 .75
145 A9 2fr ultramarine .75 .75
146 A9 2.25fr dark bl ('39) 1.10 1.10
147 A9 2.50fr rose red ('40) 1.10 1.10
148 A9 3fr green .75 .75
149 A9 5fr chocolate .75 .75
150 A9 10fr violet 1.10 1.10
151 A9 20fr copper red 1.50 1.50
Nos. 112-151 (41) 35.65 29.15

For types A7, A8 and A9 without "RF," see Nos. 166A-166D.
For surcharges see Nos. B8-B11.

Paris International Exposition Issue

Common Design Types

1937 ***Perf. 13***

152 CD74 20c deep violet 2.00 2.00
153 CD75 30c dark green 2.00 2.00
154 CD76 40c car rose 2.00 2.00
155 CD77 50c dk brn & bl 1.60 1.60
156 CD78 90c red 1.60 1.60
157 CD79 1.50fr ultra 2.00 2.00
Nos. 152-157 (6) 11.20 11.20

Colonial Arts Exhibition Issue

Souvenir Sheet
Common Design Type

1937 ***Imperf.***

158 CD76 3fr sepia 11.00 *15.00*

Louis Gustave Binger A10

1937 ***Perf. 13***

159 A10 65c red brown .35 .35

Death of Governor General Binger; 50th anniv. of his exploration of the Niger.

Caillie Issue

Common Design Type

1939 **Engr.** ***Perf. 12½x12***

160 CD81 90c org brn & org .35 .75
161 CD81 2fr bright violet .35 .90
162 CD81 2.25fr ultra & dk bl .35 .90
Nos. 160-162 (3) 1.05 2.55

New York World's Fair Issue

Common Design Type

1939

163 CD82 1.25fr carmine lake .75 1.50
164 CD82 2.25fr ultramarine .75 1.50

Catalogue values for unused stamps in this section, from this point to the end of the section, are for Never Hinged items.

Ebrié Lagoon and Marshal Pétain A11

1941

165 A11 1fr green .80 —
166 A11 2.50fr deep blue .85 —

For surcharges, see Nos. B14A-B14B.

Types of 1936-40 Without "RF"

1944 ***Perf. 13***

166A A7 30c brown 2.25
166B A8 60c car rose 2.25
166C A8 1fr dark violet 2.25
166D A9 20fr copper red 4.50
Nos. 166A-166D (4) 11.25

Nos. 166A-166D were issued by the Vichy government in France, but were not placed on sale in Ivory Coast.

For other stamps inscribed Cote d'Ivoire and Afrique Occidental Francaise see French West Africa Nos. 58, 72, 77.

Republic

Elephant — A12

1959, Oct. 1 **Engr.** ***Perf. 13***

167 A12 10fr black & emerald .85 .35
168 A12 25fr vio brn & olive 1.25 .50
169 A12 30fr ol blk & grnsh bl 1.50 1.00
Nos. 167-169 (3) 3.60 1.85

Imperforates

Most Ivory Coast stamps from 1959 onward exist imperforate in issued and trial colors, and also in small presentation sheets in issued colors.

President Felix Houphouet-Boigny A13

1959, Dec. 4 **Unwmk.**

170 A13 25fr violet brown 1.00 .60

Proclamation of the Republic, 1st anniv.

Bété Mask — A14

Designs: Masks of 5 tribes: Bété, Gueré, Baoulé, Senufo and Guro. Nos. 174-176 horiz.

1960 ***Perf. 13***

171 A14 50c pale brn & vio brn .25 .25
172 A14 1fr violet & mag .25 .25
173 A14 2fr ultra & bl grn .25 .25
174 A14 4fr dk grn & org .25 .25
175 A14 5fr ver & brown .40 .30
176 A14 6fr dark brn & vio .50 .40
177 A14 45fr dk grn & brn vio 1.80 1.00
178 A14 50fr dk brn & grnsh bl 2.75 1.20
179 A14 85fr car & slate grn 5.00 2.25
Nos. 171-179 (9) 11.45 6.15

C.C.T.A. Issue

Common Design Type

1960, May 16 **Engr.** ***Perf. 13***

180 CD106 25fr grnsh bl & vio 1.10 .50

Emblem of the Entente — A14a

1960, May 29 **Photo.** ***Perf. 13x13½***

181 A14a 25fr multicolored 1.10 1.00

1st anniv. of the Entente (Dahomey, Ivory Coast, Niger and Upper Volta).

Young Couple with Olive Branch and Globe — A15

1961, Aug. 7 **Engr.** ***Perf. 13***

182 A15 25fr emer, bister & blk 1.00 .50

First anniversary of Independence.

Blood Lilies — A16

Designs: Various Local Plants & Orchids.

1961-62

183 A16 5fr dk grn, red & org ('62) 1.00 .35
184 A16 10fr ultra, claret & yel .60 .35
185 A16 15fr org, rose lil & green ('62) 1.80 .50
186 A16 20fr brn, dk red & yel 1.00 .50
187 A16 25fr grn, red brn & yel 1.00 .50
188 A16 30fr blk, car & green 1.25 .75
189 A16 70fr green, ver & yel 3.25 1.60
190 A16 85fr brn, lil, yel & grn 5.25 2.00
Nos. 183-190 (8) 15.15 6.55

Early Letter Carrier and Modern Mailman — A17

1961, Oct. 14 Unwmk. *Perf. 13*
191 A17 25fr choc, emer & bl 1.00 .70

Issued for Stamp Day.

Ayamé Dam — A18

1961, Nov. 18 Engr.
192 A18 25fr grnsh bl, blk & grn 1.10 .50

Swimming Race A19

1961, Dec. 23 Unwmk. *Perf. 13*
193 A19 5fr shown .45 .25
194 A19 20fr Basketball .65 .30
195 A19 25fr Soccer 1.10 .45
Nos. 193-195 (3) 2.20 1.00

Abidjan Games, Dec. 24-31. See No. C17.

Palms — A20

1962, Feb. 5 Photo. *Perf. 12x12½*
196 A20 25fr brn, blue & org 1.10 .45

Commission for Technical Co-operation in Africa South of the Sahara, 17th session, Abidjan, 2/5-16.

Fort Assinie and Assinie River — A21

1962, May 26 Engr. *Perf. 13*
197 A21 85fr Prus grn, grn & dl red brn 3.25 1.50

Centenary of the Ivory Coast post.

African and Malagasy Union Issue
Common Design Type

1962, Sept. 8 Photo. *Perf. 12½x12*
198 CD110 30fr multicolored 2.10 .75

African and Malagasy Union, 1st anniv.

Fair Emblem, Cotton and Spindles — A22

1963, Jan. 26 Engr. *Perf. 13*
199 A22 50fr grn, brn org & sepia 2.75 1.25

Bouake Fair, Jan. 26-Feb. 4.

Stylized Map of Africa A23

1963, May 25 Photo. *Perf. 12½x12*
200 A23 30fr ultra & emerald 1.10 .90

Conference of African heads of state for African unity, Addis Ababa.

Hartebeest — A24

Designs: 1fr, Yellow-backed duiker, horiz. 2fr, Potto. 4fr, Beecroft's hyrax, horiz. 5fr, Water chevrotain. 15fr, Forest hog, horiz. 20fr, Wart hog, horiz. 25fr, Bongo (antelope). 45fr, Cape hunting dogs, or hyenas, horiz. 50fr, Black-and-white colobus (monkey).

1963-64 Engr. *Perf. 13*
201 A24 1fr choc, grn & yel ('64) .75 .25
202 A24 2fr blk, dk bl, gray ol & brown ('64) .75 .25
203 A24 4fr red brn, dk bl, brn & black ('64) .65 .30
204 A24 5fr sl grn, brn & citron ('64) .65 .30
205 A24 10fr ol grn & ocher .85 .30
206 A24 15fr red brn, grn & black ('64) 1.40 .45
207 A24 20fr red org grn & blk 1.75 .45
208 A24 25fr red brn & green 2.40 .60
209 A24 45fr choc, bl grn & yel green 5.00 1.50
210 A24 50fr red brn, grn & blk 7.00 2.00
a. Min. sheet of 4, #205, 207, 209-210 25.00 25.00
Nos. 201-210 (10) 21.20 6.40

See Nos. 218-220.

UNESCO Emblem, Scales and Globe — A25

1963, Dec. 10 Unwmk.
211 A25 85fr dk bl, blk & org 2.00 .80

Universal Declaration of Human Rights, 15th anniv.

Sun Radiating from Ivory Coast over Africa — A26

1964, Mar. 17 Photo. *Perf. 12x12½*
212 A26 30fr grn, dl vio & red 1.10 .45

Inter-African Conference of Natl. Education Ministers.

Weather Station and Balloon — A27

1964, Mar. 23 *Perf. 13x12½*
213 A27 25fr multicolored 1.25 .60

World Meteorological Day, Mar. 23.

Physician Vaccinating Child — A28

1964, May 8 Engr. *Perf. 13*
214 A28 50fr dk brn, bl & red 1.90 .70

Issued to honor the National Red Cross.

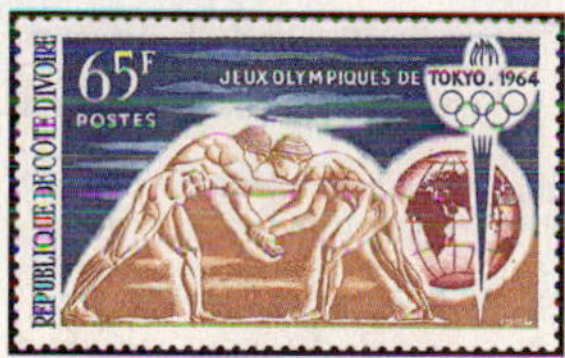

Wrestlers, Globe and Torch — A29

35fr, Globe, torch, athletes, vert.

1964, June 27 Unwmk. *Perf. 13*
215 A29 35fr multicolored 1.50 .55
216 A29 65fr shown 2.75 1.10

18th Olympic Games, Tokyo, Oct. 10-25.

Europafrica Issue, 1964
Common Design Type

Design: 30fr, White man and black man beneath tree of industrial symbols.

1964, July 20 Photo. *Perf. 12x13*
217 CD116 30fr multicolored 1.10 .35

Animal Type of 1963-64

Designs: 5fr, Manatee, horiz. 10fr, Pygmy hippopotamus, horiz. 15fr, Royal antelope.

1964, Oct. 17 Engr. *Perf. 13*
218 A24 5fr yel grn, sl grn & brn .75 .30
219 A24 10fr sep, Prus grn & dp cl 1.75 .45
220 A24 15fr lil rose, grn & org brn 2.75 .45
Nos. 218-220 (3) 5.25 1.20

Co-operation Issue
Common Design Type

1964, Nov. 7 Unwmk. *Perf. 13*
221 CD119 25fr grn, dk brn & red 1.10 .35

Korhogo Mail Carriers with Guard, 1914 — A30

1964, Nov. 28 Engr.
222 A30 85fr blk, brn, bl & brn red 2.75 1.40

Issued for Stamp Day.

Potter A31

Artisans: 10fr, Wood carvers. 20fr, Ivory carver. 25fr, Weaver.

1965, Mar. 27 Engr. *Perf. 13*
223 A31 5fr mag, green & blk .40 .25
224 A31 10fr red lil, grn & blk .50 .25
225 A31 20fr bis, dp bl & dk brn .90 .30
226 A31 25fr brn, olive & car 1.10 .45
Nos. 223-226 (4) 2.90 1.25

Unloading Mail, 1900 A32

1965, Apr. 24 Unwmk. *Perf. 13*
227 A32 30fr multicolored 1.25 .70

Issued for Stamp Day.

A32a

ITU emblem, old and new telecommunication equipment.

1965, May 17
228 A32a 85fr mar, brt grn & dk bl 2.25 .70

ITU, centenary.

Abidjan Railroad Station A33

1965, June 12 Engr. *Perf. 13*
229 A33 30fr mag, bl & brn ol 1.25 .80

Pres. Felix Houphouet-Boigny and Map of Ivory Coast — A34

1965, Aug. 7 Photo. *Perf. 12½x13*
230 A34 30fr multicolored .90 .45

Fifth anniversary of Independence.

Hammerhead Stork — A35

Birds: 1fr, Bruce's green pigeon, horiz. 2fr, Spur-winged goose, horiz. 5fr, Stone partridge. 15fr, White-breasted guinea fowl. 30fr, Namaqua dove, horiz. 50fr, Lizard buzzard, horiz. 75fr, Yellow-billed stork. 90fr, Forest (or Latham's) francolin.

1965-66 Engr. *Perf. 13*

231 A35 1fr yel grn, pur & yel ('66) 1.00 .30
232 A35 2fr slate grn, blk & red ('66) 1.00 .40
233 A35 5fr dk ol, dk brn & brn red ('66) 1.25 .45
234 A35 10fr red lil, blk & red brn 1.40 .30
235 A35 15fr sl grn, gray & ver 1.50 .40
236 A35 30fr sl grn, mar & red brown 2.00 .65
237 A35 50fr brn, blk & chlky bl 3.50 1.00
238 A35 75fr org, mar & sl grn 6.25 1.50
239 A35 90fr emer, blk & brn ('66) 7.25 3.00
Nos. 231-239 (9) 25.15 8.00

Mail Train, 1906 — A36

1966, Mar. 26 Engr. *Perf. 13*

240 A36 30fr grn, blk & mar 2.90 1.00

Issued for Stamp Day.

Baoulé Mother and Child, Carved in Wood — A37

Designs: 10fr, Unguent vessel, Wamougo mask lid, 20fr, Atié carved drums. 30fr, Bété female ancestral figure.

1966, Apr. 9 Unwmk.

241 A37 5fr blk & emerald .45 .25
242 A37 10fr purple & blk .75 .30
243 A37 20fr orange & blk 2.00 .75
244 A37 30fr red & black 2.50 1.00
Nos. 241-244 (4) 5.70 2.30

Intl. Negro Arts Festival, Dakar, Senegal, 4/1-24.

Hotel Ivoire A38

1966, Apr. 30 Engr. *Perf. 13*

245 A38 15fr bl, grn, red & olive .90 .40

Farm Tractor A39

1966, Aug. 7 Photo. *Perf. 12½x12*

246 A39 30fr multicolored 1.00 .55

6th anniversary of independence.

Uniformed Teacher and Villagers A40

1966, Sept. 1 Engr. *Perf. 13*

247 A40 30fr dk red, indigo & dk brn 1.00 .50

National School of Administration.

Veterinarian Treating Cattle A41

1966, Oct. 22 Engr. *Perf. 13*

248 A41 30fr ol, bl & dp brn 1.10 .50

Campaign against cattle plague.

Man, Waves, UNESCO Emblem — A42

1966, Nov. 14 Engr. *Perf. 13*

249 A42 30fr dp bl & vio brn 1.00 .55

UNESCO, 20th anniv.

Delivery of Gift Parcels — A43

1966, Dec. 11 Engr. *Perf. 13*

250 A43 30fr dk bl, brn & blk 1.00 .55

UNICEF, 20th anniv.

Bouaké Hospital and Red Cross A44

1966, Dec. 20

251 A44 30fr red brn, red & lilac 1.00 .55

Sikorsky S-43 Seaplane and Boats — A45

1967, Mar. 25 Engr. *Perf. 13*

252 A45 30fr indigo, bl grn & brn 3.00 1.20

Stamp Day. 30th anniv. of the Sikorsky S-43 flying boat route.

Pineapple Harvest A46

1967 Engr. *Perf. 13*

253 A46 20fr shown .60 .40
254 A46 30fr Cabbage tree .85 .45
255 A46 100fr Bananas 3.50 1.10
Nos. 253-255 (3) 4.95 1.95

Issue dates: 30fr, June 24; others, Mar. 25.

Genie, Protector of Assamlangangan A47

1967, July 31 Engr. *Perf. 13*

256 A47 30fr grn, blk & maroon 1.00 .55

Intl. PEN Club (writers' organization), 25th Congress, Abidjan, July 31-Aug. 5.

Old and New Houses A48

1967, Aug. 7 Photo. *Perf. 12½x12*

257 A48 30fr multicolored 1.00 .55

7th anniversary of independence.

Lions Emblem and Elephant's Head A49

1967, Sept. 2 Photo. *Perf. 12½x13*

258 A49 30fr lt bl & multi 1.50 .60

50th anniversary of Lions International.

Monetary Union Issue

Common Design Type

1967, Nov. 4 Engr. *Perf. 13*

259 CD125 30fr car, slate grn & blk .85 .40

Allegory of French Recognition of Ivory Coast — A50

1967, Nov. 17 Photo. *Perf. 13x12½*

260 A50 90fr multicolored 2.50 .95

Days of Recognition, 20th anniv. See No. 298.

Tabou Radio Station — A51

1968, Mar. 9 Engr. *Perf. 13*

261 A51 30fr dk grn, brn & brt grn 1.10 .55

Issued for Stamp Day.

Cotton Mill — A52

Designs: 5fr, Palm oil extraction plant. 15fr, Abidjan oil refinery. 20fr, Unloading raw cotton and spinning machine, vert. 30fr, Flour mill. 50fr, Cacao butter extractor. 70fr, Instant coffee factory, vert. 90fr, Saw mill and timber.

1968 Engr. *Perf. 13*

262 A52 5fr ver, slate grn & blk .40 .25
263 A52 10fr dk grn, gray & ol bis .70 .25
264 A52 15fr ver, lt ultra & blk 1.50 .65
265 A52 20fr Prus blue & choc 1.10 .55
266 A52 30fr dk grn, brt bl & brown 1.10 .65
267 A52 50fr red, brt grn & blk 1.90 .90
268 A52 70fr dk brn, bl & brn 2.50 1.00
269 A52 90fr dp bl, blk & brn 3.25 1.60
Nos. 262-269 (8) 12.45 5.85

Issued: 5fr, 15fr, June 8; 10fr, 20fr, 90fr, Mar. 23; others, Oct. 5.

Canoe Race A53

1968, Apr. 6 Engr. *Perf. 13*

270 A53 30fr shown 1.00 .50
271 A53 100fr Runners 3.00 .90

19th Olympic Games, Mexico City, 10/12-27.

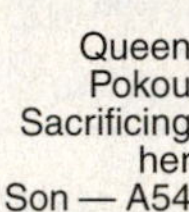

Queen Pokou Sacrificing her Son — A54

1968, Aug. 7 Photo. *Perf. 12½x12*

272 A54 30fr multicolored 1.10 .50

8th anniversary of independence.

Vaccination, WHO Emblem and Elephant's Head A55

1968, Sept. 28 Engr. *Perf. 13*

273 A55 30fr choc, brt bl & mar 1.00 .50

WHO, 20th anniversary.

Antelope in Forest — A56

1968, Oct. 26 Engr. *Perf. 13*
274 A56 30fr ultra, brn & olive 5.75 1.25

Protection of fauna and flora.

Abidjan Anthropological Museum and Carved Screen — A57

1968, Nov. 2
275 A57 30fr vio bl, ol & rose mag 1.00 .50

Human Rights Flame and Statues of "Justitia" A58

1968, Nov. 9 Engr. *Perf. 13*
276 A58 30fr slate, org & dk brn 1.00 .50

International Human Rights Year.

"Ville de Maranhao" at Grand Bassam A59

1969, Mar. 8 Engr. *Perf. 13*
277 A59 30fr brn, brt bl & grn 1.75 .55

Issued for Stamp Day.

Opening of Hotel Ivoire, Abidjan — A60

1969, Mar. 29
278 A60 30fr ver, bl & grn 1.25 .50

Carved Figure — A61

1969, July 5 Engr. *Perf. 13*
279 A61 30fr red lil, blk & red org 1.10 .60

Ivory Coast art exhibition, Fine Arts Museum, Vevey, Switzerland, 7/12-9/22.

Mountains and Radio Tower, Man — A62

1969, Aug. 7 Engr. *Perf. 13*
280 A62 30fr dl brn, sl & grn 1.25 .50

9th anniversary of independence.

Development Bank Issue
Common Design Type

Design: Development Bank emblem and Ivory Coast coat of arms.

1969, Sept. 6
281 CD130 30fr ocher, grn & mar .70 .40

Arms of Bouake — A63

Coats of Arms: 15fr, Abidjan. 30fr, Ivory Coast.

1969 Photo. *Perf. 13*
282 A63 10fr multicolored .40 .25
283 A63 15fr multicolored .50 .25
284 A63 30fr multicolored .85 .25
Nos. 282-284 (3) 1.75 .75

Issued: 10fr, 10/25; 15fr, 12/27; 30fr, 12/20.
See Nos. 335-336, 378-382, design A297.

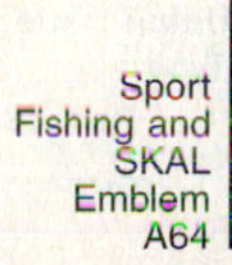

Sport Fishing and SKAL Emblem A64

100fr, Vacation village, SKAL emblem.

1969, Nov. 22 Engr. *Perf. 13*
285 A64 30fr shown 3.75 .55
286 A64 100fr multi 4.75 1.40

1st Intl. Congress in Africa of the SKAL Tourist Assoc., Abidjan, Nov. 23-28.

ASECNA Issue
Common Design Type

1969, Dec. 13 Engr. *Perf. 13*
287 CD132 30fr vermilion .90 .40

University Center, Abidjan — A65

1970, Feb. 26 Engr. *Perf. 13*
288 A65 30fr indigo & yel grn .90 .50

Higher education in Ivory Coast, 10th anniv.

Gabriel Dadié and Telegraph Operator A66

1970, Mar. 7 Engr. *Perf. 13*
289 A66 30fr dk red, sl grn & blk .70 .35

Stamp Day; Gabriel Dadié (1891-1953) 1st native-born postal administrator.

University of Abidjan — A67

1970, Mar. 21 Photo.
290 A67 30fr Prus bl, dk pur & dk yel grn .90 .50

3rd General Assembly of the Assoc. of French-language Universities (A.U.P.E.L.F.).

Safety Match Production — A68

20fr, Textile industry. 50fr, Shipbuilding.

1970, May 9 Engr. *Perf. 13*
291 A68 5fr shown .40 .45
292 A68 20fr multi .60 .40
293 A68 50fr multi 1.60 .50
Nos. 291-293 (3) 2.60 1.35

Radar, Classroom with Television — A69

1970, May 17
294 A69 40fr red, grn & gray ol 1.10 .55

Issued for World Telecommunications Day.

UPU Headquarters Issue
Common Design Type

1970, May 20
295 CD133 30fr lil, brt grn & olive 1.10 .50

UN Emblem, Lion, Antelopes and Plane A70

1970, June 27 Engr. *Perf. 13*
296 A70 30fr dk red brn, ultra & dk green 3.25 1.25

25th anniversary of the United Nations.

Coffee Branch and Bags Showing Increased Production A71

1970, Aug. 7 Engr. *Perf. 13*
297 A71 30fr org, bluish grn & gray 1.50 .50

Tenth anniversary of independence.

Type of 1967

1970, Oct. 29 Photo. *Perf. 12x12½*
298 A50 40fr multicolored 1.00 .50

Ivory Coast Democratic Party, 5th Congress.

Power Plant at Uridi — A73

1970, Nov. 21 Engr. *Perf. 13*
299 A73 40fr multicolored 2.00 .40

Independence, 10th Anniv. — A73a

Designs: Nos. 299A, 299D, Pres. Houphouet-Boigny, Gen. Charles DeGaulle. Nos. 299B, 299F, Pres. Houphouet-Boigny, elephants. Nos. 299C, 299E, Coat of arms.

1970, Nov. 27 Embossed *Perf. 10½*
Die Cut
299A A73a 300fr Silver *15.00 15.00*
299B A73a 300fr Silver *15.00 15.00*
299C A73a 300fr Silver *15.00 15.00*
g. Pair, #299B-299C *35.00 35.00*
299D A73a 1000fr Gold *45.00 45.00*
299E A73a 1000fr Gold *45.00 45.00*

Litho. & Embossed
299F A73a 1200fr Gold & multi *45.00 45.00*
h. Pair, #299E-299F *100.00 100.00*

Nos. 299B, 299F are airmail.

Postal Service Autobus, 1925 A74

1971, Mar. 6 Engr. *Perf. 13*
300 A74 40fr dp grn, dk brn & gldn brn 2.75 .50

Stamp Day.

Marginella Desjardini A75

Marine Life: 1fr, Aporrhaispes gallinae. 5fr, Neptunus validus. 10fr, Hermodice carunculata, vert. No. 305, Natica fanel, vert. No. 306, Goniaster cuspidatus, vert. No. 307, Xenorhora digitata. 25fr, Conus prometheus. 35fr, Polycheles typhlops, vert. No. 310, Conus genuanus. No. 311, Chlamys flabellum. 45fr, Strombus bubonius. 50fr, Enoplometopus callistus, vert. 65fr, Cypraea stercoraria.

1971-72 Engr. *Perf. 13*
301 A75 1fr olive & multi .50 .25
302 A75 5fr red & multi .50 .30
303 A75 10fr emer & multi 1.00 .30
304 A75 15fr brt bl & multi 1.00 .35
305 A75 15fr dp car & multi 1.50 .40
306 A75 20fr ocher & car 1.90 .50
307 A75 20fr ver & multi 2.25 .65
308 A75 25fr dk car, rose brn & black 1.25 .35
309 A75 35fr yel & multi 2.50 .75
310 A75 40fr emer & multi 4.00 1.25
311 A75 40fr brown & multi 3.25 1.10
312 A75 45fr multi 4.50 1.50
313 A75 50fr green & multi 5.00 1.60

314 A75 65fr bl, rose brn & sl grn 3.50 1.50
Nos. 301-314 (14) 32.65 10.80

Issued: Nos. 304, 306, 310, 4/24/71; 5fr, 35fr, 50fr, 6/5/71; 1fr, 10fr, No. 311, 10/23/71; 25fr, 65fr, 1/29/72; Nos. 305, 307, 45fr, 4/3/72.

Submarine Cable Station, 1891 A76

1971, May 17
315 A76 100fr bl, ocher & olive 2.25 .85

3rd World Telecommunications Day.

Apprentice and Lathe — A77

1971, June 19 **Engr.** ***Perf. 13***
316 A77 35fr grn, slate & org brn .90 .40

Technical instruction and professional training.

Map of Africa and Telecommunications System — A78

1971, June 26 ***Perf. 13x12½***
317 A78 45fr magenta & multi .85 .40

Pan-African Telecommunications system.

Bondoukou Market — A79

1971, Aug. 7 **Engr.** ***Perf. 13***
Size: 48x27mm
318 A79 35fr ultra, brn & slate 1.00 .45

11th anniv. of independence. See No. C46.

White, Black and Yellow Girls — A80

1971, Oct. 10 **Photo.** ***Perf. 13***
319 A80 40fr shown .80 .25
320 A80 45fr Boys around globe .80 .25

Intl. Year Against Racial Discrimination.

Gaming Table and Lottery Tickets A81

1971, Nov. 13 ***Perf. 12½***
321 A81 35fr green & multi 1.00 .50

National lottery.

Electric Power Installations — A82

1971, Dec. 18 ***Perf. 13***
322 A82 35fr red brn & multi 2.00 .50

Cogwheel and Workers A83

1972, Mar. 18 **Engr.** ***Perf. 13***
323 A83 35fr org, bl & dk brn .70 .40

Technical Cooperation Week.

"Your Heart is Your Health" — A84

1972, Apr. 7 **Photo.** ***Perf. 12½x13***
324 A84 40fr blue, olive & red .85 .50

World Health Day.

Girls Reading, Book Year Emblem — A85

35fr, Boys reading, horiz.

Perf. 12½x13, 13x12½
1972, Apr. 22 **Engr.**
325 A85 35fr multi .70 .25
326 A85 40fr shown .90 .40

International Book Year.

Postal Sorting Center, Abidjan A86

1972, May 13 ***Perf. 13***
327 A86 40fr dk grn, rose lil & bis 1.10 .40

Stamp Day.

Radio Tower, Abobo, and ITU Emblem — A87

1972, May 17 **Engr.** ***Perf. 13***
328 A87 40fr blue, red & grn 2.00 .65

4th World Telecommunications Day.

Computer Operator, Punch Card A88

1972, June 24
329 A88 40fr brt grn, bl & red 2.00 .60

Development of computerized information.

View of Odienné — A89

1972, Aug. 7 **Engr.** ***Perf. 13***
330 A89 35fr bl, grn & brn 1.00 .60

12th anniversary of independence.

West African Monetary Union Issue
Common Design Type

1972, Nov. 2 **Engr.** ***Perf. 13***
331 CD136 40fr brn, gray & red lilac 1.00 .50

Diamond and Diamond Mine — A90

1972, Nov. 4
332 A90 40fr Prus bl, slate & org brn 3.25 1.60

Pasteur Institute, Louis Pasteur A91

1972, Nov. 21
333 A91 35fr vio bl, grn & brn 1.10 .50

Pasteur (1822-1895), chemist and bacteriologist.

Children at Village Pump A92

1972, Dec. 9 **Engr.** ***Perf. 13***
334 A92 35fr dk red, grn & blk 1.25 .40

Water campaign. See No. 360.

Arms Type of 1969

1973 **Photo.** ***Perf. 12***
335 A63 5fr Daloa .45 .25
336 A63 10fr Gagnoa .45 .25

Nos. 335-336 are 16½-17x22mm and have "DELRIEU" below design at right. Nos. 282-284 are 17x23mm and have no name at lower right.

Dr. Armauer G. Hansen — A93

1973, Feb. 3 **Engr.** ***Perf. 13***
342 A93 35fr lil, dp bl & brn 1.10 .40

Centenary of the discovery of the Hansen bacillus, the cause of leprosy.

Lake Village Bletankoro — A94

1973, Mar. 10 **Engr.** ***Perf. 13***
343 A94 200fr choc, bl & grn 4.75 2.00

Balistes Capriscus A95

Fish: 20fr, Pseudupeneus prayensis. 25fr, Cephalopholis taeniops. 35fr, Priacanthus arenatus. 50fr, Xyrichthys novacula.

1973-74 **Engr.** ***Perf. 13***
344 A95 15fr ind & slate grn 1.50 .60
345 A95 20fr lilac & multi 2.50 .75
346 A95 25fr slate grn & rose ('74) 3.75 .80
347 A95 35fr rose red & slate grn 2.75 1.10
348 A95 50fr blk, ultra & rose red 4.00 1.20
Nos. 344-348 (5) 14.50 4.45

Issued: 50fr, 3/24; 15fr, 20fr, 7/7; 35fr, 12/1; 25fr, 3/2.

Children A96

1973, Apr. 7 **Engr.** ***Perf. 13***
354 A96 40fr grn, blk & dl red 1.10 .45

Establishment of first children's village in Africa (SOS villages for homeless children).

Parliament, Abidjan — A97

1973, Apr. 24 **Photo.** ***Perf. 13x12½***
355 A97 100fr multicolored 1.25 .45

112th session of the Inter-parliamentary Council.

Teacher and PAC Store A98

1973, May 12 Photo. ***Perf. 13x12½***
356 A98 40fr multicolored .70 .25

Commercial Action Program (PAC).

Mother, Typist, Dress Form and Pot — A99

1973, May 26
357 A99 35fr multicolored .90 .40

Technical instruction for women.

Farmers, African Scout Emblem A100

1973, July 16 Photo. ***Perf. 13x12½***
358 A100 40fr multicolored 1.00 .60

24th Boy Scout World Conference, Nairobi, Kenya, July 16-21.

Party Headquarters, Yamoussokro — A101

1973, Aug. 7 Photo. ***Perf. 13***
359 A101 35fr multicolored .70 .50

Children at Dry Pump A102

1973, Aug. 16 Engr.
360 A102 40fr multicolored 1.25 .45

African solidarity in drought emergency.

African Postal Union Issue
Common Design Type

1973, Sept. 12 Engr. ***Perf. 13***
361 CD137 100fr pur, blk & red 2.50 1.00

Decorated Arrow Heads, Abidjan Museum — A103

1973, Sept. 15 Photo. ***Perf. 12½x13***
362 A103 5fr blk, brn red & brn .55 .25

Ivory Coast No. 1 — A104

1973, Oct. 9 Engr. ***Perf. 13***
363 A104 40fr emer, blk & org 1.25 .60

Stamp Day.

Highway Intersection A105

1973, Oct. 13
364 A105 35fr blue, blk & grn .90 .45

Indenie-Abidjan intersection.

Map of Africa, Federation Emblem — A106

1973, Oct. 26 Photo. ***Perf. 13***
365 A106 40fr ultra, red brn & vio bl .65 .30

Intl. Social Security Federation, 18th General Assembly, Abidjan, Oct. 26-Nov. 3.

Elephant Emblem — A107

1973, Nov. 19
366 A107 40fr blk & bister .75 .30

7th World Congress of the Universal Federation of World Travel Agents' Associations, Abidjan.

Kong Mosque — A108

1974, Mar. 9
367 A108 35fr bl, grn & brn 1.10 .60

People and Sun A109

1974, Apr. 20 Photo. ***Perf. 13***
368 A109 35fr multicolored .65 .35

Permanent Mission to UN.

Grand Lahou Post Office — A110

1974, May 17 Engr. ***Perf. 13***
369 A110 35fr multicolored 1.00 .60

Stamp Day.

Map and Flags of Members A110a

1974, May 29 Photo. ***Perf. 13x12½***
370 A110a 40fr blue & multi .70 .25

15th anniversary of the Council of Accord.

Pres. Houphouet-Boigny
A111 A112

1974-76 Engr. ***Perf. 13***
371 A111 25fr grn, org & brn .65 .25
a. Booklet pane of 10 6.50
b. Booklet pane of 20 13.00
373 A112 35fr org, grn & brn 1.00 .25
a. Booklet pane of 10 10.00
b. Booklet pane of 20 20.00
374 A112 40fr grn, org & brn 1.00 .25
a. Booklet pane of 10 10.00
375 A112 60fr bl, car & brn ('76) .90 .40
376 A112 65fr car, bl & brn ('76) .90 .40
Nos. 371-376 (5) 4.45 1.55

See Nos. 783-792.

Ivory Coast Arms Type of 1969 with smaller "P" and "s" in "Postes"

1974, June 29 Photo. ***Perf. 12***
378 A63 35fr brn, emer & gold .70 .25
a. Booklet pane of 10 7.50
b. Booklet pane of 20 15.00
379 A63 40fr vio, bl, emer & gold .90 .25
a. Booklet pane of 10 10.00
b. Booklet pane of 20 20.00

Inscribed: "COTE D'IVOIRE"

1976, Jan.
380 A63 60fr car, gold & emer .90 .25
381 A63 65fr grn, gold & emer .90 .30
382 A63 70fr bl, gold & emer 1.00 .40
Nos. 378-382 (5) 4.40 1.45

See design A297.

WPY Emblem — A114

1974, Aug. 19 Engr. ***Perf. 13***
383 A114 40fr emerald & blue .80 .30

World Population Year.

Cotton Harvest — A115

1974, Sept. 21 Litho. ***Perf. 12½x13***
384 A115 50fr multicolored 1.10 .50

UPU Centenary A116

1974, Oct. 9 Engr. ***Perf. 13***
385 A116 40fr multicolored .80 .30

See Nos. C59-C60.

Plowing Farmer, Service Emblem A117

1974, Dec. 7 Photo. ***Perf. 13***
386 A117 35fr multicolored .75 .30

14th anniversary of independence.

National Library, First Anniv. — A118

1975, Jan. 9 Photo. ***Perf. 13***
387 A118 40fr multicolored .70 .30

Raoul Follereau and Blind Students — A119

1975, Jan. 26 Engr. ***Perf. 13***
388 A119 35fr multicolored 1.75 .80

Follereau, educator of the blind and lepers.

Congress Emblem — A120

1975, Mar. 4 Photo. ***Perf. 12½x13***
389 A120 40fr blk & emerald .75 .30

52nd Congress of the Intl. Assoc. of Seed Crushers, Abidjan, Mar. 2-7.

Coffee Cultivation A121

5fr, Flowering branch. 10fr, Branch with beans.

1975, Mar. 15 *Perf. 13½x13*
390 A121 5fr multicolored .35 .25
391 A121 10fr multicolored .65 .25

Sassandra Wharf — A122

1975, Apr. 19 **Engr.** *Perf. 13*
392 A122 100fr multicolored 2.25 1.25

Letter Sorting A123

1975, Apr. 26 **Photo.** *Perf. 13*
393 A123 40fr multicolored 1.10 .60

Stamp Day.

Cotton Flower — A124

Cotton Bolls — A125

1975, May 3 **Photo.** *Perf. 13*
394 A124 5fr multicolored .45 .35
395 A125 10fr multicolored .70 .35

Cotton cultivation.

Marie Kore, Women's Year Emblem — A126

1975, May 19 **Engr.** *Perf. 13*
396 A126 45fr lt bl, yel grn & brn .75 .50

International Women's Year.

Fort Dabou — A127

1975, June 7 **Engr.** *Perf. 13*
397 A127 50fr multicolored .90 .60

Abidjan Harbor — A128

40fr, Grand Bassam wharf, 1906. 100fr, Planned harbor expansion on Locodjro.

1975, July 1 **Photo.** *Perf. 13*
398 A128 35fr multicolored 1.10 .60

Miniature Sheet

399 Sheet of 3 9.50 9.50
a. A128 40fr multi, vert. 3.75 3.75
b. A128 100fr multi 4.00 4.00

25th anniversary of Abidjan Harbor. No. 399 contains Nos. 398, 399a, 399b.

Cacao Pods on Tree — A129

1975, Aug. 2
400 A129 35fr multicolored 2.25 .65

Farm Workers A130

1975, Oct. 4 **Photo.** *Perf. 13x12½*
401 A130 50fr multicolored .85 .60

Natl. Org. for Rural Development.

Railroad Bridge, N'zi River — A131

1975, Dec. 7 **Photo.** *Perf. 13*
402 A131 60fr multicolored 4.75 1.25

15th anniversary of independence.

Baoulé Mother and Child, Carved in Wood — A132

1976, Jan. 24 **Litho.** *Perf. 13*
403 A132 65fr black & multi 2.00 .65

Baoulé Mask A133

Chief Abron's Chair A133a

1976, Feb. 7 **Photo.** *Perf. 12½*
404 A133 20fr multicolored .60 .30
405 A133a 150fr multicolored 3.00 1.00

Senufo Statuette — A134

1976, Feb. 21 *Perf. 13x13½*
406 A134 25fr ocher & multi .75 .45

Telephones 1876 and 1976 — A135

1976, Mar. 10 **Litho.** *Perf. 12*
407 A135 70fr multicolored 1.10 .65

Centenary of first telephone call by Alexander Graham Bell, Mar. 10, 1876.

Ivory Coast Map, Pigeon, Carving A136

1976, Apr. 10 **Photo.** *Perf. 12½*
408 A136 65fr multicolored 1.25 .60

20th Stamp Day.

Smiling Trees and Cat — A137

1976, June 5 **Litho.** *Perf. 12½*
409 A137 65fr multicolored 1.25 .60

Nature protection.

Children with Books — A138

1976, July 3 **Photo.** *Perf. 12½x13*
410 A138 65fr multicolored 1.10 .60

Runner, Maple Leaf, Olympic Rings — A139

1976, July 17 **Litho.** *Perf. 12*
411 A139 60fr Javelin, vert. 1.00 .55
412 A139 65fr shown 1.00 .55

21st Olympic Games, Montreal, Canada, July 17-Aug. 1.

Mohammad Ali Jinnah — A139a

1976, Aug. 14 **Litho.** *Perf. 13*
412A A139a 50fr multicolored *65.00 15.00*

1st Governor-General of Pakistan.

Cashew
A140

1976, Sept. 18 *Perf. 12½*
413 A140 65fr blue & multi 1.90 .70

Highway and Conference Emblem — A141

1976, Oct. 25 Litho. *Perf. 12½x12*
414 A141 60fr multicolored .90 .50

3rd African Highway Conference, Abidjan, July 25-30.

Pres. Houphouet-Boigny
A142

1976-77 Photo. *Perf. 13½x12½*
415 A142 35fr brn, red lil & blk ('77) 125.00 —
416 A142 40fr brt grn, ocher & brn blk 4.50 .75
a. Bklt. pane of 12 (8#416, 4#417) 55.00
417 A142 45fr ocher, brt grn & brn blk 4.50 1.00
418 A142 60fr brn, mag & brn blk 6.00 1.00
419 A142 65fr grn, org & brn blk 7.00 1.50
Nos. 416-419 (4) 22.00 4.25

The 40fr and 45fr issued in booklet and coil; 35fr, 60fr and 65fr in coil only. No. 416 coil sells for about the same as No. 415.

Stamps from booklets are imperf. on one side or two adjoining sides. Coils have control number on back of every 10th stamp.

John Paul Jones, American Marine and Ship — A143

American Bicentennial: 125fr, Count de Rochambeau and grenadier of Touraine Regiment. 150fr, Admiral Count Jean Baptiste d'Estaing and French marine. 175fr, Lafayette and grenadier of Soissons Regiment. 200fr, Jefferson, American soldier, Declaration of Independence. 500fr, Washington, US flag, Continental officer.

1976, Nov. 27 Litho. *Perf. 11*
421 A143 100fr multicolored 1.50 .30
422 A143 125fr multicolored 1.75 .45
423 A143 150fr multicolored 2.00 .55
424 A143 175fr multicolored 2.00 .70
425 A143 200fr multicolored 2.50 .75
Nos. 421-425 (5) 9.75 2.75

Souvenir Sheet

426 A143 500fr multicolored 7.00 2.50

"Development and Solidarity" — A144

1976, Dec. 7 Photo. *Perf. 13*
427 A144 60fr multicolored .90 .60

16th anniversary of independence.

Benin Head, Ivory Coast Arms — A145

1977, Jan. 15 Photo. *Perf. 13*
428 A145 65fr gold, dk brn & grn 1.10 .75

2nd World Black and African Festival, Lagos, Nigeria, Jan. 15-Feb. 12.

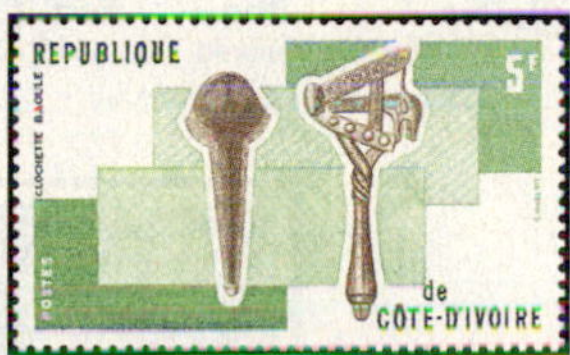

Musical Instruments — A146

5fr, Baoule bells. 10fr, Senufo balafon. 20fr, Dida drum.

1977, Mar. 5 Engr. *Perf. 13*
429 A146 5fr multi .35 .25
430 A146 10fr multi .35 .25
431 A146 20fr multi .55 .25
Nos. 429-431 (3) 1.25 .75

Air Afrique Plane Unloading Mail
A147

1977, Apr. 9 Litho. *Perf. 13*
432 A147 60fr multicolored 1.25 .60

Stamp Day.

Sassenage Castle, Grenoble — A148

1977, May 21 Litho. *Perf. 12½*
433 A148 100fr multicolored 2.00 .75

Intl. French Language Council, 10th anniv.

Orville and Wilbur Wright, "Wright Flyer," 1903 — A149

History of Aviation: 75fr, Louis Bleriot crossing English Channel, 1909. 100fr, Ross Smith and Vickers-Vimy (flew England-Australia, 1919). 200fr, Charles A. Lindbergh and "Spirit of St. Louis" (flew New York-Paris, 1927). 300fr, Supersonic jet Concorde, 1976. 500fr, Lindbergh in flying suit and "Spirit of St. Louis."

1977, June 27 Litho. *Perf. 14*
434 A149 60fr multi 1.00 .30
435 A149 75fr multi 1.10 .30
436 A149 100fr multi 1.25 .30
437 A149 200fr multi 3.00 .75
438 A149 300fr multi 4.00 1.25
Nos. 434-438 (5) 10.35 2.90

Souvenir Sheet

439 A149 500fr multi 6.50 2.00

Santos Dumont's "Ville de Paris," 1907 — A150

65fr, LZ1 at takeoff. 150fr,"Schwaben" LZ10 over Germany. 200fr, "Bodensee" LZ120, 1919. 300fr, LZ127 over Sphinx & pyramids.

1977, Sept. 3 Litho. *Perf. 11*
440 A150 60fr multi 1.00 .25
441 A150 65fr multi 1.00 .35
442 A150 150fr multi 2.00 .55
443 A150 200fr multi 3.00 1.00
444 A150 300fr multi 4.00 1.25
Nos. 440-444 (5) 11.00 3.40

History of the Zeppelin. Exist imperf.
See No. C63.

Congress Emblem — A151

1977, Sept. 12 Photo. *Perf. 12½*
445 A151 60fr lt & dk grn .80 .50

17th Intl. Congress of Administrative Sciences in Africa, Abidjan, Sept. 12-16.

A152

1977, Nov. 12 Photo. *Perf. 13½x14*
446 A152 65fr multicolored 3.25 .75

Yamoussoukro, 1st Ivory Coast container ship.

Butterflies
A152a

Designs: 30fr, Epiphora rectifascia boolana. 60fr, Charaxes jasius epijasius. 65fr, Imbrasia arata. 100fr, Palla decius.

1977, Nov. Photo. *Perf. 14x13*
446A A152a 30fr multi — 2.25
446B A152a 60fr multi — 17.50
446C A152a 65fr multi — 4.00
446D A152a 100fr multi — 6.00
Nos. 446A-446D (4) 29.75
Set, unused 280.00

A153

Hand Holding Produce, Generators, Factories.

1977, Dec. 7 Photo. *Perf. 13½*
447 A153 60fr multicolored .90 .65

17th anniversary of independence.

Flowers — A153a

5fr, Strophanthus hispidus. 20fr, Anthurium cultorum. 60fr, Arachnis flos-aeris. 65fr, Renanthera storiei.

1977 Photo. *Perf. 13x14*
447A A153a 5fr multi 125.00 62.50
447B A153a 20fr multi 125.00 62.50
447C A153a 60fr multi 125.00 62.50
447D A153a 65fr multi 125.00 62.50
Nos. 447A-447D (4) 500.00 250.00

Presidents Giscard d'Estaing and Houphouet-Boigny — A154

1978, Jan. 11 *Perf. 13*
448 A154 60fr multicolored 1.00 .35
449 A154 65fr multicolored 1.25 .35
450 A154 100fr multicolored 1.60 .75
a. Souvenir sheet, 500fr 9.25 9.25
Nos. 448-450 (3) 3.85 1.45

Visit of Pres. Valery Giscard d'Estaing. No. 450a contains one stamp.

St. George and the Dragon, by Rubens A155

Paintings by Peter Paul Rubens (1577-1640): 150fr, Child's head. 250fr, Annunciation. 300fr, The Birth of Louis XIII. 500fr, Virgin & Child.

1978, Mar. 4 Litho. *Perf. 13½*

451	A155	65fr gold & multi	.90	.35
452	A155	150fr gold & multi	2.00	.60
453	A155	250fr gold & multi	3.00	1.00
454	A155	300fr gold & multi	4.25	1.50
		Nos. 451-454 (4)	10.15	3.45

Souvenir Sheet

455	A155	500fr gold & multi	7.00	3.25

Royal Guards — A156

65fr, Cosmological figures.

1978, Apr. 1 Litho. *Perf. 12½*

456	A156	60fr shown	1.25	.40
457	A156	65fr multicolored	1.25	.40

Rural Postal Center — A157

1978, Apr. 8

458	A157	60fr multicolored	1.00	.60

Stamp Day.

Antenna, ITU Emblem A158

1978, May 17 *Perf. 13*

459	A158	60fr multicolored	.90	.50

10th World Telecommunications Day.

Svante August Arrhenius, Electrolytic Apparatus — A159

Nobel Prize Winners: 75fr, Jules Bordet, child, mountains, eagle and Petri dish. 100fr, André Gide, and St. Peter's, Rome. 200fr, John Steinbeck and horse farm. 300fr, Children with flowers and UNICEF emblem. 500fr, Max Planck, rockets and earth.

1978, May 27 Litho. *Perf. 13½*

460	A159	60fr multi	.75	.25
461	A159	75fr multi	1.00	.30
462	A159	100fr multi	1.00	.35
463	A159	200fr multi	2.00	.70
464	A159	300fr multi	4.00	1.00
		Nos. 460-464 (5)	8.75	2.60

Souvenir Sheet

465	A159	500fr multi	5.50	2.00

Soccer Ball, Player and Argentina '78 Emblem — A160

Soccer Ball, Argentina '78 Emblem and: 65fr, Player, vert. 100fr, Player, diff. 150fr, Goalkeeper. 300fr, Ball as sun, and player, vert. 500fr, Ball as globe with Argentina on map of South America.

1978, June 17

466	A160	60fr multi	.70	.25
467	A160	65fr multi	.85	.30
468	A160	100fr multi	1.00	.55
469	A160	150fr multi	1.50	.60
470	A160	300fr multi	3.00	.95
		Nos. 466-470 (5)	7.05	2.65

Souvenir Sheet

471	A160	500fr multi	5.00	2.00

11th World Cup Soccer Championship, Argentina, June 1-25.

Miniodes Discolor A161

Butterflies: 65fr, Charaxes lactetinctus. 100fr, Papilio zalmoxis. 200fr, Papilio antimachus.

1978, July 8 Photo. *Perf. 14x13*

472	A161	60fr multicolored	3.75	1.00
473	A161	65fr multicolored	3.75	1.00
474	A161	100fr multicolored	5.50	1.75
475	A161	200fr multicolored	10.00	4.00
		Nos. 472-475 (4)	23.00	7.75

Cricket A162

Insects: 20fr, 60fr, Various hemiptera. 65fr, Goliath beetle.

1978, Aug. 26 Litho. *Perf. 12½*

476	A162	10fr multicolored	1.10	.40
477	A162	20fr multicolored	1.75	.40
478	A162	60fr multicolored	3.50	1.00
479	A162	65fr multicolored	5.00	1.25
		Nos. 476-479 (4)	11.35	3.05

Stylized Figures Emerging from TV Screen A163

65fr, Passengers on train made up of TV sets.

1978, Sept. 18 *Perf. 13*

480	A163	60fr multicolored	.90	.30
481	A163	65fr multicolored	1.10	.35

Educational television programs.

Map of Ivory Coast, Mobile Drill Platform Ship A164

Map of Ivory Coast, Ram at Discovery Site and: 65fr, Gold goblets. 500fr, Pres. Houphouet-Boigny holding gold goblets.

1978, Oct. 18 Litho. *Perf. 12½x12*

482	A164	60fr multicolored	1.40	.50
483	A164	65fr multicolored	1.40	.50

Souvenir Sheet

484	A164	500fr multicolored	12.00	12.00

Announcement of oil discovery off the coast of Ivory Coast, 1st anniv.

National Assembly, Paris, UPU Emblem A165

1978, Dec. 2 Litho. *Perf. 13½*

485	A165	200fr multicolored	2.00	.90

Congress of Paris, centenary.

Drummer A166

1978, Dec. 7 Photo. *Perf. 12½x13*

486	A166	60fr multicolored	1.10	.60

18th anniversary of independence.

Poster — A167

Design: 65fr, Arrows made of flags, and television screen.

1978, Dec. 12

487	A167	60fr multicolored	.90	.40
488	A167	65fr multicolored	.90	.40

Technical cooperation among developing countries with the help of educational television.

Plowing — A168

1979, Jan. 27 Photo. *Perf. 13*

489	A168	100fr multicolored	2.00	.60

King Hassan II, Pres. Houphouet-Boigny, Flags and Map of Morocco and Ivory Coast — A169

1979, Jan. 27 Photo. *Perf. 13*

490	A169	60fr multicolored	*2.50*	1.00
491	A169	65fr multicolored	*3.50*	1.25
492	A169	500fr multicolored	*17.50*	7.50
		Nos. 490-492 (3)	*23.50*	9.75

Visit of King Hassan of Morocco to Ivory Coast. The visit never took place and the stamps were not issued. To recover the printing costs the stamps were sold in Paris for one day.

Horus — A170

500fr, Vulture with ankh, cartouches.

1979, Feb. 17 Litho. *Perf. 12½*

493	A170	200fr silver, turq & grn	3.00	1.25
494	A170	500fr gold, org & brn	6.50	3.25

UNESCO drive to save Temples of Philae.

Flowers — A171

30fr, Locranthus. 60fr, Vanda Josephine. 65fr, Renanthera storiei.

1979, Feb. 24

495	A171	30fr multicolored	1.00	.50
496	A171	60fr multicolored	1.50	.60
497	A171	65fr multicolored	1.75	.80
		Nos. 495-497 (3)	4.25	1.90

Wildlife Protection A172

1979, Mar. 24 Photo. *Perf. 13x13½*

498	A172	50fr Hippopotamus	2.25	.70

Globe and Emblem — A173

Child Riding Dove — A174

1979, Apr. 1	Litho.	*Perf. 12x12½*	
499 A173	60fr multicolored	.60	.45
500 A174	65fr multicolored	.70	.50
501 A173	100fr multicolored	1.50	.90
502 A174	500fr multicolored	5.50	3.00
	Nos. 499-502 (4)	8.30	4.85

International Year of the Child.

Rural Mail Delivery — A175

1979, Apr. 7		*Perf. 12½*	
503 A175	60fr multicolored	1.10	.35

Stamp Day.

Korhogo Cathedral — A176

1979, Apr. 9		*Perf. 13*	
504 A176	60fr multicolored	.90	.45

Arrival of Catholic missionaries, 75th anniv.

Crying Child — A177

1979, May 17	Litho.	*Perf. 12½*	
505 A177	65fr multicolored	.90	.50

10th anniv. of SOS Village (for homeless children).

Euphaedra Xypete A178

Butterflies: 65fr, Pseudacraea bois duvali. 70fr, Auchenisa schausi.

1979, May 26		*Perf. 13x13½*	
506 A178	60fr multicolored	2.50	1.00
507 A178	65fr multicolored	3.00	1.00
508 A178	70fr multicolored	4.50	1.50
	Nos. 506-508 (3)	10.00	3.50

Endangered Animals — A179

5fr, Antelopes. 20fr, Duikerbok. 60fr, Aardvark.

1979, June 2			
509 A179	5fr multicolored	.75	.35
510 A179	20fr multicolored	1.25	.45
511 A179	60fr multicolored	4.00	1.40
	Nos. 509-511 (3)	6.00	2.20

UPU Emblem, Radar, Truck and Ship — A180

No. 513, Ancestral figure & antelope, vert.

1979, June 8	Engr.	*Perf. 13*	
512 A180	70fr multicolored	3.00	2.00

Photo.

513 A180	70fr multicolored	3.00	2.00

Philexafrique II, Libreville, Gabon, June 8-17. Nos. 512, 513 each printed in sheets of 10 with 5 labels showing exhibition emblem.

Rowland Hill, Steam Locomotive, Great Britain No. 75 — A181

Rowland Hill, Locomotives and: 75fr, Ivory Coast #125. 100fr, Hawaii #4. 150fr, Japan #30, syll. 3. 300fr, France #2. 500fr, Ivory Coast #123.

1979, July 7	Litho.	*Perf. 13½*	
514 A181	60fr multi	.70	.25
515 A181	75fr multi	.80	.30
516 A181	100fr multi	1.25	.40
517 A181	150fr multi	1.50	.65
518 A181	300fr multi	3.25	.85
	Nos. 514-518 (5)	7.50	2.45

Souvenir Sheet

519 A181	500fr multi	6.75	3.00

Sir Rowland Hill (1795-1879), originator of penny postage.

Insects — A181a

30fr, Wasp. 60fr, Praying mantis, vert. 65fr, Cricket.

1979	Photo.	*Perf. 14x13, 13x14*	
519A A181a	30fr multi	*15.00*	*2.50*
519B A181a	60fr multi	*30.00*	*4.00*
519C A181a	65fr multi	*40.00*	*4.00*
	Nos. 519A-519C (3)	*85.00*	*10.50*

A181b

Musical instruments: 100fr, Harp. 150fr, Whistles.

1979	Photo.	*Perf. 13x14*	
519D A181b	100fr multi	*35.00*	*14.00*
519E A181b	150fr multi	*50.00*	*20.00*

"TELECOM 79" — A182

1979, Sept. 20	Litho.	*Perf. 13x12½*	
520 A182	60fr multicolored	.90	.40

3rd World Telecommunications Exhibition, Geneva, Sept. 20-26.

Culture Day — A183

1979, Oct. 13		*Perf. 12½*	
521 A183	65fr multicolored	.90	.40

Fish — A183a

60fr, Pterois volitans. 65fr, Coelacanth.

1979	Photo.	*Perf. 14x13*	
521A A183a	60fr multi	*150.00*	—
521B A183a	65fr multi	*150.00*	—

Boxing — A184

65fr, Running. 100fr, Soccer. 150fr, Bicycling. 300fr, Wrestling. 500fr, Gymnastics.

1979, Oct. 27	Litho.	*Perf. 14x13½*	
522 A184	60fr shown	.60	.25
523 A184	65fr multicolored	.65	.25
524 A184	100fr multicolored	1.00	.35
525 A184	150fr multicolored	1.50	.45
526 A184	300fr multicolored	3.25	1.25
	Nos. 522-526 (5)	7.00	2.55

Souvenir Sheet

527 A184	500fr multicolored	6.00	2.00

Pre-Olympic Year.

Wildlife Fund Emblem and Jentink's Duiker — A185

Wildlife Protection: 60fr, Colobus Monkey. 75fr, Manatees. 100fr, Epixerus ebii. 150fr, Hippopotamus. 300fr, Chimpanzee.

1979, Nov. 3	Litho.	*Perf. 14½*	
528 A185	40fr multi	*3.00*	.30
529 A185	60fr multi	*3.25*	.50
530 A185	75fr multi	*4.00*	.60
531 A185	100fr multi	*4.75*	.85
532 A185	150fr multi	*6.50*	1.25
533 A185	300fr multi	*15.00*	2.50
	Nos. 528-533 (6)	*36.50*	6.00

Raoul Follerau Institute, Adzope — A186

1979, Dec. 6	Litho.	*Perf. 12½*	
534 A186	60fr multicolored	1.40	.60

Independence, 19th Anniversary A187

1979, Dec. 7	Litho.	*Perf. 14x13½*	
535 A187	60fr multicolored	1.10	.35

Fireball A188

Local Flora: 5fr, Clerodendron thomsonae, vert. 50fr, Costus incanusiamus, vert. 60fr, Ficus elastica abidjan, vert.

1980	Litho.	*Perf. 12½*	
536 A188	5fr multicolored	.30	.25
537 A188	10fr multicolored	.40	.25
538 A188	50fr multicolored	1.10	.30
539 A188	60fr multicolored	1.25	.30
	Nos. 536-539 (4)	3.05	1.10

Issued: 5fr, 10fr, Jan. 26; 50fr, 60fr, Feb. 16.

Rotary Intl., 75th Anniv. — A189

1980, Feb. 23	Photo.	*Perf. 13½*	
540 A189	65fr multicolored	.90	.50

International Archives Day — A190

1980, Feb. 26 **Litho.**

541 A190 65fr multicolored .90 .50

Astronaut Shaking Hands with Boy — A191

Path of Apollo 11 — A192

1980, July 6 **Photo.**

542 A191 60fr multicolored .90 .50
543 A192 65fr multicolored .90 .50
544 A191 70fr multicolored 1.75 .75
545 A192 150fr multicolored 3.00 1.75
Nos. 542-545 (4) 6.55 3.50

Apollo 11 moon landing, 10th anniv. (1979).

Jet and Map of Africa A193

1980, Mar. 22 ***Perf. 12½***

546 A193 60fr multicolored .90 .45

ASECNA (Air Safety Board), 20th anniv.

Boys and Stamp Album, Globe — A194

1980, Apr. 12 **Litho.** ***Perf. 12½***

547 A194 65fr bl grn & red brn 1.10 .50

Stamp Day; Youth philately.

Missionary and Church, Abioisso A195

1980, Apr. 26 **Photo.** ***Perf. 13x13½***

548 A195 60fr multicolored 1.10 .50

Settlement of the Holy Fathers at Aboisso, 75th anniversary.

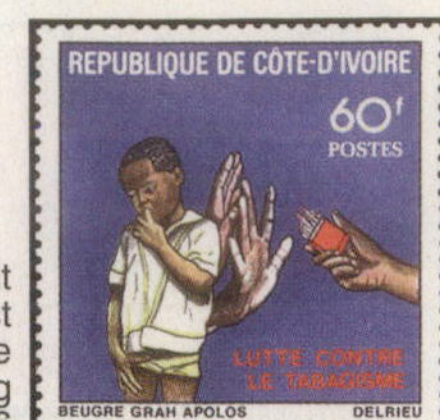

Fight Against Cigarette Smoking A196

1980, May 3 ***Perf. 12½***

549 A196 60fr multicolored 1.10 .50

Pope John Paul II, Pres. Houphouet-Boigny — A197

1980, May 10 **Photo.** ***Perf. 13***

550 A197 65fr multicolored 2.50 1.00

Visit of Pope John Paul II to Ivory Coast.

Le Belier Locomotive A198

65fr, Abidjan Railroad Station, 1904. 100fr, Passenger car, 1908. 150fr, Steam locomotive, 1940.

1980, May 17 **Litho.** ***Perf. 13***

551 A198 60fr shown .70 .35
552 A198 65fr multicolored .80 .35
553 A198 100fr multicolored 1.60 .60
554 A198 150fr multicolored 2.00 1.00
Nos. 551-554 (4) 5.10 2.30

Central Bank of West African States, 1st Anniversary A199

1980, May 26 **Litho.** ***Perf. 12x12½***

555 A199 60fr multicolored .90 .50

Lujtanus Sebae A200

65fr, Monodactylus sebae, vert. 100fr, Colisa fasciata.

1980, Apr. 19 **Photo.** ***Perf. 14***

556 A200 60fr shown 3.25 .65
557 A200 65fr multicolored 3.50 1.00
558 A200 100fr multicolored 3.75 1.40
Nos. 556-558 (3) 10.50 3.05

Snake — A201

1980, July 12 **Litho.** ***Perf. 12½***

559 A201 60fr shown 2.00 .75
560 A201 150fr Toad 4.75 1.75

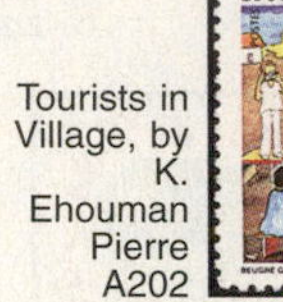

Tourists in Village, by K. Ehouman Pierre A202

Conference Emblem — A203

1980, Aug. 9

561 A202 60fr multicolored .75 .30
562 A203 65fr multicolored .75 .30

National Tourist Office, Abidjan; World Tourism Conference, Manila.

Insects A204

60fr, Forticula auricularia (Common Earwig). 65fr, Mantis religiosa (Praying mantis), vert.

Perf. 14x13, 13x14

1980, Sept. 6 **Photo.**

563 A204 60fr shown 5.00 2.00
564 A204 65fr multicolored 5.00 2.00

Cicadas — A204a

60fr, Cicada (Cicadidae sp.). 200fr, Cicada (Cicadidae sp.), with wings.

Perf. 13½x13, 13x13½

1980, Oct. 11 **Photo.**

565 A204a 60fr multi, vert. 2.50 1.25
566 A204a 200fr multi 7.50 3.50

Hands Free from Chain, Map of Ivory Coast, Pres. Houphouet-Boigny — A205

Pres. Houphouet-Boigny, Symbols of Development — A206

Perf. 12½x13, 14x14½ (A206)

1980, Oct. 18

567 A205 60fr shown 1.25 .75
568 A206 65fr shown 1.25 .75
569 A205 70fr Map, colors, document 1.75 1.00
570 A205 150fr like #567 4.25 2.75
571 A206 300fr like #568 7.50 4.25
Nos. 567-571 (5) 16.00 9.50

Pres. Houphouet-Boigny, 75th birthday.

7th PDCI and RDA Congress A207

1980, Oct. 25 ***Perf. 12½***

572 A207 60fr multicolored .90 .40
573 A207 65fr multicolored .90 .40

River Cruise Boat Sotra A208

1980, Dec. 6 **Litho.** ***Perf. 13x13½***

574 A208 60fr multicolored 1.10 .60

View of Abidjan — A209

1980, Dec. 7 ***Perf. 13x12½***

575 A209 60fr multicolored .90 .30

20th anniversary of independence.

Universities Association Emblem — A210

1980, Dec. 16 ***Perf. 12½***

576 A210 60fr multicolored .90 .50

African Universities Assoc., 5th General Conf.

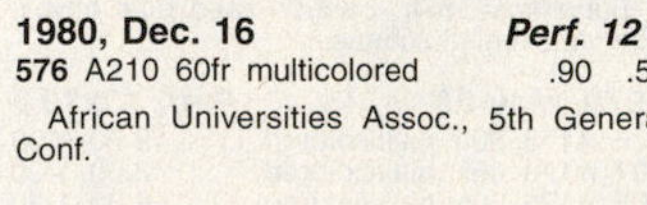

African Postal Union, 5th Anniversary A211

1980, Dec. 24 Photo. *Perf. 13½*
577 A211 150fr multi 1.50 .60

Herichtys Cyanoguttatum — A212

65fr, Labeo bicolor. 200fr, Tetraodon fluviatilis.

1981, Mar. 14 Litho. *Perf. 12½*
578 A212 60fr shown 1.10 .65
579 A212 65fr multicolored 1.25 .75
580 A212 200fr multicolored 3.25 1.75
Nos. 578-580 (3) 5.60 3.15

Birds — A212a

No. 580A, Spreo superbus. No. 580B, Tockus camurus. No. 580C, Balearica pavonina. No. 580D, Ephippiorhyn-chus.

1980, Dec. 30 Photo. *Perf. 14½x14*
580A A212a 60fr multi 300.00 60.00
580B A212a 65fr multi 300.00 60.00
580C A212a 65fr multi 300.00 60.00
580D A212a 100fr multi 300.00 60.00
Nos. 580A-580D (4) 1,200. 240.00

Post Office, Grand Lahou A213

25th Anniv. of Ivory Coast Philatelic Club A214

1981, May 2 Litho. *Perf. 12½*
581 A213 60fr multicolored .90 .30
582 A214 65fr multicolored .90 .30

Stamp Day.

13th World Telecommunications Day — A215

1981, May 17
583 A215 30fr multicolored .45 .25
584 A215 60fr multicolored .90 .35

Viking Satellite Landing, 1976 — A216

Space Conquest: Columbia space shuttle.

1981, June 13 Litho. *Perf. 13½*
585 A216 60fr multi .65 .25
586 A216 75fr multi .85 .30
587 A216 125fr multi 1.25 .55
588 A216 300fr multi 2.75 1.25
Nos. 585-588 (4) 5.50 2.35

Souvenir Sheet

589 A216 500fr multi 5.25 1.25

Local Flowers — A217

50fr, Amorphophallus. 60fr, Sugar Cane. 100fr, Heliconia ivoirea.

1981, July 4 Photo. *Perf. 14½x14*
590 A217 50fr multicolored 1.60 .55
591 A217 60fr multicolored 1.90 1.00
592 A217 100fr multicolored 3.75 1.50
Nos. 590-592 (3) 7.25 3.05

Prince Charles and Lady Diana, Coach — A218

Royal Wedding: Couple and coaches.

1981, Aug. 8 Litho. *Perf. 12½*
593 A218 80fr multi .80 .25
594 A218 100fr multi 1.00 .50
595 A218 125fr multi 1.50 .85
Nos. 593-595 (3) 3.30 1.60

Souvenir Sheet

596 A218 500fr multi 5.50 2.00

For overprints see Nos. 642-645.

Elephant on Flag and Map — A219

1981, Sept. Litho. *Perf. 12½*
597 A219 80fr multicolored .75 .25
598 A219 100fr multicolored 1.00 .50
599 A219 125fr multicolored 1.25 .60
Nos. 597-599 (3) 3.00 1.35

See Nos. 662-666, 833.

Soccer Players A220

Soccer players.

1981, Sept. 19 *Perf. 14*
600 A220 70fr multi, horiz. .65 .35
601 A220 80fr multi, horiz. .75 .45
602 A220 100fr multi .90 .55
603 A220 150fr multi 1.25 .85
604 A220 350fr multi 3.25 1.60
Nos. 600-604 (5) 6.80 3.80

Souvenir Sheet

605 A220 500fr multi, horz. 4.75 2.00

ESPANA '82 World Cup Soccer Championship.
For overprints see Nos. 651-656.

West African Rice Development Assoc., 10th Anniv. — A221

1981, Oct. 3 *Perf. 12½*
606 A221 80fr multicolored 1.10 .50

World Food Day A222

1981, Oct. 18
607 A222 100fr multicolored 1.10 .60

Post Day — A223

1981, Oct. 9 Litho. *Perf. 12½*
608 A223 70fr multicolored .65 .30
609 A223 80fr multicolored .75 .45
610 A223 100fr multicolored .95 .55
Nos. 608-610 (3) 2.35 1.30

75th Anniv. of Grand Prix — A224

Winners and their cars: 15fr, Felice Nazarro, 1907. 40fr, Jim Clark, 1962. 80fr, Fiat, 1907. 100fr, Auto Union, 1936. 125fr, Ferrari, 1961. 500fr, 1933 car.

1981, Nov. 21 *Perf. 14*
611 A224 15fr multi .25 .25
612 A224 40fr multi .50 .25
613 A224 80fr multi 1.00 .45
614 A224 100fr multi 1.25 .50
615 A224 125fr multi 1.50 .60
Nos. 611-615 (5) 4.50 2.05

Souvenir Sheet

616 A224 500fr multi 5.75 2.75

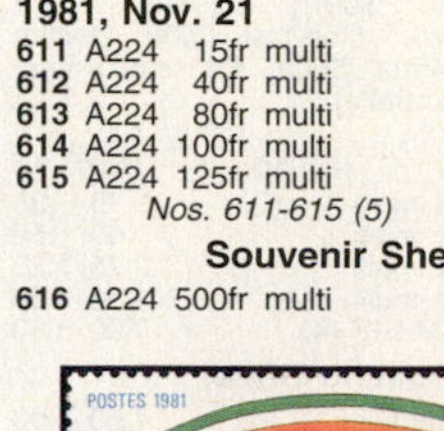

21st Anniv. of Independence — A225

1981, Dec. 7 *Perf. 13x12½*
617 A225 50fr multicolored .60 .30
618 A225 80fr multicolored 1.10 .50

Traditional Hairstyle — A226

Designs: Various hairstyles.

1981, Dec. 19 Photo. *Perf. 14½x14*
619 A226 80fr multicolored 1.50 .75
620 A226 100fr multicolored 2.50 1.10
621 A226 125fr multicolored 3.25 1.50
Nos. 619-621 (3) 7.25 3.35

Stamp Day Africa — A227

100fr, Bingerville P.O., 1902.

1982, Apr. 3 Litho. *Perf. 12½x12*
622 A227 100fr multicolored 1.10 .60

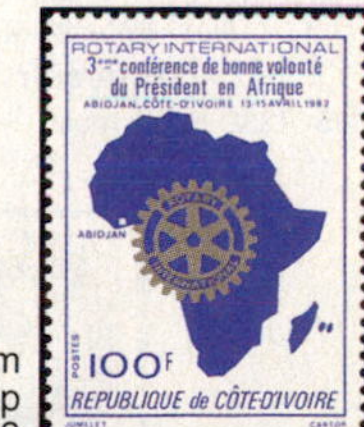

Rotary Emblem on Map of — A228

1982, Apr. 13 *Perf. 12½*
623 A228 100fr ultra & gold 1.10 .60

Pres. Houphouet-Boigny's Rotary Goodwill Conference, Abidjan, Apr. 13-15.

250th Birth Anniv. of George Washington — A229

Anniversaries: 100fr, Auguste Piccard (1884-1962), Swiss physicist. 350fr, Goethe (1749-1832). 450fr, 500fr, Princess Diana, 21st birthday (portraits).

1982, May 15 Litho. *Perf. 13*

624 A229 80fr multi .75 .35
625 A229 100fr multi 1.00 .50
626 A229 350fr multi 3.75 1.25
627 A229 450fr multi 4.50 1.50
Nos. 624-627 (4) 10.00 3.60

Souvenir Sheet

628 A229 500fr multi 4.50 2.00

Visit of French Pres. Mitterand, May 21-24 — A230

1982, May 21 Photo. *Perf. 13½*

629 A230 100fr multicolored 1.40 .55

14th World Telecommunications Day — A231

1982, May 29 Litho. *Perf. 13*

630 A231 80fr multicolored .85 .30

Scouting Year — A232

Scouts sailing, diff. 80fr, 150fr, 350fr, 500fr vert.

1982, May 29 *Perf. 12½*

631 A232 80fr multi .85 .30
632 A232 100fr multi 1.25 .35
633 A232 150fr multi 1.50 .60
634 A232 350fr multi 3.50 1.25
Nos. 631-634 (4) 7.10 2.50

Souvenir Sheet

635 A232 500fr multi 6.00 2.50

TB Bacillus Centenary A233

1982, June 5 Photo. *Perf. 13x13½*

636 A233 30fr brown & multi .70 .30
637 A233 80fr lt grn & multi 1.10 .50

UN Conference on Human Environment, 10th Anniv. — A234

1982, July Photo. *Perf. 13½x13*

638 A234 40fr multicolored .70 .30
639 A234 80fr multicolored 1.25 .45

League of Ivory Coast Secretaries, First Congress — A235

1982, Aug. 9 Litho. *Perf. 12½x13*

640 A235 80fr tan & multi 1.00 .40
641 A235 100fr silver & multi 1.25 .50

593-596 Overprinted in Blue "NAISSANCE / ROYALE 1982"

1982, Aug. 21 *Perf. 12½*

642 A218 80fr multi .85 .45
643 A218 100fr multi 1.00 .55
644 A218 125fr multi 1.25 .65
Nos. 642-644 (3) 3.10 1.65

Souvenir Sheet

645 A218 500fr multi 4.50 4.50

Birth of Prince William of Wales, June 21.

La Colombe de l'Avenir, 1962, by Pablo Picasso (1881-1973) — A236

Picasso Paintings: 80fr, Child with Dove, 1901. 100fr, Self-portrait, 1901. 185fr, Les Demoiselles d'Avignon, 1907. 350fr, The Dream, 1932. Nos. 646-649 vert.

1982, Sept. 4 Litho. *Perf. 13*

646 A236 80fr multi .85 .35
647 A236 100fr multi 1.00 .40
648 A236 185fr multi 2.50 .65
649 A236 350fr multi 4.00 1.25
650 A236 500fr multi 6.00 1.75
Nos. 646-650 (5) 14.35 4.40

Nos. 600-605 Overprinted with World Cup Winners 1966-1982 in Black on Silver

1982, Oct. 9 Litho. *Perf. 14*

651 A220 70fr multi .65 .30
652 A220 80fr multi .80 .50
653 A220 100fr multi 1.00 .55
654 A220 150fr multi 1.50 .90
655 A220 350fr multi 3.50 1.50
Nos. 651-655 (5) 7.45 3.75

Souvenir Sheet

656 A220 500fr multi 5.50 5.50

Italy's victory in 1982 World Cup.

13th World UPU Day — A237

Designs: 80fr, P.O. counter. 100fr, Postel-2001 building, Abidjan, vert. 350fr, Postal workers. 500fr, Postel-2001 interior.

1982, Oct. 23 *Perf. 12½*

657 A237 80fr multi .75 .45
658 A237 100fr multi 1.25 .50
659 A237 350fr multi 3.25 1.50

Size: 48x37mm

Perf. 13

660 A237 500fr multi 4.50 2.25
Nos. 657-660 (4) 9.75 4.70

22nd Anniv. of Independence — A238

1982, Dec. 7 *Perf. 13*

661 A238 100fr multicolored 1.10 .60

Elephant Type of 1981

1982-84

662 A219 5fr multicolored .25 .25
662A A219 10fr multi ('84) .45 .25
662B A219 20fr multicolored .45 .25
663 A219 25fr multicolored .35 .25
664 A219 30fr multicolored .35 .25
665 A219 40fr multicolored .55 .25
666 A219 50fr multicolored .55 .25
Nos. 662-666 (7) 2.95 1.75

Man Waterfall A238a

No. 666B, Boisee Savanna.

1982 Photo. *Perf. 15x14*

666A A238a 80fr shown *20.00 2.00*
666B A238a 80fr multi *30.00 1.75*
666C A238a 500fr like #666A *65.00 7.00*
Nos. 666A-666C (3) 115.00 10.75

Issued: No. 666B, 12/18; others, 11/27.

20th Anniv. of West African Monetary Union A239

1982, Dec. 21 Litho. *Perf. 12½*

667 A239 100fr Emblem 1.10 .55

Abouissa Children's Village A240

1983, Mar. 5 Photo. *Perf. 13½x13*

668 A240 125fr multicolored 1.50 .60

Fauna A241

35fr, Pangolin manis (Scaly Anteater), vert. 90fr, Potamochoerus porcus (Red River Hog). 100fr, Colobus guereza (Colobus monkey), vert. 125fr, Syncerus caffer (African Buffalo).

1983, Mar. 12 Litho. *Perf. 12½x13*

669 A241 35fr multi .55 .40
670 A241 90fr shown 1.00 .50
671 A241 100fr multi 1.25 .60
672 A241 125fr multi 1.50 .75
Nos. 669-672 (4) 4.30 2.25

Stamp Day — A242

100fr, Grand Bassam P.O., 1903.

1983, Mar. 19 Litho. *Perf. 12½*

673 A242 100fr multi 1.10 .60

Easter 1983 A243

Paintings by Rubens (1577-1640) 100fr, Descent from the Cross, vert. 125fr, Resurrection. 350fr, Crucifixion. 400fr, Piercing of the Sword, vert. 500fr, Descent, diff., vert.

1983, Apr. 9 *Perf. 13*

674 A243 100fr multi 1.00 .30
675 A243 125fr multi 1.25 .45
676 A243 350fr multi 3.25 1.00
677 A243 400fr multi 4.00 1.25
678 A243 500fr multi 4.75 1.50
Nos. 674-678 (5) 14.25 4.50

25th Anniv. of UN Economic Commission for Africa — A244

1983, Apr. 29 Litho. *Perf. 13x12½*

679 A244 100fr multicolored 1.10 .55

Gray Parakeet A245

100fr, Fish eagle, vert. 150fr, Touracoes.

1983, June 11

680 A245 100fr multi 2.00 1.00
681 A245 125fr shown 2.75 .75
682 A245 150fr multi 4.25 1.00
Nos. 680-682 (3) 9.00 2.75

World Communications Year — A245a

Designs: 100fr, Tower, telephone, operators. 125fr, Buildings, satellite dish.

1983, July 16 *Perf. 12½x13*

682A A245a 100fr multi *125.00* —
682B A245a 125fr multi *125.00* —

A246

50fr, Flali, Gouro. 100fr, Masked dancer, Guere. 125fr, Stilt dancer, Yacouba.

1983, Sept. 3 Litho. *Perf. 12½*
683 A246 50fr multi .50 .30
684 A246 100fr multi 1.10 .45
685 A246 125fr multi 1.50 .55
Nos. 683-685 (3) 3.10 1.30

20th Anniv. of the Ivory Hotel, Abidjan — A249

1983, Sept. 7 *Perf. 13*
693 A249 100fr multicolored 1.10 .60

Ecology in Action A250

25fr, Forest after fire. 100fr, Animals fleeing. 125fr, Animals grazing.

1983, Oct. 24 Litho.
694 A250 25fr multi .65 .35
695 A250 100fr multi 1.75 .75
696 A250 125fr multi 2.25 1.10
Nos. 694-696 (3) 4.65 2.20

Raphael (1483-1520), 500th Birth Anniv. — A252

Paintings: 100fr, Christ and St. Peter. 125fr, Study for St. Joseph, vert. 350fr, Virgin of the House of Orleans, vert. 500fr, Virgin with the Blue Diadem, vert.

1983, Nov. 5 Litho. *Perf. 13*
698 A252 100fr multi 1.00 .35
699 A252 125fr multi 1.25 .50
700 A252 350fr multi 3.00 1.50
701 A252 500fr multi 4.50 2.00
Nos. 698-701 (4) 9.75 4.35

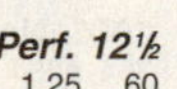
Auto Race A253

1983, Oct. 24 Litho. *Perf. 12½*
702 A253 100fr Car, map 1.25 .60

Flowers — A254

100fr, Fleurs d'Ananas (Pineapple flower). 125fr, Heliconia Rostrata (Hanging lobster claw). 150fr, Rose de Porcelaine (Porcelain rose).

1983, Nov. 26 Photo. *Perf. 14x15*
703 A254 100fr multi *150.00* —
704 A254 125fr multi *10.00 3.00*
705 A254 150fr multi *10.00 3.00*
Nos. 703-705 (3) 170.00

23rd Anniv. of Independence — A255

1983, Dec. 7
706 A255 100fr multicolored 1.10 .50

First Audio-visual Forum, Abidjan — A256

1984, Jan. 25 Litho. *Perf. 13x12½*
707 A256 100fr Screen, arrow 1.10 .50

14th African Soccer Cup — A257

100fr, Emblem. 200fr, Maps shaking hands.

1984, Mar. 4 Photo. *Perf. 12½*
708 A257 100fr multi 1.00 .40
709 A257 200fr multi 2.00 .85

Local Insects A258

100fr, Argiope, vert. 125fr, Polistes gallicus.

1984, Mar. 24 Litho. *Perf. 13*
710 A258 100fr multi 2.00 .70
711 A258 125fr multi 2.25 .90

Stamp Day — A259

100fr, Abidjan P.O., 1934.

1984, Apr. 7 Litho. *Perf. 12½*
712 A259 100fr multi 1.10 .55

Lions Emblem A260

1984, Apr. 27 *Perf. 13½x13*
713 A260 100fr multicolored 1.00 .50
714 A260 125fr multicolored 1.50 .65

3rd Convention of Multi-district 403, Abidjan, Apr. 27-29.

16th World Telecommunications Day — A261

1984, May 17 *Perf. 12½*
715 A261 100fr multi 1.10 .55

Council of Unity, 25th Anniv. — A262

1984, May 29
716 A262 100fr multicolored 1.00 .35
717 A262 125fr multicolored 1.25 .45

First Governmental Palace, Grand-Bassam — A263

125fr, Palace of Justice, Grand-Bassam.

1984, July 14 Litho. *Perf. 12½*
718 A263 100fr shown 1.00 .35
719 A263 125fr multi 1.25 .50

Men Playing Eklan — A264

1984, Aug. 11 *Perf. 13*
720 A264 100fr Board 1.40 .35
721 A264 125fr shown 1.50 .55

Locomotive "Gazelle" — A265

No. 723, Cargo ship. No. 724, Superpacific. No. 725, Cargo ship, diff. No. 726, Pacific type 10. No. 727, Ocean liner. No. 728, Mallet class GT2. No. 729, Ocean liner, diff.

1984 *Perf. 12½*
722 A265 100fr shown 1.00 .40
723 A265 100fr multicolored 1.00 .40
724 A265 125fr multicolored 1.75 .50
725 A265 125fr multicolored 1.25 .50
726 A265 350fr multicolored 4.00 1.25
727 A265 350fr multicolored 3.50 1.25
728 A265 500fr multicolored 5.50 1.75
729 A265 500fr multicolored 5.50 1.75
Nos. 722-729 (8) 23.50 7.80

Issue dates: trains, Aug. 25; ships, Sept. 1.

Stamp Day A266

100fr, Map, post offices.

1984, Oct. 20 Litho. *Perf. 12½*
730 A266 100fr multicolored 1.50 .60

10th Anniv., West African Union A267

100fr, Map, member nations.

1984, Oct. 27 Litho. *Perf. 13½*
731 A267 100fr multicolored 1.00 .50

Wildlife — A267a

100fr, Tragelaphus scriptus. 150fr, Felis serval.

1984, Nov. 3 Photo. *Perf. 14½x15*
731A A267a 100fr multi *75.00 12.00*
731B A267a 150fr multi *75.00 12.00*

Tourism A267b

50fr, Le Club Valtur. 100fr, Grand Lahou.

1984, Nov. 10 Photo. *Perf. 15x14½*
731C A267b 50fr multi *65.00 11.00*
731D A267b 100fr multi *65.00 11.00*

Flowers — A267c

100fr, Allamanda carthartica. 125fr, Baobob.

1984, Nov. 17	Photo.	*Perf. 14½x15*	
731E A267c 100fr multi		*75.00*	*12.00*
731F A267c 125fr multi		*75.00*	*12.00*

90th Anniv., Ivory Coast Postage Stamps A268

1984, Nov. 23	Litho.	*Perf. 12½*	
732 A268 125fr Book cover		1.40	.75

24th Anniv. of Independence — A269

100fr, Citizens, outline map.

1984, Dec. 7	Litho.	*Perf. 12½*	
733 A269 100fr multicolored		1.00	.60

Rotary Intl. Conf. — A270

1985, Jan. 16	Litho.	*Perf. 12½x13*	
734 A270 100fr multicolored		.90	.50
735 A270 125fr multicolored		1.10	.55

Traditional Costumes A271

90fr, Dan le Babou. 100fr, Post-natal gown.

1985, Feb. 16	Litho.	*Perf. 13½*	
736 A271 90fr multicolored		1.50	.45
737 A271 100fr multicolored		1.50	.55

Birds — A271a

25fr, Marabout. 100fr, Jacana. 350fr, Ibis.

1985	Photo.	*Perf. 14½x15*	
737A A271a 25fr multi		*150.00*	*17.50*
737B A271a 100fr multi		*150.00*	*17.50*
737C A271a 350fr multi		*150.00*	*17.50*
Nos. 737A-737C (3)		*450.00*	*52.50*

Issued: Nos. 737A, 737B, Mar. No. 737C, 8/17.

Stamp Day — A272

100fr, Riverboat Adjame.

1985, Apr. 13	Litho.	*Perf. 12½*	
738 A272 100fr multicolored		2.25	.80

18th District of Zonta Intl., 7th Conference, Abidjan, Apr. 25-27 — A273

125fr, Zonta Intl. emblem.

1985, Apr. 25	Litho.	*Perf. 13½*	
739 A273 125fr multicolored		1.25	.60

Bondoukou — A273a

100fr, Marche de Bondoukou. 125fr, Mosque, Samatiguila.

1985	Litho.	*Perf. 14½x13½*	
739A A273a 100fr multi		*140.00*	*9.00*
739B A273a 125fr multi		*140.00*	*9.00*
739C A273a 200fr multi		*140.00*	*9.00*
Nos. 739A-739C (3)		*420.00*	*27.00*

PHILEXAFRICA '85, Lome — A274

No. 740, Factory, jet, van. No. 741, Youth sports, farming.

1985, May 15		*Perf. 13*	
740 A274 200fr multicolored		2.00	1.10
741 A274 200fr multicolored		2.00	1.10
a. Pair, Nos. 740-741 + label		6.00	6.00

African Development Bank, 20th Anniv. — A275

100fr, Senegal chemical industry. 125fr, Gambian tree nursery.

1985, June 18			
742 A275 100fr multicolored		.95	.45
743 A275 125fr multicolored		1.10	.65

Intl. Youth Year — A276

125fr, Map, profiles, dove.

1985, July 20		*Perf. 12½*	
744 A276 125fr multicolored		1.20	.65

Natl. Armed Forces, 25th Anniv. — A277

Emblems: No. 745, Presidential Guard. No. 746, F.A.N.C.I. 125fr, Air Transport & Liaison Group, G.A.T.L. 200fr, National Marines. 350fr, National Gendarmerie.

1985, July 27		*Perf. 12½x13*	
745 A277 100fr dp rose lil & gold		.85	.45
746 A277 100fr dark bl & gold		.90	.50
747 A277 125fr blk brn & gold		1.10	.55
748 A277 200fr blk brn & gold		1.75	1.00
749 A277 350fr brt ultra & sil		2.75	1.75
Nos. 745-749 (5)		7.35	4.25

1986 World Cup Soccer Preliminaries, Mexico — A279

100fr, Heading the ball. 150fr, Tackle. 200fr, Dribbling. 350fr, Passing.
500fr, Power shot.

1985, Aug.		*Perf. 13*	
751 A279 100fr multicolored		.80	.45
752 A279 150fr multicolored		1.25	.75
753 A279 200fr multicolored		1.50	1.00
754 A279 350fr multicolored		3.00	1.75
Nos. 751-754 (4)		6.55	3.95

Souvenir Sheet

755 A279 500fr multicolored		4.25	2.00

Ivory Coast Sovereign Military Order of Malta Postal Convention, Dec. 19, 1984 — A280

125fr, National arms. 350fr, S.M.O.M. arms.

1985, Aug. 31		*Perf. 13x12½*	
756 A280 125fr multi		1.00	.65
757 A280 350fr multi		3.00	1.75

Visit of Pope John Paul II — A281

100fr, Portrait, St. Paul's Cathedral, Abidjan.

Overprint in Black

1985, Sept. 24		*Perf. 13*	
758 A281 100fr multicolored		2.00	1.00

The overprint, "Consecration de la Cathedrale Saint Paul d'Abidjan," was added to explain the reason for the visit of the Pope. Stamps without overprint exist but were not issued.

UN Child Survival Campaign A282

No. 759, Breast-feeding. No. 760, Oral rehydration therapy. No. 761, Mother and child. No. 762, Vaccination.

1985, Oct. 5	Litho.	*Perf. 13½x14*	
759 A282 100fr multi		.90	.50
760 A282 100fr multi		.90	.50
761 A282 100fr multi		.90	.50
762 A282 100fr multi		.90	.50
Nos. 759-762 (4)		3.60	2.00

UN 40th Anniv. — A283

1985, Oct. 31		*Perf. 13*	
763 A283 100fr multicolored		1.00	.60

Admission to UN, 25th anniv.

World Wildlife Fund — A284

Striped antelopes.

1985, Nov. 30			
764 A284 50fr multicolored		*7.00*	1.00
765 A284 60fr multicolored		*9.00*	2.00
766 A284 75fr multicolored		*18.00*	3.00
767 A284 100fr multicolored		*27.50*	5.00
Nos. 764-767 (4)		*61.50*	*11.00*

City Skyline — A285

1985, Nov. 21 Litho. *Perf. 13*
768 A285 125fr multicolored 1.25 .65

Expo '85 national industrial exhibition.

Return to the Land Campaign A286

1985, Dec. 7 *Perf. 12½*
769 A286 125fr multicolored 1.25 .65

Natl. independence, 25th anniv.

Flowers — A286a

100fr, L'Amorphophallus staudtii. 125fr, Crinum scillifolium. 200fr, Triphyophyllum peltatum.

1985, Dec. 28 Litho. *Perf. 14x15*
769A A286a 100fr multi 140.00 10.00
769B A286a 125fr multi 140.00 10.00
769C A286a 200fr multi 140.00 10.00
Nos. 769A-769C (3) 420.00 30.00

Handicrafts A287

125fr, Spinning thread. 155fr, Painting.

1986, Jan. *Perf. 13½*
770 A287 125fr multicolored 1.25 .55
771 A287 155fr multicolored 1.50 .75

Flora — A288

40fr, Omphalocarpum elatum. 50fr, Momordica charantia. 125fr, Millettia takou. 200fr, Costus afer.

1986, Feb. 22 Litho. *Perf. 13½*
772 A288 40fr multicolored .45 .25
773 A288 50fr multicolored .55 .30
774 A288 125fr multicolored 1.25 .75
775 A288 200fr multicolored 2.00 1.00
Nos. 772-775 (4) 4.25 2.30

Cooking Utensils, Natl. Museum, Abidjan — A289

20fr, We bowl. 30fr, Baoule bowl. 90fr, Baoule platter. 125fr, Dan scoop. 440fr, Baoule lidded pot.

1986, Mar. 6 *Perf. 13x12½, 12½x13*
776 A289 20fr multi .25 .25
777 A289 30fr multi .30 .25
778 A289 90fr multi 1.00 .45
779 A289 125fr multi 1.25 .65
780 A289 440fr multi 4.00 2.25
Nos. 776-780 (5) 6.80 3.85

Nos. 776-778 horiz.

Natl. Pedagogic and Vocational School, 10th Anniv. — A290

1986, Mar. 20 *Perf. 13½*
781 A290 125fr multicolored 1.40 .60

Cable Ship Stephan, 1910 — A291

1986, Apr. 12 Litho. *Perf. 12½*
782 A291 125fr multicolored 2.25 .60

Stamp Day.

Houphouet-Boigny Type of 1974-76

1986, Apr. Engr. *Perf. 13*
783 A112 5fr dk red, dp rose lil & brn .25 .25
784 A112 10fr gray grn, brt bl & brn .25 .25
785 A112 20fr brt ver, blk brn & brn .25 .25
786 A112 25fr bl, dp rose lil & brn .30 .25
787 A112 30fr brt ver, blk brn & brn .30 .25
789 A112 50fr lake, dk vio & brn .50 .25
790 A112 90fr dk brn vio, rose lake & brn .90 .40
791 A112 125fr brt lil rose, brt ver & brn 1.25 .50
792 A112 155fr dk brn vio, Prus bl & brn 1.25 .60
Nos. 783-792 (9) 5.25 3.00

The 1986 printing of the 40fr is in slightly darker colors than No. 374.

Natl. Youth and Sports Institute, 25th Anniv. — A293

1986, May 9 Litho. *Perf. 12½*
793 A293 125fr brt org & dk yel grn 1.10 .60

Fish A294

5fr, Polypterus endlicheri. 125fr, Synodontis punctifer. 150fr, Protopterus annectens. 155fr, Synodontis koensis. 440fr, Malapterurus electricus.

1986, July 5 Litho. *Perf. 14½x13½*
794 A294 5fr multi .25 .25
795 A294 125fr multi 1.25 .55
796 A294 150fr multi 1.75 .75
797 A294 155fr multi 2.00 .75
798 A294 440fr multi 5.00 2.00
Nos. 794-798 (5) 10.25 4.30

Enthronement of a Chief, Agni District — A295

50fr, Drummer, vert. 350fr, Chief in litter. 440fr, Royal entourage.

1986, July 19 *Perf. 13½x14½*
799 A295 50fr multi .45 .40
800 A295 350fr multi 3.50 2.00
801 A295 440fr multi 4.50 3.00
Nos. 799-801 (3) 8.45 5.40

Rural Houses — A296

125fr, Baoule aoulo. 155fr, Upper Antiam eva. 350fr, Lobi soukala.

1986, Aug. 2 Litho. *Perf. 14x15*
802 A296 125fr multi 1.25 .60
803 A296 155fr multi 1.50 .80
804 A296 350fr multi 3.00 1.75
Nos. 802-804 (3) 5.75 3.15

Coat of Arms — A297

1986-87 Engr. *Perf. 13*
807 A297 50fr bright org .40 .25
808 A297 125fr dark green 1.25 .35
809 A297 155fr crimson 1.50 .35
810 A297 195fr blue ('87) 1.75 .35
Nos. 807-810 (4) 4.90 1.30

Issue dates: 50fr, 125fr, 155fr, Aug. 23.

Coastal Landscapes A298

125fr, Grand Bereby. 155fr, Sableux Boubele, horiz.

Perf. 14x15, 15x14
1986, Aug. 30 Litho.
820 A298 125fr multi 1.50 .75
821 A298 155fr multi 2.00 1.00

Oceanographic Research Center — A299

125fr, Fishing grounds. 155fr, Net fishing.

Perf. 14½x13½
1986, Sept. 13 Litho.
822 A299 125fr multicolored 1.10 .60
823 A299 155fr multicolored 1.50 .80

Intl. Peace Year — A300

1986, Oct. 16 Litho. *Perf. 14x13½*
824 A300 155fr multicolored 1.40 .75

Research and Development — A301

1986, Nov. 15 *Perf. 13½x14*
825 A301 125fr Bull 1.50 .90
826 A301 155fr Wheat 1.50 .90

Natl. Independence, 26th Anniv. — A302

1986, Dec. 6 Litho. *Perf. 13½x14*
827 A302 155fr multicolored 1.50 .75

Rural Housing A303

190fr, Guesseple Dan. 550fr, M'Bagui Senoufo.

1987, Mar. 14 Litho. *Perf. 13½x14*
828 A303 190fr multi 2.00 1.10
829 A303 550fr multi 5.50 3.00

Stamp Day — A304

155fr, Mailman, 1918.

1987, Apr. 4 *Perf. 13x13½*
830 A304 155fr multicolored 1.40 .80

Jean Mermoz College, 25th Anniv. — A305

40fr, Cock, elephant. 155fr, Dove, children.

1987, Apr. 9 *Perf. 13*
831 A305 40fr multicolored .40 .30
832 A305 155fr multicolored 1.50 .70

Elephant Type of 1981

1987, Apr. 9
833 A219 35fr multicolored .50 .25

Fouilles, by Krah N'Guessan A306

Paintings by local artists: 500fr, Cortege Ceremonial, by Santoni Gerard.

1987, Aug. 14 Litho. *Perf. 14½x15*
841 A306 195fr multi 1.75 1.00
842 A306 500fr multi 4.50 2.75

World Post Day, Express Mail Service A307

1987, Oct. 9 *Perf. 13½*
843 A307 155fr multi 1.50 .95
844 A307 195fr multi 1.75 1.00

Intl. Trade Cent. A308

1987, Oct. 24
845 A308 155fr multi 2.10 1.00

A309

1987, Dec. 5 Litho. *Perf. 14x13½*
846 A309 155fr multicolored 1.40 .90

Natl. Independence, 27th anniv.

A310

1988, Feb. 20 Litho. *Perf. 14x13½*
847 A310 155fr multicolored 1.40 .85

Lions Club for child survival.

The Modest Canary, by Monne Bou A311

Paintings by local artists: 20fr, The Couple, by K.J. Houra, vert. 150fr, The Eternal Dance, by Bou, vert. 155fr, La Termitiere, by Mathilde Moro, vert. 195fr, The Sun of Independence, by Michel Kodjo, vert.

1988, Jan. 30 *Perf. 12½x13, 13x12½*
848 A311 20fr multi .30 .25
849 A311 30fr shown .30 .25
850 A311 150fr multi 1.50 .75
851 A311 155fr multi 1.60 .85
852 A311 195fr multi 2.00 1.00
Nos. 848-852 (5) 5.70 3.10

Stamp Day A312

155fr, Bereby P.O., c. 1900.

1988, Apr. 4 Litho. *Perf. 13*
853 A312 155fr multicolored 1.40 .90

A313

1988, Apr. 18 Litho. *Perf. 15x14*
854 A313 195fr blk & dark red 2.25 1.40

15th French-Language Nations Cardiology Congress, Abidjan, Apr. 18-20.

A314

1988, May 21 Litho. *Perf. 12x13*
855 A314 195fr multicolored 2.00 1.00

Intl. Fund for Agricultural Development (IFAD), 10th anniv.

1st Intl. Day for the Campaign Against Drug Abuse and Drug Trafficking A315

1988, Aug. 27 Litho. *Perf. 13½*
856 A315 155fr multi 1.75 1.00

Stone Heads — A316

Various stone heads from the Niangoran-Bouah Archaeological Collection.

Litho. & Engr.

1988, July 9 *Perf. 13x14½*
857 A316 5fr beige & sep .25 .25
858 A316 10fr buff & sep .25 .25
859 A316 30fr pale grn & sep .30 .25
860 A316 155fr pale yel & sep 1.50 .85
861 A316 195fr pale yel grn & sep 2.00 .95
Nos. 857-861 (5) 4.30 2.55

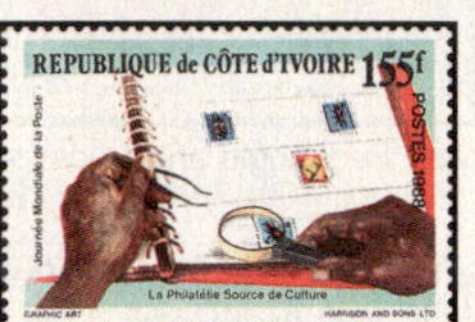

World Post Day — A317

1988, Oct. 15 Litho. *Perf. 14*
862 A317 155fr multi 1.50 .90

Natl. Independence 28th Anniv. — A318

Year of the Forest: 40fr, Healthy trees. No. 864, Stop forest fires. No. 865, Planting trees.

1988, Dec. 6 *Perf. 11½x12*
863 A318 40fr multi .50 .25
864 A318 155fr multi 2.00 .90
865 A318 155fr multi 2.00 .90
Nos. 863-865 (3) 4.50 2.05

History of Money A319

195fr, Senegal bank notes, 1854, 1901.

1989, Feb. 25 Litho. *Perf. 12x11½*

Granite Paper

866 A319 50fr shown 1.00 .25
867 A319 195fr multicolored 2.50 1.25

See Nos. 885-886, 896-898, 915. For surcharges see Nos. 904-905.

"Valeur d'echange 0fr.25" on 25c Type A5, 1920 A320

1989, Apr. *Perf. 12½*
868 A320 155fr multicolored 1.75 .95

Stamp Day.

Jewelry from the National Museum Collection A321

90fr, Voltaic bracelets. 155fr, Anklets.

1989, Mar. 25 Litho. *Perf. 14*
869 A321 90fr multicolored 1.00 .60
870 A321 155fr multicolored 2.00 1.25

Sculptures by Christian Lattier A322

40fr, The Old Man and the Infant, vert. 155fr, The Saxophone Player, vert. 550fr, The Panther.

Perf. 11½x12, 12x11½

1989, May 13 **Granite Paper**
871 A322 40fr multicolored .50 .25
872 A322 155fr multicolored 1.75 1.00
873 A322 550fr multicolored 4.25 2.75
Nos. 871-873 (3) 6.50 4.00

For surcharge see No. 903.

Council for Rural Development, 30th Anniv. — A323

75fr, Flags, well, tractor, field.

1989, May 29 *Perf. 15x14*
874 A323 75fr multicolored 1.40 .50

See Togo No. 1526.

Intl. Peace Congress — A324

1989, June Litho. *Perf. 13*
875 A324 195fr multicolored 1.75 1.00

Rural Habitat A325

155fr, Hut, Sirikukube Dida.

1989, June 10 Litho. *Perf. 14*
876 A325 155fr multicolored 1.75 1.00

For surcharge see No. 902.

Sekou Watara, King of Kong (1710-1745) — A326

Designs: No. 878, Bastille, Declaration of Human Rights and Citizenship.

1989, July 7 Litho. *Perf. 13*

877	A326	200fr shown	2.75	1.50
878	A326	200fr multicolored	2.75	1.50
a.		Pair, Nos. 877-878 + label	8.50	7.50

PHILEXFRANCE '89, French revolution bicent.

Endangered Species — A327

25fr, Varanus niloticus. 100fr, Crocodylus niloticus.

1989, Sept. 16 *Perf. 12x11½*
Granite Paper

879	A327	25fr multicolored	.50	.30
880	A327	100fr multicolored	2.00	.90

World Post Day A328

1989, Oct. 9 Litho. *Perf. 12½x13*

881	A328	195fr multicolored	1.75	.90

CAPTEAO, 30th Anniv. A329

1989, Oct. 28 Litho. *Perf. 12½*

882	A329	155fr multicolored	1.50	.90

Conference of Postal and Telecommunication Administrations of West African Nations.

A330

1989, Dec. 7 *Perf. 13*

883	A330	155fr multicolored	1.50	.85

Natl. independence, 29th anniv.

A331

1990, Jan. 18 Litho. *Perf. 13*

884	A331	155fr multicolored	1.25	.85

Pan-African Union, 10th anniv.

History of Money Type of 1989

155fr, 1923 25fr note. 195fr, 1, 2, 5fr notes.

1990, Mar. 17 Litho. *Perf. 12x11½*
Granite Paper

885	A319	155fr grn & black	1.50	.85
886	A319	195fr org & black	2.50	1.25

Stamp Day A332

1990, Apr. 21 Litho. *Perf. 13x12½*

887	A332	155fr Packet Africa	1.75	.90

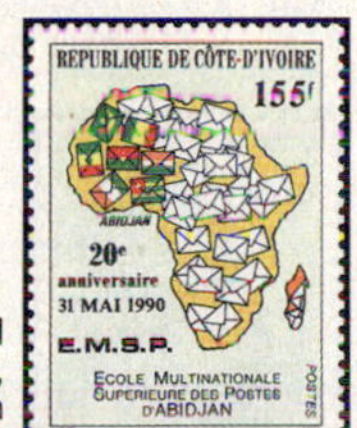

Multinational Postal School, 20th Anniv. — A333

1990, May 31 *Perf. 12½*

888	A333	155fr multicolored	1.50	.80

Rural Village A334

1990, June 30 *Perf. 14*

889	A334	155fr multicolored	1.50	.60

Intl. Literacy Year A335

1990, July 28 *Perf. 15x14*

890	A335	195fr multicolored	1.75	.90

Dedication of Basilica of Notre Dame of Peace, Yamoussoukro — A336

1990, Sept. 8 *Perf. 14½x13½*

891	A336	155fr shown	1.50	.80
892	A336	195fr Basilica, diff.	2.50	1.25

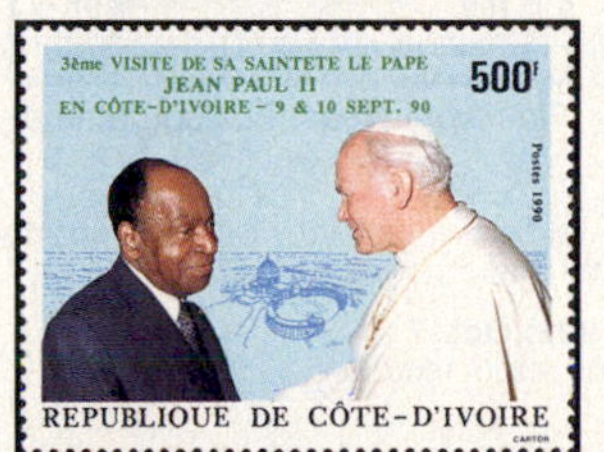

Visit of Pope John Paul II — A337

1990, Sept. 9 *Perf. 13*

893	A337	500fr multicolored	5.00	2.75

World Post Day — A338

1990, Oct. 9 Litho. *Perf. 14x15*

894	A338	195fr multicolored	3.25	1.50

Independence, 30th Anniv. — A339

1990, Dec. 6 Litho. *Perf. 13½x14½*

895	A339	155fr multicolored	1.75	.90

History of Money Type of 1989

40fr, French West Africa 1942 5fr, 100fr notes. 195fr, French West Africa & Togo 50fr, 500fr notes.

1991, Mar. 1 Litho. *Perf. 11½*
Granite Paper

896	A319	40fr yel & black	.45	.25
897	A319	155fr like #896	1.60	.85
898	A319	195fr mag & black	2.00	1.25
		Nos. 896-898 (3)	4.05	2.35

For surcharges see Nos. 904-905.

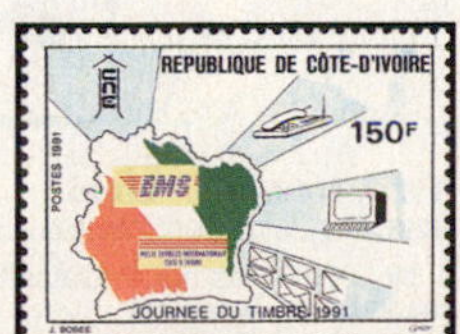

Stamp Day A340

1991, May 18 Litho. *Perf. 13½*

899	A340	150fr multicolored	1.50	.55

Miniature Sheets

French Open Tennis Championships, Cent. — A341

Tennis Players: No. 900a, Henri Cochet. b, Rene Lacoste. c, Jean Borotra. d, Don Budge. e, Marcel Bernard. f, Ken Rosewall. g, Rod Laver. h, Bjorn Borg. i, Yannick Noah.

No. 901a, Suzanne Lenglen. b, Helen Wills Moody. c, Simone Mathieu. d, Maureen Connolly. e, Francoise Durr. f, Margaret Court. g, Chris Evert. h, Martina Navratilova. i, Steffi Graf.

1991, May 24 Litho. *Perf. 13½*

900	A341	200fr #a.-i.	22.50	22.50
901	A341	200fr #a.-i.	22.50	22.50

Nos. 872, 876, 897-898 Surcharged

Perfs. as Before

1991, July 15 Litho.

902	A325	150fr on 155fr #876	1.75	.55

Granite Paper

903	A322	150fr on 155fr #872	1.75	.55
904	A319	150fr on 155fr #897	1.75	.65
905	A319	200fr on 195fr #898	2.25	.80
		Nos. 902-905 (4)	7.50	2.55

Location of obliterator and surcharge varies.

Packet Boats A342

1991, June 28 Litho. *Perf. 12x11½*
Granite Paper

906	A342	50fr Europe	.55	.25
907	A342	550fr Asia	5.25	2.75

World Post Day A343

1991, Oct. 9 *Perf. 13*

908	A343	50fr shown	.55	.25
909	A343	100fr SIPE, globe	.95	.50

Tribal Drums — A344

5fr, We. 25fr, Krou, Soubre region. 150fr, Sinematiali. 200fr, Akye, Alepe region.

1991 Litho. *Perf. 14x15*

910 A344 5fr plum & dull mauve .25 .25
911 A344 25fr red & rose .25 .25
912 A344 150fr bl grn & turq grn 1.75 1.10
913 A344 200fr grey ol & sage grn 2.00 1.25
Nos. 910-913 (4) 4.25 2.85

Independence, 31st Anniv. — A345

1991, Dec. 7 Litho. *Perf. 13½x14½*

914 A345 150fr multicolored 1.75 .80

History of Money Type of 1989

1991, Dec. 8 *Perf. 12x11½*

Granite Paper

915 A319 100fr like #898 1.00 .70

Flowers A346

Various flowers.

1991, Dec. 20 Engr. *Perf. 13*

916 A346 150fr grn, blk & mag, vert. 1.50 .50
917 A346 200fr grn, olive & rose car 1.90 .85

African Soccer Championships — A347

Designs: 150fr, Elephants holding trophy, map, soccer ball, vert.

1992, Apr. 22 Litho. *Perf. 13*

918 A347 20fr multicolored .35 .25
919 A347 150fr multicolored 1.75 1.25

Animals A348

5fr, Viverra civetta. 40fr, Nandinia binotata. 150fr, Tragelaphus euryceros. 500fr, Panthera pardus.

1992, May 5 Engr. *Perf. 13x12½*

920 A348 5fr multi .25 .25
921 A348 40fr multi .55 .25
922 A348 150fr multi 2.00 .80
923 A348 500fr multi 5.00 3.25
Nos. 920-923 (4) 7.80 4.55

World Post Day — A349

1992, Oct. 7 Litho. *Perf. 13*

924 A349 150fr black & blue 1.50 .80

First Ivory Coast Postage Stamp, Cent. — A350

Designs: a, #3, #197. b, #182, #909 with mail trucks, post office boxes.

1992, Oct. 7

925 A350 150fr Pair, #a.-b. + label 5.00 3.50

Funeral Monuments A351

Various grave site monuments.

1992, Dec. 30 Engr. *Perf. 13*

926 A351 5fr multicolored .25 .25
927 A351 50fr multicolored .65 .25
928 A351 150fr multicolored 1.60 .80
929 A351 400fr multicolored 3.75 1.75
Nos. 926-929 (4) 6.25 3.05

Intl. Abidjan Marathon A351a

150fr, Flags, runners. 200fr, Runners.

1992, Nov. 20 Litho. *Perf. 11½*

Granite Paper

929A A351a 150fr multi 1.10 .50
929B A351a 200fr multi 2.25 .75

Nos. 929A-929B were not available in the philatelic market until Apr. 1994.

Gold Mine of Ity, 1st Anniv. — A351b

1992, Nov. 8 Litho. *Perf. 14x15*

929C A351b 200fr multicolored 2.00 .75

No. 929C was not available in the philatelic market until Apr. 1994.

32nd Anniv. of Independence A351c

150fr, People, flag, Statue of Liberty, map.

1992, Dec. 4

929D A351c 30fr shown .35 .35
929E A351c 150fr multicolored 1.75 .75

Nos. 929D-929E were not available in the philatelic market until Apr. 1994.

Tourist Attractions — A351d

10fr, Modern hotel, horiz. 25fr, Dent de Man. 100fr, Resort, horiz. 200fr, Map of tourist sites.

Perf. 14x15, 15x14

1992, Sept. 4 Litho.

929F A351d 10fr multi — —
929G A351d 25fr multi *35.00* —
929H A351d 100fr multi *45.00* 10.00
929I A351d 200fr multi *65.00* 10.00

Environmental Summit — A351e

200fr, Prevent water pollution, horiz.

Perf. 11½x12, 12x11½

1992, June 5 Litho.

Granite Paper

929J A351e 150fr multicolored *70.00* 2.00
929K A351e 200fr multicolored *70.00* 5.00

Stamp Day A352

Designs showing children interested in philately: No. 930, Girl, stamp collection, #169. No. 931, Girl, #431, #446B, #186, and #920. 150fr, Boy sitting under tree, stamp exhibition.

1993, Apr. 17 Litho. *Perf. 13½*

930 A352 50fr multicolored .45 .25
931 A352 50fr multicolored .45 .25
932 A352 150fr multicolored 1.75 .75
Nos. 930-932 (3) 2.65 1.25

A353

Medicinal plants: 5fr, Argemone mexicana. 20fr, Hibiscus esculentus. 200fr, Cassia alata.

1993, May 14 Litho. *Perf. 11½x12*

Granite Paper

933 A353 5fr multi .35 .25
934 A353 20fr multi .45 .25
935 A353 200fr multi 2.00 1.25
Complete booklet, 10 #935 —
Nos. 933-935 (3) 2.80 1.75

A354

Orchids: 10fr, Calyptrochilum emarginatum. 50fr, Plectrelminthus caudathus. 150fr, Eulophia guineensis.

1993, Aug. 27 Photo. *Perf. 12x11½*

Granite Paper

936 A354 10fr multicolored .25 .25
937 A354 50fr multicolored .40 .30
938 A354 150fr multicolored 1.50 .90
Nos. 936-938 (3) 2.15 1.45

Ivory Coast Colony, Cent. A355

25fr, Organization charter. 100fr, Colonial Governor Louis Gustave Binger, Pres. F. Houphouet-Boigny. 500fr, Natives selecting goods for trade.

1993, Sept. 17 *Perf. 13x12½*

939 A355 25fr green & black .35 .25
940 A355 100fr blue & black 1.10 .75
941 A355 500fr brown & black 5.00 3.50
Nos. 939-941 (3) 6.45 4.50

Elimination Round of 1994 World Cup Soccer Championships, US — A356

Designs: 150fr, Cartoon soccer players. 200fr, Three players. 300fr, Two players. 400fr, Cartoon players, diff.

1993, Sept. 24 Litho. *Perf. 14x15*

942 A356 150fr multicolored 1.10 .45
943 A356 200fr multicolored 2.25 .85
944 A356 300fr multicolored 3.00 1.75
945 A356 400fr multicolored 4.00 2.25
Nos. 942-945 (4) 10.35 5.30

World Post Day A357

Designs: 30fr, Map of Ivory Coast. 200fr, Post office, Bouake.

1993, Oct. 9 *Perf. 13x13½*

946 A357 30fr multicolored .35 .25
947 A357 200fr multicolored 2.00 1.25

African Biennial of Plastic Arts, Abidjan A358

Perf. 14½x13½

1993, Nov. 24 **Litho.**

948	A358	200fr multicolored	1.75	.90

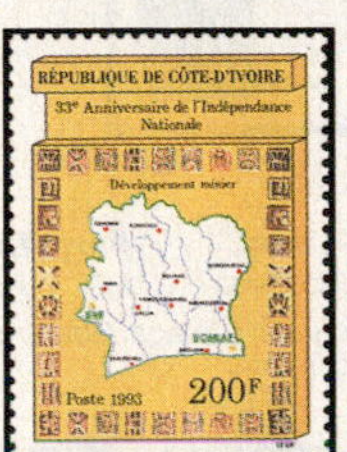

Independence, 33rd Anniv. — A359

1993, Dec. 7 **Litho.** ***Perf. 13½x13***

950	A359	200fr multicolored	2.00	.95

Pres. Felix Houphouet-Boigny (1905-93) — A360

Pres. Houphouet-Boigny and: Nos. 951a, 952a, 953a, Modern buildings, technology. Nos. 951b, 952b, 953b, Agriculture, shipping. Nos. 951c, 952c, 953c, Dove, rainbow, Presidential palace.

1994, Feb. 5 **Litho.** ***Perf. 13***

951	A360	150fr Strip of 3, #a.-c.	3.00	2.00
952	A360	200fr Strip of 3, #a.-c.	4.00	3.00

Souvenir Sheet

Perf. 12

953	A360	500fr Sheet of 3, #a.-c.	10.00	10.00

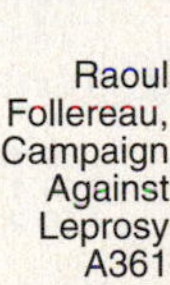

Raoul Follereau, Campaign Against Leprosy A361

1994, Feb. 20 **Litho.** ***Perf. 13***

954	A361	150fr multicolored	1.10	.85

RASCOM (Regional African Satellite Communications Organization), 1st Meeting, Abidjan — A362

1994, Jan. 19 **Litho.** ***Perf. 14x13***

955	A362	150fr multicolored	.85	.50

Woman Carrying Basket — A363

Litho. & Engr.

1994-95 ***Perf. 13½x13***

Color of Border

956	A363	5fr orange	.25	.25
956A	A363	10fr green	.25	.25
956B	A363	20fr red	.25	.25
957	A363	25fr blue	.25	.25
957A	A363	30fr olive bister	.25	.25
958	A363	40fr yellow green	.25	.25
959	A363	50fr brown	.25	.25
960	A363	75fr lilac rose	.30	.25
961	A363	150fr bright green	.70	.35
961A	A363	180fr pale lake	.95	.50
961B	A363	280fr gray	1.40	.70
962	A363	300fr violet	1.40	.70
		Nos. 956-962 (12)	6.50	4.25

Issued: 30fr, 180fr, 280fr, 5/16/95, dated 1994; others, 11/4/94.

Stained Glass Windows, Basilica of Notre Dame of Peace, Yamoussoukro A364

Designs: 25fr, Christ, world map. 150fr, Christ, fishermen. 200fr, Madonna and Child. 600fr, Aerial view of Cathedral, Yamoussoukro.

1994, Nov. 18 **Litho.** ***Perf. 14***

963	A364	25fr lilac rose & multi	.35	.25
964	A364	150fr pale org & multi	1.00	.60
965	A364	200fr yellow & multi	1.25	.80
a.		Booklet pane of 10	—	
		Complete booklet #965a	—	
		Nos. 963-965 (3)	2.60	1.65

Souvenir Sheet

966	A364	600fr multicolored	5.00	5.00

Natl. Independence, 34th Anniv. — A365

1994, Dec. 6 **Litho.** ***Perf. 12***

967	A365	150fr multicolored	1.00	.40

Snakes A366

Designs: 10fr, Python regius. 20fr, Philothamnus semivariegatus. 100fr, Dendroaspis veridis. 180fr, Bitis arietans. 500fr, Bitis nasicornis.

1995, June 23 **Litho.** ***Perf. 13***

968	A366	10fr multicolored	.25	.25
969	A366	20fr multicolored	.25	.25
970	A366	100fr multicolored	.65	.25
971	A366	180fr multicolored	1.40	.75
972	A366	500fr multicolored	3.00	1.50
		Nos. 968-972 (5)	5.55	3.00

FAO, 50th Anniv. — A367

UN, 50th Anniv. — A368

1995, Aug. 4 **Litho.** ***Perf. 11½***

973	A367	100fr multicolored	.75	.35
974	A368	280fr multicolored	2.50	.75

Mushrooms A369

Designs: 30fr, Lentinus tuber-regium. 50fr, Volvariella volvacea. 180fr, Dictyophora indusiata. 250fr, Termitomyces schimperi.

1995, Sept. 8 ***Perf. 14x13½***

975	A369	30fr multicolored	.45	.35
976	A369	50fr multicolored	.85	.70
977	A369	180fr multicolored	2.50	1.00
978	A369	250fr multicolored	2.75	2.00
a.		Block of 4, #975-978	8.50	6.00
b.		Dated "1997"	—	

No. 978a was issued in sheets of 16 stamps.

Louis Pasteur (1822-95) A370

1995, Sept. 28 ***Perf. 11½***

979	A370	280fr multicolored	1.50	.80

School Philatelic Clubs A371

1995, Oct. 6 ***Perf. 13½***

980	A371	50fr GSR	.50	.25
981	A371	180fr LBP	1.75	.80

Butterflies

Designs: 180fr, Pala decius. 280fr, Papilio dardanus. 550fr, Papilio menestheus.

1995 **Litho.** ***Perf. 15x14***

981A	A371a	180fr multicolored	*13.50*	*2.00*
981B	A371a	280fr multicolored	*19.00*	*3.00*
981C	A371a	550fr multicolored	*24.00*	*4.00*
		Nos. 981A-981C (3)	*56.50*	*9.00*

Transportation in Abidjan — A372

Designs: 180fr, People pushing, pulling cart of grain, automobiles, bus on street. 280fr, People getting into bus in middle of traffic.

1996, May 24 ***Perf. 13½***

982	A372	180fr multicolored	1.10	.60
983	A372	280fr multicolored	1.75	1.00

Fish A373

Designs: 50fr, Heterotis niloticus. 180fr, Auchenoglanis occidentalis. 700fr, Schilbe mandibularis.

1996, June

984	A373	50fr multicolored	.35	.30
985	A373	180fr multicolored	1.25	.65
986	A373	700fr multicolored	4.50	2.50
		Nos. 984-986 (3)	6.10	3.45

A374

Orchids: 40fr, Cyrtorchis arcuata. 100fr, Eulophia horsfalii. 180fr, Eulophidium maculatum. 200fr, Ansellia africana.

1996, July 12 **Litho.** ***Perf. 13½x13***

987	A374	40fr multicolored	.35	.30
988	A374	100fr multicolored	.75	.45
989	A374	180fr multicolored	1.50	1.00
990	A374	200fr multicolored	1.60	1.10
		Nos. 987-990 (4)	4.20	2.85

A375

200fr, Boxing. 280fr, Running. 400fr, Long jump. 500fr, Natl. Olympic Committee emblem.

1996, Nov. 19

991	A375	200fr multicolored	1.10	.60
992	A375	280fr multicolored	1.75	1.00
993	A375	400fr multicolored	2.25	1.25
994	A375	500fr multicolored	2.75	1.75
		Nos. 991-994 (4)	7.85	4.60

1996 Summer Olympic Games, Atlanta.

Carved Canes A376

180fr, Cane of Birifor hunter. 200fr, Cane of Chief Lobi. 280fr, Cane of Chief Lobi (Gbobéri).

1996, Sept. 20 **Litho.** ***Perf. 11½***

995	A376	180fr black & green	1.20	.60
996	A376	200fr black & org yel	1.20	.70
997	A376	280fr black & lilac	1.75	1.00
		Nos. 995-997 (3)	4.15	2.30

Water Flowers A377

Designs: 50fr, Nelumbo nucifera. 180fr, Nymphea lotus. 280fr, Nymphea capensis. 700fr, Nymphea alba.

1997, June 20 Litho. ***Perf. 13½x14***

998	A377	50fr multicolored	.30	.25
999	A377	180fr multicolored	1.10	.60
1000	A377	280fr multicolored	1.75	1.00
1001	A377	700fr multicolored	4.00	2.50
		Nos. 998-1001 (4)	7.15	4.35

Basilica of Our Lady of Peace, Yamoussoukro — A378

a, 180fr, Pres. Felix Houphouet-Boigny, exterior view of basilica. b, 200fr, Interior view. c, 280fr, Aerial view, Pope John Paul II.

1997, July 8 Litho. ***Perf. 13***

1002	A378	Strip of 3, #a.-c.	5.00	4.00

Traditional Jewelry — A379

Various beaded necklaces.

1997, Aug. 22 ***Perf. 11½***

1003	A379	50fr plum & black	.35	.25
1004	A379	100fr plum & black	.55	.50
1005	A379	180fr plum & black	1.10	.75
		Nos. 1003-1005 (3)	2.00	1.50

A379a

Various stone heads of Gohitafla.

1997, Oct. 10 Litho. ***Perf. 11½***

Granite Paper

1006	A379a	100fr red & multi	.55	.25
1007	A379a	180fr blue & multi	1.10	.75
1008	A379a	500fr green & multi	2.75	1.50
		Nos. 1006-1008 (3)	4.40	2.50

A380

Work tools: 180fr, Pulley. 280fr, Comb. 300fr, Navette, horiz.

1997, Nov. 28 ***Perf. 13½***

1009	A380	180fr orange & multi	1.10	.50
1010	A380	280fr green & multi	1.50	.75
1011	A380	300fr blue & multi	1.60	.75
		Nos. 1009-1011 (3)	4.20	2.00

Endangered Species A381

Designs: 180fr, African manatee. 280fr, Jentink's duiker. 400fr, Kob antelope.

1997, Dec. 19 Photo. ***Perf. 11½***

1012	A381	180fr multicolored	1.60	1.00
1013	A381	280fr multicolored	1.75	1.00
1014	A381	400fr multicolored	2.25	1.25
		Nos. 1012-1014 (3)	5.60	3.25

1998 World Cup Soccer Championships, France — A382

Paris landmarks in background and: 180fr, Player, ball depicted with angry face. 280fr, Flags of nations inside outline of player. 400fr, Player taking shot on goal. 500fr, Two players, mascot, vert.

Perf. 13x13½, 13½x13

1998, June 5 Litho.

1015	A382	180fr multicolored	1.10	.55
1016	A382	280fr multicolored	1.60	1.00
1017	A382	400fr multicolored	2.25	1.25
1018	A382	500fr multicolored	2.75	1.40
		Nos. 1015-1018 (4)	7.70	4.20

Mushrooms A383

50fr, Agaricus bingensis. 180fr, Lactarius gymnocarpus. 280fr, Termitomyces le testui.

1998, June 26 Litho. ***Perf. 13½x13***

1019	A383	50fr multicolored	.60	.40
1020	A383	180fr multicolored	1.25	1.00
1021	A383	280fr multicolored	2.10	1.25
		Nos. 1019-1021 (3)	3.95	2.65

See No. B20A.

Endemic Plants — A384

Designs: 40fr, Hutchinsonia barbata. 100fr, Synsepalum aubrevillei. 180fr, Cola lorougnonis.

1998, July 10 ***Perf. 12***

Granite Paper

1022	A384	40fr multicolored	.45	.25
1023	A384	100fr multicolored	.75	.50
1024	A384	180fr multicolored	1.10	.75
		Nos. 1022-1024 (3)	2.30	1.50

See No. B20A.

Traditional Costumes from Grand-Bassam Museum — A385

1998, Nov. 13 Litho. ***Perf. 13½x13***

1025	A385	180fr Tapa	1.10	.75
1026	A385	280fr Raffia	1.60	1.10

See No. B20C.

Trains of Africa A386

180fr, South African Railway, 1918. 280fr, Garret 2-8-2+2-8-2 Beyer Peacock, 1925. 500fr, Cecil Rhodes.

1999, Feb. 26 Litho. ***Perf. 13½***

1027	A386	180fr multicolored	1.10	.75
1028	A386	280fr multicolored	1.75	1.10

Souvenir Sheet

1029	A386	500fr multicolored	2.50	2.50

See No. B20B.

PhilexFrance '99, World Philatelic Exhibition — A387

Animals: 180fr+20fr, Loxodonta africana. 250fr, Syncerus caffer. 280fr, Pan troglodytes. 400fr, Cercopithecus aethiops.

1999, July 2 Litho. ***Perf. 13x13¼***

1030	A387	180fr +20fr multi	1.50	1.10
1031	A387	250fr multicolored	1.60	1.25
1032	A387	280fr multicolored	1.75	1.25
1033	A387	400fr multicolored	2.25	1.75
		Nos. 1030-1033 (4)	7.10	5.35

UPU, 125th Anniv. A388

UPU emblem and: 180fr+20fr, Carved heads. 280fr, Methods of delivering mail.

1999, June 25 ***Perf. 11¾x11½***

1034	A388	180fr +20fr multi	1.10	.75
1035	A388	280fr multicolored	1.50	1.10

Flowers — A389

Designs: 100fr, Ancistrochilus rothschilianus. 180fr+20fr, Brachycorythis pubescens. 200fr, Bulbophyllum barbigerum. 280fr, Habenaria macrandra.

1999, July 27 Litho. ***Perf. 13¼x13***

1036	A389	100fr multicolored	.55	.35
1037	A389	180fr +20fr multi	1.40	1.00
1038	A389	200fr multicolored	1.50	1.10
1039	A389	280fr multicolored	1.75	1.25
		Nos. 1036-1039 (4)	5.20	3.70

Ahouakro Rock Formations — A390

Various rock formations.

Perf. 13¼x14, 14x13¼

1999, Aug. 6 Litho.

1040	A390	180fr +20fr multi, horiz.	1.60	.75
1041	A390	280fr multi, horiz.	1.60	1.00
1042	A390	400fr multi	2.40	1.50
		Nos. 1040-1042 (3)	5.60	3.25

PhilexFrance 99 — A391

1999, July 2 Litho. ***Perf. 13***

1043	A391	280fr multicolored	2.75	2.75

No. 1043 has a holographic image. Soaking in water may affect hologram.

Birds — A392

Designs: 50fr, Oriolus auratus. 180fr + 20fr, Nectarinia cinnyris venusta. 280fr, Trenon vinago australis. 300fr, Psittacus eithacus.

1999, Oct. 29 Litho. ***Perf. 13¼x13***

1044	A392	50fr multi	.45	.25
1045	A392	180fr + 20fr multi	1.50	1.00
1046	A392	280fr multi	2.25	1.25
1047	A392	300fr multi	2.25	1.25
		Nos. 1044-1047 (4)	6.45	3.75

Fish A393

Designs: 100fr, Synodontis schall. 180fr + 20fr, Chromidotilapia guntheri. 280fr, Distichodus rostratus.

1999, Nov. 19 ***Perf. 13½x13¼***

1048	A393	100fr multi	.75	.35
1049	A393	180fr +20fr multi	1.50	1.00
1050	A393	280fr multi	2.25	1.50
		Nos. 1048-1050 (3)	4.50	2.85

Challenges for Ivory Coast in Third Millennium — A394

Designs: 100fr, Education. 180fr +20fr, Agriculture. 200fr, Industry. 250fr, Information. 280fr, Peace. 400fr, Culture.

1999, Dec. 10 ***Perf. 13½x13¾***

1051	A394	100fr multi	.55	.35
1052	A394	180fr +20fr multi	1.10	.75
1053	A394	200fr multi	1.10	.75
1054	A394	250fr multi	1.40	1.00
1055	A394	280fr multi	1.50	1.00
1056	A394	400fr multi	1.75	1.50
		Nos. 1051-1056 (6)	7.40	5.35

Native Masks A395

50fr, Wambélé. 180fr+20fr, Djè. 400fr, Korobla, vert.

Perf. 13½x13¼, 13¼x13½

2000, June 30 **Litho.**

1057 A395 50fr multi	.35	.25
1058 A395 180fr +20fr multi	1.25	.80
1059 A395 400fr multi	2.25	1.75
Nos. 1057-1059 (3)	3.85	2.80

Edible Plants — A396

Designs: 30fr, Blighia sapida. 180fr+20fr, Ricinodendron heudelotii. 300fr, Telfaira occidentalis. 400fr, Napoleonaea vogelii.

2000, July 14 *Perf. 13¼x13½*

1060 A396 30fr multi	.35	.25
1061 A396 180fr +20fr multi	1.40	.80
1062 A396 300fr multi	1.75	1.25
1063 A396 400fr multi	2.25	2.00
Nos. 1060-1063 (4)	5.75	4.30

Pres. Robert Guei, Elephant, Map and Dove — A397

2000, Aug. 4 *Perf. 13¾x13¼*

1064 A397 180fr +20fr red & multi	1.50	.80
1065 A397 400fr yel & multi	2.75	1.75

Independence, 40th anniv., coup d'etat of Robert Guei.

Cacao — A398

Frame colors: 5fr, Dark blue green. 10fr, Light brown. 20fr, Claret. 25fr, Blue. 30fr, Greenish black. 40fr, Cerise. 50fr, Golden brown. 100fr, Brown. 180fr+20fr, Orange. 300fr, Blue violet. 350fr, Prussian blue. 400fr, Emerald. 600fr, Olive green.

Perf. 11½x11¾

2000, Aug. 25 **Photo.**

Granite Paper

1066-1078 A398 Set of 13	11.50	8.00

National Lottery, 30th Anniv. — A399

Denominations: 180fr+20fr, 400fr.

2000, Aug. 30 **Litho.** *Perf. 13¼x13*

1079-1080 A399 Set of 2	4.25	2.75

2000 Summer Olympics, Sydney A400

Designs: 180fr+20fr, Soccer. 400fr, Kangaroo. 600fr, Runners. 750fr, Bird over stadium.

2000, Sept. 8 *Perf. 13½x13¼*

1081-1084 A400 Set of 4	12.00	9.00

Hairstyles — A401

Various hairstyles: 180fr+20fr, 300fr, 400fr, 500fr.

2000, Sept. 22 *Perf. 13¾x13¼*

1085-1088 A401 Set of 4	8.50	6.50

Release of Nelson Mandela, 10th Anniv. — A402

2000, Oct. 6 **Photo.** *Perf. 12x11¾*

1089 A402 300fr multi	2.10	1.25

Historic Monuments A403

Designs: 180fr+20fr, Queen Pokou. 400fr, Akwaba. 600fr, Invocation of the Spirits.

2000, Nov. 10 **Litho.** *Perf. 13½x13*

1090-1092 A403 Set of 3	7.00	6.00

UN High Commisioner for Refugees, 50th Anniv. — A404

2000, Dec. 8 **Photo.** *Perf. 11¾x12*

1093 A404 400fr multi	2.50	1.75

Abokouamekro Animal Park — A405

Designs: 50fr, Cattle. 100fr, Rhinoceroses. 180fr+20fr, Rhinoceros. 400fr+20fr, Cattle.

2001, May 14 **Litho.** *Perf. 13½x13¼*

1094-1097 A405 Set of 4	6.50	3.25

Sculpted Columns in National Museum — A406

Designs: 100fr, Alingué, Wouo Anouman. 180fr+20fr, Blolo Bian, Blolo B1a. 300fr+20fr, Botoumo. 400fr+20fr, Odi Oka.

2001, June 18 *Perf. 13¼x13*

1098-1101 A406 Set of 4	5.00	5.00

Elimination Rounds for World Cup Soccer Championships — A407

Various soccer plays: 180fr + 20fr, 400fr + 20fr, 600fr + 20fr, 700fr.

2001, Aug. 21 **Litho.** *Perf. 13x13¼*

1102-1105 A407 Set of 4	10.00	10.00

The following items inscribed "Republique de Cote d'Ivoire" have been declared "illegal" by Ivory Coast postal authorities:

Sheets of nine 100fr stamps: Marilyn Monroe (2 different).

Sheets of six 100fr stamps: Shells and Rotary emblem (2 different), Dogs and Scouting emblem (2 different), Butterflies and Scouting emblem (2 different), Orchids (2 different), Motorbike races and Rotary emblem (2 different), Table tennis players (2 different), Old fire engines (2 different), Elvis Presley (2 different), Marilyn Monroe, Pope John Paul II.

Sheets of six stamps: Trains (4 different).

Souvenir sheets of one stamp: Trains (4 different).

Sheet of ten 200fr Stamps: Birds.

Sheets of nine stamps of various denominations: Japanese Women, Earle K. Bergey, Julie Bell, Michael Möbius, Nudes.

Sheet of eight stamps of various denominations: Nature Conservancy.

Sheets of eight 300fr stamps: Owls and Mushrooms, Lighthouses and Penguins.

Sheets of eight 100fr stamps: Anthony Hopkins, Ben Affleck, Eminem.

Sheets of six stamps of various denominations: Spirited Away, Nature Conservancy, Nudes

Sheets of six 500fr stamps: History of World Aircraft (5 different), Red Cross and Rotary emblem, Japanese Women, Actresses, Women Tennis Players, Marilyn Monroe.

Sheet of six 450fr stamps: The Lord of the Rings.

Sheets of six 400fr stamps: Beatles (2 different).

Sheets of six 350fr stamps: Uniforms of World War II (5 different).

Sheets of Six 300fr stamps: Harry Potter (3 different), Fire Engines (2 different), Owls and Mushrooms.

Sheets of six 200fr stamps: Dogs and Scouting emblem, Lighthouses and Rotary emblem.

Sheets of six 100fr stamps: Pope John Paul II, Celine Dion, Pierce Brosnan, Classic Automobiles.

Sheets of four 100fr stamps: AC/DC, Backstreet Boys, Bee Gees, Beatles, Doors, Freddie Mercury, KISS, Madonna, Metallica, Queen, Rolling Stones.

Sheets of three stamps of various denominations: Nature Conservancy (2 different), Fairy Tales, Fantasy Tales, Dinosaurs, Steam Railways.

Sheet of two 1000fr stamps: Pope John Paul II.

Sheets of Two 500fr stamps: Nature Conservancy, Mother Teresa and Pope John Paul II.

Sheets of two 250fr stamps: Pope John Paul II (3 different).

Souvenir sheets of one 1000fr stamp: Dinosaurs, Fish, Owl and Scouting emblem.

Souvenir sheets of one 500fr stamp: Snow White, Nature Conservancy, Pope John Paul II.

Souvenir sheets of one 300fr stamp: Harry Potter (2 different).

Souvenir sheets of one 250fr stamp: Disney Cartoons and Scouting emblem (10 different).

Souvenir sheets of one 150fr stamp: Fire Engines and Scouting emblem (5 different).

Souvenir sheets of one 100fr stamp: Sorayama (5 different), Locomotives (2 different).

Korhogo Art A408

Designs: 100fr, Shown. 180fr+20fr, Hunters and wildlife. 400fr+20fr, Painter, vert.

2001, Nov. 27 **Litho.** ***Perf. 14***
1106-1108 A408 Set of 3 4.00 4.00

A409

2002 World Cup Soccer Championships, Japan and Korea — A410

Design: 300fr+20fr, Caricatures of soccer players in action, horiz.

Perf. 13¾, 13x13¼ (#1110), 13¼x13 (#1112)

2002, June 6 **Litho.**
1109 A409 180fr +20fr grn & multi 1.25 1.25
1110 A410 300fr +20fr multi 2.25 2.25
1111 A409 400fr +20fr red & multi 2.75 2.75
Complete booklet, 10 #1111 30.00 30.00
1112 A410 600fr +20fr shown 4.00 4.00

Souvenir Sheet

1113 A409 500fr red & multi 3.50 3.50

Ivory Coast — People's Republic of China Diplomatic Relations, 20th Anniv.
A411

2003, July 9 **Litho.** ***Perf. 12***
1114 A411 180fr grn & multi 1.25 1.25
1115 A411 400fr org & multi 2.25 2.25
1116 A411 650fr red & multi 3.75 3.75
Nos. 1114-1116 (3) 7.25 7.25

Sculpted Columns in Museum of Civilizations
A412

Designs: 20fr, Alinguè Bia column. 100fr, Laliè column. 180fr+20fr, Tre Ni Tre column. 300fr+20fr, Golikplé-Kplé column.

2003, Nov. 27 **Litho.** ***Perf. 13½x13***
1117 A412 20fr multi .25 .25
1118 A412 100fr multi .50 .50
1119 A412 180fr +20fr shown 1.00 1.00
1120 A412 300fr +20fr multi 1.50 1.50
Nos. 1117-1120 (4) 3.25 3.25

Paintings by Unknown Artists — A413

Designs: 50fr, Au Revoir. 100fr, Ballet. 250fr, Le Chef, horiz. 500fr, Ligne de Main, horiz. 825fr, Appel, horiz.

Perf. 13¼x13, 13x13¼

2004, June 15 **Litho.**
1121-1125 A413 Set of 5 *20.00* —

Independence, 44th Anniv. — A414

Denominations: 100fr, 250fr.

2004, Aug. 7 ***Perf. 13¼x13***
1126-1127 A414 Set of 2 — —

2004 Summer Olympics, Athens
A415

Designs: 50fr, Sprint race. 100fr, Greco-Roman wrestling, vert. 250fr, Torch bearer, vert. 825fr, Discus throw, vert. 1000fr, Sprint race.

Perf. 13x13¼, 13¼x13

2004, Aug. 13
1128-1131 A415 Set of 4 — —

Souvenir Sheet

1131A A415 1000fr multi 8.25 8.25

National Reconciliation
A416

2004, Sept. 28 **Litho.** ***Perf. 13¼x13***
1132 A416 50fr shown *3.50* —
1133 A416 250fr multi *9.00* —

Promotion of Women
A417

2004, Nov. 26 **Litho.** ***Perf. 14x13½***
1134 A417 250fr multi — —

Molothrus Bonariensis
A418

Perf. 14¼x13½

2004, Dec. 22 **Litho.**
1135 A418 50fr multi —

Trichosurus Vulpecula
A419

2004, Dec. 22 ***Perf. 14x13¼***
1136 A419 100fr multi 2.25 2.25

Flora — A420

Design: 250fr, Cassia tuhovaliana. 500fr, Schumanniophyton problematicum.

2004, Dec. 22 ***Perf. 13½x14¼***
1137 A420 250fr multi —
1138 A420 500fr multi —

Tenth General Assembly of African Organization of Supreme Audit Institutions
A421

Frame color: 250fr, Blue. 350fr, Purple.

2005, July 18 **Litho.** ***Perf. 13¼***
1139-1140 A421 Set of 2 *10.00* —

"Culture and Excellence" — A422

Designs: 100fr, Dan spoon. 250fr, Sénoufo cane, vert.

2005, July 25 ***Perf. 13x13½, 13½x13***
1141-1142 A422 Set of 2 — —

World Summit on the Information Society, Tunis — A423

Frame color: 30fr, Red. 220fr, Green.

2005, Sept. 28 ***Perf. 13¼***
1143-1144 A423 Set of 2 — 2.50

Women's Hairstyles
A424

Various hairstyles: 70fr, 100fr, 250fr, 350fr.

2005, Nov. 3
1145-1148 A424 Set of 4 — —

Kings and Chiefs — A425

Designs: 30fr, Tchaman chief standing. 70fr, Tchaman chief, diff. 80fr, Yacouba, Baoulé and Abron chiefs, horiz. 250fr, Akan king and staff-bearer, horiz. 1000fr, Yacouba, Baoulé, and Abron chiefs, horiz.

2005, Nov. 22
1149-1152 A425 Set of 4 — —

Souvenir Sheet

1152A A425 1000fr multi 8.25 8.25

Masks — A426

Designs: 70fr, Dan. 220fr, Gu. 250fr, Zamblé.

2005, Dec. 22
1153-1155 A426 Set of 3 *15.00* —

Europa Stamps, 50th Anniv. (in 2006) — A427

Map of Ivory Coast and: 30fr, Corn and map of Ireland. 70fr, Rubber tree and map of Germany. 80fr, Cotton plant and map of Poland. 220fr, Bananas and map of Netherlands. 250fr, Pineapple and map of Czech Republic. 350fr, Cacao and map of Belgium. 400fr, Sweet potatoes and map of Great Britain. 650fr, Coffee beans and map of Italy. 1000fr, Peanuts and map of Portugal. 2775fr, Palm nut and map of Spain.

2005, Dec. 23 **Litho.** ***Perf. 13¼***
1156-1165 A427 Set of 10 22.00 22.00
1160a Miniature sheet, #1156-1160 2.40 2.40
1165a Miniature sheet, #1161-1165 19.50 19.50
1165b Miniature sheet, #1156-1165 22.00 22.00

Coffee Branches, Flowers and Cherries — A428

Designs: 220fr, Coffea arabusta. 250fr, Coffea liberica.

2005, Dec. 28 **Litho.** ***Perf. 13¼***
1166-1167 A428 Set of 2 — —

Mushrooms
A429

Designs: 220fr, Marasmius zenkeri. 250fr, Cantharellus rufopunctatus.

2005, Dec. 28

1168-1169	A429	Set of 2	—	—

Endangered Plants — A430

Designs: 30fr, Dorstenia astyanactis. 70fr, Monosalpinx guillaumetii. 80fr, Monanthotaxis capea. 100fr, Okoubaka aubrevillei.

2005, Dec. 28 Litho. *Perf. 13¼*

1170	A430	30fr multi	—	—
1171	A430	70fr multi	—	—
1172	A430	80fr multi	—	—
1173	A430	100fr multi	—	—

Urban Transportation — A431

Designs: 30fr, Buses, automobiles, ferry. 80fr, Buses, automobiles, ferry, diff.

2005, Dec. 29 Litho. *Perf. 13¼*

1174-1175	A431	Set of 2	—	—

Léopold Sédar Senghor (1906-2001), First President of Senegal — A432

Denominations: 50fr, 250fr.

2006, Mar. 20 Litho. *Perf. 13½*

1176-1177	A432	Set of 2	2.40	2.40

A433

2006 World Cup Soccer Championships, Germany — A434

Designs: 50fr, Emblem. 100fr, Goalie making save. 200fr, World Cup. 250fr, Mascot. 1000fr, Mascot.

2006, June 9 Litho. *Perf. 13x13¼*

1178	A433	50fr multi	—	—
1179	A434	100fr multi	—	2.00
1180	A433	200fr multi	—	2.00
1181	A433	250fr multi	—	—

Souvenir Sheet

Perf. 13¾

1182	A433	1000fr multi	—	—

China-Africa Forum, Beijing
A435

Designs: 250fr, Map of Africa and China. 650fr, Forum venue.

2006, Nov. 28 *Perf. 12x12¼*

1183-1184	A435	Set of 2	7.50	7.50

Pardon
A436

Denominations: 50fr, 250fr.

2008, June 25 *Perf. 13x13¼*

1185-1186	A436	Set of 2	—	—

Diplomatic Relations Between Ivory Coast and People's Republic of China, 30th Anniv. — A437

No. 1187 — Flags of Ivory Coast and People's Republic of China and: a and c, Temple of Heaven, Beijing, Basilica of Our Lady of Peace, Yamoussoukro. b and d, Giant pandas and elephants.

500fr, Pres. Laurent Gbagbo and Chinese Prime Minister Wen Jiabao shaking hands.

2013, Mar. 2 Litho. *Perf. 12*

1187		Horiz. strip of 4	5.25	5.25
a.		A437 50fr multi	.35	.35
b.		A437 100fr multi	.70	.70
c.		A437 250fr multi	1.75	1.75
d.		A437 350fr multi	2.40	2.40

Souvenir Sheet
On Plastic
Without Gum

1188	A437	500fr multi	—	—
a.		As No. 1188, on plain paper, imperf.	—	—

Nos. 1188 and 1188a contain one 76x50mm stamp.

Historic Structures
A438

Designs: 100fr, Great Mosque, Kong. 400fr, Old Governor's Palace, Bingerville, horiz. 825fr, Bandama-Tissalé Bridge, horiz.

Perf. 13½x13, 13x13½

2013, Aug. 1 Litho.

1189-1191	A438	Set of 3	6.25	6.25

Turtle and Waterfall
A439

2013, Aug. 12 Litho. *Perf. 13x13½*

1192	A439	700fr multi	3.50	3.50

Flora — A440

Designs: 50fr, Tapinanthus belvisii. 250fr, Thonningia sanguinea. 650fr, Ottelia ulvifolia.

2013, Aug. 12 Litho. *Perf. 13½x13*

1193-1195	A440	Set of 3	4.75	4.75

Animals — A441

No. 1196 — Crocuta crocuta: a, 250fr, Hyena. b, 350fr, Hyena, diff. c, 500fr, Hyena, diff. d, 750fr, Hyena, diff.

No. 1197 — Syncerus caffer: a, 250fr, Facing left. b, 350fr, Hind leg raised. c, 500fr, Facing forward. d, 750fr, Two birds on back.

No. 1198 — Hippopotamus amphibius: a, 250fr, Adult and juvenile, juvenile at left. b, 350fr, Adult with mouth closed. c, 500fr, Adult with mouth open. d, 750fr, Adult and juvenile, juvenile at right.

No. 1199 — Primates: a, 250fr, Colobus polykomos. b, 350fr, Cercocebus torquatus. c, 500fr, Procolobus badius. d, 750fr, Cercopithecus diana.

No. 1200 — Bats: a, 250fr, Lavia frons. b, 350fr, Pipistrellus tenuipinnis. c, 500fr, Nycticeinops schlieffeni. d, 750fr, Micropteropus pusillus.

No. 1201 — Panthera leo: a, 250fr, Lion facing forward. b, 350fr, Lion climbing rock. c, 500fr, Lion looking left. d, 750fr, Lion looking right.

No. 1202 — Panthera pardus pardus: a, 250fr, Leopard on branch. b, 350fr, Leopard sitting with tail up. c, 500fr, Leopard sitting tail down. d, 750fr, Leopard walking left.

No. 1203 — Loxodonta africana: a, 250fr, Elephant front leg bent. b, 350fr, Elephant facing forward. c, 500fr, Elephant looking left trunk bent. d, 750fr, Elephant looking left trunk straight.

No. 1204 — Dolphins: a, 250fr, Sousa teuszii. b, 350fr, Steno bredanensis. c, 500fr, Stenella clymene. d, 750fr, Stenella frontalis.

No. 1205 — Whales: a, 250fr, Megaptera novaeangliae. b, 350fr, Feresa attenuata. c, 500fr, Globicephala macrorhynchus. d, 750fr, Pseudorca crassidens.

No. 1206 — Pigeons and doves: a, 250fr, Streptopelia senegalensis. b, 350fr, Treron calvus. c, 500fr, Columba guinea. d, 750fr, Turtur tympanistria.

No. 1207 — Water birds: a, 250fr, Phoenicopterus minor. b, 350fr, Scopus umbretta. c, 500fr, Plegadis falcinellus. d, 750fr, Phoenicopterus roseus.

No. 1208 — Owls: a, 250fr, Scotopelia peli. b, 350fr, Bubo shelleyi. c, 500fr, Glaucidium capense. d, 750fr, Otus icterorhynchus.

No. 1209 — Birds of prey: a, 250fr, Polyboroides typus. b, 350fr, Gyps rueppellii. c, 500fr, Aquila pennata. d, 750fr, Haliaeetus vocifer.

No. 1210 — Cuckoos: a, 250fr, Clamator levaillantii. b, 350fr, Clamator glandarius. c, 500fr, Chrysococcyx klaas. d, 750fr, Clamator jacobinus.

No. 1211 — Bee-eaters: a, 250fr, Merops albicollis. b, 350fr, Merops malimbicus. c, 500fr, Merops bulocki. d, 750fr, Merops orientalis.

No. 1212 — Wood hoopoes: a, 250fr, Phoeniculus purpureus. b, 350fr, Phoeniculus castaneiceps. c, 500fr, Rhinopomastus aterrimus. d, 750fr, Phoeniculus purpureus, diff.

No. 1213 — Butterflies: a, 250fr, Charaxes zingha. b, 350fr, Euphaedra cyparissa. c, 500fr, Charaxes imperialis. d, 750fr, Papilio menestheus.

No. 1214 — Fish: a, 250fr, Abudefduf saxatilis. b, 350fr, Anthias nicholsi. c, 500fr, Astronotus ocellatus. d, 750fr, Antigonia capros.

No. 1215 — Turtles: a, 250fr, Eretmochelys imbricata. b, 350fr, Lepidochelys olivacea. c, 500fr, Lepidochelys olivacea, diff. d, 750fr, Chelonoidis carbonaria.

No. 1216 — Snakes and lizards: a, 250fr, Hapsidophrys smaragdina. b, 350fr, Trachylepis affinis. c, 500fr, Squamata amphisbaena. d, 750fr, Leptotyphlops albiventer.

No. 1217 — Frogs: a, 250fr, Hylarana occidentalis. b, 350fr, Hildebrandtia ornata. c, 500fr, Hyperolius fusciventris. d, 750fr, Phrynomantis microps.

No. 1218 — Dinosaurs: a, 250fr, Carcharodontosaurus. b, 350fr, Ceratosaurus. c, 500fr, Allosaurus. d, 750fr, Suchomimus.

No. 1219 — Endangered animals: a, 250fr, Cephalophus jentinki. b, 350fr, Pan troglodytes. c, 500fr, Gyps africanus. d, 750fr, Choeropsis liberiensis.

No. 1220, 2500fr, Crocuta crocuta, diff. No. 1221, 2500fr, Syncerus caffer, diff. No. 1222, 2500fr, Hippopotamus amphibius adult and juvenile, diff. No. 1223, 2500fr, Pan troglodytes, diff. No. 1224, 2500fr, Rousettus aegyptiacus. No. 1225, 2500fr, Panthera leo, diff. No. 1226, 2500fr, Panthera pardus pardus, diff. No. 1227, 2500fr, Loxodonta africana, diff. No. 1228, 2500fr, Delphinus delphis. No. 1229, 2500fr, Physeter macrocephalus. No. 1230, 2500fr, Oena capensis. No. 1231, 2500fr, Phalacrocorax carbo. No. 1232, 2500fr, Tyto alba. No. 1233, 2500fr, Elanus axillaris. No. 1234, 2500fr, Chrysococcyx cupreus. No. 1235, 2500fr, Merops muelleri. No. 1236, 2500fr, Phoeniculus bollei. No. 1237, 2500fr, Charaxes hansali. No. 1238, 2500fr, Balistes punctatus. No. 1239, 2500fr, Dermochelys coriacea. No. 1240, 2500fr, Trachylepis quinquetaeniata. No. 1241, 2500fr, Kassina arboricola. No. 1242, 2500fr, Afrovenator. No. 1243, 2500fr, Loxodonta cyclotis.

Litho. & Embossed

2014, Mar. 10 *Perf. 13¼*

Sheets of 4, #a-d

1196-1219	A441	Set of 24	185.00	185.00

Souvenir Sheets

1220-1243	A441	Set of 24	250.00	250.00

New Year 2014 (Year of the Horse)
A442

2014, Mar. 10 Litho. *Perf. 13x13¼*

1243A	A442	250fr multi	1.10	1.10

Souvenir Sheet

Perf. 13¼

1243B	A442	2500fr multi	10.50	10.50

No. 1243B contains one 47x36mm stamp.

First Post Office, Grand-Bassam — A443

Denominations: 250fr, 500fr.

2015, Aug. 27 Litho. *Perf. 13x13¼*

1244-1245	A443	Set of 2	4.00	4.00

UPU Strategy Conference, Geneva.

Economic Community of West African States, 40th Anniv. A444

2015, Dec. 17 Litho. Perf. 13x13¼
1246 A444 250fr multi 1.50 1.50

SEMI-POSTAL STAMPS

No. 47 Surcharged in Red

1915 Unwmk. Perf. 14x13½
B1 A5 10c + 5c 1.60 1.60
a. Double surcharge 80.00 80.00

Curie Issue
Common Design Type

1938 Perf. 13
B2 CD80 1.75fr + 50c brt ultra 11.00 7.50

French Revolution Issue
Common Design Type

1939 Photo.
Name and Value Typo. in Black
B3 CD83 45c + 25c grn 8.75 8.75
B4 CD83 70c + 30c brn 8.75 8.75
B5 CD83 90c + 35c red org 8.75 8.75
B6 CD83 1.25fr + 1fr rose pink 8.75 8.75
B7 CD83 2.25fr + 2fr blue 8.75 8.75
Nos. B3-B7 (5) 43.75 43.75

Catalogue values for unused stamps in this section, from this point to the end of the section, are for Never Hinged items.

Stamps of 1936-38 Surcharged in Red or Black

1941
B8 A7 50c + 1fr plum (Bk) 3.75 3.75
B9 A8 80c + 2fr blk brn (R) 11.00 11.00
B10 A8 1.50fr + 2fr ultra (R) 11.00 11.00
B11 A9 2fr + 3fr ultra (Bk) 11.00 11.00
Nos. B8-B11 (4) 36.75 36.75

Common Design Type and

Native Engineer SP1

Senegalese Light Artillery SP2

1941 Photo. Perf. 13½
B12 SP1 1fr + 1fr red 1.50
B13 CD86 1.50fr + 3fr claret 1.50
B14 SP2 2.50fr + 1fr blue 1.50
Nos. B12-B14 (3) 4.50

Nos. B12-B14 were issued by the Vichy government in France, but were not placed on sale in Ivory Coast.

Nos. 165-166 Surcharged in Black or Red

1944 Engr. Perf. 12½x12
B14A 50c + 1.50fr on 2.50fr deep blue (R) .80
B14B + 2.50fr on 1fr green .80

Colonial Development Fund.

Nos. B14A-B14B were issued by the Vichy government in France, but were not placed on sale in Ivory Coast.

Republic
Anti-Malaria Issue
Common Design Type

1962, Apr. 7 Engr. Perf. 12½x12
B15 CD108 25fr + 5fr ol grn 1.25 1.25

Freedom from Hunger Issue
Common Design Type

1963, Mar. 21 Perf. 13
B16 CD112 25fr + 5fr red lil, dk vio & brn 1.50 1.50

Red Cross - Red Crescent Soc., Child Survival Campaign — SP3

1987, May 8 Litho. Perf. 13½
B17 SP3 195fr +5fr multi 2.50 2.50

No. B17 surcharged "+5fr" in red. Not issued without surcharge. Surtax for the Red Cross - Red Crescent Soc.

Organization of African Unity, 25th Anniv. — SP4

1988, Nov. 19 Litho. Perf. 12½x13
B18 SP4 195fr +5fr multi 2.25 2.25

Marie Therese Houphouet-Boigny and N'Daya Intl. Emblem — SP5

1988, Dec. 9 Litho. Perf. 13
B19 SP5 195fr +5fr multi 2.25 2.25

N'Daya Intl., 1st anniv.

See postage issues, beginning with No. 1030, for semi-postal stamps that are part of sets with regular postage stamps.

Council of Understanding, Solidarity & Rural Development, 40th Anniv. — SP6

1999, May 29 Litho. Perf. 13x13½
B20 SP6 180fr +20fr multi 1.20 1.20

Postage Types of 1998-99 With Added Surtax

1999 ? Litho. Perf. 12
Granite Paper (#B20A)
B20A A384 180fr +20fr Like #1024 —

Perf. 13½
B20B A386 180fr +20fr Like #1027 —

Nos. B20A-B20B apparently were not issued with Nos. 1022-1024 and 1027-1029.

Postage Type of 1998 With Added Surtax

1999 ? Litho. Perf. 13½x13
B20C A385 180fr +20fr Like #1025 —

Independence, 41st Anniv. — SP7

2001, Aug. 7 Litho. Perf. 13¼x13½
B21 SP7 180fr +20fr multi 1.10 1.10

Year of Dialogue Among Civilizations SP8

2001, Oct. 9 Perf. 13x13¼
B22 SP8 400fr +20fr multi 2.25 2.25

Second Republic, 1st Anniv. SP9

2001, Oct. 26
B23 SP9 180fr +20fr multi 1.10 1.10

Planned 2004 Universal Postal Union Congress, Abidjan — SP10

Vignette size: 180fr+20fr, 23x37mm. 400fr+20fr, 26x37mm. 600fr+20fr, 36x49mm.

Perf. 13, 13¼x13 (#B25)

2001, Dec. 21 Litho.
B24 SP10 180fr +20fr multi 1.00 1.00
a. Souvenir sheet of 1 5.00 5.00
B25 SP10 400fr +20fr multi 2.25 2.25
B26 SP10 600fr +20fr multi 3.25 3.25

On Nos. B24-B26 and B24a portions of the design were applied by a thermographic process producing a shiny raised effect. No. B24a sold for 1000fr and contains imperforate examples of Nos. B25 and B26 in the margin, which are surmised to be invalid for postage as the face value of these two stamps exceeds the selling price of the sheet. The 2004 UPU Congress was moved from Abidjan to Bucharest, Romania due to political unrest in the Ivory Coast.

St. Valentine's Day — SP11

Serpentine Die Cut
2002, Feb. 14 Litho.
Booklet Stamp
Self-Adhesive
B27 SP11 180fr +20fr multi 1.10 1.10
a. Booklet pane of 8 9.00

Jean Mermoz Intl. College, Abidjan, 40th Anniv. SP12

Panel color: 180fr+20fr, Tan. 400fr+20fr, Red.

2002, Apr. 19 Perf. 13½x13¼
B28-B29 SP12 Set of 2 3.00 3.00

Decentralization SP14

Denomination color: 180fr+20fr, Green. 400fr+20fr, Blue.

2002, Dec. 4 Litho. Perf. 13¼x13
B34-B35 SP14 Set of 2 3.00 3.00

SP15

Campaign Against AIDS — SP16

2003, Dec. 22 Litho. ***Perf. 13¼***
B36 SP15 180fr +20fr multi 1.00 1.00

Perf. 13¾

B37 SP16 400fr +20fr multi 2.00 2.00

Values for No. B37 are for stamps with surrounding selvage.

AIR POST STAMPS

Common Design Type

1940 Unwmk. Engr. ***Perf. 12½x12***

C1 CD85 1.90fr ultramarine .40 .40
C2 CD85 2.90fr dark red .40 .40
C3 CD85 4.50fr dk gray grn .75 .75
C4 CD85 4.90fr yel bister .75 .75
C5 CD85 6.90fr deep orange 1.50 1.50
Nos. C1-C5 (5) 3.80 3.80

Catalogue values for unused stamps in this section, from this point to the end of the section, are for Never Hinged items.

Common Design Types

1942

C6 CD88 50c car & blue .35
C7 CD88 1fr brn & black .75
C8 CD88 2fr dk grn & red brn 1.10
C9 CD88 3fr dk blue & scar 1.10
C10 CD88 5fr vio & dk red 1.10

Frame Engraved, Center Typographed

C11 CD89 10fr multicolored 1.50
C12 CD89 20fr multicolored 2.25
C13 CD89 50fr multicolored 3.00
Nos. C6-C13 (8) 11.15

There is doubt whether Nos. C6-C12 were officially placed in use.

Republic

Lapalud Place and Post Office, Abidjan — AP1

Designs: 200fr, Houphouet-Boigny Bridge. 500fr, Ayamé dam.

1959, Oct. 1 Engr. ***Perf. 13***

C14 AP1 100fr multicolored 3.00 .75
C15 AP1 200fr multicolored 5.00 2.25
C16 AP1 500fr multicolored 11.00 4.50
Nos. C14-C16 (3) 19.00 7.50

Sports Type of 1961

1961, Dec. 23

C17 A19 100fr High jump 4.50 2.25

Air Afrique Issue

Common Design Type

1962, Feb. 17 Unwmk. ***Perf. 13***

C18 CD107 50fr Prus bl, choc & org brn 2.00 1.25

Village in Man Region — AP2

200fr, Street in Odienne, vert.

1962, June 23 Engr. ***Perf. 13***

C19 AP2 200fr multi 5.50 2.75
C20 AP2 500fr shown 11.00 5.00

UN Headquarters, New York — AP3

1962, Sept. 20 ***Perf. 13***

C21 AP3 100fr multi 2.75 1.25

Admission to the UN, 2nd anniv.

Sassandra Bay — AP4

50fr, Moossou bridge. 200fr, Comoe River.

1963 Unwmk. ***Perf. 13***

C22 AP4 50fr multi 2.25 .75
C23 AP4 100fr shown 3.25 1.75
C24 AP4 200fr multi 6.00 2.75
Nos. C22-C24 (3) 11.50 5.25

African Postal Union Issue

Common Design Type

1963, Sept. 8 Photo. ***Perf. 12½***

C25 CD114 85fr org brn, ocher & red 2.50 1.50

1963 Air Afrique Issue

Common Design Type

1963, Nov. 19 Unwmk. ***Perf. 13x12***

C26 CD115 25fr crim, gray, blk & grn 1.00 .50

Ramses II and Queen Nefertari — AP5

1964, Mar. 7 Engr. ***Perf. 13***

C27 AP5 60fr car, blk & red brn 2.50 1.50

UNESCO campaign to save historic monuments in Nubia.

Arms of Republic — AP6

1964, June 13 Photo.

C28 AP6 200fr ultra, yel grn & gold 5.00 2.25

President John F. Kennedy (1917-63) — AP7

1964, Nov. 14 Unwmk. ***Perf. 12½***

C29 AP7 100fr gray, cl brn & blk 2.75 1.50
a. Souvenir sheet of 4 13.00 13.00

Liana Bridge, Lieupleu — AP8

1965, Dec. 4 Engr. ***Perf. 13***

C30 AP8 100fr ol grn, dk grn & dk red brn 3.50 1.75

Street in Kong — AP9

1966, Mar. 5 Engr. ***Perf. 13***

C31 AP9 300fr brt bl, bis brn & vio brn 8.00 4.50

Air Afrique Issue, 1966

Common Design Type

1966, Aug. 20 Photo. ***Perf. 13***

C32 CD123 30fr dk grn, blk & gray 1.00 .60

Air Afrique Headquarters AP10

1967, Feb. 4 Engr. ***Perf. 13***

C33 AP10 500fr emer, ind & ocher 11.50 5.50

Opening of Air Afrique headquarters in Abidjan.

African Postal Union Issue, 1967

Common Design Type

1967, Sept. 9 Engr. ***Perf. 13***

C34 CD124 100fr blk, vio & car lake 3.50 1.50

Senufo Village — AP11

1968 Engr. ***Perf. 13***

C35 AP11 100fr shown 3.25 1.25
C36 AP11 500fr Tiegba village 11.50 4.50

Issue dates: 100fr, Feb. 17; 500fr, Apr. 27.

PHILEXAFRIQUE Issue

Street in Grand Bassam, by Achalme — AP12

1969, Jan. 11 Photo. ***Perf. 12x12½***

C37 AP12 100fr grn & multi 4.25 4.25

PHILEXAFRIQUE Phil. Exhib., Abidjan, Feb. 14-23. Printed with alternating green label. Value, single with attached label, $6.

2nd PHILEXAFRIQUE Issue

Common Design Type

50fr, Ivory Coast #130 & view of San Pedro. 100fr, Ivory Coast #149 & man wearing chief's garments, vert. 200fr, Ivory Coast #77 # Exhibition Hall, Abidjan.

1969, Feb. 14 Engr. ***Perf. 13***

C38 CD128 50fr grn, brn red & deep bl 3.00 3.00
C39 CD128 100fr brn, org & dp blue 4.50 4.50
C40 CD128 200fr brn, gray & dp blue 7.00 7.00
a. Min. sheet of 3, #C38-C40 18.50 18.50
Nos. C38-C40 (3) 14.50 14.50

Opening of PHILEXAFRIQUE.

Man Waterfall — AP13

Mount Niangbo — AP14

1970 Engr. ***Perf. 13***

C41 AP13 100fr multicolored 3.25 1.50
C42 AP14 200fr multicolored 4.25 2.00

Issue dates: 100fr, Jan. 6; 200fr, July 18.

San Pedro Harbor — AP15

1971, Mar. 21 Engr. ***Perf. 13***

C43 AP15 100fr multicolored 2.25 1.00

Treichville Swimming Pool — AP16

1971, May 29 Photo. ***Perf. 12½***

C44 AP16 100fr multicolored 3.00 1.25

Aerial View of Coast Line — AP17

1971, July 3 Engr. *Perf. 13*
C45 AP17 500fr multi 12.00 6.00

Tourist publicity for the African Riviera.

Bondoukou Market Type of Regular Issue

Design: 200fr, Similar to No. 318, but without people at left and in center.

Embossed on Gold Paper
1971, Aug. 7 *Perf. 12½*
Size: 36x26mm
C46 A79 200fr gold, ultra & blk 4.75 2.50

African Postal Union Issue, 1971
Common Design Type

Design: 100fr, Ivory Coast coat of arms and UAMPT building, Brazzaville, Congo.

1971, Nov. 13 Photo. *Perf. 13x13½*
C47 CD135 100fr bl & multi 2.00 1.00

Lion of St. Mark
AP18

200fr, Waves, St. Mark's Basilica, Venice.

1972, Feb. 5 Photo. *Perf. 12½*
C48 AP18 100fr shown 3.50 1.75
C49 AP18 200fr multi 6.00 3.25

UNESCO campaign to save Venice.

Kawara Mosque — AP19

1972, Apr. 29 Engr. *Perf. 13*
C50 AP19 500fr bl, brn & ocher 12.00 6.00

View of Gouessesso — AP20

200fr, Jacqueville Lake. 500fr, Kossou Dam.

1972 Engr. *Perf. 13*
C51 AP20 100fr shown 3.25 1.25
C52 AP20 200fr multi 4.75 1.75
C53 AP20 500fr multi 10.00 6.00
Nos. C51-C53 (3) 18.00 9.00

Issued: 100fr, 6/10; 200fr, 1/8; 500fr, 11/17.

Akakro Radar Earth Station — AP21

1972, Nov. 27 Engr. *Perf. 13*
C54 AP21 200fr brt bl, sl grn & choc 4.50 1.75

The Judgment of Solomon, by Nandjui Legue — AP22

1973, Aug. 26 Photo. *Perf. 13*
C55 AP22 500fr multi 12.00 5.75

6th World Peace Conference for Justice.

Sassandra River Bridge — AP23

1974, May 4 Engr. *Perf. 13*
C56 AP23 100fr blk & yel grn 2.25 .75
C57 AP23 500fr slate grn & brn 12.00 4.25

Vridi Soap Factory, Abidjan — AP24

1974, July 6 Photo. *Perf. 13*
C58 AP24 200fr multi 3.50 1.75

UPU Emblem, Ivory Coast Flag, Post Runner and Jet — AP25

1974, Oct. 9 Photo. *Perf. 13*
C59 AP25 200fr multi 5.00 3.00
C60 AP25 300fr multi 6.00 4.00

Centenary of Universal Postal Union.

Fly Whisk and Panga Knife, Symbols of Akans Royal Family — AP26

1976, Apr. 3 Photo. *Perf. 12½x13*
C61 AP26 200fr brt bl & multi 4.75 2.00

Tingrela Mosque — AP27

1977, May 7 Engr. *Perf. 13*
C62 AP27 500fr multi 7.50 4.50

Zeppelin Type of 1977
Souvenir Sheet

"Graf Zeppelin" LZ 127 over New York.

1977, Sept. 3 Litho. *Perf. 11*
C63 A150 500fr multi 6.25 1.90

Exists imperf.

Philexafrique II - Essen Issue
Common Design Types

#C64, Elephant and Ivory Coast No. 239. #C65, Pheasant and Bavaria No. 1.

1978, Nov. 1 Litho. *Perf. 13x12½*
C64 CD138 100fr multi 3.50 2.50
C65 CD139 100fr multi 3.50 2.50
a. Pair, #C64-C65 + label 9.00 9.00

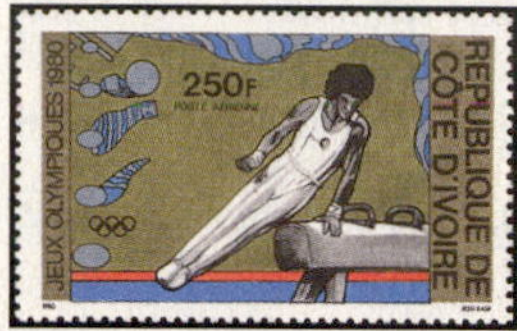

Gymnast, Olympic Rings — AP28

Various gymnasts. 75fr, 150fr, 350fr, vert.

1980, July 24 Litho. *Perf. 14½*
C66 AP28 75fr multi .90 .25
C67 AP28 150fr multi 1.25 .45
C68 AP28 250fr multi 3.00 1.00
C69 AP28 350fr multi 3.50 1.25
Nos. C66-C69 (4) 8.65 2.95

Souvenir Sheet
C70 AP28 500fr multi 5.50 2.00

22nd Summer Olympic Games, Moscow, July 19-Aug. 3.

President Houphouet-Boigny, 75th Birthday AP28a

Embossed Die Cut
1980, Oct. 18 *Perf. 10½*
C70A AP28a 2000fr Silver *20.00 20.00*
C70B AP28a 3000fr Gold *35.00 35.00*

Manned Flight Bicentenary — AP29

Various balloons: 100fr, Montgolfier, 1783, vert. 125fr, Hydrogen, 1783, vert. 150fr, Mail transport, 1870. 350fr, Double Eagle II, 1978, vert. 500fr, Dirigible.

1983, Apr. 2 Litho. *Perf. 13*
C71 AP29 100fr multi 1.00 .35
C72 AP29 125fr multi 1.50 .45
C73 AP29 150fr multi 1.75 .50
C74 AP29 350fr multi 4.50 1.00
C75 AP29 500fr multi 6.50 1.75
Nos. C71-C75 (5) 15.25 4.05

Pre-Olympic Year — AP30

Various swimming events: 100fr, Crawl. 125fr, Diving. 350fr, Backstroke. 400fr, Butterfly.
500fr, Water polo.

1983, July 9 Litho. *Perf. 14*
C76 AP30 100fr multi .95 .35
C77 AP30 125fr multi 1.25 .45
C78 AP30 350fr multi 2.00 .75
C79 AP30 400fr multi 4.00 1.40
Nos. C76-C79 (4) 8.20 2.95

Souvenir Sheet
C80 AP30 500fr multi 5.50 2.00

1984 Summer Olympics — AP31

Pentathlon: 100fr, Swimming. 125fr, Running. 185fr, Shooting. 350fr, Fencing.
500fr, Equestrian.

1984, Mar. *Perf. 12½*
C81 AP31 100fr multi 1.00 .30
C82 AP31 125fr multi 1.25 .40
C83 AP31 185fr multi 1.75 .60
C84 AP31 350fr multi 3.75 1.25
Nos. C81-C84 (4) 7.75 2.55

Souvenir Sheet
C85 AP31 500fr multi 5.50 2.00

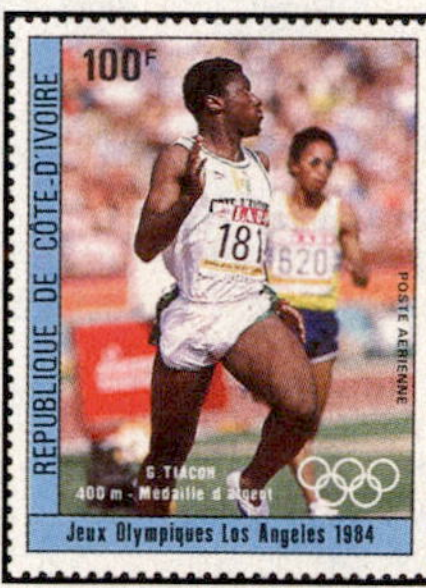

Los Angeles Olympics Winners AP32

100fr, Tiacoh, silver. 150fr, Lewis, gold. 200fr, Babers, gold. 500fr, Cruz, gold.

1984, Dec. 15 Litho. *Perf. 13*
C86 AP32 100fr multi 1.00 .25
C87 AP32 150fr multi 1.50 .40
C88 AP32 200fr multi 2.00 .75
C89 AP32 500fr multi 4.25 1.50
Nos. C86-C89 (4) 8.75 2.90

Christmas AP33

Paintings: 100fr, Virgin and Child, by Correggio. 200fr, Holy Family with Angels, by Andrea del Sarto. 400fr, Virgin and Child, by Bellini.

1985, Jan. 12 *Perf. 13*

C90 AP33 100fr multi 1.00 .35
C91 AP33 200fr multi 1.75 .85
C92 AP33 400fr multi 3.75 1.75
Nos. C90-C92 (3) 6.50 2.95

Nos. C91-C92 have incorrect frame inscriptions.

Audubon Birth Bicentenary — AP34

Birds: 100fr, Mergus serrator. 150fr, Pelecanus erythrorhynchos. 200fr, Mycteria americana. 350fr, Melanitta deglandi.

1985, June 8 **Litho.** *Perf. 13*

C93 AP34 100fr multi 1.00 .45
C94 AP34 150fr multi, vert. 1.50 .70
C95 AP34 200fr multi, vert. 2.50 1.00
C96 AP34 350fr multi 3.50 1.75
Nos. C93-C96 (4) 8.50 3.90

PHILEXAFRICA '85, Lome, Togo — AP35

No. C98, Soccer, boys and deer.

1985, Nov. 16 **Litho.** *Perf. 13*

C97 AP35 250fr shown 3.00 2.00
C98 AP35 250fr multi 3.00 2.00
a. Pair, #C97-C98 + label 9.00 6.00

Edmond Halley, Computer Drawing of Comet — AP36

Return of Halley's Comet: 155fr, Sir William Herschel, Uranus. 190fr, Space probe, comet. 350fr, MS T-5 probe, comet. 440fr, Skylab, Kohoutek comet.

1986, Jan. **Litho.** *Perf. 13*

C99 AP36 125fr shown 1.00 .50
C100 AP36 155fr multi 1.25 .75
C101 AP36 190fr multi 1.75 .90
C102 AP36 350fr multi 3.00 1.60
C103 AP36 440fr multi 3.75 2.10
Nos. C99-C103 (5) 10.75 5.85

1986 World Cup Soccer Championships, Mexico — AP37

Various soccer plays.

1986, Apr. 26 **Litho.** *Perf. 13*

C104 AP37 90fr multi .80 .40
C105 AP37 125fr multi 1.25 .60
C106 AP37 155fr multi 1.50 .70
C107 AP37 440fr multi 4.00 2.10
C108 AP37 500fr multi 4.50 2.50
Nos. C104-C108 (5) 12.05 6.30

Souvenir Sheet

Perf. 13½x13

C109 AP37 600fr multi 6.25 2.50

AP38

1988 Summer Olympics, Seoul — AP39

Sailing sports: 155fr, Soling Class. 195fr, Windsurfing. 250fr, 470 Class. 550fr, Windsurfing, diff.
650fr, 470 Class, diff.

1987, May 23 **Litho.** *Perf. 12½*

C110 AP38 155fr multi 1.50 .60
C111 AP38 195fr multi 2.25 .75
C112 AP38 250fr multi 3.00 1.00
C113 AP38 550fr multi 6.00 2.50
Nos. C110-C113 (4) 12.75 4.85

Souvenir Sheet

C114 AP39 650fr multi 7.00 2.25

1988 Summer Olympics, Seoul — AP40

100fr, Gymnastic rings. 155fr, Women's handball. 195fr, Boxing. No. C118, 500fr, Parallel bars.
No. C119, 500fr, Horizontal bar.

1988, June 18 **Litho.** *Perf. 13*

C115 AP40 100fr multi .90 .40
C116 AP40 155fr multi 1.25 .60
C117 AP40 195fr multi 2.00 .75
C118 AP40 500fr multi 5.00 2.00
Nos. C115-C118 (4) 9.15 3.75

Souvenir Sheet

C119 AP40 500fr multi 14.00 2.00

1990 World Cup Soccer Championships, Italy — AP41

Italian monuments and various athletes: 195fr, Milan Cathedral. 300fr, Columbus Monument, Genoa. 450fr, Turin. 550fr, Bologna.

1989, Nov. 25 **Litho.** *Perf. 13*

C120 AP41 195fr multi 1.75 .75
C121 AP41 300fr multi 2.50 1.25
C122 AP41 450fr multi 3.50 1.75
C123 AP41 550fr multi 5.00 2.00
Nos. C120-C123 (4) 12.75 5.75

World Cup Soccer Championships, Italy — AP42

Various plays.

1990, May 31 **Litho.** *Perf. 13*

C124 AP42 155fr multicolored 1.50 .60
C125 AP42 195fr multicolored 1.75 .85
C126 AP42 500fr multicolored 4.25 2.00
C127 AP42 600fr multicolored 5.75 2.50
Nos. C124-C127 (4) 13.25 5.95

AIR POST SEMI-POSTAL STAMPS

Types of Dahomey Air Post Semi-Postal Issue

Perf. 13½x12½, 13 (#CB3)

Photo, Engr. (#CB3)

1942, June 22

CB1 SPAP1 1.50fr + 3.50fr green 1.00 5.50
CB2 SPAP2 2fr + 6fr brown 1.00 5.50
CB3 SPAP2 3fr + 9fr car red 1.00 5.50
Nos. CB1-CB3 (3) 3.00 16.50

Native children's welfare fund.

Colonial Education Fund

Common Design Type

Perf. 12½x13½

1942, June 22 **Engr.**

CB4 CD86a 1.20fr + 1.80fr blue & red 1.00 5.50

POSTAGE DUE STAMPS

Natives — D1

Perf. 14x13½

1906-07 **Unwmk.** **Typo.**

J1 D1 5c grn, *greenish* 4.00 4.00
J2 D1 10c red brown 4.00 4.00
J3 D1 15c dark blue 6.50 6.50
J4 D1 20c blk, *yellow* 9.50 9.50
J5 D1 30c red, *straw* 9.50 9.50
J6 D1 50c violet 7.25 7.25
J7 D1 60c black, *buff* 32.50 32.50
J8 D1 1fr blk, *pinkish* 35.00 35.00
Nos. J1-J8 (8) 108.25 108.25

D2

1914

J9 D2 5c green .25 .25
J10 D2 10c rose .30 .30
J11 D2 15c gray .30 .30
J12 D2 20c brown .55 .55
J13 D2 30c blue .55 .55
J14 D2 50c black .90 .90
J15 D2 60c orange 1.25 1.25
J16 D2 1fr violet 1.50 1.50
Nos. J9-J16 (8) 5.60 5.60

Type of 1914 Issue Surcharged

1927

J17 D2 2fr on 1fr lilac rose 2.75 2.75
J18 D2 3fr on 1fr org brown 2.75 2.75

Catalogue values for unused stamps in this section, from this point to the end of the section, are for Never Hinged items.

Republic

Guéré Mask — D3

1960 **Engr.** *Perf. 14x13*

Denomination Typographed in Black

J19 D3 1fr purple .25 .25
J20 D3 2fr bright green .25 .25
J21 D3 5fr orange yellow .50 .50
J22 D3 10fr ultramarine .90 .90
J23 D3 20fr lilac rose 1.60 1.60
Nos. J19-J23 (5) 3.50 3.50

Mask — D4

Various masks and heads, Bingerville school of art.

1962, Nov. 3 **Typo.** *Perf. 13½x14*

J24 D4 1fr org & brt blue .25 .25
J25 D4 2fr black & red .30 .30
J26 D4 5fr red & dark grn .40 .40
J27 D4 10fr green & lilac .90 .90
J28 D4 20fr dark pur & blk 1.60 1.60
Nos. J24-J28 (5) 3.45 3.45

Baoulé Weight — D5

Various Baoulé weights.

1968, May 18 **Photo.** *Perf. 13*

J29 D5 5fr cit, brn & bl grn .25 .25
J30 D5 10fr lt bl, brn & bl grn .30 .30
J31 D5 15fr sal, brn & bl grn .80 .80
J32 D5 20fr gray, car & bl grn 1.10 1.10
J33 D5 30fr bis, brn & bl grn 1.50 1.50
Nos. J29-J33 (5) 3.95 3.95

Gold Weight — D6

Various gold weights.

1972, May 27 **Engr.**

J34 D6 20fr vio bl & org red .90 .90
J35 D6 40fr ver & ocher 1.50 1.50
J36 D6 50fr orange & chocolate 2.00 2.00
J37 D6 100fr slate grn & ocher 4.00 4.00
Nos. J34-J37 (4) 8.40 8.40

It has been reported that Nos. J34-J37 were used briefly as regular postage for domestic use. Examples of use as postage to foreign addresses exists.

MILITARY STAMP

The catalogue value for the unused stamp in this section is for Never Hinged.

Coat of Arms — M1

Perf. 13x14

1967, Jan. 1 **Unwmk.** **Typo.**

M1 M1 multi 3.50 3.50

OFFICIAL STAMPS

Catalogue values for unused stamps in this section are for Never Hinged items.

Ivory Coast Coat of Arms — O1

1974, Jan. 1 **Photo.** ***Perf. 12***

O1 O1 (35fr) green & multi .75 .25
O2 O1 (75fr) orange & multi 1.20 .45
O3 O1 (100fr) lil rose & multi 1.50 .80
O4 O1 (250fr) violet & multi 4.00 1.50
Nos. O1-O4 (4) 7.45 3.00

PARCEL POST STAMPS

Postage Due Stamps of French Colonies Overprinted

Overprinted In Black

1903 **Unwmk.** ***Imperf.***

Q1 D1 50c lilac 42.50 40.00
Q2 D1 1fr rose, *buff* 42.50 40.00

Overprinted In Black

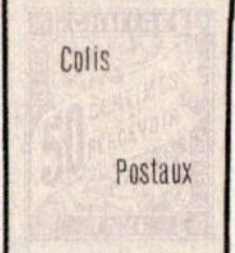

Q3 D1 50c lilac *3,300. 3,400.*
Q4 D1 1fr rose, *buff* *3,300. 3,400.*

Accents on "O" of "COTE"

Nos. Q7-Q8, Q11-Q12, Q15, Q17-Q18, Q21-Q22, Q24-Q25 exist with or without accent.

Overprinted In Red and Black

Red Overprint

Q5 D1 50c lilac 120.00 120.00
a. Inverted overprint 425.00 425.00

Blue Black Overprint

Q6 D1 1fr rose, *buff* 87.50 87.50
a. Inverted overprint 350.00 350.00

Surcharged in Black

a

b

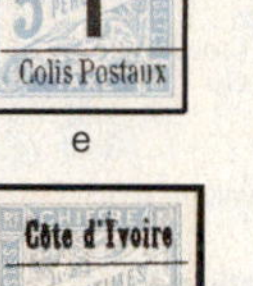

c

d

e

f

g

h

1903

Q7 D1 50c on 15c pale grn 16.00 16.00
a. Inverted surcharge 225.00 225.00
Q8 D1 50c on 60c brn, *buff* 35.00 35.00
a. Inverted surcharge 225.00 225.00
Q9 (a) 1fr on 5c blue *4,400.* *3,600.*
Q10 (b) 1fr on 5c blue *4,400.* *2,800.*
Q11 (c) 1fr on 5c blue 18.00 16.00
a. Inverted surcharge 950.00 950.00
Q12 (d) 1fr on 5c blue 27.50 24.00
Q13 (e) 1fr on 5c blue *4,800.* *4,000.*
Q14 (f) 1fr on 5c blue *12,000.* *9,500.*
Q15 (g) 1fr on 5c blue 110.00 110.00
Q16 (h) 1fr on 5c blue *3,750.* *3,850.*
Q17 (c) 1fr on 10c gray brn 27.50 24.00
a. Inverted surcharge 325.00 325.00
Q18 (d) 1fr on 10c gray brn 47.50 45.00
a. Inverted surcharge 475.00 475.00
Q19 (g) 1fr on 10c gray brn *4,000.* *3,850.*
Q20 (h) 1fr on 10c gray brn *46,000.*

Some authorities regard Nos. Q9 and Q10 as essays. A sub-type of type "a" has smaller, bold "XX" without serifs.

Surcharged in Black

j

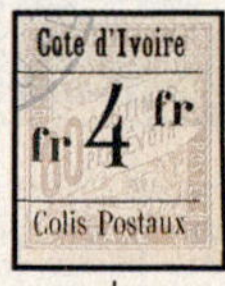

k

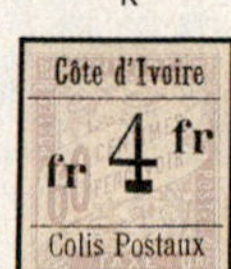

l

Q21 (j) 4fr on 60c brn, *buff* 140.00 140.00
a. Double surcharge 5,600.
Q22 (k) 4fr on 60c brn, *buff* 375.00 375.00
Q23 (l) 4fr on 60c brn, *buff* 1,200. 1,000.

Surcharged in Black

Q24 D1 4fr on 15c green 130.00 130.00
a. One large star 525.00 525.00
b. Two large stars 300.00 300.00
Q25 D1 4fr on 30c rose 130.00 130.00
a. One large star 525.00 525.00
b. Two large stars 300.00 300.00

Overprinted in Black

1904

Q26 D1 50c lilac 45.00 45.00
a. Inverted overprint
Q27 D1 1fr rose, *buff* 45.00 45.00
a. Inverted overprint

Overprinted in Black

Q28 D1 50c lilac 42.50 42.50
a. Inverted overprint 225.00 225.00
Q29 D1 1fr rose, *buff* 42.50 42.50
a. Inverted overprint 225.00 225.00

Surcharged in Black

Q30 D1 4fr on 5c blue 240.00 240.00
Q31 D1 8fr on 15c green 240.00 240.00

Overprinted in Black

1905

Q32 D1 50c lilac 92.50 92.50
Q33 D1 1fr rose, *buff* 92.50 92.50

Surcharged in Black

Q34 D1 2fr on 1fr rose, *buff* 240.00 240.00
Q35 D1 4fr on 1fr rose, *buff* 240.00 240.00
a. Italic "4" 2,200. 2,200.
Q36 D1 8fr on 1fr rose, *buff* 700.00 700.00

GET SOMEONE STARTED COLLECTING!

Thinking about starting a stamp collection? Here are the albums and the resources to get started.

MINUTEMAN ALBUM

America's number one stamp album makes collecting easy and fun. Album spaces are identified by Scott numbers and many of the spaces feature historic vignettes about the stamps. The three ring binder has been custom designed for the album pages. Now even the intermediate or beginner collector can have an album to fit their collecting interest without spending a small fortune. Save even more when you take advantage of money saving packages that are available!

ITEM	DESCRIPTION (PAGES ONLY)	RETAIL	AA*
180PMM19	**19th Century 1840-1899**	$19.99	**$16.99**
180PMM20	**20th Century 1900-1999**	$69.99	**$59.49**
180PMM21	**21st Century 2000-2003**	$49.99	**$42.49**
180PMM21A	**Pages 2004-2009**	$69.99	**$59.49**

(Part and kit pages fit 3-ring binder only.)

MINUTEMAN ALBUM KIT

Includes all Minuteman album pages covering U.S. Stamps 1840-2015, as well as two Minuteman 3-ring binders.

ITEM	DESCRIPTION	RETAIL	AA*
180MMKIT	**Minuteman Kit**	$219.99	**$169.99**

MINUTEMAN 20TH CENTURY ALBUM KIT

Includes Minuteman pages covering U.S. stamps from 1900 - 1999, as well as Minuteman 3-ring binder.

ITEM	DESCRIPTION	RETAIL	AA*
180AMM20	**20th Century Album Plus 3-Ring Binder**	$69.99	**$59.49**

MINUTEMAN SUPPLEMENTS & ACCESSORIES

ITEM	DESCRIPTION	RETAIL	AA*
180S010	**2010 Supplement** (pages only)	$19.99	**$16.99**
180S011	**2011 Supplement** (pages only)	$19.99	**$16.99**
180S012	**2012 Supplement** (pages only)	$19.99	**$16.99**
180S013	**2013 Supplement** (pages only)	$19.99	**$16.99**
180S014	**2014 Supplement** (pages only)	$19.99	**$16.99**
180S015	**2015 Supplement** (pages only)	$19.99	**$16.99**
180S016	**2016 Supplement** (pages only)	$22.99	**$19.99**
180S017	**2017 Supplement** (pages only)	$22.99	**$19.99**
180Z003	**Minuteman Blank Pages Pack** Fits both 2-post and 3-ring binders	$19.99	**$16.99**

Starting with 2003, supplements fit both the 2-post Minuteman and 3-ring binders.

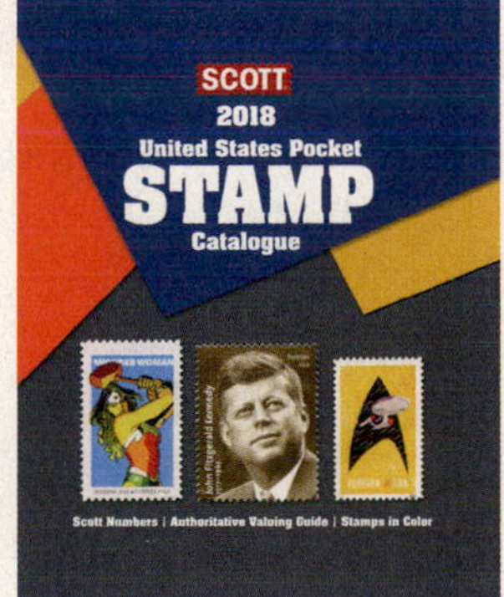

2018 U.S. STAMP POCKET CATALOGUE

With pages designed to be a convenient inventory checklist, the Scott U.S. Pocket Stamp Catalogue is a perfect compact companion at shows, club meetings, and your desk. Full-color stamp illustrations accompany listings and values for more than 4,000 U.S. stamps, all identified by Scott catalog numbers. Get your copy today!

ITEM	DESCRIPTION	RETAIL	AA*
P112018	**2018 U.S. Pocket Stamp Catalogue**	$32.50	**$26.99**

Get yours today by visiting **AmosAdvantage.com**

Or Call **1-800-572-6885** Outside U.S. & Canada Call: **1-937-498-0800**

P.O. Box 4129, Sidney, OH 45365

ORDERING INFORMATION: *AA prices apply to paid subscribers of Amos Media titles, or for orders plwaced online. Prices, terms and product availability subject to change. Taxes will apply in CA, OH, & IL. **SHIPPING & HANDLING: United States –** Order total $0-$10.00 charged $3.99 shipping; Order total $10.01-$79.99 charged $7.99 shipping; Order total $80.00 or more charged 10% of order total for shipping. Maximum Freight Charge $45.00. **Canada –** 20% of order total. Minimum charge $19.99 Maximum charge $200.00. **Foreign –** Orders are shipped via FedEx Int'l. or USPS and billed actual freight.

Illustrated Identifier

This section pictures stamps or parts of stamp designs that will help identify postage stamps that do not have English words on them.

Many of the symbols that identify stamps of countries are shown here as well as typical examples of their stamps.

See the Index and Identifier for stamps with inscriptions such as "sen," "posta," "Baja Porto," "Helvetia," "K.S.A.", etc.

Linn's Stamp Identifier is now available. The 144 pages include more than 2,000 inscriptions and more than 500 large stamp illustrations. Available from Linn's Stamp News, P.O. Box 4129, Sidney, OH 45365-4129, or amosadvantage.com

1. HEADS, PICTURES AND NUMERALS

GREAT BRITAIN

Great Britain stamps never show the country name, but, except for postage dues, show a picture of the reigning monarch.

Victoria

Edward VII George V Edward VIII

George VI

Elizabeth II

Some George VI and Elizabeth II stamps are surcharged in annas, new paisa or rupees. These are listed under Oman.

Silhouette (sometimes facing right, generally at the top of stamp)

The silhouette indicates this is a British stamp. It is not a U.S. stamp.

VICTORIA

Queen Victoria

INDIA

Other stamps of India show this portrait of Queen Victoria and the words "Service" (or "Postage") and "Annas."

AUSTRIA

YUGOSLAVIA

(Also BOSNIA & HERZEGOVINA if imperf.)

BOSNIA & HERZEGOVINA

Denominations also appear in top corners instead of bottom corners.

HUNGARY

Another stamp has posthorn facing left

BRAZIL

AUSTRALIA

Kangaroo and Emu

GERMANY

Mecklenburg-Vorpommern

SWITZERLAND

PALAU

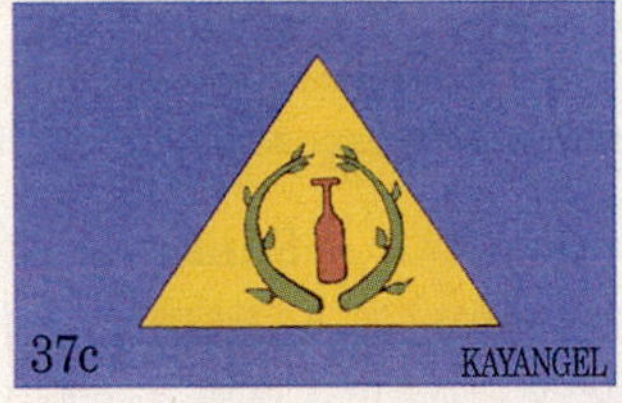

2. ORIENTAL INSCRIPTIONS

CHINA

Any stamp with this one character is from China (Imperial, Republic or People's Republic). This character appears in a four-character overprint on stamps of Manchukuo. These stamps are local provisionals, which are unlisted. Other overprinted Manchukuo stamps show this character, but have more than four characters in the overprints. These are listed in People's Republic of China.

Some Chinese stamps show the Sun.

Most stamps of Republic of China show this series of characters.

Stamps with the China character and this character are from People's Republic of China. 人

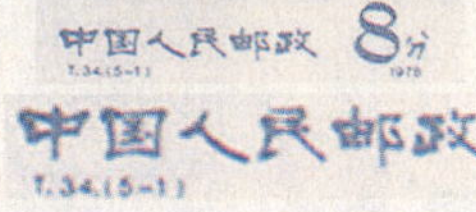

Calligraphic form of People's Republic of China

(一)	(二)	(三)	(四)	(五)	(六)
1	2	3	4	5	6
(七)	(八)	(九)	(十)	(十一)	(十二)
7	8	9	10	11	12

Chinese stamps without China character

REPUBLIC OF CHINA

PEOPLE'S REPUBLIC OF CHINA

Mao Tse-tung

MANCHUKUO

Temple

Emperor Pu-Yi

The first 3 characters are common to many Manchukuo stamps.

The last 3 characters are common to other Manchukuo stamps.

Orchid Crest

Manchukuo stamp without these elements

JAPAN

Chrysanthemum Crest

Country Name

Japanese stamps without these elements

The number of characters in the center and the design of dragons on the sides will vary.

RYUKYU ISLANDS

Country Name

PHILIPPINES (Japanese Occupation)

Country Name

NETHERLANDS INDIES (Japanese Occupation)

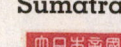

Indicates Japanese Occupation

Java

Sumatra

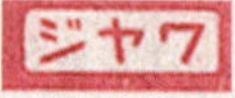

Country Name

Country Name

Moluccas, Celebes and South Borneo

Country Name

NORTH BORNEO (Japanese Occupation)

Indicates Japanese Occupation

Country Name

MALAYA (Japanese Occupation)

Indicates Japanese Occupation

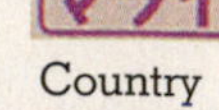

Country Name

BURMA

Union of Myanmar

ပြည်ထောင်စုမြန်မာနိုင်ငံတော်

Union of Myanmar

(Japanese Occupation)

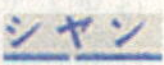

Indicates Japanese Occupation

Country Name

Other Burma Japanese Occupation stamps without these elements

Burmese Script

KOREA

These two characters, in any order, are common to stamps from the Republic of Korea (South Korea) or of the People's Democratic Republic of Korea (North Korea).

조선우표

조선우표

This series of four characters can be found on the stamps of both Koreas. Most stamps of the Democratic People's Republic of Korea (North Korea) have just this inscription.

대한민국우표

Indicates Republic of Korea (South Korea)

South Korean postage stamps issed after 1952 do not show currency expressed in Latin letters. Stamps wiith " HW," "HWAN," "WON," "WN," "W" or "W" with two lines through it, if not illustrated in listings of stamps before this date, are revenues. North Korean postage stamps do not have currency expressed in Latin letters.

Yin Yang appears on some stamps.

South Korean stamps show Yin Yang and starting in 1966, 'KOREA" in Latin letters

Example of South Korean stamps lacking Latin text, Yin Yang and standard Korean text of country name. North Korean stamps never show Yin Yang and starting in 1976 are inscribed "DPRK" or "DPR KOREA" in Latin letters.

THAILAND

Country Name

King Chulalongkorn

King Prajadhipok and Chao P'ya Chakri

3. CENTRAL AND EASTERN ASIAN INSCRIPTIONS

INDIA - FEUDATORY STATES

Alwar

Bhor

Bundi

Similar stamps come with different designs in corners and differently drawn daggers (at center of circle).

Dhar

Duttia

Faridkot

Hyderabad

Similar stamps exist with different central design which is inscribed "Postage" or "Post & Receipt."

Indore

Jammu & Kashmir

Text varies.

Jasdan

Jhalawar

Kotah

Size and text varies

Nandgaon

Nowanuggur

Poonch

Similar stamps exist
in various sizes with different text

Rajasthan

Rajpeepla

Soruth

Tonk

BANGLADESH

Country Name

NEPAL

Similar stamps are smaller, have squares in upper corners and have five or nine characters in central bottom panel.

TANNU TUVA

ISRAEL

GEORGIA

This inscription is found on other pictorial stamps.

Country Name

ARMENIA

The four characters are found somewhere on pictorial stamps. On some stamps only the middle two are found.

4. AFRICAN INSCRIPTIONS

ETHIOPIA

5. ARABIC INSCRIPTIONS

١ ٢ ٣ ٤ ٥
1 2 3 4 5

٦ ٧ ٨ ٩ ٠
6 7 8 9 0

AFGHANISTAN

Many early Afghanistan stamps show Tiger's head, many of these have ornaments protruding from outer ring, others show inscriptions in black.

Arabic Script

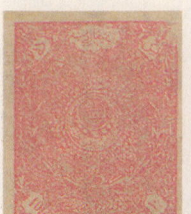

Crest of King Amanullah

Mosque Gate & Crossed Cannons

The four characters are found somewhere on pictorial stamps. On some stamps only the middle two are found.

BAHRAIN

EGYPT

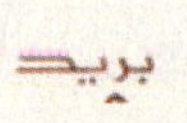

Postage

IRAN

Country Name

Royal Crown

Lion with Sword

Symbol

Emblem

IRAQ

JORDAN

LEBANON

Similar types have denominations at top and slightly different design.

LIBYA

Country Name in various styles

Other Libya stamps show Eagle and Shield (head facing either direction) or Red, White and Black Shield (with or without eagle in center).

Without Country Name

SAUDI ARABIA

Tughra (Central design)

Palm Tree and Swords

SYRIA

Arab Government Issues

THRACE **YEMEN**

PAKISTAN

PAKISTAN - BAHAWALPUR

Country Name in top panel, star and crescent

TURKEY

Star & Crescent is a device found on many Turkish stamps, but is also found on stamps from other Arabic areas (see Pakistan-Bahawalpur)

Tughra (similar tughras can be found on stamps of Turkey in Asia, Afghanistan and Saudi Arabia)

Mohammed V

Mustafa Kemal

Plane, Star and Crescent

TURKEY IN ASIA

Other Turkey in Asia pictorials show star & crescent. Other stamps show tughra shown under Turkey.

6. GREEK INSCRIPTIONS

GREECE

Country Name in various styles (Some Crete stamps overprinted with the Greece country name are listed in Crete.)

Lepta

Drachma Drachmas Lepton

Abbreviated Country Name

Other forms of Country Name

No country name

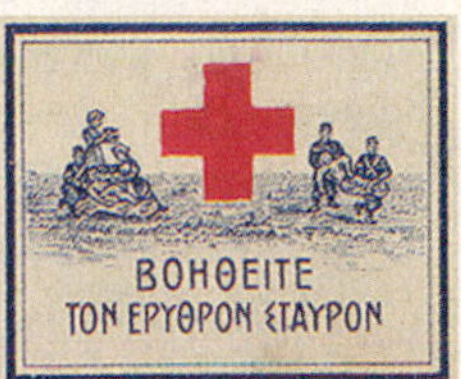

CRETE

Country Name

Crete stamps with a surcharge that have the year "1922" are listed under Greece.

EPIRUS

Similar stamps have text above the eagle.

IONIAN IS.

7. CYRILLIC INSCRIPTIONS

RUSSIA

Postage Stamp

Imperial Eagle

Postage in various styles

Abbreviation for Kopeck

Abbreviation for Ruble

Russia

Abbreviation for Russian Soviet Federated Socialist Republic RSFSR stamps were overprinted (see below)

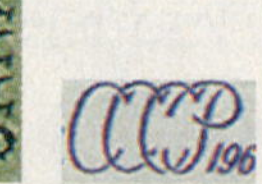

Abbreviation for Union of Soviet Socialist Republics

This item is footnoted in Latvia

RUSSIA - Army of the North

"OKCA"

RUSSIA - Wenden

RUSSIAN OFFICES IN THE TURKISH EMPIRE

These letters appear on other stamps of the Russian offices.

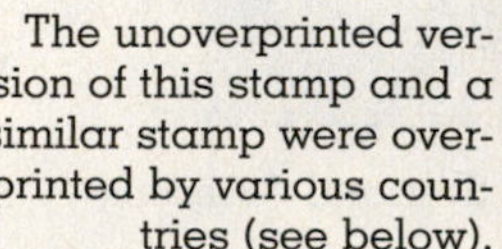

The unoverprinted version of this stamp and a similar stamp were overprinted by various countries (see below).

ARMENIA

BELARUS

FAR EASTERN REPUBLIC

Country Name

FINLAND

Circles and Dots on stamps similar to Imperial Russia issues

SOUTH RUSSIA

Country Name

BATUM

Forms of Country Name

TRANSCAUCASIAN FEDERATED REPUBLICS

Abbreviation for Country Name

KAZAKHSTAN

КАЗАКСТАН

Country Name

KYRGYZSTAN

КЫРГЫЗСТАН

Country Name

ROMANIA

TAJIKISTAN

Тадж.

Country Name & Abbreviation

UKRAINE

Пошта України

України

Україhu

Country Name in various forms

The trident appears on many stamps, usually as an overprint.

Abbreviation for Ukrainian Soviet Socialist Republic

WESTERN UKRAINE

Abbreviation for Country Name

AZERBAIJAN

AZƏRBAYCAN

Country Name

A.C.C.P. Abbreviation for Azerbaijan Soviet Socialist Republic

MONTENEGRO

ЦРНЕГОРЕ

ЦРНА ГОРА

Country Name in various forms

Ц.Р.ГОРЕ

Abbreviation for country name

No country name (A similar Montenegro stamp without country name has same vignette.)

SERBIA

СРПСКА СРБИЈА

Country Name in various forms

СРП К.С.

Abbreviation for country name

No country name

MACEDONIA

Country Name

МАКЕДОНСКИ

Different form of Country Name

SERBIA & MONTENEGRO

YUGOSLAVIA

ЈУГОСЛАВИЈА

Showing country name

No Country Name

BOSNIA & HERZEGOVINA (Serb Administration)

РЕПУБЛИКА СРПСКА

Country Name

РЕПУБЛИКЕ СРПСКЕ

Different form of Country Name

No Country Name

BULGARIA

Country Name Postage

Stotinka

Stotinki (plural) Abbreviation for Stotinki

Country Name in various forms and styles

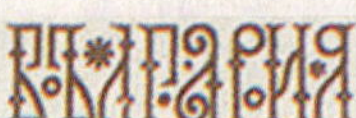

No country name

Abbreviation for Lev, leva

MONGOLIA

Country name in one word Tugrik in Cyrillic

Country name in two words Mung in Cyrillic

Mung in Mongolian

Tugrik in Mongolian

Arms

No Country Name

INDEX AND IDENTIFIER

All page numbers shown are those in this Volume 3B.

Postage stamps that do not have English words on them are shown in the Illustrated Identifier.

COVER SUPPLIES

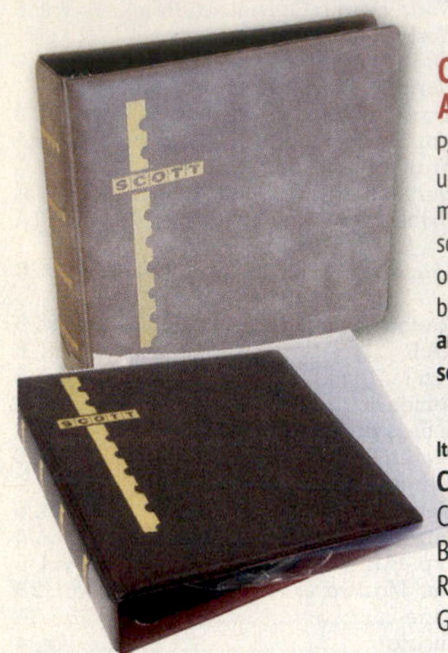

COVER BINDERS AND PAGES

Padded, durable, 3-ring binders will hold up to 100 covers. Features the "D" ring mechanism on the right hand side of album so you don't have to worry about creasing or wrinkling covers when opening or closing binder. Cover pages sold separately. **Binders and pages are also sold in a money saving sets. Call or go online for more details.**

Item	Retail	AA*
COVER BINDERS	$16.99	**$12.99**

Choose from four classic colors: Black (CBBK); Blue (CBBL); Red/Burgundy (CBRD); Gray (CBGY)

COVER ALBUM PAGES WITH BLACK BACKGROUNDS

Item	Description	Retail	AA*
T2	Double-sided Page, 2 Pocket (25/pack)	$9.99	**$8.99**
SS2PG1B	Supersafe Page, 1 Pocket (10/pack)	$5.75	**$4.75**

COVER SLEEVES

Clear polyethylene sleeves protect your covers. **Sold in packages of 100.**

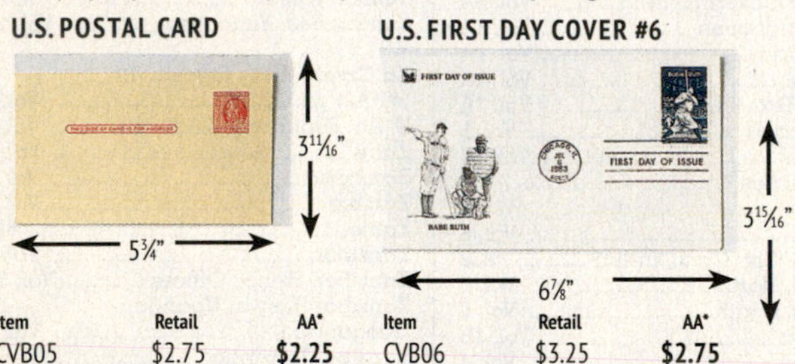

U.S. POSTAL CARD — 5¾" × 3 11/16"

Item	Retail	AA*
CVB05	$2.75	**$2.25**

U.S. FIRST DAY COVER #6 — 6⅞" × 3 15/16"

Item	Retail	AA*
CVB06	$3.25	**$2.75**

CONTINENTAL POSTCARD — 6" × 4⅜"

Item	Retail	AA*
CVB07	$3.50	**$2.99**

EUROPEAN FIRST DAY COVER — 7 13/16" × 5⅛"

Item	Retail	AA*
CVB09	$4.25	**$3.95**

#10 BUSINESS ENVELOPE

9⅝" × 4⅛"

Item	Retail	AA*
CVB10	$5.75	$4.95

MINT SHEET BINDERS & PAGES

Keep those mint sheets intact in a handsome, 3-ring binder. Just like the cover album, the Mint Sheet album features the "D" ring mechanism on the right hand side of binder so you don't have to worry about damaging your stamps when turning the pages.
Binders and pages are also sold in a money saving sets. Call or go online for more details.

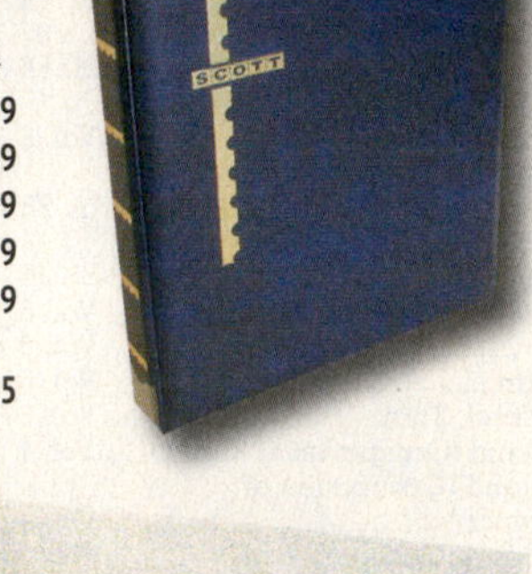

Item		Retail	AA*
MBRD	Red (Burgundy)	$21.99	**$17.99**
MBBL	Blue	$21.99	**$17.99**
MBGY	Gray	$21.99	**$17.99**
MBBK	Black	$21.99	**$17.99**
MS1	BLACK Mint Sheet Pages (25 per pack)	$16.99	**$14.99**
SSMP3C	CLEAR Mint Sheet Pages (12 per pack)	$9.95	**$8.95**

GLASSINE ENVELOPES

Perfect for organizing duplicates and sending approvals or mailing stamps. **Sold in packages of 100.**

Item	Size (Dimensions)	Retail	AA*
GE01	#1 (1¾" x 2⅞")	$4.99	**$4.49**
GE02	#2 (2 5/16" x 3⅝")	$5.49	**$4.99**
GE03	#3 (2½" x 4¼")	$5.99	**$5.49**
GE04	#4 (3¼" x 4⅞")	$6.99	**$5.99**
GE4H	#4½ (3⅛" x 5 1/16")	$5.95	**$5.25**
GE05	#5 (3½" x 6")	$8.99	**$7.99**
GE06	#6 (3¾" x 6¾")	$9.50	**$8.50**
GE07	#7 (4⅛" x 6¼")	$10.00	**$9.00**
GE08	#8 (4½" x 6⅝")	$10.50	**$9.50**
GE10	#10 (4⅛" x 9½")	$16.99	**$14.99**
GE11	#11 (4½" x 10⅜")	$17.99	**$16.99**

GLASSINE BAGS

These larger glassine bags are ideal for storing panes, covers or prestige booklets. A handy accessory to keep around for all your collecting needs. Available in five different sizes. **Sold in packages of 100.**

Item	Size (Dimensions)	Retail	AA*
GB12	#12 (4⅝" x 6⅝")	$8.99	**$7.99**
GB13	#13 (5¾" x 7¾")	$9.99	**$8.99**
GB13A	#13A (6¾" x 9")	$10.99	**$9.99**
GB14	#14 (7¾" x 9¾")	$16.99	**$14.99**
GB15	#15 (8½" x 11")	$18.99	**$15.99**
GB16	#16 (11½" x 14")	$33.99	**$28.99**

Glassines are also available in boxes of 1,000 – call for pricing.

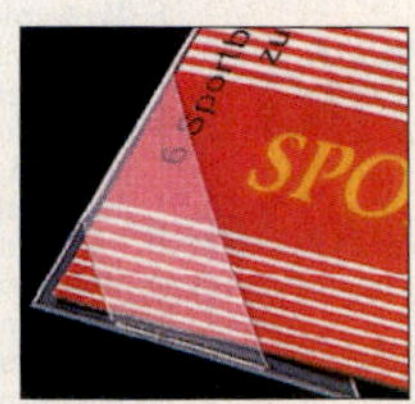

PRINZ CORNER MOUNTS

Clear, self-adhesive corner mounts are ideal for postal cards and covers. Mounts measure ⅞" each side and are made from transparent glass foil. There are 250 mounts in each pack.

Item	Retail	AA*
ACC176	$11.99	**$8.99**

AmosAdvantage.com • 1-800-572-6885

Outside U.S. and Canada, call (937) 498-0800
Mail to PO Box 4129, Sidney, OH 45365-4129

ORDERING INFORMATION: *AA prices apply to paid subscribers of Amos Media titles, or orders placed online. Prices, terms and product availability subject to change. Shipping and handling rates will apply. Taxes apply in CA, OH & IL.

SHIPPING & HANDLING: United States: Order total $0-$10.00 charged $3.99 shipping. Order total $10.01-$79.99 charged $7.99 shipping. Order total $80.00 or more charged 10% of order total for shipping. Maximum Freight Charge $45.00. **Canada:** 20% of order total. Minimum charge $19.99 Maximum charge $200.00. **Foreign:** Orders are shipped via FedEx Intl. or USPS and billed actual freight.

Vols. 3A-3B Number Additions, Deletions & Changes

Georgia

Number in 2018 Catalogue	Number in 2019 Catalogue
new	54b

Ghana

Number in 2018 Catalogue	Number in 2019 Catalogue
new	2770A

Great Britain

Number in 2018 Catalogue	Number in 2019 Catalogue
new	521b
new	1111a
new	BK142a
BK572	deleted

Greece

Number in 2018 Catalogue	Number in 2019 Catalogue
new	455b
new	456a
new	456b
new	458a
new	459a
new	462a
new	463a
new	464a
new	466a
new	467a
new	468b
new	473c
new	473Ba
new	474a
new	477c
new	480a
new	482b
new	483b
new	484a
new	485c
new	488a
new	489b
new	502a
new	506a
new	507a
new	508a
new	509a
new	510a
new	514a
new	517a
new	526a
new	530a
new	550a
new	553a
new	634a
1546a	1546A
1547a	1547A
1548a	1548A
1549a	1549A
1550a	1550A
1551a	1551A
1552a	1552A
1553a	1553A
1554a	1554A
1555a	1555A
1556a	1556A
1557a	1557A
1568a	1568A
1569b	1569B
1581a	1581A
1582a	1582A
1583a	1583A
1584a	1584A
1585a	1585A
1586a	1586A
1587a	1587A
1588a	1588A
1589a	1589A
1590b	1590B
1616a	1616A
1617a	1617A
1618a	1618A
1619a	1619A
1620a	1620A
1621a	1621A
1622b	1622B
1623a	1623A
1624a	1624A
1625a	1625A
1626a	1626A
1627b	1627B
1628a	1628A
1629a	1629A
1630a	1630A
1631a	1631A
1632a	1632A
1633a	1633A
1634a	1634A
1635a	1635A
1636a	1636A
1637a	1637A
1638a	1638A
1639a	1639A
1640a	1640A
1641b	1641A
1641a	1641b
1642a	1642A
1643a	1643A
1644a	1644A
1645a	1645A
1646a	1646A
1647a	1647A
1648a	1648A
1649a	1649A
1650a	1650A
1652a	1652A
1653a	1653A
1654a	1654A
1655a	1655A
1656b	1656B
1657a	1657A
1657b	1657B
1658b	1658B
1658e	1658E
1659a	1659A
1660a	1660A
1661a	1661A
1662a	1662A
1663a	1663A
1678a	1678A
1679b	1679B
1685a	1685A
1686a	1686A
1687a	1687A
1688a	1688A
1689a	1689A
1690a	1690A
1691a	1691A
1692a	1692A
1693a	1693A
1694a	1694A
1695a	1695A
1696a	1696A
1697a	1697A
1698a	1698A
1699a	1699A
1715a	1715A
1716b	1716B
1738a	1738A
1739b	1739B
1749a	1749A
1750a	1750A
1751a	1751A
1752a	1752A
1753a	1753A
1754a	1754A
1755a	1755A
1756a	1756A
1757a	1757A
1758a	1758A
1759a	1759A
1760a	1760A
1772a	1772A
1773b	1773B
1784a	1784A
1785b	1785B
1792a	1792A
1793a	1793A
1794a	1794A
1795a	1795A
1796a	1796A
1797a	1797A
1798a	1798A
1799a	1799A
1800a	1800A
1801a	1801A
1810a	1810A
1811b	1811B
1835a	1835A
1836b	1836B
1843a	1843A
1844a	1844A
1845a	1845A
1846a	1846A
1847a	1847A
1848a	1848A
1849a	1849A
1850a	1850A
1851a	1851A
1873a	1873A
1874b	1874B
1906a	1906A
1907b	1907B
1908a	1908A
1909a	1909A
1910a	1910A
1911a	1911A
1912a	1912A
1913a	1913A
1914a	1914A
1915a	1915A
1916a	1916A
1917a	1917A
1935a	1935A
1936b	1936B
1959a	1959A
1992c	1992C
2004a	2004A
2005a	2005A
2006a	2006A
2007a	2007A
2008a	2008A
2009a	2009A
2010a	2010A
2011a	2011A
2012a	2012A
2013a	2013A
2014a	2014A
2015a	2015A
2016a	2016A
2017a	2017A
2018a	2018A
2019a	2019A
2020a	2020A
2021a	2021A
2022a	2022A
2023a	2023A
2024a	2024A
2031c	2031C
2061c	2061C
new	2103a
2110c	2110C
2165a	2165A
2166a	2166A
2167a	2167A
2168a	2168A
2169a	2169A
2170a	2170A
2171a	2171A
2172a	2172A
2173a	2173A
2174a	2174A
2192c	2192C
2254c	2254C
2261a	2261A
2262a	2262A
2263a	2263A
2264a	2264A
2265a	2265A
2266a	2266A
2267a	2267A
2268a	2268A
2269a	2269A
2270a	2270A
2306c	2306C
2330a	2330A
2331a	2331A
2332a	2332A
2333a	2333A
2334a	2334A
2335a	2335A
2336a	2336A
2337a	2337A
2338a	2338A
2339a	2339A
2350c	2350C
2392c	2392C
2429c	2429C
2447a	2447A
2448a	2448A
2449a	2449A
2450a	2450A
2451a	2451A
2452a	2452A
2453a	2453A
2454a	2454A
2455a	2455A
2456a	2456A
2489c	2489C
2519a	2519A
2520a	2920A
2521a	2521A
2522a	2522A
2523a	2523A
2524a	2524A
2525a	2525A
2526a	2526A
2527a	2527A
2528a	2528A
2537c	2537C
2572c	2572C
2621a	2621A
2622a	2622A
2623a	2623A
2624a	2624A
2625a	2625A
2626a	2626A
2627a	2627A
2628a	2628A
2629a	2629A
2630a	2630A
2631a	2631A
2632a	2632A
2635c	2635C
2684c	2684C
2738a	2738A
2739a	2739A
2748a	2748A

Hungary

Number in 2018 Catalogue	Number in 2019 Catalogue
new	25a
new	435a
new	O21a
new	O22a
new	O23a
new	O24a
new	O25a

Iceland

Number in 2018 Catalogue	Number in 2019 Catalogue
O21h	deleted
new	O22a
O28b	deleted

India

Number in 2018 Catalogue	Number in 2019 Catalogue
new	15c
new	23c
new	308a

Ireland

Number in 2018 Catalogue	Number in 2019 Catalogue
new	1b

Italian States

Modena

Number in 2018 Catalogue	Number in 2019 Catalogue
11a	11A

SHOWGARD MOUNTS

Showgard mounts are manufactured with the highest archival qualities in mind. The foil used to produce the mounts is acid free and stronger than other mounts for maximum protection and durability. Selecting the right size mount for your stamp is easy. Simply use a millimeter ruler to measure the stamps' width then the height. Showgard incorporates these measurements into their product numbers to insure you get the right size. Mounts available with clear (c) or black (b) backgrounds, with a few exceptions. Please specify background preference when ordering.

Item	*Description*	*Mounts*	*Retail*	*AA**
SGC50X31	50/31 U.S. Jumbo Singles - Horizontal	40	$3.95	**$2.85**
SGCV31X50	31/50 U.S. Jumbo Singles - Vertical	40	$3.95	**$2.85**
SGJ40X25	40/25 U.S. Commem. - Horizontal	40	$3.95	**$2.85**
SGJV25X40	25/40 U.S. Commem. - Vertical	40	$3.95	**$2.85**
SGE22X25	22/25 U.S. Regular Issues - Vertical	40	$3.95	**$2.85**
SGEH25X22	25/22 U.S. Regular Issues - Horizontal	40	$3.95	**$2.85**
SGT25X27	25/27 U.S. Famous Americans	40	$3.95	**$2.85**
SGU33X27	33/27 U.N., Germany	40	$3.95	**$2.85**
SGN40X27	40/27 United Nations	40	$3.95	**$2.85**
SGAH41X31	41/31 U.S. Semi Jumbo - Horizontal	40	$3.95	**$2.85**
SGAV31X41	31/41 U.S. Semi Jumbo - Vertical	40	$3.95	**$2.85**
SGDH52X36	52/36 U.S. Duck Stamps	30	$3.95	**$2.85**
SGS31X31	31/31 U.S. Celebrate the Century	30	$3.95	**$2.85**
SGUS2	Cut Style with Tray-8 Sizes	320	$32.95	**$23.50**
SGUS3	Strip Style w/Tray-No. 22 thru No. 52	75	$49.95	**$35.75**
SGUS1	U.S. Strip Sizes No. 22 thru No. 52	50	$24.50	**$17.50**
SG67X25	67/25 U.S. Coil Strips of 3	40	$8.35	**$5.95**
SG57X55	57/55 U.S. Regular Issue	25	$8.35	**$5.95**
SG106X55	106/55 U.S. 3¢, 4¢ Commemoratives	20	$8.35	**$5.95**
SG105X57	105/57 U.S. Giori Press Issues	20	$8.35	**$5.95**
SG127X70	127/70 U.S. Jumbo Issues	10	$8.35	**$5.95**
SG140X89	140/89 Postcards, Souvenir Sheets	10	$8.35	**$5.95**
SG165X94	165/94 First Day Covers	10	$8.35	**$5.95**
SG20	215/20 U.S. Mini Stamps, etc.	22	$9.75	**$6.95**
SG22	215/22 Narrow U.S. Airs	22	$9.75	**$6.95**
SG24	215/24 U.K. and Canada, early U.S.	22	$9.75	**$6.95**
SG25	215/25 U.S. Commem. & Regular Issues	22	$9.75	**$6.95**
SG27	215/27 U.S. Famous Americans, U.N.	22	$9.75	**$6.95**
SG28	215/28 Switzerland, Liechtenstein	22	$9.75	**$6.95**
SG30	215/30 U.S. Special Stamps, Jamestown	22	$9.75	**$6.95**
SG31	315/31 U.S. Squares & Semi Jumbo	22	$9.75	**$6.95**
SG33	215/33 U.K. Issues, Misc. Foreign	22	$9.75	**$6.95**
SG36	215/36 Duck Stamps, Misc. Foreign	15	$9.75	**$6.95**
SG39	215/39 U.S. Magsaysay, Misc. Foreign	15	$9.75	**$6.95**
SG41	215/41 U.S. Vertical Commem. Israel Tabs	15	$9.75	**$6.95**
SG44	215/44 Booklet Panes, Hatteras Quartet	15	$9.75	**$6.95**
SG48	215/48 Canada Reg. Issue & Comm Blocks	15	$9.75	**$6.95**
SG50	215/50 U.S. Plain Blocks of 4	15	$9.75	**$6.95**
SG52	215/52 France Paintings, Misc. Foreign	15	$9.75	**$6.95**
SG57	215/57 U.S. Commem. Plate Blocks	15	$9.75	**$6.95**
SG61	215/61 Souvenir Sheets, Tab Singles, etc.	15	$9.75	**$6.95**
SG63	240/63 U.S. Semi Jumbo Blocks	10	$11.95	**$8.75**
SG66	240/66 U.S. ATM Panes, SA Duck Panes	10	$11.95	**$8.75**
SG68	240/68 Canadian Plate Blocks, etc.	10	$11.95	**$8.75**
SG74	240/74 U.N. Inscription Blocks of 4	10	$11.95	**$8.75**
SG80	240/80 U.S. Commem. Blocks	10	$11.95	**$8.75**
SG82	240/82 U.N. Chagall SS, Canada Plate Blocks	10	$11.95	**$8.75**
SG84	240/84 Israel Plate Blocks, etc.	10	$11.95	**$8.75**
SG89	240/89 U.N. Inscription Blocks of 6	10	$11.95	**$8.75**
SG100	240/100 U.S. Squares Plate Blocks	7	$11.95	**$8.75**
SG120	240/120 Miniature Sheets	7	$11.95	**$8.75**
SG70	264/70 U.S. Jumbo Plate Blocks	10	$16.25	**$11.50**
SG91	264/91 U.K. Souvenir Sheets	10	$16.25	**$11.50**
SG105	264/105 U.K. Blocks, Covers, etc.	10	$16.25	**$11.50**
SG107	264/107 U.S. Plate No. Strip of 20	10	$16.25	**$11.50**
SG111	264/111 U.S. Floating Plate No. Strips of 20	5	$10.75	**$7.75**
SG127	264/127 Modern U.S. Definitive Sheets of 20	5	$11.95	**$8.50**
SG137	264/137 U.N. SS, U.K. Coronation	5	$12.95	**$9.50**
SG158	264/158 Miniature Sheets, Apollo Soyuz PB	5	$14.50	**$10.50**
SG175	264/175 U.S. Sheets-Pan American Reissues	5	$15.95	**$11.75**
SG188	264/188 U.S. Miniature Sheets-Hollywood, etc.	5	$16.95	**$11.95**
SG198	264/198 U.S. Miniature Sheets	5	$17.25	**$12.50**
SGMPK	Assortment No. 22 thru No. 41	12	$7.50	**$5.50**
SGMPK2	Assortment No. 76 thru No. 171	15	$32.75	**$23.75**
SGAB	U.S. SS to 1975-except White Plains	11	$8.75	**$6.50**
SGWSE	World Stamp Expo Souvenir Sheets	3	$2.75	**$1.95**
SGRP94	U.S. 1994 Souvenir Sheets (*Black Only*)	5	$10.25	**$7.50**
SGRPAC97	Pacific 97 Issues	7	$5.75	**$4.25**
SGDC2006	Washington 2006 Souvenir Sheets (*Black Only*)	4	$7.95	**$5.75**
SGTM	Trans-Mississippi Issues	11	$5.75	**$4.25**
SGSPC	Space Exploration Sheets	5	$7.25	**$5.25**
SGNY2016	New York 2016 WWS Releases		$12.50	**$10.00**
SG265X231	265/231 U.S. Full Sheets & Souvenir Cards	5	$21.25	**$15.25**
SG260X25	260/25 U.S. Coil Strips of up to 11 stamps	25	$12.75	**$8.95**
SG293X30	293/30 U.S. American Eagle Coil Strips of up to 11 stamps	5	$4.25	**$3.25**

Item	*Description*	*Mounts*	*Retail*	*AA**
SG260X40	260/40 U.S. Postal People Full Strip	10	$10.50	**$7.50**
SG260X46	260/46 U.S. Vending Booklets	10	$10.50	**$7.50**
SG260X55	260/55 U.S. 13¢ Eagle Full Strip	10	$10.50	**$7.50**
SG260X59	260/59 U.S. Double Press Reg. Iss. Strips of 20	10	$10.50	**$7.50**
SG111X91	111/91 U.S. Columbian Souvenir Sheets	6	$5.50	**$3.95**
SG229X131	229/131 U.S. WWII Sheets, Looney Tunes	5	$10.75	**$7.75**
SG187X144	187/144 U.N. Flag Sheetlets	10	$18.50	**$12.95**
SG204X153	204/153 U.S. Commem. Sheets, Bicentennial	5	$11.25	**$8.25**
SG120X207	120/207 U.S. Ameripex Presidential Sheetlets	4	$7.75	**$5.75**
SG192X201	192/201 U.S. Classics Mini-Sheets	5	$13.50	**$9.75**
SG280X228	280/228 U.S. Greetings From America Sheets	5	$20.50	**$14.75**
SG191X229	191/229 U.S. Celebrate The Century Sheets	5	$15.25	**$11.25**
SG89X83	89/83 Washington 2006 Souvenir sheet and other miniature panes	3	$2.50	**$1.89**
SG146X84	146/84 Distinguished Americans, Cycling Souvenir Sheet and other miniature panes	3	$3.75	**$2.75**
SG203X146	203/146 Hanukkah, Kwanzaa, Eid, Wedding Cake Series, Ronald Reagan, Dogs at Work, Jose Ferrer, Samuel de Champlain SS, etc.	3	$7.50	**$5.50**
SG178X181	178/181 Butterfly Series, Carmel Mission Express Mail, Celebrate Scouting, Cranes, etc.	3	$7.50	**$5.50**
SG148X196	148/196 $5.00 Waves of Color, Moon Landing 25th Anniversary, etc.	3	$7.50	**$5.50**
SG76	264/76 BEP SS, Booklets, Plate Blocks	5	$11.95	**$8.75**
SG96	264/96 Souvenir Sheets, Panes	5	$11.95	**$8.75**
SG109	264/109 Foreign Miniature Sheets	5	$11.95	**$8.75**
SG115	264/115 Foreign Miniature Sheets	5	$11.95	**$8.75**
SG117	264/117 Foreign Miniature Sheets	5	$11.95	**$8.75**
SG121	264/121 Foreign Miniature Sheets	5	$11.95	**$8.75**
SG131	264/131 Looney Toons, Misc. Sheetlets	5	$11.95	**$8.75**
SG135	264/135 Foreign Miniature Sheets	5	$11.95	**$8.75**
SG139	264/139 White House Pane, etc.	5	$11.95	**$8.75**
SG143	264/143 Victorian Love, Misc. Sheets	5	$11.95	**$8.75**
SG147	264/147 Cinco de Mayo, etc.	5	$14.95	**$10.75**
SG151	264/151 Antique Auto, Communication, etc.	5	$15.50	**$11.08**
SG163	264/163 Tropical Flowers, UN Human Rights	5	$14.95	**$10.75**
SG167	264/167 Misc. U.S. Sheetlets	5	$14.95	**$10.75**
SG171	264/171 Helping Children Learn, etc.	5	$14.95	**$10.75**
SG181	264/181 U.S. Sheets–Calder, All Aboard, etc.	5	$18.50	**$13.25**
SG201	264/201 Dinosaurs, etc.	5	$18.50	**$13.25**
SG215	264/215 U.S. Sheets–Arctic Animals, Ballet, etc.	5	$18.50	**$13.25**

7" LIGHTHOUSE STAMP MOUNT CUTTER

This affordable and versatile mount cutter features an attachable measuring scale up to 7" (180mm) with an adjustable stop for accurate and clean cuts every time.

Item	*Retail*	*AA**
LH180MC	$23.99	**$19.99**

AMOS ADVANTAGE

Call **1-800-572-6885**

Outside U.S. & Canada: (937) 498-0800

Visit **AmosAdvantage.com**

Mail orders to: P.O. Box 4129, Sidney, OH 45365

ORDERING INFORMATION: *AA prices apply to paid subscribers of Amos Media titles, or orders placed online. Prices, terms and product availability subject to change. Taxes will apply in CA, OH, & IL. Shipping and handling rates will apply.

SHIPPING & HANDLING: United States: Order total $0-$10.00 charged $3.99 shipping; Order total $10.01-$79.99 charged $7.99 shipping; Order total $80.00 or more charged 10% of order total for shipping. Maximum Freight Charge $45.00. **Canada:** 20% of order total. Minimum charge $19.99; maximum charge $200.00. **Foreign:** Orders are shipped via FedEx Int'l. or USPS and billed actual freight.

INDEX TO ADVERTISERS
2019 VOLUME 3B

2019
VOLUME 3B
DEALER DIRECTORY
YELLOW PAGE LISTINGS

This section of your Scott Catalogue contains advertisements to help you conveniently find what you need, when you need it...!

Appraisals

DR. ROBERT FRIEDMAN & SONS STAMP & COIN BUYING CENTER
2029 W. 75th St.
Woodridge, IL 60517
PH: 800-588-8100
FAX: 630-985-1588
stampcollections@drbobstamps.com
www.drbobfriedmanstamps.com

Argentina

GUILLERMO JALIL
Maipu 466,local 4
1006 Buenos Aires
Argentina
guillermo@jalilstamps.com
philatino@philatino.com
www.philatino.com
www.jalilstamps.com

Auctions

DUTCH COUNTRY AUCTIONS
The Stamp Center
4115 Concord Pike
Wilmington, DE 19803
PH: 302-478-8740
FAX: 302-478-8779
auctions@dutchcountryauctions.com
www.dutchcountryauctions.com

British Commonwealth

COLLECTORS EXCHANGE ORLANDO STAMP SHOP
1814A Edgewater Drive
Orlando, FL 32804
PH: 407-620-0908
PH: 407-947-8603
FAX: 407-730-2131
jlatter@cfl.rr.com
www.BritishStampsAmerica.com
www.OrlandoStampShop.com

WORLDSTAMPS/ FRANK GEIGER PHILATELISTS
PO Box 4743
Pinehurst, NC 28374
PH: 910-295-2048
info@WorldStamps.com
www.WorldStamps.com

ARON R. HALBERSTAM PHILATELISTS, LTD.
PO Box 150168
Van Brunt Station
Brooklyn, NY 11215-0168
PH: 718-788-3978
arh@arhstamps.com
www.arhstamps.com

British Commonwealth

ROY'S STAMPS
PO Box 28001
600 Ontario Street
St. Catharines, ON
CANADA L2N 7P8
Phone: 905-934-8377
Email: roystamp@cogeco.ca

THE STAMP ACT
PO Box 1136
Belmont, CA 94002
PH: 650-703-2342
thestampact@sbcglobal.net

Buying

DR. ROBERT FRIEDMAN & SONS STAMP & COIN BUYING CENTER
2029 W. 75th St.
Woodridge, IL 60517
PH: 800-588-8100
FAX: 630-985-1588
stampcollections@drbobstamps.com
www.drbobfriedmanstamps.com

Canada

CANADA STAMP FINDER
PO Box 92591
Brampton, ON L6W 4R1
PH: 514-238-5751
Toll Free in North America:
877-412-3106
FAX: 323-315-2635
canadastampfinder@gmail.com
www.canadastampfinder.com

ROY'S STAMPS
PO Box 28001
600 Ontario Street
St. Catharines, ON
CANADA L2N 7P8
Phone: 905-934-8377
Email: roystamp@cogeco.ca

China

THE STAMP ACT
PO Box 1136
Belmont, CA 94002
PH: 650-703-2342
thestampact@sbcglobal.net

Collections

DR. ROBERT FRIEDMAN & SONS STAMP & COIN BUYING CENTER
2029 W. 75th St.
Woodridge, IL 60517
PH: 800-588-8100
FAX: 630-985-1588
stampcollections@drbobstamps.com
www.drbobfriedmanstamps.com

Ducks

MICHAEL JAFFE
PO Box 61484
Vancouver, WA 98666
PH: 360-695-6161
PH: 800-782-6770
FAX: 360-695-1616
mjaffe@brookmanstamps.com
www.brookmanstamps.com

Germany

WORLDSTAMPS/ FRANK GEIGER PHILATELISTS
PO Box 4743
Pinehurst, NC 28374
PH: 910-295-2048
info@WorldStamps.com
www.WorldStamps.com

HENRY GITNER PHILATELISTS, INC.
PO Box 3077-S
Middletown, NY 10940
PH: 845-343-5151
PH: 800-947-8267
FAX: 845-343-0068
hgitner@hgitner.com
www.hgitner.com

Great Britain

WORLDSTAMPS/ FRANK GEIGER PHILATELISTS
PO Box 4743
Pinehurst, NC 28374
PH: 910-295-2048
info@WorldStamps.com
www.WorldStamps.com

Guyana

AUKTIONSHAUS CHRISTOPH GÄRTNER GMBH AND CO KG
Steinbeisstr 6 + 8
74321 Bietigheim-Bissingen
Germany
PH: +49-(0)7142-789400
FAX: +49-(0)7142-789410
info@auktionen-gaertner.de
www.auktionen-gaertner.de

WORLDSTAMPS/ FRANK GEIGER PHILATELISTS
PO Box 4743
Pinehurst, NC 28374
PH: 910-295-2048
info@WorldStamps.com
www.WorldStamps.com

Hong Kong

THE STAMP ACT
PO Box 1136
Belmont, CA 94002
PH: 650-703-2342
thestampact@sbcglobal.net

Hungary

WORLDSTAMPS/ FRANK GEIGER PHILATELISTS
PO Box 4743
Pinehurst, NC 28374
PH: 910-295-2048
info@WorldStamps.com
www.WorldStamps.com

British Commonwealth

THE BRITISH COMMONWEALTH O·F N·A·T·I·O·N·S

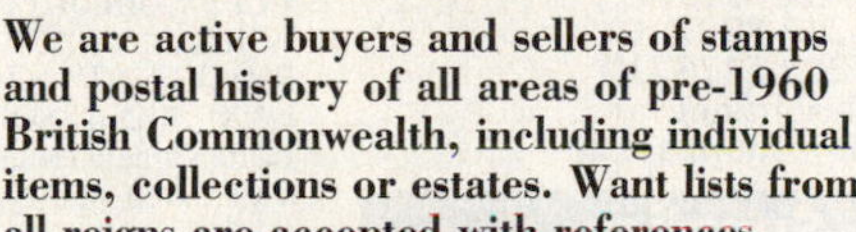

We are active buyers and sellers of stamps and postal history of all areas of pre-1960 British Commonwealth, including individual items, collections or estates. Want lists from all reigns are accepted with references.

L. W. Martin, Jr.

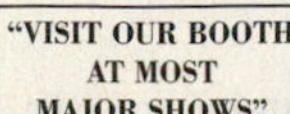

CROWN COLONY STAMPS
P.O. Box 1198
BELLAIRE, TEXAS 77402
PH. (713) 781-6563 • FAX (713) 789-9998
E-mail: lwm@crowncolony.com

British Commonwealth

British Empire 1840 - 1935

Aden to Zululand Mint & Used
Most complete stock in North America

44(10)

For over 40 years, we have built some of the world's finest collections. Our expert ***Want List Services*** can do the same for you. Over 50 volumes filled with singles, sets and rare stamps, we are sure we have what you need. We welcome your Want Lists in Scott or Stanley Gibbons numbers.

Put our expertise to work for you today!
You'll be glad you did!

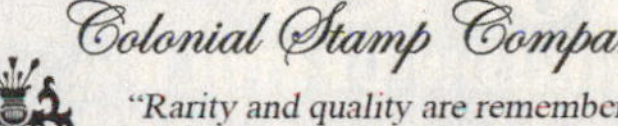

"Rarity and quality are remembered ...long after price is forgotten."

5757 Wilshire Blvd., Penthouse 8
Los Angeles, CA 90036 USA
Tel: +1 (323) 933-9435 Fax: +1 (323) 939-9930
Email: *Info@ColonialStamps.com*
www.ColonialStamps.com

Ask for your free Public Auction Catalogue today!

Iceland

**WORLDSTAMPS/
FRANK GEIGER PHILATELISTS**
PO Box 4743
Pinehurst, NC 28374
PH: 910-295-2048
info@WorldStamps.com
www.WorldStamps.com

India

**WORLDSTAMPS/
FRANK GEIGER PHILATELISTS**
PO Box 4743
Pinehurst, NC 28374
PH: 910-295-2048
info@WorldStamps.com
www.WorldStamps.com

Ireland

**WORLDSTAMPS/
FRANK GEIGER PHILATELISTS**
PO Box 4743
Pinehurst, NC 28374
PH: 910-295-2048
info@WorldStamps.com
www.WorldStamps.com

Israel

**HENRY GITNER
PHILATELISTS, INC.**
PO Box 3077-S
Middletown, NY 10940
PH: 845-343-5151
PH: 800-947-8267
FAX: 845-343-0068
hgitner@hgitner.com
www.hgitner.com

Italy

**WORLDSTAMPS/
FRANK GEIGER PHILATELISTS**
PO Box 4743
Pinehurst, NC 28374
PH: 910-295-2048
info@WorldStamps.com
www.WorldStamps.com

**HENRY GITNER
PHILATELISTS, INC.**
PO Box 3077-S
Middletown, NY 10940
PH: 845-343-5151
PH: 800-947-8267
FAX: 845-343-0068
hgitner@hgitner.com
www.hgitner.com

Korea

THE STAMP ACT
PO Box 1136
Belmont, CA 94002
PH: 650-703-2342
thestampact@sbcglobal.net

New Issues

DAVIDSON'S STAMP SERVICE
Personalized Service since 1970
PO Box 36355
Indianapolis, IN 46236-0355
PH: 317-826-2620
ed-davidson@earthlink.net
www.newstampissues.com

**WORLDSTAMPS/
FRANK GEIGER PHILATELISTS**
PO Box 4743
Pinehurst, NC 28374
PH: 910-295-2048
info@WorldStamps.com
www.WorldStamps.com

South America

**WORLDSTAMPS/
FRANK GEIGER PHILATELISTS**
PO Box 4743
Pinehurst, NC 28374
PH: 910-295-2048
info@WorldStamps.com
www.WorldStamps.com

Stamp Stores

California

**BROSIUS STAMP, COIN &
SUPPLIES**
2105 Main St.
Santa Monica, CA 90405
PH: 310-396-7480
FAX: 310-396-7455
brosius.stamp.coin@hotmail.com

Delaware

DUTCH COUNTRY AUCTIONS
The Stamp Center
4115 Concord Pike
Wilmington, DE 19803
PH: 302-478-8740
FAX: 302-478-8779
auctions@dutchcountryauctions.com
www.dutchcountryauctions.com

Worldwide

Stamp Stores

Florida

**DR. ROBERT FRIEDMAN &
SONS STAMP & COIN
BUYING CENTER**
PH: 800-588-8100
FAX: 630-985-1588
stampcollections@drbobstamps.com
www.drbobfriedmanstamps.com

Illinois

**DR. ROBERT FRIEDMAN &
SONS STAMP & COIN
BUYING CENTER**
2029 W. 75th St.
Woodridge, IL 60517
PH: 800-588-8100
FAX: 630-985-1588
stampcollections@drbobstamps.com
www.drbobfriedmanstamps.com

Indiana

KNIGHT STAMP & COIN CO.
237 Main St.
Hobart, IN 46342
PH: 219-942-4341
PH: 800-634-2646
knight@knightcoin.com
www.knightcoin.com

New Jersey

**BERGEN STAMPS &
COLLECTIBLES**
306 Queen Anne Rd.
Teaneck, NJ 07666
PH: 201-836-8987
bergenstamps@gmail.com

TRENTON STAMP & COIN CO
Thomas DeLuca
Store: Forest Glen Plaza
1804 Highway 33
Hamilton Square, NJ 08690
Mail: PO Box 8574
Trenton, NJ 08650
PH: 609-584-8100
FAX: 609-587-8664
TOMD4TSC@aol.com

New York

CHAMPION STAMP CO., INC.
432 West 54th St.
New York, NY 10019
PH: 212-489-8130
FAX: 212-581-8130
championstamp@aol.com
www.championstamp.com

CK STAMPS
42-14 Union St. # 2A
Flushing, NY 11355
PH: 917-667-6641
ckstampsllc@yahoo.com

Ohio

HILLTOP STAMP SERVICE
Richard A. Peterson
PO Box 626
Wooster, OH 44691
PH: 330-262-8907 (0)
PH: 330-262-5378 (H)
hilltop@bright.net
www.hilltopstamps.com

Supplies

**BROOKLYN GALLERY COIN &
STAMP, INC.**
8725 4th Ave.
Brooklyn, NY 11209
PH: 718-745-5701
FAX: 718-745-2775
info@brooklyngallery.com
www.brooklyngallery.com

Topicals

**WORLDSTAMPS/
FRANK GEIGER PHILATELISTS**
PO Box 4743
Pinehurst, NC 28374
PH: 910-295-2048
info@WorldStamps.com
www.WorldStamps.com

E. JOSEPH McCONNELL, INC.
PO Box 683
Monroe, NY 10949
PH: 845-783-9791
FAX: 845-782-0347
ejstamps@gmail.com
www.EJMcConnell.com

Topicals - Columbus

MR. COLUMBUS
PO Box 1492
Fennville, MI 49408
PH: 269-543-4755
David@MrColumbus1492.com
www.MrColumbus1492.com

United Nations

BRUCE M. MOYER
Box 99
East Texas, PA 18046
PH: 610-395-8410
FAX: 610-421-8020
moyer@unstamps.com
www.unstamps.com

United States

KEITH WAGNER
ACS Stamp Company
2914 W 135th Ave
Broomfield, Colorado 80020
303-841-8666
www.ACSStamp.com

BROOKMAN STAMP CO.
PO Box 90
Vancouver, WA 98666
PH: 360-695-1391
PH: 800-545-4871
FAX: 360-695-1616
info@brookmanstamps.com
www.brookmanstamps.com

U.S. Classics/Moderns

BARDO STAMPS
PO Box 7437
Buffalo Grove, IL 60089
PH: 847-634-2676
jfb7437@aol.com
www.bardostamps.com

U.S.-Collections Wanted

DUTCH COUNTRY AUCTIONS
The Stamp Center
4115 Concord Pike
Wilmington, DE 19803
PH: 302-478-8740
FAX: 302-478-8779
auctions@dutchcountryauctions.com
www.dutchcountryauctions.com

**DR. ROBERT FRIEDMAN &
SONS STAMP & COIN
BUYING CENTER**
2029 W. 75th St.
Woodridge, IL 60517
PH: 800-588-8100
FAX: 630-985-1588
stampcollections@drbobstamps.com
www.drbobfriedmanstamps.com